SUBJECT INDEX TO

POETRY

FOR CHILDREN AND YOUNG PEOPLE

———

1957-1975

SUBJECT INDEX TO

POETRY

FOR CHILDREN AND YOUNG PEOPLE

———————

1957-1975

Compiled by
DOROTHY B. FRIZZELL SMITH
and
EVA L. ANDREWS

AMERICAN LIBRARY ASSOCIATION/CHICAGO
1977

Library of Congress Cataloging in Publication Data

Smith, Dorothy B   Frizzell.
   Subject index to poetry for children and young
people, 1957-1975.

   1. Children's poetry--Indexes. I. Andrews,
Eva, joint author. II. Title.
PN1023.S6   016.80881   77-3296
ISBN 0-8389-0242-1

Printed in the United States of America

Preface

This supplement to the 1957 edition of Subject Index to Poetry for Children and Young People has many of the same purposes and uses as the earlier edition: to help the librarian, the teacher, the young person, and the general reader locate quickly and easily poems under a broad range of subjects. Public speakers (such as clergy, radio and television writers and performers), literary consultants, persons seeking choral readings, as well as those planning activities around a subject or an interest, such as a country, a person, a place, or an occasion will have a resource in this index.

Because poetry collections are seldom discarded, the 1957 index and the anthologies included in it will continue to be useful. The Supplement, 1957-1975, does not supersede the 1957 edition, as no anthologies indexed in that volume are included in the new one.

For the most part the subject headings have been drawn from Sears List of Subject Headings, 10th edition, with added entries of scientific, biographical, geographical, ethnic, and current interest as found in Readers' Guide to Periodical Literature; The Encyclopaedia Britannica, 1967; Columbia-Viking Desk Encyclopedia, 2nd edition; and Eakin, Mary K., Subject Index to Books for Intermediate Grades, 1963. Authentication of the subject headings was supplied by The American Heritage Dictionary, 1969, Current Biography, The New Century Cyclopedia of Names, Webster's Biographical Dictionary, and Webster's New Geographical Dictionary.

The growing interest and pride in ethnic, cultural, and national origins has prompted the use of a wide-ranging selection of the poetry of African and American Indian (Central, North and South) tribal and language groups, Pacific island peoples, and Asian cultures, as well as translations from various European languages as an enrichment for this supplement. This index will be the more useful because of subject headings of contemporary significance, such as ROCK MUSIC AND SONGS and COUNTER CULTURE; names of persons of recent interest, as TILL, EMMETT and KENNEDY, JOHN FITZGERALD; and events, as VIETNAMESE WAR, 1957-1975.

The 263 new anthologies have been chosen with care. The assistance of consultants in children's work, selected by the American Library Association, was most helpful. Sources such as <u>Center for Children's Books Bulletin</u> and <u>Booklist</u>, to name only two of many, provided more titles. <u>The Children's Catalog</u>, <u>The Junior High School Library Catalog</u>, and <u>The Senior High School Library Catalog</u> were prime sources and are indicated in "List of Books Indexed" as CC, JHS, SHS. Recommendations for purchase have not been indicated because of differences in libraries and patrons.

The compilers have received invaluable assistance during the seven years of compilation from these persons and libraries: Mildred Dorsey for suggesting names of co-compilers; Emma Lou Linsenmayer in the choice of anthologies; Shirley Lavenberg in checking cross references; the staff of Felipe de Neve Branch Library in Los Angeles for providing storage and working space, as well as reference assistance; Helen O'Connell, whose judgment, experience in editing, and outstanding excellence as the typist made this a more accurate and usable book; D. G. O'Connell for his many kindnesses; Dorothy Barclay, children's librarian of the Palos Verdes (California) Library District, who with her staff was unfailingly helpful and provided books for extended loan through the many years of preparation; the information sources of the Los Angeles Public Library and the Los Angeles County Public Library; the consultants appointed by the American Library Association, Dr. Rose Agree, Lois Fetterman, and Jean Fisher for their advice and suggestions. Particular thanks should go to the publishing services of the American Library Association, and especially to Herbert Bloom, senior editor, and to Vladimir Reichl, planning and design manager.

Dorothy B. Frizzell Smith and Eva L. Andrews, compilers.

Preface to 1957 Volume

Librarians working with children and young people have long felt the need for a comprehensive subject index to poetry, arranged under topics of appeal and interest to those age groups and suitable to curriculum requirements. The Subject Index to Poetry for Children and Young People is designed to fill this need — to help the librarian, the teacher, the pupil, and the general reader locate quickly and easily poems under a wide-ranging variety of subjects.

Although intended primarily for librarians to use with children and young people from kindergarten through high school, the Subject Index to Poetry for Children and Young People will assist parents, teachers, leaders of youth groups, ministers and others searching for poems on specific topics, universal concepts, persons, places, and things as well as for poems for special occasions or programs.

The 157 poetry collections indexed (many of which are not indexed elsewhere) were selected with the assistance of children's, young people's, and school librarians throughout the United States and represent titles of proven worth, usage, and interest. Out-of-print titles have been included only if they are apt to be in most libraries. In addition to anthologies, the Index includes the collected and selected works of several individual poets but not their complete works.

The grade level, or more accurately, the interest level of each title indexed is indicated in the "List of Books Indexed" as an aid to quick and easy use. Page numbers are given each entry in the Index to eliminate steps in locating a poem in an anthology.

The subject headings, chosen on the basis of children's and young people's needs and interests, were derived largely from a study of those in Rue's Subject Index to Books for Intermediate Grades. These headings are, it was found, sufficiently simple for use in the primary grades yet broad enough to include topics applicable to upper grade work. The Readers' Guide and the Essay and General Literature Index were consulted for additional headings. Poems are also indexed under such form headings as "Ballads," "Dialects," "Conceits," "Japanese Verse," "Chinese Verse," etc., because of the demand for poems in these categories. Where

well-known prose, e.g., Lincoln's "Gettyburg
Address," appears in a collection it has been included under appropriate subject headings.

The compilers, in the more than ten years that
this work has been in preparation, have received
valuable assistance from many more persons and
sources than can be recognized adequately in these
pages. However, particular acknowledgment is due
to M. Genevieve Wilson, retired junior high school
librarian of Oakland, California, for her early
work on the Index; the Long Beach Public library,
the Long Beach public school libraries, the Long
Beach State College library, and the California
State library for their generosity in lending
books to be indexed; the staff of the North branch
of the Long Beach Public library who so unself-
ishly loaned their staff room facilities for a
typing office and for the overflow of indexing
materials; Aiko Takeshita and Miho Shiroishi for
their excellent work in typing the manuscript;
Helen Chase, Marcella Corbett, Elizabeth
Feigenbutz, Frances Henselman, Gloria Patten,
Fay Tunison, and Hazel Van Marter for their
assistance in filing; Lois Fannin, Helen R. Fuller,
Marion Horton, and Gwendolen Shakeshaft for their
helpful suggestions; and Chase Dane, Everett O.
Fontaine, Pauline J. Love, and Elizabeth Redmond
of the A.L.A. Publishing Department for their
help and encouragement in compiling this index.

<u>Violet Sell</u>, Branch Librarian, North Branch,
  Long Beach Public Library, Long Beach,
  California

<u>Dorothy B. Frizzell Smith</u>, Librarian, Long
  Beach City College, Long Beach, California

<u>Ardis Sarff O'Hoyt</u>, Children's Librarian, Long
  Beach Public Library, Long Beach, California

<u>Mildred Bakke</u>, Librarian, Hamilton Junior
  High School, Long Beach, California

List of Books Indexed

KEY

The list is arranged alphabetically by coded symbols which represent two letters of the editor's name and distinguishing letters in the title; thus, Rd-OA refers to REED, GWENDOLYN, ed., *Out of the Ark*. Following the coded symbol are the editor's full name, the title of the book, the publisher, date of publication, grade level, and CC, JHS, SHS, indicating that the title is in *Children's Catalog, Junior High School Library Catalog, Senior High School Library Catalog.*

Ab-MO   ABDUL, RAOUL, ed. The Magic of Black Poetry. Dodd, 1972. (7-up)

Ad-BO   ✓ADOFF, ARNOLD, ed. Black Out Loud: An Anthology of Modern Poems by Black Americans. Macmillan, 1970. (4-up) JHS

Ad-CI   ADOFF, ARNOLD, ed. City in All Directions. Macmillan, 1969. (7-up)

Ad-IA   ADOFF, ARNOLD, ed. I Am the Darker Brother: An Anthology of Modern Poems by Negro Americans. Macmillan, 1968. (7-up) JHS

Ad-II   ADOFF, ARNOLD, ed. It Is the Poem Singing into Your Eyes: Anthology of New Young Poets. Har-Row, 1971. (7-up) JHS

Ad-PB   ADOFF, ARNOLD, ed. The Poetry of Black America: Anthology of the Twentieth Century. Har-Row, 1973. (7-up)

Ad-PE   ADAMS, ADRIENNE. Poetry of Earth. Scribner, 1972. (1-4)

Ag-HE   AGREE, ROSE. How to Eat a Poem and Other Morsels: A Collection of Food Poems for Children. Pantheon, 1967. (2-5)

Al-PI   ALDAN, DAISY, tr. Poems from India. Crowell, 1969. (4-up) SHS

Al-VBP   ALDINGTON, RICHARD, ed. The Viking Book of Poetry of the English-Speaking World. Viking, 1958. 2v. (5-up)

Al-WW   ALLEN, TERRY, ed. The Whispering Wind: Poetry by Young American Indians. Doubleday, 1972. (5-up)

An-IP   ANGLUND, JOAN W. In a Pumpkin Shell: A Mother Goose ABC. HarBraceJ, 1960. (K-3)

An-TC   BISHOP, ELIZABETH and BRASIL, EMANUEL, eds. An Anthology of Twentieth-Century Brazilian Poetry. Wesleyan, 1972. (7-up)

Ar-TP3   ✓ARBUTHNOT, MAY HILL and ROOT, SHELDON I, JR. Time for Poetry. 3rd ed. Scott, Foresman, 1968. (1-up) CC

Au-SP   AUSTIN, MARY. The Sound of Poetry. Allyn, 1965. (1-up)

Ba-HI   BARON, VIRGINIA OLSEN, ed. Here I Am: An Anthology of Poems Written by Young People in Some of America's Minority Groups. Dutton, 1969. (1-up) CC

Ba-PO   BATES, SCOTT, ed. Poems of War Resistance from 2300 B.C. to the Present. Grossman, 1969. (8-up)

Ba-ST   BARON, VIRGINIA OLSEN, ed. The Seasons of Time: Tanka Poetry of Ancient Japan. Dial, 1968. (7-up) CC

Be-AP   BEIER, ULLI. African Poetry. Cambridge, 1966. (8-up)

Be-CS   ✓BEHN, HARRY, tr. Cricket Songs: Japanese Haiku. Brace World, 1964. (4-up) CC

Be-EB   BEERMAN, MIRIAM, ed. The Enduring Beast. Doubleday, 1972. (4-up)

Be-MA   BELL, BERNARD W., ed. Modern and Contemporary Afro-American Poetry. Allyn, 1972. (9-up)

Be-MC   BEHN, HARRY, tr. More Cricket Songs: Japanese Haiku. HarBraceJ, 1971. (4-up) CC

Be-UL   BENEDETTI, MARIO, ed. Unstill Life: An Introduction to the Spanish Poetry of Latin America. HarBraceJ, 1969. (9-up)

Bi-IT   BIERHORST, JOHN, ed. In the Trail of the Wind: American Indian Poems and Ritual Orations. Farrar, 1971. (7-up)

Bl-FP   BLY, ROBERT, ed. Forty Poems Touching on Recent American History. Beacon, 1970. (8-up)

Bl-OB   BLISHEN, EDWARD, ed. Oxford Book of Poetry for Children. Watts, 1964. (K-3)

Bo-AN   BONTEMPS, ARNA, ed. American Negro Poetry. Hill & Wang, 1963. (7-up)

Bo-CO   BOLTON, HENRY CARRINGTON. The Counting-Out Rhymes of Children. Singing Tree, 1969. (1-up)

Bo-FP   BOUTON, JOSEPHINE. Favorite Poems for the Children's Hour. Platt Munk, 1967. (1-5)

Bo-GJ   BOGAN, LOUISE and SMITH, WILLIAM J., eds. Golden Journey: Poems for Young People. Reilly & Lee, 1965. (PS-7) CC

Bo-HF   BONTEMPS, ARNA. Hold Fast to Dreams. Follett, 1969. (4-up)

Bo-RU   BOSLEY, KEITH, ed. Russia's Underground Poets. Praeger, 1969. (8-up)

Br-AF   BREWTON, SARA and BREWTON, JOHN E., eds. America Forever New: A Book of Poems. Crowell, 1968. (4-up) JHS

Br-BC   BREWTON, SARA and BREWTON, JOHN E. Birthday Candles Burning Bright, a Treasury of Birthday Poetry. Macmillan, 1960. (4-6)

Br-FF   BRIGGS, RAYMOND. Fee-Fi-Fo-Fum. Coward, 1964. (K-2)

Br-FW   BRANNEN, NOAH and ELLIOTT, WILLIAM, trs. Festive Wine: Ancient Japanese Poems from the Kinkafu. Weatherhill, 1969. (9-up)

Br-LL   BREWTON, SARA and BREWTON, JOHN E., eds. Laughable Limericks. Crowell, 1965. (4-up)

Br-MW BRANDON, WILLIAM, ed. The Magic World: American Indian Songs and Poems. Morrow, 1971. (7-up)

Br-SG BRAMBLETT, ELLA, ed. Shoots of Green, Poems for Young Gardeners. Crowell, 1968. (K-5)

Br-SM BREWTON, SARA and BREWTON, JOHN E., eds. Shrieks at Midnight: Macabre Poems, Eerie and Humorous. Crowell, 1969. (4-up) CC JHS

Br-SS BREWTON, SARA and BREWTON, JOHN E. Sing a Song of Seasons. Macmillan, 1955. (4-6)

Br-TC BRINNIN, JOHN MALCOLM and READ, BILL. Twentieth Century Poetry: American and British. McGraw, 1970. (9-up) SHS

Bu-DY BURROUGHS, MARGARET TAYLOR, comp. Did You Feed My Cow? Follett, 1969. (1-5)

Ca-BF CASSEDY, SYLVIA and SUETAKE, KUNIHIRO. Birds, Frogs, and Moonlight. Doubleday, 1967. (3-5) CC

Ca-BP CARRUTH, HAYDEN, ed. The Bird/Poem Book. McCall, 1970. (2-up)

Ca-MB CAUSLEY, CHARLES. Modern Ballads and Story Poems. Watts, 1964. JHS

Ca-MR CARLISLE, OLGA ANDREYEV and STYRON, ROSE, trs. Modern Russian Poetry. Viking, 1972. (7-up)

Ca-MU CASSEDY, SYLVIA and THAMPI, PARVATHI, trs. Moon Uncle, Moon Uncle: Rhymes from India. Doubleday, 1973. (K-3)

Ca-VT CARRUTH, HAYDEN, ed. The Voice That Is Great Within Us. Bantam, 1970. (10-up)

Ch-B FUJIKAWA, GYO, illus. A Child's Book of Poems. Grosset & Dunlap, 1969. (K-6)

Cl-DT CLARK, LEONARD, ed. Drums and Trumpets. DuFour, 1963. (4-8)

Cl-FC CLARK, LEONARD. Flutes and Cymbals. Crowell, 1969. (4-8) CC

Co-BB COLE, WILLIAM, ed. Beastly Boys and Ghastly Girls. Collins-World, 1964. (K-12)

Co-BBW COLE, WILLIAM, ed. The Birds and the Beasts Were There. Collins-World, 1963. (K-12)

Co-BL COLE, WILLIAM, ed. A Book of Love Poems. Viking, 1965. (7-up) JHS SHS

Co-BN COLE, WILLIAM, ed. A Book of Nature Poems. Viking, 1969. (6-up) CC JHS

Co-EL COLE, WILLIAM, ed. Eight Lines and Under. Macmillan, 1967. (6-up)

Co-FB COLE, WILLIAM, ed. The Fireside Book of Humorous Poetry. Simon & Schuster, 1959. (6-up)

Co-HP COLE, WILLIAM, ed. Humorous Poetry for Children. Collins-World, 1955. (4-10)

Co-IW COLE, WILLIAM. I Went to the Animal Fair, a Book of Animal Poems. Collins-World, 1958. (2-5)

Co-OH COLE, WILLIAM. Oh, How Silly! Viking, 1970. (4-6)

Co-OT COLE, WILLIAM. Oh, That's Ridiculous! Viking, 1972. (4-7)

Co-OW COLE, WILLIAM, ed. Oh, What Nonsense! Viking, 1966. (4-6)

Co-PI COLE, WILLIAM. Poems from Ireland. Crowell, 1972. CC JHS SHS

Co-PM COLE, WILLIAM, ed. Poems of Magic and Spells. Collins-World, 1960. (4-up) JHS

Co-PS COLE, WILLIAM, ed. Poems for Seasons and Celebrations. Collins-World, 1961. (K-12)

Co-PT COLE, WILLIAM, ed. The Poet's Tales, a New Book of Story Poems. Collins-World, 1971. (K-12) CC JHS

Co-PU COLE, WILLIAM, ed. Pick Me Up: A Book of Short, Short Poems. Macmillan, 1972. (5-up)

Co-RG COLUM, PADRAIC. Roofs of Gold: Poems to Read Aloud. Macmillan, 1964. CC JHS

Co-RM COLE, WILLIAM. Rough Men, Tough Men. Viking, 1969. (7-up)

Co-SS COLE, WILLIAM. The Sea, Ships and Sailors. Viking, 1967. JHS

Cr-SS CRAIG, M. JEAN, ed. The Sand, the Sea, and Me. Walker, 1972. (K-3)

Cr-WS CROMIE, ROBERT, ed. Where Steel Winds Blow. McKay, 1968. (8-up)

Da-SC DAY, A. GROVE, ed. The Sky Clears: Poetry of the American Indians. U of Nebraska, 1964. (4-12) SHS

De-CH DE LA MARE, WALTER. Come Hither, a Collection of Rhymes and Poems for the Young of All Ages. Knopf, 1957. (3-up) CC JHS

De-FS DERLETH, AUGUST, ed. Fire and Sleet and Candlelight. Arkham, 1961. (7-up)

De-PO DE ANGELI, MARGUERITE. A Pocket Full of Posies. Doubleday, 1961. (K-3)

De-PP DeFOREST, CHARLOTTE B. The Prancing Pony: Nursery Rhymes from Japan. Weatherhill, 1968. (1-7)

De-TT DE LA MARE, WALTER. Tom Tiddler's Ground. Knopf, 1962. (4-up)

Do-CH DOOB, LEONARD W. A Crocodile Has Me by the Leg. Walker, 1967. (4-up)

Do-TS Don't Tell the Scarecrow and Other Japanese Poems. Four Winds Pr., 1969. (K-4) CC

Do-WH DOWNIE, MARY ALICE. The Wind Has Wings: Poems from Canada. Walck, 1968. (4-7)

Du-RG DUNNING, STEPHEN, et al., eds. Reflections on a Gift of Watermelon Pickle and Other Modern Verse. Lothrop, 1967. (7-12) CC JHS

Du-SH DUNNING, STEPHEN, et al., eds. Some Haystacks Don't Even Have Any **Needle**: And Other Complete Modern Poems. Lothrop, 1969. (7-12) JHS

Em-AF EMRICH, DUNCAN. American Folk Poetry: An Anthology. Little, 1974. (4-up)

En-PC ENGLE, PAUL and LANGLAND, JOSEPH, eds. Poet's Choice. Dial, 1962. SHS

Er-FA ERNEST, P. EDWARD, ed. The Family Album of Favorite Poems. Grosset, 1959. (7-9)

Fe-FP FERRIS, HELEN, ed. Favorite Poems, Old and New. Doubleday, 1957. (4-up) CC JHS

Fe-PL FELLEMAN, HAZEL, ed. Poems That Live Forever. Doubleday, 1965. SHS

Fi-BG FIFE, AUSTIN and FIFE, ALTA, eds. Ballads of the Great West. Am. West, 1970. SHS

Fl-HH FLEMING, ALICE. Hosanna the Home Run: Poems about Sports. Little, 1972. (7-up)

Fo-OG FORBERG, ATI. On a Grass-Green Horn. Atheneum, 1965. JHS

Fr-MP FRANK, JOSETTE, ed. More Poems to Read to the Very Young. Random, 1968. (K-2)

Fr-WO FRANKENBERG, LLOYD. Wings of Rhyme. Funk, 1967. (K-4) CC

Ga-FB GANNETT, LEWIS, ed. The Family Book of Verse. Har-Row, 1961. (6-up)

Ga-S GARNETT, EMMELINE. Seasons; a Cycle of Verse. Farrar, 1966. (7-up)

Ge-TR GEREZ, TONI DE. Two-Rabbit, Seven-Wind; Poems from Ancient Mexico. Viking, 1971. (7-up)

Go-BP GOUDGE, ELIZABETH. A Book of Peace. Coward, 1967. (7-up)

Gr-BB GREEN, NORMA B. Bears, Bees, and Birch Trees: Russian Riddles and Rhymes. Doubleday, 1973. (1-5)

Gr-BT GREAVES, GRISELDA, ed. The Burning Thorn. Macmillan, 1971. (7-up)

Gr-CC GREGORY, HORACE and ZATURENSKA, MARYA. The Crystal Cabinet: An Invitation to Poetry. Holt, 1962. (5-7) JHS

Gr-CT GRIGSON, GEOFFREY, ed. The Cherry Tree. Vanguard, 1959. (7-up)

Gr-EC GROSS, SARAH CHOKLA. Every Child's Book of Verse. Watts, 1968. (4-8)

Gr-GB GRIGSON, GEOFFREY. The Gambit Book of Popular Verse. Gambit, 1971. (5-up)

Gr-SS GREGORY, HORACE and ZATURENSKA, MARYA. The Silver Swan: Poems of Romance and Mystery. Holt, 1966. (7-9)

Gr-TG GRAHAM, ELEANOR. A Thread of Gold, an Anthology of Poetry. Bodley Head, 1964. (6-up)

Ha-LO HANNUM, SARA and REED, GWENDOLYN. Lean Out of the Window. Atheneum, 1965. CC

Ha-PO HALL, DONALD. A Poetry Sampler. Watts, 1962. (6-up) JHS

Ha-TP HANNUM, SARA and CHASE, JOHN T., eds. To Play Man Number One. Atheneum, 1969. (8-up)

Ha-WR HANNUM, SARA and CHASE, JOHN T., eds. The Wind Is Round. Atheneum, 1970. (6-up)

Ha-YA HAZELTINE, ALICE I. and HAZELTINE, SMITH, comps. The Year Around: Poems for Children. Abingdon, 1956. (2-6)

Hi-FO HINE, AL, ed. From Other Lands: Poetry That Makes Poetry Live. Lippincott, 1969. (7-up)

Hi-GD HIMMLER, RONALD, ed. Glad Day and Other Classical Poems for Children. Putnam, 1972. (1-up)

Hi-TL HINE, AL, ed. This Land Is Mine: An Anthology of American Verse. Lippincott, 1965. (5-9) CC JHS

Hi-WP I HINDLEY, WINIFRED. A Wealth of Poetry. Basil Blackwell, 1963. Part I. (5-up)

Hi-WP II HINDLEY, WINIFRED. A Wealth of Poetry. Basil Blackwell, 1963. Part II. (5-up)

Ho-CS HOPKINS, LEE BENNETT, ed. The City Spreads Its Wings. Watts, 1970. (K-3)

Ho-CT HOPKINS, LEE BENNETT. City Talk. Knopf, 1970. (3-7)

Ho-GC HOPKINS, LEE BENNETT. girls can, too. Watts, 1972. (K-3)

Ho-LP HOWARD, CORALIE. Lyric Poems. Watts, 1968. (7-up) JHS

Ho-ME HOPKINS, LEE BENNETT. me! A Book of Poems. Seabury, 1970. (K-3)

Ho-P HOWARD, RICHARD. Preferences: Fifty-One American Poets Choose Poems from Their Own Work and from the Past. Viking, 1974. (7-up)

Ho-SD HOUSTON, JAMES, ed. Songs of the Dream People: Chants and Images from the Indians and Eskimos of North America. Atheneum, 1972. (4-up)

Ho-TH HOPKINS, LEE BENNETT, comp. Take Hold! An Anthology of Pulitzer Prize Winning Poems. Nelson, 1974. (9-up)

Ho-TY HOWE, IRVING and GREENBERG, ELIEZER, eds. A Treasury of Yiddish Poetry. Holt, 1969. SHS

Ho-WR HOLLANDER, JOHN and BLOOM, HAROLD, eds. The Wind and the Rain. Doubleday, 1961. (5-up)

Hs-TC HSU, KAI-YU, ed. and tr. Twentieth Century Chinese Poetry: An Anthology. Cornell, 1963. (7-up)

Hu-MP HUFFARD, GRACE THOMPSON, et al., eds. My Poetry Book: An Anthology of Modern Verse for Boys and Girls. Holt, 1956. (7-up) CC

Hu-NN HUGHES, LANGSTON, ed. New Negro Poets: U.S.A. Indiana, 1964. (7-up)

Hu-PN HUGHES, LANGSTON and BONTEMPS, ARNA, eds. The Poetry of the Negro, 1746-1970. Doubleday, 1970. JHS

Ir-BB IRESON, BARBARA. The Barnes Book of Nursery Verse. Barnes, 1960. (PS-2)

It-HB ITSE, ELIZABETH M., comp. Hey Bug! and Other Poems about Little Things. American Heritage, 1972. (K-up)

Ja-HH JACOBS, LELAND BLAIR, comp. Holiday Happenings in Limerick Land. Garrard, 1972. (2-4)

Ja-PA JACOBS, LELAND BLAIR, ed. Poetry for Autumn. Garrard, 1968. (2-4)

Ja-PC JACOBS, LELAND BLAIR, ed. Poetry for Chuckles and Grins. Garrard, 1968. (2-4)

Jo-SA JORDAN, JUNE, ed. Soulscript: Afro-American Poetry. Doubleday, 1970. (7-up)

Jo-TS JONES, HETTIE, comp. The Trees Stand Shining: The Poetry of the North American Indians. Dial, 1971. (1-up)

Jo-VC JORDAN, JUNE and BUSH, TERRI, eds. The Voice of the Children. Holt, 1970. (6-up) JHS

Ju-CP JUSTUS, MAY T. The Complete Peddler's Pack: Games, Songs, Rhymes and Riddles from Mountain Folklore. U of Tenn. Pr., 1967. (2-6)

Ke-PP KENSETH, ARNOLD, ed. Poems of Protest Old and New. Macmillan, 1968. (9-up)

Ke-TF KEYES, FRANCES PARKINSON. A Treasury of Favorite Poems. Hawthorn, 1963. (8-up)

Kh-VA KHERDIAN, DAVID, ed. Visions of America by the Poets of Our Time. Macmillan, 1973. (7-up)

Kr-OF KRAMER, AARON, ed. On Freedom's Side: An Anthology of American Poems of Protest. Macmillan, 1972. (7-up)

La-GI LARRICK, NANCY, ed. Green Is like a Meadow of Grass. Garrard, 1968. (1-7) CC

La-IH LARRICK, NANCY. I Heard a Scream in the Street: Poetry by Young People in the City. Evans, 1970. (5-10) CC JHS

La-OC LARRICK, NANCY, ed. On City Streets: An Anthology of Poetry. Evans, 1968. (5-8) JHS

La-PH LARRICK, NANCY, ed. Poetry for Holidays. Garrard, 1966. (3-5)

La-PP   LARRICK, NANCY, ed. Piper, Pipe That Song Again. Random, 1965. (3-7) CC

La-PV   LARRICK, NANCY, ed. Piping down the Valleys Wild; Poetry for the Young of All Ages. Delacorte, 1968. (3-up) CC JHS

808.81 P661

La-RM   LARRICK, NANCY, ed. Room for Me and a Mountain Lion: Poetry of Open Space. Evans, 1974. (5-9)

Le-IB   LEWIS, RICHARD, ed. I Breathe a New Song: Poems of the Eskimo. Simon & Schuster, 1971. (4-up) JHS

Le-IS   LEWIS, RICHARD, ed. In a Spring Garden. Dial, 1965. (4-up) CC

Le-M   LEWIS, RICHARD. Miracles: Poems by the Children of the English-Speaking World. Simon & Schuster, 1966. CC JHS

Le-MW   LEWIS, RICHARD. Moment of Wonder: A Collection of Chinese and Japanese Poetry. Dial, 1963. (7-up) CC

Le-OE   LEWIS, RICHARD. Out of the Earth I Sing. Norton, 1968. (4-up)

Le-SW   LEWIS, RICHARD. Still Waters of the Air: Poems by Three Modern Spanish Poets. Dial, 1970. (8-up) SHS

Le-TA   LEWIS, RICHARD. There Are Two Lives: Poems by the Children of Japan. Simon & Schuster, 1970. (3-up)

Le-WR   LEWIS, RICHARD. The Wind and the Rain, Children's Poems. Simon & Schuster, 1968. (3-7) CC

Li-LB   LINES, KATHLEEN, ed. Lavender's Blue. Watts, 1964. (K-3)

Li-LC   LIVINGSTON, MYRA COHN, ed. Listen, Children, Listen: An Anthology of Poems for the Very Young. HarBraceJ, 1972. (K-4)

Li-SR   LIVINGSTON, MYRA COHN. Speak Roughly to Your Little Boy: A Collection of Parodies and Burlesques. HarBraceJ, 1971. (7-up)

Li-TU   LIVINGSTON, MYRA COHN. A Tune Beyond Us: A Collection of Poetry. HarBraceJ, 1968. (6-up) JHS

Lo-IT   LOWENFELS, WALTER. In a Time of Revolution: Poems from Our Third World. Random, 1969. (9-up)

Lo-LL   LOVE, KATHERINE, ed. A Little Laughter. Crowell, 1957. (4-up) CC

Lo-TY   LOMAX, ALAN and ABDUL, RAOUL, eds. 3000 Years of Black Poetry. Dodd, 1970. SHS

Ls-NY   LASK, THOMAS, ed. The New York Times Book of Verse. Macmillan, 1970. (7-up)

Ma-BB   MANNING-SANDERS, RUTH, ed. A Bundle of Ballads. Lippincott, 1959. (6-10) JHS

Ma-BH   MARY-ROUSSELAIRE, GUY, illus. Beyond the High Hills. Collins-World, 1971. (3-7) CC

Ma-FO   MANNHEIM, GRETE. Feather or Fur. Knopf, 1967. (K-4)

808.81 M192F

Ma-FW   MACKAY, DAVID, ed. A Flock of Words: An Anthology of Poetry for Children and Others. HarBraceJ, 1970. (6-up)

Ma-YA   MARSHALL, SHIRLEY E. A Young American's Treasury of English Poetry: From the Early Middle Ages to the Twentieth Century. Washington Square, 1967. (9-up)

Mc-AC   McGREGOR-HASTIE, ROY, ed. Anthology of Contemporary Romanian Poetry. Dufour, 1969. (9-up)

Mc-AW   McEWEN, CATHERINE SCHAEFER. Away We Go! One Hundred Poems for the Very Young. Crowell, 1956. (PS-3)

Mc-EA   McCULLOUGH, FRANCES MONSON. Earth, Air, Fire and Water. Coward, 1971. (6-up)

Mc-PR   McFERRAN, ANN, ed. Poems to Be Read Aloud. Nelson, 1965. (4-up)

Mc-WK   McDONALD, GERALD D., comp. A Way of Knowing: A Collection of Poems for Boys. Crowell, 1959. JHS

Mc-WS   McGINLEY, PHYLLIS, ed. Wonders and Surprises: A Collection of Poems. Lippincott, 1968. (7-up) JHS

Me-PH   MEZEY, ROBERT, ed. Poems from the Hebrew. Crowell, 1973. (9-up)

Me-WF   MENDOZA, GEORGE, comp. The World from My Window. Hawthorn, 1969. (9-up)

Mo-BG   MOLLOY, PAUL, ed. Beach Glass and Other Poems. Four Winds, 1970. (7-up)

Mo-CC   HOFFMANN, HILDE. The City and Country Mother Goose. American Heritage, 1969. (1-2)

Mo-GR   MORSE, DAVID. Grandfather Rock: The New Poetry and the Old. Delacorte, 1972. (7-up)

Mo-MGT   Mother Goose Treasury. Coward, 1966. (PS-3) CC

Mo-MI   MORTON, MIRIAM. The Moon Is like a Silver Sickle: A Celebration of Poetry by Russian Children. Simon & Schuster, 1972. (5-up)

Mo-NR   Mother Goose Nursery Rhymes. Watts, 1969. (4-6) CC

Mo-SD   MORRISON, LILLIAN, comp. Sprints and Distances: Sports in Poetry and the Poetry in Sport. Crowell, 1965. (4-up) CC JHS

Mo-TB   MORRISON, LILLIAN. Touch Blue. Crowell, 1958. (4-up)

Mo-TL   MONTGOMERIE, NORAH, ed. This Little Pig Went to Market. Watts, 1966. (K-3)

Mo-TS   MOORE, LILLIAN and THURMAN, JUDITH, comps. To See the World Afresh. Atheneum, 1974. (6-up)

Na-EO   NASH, OGDEN, comp. Everybody Ought to Know. Lippincott, 1961. JHS SHS

Ne-AM   NESS, EVALINE. Amelia Mixed the Mustard and Other Poems. Scribner, 1975. (1-5)

Ni-CD   NIATUM, DUANE, ed. Carriers of the Dream Wheel. Har-Row, 1975. (9-up)

Ni-JP   NIEBLING, RICHARD F., ed. A Journey of Poems. Delacorte, 1964. (5-up)

No-CL   NORMAN, CHARLES. Come Live with Me. McKay, 1966. (7-up)

On-TW   One, Two, Buckle My Shoe. Doubleday, 1964. (K-3)

Op-ON   OPIE, IONA and OPIE, PETER, eds. The Oxford Dictionary of Nursery Rhymes. Clarendon, 1962. (PS-3)

Ox-BB   Oxford Book of Ballads. Ed. by James Kinsley. Clarendon, 1969. (6-up)

Ox-BC   OPIE, IONA and OPIE, PETER, eds. The Oxford Book of Children's Verse. Oxford, 1973. (3-7)

Ox-BN   The Oxford Book of Nineteenth-Century English Verse. Ed. by John Hayward. Clarendon, 1964. (8-up) SHS

821.7082 Ox2

Pa-AP   PARSONS, VIRGINIA. Animal Parade. Doubleday, 1970. (1-5)

Pa-GTB   PALGRAVE, FRANCIS. Golden Treasury of the Best Songs and Lyrical Poems in the English Language. Clarendon, 1964. (5-up) JHS SHS

821.082 P175 G5

Pa-HT PARKER, ELINOR, ed. Here and There;
       100 Poems about Places. Crowell,
       1967. (4-up) JHS

Pa-MV PALANDRI, ANGELA C. Y. Jung, tr.
       Modern Verse from Taiwan.
       U of California. (9-up)

Pa-OM PARKER, ELINOR, ed. 100 More Story
       Poems. Crowell, 1960. (7-up)
       CC JHS

Pa-RE PALMER, GEOFFREY and LLOYD, NOEL, eds.
       Round about Eight: Poems for
       Today. Warne, 1972. CC

Pa-SG PARKER, ELINOR, comp. The Singing and
       the Gold: Poems Translated from
       World Literature. Crowell, 1962.
       CC JHS

Pe-FB PETERSON, ISABEL. The First Book of
       Poetry. Watts, 1954. (4-7)

Pe-M   PECK, RICHARD, ed. Mindscapes: Poems
       for the Real World. Delacorte,
       1971. (7-up)

Pe-OA PERRINE, LAURENCE and REID, JAMES M.,
       eds. One Hundred American Poems
       of the Twentieth Century.
       HarBraceJ, 1966. (9-12)

Pe-SS PECK, RICHARD. Sounds and Silences:
       Poetry for Now. Delacorte, 1970.
       (6-up)

Pl-EI PLOTZ, HELEN, ed. The Earth Is the
       Lord's: Poems of the Spirit.
       Crowell, 1965. (4-up) CC JHS

Pl-IO PLOTZ, HELEN, ed. Imagination's Other
       Place: Poems of Science and Mathe-
       matics. Crowell, 1955. (7-11) JHS

Pl-ML PLOTZ, HELEN. The Marvellous Light:
       Poets and Poetry. Crowell, 1970.
       (6-up) JHS

Pl-US PLOTZ, HELEN, ed. Untune the Sky:
       Poems of Music and the Dance.
       Crowell, 1957. (7-up) JHS

Ra-BP RANDALL, DUDLEY, ed. The Black Poets.
       Bantam, 1971. (9-up)

Rd-OA REED, GWENDOLYN, ed. Out of the Ark:
       An Anthology of Animal Poems.
       Atheneum, 1968. (5-up) CC JHS

Rd-SS REED, GWENDOLYN, ed. Songs the Sandman
       Sings. Atheneum, 1969. (PS-3)

Re-BS REED, GWENDOLYN, ed. Bird Songs.
       Atheneum, 1969. (2-7) CC

Re-PF REES, ENNIS. Pun Fun. Abelard, 1965.
       (2-6)

Re-RR REES, ENNIS. Riddles, Riddles Every-
       where. Abelard, 1964. (3-7)

Re-TW READ, HERBERT, ed. This Way, Delight.
       Pantheon, 1956. (4-9) CC JHS

Rv-CB REEVES, JAMES, ed. Cassell Book of
       English Verse. Har-Row, 1965.
       (9-12) SHS

Rv-ON REEVES, JAMES, comp. One's None.
       Watts, 1968. (K-3)

Rx-LT REXROTH, KENNETH. Love and the Turning
       Year: One Hundred More Poems from
       the Chinese. New Directions, 1970.
       (7-up)

Rx-OH REXROTH, KENNETH, tr. One Hundred
       Poems from the Chinese. New
       Directions, 1967. (7-up)

Sa-B   SALKEY, ANDREW, ed. Breaklight: The
       Poetry of the Caribbean.
       Doubleday, 1971. (8-up)

Sc-TN SCHREIBER, RON. 31 New American Poets.
       Hill, 1969. SHS

Se-PR SECHRIST, ELIZABETH HOUGH. Poems for
       Red Letter Days. Macrae, 1951.
       (3-7)

Sh-AM SHIFFERT, EDITH and SAWA, YUKI, trs.
       Anthology of Modern Japanese Poetry.
       Tuttle, 1972. (7-up)

Sh-AP SHAPIRO, KARL. American Poetry.
       Crowell, 1960. (9-up)

Sh-RP SHELDON, WILLIAM D. The Reading of
       Poetry. Allyn, 1963. (4-7)

Sm-LG SMITH, JANET ADAM, comp. The Looking
       Glass Book of Verse. Random, 1959.
       (6-up)

Sm-MK SMITH, JOHN, ed. My Kind of Verse.
       Macmillan, 1968. (5-7)

Sm-PT SMITH, CHARD PONERS, ed. Poets of the
       Twenties: 100 Great Poems.
       McCutcheon, 1967. (8-up)

Sp-AS SPIER, PETER. And So My Garden Grows.
       Doubleday, 1969. (K-3)

Sp-HW SPIER, PETER, illus. Hurrah, We're
       Outward Bound. Doubleday, 1968.
       (2-4) CC

Sp-OG SPAULDING, SUSAN THOMPSON and SPAULDING,
       FRANCIS T. Open Gates. Books for
       Libraries, 1970. (4-8)

Sp-TM SPIER, PETER, illus. To Market! To
       Market! Doubleday, 1967. (2-4) CC

St-FS STEPHENSON, MARJORIE, comp. Fives,
       Sixes, and Sevens. Warne, 1968.
       (K-3)

St-H   STRYK, LUCIEN, ed. Heartland: Poets
       of the Midwest. Northern Illinois,
       1967. (9-up)

Su-FVI SUMMERFIELD, GEOFFREY. First Voices.
       Knopf, 1970. (K-4)

Te-FC TEDLOCK, DENNIS, tr. Finding the
       Center: Narrative Poetry of the
       Zuni Indians. Dial, 1972. (7-up)

Th-AS THOMPSON, BLANCHE JENNINGS, ed. All
       the Silver Pennies. Macmillan,
       1967. (1-6) CC

To-MP TOWNSEND, JOHN ROWE. Modern Poetry:
       A Selection. Lippincott, 1974.
       (7-up)

Tr-CB TRASK, WILLARD R., ed. Classic Black
       African Poems. Eakins, 1971.
       (5-up)

Tr-MR TRAPP, JACOB, ed. Modern Religious
       Poems: A Contemporary Anthology.
       Har-Row, 1964. (7-up)

Tr-US I TRASK, WILLARD R. The Unwritten Song:
       Poetry of the Primitive and Tradi-
       tional Peoples of the World.
       Macmillan, 1966. Volume I. (7-up)

Tr-US II TRASK, WILLARD R. The Unwritten Song:
       Poetry of the Primitive and Tradi-
       tional Peoples of the World.
       Macmillan, 1966. Volume II. (7-up)

Tu-WW TUDOR, TASHA, ed. Wings from the Wind:
       An Anthology of Poetry. Lippincott,
       1964. (K-6) CC

Un-GB UNTERMEYER, LOUIS. The Golden Book of
       Poems for the Very Young. Western,
       1971. (PS-3)

Un-GF UNTERMEYER, LOUIS. The Golden Book of
       Fun and Nonsense. Golden, 1970.
       (4-up)

Un-GT UNTERMEYER, LOUIS. The Golden Treasury
       of Poetry. Golden, 1959. CC

Un-MA UNTERMEYER, LOUIS, ed. Modern American
       Poetry. HarBraceJ, 1962. (9-up) JHS

Un-MB UNTERMEYER, LOUIS, ed. Modern British
       Poetry. HarBraceJ, 1962. (9-up) JHS

Un-MW UNTERMEYER, LOUIS. Men and Women: The
       Poetry of Love. American Heritage,
       1970. (9-up)

Un-R   UNTERMEYER, JEAN STARR, comp. and tr.
       Re-Creations. Norton, 1971. (9-up)

Vi-PP VINCENT, JEAN ANNE, comp. Patriotic

Poems America Loves: 125 Poems Commemorating Stirring American Events
and American Ideals. Doubleday,
1968. (5-up)

We-PZ   WEISS, RENÉE KAROL, ed. A Paper Zoo, A
Collection of Animal Poems by Modern
American Poets. Macmillan, 1968.
(K-2)

Wi-LT   WILLIAMS, OSCAR, ed. A Little Treasury
of Modern Poetry: English and
American. Scribner, 1970. CC JHS SHS

Wi-MG   WILDSMITH, BRIAN, illus. Mother Goose,
A Collection of Nursery Rhymes.
Watts, 1964. (K-3) CC

Wo-HS   WOOD, NANCY. Hollering Sun. Simon &
Schuster, 1972. (5-up)

Wo-JR   WORSTELL, EMMA VIETOR. Jump the
Rope Jingles. Macmillan, 1961.
(K-up)

Wr-RM   WRIGHT, BLANCHE FISHER. The Real
Mother Goose. Hale, 1965. (K-2) CC

Wy-CM   WYNDHAM, ROBERT, ed. Chinese Mother
Goose Rhymes. Collins-World, 1968.
(PS-3)

Subject Index

HOW TO USE THIS INDEX

The subject headings are in capital letters and are arranged alphabetically, with cross references serving as guides to additional or substitute headings.

The titles of poems are arranged alphabetically under the subject headings. The author's name follows; there is no indication of an anonymous author. The title and the author's name are given as they appear in the anthology. If the title varied in collections the one most frequently used was chosen. The coded symbols for the anthologies in which this poem appears and the pages on which it appears conclude the citation.

A complete book or part of a book about one subject is indicated at the end of the citations on that subject, as follows:

SKIPPING ROPE
See also Wo-JR

ABARIM MOUNTAINS
   Mount Avarim. J. Halevi. Me-PH:60
ABBEY THEATRE
   An Old Woman, Outside the Abbey
      Theater. L. Strong. Co-FB:352,
      Un-MB:393
ABBEYS: see CATHEDRALS; CONVENTS AND
      NUNNERIES; and names of abbeys,
      as WESTMINSTER ABBEY
ABBOTS: see MONKS
ABBREVIATIONS: see HUMOR - ABBREVIATIONS
ABDUCTION: see KIDNAPPING
ABEL: see CAIN AND ABEL
ABÉLARD AND HÉLOÏSE
   Eloise to Abelard. A. Pope.
      Al-VBP:535
ABERFELDY, SCOT.
   The Birks of Aberfeldy. R. Burns.
      Al-VBP:643
ABILITY: see also LEADERSHIP; SKILL
   Hide Not Your Talents. . . .
      B. Franklin. Un-GT:25
   I Bless This Man. Pindar. Mo-SD:181
   The Radiance of Creativity.
      O. Beshenkovskaya. Mo-MI:82
   Rue St. Honore. P. Williamson.
      Ls-NY:242
   What a Piece of Work Is Man.
      Sophocles. Pa-SG:194
ABOLITIONISTS: see names of abolition-
      ists, as TUBMAN, HARRIET ROSS
ABOMINABLE SNOWMEN: see HUMOR -
      ABOMINABLE SNOWMEN
ABORIGINES: see names of native races
ABORTION: see also THE UNBORN
   The Abortion. A. Sexton. Ca-VT:636
   the mother. G. Brooks. Be-MA:79
   The Vow. A. Hecht. En-PC:199
ABRAHAM: see also HAGAR; ISAAC;
      MELCHIZEDEK, KING OF SALEM;
      SARAH, WIFE OF ABRAHAM
   Abraham. E. Muir. Tr-MR:67
   Abraham and Isaac. Ga-S:40, Ma-FW:78
   Abraham Takes Isaac to the Sacrifice.
      I. Manger. Ho-TY:275

Ballad of the Trial of Sodom. V. Watkins.
      Tr-MR:68
Hagar's Last Night in Abraham's House.
      I. Manger. Ho-TY:277
The Parable of the Old Men and the
      Young. W. Owen. Go-BP:207,
      Ma-FW:250, Mo-GR:18
Story of Isaac. L. Cohen. Mo-GR:16
ABSALOM
   Evening. E. Sitwell. Ca-MB:55
   The Love of King David and the Fair
      Bethsabe, 1. G. Peele. Al-VBP:137
ABSENCE: see also LONGING
   Absence. R. Bridges. Go-BP:130
   Absence. J. Burden. Ls-NY:10
   The Absence. S. Warner. Un-MB:32
   Absences. P. Larkin. En-PC:202
   Adrian Henri's Talking after Christmas
      Blues. A. Henri. Gr-BT:73
   For a Husband Away. Tr-CB:45,
      Tr-US I:46
   In Honor of Maros During His Absence
      at Sea. Tr-US I:216
   Letter to N. Y. E. Bishop.
      Br-TC:47, Mc-WS:116
   The Mistress. J. Wilmot. Al-VBP:502
   Present in Absence. Pa-GTB:6
   Remember. C. Rossetti. Al-VBP:995,
      De-CH:264, Fe-PL:98, Ga-FB:68,
      Hi-WP I:87, OX-BN:705, Un-MW:90
   Robin Adair. C. Keppel. De-TT:154
   A Song. J. Wilmot. Al-VBP:503
   Song for Someone Who Is Absent.
      Co-CH:(42)
   Sonnets XCVIII. W. Shakespeare.
      Al-VBP:206, Gr-CT:46
   The Sonnets. W. Shakespeare. No-CL:88,
      Pa-GTB:8, RV-CB:237, Un-MW:182
   The Spring. A. Cowley. No-CL:274
   To a Distant Friend. W. Wordsworth.
      Pa-GTB:189, Rv-CB:651
   To Amoret Gone from Him. H. Vaughan.
      Rv-CB:407
   To Lucasta, on Going Beyond the Seas.
      R. Lovelace. Al-VBP:445, Pa-GTB:82

ABSENCE — cont'd.
  Winter Remembered. J. Ransom.
    Ca-VT:147, Rv-CB:985
  Without Her. D. Rossetti. Al-VBP:989
    Rv-CB:881
ACACIA TREES
  And Mr. Ferritt. J. Wright. Un-MB:516
  Esthetique du Mal, II. W. Stevens.
    Wi-LT:151
ACCIDENTS: see also AMBULANCES; HUMOR -
    ACCIDENTS
  The Accident. R. Patterson. Ad-CI:102
  The Armful. R. Frost. Li-TU:163
  At 79th and Park. B. Howes. Pe-M:16
  Auto Wreck. K. Shapiro. Ca-VT:471,
    Ma-FW:131, Mo-BG:30, Pe-OA:224,
    Pe-SS:70, Wi-LT:535
  The Ballad of Billy Rose. L. Norris,
    Ca-MB:83
  Beautiful V Shape. Lo Men. Pa-MV:126
  Buff. Mo-MGT:212
  Bump, Bump, Please Go Away. Wy-CM:36
  Bump on My Knee. M. Livingston.
    Ho-ME:26
  Charm to Cure Burns. Su-FVI:48
  Choti Lal. Ca-MU:25
  Death of a Dog. B. Deutsch.
    Du-SH:119
  The Death of the Sports-Car Driver.
    J. Aaron. Pe-M:91
  Death on a Live Wire. M. Baldwin.
    Ca-MB:88
  The Deaths at Paragon, Indiana. J.
    Woods. St-H:250
  Doctor Foster. Bo-FP:133, Co-OW:42,
    Fr-WO:22, Ir-BB:42, Li-LB:70,
    Mo-MGT:43, Mo-NR:22, Wi-MG:14,
    Wr-RM:36
  Falling in the Creek. I. Heke. Le-M:65
  A Farmer Went Trotting. Ar-TP3:122,
    Br-FF:(28), Gr-EC:285, Li-LB:144,
    Mo-MGT:129, Mo-NR:67, Na-EO:123,
    Wr-RM:123
  Father and Mother and Uncle John.
    Mo-TL:83, Sp-TM:17
  The Game. Ca-MU:25
  Ginevra. S. Rogers. Fe-PL:13
  Ginger. Mo-MGT:88
  Hic, Hoc, the Carrion Crow. Ir-BB:149
  I Want to Laugh. Ho-SD:69, Le-IB:72
  It's Here in the. R. Atkins.
    Ad-PB:197, Bo-AN:171, Jo-SA:98,
    Pe-SS:149
  It's Raining. Ir-BB:211, Mo-CC:(48),
    Mo-MGT:75
  Jack and Jill. Au-SP:7, Bo-FP:104,
    De-PO:26, Er-FA:504, Fr-WO:9,
    Ir-BB:93, Li-LB:37, Mo-CC:(24),
    Mo-MGT:46, Mo-NR:18, Wi-MG:58,
    Wr-RM:16
  Jenny. Mo-MGT:183
  Malfunction. R. Albert. Du-SH:165,
    Pe-M:94

  The Milkman. Mo-MGT:158
  Now We Are Sick. J. Morton. Co-PU:29,
    Li-SR:63
  Obituary. K. Fearing. Ca-VT:237
  'Out, Out--' R. Frost. Ca-VT:11,
    Gr-BT:18, Pe-M:100
  Pickeleem, Pickeleem. Ir-BB:149
  Pussy-Cat Mew. Bo-FP:30, Ir-BB:167,
    Wr-RM:83
  Robin-A-Bobbin. Mo-MGT:94, Wr-RM:33
  The Scarred Girl. J. Dickey. Du-SH:69
  The Story of Johnny Head-in-Air.
    H. Hoffmann. Ox-BC:206
  To a Mouse. R. Burns. Co-BBW:36,
    Er-FA:226, Fe-PL:367, Hu-MP:190,
    Mc-WK:60, Pa-GTB:141, Rd-OA:24,
    Rv-CB:616, Sp-OG:297
  The Yachts. W. Williams. Al-VBP:1154,
    Fl-HH:27, Ma-FW:51, Pe-OA:73,
    Pe-SS:72, Sm-PT:112, Un-MA:262,
    Wi-LT:194
ACCORDIONS
  A Man with a Little Pleated Piano.
    W. Welles. Fe-FP:249
ACHIEVEMENT: see also SUCCESS
  Action. S. Davis. Ke-TF:251
  Canto LXXXI. E. Pound. Al-VBP:1165,
    Pe-OA:83
  Critics and Connoisseurs. M. Moore.
    Pe-OA:98
  The Farmer's Boy. Cl-DT:83
  The Heart's Desire Is Full of Sleep.
    R. Pitter. Go-BP:223
  It Couldn't Be Done. E. Guest. Er-FA:7
  It Is Too Late. H. Longfellow.Fe-PL:304
  Notes Found near a Suicide: To James.
    F. Horne. Bo-AN:45, Bo-HF:90,
    Br-BC:124, Ra-BP:73
  The Sum of All Known Reverence.
    W. Whitman. Tr-MR:161
  We Never Know How High. E. Dickinson.
    Mc-WK:98, Sh-AP:131
  Where There's a Will There's a Way.
    E. Cook. Er-FA:26
ACHILLES: see HUMOR - ACHILLES
ACORNS
  Acorn Bill. R. Ainsworth. St-FS:15
ACROBATS: see also AGILITY; CIRCUSES;
    SOMERSAULTS
  The Acrobat from Xanadu Disdained All
    Nets. D. Georgakas. Sc-TN:60
  A Circus Garland. R. Field. Au-SP:124
  The Man on the Flying Trapeze.
    Co-PT:198, Er-FA:448, Sm-LG:357
  The Performance. J. Dickey. Wi-LT:688
  Trapezists. D. Aldan. Ls-NY:278
ACROSTICS
  The Feast Day. A. McDonnall. Bo-FP:159
ACTION RHYMES: see also CLAPPING GAMES;
    COUNTING-OUT RHYMES; DANDLING RHYMES;
    FACE RHYMES; FEEDING RHYMES; FINGER
    AND HAND PLAY; FOOT PLAY; GAME RHYMES;
    JOGGING RHYMES; ROCKING RHYMES;

SEARCHING AND FINDING RHYMES; SINGING
GAMES; TICKLING GAMES; TOSSING AND
CATCHING RHYMES
Charlie Chaplin Went to France.
Er-FA:499
Jenny Wren.   Wr-RM:110
The Lost Shoe.   Wr-RM:121
See also Em-AF:27-50
ACTORS AND ACTING: see also names of
actors, as CHAPLIN, CHARLES
Between the Acts.   S. Kunitz.   Co-EL:101
David Garrick.   O. Goldsmith.   Rv-CB:543
Hamlet.   B. Pasternak.   Ca-MR:174
Mad Actor.   J. Montague.   Ls-NY:136
A Memory of the Players in a Mirror at
Midnight.   J. Joyce.   Al-VBP:1151
Sarah Bernhardt.   B. Akhmadulina.
Bo-RU:3
ADAM AND EVE: see also EDEN; HUMOR -
ADAM AND EVE; LILITH
Adam.   R. Rilke.   Tr-MR:64
Adam and Eve.   J. Milton, No-CL:52
Adam and Eve.   K. Shapiro.   Sh-AP:217
Adam Lay Ibounden.   De-CH:468, Ga-S:39,
Gr-CT:83, Gr-TG:82, Ma-YA:26, Rv-CB:9
The Animals Mourn with Eve.
C. Rossetti.   Rd-OA:197
The Discovery.   M. Gibbon.   Co-PI:49
Eve.   Y. Fichman.   Me-PH:82
Eve.   D. Gascoyne.   Pa-GTB:550
Eve.   R. Hodgson.   De-CH:465, Ha-PO:41,
Hi-WP II:95, Na-EO:105, Pa-OM:286,
Sm-MK:58, Un-MB:186, Wi-LT:123
Eve.   R. Rilke.   Tr-MR:65
Eve.   C. Rossetti.   De-CH:466,
Pa-GTB:375
The Fourth God.   C. Smith.   Sm-PT:83
The Garden.   A. Marvell.   Al-VBP:457,
Fe-PL:381, Ha-PO:202, Pa-GTB:92,
Rv-CB:403
I Am Eve.   Co-PI:133, De-CH:767
Imperial Adam.   A. Hope.   Un-MW:126
Never Again Would Birds' Songs Be the
Same.   R. Frost.   Ca-VT:19
Paradise Lost 2.   J. Milton.
Al-VBP:410
Song with Words.   J. Agee.   Un-MA:606
These Bones Gwine to Rise Agin.
Ga-S:24
Thus Eve to Adam.   J. Milton.
Ga-FB:42
Vampire Bride.   F. Stefanile.
De-FS:190
The World Was Meant to Be Peaceful.
V. Bryant.   Ba-HI:47
ADAMS, JOHN
America Was Promises.   A. MacLeish.
Br-AF:250, Vi-PP:229
John Adams.   R. & S. Benet.   Vi-PP:142
ADAPTABILITY
Ben Franklin's Head (1728).   M. Howe.
Mc-WK:89

I'll Walk the Tightrope.   M. Danner.
Bd-MA:87
Iron.   B. Brecht.   Ho-LP:39
The Manoeuvre.   W. Williams.   Ha-LO:28
Pavlov.   N. Madgett.   Ra-BP:196
To Turn Back.   J. Haines.   Co-BN:227
White Season.   R. Frost.   Ar-TP3:62,
Co-BBW:38, Fe-FP:167
ADDISON, JOSEPH: see SATIRE - ADDISON,
JOSEPH
ADJUSTMENT: see ADAPTABILITY
ADMIRALS
Admiral Benbow.   Co-RM:66, Rv-CB:420
Admirals All.   H. Newbolt.   Co-RM:51
ADMIRALTY ISLANDS
Song of a Woman Named Hi Pak.   Hi Pak.
Tr-US I:207
ADOLESCENCE: see also BOYS; GIRLS
Mysteries.   Y. Yevtushenko.   Ca-MR:52
Portrait of a Girl with a Comic Book.
P. McGinley.   Pe-OA:198, Pe-SS:39
Sunday Afternoon.   D. Levertov.
Pe-SS:55
ADONIS
Venus and Adonis.   W. Browne.   No-CL:57
"Venus with Young Adonis. . . ."
B. Griffin.   Al-VBP:91
ADVENTURE AND ADVENTURERS: see also ESCAPE;
EXPLORERS; HEROES AND HEROISM; HUMOR -
ADVENTURE AND ADVENTURERS; PIONEERS AND
PIONEER LIFE; QUESTS; SATIRE - ADVENTURE
AND ADVENTURERS; SEAFARING LIFE;
WANDERLUST
Adventures.   A. Kramer.   Br-BC:116
The Bearer of Evil Tidings.   R. Frost.
Rv-CB:968
The Belfry.   L. Binyon.   De-CH:200
The Boy.   R. Rilke.   Sm-MK:165
Boys Will Be Princes.   W. Heyen.
Ls-NY:92
The Child and the Mariner.   W. Davies.
De-CH:383
Childe Harold.   M. Kulbak.   Ho-TY:205
Creep.   L. Kershaw.   Le-M:63
Down the Glimmering Staircase.
S. Sassoon.   Fe-PL:413
Eldorado.   E. Poe.   Ho-WR:248,
Mc-PR:177, Mc-WK:174, Mo-BG:11,
Pa-HT:153, Sh-RP:284, Sm-LG:204
The Emperor's Double.   R. Gittings.
Ls-NY:142
For to Admire.   R. Kipling.   Un-MB:140
A Gest of Robyn Hode, The Seventh
Fytte.   Ox-BB:475
I Want to Go Wandering.   V. Lindsay.
Pa-HT:72
I'll Sail upon the Dog-Star.
T. Durfey.   Ir-BB:107, Pa-RE:89,
Rv-CB:481, Sm-LG:205
The Insult.   Co-RM:20
Ithaka.   C. Cavafy.   Ni-JP:15
The Janitor's Boy.   N. Crane.   Fe-PL:236,
Un-GT:165

ADVENTURE AND ADVENTURERS — cont'd.
Jock o' Hazeldean. W. Scott.
  De-TT:109, Pa-GTB:183
Johnny Fife and Johnny's Wife.
  M. Meigs. Ar-TP3:95, Au-SP:161
Kilroy. P. Viereck. Hi-TL:211,
  Un-MA:657
The Ladies. R. Kipling. Ke-TF:243,
  Un-MB:128
The Laird o' Logie. De-CH:412,
  Rv-CB:49
The Land of Story-Books. R. Stevenson.
  Ar-TP3:114, Fe-FP:12, Hu-MP:23,
  Ja-PA:50, Un-GB:30, Un-GT:12
Legend. J. Wright. Co-PT:179,
  Ma-FW:192
Lone Founts. H. Melville.
  Al-VBP:955
Madman's Song. E. Wylie. Ha-LO:90,
  Th-AS:213, Un-MA:275
My Hat. S. Smith. Sm-MK:78
O Boys! O Boys! O. Gogarty.
  Co-PI:50
Old Gray Squirrel. A. Noyes.
  Co-SS:215
The Peddler's Caravan. W. Rands.
  Au-SP:150, Bl-OB:145, Bo-FP:130,
  Hu-MP:166
Pirate Story. R. Stevenson. Ar-TP3:114,
  Fe-FP:108, Un-GB:9, Un-GT:10
Reveille. A. Housman. Er-FA:20,
  Fe-PL:398, No-CL:121, Un-MB:93,
  Wi-LT:59
Rose the Red and White Lilly. Ox-BB:189
Rumilda's Chant. G. Darley. Co-PI:33,
  Co-SS:31, Gr-CT:222
Sea Fever. J. Masefield. Ar-TP3:90,
  Co-SS:55, Fe-FP:190, Fe-PL:440,
  Ga-FB:182, Hu-MP:174, La-PV:185,
  Ma-YA:232, Mc-PR:134, Pe-FB:43,
  Sh-RP:33, Th-AS:127, Un-MB:221
The Secret of the Sea. H. Longfellow.
  Un-GT:261
A Ship for Singapore. D. Hicky.
  Th-AS:129
Sons of the Kings. J. Agnew. Br-BC:62
A Swing Song. W. Allingham. Ch-B:111,
  Fe-FP:110, Hu-MP:35, Pe-FB:66
There Is No Frigate like a Book.
  E. Dickinson. Bo-GJ:218, Br-SS:76,
  Fe-FP:13, Fe-PL:297, Gr-EC:126,
  Ha-YA:131, Hu-MP:26, Un-MA:97
To My Son. S. Sassoon. Mc-WS:137
Tony O. C. Francis. Bl-OB:19,
  Ch-B:72, Co-PM:147, De-CH:357
Travel. E. Millay. Ar-TP3:87,
  Bo-HF:43, Fe-FP:190, Hu-MP:169,
  La-PP:40, Sh-RP:99, Th-AS:151
Travel. R. Stevenson. Ar-TP3:96,
  Bo-HF:26, Fe-FP:459, Hu-MP:178,
  Mc-WK:190, Pa-HT:84, Sm-LG:104,
  Un-GT:263
The Two Travellers. C. Boland. Co-PI:11

Voices. J. Hearst. Th-AS:128
When I Came from Colchis. W. Merwin.
  Ca-VT:612
When I Grow Up. R. Holland. Br-BC:116
The Wraggle Taggle Gipsies. Ar-TP3:15,
  De-CH:75, Fe-FP:509, Ho-WR:48, Hu-MP:
  155, Mc-WS:163, Na-EO:33, Re-TW:124,
  Rv-CB:436, Un-GT:96
ADVERTISING: see HUMOR - ADVERTISING;
  SATIRE - ADVERTISING
ADVICE: see also HUMOR - ADVICE; SATIRE -
  ADVICE; WARNINGS
Abraham Scolds Lot. I. Manger.
  Ho-TY:274
Address to My Soul. E. Wylie.
  Tr-MR:252, Wi-LT:208
Advice to a Girl. T. Campion.
  Al-VBP:215, Ma-YA:72, Un-MW:35
Advice to a Prophet. R. Wilbur.
  Un-MA:677
Advice to Children and Their Parents.
  Gr-TG:13
Advice to Small Children. E. Anthony.
  Un-GT:26
Advice to Travelers. W. Gibson.
  Du-RG:42
Against Quarrelling and Fighting.
  I. Watts. Ox-BC:49
Alumnus Football. G. Rice. Fe-PL:56
Always. L. Pepper. Ho-CT:32
Always Begin Right Where You Are.
  T. Ferril. Ca-VT:201
Ballad of the Soldier. B. Brecht.
  Li-TU:231
Battle Won Is Lost. P. George.
  Al-WW:114
Be Not Too Wise. De-CH:621
Be Still, My Soul. Archilochus.
  Pa-SG:177
A Children's Don't. H. Graham.
  Co-BB:90
Civilizing the Child. L. Mueller.
  Ha-TP:118
Colder Fire. R. Warren. Wi-LT:835
A Counsel of Moderation. F. Thompson.
  Un-MB:85
Counsel to Girls. R. Herrick.
  Al-VBP:328, Er-FA:104, Ga-FB:41,
  Gr-CT:51, Ha-PO:161, Hi-WP II:140,
  Li-SR:21, Ma-YA:86, Pa-GTB:71,
  Un-MW:19
Cowboy's Salvation Song. R. Carr.
  Fi-BG:191
Dance Songs, VII. Tr-US II:164
Direction. A. Lopez. Al-WW:10
Directions to a Rebel. W. Rodgers.
  Wi-LT:488
Discretion. Rv-CB:18
Do It Now. Er-FA:24
Do Not, Oh Do Not Prize. Rv-CB:122
Don't Give Up. P. Cary. Ch-B:81
Don't Tell All You Know. Bo-FP:119
Don'ts. D. Lawrence. Wi-LT:220

Early Thoughts of Marriage. N. Cotton.
  Ox-BC:65
An Elder's Reproof to His Wife.
  A. Muuse. Lo-TY:57
Epigraph. W. Blake. Ox-BN:46
Every Day. F. Mendelssohn. Bo-FP:300,
  Ch-B:97
Every Day Thou Might Lere. Ma-YA:27
The Exhortation of a Father to His
  Children. R. Smith. Ox-BC:13
Expostulation and Reply.
  W. Wordsworth. Rv-CB:640
Faery Song. J. Keats. De-CH:267,
  Sp-OG:170
Farewell Advice. C. Kingsley. Ke-TF:64
First Fight. Then Fiddle. G. Brooks.
  Hu-PN:337
The First Step. C. Cavafy. Pl-ML:34
The Fisherman. Fe-FP:473
Five Little Chickens. Ch-B:85,
  Fe-FP:282, Gr-EC:182, La-PV:198,
  St-FS:78, Un-GB:15, Un-GT:67
For a Six-Year Old. F. Rodman.
  Ke-TF:250
Forget It. Fe-PL:294
Freedom and Love. T. Campbell.
  Pa-GTB:184
Generations. R. Korn. Ho-TY:304
George. H. Belloc. Co-FB:109,
  Co-HP:32, Co-OH:40, Ir-BB:159,
  Un-GT:216
Girls and Boys, Young Ladies and
  Gentlemen. R. Fernàndez Retamar.
  Be-UL:119
Go to the Ant. Bible. O.T. Proverbs.
  Ch-B:61, Fe-FP:125
Going to Bed. Mo-MGT:49
Good Advice. T. Carew. Un-MW:36
Good Advice. L. Untermeyer. Ar-TP3:209
Good Advice. Mo-NR:19, Wr-RM:77
Good and Bad Children. R. Stevenson.
  Bl-OB:31, Co-BB:98, Er-FA:494,
  Gr-TG:19, Sm-LG:98
He That Would Thrive. Ir-BB:229,
  Mo-MGT:131, Sp-TM:1
He Who Knows. Un-GT:305
Hermit Hoar. S. Johnson. Al-VBP:554,
  No-CL:132
How to Walk in a Crowd. R. Hershon.
  Sc-TN:97
Humility and Patience in Adversity.
  T. a Kempis. Go-BP:268
I Thee Advise. G. Turberville.
  De-CH:621
If. R. Kipling. Er-FA:5, Hi-WP I:118,
  Un-GT:314
If a Jackal Bothers You. . . . Du-CH:(12)
If You Are Lazy. Ho-SD:13
If You Ever. Co-IW:23
If You Want to Go to Heben. Gr-GB:299
In a Girl's Album. C. Dover.
  Hi-WP II:149

In Glencullen. J. Synge. Co-EL:24,
  Co-PI:186, Co-PM:103, Pa-RE:50,
  Re-BS:42, Re-TW:13
Japanese Folk-Song from Hyogo. Pa-RE:64
John Wesley's Rule. J. Wesley.
  Bo-FP:301, Er-FA:29
Kimpa. Tr-US I:61
The Land. R. Kipling. Ni-JP:134,
  Pa-OM:190, Un-MB:138
Lesson. H. Behn. Br-SG:12
Lesson from a Sundial. Ar-TP3:208
Letter to My Sister. A. Spencer.
  Ad-PB:16, Bo-AN:19, Hu-PN:61
Limitations. S. Sassoon. Un-MB:316
Listen to My Words. Le-IB:114
Little Children. T. Tsosie. Ba-HI:142
Long-Expected One-and-Twenty.
  S. Johnson. No-CL:118
Look Not Thou. W. Scott. Rv-CB:656
Look Up! E. Hale. Er-FA:29
Love in Thy Youth. Al-VBP:363
Love Songs, II. Tr-US II:225
Love Thy Country. G. Dodington.
  Rv-CB:514
A Moral Poem. J. Cunningham. Ca-VT:323
A Moral Tetrastitch. Co-PM:149
Mother to Son. L. Hughes. Ab-MO:97,
  Be-MA:38, Bo-AN:67, Bo-HF:177,
  Br-BC:123, Hu-PN:186, Jo-SA:19,
  La-OC:94, Lo-TY:225, Pe-FB:70, Pe-SS:7
My Daughter. Ge-TR:44
My Sailor of Seven. G. Brenan. Br-BC:73
My Son. Ge-TR:41
The Name. R. Creeley. Pe-SS:4
Never Get Up till the Sun Gets Up.
  Do-CH:(11)
Notes Found near a Suicide: To "Chick."
  F. Horne. Bo-AN:43, Ra-BP:71
Notes Found near a Suicide: To James.
  F. Horne. Bo-AN:45, Bo-HF:90,
  Br-BC:124, Ra-BP:73
October Journey. M. Walker. Ad-PB:146
On Censure. J. Swift. Rv-CB:494
Old Black Men Say. J. Emanuel.
  Ad-PB:180
Out in the Woods with Father.
  D. McCord. Gr-TG:24
Perhaps You Expect. Ho-SD:64
The Periwinkle Diggers. Ir-BB:38
Poem. K. Cuestas. Jo-SA:85
Preparedness. E. Markham. Er-FA:29,
  Un-MA:108
Press Onward. Er-FA:22
The Priest and the Mulberry-Tree.
  T. Peacock. De-TT:119, Ha-PO:297,
  Sp-OG:224
Proverbs of King Alfred. King Alfred.
  Mc-MK:222
A Psalm of Life. H. Longfellow.
  Er-FA:32, Fe-PL:303, Sp-OG:322
Root, Hog, or Die. Fi-BF:65
Service Is No Heritage. Rv-CB:17

ADVICE — cont'd.
  Silence. M. Moore. Al-VBP:1174,
    Ha-PO:219, Ho-LP:72, Ma-FW:621,
    Mc-WS:77, Mo-BG:81
  Sir Halewyn. Ox-BB:690
  Sister Lou. S. Brown. Ad-PB:66,
    Bo-AN:53, Hu-NP:174
  Some Boys. J. Penkethman. Ox-BC:27
  Song. T. Lodge. No-CL:117
  Song after a Man Dies. Tr-US II:293
  Song for the Lazy. Do-CH:(10)
  Song of the Wolf. Sitting Bull.
    Da-SC:113
  Songs, III. Tr-US II:144
  Speak Gently. D. Bates. Li-SR:3
  Speech to a Crowd. A. MacLeish.
    Un-MA:462
  Staying Alive. D. Wagoner. Co-BN:160,
    Du-SH:183, Pe-M:38
  The Sweet Red Rose. M. Dodge.
    Br-BC:119
  Symon's Lessons of Wisdom for All
    Manner of Children. Ox-BC:9
  The Texas Ranger. Fi-BG:112
  This Above All. W. Shakespeare.
    Mc-PR:75
  Three Things There Be. . . .
    W. Raleigh. De-CH:535, Rv-CB:159
  To a Child with Eyes. M. Van Doren.
    Bo-FP:95, Ha-LO:78
  To a Negro Boy Graduating.
    E. Maleska. Hu-PN:569
  To a Young Girl. Tr-US I:128
  To His Child. W. Bullokar. Ox-BC:16
  To Kate, Skating Better Than Her Date.
    D. Daiches. Co-FB:402, Mo-SD:150
  To My Infant Daughter. Y. Winters.
    Ca-VT:226
  To My Son. S. Sassoon. Mc-WS:137
  To Thine Own Self Be True.
    W. Shakespeare. Er-FA:84
  Truth. G. Chaucer. Al-VBP:18, Rv-CB:60
  Try Smiling. Er-FA:13
  Vernal Equinox. R. Stone. Un-MA:655
  What Shall They Tell That Son?
    C. Sandburg. Pe-SS:10
  When I Was One-and-Twenty. A. Housman.
    Al-VBP:1080, Bo-HF:92, Co-BL:61,
    Er-FA:153, Fe-PL:118, Ga-FB:72,
    Ho-LP:12, Ke-TF:93, Ma-YA:222,
    Pe-M:150, Un-MB:94, Um-MW:55,
    Wi-LT:59
  the will's love. B. Brigham. Sc-TN:24
  Woman. E. Loftin. Ad-PB:514
  The Woman of Three Cows. Co-PI:125
  Young Companions. Fi-BG:211
  The Young Girl's Song. A. Gordon.
    Pe-M:140
  Young Lady. Do-CH:(12)
  Young Soul. I. Baraka. Mc-EA:32,
    Ra-BP:220

AEGEAN SEA
  Santorin. J. Flecker. Bo-GJ:183,
    Gr-CC:97, No-CL:58
  Sunset over the Aegean. G. Byron.
    Ox-BN:240
AENEAS: see also DIDO; TROJAN WAR
  Dido. T. Campion. Rv-CB:266
  Dido of Tunisia. P. McGinley.
    Cr-WS:18
  Falling Asleep over the Aeneid.
    R. Lowell. Un-MA:666
AEOLUS (GOD)
  Aeolus. R. Humphries. Sh-RP:164
AERONAUTICS: see AVIATION; FLYING
    SAUCERS; PARACHUTES
AFFECTATION: see also HUMOR -
    AFFECTATION; SNOBS AND SNOBBISHNESS
  The Academy Disporting. J. Nims.
    St-H:159
  The Bourgeois Poet, #29.
    K. Shapiro. St-H:202
  Brainwashing Dramatized.
    D. Johnson. Hu-PN:436
  Bussy d'Ambois. G. Chapman. Al-VBP:145
  But He Was Cool. D. Lee.
    Ad-PB:426, Be-MA:160, Ra-BP:299
  Don't Say You Like Tchaikowsky.
    P. Rosner. Co-FB:461
  Goodbye Now, or, Pardon My Gauntlet.
    O. Nash. Co-FB:481
  Government Injunction. J. Miles.
    Hu-PN:554
  Matinees. J. Merrill. Ho-P:187
  Mourning Dove. C. Calkins. Un-MW:60
  Othello Jones Dresses for Dinner.
    E. Roberson. Ad-PB:349, Hu-PN:429
  Pretences. Ibn Rashiq. Lo-TY:44
  Put Down. L. Damas. Lo-TY:121
  The Sundays of Satin-Legs Smith.
    G. Brooks. St-H:14
  Thoughts While Driving Home. J. Updike.
    Pe-SS:111
  To a Fat Lady Seen from a Train.
    F. Cornford. Bo-GJ:106, Co-EL:100,
    Co-PM:132, Hi-WP I:109, Li-SR:20,
    Sm-MK:99, Un-MB:306
  We Delighted, My Friend. L. Senghor.
    Lo-TY:133
AFRICA: see also HUMOR - AFRICA; names of
    countries, as EGYPT; and tribes, as
    HOTTENTOTS
  Afar in the Desert. T. Pringle.
    Rd-OA:168
  Africa. D. Diop. Lo-TY:137
  The African Affair. B. Wright.
    Ad-PB:171, Hu-PN:357
  African Dance. L. Hughes. Fe-FP:480,
    Sh-RP:8, Th-AS:159
  African Dream. B. Kaufman. Ad-PB:263,
    Be-MA:129
  African Memories. J. Oppenheimer. Lo-IT:100

African Sunrise. G. Lutz. Du-RG:46
Africa's Plea. R. Dempster. Lo-TY:168
Appeal. N. de Sousa. Lo-TY:188
The Babiaantje. F. Prince. Un-MB:488
Breath. B. Diop. Lo-TY:139
Change Is Not Always Progress. D. Lee.
    Be-MA:163
Dawn in the Heart of Africa.
    P. Lumumba. Lo-TY:150
Dry Your Tears, Africa. B. Dadie.
    Lo-TY:143
Enchantment, II, Medicine Dance.
    L. Alexander. Ad-PB:59
Etta Moten's Attic. M. Danner.
    Ad-PB:136, Be-MA:90, Bo-AN:156
Father Elephant. Tr-CB:34, Tr-US I:67
Heritage. G. Bennett. Ad-PB:81,
    Bo-AN:73
Heritage. C. Cullen. Ad-PB:88,
    Be-MA:47, Bo-AN:83, Ga-FB:274,
    Lo-TY:230, Ra-BP:95, Un-MA:571
I Am a Negro. M. Al-Fituri. Lo-TY:54
The Lonely Traveller. K. Brew.
    Lo-TY:166
Morning Light. E. Newsome. Ad-PB:21,
    Bo-AN:19, Hu-PN:70
O Daedalus, Fly Away Home. R. Hayden.
    Ad-PB:116, Bo-HF:158, Hu-PN:288,
    Jo-SA:120
old laughter. G. Brooks. Ho-TH:52
A Poem for a Poet. D. Lee. Ad-PB:425
A Poem for Integration. A. Saxon.
    Ad-PB:495
Ula Masondo's Dream. W. Plomer.
    Ca-MB:73
The Unicorn. E. Rieu. Co-BBW:286
The Vultures. D. Diop. Lo-TY:138
We Delighted, My Friend. L. Senghor.
    Lo-TY:133
Who Knows? A. Milner-Brown. Lo-TY:167
AFRICAN VERSE
    Cricket, Come Back! Le-OE:53
    Drum Song in Three Parts from the
        Funeral Ceremony for a Hero.
        Tr-US I:56
    For a Husband Away. Tr-CB:45,
        Tr-US I:46
    From the Rain-Making Ceremony.
        Tr-US I:104
    Hidesong. A. Higo. Lo-TY:159
    Home-Coming Song of Fighting Men
        after a Raid. Tr-US I:69
    Hunger. Lo-TY:156
    I Am a Negro. M. Al-Fituri. Lo-TY:54
    I Am a Wanderer. . . . Ho-SD:24,
        Le-OE:127
    In Air. P. Clarke. Ab-MO:38
    The Knell. M. Al-Fituri. Lo-TY:53
    Koko Oloro. W. Soyinka. Gr-BT:16
    Life in Our Village. M. Markwei.
        Ab-MO:20

Love Praise. Tr-CB:42, Tr-US I:69
New York Skyscrapers. J. Mbiti.
    Ab-MO:49
On the Death of a Wife. Le-OE:133
Pass Office Song. Lo-TY:17
The Rain-Man Praises Himself.
    Tr-CB:38, Tr-US I:71
Raindrops. Bo-FP:262
Season. W. Soyinka. Ma-FW:127
Song for the Dead, III. Lo-TY:13
Song to the Xylophone at a Fighting
    Man's Funeral. Tr-US I:42
Spear-Blessing. Tr-US I:103
Spring Blossom. E. Attah. Ab-MO:24
Telephone Conversation. W. Soyinka.
    Lo-TY:161, Ma-FW:134
Where the Rainbow Ends. R. Rive.
    Ab-MO:107, Lo-TY:180
Why Dost Thou Weep, My Child?
    Le-OE:29
Women's Song for Fighting Men Delayed
    on a Raid. Tr-US I:95
See also Do-CH; Tr-CB
AFRICAN VERSE - ACHOLI
    Battle Hymn. Tr-US I:101
AFRICAN VERSE - AKAN
    The Creator. Be-AP:19
    Dirges, I. Tr-US I:47
    Dirges, II. On a Ruler. Tr-US I:47
    Lament. Be-AP:28
    Lullaby. Be-AP:63
AFRICAN VERSE - AMHARIC
    King Tekla Haimont Learns that His
        Daughter Mentaub Has Been Captured
        by the Enemy. Tr-US I:112
    The Worthless Lover. Be-AP:52,
        Lo-TY:48
AFRICAN VERSE - ASHANTI
    Address on the Talking Drums to Asase
        Yaa, the Spirit of Earth. Tr-US I:47
    Song to Instruments. Tr-CB:22,
        Tr-US I:48
AFRICAN VERSE - BAGIRMI
    Love Song. Be-AP:51
AFRICAN VERSE - BANTU
    Courtship and Wedding Songs. Tr-US I:99
    Dance Song in Praise of a Dancer.
        Tr-US I:88
    Death. Be-AP:25
    The Elephant II. Lo-TY:3
    Glory to Moshesh. Be-AP:39
    Her Sister-in-Law Answers the Greeting
        Song. . . . Tr-CB:36, Tr-US I:93
    Hippopotamus Hunter's Song. Tr-US I:96
    Hunting Song. Le-OE:61
    Hyena. Lo-TY:9
    Hymn of the Afflicted. Tr-US I:81
    Invocation. Pa-SG:198
    Kimpa. Tr-US I:61
    Lament. Tr-US I:86
    Lament. Tr-US I:95

AFRICAN VERSE - BANTU — cont'd.
  Love Longing. Tr-CB:54
  Lullaby. Tr-US I:97, Tr-CB:13
  Man's Dance Song. Tr-US I:94
  The Missionary. Tr-US I:82, Tr-CB:20
  Mock Lament over a Dead Slave.
    Tr-US I:55
  Mugala's Song. Tr-CB:14, Tr-US I:92
  National Song of the Matabele. Tr-US I:85
  Night. S. Sutu. Lo-TY:175
  Old Praise Song of the Crocodile.
    Tr-US I:84
  Owl, Crevice-Sitter. Le-OE:42
  Paddling Song. Le-OE:52
  Plaint. Tr-US I:91
  Praise of Chief Mosenene. Be-AP:37
  Praise of King Mtesa. Tr-US I:102
  Praise Song for a Chief. Tr-US I:87
  Praise Song for a Chief. Tr-US I:94
  Song. Be-AP:63
  Song. Be-AP:66
  Song Commemorating the Death of a
    Hunter. Tr-US I:93
  Song Composed under a Tyrannical King.
    Tr-US I:102
  Song for a War Dance. Tr-US I:92
  A Song Made by Dancers on Hearing a
    Woman Mourning for Her Child.
    Tr-US I:86
  Song of a Mother Whose Child Has Been
    Left Behind on the Caravan Trail.
    Tr-US I:61
  Song of the Bridegroom in Praise of His
    Bride. Tr-US I:70
  Song of the Poor Man. Lo-TY:49
  Song of the Unburied. Tr-US I:81
  To the New King Mutara II Rwogera.
    Tr-US I:97
  The Train. Lo-TY:9
  War Song of Goloane. Goloane.
    Tr-US I:82
  War Song of the Nkuna Clan. Tr-US I:89
  Wedding Song. Tr-US I:102
AFRICAN VERSE - BEMBA
  The Pregnant Woman. Tr-US I:90
AFRICAN VERSE - BERBER: see also BALLADS,
    BERBER
  At a Noon Halt on a Journey. Kanimana
    oult Ourzig. Tr-US I:137
  Ballad. Tr-US I:125
  Dance Song. Tr-US I:130
  Drought. Kamid agg Afiser. Tr-US I:135
  Fighting Frenzy. Ebbeki ag Bouken.
    Tr-US I:135
  Girl's Song. Tr-US I:136
  Girl's Song at a Wedding. Tr-US I:128
  Gnomes, I. Tr-US I:124
  Gnomes, II. Tr-US I:124
  Gnomes, III. Tr-US I:125
  In Praise of Abazza ag Mekiia.
    Tekadeit oult Ag-Eklan. Tr-US I:135
  Koukaa. Tr-US I:133

  Learning French. Tr-US I:132
  Love Songs. Tr-US I:129
  Love Songs (I Left). Tr-US I:129
  Love Songs (I Weep). Tr-US I:131
  Love Songs (I Wish I Could Die).
    Tr-US I:129
  Love Songs (I Wish I Could Put).
    Tr-US I:126
  Love Songs (O My). Tr-US I:126
  Love Songs (When I). Tr-US I:126
  Love Songs (Who Told). Tr-US I:131
  Memorial. Tr-Us I:126
  Men's Song at a Wedding. Tr-US I:127
  An Old Man's Night Thoughts.
    Tr-US I:134
  Old War Song. Tr-US I:132
  On a Victory. Tr-US I:127
  On the Tuareg Violin. Tr-US I:133
  Pilgrims' Song. Tr-US I:129
  The Poetess Reproaches Mohammed ag
    Mekiia. Eberkaou oult Belou.
    Tr-US I:136
  Remonstrance. Rotman ag El-hadj Bekri.
    Tr-US I:134
  Song Composed by a Fighting Man Lying
    Wounded in the Desert. Tr-US I:133
  Song of Exile. Tr-US I:130
  Song on Drums and Pipe. Tr-US I:124
  To a Young Girl. Tr-US I:128
  Wisdom. Tr-CB:17
AFRICAN VERSE - BERGDAMA
  Despair. Tr-CB:41, TR-US I:74
  Journey Song. Tr-US I:74
  Lament of a Widow over Her Dead
    Husband. Tr-US I:72
  Leave-Taking. Tr-US I:74
  The Ostrich. Tr-CB:21, Tr-US I:75
AFRICAN VERSE - BINI
  The Oba of Benin. Be-AP:43
AFRICAN VERSE - BUSHMAN
  The Broken String. Tr-CB:51,
    Tr-US I:76
  The Day We Die. Le-OE:130
  Hunting Prayer. Le-OE:58
  New Moon Come Out. . . . Le-OE:70
  Oh! Oh! Le-OE:47
  Please Don't Kill My Antelope. Le-OE:49
  Prayer to the Moon. Le-OE:63
  Prayer to the Moon. Be-AP:23
  The Song of the Rain. Le-OE:71
  The Wind Was Once a Man. Le-OE:106
AFRICAN VERSE - DIDINGA
  Auranomoi's Song of Praise for His Bull
    Akorikono. Tr-US I:107
  Girls' Song for the Game of "Pots."
    Do-CH:(32), Tr-CB:46, Tr-US I:109
  A Mother to Her First-Born. Tr-CB:27,
    Tr-US I:105
AFRICAN VERSE - DINKA
  Chant. Tr-CB:57, Tr-US I:110
  Herder's Song. Be-AP:59, Tr-US I:111

AFRICAN VERSE - DOGON
Encouraging a Dancer.   Tr-CB:18,
  Tr-US I:38
AFRICAN VERSE - EGYPTIAN
Adoration of the Disk.   King Akhnaten
  and Princess Nefer Nefuriu Aten.
  Fe-FP:478
The Battle Of Kadesh.   Be-AP:46
Beyond the Window.   S. Jahin. Lo-TY:51
The Bird Catcher.   Be-AP:49, Lo-TY:28
The Creator.   Bo-FP:160
The Dead Man Ariseth and Singeth a
  Hymn.   The Book of the Dead.
  Pa-SG:210
Death as the Lotus Flower.   Be-AP:31,
  Lo-TY:27, Pl-EI:24
Death Is Before Me To-Day.   De-CH:635
A Dispute over Suicide.   Lo-TY:26
Excuses.   Be-AP:53
From the Fang of Time.   S. Jahin.
  Lo-TY:51
The Hymn to the Sun.   Ab-MO:3,
  Lo-TY:21
If There Was Peace.   S. Jahin.
  Lo-TY:52
The Irresponsible Student.   Be-AP:56
Love Lyric.   Ho-LP:1
Love Song (I Passed).   Ab-MO:23,
  Lo-TY:30
Love Song (The Little).   Lo-TY:29
Love Song (My Boat).   Lo-TY:31
Love Song (My Love).   Lo-TY:28
Love Song (My Loved).   Lo-TY:31
Marble Mausoleum.   S. Jahin. Lo-TY:51
My Heart Got Stuck.   S. Jahin.
  Lo-TY:51
Prayer to the God Thot.   Be-AP:18,
  Lo-TY:28
Spring Came Bouncing.   S. Jahin.
  Lo-TY:52
Winter Stormed In.   S. Jahin.
  Lo-TY:52
AFRICAN VERSE - ETHIOPIC
The Marital Journey.   H. Araaya.
  Pe-M:152
The Potter.   Lo-TY:47
AFRICAN VERSE - EWE
A Baby Is a European.   Be-AP:64
The Dead Man Asks for a Song.
  Le-OE:129, Tr-CB:44, Tr-US I:49
Death Song.   Tr-US I:50
Dirge.   Tr-CB:30, Tr-US I:50
Girls Mocking White Men's Serving Boys.
  Tr-CB:50, Tr-US I:52
Lament for the Dead Mother.   Be-AP:28
Loneliness.   Be-AP:36
Longing for Death.   Be-AP:30
Sadness of Life.   Be-AP:34
The Sky.   Ab-MO:6, Be-AP:64, Le-OE:109,
  Lo-TY:8
Song.   Tr-US I:50

Song of the Telegraph.   Tr-US I:51
The Sun.   Be-AP:64
To Destiny.   Pl-EI:184
AFRICAN VERSE - FANG
Fire Song at an Expiation Ceremony.
  Tr-US I:59
The Honey Bird's Song.   Tr-US I:60
Hymn to the Sun.   Be-AP:22, Le-OE:9
Ombrure Calls up the Forest Spirits.
  Tr-US I:60
Song at a Deathbed.   Tr-US I:57
Song of the Last Moments.   Tr-US I:58
The Will-o'-the-Wisp.   Tr-CB:31,
  Tr-US I:59
AFRICAN VERSE - FON
For the Earth God.   Pl-EI:174,
  Tr-US I:52
In Praise of Bow and Arrow.
  Tr-CB:23, Tr-US I:54
King Agongola's Song.   Tr-CB:56,
  Tr-US I:55
Song for the Dead.   Tr-US I:53
To the Envious.   Pl-EI:25, Tr-CB:53,
  Tr-US I:53
To the Sun-God.   Tr-CB:52, Tr-US I:52
War Chant.   Be-AP:45
AFRICAN VERSE - FULANI
The Beloved.   Be-AP:50
Herder's Song.   Tr-US I:39
War Song.   Tr-US I:40
AFRICAN VERSE - GALLA
Caravaners.   Tr-CB:26, Tr-US I:113
Love Songs (If I).   Tr-US I:114
Love Songs (A Javelin).   Tr-US I:114
Love Songs (O Merchant).   Tr-US I:115
Love Songs (That Which).   Tr-US I:114
The Negligent Lover.   Be-AP:52
Prayer.   Be-AP:19
The Victorious Fighting Man's Home-
  Coming.   Tr-US I:113
AFRICAN VERSE - HAUSA
For a Hunter.   Tr-CB:48, Tr-US I:42
"Praise Song" by a Woman Possessed
  by a Spirit.   Tr-US I:43
AFRICAN VERSE - HOTTENTOT
The Ancestors.   Be-AP:20
Giraffe.   Ab-MO:39
How Death Came.   Lo-TY:5
Invocation.   Tr-US I:76
A Mother Praises Her Baby.   Tr-US I:77
Praise Songs for the Baboon. Tr-US I:78
Prayer Before a Dead Body.   Be-AP:26
Prayer of a Hunter at a Grave of
  Heitsi-Eibib.   Tr-US I:77
Song for the Sun that Disappeared
  Behind the Rainclouds.   Be-AP:22,
  Lo-TY:5
Song of a Lioness Warning Her Cub.
  Be-AP:60, Tr-US I:79
Song of Greeting to a Missionary's Wife.
  Tr-US I:79

AFRICAN VERSE - IBO
  Distances. C. Okibgo. Lo-TY:160
  Funeral Song. Be-AP:29
  Girl's Song. Tr-US I:42
  Melting Pot. M. Echeruo. Lo-TY:163
  The Mystic Drum. G. Okara. Lo-TY:157
  Piano and Drums. G. Okara. Lo-TY:158
  The Stars Have Departed. C. Okigbo.
    Ab-MO:6
AFRICAN VERSE - ITESO
  The Train. Be-AP:35
AFRICAN VERSE - MANDE
  Song after Defeat. Tr-US I:37
AFRICAN VERSE - MBUNDU
  Song of the Fishermen. Le-OE:60
AFRICAN VERSE - MENDE
  Home-Sick Songs (Let Us). Tr-US I:45
  Home-Sick Songs (O They). Tr-US I:45
  I Am Rich. Do-CH:(18), Le-OE:122
  Prologue to a Yomeh Ballad. Tr-US I:44
AFRICAN VERSE - MOSSI
  Drum Song. Tr-US I:41
AFRICAN VERSE - NUER
  Beginning of a Girls' Song. Tr-US I:11
AFRICAN VERSE - PEUL
  At Twilight. Tr-CB:37, Tr-US I:41
  Girls' Song. Tr-US I:44
  Song. Tr-US I:43
AFRICAN VERSE - PYGMY
  Against Exploiters. Tr-CB:33,
    Tr-US I:65
  The Animal World. Tr-CB:24
  Dance of the Animals. Do-CH:(44),
    Le-OE:21
  Dirge in Dialogue. Lo-TY:3,
    Tr-US I:64
  Father Elephant. Tr-CB:34, Tr-US I:67
  Freedom. Tr-CB:58, Tr-US I:64
  Invocation to the Rainbow. Tr-US I:63
  Moon, O Mother Moon. Le-OE:5
  My Heart Is All Happy. Le-OE:87
  O Sun, O Sun. Le-OE:135
  Ritual Song. Tr-US I:62
  Sleep, Sleep, Little One. . . .
    Le-OE:111
  Song of a Marriageable Girl.
    Tr-CB:40, Tr-US I:62
  Song of Expiation. Tr-US I:64
  Song of the Animal World. Ab-MO:11,
    Tr-US I:66
  Song Sung by a Woman Giving Birth.
    Tr-CB:55, Tr-US I:65
AFRICAN VERSE - SOMALI
  All Your Young Beauty. . . .
    Le-OE:87
  An Elder's Reproof to His Wife.
    A. Muuse. Lo-TY:57
  Improvised Song Against a White Man.
    Tr-US I:118
  The Limits of Submission. F. Nuur.
    Ab-MO:29, Lo-TY:58

  Love Song. Tr-US I:116
  Modern Love Songs. F. Nuur.
    Lo-TY:59
  Modern Song. Ab-MO:31
  Songs to Horses, I. Tr-US I:115
  Songs to Horses, II. Tr-US I:116
AFRICAN VERSE - SOUSSOU
  The Moon. Ab-MO:3, Be-AP:68
  The Sweetest Thing. Ab-MO:102,
    Be-AP:68, Lo-TY:7
  The Well. Be-AP:69
AFRICAN VERSE - SWAHILI
  A Caravan Porter's Song. Tr-US I:96
  Home-Sick Song. Tr-US I:97
  The Plover. Pa-SG:134
  The Poor Man. Be-AP:55
AFRICAN VERSE - TEMNE
  Love Song. Tr-CB:16, Tr-US I:45
AFRICAN VERSE - TWI
  Prelude to Akwasidae. Lo-TY:14
  The Wandering Story-Teller.
    Tr-CB:39, Tr-US I:46
  Women's Song. Tr-US I:46
AFRICAN VERSE - YORUBA
  The Almighty. Be-AP:18
  Colobus Monkey. Be-AP:61
  Duck, You Are Merely Boasting.
    Le-OE:39
  The Elephant. Lo-TY:11, Rd-OA:121
  The God of War. Be-AP:45
  Invocation of the Creator. Be-AP:17
  Kob Antelope. Be-AP:60
  The Lazy Man. Be-AP:57
  The Moon Cannot Fight. Le-OE:103
  Oriki Erinle. Lo-TY:11
  Shango I. Lo-TY:12
  Shango II. Lo-TY:12
  Three Friends. U. Beier. Be-AP:31,
    Hu-PB:19
  The Time of Ede. Be-AP:42
  Viper. Be-AP:62
AFRICAN VERSE - ZULU
  He Who Bathes among Crocodiles.
    Le-OA:40
  In Honor of Senzangakona. Tr-US I:79
  In the Gold Mines. B. Vilakazi.
    Lo-TY:176
  Love Song. Le-OE:83, Tr-US I:80
  Love Song. Be-AP:51
  Shaka, King of the Zulus. Lo-TY:16
  Song at Separation. Tr-US I:80
  Unamina. B. Vilikazi. Pa-SG:38
AFTER LIFE: see FUTURE LIFE; IMMORTALITY;
  REINCARNATION
AFTERNOON
  Afternoon. D. O'Grady. Co-PI:160
  Afternoon. M. Stearns. Ar-TP3:176
  Afternoon, Amagansett Beach.
    J. Wheelock. Co-BN:79, Ha-WR:33
  August Afternoon. M. Edey. Ha-YA:90
  Clouds' Work. F. Gullar. An-TC:171
  The Green Afternoon. H. Rago. Ca-VT:425

Parameter. M. Reis. An-TC:169
Prelude IV. T. Eliot. Br-TC:106,
   Ca-VT:130, Pe-OA:104, Sh-AP:183
Run, Child, Run Fast. C. Williams.
   La-IH:18
The Sun Is a Globe of Fire.
   A. Machado. Le-SW:45
Wisteria Trellis. Fang Hsin. Pa-MV:84
AFTON RIVER
Sweet Afton. R. Burns. Co-BN:73,
   Er-FA:428, Mc-PR:17, Un-MW:154
AGAMEMNON, MYTHOLOGICAL KING OF MYCENAE
Nemea. L. Durrell. Pa-GTB:525
Sweeney among the Nightingales.
   T. Eliot. Wi-LT:285
AGASSIZ, JEAN LOUIS RODOLPHE
A Farewell to Agassiz. O. Holmes.
   Pl-IO:163
The Fiftieth Birthday of Agassiz.
   H. Longfellow. Pl-IO:161
AGE: see MIDDLE AGE; OLD AGE; YOUTH;
   YOUTH AND AGE
AGILITY: see also ACROBATS, JUGGLERS
   AND JUGGLING
How Many Miles to Babylon? Bo-FP:30,
   Cl-DT:33, De-PO:10, Gr-GB:25,
   Ir-BB:241, Ke-TF:69, Li-LB:38,
   Mo-MGT:108, Mo-NR:105, On-TW:61,
   Rv-CB:456, Sm-LG:241, Tu-WW:14,
   Wr-RM:57
Jack Be Nimble. An-IP:(15), Ar-TP3:101
   Au-SP:7, Bo-FP:38, Li-LB:38,
   Mo-MGT:38, Mo-NR:21, Wi-MG:58,
   Wr-RM:16
AGINCOURT, BATTLE, 1415
Agincourt. M. Drayton. De-CH:501,
   Hi-FO:91, Rv-CB:183, Sm-LG:245
Before Agincourt. W. Shakespeare.
   Gr-CT:337
Henry Before Agincourt. J. Lydgate.
   De-CH:179
AGING: see GROWING OLD; GROWING UP; OLD
   AGE; YOUTH AND AGE
AGNOSTICISM
Myself When Young Did Eagerly Frequent.
   O. Khayyam. Pl-EI:66
On the Death of a Metaphysician.
   G. Santayana. Al-VBP:1088
Silver Jack's Religion. J. Jones.
   Fi-BG:185
There Are No Gods. Euripides. Pl-EI:70
AGRICULTURE: see FARM LIFE; HARVEST;
   PLANTS AND PLANTING; PLOWING;
   and names of agricultural products,
   as CORN
AIMLESSNESS: see also FUTILITY
An Arrow Flying Past. G. Bécquer.
   Pa-SG:181
Ex-Basketball Player. J. Updike.
   Du-SH:79, Ha-TP:38, Mo-BG:53,
   Ni-JP:32, Pe-M:60

Man. H. Vaughan. Rv-CB:412
Street Corner College. K. Patchen.
   Un-MA:609
AIR: see also WINDS
After the Party. F. Cornford.
   Co-EL:115
Air. K. Raine. Un-MB:485
Fire Fire of the First World. Wo-HS:(61)
I Am the Blood. I. Rosenberg.
   Un-MB:352
I Taste a Liquor Never Brewed.
   E. Dickinson. Ga-FB:9, Mo-BG:128,
   Na-EO:153, Sh-AP:127, Un-MA:94,
   Wi-LT:3
I'm Glad the Sky Is Painted Blue.
   Au-SP:320, Ch-B:110, Fr-MP:12,
   Lo-LL:107
Physical Geography. L. Nicholl.
   Li-TU:29, Pl-IO:52
Spring Air. G. Derwood. Er-FA:113
AIR PLANTS
The Air Plant. H. Crane. Un-MA:533
AIR RAID SHELTERS
Reflections upon a Recurrent Suggestion
   by Civil Defense Authorities that I
   Build a Bombshelter in My Backyard.
   R. Whittemore. Ba-PO:28, Cr-WS:49,
   En-PC:177
AIR RAIDS
Air Raid Across the Bay of Plymouth.
   S. Spender. Ha-TP:80
Alert: London. M. Bracker. Ke-TF:254
The Angels at Hamburg. R. Jarrell.
   Sh-AP:224
B-52's. A. Kenseth. Ke-PP:84.
Broken Glasses. S. Takahashi.
   Sh-AM:97
Brother Fire. L. MacNeice. Ba-PO:177,
   Ha-TP:83, Hi-FO:269
Come to the Stone. R. Jarrell.
   Ca-VT:399
Five Minutes after the Air Raid.
   M. Holub. Gr-BT:104
A Front. R. Jarrell. Ca-VT:399
Funeral Moment. C. Theodorescu.
   Mc-AC:102
Homage to Wren. L. MacNeice. Cr-WS:121
Losses. R. Jarrell. Sh-AP:223,
   Wi-LT:562
A Man-Made World. S. Spender. Tr-MR:185
My Spoon Was Lifted. N. Replansky.
   Co-PM:73
Night Bombers. P. Mowrer. Cr-WS:122
Prayer in Blackout. G. Code. De-FS:66
The Raider. W. Rodgers. Un-MB:481
Still Falls the Rain. E. Sitwell.
   Br-TC:389, Ga-S:161, Tr-MR:131,
   Un-MB:336, Wi-LT:642
The Tempering of Steel. Jen Chun.
   Hs-TC:393
Thoughts During an Air Raid. S. Spender.
   Al-VBP:1234, Un-MB:479

AIR RAIDS — cont'd.
  Vapor Trail Reflected in the Frog Pond.
    G. Kinnell. Ca-VT:604, Pe-SS:102
AIRPLANES: see also HUMOR - AIRPLANES;
    SONIC BOOMS
  Aeroplane. M. Green. Ar-TP3:87,
    Au-SP:174, Pe-FB:44
  The Airplane. R. Bennett. Fe-FP:197
  The Airplane. R. Bennett. Fr-MP:11
  Field and Forest. R. Jarrell.
    Ca-VT:403
  From the Window of a Plane.
    A. Voznesensky. Ca-MR:71
  Looking Up at Airplanes, Always.
    R. Humphries. Sh-RP:163
  Malfunction. R. Albert. Du-SH:165,
    Pe-M:94
  The Man in the Dead Machine. D. Hall.
    Du-SH:96
  Night Plane. F. Frost. Ar-TP3:88,
    Fe-FP:201, La-PV:60
  Riding in an Airplane. D. Baruch.
    Fe-FP:200
  A San Diego Poem: January-February 1973.
    S. Ortiz. Ni-CD:146
  Taking Off. Ar-TP3:87, Au-SP:175,
    Mc-AW:26
  To Beachey, 1912. C. Sandburg.
    Ar-TP3:88
  Up in the Air. J. Tippett. Ar-TP3:87,
    Au-SP:173, Gr-EC:274
  Vapor Trails. G. Snyder. Du-SH:166,
    Mo-BG:129
AIRPORTS
  At the Airport. H. Nemerov.
    Du-SH:163, Mc-WS:115
  The Landscape near an Aerodrome.
    S. Spender. Un-MB:475, Wi-LT:499
  A San Diego Poem: January-February 1973.
    S. Ortiz. Ni-CD:146
AIRSHIPS: see also AIRPLANES; AVIATION;
    BALLOONS (AIRSHIPS)
  The Dirigible. R. Bergengren.
    Au-SP:173, Fe-FP:198
  An Elegy. Y. Winters. Ca-VT:229
  The Landscape near an Aerodrome.
    S. Spender. Un-MB:475, Wi-LT:499
AIS: see SLOTHS
AJANTA CAVES
  Ajanta. M. Rukeyser. Un-MA:630,
    Wi-LT:806
AJAX, MYTHOLOGICAL KING OF SALAMIS
  The Great Hector Was Killed by Arrows.
    J. Brodsky. Ca-MR:32
AKHMADULINA, BELLA
  To Bella Akhmadulina. A. Voznesensky.
    Ca-MR:79
ALABAMA: see also names of towns, as
    BIRMINGHAM, ALA.
  Alabama. J. Fields. Ad-PB:319,
    Hu-PN:420
  Alabama. J. Tutwiler. Se-PR:250
  Alabama Centennial. N. Madgett.
    Ra-BP:197
  Alabama Earth. L. Hughes. Br-AF:48
  Daybreak in Alabama. L. Hughes.
    Br-AF:47
  i remember how she sang. R. Penny.
    Ad-PB:388
  March on the Delta. A. Berger.
    Lo-IT:9
  The Trial. M. Rukeyser. Hu-PN:560
THE ALAMO: see also BOWIE, JAMES;
    CROCKETT, DAVID (DAVY); HUMOR -
    THE ALAMO
  The Defence of the Alamo. J. Miller.
    Pa-OM:173
  Lament for the Alamo. A. Guiterman.
    Br-AF:69, Sh-RP:260
  The Men of the Alamo. J. Roche.
    Hi-TL:86
ALASKA: see also ESKIMOS; HUMOR -
    ALASKA; names of towns, as
    BARROW, ALSK.
  Alaska. J. Miller. Hi-TL:133
  Alaska. G. Nichols. Ba-HI:106
  Alaska. Se-PR:293
  Song Composed at the Beginning of an
    Autumn Festival. Le-IB:106,
    Tr-US I:31
  Winter in Alaska. F. Washington.
    Ba-HI:70
ALBATROSSES
  The Albatross. J. Biram. Ls-NY:202
  The Albatross. R. Lister. Co-SS:133
  The Rime of the Ancient Mariner.
    S. Coleridge. Al-VBP:679, Co-RG:60,
    Co-SS:131, De-CH:364, Er-FA:318,
    Ga-FB:105, Ha-PO:15, Hi-WP II:68,
    Ma-YA:146, Ni-JP:52, Ox-BN:139,
    Rv-CB:658, Sm-LG:312
ALBERT, PRINCE CONSORT OF ENGLAND:
    see HUMOR - ALBERT, PRINCE
    CONSORT OF ENGLAND
ALCIPHRON
  Modo and Alciphron. S. Warner.
    Un-MB:375
ALCOHOL: see DRINKERS AND DRINKING
ALDEN, JOHN
  American History. M. Adams. Se-PR:219
ALE
  Back and Side Go Bare. J. Still.
    Al-VBP:64, Ho-WR:236
  Bring Us in Good Ale. Al-VBP:24,
    Cl-FC:94, De-CH:64
  The Brown Jug. F. Fawkes. Al-VBP:570,
    Rv-CB:534
  Heather Ale. R. Stevenson.
    Co-PT:117, Sp-OG:162
  In Praise of Ale. Al-VBP:376
  Sally Birkett's Ale. Gr-CT:469
  Terence, This Is Stupid Stuff. A. Housman.
    Ma-YA:224, Un-MB:100, Wi-LT:63

ALEHOUSES: see INNS AND TAVERNS; also
    names, as MERMAID TAVERN
ALEXANDER THE GREAT
  Alexander the Great. De-CH:180
  Alexander's Feast. J. Dryden.
    Ho-WR:100, Ma-YA:107, Pa-GTB:105
  Santorin. J. Flecker. Bo-GJ:183,
    Gr-CC:97, No-CL:58
ALEXANDRIA, EGY.
  Alexandrian Kings. C. Cavafy.
    Gr-CC:109
ALFRED THE GREAT, KING OF WESSEX
  A Fact and an Imagination.
    W. Wordsworth. Hi-FO:67
  Proverbs of King Alfred. King Alfred.
    Mc-WK:222
ALGEBRA: see MATHEMATICS
ALI, MUHAMMED: see CLAY, CASSIUS
    MARCELLUS
ALICE IN WONDERLAND
  Alice 1963. G. Bishop-Dubjinsky.
    Sc-TN:11
  Last Days of Alice. A. Tate.
    Sh-AP:200
ALIENATION: see LONELINESS
ALIENS
  Dancers at Banstead. M. Oliver.
    St-H:165
  Man I Thought I Was Talking Another
    Language That Day. V. Cruz.
    Ad-BO:65
  This Landscape, These People.
    Z. Ghose. To-MP:124
  Untitled. J. Smith. Ad-II:118
ALL SOULS' DAY
  All Souls. Y. Gillespie. Ke-TF:177
  All Souls. L. Romano. De-FS:156
  The One Forgotten. D. Sigerson.
    Se-PR:197
  Pray for the Dead. A. Eaton.
    Se-PR:197
  The Souling Song. Gr-SS:151
ALLAH
  Call to Prayer. Bilal. Ab-MO:61
  The Easterner's Prayer. Fe-PL:130,
    Ke-TF:208
  El Hajj El-Shabazz. R. Hayden.
    Ad-PB:123
  Songs of Nature, I. Tr-US II:137
ALLEGORIES: see also FABLES
  Comparison. J. Bunyan. Ox-BC:39
  The Emancipation of George-Hector.
    M. Evans. Ab-MO:40, Bo-AN:165
  The Pelican. P. de Thaun. Mc-WK:43
  The Pilgrimage. G. Herbert.
    Gr-CT:282
  The Ribs and Terrors. H. Melville.
    Al-VBP:950, Pl-EI:207
  Second Fig. E. Millay. Ho-TH:21,
    Sh-AP:186
  Shiva. R. Jeffers. Gr-SS:69,
    Ls-NY:36

ALLEN, ETHAN
  Green Mountain Boy. F. Smyth.
    Gr-EC:231
  Ticonderoga. V. Wilson. Vi-PP:122
ALLEN-A-DALE
  Allen-a-Dale. W. Scott. Co-PT:231
  Robin Hood and Allan a Dale.
    Gr-GB:247, Ma-BB:44, Un-GT:115
ALLERGIES
  And Mr. Ferritt. J. Wright. Un-MB:516
ALLIGATORS: see CROCODILES
ALLITERATION: see also HUMOR -
    ALLITERATION
  An Austrian Army. Co-FB:415, Gr-CT:336
  Chimes. D. Rossetti. Ox-BN:686
  The Lacquer Liquor Locker. D. McCord.
    Co-FB:436
ALMANACS: see also CALENDARS
  The Child Reads On. F. James.
    Fe-FP:470
ALMOND TREES
  Bare Almond-Trees. D. Lawrence.
    Ma-FW:274
  Mythistorema XXIII. G. Seferis.
    Gr-BT:147
ALPHABETS: see also CALLIGRAPHY; HUMOR -
    ALPHABETS
  A Apple-Pie. Mother Goose. De-TT:25,
    Mo-NR:45
  "A" for Apple. Bu-DY:23
  A Is for Abracadabra. E. Farjeon.
    Gr-EC:252
  A Was an Apple-Pie. Bo-FP:55,
    Gr-EC:251, Li-LB:108, Mo-MGT:137
  A Was an Archer. Mother Goose.
    Gr-EC:253, Ir-BB:43, Li-LB:110,
    Mo-MGT:214, Mo-NR:28
  A Was an Archer. Ox-BC:43
  An ABC. Gr-GB:309
  The ABC Bunny. W. Gag. Ar-TP3:104
  A B C Objects. Gr-EC:250
  A B C of Names. Ir-BB:96
  AEIOU. J. Swift. Bl-OB:21, De-TT:28
  The Alphabet. K. Shapiro. Tr-MR:64
  The Alphabet. Bo-FP:11
  The Alphabet. Wr-RM:49
  Alphabet of Christmas Cheer.
    E. Weston. Gr-EC:264
  And with the Sorrows of This Joyousness.
    K. Patchen. Gr-EC:266
  An Animal Alphabet. Gr-EC:256
  Double-U. De-TT:28
  The Five. J. Swift. Gr-EC:124,
    Ir-BB:53
  Gifts. H. Harris. Br-BC:32
  Great A. De-PO:8, Li-LB:106, Mo-MGT:146,
    Mo-NR:49, Wr-RM:55
  A Jamboree for J. E. Merriam. Gr-EC:266
  Line-Up for Yesterday. O. Nash. Mo-SD:21
  Some Days Are Rainy. Re-RR:10
ALPHEUS (GOD)
  Arethusa. P. Shelley. Ho-WR:136

ALPS: see names of mountains, as
    MATTERHORN
ALTAIC VERSE - ALTAIAN
    Ceremonial Chants of a Shaman.
        Tr-US II:128
    Improvised Songs, I.   Tr-US II:130
    Improvised Songs, II.   Tr-US II:130
    Improvised Songs, III.   Tr-US II:130
    Praise Song of the Wind.   Tr-US II:131
ALTAIC VERSE - BURYAT
    The Kalmyk Mourns for His Country.
        Tr-US II:133
    Song for the Arrival of Guests and the
        Bride.   Tr-US II:134
ALTAIC VERSE - MONGOLIAN
    Complaint of the Wild Goose.
        Tr-US II:135
    Shaman's Chant at a Wedding.
        Tr-US II:134
    Songs, I.   Tr-US II:135
ALTAIC VERSE - YAKUT
    Ceremonial Chant of a Shaman.
        Tr-US II:126
ALTGELD, JOHN PETER
    The Eagle That Is Forgotten.
        V. Lindsay.   Al-VBP:1139, Sh-AP:166,
        Tr-MR:171, Un-MA:223
    Paterson: Book II.   W. Williams.
        Bl-FP:61
ALUM
    Alum.   R. Burns.   Ls-NY:168
AMAGANSETT, N.Y.
    Afternoon, Amagansett Beach.
        J. Wheelock.   Co-BN:79, Ha-WR:33
AMBASSADORS: see DIPLOMATS
AMBER
    The Amber Bead.   R. Herrick.
        Gr-CT:109, Ho-LP:38, Ho-WR:141
AMBITION: see also DETERMINATION; HUMOR -
    AMBITION; SATIRE - AMBITION; SUCCESS
    Ambition.   W. Davies.   Un-MB:176
    Ambition.   P. George.   Al-WW:120
    Are Things Really Changing?   B. Davis.
        Me-WF:59
    At the Bottom of the Well.
        L. Untermeyer.   Bo-GJ:218
    At the Washing of My Son.   Su Tung P'o.
        Rx-OH:84
    Ball Game.   R. Eberhart.   Pe-M:5
    Beyond the End.   D. Levertov.
        Ca-VT:508
    Billiards.   G. Dumitrescu.   Mc-AC:122
    The Bishop Orders His Tomb at Saint
        Praxed's Church.   R. Browning.
        Al-VBP:895, Mo-GR:57
    Black Is Beautiful.   A. Burns.   Ba-HI:18
    The Boy.   R. Rilke.   Li-TU:170
    Camoens.   H. Melville.   Al-VBP:957
    The Catfish.   J. Mathews.   Ha-TP:115
    The Chambered Nautilus.   O. Holmes.
        Er-FA:479, Fe-PL:297, Mc-PR:130,
        Sh-AP:63, Sp-OG:366

The Clerk.   E. Robinson.   Un-MA:126
Climb.   W. Welles.   Br-BC:128
The Colossus.   S. Plath.   Wi-LT:787
Cortez.   W. Seymour.   Sm-MK:64
Critics and Connoisseurs.   M. Moore.
    Pe-OA:98
Daedalus and Icarus.   L. Coxe.
    Ls-NY:228
Davis Matlock.   E. Masters.   Wi-LT:117
Dreams.   N. Giovanni.   Ad-PB:454
The Duel.   E. Dickinson.   Li-TU:172
Eagle Song.   G. Bottomley.   Un-MB:213
The Eastern Gate.   Le-MW:120, Ma-FW:88
Excelsior.   H. Longfellow.   Fe-FP:566,
    Li-SR:49, Pa-OM:223
First Fight.   Then Fiddle.   G. Brooks.
    Hu-PN:337
Follow the Gleam.   A. Tennyson.
    Mc-PR:38, Se-PR:320
For Eusi, Ayi Kwei & Gwen Brooks.
    K. Kgositsile.   Ad-PB:325
Get Up, Blues.   J. Emanuel.   Ad-BO:62,
    Ad-PB:179, Bo-AN:175, Li-TU:173
Go Away.   Hsu Chih-mo.   Hs-TC:87
Good, Better, Best.   Sp-AS:(35)
Homage to Aesop.   C. Faerstein.
    Ls-NY:42
I Am Waiting.   M. Goode.   Jo-SA:5,
    Jo-VC:88
I Cannot Tell My Future.   A. Holmes.
    Jo-VC:35
I Come from the Nigger Yard.   M. Carter.
    Sa-B:96
I Saw a Man Pursuing the Horizon.
    S. Crane.   Mo-BG:195, Sm-LG:389,
    Un-MA:147, Wi-LT:118
Idle Chatter.   C. Cooper.   Ad-BO:8
Imperial Valley, Calif.   J. Kessler.
    Ls-NY:253
In Search of a Bright Star.
    Hsu Chih-mo.   Hs-TC:86
In These Dissenting Times.   A. Walker.
    Ad-PB:475
It Is Too Late.   H. Longfellow.
    Fe-PL:304
Keep on Pushing.   D. Henderson.
    Ad-PB:408
Life.   Cheng Min.   Hs-TC:237
Life Is Long.   Rx-LT:8
The Life That Counts.   Er-FA:24
The Lifting Hill.   J. Merchant.
    Ke-TF:177
A Little Learning.   A. Pope.
    Er-FA:99, Gr-CT:435
A Little Song of Life.   L. Reese.
    Fe-FP:18, Gr-TG:23, Hu-MP:61,
    Th-AS:179
Living among the Toilers.   H. Percikow.
    La-OC:146
The Long Hill.   S. Teasdale. Un-MA:265
Looking at Your Hands.   M. Carter.
    Sa-B:134

A Man.   N. Cassian.   Mc-AC:132

A Man of the Middle Class.   G. Brooks.
   St-H:12

The Marigold.   G. Wither.   Rv-CB:333

Measure Me, Sky.   L. Speyer.   Ad-PE:46,
   Br-BC:129, Fe-FP:22, Hu-MP:63

Moods.   S. Teasdale.   Mc-PR:62

Mother to Son.   L. Hughes.   Ab-MO:97,
   Be-MA:38, Bo-AN:67, Bo-HF:177,
   Br-BC:123, Hu-PN:186, Jo-SA:19,
   La-OC:94, Lo-TY:225, Pe-FB:70,
   Pe-SS:7

The Mouse That Gnawed the Oak-Tree Down.
   V. Lindsay.   Ha-LO:74

Move Un-noticed to Be Noticed.
   N. Giovanni.   Be-MA:166

The Music Makers.   A. O'Shaughnessy.
   Al-VBP:1063, Co-PI:163, Ga-FB:133,
   Mc-PR:72, Se-PR:324

The New Duckling.   A. Noyes.
   Fe-FP:283, Hu-MP:241

Nocturnal Song (IV).   Ho Ch'i-fang.
   Hs-TC:224

Nothing Is Enough.   L. Binyon.
   Un-MB:156

Ocean.   R. Jeffers.   Pe-OA:87

Ode on Indolence.   J. Keats.   Ox-BN:374

Ode to the West Wind.   P. Shelley.
   Al-VBP:748, Co-BN:127, De-CH:212,
   Er-FA:244, Fe-PL:390, Ga-FB:15,
   Ha-PO:96, Ma-YA:177, Ox-BN:280,
   Pa-GTB:295, Rv-CB:696

Once to Every Man and Nation.
   J. Lowell.   Vi-PP:68

The People Will Live On.   C. Sandburg.
   Un-MA:214

A Pig-Tale.   L. Carroll.   Ch-B:65,
   Fe-FP:346, Ho-WR:80, Pa-RE:27,
   Rd-OA:94

poem.   J. Gill.   Sc-TN:69

The Poems of Our Climate.   W. Stevens.
   Br-TC:411, Sh-AP:182

Poems of Shape and Motion.   M. Carter.
   Sa-B:136

"pygmies are pygmies still, though
   percht on Alps."   G. Brooks.   Hu-PN:336

The Scales.   W. Empson.   Wi-LT:441

Similar Cases.   C. Gilman.   Fe-PL:191

Sleep, Sleep, Little One. . . .
   Le-OE:111

Song.   Bi-IT:164, Tr-US I:27

Song of a Man Who Has Come Through.
   D. Lawrence.   Al-VBP:1158, Go-BP:69,
   Pa-GTB:458, Wi-LT:212

A Song of Greatness.   Ar-TP3:35,
   Br-AF:37, Br-BC:126, Fe-FP:24,
   Sh-RP:103

splitting the silence.   C. Burchardt.
   Ad-II:31

Standing or Sitting.   Ba-ST:31

Sun and Rain and Dew from Heaven.
   A. Gordon.   Fe-PL:313

Tamburlaine the Great.   C. Marlowe.
   Al-VBP:172

Teddy's Wonderings.   J. Bangs.
   Br-BC:109

There Isn't Time.   E. Farjeon.
   Fe-FP:323, Sh-RP:160

To Fling Songs into the Air.
   Y. Grizlov.   Mo-MI:34

To Fly Higher than the Eagle.   Wo-HS:(42)

To Get There.   I. Brodsky.   Bo-RU:21

To Infinite Heights.   V. Lapin.
   Mo-MI:38

To My Son Parker, Asleep in the Next
   Room.   B. Kaufman.   Ad-PB:265,
   Br-TC:230, Ca-VT:539, Jo-SA:30

The Tradesman.   Bo-FP:116

Vickery's Mountain.   E. Robinson.
   Un-MA:120

Victory.   M. Miller.   Sh-RP:283

Want to Be Someone.   H. Yazzie.
   Ba-HI:15

What I Am I Must Become.   Wo-HS:(70)

When I Am a Man.   Da-SC:9, Ho-SD:56

When I Have Fears that I May Cease to
   Be.   J. Keats.   Go-BP:148, Ha-PO:129,
   Ma-YA:187, No-CL:6, Ox-BN:369,
   Pa-GTB:198, Rv-CB:747, Un-GT:313

When Smoke Stood Up from Ludlow.
   A. Housman.   Un-MB:95

Will I Make It?   J. Holland.   Jo-VC:91

With Wavering Feet I Walked.
   V. Solovyov.   Pa-SG:118

Word Poem.   N. Giovanni.   Ad-BO:9,
   Ad-PB:450

You Too.   P. Irving.   Al-WW:79

Your World.   G. Johnson.   Bo-AN:23,
   Bo-HF:170

Youth and Art.   R. Browning.   Al-VBP:909

The Youth Dreams.   R. Rilke.   Pa-SG:142

AMBULANCES: see also HUMOR - AMBULANCES

Auto Wreck.   K. Shapiro.   Ca-VT:471,
   Ma-FW:131, Mo-BG:30, Pe-OA:224,
   Pe-SS:70, Wi-LT:535

The Deaths at Paragon, Indiana.
   J. Woods.   St-H:250

AMEBAS: see AMOEBAS

AMERICA: see also BALLADS, AMERICAN;
   CANADA; COLONIAL PERIOD IN
   AMERICA; DISCOVERY PERIOD IN
   AMERICA; HUMOR - AMERICA; INDIANS
   OF NORTH AMERICA; LATIN AMERICA;
   PAN-AMERICANISM; SATIRE - AMERICA;
   SOUTH AMERICA; UNITED STATES

America.   S. Dobell.   Vi-PP:17

America.   H. Dumas.   Ad-BO:40,
   Ad-PB:267, Co-PM:61

America.   C. McKay.   Ad-PB:26, Be-MA:15,
   Bo-HF:40, Hu-PN:100, Lo-TY:119

America.   S. Smith.   Er-FA:293,
   Fe-FP:423, Fe-PL:158, Se-PR:131,
   Vi-PP:11

America.   B. Taylor.   Vi-PP:37

AMERICA — cont'd.
America for Me. H. Van Dyke.
  Er-FA:292, Hu-MP:403, Sh-RP:214,
  Th-AS:168, Vi-PP:39
America, the Beautiful. K. Bates.
  Bo-FP:302, Er-FA:293, Fe-FP:402,
  Ga-FB:278, Hu-MP:363, Pl-EI:164,
  Se-PR:127, Vi-PP:30
America Was Promises. A. MacLeish.
  Br-AF:250, Vi-PP:229
America Was Schoolmasters. R. Coffin.
  Mc-WK:173, Vi-PP:191
American Letter. A. MacLeish.
  Br-AF:3
American Names. S. Benét. Br-AF:6,
  Mc-WK:157, Pa-HT:3, Sh-AP:194,
  Sm-LG:145
Boston Hymn. R. Emerson. Vi-PP:76
Brown River, Smile. J. Toomer.
  Ad-PB:31, Bo-AN:34, Hu-PN:107,
  Jo-SA:72
Cape Hatteras. H. Crane. Sm-PT:102
Chorus for Survival. H. Gregory.
  Sm-PT:115
Dear Land of All My Love. S. Lanier.
  Hu-MP:404
England. M. Moore. Un-MA:350
England and America in 1782.
  A. Tennyson. Vi-PP:136
The Gift Outright. R. Frost.
  Br-AF:29, Mc-WK:184, Mo-BG:109,
  Sh-AP:153, Sh-RP:267, Sm-LG:144,
  Un-MA:195, Vi-PP:29, Wi-LT:179
Here Down on Dark Earth. J. Kerouac.
  Kh-VA:1
I Hear America Singing. W. Whitman.
  Ar-TP3:47, Bo-FP:304, Br-AF:44,
  Co-PS:118, Er-FA:289, Fe-FP:451,
  Ga-FB:247, Hu-MP:369, La-PV:103,
  Mc-PR:33, Sm-LG:40, Un-GT:306,
  Un-MA:40
I Sing America Now! J. Stuart.
  Br-AF:248
I Wish the Wood-Cutter Would Wake Up.
  P. Neruda. Bl-FP:51
Land of the Free. N. Hosking.
  Vi-PP:22
Land of the Free. A. MacLeish.
  Br-AF:243
Let America Be America Again.
  L. Hughes. Hu-PN:193
Moving in a Caravan (1). R. Bly.
  Mc-EA:46
Musica. G. Montgomery. Lo-IT:94
My America. O. La Crone. Hu-NN:36
A National Hymn. J. DeForest.
  Vi-PP:13
The New Colossus. E. Lazarus.
  Bo-HF:35, Br-AF:247, Er-FA:289,
  Fe-FP:448, Fe-PL:153, Ga-FB:265,
  Vi-PP:187
The New World. E. Masters. Br-AF:246

Night Journey. T. Roethke.
  Bl-FP:80, Bo-HF:36, Br-AF:231,
  Gr-EC:239, Ha-TP:25
Ode in a Night of Overhanging Weather.
  V. McHugh. Mc-WK:175
Of Those Who See Through This Riddle.
  Re-RR:82
Plain-Chant for America. K. Chapin.
  Vi-PP:34
The Poet. W. Whitman. Un-MA:79
The River. H. Crane. Bl-FP:81
So Long! W. Whitman. Sh-AP:111
Song of Myself. W. Whitman.
  Al-VBP:928, Sh-AP:69, Un-MA:44
The Topography of History. T. McGrath.
  St-H:119
The United States. Goethe. Bl-FP:72
Verses on the Prospect of Planting Arts
  and Learning in America. G. Berkeley.
  Al-VBP:521, Er-FA:458
Whenever I Say "America." N. Turner.
  Ha-YA:77
AMERICAN INDIAN DAY: see INDIANS OF
  NORTH AMERICA; and names of tribes
AMERICAN REVOLUTION: see REVOLUTIONARY
  WAR IN AMERICA, 1776-1781
AMERICANS: see also SATIRE - AMERICANS;
  UNITED STATES
America. B. Taylor. Vi-PP:37
American Laughter. K. Robinson.
  Br-AF:118
American Letter. A. MacLeish. Br-AF:3
Brooklyn Heights. J. Wain. Wi-LT:834
The Coming American. S. Foss.
  Br-AF:33, Mc-WK:160
Depot in a River Town. M. Williams.
  Du-SH:131
Europe and America. D. Ignatow.
  Br-AF:41
Four Sheets to the Wind and a One-Way
  Ticket to France. C. Rivers.
  Ad-PB:234, Bo-AN:176, Hu-NN:107,
  Ra-BP:199
Fourth of July Ode. J. Lowell.
  Se-PR:158, Vi-PP:67
I Am an American. E. Lieberman.
  Fe-FP:448, Fe-PL:162, Vi-PP:190
Irish-American Dignitary.
  A. Clarke. Co-PI:26
My America. O. La Crone. Hu-NN:36
Rari for the Americans. Eina'a.
  Tr-US II:94
Song of Myself. W. Whitman.
  Al-VBP:928, Sh-AP:69, Un-MA:44
The Sound Track. A MacLeish. Li-TU:265
Tribute to America. P. Shelley.
  Vi-PP:36
Two 'Mericana Men. T. Daly. Hu-MP:150
Western Star. S. Benét. Br-AF:225
AMMON
The Sphinx. O. Wilde. Un-MB:69
AMNESIA: see FORGETTING; SELF

AMOEBAS: see HUMOR - AMOEBAS
AMPUTATIONS
The Leg. K. Shapiro. Ha-TP:84,
Un-MA:634
AMSTERDAM, NETH.
Robinson Crusoe Returns to Amsterdam.
F. Jammes. Fe-FP:472
The Weepers Tower in Amsterdam.
P. Goodman. Ca-VT:334
AMU DARYA RIVER: see OXUS RIVER
AMUSEMENTS: see also CIRCUSES; FORTUNE
TELLING; GAMES; HOBBIES; MAGICIANS;
MOVING PICTURES; PENNY ARCADES; PLAY;
SPORTS; TELEVISION; TOYS; VAUDEVILLE;
VENTRILOQUISTS
Blind Date. C. Aiken. Al-VBP:1189
Edward the Second. C. Marlowe.
Al-VBP:179
Houses Have No Fun. D. Hendell.
Me-WF:18
Jill Came from the Fair. E. Farjeon.
Ar-TP3:116
Negro Servant. L. Hughes. Ca-VT:240
A Night Out. D. Abse. Gr-BT:158
Polite Song. T. Spenser. No-CL:201
The Poppet-Show. Rv-ON:65
Street Performers, 1851. T. Tiller.
Pa-GTB:551
Swineherd. E. Chuilleanáin. Co-PI:24
To See a Quaint Outlandish Fowl.
H. Farley. Al-VBP:276
Winter. T. Campion. Al-VBP:218,
Ma-FW:277, No-CL:280, Rv-CB:272
AN-SHAN, CHINA
I Sing of Anshan Steel. Feng Chih.
Hs-TC:158
ANARCHY
Carl Hamblin. E. Masters. Kr-OF:113,
Sh-AP:137, Wi-LT:114
The Masque of Anarchy. P. Shelley.
Hi-FO:206
The Second Coming. W. Yeats.
Mo-GR:89, Pa-GTB:424, Pl-EI:28,
Tr-MR:236, Un-MB:117, Wi-LT:72
ANATOMY: see BODY, HUMAN; HUMOR -
ANATOMY
ANCESTORS AND ANCESTRY: see also HUMOR -
ANCESTORS AND ANCESTRY
The Ancestors. Be-AP:20
The Cliffs of Moher. W. Stevens.
Ca-VT:41
Country Graveyard. D. Etter.
Sc-TN:44
Funnel. A. Sexton. Un-MA:688
Generations. R. Korn. Ho-TY:304
The House. R. Debee. Al-PI:84
I Am an American. E. Lieberman.
Fe-FP:448, Fe-PL:162, Vi-PP:190
The Idea of Ancestry. E. Knight.
Ad-PB:229, Be-MA:108, Ra-BP:203
My Father's Face Is in the Rock.
Wo-HS:(42)

Pedigree. E. Dickinson. Ch-B:41,
Ga-FB:291, Mc-PR:108, Mo-BG:124,
Un-GT:24
Prayer at the Offering of Food to the
Ancestors. Tr-US II:255
Stark Boughs on the Family Tree.
M. Oliver. Pe-SS:14
Totem. L. Senghor. Gr-BT:32
Upon the Round Tower. W. Yeats.
Gr-SS:55
Women Songs, I. K. Molodowsky.
Ho-TY:284
ANDAMANESE VERSE
My Bow, Its Lower Part I Draw Back.
Le-OE:59
Pig-Hunting Song. Tr-US II:181
Song for a Dead Mother. Tr-US II:181
Song on Cutting a Bow. Tr-US II:180
ANDERSON, MARIAN
For Marian Anderson. F. Bock.
Ls-NY:159
Singing in the Dark. I. Wassall.
Hu-PN:546
ANDERSON, SHERWOOD
To Sherwood Anderson in Heaven.
F. Eckman. St-H:46
ANDES
The Christ of the Andes. E. Markham.
Se-PR:85
ANDRÉ, JOHN
Major Andre. Em-AF:428
ANDRÉA DEL SARTO
Andrea del Sarto. R. Browning.
Ke-TF:310
ANDROMACHE: see also HECTOR
The Sixth Book of Homer's Illiads.
Homer. Al-VBP:148
ANEMONES
Anemone. F. Sherman. Mc-PR:116
The Anemones of Collioure.
J. Unterecker. Sc-TN:211
Long Ago I Went to Rome. M. Furse.
De-CH:578
Song of the Pasque Flower. Tr-US II:235
ANGELICO, FRA
Giocanni da Fiesole on the Sublime.
R. Howard. Ho-P:117
ANGELS: see also JESUS CHRIST - NATIVITY;
and names of angels, as GABRIEL
Ambushed by Angels. G. Davison.
De-FS:71
Angel Spirits of Sleep. R. Bridges.
De-CH:455
Angels. E. Spenser. Ga-S:5
The Angels Came a-Mustering. Pl-EI:100
The Call. U. Birnbaum. Un-R:78
The Flaming Terrapin. R. Campbell.
Ga-S:3
I Heard an Angel Singing. W. Blake.
Rv-CB:621
Jacob and the Angel. Brother Antoninus.
Tr-MR:72

ANGELS — cont'd.
  Joseph's Suspicion. R. Rilke.
    Tr-MR:99
  Michael, Archangel. Alcuin. Ga-S:4
  Miracles. C. Aiken. Un-MA:472
  The Monk in the Kitchen. A. Branch.
    Un-MA:152
  My Angel. J. Brooks. Hu-PN:238
  Night. W. Blake. Br-SG:33, Ch-B:13,
    Co-BN:111, De-CH:432, Fe-FP:53,
    Fe-PL:404, Ho-WR:197, Rd-SS:29,
    Rv-CB:592. Un-GT:263
  The Olive Garden. R. Rilke. Go-BP:293
  Out of Paradise. J. Milton. Ga-S:35
  Revelation. L. Clark. Sm-MK:218
  The Sea of Death. De-CH:389
  Song. H. Killigrew. De-CH:447
  Swedish Angel. W. Scott. Wi-LT:810
  Up in Heaven. On-TW:29
ANGER: see also HUMOR - ANGER;
    IRASCIBILITY
  Anger. C. & M. Lamb. Gr-TG:60
  Angry Old Men. B. Payne. Co-PI:167
  Apostrophe to Man. E.Millay.Du-SH:86
  Childhood's Trials. Mrs. C. Alexander.
    Gr-TG:20
  Fighting Frenzy. Ebbeki ag Bouken.
    Tr-US I:135
  Piano after War. G. Brooks. Bo-AN:142
  The Poetess Reproaches Mohammed ag
    Mekiia. Eberkaou oult Beleou.
    Tr-US I:136
  A Poison Tree. W. Blake. Co-PM:29,
    Er-FA:64, Ga-S:133, Gr-SS:77,
    Rv-CB:607
  The Rage That Shatters Man into
    Children. C. Vallejo. Be-UL:41
  Return to My Native Land. A. Cesaire.
    Lo-TY:123
  Rubaiyat. Omar Khayyam. Ba-PO:169
  The Sleeping Fury. L.Bogan.Wi-LT:380
  A Soft Answer Turneth Away Wrath.
    Bible. O.T. Proverbs. Ar-TP3:209
  Take This Remark. . . . B. Franklin.
    Un-GT:26
  Temper in October. V. Edminson.
    Go-BP:31
  The White House. C. McKay. Ad-PB:28,
    Be-MA:15, Bo-AN:31, Hu-PN:101,
    Jo-SA:119
ANGLERFISH
  The Goose Fish. H. Nemerov. Wi-LT:590
ANGLO-SAXON VERSE
  Beowulf. Al-VBP:1, Ma-YA:14
  Beowulf's Voyage to Denmark.
    Ma-FW:45
  Book-Moth. Ma-YA:3, Rd-OA:29
  The Dream of the Rood. Ga-S:153
  Eastward I Stand, Mercies I Beg.
    Pl-EI:173
  Elene. Cynewulf. Ma-YA:11
  Genesis A. Ma-YA:8

  The Happy Land. Ga-S:21
  Hymn. Caedmon. Ma-YA:7
  Proverbs of King Alfred. King Alfred.
    Mc-MK:222
  Riddle #29. The Moon and the Sun.
    Bo-GJ:244
  The Ruin. Ma-YA:4
  The Seafarer. E. Pound. Sh-AP:171
  The Seafarer. Ma-YA:5
  The Swan. De-TT:58
  The Whale. Rd-OA:151
ANGOLA
  Angola Question Mark. L. Hughes.
    Lo-TY:230, Ra-BP:89
  Monangamba. A. Jacinto. Lo-TY:181
ANIMAL COMMUNICATION AND SOUNDS: see also
    HUMOR - ANIMAL COMMUNICATION AND
    SOUNDS
  Bow-Wow. An-IP:(22), Mo-CC:(22),
    Mo-MGT:116, Pa-AP:8
  The Fox. Su-FVI:62
  The Hens. E. Roberts. Ar-TP3:73,
    Au-SP:50, Bo-GJ:51, Co-BBW:166,
    Co-IW:20, Fe-FP:281, Hu-MP:239,
    La-PV:129, Li-LC:27, Pe-FB:21,
    Th-AS:47, Tu-WW:96, Un-GB:14,
    Un-GT:66
  I Bought Me a Cat. Su-FVI:52
ANIMAL TRACKS: see also TRACKING AND
    TRAILING
  Invisible Tree. R. Tamura. Mo-TS:20
  The Open Door. E. Coatsworth.
    Gr-EC:76
  The Presence. M. Kumin. Mo-TS:67
  Raccoons. A. Fisher. La-PP:47,
    La-PV:149
  A Story in the Snow. P. Crouch.
    Ar-TP3:62, Au-SP:60, Hu-MP:322
  Tracks in the Snow. M. Chute.
    Br-SS:90
ANIMALS: see also ANIMAL COMMUNICATION
    AND SOUNDS; COMPANIONSHIP OF MEN AND
    ANIMALS; HIBERNATION; HUMOR - ANIMALS;
    JESUS CHRIST - NAVITY; MYTHICAL
    ANIMALS AND BIRDS; PETS; PREHISTORIC
    ANIMALS; and names of animals, as DOGS
  Afar in the Desert. T. Pringle.
    Rd-OA:168
  Allie. R. Graves. Bo-GJ:81,
    Fe-FP:100, Ha-LO:103
  And Did the Animals. M. Van Doren.
    Ca-VT:196
  An Animal Alphabet. Gr-EC:256
  Animals. L. Anderson. Me-WF:91
  The Animals. L. MacAdams. Mc-EA:65
  The Animals. E. Muir. Gr-CC:143,
    Un-MB:342
  Animals' Houses. J. Reeves. St-FS:96
  The Animals in the Ark. Gr-CT:93,
    Gr-GB:74
  At the Zoo. A. Milne. Fe-FP:251,
    Fr-MP:17

Beasts. R. Wilbur. Br-TC:472
Beasts and Birds. A. O'Keeffe.
  Ox-BC:124
Bed-Time Story. M. Cane. Un-GT:81
The Butterfly's Ball. W. Roscoe.
  Un-GT:74
The Call. B. Björnson. Ch-B:16
Christmas Eve Legend. F. Frost.
  Br-BC:169
Christmas in the Woods. F. Frost.
  Ar-TP3:197
Christmas Song. E. Long. Br-SS:107
The Circus-Postered Barn. E. Coatsworth.
  Un-MA:464
The Combat. E. Muir. Un-MB:342
The Coyote Lived at Sun House.
  Wo-HS:(14)
Dance of the Animals. Do-CH:(44),
  Le-OE:21
Dear Father. M. Brown. La-PV:140
Deities and Beasts. J. Updike.
  Co-EL:26
The Dog Will Come When He Is Called.
  A. O'Keeffe. Bl-OB:122
Easter in the Woods. F. Frost.
  Br-SS:138
The Egg. L. Richards. Ar-TP3:71,
  Hu-MP:239
Evening at the Farm. J. Trowbridge.
  Fe-FP:237, Hu-MP:308
Excuse Us, Animals in the Zoo.
  A. Wynne. Ar-TP3:78
Eyes Are Lit Up. R. Coffin. Sm-MK:157
A Farmyard Song. M. Hastings.
  Au-SP:228
The Flaming Terrapin. R. Campbell.
  Co-BBW:210, Rd-OA:134
The Gifts of the Animals to Man.
  P. Sidney. Rd-OA:38
Green Hill Neighbors. F. Frost.
  Ar-TP3:76
His Shield. M. Moore. Wi-LT:275
How They Sleep. Ch-B:28
I Sing for the Animals. Da-SC:23,
  Le-OE:36
If a Jackal Bothers You. . . .
  Du-CH:(12)
If They Spoke. M. Van Doren.
  Pl-IO:102
In Come de Animuls Two by Two.
  Gr-GB:75
In Fur. W. Stafford. La-RM:113
In Spring in Warm Weather. D. Aldis.
  Br-BC:9
In the Fashion. A. Milne. La-PP:56,
  Sh-RP:31
The Indolent Gardener. M. Kennedy.
  Co-BN:51
The Law of the Jungle. R. Kipling.
  Rd-OA:128
Lazy Balan. Ca-MU:12

Let No One Suppose. J. Reeves.
  Co-BBW:283
Little Donkey, Close Your Eyes.
  M. Brown. La-PP:76, La-PV:18
Man Is a Lumpe Where All Beasts
  Kneaded Be. C. Lewis. Go-BP:102
Minstrel's Song. Do-CH:(39)
The Monster. D. Quick. De-FS:151
My Father Kept a Horse. Gr-GB:54
Of Seals and Arms. J. Taylor.
  Rv-CB:318
On Christmas Morn. R. Sawyer.
  Fe-FP:89, La-PH:26, La-PV:88
On Hardscrabble Mountain. G. Kinnell.
  Du-SH:107
One More River. Cl-DT:52
The Reason. D. Aldis. Ar-TP3:167
Reluctances. H. Witt. Ls-NY:320
The Rousing Canoe Song. H. Fraser.
  Do-WH:58
Serenade. Ca-MU:9
Sing a Song of Moonlight. I. Eastwick.
  Br-SS:33
Sing a Song of Sunshine. I. Eastwick.
  Br-SS:16
Somebody Stole. Ju-CP:34
Song of Myself. W. Whitman. Co-BBW:274
A Story. W. Stafford. Co-PT:142
Their Thanksgiving Day. L. Driscoll.
  Bo-FP:161
There's a Fire in the Forest. W. Ross.
  Do-WH:57
Twilight Calm. C. Rossetti.
  Co-BN:109, Ox-BN:709
Variations on a Sentence. L. Bogan.
  Ho-LP:44, Pl-IO:111
The Virtuous Fox and the Self-Righteous
  Cat. J. Cunningham. Pa-OM:334
What in the World? E. Merriam. Gr-EC:14
When the Animals Were Let Out of the Ark
  after the Flood. Cl-FC:76, Pa-RE:113
Who's In? E. Fleming. Bl-OB:145,
  Cl-FC:61, Pe-FB:22, Th-AS:41
Wild Beasts. Cheng Min. Hs-TC:240
The Wolf Also Shall Dwell. . . .
  Bible. O.T. Isaiah. Fe-FP:179,
  Go-BP:103, La-PV:158
Wolf and Tiger Dining, A.B. J. Keith.
  De-FS:118
The Zoo. H. Wolfe. Co-HP:117,
  Mc-WK:78
Zoo Manners. E. Mathias. St-FS:52
ANIMALS, CAPTIVE: see also BIRDS,
  CAPTIVE; ZOOS
At the Lion's Cage. P. Dufault.
  Co-BBW:202
Au Jardin des Plantes. J. Wain.
  Co-BBW:199, Ma-FW:220
The Bear. R. Frost. Sh-AP:154, Un-MA:184
The Bear on the Delhi Road. E. Birney.
  En-PC:55

ANIMALS, CAPTIVE — cont'd.
  Bird Thou Never Wert. P. Bennett.
    Co-BBW:204
  Black Hair Rope Is What You Used.
    Ho-SD:42
  The Bull. W. Williams. Br-TC:483,
    Wi-LT:199
  The Captive Lion. W. Davies.
    Co-BBW:198
  Circus Lion. C. Day Lewis. To-MP:114
  Encounter in the Cage Country.
    J. Dickey. Ha-TP:102
  Exile. V. Sheard. Co-BBW:205
  False Country of the Zoo. J. Garrigue.
    Wi-LT:711
  Greed. P. Bennett. Co-BBW:184
  The Jaguar. J. Hollander. Wi-LT:736
  The Lion. H. Asquith. Li-TU:191
  Lion. M. Swenson. Pe-OA:249,
    Wi-LT:827
  Mr. Zookeeper. L. Hopkins. Ho-CS:27
  Monkeys. P. Colum. Co-BBW:203
  A Mouse's Petition. A. Barbauld.
    Ox-BC:79
  The Panther. R. Rilke. Ma-FW:61,
    Rd-OA:120
  Truth Will Out. P. Bennett. Co-BBW:201
  Where More Is Meant. C. Morley.
    Sh-RP:70
  Willy. R. Moore. Du-SH:117
ANIMALS, CRUELTY TO: see also BIRDS,
    CRUELTY TO; HUMOR - ANIMALS,
    CRUELTY TO
  Apology for Bad Dreams. R. Jeffers.
    Sh-AP:175, Un-MA:363
  Armadillo. E. Bishop. Ca-VT:319
  Auguries of Innocence. W. Blake.
    Al-VBP:621, Ch-B:36, Co-BBW:278,
    Er-FA:69, Ga-FB:96, Ma-YA:130,
    Ox-BN:28, Pl-IO:5, Sh-RP:76, Sm-LG:67,
    Sm-MK:220, Un-GT:305
  The Baby Tigers. K. Raikin. Mo-MI:53
  Badger. J. Clare. Cl-FC:67, Co-BBW:50,
    Ho-WR:213, Rv-CB:720
  The Bells of Heaven. R. Hodgson.
    Bo-GJ:20, Br-SS:152, Co-BBW:280,
    De-TT:82, Ha-PO:109, Ke-PP:104,
    Pl-EI:131, Th-AS:51, Un-MB:192,
    Wi-LT:125
  Bête Humaine. F. Young. De-CH:86
  Beth Gêlert. W. Spencer. Un-GT:138
  The Broncho That Would Not Be Broken.
    V. Lindsay. Ar-TP3:255, Co-BBW:147,
    Co-RG:108
  The Bull Calf. I. Lawton. Co-BBW:168
  Childhood and School-Time.
    W. Wordsworth. Ox-BN:93
  Country Idyll. F. Cornford. Co-BBW:176,
    Co-PM:95
  Ding, Dong, Bell. Ar-TP3:131, Au-SP:14,
    De-PO:20, Li-LB:95, Mo-MGT:119,
    Mo-NR:36, Wi-MG:37, Wr-RM:122

Dolphin. J. Unternecker. Sc-TN:216
The Fawn in the Snow. W. Benét.
  Rd-OA:183, Un-MA:323
The Field of Waterloo. T. Hardy.
  Sm-LG:257
Four Little Foxes. L. Sarett.
  Ar-TP3:64, Bo-HF:71, Co-BBW:35,
  Co-PS:54, Du-RG:98, Fe-FP:173,
  Ha-YA:40, La-PV:150, Mc-WK:64,
  Sh-RP:203, Un-GT:31
A Fox Jumped Up. Mo-MGT:206, Sm-MK:72
Fragment of a Bylina. A. Pushkin.
  Li-TU:83
Gallows. E. Thomas. Co-BBW:27,
  Un-MB:217
The Gray Squirrel. H. Wolfe.
  Bo-GJ:65, Co-BBW:39, Un-MB:303
Horse and Hammer. P. Dufault.
  Co-BBW:157
The Hound. S. Lanier. Co-PM:113
A Hunted Deer. De-PP:41
I Had a Little Pony. Mother Goose.
  Au-SP:19, Bl-OB:115, Bo-FP:131,
  De-TT:20, Li-LB:82, Mo-MGT:179,
  Mo-NR:128, Mo-TL:82, Wr-RM:83
January. R. Thomas. Co-BBW:49,
  Co-EL:24, Co-PM:91
The Lament of the Mole-Catcher.
  O. Sitwell. Co-BBW:22
The Little Fish Cries. D. Recht.
  Le-M:109
Little Things. J. Stephens. Ad-PE:47,
  Ar-TP3:65, Bo-GJ:19, Br-SS:151,
  Co-BBW:55, Co-PM:70, Fe-FP:149,
  Gr-EC:40, Hi-WP I:33, Hu-MP:200,
  La-PV:160, Pl-EI:130, Un-MB:263
Love on the Farm. D. Lawrence.
  Ga-FB:80, Un-MB:288, Un-MW:122
Molecatcher. A. Mackie. Co-BBW:40
Myxomatosis. P. Larkin. Co-EL:30
Nightmare. A. Marx. De-FS:136
Original Sin. R. Jeffers. Un-MA:373
Poor Old Horse. De-CH:84
The Rabbit. W. Davies. Hi-WP I:32
The Rabbit Hunter. R. Frost. Ho-TH:46
Song of Horses. M. Beniuc. Mc-AC:96
The Snare. P. MacDonough. Co-BBW:55
The Snare. J. Stephens. Ad-PE:22,
  Ar-TP3:62, Bl-OB:130, Co-BBW:21,
  Co-IW:28, De-CH:89, Gr-EC:32,
  La-PP:51, La-PV:151, Mc-WS:44,
  Se-PR:300, Sm-MK:159, Th-AS:50
The Sound of a Gun. A. Taylor.
  De-TT:82
A Sparrow-Hawk. De-CH:101
Sport. W. Davies. Co-BBW:47,
  Co-PM:120
Stray Dog. C. Mish. Fe-PL:359
There Was a Presbyterian Cat. Sm-LG:77
Tit for Tat. W. de la Mare. Co-BBW:273
To a Dog Injured in the Street.
  W. Williams. Wi-LT:203

The Unicorn's Hoofs. Rd-OA:169,
  Sm-LG:43
Wild Horse. H. Allen. Le-M:99
ANIMALS - DEATH: see also BIRDS - DEATH;
  HUMOR - ANIMALS - DEATH; SATIRE -
  ANIMALS - DEATH
After Shooting a Cock Pheasant Last
  Friday. P. Mayer. St-H:139
Argus and Ulysses. E. Farjeon.
  Gr-EC:84
Ay Me, Alas. De-CH:85, Sm-LG:69
Badger. J. Clare. Cl-FC:67,
  Co-BBW:50, Ho-WR:213, Rv-CB:720
Ballad of Another Ophelia.
  D. Lawrence. Gr-CT:79
Ballad of Red Fox. M. La Follette.
  Ad-PE:43, Ha-LO:42
The Bear. G. Kinnell. Ca-VT:605,
  La-RM:25, Mc-EA:55
Best Loved of Africa. M. Danner.
  Ad-PB:137, Hu-PN:162
Bête Humaine. F. Young. De-CH:86
Blue Moon Butterfly. P. Williams.
  Le-M:88
The Broncho That Would Not Be Broken.
  V. Lindsay. Ar-TP3:255, Co-BBW:147,
  Co-RG:108
The Buck in the Snow. E. Millay.
  Ad-PE:29, Sm-PT:152
The Bull Calf. I. Layton. Co-BBW:168
Cat's Funeral. E. Rieu. Ar-TP3:53,
  Gr-EC:78, Mc-WS:43
Colly, My Cow. Na-EO:128, Rv-ON:33
Day of the Wolf. K. Wilson. Ha-WR:76
Dead Doe. J. Harrison. Ho-LP:23
The Dead Horse. C. Meireles. An-TC:43
A Dead Mole. A. Young. Co-BBW:43,
  Pa-GTB:466
Death of a Frog. S. Hagiwara. Sh-AM:48
The Death of a Snake. W. Plomer.
  Co-EL:23
Death of the Cat. I. Serraillier.
  Co-BBW:126
Death Was a Trick. J. Mazzaro. Mc-EA:65
The Deer and the Snake. K. Patchen.
  Un-MA:609
The Discarded Horse. H. Anzai.
  Sh-AM:118
The Dolphin's Tomb. Anyte. Rd-OA:147
Done For. W. de la Mare. Bl-OB:131
Donkey. M. Van Doren. Pl-EI:126
Elegy for Jog. J. Ciardi. Du-RG:87
Epitaph for a Cat. M. Bruner.
  Fe-PL:352
Epitaph for a Lighthouse-Keeper's
  Horse. J. Morton. Co-PM:156
Epitaph for a Pet. F. Rodman. Ke-TF:327
Epitaph on a Dormouse Which Some
  Children Were to Bury. Ox-BC:77
For a Dead Kitten. S. Hay. Du-RG:92
For a Lamb. R. Eberhart. Pe-SS:67,
  Wi-LT:430

The Fox. E. Ford. Ke-TF:331, Ls-NY:199
The Fox. K. Patchen. To-MP:32
From My Rural Pen. T. Watt. Co-FB:221
The Heaven of Animals. J. Dickey.
  Kh-VA:42, Wi-LT:687
Hey Diddle Diddle. P. Dehn. Co-FB:451,
  Du-RG:80
The House Dog's Grave. R. Jeffers.
  Co-BBW:108
Improvised Song of the Baby Coconut-
  Monkey. Tr-US II:202
John Cook Had a Grey Mare. Bl-OB:115,
  De-TT:20, Mo-TL:84, Rv-ON:29, Wi-MG:56
Johnny Armstrong. Rv-ON:32
The Kangaroo. Su-FVI:60
Landscape, Deer Season. B. Howes.
  Bo-GJ:253, Pe-M:111
Letter to the City Clerk. F. Wright.
  Er-FA:224
A Little Dog-Angel. N. Holland.
  Fe-PL:361
Loneliness. J. Pomroy. Su-FVI:11
A Maltese Dog. Tymnés. Ar-TP3:50,
  Co-BBW:99, Gr-EC:86, Sm-LG:85
Memorandum for St. Peter. E. Chaffee.
  Ke-TF:328
Mountain Lion. D. Lawrence. La-RM:20
My Dog Is Dead. Ke-TF:207
The Nymph Complaining for the Death of
  Her Fawn. A. Marvell. De-CH:92,
  Rd-OA:191, Rv-CB:402, Sm-LG:71
Old Blue. Mo-SD:115
Old Dog. A. Covici. Ch-B:29
The Old Grey Goose. Bl-OB:154,
  Gr-CT:108
On a Hare. Bl-OB:121, Co-BBW:47,
  Go-BP:94
On the Skeleton of a Hound. J. Wright.
  Wi-LT:844
Our Lucy (1956-1960). P. Goodman.
  Co-BBW:100
Plague of Dead Sharks. A. Dugan.
  Wi-LT:692
The Rabbit. E. Millay. Co-BBW:28
The Rabbit Hunter. R. Frost. Be-EB:28
Raccoon on the Road. J. Brennan.
  Gr-EC:40
The Rat. A. Young. Hi-WP II:43
Reapers. J. Toomer. Ad-PB:29,
  Jo-SA:63, Ra-BP:68
Rest in Peace. W. Funk. Fe-PL:364
A Runnable Stag. J. Davidson.
  Co-BBW:195, Ho-WR:77, Mo-SD:123,
  Na-EO:63, Rd-OA:177
The Ruthless Moon. B. Reece. Ls-NY:99
A Salmon Trout to Her Children.
  Le-IB:45, Su-FVI:69, Tr-US I:3
Samuel. B. Katz. Ho-GC:19
The Shark's Parlor. J. Dickey. Pe-M:116
Skipper. G. Brooks. Ho-ME:18
Song of the Fallen Deer. Bi-IT:57,
  Da-SC:88

ANIMALS - DEATH — cont'd.
  The Stricken Colts. L. Peck. Ls-NY:211
  The Tantanoola Tiger. M. Harris.
    Ca-MB:66
  To a Dog Injured in the Street.
    W. Williams. Wi-LT:203
  Traveling Through the Dark. W. Stafford
    Co-PT:126, Ma-FW:225, Mo-BG:144,
    Mo-TS:71, Pe-SS:76, Wi-LT:826
  View of a Pig. T. Hughes. Br-TC:210,
    Ma-FW:229, Wi-LT:738
  Wolves. G. Kinnell. Co-RM:95
  The Wounded Doe. D. Schmitz. St-H:197
ANIMALS, KINDNESS TO: see also COMPAN-
    IONSHIP OF MEN AND ANIMALS; HUMOR -
    ANIMALS, KINDNESS TO; JESUS CHRIST
    - NATIVITY
  Anne and the Field Mouse.
    I. Serraillier. Pa-RE:106
  Ding, Dong, Bell. Ar-TP3:131, Au-SP:14,
    De-PO:20, Li-LB:95, Mo-MGT:119,
    Mo-NR:36, Wi-MG:37, Wr-RM:122
  The Dog. M. Owgang. Me-WF:54
  The Donkey. Mo-MGT:21, Wi-MG:52
  The Donkey. Br-BC:10, Co-BBW:154,
    Gr-EC:37, Ma-FO:(31)
  A Fairy Went a-Marketing. R. Fyleman.
    Au-SP:293
  Fall. R. Francis. Ca-VT:233
  Feather or Fur. J. Becker. Ar-TP3:65,
    Bo-FP:75, Fe-FP:121, Ma-FO:(1),
    Sh-RP:25
  Four Little Foxes. L. Sarett.
    Ar-TP3:64, Bo-HF:71, Co-BBW:35,
    Co-PS:54, Du-RG:98, Fe-FP:173,
    Ha-YA:40, La-PV:150, Mc-WK:64,
    Sh-RP:203, Un-GT:31
  The Horse's Prayer. Mo-TB:123
  Hurt No Living Thing. C. Rossetti.
    Au-SP:88, Bo-FP:96, Br-SG:50,
    Br-SS:149, Ch-B:16, Fe-FP:149,
    Gr-EC:39, Gr-TG:14, La-PV:158,
    Pa-RE:103, Se-PR:300
  I Love a Little Pussy. Bo-FP:6,
    Li-LB:92, Mo-MGT:176, Mo-NR:23,
    Mo-TL:69, Wi-MG:59
  Kindness to Animals. Au-SP:89, Ch-B:17,
    Cl-FC:65, De-TT:40, Un-GT:80
  The Lambs of Grasmere, 1860.
    C. Rossetti. Co-BBW:165
  Lovely Big Cow. J. Morton. Pa-RE:67
  The Mole. R. Daniells. Do-WH:83
  Nature's Friend. W. Davies. Se-PR:299
  Old Mother Hubbard. An-IP:(8), Au-SP:3,
    Fr-WO:21, Ir-BB:171, Li-LB:153,
    Mo-MGT:8, Mo-NR:108, Pa-OM:336,
    Un-GT:102, Wi-MG:50, Wr-RM:43
  Pussy. Ox-BC:166
  Sanctuary. J. Boothroyd. Co-FB:28
  The Tree. J. Rose. La-GI:16
ANNE, QUEEN OF ENGLAND: see HUMOR - ANNE,
    QUEEN OF ENGLAND
ANNIVERSARIES: see HOLIDAYS

ANNOYANCE
  Epic Song. Tr-US I:236
  The Oyster. A. Herbert. Co-BBW:63
ANONYMITY: see also SATIRE - ANONYMITY
  Anonymous. R. Potash. Ho-TY:358
  Anonymous Gravestone. E. Kästner.
    Co-EL:77
  anyone lived in a pretty how town.
    E. Cummings. Br-TC:80, Ca-VT:182,
    Ha-PO:241, Na-EO:73, Pe-OA:152,
    Un-MA:477, Wi-LT:365
  Being Nobody. K. Crawford. Le-M:163
  The Electric Train. M. Nakagiri.
    Sh-AM:120
  The Grave. S. Tchernichovsky. Me-PH:79
  Hokku Poems. R. Wright. Ad-PB:108,
    Bo-AN:104
  Missing. J. Pudney. Hi-WP I:24
  Self. N. Pritchard. Ad-PB:359
  To the Portrait of an Unknown Man.
    A. Scruggs. Ls-NY:144
  The Tourist from Syracuse. D. Justice.
    Br-TC:226
  Unkept Good Fridays. T. Hardy.
    Tr-MR:128
  Unknown Man in the Morgue. M. Moore.
    Un-MA:576
  What Was Her Name? J. Ciardi. Pe-M:137
ANTELOPES: see also GNUS; HUMOR -
    ANTELOPES
  Gambling Songs, II. Tr-US II:252
  Gazelles and Unicorn. J. Gay. Gr-CT:115
  Kob Antelope. Be-AP:60
  Please Don't Kill My Antelope.
    Le-OE:49
ANTHONY, SAINT
  Saint of the Lost. E. Morrow. Ke-TF:211
ANTICHRIST
  The Antichrist. E. Muir. Pl-EI:72
ANTICIPATION: see also LOVE - ANTICIPA-
    TION; SATIRE - ANTICIPATION
  Another Song from Arsut. Tr-US I:5
  At the New Year. K. Patchen. Wi-LT:784
  Coming. P. Larkin. Un-MB:526
  The Day Will Bring Some Lovely Thing.
    G. Crowell. Ar-TP3:218
  Early Spring. M. Chute. Br-SG:5
  Evening Appointment. Cheng Min.
    Hs-TC:242
  The Expectation. R. Gales. Ga-S:58
  For a Child Expected. A. Ridler
    Gr-BT:3, Wi-LT:804
  The French Revolution. W. Wordsworth.
    Hi-FO:181
  From My Study at the Mouth of the
    Valley. Ch'ien Ch'i. Le-MW:53
  Gift. C. Freeman. Ab-MO:75, Ad-PB:397,
    Hu-PN:435, Lo-TY:255
  Going to the Heavenly Bridge.
    Li Kuant-T'ien. Hs-TC:205
  Graduation. D. Richardson. Ke-TF:87
  Growing Up. A. Guiterman. Br-BC:81
  Half of My Life. C. O'John. Al-WW:64

He's Coming. M. Van Doren. Ga-FB:85
I Bid You Keep Some Few Small Dreams.
   H. Frazee-Bower. Th-AS:210
I Heard a Bird Sing. O. Herford.
   Ar-TP3:212, Au-SP:352, Br-SS:88,
   Co-BBW:256, Fe-PL:389, Ha-YA:151,
   La-PP:8, La-PV:128, Li-LC:71, Th-AS:49
I Never Shall Love the Snow Again.
   R. Bridges. De-CH:258, Ga-FB:150
I Sing No New Songs. F. Davis.
   Ad-PB:98, Hu-PN:252
In February. J. Symonds. Ha-YA:171
January Night. R. Arrieta. Pa-SG:30
A Man Waiting for the Sunrise.
   M. Beniuc. Mc-AC:98
The May Queen. A. Tennyson. Ch-B:76,
   Hu-MP:336, Se-PR:111
Midwinter. O. Wilde. Bo-FP:179
Next, Please. P. Larkin. Un-MB:526
Pantuns, VI. Tr-US II:203
Prophecy. Ho Ch'i-fang. Hs-TC:218
Reconnaissance. A. Bontemps.
   Bo-AN:80, Bo-HF:54, Ra-BP:92
The Return. E. Dickinson. Un-MA:103
The Road Looks Longer. Le-OE:85
Six in June. M. Davies. Br-BC:57
Someone I Know. . . . Mo-MI:36
The Song of Youth. Ai Ch'ing.
   Hs-TC:297
A Sure Sign. N. Turner. Ar-TP3:199,
   Au-SP:360, Bo-FP:291
Sword and Flower. T. Utan. Mc-AC:144
The Trees Are Bare. E. Brontë.
   De-TT:158
Turkey Time. Bo-FP:156, Ch-B:92
The Twenty-Fourth of December.
   Bo-FP:183, Ch-B:52
Ulysses. A. Tennyson. Al-VBP:863,
   Ha-PO:40, Ke-TF:262, Ni-JP:16,
   Rv-CB:793
Vickery's Mountain. E. Robinson.
   Un-MA:120
The Visit of the Professor of
   Aesthetics. M. Danner. Ad-PB:135,
   Be-MA:89, Bo-AN:155, Hu-NN:31
Waiting. R. Jacob. Br-BC:103
Waiting for Audience on a Spring Night.
   Tu Fu. Rx-OH:10
What I Expected. S. Spender. Un-MB:472
What Makes Life Interesting.
   M. Montgomery. Ls-NY:340
When I Was Young. Le-OE:119, Ma-BH:26
When My Ship Comes In. R. Burdett.
   Er-FA:30
Winter Field. K. Ozaki. Sh-AM:58
Winter Song. J. Jiminez. Le-SW:73
Work Without Hope. S. Coleridge.
   Co-BN:199, Ma-YA:166
ANTIETAM, BATTLE, 1862
   The Battle of Antietam Creek. Em-AF:451
ANTIGONE
   For the Antigone. A. Hamori.
   Ls-NY:27

ANTIPATHIES: see PREJUDICES AND
   ANTIPATHIES
ANTONY, MARK: see also CLEOPATRA
   Early in the Morning. L. Simpson.
   Ha-PO:158
ANTRIM COUNTY, IRE., N.
   Antrim. R. Jeffers. Ca-VT:124
ANTS: see also HUMOR - ANTS
   The Ant. J. Kransnai. La-GI:55
   The Ant and the Cricket. Aesop.
   De-TT:59, Un-GT:78
   An Ant Came Out. Wo-HS:(9)
   The Ant Village. M. Edey & D. Grider.
   Ar-TP3:70, Fe-FP:124
   Ants, Although Admirable, Are Awfully
   Aggravating. W. Brooks. It-HB:17
   The Bee, the Ant, and the Sparrow.
   N. Cotton. Ox-BC:67
   Departmental. R. Frost. Du-SH:114,
   Mc-WS:48, Sh-AP:154, Un-MA:190
   A Dream. W. Blake. De-CH:456,
   Hu-MP:127, Rd-OA:13, Rv-CB:585
   Four Things. Bible. O.T. Proverbs.
   Fe-FP:124, Un-GT:30
   A Garden Path. M. Justus. Bo-FP:241,
   Br-SG:49
   Go to the Ant. Bible. O.T. Proverbs.
   Ch-B:61, Fe-FP:125
   Jungles of Grass. A. Fisher. It-HB:37
   The Odyssey of a Snail. F. Garcia Lorca.
   Ma-FW:211
   On the Bales. E. Coupland. Su-FVI:65
   The People. E. Roberts. Bo-GJ:105
   A War Between Two Races of Ants.
   H. Thoreau. Kr-OF:69
ANXIETY: see WORRY
AOUDADS: see SHEEP
APACHE INDIANS: see also INDIANS OF NORTH
   AMERICA - VERSE - APACHE
   Geronimo. E. McGaffey. Co-RM:15,
   Fi-BG:48, Hi-TL:168
APARTMENT HOUSES
   Apartment House. G. Raftery.
   Br-AF:210, Du-RG:39, La-OC:108
   Apartment House. M. Usami. Le-TA:44
   Flight. J. Tate. La-OC:106
APATHY: see INDIFFERENCE
APES: see also BABOONS; CHIMPANZEES;
   MONKEYS; ORANG-UTANS
   Au Jardin des Plantes. J. Wain.
   Co-BBW:199, Ma-FW:220
   Best Loved of Africa. M. Danner.
   Ad-PB:137, Hu-PN:162
APHRODITE: see VENUS (GODDESS)
APOLLO (GOD)
   The Song of the Muses. M. Arnold.
   Gr-CT:444, Ho-WR:249
APOLOGIES
   Brazen Tongue. W. Benét. Un-MA:327
   Excuse Me. E. Dailey. Ba-HI:32
APOSTLES
   Emmaus. R. Rilke. Go-BP:302
   The Last Supper. R. Rilke. Tr-MR:121

APOSTLES — cont'd.
  The Last Supper. O. Williams.
    Er-FA:466, Tr-MR:120, Wi-LT:411
  Peter and John. E. Wylie.
    Ca-MB:46, Tr-MR:87, Un-MA:279
  Starlight like Intuition Pierced the
    Twelve. D. Schwartz. En-PC:128,
    Sh-AP:222, Tr-MR:94
  The Transfiguration. E. Muir.
    Go-BP:291
APPALACHIAN MOUNTAINS: see also BLUE
    RIDGE MOUNTAINS; CUMBERLAND GAP
  Appalachian Front. R. Weeks. Br-AF:135
  Uncle Ambrose. J. Still. Br-AF:133
APPARITIONS: see also GHOSTS; HUMOR -
    APPARITIONS
  Ambushed by Angels. G. Davidson.
    De-FS:71
  Black Spirit. T. Poots. De-FS:150
  Grand Finale. S. Carleton. De-FS:43
  Lyric of Doubt. D. Wandrei. De-FS:215
  The Man I Met. J. Brennan. De-FS:35
  The Night Song. Wen I-to. Hs-TC:66
  Nightmare. J. Emanuel. Ra-BP:88
  Song of a Sunrise Chinoi. Tr-US II:201
  Song of the Chinoi as They Come Out of
    Flowers. Tr-US II:201
  Sorceress. G. Claytor. De-FS:50
  spirits. V. Cruz. Ad-PB:509
  Spirits. Bi-IT:94
  The Stair. G. Claytor. De-FS:50
  Thoughts of Thomas Hardy. E. Blunden.
    En-PC:31
  To a Conscript of 1940. H. Read.
    Wi-LT:633
  The Two Spirits. P. Shelley.
    De-CH:323, Ho-WR:189
  We Spirits Dance. Bi-IT:95
  The Wind Has Wings. Do-WH:54
  Within the Blackened Sea. F. Saito.
    Sh-AM:151
APPETITE: see also HUMOR - APPETITE
  The Heavy Bear. D. Schwartz.
    Br-TC:356, Pe-OA:218, Wi-LT:520
  O for a Bowl of Fat Canary.
    T. Middleton. Al-VBP:232
APPLE BLOSSOMS
  Apple Blossoms. L. Larcom. Ha-YA:57
  A Comparison. J. Farrar. Fe-FP:214,
    Hu-MP:277
APPLE TREES; see also HUMOR - APPLE TREES
  The Apple Tree. B. Brown. Br-SS:142
  The Comfortable Apple Trees.
    G. Hallock. Sh-RP:163
  Garden Abstract. H. Crane. Gr-CC:53
  Here's to Thee. Bl-OB:139, Bo-FP:144,
    Ch-B:100, Mo-MGT:191, Mo-TB:120,
    Tu-WW:17
  Johnny Appleseed. S. Benét. Hu-MP:390
  Mine Host of the "Golden Apples."
    T. Westwood. Gr-EC:46
  My Apple Tree. F. Garcia Lorca. Lo-SW:33

A Pastoral. R. Hillyer. Co-BN:155
The Planting of the Apple Tree.
  W. Bryant. Co-PS:73, Hu-MP:276
Somewhere Around Christmas. J. Smith.
  Ma-FW:278
Talking in Their Sleep. E. Thomas.
  Co-BN:29
Under a Wiltshire Apple Tree.
  A. De Bary. De-CH:150
Yer's tu Thee. De-TT:73
APPLES
  After Apple-Picking. R. Frost.
    Al-VBP:1126, Co-RG:163, Sh-AP:146,
    Un-MA:176
  The Apple. J. Halevi. Me-PH:61
  The Apple-Barrel of Johnny Appleseed.
    V. Lindsay. Br-AF:118
  Apple Blight. P. Zimmer. Ca-VT:693
  An Apple for Isaac. S. Ibn Gabirol.
    Me-PH:58
  An Apple Gathering. C. Rossetti.
    Co-BL:42, Gr-CC:25, Ox-BN:707
  Apple Season. F. Frost. Br-SS:64
  Apple Song. F. Frost. Fe-FP:239
  The Apple Tree. Mo-MGT:91
  Apples. L. Lee. Hi-WP II:48
  Apples in New Hampshire. M. Gilchrist.
    Co-BN:137
  Apples to Keep. F. Frost. Gr-EC:109
  August. A. Swinburne. Ho-WR:109
  Autumn. P. Hubbell. La-PV:85
  A Ballad of Johnny Appleseed.
    H. Oleson. Ar-TP3:41, Br-SS:142
  Beauty. D. Rossetti. Al-VBP:992
  The Boys and the Apple-Tree.
    A. O'Keeffe. De-TT:120
  Cider Song. M. Weston. Co-BN:140
  The Cow in Apple Time. R. Frost.
    Fe-PL:365, Rd-OA:72, Un-MA:171
  Dividing. D. McCord. Ag-HE:47
  The Faery Queen, Book 2, Canto 7.
    E. Spenser. Al-VBP:118
  Garden Abstract. H. Crane. Gr-CC:53
  Here's to Thee. Bl-OB:139, Bo-FP:144,
    Ch-B:100, Mo-MGT:191, Mo-TB:120,
    Tu-WW:17
  Hot Codlins. Wr-RM:121
  If I Were an Apple. An-IP:(4),
    Ja-PC:29
  In the Apple Orchard. I. Schwartz.
    Ho-TY:149
  The Lotos Eaters. A. Tennyson.
    Bo-FP:143, Cl-FC:42
  The Milkman. I. Gardner. St-H:70
  Moonlit Apples. J. Drinkwater.
    Co-BN:132, Go-BP:113
  Riddle. C. Rossetti. Au-SP:372
  Stand Fast Root. De-CH:669
  Two Apple-Howling Songs, Surrey.
    Bo-FP:143
  Toward Harvest. S. Morse. Ls-NY:56
  Unharvested. R. Frost. Co-BN:154

Upon Paul's Steeple. Li-LB:46
Yer's tu Thee. De-TT:73
APPLESEED, JOHNNY: see CHAPMAN, JOHN
   (JOHNNY APPLESEED)
APPROVAL: see also SATIRE - APPROVAL
   Do It Now. B. Braley. Er-FA:12
APRICOT BLOSSOMS
   Two Songs of Spring Wandering, I.
      Wang Wei. Le-MW:72
APRIL.
   April. R. Emerson. Al-VBP:806
   April. T. Garrison. Hu-MP:292
   April. M. Masters. Du-RG:95
   April. T. Robinson. Un-GT:273
   April. M. Stancher. Ho-CT:9
   April. S. Teasdale. Ar-TP3:203,
      Au-SP:319, Bo-FP:222, Co-PS:54,
      Fe-FP:74, Ha-YA:45, La-PV:81
   April. E. Tietjens. Au-SP:347,
      Ha-YA:47
   An April Child. De-PP:33
   April Mortality. L. Adams. Un-MA:542
   April Rise. L. Lee. Ma-FW:13,
      Ro-OM:190, To-MP:57
   April Showers. T. Tribilla. La-GI:24
   April Weather. M. Watts. Mc-AW:37
   April's Amazing Meaning. G. Dillon.
      Co-BL:17
   Bel M'es Quan lo M'alena. A. Daniel.
      Pa-SG:70
   The Concert. P. McGinley. Ha-YA:47
   Early April. R. Frost. Ha-YA:45
   Edict. H. Vinal. Ls-NY:49
   The Flowering Forest. E. Sitwell.
      Gr-SS:51
   Gale in April. R. Jeffers. Un-MA:362
   Home-Thoughts from Abroad. R. Browning.
      Bo-FT:230, Co-BN:19, Er-FA:266,
      Fe-FP:460, Fe-PL:376, Ga-FB:229,
      Ke-TF:366, Ma-YA:202, Mc-PR:106,
      Ox-BN:534, Pa-HT:117
   I Shall Not Care. S. Teasdale.
      Un-MA:265
   Lady April. R. Le Gallienne. Ha-YA:46
   Like an April Day. J. Wellhaven.
      Pa-SG:30
   Mamble. J. Drinkwater. Hi-WP I:5
   Now the Noisy Winds Are Still.
      M. Dodge. Ha-YA:44
   Ode on the Pleasure Arising from
      Vicissitude. T. Gray. Pa-GTB:109
   Pennines in April. T. Hughes.
      Hi-WP II:49
   The Prologue to the Canterbury Tales.
      G. Chaucer. Al-VBP:6, Gr-CT:281,
      Ma-FW:17, Ma-YA:28
   Proud Songsters. T. Hardy. Ha-PO:105,
      Ma-FW:90
   Sheep and Lambs. K. Hinkson,
      Go-BP:91, Se-PR:74
   The Shepherd's Calendar, April.
      E. Spenser. Al-VBP:98

Sir Robin. L. Larcom. Hu-MP:221
Song. W. Watson. Co-PS:53,
   Ga-FB:232, Se-PR:79, Un-GT:273
Spring. E. Millay. Gr-BT:132,
   Mo-BG:113, Un-MA:444
Spring Families. F. Frost. Sh-RP:198
Spring in New Hampshire. C. McKay.
   Bo-HF:52, Hu-PN:97, Ra-BP:59
This Fevers Me. R. Eberhart. Tr-MR:38
Two Tramps in Mud Time. R. Frost.
   Un-MA:189, Wi-LT:176
The Waste Land. T. Eliot. Pe-OA:112,
   Un-MA:386
The West Wind. J. Masefield.
   Er-FA:242, Un-MB:223, Wi-LT:188
When Faces Called Flowers. E. Cummings.
   Co-BN:22
A World Still Young. W. Henley.
   Un-MW:8
The Worm. R. Souster. Do-WH:71
Yellow Spring. J. Jiminez. Le-SW:21
APRIL FOOLS' DAY
   All Fools' Day. Au-SP:367, Bo-FP:222,
      Br-SS:145, Ch-B:60, Se-PR:80
   An April First Happening. Ja-HH:21
   April Fool. E. Coatsworth. Ha-YA:48,
      Sh-RP:200
   April Fool. E. Hammond. Au-SP:367
   April Fool! B. Lee. Ja-HH:20
   April Fool's Day. M. Pomeroy.
      Co-PS:69
   The First of April. W. Hone. Se-PR:80
   The First of April. G. Johnson.
      Se-PR:81
   Oh Did You Hear? S. Silverstein.
      Co-PS:71
   The Rain. Ch-B:84
AQUARIUMS
   The Aquarium Dream. F. Trefethen.
      Ls-NY:100
   At the Aquarium. M. Eastman.
      Fe-FP:252, Ni-JP:81
   Where the Manatee Plays and the Manta
      Ray Flutters. H. Witt. Ls-NY:190
ARABIC VERSE
   Bubbling Wine. Abu Zakariya. Lo-TY:46
   Call to Prayer. Bilal. Ab-MO:61
   Dates. Fe-FP:478, Ho-LP:26
   The Fountain. al-Mu'tamid. Ho-LP:39
   Haroun's Favorite Song. Pa-SG:64
   Humorous Verse. Abu Dolama. Ab-MO:33,
      Lo-TY:43
   If . . . Tr-US I:121
   Love. Pa-SG:47
   The Mu'allaqa of Antar. Antar.
      Lo-TY:37
   Muhammedan Call to Prayer. Bilal.
      Lo-TY:43
   My Garden. Mu'tamid, King of Seville.
      Pa-SG:29
   My Little Birds. Fe-FP:477
   The Oranges. Abu Dharr. Lo-TY:45

ARABIC VERSE — cont'd.
  Poem Sung at a Mystical Exercise.
    Tr-US I:122
  Popular Song. Tr-US I:122
  The Power of Love. Pa-SG:44
  The Preacher. Al-Mahdi. Lo-TY:45
  Pretences. Ibn Rashiq. Lo-TY:44
  The Romance of Antar. Antar. Ab-MO:66
  Song. Tr-US I:123
  Song. Tr-US I:121
  The Storm. Ibn Suhaid. Bl-SH:5
  The Sword. Abu Bakr. Lo-TY:44
  Women's Grinding Song. Tr-US I:123
ARABS: see ARABIC VERSE; BEDOUINS;
    MOORS (ARABS)
ARAN ISLANDS, IRE.
  Arran. Gr-CT:238, Sm-LG:139
  Isle of Arran. A. Reid. Ha-WR:19
ARAPAHO INDIANS: see INDIANS OF NORTH
    AMERICA - VERSE - ARAPAHO; SAND
    CREEK, BATTLE, 1864
ARBOR DAY: see also TREES
  Arbor Day. D. Thompson. Br-SG:100,
    Br-SS:141, McAW:94
  An Arbor Day Tree. Sh-RP:207
  Motto for a Tree-Planting. R. Gilder.
    Se-PR:95
  Planting a Tree. N. Turner. Ha-YA:53,
    Sh-RP:209
  Planting Trees. V. Friedlaender.
    Co-BN:146
  What Do We Plant? H. Abbey.
    Ar-TP3:205, Fe-FP:211, Hu-MP:269
  Woodman, Spare That Tree. G. Morris.
    Er-FA:243, Fe-FP:546, Hu-MP:267
ARBORVITAE TREES
  Arbor Vitae. C. Patmore. Ox-BN:656
ARBUTUS
  Pink, Small and Punctual (Arbutus).
    E. Dickinson. Ga-FB:284
ARC, JOAN OF: see JOAN OF ARC
ARCADIA, GR.
  In Arcadia. L. Durrell. Un-MB:490
ARCHAEOLOGY: see also RUINS
  Long I Have Loved to Stroll.
    T'ao Ch'ien. Gr-CT:331
  Vil for the Layman. M. Piercy.
    Sc-TN:187
ARCHERY: see BOWS AND ARROWS
ARCHITECTS AND ARCHITECTURE: see also
    BUILDERS AND BUILDING; BUILDINGS;
    HUMOR - ARCHITECTS AND ARCHITECTURE;
    and names of architects, as WREN,
    SIR CHRISTOPHER
  Columns. M. Paraschivescu. Mc-AC:110
  Within King's College Chapel, Cam-
    bridge. W. Wordsworth. Ox-BN:81,
    Pa-GTB:300
ARCTIC REGIONS: see also ALASKA; DOG SLEDS;
    ESKIMOS; HUMOR - ARCTIC REGIONS;

LAPPISH VERSE
  An Empty Threat. R. Frost. La-RM:209
  Far, Far Will I Go. Ma-BH:30
  Hard Times, Dearth Times. Ma-BH:13
  Hunting Songs, 1. Walrus Hunting.
    Ma-BH:17, Tr-US I:12
  I Sighted a Bear. Ma-BH:14
  I Will Walk. Le-IB:36, Ma-BH:8
  The Ice King. A. De Mille. Do-WH:68
  In Fur. W. Stafford. La-RM:113
  The Lands Around My Dwelling.
    Bi-IT:49, Br-MW:141, Ma-BH:23
  Magic Prayer. Le-IB:30, Le-OE:19,
    Ma-BH:7, Tr-US I:9
  A North Pole Story. M. Smedley.
    Ox-BC:251
  Religious Hymn to Be Sung Wearing a
    Head Decoration. Le-IB:95,
    Ma-BH:15, Tr-US I:20
  Song of Caribou, Musk Oxen.
    Br-MW:140, Ho-SD:67, Le-IB:34,
    Ma-BH:21, Tr-US I:26
  There Is Fear. Ma-BH:11, Tr-US I:24
  The Train Dogs. P. Johnson. Do-WH:59
  A View from Here. W. Stafford.
    La-RM:123
ARCTURUS (STAR)
  Arcturus Is His Other Name.
    E. Dickinson. Ga-FB:148
ARETHUSA (NYMPH)
  Arethusa. P. Shelley. Ho-WR:136
ARGENTINA
  The Christ of the Andes. E. Markham.
    Se-PR:85
ARGUMENTS: see CONTROVERSY; QUARRELS
ARISTOCRACY: see also HUMOR - ARISTOCRACY;
    KINGS AND RULERS; KNIGHTS AND KNIGHT-
    HOOD; PRINCES AND PRINCESSES; SOCIAL
    CLASSES
  Flammonde. E. Robinson. Wi-LT:105
ARISTOTLE
  Among School Children. W. Yeats.
    Pa-GTB:428, Un-MB:114, Wi-LT:72
  The Motto. A. Cowley. No-CL:6
ARITHMETIC: see also HUMOR - ARITHMETIC;
    MATHEMATICS
  Multiplication Is Vexation.
    Un-GT:23, Wr-RM:113
  Nine Times Nine. On-TW:33
  Seven Times One. J. Ingelow. Br-BC:71,
    Fe-FP:50, Gr-TG:47, Hu-MP:70
    Ke-TF:41, Ox-BN:720, Un-GT:14
  "To Think that Two and Two Are Four."
    A. Housman. Pl-IO:77
ARIZONA: see also HUMOR - ARIZONA
  Arizona. M. Clifford. Se-PR:252
  Arizona. Em-AF:758
  Arizona Village. R. Davieau. Br-AF:148
  The Painted Hills of Arizona.
    E. Curran. Pa-HT:57

ARK: see NOAH
ARKANSAS: see also names of towns, as
    LITTLE ROCK, ARK.
  The Arkansas Traveler. S. Faulkner.
    Se-PR:253
  The Old Section Boss. Ra-BP:17
ARMADAS: see SPANISH ARMADA
ARMADILLOS: see also HUMOR - ARMADILLOS
  The Armadillo. E. Bishop. Ca-VT:319
ARMAGEDDON: see END OF THE WORLD
ARMAGH, IRE., N.
  Armagh. W. Rodgers. Co-PI:171
ARMED FORCES DAY: see HEROES AND HEROISM;
    PATRIOTISM; UNITED STATES - HISTORY
    AND PATRIOTISM
ARMENIANS IN THE UNITED STATES
  For My Father. D. Kherdian. Kh-VA:11
ARMIES: see also MILITARY SERVICE,
    COMPULSORY; SOLDIERS
  An Army Corps on the March. W. Whitman.
    Fe-PL:171, Vi-PP:147
  Bivouac on a Mountain Side. W. Whitman.
    Fe-PL:170, Gr-CT:338, Li-TU:236,
    Sh-AP:118, Vi-PP:148
  Charlemagne. H. Longfellow. Er-FA:310
  The Reveille. B. Harte. Se-PR:121,
    Sp-OG:192, Vi-PP:199
  Vae Victis. R. Humphries. Ni-JP:123
ARMISTICE DAY: see VETERANS DAY
ARMISTICES
  And There Was a Great Calm. T. Hardy.
    Gr-CT:345, Tr-MR:181, Wi-LT:26
  Everyone Sang. S. Sassoon. Co-PS:144,
    Ga-FB:218, Ga-S:171, Ha-LO:71,
    Mc-WK:13, Ni-JP:79, Pa-GTB:453,
    Sh-RP:88, Sm-MK:211, Un-MB:314
ARMS AND ARMOR: see also ATOMIC WEAPONS;
    BOMBS; BOWS AND ARROWS; GUNS; HUMOR -
    ARMS AND ARMOR; HYDROGEN WEAPONS;
    MINES (EXPLOSIVE); SATIRE - ARMS AND
    ARMOR; SPEARS; SWORDS
  Another Rotating Thing. K. Takamura.
    Sh-AM:45
  The Arsenal at Springfield. H. Longfellow.
    Ba-PO:96, Cr-WS:24
  Avenger, What Wrong? J. Rorty.
    Sm-PT:128
  Charlemagne. H. Longfellow. Er-FA:310
  The Faerie Queene. E. Spenser.
    Ma-YA:55
  A Fairy in Armor. J. Drake. Fe-FP:380
  Haiku. R. Lockett. La-IH:132
  Rearmament. R. Jeffers. Bl-FP:50
  The Shield. C. Stetson. Sp-OG:34
  Weapons. A. Wickham. Un-MB:278
ARMSTRONG, LOUIS (SATCHMO)
  Lambda. M. Tolson. Be-MA:24, Hu-PN:141
  Satchmo. M. Tolson. Ra-BP:119
ARMY LIFE: see MILITARY LIFE; SOLDIERS
ARNOLD, BENEDICT
  Major André. Em-AF:428
ARNOLD, MATTHEW: see SATIRE - ARNOLD,
    MATTHEW

ARNOLD, THOMAS
  Rugby Chapel—November, 1857. M. Arnold.
    Rv-CB:874
AROUET, FRANCOIS MARIE: see VOLTAIRE
    (FRANCOIS MARIE AROUET)
ARRIVALS: see also GREETINGS; HOMECOMING;
    MEETINGS (ENCOUNTERS); RETURNING
  Arrivals, Departures. P. Larkin.
    Un-MB:527
ART AND ARTISTS: see also ARCHITECTS AND
    ARCHITECTURE; CUBISM; HUMOR - ART AND
    ARTISTS; ILLUMINATION OF BOOKS AND
    MANUSCRIPTS; PAINTINGS; SATIRE - ART
    AND ARTISTS; SCULPTORS AND SCULPTURE;
    STATUES; and names of artists, as
    MARIN, JOHN
  Abstract Painter. G. Kennedy.
    Ls-NY:171
  Abstract Painter in Spring. R. Haas.
    Ls-NY:151
  Addressed to Haydon. J. Keats.
    Ox-BN:335
  Ajanta. M. Rukeyser. Un-MA:630,
    Wi-LT:806
  Andrea del Sarto. R. Browning.
    Ke-TF:310
  Art. H. Melville. Al-VBP:955
  Ballad of Tramway Art. A. Aronov.
    Bo-RU:8
  The Chicago Picasso. G. Brooks.
    Ra-BP:169, Wi-LT:665
  The Conundrum of the Workshops.
    R. Kipling. Un-MB:131
  The Convert. M. Danner. Ra-BP:149
  Les Deux Arts. M. Ward. Ke-TF:242
  A Disappearance in West Cedar Street.
    L. Sissman. Br-TC:383
  "Don't Let That Horse."
    L. Ferlinghetti. Mo-BG:82
  Edward Hopper's "House by the Tracks."
    R. Cuscaden. St-H:33
  The Elfin Artist. A. Noyes. Sp-OG:168
  First Lesson. N. Willard. Sc-TN:234
  Fra Lippo Lippi. R. Browning.
    Al-VBP:898, Ho-P:118
  Giocanni da Fiesole on the Sublime.
    R. Howard. Ho-P:117
  El Greco. C. Trypanis. Ls-NY:177
  Homage to Chagall. D. Niatum. Ni-CD:135
  I Paint What I See. E. White. Mo-BG:64
  The Image-Maker. O. Gogarty. Go-BP:63
  In Santa Maria del Popolo. T. Gunn.
    Pa-GTB:563
  Keorapsetse Kgositsile. G. Brooks.
    Ra-BP:172
  Lapis Lazuli. W. Yeats. Wi-LT:89
  The Laughing Hyena, by Hokusai.
    D. Enright. Br-TC:117
  Musée des Beaux Arts. W. Auden.
    To-MP:31
  On a Picture by Pippin, Called "The Den."
    S. Rodman. Hu-PN:544

ART AND ARTISTS — cont'd.
  On Kuan Shan-Yueh's Painting.
    Kuo Mo-jo. Hs-TC:42
  One Word More. R. Browning.
    Al-VBP:911
  The Painter's Philosophy. R. Browning.
    Ga-S:117
  Paul Klee. J. Haines. Sc-TN:74
  Portrait of the Boy as an Artist.
    B. Howes. Un-MA:653
  Retort to the Anti-Abstractionists.
    E. Jennings. Go-BP:64
  The Slave and the Iron Lace. M. Danner.
    Bo-AN:157, Ra-BP:154
  The Story of Soutine. J. Schevill.
    En-PC:188
  Under Ben Bulben. W. Yeats. Wi-LT:96
  Ungainly Things. R. Wallace. Du-SH:34
  Youth and Art. R. Browning. Al-VBP:909
ART GALLERIES: see also MUSEUMS
  The Municipal Gallery Revisited.
    W. Yeats. Pa-GTB:432
  Musée des Beaux Arts. W. Auden.
    Br-TC:20, Er-FA:64, Ha-PO:223,
    Pa-GTB:510, Wi-LT:467
ARTAGNAN, CHARLES DE BAATZ D': see THREE
    MUSKETEERS
ARTEMIS: see DIANA
ARTHUR, KING
  The Boy and the Mantle. Ox-BB:31
  Cablegram. A. Kramer. Ls-NY:34
  Idylls of the King, Guinevere.
    A. Tennyson. Ma-YA:198
  The Passing of Arthur. A. Tennyson.
    Ni-JP:158, Ox-BN:511
  Prayer. A. Tennyson. Go-BP:188
  When Good King Arthur Ruled. Bo-FP:53,
    Br-FF:(6), De-TT:93, Ir-BB:272,
    Li-LB:50, Mo-MGT:168, Mo-NR:54,
    On-TW:13
ARTICHOKES
  Artichoke. P. Neruda. Li-TU:53
ARTIFICIAL SATELLITES
  Little Satellite. J. Krows. Au-SP:176
ARTISTS: see ART AND ARTISTS
ARTS AND CRAFTS: see also CARVING (ART);
    ILLUMINATION OF BOOKS AND MANUSCRIPTS;
    WEAVING
  Artificer. X. Kennedy. Br-TC:233
ARUNDEL FAMILY
  An Arundel Tomb. P. Larkin. To-MP:79
ASH TREES: see also MOUNTAIN ASH TREES
  Alms in Autumn. R. Fyleman. Bo-FP:149
  Ash-Boughs. G. Hopkins. Go-BP:30
  Discord in Childhood. D. Lawrence.
    Co-EL:147, Rv-CB:978
  Trees. W. de la Mare. Mc-PR:199
ASH WEDNESDAY: see LENT
ASPEN TREES
  Binsey Poplars Felled 1879. G. Hopkins.
    Co-BN:153, Ma-FW:104
    Rain in the Aspens. Su-Tung P'o.
  Rx-OH:87

ASPIRATION: see AMBITION; HOPE
ASSASSINATIONS: see also MURDER
  April 4, 1968. M. Goode. Jo-SA:6,
    Jo-VC:57
  The Assassin. D. Hall. Ha-TP:31
  Assassination. D. Lee. Ad-BO:29,
    Ad-PB:423
  Booth Killed Lincoln. Em-AF:459
  Channel U.S.A.—Live. A. Stoutenburg.
    Br-AF:93, Hi-TL:234
  Charles Guiteau. Em-AF:460
  Garfield's Murder. Hi-TL:142
  In America There Is Mourning.
    A. Karlov. Mo-MI:78
  White Weekend. Q. Troupe. Kr-OF:164
  Zolgotz. Em-AF:462
ASSES: see DONKEYS; MULES
ASSURANCE
  Assurance. G. Crowell. Se-PR:75
  The Collar. G. Herbert. Al-VBP:341,
    Go-BP:181, Pl-EI:92, Rv-CB:355
  Comfort Ye My People. Bible. O.T.
    Isaiah. Ga-S:65, Pl-EI:175
  The Flight into Egypt. W. Auden.
    Ga-S:113, Pl-EI:61
  Hammer and Anvil. S. Cole. Fe-PL:333
  I Will Lift Up Mine Eyes. Bible. O.T.
    Psalms. Bo-FP:305, Cl-DT:43,
    Rv-CB:129
  The Lord Is My Shepherd. Bible. O.T.
    Psalms. Ar-TP3:189, Bo-FP:107,
    Fe-FP:25, Fe-PL:346, Ga-S:213,
    Rv-CB:130, Sh-RP:92
  O Heart, Hold Thee Secure. W. de la Mare.
    Go-BP:183
  Remember Thy Covenant. E. Pierce.
    Tr-MR:192
  S.S. "Lusitania." M. Arnold. Rv-CB:865
  Sweet Baby, Sleep. G. Wither. Cl-DT:32
ASSURBANIPAL: see SARDANAPALUS
ASSYRIA
  After Reading Translations of Ancient
    Texts on Stone and Clay.
    C. Reznikoff. Gr-SS:170
  The Destruction of Sennacherib.
    G. Byron. Er-FA:347, Fe-FP:511,
    Fe-PL:431, Hi-FO:27, Hu-MP:416,
    Mc-PR:25, Na-EO:50, Ni-JP:75,
    Pa-OM:146, Sm-LG:256, Sp-OG:183,
    Un-GT:143
  Sardanapalus. H. Howard. Hi-FO:29
ASTROLOGY: see also FORTUNE TELLING;
    PROPHETS AND PROPHECIES; ZODIAC
  An Astrologer's Song. R. Kipling.
    Un-MB:135
  For the Conjunction of Two Planets.
    A. Rich. Pl-IO:30
  Symmetries and Asymmetries. W. Auden.
    Ma-FW:109
  Verses of an Inca Poet and Astrologer.
    Tr-US II:300
ASTRONAUTS: see also HUMOR - ASTRONAUTS;

SPACE EXPLORATION
Outward. L. Simpson.   Li-TU:253
ASTRONOMERS AND ASTRONOMY: see also
   ASTROLOGY; COMETS; CONSTELLATIONS;
   ECLIPSES; EQUINOX; GALAXIES; HUMOR –
   ASTRONOMERS AND ASTRONOMY; LIFE ON
   OTHER PLANETS; METEORS; MOON;
   PLANETARIUMS; PLANETS; QUASARS;
   SATIRE – ASTRONOMERS AND ASTRONOMY;
   SKY; SPACE (OUTER); STARS; SUN; TELE-
   SCOPES; TIDES; UNIVERSE; ZODIAC
Driving Clock. H. Flanner. Sm-PT:57
For the Conjunction of Two Planets.
   A. Rich. Pl-IO:30
Ode to the Hayden Planetarium.
   A. Guiterman. Pl-IO:29
The Star-Splitter. R. Frost. Pl-IO:173
Troilus and Cressida. W. Shakespeare.
   Pl-IO:22
A Welcome to Dr. Benjamin Apthorp
   Gould. O. Holmes. Pl-IO:169
ASYLUMS: see also MADNESS
Counting the Mad. D. Justice.
   Ke-PP:105
I'm like a Count. L. Batshev.
   Bo-RU:15
Madhouse. C. Hernton. Ad-PB:238,
   Hu-NN:102, Hu-PN:403, Jo-SA:81
Ringing the Bells. A. Sexton.
   Ca-VT:635
Sometimes I Go to Camarillo & Sit in
   the Lounge. K. Lyle. Ad-PB:464
A Visit to Van Gogh. C. Causley.
   En-PC:158
Visits to St. Elizabeths. E. Bishop.
   Ca-VT:320, Mc-EA:154
Waking in the Blue. R. Lowell.
   Un-MA:667
You, Doctor Martin. A. Sexton.
   Un-MA:686
ATALANTA
Atalanta in Calydon. A. Swinburne.
   Al-VBP:1038, Ga-FB:230, Ha-PO:237,
   Ma-YA:216, Na-EO:58, Pa-GTB:388
ATHEISM: see AGNOSTICISM
ATHENA (GODDESS): see MINERVA (GODDESS)
ATHENS, GR.
Caryatid. L. Adams. Wi-LT:603
The Night There Was Dancing in the
   Streets. E. Olson. St-H:174
Paradise Regained. J. Milton.
   Al-VBP:412
ATHLETES: see also names of athletes, as
   GEHRIG, HENRY LOUIS (LOU); and sports,
   as BASEBALL; OLYMPIC GAMES
After the Record Is Broken.
   J. Emanuel. Ls-NY:40
The Ageing Athlete. N. Weiss. Mo-SD:173
Athletes. W. Gibson. Mo-SD:177
The Breed of Athletes. Euripides.
   Mo-SD:163

To an Athlete Dying Young. A. Housman.
   Ha-PO:140, Ma-YA:223, Mo-SD:168,
   Ni-JP:33, Pe-M:58, Un-MB:94, Wi-LT:60
ATLANTA, GA.
Give Us the Sign! W. Du Bois.
   Kr-OF:149
A Litany at Atlanta. W. Du Bois.
   Hu-PN:20
ATLANTIC CABLE: see CABLES, SUBMARINE
ATLANTIC CHARTER
Atlantic Charter, A.D. 1620-1942.
   F. Young. Ar-TP3:39, Br-AF:86,
   Vi-PP:221
ATLANTIC OCEAN
Atlantic Ocean. V. Mayakovsky.
   Ca-MR:118
I Found Her Out There. T. Hardy.
   De-CH:257
ATLANTIS
The Atlantides. H. Thoreau. Al-VBP:918
Atlantis. C. Aiken. Gr-SS:180
Atlantis. S. Coblentz. De-FS:56
ATOMIC BOMBS: see ATOMIC WEAPONS
ATOMIC ENERGY: see also SATIRE – ATOMIC
   ENERGY
Pentagonia. G. Bates. Li-SR:133
ATOMIC WEAPONS: see also HEAVY WATER;
   HIROSHIMA, JAPAN; HUMOR – ATOMIC
   WEAPONS; HYDROGEN WEAPONS;
   NAGASAKI, JAPAN; SATIRE – ATOMIC
   WEAPONS
Advice to a Prophet. R. Wilbur.
   Tr-MR:233
And the Lord Was Not in the Whirlwind.
   L. MacNeice. Pl-EI:154
At Hiroshima. L. Hubbell. Ba-PO:52,
   Cr-WS:148
At the Bomb Testing Site. W. Stafford.
   Ba-PO:56, Bl-FP:55, Wi-LT:827
The Autumn of the Bomb. R. Ellison.
   Ba-PO:58
Back Again from Yucca Flats. R. Kelley.
   Br-AF:92
Dirge for the New Sunrise. E. Sitwell.
   Pl-EI:144, Tr-MR:189, Un-MB:338
For the Lost Generation. G. Kinnell.
   Ke-PP:58
Ghosts. Fire. Water. J. Kirkup.
   Go-BP:215
The Gift to Be Simple. H. Moss.
   Br-TC:307, Pl-IO:181, Tr-MR:174
Hiroshima. M. Rockwell. Ba-PO:53,
   Ke-PP:9
Hour of Concern. L. Hubbell. Ba-PO:52
In a Surrealist Year. L. Ferlinghetti.
   Ke-PP:3
The Inquisitors. R. Jeffers.
   Un-MA:372
Little Johnny's Foolish Invention.
   B. Patten. Gr-BT:142
Pentagonia. G. Bates. Li-SR:133

ATOMIC WEAPONS — cont'd.
  A Poem on the Nuclear War, from Pompeii.
    R. Tillinghast. Ba-PO:55
  The Progress of Faust. K. Shapiro.
    Pe-OA:220
  Relative Sadness. C. Rowbotham.
    Gr-BT:119
  Rhymes for a Modern Nursery. P. Dehn.
    Br-SM:65, Co-FB:451, Du-RG:80
  Ring-a-Ring o' Neutrons. P. Dehn.
    Li-SR:129
  what if a much of a which of a wind.
    E. Cummings. Al-VBP:1203, Er-FA:94,
    Un-MA:477, Wi-LT:368
ATOMS: see also HUMOR - ATOMS; SATIRE -
    ATOMS
  "Atom from Atom." R. Emerson. Pl-IO:8
  No Single Thing Abides. T. Lucretius
    Carus. Pl-IO:9
ATTICA, N.Y.
  If We Cannot Live as People. C. Lynch.
    Ad-PB:461
ATTICS
  The Attic. R. Fyleman. Bo-FP:23
  Etta Moten's Attic. M. Danner.
    Ad-PB:136, Be-MA:90, Bo-AN:156
  Fun in a Garret. E. Dowd. Ar-TP3:113
  My Father's Trunk. R. Roseliep.
    St-H:188
ATTILA (THE HUN)
  Attila. W. Everson. Gr-WS:4
AVON RIVER
  The Ebb Tide. R. Southey. Ox-BN:176
AUCTIONS: see also HUMOR - AUCTIONS
  The Auction Sale. H. Reed. Un-MB:509
  Auctioneer. C. Sandburg. La-PV:57
  Horse and Hammer. P. Dufault.
    Co-BBW:157
  A Sheep Fair. T. Hardy. Ho-P:206
AUDEN, WYSTAN HUGH
  To Auden on His Fiftieth. R. Eberhart.
    Pl-ML:74
  To W. H. Auden on His Fiftieth Birthday.
    B. Howes. Pl-ML:76
AUDUBON, JOHN JAMES
  John James Audubon. S. Benét. Hi-TL:82
AUDUBON, LUCY BAKEWELL: see AUDUBON,
    JOHN JAMES
AUGUST
  August. F. Garcia Lorca. Le-SW:47
  August. F. Ledwidge. Gr-SS:41
  August. M. Lewis. Un-GT:277
  August. A. Swinburne. Ho-WR:109
  August. C. Thaxter. Fe-FP:77, Ha-YA:90
  August. H. Winslow. Ha-YA:86
  August. E. Wylie. Un-MA:277
  August from My Desk. R. Flint.
    Br-AF:156, Du-RG:49
  August Night. E. Roberts. Ha-YA:89
  August Night. S. Teasdale.
    Un-MA:267

August Smiles. E. Coatsworth.
  Br-SS:177
Blackberry-Picking. S. Heaney.
  Co-BN:100
Cold August. J. Harrison. Ls-NY:284
Daisy. W. Williams. Un-MA:257
A Dog Day. R. Field. Br-SS:178
End of Summer, Georgia. A. Scruggs.
  Ke-TF:443
The Golden Month. M. Doyle. Ha-YA:92
Hymn to the Sun. M. Roberts. Sm-LG:56
In August. M. Chute. Mc-AW:46
In August. W. Howells. Se-PR:164
In the Fields. C. Mew. Co-BN:208,
  Sm-MK:221, Un-MB:159
Mid-August. L. Driscoll. Ha-YA:88
Mid-August at Sourdough Mountain
  Lookout. G. Snyder. Kh-VA:28,
  Mc-EA:41
The Month of Falling Stars.
  E. Higginson. Ha-YA:91
AUKS: see HUMOR - AUKS
AUNTS: see also HUMOR - AUNTS
  Aunt Alice in April. W. Matchett.
    Ha-TP:128
  Aunt Dvorah. J. Segal. Ho-TY:157
  Aunt Edna. J. Tate. St-H:229
  Aunt Helen. T. Eliot. Ha-PO:68,
    Mc-WS:146, Pe-SS:158
  Aunt Julia. N. Maccaig. To-MP:185
  Aunt Selina. C. Haynes. Hu-MP:15,
    Ja-PC:44
  Auntie's Skirts. R. Stevenson.
    Hu-MP:135
  Aunts Watching Television. J. Pudney.
    To-MP:71
  The Fox Rhyme. I. Serraillier.
    Co-BBW:29, Co-EL:28, Sm-MK:197
  Girl's-Eye View of Relatives.
    P. McGinley. Ke-TF:90, Mc-WS:145
  Great Aunts. S. O'Críadáin. Co-PI:157
  The Heir. Pa-RE:56
  Lizards and Snakes. A. Hecht.
    Br-TC:183, Ha-TP:39
  Manners. M. Van Rensselaer.
    Fe-FP:44, Hu-MP:16
  My Last Afternoon with Uncle Devereux
    Winslow. R. Lowell. Ca-VT:447
  My Old Maid Aunt. D. Schultz.
    Du-SH:137
  Out to Old Aunt Mary's. J. Riley.
    Er-FA:143
  Some Foreign Letters. A. Sexton.
    En-PC:274, Un-MA:687
  Songs, I. Tr-US II:123
  There Were Three Sisters. On-TW:13
  To Aunt Rose. A. Ginsberg. Ca-VT:575,
    Wi-LT:719
  The Visits of My Aunt. J. Woods.
    St-H:244
AURORA BOREALIS: see AURORAS

AURORAS
  Aurora. Lo Men. Pa-MV:123
  We Will Watch the Northern Lights.
    Ho-SD:2, La-RM:122
  When I See. H. Panigeo. Ba-HI:71
  Wild March. C. Woolson. Ha-YA:36
AUSCHWITZ, POL.: see CONCENTRATION CAMPS
AUSTRALIA: see also AUSTRALIAN ABORIGINAL
    VERSE; BALLADS, AUSTRALIAN; DIALECTS,
    AUSTRALIAN; HUMOR - AUSTRALIA; RANCH
    LIFE
  At Cooloolah. J. Wright. Un-MB:516
  The Banks of the Condamine. Gr-GB:212
  The Bunyip. D. Stewart. Rd-OA:66
  From the "Goulburn Island" Love Cycle.
    Tr-US I:246
  From the Sacred Dulngulg Cycle.
    Tr-US I:243
  The Gidgid-Bird. Tr-US I:245
  Hunter's Chant Sung While Spearing
    Turtles. Tr-US I:241
  Jim Jones at Botany Bay. Co-RM:139,
    Gr-GB:257
  Kangaroo. D. Lawrence. Ma-FW:214,
    Rd-OA:139
  Native-Cat Songs. Tr-US I:254
  Of Those Who See Through This Riddle.
    Re-RR:82
  The Railway Train. Tr-US I:260
  Recited Before Going to the Beach to
    Fish. Tr-US I:241
  Sacred Song of the Jackeroo Cult.
    Tr-US I:258
  The Sick Stockrider. A. Gordon.
    Hi-FO:233
  Some Know Whom Australia. Re-RR:103
  Song of a Widow for Her Dead Husband.
    Tr-US I:242
  Song of a Woman Crying for the Dead
    Baby Son of Her Daughter. Tr-US I:244
  Song of Departure and Farewell.
    Tr-US I:245
  Stir the Wallaby Stew. Hi-FO:253
  The Tantanoola Tiger. M. Harris.
    Ca-MB:66
  A Triptych on the Dugong. Tr-US I:242
  Umbara's Song. Umbara. Tr-US I:260
  Waltzing Matilda. A. Paterson.
    Gr-CT:138, Gr-GB:259,
    Ha-PO:238, Mc-WK:147
  Waves Coming Up Against the Rocks.
    Le-OE:85, Tr-US I:244
  Wenberri's Song. Tr-US I:261
  What Island Was Largest. Re-RR:20
  The Wild Colonial Boy. Co-RM:171
AUSTRALIAN ABORIGINAL VERSE
  Be Kind. Le-OE:33
  From the "Goulburn Island" Love Cycle.
    Tr-US I:246
  From the Sacred Dulngulg Cycle.
    Tr-US I:243
  The Gidgid-Bird. Tr-US I:245

  Hunter's Chant Sung While Spearing
    Turtles. Tr-US I:241
  The Narba-Bird. Tr-US I:245
  Native-Cat Songs. Tr-US I:254
  Over the Sun-Darkened River Sands.
    Le-OE:73
  Paddling We Saw That Turtle, Saw Its
    Eyes Open. Le-OE:45
  Poor Fellow Me. Le-OE:123
  The Railway Train. Tr-US I:260
  Recited Before Going to the Beach to
    Fish. Tr-US I:241
  Sacred Song of the Avocet Cult.
    Tr-US I:256
  Sacred Song of the Jackeroo Cult.
    Tr-US I:258
  Song Cycle of the Moon-Bone. Tr-US I:246
  Song of a Widow for Her Dead Husband.
    Tr-US I:242
  Song of a Woman Crying for the Dead
    Baby Son of Her Daughter. Tr-US I:244
  Song of Departure and Farewell.
    Tr-US I:245
  There Are the Eagles Crying. Le-OE:46
  A Triptych on the Dugong. Tr-US I:242
  Umbara's Song. Umbara. Tr-US I:260
  Waves Coming Up Against the Rocks.
    Le-OE:85, Tr-US I:244
  Wenberri's Song. Tr-US I:261
AUSTRALIANS
  The Dead Swagman. N. Cato. Co-RM:140
  The Man from Ironbark. A. Peterson.
    Co-RM:146
AUTHORS: see also HUMOR - AUTHORS;
    SATIRE - AUTHORS; and names of
    authors, as ELIOT, THOMAS STEARNS
  An Advertisement to the Reader.
    J. Bunyan. De-CH:616
  The Crystal. S. Lanier. Sh-AP:133
  Digging. S. Heaney. Br-TC:173
  Dream with an Angel. M. Banus.
    Mc-AC:113
  Epigraph. W. Blake. Ox-BN:46
  Henry James. R. Stevenson. Ox-BN:891
  Important Statement. P. Kavanagh.
    En-PC:65
  It Is Too Late. H. Longfellow.
    Fe-PL:304
  Limitations. S. Sassoon. Un-MB:316
  The Person from Porlock. R. Graves.
    Pl-ML:8
  Prologue to Aureng-zebe. J. Dryden.
    Rv-CB:464
  Sat Est Scripsisse. A. Dobson.
    Go-BP:66
  Shaman Song 2. G. Fowler. Sc-TN:52
  Shut Not Your Doors. W. Whitman.
    Pl-ML:29
  Testament. T. Arghezi. Mc-AC:25
  The Troubles of a Book. L. Riding.
    Ls-NY:334
  Weapons. A. Wickham. Un-MB:278

AUTOMATION
  A Valedictory to Standard Oil of Indiana.
    D. Wagner. Du-SH:146
AUTOMOBILE DRIVERS: see also HUMOR -
    AUTOMOBILE DRIVERS
  The Autostrada. G. Johnson. Ls-NY:250
  Journey to the Interior. T. Roethke.
    Ca-VT:297
  Midsummer Nights. S. Sandy. Be-EB:34
  North on One-Eleven. J. Knoepfle.
    St-H:98
  The Sunday Driver in Search of Himself.
    J. Tate. St-H:233
  Turnpike. R. Sward. St-H:225
AUTOMOBILE RACING
  Scrapyard. M. Benson. Le-M:71
AUTOMOBILES: see also HUMOR - AUTOMOBILES;
    SERVICE STATIONS; TAXICABS
  Automobile Mechanics. D. Baruch.
    Ar-TP3:4, Au-SP:103, Fe-FP:35
  Buick. K. Shapiro. Al-VBP:1242
  "Cars Once Steel and Green, Now Old."
    L. Zukovsky. Ca-VT:249
  Central Park Tourney. M. Weston.
    Br-AF:195, Du-RG:47, La-OC:123,
    Pe-M:129
  The Death of the Sports-Car Driver.
    J. Aaron. Pe-M:91
  The Flat. L. Lieberman. Du-SH:70
  Funny the Way Different Cars Start.
    D. Baruch. Fe-FP:186
  Highway: Michigan. T. Roethke.
    Du-SH:68
  It's a Lean Car. C. Sandburg.
    Su-FVI:39
  Lines Based on a 1924 Advertisement.
    G. Lehmann. Ls-NY:264
  The Misery of Mechanics. P. Booth.
    Du-SH:151
  Model T. A. Stoutenburg. Du-SH:71
  Motor Cars. R. Bennett. Ar-TP3:92,
    Au-SP:163, Fe-FP:245, La-PP:35
  Song of the Blue Roadster. R. Field.
    Fe-FP:184
  Southbound on the Freeway. M. Swenson.
    Br-AF:236, Du-RG:82, Pe-SS:96
  Stop-Go. D. Baruch. Ar-TP3:91,
    Fe-FP:185
  This Dim and Ptolemaic Man. J. Bishop.
    Pl-IO:25, Wi-LT:607
  To Bella Akhmadulina. A. Voznesensky.
    Ca-MR:79
  What Has a Horn. Re-RR:60
AUTOMOBILES - TRAILERS
  Johnny Fife and Johnny's Wife.
    M. Merryman. Ar-TP3:95, Au-SP:161
AUTUMN: see also EQUINOX; HARVEST;
    INDIAN SUMMER; and names of months,
    as OCTOBER
  Alms in Autumn. R. Fyleman. Bo-FP:149
  Alone. Chu Shu Chen. Rx-OH:134
  Another September. T. Kinsella. En-PC:270

Antique Harvesters. J. Ransom.
  Un-MA:413
As Imperceptibly As Grief. E. Dickinson.
  Wi-LT:15
At Thanksgiving. J. Leichliter.
  Ls-NY:288
Autumn. R. Campbell. Pa-GTB:498,
  Un-MB:418
Autumn. W. Carruth. Hu-MP:314
Autumn. J. Clare. Co-BN:135
Autumn. V. Contoski. Sc-TN:27
Autumn. W. de la Mare. Gr-CC:46
Autumn. E. Dickinson. Ar-TP3:185,
  Bo-FT:142, Bo-HF:127, Ch-B:92,
  Co-BN:129, Fe-FP:81, Ha-YA:96,
  Hu-MP:314, Pe-FB:86, Tu-WW:73
Autumn. D. Dore. Ho-CT:28
Autumn. Ho Ch'i-fang. Hs-TC:220
Autumn. T. Hood. Al-VBP:795,
  Cl-DT:88, De-CH:620, Ox-BN:420
Autumn. P. Hubbell. La-PV:85
Autumn. T. Hulme. Al-VBP:1152,
  Ha-LO:102, Ja-PA:7, Sm-MK:13
Autumn. Manovinoda. Al-PI:38
Autumn. F. O'Connor. Co-PS:129
Autumn. R. Rilke. Pa-SG:97
Autumn. V. Scannell. Ma-FW:264,
  To-MP:176
Autumn. P. Shelley. De-CH:208
Autumn. W. Smith. Sh-RP:219
Autumn. Su Tung P'o. Rx-OH:88
Autumn. R. Tagore. Go-BP:26
Autumn. Tsang K'o-chia. Hs-TC:285
Autumn! N. Turner. Ha-YA:95, Ja-PA:10
Autumn. J. Untermeyer. Un-MA:332
Autumn. Wang Wei. Rx-LT:56
Autumn. H. Wolfe. Fe-PL:268
Autumn Birds. J. Clare. Rd-OA:182
Autumn Color. T. Robinson. Ha-YA:97
Autumn Colors. Wen I-to. Hs-TC:52
Autumn Dawning. A. Machado. Le-SW:71
Autumn Evening. J. Clare. Re-TW:104
Autumn Evening Beside the Lake.
  Li Ch'ing Chao. Rx-OH:93
Autumn Fancies. Fe-FP:212, Hu-MP:279,
  Ja-PA:15
Autumn Fashions. E. Thomas. Ha-YA:99
Autumn Fires. R. Stevenson. Ar-TP3:184,
  Br-SG:93, Ha-YA:101, Ja-PA:10,
  Mc-PR:100
Autumn Flight. A. Karanikas.
  Bo-HF:126
Autumn Haze. R. Munkittrick. Se-PR:169
Autumn Leaves. J. Heyward. Hu-MP:281
Autumn Leaves. M. Sutphen. Bo-FP:147
Autumn Morning. F. Frost. Sh-RP:225
Autumn on the Yangtze River. Chi Hsuan.
  Pa-MV:46
Autumn Rain. A. Fisher. Sh-RP:220
Autumn Scene. B. Dowling. Co-BN:133
An Autumn Sky. K. Takahama. Sh-AM:162

Autumn Song.   E. Long.   Br-SS:53,
   Ja-PA:11
Autumn Song.   C. Rossetti.   Al-VBP:987,
   Ma-YA:212
The Autumn Storm.   Basho.   Sh-RP:63
Autumn Thoughts.   Lu Yu.   Rx-OH:112
The Autumn Wind.   J. Clare.   Co-BN:130
Autumn Wind.   Emperor Wu.   Rx-LT:4,
   Sm-LG:398
Autumn Woods.   J. Tippett.   Ar-TP3:184,
   Ja-PA:14, Mc-AW:48, St-FS:102
Autumnal.   E. Dowson.   Ox-BN:942
Autumnal.   R. Humphries.   Tr-MR:273
Autumnal Ode.   A. De Vere.   Ox-BN:587
Autumnal Spring Song.   V. Miller.
   Ha-PO:99
Autumn's Fete.   A. McGeorge.   Ha-YA:96
Autumn's Passing.   H. Rostrom.
   St-FS:66
Beech Leaves.   J. Reeves.   Pa-RE:108,
   Sh-RP:222
Before the Coming of Winter.
   D. Schmitz.   St-H:198
Berries.   I. Eastwick.   Br-SG:91
Blue Smoke.   F. Frost.   Br-SS:65
   Sh-RP:229
The Burning of the Leaves.   L. Binyon.
   Pa-GTB:434
Butternuts.   E. Astley.   Ke-TF:446
Chant for Skippers.   K. Gallagher.
   Br-SS:54
Cider.   P. Booth.   Ha-WR:70
City Autumn.   J. March.   La-OC:34
The City of Falling Leaves.   A. Lowell.
   Ar-TP3:184
Clear after Rain.   Tu Fu.   Rx-OH:16
Come, Little Leaves.   G. Cooper.
   Bo-FP:147, Fe-FP:541, Hu-MP:280
The Cranes.   Po-Chu-i.   Gr-EC:178,
   Pa-SG:99
A Day in Autumn.   R. Thomas.
   Co-BN:139, Hi-WP II:134
Dead Metaphors.   D. Holbrook.
   Ls-NY:287
The Death of the Flowers.   W. Bryant.
   Co-BN:188, Fe-PL:271
The Deer That Lives.   Onakotomi
   Yoshinobu.   Ba-ST:40, Le-MW:80
Down! Down!   E. Farjeon.   Ar-TP3:184,
   Au-SP:325
Each in His Own Tongue.   Ke-TF:246
The End of Summer.   Basho.   Sh-RP:64
End of Summer.   S. Kunitz.
   Ca-VT:264, Un-MA:593
The End of Summer.   E. Millay.
   Co-BN:102
End-of-Summer Poem.   R. Bennett.
   Br-SS:179, Fe-FP:148, Ja-PA:5
Evening Clouds.   Chang Ch'ou-yü.
   Pa-MV:40
Exeunt.   R. Wilbur.   Co-EL:113, Co-BN:103,
   Fe-PL:334, Ha-WR:68, Ho-LP:31

A Fabulous Autumn.   A. Akhmatova.
   Ca-MR:184
Fall.   A. Fisher.   Ar-TP3:185,
   Br-SG:90, Ha-YA:113, Ja-PA:27
Fall Comes to Back-Country Vermont.
   R. Warren.   Ca-VT:278
Fall Days.   M. Conger.   Br-SS:54
Fall, Leaves, Fall.   E. Bronte.
   De-CH:210, Ga-FB:9, Sm-LG:59
Fall Mornings.   M. Cannon.   Ja-PA:28
The Fall of the Leaf.   H. Thoreau.
   Sh-AP:68
Father, the Year Is Fallen.   A. Lorde.
   Ad-PB:246
Field of Autumn.   L. Lee.   Wi-LT:757
The Fields Are Golden.   Gr-BB:20
The First Autumn.   M. Schacht.   Tr-MR:25
The First Night of Fall and Falling
   Rain.   D. Schwartz.   Ls-NY:298
Foam Flowers.   Yashuhide.   Le-MW:82
For a Wine Festival.   V. Watkins.
   Ls-NY:301
For Autumn.   E. Farjeon.   Gr-TG:32
Forest Leaves in Autumn.   J. Keble.
   Ox-BN:306
From My Study at the Mouth of the
   Valley.   Ch'ien Ch'i.   Le-MW:53
Gathering Leaves.   R. Frost.   Br-SG:95,
   Ca-VT:17, Ha-LO:34, Sh-RP:223
The Geese.   R. Peck.   Pe-SS:9
The Gentian Weaves Her Fringes.
   E. Dickinson.   Ho-PR:105
The Georgics.   Virgil.   Ma-FW:261
God's World.   E. Millay.   Co-PS:124,
   Ga-FB:3, Sh-RP:103, Tr-MR:26,
   Tu-WW:48, Un-GT:245, Un-MA:443
Golden Bough.   E. Wylie.   Un-MA:276
The Golden Rod.   F. Sherman.
   Fe-FP:221, Ja-PA:6
The Golden Tickseed.   G. Davidson.
   Bo-HF:128
Harvest Home.   A. Guiterman.   Ha-YA:109
The Harvest Moon.   Sodo.   Do-TS:36
Horse-Chestnut Time.   K. Staybird.
   La-PV:84
How Do You Know It's Spring?   M. Brown.
   Br-SG:102
How the Leaves Came Down.   S. Coolidge.
   Hu-MP:281
The Huntress.   G. Johnston.   Do-WH:90
Hurrahing in Harvest.   G. Hopkins.
   Co-BN:130, Gr-CT:313, Ma-FW:126,
   Rv-CB:946, Un-MB:43
I Like Fall.   A. Fisher.   La-PH:17
Immortal Autumn.   A. MacLeish.
   Gr-SS:44, Un-MA:456
In Autumn.   G. Derwood.   Ls-NY:283
In Autumn.   T. Dinsburg.   Mo-MI:21
In Memoriam.   A. Tennyson.   Gr-CT:315,
   Hi-WP II:143, Ox-BN:495
In My Loneliness.   Ryōzen.
   Ba-ST:42

AUTUMN — <u>cont'd.</u>
In the Apple Orchard. I. Schwartz.
  Ho-TY:149
In the Clear Cold. S. Yesenin.
  Pa-SG:100
In the Evening. Minamoto No Tsunenobu.
  Ba-ST:42
In the Garden of Paradise Others May
  Bask. A. Akhmatova. Ca-MR:186
In the Mountains as Autumn Begins.
  Wen T'ing Yen. Rx-LT:86
It's Fall. M. Campbell. Ho-CT:36
Junker Schmidt. Co-EL:101
Keeping Store. M. Butts. Bo-FP:140
The Last Flower. J. Moore. Co-PS:126
The Last Leaf. H. Behn. Sh-RP:231
Last Week in October. T. Hardy.
  Co-PM:144
Late Autumn in Montreal. J. Segal.
  Ho-TY:153
Late October. S. Teasdale. Co-PS:125,
  Ha-YA:112
The Latter Rain. J. Very. Sh-AP:65
Leaf Falling on Leaf. Gyodai.
  Be-CS:54
Leaf That Falls Yellow. . . . Wo-HS:(62)
A Leaf-Treader. R. Frost. Un-MA:188
Leaves. C. Cullen. Bo-HF:62
The Leaves. O. Lermand. Ho-CT:28
The Leaves. St-FS:125
Legacy. C. Morley. Du-RG:130
Limited View. J. Hearst. St-H:76
The Lone Tree and Others. Liu-Ta-pai.
  Hs-TC:9
The Man with the Rake. C. Morley.
  Na-EO:55
Marigold. L. Nicholl. Sh-RP:221
Marjorie's Almanac. T. Aldrich.
  Br-SG:101, Fe-FP:62, Hu-MP:298
Merry Autumn Days. C. Dickens.
  Bo-FP:145, Ch-B:93
Metamorphosis. W. Stevens. Ca-VT:37
The Mist and All. D. Willson.
  Au-SP:329, Fe-FP:82, Ha-YA:129,
  Hu-MP:318, Ja-PA:43, Pe-FB:88
Moon Festival. Tu-Fu. Rx-OH:8
Never Was the Autumn. T. Arghezi.
  Mc-AC:29
New Moon. Tu-Fu. Rx-OH:17
New York-Albany. L. Ferlinghetti.
  En-PC:171
Ninth Moon. Li Ho. Pa-SG:95
November. J. Clare. Bo-FP:148,
  Ch-B:92, Cl-FC:44
November. A. Fisher. Br-SS:84
November Day. E. Averitt. Du-RG:121
November Rain. M. Uschold. Ha-YA:123
Now Gaze the Stags. E. Thurlow.
  De-CH:619
October. R. Fyleman. Br-SG:94,
  Br-SS:61, Ja-PA:25, Sh-RP:225

October Night. A. Dean. Ha-YA:111
The October Redbreast. A. Meynell.
  Un-MB:64
October's Song. E. Farjeon.
  Co-PS:123, Ja-PA:24
Ode to the West Wind. P. Shelley.
  Al-VBP:748, Co-BN:127, De-CH:212,
  Er-FA:244, Fe-PL:390, Ga-FB:15,
  Ha-PO:96, Ma-YA:177, Ox-BN:280,
  Pa-GTB:295, Rv-CB:696
On a Bare Branch. Matsuo Basho.
  Ma-FW:264
On Distant Mountains. K. Takahama.
  Sh-AM:163
One Paulownia Leaf. K. Takahama.
  Sh-AM:162
One Word. Chang Hsiu-ya. Pa-MV:36
Over Coarse Rock in the Middle of the
  Square. A. Machado. Le-SW:63
Overlooking the Desert. Tu Fu.
  Rx-OH:18
A Passing Shower. Ba-ST:35
Pencil and Paint. E. Farjeon.
  La-PV:86
Pirate Wind. M. Carr. Br-SS:53
Quail Sky. Li Ch'ing Chao. Rx-OH:95
Rain in the Aspens. Su Tung P'o.
  Rx-OH:87
Red in Autumn. E. Gould. St-FS:94
Reflection. Tomonori. Le-MW:83
Reluctance. R. Frost. Un-MA:170
Remembering Shi Ch'a Hai. Chang
  Hsiu-ya. Pa-MV:29
The Reunion. O. Dodson. Bo-HF:129
Rich Days. W. Davies. Co-BN:135
The Ripe and Bearded Barley. Cl-DT:86,
  Co-BN:126, Gr-CT:313, Gr-GB:46
River of Ice. S. Tsuboi. Sh-AM:68
River Travel. Ts'ui Hao. Le-MW:82
Robin Redbreast. W. Allingham.
  Ja-PA:16
Rushes in a Watery Place. C. Rossetti.
  Gr-CT:314, Mc-PR:101
Scene in a Garden. R. Browning.
  Bo-FP:142
The Scent of Autumn. Li Kuang-t'ien.
  Hs-TC:202
September. E. Fallis. Br-SG:102,
  Ha-YA:103
September. H. Jackson. Bo-GJ:250,
  Fe-FP:76, Fe-PL:385, Ha-YA:104,
  Hu-MP:315, Mc-PR:93, Se-PR:165,
  Un-GT:277
September. K. Pyle. Bo-FP:139
The Sheaves. E. Robinson. Un-MA:127
Simple Autumnal. L. Bogan. Un-MA:491
Sleep Impression. C. Sandburg.
  Sh-RP:60
Slieve Gua. Gr-CT:318
Something Told the Wild Geese. R. Field.

Ar-TP3:187, Au-SP:331, Br-SS:59,
Co-BBW:234, Co-PS:124, Ha-YA:100,
Ho-LP:32, La-PV:135, Mc-WK:27,
Sm-MK:140, Tu-WW:106
Song. R. Dixon. Bl-OB:134,
Co-BN:133, De-CH:210, Gr-CT:316,
Ha-YA:122, Ox-BN:751, Pa-GTB:37,
Re-TW:45, Rv-CB:926, Sm-LG:38
Song Composed at the Beginning of an
Autumn Festival. Le-IB:106,
Tr-US I:31
Song of Autumn. P. Verlaine. Pa-SG:96
Sonnet II. Feng Chih. Hs-TC:148
A Spell Before Winter. H. Nemerov.
Ha-WR:56, Wi-LT:593
Splinter. C. Sandburg. Ar-TP3:185,
Fe-FP:129, Sh-RP:82
The Spring and the Fall. E. Millay.
Co-BL:141
Spring, I Suppose. Re-RR:44
Standing at the Foot of the Steps at
Night. Yuan Mei. Ma-FW:259
Stars and Moon on the River. Tu Fu.
Rx-OH:32
"The Storm Is Over. . . ." R. Bridges.
Pa-GTB:416, Wi-LT:56
Summer Is Gone. Sm-LG:58
Summer's Green. L. Haberly. Cl-DT:87
Sundown. L. Adams. Un-MA:548
Then Settle, Frost! Otomo Oemaru.
Ma-FW:264
Thou Shalt See the Field-Mouse Peep.
J. Keats. Rd-OA:181
Threnody. J. Farrar. Ja-PA:17
To Autumn. W. Blake. Co-BN:136,
Ho-WR:115, No-CL:278
To Autumn. J. Keats. Al-VBP:777,
Co-BN:125, Co-RG:126, De-CH:206,
De-TT:163, Fe-PL:384, Ga-FB:225,
Go-BP:25, Ha-PO:85, Hi-WP II:34,
Mc-PR:84, Ox-BN:359, Pa-GTB:261,
Rv-CB:736, Sp-OG:369, Un-GT:279
To Meadows. R. Herrick. Al-VBP:336,
De-CH:205, Rv-CB:340
To the Tune "Cutting a Flowering Plum
Branch." Li Ch'ing Chao. Rx-LT:95
Tree. J. Hunter. Le-M:123
Trees. R. Johnson. Me-WF:5
Tropes of One Season. C. Eaton.
De-FS:85
Two Lives and Others. W. Scott.
Du-RG:119
The Unfound Door. D. Etter. St-H:64
A Vagabond Song. B. Carman.
Co-PS:122, Fe-FP:81, Hu-MP:316,
Sh-RP:116, Sp-OG:251, Un-GT:277
Wait. E. Botta. Mc-AC:111
When I Count. Minamoto No Shitago.
Ba-ST:39
Whose Scarf Could This Be. Buson.
Be-CS:56

The Willows of Massachusetts.
D. Levertov. Ha-WR:84
Winter Soon Is Coming. E. Coatsworth.
Gr-EC:53
Words for the Raker of Leaves. L. Adams.
En-PC:35
The Yellow Season. W. Williams.
Un-MA:263
AVARIM MOUNTAINS: see ABARIM MOUNTAINS
AVES ISLANDS, VENEZ.
The Old Buccaneer. C. Kingsley.
Co-RM:60, Na-EO:48, Un-GT:140
AVIATION: see also AIR RAIDS; AIRPLANES;
AIRSHIPS; BALLOONS (AIRSHIPS);
FLIGHT; SATIRE - AVIATION; WRIGHT,
ORVILLE AND WILBUR
An Airstrip in Essex. D. Hall.
Cr-WS:168, En-PC:268, Wi-LT:727
The Campers at Kitty Hawk.
J. Dos Passos. Mo-BG:59
For I Dipped into the Future.
A. Tennyson. Fe-PL:432
Power: Cape Hatteras. H. Crane.
Un-MA:528
The Raider. W. Rodgers. Un-MB:481
AVIATION, MILITARY: see AVIATION
AVIATORS: see also ASTRONAUTS; HUMOR -
AVIATORS
The Blue Wings. A. Karlov. Mo-MI:25
The Death of the Ball Turret Gunner.
R. Jarrell. Ba-PO:186, Ca-VT:400,
Co-EL:82, Cr-WS:100, Pe-SS:138,
Un-MA:647, Wi-LT:561
Ego. P. Booth. Br-TC:59, Du-SH:164,
Pe-SS:81
Eighth Air Force. R. Jarrell.
En-PC:140, Mo-BG:172
Flight. H. Vinal. Fe-FP:203, Hu-MP:402
A Front. R. Jarrell. Ca-VT:399
An Irish Airman Foresees His Death.
W. Yeats. Bo-GJ:191, Gr-CC:129,
Ho-LP:87, Pa-GTB:424, Pe-SS:138,
Sm-LG:270, Un-MB:116, Wi-LT:70
Lindbergh. Em-AF:770
The Old Pilot's Death. J. Hall.
Cr-WS:167, Ha-TP:44, To-MP:148
A Pilot from the Carrier. R. Jarrell.
Ha-TP:79
Pilots, Man Your Planes. R. Jarrell.
Un-MA:645
Prayer for a Pilot. C. Roberts.
Fe-FP:202
The Raider. W. Rodgers. Un-MB:481
Second Air Force. R. Jarrell. Wi-LT:563
To an Aviator. D. Hicky. Th-AS:191
Trails of Smoke. R. Bennett. Hu-MP:78
AVILA, SP.: see also THERESA, SAINT
Avila. F. Keyes. Ke-TF:395
AVOCETS
Sacred Song of the Avocet Cult.
Tr-US I:256

AWAKENING: see WAKE-UP VERSES; WAKENING
AWARENESS
  About Myself.   S. Mernit.   Ad-II:16
  Being.   K. Ozaki.   Sh-AM:59
  Canal Bank Walk.   P. Kavanagh.
    Un-MB:431
  For Poets.   A. Young.   La-RM:178
  Hast Never Come to Thee an Hour.
    W. Whitman.   Rv-CB:852
  I Read a Tight-Fisted Poem Once.
    N. Woods.   La-RM:177
  It Was Not Death.   E. Dickinson.
    Rv-CB:922
  To Look at Any Thing.   J. Moffitt.
    La-RM:175
  When You Walk.   J. Stephens.
    Gr-EC:64, La-PV:189, Mc-WK:21
AWE: see WONDER
AWKWARDNESS: see HUMOR - AWKWARDNESS
AXES: see also PICKAXES
  The Axe-Helve.   R. Frost.   Ni-JP:89
  The Broad-Ax.   W. Whitman.   Un-MA:65
  Sixth-Month Song in the Foothills.
    G. Snyder.   Ha-WR:7
  This One Has Often Been Guessed.
    Re-RR:23
  What Lies Out Back.   Re-RR:28
AYLER, ALBERT
  Albert Ayler: Eulogy for a Decomposed
    Saxophone Player.   S. Crouch.
    Ad-PB:486
AZTECS: see also INDIANS OF CENTRAL
    AMERICA - VERSE - NAHUATL
  The Aztec City.   E. Ware.   Pa-HT:69
  Aztec Song.   Br-WM:4, Le-OE:128
  The Carver and the Rock Are One.
    B. Brigham.   Sc-TN:31
  From the Aztec Ceremonial Calendar.
    Br-MW:9
  Hymn of the High Priest of Xipe Totec.
    Da-SC:171
BABEL, TOWER OF
  The Tower of Babel.   N. Crouch.
    Ox-BC:42
BABIES: see also BABY CARRIAGES; BIRTH;
    HUMOR - BABIES; PARENT AND CHILD
  Address to His Infant Daughter.
    W. Wordsworth.   Na-EO:140
  Adgule, Madgulé.   Ca-MU:8
  Anniversary in September.   B. Brown.
    Br-BC:146
  An April Child.   De-PP:33
  At the Washing of My Son.   Su Tung P'o.
    Rx-OH:84
  Babies Are Crying.   P. John.   Ba-HI:85
  Baby.   G. Macdonald.   Br-BC:14,
    Er-FA:485, Fe-FP:528, Hu-MP:7
  A Baby Asleep after Pain.   D. Lawrence.
    Go-BP:117
  A Baby Is a European.   Be-AP:64

  Baby Playing.   R. Clarke.   Le-M:73
  A Baby-Tending Song.   S. Muro Sh-AM:54
  A Baby's Foot.   A. Swinburne.   Fe-FP:38
  Baby's Hands.   Gomei.   Hu-MP:8
  Baby's World.   R. Tagore.   Ma-FW:67
  Bartholomew.   N. Gale.   Br-BC:42,
    Th-AS:54
  Be Quiet, My Baby.   Do-CH:(6)
  Be Still, My Child.   Do-CH:(6)
  Blessings upon an Infant.   Do-CH:(2)
  Brother.   T. Ikenaga.   Le-TA:23
  A Bunch of Roses.   J. Tabb.   Th-AS:58
  Christmas Lullaby for a New-Born Child.
    Y. Gregory.   Bo-AN:153
  Cradle Song.   A. Tennyson.   Ox-BC:213
  The Crib.   C. Morley.   Br-BC:157
  Dear Little Baby.   Wy-CM:27
  Don't Cry, My Little One.
    Wang T'ung-chao.   Hs-TC:259
  The Evil Eye.   J. Ciardi.   Ca-MB:19
  The First Tooth.   C. and M. Lamb.
    Ox-BC:143
  For a Child Expected.   A. Ridler.
    Gr-BT:3, Wi-LT:804
  The Forsaken.   D. Scott.   Do-WH:63,
    Ha-PO:159
  Frost at Midnight.   S. Coleridge.
    Ox-BN:162, Rv-CB:661
  Gaelic Lullaby.   Ch-B:117, Ke-TF:40
  A Girl in the Army.   Mo-MGT:15
  Good Night.   J. Taylor.   Ch-B:109
  He Is Round.   Le-IB:62
  Ho! Ye Sun, Moon, Stars.   Da-SC:104,
    Ho-SD:18
  How They Sleep.   Ch-B:28
  Hush, My Child.   Do-CH:(5)
  If Your Mother Has Set Out to Fish.
    Do-CH:(7)
  In a Surgery Room.   T. Yamamoto.
    Sh-AM:128
  In the Baby Carriage.   K. Nakamura.
    Sh-AM:172
  Infant Joy.   W. Blake.   Al-VBP:614,
    Bo-GJ:132, Br-BC:41, Br-SS:41,
    Fe-FP:37, Fe-PL:245, Ga-S:97,
    Re-TW:39, Rv-CB:571, Tu-WW:13,
    Un-GT:10
  Infant Sorrow.   W. Blake.   Ox-BN:25,
    Rv-CB:572
  Little.   D. Aldis.   Ar-TP3:5, Fe-FP:38
  Little Brand New Baby.   T. Paxton.
    Pe-SS:3
  Little Brown Baby.   P. Dunbar.
    Ab-MO:100, Hu-PN:40
  Little Papoose.   H. Conkling.
    Fe-FP:306
  Lord Christ, My Darling Is So Dear.
    C. Hansen-Bay.   Gr-TG:66
  Lullaby.   Le-IB:63
  Morning Song.   S. Plath.   Mc-EA:103

Moses.   Mo-MGT:202
Mother Moon, Bless Baby.   Le-OE:104
A Mother Praises Her Baby.   Tr-US I:77
A Mother to Her First-Born.   Tr-CB:27,
   Tr-US I:105
Mundus et Infans.   W. Auden.   Un-MB:462,
   Wi-LT:474
Mutterings over the Crib of a Deaf
   Child.   J. Wright.   Du-SH:139
My Brother.   M. Ridlon.   Ho-GC:13
Neighbors, Friends, Two Gypsies, et al.,
   Arrive.   J. de Melo Neto.   An-TC:139
O Can Ye Sew Cushions?   Sm-LG:97
On an Infant Dying as Soon as Born.
   C. Lamb.   Pa-GTB:237
Petting Song (Modern).   Da-SC:42
A Poet's Welcome to His Love-Begotten
   Daughter.   R. Burns.   Al-VBP:625
Presenting an Infant to the Sun.
   Bi-IT:113
Ringely, Ringely.   E. Follen.   Br-BC:15
Short History of Man.   J. Holmes.
   Mc-WS:138
Six Weeks Old.   C. Morley.   Br-BC:41
Sleep! Sleep! Beauty Bright.
   Fe-PL:246, Rv-CB:570
Slippery.   C. Sandburg.   Br-BC:42,
   Fe-FP:39
Sung by a Little Girl to Soothe a
   Crying Baby.   Le-IB:62, Ma-BH:27,
   Tr-US I:10
Sweetes' Li'l Feller.   F. Stanton.
   Er-FA:503
Taking Out Jim.   J. Walsh.   Pa-RE:52
Taking Steps at Thirteen Months.
   H. Miller.   Ls-NY:219
To Baby.   K. Greenaway.   Hu-MP:8
To Our Babies, I.   Le-IB:60
To Our Babies, II.   Le-IB:60
To Rose.   S. Teasdale.   Br-BC:147
Upon My Lap My Sovereign Sits.
   R. Rowlands.   Al-VBP:210, De-CH:20
Watching a Petal.   Kubutsu.   Be-MC:44
Weep Not, My Wanton.   R. Greene.
   Al-VBP:141, Rv-CB:172
Where Did You Come from, Baby Dear?
   G. Macdonald.   Ox-BC:273
Why Do You Cry?   Do-CH:(4)
BABOONS: see also HUMOR - BABOONS,
   MONKEYS
Praise Songs for the Baboon.   Tr-US I:78
BABY CARRIAGES
Around the World.   K. Greenaway.
   Ch-B:85, Fe-FP:38
BABYLON: see also BELSHAZZAR
Babylon.   L. Benét.   De-FS:20
Babylon.   S. Sassoon.   Tr-MR:235
Babylon.   Gr-CT:275
By the Rivers of Babylon.   Bible.   O.T.
   Psalms.   Me-PH:30
The Destruction of Jerusalem by the
   Babylonian Hordes.   I. Rosenberg.
   Gr-SS:172

How Many Miles to Babylon?   Bo-FP:30,
   Cl-DT:33, De-PO:10, Gr-GB:25,
   Ir-BB:241, Ke-TF:69, Li-LB:38,
   Mo-MGT:108, Mo-NR:105, On-TW:61,
   Rv-CB:456, Sm-LG:241, Tu-WW:14,
   Wr-RM:57
Psalm 137.   W. Empson.   En-PC:83
BACCHUS
The Ballad of Hampstead Heath.
   J. Flecker.   Un-MB:275
Come, Thou Monarch.   W. Shakespeare.
   Al-VBP:194
Endymion 4.   J. Keats.   Al-VBP:790
BACH, JOHANN SEBASTIAN
All These Hymnings Up to God.   A. Evans.
   Tr-MR:197
Homage to J. S. Bach.   J. Heath-Stubbs.
   Go-BP:65
Sheldonian Symphony.   S. Sassoon.
   Pl-US:82
To J. S. Bach.   M. Thwaites.   Tr-MR:196
BACHELORS: see also HUMOR - BACHELORS
Green Bedroom.   R. Roseliep.   St-H:182
Jack Jingle.   Wr-RM:98
A New England Bachelor.   R. Eberhart.
   Un-MA:589
BACTERIA
The Minimal.   L. Roethke.   Li-TU:195
BADGERS
The Badger.   P. Chalmers.   Go-BP:96
Badger.   J. Clare.   Cl-FC:67,
   Co-BBW:50, Ho-WR:213, Rv-CB:720
The Combe.   E. Thomas.   Pa-GTB:443
The Six Badgers.   Bo-GJ:76, Co-BBW:33,
   Co-IW:19, Ir-BB:22, Pa-RE:41
The Women and the Men.   Te-FC:87
BAGAMOYO, TANZANIA
Bwagamoyo.   L. Bethune.   Ad-PB:310
BAGELS
The Bagel.   D. Ignatow.   Br-TC:214,
   Du-SH:23, Mo-BG:10
BAGPIPES: see also HUMOR - BAGPIPES
Bagpipes.   Mo-MGT:205
A Cat Came Fiddling.   Bo-FP:94,
   De-TT:29, Gr-EC:70, Ir-BB:27,
   Wi-MG:18
King Orfeo.   Ma-BB:152, Ox-BB:62
The Pipes at Lucknow.
   J. Whittier.   Hi-FO:241
The Relief of Lucknow.   R. Lowell.
   Co-PT:221
Scotch Rhapsody.   E. Sitwell.
   Br-TC:190
BAKERS AND BAKERIES: see also BREAD;
   CAKES AND COOKIES; HUMOR - BAKERS
   AND BAKERIES
The Baker's Boy.   M. Newsome.   Ag-HE:23
Charley, Charley.   Br-FF:14, Wi-MG:63
Lament.   A. Bergman.   Kr-OF:198
Pat-a-Cake, Pat-a-Cake, Baker's Man.
   Bo-FP:118, De-PO:6, Li-LB:18,
   Mo-CC:(52), Mo-MGT:5, Mo-NR:5,
   Mo-TL:74, Wi-MG:43, Wr-RM:14

BAKEWELL, LUCY: see AUDUBON, JOHN JAMES
BALAAM
    Balaam. J. Kreble. Ox-BN:304
BALAKLAVA, BATTLE, 1854
    The Charge of the Light Brigade.
        A. Tennyson. Er-FA:183, Fe-FP:564,
        Ga-FB:206, Hi-FO:238, Ma-YA:196,
        Mc-PR:184, Sp-OG:49
BALDNESS: see also HUMOR - BALDNESS
    On the Top of the Hill. Wy-CM:31
    You Surely Haven't Got It Yet. Re-RR:48
BALKIS: see SHEBA, QUEEN OF
BALLADS
    Another Song. D. Justice. Ca-VT:536
    At the Setting of the Sun. Rv-CB:440
    Ballad: "O What Is That Sound. . ."
        W. Auden. Al-VBP:1227, Gr-SS:70,
        Ma-FW:254, Pe-M:98, Un-MB:455
    The Ballad of Mrs. Noah. R. Duncan.
        To-MP:106
    The Ballad of Reading Gaol. O. Wilde.
        Al-VBP:1072, Er-FA:87, Un-MB:70
    The Ballad of the Billycock. A. Deane.
        Co-SS:28
    Blow the Winds, I-Ho. Gr-GB:110
    The Burnt Bridge. L. MacNeice.
        Gr-SS:111
    The Bushrangers. E. Harrington.
        Co-PT:244
    El Capitan-General. C. Leland.
        Co-SS:25
    The Crafty Farmer. Ar-TP3:16
    The Death of Robin Hood. E. Field.
        Co-PT:239
    The Demon of the Gibbet. F. O'Brien.
        Co-PM:134
    The Farmer's Boy. Cl-DT:83
    The Gay Goshawk. Ma-BB:183, Ox-BB:222
    Gunga Din. R. Kipling. Er-FA:371,
        Go-BP:54, Hi-WP I:69, Ma-YA:226,
        Pa-OM:230, Un-MB:122
    The Jovial Gentlemen. D. Hoffman.
        Ca-MB:62
    The Ratcatcher's Daughter. Gr-GB:134
    The Revolving Door. N. Levy.
        Br-SM:45, Co-HP:91
    Three Jolly Huntsmen. Un-GT:217
    The River of Stars. A. Noyes. Pa-OM:131
    The Smithfield Market Fire. F. Dallas.
        Hi-WP I:84
    See also Em-AF:3-774
BALLADS, AMERICAN: see also BALLADS,
    COWBOY; BALLADS, NEGRO
    Abdulla Bulbul Amir. Co-RM:193
    Ain't Got No Home in This World Anymore.
        W. Guthrie. Kr-OF:194
    A Ballad of China. L. Richards. Sh-RP:5
    A Ballad of Dead Girls. D. Burnet.
        Kr-OF:174
    The Ballad of the Boll Weevil. Hi-TL:163
    A Ballad of the Boston Tea-Party.
        O. Holmes. Hi-TL:42, Vi-PP:90

The Ballad of the Oysterman. O. Holmes.
    Er-FA:306, Sm-MK:69
The Ballad of Tonopah Bill. Fi-BG:61
The Ballad of William Sycamore.
    S. Benét. Co-RM:228, Hu-MP:387,
    Un-MA:498
The Big Rock Candy Mountain. Gr-CT:280,
    Gr-GB:228, Hi-WP I:96, Pe-SS:86
Billy the Kid. Co-RM:164, Fi-BG:53
Bishop Cody's Last Request. T. Paxton.
    Mo-GR:55
Brady's Bend. M. Keller. Co-PT:217
The Briefless Barrister. J. Saxe.
    Br-SM:39
Bung Yer Eye. S. White. Sh-RP:18
Casey at the Bat. E. Thayer.
    Fe-FP:549, Mo-SD:11
Casey Jones. Bl-OB:76, Ga-FB:267,
    Hi-TL:141, Mc-WS:155
Casey Jones, the Union Scab. J. Hill.
    Kr-OF:177
Cecilia. Do-WH:34
Cocaine Lil. Gr-GB:266, Pe-M:138
The Colorado Trail. Mc-WS:120
Come and I Will Sing You. Ga-S:16
The Cremation of Sam McGee. Ar-TP3:143,
    Br-SM:140, Er-FA:399, Fe-PL:6,
    Ha-PO:96
Cumberland Gap. Br-AF:112
Daniel. V. Lindsay. Co-RM:238,
    Ga-S:49, Gr-CT:143, Hi-WP I:80,
    Rv-CB:972, Sm-MK:75
Dorlan's Home Walk. A. Guiterman.
    Co-PT:90
Flash: the Fireman's Story.
    W. Carleton. Se-PR:317
Folk-Song. L. Untermeyer. Un-MW:102
Frankie and Johnny. Er-FA:402
The Ghost That Jim Saw. B. Harte.
    Br-SM:6, Co-PM:84
Hawicks Crossing. J. Stuart. De-FS:193
How Bill Went East. G. Bryan. Co-PT:82
How Old John Brown Took Harper's Ferry.
    E. Stedman. Hu-PN:493, Pa-OM:175
In a Prominent Bar in Secaucus One Day.
    X. Kennedy. En-PC:234
In Praise of Johnny Appleseed.
    V. Lindsay. Se-PR:99
Isabel. Do-WH:32
Jesse James. W. Benét. Ha-PO:208,
    Hi-TL:145, Un-MA:327
Jesse James. Ho-WR:116, Mc-WS:161
John Hardy. Co-RM:16
John Henry. Ab-MO:81, Bo-HF:104,
    Co-RM:225, Er-FA:407, Ga-S:124,
    Hi-TL:159, Ra-BP:12
The Juniper Tree. W. Watson.
    Co-BL:162, Do-WH:36
Kit Carson's Ride. J. Miller.
    Fi-BG:161
Lewis and Clark. S. Benét.
    Sh-RP:296

Love Me, Love My Dog. I. Crawford.
  Do-WH:30
The Luck of Edenhall. H. Longfellow.
  Co-PT:151
The Mountain Whippoorwill. S. Benét.
  Co-PT:110
My Last Illusion. Dum-Dum. Co-FB:318
New England's Chevy Chase. E. Hale.
  Se-PR:88, Vi-PP:103
Old Christmas. R. Helton. Co-PM:94,
  Un-MA:346
On Top of Old Smoky. Er-FA:451
The Puritan's Ballad. E. Wylie.
  Co-BL:92
The Rattlesnake. J. & A. Lomax.
  Sh-RP:19
The Revenge of Hamish. S. Lanier.
  Ni-JP:46, Sp-OG:141
Samuel Hall. Co-RM:98
Shenandoah. Br-AF:189
The Shooting of Dan McGrew. R. Service.
  Co-RM:129, Do-WH:22, Er-FA:382,
  Fe-PL:9
The Singing Leaves. J. Lowell.
  Hu-MP:410
The Skeleton in Armor. H. Longfellow.
  Mc-PR:56, Sp-OG:103, Un-GT:173
Slave Story. H. Carter. Hu-PN:540
Sourwood Mountain. Gr-GB:124
Spanish Johnny. W. Cather. Co-RM:26,
  Fe-FP:436, Hu-MP:154, Mc-WK:140,
  Mc-WS:160, Sh-RP:41
Stranger. E. Roberts. Un-MA:270
The Strong Swimmer. W. Benét.
  Hu-PN:500
Times Are Gettin' Hard. L. Mays.
  Kr-OF:168
The <u>Titanic</u>. Co-SS:135
Waltz. R. Sherry. De-FS:176
The White Drake. Do-WH:35
Willie and Nellie's Wish. J. Moore.
  Co-FB:302
BALLADS, CANADIAN: see BALLADS, AMERICAN
BALLADS, AUSTRALIAN
The Griesly Wife. J. Manifold.
  Ca-MB:25, Un-MB:513
The Kangaroo. Su-FVI:60
The Man from Snowy River. A. Paterson.
  Hi-WP II:91
The Wild Colonial Boy. Co-RM:171
BALLADS, BERBER
Ballad. Tr-US I:125
BALLADS, CHINESE
Ashima. Hs-TC:447
Building Pumpkin Trellis. Hs-TC:453
Can't Kill Him. Chang Chih-min.
  Hs-TC:426
Monkey Sun Descends to Earth.
  Hs-TC:451
Rendezvous. Chang Chih-min. Hs-TC:429

The Rhinoceros Mountain. Hs-TC:453
A Sweet Potato Rolls off the Hill.
  Hs-TC:454
BALLADS, COWBOY
Alaska, or Hell of the Yukon. Fi-BG:43
The Ballad of Pug-Nosed Lil.
  R. Fletcher. Fi-BG:231
Ballad of the Broomtails. Fi-BG:143
Bill and Parson Sim. Fi-BG:199
Bill Roy. Fi-BG:206
Boomer Johnson. Fi-BG:84
The Broken Wedding Ring. Fi-BG:216
The Buffalo Skinners. Gr-GB:220,
  Hi-TL:150
The Buffalo Skinners. Co-RM:232
The Bullwhacker. Co-RM:18
The Cow Girl. Fi-BG:140
Cowboy Dance Song (No. 2). Fi-BG:169
Cowboy Song. C. Causley. Co-RM:27,
  Ha-PO:10, Pe-M:36
Curly Joe. Fi-BG:214
'Dobe Bill. Co-RM:31
The Flying Outlaw. C. Fletcher.
  Fi-BG:94
The Glory Trail. B. Clark. Co-PT:129
Greer County. Co-RM:15
Hell in Texas. Co-RM:30
A Home on the Range. J. Lomax.
  Er-FA:447, Hu-MP:204, Se-PR:262
The Insult. Co-RM:20
Lasca. F. Desprez. Fi-BG:208
The Legend of Boastful Bill. C. Clark.
  Fi-BG:92
The Man from Snowy River. A. Paterson.
  Hi-MP II:91
Night Herding Song. H. Stephens.
  Sh-RP:79
Old Dolores. Pe-M:34
On the Trail to Idaho. Se-PR:147
Passing of the Wrangler. H. Fellow.
  Fi-BG:151
Rattlin' Joe's Prayer. J. Crawford.
  Fi-BG:187
The Raven Visits Rawhide. Fi-BG:182
Red River Valley. Er-FA:445
Silver Jack's Religion. J. Jones.
  Fi-BG:185
The Stampede. A. Caldwell. Fi-BG:100
The Stampede. F. Miller. Fi-BG:159
The Streets of Laredo. Co-RM:28,
  Er-FA:337, Gr-CT:137, Gr-GB:321,
  Hi-TL:162, Mc-WK:169, Mc-WS:153
The Texas Ranger. Fi-BG:112
Two-Gun Percy. Fi-BG:136
Two Ponies Shy. Fi-BG:142
Waring of Sonoratown. H. Knibbs.
  Fi-BG:141
Whiskey Bill. Co-RM:13
Whoopee Ti Yi Yo, Git Along Little
  Dogies. J. Lomax. Ar-TP3:34, Fe-FP:435,
  Fi-BG:157, 158, Hu-MP:209, Mc-WK:72

BALLADS, COWBOY — cont'd.
 The Wrangler Kid. Fi-BG:102
 Young Companions. Fi-BG:211
 The Zebra Dun. Co-PT:144, Sh-RP:49
 See also Em-AF:635-647
BALLADS, EAST INDIAN
 The Rise of Shivaji. Z. Ghose. Ca-MB:59
BALLADS, ENGLISH AND SCOTTISH
 Adam Bell, Clym of the Clough, and
   William of Cloudesley. Ma-BB:157,
   Ox-BB:380
 Alice Brand. W. Scott. Pa-OM:248
 Alison Gross. De-CH:406, Fo-OG:36,
   Ma-BB:108, Ox-BB:54
 All. All a-Lonely. Gr-CT:159
 Allen-a-Dale. W. Scott. Co-PT:231
 Annan Water. De-CH:311, Ma-BB:214
 Annie of Lochroyan. Ma-BB:202
 Archie of Cawfield. Ma-BB:20
 As I Walked Out One Night. De-CH:596
 Auld Robin Gray. A. Lindsay.
   Al-VBP:603, De-CH:344, Pa-GTB:152
 The Babes in the Wood. Bl-OB:70,
   De-CH:546, De-TT:44, Gr-EC:152
 Babylon. Ma-BB:143, Ox-BB:199
 The Bailiff's Daughter of Islington.
   Ox-BB:342, Sh-RP:250, Un-GT:114
 A Ballad of a Mine. R. Skelton.
   Ca-MB:77
 Ballad of East and West. R. Kipling.
   Ar-TP3:25, Ga-FB:211
 A Ballad of Hell. J. Davidson.
   Un-MB:72
 The Ballad of Reading Gaol. O. Wilde.
   Ox-BN:896
 The Ballad of Semmerwater. W. Watson.
   Bl-OB:81
 A Ballad of Sir John Franklin. G. Baker.
   Pa-OM:109
 The Ballad of the "Bolivar."
   R. Kipling. Sp-OG:79
 Ballad of the Flood. E. Muir. Ca-MB:34
 A Ballad of the Good Lord Nelson.
   L. Durrell. Wi-LT:697
 Ballad of the Two Tapsters. V. Watkins.
   Ca-MB:91
 Barbara Allen. Al-VBP:55, Er-FA:315,
   Mc-PR:156, Rv-CB:434, Un-MW:112
 The Baron of Braikley. Ox-BB:618
 The Baron of Leys. Ox-BB:270
 The Battle of Bothwell Bridge. Ox-BB:621
 The Battle of Otterburn. Ox-BB:491,
   Pa-OM:148
 La Belle Dame sans Merci. J. Keats.
   Al-VBP:779, Bo-GJ:163, Bo-HF:22,
   De-CH:121, De-TT:200, Er-FA:409,
   Gr-CT:178, Gr-SS:108, Ha-PO:6,
   Hi-WP II:106, Mc-WK:8, Ni-JP:98,
   No-CL:65, Ox-BN:376, Pa-GTB:193,
   Rv-CB:735, Sm-LG:217, Sm-MK:46,
   Sp-OG:113, Un-GT:126
 The Bents and Broom. Ox-BB:187

Bessy Bell and Mary Gray. De-CH:520,
   Ox-BB:617
Beth Gêlert. W. Spencer. Un-GT:138
Binnorie. Ma-BB:25, Ox-BB:69
Birkett's Eagle. D. Howard. Ca-MB:27
The Birth of Robin Hood. Al-VBP:37
The Birth of Robin Hood. Ma-BB:41,
   Ox-BB:377
The Bitter Withy. Gr-CT:145, Gr-GB:303
Bonnie Annie Livieston. Ox-BB:254
Bonnie George Campbell. Al-VBP:54
   De-CH:41, Fo-OG:20, Gr-GB:250,
   Ox-BB:341, Rv-CB:419
Bonny Barbara Allan. De-CH:338,
   Ox-BB:353
The Bonny Brown Girl. OX-BB:355
The Bonny Earl of Livingston. Ox-BB:309
The Bonny Earl of Murray. Bl-OB:152,
   Co-RM:206, Ma-BB:36, Ox-BB:594,
   Rv-CB:35, Sm-LG:271
The Bonny Heyn. Ox-BB:201
The Bonny House of Airlie. Ma-BB:130,
   Ox-BB:614
The Boy and the Mantle. Ox-BB:31
The Braes of Yarrow. Ox-BB:590
Bristowe Tragedie. Ox-BB:656
Broom, Green Broom. Bl-OB:38,
   De-CH:139, Fo-OG:8, Ha-PO:54
The Broomfield Hill. Ox-BB:72
Brown Adam. Ma-BB:154, Ox-BB:162
Brown Robin. Ox-BB:227
Brown Robyn's Confession. De-CH:399,
   Gr-GB:314
A Carol for Saint Stephen's Day.
   De-CH:225, Ox-BB:3
Chevy Chase. Al-VBP:43, Ma-BB:97
   Ox-BB:496
Chevy Chase, The Second Fytte. Ma-BB:101
Child Waters. Ox-BB:149
Clark Sanders. Ox-BB:76, Rv-CB:34
Clerk Colvill. Ma-BB:212, Ox-BB:85
Clootie. Ma-BB:94
Clyde's Waters. Ox-BB:331
The Coasts of High Barbary. Bl-OB:50
Corpus Christi Carol (The Falcon).
   Al-VBP:36, Ga-S:200, Gr-CC:163,
   Gr-CT:186, Gr-GB:308. Ma-FW:257,
   Rv-CB:13, Sm-MK:36
The Courteous Knight. Ox-BB:246
The Craft Miss of London. Ox-BB:646
The Cruel Brother. Ma-YA:38, Ox-BB:236
The Cruel Mother. Ox-BB:68
The Cunning Clerk. Ox-BB:631
The Death of Admiral Benbow. Bl-OB:44,
   Gr-GB:239, Rv-CB:420
The Death of Ben Hall. W. Ogilvie.
   Co-PT:214
The Death of Lord Warriston. Ox-BB:603
The Death of Robin Hood. Al-VBP:38
The Death of Robin Hood. Ma-BB:77,
   Ma-FW:156
Deeply Gone. J. Silkin. De-FS:177

The Demon Lover.   Co-PM:201, Fo-OG:44,
  Ma-BB:188, Ma-FW:199, Ox-BB:83,
  Rv-CB:45
Dick o' the Cow.   Ox-BB:538
The Diverting History of John Gilpin.
  W. Cowper.   Al-VBP:588, Co-RG:88,
  Hi-WP I:47, Sp-OG:215
Dives and Lazarus.   Ga-S:202,
  Ma-FW:165, Ox-BB:5
Donald of the Isles.   Ox-BB:258
The Douglas Tragedy.   Ox-BB:118,
  Un-MW:109
The Drowned Lady.   Gr-CT:139
The Duke o' Athole's Nurse.   Ox-BB:344
The Duke of Gordon's Daughter.
  Ma-BB:217
Duriesdyke.   Ox-BB:686
Earl Brand.   Ox-BB:115
Earl Haldan's Daughter.   C. Kingsley.
  Sp-OG:101
The Earl of Mar's Daughter.   De-CH:290,
  Fo-OG:21, Ma-BB:146
Edom o' Gordon.   Ox-BB:598
Edward, Edward.   De-CH:410, Ha-PO:1,
  Ma-BB:39, Ox-BB:239, Rv-CB:39
Eppie Morrie.   Ox-BB:251
Erlington.   Ma-BB:9
Evening.   E. Sitwell.   Ca-MB:55
Fair Annie.   De-CH:414
Fair Annie.   Ox-BB:138
The Fair Flower of Northumberland.
  Ma-BB:222, Ox-BB:272
Fair Flowers in the Valley.   Rv-CB:46
Fair Helen.   Al-VBP:53, De-CH:418,
  Er-FA:338, Hi-WP I:16, Pa-GTB:89,
  Rv-CB:43
Fair Isabell of Rochroyall.   Ox-BB:144
Fair Janet.   Ox-BB:173
The Fair Lass of Islington.   Ox-BB:649
Fair Margaret and Sweet William.
  Ox-BB:231
Faithless Nelly Gray.   T. Hood.
  Br-SM:33, Co-HP:78, Hi-WP I:100
The False Knight upon the Road.
  De-CH:316, Gr-GB:288
The False Lover.   Ox-BB:277
The Famous Flower of Serving-Men.
  Ox-BB:182
Fa'se Footrage.   Ox-BB:279
The Fire of Frendraught.   Ox-BB:610
Flannan Isle.   W. Gibson.   Bl-OB:78,
  Co-SS:200, De-CH:395, Ha-PO:154,
  Hi-WP I:76
The Fox.   Bl-OB:114, Co-PT:137,
  Ha-PO:137, Un-GT:32
The Fox.   Su-FVI:62
The Gaberlunzie-Man.   Ox-BB:626
The Gardener.   Rv-CB:48
Gentle Alice Brown.   W. Gilbert.
  Co-FB:147
Geordie.   Ox-BB:557
A Gest of Robyn Hode.   Ox-BB:420

A Gest of Robyn Hode, The Second Fytte.
  Ox-BB:433
A Gest of Robyn Hode, The Third Fytte.
  Ox-BB:443
A Gest of Robyn Hode, The Fourth Fytte.
  Ox-BB:452
A Gest of Robyn Hode, The Fifth Fytte.
  Ox-BB:464
A Gest of Robyn Hode, The Sixth Fytte.
  Ox-BB:469
A Gest of Robyn Hode, The Seventh Fytte.
  Ox-BB:475
A Gest of Robyn Hode, The Eighth Fytte.
  Ox-BB:484
Get Up and Bar the Door.   Al-VBP:56,
  Ar-TP3:17, Bl-OB:19, Fo-OG:49,
  Ha-PO:75, La-PV:214, Pa-OM:94,
  Un-GT:123
Gil Brenton.   Ox-BB:38
Gil Morrice.   Ox-BB:156
The Gipsy Laddie.   Bl-OB:70, Sm-LG:185
Glasgerion.   Ox-BB:123
Glenlogie.   Ma-BB:120
The Golden Vanity.   Bl-OB:55, Co-SS:193,
  De-CH:398, Fo-OG:10, Ho-WR:128,
  Rv-CB:438
Graeme and Bewick.   Ox-BB:356, Rv-CB:47
The Great Silkie of Sule Skerrie.
  Gr-CT:206, Gr-GB:282, Ma-BB:18
Greensleeves.   C. Robinson.   Un-MW:74
The Grey Selchie of Sule Skerry.
  Ox-BB:91
The Haystack in the Floods.   W. Morris.
  Ni-JP:41, Ox-BN:779
Heather Ale.   R. Stevenson.
  Co-PT:117, Sp-OG:162
The Heir of Linne.   Ma-BB:110
Henry Martyn.   Fo-OG:18, Rv-CB:439
The Highwayman.   A. Noyes.   Ar-TP3:24,
  Co-BL:155, Er-FA:343, Fe-FP:449,
  Fe-PL:16, Un-GT:131
Hind Etin.   Ox-BB:97
Hobie Noble.   Ox-BB:572
Hugh of Lincoln.   De-CH:408, Ox-BB:317
Hughie Graham.   Ox-BB:579
Hynd Etin.   Ma-BB:192
Hynd Horn.   Ma-BB:229, Ox-BB:112
Jack Hall.   Co-RM:99
Jackie Faa.   Gr-CT:162, Ma-BB:106,
  Ox-BB:249
Jamie Telfer of the Fair Dodhead.
  Ox-BB:549
Jellon Grame.   Ox-BB:164
Jock o' the Side.   Ox-BB:567
John Dory.   Ma-BB:122
Johnie o'Cocklesmuir.   Ox-BB:535
Johnnie Armstrang.   Ox-BB:520
Johnnie Blunt.   Ox-BB:630
The Jolly Beggar.   Ox-BB:624
Judas.   Ma-FW:160
Katherine Jaffray.   Ox-BB:300
Katherine Johnstone.   Ma-BB:232

BALLADS, ENGLISH AND SCOTTISH — cont'd.
 Keith of Ravelston. S. Dobell.
  De-CH:299, De-TT:189, Ox-BN:661
 Kellyburnbraes. Ox-BB:634
 Kemp Oweyne. Fo-OG:13, Ma-BB:33,
  Rv-CB:50
 Kempion. Ox-BB:56
 King Estmere. Ma-BB:133, Ox-BB:127
 King Henry. Ox-BB:64
 King John and the Abbot of Canterbury.
  Sp-OG:147; Un-GT:120
 King Orfeo. Ma-BB:152, Ox-BB:62
 Kinmont Willie. Ox-BB:559
 The Knight's Leap. C. Kingsley.
  Co-PT:230
 Lady Clare. A. Tennyson. Co-PT:189,
  Sp-OG:122
 Lady Elspat. Ma-BB:199
 The Lady Isabella's Tragedy. Gr-GB:251
 Lady Maisry. Ox-BB:295
 The Laily Worm and the Machrel of the
  Sea. Gr-CT:135, Ox-BB:59, Rd-OA:200
 The Laird o' Cockpen. C. Nairne.
  Co-PT:201
 The Laird o' Logie. De-CH:412, Rv-CB:49
 The Laird o' Ochiltree Wa's. Ox-BB:266
 The Lament of the Border Widow.
  De-CH:419, Gr-GB:246, Ox-BB:525
 Lamkin. Ox-BB:313, Rv-CB:44
 A Lincolnshire Tale. J. Betjeman.
  De-FS:21
 Little Billee. W. Thackeray.
  Bl-OB:72, Br-SM:72, Co-SS:15,
  De-TT:126, Gr-EC:244, Hu-MP:452,
  Ir-BB:42, Ox-BB:678, Sm-LG:186
 Little Mousgrove and the Lady Barnet.
  Ox-BB:168
 Lochinvar. W. Scott. Co-FB:230,
  Co-PT:207, Co-RG:33, Er-FA:316,
  Fe-FP:504, Ga-FB:54, Gr-EC:132,
  Ma-YA:143, Mc-PR:154, Na-EO:133,
  Ox-BN:128, Sp-OG:126, Un-GT:134
 The Lochmabyn Harper. Ma-BB:208,
  Ox-BB:582
 Lord Douglas. Ox-BB:324
 Lord Livingston. Ox-BB:206
 Lord Lovel. Co-PM:205, Fe-FP:508
 Lord Maxwell's Last Goodnight.
  Ox-BB:607
 The Lord of Lorn and the Fals Steward.
  Ox-BB:285
 Lord Randal. Cl-FC:85, Fo-OG:7,
  Ox-BB:243, Rv-CB:37, Un-MW:108
 Lord Thomas and Fair Annet. Ox-BB:178
 Lord Thomas and Fair Eleanor. Ma-FW:151
 Lord Ullin's Daughter. T. Campbell.
  Co-RG:50, Fe-FP:520, Pa-GTB:182
 Lowlands Away. Gr-GB:132
 The Lowlands o' Holland. De-CH:345,
  Fo-OG:51, Ox-BB:348
 Lucy Gray. W. Wordsworth. De-CH:222,
  De-TT:85
 A Lytell Geste of Robyn Hode. Ma-YA:43

 McNaughton. Ox-BB:304
 The Maid Freed from the Gallows.
  Gr-EC:134
 The Maid of Neidpath. W. Scott.
  Pa-GTB:196
 Maiden in the Moor. Ma-BB:82
 Mary Hamilton. Ox-BB:328
 Mary Hamilton. Rv-CB:131
 The Massacre of the MacPherson.
  W. Aytoun. Gr-CT:17
 May Colven. Ma-BB:117, Ox-BB:49
 The Merchant and the Fidler's Wife.
  Ox-BB:640
 The Mermaid. De-CH:403, Fo-OG:39
 Moy Castle. Un-GT:112
 Muckle-Mouth Meg. R. Browning.
  Un-MW:118
 My Handsome Gilderoy. De-CH:78
 The North Ship. P. Larkin. Ma-FW:50
 Northumberland Betrayed by Dowglas.
  Ox-BB:526
 Oh! Dear, What Can the Matter Be?
  De-CH:70, Mc-WS:165, Mo-MGT:200,
  Mo-TL:34, Wr-RM:127
 "O Wha Will Shoe My Bonny Foot?"
  De-CH:514
 O Wha's the Bride? H. MacDiarmid.
  Wi-LT:626
 O What Is That Sound. . . . W. Auden.
  To-MP:29
 The Old Cloak. Ma-BB:226
 The Old Farmer and His Young Wife.
  Co-PT:311, Gr-GB:158
 One Friday Morn. De-CH:400, Pa-OM:294
 The Outlandish Knight. Br-SM:36,
  Un-GT:111
 The Outlaw Murray. Ox-BB:363
 The Parklands. S. Smith. Ca-MB:94
 Percy Reed. Ox-BB:586
 Prince Robert. Ox-BB:203
 Proud Margret. Ox-BB:74
 Rare Willie Drowned in Yarrow.
  Gr-GB:133, Ox-BB:593
 Red Harlaw. Ox-BB:676
 The Relief of Lucknow. R. Lowell.
  Co-PT:221
 Robin Hood and Allan a Dale.
  Gr-GB:247, Ma-BB:44, Un-GT:115
 Robin Hood and Guy of Gisborne.
  Ma-BB:54
 Robin Hood and the Bishop of Hereford.
  Bl-OB:73, Ma-BB:74
 Robin Hood and the Butcher. Ma-BB:62
 Robin Hood and the Curtal Friar.
  Ma-BB:48
 Robin Hood and the Monk. Al-VBP:37,
  De-CH:135, Ox-BB:405
 Robin Hood and the Widow's Three Sons.
  Ar-TP3:17, Co-PT:224, Ma-BB:70,
  Pa-OM:86, Sp-OG:157, Un-GT:119
 Robin Hood and Two Priests. Ma-BB:66

Robyn and Gandeleyn. Ox-BB:374
Room for a Jovial Tinker. Ox-BB:636
Rosabelle. W. Scott. Pa-GTB:236
Rose the Red and White Lilly. Ox-BB:189
The Royal Fisherman. Gr-CT:128
The Runaway Slave at Pilgrim's Point.
    E. Browning. Hu-PN:448
The Sands of Dee. C. Kingsley.
    Bl-OB:153, Cl-FC:88, Co-PM:111,
    Co-SS:43, De-CH:211, De-TT:182,
    Fe-FP:511, Hu-MP:430, Sp-OG:84
Screaming Tarn. R. Bridges. Co-PT:26
The Seaman's Happy Return. Gr-CT:64,
    Gr-GB:119
Shameful Death. W. Morris. Gr-CT:129,
    Gr-SS:174, Pa-GTB:380, Un-GT:136
Sheath and Knife. De-CH:54
The Shepherd's Dochter. Ox-BB:263
Sir Aldinger. Ox-BB:23
Sir Andrew Bartton. Ox-BB:508
Sir Colin. Ox-BB:20
Sir Halewyn. Ox-BB:690
Sir Patrick Spens. Al-VBP:35, Ar-TP3:19,
    Bl-OB:47, Bo-GJ:159, Co-RG:58,
    Co-SS:129, De-CH:405, Ha-PO:3,
    Ma-BB:1, Ma-FW:46, Ma-YA:41, Ox-BB:311,
    Rv-CB:38, Sm-LG:307, Sp-OG:98
Sir William Deloraine at the Wizard's
    Tomb. W. Scott. Ox-BN:118
Song David. Ox-BB:241
Squire and Milkmaid. OX-BB:652
Stratton Water. Ox-BB:680
Sweet William's Ghost. De-CH:423,
    Ma-BB:115
Sweet Willie. Ox-BB:45
Tam Lin. Ma-BB:124, Ox-BB:13
Tammie Doodle. Fo-OG:12
There Gowans Are Gay. Gr-GB:97
There Was a Knight. De-CH:315,
    Gr-GB:277
Thomas the Rhymer. Al-VBP:40,
    De-CH:119, Fo-OG:3, Gr-CT:175,
    Ha-PO:51, Ma-BB:5, Ma-FW:181,
    Pa-OM:275, Rv-CB:40, Un-GT:124
The Three Butchers. Co-RM:102
Three Knights from Spain. Bl-OB:36,
    De-CH:328, Fo-OG:42, Gr-GB:26,
    Rv-ON:106
The Three Ravens. Al-VBP:39, Fo-OG:34,
    Gr-CT:165, Gr-GB:245, Ox-BB:245
A Trampwoman's Tragedy. T. Hardy.
    Ox-BN:825
The True Lover. A. Housman. Un-MW:121
The Trumpeter of Fyvie. Ox-BB:349
The Twa Brothers. De-CH:52, Ox-BB:234
The Twa Corbies. De-CH:102, Ha-PO:127,
    Ma-BB:132, Ma-FW:256, Pa-GTB:90,
    Rv-CB:55, Sm-LG:268, Sp-OG:115
The Twa Magicians. Ox-BB:51
The Twa Sisters. De-CH:421, Rv-CB:42
Two Red Roses Across the Moon.
    W. Morris. Rv-CB:927

The Unfortunate Miller. Ox-BB:643
The Unquiet Grave. Al-VBP:39,
    De-CH:342, Gr-GB:131, Hi-WP II:17,
    Ox-BB:96, Rv-CB:51
Verses on Daniel Good. Ox-BB:654
Villikins and His Dinah. S. Cowell.
    Co-PT:184
The Walloping Window-Blind. C. Carryl.
    Co-HP:48, Fe-FP:343, Hu-MP:450,
    Lo-LL:90, Sh-RP:123, Un-GF:30,
    Un-GT:220
Waly, Waly. Al-VBP:51, Gr-GB:144,
    Ox-BB:327, Pa-GTB:87
The Water o' Wearie's Well. De-CH:730
The Wee Wee Man. De-CH:277, Fo-OG:28,
    Gr-GB:286, Ma-BB:12, Ox-BB:11
Widdecombe Fair. Co-PM:213, De-CH:72
The Wife of Usher's Well. Ar-TP3:20,
    De-CH:424, De-TT:171, Gr-CT:134,
    Ma-BB:37, Ox-BB:94, Pa-OM:91, Rv-CB:36
William Bond. Ox-BB:674
Willie and Lady Margerie. Ox-BB:121
Willie Mackintosh. Ma-BB:8, Ox-BB:597,
    Rv-CB:125
The Witches' Ballad. W. Scott.
    De-CH:306, Na-EO:24
The Wraggle Taggle Gipsies. Ar-TP3:15,
    De-CH:75, Fe-FP:509, Ho-WR:48,
    Hu-MP:155, Mc-WS:163, Na-EO:33,
    Re-TW:124, Rv-CB:436, Un-GT:96
The Yarn of the Loch Achray.
    J. Masefield. Co-SS:139, Ha-PO:252
Young Beichan. Ma-FW:146, Pa-OM:240
Young Bekie. Ma-BB:13, Ox-BB:103
Young Benjie. Ox-BB:337
The Young Cordwainer. R. Graves.
    Ca-MB:30
Young Hunting. Ox-BB:87
Young John. Ma-BB:30
Young Johnstone. Ox-BB:212
Young Waters. Fo-OG:31, Ox-BB:321
Younge Andrew. Ox-BB:216
BALLADS, GERMAN
    The Erl-King. J. von Goethe. Sp-OG:111
BALLADS, INDIAN: see INDIANS OF NORTH
    AMERICA - VERSE
BALLADS, IRISH
    The Abbot of Inisfalen. W. Allingham.
        Pa-OM:104
    The Ballad of Father Gilligan. W. Yeats.
        Hi-WP I:72, Mc-MK:132, Mc-WS:157,
        Pl-EI:114, Un-MB:112
    Brennan on the Moor. Co-RM:165,
        Gr-GB:254
    Brian Boy Magee. F. Carbery. Co-PI:21
    The Cow Ate the Piper. Gr-GB:88
    The Croppy Boy. Rv-CB:437
    The Death of Cuchulain. W. Yeats.
        Gr-CT:146
    The Host of the Air. W. Yeats.
        De-CH:295, Li-TU:90

BALLADS, IRISH — cont'd.
  I Know Where I'm Going. Al-VBP:1122,
    Gr-CC:14, Gr-GB:117, Un-MW:189
  Johnny, I Hardly Knew Ye. Gr-GB:241
  A Kiss in the Morning Early. Gr-GB:126
  Kitty of Coleraine. Co-PT:188
  A Longford Legend. Co-PT:153
  The Love-Talker. E. Carbery.
    Co-PI:20, De-CH:296, Ha-PO:192
  The Shan Van Vocht. Gr-GB:194
  The Whistling Thief. Co-PT:202
BALLADS, NEGRO: see also SPIRITUALS
  Ballad of Birmingham. D. Randall.
    Be-MA:71, Ra-BP:143
  The Ballad of Joe Meek. S. Brown.
    Be-MA:31
  The Ballad of Rudolph Reed. G. Brooks.
    Jo-SA:46
  The Blue-Tail Fly. Er-FA:450, Gr-GB:324
  Blues for Bessie. M. O'Higgins.
    Hu-PN:347, Kr-OF:50
  Joseph Mica. Mo-GR:53
  Old Marse John. Lo-TY:198
  The Old Section Boss. Ra-BP:17
  Stagolee. Lo-TY:201
BALLADS, ROCK
  I've Got to Know. W. Guthrie. Pe-SS:142
  Where Have All the Flowers Gone?
    P. Seeger. Pe-SS:132
BALLADS, RUMANIAN
  Ballad of Death. G. Topirceanu.
    Mc-AC:51
  Ballad of the Priest of Rudeni.
    G. Topirceanu. Mc-AC:49
  John the Innkeeper. O. Goga. Mc-AC:36
BALLADS, RUSSIAN
  The God. B. Akhmadulina. Bo-RU:2
BALLADS, SCOTTISH: see BALLADS, ENGLISH
    AND SCOTTISH
BALLADS, SEA: see SEA SONGS
BALLADS, SIERRA LEONE
  Prologue to a Yomeh Ballad. Tr-US I:44
BALLADS, SPANISH
  As Mary Was A-Walking. Ga-S:107
BALLADS, WELSH
  The Ballad of Billy Rose. L. Norris.
    Ca-MB:83
BALLADS, WESTERN: see BALLADS, AMERICAN;
    BALLADS, COWBOY
BALLET: see also DANCERS AND DANCING;
    HUMOR - BALLET; and names of dancers,
    as PAVLOVA, ANNA
  Arthur Mitchell. M. Moore. Hu-PN:506
  Ballet School. B. Deutsch. Ho-LP:60
  Homage to Vaslav Nijinsky. J. Kirkup.
    Pl-US:120
  The Swan. S. Spender. Pl-US:118
  Les Sylphides. L. MacNeice. Gr-BT:81
  To Potapovitch. H. Crane. Pl-US:117
BALLOONS (AIRSHIPS): see also HUMOR -
    BALLOONS (AIRSHIPS)
  The Balloon. A. Tennyson. Co-RG:137

  Balloon. S. Tsuboi. Sh-AM:72
  The Balloon. Wr-RM:121
  Who Knows if the Moon's. E. Cummings.
    Co-PM:42, Ha-LO:47
BALLONS (TOYS): see also HUMOR -
    BALLOONS (TOYS)
  The Balloon. K. Kuskin. La-PV:6
  The Balloon Man. D. Aldis. Ar-TP3:12
  The Balloon Man. R. Fyleman. Au-SP:145
  Balloon Man. J. North. Au-SP:146
  Balloons. S. Plath. Ha-TP:22, To-MP:97
  In Just. E. Cummings. Ad-CI:72,
    Bo-FP:224, Co-HP:55, Du-RG:96,
    Fe-FP:73, Ga-FB:283, Ir-BB:25,
    Re-TW:53, Sh-RP:30, Un-GT:272,
    Un-MA:472
  Multi-Colored Balloon. H. Greggs.
    Ab-MO:16
  Timothy Boon. I. Eastwick.
    Au-SP:208, Ir-BB:148
BALLS (TOYS)
  Ball. K. Greenaway. Bo-FP:4
  The Ball Poem. J. Berryman.
    La-OC:86, Un-MA:641
  Bouncing Ball. S. Watson. Au-SP:193
  Heel, Toe, Stamp and Over. Bu-DY:87
  I Love Coffee. Bu-DY:84
  Jack, Jack, Pump the Water. Bu-DY:85
  The Lost Ball. L. Mitchell. Ir-BB:18
  Song of the Playing Ball. I. Adigal.
    Al-PI:70
  Where Are You Going, Ruth? Bu-DY:86
BALLYBUNION, IRE.
  The Black Cliffs, Ballybunion.
    B. Kennelly. Co-PI:83
BALLYJAMESDUFF, IRE.
  Come Back, Paddy Reilly. P. French.
    Co-PI:48
BALTIMORE, MD.
  The Dome of Sunday. K. Shapiro.
    Un-MA:637, Wi-LT:532
  Incident. C. Cullen. Ab-MO:94,
    Ad-PB:91, Be-MA:51, Ca-VT:241,
    Ho-LP:58, Hu-PN:232, Jo-SA:107,
    Kr-OF:50, Mo-BG:78, Pe-OA:190,
    Ra-BP:98, Th-AS:193
BALUCHI VERSE: see IRANIAN VERSE - BALUCHI
BALZAC, HONORÉ DE: see also EUGÉNE DE
    RASTIGNAC
  Balzac. D. Gottlieb. Ls-NY:148
BAMBOO
  The Bamboo by Li Ch'e Yun's Window.
    Po Chu I. Rx-LT:73
  Languishing. Br-FW:2
  Song for a Ceremonial Dance. Tr-US I:183
BANANAS: see also HUMOR - BANANAS
  The Song of the Banana Man. E. Jones.
    Co-RM:242, Sa-B:101, To-MP:168
  Though They Have Been Known. Re-RR:20
BANBURY, ENG.
  As I Was Going to Banbury. Ir-BB:123,
    Mo-MGT:185, Pa-AP:38

BANCROFT, GEORGE
  A Decanter of Madeira, Aged 86, to
    George Bancroft, Aged 86.
    S. Mitchell. Al-VBP:992
BANDITS: see OUTLAWS
BANDS (MUSIC): see also HUMOR - BANDS
    (MUSIC); and names of musical
    instruments, as DRUMS
  The Colored Band. P. Dunbar. Hu-MP:149
  Concert. R. Sward. Ca-VT:681
  Dances. D. Meltzer. Lo-IT:90
  The High School Band. R. Whittemore.
    Pe-M:9
  Italian Music in Dakota. W. Whitman.
    Sh-AP:120
  Summer Concert. R. Whittemore.
    Br-AF:216
  Ten Tom-Toms. On-TW:35
BANISHMENT: see EXILES
BANJOS
  The Banjo Player. F. Johnson. Hu-PN:86
BANKS AND BANKING: see also HUMOR- BANKS
    AND BANKING
  At the Bank. R. Field. Mc-PR:183
BANKS ISLANDS (MELANESIA)
  In Honor of Maros During His Absence
    at Sea. Tr-US I:216
BANNOCKBURN, BATTLE, 1314
  Scots Wha Hae. R. Burns. Hi-FO:83,
    Ma-YA:135, Sm-LG:154, Sp-OG:189
BAPTISM: see also GODPARENTS AND
    GODCHILDREN
  At a Child's Baptism. V. Miller.
    Bo-GJ:28, Ls-NY:119
  Baptism. C. Bell. Br-AF:140
  Baptism. W. Langland. Ga-S:181
  Ceremony for Birth and Naming.
    R. Torrence. Tr-MR:206
  Charm. Ga-S:181
  The Christening. W. de la Mare.
    Br-BC:30
  The Christening. A. Milne. Br-BC:38
  The Evil Eye. J. Ciardi. Ca-MB:19
  The Font. C. Sansom. Ga-S:180,
    Gr-BT:5
  For a Christening. V. Watkins.
    Tr-MR:208
  Gifts. H. Harris. Br-BC:32
  It Really Happened. E. Henley.
    Br-BC:31
  To Patricia on Her Christening Day.
    E. Price. Br-BC:29
BARBADOS
  Poem. E. Brathwaite. Sa-B:169
BARBERRIES
  Song Against Children. A. Kilmer.
    Th-AS:65
BARBERS: see also HUMOR - BARBERS
  The Barber's. W. de la Mare. Au-SP:139,
    Bo-FP:118, Bo-GJ:25, Hu-MP:146
  Barber's Clippers. D. Baruch.
    Au-SP:140

haircut. W. Packard. Ad-CI:70
Haircut. K. Shapiro. Br-TC:372
The Man from Ironbark. A. Peterson.
  Co-RM:146
To a Child Trapped in a Barber Shop.
  P. Levine. Ca-VT:633
BARCELONA, SP.
  Barcelona. C. McKay. Ab-MO:46
BARGES: see BOATS AND BOATING; CARGOES;
    FREIGHTERS
BARKING
  Dog, Midwinter. R. Souster. Co-BBW:112
  Getting On. S. Sandy. Ad-CI:92
  A Man Lost His Dog. Re-RR:22
  Night Song. F. Cornford. Co-BBW:112,
    Co-IW:41
  To a Dog Barking at Night. F. Maguire.
    Ls-NY:326
BARLEY
  John Barleycorn. R. Burns. Sm-LG:212
  The Ripe and Bearded Barley. Cl-DT:86,
    Co-BN:126, Gr-CT:313, Gr-GB:46
  Sir John Barleycorn. Rv-CB:492
BARMECIDES
  The Time of the Barmecides. J. Mangan.
    Co-RG:8
BARNEGAT BAY, N.J.
  Patrolling Barnegat. W. Whitman.
    Rv-CB:848
BARNES, WILLIAM
  The Last Signal. T. Hardy. Pl-ML:159
BARNS
  The Barn. E. Blunden. Un-MB:397
  Elegy for the Monastery Barn.
    T. Merton. Ca-VT:420
  The Hayloft. R. Stevenson. Bo-FP:94
  Human Things. H. Nemerov. Co-BN:200
  Lamplighter Barn. M. Livingston.
    Ar-TP3:105
  The Little Boy. Mo-MGT:10
  The Satin Mice Creaking Last Summer's
    Grass. R. Coffin. Rd-OA:90
  The Wagon in the Barn. J. Drinkwater.
    Pe-FB:30, Th-AS:70
BARNUM, IRENA TAYLOR
  Nancy Hanks, Mother of Abraham Lincoln.
    V. Lindsay. Hi-TL:96
BARROW, ALSK.
  Barrow. L. Adams. Ba-HI:105
BARS: see INNS AND TAVERNS; RESTAURANTS
    AND BARS
BARSTOW, CALIF.
  At Barstow. C. Tomlinson. Br-TC:446
BARTHÉLEMON, FRANCOIS HIPPOLYTE
  Barthélémon at Vauxhall. T. Hardy.
    Pl-US:89
BARTON, SIR ANDREW
  Sir Andrew Bartton. Ox-BB:508
BARTON, BRUCE: see SATIRE - BARTON, BRUCE
BASEBALL: see also HUMOR - BASEBALL;
    STICKBALL
  Ball Game. R. Eberhart. Pe-M:5

BASEBALL — cont'd.
  The Base Stealer. R. Francis.
    Ar-TP3:107, Bo-GJ:212, Du-RG:112,
    Fl-HH:3, Mo-SD:2
  Baseball. J. Wagner.   Ho-CT:10
  Casey at the Bat. E. Thayer.
    Fe-FP:549, Mo-SD:11
  Cobb Would Have Caught It.
    R. Fitzgerald. Br-TC:128, Du-SH:75,
    Mo-BG:35, Mo-SD:15
  The Double Play. R. Wallace.
    Fl-HH:62, Mo-SD:16
  Dream of a Baseball Star. G. Corso.
    Ca-VT:658, Fl-HH:18, Mo-SD:17
  Hits and Runs. C. Sandburg.
    Fl-HH:41, Mo-SD:3
  I Like to Go to the Moon. G. Gotthardt.
    La-GI:46
  It Is an Outfielder. R. Loewinsohn.
    Kh-VA:76
  Line-Up for Yesterday. O. Nash.
    Mo-SD:21
  Night Game. R. Humphries. Mo-BG:28,
    Ni-JP:87
  Nuns at Eve. J. Brinnin. Br-TC:64
  Pitcher. R. Francis. Du-SH:77,
    Mo-SD:4, Ni-JP:95
  Polo Grounds. R. Humphries.
    Mo-SD:9, Ni-JP:124
  To Lou Gehrig. J. Kieran. Mo-SD:19
  To Satch. S. Allen. Ab-MO:89,
    Ad-PB:167, Bo-AN:140, Gr-BT:178,
    Hu-PN:343, Jo-SA:58, Lo-TY:244,
    Mc-EA:71, Mo-SD:18
  The Umpire. W. Gibson. Fl-HH:45,
    Mo-SD:6
  Villanelle. M. Feld. Mo-SD:159
  Where, O Where? M. Bracker. Mo-SD:20
BASHFULNESS: see LOVE - BASHFULNESS;
    TIMIDITY
BASKETBALL
  Basketball: A Love Song Because It Is.
    T. Meschery. Fl-HH:25
  Ex-Basketball Player. J. Updike.
    Du-SH:79, Ha-TP:38, Mo-BG:53,
    Ni-JP:32, Pe-M:60
  Foul Shot. E. Hoey. Du-RG:112,
    Fl-HH:53
  Jump Shot. R. Peck. Pe-M:8
BASTARDY: see ILLEGITIMACY
BATHS: see also HUMOR - BATHS
  After a Bath. A. Fisher. Ho-ME:13,
    Mc-AW:88, St-FS:31
  Business Girls. J. Betjeman.
    Hi-WP II:167
  The Candle's Light. A. Nakamura.
    Le-TA:46
  Charm at a Ceremonial Bathing to Make One
    Beautiful and Irresistible. Tr-US I:197
  I Wonder What It Feels Like to Be
    Drowned. R. Graves. Un-MB:386

  In the Tub We Soak Our Skin. E. Horn.
    Co-EL:124, Co-PM:133
  An Indignant Male. A. Ross.
    Ho-ME:12, Hu-MP:14
  Pater's Bathe. E. Parry. Ox-BC:309
  Slippery. C. Sandburg. Br-BC:42,
    Fe-FP:39
  The Tub. G. Chappell. St-FS:91
  The Voyage of Jimmy Poo. J. Emanuel.
    Bo-AN:174, Hu-NN:97, Ls-NY:220
BATHSHEBA
  The Love of King David and Fair Bethsabe.
    G. Peele. Al-VBP:138
BATS (ANIMALS)
  All but Blind. W. de la Mare.
    Fe-FP:138, Ga-S:48, Hi-WP I:121,
    La-PV:152, Mc-WK:99, Ni-JP:82,
    Un-MB:291
  The Barefoot Bat. De-PP:17
  The Bat. Buson. Le-IS:18
  Bat. J. Clare. Rd-OA:77
  The Bat. A. Guiterman. Co-BBW:21
  The Bat. R. Herschberger. Du-RG:34
  Bat. D. Lawrence. Pa-GTB:458
  The Bat. R. Pitter. Co-BBW:52,
    Hi-WP II:44
  The Bat. T. Roethke. Bo-FP:82,
    Bo-GJ:80, Co-BBW:45, Du-RG:35,
    Gr-EC:8, La-PV:147, Ls-NY:104,
    Ma-FW:209, Pa-RE:111, Pe-SS:66,
    Sm-MK:154, Un-GT:56
  The Bat. Sun Yü-t'ang. Hs-TC:119
  Bat, Bat. Ir-BB:191, Mo-MGT:85,
    Wr-RM:73
  The Bat Is Dun. E. Dickinson. Be-EB:23
  The Bats. W. Bynner. Bo-HF:68
  Bats. R. Jarrell. Ad-PE:10, Du-SH:162,
    La-RM:138, Mc-WS:50, Mo-TS:61,
    Pa-RE:19, Rd-OA:10, To-MP:156,
    We-PZ:22
  Dance Songs, X. Tr-US II:165
  The End of the Weekend. A. Hecht.
    Wi-LT:731
  The Mad Hatter's Song. L. Carroll.
    Bo-FP:82, Ir-BB:121
  Mind. R. Wilbur. Ha-PO:230
  Professor Nocturnal. R. Roseliep.
    De-FS:158
  A Round Trip. De-PP:35
  The Sun Is Slowly Departing. Hs-TC:41
  Sunset. Tai Wang-shu. Hs-SD:41
  The Witch of Willoughby Wood.
    R. Bennett. Co-PM:27, Sh-RP:228
BATTLES: see also HUMOR - BATTLES; NAVAL
    BATTLES; RAIDS; SATIRE - BATTLES; and
    names of battles, as CRECY, BATTLE,
    1346
  All That Is Left. Basho. Ba-PO:25,
    Pa-SG:9
  The Ash and the Oak. L. Simpson.
    Cr-WS:3, Mo-BG:168

Battle. R. Jeffers. Un–MA:371,
  Wi–LT:260
Battle Song. Sitting Bull. Da–SC:113
Before Sedan. A. Dobson. Ke–TF:52
Carentan O Carentan. L. Simpson.
  Bl–FP:46, Ca–MB:117, Co–RM:202,
  To–MP:49
Carmen Bellicosum. G. McMaster.
  Vi–PP:114
Chant on the Return from a Successful
  Head–Taking Raid. Tr–US I:142
Counter–Attack. S. Sassoon. Ba–PO:136,
  Co–RM:204, Cr–WS:87, Un–MB:312
The Day of Battle. A. Housman. Cr–WS:90
The Fighting Race. J. Clarke. Co–RM:111
Grass. C. Sandburg. Cr–WS:19,
  Fe–PL:155, Ga–FB:219, Un–MA:200
Henry's Address to His Troops.
  W. Shakespeare. Mc–WS:100
Horatius. T. Macaulay. Er–FA:387,
  Fe–PL:64, Hi–FO:32, Sm–LG:161
McNaughton. Ox–BB:304
The Myth of Numputul, the Self–Beheaded.
  Tr–US I:178
Names from the War. B. Catton.
  Br–AF:78
Near Mons. N. Myers. Ls–NY:256
Night in the House by the River.
  Tu Fu. Rx–OH:29
On a Victory. Tr–US I:127
The Oranges. Abu Dharr. Lo–TY:45
The Portrait of a Chinese Soldier.
  Wang Ya–p'ing. Hs–TC:354
Range–Finding. R. Frost. Ha–TP:77
Red Harlaw. Ox–BB:676
Retreat. J. Clark. Ls–NY:87
Riding Together. W. Morris. Cl–FC:79
The Romance of Antar. Antar. Ab–MO:66
Seravezza. H. Fuller. Ad–PB:200
Sixteen–Syllable Stanza. Mao Tse–tung.
  Hs–TC:362
Song for a Seated Dance: Victory of
  the Mea. Tr–US I:219
Thermopylae 1941. C. Trypanis.
  Cr–WS:33
Two Red Roses Across the Moon.
  W. Morris. Rv–CB:927
Under the Frontier Post. Wang Chang–Ling.
  Gr–CT:340
The Valley of the Black Pig. W. Yeats.
  Gr–CT:335
BAUCIS AND PHILEMON
Baucis and Philemon. J. Swift.
  Sp–OG:153
BAUDELAIRE, CHARLES PIERRE
Ave atque Vale. A. Swinburne.
  Al–VBP:1033, Ox–BN:814
Baudelaire. D. Schwartz. Br–TC:357,
  Pl–ML:14
The Bourgeois Poet, #69. K. Shapiro.
  St–H:206

BAVARIA, GER.
Lines on Leaving a Scene in Bavaria.
  T. Campbell. Ox–BN:198
Two Poems on the Catholic Bavarians, I.
  E. Bowers. En–PC:220
Two Poems on the Catholic Bavarians, II.
  E. Bowers. En–PC:221
BAY TREES
Song. C. Rossetti. Al–VBP:995,
  Pa–GTB:374
BAYOUS: see MARSHES
BAZAARS (STREET)
In the Bazaars of Hyderabad. S. Naidu.
  Al–PI:102, Fe–FP:489, Sh–RP:56,
  Th–AS:156
BEACHES: see SEASHORE
BEADS
Overheard on a Saltmarsh. H. Monro.
  Ad–PE:17, Ar–TP3:153, Bo–GJ:227,
  Co–PM:125, De–CH:116, Du–RG:67,
  Fe–FP:388, Gr–EC:269, Li–LC:41,
  Mc–WS:29, Re–TW:25, Su–FVI:16,
  Th–AS:14
BEAN, ROY
The Law West of the Pecos. S. Barker.
  Fi–BG:64
BEANS
The Butterbean Tent. E. Roberts.
  Bo–GJ:48, Br–SG:51
How to Sow Beans. Br–SG:11
BEARDS: see also HUMOR – BEARDS
A Beard Wishes to Escape. A. Lutzky.
  Ho–TY:265
Whiskers. J. Brown. Le–M:144
BEARS: see also HUMOR – BEARS
The Bear. J. Carpenter. Ls–NY:86
The Bear. R. Frost. Sh–AP:154,
  Un–MA:184
The Bear. G. Kinnell. Ca–VT:605,
  La–RM:25, Mc–EA:55
The Bear. N. Momaday. Ni–CD:91
The Bear on the Delhi Road. E. Birney.
  En–PC:55
Bears. A. Rich. Ha–TP:120
The Brown Bear. M. Austin. Co–PS:62,
  Fe–FP:169, Hu–MP:202, Mc–PR:118,
  Mc–WK:70
Brown Bear's Honey Song. K. Jackson.
  Mc–AW:86, Sh–RP:36
Color. R. Bennett. Hu–MP:185
Fall Comes to Back–Country Vermont.
  R. Warren. Ca–VT:278
Four–Footed Poems. E. Greenberg.
  Ho–TY:312
Four for Sir John Davies. T. Roethke.
  Pl–US:104, Un–MA:599
Fragment of a Bylina. A. Pushkin.
  Li–TU:83
Furry Bear. A. Milne. Au–SP:236,
  Co–IW:25, Pe–FB:13
Grizzly. B. Harte. Co–BBW:207, Rd–OA:48

BEARS — cont'd.
How Shall We Hide.   Ho-SD:58
Hunting Songs, 2. Bear Song.   Tr-US I:12
I Remember the White Bear.   Le-IB:54
I Sighted a Bear.   Ma-BH:14
I Took a Bow and Arrow.   J. Ciardi.
   Na-EO:116
Infant Innocence.   A. Housman.
   Er-FA:219, Gr-CT:23, Sm-LG:102
March.   J. Wright.   Ho-TH:89
The Marvellous Bear Shepherd.   Ma-FW:216
Orpingalik's Song: My Breath.
   Tr-US I:17
Part of the Darkness.   I. Gardner.
   St-H:73
Self-Portrait, as a Bear.   D. Hall.
   Ha-TP:94
Signal Song on Capture of Polar Bear.
   Le-IB:53
Song of a Bear.   Tr-US II:252
Ten Trained Bears on Roller Skates.
   On-TW:52
Two Little Men with Equal Feet.
   Fr-WO:54
Waiting.   H. Behn.   Ar-TP3:199,
   Br-SG:109, Br-SS:92
Was Not the Lost Dauphin.   R. Warren.
   Be-EB:40
"Who Are You?" Asked the Cat of the
   Bear.   E. Coatsworth.   Ar-TP3:54
Willy.   R. Moore.   Du-SH:117
BEAT GENERATION: see COUNTER CULTURE
BEATRICE PORTINARI
Love Is a Keeper of Swans.   H. Wolfe.
   Un-MB:303
BEAUMONT, SIR GEORGE HOWLAND
Elegiac Stanzas.   W. Wordsworth.
   Ox-BN:81, Pa-GTB:297
BEAUTY: see also BEAUTY, PERSONAL; HUMOR —
   BEAUTY; NATURE, BEAUTY; SATIRE — BEAUTY
The Act.   W. Williams.   Ca-VT:62,
   Co-EL:122
Adam's Curse.   W. Yeats.   Co-PI:205
An Agony. As Now.   I. Baraka.
   Ra-BP:211, Wi-LT:743
Alas.   W. de la Mare.   No-CL:71
Altar Smoke.   R. Grayer.   Un-GT:266
An Angel in the House.   C. Patmore.
   Pa-GTB:368
Appoggiatura.   D. Hayes.   Ad-PB:94,
   Bo-AN:90, Hu-PN:246
Aware.   D. Lawrence.   Co-BN:118,
   Co-PM:57, Un-MB:297
Barter.   S. Teasdale.   Fe-FP:21,
   Ga-FB:5, Hu-MP:71, Th-AS:199
The Beautiful.   W. Davies.   Co-EL:92,
   Co-PM:133
The Beautiful.   Le-OE:138
Beauty.   L. Binyon.   Un-MB:157
Beauty.   E-Yeh-Shure.   Ar-TP3:213,
   Fe-FP:20
Beauty.   D. Rossetti.   Al-VBP:992

Beauty, a Silver Dew.   Rv-CB:107
Beauty Clear and Fair.   J. Fletcher.
   Al-VBP:282, Rv-CB:313
Beetle.   H. Finn.   Co-BBW:216
Begonias.   Su Tung P'o.   Rx-OH:86
Boats in a Fog.   R. Jeffers.   Mo-BG:143
Brittania's Pastorals.   W. Browne.
   Al-VBP:320
By T'ing Yang Waterfall.   Hsieh Ling
   Yuen.   Rx-LT:34
Can You Paint a Thought?   J. Ford.
   Al-VBP:308, Rv-CB:332
Caryatid.   L. Adams.   Wi-LT:603
The Choice.   J. Masefield.   Un-MB:229
The Coin.   S. Teasdale.   Ar-TP3:213,
   Sh-RP:108, Th-AS:217
The Cross-Eyed Lover.   D. Finkel.
   Ho-P:79
The Cuckoo Calls from the Bamboo Grove.
   Rx-LT:12
Dawn Boy's Song.   Da-SC:64, Ga-FB:247
The Day Will Bring Some Lovely Thing.
   G. Crowell.   Ar-TP3:218
Divinely Superfluous Beauty.
   R. Jeffers.   Un-MA:369
The Door.   L. Strong.   Un-MB:394
Drop Me the Seed.   J. Masefield.
   Tr-MR:56
Each and All.   R. Emerson.   Sh-AP:25
Ella.   G. Brooks.   Ag-HE:39
The Enamel Girl.   G. Taggard.   Un-MA:478
Endymion.   J. Keats.   Al-VBP:788,
   Er-FA:264, Ma-YA:186, Mc-PR:89,
   Ox-BN:335
Envoi.   E. Pound.   Ca-VT:86, No-CL:27,
   Un-MA:296
The Eternal.   E. Tegnér.   Pa-SG:206
Euclid Alone.   E. Millay.   Er-FA:88,
   Ga-FB:3, Pl-IO:75, Un-MA:448
Fair and Unfair.   R. Francis.   Ca-VT:235
Fair Is My Love.   B. Griffin.   Al-VBP:91,
   Rv-CB:144
Fare Well.   W. de la Mare.   Pa-GTB:439
For Jim. Easter Eve.   A. Spencer.
   Bo-AN:17, Hu-PN:65
Forms of the Earth at Abiquiu.
   N. Momaday.   Ni-CD:88
From the Night Chant.   Br-MW:62
Gale in April.   R. Jeffers.   Un-MA:362
Gay Head.   N. Abeel.   Pa-HT:30
Ghazal.   J. Morabandi.   Al-PI:151
Give Beauty All Her Right.   T. Campion.
   Al-VBP:214, No-CL:201, Un-MW:14
Go, Lovely Rose!   E. Waller.   Al-VBP:386,
   Bo-GJ:128, Ha-PO:164, No-CL:29,
   Pa-GTB:76, Rv-CB:365, Un-MW:162
God's Grandeur.   G. Hopkins.   Er-FA:467,
   Ox-BN:867, Tr-MR:22, Un-MB:42,
   Wi-LT:40
The Great Breath.   "AE"
   Un-MB:143

Her Words.   A. Branch.   Ar-TP3:4,
   Br-SS:154, Fe-FP:32, Ha-YA:59
Here in the Self Is All That Man Can
   Know.   J. Masefield.   Go-BP:288
How to Choose a Mistress.   E. Prestwich.
   No-CL:140
Hurrahing in Harvest.   G. Hopkins.
   Co-BN:130, Gr-CT:313, Ma-FW:126,
   Rv-CB:946, Un-MB:43
Hymn to Intellectual Beauty.
   P. Shelley.   Ox-BN:276
I Died for Beauty.   E. Dickinson.
   Er-FA:85, Un-MA:95, Wi-LT:9
Independence Day.   W. Smith. Br-TC:394
Institute Poems, I-A.   M. Bruce.
   Ad-II:18
Invocation to Dsilyi Neyani. Da-SC:75,
   Tr-US II:250
The Islands.   H.D.   Un-MA:339
It Is Not Growing like a Tree. B. Jonson.
   Co-PM:69, Gr-CT:375, Hi-WP I:113,
   Ma-YA:82, Pa-GTB:63
The Judgment of the May.   R. Dixon.
   Ox-BN:750
The Lady with the Unicorn. V. Watkins.
   Br-TC:459
Last Lines — 1916.   P. Pearse.
   Co-PI:168
The Leaden Echo and the Golden Echo.
   G. Hopkins.   Er-FA:169, Ox-BN:867,
   Pa-GTB:393, Un-MB:40, Wi-LT:46
Look, How Beautiful.   R. Jeffers.
   Tr-MR:148
Lovely Dames.   W. Davies.   Gr-SS:103
Madrigal.   W. Drummond.   Al-VBP:302
Moonlight.   S. Teasdale.   Ca-VT:76,
   Co-PM:154
Most Lovely Shade.   E. Sitwell.
   Pa-GTB:473
Music.   R. Emerson.   Ga-FB:13, Un-GT:309
My Tired Old Nag.   Issa.   Be-MC:20
Not by Bread Alone.   J. White. Fe-PL:105
Nova.   R. Jeffers.   Pe-OA:90
Ode on a Grecian Urn.   Al-VBP:772,
   Er-FA:80, Ha-PO:228, Ke-TF:59,
   Ox-BN:355, Rv-CB:742
Of What Use Are Twigs.   Buson. Be-CS:15
The Old Summerhouse.   W. de la Mare.
   Pa-GTB:439
Old Tityrus to Eugenia.   C. Cotton.
   Al-VBP:474
On Growing Old.   J. Masefield.
   Al-VBP:1136, Er-FA:149, Fe-PL:263,
   Tr-MR:55, Un-MB:227, Wi-LT:193
On the Marriage of a Beauteous Young
   Gentlewoman with an Ancient Man.
   F. Beaumont.   Al-VBP:300
Orchard.   H.D.   Un-MA:337, Wi-LT:619
Oricessional Song from the Night Chant.
   Tr-US II:251
Ownership.   L. Reese.   Un-MA:111
Panope.   E. Sitwell.   Un-MB:333

Pericles and Aspasia.   W. Landor.
   Al-VBP:709, Ox-BN:192
Peter Quince at the Clavier. W. Stevens.
   Al-VBP:1142, Br-TC:415, Gr-CC:62,
   No-CL:43, Pe-OA:66, Un-MA:240,
   Wi-LT:142
Piazza Piece.   J. Ransom.   Gr-SS:122,
   Ha-PO:46, Rv-CB:984, Un-MA:414
Pied Beauty.   G. Hopkins.   Al-VBP:1062,
   Bo-GJ:47, Er-FA:461, Ga-S:16,
   Hi-WP II:37, Ho-LP:47, Ma-FW:101,
   Mc-PR:182, Mc-WK:16, No-CL:269,
   Ox-BN:865, Pa-GTB:390, Pl-EI:124,
   Re-TW:89, Sm-MK:222, Tr-MR:25,
   Un-GT:246, Un-MB:39, Wi-LT:42
Portrait of a Girl.   C. Aiken.
   Bo-GJ:123, Un-MA:425
Precious Stones.   C. Rossetti.
   Ar-TP3:210, De-TT:62, Un-GT:306
Reflection.   L. Sarett.   Th-AS:87
Renascence.   E. Millay.   Er-FA:95,
   Un-MA:440
The Revenger's Tragedy.   C. Tourneur.
   Al-VBP:274
The Rhodora.   R. Emerson.   Co-BN:59,
   De-CH:577, Er-FA:468, Ga-FB:289,
   Hu-MP:264, Sp-OG:359, Un-GT:257
Roadways.   J. Masefield.   Pa-HT:78,
   Sh-RP:157
The Rose and the Gardener.   H. Dobson.
   Hu-MP:248
The Rose of the World.   W. Yeats.
   Un-MB:111
Second Rose Motif.   C. Meireles.
   An-TC:35
The Sense of the Sleight-of-Hand Man.
   W. Stevens.   Pe-OA:70, Un-MA:252,
   Wi-LT:147
Sestina.   Dante Alighieri.   Gr-SS:93
Shall I Compare Thee to a Summer's Day?
   W. Shakespeare.   Al-VBP:200,
   Er-FA:126, Fe-PL:99, Ga-FB:32,
   Ha-PO:253, Hi-WP II:53, Ke-TF:102,
   Ma-YA:65, Ni-JP:126, Pa-GTB:12,
   Rv-CB:208, Un-MW:181
Song.   P. Massinger.   Al-VBP:298
The Song about the Bird.   V. Kalugin.
   Bo-RU:42
Sonnet.   J. Masefield.   Un-MB:228,
   Wi-LT:191
Sonnet II.   G. Bennett.   Ad-PB:82,
   Bo-AN:75, Hu-PN:206
Sonnet, xliii.   E. Millay.   Sm-PT:51
Sonnets 2.   S. Daniel.   Al-VBP:157
Sonnets LIV.   W. Shakespeare.
   Al-VBP:202
Spring Night.   S. Teasdale. Co-BL:38,
   Un-MA:264
The Spring Waters, 33.   Ping Hsin.
   Hs-TC:22
Swift Things Are Beautiful.
   E. Coatsworth. Ar-TP3:213, Du-RG:101

BEAUTY — cont'd.
  Taught Me Purple.   E. Hunt.   La-OC:93,
    Pe-SS:6
  There Was a Time.   E. Coatsworth.
    Mo-BG:111
  Thou Art Not Fair.   T. Campion.
    Al-VBP:214
  To Colin Clout.   A. Munday.
    Al-VBP:120, Pa-GTB:12, Rv-CB:164
  To Entertain Divine Zenocrate.
    C. Marlowe.   Al-VBP:174, Gr-CT:180
  To L.S.C.L.M.   R. Bridges.   Al-VBP:1064
  "To Me, Fair Friend, You Never Can Be
    Old."   W. Shakespeare.   Al-VBP:207,
    Pa-GTB:9
  The Triumph of Charis.   B. Jonson.
    Al-VBP:235, Rv-CB:283
  The Unknown God.   "AE"   Un-MB:144
  The Viper.   R. Pitter.   Gr-CC:144
  Washed in Silver.   J. Stephens.
    Co-EL:151
  The Waters of Life.   H. Wolfe.
    Un-MB:304
  The Weaving.   H. Cook.   Th-AS:119
  When in the Chronicle of Wasted Time.
    W. Shakespeare.   Al-VBP:207, Ga-FB:32,
    Gr-CC:80, No-CL:89, Pa-GTB:13,
    Rv-CB:238, Sm-LG:353
  When You Are Old.   W. Yeats.
    Bo-GJ:233, Co-BL:80, Er-FA:172,
    Fe-PL:94, Ga-FB:74, Go-BP:151,
    Ha-PO:179, Hi-MP I:43, Ma-FW:289,
    Un-MB:109, Un-MW:98, Wi-LT:68
  Wherever Beauty Has Been Quick in Clay.
    J. Masefield.   Tr-MR:41
  The White Bouquet.   Chung Ting-wen.
    Pa-MV:79
BEAUTY, PERSONAL: see also HUMOR -
    BEAUTY, PERSONAL; SATIRE - BEAUTY,
    PERSONAL
  Aeglamour's Lament.   B. Jonson.
    De-CH:334, No-CL:199
  The Air to Gi'e Your Cheäks a Hue.
    W. Barnes.   De-CH:614
  All Your Young Beauty.   Le-OE:87
  The Apple.   J. Halevi.   Me-PH:61
  Approaching and Departing.   N. Lenau.
    Un-R:125
  Art Thou That She.   Al-VBP:353
  As to His Choice of Her.   W. Blunt.
    Al-VBP:1052
  At Flock Mass.   F. Higgins.   Co-PI:65
  The Autumnal.   J. Donne.   Al-VBP:254
  Ayii, Ayii, Ayii (I Am Goodlooking).
    Ho-SD:82
  A Ballad of the Mulberry Road.
    E. Pound.   Ha-LO:93
  Ballatetta.   E. Pound.   Ca-VT:81
  Beauty Extolled.   H. Noel.   Gr-CT:62
  The Beauty of Job's Daughters.
    J. MacPherson.   En-PC:289
  Black Diamond.   N. Gumilyov.   Pa-SG:24

  Black Woman.   L. Curry.   Jo-VC:64
  Black Woman.   L. Senghor.   Lo-TY:134
  Blue Girls.   J. Ransom.   Ca-VT:150,
    Gr-CC:79, Gr-CT:51, Ha-PO:183,
    Mc-WS:75, Pe-OA:137, Sh-AP:182,
    Un-MA:409
  Boys' Dance Song on the Departure of an
    Older Girl Named Yiluai.   Tr-US II:6
  Brown Is My Love.   Rv-CB:110
  By the City Gate.   Ts'ui Hao.   Rx-LT:63
  Cherry-Ripe.   T. Campion.   Al-VBP:217,
    Bo-GJ:125, De-CH:142, Ke-TF:98,
    Pa-GTB:77, Re-TW:67
  Cleopatra.   W. Shakespeare.   Hi-FO:51,
    No-CL:60
  Dagonet's Canzonet.   E. Rhys.   Gr-SS:86
  Dance Figure.   E. Pound.   Un-MA:294
  Deirdre.   J. Stephens.   Al-VBP:1151,
    Gr-CC:91
  Dew Sate upon Julia's Hair.
    R. Herrick.   De-CH:733
  Disdain Returned.   T. Carew.
    Al-VBP:349, Ga-FB:41, Pa-GTB:75
  Do Not, Oh Do Not Prize.   Rv-CB:122
  Encouraging a Dancer.   Tr-CB:18,
    Tr-US I:38
  The Eve of Crécy.   W. Morris.   Gr-SS:95
  The Face of Helen.   C. Marlowe.
    Al-VBP:176, Er-FA:106, Ga-FB:31
  Fidele's Song.   A. Munday.   Rv-CB:162
  The First Part of Tamurlaine the Great.
    C. Marlowe.   Al-VBP:173
  The Folly of Being Comforted.
    W. Yeats.   Go-BP:130
  Gee, You're So Beautiful that It's
    Starting to Rain.   R. Brautigan.
    Kh-VA:14
  Girls on the Yueh River.   Li Po.
    Gr-CT:62, Ho-LP:62
  Grieve Not, Ladies.   A. Branch.
    Er-FA:156
  Haroun's Favorite Song.   Pa-SG:64
  He Compares All Things with His Lady
    and Finds Them Wanting.
    G. Cavalcanti.   Pa-SG:73
  Her, a Statue.   T. Stoddart.   Ox-BN:531
  Her Perfections.   P. Sidney.   No-CL:208
  Her Powder-Box.   W. Stead.   Ls-NY:324
  Hymn to the Spirit of Nature.
    P. Shelley.   Al-VBP:742, De-CH:335,
    Pa-GTB:281
  I Know that All Beneath the Moon Decays.
    W. Drummond.   De-CH:624
  I Saw My Lady Weep.   Al-VBP:355,
    Rv-CB:112
  If Souls Should Only Shine as Bright.
    W. Barnes.   De-CH:636
  If the Heart of a Man.   J. Gay.
    Rv-CB:394
  Judith of Bethulia.   J. Ransom.
    Wi-LT:313
  A Lady.   A. Lowell.   Un-MA:156

Laura. T. Campion. Al-VBP:221,
   Go-BP:119, Gr-SS:98, Pl-US:49
Laura Sleeping. C. Cotton. Al-VBP:476
Love Song for Nneka. Do-CH:(35)
Lovel's Song. B. Jonson. Ho-LP:9
The Lover Praises His Lady's Bright
   Beauty. S. O'Sheel. Co-BL:70
Memorial. C. Smith. De-FS:185
Merciless Beauty: A Triple Rondel.
   G. Chaucer. No-CL:148, Rv-CB:59
The Morning Sun Shines.
   Emperor Wu. Rx-LT:9
My Love. e. cummings. Ca-VT:171,
   Wi-LT:358
My Mistress Is as Fair as Fine.
   De-CH:333
No Images. W. Cuney. Bo-AN:98,
   Bo-HF:92, Lo-TY:237
"Not Marble nor the Gilded Monuments."
   A. MacLeish. Al-VBP:1194, Br-TC:277,
   Un-MW:143
On Getting a Natural. D. Randall.
   Ad-PB:141
On His Mistress, the Queen of Bohemia.
   H. Wotton. Al-VBP:222, Pa-GTB:73,
   Rv-CB:278
Parthenope. B. Barnes. Rv-CB:279
Persuasions to Love. T. Carew.
   Al-VBP:348
Philip Sparrow. J. Skelton. Al-VBP:26
Piazza de Spagna: Early Morning.
   R. Wilbur. Ca-VT:485
The Picture of Little T.C. in a
   Prospect of Flowers. A. Marvell.
   Rv-CB:406
The Planter's Daughter. A. Clarke.
   Co-PI:25
A Prayer for My Daughter. W. Yeats.
   Al-VBP:1090, Fe-PL:137, Tr-MR:49,
   Wi-LT:73
Puella Mea. E. Cummings. No-CL:212
A Question. Rv-CB:136
Radhadevi's Dance. Nayacandra Suri.
   Al-PI:53
The Rape of the Lock. A. Pope.
   Al-VBP:531
Samela. R. Greene. Al-VBP:141
She Walked Unaware. P. MacDonogh.
   Co-BL:135, Co-PI:109
She Walks in Beauty. G. Byron.
   Co-RG:148, Er-FA:105, Hi-WP II:54,
   Ke-TF:107, Mc-PR:91, Ni-JP:96,
   Ox-BN:251, Pa-GTB:177, Rv-CB:688,
   Sh-RP:89, Un-MW:166
She Was a Phantom of Delight.
   W. Wordsworth. Al-VBP:656, Er-FA:109,
   Ga-FB:49, Pa-GTB:178, Rv-CB:638
Shee Was Brighter of Her Blee.
   De-CH:766
Song. L. Abercrombie. Un-MB:253
Song. T. Carew. Al-VBP:350,
   De-CH:144, Er-FA:107, Un-MW:163
Song. H.D. Un-MA:337, Wi-LT:618

Song. G. Vicente. Pa-SG:41
Sonnet 19. W. Shakespeare. Gr-CT:61,
   Ho-LP:8, Rv-CB:209, Un-MW:182
Sonnet 20. W. Shakespeare. Rv-CB:210
Sonnet CIV. W. Shakespeare. Ho-P:130
Sonnet 127. W. Shakespeare. Rv-CB:245
Sonnets, v. E. Wylie. Sm-PT:70
Spectrum. W. Dickey. Co-EL:96
The Stranger. J. Garrigue. Br-TC:142,
   Wi-LT:709
That Ever I Saw. Rv-CB:7
There Be None of Beauty's Daughters.
   G. Byron. De-TT:152, Pa-GTB:176,
   Rv-CB:691
The Three Cherry Trees. W. de la Mare.
   Gr-SS:35
To a Fair Lady, Playing with a Snake.
   E. Waller. Gr-CC:86
To a Golden-Haired Girl in a Louisiana
   Town. V. Lindsay. Un-MA:221
To a Lady. W. Dunbar. No-CL:149
To a Lady Seen for a Few Moments at
   Vauxhall. J. Keats. No-CL:162
To a Very Young Lady. G. Etherege.
   Al-VBP:496
To Cynthia. F. Kynaston. Al-VBP:310
To Dianeme. R. Herrick. Al-VBP:326,
   Pa-GTB:76, Rv-CB:335
To Helen. E. Poe. Al-VBP:878,
   Co-BL:76, De-CH:347, Er-FA:123,
   Fe-PL:101, Fr-WO:84, Ga-FB:62,
   Gr-CT:440, No-CL:56, Rv-CB:802,
   Sh-AP:53, Un-MW:168
To Ianthe. G. Byron. Ox-BN:241
To Judith Asleep. J. Ciardi.
   Wi-LT:669
To One Admiring Herself in a Looking
   Glass. T. Randolph. Al-VBP:381,
   No-CL:205
The Tribute. C. Patmore. Ox-BN:651
Unamina. B. Vilikazi. Pa-SG:38
Unthrifty Loveliness (Sonnet IV).
   W. Shakespeare. Mo-GR:123
Upon a Maid. R. Herrick. Gr-CT:354,
   Sm-LG:273
Water Music. L. Durrell. Ha-TP:60
The Weeping Cherry. R. Herrick.
   Hi-WP II:1
What Is Your Substance. W. Shakespeare.
   Al-VBP:202, Er-FA:117
When I Do Count the Clock.
   W. Shakespeare. Al-VBP:200,
   Er-FA:262, Rv-CB:207
When Sue Wears Red. L. Hughes.
   Lo-TY:228
When the Light Falls. S. Kunitz.
   Un-MA:593
When Thy Beauty Appears. T. Parnell.
   Rv-CB:500
When Yon Full Moon. W. Davies.
   Un-MB:177
The Whummil Bore. De-CH:329
Why Try? T. Joans. Br-MA:101

BEAUTY, PERSONAL — <u>cont'd.</u>
Wishes. To His Supposed Mistress.
  R. Crashaw. Al-VBP:432, Pa-GTB:67
Woman Recipe. V. de Moraes. An-TC:105
Woman's Beauty. L. Abercrombie.
  Un-MB:255
Women's Grinding Song. Tr-US I:123
BEAVERS
A Bedtime Song for Children. Br-MW:90
Over in the Meadow. Au-SP:223,
  Ir-BB:24, On-TW:38
Paddy the Beaver. T. Burgess.
  Sh-RP:343
You Talk about and Fear Me. Ho-SD:31
BEDBUGS
Bedbug. Ab-MO:41
The Lightning Bug Has Wings of Gold.
  La-OC:129
BEDIVERE, SIR
The Passing of Arthur. A. Tennyson.
  Ni-JP:158, Ox-BN:511
BEDOUINS
Bedouin Song. B. Taylor. Co-BL:39,
  Sh-AP:124
The Desert. S. Crane. Wi-LT:119
BEDS AND BEDDING: see also HUMOR - BEDS
  AND BEDDING
Blanket Street. I. Hogan. Br-BC:56
Good Night. T. Hood. Au-SP:93,
  Br-SS:36, Hu-MP:109, Su-FV I:84
Kivers. A. Cobb. Br-AF:133
Moon-Come-Out. E. Farjeon. Ar-TP3:139,
  Mc-AW:123
My Bed. L. Mitchell. Au-SP:94
My Bed Is a Boat. R. Stevenson.
  Bo-FP:40
Rock, Ball, Fiddle. De-CH:446, De-TT:52,
  Ir-BB:231, Mo-MGT:39, Rv-CB:454
Star Quilt. R. Hill. Ni-CD:79
Two in a Bed. A. Ross. Ar-TP3:5,
  Au-SP:95, Ch-B:105, Fe-FP:40, Hu-MP:9
Wooden Hill. Mo-MGT:169
Woolly Blanket. K. Goddard. Fr-MP:22
BEDTIME: see also HUMOR - BEDTIME;
  LULLABIES; SANDMAN
Afraid. W. de la Mare. Gr-TG:58
And Now Goodnight. Mother Goose.
  Pa-AP:54
The Attack. L. Clark. Pa-RE:15
B. Bed. An-IP:(6)
Bed in Summer. R. Stevenson. Bo-FP:35,
  Bo-GJ:100, De-TT:90, Fr-WO:34,
  Ke-TF:71, Ox-BC:293
Bedtime. E. Farjeon. Ar-TP3:114,
  Au-SP:92, Pe-FB:38, Rd-SS:3
Bedtime. K. Goddard. Fr-MP:22
Bedtime. D. Levertov. Mc-EA:97
Bedtime. Bo-FP:108, Mo-MGT:207,
  Rd-SS:5, Wr-RM:101
Bedtime. Mo-MGT:36
A Candle. L. Jackson. Bo-FP:37
Child and Mother. E. Field. Hu-MP:126

Come. Let's To Bed. Mother Goose.
  De-TT:52, Gr-GB:19, Li-LB:72,
  Mo-MGT:13, Mo-NR:76
Come, Let's to Bed. Wr-RM:108
Copper Song. E. Scheffauer. Co-PM:150
Crawl into Bed. Q. Prettyman. Ad-BO:74
The Critic. J. Farrar. Au-SP:92
Disillusionment of Ten O'Clock.
  W. Stevens. Ha-LO:55, Ha-PO:236,
  Sh-AP:159
Early Supper. B. Howes. Bo-GJ:27
Early to Bed. An-IP:(10), Bo-FP:36,
  Ch-B:117, Ir-BB:231, Li-LB:162,
  Mo-NR:122
Escape at Bedtime. R. Stevenson.
  Ar-TP3:178, Bo-FP:34, Pe-FB:64,
  Rd-SS:31, Un-GT:13
The Fairy Book. A. Brown. Hu-MP:24
Fire-Fly, Fire-Fly, Bright Little
  Thing. Da-SC:28
Girls and Boys, Come Out to Play.
  I. Serrailler. Ir-BB:17
Go to Bed First. Gr-CT:410, Gr-GB:17,
  Mo-MGT:39, On-TW:63, Rd-SS:7,
  Rv-ON:46
God's Saints Are Shining Lights.
  H. Vaughan. Gr-TG:57
Going to Bed. M. Chute. Ho-GC:42,
  La-PP:66, La-PV:20
Going to Bed. E. Turner. Rd-SS:2
Going to Bed. Mo-MGT:49
Good Night! E. Farjeon. Gr-TG:54
Good Night. T. Hood. Au-SP:93,
  Br-SS:36, Hu-MP:109, Su-FV I:84
Good Night! J. Tabb. Gr-TG:56
Goodnight, Little People. T. Hood.
  Fr-MP:23
Hippity Hop to Bed. L. Jackson.
  Ar-TP3:100, Rd-SS:3
Household of Eight. A. Reisen.
  Ho-TY:70
The Huntsmen. W. de la Mare. Ar-TP3:109,
  Br-SS:37
I Feel Relaxed and Still. K. Anderson.
  Le-M:160
Jesus, Tender Shepherd, Hear Me.
  M. Duncan. Gr-TG:57
Keep a Poem in Your Pocket.
  B. de Regniers. Au-SP:97
Let's Go to Bed. Gr-CT:10, Rd-SS:4
Little Donkey, Close Your Eyes.
  M. Brown. La-PP:76, La-PV:18
Little Fred. Wr-RM:58
Lullaby. E. Ford. Rd-SS:25
Mrs. Brown. R. Fyleman. Ar-TP3:115
The Night. A. Goodman. Le-M:213
Nurse's Song. W. Blake. Cl-FC:60,
  De-CH:433, De-TT:89, Fe-FP:99,
  Hu-MP:109, Ox-BC:88, Rd-SS:6,
  Re-TW:75, Rv-CB:574, Un-GT:11
On the Staircase. E. Farjeon.
  Br-SS:35

The Plumpuppets. C. Morley. Ar-TP3:150,
  Fe-FP:395, Hu-MP:117, Rd-SS:10
The Remorseful Cakes. E. Field.
  Ir-BB:102
The Rock-A-By Lady. E. Field.
  Bo-FP:43, Hu-MP:116
The Southern Room over the River.
  Su Tung P'o. Rx-OH:83
Ten o-Clock. P. Hubbell. La-OC:80
Vespers. A. Milne. Ke-TF:77, Li-SR:62
Wee Willie Winkie. Au-SP:8, Bo-FP:39,
  Br-SS:36, Cl-DT:31, De-PO:28,
  Er-FA:492, Li-LB:39, Mo-CC:(36),
  Mo-MGT:17, Mo-NR:106, Ox-BC:172,
  Rd-SS:7, Wi-MG:35, Wr-RM:33
Where. W. de la Mare. Co-PM:136,
  Ir-BB:135
Where Are You Now? M. Miller. Gr-EC:102
Winter Night. Yuan Mei. Rx-LT:115
BEECH TREES
  The Beech. A. Young. Co-BN:153
  Beech and Oak. T. Peacock. Rv-CB:687
  Beech Leaves. J. Reeves. Pa-RE:108,
    Sh-RP:222
  A Boundless Moment. R. Frost. Ke-TF:420
  Ghostly Tree. L. Adams. Un-MA:545
BEECHER, HENRY WARD: see HUMOR - BEECHER,
  HENRY WARD
BEELZEBUB: see also HUMOR - BEELZEBUB
BEER: see also HUMOR - BEER
  The Grenadier. Gr-GB:238
  Hermit Hoar. S. Johnson. Al-VBP:554,
    No-CL:132
BEES: see also HONEY; HUMOR - BEES
  Agamemnon's Tomb. S. Sitwell.
    Un-MB:402
  The Arrival of the Bee Box. S. Plath.
    Ha-TP:99
  A Bee. Chang Hsiu-ya. Pa-MV:35
  The Bee. E. Dickinson. Mc-PR:190,
    Un-MA:104
  The Bee. I. Watts. Au-SP:76,
    Bo-FT:99, Fe-FP:125, Li-SR:97,
    Ma-YA:115, Ox-BC:49, Un-GT:69
  The Bee. R. Weiss. La-GI:57
  The Bee. Bo-FP:87, Ch-B:65, Gr-EC:21
  The Bee-Orchis. A. Young. Cl-DT:79,
    Gr-CT:249
  A Bee Sets Sail. K. Morse. It-HB:44
  Bee Song. C. Sandburg. La-PV:143
  The Bee, the Ant, and the Sparrow.
    N. Cotton. Ox-BC:67
  A Bee Thumps Against the Dusty Window.
    R. Sund. Co-PM:99
  Beehive. J. Toomer. Ad-PB:29,
    Be-MA:17, Lo-TY:211
  The Beekeeper. J. Matthews. Ls-NY:138
  The Bees. L. Ridge. Fe-FP:126, Hu-MP:307
  Beside the Sierra in Flower. A. Machado.
    Le-SW:43
  Bumble Bee. M. Brown. La-PV:143
  Bumblebee. E. Wood. Bo-FP:255

Burnie Bee. Wr-RM:25
Busy Craftsmen in Their Homes. Gr-BB:15
By Chance I Walk. . . . Yuan Mei.
  Pe-M:7
Charm Against a Swarm of Bees. Ma-YA:3
Corn-Grinding Songs, II. Tr-US II:258
Farewell! Like a Bee. Basho. Be-CS:62
Fiddle-de-Dee; Fiddle-de-Dea. Mother
  Goose. Mo-NR:130, Pa-AP:48
The First Bee. M. Webb. De-TT:55
Flowers. H. Behn. Br-SG:54, Fe-FP:222
The Georgics. Virgil. Ma-FW:113
The Happy World. W. Rands. Bo-FP:87
Honey-Bees. W. Shakespeare. Co-BBW:219
The Honey Bird's Song. Tr-US I:60
The Honeybee. H. Bevington. Ls-NY:174
The Humble-Bee. R. Emerson. Fe-FP:125
I Would Like to Be a Bee. D. Baruch.
  Br-BC:92
If Bees Stay at Home. Ir-BB:230,
  Un-GT:23
In a Cornfield. E. Markham. Mc-PR:120
Insect Riddles I. Gr-GB:70
Julius Caesar and the Honey-Bee.
  C. Turner. Rd-OA:160
Kachina Song. Br-MW:43, Da-SC:84,
  Pa-SG:128
Leaving the House of a Friend.
  Basho. Sh-RP:63
March. J. Clare. Rd-OA:187
1-2. T. McNeill. Sa-B:156
Over in the Meadow. Au-SP:223,
  Ir-BB:24, On-TW:38
Pedigree. E. Dickinson. Ch-B:41,
  Ga-FB:291, Mc-PR:108, Mo-BG:124,
  Un-GT:24
The Poor Little Bee. Ho-SD:32,
  Hu-MP:304, Le-OE:51
Quandary. H. Gleason. Ke-TF:171
Red-Currant Jelly. M. Stephenson.
  St-FS:67
Resting from the Noon Sun. Gonsui.
  Be-MC:60
Robbing the Tree Hive. E. Moll.
  Co-PT:140
Solomon and the Bees. J. Saxe.
  Un-GT:142
A Spring Lilt. Hu-MP:303
Swallows, Spare Those Bees. Basho.
  Be-MC:13
A Swarm of Bees in May. Ir-BB:228,
  Li-LB:160, Mo-TB:119, Wr-RM:17
The Swarming Bees. J. Laughlin.
  Ca-VT:410
There Was a Bee Sat on a Wall.
  Sp-AS:(8)
Thou Shalt See the Field-Mouse Peep.
  J. Keats. Rd-OA:181
Three More Riddles. Gr-CT:12
Waiting. H. Behn. Ar-TP3:199,
  Br-SG:109, Br-SS:92
What Is Buzz? M. O'Neill. It-HB:50

BEES — cont'd.
  Wild Bees. J. Clare. Go-BP:82
BEETHOVEN, LUDWIG VAN
  Beethoven's Death Mask. S. Spender.
    Li-TU:219, Pl-US:86
  Beethoven's Ninth Symphony in Wartime.
    E. Pierce. Cr-WS:59
BEETLES: see also BOLL WEEVILS; HUMOR -
    BEETLES; LADYBUGS
  Beetle. H. Finn. Co-BBW:216
  The Beetle. J. Riley. Fe-FP:126
  The Beetle in the Country Bathtub.
    J. Wheelock. Ha-WR:65
  The Beetle in the Wood. B. Reece.
    Co-PT:40
  Black Beetle. Ca-MU:13
  Black, but Not a Raven. Gr-BB:14
  Forgiven. A. Milne. Au-SP:73, Pe-FB:18
  A Good World. Issa. Le-MW:5
  The Harnet and the Bittle. J. Akerman.
    Gr-CT:15
  I Wish I Were. Er-FA:502
  Jungles of Grass. A. Fisher. It-HB:37
  Lullaby. Le-OE:43
  Mary Arnold, the Female Monster.
    Gr-GB:271
  Mrs. Brownish Beetle. A. Fisher.
    It-HB:33
  Wee Man o'Leather. Gr-CT:12, Gr-GB:70,
    Ir-BB:48
BEGGARS
  Atman. D. Saxon. Lo-IT:123
  Beggar. N. Parra. Ad-CI:101
  The Beggar Man. L. Aikin. Ox-BC:109
  Beggars. F. Davidson. De-CH:77
  Beggar's Rhyme. Ar-TP3:192, Au-SP:375,
    Bo-FP:181, Cl-DT:23, La-PH:33,
    Mo-MGT:109, Wr-RM:123
  Blind and Deaf Old Woman. C. Major.
    Ad-PB:300, Jo-SA:49
  Cast Our Caps and Cares Away.
    J. Fletcher. Al-VBP:280, Sm-MK:17
  Dives and Lazarus. Ga-S:202, Ma-FW:165,
    Ox-BB:5
  Dream. S. Edwards. Hu-NN:75, Hu-PN:402
  The Gaberlunzie-Man. Ox-BB:626
  Good Master and Mistress. Na-EO:162
  Hark, Hark, the Dogs Do Bark.
    An-IP:(20), Ar-TP3:132, Bo-FP:114,
    Br-FF:(31), Cl-DT:16, De-PO:20,
    Gr-GB:228, Li-LB:74, Mo-MGT:153,
    Mo-NR:56, Wi-MG:9, Wr-RM:75
  The Horse Trader's Song. Em-AF:762
  Jerusalem Beggars. R. Potash. Ho-TY:357
  The Jolly Beggar. Ox-BB:634
  The Jovial Beggar. Cl-DT:82
  Kid. R. Hayden. Ad-CI:68
  Monk Begging, Kyoto. E. Shiffert.
    Ls-NY:140
  November Morning. E. Blunden. Hi-WP II:132
  O for Doors to Be Open. W. Auden.
    Al-VBP:1226

  Running to Paradise. W. Yeats. Ha-LO:13
  Serves You Right, Beggar. Hsü Chih-mo.
    Hs-TC:77
  The Souling Song. Gr-SS:151
  The Suppliant. G. Johnson. Ad-PB:23,
    Hu-PN:76
  There Goes a Beggar. Kikaku. Be-MC:25
  Tom o'Bedlam's Song. Al-VBP:305,
    Gr-CT:172, Ha-PO:56, Ho-WR:89,
    Na-EO:97, Rv-CB:114
  A True Story. A. Taylor. De-TT:102
  Under the Round Tower. W. Yeats.
    Gr-SS:55
  Wait's Carol. B. Young. Th-AS:107
BEGONIAS
  Begonias. Su Tung P'o. Rx-OH:86
BEHAVIOR: see also special aspects, as
    COURTESY; HUMOR - BEHAVIOR
  Advice to Children and Their Parents.
    Gr-TG:13
  Against Quarrelling and Fighting.
    I. Watts. Ox-BC:49
  Always. R. Groppuso. Me-WF:17
  Am I Stupid? H. Ooguro. Le-TA:92
  Ann. K. Starbird. Gr-EC:200, Ho-GC:22
  The Ballad of Joe Meek. S. Brown.
    Be-MA:31
  Be Not Too Wise. De-CH:621
  Blue Blood. J. Stephens. Un-MB:266
  A Boy Serving at Table. J. Lydgate.
    Ox-BC:4
  The Brothers. A. Groesbeck. De-FS:102
  The Camel's Hump. R. Kipling.
    Ir-BB:104, Na-EO:137
  Christmas. M. Chute. Br-SS:101,
    Fr-MP:9
  Cruel Frederick. H. Hoffman. Li-SR:24
  The Cupboard. W. de la Mare. Ar-TP3:7,
    Au-SP:131, Bo-FP:51, Fe-FP:42,
    Fr-MP:8, St-FS:76
  Dalyaunce. De-CH:26
  Discretion. Rv-CB:18
  Every Day Thou Might Lere. Ma-YA:27
  Extremes. J. Riley. Bo-FT:18,
    Ch-B:80, Fe-FP:104, Gr-EC:201,
    Hu-MP:55
  Felicia Ropps. G. Burgess. Co-BB:40,
    Fe-FP:309
  First Travels of Max. J. Ransom.
    Un-MA:412
  Four Children. Mo-MGT:104
  Fräulein Reads Instructive Rhymes.
    M. Kumin. Li-SR:29
  Godfrey Gordon Gustavus Gore. W. Rands.
    Ar-TP3:136, Co-BB:111, Co-OT:42,
    Fe-FP:308, Hu-MP:451, Ir-BB:109,
    Pe-FB:92
  Going to Bed. E. Turner. Rd-SS:2
  The Golden Rule. Ch-B:108
  Good Advice. Mo-NR:19, Wr-RM:77
  Good and Bad. De-PP:17

Good and Bad Children.   R. Stevenson.
  Bl-OB:31, Co-BB:98, Er-FA:494,
  Gr-TG:19, Sm-LG:98
He That Spendeth Much.   H. Rhodes.
  De-CH:634
Here in This Book.   W. Cole. Co-BB:11
Higglety, Pigglety, Pop!   Ir-BB:184,
  Lo-LL:30, Mo-MGT:129, St-FS:22
I, a Justified Sinner.   A. Price.
  Ls-NY:90
I Woke Up This Morning.   K. Kuskin.
  Ho-GC:44
If I Were King.   A. Milne.   Sh-RP:2
I'm No Animal.   C. Minor.   Jo-VC:36
The Isle of Man.   Gr-GB:166
It's in Your Face.   Fe-PL:299
James and the Shoulder of Mutton.
  A. O'Keeffe.   De-TT:46
Jest 'fore Christmas.   E. Field.
  Er-FA:513, Fe-FP:538, Fe-PL:201,
  Ga-FB:176, Hu-MP:359
Jim.   H. Belloc.   Br-SM:113, Co-BB:70,
  Gr-CT:22, Ir-BB:161, Lo-LL:80,
  Na-EO:150, Ox-BC:312
Lazy Lou.   M. Dodge.   Co-BB:39
Letter to My Sister.   A. Spencer.
  Ad-PB:16, Bo-AN:19, Hu-PN:61
A Letter to the Child Lady Margaret Caven-
  dish Holles-Harley.   M. Prior.   Ox-BC:53
Little Jack Horner.   De-TT:49, Li-LB:42
Little Jack Horner Sat in a Corner.
  Au-SP:6, Bo-FP:197, De-PO:12,
  Er-FA:506, Fr-WO:11, Hi-FO:117,
  Mo-CC:(31), Mo-MGT:125, Mo-NR:77,
  Mo-TL:70, Wi-MG:33, Wr-RM:90
Little Things.   J. Carney.   An-IP:(31),
  Ch-B:89, Er-FA:239, Fe-FP:540,
  Mo-CC:(2), Un-GT:306
Lollocks.   R. Graves.   Gr-CT:155,
  Ma-FW:196, Na-EO:135
Lucy McLockett.   P. McGinley.   Br-BC:54
Manners.   M. Van Rensselaer.   Fe-FP:44,
  Hu-MP:16
Matilda.   H. Belloc.   Bl-OB:30,
  Co-PT:305, Ox-BC:314, Pa-OM:6,
  Sm-LG:100
Meddlesome Mattie.   A. Taylor.   Ox-BC:115,
  Pa-OM:71
Mode of Maidens.   Br-FW:5
Modifications.   R. Koertge.   Du-SH:42,
  Pe-M:22
A Moral Poem.   J. Cunningham.   Ca-VT:323
Mouths.   D. Aldis.   Ag-HE:75
My Dog.   S. Lewis.   St-FS:98
My Fairy.   Ch-B:80
My Sort of Man.   P. Dunbar.   Bo-AN:6
The Night Wind.   E. Field.   Fe-FP:70
Old Mother Frost.   E. Fleming.
  Ir-BB:106
One, Two, Three, Four, Five, Six,
  Seven.   On-TW:62

Otto.   G. Brooks.   La-PH:37, La-PV:101
Political Reflection.   H. Nemerov.
  Co-EL:104
The Quiet Child.   R. Field.   Rd-SS:39
Rebecca.   H. Belloc.   Du-RG:65,
  Ir-BB:156, Tu-WW:116, Un-GF:61
The Schoolboy, the Pedant, and the Man
  with a Garden.   J. de la Fontaine.
  Un-R:82
Seein' Things.   E. Field.   Hu-MP:130
Seven Gifts.   De-PP:33
Some Boys.   J. Penkethman.   Ox-BC:27
Song Against Children.   A. Kilmer.
  Th-AS:65
A Song of Wetting the Bed.   Y. Tanaka.
  Le-TA:87
The Story of Augustus.   H. Hoffman.
  Ag-HE:62, Ar-TP3:135, Bo-GJ:114,
  Br-SM:71, Co-BB:48, De-TT:93,
  Ir-BB:101, Li-SR:25
The Story of Fidgety Philip.
  H. Hoffmann.   Ox-BC:208
The Story of Little Suck-a-Thumb.
  H. Hoffmann.   Ir-BB:95, Li-SR:27,
  Na-EO:154
Success.   Er-FA:17
Sulky Sue.   De-PO:26, Mo-CC:(50),
  Mo-MGT:72, Wr-RM:68
Supper.   Y. Ashibe.   Le-TA:25
There Was a Little Girl.   An-IP:(12),
  Bl-OB:29, Co-BB:69, De-PO:12,
  Er-FA:492, Fr-WO:28, Mo-MGT:200,
  Na-EO:168, Sm-LG:99, Un-GT:101,
  Wi-MG:45, Wr-RM:84
There Was a Young Hopeful Named Sam.
  E. Ripley.   Fr-MP:5
There Was an Old Man of the East.
  E. Lear.   Ag-HE:71
This Little Fellow.   Wy-CM:13
The Three Little Kittens.   An-IP:(16),
  Au-SP:22, Bo-FP:91, Fe-FP:526,
  Li-LB:146, Mo-MGT:212, Mo-NR:15,
  On-TW:16
Tom at Dinner.   A. O'Keeffe.   De-TT:101
Two People.   E. Rieu.   Co-BB:24,
  Gr-EC:210
Under-the-Table Manners.   St-FS:93
When I Was Six.   Z. Cross.   Br-BC:60,
  Fe-FP:486
When Jacky's a Very Good Boy.
  Ag-HE:61, Mo-MGT:107, Na-EO:70
Whole Duty of Children.   R. Stevenson.
  Gr-TG:14, Na-EO:138
Why Did the Children.   C. Sandburg.
  Su-FVI:12
Willie.   M. Adeler.   Co-BB:100
Wise Sarah and the Elf.   E. Coatsworth.
  Co-PM:36
Zoo Manners.   E. Mathias.   St-FS:52
BELFAST, IRE., N.
  In This Year of Grace. J. Hewitt. Co-PI:62

BELFRIES: see BELLS; CATHEDRALS; CHURCHES;
    STEEPLES; TOWERS
BELGIUM: see also FLANDERS; and names of
    towns, as BRUGES, BELG.
    The Moon and the Night and the Men.
    J. Berryman.   Ca-VT:380
BELGRADE, YUGOS.
    An Austrian Army.   Co-FB:415, Gr-CT:336
BELIEF: see FAITH
BELISARIUS
    Belisarius.   H. Longfellow. Ho-WR:120
BELL, ALEXANDER GRAHAM
    Alexander Graham Bell Did Not Invent
        the Telephone. R. Coffin. Ar-TP3:46
BELLE ISLE, STRAIT OF
    Belle Isle. Rv-ON:68, Wr-RM:81
BELLS: see also HUMOR - BELLS
    After the Bells Hummed. Basho.
        Be-CS:34
    Against Oblivion. H. Newbolt.
        De-CH:202, De-TT:193
    The Belfry. L. Binyon. De-CH:200
    The Belfry of Bruges. H. Longfellow.
        Pa-HT:113
    The Bell-Man. R. Herrick. De-CH:202,
        Rv-CB:341
    Bell Speech. R. Wilbur. Un-MA:675
    Bell Tower. L. Adams. Un-MA:547
    The Bells. Wr-RM:105
    The Bells. E. Poe. Bo-FP:177,
        Bo-HF:162, Er-FA:277, Fe-FP:64,
        Fe-PL:433, Li-SR:72, Sp-OG:339
    Bells in the Country. R. Nathan.
        Bo-FP:109
    The Bells of London. Mother Goose.
        Bo-FP:125, De-PO:24, Gr-CT:296,
        Ir-BB:116, Li-LB:132, Mc-PR:110,
        Mo-MGT:138, Mo-NR:84, Na-EO:167
    The Bells of Peace. A. Fisher.
        Br-SS:75
    The Bells of Shandon. F. Mahony.
        Co-PI:122, Co-RG:124, De-CH:197,
        Gr-CT:34, Pa-HT:141
    Beyond Stillness. Kyorai. Be-MC:42
    Bredon Hill. A. Housman. Cl-DT:44,
        No-CL:125, Un-MB:98, Un-MW:99
    The Broken Doll. C. Rossetti.
        Ar-TP3:106, Ch-B:114, Hu-MP:52
        Li-LC:38
    The Broken Tower. H. Crane.
        Sh-AP:196, Un-MA:535, Wi-LT:399
    The Calls. W. Owen. Go-BP:48
    A Cat Called Little Bell. De-PP:39
    The Children's Bells. E. Farjeon.
        De-CH:164
    Chimes. A. Meynell. De-CH:202,
        Tu-WW:70, Un-MB:62
    Christ Church Bells. H. Aldrich.
        Rv-CB:480
    Christmas Bells. H. Longfellow.
        Ch-B:55, Co-PS:162, Er-FA:515,
        Fe-FP:85, Hu-MP:349, La-PH:43,
        Se-PR:230, Sh-RP:244, Un-GT:295

    Country Thought.   S. Warner. Un-MB:371
    Doorbells. R. Field. Ar-TP3:9,
        Fe-FP:323
    Drawing Details in an Old Church.
        T. Hardy.   No-CL:160
    Easter. H. Conkling.   Ar-TP3:204
    For a Child Named Katherine. L. Nicholl.
        Th-AS:16
    For Whom the Bell Tolls. J. Donne.
        Fe-PL:300
    The Green Gnome. R. Buchanan.
        Co-PT:47
    The High Tide on the Coast of
        Lincolnshire. J. Ingelow. De-TT:183,
        Pa-OM:118, Sp-OG:85
    Independence Bell. Vi-PP:80
    Jingle Bells. J. Pierpont.   Er-FA:510,
        Mo-CC:(35), Mo-MGT:158
    Limericks. E. Lear. Bo-GJ:9
    Men's Death I Tell. De-CH:617
    Night at Anchor by Maple Bridge.
        Chang Chi. Rx-LT:64
    Night at Yen Chou. Chou Shang Ju.
        Le-MW:55
    The Nightingales Sing. Uko. Le-IS:27
    Oranges and Lemons. Sm-MK:203,
        Wi-MG:79
    The Pale Temple Bell. Mu Mu-t'ien.
        Hs-TC:188
    Riddle. Gr-GB:91
    Ring Out, Wild Bells. A. Tennyson.
        Bo-FP:177, Fe-FP:64, Ho-WR:241
    Ringing the Bells. A. Sexton.
        Ca-VT:635
    School-Bell. E. Farjeon. Br-SS:55,
        Fe-FP:19
    The School Servant. Suifu. Le-MW:107
    Sleigh Bells at Night. E. Coatsworth.
        Br-SS:95
    The Song of the Wind Bell.
        Ch'en Meng-Chia. Le-MW:49
    The Spring Waters, 168. Ping Hsin.
        Hs-TC:24
    Sunset. E. Cummings. Un-MA:470
    Tanka. Y. Aizu. Sh-AM:142
    The Temple Bells of Yun Sui.
        Yang Wan-Li. Le-MW:48
    Upon a Ring of Bells. J. Bunyan.
        De-CH:198
    Wantage Bells. J. Betjeman. Hi-WP I:111
    Why Do the Bells of Christmas Ring?
        E. Field. Ar-TP3:195, Au-SP:381,
        Bo-FP:200, Ha-YA:155, La-PH:23
BELSHAZZAR, KING OF BABYLON
    Belshazzar. E. Dickinson. Rv-CB:902,
        Tr-MR:84
    Country Words. W. Stevens. Ls-NY:328
    Vision of Belshazzar. G. Byron.
        Co-RG:3, Hi-FO:30, Pa-OM:115
BENBOW, JOHN
    Admiral Benbow. Co-RM:66, Rv-CB:420
    The Death of Admiral Benbow.
        Bl-OB:44, Gr-GB:239, Rv-CB:420

BENEDICT, SAINT
Good Saint Benedict. Ab-MO:58
BENEDICTIONS: see BLESSINGS; PRAYERS
BENET, STEPHEN VINCENT - *Benét*
Love to Stephen. E. Wylie. Pl-ML:80
BENNETT, ENOCH ARNOLD
Hugh Selwyn Mauberly, Mr. Nixon.
E. Pound. Un-MA:303
BEQUESTS: see GIFTS AND GIVING; WILLS
BERENICE: see TITUS AND BERENICE
BERKELEY, GEORGE
The Fountain. D. Davie. Pa-GTB:554
BERLIN, GER.
Childe Harold. M. Kulbak. Ho-TY:205
BERMUDA
Bermudas. A. Marvell. Al-VBP:455,
De-CH:362, Gr-CT:277, Hi-TL:17,
Pa-GTB:103, Rv-CB:399, Sm-LG:296
BERNARD OF CLAIRVAUX, SAINT
The One Thing Needful. V. Miller.
En-PC:226
BERNHARDT, SARAH
Sarah Bernhardt. B. Akhmadulina.
Bo-RU:3
BERRIES: see also names of individual
berries, as BLACKBERRIES
Berries. I. Eastwick. Br-SG:91
Strawberry Fair. Cl-DT:59
The Thorn Trees. R. Field. Br-SG:92
Winter Feast. F. Frost. Br-SG:107,
Ha-YA:146
BETHESDA (POOL)
Nocturne at Bethesda. A. Bontemps.
Be-MA:43, Bo-AN:81, Hu-PN:211
BETHLEHEM
Bethlehem. W. Canton. Ha-YA:158
Bethlehem. P. Hartnoll. Ga-S:108
Bethlehem of Judea. Br-BC:176
A Carol. F. Weatherly. Ha-YA:154
Christmas Morning. E. Roberts.
Bo-FP:194, Co-PS:172, Hu-MP:348,
Sh-RP:240, Un-GT:289, Un-MA:269
The Light of Bethlehem. J. Tabb.
Se-PR:222
Long, Long Ago. Ar-TP3:196, Co-PS:176,
Fe-FP:91, Hu-MP:347, La-PH:24,
La-PV:87, Mc-AW:76, Pa-RE:104
O Little Town of Bethlehem. P. Brooks.
Bo-FP:190, Er-FA:518, Fe-FP:94,
Ga-S:85, Ke-TF:221
On Christmas Morn. R. Sawyer.
Fe-FP:89, La-PH:26, La-PV:88
Ox and Donkey's Carol. Sister Maris
Stella. Se-PR:223
Prayer. J. Farrar. Se-PR:222
BETHUNE, MARY MCLEOD
For Mary McLeod Bethune. M. Walker.
Hu-PN:326
BETRAYAL: see also LOVE - BETRAYAL;
TREACHERY
The Boys of Mullaghbawn.
Gr-GB:256

The Confessional (Spain). R. Browning.
Al-VBP:885
The Croppy Boy. Rv-CB:437
Deceptions. P. Larkin. Pa-GTB:557
God's Price and Man's Price.
R. Herrick. Ga-S:167
he's doing natural life. Conyus.
Ad-PB:403
I Must Go Walk the Woods. Ho-WR:158,
Rv-CB:30
In the Servant's Quarters. T. Hardy.
Tr-MR:92, Un-MB:26
It Was a Funky Deal. E. Knight.
Ad-BO:32, Ad-PB:232, Ra-BP:207
Judas. Ma-FW:160
The Lost Leader. R. Browning.
Al-VBP:884, Hi-FO:225, Ke-TF:56,
Pl-ML:58
Ruth: or the Influence of Nature.
W. Wordsworth. Pa-GTB:283
Sonnet 34. W. Shakespeare. Rv-CB:216
"Where Shall the Lover Rest." W. Scott.
Al-VBP:670, De-CH:263, Pa-GTB:191
BEZHETZK, U.S.S.R.
Bezhetzk. A. Akhmatova. Ca-MR:183
BIAFRA: see also AFRICAN VERSE - IBO
Biafra. N. Kaplan. Ad-II:104
Biafra. L. Mack. Ad-PB:499
I Had a Dream Last Night. C. Meyer.
Jo-VC:19
Negatives. D. Walcott. Sa-B:183
BIBLE STORIES: see also HUMOR - BIBLE
STORIES; and names of Bible
characters, as MOSES
Ballad of the Trial of Sodom.
V. Watkins. Tr-MR:68
Bible Stories. L. Reese. Hu-MP:25,
Th-AS:102
How Samson Bore Away the Gates of Gaza.
V. Lindsay. Tr-MR:76
Jacob and the Angel. Brother Antoninus.
Tr-MR:72
Jepthah's Daughter. A. Tennyson.
Hi-FO:17
Three Helpers in Battle. M. Coleridge.
Pl-EI:99
Warm Babies. K. Preston. Co-FB:225,
Ga-S:53
BICYCLE RACING: see HUMOR - BICYCLE
RACING
BICYCLES AND BICYCLING: see also BICYCLE
RACING; MOTORCYCLES
The Bicycle. J. Harasymowicz. Du-SH:22
Bicycles. A. Voznesensky. Li-TU:40
Broncho Versus Bicycle. J. Crawford.
Fi-BG:117
A Certain Age. P. McGinley. Du-SH:44
Different Bicycles. D. Baruch.
Ar-TP3:107, Fe-FP:107
My Bicycle and Me. L. Kulichkova.
Mo-MI:20
On a Bicycle. Y. Yevtushenko.
Li-TU:19

BIG DIPPER: see URSA MAJOR
BIGHORNS
  The Rocky Mountain Sheep. M. Austin.
    Hu-MP:206
BILLIARDS: see also POOL (GAME)
  Billiards. G. Dumitrescu. Mc-AC:122
  Poolroom. J. Nims. St-H:152
BILLY BUDD
  Billy in the Darbies. H. Melville.
    Mo-BG:160, Rv-CB:835
  The Hanging of Billy Budd. K. Wilson.
    Sc-TN:242
BILLY THE KID: see BONNEY, WILLIAM H.
BIOGRAPHY: see also HUMOR - BIOGRAPHY
  A Living Pearl. K. Rexroth. Wi-LT:798
BIRCH TREES
  Birch. L. Simpson. Co-EL:90
  Birch. Br-FW:15
  Birches. R. Frost. Fe-PL:437, Ga-FB:299,
    Mo-BG:114, Pe-OA:33, Sm-LG:61,
    Sp-OG:357, Un-MA:177, Wi-LT:166
  The Birks of Aberfeldy. R. Burns.
    Al-VBP:643
  Hiawatha's Sailing. H. Longfellow.
    Bo-FP:230
  Improvised Songs, I. Tr-US II:130
  In Autumn. T. Dinsburg. Mo-MI:21
  Little Birches. E. Newsome. Hu-PN:72
  On the White Birches. S. Mizuhara.
    Sh-AM:167
  Parenthood. J. Farrar. Hu-MP:274
  Seven Poems 3. L. Niedecker.
    Ca-VT:244
  The Spirit of the Birch. A. Ketchum.
    Hu-MP:274, Th-AS:135
  Standing in the Fields. Gr-BB:22
  Three Little Birches. M. Nikogosian.
    Mo-MI:47
  A Young Birch. R. Frost. Co-BN:152
BIRD DAY: see BIRDS
BIRD WATCHING: see BIRDS
BIRDS: see also FEATHERS; HUMOR - BIRDS;
    MYTHICAL ANIMALS AND BIRDS; WATER
    BIRDS; and names of birds, as ROBINS
  Acceptance. R. Frost. Tr-MR:275
  All Morning. T. Roethke. Ca-BP:48
  All These Birds. R. Wilbur. Ho-P:313
  Allie. R. Graves. Bo-GJ:81, Fe-FP:100,
    Ha-LO:103
  The Animal World. Tr-CB:24
  Any Bird. I. Orleans. Br-SG:62
  Augury. S. George. Gr-SS:68
  Autumn Birds. J. Clare. Rd-OA:182
  Avondale. S. Smith. Pa-RE:9
  Beasts and Birds. A. O'Keeffe.
    Ox-BC:124
  Because the Songbird. T. Takaori.
    Sh-AM:155
  The Bestiary. W. Benét. Rd-OA:126
  The Bird. R. Tagore. Pa-SG:132
  The Bird and the Butterfly. Tr-US II:281
  Bird and Toad Play Hide and Seek.Br-MW:50

  Bird at Dawn. H. Monro. Un-GT:58,
    Un-MB:234
  The Bird-Man. W. Davies. Sm-MK:167
  Bird Riddles. Gr-GB:65
  The Birds. W. Blake. De-CH:105
  Birds. R. Fabrizio. Sm-MK:166
  The Birds. K. Finnell. Ho-CT:24
  Birds at Winter Nightfall. T. Hardy.
    Co-EL:25, Un-MB:31
  The Birds from the Mountain. Chang Chi.
    Rx-LT:65
  Birds in Summer. M. Howitt. Hu-MP:215
  The Birds of America. J. Broughton.
    Br-AF:25
  The Birds of Killingworth.
    H. Longfellow. Pa-OM:308
  Birds of Passage. Issa. Ba-PO:26
  The Birds of the Air. Rv-ON:109
  Bridal Song. J. Fletcher. Al-VBP:285,
    Rv-CB:314
  Calico Pie. E. Lear. Au-SP:225,
    Bl-OB:12, Fe-FP:356, Hu-MP:461,
    Ir-BB:88, It-HB:57, Li-LC:67,
    Lo-LL:67, Pa-RE:109, Rv-CB:811,
    Sm-LG:87, Tu-WW:114, Un-GB:29,
    Un-GF:33, Un-GT:225
  The Call. B. Björnson. Ch-B:16
  Cape Ann. T. Eliot. Bo-GJ:53,
    Ho-LP:50, Na-EO:35, Re-TW:83,
    Sm-LG:143
  City Bird. T. Kenyon. Gr-EC:176
  Come, Little Bird. Ca-MU:32
  Cradle Song. A. Tennyson. Ox-BC:213
  Dawn. G. Bottomley. Re-BS:40,
    Un-MB:213
  Deities and Beasts. J. Updike.
    Co-EL:26
  The Distances They Keep. H. Nemerov.
    Ca-BP:40
  Exercise Book. P. Dehn. Hi-WP II:8
  Eyes Are Lit Up. R. Coffin. Sm-MK:157
  A Fairy Went a-Marketing. R. Fyleman.
    Au-SP:293, Ox-BC:337
  Feel like a Bird. M. Swenson.
    Be-EB:11
  Field Glasses. A. Young. Pa-GTB:467,
    Rv-CB:979
  Five Eager Little Squirrels. On-TW:23
  A Foreigner Comes to Earth on Boston
    Common. H. Gregory. Pl-EI:111
  The Girl and the Birds. Wr-RM:109
  Goat Songs, II. R. Drew. Kh-VA:44
  Golden Birds. E. Greenberg. Ho-TY:314
  Good Morning. M. Sipe. Ar-TP3:70,
    Au-SP:87
  Ha-Tima Tim-Tim. Ca-MU:14
  Hail, Bishop Valentine. J. Donne.
    Gr-CT:39
  A Health to the Birds. S. MacManus.
    Co-PI:112
  The Hermit's Song. Pa-SG:158
  Hiawatha's Chickens. H. Longfellow.
    Bo-SP:276

The Hill Wife: Her Word. R. Frost.
  Ca-VT:10
A Hint to the Wise. P. Barret. Bo-FP:254
How Many Birds? Rv-ON:54
How They Sleep. Ch-B:28
How to Paint the Portrait of a Bird.
  J. Prevert. Ma-FW:96, Sm-MK:168
I Bear, in Sign of Love. F. Andrewes.
  Re-BS:10
I Like the Birds. Z. White. Ba-HI:69
I Will Go with My Father a-Ploughing.
  J. Campbell. Ar-TP3:202, Br-SS:166,
  Fe-FP:231
In February. J. Symonds. Ha-YA:171
The Last Corn Shock. G. Dresbach.
  Fe-FP:236
Little Brother. A. Fisher. Br-BC:48,
  Mc-AW:91
A Little Tune. Tai Wang-shu.
  Hs-TC:183
A Living. D. Lawrence. Co-BBW:249,
  La-RM:169
Look, Spring Is Coming. Gr-BB:11
Moods. S. Teasdale. Mc-PR:62
The Nightingale. M. Stearns.
  Ar-TP3:176
No Shop Does the Bird Use.
  E. Coatsworth. Gr-TG:29, Mc-PR:94
November. R. Bridges. Ox-BN:879
Of Seals and Arms. J. Taylor.
  Rv-CB:318
Of the Child with the Bird on the Bush.
  J. Bunyan. Ox-BC:37, Rv-CB:461
On Finding a Bird's Bones in the Woods.
  L. Mueller. St-H:144
Once I Nearly Touched a Bird. M. Carr.
  Sh-RP:338
The Orphan's Song. S. Dobell.
  De-CH:41, Ox-BN:668
The Ousel Cock. W. Shakespeare.
  Al-VBP:184, Sm-MK:149
Out of the Cradle Endlessly Rocking.
  W. Whitman. Al-VBP:936, Un-MA:66
The Peacock "At Home." C. Dorset.
  Ox-BC:132
Pleasant Sounds. J. Clare. Go-BP:110,
  Rv-CB:723
Poor Bird. W. de la Mare. Ma-FW:93
The Poppet-Show. Rv-ON:65
Rari about the Faufe's Bird. Puko'i.
  Tr-US II:93
Remembering the Winter. R. Bennett.
  Br-SS:74
River Roads. C. Sandburg. Ca-VT:22
The Robin of the Red Breast.
  Co-PM:212, De-CH:547
Saint Francis and the Birds. S. Heaney.
  Ma-FW:89
Seasons. C. Rossetti. Ha-YA:18
Silence. W. Williams. Re-BS:53
Sitting. T. Tsosie. Ba-HI:57
Small Birds. P. Quennell. Re-BS:54

A Small Bird's Sky. S. Murano.
  Sh-AM:91
A Son Just Born. M. Miller. Ar-TP3:70
Song. J. Jiménez. Le-SW:57
Song of Myself. W. Whitman. Co-BBW:274
Song of the Animal World. Ab-MO:11,
  Tr-US I:66
Songs from Cyprus. H.D. Un-MA:338
Songs of Dancing Women Personifying
  Birds. Tr-US II:303
The Soul of Birds. P. Mitra. Al-PI:85
Sparrows. A. Fyfe. Ls-M:100
Spring's Arrival. Fe-FP:471
Statue and Birds. L. Bogan. Un-MA:491
A Summer Wish. C. Rossetti. Ox-BN:706
Ten Little Dicky-Birds. A. Baldwin.
  St-FS:12
There Is an Eagle in Me. Wo-HS:(47)
They Say on Leaving Eden. M. Dunster.
  Ls-NY:47
To a Vine-Clad Telegraph Pole.
  L. Untermeyer. Un-MA:307
To Cheer Our Minds. W. Ronksley.
  Ox-BC:48
Twilight Calm. C. Rossetti.
  Co-BN:109, Ox-BN:709
Two Birds. Mo-MGT:85, On-TW:11,
  Rv-ON:14, Sp-AS:27, Wr-RM:23
Two Little Dicky Birds. Li-LB:14,
  Mo-TL:52, On-TW:11, Wi-MG:21
Waking Time. J. Eastwick. Ar-TP3:239,
  Br-SS:7
Who'll That Be. K. Patchen. Mc-WK:94
Why Chidest Thou the Tardy Spring.
  R. Emerson. Re-BS:19
The Wood-Pile. R. Frost. Ca-VT:8,
  Ni-JP:88, Sh-AP:146, Sp-OG:285
Yardbird's Skull. O. Dodson.
  Ad-PB:132, Bo-AN:125, Ca-VT:387
BIRDS - CALLS: see also HUMOR - BIRDS -
  CALLS
Always with Us! - the Black Preacher.
  H. Melville. Re-BS:51
As Evening Falls. Shunzei. Ba-ST:39
Bird and Waterfall Music. Wang Wei.
  Rx-LT:59
The Bird of Night. R. Jarrell.
  Ad-PE:32, La-RM:55, Mo-TS:65,
  Re-BS:45
Blue Jay. H. Conkling. Co-BBW:261,
  Re-BS:29
Bobwhite. R. Hillyer. Co-BBW:254
Bow-Wow. An-IP:(22), Mo-CC:(22),
  Mo-MGT:116, Pa-AP:8
Chanticleer. K. Tynan. Ar-TP3:72,
  Hu-MP:219, Tu-WW:86
Chickadee. R. Emerson. Bo-FP:175
The Corncrake. J. Cousins. Co-PI:31
Crow's Ditty. Gr-GB:61
Cuckoo. A. Young. Gr-CT:49
The Cuckoo. Co-BBW:253, Pa-RE:34
The Cuckoo's Song. Josui. Hu-MP:223

BIRDS - CALLS — <u>cont'd.</u>
  The Echoing Cliff.   A. Young. Re-BS:33
  A Gull's Ghostly Call. S. Hopkins.
    Le-M:108
  Hoopoe. G. Darley. Ox-BN:393
  The Mother Bird. W. de la Mare.
    Sp-OG:297
  The Narba-Bird. Tr-US I:245
  Once I Was a Monarch's Daughter.
    De-CH:98, De-TT:81
  Out in the Marsh Reeds. Tsurayuki.
    Ba-ST:39
  The Owl. B. Procter. Co-BBW:262
  The Owl. E. Thomas. Gr-CT:107,
    Ha-PO:105, Pa-GTB:441, Re-BS:47
  The Peabody Bird. R. Field. Gr-EC:172
  The Pigeons. M. Burnham. Bo-FP:219
  The Praise of Philip Sparrow.
    G. Gascoigne. Al-VBP:81, De-CH:93,
    Rd-OA:102
  Rooks. C. Sorley. Un-MB:380
  The Sea-Bird's Cry. R. Hawker.
    Hi-WP II:36
  The Song of the Birds. Tr-US II:288
  Startled. Saigyo Hoshi. Ba-ST:39
  Swans at Night. M. Gilmore. Co-BBW:239
  Sweet Suffolk Owl. T. Vautor.
    De-CH:97, Gr-CT:107, Rv-CB:262
  The Tiny Bird. Re-BS:30
  The Unwise Owl. Ir-BB:124
  Vespers. T. Brown. Co-BBW:259
  Weaving the Morning. J. de Melo Neto.
    An-TC:151
  What's o'Clock XVI. A. Lowell.
    Ho-TH:24
  Whippoorwill. M. Miller. Co-BBW:247
  Who? Who? De-CH:98
BIRDS, CAPTIVE
  The Birdcage. C. Aiken. Re-BS:26
  The Caged Skylark. G. Hopkins.
    Un-MB:43, Wi-LT:42
  The Captive Eagle. H. Ishida.
    Sh-AM:173
  Come Wary One. R. Manning-Sanders.
    De-CH:104
  Hawks. S. Bates. Ba-PO:196
  How Sadly the Bird in His Cage. Issa.
    Do-TS:23
  I Had a Dove. J. Keats. Bl-OB:64,
    Co-BBW:252, Co-IW:40, De-CH:100,
    De-TT:158, Fe-FP:289, Re-BS:25,
    Re-TW:30
  The Liberator. Wu-ti. Re-BS:25
  Mary's Canary. De-TT:38, Sp-AS:23,
    Wr-RM:93
  O Lapwing. W. Blake. Gr-CT:108,
    Re-BS:27
  Political Reflection. H. Nemerov.
    Co-EL:104
  The Red Cockatoo. Po Chü-i.
    Co-PM:105, Gr-CT:98, Rd-OA:37

  Some Brown Sparrows. B. Fearing.
    Co-BBW:258, Du-RG:27
  Take Any Bird. G. Chaucer. De-CH:552,
    Rd-OA:17
  To a Linnet in a Cage. F. Ledwidge.
    Co-RG:143
  Tom's Sleeping Song. M. Van Doren.
    Ha-LO:72
  A True Story. J. Smith. Sm-MK:111
  Upon the Lark and the Fowler. J. Bunyan.
    Co-BBW:256, De-CH:104
BIRDS, CRUELTY TO
  The Bird Scarer. Gr-EC:177, Wr-RM:90
  The Blinded Bird. T. Hardy. Co-BBW:251,
    Pl-EI:128, Wi-LT:20
  Chain. P. Petrie. Co-BBW:242
  The Farmer's Gun. A. Young. Rd-OA:35
  Forgive My Guilt. R. Coffin. Ba-PO:165,
    Du-RG:76
  Gallows. E. Thomas. Co-BBW:27,
    Un-MB:217
  In Glencullen. J. Synge. Co-EL:24,
    Co-PI:186, Co-PM:103, Pa-RE:50,
    Re-BS:42, Re-TW:13
  In London Town. M. Coleridge.
    Pa-RE:77
  O What if the Fowler? C. Dalmon.
    Co-BBW:240, De-CH:337, Re-BS:24
  The Peacock. I. Barbu. Mc-AC:63
  Still, Citizen Sparrow. R. Wilbur.
    Wi-LT:597
  Stupidity Street. R. Hodgson.
    Br-SS:149, Co-BBW:268, De-CH:103,
    De-TT:58, Ha-LO:60, La-PV:138,
    Th-AS:52, Un-MB:192, Wi-LT:125
  Swan Curse. A. Sullivan. Ls-NY:213
  Three Things to Remember. W. Blake.
    Br-SS:150, Ch-B:89, Fe-FP:280,
    Gr-EC:178, Gr-TG:31, Hi-GD:13,
    Hi-WP II:170
  The White Dove. Rv-ON:25
BIRDS - DEATH: see also HUMOR - BIRDS -
    DEATH
  Albert. D. Abse. Sm-MK:109
  The Ballad of the Light-Eyed Little
    Girl. G. Brooks. Li-TU:140,
    Pe-SS:28
  Beau's Reply. W. Cowper. Rd-OA:108
  A Bird's Epitaph. M. Armstrong.
    De-CH:95, Re-BS:55
  The Birds of Killingworth.
    H. Longfellow. Pa-OM:308
  Burial. R. Raymond. Ls-NY:224
  The Burial of the Linnet. J. Ewing.
    Ox-BC:254
  Cherry Robbers. D. Lawrence.
    Un-MB:287
  The Container. C. Corman. Ca-VT:525
  Dance Song. Tr-US I:232
  A Dead Bird. A. Young. Co-BBW:245,
    Re-BS:56
  The Dead Sparrow. W. Cartwright. De-CH:95

Dead Titmouse. E. Gullevic. Be-EB:26
The Death and Burial of Cock Robin.
   De-TT:41, Ir-BB:114, Mo-MGT:60,
   Mo-NR:143, Un-GT:62, Wr-RM:124
The Dying Crane. M. Drayton. Rd-OA:190
The Dying Swan. A. Tennyson. Ho-WR:139
The Dying Swan. Gr-CT:98
Early Snow. R. Huff. St-H:84
Elegy of the Bird. J. Pasos. Be-UL:77
The Epic of Dengei. Tr-US I:233
Epitaph on Lady Ossory's Bullfinch.
   H. Walpole. Gr-CT:109, Rd-OA:114
Feathers and Moss. J. Ingelow.
   Li-SR:33
Hurt Hawks. R. Jeffers. Co-BBW:236,
   Ni-JP:115, Pe-SS:150, Sh-AP:177,
   Un-MA:369, Wi-LT:258
I Had a Dove. J. Keats. Bl-OB:64,
   Co-BBW:252, Co-IW:40, De-CH:100,
   De-TT:158, Fe-FP:289, Re-BS:25,
   Re-TW:30
The Icebound Swans. Rd-OA:199
In London Town. M. Coleridge.
   Pa-RE:77
Last Rites. C. Rossetti. Ox-BC:280
The Lives of Gulls and Children.
   H. Nemerov. Ni-JP:116
Look, See the Cat. N. Price. Ls-NY:99
My Little Parrot. W. Wood. Co-PM:103
O Cat of Carlish Kind. J. Skelton.
   Gr-CT:118, Ha-PO:100, Rd-OA:105
The Old Gray Goose. Gr-GB:57
On a Spaniel, Called Beau, Killing a
   Young Bird. W. Cowper. Rd-OA:107
One-Eyed Gunner. Rv-ON:31
Peace. C. Bukowski. Kh-VA:32
Perfect. G. Jones. Ma-FW:92
The Pheasant. R. Coffin. Ar-TP3:58,
   Du-RG:120, Ho-TH:37
The Phoenix and the Turtle.
   W. Shakespeare. Rv-CB:256
The Produce District. T. Gunn.
   Du-SH:148
The Redwing. P. Dickinson. Go-BP:77
Requiem for a Personal Friend.
   E. Boland. Co-PI:13
The Robin. T. Hardy. Pa-RE:14
A Robin's Epitaph. S. Rogers.
   Rv-CB:627
The Silver Swan. Co-PM:145, Gr-CT:98,
   Gr-SS:25, Sm-LG:91
Some Western Haikus, I. J. Kerouac.
   Kh-VA:12
The Sparrow's Dirge. J. Skelton.
   Sm-LG:85
The Sparrow's Skull. R. Pitter.
   Pl-EI:141
Swan Curse. A. Sullivan. Ls-NY:213
To Christ Our Lord. G. Kinnell. Br-TC:239,
   Ha-WR:92, La-RM:120, Pe-M:112
To Kill the Eagle. . . . Wo-HS:(54)
Why Must You Know. J. Wheelwright. Ca-VT:205

BIRDS - EGGS AND NESTS: see also HUMOR -
   BIRDS - EGGS AND NESTS
Birds. L. Kitagaki. Ba-HI:56
The Bird's Nest. J. Drinkwater.
   Au-SP:66, La-PV:131, Mc-AW:62,
   Na-EO:130
Birds' Nests. J. Clare. Re-BS:13
The Birds' Nests. Hu-MP:236
The Boy with the Little Bare Toes.
   F. Harvey. St-FS:118
The Emperor's Bird's-Nest.
   H. Longfellow. Hu-MP:419, Re-BS:14
Feathers and Moss. J. Ingelow.
   Li-SR:33
The Green Grass Growing All Around.
   Gr-EC:47, Hu-MP:237
Hymn for Saturday. C. Smart. Ox-BC:74,
   Rv-CB:539, Sm-LG:68
Kriss Kringle. T. Aldrich. Hu-MP:360
The Linnet. R. Burns. De-TT:59,
   Re-BS:12
Little Knowing. Issa. Do-TS:32
Look at Six Eggs. C. Sandburg.
   Fe-FP:291
Lullaby. W. Barnes. De-TT:54, Rd-SS:26
Malison of the Stone-Chat. Gr-GB:63
The Marvel of Birds. W. Langland.
   Ga-S:13
The Mother Bird. W. de la Mare.
   Sp-OG:297
The Mourning Dove. M. Livingston.
   Gr-EC:178
My Garden. W. Davies. Co-BN:52
The Nesting Ground. D. Wagoner.
   En-PC:249
Nesting Time. A. Guiterman. Gr-EC:180
No Communication. M. Van Doren.
   Re-BS:6
One Day I Went Down in the Golden
   Harvest Field. Gr-GB:65
The Osprey's Nest. D. Wagoner.
   Ca-BP:10
The Pettichap's Nest. J. Clare.
   Go-BP:74
The Red Sun Sinks Low. Boncho.
   Be-CS:11
Robert of Lincoln. W. Bryant.
   Bo-FP:276, Co-BBW:263, Fe-FP:287,
   Hu-MP:227
The Robin and the Wren. Bl-OB:64,
   Ch-B:49, De-CH:547, De-TT:43,
   Ir-BB:226
The Secret. Ar-TP3:55, Au-SP:64,
   Gr-EC:172, Hu-MP:213
The Swallow. C. Gasztold. Re-BS:31
The Swan's Nest. P. Griffin. Go-BP:80
"Talents Differ." L. Richards. Ar-TP3:55
Thou Shalt See the Field-Mouse Peep.
   J. Keats. Rd-OA:181
The Thrush's Nest. J. Clare. Bl-OB:67,
   Bo-GJ:91, Ha-PO:84, Ma-FW:12, Re-TW:94,
   Se-PR:109, Sm-MK:143, Un-GT:64

BIRDS - EGGS AND NESTS — cont'd.

The Thrush's Nest. R. Ryan.   Co-PI:174
Two Guests from Alabama. W. Whitman.
  Rd-OA:27
The Two Nests. F. Carlin. Re-BS:13
What the Robin Told. G. Cooper.
  Ar-TP3:55, Ch-B:67, Fe-FP:285,
  Hu-MP:221
When Building My House. Re-RR:42
Who Stole the Nest? Ir-BB:87, St-FS:112
Without Hammer or Hands. Gr-BB:14

BIRDS - FEEDING

A Bird Came down the Walk. E. Dickinson.
  Ar-TP3:57, Au-SP:65, Bo-GJ:77,
  Br-SG:61, Ca-BP:6, Ch-B:49, Co-BBW:267,
  Co-IW:9, Fe-FP:279, Fe-PL:350,
  Hu-MP:212, La-PP:13, La-PV:128,
  Tu-WW:103, Un-MA:94, Wi-LT:5
Birds at Winter Nightfall. T. Hardy.
  Co-PM:101, Re-BS:19, Un-MB:31
Birds in the Garden. Gr-TG:30,
  St-FS:30
Crumbs. W. de la Mare. Au-SP:66
December Bird. A. Fisher. La-PH:40
Ducks at Dawn. J. Tippett. Ar-TP3:73,
  Au-SP:52, Br-SS:21
Gull. B. Stuart. Ls-NY:214
The Heron. T. Roethke. Co-BBW:259,
  Ho-LP:46, La-PV:137, Re-BS:34
Invitation. H. Behn. Au-SP:63,
  Fe-FP:287
Joe. D. McCord. Ar-TP3:60
A Little Bird. A. Fisher. Au-SP:101
Midsummer. S. Calverley. Re-BS:23
Often along the Bathing Beach One Sees.
  J. Urzidil. Un-R:51
On a Cold Day. W. Davies. Go-BP:78
The Parrot. Ca-MU:11
Pigeon Playmates. De-PP:54
The Redwing. P. Dickinson. Go-BP:77
Rover and the Bird. N. Crossland.
  De-TT:44
The Seed Eaters. R. Francis. Ca-BP:7
The Snow Lies Light upon the Pine.
  W. Christman. Re-BS:18
Still Life: Lady with Birds.
  Q. Prettyman. Ad-CI:50, Ad-PB:259
The Swallow. C. Gasztold. Re-BS:31
We've Plowed Our Land, We've Sown Our
  Seed. Sp-AS:(36)
Winter. C. Rossetti. Bo-FP:167,
  Ch-B:54, Rv-CB:891, St-FS:38
Winter Feast. F. Frost. Br-SG:107,
  Ha-YA:146
The Yellow Bird. Re-BS:44

BIRDS - FLIGHT

Arctic Tern in a Museum. E. Newsome.
  Hu-PN:71
As When Emotion Too Far Exceeds Its
  Cause. G. Oden. Be-MA:96, Bo-AN:160
Be like the Bird. V. Hugo. Ar-TP3:212,
  Ch-B:17, Ma-FO:(4)

A Bird Came down the Walk. E. Dickinson.
  Ar-TP3:57, Au-SP:65, Bo-GJ:77,
  Br-SG:61, Ca-BP:6, Ch-B:49, Co-BBW:267,
  Co-IW:9, Fe-FP:279, Fe-PL:350,
  Hu-MP:212, La-PP:13, La-PV:128,
  Tu-WW:103, Un-MA:94, Wi-LT:5
A Bird in My Hand. J. Spicer. Ma-FO:(3)
The Birdcatcher. R. Hodgson. Un-MB:187
Birds. R. Jeffers. Ca-BP:29, Ca-VT:120
The Children of the Wind. C. Sandburg.
  Hi-WP II:41, Re-BS:57
Description Is a Bird. M. Ondaatje.
  Ca-BP:8
Eagle Flight. A. Lopez. Al-WW:7
The Flight of Birds. J. Clare.
  Co-BBW:238
Flight of the Sparrows. M. Zaturenska.
  Ha-TP:20
The Great Scarf of Birds. J. Updike.
  Mo-BG:134
Hawk Remembered. J. Phoenice.
  Ls-NY:210
How They Came from the Blue Snows.
  A. Kenseth. Ke-PP:54
I Have Not So Much Emulated.
  W. Whitman. La-RM:170
In Air. P. Clarke. Ab-MO:38
Late at Night. W. Stafford. La-RM:154
Little Bird Flitting. Basho. Be-CS:38
A Little Cock Sparrow. Ir-BB:26,
  Li-LB:87, Mo-MGT:171, Mo-NR:48,
  Mo-TL:57, Wi-MG:36, Wr-RM:66
The Longspur's Incantation. Le-IB:44
Love Is. A. Darr. Pe-M:119
Mallard. R. Warner. Co-BBW:237
The Missel-Thrush. A. Young. Re-BS:37
The Narba-Bird. Tr-US I:245
Often along the Bathing Beach One Sees.
  J. Urzidil. Un-R:51
On a River in Late Autumn. Liu Ta-pai.
  Hs-TC:8
Once I Saw a Little Bird. Fr-MP:20,
  Mo-TL:56, Wr-RM:93
Sandpipers. H. Nemerov. Mo-BG:130
The Sea Gull. Ch-B:91, Ma-FO:(6)
The Sixteen Circuits of the Lodge - Third
  Song. Da-SC:103
Skimmers. P. Newman. Ca-BP:47
The Swallow. L. Aikin. Ox-BC:110
The Swallow. C. Gasztold. Re-BS:31
The Swallows. A. Young. Co-BBW:245
Two Birds Flying. De-PP:60
Washing My Rice Hoe. Buson. Be-CS:13
When Sea Birds Fly to Land. Sp-HW:11
The White Bird. H. Chattopadhyaya.
  Al-PI:92
Wild Geese Flying. De-PP:37
With His Apology. S. Karai. Ma-FW:93

BIRDS, KINDNESS TO

The Emperor's Bird's-Nest.
  H. Longfellow. Hu-MP:419, Re-BS:14

Lady Lost. J. Ransom. Ha-PO:69,
Rd-OA:196, Un-MA:409
Let Ye Then My Birds Alone. J. Clare.
Re-BS:27
The Liberator. Wu-ti. Re-BS:25
My Little Birds. Fe-FP:477
BIRDS - MIGRATION
Always with Us! - the Black Preacher.
H. Melville. Re-BS:51
Autumn Flight. A. Karanikas. Bo-HF:126
Fall. S. Andresen. Du-RG:123
The Great Scarf of Birds. J. Updike.
Mo-BG:134
A Gryphon Sighted in an Iowa Flyway.
N. Westerfield. Ls-NY:192
I Know the Trusty Almanac. R. Emerson.
Re-BS:20
I Too! I Too! J. Wheelock. Sm-MK:32
The Last Word of a Bluebird. R. Frost.
Ar-TP3:187, Bo-GJ:13, Fe-FP:286,
Gr-TG:33, Ir-BB:33, Ja-PA:8,
Li-LC:55, Pa-RE:58, Tu-WW:92
Late October. S. Teasdale. Co-PS:125,
Ha-YA:112
The Man Who Married the Birds.
Br-MW:84
Remembering the Winter. R. Bennett.
Br-SS:74
Ruins under the Stars. G. Kinnell.
Ha-WR:82, La-RM:152
Something Told the Wild Geese.
R. Field. Ar-TP3:187, Au-SP:331,
Br-SS:59, Co-BBW:234, Co-PS:124,
Ha-YA:100, Ho-LP:32, La-PV:135,
Mc-WK:27, Sm-MK:140, Tu-WW:106
Tampa Robins. S. Lanier. Se-PR:108
Traveling Light. M. Upton. Bo-FP:151
Two Little Birds Fly. Gr-BB:26
Wild Geese. E. Chipp. Ar-TP3:57,
Fe-FP:284, Hu-MP:236, Sh-RP:341
Wild Goose. C. Heath. Du-RG:123
Words for the Raker of Leaves. L. Adams.
En-PC:35
BIRDS - NESTS: see BIRDS - EGGS AND
NESTS
BIRDS - SONGS: see also BIRDS - CALLS;
HUMOR - BIRDS - SONGS
The Abbot of Inisfalen. W. Allingham.
Pa-OM:104
Above the Meadow. Chiyo. Be-MC:40
Address to a Lark Singing in Winter.
J. Clare. Re-BS:48
After the Goddess Sang. Onitsura.
Be-MC:35
After Yesterday. A. Ammons. Mo-TS:50
Alle Vögel Sind Schon Da.
F. Chesterton. Pl-US:64
Answer to a Child's Question.
S. Coleridge. Bl-OB:68, Co-BBW:266,
Gr-EC:224, Gr-TG:67, Hi-GD:12,
Ox-BC:111, Re-BS:10, Re-TW:31
At Common Dawn. V. Ellis. De-CH:352

At Half-Past Three a Single Bird.
E. Dickinson. Un-MA:105
A Baby Warbler. Kikaku. Be-CS:42
Ballata. Pl-US:62
The Barrel-Organ. A. Noyes. Ga-FB:234,
Un-MB:245
The Bird. E. Wylie. Mc-WS:41
The Bird Fancier. J. Kirkup. Gr-EC:71
A Bird Song in the Ravine. Wang Wei.
Le-MW:22
A Bird that Calls Before Dawn.
Tr-US I:194
Birds Must Sing. A. Rye. Sm-MK:152
The Birds of Killingworth.
H. Longfellow. Pa-OM:308
Birds Waking. W. Merwin. Ca-BP:21
The Blackbird. H. Wolfe. Ar-TP3:57,
Bo-FP:248, Bo-GJ:75, Fe-FP:285,
Hu-MP:225, Pa-RE:94, Sh-RP:340
The Blackbird by Belfast Lough.
Gr-EC:167, Pa-SG:117, Re-BS:38
A Blackbird Singing. R. Thomas.
Co-BBW:255, Hi-WP I:35, Ma-FW:90
A Blackbird Suddenly. J. Auslander.
Ar-TP3:212, Hu-MP:225, Se-PR:107,
Sh-RP:73, Tu-WW:104
Blackbird's Song. Gr-GB:62
The Blind Man. A. Young. Re-BS:41
The Blinded Bird. T. Hardy.
Co-BBW:251, Pl-EI:128, Wi-LT:20
The Bluebird. E. Miller. Hu-MP:225
Bob White. G. Cooper. Hu-MP:226,
Un-GT:60
The Bower of Bliss. E. Spenser.
De-CH:144
The Brown Thrush. L. Larcom.
Fe-FP:295, Hu-MP:224
Cape Ann. T. Eliot. Bo-GJ:53,
Ho-LP:50, Na-EO:35, Re-TW:83,
Sm-LG:143
The Cardinal's Valentine. Ja-HH:14
The Carnival of Animals. O. Nash.
Pl-US:92
The Chickadee. R. Emerson. Fe-FP:290,
Mc-PR:129
Claritas. D. Levertov. Ca-BP:27,
Ca-VT:512
Come, Come Away! R. Brome. Re-BS:22
Come In. R. Frost. Co-BN:157,
Ga-FB:292, Hi-WP I:4, Un-MA:19,
Wi-LT:179
The Cuckoo. Kodo. Le-MW:23, Ma-FW:10
The Cuckoo. Gr-GB:60
The Daisies. B. Carman. Co-BN:58
Dance Song. Tr-US I:232
The Darkling Thrush. T. Hardy.
Co-RG:170, Er-FA:455, Ha-PO:106,
Na-EO:56, Ox-BN:824, Un-MB:25,
Wi-LT:17
Dawn. W. Williams. Un-MA:256
Daylight Song. Da-SC:66
Desolate. S. Dobell. Ox-BN:659, Rv-CB:879

BIRDS - SONGS — cont'd.

The Dove. W. Barnes.   Re-BS:36

The Dove's Song. St-FS:24

The Dying Swan. A. Tennyson.
  Ho-WR:139

A Fiddler. W. de la Mare. Ha-LO:32,
  Pl-US:30

Flute-Priest Song for Rain. A. Lowell.
  Pl-US:132

For Keats and the Florentine Night.
  G. Kennedy. Ls-NY:141

Gay Comes the Singer. Sm-MK:142

Gic to Har. K. Rexroth. Ca-BP:23,
  Kh-VA:68

A Great Time. W. Davies. Hi-WP I:1,
  Un-MB:178

The Happy Nightingale. Ox-BC:70

Hark! De-TT:38

High on a Mountain. Basho. Be-CS:21

I Heard a Bird Sing. O. Herford.
  Ar-TP3:212, Au-SP:352, Br-SS:88,
  Co-BBW:256, Fe-PL:389, Ha-YA:151,
  La-PP:8, La-PV:128, Li-LC:71,
  Th-AS:49

I Rose Anon. J. Lydgate. De-CH:489

I Sing an Old Song. O. Williams.
  Wi-LT:412

In Heavy Mind. J. Agee. Un-MA:606

In Praise of May. Re-BS:22

In the Swamp. W. Whitman. La-RM:151

Interlude. E. Sitwell. Un-MB:330

Is It the Morning? Is It the Little
  Morning? D. Schwartz. Co-EL:152

Jenny Wren. W. Davies. Co-BBW:257,
  Re-BS:7, Un-MB:176

Jenny Wren. W. de la Mare. Re-BS:5

Joy of the Morning. E. Markham.
  Fe-FP:279, Hu-MP:214, Se-PR:107

Ko-Ko's Song. W. Gilbert. Er-FA:438

The Koocoo. De-CH:489, Gr-GB:60

The Lamentation of Beulah over Ololon.
  W. Blake. Ho-WR:60, Ox-BN:41

Lark Ascending. G. Meredith.
  Ho-WR:66, Rd-OA:53

The Lark in the Morning. Gr-CT:41,
  Gr-GB:44, Re-BS:49

A Little Morning Music. D. Schwartz.
  Co-BN:212

Look at Six Eggs. C. Sandburg.
  Fe-FP:291

Looking for a Sunset Bird in Winter.
  R. Frost. Re-BS:17

Magic Casements. J. Keats. Ga-FB:13,
  Ke-TF:333

The Magpie Singing His Delight.
  D. Campbell. Re-BS:34

The Making of Birds. K. Tynan.
  Re-BS:54

Mary's Canary. De-TT:38, Sp-AS:23,
  Wr-RM:93

The Mass of the Grove. D. ap Gwilym
  Go-BP:73

The Midges Dance aboon the Burn.
  R. Tannahill. Co-BN:108

A Minor Bird. R. Frost. Co-PM:108,
  De-CH:546, Ha-LO:68

The Mockingbird. R. Jarrell.
  La-RM:146

Most She Touched Me by Her Muteness.
  E. Dickinson. Re-BS:42

Music's Duel. R. Crashaw. No-CL:31

Never Again Would Birds' Songs Be the
  Same. R. Frost. Ca-VT:19

The Nightingale. W. Henley.
  Al-VBP:1068, Un-MB:53, Un-MW:9

The Nightingale. M. Stearns.
  Ar-TP3:176

Nightingales. R. Bridges. Gr-SS:52,
  Ox-BN:877, Rd-OA:194, Un-MB:51,
  Wi-LT:57

The Nightingale's Song Is Beautiful.
  Issa. Do-TS:29

Notes Toward a Supreme Fiction.
  W. Stevens. Wi-LT:162

Now Close the Windows. G. Hopkins.
  Hi-WP II:37

Now It Is Spring. Yakamochi. Ba-ST:16

now (more near ourselves than we).
  e. cummings. Gr-CC:74, We-PZ:9

Now Welcome Summer. G. Chaucer.
  Rv-CB:58

Ode to a Nightingale. J. Keats.
  Al-VBP:769, Er-FA:89, Gr-CT:102,
  Li-SR:138, Ox-BN:352, Pa-GTB:248

On Summer Nights. Tsurayuki. Ba-ST:29

One Morning, Oh So Early! J. Ingelow.
  Ox-BC:271

The Oven Bird. R. Frost. Pl-US:63

Overtones. W. Percy. Bo-HF:136

Pack, Clouds, Away! T. Heywood.
  Al-VBP:271, Bl-OB:42, De-CH:7,
  Pa-GTB:32, Re-BS:9, Re-TW:52,
  Tu-WW:11, Un-MW:6

Peacock and Nightingale. R. Finch.
  Co-BBW:248

People Buy a Lot of Things. A. Wynne.
  Au-SP:67, La-PV:137

Prelude. W. Gibson. Un-MB:241

Proud Songsters. T. Hardy. Ha-PO:105,
  Ma-FW:90

The Red Robin. J. Clare. Pa-RE:30,
  Re-BS:4

The Relic. R. Hillyer. Pl-US:145

Resolution and Independence.
  W. Wordsworth. Co-BN:214, Ma-FW:36,
  Ox-BN:71, Rv-CB:654

The Rivals. J. Stephens. Fe-FP:280,
  Mc-PR:191, Pa-RE:42, Re-BS:43,
  Th-AS:53

Robert of Lincoln. W. Bryant.
  Bo-FP:276, Co-BBW:263, Fe-FP:287,
  Hu-MP:227

The Robin. E. Dickinson. Ga-FB:284,
  Re-BS:1

The Robin and the Cows. W. Howells.
  Un-GT:60
The Robin's Song. R. Honeywood.
  Gr-EC:222, Pa-RE:83
Robin's Song. E. King. Ar-TP3:201
Rookery: Brookfield Zoo. L. Mueller.
  St-H:143
Rover and the Bird. N. Crossland.
  De-TT:44
The Saddest Noise, the Sweetest Noise.
  E. Dickinson. Cl-FC:39
Sedge-Warblers. E. Thomas. Re-BS:33
The Silver Swan. Co-PM:145, Gr-CT:98,
  Gr-SS:25, Sm-LG:91
Sing in the Silent Sky. C. Rossetti.
  Re-BS:56
Sing, Little Bird. M. Hastings.
  Au-SP:67
The Singers in a Cloud. R. Torrence.
  Pl-US:56
Singing. R. Stevenson. Bo-FP:133,
  Fr-MP:13
The Singing Bird. Ju-CP:36
The Skylark. C. Rossetti. Pa-RE:26,
  Un-GT:61
Skylark. Seien. Le-MW:24
Small Bird, Forgive Me. Be-MC:62
Snow Bunting. T. Miyoshi. Sh-AM:81
The Snowy Owl. E. Kroll. Co-BBW:244
Song. S. Coleridge. Co-PS:83,
  De-CH:355, De-TT:148
Song. Koma Doube Pio. Tr-US I:192
Song for a Summer Afternoon.
  V. Miller. Ca-BP:46
The Song of Honor. R. Hodgson.
  Un-MB:188
The Song of the Birds. Tr-US II:288
Song of the Chickadee. Bo-FP:167
The Song of the Reed Sparrow. Ox-BC:81
The Song Sparrow. H. van Dyke.
  Hu-MP:229
Songs of Birds. Bi-IT:111
Spring. W. Allingham. Ox-BN:673
Spring. W. Blake. Ar-TP3:203,
  Ch-B:99, Fe-FP:71, Ha-YA:25,
  Li-LC:70, Sm-LG:53, Un-GB:7,
  Un-GT:271
Spring. T. Nashe. Al-VBP:210,
  Bl-OB:102, Bo-FP:235, Co-BN:21,
  De-CH:14, De-TT:55, Ho-WR:35,
  Ma-FW:6, Ma-YA:73, Pa-GTB:1,
  Pa-RE:82, Rv-CB:275, Tu-WW:57
Spring Sorrow. Ch'n Ch'ang Siu.
  Rx-LT:60
Sun. D. Wakoski. Kh-VA:13
The Sun Has Long Been Set.
  W. Wordsworth. Ha-YA:72
Swallow Song. Da-SC:97, Tr-US II:266
There, where the Skylark's Singing.
  Kyorai. Be-MC:43
The Throstle. A. Tennyson.
  Co-BBW:241, Co-BN:97, Co-PS:106,
  Fe-FP:294, Mc-WK:25, Se-PR:155

Thrush. C. Simic. Mc-EA:39
A Thrush Before Dawn. A. Meynell.
  Un-MB:64
The Thrush in February. G. Meredith.
  Ox-BN:694
The Thrush's Song. W. McGillivray.
  De-CH:97, Un-GT:64
To a Skylark. P. Shelley.
  Co-RG:139, Er-FA:228, Fe-FP:293,
  Fe-PL:356, Ga-FB:18, Hu-MP:230,
  Ox-BN:283, Pa-GTB:243, Sp-OG:353
To the Cuckoo. W. Wordsworth.
  Er-FA:225, Fe-PL:353, Pa-GTB:247,
  Rv-CB:634, Un-GT:61
The Tree of Life. Re-BS:58
An Unseen Skylark. Shiki. Be-CS:17
Walking. T. Tsosie. Ba-HI:56
What Bird So Sings. J. Lyly.
  Al-VBP:121, Bl-OB:67, De-CH:14,
  Re-TW:54
When a Cuckoo Sings. Basho. Be-MC:8
When Daffodils Begin to Peer.
  W. Shakespeare. Al-VBP:195,
  Gr-CT:42, Rv-CB:205, Sm-LG:55
When Nightingales Burst into Song.
  Jurin. Be-MC:58
When Smoke Stood Up from Ludlow.
  A. Housman. Un-MB:95
Where's Mary? I. Eastwick. Ar-TP3:7
Who Is't Now We Hear? J. Lyly.
  Re-BS:49
The Wild. W. Berry. Ca-VT:683
Winter Song. J. Jiménez. Le-SW:73
Ye Little Birds. . . . Al-VBP:359
BIRDS OF PARADISE
  Bird of Paradise. R. Graves. Go-BP:81
  The Birds of Paradise. J. Bishop.
    Bo-GJ:67
  The Captive Bird of Paradise.
    R. Pitter. Gr-SS:50
  In London Town. M. Coleridge.
    Pa-RE:77
BIRMINGHAM, ALA.
  Ballad of Birmingham. D. Randall.
    Be-MA:71, Ra-BP:143
  Birmingham. M. Walker. Ad-PB:149
  Birmingham 1963. R. Patterson.
    Ad-PB:209, Kr-OF:163
  Birmingham Sunday. L. Hughes.
    Hu-PN:200
  A Young David: Birmingham.
    H. Brooks. Hu-PN:276
BIRMINGHAM, ENG.
  Birmingham. L. MacNeice. Un-MB:445
BIRTH: see also ABORTION; HUMOR - BIRTH;
    SATIRE - BIRTH; THE UNBORN
  The Babies Are Born. M. Bryant.
    Ba-HI:83
  Becoming a Dad. E. Guest. Fe-PL:141
  Behind Memory. M. Montes de Oca.
    Be-UL:127
  Birth. A. Gilboa. Me-PH:116
  Birth. Tr-US II:36

BIRTH — <u>cont'd.</u>
Birth of Mary. R. Rilke. Tr-MR:98
The Bonny Earl of Livingston. Ox-BB:309
C. L. M. J. Masefield. Un-MB:225,
    Wi-LT:190
Escape. T. McGrath. St-H:123
Fable for When There's No Way Out.
    M. Swenson. Pe-M:82
The Family Poem. M. Rawitch. Ho-TY:202
From the Moment. A. Blandiana.
    Mc-AC:162
The Hatch. N. Farber. Ho-LP:100
Imperial Adam. A. Hope. Un-MW:126
In Spring in Warm Weather. D. Aldis.
    Br-BC:9
In These Dissenting Times. A. Walker.
    Ad-PB:475
Infant Sorrow. W. Blake. Ox-BN:25,
    Rv-CB:572
John Brown's Body. S. Benét.
    Ke-TF:114, Un-MA:499
The Land in My Mother. N. Hashimoto.
    Le-TA:17
Manhattan Lullaby. R. Field.
    Br-AF:193, Br-BC:145, La-OC:127
May 10th. M. Kumin. Co-BN:25
Multipara: Gravida 5. M. Ponsot.
    Ca-VT:488
The Nativity Chant. W. Scott.
    Gr-CT:167, Sm-LG:233
Neighbors, Friends, Two Gypsies, et al.,
    Arrive. J. de Melo Neto. An-TC:139
Now That I Am Forever with Child.
    A. Lorde. Ad-PB:246
O Sun, O Sun. Le-OE:135
Ode on Intimations of Immortality.
    W. Wordsworth. Br-BC:18, Ga-FB:101,
    Gr-CT:436, Ha-PO:206, Pl-EI:59
Pro Sua Vita. R. Warren. Un-MA:584
Saturday's Child. C. Cullen.
    Ad-PB:86, Bo-HF:88, Wi-LT:616
Second Son. B. Weinstein. Ho-TY:292
The Snow. D. Hall. Mc-EA:49
Song. Bi-IT:123
Song Sung by a Woman Giving Birth.
    Tr-CB:55, Tr-US I:65
Songs, II. Tr-US II:124
Sonnets I, II. J. Agee. Un-MA:604
This Is to Make Children Jump Down.
    Da-SC:143
To Insure Survival. S. Ortiz.
    Ni-CD:143
To Our Babies, III. Le-IB:60
Whenever a Little Child Is Born.
    A. Mason. Br-BC:4
Words Spoken by a Mother to Her
    Newborn Son. Bi-IT:112
BIRTH CONTROL: see also ABORTION
The Pill Versus the Springhill Mine
    Disaster. R. Brautigan. Mc-EA:27
BIRTHDAY CAKES: see BIRTHDAYS
BIRTHDAY GIFTS: see BIRTHDAYS

BIRTHDAYS
Amy Margaret. W. Allingham. Br-BC:53
Anniversary in September. B. Brown.
    Br-BC:146
Another Birthday. B. Jonson. Ho-WR:71
Betsy Jane's Sixth Birthday. A. Noyes.
    Br-BC:101, Br-SS:45
Birthday. E. Emans. Br-BC:138
A Birthday. R. Field. Br-BC:85,
    Br-SS:41
A Birthday. C. Rossetti. Al-VBP:997,
    Bl-OB:41, Co-BL:107, De-CH:334,
    Er-FA:116, Ho-WR:70, Re-TW:46,
    Un-MW:137
The Birthday Bus. M. Hoberman.
    Ar-TP3:92, Br-BC:98
The Birthday Cake. V. Chase. Br-BC:86
Birthday Cake. I. Eastwick. Br-BC:88
Birthday Cake. A. Fisher. Br-BC:88,
    La-PV:118
The Birthday-Cake Glockenspiel.
    E. Henley. Br-BC:90
Birthday Candles. G. Johnson.
    Ke-TF:155
Birthday Candles. L. Scott. Br-BC:86
The Birthday Child. R. Fyleman.
    Br-BC:3, Br-SS:50, Fe-FP:50,
    La-PH:59
Birthday Garden. I. Eastwick.
    Br-BC:58
Birthday Gifts. H. Asquith. Br-BC:100,
    Br-SS:49
Birthday Gifts. L. Scott. Br-BC:99
A Birthday Song. R. Gilder. Se-PR:237
Birthday Verses Written in a Child's
    Album. J. Lowell. Ox-BC:282
Birthdays. M. Chute. Br-BC:78,
    Br-SS:48
Cake. M. Potter. Br-BC:85
Christmas Birthday. G. Glaubitz.
    Br-BC:77, Br-SS:47
Crab-Apple. E. Talbot. Ar-TP3:149,
    Bo-FP:328, Br-BC:8
Dandelions. M. Chute. Br-BC:102,
    Mc-AW:67
Dying Speech of an Old Philosopher.
    W. Landor. Al-VBP:704, Gr-CT:435,
    Ha-PO:209, Ma-YA:169, Ox-BN:194,
    Pa-GTB:318
Experience. A. Kilmer. Br-BC:46
February Birthday. N. Turner.
    Br-BC:154
Fiftieth Birthday. P. Viereck.
    Ls-NY:68
Five Years Old. M. Allen. Br-BC:52
For a Birthday. E. Emans. Br-BC:152
For K. R. on Her Sixtieth Birthday.
    R. Wilbur. Pl-ML:77
For the Eightieth Birthday of a Great
    Singer. E. Shanks. Pl-US:58

Grandmamma's Birthday. H. Belloc.
   Co-EL:56, Co-FB:189
Growing Up. Br-BC:48, Fr-MP:3
Hal's Birthday. L. Larcom. Br-BC:51
Her Birthday. Feng Yen-Chi.
   Le-MW:112
How Soon Hath Time. J. Milton.
   Al-VBP:388, Ma-YA:93
Hurry Tomorrow. I. Eastwick. Br-BC:43
I Would Like to Be a Bee. D. Baruch.
   Br-BC:92
If You Saw a Negro Lady. J. Meyer.
   Jo-SA:54, Lo-IT:92
It's Somebody's Birthday. L. Norris.
   Ls-NY:80
January 3, 1970. M. Jackson.
   Ad-PB:499
Kentucky Birthday, February 12, 1815.
   F. Frost. Br-SS:116, Ha-YA:173
Little Brother's Secret. K. Mansfield.
   Ar-TP3:6, Fe-FP:49, Th-AS:64
The Miracle. E. Fowler. Br-BC:87
Monday's Child. . . . Au-SP:5,
   De-PO:14, Gr-EC:129, Ir-BB:226,
   Li-LB:164, Mo-CC:(11), Mo-MGT:16,
   Mo-NR:19, Mo-TB:107, Rv-CB:452,
   Sm-LG:97, Un-GT:22, Wi-MG:58, Wr-RM:87
My Birthday. T. Moore. Se-PR:239
My Birthday's in Winter. Z. Gay.
   Br-BC:59
Nature at Three. B. Breeser. Br-BC:46
Oh! to Have a Birthday. L. Lenski.
   Br-BC:85
Ode for My Father's Eightieth Birthday.
   R. Potash. Ho-TY:358
On a Birthday. J. Synge. Gr-CT:42
On His Thirty-Third Birthday.
   Ch'ang Kuo Fang. Rx-LT:118
On My Birthday. Y. Amichai. Me-PH:128
On This Day I Complete My Thirty-Sixth
   Year. G. Byron. Al-VBP:738,
   Ma-YA:175
One, Two, Buckle My Shoe. O. Nash.
   Br-BC:44, Ir-BB:92
The Only Card I Got on My Birthday Was
   from an Insurance Man. W. Stafford.
   St-H:214
Our Birthday. M. Edey. Br-BC:57,
   Br-SS:44
A Party. L. Richards. Au-SP:119,
   Br-BC:93, Br-SS:49
Poem at Thirty. S. Sanchez. Ad-PB:286,
   Ra-BP:231
Poem in October. D. Thomas. Gr-CC:42,
   Hi-WP II:135, To-MP:54
Present. M. Potter. Br-BC:101
Richer. A. Fisher. Br-BC:5
Seven Times One. J. Ingelow. Br-BC:71,
   Fe-FP:50, Gr-TG:47, Hu-MP:70,
   Ke-TF:41, Ox-BN:720, Un-GT:14
Seven Times One Are Seven. R. Hillyer.
   Br-BC:156
Seven Today. I. Eastwick. Br-BC:70

Six Birthday Candles Shining. M. Carr.
   Br-BC:91
Somebody's Birthday. A. Brown. Br-BC:5
Someone. J. Ciardi. Br-BC:16
Something Very Elegant. A. Fisher.
   Br-BC:74
Sons of the Kings. J. Agnew. Br-BC:62
The Squad Car. M. Neville. Su-FVI:33
Telegram. W. Wise. Ar-TP3:105
To a Little Sister, Aged Ten.
   A. Cummings. Br-BC:79
To Auden on His Fiftieth. R. Eberhart.
   Pl-ML:74
To Dick, on His Sixth Birthday.
   S. Teasdale. Br-BC:59
To T. S. Eliot on His Sixtieth Birthday.
   W. Auden. Pl-ML:71
To W. H. Auden on His Fiftieth Birthday.
   B. Howes. Pl-ML:76
Tree Birthdays. M. Davies. Br-BC:9
Two Days. M. de Veaux. Ho-CT:6
Un-Birthday Cake. A. Fisher. Br-BC:89
Verses for a First Birthday.
   G. Barker. Un-MB:495
When a Fellow's Four. M. Carr.
   Br-BC:49
When I Was Six. Z. Cross. Br-BC:60,
   Fe-FP:486
Who Wants a Birthday? D. McCord.
   Br-BC:3
The Wish. A. Friday. La-PH:58
Written on the Road. M. Dodge.
   Br-BC:145
BISHOPS: see also HUMOR - BISHOPS;
   SATIRE - BISHOPS
Bishop Blougram's Apology. R. Browning.
   Ox-BN:547
The Bishop Orders His Tomb at Saint
   Praxed's Church. R. Browning.
   Al-VBP:895, Mo-GR:57
Heriger, Bishop of Mainz. Li-TU:152
Latimer and Ridley. W. Wordsworth.
   Hi-FO:118
The Loyal Scot. A. Marvell. Al-VBP:461
BISON: see also HUMOR - BISON
Ayii, Ayii, Ayii, Ayii (Wondering).
   Ho-SD:68
The Buffalo Coat. T. McGrath. St-H:124
Buffalo Dance Song. Br-MW:72
Buffalo Dusk. C. Sandburg. Ad-PE:14,
   Ar-TP3:37, Ho-TH:57, La-PV:156,
   La-RM:80, Pe-M:33, Rd-OA:29
Buffalo Myth. Br-MW:73
The Buffalo Skinners. Co-RM:232,
   Gr-GB:220, Hi-TL:150
Buffalo Song. Br-MW:79
The Flower-Fed Buffaloes. V. Lindsay.
   Ar-TP3:83, Bo-GJ:203, Br-AF:151,
   Ca-VT:30, Co-BBW:198, Fe-FP:433,
   Gr-CT:124, Ha-PO:157, Hu-MP:203,
   Ke-PP:86, La-RM:78, Mc-WK:76,
   Mo-BG:139, Re-TW:99, Sh-RP:77,
   Sm-LG:83, Un-MA:228

BISON — <u>cont'd.</u>
  Gates of the Rockies. J. Daugherty.
    Sh-RP:301
  The Ghosts of the Buffaloes. V. Lindsay.
    Sh-RP:46, Un-MA:223
  Hunting Song. Le-OE:59
  Monument in Bone. P. George. Al-WW:122
  The Rising of the Buffalo Men.
    Da-SC:109, Ho-SD:23
  We Put on the Buffalo. R. Coffin.
    Sh-RP:289
  What Great Difference Can You See.
    Re-RR:107
  The Whole World Is Coming. Da-SC:121,
    Ho-SD:12
  Wolves. G. Kinnell.   Co-RM:95
BITTERNESS
  À Terre.   W. Owen.   Wi-LT:352
  The Ballad of Reading Gaol. O. Wilde.
    Al-VBP:1072, Er-FA:87, Un-MB:70
  Blues and Bitterness. L. Bennett.
    Ad-PB:202, Hu-NN:53
  The Heart. S. Crane.   Un-MA:148,
    Wi-LT:117
  Henry C. Calhoun. E. Masters.
    Sh-AP:138, Wi-LT:115
  My Heart Has Known Its Winter.
    A. Bontemps. Be-MA:45
  My Soul Is Weary of My Life.   Bible.
    O.T. Job. Pl-EI:67
  Poem (No Name No. 2). N. Giovanni.
    Ad-BO:9
  Tragedy. AE. Un-MB:143
  Transformation. L. Alexander.
    Hu-PN:160
  We Were Not like Dogs. U. Greenberg
    Me-PH:98
  Wisdom. Tr-CB:17
BITTERROOT
  Montana. C. Cohan. Se-PR:272
BLACK (COLOR)
  The African Affair. B. Wright.
    Ad-PB:171, Hu-PN:357
  Amen. R. Thomas. Ad-PB:372
  The Black Finger. A. Grimke.
    Ad-PB:15, Bo-AN:17
  Black Is a Soul. J. White. Ad-PB:261
  Black Is Beautiful. La-IH:99
  The Black Me. Chi Hsüan. Pa-MV:46
  Coal. A. Lorde. Ad-PB:244
  Color. V. Castro. Ba-HI:37
  Crow, with Shiny Clothes. B. Jones.
    Ba-HI:19
  Evil Is No Black Thing. S. Fabio.
    Ad-PB:205
  Negritude. J. Emanuel. Ra-BP:189
  The Song of the Smoke. W. Du Bois.
    Ad-PB:1
  Sonnet 127. W. Shakespeare. Rv-CB:245
  The Undertaker's Club. Gr-GB:325
  Vive Noir! M. Evans. Ad-PB:188

BLACK HAWK, CHIEF
  Deny It, but It Is So. E. Smith.
    Kr-OF:13
BLACK KETTLE, CHIEF
  Black Kettle Raises the Stars and
    Stripes. L. Simpson. Cr-WS:24
BLACK MAGIC: see MAGIC; VOODOO; WITCHES
  AND WITCHCRAFT
BLACK PANTHERS: see also SEALE, BOBBY G.
  My Name Is Afrika. K. Kgositsile.
    Ad-PB:326
  Newsletter from My Mother. M. Harper.
    Ad-PB:315
BLACK POWER: see NEGROES
BLACKBERRIES
  Berries. W. de la Mare. Un-MB:200
  The Blackberry. N. Nicholson.
    Un-MB:504
  Blackberry-Picking. S. Heaney.
    Co-BN:100
  Blackberrying. S. Plath. To-MP:98
  Fruit, Flower and Tree Riddles.
    Gr-GB:72
  This You May Answer. Re-RR:52
BLACKBIRDS
  The Blackbird. D. Craik. Un-GT:59
  The Blackbird. H. Wolfe. Ar-TP3:57,
    Bo-FP:248, Bo-GJ:75, Fe-FP:285,
    Hu-MP:225, Pa-RE:94, Sh-RP:340
  The Blackbird by Belfast Lough.
    Gr-EC:167, Pa-SG:117, Re-BS:38
  A Blackbird Singing. R. Thomas.
    Co-BBW:255, Hi-WP I:35, Ma-FW:90
  A Blackbird Suddenly. J. Auslander.
    Ar-TP3:212, Hu-MP:225, Se-PR:107,
    Sh-RP:73, Tu-WW:104
  Blackbird's Song. Gr-GB:62
  Child's Song. K. Greenaway. Bo-FP:260
  A Health to the Birds. S. McManus.
    Co-PI:112
  In the Blue. A. Machado. Le-SW:75
  The Nightingale. W. Henley.
    Al-VBP:1068, Un-MB:53, Un-MW:9
  Nursery Song in Pidgin English.
    Li-SR:130
  O What if the Fowler? C. Dalmon.
    Co-BBW:240, De-CH:337, Re-BS:24
  October. D. Thomas. Ha-YA:110
  The Redwing. P. Dickinson. Go-BP:77
  River Roads. C. Sandburg. Ca-VT:22
  Secrets. L. Hewitt. Bo-FP:240
  Seven Little Blackbirds. Ju-CP:77
  Shadows. E. Farjeon. De-TT:149
  Sing a Song of Sixpence. Mother Goose.
    Bo-FP:9, Br-FF:(18), De-PO:22,
    Fr-WO:16, Ir-BB:262, Li-SR:129,
    Mo-MGT:19, Mo-NR:10, On-TW:57,
    Sm-MK:19
  Sing a Song of Sixpence. Au-SP:16,
    Li-LB:100, Wi-MG:72, Wr-RM:62
  Sing a Song of Sunshine. I. Eastwick.
    Br-SS:16

Song. L. Kemp. Ls-NY:16
There Were Two Blackbirds. De-PO:10
Thirteen Ways of Looking at a Blackbird.
 W. Stevens. Ha-PO:233, Mc-EA:150,
 Mo-TS:80, Wi-LT:144
Two Little Blackbirds. Ir-BB:137,
 Mo-MGT:145, Sm-MK:74
Vespers. T. Brown. Co-BBW:259
BLACKOUTS: see AIR RAIDS; CIVIL DEFENSE
BLACKS: see NEGROES
BLACKSMITHING: see also HUMOR -
 BLACKSMITHING
 The Blacksmith. Sp-TM:30, Wr-RM:80
 The Blacksmith. Mo-TL:28, On-TW:8,
 Rv-ON:87, Wr-RM:33
 Blacksmiths. Ho-WR:99
 The Blacksmith's Song. Gr-GB:208
 Felix Randal. G. Hopkins. Co-RG:158,
 Ox-BN:866, Pa-GTB:392, Un-MB:44,
 Wi-LT:43
 The Forge. S. Heaney. Co-PI:59
 The Smith. L. Uhland. Un-R:95
 Tubal Cain. C. Mackay. Hu-MP:407
 The Unemployed Blacksmith. J. Woods.
 Mc-WS:147
 The Village Blacksmith. H. Longfellow.
 Ch-B:86, Er-FA:275, Fe-FP:545,
 Sp-OG:323, Tu-WW:22, Un-GT:96
BLAGA, LUCIAN
 Self-Portrait. L. Blaga. Mc-AC:72
BLAKE, WILLIAM
 William Blake. R. Iceland. Ho-TY:116
 William Blake. J. Thomson. Rv-CB:931
BLARNEY CASTLE, IRE.
 The Groves of Blarney. R. Millikin.
 Rv-CB:629
BLENHEIM, BATTLE, 1704
 The Battle of Blenheim. R. Southey.
 Cr-WS:21, Fe-PL:182, Ga-FB:203,
 Ha-PO:13, Hi-FO:165, Ox-BN:177,
 Pa-GTB:213, Sp-OG:184, Un-GT:146
BLENHEIM PALACE
 On Blenheim House. A. Evans. Rv-CB:501
BLENNERHASSET, HARMAN
 Blennerhassett's Island. T. Read.
 Hi-TL:60
BLENNERHASSET ISLAND, W. VA.
 Blennerhassett's Island. T. Read.
 Hi-TL:60
BLESSINGS: see also HUMOR - BLESSINGS;
 SATIRE - BLESSINGS
 Amends to the Tailors and Soutars.
 W. Dunbar. Rv-CB:70
 Beggar's Rhyme. Ar-TP3:192, Au-SP:375,
 Bo-FP:181, Cl-DT:23, La-PH:33,
 Mo-MGT:109, Wr-RM:123
 Blessed Are They That Sow.
 A. Ben Yitzhak. Me-PH:83
 A Blessing. Bible. O.T. Numbers.
 Gr-TG:58
 Blessing for Light.
 Th-AS:176

A Blessing on the Cows. S. O'Sullivan.
 Co-PI:166
Blessing over Food. H. Bialik.
 Ha-YA:133
Blessings upon an Infant. Do-CH:(2)
A Child's Grace. R. Burns. Bo-FP:158,
 Fe-FP:45, Hi-WP I:117, Hu-MP:16,
 Sm-LG:123
Close Eyes, Bow Head. Gr-TG:36
Evening Hymn. E. Roberts. Ar-TP3:177
For All the Joys of Harvest. E. Vipont.
 Br-SG:104
God Bless the Master of This House.
 Ar-TP3:197, Br-SS:111, De-PO:28,
 Sh-RP:246
Good Wish. Sm-LG:240
Grace. W. de la Mare. Gr-TG:35
Grace. B. Jonson. De-CH:590
Grace Before Sleep. S. Teasdale.
 Tr-MR:52
Grace for a Child. R. Herrick.
 Al-VBP:336, Bo-GJ:29, De-CH:495,
 De-TT:46, Fe-FP:25, Fr-WO:91,
 Gr-CT:168, Gr-TG:37, Mc-PR:39,
 Ox-BC:31, Pl-EI:190, Re-TW:79,
 Sm-LG:117, Sm-MK:215
A Grace for Children. R. Herrick.
 Ox-BC:31
Grace for Light. M. O'Neill.
 Th-AS:174
The Grasshopper's Song. H. Bialik.
 Fe-FP:476, Ha-YA:65
Greeting. Gr-TG:42
Happy New Year! Co-PS:22
Ho! Ye Sun, Moon, Stars. Da-SC:104,
 Ho-SD:18
House Blessing. A. Guiterman.
 Ar-TP3:216
House Blessing. Bi-IT:48
I See the Moon. Ar-TP3:180, Au-SP:94,
 Bo-FP:47, De-CH:743, Gr-GB:39,
 Mo-MGT:207, Rd-SS:32, Sm-MK:215,
 Un-GT:23
It Is Very Nice to Think. R. Stevenson.
 Gr-TG:36
The Jackdaw of Rheims. R. Barham.
 Pa-OM:322
Matthew, Mark, Luke and John.
 Bo-FP:36, De-CH:446, De-PO:28,
 De-TT:202, Gr-GB:298, Gr-TG:55,
 Hi-GD:23, Mo-MGT:28, Mo-NR:99,
 On-TW:18, Rd-SS:40, Rv-CB:451
 Sm-LG:385, Un-GT:23
Mother Moon, Bless Baby. Le-OE:104
An Old Grace. Cl-FC:91
The Players Ask for a Blessing on the
 Psalteries and on Themselves.
 W. Yeats. Pl-US:10
A Prayer to Be Restored to the Sanctuary.
 Bible. O.T. Psalms. Me-PH:22
The Robin's Song. R. Honeywood.
 Gr-EC:222, Pa-RE:83

BLESSINGS — cont'd.
   Saint Francis and Saint Benedight.
     W. Cartright.   Gr-CT:167, Mo-TB:77,
     Pl-EI:189
   Song of the Mayers.   De-CH:12, Gr-GB:42
   The Souling Soul.   Gr-SS:151
   Spear-Blessing.   Tr-US I:103
   Thank You for the World So Sweet.
     R. Leatham.   Gr-TG:36
   Three Blessings.   Go-BP:278
   X-Ray.   L. Speyer.   Pl-IO:146
BLINDNESS
   À Terre.   W. Owen.   Wi-LT:352
   All but Blind.   W. de la Mare.
     Fe-FP:138, Ga-S:48, Hi-WP I:121,
     La-PV:152, Mc-WK:99, Ni-JP:82,
     Un-MB:291
   As Mary Was A-Walking.   Ga-S:107
   The Ballad of Billy Rose.   L. Norris.
     Ca-MB:83
   The Blind Boy.   C. Cibber.
     Co-RG:134, Ox-BC:58, Pa-GTB:111
   Blind Man.   J. Miller.   Sc-TN:169
   The Blind Man.   A. Young.   Re-BS:41
   The Blind Men and the Elephant.
     Bo-HF:73, Gr-EC:150, Ha-PO:302,
     Pa-OM:330, Un-GT:200
   The Blinded Bird.   T. Hardy.
     Co-BBW:251, Pl-EI:128, Wi-LT:20
   Charles.   L. Clark.   Ma-FW:180
   Drum Song.   Tr-US I:41
   The Fog.   W. Davies.   Ar-TP3:172,
     La-OC:133, Mc-WK:34
   Having Eyes That See.   M. Morris.
     Sa-B:221
   The Horse Show.   W. Stevens.
     Ca-VT:66, Pe-OA:79
   I Know My Soul Hath Power.   J. Davies.
     De-CH:585
   An Idle Poet.   C. Patmore.   Al-VBP:973,
     De-CH:584, Ox-BN:652, Pa-GTB:367
   In the Old Man's Eyes.   K. Takahama.
     Ma-FW:179
   The Irish Harper and His Dog.
     T. Campbell.   De-CH:83, De-TT:66,
     Hu-MP:194, Rv-CB:678, Un-GT:41
   The Lament of the Mole-Catcher.
     O. Sitwell.   Co-BBW:22
   Mary Arnold, the Female Monster.
     Gr-GB:271
   A Music.   W. Berry.   Ca-VT:683
   On His Blindness.   J. Milton.
     Al-VBP:408, Er-FA:31, Fe-PL:321,
     Ga-FB:92, Gr-CT:434, Ke-TF:58,
     Ma-FW:181, Ma-YA:93, Mc-PR:79,
     Pa-GTB:62, Rv-CB:374, Sp-OG:332
   Out of Blindness.   L. Blades.
     Du-SH:141
   Paradise Lost.   J. Milton. Al-VBP:408
   Poet.   S. Halkin.   Ho-TY:187
   Samson Agonistes.   J. Milton.
     Al-VBP:413, Ga-S:47

   Sight.   W. Gibson.   Un-MB:242
   Singing in the Dark.   I. Wassall.
     Hu-PN:546
   A Solitude.   D. Levertov.   Du-SH:142,
     Mo-BG:36
   The Spring Waters.   Ping Hsin.
     Hs-TC:22
   Tim Turpin.   T. Hood.   Ho-WR:84
   To a Mole.   L. Darcy.   Ls-NY:198
   To Homer.   J. Keats.   Rv-CB:748
   The Train.   Be-AP:35
BLISS: see HAPPINESS
BLIZZARDS: see STORMS
BLOOD BANKS: see also HUMOR — BLOOD
    BANKS
   Just Making It.   R. Thomas.   Hu-PN:432
BLOOMER, AMELIA JENKS
   Crinolines and Bloomers.   Hi-TL:174
BLOSSOMS: see FLOWERS
BLUE (COLOR)
   Blue Flowers.   R. Field.   Br-SG:32,
     Mc-PR:161
   Blue Is Like the Wind.   S. Hawes.
     La-GI:30
   Blue Winter.   R. Francis.   Ho-LP:34
   Little Blue Ben.   Mo-MGT:75
   November Blue.   A. Meynell.   Un-MB:62
   Variations on a Sentence.   L. Bogan.
     Ho-LP:44, Pl-IO:111
BLUE JAYS
   Blue Jay.   H. Conkling.   Co-BBW:261,
     Re-BS:29
   Blue Jay.   R. Francis.   Co-EL:34
   Blue on White.   E. Coatsworth.
     Sh-RP:339
   crazy jay blue.   e. cummings.
     Co-BBW:246
   Invitation.   H. Behn.   Au-SP:63,
     Fe-FP:287
BLUE RIDGE MOUNTAINS
   The Blue Ridge.   H. Monroe.   Bo-HF:20
BLUEBELLS: see also HAREBELLS
   Bluebells.   P. Dickinson.   Go-BP:112
   Bluebells.   J. Szabo.   La-GI:14
   Secrets.   L. Hewitt.   Bo-FP:240
BLUBERRIES
   Bleeberrying.   J. Denwood.
     Ca-MB:17
   The Hermit Picks Berries.   M. Kumin.
     La-RM:140
   They Ripen in the Sun.   Gr-BB:8
BLUEBIRDS
   The Blue Bird.   M. Coleridge.
     De-CH:99, Hi-WP I:108
   The Bluebird.   E. Miller.   Hu-MP:225
   Daylight Song.   Da-SC:66
   The Last Word of a Bluebird.   R. Frost.
     Ar-TP3:187, Bo-GJ:13, Fe-FP:286,
     Gr-TG:33, Ir-BB:33, Ja-PA:8,
     Li-LC:55, Pa-RE:58, Tu-WW:92
   Little Horned Toad.   Fe-FP:144
BLUES: see DESPAIR; MELANCHOLY

BLUES (MUSIC): see also HUMOR - BLUES
   (MUSIC)
   Black Is a Soul. J. White. Ad-PB:261
   Blues. T. Matthews. Sa-B:94
   Blues and Bitterness. L. Bennett.
      Ad-PB:202, Hu-NN:53
   Blues for Bessie. M. O'Higgins.
      Hu-PN:347, Kr-OF:50
   Blues Note. B. Kaufman. Ad-PB:263,
      Be-MA:131, Jo-SA:36
   The Blues Today. M. Jackson. Ad-BO:63,
      Ad-PB:496
   Effendi. M. Harper. Ad-PB:318
   Elegy for a Jazz Musician. E. Kroll.
      Du-SH:138
   Get Up, Blues. J. Emanuel. Ad-BO:62,
      Ad-PB:179, Bo-AN:175, Li-TU:173
   Go 'Way from My Window. Ab-MO:51
   Haiku 4. E. Knight. Ra-BP:206
   Homage to the Empress of the Blues.
      R. Hayden. Ad-PB:117, Be-MA:64,
      Hu-PN:290, Mo-BG:46
   i remember how she sang. R. Penny.
      Ad-PB:388
   Lead. J. Cortez. Ad-PB:343
   Riding Across John Lee's Finger.
      S. Crouch. Ad-PB:485
   Satchmo. M. Tolson. Ra-BP:119
   Song of Dry Bones. T. Matthews.
      Sa-B:92
   Soul. D. Graham. Ad-PB:482
   The Sound of Afroamerican History.
      S. Anderson. Ad-PB:441
   The Weary Blues. L. Hughes. Be-MA:39,
      Ga-FB:276, Hu-PN:184, Pl-US:90
   See also Em-AF:742-754.
BOA CONSTRICTORS: see HUMOR - BOA
   CONSTRICTORS
BOADICEA. QUEEN OF ANCIENT BRITONS
   Boadicea. W. Cowper. Hi-FO:56
BOARD MEETINGS: see COMMITTEES AND
   COMMITTEE MEETINGS
BOARS
   The Boar. W. Shakespeare. Co-BBW:206
   The Boar and the Dromedary. H. Beissel.
      Do-WH:11
   The Boar Hunt. Homer. Ma-FW:230
   The Borys Hede That We Bryng Here.
      Ma-YA:24
   The Stars Go over the Lonely Ocean.
      R. Jeffers. Wi-LT:259
   The Wild Boar and the Ram. J. Gay.
      Ke-PP:37
BOASTING: see also EXAGGERATION; HUMOR -
   BOASTING; TALL TALES
   An Afternoon like This. Fi-BG:82
   Bitter Creek. Fi-BG:83
   Braggin' Bill's Fortytude. C. Hallock.
      Fi-GB:79
   Conquistador. E. Coatsworth.
      Un-GT:93

Fable. R. Emerson. Bo-FP:71, Bo-GJ:26,
   Bo-HF:69, Ch-B:27, Er-FA:496,
   Fe-FP:530, Ga-FB:317, Hu-MP:210,
   Pa-OM:333, Rd-OA:91, Sh-AP:27,
   Sp-OG:303, Un-GT:57
Four Preludes on Playthings of the Wind:
   The Past Is a Bucket of Ashes.
   C. Sandburg. Un-MA:201
The High Loping Cowboy. C. Fletcher.
   Fi-BG:76
It Is My Form and Person. Da-SC:153
The Legend of Boastful Bill. C. Clark.
   Fi-BG:92
The Mu'allaqa of Antar. Antar.
   Lo-TY:37
Peacock and Nightingale. R. Finch.
   Co-BBW:248
Potlatch Boasts. Br-MW:137
Song of QWAXILA. Da-SC:86
Song of the New-Rich. Da-SC:56
A Texas Idyl. Fi-BG:81
The Wicked Little Kukook. Le-IB:87
The Wind and the Moon. G. MacDonald.
   Bo-GJ:35, Ir-BB:127, Li-LC:79,
   Pa-OM:268, Un-GT:258
The Wolf and the Lioness. E. Rees.
   Ar-TP3:81
BOAT RACING
   The Boat Race. Virgil. Fl-HH:43,
      Mo-SD:64
   Eight Oars and a Coxswain. A. Guiterman.
      Fl-HH:58, Mo-SD:62
   The Yachts. W. Williams. Al-VBP:1154,
      Fl-HH:27, Ma-FW:51, Pe-OA:73,
      Pe-SS:72, Sm-PT:112, Un-MA:262,
      Wi-LT:194
BOATS AND BOATING: see also CANOES AND
   CANOEING; FERRIES; FREIGHTERS; HUMOR -
   BOATS AND BOATING; KAYAKS; SAILING;
   SHIPS; TUGBOATS; YACHTS AND YACHTING
   Bab-Lock-Hythe. L. Binyon.
      Hi-WP II:38, Mo-SD:132
   Boatmen. I Men. Hs-TC:417
   Boats. R. Bennett. Ar-TP3:88,
      Au-SP:180
   A Boatwoman. Chao Yeh. Le-MW:114
   The Bonny Keel Laddie. Gr-GB:215
   But That Was Yesterday. A. Fisher.
      Au-SP:203
   Canadian Boat Song. J. Galt.
      Ox-BN:204, Rv-CB:683, Sm-LG:140
   Carrying Their Coracles. A. Marvell.
      Gr-CT:221
   The Coracle. M. Lucan. Gr-CT:221
   The Coracle Fishers. R. Bloomfield.
      Ox-BN:57
   Crew Cut. D. McCord. Mo-SD:63
   The Excursion. Tu Fu. Mo-SD:138
   The Fishing Boat. M. Howitt. Mc-PR:152
   A Flock of Little Boats. S. Menashe.
      Sm-MK:16

BOATS AND BOATING — cont'd.
  Holidays in Childhood. C. Dyment.
    Go-BP:64
  Hospital Barge at Cérisy. W. Owen.
    Rv-CB:988
  In Old Age. B. Chamberlain. Ls-NY:179
  Jim Bludso. J. Hay. Co-RM:234,
    Er-FA:307, Fi-BG:129, Sp-OG:34
  Landscape by Ch'eng Sui. J. Kirkup.
    Go-BP:162
  Lost. C. Sandburg. Du-RG:69,
    La-PV:184, Mc-PR:108, Sh-RP:76
  Morning on the Lièvre. A. Lampman.
    Mo-SD:130
  Music. C. Baudelaire. Pa-SG:135
  My Boat Swings Out and Back. L. Binyon.
    Hi-WP II:129
  My Plan. W. Chute. Br-BC:115,
    Fe-FP:112
  Offshore. P. Booth. Mo-SD:137
  The Other Little Boats. E. Shanks.
    Hi-FO:267
  Paper Boats. R. Tagore. Bo-FP:108,
    Bo-HF:28, Fe-FP:114, Ma-FW:236,
    Pa-RE:36, Th-AS:72
  The Passage at Night--the Blaskets.
    R. Flower. Co-PI:45
  Pier. J. Scully. Ha-WR:21
  Pirate Story. R. Stevenson. Ar-TP3:114,
    Fe-FP:108, Un-GB:9, Un-GT:10
  The Prelude. W. Wordsworth. Ma-FW:121
  The Queen of Connemara. F. Fahy.
    Co-PI:38
  Rain on Castle Island. H. Kitahara.
    Ma-FW:118
  Riding in a Motor Boat. D. Baruch.
    Fe-FP:194, Hu-MP:171
  The River Boats. D. Hickey. Br-AF:172
  River Night. F. Frost. La-OC:36
  River Travel. Ts'ui Hao. Le-MW:82
  The Rowers. L. Benét. De-FS:19
  Sailboat. Your Secret. R. Francis.
    Mo-SD:140
  Sampan. Hi-WP I:1
  Sea Way! S. Briody. Ho-CT:34
  Song on the Water. T. Beddoes.
    Sm-LG:52
  The Spirit of Spring. Liu Ta-pai.
    Hs-TC:7
  The Spring Waters. Ping Hsin.
    Hs-TC:24
  To Be Sung on the Water. L. Bogan
    Ca-VT:204
  Umbara's Song. Umbara. Tr-US I:260
  Where Go the Boats? R. Stevenson.
    Ar-TP3:110, Au-SP:201, Bo-GJ:177,
    Hu-MP:173, Li-LC:74, Mc-PR:132,
    Ox-BC:294, Sm-LG:103
  Whistles. R. Field. Ar-TP3:89
  Young Argonauts. S. Wingfield. Mo-SD:138
BOBOLINKS
  Robert of Lincoln. W. Bryant. Bo-FP:276,
    Co-BBW:263, Fe-FP:287, Hu-MP:227

BOBWHITES: see QUAILS
BOCCACCIO, GIOVANNI
  Emmy. A. Symons. Ox-BN:934
BODENHEIM, MAXWELL
  Afterwards, They Shall Dance. B. Kaufman.
    Br-TC:229, Ca-VT:538, Hu-PN:409
BODY, HUMAN: see also HUMOR - BODY, HUMAN
    and names of parts of the body as
    HANDS
  The Alchemist. L. Bogan. Un-MA:491
  Body. M. Takahashi. Le-TA:86
  The Ecstasy. J. Donne. Al-VBP:250,
    Rv-CB:303
  Eyes. M. Paraschivescu. Mc-AC:109
  The Flesh and the Spirit.
    A. Bradstreet. Sh-AP:9
  Frances. J. Gill. Sc-TN:65
  Gone Away. D. Levertov. Pe-SS:57
  Homage to Aesop. C. Faerstein.
    Ls-NY:42
  The Immortal Past. A. Housman.
    Un-MB:97
  In This Strange House. C. Drewry.
    Tr-MR:281
  Longing. S. Teasdale. Sm-PT:161
  Man Carrying Bale. H. Monro.
    Un-MB:238
  Mountains, Give Me a Body. L. Blaga.
    Mc-AC:68
  On the Bright Side. A. Raymond.
    Sa-B:104
  Painting: A Head. J. Ransom.
    Un-MA:418, Wi-LT:321
  Question. May Swenson. Ca-VT:480,
    Wi-LT:829
  Seven Poems. L. Niedecker. Ca-VT:243
  A Small Thought Speaks for the Flesh.
    C. Drewry. Tr-MR:226
  Soldiers Bathing. F. Prince.
    Pà-GTB:528, Un-MB:486, Wi-LT:793
  Thanksgiving for the Body. T. Traherne.
    Pl-IO:145
  This Corruptible. E. Wylie.
    Tr-MR:257, Un-MA:282
  Tramp. R. Hughes. Un-MB:407
  X-Ray. L. Speyer. Pl-IO:146
BOER WAR, 1899-1902
  I Heard a Soldier. H. Trench.
    De-CH:160
BOLEYN, ANNE, QUEEN OF ENGLAND
  Defiled Is My Name. A. Boleyn.
    Hi-FO:116
BOLIVAR, SIMON
  Simon: How Many Bolivars?
    C. Lushington. Sa-B:194
BOLL WEEVILS
  The Ballad of the Boll Weevil.
    Hi-TL:163
BOLSHEVISM: see also LENIN, VLADIMIR
    ILICH (NIKOLAI)
  Bolsheviks. A. Stolzenberg. Ho-TY:269
BOMBS: see also SATIRE - BOMBS
  Of Bombs and Boys. R. Corbin. Pe-SS:136

Ruins. E. Pierce. Cr-WS:51
BONES: see also ANATOMY; HUMOR - BONES
Bone Thoughts on a Dry Day. G. Starbuck.
   Br-TC:407
Bone Yard. J. Barnes. Ni-CD:21
The Bones. W. Merwin. Wi-LT:767
Didn't It Rain? Bu-DY:52
The Dinosaur Bones. C. Sandburg.
   Du-SH:108, Ho-TH:56
Hie, Hie. Rv-ON:23
BONFIRES
Beach Fire. F. Frost. Ar-TP3:110,
   Pe-FB:24
The Burning of the Leaves. L. Binyon.
   Pa-GTB:434
BONNEY, WILLIAM H. (BILLY THE KID)
The Ballad of Billy the Kid. H. Knibbs.
   Fi-BG:179
Billy the Kid. Co-RM:164, Fi-BG:53
Billy the Kid. Hi-TL:144
Pizen Pete's Mistake. M. Honey.
   Fi-BG:67
BONNIE PRINCE CHARLIE: see STUART,
   CHARLES EDWARD (BONNIE PRINCE
   CHARLIE)
BONNIVARD, FRANCOIS DE
The Prisoner of Chillon. G. Byron.
   Fe-PL:22
Sonnet on Chillon. G. Byron.
   Ma-YA:173, Pa-GTB:209
BONONCINI, GIOVANNI MARIA
Epigram on Handel and Bononcini.
   J. Byrom. Pl-US:77, Rv-CB:517
BOOK WEEK: see BOOKS AND READING
BOOKS AND READING: see also HUMOR -
   BOOKS AND READING; LIBRARIES;
   SATIRE - BOOKS AND READING
Adventures. A. Kramer. Br-BC:116
And As for Me. G. Chaucer. Al-VBP:17,
   De-CH:13
At the British Museum. R. Aldington.
   Un-MB:354
A Book. H. More. Co-PS:141, Se-PR:306
A Book. L. Reese. Ha-YA:132
Books. E. Farjeon. Ha-YA:132
Books Are Keys. E. Poulsson. Br-SS:80
The British Museum Reading Room.
   L. MacNeice. Un-MB:442, Wi-LT:460
A Classical Quotation. P. Goodman.
   Ca-VT:333
Dedication on the Gift of a Book to a
   Child. H. Belloc. Gr-TG:21
Dickens in Camp. B. Harte. Se-PR:308
Emerson. M. Dodge. Se-PR:310
The Eve of Saint Mark. J. Keats.
   De-CH:447
A Fountain, a Bottle, a Donkey's Ears,
   and Some Books. R. Frost. Ca-VT:12
Go, Little Book. R. Stevenson.
   Mc-PR:87, Se-PR:306, Un-MB:59
Golden Spurs. V. Miner. Br-SS:77,
   Se-PR:304
Good from a Book. E. Browning.
   Se-PR:305

Greek Anthology, III. Un-MW:174
Hamilton. J. Schevill. Du-SH:157
He Ate and Drank the Precious Words.
   E. Dickinson. Sh-RP:101
The House Was Quiet and the World Was
   Calm. W. Stevens. Ca-VT:40
"I," Says the Poem. Ar-TP3:222
If Someone Asks You. M. Donian.
   Co-PS:142
I've Got a New Book from My Grandfather
   Hyde. L. Jackson. Br-SS:79,
   Fe-FP:45, Sh-RP:146
The Land of Story-Books. R. Stevenson.
   Ar-TP3:114, Fe-FP:12, Hu-MP:23,
   Ja-PA:50, Un-GB:30, Un-GT:12
The Land Was White. Gr-CT:10,
   Ir-BB:50, Mo-MGT:156
The Library. B. Huff. Fe-FP:250,
   Ja-PA:52
The Lion. W. Turner. Un-MB:346
Looking at Your Hands. M. Carter.
   Sa-B:134
Lovely Dames. W. Davies. Gr-SS:103
Mary Make the Butter. I. Eastwick.
   Ja-PA:53
National Library. O. de Andrade.
   An-TC:11
O for a Booke. J. Wilson. Bo-FP:24,
   Br-SS:80, Cl-DT:64, Co-PS:142,
   De-CH:138
Old Susan. W. de la Mare. Se-PR:306,
   Un-MB:198
On a Booklover's Shelves. S. Coblentz.
   Ke-TF:302
On First Looking into Chapman's Homer.
   J. Keats. Al-VBP:769, Co-RG:17,
   De-CH:361, Er-FA:75, Ga-FB:14,
   Gr-CT:442, Ke-TF:61, Ma-YA:182,
   Mc-PR:78, Ni-JP:19, No-CL:18,
   Ox-BN:334, Pa-GBT:169, Pl-ML:91,
   Rv-CB:739, Sm-LG:36
On Opening a New Book. A. Brown.
   Ha-YA:131
One. A. Young. La-IH:21
The Parliament of Fowls. G. Chaucer.
   Al-VBP:15
Shut Not Your Doors. W. Whitman.
   Pl-ML:29
The Summer Rain. H. Thoreau. Sh-AP:67
Tales of My Nursery. De-CH:571
There Is No Frigate like a Book.
   E. Dickinson. Bo-GJ:218, Br-SS:76,
   Fe-FP:13, Fe-PL:297, Gr-EC:126,
   Ha-YA:131, Hu-MP:26, Un-MA:97
To a Dead Poet, His Book. D. Berrigan.
   Pl-ML:147
To His Book. W. Walsh. No-CL:139
Troilus and Criseyde. G. Chaucer.
   Al-VBP:15
The Troubles of a Book. L. Riding.
   Ls-NY:334
The Two Boys. M. Lamb. Rv-CB:628
When Mother Reads Aloud. Fe-FP:31,
   Hu-MP:25

BOOKS AND READING — cont'd.
When Terry Reads. B. Lee. Ja-HH:42
Who Hath a Book. W. Nesbit.
  Ar-TP3:216, Br-SS:79
Why Not a Book? A. Herbert. Ke-TF:286
Winter Night. Yuan Mei. Rx-LT:115
A Winter Wish. R. Messinger.
  Al-VBP:882
BOOKWORMS: see WORMS
BOOMERANGS: see HUMOR - BOOMERANGS
BOONE, DANIEL
Cumberland Gap. Br-AF:112
Daniel Boone. A. Guiterman.
  Fe-FP:428, Hu-MP:385
Daniel Boone, 1735-1820.
  R. and S. Benét. Br-AF:63, Ho-LP:89
BOOTBLACKS
Here's Finikey Hawkes. Bo-FP:121,
  Ir-BB:37, Mo-CC:(19)
BOOTH, JOHN WILKES
Booth Killed Lincoln. Em-AF:459
BOOTH, WILLIAM
General William Booth Enters into
  Heaven. V. Lindsay. Ga-S:221,
  Un-MA:221, Wi-LT:624
BOOTS: see SHOES
BORDEN, LIZZIE ANDREW: see HUMOR -
  BORDEN, LIZZIE ANDREW
BORDER WARS: see also ENGLAND - HISTORY
  AND PATRIOTISM; SCOTLAND - HISTORY
  AND PATRIOTISM
The Battle of Bothwell Bridge.
  Ox-BB:621
Chevy Chase. Al-VBP:43, Ma-BB:97,
  Ox-BB:496
Edom o' Gordon. Ox-BB:598
A Father's Notes of Woe. W. Scott.
  Ox-BN:125
Graeme and Bewick. Ox-BB:356, Rv-CB:47
Hobie Nobel. Ox-BB:572
Jock o' the Side. Ox-BB:567
Johnnie Armstrang. Ox-BB:520
Kinmont Willie. Ox-BB:559
Northumberland Betrayd by Dowglas.
  Ox-BB:526
Parcy Reed. Ox-BB:586
BORES AND BOREDOM: see also HUMOR -
  BORES AND BOREDOM
Afternoon. M. Stearns. Ar-TP3:176
Cassandra. L. Bogan. Ca-VT:203,
  Un-MA:492
Dream Song. J. Berryman. Br-TC:38,
  Mc-EA:69, Wi-LT:571
Epistrophe. L. Jones. Ad-CI:107,
  Hu-NN:73, Hu-PN:407
The Garden. E. Pound. Br-TC:331,
  Un-MA:289
A Monk. Pien Chih-lin. Hs-TC:161
Night Game. R. Humphries. Mo-BG:28,
  Ni-JP:87
Pleasures of the Soul. Z. Landau.
  Ho-TY:99

Secret Thoughts. C. Morley. Na-EO:55
To the Reader. C. Baudelaire.
  Mo-GR:30
What a Terrible Day. B. Ovens.
  Le-WR:23
Window, 3rd Story, 5th to the Right,
  Morning. R. Drapeau. La-IH:56
BORGES, JORGE LUIS
In Some Seer's Cloud Car. C. Middleton.
  Br-TC:293
BORNEO
See Tr-US I:141-153
BORODINO, BATTLE, 1812
Mural of Borodino. L. Adler.
  Ls-NY:175
BORROWING AND LENDING: see also HUMOR -
  BORROWING AND LENDING
A Gest of Robyn Hode, the Fourth Fytte.
  Ox-BB:52
He That Goes a-Borrowing. B. Franklin.
  Un-GT:26
Widdecomb Fair. Co-PM:213, De-CH:72
BOSTON, ENG.: see SATIRE - BOSTON, ENG.
BOSTON, MASS.: see also HUMOR - BOSTON,
  MASS.; SATIRE - BOSTON, MASS.
Boston. J. Bossidy. Br-AF:198
Christmas Eve under Hooker's Statue.
  R. Lowell. Ba-PO:202, Hi-TL:214
Death from Cancer. R. Lowell.
  Br-TC:265, Ha-PO:125
The Fall of J. W. Beane. O. Herford.
  Co-PT:21
For the Union Dead. R. Lowell.
  Br-TC:265, Pe-OA:244, Wi-LT:583
A Foreigner Comes to Earth on Boston
  Common. H. Gregory. Pl-EI:111
In the Boston Public Garden.
  S. Gottlieb. Ke-TF:354
The New Order. P. McGinley. Br-AF:199
Night in Boston. J. Harrison.
  Sc-TN:86
A Revivalist in Boston. A. Rich.
  Pl-EI:107
Sunday Evening in the Common.
  J. Wheelock. No-CL:257, Un-MA:342
Unhappy Boston. P. Revere. Kr-OF:131
Where the Rainbow Ends. R. Lowell.
  Sh-AP:230, Un-MA:665
BOSTON TEA PARTY, 1773
A Ballad of the Boston Tea-Party.
  O. Holmes. Hi-TL:42, Vi-PP:90
BOSWORTH FIELD, BATTLE, 1485
Richard III. W. Shakespeare. Hi-FO:102
BOTANY: see HUMOR - BOTANY
BOTHWELL BRIDGE, BATTLE, 1679
The Battle of Bothwell Bridge.
  Ox-BB:621
BOTTLES: see also HUMOR - BOTTLES
Around the Rick. Mo-MGT:155
Poem to Be Cast into the Sea in a
  Bottle. J. Kirkup. Go-BP:217
The Song of the Bottle. Tr-US I:117

The Vial. D. Galler. Ls-NY:266
BOUGAINVILLAEA
On a Bougainvillea Vine at the Summer
Palace. B. Howes. Un-MA:653
BOUILLABAISSE
The Ballad of Bouillabaisse.
W. Thackeray. Al-VBP:879
BOUNCING BETS
The Faithless Flowers. M. Widdemer.
Hu-MP:258, Th-AS:84
BOWIE, JAMES
The Defence of the Alamo. J. Miller.
Pa-OM:173
BOWLES, WILLIAM LISLE
William Lisle Bowles. G. Byron.
Ox-BN:239
BOWLING
english. D. Lourie. Sc-TN:152
BOWS AND ARROWS: see also SATIRE –
BOWS AND ARROWS
Adam Bell, Clym of the Clough, and
William of Cloudesley. Ma-BB:157,
Ox-BB:380
The Archer. C. Scollard. Fe-FP:109
Arrow Song. Da-SC:157
Chevy Chase. Al-VBP:43, Ma-BB:97,
Ox-BB:496
A Flight Shot. M. Thompson. Co-RM:72
A Gest of Robyn Hode, the Fifth Fytte.
Ox-BB:464
He Constantly Bends It. Le-IB:49
I Have No Wings, but Yet I Fly.
M. Austin. Ar-TP3:99
I Took a Bow and Arrow. J. Ciardi.
Na-EO:116
In Praise of Bow and Arrow. Tr-CB:23,
Tr-US I:54
A Lytell Geste of Robyn Hode. Ma-YA:43
My Bow, Its Lower Part I Draw Back.
Le-OE:59
Prayer to the Moon. Le-OE:63
Robin Hood and Guy of Gisborne.
Ma-BB:54
Robin Hood and the Curtal Friar.
Ma-BB:48
Robyn and Gandeleyn. Ox-BB:374
Song on Cutting a Bow. Tr-US II:180
The Zen Archer. J. Kirkup. Pl-EI:22
BOXES
Boxes and Bags. C. Sandburg.
Sh-RP:159
If I Had a Cardboard Box. A. Fisher.
Mc-AW:7
BOXING: see also names of boxers, as
PARET, BERNARDO (KID)
The Ballad of Billy Rose. L. Norris.
Ca-MB:83
Boxer. A. Katz. Ho-TY:294
Boxers. J. Clancy. Co-RM:185, Mo-SD:72
The Boxer's Face. Lucilius. Mo-SD:79
The Boxing Match. Virgil. Fl-HH:7,
Mo-SD:78

The Fancy. W. Benét. Mo-SD:74
First Fight. V. Scannell. Co-RM:188,
Sm-MK:89
Gallantly Within the Ring. J. Reynolds.
Mo-SD:71
The Loser. C. Bukowski. Pe-M:64
Mastering the Craft. V. Scannell.
Co-RM:186
The Memory of Boxer Benny (Kid) Paret.
F. Lima. Hu-PN:587
My Lord, What a Morning. W. Cuney.
Ab-MO:90, Lo-TY:236
The Nonpareil's Grave. M. McMahon.
Mo-SD:76
On Hurricane Jackson. A. Dugan.
Mo-BG:48, Mo-SD:80, Pe-M:63
Peerless Jim Driscoll. V. Scannell.
Co-RM:231
The World's Worst Boxer. Lucilius.
Mo-SD:81
BOY SCOUTS
Rules for the Road. E. Markham.
Se-PR:313, Sh-RP:102
BOYS: see also BROTHERS; CHIMNEY SWEEPS;
HUMOR – BOYS; NEWSBOYS; SONS; YOUTH
Albert. D. Abse. Sm-MK:109
April's Amazing Meaning. G. Dillon.
Co-BL:17
Arms and the Boy. W. Owen. Er-FA:192,
Ni-JP:78, Un-MB:367, Wi-LT:349
At the Bottom of the Well.
L. Untermeyer. Bo-GJ:218
At the Railway Station, Upway. T. Hardy.
Ma-FW:71
August from My Desk. R. Flint.
Br-AF:156, Du-RG:49
The Aura. J. Dickey. Du-SH:55
A Barefoot Boy. J. Riley.
Er-FA:137
The Barefoot Boy. J. Whittier.
Ch-B:65, Fe-FP:544, Fe-PL:249
Bea's Bee. M. Ray. Ho-GC:16
The Big Boy. Mo-MGT:76
Bill. J. Salzburg. Br-BC:50
Billy, Billy. Wr-RM:89
Birches. R. Frost. Fe-PL:437,
Ga-FB:299, Mo-BG:114, Pe-OA:33,
Sm-LG:61, Sp-OG:357, Un-MA:177,
Wi-LT:166
The Birthday Cake. V. Chase. Br-BC:86
The Birthday-Cake Glockenspiel.
E. Henley. Br-BC:90
Birthday Gift. E. de Vito. Br-BC:153
Black Is Beautiful. A. Burns. Ba-HI:18
Blanket Street. I. Hogan. Br-BC:56
The Bold Unbiddable Child. W. Letts.
Co-PI:94
The Boy. E. Field. Gr-EC:199
A Boy. B. Graves. Le-M:142
A Boy. T. Miyoshi. Sh-AM:80
The Boy. R. Rilke. Sm-MK:165
A Boy and a Pup. A. Guiterman. Hu-MP:40

BOYS — cont'd.
Boy and Girl. Mo-NR:32, Wr-RM:118
Boy at the Window. R. Wilbur.
Ho-TH:65, Pe-SS:27
The Boy Fishing. E. Scovell.
Cl-FC:77, Sm-MK:183
Da Boy from Rome. T. Daly. Fe-FP:304,
Hu-MP:158
Boy in a Pond. J. Whaler. Rd-OA:47
Boy into Heron. C. Randall. Sm-MK:186
Boy, Walking and Whistling. A. Armour.
Ke-TF:82
The Boy with the Little Bare Toes.
F. Harvey. St-FS:118
The Boys and the Apple-Tree. A. O'Keeffe.
De-TT:120
Boy's Day. R. Henderson. Br-BC:151
Boys Don't Cry. L. Martinez. La-IH:80
A Boy's Need. H. Johnson. Hu-PN:283
A Boy's Song. J. Hogg. Bl-OB:138,
Bo-FP:258, Ch-B:62, De-CH:132,
De-TT:75, Fe-FP:301, Ho-WR:69,
Ke-TF:45, Mc-PR:114, Mc-WK:84,
Ox-BC:156
A Boy's Summer Song. P. Dunbar.
Br-SS:171, Sh-RP:17
Boys Will Be Princes. W. Heyen.
Ls-NY:92
Boys with Frogs. S. Kahn. Du-RG:30
The Brothers: Two Saltimbanques.
J. Logan. Du-SH:46
The Cave. G. Dresbach. Le-RM:35,
Pa-SS:42
The Centaur. M. Swenson. Br-TC:425,
Du-SH:44, Li-TU:107, Mo-BG:72
Child on Top of a Greenhouse.
T. Roethke. Ca-VT:286, Co-EL:137,
Du-RG:54, Gr-BT:12, Ha-LO:101,
Hi-WP I:110
A Child's Christmas Song. T. Daly.
Br-BC:173
Circus Hand. P. Dehn. Sm-MK:164
Crossing a Creek. H. Johnson.
Hu-PN:284
Dance Songs, III. Tr-US II:163
Darius Green and His Flying Machine.
J. Trowbridge. Fe-PL:204, Ox-BC:260
Dark Danny. I. Eastwick. Ar-TP3:14,
Fe-FP:397
Dirty Jack. De-TT:24
Dog with Schoolboys. J. Follain.
Co-PM:64
The Dunce. J. Prevert. Ma-FW:72
Eleven. A. MacLeish. Ni-JP:26
Envy. Y. Yevtushenko.. Ma-FW:139
The False Knight on the Road.
De-CH:316, Gr-GB:288, Ma-BB:84,
Rv-CB:52
Farm Child. R. Thomas. Co-BN:206,
Co-PM:118, Hi-WP II:134, Ma-FW:77
A Feller I Know. M. Austin. Br-AF:38,
Fe-FP:306

Fern Hill. D. Thomas. Al-VBP:1246,
Bo-GJ:53, Br-TC:440, Co-RG:160,
Fe-PL:251, Ga-FB:166, Hi-WP II:46,
Mc-EA:42, Mc-WK:10, Na-EO:45,
Pa-GBT:542, Pe-SS:162, Re-TW:100,
Sm-LG:108, Un-MB:502, Wi-LT:559
Fifteen Boys. B. Akhmadulina.
Bo-RU:5, Ca-MR:39, Gr-BT:65
The Fisherman. D. McCord. La-PV:8
Fräulein Reads Instructive Rhymes.
M. Kumin. Li-SR:29
The Fruit Plucker. S. Coleridge.
De-CH:320, De-TT:150, Ox-BN:175,
Sm-LG:110
Fun with Fishing. E. Tietjens.
Fe-FP:484
Girl, Boy, Flower, Bicycle. M. Joseph.
Pe-M:149
Girls Can, Too. L. Hopkins. Ho-GC:26
Going into Breeches. C. and M. Lamb.
Ox-BC:145
Growing. F. Frost. Br-BC:72
Hal's Birthday. L. Larcom. Br-BC:51
Hard but Soft. W. Barbour. La-IH:29
The Horse Chestnut Tree. R. Eberhart.
Pe-OA:194, Un-MA:578, Wi-LT:437
I Am a Nice Nice Boy. M. O'Connor.
Le-M:154
I Knew a Boy Who Ran with the Dogs.
N. Willard. Sc-TN:230
I Wonder in What Fields Today.
Kaga no Chiyo. Le-MW:99
Improvisation of the Dead Boy.
M. de Andrade. An-TC:21
The Inky Boys. H. Hoffman. De-TT:21
Jake Hates All the Girls. E. Cummings.
Du-SH:65
Jenny White and Johnny Black.
E. Farjeon. Fe-FP:303
Jeremy's Secrets. B. Todd. Br-BC:61
Jest 'fore Christmas. E. Field.
Er-FA:513, Fe-FP:538, Fe-PL:201,
Ga-FB:176, Hu-MP:359
Jim. H. Belloc. Ox-BC:312
Kansas Boy. R. Lechlitner.
Br-AF:150, Du-RG:50
The Leak in the Dike. P. Cary.
Er-FA:348, Fe-FP:554
The Little Boy. Mo-MGT:10
Little Boy Lost. W. Blake. Rv-CB:581
Little Brother. A. Fisher. Br-BC:48,
Mc-AW:91
Little Jack Horner. De-TT:49, Li-LB:42
The Lonesome Boy. V. White. La-IH:24
Look, Edwin! E. Millay. Bo-FP:116,
Bo-GJ:115
The Main Truck; or a Leap for Life.
G. Morris. Fe-PL:55
Me. M. Goode. Ba-HI:14
Midnight on the Great Western. T. Hardy.
De-CH:24
Morning. D. Gallagher. Br-SS:20

Morning Light.   E.Newsome.   Ad-PB:21,
   Bo-AN:19, Hu-PN:70
My Sailor of Seven.   G. Brenan.
   Br-BC:73
My Turn.   M. Ray.   Ho-GC:10
Nature at Three.   B. Breeser. Br-BC:46
New Blast Furnace.   B. Akhmadulina.
   Ca-MR:37
Nursery Rhyme of Innocence and
   Experience.   C. Causley. Bo-GJ:170,
   Hi-WP I:82
Nutting.   W. Wordsworth.   Rv-CB:637
The October Redbreast.   A. Meynell.
   Un-MB:64
Ode on a Distant Prospect of Clapham
   Academy.   T. Hood.   Rv-CB:763
Ode on a Distant Prospect of Eton
   College.   T. Gray.   Al-VBP:563,
   Pa-GTB:158
Of Kings and Things.   L. Morrison.
   Ad-CI:67
Of the Boy and the Butterfly.
   J. Bunyan.   Ox-BC:35
On a Little Boy Endeavouring to Catch
   a Snake.   T. Foxton.   Ox-BC:56
On His Very First Hunt.   Le-IB:51
Out, Out--.   R. Frost.   Ca-VT:11,
   Gr-BT:18, Pe-M:100
A Party.   L. Richards.   Au-SP:119,
   Br-BC:93, Br-SS:49
Petting Song (Modern).   Da-SC:42
Poem.   H. Johnson.   Ad-PB:93, Bo-AN:100
Portrait of the Boy as an Artist.
   B. Howes.   Un-MA:653
Railroad Reverie.   E. Young. Gr-EC:241
The School Boy Reads His Iliad.
   D. Morton.   Cr-WS:135
The Schoolboy, the Pedant, and the Man
   with a Garden.   J. de la Fontaine.
   Un-R:82
Schoolboys in Winter.   J. Clare.
   Fr-WO:82, Rv-CB:732
The Sea Boy.   W. de la Mare. Cr-SS:32
Seven Times One Are Seven. R. Hillyer.
   Br-BC:156
Sick Boy.   A. Ridler.   Ls-NY:225
Six and Thirty.   D. Stevenson.
   Br-BC:65
Small Colored Boy in the Subway.
   B. Deutsch.   Hu-PN:513
A Snowy Day in School.   D. Lawrence.
   Ma-FW:75
Somebody's Mother.   M. Brine. Er-FA:139
Son.   J. Emmanuel.   Bo-HF:24, Hu-PN:376
The Song of Kuk-Ook, the Bad Boy.
   Da-SC:47
The Song of Senia and Monia.
   Tr-US II:25
Stalky Jack.   W. Rands.   Ir-BB:102
The Story of Augustus.   H. Hoffmann.
   Ox-BC:205

The Story of Fidgety Philip.
   H. Hoffmann.   Ox-BC:208
The Sweet o' the Year.   G. Meredith.
   Co-BN:23
Ten Little Indian Boys.   M. Hutchinson.
   Au-SP:153, Ir-BB:110
That Is Tad.   M. Korte.   Sc-TN:118
There Was a Naughty Boy.   J. Keats.
   Bo-FP:113, Ch-B:77, Co-HP:84,
   Fr-WO:69, Gr-EC:215, Ir-BB:97,
   Ma-YA:183, Ox-BC:148, Pl-ML:18,
   Sm-LG:291, Sm-MK:131, Un-GF:18
Those Boys That Ran Together.
   L. Clifton.   Ad-PB:307
Timothy Dan.   J. Sheridan. St-FS:47
Timothy Winters.   C. Causley.
   Sm-MK:123, To-MP:73
To a Child Trapped in a Barber Shop.
   P. Levine.   Ca-VT:633
To Christ Our Lord.   G. Kinnell.
   Br-TC:239, Ha-WR:92, La-RM:120,
   Pe-M:112
To Dick, on His Sixth Birthday.
   S. Teasdale.   Br-BC:59
Tom at Dinner.   A. O'Keeffe. De-TT:101
Treasure.   E. Long.   Br-BC:65
The Two Boys.   M. Lamb.   Rv-CB:628
Two Indian Boys.   J. Concha. Ba-HI:98
Upon Boys Diverting Themselves in the
   River.   T. Foxton.   Ox-BC:55
Upon Pagget.   R. Herrick.   Sm-LG:111
What Are Little Boys Made Of.   Mother
   Goose.   De-PO:14, Er-FA:205,
   Ir-BB:92, Mo-CC:(13), Mo-MGT:59,
   Mo-NR:111, Wi-MG:31, Wr-RM:108
What's a Student.   A. Round.   Ke-TF:82
When a Fellow's Four.   M. Carr.
   Br-BC:49
When I Was a Little Boy.   Mother Goose.
   Tu-WW:15
Whistling Boy.   J. Quinn.   Br-BC:77
Whistling Boy.   N. Waterman. Fe-PL:301
Wonders of Nature.   Gr-TG:18
The Workhouse Boy.   Gr-GB:265
A World to Do.   T. Weiss.   Gr-SS:136
A Young David: Birmingham.   H. Brooks.
   Hu-PN:276
BOZZARIS, MARCO
   Marco Bozzaris.   F. Halleck. Hi-FO:208
BRADDOCK, EDWARD
   Braddock's Fate, with an Incitement to
      Revenge.   S. Tilden.   Hi-TL:33
BRADSTREET, ANNE
   Homage to Mistress Bradstreet.
      J. Berryman.   Sh-AP:225
BRAGGING: see BOASTING
BRAHMA
   Brahma.   R. Emerson.   Al-VBP:807,
      Mo-BG:52, Pl-EI:23, Rv-CB:776,
      Sh-AP:34

BRAHMINS AND BRAHMINISM: see also HINDUISM
  Dhammapada. Buddha. Ba-PO:19
  Mohini Chatterjee. W. Yeats. Tr-MR:278
BRAHMS, JOHANNES: see HUMOR - BRAHMS,
  JOHANNES
BRAIN: see also HUMOR - BRAIN; MIND
  My Brain. A. Laurance. Le-M:164
  A Small Thought Speaks for the Flesh.
    C. Drewry. Tr-MB:226
BRANCUSI, CONSTANTIN
  First Lesson. N. Willard. Sc-TN:234
BRATHWAITE, EDWARD
  The Children. T. McNeill. Sa-B:211
  Spring Poem: Brown's Town. T. McNeill.
    Sa-B:209
BRAVERY: see COURAGE; HEROES AND HEROISM
BRAWNE, FANNY
  To Fanny. J. Keats. No-CL:155,
    Un-MW:81
BRAZIL: see also PORTUGUESE VERSE
  Brazilian Happenings. R. O'Connell.
    Du-SH:97
  The Death and Life of a Severino.
    J. de Melo Neto. An-TC:127
  Good Saint Benedict. Ab-MO:58
  He Meets Two Men Carrying a Corpse in a
    Hammock. J. de Melo Neto. An-TC:131
  A Private Letter to Brazil. G. Oden.
    Bo-AN:158, Hu-NN:91, Hu-PN:383
  Sea Horse. Ab-MO:60
  Song of Exile. A. Dias. Lo-TY:78
BRAZIL - COUNTRYSIDE
  Map. M. Reis. An-TC:167
BREAD: see also HUMOR - BREAD
  Baking Day. R. Joseph. To-MP:142
  Blow, Wind, Blow. Ar-TP3:163, Au-SP:11,
    Bo-FP:77, De-PO:26, Mo-MGT:88
  Hot Cross Buns! Mother Goose.
    Au-SP:11, Bo-FP:244, De-PO:10,
    Mo-MGT:109, Mo-NR:120, Mo-TL:75,
    On-TW:10, Wi-MG:39, Wr-RM:127
  I Eat a Slice of Bread. P. Mayer.
    St-H:132
  The Johnnycake. Hu-MP:19
  A Man's Bread. J. Peabody. Ha-YA:107
  A Song of Bread and Honey.
    R. Le Gallienne. Bo-FP:62
  Thank You Note. Ke-TF:127
  To Market, to Market. De-PO:8
BREAKFAST: see also HUMOR - BREAKFAST;
    SATIRE - BREAKFAST
  At Breakfast. M. Swenson. Pe-SS:62
  A Bowl of October. H. Bevington.
    Sh-RP:129
  Breakfast Time. J. Stephens. Gr-EC:66
  The Child and the Snake. M. Lamb.
    De-TT:63, Ox-BC:142
  The King's Breakfast. A. Milne.
    Ox-BC:341
  A Little Bird. A. Fisher. Au-SP:101
  Little Gustava. C. Thaxter. Fe-FP:535
  My Turn. M. Ray. Ho-GC:10

  Pancakes. G. Jacoby. La-GI:47
  Winter. C. Rossetti. Bo-FP:167,
    Ch-B:54, Rv-CB:891, St-FS:38
BREATHING: see also HUMOR - BREATHING
  The Breathing. D. Levertov. La-RM:135
  The Song of Breath. S. Benet.
    Sh-AP:194
BREEZES: see WINDS
BREUGHEL, PIETER: see BRUEGHEL, PIETER
BREVITY OF LIFE: see LIFE - BREVITY
BRIBERY: see CORRUPTION
BRIDES AND BRIDEGROOMS: see also HUMOR -
    BRIDES AND BRIDEGROOMS
  As the Sun Rose over the Mountain.
    Wy-CM:33
  At the Altar Rail. T. Hardy. Un-MB:30
  Ballade for a Bridegroom. F. Villon.
    Un-MW:131
  Beat the Drum! Wy-CM:34
  Bridal Song. J. Fletcher. Al-VBP:285,
    Rv-CB:314
  The Bride. J. Suckling. Un-MW:18
  Bride's Song. Tr-US I:166
  Bride's Song on the Way to Her Husband's
    House. Tr-US II:139
  By What Name Is Thy Bride Known?
    Ho-SD:21
  Courtship and Wedding Songs. Tr-US I:99
  Epithalamion. E. Spenser. Al-VBP:104
  The Farmer's Bride. C. Mew. Un-MB:161
  In the Room of the Bride-Elect.
    T. Hardy. Ga-BT:84
  Light for a Bride. De-PP:58
  Love and a Question. R. Frost.
    Ca-MB:16
  Mammon Marriage. G. MacDonald.
    Rv-CB:878
  Marriage Poems, I. Tr-US II:162
  Marriage Poems, II. Tr-US II:162
  A Nuptial Eve. S. Dobell. Ox-BN:660
  Song of the Bridegroom in Praise of
    His Bride. Tr-US I:70
  Songs, III. Tr-US II:171
  A Wedding. Bo-FP:294, Ch-B:114,
    De-CH:34
  Wedding Morn. D. Lawrence. Un-MB:290
  A Young Bride. Sappho. Pa-SG:50
BRIDGE (GAME):   see HUMOR - BRIDGE (GAME)
BRIDGES, ROBERT
  To R. B. G. Hopkins. Pa-GTB:398,
    Pl-ML:50, Rv-CB:943
BRIDGES: see also names of bridges, as
    BROOKLYN BRIDGE
  The Bridge. S. Murano. Sh-AM:94
  Bridges. R. Bacmeister. Au-SP:160,
    Mc-AW:27
  The Bridges. J. Rimbaud. Ma-FW:265
  Covered Bridge. R. Coffin. Br-AF:125
  Horatius. T. Macaulay. Er-FA:387,
    Fe-PL:64, Hi-FO:32, Sm-LG:161
  If You Chance to Be Crossing. Wy-CM:17

The Old Bridge.　H. Conkling.
　Hu-MP:172, Th-AS:95
The Old Bridge at Florence.
　H. Longfellow.　Pa-HT:111
On the Bridge.　K. Greenaway.　Hu-MP:66
Potomac Town in February.　C. Sandburg.
　Li-LC:67, Mc-WK:104, Na-EO:117
Seagulls.　P. Hubbell.　La-PV:136
The Tay River Bridge Disaster.
　W. McGonagall.　Na-EO:78
Trip: San Francisco.　L. Hughes.
　Br-AF:209
BRINLEY, JOHN
Jno Brinlyes Body Here Doth Ly.
　De-CH:653
BRITISH COMMONWEALTH OF NATIONS:　see
　names of dominions, as CANADA
BRITISH ISLES:　see ENGLAND; IRELAND;
　SCOTLAND; WALES
BRITISH MUSEUM
At the British Museum.　R. Aldington.
　Un-MB:354
The British Museum Reading Room.
　L. MacNeice.　Un-MB:442, Wi-LT:460
Homage to the British Museum.
　W. Empson.　Un-MB:435, Wi-LT:444
BRITTANY, FR.
The Calvaries.　P. Williamson.
　Ls-NY:108
In Brittany.　N. Willard.　Sc-TN:228
BRONCOS:　see HORSES
BRONTË, ANNE
On the Death of Anne Brontë.
　C. Brontë.　Al-VBP:916
BRONTË, EMILY
Emily Brontë.　C. Lewis.　Pa-GTB:497
BROOKLYN, N.Y.:　see also DIALECTS,
　BROOKLYN
Brooklyn Heights.　J. Wain.　Wi-LT:834
The Brooklyn Theater Fire.　Em-AF:467
Geography: A Song.　H. Moss.　Ad-CI:26
Number 7.　L. Ferlinghetti.　Ad-CI:18,
　Du-RG:102, Kh-VA:74, La-OC:85,
　Pe-SS:156
BROOKLYN BRIDGE
Brooklyn Bridge.　V. Mayakovsky.
　Li-TU:254
Brooklyn Bridge at Dawn.
　R. LeGallienne.　Ar-TP3:173
To Brooklyn Bridge.　H. Crane.
　Hi-TL:167, Pa-HT:33, Sh-AP:197,
　Sm-PT:9, Un-MA:518, Wi-LT:383
Walking Across Brooklyn Bridge.
　J. Marshall.　Mc-EA:78
BROOKS
All That's Past.　W. de la Mare.
　Al-VBP:1119, Bo-GJ:202, Re-TW:85
As to the Restless Brook.　J. Bangs.
　Co-OW:53
The Brook.　L. Alaverdoshvili.
　Mo-MI:26

The Brook.　A. Tennyson.　Bl-OB:134,
　Bo-FP:72, Bo-GJ:42, Cl-DT:60,
　Cl-FC:51, Co-BN:64, De-TT:145,
　Er-FA:259, Fe-FP:272, Ga-FB:227,
　Hu-MP:293, Mc-PR:99, Sp-OG:282
The Brook in February.　C. Roberts.
　Co-BN:68, Do-WH:71
The Brook of the Heart.　E. Dickinson.
　Co-BL:28, Gr-FB:67
The Brook-Song.　J. Riley.　Sp-OG:281
Divided.　J. Ingelow.　Li-SR:35
The Hurrying Brook.　E. Blunden.
　Co-BN:66
Hyla Brook.　R. Frost.　Co-BN:66
I'm Like You.　Re-RR:120
March 8, 1849.　H. Thoreau.　Ka-RM:158
A Mountain Spring.　Ch'u Ch'uang I.
　Rx-LT:51
The Resolve.　D. Levertov.　Ha-WR:10,
　La-RM:56
Song.　J. Jimenez.　Le-SW:57
West-Running Brook.　R. Frost.
　Sh-AP:151, Sm-PT:138, Un-MA:182
BROOKS, GWENDOLYN
On Getting a Natural.　D. Randall.
　Ad-PB:141
When I Heard Dat White Man Say.
　Z. Gilbert.　Ad-PB:195
BROOKS, VAN WYCK
Sunday Evening in the Common.
　J. Wheelock.　No-CL:257, Un-MA:342
BROOM (SHRUB)
Broom, Green Broom.　Bl-OB:38,
　De-CH:139, Fo-OG:8, Ha-PO:54
BROOMS
The Fate of a Broom--an Anticipation.
　T. Peacock.　Rv-CB:685
Who Liveth So Merry.　De-CH:573
BROTHERHOOD:　see also HUMOR -
　BROTHERHOOD; RACE RELATIONS;
　SATIRE - BROTHERHOOD
Abou Ben Adhem.　L. Hunt.　Er-FA:6,
　Fe-FP:565, Ga-FB:127, Gr-EC:142,
　Ma-YA:172, Mc-PR:187, Sp-OG:321,
　Un-GT:315
All of Us a Family.　C. Meyer.　Jo-VC:18
All One People.　C. Sandburg.　Br-AF:33
Any Human to Another.　C. Cullen.
　Tr-MR:160
At a Calvary near the Ancre.　W. Owen.
　Tr-MR:187
Babi Yar.　Y. Yevtushenko.　Ca-MR:54
Ballad of East and West.　R. Kipling.
　Ar-TP3:25, Ga-FB:211
Beethoven's Ninth Symphony in Wartime.
　E. Pierce.　Cr-WS:59
The Black Cottage.　R. Frost.　Ca-VT:5
The Body Politic.　D. Hall.　Br-TC:167,
　Pe-OA:272, Pe-SS:104
Borders.　S. Mosova.　Mo-MI:74
Brotherhood.　E. Markham.　Se-PR:185

BROTHERHOOD — cont'd.
The Cable Hymn. J. Whittier. Hi-TL:131
Carol of the Brown King. L. Hughes.
    La-PH:31, Li-LC:86
Children's Crusade, 1939. B. Brecht.
    Ca-MB:106
Christmas 1945. A. Hine. Hi-TL:219
The City. E. Jarrett. Sc-TN:111
Coexistence. M. Syrkin. Ls-NY:97
Conscientious Objector. E. Millay.
    Ba-PO:4, Cr-WS:137
A Consecration. J. Masefield.
    Un-MB:221
The Contemplative. Sister M. Thérése.
    Tr-MR:210
The Copperfaces. C. Sandburg.
    Sh-RP:269
Credo. E. Debs. Kr-OF:117
A Creed. E. Markham. Er-FA:94,
    Mc-PR:68, Se-PR:185
Cruciform. W. Welles. Ho-LP:92,
    Sm-PT:137
Daybreak in Alabama. L. Hughes.
    Br-AF:47
The Drayman. W. Whitman. Hu-PN:469
Elegiac Statement for Two Human Beings
    Named Rosenberg. L. Hedley.
    Kr-OF:124
Face. F. Kitagawa. Sh-AM:84
The Fatherland. J. Lowell. Se-PR:189
Fear No More. W. Shakespeare.
    Al-VBP:195, Bo-HF:179, Co-RG:144,
    De-CH:250, De-TT:193, Er-FA:260,
    Gr-CT:332, Ha-PO:251, Hi-WP II:19,
    No-CL:73, Pa-GTB:28, Rv-CB:201,
    Sm-LG:267
Fellow-Creatures. R. Pitter. Ls-NY:106
Five Vignettes, 5. J. Toomer. Ad-PB:35
For Denis Who Was a Drum. M. Maxwell.
    Sa-B:172
For Whom the Bell Tolls. J. Donne.
    Fe-PL:300
Four Winds Blow the Wide World O'er.
    On-TW:19
From Far. A. Housman. Go-BP:186,
    Ho-LP:103, Un-MB:102
From the Walum Olum. Br-MW:100
Ghosts. Fire. Water. J. Kirkup.
    Go-BP:215
Gloucester Moors. W. Moody,
    Pa-HT:19, Sp-OG:362
The Gum-Gatherer. R. Frost. Mo-BG:60
Hands. G. Thompson. Jo-SA:9, Jo-VC:15
Hate. J. Stephens. Un-MB:265
Here Is Thy Footstool. R. Tagore.
    Go-BP:288
High Tide. D. Palmer. Sc-TN:179
The Hill Farmer Speaks. R. Thomas.
    To-MP:62
The House by the Side of the Road.
    S. Foss. Er-FA:18

Hymn to Intellectual Beauty.
    P. Shelley. Ox-BN:276
I Dream a World. L. Hughes. Bo-AN:71,
    Bo-HF:29
I Know Neither English Nor French.
    A. Stolzenberg. Ho-TY:269
I Mix in Life. S. Coleridge. Rv-CB:659
I Stood upon a High Place. S. Crane.
    Sh-AP:143
I Want You to Read. E. Schwager.
    Ad-II:15
Identity. D. Botez. Mc-AC:61
If Everybody Was Black. J. Holland.
    Jo-VC:50
If War Should Come. B. Musser.
    Ba-PO:168
In a Bar near Shibuya Station, Tokyo.
    P. Engle. Ad-CI:84, Br-AF:88
In a Field. D. Palmer. Sc-TN:177
In a Grave-Yard. W. Braithwaite.
    Ad-PB:13
In Distrust of Merits. M. Moore.
    Al-VBP:1176, Pl-EI:146, Se-PR:207,
    Sm-PT:126, Un-MA:354, Wi-LT:272
In the Immense Cathedral. J. Wheelock.
    Tr-MR:38
In the Mourning Time. R. Hayden.
    Ra-BP:138
Incense. V. Lindsay. Tr-MR:196
The Indian Woman. W. Whitman.
    Bo-FP:21
Innumerable Friend. M. Sarton.
    Mc-WK:186
International Hymn. G. Huntington.
    Fe-PL:161
Interracial. G. Johnson. Hu-PN:78,
    Lo-TY:210
Is There No Thread to Bind Us?
    M. Peake. Gr-BT:102
Jew. J. Randall. Ra-BP:278
Jhesu, for Thy Wondes Fyff. Ba-PO:6
The Last Riot. V. Howard. Jo-VC:8
Lenox Avenue. S. Alexander. Hu-PN:556
Let Us Move Evenly Together. Wo-HS:(32)
Liberty for All. W. Garrison. Kr-OF:30
The Little Black Boy. W. Blake.
    De-CH:20, Hu-PN:445, Ox-BC:85,
    Ox-BN:21, Rv-CB:590, Sm-LG:106
Locksley Hall. A. Tennyson. Er-FA:56
Loneliness. I Men. Hs-TC:415
The Long Shadow of Lincoln. C. Sandburg.
    Ha-TP:141
The Long War. L. Lee. Go-BP:216,
    Gr-BT:100
The Lost Black Man. L. Baez. Jo-VC:28
The Lost Tribe. R. Pitter. Ho-LP:80
Love the Samaritan. W. Langland.
    Ga-S:205
Malachi. E. Marlatt. Tr-MR:80
The Man He Killed. T. Hardy.
    Ba-PO:131, Co-RM:218, Cr-WS:107,
    Er-FA:182, Un-MB:26, Wi-LT:18

A Man's a Man for A' That. R. Burns.
    Al-VBP:653, Bo-HF:142, Er-FA:268,
    Sp-OG:330
Most Men Know Love but as a Part of
    Life. H. Timrod. Sh-AP:125
Moving in a Caravan (1). R. Bly.
    Mc-EA:46
My Father Moved Through Dooms of Love.
    e. cummings. En-PC:22, Sh-AP:193
My People. L. Hughes. Jo-SA:18
My People. D. Palmer. Sc-TN:175
Near and Far. K. Goddard. Fr-MP:12
A Net to Snare the Moonlight.
    V. Lindsay. Fe-PL:420
Nice Day for a Lynching. K. Patchen.
    Hu-PN:555, Kr-OF:160
Not in Vain. E. Dickinson. Bo-HF:140,
    Fe-PL:297
Oh World. L. Blair. Ja-PA:33
Ode: Salute to the French Negro Poets.
    F. O'Hara. Hu-PN:581
On a Certain Engagement South of Seoul.
    H. Carruth. Br-AF:89
On Another's Sorrow. W. Blake.
    Al-VBP:614, Ga-FB:100, Rv-CB:591
Our Family. L. Clark. Pa-RE:44
Out Fishin'. E. Guest. Fe-PL:419
Outwitted. E. Markham. Co-EL:110,
    Co-PM:25, Un-MA:106
Ovid's Island. C. Theodorescu.
    Mc-AC:101
Peace Universal. A. Thorne. Se-PR:186
The Pebble. E. Wylie. Tr-MR:156,
    Un-MA:281
Pioneers! O Pioneers! W. Whitman.
    Hu-MP:381
Poem at Thirty. A. Sanchez. Ad-PB:286,
    Ra-BP:231
A Poem for a Poet. D. Lee. Ad-PB:425
Poem for Flora. N. Giovanni. Ne-AM:34
Poem to Negro and White. M. Bodenheim.
    Hu-PN:511
Poems of Shape and Motion. M. Carter.
    Sa-B:136
Porgy, Maria, and Bess. D. Heyward.
    Hu-PN:499
Prayer. Chou Meng-tich. Pa-MV:71
Preliminary Draft of a World Constitution.
    Ba-PO:115
The Prisoner of Chillon. G. Byron.
    Fe-PL:22
Prophecy. Bi-IT:140, Br-MW:104
Quiet Night. Wen I-to. Hs-TC:63
the real people loves one another.
    R. Penny. Ad-PB:388
Recitative - A Lakeshore Poem.
    M. Kaneko. Sh-AM:64
Reconciliation. W. Whitman. Ba-PO:123
Refugee in America. L. Hughes.
    Bo-HF:44, Br-AF:249, Mc-WK:185,
    Ra-BP:87

The Rime of the Ancient Mariner.
    S. Coleridge. Al-VBP:679, Co-RG:60,
    Co-SS:131, De-CH:364, Er-FA:318,
    Ga-FB:105, Ha-PO:15, Hi-WP II:68,
    Ma-YA:146, Ni-JP:52, Ox-BN:139,
    Rv-CB:658, Sm-LG:312
Ring Around the World. A. Wynne.
    Ar-TP3:95, Ja-PA:32
The Ritual to Read to Each Other.
    W. Stafford. Pe-SS:115
The Runaway Slave. W. Whitman.
    Hu-PN:467, Kr-OF:39, Un-MA:49
Santos, New Mexico. M. Sarton.
    Pl-EI:116
Self-Portrait. N. Cassian. Mc-AC:132
She Came with Lips of Brown. B. Cox.
    La-IH:100
Shiloh, a Requiem. H. Melville.
    Al-VBP:952, Br-AF:72, Ho-WR:120,
    Pa-HT:42, Rv-CB:838, Vi-PP:149
Simultaneously. D. Ignatow. Ha-TP:23
Somebody's Birthday. A. Brown.
    Br-BC:5
Something in Common. R. Church.
    Tr-MR:152
Song. M. Holman. Jo-SA:86
Song for All Seas, All Ships.
    W. Whitman. De-CH:167
A Song for the States. W. Whitman.
    Se-PR:246
Song of Myself. W. Whitman. Al-VBP:928,
    Mo-GR:106, Sh-AP:69, Un-MA:44
The Song of the Good Samaritan.
    V. Watkins. Wi-LT:450
Sonnet to Negro Soldiers. J. Cotter.
    Ad-PB:35
Space. W. Burford. Ho-LP:81
Special Starlight. C. Sandburg.
    Tr-MR:101
Stanzas on Freedom. J. Lowell.
    Hu-PN:464, Kr-OF:31
The Stars, 12. Ping Hsin. Hs-TC:21
Stepping Westward. W. Wordsworth.
    De-CH:436
A Strange Meeting. W. Davies.
    Bl-OB:148
Street Scene - 1946. K. Porter.
    Hu-PN:539
The Sun That Warms You. E. Farjeon.
    Ga-S:204
Supernatural. J. Holland. Jo-VC:85
Tableau. C. Cullen. Ad-PB:92,
    Br-AF:248
Then as Now. W. de la Mare. Li-TU:250,
    Mc-WK:116
There's a Certain Illness. A. Blackwell.
    Jo-VC:61
This Moment Yearning and Thoughtful.
    W. Whitman. Sh-RP:94
To a Beautiful Girl Whose Name I Don't
    Know. A. Brooks. Ad-II:112

BROTHERHOOD — cont'd.
To Him That Was Crucified. W. Whitman.
   Tr-MR:177
The Tree of Great Peace. Dekanawideh.
   Br-MW:102
The Triumph of Freedom. W. Garrison.
   Ba-PO:100
True Religion. Tulsidas. Ba-PO:3
The Tuft of Flowers. R. Frost.
   Rv-CB:966, Sh-AP:150, Un-MA:168
Two Armies. S. Spender. Ba-PO:121
Two Girls of Twelve or So. . . .
   C. Reznikoff. La-OC:90
Two 'Mericana Men. T. Daly. Hu-MP:150
Uptown. A. Ginsburg. Br-TC:150
Utopia. J. Amini. Ra-BP:230
A Wanderer. N. Ayukawa. Sh-AM:123
We Can Be Together. P. Kantner.
   Mo-GR:105
We Shall Live Together. Wo-HS:(29)
We Shall Overcome. Ba-PO:199,
   Hi-TL:228, Pl-EI:165
Where the Rainbow Ends. R. Rive.
   Ab-MO:107, Lo-TY:180
A Whim of Time. S. Spender. Un-MB:471
White Magic. W. Braithwaite.
   Hu-PN:49
White Man and Black Man Are Talking.
   M. Goode. Jo-VC:48
Who Are They? Bi-IT:145
With the Herring Fishers. H. MacDiarmid.
   Wi-LT:627
Wooden Ships. D. Crosby. Mo-GR:108
The Wounded Person. W. Whitman.
   Hu-PN:468
You, Whoever You Are. W. Whitman.
   Br-AF:49
Youth's Question - Revenge's Answer.
   R. Groppuso. Me-WF:25
BROTHERS: see also HUMOR - BROTHERS
Abel. D. Capetanakis. Pa-GTB:523
Archie of Cawfield. Ma-BB:20
The Battle of Antietam Creek. Em-AF:451
Big Brother. E. Roberts. Fe-FP:41,
   Hu-MP:9
Bishop Cody's Last Request. T. Paxton.
   Mo-GR:55
The Bonny Heyn. Ox-BB:201
Boy with His Hair Cut Short.
   M. Rukeyser. Br-TC:350, Ca-VT:361,
   Co-RG:159, Wi-LT:805
The Braes of Yarrow. Ox-BB:590
Brother. T. Ikenaga. Le-TA:23
Brother and Sister. W. Wordsworth.
   De-TT:33
The Brothers. A. Groesbeck. De-FS:102
The Brothers: Two Saltimbanques.
   J. Logan. Du-SH:46
Clark Sanders. Ox-BB:76, Rv-CB:34
The Collier. V. Watkins. To-MP:24
Cradle-Song for a Boy. Da-SC:57,
   Ho-SD:65

The Cruel Brother. Ma-YA:38, Ox-BB:236
Dirge. Tr-CB:30, Tr-US I:50
The Duke o' Athole's Nurse. Ox-BB:344
Earl Brand. Ox-BB:115
The First Grief. F. Hemans. De-CH:45
A Flight Shot. M. Thompson. Co-RM:72
Hymn of the Afflicted. Tr-US I:81
I Would Like to Be a Bee. D. Baruch.
   Br-BC:92
In Memory. II. L. Johnson. Ox-BN:948
It Shall Be. Ho-SD:13
Joan's Door. E. Farjeon. Br-BC:80
Little. D. Aldis. Ar-TP3:5, Fe-FP:38
Love. P. Solomon. Jo-VC:4
Love. An-IP:(18)
Lu Yün's Lament. H. Read. Pl-ML:26
Mourning Song for a Brother Drowned at
   Sea. Br-MW:139
My Brother. D. Aldis. Ar-TP3:185,
   Au-SP:191
My Brother. M. Ridlon. Ho-GC:13
Nonsense. N. Koralova. Mo-MI:54
Older Brother. T. Maruyama. Le-TA:29
Older Brother. F. Yamashita. Le-TA:30
The Portrait of a Chinese Soldier.
   Wang Ya-p'ing. Hs-TC:354
The Prodigal Son. E. Robinson.
   Un-MA:136
Proud Margret. Ox-BB:74
A Puzzling Example. V. Benjamin.
   Br-BC:55
The Quarrel. E. Farjeon. Fe-FP:41
Seven Brothers. M. Leib. Ho-TY:91
Seven Brothers Have One Sister.
   Gr-BB:30
Song David. Ox-BB:241
Swinging on a Gate. On-TW:31
The Table. C. de Andrade. An-TC:67
The Tale of the Jealous Brother.
   Br-MW:120
Three Old Brothers. F. O'Connor.
   Co-PI:150
To a Little Sister, Aged Ten.
   A. Cummings. Br-BC:79
To My Brother Miguel. C. Vallejo.
   Pe-M:13
Tour. In Rain. R. Roseliep.
   De-FS:164, St-H:186
The Twa Brothers. De-CH:52, Ox-BB:234
Two in a Bed. A. Ross. Ar-TP3:5,
   Au-SP:95, Ch-B:105, Fe-FP:40, Hu-MP:9
"Vale" from Carthage. P. Viereck.
   Cr-WS:102, Pe-OA:238, Un-MA:658,
   Wi-LT:832
You Were at the Dead River. G. Abbe.
   De-FS:3
Young Johnstone. Ox-BB:212
Younger Brother. T. Suzuki. La-TA:28
BROWN, JOHN: see also MARTINS FERRY, O.
Brown of Ossawatomie. J. Whittier.
   Hi-TL:98
Harpers Ferry. S. Rodman. Hu-PN:545

How Old John Brown Took Harper's Ferry.
  E. Stedman. Hu-PN:493, Pa-OM:175
John Brown. V. Lindsay. Un-MA:227
John Brown's Body. Er-FA:448, Hi-TL:99
John Brown's Prayer. S. Benét.
  Hu-PN:517
More Alive than Ever. H. Thoreau.
  Kr-OF:110
Narrative. R. Atkins. Ad-PB:198
A Negro Mother's Lullaby. C. Cullen.
  Mc-PR:153
October 16: The Raid. L. Hughes.
  Ad-BO:36, Ad-PB:78
The Portent. H. Melville. Ho-WR:196,
  Kr-OF:109, Rv-CB:836
The Soul and Body of John Brown.
  M. Rukeyser. Un-MA:624
The Virginia Scaffold. E. Proctor.
  Kr-OF:109
BROWN (COLOR)
At Thanksgiving. J. Leichliter.
  Ls-NY:288
Brown. C. Pivnichny. La-GI:33
Brown Is Sad. R. Kerecz. La-GI:32
Why Try? T. Joans. Br-MA:101
BROWNIES (FAIRIES)
Orkney Lullaby. E. Field. Un-GT:300
Sweet Willie. Ox-BB:45
BROWNING, ROBERT
Life-Long, Poor Browning. A. Spencer.
  Hu-PN:60
To Robert Browning. W. Landor.
  Al-VBP:702, Se-PR:307
BRUEGHEL, PIETER
The Dance. W. Williams. Bo-GJ:137,
  Sh-AP:168, Sm-LG:44, Wi-LT:200
Hunters in the Snow: Brueghel.
  J. Langland. Wi-LT:753
Musée des Beaux Arts. W. Auden.
  Br-TC:20, Er-FA:64, Ha-PO:223,
  Pa-GTB:510, To-MP:31, Wi-LT:467
Winter Landscape. J. Berryman.
  Br-TC:37, Mo-BG:112, Un-MA:640,
  Wi-LT:566
BRUGES, BELG.
The Belfry of Bruges. H. Longfellow.
  Pa-HT:113
BRUNANBURH, BATTLE, 937
The Battle of Brunanburh. A. Tennyson.
  Hi-FO:63
BRUTUS, MARCUS
Brutus. W. Shakespeare. Er-FA:63,
  Un-GT:85
Julius Caesar. W. Shakespeare.
  Hi-FO:49
BRYAN, WILLIAM JENNINGS
Bryan's Last Battle (The Scopes Trial).
  Em-AF:769
Free Silver. Em-AF:768
BUCCANEERS: see PIRATES

BUCHANAN, JAMES
Kansas Curses the President. J. Howe.
  Kr-OF:143
While There Is a Country to Save.
  R. Emerson. Kr-OF:142
BUCKINGHAM, GEORGE VILLIERS, 2ND DUKE OF:
  see VILLIERS, GEORGE, 2ND DUKE OF
  BUCKINGHAM
BUCKINGHAM PALACE: see also HUMOR –
  BUCKINGHAM PALACE
Buckingham Palace. A. Milne.
  Ke-TF:73, La-PV:206, Ox-BC:340
BUCKINGHAMSHIRE, ENG.
Buckinghamshire. Gr-GB:169
BUCKLAND, WILLIAM
A Serio-Comic Elegy. R. Whately.
  Br-SM:162
BUDDHA
Buddha. S. Hagiwara. Sh-AM:51
Disarmament. J. Whittier. Ba-PO:103,
  Cr-WS:157
My Little Golden Sister. Wy-CM:39
Tanka. Y. Aizu. Sh-AM:142
3 Meditations. G. Fowler. Sc-TN:55
BUDDHISM
Ajanta. M. Rukeyser. Un-MA:630,
  Wi-LT:806
Dhammapada. Buddha. Ba-PO:19
A Drape. Feng Chih. Hs-TC:143
A Monk. Pien Chih-lin. Hs-TC:161
Morning at the Temple of Kobai.
  E. Shiffert. Ls-NY:257
The Zen Archer. J. Kirkup. Pl-EI:22
BUDS: see FLOWERS
BUFFALO, N.Y.
Fish. J. Unternecker. Sc-TN:219
BUFFALO BILL: see CODY, WILLIAM
  FREDERICK
BUFFALOES: see BISON
BUGANDA: see MUTESA, KING OF BUGANDA
BUGLES: see also HUMOR – BUGLES
The Calls. W. Owen. Go-BP:48
The Splendor Falls on Castle Walls.
  A. Tennyson. Al-VBP:858, Ar-TP3:217,
  Bo-GJ:139, Co-RG:145, De-CH:113,
  De-TT:196, Fe-FP:373, Ga-FB:11,
  Gr-CT:444, Hi-WP I:106, Ho-WR:162,
  Hu-MP:95, Mc-PR:65, Ox-BN:485,
  Pl-US:26, Re-TW:72, Rv-CB:791,
  Sm-LG:39
BUGS: see INSECTS
BUILDERS AND BUILDING: see also
  ARCHITECTS AND ARCHITECTURE;
  HUMOR – BUILDERS AND BUILDING
The Assassin. D. Hall. Ha-TP:31
Ballad of the Common Man. A. Kreymborg.
  Vi-PP:144
The Birds of the Air. Rv-ON:109
Castles. M. Ridlon. Ho-CS:44
Construction. P. Hubbell. La-OC:111
The Cycle Repeated. K. Chapin. Ls-NY:258

BUILDERS AND BUILDING — cont'd.
Dedication for a Building. A. Dugan.
  Ad-CL:89
Dividing the Wheat. F. Saito.
  Sh-AM:152
For the New Railway Station in Rome.
  R. Wilbur. Pe-OA:257
Homo Faber: the Shell Game.
  M. Piercy. Sc-TN:190
Love Song: I and Thou. A. Dugan.
  Gr-BT:139
New House. B. Buchanan. Ke-TF:409
On Watching the Construction of a
  Skyscraper. B. Raffel. Du-RG:38,
  La-OC:112
One, Two. R. Ainsworth. St-FS:10
Prayers of Steel. C. Sandburg.
  Fe-FP:255, Hu-MP:403, La-OC:151,
  La-PV:194, Mo-BG:26, Un-MA:203
Questions of a Studious Working Man.
  B. Brecht. Sm-MK:224
Sand Hill Road. M. Grosser. Pe-SS:85
Song of the Builders. J. Murton.
  Br-AF:212
Sound. J. Harrison. Ca-VT:711
Summon the Workers. C. Lambert.
  Hu-MP:400
We Are All Workmen. R. Rilke. Pl-EI:56
Which Are You? Fe-PL:299
BUILDINGS: see SKYSCRAPERS; and names of
  buildings, as EMPIRE STATE BUILDING
BULBS (PLANTS)
A Bulb. R. Munkittrick. Co-PM:45
BULL RUN, BATTLES, 1861, 1862
The Battle of Bull Run. Em-AF:447
BULLDOZERS
The Chant of the Awakening Bulldozers.
  P. Hubbell. Su-FVI:44
Near and Far. H. Behn. Li-LC:56
BULLFIGHTS AND BULLFIGHTERS
Juan Belmont, Torero. D. Finkel.
  Co-RM:228
BULLFINCHES: see FINCHES
BULLS
Anecdotes of Four Gentlemen. Ox-BC:152
Auranomoi's Song of Praise for His Bull
  Akorikono. Tr-US I:107
The Bull. R. Hodgson. Rd-OA:122,
  Un-MB:190, Wi-LT:125
The Bull. W. Williams. Br-TC:483,
  Wi-LT:199
The Bull Calf. I. Layton. Co-BBW:168
Conjecture. A. Raha. Al-PI:86
Herder's Song. Be-AP:59, Tr-US I:111
Hoosen Johnny. Fe-FP:165
Rodeo. E. Lueders. Co-RM:24,
  Du-RG:133
BUMBLEBEES: see BEES
BUMS: see TRAMPS
BUNKER HILL, BATTLE, 1775
Grandmother's Story of Bunker Hill
  Battle. O. Holmes. Un-GT:178

On the Eve of Bunker Hill. C. Scollard.
  Se-PR:150
Warren's Address at Bunker Hill.
  J. Pierpont. Vi-PP:106
BUNTINGS
Snow Bunting. T. Miyoshi. Sh-AM:81
The Song of the Reed Sparrow. Ox-BC:81
Winter in Vermont. H. Carruth.
  Ca-BP:41
BUNYAN, JOHN
An Advertisement to the Reader.
  J. Bunyan. De-CH:616
BUNYAN, PAUL: see PAUL BUNYAN
BUONARROTI, MICHELANGELO: see
  MICHELANGELO
BUOYS
Beginning to Squall. M. Swenson.
  La-RM:88, Ls-NY:308
In Winter. R. Wallace. Co-BN:182
The Inchcape Rock. R. Southey.
  Gr-CT:141, Un-GT:161
BUREAUCRACY: see also HUMOR - BUREAUCRACY;
  SATIRE - BUREAUCRACY
Loves of Public Servants. R. Hershon.
  Sc-TN:96
BURIALS: see FUNERALS
BURIED TREASURE: see TREASURE-TROVES
BURMESE VERSE: see KAREN VERSE
BURNS, ROBERT
On the Author. R. Burns. Rv-CB:620
BURR, AARON
Blennerhassett's Island. T. Read
  Hi-TL:60
BURROS: see DONKEYS
BURROUGHS, JOHN
To the Memory of John Burroughs.
  C. Parmenter. Se-PR:98
BURYAT VERSE: see ALTAIC VERSE - BURYAT
BUSES: see also HUMOR - BUSES
Beautiful V Shape. Lo Men. Pa-MV:126
The Birthday Bus. M. Hoberman.
  Ar-TP3:92, Br-BC:98
B's the Bus. P. McGinley. Ar-TP3:92,
  Au-SP:162, Fe-FP:187, Lo-LL:89
The Bus. L. Cohen. Ad-CI:9
Bus Ride. S. Robinson. Fe-FP:246
Good Green Bus. R. Field. Mc-PR:95
The Last Bus. M. Strand. Br-TC:422
Night Ride. H. Read. Co-BL:111,
  Hi-WP II:61
BUSHES: see SHRUBS
BUSHMEN: see also AFRICAN VERSE - BUSHMAN
Ula Masondo's Dream. W. Plomer.
  Ca-MB:73
BUSINESS: see INVESTMENTS AND INVESTORS;
  SATIRE - BUSINESS
BUSINESSMEN: see MERCHANTS
BUSYNESS: see also HUMOR - BUSYNESS;
  SATIRE - BUSYNESS
A Busy Person. A. Hilton. Bo-FP:35
Little Bird Flitting. Basho. Be-CS:38
One Man and One Fly. Issa. Be-CS:34

Portrait. M. Chute. Mc-AW:15
Three Wonderful Women III. Ox-BC:152
A World to Do. T. Weiss. Gr-SS:136
BUTCHERS AND BUTCHERING: see also
   HUMOR - BUTCHERS AND BUTCHERING
A Butcher. T. Hood. Co-RM:241
Clear Night. Ai Ch'ing. Hs-TC:295
Nights of Crisis. J. Sternberg.
   Ho-TY:194
Reuben Bright. E. Robinson. Co-RM:233,
   Sh-AP:141, Un-MA:119
Robin Hood and the Butcher. Ma-BB:62
Shopping for Meat in the Winter.
   O. Williams. Ho-LP:35, Pe-M:115,
   Wi-LT:420
Song from the Bride of Smithfield.
   S. Warner. Un-MB:374
The Three Butchers. Co-RM:102
BUTLER, SAMUEL, 1612-1680
On the Setting Up of Mr. Butler's
   Monument in Westminster Abbey.
   S. Wesley. Ke-PP:51, Rv-CB:516
BUTLERS: see SERVANTS
BUTTE, MONT.: see HUMOR - BUTTE, MONT.
BUTTER
Betty Botter's Batter. Mo-MGT:182
Churning. De-CH:670, Mo-MGT:85
The King's Breakfast. A. Milne.
   Ox-BC:341
BUTTERCUPS
Buttercup. M. Dodge. Gr-EC:291
Buttercups. W. Thorley. Fe-FP:381
Buttercups and Daisies. M. Howitt.
   Ox-BC:159
Kingcups. S. Sitwell. Un-MB:401
Three Things. J. Auslander. Hu-MP:198
BUTTERFLIES: see also HUMOR - BUTTERFLIES
Annual Legend. W. Scott. Wi-LT:811
Another Song of a Fool. W. Yeats.
   Rd-OA:195
Asleep in the Sun. Buson. Be-CS:6
Away Floats the Butterfly. Wy-CM:9
Because a Tunnel. F. Saito. Sh-AM:152
The Bird and the Butterfly.
   Tr-US II:281
Blue-Butterfly Day. R. Frost.
   Br-SG:4, La-RM:133
Blue Moon Butterfly. P. Williams.
   Le-M:88
A Brimstone Butterfly. A. Young.
   Cl-DT:72
Brother and Sister. W. Wordsworth.
   De-TT:33
Butterflies. Chu Miao Tuan.
   Le-MW:19, Ma-FW:14
Butterflies. W. Davies. Go-BP:83
Butterflies, Beware! Shosen. Be-MC:55
Butterflies Dancing. Oemaru. Do-TS:46
The Butterfly. J. Benitez. Me-WF:26
Butterfly. H. Conkling. Ar-TP3:66
Butterfly. W. Smith. Ar-TP3:66,
   Bo-GJ:92, Co-IW:46, Sh-RP:337

The Butterfly and the Caterpillar.
   J. Lauren. Pa-OM:342
Butterfly in the Fields. J. Campbell.
   Co-PI:18
Butterfly Song. Bi-IT:110, Jo-TS:14,
   Tr-US II:259
Butterfly, These Words. Soseki.
   Be-CS:18
A Butterfly's. K. Takahama. Sh-AM:163
Climbing a Steep Hill. Kwaso.
   Be-MC:44
The Example. W. Davies. Rd-OA:69,
   Un-MB:176
Flowers. H. Behn. Br-SG:54, Fe-FP:222
Flying Crooked. R. Graves. Br-TC:152,
   Co-PM:99, Ho-LP:44, Ma-FW:208,
   Rd-OA:18, Wi-LT:371
Fuzzy Wuzzy, Creepy Crawly. L. Vanada.
   Ar-TP3:65, Au-SP:72, It-HB:29
Ha! the Butterfly. Le-IS:20
A Heavy Cart Rumbles. S. Kuroyanagi.
   Ma-FW:114
How Soft the Sound. Kyoshi. Do-TS:35
I Think. Tai Wang-shu. Hs-TC:184
Insect Riddles III. Gr-GB:70
Kachina Song. Br-MW:43, Da-SC:84,
   Pa-SG:128
The King of Yellow Butterflies.
   V. Lindsay. Co-BBW:215
A Magic Carpet. T. Weiss. We-PZ:30
March. J. Clare. Rd-OA:187.
Now. G. Bishop-Dubjinsky. Sc-TN:12
O Butterfly. Chiyo-ni. Le-MW:18
Of the Boy and the Butterfly.
   J. Bunyan. Ox-BC:35
The Painted Lady. M. Danner.
   Ra-BP:152
Pod of the Milkweed. R. Frost.
   Wi-LT:186
The Prayer of the Butterfly.
   C. Gasztold. Li-TU:198
A Secret Code. S. Kurahara. Sh-AM:78
Softly. Issa. Le-MW:17
Sparrows or Butterflies? De-PP:23
Summer. R. Aldington. Cl-FC:40
A Temple Room. S. Takano. Sh-AM:168
Tilda Tilbury. L. Allen. Pa-RE:45
To a Butterfly. W. Wordsworth.
   Br-SG:55, Co-BBW:226, Mc-PR:204,
   Un-GT:74
Trap. A. Ammons. Ls-NY:106
The Tuft of Flowers. R. Frost.
   Rv-CB:966, Sh-AP:150, Un-MA:168
Up the Barley Rows. Sora. Au-SP:320
Wake Up! Wake Up! Basho. Au-SP:72,
   Be-CS:22
Was Worm. M. Swenson. Un-GT:73
What a Sad Sight. Shiki. Do-TS:24
What Is a Butterfly? B. Franklin. Un-GT:25
White Butterflies. A. Swinburne. Ad-PE:13,
   Bo-FP:278, Bo-GJ:79, Ch-B:116, Fe-FP:129,
   Hu-MP:307, La-PV:145, Ma-FO:(35),
   Mc-PR:45

BUTTERFLIES — cont'd.
  White Butterfly. Tai Wang-shu.
    Hs-TC:184
  With Wings That Will Not Ever.
    F. Saito. Sh-AM:151
  The Women and the Man. Te-FC:87
BUTTERNUT TREES
  Butternuts. E. Astley. Ke-TF:446
BUTTONS
  About Buttons. D. Aldis. Th-AS:59
  The Button-Seller. Ir-BB:36,
    Wr-RM:61
BUYING AND SELLING: see also SHOPPING
  My Father Died, but I Can't Tell You
    How. Bl-OB:22, Ir-BB:124, On-TW:25,
    Pa-RE:46
BUZZARDS
  Myth. Br-MW:81
  Pondy Woods. R. Warren. Un-MA:582
BYRON, GEORGE NOEL GORDON, LORD: see
    also HUMOR - BYRON, GEORGE NOEL
    GORDON, LORD
  Byron Recollected at Bologna.
    S. Rogers. Ox-BN:51
BYZANTIUM
  Byzantium. W. Yeats. Un-MB:117,
    Wi-LT:87
  Protus. R. Browning. Hi-FO:86
  Sailing to Byzantium. W. Yeats.
    Al-VBP:1093, Er-FA:152, Go-BP:168,
    Pa-GTB:425, Rv-CB:956, Tr-MR:290,
    Un-MB:114, Wi-LT:75
CABARETS: see NIGHT CLUBS
CABBAGES
  Cabbages. T. Hooley. Ga-S:11
  Vegetable Fantasies. H. Hoyt.
    Ir-BB:16; 17
CABIN CREEK, KEN.
  The Cabin Creek Flood. Em-AF:476
CABLES, SUBMARINE
  The Cable Hymn. J. Whittier.
    Hi-TL:131
CABOT, RICHARD CLARKE
  The White-Haired Man: for Richard
    Cabot. M. Sarton. Tr-MR:173
CADMUS AND HARMONIA
  Empedocles on Etna. M. Arnold.
    Pa-GTB:366
CAESAR, GAIUS JULIUS
  Julius Caesar. W. Shakespeare.
    Hi-FO:49
  Julius Caesar and the Honey-Bee.
    C. Turner. Rd-OA:160
  Long-Legged Fly. W. Yeats. Wi-LT:92
  Res Publica. J. McKellar. Ni-JP:121
CAFES: see RESTAURANTS AND BARS
CAGES
  The Squirrel. De-TT:19, Mo-MGT:97
CAIN AND ABEL
  Abel. D. Capetanakis. Pa-GTB:523
  Cain and Abel. H. Leivick. Ho-TY:125
  Cain and Abel. I. Manger. Ho-TY:278

  The Discovery. M. Gibbon. Co-PI:49
CAIRO, EGY.
  Egypt. Z. Ghose. Ls-NY:246
CAKES AND COOKIES: see also HUMOR -
    CAKES AND COOKIES; and names of
    cakes, as PLUMCAKE
  A Birthday. R. Field. Br-BC:85,
    Br-SS:41
  The Birthday Cake. V. Chase. Br-BC:86
  Birthday Cake. I. Eastwick. Br-BC:88
  Birthday Cake. A. Fisher. Br-BC:88,
    La-PV:118
  The Birthday-Cake Glockenspiel.
    E. Henley. Br-BC:90
  Birthday Candles. L. Scott. Br-BC:86
  Cake. M. Potter. Br-BC:85
  Cake Recipe Rhyme. Ju-CP:7
  Catherine. K. Kuskin. La-PV:97
  Christmas Cookies. A. Fisher.
    Ag-HE:24
  The Cupboard. W. de la Mare.
    Ar-TP3:7, Au-SP:131, Bo-FP:51,
    Fe-FP:42, Fr-MP:8, St-FS:76
  Goody O'Grumpity. C. Brink.
    Fe-FP:312, Sh-RP:37
  Hot Cakes. Shu Hsi. Cl-FC:90,
    Ma-FW:280
  Lickety-Lick. M. Justus. Fr-MP:9,
    Mc-AW:28
  The Miracle. E. Fowler. Br-BC:87
  Mix a Pancake. C. Rossetti. Ag-HE:6,
    Au-SP:10, Bo-FP:53, Ch-B:80,
    Cl-FC:94, Li-LC:45
  The Oven Bricks Are Ready. Gr-BB:19
  Pancakes. G. Jacoby. La-GI:47
  Seven Times One Are Seven. R. Hillyer.
    Br-BC:156
  Spice Cake. A. Fisher. Ag-HE:25
  Un-Birthday Cake. A. Fisher. Br-BC:89
  Who Wants a Birthday? D. McCord.
    Br-BC:3
CALCUTTA, INDIA
  Calcutta. A. Chakravarty. Al-PI:77
CALENDARS: see also ALMANACS; HUMOR -
    CALENDARS
  The Calendar. B. Todd. Ir-BB:23
  The Crows. Gr-GB:62, Mo-MGT:185
  Fragments. Br-MW:130
  From the Aztec Ceremonial Calendar.
    Br-MW:9
  The Garden Year. S. Coleridge.
    Ar-TP3:183, Bo-FP:204, Ch-B:30,
    De-TT:35, Hu-MP:289, Ir-BB:227,
    Mc-PR:30, Ox-BC:169, Sh-RP:188,
    Un-GB:8, Un-GT:268
  Happy New Year. M. Roberts. Mc-AW:64
  Thirty Days Hath September. Au-SP:323,
    Bo-FP:139, Li-LB:165, Mo-MGT:172,
    Mo-NR:101, On-TW:59, Un-GT:22,
    Wi-MG:30, Wr-RM:17
CALIFORNIA: see also CALIFORNIA -
    MISSIONS; CAMINO REAL;
    SATIRE - CALIFORNIA; and names

of towns, as SAN FRANCISCO, CALIF.
All the Little Hoofprints. R. Jeffers.
  Ni-JP:109
Apology for Bad Dreams. R. Jeffers.
  Sh-AP:175, Un-MA:363
Ascent to the Sierras. R. Jeffers.
  Pa-HT:61, Sm-LG:148
The Bourgeois Poet. K. Shapiro.
  St-H:204
California Winter. K. Shapiro.
  Br-AF:164
Hay for the Horses. G. Snyder.
  Du-SH:144, Mo-BG:56
In California There Are Two Hundred
  Fifty Six Religions. R. Albert.
  Du-SH:102
The King's Highway. J. McGroarty.
  Pa-HT:66
Song of the Redwood Tree. W. Whitman.
  Pa-HT:64
Strength Through Joy. K. Rexroth.
  Ca-VT:268
Time Is the Mercy of Eternity.
  K. Rexroth. Ca-VT:272
To the Holy Spirit. Y. Winters.
  Ca-VT:231, Un-MA:551
CALIFORNIA - GOLD DISCOVERIES: see also
  GHOST TOWNS; HUMOR - CALIFORNIA -
  GOLD DISCOVERIES
Californy Stage. Fi-BG:132
How Bill Went East. G. Bryan.
  Co-PT:82
John Sutter. Y. Winters. Ha-PO:72,
  Un-MA:549
A Peck of Gold. R. Frost. Bo-HF:21,
  La-PV:196
The Society upon the Stanislaus.
  B. Harte. Co-RM:22
The Spelling Bee at Angels. B. Harte.
  Co-PT:241
Walk, Damn You, Walk! W. De Vere.
  Fe-PL:51
See also Em-AF:560-576
CALIFORNIA - MISSIONS: see also CAMINO
  REAL; SPANIARDS IN AMERICA
The Path of the Padres. E. Osborne.
  Br-AF:60
CALLA LILIES: see LILIES
CALLIGRAPHY
Lightly a New Moon. Kyoshi. Be-CS:26
The Steel Pen. Chung Ting-wen.
  Pa-MV:76
The Writing Brush. Chung Ting-wen.
  Pa-MV:75
CALLIMACHUS (SCULPTOR)
Lapis Lazuli. W. Yeats. Wi-LT:89
CALLIOPE (MUSE)
To Calliope. R. Graves. Ls-NY:165
CALM: see PEACE; PEACE OF MIND
CALORIES: see DIET; FOOD AND EATING
CALUMETS: see PEACE PIPES
CALVES: see COWS

CALYPSOS
Calypsonian. F. Charles. Sa-B:91
Cordelia Brown. Ab-MO:57
Jaffo the Calypsonian. I. MacDonald.
  Sa-B:34
CAM RIVER
The Old Vicarage, Grantchester.
  R. Brooke. Hi-WP II:129, Pa-HT:120
CAMARGUE: see LA CAMARGUE, FR.
CAMBODIAN VERSE
Song. Tr-US II:194
CAMBRIDGE, ENG.: see also CAM RIVER;
  CAMBRIDGE UNIVERSITY
On the Death of William Hervey.
  A. Cowley. Al-VBP:447, Rv-CB:395
Second Farewell to Cambridge.
  Hsü Chih-mo. Hs-TC:83
CAMBRIDGE, MASS.: see also HARVARD
  UNIVERSITY
The Cambridge Ladies. e. cummings.
  Al-VBP:1202, Ha-PO:243, Ke-PP:93,
  Rv-CB:991
A Sound in Cambridge, Mass.
  R. Whitman. Ls-NY:327
CAMBRIDGE UNIVERSITY
Cambridge. F. Cornford. Cl-FC:57
Sunday Morning, King's Cambridge.
  J. Betjeman. Pl-EI:12
Within King's College Chapel, Cambridge.
  W. Wordsworth. Ox-BN:81, Pa-GTB:300
CAMBRIDGESHIRE, ENG.
The Old Vicarage, Grantchester.
  R. Brooke. Hi-WP II:129, Pa-HT:120
CAMELLIAS
The Camellia. Basho. Sh-RP:63
CAMELS: see also CARAVANS; HUMOR -
  CAMELS
African Sunrise. G. Lutz. Du-RG:46
At the Zoo. A. Smith. Bo-FP:266
Baby Camel. V. Korostylev. Co-BBW:186
The Boar and the Dromedary. H. Beissel.
  Do-WH:11
The Camel. C. de Gasztold. Rd-OA:161
A Camel. S. Muro. Sh-AM:54
Camel. J. Stallworthy. Ls-NY:201
Exile. V. Sheard. Co-BBW:205
Twelfth Night Song of the Camels.
  E. Coatsworth. Bo-HF:72, Fe-FP:171
CAMEROON
Autobiography. M. Dipoko. Lo-TY:142
CAMINO REAL: see also CALIFORNIA -
  MISSIONS; COLONIAL PERIOD IN AMERICA;
  SPANIARDS IN AMERICA
The King's Highway. J. McGroarty.
  Pa-HT:66
CAMOMILE
An Autumn Sky. K. Takahama. Sh-AM:162
CAMPING: see also HUMOR - CAMPING
At Cove on the Crooked River.
  W. Stafford. Wi-LT:825
Eat-It-All Elaine. K. Starbird.
  La-PV:99

CAMPING — cont'd.
The River. D. Short. Du-SH:129
Song Cycle of the Moon-Bone.
Tr-US I:246
Song for a Camper. J. Farrar. Ha-YA:66
CANADA: see also BALLADS, AMERICAN;
DIALECTS, FRENCH - CANADIAN; and names
of cities, as MONTREAL, CAN.; and
regions, as KLONDIKE, CAN.
Canadian Boat Song. J. Galt.
Ox-BN:204, Rv-CB:683, Sm-LG:140
Canadian Folk Song. W. Campbell.
Bo-FP:171
CANARIES: see also HUMOR - CANARIES
The Canary. E. Turner. Ox-BC:136
Mary's Canary. De-TT:38, Sp-AS:23,
Wr-RM:93
To a Young Brother. M. Jewsbury.
Ox-BC:168
When My Canary. Shiki. Ar-TP3:54,
Be-CS:45
CANCER (MALIGNANCY)
The Cancer Cells. R. Eberhart.
Wi-LT:435
Death from Cancer. R. Lowell.
Br-TC:265, Ha-PO:125
My Old Maid Aunt. D. Schultz.
Du-SH:137
CANDLEMAS
Candlemas. A. Brown. Se-PR:43
A Ceremony for Candlemas Day. R. Herrick.
Se-PR:42
The Ground Hog. E. Jay. Ja-HH:9
Ground Hog Day. M. Pomeroy.
Co-BBW:32, Co-PM:83, Co-PS:29
The Ground Hog's Complaint. J. Lee.
Ja-HH:8
If Candlemas Day Be Fair and Bright.
Co-PS:30, Se-PR:42
CANDLES
Ash Wednesday. R. Marinoni. Se-PR:69
A Birthday. R. Field. Br-BC:85,
Br-SS:41
Birthday Cake. I. Eastwick. Br-BC:88
Birthday Candles. G. Johnson.
Ke-TF:155
Birthday Candles. L. Scott. Br-BC:86
Cake. W. Potter. Br-BC:85
Candle and Star. E. Coatsworth.
Br-BC:168
A Candle Burning in the Night.
S. Warner. Gr-TG:46
The Candle Indoors. G. Hopkins.
Ma-FW:124, Wi-LT:43
Candle-Saving. De-TT:63, Wr-RM:85
Candle Talk. Ja-HH:53
Candles. C. Cavafy. Sm-MK:217
Candles. S. Heitler. Le-M:209
Candles. Ho-CT:43
The Candle's Light. A. Nakamura. Le-TA:46
The Christmas Candle. K. Brown.
Au-SP:380, Se-PR:224

Christmas Chant. I. Shaw. Br-SS:108,
La-PH:42
Fairy Thief. W. Welles. Br-SG:84
First Fig. E. Millay. Bo-FP:45,
Er-FA:220, Fe-PL:417, Ga-FB:3,
Ho-TH:21, Sh-AP:186
Kinship. M. Doyle. Ke-TF:439
Little Nancy Etticoat. Ar-TP3:99,
Au-SP:25, Bo-FP:36, Gr-CT:3,
Ir-BB:48, Li-LB:169, Mo-MGT:154,
Mo-NR:99, Wr-RM:39
O Jesus, Keep My Candle Burning
Bright. Gr-TG:46
Seven Times One Are Seven. R. Hillyer.
Br-BC:156
Six Birthday Candles Shining. M. Carr.
Br-BC:91
Six Little Candles Burning Bright.
On-TW:27
Un-Birthday Cake. A. Fisher. Br-BC:89
What Is It That Sits. . . . Ju-CP:12
Where Could You Put a Candle. Re-RR:99
A Winter Night. B. Pasternak.
Ca-MR:174
CANDY: see also HUMOR - CANDY
The Ambitious Mouse. J. Farrar.
Bo-FP:59
Choice. J. Farrar. Br-SS:175
The Cupboard. W. de la Mare.
Ar-TP3:7, Au-SP:131, Bo-FP:51,
Fe-FP:42, Fr-MP:8, St-FS:76
Hippety Hop to the Barber Shop.
Ar-TP3:100, Au-SP:9, Ir-BB:13
Hippity-Hop to the Sweetie Shop.
Mo-TL:79
I'd Like a Little. Er-FA:498
Lollipop, Lollipop. Re-RR:58
The Lollypops. C. Thomas. Au-SP:220
Nauty Pauty. Mother Goose. Ag-HE:38,
Mo-MGT:135
The Pennycandystore Beyond the El.
L. Ferlinghetti. Ad-CI:17,
Mo-BG:19, Pe-SS:80
The Sugar-Plum Tree. E. Field.
Au-SP:302, Bo-FP:200, Ch-B:20,
Er-FA:489, Hu-MP:118, Ir-BB:66,
Ke-TF:76, Mc-PR:96, Ox-BC:304
CANIS MAJOR AND MINOR
A Sky Pair. R. Frost. Un-MA:181
CANNIBALS: see also HEAD-HUNTERS; HUMOR -
CANNIBALS
Song of the Victim at a Cannibal Feast.
Tr-US II:302
CANNING AND PRESERVING: see also HUMOR -
CANNING AND PRESERVING
Autumn. J. Untermeyer. Un-MA:332
CANNONS: see GUNS
CANOES AND CANOEING
Canoe. P. Anderson. Mo-SD:135
Canoe Song. Tr-US I:202
The Canoe Speaks. R. Stevenson.
Mo-SD:134

Lullaby. R. Hillyer. Du-RG:111,
   Fe-FP:113, Ha-LO:22, Rd-SS:16
Paddling Song. Le-OE:52
The Song My Paddle Sings. E. Johnson.
   Fe-FP:493, Se-PR:321
The Song of the Aotea Canoe.
   Tr-US II:108
Women's Ur-Dance Song. Tr-US II:12
CANOPUS: see STARS
CANUTE, KING OF ENGLAND, DENMARK, NORWAY
   A Fact and an Imagination.
   W. Wordsworth. Hi-FO:67
CANYONS: see names of canyons, as
   GRAND CANYON
CAPE COD: see HUMOR - CAPE COD
CAPE HATTERAS
   Hatteras Calling. C. Aiken. Co-BN:178
CAPE HORN
   Rounding the Horn. J. Masefield.
   Un-MB:223
CAPELLA (STAR)
   See Where Capella with Her Golden Kids.
   E. Millay. Ni-JP:122
CAPITAL PUNISHMENT: see EXECUTIONS AND
   EXECUTIONERS
CAPS: see HATS
CAPTIVES AND CAPTIVITY: see PRISONS AND
   PRISONERS
CARAVAGGIO, MICHELANGELO, MERISI DA
   In Santa Maria del Popolo. T. Gunn.
   Pa-GTB:563
CARAVANS
   Caravaners. Tr-CB:26, Tr-US I:113
   Caravans. H. Borland. Th-AS:150
   Caravans. I. Thompson. St-FS:99
   The Golden Journey to Samarkand.
   J. Flecker. Bo-GJ:229, Pa-HT:91
   The Snow-Leopard. R. Jarrell.
   Br-TC:221, Wi-LT:560
   Timbuctu. E. Brathwaite. To-MP:164
CARCASSONNE, FR.
   Carcassonne. G. Nadaud. Pa-HT:116
CARD GAMES: see also CARDS (PLAYING)
   Cupid and Campaspe. J. Lyly.
   Al-VBP:121, Ma-YA:60, Pa-GTB:31,
   Un-MW:37
   A Game of Cards. E. Jennings.
   Ls-NY:15
   Poker. Fi-BG:205
   Whist. E. Ware. Fe-PL:311
CARDINALS (BIRDS)
   The Cardinal. R. Warren. Re-BS:36
   Cardinals. J. Harrison. Ha-WR:4
   The Cardinal's Valentine. Ja-HH:14
CARDS (PLAYING): see also FORTUNE
   TELLING
   The Card Players. D. Ray. Ca-VT:678
   A House of Cards. C. Rossetti.
   Bo-FP:18
   I Give to You. Re-RR:27
   The Playing Cards. A. Pope. Gr-CT:28
   Rattlin' Joe's Prayer. J. Crawford.
   Fi-BG:187

CAREERS: see OCCUPATIONS
CAREFULNESS: see SAFETY
CARELESSNESS: see also HUMOR -
   CARELESSNESS
   Diddle, Diddle, Dumpling.
   Bo-FP:37, De-PO:28, Ir-BB:191,
   Li-LB:71, Mo-CC:(21), Mo-MGT:36,
   Mo-TL:41, Wi-MG:13, Wr-RM:37
   "Don't Care" and "Never Mind."
   J. Bangs. Er-FA:16
   Little Polly Flinders. Mother Goose.
   Li-LB:26, Mo-MGT:87, Mo-NR:90,
   Wi-MG:64, Wr-RM:26
   Lollocks. R. Graves. Gr-CT:155,
   Ma-FW:196, Na-EO:135
   Lucy Locket. Bo-FP:121, De-PO:18,
   Hi-FO:160, Li-LB:45, Mo-MGT:132,
   Wr-RM:23
   The Story of Johnny Head-in-Air.
   H. Hoffmann. Ox-BC:206
   Vain and Careless. R. Graves.
   Ha-LO:20
CARENTAN, FR.
   Carentan O Carentan. L. Simpson.
   Bl-FP:46, Ca-MB:117, Co-RM:202,
   To-MP:49
CAREW, THOMAS
   On Thomas Carew. Rv-CB:415
CARGOES: see also FREIGHTERS; HUMOR -
   CARGOES
   A Caravan from China Comes.
   R. Le Gallienne. Th-AS:152
   Cargoes. J. Masefield. Ar-TP3:90,
   Bo-FP:134, Co-RG:56, Co-SS:75,
   Fe-FP:196, Ga-FB:182, Hi-MP I:109,
   Mc-PR:135, Th-AS:130, Un-MB:225,
   Wi-LT:189
   Chaucer's Thames. W. Morris. Cl-FC:25
   I'm a Longshoreman. Hs-TC:451
   Mine Argosy from Alexandria.
   C. Marlowe. Gr-CT:219
   Mulholland's Contract. R. Kipling.
   Co-SS:210
   An Old Song Re-Sung. J. Masefield.
   Gr-EC:243, Na-EO:68
   Sheep. W. Davies. Cl-FC:68,
   Ha-PO:125, Pa-RE:29, Rd-OA:76,
   Un-MB:177, Wi-LT:618
   A Ship a-Sailing. G. Setoun.
   Ar-TP3:122, Au-SP:19, Bo-FP:200,
   Co-SS:85, De-TT:48, Gr-EC:242,
   Hi-GD:16, Hu-MP:175, Ir-BB:241,
   Li-LB:86, Mo-MGT:174, Mo-NR:103,
   Pa-AP:44, Sm-MK:199, Sp-HW:25,
   Wi-MG:53, Wr-RM:73
   The Ships of Yule. B. Carman.
   Br-BC:126, Do-WH:16, Sh-RP:168
   Song of the Truck. D. Frankel.
   Br-AF:235
   Timbuctu. E. Brathwaite. To-MP:164
   The Train Dogs. P. Johnson.
   Do-WH:59

CARIBBEAN SEA: see also WEST INDIES
  O Carib Isle! H. Crane. Ca-VT:216
  Voyages II. H. Crane. Al-VBP:1210,
    Un-MA:519, Wi-LT:398
CARIBOUS: see DEER
CARLYLE, THOMAS: see HUMOR - CARLYLE,
  THOMAS
CARMEL, CALIF.
  At Carmel. M. Austin. Br-AF:210
  Autumn in Carmel. G. Sterling.
    Pa-HT:63
  Carmel Point. M. MacSweeney. Du-RG:75
  In Memory of Robinson Jeffers.
    E. Barker. Ls-NY:135
CARNATIONS
  The Feel of Fineness. J. Wildman.
    Ls-NY:58
  The Poems of Our Climate. W. Stevens.
    Br-TC:411, Sh-AP:182
CARNIVALS: see FAIRS
CAROLS: see CHRISTMAS SONGS
CAROUSELS: see MERRY-GO-ROUNDS
CARPENTERS AND CARPENTRY: see also
  HAMMERS; HUMOR - CARPENTERS AND
  CARPENTRY; WOODWORK
  Busy Carpenters. J. Tippett.
    Au-SP:138
  Carpenters. Ch-B:41
  He Who Hanged Himself. Tsou Ti-fan.
    Hs-TC:341
  In the Carpenter Shop. Un-GT:92
CARPETS: see RUGS
CARRIAGES: see also HUMOR - CARRIAGES;
  STAGECOACHES
  A Carriage from Sweden. M. Moore.
    Br-TC:297, Wi-LT:271
CARROLL, LEWIS: see also ALICE IN
  WONDERLAND
  In Memory of Lewis Carroll. Se-PR:308
  Lewis Carroll. E. Farjeon. Ox-BC:331
CARROTS
  Fruit, Flower and Tree Riddles V.
    Gr-GB:72
CARSON, CHRISTOPHER (KIT)
  Kit Carson's Ride. J. Miller.
    Fi-BG:161
CARTHAGE, N. AF.
  Dido of Tunisia. P. McGinley.
    Cr-WS:18
CARVING (ART)
  Kosumi, the Carver. Yehoash. Ho-TY:75
CARYATIDS: see STATUES
CASABIANCA, GIACOMO JOCANTE
  Casabianca. E. Bishop. Gr-SS:104
  Casabianca. F. Hemans. Er-FA:184,
    Fe-FP:552, Hi-FO:189, Un-GT:159
CASSANDRA
  Cassandra. L. Bogan. Ca-VT:203,
    Un-MA:492
  Cassandra. R. Jeffers. Wi-LT:266
  Rebecca. V. Andreyev. Ca-MR:97
CASSOWARIES: see HUMOR - CASSOWARIES

CASTAWAYS: see SHIPWRECKS
CASTLEREAGH, VISCOUNT: see STEWART,
  ROBERT, VISCOUNT CASTLEREAGH
CASTLES: see also names of castles, as
  CHILLON CASTLE
  Captivity. S. Rogers. Ox-BN:47
  Carcassonne. G. Nadaud. Pa-HT:116
  The Castle Yonder. J. Dudley. Le-M:62
  Castles and Candelight. J. Reeves.
    Co-PT:183
  Elegiac Stanzas. W. Wordsworth.
    Ox-BN:81, Pa-GTB:297
  Grongar Hill. J. Dyer. Al-VBP:544,
    Cl-FC:26
  Psalm Concerning the Castle.
    D. Levertov. Br-TC:256
  The Ruin. Ma-YA:4
CASTRO, FIDEL
  One Thousand Fearful Words for Fidel
    Castro. L. Ferlinghetti. Ca-VT:476
CATALPA TREES
  Catalpa Trees. P. Colum. Ls-NY:270
CATASTROPHES: see DISASTERS
CATBIRDS
  Air: Catbird Singing. R. Creeley.
    Ho-P:41
  The Cat Heard the Cat-Bird. J. Ciardi.
    Gr-EC:70
CATCHING RHYMES: see TOSSING AND CATCHING
  RHYMES
CATERPILLARS (LARVAE)
  The Butterfly and the Caterpillar.
    J. Lauren. Pa-OM:342
  The Caterpillar. A. Noyes. Go-BP:83
  The Caterpillar. C. Rossetti.
    Au-SP:73, Bo-GJ:90, Br-SG:50,
    Ch-B:48, Co-BBW:229, Fe-FP:127,
    Hu-MP:306, La-PP:10, Mc-PR:93,
    Ox-BC:279, Un-GB:16, Un-GT:73
  Caterpillars. A. Fisher. It-HB:28
  Cocoon. D. McCord. It-HB:29
  Fuzzy Wuzzy, Creepy Crawly. L. Vanada.
    Ar-TP3:65, Au-SP:72, It-HB:29
  My Friend the Caterpillar. D. Russell.
    Ls-NY:331
  Now that Night Is Gone. Buson.
    Be-MC:48
  Only My Opinion. M. Shannon.
    Ar-TP3:124, Au-SP:232, Fe-FP:128,
    Hu-MP:457, Ir-BB:80
  The Tickle Rhyme. I. Serraillier.
    Au-SP:232, Co-OW:56, Ir-BB:57,
    La-PP:10
  You Can See the Morning Breeze.
    Buson. Do-TS:15
CATFISH
  The Catfish. J. Mathews. Ha-TP:115
CATHEDRALS: see also GARGOYLES
  The Cathedral of St. Louis. C. Carmer.
    Th-AS:167
  Chartres Cathedral. D. Babcock.
    Ls-NY:239

Divina Commedia. H. Longfellow.
   Al-VBP:828, Sh-AP:37, 38
Return to Chartres. M. Sarton.
   Ke-TF:379
St. Isaac's Church, Petrograd. C. McKay.
   Ad-PB:27, Be-MA:15, Bo-AN:29
Siena, from a Northern Slope.
   J. Ackerson. Ke-TF:381
CATHERINE OF ALEXANDRIA, SAINT
   For A Marriage of St. Catherine.
   D. Rossetti. Gr-SS:162
CATHLEEN NI HOULIHAN
   Red Hanrahan's Song about Ireland.
   W. Yeats. Sm-LG:141
CATHOLIC CHURCH: see also BISHOPS;
   CATHEDRALS; MONKS; NUNS; POPES;
   PRIESTS; SAINTS; and names of
   saints, as THERESA, SAINT
   Bishop Blougram's Apology. R. Browning.
   Ox-BN:547
   Two Poems on the Catholic Bavarians, I.
   E. Bowers. En-PC:220
   Two Poems on the Catholic Bavarians, II.
   E. Bowers. En-PC:221
CATS: see also HUMOR - CATS
   The Ad-Dressing of Cats. T. Eliot.
   Un-GT:54
   Affinities. A. Stoutenberg. Mo-TS:60
   Alas, You Cannot. Kyoshi. Ca-BF:7
   Avondale. S. Smith. Pa-RE:9
   The Bad Kittens. E. Coatsworth.
   Fe-FP:160, Hu-MP:186, Se-PR:195,
   Sh-RP:40, Th-AS:105
   Bimbo's Pome. P. Klee. Ma-FW:60
   The Bird Fancier. J. Kirkup. Gr-EC:71
   Brothers. S. Edwards. Hu-NN:70
   Butting, Tumbling Cat. Kikaku.
   Ca-BF:39
   Calling in the Cat. E. Coatsworth.
   Rd-OA:16
   The Cat. J. Brennan. Br-SM:11
   The Cat. C. Calverley. Gr-CT:118
   The Cat. Chung Ting-wen. Pa-MV:79
   Cat. J. Das. Al-PI:80
   The Cat. W. Davies. Bl-OB:108
   Cat! E. Farjeon. Bl-OB:104,
   Co-BBW:119, Pa-RE:20
   A Cat. J. Gittings. Le-M:102
   The Cat. O. Herford. Ga-FB:331
   Cat. S. Lewis. Ma-FO:(13), Un-GT:49
   Cat. M. Miller. Ar-TP3:54, Au-SP:31,
   Co-BBW:130, Li-LC:30, Pe-FB:3,
   St-FS:73
   Cat. J. Struther. Un-GT:50
   A Cat. E. Thomas. Bl-OB:108
   Cat. J. Tolkien. Gr-EC:68
   The Cat and the Bird. G. Canning.
   Gr-CT:118, Gr-EC:76, Re-BS:4
   The Cat and the Miser. M. Van Doren.
   Ha-TP:37

The Cat and the Moon. W. Yeats.
   Bo-FP:92, Bo-GJ:245, Co-BBW:135,
   Co-PI:200, Co-PM:194, Co-RG:102,
   Ha-LO:30, Hi-WP I:2, Li-TU:200,
   Ma-FW:57, Re-TW:18, Sm-LG:72
Cat & the Weather. M. Swenson.
   Co-BBW:120, Ha-WR:90, Pe-M:108
Cat at the Cream. Gr-GB:55
A Cat Called Little Bell. De-PP:39
A Cat Has No Tail. B. Williams.
   Me-WF:28
The Cat Heard the Cat-Bird. J. Ciardi.
   Gr-EC:70
Cat in the Long Grass. A. Dixon.
   Ma-FW:58
A Cat May Look at a King. L. Richards.
   Co-IW:26
The Cat of Cats. W. Rands. Ox-BC:236
Cat on a Couch. B. Howes. Co-BBW:136,
   Ha-PO:114
Catalogue. R. Moore. Du-RG:89,
   Un-GT:50
Cats. M. Chute. Au-SP:31
Cats. E. Farjeon. Gr-EC:75, Gr-TG:53,
   La-PV:109, St-FS:46
The Cats. J. Struther. Co-BBW:133
A Cat's Conscience. Fe-PL:352
Cat's Funeral. E. Rieu. Ar-TP3:53,
   Gr-EC:78, Mc-WS:43
The Cats Have Come to Tea.
   K. Greenaway. Bo-FP:58, Ch-B:101
The Cat's Song. Gr-GB:55
The Cat's Tea-Party. F. Weatherley.
   Ar-TP3:119, Co-IW:34, Ir-BB:182,
   On-TW:22
The Cattie Rade to Paisley. Mo-TL:78
A Change of Heart. V. Hobbs. Br-SS:151
Cheetie Pussie. Mo-TL:21
Choosing a Kitten. Ch-B:43
Christmas Wishes. J. Lee. Ja-HH:54
Cosy Cat Nap. J. Kirkup. Pa-RE:13
Country Cat. E. Coatsworth.
   Un-GB:19, Un-GT:53
Cruel Clever Cat. G. Taylor. Gr-CT:122
A Curse on the Cat. J. Skelton.
   Na-EO:94
Dame Trot. Ir-BB:169, Mo-CC:(50),
   Mo-MGT:133, St-FS:36, Wr-RM:13
Death of the Cat. I. Serraillier.
   Co-BBW:126
Diddlety, Diddlety, Dumpty. Mother
   Goose. Li-LB:91, Mo-CC:(21),
   Mo-NR:32
Ding, Dong, Bell. Ar-TP3:131,
   Au-SP:14, De-PO:20, Li-LB:95,
   Mo-MGT:119, Mo-NR:36
A Dog and a Cat Went Out Together.
   Mother Goose. Bo-FP:225, Ir-BB:237
The Dog and the Cat. G. Hallock.
   Sh-RP:330
Double Dutch. W. de la Mare. Cl-FC:66

CATS — cont'd.
  Epitaph. J. Whittier. Gr-EC:78
  Epitaph for a Cat. M. Bruner. Fe-PL:352
  The Fighter. C. Schmid. Ke-TF:326
  The First Friend. R. Kipling. Hu-MP:192
  Five Eyes. W. de la Mare. Co-BBW:133,
    Co-IW:18, Ir-BB:28
  For a Dead Kitten. S. Hay. Du-RG:92
  Four-Footed Poems. E. Greenberg.
    Ho-TY:312
  Four-Paws. H. Eden. De-TT:65
  Fourteen Ways of Touching the Peter.
    G. MacBeth. Ma-FW:59
  Garden-Lion. E. Hayes. Gr-CT:122
  Hearth. P. Bacon. Fe-FP:160, Hu-MP:186
  Hie, Hie. Rv-ON:23
  Higglety, Pigglety, Pop! Ir-BB:184,
    Lo-LL:30, Mo-MGT:129, St-FS:22
  Hoddley, Poddley. Ir-BB:88, Mo-MGT:162
  I Love a Little Pussy. Bo-FP:6,
    Li-LB:92, Mo-MGT:176, Mo-NR:23,
    Mo-TL:69, Wi-MG:59
  I Love Little Pussy. J. Taylor.
    Ar-TP3:52, Fe-FP:526, Pa-AP:22,
    Un-GT:48, Wr-RM:62
  I Wouldn't. J. Ciardi. Gr-EC:74
  In Honour of Taffy Topaz. C. Morley.
    Ar-TP3:53
  The Innkeeper's Cat. U. Troubetzkoy.
    Ke-TF:325
  Jubilate Agno. C. Smart. Ho-P:55
  A Kitten. E. Farjeon. Ar-TP3:52,
    Pa-RE:40
  The Kitten. Issa. Do-TS:38
  The Kitten. O. Nash. Co-BBW:122,
    Fe-FP:363
  The Kitten and the Falling Leaves.
    W. Wordsworth. Bl-OB:106, Ch-B:23,
    Co-BBW:124, Fe-FP:157, Hu-MP:208,
    Un-GB:18, Un-GT:52
  A Kitten Is a Little Thing. J. Parr.
    La-GI:60
  Kitten's Night Thoughts. O. Herford.
    HU-MP:186
  Kitty. E. Prentiss. Hu-MP:184
  Kitty: What She Thinks of Herself.
    W. Rands. Co-PM:100, Hi-GD:22
  Lady Feeding Cats. D. Stewart.
    Ma-FW:61
  Lat Take a Cat. G. Chaucer. Gr-CT:117
  The Lavender Kitten. A. Lopez.
    Al-WW:11
  A Letter from the Front. H. Newbolt.
    Cr-WS:79
  The Little Kittens. E. Follen.
    Ar-TP3:118
  The Lonely Man. R. Jarrell. To-MP:85
  Look, See the Cat. N. Price. Ls-NY:99
  The Lost Cat. E. Rieu. Ar-TP3:53,
    Co-BBW:122
  Mary and Her Kitten. E. Farjeon.
    De-TT:29
  Midwife Cat. M. Van Doren. Rd-OA:83
  Milk for the Cat. H. Monro. Bl-OB:109,
    Co-BBW:137, Er-FA:233, Ga-BP:97,
    Re-TW:16, Sm-MK:160, Un-GT:47,
    Un-MB:236
  The Milk Jug. O. Herford. Bo-FP:56,
    Ch-B:43
  The Monk and His Cat. Co-PI:43,
    De-CH:90, Pa-SG:154, Rd-OA:110,
    Sm-LG:73
  Moon. W. Smith. La-PV:112
  My Cat. L. Syrett. Pa-RE:35
  My Cat Jeoffry. C. Smart. Bl-OB:107,
    Cl-DT:48, Co-BBW:127, Gr-CT:120,
    Ha-PO:111, Ho-WR:244, Un-GT:46
  My Kitten. Mo-TL:43, Wr-RM:53
  My Kitty-Cat Has Nine Lives. On-TW:32
  The Mysterious Cat. V. Lindsay.
    Ar-TP3:54, Au-SP:33, Bo-GJ:88,
    Co-IW:12, Fe-FP:158, Gr-CT:119,
    Hu-MP:187, Ir-BB:174, Pe-FB:10,
    Th-AS:42
  The Naming of Cats. T. Eliot. Bo-FP:7,
    Co-HP:56, Sh-RP:324, We-PZ-17
  Night. L. McKay. Br-SS:30
  Nipping Pussy's Feet in Fun. S. Smith.
    Sm-MK:11
  O Cat of Carlish Kind. J. Skelton.
    Gr-CT:118, Ha-PO:100, Rd-OA:105
  Of the Mean and Sure Estate. T. Wyatt.
    Rd-OA:98
  The Old Gumbie Cat. T. Eliot.
    Ir-BB:168, Un-GT:45
  On a Night of Snow. E. Coatsworth.
    Co-BBW:123, Du-RG:91, Un-GT:48,
    Un-MA:465
  On Lutestrings Cat-Eaten. T. Masters.
    No-CL:36
  The Only One Who Understands Me.
    G. Chinchilla. Me-WF:2
  The Open Door. E. Coatsworth.
    Gr-EC:76
  Our Cat. V. Lapin. Mo-MI:30
  The Pets. R. Farren. Gr-EC:30,
    Rd-OA:6
  Philological. J. Updike. Co-EL:32
  Poem. W. Williams. Co-BBW:125,
    Du-RG:90, Fe-FP:159, Ha-LO:18,
    La-PV:114, Re-TW:19
  The Prayer of the Cat. C. Gasztold.
    Ar-TP3:82, La-PV:113
  The Puddy and the Mouse. Gr-GB:68
  Pussy. Ox-BC:166
  Pussy at the Fireside. Sm-MK:4
  Pussy-Cat and the Dumplings. Mo-MGT:128,
    Wr-RM:92
  Pussy-Cat by the Fire. Wr-RM:128
  Pussy-Cat Mew. Bo-FP:30, Ir-BB:167,
    Wr-RM:83
  Pussy Cat, Pussy Cat. Mo-TL:21
  Pussy Cat, Pussy Cat, Where Have You
    Been? Ar-TP3:52, Au-SP:15, Bo-FP:6,

De-PO:18, Er-FA:506, Ir-BB:269,
Li-LB:88, Mo-MGT:163, Mo-NR:100,
Pa-AP:50, Wi-MG:34, Wr-RM:26
Pussy Has a Whiskered Face.
C. Rossetti. Ar-TP3:48
Pussycat Sits on a Chair. E. Horn.
Co-EL:27
Requiem for a Personal Friend.
E. Boland. Co-PI:13
The Rescue. H. Summers. Co-PT:131
Robin Redbreast. Hu-MP:185, Li-LB:83,
Wr-RM:14
Run, Kitty, Run! J. Garthwaite.
Co-BB:100
The Sage. D. Levertov. Kh-VA:27
Scenes from the Life of the Peppertrees.
D. Levertov. Wi-LT:761
She Sights a Bird. E. Dickinson.
Rd-OA:171
Sing, Sing. Li-LB:95, Mo-MGT:124,
Mo-NR:22, Pa-AP:6, Wr-RM:120
Six Little Mice Sat Down to Spin.
Mo-CC:(52), Mo-MGT:90, On-TW:27,
Sm-MK:192, St-FS:6
Sleeping, Waking. Issa. Le-MW:31,
Ma-FW:58
Snow in the Suburbs. T. Hardy.
Bo-GJ:254, Co-BN:192, Hi-WP I:127,
Re-TW:105, Un-MB:34
Some Little Mice Sat in a Barn to Spin.
Mo-NR:120
Some Western Haikus, III. J. Kerouac.
Kh-VA:12
Song for a Child. H. Davis. Au-SP:30
The Song of the Jellicles. T. Eliot.
Bl-OB:105, Ir-BB:175, Li-LC:28,
Li-TU:114, Lo-LL:50, Mc-WS:177,
Ox-BC:347, Sm-LG:75, Un-GF:92
A Sound in Cambridge, Mass. R. Whitman.
Ls-NY:327
Sparrows. A. Fyfe. Le-M:100
Story of the Pennies. A. Lutzky.
Ho-TY:267
A Stray Cat. Taigi. Do-TS:7
Sunday. E. Coatsworth. Br-AF:213,
La-OC:32, Mc-WK:56
The Tale of the Skunk and Poor Jez.
J. Becker. Sh-RP:133
Ten Little Mice. Ir-BB:25
A Thanksgiving Fable. O. Herford.
Ja-PA:58
That Little Black Cat. D. Thompson.
Ox-BC:231
There Was a Presbyterian Cat. Sm-LG:77
There Was a Wee Bit Mousikie.
Bl-OB:105, De-CH:544
The Three Cats. De-TT:30, Rv-ON:120
The Three Little Kittens. An-IP:(16),
Au-SP:22, Bo-FP:91, Fe-FP:526,
Li-LB:146, Mo-MGT:212, Mo-NR:15,
On-TW:16
Three Mice Went into a Hole to Spin.
Mo-TL:68

Three Young Rats. Fr-WO:35, Gr-CT:31,
Gr-EC:11, Gr-GB:92, Ir-BB:234,
Lo-LL:41, Mo-MGT:187, On-TW:15,
Sm-MK:193
Tiger-Cat Tim. E. Chase. Ar-TP3:52,
Au-SP:35
To a Cat. Co-BBW:139
The Two Gray Kits. Ir-BB:153, Wr-RM:80
Two Little Kittens. Ox-BC:285
Two Songs of a Fool. W. Yeats. Rd-OA:14
Under-the-Table Manners. St-FS:93
We Keep a Dog to Guard the House.
Wy-CM:30
We're All in the Dumps. Bl-OB:10,
Gr-GB:93, Ir-BB:133
What in the World? E. Merriam.
Gr-EC:14
What the Gray Cat Sings. A. Guiterman.
Co-PM:80, Hu-MP:188, Li-TU:112,
Rd-SS:24, Se-PR:194
Wherever the Cat of the House. De-CH:545
White Cat. R. Knister. Do-WH:82
"Who Are You?" Asked the Cat of the
Bear. E. Coatsworth. Ar-TP3:54
Who Was It? Ca-MU:19
Who's That Ringing at My Doorbell?
Ir-BB:166, Sm-LG:77
Winter Tryst. O. de Kay. Un-MW:145
Witch Cat. R. Bennett. Br-SS:69
The Yellow Cat. L. Jennings. De-FS:110
CATTLE: see also COWS; MILK
Cattle. Banko. Au-SP:45, Hu-MP:196
Cattle. B. Nance. Fi-BG:35
Cattle Show. H. MacDiarmid. Un-MB:360
Cowboy's Salvation Song. R. Carr.
Fi-BG:191
A Drover. P. Colum. Al-VBP:1148,
Co-PI:26, Pa-HT:139, Un-MB:250
Lasca. F. Desprez. Fi-BG:208
Midsummer. J. Scully. Br-TC:359,
Pe-OA:270
Mulholland's Contract. R. Kipling.
Co-SS:210
Old Blue. R. Coffin. Rd-OA:79
Run Little Dogies. Fi-BG:156
The Stampede. A. Caldwell. Fi-BG:100
The Stampede. F. Miller. Fi-BG:159
The War-Song of Dinas Vawr. T. Peacock.
Al-VBP:716, Ha-PO:220, Ho-WR:106,
Mc-WS:105, Na-EO:110, Pa-OM:197
Whoopee Ti Yi Yo, Git Along Little
Dogies. J. Lomax. Ar-TP3:34,
Fe-FP:435, Fi-BG:157, Hu-MP:209,
Mc-WK:72
Wires. P. Larkin. Pe-M:32
CATULLUS, GAIUS VALERIUS
Frater Ave atque Vale. A. Tennyson.
Gr-CT:444, Pa-GTB:341
On Catullus. W. Landor. Al-VBP:703
CAULIFLOWERS
The Cauliflower. J. Haines.
Sc-TN:73

CAUSES (CONCERNS):   see HUMOR - CAUSES
    (CONCERNS)
CAVALRY: see COSSACKS; U.S. CAVALRY
CAVES: see also names of caves, as
    AJANTA CAVES
  The Cave. G. Dresbach. La-RM:35,
    Pe-SS:42
  A Cave. J. Kirkup. Go-BP:32
  Grim and Gloomy. J. Reeves. Sh-RP:183
  The Secret Cavern. M. Widdemer.
    Fe-FP:11, Hu-MP:43, Sh-RP:110
  Staffa. J. Keats. Gr-SS:163
  Ula Masondo's Dream. W. Plomer.
    Ca-MB:73
CECILIA, SAINT
  Anthem for St. Cecilia's Day. W. Auden.
    Br-TC:20
  A Song for St. Cecilia's Day, 1687.
    J. Dryden. Pa-GTB:49, Pl-US:152,
    Rv-CB:466
CEDAR CREEK, BATTLE, 1864
  Sheridan's Ride. T. Read.   Er-FA:185,
    Ga-FB:261, Sp-OG:44
CEDAR TREES
  The House That Was. L. Binyon.
    Un-MB:157
  To the Cedar Tree. Jo-TS:16
CEDAR WAXWINGS
  Cedar Waxwings. W. Matchett. Co-EL:31,
    Ha-WR:61
CELANDINES
  A Lesson. W. Wordsworth. Pa-GTB:222
CELEBRATIONS: see FESTIVALS
CELERY
  Celery. O. Nash. Fe-FP:364,
    Hi-WP II:14, Sh-RP:143
CELLARS
  The Cellar. H. Conkling. Bo-FP:14
  Root Cellar. T. Roethke. Co-BN:219,
    Ho-LP:43
CEMENT: see CONCRETE MIXERS; HUMOR -
    CEMENT
CEMETERIES: see also EPITAPHS; HUMOR -
    CEMETERIES; SATIRE - CEMETERIES;
    TOMBS
  At the British War Cemetery, Bayeux.
    C. Causley. Go-BP:210
  At the Grave of John Clare. C. Causley.
    Ma-FW:171
  At the Indian Killer's Grave.
    R. Lowell. Ca-VT:443
  Aunt Dvorah. J. Segal. Ho-TY:157
  Brief Biography. M. George. De-FS:94
  The Cemetery. M. Tsvetayeva. Ca-MR:133
  Cemetery in Pernambuco. J. de Melo Neto.
    An-TC:123
  Cemetery of Childhood. J. Cardozo.
    An-TC:29
  The Churchyard on the Sands.
    Lord De Tabley. De-CH:346, Ox-BN:792
  Country Graveyard. D. Etter. Sc-TN:44
  Dorset. J. Betjeman. To-MP:20

Dunbarton. R. Lowell. To-MP:87
Edgar Allan Poe. R. Barlow. De-FS:11
Elegy Written in a Country Churchyard.
  T. Gray. Al-VBP:559, De-TT:83,
  Er-FA:462, Fe-PL:281, Ha-PO:144,
  Ma-YA:125, Pa-GTB:145, Rv-CB:533
Epitaph for a Negro Woman. O. Dodson.
  Hu-PN:301
Five for the Grace of Man 3. W. Scott.
  Ca-VT:313
For the Unknown Seamen of the 1939-45
  War Buried in Iona Churchyard.
  I. Smith. Go-BP:212
The Forgotten Graveyard. D. Etter.
  St-H:63
Fort McKinley. Lo Men. Pa-MV:125
God's Acre. H. Longfellow. Se-PR:198
Grave Visiting. S. Murano. Sh-AM:88
Graves at Inishbofin. R. Murphy.
  Ls-NY:110
Graveyard. R. Coffin. Br-AF:127
Griefs for Dead Soldiers. T. Hughes.
  Go-BP:211
Hide-and-Seek. R. Francis. Ha-PO:128
The Hill. E. Masters. Al-VBP:1104,
  Sh-AP:138, Wi-LT:113
Home Burial. R. Frost. Pe-SS:15
In a Grave-Yard. W. Braithwaite.
  Ad-PB:13
In Front of the Landscape. T. Hardy.
  Ox-BN:832
In Kerry. J. Synge. Un-MB:181
The Indian Burying Ground. P. Freneau.
  Fe-PL:279, Hi-TL:8, Rv-CB:559,
  Sh-AP:15
International Cemetery. Tsang K'o-chia.
  Hs-TC:279
The Jewish Cemetery at Newport.
  H. Longfellow. Ke-PP:69, Pa-HT:22,
  Sh-AP:34
A Jewish Cemetery near Leningrad.
  I. Brodsky. Bo-RU:18
Lines Written at the Grave of Alexandre
  Dumas. G. Bennett. Hu-PN:208
New England Churchyard. M. Adams.
  Ke-TF:349
Ode to the Confederate Dead. A. Tate.
  Al-VBP:1215, Un-MA:536, Wi-LT:402
Ode to the Confederate Dead in Magnolia
  Cemetery. H. Timrod. Se-PR:134,
  Sh-AP:126, Vi-PP:165
The Old Churchyard at Bonchurch.
  P. Marston. Ox-BN:888
Oldest Cemetery. M. Van Doren.
  De-FS:205
On the Death of Keats. J. Logan.
  Ho-P:169
Part-Time Tenant. E. Meudt. De-FS:141
The Pauper's Funeral. G. Crabbe.
  Ox-BN:1
Peace. L. Hughes. Ra-BP:82

The Poet's Final Instructions.
   J. Berryman.   Ca-VT:384
The Quaker Graveyard in Nantucket.
   R. Lowell.   Al-VBP:1248, Pa-HT:25,
   Wi-LT:573
Rainy Mountain Cemetery.   N. Momaday.
   Ni-CD:99
Refrigerium.   J. Newman.   Ox-BN:436
Sleeping Village.   H. Vinal.   De-FS:207
The Soul Longs to Return Whence It
   Came.   R. Eberhart.   Sh-AP:208
The Street of Crosses.   A. Stringer.
   Ke-TF:179
They Resemble Stakes.   S. Takayanagi.
   Sh-AM:176
This Quiet Dust.   E. Dickinson.
   Al-VBP:1003, Mc-WS:80, Un-MA:100
To the Holy Spirit.   Y. Winters.
   Ca-VT:231, Un-MA:551
The Town Without a Market.   J. Flecker.
   Un-MB:274
Trinity Place.   P. McGinley.   La-OC:120,
   Un-MA:596
Voices of Heroes.   H. Gregory.
   Gr-CC:104
Wake, All the Dead!   W. Davenant.
   De-CH:639, Rv-CB:366, Sm-LG:277
Waldheim Cemetery.   R. Sward.   St-H:217
Week-End by the Sea.   E. Masters.
   Un-MA:140
What Did You See?   J. Perez.   Me-WF:30
The Wooden Crosses.   H. Sahl.   Un-R:59
Wordsworth's Grave.   W. Watson.
   Ox-BN:910
CENSORSHIP
After a Symphony Concert.   V. Uflyand.
   Bo-RU:86
Dream with an Angel.   M. Banus.
   Mc-AC:113
Unicorns at Harvard.   N. Farber.
   De-FS:89
CENSUS: see HUMOR - CENSUS
CENTAURS: see also HUMOR - CENTAURS
The Centaur Overheard.   E. Bowers.
   Ls-NY:193
The Centaurs.   J. Stephens. Co-BBW:292,
   Co-PI:175
CENTIPEDES: see HUMOR - CENTIPEDES
CENTRAL AMERICA: see INDIANS OF CENTRAL
   AMERICA; LATIN AMERICA
CEREMONIES: see RITES AND CEREMONIES
CERES
Song.   T. Heywood.   No-CL:51
CERVANTES SAAVEDRA, MIGUEL DE
Cervantes.   E. Bentley.   Co-FB:127,
   Na-EO:54
CÉSAIRE, AIMÉ
Song for Aimé Césaire.   K. Kgositsile.
   Be-MA:146
CHAD, LAKE
Chad.   E. Brathwaite.   To-MP:163

CHAGALL, MARC
Don't Let That Horse.   L. Ferlinghetti.
   Mo-BG:82
Homage to Chagall.   D. Niatum. Ni-CD:135
CHAGRES RIVER
Beyond the Chagres.   J. Gilbert.
   Fe-PL:429
CHAIRS: see also HUMOR - CHAIRS
The Chair-Mender.   Mother Goose.
   Er-FA:505, Gr-EC:280, Ir-BB:40,
   Li-LB:63, Mo-MGT:124, Mo-NR:59,
   Wr-RM:19
I Have Legs.   St-FS:38
CHALLENGES
America.   C. McKay.   Ad-PB:26,
   Be-MA:15, Bo-HF:40, Hu-PN:100,
   Lo-TY:119
The Ascent.   J. Wade.   Sc-TN:225
Beyond the Panther.   J. Wade. Sc-TN:224
Brave Buffalo.   Jo-TS:20
The Challenger.   D. Wandrei. De-FS:214
Death as History.   J. Wright.
   Ad-PB:280, Sc-TN:249
King Henry the Fifth.   W. Shakespeare.
   Co-RM:199, Ga-FB:195, Ha-PO:255,
   Ke-TF:54
The Loser.   C. Bukowski.   Pe-M:64
Manifesto of Man.   Y. Galanskov.
   Bo-RU:29
People, Listen!   A. Shchukin. Bo-RU:73
The Pipe.   H. Plisetsky.   Bo-RU:65
The Word.   A. Timofeyevsky.   Bo-RU:84
CHAMELEONS: see also HUMOR - CHAMELEONS
The Chameleon.   A. Herbert.   Co-BBW:94,
   Co-IW:44, Fe-FP:129
The Chameleon.   J. Merrick.   Cl-FC:74
On a Bougainvillea Vine at the Summer
   Palace.   B. Howes.   Un-MA:653
CHANCE: see also GAMBLING; HUMOR -
   CHANCE
A Is for Abracadabra.   E. Farjeon.
   Gr-EC:252
Brown Penny.   W. Yeats.   Co-BL:18,
   Co-PI:203, Gr-CC:18, No-CL:142,
   Sm-LG:361
Brown Robyn's Confession. De-CH:399,
   Gr-GB:314
By the Hoof of the Wild Goat.
   R. Kipling.   Ox-BN:928
Circumstance.   P. Shelley.   Rv-CB:711
Circumstance.   A. Tennyson.   Sp-OG:277
The Coming of Good Luck.   R. Herrick.
   Co-EL:157, Gr-EC:163, Rv-CB:346
A Coney Island Life.   J. Weil. Br-AF:196,
   Du-RG:74
The Convergence of the Twain.   T. Hardy.
   Ni-JP:119, Un-MB:35, Wi-LT:19
Ecclesiastes IX.   Bible.   O.T.
   Ecclesiastes.   Ho-P:320
The Flat.   L. Lieberman.   Du-SH:70
Flux.   R. Eberhart.   Ca-VT:247

CHANCE — <u>cont'd</u>.
  For Ever, Fortune. . . . J. Thomson.
    Pa-GTB:130, Rv-CB:522
  The Great Coincidence. J. Hearst.
    St-H:80
  Hap. T. Hardy. Ke-PP:94, Pl-EI:65,
    Un-MB:35
  A Hero in the Land of Dough.
    R. Clairmont. Mc-WK:93
  Hope. R. Fanshawe. Rv-CB:368
  House in St. Petersburg. S. Burnshaw.
    Gr-SS:72
  Illness. B. Pasternak. Ca-MR:170
  Irritable Song. R. Atkins. Bo-AN:170
  Juxtaposition. A. Clough. Ox-BN:613
  Little Dame Crump. Bo-FP:89, Pa-RE:91
  A Lost Chord. A. Procter. Er-FA:437,
    Sp-OG:338
  The Luck of Edenhall. H. Longfellow.
    Co-PT:151
  Luck Tips the Balance. E. Greenberg.
    Ho-TY:309
  Marriage. Gr-GB:151
  Marvel No More. T. Wyatt. Rv-CB:81
  Mugala's Song. Tr-CB:14, Tr-US I:92
  A Nickle Bet. E. Knight. Ad-CI:43
  Old Fortunatus, 1. T. Dekker.
    Al-VBP:228
  On a Friday Morn. De-TT:130
  On Luck. M. Goldman. Ls-NY:32
  One I Love, Two I Loathe. On-TW:58
  A Portrait in the Guards. L. Whistler.
    Pa-GTB:531
  See a Pin and Pick It Up. Ir-BB:226,
    Li-LB:161, Mo-MGT:172, Mo-NR:119,
    Mo-TB:55, Un-GT:23, Wr-RM:41
  The Sense of the Sleight-of-Hand Man.
    W. Stevens. Pe-OA:70, Un-MA:252,
    Wi-LT:147
  That City. Li Kuang-t'ien. Hs-TC:211
  To a Mouse. R. Burns. Co-BBW:36,
    Er-FA:226, Fe-PL:367, Hu-MP:190,
    Mc-WK:60, Pa-GTB:141, Rd-OA:24,
    Rv-CB:616, Sp-OG:297
  A Trucker. T. Gunn. Ha-TP:26
  Well Met. A. Evans. Co-PM:11
  Whist. E. Ware. Fe-PL:311
  Yellow Stones on Sunday. Mo-TB:113
CHANGE: see also ADAPTABILITY; FICKLENESS;
    GROWING OLD; GROWING UP; HUMOR -
    CHANGE; IMPERMANENCE; MOVING (HOUSE-
    HOLD); SATIRE - CHANGE
  Address to a Mummy. H. Smith. Co-RG:5
  After Swimming Across the Yangtze
    River. Mao Tse-tung. Hs-TC:365
  All, All of a Piece Throughout. J. Dryden.
    Al-VBP:494, Co-EL:141, Gr-CT:349,
    No-CL:247, Rv-CB:469
  Alone. S. Sassoon. Hi-WP I:121, Un-MB:318
  And Through the Caribbean Sea.
    M. Danner. Ra-BP:152

And with the Sorrows of This Joyousness.
    K. Patchen. Gr-EC:266
And Yet the Earth Remains Unchanged.
    Bi-IT:101
And You Know It. W. Day. Lo-IT:27
Answering a Letter from a Younger Poet.
    B. Ghiselin. En-PC:50
Are Things Really Changing? B. Davis.
    Me-WF:59
August. L. MacNeice. Wi-LT:456
August 2. N. Jordan. Ad-PB:323
Autobiography. M. Dipoko. Lo-TY:142
Autumn. Su Tung P'o. Rx-OH:88
Aztec Song. Br-MW:4, Le-OE:128
The Ballad of Joe Meek. S. Brown.
    Be-MA:31
Beasts. R. Wilbur. Br-TC:472
Before the World Was Made. W. Yeats.
    Pa-GTB:431
Believe Me, if All Those Endearing Young
    Charms. T. Moore. Er-FA:103,
    Ga-FB:50, Ma-YA:171, Ox-BN:212,
    Rv-CB:681
Blackman/an unfinished history.
    D. Lee. Be-MA:161
The Broken String. Tr-CB:51,
    Tr-US I:76
The Butterfly and the Caterpillar.
    J. Lauren. Pa-OM:342
By the Deep Sea. G. Byron. Ox-BN:249
Can It Be. . . . Narihira. Ba-ST:21
Change. J. Donne. Al-VBP:253
A Change of Heart. V. Hobbs. Br-SS:151
Change of Seasons. J. Smith. Mc-AW:33
A Change of World. A. Rich. Ha-PT:33
Change Toward Certainty. J. Hearst.
    St-H:79
change-up. D. Lee. Ad-PB:428
Changes. R. Bulwer-Lytton. Fe-PL:307
Child-Mother in Metamorphosis.
    S. Clarke. Sa-B:32
The Children. H. Applebaum. Ke-TF:80
The Cloud. P. Shelley. Al-VBP:752,
    Bo-FP:261, Fe-FP:76, Hu-MP:295,
    Pl-IO:46, Rv-CB:708, Sh-RP:67,
    Sp-OG:349
Conservative. W. Stafford. St-H:212
Customs Change. Ox-BC:6
A Day in Autumn. R. Thomas.
    Co-BN:139, Hi-WP II:134
The Days and Months Do Not Last Long.
    Pai Ta-Shun. Le-MW:95
The Deceptive Present, the Phoenix Year.
    D. Schwartz. Co-BN:99
The Deserted Village. O. Goldsmith.
    Al-VBP:585, Er-FA:410, Hi-FO:178
Did the Harebell. E. Dickinson.
    Ga-FB:67
Discovery. Wen I-to. Hs-TC:58
Do Not, Oh Do Not Prize. Rv-CB:122
The Dreary Change. W. Scott.
    Ox-BN:134

During Wind and Rain. T. Hardy.
   Ha-PO:153, Pa-GTB:411
Early April. R. Frost. Ha-YA:45
East Coker. T. Eliot. Ca-VT:140
The Ebb Tide. R. Southey. Ox-BN:176
Egan O'Rahilly. J. Stephens. Rv-CB:974
Elegiac Stanzas. W. Wordsworth.
   Ox-BN:81, Pa-GTB:297
The Elements. W. Davies. Mc-WK:19,
   Sh-RP:111, Un-MB:178
The Embankment. T. Hulme. Co-EL:123
Exile. D. Scott. Sa-B:59
Extracts from Addresses to the Academy
   of Fine Ideas. W. Stevens. Wi-LT:148
Face to Face. A. Rich. Ha-TP:52,
   Wi-LT:803
Feigned Courage. C. and M. Lamb.
   Ox-BC:146
The Fickle Wind. C. Schonhaut. Le-M:128
A Field of Light. T. Roethke. Wi-LT:484
The Fire of Drift-Wood. H. Longfellow.
   Mo-BG:148
The First Day's Night Had Come.
   E. Dickinson. Wi-LT:6
Flowers at an Airport. W. Stafford.
   Mc-EA:128
For Denis Who Was a Drum. M. Maxwell.
   Sa-B:172
For the Union Dead. R. Lowell.
   Br-TC:265, Pe-OA:244, Wi-LT:583
The Forest. D. Quick. De-FS:153
Fruit, Flower and Tree Riddles.
   Gr-GB:72
Full Fathom Five. . . . W. Shakespeare.
   Al-VBP:197, Bl-OB:52, Bo-GJ:141,
   Cl-DT:39, Co-SS:159, De-CH:719,
   Fr-WO:86, Gr-CT:231, Ma-FW:42,
   Ma-YA:70, Na-EO:44, No-CL:43,
   Pa-GTB:29, Re-TW:70, Rv-CB:193,
   Sm-MK:37
Furniture. P. Harris. Ha-TP:32
Fuzzy Wuzzy, Creepy Crawly. L. Vanada.
   Ar-TP3:65, Au-SP:72, It-HB:29
The Gallery. A. Marvell. Gr-SS:87
Garnishing the Aviary. M. Danner.
   Ad-PB:134, Be-MA:88, Bo-AN:153,
   Hu-NN:29, Ra-BP:149
Genealogy. V. Felea. Mc-AC:130
The Glass of Water. W. Stevens.
   Un-MA:252
The Good Man in Hell. E. Muir.
   Tr-MR:159, Un-MB:339
The Groundhog. R. Eberhart.
   Er-FA:62, Ha-PO:121, Pe-OA:192,
   Sh-AP:208, Un-MA:579, Wi-LT:430
Harlem 1960 & 1968. P. Bird.
   La-IH:95
Here I Am. A. Morrissett. Co-BL:29
His Picture. J. Donne. Rv-CB:307
Hour of Memories. A. Shamri. Ho-TY:362
How Still, How Happy! E. Brontë.
   Ox-BN:598
How Time Consumeth All Earthly Things.
   T. Proctor. Gr-CT:243
Hymn to Proserpine. A. Swinburne.
   Hi-FO:58, Ox-BN:797
I Could Give All to Time. R. Frost.
   Sm-PT:169, Tr-MR:283
I Wage Not Any Feud with Death.
   A. Tennyson. Ke-PP:79
In a Drear-Nighted December. J. Keats.
   De-CH:216, Ox-BN:373, Pa-GTB:191,
   Rv-CB:737
In Due Season. W. Auden. Ho-P:15
In Early Spring. R. Aldridge. Ls-NY:295
In Memoriam XXXV. A. Tennyson.
   Al-VBP:861
In Time of "The Breaking of Nations."
   T. Hardy. Ha-PO:185, Tr-MR:188,
   Un-MB:25, Wi-LT:23
Indian Summer. D. Parker. Ke-TF:128
Interior. P. Colum. Co-PI:28,
   Un-MB:250
It Is Not Now. Ho-SD:64
It Must All Be Done Over. . . .
   J. Haines. Sc-TN:72
January. F. Sherman. Ha-YA:161
Juncture. R. Duncan. Hu-PN:574
Landmark. J. Hearst. St-H:77
Leaves. C. Cullen. Bo-HF:62
Let Her Give Her Hand. Co-BL:56
Letter to Yesenin. S. Yesenin.
   Ca-MR:108
The Little Maple. C. Zolotow.
   Br-SG:106
Longing. S. Teasdale. Sm-PT:161
Marvel No More. T. Wyatt. Rv-CB:81
Maturity. D. Gallup. Mc-EA:146
The Melodies of Time. T. Hood.
   Ox-BN:413
The Metamorphoses. R. Jarrell.
   Ha-TP:87
Metamorphosis. W. Stevens. Ca-VT:37
Milk. J. Schuyler. Mc-EA:142
Modern Love. G. Meredith. Ox-BN:689
The Moon Is Full. Liu Ta-Pai.
   Hs-TC:6
The Motive for Metaphor. W. Stevens.
   Un-MA:253
Music of Colours. V. Watkins.
   Wi-LT:453
Mutability. P. Shelley. Rv-CB:705
Negro Servant. L. Hughes. Ca-VT:240
no dawns. J. Perry. Ad-PB:516
Nobody Loves Me. C. Zolotow. Ho-ME:24
Nostalgia. Yang Huan. Pa-MV:159
Nothing Gold Can Stay. R. Frost.
   Bo-HF:56, Ca-VT:16, Mo-BG:133,
   Mo-TS:54, Un-MA:187
Nothing Is. Sun Ra. Ad-PB:207
Ode on the Pleasure Arising from
   Vicissitude. T. Gray. Pa-GTB:109
Old and New Year Ditties, III.
   C. Rossetti. Ox-BN:713

CHANGE — cont'd.
The Old Knight. G. Peele. Al-VBP:135
  Gr-CT:346, Ha-PO:172, Rv-CB:173
On the Pei-Tai River. Mao Tse-tung.
  Hs-TC:365
One Foot in Eden. E. Muir. Pa-GTB:470
Only a Beauty, Only a Power.
  J. Masefield. Tr-MR:282
Our Father. R. Swartz. Tr-MR:216
The Passing Strange. J. Masefield.
  Un-MB:229
Phases of the Moon. R. Browning.
  Gr-CT:406
Photograph. Q. Prettyman. Ad-PB:258
Pleasant Changes. J. Browne. Ox-BC:225
Poem for Psychologists and/or
  Theologians. C. Lewis. Gr-BP:159
a poem to complement other poems.
  D. Lee. Be-MA:158, Ra-BP:300
The Poplar Field. W. Cowper.
  Co-RG:117, De-CH:46, De-TT:161,
  Gr-CT:239, Ha-PO:151, Ho-WR:159,
  Ma-FW:105, Pa-GTB:140, Rv-CB:548
Prayers for the First Forty Days of the
  Dead. S. Yesenin. Ca-MR:109
Precedents. I. Newman. Ls-NY:274
Prediction. B. Esbensen. Ar-TP3:187
Prescription of Painful Ends.
  R. Jeffers. Un-MA:370
The Procession. M. Widdemer. Ha-YA:19
Prometheus Unbound. P. Shelley.
  Pl-IO:12
Proposition. N. Guillén. Ab-MO:4,
  Fe-FP:487, Lo-TY:104
Puzzles. J. Drinkwater. Mc-WK:107
Quail Sky. Li Ch'ing Chao. Rx-OH:95
The Quiet Child. R. Field. Rd-SS:39
The Return. R. Kipling. Un-MB:130
Rising Five. N. Nicholson. To-MP:69
The Rubaiyat of Omar Khayyam of
  Naishapur. E. Fitzgerald. Ha-PO:210
The Second Coming. W. Yeats.
  Mo-GR:89, Pa-GTB:424, Pl-EI:28,
  Tr-MR:236, Un-MB:117, Wi-LT:72
Seven Poems 2. L. Niedecker. Ca-VT:243
Shadow. Ch'en Meng-chia. Hs-TC:116
Shiva. R. Jeffers. Gr-SS:69, Ls-NY:36
Short Song to Greet the New Year.
  Tsang K'o-chia. Hs-TC:291
The Silent Generation. L. Simpson.
  Hi-TL:224
Soft Wood. R. Lowell. Wi-LT:581
Song. D. Moraes. Go-BP:138
Song. E. Sitwell. Gr-CC:34
Songs for a Colored Singer. E. Bishop.
  Hu-PN:550
Sonnet III. Feng Chih. Hs-TC:149
Sonnet 60. W. Shakespeare. Al-VBP:203,
  Er-FA:261, Gr-CT:196, Pa-GTB:19,
  Rv-CB:226
The Sonnets. W. Shakespeare. No-CL:87
Soonest Mended. J. Ashbery. Ho-P:9

South End. C. Aiken. Pe-OA:144
Spring. C. Rossetti. Ox-BN:704
Spring and Fall. G. Hopkins.
  Bo-GJ:249, Gr-CT:317, Ha-PO:148,
  Ke-PP:99, Pa-GTB:392, Re-TW:62,
  Wi-LT:44
Spring Ending. Hsü Chih-mo.
  Hs-TC:92
spring is like a perhaps hand.
  e. cummings. Ca-VT:175,
  Ma-FW:7
Spring to Winter. G. Crabbe.
  Gr-CT:316
The Spring Waters. Ping Hsin.
  Hs-TC:22
Starlight like Intuition Pierced the
  Twelve. D. Schwartz. En-PC:128,
  Sh-AP:222, Tr-MR:94
Summer. D. Wakoski. Ca-VT:714
Summer Holiday. R. Jeffers. Pe-M:85,
  Un-MA:366
The Tame Stag. J. Gay. Rv-CB:503
There Was a Time. E. Coatsworth.
  Mo-BG:111
Those Boys That Ran Together.
  L. Clifton. Ad-PB:307
The Three Cherry Trees. W. de la Mare.
  Gr-SS:35
Times o' Year. W. Barnes. Co-BN:226
To a Young Lady. R. Savage. Rv-CB:521
To the Tune "The Fair Maid of Yu."
  Chiang Chieh. Rx-LT:109
The Transfiguration. E. Muir. Go-BP:291
Transformation. L. Alexander.
  Hu-PN:160
The Tree and the Lady. T. Hardy.
  Un-MB:33
Unrest. R. Dixon. Ox-BN:753
A Valedictory to Standard Oil of
  Indiana. D. Wagner. Du-SH:146
A Visit from Abroad. J. Stephens.
  Co-PM:156, Ha-LO:40
Visiting Second Avenue. E. Greenberg.
  Ho-TY:311
The Visitor. M. Goldman. Ha-WR:69
The Voice. T. Hardy. Ox-BN:842,
  Pa-GTB:406
The Wall. A. Brownjohn. Ls-NY:260
Watch Long Enough, and You Will See
  the Leaf. C. Aiken. Ho-LP:101
What Strange Pleasure Do They Get Who'd.
  L. Welch. Kh-VA:70
What the Gray Cat Sings. A. Guiterman.
  Co-PM:80, Hu-MP:188, Li-TU:112,
  Rd-SS:24, Se-PR:194
A Whim of Time. S. Spender. Un-MB:471
White Primit Falls. Virgil. Gr-CT:50
The Whole World Is Coming. Da-SC:121,
  Ho-SD:12
Years. A. Margolin. Ho-TY:162
You Earth. Le-IB:119
Youth and Age. W. Yeats. Co-EL:135
Zephyr. E. Ware. Fe-PL:430

CHANGELINGS: see also HUMOR - CHANGELINGS
  Bewitched. W. de la Mare. Co-PM:44
  The Changeling. C. Mew. De-CH:293,
    Hu-MP:95
  Changeling. B. Young. Th-AS:136
  The Fairies Feast. C. Doughty.
    De-CH:124
  Lady Clare. A. Tennyson. Fe-FP:517,
    Pa-OM:253, Un-GT:144
  The Moon-Child. F. Macleod.
    De-CH:402
  The Return of the Fairy. H. Wolfe.
    Co-PM:178
  The Stolen Child. W. Yeats. Co-PM:197
    Hu-MP:82
  Stranger Bride. J. Sloan. De-FS:182
  When Larks Gin Sing. De-CH:660
CHANNING, WILLIAM HENRY
  Ode. R. Emerson. Ke-PP:65, Sh-AP:31
CHANTEYS: see SEA SONGS
CHANUKAH: see HANUKKAH
CHAOS AND ORDER: see also ANARCHY;
    HUMOR - CHAOS AND ORDER
  Address to My Soul. E. Wylie.
    Tr-MR:252, Wi-LT:208
  Chant. O. Williams. Tr-MR:34
  Chaos and Exactitude. M. Paraschivescu.
    Mc-AC:110
  Connoisseur of Chaos. W. Stevens.
    Wi-LT:146
  The Creation. Ovid. Cl-FC:78
  The Dunciad. A. Pope. Al-VBP:541
  Entropy. T. Spencer. Pl-IO:90
  Esthetique du Mal, XI. W. Stevens.
    Wi-LT:157
  God's Virtue. B. Barnes. Go-BP:22
  Hudibras. S. Butler. Pl-IO:23
  The Idea of Order at Key West.
    W. Stevens. Sh-AP:160, Un-MA:349
  Lightly Stepped a Yellow Star.
    E. Dickinson. Un-MA:101
  The Lost Telescope. Chi Hsüan.
    Pa-MV:50
  Man. H. Vaughan. Rv-CB:412
  The Monk in the Kitchen. A. Branch.
    Un-MA:152
  My Father's Watch. J. Ciardi.
    Pl-IO:24
  The Pleasures of Merely Circulating.
    W. Stevens. Ha-LO:12
  The Room. C. Aiken. Un-MA:424,
    Wi-LT:332
  A Slant of Sun. S. Crane. Sh-AP:145,
    Wi-LT:120
  Sonnet. J. Masefield. Un-MB:228,
    Wi-LT:191
  Sonnet XXVII. Feng Chih. Hs-TC:155
  Troilus and Cressida. W. Shakespeare.
    Pl-IO:22
  Undersong. M. Van Doren. En-PC:25
  Upon Nothing. J. Wilmot. Al-VBP:504
  We Shall Live Together. Wo-HS:(29)
  Wealth. R. Emerson. Pl-IO:34
  Zone. L. Bogan. En-PC:33
CHAPELS: see CHURCHES
CHAPERONS: see HUMOR - CHAPERONS
CHAPLAINS: see CLERGY
CHAPLIN, CHARLES
  Chaplinesque. H. Crane. Ca-VT:212,
    Wi-LT:395
  Patriotic Ode on the Fourteenth
    Anniversary of the Persecution of
    Charlie Chaplin. B. Kaufman.
    Ad-PB:264
CHAPLIN, RALPH
  Because He Was a Man. J. Pierpont.
    Kr-OF:107
CHAPMAN, GEORGE
  On First Looking into Chapman's Homer.
    J. Keats. Al-VBP:769, Co-RG:17,
    De-CH:361, Er-FA:75, Ga-FB:14,
    Gr-CT:442, Ke-TF:61, Ma-YA:182,
    Mc-PR:78, Ni-JP:19, No-CL:18,
    Ox-BN:334, Pa-GBT:169, Pl-ML:91,
    Rv-CB:739, Sm-LG:36
  Was It the Proud Full Sail of His Great
    Verse. W. Shakespeare. Pl-ML:56,
    Rv-CB:233
CHAPMAN, JOHN, (JOHNNY APPLESEED)
  The Apple-Barrel of Johnny Appleseed.
    V. Lindsay. Br-AF:118
  A Ballad of Johnny Appleseed.
    H. Oleson. Ar-TP3:41, Br-SS:142
  In Praise of Johnny Appleseed.
    V. Lindsay. Se-PR:99
  Johnny Appleseed. S. Benét. Hu-MP:390
  Johnny Appleseed. V. Lindsay. Fe-FP:431
  Johnny Appleseed's Hymn to the Sun.
    V. Lindsay. Tr-MR:29
CHARACTER
  Addressed to Haydon. J. Keats.
    Rv-CB:740
  And when I Am Entombed. R. Emerson.
    Al-VBP:800
  The Answer. R. Jeffers. Tr-MR:222
  As Kingfishers Catch Fire. G. Hopkins.
    Pl-EI:134, Tr-MR:286, Un-MB:45,
    Wi-LT:45
  Beowulf. Al-VBP:1, Ma-YA:14
  Birthday Verses Written in a Child's
    Album. J. Lowell. Ox-BC:282
  A Builder's Lesson. J. O'Reilly.
    Fe-PL:295
  The Captive. R. Kipling. Go-BP:53
  Character of a Happy Life. H. Wotton.
    Al-VBP:221, Ni-JP:169, Pa-GTB:63
  Character of the Happy Warrior.
    W. Wordsworth. Er-FA:85
  Cliff Klingenhagen. E. Robinson.
    Mo-BG:49, Sh-AP:140, Un-MA:117
  The Climb to Virtue. Simonides.
    Pa-SG:209
  The Coming American. S. Foss.
    Br-AF:33, Mc-WK:160

CHARACTER — cont'd.
  Disdain Returned. T. Carew. Al-VBP:349,
    Ga-FB:41, Pa-GTB:75
  Duty. R. Emerson. Er-FA:29
  Epilogue. S. Spender. Un-MB:472
  Forbearance. R. Emerson.
    Al-VBP:801, Hu-MP:307, Se-PR:314
  Four-Leaf Clover. E. Higginson.
    Fe-FP:540
  Give All to Love. R. Emerson.
    Al-VBP:802, Er-FA:121, Fe-PL:102,
    Mc-WK:219, No-CL:151, Sh-AP:32
  Gradatim. J. Holland. Er-FA:4
  Humility and Patience in Adversity.
    T. à Kempis. Go-BP:268
  I Bless This Man. Pindar. Mo-SD:181
  I Paint What I See. E. White.
    Mo-BG:64
  I Think Continually of Those Who Were
    Truly Great. S. Spender.
    Al-VBP:1235, Gr-CT:377, Ha-PO:222,
    Pl-EI:158, Tr-MR:166, Un-MB:477,
    Wi-LT:496
  If. R. Kipling. Er-FA:5, Hi-WP I:118,
    Ox-BC:324, Un-GT:314
  In an Age of Fops and Toys.
    R. Emerson. Fe-FP:167
  Invictus. W. Henley. Al-VBP:1067,
    Co-RM:245, Er-FA:460, Ga-FB:132,
    Ke-TF:253, Mc-PR:69, Ox-BN:883,
    Sp-OG:332, Un-GT:316, Un-MB:53
  It Is Not Growing like a Tree.
    B. Jonson. Co-PM:69, Gr-CT:375,
    Hi-WP I:113, Ma-YA:82, Pa-GTB:63
  It's in Your Face. Fe-PL:299
  Keep a Stiff Upper Lip. P. Cary.
    Er-FA:19
  The Life That Counts. Er-FA:24
  Little Things. J. Carney. An-IP:(31),
    Ch-B:89, Er-FA:239, Fe-FP:540,
    Mo-CC:(2), Ox-BC:182, Un-GT:306
  The Measure of a Man. Fe-PL:312
  Move Un-noticed to be Noticed.
    N. Giovanni. Be-MA:166
  My Sort of Man. P. Dunbar. Bo-AN:6
  A Nation's Strength. R. Emerson.
    Br-AF:35, Fe-FP:452, Vi-PP:65
  The Need of the Hour. E. Markham.
    Vi-PP:224
  The Noble. W. Wordsworth. Gr-CT:377
  On Freedom. J. Lowell. Mc-WK:185,
    Vi-PP:66
  Once to Every Man and Nation.
    J. Lowell. Vi-PP:68
  Prayer. L. Untermeyer. Un-GT:308,
    Un-MA:305
  Recessional. R. Kipling. Al-VBP:1101,
    Er-FA:472, Ga-FB:242, Ma-YA:229,
    Ox-BN:867, Sp-OG:214, Un-MB:135
  The Rich Interior Life. R. Eberhart.
    Tr-MR:250
  Rounding the Horn. J. Masefield. Un-MB:223

  Rugby Chapel — November, 1857.
    M. Arnold. Rv-CB:874
  Say Not the Struggle Nought Availeth.
    A. Clough. Al-VBP:926, Er-FA:460,
    Ga-FB:132, Ke-TF:57, Ox-BN:610,
    Pa-GTB:358, Pl-EI:121, Rv-CB:842,
    Tu-WW:44
  Shrine to What Should Be. M. Evans.
    Hu-NN:77
  A Song. L. Binyon. Un-MB:157
  Success. Er-FA:17
  Summer Oracle. A. Lorde. Ad-PB:245,
    Be-MA:123, Jo-SA:88
  A Thought. S. Ukachev. Mo-MI:83
  Thought. Al-PI:20
  To Be Honest, to Be Kind.
    R. Stevenson. Fe-PL:311
  Tolerance. T. Hardy. Tr-MR:158
  Trees. H. Nemerov. Co-BN:159
  The Way of Life. Laotzu. Mc-MK:220
CHARACTER EDUCATION: see BEHAVIOR;
    CHARACTER; VALUE AND VALUES
CHARCOAL BURNERS
  The Penny Whistle. E. Thomas.
    Un-MB:216
CHARIOT RACING
  The Chariot Race. Virgil. Mo-SD:69
CHARITY: see also FORGIVENESS; HUMOR -
    CHARITY; SATIRE - CHARITY
  Essay on Man. A. Pope. Al-VBP:536
  For Johnny. J. Pudney. Hi-WP I:24
  For Modes of Faith Let Graceless
    Zealots Fight. A. Pope. Go-BP:179
  Shiv and the Grasshopper.
    R. Kipling. Go-BP:84
  The Vision of Sir Launfal. J. Lowell.
    Pa-OM:210
CHARLEMAGNE, EMPEROR, HOLY ROMAN EMPIRE
  Charlemagne. H. Longfellow.
    Er-FA:310
CHARLES I, KING OF ENGLAND
  As I Was Going by Charing Cross.
    Bl-OB:146, De-CH:177, De-TT:181,
    Gr-GB:188, Ir-BB:261, Sm-LG:153
  By the Statue of King Charles at
    Charing Cross. L. Johnson.
    Co-RG:18, Ni-JP:165, Ox-BN:946,
    Un-MB:153
  Charing Cross. Rv-CB:447
  His Metrical Vow. J. Graham.
    Al-VBP:425
  A Horation Ode upon Cromwell.
    A. Marvell. Al-VBP:459, Pa-GTB:51
  King Charles upon the Scaffold.
    A. Marvell. Gr-CT:378
CHARLES II, KING OF ENGLAND: see also
    HUMOR - CHARLES II, KING OF ENGLAND
  Charles the Second. J. Wilmot.
    Hi-FO:157
  On Charles II. J. Wilmot. Ha-PO:59
CHARLES VII, KING OF FRANCE
  Henry VI, Part 1. W. Shakespeare. Hi-FO:9[

CHARLES II, KING OF SPAIN
  The Emperor's Bird's-Nest.
    H. Longfellow. Hu-MP:419, Re-BS:14
CHARLES XII, KING OF SWEDEN
  The Vanity of Human Wishes. S. Johnson.
    Al-VBP:552, Hi-FO:171
CHARLES EDWARD STUART: see STUART,
    CHARLES EDWARD (BONNIE PRINCE CHARLIE)
CHARLES, RAY
  The Bishop of Atlanta: Ray Charles.
    J. Bond. Bo-AN:184, Mo-BG:54
  Blues Note. B. Kaufman. Ad-PB:263,
    Be-MA:131, Jo-SA:36
  Charles. L. Clark. Ma-FW:180
CHARLES RIVER
  Some Refrains at the Charles River.
    P. Viereck. En-PC:154
CHARLESTON, S.C.
  Charleston. H. Timrod. Sh-AP:125
  Charleston - Post Confederate.
    A. Deas. Ke-TF:360
  Dusk. D. Heyward. Pa-HT:43
CHARMS: see also HUMOR - CHARMS
  Against Witches. Gr-GB:290
  All Hail to Thee Moon. De-CH:668
  An Amulet. S. Menashe. Sm-MK:15
  A Charm. J. Dryden. Gr-CT:151
  A Charm. R. Herrick. Gr-CT:167
  Charm. Tr-US II:108
  Charm Against a Swarm of Bees. Ma-YA:3
  A Charm Against Cough. Al-PI:18
  A Charm Against the Stitch. Ma-FW:233
  A Charm Against the Toothache.
    J. Heath-Stubbs. Br-TC:177,
    Go-BP:49, Ma-FW:231, Sm-MK:194
  Charm at a Ceremonial Bathing to Make
    One Beautiful and Irresistible.
    Tr-US I:197
  Charm for a Rebab. Tr-US II:207
  Charm for Going a-Hunting. M. Austin.
    Sh-RP:341
  Charm for Rain. Tr-US I:214
  A Charm for Spring Flowers. R. Field.
    Ar-TP3:211, Tu-WW:58
  Charm for Striking Fear into a Tiger.
    Tr-US II:205
  A Charm for the Ear-Ache. J. Kirkup.
    Go-BP:48
  Charm for the Oil. Tr-US II:208
  Charm of the Rice-Reapers.
    Tr-US II:207
  A Charm, or an Allay for Love.
    R. Burns. Sm-LG:236
  Charm to Cure Burns. Su-FVI:48
  Charm to Cure Fevers. Su-FVI:48
  Charm to Cure Warts. Su-FVI:49
  Charm to Restore a Dying Man.
    Tr-US I:189
  Charms. Bi-IT:92
  Charms Against the Demon. Tr-US II:206
  Churning. De-CH:670, Mo-MGT:85
  The Coconut-Monkey. Tr-US II:198

Come You. Ho-SD:27
A Conjuration to Electra. R. Herrick.
  Gr-SS:145
Devil Doll. L. Grenelle. De-FS:99
The Dove. Gr-CT:93, Gr-GB:61
The Dream. L. Bogan. Pe-OA:146,
  Un-MA:492, Wi-LT:382
The Evil Eye. J. Ciardi. Ca-MB:19
Evocation. H. King. De-FS:129
The First of May. Bo-FP:235, Ir-BB:226,
  Mo-MGT:121, Mo-NR:91, Rv-ON:44,
  Wr-RM:66
Flute-Priest Song for Rain. A. Lowell.
  Pl-US:132
Formula for Obtaining Long Life.
  Da-SC:141
Formula for Young Children. Da-SC:143
Gipsy Song. B. Jonson. Sm-LG:236
He That Would Live. De-CH:671
Hear, Sweet Spirit. S. Coleridge.
  Al-VBP:700, De-CH:313
Hempseed. Rv-ON:45
Herb Pimpernell. De-CH:667
Herbs and Simples. M. Keller.
  De-FS:123
Here's to Thee. Bl-OB:139, Bo-FP:144,
  Ch-B:100, Mo-MGT:191, Mo-TB:120,
  Tu-WW:17
The Hopis and the Famine. Te-FC:35
I Love Animals and Dogs. H. Farley.
  Le-M:89
I Sought a Vision. Ho-SD:14
Incantation Used by a Jealous Woman.
  Tr-US II:124
Kiph. W. de la Mare. Ar-TP3:151
Koko Oloro. W. Soyinka. Gr-BT:16
Learning the Spells: A Diptych.
  A. Probst. Ni-CD:170
Litany for Halloween. Au-SP:371,
  Br-SM:3, Br-SS:72, Co-PS:140,
  Mo-TB:77, Se-PR:192
Love Charm. Br-MW:112
Love Charm. Tr-US II:205
Love-Charm Song. Br-MW:99
Love-Charm Songs. Da-SC:152,
  Tr-US II:223
Love-Charm Songs, I, II. Br-MW:6
Love Incantation. Tr-US I:201
Love Incantations. Tr-US II:232
Love-Magic Spell. Tr-US I:205
Luck for Halloween. M. Justus.
  Ja-PA:36, Ju-CP:81
Magic Formula. Bi-IT:163
Magic Formula Against Disease.
  Bi-IT:151
Magic Formula to Destroy Life.
  Bi-IT:98
Magic Formula to Fix a Bride's
  Affections. Bi-IT:79
Magic Formula to Make an Enemy
  Peaceful. Bi-IT:69

CHARMS — cont'd.
  Magic Song for Him Who Wishes to Live.
    Le-IB:27, Tr-US I:3
  Magic Words. Le-IB:28, Tr-US I:9
  Magic Words to Bring Luck when Hunting
    Caribou. Le-IB:67
  Magical Chant. Tr-US II:209
  Medicine Song for Snake Sickness.
    Da-SC:145
  My Name Is John Wellington Wells.
    W. Gilbert. Co-PM:72
  The Nativity Chant. W. Scott.
    Gr-CT:167, Sm-LG:233
  Our Savior Was of Virgin Born.
    De-CH:670
  The Peddler of Spells. Lu Yu.
    Le-MW:127
  Plague Charm. Hi-FO:153
  The Protective Grigri. T. Joans.
    Ad-PB:207
  Right Cheek! Left Cheek! De-CH:669
  Runes IX. H. Nemerov. Du-SH:100
  The Shaman Aua's Song to Call His
    Spirits. Tr- US I:10
  Snake Medicine Song. Da-SC:144
  Song. B. Jonson. Gr-SS:138
  A Spell. J. Dryden. Gr-SS:153,
    Ho-WR:226
  A Spell. G. Peele. Gr-CT:153
  Spell Called "The Lifting of the Head."
    Tr-US II:27
  A Spell of Invisibility. C. Marlowe.
    Gr-CT:154
  A Spell to Destroy Life. Br-MW:111
  Spells. J. Reeves. Co-PM:143,
    Sm-MK:54
  Stand Fast Root. De-CH:669
  Storm Tide on Mejit. Tr-US II:31
  The Sunrise. Da-SC:87
  Ten Commandments, Seven Deadly Sins,
    and Five Wits. Gr-CT:168
  There Came Two Angels. De-CH:671
  Thief's Spell. Tr-US I:207
  This Is to Make Children Jump Down.
    Da-SC:143
  This Knot I Knot. De-CH:668, Gr-GB:148
  Those Dressed in Blue. De-CH:669
  Thrice Toss These Oaken Ashes.
    T. Campion. Al-VBP:216, Gr-SS:146,
    Sm-LG:236
  To Frighten a Storm. G. Cardiff.
    Ni-CD:54
  To Frighten a Storm. Da-SC:143
  Two Apple-Howling Songs, Surrey.
    Bo-FP:143
  Two Charms to Cure Hiccups, I, II.
    Su-FVI:48
  Underneath This Hazelin Mote. De-CH:670
  A Voice Speaks from the Well. G. Peele.
    Rv-CB:176, Sm-LG:237
  Weather Chant. Le-IB:118
  Weather Incantation. Le-IB:31
  The Witch of Willoughby Wood.
    R. Bennett. Co-PM:27, Sh-RP:228
  Witches' Charm. B. Jonson. Bl-OB:88,
    Sm-LG:234
  The Witches' Charms. B. Jonson.
    Co-PM:107, Re-TW:26
  Witch's Broomstick Spell. Gr-GB:290
  Witch's Milking Charm. Gr-CT:159,
    Gr-GB:290
  With a Four-Leaved Clover. De-CH:670
  A Woman's First Sewing after a Mourning.
    Da-SC:40
  The Woods Grow Darker. L. Drake.
    De-FS:75
  Yarrow, Sweet Yarrow. De-CH:669
  See also Mo-TB:79-81
CHARON
  Dirce. W. Landor. Al-VBP:707,
    Gr-CT:80, Ox-BN:190, Rv-CB:668
CHARTISM
  The Old Chartist. G. Meredith.
    Hi-FO:244
CHARTRES, FR.
  Chartres Cathedral. D. Babcock.
    Ls-NY:239
  Return to Chartres. M. Sarton.
    Ke-TF:379
CHASE: see HUNTING
CHATTAHOOCHEE RIVER
  Song of the Chattahoochee. S. Lanier.
    Br-AF:176, Co-BN:70, Ga-FB:311,
    Mc-PR:195, Sh-AP:131
CHAUCER, GEOFFREY
  Chaucer. H. Longfellow. No-CL:12,
    Pl-ML:98, Rv-CB:780, Sh-AP:39
  "The Lyf So Short. . . ."
    W. Stafford. Pl-ML:97
  Sir Geoffrey Chaucer. R. Greene.
    De-CH:488, Hi-WP II:123, Sm-LG:127
CHEATING: see DECEPTION
CHEERS AND CHEERLEADING
  Cheers. E. Merriam. Du-RG:115
  Strawberry Shortcake, Blueberry Pie.
    Sm-LG:122
CHEESE: see also HUMOR - CHEESE
  Turn, Cheeses, Turn. Rv-ON:17
CHEMISTRY: see also HUMOR - CHEMISTRY
  The Naked World. Sully-Prudhomme.
    Pl-IO:69
CHEROKEE INDIANS: see also INDIANS OF
    NORTH AMERICA - VERSE - CHEROKEE
  In the Name of God. R. Emerson.
    Kr-OF:11
  Wail! For Our Nation. J. Lowell.
    Kr-OF:10
CHERRIES: see also HUMOR - CHERRIES
  Bread and Cherries. W. de la Mare.
    Br-SG:71
  Cherries a Ha'penny a Stick.
    De-CH:573
  A Cherry. Wr-RM:121
  Cherry Robbers. D. Lawrence. Un-MB:287

Cherry-Stones. E. Farjeon. Ag-HE:52
The Child and the Sparrow. T. Westwood.
   Re-BS:39
Eardrops. W. Davies. Gr-CC:16
Pan and the Cherries. P. Fort.
   Co-PM:67
Riddle Me. Mo-MGT:154
Round and Sound. De-CH:572
Round as a Marble. Gr-BB:9
Under the Boughs. G. Baro. Co-BN:156
CHERRY BLOSSOMS
   As Now I Come. Nöin. Ba-ST:25
   Blossoms and Storm. Sadaiye. Pa-SG:90
   The Cherry-Blossom Wand. A. Wickham.
      Un-MB:281, Un-MW:25
   The Cherry Blossoms. Yekei Hoshi.
      Ba-ST:22
   The Child Sways on the Swing. Issa.
      Le-MW:104
   The Prancing Pony. De-PP:31
   What a Thing to See! Be-CS:61
CHERRY TREES: see also HUMOR - CHERRY
   TREES
   The Cherry Tree Blossomed. Tomonori.
      Le-MW:129
   Kosumi, the Carver. Yehoash. Ho-TY:75
   Loveliest of Trees. A. Housman.
      Al-VBP:1079, Bl-OB:136, Bo-FP:246,
      Co-BN:145, Er-FA:153, Fe-PL:371,
      Ga-FB:232, Go-BP:28, Gr-CT:47,
      Hu-MP:276, Ma-FW:13, Ma-YA:222,
      Sh-RP:208, Sm-MK:172, Tu-WW:52,
      Un-MB:95, Wi-LT:58
   Oh, Fair to See. C. Rossetti.
      Ar-TP3:204, Ch-B:107, Fe-FP:215,
      Gr-EC:44, Ha-YA:46, Hu-MP:277
   The Three Cherry Trees. W. de la Mare.
      Gr-SS:35
   The Weeping Cherry. R. Herrick.
      Hi-WP II:1
   Weeping Cherry Trees. De-PP:27
CHERUBS: see ANGELS
CHESAPEAKE (SHIP)
   The "Shannon" and the "Chesapeake."
      De-TT:134
CHESS
   The Game of Chess. E. Pound. Li-TU:42
CHESTNUT TREES
   Above the Ruins. Basho. Be-CS:23
CHESTNUTS
   Chestnut Stands. R. Field. Br-SS:73
   Horse-Chestnut Time. K. Staybird.
      La-PV:84
   The Horse Chestnut Tree. R. Eberhart.
      Pe-OA:194, Un-MA:578, Wi-LT:437
   What Nut Is There. Re-RR:54
CHIATURA, U.S.S.R.
   A Funeral in Tchiatura. A. Mezhirov.
      Ca-MR:89
CHICAGO, ILL.: see also HUMOR - CHICAGO,
   ILL.; SATIRE - CHICAGO, ILL.
   Aunt Jane Allen. F. Johnson. Ad-PB:24,
      Hu-PN:89

The Bourgeois Poet. K. Shapiro.
   St-H:204
Chicago. J. Gill. Sc-TN:64
Chicago. B. Harte. Hi-TL:136
Chicago. C. Sandburg. Al-VBP:1137,
   Ca-VT:20, Ga-FB:271, Pa-HT:45,
   Pe-OA:52, Sm-LG:147, Un-MA:199,
   Wi-LT:638
Chicago. J. Whittier. Se-PR:316
Free at Last. A. Alenik. La-IH:126
Heels Wear Down. R. Roseliep. St-H:187
Night. C. Sandburg. La-OC:132
Ode of the Angels of Chicago Who Move
   Perpetually. P. Carroll. St-H:20
One-Sided Shoot-Out. D. Lee.
   Ad-PB:423, Ra-BP:302
Sitting upon the Koala Bear Statue.
   J. Tomasello. La-IH:120
Swallow the Lake. C. Major. Ad-PB:302
Tonight in Chicago. . . . Br-AF:204
CHICAGO, ILL. - HISTORY
   Before the Judge. D. Edelshtat.
      Kr-OF:111
CHICKADEES
   Chickadee. H. Conkling. Ar-TP3:56
   Chickadee. R. Emerson. Bo-FP:175,
      Fe-FP:290, Mc-PR:129
   Christmas Tree. A. Fisher. La-PH:38,
      La-PV:173
   Song of the Chickadee. Bo-FP:167
CHICKENS: see also COCKFIGHTS; HUMOR -
   CHICKENS
   Baby Chick. A. Fisher. Co-IW:36
   Ballad of Another Ophelia. D. Lawrence.
      Gr-CT:79
   A Bantam Rooster. Kikaku. Be-MC:25
   Before the Barn-Door Crowing. J. Gay.
      Co-EL:14, Rv-CB:505
   Biddy. F. Lape. Co-BBW:179
   Birthday Gifts. L. Scott. Br-BC:99
   A Bright Red Flower He Wears on His Head.
      Wy-CM:20
   Calypsos III. W. Williams. Ho-TH:72
   Chanticleer. W. Austin. Ga-S:77
   Chanticleer. J. Farrar. Ar-TP3:72,
      Au-SP:50, Bo-FP:65
   Chanticleer. K. Tynan. Ar-TP3:72,
      Hu-MP:219, Tu-WW:86
   Chicken. W. de la Mare. Ar-TP3:72
   The Chicken. Le-IS:12
   Chicken Come Clock. Rv-ON:27
   Chicken in the Bread Tray. Bu-DY:39
   The Chicken Wants. S. Karai. Ma-FW:93
   The Chickens. Ar-TP3:71
   Chicks and Ducks. St-FS:122
   The Clucking Hen. A. Hawkshawe.
      Ch-B:45, Ir-BB:28
   The Cock. A. Buttigirg. Pa-RE:121
   The Cock. M. Mota. An-TC:113
   The Cock. Mother Goose. Ar-TP3:174,
      Bo-FP:65
   Cock. A. Ostroff. Ls-NY:105

CHICKENS — cont'd.
  Cock-a-Doodle-Doo! Ir-BB:120,
    Li-LB:96, Mo-MGT:125, Mo-TL:88
  The Cock Again. Kikaku. Au-SP:49
  The Cock and the Fox. J. de la Fontaine.
    Mc-PR:14
  Cock-Crow. E. Thomas. Pa-GTB:444,
    Un-MB:215
  The Cock Crows. Ca-MU:11
  Cocks Crow in the Morn. Ar-TP3:174,
    Sp-TM:1, Un-GT:22, Wr-RM:78
  Come and See! Wy-CM:22
  The Complete Hen. E. Coatsworth.
    Un-GT:66
  A Dog and a Cock. Ir-BB:237
  Five Hens. Gr-GB:58, Mo-MGT:135
  Five Little Chickens. Ch-B:85,
    Fe-FP:282, Gr-EC:182, La-PV:198,
    St-FS:78, Un-GB:15, Un-GT:67
  Four-Footed Poems. E. Greenberg.
    Ho-TY:312
  The Fox and the Rooster. E. Rees.
    Ar-TP3:82
  The Goose and the Gander. Gr-GB:57
  He Leaves the Nest. Su-FVI:68
  Hen and Cock. Gr-GB:58
  The Hen and the Carp. I. Serraillier.
    Co-BBW:62
  The Hens. E. Roberts. Ar-TP3:73,
    Au-SP:50, Bo-GJ:51, Co-BBW:166,
    Co-IW:20, Fe-FP:281, Hu-MP:239,
    La-PV:129, Li-LC:27, Pe-FB:21,
    Th-AS:47, Tu-WW:96, Un-GB:14,
    Un-GT:66
  Hens in Winter. R. Coffin. Ho-TH:36
  Hen's Nest. J. Clare. Rd-OA:71
  Hickety, Pickety, My Black Hen. Mother
    Goose. An-IP:(13), Ar-TP3:103,
    Au-SP:16, Bo-FP:89, De-PO:20,
    Li-LB:93, Mo-MGT:120, Mo-NR:23,
    On-TW:34, Wi-MG:11, Wr-RM:39
  I Had a Little Hen. Ir-BB:66, Li-LB:90,
    Pa-AP:12, Wr-RM:21
  I Have a Gentle Cock. Al-VBP:23,
    Gr-GB:100, Rv-CB:23
  I Pray You, Rooster. Br-FW:9
  In the Barnyard. D. Aldis. Sh-RP:330
  Janet Waking. J. Ransom. Pe-SS:32,
    Re-TW:21, Sh-AP:181, Un-MA:410
  Linked Pantuns. Tr-US I:177
  Little Cock, Little Cock. Gr-BB:5
  A Little Egg. T. Anthony. Le-M:30
  The Maid to Her Cock. Bo-FP:67
  The Mouse, the Frog, and the Little
    Red Hen. Gr-EC:31, Ir-BB:89
  Near and Far. H. Behn. Li-LC:56
  The Prayer of the Cock. C. Gasztold.
    Ar-TP3:82
  A Pullet in the Pen. Mother Goose.
    Ag-HE:19, Ir-BB:226
  Red Rooster. H. Conkling. Ir-BB:74
  Rooster. F. Belkin. Co-BBW:172

  Roosters. E. Bishop. Wi-LT:506
  See-Saw, Margery Daw. Au-SP:6,
    Ir-BB:11, Li-LB:130, Mo-MGT:28,
    Mo-NR:3, Mo-TL:16
  Song of the Battery Hen. E. Brock.
    To-MP:116
  Though Not a Soldier. Re-RR:40
  Weaving the Morning. J. de Melo Neto.
    An-TC:151
  What the Cock and Hen Say. Mo-MGT:78,
    Rv-ON:26, Sp-TM:6
  What They Do. E. Farjeon. Gr-TG:44
  Which Animal Travels Lightest.
    Re-RR:30
  Who Stole the Nest? Ir-BB:87,
    St-FS:112
  Wild Spurs. Owen. Le-M:98
CHIEFS: see INDIANS OF NORTH AMERICA -
    CHIEFS
CHILD LABOR
  Child Labor. C. Gilman. Kr-OF:173
  The Cry of the Children. E. Browning.
    Al-VBP:819, Cl-FC:27
  The Golf Links. S. Cleghorn.
    Er-FA:268, Fe-PL:421, Ke-PP:61,
    Kr-OF:180
CHILDHOOD: see also CHILDHOOD RECOLLEC-
    TIONS; CHILDREN; SATIRE - CHILDHOOD
  The Birth in a Narrow Room. G. Brooks.
    Ha-TP:117, Hu-PN:335
  Cemetery of Childhood. J. Cardozo.
    An-TC:29
  Child. S. Plath. Ma-FW:66
  A Child-Thought. W. Thorley. Bo-FP:273
  Childhood. Ma-FW:67
  Children Are Game. I. Gardner. St-H:66
  Dedication on the Gift of a Book to a
    Child. H. Belloc. Gr-TG:21
  Down the Glimmering Staircase.
    S. Sassoon. Fe-PL:413
  The Echoing Green. W. Blake.
    Bo-FP:237, Ch-B:115, Co-PS:59,
    De-CH:21, Ho-WR:161, Rv-CB:589
  Eleven. A. MacLeish. Ni-JP:26
  Escape. T. McGrath. St-H:123
  For a Six-Year Old. F. Rodman.
    Ke-TF:250
  From a Childhood. R. Rilke. Gr-SS:133
  From Early Childhood Even as Hath Been
    Said. W. Wordsworth. Go-BP:273
  Her Christmas Tree. E. Maleska.
    Ke-TF:228
  Hiawatha's Childhood. H. Longfellow.
    Ar-TP3:36, Fe-FP:405, Ga-FB:248,
    Gr-EC:100, Hu-MP:422, Li-SR:54,
    Mc-PR:80, Sh-RP:272
  Long Time a Child. H. Coleridge.
    Ox-BN:398, Rv-CB:758
  Measure Me, Sky. L. Speyer. Ad-PE:46,
    Br-BC:129, Fe-FP:22, Hu-MP:63
  Mutterings over the Crib of a Deaf
    Child. J. Wright. Du-SH:139

Once. W. de la Mare. Go-BP:170
Out of Bounds. J. Stallworthy.
  Ha-TP:121
Portrait of a Girl with a Comic Book.
  P. McGinley. Pe-OA:198, Pe-SS:39
The Sleeping Giant. D. Hall.
  Br-TC:165, Ni-JP:25
The Stars. Ping Hsin. Hs-TC:21
The Stone Frog. G. Pritchard.
  Co-PM:8, Ls-NY:226
Sword and Flower. T. Utan. Mc-AC:144
A Thought. A. Milne. Gr-TG:20
To a Child Dancing in the Wind.
  W. Yeats. Co-PI:202
Tree-Sleeping. R. Coffin. Ha-LO:54
The Truth about My Sister and Me.
  A. Probst. Ni-CD:166
Washington. N. Turner. Ar-TP3:92,
  Au-SP:362, Fe-FP:413, Gr-EC:230,
  Ha-YA:183, Hu-MP:376, Pe-FB:33
When I Was Young. Le-OE:119, Ma-BH:26
The Wise Child. E. Lucie-Smith.
  Ls-NY:229
Youth. A. W. Hu-MP:65
CHILDHOOD RECOLLECTIONS: see also HUMOR –
  CHILDHOOD RECOLLECTIONS; MEMORIES
Above the Moving River. D. Kherdian.
  Kh-VA:72
Adults Only. W. Stafford. St-H:215
All Day It Has Rained. A. Lewis.
  Hi-WP I:28, Pa-GTB:543
Among Many Heaps of Ashes.
  Cho Sung Kyun. Ba-PO:156, Cr-WS:6
Among School Children. W. Yeats.
  Pa-GTB:428, Un-MB:114, Wi-LT:72
Arrowhead Field. L. Herrick. Ha-TP:124
Auld Lang Syne. R. Burns. Bo-FP:209,
  Er-FA:425, Fe-PL:129, Ma-YA:133,
  Sp-OG:260
Autobiographical Note. V. Scannell.
  To-MP:127
Autobiography. M. Dipoko. Lo-TY:142
Autobiography. L. MacNeice. Gr-BT:13,
  Ma-FW:193
Autumn. E. Roberts. Co-PT:285,
  Ja-PA:49
Autumn. J. Untermeyer. Un-MA:332
The Babiaantje. F. Prince. Un-MB:488
Baking Day. R. Joseph. To-MP:142
The Barefoot Boy. J. Whittier.
  Ch-B:65, Fe-FP:544, Fe-PL:249
Bears. A. Rich. Ha-TP:120
Before the Big Storm. W. Stafford.
  St-H:214
Ben Bolt. T. English. Er-FA:342
Birches. R. Frost. Fe-PL:437,
  Ga-FB:299, Mo-BG:114, Pe-OA:33,
  Sm-LG:61, Sp-OG:357, Un-MA:177,
  Wi-LT:166
Birthday Candles. G. Johnson. Ke-TF:155
Birthplace Revisited. G. Corso. Ad-CI:63,
  Ca-VT:655, Kh-VA:65, La-OC:58

Block City. R. Stevenson. Au-SP:210,
  Bo-FP:17, Fe-FP:103, Hu-MP:44
The Bourgeois Poet, #54. K. Shapiro.
  St-H:205
Brother and Sister. W. Wordsworth.
  De-TT:33
Cathexis. F. Bryant. Ad-PB:406
The Cave. G. Dresbach. La-RM:35,
  Pe-SS:42
The Centaur. M. Swenson. Br-TC:425,
  Du-SH:44, Li-TU:107, Mo-BG:72
Chicago. J. Gill. Sc-TN:64
Childhood. H. Percikow. La-OC:75
Childhood. M. Walker. Ad-BO:73,
  Ad-PB:148, Be-MA:77
Childhood and School-Time.
  W. Wordsworth. Ox-BN:93
Christmas Eve. C. Day Lewis.
  Pl-EI:29
The Chums. T. Roethke. Du-SH:41
Clifton Grove. H. White. Ox-BN:228
The Collier. V. Watkins. Ma-FW:197,
  To-MP:24
Colonel Fantock. E. Sitwell. Un-MB:334
Coming Back Home. R. Young Bear.
  Ni-CD:280
Commander Lowell. R. Lowell. Ca-VT:451
Conversation about Christmas. D. Thomas.
  Li-TU:28, 37
Crane. J. Langland. St-H:109
Crystal Moment. R. Coffin. Gr-EC:162,
  Pe-SS:74
Debate Question, Quarry Dream.
  R. Warren. Ca-VT:277
Digging for China. R. Wilbur.
  Bo-GJ:224, Br-TC:471, Gr-BT:11,
  Ha-LO:88, Ho-TH:66
Early Friends. M. Mansfield. Ke-TF:74
Earth Dweller. W. Stafford. Mc-EA:118
Echoes of Childhood. A. Corbin.
  Hu-PN:491
The Echoing Green. W. Blake.
  Bo-FP:237, Ch-B:115, Co-PS:59,
  De-CH:21, Ho-WR:161, Rv-CB:589
Elegy for the Rev. Mr. James B. Hodgson.
  J. Logan. St-H:111
The Elementary Scene. R. Jarrell.
  Pe-SS:161
Fairy Days. W. Thackeray. Un-GT:16
Family Prime. M. Van Doren. Ca-VT:195
Fern Hill. D. Thomas. Al-VBP:1246,
  Bo-GJ:53, Br-TC:440, Co-RG:160,
  Fe-PL:251, Ga-FB:166, Hi-WP II:46,
  Mc-EA:42, Mc-WK:10, Na-EO:45,
  Pa-GBT:542, Pe-SS:162, Re-TW:100,
  Sm-LG:108, Un-MB:502, Wi-LT:559
The 1st. L. Clifton. Mo-TS:6
First Blood. J. Stallworthy.
  Ha-TP:104
Fish. J. Unternecker. Sc-TN:219
Flame-Heart. C. McKay. Bo-AN:30,
  Hu-PN:104

CHILDHOOD RECOLLECTIONS — cont'd.
  Fra Lippo Lippi. R. Browning.
    Al-VBP:898
  Frost at Midnight. S. Coleridge.
    Ox-BN:162, Rv-CB:661
  Gic to Har. K. Rexroth. Ca-BP:23,
    Kh-VA:68
  Gift. C. Freeman. Ab-MO:75,
    Ad-PB:397, Hu-PN:435, Lo-TY:255
  Glimpses #xii. L. McGaugh. Ad-BO:74
  Golden Fishes. Br-FF:(38), Mo-MGT:79
  The Grandmother. E. Roberts. Hu-MP:14
  Grandmother's Story of Bunker Hill
    Battle. O. Holmes. Un-GT:178
  The Green Door. L. Drake. Br-BC:155
  Halloween. J. Benton. Se-PR:192
  Here Lives the Jewish People.
    H. Leivick. Ho-TY:120
  Horses. E. Muir. Sm-LG:80
  House in Denver. T. Ferril. Br-AF:208
  I Know a Secret. C. Morley. Hu-MP:27
  I Remember. T. Hood. De-CH:23,
    De-TT:100, Er-FA:148, Fe-FP:542,
    Ga-FB:159, Hu-MP:2, Pa-GTB:223,
    Rv-CB:761, Un-GT:95
  i used to wrap my white doll up in.
    M. Jackson. Ad-BO:72, Ad-PB:498
  Improvisations: Light and Snow.
    C. Aiken. Co-BN:189
  In School Days. J. Whittier.
    Fe-FP:543, Hu-MP:406
  In the Kitchen of the Old House.
    D. Hall. To-MP:144
  In These Dissenting Times. A. Walker.
    Ad-PB:475
  Incident. C. Cullen. Ab-MO:94,
    Ad-PB:91, Be-MA:51, Ca-VT:241,
    Ho-LP:58, Hu-PN:232, Jo-SA:107,
    Kr-OF:50, Mo-BG:78, Pe-OA:190,
    Ra-BP:98, Th-AS:193
  Indian Reservation: Caughnawaga.
    A. Klein. Wi-LT:748
  The Indian Woman. W. Whitman.
    Bo-FP:21
  Infancy. C. de Andrade. An-TC:87
  Intimations of an Autobiography.
    J. Tate. St-H:226
  Isaac and Archibald. E. Robinson.
    Ni-JP:145, Pe-OA:9
  Jigsaw. J. Wade. Sc-TN:224
  Jimmy's Father. J. Wade. Sc-TN:225
  Kaddish. A. Ginsberg. Lo-IT:58
  Keepsake Mill. R. Stevenson.
    Tu-WW:27
  Kind Sir: These Woods. A. Sexton.
    Ha-TP:93
  Kindergarten. R. Rogers. Al-WW:87
  Knoxville, Tennessee. N. Giovanni.
    Ad-BO:58, Ad-PB:450, Ra-BP:322
  Landmark. J. Hearst. St-H:77
  The Lime-Tree. E. Lucie-Smith.
    Gr-BT:15

  Lines on Receiving His Mother's Picture.
    W. Cowper. De-CH:38
  Lion. M. Swenson. Pe-OA:249,
    Wi-LT:827
  A Little Boy Lost. J. Rothenberg.
    Kh-VA:20
  A Little More Traveling Music.
    A. Young. Mc-EA:28
  Locked Out. R. Frost. Li-TU:31
  The Midnight Snack. J. Merrill.
    Mo-BG:80
  Modifications. R. Koertge. Du-SH:42,
    Pe-M:22
  My Father in the Night Commanding No.
    L. Simpson. Br-MP:330, Br-TC:380,
    Ca-VT:520, Hi-WP II:357
  My Father's Trunk. R. Roseliep.
    St-H:188
  My Last Afternoon with Uncle Devereux
    Winslow. R. Lowell. Ca-VT:447
  My Lost Youth. H. Longfellow.
    Al-VBP:825, Bo-GJ:178, Co-RG:114,
    Er-FA:163, Fe-FP:547, Fe-PL:253,
    Ga-FB:160, Hu-MP:73, No-CL:257,
    Pa-HT:9
  My Mother's Breast. J. Okito.
    Le-TA:21
  My Parents Kept Me from Children Who
    Were Rough. S. Spender. Ho-LP:59,
    Ma-FW:62, Pe-SS:26
  My Playmate. J. Whittier. De-TT:88
  My Trust. J. Whittier. Se-PR:118
  The Night Mirror. J. Hollander.
    Ho-P:111
  Nikki-Rosa. N. Giovanni. Ad-CI:20,
    Ad-PB:451, Be-MA:169, Jo-SA:22
  No Finis. D. Schubert. Mc-EA:169
  No One Remembers Abandoning the Village
    of White Fir. D. Niatum. Ni-CD:124
  Number 7. L. Ferlinghetti. Ad-CI:18,
    Du-RG:102, Kh-VA:74, La-OC:85,
    Pe-SS:156
  Nutting. W. Wordsworth. Rv-CB:637
  Ode on a Distant Prospect of Clapham
    Academy. T. Hood. Rv-CB:763
  Ode on a Distant Prospect of Eton
    College. T. Gray. Al-VBP:563,
    Pa-GTB:158
  Ode on Intimations of Immortality.
    W. Wordsworth. Al-VBP:662, Br-BC:18,
    Er-FA:157, Ga-FB:101, Gr-CT:436,
    Ha-PO:206, Ox-BN:84, Pa-GTB:308,
    Pl-EI:59
  Odyssey of a Slum. V. Howard.
    La-IH:124
  Of Flesh and Bone. I. Gardner.
    St-H:67
  Old Gray Squirrel. A. Noyes.
    Co-SS:215
  The Old Oaken Bucket. S. Woodworth.
    Er-FA:138, Fe-FP:543

The Old Oaken Bucket. Er-FA:208
The Old Swimmin'-Hole. J. Riley.
   Er-FA:241
On the Appeal from the Race of Sheba:II.
   L. Senghor. Lo-TY:134
Once a Child. E. Dickinson. Pl-IO:21
Once upon a Great Holiday. A. Wilkinson.
   Do-WH:15
The Orange Bears. K. Patchen. Kh-VA:7
Our House. O. Goga. Mc-AC:39
Out of the Cradle Endlessly Rocking.
   W. Whitman. Al-VBP:936, Un-MA:66
Out to Old Aunt Mary's. J. Riley.
   Er-FA:143
Pagan Saturday. J. Logan. St-H:114
Paradigm of a Hero. J. Mathews.
   Ha-TP:56
The Pennycandystore Beyond the El.
   L. Ferlinghetti. Ad-CI:17,
   Mo-BG:19, Pe-SS:88
Piano. D. Lawrence. Pa-GTB:457,
   Rv-CB:977, Un-MB:289
Picture in an Old Frame.
   E. Chaffee. Ke-TF:68
The Place's Fault. P. Hobsbaum.
   To-MP:131
Poem. S. Clarke. Sa-B:229
Poem in October. D. Thomas. Gr-CC:42,
   Hi-WP II:135, To-MP:54
Poem to Americans. G. Jackson.
   Lo-IT:58
A Recollection. F. Cornford. Co-EL:76,
   Co-PM:145
Reflections on a Gift of Watermelon
   Pickle Received from a Friend Called
   Felicity. J. Tobias. Du-RG:134
Reflections upon a Recurrent Suggestion
   by Civil Defense Authorities that I
   Build a Bombshelter in My Backyard.
   R. Whittemore. Ba-PO:28, Cr-WS:49,
   En-PC:177
The Retreat. H. Vaughan. Al-VBP:466,
   Pa-GTB:65, Rv-CB:408
The Review. T. Traherne. Rv-CB:471
The Riders. A. Stanford. Ha-TP:118
The River. D. Short. Du-SH:129
The Roads into the Country. T. McGrath.
   St-H:121
Robbing the Tree Hive. E. Moll.
   Co-PT:140
Rock Me to Sleep. E. Allen. Er-FA:171
Romance. W. Turner. Bo-GJ:220,
   Hi-WP I:7, Mc-WS:113, Ni-JP:24,
   No-CL:251, Un-MB:345
Rustic Childhood. W. Barnes. Ox-BN:428
Sang-Kan River. Ya Hsüan. Pa-MV:149
The Scissors Grinder. R. Roseliep.
   De-FS:162
The Secret Heart. R. Coffin. Co-PS:103
   Se-PR:152
The Ships of Yule. B. Carman.
   Br-BC:126, Do-WH:16, Sh-RP:168

A Snowy Day in School. D. Lawrence.
   Ma-FW:75
Songs for My Mother: Her Hands.
   A. Branch. Hu-MP:4, Se-PR:117
The Stenographers. P. Page. Wi-LT:782
A Storm in Childhood. T. Jones.
   Ma-FW:35
sugarfields. B. Mahone. Ad-PB:473
Summertime and the Living. . . .
   R. Hayden. Ad-PB:118, Br-TC:169,
   Ra-BP:103
A Sunday. W. de la Mare. Ls-NY:50
Sunday Morning. W. Moreland. Ad-PB:502
The Swimmers. A. Tate. Pe-OA:180,
   Un-MA:540
Tales of My Nursery. De-CH:571
Tintern Abbey. W. Wordsworth. Al-VBP:667
To Aunt Rose. A. Ginsberg. Ca-VT:575,
   Wi-LT:719
Twenty-Five. R. McKuen. Du-SH:66
Uncle Ananias. E. Robinson. Un-MA:137
Under Your Voice, among Legends.
   P. Harris. Sc-TN:81
The Vanity of Human Wishes. J. Leax.
   Pe-M:65
Van Winkle. H. Crane. Ga-FB:269,
   Sh-AP:199, Un-MA:521
Waldheim Cemetery. R. Sward. St-H:217
We Who Were Born. E. Lewis. Br-BC:11,
   Fe-FP:465
A Wedding at Harvest Time. N. Bomze.
   Ho-TY:227
West of Childhood. I. Gardner. St-H:65
The Whale, His Bulwark. D. Walcott.
   Lo-TY:113
When Gathering Up on a Wet Mountain
   Morning. G. Dubrow. Ad-II:46
When I Chance to Think of My Childhood.
   Ma-BH:29
When I Learned to Whistle. G. Lea.
   Le-M:67
With a Happiness Continuing.
   B. Tsuchiya. Sh-AM:148
Woodman, Spare That Tree. G. Morris.
   Er-FA:243, Fe-FP:546, Hu-MP:267
Young. A. Sexton. To-MP:100
Zima Junction. Y. Yevtushenko.
   Li-TU:31
THE CHILDLESS
The Empty Woman. G. Brooks. Pe-SS:13
CHILDREN: see also BABIES; BOYS; DEATH -
   CHILDREN; DIALECTS, CHILDREN'S;
   GIRLS; HUMOR - CHILDREN; NURSERIES
   (FOR CHILDREN); ORPHANS; PARENT AND
   CHILD
Ah, How We Loved. O. Mandelstam.
   Ca-MR:58
Allie. R. Graves. Bo-GJ:81, Fe-FP:100,
   Ha-LO:103
At the Edge. M. Korte. Sc-TN:116
At the Garden Gate. D. McCord.
   Fe-FP:122

CHILDREN — cont'd.
Avondale. S. Smith. Pa-RE:9
The Ballad of Chocolate Mabbie.
  G. Brooks. Pe-SS:30
The Ballad of the Little Square.
  F. Garcia Lorca. Li-TU:222
The Black Pebble. J. Reeves.
  La-PV:208
Boys and Girls, Come Out to Play.
  De-CH:742, Mo-CC:56, Mo-MGT:181,
  Sm-MK:136
A Carol for Children. O. Nash.
  Pl-EI:150
The Carol of the Poor Children.
  R. Middleton. Sm-MK:219
The Castle. S. Alexander. Hu-PN:559
Child-Naming Rite of the Bow People.
  Da-SC:107
A Child Stretched Forth. Torai.
  Le-MW:71
The Children. H. Applebaum. Ke-TF:80
Children Are Slaves. I. Velez.
  Jo-VC:32
Children Are the Children of the Wind.
  Santaro. Le-MW:98
Children at Night. S. Morse.
  Ls-NY:230
Children's Crusade, 1939. B. Brecht.
  Ca-MB:106
The Children's Orchestra. M. Johnson.
  De-CH:710
The Child's Hymn. M. Howitt. Un-GT:20
A Child's Laughter. A. Swinburne.
  Br-BC:69, Fe-PL:246
The Child's Morning. W. Scott.
  Du-RG:97
The Child's Sight. H. Sobiloff.
  Ca-VT:354
Christabel. S. Coleridge. Al-VBP:698
Christmas Birthday. G. Glaubitz.
  Br-BC:77, Br-SS:47
Cities #8. V. Cruz. Ad-BO:68
Clear. A. Lewis. Ad-II:78, Ad-PB:513
Come to the Stone. R. Jarrell.
  Ca-VT:399
Come You Four Winds. Wo-HS:(67)
The Companion. Y. Yevtushenko.
  Cr-WS:127, Ma-FW:252
Comparison. M. Hoberman. Br-BC:110
Declaration of Independence. W. Gibbs.
  Pe-SS:23
Dalyaunce. De-CH:26
Ditty for a Child Losing His First
  Tooth. Do-CH:(7)
Doctor Spock. Y. Yevtushenko.
  Ca-MR:60
Documentary. R. Beum. Cr-WS:130
The Doors. B. Andrews. Le-M:166
Drawing by Ronnie C., Grade One.
  R. Lechlitner. Pe-SS:24
The Dreamer. W. Childress. Du-SH:48,
  Pe-SS:41

Early Supper. B. Howes. Bo-GJ:27
An Elementary School Class Room in a
  Slum. S. Spender. To-MP:26
The First Tooth. C. and M. Lamb.
  Ox-BC:143
Five. C. Tringress. St-FS:3
A Flower Is Looking. H. Monro.
  Un-MB:236
Foreign Children. R. Stevenson.
  Bo-GJ:105, Hu-MP:137
Four and Eight. ff. Wolfe. Br-BC:76,
  Br-SS:43
The Gardeners. D. Ignatow. Ls-NY:226
Germinal. "AE." Un-MB:146
A Girl Speaks to Her Playmate.
  Al-PI:66
Going to the Heavenly Bridge.
  Li Kuang-t'ien. Hs-TC:205
Good and Bad Children. R. Stevenson.
  Bl-OB:31, Co-BB:98, Er-FA:494,
  Gr-TG:19, Ox-BC:296, Sm-LG:98
Good Master and Mistress. Na-EO:162
A Goodly Child. Ox-BC:6
Guide, O Christ, This Little Hand.
  Gr-TG:59
Heart's Needle: Child of My Winter.
  W. Snodgrass. Un-MA:682
Holy Thursday. W. Blake. De-CH:62,
  Ma-YA:127, Rv-CB:584
Hopi Owl Song. Da-SC:95
Housekeeping Problems. L. Haft.
  Le-M:139
I Think when I Read That Sweet Story of
  Old. J. Luke. Bo-FP:48
The Ideal Age for a Man. M. Shannon.
  Br-BC:43
In Just. E. Cummings. Ad-CI:72,
  Bo-FP:224, Co-HP:55, Du-RG:96,
  Fe-FP:73, Ga-FB:283, Ir-BB:25,
  Re-TW:53, Sh-RP:30, Un-GT:272,
  Un-MA:472
In London Town. M. Coleridge. Pa-RE:77
Infidelities. D. Scott. Sa-B:3
Intaglio. H. Coulette. En-PC:252
It Is Impossible. R. Falconer.
  Gr-BT:9
Kids. W. Stafford. Du-SH:187
Lady of the Land. Rv-ON:100
Landscape near a Steel Mill. H. Horn.
  Ke-PP:110
A Lesson for Mamma. S. Dayre. Ox-BC:286
Letty's Globe. C. Turner. Rv-CB:787
The Little Black Boy. W. Blake.
  De-CH:20, Hu-PN:445, Ox-BC:85,
  Ox-BN:21, Rv-CB:590, Sm-LG:106
Little Blue Shoes. K. Greenaway.
  Ar-TP3:5, Hu-MP:8
A Little Boy Lost. W. Blake.
  Al-VBP:618, Rv-CB:583
The Little Dancers. L. Binyon.
  De-CH:185, Un-MB:156
Little Orphant Annie. J. Riley. Ox-BC:300

The Lives of Gulls and Children.
H. Nemerov. Ni-JP:116
The Lonely House. A. Mezquida.
Ke-TF:152
Lord, Look upon a Little Child.
J. Taylor. Gr-TG:59
Loving Jesus, Gentle Lamb. C. Wesley.
Gr-TG:59
Lucy Lavender. I. Eastwick.
Br-BC:47, Br-SS:42
Lullaby of the Cannibal Giants.
Da-SC:95
The Man Who Hid His Own Front Door.
E. MacKinstry. Fe-FP:374
Manners at Table When Away from Home.
Ox-BC:7
Middle-Aged Child. I. Hogan. Br-BC:74
Mrs. Santa Claus' Christmas Present.
A. Morris. Co-PS:166
Navajo Children, Canyon de Chelly,
Arizona. C. Middleton. Ma-FW:69
No New Music. S. Crouch. Ad-PB:484
Nobody. J. Wade. Sc-TN:222
Number 7. L. Ferlinghetti. Ad-CI:18,
Du-RG:102, Kh-VA:74, La-OC:85,
Pe-SS:156
Nurse's Song. W. Blake. Ox-BC:88
O Father, Bless Me Good or Bad.
Gr-TG:60
Old-Age Chant. Da-SC:105
On a Child Beginning to Talk.
T. Bastard. Rv-CB:261
On the Gifts of God. Bible. O.T.
Psalms. Me-PH:29
On the Seashore. R. Tagore. Al-PI:89
The Orchard and the Heath. G. Meredith.
Ox-BN:691
The Party. R. Whittemore. Ad-CI:71
The Pied Piper of Hamelin. R. Browning.
Ox-BC:173
The Plaza and the Flaming Orange Trees.
A. Machado. Le-SW:23
Pockets. S. Williams. St-FS:51
Polly. W. Rands. Un-GT:101
Portrait Philippines. A. Duckett.
Hu-PN:358
Recital. L. Nicholl. Pl-US:22
Reconciliation. AE. Tr-MR:250
Ring Around the World. A. Wynne.
Ar-TP3:95, Ja-PA:32
The Secret Garden. T. Kinsella.
Br-TC:241
Shells. W. Wordsworth. Go-BP:111
A Sick Child. R. Jarrell. Ca-VT:402
The Snow Thaws. Issa. Le-MW:90,
Ma-FW:11
So Run Along and Play. D. McCord.
Ar-TP3:5
Song. Be-AP:66
Spring. W. Blake. Ar-TP3:203,
Ch-B:99, Fe-FP:71, Ha-YA:25,
Li-LC:70, Sm-LG:53, Un-GB:7,
Un-GT:271

Statues. R. Wilbur. Ha-TP:17
Symon's Lessons of Wisdom for All
Manner of Children. Ox-BC:9
Table Rules for Little Folks.
Ox-BC:226
Taking Out Jim. J. Walsh. Pa-RE:52
There Was a Child Went Forth.
W. Whitman. Br-BC:128, La-RM:164,
Un-GT:307
The Thoughts of a Child. D. Embry.
La-IH:94
To a Child. C. Morley. Br-BC:148
To a Child of Quality, Five Years Old.
M. Prior. Rv-CB:485
To a Child Running with Outstretched
Arms in Canyon de Chelly.
N. Momaday. Ni-CD:92
To a Child with Eyes. M. Van Doren.
Bo-FP:95, Ha-LO:78
To Another Poet a Thousand Years Hence.
C. Norman. Cr-WS:131
To Charlotte Pulteney. A. Philips.
Pa-GTB:113
The Truants. W. de la Mare. Un-MB:197
The Ugly Child. E. Jennings. Pa-RE:31
Vespers. A. Milne. Ke-TF:77,
Li-SR:62, Ox-BC:344
The Victory. J. Gelman. Be-UL:123
Village Before Sunset. F. Cornford.
Co-BN:108, Co-PM:143, Sm-LG:50
Waking Time. J. Eastwick. Ar-TP3:239,
Br-SS:7
Water and Shadow. M. Zaturenska.
Gr-SS:132
We Are Seven. W. Wordsworth.
Li-SR:116, Ox-BC:100
Wee Willie Winkie. Au-SP:8, Bo-FP:39,
Br-SS:36, Cl-DT:31, De-PO:28,
Er-FA:492, Li-LB:39, Mo-CC:(36),
Mo-MGT:17, Mo-NR:106, Ox-BC:172,
Rd-SS:7, Wi-MG:35, Wr-RM:33
When I Was a Little Girl. A. Milligan.
Co-PI:139
When You and I Grow Up. K. Greenaway.
Bo-FP:135, Ch-B:108, Hu-MP:174
Where Does He Wander. Chiyo. Be-CS:46
Who Will Shoe My Little Feet. Ju-CP:24
Whole Duty of Children. R. Stevenson.
Gr-TG:14, Na-EO:138, Ox-BC:293
Why Dost Thou Weep, My Child? Le-OE:29
The Winning of the TV West. J. Alexander.
Bo-HF:97, Br-AF:153, Mc-WK:172

CHILDREN AS POETS

Autumn Leaves. M. Sutphen. Bo-FP:147
Blue Jay. H. Conkling. Co-BBW:261,
Re-BS:29
Conversion. J. Lillie. Co-BBW:74
Explanation on Coming Home Late.
R. Hughes. Co-EL:155, Co-PM:130,
Re-TW:8
Garden. M. Drouet. Gr-EC:270
In the Market on Monday Morning.
Co-PM:6

CHILDREN AS POETS — cont'd.
  Interesting Things. S. Cross.
    Su-FVI:1
  Jane, Do Be Careful. I. Page.
    Co-BB:54
  King Arthur and His Knights.
    R. Williams. Co-OT:17
  Little Rain Men. R. Hussey. Bo-FP:263
  A Little Squirrel. Ar-TP3:60
  Loneliness. J. Pomroy. Su-FVI:11
  May-Time. M. Gant. Bo-FP:236
  A Melancholy Lay. M. Fleming.
    Co-FB:300, Re-TW:22, Sm-LG:70
  My Teddy Bear. B. Olgin. Mc-AW:10
  My Thoughts. S. Gristwood. Su-FVI:4
  On the Bales. E. Coupland. Su-FVI:65
  Red Rooster. H. Conkling. Ir-BB:74
  Reflections. V. Howard. Jo-SA:2
  The Snake. Valerie. Su-FVI:64
  Softly. P. Sandell. Su-FVI:67
  The Song of the Mischievous Dog.
    D. Thomas. Er-FA:236
  Spring Song. H. Conkling. Co-PS:57,
    Hu-MP:246
  Tears. W. Kraus. Su-FVI:10
  That Duck. B. Mac I. Mc-AW:98
  To a Monkey. M. Fleming. Co-FB:300,
    Er-FA:227, Un-GT:55
  Tragedy. W. Cheney. Co-OW:57
  War. W. McLean, Jr. Ad-BO:53
  Xmas Time. W. Karsner. Co-EL:142,
    Co-PM:30
  See also Ba-HI, Ho-CT, Jo-VC, La-GI,
    La-IH, Le-M, Le-TA, Le-WR, Me-WF,
    Mo-MI
CHILDREN OF OTHER LANDS
  Foreign Children. R. Stevenson.
    Bo-GJ:105, Hu-MP:137
  Japanese Children. J. Kirkup.
    Ma-FW:68, Pa-RE:125
  Look, Edwin! E. Millay. Bo-FP:116,
    Bo-GJ:115
  Our Family. L. Clark. Pa-RE:44
  Welcome. R. Waldo. Au-SP:133,
    Hu-MP:38
CHILDREN'S CRUSADE: see CRUSADES
CHILE
  The Christ of the Andes. E. Markham.
    Se-PR:85
  What Country? Re-RR:18
CHILLON CASTLE, SWITZ.
  The Prisoner of Chillon. G. Byron.
    Fe-PL:22
  Sonnet on Chillon. G. Byron.
    Ma-YA:173, Pa-GTB:209
CHIMERAS
  Chimera. B. Howes. Br-TC:205
CHIMES: see BELLS
CHIMNEY SWEEPS
  The Chimney Sweeper. W. Blake.
    Ma-YA:128, Rv-CB:580
  The Chimney Sweeper. W. Blake. De-CH:40
    De-TT:107, Ox-BC:86, Rv-CB:579

Jack Hall. Co-RM:99
Oh! Sweep Chimney, Sweep! De-CH:513
Who Liveth So Merry. De-CH:573
Willy the Weeper. Gr-GB:270
Wmffre the Sweep. R. Humphries.
  Pl-EI:197
CHIMNEYS
  Black Within. De-CH:676, Gr-GB:17,
    Mo-MGT:155, Wr-RM:87
  Christmas Eve Rhyme. C. McCullers.
    Ho-ME:28
  What the Chimney Sang. B. Harte.
    Sp-OG:307
CHIMPANZEES: see HUMOR - CHIMPANZEES
CHINA: see also ALTAIC VERSE;
  BALLADS, CHINESE; CHINESE VERSE;
  HUMOR - CHINA; LEGENDS, CHINESE;
  SATIRE - CHINA; WALL OF CHINA;
  and names of cities and places,
  as PEKING, CHINA
Autumn. Ho Ch'i-fang. Hs-TC:220
Autumn. Tsang K'o-chia. Hs-TC:285
Autumn Twilight in the Mountains.
  Wang Wei. Rx-LT:55
Ballad of the Western Island in the
  North Country. Gr-SS:187
Boatmen. I Men. Hs-TC:17
Can't Afford to Live. Yüan Shui-p'ai.
  Hs-TC:412
Can't Understand. Yüan Shui-p'ai.
  Hs-TC:411
The Chinese Nightingale. V. Lindsay.
  Un-MA:229
The Ch'ing Ming Festival. Feng Hsüeh-feng.
  Hs-TC:368
Clear Night. Ai Ch'ing. Hs-TC:295
The Day of Cold Food. Li Ch'ing Chao.
  Rx-OH:98
The Deserted Village. Feng Hsüeh-feng.
  Hs-TC:371
Digging for China. R. Wilbur.
  Bo-GJ:224, Br-MP:394, Br-TC:471,
  Gr-BT:11, Ha-LO:88, Ho-TH:66
Discovery. Wen I-to. Hs-TC:58
Don't Cry, My Little One.
  Wang T'ung-chao. Hs-TC:259
Dreaming that I Went with Li and Yu to
  Visit Yüan Chën. Po Chü-i. Pa-SG:19
The Drought. Cheng Min. Hs-TC:238
The Electric Lights Shine in Everybody's
  Heart. Hs-TC:452
An Enjoyable Evening in the Village
  near the Lake. Lin Ho Ching.
  Ma-FW:120
The Execution Ground. Tsang K'o-chia.
  Hs-TC:286
Five Short Stanzas, I. Chariot.
  Tsou Ti-fan. Hs-TC:347
Five Short Stanzas, III. Spring.
  Tsou Ti-fan. Hs-TC:348
The Flower Market. Po-Chu-I. Ke-PP:10

The Golden Palace.   Gr-CC:181
The Harper of Chao.   Po Chü-i.
   Pl-US:23
Having Climbed to the Topmost Peak of
   the Incense-Burner Mountain.
   Po Chü-I.   Mo-SD:94
He Who Hanged Himself.   Tsou Ti-fan.
   Hs-TC:341
The Heart of a Warrior.   Tsang K'o-chia.
   Hs-TC:284
The Heart of the Ancient City.
   Pien Chih-lin.   Hs-TC:166
I Seem to Hear the Roar of the Waves.
   Ho Ch'i-fang.   Hs-TC:227
I Stand on Mountain High.   Hs-TC:450
I Walk Out into the Country at Night.
   Lu Yu.   Rx-OH:108
I'm a Newcomer.   Chung Hsüan.
   Hs-TC:433
The Journey.   Hu Feng.   Hs-TC:375
A Journey.   Li Kuang-t'ien.   Hs-TC:203
Kowtow.   Yüan Shui-p'ai.   Hs-TC:412
Landscape by Ch'eng Sui.   J. Kirkup.
   Go-BP:162
Lava.   Chang Chien.   Pa-MV:24
Leaving the Monastery Early in the
   Morning.   Lu Yu.   Rx-OH:105
Lo-Yang.   Ch'ien Wen-tu.   Gr-CC:182
Love Songs of Turfan.   Wen Chieh.
   Hs-TC:437
Man and Mountain.   T'ien Chien.
   Hs-TC:334
The Most Sacred Mountain.   E. Tietjens.
   Pa-HT:87, Tr-MR:202
New Year.   Wang Ya-p'ing.   Hs-TC:352
Night.   Ai Mu.   Hs-TC:436
The Night of Terror.   Wang Ya-p'ing.
   Hs-TC:353
Nocturnal Song (IV).   Ho Ch'i-fang.
   Hs-TC:224
No. 7, Stone Tiger Lane.   Hsü Chih-mo.
   Hs-TC:85
Old Mother Blinds Her Own Son.
   Yüan Shui-p'ai.   Hs-TC:410
One Step Covers Ten Thousand Li.
   Hs-TC:452
Opinions of the New Student.
   R. Pedroso.   Lo-TY:102
Portrait of Life.   Tsang K'o-chia.
   Hs-TC:287
The Red Cliff.   Su Tung P'o.   Rx-OH:65
Reminiscence.   Chu Hsiang.   Hs-TC:99
The Ricksha Puller.   Cheng Min.
   Hs-TC:233
The River.   Tsou Ti-fan.   Hs-TC:338
The Road to China.   O. Miller.
   Hu-MP:180, St-FS:105
The Road to Pengya.   Tu Fu.   Ho-P:75
Several Individuals.   Pien Chih-lin.
   Hs-TC:164
Short Song to Greet the New Year.
   Tsang K'o-chia.   Hs-TC:291

The Song of a Vagabond Son.   Fang Ching.
   Hs-TC:385
Spring Sun.   Chu Hsi.   Rx-OH:118
Stars in a May Night.   Wang T'ung-chao.
   Hs-TC:266
Story of the Flowery Kingdom.
   J. Cabell.   Pa-OM:9
A Sweet Potato Rolls off the Hill.
   Hs-TC:454
That City.   Li Kuang-t'ien.   Hs-TC:211
To India.   Yüan Shui-p'ai.   Hs-TC:413
To the Young Pioneers of the Northwest.
   Pien Chih-lin.   Hs-TC:169
The Tower of Genghis Khan.   H. Allen.
   Pa-HT:85
Twilight in the River Pavilion.
   Chiang She Ch'uan.   Rx-LT:117
Under the Moon.   Hsü Hsü.   Hs-TC:275
Verse on the Wall.   Chang Chih-min.
   Hs-TC:431
"Very Interesting" Death.   Yüan Shui-p'ai.
   Hs-TC:408
A Walk in the Country.   Su Tung P'o.
   Rx-OH:76
The Wall of China.   P. Colum.
   Co-RG:110
The War Year.   Ts'ao Sung.   Ba-PO:172,
   Cr-WS:15, Ke-PP:12
Western Ch'ang-An Street.   Pien Chih-lin.
   Hs-TC:162
What Kind of Troops Are These.
   Chang Chih-min.   Hs-TC:430
Winter in the City.   Wang Ya-p'ing.
   Hs-TC:351
Yang-Ze-Fu.   Yehoash.   Ho-TY:77
The Zero Degree of Life.   Tsang K'o-chia.
   Hs-TC:289
CHINA - COUNTRYSIDE
An Abandoned Road to the Chi-Ming
   Temple.   Ch'en Meng-chia. Hs-TC:115
After Rain.   Tu Fu.   Ho-LP:29
After the Rain.   Chang Chih-min.
   Hs-TC:426
Autumn Colors.   Wen I-to.   Hs-TC:52
Beautiful Is the Land South of the
   Yangtze River.   Wang T'ung-chao.
   Hs-TC:265
The Deserted Village.   Wen I-to.
   Hs-TC:61
The Farm by the Lake.   Chu Hsi.
   Rx-OH:119
Green Jade Plum Trees in Spring.
   Ou Yang Hsiu.   Rx-OH:53
The Green Spring.   Shan Mei.
   Hs-TC:436
He Died a Second Time, 6.   In the
   Countryside.   Ai Ch'ing.   Hs-TC:306
Homecoming.   Chu Hsiang.   Hs-TC:100
I Come to the Shore of the Yangtze
   River to Buy a Handful of Lotus
   Seeds.   Hsü Chih-mo.   Hs-TC:87
In the Hills.   Wang Wei.   Ho-LP:29

CHINA - COUNTRYSIDE — cont'd.
Mount Kuanyin. Yü Kuan-chung.
   Pa-MV:188
On the Siu Cheng Road. Su Tung P'o.
   Rx-OH:80
The Pale Temple Bell. Mu Mu-t'ien.
   Hs-TC:188
Pilgrimage. Jao Meng-k'an.
   Hs-TC:108
Rainy Night. Feng Chih. Hs-TC:141
Sailing on the Lake to the Ching River.
   Lu Yu. Rx-OH:113
The Snow. Mao Tse-tung. Hs-TC:363
The Song of the Setting Sun. Hu Feng.
   Hs-TC:378
The Songs of Spring (II).
   Feng Hsüeh-feng. Hs-TC:368
The Southern Wind. Kuo Mo-jo.
   Hs-TC:37
The Terrace in the Snow. Su Tung P'o.
   Rx-OH:71
Village at Dusk. Mu Mu-t'ien.
   Hs-TC:187
Wilderness. Ai Ch'ing. Hs-TC:314
CHINA - HISTORY AND PATRIOTISM
About to Sail for Home. Wang Tu-ch'ing.
   Hs-TC:196
After Swimming Across the Yangtze
   River. Mao Tse-tung. Hs-TC:365
The Battle Hymn of Shanghai.
   Wang T'ung-chao. Hs-TC:269
Freedom Is Walking Toward Us.
   T'ien Chien. Hs-TC:330
The Glowing Years. Jen Chün.
   Hs-TC:392
He Died a Second Time, 1. On the Litter.
   Ai Ch'ing. Hs-TC:302
He Died a Second Time, 2. Hospital.
   Ai Ch'ing. Hs-TC:303
He Died a Second Time, 8. Exchange.
   Ai Ch'ing. Hs-TC:308
He Died a Second Time, 9. Send-off.
   Ai Ch'ing. Hs-TC:308
He Died a Second Time, 10. A Thought.
   Ai Ch'ing. Hs-TC:309
He Died a Second Time, 11. Forward
   March. Ai Ch'ing. Hs-TC:310
He Died a Second Time, 12. He Fell.
   Ai Ch'ing. Hs-TC:311
Headline Music. Yüan Shui-p'ai.
   Hs-TC:402
I Get Up at Dawn. Lu Yu. Rx-OH:111
I Sing of May. Jen Chün. Hs-TC:395
I Sing of My Fatherland. T'ien Chien.
   Hs-TC:334
March 18. Jao Meng-k'an. Hs-TC:106
The Moon at the Fortified Pass. Li Po.
   Cr-WS:9
My Friend, You Must Have Smelt This
   Stench. Wang T'ung-chao. Hs-TC:267
The Nefarious War. Li Po. Ba-PO:153,
   Cr-WS:14, Li-TU:241

The Northland. Ai Ch'ing. Hs-TC:299
Northward March. Tsou Ti-fan.
   Hs-TC:340
On the Liu-P'an Mountain. Mao Tse-tung.
   Hs-TC:363
On the Pei-Tai River. Mao Tse-tung.
   Hs-TC:365
One Sentence. Wen I-to. Hs-TC:64
The Portrait of a Chinese Soldier.
   Wang Ya-p'ing. Hs-TC:354
Prayer. Wen I-to. Hs-TC:63
The Ruined City. Pao Chao. Ma-FW:240
The Sandaled Soldier. Tu Yün-hsieh.
   Hs-TC:245
Smash the Blockade. Jen Chün.
   Hs-TC:398
The Snow. Mao Tse-tung. Hs-TC:363
Some More. T'ien Chien. Hs-TC:331
The Song of Joy. Hu Feng. Hs-TC:379
The Song of Ling Shan. Feng Hsüeh-feng.
   Hs-TC:369
A Song of War Chariots. Tu Fu.
   Cr-WS:10
The Tempering of Steel. Jen Chün.
   Hs-TC:393
To Those Who Fight. T'ien Chien.
   Hs-TC:322
Under the Frontier Post. Wang Chang-Ling.
   Gr-CT:340
War. Li Po. Gr-CT:341
War in Chang-An City. Wang Tsan.
   Ba-PO:41, Cr-WS:12, Ke-PP:8
The White Horse. Tu Fu. Gr-CT:343
With My Maimed Hand. Tai Wang-Shu.
   Hs-TC:185
Written on a Prison Wall. Tai Wang-shu.
   Hs-TC:184
The Yellow Crane Pavilion.
   Mao Tse-tung. Hs-TC:364
Yen Hsi-shan's Tax Agent. Liu Chia.
   Hs-TC:434
CHINA (PORCELAIN): see POTTERY
THE CHINESE: see also HUMOR - THE
   CHINESE
African China. M. Tolson. Ad-PB:45
As I Step over a Puddle at the End of
   Winter I Think on an Ancient Chinese
   Governor. J. Wright. Kh-VA:73,
   St-H:254
A Ballad of the Mulberry Road.
   E. Pound. Ha-LO:93
Ballad of the Western Island in the
   North Country. Gr-SS:187
A Big Mountain Is Moved Away.
   Hs-TC:442
A Boatwoman. Chao Yeh. Le-MW:114
Border Songs. Lu Lun. Le-MW:122
Can't Kill Him. Chang Chih-min.
   Hs-TC:426
Chinese Lullaby. Ir-BB:127
A Dead Turk. Li Kuang-t'ien.
   Hs-TC:208

Dreaming in the Shanghai Restaurant.
D. Enright. To-MP:123
Girls on the Yueh River. Li Po.
Gr-CT:62, Ho-LP:62
The Golden Palace. Gr-CC:181
Haystack. Hs-TC:454
He Who Hanged Himself. Tsou Ti-fan.
Hs-TC:341
The Hermit. Hsu Pen. Le-MW:130,
Ma-FW:85
Hymnus ad Patrem Sinensis. P. Whalen.
Kh-VA:45
I Seem to Hear the Roar of the Waves.
Ho Ch'i-fang. Hs-TC:227
I'm a Longshoreman. Hs-TC:451
It Can Bend the Huge River. Hs-TC:443
Life. Lu Li. Hs-TC:422
Many, Many Are the Songs of Good
Harvest. Hs-TC:442
Mar Quong, Chinese Laundryman.
C. Morley. Hu-MP:144
Moon Door. M. Kennedy. Co-BL:154
Neighbors. Tu Fu. Le-MW:117
The Northland. Ai Ch'ing. Hs-TC:299
Official Visit to Shih Hao Village.
Tu Fu. Ba-PO:154, Cr-WS:13
Old Soldier. I Men. Hs-TC:419
Our Songs Make the Yangtze River Flow
Backward. Hs-TC:444
The Peddler of Spells. Lu Yu.
Le-MW:127
Prayer. Wen I-to. Hs-TC:63
Rendezvous. Chang Chih-min. Hs-TC:429
The River Merchant's Wife: A Letter.
Li T'ai-Po. Bo-HF:120, Br-TC:332,
Co-BL:101, Gr-CC:22, Ha-PO:184,
Li-TU:181, Mo-BG:98, Pe-SS:126,
Sh-AP:171, Un-MA:290
Several People. Pien Chih-Lin.
Le-MW:108
Sewing. Chang Chih-min. Hs-TC:430
The Spirit of Spring. Liu Ta-pai.
Hs-TC:7
Tomorrow We Take Over the Heavenly
Palace. Hs-TC:443
Water Flows Around Our Village.
Hs-TC:450
A Wee Little Boy Has Opened a Store.
Wy-CM:11
White Stone Bank. Wang Wei. Le-MW:118
With One Stroke I Dig Through the
Crystal Palace. Hs-TC:442
Women Transport Corps. Hs-TC:441
CHINESE IN THE UNITED STATES
The Chinese Nightingale. V. Lindsay.
Un-MA:229
Laundry Song. Wen I-to. Hs-TC:55
CHINESE VERSE: see also BALLADS, CHINESE
After Rain. Tu Fu. Ho-LP:29
As the Sun Rose over the Mountain.
Wy-CM:33
Autumn Wind. Emperor Wu. Rx-LT:4,
Sm-LG:398

The Bald Old Woman. Ir-BB:202
Ballad of the Western Island in the
North Country. Gr-SS:187
Both Sides of the Yellow River
Recaptured by the Imperial Army.
Tu Fu. Cr-WS:10
By Chance I Walk. . . . Yuan Mei.
Pe-M:7
A Chinese Poem Written B.C. 1121.
Hi-WP II:63
A Chinese Poem Written in B.C. 718.
Hi-WP II:105
The Ching-Ting Mountain. Li Po.
Li-TU:39
Chopsticks. Yuan Mei. Ma-FW:233
Clearing at Dawn. Li T'ai-po.
Pa-SG:83
Complaint of a New Wife. Tr-US II:188
The Confession. Wen Yi-tuo. Gr-CT:463
Conversation in the Mountains. Li Po.
Pa-SG:192
The Cow. Ir-BB:141
The Cranes. Po-Chü-i. Gr-EC:178,
Pa-SG:99
The Cricket. Ir-BB:70
Crossing the River. Pa-SG:47
Dancing. Yang Kuei-Fei. Fe-FP:481
Dreaming that I Went with Li and Yü
to Visit Yüan Chën. Po Chü-i.
Pa-SG:19
The Eastern Gate. Le-MW:120, Ma-FW:88
An Enjoyable Evening in the Village
near the Lake. Lin Ho Whing.
Ma-FW:120
The Excursion. Tu Fu. Mo-SD:138
Fifteen Poems of My Heart. Juan Chi.
Ma-FW:184
Fighting South of the Ramparts.
Cr-WS:7, Ma-FW:249, Pa-SG:3
The Flower Market. Po-Chu-I. Ke-PP:10
The Gardener. Po-Chu-I.
Co-BN:209, Pa-SG:166
Getting Up Early on a Spring Morning.
Po-Chu-i. Ma-FW:9
Girls on the Yueh River. Li Po.
Gr-CT:62, Ho-LP:62
The Golden Palace. Gr-CC:181
Grass Withers. Ba-PO:92
A Green Stream. Wang Wëi. Mo-SD:108
The Harper of Chao. Po Chü-i.
Pl-US:23
Having Climbed to the Topmost Peak of
the Incense-Burner Mountain.
Po Chü-I. Mo-SD:94
He Ran up the Candlestick. Ir-BB:84
Hearing the Early Oriole. Po Chü-i.
Pl-US:128
The Herd-Boy's Song. Chen Shan-min.
Pa-SG:126
Hot Cake. Shu Hsi. Cl-FC:90,
Ma-FW:280
The Hundred Names. Ba-PO:117
I Built My Hut. Tao Ch'ien. Pa-SG:157

CHINESE VERSE — cont'd.
In the Hills. Wang Wei. Ho-LP:29
In the Mountains on a Summer Day.
  Li Po. Ma-FW:116, Mo-SD:93
Lament of a Frontier Guard. Rihaku.
  Ca-VT:83
The Liberator. Wu-ti. Re-BS:25
Lines. Shen Ch'uan-ch'i. Cr-WS:9
The Little Cart. Ch'en Tzu-lung.
  Ma-FW:89
The Little Rain. Tu Fu. Fe-FP:480
Lo-Yang. Ch'ien Wen-tu. Gr-CC:182
The Locust Swarm. Hsu Chao. Cr-WS:5,
  Rx-OH:123
Long I Have Loved to Stroll. T'ao Ch'ien.
  Gr-CT:331
A Long Time Ago. T'ao Ch'ien.
  Sm-LG:303
Looking at the Moon and Thinking of
  One Far Away. Chang Ching-ling.
  Pa-SG:145
A Mad Poem Addressed to My Nephews and
  Nieces. Po Chu-i. Gr-BT:165
Madly Singing in the Mountains.
  Po Chu-i. Rv-CB:987
A Mistake. Ir-BB:199
Mixed. Ir-BB:71
The Moon at the Fortified Pass.
  Li Po. Cr-WS:9
The Moon in the Mountains.
  Chen Shan-min. Pa-SG:165
The Morning Glory. Confucius.
  Ga-S:175, Pa-SG:50
The Mouse. Bo-FP:59, Wy-CM:15
My Little Golden Sister. Wy-CM:39
Name or Person. Lao Tzu. Sm-MK:223
Nature Songs, I. Tr-US II:185
Nature Songs, II. Tr-US II:186
The Nefarious War. Li Po.
  Ba-PO:153, Cr-WS:14, Li-TU:241
New Corn. T'ao Ch'ien. Pa-SG:91
Ninth Moon. Li Ho. Pa-SG:95
Official Visit to Shih Hao Village.
  Tu Fu. Ba-PO:154, Cr-WS:13
Old Chang, the Crab. Bo-FP:279,
  Wy-CM:16
Old Mother Wind. Bo-FP:259
On a Mountain Road. Wu Ch'ing-jen.
  Pa-SG:99
On Hearing a Flute at Night from the
  Wall of Shou-Hsiang. Li Yi.
  Pl-US:11
On Hearing Someone Sing a Poem by
  Yuan Chen. Po Chu-i. Pl-ML:150
On the Birth of His Son. Su Tung-P'o.
  Gr-BT:7
Only Be Willing to Search for Poetry.
  Yuan Mei. La-PV:224
Overnight in the Apartment by the
  River. Tu Fu. Gr-CT:344
Parting. Wang Wei. Ar-TP3:97,
  Le-MW:121

A Peacock Feather. Ir-BB:29, Wy-CM:46
Pear-Trees by the Fence. Su Tung-p'o.
  Pa-SG:90
People Hide Their Love. Wu-Ti.
  Pa-SG:46
The People of Tao-Chou. Po Chu-i.
  Gr-CT:374
The Pine-Trees in the Courtyard.
  Po Chü-i. Pa-SG:162
Plucking the Rushes. Co-PM:75,
  Gr-BT:45
The Poem on the Wall. Po Chü-i.
  Pl-ML:85
A Protest in the Sixth Year of
  Chi'en Fu. Ts'ao Sung. Ga-FB:193
Pruning Trees. Po Chü-i. Ma-FW:107,
  Pa-SG:169
A Rare Tree. Pa-SG:69
Reading the Book of Hills and Sea.
  Tao Ch'ien. Pa-SG:171
The Red Cockatoo. Po Chü-i.
  Co-PM:105, Gr-CT:98, Rd-OA:37
The Rice Seller. Bo-FP:129
The River Merchant's Wife: A Letter.
  Li T'ai-Po. Bo-HF:120, Br-TC:332,
  Co-BL:101, Gr-CC:22, Ha-PO:184,
  Li-TU:181, Mo-BG:98, Pe-SS:126,
  Sh-AP:171, Un-MA:290
The Road to Pengya. Tu Fu. Ho-P:75
The Ruined City. Pao Chao. Ma-FW:240
Sailing Homeward. Chan Fang-Sheng.
  Ar-TP3:97, Le-MW:43, Pa-SG:180,
  Sm-LG:298, Th-AS:158
Sampan. Hi-WP I:1
The Snail. Bo-FT:85, Wy-CM:19
Song. Sung Tzü-hou. Pa-SG:84
Song of a Young Man about to Be Married.
  Tr-US II:186
A Song of Dagger Dancing. Tu Fu.
  Pl-US:105
A Song of War Chariots. Tu Fu.
  Cr-WS:10
South Wind. Tu Fu. Ar-TP3:203,
  Ma-FW:100
Spring Night. Su Tung-P'o. Ho-P:250
Spring Rain. Tu Fu. Pa-SG:83,
  Rx-LT:62
Standing at the Foot of the Steps at
  Night. Yuan Mei. Ma-FW:259
Tell Me Now. Wang Chi. Sm-LG:391
Thinking of a Friend Lost in the
  Tibetan War. Chang Chi. Cr-WS:8
To His Friend, Wei, . . . Li Po.
  Li-TU:234
To Pi Ssu Yao. Tu Fu. Pl-ML:79,
  Rx-OH:15
Turkestan. Ch'en T'ao. Cr-WS:8
Under the Frontier Post. Wang Chang-
  Ling. Gr-CT:340
The Unicorn's Hoofs. Rd-OA:169,
  Sm-LG:43
Up You Go. Ir-BB:107, Wy-CM:49

War. Li Po. Gr-CT:341
War in Chang-An City. Wang Tsan.
    Ba-PO:41, Cr-WS:12, Ke-PP:8
The War Year. Ts'ao Sung.
    Ba-PO:172, Cr-WS:15, Ke-PP:12
The Way of Life. Laotse. Ba-PO:7,
    Mc-MK:220
The White Egret. Li Po. Pa-SG:98
The White Horse. Tu Fu. Gr-CT:343
Wild Geese. Shen Yo. Pa-SG:87
Winter Night. Hi-WP II:145
The Yellow Bird. Re-BS:44
    See also Hs-TC, Le-MW, Pa-MV, Rx-LT,
    Rx-OH, Wy-CM
CHIPMUNKS
The Chipmunk. M. Brand. Ls-NY:100
Chipmunk. M. Welch. Sh-RP:36
Chipmunks. M. Pomeroy. Co-BBW:26
The Chipmunk's Song. R. Jarrell.
    La-PV:142
Little Charlie Chipmunk. H. Le Cron.
    Ar-TP3:61, Au-SP:69, Fe-FP:128,
    Ir-BB:77, Pe-FB:11
Winter Noon. S. Teasdale. Ha-YA:146,
    Sh-RP:238
CHIPPEWA INDIANS: see OJIBWA INDIANS
CHIVALRY: see also CRUSADES; HUMOR -
    CHIVALRY; KNIGHTS AND KNIGHTHOOD;
    SATIRE - CHIVALRY; and names of
    persons, as ARTHUR, KING
Andrew Jackson. M. Keller.
    Br-AF:67, Co-RM:212, Un-GT:92
Chivalry. AE. Al-VBP:1103, Tr-MR:181
Fast Rode the Knight. S. Crane.
    Li-TU:236
The Glove. J. von Schiller.
    Sp-OG:138
Idylls of the King, Guinevere.
    A. Tennyson. Ma-YA:198
A Knight, Canterbury Tales.
    G. Chaucer. Un-GT:86
Sir Galahad. A. Tennyson.
    Co-RM:78, Sp-OG:134
A Squire, Canterbury Tales. G. Chaucer.
    Hi-WP II:121, Un-GT:87
CHIVINGTON, JOHN MILTON
Black Kettle Raises the Stars and
    Stripes. L. Simpson. Cr-WS:24
CHOICES: see also HUMOR - CHOICES
Andre. G. Brooks. Ar-TP3:5, Sh-RP:97
As to His Choice of Her. W. Blunt.
    Al-VBP:1052
Birds of a Feather. Un-GT:22, Wr-RM:93
Birthday Gifts. H. Asquith. Br-BC:100,
    Br-SS:49
Bunches of Grapes. W. de la Mare.
    Ar-TP3:7, Bo-GJ:23, Hi-GD:14,
    Ir-BB:123, Li-LC:44, Ox-BC:326
Choice. J. Farrar. Br-SS:175
The Choice. W. Letts. Co-PI:95
Choice. R. Mal'kova. Mo-MI:37
Choice. A. Morgan. Fe-PL:106, Ke-TF:117

The Choice. D. Parker. Co-BL:95
Choosing. E. Farjeon. Ar-TP3:104
Choosing a Homesite. P. Booth.
    Ha-TP:13
Choosing Shoes. F. Wolfe. Ar-TP3:111,
    Au-SP:111, St-FS:77
The Cross-Roads of the World.
    M. Dragomir. Mc-AC:121
The Death of Vitellozzo Vitelli.
    I. Feldman. Br-TC:121
The Decision. O. Dodson. Hu-PN:302
Dividing. D. McCord. Ag-HE:47
An Easy Decision. K. Patchen.
    Du-SH:21, Ha-LO:44
Greedy Jane. Gr-EC:106, Ox-BC:328
The Haystack in the Floods. W. Morris.
    Ni-JP:41, Ox-BN:779
Hey, Wully Wine. De-CH:330
His Choice. A. Baker. Ke-TF:252
How to Choose a Mistress. E. Prestwich.
    No-CL:140
If. R. Kipling. Er-FA:5, Hi-WP I:118,
    Ox-BC:324, Un-GT:314
Land of My Heart. W. Foulke. Vi-PP:21
Lines Written in Windsor Forest.
    A. Pope. Gr-SS:100
The Lovely Shall Be Choosers. R. Frost.
    Sh-AP:155, Un-MA:185
A Matter of Taste. E. Merriam.
    Ag-HE:31
Not I. R. Stevenson. Ch-B:97,
    Hi-WP I:117
Not Self-Denial. E. Gibbs. Ls-NY:334
Once to Every Man and Nation.
    J. Lowell. Vi-PP:68
Passing Remark. W. Stafford. Kh-VA:30
Places, Loved Ones. P. Larkin.
    Pe-SS:123
Pruning Trees. Po Chu-i. Ma-FW:107,
    Pa-SG:169
The Repetitive Heart. D. Schwartz.
    Al-VBP:1241
The Road Not Taken. R. Frost.
    Br-TC:136, Er-FA:180, Fe-PL:317,
    Gr-CT:314, La-RM:48, Na-EO:14,
    Sm-LG:301, Un-MA:187, Wi-LT:165
The Road of Life. W. Morris. Ox-BN:786
Sailor and Tailor. De-TT:127
Sensible People. J. Stephens.
    Pa-RE:122
Song for the Heroes. A. Comfort.
    Cr-WS:163, Un-MB:521
Take Notice. R. Robin. Ls-NY:325
The Visitation. R. Graves. Go-BP:135
The Ways. J. Oxenham. Fe-PL:300
Which Are You? Fe-PL:299
Wine and Cakes. Mo-MGT:209
CHOIRS (MUSIC)
Sunday Morning, King's Cambridge.
    J. Betjeman. Pl-EI:12
CHOOSING: see CHOICES

CHOPSTICKS
  Chopsticks. Yuan Mei. Ma-FW:233
CHORAL READINGS: see Ar-TP3:233-246,
    Sh-RP:2-59, and many other poems
    suitable for choral reading
CHRIST: see JESUS CHRIST
CHRISTENING: see BAPTISM
CHRISTIANITY: see also CATHOLIC CHURCH;
    CONVERSION; JESUS CHRIST; PURITANS
    AND PURITANISM; REVIVALS; SALVATION;
    SATIRE - CHRISTIANITY; and the rites
    listed under the heading SACRAMENTS
  Everywhere, Everywhere Christmas Tonight.
    P. Brooks. Se-PR:225
  Hymn to Proserpine. A. Swinburne.
    Hi-FO:58, Ox-BN:797
  Hynd Etin. Ma-BB:192
  On Being Brought from Africa to
    America. P. Wheatley. Lo-TY:205
  Onward, Christian Soldiers.
    S. Baring-Gould. Bo-FP:305,
    Er-FA:481, Ke-TF:186
  Watchman, What of the Night?
    A. Swinburne. Ho-WR:200
  Why Should Men Love the Church.
    T. Eliot. Tr-MR:199
CHRISTMAS: see also BETHLEHEM; CANDLES;
    EPIPHANY; HOLLY TREES; HUMOR -
    CHRISTMAS; JESUS CHRIST - NATIVITY;
    JOSEPH, SAINT; MARY, VIRGIN;
    MISTLETOE; SANTA CLAUS; SATIRE -
    CHRISTMAS
  Adrian Henri's Talking after Christmas
    Blues. A. Henri. Gr-BT:73
  After Christmas. W. Auden. Ga-S:90,
    Un-MB:467
  Alphabet of Christmas Cheer.
    E. Weston. Gr-EC:264
  As I Went Out on Christmas Day.
    Rv-CB:20
  As Lucy Went a-Walking. W. de la Mare.
    Sm-MK:50
  Awake! Glad Heart! H. Vaughan.
    Un-GT:294
  Beggar's Rhyme. Ar-TP3:192, Au-SP:375,
    Bo-FP:181, Cl-DT:23, La-PH:33,
    Mo-MGT:109, Wr-RM:123
  Bundles. J. Farrar. Ar-TP3:192,
    Bo-FP:182
  The Burning Babe. R. Southwell.
    Al-VBP:150, De-CH:227, Ma-FW:288,
    Rv-CB:178, Sm-LG:371
  Chanticleer. W. Austin. Ga-S:77
  A Child's Christmas Song. T. Daly.
    Br-BC:173
  A Child's Song of Christmas.
    M. Pickthall. Ha-YA:160
  Christmas. J. Betjeman. Hi-WP I:134
  Christmas. M. Dodge. Br-BC:173
  Christmas. A. Fair. Ho-CT:45
  Christmas. A. Kilmer. Ke-TF:226
  Christmas. O. Lermand. Ho-CT:45

  Christmas. W. Scott. Bo-FP:184
  Christmas at Sea. R. Stevenson.
    Co-SS:207, De-CH:28, Ga-FB:183,
    Ha-PO:251, Ma-YA:220, Sp-OG:257
  A Christmas Banquet. C. Lushington.
    Sa-B:53
  Christmas Birthday. G. Glaubitz.
    Br-BC:77, Br-SS:47
  The Christmas Candle. K. Brown.
    Au-SP:380, Se-PR:224
  A Christmas Carol. P. Brooks.
    Au-SP:382, Bo-FP:199, Er-FA:517,
    Se-PR:225, Un-GT:295
  Christmas Carol. K. Grahame.
    Fe-FP:88, Hu-MP:352
  The Christmas Child. Bo-FP:189
  A Christmas Cross. W. Allen. Ke-TF:227
  Christmas Day. C. Smart. Gr-CT:417
  Christmas Day. A. Young. Cl-DT:25
  Christmas Eve. The Bible. N.T. Luke.
    Au-SP:381, Bo-FP:190, Br-BC:162,
    Br-SS:106, Fe-FP:91, Se-PR:221
  Christmas Eve. J. Davidson. Hu-MP:351
  Christmas Eve. C. Day Lewis. Pl-EI:29
  Christmas Eve. M. Edey. Ha-YA:153,
    La-PH:22
  Christmas Eve. J. Freeman. Ke-TF:226
  Christmas Eve Rhyme. C. McCullers.
    Ho-WE:28
  Christmas Hearth Rhyme. Bo-FP:204,
    Ch-B:53
  Christmas in the Heart. Br-SS:99,
    Sh-RP:244
  Christmas Is Remembering. E. Binns.
    Br-BC:175, Br-SS:109
  Christmas Landscape. L. Lee.
    Go-BP:284, Ma-FW:278
  Christmas Mourning. V. Miller.
    Un-MA:679
  Christmas 1945. A. Hine. Hi-TL:219
  A Christmas Party. C. Bailey.
    Bo-FP:186
  Christmas Poem. V. de Moraes. An-TC:101
  Christmas Song. R. Leonhard. Un-R:57
  Christmas Song. E. Long. Br-SS:107
  Christmas Wishes. J. Lee. Ja-HH:54
  Come, Ride with Me to Toyland.
    R. Bennett. Br-SS:103
  Dame, Get Up and Bake Your Pies.
    Wi-MG:57
  Do Rabbits Have Christmas? A. Fisher.
    Mc-AW:82
  The Earth Has Grown Old. P. Brooks.
    Ke-TF:221
  Eddi's Service. R. Kipling. Go-BP:41
  Eighth Street West. R. Field. Br-SS:100
  The End of the Play. W. Thackeray.
    Er-FA:520
  The Expectation. R. Gales. Ga-S:58
  For Daphne at Christmas. J. Nims.
    St-H:157
  For Them. E. Farjeon. Gr-TG:72

Gift. C. Freeman. Ab-MO:75, Ad-PB:397,
Hu-PN:435, Lo-TY:255
Gladde Things. Ar-TP3:197
The House of Christmas. G. Chesterton.
Go-BP:254
How Grand and How Bright. Gr-GB:302
I Saw Three Ships. Cl-DT:24, Sh-RP:28,
Un-GT:294
If Ye Would Hear the Angels Sing.
D. Greenwell. Ga-S:71
I'm Wishing the Whole World Christmas.
A. Wynne. Th-AS:108
In Terra Nostra. A. Tarbat. Go-BP:283
Jest 'fore Christmas. E. Field.
Er-FA:513, Fe-FP:538, Fe-PL:201,
Ga-FB:176, Hu-MP:359
The Jew at Christmas Eve. K. Shapiro.
Ca-VT:373
Jolly Jankin. Gr-GB:141
Kid Stuff. F. Horne. Ab-MO:76,
Ad-PB:56, Bo-AN:41, Bo-HF:109,
Hu-PN:148, Li-TU:247
Know It Is Christmas. L. Snelling.
Br-BC:175
Little Christmas. M. Caruthers.
Ke-TF:230
Little Jack Horner Sat in a Corner.
Au-SP:6, Bo-FP:197, De-PO:12,
Er-FA:506, Fr-WO:11, Hi-FO:117,
Mo-CC:(31), Mo-MGT:125, Mo-NR:77,
Mo-TL:70, Wi-MG:33, Wr-RM:90
Long, Long Ago. Ar-TP3:196, Co-PS:176,
Fe-FP:91, Hu-MP:347, La-PH:24,
La-PV:87, Mc-AW:76, Pa-RE:104
The Months. Gr-CT:425
Night of Marvels. Sister Violante do Ceo.
Ga-S:71
Ode on the Morning of Christ's Nativity.
J. Milton. Ma-YA:93, Pa-GTB:42
An Old Christmas Greeting. Ar-TP3:192,
Br-SS:98, Ch-B:53, Fe-FP:88,
Hu-MP:344
Old Polly. Ja-HH:61
Santa Claus. Au-SP:374
The Satin Mice Creaking Last Summer's
Grass. R. Coffin. Rd-OA:90
Shine Out, Fair Sun, with All Your Heat.
G. Chapman. Gr-CT:414
Signs of Christmas. M. Justus.
Mc-AW:72
Some Say. . . . W. Shakespeare.
Ar-TP3:197, Gr-CT:13
Song for a Christmas Celebration.
Tr-US I:31
Sonnets at Christmas. A. Tate.
Ca-VT:220, Sh-AP:206, Wi-LT:405
Star of the East. E. Field. Se-PR:224
Stay, Christmas! I. Eastwick.
Br-SS:111
Taking Down the Tree. A. Fisher.
Sh-RP:246
There Was a Pig. Rv-ON:110

The Three Kings. H. Longfellow.
Pa-OM:357, Sp-OG:314, Un-GT:290
Trio. E. Morgan. To-MP:191
The Twenty-Fourth of December.
Bo-FP:183, Ch-B:52
Village Christmas. M. Widdemer.
Sh-RP:239
A Visit from St. Nicholas. C. Moore.
Ar-TP3:193, Bo-FP:187, Br-SS:104,
Er-FA:511, Fe-FP:86, Ga-FB:177,
Hu-MP:357, Ox-BC:154, Pa-OM:346,
Sh-RP:242, Un-GT:292
Welcome Yule. De-CH:229
Why Do the Bells of Christmas Ring.
E. Field. Ar-TP3:195, Au-SP:381,
Bo-FP:200, Ha-YA:155, La-PH:23
Xmas Time. W. Karsner. Co-EL:142,
Co-PM:30
Yule-Tide Fires. Bo-FP:199, Se-PR:232
Yule's Come and Yule's Gane. Gr-GB:49
CHRISTMAS CAROLS: see CHRISTMAS SONGS
CHRISTMAS CUSTOMS: see also HUMOR -
CHRISTMAS CUSTOMS
Bezhetzk. A. Akhmatova. Ca-MR:183
The Borys Hede That We Bryng Here.
Ma-YA:24
Ceremonies for Christmas. R. Herrick.
Ar-TP3:194
Christmas. M. Chute. Br-SS:101,
Fr-MP:9
Christmas Chant. I. Shaw. Br-SS:108,
La-PH:42
Christmas in the Olden Time. W. Scott.
Ar-TP3:192, Bo-FP:198, Br-SS:98,
Ch-B:53, Hu-MP:355, Se-PR:231
The Christmas Pudding. Ar-TP3:192,
La-PH:35
Christmas Singing. E. Chandler.
Br-SS:97
Christmas Time. W. Scott. Cl-FC:92
Conversations about Christmas.
D. Thomas. Li-TU:28
For Christmas Day. E. Farjeon.
Ar-TP3:195
In the Week when Christmas Comes.
E. Farjeon. Ar-TP3:194, Br-SS:96,
La-PH:32, La-PV:89, Li-LC:85
Little Jack Horner. De-TT:49, Li-LB:42
Our Joyful Feast. G. Wither.
Al-VBP:315, Br-SS:99
Wassail. Wassail. J. Bale. Gr-CT:425
CHRISTMAS DECORATIONS
Burning the Christmas Greens.
W. Williams. Wi-LT:200
Christmas. J. Betjeman. Hi-WP I:134
Christmas Tree Angel. M. Millet.
Ja-HH:52
little tree. E. Cummings. Bo-FP:184,
Co-PS:163, Co-RG:128, Fr-WO:89,
Ha-LO:49, La-PV:172, Li-LC:83,
Ma-FW:286, Pa-RE:84
Roundelay. I. Gardner. Ho-LP:41

CHRISTMAS DECORATIONS — cont'd.
  Swedish Angel. W. Scott. Wi-LT:810
  Taking Down the Tree. A. Fisher.
    Sh-RP:246
  The Thorn Trees. R. Field. Br-SG:92
  What the Christmas Tree Thinks.
    M. Davies. Bo-FP:196
CHRISTMAS DINNERS: see also HUMOR -
    CHRISTMAS DINNERS
  To Christ Our Lord. G. Kinnell.
    Br-TC:239, Ha-WR:92, La-RM:120,
    Pe-M:112
  Virginia. P. McGinley. Ag-HE:8
CHRISTMAS ENTERTAINMENTS: see HUMOR -
    CHRISTMAS ENTERTAINMENTS
CHRISTMAS GIFTS: see also HUMOR -
    CHRISTMAS GIFTS
  Birthday Presents. E. Thomas. Mc-AW:75
  Christmas. J. Betjeman. Hi-WP I:134
  The Coming of Mary Louise. G. Urquhart.
    Bo-FP:195
  The Gift. W. Williams. Pe-OA:76,
    Tr-MR:105
  If. C. Bailey. Bo-FP:182
  Mrs. Santa Claus' Christmas Present.
    A. Morris. Co-PS:166
  My Gift. C. Rossetti. Br-BC:174,
    Br-SS:108, Ch-B:52, Fe-FP:23,
    La-PH:29, Li-LC:87
  Otto. G. Brooks. La-PH:37, La-PV:101
  Presents. M. Chute. Br-SS:109,
    La-PH:36, La-PP:60, Na-EO:130
  The Shepherds at Bethlehem. Gr-CT:418
  Take Frankincense, O God.
    C. Fitz-Geffry. Gr-CT:426
  The Twelve Days of Christmas.
    Er-FA:518, La-PH:41, Li-LB:119,
    Mo-MGT:50, On-TW:46, Sh-RP:27
  What the Christmas Tree Thinks.
    M. Davies. Bo-FP:196
CHRISTMAS LEGENDS: see also SANTA CLAUS
  Babushka. E. Thomas. Hu-MP:432,
    Pa-OM:362
  Christmas Eve Legend. F. Frost.
    Br-BC:169
  The Mystic Magi. R. Hawker. Gr-CT:425
  The Oxen. T. Hardy. Ga-S:86,
    Go-BP:92, Ha-PO:117, No-CL:281,
    Tr-MR:109, Un-MB:33, Wi-LT:21
CHRISTMAS PRAYERS
  A Christmas Carol. G. Thomas.
    Tr-MR:108
  God Bless the Little Things. M. Murray.
    Ke-TF:228
  God Bless the Master of This House.
    Ar-TP3:197, Br-SS:111, De-PO:28,
    Sh-RP:246
  Moonless Darkness Stands Between.
    G. Hopkins. Hi-WP II:176
  Now Let Us Pray. Ba-PO:89
CHRISTMAS SHOPPING: see HUMOR -
    CHRISTMAS SHOPPING

CHRISTMAS SONGS: see also SATIRE -
    CHRISTMAS SONGS
  A-Caroling on Christmas Eve.
    J. Tippett. Mc-AW:73
  Ane Sang of the Birth of Christ. . . .
    J. Wedderburn. Gr-CT:423
  As I Sat on a Sunny Bank. Gr-CT:414,
    Gr-GB:300
  As I Sat under a Sycamore Tree.
    Al-VBP:60, Sm-MK:227
  As Joseph Was Awakening. Al-VBP:59,
    De-TT:174, Gr-TG:75
  At Christmas. Cl-FC:89
  Away in a Manger. M. Luther.
    Ar-TP3:195, Bo-FP:193, Br-BC:165,
    Fe-FP:93, Gr-TG:78, Hu-MP:347,
    Ke-TF:78, La-PH:25, Mc-AW:78,
    Un-GT:301
  A Babe Is Born. Ga-S:100
  Burgundian Carol. B. de la Monnoye.
    Pl-US:109
  Carol. W. Rodgers. Ma-FW:285
  Carol. J. Short. Sm-LG:371
  Carol, Brothers, Carol. W. Muhlenberg.
    Ar-TP3:192
  The Carol of the Poor Children.
    R. Middleton. Sm-MK:219
  The Cherry-Tree Carol. Al-VBP:58,
    Ga-S:64, Gr-CT:127, Gr-GB:299,
    Ke-TF:47, Ox-BB:1, Pa-OM:349,
    Rv-CB:53
  Child's Carol. E. Farjeon. Sh-RP:13
  A Child's Christmas Song. T. Daly.
    Br-BC:173
  A Christmas Carol. H. Behn. Br-BC:164
  A Christmas Carol. G. Chesterton.
    Ar-TP3:196, Er-FA:517, Se-PR:233
  Christmas Carol. K. Grahame.
    Fe-FP:88, Hu-MP:352
  A Christmas Carol. J. Lowell. Sp-OG:319
  A Christmas Carol. C. Rossetti.
    Br-BC:163, Rv-CB:893, Un-GT:287
  A Christmas Carol. Al-VBP:61,
    Bo-FP:202, Er-FA:516, Ga-S:88,
    Ke-TF:46
  A Christmas Caroll. R. Herrick.
    Bo-GJ:256, Hu-MP:354
  A Christmas Folk Song. L. Reese.
    Ar-TP3:196, Fe-FP:93, Gr-TG:77,
    Hu-MP:348, Pa-OM:352, Se-PR:228,
    Th-AS:106
  A Christmas Hymn. R. Wilbur. To-MP:103
  December. C. Rossetti. Ha-YA:150
  The First Nowell. Al-VBP:62
  From Far Away. Sp-OG:317
  Good King Wenceslaus. J. Neale.
    Pa-OM:355, Se-PR:234
  Good Tidings of Great Joy!
    Mrs. C. Alexander. Gr-TG:76,
    Ke-TF:183
  Hark How All the Welkin Rings.
    C. Wesley. Ga-S:87

Hark the Herald Angels Sing. C. Wesley.
  Bo-FP:202
Here We Come A-Caroling. Ar-TP3:194,
  Fe-FP:90, Hu-MP:353
Hey the Gift, Ho the Gift. Ga-S:67
The Holly and the Ivy. De-CH:228,
  De-TT:114, Gr-CT:421, Gr-GB:301
How Many Miles to Bethlehem.
  F. Chesterton. De-TT:176, Ke-TF:217
It Came upon the Midnight Clear.
  E. Sears. Bo-FP:192, Er-FA:510,
  Fe-FP:94, Ke-TF:223
Joy to the World! The Lord Is Come.
  I. Watts. Ke-TF:216
Lullay, Lullay, Thou Lytil Child.
  De-CH:627
Masters, in This Hall. W. Morris.
  Gr-CT:419
Now Every Child. E. Farjeon. Br-BC:167
Nowell Sing We. Gr-CT:419
O Come, All Ye Faithful. Er-FA:514,
  Ke-TF:225
O Little Town of Bethlehem. P. Brooks.
  Bo-FP:190, Er-FA:518, Fe-FP:94,
  Ga-S:85, Ke-TF:221
Sans Day Carol. Ga-S:86
The Shepherd and the King. E. Farjeon.
  Ar-TP3:196
Silent Night. J. Mohr. Er-FA:515
The Twelve Days of Christmas.
  Er-FA:518, La-PH:41, Li-LB:119,
  Mo-MGT:50, On-TW:46, Sh-RP:27
Wait's Carol. B. Young. Th-AS:107
Wassail Song. Co-PS:21, De-TT:92
Wassail, Wassail. J. Bale. Gr-CT:425
What Can I Give Him? C. Rossetti.
  Cl-DT:19, Gr-CT:422, Gr-TG:79
When Crist Was Born of Mary Free.
  Ma-YA:26
While Shepherds Watched Their Flocks by
  Night. N. Tate. Bo-FP:192,
  Ke-TF:224
The Yule Days. Gr-CT:415, Gr-GB:47,
  Rv-ON:121
See also Em-AF:401-416
CHRISTMAS STOCKINGS
Christmas Stocking. E. Farjeon.
  La-PH:34
Santa Claus and the Mouse.
  E. Poulsson. Ch-B:56
Triolet on a Dark Day. M. Fishback.
  Co-PS:161
CHRISTMAS TREES: see also HUMOR −
  CHRISTMAS TREES
Christmas. M. Dodge. Br-BC:173
Christmas. A. Kilmer. Ke-TF:226
Christmas Cookies. A. Fisher. Ag-HE:24
Christmas Mouse. A. Fisher. La-PH:39
The Christmas Robin. R. Graves.
  Gr-CC:48
The Christmas Tree. C. Day Lewis.
  Ga-S:89

Christmas Tree. A. Fisher. La-PH:38,
  La-PV:173
December Bird. A. Fisher. La-PH:40
Earth and Sky. E. Farjeon. Br-SG:108,
  Co-PS:173
Her Christmas Tree. E. Maleska.
  Ke-TF:228
If. C. Bailey. Bo-FP:182
little tree. e. cummings. Bo-FP:184,
  Co-PS:163, Co-RG:128, Fr-WO:89,
  Ha-LO:49, La-PV:172, Li-LC:83,
  Ma-FW:286, Pa-RE:84
The Outdoor Christmas Tree. A. Fisher.
  Br-SS:102
Round and Round. D. Thompson.
  Br-BC:172, Mc-AW:74
What the Christmas Tree Thinks.
  M. Davies. Bo-FP:196
CHRISTOPHE, HENRI
Black Majesty. C. Cullen. Ad-PB:92,
  Ca-VT:242
Christophe. R. Atkins. Ab-MO:82,
  Hu-PN:391
CHRYSANTHEMUMS
Ceremony. J. De Longchamps. Ls-NY:91
Chrysanthemum Colors. De-PP:33
The Hostess. Wang Mou Fang. Le-MW:101
My Existence. S. Mizuhara. Sh-AM:167
Reflection. Tomonori. Le-MW:83
The White Chrysanthemum. Mitsune.
  Ba-ST:47
Winter Chrysanthemum. S. Mizuhara.
  Sh-AM:167
CHUKCHI VERSE
Incantation Used by a Jealous Woman.
  Tr-US II:124
Prayer to the Creator. Tr-US II:124
Prayer to the Sea. Tr-US II:124
Songs, I. Tr-US II:123
Songs, II. Tr-US II:124
CHURCHES: see also CATHEDRALS; HUMOR −
  CHURCHES; SATIRE − CHURCHES;
  SYNAGOGUES; TEMPLES
The Belfry. R. Thomas. Ga-BP:189
Building in Stone. S. Warner.
  Un-MB:377
The Church. E. Muir. Tr-MR:204
The Church. N. Willard. Sc-TN:231
Church Going. P. Larkin. Br-TC:251,
  Pa-GTB:557, Un-MB:528, Wi-LT:754
Church of Rose of Lima, Cincinnati.
  J. Knoepfle. St-H:95
The Church Windows. G. Herbert.
  Rv-CB:351
Drawing Details in an Old Church.
  T. Hardy. No-CL:160
Dread. J. Synge. Un-MB:182
Ghost Church. H. Elliott. Ke-TF:423
i am a little church (no great
  cathedral). E. Cummings. Tr-MR:201
In Church. W. Barnes. Hi-WP I:140
In Church. R. Thomas. Go-BP:226

CHURCHES — cont'd.
  In These Dissenting Times. A. Walker.
    Ad-PB:475
  The Kirk of the Birds, Beasts and
    Fishes. Gr-GB:76
  Las Trampas, U.S.A. C. Tomlinson.
    Br-TC:443
  Meeting-House Hill. A. Lowell.
    Sm-LG:146, Un-MA:155
  The Moon and the Yew Tree. S. Plath.
    Mo-BG:146
  Poem for Flora. N. Giovanni.
    Ad-PB:456
  The Problem. R. Emerson. Sh-AP:26
  Saint Apollinare in Classe. R. Wilson.
    No-CL:260
  Sunday Morning, King's Cambridge.
    J. Betjeman. Pl-EI:12
  Tudor Church Music. S. Warner.
    Pl-US:16
  Why Should Men Love the Church.
    T. Eliot. Tr-MR:199
  Within King's College Chapel,
    Cambridge. W. Wordsworth.
    Ox-BN:81, Pa-GTB:300
CHURCHILL, JOHN: see MARLBOROUGH, JOHN
  CHURCHILL, 1ST DUKE OF
CHURCHILL, SIR WINSTON LEONARD SPENCER
  The Unkillable Knowledge.
    W. Everson. Ba-PO:181
CICADAS: see also LOCUSTS
  Cicada. A. Stoutenburg. La-RM:136
  Cicada-Shell. Basho. Au-SP:77
  Cicadas. L. Mueller. St-H:145
  The Cicadas. J. Wright. Ma-FW:102
  Cicadas Buzzing. Basho. Be-CS:9
  Four Things. Bible. O.T. Proverbs.
    Fe-FP:124, Un-GT:30
  Nothing in the Voice. Basho. Ma-FW:102
  On the Dewy Trunk. Kyoshi. Ca-BF:11
  Parched by the Shrill Song. Soseki.
    Be-MC:37
  The Singing Cicada. Kuo Mo-jo.
    Hs-TC:35
  Song of Old Age and a White Head.
    Tr-US I:193
CICERO
  The Motto. A. Cowley. No-CL:6
THE CID
  The Cid's Rising. F. Hemans. Hi-FO:72
CIDER: see also HUMOR - CIDER
  Cider Song. M. Weston. Co-BN:140
  Great Things. T. Hardy. Pa-GTB:409
CIGARS: see SMOKING
CIMARRON RIVER
  The Cimarron. B. Cutler. St-H:42
CINCINNATI, O.
  Church of Rose of Lima, Cincinnati.
    J. Knoepfle. St-H:95
CINDERELLA
  After All and After All. M. Davies.
    Ar-TP3:117, Hu-MP:68, Th-AS:148

Cinderella's Song. E. Roberts.
    Ir-BB:119
CIRCLES: see also HUMOR - CIRCLES
  The Circus; or One View of It.
    T. Spencer. Pe-OA:188
  Discovery. M. Livingston. Li-LC:22
  The Pleasures of Merely Circulating.
    W. Stevens. Ha-LO:12
  Rings in a Roundness. C. Drewry.
    Ls-NY:71
CIRCUSES: see also ACROBATS; CLOWNS;
    HUMOR - CIRCUSES; PARADES; also
    names of circus animals, as
    ELEPHANTS
  The Big Tent under the Roof. O. Nash.
    Sh-RP:253
  C Is for the Circus. P. McGinley.
    Ar-TP3:115, Au-SP:123
  The Circus. F. Davis. Bo-FP:237
  Circus. E. Farjeon. Hu-MP:57
  Circus. J. Heinegg. Ad-II:65
  The Circus. E. Roberts. Fe-FP:254,
    Hu-MP:58
  A Circus Garland. R. Field. Au-SP:124
  Circus Lion. C. Day Lewis. To-MP:114
  The Circus Parade. O. Miller.
    Ar-TP3:115, Au-SP:126
  The Circus-Postered Barn.
    E. Coatsworth. Un-MA:464
  The End of the World. A. MacLeish.
    Ca-VT:164, Ha-PO:48, Mc-WS:27,
    Pe-OA:162, Un-MA:457, Wi-LT:341
  What Happens. J. Jordan. Ra-BP:249
  A Windy Circus. L. Ray. Al-PI:107
CISTERNS: see WELLS
CITIES AND TOWNS: see also APARTMENT
    HOUSES; CITY TRAFFIC; FACTORIES;
    GHETTOS; HUMOR - CITIES AND TOWNS;
    MUSEUMS; PARKS; PLAYGROUNDS;
    SATIRE - CITIES AND TOWNS;
    SKYSCRAPERS; SLUMS AND SLUM LIFE;
    TENEMENT HOUSES; and names of
    cities, as CHICAGO, ILL.
  Afternoon. D. O'Grady. Co-PI:160
  Against Borders. Y. Yevtushenko.
    Ad-CI:80
  Air. C. Major. Jo-SA:96
  All Tropic Places Smell of Mold.
    K. Shapiro. Ca-VT:375
  L'Allegro. J. Milton. Al-VBP:389,
    Er-FA:37, Pa-GTB:94, Rv-CB:369
  American Rhapsody. K. Fearing.
    Pe-M:20, Un-MA:556
  Approach to a City. W. Williams.
    Ad-CI:25
  At 79th and Park. B. Howes. Pe-M:16
  August 24, 1963 - 1:00 a.m. - Omaha.
    D. Whitewing. Al-WW:57
  Autobiography: Last Chapter. J. Barnes.
    Ni-CD:27
  The Avenue Bearing the Initial of Christ
    into the New World. G. Kinnell.
    Ad-CI:11, Wi-LT:746

The Bard. M. Leib. Ho-TY:94
Based on City Rhythms. L. McDowell.
  Me-WF:7
Beggar. N. Parra. Ad-CI:101
Beleaguered Cities. F. Lucas. Cl-FC:31
Beneath the Aging Buildings.
  M. Deighton. La-IH:62
Blue Island Intersection. C. Sandburg.
  Un-MA:203
Bring the Soul Blocks. V. Cruz.
  Ad-CI:60
Broadway: Twilight. T. Prideaux.
  La-OC:19
Brownstone. R. McKuen. Ha-TP:8
The Bus. L. Cohen. Ad-CI:9
Bus Ride. S. Robinson. Fe-FP:246
Business Girls. J. Betjeman.
  Hi-WP II:167
A Call to the Wild. Lord Dunsany.
  Co-PI:36
Cities and Science. D. McCord.
  Br-AF:221
The City. J. Bryant. Ba-HI:109,
  La-IH:15
City. L. Hughes. Br-AF:209, Gr-EC:96,
  Ho-CS:7, 46, La-PP:33, La-PV:188,
  Li-LC:41
The City. D. Ignatow. Co-PM:63
The City. E. Jarrett. Sc-TN:111
The City. V. Pitt. Ho-CS:11
City Afternoon. B. Howes. Br-AF:211,
  Ha-TP:9
City Bird. T. Kenyon. Gr-EC:176
City Blockades. L. Hopkins. Ho-CS:33
City Child. E. McCormick. La-IH:83
A City Flower. A. Dobson. Go-BP:124
The City Is Big. T. Heard. Me-WF:10
The City Is Burning. H. Lewis.
  La-IH:32
City Life. D. Lawrence. Ad-CI:88
City Lights. R. Field. Fe-FP:254,
  La-PP:34, La-PV:188
The City Mouse and the Garden Mouse.
  C. Rossetti. Ar-TP3:59, Bo-FP:15,
  Br-SG:66, Ch-B:25, Fe-FP:138,
  Hu-MP:189, It-HB:26, Un-GB:14,
  Un-GT:56
City Number. C. Sandburg. La-OC:109
A City Park. A. Brody. La-OC:118
City Rain. R. Field. Ar-TP3:169,
  Au-SP:309, Gr-EC:63
City Sparrow. A. Kreymborg. La-OC:119
City-Storm. H. Monro. Un-MB:239
City Streets and Country Roads.
  E. Farjeon. Ar-TP3:93, Au-SP:165,
  Pe-FB:46
City Trees. E. Millay. Bo-HF:64,
  Fe-FP:250, La-OC:23, Sh-RP:108
Cockpit in the Clouds. D. Dorrance.
  Ar-TP3:88, Fe-FP:201
The Complacent Cliff-Dweller.
  M. Fishback. Fe-PL:200

Connecticut Road Song. A. Branch.
  Pa-HT:31
The Continuity. P. Blackburn.
  Ad-CI:105
Corner. R. Pomeroy. Ad-CI:64,
  Du-SH:39
Corner Meeting. L. Hughes. Ad-CI:31
The Country Mouse and the City Mouse.
  R. Sharpe. Ox-BC:139
Dances. D. Meltzer. Lo-IT:90
Definition of Nature. E. Redmond.
  Ad-PB:311
A Description of a City Shower.
  J. Swift. Al-VBP:515
A Description of the Morning.
  J. Swift. Al-VBP:515, Ho-P:62
Despisals. M. Rukeyser. Ho-P:223
Dog Around the Block. E. White.
  La-OC:28, Mc-WS:42
The Dome of Sunday. K. Shapiro.
  Un-MA:637, Wi-LT:532
Driving to Town Late to Mail a Letter.
  R. Bly. Ca-VT:558, Co-BN:201,
  Co-EL:156, Mo-TS:55
dry july. A. Adoff. Ad-CI:47
Elegy on an Empty Skyscraper.
  J. Fletcher. Sh-AP:173
Emigrant's Iconoclasm. T. Baybars.
  Ls-NY:249
Escape the Ghettos of New York.
  V. Howard. La-IH:22
Essay on Solitude. A. Cowley.
  Al-VBP:451
Faces. S. McCoy. La-IH:16
Faces. S. Teasdale. La-OC:69
Far from the Madding Crowd. N. Waterman.
  Hu-MP:60
Fools Gaze at Painted Courts.
  M. Drayton. Gr-CT:310
From Country to Town. H. Coleridge.
  Rv-CB:759
From My. A. Dunlap. La-IH:55
Get 'Em Here. L. Hopkins. Ho-CS:20
Get the Gasworks. D. Ignatow. Kh-VA:57,
  Mo-BG:181
A Girl Skipping Rope in Flushing.
  S. Stepanchev. Ls-NY:287
Give Me the Splendid Silent Sun.
  W. Whitman. Co-BN:232, Fe-FP:263,
  Mo-BG:20, Un-MA:84
Good Green Bus. R. Field. Mc-PR:95
The Greatest City. W. Whitman.
  La-OC:71, Sh-RP:263
Hampton Road. J. Knoepfle. St-H:93
Hearing Men Shout at Night on McDougal
  Street. R. Bly. Ad-CI:34, Mc-EA:117
Hearing of Harvests Rotting in the
  Valleys. W. Auden. Un-MB:457
The Heart of the Ancient City.
  Pien Chih-lin. Hs-TC:166
Hidden Treasure. B. Katz. Ho-CS:9
The Hold-Up. D. Wagoner. Ha-TP:19

CITIES AND TOWNS — cont'd.
Hot Afternoons. P. Blackburn. Ca-VT:555
Hot Night on Water Street. L. Simpson.
   Br-TC:379
Hotel Paradiso e Commerciale.
   J. Brinnin. Br-TC:61, En-PC:147
The House-Top. H. Melville. Ho-P:176
I Am Cool Brother Cool. W. McLean.
   Ad-II:116
I Stand Here Against This Lamp Post.
   R. Chafetz. La-IH:85
I Went to Noke. Gr-GB:172
I Wonder How Many People in the City.
   L. Cohen. Ad-CI:8, Co-EL:99,
   Co-PM:41
The Ice-Cream Man. R. Field.
   Au-SP:148, Br-SS:176, Fe-FP:249
If You Saw a Negro Lady. J. Meyer.
   Jo-SA:54, Lo-IT:92
An Impression of Shanghai. Kuo Mo-jo.
   Hs-TC:36
Impressions. e. cummings. Ad-CI:6,
   Sm-PT:80, Un-MA:470
The Imprisoned II. R. Fitzgerald.
   Br-TC:126
The Imprisoned IV. R. Fitzgerald.
   Br-TC:127
In the Inner City. L. Clifton.
   Be-MA:139, Mo-TS:7
In the Street I Have Just Left.
   C. Reznikoff. La-OC:26
In This City. A. Brownjohn. Ad-CI:106
Joralemon Street. P. Hubbell.
   La-OC:22
July. A. Dobson. Pa-RE:37
A Kingdom of Clouds. M. Copeland.
   Le-M:83
Last Look at La Plata, Missouri.
   J. Barnes. Ni-CD:18
Legsby, Lincolnshire. Gr-GB:174
Letter to N.Y. E. Bishop. Br-TC:47,
   Mc-WS:116
Listen. Put on Morning. Wi-LT:720
A Little Boy Lost. J. Rothenberg.
   Kh-VA:20
A London Plane-Tree. A. Levy.
   Hi-WP I:125
A London Thoroughfare Two A.M.
   A. Lowell. Ni-JP:131
The Lonesome Boy. V. White. La-IH:24
Manhattan Lullaby. R. Field.
   Br-AF:193, Br-BC:145, La-OC:127
Map. M. Reis. An-TC:167
Midwest Town. R. Peterson. Br-AF:219
Montana Wives. G. Haste. Br-AF:159
Morning at the Window. T. Eliot.
   Ad-CI:10, Ho-LP:73
Morning in Spring. L. Ginsburg.
   Gr-EC:65
Morning Sun. L. MacNeice. Br-TC:281,
   Un-MB:445

The Mouth of the Hudson. R. Lowell.
   Ad-CI:29, Br-AF:181, Ha-TP:12,
   La-OC:39
Murphy in Manchester. J. Montague.
   Co-PI:142
My Town. K. Itta. Ba-HI:104
Neighborhood. G. Isaacs. La-IH:43
New England Landscape. E. Chaffee.
   Ke-TF:348
New York. V. Jones. Me-WF:12
Newark, for Now (68). C. Rodgers.
   Ad-PB:430
The News Around Midnight. T. McGrath.
   St-H:126
News Report. D. Ignatov. Br-TC:214
The News Stand. D. Berrigan. Ad-CI:35
Night Game. R. Humphries. Mo-BG:28,
   Ni-JP:87
No One. Barbara. La-IH:68
Obsessions. D. Levertov. Wi-LT:760
Ode of the Angels of Chicago Who Move
   Perpetually. P. Carroll. St-H:20
An Ode to Mr. Anthony Stafford to
   Hasten Him into the Country.
   T. Randolph. Al-VBP:378
Of the Mean and Sure Estate. T. Wyatt.
   Rd-OA:98
The Old City. R. Manning-Sanders.
   De-CH:322
Ombres Chinoises. B. Deutsch.
   Ha-TP:23
On Dwelling. R. Graves. Rv-CB:994
On Nights like This All Cities Are the
   Same. R. Rilke. Gr-CC:81
On the El. Z. Landau. Ho-TY:100
On the Expressway. R. Dana. La-OC:143
On Walking to School. T. Carter.
   Me-WF:69
Once I Passed Through a Populous City.
   W. Whitman. Pe-M:30
Our Largest and Smallest Cities.
   N. Rhodes. La-OC:144
Penny Arcade. J. Nims. St-H:151
The Pennycandystore Beyond the El.
   L. Ferlinghetti. Ad-CI:17,
   Mo-BG:19, Pe-SS:80
People. L. Lenski. Au-SP:130,
   Fe-FP:247, Ho-CS:16, La-OC:43
Pigeon Woman. M. Swenson. Mo-BG:50
Poem. J. Sloman. Sc-TN:200
Police Station. D. Dzwonkoski.
   Ad-II:86
Prelude I. T. Eliot. Ar-TP3:177,
   Br-TC:103, Ca-VT:128, Hi-WP II:162,
   La-OC:130, Pe-OA:103, Sh-AP:182
Prelude II. T. Eliot. Br-TC:105,
   Ca-VT:129, Pe-OA:103, Sh-AP:182
Prelude III. T. Eliot. Br-TC:105,
   Ca-VT:129, Sh-AP:182
Prelude IV. T. Eliot. Br-TC:106,
   Ca-VT:130, Pe-OA:104, Sh-AP:183

The Purse-Seine. R. Jeffers. Pe-OA:92
Q Is for Quietness. P. McGinley.
    La-OC:31
Rain after a Vaudeville Show. S. Benét.
    Mo-BG:29, Un-MA:497
The Rainwalkers. D. Levertov.
    Ad-CI:109, Du-SH:145
Reading Yeats I Did Not Think.
    L. Ferlinghetti. Pl-ML:117
Roller Skates. J. Farrar. Fe-FP:106
Run, Child, Run Fast. C. Williams.
    La-IH:18
A Sad Song about Greenwich Village.
    F. Park. La-OC:66
Sal's Atomic Submarines. L. Sissman.
    Mo-BG:25
The Sea Eats the Land at Home.
    K. Awoonor. Ad-CI:82
Several Individuals. Pien Chih-lin.
    Hs-TC:164
The Shore of Life. R. Fitzgerald.
    Ca-VT:302
Sing a Song of the Cities. M. Bishop.
    Ad-CI:79
The Sins of Kalamazoo. C. Sandburg.
    Ca-VT:23
Sioux City: January - Very Late.
    R. Rogers. Al-WW:89
Skyscraper Is a City's House.
    C. Lambert. Hu-MP:400
Small Quiet Song. R. Smith. Ad-CI:15
Smoke. P. Murphy. Me-WF:37
Snow in the City. R. Field.
    Ar-TP3:190, Gr-EC:63, La-PP:32
Snowy Morning. L. Moore. Un-GB:11
Song. F. O'Hara. Ad-CI:28
A Song of the Moon. C. McKay.
    Hu-PN:98
Sonnet. A. Nelson. Ad-PB:12,
    Hu-PN:46
South End. C. Aiken. Pe-OA:144
Spring. V. Mayakovsky. Ad-CI:90
Squares and Angles. A. Storni.
    La-OC:100
A Step Away from Them. F. O'Hara.
    Ca-VT:586
Stickball. L. Thompson. Ad-II:117
The Stinky City. R. Isaac. La-GI:49
The Stone. P. Blackburn. Du-SH:24
Stone Too Can Pray. C. Aiken.
    Pl-EI:177, Sm-MK:229, Tr-MR:23
The Streetcleaner's Lament.
    P. Hubbell. La-OC:27
The Subway. C. Rivers. Be-MA:106
Summer Concert. R. Whittemore.
    Br-AF:216
Summer in the City. D. McNally.
    La-IH:64
Summer: West Side. J. Updike.
    Pe-SS:68
Sunday. V. Rutsala. Du-SH:101

Sunday. E. White. Mc-WS:123
Tall City. S. Pulsifer. La-OC:99
The Telephone. E. Field. Ad-CI:104
That City. Li Kuang-t'ien. Hs-TC:211
This Shall Be Sufficient. K. Rexroth.
    Ad-CI:27
To Nowhere. D. Ignatow. Ad-CI:44
To the City in Snow. A. Ruggeri.
    Th-AS:125
The Tower. Y. Sasazawa. Sh-AM:76
Town and Country. T. Moult. Cl-FC:23
Transcontinent. D. Hall. Du-RG:41,
    La-OC:145, Pe-M:31
The Tropics in New York. C. McKay.
    Ad-PB:25, Bo-AN:28, Bo-HF:167,
    Hu-PN:95, Lo-TY:118
The Tunnel. H. Crane. Sh-AP:203,
    Un-MA:529
An Unfinished Poem. S. Muro. Sh-AM:56
Until We Built a Cabin. A. Fisher.
    Ar-TP3:179
Up at a Villa - Down in the City.
    R. Browning. Pa-GTB:342, Rv-CB:824
Victoria. E. Farjeon. Bl-OB:142
Voices Gay. A. Fair. Ho-CT:8
Waiting for the Bus. H. Ishida.
    Sh-AM:173
Walk down My Street. V. Dorset.
    La-IH:39
Wanting to Be Walking among the Crowds.
    S. Hagiwara. Sh-AM:50
Wet Night on a Pavement. A. Tessimond.
    Hi-WP I:129
What Is a City? M. Tobin. La-IH:34
What They Are For. D. Aldis.
    Au-SP:188
The Wind Blows the Rain into Our Faces.
    C. Reznikoff. La-OC:29
Winter in the City. Wang Ya-p'ing.
    Hs-TC:351
The Wish. A. Cowley. Al-VBP:450,
    De-CH:524
Wishes. E. Guest. Ke-TF:238
Wonder Wander. L. Kandel. Du-RG:51
Yorkville. D. Aldan. Lo-IT:3
CITIZENSHIP: see also SATIRE -
    CITIZENSHIP
Song Concerning a Message from Washington.
    Tr-US II:240
CITY LIFE: see CITIES AND TOWNS
CITY TRAFFIC: see also HUMOR - CITY
    TRAFFIC; STREETS; TRAFFIC LIGHTS
Apology. E. Herrick. Ls-NY:296
Birmingham. L. MacNeice. Un-MB:445
Blue Island Intersection. C. Sandburg.
    Un-MA:203
Bobby Blue. J. Drinkwater. Au-SP:135,
    Fe-FP:247
Central Park Tourney. M. Weston.
    Br-AF:195, Du-RG:47, La-OC:123,
    Pe-M:129

CITY TRAFFIC — <u>cont'd.</u>
  The Child on the Curbstone. E. Wylie.
    La-OC:92
  City Traffic. E. Merriam. La-OC:20,
    La-PV:190
  The Donkey in the Nyevsky Prospekt.
    G. Garbovsky. Bo-RU:35
  Highway: Michigan. T. Roethke.
    Du-SH:68
  I'm the Police Cop Man, I Am.
    M. Morrison. Au-SP:204
  In the Naked Bed, in Plato's Cave.
    D. Schwartz. Ca-VT:365, Un-MA:619,
    Wi-LT:515
  J's the Jumping Jay-Walker.
    P. McGinley. Ar-TP3:92, La-PP:37
  Motor Cars. R. Bennett. Ar-TP3:92,
    Au-SP:163, Fe-FP:245, La-PP:35
  Reason. J. Miles. En-PC:107,
    Mo-BG:34
  Stop-Go. D. Baruch. Ar-TP3:91,
    Fe-FP:185
CIVETS: see also SKUNKS
  From an Angba. Tr-US I:181
CIVIL DEFENSE: see also AIR RAID
    SHELTERS; CONSCIENTIOUS OBJECTORS
  For the Record. R. Thomas. Go-BP:217,
    To-MP:43
  Noon Hour. J. Finnigan. Gr-BT:115
  Watching Post. C. Day Lewis. To-MP:38
CIVIL RIGHTS: see also FREEDOM; JUSTICE;
    PROTESTS; SATIRE - CIVIL RIGHTS
  Epitaph. Ba-PO:72
  For Andy Goodman - Michael Schwerner -
    and James Chaney. M. Walker.
    Ra-BP:158
  Mine. A. Jackson. La-IH:103
  Street Demonstration. M. Walker.
    Ra-BP:156
CIVIL WAR - UNITED STATES, 1861-1865:
    see also EMANCIPATION PROCLAMATION;
    MEMORIAL DAY; MORGAN'S RAIDS, 1862-
    1864; SATIRE - CIVIL WAR - U.S.,
    1861-1865; SLAVERY; and the names of
    persons, as LINCOLN, ABRAHAM, and
    names of battles, as GETTYSBURG,
    BATTLE, 1863
  Achilles Deatheridge. E. Masters.
    Br-AF:73
  The Aged Stranger. B. Harte. Br-AF:74
  Banty Tim. J. Hay. Kr-OF:45
  Barbara Frietchie. J. Whittier.
    Co-PS:97, Er-FA:380, Fe-FP:442,
    Fe-PL:167, Ga-FB:258, Hi-TL:112,
    Mc-PR:170, Sp-OG:40, Un-GT:190,
    Vi-PP:150
  Battle Hymn of the Republic. J. Howe.
    De-CH:159, Er-FA:469, Fe-FP:441,
    Hi-TL:100, Ke-TF:53, Pl-EI:160,
    Un-GT:311, Vi-PP:145
  The Battle of Antietam Creek.
    Em-AF:451

Beat! Beat! Drums! W. Whitman.
    Fe-PL:170, Ga-FB:208
The Blue and the Gray. F. Finch.
    Hi-TL:129, Sp-OG:206, Vi-PP:163
The Bonnie Blue Flag. A. Ketchum.
    Hi-TL:101
The Brigade Must Not Know, Sir!
    Hi-TL:120
Brother Green. Em-AF:455
Brother Jonathan's Lament for Sister
    Caroline. O. Holmes. Hi-TL:102
Carry Me Back. J. Holmes. Br-AF:21
Cavalry Crossing a Ford. W. Whitman.
    Co-PM:137, Gr-CT:338, Mo-BG:167,
    Ni-JP:76, Rv-CB:847, Sh-AP:118,
    Sh-RP:312
Charleston. H. Timrod. Sh-AP:125
Craven. H. Newbolt. Sp-OG:78
The Cripple for Life. Em-AF:457
The Cruise of the Monitor. G. Boker.
    Hi-TL:110
The Cumberland and the Merrimac.
    Em-AF:443
The Cumberland's Crew. Em-AF:442
Dan Ellis's Boys. Em-AF:452
Ethiopia Saluting the Colors.
    W. Whitman. Hu-PN:470, Sh-AP:119
Farragut. W. Meredith. Hi-TL:108
Goin' 'Cross the Mountain. Em-AF:452
History among the Rocks. R. Warren.
    Un-MA:565
The House-Top. H. Melville. Ho-P:176
Jack Ellyat Heard the Guns. S. Benét.
    Fe-PL:172
John Brown's Body. S. Benét.
    Hi-TL:105
John Burns of Gettysburg. B. Harte.
    Sp-OG:36, Vi-PP:156
Kentucky Belle. C. Woolson.
    Ha-PO:133, Un-GT:192
Killed at the Ford. H. Longfellow.
    Sp-OG:194
Knowlt Hoheimer. E. Masters.
    Ba-PO:81, Ho-LP:89
The Last Fierce Charge. Em-AF:456
Lee in the Mountains, 1865-1870.
    D. Davidson. Sm-PT:92
Looking into History. R. Wilbur.
    Ca-VT:485
Maggie Mac. Em-AF:445
The March into Virginia. H. Melville.
    Al-VBP:951, Sh-AP:121
Misgivings. H. Melville. Rv-CB:837
My Maryland. J. Randall. Er-FA:441
Names from the War. B. Catton.
    Br-AF:78
Negro Soldier's Civil War Chant.
    Ra-BP:7
Ode to the Confederate Dead. A. Tate.
    Al-VBP:1215, Un-MA:536, Wi-LT:402
The Old Man and Jim. J. Riley.
    Co-PT:232, Sp-OG:197

One-and-Twenty.   Em-AF:458
The Picket-Guard.   E. Beers.   Er-FA:187,
  Sp-OG:196
A Prayer for Our Nation.   Ba-PO:70
The Red, White, and Red.   Em-AF:447
Reviewing Negro Troops Going South
  Through Washington, April 26, 1864.
  P. Horgan.   Cr-WS:23
Running the Batteries.   H. Melville.
  Hi-TL:118
Sheridan's Ride.   T. Read.   Er-FA:185,
  Ga-FB:261, Sp-OG:44
Shiloh, a Requiem.   H. Melville.
  Al-VBP:952, Br-AF:72, Ho-WR:120,
  Pa-HT:42, Rv-CB:838, Vi-PP:149
A Sight in Camp in the Daybreak Gray
  and Dim.   W. Whitman.   Ha-PO:62
Tenting on the Old Camp Ground.
  W. Kittredge.   Ba-PO:198
Uncle Frank.   L. Bacon.   Cr-WS:34
The Unsung Heroes.   P. Dunbar.   Ra-BP:54
Virginia's Bloody Soil.   Em-AF:446
We're Tenting To-Night.   W. Kittredge.
  Vi-PP:160
When Dey 'Listed Colored Soldiers.
  P. Dunbar.   Ra-BP:48
When Lilacs Last in the Dooryard
  Bloom'd.   W. Whitman.   Al-VBP:940,
  Sh-AP:113, Un-MA:71, Vi-PP:172
When This Cruel War Is Over.   Em-AF:454
Whisperin' Bill.   I. Bacheller.
  Fe-PL:156
White Magic.   W. Braithwaite.   Hu-PN:49
CIVIL WAR - UNITED STATES - RECONSTRUCTION
The Rebel.   I. Randolph.   Co-RM:208
  Hi-TL:128
CIVILIZATION: see also CULTURE; HISTORY;
  SATIRE - CIVILIZATION
Chorus for Survival.   H. Gregory.
  Sm-PT:115
Piano and Drums.   G. Okara.   Lo-TY:158
The Purse-Seine.   R. Jeffers.   Pe-OA:92
Song: Fish in the Unruffled Lakes.
  W. Auden.   Un-MB:464
To the Western World.   L. Simpson.
  Wi-LT:817
Wealth.   R. Emerson.   Pl-IO:34
CLAMS: see also HUMOR - CLAMS
The Clam.   S. Silverstein.   Co-BBW:72
Clam-Digging Song.   M. Kumin.   Cr-SS:6
The Sea Is Full of Clams.   I. Georgoff.
  La-GI:40
CLANS: see SCOTLAND - CLANS
CLAPPING GAMES
Boogie Chant and Dance.   Bu-DY:67
Clap Handies.   Mo-TL:73, Wr-RM:28
Clap Hands, Clap Hands.   Mo-TL:73
Ha Ha Thisaway.   Bu-DY:33
Hands Clapping. . . .   Gr-BB:16
Handy, Pandy, Jack-a-Dandy.   Mo-TL:73,
  Wr-RM:49
Handy Spandy.   Au-SP:11, Bo-FP:117

Head and Shoulders, Baby.   Bu-DY:58
Li'l Liza Jane.   Bu-DY:55
Ma's Gonna Buy Me.   Bu-DY:24
Miss Mary Mac.   Bu-DY:68
Parrot, Parrot.   Ca-MU:21
Pat-a-Cake, Pat-a-Cake, Baker's Man.
  Bo-FP:118, De-PO:6, Li-LB:18,
  Mo-CC:(52), Mo-MGT:5, Mo-NR:5,
  Mo-TL:74, Wi-MG:43, Wr-RM:14
Pease-Porridge Hot.   Ar-TP3:103,
  Au-SP:10, Bo-FP:53, De-PO:10,
  Ir-BB:192, Li-LB:130, Mo-CC:(20),
  Mo-MGT:119, On-TW:33, Wi-MG:31,
  Wr-RM:102
Pease Pudding Hot.   Mother Goose.
  Er-FA:506, Mo-NR:25, Mo-TL:76
Peter Simon Suckegg.   Bu-DY:66
Who Did?   Bu-DY:45
CLARE, JOHN
At the Grave of John Clare.   C. Causley.
  Ma-FW:171
Vain Dream for John Clare.   J. Hutton.
  Ls-NY:129
CLASS DISTINCTIONS: see SOCIAL CLASSES
CLAVICHORDS
The Clavichord.   M. Sarton.   Pl-US:18
CLAY, CASSIUS MARCELLUS
Ali.   Djangatolum.   Ad-BO:26, Ad-PB:511
CLEANLINESS: see also BATHS; HUMOR -
  CLEANLINESS
Cleanliness.   C. and M. Lamb.   Ox-BC:144
Get This Garbage Out of My Life.
  P. Goggins.   Ba-HI:132
I Lay on the Rock in the Stream.
  Wo-HS:(56)
Love Song.   W. Williams.   Un-MA:255
CLEMENS, JANE LAMPTON
Nancy Hanks, Mother of Abraham Lincoln.
  V. Lindsay.   Hi-TL:96
CLEOPATRA, QUEEN OF EGYPT: see also
  ANTONY, MARK
Cleopatra.   W. Shakespeare.   Hi-FO:51,
  No-CL:60
Discordants III.   C. Aiken.   Co-BL:36
Early in the Morning.   L. Simpson.
  Ha-PO:158
CLERGY: see also BISHOPS; HUMOR - CLERGY;
  MONKS; PREACHERS AND PREACHING;
  PRIESTS; SATIRE - CLERGY
The Country Clergy.   R. Thomas.
  Go-BP:44, Pa-GTB:537
Elegy for the Rev. Mr. James B. Hodgson.
  J. Logan.   St-H:111
Irish-American Dignitary.   A. Clarke.
  Co-PI:26
The Jackdaw of Rheims.   R. Barham.
  Pa-OM:322
The Old Pastor.   J. Tabb.   Sh-AP:136
The Parson.   O. Goldsmith.   Hi-WP II:125
Soldier's Song.   W. Scott.   Al-VBP:673
The Vicar of Bray.   Al-VBP:608,
  Gr-GB:198

CLERGY — cont'd.
Watchman, What of the Night?
A. Swinburne. Ho-WR:200
CLERKS AND CLERKING: see also SATIRE -
CLERKS AND CLERKING
The Clerk. E. Robinson. Un-MA:126
CLEVELAND, O.
Ode to Mayor Locker. D. Levy. Lo-IT:78
CLIMBING: see also HUMOR - CLIMBING
At Castle Boterel. T. Hardy.
Ha-PO:186, Ox-BN:844, Pa-GTB:408
At Heron Lodge. Wang Chih-Huan.
Le-MW:51
Burning. G. Snyder. Ma-FW:140
Climbing. A. Fisher. Ar-TP3:102
Climbing in Glencoe. A. Young.
Mo-SD:89
Cold Mountain Is Full of Weird Sights.
Han-Shan. Le-MW:45
Conclusion. W. Wordsworth. Ox-BN:112
18,000 Feet. E. Roberson. Hu-PN:430
Every Time I Climb a Tree. D. McCord.
Ar-TP3:103, Au-SP:192, Ho-GC:34,
La-PP:62, La-PV:4, Un-GT:253
Finding a Poem. E. Merriam. La-RM:25
Foreign Lands. R. Stevenson. Bo-FP:86,
Hu-MP:179
Having Climbed to the Topmost Peak of
the Incense-Burner Mountain.
Po Chü-I. Mo-SD:94
Here in Katmandu. D. Justice.
La-RM:38
The Hike. N. Weiss. Mo-SD:87
I Can Climb Our Apple Tree. J. Jones.
Sh-RP:106
The Mountain. R. Frost. Ga-FB:292,
Pa-HT:13
Mythistorema XXIII. G. Seferis.
Gr-BT:147
On Middleton Edge. A. Young. Co-EL:68,
Mo-SD:95
Strength Through Joy. K. Rexroth.
Ca-VT:268
Summer Solstice. A. Garner. Gr-BT:155
Tree Climbing. K. Fraser. Ho-ME:10
Victory. M. Miller. Sh-RP:283
Zermatt. T. Hardy. Ox-BN:823
CLIPPER SHIPS
Citizens in the Round. R. Coffin.
Sh-RP:290
Clipper Ships and Captains. S. Benét.
Sh-RP:298
Picture in an Old Frame. E. Chaffee.
Ke-TF:68
CLOCKS AND WATCHES: see also HUMOR -
CLOCKS AND WATCHES; SUNDIALS;
TELLING TIME
After My Grandfather's Death: A Poem
of the China Clock. M. Oliver.
St-H:167
The Alarm Clock. M. Evans. Ad-BO:6
The Alarum. S. Warner. Un-MB:372

The Big Clock.   Ar-TP3:174, Au-SP:99
The Clock. J. Jaszi. Au-SP:97
The Clock. Bo-FP:3
The Clock. Wr-RM:12
The Clock Tower. C. Thibaudeau.
Do-WH:87
Clocks and Watches. St-FS:27
Contract. F. Nicklaus. Ls-NY:5
Elder Belder. Rv-ON:61
Fall, 1961. R. Lowell. Ca-VT:453,
Ha-TP:135
Four Quartz Crystal Clocks. M. Moore.
Br-TC:302, Pl-IO:67
Grandfather's Clock. H. Work.
Er-FA:351
Hickory, Dickory, Dock. An-IP:(7),
Au-SP:17, Bo-FP:16, De-PO:20,
Er-FA:505, Fr-WO:17, Li-LB:102,
Mo-CC:(15), Mo-MGT:77, Mo-NR:24,
Mo-TL:22, Wi-MG:58, Wr-RM:125
The Horologe. C. Smith. De-FS:186
Housekeeping Problems. L. Haft.
Le-M:139
Mr. Coggs, Watchmaker. E. Lucas.
Fe-FP:315, Hu-MP:145
My Father's Watch. J. Ciardi.
Pl-IO:24
The Old Clock on the Stairs.
H. Longfellow. Sp-OG:309
Our Clock. F. Eakman. Br-SS:6
Someone Slow. J. Ciardi. Un-GB:21
Song for a Little Cuckoo Clock.
E. Coatsworth. Br-SS:6
A Stopwatch and an Ordnance Map.
S. Spender. Ca-MB:99
The Sun-Dial. T. Peacock. Ox-BN:231
Tickle Tockle. Re-RR:18
Time Piece. W. Cole. Co-EL:110
To His Watch. G. Hopkins. Un-MB:44
Town and Country. De-PP:36
The Twenty-Fourth of December.
Bo-FP:183, Ch-B:52
The Watch. F. Cornford. Un-MB:306
The Watch. M. Swenson. Co-PT:69
CLONMACNOISE, IRE.
The Dead at Clonmacnoise. T. Rolleston.
Co-PI:172, Pa-HT:144
CLOTHING AND DRESS: see also BUTTONS;
COATS; DRESSMAKING; FASHION; HATS;
HUMOR - CLOTHING AND DRESS; JEWELRY;
SHOES
Auntie's Skirts. R. Stevenson.
Hu-MP:135
Away with Silks. R. Herrick. Un-MW:22
The Baker's Boy. M. Newsome. Ag-HE:23
The Ballad of the Harp-Weaver.
E. Millay. Ar-TP3:156, Co-PT:64
A Ballad of the Mulberry Road.
E. Pound. Ha-LO:93
Black Jackets. T. Gunn. Br-TC:162
Canterbury Tales. G. Chaucer.
Al-VBP:10

Clothes.   E. Jennings.   Pa-RE:61
Delight in Disorder.   R. Herrick.
   Al-VBP:325, Ga-FB:39, Ha-PO:171,
   Pa-GTB:78, Rv-CB:339, Un-MW:21
Dressing.   R. Gay.   Fr-MP:4
Eighteenth Century Lady.   R. O'Neill.
   Ls-NY:316
Happiness.   A. Milne.   Ar-TP3:111
I Have a Garment.   A. Ibn Ezra.
   Me-PH:65
If I Had as Much Money as I Could
   Spend.   Mother Goose.   Er-FA:505
I'll Wear Me a Cotton Dress. Ra-BP:11
In My New Clothing.   Bashö.   Au-SP:102,
   Su-FVI:10
Little Blue Ribbons.   A. Dobson.
   Br-BC:54
Look, Edwin!   E. Millay.   Bo-FP:116,
   Bo-GJ:115
McDonogh Day in New Orleans.
   M. Christian.   Bo-AN:52, Hu-PN:157
Minstrel's Song.   Do-CH:(39)
Mother.   R. Fyleman.   Br-SS:152,
   Hu-MP:5
My Love in Her Attire.   Al-VBP:356,
   No-CL:200, Pa-GTB:79, Un-MW:13
My Love Is in a Light Attire. J. Joyce.
   Ha-LO:91
My Sort of Man.   P. Dunbar.   Bo-AN:6
My Zipper Suit.   M. Allen.   Ar-TP3:98
On a Girdle.   E. Waller.   Al-VBP:385,
   Pa-GTB:79, Un-MW:164
On the Gift of a Cloak.   Hugo of
   Orleans.   Li-TU:44
Ready for Winter.   C. Booth.   Mc-AW:5
Red Stockings.   Mo-MGT:163
The Satin Dress.   D. Parker.   Ke-TF:173
Sir Gawain and the Green Knight.
   Ma-YA:21
Solution.   L. Jacobs.   Fr-MP:4
Songs, II.   Tr-US II:147
A Spring Song.   Fe-PL:371
Still to Be Neat.   B. Jonson.
   Al-VBP:240, Ha-PO:58, Ma-YA:83,
   Rv-CB:282, Un-MW:15
Stocking and Shirt.   J. Reeves.
   Gr-EC:114
Talking Designs.   L. Bahe.   Ni-CD:10
Ten of Chaucer's People: The Wife of
   Bath.   G. Chaucer.   Ha-PO:53
Turvey.   Rv-ON:92
Two Hundred Girls in Tights & Halters.
   D. Hoffman.   Co-EL:153
Upon Julia's Clothes.   R. Herrick.
   Al-VBP:328, Er-FA:112, Ga-FB:40,
   Gr-CT:62, Ho-LP:63, Li-SR:23,
   Pa-GTB:78, Rv-CB:337, Un-MW:21
The Vesture of the Soul.   G. Russell.
   Co-PI:174
What Curious Dresses All Men Wear.
   D. Schwartz.   Co-EL:38

What, My Son, Does Your Blanket Mean?
   Wo-HS:(30)
The Wife of Bath.   G. Chaucer.
   Hi-WP II:122
Winter.   C. Rossetti.   Bo-FP:167,
   Ch-B:54, Rv-CB:891, St-FS:38
The Woman at the Washington Zoo.
   R. Jarrell.   Br-TC:220, Wi-LT:565
CLOUDS: see also FOG; HAZE; MIST
Among the Millet.   A. Lampman.   Do-WH:78
Anatomy of a Cloud.   Lin Ling.   Pa-MV:110
Boats Sail on the Rivers.   C. Rossetti.
   Ar-TP3:172, Bo-FP:263, Ox-BC:278,
   Pe-FB:73
Black Clouds.   T. Brame.   Pa-RE:72
The Cloud.   P. Shelley.   Al-VBP:752,
   Bo-FP:261, Fe-FP:76, Hu-MP:295,
   Pl-IO:46, Rv-CB:708, Sh-RP:67,
   Sp-OG:349
The Cloud Messenger.   Kalidasa.
   Al-PI:46
The Cloud-Mobile.   M. Swenson.
   Un-GT:255
Clouds.   D. Aldis.   Au-SP:322
The Clouds.   J. de Melo Neto.   An-TC:145
Clouds.   J. Jaszi.   Sh-RP:74
Clouds.   P. Kuramoto.   Le-M:37
Clouds.   J. Reaney.   Do-WH:79
Clouds.   C. Rossetti.   Ar-TP3:166,
   Au-SP:352, Bo-FP:260, Ch-B:108,
   Gr-GB:37, La-PP:18
The Clouds.   W. Williams.   Ca-VT:62
Clouds Across the Canyon.   J. Fletcher.
   Pa-HT:56
The Clouds Go over the Sun.   Puti.
   Le-WR:42
Clouds in a Wild Storm.   D. May.
   Le-M:50
Clouds of Evening.   R. Jeffers.
   Un-MA:362
Clouds' Work.   F. Gullar.   An-TC:171
Dancing.   Yang Kuei-Fei.   Fe-FP:481
The Dark Gray Clouds.   N. Belting.
   La-PV:40
Don't You Ever.   Jo-TS:7
Dreaming.   T. Miles.   Ho-CT:5
Ella.   G. Brooks.   Ag-HE:39
An Enchanted Garden.   C. Webb.   Le-M:158
Evening Clouds.   D. Bharati.   Al-PI:114
Green Symphony.   J. Fletcher.   Un-MA:314
I Wonder.   J. Lawton.   Le-M:170
I Wonder.   J. Ricci.   La-GI:19
Irradiations.   J. Fletcher.   Un-MA:313
Job.   Bible.   O.T. Job.   Pl-IO:45
A Kingdom of Clouds.   M. Copeland.
   Le-M:83
A Legacy.   J. Tabb.   Mc-PR:147
Lines for a Night Driver.   P. Dufault.
   Ha-WR:53
The Loaves.   R. Everson.   Do-WH:79
London Nightfall.   J. Fletcher.
   Un-MA:317

CLOUDS — cont'd.
Lost in Heaven. R. Frost. Un-MA:188
Low-Anchored Cloud. H. Thoreau.
   Al-VBP:917, Pl-IO:49
A Memory. Emperor Hirohito. Th-AS:155
Mount Koonak: A Song of Arsut.
   Da-SC:36
Night Clouds. A. Lowell. Ho-TH:24,
   Mo-BG:147, Sh-RP:88, Th-AS:142,
   Un-MA:159
On the Sea of Heaven. . . . Hitomaro.
   Ba-ST:32
A Piece of Colored Cloud. Chien Hsu.
   Le-MW:35
The Ragged Phantom. Boncho. Be-MC:36
The Rainbow Fairies. L. Hadley.
   St-FS:65
The Scared Clouds. H. Hodgins.
   Le-M:46
Sea Surface Full of Clouds. W. Stevens.
   Ca-VT:32, Un-MA:245
Song of the Red Cloud. Tr-US II:250
Substantiations. Vallana. Al-PI:40
That Nature Is a Heraclitean Fire and
   of the Comfort of the Resurrection.
   G. Hopkins. Pa-GTB:396
This Little Cloud, and This.
   Do-CH:(19)
Trees and Evening Sky. N. Momaday.
   Ni-CD:102
Untitled. Chung Ting-wen. Pa-MV:74
Watching Clouds. J. Farrar. Au-SP:351
Weather Incantation. Le-IB:31
When Clouds Appear. . . . Un-GT:23
The Wind Is Half the Flower. D. Cairns.
   Le-M:43, Le-WR:34
The Wind Is like the Yeast in Bread.
   R. Tanaka. Le-M:44, Le-WR:14
CLOUGH, ARTHUR HUGH
Thyrsis. M. Arnold. Ox-BN:637
CLOVER
Clover for Breakfast. F. Frost.
   Sh-RP:333
Clover Swaths. J. Hearst. St-H:83
Four-Leaf Clover. E. Higginson.
   Fe-FP:540
I Found. M. Livingston. Br-SG:84
Luck for Halloween. M. Justus.
   Ja-PA:36, Ju-CP:81
Purple Crown. E. Dickinson. Un-MA:104
CLOVES
The Alley in the Rain. Tai Wang-shu.
   Hs-TC:180
CLOWNS
The Clown. D. Aldis. La-PV:92
The Clown. N. Alexander. Me-WF:78
The Clown. M. Rose. Au-SP:144
Quite a Clown. J. Lee. Ja-HH:12
CLUMSINESS: see HUMOR - CLUMSINESS
CLYDE RIVER
Clyde's Waters. Ox-BB:331

COACHES AND COACHMEN: see CARRIAGES;
   STAGECOACHES
COAL: see also MINERS AND MINING
Banking Coal. J. Toomer. Bo-HF:132,
   Hu-PN:106
Black I Am. Mo-MGT:154
The Bonny Keel Laddie. Gr-GB:215
Coal Fire. L. Untermeyer. Un-GT:256
Coal for Mike. B. Brecht. Li-TU:142
The Collier. V. Watkins. To-MP:24
Happiness. N. Mitchell. Me-WF:38
The Mine. B. Mason. Le-M:70
Miners. W. Owen. Un-MB:366
COATS
The Buffalo Coat. T. McGrath.
   St-H:124
The Coat. C. Grade. Ho-TY:338
The Coat. E. Jebeleanu. Mc-AC:107
COAXING
Bedtime. E. Farjeon. Ar-TP3:114,
   Au-SP:92, Pe-FB:38, Rd-SS:3
Of the Child with the Bird on the Bush.
   J. Bunyan. Ox-BC:37
COBALT: see HUMOR - COBALT
COBBLERS: see SHOEMAKERS
COBWEBS: see also SPIDERS
A Bit of Cobweb. L. Sarchuk. Mo-MI:20
Cold Snuggle. J. Lloyd. Le-WR:33
Dew on a Spider Web. M. Stone.
   Le-M:97
The Gossamer. C. Smith. Al-VBP:602
Little City. R. Horan. Co-BBW:219
The Spider. J. Jenkins. Le-M:91
Spider Silverlegs. C. Bailey.
   Bo-FP:326
Spider Webs. R. Fabrizio. Sm-MK:21
A Spider's Web. S. Takano. Sh-AM:168
Tangled over Twigs. Onitsura.
   Be-MC:34
There Was an Old Woman. Au-SP:2,
   Bo-FT:215, Gr-EC:211, Ir-BB:252,
   La-PV:197, Li-LB:58, Mo-MGT:145,
   Mo-NR:92, Na-EO:100, Wr-RM:66
Webs. C. Sandburg. Ho-TH:56
What a Sad Sight. Shiki. Do-TS:24
COCHITI, N.M.
A Dance for Rain. W. Bynner. Pa-HT:58
COCKATOOS: see PARROTS
COCKFIGHTS
The Bonny Grey. Gr-GB:59
COCKROACHES: see also HUMOR -
   COCKROACHES
I Wish I Were. Er-FA:502
A New Year Idyl. E. Field. Co-PS:28
Nursery Rhymes for the Tender-Hearted.
   C. Morley. Co-BBW:227, Er-FA:231
The Roach. J. Raven. Ra-BP:259
COCKSCOMBS (FLOWERS)
Aubade. E. Sitwell. Hi-WP II:6,
   Un-MB:330

COCOA
  Animal Crackers. C. Morley. Au-SP:118,
    Fe-FP:43, Fr-MP:5, Hu-MP:16, Th-AS:62
COCONUTS: see HUMOR - COCONUTS
COCOONS: see BUTTERFLIES; CATERPILLARS
    (LARVAE); MOTHS; SILKWORMS
CODLINGS: see APPLES
CODRINGTON, SIR EDWARD
  The Glorious Victory of Navarino.
    Hi-FO:214
CODY, MARY ANN LEACOCK
  Nancy Hanks, Mother of Abraham Lincoln.
    V. Lindsay. Hi-TL:96
CODY, WILLIAM FREDERICK (BUFFALO BILL)
  Buffalo Bill's. E. Cummings.
    Br-AF:113, Ca-VT:172, Gr-CC:128,
    Ho-LP:91, Li-TU:144, Mc-EA:158,
    Mo-BG:157, Mo-GR:76, Un-MA:473
COFFEE: see also HUMOR - COFFEE
  Coffee. J. Cunningham. Ca-VT:325,
    Un-MA:615
  Coffee and Tea. Wr-RM:83
COFFINS: see also HUMOR - COFFINS
  Two Riddles. Gr-GB:323
COINS: see also HUMOR - COINS; MONEY
  Henry Turnbull. W. Gibson. Co-EL:76
  I Love Sixpence. Gr-EC:226, Ir-BB:121,
    Li-LB:122, Mo-NR:62, On-TW:26,
    Wr-RM:77
  Little Dame Crump. Bo-FP:89, Pa-RE:91
  The Penny. L. Benét. Bo-FP:122
  Sing Song Merry Go Round. Ir-BB:124
  Story of the Pennies. A. Lutzky.
    Ho-TY:267
COLD: see also FREEZING; HUMOR - COLD
  After He Has Gone. S. Warner. Un-MB:373
  All Animals Like Me. R. Souster.
    Do-WH:70
  The Ballad of the Harp-Weaver.
    E. Millay. Ar-TP3:156, Co-PT:64
  The Banks of Newfoundland. Gr-GB:219
  Black and White Spring. C. Hampton.
    Ls-NY:237
  Black Clouds. T. Brame. Pa-RE:72
  The Chiming River. Rokwa. Be-MC:53
  Cold. B. Donohoo. Me-WF:74
  The Cold. L. Henson. Ni-CD:63
  Cold August. J. Harrison. Ls-NY:284
  Cold Blows the Wind. J. Hamilton.
    Cl-FC:33
  Cold Snuggle. J. Lloyd. Le-WR:33
  Contract. F. Nicklaus. Ls-NY:5
  December. J. Lowell. Un-GT:283
  Dirge in Dialogue. Lo-TY:3, Tr-US I:64
  The End of the World. G. Bottomley.
    De-CH:390, Un-MB:212
  Exposure. W. Owen. Go-BP:207
  Frozen Hands. J. Bruchac. Ni-CD:35
  Gone Were But the Winter Cold.
    A. Cunningham. De-CH:224
  He Who Hanged Himself. Tsou Ti-fan.
    Hs-TC:341

Ice Cold. D. Adams. Ho-CT:40
In the Clear Cold. S. Yesenin.
  Pa-SG:100
Kingdom of Heaven. L. Adams. Un-MA:547
Late Winter. Laksmidhara. Al-PI:41
A Man Is Buried where the Cold Winds
  Blow. D. Matumeak. Ba-HI:73
The Night Is Freezing Fast. A. Housman.
  Wi-LT:66
The North Wind Doth Blow. Au-SP:62,
  Bl-OB:97, Bo-FP:152, Cl-DT:19,
  De-CH:625, Hi-GD:21, Ir-BB:29,
  Li-LB:102, Mo-MGT:20, Mo-NR:86,
  Pa-AP:16, Sm-MK:2, Wi-MG:20,
  Wr-RM:114
Old January. E. Spenser. Ha-YA:163
On a Cold Day. W. Davies. Go-BP:78
On a Mountain Road. Wu Ch'ing-jen.
  Pa-SG:99
Phantoms of the Steppe. A. Pushkin.
  Ab-MO:63
Ready for Winter. C. Booth. Mc-AW:5
Rounding the Horn. J. Masefield.
  Un-MB:223
Second Half. D. McCord. Mo-SD:25
Siberia. J. Mangan. Co-RG:132,
  Hi-FO:221
Skating. W. Wordsworth. Sm-LG:60,
  Un-GT:281
The Snow-Leopard. R. Jarrell.
  Br-TC:221, Wi-LT:560
The Snow Man. W. Stevens. Bo-GJ:226
A Snowy Day. D. ap Gwilym. Pa-SG:100
A Song of Winter. De-CH:217
Spider. M. Foster. Le-M:200
Star Talk. R. Graves. Bo-GJ:242,
  Co-BN:115, Un-MB:385
The Subalterns. T. Hardy. Un-MB:33
Summer Is Gone. Sm-LG:58
There Is Fear. Ma-BH:11, Tr-US I:24
There's Snow on the Fields.
  C. Rossetti. De-TT:39
This Evening So Cold and Chill.
  Prince Shiki. Ba-ST:50
Travelling Northward. Tu Fu. Rx-OH:10
Twin Lakes Hunter. A. Guthrie, Jr.
  Du-RG:127, Ha-PO:143
The Watercress Seller. T. Miller.
  Ox-BC:211
The Waves Are So Cold. Basho.
  Be-MC:12
The Windham Thaw. A. Guiterman.
  Gr-EC:58
Winter. R. Hughes. Re-TW:112
Winter. C. Mair. Co-PS:153
Winter Holding off the Coast of North
  America. N. Momaday. Ni-CD:91
A Winter Night. J. Velez. Pa-HI:72
Winter-Time. R. Stevenson. Un-GT:280,
  Un-MB:58
A Winter's Dream.
  De-PP:45

COLD — cont'd.
  Your Load Being Taken Off. S. Ogiwara.
    Sh-AM:165
COLDS: see also HUMOR - COLDS;
    INFLUENZA; SNEEZING
  Blanket Street. I. Hogan. Br-BC:56
  A Charm Against Cough. Al-PI:18
  A Child That Has a Cold. T. Dibdin.
    Co-PM:18, Gr-CT:392
  My Nose. D. Aldis. Ho-ME:14
  Song of Coughing. Tr-US II:195
  Such Is Holland! P. de Genestet.
    Ma-FW:42
COLERIDGE, SAMUEL TAYLOR
  The Man from Porlock. H. Bevington.
    Na-EO:38
  O, Lift One Thought. S. Coleridge.
    De-CH:254
  To Coleridge. P. Shelley. Rv-CB:700
  To Coleridge in Sicily. W. Wordsworth.
    Ox-BN:103
COLLECTIVE BARGAINING: see HUMOR -
    COLLECTIVE BARGAINING; LABOR UNIONS
COLLECTORS AND COLLECTING
  Ferrore. J. Schevill. Du-SH:155
  My Grandmother. E. Jennings.
    To-MP:111
  My Uncle Jack. D. Amey. Le-M:145
  To a Lady on Her Passion for Old China.
    J. Gay. Er-FA:141
COLLEGE LIFE: see COLLEGES AND
    UNIVERSITIES
COLLEGES AND UNIVERSITIES: see also
    COMMENCEMENTS; HUMOR - COLLEGES AND
    UNIVERSITIES; SATIRE - COLLEGES AND
    UNIVERSITIES; SCHOLARS AND SCHOLAR-
    SHIP; STUDENTS
  Epilogue. H. Keyes. Ke-TF:452
  Hail! Minnesota! T. Rickard.
    Se-PR:270
  Here We Have Idaho. H. Powell.
    Se-PR:258
  I Sing of Lienta. Cheng Min.
    Hs-TC:236
  In and Out: Severance of Connections,
    1946. L. Sissman. Br-TC:384
  Kent State, May 4, 1970. P. Goodman.
    Mo-TS:41
  University Examinations in Egypt.
    D. Enright. Br-TC:119
  Valediction to My Contemporaries.
    H. Gregory. Un-MA:506
COLM, SAINT: see COLUMBA, SAINT
COLONIAL PERIOD IN AMERICA: see also
    CAMINO REAL; PILGRIM FATHERS;
    PURITANS AND PURITANISM; SATIRE -
    COLONIAL PERIOD IN AMERICA;
    THANKSGIVING DAY; and names of
    colonists, as ALDEN, JOHN, and
    native tribes, as SIOUAN INDIANS
  Atlantic Charter, A.D. 1620-1942.
    F. Young. Ar-TP3:39, Br-AF:86, Vi-PP:221

Bar's Fight, August 28, 1746. L. Terry.
    Hu-PN:3, Ra-BP:37
  Citadel. E. Brathwaite. Sa-B:241
  First Thanksgiving of All. N. Turner.
    Br-SS:80, Fe-FP:410, Sh-RP:232,
    Vi-PP:52
  Homage to Mistress Bradstreet.
    J. Berryman. Sh-AP:225
  The Landing of the Pilgrim Fathers.
    F. Hemans. Ar-TP3:39, Bo-FP:159,
    Er-FA:296, Fe-FP:409, Ga-FB:252,
    Gr-EC:228, Hi-TL:23, Se-PR:217,
    Sp-OG:23, Un-GT:176, Vi-PP:50
  The New World. P. Engle. Br-AF:58
  The Plymouth Harvest. W. Bradford.
    Bo-FP:154
  School Days in New Amsterdam.
    A. Guiterman. Fe-FP:411
  Southern Ships and Settlers, 1606-1732.
    R. & S. Benét. Br-AF:56
  Virginia. P. McGinley. Ag-HE:8
  Who Are They? Bi-IT:145
COLONIALISM: see IMPERIALISM
COLONNA, VITTORIA
  Vittoria Colonna. H. Longfellow.
    Gr-CC:87
COLONNA, CAPE: see SUNIUM, CAPE
COLOR: see also DYES AND DYING; HUMOR -
    COLOR; SATIRE - COLOR; and names of
    individual colors, as SILVER (COLOR)
  Autumn Color. T. Robinson. Ha-YA:97
  Autumn Colors. Wen I-to. Hs-TC:52
  Autumn Fancies. Fe-FP:212, Hu-MP:279,
    Ja-PA:15
  Autumn Fashions. E. Thomas. Ha-YA:99
  Blue Is True. Un-GT:22
  The Chameleon. J. Merrick. Cl-FC:74
  Color. M. Cane. Sh-RP:222
  Colours. F. Evans. Pa-RE:25
  Green Red Brown and White. M. Swenson.
    Ca-VT:481
  Hymn to Colour. G. Meredith. Ox-BN:700
  In California There Are Two Hundred
    Fifty Six Religions. R. Albert.
    Du-SH:102
  In October. B. Carman. Ha-YA:110
  Indian Summer. A. Draper. Ha-YA:102
  Legacy. C. Morley. Du-RG:130
  The Map. G. Oden. Be-MA:97, Bo-AN:161,
    Hu-NN:47, Hu-PN:385
  No Meaning. T. Brame. Pa-RE:52
  Ombres Chinoises. B. Deutsch.
    Ha-TP:23
  The Red Wheelbarrow. W. Williams.
    Ma-FW:111, Mc-EA:52, Mo-TS:49,
    Na-EO:115, Re-TW:12, Un-MA:261,
    Wi-LT:199
  Reel One. A. Stoutenburg. Du-SH:40,
    Pe-M:4
  Spectrum. W. Dickey. Co-EL:96
  Spectrum. M. Evans. Ra-BP:186
  Summer Shower. S. Robinson. Th-AS:118

This Is a World Full. . . . D. Peterson.
Ba-HI:41
Those Dressed in Blue. De-CH:669
To the Sun. R. Campbell. Ga-S:188,
Pl-EI:21
Variations on a Sentence. L. Bogan.
Ho-LP:44, Pl-IO:111
What Is Pink? C. Rossetti.
Ar-TP3:207, Au-SP:322, Bo-GJ:3,
Br-SG:30, Ch-B:78, Ox-BC:280
COLORADO: see also names of towns, as
DENVER, COLO.
The Colorado Trail. Mc-WS:120
Holding the Sky. W. Stafford. La-RM:37
COLORADO RIVER: see also GRAND CANYON
Indian Legend of the Canyon.
J. Mahoney. Fi-BG:49
COLTRANE, JOHN
John Coltrane, an Impartial Review.
A. Spellman. Ad-PB:283, Be-MA:125,
Hu-NN:57
JuJu. A. Touré. Ad-PB:340
COLTS: see HORSES
COLUMBIA RIVER
The Fish Counter at Bonneville.
W. Stafford. Br-AF:157
John Day, Frontiersman. Y. Winters.
Ha-PO:73
COLUMBA, SAINT
The Pets. R. Farren. Gr-EC:30,
Rd-OA:6
COLUMBUS, CHRISTOPHER: see also DISCOVERY
PERIOD IN AMERICA; HUMOR - COLUMBUS,
CHRISTOPHER
Christopher Columbus. R. & S. Benét.
Pe-FB:34, Sh-RP:294
Christopher Columbus. A. Wynne.
Ja-PA:29
Columbian Ode. P. Dunbar. Se-PR:180
Columbus. A. Clough. Br-AF:53,
Co-PS:131
Columbus. L. Jackson. Br-SS:63
Columbus. J. Miller. Ar-TP3:38,
Er-FA:298, Fe-FP:403, Ha-YA:116,
Hi-TL:13, Hu-MP:370, Mc-PR:180,
Mc-WK:161, Se-PR:182, Sp-OG:59,
Vi-PP:42
Columbus. L. Simpson. To-MP:157
Columbus. A. Wynne. Ar-TP3:38,
Hu-MP:372
Dark-Eyed Lad Columbus. N. Turner.
Br-SS:62
The Discovery. J. Squire. Br-AF:54,
Cl-FC:83, Co-PS:132, De-CH:361,
Fe-FP:404, Mc-WK:163
Have You the Slightest Notion. Re-RR:24
Immortal Morn. H. Butterworth.
Se-PR:179
Light in the Darkness. A. Fisher.
Ha-YA:115, Ja-PA:30
Mysterious Biography. C. Sandburg.
Br-SS:63

The Prayer of Columbus. W. Whitman.
Se-PR:180
Prologue. A. MacLeish. Un-MA:454
To Columbus. R. Dario. Lo-TY:86
Voyage. J. Miles. Wi-LT:774
COLUMBUS DAY: see COLUMBUS, CHRISTOPHER
COLVILLE INDIANS: see INDIANS OF NORTH
AMERICA - VERSE - SALISHAN
COMBS
Combing. G. Cardiff. Ni-CD:50
I Have Teeth. St-FS:38
COMETS
Go Fly a Saucer. D. McCord.
Fe-FP:198, Li-TU:47, Pl-IO:27
I Am like a Slip of Comet. G. Hopkins.
Li-TU:175
COMFORT, ALEXANDER
Letter to Alex Comfort. D.Abse.Br-TC:1
COMFORT
All Animals Like Me. R. Souster.
Do-WH:70
Choti Lal. Ca-MJ:25
Cloudy Days. A. Coor. Ho-CT:43
Composed While under Arrest.
M. Lermontov. Pa-SG:204
Cry Silent. D. Whitewing. Al-WW:56
"Don't Care" and "Never Mind."
J. Bangs. Er-FA:16
(Drums and Drumming.) B. Brown.
Ba-HI:131
The Embankment. T. Hulme. Co-EL:123
From Thee to Thee. S. Gabirol.
Pl-EI:48
Golden Birds. E. Greenberg. Ho-TY:314
Grieve Not, Ladies. A. Branch.
Er-FA:156
His Litany to the Holy Spirit.
R. Herrick. Fe-PL:343
Inscription for the Entrance to a Wood.
W. Bryant. Sh-AP:19
A Life-Lesson. J. Riley. Fe-PL:247
Nelly Trim. S. Warner. Sm-PT:33
The Peace of Wild Things. W. Berry.
Ca-VT:685, Ls-NY:62
The Rain. R. Creeley. Ca-VT:563,
Mc-EA:37
The River. M. Arnold. Rv-CB:866
Should You Go First. A. Rowswell.
Fe-PL:277
A Song. A. Reisen. Ho-TY:71
Song of Thyrsis. P. Freneau.
Al-VBP:606
Sonnet. W. Drummond. Al-VBP:302
Sung by a Little Girl to Soothe a
Crying Baby. Le-IB:62, Ma-BH:27,
Tr-US I:10
Trifle. G. Johnson. Bo-AN:21,
Bo-HF:20
Turn Again to Life. M. Hall. Fe-PL:336
Under the Holly-Bough. C. Mackay.
Ke-TF:48
Weep No More. J. Fletcher.
Al-VBP:284, De-CH:420

COMFORT — cont'd.
Weep You No More. Al-VBP:357,
   De-CH:266, Go-BP:145, Gr-CT:410
The White Bouquet. Chung Ting-wen.
   Pa-MV:79
Windy Morning. H. Behn. Ar-TP3:164
The World and I. A. Reisen. Ho-TY:69
Ye That Do the Master's Will.
   C. Wesley. Go-BP:181
COMMANDMENTS: see TEN COMMANDMENTS
COMMENCEMENTS
At Graduating Time. Se-PR:240
At School-Close. J. Whittier. Se-PR:241
Graduation. J. Heinegg. Ad-II:64
Graduation. D. Richardson. Ke-TF:87
To a Negro Boy Graduating. E. Maleska.
   Hu-PN:569
COMMITTEES AND COMMITTEE MEETINGS:
   see HUMOR - COMMITTEES AND
   COMMITTEE MEETINGS
COMMON SENSE: see also WISDOM
The Pessimist. B. King. Bl-OB:14,
   Co-HP:84, Er-FA:205, Hi-WP II:13,
   Mc-WK:85, Sm-MK:115
Plain Talk. W. Smith. Co-FB:51,
   Un-MA:671
COMMONPLACENESS: see also HUMOR -
   COMMONPLACENESS; MEDIOCRITY
Ameinias. J. Simon. Co-EL:53
Black Rook in Rainy Weather. S. Plath.
   Wi-LT:788
Continual Conversation with a Silent
   Man. W. Stevens. Wi-LT:160
Diary of a Nondescript. G. Oppenheim.
   Ls-NY:148
Lord of All Pots and Pans. Ke-TF:205
The Man in the Bowler Hat. P. Black.
   Gr-BT:135
Not in the Guide-Books. E. Jennings.
   Wi-LT:742
The Trouble with the Times.
   T. McGrath. St-H:122
The Valley of Men. U. Greenberg.
   Me-PH:93
COMMUNICATION: see also LANGUAGE; NEWS;
   NEWSPAPERS; PONY EXPRESS; POSTAL
   SERVICE; RADIO; SATIRE - COMMUNICA-
   TION; SPEECH; TELEGRAPH; TELEPHONES;
   TELEVISION
The Buried Life. M. Arnold. Go-BP:126
The Cable Hymn. J. Whittier. Hi-TL:131
Councils. M. Piercy. Mo-TS:44
Effort at Speech. W. Meredith.
   Ho-P:181
Effort at Speech Between Two People.
   M. Rukeyser. Br-TC:351, Un-MA:623
Encountering. M. Fuller. Ba-HI:92
The Generation Gap. E. Alexander.
   La-IH:86
The Horse Show. W. Stevens. Ca-VT:66,
   Pe-OA:79
The House of Life. K. Tynan. Go-BP:133

In One Petal. Hirotsugu. Ba-ST:22
It Is Impossible. R. Falconer.
   Gr-BT:9
Lack of Communication. A. Philippide.
   Mc-AC:82
Long Distance. F. Eckman. St-H:49
My Secret. J. Tabb. Mc-WK:83
My Voice. J. Jiménez. Li-TU:213
Poem. W. Williams. Ca-VT:67
Their Lonely Betters. W. Auden.
   Bo-GJ:87, Ha-LO:64
There Are Things to Be Said. C. Corman.
   Ca-VT:528
There Was a Man. S. Crane. Un-MA:148
Within One Petal. Ba-ST:22
Without a Speaking Tongue. W. Sorell.
   Ls-NY:120
COMMUNION: see LORD'S SUPPER
COMMUNISM: see also SATIRE - COMMUNISM
A Big Mountain Is Moved Away. Hs-TC:442
Boatmen. I Men. Hs-TC:417
Can't Kill Him. Chang Chih-min.
   Hs-TC:426
The Electric Lights Shine in Everybody's
   Heart. Hs-TC:452
I Stand on Mountain High. Hs-TC:450
I'm a Longshoreman. Hs-TC:451
It Can Bend the Huge River. Hs-TC:443
Lava. Chang Chien. Pa-MV:24
Life. Lu Li. Hs-TC:422
Many, Many Are the Songs of Good
   Harvest. Hs-TC:442
One Step Covers Ten Thousand Li.
   Hs-TC:452
Our Songs Make the Yangtze River Flow
   Backward. Hs-TC:444
Please Take Good Care of My Home.
   Hs-TC:444
Poems, 1930-1940. H. Gregory.
   Sm-PT:118
Rendezvous. Chang Chih-min. Hs-TC:429
The Rhinoceros Mountain. Hs-TC:453
Sewing. Chang Chih-min. Hs-TC:430
Smash the Blockade. Jen Chun.
   Hs-TC:398
A Sweet Potato Rolls off the Hill.
   Hs-TC:454
Tomorrow We Take Over the Heavenly
   Palace. Hs-TC:443
Verse on the Wall. Chang Chih-min.
   Hs-TC:431
Water Flows Around Our Village.
   Hs-TC:450
What Kind of Troops Are These.
   Chang Chih-min. Hs-TC:430
With One Stroke I Dig Through the
   Crystal Palace. Hs-TC:442
Women Transport Corps. Hs-TC:441
COMMUTERS: see also HUMOR - COMMUTERS
Fatigue. P. Bacon. La-OC:62
COMORIN, CAPE
Kanya-Kumari. K. Subramanyan. Al-PI:146

COMPANIONSHIP: see FELLOWSHIP; FRIENDSHIP
COMPANIONSHIP OF MAN AND NATURE: see also
   SATIRE - COMPANIONSHIP OF MAN AND
   NATURE
   After the Death of Elder Klallum.
      D. Niatum.   Ni-CD:136
   All These Birds.   R. Wilbur.   Ho-P:313
   Answer.   D. Quick.   Ke-TF:425
   The Beatific Vision.   G. Chesterton.
      Tr-MR:244
   The Ching-Ting Mountain.   Li Po.
      Li-TU:39
   Companions.   A. Stoutenberg.   Ha-WR:83
   Earth-Born.   R. Howard.   De-FS:108
   Farm Child.   R. Thomas.   Co-BN:206,
      Co-PM:118, Hi-WP II:134, Ma-FW:77
   Fed.   E. Bragdon.   Ke-TF:426
   From Early Childhood Even as Hath Been
      Said.   W. Wordsworth.   Go-BP:273
   From the Walum Olum.   Br-MW:100
   The Geranium.   T. Roethke.   To-MP:141
   Green Things Growing.   D. Craik.
      Er-FA:247
   Held by the Land.   C. Rainsford.
      Ke-TF:425
   The Hermit.   Hsü Pên.   La-RM:168
   Hollyhocks.   D. Etter.   St-H:61
   I Know a Star.   P. Nardella.   La-GI:47
   In Dreamy Swoon.   G. Darley.   Ox-BN:388
   The Lime-Tree Bower My Prison.
      S. Coleridge.   Rv-CB:660
   Lines Composed above Tinturn Abbey.
      W. Wordsworth.   Go-BP:21, Ho-P:125
   Nonentity.   D. Lawrence.   Go-BP:164
   Nutting.   W. Wordsworth.   Rv-CB:637
   Ode on Intimations of Immortality from
      Recollections of Early Childhood.
      W. Wordsworth.   Ho-P:88
   On the Death of a Recluse.   G. Darley.
      Rv-CB:755
   Poets Love Nature.   J. Clare.   Rv-CB:727
   Saying.   A. Ammons.   Mo-TS:51
   The South Wind.   R. Bridges.   Ox-BN:877
   The Tables Turned.   W. Wordsworth.
      Rv-CB:641
   There Was a Boy.   W. Wordsworth.
      Go-BP:119, Ox-BN:101, Sm-LG:107
   The Voice.   R. Brooke.   Gr-BT:59
   Wales Visitation.   A. Ginsberg.
      Ho-P:85
   The Waters of Spring.   Ping Hsin.
      Hs-TC:25
COMPANIONSHIP OF MEN AND ANIMALS: see
   also HUMOR - COMPANIONSHIP OF MEN
   AND ANIMALS; PETS; SATIRE - COM-
   PANIONSHIP OF MEN AND ANIMALS
   The Adventures of Tom Bombadil.
      J. Tolkien.   Li-TU:92
   All Morning.   T. Roethke.
      Ca-BP:48

The Animals Mourn with Eve.
   C. Rossetti.   Rd-OA:197
Ay Me, Alas.   De-CH:85, Sm-LG:69
The Babes in the Wood.   Bl-OB:70,
   De-CH:546, De-TT:44, Gr-EC:152,
   Ox-BC:97
The Barnyard.   M. Burnham.   Ar-TP3:70,
   Bo-FP:105
The Bat.   R. Pitter.   Co-BBW:52,
   Hi-WP II:44
Beasts.   P. Engle.   En-PC:92
Beau's Reply.   W. Cowper.   Rd-OA:108
The Bells of Heaven.   R. Hodgson.
   Bo-GJ:20, Br-SS:152, Co-BBW:280,
   De-TT:82, Ha-PO:109, Ke-PP:104,
   Pl-EI:131, Th-AS:51, Un-MB:192,
   Wi-LT:125
Bird at Dawn.   H. Monro.   Un-GT:58,
   Un-MB:234
Birthdays.   M. Chute.   Br-BC:78,
   Br-SS:48
A Blessing.   J. Wright.   Br-TC:485,
   Du-SH:122, Kh-VA:31, Ma-FW:226,
   Mc-EA:53, St-H:261
The Boy and the Deer.   Te-FC:3
The Boy and the Parrot.   J. Frere.
   Ox-BC:150
Boy in a Pond.   J. Whaler.   Rd-OA:47
Bread from Our Pockets.   J. Rolnick.
   Ho-TY:164
Burro with the Long Ears.   Fe-FP:163
Charm for Going a-Hunting.   M. Austin.
   Sh-RP:341
The Child and the Snake.   M. Lamb.
   De-TT:63, Ox-BC:142
Children's Arms.   R. Jarrell.   Li-TU:25
The Church.   N. Willard.   Sc-TN:231
Concert Champêtre.   F. O'Hara.
   Kh-VA:16
Conversation with a Giraffe at Dusk in
   the Zoo.   D. Livingstone.   To-MP:196
Country Letter.   J. Clare.   Rv-CB:733
The Crayfish.   R. Wallace.   Co-BBW:74,
   Mc-WK:45
The Creation, Part II.   Te-FC:275
Dame Trot.   Ir-BB:169, Mo-CC:(50),
   Mo-MGT:133, St-FS:36, Wr-RM:13
Dame Wiggins of Lee.   Ox-BC:153
The Dead Sparrow.   W. Cartwright.
   De-CH:95
A Dirge.   J. Webster.   Al-VBP:288,
   Bl-OB:153, De-CH:251, Gr-CT:363,
   Pa-GTB:29, Re-TW:23, Rv-CB:315,
   Sm-LG:267
Do Not Believe Your Shakespeare's Grief.
   C. Aiken.   Co-PM:68, Rd-OA:32
Dog, Midwinter.   R. Souster.   Co-BBW:112
A Dog Named Ego, the Snowflakes as
   Kisses.   D. Schwartz.   Wi-LT:521
Dogs.   F. Cornford.   Gr-TG:25,
   Ma-FO:(15), St-FS:25

COMPANIONSHIP OF MEN AND ANIMALS — cont'd.
Doney Gal. Fi-BG:165
A Dream. W. Blake. De-CH:456,
    Hu-MP:127, Rd-OA:13, Rv-CB:585
Dust of Snow. R. Frost. Ad-PE:19,
    Ar-TP3:212, Hi-WP I:4, La-PV:133,
    Mo-TS:22, Re-BS:52, Tu-WW:42
Epitaph for a Lighthouse-Keeper's
    Horse. J. Morton. Co-PM:156
Familiar Friends. J. Tippett.
    Au-SP:42, St-FS:120
Fidelity. W. Wordsworth. Cl-FC:70
The First Friend. R. Kipling.
    Hu-MP:192
The Fish. E. Bishop. Al-VBP:1238,
    Bo-GJ:67, Co-BBW:69, Pe-OA:210,
    Un-GT:128, Un-MA:611, Wi-LT:510
Foot, Fin or Feather. C. Smart.
    Rd-OA:163
Forgiven. A. Milne. Au-SP:73,
    Pe-FB:18
Four Little Foxes. L. Sarett. La-RM:53
The Fox. K. Patchen. To-MP:32
From the Mountain's Summit. Ho-SD:40
Gecko. N. Lloyd. Pa-RE:18
Getting On. S. Sandy. Ad-CI:92
A Gigantic Beauty of a Stallion. . . .
    W. Whitman. Co-BBW:149, La-PV:124
The Girl and the Birds. Wr-RM:109
Gluskap's Hound. T. Roberts. Do-WH:61
Goat. S. Johnson. Gr-EC:6
Good Morning. M. Sipe. Ar-TP3:70,
    Au-SP:87
The Gracious and the Gentle Thing.
    R. Coffin. Rd-OA:84
Green Hill Neighbors. F. Frost.
    Ar-TP3:76
The Green Silk Bug. A. Fisher.
    Mc-AW:61
Growing. F. Frost. Br-BC:72
Hardweed Path Going. A. Ammons.
    Ca-VT:552
Hector the Dog. K. Barnes. Co-BBW:110
Herder's Song. Be-AP:59, Tr-US I:111
Hiawatha's Brothers. H. Longfellow.
    Bo-FP:265
Hiawatha's Chickens. H. Longfellow.
    Bo-FP:276
Ho, for the May Rains. Sanpu. Be-CS:51
Hop Out of My Way. Chora. Be-CS:27
The House Dog's Grave. R. Jeffers.
    Co-BBW:108
How They Brought the Good News from
    Ghent to Aix. R. Browning.
    Ar-TP3:31, Co-RG:31, Er-FA:378,
    Gr-EC:156, Hi-WP I:66, Li-SR:12,
    Sp-OG:29, Un-GT:149
I Doubt, I Doubt. Rv-ON:67
I Had a Little Hen. Ir-BB:66,
    Li-LB:90, Pa-AP:12, Wr-RM:21
I Have a Fawn. T. Moore.
    Cl-FC:72

I Have Found Out a Gift for My Fair.
    W. Shenstone. Re-BS:11
I Held a Lamb. K. Worthington.
    Au-SP:49
I Knew a Boy Who Ran with the Dogs.
    N. Willard. Sc-TN:230
I Love a Little Pussy. Bo-FP:6,,
    Li-LB:92, Mo-MGT:176, Mo-NR:23,
    Mo-TL:69, Wi-MG:59
I Remember the White Bear. Le-IB:54
I Would Like You for a Comrade.
    E. Parry. Ne-AM:20, Ox-BC:309
If I Were Only Able. B. Lapin.
    Mo-MI:78
If Things Were Better. Issa. Be-CS:32
Immalee. C. Rossetti. Bl-OB:136,
    Co-BN:207, Re-TW:61
In the Deep Museum. A. Sexton.
    Ho-P:229
In the Wilderness. R. Graves.
    De-CH:102, Ga-S:144, Pl-EI:105,
    Un-MB:388
The Irish Harper and His Dog.
    T. Campbell. De-CH:83, De-TT:66,
    Hu-MP:194, Rv-CB:678, Un-GT:41
The Kentucky Thoroughbred. J. Riley.
    Co-EL:52
A Kitten Is a Little Thing. J. Parr.
    La-GI:60
Lady Feeding Cats. D. Stewart.
    Ma-FW:61
The Lark in the Morning. Gr-CT:41,
    Gr-GB:44, Re-BS:49
Like as a Huntsman. E. Spenser.
    Ha-PO:108
A Little Dog-Angel. N. Holland.
    Fe-PL:361
The Little Dog under the Wagon.
    Fe-PL:360
Little Fly. W. Blake. Be-EB:36,
    Bl-OB:130, De-CH:539, Ha-PO:115,
    Ma-YA:128, Rv-CB:608, Un-GT:81
A Little Girl. Ir-BB:111, Mo-MGT:188,
    Sm-MK:10
Little Gustava. C. Thaxter. Fe-FP:535
Little Horned Toad. Fe-FP:144
Little Horse. W. Merwin. Ho-TH:87
Little Miss and Her Parrot. J. Marchant.
    Ox-BC:61
Little Puppy. Fe-FP:156
Little Things. J. Stephens. Ad-PE:47,
    Ar-TP3:65, Bo-GJ:19, Br-SS:151,
    Co-BBW:55, Co-PM:70, Fe-FP:149,
    Gr-EC:40, Hi-WP I:33, Hu-MP:200,
    La-PV:160, Pl-EI:130, Un-MB:263
The Lonely Man. R. Jarrell. To-MP:85
Lost Dog. F. Rodman. Se-PR:301
Make Me a Man. P. George. Al-WW:121
Making Friends. V. Lapin. Mo-MI:51
Man Is a Lumpe where All Beasts Kneaded
    Be. C. Lewis. Go-BP:102
The Marvellous Bear Shepherd. Ma-FW:216

Mary's Lamb. S. Hale.   Au-SP:17,
    De-PO:12, Er-FA:504, Fe-FP:529,
    Fr-WO:25, Li-LB:94, Mo-CC:(38),
    Mo-MGT:120, Ox-BC:166, Un-GT:34,
    Wi-MG:67
The Meadow Mouse. T. Roethke. Mo-TS:58
Meeting. C. Dyment. Co-BBW:46
Mick. J. Reeves. Co-BBW:111, Pa-RE:12
Mr. Rabbit. D. Wilson. Fr-MP:21
Mrs. Malone. E. Farjeon. Co-PM:61,
    Ox-BC:332
The Monk and His Cat. Co-PI:43,
    De-CH:90, Pa-SG:154, Rd-OA:110,
    Sm-LG:73
The Mousetrap. C. Morgenstern.
    Rd-OA:30
My Airedale Dog. W. Mason. Au-SP:38,
    Pe-FB:14
My Dog. J. Robinson. Au-SP:39
Nicholas Nye. W. de la Mare.
    Bl-OB:120, Cl-DT:50, Co-BBW:150,
    Rd-OA:73
A Night with a Wolf. B. Taylor.
    Un-GT:33
No Mother! No Father! Issa. Do-TS:2
Noonday Sun. K. & B. Jackson.
    Ar-TP3:33, Fe-FP:161
Of the Child with the Bird on the Bush.
    J. Bunyan. Ox-BC:37, Rv-CB:461
Old Blue. Mo-SD:115
The Old Cowboy. Kao Chi. Rx-LT:111
Old Dog Tray. S. Foster. Co-BBW:109
Old Friends. A. Muir. Co-BBW:272
Old Jake Sutter. K. Starbird.
    Ar-TP3:13
Old Joe Jones. L. Richards. Ag-HE:17
Old Man, Phantom Dog. F. Eckman.
    St-H:49
Old Mother Hubbard. An-IP:(8),
    Au-SP:3, Fr-WO:21, Ir-BB:171,
    Li-LB:153, Mo-MGT:8, Mo-NR:108,
    Ox-BC:126, Pa-OM:336, Un-GT:102,
    Wi-MG:50, Wr-RM:43
On a Hare. W. Cowper. Bl-OB:121,
    Co-BBW:47, Go-BP:94
On a Squirrel Crossing the Road in
    Autumn, in New England. R. Eberhart.
    En-PC:60, Ho-TH:81, Pe-OA:196,
    Wi-LT:439
On the Skeleton of a Hound. J. Wright.
    Wi-LT:844
Once I Nearly Touched a Bird. M. Carr.
    Sh-RP:338
One Man and One Fly. Issa. Be-CS:34
The Only One Who Understands Me.
    G. Chinchilla. Me-WF:2
Onto a Boy's Arm. Ho-SD:77
Orphan. Le-IB:69
The Orphan's Song. S. Dobell.
    De-CH:41, Ox-BN:668
Our Lucy (1956-1960). P. Goodman.
    Co-BBW:100

Parley of Beasts. H. MacDiarmid.
    Rd-OA:22, Un-MB:359
The Peopled Air. T. Gray. Rd-OA:81
The Pet Lamb. W. Wordsworth.
    Ox-BC:103
Pigeon Woman. M. Swenson. Mo-BG:50
Pigeons. B. Meyers. Ca-BP:32
Poem. P. Markish. Ho-TY:182
Practical Concerns. W. Harris.
    Ad-PB:440
The Praise of Philip Sparrow.
    G. Gascoigne. Al-VBP:81, De-CH:93,
    Rd-OA:102
A Prayer to Go to Heaven with the
    Donkeys. F. Jammes. Ar-TP3:83,
    Co-BBW:149, Go-BP:255, Pl-EI:124,
    Rd-OA:20, Tr-MR:52
Puppy and I. A. Milne. Ar-TP3:49,
    Au-SP:39, Fr-MP:6, La-PV:10,
    Pe-FB:4
The Rat. W. Davies. Go-BP:91
The Rime of the Ancient Mariner.
    S. Coleridge. Al-VBP:679,
    Bo-FP:301, Co-RG:60, Co-SS:131,
    De-CH:364, Er-FA:318, Fe-FP:147,
    Ga-FB:105, Gr-TG:61, Ha-PO:15,
    Hi-WP II:68, Ma-YA:146, Ni-JP:52,
    Ox-BN:139, Rv-CB:658, Sm-LG:312,
    Un-GT:30
The Road to Vagabondia. D. Burnet.
    Fe-PL:410
Robin Redbreast. S. Kunitz. Ho-P:151
Roo. M. Oliver. Ls-NY:195
Saint Francis and the Birds. S. Heaney.
    Ma-FW:89
The Sale of the Pet Lamb. M. Howitt.
    De-CH:87
The Same Old Law. W. Whitman. Rd-OA:23
The Seed Eaters. R. Francis. Ca-BP:7
The Shepherd. J. Baxter. Gr-EC:216
The Shepherd. W. Wordsworth. Ox-BN:101
The Shepherd Dog of the Pyrenees.
    E. Murray. Se-PR:302
A Small Bird's Sky. S. Murano.
    Sh-AM:91
Snake. D. Lawrence. Ar-TP3:68,
    Co-BBW:85, Ha-PO:102, Ni-JP:112,
    Wi-LT:212
Song of Myself. W. Whitman. Be-EB:44,
    Ca-BP:3, Co-BBW:271, 274, Er-FA:225,
    Ke-PP:85, Li-TU:187, Ni-JP:101,
    Rv-CB:895, Sh-AP:87, Sm-MK:158,
    Un-MA:56
Songs to Horses, I. Tr-US I:115
Songs to Horses, II. Tr-US I:116
The Soul of Birds. P. Mitra. Al-PI:85
A Sound in Cambridge, Mass. R. Whitman.
    Ls-NY:327
The Sparrow's Dirge. J. Skelton.
    Sm-LG:85
Spiel of the Three Mountebanks.
    J. Ransom. Un-MA:411

COMPANIONSHIP OF MEN AND ANIMALS — cont'd.
Spring Quiet. C. Rossetti. Co-BN:16,
   De-CH:235, Gr-TG:26, Pa-GTB:373,
   Re-BS:21
A Story for a Child. B. Taylor.
   Co-BBW:188
The Story of the Baby Squirrel.
   D. Aldis. Ar-TP3:60
A Tall Man Executes a Jig. I. Layton.
   En-PC:119
There Lived a Little Man. St-FS:19
There Was a Boy. W. Wordsworth.
   Go-BP:119, Ox-BN:101, Sm-LG:107
Three Things to Remember. W. Blake.
   Br-SS:150, Ch-B:89, Fe-FP:280,
   Gr-EC:178, Gr-TG:31, Hi-GD:13,
   Hi-WP II:170
Tim, an Irish Terrier. W. Letts.
   Co-BBW:104
Tired Equinox. R. Roseliep. St-H:183
To a Butterfly. W. Wordsworth.
   Br-SG:55, Co-BBW:226, Mc-PR:204,
   Un-GT:74
To a Dog Injured in the Street.
   W. Williams. Wi-LT:203
To a Mouse. R. Burns. Co-BBW:36,
   Er-FA:226, Fe-PL:367, Hu-MP:190,
   Mc-WK:60, Pa-GTB:141, Rd-OA:24,
   Rv-CB:616, Sp-OG:297
To a Squirrel at Kyle-Na-No. W. Yeats.
   Ad-PE:28, Be-EB:38, Bl-OB:131,
   Co-BBW:43, Co-PM:85, Fe-FP:167,
   La-PV:140, Li-LC:23, Re-TW:34
To a Starved Hare in the Garden in
   Winter. C. Turner. Sm-MK:182
To K. de M. R. Stevenson. Ox-BN:891
To My Dog "Blanco." J. G. Holland.
   Fe-PL:362
To Scott. W. Letts. Fe-PL:364
To the Snake. D. Levertov. Co-BBW:92,
   Wi-LT:760
The Turkish Trench Dog. G. Dearmer.
   Co-BBW:101
Two Look at Two. R. Frost. Un-MA:180
Two Songs of a Fool. W. Yeats.
   Rd-OA:14
Vern. G. Brooks. Ar-TP3:50, Ho-CS:36,
   La-OC:82
Wake Up! Wake Up! Bashö. Au-SP:72,
   Be-CS:22
A Waltzer in the House. S. Kunitz.
   Co-BBW:25, We-PZ:33
The War God's Horse Song. Br-MW:60,
   Sm-LG:78
Well! Hello Down There. Issa.
   Be-CS:25
When My Canary. Shiki. Ar-TP3:54,
   Be-CS:45
The White Bird. H. Chattopadhyaya.
   Al-PI:92
The White-Footed Deer. W. Bryant.
   Sp-OG:178

The Women and the Man. Te-FC:87
You Frogs. S. Hagiwara. Sh-AM:49
You Talk about and Fear Me. Ho-SD:31
The Young Calves. R. Coffin.
   Ar-TP3:75
COMPASSES: see also HUMOR - COMPASSES
A Compass Needle. F. Quarles.
   Ga-S:54, Rv-CB:347
COMPASSION: see MERCY; PITY; SYMPATHY
COMPENSATION: see also RETRIBUTION;
   REWARDS
The Country Clergy. R. Thomas.
   Go-BP:44, Pa-GTB:537
The Debt. P. Dunbar. Bo-AN:5,
   Bo-HF:176
Fable. R. Emerson. Bo-FP:71,
   Bo-GJ:26, Bo-HF:69, Ch-B:27,
   Er-FA:496, Fe-FP:530, Ga-FB:317,
   Hu-MP:210, Pa-OM:333, Rd-OA:91,
   Sh-AP:27, Sp-OG:303, Un-GT:57
Roses and Thorns. S. Betai. Al-PI:109
Sometimes with One I Love. W. Whitman.
   Rv-CB:849
COMPETITION: see also HUMOR - COMPETITION;
   LOVE - RIVALRY; SPORTS; TRACK ATHLETICS
Aware, Aware. T. Combs. Br-TC:75
Bea's Bee. M. Ray. Ho-GC:16
Brother. T. Ikenaga. Le-TA:23
A Flight Shot. M. Thompson. Co-RM:72
A Gest of Robyn Hode, The Fifth Fytte.
   Ox-BB:464
Girls Can, Too. L. Hopkins. Ho-GC:26
Graeme and Bewick. Ox-BB:356, Rv-CB:47
Holly and Ivy. Rv-CB:21
The Horse and the Mule. J. Wynne.
   Ox-BC:78
Idaho Jack. J. Lee. Fi-BG:90
In a Wood. T. Hardy. Ox-BN:821
John Henry. Ab-MO:81, Bo-HF:104,
   Co-RM:225, Er-FA:407, Ga-S:124,
   Hi-TL:159, Ra-BP:12
Love among the Manchees. W. Dickey.
   En-PC:266
Lu Yün's Lament. H. Read. Pl-ML:26
Mutual Nith-Song Between Savladt and
   Pulangitsissok. Tr-US I:5
My Turn. M. Ray. Ho-GC:10
Phoebus and Boreas. J. de la Fontaine.
   Un-R:87
Song Contest. Tr-US II:175
The Wind and the Moon. G. MacDonald.
   Bo-GJ:35, Ir-BB:127, Li-LC:79,
   Pa-OM:268, Un-GT:258
COMPLAINTS: see also DISCONTENT; HUMOR -
   COMPLAINTS; LOVE - COMPLAINTS AND
   PROTESTS
Against Exploiters. Tr-CB:33, Tr-US I:6
Alone Walking. Rv-CB:2
The Ant. J. Kransnai. La-GI:55
Complaint over Bad Hunting. Da-SC:45,
   Le-IB:71

The Complaint to God. Bible. O.T.
Job. Me-PH:18
For the Earth God. Pl-EI:174,
Tr-US I:52
I Hear America Griping. M. Bishop.
Br-AF:43
I Return to My Little Song. Le-IB:76
The Inventor's Wife. E. Corbett.
Fe-PL:219
The Man in the Ocelot Suit.
C. Brookhouse. Ad-CI:108
The Mermaid's Song. Hu P'in-ch'ing.
Pa-MV:102
The Mouse. E. Coatsworth. Ar-TP3:59,
Au-SP:56, Co-IW:29, Fe-FP:136,
Ir-BB:86, Rd-SS:33, Th-AS:38
Plaint. Tr-US I:91
Plaint. C. Carryl. Au-SP:83,
Co-IW:39, Fe-FP:341, Ir-BB:80,
Na-EO:164, Ox-BC:305, Pe-FB:16,
Th-AS:45, Un-GT:37
Presents. M. Chute. Br-SS:109,
La-PH:36, La-PP:60, Na-EO:130
A Roman Soldier on the Wall. W. Auden.
Hi-WP I:122, Sm-MK:98
The Shades of the Newly Dead to the
Gods. Tr-US I:227
some friends. J. Gill. Sc-TN:68
Too Late. F. Ludlow. Fe-PL:261
Washing. J. Drinkwater. Fe-FP:6
Young Men's Song. Tr-US I:187
COMPOSERS: see also HUMOR - COMPOSERS;
and names of composers, as
HAYDN, FRANZ JOSEPH
Barthélémon at Vauxhall. T. Hardy.
Pl-US:89
The Composer. W. Auden. Pl-US:70
Ives. M. Rukeyser. Pl-US:87
Mozart. J. Mayhall. Ls-NY:132
Portrait of the Boy as an Artist.
B. Howes. Un-MA:653
To Mr. Henry Lawes. E. Waller.
No-CL:28,
COMPROMISE: see GIVE-AND-TAKE
COMPUTERS: see also HUMOR - COMPUTERS;
SATIRE - COMPUTERS
Univac to Univac. L. Salomon. Du-SH:89
COMRADESHIP: see FELLOWSHIP; FRIENDSHIP
CONCEIT: see also BOASTING; HUMOR -
CONCEIT
The Ant's a Centaur. . . . E. Pound.
Ha-PO:220
The Cock. A. Buttigieg. Pa-RE:121
The Dog. A. Buttigieg. Pa-RE:121
Ego Swamp. K. Kuka. Al-WW:74
Indispensability. A. Guiterman.
Mc-WK:124
The Lamp. A. Buttigieg. Pa-RE:120
Look at That Strutting Crow. Issa.
Be-MC:21
The Love of King David and the Fair
Bethsabe. G. Peele. Al-VBP:137

A Man Said to the Universe. S. Crane.
Pl-IO:139, Wi-LT:120
The Most Important. D. Almore.
Me-WF:11
Posturing. C. Lewis. Go-BP:184
Proud Margret. Ox-BB:74
Queen Mary, Queen Mary, My Age Is
Sixteen. De-CH:696
Reflections. C. Gardner. Ad-PB:217,
Hu-NN:98
Robin Redbreast's Testament. Gr-GB:66
She Was a Pretty Little Girl.
R. de Ayada. Fe-FP:473
Song of Myself. W. Whitman.
Al-VBP:928, Sh-AP:69, Un-MA:44
To Vanity. D. Turner. Hu-PN:401
Two Kinds, Bold and Shy. J. Holmes.
Mc-WS:71
Vain and Careless. R. Graves.
Ha-LO:20
CONCENTRATION CAMPS: see also JEWS -
PERSECUTION
Annotations of Auschwitz. P. Porter.
Hi-FO:264
The Black Rock. J. Berryman.
Ca-VT:385
A Camp in the Prussian Forest.
R. Jarrell. Pe-OA:227, Un-MA:644
The Funeral. M.J. Ba-PO:180
The Gift. J. Ciardi. Wi-LT:670
I Sit with My Dolls. Ba-PO:179,
Cr-WS:131
More Light, More Light. A. Hecht.
Br-TC:182, Ca-VT:505
My Father's Boots. I. Spiegel.
Ho-TY:349
A Night Out. D. Abse. Gr-BT:158
Poem - 1959. S. Halkin. Ho-TY:187
Security. M. Hamburger. En-PC:223
Smoke. J. Glatstein. Ho-TY:331
CONCERN (CARE)
Doctor Spock. Y. Yevtushenko. Ca-MR:60
Homecoming. A. Kramer. Ls-NY:94
If Your Mother Has Set Out to Fish.
Do-CH:(7)
The Little Boy Found. W. Blake.
Rv-CB:582
The Little Girl Found. W. Blake.
Rv-CB:593
Man Is a Lumpe where All Beasts Kneaded
Be. C. Lewis. Go-BP:102
The New Platitudes. R. Whittemore.
Ba-PO:28
Place Midnight in the Care of My Hands.
Y. Vinokurov. Ca-MR:88
Puzzles. J. Drinkwater. Mc-WK:107
Seven Poems. L. Niedecker. Ca-VT:245
Sick Boy. A. Ridler. Ls-NY:225
Under Such Blows. O. Mandelstam.
Ca-MR:160
CONCERTS: see also HUMOR - CONCERTS
After a Music Concert. S. Muro. Sh-AM:52

CONCERTS — cont'd.
  Concert Interpretation (Le Sacré de
    Printemps). S. Sassoon. Rv-CB:981
  Summer Concert. R. Whittemore.
    Br-AP:216
CONCORD, MASS.
  Concord Hymn. R. Emerson. Al-VBP:805,
    Br-AF:61, Er-FA:188, Fe-FP:422,
    Hi-TL:52, Hu-MP:379, Ke-TF:256,
    Mc-PR:22, Pa-HT:18, Se-PR:87,
    Sh-AP:25, Sp-OG:193, Tu-WW:30,
    Vi-PP:99
CONCORD RIVER
  Two Rivers. R. Emerson. Gr-CC:36
CONCRETE MIXERS
  The Concrete Mixer. T. Langley.
    Ho-CS:31, Le-M:69
  Concrete Mixers. P. Hubbell. La-PV:192
  The Pigeon. R. Church. Hi-WP II:166
CONDORS: see also HUMOR - CONDORS
  Condors. P. Colum. Bo-GJ:75
CONFEDERATE STATES OF AMERICA: see also
    CIVIL WAR - UNITED STATES,
    1861-1865
  The Battle of Shiloh. Em-AF:448
  Fare You Well, My Darling. Em-AF:453
  The Red, White, and Red. Em-AF:447
CONFESSIONS: see also HUMOR - CONFESSIONS
  Boy Driving His Father to Confession.
    S. Heaney. Gr-BT:23
  The Confidence. E. Jennings. Ga-BP:186
  Fire Song at an Expiation Ceremony.
    Tr-US I:59
  Lines for a Young Man Who Talked.
    J. Logan. St-H:116
  Psalm XCIX. Bible. O.T. Psalms.
    Ma-YA:75
  Third Degree. L. Hughes. Gr-BT:123,
    Ra-BP:80
CONFIDENCE: see FAITH
CONFORMITY: see also HUMOR - CONFORMITY;
    SATIRE - CONFORMITY
  Back Again, Home. D. Lee. Ra-BP:295
  Bottled: New York. H. Johnson.
    Ad-PB:104
  The Bourgeois Poet. K. Shapiro.
    St-H:199
  Butterfly Bones. M. Avison. Wi-LT:661
  A Certain Age. P. McGinley. Du-SH:44
  The Citizen. V. Howard. Hu-NN:58
  Dipsychus. A. Clough. Ox-BN:616
  Disillusionment at Ten O'Clock.
    W. Stevens. Ha-LO:55, Ha-PO:236,
    Sh-AP:159
  The Enamel Girl. G. Taggard. Un-MA:478
  Escape. T. McGrath. St-H:123
  The Fired Pot. A. Wickham. Un-MW:125
  The Fresh Start. A. Wickham. Al-VBP:1155
  From the Embassy. R. Graves. Ha-TP:95
  Garnishing the Aviary. M. Danner.
    Ad-PB:134, Be-MA:88, Bo-AN:153,
    Hu-NN:29, Ra-BP:149

the greedy the people. E. Cummings.
    Pe-OA:155
Hoo, Suffolk. Gr-GB:175
In the Suburbs. L. Simpson. Ho-TH:76
Jonas Kindred's Household. G. Crabbe.
    Ox-BN:15
Leap Before You Look. W. Auden.
    Ha-TP:137
Little Boxes. M. Reynolds. Pe-SS:98
The Love Song of J. Alfred Prufrock.
    T. Eliot. Al-VBP:1180, Br-TC:106,
    Pe-OA:105, Rv-CB:986, Un-MA:379,
    Wi-LT:278
A Man of the Middle Class. G. Brooks.
    St-H:12
Modifications. R. Koertge. Du-SH:42,
    Pe-M:22
Morning Song from "Senlin." C. Aiken.
    Pe-OA:141, Sh-AP:185, Un-MA:422,
    Wi-LT:325
Much Madness Is Divinest Sense.
    E. Dickinson. Co-EL:143, Ho-LP:75,
    Mo-BG:191, Rv-CB:899, Wi-LT:8
The Observation. D. Leitch. Mo-GR:80
The Parents: People Like Our Marriage,
    Maxie and Andrew. G. Brooks.
    Ha-TP:47
Patterns. A. Lowell. Bo-HF:116,
    Co-BL:142, Cr-WS:115, Er-FA:65,
    Mo-GR:39, Pa-OM:262, Pe-OA:47,
    Sm-PT:18, Un-MA:156
Plea to a Particular Soft-Handed
    Goddess. P. Mayer. St-H:134
Poetry of Departures. P. Larkin.
    Br-TC:249
Portrait. K. Fearing. Pe-OA:184,
    Un-MA:556
Precedents. I. Newman. Ls-NY:274
The Princess and the Gypsies.
    F. Cornford. Co-PT:57
A Question of Weather. K. Katrak.
    Al-PI:98
Respectability. R. Browning.
    Al-VBP:889
The Revolutionary. V. Watkins.
    Ls-NY:118
Souls. F. Davis. Th-AS:202
Squares and Angles. A. Storni.
    La-OC:100
Thirty Bob a Week. J. Davidson.
    Er-FA:271, Ox-BN:900
The Unknown Citizen. W. Auden.
    Du-SH:95, Gr-BT:133, Ke-PP:33,
    Mo-BG:194, Ni-JP:30, Pe-SS:106,
    Tr-MR:232, Wi-LT:471
What Strange Pleasures They Do Get.
    L. Welch. Kh-VA:70
Wild Thyme. E. Farjeon. Br-SS:3
Women. L. Bogan. Br-TC:55, Ca-VT:202,
    Mc-EA:87, Un-MA:490
The Words. D. Wagoner. Du-SH:30,
    Mo-TS:52

Young Poet. M. O'Higgins. Ad-PB:170,
Hu-PN:351
CONFRONTATION: see PROTEST; REBELLION;
VIOLENCE
CONFUCIUS
The Most-Sacred Mountain. E. Tietjens.
Pa-HT:87, Tr-MR:202
CONGO, AF.
Bedtime Story. G. Macbeth. To-MP:152
The Congo. V. Lindsay. Er-FA:300,
Hi-WP II:98, Hu-PN:484, Pe-OA:55,
Sh-AP:163, Un-MA:218
Dawn in the Heart of Africa.
P. Lumumba. Lo-TY:150
Mmenson. E. Brathwaite. To-MP:162
CONNECTICUT: see also HUMOR -
CONNECTICUT
Abraham Davenport. J. Whittier.
Sp-OG:31
Connecticut Road Song. A. Branch.
Pa-HT:31
Midsummer. J. Scully. Br-TC:359,
Pe-OA:270
The River of Rivers in Connecticut.
W. Stevens. Ca-VT:42
The State We Honor. F. Crosby.
Se-PR:254
Words from England. D. Hall. Ke-TF:445
CONQUESTS: see also IMPERIALISM; SATIRE -
CONQUESTS; VICTORY
El Archivo General de Indias. I. Wright.
Ke-TF:386
At Cooloolah. J. Wright. Un-MB:516
Belisarius. H. Longfellow. Ho-WR:120
The Bloody Conquests of Mighty
Tamburlaine. C. Marlowe. Gr-CT:335
The Chronicle of the Drum.
W. Thackeray. Al-VBP:878
Conquistador. E. Coatsworth. Un-GT:93
Conquistador. A. MacLeish. Hi-TL:15
Cortez. W. Seymour. Sm-MK:64
The Destruction of Jerusalem by the
Babylonian Hordes. I. Rosenberg.
Gr-SS:172
The First Part of Tamburlaine the Great.
C. Marlowe. Al-VBP:173
From the Prophecy of Katun 9 Ahau.
Br-MW:28, Da-SC:163
Fuzzy-Wuzzy. R. Kipling. Un-MB:126
Imperator Victus. H. Crane. Bl-FP:36
Prophecy. Bi-IT:140, Br-MW:104
The Second Part of Tamburlaine the Great.
C. Marlowe. Al-VBP:175
This Was Our Land. Wo-HS:(35)
The Vanity of Human Wishes. S. Johnson.
Al-VBP:552, Hi-FO:171
CONSCIENCE: see also DUTY; HUMOR -
CONSCIENCE; SATIRE - CONSCIENCE
Belshazzar. E. Dickinson. Rv-CB:902,
Tr-MR:84
Black Are the Stars. R. Roseliep.
De-FS:160

Childhood and School-Time.
W. Wordsworth. Ox-BN:93
The Conspiracy of Charles, Duke of
Byron. G. Chapman. Al-VBP:147
The Dirty Word. K. Shapiro. En-PC:132
Ere Sleep Comes Down to Soothe the
Weary Eyes. P. Dunbar. Hu-PN:43
For the Existentialist. W. Palmer.
Ls-NY:339
The Gardener and the Mole. W. Landor.
Rd-OA:115
A Good-Night. F. Quarles. Rd-SS:41
Haukyn's Coat. W. Langland. Ga-S:135
In Answer to a Question. W. Blunt.
Al-VBP:1053
Keep Conscience Clear. B. Franklin.
Un-GT:25
Like a Murderer. I. Manger. Ho-TY:272
Love Unknown. G. Herbert. Ho-P:29
The Midnight Snack. J. Merrill.
Mo-BG:80
My Spectre Around Me. W. Blake.
Rv-CB:611
On a Quiet Conscience. Charles I.
De-CH:446
The Praying Mantis Visits a Penthouse.
O. Williams. Er-FA:235, Wi-LT:417
Return to Hiroshima. L. Stryk.
Cr-WS:148
The Rime of the Ancient Mariner.
S. Coleridge. Al-VBP:679, Co-RG:60,
Co-SS:131, De-CH:364, Er-FA:318,
Ga-FB:105, Ha-PO:15, Hi-WP II:68,
Ma-YA:146, Ni-JP:52, Ox-BN:139,
Rv-CB:658, Sm-LG:312
Song by Mr. Cypress. T. Peacock.
Ox-BN:233
Song: Fish in the Unruffled Lakes.
W. Auden. Un-MB:464
To Christ Our Lord. G. Kinnell.
Br-TC:239, Ha-WR:92, La-RM:120,
Pe-M:112
CONSCIENTIOUS OBJECTORS
Conscientious Objector. E. Millay.
Ba-PO:4, Cr-WS:137
The Conscientious Objector. K. Shapiro.
Ba-PO:166, Pe-SS:140
Dooley Is a Traitor. J. Michie.
Co-RM:119
For the One Who Would Take Man's Life
in His Hands. D. Schwartz. Ca-VT:366,
Hi-TL:218, Un-MA:618, Wi-LT:517
I Sing of Olaf. e. cummings. Ca-VT:179,
Ke-PP:113, Sh-AP:190, Wi-LT:362
If War Should Come. B. Musser.
Ba-PO:168
Jail. T. Barnes. La-IH:131
Of Late. G. Starbuck. Ca-VT:667
CONSCRIPTION, MILITARY: see MILITARY
SERVICE, COMPULSORY
CONSERVATION: see also POLLUTION
Big Dam. W. Moses. Br-AF:188

CONSERVATION — <u>cont'd.</u>
  Above the Moving River. D. Kherdian.
    Kh-VA:72
  Binsey Poplars Felled 1879. G. Hopkins.
    Co-BN:153, Ma-FW:104
  The Crow. H. Thoreau. Re-BS:50
  In These Fair Vales. W. Wordsworth.
    Rv-CB:652
  Inversnaid. G. Hopkins. Fr-WO:88,
    Pa-GTB:393, Un-MB:45, Wi-LT:45
  Revolutionary Letter #16. D. di Prima.
    Kh-VA:69
  The River. P. Lorentz. Br-AF:182
  To the Wayfarer. Ar-TP3:217, Br-SS:144
CONSERVATISM: see also CONFORMITY;
    HUMOR - CONSERVATISM;
  Hawk Roosting. T. Hughes. Br-TC:209,
    Pa-GTB:564, Rd-OA:145, Wi-LT:735
  A Human Instinct. C. Morley. Na-EO:54
  I Paint What I See. E. White.
    Mo-BG:64
  Two Voices in a Meadow. R. Wilbur.
    Pe-SS:56
CONSOLATION: see COMFORT; SYMPATHY
CONSPIRACY: see also HUMOR - CONSPIRACY
  Blennerhassett's Island. T. Read.
    Hi-TL:60
  Guy Fawkes Day. Hi-FO:144, Li-LB:161,
    Mo-MGT:203
CONSTANCY: see LOYALTY
CONSTANTINE I, THE GREAT
  Elene. Cynewulf. Ma-YA:11
CONSTANTINOPLE: see BYZANTIUM;
    CONSTANTINE I, THE GREAT
CONSTELLATIONS: see also HUMOR - CON-
    STELLATIONS; STARS; and names of
    constellations, as ORION (CON-
    STELLATION)
  Among the Stars. W. Blake. Re-TW:129,
    Un-GT:264
  The Child Reads On. F. James. Fe-FP:470
  Escape at Bedtime. R. Stevenson.
    Ar-TP3:178, Bo-FP:34, Pe-FB:64,
    Rd-SS:31, Un-GT:13
  The God of Galaxies. M. Van Doren.
    Pl-IO:19, Tr-MR:138
  A Letter to Yvor Winters. K. Rexroth.
    Pl-ML:53
  Mythological Sonnets, VIII. R. Fuller.
    Pa-GTB:527
  Peace on Earth. W. Williams.
    Al-VBP:1153, Ha-LO:24
  The Ride-by-Nights. W. de la Mare.
    Ar-TP3:186, Br-SS:66, Fe-FP:394
  Shut Out That Moon. T. Hardy.
    Al-VBP:1047
  Star Talk. R. Graves. Bo-GJ:242,
    Co-BN:115, Un-MB:385
  The Starlight Night. G. Hopkins.
    Al-VBP:1061, Cl-DT:38, Pa-GTB:389,
    Re-TW:84, Un-MB:42, Wi-LT:40

  Troilus and Cressida. W. Shakespeare.
    Pl-IO:22
  Ursa Major. J. Kirkup. Pl-IO:32
CONSTITUTION - UNITED STATES: see UNITED
    STATES - CONSTITUTION
CONSTITUTION (SHIP)
  The Constitution and the Guerriére.
    Em-AF:434
  The Main Truck; or a Leap for Life.
    G. Morris. Fe-PL:55
  Old Ironsides. O. Holmes. Co-SS:60,
    Er-FA:189, Fe-FP:548, Hi-TL:82,
    Mc-PR:23, Se-PR:123, Sp-OG:75,
    Vi-PP:195
CONTEMPT: see also HUMOR - CONTEMPT
  and we conquered. R. Penny. Ad-PB:391
  be cool, baby. R. Penny. Ad-PB:390
  The Bonny Brown Girl. Ox-BB:355
  Despisals. M. Rukeyser. Ho-P:223
  The Field of Glory. E. Robinson.
    Un-MA:125
  Girls Mocking White Men's Serving Boys.
    Tr-CB:50, Tr-US I:52
  The Glove. J. von Schiller. Sp-OG:138
  he's doing natural life. Conyus.
    Ad-PB:403
  Hughie Graham. Ox-BB:579
  Hunting Songs. Bear Song. Tr-US I:12
  Man's Song Against a Woman.
    Tr-US I:213
  Miniver Cheevy. E. Robinson.
    Er-FA:384, Fe-PL:33, Ga-FB:328,
    Gr-CT:467, Ha-PO:63, Li-SR:75,
    No-CL:243, Pe-OA:3, Rv-CB:958,
    Sm-LG:130, Un-MA:117, Wi-LT:103
  Noah. H. Hagedorn. Tr-MR:66
  A Sketch from Private Life. G. Byron.
    Ox-BN:253
  Sometimes I Dream. N. Bomze. Ho-TY:228
  Song. Tr-US I:43
  Song Contest. Tr-US II:175
  Taunt Song. Tr-US II:105, 112
  Taunt Song Against a Clumsy Kayak
    Paddler. Le-IB:111, Tr-US I:3
  To a Traitor. Tr-US II:301
  The Twa Magicians. Ox-BB:51
  Victory Song. Tr-US II:244
CONTENTMENT: see also HUMOR - CONTENTMENT;
    PEACE OF MIND
  Address to a Child During a Boisterous
    Winter Evening. D. Wordsworth.
    Bl-OB:100
  Almswomen. E. Blunden. Do-BP:51
  Altar Smoke. R. Grayer. Un-GT:266
  Any Bird. I. Orleans. Br-SG:62
  Art Thou Poor. T. Dekker. Al-VBP:226,
    De-CH:237, De-TT:104, Pa-GTB:37,
    Re-TW:48, Rv-CB:258
  Ask No Return! H. Gregory. Ca-VT:209,
    Sm-PT:120, Un-MA:508
  At Twilight. Shiki. Be-MC:31
  Autumn. Wang Wei. Rx-LT:56

Autumn Evening. F. Cornford. De-CH:502
The Barefoot Boy. J. Whittier. Ch-B:65,
  Fe-FP:544, Fe-PL:249
Bedtime. D. Levertov. Mc-EA:97
Better than Gold. A. Ryan. Er-FA:9
By the Fire. E. Coatsworth. Sh-RP:72
Cattle. Banko. Au-SP:45, Hu-MP:196
Comfort. W. Stafford. Du-SH:187
The Conquered One. D. Jackson.
  Ba-HI:30
Contentment. N. Cotton. Ox-BC:64
Coridon's Song. J. Chalkhill.
  Al-VBP:271
Destiny. N. Crane. Un-GT:305
A Dialogue of Self and Soul. W. Yeats.
  Un-MB:118, Wi-LT:84
Dipsychus. A. Clough. Ox-BN:616
Dying Speech of an Old Philosopher.
  W. Landor. Al-VBP:704, Gr-CT:435,
  Ha-PO:209, Ma-YA:169, Ox-BN:194,
  Pa-GTB:318
The Eastern Gate. Le-MW:120,
  Ma-FW:88
The Embankment. T. Hulme. Co-EL:123
The Example. W. Davies. Rd-OA:69,
  Un-MB:176
A Farmer's Life. Pa-RE:24
Five Short Stanzas, IV. A Bud.
  Tsou Ti-fan. Hs-TC:348
The Garden. A. Marvell. Al-VBP:457,
  Fe-PL:381, Ha-PO:202, Pa-GTB:92,
  Rv-CB:403
Gladly I'll Live in a Poor Mountain Hut.
  Le-MW:111
A Goldfinch. W. de la Mare. Re-BS:38
The Great Lover. R. Brooke. Er-FA:73,
  Hi-WP I:108, Un-MB:320, Wi-LT:613
The Happy Farmer. Un-GT:94
The Happy Life. W. Thompson.
  Al-VBP:555
Heart's Desire. Omar Khayyam. Un-MW:193
The Herd-Boy's Song. Chen Shan-min.
  Pa-SG:126
The Hermit's Song. Pa-SG:158
Himalaya. Po Fei Huang. Ls-NY:248
His Grange or Private Wealth. R. Herrick.
  Bo-FP:65, Bo-GJ:22, Ma-YA:88
Hope. W. Shenstone. Co-BN:215
The Hundred Names. Ba-PO:117
I Feel So Muggy. C. Reed. Ad-II:14
I Return to the Place where I Was Born.
  T'ao Yuan Ming. Rx-LT:33
I Shall Have Had My Day. A. Tennyson.
  Un-MW:137
The Idle Life I Lead. R. Bridges.
  Wi-LT:56
Idleness. Lu Yu. Rx-OH:109
In the Silence. Stephany. Ra-BP:330
It's Little for Glory I Care.
  C. Lever. Co-PI:96
Jolly Miller. I. Bickerstaffe.
  Al-VBP:598, Co-PI:10, Li-LB:73,
  Mo-MGT:170, Un-GT:94, Wi-MG:48

The Jolly Thresherman. Em-AF:773
The Kingdom. L. MacNeice. Wi-LT:463
Knee-Deep in June. J. Riley. Sp-OG:291
The Lands Around My Dwelling. Bi-IT:49,
  Br-MW:141, Ma-BH:23
Lazy. Lu Yu. Rx-LT:102
Let Me Go Warm. L. de Góngora.
  Mc-PR:47
M. Antonio Flaminio: To His Farm.
  J. Ashmore. No-CL:272
Mad as Mist and Snow. W. Yeats.
  Gr-CT:395
A Mad Poem Addressed to Nephews and
  Nieces. Pu Chü-i. Gr-BT:165
The Means to Attain a Happy Life.
  H. Howard. Al-VBP:79
The Miller. J. Clerk. Gr-CT:84
The Miller of Dee. Gr-GB:214
A Mind Content. R. Greene. Al-VBP:142
The Mist and All. D. Willson.
  Au-SP:329, Fe-FP:82, Ha-YA:129,
  Hu-MP:318, Ja-PA:43, Pe-FB:88
Moon, Flowers, Man. Su Tung P'o.
  Rx-OH:85
My Mind to Me a Kingdom Is. E. Dyer.
  Al-VBP:89, Ha-PO:193, Sp-OG:333
Night Words: The Ravishing. M. McClure
  Kh-VA:34
Nimium Fortunatus. R. Bridges.
  Un-MB:51
November Moratorium, Washington.
  C. Burchardt. Ad-II:32
O Happy! De-TT:105, Sp-AS:28
Oh, Sweet Content. W. Davies.
  De-CH:238
Ode. G. Santayana. Al-VBP:1087
Ode on Solitude. A. Pope. Al-VBP:529,
  Er-FA:248, Go-BP:45, Ho-P:48,
  Ma-FW:85, Mc-PR:203, Ni-JP:137,
  Pa-GTB:110, Rv-CB:510
Ode to Maecenas. Horace. Pa-SG:173,
  Un-GT:236
Ode to Solitude. J. Grainger.
  Al-VBP:570
Of the Mean and Sure Estate. T. Wyatt.
  Rd-OA:98
Old Jake Sutter. K. Starbird.
  Ar-TP3:13
The Old Man's Comforts and How He Gained
  Them. R. Southey. Li-SR:90,
  Ma-YA:167, Ox-BC:93
Old Winter. T. Noël. Co-PS:152
On Himself. R. Herrick. Gr-CT:272
Peace and Rest. W. Davies. Go-BP:29
Planting Song. Da-SC:109, Ho-SD:23
Poem in Prose. A. MacLeish. Mc-WS:149
The Pope He Leads a Happy Life.
  C. Lever. Co-PI:96
Rarely, Rarely Comest Thou. P. Shelley.
  De-CH:238, Ox-BN:294, Pa-GTB:225,
  Rv-CB:701
Reading the Book of Hills and Sea.
  Tao Ch'ien. Pa-SG:171

CONTENTMENT — cont'd.
  Rubaiyat of Omar Khayyam. E. Fitzgerald.
    Al-VBP:832, Er-FA:43, Fe-FP:479,
    Ha-PO:210, Ox-BN:526, Pa-SG:120
  Running to Paradise. W. Yeats.
    Ha-LO:13
  The Shepherd Boy's Song. J. Bunyan.
    Gr-TG:17, Pl-EI:204, Rv-CB:459,
    Un-GT:308
  The Shepherd's Wife's Song. R. Greene.
    Al-VBP:139
  A Song of Bread and Honey.
    R. Le Gallienne. Bo-FP:62
  Songs of Joy. W. Davies. Un-MB:178
  Spring Comes to a Little Temple.
    Ch'en Meng-chia. Hs-TC:117
  Spring in My Hut. Sodo. Sh-RP:67
  Such Lazy Shadows under the Sun.
    Tai Wang-shu. Hs-TC:179
  Sunset. Tu Fu. Rx-OH:21
  Sweet Stay-at-Home. W. Davies.
    De-CH:36
  A Thanksgiving to God for His House.
    R. Herrick. Al-VBP:337, De-TT:168,
    Gr-CT:269
  There Is a Jewel. De-CH:634
  To Each His Own. M. Bracker. Ke-TF:138
  To Mr. Izaak Walton. C. Cotton.
    Al-VBP:472, Go-BP:19
  Tollable Well. F. Stanton. Er-FA:22
  Tomorrow. J. Collins. Pa-GTB:167
  Under the Greenwood Tree. W. Shakespeare.
    Al-VBP:186, Ar-TP3:204, Bo-FP:259,
    Co-BN:206, De-CH:134, De-TT:147,
    Er-FA:263, Fe-FP:211, Gr-EC:48,
    Ho-WR:74, Hu-MP:268, Mc-PR:30,
    Pa-GTB:5, Rv-CB:196, Tu-WW:61
  Upon the Downs. G. Etherege. Al-VBP:495
  Visitors. Tu Fu. Rx-OH:19
  Walk in the Rain. F. Frost. Ke-TF:85
  Waves of Thought. Panikkar. Al-PI:127
  What Makes Me Different.
    B. Akhmadulina. Bo-RU:6
  Who Bides His Time. J. Riley.
    Sp-OG:329
  Who Loves the Rain. F. Shaw.
    Hu-MP:298, Th-AS:113
  Who's In? E. Fleming. Bl-OB:145,
    Cl-FC:61, Pe-FB:22, Th-AS:41
  A Widow's Weeds. W. de la Mare.
    Ga-FB:238
  Winter. A. Tennyson. Bo-FP:176
  The Wish. A. Cowley. Al-VBP:450,
    De-CH:524
  A Wish. S. Rogers. Pa-GTB:143
  A Woman's Last Word. R. Browning.
    Er-FA:118, Rv-CB:823, Un-MW:190
  Woolly Blanket. K. Goddard. Fr-MP:22
  Work. H. Van Dyke. Ke-TF:204,
    Se-PR:67, Th-AS:209
  You Tell Me that Times Are Changing.
    Wo-HS:(38)

CONTESTS: see COMPETITION; TOURNAMENTS
CONTRARINESS: see also OBSTINACY
  All's Well that Ends Well. Er-FA:211
  The Contrary Boy. G. Drake. Co-BB:82
  Contrary Mary. N. Turner. Ir-BB:104
  Cross-Patch. De-PO:12, Gr-CT:10,
    Gr-GB:19, Li-LB:55, Mo-MGT:161,
    Mo-MR:53, Na-EO:73, Wi-MG:74,
    Wr-RM:13
  I Woke Up This Morning. K. Kuskin.
    Ho-GC:44
  Japanese Folk-Song from Hyogo. Pa-RE:64
  Man Is a Fool. Er-FA:220
  Mary, Mary, Quite Contrary.
    Au-SP:7, Bo-FP:253, De-PO:12,
    Er-FA:505, Ir-BB:117, Li-LB:42,
    Mo-CC:(12), Mo-MGT:153, Mo-NR:34,
    Sp-AS:(7), Wi-MG:10, Wr-RM:90
  Matilda. F. Evans. Co-BB:84
  On Being a Woman. D. Parker. Fe-PL:414
  Rules of Contrary. Rv-ON:20
  The Rum Tum Tugger. T. Eliot.
    Ar-TP3:120, Fe-FP:157, Ga-FB:330,
    La-PV:110, Na-EO:21
  There Was a Little Girl. H. Longfellow.
    An-IP:(12), Bl-OB:29, Co-BB:69,
    De-PO:12, Er-FA:492, Fr-WO:28,
    Mo-MGT:200, Na-EO:168, Ox-BC:226,
    Sm-LG:99, Un-GT:101, Wi-MG:45,
    Wr-RM:84
CONTROVERSY: see also HUMOR - CONTROVERSY
  Bishop Blougram's Apology. R. Browning.
    Ox-BN:547
  The Blind Men and the Elephant.
    J. Saxe. Bo-HF:73, Gr-EC:150,
    Ha-PO:302, Pa-OM:330, Un-GT:200
  Booker T. and W.E.B. D. Randall.
    Ab-MO:84, Be-MA:69
  The Chameleon. J. Merrick. Cl-FC:74
  Contest. F. Victor. Mo-SD:127
  Dialogue at Night. E. Greenberg.
    Ho-TY:308
  Dooley Is a Traitor. J. Michie.
    Co-RM:119
  The Flesh and the Spirit.
    A. Bradstreet. Sh-AP:9
  From Plane to Plane. R. Frost.
    Un-MA:191
  The Opposition. S. Hazo. Ls-NY:273
  Poets Hitchhiking on the Highway.
    G. Corso. Du-RG:19
  A Psalm of Montreal. S. Butler.
    Rv-CB:933
  Witchcraft: New Style. L. Abercrombie.
    Un-MB:256
  A Woman's Last Word. R. Browning.
    Er-FA:118, Rv-CB:823, Un-MW:190
CONUNDRUMS: see RIDDLES
CONVENTIONALITY: see CONFORMITY
CONVENTS AND NUNNERIES
  The Convent. S. O'Sullivan. Co-PI:166
  A Drape. Feng Chih. Hs-TC:143

CONVERSATION: see also HUMOR - CONVERSA-
TION; SATIRE - CONVERSATION
After Long Silence. W. Yeats.
Co-EL:122, Wi-LT:89
Be Different to Trees. M. Davies.
Fe-FP:208, Hu-MP:269
Conversation with a Friend. G. Abbe.
Ls-NY:65
From Plane to Plane. R. Frost.
Un-MA:191
In Memoriam. A. Tennyson. Ox-BN:501
Little Talk. A. Fisher. Fe-FP:147,
La-PP:11
Looking into a Face. R. Bly. Mo-TS:12
The Oath. A. Tate. Wi-LT:408
Talk. D. Lawrence. Cl-FC:21
"The Time Has Come," the Walrus Said.
L. Carroll. Ar-TP3:126
A Time to Talk. R. Frost. Sp-OG:248
Voices. W. Bynner. Bo-FP:158
CONVERSION: see also HUMOR - CONVERSION;
SALVATION
The Congo. V. Lindsay. Er-FA:300,
Hi-WP II:98, Hu-PN:484, Pe-OA:55,
Sh-AP:163, Un-MA:218
Conversion. F. Angermayer. Fe-PL:334
Conversion. J. Toomer. Be-MA:17
Elene. Cynewulf. Ma-YA:11
I Met the Master. Fe-PL:337
A Little Indian Maid. Fi-BG:196
The Supper after the Last. G. Kinnell.
En-PC:255
Two Sonnets. E. Robinson. Sm-PT:148
COOK, JAMES (CAPTAIN COOK)
Captain Cook. A. Domett. Hi-FO:180
COOK ISLANDS
See Tr-US II:53-64
COOKS AND COOKERY: see also BAKERS AND
BAKERIES; CANNING AND PRESERVING;
DIET; HUMOR - COOKS AND COOKERY
Baking Day. R. Joseph. To-MP:142
Dedication of the Cook. A. Wickham.
Un-MB:279
Goody O'Grumpity. C. Brink. Fe-FP:312,
Sh-RP:37
I Like. C. Tringress. St-FS:104
The Miracle. E. Fowler. Br-BC:87
Mix a Pancake. C. Rossetti. Ag-HE:6,
Au-SP:10, Bo-FP:53, Ch-B:80,
Cl-FC:94, Li-LC:45
Mother's Biscuits. F. Quenneville.
Du-RG:118
Ten of Chaucer's People: A Tasty Cook.
G. Chaucer. Ha-PO:52
Thanksgiving Magic. R. Bennett.
Br-SS:82
Three Cooks. Ir-BB:37, Mo-MGT:75
What Happened. D. Aldis. Gr-EC:220
COONS: see RACCOONS
COOPERATION: see HUMOR - COOPERATION
COPENHAGEN, BATTLE, 1801
Battle of the Baltic. T. Campbell.
Co-RG:46, Hi-FO:193, Pa-GTB:205,
Rv-CB:675
COPHETUA, MYTHICAL KING OF AFRICA
The Beggar Maid. A. Tennyson.
Pa-OM:257
COPLEY, JOHN SINGLETON
On a Portrait by Copley. A. Freeman.
Co-RM:215, Cr-WS:54
COQUETTES
Amoret. W. Congreve. Al-VBP:519
Complaint. Sun Yü-t'ang. Hs-TC:120
The Coquet. A. Behn. Al-VBP:499
A Reaping Song. Tr-US II:153
A Trampwoman's Tragedy. T. Hardy.
Ox-BN:825
CORACLES: see BOATS AND BOATING
CORALS
The Atoll in the Mind. A. Comfort.
Wi-LT:671
The Coral Grove. J. Percival.
Un-GT:262
CORMORANTS
The Common Cormorant. Bl-OB:66,
Co-FB:371, Co-HP:21, Gr-CT:21,
Gr-EC:28, Ir-BB:82, Lo-LL:33,
Pa-RE:66, Sm-LG:90, Sm-MK:192,
Un-GT:223
Cormorants. J. Blight. Ma-FW:94
In the Evening I Walk by the River.
Hsiu Ou-Yang. Le-MW:88, Rx-OH:51
Late. L. Bogan. Ca-VT:203
The Sea-Bird's Cry. R. Hawker.
Hi-WP II:36
CORN: see also HUMOR - CORN
America Is Corn. R. Coffin. Mc-WK:158
The Beginning, Part I. Te-FC:225
Blue Evening Falls. Ho-SD:49, Le-OE:99
A Cloud on Top of Evergreen Mountain.
Ho-SD:47, Tr-US II:273
Corn. E. Antin. Br-SG:43
Corn Ceremony. Da-SC:83
Corn-Grinding Song. Sh-RP:80
Corn-Grinding Songs, I. Tr-US II:257
The Corn Grows Up. Le-OE:78
Corn Must Be Sown. T. Carlyle.
Gr-TG:27
The Cornfield. E. Roberts. Bo-GJ:46
The Creation, Part II. Te-FC:275
Ear-of-Corn. Ge-TR:39
From a Seasonal Prayer. Tr-US II:254
Harvest. C. Sandburg. Ha-WR:81
I Am the Corncob. Ge-TR:49
An Indian Hymn of Thanks to Mother
Corn. Bo-FP:154
It Is Raining Up There. Ho-SD:49
Kachina Song. Br-MW:43, Da-SC:84,
Pa-SG:128
The Last Corn Shock. G. Dresbach.
Fe-FP:236
Miss Elderli Dora DesMoines - One
March. R. Sward. St-H:224
My Great Corn Plants. Ho-SD:37
Plow the Corn. Ju-CP:6

CORN — cont'd.
  Raise Your Hands to the Sky. A. Lopez.
    Al-WW:9
  Season. W. Soyinka. Ma-FW:127
  Song Concerning the Corn Harvest.
    Tr-US II:261
  The Song of a Dream. Bi-IT:127
  Songs in the Garden of the House God.
    Bi-IT:115, Da-SC:86
  Winter Dance Song. Tr-US II:259
  Woman's Song of Corn Growing.
    Tr-US II:247
CORNCRAKES: see RAILS (BIRDS)
CORNWALL, ENG.: see also DIALECTS,
    CORNISH
  A Ballad of a Mine. R. Skelton.
    Ca-MB:77
  Cornish Cliffs. J. Betjeman. To-MP:177
  Cornish Magic. A. Durell. Fe-FP:372
  Cornwall. C. Bond. Le-M:33
  Table d'Hote. R. Esler. Ls-NY:154
  Trebetherick. J. Betjeman. Na-EO:160
COROMANDEL COAST, INDIA
  The Coromandel Fishers. S. Naidu.
    Sh-RP:26
  The Courtship of the Yonghy-Bonghy-Bo.
    E. Lear. Ho-WR:50, Na-EO:171,
    Pa-OM:59, Un-GT:213
  On the Coast of Coromandel. O. Sitwell.
    Un-MA:358
CORPSES: see THE DEAD
CORRIB RIVER, IRE.
  Corrib. An Emblem. D. Davie. En-PC:197
CORRUPTION: see also DEGENERACY; HUMOR —
    CORRUPTION; POLITICS
  Consider These, for We Have Condemned
    Them. C. Day-Lewis. Wi-LT:428
  A Denunciation of the Princes and the
    Prophets. Bible. O.T. Micah.
    Me-PH:51
  Epigram. J. Wolcot. Co-EL:51
  For More Public Fountains in New York
    City. A. Dugan. Ho-P:61
  Friars. W. Langland. Ke-PP:14
  The Heart of the Ancient City.
    Pien Chih-lin. Hs-TC:166
  Jack and the Beanstalk. P. Goedicke.
    Du-SH:50
  Judgment. T. Palmanteer. Al-WW:46
  The Lie. W. Raleigh. Al-VBP:95,
    Gr-CT:372, Ke-PP:16, Rv-CB:157
  Only the Beards Are Different. B. Dawe.
    Cr-WS:44
  Sardanapalus. H. Howard. Hi-FO:29
  Shame. R. Wilbur. Cr-WS:173
  Shine, Perishing Republic. R. Jeffers.
    Al-VBP:1170, Ca-VT:121, Sh-AP:177,
    Un-MA:369, Wi-LT:257
  Since We Are Property. L. Lorraine.
    De-FS:133
  A Sketch from Private Life. G. Byron.
    Ox-BN:253

  There Are No Good Giants. W. Benton.
    Cr-WS:52
  This Compost. W. Whitman. Un-MA:86
  This Hour. O. La Grone. Hu-NN:37,
    Hu-PN:327
  The Vanity of the World. F. Quarles.
    Ke-PP:28
  War Is the Statesman's Game.
    P. Shelley. Ba-PO:157, Ke-PP:57
  Will the Wig Be Big Enough?
    P. Crawford. La-IH:128
CORTEZ, HERNANDO
  Cortez. W. Seymour. Sm-MK:64
COSMETICS: see GROOMING, PERSONAL;
    PERFUMES
COSSACKS
  The Young Cossack. A. Kamensky.
    Mo-MI:18
COST OF LIVING: see SATIRE — COST OF
    LIVING
COTTON
  Cotton Songs. J. Toomer. Ra-BP:68
  Pantuns, III. Tr-US II:203
  Snapshots of the Cotton South.
    F. Davis. Ad-PB:98
COTTON BLOSSOMS
  November Cotton Flower. J. Toomer.
    Jo-SA:121
COTTONWOOD TREES
  Summer Storm. R. Cuscaden. St-H:32
COUÉ, EMILE: see HUMOR — COUÉ, EMILE
COUGARS: see MOUNTAIN LIONS
COUGHING: see COLDS
COUNTER CULTURE: see also HUMOR —
    COUNTER CULTURE; SATIRE — COUNTER
    CULTURE; YOUTH AND AGE
  Furniture. P. Harris. Ha-TP:32
  Howl. A. Ginsberg. Sh-AP:233
  Love among the Manchees. W. Dickey.
    En-PC:266
  Mandylion. P. Harris. Sc-TN:78
  Sonnet XV. Feng Chih. Hs-TC:152
  Tonight at Noon. A. Henri. To-MP:192
  See also Bo-RU, Jo-SA, Sc-TN
COUNTING-OUT RHYMES
  As I Was Walking down the Lake.
    Ir-BB:19
  Ball. K. Greenaway. Bo-FP:4
  Cherry Stones. Mo-MGT:148
  Cinderella. Co-OW:36
  The Counting Man. W. Moody. Ch-B:64,
    Co-PM:127
  Counting-Out Rhyme. E. Millay.
    Bo-GJ:7, Du-RG:99
  Counting Out Rhyme. Li-SR:125
  A Counting-Out Rhyme. Wr-RM:60
  Counting Rhymes. Mo-MGT:192
  Dips or Counting Out Rhymes. Gr-GB:20, 21
  Draw a Pail of Water. Ir-BB:264,
    Li-LB:135
  Ducks and Drakes. De-CH:685, Ir-BB:33,
    Wr-RM:104

Eena, Deena, Deina, Duss.   De-CH:684,
   Mo-NR:82
Eenie, Meenie, Minie Mo.   Fe-FP:117,
   Ir-BB:19
Eenity, Feenity, Fickety Feg.   De-CH:685
Eeny, Pheeny, Figgery, Fegg.   Ir-BB:19,
   Su-FVI:80
Ena, Mena, Bora Mi.   De-CH:685
Engine, Engine, Number Nine.   Ir-BB:19
Ex and Squarey.   Gr-CT:166, Gr-GB:20
Fireman, Fireman.   Bu-DY:73
The Five Students.   T. Hardy.   Pa-GTB:410
Hinty, Minty, Cuty, Corn.   Ch-B:64,
   De-CH:684, Fe-FP:117
Hoky, Poky, Winky Wum.   Ir-BB:19,
   Su-FVI:80
I Sent a Letter to My Love.   Li-LB:134
I Walked under an Apple Tree.   Ju-CP:15
Ibbity, Bibbity, Sibbity.   Bu-DY:91,
   Ir-BB:19, Su-FVI:80
Icker-Backer.   Ir-BB:19, Su-FVI:81
Intery, Mintery, Cutery Corn.
   Ar-TP3:103, Bo-FP:140, Cl-FC:19,
   De-TT:28, Gr-EC:283, Tu-WW:15,
   Wr-RM:88
Inty, Tinty, Tethery, Methery.   Ir-BB:19
Jumping Joan.   Mother Goose.   Ne-AM:32
A Knife and a Razor.   De-CH:686,
   Ir-BB:269
Lady of the Land.   Rv-ON:100
Linnet, Linnet, Come This Minute.
   Ju-CP:15
Mena, Deena, Deina, Duss.   Li-LB:118
Old Dan Tucker.   De-CH:686, Ir-BB:148
One-ery, Ore-ery, Ickery, Ann.
   Fe-FP:117, Ir-BB:19, Su-FVI:81
One-ery, Two-ery, Dickery, Dee.
   Ir-BB:19, Su-FVI:80
One-ery, Two-ery, Ickery, Ann.
   Ch-B:64, Mo-MGT:192
One, He Loves.   Wi-MG:30, Wr-RM:73
One I Love, Two I Loathe.   On-TW:58
One I Love, Two I Love.   Ir-BB:18,
   Li-LB:118
One Little Man a-Driving Cattle.
   Ju-CP:15
One Potato, Two Potato.   Ch-B:64,
   Fe-FP:117
One to Make Ready.   Mother Goose.
   Bo-FP:264, Li-LB:118, Mo-MGT:173,
   Mo-NR:25, Mo-SD:68, Pa-AP:5
One to Ten.   Wr-RM:107
One, Two.   Mother Goose.   De-TT:27,
   Li-LB:116, Mo-MGT:40, Un-GT:23
One Two Three.   Co-OW:38, On-TW:63
One - Two - Three.   De-TT:26
One, Two, Three, Four.   Mother Goose.
   Bo-FP:67, Ju-CP:16, Li-LB:124,
   Mo-NR:123, On-TW:62
One, Two, Three, Four, Five.
   Mo-TL:67, Wi-MG:30, Wr-RM:41

One, Two, Three, Four, Five.   Mother
   Goose.   Mo-CC:(45)., Mo-MGT:149,
   Mo-NR:34, Sm-MK:18
One Two Three Four Five, Six Seven
   Eight Nine Ten.   Li-LB:125
One, Two, Three, O'Leary.   On-TW:58
Out Goes the Rat.   Ch-B:64, Fe-FP:117
A Pretty Maid.   Mo-MGT:151
Robbers.   Gr-EC:282
Salt, Mustard, Vinegar, Pepper.
   Su-FVI:76
This Little Pig Got into the Barn.
   Mo-TL:16
This Little Pig Went to Market.
   Au-SP:18, Bo-FP:8, De-CH:497,
   De-PO:8, Ir-BB:10, Li-LB:20,
   Mo-CC:(48), Mo-MGT:54, Mo-NR:78,
   Mo-TL:15, Sp-TM:23, Wi-MG:73,
   Wr-RM:35
Three Potatoes in a Pot.   Ju-CP:15
Tinker, Tailor.   Ir-BB:36
Tit-Tat-Toe.   Mother Goose.   Ir-BB:36,
   Mo-MGT:196, Mo-NR:123, Mo-TL:30
Who Picked Peppers.   Ju-CP:16
Wire, Briar, Limber-Lock.   Ir-BB:19
Zeenty, Peenty, Heathery, Mithery.
   Gr-CT:166, Gr-GB:21, Su-FVI:80
See also Bo-CO, On-TW
COUNTRY LIFE: see also DIALECTS, COUNTRY;
   FARM LIFE; OUTDOOR LIFE; SATIRE -
   COUNTRY LIFE
Air.   C. Major.   Jo-SA:96
L'Allegro.   J. Milton.   Al-VBP:389,
   Er-FA:37, Ga-FB:26, Pa-GTB:94,
   Rv-CB:369
Arriving in the Country Again.   J. Wright.
   Co-PM:139
At Thanksgiving.   J. Leichliter.
   Ls-NY:288
Autumn Morning.   F. Frost.   Sh-RP:225
A Barefoot Boy.   J. Riley.   Er-FA:137
The Barefoot Boy.   J. Whittier.
   Ch-B:65, Fe-FP:544, Fe-PL:249
Barefoot Days.   R. Field.   Fe-FP:229,
   Ha-YA:66
The Beginning of Day.   Euripides.
   Pa-SG:104
Being.   K. Ozaki.   Sh-AM:59
Bells in the Country.   R. Nathan.
   Bo-FP:109
A Boy's Song.   J. Hogg.   Bl-OB:138,
   Bo-FP:258, Ch-B:62, De-CH:132,
   De-TT:75, Fe-FP:301, Ho-WR:69,
   Ke-TF:45, Mc-PR:114, Mc-WK:84,
   Ox-BC:156
Break of Day.   J. Clare.   Rv-CB:731
The Breathing.   D. Levertov.   Ha-WR:73
Change Toward Certainty.   J. Hearst.
   St-H:79

COUNTRY LIFE — cont'd.
  The City Mouse and the Garden Mouse.
    C. Rossetti. Ar-TP3:59, Bo-FP:15,
    Br-SG:66, Ch-B:25, Fe-FP:138,
    Hu-MP:189, It-HB:26, Un-GB:14,
    Un-GT:56
  City Streets and Country Roads.
    E. Farjeon. Ar-TP3:93, Au-SP:165,
    Pe-FB:46
  City Trees. E. Millay. Bo-HF:64,
    Fe-FP:250, La-OC:23, Sh-RP:108
  Coridon's Song. J. Chalkhill.
    Al-VBP:271
  Country Burying. R. Warren. Wi-LT:837
  A Country God. E. Blunden. Un-MB:396
  A Country Life. R. Jarrell. Un-MA:149
  The Country Mouse and the City Mouse.
    R. Sharpe. Ox-BC:139
  Country Summer. L. Adams. Al-VBP:1218,
    Bo-GJ:98, Un-MA:546, Wi-LT:604
  Country Vegetables. E. Farjeon.
    Bo-FP:83, Br-SG:37, Fe-FP:233
  Country Woman. B. Van Slyke. Ke-TF:424
  Dabbling in the Dew. De-CH:194
  Daphnis to Ganymede. R. Barnfield.
    Re-TW:42
  A Deserted Home. S. Lysaght. De-CH:50
  Dog-Tired. D. Lawrence. Gr-BT:50
  Driving Toward the Lac Qui Parle River.
    R. Bly. St-H:3
  Early Morning Meadow Song. C. Dalmon.
    De-CH:193
  The End of the Weekend. A. Hecht.
    Wi-LT:731
  Essay on Solitude. A. Cowley.
    Al-VBP:451
  Fall Comes to Back-Country Vermont.
    R. Warren. Ca-VT:278
  February. J. Clare. Ox-BN:309
  Figures in the Field Against the Sky.
    A. Machado. Le-SW:61
  Fools Gaze at Painted Courts.
    M. Drayton. Gr-CT:310
  The Fresh Air. H. Monro. De-CH:9
  Give Me the Splendid Silent Sun.
    W. Whitman. Co-BN:232, Fe-FP:263,
    Mo-BG:20, Un-MA:84
  The Goat Paths. J. Stephens.
    Ad-PE:30, Bo-GJ:56, De-CH:149,
    Go-BP:93, Rd-OA:55
  A Great Time. W. Davies. Hi-WP I:1,
    Un-MB:178
  Haymakers, Rakers. T. Dekker.
    Al-VBP:227
  Heart's Needle; Child of My Winter.
    W. Snodgrass. Un-MA:682
  Hen's Nest. J. Clare. Rd-OA:71
  The Hermit's Song. Pa-SG:158
  High Summer. J. Clare. Gr-CC:35
  The Hills. F. Cornford. Un-MB:308
  Hills. G. Foster. Le-M:122

  The Hock-Cart. R. Herrick. Al-VBP:328,
    Ga-S:211
  The Horses. T. Hughes. Go-BP:99,
    Ha-WR:74
  A House and Grounds. J. Hunt.
    Rv-CB:684
  I Return to the Place Where I Was Born.
    T'ao Yuan Ming. Rx-LT:33
  I Want a Pasture. R. Field. Sh-RP:109
  In August. W. Howells. Se-RP:164
  In the Summer. D. Aldis. Mc-AW:41
  It Was a Lover and His Lass.
    W. Shakespeare. Al-VBP:188,
    Bo-FP:214, De-CH:188, Ma-YA:67,
    No-CL:127, Pa-GTB:6, Rv-CB:198,
    Un-MW:4
  July. A. Dobson. Pa-RE:37
  June Twilight. J. Masefield.
    Go-BP:131
  Knee-Deep in June. J. Riley. Sp-OG:291
  Landscape. J. Cunha. Be-UL:65
  Let Me Go Warm. L. de Góngora.
    Mc-PR:47
  The Lime-Tree Bower My Prison.
    S. Coleridge. Rv-CB:660
  A Little Boy Lost. J. Rothenberg.
    Kh-VA:20
  Love on the Farm. D. Lawrence.
    Ga-FB:80, Un-MB:288, Un-MW:122
  M. Antonio Flaminio: To His Farm.
    J. Ashmore. No-CL:272
  A May Day. H. Wotton. De-CH:15
  May-Pole Dance. Gr-GB:40, Hi-WP I:38
  Meeting Mary. E. Farjeon. Br-BC:72
  The Merry Country Lad. N. Breton.
    Al-VBP:84, De-CH:137, Rd-OA:39,
    Rv-CB:148
  Midsummer Jingle. N. Levy. Co-BN:96,
    Co-PM:47
  Midsummer Pause. F. Lape. Co-PS:107
  A Midsummer Song. R. Gilder.
    Co-BN:92, Ke-TF:44
  Milking Pails. De-CH:67
  Milking Time. C. Rossetti. Hu-MP:310
  The Minstrel. J. Beattie. Al-VBP:598
  Montana Wives. G. Haste. Br-AF:159
  Morning. D. Gallagher. Br-SS:20
  Morning. J. Harrison. Ha-WR:44
  My Early Home. J. Clare. Fe-PL:146
  My Maid Mary. Bo-FP:68, Hi-GD:11,
    Mo-MGT:149, Wr-RM:76
  The News Around Midnight. T. McGrath.
    St-H:126
  Nicholas Nye. W. de la Mare.
    Bl-OB:120, Cl-DT:50, Co-BBW:150,
    Rd-OA:73
  The North Country. R. Browning.
    Bo-FP:70
  Not Love, Not War. W. Wordsworth.
    No-CL:10
  November. J. Clare. Ma-FW:266

O Country People. J. Hewitt. Co-PI:60
Oh, Fairest of the Rural Maids!
  W. Bryant. Al-VBP:767
The Oak and the Ash. Sm-LG:138
Obsessions. D. Levertov. Wi-LT:760
An Ode to Mr. Anthony Stafford to
  Hasten Him into the Country.
  T. Randolph. Al-VBP:378
Of Bloom. L. Goldberg. Me-PH:113
Of the Mean and Sure Estate. T. Wyatt.
  Rd-OA:98
The Old Man's Wish. W. Pope. Go-BP:47
The Old Squire. W. Blunt. Mo-SD:110
On Dwelling. R. Graves. Rv-CB:994
On Eastnor Knoll. J. Masefield.
  De-CH:25, Ma-FW:122
Out in the Fields with God. L. Guiney.
  Hu-MP:64, Mc-PR:183, Un-GT:264
Out to Old Aunt Mary's. J. Riley.
  Er-FA:143
Ox Driver. B. Cutler. St-H:40
Pastoral. E. Millay. Sh-RP:218
Pastoral. W. Trask. No-CL:262
Pastoral. V. Wilder. Ke-TF:442
The Pasture. R. Frost. Al-VBP:1125,
  Ar-TP3:75, Au-SP:45, Bo-GJ:44,
  Co-BBW:162, Fe-FP:230, La-PP:23,
  La-PV:166, Li-LC:75, Mc-PR:121,
  Pa-RE:115, Pe-FB:2, Su-FVI:57,
  Th-AS:75, Un-MA:168
Patch-Shaneen. J. Synge. Co-PI:188
Peader Og Goes Courting. J. Stephens.
  Co-BL:19
The Pentland Hills. Gr-GB:175
Pleasant Sounds. J. Clare. Go-BP:110,
  Rv-CB:723
Poem. T. McGrath. St-H:125
Reading the Book of Hills and Sea.
  Tao Ch'ien. Pa-SG:171
Remember That Country. J. Garrigue.
  Ca-VT:389
Return to the Farm. M. Taylor.
  Ke-TF:352
The Roads into the Country. T. McGrath.
  St-H:121
Rudolph Is Tired of the City. G. Brooks.
  La-PV:101, Sh-RP:99, Un-GB:20
September. H. Jackson. Bo-GJ:250,
  Fe-FP:76, Fe-PL:385, Ha-YA:104,
  Hu-MP:315, Mc-PR:93, Se-PR:165,
  Un-GT:277
A Song of the Moon. C. McKay.
  Hu-PN:98
Sonnet. A. Nelson. Ad-PB:12, Hu-PN:46
Sonnet of Intimacy. V. de Moraes.
  An-TC:103
Sowing. E. Thomas. Cl-FC:29
Spring. A. De Vere. Ox-BN:586
The Spring Walk. T. Miller. De-TT:32
Stool Ball. De-CH:67
Stranger. E. Roberts. Un-MA:270

Summer. J. Clare. Rv-CB:718
The Summer Countries. H. Rago.
  Ca-VT:425
Summer Images. J. Clare. Gr-CT:117,
  Ox-BN:318, Rv-CB:716
Summer Morning. J. Clare. Co-PS:111,
  Rv-CB:714
Sun and Rain and Dew from Heaven.
  A. Gordon. Fe-PL:313
The Sun Has Long Been Set.
  W. Wordsworth. Ha-YA:72
A Sweet Country Life. Rv-ON:42
Three Kinds of Pleasure. R. Bly.
  Mo-BG:110, St-H:1
Thrice Happy He. W. Drummond.
  Co-BN:211
Time for Ripening. A. Laszlofy.
  Mc-AC:158
To a Young Lady. A. Pope. Hi-WP II:124
To Christ Our Lord. G. Kinnell.
  Br-TC:239, Ha-WR:92, La-RM:120,
  Pe-M:112
To Meadows. R. Herrick. Al-VBP:336,
  De-CH:205, Rv-CB:340
To Mr. Izaak Walton. C. Cotton.
  Al-VBP:472, Go-BP:19
To One Who Has Been Long in City Pent.
  J. Keats. Go-BP:25, Rv-CB:738
Town and Country. T. Moult. Cl-FC:23
Troubles of the Day. W. Barnes.
  Pa-GTB:323
Turf-Stacks. L. MacNeice. Wi-LT:455
Twilight Calm. C. Rossetti.
  Co-BN:109, Ox-BN:709
Under the Greenwood Tree. Gr-GB:44
Until We Built a Cabin. A. Fisher.
  Ar-TP3:179
Up at a Villa – Down in the City.
  R. Browning. Pa-GTB:342, Rv-CB:824
Upon Boys Diverting Themselves in the
  River. T. Foxton. Ox-BC:55
Village Before Sunset. F. Cornford.
  Co-BN:108, Co-PM:143, Sm-LG:50
The Vineyard. I. Pillat. Mc-AC:56
The Wagon in the Barn. J. Drinkwater.
  Pe-FB:30, Th-AS:70
We Who Were Born. E. Lewis. Br-BC:11,
  Fe-FP:465
Week-End. H. Monro. Un-MB:233
Weekend Stroll. F. Cornford. Co-BN:94
Wheat. R. Cuscaden. St-H:35
Wiltshire Downs. A. Young. Pa-GTB:465
Winter Encounters. C. Tomlinson.
  Wi-LT:829
Winter Field. K. Ozaki. Sh-AM:58
Wishes. E. Guest. Ke-TF:238
Yankee Cradle. R. Coffin. Gr-EC:234,
  Na-EO:102
Yes, I Grew Up with the Poppies.
  Z. Stancu. Mc-AC:86
Young Lambs. J. Clare. Mc-PR:55,
  Un-GT:35

COURAGE: see also HEROES AND HEROISM;
    HUMOR - COURAGE; SATIRE - COURAGE
  Abraham Davenport.   J. Whittier.
    Sp-OG:31
  The Acrobat from Xanadu Disdained All
    Nets. D. Georgakas. Sc-TN:60
  Adam Bell, Clym of the Clough, and
    William of Cloudesley. Ma-BB:157,
    Ox-BB:380
  Admiral Benbow.   Co-RM:66, Rv-CB:420
  Alec Yeaton's Son.   T. Aldrich.
    Sp-OG:92
  Alice Brand. W. Scott. Pa-OM:248
  Allen-a-Dale. W. Scott. Co-PT:231
  And When I Am Entombed. R. Emerson.
    Al-VBP:800
  April 4, 1968. M. Goode. Jo-SA:6,
    Jo-VC:57
  Autumnal. R. Humphries. Tr-MR:273
  The Ballad of Kon-Tiki. I. Serraillier.
    Co-SS:223
  Ballade by the Fire. E. Robinson.
    Bo-HF:174
  Baptism. C. McKay. Hu-PN:103
  Be Still, My Soul. Archilochus.
    Pa-SG:177
  Be Strong. M. Babcock. Er-FA:23
  Beautiful Black Women. . . .
    I. Baraka. Ra-BP:213
  A Bee Sets Sail. K. Morse. It-HB:44
  The Blind Boy. C. Cibber. Co-RG:134,
    Ox-BC:58, Pa-GTB:111
  Boot and Saddle. R. Browning.
    Bo-FP:300
  The Brave at Home. T. Read. Sp-OG:201
  The Brave Man. W. Stevens. Li-TU:206
  Bristowe Tragedie. Ox-BB:656
  The Broken Dike, the Levee Washed Away.
    E. Millay. Ni-JP:128
  Burning. G. Snyder. Ma-FW:140
  Call to Youth. Horace. Pa-SG:4
  The Captain Stood on the Carronade.
    F. Marryat. De-CH:597
  Casabianca. F. Hemans. Er-FA:184,
    Fe-FP:552, Hi-FO:189, Un-GT:159
  Character of the Happy Warrior.
    W. Wordsworth. Er-FA:85
  The Charge of the Light Brigade.
    A. Tennyson. Er-FA:183, Fe-FP:564,
    Ga-FB:206, Hi-FO:238, Ma-YA:196,
    Mc-PR:184, Sp-OG:49
  Charm for Striking Fear into a Tiger.
    Tr-US II:205
  Chevy Chase, The Second Fytte.
    Ma-BB:101
  The Child on the Curbstone. E. Wylie.
    La-OC:92
  The Childless Father. W. Wordsworth.
    De-CH:260
  The Choice. H. Corke. Cr-WS:170,
    Ni-JP:129

  The City of Dreadful Night. J. Thomson.
    Pa-GTB:382
  Columbus. J. Miller. Ar-TP3:38,
    Er-FA:298, Fe-FP:403, Ha-YA:116,
    Hi-TL:13, Hu-MP:370, Mc-PR:180,
    Mc-WK:161, Se-PR:182, Sp-OG:59,
    Vi-PP:42
  A Commemoration for the Physicist X.
    P. Oppenheimer. Ls-NY:130
  The Companion. Y. Yevtushenko.
    Cr-WS:127, Ma-FW:252
  Conquest. G. Johnson. Bo-AN:24,
    Bo-HF:102
  The Conspiracy of Charles, Duke of
    Byron. G. Chapman. Al-VBP:147
  Courage. A. Earhart. Th-AS:190
  Courage. G. Herbert. Bo-FP:299,
    Ch-B:97, Un-GT:305
  Courage Has a Crimson Coat. N. Turner.
    Bo-FP:299, Th-AS:212
  Craven. H. Newbolt. Sp-OG:78
  The Cumberland and the Merrimac.
    Em-AF:443
  The Cumberland's Crew. Em-AF:442
  Curfew Must Not Ring Tonight. R. Thorpe.
    Fe-FP:559
  Custer's Last Charge. F. Whittaker.
    Fe-PL:173, Hi-TL:37, Pa-OM:183
  D'Artagnan. V. Starrett. Cr-WS:17
  The Day of Battle. A. Housman.
    Cr-WS:90
  Dear God. C. O'Riordan. De-CH:656
  Death and General Putnam. A. Guiterman.
    Co-PM:77, Co-RM:219, Cr-WS:55
  Death of a Comrade. M. Carter.
    Sa-B:163
  The Death of Admiral Benbow.
    Bl-OB:44, Gr-GB:239, Rv-CB:420
  Death of an Aircraft. C. Causley.
    Ca-MB:115
  The Difficult Land. E. Muir. Go-BP:228
  Do You Fear the Wind? H. Garland.
    Ar-TP3:165, Hu-MP:317, Ja-PA:45,
    Th-AS:115
  Earl Brand. Ox-BB:115
  The Eleventh Hour. F. Morris.
    Hi-WP II:146
  Elysium Is as Far. E. Dickinson.
    Un-MA:95
  Epilogue. R. Browning. Al-VBP:916,
    Ga-FB:131, Ox-BN:586
  Epilogue. S. Spender. Un-MB:472
  Epitaph for Chaeroneia. Aristotle.
    Pa-SG:7
  The Explorer. R. Kipling. Sp-OG:54
  The Fish. E. Bishop. Al-VBP:1238,
    Bo-GJ:67, Co-BBW:69, Pe-OA:210,
    Un-GT:128, Un-MA:611, Wi-LT:510
  Floodtide. A. Toure. Ad-PB:336,
    Hu-PN:424
  For a Six-Year Old. F. Rodman. Ke-TF:250

For God Hath Not Given Us the Gift of
  Fear. Bible. N.T. Timothy.
  Ar-TP3:209
Frederick Douglass. P. Dunbar.
  Ad-PB:9
Frederick Douglass, 1817-1895.
  L. Hughes. Ra-BP:87
Fuzzy-Wuzzy. R. Kipling. Un-MB:126
God Said. Bible. O.T. Joshua.
  Gr-TG:84
The Golden Vanity. Bl-OB:55,
  Co-SS:193, De-CH:398, Fo-OG:10,
  Ho-WR:128, Rv-CB:438
Good and Bad. J. Stephens. Un-MB:267
The Guards Came Through. A. Doyle.
  Sp-OG:52
Gunga Din. R. Kipling. Er-FA:371,
  Go-BP:54, Hi-WP I:69, Ma-YA:226,
  Pa-OM:230, Un-MB:122
Harlem Freeze Frame. L. Bethune.
  Ad-PB:309
A Hat of Eagle Feathers. Ho-SD:17
The Haystack in the Floods. W. Morris.
  Ni-JP:41, Ox-BN:779
He Died a Second Time. Ai Ch'ing.
  Hs-TC:310
He Got Up. Ai Ch'ing. Hs-TC:299
He Loves and Rides Away. S. Dobell.
  Ox-BN:663
Heather Ale. R. Stevenson. Co-PT:117,
  Sp-OG:162
Held by the Land. C. Rainsford.
  Ke-TF:425
The Hero. L. Jackson. Br-SS:164
The Highwayman. A. Noyes. Ar-TP3:24,
  Co-BL:155, Er-FA:343, Fe-FP:449,
  Fe-PL:16, Un-GT:131
His Cavalier. R. Herrick. Bo-GJ:109,
  Gr-CC:120
His Choice. A. Baker. Ke-TF:252
El Hombre. W. Williams. Ho-LP:56
Horatius. T. Macaulay. Er-FA:387,
  Fe-PL:64, Hi-FO:32, Sm-LG:161
How Can a Man Die Better. Tyrtaeus.
  Pa-SG:6
How Far. M. Nakagawa. Sh-AM:149
How They Brought the Good News from
  Ghent to Aix. R. Browning.
  Ar-TP3:31, Co-RG:31, Er-FA:378,
  Gr-EC:156, Hi-WP I:66, Li-SR:12,
  Sp-OG:29, Un-GT:149
Hughie Graham. Ox-BB:579
Hyena. Lo-TY:9
I Don't Mind. C. Jackson. Le-M:168
I Go Forth to Move about the Earth.
  A. Lopez. Al-WW:8
I Think I Understand. J. Mitchell.
  Mo-GR:126
I to My Perils. A. Housman. Al-VBP:1081
If. R. Kipling. Er-FA:5, Hi-WP I:118,
  Un-GT:314
If We Must Die. C. McKay. Ad-PB:25,
  Be-MA:13, Bo-AN:31, Ga-FB:277,
  Hu-PN:102, Jo-SA:135, Kr-OF:48,
  Lo-TY:118, Ra-BP:63
Incident of the French Camp.
  R. Browning. Co-RG:28, Mc-PR:144,
  Sp-OG:43, Un-GT:148
An Infantryman. E. Blunden.
  Al-VBP:1208
Interim. C. Delaney. Hu-PN:181
Invictus. W. Henley. Al-VBP:1067,
  Co-RM:245, Er-FA:460, Ga-FB:132,
  Ke-TF:253, Mc-PR:69, Ox-BN:883,
  Sp-OG:332, Un-GT:316, Un-MB:53
John Burns of Gettysburg. B. Harte.
  Sp-OG:36, Vi-PP:156
Judith of Bethulia. J. Ransom.
  Wi-LT:313
Keep a Stiff Upper Lip. P. Cary.
  Er-FA:19
King Henry the Fifth. W. Shakespeare.
  Co-RM:199, Ga-FB:195, Ha-PO:255,
  Ke-TF:54
The Knight's Leap. C. Kingsley.
  Co-PT:230
The Laird o' Logie. De-CH:412,
  Rv-CB:49
Last Word. H. Kemp. Ke-TF:252
The Leak in the Dike. P. Cary.
  Er-FA:348, Fe-FP:554
The Little House. Alesha. Mo-MI:77
Maggie Mac. Em-AF:445
The Main Truck; or a Leap for Life.
  G. Morris. Fe-PL:55
The Man from Snowy River. A. Paterson.
  Co-RM:141, Hi-WP II:91
The Man of Life Upright. T. Campion.
  Al-VBP:219, De-CH:637, Go-BP:44,
  Ha-PO:197, Rv-CB:273
Martin's Blues. M. Harper.
  Ad-PB:312
Medger Evers. G. Brooks. Ad-PB:158
The Minstrel Boy. T. Moore.
  Cl-FC:84, Co-RG:30, Er-FA:182,
  Un-GT:313
Molly Pitcher. K. Sherwood.
  Un-GT:183, Vi-PP:116
My Intrigue. J. Holland. Jo-VC:90
No Enemies. C. Mackay. Un-GT:316
No Worst, There Is None. G. Hopkins.
  Ke-PP:5, Ox-BN:870, Pa-GTB:395,
  Rv-CB:944, Un-MB:46, Wi-LT:49
Norman Conquest. P. Mackaye.
  Ke-TF:260
A North Pole Story. M. Smedley.
  Ox-BC:251
O Heart, Hold Thee Secure.
  W. de la Mare. Go-BP:183
One. C. Rodgers. Ra-BP:261
One Who Mobs the Mob. R. Emerson.
  Kr-OF:136

COURAGE — cont'd.
  Opportunity. E. Sill. Co-RM:71,
    Sp-OG:46, Un-GT:310
  The Painted Lady. M. Danner.
    Ra-BP:152
  Paternal. E. Wilson. Hu-PN:370
  The Patriot's Pass-Word.
    J. Montgomery. Sp-OG:19
  Philip Dagg. W. Gibson. Cr-WS:106
  Picture in an Old Frame.
    E. Chaffee. Ke-TF:68
  The Pilgrim. J. Bunyan. Ar-TP3:210,
    Cl-FC:22, De-TT:178, Ho-WR:47,
    Mc-WK:207, Na-EO:96, Rv-CB:460
  Poem at Thirty. S. Sanchez.
    Ad-PB:286, Ra-BP:231
  A Poem Beginning with a Line by
    Pindar. R. Duncan. Bl-FP:74
  Prayer. L. Untermeyer.
    Un-GT:308, Un-MA:305
  Preparedness. E. Markham.
    Er-FA:29, Un-MA:108
  Press Onward. Er-FA:22
  Prospice. R. Browning. Fe-PL:287,
    Ga-FB:129, Rv-CB:829
  Red Harlaw. Ox-BB:676
  The Rest. E. Pound. Sh-AP:173,
    Un-MA:296
  The Revenge. A. Tennyson. Co-RM:45,
    Hi-FO:134, Pa-OM:154, Sp-OG:60
  Robyn and Gandeleyn. Ox-BB:374
  Say Not the Struggle Nought Availeth.
    A. Clough. Al-VBP:926, Er-FA:460,
    Ga-FB:132, Ke-TF:57, Ox-BN:610,
    Pa-GTB:358, Pl-EI:121, Rv-CB:842,
    Tu-WW:44
  Seaside Storm. M. Craig. Cr-SS:18
  Sheridan's Ride. T. Read.
    Er-FA:185, Ga-FB:261, Sp-OG:44
  The Shield. C. Stetson. Sp-OG:34
  The Ship of Death. D. Lawrence.
    Pa-GTB:462
  Sir Eglamour. S. Rowlands.
    Bl-OB:25, Co-RM:80, Gr-EC:143,
    Mc-WK:134, Sm-LG:181
  The Sixth Book of Homer's Iliads.
    Homer. Al-VBP:148
  Soldier's Prayer. A. Giles.
    Ke-TF:203
  Song. M. Sarton. Tr-MR:175
  Song of Encouragement. Bi-IT:64
  Song of the Brave. L. Altgood.
    Vi-PP:205
  Spirits Unchained. K. Kgositsile.
    Ad-PB:323
  Stick to It. E. Guest. Er-FA:23
  Still Here. L. Hughes. Gr-BT:151,
    Ra-BP:83
  Strange Legacies. S. Brown.
    Ad-PB:62, Lo-TY:218
  The Strong Swimmer. W. Benét. Hu-PN:500

Sun and Rain and Dew from Heaven.
    A. Gordon. Fe-PL:313
  Symmetries and Asymmetries.
    W. Auden. Ma-FW:107
  Tempt Me No More. C. Day Lewis.
    Un-MB:423
  There Is an Old Horse.
    Jao Meng-k'an. Hs-TC:107
  These Are the Boys. A. Herbert.
    Cr-WS:123
  Three Fragments, II. Br-MW:96
  To a Friend Whose Work Has Come to
    Nothing. W. Yeats. Un-MB:116,
    Wi-LT:69
  To an Oak Tree. W. Scott. Ox-BN:135
  To His Heart Bidding It to Have No
    Fear. W. Yeats. Go-BP:183
  To Those Who Fight. T'ien Chien.
    Hs-TC:322
  Tomorrow. J. Masefield.
    Un-MB:222
  Ulysses. A. Tennyson. Al-VBP:863,
    Ha-PO:40, Ke-TF:262, Ni-JP:16,
    Rv-CB:793
  Untitled. Kao Meng-k'an. Hs-TC:106
  Upstream. C. Sandburg. Pe-M:45,
    Tr-MR:176, Un-MA:209
  Vitai Lampada. H. Newbolt. Sp-OG:17
  A Voice. Jo-TS:24, Tr-US II:235
  Walk. F. Horne. Ra-BP:75
  Walk Together Children. Ra-BP:1
  The War for Truth. W. Bryant.
    Kr-OF:133
  The War Horse. Bible. O.T. Job.
    Co-BBW:158
  War Song on a Brave Woman. Tr-US II:227
  What Are Years? M. Moore. Ha-TP:140,
    Pe-OA:101, Pl-EI:138, Sh-AP:179,
    Sm-PT:10
  What if Some Paine the Passage Have.
    E. Spenser. De-CH:179
  Will I Make It? J. Holland.
    Jo-VC:91
  Willie and Lady Margerie. Ox-BB:121
  Willie Mackintosh. Ma-BB:8,
    Ox-BB:597, Rv-CB:125
  The Wind. Da-SC:149, Ho-SD:7
  Without One Particle of Sentiment in
    His Being. M. Ooka. Sh-AM:134
  The Woman Who Understands.
    L. Appleton. Fe-PL:117
  You Are the Brave. R. Patterson.
    Ad-PB:209, Jo-SA:45
  Young Jack Snyder. J. Adams.
    Fi-BG:223
COURT LIFE: see CHIVALRY; KINGS AND
    RULERS
COURTESY: see also ETIQUETTE; HUMOR -
    COURTESY; TACT
  Bobby Blue. J. Drinkwater.
    Au-SP:135, Fe-FP:247
  A Child's Prayer. J. Tabb. Fe-FP:24

Consideration for Others. C. Smart.
Ox-BC:75
Excuse Us, Animals in the Zoo.
A. Wynne. Ar-TP3:78
Go to the Barn for Courtesy.
T. Coffin. Ke-TF:339
Little Maid, Little Maid, Where Have
You Been? Sp-TM:31
Of Courtesy. A. Guiterman.
Ar-TP3:209
On a Dead Hostess. H. Belloc.
Un-MB:172
Others. H. Behn. Au-SP:114
Politeness. Bo-FP:11
A Prayer for My Daughter. W. Yeats.
Al-VBP:1090, Fe-PL:137, Tr-MR:49
Riding. W. Allingham. Ox-BC:216
COURTS (LAW): see also JUDGES AND
JUDGING; LAWYERS; SATIRE -
COURTS (LAW); TRIALS
In the Dock. W. de la Mare.
Wi-LT:133
The Inquest. W. Davies. Pa-GTB:435,
Rv-CB:961
Last Speech to the Court.
B. Vanzetti. Mo-BG:170
COURTSHIP: see also COQUETTES; DATING;
HUMOR - COURTSHIP; KISSES AND
KISSING; LOVE; MARRIAGE PROPOSALS
All Year Long. Rx-LT:24
Allen-a-Dale. W. Scott. Co-PT:231
Alphabet Spring. L. Nagan. Ad-II:72
Anne. Rv-ON:100
At Early Morn. C. Mendes. Hu-PN:94
At the Silent Movies. Z. Landau.
Ho-TY:101
The Birds. W. Blake. De-CH:105
Birmingham Jail. Er-FA:235,
Gr-GB:264
Black Magic. S. Sanchez. Ra-BP:233
Bleeberrying. J. Denwood. Ca-MB:17
Boatmen's Song. Tr-US I:176
Bonny Lassie O! J. Clare. De-CH:195
Boy and Girl. Mo-NR:32, Wr-RM:118
By Ferry to the Island. I. Smith.
To-MP:95
By What Name Is Thy Bride Known?
Ho-SD:21
The Call. J. Hall. Al-VBP:471
The Cameo. E. Millay. Un-MA:449
Charlie, He's My Darling. R. Burns.
Al-VBP:652, De-CH:174
Come Down, O Maid. A. Tennyson.
Al-VBP:860, Go-BP:124, Ox-BN:488,
Rv-CB:798
Come into the Garden, Maud.
A. Tennyson. Co-BL:74, Ga-FB:57,
Rv-CB:799
Confessions. R. Browning.
Al-VBP:908, Pa-GTB:355
A Conjuration to Electra. R. Herrick.
Gr-SS:145

Counting the Beats. R. Graves.
Al-VBP:1206, Pa-GTB:490
Courting Song and Reply. Tr-US I:190
Dance Song. Tr-US II:127
Dance Songs, V. Tr-US II:164
Dance Songs, VI. Tr-US II:164
Dark Rosaleen. J. Mangan.
Al-VBP:812, Co-PI:128, De-CH:172
Dialogue. Tr-US II:151
Dialogues, I. Tr-US I:118
Donald of the Isles. Ox-BB:258
Down by the River. Mo-MGT:170
Down in a Garden. Rv-CB:134
Down in Yonder Meadow. De-CH:331,
Ir-BB:32
Earl Haldan's Daughter. C. Kingsley.
Sp-OG:101
Fa La La. De-CH:187
Fair Iris and Her Swain. J. Dryden.
Al-VBP:484
Fantasy under the Moon.
E. Boundzekei-Dongala. Lo-TY:148
Flowers in the Valley. Bl-OB:40,
Gr-EC:136, Gr-SS:29
For Daphne at Christmas. J. Nims.
St-H:157
The Gaberlunzie-Man. Ox-BB:626
Girl, Boy, Flower, Bicycle.
M. Joseph. Pe-M:149
Girl's Song. Tr-US II:21
Go Little Ring. Rv-CB:29
Greek Anthology, V. Un-MW:174
Green Grow the Rashes. R. Burns.
Al-VBP:642, Er-FA:426
The Grey Selchie of Sule Skerry.
Ox-BB:91
Here Comes a Lusty Wooer. De-CH:327
Howdy, Honey, Howdy. P. Dunbar.
Fe-PL:425
I Am Conscious. T. Clark. Mc-EA:85
I Am Cool Brother Cool. W. McLean.
Ad-II:116
I Call and I Call. R. Herrick.
Gr-CT:50
I Heard a Linnet Courting. R. Graves.
Rd-OA:41, Wi-LT:51
I Loved a Lass. G. Wither.
Al-VBP:312, De-CH:190, No-CL:121
If Doughty Deeds. . . . Graham of
Gartmore. Pa-GTB:128
In a Gondola. R. Browning.
Al-VBP:891
It Is My Form and Person. Da-SC:153
Jason and Medea. A. Lewis.
Rv-CB:1001
Johnie Cam to Our Toun. Gr-GB:99
A Joyful Chant. Le-OE:82
Jungle Songs, III. Tr-US II:160
King Estmere. Ma-BB:133, Ox-BB:127
A Knight Came Riding from the East.
Bl-OB:39
Lady Maisry. Ox-BB:295

COURTSHIP — cont'd.
  The Licorice Fields of Pontefract.
    J. Betjeman. To-MP:66
  The Lie. H. Moss. Wi-LT:776
  Love. S. Coleridge. Pa-GTB:171
  Love-Charm Song. Br-MW:99
  Love in a City in Spring. A. Miller.
    Ke-TF:358
  Love Me, Love My Dog. I. Crawford.
    Do-WH:30
  Love on the Farm. D. Lawrence.
    Ga-FB:80, Un-MB:288, Un-MW:122
  Love Song. Bi-IT:80
  Love Song. Tr-US II:263
  Love Songs of Turfan. Wen Chieh.
    Hs-TC:437
  Love's Philosophy. P. Shelley.
    Co-BL:40, Ga-FB:52, Hi-WP II:55,
    Pa-GTB:185, Un-MW:189
  Mark Antony. J. Cleveland.
    Al-VBP:440
  Marriage Songs, III. Tr-US II:159
  May Colven. Ma-BB:117, Ox-BB:49
  Melhill Feast. W. Barnes.
    Ox-BN:433, Rv-CB:766
  Men Loved Wholly Beyond Wisdom.
    L. Bogan. Ca-VT:202, Wi-LT:379
  The Milkmaid. Mo-MGT:190
  My Boy Tammy. H. Macneill. De-CH:33
  My Heart Is All Happy. Le-OE:87
  A Negro Love Song. P. Dunbar.
    Ab-MO:21, Hu-PN:36
  O My Bonny, Bonny May. Gr-GB:103
  Oh, See How Thick the Goldcup Flowers.
    A. Housman. Co-BL:153, Ga-FB:72,
    Ke-TF:94, No-CL:129, Un-MB:96,
    Un-MW:56
  O, the Month of May. T. Dekker.
    Al-VBP:225
  Old Mother Goose and the Golden Egg.
    Li-LB:48, Mo-MGT:2
  One I Love, Two I Loathe. On-TW:58
  Over the Water. De-TT:30,
    Sp-HW:4, Wr-RM:85
  Paired Reverberation. C. Baltag.
    Mc-AC:159
  Peader Og Goes Courting. J. Stephens.
    Co-BL:19
  Penal Law. A. Clarke. Pa-GTB:493
  The Phantom Wooer. T. Beddoes.
    Al-VBP:811, Ho-WR:191
  Piazza Piece. J. Ransom. Gr-SS:122,
    Ha-PO:46, Rv-CB:984, Un-MA:414
  Poem. J. Friedman. Ho-TY:368
  The Rigs o' Barley. R. Burns.
    Al-VBP:641, Rv-CB:617
  Rondel. A. Swinburne. Al-VBP:1027
  Roses Are Red. Ch-B:96, Mo-MGT:22
  Sally in Our Alley. H. Carey.
    Al-VBP:527, Co-PS:38, Er-FA:125,
    Pa-GTB:126, Rv-CB:498, Sp-OG:268

The Shepherdess.   Cheng Ch'ou-yü.
    Pa-MV:40
The Siege. J. Suckling. Al-VBP:416
Soldier, Soldier, Won't You Marry Me?
    Bl-OB:35
Song. Tr-US II:301
Song. Tr-US II:306
Song at a Public Courtship Ceremony.
    Tr-US I:188
Song for a Kachua Dance. Tr-US I:175
Song of a Chief's Daughter.
    Bi-IT:81, Ho-SD:57
Song of Caribou, Musk Oxen.
    Br-MW:140, Ho-SD:67, Le-IB:34,
    Ma-BH:21, Tr-US I:26
Song: Weekend's Over. M. Halpern.
    Ho-TY:106
Songs and Dance Songs, I.
    Tr-US II:152
Sonnets from the Portuguese.
    E. Browning. Ox-BN:466
Sonnets from the Portuguese XXVIII.
    E. Browning. Al-VBP:816
Spring Festival Songs, V.
    Tr-US II:172
Strange Fits of Passion.
    W. Wordsworth. Al-VBP:655,
    Ox-BN:61, Rv-CB:630
A Subaltern's Love-Song. J. Betjeman.
    Br-TC:43, Mc-WS:58, Na-EO:147,
    Un-MW:62
Sweet Cupid, Ripen Her Desire.
    Al-VBP:362
Les Sylphides.   L. MacNeice.
    Gr-BT:81
Tale.   Br-MW:44
There Was a Maid Went to the Mill.
    Gr-GB:107
This Morning Our Boat Left. Rx-LT:10
Three Knights from Spain.
    Bl-OB:36, De-CH:328, Fo-OG:42,
    Gr-GB:26, Rv-ON:106
To a Weeping Willow. L. Untermeyer.
    Un-MW:141
To His Coy Mistress.   A. Marvell.
    Al-VBP:456, Er-FA:123, Fe-PL:115,
    Ga-FB:44, Ha-PO:162, Ma-YA:103,
    No-CL:176, Rv-CB:400, Un-MW:185
Two in the Campagna. R. Browning.
    Ke-TF:134, Ox-BN:540, Pa-GTB:348,
    Un-MW:114
Unamina. B. Vilikazi. Pa-SG:38
Wasn't It You? K. Narasimkaswamy.
    Al-PI:125
What Faire Pompe. T. Campion. Ho-P:16
What Slender Youth. Horace.
    Ho-WR:185, No-CL:172
The Wheatear and the Snowbird.
    Da-SC:46, Le-IB:42
Whistle an' I'll Come. R. Burns.
    Al-VBP:651, Co-BL:99, Hi-WP I:41,
    Un-MW:188

The Whistling Thief. Co-PT:202
White an' Blue. W. Barnes.
   Pa-GTB:322
The Wicked Little Kukook. Le-IB:87
Willie and Lady Margerie. Ox-BB:121
The Willing Mistress. A. Behn.
   Al-VBP:500
Winter Winds Cold and Blea. J. Clare.
   Ox-BN:317
Ye Little Birds. . . . Al-VBP:359
The Yellow-Haired Laddie. Gr-GB:101
You Shall Be Queen. Bo-FP:292,
   Li-LB:170, Mo-MGT:10
A Young Man Going to War. Jo-TS:16
Your Kisses. A. Symons. Un-MW:194
COUSINS
   Cities #8. V. Cruz. Ad-BO:68
   Dead Boy. J. Ransom. Br-TC:336
   Girl's-Eye View of Relatives.
      P. McGinley. Ke-TF:90, Mc-WS:145
COVETOUSNESS: see GREED
COWARDICE: see also HUMOR - COWARDICE
   The Coward. E. Merriam. Ba-PO:204
   The Day of Battle. A. Housman.
      Cr-WS:90
   From the Greek of Julianus.
      W. Cowper. Sp-OG:49
   The Hero. S. Sassoon. Co-RM:208
   How Can a Man Die Better.
      Tyrtaeus. Pa-SG:6
   If You Are Lazy. Ho-SD:13
   Mourn Not the Dead. R. Chaplin.
      Al-VBP:1147, Ba-PO:146, Cr-WS:120,
      Kr-OF:117
   On Freedom. J. Lowell.
      Mc-WK:185, Vi-PP:66
   Skipper Ireson's Ride. J. Whittier.
      Co-SS:147, Fe-PL:45, Hi-TL:73,
      Sh-AP:40, Sp-OG:226
   Song of Reproach. Bi-IT:63
   Strong Men, Riding Horses. G. Brooks.
      Ad-PB:157
COWBOYS: see also BALLADS, COWBOY;
   CATTLE; DIALECTS, WESTERN;
   HUMOR - COWBOYS; RANCH LIFE;
   RODEOS
   Across the Range. Fi-BG:175
   An Afternoon like This. Fi-BG:82
   Bitter Creek. Fi-BG:83
   Braggin' Bill's Fortytude.
      C. Hallock. Fi-BG:79
   The Broncho Buster. Fi-BG:89
   Buckskin Sam's Tribute to Texas
      Jack. Fi-BG:174
   The Bullwhacker. Co-RM:18
   The Campfire Has Gone Out.
      B. Arnold. Fi-BG:106
   The Closing of the Rodeo. W. Smith.
      Br-TC:395, Ho-LP:73, Mc-WS:111,
      Mo-SD:70, Sh-RP:306
   Cowboy. J. Antrobus. Fi-BG:73

The Cowboy. J. Antrobus.
   Fe-FP:434, Fi-BG:122, Se-PR:148
The Cowboy. Fi-BG:71
A Cowboy Dance. N. Bachman.
   Fi-BG:167
Cowboy Dance Call. Fi-BG:170
Cowboys: One. R. McKuen. Pe-M:66
Cowboys: Two. R. McKuen. Pe-M:67
Cowboys: Three. R. McKuen. Pe-M:68
The Cowboy's Life. J. Adams.
   Ar-TP3:35, Au-SP:152, Br-AF:152,
   Hu-MP:153
Cowboy's Salvation Song. R. Carr.
   Fi-BG:191
The Cowboy;s Wishes. D. White.
   Fi-BG:72
Doney Gal. Fi-BG:165
Empty Saddles. Fi-BG:192
Git Along, Cayuse. H. Knibbs.
   Fi-BG:202
The High Loping Cowboy. C. Fletcher.
   Fi-BG:76
Idaho Jack. J. Lee. Fi-BG:90
Lament for the Cowboy Life.
   J. Mitchell. Co-RM:21
A Living Pearl. K. Rexroth.
   Wi-LT:798
Mongolian Pastoral. Hs-TC:446
Night Herding Song.
   H. Stephens. Sh-RP:79
Old Blue. R. Coffin. Rd-OA:79
On Salt Plains. D. Coldiron.
   Fi-BG:47
On the Trail from a Puncher's Point
   of View. Fi-BG:149
Passing of the Wrangler. H. Fellow.
   Fi-BG:151
The Philosophical Cowboy.
   J. H. S. Fi-BG:148
The Poor Lonesome Cowboy. Fi-BG:147
Proud Riders. H. Davis. Co-RM:24
Ranch Life, or Idyl of the Plains.
   Fi-BG:78
The Range Rider's Soliloquy.
   Fi-BG:194
Rodeo. E. Lueders. Co-RM:24,
   Du-RG:133
Run Little Dogies. Fi-BG:156
The Sick Stockrider. A. Gordon.
   Hi-FO:233
Silver Screen. L. Clark. Pa-RE:80
The Stampede. F. Miller. Fi-BG:159
The Streets of Laredo. Co-RM:28,
   Er-FA:337, Gr-CT:137, Gr-GB:321,
   Hi-TL:162, Mc-WK:169, Mc-WS:153
Texas. A. Lowell. Br-AF:143
A Texas Idyl. Fi-BG:81
Texas Trains and Trails. M. Austin.
   Ar-TP3:85, Au-SP:154
The Trail Herd. Fi-BG:145
Tywater. R. Wilbur. Ha-PO:124,
   Wi-LT:593

COWBOYS — cont'd.
Vaquero. E. Dorn. Kh-VA:29
When Broncho Jack Was Spliced.
    J. Adams. Fi-BG:172
Whiskey Bill. Co-RM:13
Whoopee Ti Yi Yo, Git Along Little
    Dogies. J. Lomax. Ar-TP3:34,
    Fe-FP:435, Fi-BG:157, 158,
    Hu-MP:209, Mc-WK:72
Wild West. R. Boylan. Du-SH:134
COWPER, WILLIAM
Cowper. N. Nicholson. Pl-ML:120
COWS: see also BULLS; BUTTER; CHEESE;
    HERDING; HUMOR - COWS; MILK
Birthday Gifts. L. Scott. Br-BC:99
A Blessing on the Cows.
    S. O'Sullivan. Co-PI:166
Buttercup Cow. E. Randall.
    Ar-TP3:74
Calling the Cows Home.
    J. Ingelow. Gr-TG:51
Charlie Warlie. Mo-MGT:25
Colly, My Cow. Na-EO:128, Rv-ON:33
Concert Champêtre. F. O'Hara.
    Kh-VA:16
Country Idyll. F. Cornford.
    Co-BBW:176, Co-PM:95
The Cow. J. Ciardi. Du-SH:120
The Cow. R. Lister. Ke-TF:337
Cow. H. Massingham. Ma-FW:227
The Cow. C. Rossetti. Mc-PR:121
The Cow. J. Stephens. Gr-EC:9
The Cow. R. Stevenson.
    Ar-TP3:74, Au-SP:43, Bl-OB:116,
    Bo-FP:70, Ch-B:50, Fe-FP:164,
    Hu-MP:187, Ox-BC:296, Sm-MK:153
The Cow in Apple Time. R. Frost.
    Fe-PL:365, Rd-OA:72, Un-MA:171
Cow Time. M. Shannon. Br-SS:9
Cows. J. Reeves. Bl-OB:118,
    Co-BBW:175, Co-PS:80, St-FS:85
Cushy Cow. L. Benét. Hu-MP:198
Cushy Cow, Bonny. Gr-GB:290,
    Mo-MGT:49, Sp-TM:13, Wr-RM:32
Drinking Time. D. O'Sullivan.
    Co-PI:164
The Farmyard. St-FS:90
Fetching Cows. N. MacCaig.
    Ma-FW:227
Four Stiff-Standers. Br-FF:(42),
    Gr-CT:13, Gr-GB:58, Ir-BB:50,
    Li-LB:168, Mo-MGT:157, Sp-TM:13
Go to the Barn for Courtesy.
    T. Coffin. Ke-TF:339
The Gracious and the Gentle Thing.
    R. Coffin. Rd-OA:84
Green Afternoon. F. Frost. Ar-TP3:76
The Hills. F. Cornford. Un-MB:308
I Stare at the Cow. P. Chase.
    Co-IW:42
I Would Like You for a Comrade.
    E. Parry. Ne-AM:20, Ox-BC:309

Johnny Armstrong. Rv-ON:32
Little Boy Blue. J. Ransom.
    We-PZ:36, Wi-LT:321
Lovely Big Cow. J. Morton.
    Pa-RE:67
Milk-White Moon, Put the Cows to
    Sleep. C. Sandburg. Fe-FP:164
Milking Time. E. Roberts. Bo-GJ:45,
    Fe-FP:239, Ma-FO:(11), Pa-RE:82
Milking Time. C. Rossetti. Hu-MP:310
Moo! R. Hillyer. Co-BBW:170,
    Ho-TH:33
The New Baby Calf. E. Chase.
    Ar-TP3:75, Au-SP:43
The New Calf. B. Bradbury.
    Ke-TF:338
Night and Noises. G. Foster.
    Le-M:86
The Old Woman's Three Cows. Mo-MGT:13
The Pasture. R. Frost. Al-VBP:1125,
    Ar-TP3:75, Au-SP:45, Bo-GJ:44,
    Co-BBW:162, Fe-FP:230, Hi-WP I:31,
    La-PP:23, La-PV:166, Li-LC:75,
    Mc-PR:121, Pa-RE:115, Pe-FB:2,
    Su-FVI:57, Th-AS:75, Un-MA:168
Philological. J. Updike. Co-EL:32
The Pleasant Cow. G. Hallock.
    Sh-RP:331
The Robin and the Cows. W. Howells.
    Un-GT:60
Thank You, Pretty Cow.
    A. and J. Taylor. Bo-FP:69,
    Hi-GD:9, Hu-MP:197, Ox-BC:123
There Was a Pig. Rv-ON:110
There Was an Old Man Who Said, "How."
    E. Lear. Bl-OB:17, Br-LL:22,
    Na-EO:103
This Little Cow Eats Grass.
    Mo-TL:17
Though This One's a Wow. Re-RR:20
Three Things. J. Auslander.
    Hu-MP:198
Who Stole the Nest? Ir-BB:87,
    St-FS:112
The Young Calves. R. Coffin.
    Ar-TP3:75
COYOTES
Coyote and Junco. Te-FC:77
The Coyote Sat. M. Tso. Ba-HI:101
Coyote's Night. P. George. Al-WW:128
Mad Coyote. Jo-TS:10
Quail Song. Da-SC:90, Le-OE:51
Rattlesnake Recitative. Da-SC:10
Song of Coyote Who Stole Fire.
    Da-SC:69
The Women and the Man. Te-FC:87
CRABBE, GEORGE
George Crabbe. E. Robinson.
    Pl-ML:113, Un-MA:122, Wi-LT:100
CRABS
Carmel Point. M. MacSweeney.
    Du-RG:75

A Dance.   Br-MW:34
The Dead Crab. A. Young. Rd-OA:157
Legend. T. Aida.   Sh-AM:110
Old Chang, the Crab. Bo-FP:279,
   Wy-CM:16
On the Shore. D. Baruch. Cr-SS:12
Sitting on the Stone, O Crab.
   Le-OE:47
Song of the Four Little Shell-
   Animals. Le-OE:41
Water Island. H. Moss. Ho-P:199
CRACKERS: see FOOD AND EATING
CRANBERRIES
The Cranberry Song. B. Reynolds.
   Em-AF:763
CRANE, (HAROLD) HART
Look, Hart, That Horse You Ride Is
   Wood. P. Vierick. Pl-ML:156
Orpheus. Y. Winters. Ca-VT:227
CRANES (BIRDS): see also HUMOR -
   CRANES (BIRDS)
Crane. J. Langland. St-H:109
The Dying Crane. M. Drayton.
   Rd-OA:190
A Hiroshima Lullaby. J. Langland.
   Ke-PP:131
I Hear the Crane. J. Sylvester.
   De-CH:624, Rd-OA:152
Ibycus. J. Heath-Stubbs.
   En-PC:165
In the Evening Calm. Ba-ST:40
My Dame Hath a Lame Tame Crane.
   Mother Goose. Pa-AP:34
Myth. Br-MW:81
Now at Evening. T. Takaori.
   Sh-AM:155
On the Dawn-Reddened. T. Takaori.
   Sh-AM:155
The Sandhill Crane. M. Austin.
   Ad-PE:39, Ar-TP3:57, Co-BBW:242,
   Gr-EC:173
Startled. Saigyo Hōshi. Ba-ST:39
When the Frost Lies White. Ba-ST:50
The Wolf and the Crane. E. Rees.
   Ar-TP3:81
CRANES AND DERRICKS
The Crane. C. Tomlinson.
   Un-MB:530
CRAPE MYRTLES
Crape Myrtles in the South.
   E. Tatum. Ke-TF:440
CRASHAW, RICHARD
On the Death of Mr. Crashaw.
   A. Cowley. Al-VBP:448
CRAVEN, TUNIS AUGUSTUS MACDONOUGH
Craven. H. Newbolt. Sp-OG:78
CRAWFISH: see CRAYFISH
CRAYFISH
The Crayfish. R. Wallace.
   Co-BBW:74, Mc-WK:45
CREATION: see also EVOLUTION; GOD;
   HUMOR - CREATION; OBATALA,

YORUBA GOD OF CREATION; SATIRE -
   CREATION; UNIVERSE
After the Flood Went Down. Bible.
   O.T. Genesis. Gr-TG:73
The Animals. E. Muir. Gr-CC:143,
   Un-MB:342
At the Time That Turned the Beat. . . .
   Le-OE:97
At the Time when the Earth. . . .
   Le-OE:2
Atalanta in Calydon. A. Swinburne.
   Al-VBP:1040, Er-FA:82, Rv-CB:936
The Beginning, Part I. Te-FC:225
Beseeching the Breath. Bi-IT:25
The Book of How. M. Moore. Un-MA:577
Breathe on Him. Bi-IT:20
Chant. Tr-CB:57, Tr-US I:110
Continent's End. R. Jeffers.
   Ga-FB:312, Pl-IO:53
The Cosmic Fabric. Y. Polonsky.
   Pl-EI:17
Cosmogony. Tr-US II:106
The Creation. C. Alexander.
   De-TT:36, Fe-FP:260, Gr-TG:22,
   Hu-MP:286, Ox-BC:200
The Creation. J. Johnson.
   Ad-PB:3, Ar-TP3:214, Ga-FB:152,
   Ga-S:6, Hi-WP I:141, Jo-SA:60,
   Pe-M:76, Un-MA:149
The Creation. Te-FC:275
The Creation According to Coyote.
   S. Ortiz. Ni-CD:144
Creation Chant. Tr-US II:79
Creation Myth. Tr-US I:159
The Creation of Man. Ab-MO:7
The Creation of the Earth. Da-SC:69
The Creator. Be-AP:19
The Cussitaws Come East. Bi-IT:13
Dead Cow Farm. R. Graves. Li-TU:244
A Different Image. D. Randall.
   Ra-BP:142
Ducks. F. Harvey. Co-BBW:163
Emergence Song. Bi-IT:10
First Man Was the First to Emerge.
   Bi-IT:9, Da-SC:68
A Forest Hymn. W. Bryant. Sh-AP:23
The Fourth God. C. Smith. Sm-PT:83
Fragment from the Child-Naming
   Rites. Br-MW:77
From the Walum Olum. Br-MW:100
Genesis. Bible. O.T. Genesis.
   Pl-IO:14
Genesis A. Ma-YA:8
Glorious the Sun in Mid-Career.
   C. Smart. Sm-LG:376
God's First Creature Was Light.
   W. Welles. Pl-IO:17
He Wove the Strands of Our Life.
   Bi-IT:8
The Heart. F. Thompson. Pa-GTB:399,
   Un-MB:79
Hymn. Caedmon. Ma-YA:7

CREATION — cont'd.
  In the Beginning. D. Thomas.
    Tr-MR:242
  Incantation Used by Rangitokona
    to Create Man. Tr-US II:120
  Job. Bible. O.T. Job. Pl-IO:39
  The Lamb. W. Blake. Ox-BC:85
  Look, How Beautiful. R. Jeffers.
    Tr-MR:148
  The Makers. R. Kell. Co-PI:82
  The Making of Birds. K. Tynan.
    Re-BS:54
  On Man. W. Landor. Ox-BN:185
  Over the Water. Bi-IT:14
  Paradise Lost. J. Milton.
    Al-VBP:410
  Popul Vuh. Da-SC:164
  Praise of Created Things.
    St. Francis of Assisi. Fe-FP:259
  Praise the Lord, O My Soul!
    Bible. O.T. Psalms. Gr-TG:86
  Prayer. Bi-IT:29
  The Princess. A. Tennyson.
    Pl-IO:33
  Reward. I. Barbu. Mc-AC:64
  The Rich Earth. Bible. O.T.
    Psalms. Un-GT:245
  Rock. K. Raine. Pl-IO:42
  The Scribe. W. de la Mare.
    Sm-LG:35, Tr-MR:24
  Shells. K. Raine. Pl-IO:43
  The Song of Bekotsidi. Da-SC:67
  The Song of Creation. Al-PI:11
  Song of Creation. Bi-IT:4,
    Ho-SD:52
  Song of the Flood. Da-SC:67
  Song of the Sun and the Moon.
    Da-SC:68, Le-OE:3
  Spell of Creation. K. Raine.
    Mc-WK:16, Sm-LG:238
  Spring Festival Songs, II.
    Tr-US II:172
  Stars. F. Edsall. Th-AS:88
  The Sun. F. Thompson. Un-MB:82
  Tahitian Chant of Creation.
    Tr-US II:67
  That Nature Is a Heraclitean Fire
    and of the Comfort of the
    Resurrection. G. Hopkins.
    Pa-GTB:396
  Then He Descended. Bi-IT:3
  These Bones Gwine to Rise Agin.
    Ga-S:24
  They Stooped Over and Came Out.
    Bi-IT:11
  This Newly Created World. Bi-IT:5
  Thus It Is Told. Bi-IT:6
  The Tiger. W. Blake. Al-VBP:616,
    Ar-TP3:80, Bl-OB:111, Co-BBW:209,
    Co-RG:146, De-CH:91, Er-FA:234,
    Fe-FP:178, Fe-PL:366, Ga-FB:95,
    Ga-S:12, Gr-CT:115, Ha-PO:116,
    Hi-WP II:171, Hu-MP:201, Li-SR:8,
    Ma-YA:129, Mc-PR:158, Ox-BN:23,
    Pl-EI:19, Rd-OA:118, Rv-CB:576,
    Sm-LG:68, Tu-WW:108, Un-GT:36
  To the Envious. Pl-EI:25,
    Tr-CB:53, Tr-US I:53
  To the Stars. T. Arghezi. Mc-AC:29
  Up from the Bed of the River.
    J. Johnson. Pl-EI:132
  Upward Going! Bi-IT:12
  The Walam Olum. Da-SC:127
  Wealth. R. Emerson. Pl-IO:34
  Whale. W. Benét. Sm-PT:22, Un-MA:323
  When the Raven. Ho-SD:80
  The Wonderful World. W. Rands.
    Ar-TP3:217, Fe-FP:260, Hu-MP:284
CREATIVITY: see GENIUS; IMAGINATION;
    INSPIRATION
CRECY, BATTLE, 1346
  The Eve of Crécy. W. Morris. Gr-SS:95
CREEDS: see also FAITH
  Credo. E. Debs. Kr-OF:117
  Credo. R. Jeffers. Un-MA:366
  Credo. G. Johnson. Ad-PB:23
  Creed. W. Lowenfels. Hu-PN:516
  His Creed. Hi-WP I:138
  My Creed. H. Walter. Er-FA:9,
    Fe-PL:311
  No Coward Soul Is Mine. E. Brontë.
    Al-VBP:925, Er-FA:459, Ox-BN:608,
    Pl-EI:4, Rv-CB:833
CREEK INDIANS: see INDIANS OF NORTH
    AMERICA - VERSE - MUSKOGEAN
CREMATION: see also HUMOR - CREMATION
  Cremation. R. Jeffers. Co-EL:75
  Cremation. Ya Hsüan. Pa-MV:149
  The Cremation Ground. Bha Vabhuti.
    Al-PI:37
  The Crematory. Chung Ting-wen.
    Pa-MV:78
CREOLES
  Creole Girl. L. Collins. Hu-PN:297
  Juba Dance. Ab-MO:14
  Mister Banjo. Ab-MO:52
CRETE
  The City. E. Jarrett. Sc-TN:111
  Death of an Aircraft. C. Causley.
    Ca-MB:115
CRICKET (GAME): see also HUMOR -
    CRICKET (GAME)
  Rythm. I. Smith. To-MP:175
  Songs from an Island in the Moon.
    W. Blake. Li-TU:24
CRICKETS
  Above the Chorus. Kyoshi. Ca-BF:9
  All Day the Cricket Waits to Sing.
    Wo-HS:(9)
  The Animal That Drank Up Sound.
    W. Stafford. Ca-VT:413
  The Ant and the Cricket. Aesop.
    De-TT:59, Un-GT:78

The Chirrupy Cricket. M. Thomas.
  Bo-FP:42
Cornwall. C. Bond. Le-M:33
The Cricket. Ir-BB:70
Cricket, Come Back! Le-OE:53
Crickets. H. Behn. It-HB:43
Crickets. D. McCord. Ja-PA:22,
  La-PV:145
A Game of Tag. Bo-FP:141,
  Ir-BB:85
The Grasshopper and the Cricket.
  L. Hunt. Bo-FP:273, Co-BBW:218,
  Ox-BN:220, Un-GT:77
The Halloween Concert. A. Fisher.
  Br-SS:70
In a Cornfield. E. Markham.
  Mc-PR:120
A Leaf Crashes Gently to the Ground.
  J. Hodgman. Le-M:125
The Little Mute Boy. F. Garcia
  Lorca. Le-SW:29
A Little Night Music. F. Stefanile.
  De-FS:188
A Little Yellow Cricket. Jo-TS:14
The Noisy Cricket. S. Watanabe.
  Ma-FW:102
Old Dame Cricket. Ch-B:61
On the Grasshopper and Cricket.
  J. Keats. Bo-FP:272, Co-BBW:228,
  Gr-EC:6, Ho-WR:66, Rd-OA:89,
  Rv-CB:741, Sp-OG:302, Un-GT:77
A Passing Shower. Ba-ST:35
Poor Crying Cricket. Kikaku.
  Be-CS:23
Splinter. C. Sandburg.
  Ar-TP3:185, Fe-FP:129, Sh-RP:82
Spring Cricket. F. Rodman.
  Br-SS:141, Fe-FP:128
Tonight in This Town. Be-CS:52
Trapped in a Helmet. Basho.
  Be-MC:12
CRIME AND CRIMINALS: see also
  ASSASSINATIONS; FINGERPRINTS;
  HUMOR - CRIME AND CRIMINALS;
  MURDER; OUTLAWS; PIRATES;
  THIEVES; VILLAINS AND VILLAINY
The Black Martyr. R. Dickens.
  La-IH:106
The Continuity. P. Blackburn.
  Ad-CI:105
Cumnor Hall. W. Mickle.
  Al-VBP:599, Ox-BB:670
Farewell. A. Housman. Un-MB:103
Jig Time: Not for Love.
  T. McGrath. Ca-VT:427
Jim Jones at Botany Bay.
  Co-RM:139, Gr-GB:257
Mary Arnold, the Female Monster.
  Gr-GB:271
Two Lean Cats. M. O'Higgins.
  Ad-PB:170, Hu-PN:350
Unwanted. E. Field. Ke-PP:78

We Real Cool. G. Brooks.
  Ab-MO:96, Ad-PB:157, Be-MA:81,
  Bo-HF:106, Gr-BT:22, Ha-TP:21,
  La-OC:59, Lo-TY:245
You Felons on Trial in Courts.
  W. Whitman. Rv-CB:853
CRIMEAN WAR, 1853-1856: see also
  NIGHTINGALE, FLORENCE
The Crimean War Heroes. W. Landor.
  Mc-WS:104
CRIPPLES: see also WAR WOUNDED
The Girl in the Lane.
  Mo-MGT:209, Mo-NR:30, Rv-ON:81,
  Wr-RM:47
Here Lives the Jewish People.
  H. Leivick. Ho-TY:120
The Hunchback in the Park.
  D. Thomas. Br-TC:437, Un-MB:504
O for Doors to Be Open. W. Auden.
  Al-VBP:1226
Second Avenue Encounter.
  R. Patterson. Jo-SA:53
Three Crooked Cripples. Rv-ON:52
CRISPIN, SAINT
King Henry V. W. Shakespeare.
  Co-RM:200, Mc-WS:100
CRITICS AND CRITICISM: see also
  HUMOR - CRITICS AND CRITICISM;
  SATIRE - CRITICS AND CRITICISM
A Choice of Weapons. S. Kunitz.
  Wi-LT:749
The Conundrum of the Workshops
  R. Kipling. Un-MB:131
The Crystal. S. Lanier. Sh-AP:133
Epistle to Dr. Arbuthnot. A. Pope.
  Al-VBP:539, Gr-CT:435
An Essay on Criticism. A. Pope.
  Al-VBP:530, Ma-YA:116
Extempore to Voltaire Criticizing
  Milton. F. Young. Al-VBP:521
The Honor Done to Poets of Old
  and Modern Poets. T. Heywood.
  No-CL:13
In Memory of W. B. Yeats.
  W. Auden. Gr-CT:431
On Being Chosen Poet of Vermont.
  R. Frost. Pl-ML:25
On Censure. J. Swift. Rv-CB:494
On Re-Reading the Complete Works
  of an Elder Poet. W. Scott.
  Pl-ML:45
On the Oxford Book of Victorian
  Verse. H. MacDiarmid.
  Un-MB:360
Sonnet 121. W. Shakespeare.
  Rv-CB:244
Terence, This Is Stupid Stuff.
  A. Housman. Ma-YA:224,
  Un-MB:100, Wi-LT:63
To a Poet, Who Would Have Me Praise
  Certain Bad Poets. W. Yeats.
  Co-PI:203, Pl-ML:60

CRITICS AND CRITICISM — cont'd.
  To Christopher North. A. Tennyson.
    Co-FB:337, Co-PM:26, Na-EO:117
  Tyrannic Love. J. Dryden.
    Al-VBP:492
  Untitled. D. Hine. Br-TC:188
  What I Think of Hiawatha. J. Morris.
    Li-SR:61
  When None Shall Rail. D. Lewis.
    Rv-CB:502
CROCKETT, DAVID (DAVY): see also
  THE ALAMO
  The Defence of the Alamo.
    J. Miller. Pa-OM:173
CROCODILES: see also HUMOR —
  CROCODILES
  The Bestiary. W. Benét. Rd-OA:126
  A Crocodile. T. Beddoes.
    Co-BBW:84
  He Who Bathes among Crocodiles.
    Le-OA:40
  How Doth the Little Crocodile.
    L. Carroll. Ar-TP3:125, Au-SP:233,
    Bl-OB:116, Bo-FP:88, Br-SM:89,
    Ch-B:83, Er-FA:209, Fe-FP:352,
    Gr-EC:9, Hu-MP:455, La-PP:55,
    Li-LC:25, Li-SR:98, Lo-LL:34,
    Ma-YA:214, Sm-LG:91, Un-GT:70
  Old Praise Song of the Crocodile.
    Tr-US I:84
  Ombrure Calls Up the Forest Spirits.
    Tr-US I:60
  Silent Logs Floating. M. Goodson.
    Le-M:90
CROCUSES
  The Crocus. W. Crane.
    Au-SP:347, Bo-FP:214, Br-SG:6
  Crocus. S. Day. Hu-MP:248
  The Crocus. N. Nicholson. Go-BP:113
  Crocuses. Jösa. Ar-TP3:202,
    Hu-MP:248
  Secrets. L. Hewitt. Bo-FP:240
  Since You Are One Who Plainly
    Knows about Plants. Re-RR:98
CROMWELL, OLIVER: see also HUMOR —
  CROMWELL, OLIVER
  Cromwell Dead. A. Marvell.
    Al-VBP:460, Gr-CT:379
  Curfew Must Not Ring Tonight.
    R. Thorpe. Fe-FP:559
  A Horatian Ode upon Cromwell.
    A. Marvell. Al-VBP:459, Pa-GTB:51
  Jonas Kindred's Household.
    G. Crabbe. Ox-BN:15
  To the Lord General Cromwell.
    J. Milton. Al-VBP:407
THE CROSS: see also JESUS CHRIST —
  CRUCIFIXION
  At a Calvary near the Ancre.
    W. Owen. Tr-MR:187
  The Calvaries. P. Williamson.
    Ls-NY:108

Cross Talk. C. Cusack. Ls-NY:88
The Dream of the Rood. Ga-S:153
The Holy Cross. R. Crashaw.
  Ga-S:167
The Making of the Cross.
  Brother Antoninus. Ca-VT:351
To a Crucifix. A. Wickham.
  Un-MB:279
CROSSBILLS
  Winter in Vermont. H. Carruth.
    Ca-BP:41
CROW INDIANS: see SIOUAN
  INDIANS
CROWDS: see also HUMOR - CROWDS;
  PEOPLE
  Crowds on a Train. H. Gibau.
    La-IH:20
  Give Me the Splendid Silent Sun.
    W. Whitman. Co-BN:232, Fe-FP:263,
    Mo-BG:20, Un-MA:84
  How to Walk in a Crowd. R. Hershon.
    Sc-TN:97
  In a Station of the Metro.
    E. Pound. Ad-CI:41, Ca-VT:83,
    Mo-BG:23, Sh-AP:173, Un-MA:294
  Music and Drum. A. MacLeish.
    Ho-TH:59, Tr-MR:186
  Night Game. R. Humphries.
    Mo-BG:28, Ni-JP:87
  Wanting to Be Walking among Crowds.
    S. Hagiwara. Sh-AM:50
CROWING: see also HUMOR - CROWING
  Chanticleer. W. Austin. Ga-S:77
  Spring Festival Songs. Tr-US II:172
CROWNS
  If You Know Any History. Re-RR:61
CROWS: see also HUMOR - CROWS;
  ROOKS
  Absolutes. G. Keyser. Du-RG:23
  Always with Us! - the Black
    Preacher. H. Melville. Re-BS:51
  The Answer. J. Wheelock. Ha-WR:80
  Beauty. Bashō. Au-SP:340
  The Carrion Crow. T. Beddoes.
    Co-BBW:250, Co-PM:26,
    Ho-WR:211, Rv-CB:773
  A Carrion Crow Sat on an Oak.
    Bl-OB:21, Li-LB:98, Mo-MGT:164,
    Mo-NR:132, Sm-MK:181, Wr-RM:29
  A Cautious Crow. Basho. Be-CS:35
  The Crow. Mrs. Alexander.
    Bo-FP:81
  The Crow. W. Canton. Un-GT:65
  The Crow. J. Clare. Hi-WP I:27
  The Crow. W. Müller. Un-R:119
  The Crow. P. Page. Do-WH:90
  The Crow. H. Thoreau. Re-BS:50
  Crow. M. Van Doren. Rd-OA:60
  The Crow. Ca-MU:8
  Crow. Ca-MU:13

Crow, with Shiny Clothes.
B. Jones.   Ba-HI:19
The Crows.   L. Drake.   Du-RG:24
Crows.   D. McCord.   Ad-PE:18,
Ar-TP3:56, Du-RG:25, La-PV:132,
La-RM:130, Tu-WW:88
The Crows.   D. McCord.   Un-MA:493
The Crows.   Gr-GB:62, Mo-MGT:185
Crow's Ditty.   Gr-GB:61
The Cry. M. Perlberg.   Co-PM:138
Detestable Crow! Bashö. Ca-BF:41
Dream Songs, III.   Tr-US II:224
Dust of Snow.   R. Frost.   Ad-PE:19,
Ar-TP3:212, Hi-MP I:4, La-PV:133,
Mo-TS:22, Re-BS:52, Tu-WW:42
Flapping into a Fog.   Gyodai.
Be-MC:53
Flight. G. Johnston.   Do-WH:66
The Frog and the Crow. Gr-GB:67
The Great Black Crow. P. Bailey.
Co-BBW:233
Hokku Poems.   R. Wright. Bo-AN:105
Horsey Gap.   Gr-GB:172
How Many Nights. G. Kinnell.
Ca-BP:45
In Air. P. Clarke.   Ab-MO:38
The Last Word of a Bluebird.
R. Frost.   Ar-TP3:187,
Bo-GJ:13, Fe-FP:286, Gr-TG:33,
Ir-BB:33, Ja-PA:8, Li-LC:55,
Pa-RE:58, Tu-WW:92
Legend of the Carrion Crow.
W. McAndrew.   Sa-B:80
Look at That Strutting Crow.
Issa.   Be-MC:21
The March Problem.   G. Garrett.
Ho-LP:36
My Sister Jane.   T. Hughes.
Ma-FW:95
Night Crow.   T. Roethke.
Ca-VT:287, Co-EL:38, Ho-LP:77,
Re-BS:52, Sh-AP:213
No Possum, No Sop, No Taters.
W. Stevens.   Ca-VT:38,
Sh-AP:162
River Roads. C. Sandburg. Ca-VT:22
Song of the Ghost Dance. Bi-IT:171
Tanka. M. Ota.   Sh-AM:141
The Twa Corbies.   De-CH:102,
Ha-PO:127, Ma-BB:132, Ma-FW:256,
Pa-GTB:90, Rv-CB:55, Sm-LG:268,
Sp-OG:115
A Warning to Crows.   De-PP:36
The Women and the Man. Te-FC:87
CRUCIFIXION: see THE CROSS; JESUS
CHRIST - CRUCIFIXION
CRUELTY: see also ANIMALS, CRUELTY
TO; BIRDS, CRUELTY TO; HUMOR -
CRUELTY
Adolescent with Bear.   A. Storni.
Be-UL:35
Annie of Lochroyan.   Ma-BB:202

Barbara Allen.   Al-VBP:55,
Er-FA:315, Mc-PR:156, Rv-CB:434,
Un-MW:112
Blow, Blow, Thou Winter Wind.
W. Shakespeare.   Al-VBP:187,
De-CH:232, De-TT:168, Er-FA:257,
Gr-CT:476, Hi-WP II:139, Ho-WR:172,
Mc-PR:50, Pa-GTB:26, Rv-CB:197
Child Waters.   Ox-BB:149
Cruel Frederick.   H. Hoffman.
Li-SR:24
The Cruel Mother.   Ox-BB:68
Deranged. P. Fiacc. Co-PI:42
A Divine Image.   W. Blake.
Ga-S:156, Gr-CT:436, Ox-BN:25
The Drowned Lady.   Gr-CT:139
1867.   J. Plunkett.   Co-PI:169
Four Thousand Days and Nights.
R. Tamura.   Sh-AM:125
Fraülein Reads Instructive Rhymes.
M. Kumin.   Li-SR:29
Gangrene. P. Levine. Ca-VT:628
The Golden Vanity.   Bl-OB:55,
Co-SS:193, De-CH:398, Fo-OG:10,
Ho-WR:128, Rv-CB:438
The Haystack in the Floods.
W. Morris. Ni-JP:41, Ox-BN:779
Hugh of Lincoln.   De-CH:408,
Ox-BB:317
In Memoriam.   A. Tennyson.
Ox-BN:500
Iris.   T. McNeill.   Sa-B:6
Iron Virgin. Kuo Mo-jo. Hs-TC:41
Jean Richepin's Song. H. Trench.
Co-PI:191, Co-PT:25, Gr-EC:127
Jellon Grame.   Ox-BB:164
Loneliness. J. Pomroy. Su-FVI:11
Man, the Man-Hunter. C. Sandburg.
Kr-OF:156
Man's Inhumanity to Man.
R. Burns.   Er-FA:274
Mary Arnold, the Female Monster.
Gr-GB:271
Millenium. J. Kohut. Lo-IT:67
My Last Duchess.   R. Browning.
Er-FA:374, Fe-PL:82, Ha-PO:39,
Ma-YA:200, Ni-JP:40, Ox-BN:545,
Pa-GTB:350, Rv-CB:817
On the Death of a Murderer.
J. Wain.   Cr-WS:113
On the Eyes of an SS Officer.
R. Wilbur.   Cr-WS:42
Parable. P. Bennett. Co-EL:137
Peter Grimes. G. Crabbe.
Hi-WP II:65
Prince Robert.   Ox-BB:203
Quietly I Shout.   A. Pratt.
Al-WW:110
Salmon-Fishing.   R. Jeffers.
Mo-SD:106
She Was a Pretty Little Girl.
R. de Ayada.   Fe-FP:473

CRUELTY — cont'd.
  Soldiers Bathing. F. Prince.
    Pa-GTB:528, Un-MB:486, Wi-LT:793
  Someone Is Beating a Woman.
    A. Voznesensky. Gr-BT:125
  Tanist. J. Stephens. Ls-NY:98
  To a Lady. W. Dunbar. No-CL:149
  To Phyllis, the Fair Shepherdess.
    T. Lodge. Al-VBP:133
  The True Story of Web-Spinner.
    M. Howitt. De-TT:122
  The Trumpeter of Fyvie. Ox-BB:349
  Vala or the Four Zoas. W. Blake.
    Al-VBP:621, Ox-BN:37
  The War-Song of Dinas Vawr.
    T. Peacock. Al-VBP:716,
    Ha-PO:220, Ho-WR:106, Mc-WS:105,
    Na-EO:110, Pa-OM:197
  Words. D. Quick. Ke-TF:129
CRUSADES
  Children's Crusade, 1939.
    B. Brecht. Ca-MB:106
  Choruses from "The Rock."
    T. Eliot. Gr-CC:112
  Crusader Chorus. C. Kingsley.
    Hi-FO:74
  Lepanto. G. Chesterton.
    Ga-FB:196, Hi-FO:119, Un-MB:205
  Loyal. F. Ticknor. Sp-OG:18
CRUSOE: see ROBINSON CRUSOE
CRYING: see also HUMOR — CRYING;
    TEARS
  Boys Don't Cry. L. Martinez.
    La-IH:80
  The Circle of Weeping.
    A. Gilboa. Me-PH:117
  Cry, Baby. Mo-NR:58, Un-GT:17,
    Wr-RM:58
  The Fable of the Piece of Glass
    and the Piece of Ice. Ox-BC:151
  Giant Bonaparte. Mo-MGT:166
  Mater Dolorosa. W. Barnes.
    De-CH:265
  A Small Discovery. J. Emanuel.
    Li-LC:13
  Weep You No More. Al-VBP:357,
    De-CH:266, Go-BP:145, Gr-CT:410
  The Weeping. F. Garcia Lorca.
    Le-SW:67
  When I Was Christened. D. McCord.
    Br-BC:29
  Winifred Waters. W. Rands.
    Ox-BC:237
  Youth. Le-M:162
CRYSTAL: see GLASS
CUBA
  Cuba Libre. J. Miller. Hi-TL:153
  A Dedication to Cuba. F. Charles.
    Sa-B:130
  Lament of the Slave. Ab-MO:54
  One Thousand Fearful Words for Fidel
    Castro. L. Ferlinghetti. Ca-VT:476
  Ten Years: 1959-1969.
    J. Carew. Sa-B:189
  Two Countries. J. Marti.
    Lo-TY:101
CUBA - HISTORY AND PATRIOTISM:
    see also CASTRO, FIDEL
  On a Monument to Marti.
    W. Roberts. Lo-TY:116
CUBANS
  The Cuban Emigrant. V. Alvarez.
    Ba-HI:20
CUBISM: see PICASSO, PABLO;
    SATIRE - CUBISM
CU CHULAINN, LEGENDARY CELTIC HERO
  Cuchulain Comforted. W. Yeats.
    Wi-LT:95
  The Death of Cuchulain.
    W. Yeats. Gr-CT:146
CUCKOOS: see also HUMOR - CUCKOOS
  Come, Come Away! R. Brome.
    Re-BS:22
  The Cuckoo. G. Hopkins.
    Co-BBW:244, Co-EL:26, Ma-FW:11,
    Un-MB:44
  The Cuckoo. Kodo. Le-MW:23,
    Ma-FW:10
  Cuckoo. A. Young. Gr-CT:49
  The Cuckoo. Gr-GB:60
  The Cuckoo. Co-BBW:253, Pa-RE:34
  The Cuckoo. Ir-BB:76, Li-LB:164,
    Mo-MGT:20, Mo-TB:92
  The Cuckoo. Gr-CT:49
  The Cuckoo. Rv-CB:433
  Cuckoo, if You Must. Soseki.
    Be-MC:37
  Cuckoo in the Pear-Tree.
    W. Rands. Re-BS:35
  Cuckoos. M. Kaneko. Sh-AM:62
  Cuckoos. A. Young. Gr-CT:50
  Cuckoo's Palace. W. Rands.
    Re-BS:32
  The Cuckoo's Song. Josui.
    Hu-MP:223
  The Fresh Air. H. Monro. De-CH:9
  A Great Time. W. Davies.
    Hi-WP I:1, Un-MB:178
  In the Leafy Treetops. Yakamochi.
    Ba-ST:29
  The Koocoo. De-CH:489, Gr-GB:60
  Little Gray Cuckoo. Basho.
    Le-MW:25
  The Living Spring. J. Taylor.
    De-TT:57
  On a Day when Jenkin. De-CH:489
  On Summer Nights. Tsurayuki.
    Ba-ST:29
  Our Clock. F. Eakman. Br-SS:6
  Song for a Little Cuckoo Clock.
    E. Coatsworth. Br-SS:6
  The Songs of Spring (II).
    Feng Hsüeh-feng.
    Hs-TC:368

Sumer Is Icumen In.   Al-VBP:2,
    Bo-FP:241, Fr-WO:74, Gr-CT:48,
    Gr-GB:40, Li-SR:123, Ma-FW:34,
    Ma-YA:25, Rv-CB:1
There, where the Skylark's Singing.
    Kyorai.   Be-MC:43
Three Cuckoo Rhymes.   De-TT:56
To the Cuckoo. M. Bruce. Al-VBP:601
To the Cuckoo. F. Townsend.
    Gr-CT:21
To the Cuckoo. W. Wordsworth.
    Er-FA:225, Fe-PL:353, Pa-GTB:247,
    Rv-CB:634, Un-GT:61
Turned Towards the Moon. Yakamochi.
    Ba-ST:35
When a Cuckoo Sings. Basho.
    Be-MC:8
Which Is the Bow?   Gr-GB:38
CUERNAVACA, MEX.
    Kid. R. Hayden.   Ad-CI:68
CULLEN, COUNTEE
    Countee Cullen. E. Maleska.
        Hu-PN:570
CULLODEN, BATTLE, 1746
    Lament for Culloden. R. Burns.
        Pa-GTB:119, Rv-CB:614
CULTURE: see also CIVILIZATION;
    HUMOR - CULTURE; SATIRE -
    CULTURE; SCHOLARS AND
    SCHOLARSHIP
    A Black Man's World. L. Loflin II.
        La-IH:109
    Coole Park and Ballylee, 1931.
        W. Yeats. Pa-GTB:430
CUMBERLAND (SHIP)
    The Cumberland and the Merrimac.
        Em-AF:443
    The Cumberland's Crew. Em-AF:442
    Maggie Mac. Em-AF:445
CUMBERLAND GAP
    Cumberland Gap. Br-AF:112
CUMULATIVE VERSE: see also
    DIMINISHING VERSE
    As I Was Going to St. Ives.
        Au-SP:26, Cl-DT:61, Ir-BB:54,
        Li-LB:168, Mo-MGT:172, Mo-NR:122,
        On-TW:29, Wi-MG:24, Wr-RM:16
    Black Monkeys. R. Ainsworth.
        St-FS:8
    Cottage. E. Farjeon. St-FS:72
    A Counting Rhyme. M. Stephenson.
        St-FS:9
    Craigbilly Fair.   Gr-CT:86,
        Gr-GB:230
    The Dilly Song. Gr-GB:28
    The Firefly. Pa-RE:68
    For Want of a Nail. Gr-EC:130,
        Ir-BB:134, Li-LB:166, Mo-MGT:132,
        Mo-NR:103, Un-GT:305, Wr-RM:101
    The House That Jack Built. Mother
        Goose. Au-SP:12, Fr-WO:12,
        Li-LB:140, Li-SR:131, Mo-MGT:30,
        Mo-NR:37, Wr-RM:68
I Bought Me a Cat.   Su-FVI:52
In Come de Animuls Two by Two.
    Gr-GB:75
The Johnnycake.   Hu-MP:19
The Key of the Kingdom. Bl-OB:158,
    De-CH:3, Er-FA:202, Gr-EC:292,
    Ho-P:107, Mo-MGT:133, Re-TW:32,
    Rv-CB:31, Sm-LG:237, Sp-AS:(10)
The Little Girl That Lost a Finger.
    G. Mistral. Fe-FP:491
A Man of Words. Bl-OB:156,
    De-TT:72, Er-FA:274, Gr-EC:208,
    Rv-CB:450, Rv-ON:115, Sm-LG:235,
    Sp-AS:35
Milking Pails. De-CH:67
Not Ragged-and-Tough. Gr-CT:4
The Old Lady Who Swallowed a Fly.
    Br-SM:105
Old Mother Hubbard.
    An-IP:(8), Au-SP:3, Fr-WO:21,
    Ir-BB:171, Li-LB:153, Mo-MGT:8,
    Mo-NR:108, Ox-BC:126, Pa-OM:336,
    Un-GT:102, Wi-MG:50, Wr-RM:43
Old Noah's Ark. Co-BBW:271
An Old Woman Was Sweeping Her House.
    Mother Goose. Li-LB:148,
    Mo-NR:68
On a Ruined House in a Romantic
    Country. S. Coleridge.
    Un-GF:16
One Old Ox. Gr-CT:31, On-TW:45
One, Two, Buckle My Shoe.
    Ar-TP3:104, Au-SP:21, Bo-FP:5,
    De-PO:14, Ir-BB:34, Mo-NR:31,
    On-TW:50, Wi-MG:30, Wr-RM:80
Pentagonia. G. Bates. Li-SR:133
The Robber. I. Eastwick. Br-SS:119
Spell of Creation. K. Raine.
    Mc-WK:16, Sm-LG:238
The Story of the Old Woman and Her
    Pig. Mo-MGT:68
Ten Little Dicky-Birds.
    A. Baldwin. St-FS:12
Ten Little Indian Boys.
    M. Hutchinson. Au-SP:153,
    Ir-BB:110
There Was an Old Woman. Su-FVI:24
The Train to Glasgow.
    W. Horsbrugh. Ir-BB:251
The Twelve Days of Christmas.
    La-PH:41, Li-LB:119, On-TW:46,
    Sh-RP:27
Visits to St. Elizabeths. E. Bishop.
    Ca-VT:320, Mc-EA:154
What's in There? De-CH:277,
    Ir-BB:143
The Yule Days. Gr-CT:415,
    Gr-GB:47, Rv-ON:121
See also Em-AF:11-15
CUNA INDIANS: see INDIANS OF CENTRAL
    AMERICA - VERSE - CHIBCHAN
CUPID
    Children of Love. H. Monro. Un-MB:235

CUPID — cont'd.
   Cupid and Campaspe. J. Lyly.
      Al-VBP:121, Ma-YA:60, Pa-GTB:31,
      Un-MW:37
   Cupid's Mistaken. M. Prior.
      Al-VBP:513
   Rosalind's Madrigal. T. Lodge.
      Al-VBP:131
   Song. J. Dryden. Al-VBP:478,
      Rv-CB:465
   Song to His Cynthia. F. Grevelle.
      Al-VBP:122
   There Is a Lady Sweet and Kind.
      Co-BL:79, De-CH:348, Er-FA:102,
      Rv-CB:260, Un-MW:160
   To Cupid. J. Suckling. Rv-CB:380
CURES: see REMEDIES AND CURES
CURFEW
   Curfew Must Not Ring Tonight.
      R. Thorpe. Fe-FP:559
CURIOSITY: see also HUMOR -
      CURIOSITY
   Bundles. J. Farrar.
      Ar-TP3:192, Bo-FP:182
   Curiosity. H. Behn. Au-SP:349
   A Dead Turk. Li Kuang-t'ien.
      Hs-TC:208
   From the Window of a Plane.
      A. Voznesensky. Ca-MR:71
   Hallo My Fancy. W. Cleland.
      De-CH:358
   I Wonder How Many People in the
      City. L. Cohen.
      Ad-CI:8, Co-EL:99, Co-PU:41
   Nature at Three. B. Breeser.
      Br-BC:46
   A New Friend. M. Anderson.
      Fr-MP:10, Mc-AW:13
   The Orient Express. R. Jarrell.
      Sh-AP:224
   The Package. A. Fisher.
      Au-SP:101
   Pandora. M. Livingston. Ne-AM:16
   Portrait of a Lady. W. Praed.
      No-CL:235
   The Rabbit. P. McIntyre. Le-M:96
   The Song of the Mad Prince.
      W. de la Mare. Bo-GJ:136,
      Gr-CC:75, Ox-BC:327, Sm-LG:287,
      Sm-MK:41
   When I Awoke. R. Patterson.
      Ad-PB:208, Hu-NN:113
CURSES: see also HUMOR - CURSES
   Alice Brand. W. Scott. Pa-OM:248
   Amor Aeternalis. C. Smith.
      De-FS:186
   Auguries of Innocence. W. Blake.
      Al-VBP:621, Ch-B:36, Co-BBW:278,
      Er-FA:69, Ga-FB:96, Ma-YA:130,
      Ox-BN:28, Pl-IO:5, Sh-RP:76,
      Sm-LG:67, Sm-MK:220, Un-GT:305

Babylon Revisited. I. Baraka.
   Ra-BP:214
The Ballad of Semmerwater.
   W. Watson. Bl-OB:81
Bruadar and Smith and Glinn.
   Co-PI:68, Mc-WS:86
By the Hoof of the Wild Goat.
   R. Kipling. Ox-BN:928
Clyde's Waters. Ox-BB:331
Coriolanus's Farewell. . . .
   W. Shakespeare. Mc-WS:90
Crazy Jane and the Bishop.
   W. Yeats. Wi-LT:88
The Cruel Mother. Ox-BB:68
Curs'd Is the Man. Homer.
   Ba-PO:169
The Curse. J. Donne. Rv-CB:300
Curse on People That Wish One
   Ill. Bi-IT:156
A Curse on the Closed Gate.
   J. Cousins. Co-PI:32
Curse Tabooing a Lake.
   Tr-US I:169
The Elder Tree. Gr-CT:166,
   Gr-GB:307
Emmy. A. Symons. Ox-BN:934
Evocation. H. King. De-FS:129
A Glass of Beer. J. Stephens.
   Co-FB:470, Mc-WS:83, Rv-CB:973,
   Un-MB:265
I Wish My Tongue Were a Quiver.
   L. Mackay. Mc-WS:92
An Imprecation Against Foes and
   Sorcerers. Al-PI:18
Insensibility. W. Owen.
   Ba-PO:xiii
Irish Curse on the Occupying
   English. M. MacEntee.
   Co-PI:112
The Jackdaw of Rheims. R. Barham.
   Pa-OM:322
Kehama's Curse. R. Southey.
   Ox-BN:180
Kempion. Ox-BB:56
The Lady of Shalott.
   A. Tennyson. Er-FA:339,
   Hi-WP I:59, Ho-WR:145, Sp-OG:128
The Lark. Gr-GB:61
Magic Formula Against Disease.
   Bi-IT:151
Malison of the Stone-Chat.
   Gr-GB:63
Nell Flaherty's Drake. Rd-OA:86
O Cat of Carlish Kind.
   J. Skelton. Gr-CT:118,
   Ha-PO:100, Na-EO:94, Rd-OA:105
Old Wife's Song. E. Farjeon.
   Sh-RP:15
Remonstrance. Rotman ag El-hadj Bekri.
   Tr-US I:134
Right Cheek! Left Cheek! De-CH:669

The Rime of the Ancient Mariner.
  S. Coleridge. Al-VBP:679,
  Bo-FP:301, Co-RG:60, Co-SS:131,
  De-CH:364, Er-FA:318, Fe-FP:147,
  Ga-FB:105, Gr-TG:61, Ha-PO:15,
  Hi-WP II:68, Ma-YA:146, Ni-JP:52,
  Ox-BN:139, Rv-CB:658, Sm-LG:312,
  Un-GT:30
The Sleeping Beauty. E. Sitwell.
  Ma-FW:189
A Spell to Destroy Life. Br-MW:111
The Stone. W. Kerr. De-FS:128
Swan Curse. A. Sullivan. Ls-NY:213
Tit for Tat. Mc-WS:93
To Secure Victory in Battle.
  Al-PI:18
To the Lord Chancellor. P. Shelley.
  Al-VBP:747
Traveller's Curse after Misdirection.
  R. Graves. Co-FB:475, Ho-LP:70,
  Un-MB:387, Wi-LT:369
Warning to Snake-Killers. R. Barlow.
  De-FS:12
Whoever It Was. Sophocles. Ba-PO:74
CUSTER, GEORGE ARMSTRONG
  Custer's Last Charge. F. Whittaker.
    Fe-PL:173, Hi-TL:37, Pa-OM:183
  Custer's Last Fight. Fi-BG:114
CUSTOMS AND DUTIES: see TARIFFS
CUTTLE FISH: see OCTOPUSES
CYCLAMENS
  Long Ago I Went to Rome. M. Furse.
    De-CH:578
CYNICISM: see also DISILLUSIONMENT;
    HUMOR - CYNICISM; MISANTHROPY
  All, All of a Piece Throughout.
    J. Dryden. Al-VBP:494,
    Co-EL:141, Gr-CT:349, No-CL:247,
    Rv-CB:469
  Another Day. I. Brown. Hu-PN:342
  The Beach in August. W. Kees.
    Mc-EA:48
  Blessing the Battle. W. Tappan.
    Cr-WS:140
  Bowery Motifs, I. A. Katz.
    Ho-TY:294
  Can't Understand. Yüan Shui-p'ai.
    Hs-TC:411
  Children's Rhymes. L. Hughes.
    Ad-BO:43, Ra-BP:86
  The Church on Comiaken Hill.
    R. Hugo. Ho-P:123
  The City. Yüan Shui-p'ai.
    Hs-TC:402
  Clarel. H. Melville. Ba-PO:91
  Dancing. A. Young. Mc-EA:88
  The Day of Battle. A. Housman.
    Cr-WS:90
  Documentary. R. Beum.   Cr-WS:130
  The Dodger. Em-AF:755
  Five Ways to Kill a Man. E. Brock.
    Cr-WS:145, Mo-TS:39

The Formalities. J. Ciardi.
  Cr-WS:143
The Four Zoas. W. Blake. Ho-P:257
The Fury of Aerial Bombardment.
  R. Eberhart. Ba-PO:178,
  Ca-VT:248, Sh-AP:209, Wi-LT:438
Hard Times.   Em-AF:767
Hugh Selwyn Mauberley. E. Pound.
  Ca-VT:84, Un-MA:301, Wi-LT:232
The Human Fold. E. Muir. Wi-LT:247
I Know a Man. R. Creeley. Bl-FP:25
In Humbleness. D. Hoffman.
  Cr-WS:139
The Invention of New Jersey.
  J. Anderson. Sc-TN:3
It Was a Goodly Co. e. cummings.
  Wi-LT:366
It's Cool. J. Sternberg. Ho-TY:196
Jehovah Buried, Satan Dead.
  E. Cummings. Pe-OA:147
The Last Laugh. W. Owen. Cr-WS:94
The Latest Decalogue. A. Clough.
  Al-VBP:926, Gr-CT:475, Ox-BN:609,
  Pa-GTB:358, Rv-CB:841
Like in the Movies. F. Eckman.
  St-H:53
Lullaby. E. Sitwell. Wi-LT:644
Mock On, Mock On. W. Blake.
  Ox-BN:26
The New Platitudes. R. Whittemore.
  Ba-PO:28
New Year's Eve. J. Berryman.
  Wi-LT:570
Ninth Philosopher's Song.
  A. Huxley. Al-VBP:1199
O Wearisome Condition. F. Greville.
  Al-VBP:124, Rv-CB:265
Octaves. E. Robinson. Sm-PT:143
Odyssey of a Slum. V. Howard.
  La-IH:124
Of the Great White War. T. Burke.
  Cr-WS:143
On a Shield Representing the Birth
  of Christ. Ba-PO:5
On a Very Young, Very Dead Soldier.
  R. Gillman. Cr-WS:101
On the Eve of New Wars.
  L. Untermeyer. Ba-PO:164
Our New National Anthem.
  W. Eggleston. Ba-PO:80,
  Cr-WS:155
Past Arenas, Sanctuaries. I. Brodsky.
  Bo-RU:19
Plan. Rod McKuen. Pe-M:3
Poem for the Subterranean Poor.
  D. di Prima. Kh-VA:53
Poems in Praise of Practically
  Nothing. S. Hoffenstein.
  Co-FB:492
Rastignac at 45. T. Gunn. Ha-TP:43
Red Atlantis. J. Haines. Sc-TN:77
Rising Five. N. Nicholson. To-MP:69

CYNICISM — <u>cont'd</u>.
  The Road of All Lives. Fang Ching.
    Hs-TC:388
  The Savage Century. C. Norman.
    Cr-WS:132
  The Scorner. T. U Tam'si.
    Lo-TY:149
  Sehnsucht. Corinna. Co-FB:495
  Shame. R. Wilbur. Cr-WS:173
  The Soul of Shanghai. Shao Hsün-mei.
    Hs-TC:127
  Spaniel's Sermons. C. Ellis.
    Cr-WS:138
  Spring 1942. R. Fuller. Wi-LT:705
  Strange Tales, Domestic Vintage.
    Yüan Shui-p'ai. Hs-TC:406
  There Was Crimson Clash of War.
    S. Crane. Cr-WS:158
  Time Is a Pair of Scissors.
    Wang Ching-chih. Hs-TC:44
  To Another Poet a Thousand Years
    Hence. C. Norman. Cr-WS:131
  To Meet, or Otherwise. T. Hardy.
    Ox-BN:836
  To Richard Wright. C. Rivers.
    Ad-PB:234, Be-MA:105, Bo-AN:177
  The Train Runs Late to Harlem.
    C. Rivers. Ad-PB:237
  Truth. AE. Un-MB:142
  Unending Sameness of Questionable
    Quality. E. Livingston.
    Sc-TN:145
  The Volunteer's Reply to the
    Poet. R. Campbell. Al-VBP:1222
  War Begets Poverty. F. Pastorius.
    Ba-PO:169
  Way Out West. I. Baraka. Ad-PB:252
  The Weaker the Wine. Su Tung P'o.
    Rx-OH:72
  We're Here Because. Ba-PO:93
  When after Many Battles Past.
    Ba-PO:170
  Why. L. Wolf. Ho-TY:222
  The Will. M. Halpern. Ho-TY:112
  The World Is a Beautiful Place.
    L. Ferlinghetti. Pe-M:10
  A Year Without Seasons.
    M. Williams. Hu-NN:68
CYNTHIA: see DIANA; MOON
CYPRESS TREES
  The Black Finger. A. Grimke.
    Ad-PB:15, Bo-AN:17
  Last Lauch. D. Young. Co-PU:148
CYPRUS
  The Fifth Sense. P. Beer.
    Ca-MB:120
CZECHOSLOVAKIA: see also
    CZECHOSLOVAKIAN VERSE
  Czecho-Slovakia. E. Millay.
    Cr-WS:45
  Poem to Czechoslovakia.
    M. Tsvetayeva. Ca-MR:139

CZECHOSLOVAKIAN VERSE
  A Boy's Head. M. Holub.
    Ma-FW:71
  Five Minutes after the Air Raid.
    M. Holub. Gr-BT:104
  A History Lesson. M. Holub.
    Gr-BT:127, Ma-FW:239
  Much Love. Bo-FP:295
  Ode to Joy. M. Holub. Gr-BT:150
  Rocking. Cl-DT:28
  St. Gregory's Day. Bo-FP:217
  Spring Song. Bo-FP:229
  Water Sprite. M. Holub.
    Su-FVI:18
CZOLGOSZ, LEON
  Zolgotz. Em-AF:462
DAEDALUS AND ICARUS
  Be Daedalus. N. Alba.
    Ad-PB:169, Hu-PN:329
  Daedalus and Icarus. L. Coxe.
    Ls-NY:228
  Icarus. R. Bottrall. Pa-GTB:503
  Musée des Beaux Arts. W. Auden.
    Br-TC:20, Er-FA:64, Ha-PO:223,
    Pa-GTB:510, To-MP:31, Wi-LT:467
  Visionary. D. Scott. Sa-B:202
  Winged Man. S. Benét. Un-MA:497
DAFFODILS
  Daffadowndilly. Ar-TP3:201
  Daffodils. W. Shakespeare.
    Ar-TP3:201, Br-SG:7, Tu-WW:54
  Daffodils. K. Sutton. La-GI:13
  Daffodils. W. Wordsworth.
    Al-VBP:657, Bl-OB:137, Bo-GJ:71,
    Bo-HF:48, Ch-B:59, Co-BN:56,
    Er-FA:258, Fe-FP:218, Ga-FB:22,
    Ha-PO:95, Hi-WP II:33, Hu-MP:252,
    Ke-TF:434, Li-SR:105, Ma-YA:140,
    Mc-PR:188, Ox-BN:65, Pa-GTB:259,
    Re-TW:102, Sm-MK:188, Sp-OG:287,
    Tu-WW:64, Un-GT:254
  Daffodils. Ar-TP3:201, Au-SP:306
  Daffodils over Night. D. Morton.
    Bo-FP:232
  Daffy-Down-Dilly. Mother Goose.
    Au-SP:307, Br-SG:7, Mo-MGT:190,
    Mo-NR:111, Sp-AS:32, Wr-RM:47
  Daffy-Down-Dilly. A. Warner.
    Hu-MP:253
  Echo's Lament for Narcissus.
    B. Jonson. Al-VBP:238,
    De-CH:236, Gr-CT:321
  For Easter. M. Millet. Ja-HH:23
  Growing in the Vale.
    C. Rossetti. Ar-TP3:201
  The Lent Lily. A. Housman.
    Co-PS:67, Hu-MP:250, Se-PR:71
  Spring Song. H. Conkling.
    Co-PS:57, Hu-MP:246
  To Daffodils. R. Herrick. Al-VBP:332,
    Bo-GJ:70, Co-BN:55, Hi-WP I:115,
    Ho-LP:94, Na-EO:15, Pa-GTB:91,
    Rv-CB:342

DAGGERS: see SWORDS
DAHLIAS
  Dahlias.   P. Colum.   Bo-GJ:81
  Frost To-Night.   E. Thomas.
    Sp-OG:360
DAHOMEY: see AFRICAN VERSE - EWE;
    AFRICAN VERSE - FON
DAIRYING: see BUTTER; COWS;
    HUMOR - DAIRYING; MILK
DAISIES
  And As for Me.   G. Chaucer.
    Al-VBP:17, De-CH:13
  August.   E. Wylie.   Un-MA:277
  Buttercups and Daisies.   M. Howitt.
    Ox-BC:159
  The Daisies.   B. Carman.   Co-BN:58
  The Daisies.   K. Greenaway.
    Hu-MP:261
  Daisies.   F. Sherman.   Ch-B:88
  Daisies.   A. Young.   Bo-GJ:241
  Daisy.   L. Reiss.   La-GI:12
  The Daisy.   A. Tennyson.
    Ox-BN:489
  Daisy.   W. Williams.   Un-MA:257
  The Daisy.   M. Zaturenska.
    Un-MA:559
  The Daisy.   Bo-FP:233
  Daisy's Song.   J. Keats.   Co-BN:58
  Double Red Daisies.   R. Graves.
    Bo-FP:13
  For the Candle Light.   A. Grimke.
    Hu-PN:55
  In a Child's Album.
    W. Wordsworth.   Bo-FP:232,
    Ch-B:17, Ox-BN:92
  The Second Brother.   T. Beddoes.
    De-CH:487
  The Sun Is Today.   I. Muller.
    Mo-MI:64
  Thoughts of a Little Girl.
    M. Enriqueta.   Fe-FP:489
  To a Daisy.   A. Meynell.   Un-MB:61
  To a Mountain Daisy.   R. Burns.
    Co-BN:57, Fe-PL:374, Hu-MP:259,
    Sp-OG:289
  To the Daisy.   W. Wordsworth.
    Pa-GTB:260
  Villanelle of Marguerites.
    E. Dowson.   Un-MB:150
  With a Daisy.   E. Dickinson.
    Pl-IO:141
DAKOTA INDIANS: see SIOUAN INDIANS
DAMIEN DE VEUSTER, JOSEPH
    (FATHER DAMIEN)
  Father Damien.   J. Tabb.   Sh-AP:136
DAMS
  Big Dam.   W. Moses.   Br-AF:188
  The Dam.   P. Dickinson.   Co-PT:165
  The Fish Counter at Bonneville.
    W. Stafford.   Br-AF:157
  The Song of Cove Creek Dam.
    Em-AF:757

DAMSON TREES: see PLUM TREES
DANCERS AND DANCING: see also
    BALLET; HUMOR - DANCERS AND
    DANCING; SATIRE - DANCERS
    AND DANCING; SQUARE DANCING
  African Dance.   L. Hughes.
    Fe-FP:480, Sh-RP:8, Th-AS:159
  Bailada.   A. Nunez.   Pa-SG:66
  A Ballad of Remembrance.   R. Hayden.
    Ad-PB:115, Bo-AN:109, Hu-PN:291,
    Ra-BP:131
  Ballad of the Ten Casino Dancers.
    C. Meireles.   An-TC:39
  Beg-Innish.   J. Synge.   Un-MB:180
  Boogie Chant and Dance.   Bu-DY:67
  Bottled: New York.   H. Johnson.
    Ad-PB:104
  Buckdancer's Choice.   J. Dickey.
    Hu-PN:579
  Buffalo Girls.   Gr-EC:118
  By the Moon.   T. Ravenscroft.
    De-CH:111
  Celebration.   A. Lopez.   Al-WW:3
  Charlie Chaplin Went to France.
    Er-FA:499
  Cottage.   S. O'Sullivan.
    Co-PI:165
  Cowboy Dance Song.   Fi-BG:169
  The Dance.   T. Campion.   Sm-LG:43
  The Dance.   R. Thomas.   Go-BP:118
  The Dance.   W. Williams.
    Bo-GJ:137, Sh-AP:168, Sm-LG:44,
    Wi-LT:200
  Dance Figure.   E. Pound.   Un-MA:294
  Dance, Little Baby.   A. Taylor.
    De-PO:6, Gr-EC:119, Ox-BC:120,
    Wr-RM:101
  Dance of the Abakweta.   M. Danner.
    Ad-PB:134, Be-MA:88, Bo-AN:154,
    Hu-NN:30, Hu-PN:163
  Dance of the Animals.   Do-CH:(44),
    Le-OE:21
  Dance Song.   Tr-US I:130
  Dance Song in Praise of a Dancer.
    Tr-US I:88
  Dance Songs, I.   Tr-US II:163
  Dance Songs, III.   Tr-US I:28
  Dance Steps.   Gr-EC:118
  The Dancer.   Koma Doube Pio.
    Tr-US I:192
  The Dancer.   I. Pillat.   Mc-AC:58
  The Dancer at Cruachan and Cro-
    Patrick.   W. Yeats.   Pl-US:100
  Dancing.   Alex M.   Le-M:68
  Dancing.   Yang Kuei-Fei.
    Fe-FP:481
  The Dancing Seal.   W. Gibson.
    Co-PM:68, Pa-OM:289
  Danse Macabre.   A. Schwab.   De-FS:174
  Dark Girl.   A. Bontemps.   Pe-SS:148
  The Deil's Awa wi' the Exciseman.
    R. Burns.   Al-VBP:649

DANCERS AND DANCING — cont'd.

The Desert. S. Crane. Wi-LT:119
The Dick Johnson Reel. J. Falstaff.
    Co-RM:14, Na-EO:94
Echoes of Childhood. A. Corbin.
    Hu-PN:491
Ecstasy. R. Taylor. Gr-SS:107
Elegy on the Death of Mme. Anna
    Pavlova. E. Meyerstein.
    Pl-US:119
The Elves' Dance. T. Ravenscroft.
    De-CH:111, De-TT:50, Fe-FP:373
Enchantment, II, Medicine Dance.
    L. Alexander. Ad-PB:59
Encouraging a Dancer.
    Tr-CB:18, Tr-US I:38
The Eve of Waterloo. G. Byron.
    Al-VBP:723, Er-FA:362, Ga-FB:205,
    Hi-FO:204, Ox-BN:243
The Fiddler of Dooney. W. Yeats.
    Ar-TP3:15, Pl-US:113, Sm-LG:42
For a Dance. E. Farjeon.
    La-PH:55
For Nijinsky's Tomb. F. Cornford.
    Pl-US:121
Four for Sir John Davies.
    T. Roethke. Pl-US:104,
    Un-MA:599
Full of the Moon. K. Kuskin.
    La-PP:25, La-PV:53
Gratiana Dancing. R. Lovelace.
    No-CL:41, Rv-CB:393
Great Things. T. Hardy.
    Pa-GTB:409
Green Grass. De-CH:191, Mo-MGT:171,
    Rv-ON:16
The Harlem Dancer. C. McKay.
    Ra-BP:59
Harp Music. R. Humphries.
    Pl-US:107
Hawicks Crossing. J. Stuart.
    De-FS:193
Hey, Nonny No! Al-VBP:353,
    De-CH:188, Gr-CT:83, Sm-LG:389,
    Sp-OG:280
Homage to Vaslav Nijinsky.
    J. Kirkup. Pl-US:120
I Am of Ireland. Gr-GB:164,
    Rv-CB:142, Sm-LG:141
I Am the Duke of Norfolk. Gr-GB:197
I Cannot Dance upon My Toes.
    E. Dickinson. Pl-US:116
In the Moonlight. N. O'Connor.
    Au-SP:298
The Inheritance. Ir-BB:122,
    St-FS:127
The Irish Dancer. Gr-BT:17
Jonathan Bing Dances for Spring.
    B. Brown. Br-SS:131
Juba Dance. Ab-MO:14
Kids. W. Stafford.   Du-SH:187

Legend of Ramapo Mountain.
    J. Palen.   De-FS:144
Let Us Be Seen.   De-CH:601
Life Is Motion. W. Stevens.
    Mo-SD:189
The Little Dancers. L. Binyon.
    De-CH:185, Un-MB:156
Little Ivory Figures Pulled with
    a String. A. Lowell.
    Al-VBP:1124
The Looking Glass. R. Kipling.
    Gr-CC:160, Na-EO:120
The Lost Dancer. J. Toomer.
    Ad-PB:34
Marrakech. R. Eberhart. Wi-LT:440
May-Pole Dance. Gr-GB:40,
    Hi-WP I:38
A Meeting. H. Heine.   Co-PM:89
Midsummer Magic. I. Eastwick.
    Ar-TP3:148
A Minuet on Reaching the Age of
    Fifty. G. Santayana. Er-FA:154
The Morris Dance. Pa-RE:97
Mu. Ma'u. Tr-US II:95
My Cousin German Came from France.
    Ir-BB:184, Sm-LG:46
My Feet Touch the Earth.
    Wo-HS:(53)
My Limbs I Will Fling. W. Strode.
    Rv-CB:361
My Papa's Waltz. T. Roethke.
    Ca-VT:286, Ha-PQ:71, Mc-FW:64,
    Mo-BG:79, Pe-OA:206, Pe-SS:12,
    Sh-AP:213, Wi-LT:478
New Strain. G. Starbuck. Br-TC:409
Old Dance Song. Tr-US I:10
The Old Woman from France.
    Wr-RM:52
On an Island. J. Synge. Un-MB:181
On the Coast of Coromandel.
    O. Sitwell. Un-MA:358
A Pavane for the Nursery. W. Smith.
    Bo-GJ:124, Co-BL:110, Co-PS:41,
    Un-MA:671
Phrases. J. Rimbaud. Ma-FW:100
A Piper. S. O'Sullivan.
    Ar-TP3:13, Co-PI:186, Co-PM:131,
    De-CH:185, Fe-FP:465, Hu-MP:147,
    La-PV:221
Poet to Dancer. B. Kavinsky.
    Pl-US:122
The Power of Music. Pindar.
    Pl-US:102
Praise of Beaches. Tr-US II:47
The Progress of Poesy. T. Gray.
    Al-VBP:566, Pa-GTB:132, Rv-CB:532
The Puppet Dreams. C. Aiken.
    Un-MA:425
Quick-Step. R. Creeley. Ca-VT:569
Radhadevi's Dance. Nayacandra Suri.
    Al-PI:53

Round about the Mushroom Ring.
  L. Haberly. Cl-DT:77
Rumba. J. Tallet. Lo-TY:102
Say There, Fellow. Bu-DY:63
The Sea Boy. W. de la Mare.
  Cr-SS:32
The Seven Fiddlers. S. Evans.
  Co-PM:57, Pa-OM:282
Shadow Dance. I. Eastwick.
  Ar-TP3:112, Au-SP:188, La-PP:75
Shake Off Your Heavy Trance.
  F. Beaumont. Al-VBP:299,
  Co-EL:151, Gr-CT:168, Pl-US:106,
  Rv-CB:326
Skip It and Trip It. De-CH:601
Slow Rhythm. E. Livingston.
  Sc-TN:147
Song for a Christmas Celebration.
  Tr-US I:31
Song for Girl Dancers. Tr-US I:163
Song from a County Fair. L. Adams.
  Bo-GJ:234
A Song of Dagger Dancing. Tu Fu.
  Pl-US:105
Song of the Priestess at a Victory
  Feast. Tr-US II:302
Sonnets to Orpheus - Second Part.
  R. Rilke. Pl-US:101
Strut Miss Sally. Bu-DY:60
The Swan. S. Spender. Pl-US:118
Tarantella. H. Belloc. De-CH:189,
  Hi-WP II:2, Li-SR:5, Pa-HT:105,
  Sm-LG:45, Th-AS:164, Un-MB:167
Theme One: The Variations.
  A. Wilson. Ad-PB:491
There'd Be an Orchestra.
  F. Fitzgerald. Bo-GJ:135,
  Co-EL:152
Throwing Them Up to the Moon.
  Le-MW:124
To Dance in a Loving Ring.
  M. Korte. Sc-TN:114
To Potapovitch. H. Crane.
  Pl-US:117
The Twist. E. Braithwaite.
  Ab-MO:13
Under the Greenwood Tree. Gr-GB:44
Undersea. M. Chute. Ja-PC:54,
  La-PP:42
Upon His Mistress Dancing.
  J. Shirley. Mc-WS:66, No-CL:188
Vaudeville Dancer. J. Wheelock.
  Pl-US:112
A Waltz in the Afternoon.
  B. Bentley. Co-BL:22
Waltzing It. W. W. Moncrieff.
  Pl-US:106
The Waters of Life. H. Wolfe.
  Un-MB:304
We Dance like Ella Riffs.
  C. Rodgers. Ad-PB:431

When a Ring's Around the Moon.
  M. Carr. Ar-TP3:148
When Trouble Comes to Me.
  Wo-HS:(53)
When Young Melissa Sweeps.
  N. Turner. Fe-FP:46
Where Shall We Dance? G. Mistral.
  Pa-SG:119
Where Shall Wisdom Be Found?
  Euripides. Pa-SG:186,
  Pl-US:108
Where the Hayfields Were.
  A. MacLeish. Ha-LO:80
The Winter's Tale.
  W. Shakespeare. Pl-US:102
The Witches' Ballad. W. Scott.
  De-CH:306, Na-EO:24
Women's Song at a Dance Festival.
  Tr-US I:209
Zalka Peetruza. R. Dandridge.
  Ad-PB:19
DANDELIONS: see also HUMOR -
  DANDELIONS
The Beatific Vision.
  G. Chesterton. Tr-MR:244
Casual Gold. M. Uschold.
  Au-SP:348, Ha-YA:30
Dandelion. H. Conkling.
  Ar-TP3:206, Br-SG:26, Fe-FP:219,
  Hu-MP:257, Ir-BB:10, La-PV:165
The Dandelion. Bo-FP:269
Dandelions. M. Chute. Br-BC:102,
  Mc-AW:67
Dandelions. F. Frost. Ar-TP3:206
Dandelions. W. Stanton. Pe-OA:282
Ho, Dandelion! M. Dodge. Mc-PR:200
Taking Out Jim. J. Walsh.
  Pa-RE:52
To the Dandelion. J. Lowell.
  Fe-FP:220, Hu-MP:254
The Young Dandelion. D. Craik.
  Hu-MP:256, Sh-RP:156, Un-GT:253
DANDLING RHYMES
Dance, Little Baby. A. Taylor.
  De-PO:6, Gr-EC:119, Ox-BC:120,
  Wr-RM:101
Dance to Your Daddy. Mother Goose.
  Ar-TP3:100, De-PO:6, Li-LB:10,
  Mo-MGT:181, Mo-NR:24, Mo-TL:86,
  Wr-RM:50
Diddle, Diddle, Dumpling.
  Bo-FP:37, De-PO:28, Ir-BB:191,
  Li-LB:71, Mo-CC:(21), Mo-MGT:36,
  Mo-TL:41, Wi-MG:13, Wr-RM:37
The Doggies Gaed to the Mill.
  De-CH:498, Mo-TL:40
A Farmer Went Trotting.
  Ar-TP3:122, Br-FF:(28), Gr-EC:285,
  Li-LB:144, Mo-MGT:129, Mo-NR:67,
  Na-EO:123, Wr-RM:123
Feetikin, Feetikin. Mo-TL:41

DANDLING RHYMES — cont'd.
  Here Goes My Lord.   Ir-BB:235,
    Mo-TL:81, Wr-RM:21
  How Many Days Has My Baby to
    Play? Mother Goose. Ar-TP3:183,
    Ir-BB:10, Mo-NR:8, Wr-RM:28
  Leg over Leg. Li-LB:83,
    Mo-NR:67, Mo-TL:39, Wr-RM:23
  My Kitten. Mo-TL:43, Wr-RM:53
  Old Farmer Giles. Ir-BB:37,
    Mo-MGT:213, Mo-TL:44
  Ride a Cock-Horse to Banbury Cross.
    Ar-TP3:100, Au-SP:15, Bo-FP:10,
    De-PO:8, Er-FA:507, Fr-WO:32,
    Ir-BB:11, Li-LB:10, Mo-MGT:149,
    Mo-NR:7, Mo-TL:77, Wi-MG:8,
    Wr-RM:30
  See-Saw, Sacradown. Bo-FP:115,
    De-PO:10, Gr-EC:238, Ir-BB:234,
    Mo-NR:20, Mo-TL:39
  This Is Bill Anderson. Mo-TL:42
  This Is the Way the Ladies Ride.
    Mother Goose. Ar-TP3:77,
    De-PO:10, Li-LB:11, Mo-MGT:189,
    Mo-NR:52, Mo-TL:81, Wi-MG:29,
    Wr-RM:102
  To Market, to Market. Mo-NR:17
  Up and down the Market. Mo-TL:39
DANGER: see also HUMOR - DANGER
  The Acrobat from Xanadu Disdained
    All Nets. D. Georgakas.
    Sc-TN:60
  At the Wood's Edge.   Bi-IT:161
  Babylon. L. Benét. De-FS:20
  Balloon. S. Tsuboi. Sh-AM:72
  Beyond the Chagres. J. Gilbert.
    Fe-PL:429
  Chorus. W. Auden. Pa-GTB:509,
    Un-MB:450
  Encounter in the Cage Country.
    J. Dickey. Ha-TP:102
  The Fear of Beasts. W. Meredith.
    Ha-TP:138
  Good Taste. C. Logue. Pa-RE:95
  Hazardous Occupations.
    C. Sandburg. Ho-LP:88
  In Love for Long. E. Muir.
    Wi-LT:256
  Irritable Song. R. Atkins.
    Bo-AN:170
  Jealousy. M. Coleridge.
    De-CH:180, Ox-BN:925
  Knock, Knock, Knock, Knock.
    On-TW:18
  Leap Before You Look. W. Auden.
    Ha-TP:137
  Loneliness. Tu Fu. Rx-OH:16
  No Man Exists. Do-CH:(16)
  No Worst, There Is None. G. Hopkins.
    Ke-PP:5, Ox-BN:870, Pa-GTB:395,
    Rv-CB:944, Un-MB:46, Wi-LT:49
  O Foolish Ducklings. Buson. Be-CS:59

On Middleton Edge. A. Young.
    Co-EL:68, Mo-SD:95
  Paper Men to Air Hopes and Fears.
    R. Francis. Du-SH:92
  Prophets for a New Day.
    M. Walker. Ra-BP:160
  The Rapid. C. Sangster. Do-WH:72
  Reconnaissance. A. Bontemps.
    Bo-AN:80, Bo-HF:54, Ra-BP:92
  The Rescue. D. Schmitz. St-H:190
  Sanctuary. E. Wylie. Un-MA:276
  A Storm at Sea. D. Valentin.
    Le-M:52, Le-WR:21
  Through Lane It Lay. E. Dickinson.
    Gr-SS:80
  To Become a Chief's Favorite.
    Do-CH:(16)
  The Way of Cape Race. E. Pratt.
    Do-WH:47
DANIEL: see also HUMOR - DANIEL
  Vision of Belshazzar. G. Byron.
    Co-RG:3, Hi-FO:30, Pa-OM:115
DANISH VERSE
  The Heather. S. Blicker. Pa-SG:172
  The Pearl. H. Andersen. Pa-SG:49
  The Plants Stand Silent round Me.
    J. Jorgensen. Ho-LP:22,
    Pa-SG:155
  There Is a Charming Land.
    A. Oehlenschlager. Fe-FP:467
DANTE ALIGHIERI
  Cervantes. E. Bentley.
    Co-FB:127, Na-EO:54
  Dante. W. Bryant. Al-VBP:768
  Litany of the Heroes. V. Lindsay.
    Tr-MR:166
  One Word More. R. Browning.
    Al-VBP:911
DAPHNE (NYMPH)
  Daphne. D. Galler. Ls-NY:317
  Daphne. S. Rodman. Hu-PN:543
  Daphne. M. Zaturenska. Gr-CC:93
  For Daphne at Christmas. J. Nims.
    St-H:157
DARKNESS: see also NIGHT
  August Night. S. Teasdale.
    Un-MA:267
  Auld Daddy Darkness. J. Ferguson.
    Ox-BC:275
  The Conquered One. D. Jackson.
    Ba-HI:30
  Crepuscular. R. Howard. Br-TC:199
  Dark. S. Partridge. De-TT:87
  Darkness. Murari. Al-PI:38
  The Darkness Darts. Janine. Le-M:214
  The Day's No Rounder than Its
    Angles Are. P. Viereck. Sh-AP:229
  God's Dark. J. Martin. Fe-PL:336
  Hidden by Darkness. Basho. Be-MC:11
  Hymn to Night. M. Cane. Un-MA:236
  In a Dark Wood. Pa-RE:116
  In the Great Night. Bi-IT:132, Ho-SD:46

In the Hours of Darkness.
   J. Flexner. Fe-FP:386,
   Hu-MP:119
In Time of Darkness. R. Roseliep.
   De-FS:161
Inversely, as the Square of Their
   Distances Apart. K. Rexroth.
   Mo-TS:24
Keep Darkness. L. Jennings.
   De-FS:110
No Moon No Star. B. Deutsch.
   Ha-WR:52
On the Staircase. W. Wellman.
   De-FS:215
Program Notes on Sibelius.
   D. Babcock. Pl-US:73
Revolution. A. Housman. Pl-IO:37
The Room. C. Aiken.
   Un-MA:424, Wi-LT:332
Song. Tr-US I:202
Visit. E. Recht. Le-M:202
Waiting in Darkness. Be-CS:31
DART RIVER
   The Dart. Gr-GB:172
   The River Dart. Gr-GB:172
D'ARTAGNAN: see THREE MUSKETEERS
DATES (FRUIT)
   Dates. Fe-FP:478, Ho-LP:26
DATING (SOCIAL CUSTOM): see
   HUMOR - DATING (SOCIAL CUSTOM)
DAUGHTERS
   Amusing Our Daughters. C. Kizer.
      Ca-VT:542
   The Beauty of Job's Daughters.
      J. MacPherson. En-PC:289
   Circuit Through the Hills.
      T. Singh. Al-PI:119
   Dirge. Tr-US II:103
   A Flower Given to My Daughter.
      J. Joyce. Go-BP:117
   For My Daughter. W. Kees.
      Mc-EA:106
   Generations. R. Korn. Ho-TY:304
   The Goodnight. L. Simpson.
      To-MP:91
   Homecoming. A. Kramer. Ls-NY:94
   Ihunui's Lament for Her Daughter
      Rangi. Ihunui. Tr-US II:115
   Missing My Daughter. S. Spender.
      Pa-GTB:521
   My Daughter. Ge-TR:44
   The Name. R. Creeley. Pe-SS:4
   O Tender under Her Right Breast.
      G. Barker. Un-MB:493
   Old Mother Frost. E. Fleming.
      Ir-BB:106
   Pain for a Daughter. A. Sexton.
      Mc-WS:142
   a poem for fathers. K. Wilson.
      Sc-TN:243
   Poems for My Daughter.
      H. Gregory. Un-MA:505

A Prayer for My Daughter.
   W. Yeats. Al-VBP:1090,
   Fe-PL:137, Tr-MR:49, Wi-LT:73
A Sense of Property. A. Thwaite.
   To-MP:139
Song. V. de Moraes. An-TC:95
Song for Naomi. I. Layton.
   Do-WH:80
tell our daughters. B. Brigham.
   Sc-TN:17
To Be Sung. P. Viereck. Ga-FB:86
What Shall I Give? E. Thomas.
   Ox-BC:330, Sm-LG:113
DAVENPORT, ABRAHAM
   Abraham Davenport. J. Whittier.
      Sp-OG:31
DAVENPORT, IA.
   Old Davenport Days. R. Cuscaden.
      St-H:34
DAVID, KING OF ISRAEL: see also
   GOLIATH; HUMOR - DAVID, KING
   OF ISRAEL
   After Goliath. K. Amis. En-PC:194
   Beauteous, Yea Beauteous More
      than These. C. Smart. Pl-EI:97
   A Boy Looking at Big David.
      M. Swenson. Li-TU:52
   David and Goliath. N. Crouch.
      Ox-BC:41
   David's Lament. Bible. O.T.
      Samuel. Gr-CT:343
   David's Lament for Jonathan.
      P. Abelard. Ga-S:162
   David's Song. R. Browning.
      Ga-FB:11
   King David. W. de la Mare.
      Li-TU:169
   King David. I. Manger. Ho-TY:278
   Little David. Ab-MO:80
   The Love of King David and Fair
      Bethsabe. G. Peele. Al-VBP:138
   The Pebble. E. Wylie. Tr-MR:156,
      Un-MA:281
   Saul. R. Browning. Hi-FO:23
   Song to David. C. Smart.
      Al-VBP:575, Gr-CT:447, Pl-US:72
   That Harp You Play So Well.
      M. Moore. Un-MA:349
DAVIES, WILLIAM HENRY
   I Am the Poet, Davies, William.
      W. Davies. Rv-CB:960
DA VINCI, LEONARDO: see LEONARDO
   DA VINCI
DAVIS, ANGELA YVONNE
   For Angela. Z. Gilbert. Ad-PB:196
   Poem of Angela Yvonne Davis.
      N. Giovanni. Ad-PB:458
DAVIS, MILES DEWEY, JR.
   Miles' Delight. T. Joans. Hu-PN:396
DAVY, SIR HUMPHRY
   Sir Humphry Davy. E. Bentley.
      Pl-IO:160

DAWN: see also SUNRISE
  Alba. D. Walcott. Bo-GJ:212
  Another September. T. Kinsella.
    En-PC:270
  At the Edge of the World.
    Jo-TS:13
  Aubade for Hope. R. Warren.
    Un-MA:589
  Ayii, Ayii, (I Think). Ho-SD:76
  Bathed Is My Blood. O. La Crone.
    Hu-NN:38
  A Bird That Calls Before Dawn.
    Tr-US I:194
  Birds Waking. W. Merwin.
    Ca-BP:21
  The Birth of Dawn. Br-MW:68
  Blue Island Intersection.
    C. Sandburg. Un-MA:203
  Break of Day. J. Clare. Rv-CB:731
  A Breeze Stirs at Dawn. Asayasu.
    Be-MC:39
  The Bright Dawn Appears. Ho-SD:52
  Brooklyn Bridge at Dawn.
    R. LeGallienne. Ar-TP3:173
  The Cock. M. Mota. An-TC:113
  Cock-Crow. E. Thomas.
    Pa-GTB:444, Un-MB:215
  Cockcrow Song. Le-MW:40
  Come All! Bi-IT:167
  Dance Songs, I. Tr-US I:199
  Dance Songs, III. Tr-US II:146
  Dance Songs, X. Tr-US II:165
  Dawn. G. Bottomley.
    Re-BS:40, Un-MB:213
  Dawn. P. Dunbar. Bo-AN:5,
    Hu-PN:35
  Dawn. O. Paz. Mo-TS:86
  Dawn. J. Sternberg. Ho-TY:194
  Dawn. W. Williams. Un-MA:256
  Dawn Is a Feeling. M. Pinder.
    Mo-GR:117
  Dawn over the Mountains. Tu Fu.
    Rx-OH:30
  Dawn Song. Tr-US II:104
  Dawn Song. Tr-US II:228
  Dawn Song. Br-MW:59, Da-SC:83,
    Le-OE:17, Tr-US II:264
  A Dawn Wind Blows. S. Morrison.
    Le-M:18
  The Day Has Risen. Bi-IT:165
  Daybreak. H. Longfellow.
    De-TT:54, Fe-PL:399, Mc-WK:30
  Daybreak. C. Sandburg.
    La-PV:48
  Daybreak in Alabama. L. Hughes.
    Br-AF:47
  Dream Song. Bi-IT:128, Da-SC:100,
    Ho-SD:12, Le-OE:107
  Dream Songs, III. Tr-US II:249
  Ducks at Dawn. J. Tippett.
    Ar-TP3:73, Au-SP:52, Br-SS:21

  The Early Morning. H. Belloc.
    Co-BN:122, Gr-EC:104, Gr-TG:41,
    Mc-WK:4
  Getting Up Early on a Spring
    Morning. Po Chu-i. Ma-FW:9
  The Greek Anthology, I.
    Un-MW:173
  Greek Epigram. E. Pound.
    Un-MA:292
  Green. D. Lawrence. Co-EL:95,
    Un-MB:290
  The Harbor Dawn. H. Crane.
    Pe-OA:178, Sh-AP:198
  Hassan. J. Flecker. Hi-WP II:39
  Hey! Now the Day Dawns.
    A. Montgomerie. De-CH:4
  The Horses. T. Hughes.
    Go-BP:99, Ha-WR:74
  How Cool Cut Hay Smells. Boncho.
    Be-CS:16
  Hymn to the Sun. Be-AP:22,
    Le-OE:9
  I Arise with Movements. Ho-SD:77
  Impressions. E. Cummings.
    Ad-CI:6, Sm-PT:80, Un-MA:470
  Is It the Morning? Is It the
    Little Morning? D. Schwartz.
    Co-EL:152
  Love-Magic Song. Tr-US II:243
  A Low Range of Mountains.
    Ho-SD:51, Le-OE:15
  Mad Song. W. Blake. Rv-CB:566
  Magic Prayer. Le-IB:30,
    Le-OE:19, Ma-BH:7, Tr-US I:9
  The Magpie! The Magpie!
    Da-SC:96, Ho-SD:44, Le-OE:15,
    Tr-US II:252
  Man Watching. A. Brownjohn.
    Ls-NY:290
  A Mask Presented at Ludlow
    Castle (Comus). J. Milton.
    Al-VBP:397, Sm-LG:51
  Mists of Daybreak. Buson.
    Hu-MP:318
  Morning. W. Blake. Sm-LG:49
  Morning Star. T. Ferril.
    Ca-VT:200
  On Summer Nights. Tsurayuki.
    Ba-ST:29
  The Owl Hooted. Da-SC:88,
    Ho-SD:20, Le-OE:11
  Pack, Clouds, Away! T. Heywood.
    Al-VBP:271, Bl-OB:42, De-CH:7,
    Pa-GTB:32, Re-BS:9, Re-TW:52,
    Tu-WW:11, Un-MW:6
  Poems for My Brother Kenneth.
    O. Dodson. Ad-PB:131,
    Hu-PN:304
  Prelude. R. Gilder. Fe-PL:395
  Red Sky in the Morning.
    Kobayashi Issa. Ma-FW:213

Riding at Daybreak.   Sun Yun Feng.
    Le-MW:39, Ma-FW:129
Roosters.   E. Bishop.   Wi-LT:506
The Salutation of the Dawn.
    Fe-PL:397
Song of the Horse Society.
    Tr-US II:236
Sound.   J. Harrison.   Ca-VT:711
Spring Festival Songs, V.
    Tr-US II:172
Summer Dawn.   W. Morris.
    Al-VBP:1010, Ox-BN:784, Rv-CB:930
A Summer Morning.   R. Field.
    Ar-TP3:175, Au-SP:319, La-PV:48,
    Pe-FB:86
Sunrise on Rydal Water.
    J. Drinkwater.   Wi-LT:621
There!   Bi-IT:166
This Shall Be Sufficient.
    K. Rexroth.   Ad-CI:27
Through Dawn's Pink Aurora.
    P. George.   Al-WW:127
To the Dawn.   Al-PI:15
Upward Going!   Bi-IT:12
The Valley's Singing Day.
    R. Frost.   Pl-US:54
War.   D. Roth.   Du-RG:71
A Wartime Dawn.   D. Gascoyne.
    Wi-LT:713
When Dawn Comes to the City:
    New York.   C. McKay.
    Bo-HF:30, La-OC:138
The World Calling on Dawn.
    Tr-US I:195
The Zebras.   R. Campbell.
    Al-VBP:1222, Co-BBW:192, Un-MB:410
DAY, JOHN
John Day, Frontiersman.
    Y. Winters.   Ha-PO:73
DAY: see also AFTERNOON; BEDTIME;
    DAWN; EVENING; MIDNIGHT;
    MOONRISE; MOONSET; MORNING;
    NIGHT; NOON; SUNRISE; SUNSET;
    TODAY; TOMORROW; YESTERDAY
A Bit of Cobweb.   L. Sarchuk.
    Mo-MI:20
Blind Angel.   D. Rokeah.   Me-PH:119
Bussy d'Ambois.   G. Chapman.
    Al-VBP:146
Daily Round.   L. Reese.   Gr-TG:34
Day and Night.   A. Lindsay.   Gr-TG:41
Day That I Have Loved.   R. Brooke.
    Fe-PL:400
The Day with a White Mark.   C. Lewis.
    Go-BP:250
The Day's No Rounder than Its Angles
    Are.   P. Viereck.   Sh-AP:229
A Feast Song.   Br-MW:41
Glad Day.   W. Robertson.   Hi-GD:6
I Look Out of My Window.   Olya.
    Mo-MI:24

Impressions.   e. cummings.
    Ad-CI:6, Sm-PT:80, Un-MA:470
An Indian Summer Day on the
    Prairie.   V. Lindsay.
    La-RM:70, Mc-WK:31
A June Day.   S. Teasdale.
    Ha-YA:70
Little Song of the Sun.
    Tr-US II:247
Magic Song for Him Who Wishes to
    Live.   Le-IB:27, Tr-US I:3
Myself.   L. Ahsoak.   Ba-HI:23
Night and Morning.   D. Aldis.
    Co-PS:89, Ha-YA:58
The Salutation of the Dawn.
    Fe-PL:397
Silent, Silent Night.   W. Blake.
    Rv-CB:604
The Sleepy Day.   H. Patel. Le-M:186
Sometimes.   R. Fyleman. Br-SS:24
Sun Goes Up.   H. Farley. Le-M:143
The Two Spirits.   P. Shelley.
    De-CH:323, Ho-WR:189
Two Splendid Horses.   Re-RR:88
The Two Stars.   W. Davies.
    Un-MB:176
A Wasted Day.   F. Cornford.
    Un-MB:306
Wee Davie Daylicht.   R. Tennant.
    Ox-BC:230
With Wavering Feet I Walked.
    V. Solovyov.   Pa-SG:118
You, Whose Day It Is.
    Ho-SD:55, Jo-TS:1, Le-OE:16
DAYDREAMS: see DREAMS; FANTASY
DAYS: see also BIRTHDAYS; CALENDARS;
    HOLIDAYS; HUMOR - DAYS; also
    names of special days, as
    CHRISTMAS
The Day.   T. Spencer. Mo-BG:71,
    Ni-JP:157
Days.   R. Emerson.   Al-VBP:805,
    Mo-BG:136, Ni-JP:30, Rv-CB:775
Days.   P. Larkin.   Sm-MK:212
Hoo, Suffolk.   Gr-GB:175
How Many Days Has My Baby to Play?
    Mother Goose.   Ar-TP3:183,
    Ir-BB:10, Mo-NR:8, Wr-RM:28
Lengthening Days.   Wr-RM:37
A Little Work.   G. du Maurier.
    Fe-PL:294
Monday's Child. . . .   Au-SP:5,
    De-PO:14, Gr-EC:129, Ir-BB:226,
    Li-LB:164, Mo-CC:(11), Mo-MGT:16,
    Mo-NR:19, Mo-TB:107, Rv-CB:452,
    Sm-LG:97, Un-GT:22, Wi-MG:58,
    Wr-RM:87
Northern View.   H. Plimpton.
    Ls-NY:293
Page IX.   G. Stein.   Mc-WK:104
Renunciation.   E. Dickinson.
    Un-MA:104

DAYS — cont'd.
  Seven Days in the Week. On-TW:28
  Sneeze on Monday. Mother Goose.
    Ir-BB:228, Ju-CP:80, Li-LB:165,
    Mo-NR:91, Mo-TB:108, Na-EO:19,
    Wr-RM:128
  Solomon Grundy. Mother Goose.
    De-PO:22, Li-LB:74, Mo-MGT:140,
    Mo-NR:35, Wi-MG:42, Wr-RM:24
  Still Branches. J. Simvovk.
    Gr-BT:156
  They That Wash on Monday. Bl-OB:145,
    Ir-BB:228, Li-LB:163, Mo-TB:110
  Thirty Days Hath September.
    Au-SP:323, Bo-FP:139, Li-LB:165,
    Mo-MGT:172, Mo-NR:101, On-TW:59,
    Un-GT:22, Wi-MG:30, Wr-RM:17
  This Day Is Over. C. O'John.
    Al-WW:67
  This Is Silver Saturday. Sp-TM:35
  Tommy Snooks and Bessy Brooks.
    Mother Goose. Bo-FP:132,
    Li-LB:35, Mo-CC:(17), Mo-MGT:14,
    Mo-NR:126, Wi-MG:4, Wr-RM:78
  Twilight Poem. C. Bialik. Me-PH:71
  The Weather. N. Taalak. Ba-HI:76
  The Week in Old New England.
    Mo-TB:111
  When the Days Begin to Lengthen.
    Un-GT:22
  Yellow Stones on Sunday. Mo-TB:113
  Yesterday Returneth Not. De-CH:485
THE DEAD: see also GHOSTS; HUMOR -
    THE DEAD; WAR DEAD
  A Solis Ortus Cardine. F. Ford.
    Al-VBP:1118
  The Absent. E. Muir. Tr-MR:273
  Autumnal Ode. A. De Vere. Ox-BN:587
  Ballade of Boot-Hill. Fi-BG:110
  Ben Bolt. T. English. Er-FA:342
  The Bride. D. Lawrence. Go-BP:244
  Burying Ground by the Ties.
    A. MacLeish. Un-MA:459
  Cemetery in Pernambuco.
    J. de Melo Neto. An-TC:123
  Coming and Going. N. Goodman.
    Ca-VT:497
  The Crematory. Ching Ting-wen.
    Pa-MV:78
  Cuchulain Comforted. W. Yeats.
    Wi-LT:95
  Dance Song. Tr-US II:7
  De Coenatione Micae. Martial.
    Sm-LG:275
  The Dead Who Climb Up to the Sky.
    Le-IB:120
  Death. W. Williams. Ca-VT:51
  Death Song. Tr-US I:50
  Death Song of a Warrior. Da-SC:157,
    Tr-US II:226
  A Dirge. Fang Ching. Hs-TC:387
  Dirge. Tr-US I:167

A Dream. W. Allingham.
  Co-PI:9, Co-PT:70
The Dream. J. Bishop. Wi-LT:608
The Dust of Love. C. Walsh.
  Ls-NY:66
Elegy to the Memory of an Unfortunate
  Woman. A. Pope. Rv-CB:511
Elizabeth. S. Warner. Un-MB:373
Epitaph of a Faithful Man.
  R. Mezey. Co-EL:79
Extempore Effusion upon the
  Death of James Hogg.
  W. Wordsworth. Rv-CB:648
Flight. H. Vinal. De-FS:206
Gather These Bones. L. Turco.
  De-FS:200
The Grave. S. Tchernichovsky.
  Me-PH:79
Henry Turnbull. W. Gibson.
  Co-EL:76
Here I Lie. M. George.
  De-FS:95
Here Lies a Prisoner. C. Mew.
  Un-MB:165
The Hill. E. Masters.
  Al-VBP:1104, Sh-AP:138, Wi-LT:113
In the Museum. I. Gardner.
  Co-EL:78
Lament of a Widow for Her Dead
  Husband. Tr-US I:189
Love-Song of the Dead. Da-SC:54
Lying in State. A. Mitchell.
  Co-EL:81
My Dead. Rachel. Me-PH:88
Obituary. K. Fearing. Ca-VT:237
The Old Churchyard at Bonchurch.
  P. Marston. Ox-BN:888
Oldest Cemetery. M. Van Doren.
  De-FS:205
On a Certain Ruler in Memory of
  Former Rulers. Da-SC:174
On the Death of a Recluse.
  G. Darley. Rv-CB:755
Our Fear. Z. Herbert. Gr-BT:120
Prayer at the Sacrifice Before
  the Coffin. Tr-US II:196
Prayer to a Dead Wife. Da-SC:73
Requiescat. O. Wilde.
  Hi-WP I:21, Ox-BN:895, Un-MB:67
Reversions. A. Dorn. De-FS:74
Ritual Song. Tr-US I:62
Safe in Their Alabaster Chambers.
  E. Dickinson. Rv-CB:924
The Shades of the Newly Dead to
  the Gods. Tr-US I:227
The Shape of Memory. W. Welles.
  Sm-PT:160
Sleeping Village. H. Vinal.
  De-FS:207
Song. E. Brontë. Ox-BN:600
Song Commemorating the Death of a
  Hunter. Tr-US I:93
Song of a Dead One. Le-IB:122

Song of a Departed Spirit.
  Tr-US II:260
Song of a Widow for Her Dead
  Husband. Tr-US I:242
Song of the Departed Spirit.
  Tr-US I:197
Song of the Unburied. Tr-US I:81
Spell Called "The Lifting of the
  Head." Tr-US II:27
A Street in Bronzeville: Southeast
  Corner. G. Brooks. Ca-VT:439
They Know. R. Goodman. De-FS:96
Those Who Go Not to Return.
  B. Galai. Me-PH:125
Through the Dear Might of Him Who
  Walked the Waves. J. Heath-Stubbs.
  Go-BP:289
To the Holy Spirit. Y. Winters.
  Ca-VT:231, Un-MA:551
Torchbearer. H. Wolfe. Go-BP:245
The Town Without a Market.
  J. Flecker. Un-MB:274
The Two Societies. J. Wheelock.
  En-PC:8
The Unreturning. W. Owen. Un-MB:365
Wide Empty Landscape with a Death
  in the Foreground. N. Momaday.
  Ni-CD:90
A Wreath for One Lost. H. Vinal.
  De-FS:208
The Yew Tree. V. Watkins.
  Pl-EI:6
DEAF MUTES: see DEAFNESS
DEAFNESS: see also HUMOR - DEAFNESS
  The Fifth Sense. P. Beer. Ca-MB:120
  The Little Mute Boy. F. Garcia
    Lorca. Le-SW:29
  Mutterings over the Crib of a Deaf
    Child. J. Wright. Du-SH:139
DEATH: see also ABORTION; ANIMALS -
  DEATH; ASSASSINATIONS; BIRDS -
  DEATH; THE DEAD; DROWNING;
  DYING; ELEGIES; EPITAPHS;
  EXECUTIONS AND EXECUTIONERS;
  FUNERALS; HUMOR - DEATH; LIFE
  AND DEATH; LOVE - DEATH;
  LYNCHINGS; MURDER; SATIRE -
  DEATH; SUICIDE; WAKES; WAR DEAD;
  WIDOWS; and the subheadings
  following DEATH
Acceptance. R. Frost. Tr-MR:275
Adieu: Farewell Earth's Bliss.
  T. Nashe. Al-VBP:211, De-CH:244,
  Gr-CT:358, Ha-PO:142, Hi-FO:141,
  Rv-CB:276, Sm-LG:276
Admiral Death. H. Newbolt. Co-RM:62
Adonais. P. Shelley. Al-VBP:759,
  Ha-PO:130, Ox-BN:287
after kent state. L. Clifton.
  Be-MA:142
Afterwards. T. Hardy. Al-VBP:1050,
  Co-BN:210, De-CH:435, Gr-CT:353,

Ni-JP:172, No-CL:284, Ox-BN:846,
  Pa-GTB:412, Rv-CB:944, Un-MB:31,
  Wi-LT:25
Age. W. Landor. Co-EL:123,
  Co-PU:150
Air Burial. J. Rorty. Sm-PT:162
Alexander the Great. De-CH:180
All Souls' Day. S. Sassoon.
  Tr-MR:276
All That Was Mortal. S. Teasdale.
  Tr-MR:286
All the Flowers of the Spring.
  J. Webster. Al-VBP:289,
  De-CH:252, Rv-CB:317
All the Hills and Vales. C. Sorley.
  Un-MB:380
Alone. C. Bialik. Me-PH:73
Anactoria. A. Swinburne.
  Al-VBP:1022
And Death Shall Have No Dominion.
  D. Thomas. Hi-WP II:31,
  Pl-EI:60, To-MP:34, Tr-MR:291,
  Un-MB:500, Wi-LT:546
And Will A' Not Come Again.
  W. Shakespeare. Al-VBP:192
The Ashtabula Disaster. J. Moore.
  Na-EO:122
The Assassination. R. Hillyer.
  Un-MA:483
At My Father's Grave. H. MacDiarmid.
  Co-EL:70, Pa-GTB:486
Atalanta in Calydon. A. Swinburne.
  Al-VBP:1041
The Atheist's Tragedy.
  C. Tourneur. Al-VBP:273
Aubade. K. Shapiro. Ca-VT:376
Aunt Jane Allen. F. Johnson.
  Ad-PB:24, Hu-PN:89
Auto Wreck. K. Shapiro.
  Ca-VT:471, Ma-FW:131, Mo-BG:30,
  Pe-OA:224, Pe-SS:70, Wi-LT:535
Autumnal. R. Humphries. Tr-MR:273
Ave atque Vale. A. Swinburne.
  Al-VBP:1033, Ox-BN:814
Ballad of Death. G. Topirceanu.
  Mc-AC:51
The Ballad of Father Gilligan.
  W. Yeats. Hi-WP I:72, Mc-MK:132,
  Mc-WS:157, Pl-EI:114, Un-MB:112
Ballade by the Fire. E. Robinson.
  Bo-HF:174
Barbara Allen. Al-VBP:55, Er-FA:315,
  Mc-PR:156, Rv-CB:434, Un-MW:112
Because that You Are Going.
  E. Dickinson. Un-MA:101
The Being Without Face. Bi-IT:89
The Bells. E. Poe. Bo-FP:177,
  Bo-HF:162, Er-FA:277, Fe-FP:64,
  Fe-PL:433, Li-SR:72, Sp-OG:339
Beside the Bed. C. Mew.
  Un-MB:162

DEATH — cont'd.
Between the World and Me.
  R. Wright.   Ad-PB:107,
  Bo-AN:103, Kr-OF:158, Pe-M:92,
  Wi-LT:657
The Bishop Orders His Tomb at
  Saint Praxed's Church.
  R. Browning.   Al-VBP:895,
  Mo-GR:57
The Blessed Damozel.   D. Rossetti.
  Li-SR:77, Ox-BN:675
The Blue-Tail Fly.   Er-FA:450.
  Gr-GB:324
The Bourgeois Poet, #18.
  K. Shapiro.   St-H:201
The Bourne.   C. Rossetti.
  Ox-BN:715
Break, Break, Break.   A. Tennyson.
  Bl-OB:51, Bo-GJ:182, De-CH:211,
  Ga-FB:128, Ha-PO:137, Ma-YA:192,
  Ox-BN:485, Pa-GTB:331, Sp-OG:267
A Bright Journey Ends.   R. Gilder.
  Ke-TF:174
The Broken String.   Tr-CB:51,
  Tr-US I:76
Buckskin Sam's Tribute to Texas
  Jack.   Fi-BG:174
C. L. M.   J. Masefield.
  Un-MB:225, Wi-LT:190
Caesar and Pompey.   G. Chapman.
  Al-VBP:146
Called Back.   E. Dickinson.
  Un-MA:105
The Chariot.   E. Dickinson.
  Ma-FW:164, Rv-CB:911, Sh-AP:130,
  Tr-MR:271, Un-MA:102, Wi-LT:13
A Cherry Fair.   Gr-CT:321
The Chestnut Roasters.   J. Brennan.
  De-FS:34
The Choice I.   D. Rossetti.
  Al-VBP:989
The Choice II.   D. Rossetti.
  Al-VBP:990
The City in the Sea.   E. Poe.
  Al-VBP:873, Gr-SS:182, Rv-CB:807,
  Sh-AP:53
Close Your Eyes!   A. Bontemps.
  Ad-PB:86, Bo-AN:76, Hu-PN:218
The Coffin-Worm.   R. Pitter.
  Un-MB:403
Come, Break with Time.   L. Bogan.
  Un-MA:492
Come to the Stone.   R. Jarrell.
  Ca-VT:399
The Comforters.   D. Shorter.
  De-CH:259
A Commemoration for the Physicist X.
  P. Oppenheimer.   Ls-NY:130
Complaint.   J. Wright.   Ca-VT:622
The Conqueror Worm.   E. Poe.   Sh-AP:55
A Contemplation upon Flowers.   H. King.
  Co-BN:44, Rv-CB:350

Cool Tombs.   C. Sandburg.
  Al-VBP:1138, Fe-PL:276, Sh-AP:157,
  Un-GB:159, Un-MA:200, Vi-PP:194
Coronach.   W. Scott.   Al-VBP:672,
  De-CH:163, Ho-WR:119, Ma-YA:145,
  Pa-GTB:235
The Country of a Thousand Years of
  Peace.   J. Marrill.   En-PC:240
The Cow Girl.   Fi-BG:140
The Cremation Ground.   Bha Vabhuti.
  Al-PI:37
Cromwell Dead.   A. Marvell.
  Al-VBP:460, Gr-CT:379
Crossing the Bar.   A. Tennyson.
  Al-VBP:865, Er-FA:477, Fe-PL:286,
  Ga-FB:127, Ma-YA:199, Mc-PR:105,
  Ox-BN:526, Sp-OG:279
A Cut Flower.   K. Shapiro.
  Co-BN:54
Dance Song of Death.   Tr-US II:3
Dance Song on the Death of a Girl
  Named Rutenag.   Tr-US II:4
Dance Songs, V.   Tr-US II:141
Darest Thou Now O Soul.
  W. Whitman.   Al-VBP:948
The Dark Angel.   L. Johnson.
  Pa-GTB:401, Un-MB:154
Dark Girl.   A. Bontemps.   Pe-SS:148
Dark Hotel.   A. Dorn.   De-FS:74
The Day We Die.   Le-OE:130
De Profundis.   L. Blaga.   Mc-AC:72
Dead.   L. Johnson.   Ox-BN:948
The Dead Knight.   J. Masefield.
  De-CH:53, Pa-GTB:440
The Dead Man Asks for a Song.
  Le-OE:129, Tr-CB:44, Tr-US I:49
The Dead Poet.   A. Douglas.
  Al-VBP:1110, No-CL:19
Dead Sea.   Sun Yü-t'ang.   Hs-TC:123
The Dead Swagman.   N. Cato.   Co-RM:140
A Dead Turk.   Li Kuang-t'ien.
  Hs-TC:208
Deadfall.   M. Keller.   Gr-EC:272
Dear Beauteous Death.
  H. Vaughan.   Ga-S:36
Dear Lord.   W. Mann.   Me-WF:20
Death.   E. Brontë.   Ox-BN:603
Death.   J. Clare.   Pa-GTB:319
Death.   J. Erwin.   Le-M:180
Death!   A. Kack.   Me-WF:89
Death.   J. Milton.   Ga-S:29
Death.   Saint Geraud.   Mc-EA:159
Death.   Be-AP:25
Death and General Putnam.
  A. Guiterman.   Co-PM:77,
  Co-RM:219, Cr-WS:55
Death and the Lady.   L. Adams.
  Un-MA:544
Death and the Maiden.
  M. Claudius.   Un-R:121
Death as History.   J. Wright.
  Ad-PB:280, Sc-TN:249

Death as the Lotus Flower.
Be-AP:31, Lo-TY:27, Pl-EI:24
Death, Be Not Proud. J. Donne.
Al-VBP:203, Er-FA:36, Ga-FB:91,
Ga-S:215, Gr-CT:381, Ha-PO:143,
Ho-LP:95, Ke-PP:24, Ma-YA:81,
Rv-CB:309
Death-Dance Song. Tr-US II:243
Death Is a Clean Cold Word. . . .
R. Richmond. Go-BP:230
Death Is a Door. J. Allcock.
Gr-BT:176
Death Is Before Me To-Day.
De-CH:635
Death of a Comrade. M. Carter. Sa-B:163
Death of a Friend. P. Murray.
Ad-PB:110
Death of a Peasant. R. Thomas.
Ma-FW:168
Death of a Schoolteacher.
B. Hirshberg. Ke-TF:171
Death of a Sister. Bi-IT:96
The Death of Kings. W. Shakespeare.
Mo-GR:93
The Death of Robin Hood. E. Field.
Co-PT:239
The Death of Robin Hood.
Al-VBP:38, Ma-BB:77, Ma-FW:156
The Death of the Flowers. W. Bryant.
Co-BN:188, Fe-PL:271
The Death of the Hired Man. R. Frost.
Pe-OA:26, Un-MA:171
The Death of the Sheriff. R. Lowell.
Un-MA:664
A Death Song. P. Dunbar.
Fe-PL:274, Hu-PN:42
Death Stands above Me. W. Landor.
De-CH:641, Ga-FB:125, Ma-YA:169,
Ox-BN:194
Death Summons Everyman. Ga-S:30
Devil Doll. L. Grenelle. De-FS:99
Dew on a Dusty Heart.
J. Untermeyer. Un-MA:333
Difficult Chieko. K. Takamura.
Sh-AM:47
Dirce. W. Landor. Al-VBP:707,
Gr-CT:80, Ox-BN:190, Rv-CB:668
Dirge. T. Beddoes. Ho-WR:188,
Ox-BN:453
A Dirge. J. Webster. Al-VBP:288,
De-CH:247, Rv-CB:316
Dirge. Tr-CB:30, Tr-US I:50
Dirge for a Chief. Tr-US II:116
Dirge in Cymbeline. W. Collins.
Al-VBP:574, No-CL:63
Dirge in Dialogue. Lo-TY:3,
Tr-US I:64
Dirge Without Music. E. Millay.
Ke-PP:80, Tr-MR:266
Dirges, I, II. Tr-US I:47
Discordants III. C. Aikens. Co-BL:36
The Discovery. M. Gibbon. Co-PI:49

A Dispute over Suicide. Lo-TY:26
Distances. C. Okigbo: Lo-TY:160
Divine Poems. J. Villa. Tr-MR:289
The Door of Death. W. Blake.
De-CH:753, Gr-CT:376
Downgoing. G. Davidson. De-FS:70
A Dream at Night. Mei Yao Ch'en.
Rx-OH:43
The Dreamer. Wen I-to. Hs-TC:54
Drum. L. Hughes. Un-MA:553
Drum Song in Three Parts from the
Funeral Ceremony for a Hero.
Tr-US I:56
Drummer Hodge. T. Hardy. Pa-GTB:404
The Duchess of Malfi. J. Webster.
Gr-CT:360
Dust. R. Brooke. Un-MB:323
Early in the Morning. L. Simpson.
Ha-PO:158
Earth upon Earth. Gr-CT:325,
Rv-CB:15
Echo. C. Rossetti. Al-VBP:998,
De-CH:452, Ox-BN:708, Un-MW:91
Eclogue. F. Prokosch. Al-VBP:1235
1867. J. Plunkett. Co-PI:169
Elegy. G. Byron. Pa-GTB:233
Elegy. E. Millay. Un-MA:446
Elegy for a Nature Poet.
H. Nemerov. Co-BN:230
Elegy for Jack Bowman. J. Bruchac.
Ni-CD:32
Elegy for Jane. T. Roethke.
Br-TC:348, Pe-OA:204, Pe-SS:160,
Sh-AP:213, Un-MA:598, Wi-LT:486
Elegy over a Tomb. Lord Herbert.
Al-VBP:296
Elegy Written in a Country
Churchyard. T. Gray.
Al-VBP:559, De-TT:83, Er-FA:462,
Fe-PL:281, Ha-PO:144, Ma-YA:125,
Pa-GTB:145, Rv-CB:533
Elisa, or an Elegy upon the Unripe
Decease of Sir Antony Irby.
P. Fletcher. Al-VBP:291
Emblems. A. Tate. Ca-VT:223
The Emperor of Ice-Cream.
W. Stevens. Al-VBP:1142, Ha-PO:141,
Mo-BG:187, Sh-AP:160
Empty Saddles. Fi-BG:192
The End. M. Van Doren. Al-VBP:1200
England Reclaimed. O. Sitwell.
Al-VBP:1192
L'Envoi. R. Kipling.
Er-FA:10, Ke-TF:453
Envoy. F. Thompson. Ga-FB:335,
Un-MB:91
Epistle to Be Left in the Earth.
A. MacLeish. Pl-IO:55,
Sm-PT:114, Un-MA:458
Epitaph. L. Abercrombie.
Al-VBP:1147, Un-MB:259

DEATH — cont'd.

Epitaph. J. Cunningham.
  Co-EL:81, En-PC:106
The Epitaph. T. Gray. Mc-PR:201
An Epitaph. S. Hawes. Al-VBP:34,
  De-CH:643, Go-BP:234, Gr-CT:382,
  Rv-CB:72
Epitaph. E. Wylie. Un-MA:280
Epitaph for a Timid Lady.
  F. Cornford. Co-EL:85
Escape. R. Graves. Cr-WS:92,
  Un-MB:387
Even Such Is Time. Al-VBP:97,
  De-CH:644, Ga-S:219, Gr-BT:167,
  Gr-CT:381, Hi-WP II:169, Na-EO:93
Excelsior. H. Longfellow.
  Fe-FP:566, Li-SR:49, Pa-OM:223
Exit. W. MacDonald. Al-VBP:1145
Exit. E. Robinson. Un-MA:116
Extended Invitation. J. Stuart.
  De-FS:197
Exultation Is the Going.
  E. Dickinson. Rv-CB:906,
  Sh-AP:127
Eyes That Last I Saw in Tears.
  T. Eliot. Al-VBP:1185
Fable. M. Moore. Du-SH:138
Fair Helen. Al-VBP:53, De-CH:418,
  Er-FA:338, Hi-WP I:16, Pa-GTB:89,
  Rv-CB:43
Fall Comes to Back-Country Vermont.
  R. Warren. Ca-VT:278
Fare Well. W. de la Mare.
  Pa-GTB:439
Farewell to the Warriors. Le-OE:125
Fate! I Have Asked. W. Landor.
  Al-VBP:704
Felix Randal. G. Hopkins. Co-RG:158,
  Ox-BN:866, Pa-GTB:392, Un-MB:44,
  Wi-LT:43
Fingernails of the Dead. J. Takami.
  Sh-AM:108
First Snowfall. G. Carducci. Pa-SG:18
Five Minutes after the Air Raid.
  M. Holub. Gr-BT:104
The Folding Fan. G. Cohoe. Al-WW:25
For a Dead Lady. E. Robinson.
  Al-VBP:1106, Un-MA:119, Wi-LT:104
For a Virgin Lady. C. Cullen.
  Un-MA:571
For Ann Scott-Moncrieff. E. Muir.
  Gr-SS:119, Pa-GTB:469
For My Funeral. A. Housman.
  Al-VBP:1081, Go-BP:237
For Sleep or Death. R. Pitter.
  Hi-WP I:144, Sm-MK:218
For the Antigone. A. Hamori.
  Ls-NY:27
For the Moment. R. Weber. Co-PI:196
The Funeral. S. Spender. Un-MB:474
A Funeral in Tchiatura. A. Mezhirov.
  Ca-MR:89

A Funeral Piece. M. Yoshioka.
  Sh-AM:114
Funeral Poem. Tr-US II:191
Funeral Song. Be-AP:29
The Garden of Proserpine.
  A. Swinburne. Al-VBP:1028,
  Ga-FB:138, Ox-BN:802
A Gesture by a Lady with an
  Assumed Name. J. Wright.
  Wi-LT:846
The Ghost Wails in the Woods at
  Night. Tu Yün-hsieh. Hs-TC:246
Ghostly Reaper. H. Vinal.
  De-FS:207
The Gift. J. Ciardi. Wi-LT:670
The Glories of Our Blood and
  State. J. Shirley.
  Al-VBP:347, Ga-S:30, Gr-CC:107,
  Gr-CT:350, Ke-PP:30, Ni-JP:121,
  Pa-GTB:61, Rv-CB:360
Go By. A. Tennyson. Ox-BN:484
Go Down Death. J. Johnson.
  Ad-PB:6, Bo-AN:2
The Goddess. T. de Banville.
  Gr-SS:125
God's Education. T. Hardy.
  Tr-MR:221
Grandfather's Clock. H. Work.
  Er-FA:351
The Grave. Gr-CT:367
The Gravedigger. B. Carman.
  Co-BN:72
The Gray-Eyed King. A. Akhmatova.
  Ca-MR:182
The Great Hector Was Killed by
  Arrows. J. Brodsky. Ca-MR:32
The Hammers. R. Hodgson.
  Bo-GJ:202, Un-MB:192
Harold Lamson. E. Masters.
  Al-VBP:1105
The Harrowing of Hell. R. Rilke.
  Go-BP:296
Hawthorne — May 23, 1864.
  H. Longfellow. Rv-CB:783
Hazardous Occupations.
  C. Sandburg. Ho-LP:88
He Fell among Thieves. H. Newbolt.
  Pa-OM:227, Sp-OG:47
He Meets Two Men Carrying a Corpse
  in a Hammock. J. de Melo Neto.
  An-TC:131
Heh Nonny No! Gr-BT:177
Heraclitus. W. Cory. Al-VBP:973,
  Co-EL:74, Co-PU:149, Hi-WP II:21,
  Ox-BN:648, Pa-SG:13, Pl-ML:143,
  Rv-CB:875
Hesiod, 1908. A. Mair. Gr-SS:60
Hester. C. Lamb. Pa-GTB:234
The Hill. R. Brooke. Al-VBP:1178,
  Co-BL:165, Hi-WP II:109,
  Un-MB:322, Un-MW:171

History among the Rocks.
R. Warren. Un-MA:565
The Hollow Men. T. Eliot.
Un-MA:395, Wi-LT:302
The Hour of Death. F. Hemans.
Ox-BN:307
The House of Falling Leaves.
W. Braithwaite. Hu-PN:47
How Annandale Went Out.
E. Robinson. Un-MA:125
The Husband. D. Finkel.
Co-EL:71
Hymen. H.D. Al-VBP:1169,
Gr-SS:118
Hymne to God My God in My
Sicknesse. J. Donne.
Gr-CT:383, Pl-US:127
I Am a Wanderer. . . .
Ho-SD:24, Le-OE:127
I Am Old Now and Covered with My
Life. Wo-HS:(69)
I Am Rich. Do-CH:(18), Le-OE:122
I Am the Blood. I. Rosenberg.
Un-MB:352
I Believe One Day. M. Classé.
Ba-HI:93
I Found Her out There. T. Hardy.
De-CH:257
I Have a Rendezvous with Death.
A. Seeger. Al-VBP:1179,
Cr-WS:58, Er-FA:191, Ga-FB:216,
Hi-TL:182, Ke-TF:168, Sp-OG:211
I Like a Look of Agony.
E. Dickinson. Rv-CB:907
I Murder Hate by Field or Flood.
R. Burns. Rv-CB:618
I Never Lost as Much but Twice.
E. Dickinson. Un-MA:95
I Never Shall Love the Snow Again.
R. Bridges. De-CH:258,
Ga-FB:150
I See the World. B. Grayson.
Me-WF:6
I Wage Not Any Feud with Death.
A. Tennyson. Ke-PP:79
I Walked over the Grave of Henry
James. R. Eberhart. Ca-VT:246
If Souls Should Only Shine as
Bright. W. Barnes. De-CH:636
If We Must Die. C. McKay.
Ad-PB:25, Be-MA:13, Bo-AN:31,
Ga-FB:277, Hu-PN:102, Jo-SA:135,
Kr-OF:48, Lo-TY:118, Ra-BP:63
If You Should Go. C. Cullen. Bo-HF:32
Ihunui's Lament for Her Daughter
Rangi. Ihunui. Tr-US II:115
Ilicet. T. Garrison. Fe-PL:306
The Image of Death. R. Southwell.
Al-VBP:152
In a Grave-Yard. W. Braithwaite.
Ad-PB:13

In Glass Petropolis We Shall Die.
O. Mandelstam. Ca-MR:151
In Memoriam XXXV. A. Tennyson.
Al-VBP:861
In Memoriam. A. Tennyson.
Ha-PO:133, Ox-BN:494, 495,
Pa-GTB:336
In Memory. L. Johnson. Ox-BN:948
In Memory of Kathleen.
K. Patchen. Un-MA:608
In Memory of Robinson Jeffers.
E. Barker. Ls-NY:135
In Memory of W. B. Yeats. W. Auden.
Al-VBP:1228, Er-FA:41, Pl-ML:163,
Un-MB:459, Wi-LT:468
In the Broad Daylight I Dream of My
Dead Wife. Mei Yao Ch'en.
Rx-OH:46
In the Garden at Swainston.
A. Tennyson. Ox-BN:493
In the Late Autumn. A. Blok.
Ca-MR:191
In This Hour. J. Johnson. Tr-MR:232
The Indian Burying Ground.
P. Freneau. Fe-PL:279, Hi-TL:8,
Rv-CB:559, Sh-AP:15
Instantaneous. V. Ayres. Hu-NN:85
Invocation. S. Sassoon. Un-MB:313
An Irish Airman Foresees His Death.
W. Yeats. Bo-GJ:191, Gr-CC:129,
Ho-LP:87, Pa-GTB:424, Pe-SS:138,
Sm-LG:270, Un-MB:116, Wi-LT:70
Isabella or The Pot of Basil.
J. Keats. Al-VBP:783
The Isle of Portland. A. Housman.
Un-MB:102
It Was Not Death. E. Dickinson.
Rv-CB:922
It's Here in the. R. Atkins.
Ad-PB:197, Bo-AN:171, Jo-SA:98,
Pe-SS:149
Janet Waking. J. Ransom. Pe-SS:32,
Re-TW:21, Sh-AP:181, Un-MA:410
John Henry. Ab-MO:81, Bo-HF:104,
Co-RM:225, Er-FA:407, Ga-S:124,
Hi-TL:159, Ra-BP:12
John Kinsella's Lament for Mrs.
Mary Moore. W. Yeats. Wi-LT:93
Journey of the Magi. T. Eliot.
Br-TC:114, Er-FA:478, Ga-S:100,
Ha-PO:43, Hi-WP II:174, Pe-OA:132,
Pl-EI:26, Sh-AP:184, Sm-LG:372,
Tr-MR:107, Un-MA:397, Wi-LT:305
Joy, Shipmate, Joy. W. Whitman.
Bo-FP:282, Sh-AP:119, Un-MA:88
Kent State, May 4, 1970.
P. Goodman. Mo-TS:41
Kimpa. Tr-US I:61
King Agongola's Song. Tr-CB:56,
Tr-US I:55
A King Is Dead. W. Shakespeare.
Gr-CT:357

DEATH — cont'd.
  The Knell. M. Al-Fituri. Lo-TY:53
  Lakes. F. Bianco. No-CL:62
  Lament. Be-AP:28
  Lament for the Dead Mother.
    Be-AP:28
  Lament for the Death of Eoghan
    Ruadh O'Neill. T. Davis.
    Co-PI:34, Hi-FO:148
  The Lament for the Makers. W. Dunbar.
    Al-VBP:32, Gr-CT:354, Pl-ML:146,
    Rv-CB:71
  Lament with Me. M. Tsvetayeva.
    Ca-MR:135
  The Last Conqueror. J. Shirley.
    Pa-GTB:60, Rv-CB:359
  The Last Invocation. W. Whitman.
    Sh-AP:119, Un-MA:87
  Last Words. S. Plath. Mc-EA:157
  Leaf after Leaf. W. Landor.
    Al-VBP:710
  Lester Young. T. Joans.
    Be-MA:101, Bo-AN:171, Mo-BG:55
  Let Be at Last. E. Dowson.
    Ha-PO:155
  Let Me Die a Youngman's Death.
    R. McGough. Gr-BT:171
  Let the Light Enter. F. Harper.
    Hu-PN:15
  Letter of a Mother. R. Warren.
    Un-MA:584
  Light Wearing a Black Nightgown.
    Lo Men. Pa-MV:124
  Lines Before Execution.
    C. Tichbourne. Al-VBP:138,
    Gr-CT:324, Ha-PO:132, Rv-CB:103
  Lines on Receiving His Mother's
    Picture. W. Cowper. De-CH:38
  Lonesome Valley. Ga-S:34
  Long Feud. L. Untermeyer.
    Un-MA:306
  Long Sleep. Le-M:181
  Longing for Death. Be-AP:30
  A Louse Crept Out of My Lady's
    Shift. G. Bottomley. Gr-CT:85
  Love and Death. B. Jonson.
    Rv-CB:288
  Lycidas. J. Milton. Al-VBP:402,
    Gr-CT:250, Pa-GTB:55
  Lydia Is Gone This Many a Year.
    L. Reese. Bo-GJ:236, De-CH:261,
    Gr-CC:11
  A Lyke-Wake Drige. De-CH:248,
    Ga-S:219, Gr-CT:366, Gr-GB:322,
    Ma-BB:236, Ma-FW:258, Na-EO:107,
    Pl-EI:139, Rv-CB:54
  The Madman Looks at His Fortune.
    D. Lourie. Sc-TN:153
  Magic Formula to Destroy Life.
    Bi-IT:98
  Malfunction. R. Albert. Du-SH:165,
    Pe-M:94

  Mammon Marriage. G. MacDonald.
    Rv-CB:878
  A Man Is Buried where the Cold
    Winds Blow. D. Matumeak.
    Ba-HI:73
  Man's Medley. G. Herbert.
    Al-VBP:340
  Margaritae Sorori. W. Henley.
    Go-BP:237, Ha-PO:127, Ox-BN:884,
    Rv-CB:948, Un-MB:57
  Marina. T. Eliot. Pa-GTB:476,
    Sh-AP:185
  May the Gravedigger Not Bury Me.
    Do-CH:(48)
  Midnight Lamentation. H. Monro.
    Al-VBP:1140
  The Midnight Skaters. E. Blunden.
    Bo-GJ:235, Hi-WP II:145,
    Pa-GTB:491, Un-MB:398
  The Mill. R. Wilbur. Pe-OA:259
  Mock Lament over a Dead Slave.
    Tr-US I:55
  Monna Innominata. C. Rossetti.
    Al-VBP:993, Ox-BN:717
  More Poems. A. Housman. Pa-GTB:419
  The Morning after Death.
    E. Dickinson. Co-EL:71, Fe-PL:285,
    Ga-FB:150, Rv-CB:910, Tr-MR:269
  Mortality. N. Madgett. Ad-PB:182,
    Be-MA:92, Hu-NN:23, Hu-PN:382
  Mortification. G. Herbert.
    Al-VBP:345
  Mourn Not the Dead. R. Chaplin.
    Al-VBP:1147, Ba-PO:146, Cr-WS:120,
    Kr-OF:117
  My Body in the Walls Captived.
    W. Ralegh. Ma-FW:172, Rv-CB:160
  My City. J. Johnson. Bo-HF:41,
    Hu-PN:31
  My Old Grandfather. J. Alumasa.
    Le-M:179
  My Soul, Consider! E. Mörike.
    Un-R:105
  Nahuatl Poem. Ho-LP:85
  The Nation's Drum Has Fallen Down.
    Da-SC:53
  Nature. H. Longfellow.
    Co-BN:229, Fe-PL:280
  Near Avalon. W. Morris. Rv-CB:929
  Nearer to Thee. S. Adams.
    Er-FA:481, Fe-PL:328
  Night. R. Jeffers. Sm-PT:155,
    Un-MA:367
  Night, Death, Mississippi.
    R. Hayden. Ca-VT:357
  The Night Is Freezing Fast.
    A. Housman. Wi-LT:66
  Night on the Prairies. W. Whitman.
    La-RM:68, Tr-MR:288
  Night Song. Tr-US II:192
  The Night Wind. E. Brontë.
    Co-RG:152, Gr-CT:403, Ha-PO:138

No Coward Soul Is Mine. E. Brontë.
  Al-VBP:925, Er-FA:459, Ox-BN:608,
  Pl-EI:4, Rv-CB:833
Nostalgia. K. Shapiro. Br-TC:371
Not for That City. C. Mew.
  Un-MB:165
Not Waving, but Drowning. S. Smith.
  Gr-BT:40, Pa-GTB:568
Notes Found near a Suicide. F. Horne.
  Ad-PB:48, Bo-AN:42, Hu-PN:151
Notes Found near a Suicide: To the
  Poets. F. Horne. Bo-AN:46
Now and Afterwards. D. Craik.
  Fe-PL:329
O Death, Rock Me on Sleep.
  A. Boleyn. Gr-CT:357
O Sun, O Sun. Le-OE:135
Oh, Why Should the Spirit of Mortal
  Be Proud? W. Knox. Er-FA:34
The Oath. A. Tate. Wi-LT:408
Oblivion. M. Coicou. Hu-PN:69
Ode on a Grecian Urn. J. Keats.
  Al-VBP:772, Er-FA:80, Ha-PO:228,
  Ke-TF:59, Ox-BN:355, Rv-CB:742
Ode to a Nightingale. J. Keats.
  Al-VBP:769, Er-FA:89, Gr-CT:102,
  Li-SR:138, Ox-BN:352, Pa-GTB:248
Ode to Hengist and Hora.
  R. Jeffers. Gr-SS:173
Of Death. S. Harding. Rv-CB:458
Of Flesh and Bone. I. Gardner.
  St-H:67
Of My Dear Son, Gervase Beaumont.
  J. Beaumont. Al-VBP:293
Of the Death of Kings.
  W. Shakespeare. Gr-CT:368
Old Abram Brown. De-TT:45,
  Rv-ON:93
Old Hundred. M. Van Doren.
  Pl-US:53
Old Men. O. Nash. Na-EO:20
The Old Pilot's Death. J. Hall.
  Cr-WS:167, Ha-TP:44
The Old Repair Man. F. Johnson.
  Bo-AN:27, Pe-M:75
Old Shepherd's Prayer. C. Mew.
  Pl-EI:176, Un-MB:163
An Old Soldier Dies. E. de Vito.
  Ke-TF:169
On a Dead Hostess. H. Belloc.
  Un-MB:172
On a Row of Nuns in a Cemetery.
  R. Howarth. Co-EL:80
On a Virtuous Young Gentlewoman
  That Died Suddenly.
  W. Cartwright. Rv-CB:384
On One Who Died Discovering Her
  Kindness. J. Sheffield. No-CL:74
On Salt Plains. D. Coldiron.
  Fi-BG:47
On Slaughter. C. Bialik.
  Me-PH:74

On the Countess Dowager of
  Pembroke. W. Browne.
  Al-VBP:325, Rv-CB:348
On the Death of an Epicure.
  R. Graves. Rv-CB:530
On the Death of Anne Brontë.
  C. Brontë. Al-VBP:916
On the Death of William Hervey.
  A. Cowley. Al-VBP:447,
  Rv-CB:395
On the Tombs in Westminster Abbey.
  F. Beaumont. Al-VBP:301,
  De-CH:252, Hi-WP II:18, Pa-GTB:60
On the University Carrier.
  J. Milton. Sm-LG:272
On This Day I Complete My Thirty-
  Sixth Year. G. Byron.
  Al-VBP:738, Ma-YA:175
One Day of Rain. J. Brennan.
  De-FS:31
Others, I Am Not the First.
  A. Housman. Un-MB:101
Our Journey Had Advanced.
  E. Dickinson. Mo-GR:127,
  Wi-LT:12
Out of the Cradle Endlessly
  Rocking. W. Whitman.
  Al-VBP:936, Un-MA:66
Out, Out-- R. Frost. Ca-VT:11,
  Gr-BT:18, Pe-M:100
The Overtakelessness of Those.
  E. Dickinson. Tr-MR:270
Passage to More than India.
  W. Whitman. Tr-MR:292
Passer Mortuus Est. E. Millay.
  Un-MA:445
The Passing of Arthur.
  A. Tennyson. Ni-JP:158,
  Ox-BN:511
Passing of the Wrangler. H. Fellow.
  Fi-BG:151
Patch-Shaneen. J. Synge. Co-PI:188
Peruvian Dance Song. Le-OE:133
Phantom. S. Coleridge. Gr-SS:116
The Phantom Wooer. T. Beddoes.
  Al-VBP:811, Ho-WR:191
Piazza Piece. J. Ransom.
  Gr-SS:122, Ha-PO:46, Rv-CB:984,
  Un-MA:414
Poet. P. Viereck. Un-MA:660
The Poet and His Book. E. Millay.
  Un-MA:443
Poor Fellow Me. Le-OE:123
A Prayer. D. Einhorn. Ho-TY:83
A Prayer. A. Shamri. Ho-TY:363
Prayer Before a Dead Body. Be-AP:26
The Prince's Progress. C. Rossetti.
  Al-VBP:995
Prophecy. E. Wylie. Ca-VT:104
Prospice. R. Browning. Fe-PL:287,
  Ga-FB:129, Rv-CB:829
Proviso. P. George. Al-WW:113

DEATH — cont'd.
The Quaker Graveyard in Nantucket.
   R. Lowell. Al-VBP:1248,
   Pa-HT:25, Wi-LT:573
Quandary. H. Gleason. Ke-TF:171
A Question. J. Synge. Co-EL:84,
   Co-PI:187, Un-MB:181
Rain or Hail. E. Cummings.
   Du-SH:136
Rainy Mountain Cemetery. N. Momaday.
   Ni-CD:99
Readen ov a Head-Stwone. W. Barnes.
   De-CH:264
The Reaper. R. Duncan. Gr-CC:68
The Recall. R. Kipling. Go-BP:236
The Recapitulation. R. Eberhart.
   Tr-MR:284
Recognition of Death. J. Brennan.
   De-FS:33
A Recollection. F. Cornford.
   Co-EL:76, Co-PU:145
Red Eagle. J. Campbell. Al-WW:31
Refrigerium. J. Newman. Ox-BN:436
Remember. C. Rossetti. Al-VBP:995,
   De-CH:264, Fe-PL:98, Ga-FB:68,
   Hi-WP I:87, Ox-BN:705, Un-MW:90
Renascence. E. Millay. Er-FA:95,
   Un-MA:440
Requickening. Bi-IT:162
Requiem. K. Fearing. Ni-JP:171
Requiescat. M. Arnold.
   Al-VBP:963, Go-BP:146, Ha-PO:128
Resolution. Cheng Ch'ou-yü.
   Pa-MV:40
The Revenger's Tragedy. C. Tourneur.
   Al-VBP:274
Review of This Morning's Graveyard.
   P. Mayer. St-H:136
Rhymes for a Modern Nursery.
   P. Dehn. Co-FB:451
Rockferns. N. Nicholson. Un-MB:505
The Rose. W. Browne. Al-VBP:324,
   De-CH:143
Rubaiyat of Omar Khayyam.
   E. Fitzgerald. Al-VBP:832,
   Er-FA:43, Fe-FP:479, Ga-FB:60,
   Ke-TF:176, Ox-BN:526, Pa-SG:120
Rumination. R. Eberhart.
   Ho-LP:96, Sm-MK:214, Wi-LT:433
Scintilla. W. Braithwaite.
   Bo-AN:15
Second Best. R. Brooke. Un-MB:324
The Serpent Waits. J. Brennan.
   De-FS:35
Shameful Death. W. Morris.
   Gr-CT:129, Gr-SS:174, Pa-GTB:380,
   Un-GT:136
The Shape of Fear. S. Russell.
   De-FS:169
She Dwelt among the Untrodden Ways.
   W. Wordsworth. Al-VBP:656,
   Ga-FB:50, Li-SR:106, Mc-PR:179
   Ox-BN:62, Pa-GTB:179, Rv-CB:631

Sheath and Knife.   De-CH:54
Ship of Death. D. Lawrence.
   Al-VBP:1160, Pa-GTB:462, Un-MB:299
Shot Who? Jim Lane! M. Moore.
   Un-MA:574
Should You Go First. A. Rowswell.
   Fe-PL:277
Shub-Ad. R. Barlow. De-FS:11
Sister Lou. S. Brown.
   Ad-PB:66, Bo-AN:53, Hu-PN:174
A Slumber Did My Spirit Seal.
   W. Wordsworth. Al-VBP:657,
   Hi-WP I:20, Ma-FW:176, Ox-BN:65,
   Pa-GTB:181, Rv-CB:643, Sm-LG:275
Small Bird, Forgive Me. Be-MC:62
Small Elegy. M. Weisenthal.
   Ls-NY:66
The Snow Dissolv'd.   Horace.
   No-CL:130
Soldier, Rest! W. Scott. De-CH:600,
   De-TT:140, Ho-PR:282, Mc-PR:67,
   Mc-WK:204, Ox-BN:130
Solstice. M. Banus. Mc-AC:114
Some Day, Some Day. H. Longfellow.
   Al-VBP:828
Some Time at Eve. E. Hardy.
   Fe-PL:273
The Son. R. Torrence. Mc-WK:131
A Song. R. Crashaw. Al-VBP:435
Song. T. Peacock. Al-VBP:714
Song. C. Rossetti. Al-VBP:994,
   Co-BL:103, De-CH:262, Er-FA:84,
   Fe-PL:97, Ha-PO:157, Hi-WP II:21,
   Rv-CB:892, Sp-OG:278, Un-MW:91
Song. Tr-US I:50
Song at a Deathbed. Tr-US I:57
Song for the Dead. Tr-US I:53
Song for the Dead. Lo-TY:13
A Song in Passing. Y. Winters.
   Ca-VT:232
The Song of Creatures.
   St. Francis of Assisi. Pa-SG:202
Song of Myself. W. Whitman.
   Al-VBP:928, Mo-GR:106, Sh-AP:69,
   Un-MA:44
Song of the Last Moments. Tr-US I:58
The Song of the Mad Prince.
   W. de la Mare. Bo-GJ:136,
   Gr-CC:75, Sm-LG:287, Sm-MK:41
Song on the Death of an Uncle.
   Tr-US II:215
Song to the Xylophone at a Fighting
   Man's Funeral. Tr-US I:42
Sonnet. H. Belloc. Un-MB:172
Sonnet. G. Bennett. Ad-PB:82,
   Bo-AN:74, Hu-PN:206
Sonnet. R. Brooke. Un-MB:323
Sonnet. W. Drummond. Al-VBP:304
Sonnet. T. Hood. Al-VBP:798,
   Ox-BN:424
Sonnet 74. W. Shakespeare.
   Rv-CB:231

Sonnet 107. W. Shakespeare.
   Rv-CB:239
Sonnet 146. W. Shakespeare.
   Al-VBP:209, Pa-GTB:38, Pl-EI:53,
   Rv-CB:253
Sonnet on Death. W. Walsh.
   Al-VBP:512, Rv-CB:483
Sonnet on Life. B. Boothby.
   Al-VBP:597
Sonnet on the Death of His Wife.
   J. Masefield. Go-BP:150
Sonnets, xxxvii. E. Millay.
   Sm-PT:153
Sorrow. Mei Yao Ch'en. Rx-OH:42
The Sparrow's Skull. R. Pitter.
   Pl-EI:141
Speed. W. Davies. Tr-MR:268
Spring Came Bouncing. S. Jahin.
   Lo-TY:52
Squatter's Rites. D. Scott.
   Sa-B:151
The Stampede. F. Miller. Fi-BG:159
Stanzas Written in Dejection,
   near Naples. P. Shelley.
   Al-VBP:745, Ga-FB:125, Pa-GTB:227,
   Rv-CB:707
Stepping Westward. W. Wordsworth.
   De-CH:436
Still Life. M. Yoshioka. Sh-AM:113
The Stirrup-Cup. S. Lanier.
   Sh-AP:132
Stop All the Clocks. W. Auden.
   Hi-WP II:29, Un-MB:465,
   Un-MW:103
The Streets of Laredo. Co-RM:28,
   Er-FA:337, Gr-CT:137, Gr-GB:321,
   Hi-TL:162, Mc-WK:169, Mc-WS:153
The Subalterns. T. Hardy. Un-MB:33
The Sun Came Out in April.
   C. Day Lewis. Ca-MB:23
Sun Goes Up. H. Farley. Le-M:143
Sunday Morning. W. Stevens.
   Sh-AP:158, Sm-PT:121, Un-MA:242,
   Wi-LT:139
Sunset Horn. M. O'Higgins.
   Bo-AN:146, Hu-PN:352
Suspiria. H. Longfellow.
   Al-VBP:825
Swing Low, Sweet Chariot.
   Gr-GB:327, Sm-LG:386
Synchronized. L. Rubin. De-FS:165
A Talisman. M. Moore. Al-VBP:1174,
   Bo-GJ:199, Ho-LP:52, Un-MA:349
Tetélestai. C. Aiken. Un-MA:431,
   Wi-LT:327
Thanatopsis. W. Bryant. Al-VBP:765,
   Co-BN:216, Er-FA:67, Sh-AP:17
That Dark Other Mountain. R. Francis.
   Mo-SD:169, Pe-SS:8
That Nature Is a Heraclitean Fire and
   of the Comfort of the Resurrection.
   G. Hopkins. Pa-GTB:396

There Is No Death.   Mc-PR:83
They Are Not Long. E. Dowson.
   Al-VBP:1102, Gr-CT:325, Ha-PO:155,
   Un-MB:151
They Found Him Sitting in a Chair.
   H. Gregory. Un-MA:504
This Houre Her Vigill.
   V. Iremonger. Co-PI:74
This Is Not Death. H. Wolfe. Un-MB:304
Thoughts During an Air Raid.
   S. Spender. Al-VBP:1234, Un-MB:479
Three Friends. U. Beier. Be-AP:31,
   Hu-PB:19
The Three Ravens.   Al-VBP:39,
   Fo-OG:34, Gr-CT:165, Gr-GB:245,
   Ox-BB:245
The Three Roses. W. Landor.
   No-CL:126
Three Years She Grew in Sun and
   Shower. W. Wordsworth.
   Ox-BN:63, Pa-GTB:180, Rv-CB:642
Threnody. W. Cuney. Bo-AN:99
To a Dead Poet, His Book.
   D. Berrigan. Pl-ML:147
To a Traveler. L. Johnson. Un-MB:154
To an Athlete Dying Young.
   A. Housman. Ha-PO:140,
   Ma-YA:223, Mo-SD:168, Ni-JP:33,
   Pe-M:58, Un-MB:94, Wi-LT:60
To Clarissa Scott Delany. A. Grimke.
   Bo-AN:15
To Entertain Divine Zenocrate.
   C. Marlowe. Al-VBP:174, Gr-CT:180
To Everlasting Oblivion. J. Marston.
   Rv-CB:311
To His Wife. J. Skelton. Rv-CB:69
To Mary. C. Wolfe. Al-VBP:739
To One in Paradise. E. Poe.
   Al-VBP:874, Fe-PL:101, Un-MW:207
To Robert Louis Stevenson.
   W. Henley. Un-MB:56
To Sleep. J. Kochanowski. Pa-SG:178
To Stella. Plato. Al-VBP:759,
   Pa-SG:13
To the Mound of Corpses in the Snow.
   U. Greenberg. Me-PH:95
The Tod's Hole. Gr-GB:320
The Tourist from Syracuse.
   D. Justice. Br-TC:226
Tree. J. Hunter. Le-M:123
The Truth the Dead Know. A. Sexton.
   Un-MA:689
The Twa Brothers. De-CH:52, Ox-BB:234
Twenty Years Hence. W. Landor.
   Al-VBP:706
The Two Fires. J. Wright. Un-MB:515
Two of the Festivities of Death.
   J. de Melo Neto. An-TC:165
Two Sonnets. C. Sorley. Un-MB:378
Ulalume. E. Poe. Al-VBP:869, Sh-AP:58
Unknown Man in the Morgue. M. Moore.
   Un-MA:576

DEATH — cont'd.
  Upon a Maid. R. Herrick. Gr-CT:354,
    Sm-LG:273
  Upon the Image of Death.
    R. Southwell. De-CH:244
  Venus and Adonis. W. Browne.
    No-CL:57
  Vigil. C. Meireles.   An-TC:37
  The Virgin Mother. D. Lawrence.
    Al-VBP:1157
  Virtue. G. Herbert. Al-VBP:343,
    De-CH:431, Ha-PO:199, Rv-CB:352
  Wake, All the Dead! W. Davenport.
    De-CH:639, Rv-CB:366, Sm-LG:277
  The Wanderer Recalls the Past.
    W. Wordsworth. Ox-BN:92
  Warning to One. M. Moore. Un-MA:575
  Watchman, What of the Night?
    A. Swinburne. Ho-WR:200
  Weep You No More. Al-VBP:357,
    De-CH:266, Go-BP:145, Gr-CT:410
  Wenberri's Song. Wenberri.
    Tr-US I:261
  What Do You Do with a Woman's
    Things? A. Miller. Ke-TF:175
  What's in the Newspaper Tonight?
    R. Holzinger. La-IH:17
  When from the World. De-CH:650
  When God Lets My Body Be.
    E. Cummings. Un-MA:470
  When I Am Dead. J. Wilson. Fe-PL:275
  When I Awoke. R. Patterson.
    Ad-PB:208, Hu-NN:113
  When I Die. F. Johnson. Hu-PN:90
  When I Have Fears that I May Cease
    to Be. J. Keats. Go-BP:148,
    Ha-PO:129, Ma-YA:187, No-CL:6,
    Ox-BN:369, Pa-GTB:198, Rv-CB:747,
    Un-GT:313
  When Lilacs Last in the Dooryard
    Bloom'd. W. Whitman. Al-VBP:940,
    Sh-AP:113, Un-MA:71, Vi-PP:172
  When You Have Gone. Le-OE:132
  Where Is Paris and Heleyne?
    Thomas of Hales. Gr-CT:321
  The White Dress. M. Zaturenska.
    Un-MA:560
  Who Comes? Le-IB:120
  Who's at My Window?
    J. Wedderburn. De-CH:640
  Why Did I Laugh Tonight? J. Keats.
    Rv-CB:751
  The Wife of Usher's Well. Ar-TP3:20,
    De-CH:424, De-TT:171, Gr-CT:134,
    Ma-BB:37, Ox-BB:94, Pa-OM:91
    Rv-CB:36
  The Wisdom of Merlyn. W. Blunt.
    Al-VBP:1056
  The Wise. C. Cullen. Hu-PN:230
  The Witch. R. Southey. Ho-WR:219
  With Rue My Heart Is Laden. A. Housman.
    Er-FA:88, Un-MB:94, Wi-LT:62

  Witness to Death. R. Lattimore.
    Ca-VT:282
  Wolf Woman. Da-SC:51, Ho-SD:60
  Women's Grinding Song. Tr-US I:123
  The World of Light. H. Vaughan.
    Al-VBP:469, De-CH:267, Gr-CT:384,
    Rv-CB:411
  Yardbird's Skull. O. Dodson.
    Ad-PB:132, Bo-AN:125, Ca-VT:387
  Years, Many Parti-Colored Years.
    W. Landor. Al-VBP:705, Rv-CB:671
  You and I Shall Go. Bi-IT:100,
    Tr-US II:248
  You Know What Will Happen.
    R. Richard. Ad-II:95
  You Were at the Dead River.
    G. Abbe. De-FS:3
  A Youth. S. Crane. Un-MA:148
DEATH - CHILDREN: see also HUMOR -
    DEATH - CHILDREN
  All. All a-Lonely. Gr-CT:159
  The Babes in the Wood.
    Bl-OB:70, De-CH:546, De-TT:44,
    Gr-EC:152, Ox-BC:97
  Ballad of Birmingham. D. Randall.
    Be-MA:71, Ra-BP:143
  Bells for John Whiteside's Daughter.
    J. Ransom. Ca-VT:148, Ke-PP:31,
    Pe-SS:159, Sh-AP:179, Un-MA:408,
    Wi-LT:311
  Birmingham Sunday. L. Hughes.
    Hu-PN:200
  The Black Rock. J. Berryman.
    Ca-VT:385
  "Blackened-Face" Dirge - Proper for
    Atiroa. Koroneu. Tr-US II:64
  Bombing Casualties: Spain.
    H. Read. Ke-PP:64
  The Boy and the Deer. Te-FC:3
  The Brothers. E. Muir. Pa-GTB:471
  Burial. M. Van Doren. Ca-MB:22
  The Child Dying. E. Muir.
    Pa-GTB:468
  The Childless Father.
    W. Wordsworth. De-CH:260
  Complaint of a Widow over Her Dying
    Son. Tr-US I:157
  The Cruel Mother. Ox-BB:68
  Dance Song. Tr-US II:7
  Dead Boy. J. Ransom. Br-TC:336
  Death of a Son. J. Silkin.
    Br-TC:375, Pa-GTB:566
  Death of a Son. Bi-IT:99
  Death of Little Boys. A. Tate.
    Br-TC:430
  Deathwatch. M. Harper. Ad-PB:317
  Dirge. Tr-US II:103
  Dirge. Tr-US II:146
  The Dream. De-TT:172
  The Dying Child. J. Clare.
    Ma-FW:169, Rv-CB:726
  Earth. M. Rosenfeld. Ho-TY:80

An Elegy for a Dead Child in the
Street. R. Rao. Al-PI:106
Empty House. S. Spender.
Hi-WP II:27
Epilogue to Rhymes and Rhythms.
W. Henley. Al-VBP:1069
An Epitaph on Salathiel Pavey.
B. Jonson. Al-VBP:233, Ha-PO:131
The Erl-King. J. von Goethe.
Sp-OG:111
First Death in Nova Scotia.
E. Bishop. Mc-EA:162
The First Grief. F. Hemans.
De-CH:45
For a Child in Death. C. Mew.
Un-MB:160
For a Very New Angel. V. Storey.
Ke-TF:200
Four Epitaphs. S. Warner.
Un-MB:371
Get the Gasworks. D. Ignatow.
Kh-VA:57, Mo-BG:181
A Greyport Legend. B. Harte.
Sp-OG:83
Hint Heavenward. A. Peach.
Ke-TF:207
A Hiroshima Lullaby. J. Langland.
Ke-PP:131
Holidays in Childhood. C. Dyment.
Go-BP:64
The Holy Innocents. R. Lowell.
Un-MA:663
Home Burial. R. Frost. Pe-SS:15
How the Gates Came Ajar. Ke-TF:42
I Wanted to Come Home. Wen I-to.
Hs-TC:59
Improvisation of the Dead Boy.
M. de Andrade. An-TC:21
In Memoriam. Yü Ta-fu. Hs-TC:272
Italian Extravaganza. G. Corso.
La-OC:91
Lament: Sea-Burial of Toga's
Daughter. Tr-US II:88
Little Boy Blue. E. Field.
Er-FA:490, Fe-FP:536, Fe-PL:248
Little Elegy. X. Kennedy.
Bo-GJ:234, Co-EL:78, Co-PU:157,
Mo-BG:162
Lucy Gray. W. Wordsworth.
De-CH:222, De-TT:85, Ox-BC:98
Lyrics. J. Agee. Un-MA:603
Margaret Love Peacock for Her
Tombstone, 1826. T. Peacock.
Ox-BN:237
The Massacre of the Innocents.
W. Smith. Pl-EI:149
Mater Dolorosa. W. Barnes.
De-CH:265
O Tender under Her Right Breast.
G. Barker. Un-MB:493
On a Dead Child. R. Bridges.
Al-VBP:1064, Ox-BN:875, Wi-LT:54

On an Infant Dying as Soon as Born.
C. Lamb. Pa-GTB:237
On the Death of a Child.
E. Silvera. Hu-PN:260
On the Death of a New Born Child.
Mei Yao Ch'en. Rx-OH:41
On the Death of His Baby Son.
Su Tung P'o. Rx-OH:69
On the Staircase. W. Wellman.
De-FS:215
Protocols. R. Jarrell. Ca-VT:308
A Refusal to Mourn the Death, by
Fire, of a Child in London.
D. Thomas. Br-TC:439, Er-FA:192,
Gr-BT:103, Pa-GTB:540, To-MP:48,
Un-MB:503, Wi-LT:550
Responsive Song for the Dead Child
of a Chief. Tr-US II:220
A Song Made by Dancers on Hearing a
Woman Mourning for Her Child.
Tr-US I:86
Song of a Dying Girl. Tr-US I:170
Song of a Mother for Her Dead Son.
Tr-US II:20
Song of a Woman Crying for the Dead
Baby Son of Her Daughter.
Tr-US I:244
The Step Mother. H. Adam. De-FS:5
Ternissa. W. Landor. Ox-BN:194
To My Brother Miguel. C. Vallejo.
Pe-M:13
The Truants. W. de la Mare.
Un-MB:197
The Turnstile. W. Barnes. De-CH:255
The Two April Mornings.
W. Wordsworth. Pa-GTB:302
Upon a Child That Died. R. Herrick.
De-CH:255, Sm-MK:211
We Are Seven. W. Wordsworth.
Li-SR:116, Ox-BC:100
A Wreath. Ho Ch'i-fang. Hs-TC:220
A Young David: Birmingham.
H. Brooks. Hu-PN:276
The Zero Degree of Life.
Tsang K'o-chia. Hs-TC:289
DEATH – DEFINITIONS
Death, Great Smoothener. M. Swenson.
Ha-TP:127
Death Is a Little Thing. G. Abbe.
De-FS:3
Ignorance of Death. W. Empson.
Wi-LT:444
The Paradox. P. Dunbar. Ad-PB:11
DEATH, DESIRED
After Dark Vapours. J. Keats.
Ox-BN:367, Rv-CB:745
Ah! Sun-Flower. W. Blake.
Al-VBP:617, Co-EL:85, Gr-CT:255,
Ox-BN:24, Rv-CB:610
Alone Walking. Rv-CB:2
Anthology. M. Bandeira. An-TC:5
Bury Me. Chu Hsiang. Hs-TC:98

DEATH, DESIRED — cont'd.
Call into Death. D. Lawrence.
  Go-BP:245
Chinook Sad Song. Da-SC:16
The City of Dreadful Night XIII.
  J. Thomson. Al-VBP:1007
Death Carol. W. Whitman. Tr-MR:266
Death of a Vermont Farm Woman.
  B. Howes. Un-MA:653
Died of Love. Rv-CB:431
Distance Spills Itself.
  Y. Bat-Miriam. Me-PH:104
The Dying Christian to His Soul.
  A. Pope. Go-BP:235
For Annie. E. Poe. Sh-AP:60
The Heart Asks Pleasure First.
  E. Dickinson. Ha-PO:149,
  Rv-CB:898, Un-MA:96
Hurt Hawks. R. Jeffers.
  Co-BBW:236, Ni-JP:115, Pe-SS:150,
  Sh-AP:177, Un-MA:369, Wi-LT:258
In Trouble and Shame. D. Lawrence.
  Go-BP:244
Jerusalem, My Happy Home. Rv-CB:108,
  Sm-LG:383
The Junk Man. C. Sandburg. Ga-S:35
A Last Word. E. Dowson. Un-MB:147
Madboy's Song. M. Rukeyser.
  Un-MA:628
The Mask. E. Browning. Ox-BN:463,
  Rv-CB:778
The Moor. R. Hodgson. Un-MB:187
Music. G. du Maurier. Rv-CB:932
My Thoughts Hold Mortal Strife.
  W. Drummond. Pa-GTB:27, Rv-CB:328
Never Weather-Beaten Sail.
  T. Campion. Gr-CT:226, Rv-CB:274
Now Full Twelve Years Twice-Told.
  De-CH:639
O Death, Rock Me Asleep. Rv-CB:105
O God, Beloved God, in Pity Send.
  J. Masefield. Go-BP:243
Old Black Joe. S. Foster. Er-FA:441
The Old Pastor. J. Tabb. Sh-AP:136
The Prayer of the Old Horse.
  C. Gasztold. La-PV:126
The Prisoner. E. Brontë. Ox-BN:607
Rest. C. Rossetti. Ox-BN:712
Return. I. Vilarino. Be-UL:81
Sleep after Toil. E. Spenser.
  Gr-CT:230
Song. P. Massinger. Al-VBP:298
A Song for Simeon. T. Eliot.
  Gr-BT:174, Pl-EI:202
The Song of Love and Death.
  A. Tennyson. Ox-BN:510
Sonnet 21. P. Goodman. Ca-VT:335
Sonnet 66. W. Shakespeare.
  Al-VBP:204, Er-FA:120, No-CL:85,
  Pa-GTB:40, Rv-CB:227
Sorrow of Mydath. J. Masefield.
  Un-MB:222

The Staircase. S. Allen. Ad-PB:167
Tithonus. A. Tennyson. Ox-BN:482,
  Rv-CB:792
The Watch. F. Cornford. Un-MB:306
The Wheel. W. Yeats. Pa-GTB:427
DEATH - PARENTS
And Be Her Mother, Just as She Was
  Mine. Ke-TF:145
Ballad. R. Fuller. Co-EL:75
Daddy. S. Plath. Br-TC:324,
  Mc-EA:164, Wi-LT:789
Death-Bed. A. Rowse. Hi-WP II:26
Dirge. Tr-US II:51
Dirges, I. Tr-US II:41
Do Not Go Gentle into That Good
  Night. D. Thomas.
  Al-VBP:1247, Br-TC:439, Er-FA:40,
  Gr-BT:173, Ha-PO:126, Hi-WP II:30,
  Ke-PP:25, Un-MB:504, Wi-LT:551
The Door. V. Golyavkin. Bo-RU:38
Elegy for My Father. H. Moss.
  Wi-LT:777
Father Son and Holy Ghost. A. Lorde.
  Ad-PB:248, Be-MA:121
The Feast of Lanterns.
  J. Yoshimura. Le-TA:35
For a Fatherless Son. S. Plath.
  Mc-EA:98
Heart-Summoned. J. Stuart. De-FS:195
Kaddish. M. Rawitch. Ho-TY:203
Lament. E. Millay. Kr-OF:183
The Lesson. E. Lucie-Smith.
  Br-TC:271, Gr-BT:20, To-MP:99
The Lost Pilot. J. Tate. Br-TC:433
Mom. G. Cohoe. Al-WW:27
Mortmain. R. Warren. En-PC:74,
  Ho-P:295
Mother, the Wardrobe Is Full of
  Infantrymen. R. McGough.
  Gr-BT:117
Poor Miner's Farewell. M. Jackson.
  Kr-OF:190
The Red-Throated. M. Saito. Sh-AM:144
Seven Brothers. M. Leib. Ho-TY:91
Soldier. W. Benét. Ke-TF:170
Song for a Dead Mother. Tr-US II:181
Two Mounds. J. Glatstein. Ho-TY:326
Very Close to Death. M. Saito.
  Sh-AM:144
When I Read My Poems. H. Takai.
  Le-TA:36
DEBS, EUGENE VICTOR
Debs. J. Oppenheim. Kr-OF:118
The Old Agitator. W. Leonard.
  Ba-PO:147
DEBTS: see also BORROWING AND LENDING;
  HUMOR - DEBTS
Baudelaire. D. Schwartz. Br-TC:357,
  Pl-ML:14
The Creditor. L. MacNeice. Pl-EI:41
The Debt. P. Dunbar. Bo-AN:5,
  Bo-HF:176

A Gest of Robyn Hode, The Seconde
Fytte. Ox-BB:433
A Gest of Robyn Hode, The Fourth
Fytte. Ox-BB:452
Han Po Chops Wood. Feng Chih.
Hs-TC:155
Lamkin. Ox-BB:313, Rv-CB:44
DECAY: see DEATH
DECEMBER
December. A. Fisher. Br-SS:95,
La-PH:21
December. J. Lowell. Un-GT:283
December. T. Ramsey. Sm-MK:137
December. C. Rossetti. Ha-YA:150
A December Day. S. Teasdale.
Ha-YA:151, Se-PR:214
December Stillness. S. Sassoon.
Tr-MR:57
How Still, How Happy! E. Brontë.
Ox-BN:598
In a Drear-Nighted December.
J. Keats. De-CH:216, Ox-BN:373,
Pa-GTB:191, Rv-CB:737
The Long Night Moon: December.
F. Frost. Ha-YA:152
Somewhere Around Christmas.
J. Smith. Ma-FW:278
Tree in December. M. Cane.
Un-MA:235
When Cold December. E. Sitwell.
Mc-WS:133
DECEPTION: see also APRIL FOOLS'
DAY; FALSEHOOD; HUMOR - DECEP-
TION; LIARS; PLAGIARISM;
QUACKS AND QUACKERY; TRICKS
The Ass in the Lion's Skin.
Aesop. Gr-EC:198, Rd-OA:167
The Bents and Broom. Ox-BB:187
Blind Love. W. Shakespeare.
Pa-GTB:24
Brown Robin. Ox-BB:227
The Buffalo Skinners. Gr-GB:220,
Hi-TL:150
Bussy d'Ambois. G. Chapman.
Al-VBP:145
Cantares II. L. Speyer. Ho-TH:26
Chief Red Jacket Addresses a
Missionary. Red Jacket. Kr-OF:4
Clark Sanders. Ox-BB:76, Rv-CB:34
The Cock and the Fox.
J. de la Fontaine. Mc-PR:14
Contemplation. F. Thompson.
Ox-BN:920
Corinna, Pride of Drury-Lane.
J. Swift. Ke-PP:34
The Crafty Farmer. Ar-TP3:16
Dawn Song. Tr-US II:228
Dialogue. Tr-US II:192
The Dishonest Miller. Em-AF:761
The Dodger. Gr-GB:201
Donald of the Isles. Ox-BB:258
The Duke o' Athole's Nurse. Ox-BB:344

False Love. W. Ralegh. Rv-CB:151
The Famous Flower of Serving-Men.
Ox-BB:182
The Fate of a Broom — an Anticipation.
T. Peacock. Rv-CB:685
The Frog and the Crow. Gr-GB:67
Full Moon. E. Wylie. Ca-VT:103,
Un-MA:280
A Gest of Robyn Hode, The Seconde
Fytte. Ox-BB:433
Hard Times. Em-AF:767
The Hero. S. Sassoon. Co-RM:208
The Horse Trader's Song. Em-AF:762
How Shall I Get Inside the Door.
Un-R:97
How Shall We Hide. Ho-SD:58
The Humbug Steamship Companies.
J. Stone. Fi-BG:134
I Almost Did — Very Nigh.
E. Turner. Gr-TG:15
Idle Fyno. Al-VBP:360, Gr-CT:18,
Rv-CB:128
The Jolly Beggar. Ox-BB:624
Juan's Song. L. Bogan. Mo-BG:87
Jungle Songs, III. Tr-US II:158
Lack of Steadfastness.
G. Chaucer. Rv-CB:62
The Leaders of the Crowd.
W. Yeats. Un-MB:116
The Lion and the Fox. E. Rees.
Ar-TP3:81
Love to Faults Is Always Blind.
W. Blake. Al-VBP:620
The Magnet. R. Stone. Un-MA:655
Man's a Bubble. R. Dodsley.
Rv-CB:523
March 18. Jao Meng-k'an.
Hs-TC:106
The Mask. E. Browning. Ox-BN:463,
Rv-CB:778
The Mask. C. Delaney. Hu-PN:177
The Mask. W. Yeats. No-CL:202
The Merchant, to Secure. . . .
M. Prior. Al-VBP:512,
Pa-GTB:130, Rv-CB:484, Un-MW:50
Movie Queen. J. Vaughn. Hu-NN:62
My Brother. D. Aldis. Ar-TP3:185,
Au-SP:191
The Nesting Ground. D. Wagoner.
En-PC:249
The Outlandish Knight. Br-SM:36,
Un-GT:111
The Pied Piper of Hamelin.
R. Browning. Ar-TP3:28, Er-FA:354,
Ox-BC:173, Sm-LG:173, Un-GT:153
A Prayer to Be Delivered from Liars
and Warmongers. Bible. O.T.
Psalms. Me-PH:27
The Revenger's Tragedy.
C. Tourneur. Al-VBP:275
Robin Hood and Allan a Dale.
Gr-GB:247, Ma-BB:44, Un-GT:115

DECEPTION — cont'd.
  Robin Hood and the Widow's Three
    Sons.   Ar-TP3:17, Co-PT:224,
    Ma-BB:70, Pa-OM:86, Sp-OG:157,
    Un-GT:119
  Silent, Silent Night.   W. Blake.
    Rv-CB:604
  Soldier, Soldier, Won't You Marry
    Me?   Bl-OB:35
  Tale.   Br-MW:44
  'Tis a Sin.   De-CH:569
  We Wear the Mask.   P. Dunbar.
    Ad-IA:86, Ad-PB:8, Bo-AN:14,
    Bo-HF:103, Jo-SA:134, Lo-TY:208,
    Mo-BG:190
  What Curious Dresses All Men Wear.
    D. Schwartz.   Co-EL:38
  Whistle an' I'll Come to Ye, My Lad.
    R. Burns.   Al-VBP:651, Co-BL:99,
    Hi-WP I:41, Un-MW:188
  Witch Doctor.   R. Hayden.   Bo-AN:110
  See also Em-AF:152-164
DECLARATION OF INDEPENDENCE
  Independence Bell.   Vi-PP:80
DECORATION DAY: see MEMORIAL DAY
DEE, RUBY
  Beautiful Black Women. . . .
    I. Baraka.   Ra-BP:213
DEE RIVER
  The Sands of Dee.   Bl-OB:153,
    Cl-FC:88, Co-PM:111, Co-SS:43,
    De-CH:211, De-TT:182, Fe-FP:511,
    Hu-MP:430, Sp-OG:84
DEEDS: see THOUGHT AND DEED
DEEP-SEA DIVING: see SKIN AND
    SCUBA DIVING
DEER
  Ah, the Peasant.   Hosokawa Yusai.
    Le-MW:116
  Akjartoq's Song of the Olden Days.
    Le-IB:110, Tr-US I:15
  All in Green Went My Love Riding.
    E. Cummings.   Al-VBP:1201,
    Bo-GJ:121, Ga-FB:82, Ma-FW:203,
    Mo-SD:186, No-CL:70, Re-TW:118,
    Wi-LT:357
  Alone.   K. Raikin.   Mo-MI:48
  The Baby Tigers.   K. Raikin.
    Mo-MI:53
  Black-Tailed Deer Song.   Bi-IT:54
  Blacktail Deer.   L. Sarett.
    Co-BBW:187
  The Boy and the Deer.   Te-FC:3
  The Buck in the Snow.   E. Millay.
    Ad-PE:29, Sm-PT:152
  Caribou Hunting.   Le-IB:71,
    Ma-BH:24, Tr-US I:13
  Child's Song.   T. Moore.
    Al-VBP:711, Co-BN:49, Gr-CC:56,
    Gr-EC:224, Sm-MK:9
  Complaint.   Tr-US I:34
  The Coyote Lived at Sun House.
    Wo-HS:(14)

The Cross of Antlers.
  M. Yeryomin.   Bo-RU:92
Crystal Moment.   R. Coffin.
  Gr-EC:162, Pe-SS:74
Dead Doe.   J. Harrison.   Ho-LP:23
The Deer.   M. Austin.   Fe-FP:171
Deer.   H. Behn.   Co-BBW:208,
  Li-TU:192
Deer.   J. Drinkwater.   De-CH:282
The Deer.   T. Miyoshi.   Sh-AM:83
A Deer.   S. Murano.   Sh-AM:93
Deer.   Ca-MU:29
The Deer.   Jo-TS:4
Deer among Cattle.   J. Dickey.
  Mo-TS:69
The Deer and the Snake.
  K. Patchen.   Un-MA:609
The Deer Is Taking Away.
  Ho-SD:19
The Deer Live at the Deer Yawn.
  Wo-HS:(14)
Deer Song.   Da-SC:81
The Deer That Lives.
  Önakotomi Yoshinobu.   Ba-ST:40,
  Le-MW:80
Earthy Anecdote.   W. Stevens.
  Bo-GJ:225, Re-TW:35
Evening Shadows Touch.   Buson.
  Be-CS:39
Fall.   R. Francis.   Ca-VT:233
The Fallow Deer at the Lonely
  House.   T. Hardy.   Bl-OB:124,
  Co-PU:87, De-CH:281
The Faun.   E. Pound.   Ma-FW:112,
  Sm-LG:72
The Fawn.   R. Holden.   Ls-NY:198
The Fawn.   E. Millay.   Co-BBW:190
The Fawn in the Snow.   W. Benét.
  Rd-OA:183, Un-MA:323
First They Shot.   Le-IB:51
For the Deer Dance.   Tr-US II:170
From the Mountain's Summit.
  Ho-SD:40
Gates of the Rockies. J. Daugherty.
  Sh-RP:301
Glorious It Is.   La-RM:112
Green Afternoon.   F. Frost.
  Ar-TP3:76
The Hart.   Gr-EC:282, Gr-GB:53,
  Mo-MGT:191, Rv-CB:448, Rv-ON:99,
  Sm-LG:291, Wr-RM:75
Hiking.   J. Bruchac.   Ni-CD:38
A Hunted Deer.   De-PP:41
Hunter's Song.   W. Scott. Rd-OA:176
Hunting Song.   Da-SC:80, Le-OA:64
Hunting Song.   Tr-US II:271
Hymn to the Southern Mountains.
  Tr-US I:33
I Have a Fawn.   T. Moore. Cl-FC:72
In Summer the Rains.   Da-SC:16,
  Ho-SD:19, Le-OE:79
In the Mountain Village.
  Minamoto No Morotada. Ba-ST:40

July. L. Tatyanicheva. Pa-SG:94
Landscape, Deer Season. B. Howes.
  Bo-GJ:253, Pe-M:111
Like as a Huntsman. E. Spenser.
  Ha-PO:108
Magic Words to Bring Luck when
  Hunting Caribou. Le-IB:67
Make Me a Man. P. George.
  Al-WW:121
Midsummer Nights. S. Sandy.
  Be-EB:34
Mrs. Santa Claus' Christmas Present.
  A. Morris. Co-PS:166
Moment. D. Berrigan. Re-EB:41
The Most of It. R. Frost.
  Ha-PO:218, Mo-BG:104
My Thoughts Went Constantly.
  Le-IB:99
The Nymph Complaining for the
  Death of Her Fawn. A. Marvell.
  De-CH:92, Rd-OA:191, Rv-CB:402,
  Sm-LG:71
O Warmth of Summer. Le-IB:37
Old Wife's Song. E. Farjeon.
  Sh-RP:15
Out in the Dark. E. Thomas.
  Cl-DT:35, De-CH:453, Pa-GTB:444,
  Un-MB:218, Wi-LT:647
Over There I Could Think of Nothing
  Else. Le-IB:50
Religious Hymn to Be Sung Wearing a
  Head Decoration. Le-IB:95,
  Ma-BH:15, Tr-US I:20
The Revenge of Hamish. S. Lanier.
  Ni-JP:46, Sp-OG:141
Robin Hood and the Butcher.
  Ma-BB:62
A Runnable Stag. J. Davidson.
  Co-BBW:195, Ho-WR:77, Mo-SD:123,
  Na-EO:63, Rd-OA:177
The Sacrament. R. Coffin. Ho-TH:38
Song. Bi-IT:53
Song of Caribou, Musk Oxen.
  Br-MW:140, Ho-SD:67, Le-IB:34,
  Ma-BH:21, Tr-US I:26
Song of the Deer. Bi-IT:56
Song of the Fallen Deer. Bi-IT:57,
  Da-SC:88
Song of the Hunter. Bi-IT:55
Songs, II. The Reindeer Herd.
  Tr-US I:33
The Tame Stag. J. Gay. Rv-CB:503
The Three Ravens. Al-VBP:39,
  Fo-OG:34, Gr-CT:165, Gr-GB:245,
  Ox-BB:245
Traveling Through the Dark.
  W. Stafford. Co-PT:126,
  Ma-FW:225, Mo-BG:144, Mo-TS:71,
  Pe-SS:76, Wi-LT:826
Two Look at Two. R. Frost. Un-MA:180
Ulivfak's Song of the Caribou.
  Le-IB:112

The White-Footed Deer. W. Bryant.
  Sp-OG:178
The White Stag. E. Pound.
  Ha-LO:97
The Wounded Doe. D. Schmitz.
  St-H:197
Young Flash the Deer. T. Burgess.
  Sh-RP:342
DEFEAT: see also FAILURE; HUMOR -
  DEFEAT
All the World Over. R. Kipling.
  Go-BP:216
Aunt Jennifer's Tigers. A. Rich.
  Ha-TP:52
Boxer. A. Katz. Ho-TY:294
The Bull. R. Hodgson. Rd-OA:122,
  Un-MB:190, Wi-LT:125
The Destruction of Sennacherib.
  G. Byron. Er-FA:347, Fe-FP:511,
  Fe-PL:431, Hi-FO:27, Hu-MP:416,
  Mc-PR:25, Na-EO:50, Ni-JP:75,
  Pa-OM:146, Sm-LG:256, Sp-OG:183,
  Un-GT:143
For the Moment. R. Weber. Co-PI:196
The Last Word. M. Arnold.
  Ha-PO:215, Ox-BN:647
Lucifer in Starlight. G. Meredith.
  Al-VBP:985, De-CH:314, Ha-PO:48,
  Ox-BN:693, Rv-CB:880
Ode to the Confederate Dead in
  Magnolia Cemetery. H. Timrod.
  Se-PR:134, Sh-AP:126, Vi-PP:165
Retreat. J. Clark. Ls-NY:87
Riding Together. W. Morris.
  Cl-FC:79
A Snapshot for Miss Bricka.
  R. Wallace. Mo-SD:35
Song after Defeat. Tr-US I:37
Success Is Counted Sweetest.
  E. Dickinson. Bo-GJ:191,
  Mo-BG:166. Rv-CB:897, Sh-AP:126,
  Un-MA:103, Wi-LT:3
The Surrender Speech of Chief
  Joseph. Chief Joseph. Bi-IT:153,
  Kr-OF:19
The Surrender Speech of Cuauhtemoc.
  Cuauhtemoc. Bi-IT:152
Taunt Sung to the Impaled Head of
  an Enemy Chief. Paenga-Huru.
  Tr-US II:112
To a Friend Whose Work Has Come to
  Nothing. W. Yeats. Un-MB:116,
  Wi-LT:69
The Vanity of Human Wishes.
  S. Johnson. Al-VBP:552,
  Hi-FO:171
Victory in Defeat. E. Markham.
  Fe-PL:301
War. Chief Joseph. Ba-PO:112
DEFIANCE: see also CHALLENGES;
  PROTEST; REBELLION
America. A. Ginsberg. Bl-FP:64

DEFIANCE — cont'd.
Arthur McBride.   Co-RM:115,
Gr-GB:236
Banty Tim. J. Hay. Kr-OF:45
Broken Heart, Broken Machine.
R. Grant. Ad-PB:505
The Broncho That Would Not Be
Broken. V. Lindsay.
Ar-TP3:255, Co-BBW:147, Co-RG:108
Cawdor. R. Jeffers. Sm-PT:25
Do Not Go Gentle into That Good
Night. D. Thomas.
Al-VBP:1247, Br-TC:439, Er-FA:40,
Gr-BT:173, Ha-PO:126, Hi-WP II:30,
Ke-PP:25, Un-MB:504, Wi-LT:551
Gone Away Blues. T. McGrath.
Cr-WS:174
Heh Nonny No! Gr-BT:177
Letter to My Sister. A. Spencer.
Ad-PB:16, Bo-AN:19, Hu-PN:61
Milton. W. Blake. Al-VBP:622,
Ga-FB:223, Ha-PO:206, Hi-FO:251,
Ke-PP:132, Na-EO:32, Ox-BN:40,
Pl-EI:162, Rv-CB:612, Sm-LG:135
The Minstrel Boy. T. Moore.
Cl-FC:84, Co-RG:30, Er-FA:182,
Un-GT:313
Night Here. G. Snyder. Bl-FP:62
O for a Man Who Is a Man!
H. Thoreau. Kr-OF:67
Ojibwa War Song. Da-SC:155,
Kr-OF:1, Le-OE:120
Once. A. Walker. Ad-PB:474
The One-Horned Ewe. Gr-GB:82
The Taming of the Shrew.
W. Shakespeare. Pl-US:14
The War for Truth. W. Bryant.
Kr-OF:133
The Wearing of the Green. Co-PS:51,
Er-FA:295, Gr-GB:193, Hi-FO:252
What Though the Field Be Lost?
J. Milton. Pl-EI:76
The White City. C. McKay.
Ra-BP:61
DEGENERACY: see also CORRUPTION
Eclipse. A. Probst. Ni-CD:178
Prescription of Painful Ends.
R. Jeffers. Un-MA:370
The Scarlet Woman. F. Johnson.
Ad-PB:24
DEIRDRE
Deirdre. J. Stephens. Al-VBP:1151,
Gr-CC:91
DE LA MARE, WALTER (JOHN): see
HUMOR - DE LA MARE, WALTER (JOHN)
DELANY, CLARISSA SCOTT
To Clarissa Scott Delany. A. Grimke.
Bo-AN:15
DELAWARE
Nocturne. F. Frost. Co-BN:202
Our Delaware. G. Hynson.
Se-PR:255

DELPHI, GR.
News for the Delphic Oracle.
W. Yeats. Wi-LT:91
DEMOCRACY: see also EQUALITY;
SATIRE - DEMOCRACY
Americans! P. Freneau. Ke-PP:45
Boston Hymn. R. Emerson. Vi-PP:76
Builders of the State. R. Gilder.
Se-PR:202
Color - Caste - Denomination.
E. Dickinson. Pl-EI:159
Freedom for All. C. Cayer.
Ad-II:93
The Glowing Years. Jen Chün.
Hs-TC:392
God Give Us Men! J. Holland.
Se-PR:200, Vi-PP:232
I Hear America Singing.
W. Whitman. Ar-TP3:47, Bo-FP:304,
Br-AF:44, Co-PS:118, Er-FA:289,
Fe-FP:451, Ga-FB:247, Hu-MP:369,
La-PV:103, Mc-PR:33, Sm-LG:40,
Un-GT:306, Un-MA:40, Vi-PP:185
Lafayette to Washington.
M. Anderson. Vi-PP:117
A Man's a Man for A' That. R. Burns.
Al-VBP:653, Bo-HF:142, Er-FA:268,
Sp-OG:330
My Sort of Man. P. Dunbar. Bo-AN:6
Not Palaces. S. Spender. Un-MB:477,
Wi-LT:500
The People Will Live On. C. Sandburg.
Un-MA:214
The Poet. W. Whitman. Un-MA:79
The Poor Voter on Election Day.
J. Whittier. Ja-PA:47, Se-PR:201,
Vi-PP:188
The Second Sermon on the Warpland.
G. Brooks. Ad-PB:163, Ra-BP:171
Song of Myself. W. Whitman.
Al-VBP:928, Sh-AP:69, Un-MA:44
Written in a Time of Crisis.
S. Benét. Vi-PP:220
DEMONS: see DEVILS; WITCHES AND
WITCHCRAFT
DEMPSEY, JACK (THE NONPAREIL)
The Nonpareil's Grave. M. McMahon.
Mo-SD:76
DENMARK: see also DANISH VERSE;
ELSINORE, DEN.
There Is a Charming Land.
A. Oehlenschlager. Fe-FP:467
DENMARK - HISTORY AND PATRIOTISM
Battle of the Baltic. T. Campbell.
Co-RG:46, Hi-FO:193, Pa-GTB:205,
Rv-CB:675
DENTISTS AND DENTISTRY: see also
HUMOR - DENTISTS AND DENTISTRY;
TEETH
The Dentist. R. Fyleman. Ar-TP3:12,
Au-SP:142

Intimations of Mortality.
P. McGinley. Un-MA:595
DENVER, COLO.
House in Denver. T. Ferril. Br-AF:208
Waltz Against the Mountains.
T. Ferril. Ca-VT:197
DEPARTURE: see FAREWELLS; LOVE –
PARTING; PARTING
DEPENDABILITY: see TRUSTWORTHINESS
THE DEPRIVED; see SOCIALLY
HANDICAPPED
DERRICKS: see CRANES AND DERRICKS
DESCARTES, RENÉ: see HUMOR –
DESCARTES, RENÉ
DESERTION, MILITARY
Communiqué from an Army Deserter
Probably Italian. S. Moss.
Cr-WS:91
James Bird. Em-AF:438
DESERTS
Arizona Village. R. Davieau.
Br-AF:148
The City of Dreadful Night.
J. Thomson. Ho-WR:207
The Desert. R. King. Ba-HI:99
Desert School Ma'am. S. Andrews.
Fi-BG:195
The Exile. M. Benaya. Ls-NY:43
The Flight in the Desert.
Brother Antoninus. Ca-VT:350
Gift of the Sego Lily. M. Jarvis.
Fi-BG:197
Green, Green, Is El Aghir.
N. Cameron. Ca-MB:114
In the Desert Sand. N. Leonard.
Ba-HI:61
My Home. J. Saltwater. Ba-HI:100
Night in the Desert. R. Southey.
Mc-PR:146
O Pioneers! J. Bishop. Ca-VT:161
The Palm. R. Campbell. Un-MB:417
Purgatory. Sun Yü-t'ang. Hs-TC:121
Wind on an Inner Mongolian Desert.
Wang T'ung-chao. Hs-TC:262
DESOLATION: see also DESPAIR; RUINS
After the War. G. Garbovsky.
Bo-RU:36
Afterward. M. Van Doren. Ho-TH:44
American Farm, 1934. G. Taggard.
Ca-VT:191
The Deserted House. M. Coleridge.
De-CH:49, De-TT:157, Pa-RE:63,
Re-TW:88
The Deserted House. J. Fairbun.
Le-M:175
The Deserted Village. O. Goldsmith.
Al-VBP:585, Er-FA:410, Hi-FO:178
The Deserted Village. Wen I-to.
Hs-TC:61
The Dismantled Ship. W. Whitman.
Cl-FC:87, Ho-LP:53, Rv-CB:846
The Drought. Cheng Min. Hs-TC:238

Empty House. E. Coatsworth.
De-FS:52
Epilogue to a Narrative Poem.
Tr-US I:164
Fall Comes to Back-Country
Vermont. R. Warren. Ca-VT:278
Former Barn Lot. M. Van Doren.
Ga-FB:296, Ha-LO:53, La-PV:166,
Un-MA:467
A Forsaken Garden. A. Swinburne.
Ox-BN:811, Pa-GTB:385, Rv-CB:937
A Fountain, a Bottle, a Donkey's
Ears, and Some Books. R. Frost.
Ca-VT:12
Frail Hands. L. Trent. De-FS:198
Ha'nacker Hill. H. Belloc.
Un-MB:170
The Haunted House. T. Hood.
Ho-WR:192
The House on Maple Hill. S. McNail.
De-FS:139
The House on the Hill. E. Robinson.
Bo-GJ:204, Bo-HF:131, Fe-FP:241,
Ha-PO:156, Ho-TH:18, Hu-MP:77,
Un-MA:118
The House That Was. L. Binyon.
Un-MB:157
I Know Some Lonely Houses.
E. Dickinson. Co-PM:50,
Mc-WK:129, Rv-CB:900, Un-MA:103
I Walked Across the Park.
B. Douglas. Me-WF:1
The Isles of Greece. D. Capetanakis.
Pa-GTB:524
Kilcash. F. O'Connor. Co-PI:155,
Hi-WP II:132, Re-TW:86
Lines for Marking Time. R. Hill.
Ni-CD:78
Liu Ch'e. E. Pound. Ca-VT:82
The Moldering Hulk. A. Machado.
Pa-SG:144
Murder House. E. Coatsworth.
De-FS:54
No Possum, No Sop, No Taters.
W. Stevens. Ca-VT:38, Sh-AP:162
Panic. A. MacLeish. Un-MA:460
The Ruin. Ma-YA:4
Ruins of a Great House. D. Walcott.
Br-TC:447
The Sea House. W. Goodreau. Ls-NY:255
Song. Tr-US I:50
The Supplanting. W. Berry. Ls-NY:115
Time's Fool. R. Pitter. Un-MB:405
The Triumph of Doubt. J. Bishop.
Pl-EI:90
Two Beers In Argyle, Wisconsin.
D. Etter. St-H:62
Vacant House. J. Bonnette. Du-SH:167
A Year Without Seasons. M. Williams.
Hu-NN:68
DE SOTO, HERNANDO
The Distant Runners. M. Van Doren.
Sm-LG:81, Un-MA:467, Wi-LT:653

DESPAIR: see also HUMOR - DESPAIR
  The Abyss. C. Baudelaire. Mo-GR:29
  Alabama. J. Fields. Ad-PB:319,
    Hu-PN:420
  And You Know It. W. Day. Lo-IT:27
  As I Grew Older. L. Hughes.
    Ha-TP:101
  Ash-Wednesday. T. Eliot.
    Ca-VT:134, Un-MA:398
  At Castle Wood. E. Brontë.
    Al-VBP:924
  At Dawn. A. Symons. Ox-BN:935
  Awake. M. Coleridge. Ox-BN:926
  Bad Moon Rising. J. Fogerty.
    Mo-GR:85
  Barren. Z. Stancu. Mc-AC:86
  Barren Spring. D. Rossetti.
    Ox-BN:685
  Be Still, My Soul, Be Still.
    A. Housman. Ox-BN:923, Un-MB:101
  Before Olympus. J. Fletcher.
    Un-MA:320
  Birmingham. J. Fields. Hu-PN:418
  Birth of a Nation. C. Sealy.
    Sa-B:29
  Blues. H. Mungin. Ad-BO:61
  The Book of Job. H. Leivick.
    Ho-TY:126
  Bowery Motifs, I-III. A. Katz.
    Ho-TY:294-296
  The Brand. Tsang K'o-chia.
    Hs-TC:280
  The Bridge of Sighs. T. Hood.
    Pa-GTB:230
  By the Winding River, II. Tu Fu.
    Rx-OH:14
  Cawdor. R. Jeffers. Sm-PT:25
  The Century when Even Death Died.
    K. Patchen. Ba-PO:ix
  Chorus for a Phonograph. K. Congdon.
    Lo-IT:21
  Chorus from a Tragedy. L. Bacon.
    Al-VBP:1173
  Cities and Seas. N. Jordan. Hu-PN:422
  City Life. D. Lawrence. Ad-CI:88
  The City of Dreadful Night.
    J. Thomson. Al-VBP:1007, Pa-GTB:382
  Cold Night. Hu Feng. Hs-TC:377
  The Complaint to God. Bible. O.T.
    Job. Me-PH:18
  The Crazy Woman. G. Brooks.
    Ab-MO:28, Bo-HF:136, Li-TU:151
  Curse God and Die, You Said to Me.
    A. MacLeish. Pl-EI:69
  Dance Songs, IV. Tr-US II:164
  Death as History. J. Wright.
    Ad-PB:280, Sc-TN:249
  death prosecuting. L. Curry.
    Jo-SA:7, Jo-VC:84
  The Descendant and the Id. A. Branch.
    Sm-PT:131

  The Descent into Hell. Y. Stefanov.
    Bo-RU:81
  Despair. Tr-CB:41, Tr-US I:74
  A Development of Idiocy. E. Jones.
    Ox-BN:619
  Dirge. Q. Troupe. Ad-PB:442
  Discordants II. C. Aiken. Co-BL:36
  Discovery. C. Link. Ke-TF:120
  A Dispute over Suicide. Lo-TY:26
  Distress. S. Tanikawa. Sh-AM:131
  Don't Cry, My Little One.
    Wang T'ung-chao. Hs-TC:259
  A Drape. Feng Chih. Hs-TC:143
  E Tenebris. O. Wilde. Un-MB:68
  Earth's Answer. W. Blake. Rv-CB:568
  Eclogue. F. Prokosch. Al-VBP:1235
  The End of the World. Bible. O.T.
    Jeremiah. Ba-PO:48, Ke-PP:2
  The Epic of Dengei. Tr-US I:233
  Epilogue to a Narrative Poem.
    Tr-US I:164
  Everyman. S. Sassoon. Un-MB:315
  Evicted. S. Funaroff. Kr-OF:200
  Ex Nihilo. D. Gascoyne. Pa-GTB:549
  Execution. J. Randall. Ra-BP:277
  Fall Down. C. Hernton. Ad-PB:243
  Falling. B. Kaufman. Ad-PB:266
  Farewell and No. J. Adoum. Be-UL:109
  Fire in the Sky. Tsang K'o-chia.
    Hs-TC:280
  Four and Twenty. S. Stills.
    Mo-GR:30
  Get Up, Blues. J. Emanuel.
    Ad-BO:62, Ad-PB:179, Bo-AN:175,
    Li-TU:173
  Ghetto Song. J. Glatstein.
    Ho-TY:332
  The Gray Sky. L. Curry. Jo-VC:80
  The Gyres. W. Yeats. Pa-GTB:432
  Habitat. J. Anderson. Sc-TN:1
  He Loves and Rides Away.
    S. Dobell. Ox-BN:663
  Heaven Haven. G. Hopkins. Go-BP:182
  Her Story. N. Madgett. Ad-PB:183
  The Hollow Men. T. Eliot.
    Un-MA:395, Wi-LT:302
  Human Soul. R. Maran. Lo-TY:71
  Hunger. B. Weinstein. Ho-TY:291
  Hunger. Le-IB:93, Tr-US I:25
  I Cannot Live with You.
    E. Dickinson. Rv-CB:923,
    Sh-AP:129, Un-MA:96, Un-MW:87
  I Know a Man. R. Creeley. Bl-FP:25
  I Said to the Leaf. C. Drewry.
    Tr-MR:270
  I Sit and Look Out. W. Whitman.
    Ke-PP:1, Mo-GB:177, Rv-CB:851
  I Wake and Feel the Fell of Dark,
    Not Day. G. Hopkins. Pa-GTB:396
  If on Account of the Political
    Situation. W. Auden. Ba-PO:50

If the Stars Should Fall. S. Allen.
  Ad-PB:168, Hu-NN:95
In Heavy Mind. J. Agee. Un-MA:606
In Memoriam: Rev. Martin Luther
  King, Jr. J. Jordan. Ad-PB:305,
  Jo-SA:115
In Texas Grass. Q. Troupe.
  Ad-PB:443
In the Night Fields. W. Merwin.
  En-PC:258
In This Hour. J. Johnson. Tr-MR:232
The Incubus of Time. C. Smith.
  De-FS:184
Independence. K. Begin. Me-WF:72
Interim. C. Delaney. Hu-PN:181
The Invention of Comics. I. Baraka.
  Ad-PB:251, Bo-AN:179, Wi-LT:744
July in Washington. R. Lowell.
  Ho-P:175
Junior Addict. L. Hughes. Ra-BP:85
A Lament. P. Shelley. Gr-CT:318,
  Pa-GTB:307
The Lament of the Mole-Catcher.
  O. Sitwell. Co-BBW:22
The Last Sunday. Wang Tu-ch'ing.
  Hs-TC:194
A Last Word. E. Dowson. Un-MB:147
The Leaden Echo and the Golden
  Echo. G. Hopkins. Er-FA:169,
  Ox-BN:867, Pa-GTB:393, Un-MB:40,
  Wi-LT:46
Lines Written During a Period of
  Insanity. W. Cowper. Ho-P:183
Loneliness. Tu Fu. Rx-OH:16
Long for Home. M. Halpern.
  Ho-TY:106
Look for You Yesterday, Here You
  Come Today. L. Jones. Be-MA:113
Lost Joy. A. Onyezhskaya.
  Bo-RU:60
The Lost Son. T. Roethke.
  Ca-VT:287, Wi-LT:479
Lullaby. Tr-US II:305
Man's Dance Song. Tr-US I:94
Many a Night. A. Reisen. Ho-TY:69
Marriage Poems, IV-V. Tr-US II:163
The Mask. E. Browning.
  Ox-BN:463, Rv-CB:778
Me Because. D. Witt. Ad-II:10
Men's Impotence. Tr-US I:23
Merciful Heaven. I. Spiegel.
  Ho-TY:350
Midcentury Love Letter. P. McGinley.
  Al-VBP:1225, Mo-BG:91
The Midnight Meditation. E. Olson.
  St-H:175
Migration. C. Clemmons.
  Ad-PB:489
Missing Dates. W. Empson.
  Al-VBP:1225
missing is the vision of sunshine.
  P. Murtha. Ad-II:39

Montana Fifty Years Ago.
  J. Cunningham. Ho-P:47
Moo! R. Hillyer. Co-BBW:170,
  Ho-TH:33
Mortality. N. Madgett. Ad-PB:182,
  Be-MA:92, Hu-NN:23, Hu-PN:382
My Angel. J. Brooks. Hu-PN:238
My Body in the Walls Captived.
  W. Ralegh. Ma-FW:172,
  Rv-CB:160
My Enemy. L. Curry. Ba-HI:42
My Father Isaac. J. Glatstein.
  Ho-TY:246
My Galley. T. Wyatt. Rv-CB:89
My Heart Moves as Heavy.
  Co-EL:139, Co-PM:66
My Soul Is Weary of My Life. Bible.
  O.T. Job. Pl-EI:67
My World. R. Diaz. Me-WF:14
Nausea Has Me in Its Grip.
  A. Timofeyevsky. Bo-RU:84
The New World. A. Reisen.
  Ho-TY:71
New Year. Wang Ya-p'ing. Hs-TC:352
No Way Out. L. Curry. Jo-SA:8,
  Jo-VC:82
No Worst, There Is None.
  G. Hopkins. Ke-PP:5, Ox-BN:870,
  Pa-GTB:395, Rv-CB:944,
  Un-MB:46, Wi-LT:49
Nobody Riding the Roads Today.
  J. Jordan. Ra-BP:248
Nocturne at Bethesda. A. Bontemps.
  Be-MA:43, Bo-AN:81, Hu-PN:211
Not Waving but Drowning. S. Smith.
  Gr-BT:40, Pa-GTB:568
O Quickly, Messiah. A. Reisen.
  Ho-TY:72
Oh Why? M. Fletcher. Me-WF:23
Octaves. E. Robinson. Sm-PT:143
off d pig. I. Reed. Jo-SA:90
Old Horse. Sun Yü-t'ang.
  Hs-TC:122
On Fanny Godwin. P. Shelley.
  Ox-BN:278
On Slaughter. C. Bialik. Me-PH:74
On the Iroquois League.
  Tr-US II:229
The One Certainty. C. Rossetti.
  Ox-BN:711
The Outcast. J. Stephens. Un-MB:267
Outside. P. Harris. Sc-TN:80
Panic. A. MacLeish. Un-MA:460
The Passing of Arthur. A. Tennyson.
  Ni-JP:158, Ox-BN:511
Poem. P. Markish.
  Ho-TY:182, 183, 184
A Poem. B. Pasternak. Bo-RU:1
A Poem Some People Will Have to
  Understand. I. Baraka. Ra-BP:216
Poor It Is. Le-IB:118

DESPAIR — cont'd.
  Preface to a Twenty Volume Suicide
    Note. L. Jones. Ad-PB:250,
    Hu-PN:406, Jo-SA:33, Kh-VA:18,
    Lo-TY:251, Pe-SS:43
  The Rain. R. Creeley. Ca-VT:563,
    Mc-EA:37
  The Raven. E. Poe. Al-VBP:865,
    Bo-GJ:165, Co-RG:103, De-CH:303,
    Er-FA:312, Ga-FB:134, Sh-AP:56,
    Sm-LG:207
  The Raven Days. S. Lanier. Rv-CB:942
  The Ricksha Puller. Tsang K'o-chia.
    Hs-TC:281
  Ritual of the Priest Chilan.
    Bi-IT:141, Br-MW:27, Da-SC:162
  The Road of All Lives. Fang Ching.
    Hs-TC:388
  Sadness of Life. Be-AP:34
  Samson Agonistes. J. Milton.
    Al-VBP:413, Ga-S:47
  Sanitorium. H. Leivick. Ho-TY:122
  The Scarlet Woman. F. Johnson.
    Ad-PB:24
  Siberia. I. Emiot. Ho-TY:316
  Silence. A. Pritam. Al-PI:141
  Silences. A. O'Shaughnessy.
    Ox-BN:851
  Simple. N. Madgett. Ad-PB:182
  Sleeplessness. Tsang K'o-chia.
    Hs-TC:279
  The Soliloquy of an Invalid.
    Harata Tangikuku. Tr-US II:119
  Solstice. M. Banus. Mc-AC:114
  Song. Br-MW:29
  Song. Tr-US I:230
  Song of a Sick Chief. Tr-US I:211
  A Song of Lamentation. Ba-PO:27,
    Bi-IT:137, Da-SC:175
  Sonnet 29. W. Shakespeare.
    Al-VBP:200, Co-BL:117, Ga-FB:34,
    Ha-PO:254, Ho-P:290, Ni-JP:96,
    Pa-GTB:8, Rv-CB:212, Un-MW:181
  Sonnets. G. Hopkins. Ox-BN:870
  Sonnets, vii, xxv. G. Santayana.
    Sm-PT:135
  Sorrow. Mei Yao Ch'en. Rx-OH:42
  The Sound of Afroamerican History.
    S. Anderson. Ad-PB:440
  Spring Festival Songs, XIV.
    Tr-US II:174
  Stanzas Written in Dejection, near
    Naples. P. Shelley. Al-VBP:745,
    Ga-FB:125, Pa-GTB:227, Rv-CB:707
  The Stone-Breaker. Nirala.
    Al-PI:118
  Stop All the Clocks. W. Auden.
    Hi-WP II:29, Un-MB:465, Un-MW:103
  A Stroll. Wang T'ing-chao. Hs-TC:257
  The Sunlight on the Garden.
    L. MacNeice. Br-TC:279, Pa-GTB:515

  Supplication. J. Cotter. Hu-PN:134
  That Lonesome Place. C. O'John.
    Al-WW:68
  There's Nane o' My Ain to Care.
    W. Ogilvie. De-CH:515
  These. W. Williams. Un-MA:261
  This Is the Dark Time, My Love.
    M. Carter. Sa-B:16
  This Land. B. Smith. Sa-B:175
  This Place. C. Graves. La-IH:133
  To a Single Shadow Without Pity.
    S. Cornish. Ad-PB:294
  To Children. L. McGaugh. Ad-PB:377
  To the Castle at Gordes.
    O. de Magny. Ba-PO:88, Cr-WS:153
  Tomorrow and Tomorrow and Tomorrow.
    W. Shakespeare. Er-FA:92,
    Gr-CT:367, Ma-YA:69
  The Trees Are Bare. E. Brontë.
    De-TT:158
  Two Legends, I, II. T. Hughes.
    Mc-EA:64
  The Two Spirits: An Allegory.
    P. Shelley. Ho-P:112
  Under the Moon. Hsü Hsü.
    Hs-TC:275
  The Unfortunate Miller.
    A. Coppard. Co-PT:19
  untitled requiem for tomorrow.
    Conyus. Ad-PB:402
  Voronezh. A. Akhmatova. Ca-MR:185
  A Weary Song to a Slow Sad Tune.
    Li Ch'ing Chao. Rx-LT:91
  What the Old Women Say.
    A. MacLeish. Ha-TP:76
  What Will Become of a Dream.
    B. Brown. Ba-HI:134
  When I Am in Grief.
    Yamanoue no Okura. Le-MW:121
  When They Call Out. S. Chudakov.
    Bo-RU:27
  When They Have Lost. C. Day Lewis.
    Un-MB:425
  Where Is the House of Quetzal
    Feathers? Ge-TR:31
  Why Must You Know? J. Wheelwright.
    Ca-VT:205
  The Wind's Arrows Shoot Ceaselessly.
    Wang Ching-chih. Hs-TC:44
  Women Songs, II. K. Molodowsky.
    Ho-TY:285
  Work Without Hope. S. Coleridge.
    Co-BN:199, Ma-YA:166
  The World and I. A. Reisen.
    Ho-TY:69
  A Year Without Seasons.
    W. Williams. Hu-NN:68
DESSALINES, JEAN JACQUES
  Black Majesty. C. Cullen.
    Ad-PB:92, Ca-VT:242
DESTINY: see FATE

DESTRUCTION
   Advice to a Prophet. R. Wilbur.
      Tr-MR:233, Un-MA:677
   The Animal That Drank Up Sound.
      W. Stafford. Ca-VT:413
   At Carnoy. S. Sassoon. Cr-WS:84
   At Dunwich. A. Thwaite.
      To-MP:182
   Babylon. S. Sassoon. Tr-MR:235
   Bam, Bam, Bam. E. Merriam.
      La-PV:193
   The Century when Even Death Died.
      K. Patchen. Ba-PO:ix
   Clover Swaths. J. Hearst.
      St-H:83
   The Cycle Repeated. K. Chapin.
      Ls-NY:258
   Dark with Power. W. Berry.
      Mc-EA:119
   Death, Look to Your Domain.
      C. Norman. Cr-WS:172
   Design for the City of Man.
      E. Jarrett. Sc-TN:107
   The End of the World. Bible.
      O.T. Jeremiah. Ba-PO:48,
      Ke-PP:2
   Evening at the Sunset.
      W. Melaney. Ad-II:100
   The Field of Waterloo. T. Hardy.
      Sm-LG:257
   The Hammers. R. Hodgson.
      Bo-GJ:202, Un-MB:192
   The Incubus of Time. C. Smith.
      De-FS:184
   Innocents. K. Hopkins. Cr-WS:130
   The Inquisitors. R. Jeffers.
      Un-MA:372
   Kilcash. F. O'Connor. Co-PI:155,
      Hi-WP II:132, Re-TW:86
   Lament for Walsingham. Gr-GB:184,
      Rv-CB:115
   The Long War. L. Lee. Go-BP:216,
      Gr-BT:100
   Look, How Beautiful. R. Jeffers.
      Tr-MR:148
   The Luck of Edenhall.
      H. Longfellow. Co-PT:151
   The Midnight Meditation. E. Olson.
      St-H:175
   Mother, the Wardrobe Is Full of
      Infantrymen. E. McGough.
      Gr-BT:117
   A Poem on the Nuclear War, from
      Pompeii. R. Tillinghast.
      Ba-PO:55
   Ritual of the Priest Chilan.
      Bi-IT:141, Br-MW:27, Da-SC:162
   The River. P. Lorentz. Br-AF:182
   Samson Agonistes. J. Milton.
      Hi-FO:20, Ma-FW:173
   The Sea Eats the Land at Home.
      K. Awoonor. Ad-CI:82

   Shiva. R. Jeffers. Gr-SS:69,
      Ls-NY:36
   A Song of Lamentation.
      Ba-PO:27, Bi-IT:137, Da-SC:175
   Star-Swirls. R. Jeffers.
      Du-SH:108
   The Supplanting. W. Berry.
      Ls-NY:115
   The Termites. R. Hillyer.
      Rd-OA:159
   They Say the Last Supper Is Badly
      Damaged. S. Yellen. Cr-WS:133
   This Excellent Machine.
      J. Lehmann. Du-SH:87
   To His Friend, Wei. . . . Li Po.
      Li-TU:234
   Triumphal Entry. C. Norman.
      Cr-WS:125
   Vae Victis. R. Humphries.
      Ni-JP:123
   The War God. Ya Hsüan. Pa-MV:148
   War in Chang-An City. Wang Tsan.
      Ba-PO:41, Cr-WS:12, Ke-PP:8
   The Weeping Spreads. Bi-IT:147
   what if a much of a which of a wind.
      E. Cummings. Al-VBP:1203,
      Er-FA:94, Un-MA:477, Wi-LT:368
   Which Are You? Fe-PL:299
   The Window. E. Muir. Wi-LT:255
DETERMINATION
   De Black Girl. Gr-GB:224
   A Blade of Grass. O. Williams.
      Ls-NY:58
   Determination. J. Clarke. Ad-PB:144
   I May, I Might, I Must. M. Moore.
      Co-EL:103, Mc-WS:118, Mo-BG:63,
      Sh-RP:303
   I Will Not Let Thee Go.
      R. Bridges. Ox-BN:872
   To the Man after the Harrow.
      P. Kavanagh. Pa-GTB:514
   We Shall Overcome. Ba-PO:199,
      Hi-TL:228, Pl-EI:165
   Where There's a Will There's a Way.
      E. Cook. Er-FA:26
DETROIT, MICH.: see also SATIRE -
      DETROIT, MICH.
   Detroit. D. Hall. Br-AF:203
   A Mother Speaks. M. Harper.
      Ra-BP:291
DEUTSCHLAND (SHIP)
   The Wreck of the Deutschland.
      G. Hopkins. Li-TU:220,
      Ox-BN:852, Wi-LT:30
DEVILFISH: see OCTOPUSES
DEVILS: see also BEELZEBUB; HUMOR -
      DEVILS; LUCIFER
   Adam and Eve. J. Milton. No-CL:52
   After Reading Certain Books.
      M. Coleridge. Pl-EI:74
   Alaska, or the Hell of the Yukon.
      Fi-BG:43

DEVILS — cont'd.
Ambushed by Angels. G. Davidson.
    De-FS:71
Chiliasm. R. Eberhart. Pl-EI:77
Clootie. Ma-BB:94
The Conundrum of the Workshops.
    R. Kipling. Un-MB:131
The Deil's Awa wi' the Exciseman.
    R. Burns. Al-VBP:649
The Demon Lover. Co-PM:201,
    Fo-OG:44, Ma-BB:188, Ma-FW:199,
    Ox-BB:83, Rv-CB:45
A Devil. Y. Kurihara. Le-TA:90
The Devil. W. Wicks. Me-WF:50
The Devil. Mo-MGT:111
Devil Doll. L. Grenelle. De-FS:99
The Devil's Bag. J. Stephens.
    Co-PI:178, Ha-PO:61, Li-TU:81
The Devil's Thoughts.
    S. Coleridge. Co-PM:40
Esthetique du Mal, VIII.
    W. Stevens. Wi-LT:155
Eve. Y. Fichman. Me-PH:82
First Travels of Max. J. Ransom.
    Un-MA:412
Ghoul Care. R. Hodgson. Un-MB:193
Hell in Texas. Co-RM:30
I Heard an Angel Singing.
    W. Blake. Rv-CB:621
Jerusalem. W. Blake. Gr-CT:295,
    Ox-BN:42
The Knight Fallen on Evil Days.
    E. Wylie. Un-MA:274
Lizards and Snakes. A. Hecht.
    Br-TC:183, Ha-TP:39
A Mighty Fortress Is Our God.
    M. Luther. Pl-EI:213
Prenatal Fantasy. W. Kerr. De-FS:126
Satan Journeys to the Garden of Eden.
    J. Milton. Gr-CT:276
Satan's Prayer. I. Manger. Ho-TY:273
Simon Legree — a Negro Sermon.
    V. Lindsay. Co-RM:182, Sm-LG:183,
    Un-MA:226
Some Say the Deil's Dead. Sm-LG:241
Someone's Opinion of Arizona.
    C. Brown. Fi-BG:42
Static. R. Humphries. Pl-US:41
Thirty Bob a Week. J. Davidson.
    Co-EL:143
To the Accuser Who Is God of This
    World. W. Blake. Al-VBP:624,
    Ox-BN:47
To the Reader. C. Baudelaire.
    Mo-GR:30
The Tragicall Historie of Doctor
    Faustus. C. Marlowe. Ma-YA:63
What Though the Field Be Lost?
    J. Milton. Pl-EI:76
When Satan Fell. D. Lawrence.
    Tr-MR:215

The Witch. R. Southey. Ho-WR:219
DEVOTION: see also LOVE - DEVOTION;
    PRAYER; WORSHIP
And She Washed His Feet with Her
    Tears, and Wiped Them with the
    Hairs of Her Head.
    E. Sherburne. Rv-CB:396
The Ashtabula Disaster. J. Moore.
    Na-EO:122
Doubt Me. . . . E. Dickinson.
    Al-VBP:1001
The Elixir. G. Herbert. Bo-FP:301,
    Ga-S:115, Gr-TG:59, Sm-LG:366
Expectans Expectavi. C. Sorley.
    Sm-LG:379
The Faithful Shepherdess.
    J. Fletcher. Al-VBP:287
The Henchman. J. Whittier.
    No-CL:64
Huswifery. E. Taylor. Ga-FB:95,
    Pl-EI:49, Sh-AP:12
It Is There that Our Hearts Are
    Set. Ho-SD:33, Le-OE:5
Love and Age. T. Peacock.
    Al-VBP:717, Ox-BN:235
To Mary. C. Wolfe. Al-VBP:739
Twenty Years Hence. W. Landor.
    Al-VBP:706
Upon the Death of Sir Albert
    Morton's Wife. H. Wotton.
    Al-VBP:223, Hi-WP II:18,
    No-CL:159, Rv-CB:277
Well I Remember. . . . W. Landor.
    Al-VBP:707, Gr-BT:78, No-CL:22,
    Ox-BN:189, Rv-CB:666
DEW
A Breeze Stirs at Dawn. Asayasu.
    Be-MC:39
The Broad Water. Rv-ON:58
The Dew. A. Epstein. Le-M:20
Dew on Young Garlic Leaves.
    T'ien Hung. Rx-LT:7
Dewdrop. T. Walker. Ls-NY:59
The Dewdrop and the Wave. G. Herwegh.
    Sp-OG:306
Dewdrops. J. Clare. Go-BP:110
A Drop of Dew. A. Marvell.
    De-TT:149
Emeralds and Diamonds. Re-RR:84
Firefly Party. De-PP:63
For a Dewdrop. E. Farjeon. De-TT:62
Grasshopper. Issa. Le-IS:5
In a Gust of Wind. Funya No Asayasu.
    Ba-ST:42
A Little Child. Issa. Le-MW:100
Now that Night Is Gone. Buson.
    Be-MC:48
Play About, Do. Baskö. Au-SP:320,
    Le-MW:79
DIALECTS, AUSTRALIAN
Biby's Epitaph. Co-FB:219

Waltzing Matilda.   A. Paterson.
  Gr-CT:138, Gr-GB:259, Ha-PO:238,
  Mc-WK:147
DIALECTS, BROOKLYN
  Thirty Purple Birds.   Hi-WP I:100
  ygUDuh.   e. cummings.   Ba-PO:188
DIALECTS, CHILDREN'S
  The Anxious Farmer.   B. Johnson.
    Co-BN:37
  Bobby's First Poem.   N. Gale.
    Co-FB:105, Co-PU:7
  Burglar Bill.   T. Guthrie. Co-FB:112
  How to Treat Elves.   M. Bishop.
    Co-FB:197
  A Tonversation with Baby.
    M. Bishop.   Co-FB:190
DIALECTS, COCKNEY
  Bill 'Awkins.   R. Kipling. Co-RM:214
  For to Admire.   R. Kipling. Un-MB:140
  Framed in a First-Story Winder.
    Co-OH:36
  Fuzzy-Wuzzy.   R. Kipling. Un-MB:126
  Gunga Din.   R. Kipling.   Er-FA:371,
    Go-BP:54, Hi-WP I:69, Ma-YA:226,
    Pa-OM:230, Un-MB:122
  The Ladies.   R. Kipling.   Ke-TF:243,
    Un-MB:128
  The Liner She's a Lady. R. Kipling.
    Ga-FB:189
  Mandalay.   R. Kipling.   Ga-FB:70,
    Un-MB:125
  The Road to Vagabondia.   D. Burnet.
    Fe-PL:410
  Sestina of the Tramp Royal.
    R. Kipling.   Ni-JP:18, Un-MB:137
  Tommy.   R. Kipling.   Ga-FB:209,
    Un-MB:127
  The Widow at Windsor. R. Kipling.
    Hi-FO:249
DIALECTS, CORNISH
  A Ballad of a Mine.   R. Skelton.
    Ca-MB:77
DIALECTS, COUNTRY
  Banty Tim.   J. Hay.   Kr-OF:45
  Blow Me Eyes! W. Irwin. Co-BL:166
  A Boy's Mother.   J. Riley. Se-PR:119
  The Brothers.   A. Groesbeck.
    De-FS:102
  Daley's Dorg Wattie.   W. Goodge.
    Co-BBW:106
  Dow's Flat.   B. Harte. Co-PT:86
  Friendly People. J. Herndon.
    Hu-MP:162
  The Gray Goose. Bu-DY:27, Du-RG:122
  A Gret Fight. R. Newell. Co-RM:179
  The Inventor's Wife.   E. Corbett.
    Fe-PL:219
  Jest 'fore Christmas.   E. Field.
    Er-FA:513, Fe-FP:538, Fe-PL:201,
    Ga-FB:176, Hu-MP:359
  Jim Bludso.   J. Hay.   Co-RM:234,
    Er-FA:307, Fi-BG:129, Sp-OG:34

Just Folks.   E. Guest.   Er-FA:134
Keep a-Goin'.   F. Stanton. Er-FA:27
Kivers.   A. Cobb.   Br-AF:133
Knee-Deep in June. J. Riley. Sp-OG:291
Little Breeches.   J. Hay.   Un-GT:198
Little Orphant Annie.   J. Riley.
  Co-BB:113, Er-FA:493, Fe-FP:532,
  Hu-MP:27, Ox-BC:300
Lonesome Water.   R. Helton.
  Br-AF:100, Co-PM:91, Mc-WK:200,
  Un-MA:347
The Man in the Moon.   J. Riley.
  Co-HP:109
Mis' Smith.   A. Paine.   Fe-PL:415
The Mountain Whippoorwill.
  S. Benét.   Co-PT:110
The New Church Organ.   W. Carleton.
  Fe-PL:233
November's Come.   J. Lincoln.
  Sh-RP:233
Old Christmas.   R. Helton. Co-PM:94,
  Un-MA:346
The Old Man and Jim.   J. Riley.
  Co-PT:232, Sp-OG:197
The Old Swimmin'-Hole.   J. Riley.
  Er-FA:241
Options.   O. Henry.   Co-FB:254
Out Fishin'.   E. Guest.   Fe-PL:419
Over the Hills to the Poor-House.
  W. Carleton.   Er-FA:266
The Raggedy Man.   J. Riley.
  Fe-FP:533, Hu-MP:142, Ox-BC:301,
  Un-GT:99
Rain.   J. Riley.   Co-BN:169
A Rainy Day.   J. Lincoln. Sh-RP:198
The Rattlesnake.   J. and A. Lomax.
  Sh-RP:19
The Runaway Boy.   J. Riley. Hu-MP:30
A Rustic Song. A. Deane. Co-FB:218
Seein' Things. E. Field. Hu-MP:130
The Spelling Bee at Angels.
  B. Harte.   Co-PT:241
This Season Our Tunnips Was Red.
  D. McCord.   Br-LL:130
Tollable Well. F. Stanton. Er-FA:22
When the Drive Goes Down.
  D. Malloch.   Br-AF:175
When the Frost Is on the Punkin.
  J. Riley.   Co-BN:134, Er-FA:132,
  Fe-PL:387, Ga-FB:298, Hu-MP:319
Whisperin' Bill.   I. Bacheller.
  Fe-PL:156
DIALECTS, COWBOY: see DIALECTS,
  WESTERN
DIALECTS, CUMBERLAND
  Bleeberrying. J. Denwood. Ca-MB:17
  Dips or Counting Out Rhymes IV.
    Gr-GB:20
DIALECTS, DEVON
  Drake's Drum.   H. Newbolt.
    Co-SS:58, De-TT:195, Hi-FO:128,
    Hi-WP I:68

DIALECTS, DEVON — cont'd.
 Wul 'E Plaize.   De-TT:92
 Yer's tu Thee.   De-TT:73
DIALECTS, DORSET
 The Aïr to Gi'e Your Cheäks a Hue.
  W. Barnes.   De-CH:614
 In Church.   W. Barnes.   Hi-WP I:140
 Mäy.   W. Barnes.   Co-PS:78
 Mäy.   W. Barnes.   Gr-CT:48
 Readen ov a Head-Stwone.   W. Barnes.
  De-CH:264
 The Rwose in the Dark.   W. Barnes.
  Rv-CB:767
 The Spring.   W. Barnes.   Co-BN:36
 Times o' Year.   W. Barnes.
  Co-BN:226
 The Turnstile.   W. Barnes.   De-CH:255
 White an' Blue.   W. Barnes.
  Pa-GTB:322
 The Wind at the Door.   W. Barnes.
  Pa-GTB:321, Rv-CB:768
 A Witch.   W. Barnes.   Co-PM:23
 The Woodlands.   W. Barnes.
  Co-BN:158
 Zummer Stream.   W. Barnes.   Co-BN:93
DIALECTS, DURHAM
 Pigs o' Pelton.   Gr-GB:176
DIALECTS, ENGLISH: see also
  dialects of regions of England,
  as DIALECTS, DEVON
 Ballad of the Flood.   E. Muir.
  Ca-MB:34
 Blow, Ye Winds.   Co-SS:105
 The Cheerful Horn.   De-CH:130
 The Chinese Bumboatman.   Co-SS:113
 A Country God.   E. Blunden.   Un-MB:396
 Danny Deever.   R. Kipling.   Co-RM:87,
  Fe-PL:84, Pa-GTB:420, Un-MB:124
 Do Li A.   Gr-GB:236
 Friends Beyond.   T. Hardy.   Pa-GTB:403
 From My Rural Pen.   T. Watt.
  Co-FB:221
 Mules.   C. Smith.   Co-RM:216
 My Sweet Sweeting.   De-CH:35
 O Sing unto My Roundelay.
  T. Chatterton.   De-CH:249,
  Ho-WR:152
 Old Shepherd's Prayer.   C. Mew.
  Pl-EI:176, Un-MB:163
 Rythm.   I. Smith.   To-MP:175
 Screw Guns.   R. Kipling.   Al-VBP:1098
 Sea Love.   C. Mew.   Al-VBP:1111,
  Co-BL:159, Co-EL:10, Co-PM:78,
  Un-MB:159, Un-MW:100
 A Smuggler's Song.   R. Kipling.
  Ox-BC:322
 Swell's Soliloquy.   Co-FB:222
 This Gurt Pig.   De-CH:497
 Villikins and His Dinah.   S. Cowell.
  Co-PT:184
 The Water o' Wearie's Well.
  De-CH:730

Whether or Not.   D. Lawrence.
 Un-MB:291
The Workhouse Boy.   Gr-GB:265
Young Beichan.   Ma-FW:146, Pa-OM:240
DIALECTS, FRENCH
 Pourquoi?   Co-BBW:103, Gr-CT:89,
  Gr-EC:79
DIALECTS, FRENCH-CANADIAN
 The Wreck of the "Julie Plant."
  W. Drummond.   Fe-FP:491, Ha-PO:177
DIALECTS, GERMAN
 Ballad of the Mermaid.   C. Leland.
  Co-FB:217
 Morning Song.   K. Stein.   Co-FB:215
 Vor a Gaugin Picture zu Singen.
  K. Stein.   Co-FB:217
DIALECTS, ILLITERATE
 A Baker's Duzzen uv Wize Saws.
  E. Sill.   Er-FA:214
 The Bashful Man.   B. Johnson.
  Co-RM:43
 The Deckhands.   Co-RM:53
 Drug Store.   J. Weaver.   Hi-TL:192
 The Ghost That Jim Saw.   B. Harte.
  Br-SM:6, Co-PM:84
 Legend.   J. Weaver.   Br-AF:197
 ?   E. Cummings.   Co-FB:494
 Rain or Hail.   E. Cummings.
  Du-SH:136
 A Ride in a Blue Chevy.
  J. Williams.   Ls-NY:160
 The Sea Serpant.   W. Irwin.
  Co-BBW:288, Co-FB:18, Co-OH:22
 Sensitive Sydney.   W. Irwin.
  Co-FB:49, Co-HP:82
 This Boy Think.   C. Pass.   Jo-VC:3
 The Weed.   R. Pitter.   Sm-MK:79
DIALECTS, IRISH
 Come Back. Paddy Reilly.
  P. French.   Co-PI:48
 The Cow Ate the Piper.   Gr-GB:88
 Father O'Flynn.   A. Graves.
  Co-PI:54
 The Gals o' Dublin Town.   Co-SS:111
 Grace for Light.   M. O'Neill.
  Th-AS:174
 Haul Away Joe.   Co-SS:99
 Hush Song.   E. Shane.   Th-AS:34
 The Irish Dancer.   Gr-BT:17
 The Irish Schoolmaster.   J. Sidey.
  Co-FB:223, Co-HP:111
 It's Little for Glory I Care.
  C. Lever.   Co-PI:96
 Maloney Remembers the Resurrection
  of Kate Finucane.   B. Kennelly.
  Co-PT:108
 Mavrone.   A. Guiterman.   Co-FB:264,
  Li-SR:149
 The Mountains of Mourne.   P. French.
  Co-PI:46
 Mush, Mush.   Co-RM:114

Oh, It's Nine Years Ago I Was Digging
in the Land.   Em-AF:760
O'Grady's Goat.   W. Hays.   Fe-PL:214
Paddy O'Rafther.   S. Lover.
Co-PI:97, Co-PT:298
The Rachray Man.   M. O'Neill.
Co-PI:162
The Wearing of the Green.   Co-PS:51,
Er-FA:295, Gr-GB:193, Ho-FO:252
DIALECTS, ITALIAN
Da Boy from Rome.   T. Daly.   Fe-FP:304,
Hu-MP:158
The Educated Love Bird.   P. Newell.
Co-FB:216
Leetla Giorgio Washeenton.   T. Daly.
Co-PS:46, Fe-FP:414, Hu-MP:377
Mia Carlotta.   T. Daly.   Hi-WP I:103
Two 'Mericana Men.   T. Daly.   Hu-MP:150
DIALECTS, LINCOLN
The High Tide on the Coast of
Lincolnshire.   J. Ingelow.
De-TT:183, Pa-OM:118, Sp-OG:85
The One-Horned Ewe.   Gr-GB:82
DIALECTS, LUMBERJACK
Bung Yer Eye.   S. White.   Sh-RP:18
DIALECTS, MIDDLE ENGLISH
And as for Me.   G. Chaucer.
Al-VBP:17, De-CH:13
Ane Sang of the Birth of Christ. . . .
J. Wedderburn.   Gr-CT:423
Against Garnesche.   J. Skelton.
Al-VBP:29
Balade.   G. Chaucer.   Gr-CT:58
The Birth of Robin Hood.   Al-VBP:37
The Borrowing Days.   Gr-GB:38
The Borys Hede That We Bryng Here.
Ma-YA:24
Bring Us In Good Ale.   Al-VBP:24,
Cl-FC:94, De-CH:64
The Bruce.   J. Barbour.   Al-VBP:5
Canterbury Tales (Prologue).
G. Chaucer.   Al-VBP:7, 9, 10, 11
A Carol for Saint Stephen's Day.
De-CH:225, Ox-BB:3
A Cherry Fair.   Gr-CT:321
Confession.   Charles d'Orleans.
Gr-CT:59
Corpus Christi Carol (The Falcon).
Al-VBP:36, Ga-S:200, Gr-CC:163,
Gr-CT:186, Gr-GB:308, Ma-FW:257,
Rv-CB:13, Sm-MK:36
Gentilesse.   G. Chaucer.   Rv-CB:61
The Grave.   Gr-CT:367
How, Butler, How.   Al-VBP:25
Hugh of Lincoln.   De-CH:408,
Ox-BB:317
I Am as Light as Any Roe.
Al-VBP:23, Gr-GB:207
I Have a Gentle Cock.   Al-VBP:23,
Gr-GB:100, Rv-CB:23
I Have a Young Sister.   De-CH:55,
Gr-GB:84

I Mun Be Married a Sunday.
N. Udall.   Gr-CC:158
In Dulci Jubilo.   J. Wedderburn.
Gr-CT:413
Jolly Jankin.   Gr-GB:141
Jolly Wat.   Al-VBP:21, Ma-BB:91
The Lament for the Makers.
W. Dunbar.   Al-VBP:32,
Gr-CT:354, Pl-ML:146, Rv-CB:71
Lat Take a Cat.   G. Chaucer.
Gr-CT:117
Lenten Is Come.   Al-VBP:4
A Lyke-Wake Dirge.   De-CH:248,
Ga-S:219, Gr-CT:366, Gr-GB:322,
Ma-BB:236, Ma-FW:258, Na-EO:107,
Pl-EI:139, Rv-CB:54
A Lytell Geste of Robyn Hode.
Ma-YA:43
Me Rueth Mary.   Gr-GB:306
Mon, in the Mone.   De-CH:742
The Months.   Gr-CT:425
Now Welcome Summer.   G. Chaucer.
Rv-CB:58
O for a Booke.   J. Wilson.
Bo-FP:24, Br-SS:80, Cl-DT:64,
Co-PS:142, De-CH:138
The Parliament of Fowls.
G. Chaucer.   Al-VBP:15
Philipp Sparrowe.   J. Skelton.
Gr-EC:177
The Reeve's Tale.   G. Chaucer.
Al-VBP:12
Robert of Gloucester's Chronicle.
Robert of Gloucester.   Ma-YA:23
Robin Hood and the Monk.
Al-VBP:37, De-CH:135, Ox-BB:405
The Shepherd upon a Hill.
Rv-CB:11
Suddenly Afraid.   Rv-CB:12
Sumer Is Icumen In.   Al-VBP:2,
Bo-FP:241, Fr-WO:74, Gr-CT:48,
Gr-GB:40, Li-SR:123, Ma-FW:34,
Ma-YA:25, Rv-CB:1
A Summer's Day.   A. Hume.
De-CH:136
Take Any Bird.   G. Chaucer.
De-CH:552, Rd-OA:17
To Rosamund.   G. Chaucer.
Rv-CB:57
Troilus and Criseyde. G. Chaucer.
Al-VBP:15
Truth.   G. Chaucer.   Al-VBP:18,
Rv-CB:60
Twelve Oxen.   Cl-DT:49, De-CH:139,
Gr-CT:114, Gr-GB:53, Re-TW:78,
Sh-RP:51
The Virgin.   Gr-GB:303
The Vision of William Concerning
Piers the Plowman. W. Langland.
Ma-YA:37
Welcome Yule.   De-CH:229

DIALECTS, MIDDLE ENGLISH — cont'd.
When Crist Was Born of Mary Free.
   Ma-YA:26
Why Come Ye Not to Courte.
   J. Skelton. Hi-FO:113
The Wife of Bath's Tale.
   G. Chaucer. Al-VBP:14
DIALECTS, NEGRO
Accountability. P. Dunbar.
   Fe-PL:427
After Winter. S. Brown.
   Ad-PB:65, Be-MA:30, Bo-HF:50,
   Hu-PN:165, Jo-SA:50
Ain' Go'n' to Study War No Mo'.
   Ba-PO:167
and we conquered. R. Penny.
   Ad-PB:391
An Ante-Bellum Sermon.
   P. Dunbar. Ra-BP:44
The Ballad of Joe Meek.
   S. Brown. Be-MA:31
Bim Bam. D. Rosenberg. Hu-PN:571
De Black Girl. Gr-GB:224
Blessing Without Company. Ra-BP:17
The Blue-Tail Fly. Er-FA:450,
   Gr-GB:324
D Blues. C. Hernton. Ad-PB:244
Blues for Bessie. M. O'Higgins.
   Hu-PN:347, Kr-OF:50
Bound No'th Blues. L. Hughes.
   Bo-AN:65
But He Was Cool. D. Lee.
   Ad-PB:426, Be-MA:160, Ra-BP:299
Carry Me Back to Old Virginny.
   J. Bland. Er-FA:444, Ga-FB:273,
   Se-PR:289
Chuck Will's Widow Song. Ra-BP:19
The Colored Band. P. Dunbar.
   Hu-MP:149
Conception. W. Cuney. Ab-MO:70
Cotton Songs. J. Toomer. Ra-BP:68
Crucifixion. Ra-BP:29
A Death Song. P. Dunbar.
   Fe-PL:274, Hu-PN:42
Dere's No Hidin' Place down Dere.
   Ra-BP:25
Dialect Quatrain. M. Christian.
   Bo-AN:53
Disgrace. Ab-MO:27
Dives and Laz'us. Lo-TY:197
Dixie. D. Emmett. Er-FA:290,
   Fe-FP:439
Done Found My Lost Sheep. Ga-S:147
Don't Tell All You Know. Bo-FP:119
Down in the Lonesome Garden.
   Ra-BP:8
Freedom in Mah Soul. D. Cannon.
   Hu-PN:281
Give Me Jesus. Ra-BP:28
Go Down, Old Hannah. Lo-TY:200
The Gospel Train. Bo-FP:120,
   Ra-BP:27

The Grey Goose. Mc-WK:62
Half Black, Half Blacker. S. Plumpp.
   Ad-PB:385
He Paid Me Seven. Ra-BP:5
Hold the Wind. Gr-GB:326
Homesick Blues. L. Hughes. Mc-WK:202,
   Un-MA:552
Hoosen Johnny. Fe-FP:165
Howdy, Honey, Howdy. P. Dunbar.
   Fe-PL:425
I Got a Home in Dat Rock. Ra-BP:25
I Got the Blues. Lo-TY:203
I Know de Moonlight. Ra-BP:23
I Thank God I'm Free at Las'.
   Ra-BP:31
I Told Jesus. S. Plumpp. Ad-PB:385
If You Want to Go to Heben. Gr-GB:299
I'll Wear Me a Cotton Dress. Ra-BP:11
imperial thumbprint. T. Weatherly.
   Ad-PB:399
In Come de Animuls Two by Two.
   Gr-GB:75
In the Morning. P. Dunbar. Ra-BP:51
An Indignation Dinner. J. Corrothers.
   Hu-PN:27
Jack and Dinah Want Freedom. Ra-BP:6
Jesus Was Crucified. C. Rodgers.
   Ad-PB:432
Joshua Fit de Battle of Jericho.
   Ra-BP:24
Juba Dance. Ab-MO:14
Lament of the Banana Man. E. Jones.
   To-MP:171
Little Brown Baby. P. Dunbar.
   Ab-MO:100, Hu-PN:40
Lonesome. P. Dunbar. Hu-MP:29, Se-PR:118
Long Gone. S. Brown. Ra-BP:112
Lullaby. P. Dunbar. Hu-MP:112
Miss Melerlee. J. Holloway.
   Hu-PN:19
Mister Banjo. Ab-MO:52
Molly Means. M. Walker. Be-MA:74,
   Bo-AN:130, Ha-PO:55, Hu-PN:309
My Sort of Man. P. Dunbar. Bo-AN:6
A Negro Love Song. P. Dunbar.
   Ab-MO:21, Hu-PN:36
Negro Soldier's Civil War Chant.
   Ra-BP:7
Never Said a Mumbalin' Word.
   Gr-GB:307
Northboun'. L. Holloway. Hu-PN:257
Oh, Freedom. Ab-MO:53
O! Susanna. S. Foster. Er-FA:431
Old Black Men Say. J. Emanuel.
   Ad-PB:180
The Old Cabin. P. Dunbar. Fe-PL:426
Old Man Know-All. Ra-BP:9
Old Marse John. Lo-TY:198
The Old Section Boss. Ra-BP:17
De Ole Sheep Dey Know de Road.
   Ra-BP:32
One o' These Mornin's. Ga-S:215

One-Sided Shoot-Out. D. Lee.
   Ad-PB:423, Ra-BP:302
The Party. P. Dunbar. Bo-AN:8
Paternal. E. Wilson. Hu-PN:370
Philosophy. P. Dunbar. Ra-BP:55
a poem for positive thinkers.
   B. Mahone. Ad-PB:473
Positives: For Sterling Plumpp.
   D. Lee. Ad-PB:427
Promises of Freedom. Ra-BP:5
Raise a "Rucus" To-Night. Ra-BP:10
the real people loves one another.
   R. Penny. Ad-PB:388
Refugee. N. Madgett. Hu-PN:379
Run, Nigger, Run! Ra-BP:5
She Hugged Me and Kissed Me.
   Ra-BP:16
Sister Lou. S. Brown. Ad-PB:66,
   Bo-AN:53, Hu-PN:174
Slave Marriage Ceremony Supplement.
   Ra-BP:16
Slim in Hell. S. Brown. Ra-BP:105
Soliloquy of a Turkey. P. Dunbar.
   Ra-BP:47
Song of the Banana Man. E. Jones.
   To-MP:168
Song to a Runaway Slave. Ra-BP:8
Southern Road. S. Brown. Ad-PB:67,
   Be-MA:29, Ra-BP:111
A Spiritual. P. Dunbar. Ra-BP:53
Steal Away to Jesus. Ra-BP:27
Swanee River. S. Foster. Er-FA:428,
   Se-PR:256
Sweetes' Li'l Feller. F. Stanton.
   Er-FA:503
Swing Low, Sweet Chariot. Br-AF:111,
   Fe-FP:441, Gr-GB:327, Sm-LG:386
Tails. Co-HP:26
That Hypocrite. Ra-BP:9
These Bones Gwine to Rise Agin.
   Ga-S:24
This Old Hammer. Su-FVI:42
This Sun Is Hot. Ra-BP:9
Turkey in the Straw. Er-FA:434,
   Gr-GB:209
The Turtle's Song. Ra-BP:18
Warm Babies. K. Preston.
   Co-FB:225, Ga-S:53
We Raise de Wheat. F. Douglass.
   Ra-BP:3
The Weary Blues. L. Hughes.
   Be-MA:39, Ga-FB:276, Hu-PN:184,
   Pl-US:90
Weeping Mary. Ga-S:142
We're Free. C. Williams. Ba-HI:124
What Yo' Gwine to Do when Yo' Lamp
   Burn Down? Ra-BP:29
When de Saints Go Ma'chin' Home.
   S. Brown. Bo-AN:55
When I Heard Dat White Man Say.
   Z. Gilbert. Ad-PB:195

When Malindy Sings. P. Dunbar.
   Ad-PB:10, Hu-PN:37
Wild Negro Bill. Ra-BP:7
DIALECTS, NEW ENGLAND
The Biglow Papers. J. Lowell.
   Ba-PO:98, Cr-WS:154, Ke-PP:83
The Deacon's Masterpiece or, The
   Wonderful "One-Hoss Shay."
   O. Holmes. Er-FA:375, Fe-PL:85,
   Sh-AP:63, Sm-LG:191, Sp-OG:229
A Farm Boy's Answer. J. Lowell.
   Kr-OF:63
Simon Soggs' Thanksgiving.
   W. Croffut. Co-PT:120
Spring. J. Lowell. Ga-FB:287
Yankee Doodle. Er-FA:434,
   Fe-FP:422, Se-PR:162, Vi-PP:107
DIALECTS, NEWFOUNDLAND
The Wreckers' Prayer. T. Roberts.
   Co-SS:127
DIALECTS, NORTHUMBERLAND
A. U. Hinny Bird. Gr-GB:170
The Bonny Keel Laddie. Gr-GB:215
Captain Bover. Gr-GB:238
Durham Old Women. Gr-GB:175
Ma Canny Hinny. Gr-GB:155
A Magpie Rhyme, Northumberland.
   Gr-GB:61
Maw Bonnie Lad. Gr-GB:133
Sair Fyel'd, Hinny. Gr-GB:319
The Waggoner. Gr-GB:213
DIALECTS, ORKNEY
The Miller's Wife's Lullaby.
   Gr-GB:16
DIALECTS, PENNSYLVANIA DUTCH
Lancaster County Tragedy. W. Kay.
   Br-SM:102
DIALECTS, PIDGIN ENGLISH
Nursery Song in Pidgin English.
   Li-SR:130
DIALECTS, SCOTTISH
Absence. De-TT:154
Adam and Eve Gaed up My Sleeve.
   Mo-TL:24
Address to a Haggis. R. Burns.
   Al-VBP:633
Address to the Unco Guid or the
   Rigidly Righteous. R. Burns.
   Al-VBP:631
Ae Fond Kiss. R. Burns.
   Al-VBP:648, Er-FA:122,
   Hi-WP II:102, Un-MW:80
An Thou Were My Ain Thing. A. Ramsay.
   Al-VBP:526
Annan Water. De-CH:311, Ma-BB:214
Annie Laurie. W. Douglass.
   Er-FA:425, Ga-FB:45
Ash Wednesday. W. Dunbar. Ga-S:142

At My Father's Grave. H. MacDiarmid.
   Co-EL:70, Pa-GTB:486
Auld Daddy Darkness. J. Ferguson.
   Ox-BC:275

DIALECTS, SCOTTISH — cont'd.
  Auld Lang Syne. R. Burns.
    Bo-FP:209, Er-FA:425, Fe-PL:129,
    Ma-YA:133, Sp-OG:260
  Auld Robin Gray. A. Lindsay.
    Al-VBP:603, De-CH:344, Pa-GTB:152
  Ballad. W. Soutar. Hi-WP I:89
  The Banks o' Doon. R. Burns.
    Un-MW:79
  The Battle of Otterburn.
    Ox-BB:491, Pa-OM:148
  Bessy Bell and Mary Gray.
    De-CH:520, Ox-BB:617
  The Birks of Aberfeldy. R. Burns.
    Al-VBP:643
  Blythsome Bridal. Gr-GB:152
  Bonnie George Campbell.
    Al-VBP:54, De-CH:41, Fo-OG:20,
    Gr-GB:250, Ox-BB:341, Rv-CB:419
  Bonnie Lesley. R. Burns.
    Pa-GTB:149, Rv-CB:625
  Bonny at Morn. Gr-GB:15
  The Bonny Moorhen. Gr-GB:191
  The Braes of Yarrow. J. Logan.
    Pa-GTB:121
  The Broomfield Hill. De-CH:292
  Cam' Ye By? De-CH:32, Gr-GB:105
  Cat at the Cream. Gr-GB:55
  The Cattie Rade to Paisley.
    Mo-TL:78
  Charlie, He's My Darling. R. Burns.
    Al-VBP:652, De-CH:174
  A Child's Grace. R. Burns.
    Bo-FP:158, Fe-FP:45, Hi-WP I:117,
    Hu-MP:16, Sm-LG:123
  Clark Sanders. Ox-BB:76, Rv-CB:34
  Cold Blows the Wind. J. Hamilton.
    Cl-FC:33, De-CH:218
  Comin' thro' the Rye. R. Burns.
    Er-FA:112
  Composed in Spring. R. Burns.
    Co-BN:141, Rv-CB:621
  The Corpus Christi Carol. Gr-GB:309
  The Cotter's Saturday Night.
    R. Burns. Fe-PL:58
  Cradle Song. Pl-EI:189
  The Cruel Brother. Ma-YA:38,
    Ox-BB:236
  Dance to Your Daddy. Ar-TP3:100,
    De-PO:6, Li-LB:10, Mo-MGT:181,
    Mo-NR:24, Mo-TL:86, Wr-RM:50
  The Deil's Awa wi' the Exciseman.
    R. Burns. Al-VBP:649
  The Doggies Gaed to the Mill.
    De-CH:498, Mo-TL:40
  The Dree Night. Gr-CT:364
  Drumdelgie. Gr-GB:210
  Duncan Gray. R. Burns. Pa-GTB:153
  The Earl of Mar's Daughter.
    De-CH:290, Fo-OG:21, Ma-BB:146
  Ech, Sic a Pairish.
    Co-FB:222

Edward, Edward. De-CH:410, Ha-PO:1,
    Ma-BB:39, Ox-BB:239, Rv-CB:39
The Elfin Knight. De-CH:276,
    Gr-GB:285, Ma-BB:181
The English. Gr-GB:163
Epigram Addressed to an Artist.
    R. Burns. Co-PU:24
Fair Annie. De-CH:414
Fair Flowers in the Valley. Rv-CB:46
Fair Helen. Al-VBP:53, De-CH:418,
    Er-FA:338, Hi-WP I:16, Pa-GTB:89,
    Rv-CB:43
The False Knight upon the Road.
    De-CH:316, Gr-GB:288
False Love. W. Scott. Al-VBP:675,
    Gr-GB:139
The Farewell. R. Burns.
    Al-VBP:377, De-CH:175
Feetikin, Feetikin. Mo-TL:41
The Flowers of the Forest. J. Elliott.
    Al-VBP:582, De-CH:176, Pa-GTB:120
The Forty-Second. Gr-GB:235
Four and Twenty White Kye.
    Gr-GB:17, Mo-TL:46
Gil Brenton. Ox-BB:38
The Goblin's Song. J. Telfer.
    Gr-CT:156
Gone Were But the Winter Cold.
    A. Cunningham. De-CH:224
The Gowden Locks of Anna. R. Burns.
    Rv-CB:624
The Great Silkie of Sule Skerrie.
    Gr-CT:206, Gr-GB:282, Ma-BB:18
Green Grow the Rashes. R. Burns.
    Al-VBP:642, Er-FA:426
Green Sleeves. Gr-GB:102
The Grey Selchie of Sule Skerry.
    Ox-BB:91
Hame, Hame, Hame. A. Cunningham.
    De-CH:169, De-TT:180
Hey-How for Hallowe'en! Sm-LG:234
Hey! Now the Day Dawns.
    A. Montgomerie. De-CH:4
Hey, Wully Wine. De-CH:330
Highland Mary. R. Burns.
    Al-VBP:650, Pa-GTB:151, Sp-OG:276
Holy Willie's Prayer. R. Burns.
    Al-VBP:626
How the First Hielandman of God
    Was Made of Ane Horse Turd in
    Argyll as Is Said. Gr-GB:166
Hush-a-Ba, Birdie. De-CH:741,
    Gr-GB:15, Mo-MGT:217, Rd-SS:20
Hush and Baloo. Gr-GB:15
I Do Confess Thou Art Sae Fair.
    R. Burns. Rv-CB:622
If Doughty Deeds. . . .
    Graham of Gartmore. Pa-GTB:128
I'm O'er Young to Marry Yet.
    R. Burns. Al-VBP:644
The Innumerable Christ.
    H. MacDiarmid. Pl-EI:156

Insect Riddles I.   Gr-GB:70
Jean.   R. Burns.   Al-VBP:645,
  Hi-WP I:41, Pa-GTB:156
Jock o' Hazeldean.   W. Scott.
  De-TT:109, Pa-GTB:183
John Anderson, My Jo.   R. Burns.
  Al-VBP:646, Ga-FB:47, Ha-PO:176,
  Pa-GTB:157, Rv-CB:619, Sp-OG:276
John Grumlie.   A. Cunningham.
  Fe-PL:235, Gr-GB:205
John Hielandman.   Gr-GB:168
Johnie Cam to Our Toun.   Gr-GB:99
Johnnie Norrie.   Mo-MGT:95
Kate Dalrymple.   Gr-GB:109
Kempion.   Ox-BB:56
King Henry.   Ox-BB:64
The Kirk of the Birds, Beasts and
  Fishes.   Gr-GB:76
Kiss'd Yestreen.   Gr-GB:101
Kissin'.   Co-BL:119, Co-FB:324,
  Un-MW:34
The Laird o' Logie.   De-CH:412,
  Rv-CB:49
A Lament.   A. Scott. De-CH:342
Lament for Culloden.   R. Burns.
  Pa-GTB:119, Rv-CB:614
The Lament of the Border Widow.
  De-CH:419, Gr-GB:246, Ox-BB:525
The Land o' the Leal.   Lady Nairn.
  Pa-GTB:157
The Lark.   Gr-GB:60
Last Lauch.   D. Young. Co-PU:148
Leezie Lindsay.   Sm-LG:361
Little Boy.   Gr-GB:169, Mo-MGT:62,
  Rv-ON:70
Lord Randal.   Cl-FC:85, Fo-OG:7,
  Ox-BB:243, Rv-CB:37, Un-MW:108
The Lowlands o' Holland.   De-CH:345,
  Fo-OG:51
Malison of the Stone-Chat.
  Gr-GB:63
M'Andrew's Hymn.   R. Kipling.
  Ga-S:119
A Man's a Man for A' That.   R. Burns.
  Al-VBP:653, Bo-HF:142, Er-FA:268,
  Sp-OG:330
March.   Gr-GB:38
Mary Hamilton.   Rv-CB:131
Mary Morison.   R. Burns. Pa-GTB:149
Mary, Queen of Scots.   R. Burns.
  Hi-FO:125
The Massacre of the MacPherson.
  W. Aytoun.   Gr-CT:17
The Meenister in the Poopit.
  Mo-TL:59
The Mermaid.   De-CH:403, Fo-OG:39
The Midges Dance aboon the Burn.
  R. Tannahill.   Co-BN:108
The Miller.   J. Clerk.   Gr-CT:84
The Mither's Lament.   S. Smith.
  Co-PU:151
Molecatcher.   A. Mackie. Co-BBW:40

Muckle-Mouth Meg.   R. Browning.
  Un-MW:118
My Auld Wife.   Gr-GB:160
My Bonie Mary.   R. Burns.
  Al-VBP:646, Gr-CC:121, Pa-GTB:127
My Boy Tammy.   H. Macneill.
  De-CH:33
My Love, She's But a Lassie Yet.
  R. Burns.   Al-VBP:647
My Luve's in Germany.   De-CH:172
The Nativity Chant.   W. Scott.
  Gr-CT:167, Sm-LG:233·
Nievie, Nievie, Nick, ·Nack.
  Mo-TL:75
O Alva Hills Is Bonny.   De-CH:518
O Can Ye Sew Cushions?   Sm-LG:97
O gin My Love Were Yon Red Rose.
  Gr-GB:117
O My Bonny, Bonny May.   Gr-GB:103
O Wert Thou in the Cauld Blast.
  R. Burns.   Un-MW:154
O Wha Will Shoe My Bonny Foot?
  De-CH:514
O Wha's the Bride?   H. MacDiarmid.
  Wi-LT:626
O What's the Rhyme to Porringer.
  Gr-GB:190
The Oak-Tree.   Rv-CB:33
On a Wag in Mauchline.   R. Burns.
  Co-EL:54, Co-FB:322
On Andrew Turner.   R. Burns.
  Co-PU:123
The Outlaw.   C. Kingsley.
  Co-RM:161
The Padda Song.   Gr-GB:283
Parley of Beasts. H. MacDiarmid.
  Rd-OA:22, Un-MB:359
Peggy.   A. Ramsay.   Al-VBP:526
A Poet's Welcome to His Love-
  Begotten Daughter. R. Burns.
  Al-VBP:625
The Puddy and the Mouse.   Gr-GB:68
Queen Mary, Queen Mary, My Age Is
  Sixteen.   De-CH:696
A Red, Red Rose.   R. Burns.
  Al-VBP:651, Ar-TP3:211, Bo-FP:292,
  Bo-HF:114, Co-BL:83, Co-PS:39,
  Er-FA:102, Fe-PL:111, Ga-FB:48,
  Gr-CT:64, Ha-PO:176, Hi-WP I:40,
  Ma-YA:136, Pa-GTB:150, Rv-CB:613,
  Se-PR:55, Sm-LG:351, Sp-OG:267,
  Un-MW:165
Riddles of the Weather IV. Gr-GB:37
The Rigs o' Barley.   R. Burns.
  Al-VBP:641, Rv-CB:617
Roon Aboot, Roon Aboot.   Mo-TL:24
Sailor and Tailor.   De-TT:127
The Sailor's Wife.   W. Mickle.
  Al-VBP:600, De-TT:110, Pa-GTB:154
Scots Wha Hae.   R. Burns. Hi-FO:83,
  Ma-YA:135, Sm-LG:154, Sp-OG:189

DIALECTS, SCOTTISH — cont'd.

The Sea Eagle. H. MacDiarmid.
Un-MB:360
Sheath and Knife. De-CH:54
Shee Was Brighter of Her Blee.
De-CH:766
Sir Colin. Ox-BB:20
Sir Patrick Spens. Al-VBP:35,
Ar-TP3:19, Bl-OB:47, Bo-GJ:159,
Co-RG:58, Co-SS:129, De-CH:405,
Ha-PO:3, Ma-BB:1, Ma-FW:46,
Ma-YA:41, Ox-BB:311, Rv-CB:38,
Sm-LG:307, Sp-OG:98
Snow. Gr-GB:36
Some Say the Deil's Deid. Sm-LG:241
A Song. Co-PU:7
The Strange Visitor. Bl-OB:86,
De-CH:677, Gr-CT:132, Gr-GB:290
Sweet Afton. R. Burns. Co-BN:73,
Er-FA:428, Mc-PR:17, Un-MW:154
Sweet Willie. Ox-BB:45
Tam o' Shanter. R. Burns.
Al-VBP:634, Sp-OG:170
There Cam' Seven Egyptians.
De-CH:534
There Gowans Are Gay. Gr-GB:97
There Once Was a Bonnie Scotch
Laddie. Br-LL:84
There Was a Knight. De-CH:315,
Gr-GB:277
There Was a Wee Bit Mousikie.
Bl-OB:105, De-CH:544
There'll Never Be Peace.
R. Burns. Rv-CB:626
There's Nane o' My Ain to Care.
W. Ogilvie. De-CH:515
This Ain Biggit the Baurn.
De-CH:497
This Is the Man That Broke the
Barn. Mo-TL:18
Thomas the Rhymer. Al-VBP:40,
De-CH:119, Fo-OG:3, Gr-CT:175,
Ha-PO:51, Ma-BB:5, Ma-FW:181,
Pa-OM:275, Rv-CB:40, Un-GT:124
Thumb Bold. Mo-TL:18
Tintock-Tap. Gr-GB:177
Tae Titly. Ir-BB:12, Mo-TL:48
To a Louse. R. Burns.
Al-VBP:629, Co-BBW:221,
Er-FA:71, Ma-YA:131, Sp-OG:300
To a Mountain Daisy. R. Burns.
Co-BN:57, Fe-PL:374, Hu-MP:259,
Sp-OG:289
To a Mouse. R. Burns.
Co-BBW:36, Er-FA:226, Fe-PL:367,
Hu-MP:190, Mc-WK:60, Pa-GTB:141,
Rd-OA:24, Rv-CB:616, Sp-OG:297
To Miss Ferrier (Enclosing the
Elegy on Sir J. H. Blair).
R. Burns. Rv-CB:623
To the Ladybug. Mo-TB:88

To the Princess Margaret Tudor.
W. Dunbar. Gr-SS:92
The Twa Brothers. De-CH:52,
Ox-BB:234
The Twa Corbies. De-CH:102,
Ha-PO:127, Ma-BB:132, Ma-FW:256,
Pa-GTB:90, Rv-CB:55, Sm-LG:268,
Sp-OG:115
The Twa Magicians. Ox-BB:51
The Twa Sisters. De-CH:421,
Rv-CB:42
The Two Rivers. Co-BN:79,
De-CH:404, Gr-CT:165, Gr-GB:176,
Ma-BB:83, Rv-CB:119
Up in the Morning Early. R. Burns.
Bl-OB:98, Bo-FP:168, Co-PS:160,
De-TT:91
Venus and Cupid. M. Boyd. Ho-P:147
Waly, Waly. Al-VBP:51, Gr-GB:144,
Ox-BB:327, Pa-GTB:87
The Wandering Spectre. Bl-OB:156,
De-CH:314, Gr-CT:155, Gr-GB:284,
Rv-CB:141, Sm-LG:238
Wee Davie Daylicht. R. Tennant.
Ox-BC:230
The Wee Wee Man. De-CH:277,
Fo-OG:28, Gr-GB:286, Ma-BB:12,
Ox-BB:11
Wee Willie Winkie. Au-SP:8,
Bo-FP:39, Br-SS:36, Cl-DT:31,
De-PO:28, Er-FA:492, Li-LB:39,
Mo-CC:(36), Mo-MGT:17,
Mo-NR:106, Ox-BC:172, Rd-SS:7,
Wi-MG:35, Wr-RM:33
We'll Go to Sea No More.
Co-SS:62, Gr-CT:220, Gr-GB:215
We're A' Dry wi' the Drinkin' o't.
Co-EL:16
Wha Lies Here? Co-FB:131,
Co-PM:159
What Will Be Our Twelve, Boys.
De-CH:629
What's in There? De-CH:277,
Ir-BB:143
Wheesht, Wheesht! H. MacDiarmid.
Co-EL:12
Whistle an' I'll Come. R. Burns.
Al-VBP:651, Co-BL:99,
Hi-WP I:41, Un-MW:188
The Whummil Bore. De-CH:329
Willie Brew'd a Peck o' Maut.
R. Burns. Al-VBP:647
Willy Drowned in Yarrow.
De-CH:728, Pa-GTB:122
The Wind. Gr-CT:389, Gr-GB:37,
Ir-BB:49, Sm-LG:64
The Witches' Ballad. W. Scott.
De-CH:306, Na-EO:24
Witch's Milking Charm. Gr-CT:159,
Gr-GB:290
With the Herring Fishers.
H. MacDiarmid. Wi-LT:627

Ye Banks and Braes. R. Burns.
  Al-VBP:648, Co-BL:141, De-CH:47,
  Hi-WP II:103, Pa-GTB:131, Rv-CB:615
The Yellow-Haired Laddie. Gr-GB:101
Yet Some Are Always Hungry.
  Gr-TG:38
See also Ox-BB
DIALECTS, SEAMAN
  Captain Pink of the Peppermint.
    W. Irwin. Co-SS:88
  Peg-Leg's Fiddle. B. Adams.
    Sh-RP:53
  The Powerful Eyes o' Jeremy Tait.
    W. Irwin. Co-FB:135, Co-SS:79,
    Ha-PO:264
DIALECTS, WESSEX
  The Pity of It. T. Hardy. Wi-LT:23
DIALECTS, WEST INDIAN
  Colonisation in Reverse.
    L. Bennett. Sa-B:51
  Husa. F. John. Sa-B:108
  The Song of the Banana Man. E. Jones.
    Co-RM:242, Sa-B:101
  Uncle Time. D. Scott. Sa-B:153
  Valley Prince. M. Morris. Sa-B:125
  The Woman's Tongue Tree.
    A. Guiterman. Co-PM:81
DIALECTS, WESTERN
  At a Cowboy Dance. J. Adams.
    Sh-RP:22
  The Big Rock Candy Mountain.
    Gr-CT:280, Gr-GB:228, Hi-WP I:96,
    Pe-SS:86
  Boomer Johnson. Fi-BG:84
  The Bullwhacker. Co-RM:18
  Californy Stage. Fi-BG:132
  'Dobe Bill. Co-RM:31
  Broncho Versus Bicycle. J. Crawford.
    Fi-BG:117
  The Legend of Boastful Bill.
    C. Clark. Fi-BG:92
  Night Herding Song. H. Stephens.
    Sh-RP:79
  Passing of the Wrangler. H. Fellow.
    Fi-BG:151
  The Trail Herd. Fi-BG:145
  Two-Gun Percy. Fi-BG:136
  Tying a Knot in the Devil's Tail.
    Co-RM:35
  Walk, Damn You, Walk! W. De Vere.
    Fe-PL:51
  Waring of Sonoratown. H. Knibbs.
    Fi-BG:141
  Western Justice. A. Rafter.
    Fi-BG:63
  When Broncho Jack Was Spliced.
    J. Adams. Fi-BG:172
DIALECTS, WILTS
  The Harnet and the Bittle.
    J. Akerman. Gr-CT:15
  Under a Wiltshire Apple Tree.
    A. De Bary. De-CH:150

DIANA (GODDESS)
  Atalanta in Calydon. A. Swinburne.
    Al-VBP:1038, Ga-FB:230,
    Ha-PO:237, Ma-YA:216, Na-EO:58,
    Pa-GTB:388
  Dianae Sumus in Fide. Catullus.
    Gr-CC:94
  Homage to Diana. W. Raleigh.
    Ho-WR:38
  Hymn to Diana. B. Jonson.
    Al-VBP:239, De-CH:441, Gr-CT:403,
    Ho-WR:39, Ma-YA:83, Pa-GTB:67,
    Rv-CB:281
  To the Moon. W. Wordsworth.
    Rv-CB:653
DICKENS, CHARLES
  Dickens in Camp. B. Harte. Se-PR:308
DICKINSON, EMILY ELIZABETH
  I Am in Danger - Sir. A. Rich.
    Pl-ML:134
  Not to Forget Miss Dickinson.
    M. Schacht. Wi-LT:642
  To Emily Dickinson. H. Crane.
    Pl-ML:133
DICTATORS: see also SATIRE -
    DICTATORS
  Haunted Caudillo. F. Charles.
    Sa-B:187
  Only the Beards Are Different.
    B. Dawe. Cr-WS:44
DICTIONARIES
  Some Days Are Rainy. Re-RR:10
DIDO: see also AENEAS
  Dido. T. Campion. Rv-CB:266
  Dido of Tunisia. P. McGinley.
    Cr-WS:18
DIET: see COOKS AND COOKERY; FOOD
    AND EATING; HUMOR - DIET
DIGGING: see also MINERS AND
    MINING
  Clam-Digging Song. M. Kumin.
    Cr-SS:6
  Digging. S. Heaney. Br-TC:173,
    To-MP:150
  Digging for China. R. Wilbur.
    Bo-GJ:224, Br-TC:471, Gr-BT:11,
    Ha-LO:88, Ho-TH:66
  Mister Beers. H. Lofting.
    Fe-FP:316, Ir-BB:202, Sh-RP:148
DIGNITY: see also HUMOR - DIGNITY;
    SELF-RESPECT
  Blackman/an unfinished history.
    D. Lee. Be-MA:161
  Haven. D. Hayes. Bo-AN:92,
    Hu-PN:245
  Let Us Move Evenly Together.
    Wo-HS:(32)
  Sonnet to a Negro in Harlem.
    H. Johnson. Bo-AN:102, Mo-BG:27
  Sonnets, xxxvii. E. Millay. Sm-PT:153
  Two Surprises. R. McAlpine. Fe-PL:88

DIGNITY — cont'd.
  WALK TALL MY BLACK CHILDREN.
    S. Boone. La-IH:114
DILIGENCE: see also BUSYNESS;
    PERSEVERANCE
  The Bee. I. Watts. Ox-BC:49
  Five Little Chickens.
    Ch-B:85, Fe-FP:282, Gr-EC:182,
    La-PV:198, St-FS:78, Un-GB:15,
    Un-GT:67
  The Gleaner. J. Taylor. Ox-BC:120
  He That Would Thrive.
    Ir-BB:229, Mo-MGT:131, Sp-TM:1
  Motto. Ar-TP3:209
DIMINISHING VERSE: see also
    CUMULATIVE VERSE
  And Then There Were None.
    E. Millay. Cr-WS:42
  The Key of the Kingdom.
    Bl-OB:158, De-CH:3, Er-FA:202,
    Gr-EC:292, Ho-P:107, Mo-MGT:133,
    Re-TW:32, Rv-CB:31, Sm-LG:237,
    Sp-AS:(10)
  The Pinwheel's Song. J. Ciardi.
    La-PV:58
  san francisco county jail cell b-6.
    Conyus. Ad-PB:400
  Ten Brothers. L. Untermeyer.
    Sh-RP:9
  Ten Trained Bears on Roller
    Skates. On-TW:52
  Two Birds. Mo-MGT:85, On-TW:11,
    Rv-ON:14, Sp-AS:27, Wr-RM:23
  Underneath This Hazelin Mote.
    De-CH:670
  What Will Be Our Twelve, Boys?
    De-CH:629
DINNERS: see SATIRE - DINNERS
DINOSAURS
  The Dinosaur. C. Junge. Au-SP:81
  The Dinosaur. B. Taylor. Pl-IO:112
  The Dinosaur Bones. C. Sandburg.
    Du-SH:108, Ho-TH:56
  Epitaph for the Race of Man.
    E. Millay. Sh-AP:187
DIOCLETIAN, ROMAN EMPEROR
  Great Diocletian. A. Cowley.
    Gr-CT:269
DIONYSIUS: see BACCHUS
DIPLOMATS: see also HUMOR -
    DIPLOMATS
  The Ambassadors. W. Burford.
    Bl-FP:77
  Embassy. W. Auden. Du-SH:81
  Imperialists in Retirement.
    E. Lucie-Smith. To-MP:149
DIRECTIONS TO PLACES: see also
    HUMOR - DIRECTIONS TO PLACES;
    SIGNS AND SIGNBOARDS
  The Shepherd's Hut. A. Young.
    Re-TW:10

  Visit. A. Ammons. Br-TC:9,
    Kh-VA:25, Mo-BG:100
  You, North Must Go.
    Ir-BB:17, St-FS:32
DIRGES: see also ELEGIES; LAMENTS;
    SATIRE - DIRGES
  Autumn. P. Shelley. De-CH:208
  "Blackened-Face" Dirge - Proper for
    Atiroa. Koroneu. Tr-US II:64
  Come Away, Come Away, Death.
    W. Shakespeare. Al-VBP:190,
    Pa-GTB:27, Rv-CB:195
  Coronach. W. Scott. Al-VBP:672,
    De-CH:163, Ho-WR:119, Ma-YA:145,
    Pa-GTB:235
  Dark Girl. A. Bontemps. Pe-SS:148
  Death of Dr. King. S. Cornish.
    Ad-PB:296
  Death Song. R. Hawker. Ox-BN:462
  Dido My Dear, Alas, Is Dead.
    E. Spenser. Gr-CT:181
  Dirge. T. Beddoes. Ox-BN:450
  A Dirge. W. Cory. Ox-BN:648
  A Dirge. Fang Ching. Hs-TC:387
  A Dirge. C. Rossetti. Gr-CT:332
  A Dirge. P. Shelley. Gr-CT:195,
    Ho-WR:234, Mo-GR:86
  A Dirge. J. Webster. Al-VBP:288,
    Bl-OB:153, De-CH:251, Gr-CT:363,
    Pa-GTB:29, Re-TW:23, Rv-CB:315,
    Sm-LG:267
  Dirge. Tr-US II:51
  Dirge. Tr-CB:30, Tr-US I:50
  Dirge. Tr-US I:167
  Dirge. Tr-US II:103
  Dirge. Tr-US II:146
  Dirge for a Chief. Tr-US II:116
  Dirge for a Son Killed in Battle.
    Tr-US I:187
  Dirge for Robin Hood. A. Munday.
    Bl-OB:152, De-CH:77, Ho-WR:116,
    Re-TW:71, Rv-CB:163
  Dirge for Two Veterans. W. Whitman.
    Un-MA:77
  Dirge in Cymbeline. W. Collins.
    Al-VBP:574, No-CL:63
  Dirge in Dialogue. Lo-TY:3,
    Tr-US I:64
  Dirges, I. Tr-US I:47
  Dirges, I. Tr-US II:41
  Dirges, II. Tr-US II:42
  Dirges II. On a Ruler. Tr-US I:47
  Fall Down. C. Hernton. Ad-PB:243
  Fear No More. W. Shakespeare.
    Al-VBP:195, Bo-HF:179, Co-RG:144,
    De-CH:250, De-TT:193, Er-FA:260,
    Gr-CT:332, Ha-PO:251, Hi-WP II:19,
    No-CL:73, Pa-GTB:28, Rv-CB:201,
    Sm-LG:267
  Full Fathom Five. W. Shakespeare.
    Al-VBP:197, Bl-OB:52, Bo-GJ:141,

Cl-DT:39, Co-SS:159, De-CH:719,
Fr-WO:86, Gr-CT:231, Ma-FW:42,
Ma-YA:70, Na-EO:44, No-CL:43,
Pa-GTB:29, Re-TW:70, Rv-CB:193,
Sm-MK:37
Funeral Poem.   Tr-US II:191
Funeral Song.   J. Fletcher. Gr-CT:359
Hear, Sweet Spirit.   S. Coleridge.
Al-VBP:700, De-CH:313
Hymn to Earth.   E. Wylie.
Un-MA:284, Wi-LT:209
Keening.   Tr-US II:309
Lament.   D. Georgakas. Sc-TN:58
A Lyke-Wake Dirge.   De-CH:248,
Ga-S:219, Gr-CT:366, Gr-GB:322,
Ma-BB:236, Ma-FW:258, Na-EO:107,
Pl-EI:139, Rv-CB:54
Madrigal.   R. Thomas. Co-EL:74
Mourning Song for a Brother Drowned
at Sea.   Br-MW:139
November Twenty-Sixth Nineteen Hundred
and Sixty-Three.   W. Berry.
Wi-LT:662
O Sing unto My Roundelay.
T. Chatterton. De-CH:249,
Ho-WR:152
Old Funeral Chant. Tr-US II:43
Ophelia's Song. W. Shakespeare.
Al-VBP:191, De-CH:343, De-TT:159,
Gr-CT:77
The Overthrow of Ruanae. Potiki.
Tr-US II:56
Pardon, Goddess of the Night.
W. Shakespeare. Al-VBP:186
Perhaps (a Dirge). Wen I-to.
Hs-TC:65
Prayer at the Sacrifice Before the
Coffin. Tr-US II:196
The Sea-Ritual. G. Darley.
De-CH:312, Gr-SS:179, Ho-WR:126,
Ox-BN:396
Song. Tr-US I:50
Song of the Last Moments. Tr-US I:58
The Sparrow's Dirge. J. Skelton.
Sm-LG:85
A Voice from the Waters. T. Beddoes.
Ox-BN:449, Rv-CB:771
DIRIGIBLES: see AIRSHIPS
DIRTINESS: see also HUMOR - DIRTINESS
Cleanliness. C. and M. Lamb.
Ox-BC:144
Dirty Jack. De-TT:24
Get This Garbage Out of My Life.
P. Goddins. Ba-HI:132
Song. F. O'Hara. Ad-CI:28
DISADVANTAGED: see HANDICAPPED;
SOCIALLY HANDICAPPED
DISAPPOINTMENT: see also FRUSTRATION
The Auction Sale. H. Reed. Un-MB:509
Ball Game. R. Eberhart. Pe-M:5
Blackberry-Picking. S. Heaney.
Co-BN:100

Blue Blood.   J. Stephens. Un-MB:266
Boys Will Be Princes.   W. Heyen.
Ls-NY:92
A Broken Appointment.   T. Hardy.
Rv-CB:940
By the Winding River, II.   Tu Fu.
Rx-OH:14
Camoëns in the Hospital (After).
H. Melville. Al-VBP:958
Dance Song.   Le-IB:77
For a Poet.   C. Cullen. Ab-MO:109,
Hu-PN:229, Lo-TY:234, Th-AS:197
Grown-Up.   E. Millay. Ho-TH:21
Half of My Life.   C. O'John.
Al-WW:64
Harpalus' Complaint.   Al-VBP:67
Hope.   G. Herbert. Gr-CC:169
I Did Not See a Mermaid.
S. Johnson. Li-LC:61
Improvisations: Light and Snow.
C. Aiken. Co-BN:189
The Little Cart.   Ch'en Tzu-lung.
Ma-FW:89
Live Man's Epitaph.   F. Hope.
Gr-BT:83
The Lost Leader.   R. Browning.
Al-VBP:884, Hi-FO:225, Ke-TF:56,
Pl-ML:58
The Magi.   W. Yeats. Co-EL:148
Midnight Raffle.   L. Hughes.
La-OC:65
Misconceptions.   R. Browning.
Rv-CB:825
My Song Was Ready.   Le-IB:79
Neglectful Edward.   R. Graves.
Un-MB:383
O I Won't Lead a Homely Life.
T. Hardy. Pl-US:33
Old Gray Squirrel.   A. Noyes.
Co-SS:215
Presents.   M. Chute. Br-SS:109,
La-PH:36, La-PP:60, Na-EO:130
Strange Meeting.   W. Owen. Ba-PO:140
Tell Him.   C. Bialik. Pa-SG:52
To the Lord Chancellor.   P. Shelley.
Al-VBP:747
Une Vie.   P. Saarikoski. Co-EL:144
The Visit of the Professor of
Aesthetics.   M. Danner.
Ad-PB:135, Be-MA:89, Bo-AN:155,
Hu-NN:31
The Way-Side Well.   J. Cotter. Hu-PN:18
The Wild Flower's Song.
W. Blake. Rv-CB:606
The World Was Meant to Be Peaceful.
V. Bryant. Ba-HI:47
DISAPPROVAL
The Breed of Athletes.   Euripides.
Mo-SD:163
Song: One Hard Look.
R. Graves. Un-MB:388

DISASTERS: see also ACCIDENTS;
    DROUGHTS; EARTHQUAKES; FAMINES;
    FIRES; FLOODS; FOREST FIRES;
    HUMOR – DISASTERS; RED CROSS;
    SHIPWRECKS; STORMS
  The Ashtabula Disaster. J. Moore.
    Na-EO:122
  At Dunwich. A. Thwaite. Ca-MB:89
  The Avondale Mine Disaster.
    Hi-TL:133
  A Ballad of a Mine. R. Skelton.
    Ca-MB:77
  The Brooklyn Theater Fire. Em-AF:467
  Tha Cabin Creek Flood. Em-AF:476
  Casey Jones. R. Hunter. Mo-GR:52
  The Dykes. R. Kipling. Ni-JP:138
  The Gresford Disaster. Gr-GB:225
  Joseph Mica. Mo-GR:53
  The Milwaukee Fire. Em-AF:469
  Miners. J. Wright. St-H:256
  The Miramichi Fire. Em-AF:464
  The Old Churchyard at Bonchurch.
    P. Marston. Ox-BN:888
  On the Pestilence That Scourged
    the Fijians after Their First
    Contact with Whites, ca. 1791.
    Tr-US I:228
  Run, Boys, Run.   Br-FF:(41),
    Mo-MGT:128
  The Santa Barbara Earthquake.
    Em-AF:472
  The Sherman Cyclone. Em-AF:471
  Song on the Great Visitation of
    Measles in 1875. Tr-US I:228
  The Tay River Bridge Disaster.
    W. McGonagall. Na-EO:78
  The Tupelo Destruction. Em-AF:474
  The Wave. D. Hine. Ho-P:99
  The West Palm Beach Story.
    Em-AF:473
  What Bright Pushbutton?
    S. Allen. Hu-PN:344
  The White Dust. W. Gibson. Un-MB:242
  You Were at the Dead River. G. Abbe.
    De-FS:3
  Zermatt. T. Hardy. Ox-BN:823
DISCIPLES, TWELVE: see APOSTLES
DISCIPLINE: see also PUNISHMENT
  Always. R. Groppuso. Me-WF:17
  Call to Youth. Horace. Pa-SG:4
  Discipline. G. Herbert. Al-VBP:342,
    Fe-PL:342, Mc-PR:92
  Of Love. K. Gibran. Fe-PL:121
  Sin. G. Herbert. Al-VBP:344
  Sonnets 1. W. Wordsworth. Al-VBP:658
  Thought. Al-PI:20
DISCOBOLUS (STATUE)
  A Psalm of Montreal. S. Butler.
    Rv-CB:933
DISCONTENT: see also HUMOR –
    DISCONTENT; PROTEST
  Ah, Poverties, Wincings, and Sulky

  Retreats.   W. Whitman. Rv-CB:855
Alone Walking.   Rv-CB:2
As for the World.   Y. Amichai.
  Me-PH:127
Baudelaire.   D. Schwartz.
  Br-TC:357, Pl-ML:14
Beginning of a Girls' Song.
  Tr-US I:111
bitchice.   E. Jenkins. Ad-II:22
The Collar.   G. Herbert.
  Al-VBP:341, Go-BP:181, Pl-EI:92,
  Rv-CB:355
From the Flats. S. Lanier. Sh-AP:132
Hearing of Harvests Rotting in the
  Valleys. W. Auden. Un-MB:457
I Am Weary of the Time. . . .
  L. Beebe. La-RM:171
Journey Song. Tr-US I:74
Life. Lord Bacon. Pa-GTB:38
The Magi. W. Yeats. Co-EL:148
Me. Danny. La-IH:89
Messo Cammin. H. Longfellow.
  Rv-CB:782
Morning. Chu Shu Chen. Rx-OH:132
Mugala's Song. Tr-CB:14,
  Tr-US I:92
Nothing Is Enough. L. Binyon.
  Un-MB:156
On My Birthday. Y. Amichai.
  Me-PH:128
Plaint. Chu Shu Chen. Rx-OH:127
Prayer. L. Untermeyer. Un-GT:308,
  Un-MA:305
Rock Me to Sleep. E. Allen.
  Er-FA:171
Sad Songs, III. Tr-US II:174
The Seekers. J. Masefield.
  Go-BP:224
Song. Tr-US II:168
Sonnet XXIX.   W. Shakespeare.
  Al-VBP:200, Co-BL:117, Ga-FB:34,
  Ha-PO:254, Ni-JP:96, Pa-GTB:8,
  Rv-CB:212, Un-MW:181
Sonnet 30. W. Shakespeare.
  Al-VBP:201, Er-FA:166, Fe-PL:130,
  Ga-FB:33, Pa-GTB:18, Rv-CB:213
A Summer Night. M. Arnold. Rv-CB:871
This Old Countryside. M. Fuller.
  Ba-HI:135
To Those Born After. B. Brecht.
  Un-R:41
The Wheel Change. B. Brecht.
  Co-EL:104
Why. V. Howard. Ba-HI:120
Why Should I Want. W. Harris.
  Ad-PB:439
Winter and Summer. S. Spender.
  Un-MB:480
The Woman at the Washington Zoo.
  R. Jarrell. Br-TC:220, Wi-LT:565
Youth's Agitations. M. Arnold.
  Rv-CB:870

DISCOVERIES: see also DISCOVERY PERIOD
    IN AMERICA; EXPLORERS; names of
    discoverers, as COLUMBUS, CHRISTOPHER
Christopher Columbus.   R. & S. Benét.
    Pe-FB:34, Sh-RP:294
Columbian Ode.   P. Dunbar. Se-PR:180
Columbus.   L. Jackson.   Br-SS:63
Columbus.   L. Simpson.   To-MP:157
Discoveries.   V. Watkins. Wi-LT:448
the discoveries of fire.
    L. Clifton.   Mo-TS:32
Fingers in the Nesting Box.
    R. Graves.   Co-BBW:162
Four Quartets.   T. Eliot. Pl-IO:6
Lines Written after the Discovery
    by the Author of the Germ of
    Yellow Fever.   R. Ross.
    Pl-IO:187
Lone Founts.   H. Melville.
    Al-VBP:955
A Morning Song.   E. Farjeon.
    Hi-WP I:6
On First Looking into Chapman's
    Homer.   J. Keats.   Al-VBP:769,
    Co-RG:17, De-CH:361, Er-FA:75,
    Ga-FB:14, Gr-CT:442, Ke-TF:61,
    Ma-YA:182, Mc-PR:78, Ni-JP:19,
    No-CL:18, Ox-BN:334, Pa-GBT:169,
    Pl-ML:91, Rv-CB:739, Sm-LG:36
The Prayer of Columbus.
    W. Whitman.   Se-PR:180
Sonnet XXVI.   Feng Chih. Hs-TC:154
Who Was It.   H. Heine. Pa-SG:34
DISCOVERY PERIOD IN AMERICA: see also
    COLONIAL PERIOD IN AMERICA;
    EXPLORERS; NORTHMEN; also names of
    discoverers, as COLUMBUS,
    CHRISTOPHER
The Discovery.   J. Squire. Br-AF:54,
    Cl-FC:83, Co-PS:132, De-CH:361,
    Fe-FP:404, Mc-WK:163
The English in Virginia.
    C. Reznikoff.   Gr-SS:62
The Night Before America.   N. Farber.
    Hi-FO:106
The Skeleton in Armor. H. Longfellow.
    Mc-PR:56, Sp-OG:103, Un-GT:173
To the Virginian Voyage.   M. Drayton.
    Al-VBP:161, Hi-TL:19, Rv-CB:184
To the Western World.   L. Simpson.
    Wi-LT:817
DISCRIMINATION: see also CIVIL
    RIGHTS; HUMOR - DISCRIMINATION;
    INDIANS OF NORTH AMERICA - TREAT-
    MENT; JEWS - PERSECUTION; RACE
    PROBLEMS; SATIRE - DISCRIMINATION;
    WOMEN - EQUAL RIGHTS
The Alarm Clock.   M. Evans. Ad-BO:6
America.   J. Whitfield. Ba-PO:17,
    Ra-BP:35

Award.   R. Durem.   Ad-PB:152,
    Hu-NN:33, Jo-SA:26, Ke-PP:118,
    Kr-OF:54, Lo-TY:243, Ra-BP:164
The Backlash Blues.   L. Hughes.
    Ra-BP:90
The Ballad of Rudolph Reed.
    G. Brooks.   Jo-SA:46
be cool, baby.   R. Penny. Ad-PB:390
Black Child.   P. Solomon. Jo-VC:51
De Black Girl.   Gr-GB:224
Blues for Bessie.   M. O'Higgins.
    Hu-PN:347, Kr-OF:50
colors for mama.   B. Mahone.
    Ad-PB:473
Come Back Blues.   M. Harper.
    Ad-PB:314
Cultural Exchange.   L. Hughes.
    Ad-PB:76, Hu-PN:203, Ra-BP:83
Dream Deferred.   L. Hughes.
    Ad-PB:76, Be-MA:42, Bo-AN:67,
    Ha-TP:21, Hu-PN:199, La-OC:149,
    Wi-LT:422
Elephant Rock.   P. St. John.
    Ad-PB:347
God Give to Men.   A. Bontemps.
    Hu-PN:225, Ra-BP:92
Harlem.   L. Hughes.   Ad-CI:32
It Happened in Montgomery.
    P. Petrie.   Ab-MO:86
Last Night Somebody Called Me
    Darky.   N. Guillen. Ab-MO:95
Legacy: My South.   D. Randall.
    Ad-PB:138, Be-MA:71, Hu-NN:43,
    Hu-PN:306
Let America Be America Again.
    L. Hughes.   Hu-PN:193
Liberty for All.   W. Garrison.
    Kr-OF:30
The Louisiana Weekly #4. D. Henderson.
    Ad-PB:421, Jo-SA:103
The Melting Pot.   D. Randall.
    Ra-BP:141
Merry-Go-Round.   L. Hughes.
    Ab-MO:94, Hu-PN:192, Kr-OF:52
Montgomery.   S. Cornish. Ad-PB:293
Now, All You Children.   R. Durem.
    Jo-SA:106
On Seeing Two Brown Boys in a
    Catholic Church.   F. Horne.
    Ad-PB:551, Hu-PN:146, Lo-TY:212
Picnic: The Liberated.   M. Holman.
    Ad-PB:176, Hu-PN:367
Poem.   D. Walcott.   Sa-B:67
Poem to Americans.   G. Jackson.
    Lo-IT:58
poll.   E. Roberson.   Ad-PB:350
Primary Lesson: The Second Class
    Citizens.   Sun Ra. Ad-PB:208
right on: white america.
    S. Sanchez.   Ad-BO:42,
    Ad-PB:287, Be-MA:135, Jo-SA:104

DISCRIMINATION — cont'd.
  Scottsboro, Too, Is Worth Its Song.
    C. Cullen. Ad-PB:93, Be-MA:52
  Snapshots of the Cotton South.
    F. Davis. Ad-PB:98
  Sonnet to Gath. E. Millay.
    Un-MA:448
  The Sorrow of Shanghai.
    Wang Tu-ch'ing. Hs-TC:198
  The Sounds of Afroamerican History.
    S. Anderson. Ad-PB:440
  Stanzas on Freedom. J. Lowell.
    Hu-PN:464, Kr-OF:31
  Status Quo. B. Dismond. Hu-PN:93
  This Is an African Worm.
    M. Danner. Ra-BP:151
  To Some Millions Who Survive
    Joseph E. Mander, Senior.
    S. Wright. Ad-PB:212
  Until They Have Stopped. S. Wright.
    Ad-PB:215
  Vietnam #4. C. Major. Ad-BO:48,
    Ad-PB:298, Ba-PO:38
  Watts. C. Rivers. Ad-BO:41,
    Ad-PB:233
  We Live in a Cage. W. Harris.
    Ad-PB:438
  Where? When? Which? L. Hughes.
    Ra-BP:88
  Who Are You - Who Are You?
    D. Clarke. Jo-VC:79
  Why Prejudice. B. Chase. Ba-HI:24
  You Know, Joe. R. Durem.
    Ad-BO:47, Hu-PN:330
DISDAIN: see CONTEMPT
DISEASES: see PLAGUES; SICKNESS;
    and names of diseases, as
    MEASLES
DISGRACE: see SHAME
DISGUISE: see DECEPTION
DISHONESTY: see DECEPTION
DISILLUSIONMENT: see also
    CYNICISM; DISAPPOINTMENT
  Adulthood. N. Giovanni. Be-MA:69
  After They Have Tired of the
    Brilliance of Cities.
    S. Spender. Wi-LT:497
  Alumnus Football. G. Rice.
    Fe-PL:56
  Always the Following Wind.
    W. Auden. Un-MB:454
  American Rhapsody. K. Fearing.
    Pe-M:20, Un-MA:556
  And What Shall You Say?
    J. Cotter. Ad-PB:35,
    Hu-PN:135, Kr-OF:49
  Anthology. M. Bandeira. An-TC:5
  Anticipation. E. Brontë. Ox-BN:604
  April 1962. P. Goodman. Ca-VT:336
  As for This World. Semimaru.
    Ba-ST:57

As when Emotion Too Far Exceeds
    Its Cause. G. Oden. Be-MA:96
    Bo-AN:160
At Midnight. J. Sloman.
    Sc-TN:202
Aubade. L. MacNeice. Al-VBP:1231
Autumnal. E. Dowson. Ox-BN:942
Babylon. L. Benét. De-FS:20
Ball Game. R. Eberhart. Pe-M:5
Before Olympus. J. Fletcher.
    Un-MA:320
Ben Jonson Entertains a Man from
    Stratford. E. Robinson.
    Un-MA:127
Blow, Blow, Thou Winter Wind.
    W. Shakespeare. Al-VBP:187,
    De-CH:232, De-TT:168, Er-FA:257,
    Gr-CT:476, Hi-WP II:139, Ho-WR:172,
    Mc-PR:50, Pa-GTB:26, Rv-CB:197
Boxer, A. Katz. Ho-TY:294
Brave New World. A. MacLeish.
    Sh-AP:189
Buffalo. H. Dumas. Ad-PB:267
Burnt Norton. T. Eliot. Wi-LT:306
The Captain. J. White. Co-RM:201
The City of Dreadful Night.
    J. Thomson. Al-VBP:1004,
    Ox-BN:754
The Counsels of O'Riordan the Rain
    Maker. T. O'Bolger. Co-PI:149
Dancers at Banstead. M. Oliver.
    St-H:165
Dirge for the New Sunrise.
    E. Sitwell. Pl-EI:144,
    Tr-MR:189, Un-MB:338
Discovery. H. Belloc. Al-VBP:1110
Dream Deferred. L. Hughes.
    Ad-PB:76, Be-MA:42, Bo-AN:67,
    Ha-TP:21, Hu-PN:199, La-OC:149,
    Wi-LT:422
Dreamer of Dreams. W. Carruth.
    Fe-PL:305
The End of Man Is His Beauty.
    L. Jones. Bo-AN:181, Jo-SA:76
Ever More and More Profound.
    F. Saito. Sh-AM:151
Failure. R. Brooke. Ke-TF:122
Finis? M. Lewis. Un-MW:106
Forgotten Dreams. E. Silvera.
    Hu-PN:259
Four Preludes on Playthings of the
    Wind: The Past Is a Bucket of
    Ashes. C. Sandburg. Un-MA:201
Going to the Heavenly Bridge.
    Li Kuang-t'ien. Hs-TC:205
Hast Never Come to Thee an Hour.
    W. Whitman. Rv-CB:852
Hawks. S. Bates. Ba-PO:196
The Hollow Men. T. Eliot.
    Un-MA:395, Wi-LT:302

Hugh Selwyn Mauberley. E. Pound.
    Ba-PO:149, Ca-VT:84, Ha-PO:122,
    Hi-TL:186, Un-MA:301, Wi-LT:232
Hymnus and Patrem Sinensis.
    P. Whalen.   Kh-VA:45
An Impression of Shanghai.
    Kuo Mo-jo.   Hs-TC:36
In Tenebris. T. Hardy.   Wo-LT:16
In the Morning. A. Housman.
    Hi-WP I:88
International Conference. C. Ellis.
    Cr-WS:138
I've Returned to My Fatherland.
    Wang Tu-ch'ing.   Hs-TC:198
Just a Smack at Auden. W. Empson.
    Un-MB:435, Wi-LT:446
The Lady's Complaint.
    T. Heath-Stubbs. Br-TC:178
The Last Day of the Year.
    Su Tung P'o.   Rx-OH:74
The Lesson for Today. R. Frost.
    Wi-LT:180
Let No Charitable Hope.   E. Wylie.
    Ca-VT:104, Un-MA:278, Wi-LT:206
Lines. H. Martin.   Ad-PB:227
The Long Hill. S. Teasdale.
    Un-MA:265
Look for You Yesterday, Here You
    Come Today. L. Jones. Be-MA:113
The Love Song of J. Alfred
    Prufrock. T. Eliot. Al-VBP:1180,
    Br-TC:106, Pe-OA:105, Rv-CB:986,
    Un-MA:379, Wi-LT:278
A Man of the Middle Class.
    G. Brooks.   St-H:12
A Man Saw a Ball of Gold in the
    Sky. S. Crane. Na-EO:41,
    Sh-AP:143
Mandela's Sermon.   K. Kgositsile.
    Be-MA:146
Mandylion. P. Harris. Sc-TN:78
The Moon and the Yew Trees.
    S. Plath. To-MP:96
Motto. L. Hughes.   Ad-PB:75,
    Co-PU:126, Hu-PN:202, Jo-SA:118
No Worst, There Is None.
    G. Hopkins. Ke-PP:5, Ox-BN:870,
    Pa-GTB:395, Rv-CB:944, Un-MB:46,
    Wi-LT:49
Nursery Rhyme of Innocence and
    Experience. C. Causley.
    Bo-GJ:170, Hi-WP I:82
O Boys! O Boys! O. Gogarty.
    Co-PI:50
Pain of the World. M. Halpern.
    Ho-TY:110
The Pale Blue Casket. O. Pitcher.
    Ad-PB:194, Hu-NN:114, Lo-TY:247
Pilgrimage. Jao Meng-k'an.
    Hs-TC:108
Pity Me Not. E. Millay. Un-MA:445

Rebecca. V. Andreyev. Ca-MR:97
Rebirth. R. Kipling. Ox-BN:933
Review from Staten Island. G. Oden.
    Ad-PB:184, Be-MA:95, Hu-NN:90
The Roads into the Country.
    T. McGrath. St-H:121
Rubaiyat of Omar Khayyam.
    E. Fitzgerald. Al-VBP:832,
    Er-FA:43, Fe-FP:479, Ha-PO:210,
    Ox-BN:526, Pa-SG:120
Saul, Afterward, Riding East.
    J. Brinnin. Ho-P:35
Sitting upon the Koala Bear
    Statue. . . . J. Tomasello.
    La-IH:120
Snake in the Strawberries.
    J. Hearst. St-H:82
Sonnet. P. Shelley. Ox-BN:279
Sonnet XI. Feng Chih. Hs-TC:150
Sonnet XV. Feng Chih. Hs-TC:152
Still Branches. J. Simvovk.
    Gr-BT:156
Sweet Winds of Love. P. Irving.
    Al-WW:77
teechur. D. Higgins. Pe-M:25
Terence, This Is Stupid Stuff.
    A. Housman. Ma-YA:224,
    Un-MB:100, Wi-LT:63
They Say the Last Supper Is Badly
    Damaged. S. Yellen. Cr-WS:133
This Evening when the Pane.
    A. Ivanov. Bo-RU:41
This Last Pain. W. Empson.
    Pa-GTB:505, Wi-LT:442
To My Son. G. Barker.
    Br-TC:26
To the Castle at Gordes.
    O. de Magny. Ba-PO:88,
    Cr-WS:153
Twilight Poem. C. Bialik. Me-PH:71
Twilights. I. Stern. Ho-TY:226
The Unkillable Knowledge.
    W. Everson. Ba-PO:181
A Valedictory to Standard Oil of
    Indiana. D. Wagner. Du-SH:146
The Voice. R. Brooke. Gr-BT:59
The Voices of Peace Are Hushed.
    S. Himmell. Cr-WS:165
The Waste Land. T. Eliot.
    Pe-OA:112, Un-MA:386
The Watchman. A. Reisen. Ba-PO:205
What I Expected. S. Spender. Un-MB:472
Why the Soup Tastes like the Daily
    News. M. Piercy. Sc-TN:182
The World out There Called to My Son.
    Wo-HS:(36)
Years. A. Margolin. Ho-TY:162
DISOBEDIENCE: see also HUMOR –
    DISOBEDIENCE
Fräulein Reads Instructive Rhymes.
    M. Kumin. Li-SR:29

DISOBEDIENCE — cont'd.
  Going to Bed. E. Turner. Rd-SS:2
  Jim. H. Belloc. Br-SM:113,
    Co-BB:70, Gr-CT:22, Ir-BB:161,
    Lo-LL:80, Na-EO:150
  Meddlesome Mattie. A. Taylor.
    Pa-OM:71
  My Mother Said. . . . Bl-OB:28,
    De-CH:535, Gr-EC:286, Ir-BB:10,
    Mo-MGT:159, Pa-RE:55
  Sarah Cynthia Sylvia Stout.
    S. Silverstein. Co-BB:73
  The Story of Little Suck-a-Thumb.
    H. Hoffmann. Ir-BB:95,
    Li-SR:27, Na-EO:154
  Why Did the Children.
    C. Sandburg. Su-FVI:12
DISPLACED PERSONS: see EXILES;
    REFUGEES
DISSENT: see also ANARCHY;
    CONTROVERSY; HUMOR - DISSENT;
    PROTEST
  As I Lay with My Head in Your Lap
    Camerado. W. Whitman. Gr-BT:27
  Deer Hunt. J. Jerome. Du-RG:36
  The Laws of God, the Laws of Men.
    A. Housman. Un-MB:102
  Much Madness Is Divinest Sense.
    E. Dickinson. Co-EL:143,
    Ho-LP:75, Mo-BG:191, Rv-CB:899,
    Wi-LT:8
  Poem. T. McGrath. St-H:125
  The Rendezvous. B. Spencer.
    Pa-GTB:519
  The Scholar Gypsy. M. Arnold.
    Al-VBP:964, Gr-CT:255, Ox-BN:628
  Subversive. W. Benét. Tr-MR:116
DITMARS, RAYMOND LEE
  Lines to Dr. Ditmars. K. Robinson.
    Pl-IO:167
DIVES AND LAZARUS
  Dives and Lazarus. Ga-S:202,
    Ma-FW:165, Ox-BB:5
  Dives and Laz'us. Lo-TY:197
DIVING: see SWIMMING AND DIVING
DIVINING ROD: see DOWSERS AND
    DOWSING
DIVORCE
  Mementos. W. Snodgrass.
    Un-MA:684, Un-MW:105
DOCKS: see also HARBORS
  Down at the Docks. K. Koch.
    Ca-VT:547
  Hastings Mill. C. Smith.
    Mc-WK:196
  The Old Wharves. R. Field.
    Au-SP:181
DOCTORS: see MEDICINE; MEDICINE
    MEN; PHYSICIANS; SURGEONS
    AND SURGERY
DODGSON, CHARLES LUTWIDGE: see ALICE
    IN WONDERLAND; CARROLL, LEWIS

DODOES
  The Dodo. H. Belloc. Co-OH:68,
    Gr-CT:21, Ir-BB:82, Lo-LL:69
DOES: see DEER
DOG SLEDS
  The Train Dogs. P. Johnson.
    Do-WH:59
DOGS: see also BARKING; HUMOR -
    DOGS
  The Accident. R. Patterson. Ad-CI:102
  The Ad-Dressing of Cats. T. Eliot.
    Un-GT:54
  Albert. D. Abse. Sm-MK:109
  The Ambiguous Dog. A. Guiterman.
    Co-BBW:113
  Annus Mirabilis. J. Dryden.
    Co-BBW:46
  Argus and Ulysses. E. Farjeon.
    Gr-EC:84
  At the Dog Show. C. Morley.
    Hu-MP:194
  Avondale. S. Smith. Pa-RE:9
  Beagles. W. Rodgers. Mo-SD:117
  Beau's Reply. W. Cowper. Rd-OA:108
  Ben Jonson Entertains a Man from
    Stratford. E. Robinson. Un-MA:127
  Beth Gêlert. W. Spencer. Un-GT:138
  Birthday Gift. E. de Vito.
    Br-BC:153
  Birthday Gifts. L. Scott. Br-BC:99
  The Bloodhound. E. Anthony.
    Un-GT:43
  Bony. S. Ortiz. Ni-CD:158
  Bow, Wow, Wow. Ar-TP3:48, Bo-FP:115,
    De-PO:18, Mo-CC:(52), Mo-MGT:16
  A Boy and a Pup. A. Guiterman.
    Hu-MP:40
  Brave Rover. M. Beerbohm.
    Rd-OA:112
  The Buccaneer. N. Turner. Ar-TP3:50
  Buff. Mo-MGT:212
  Caesar's Song. Wr-RM:88
  A Cat's Conscience. Fe-PL:352
  Children's Arms. R. Jarrell. Li-TU:25
  Children's Crusade, 1939. B. Brecht.
    Ca-MB:106
  Chums. A. Guiterman. Fr-MP:20
  The Collies. E. Anthony. Un-GT:43
  Country Letter. J. Clare. Rv-CB:733
  Crepuscular. R. Howard. Br-TC:199
  Cruel Frederick. H. Hoffman. Li-SR:24
  Crystal Moment. R. Coffin.
    Gr-EC:162, Pe-SS:74
  The Dachshund. E. Anthony. Un-GT:43
  Daley's Dorg Wattie. W. Goodge.
    Co-BBW:106
  Death of a Dog. B. Deutsch. Du-SH:119
  Death Was a Trick. J. Mazzaro.
    Mc-EA:65
  Denise. R. Hale. Co-BBW:114,
    Ke-TF:329
  The Dog. A. Buttigieg. Pa-RE:121

The Dog. W. Davies. Un-MB:176
Dog. H. Monro. Un-GT:39,
   Un-MB:237
The Dog. M. Owgang. Me-WF:54
Dog. W. Smith. Bo-GJ:90
A Dog and a Cat Went Out Together.
   Mother Goose. Bo-FP:225,
   Ir-BB:237
A Dog and a Cock. Ir-BB:237
The Dog and the Cat. G. Hallock.
   Sh-RP:330
Dog Around the Block. E. White.
   La-OC:28, Mc-WS:42
Dog at Night. L. Untermeyer.
   Pe-M:110, Un-GT:42
Dog in a Car. D. McCord. Sh-RP:326
The Dog in the River. Plato.
   Mc-PR:27
Dog, Midwinter. R. Souster.
   Co-BBW:112
A Dog Named Ego, the Snowflakes
   as Kisses. D. Schwartz.
   Wi-LT:521
Dog, Sleeping Late. M. Madsen.
   Ke-TF:330
Dog with Schoolboys. J. Follain.
   Co-PU:64
Dogs. F. Cornford. Gr-TG:25,
   Ma-FO:(15), St-FS:25
Dogs and Weather. W. Welles.
   Ar-TP3:51, Fe-FP:155, Ma-FO:(18)
Doldrums. C. O'John. Al-WW:65
Elegy for Jog. J. Ciardi. Du-RG:87
An Englyn on a Yellow Hound.
   W. Barnes. Rd-OA:146
Epitaph for a Pet. F. Rodman.
   Ke-TF:327
Epitaph on a Dog. Gr-EC:86
Every Time I Come to Town. Un-GT:18
The Extraordinary Dog. N. Turner.
   Ar-TP3:48
A Farmer's Dog. Bl-OB:115
Fidelity. W. Wordsworth. Cl-FC:70
The First Friend. R. Kipling.
   Hu-MP:192
Four-Footed Poems. E. Greenberg.
   Ho-TY:312
Full of the Moon. K. Kuskin.
   La-PP:25, La-PV:53
German Shepherd. M. Livingston.
   La-RM:96
A Girl in the Army. Mo-MGT:15
Gluskap's Hound. T. Roberts.
   Do-WH:61
Good Morning. M. Sipe. Ar-TP3:70,
   Au-SP:87
Haiku. D. Lippa. Le-M:192
The Hairy Dog. H. Asquith.
   Ar-TP3:51, Au-SP:37, Fe-FP:154,
   Gr-EC:83, La-PP:59, La-PV:107,
   Ma-FO:(17), Pe-FB:6
Hector the Dog. K. Barnes. Co-BBW:110

Higglety, Pigglety, Pop! Ir-BB:184,
   Lo-LL:30, Mo-MGT:129, St-FS:22
Hoddley, Poddley. Ir-BB:88,
   Mo-MGT:162
Hokku Poems. R. Wright. Bo-AN:105
The Hound. S. Lanier. Co-PM:113
The House. R. Young Bear. Ni-CD:292
The House Dog's Grave. R. Jeffers.
   Co-BBW:108
Hunting Song. D. Finkel. Ca-MB:65,
   Co-BBW:19, Du-RG:106, We-PZ:21
I Had a Little Doggy. Ch-B:43,
   Hu-MP:191
I Knew a Boy Who Ran with the Dogs.
   N. Willard. Sc-TN:230
An Introduction to Dogs. O. Nash.
   Un-GT:38
The Irish Harper and His Dog.
   T Campbell. De-CH:83, De-TT:66,
   Hu-MP:194, Rv-CB:678, Un-GT:41
The Kill. D. Hall. Ha-WR:45
Let Dogs Delight. I. Watts.
   Ch-B:114, Gr-TG:69, Un-GT:69
Letter to the City Clerk.
   F. Wright. Er-FA:224
The Little Black Dog. E. Reynolds.
   Fe-PL:362
The Little Black Dog. Ir-BB:82,
   Mo-MGT:82
A Little Dog-Angel. N. Holland.
   Fe-PL:361
The Little Dog under the Wagon.
   Fe-PL:360
Little Puppy. Fe-FP:156
Lone Dog. I. McLeod. Ar-TP3:51,
   Co-BBW:103, De-TT:68, Fe-FP:155,
   Hu-MP:195, La-PV:108, Th-AS:186
The Lonely Man. R. Jarrell.
   To-MP:85
Lost Dog. F. Rodman. Se-PR:301
Love Me, Love My Dog. I. Crawford.
   Do-WH:30
A Maltese Dog. Tymnés. Ar-TP3:50,
   Co-BBW:99, Gr-EC:86, Sm-LG:85
Meditatio. E. Pound. Ar-TP3:132,
   Du-RG:61, Ga-S:133, Ha-LO:63,
   Hi-WP II:11, Sm-LG:390
Memorandum for St. Peter.
   E. Chaffee. Ke-TF:328
Mick. J. Reeves. Co-BBW:111,
   Pa-RE:12
Morning Overture: Chorus of Dogs.
   P. Strachan. Un-GT:42
My Airedale Dog. W. Mason.
   Au-SP:38, Pe-FB:14
My Dog. J. Bangs. Hu-MP:192
My Dog. M. Chute. Ar-TP3:50,
   Au-SP:37, Fe-FP:154, La-PV:107,
   Mc-AW:52, Pe-FB:20, Th-AS:40
My Dog. S. Lewis. St-FS:98
My Dog. J. Robinson.
   Au-SP:39

DOGS — cont'd.
  The Night Hunt. T. MacDonagh.
    Co-BBW:105, Co-PI:102
  Night Song. F. Cornford. Co-BBW:112,
    Co-IW:41
  Now the Man Has a Child. S. Karai.
    Ma-FW:67
  Oh Where, Oh Where Has My Little
    Dog Gone. Mother Goose.
    Mo-CC:(54), Mo-MGT:29, Mo-TL:70,
    Wi-MG:46
  Of an Ancient Spaniel in Her Fifteenth
    Year. C. Morley. Mc-WK:57
  The Old Coon-Dog Dreams. K. Porter.
    Un-GT:40
  Old Dog. A. Covici. Ch-B:29
  Old Dog Tray. S. Foster. Co-BBW:109
  Old Man, Phantom Dog. F. Eckman.
    St-H:49
  Old Mother Hubbard. An-IP:(8),
    Au-SP:3, Fr-WO:21, Ir-BB:171,
    Li-LB:153, Mo-MGT:8, Mo-NR:108,
    Ox-BC:126, Pa-OM:336, Un-GT:102,
    Wi-MG:50, Wr-RM:43
  Old Rattler. Bu-DY:41
  On a Spaniel, Called Beau, Killing a
    Young Bird. W. Cowper. Rd-OA:107
  On the Skeleton of a Hound.
    J. Wright. Wi-LT:844
  The Ordinary Dog. N. Turner.
    Ar-TP3:49
  Our Dumb Friends. R. Wotherspoon.
    Co-BBW:113
  Our Heritage. J. Stuart. Br-AF:4
  Our Lucy (1956-1960). P. Goodman.
    Co-BBW:100
  Our Old Family Dog. Issa. Be-MC:16
  The Peacemaker. W. Davies. Go-BP:99
  The Perfect Greyhound. Bo-FP:132
  pete at the seashore. D. Marquis.
    Co-BBW:115
  The Picnic Box. A. Fisher. Mc-AW:60
  Pourquoi You Greased. Co-BBW:103,
    Gr-CT:89, Gr-EC:79
  Puppy. A. Fisher. Au-SP:36
  Puppy. R. Tyler. Du-RG:86
  Puppy and I. A. Milne. Ar-TP3:49,
    Au-SP:39, Fr-MP:6, La-PV:10,
    Pe-FB:4
  The Puppy Asleep. Issa. Le-IS:19
  Pussy-Cat by the Fire. Wr-RM:128
  Pussy Has a Whiskered Face.
    C. Rossetti. Ar-TP3:48
  The Rabbit Hunter. R. Frost.
    Be-EB:28, Ho-TH:46
  The Rainwalkers. D. Levertov.
    Ad-CI:109, Du-SH:145
  Rest in Peace. W. Funk. Fe-PL:364
  The Road to Vagabondia. D. Burnet.
    Fe-PL:410
  Roo. M. Oliver. Ls-NY:195
  Round About, Round About. Mo-TL:23

  A Scholar and His Dog. J. Marston.
    Go-BP:98
  The Shepherd Dog of the Pyrenees.
    E. Murray. Se-PR:302
  Sonnet: To Tartar, a Terrier
    Beauty. T. Beddoes. Ox-BN:455
  Snow Everywhere. I. Eastwick.
    Fr-MP:21
  The Span of Life. R. Frost.
    Ma-FW:228, Wi-LT:179
  Spiel of the Three Mountebanks.
    J. Ransom. Un-MA:411
  A Story in the Snow. P. Crouch.
    Ar-TP3:62, Au-SP:60, Hu-MP:322
  Stray Dog. C. Mish. Fe-PL:359
  Sun Goes Up. H. Farley. Le-M:143
  Sunning. J. Tippett. Ar-TP3:51,
    Br-SS:178, Du-RG:86, Gr-EC:82
  The Tale of a Dog. J. Lambert, Jr.
    Co-IW:16
  There Was a Little Dog. Ir-BB:148,
    St-FS:80
  There Was an Old Dog. De-TT:67
  There Was an Old Woman as I've
    Heard Tell. Ar-TP3:132,
    Co-PS:70, Co-PT:281, De-TT:69,
    Gr-EC:204, Ha-PO:281, Li-LB:156,
    Mo-NR:63, Pa-OM:5, Un-GT:103,
    Wr-RM:71
  The Thorn. B. Christman. Ke-TF:331
  Three Young Rats. Fr-WO:35,
    Gr-CT:31, Gr-EC:11, Gr-GB:92,
    Ir-BB:234, Lo-LL:41, Mo-MGT:187,
    On-TW:15, Sm-MK:193
  Through a Wide Field of Stubble.
    R. Sund. Co-PU:129
  Tied Dogs. S. Coblentz. Ke-TF:330
  Tim, an Irish Terrier. W. Letts.
    Co-BBW:104
  Tired Equinox. R. Roseliep.
    St-H:183
  To My Dog "Blanco." J. Holland.
    Fe-PL:362
  To Scott. W. Letts. Fe-PL:364
  Tom's Little Dog. W. de la Mare.
    Ar-TP3:50, Co-BBW:99
  The Turkish Trench Dog.
    G. Dearmer. Co-BBW:101
  The Two Dogs. Bo-FP:30, On-TW:9
  Two Puppies. De-PP:38
  Uncle Dog; the Poet at 9. R. Sward.
    Ca-VT:680
  Under the Willow. Issa. Do-TS:(3),
    Le-MW:33, Ma-FW:228
  Unsatisfied Yearning.
    R. Munkittrick. Du-RG:85
  Vern. G. Brooks. Ar-TP3:50,
    Ho-CS:36, La-OC:82
  Waves Against a Dog. T. Baybars.
    Sm-MK:176
  We Keep a Dog to Guard the House.
    Wy-CM:30

What Has Feet like Plum Blossoms.
  Wy-CM:20
Who Stole the Nest? Ir-BB:87,
  St-FS:112
Who'll That Be. K. Patchen.
  Mc-WK:94
Wonder. B. Raymund. Co-BBW:102
The Woodman's Dog. W. Cowper.
  Bo-FP:101, Co-BBW:108, Co-EL:33,
  Co-PU:93, De-TT:69
Yolp, Yolp, Yolp, Yolp. Rd-OA:50
Zephyr. E. Ware. Fe-PL:430
DOGWOOD BLOSSOMS
  The Newlyweds. C. Criswell.
    Fe-PL:96
DOLLS
  Baby Dolly. Wr-RM:17
  The Broken Doll. C. Rossetti.
    Ar-TP3:106, Ch-B:114, Hu-MP:52,
    Li-LC:38
  A Busy Person. A. Hilton. Bo-FP:35
  The Coming of Mary Louise.
    G. Urquhart. Bo-FP:195
  The Doll. R. Friend. Ls-NY:118
  Doll Song. L. Carroll. Au-SP:202
  Doll's Walk. Ch-B:72
  The Dolls' Wash. J. Ewing. Ox-BC:257
  The Little Moppet. Mo-MGT:42,
    Rv-ON:88, Wr-RM:72
  The Lost Doll. C. Kingsley.
    Au-SP:203, Fe-FP:108, Gr-EC:147,
    Hu-MP:51, Ke-TF:39, Ox-BC:228
  The Old Doll. W. Seegmiller.
    Hu-MP:51
  The Step Mother. H. Adam. De-FS:5
DOLPHINS: see also HUMOR - DOLPHINS;
    PORPOISES
  Dolphin. J. Unternecker. Sc-TN:216
  Dolphins at Cochin. T. Buchan.
    Co-SS:176
  The Dolphin's Tomb. Anyte. Rd-OA:147
DOMINICAN REPUBLIC - HISTORY AND
    PATRIOTISM
  Toussaint L'Ouverture. J. Carew.
    Sa-B:11
DON QUIXOTE
  Litany of Our Sire, Don Quixote.
    R. Darió. Be-UL:19
DONEGAL COUNTY, IRE., N.
  Rain. S. O'Sullivan. Co-PI:165
DONKEYS: see also HUMOR - DONKEYS
  Advice to Travelers. W. Gibson.
    Du-RG:42
  The Ass in the Lion's Skin. Aesop.
    Gr-EC:198, Rd-OA:167
  Asses. P. Colum. Ha-LO:27
  Burro with the Long Ears. Fe-FP:163
  Dance of Burros. D. Laing.
    Co-BBW:155
  The Donkey. G. Chesterton.
    Fe-PL:330, Ga-FB:7, Se-PR:72,
    Un-MB:209

Donkey. V. Popa.   Mo-TS:70
Donkey. M. Van Doren. Pl-EI:126
The Donkey.   Br-BC:10, Co-BBW:154,
  Gr-EC:37, Ma-FO:(31)
The Donkey. Mo-MGT:21, Wi-MG:52
The Donkey. Ir-BB:33, Mo-MGT:213,
  Sp-AS:20, Wr-RM:104
Donkey, Donkey, Do Not Bray.
  Mother Goose. Pa-AP:20
The Donkey in the Nyevsky Prospekt.
  G. Garbovsky. Bo-RU:35
Donkey Riding. Do-WH:19, Ir-BB:253,
  Pa-RE:49, St-FS:125
The Donkey's Owner. C. Sansom.
  Ga-S:152
My Donkey. Ar-TP3:123, Ir-BB:175
Nicholas Nye. W. de la Mare.
  Bl-OB:120, Cl-DT:50, Co-BBW:150,
  Rd-OA:73
Pegasus Lost. E. Wylie. Un-MA:275
The Prayer of the Donkey.
  C. Gasztold. Ar-TP3:83
A Prayer to Go to Heaven with the
  Donkeys. F. Jammes. Ar-TP3:83,
  Co-BBW:149, Go-BP:255, Pl-EI:124,
  Rd-OA:20, Tr-MR:52
Progress. E. Agnew. Br-AF:233
Time Out. J. Montague. Co-PI:143,
  Ls-NY:196
Why Did the Little Boy. Re-RR:96
Wild Ass. P. Colum. Un-MB:251
DONNE, JOHN
  Great Elegy for John Donne.
    J. Brodsky. Ca-MR:27
  On Donne's Poetry. S. Coleridge.
    Rv-CB:663
  On John Donne's Books of Poems.
    J. Marriot. De-CH:254
  To England. R. Brautigan.
    Mc-EA:142
DOOMSDAY: see END OF THE WORLD
DOON RIVER, SCOT.
  Ye Banks and Braes. R. Burns.
    Al-VBP:648, Co-BL:141, De-CH:47,
    Hi-WP II:103, Pa-GTB:131,
    Rv-CB:615
DOORS: see also HUMOR - DOORS
  The Door. V. Golyavkin. Bo-RU:38
  The Door. R. Morton. Me-WF:52
  A Door Has Feelings. K. Hanis.
    Me-WF:58
  Doorbells. R. Field. Ar-TP3:9,
    Fe-FP:323
  The Doors. B. Andrews. Le-M:166
  Doors. C. Sandburg. Ha-LO:16
  The Green Door. L. Drake.
    Br-BC:155
  Joan's Door. E. Farjeon. Br-BC:80
  Opening Door. W. Burr. De-FS:41
  Plans. H. Brooks. Hu-NN:109,
    Hu-PN:274
  Regarding a Door. D. Antin. Du-SH:26

DORMICE
  The Christening. A. Milne. Br-BC:38
  The Dormouse. P. Hill. Co-BBW:56
  The Dormouse. M. Stephenson.
    St-FS:97
  The Dormouse and the Frog.
    R. Goodchild. Ir-BB:81
  Dormy, Dormy, Dormouse. Mo-TL:35
  The Elf and the Dormouse. O. Herford.
    Ar-TP3:153, Au-SP:285, Bo-FP:225,
    Ch-B:60, Fe-FP:345, Hu-MP:92,
    Mc-PR:31, Pa-OM:50, Pe-FB:53,
    Th-AS:11, Un-GB:13, Un-GT:15
  Epitaph on a Dormouse Which Some
    Children Were to Bury. Ox-BC:77
DOROTHEA, SAINT
  For a Picture of Saint Dorothea.
    G. Hopkins. Gr-CC:140
DORSETSHIRE, ENG: see also DIALECTS,
    DORSET; DIALECTS, WESSEX
  Dorset. J. Betjeman. To-MP:20
  The Green Valley. S. Warner.
    Un-MB:377
  Wessex Heights. T. Hardy. Ox-BN:839
DOUBT: see also HUMOR - DOUBT;
    UNBELIEF
  Adjuration. C. Wheeler. Bo-AN:105,
    Hu-PN:272
  Advice. H. Rhodes. Un-GT:310
  After Goliath. K. Amis. En-PC:194
  And What Will Happen.
    K. Molodowsky. Ho-TY:286
  Belief and Unbelief. R. Browning.
    Ga-FB:130
  Bishop Blougram's Apology.
    R. Browning. Ox-BN:547
  The Boy Who Laughed at Santa Claus.
    O. Nash. Co-BB:16, Ha-PO:291
  A Christmas Sonnet. E. Robinson.
    Pl-EI:89, Sm-PT:188
  Davis Matlock. E. Masters.
    Wi-LT:117
  The Death of Lord Warriston.
    Ox-BB:603
  Dipsychus. A. Clough. Ox-BN:616
  Doubting Thomas. Ga-S:176
  Dover Beach. M. Arnold.
    Al-VBP:972, Cl-FC:48, Co-BL:84,
    Er-FA:454, Ga-FB:66, Go-BP:147,
    Ha-PO:187, Hi-WP II:35, Ho-P:201,
    Ke-PP:87, Ma-FW:53, Ma-YA:209,
    Mc-PR:70, Mo-GR:35, Ox-BN:645,
    Pa-GTB:305, Pl-EI:78, Rv-CB:863,
    Un-MW:120
  Easter Hymn. A. Housman. Pl-EI:87
  Epilogue. W. Auden. Sm-LG:303,
    Wi-LT:465
  Epilogue. H. Melville. Pl-IO:128
  Esthetique du Mal, VIII, IX.
    W. Stevens. Wi-LT:155, 156
  Ever More and More Profound.
    F. Saito. Sh-AM:151

  Faith Is a Fine Invention.
    E. Dickinson. Co-EL:107,
    Ga-FB:150, Rv-CB:916
  False Gods. W. de la Mare.
    Pl-EI:83
  For All Sorts and Conditions.
    N. Nicholson. Pl-EI:181
  For Life I Had Never Cared Greatly.
    T. Hardy. Wi-LT:22
  I Asked for Peace. D. Dolben.
    Go-BP:180
  The Impercipient (at a Cathedral
    Service). T. Hardy. Al-VBP:1045
  In Memorian. A. Tennyson.
    Ox-BN:498, 499
  Inbound. B. Eaton. De-FS:82
  Journal. E. Millay. Pl-IO:133
  My Shadow. J. Rubinstein.
    Ho-TY:240
  O Weary Pilgrims. R. Bridges.
    Un-MB:49
  Of All the Faces. R. Zychlinska.
    Ho-TY:231
  On Lavater's Song of a Christian
    to Christ. J. von Goethe.
    Co-EL:53
  Poems, III. E. Blum-Alquit.
    Ho-TY:263
  Praise Doubt. M. Van Doren.
    Pl-EI:80, Tr-MR:214
  Sonnets. G. Hopkins. Ox-BN:870
  Spring 1943. R. Fuller. Wi-LT:705
  The Triumph of Doubt. J. Bishop.
    Pl-EI:90
  Vision and Prayer. D. Thomas.
    Wi-LT:553
  The Way. E. Muir. Gr-SS:191,
    Ha-LO:75
  When I Awoke. R. Patterson.
    Ad-PB:208, Hu-NN:113
  When I Pray. M. Classé. Ba-HI:141
  While Sitting Here Looking at the
    Stars. L. Curry. Ba-HI:144
DOUGLAS, SIR JAMES, "THE GOOD"
    (BLACK DOUGLAS)
  Black Douglas. H. Mullins. Cr-WS:31
  Loyal. F. Ticknor. Sp-OG:18
DOUGLAS, JAMES, 2nd EARL OF DOUGLAS
  The Battle of Otterburn.
    Ox-BB:491, Pa-OM:148
  Chevy Chase. Al-VBP:43, Ma-BB:97,
    Ox-BB:496
  Chevy Chase, The Second Fytte.
    Ma-BB:101
DOUGLASS, FREDERICK
  Frederick Douglass. S. Cornish.
    Ad-PB:294
  Frederick Douglass. P. Dunbar. Ad-PB:9
  Frederick Douglass. R. Hayden.
    Ab-MO:83, Ad-PB:120, Be-MA:56,
    Bo-AN:119, Hu-PN:296, Jo-SA:41,
    Lo-TY:237

Frederick Douglass, 1817-1895.
  L. Hughes. Ra-BP:87
DOVER, ENG.
  At Dover Cliffs, July 20, 1787.
    W. Bowles. Al-VBP:654
  Dover Beach. M. Arnold. Al-VBP:972,
    Cl-FC:48, Co-BL:84, Er-FA:454,
    Ga-FB:66, Go-BP:147, Ha-PO:187,
    Hi-WP II:35, Ho-P:201, Ke-PP:87,
    Ma-FW:53, Ma-YA:209, Mc-PR:70,
    Mo-GR:35, Ox-BN:645, Pa-GTB:305,
    Pl-EI:78, Rv-CB:863, Un-MW:120
  The Dover Bitch. A. Hecht. Ca-VT:504
  Dover Cliffs. W. Bowles. Al-VBP:654
  I Have Loved England. A. Miller.
    Fe-PL:181
DOVES: see also HUMOR - DOVES;
    PIGEONS
  Cecilia. Do-WH:34
  The Dove. W. Barnes. Re-BS:36
  The Dove. Gr-CT:93, Gr-GB:61
  The Dove and the Wren. De-TT:38,
    Mo-MGT:17, On-TW:56, Wr-RM:41
  The Dove's Loneliness. G. Darley.
    Ox-BN:384
  The Dove's Song. St-FS:24
  Four-Footed Poems. E. Greenberg.
    Ho-TY:312
  High in the Pine Tree. Sp-AS:(27)
  I Had a Dove. J. Keats.
    Bl-OB:64, Co-BBW:252, Co-IW:40,
    De-CH:100, De-TT:158, Fe-FP:289,
    Re-BS:25, Re-TW:30
  Marriage Songs, I. Tr-US II:159
  The Milk-White Dove. Gr-CT:159,
    Gr-GB:251
  The Mourning Dove. M. Livingston.
    Gr-EC:178
  The Old Sweet Dove of Wiveton.
    S. Smith. Rd-OA:4
  Peace. C. Bukowski. Kh-VA:32
  The Phoenix and the Turtle.
    W. Shakespeare. Rv-CB:256
  See How the Doves Flutter and
    Huddle. Do-CH:(15)
  Serenade of a Loyal Martyr.
    G. Darley. Ox-BN:395
  Song for a Summer Afternoon.
    V. Miller. Ca-BP:46
  Song of Fixed Accord. W. Stevens.
    Rd-OA:204
  Song of Thyrsis. P. Freneau.
    Al-VBP:606
  The White Dove. Rv-ON:25
DOWSERS AND DOWSING
  The Well-Finder. H. Vinal. De-FS:211
DRAFT, MILITARY: see MILITARY
    SERVICE, COMPULSORY
DRAGONFLIES
  At the Rainbow Spring. Jo-TS:2
  Bête Humaine. F. Young.
    De-CH:86

By a Rich Fast Moving Stream.
  J. Tagliabue. Co-EL:39
Catching Dragonflies. De-PP:34
A Dragon-Fly. E. Farjeon.
  Fe-FP:130, La-PV:144, Ma-FO:(36)
The Dragon-Fly. A. Tennyson.
  Rd-OA:70
Dragonfly. H. Behn. Li-TU:192
The Dragonfly. Chisoku. Au-SP:75
The Dragonfly. W. Davies. Go-BP:84
The Elfin Plane. R. Bennett.
  Hu-MP:80
The Face of the Dragonfly. Chisoku.
  Do-TS:(12), Le-MW:10, Ma-FW:206
A Hundred Mountains. Issa.
  Be-MC:20
I Would I Were. Le-OE:43
In a Cornfield. E. Markham.
  Mc-PR:120
In the West the Dragonfly Wanders.
  Ho-SD:30
Lines to a Dragon Fly. W. Landor.
  Ox-BN:190
Red Dragonfly. . . . Sôseki.
  Ca-BF:23
Secrets. L. Hewitt. Bo-FP:240
Tonight. Br-FW:8
Where Does He Wander. Chiyo.
  Be-CS:46
DRAGONS: see also HUMOR - DRAGONS
  As the Sun Came Up. Wy-CM:6
  Davy Doldrum Dreamed He Drove a
    Dragon. Mother Goose. Pa-AP:36
  The Faerie Queene. E. Spenser.
    Ma-YA:55
  In That Dark Cave. S. Silverstein.
    Co-EL:58, Co-PU:135
  A Knight and a Lady. Gr-EC:138
  Story of the Flowery Kingdom.
    J. Cabell. Pa-OM:9
DRAKE, SIR FRANCIS
  The Admiral's Ghost. A. Noyes.
    Ar-TP3:22, Co-PM:129
  Drake's Drum. H. Newbolt.
    Co-SS:58, De-TT:195, Hi-FO:128,
    Hi-WP I:68
  Of the Great and Famous.
    R. Hayman. De-CH:177
  On Sir Francis Drake. Rv-CB:124
  Sir Francis Drake. Hi-FO:224
  Sir Francis Drake; or Eighty-Eight.
    Gr-GB:185
DRAMA: see also ACTORS AND ACTING;
    HUMOR - DRAMA; MOVING PICTURES;
    MUSICAL COMEDIES; PUPPETS;
    THEATERS
  L'Allegro. J. Milton. Al-VBP:389,
    Er-FA:37, Ga-FB:26, Pa-GTB:94,
    Rv-CB:369
  I Shall Not See the Famous Phêdre.
    O. Mandelstam. Ca-MR:150
  Love's Labour Lost. R. Tofte. No-CL:143

DRAMA — cont'd.
  Prologue to Aureng-zebe. J. Dryden.
    Rv-CB:464
DRAYMEN
  The Drayman. W. Whitman. Hu-PN:469
DRAYTON, MICHAEL
  Do Pious Marble. F. Quarles.
    De-CH:652
DREAD: see FEAR
DREAMS: see also HUMOR - DREAMS;
    NIGHTMARES; VISIONS
  African Dream. B. Kaufman.
    Ad-PB:263, Be-MA:129
  Ah, How We Loved. O. Mandelstam.
    Ca-MR:58
  And God Be Witness. B. Akhmadulina.
    Ca-MR:35
  Andre. G. Brooks. Ar-TP3:5,
    Sh-RP:97
  The Angel. W. Blake. De-CH:454
  Annie of Lochroyan. Ma-BB:202
  The Aquarium Dream. F. Trefethen.
    Ls-NY:100
  Ballad of the Two Tapsters.
    V. Watkins. Ca-MB:91
  Bankrupt. C. Sayres. Fe-PL:295
  Beasts. R. Wilbur. Br-TC:472
  The Bridge of Dreams. Teika.
    Ba-ST:25
  The Cave-Boy. L. Richards.
    Fe-FP:17
  Cheers. E. Merriam. Du-RG:115
  A Child Half-Asleep. T. Connor.
    Go-BT:8
  Children at Night. S. Morse.
    Ls-NY:230
  Chimera. B. Howes. Br-TC:205
  The Chimney Sweeper. W. Blake.
    De-CH:40, De-TT:107, Ox-BC:86,
    Rv-CB:579
  Christmas Lullaby for a New-Born
    Child. Y. Gregory. Bo-AN:153
  Cortez. W. Seymour. Sm-MK:64
  Crab-Apple. E. Talbot.
    Ar-TP3:149, Bo-FP:328, Br-BC:8
  A Cradle Song. W. Blake.
    Al-VBP:612, Rv-CB:569
  Cradle Song. S. Naidu. Fe-FP:54,
    Hu-MP:123, Th-AS:35
  A Cry. F. Bianco. No-CL:261
  Daddy in the Dream.
    M. Yamaguchi. Le-TA:31
  The Dancing Seal. W. Gibson.
    Co-PM:68, Pa-OM:289
  Dark-Eyed Lad Columbus.
    N. Turner. Br-SS:62
  Davy Doldrum Dreamed He Drove a
    Dragon. Mother Goose. Pa-AP:36
  The Dead Poet. A. Douglas.
    Al-VBP:1110, No-CL:19
  Disillusionment of Ten O'Clock.
    W. Stevens. Ha-LO:55,
    Ha-PO:236, Sh-AP:159

  Do Not Dream. N. Zach. Gr-BT:160
  The Dream. H. Behn. Li-TU:221
  A Dream. W. Blake. De-CH:456,
    Hu-MP:127, Rd-OA:13, Rv-CB:585
  The Dream. L. Bogan. Pe-OA:146,
    Un-MA:492, Wi-LT:382
  The Dream. G. Byron. Mo-GR:118
  A Dream. J. Duerr. Ho-CT:46
  A Dream. I. Nez. Ba-HI:129
  The Dream. T. Roethke.
    Sh-AP:213
  A Dream. M. Stiker. Ho-TY:281
  The Dream. De-TT:172
  The Dream. Le-IB:83
  The Dream-Daemon. L. Carter.
    De-FS:46
  Dream Deferred. L. Hughes.
    Ad-PB:76, Be-MA:42, Bo-AN:67,
    Ha-TP:21, Hu-PN:199, La-OC:149,
    Wi-LT:422
  Dream in a Storm. Chu Ta-nan.
    Hs-TC:131
  Dream of a Baseball Star. G. Corso.
    Ca-VT:658, Fl-HH:18, Mo-SD:17
  A Dream Party. De-PP:47
  Dream-Pedlary. T. Beddoes.
    Al-VBP:808, De-CH:429, Ho-WR:95,
    Li-LC:45, Ox-BN:455, Rv-CB:772,
    Un-GB:25
  Dream Signs. Ju-CP:82
  Dream Song. L. Alexander.
    Ad-PB:59, Hu-PN:159
  Dream Song. Bi-IT:130
  Dream Song of a Canoe-Builder.
    Tr-US II:72
  The Dream Woman. P. Hubbell.
    Ar-TP3:150
  Dreamer of Dreams. W. Carruth.
    Fe-PL:305
  Dreamers. S. Sassoon. Cr-WS:83,
    Un-MB:310
  Dreaming. T. Miles. Ho-CT:5
  Dreaming that I Went with Li and Yü
    to Visit Yüan Chën. Po Chü-i.
    Pa-SG:19
  Dreams. C. Cooper. Ad-PB:505
  Dreams. L. Hughes. Bo-HF:19,
    Du-RG:129, Mc-WS:38
  Dreams. E. Poe. Rv-CB:803
  Dreams. Wr-RM:84
  Drug Store. J. Weaver. Hi-TL:192
  Early Waking. L. Adams. Wi-LT:603
  Echo. C. Rossetti. Al-VBP:998,
    De-CH:452, Ox-BN:708, Un-MW:91
  Egypt's Might Is Tumbled Down.
    M. Coleridge. De-CH:349
  Fairies. H. Conkling.
    Ar-TP3:146, Th-AS:5
  Falling Asleep over the Aeneid.
    R. Lowell. Un-MA:666
  Fantasia. W. Letts. Co-PI:93
  Farewell in a Dream. S. Spender.
    Un-MB:470

Father and Son. S. Kunitz.
  Br-TC:247
The First of All My Dreams Was of.
  E. Cummings. Ca-VT:185,
  Gr-SS:57
The Fly-Away Horse. E. Field.
  Un-GB:32, Un-GT:298
Forgotten Dreams. E. Silvers.
  Hu-PN:259
From the Hills of Dream.
  F. Macleod. Th-AS:140
A Funeral in Tchiatura. A. Mezhirov.
  Ca-MR:89
The Ghosts of the Buffaloes.
  V. Lindsay. Sh-RP:46, Un-MA:223
Going Back Again. R. Lytton.
  Co-FB:306, Na-EO:47
Green Bedroom. R. Roseliep.
  St-H:182
Havana Dreams. L. Hughes.
  Hu-PN:189
He Wishes for the Cloths of Heaven.
  W. Yeats. Go-BP:130, Ho-LP:13,
  Th-AS:144, Un-MB:108
Hold Fast Your Dreams.
  L. Driscoll. Ar-TP3:214,
  Au-SP:356, Br-BC:123, Fe-FP:22,
  Hu-MP:73
The Hope I Dreamed of.
  C. Rossetti. Un-MW:90
I Dream a World. L. Hughes.
  Bo-AN:71, Bo-HF:29
I Had a Boat. M. Coleridge.
  Sm-MK:30
I Hear an Army. J. Joyce.
  Al-VBP:1150, Un-MB:269, Wi-LT:623
In After Time. R. Eberhart.
  Tr-MR:287
In Procession. R. Graves.
  Br-TC:155
In the Smoking Car. R. Wilbur.
  Un-MA:677, Wi-LT:599
In Youth Is Pleasure. R. Wever.
  Rv-CB:143
The Journey. Hu Feng. Hs-TC:375
The Jovial Gentlemen. D. Hoffman.
  Ca-MB:62
The Juniper Tree. N. Zabolotzky.
  Ca-MR:102
Kansas Boy. R. Lechlitner.
  Br-AF:150, Du-RG:50
Kitchenette Building. G. Brooks.
  Hu-PN:334, Ra-BP:166
The Land of Dreams. W. Blake.
  De-CH:457
The Land of Nod. R. Stevenson.
  Hu-MP:108, Ir-BB:256, Un-GT:303
last poem i'm gonna write about us.
  S. Sanchez. Be-MA:136
Laziness and Silence. R. Bly.
  St-H:6
The Lime-Tree. E. Lucie-Smith.
  Gr-BT:15

Little Dreams. L. Hughes. Ls-NY:53
Longing. M. Arnold. Fe-PL:97,
  Go-BP:129, Rv-CB:867
Longing Pleases Me like Sweet
  Fragrance. Do-CH:(31)
My Dream. Ch'in Tzu-hao. Pa-MV:59
My Father's Watch. J. Ciardi.
  Pl-IO:24
My Granny Is a Witch. A. Mikhailov.
  Bo-RU:52
The Night a Sailor Came to Me in a
  Dream. D. Wakoski. Ca-VT:714
Nightmare. J. Emanuel. Ra-BP:188
An Ocean Holds the Globe.
  F. Tyutchev. Pa-SG:124
On a Dream (after Reading Dante's
  Episode of Paolo and Francesca).
  J. Keats. Rv-CB:754
Once Only. Ato-Tobira. Pa-SG:42
One Stormy Night. V. Jones.
  Ba-HI:130
Paper Boats. R. Tagore.
  Bo-FP:108, Bo-HF:28, Fe-FP:114,
  Ma-FW:236, Pa-RE:36, Th-AS:72
Pegasus Lost. E. Wylie. Un-MA:275
Peter and John. E. Wylie.
  Ca-MB:46, Tr-MR:87, Un-MA:279
A Pinch of Salt. R. Graves.
  Go-BP:166, Un-MB:385
Poem. H. von Hofmannsthal.
  Pa-SG:136
Postcript. W. Auden. Ma-FW:176
Prayer. J. Farrar. Se-PR:222
Prayer after World War.
  C. Sandburg. Ca-VT:26
Prophecy. W. Shedlofsky. De-FS:175
Queen Mab. T. Hood. Bo-FP:327,
  Ch-B:75
Queen Mab. W. Shakespeare.
  Fe-FP:382, Hu-MP:87, Ma-FW:186,
  Mc-PR:28
Quiet Night. Liu Ta-pai. Hs-TC:8
The Quiet One. Fang Wei-teh.
  Hs-TC:136
A Real Dream. S. Brown. Ba-HI:133
A Rhyme of the Dream-Maker Man.
  W. White. Fe-PL:94
The Rock-a-By Lady. E. Field.
  Bo-FP:43, Hu-MP:116
The Slave's Dream. H. Longfellow.
  Hi-WP I:18, Hu-PN:459
Sleep Brings Pearl Necklaces. . . .
  Le-OE:100
Sleepy John. C. Tringress.
  St-FS:74
Since I Am Convinced.
  Saigyo Hishi. Ba-ST:58
Sometimes I Dream. N. Bomze.
  Ho-TY:228
A Song of Fallen Leaves.
  Hsü Chih-mo. Hs-TC:84
Sonnet 44. W. Shakespeare.
  Rv-CB:223

DREAMS — cont'd.
  The Soul and Body of John Brown.
    M. Rukeyser. Un-MA:624
  This Old Countryside.
    M. Fuller. Ba-HI:135
  Three Fragments, II. Br-MW:96
  Through Nightmare. R. Graves.
    Go-BP:166
  Thus Spoke My Love. P. Hooft.
    Pa-SG:25
  to L.V. L. Batshev. Bo-RU:16
  To Make a Prairie. E. Dickinson.
    Bo-HF:21
  Tom, Tom, the Piper's Son.
    J. Ransom. Al-VBP:1186
  Trains. R. Burgunder. Ar-TP3:85
  Trifle. G. Johnson.
    Bo-AN:21, Bo-HF:20
  Under the Round Tower. W. Yeats.
    Gr-SS:55
  Us Idle Wenches. De-CH:484,
    Gr-CC:13
  Vendor. R. Roseliep. De-FS:157,
    St-H:179
  Waking Up from a Dream.
    Chu Ta-nan. Hs-TC:132
  Wandering, Dreaming. Basho.
    Be-MC:16
  What Dreamed I? Rv-CB:104
  What Makes Life Interesting.
    M. Montgomery. Ls-NY:340
  What Will Become of a Dream.
    B. Brown. Ba-HI:134
  What's Night to Me. S. Gilford.
    Le-M:210
  Willy the Weeper. Gr-GB:270
  The Wind. C. Wilson. La-GI:17
  A Winter's Dream. De-PP:45
  Wynken, Blynken, and Nod. E. Field.
    Au-SP:253, Bo-FP:41, Ch-B:18,
    Er-FA:487, Fe-FP:55, Gr-EC:98,
    Hu-MP:128, Ir-BB:244, Ox-BC:303,
    Un-GT:302
  The Youth Dreams. R. Rilke.
    Pa-SG:142
DREIDELS: see TOPS (TOYS)
DRESS: see CLOTHING AND DRESS
DRESSING UP
  Hallowe'en Scare. C. Cutler.
    Mc-AW:70
DRESSMAKING
  A Dressmaker. J. Kenward. Sm-MK:103
DRILLS AND MARCHES: see MARCHING
DRINKERS AND DRINKING: see also
    DRINKING SONGS; HUMOR - DRINKERS
    AND DRINKING; INNS AND TAVERNS;
    INTOXICATION; RESTAURANTS AND
    BARS; see also names of drinks,
    as ALE
  After They Put Down Their Overalls.
    L. Peters. Lo-TY:170
  Ai Viva Tequila. Fi-BG:198

  Alcohol. L. MacNeice. Wi-LT:462
  Back and Side Go Bare. J. Still.
    Al-VBP:64, Ho-WR:236
  Bowery. D. Ignatow. Pe-M:70
  Bremerton, January 18, 1969.
    A. Pratt. Al-WW:99
  Bring Us In Good Ale. Al-VBP:24,
    Cl-FC:94, De-CH:64
  By the Winding River. Tu Fu.
    Rx-OH:13
  Casual Lines. Su Shih. Le-MW:128,
    Ma-FW:87
  The Chestnut Casts His Flambeaux.
    A. Housman. No-CL:132,
    Un-MB:99
  Clear Night. Ai Ch'ing. Hs-TC:295
  Drink To-Day. J. Fletcher.
    Al-VBP:282
  Drinking. A. Cowley. Ha-PO:250,
    Hi-WP II:141, Ho-WR:64
  Drinking Vessels. L. Richards.
    Lo-LL:4
  Drinking with Friends Amongst the
    Blooming Peonies. Liu Yu Hsi.
    Rx-LT:71
  The Drunk in the Furnace. W. Merwin.
    Br-TC:292, Wi-LT:769
  Elinor Rumming. J. Skelton.
    Al-VBP:27
  A Friend Advises Me to Stop
    Drinking. Mei Yao Ch'en.
    Rx-OH:48
  Fueling. Chu Ta-nan. Hs-TC:130
  A Glass of Beer. J. Stephens.
    Co-FB:470, Mc-WS:83, Rv-CB:973,
    Un-MB:265
  Hey, Nonny No! Al-VBP:353, De-CH:188,
    Gr-CT:83, Sm-LG:389, Sp-OG:280
  How, Butler, How. Al-VBP:25
  If All the World Were Paper.
    Ag-HE:27, Bl-OB:20, Gr-GB:91,
    Ir-BB:119, Mo-MGT:99, Rv-CB:139,
    Sp-HW:6, Wi-MG:59
  In Praise of Ale. Al-VBP:376
  Interview with Doctor Drink.
    J. Cunningham. Ca-VT:329
  John Barleycorn. R. Burns.
    Sm-LG:212
  King Agongola's Song.
    Tr-CB:56, Tr-US I:55
  The Last Resort. J. Woods. St-H:249
  Lord Alcohol. T. Beddoes.
    Al-VBP:810, Ho-WR:237
  The Mad Lover. A. Brome. Rv-CB:398
  The Men of Gotham. T. Peacock.
    Al-VBP:715, De-CH:193, Hi-WP I:91
    Ho-WR:108, Sp-OG:344
  Miniver Cheevy. E. Robinson.
    Er-FA:384, Fe-PL:33, Ga-FB:328,
    Gr-CT:467, Ha-PO:63, Li-SR:75,
    No-CL:243, Pe-OA:3, Rv-CB:958,
    Sm-LG:130, Un-MA:117, Wi-LT:103

Moon, Flowers, Man.   Su Tung P'o.
    Rx-OH:85
Mounsier Mingo.   Rv-CB:120
Ode.   C. Cotton.   Al-VBP:477
Old Boniface.   Mo-MGT:134
Paddy Murphy.   Co-RM:118
The Parting Glass.   P. Freneau.
    Sh-AP:15
The Rubaiyat of Omar Khayyam of
    Naishapur.   E. Fitzgerald.
    Ha-PO:210
Sally Birkett's Ale.   Gr-CT:469
Sir John Barleycorn.   Rv-CB:492
Song.   O. Goldsmith.   Al-VBP:587
Song.   T. Peacock.   Al-VBP:714
The Song of the Bottle.   Tr-US I:117
Survey of Literature.   J. Ransom.
    Br-TC:335, Ca-VT:151, Sm-LG:36
Tarpauling Jacket.   Co-RM:64
Terence, This Is Stupid Stuff.
    A. Housman.   Ma-YA:224,
    Un-MB:100, Wi-LT:63
What Someone Told Me about Bobby
    Link.   J. Ciardi.   Ag-HE:26
Where Didst Thou Find, Young
    Bard. . . .   J. Keats. Rv-CB:753
The Wild Flower Man.   Lu Yu.
    Rx-OH:103
The Wind Blows Cold.   De-CH:633
Wine and Water.   G. Chesterton.
    Al-VBP:1121, Co-FB:83, Un-MB:209
A Winter Wish.   R. Messinger.
    Al-VBP:882
DRINKING FOUNTAINS
  Drinking Fountain. M. Chute. Mc-AW:23
DRINKING SONGS
  Back and Side Go Bare.   J. Still.
    Al-VBP:64, Ho-WR:236
  The Barley Mow.   Cl-DT:84
  Bring Us In Good Ale.   Al-VBP:24,
    Cl-FC:94, De-CH:64
  Chorus.   T. Peacock.   Al-VBP:716
  Cold's the Wind.   T. Dekker.
    Al-VBP:226
  Come, Thou Monarch.
    W. Shakespeare.   Al-VBP:194
  Dreaming Liquor Songs.   Tr-US II:270
  Drink To-Day.   J. Fletcher.
    Al-VBP:282
  A Drinking Song.   W. Yeats. No-CL:40
  Early Morning Meadow Song. C. Dalmon.
    De-CH:193
  The Ghosts.   T. Peacock.
    Al-VBP:719, Sm-MK:45
  How, Butler, How.   Al-VBP:25
  Invitation to Drink Cactus Liquor
    at a Rain-Bringing Ceremony.
    Tr-US II:269
  Kava Drinking Song.   Tr-US II:51
  Little Brown Jug.
    Er-FA:430

The Men of Gotham.   T. Peacock.
    Al-VBP:715, De-CH:193, Hi-WP I:91,
    Ho-WR:108, Sp-OG:344
  A Round.   W. Browne.   Al-VBP:323
  Soldier's Song.   W. Scott. Al-VBP:673
  Song.   O. Goldsmith.   Al-VBP:587
  'Tis Late and Cold.   J. Fletcher.
    Al-VBP:281
  Wassail Song.   Gr-GB:35
  We Be Soldiers Three.   Gr-CC:119,
    Gr-CT:87, Gr-GB:235
  West Sussex Drinking Song.   H. Belloc.
    Un-MB:167
  Willie Brew'd a Peck o' Maut.
    R. Burns.   Al-VBP:647
DRISCOLL, JEM
  Peerless Jim Driscoll.
    V. Scannell.   Co-RM:231
DRIVING: see AUTOMOBILES
DROMEDARIES: see CAMELS
DROPOUTS
  Little Boy Blue.   J. Johnson.
    Me-WF:29
DROUGHTS
  Bone Yard.   J. Barnes.   Ni-CD:21
  The Drought.   Cheng Min. Hs-TC:238
  Drought.   Kamid agg Afiser.
    Tr-US I:135
  Dry and Parched.   A. Lopez.
    Al-WW:9
  Floodtide.   A. Touré.   Ad-PB:336,
    Hu-PN:424
  I Am Crying from Thirst.
    A. Lopez.   Al-WW:8
  I Have Given Up Singing about Men.
    Do-CH:(21)
  Purgatory.   Sun Yü-t'ang.   Hs-TC:121
  The Skeptic. L. Williams. De-FS:220
  Summer.   T. Tsosie.   Ba-HI:62
  Thirst.   G. Cohoe.   Al-WW:23
  This Little Cloud, and This.
    Do-CH:(19)
DROWNING: see also HUMOR - DROWNING
  Annan Water.   De-CH:311, Ma-BB:214
  Avery Anameer.   J. Brennan.
    De-FS:38
  Ballad.   J. Gay.   Al-VBP:522
  Ballad.   W. Souten.   Hi-WP I:89
  The Braes of Yarrow.   J. Logan.
    Pa-GTB:121
  The Castaway.   W. Cowper. Ha-PO:135,
    Rv-CB:551
  Child Wife.   J. Keith.   De-FS:115
  The Dead Man Dragged from the Sea.
    C. Gardner.   Ad-PB:216, Lo-IT:37
  Death Song.   R. Hawker.   Ox-BN:462
  Dirges, I.   Tr-US II:41
  A Dream of Wrecks. W. Shakespeare.
    Gr-CT:229
  The Drowned Lady.   Gr-CT:139
  Elegy on Gordon Barber. G. Derwood.
    Er-FA:193, Wi-LT:683

DROWNING — cont'd.
  Full Fathom Five. W. Shakespeare.
    Al-VBP:197, Bl-OB:52, Bo-GJ:141,
    Cl-DT:39, Co-SS:159, De-CH:719,
    Fr-WO:86, Gr-CT:231, Ma-FW:42,
    Ma-YA:70, Na-EO:44, No-CL:43,
    Pa-GTB:29, Re-TW:70, Rv-CB:193,
    Sm-MK:37
  A Funeral Piece. M. Yoshioka.
    Sh-AM:114
  The Golden Vanity. Bl-OB:55,
    Co-SS:193, De-CH:398, Fo-OG:10,
    Ho-WR:128, Rv-CB:438
  The Great Hector Was Killed by
    Arrows. J. Brodsky. Ca-MR:32
  The High Tide on the Coast of
    Lincolnshire. J. Ingelow.
    De-TT:183, Pa-OM:118, Sp-OG:85
  How's My Boy? S. Dobell. De-CH:31
  An Inscription by the Sea.
    E. Robinson. Co-EL:68,
    Co-PU:153, Co-SS:179, Gr-CT:231
  Lake Water. T. Miyoshi. Sh-AM:79
  Letter from Slough Pond.
    I. Gardner. Co-EL:12, St-H:72
  Live Man's Epitaph. F. Hope.
    Gr-BT:83
  Lord Ullin's Daughter. T. Campbell.
    Co-RG:50, Fe-FP:520, Pa-GTB:182
  Loss of the Royal George.
    W. Cowper. Co-RG:44, Co-SS:137,
    Pa-GTB:123, Rv-CB:552, Sp-OG:73
  Lowlands. Gr-CT:229
  The Lowlands o' Holland.
    De-CH:345, Fo-OG:51, Ox-BB:348
  Maw Bonnie Lad. Gr-GB:133
  Mourning Song for a Brother
    Drowned at Sea. Br-MW:139
  Mourning Song for Modana.
    Da-SC:54, Tr-US II:217
  On a Friend's Escape from Drowning
    off the Norfolk Coast.
    G. Barker. To-MP:67
  On an Engraved Gem of Leander.
    J. Keats. Rv-CB:746
  Ophelia. A. Rimbaud. Gr-CT:78
  Ophelia's Death. W. Shakespeare.
    Gr-CT:77
  Pont and Blyth. Gr-GB:176
  Rare Willie Drowned in Yarrow.
    Gr-GB:133, Ox-BB:593
  A River. A. Ramanujan. To-MP:166
  Rosabelle. W. Scott. Pa-GTB:236
  A Runnable Stag. J. Davidson.
    Co-BBW:195, Ho-WR:77, Mo-SD:123,
    Na-EO:63, Rd-OA:177
  The Sands of Dee. C. Kingsley.
    Bl-OB:153, Cl-FC:88, Co-PM:111,
    Co-SS:43, De-CH:211, De-TT:182,
    Fe-FP:511, Hu-MP:430, Sp-OG:84
  The Sea-Ritual. G. Darley. De-CH:312,
    Gr-SS:179, Ho-WR:126, Ox-BN:396

  Sir Patrick Spens. Al-VBP:35,
    Ar-TP3:19, Bl-OB:47, Bo-GJ:159,
    Co-RG:58, Co-SS:129, De-CH:405,
    Ha-PO:3, Ma-BB:1, Ma-FW:46,
    Ma-YA:41, Ox-BB:311, Rv-CB:38,
    Sm-LG:307, Sp-OG:98
  Song. A. Lewis. Wi-LT:763
  The Three Fishers. C. Kingsley.
    Co-SS:205, Fe-PL:418, Pa-OM:117,
    Sp-OG:91
  Through the Dear Might of Him Who
    Walked the Waves. J. Heath-Stubbs.
    Go-BP:289
  To Some Millions Who Survive Joseph
    E. Mander, Senior. S. Wright.
    Ad-PB:212
  The Twa Sisters. De-CH:421,
    Rv-CB:42
  The Two Rivers. Co-BN:79, De-CH:404,
    Gr-CT:165, Gr-GB:176, Ma-BB:83,
    Rv-CB:119
  Water Island. H. Moss. Ho-P:199
  The Water o' Wearie's Well. De-CH:730
  Willy Drowned in Yarrow. De-CH:728,
    GTB:122
  Within the Blackened Sea. F. Saito.
    Sh-AM:151
  The Wreck of the Deutschland.
    G. Hopkins. Li-TU:220, Ox-BN:852,
    Wi-LT:30
  The Yachts. W. Williams.
    Al-VBP:1154, Fl-HH:27, Ma-FW:51,
    Pe-OA:73, Pe-SS:72, Sm-PT:112,
    Un-MA:262, Wi-LT:194
DROWSINESS
  Falling Asleep. S. Sassoon.
    Un-MB:315
  Myself. L. Ahsoak. Ba-HI:23
DRUG STORES: see also PHARMACISTS
  Drug Store. K. Shapiro.
    Br-TC:373, Pe-OA:225
  Drug Store. J. Weaver. Wi-TL:192
DRUGGISTS: see PHARMACISTS
DRUGS: see HUMOR - DRUGS; NARCOTICS
DRUMS
  African Dance. L. Hughes.
    Fe-FP:480, Sh-RP:8, Th-AS:159
  Burgundian Carol. B. de la Monnoye.
    Pl-US:109
  Dancing. Alex M. Le-M:68
  Darby Kelly. T. Dibdin. Cl-DT:12
  The Drum. J. Scott. Al-VBP:588,
    Ba-PO:67, Ke-PP:39, Rv-CB:545
  The Drum Maker. J. Bruchac.
    Mo-TS:28
  Drum Song. Tr-US I:41
  The Drummer Boy of Shiloh. Em-AF:450
  Drums and Drumming. B. Brown.
    Ba-HI:131
  Drums of Freedom. G. Thompson.
    Jo-VC:21

From Jazz for Five, 3:Colin Barnes,
   Drums. J. Smith.   To-MP:194
Full of Beats.   Re-RR:33
Hear a War Drum Sound.
   S. Takayanagi.   Sh-AM:176
How Happy the Soldier. Sm-LG:262
Marrakech. R. Eberhart. Wi-LT:440
The Mystic Drum. G. Okara.
   Lo-TY:157
Once Again. L. Bahe.   Ni-CD:12
Oom-Pah. H. Lofting.   Ir-BB:42
Piano and Drums. G. Okara.
   Lo-TY:158
Praise Song for a Drummer.
   Do-CH:(36)
Prelude to Akwasidae. Lo-TY:14
See the Conquering Hero Comes.
   N. Lee. Cl-DT:12
Song about the Drummer.
   B. Okujava. Bo-RU:59
A Song for St. Cecilia's Day.
   J. Dryden. Pa-RE:97
Talking to His Drum.
   E. Mitchell.   Al-WW:96
They Came This Evening.
   L. Damas. Lo-TY:120
Until Then. P. George. Al-WW:126
Whoops a Daisy. T. Carr. Le-M:80
DRUNKENNESS: see INTOXICATION
DRYADS: see NYMPHS
DRYDEN, JOHN
   The Progress of Poesy.   T. Gray.
   Al-VBP:566, Pa-GTB:132, Rv-CB:532
DUBLIN, IRE.
   Dublin. L. MacNeice. Co-PI:114
   Dublin Made Me. D. MacDonagh.
   Co-PI:100
DUBOIS, WILLIAM EDWARD BURGHARDT
   Booker T. and W.E.B. D. Randall.
   Ab-MO:84, Be-MA:69
   For William Edward Burghardt
      Dubois on His Eightieth
      Birthday. B. Latimer.
   Ad-PB:199, Hu-PN:392
   The Negro Speaks of Rivers.
      L. Hughes. Ad-PB:72, Be-MA:38,
      Br-AF:176, Hu-PN:187, Li-TU:179,
      Lo-TY:225, Mo-TS:38, Pe-SS:49,
      Ra-BP:78
   On the Death of William Edward
      Burghardt Du Bois by African
      Moonlight and Forgotten Shores.
      C. Rivers. Ad-PB:235
DUBUQUE, IA.
   Old Dubuque. D. Etter. Br-AF:206
DUCKS: see also HUMOR - DUCKS
   Chicks and Ducks. St-FS:122
   Dame Duck's Lecture. St-FS:94
   Dilly Dilly. Ag-HE:18
   The Duck. O. Nash.   Ir-BB:76,
      Pa-RE:39

Duck-Chasing. G. Kinnell.
   Br-TC:238, Ca-VT:599 .
Duck, You Are Merely Boasting.
   Le-OE:39
Ducks. F. Harvey. Cl-DT:57,
   Co-BBW:163
The Ducks. A. Wilkins.   Ar-TP3:73
Ducks at Dawn. J. Tippett.
   Ar-TP3:73, Au-SP:52, Br-SS:21
Ducks' Ditty. K. Grahame.
   Ar-TP3:73, Au-SP:51, Bo-FP:68,
   Bo-GJ:50, Co-BBW:169, Fe-FP:182,
   Hu-MP:241, Ir-BB:78, La-PP:4,
   La-PV:130, Mc-WK:40, Ox-BC:328,
   Pe-FB:12, Tu-WW:84
Four Ducks on a Pond. W. Allingham.
   Bl-OB:66, Ch-B:28, De-CH:517,
   Du-RG:99, Re-TW:11
A Fox Started Out in a Hungry
   Plight. Mo-NR:146
How Far. M. Nakagawa. Sh-AM:149
The Hunter. O. Nash. Co-BBW:248,
   Ke-TF:291, Mo-SD:126, Na-EO:112
Hunting. J. Aluskak. Ba-HI:67
In the Barnyard. D. Aldis.
   Sh-RP:330
It May Be. Re-RR:16
It Very Well May Be. Re-RR:38
I've Seen Everything. J. Naito.
   Ma-FW:93
The Little Duck. Joso. Au-SP:54,
   Le-IS:9, Su-FVI:72
Mallard. R. Warner. Co-BBW:237
My Boat Is Turned Up at Both Ends.
   Wy-CM:18
Natura in Urbe. E. White. Mc-WK:41
Nell Flaherty's Drake. Rd-OA:86
The New Duckling. A. Noyes.
   Fe-FP:283, Hu-MP:241
O Foolish Ducklings. Buson.
   Be-CS:59
A Pair. M. Swenson. La-RM:58
The Prayer of the Little Ducks.
   C. Gasztold. Ad-PE:38, Ar-TP3:82,
   Gr-TG:63, La-PV:131, Su-FVI:72
The Ptarmigan Sings to the Long-
   Tailed Duck. Le-IB:43
Quack! W. de la Mare. Ar-TP3:74,
   Co-BBW:268, Co-IW:14, Ma-FO:(9)
Regent's Park. R. Fyleman. Au-SP:54
Sing-Song Rhyme. Br-SS:58
Song Cycle of the Moon-Bone.
   Tr-US I:246
Song from a Story. Tr-US I:30
Swimming. C. Scollard.
   Fe-FP:112, Hu-MP:41
That Duck. B. Mac I. Mc-AW:98
That Duck, Bobbing Up. Joso.
   Be-CS:57

DUCKS — cont'd.
   Three Young Rats. Fr-WO:35,
      Gr-CT:31, Gr-EC:11, Gr-GB:92,
      Ir-BB:234, Lo-LL:41, Mo-MGT:187,
      On-TW:15, Sm-MK:193
   A Trueblue Gentleman. K. Patchen.
      Pa-RE:57, Rd-OA:75, Su-FVI:20
   Two Ducks. Hiroshige. Le-MW:14
   The White Drake. Do-WH:35
   Who Likes the Rain. C. Bates.
      Ar-TP3:167, Bo-FP:226, St-FS:18
   Wild Duck. T. Aida. Sh-AM:109
   Wild Ducks Have Eaten. Yasui.
      Be-CS:58
   With His Apology. S. Karai. Ma-FW:93
DUELS: see also FENCING; HUMOR - DUELS
   Monument to Pushkin. I. Brodsky.
      Bo-RU:22
DUGONGS
   Song Cycle of the Moon-Bone.
      Tr-US I:246
   A Triptych on the Dugong.
      Tr-US I:242
DUKE OF YORK ISLANDS
   Men's Song. Tr-US I:208
   Men's Song. Tr-US I:209
   A Song of a Men's Secret Society.
      Tr-US I:208
   Women's Song. Tr-US I:209
   Women's Song at a Dance Festival.
      Tr-US I:209
   Women's Song at a Wedding Feast.
      Tr-US I:208
DUMAS, ALEXANDRE
   Lines Written at the Grave of
      Alexandre Dumas. G. Bennett.
      Hu-PN:208
DUMPLINGS
   Davy Dumpling. Mo-MGT:90
DUNBAR, PAUL LAURENCE
   For Paul Laurence Dunbar. C. Cullen.
      Ad-PB:91, Bo-AN:89, Bo-HF:141
   Paul Laurence Dunbar.
      J. Corrothers. Hu-PN:25
DUNGEONS: see PRISONS AND PRISONERS
DUNKIRK, FR.
   The Other Little Boats.
      E. Shanks. Hi-FO:267
DUNS SCOTUS, JOHN
   Duns Scotus's Oxford. G. Hopkins.
      Pa-GTB:391
DUNSTAN, SAINT
   The Devil. Mo-MGT:111
DUNWICH, ENG.
   At Dunwich. A. Thwaite. To-MP:182
DUSK: see TWILIGHT
DUST
   Common Dust. G. Johnson.
      Ad-PB:22, Bo-AN:20, Lo-TY:209
   Dust. R. Brooke. Un-MB:323
   Dust. S. Russell. Br-SM:116,
      Du-RG:64

Dust. Yu Kuang-chung. Pa-MV:179
Earth. J. Wheelock. Tr-MR:42,
   Un-MA:343
The Hour-Glass. B. Jonson.
   Rv-CB:284
In Praise of Dust. G. Chesterton.
   Un-MB:209
In Praise of Dust. R. Field.
   Sh-RP:132
A Peck of Gold. R. Frost.
   Bo-HF:21, La-PV:196
Mrs. Southern's Enemy. O. Sitwell.
   Al-VBP:1190
Taking Off. R. Rogers. Al-WW:85
This Quiet Dust. J. Wheelock.
   Un-MA:344
The Wall. A. Brownjohn. Ls-NY:260
The White Dust. W. Gibson.
   Un-MB:242
THE DUTCH
   The Character of Holland.
      A. Marvell. Gr-CT:204
DUTCH VERSE
   Jonathan. R. Fyleman. Ar-TP3:133,
      Ja-PC:27
   Prayer. W. Bilderdÿk. Pa-SG:200
   Such Is Holland. P. de Genestet.
      Ma-FW:42
   Thus Spoke My Love. P. Hooft.
      Pa-SG:25
DUTIES (IMPORTS): see TARIFFS
DUTY: see also CONSCIENCE; HUMOR -
   DUTY
   Abraham Davenport. J. Whittier.
      Sp-OG:31
   The Builders. H. Longfellow.
      Er-FA:8, Sp-OG:327
   Compromise. C. Stetson. Sp-OG:331
   Daily Round. L. Reese. Gr-TG:34
   Duty. R. Emerson. Er-FA:29
   Four Things. H. Van Dyke.
      Fe-PL:291, Un-GT:305
   The Girl Who Took Care of the
      Turkeys. Te-FC:67
   In an Age of Fops and Toys.
      R. Emerson. Fe-FP:167
   In Spite of All This Much Needed
      Thunder. Z. Gilbert. Hu-PN:390
   The Looker-On. C. Stetson. Sp-OG:325
   Mary Make the Butter. I. Eastwick.
      Ja-PA:53
   Ode to Duty. W. Wordsworth.
      Pa-GTB:207
   The Small Task. M. Lindsay. Ke-TF:241
   Stopping by Woods on a Snowy Evening.
      R. Frost. Ad-PE:31, Al-VBP:1134,
      Ar-TP3:198, Bo-FP:170, Bo-GJ:257,
      Br-SS:88, Br-TC:135, Cl-DT:20,
      Co-BN:151, Co-PS:160, De-CH:625,
      Er-FA:257, Fe-FP:67, Ga-FB:299,
      Gr-EC:273, Ha-PO:90, Ke-TF:420,
      La-PP:29, La-PV:167, Ma-FW:276,

Mc-PR:124, Mc-WK:32, Pe-FB:80,
   Re-TW:123, Sh-AP:150, Sh-RP:52
   Sm-LG:63, Sm-PT:8, Un-MA:187,
   Wi-LT:174
A Voice. H. Leivick. Ho-TY:124
Whole Duty of Children.
   R. Stevenson. Gr-TG:14,
   Na-EO:138, Ox-BC:293
Work. H. Van Dyke. Ke-TF:204,
   Se-PR:67, Th-AS:209
DWARFS (FAIRIES)
Alice Brand. W. Scott. Pa-OM:248
Dwarves' Song. J. Tolkien.
   Li-TU:89
DWARFS (MIDGETS)
The People of Tao-Chou.
   Po Chu-i. Gr-CT:374
DYES AND DYEING: see HUMOR -
   DYES AND DYEING
DYING: see also EXTREME UNCTION;
Across the Range. Fi-BG:175
Bury Me Not on the Lone Prairie.
   Er-FA:445, Ga-FB:269
The Choice. H. Corke.
   Cr-WS:170, Ni-JP:129
Christ's Descent into Hell.
   R. Rilke. Ho-P:231
Come in Kayaks. Le-IB:115
Confessions. R. Browning.
   Al-VBP:908, Pa-GTB:355
The Cottage Hospital. J. Betjeman.
   Pa-GTB:502, Un-MB:438
The Death-Bed. T. Hood.
   Ox-BN:425, Pa-GTB:235
The Death-Bed. S. Sassoon.
   Wi-LT:640
Death from Cancer. R. Lowell.
   Br-TC:265, Ha-PO:125
The Death of a Toad. R. Wilbur.
   Sh-AP:231, Wi-LT:598
The Death of Artemidora. W. Landor.
   Al-VBP:709, Ox-BN:193
The Death of Hoelderlin.
   P. Oppenheimer. Ls-NY:167
The Death Song of White Antelope.
   White Antelope. Br-MW:92
The Dree Night. Gr-CT:364
Drum Song in Three Parts from the
   Funeral Ceremony for a Hero.
   Tr-US I:56
The Dying Man in His Garden.
   G. Sewell. Pa-GTB:166
Dying Speech of an Old Philosopher.
   W. Landor. Al-VBP:704,
   Gr-CT:435, Ha-PO:209, Ma-YA:169,
   Ox-BN:194, Pa-GTB:318
Elegy Dream Song. Br-MW:42
Endless Sleep. C. Minor. Jo-VC:68
Exit Molloy. D. Mahon. Co-PI:119
Farewell, My Younger Brother.
   Ho-SD:38

A Flat One. W. Snodgrass.
   En-PC:244, Wi-LT:822
For One Shortly to Die.
   W. Whitman. Rv-CB:854
The Heavenly Song. Le-IB:124
Holographic Testament.
   S. Salazar Bondy. Be-UL:85
hospital/poem. S. Sanchez.
   Ad-PB:289
I Heard a Fly Buzz when I Died.
   E. Dickinson. Mo-BG:163,
   Un-MA:98, Wi-LT:9
Inevitable. J. Betjeman. Un-MB:440
I've Seen a Dying Eye.
   E. Dickinson. Fe-PL:285
Lament. A. Bergman. Kr-OF:198
The Last Night That She Lived.
   E. Dickinson. Rv-CB:909,
   Sh-AP:130
Let the Light Enter. F. Harper.
   Hu-PN:15
The Man in White. W. Percy.
   Ke-TF:166
Messages. F. Thompson. De-CH:246
Monologue of a Dying Man.
   J. Datta. Al-PI:82
Mortmain. R. Warren. En-PC:74,
   Ho-P:295
Mother and Son. A. Tate.
   Un-MA:538
Music. G. du Maurier. Rv-CB:932
Nekros. J. Tabb. Sh-AP:135
The Old Men. I. Feldman. Br-TC:122
On the Death of Keats. J. Logan.
   Ho-P:169
The Palm of the Hand. F. Saito.
   Sh-AM:150
Plaint. Tr-US I:91
Quintana Lay in the Shallow Grave
   of Coral. K. Shapiro. Ca-VT:374
Reconciliation. C. Day Lewis.
   Br-TC:260
Remorse. J. Betjeman. Un-MB:440
Round Apples. Rv-ON:96
Sept. 16, 1961, Poem. J. Kerouac.
   Kh-VA:38
The Ship of Death. D. Lawrence.
   Al-VBP:1160, Pa-GTB:462, Un-MB:299
The Sick Stockrider. A. Gordon.
   Hi-FO:233
So Might It Be. J. Galsworthy.
   Fe-PL:277
Song after a Man Dies. Tr-US II:293
Song at a Deathbed. Tr-US I:57
Song of a Dying Girl. Tr-US I:170
Song of Tukulua. Tukulua.
   Tr-US II:48
The Spring of Lime. R. Nichols.
   Pa-GTB:454
The Sun Came Out in April.
   C. Day Lewis. Ca-MB:23

DYING — cont'd.
  Testament. Sister M. Thérése.
    Tr-MR:169
  There Is an Old Horse.
    Jao Meng-k'an. Hs-TC:107
  To a Single Shadow Without Pity.
    S. Cornish. Ad-PB:294
  Two Fragments of Songs, II.
    Br-MW:48
  Variation on a Polish Folk Song.
    M. Zaturenska. Gr-CC:137
  Whom the Gods Love. M. Bruner.
    Fe-PL:261
  Winter Nightfall. R. Bridges.
    Un-MB:50
  The World Feels Dusty.
    E. Dickinson. Un-MA:100
DYKES
  The Dykes. R. Kipling. Ni-JP:138
  The Leak in the Dike. P. Cary.
    Er-FA:348, Fe-FP:554
EAGLES
  Birkett's Eagle. D. Howard.
    Ca-MB:27
  The Captive Eagle. H. Ishida.
    Sh-AM:173
  Cawdor. R. Jeffers. Sm-PT:25
  The Clouds Float By.
    J. O'Donnell. Le-M:94
  The Dalliance of the Eagles.
    W. Whitman. Co-PU:102
  The Eagle. M. Rosenfeld.
    Ho-TY:81
  The Eagle. A. Tennyson.
    Ad-PE:26, Ar-TP3:58, Bl-OB:66,
    Bo-FP:278, Bo-GJ:74, Ch-B:90,
    Cl-DT:58, Co-BBW:260, De-CH:101,
    Fe-FP:291, Hi-WP I:27, Ho-WR:215,
    La-PV:134, Mc-PR:129, Pa-GTB:331,
    Re-TW:96, Rv-CB:801, Sm-LG:90,
    Tu-WW:82, Un-GT:58
  The Eagle. A. Young. Co-EL:30,
    Hi-WP I:33
  The Eagle. Ho-SD:50, Le-OE:13
  The Eagle above Us. Tr-US II:285
  The Eagle and the Mole. E. Wylie.
    Al-VBP:1166, Rd-OA:158, Un-MA:274,
    Wi-TL:205
  The Eagle-Feather Fan. N. Momaday.
    Ni-CD:98
  An Eagle Feather I See. Jo-TS:20
  Eagle Flight. A. Lopez. Al-WW:7
  Eagle Plain. R. Francis. Br-AF:24
  Eagle Song. G. Bottomley.
    Un-MB:213
  The Eagle Speaks. Jo-TS:13
  Eagles. V. Bashkin. Co-BBW:239
  The Folding Fan. G. Cohoe. Al-WW:25
  From the Edge of the Hole in the Sky.
    Wo-HS:(5)
  A Hat of Eagle Feathers.
    Ho-SD:17

  Hi-ihiya Naiho-o! Da-SC:77,
    Ho-SD:41
  I Hear the Eagle Bird. Ho-SD:3
  I Want to Go Wandering. V. Lindsay.
    Pa-HT:72
  Man Is Nothing But.
    S. Tchernichovsky. Me-PH:76
  Nesting Time. A. Guiterman.
    Gr-EC:180
  Plato's Tomb. Sm-LG:275
  The Sea Eagle. H. MacDiarmid.
    Un-MB:360
  See How the Doves Flutter and
    Huddle. Do-CH:(15)
  The Shape God Wears. S. Hay.
    Un-GT:82
  The Sixteen Circuits of the Lodge -
    Third Song. Da-SC:103
  The Song of the Reim-kennar.
    W. Scott. Ox-BN:137
  The Story of a Well-Made Shield.
    N. Momaday. Ni-CD:104
  There Are the Eagles Crying.
    Le-OE:46
  There Is an Eagle in Me.
    Wo-HS:(47)
  To Kill the Eagle. . . .
    Wo-HS:(54)
  Two Fragments of Songs, I.
    Br-MW:48
  The Women and the Man. Te-FC:87
EARS: see also HUMOR - EARS;
    LISTENING
  A Charm for the Ear-Ache.
    J. Kirkup. Go-BP:48
  I Am Conscious. T. Clark. Mc-EA:85
  King Juke. K. Fearing.
    Mo-BG:32, Ni-JP:92
  On Wearing Ears. W. Harris.
    Ad-BO:70
  A Way of Touching the World.
    Me-WF:75
EARTH: see also CREATION; HUMOR -
    EARTH; WORLD
  Address on the Talking Drums to
    Asase Yaa, the Spirit of Earth.
    Tr-US I:47
  After. R. Hodgson. Un-MB:187
  Among the Stars. W. Blake.
    Re-TW:129, Un-GT:264
  Antonio and Mellida. J. Marston.
    Al-VBP:268
  The Beautiful. Le-OE:138
  Black Mouth Society Song.
    Tr-US II:234
  The Cosmic Fabric. Y. Polonsky.
    Pl-EI:17
  The Dancing Sea. J. Davies.
    Gr-CT:191
  The Death Song of White Antelope.
    White Antelope. Br-MW:92
  The Earth. J. Very. Sh-AP:65

Earth.   J. Wheelock.   Tr-MR:42,
   Un-MA:343
Earth and Sea.   A. Pushkin.
   Pa-SG:368
Earth and Sky.   Euripides. Pl-EI:180
Earth Cure Me.   Earth Receive My Woe.
   Wo-HS:(55)
The Earth Is Not an Old Woman.
   D. Satyarthi. Al-PI:142
The Earth Is the Lord's.   Bible.
   O.T. Psalms. Ar-TP3:188,
   Bo-FP:249, Fe-FP:232, Pa-SG:198,
   Pl-EI:214
Earth Song.   R. Emerson. Sh-AP:30
Earth upon Earth.   Gr-CT:325,
   Rv-CB:15
Earth Woman with Hands.   Wo-HS:(8)
Earth's Answer.   W. Blake. Rv-CB:568
Earth's Bondman.   B. Dabney.
   Gr-EC:275
Elegy for Maria Alves.   J. Cardozo.
   An-TC:33
Epistle to Be Left in the Earth.
   A. MacLeish. Pl-IO:55,
   Sm-PT:114, Un-MA:458
Epitaph for Us.   E. Masters.
   Sm-PT:158
Fear of the Earth.   A. Comfort.
   Un-MB:519
Fire Fire of the First World.
   Wo-HS:(61)
For Once in a Dream or Trance, I
   Saw the Gods.   E. Muir.
   Go-BP:155
The Good Earth.   K. Itta. Ba-HI:107
La Guerre II.   E. Cummings.
   Un-MA:471
Hamatreya.   R. Emerson.   Sh-AP:30
Heaven and Earth.   James I, King
   of England.   Gr-CT:235
Heaven Is Heaven.   C. Rossetti.
   Ha-YA:69
Housemates.   O. Shepard.   Tr-MR:192
Hymn to Earth.   E. Wylie.
   Un-MA:284, Wi-LT:209
I Am He That Walks with the Tender
   and Growing Night.   W. Whitman.
   Gr-CT:236
In Response to a Question.
   W. Stafford. Mc-EA:54, St-H:213
In the Immense Cathedral.
   J. Wheelock. Tr-MR:38
In the Middle of This Century.
   Y. Amichai. Me-PH:136
The Landsman.   Moschus. Pa-SG:174
Let Me Enjoy.   T. Hardy. Al-VBP:1049,
   Ga-FB:10, Tr-MR:53
Mask.   S. Spender.   Un-MB:476
The New Year Came.   Ja-HH:7
No Single Thing Abides.
   T. Lucretius Carus. Pl-IO:9
Offering.   Bi-IT:108

The Old Men.   Jo-TS:10, Tr-US II:237
Physical Geography.   L, Nicholl.
   Li-TU:29, Pl-IO:52
The Plane: Earth.   Sun Ra.
   Ad-PB:207
Preparation.   R. Francis. Du-RG:131
The Recall.   R. Kipling. Go-BP:236
Renascence.   E. Millay.   Er-FA:95,
   Un-MA:440
The Return.   E. Millay.   Un-MA:450
Song of the Sky Loom.   Br-MW:49,
   Da-SC:76, Le-OE:6, Tr-US II:256
Song of the Wolf Society.
   Tr-US II:242
The Soul Longs to Return Whence It
   Came.   R. Eberhart.   Sh-AP:208
The Spectacle.   W. de la Mare.
   Go-BP:249
A Spring Song.   Fe-PL:371
Strange Meetings.   H. Monro.
   Un-MB:235
Stuff.   A. Mitchell.   Sm-MK:190
Thanksgiving for the Earth.
   E. Goudge.   Ha-YA:138
This Compost.   W. Whitman.
   Un-MA:86
This Newly Created World. Bi-IT:5
To a Traveler.   L. Johnson.
   Un-MB:154
This Was Our Land.   Wo-HS:(35)
Under Ground.   J. Reeves. Sh-RP:182
Under the Ground.   R. Bachmeister.
   It-HB:39
What I Tell Him.   S. Ortiz. Ni-CD:151
Who Are the Two from Whom We Beg.
   Re-RR:31
EARTHQUAKES: see also HUMOR -
   EARTHQUAKES; TSUNAMIS; VOLCANOES
   Earthquake.   Kuo Mo-jo. Hs-TC:38
   The Santa Barbara Earthquake.
   Em-AF:472
THE EAST: see NEW ENGLAND; ORIENT; and
   names of states, as NEW JERSEY
EAST INDIAN VERSE: see also BALLADS,
   EAST INDIAN
   The Coromandel Fishers.   S. Naidu.
   Sh-RP:26
   Dialogue.   Tr-US II:151
   The Man on My Back.   P. Sen.
   Gr-BT:136
   Mother Moon, Bless Baby.   Le-OE:104
   Sitting on the Stone, O Crab.
   Le-OE:47
   Song.   Tr-US II:168
   Song.   Tr-US II:150
   Songs, I, II, III.   Tr-US II:165, 166
   Songs and Dance Songs, I. Tr-US II:152
   Songs at a Wedding, II.   Tr-US II:167
   To the Poets of India.   F. Scott.
   Ls-NY:168
   Wasn't It You? K. Narasimhaswamy.
   Al-PI:125
   Women's Dance Song.   Tr-US II:151

EAST INDIAN VERSE - ASSAMESE
  I Shall Be a Swan. . . . Le-OE:90
  Sad Songs, I. Tr-US II:174
  Sad Songs, II, III. Tr-US II:174
  A Snapshot. H. Barua. Al-PI:75
  Spring Festival Songs.
    Tr-US II:172-174
EAST INDIAN VERSE - BENGALI
  Baby's World. R. Tagore. Ma-FW:67
  Calcutta. A. Chakravarty.
    Al-PI:77
  Cat. J. Das. Al-PI:80
  Conjecture. A. Raha. Al-PI:86
  An Evening Air. S. Sen. Al-PI:87
  For Strength. R. Tagore. Tr-MR:52
  Frogs. B. Bose. Al-PI:78
  The Home. R. Tagore. Bo-GJ:xix
  Let This Be My Parting Word.
    R. Tagore. Tr-MR:284
  A Little Girl, Rumi's Fancy.
    N. Guha. Al-PI:81
  Monologue of a Dying Man.
    J. Datta. Al-PI:82
  On the Seashore. R. Tagore.
    Al-PI:89
  Paper Boats. R. Tagore. Bo-FP:108,
    Bo-HF:28, Fe-FP:114, Ma-FW:236,
    Pa-RE:36, Th-AS:72
  The Rainy Day. R. Tagore.
    Al-PI:90, Ma-FW:117
  A Song of Kabir. R. Tagore.
    Ga-S:126
  The Soul of Birds. P. Mitra.
    Al-PI:85
  Unfathomed Past. R. Tagore.
    Al-PI:88
  Yours. R. Tagore. Tr-MR:33
EAST INDIAN VERSE - BHIL
  Bride's Song on the Way to Her
    Husband's House. Tr-US II:139
  Song for the Feast of Krishna.
    Tr-US II:139
  Song of a Woman to Her Lover.
    Tr-US II:140
EAST INDIAN VERSE - BIHARI
  Dance Songs, I-X. Tr-US II:163-165
  Dialogue Between a Newly Married
    Couple. Tr-US II:156
  Festival Songs, I-II.
    Tr-US II:155, 157, 158
  Jungle Songs, I-V.
    Tr-US II:158-160
  Lament. Tr-US II:155
  Marriage Poems, I, II, III.
    Tr-US II:162, 163
  Marriage Songs. Tr-US II:159
  Songs and Dance Songs.
    Tr-US II:152-153
EAST INDIAN VERSE - DAFLA
  Love Songs, I, II.
    Tr-US II:171

EAST INDIAN VERSE - GONDI
  The Birth of the Goddess Jangu Bai.
    Tr-US II:148
  Dance Songs. Tr-US II:140-146
  Dirge. Tr-US II:146
  Fertility. Tr-US II:144
  Men's Stick-Dance Songs, I.
    Tr-US II:142
  Men's Stick-Dance Songs, II.
    Tr-US II:142
  Song of an Old Man. Tr-US II:144
  Songs. Tr-US II:142-148
  Songs at a Wedding, I. Tr-US II:166
  Women's Dance Song. Tr-US II:143
EAST INDIAN VERSE - GUJARATI
  As a Flower I Come. Sundaram.
    Al-PI:112
  Roses and Thorns. S. Betai.
    Al-PI:109
  The Washerman. U. Joshi. Al-PI:110
EAST INDIAN VERSE - HINDI
  Arjuna's Paean to Krishna.
    Al-PI:25
  A Charm Against Cough. Al-PI:18
  Circuit Through the Hills.
    T. Singh. Al-PI:119
  Dance Song. Tr-US II:154
  Evening at the Seashore.
    N. Sharma. Al-PI:122
  Evening Clouds. D. Bharati.
    Al-PI:114
  The Family. Visvaneth. Al-PI:123
  An Imprecation Against Foes and
    Sorcerers. Al-PI:18
  The Meaning of Atman. Al-PI:19
  Old Age. Al-PI:22
  Precepts. Al-PI:24
  Since I Left the Ocean. Navin.
    Al-PI:120
  Song. Tr-US II:154
  The Song of Creation. Al-PI:11
  Spring Wind. K. Agrawal. Al-PI:115
  The Stone-Breaker. Nirala.
    Al-PI:118
  Thought. Al-PI:20
  To Agni. Al-PI:14
  To Secure Victory in Battle.
    Al-PI:18
  To the Dawn. Al-PI:15
  To the Maruts. Al-PI:13
  To the Waters. Al-PI:17
  To the Wind. Al-PI:16
  The True and Tender Wife. Al-PI:29
  Who Is the Man of Poise? Al-PI:26
EAST INDIAN VERSE - MALAYALAM
  Waves of Thought. Panikkar.
    Al-PI:127
EAST INDIAN VERSE - MARATHI
  Carving Away in the Mist.
    M. Padgaonkar. Al-PI:133
  In a Mirage I Filled My Pitcher.
    V. Karandikar. Al-PI:130

Now and Then. S. Muktibodh.
  Al-PI:132
Poem. B. Mardhekar. Al-PI:131
Steel. Rege. Al-PI:134
Then Go at Once. V. Bapat.
  Al-PI:129
The Trail. Anil. Al-PI:128
EAST INDIAN VERSE - ORIYA
The Doves of My Eyes. G. Mohanty.
  Al-PI:138
For the Deer Dance. Tr-US II:170
For the Peacock Dance. Tr-US II:169
For the Vulture Dance. Tr-US II:169
If I Die Tomorrow. G. Mahapatra.
  Al-PI:135
Music of Stones. G. Misra.
  Al-PI:137
Songs. Tr-US II:168
Songs, I. Tr-US II:170
Songs, II. Tr-US II:171
Songs, III. Tr-US II:171
EAST INDIAN VERSE - PUNJABI
The Earth Is Not an Old Woman.
  D. Satyarthi. Al-PI:142
Silence. A. Pritam. Al-PI:141
A Village Girl. M. Singh. Al-PI:144
EAST INDIAN VERSE - SANSKRIT
All These Hurt. Vainateya. Al-PI:58
Arrows of Love. Chauras. Pa-SG:51
Autumn. Manovinoda. Al-PI:38
The Bird. R. Tagore. Pa-SG:132
The Blossoming of Love.
  Dharmakirti. Al-PI:36
Characterization. Yogesvara.
  Al-PI:37
The Cloud Messenger. Kalidasa.
  Al-PI:46
The Cremation Ground. Bha Vabhuti.
  Al-PI:37
The Dalliance of the Leopards.
  Ho-LP:3
Darkness. Murari. Al-PI:38
Dhammapada. Buddha. Ba-PO:19
Epigram. Viryamitra. Al-PI:39
Even Now. . . . Bilhana.
  Al-PI:48, Pa-SG:65
Funeral Hymn. Pa-SG:9
Good Men. Bhartrihari. Al-PI:35
He Leaves the Nest. Su-FVI:68
In Praise of Celibacy. Al-PI:51
Is Poetry Always Worthy when It's
  Old. Kalidasa. Gr-BT:i
Krishna's Longing. Jayadeva.
  Al-PI:56
Late Winter. Laksmidhara. Al-PI:41
Love in Moonlight. Bhartrihari.
  Pa-SG:64
The Moon. Bhasa. Pa-SG:114
Peace. Bhartrihari. Pa-SG:161
Radhadevi's Dance.
  Nayacandra Suri. Al-PI:53

The Salutation of the Dawn.
  Fe-PL:397
A Song-Offering. R. Tagore.
  Pa-SG:43
Substantiations. Vallana. Al-PI:40
Summer. Bana. Al-PI:35
Tell Me, O Swan. Kabir. Al-PI:55
Time a River. Vainateya. Al-PI:45
To What Shore Would You Cross. . . .
  Kabir. Al-PI:59
True Friendship. Pa-SG:20
True Religion. Tulsidas. Ba-PO:3
Villains. Abhinanda. Al-PI:38
Women's Eyes. Bhartrihari.
  Pa-SG:46
EAST INDIAN VERSE - TAMIL
A Description of Famine. Al-PI:69
A Girl Speaks to Her Playmate.
  Al-PI:66
Kanya-Kumari. K. Subramanyan.
  Al-PI:146
Love. Tiruvalluvar. Al-PI:67
The Lover's Song. I. Adigal.
  Al-PI:71
Observations. Naladiyar. Al-PI:68
Song of the Playing Ball.
  I. Adigal. Al-PI:70
What Her Friend Said.
  Varumulaiyaritti. Al-PI:64
What She Said.
  Milaipperun Kantan. Al-PI:65
What the Girl Said. Kapilar.
  Al-PI:63
What the Lover Said.
  A. Nanmullaiyar. Al-PI:63
EAST INDIAN VERSE - URDU
Ghazal. J. Morabandi. Al-PI:151
EAST INDIAN VERSE - VEDDA
Lullaby. Tr-US II:178
Song. Le-OE:84, Tr-US II:179
EAST INDIANS: see also BALLADS,
  EAST INDIAN; EAST INDIAN
  VERSE; HINDUS; INDIA -
  SOCIAL LIFE AND CUSTOMS
Americans Are Afraid of Lizards.
  K. Shapiro. Br-AF:45
EAST INDIANS - RELIGION: see also
  HINDUISM
The Indian upon God. W. Yeats.
  Un-MB:110
EAST RIVER, N.Y.
East River. R. Thomas. Br-AF:179
The Tunnel. H. Crane. Sh-AP:203,
  Un-MA:529
EASTER: see also HUMOR - EASTER;
  JESUS CHRIST - CRUCIFIXION;
  LENT; LILIES; RESURRECTION;
  SATIRE - EASTER
Alleluia! Alleluia! Let the Holy
  Anthem Rise. Co-PS:66

EASTER — cont'd.
  Alleluia, Hearts to Heaven and
    Voices Raise. C. Wordsworth.
    Ke-TF:195
  Assurance. G. Crowell. Se-PR:75
  At Easter Time. L. Richards.
    Hu-MP:334
  Belief. E. Jay. Ja-HH:27
  Canticle of the Sun Dancing on
    Easter Morning.
    J. Heath-Stubbs. Go-BP:298
  The Corpus Christi Carol. Gr-GB:308
  Down a Sunny Easter Meadow.
    N. Turner. Au-SP:363, Br-SS:140
  Early, Early Easter Day. A. Fisher.
    Br-SS:137, Mc-AW:66
  Easter. E. Coatsworth. Ha-YA:50
  Easter. H. Conkling. Ar-TP3:204
  Easter. G. Herbert. Bo-FP:248,
    De-CH:16, Ga-S:173
  Easter. G. Hopkins. Ga-S:179
  Easter. J. Kilmer. Ar-TP3:204,
    Au-SP:366, Hu-MP:333, La-PH:51,
    La-PV:82
  Easter. E. Sabin. Co-PS:68,
    Se-PR:78
  Easter Bonnet. E. Jay. Ja-HH:24
  An Easter Carol. C. Rossetti.
    Bo-FP:245, Hu-MP:334, Se-PR:77
  Easter Gloves. Bo-FP:246,
    De-PO:24
  Easter Hymn. M. Thwaites.
    Tr-MR:133
  Easter Hymn. H. Vaughan.
    Ga-S:171
  Easter in the Woods. F. Frost.
    Br-SS:138
  Easter Joy. N. Turner. Ha-YA:49
  Easter Lily. M. Miller. La-PH:51
  Easter Morning. A. Fisher.
    La-PH:52
  Easter Music. M. Deland. Se-PR:76
  Easter Song. K. Leslie. Tr-MR:134
  Easter Sunday. Sedulius Scottus.
    Li-TU:218
  For Easter. M. Millet. Ja-HH:23
  If Easter Eggs Would Hatch.
    D. Malloch. Au-SP:364, Hu-MP:335
  In Memoriam (Easter 1915).
    E. Thomas. Pa-GTB:444
  Meeting the Easter Bunny.
    R. Bennett. Ar-TP3:203,
    Au-SP:365, Br-SS:139
  O Filii et Filiae. Ga-S:174
  On Easter Day. C. Thaxter.
    Fe-FP:74, Ha-YA:51
  Prothalamion. R. Hillyer.
    Un-MA:482
  The Reason. L. Blair. Ja-HH:26
  Rest Remaineth. R. Browning.
    Se-PR:75
  Seven Stanzas at Easter.
    J. Updike. Pl-EI:36
  Some Things That Easter Brings.
    E. Parrish. Au-SP:366
  The Third Day. E. Pierce.
    Tr-MR:133
  Time for Rabbits. A. Fisher.
    La-PH:50
  Upon an Easter Morning.
    E. Farjeon. Co-PS:65
EASTER LILIES: see LILIES
EATING: see FOOD AND EATING;
    RESTAURANTS AND BARS
EAVESDROPPING: see also HUMOR -
    EAVESDROPPING
  Confession Overheard in a Subway.
    K. Fearing. Pe-SS:112,
    Wi-LT:699
ECHO (NYMPH)
  The Ballad of Hampstead Heath.
    J. Flecker. Un-MB:275
  Echo. J. Milton. Al-VBP:399,
    Rv-CB:371
  Echo's Lament for Narcissus.
    B. Jonson. Al-VBP:238,
    De-CH:236, Gr-CT:321
ECHOES: see also HUMOR - ECHOES
  The Chase. W. Rowley. De-CH:356,
    Gr-CT:276, Re-TW:49
  Echo. W. de la Mare. Mc-WS:23
  Echo. Viscountess Gray.
    De-CH:113
  Echo. M. Weston. Co-BN:224
  Echoes. T. Moore. Pa-GTB:186,
    Rv-CB:679
  Heaven. G. Herbert. Gr-CC:139
  I Break the Sky. O. Dodson.
    Ad-PB:133
  I'm Sometimes Strong. Re-RR:76
  The Instruments. C. Smart.
    Ho-WR:97
  Into a Forest. Otsuji. Be-MC:59
  The Leaden Echo and the Golden
    Echo. G. Hopkins. Er-FA:169,
    Ox-BN:867, Pa-GTB:393, Un-MB:40,
    Wi-LT:46
  Melander Supposed to Love Susan,
    but Did Love Ann. E. Herbert.
    Gr-CC:186
  O Woodland Cool. C. Brentano.
    Pa-SG:44
  The Splendor Falls on Castle Walls.
    A. Tennyson. Al-VBP:858,
    Ar-TP3:217, Bo-GJ:139, Co-RG:145,
    De-CH:113, De-TT:196, Fe-FP:373,
    Ga-FB:11, Gr-CT:444, Hi-WP I:106,
    Ho-WR:162, Hu-MP:95, Mc-PR:65,
    Ox-BN:485, Pl-US:26, Re-TW:72,
    Rv-CB:791, Sm-LG:39
  There Was a Boy. W. Wordsworth.
    Go-BP:119, Ox-BN:101, Sm-LG:107

ECLIPSES
On the Eclipse of the Moon of
October 1865.
C. Tennyson-Turner.   Ox-BN:471
ECOLOGY: see CONSERVATION;
POLLUTION
ECSTASY: see HAPPINESS; JOY
EDEN: see also ADAM AND EVE
Adam and Eve.   K. Shapiro.
Sh-AP:217
And the Lord God Planted a Garden.
Bible. O.T. Genesis. Cl-DT:68
Balme. E. Spenser. De-CH:471
Eve. R. Hodgson. De-CH:465,
Ha-PO:41, Hi-WP II:95, Na-EO:105,
Pa-OM:286, Sm-MK:58, Un-MB:186,
Wi-LT:123
Eve.   C. Rossetti.   De-CH:466,
Pa-GTB:375
Expulsion from Paradise.
J. Milton. Gr-CT:277
The Garden. J. Very. Sh-AP:66
The Happy Land. Ga-S:21
One Foot in Eden. E. Muir.
Pa-GTB:470
Out of Paradise. J. Milton.
Ga-S:35
Paradise Lost. J. Milton.
Al-VBP:410
Poem for Psychologists and/or
Theologians. C. Lewis. Gr-BP:159
Satan Journeys to the Garden of
Eden. J. Milton. Gr-CT:276
The Task. R. Pitter. Un-MB:403
These Bones Gwine to Rise Agin.
Ga-S:24
Thoughts in a Garden. A. Marvell.
Ga-S:22
To the Garden of the World.
W. Whitman. Mo-GR:103
Trees. B. Carman. Se-PR:95
EDINBURGH, SCOT.
The Chain of Princes Street.
E. Fleming. Bo-FP:136
Edinburgh. A. Noyes. Pa-HT:145
EDISON, THOMAS ALVA
And Yet Fools Say. G. Holmes.
Ar-TP3:46
EDITORS: see JOURNALISM;
NEWSPAPERS
EDUCATION: see also COLLEGES AND
UNIVERSITIES; HUMOR - EDUCA-
TION; SATIRE - EDUCATION;
SCHOLARS AND SCHOLARSHIP;
STUDENTS; TEACHERS AND
TEACHING
At School-Close. J. Whittier.
Se-PR:241
The Boy Washington. D. Thompson.
Br-SS:122
Education by Stone.
J. de Melo Neto.   An-TC:149

He That Ne'er Learns His A.B.C.
Gr-GB:28
The Lord of Lorn and the Fals
Steward. Ox-BB:285
Soonest Mended. J. Ashbery.
Ho-P:9
Statement on Our Higher Education.
W. Ransom. Ni-CD:198
The Tables Turned.
W. Wordsworth. Rv-CB:641
The Waking. T. Roethke. Br-TC:349,
Mc-EA:72, Un-MA:599, Wi-LT:487
Young Soul. I. Baraka. Mc-EA:32,
Ra-BP:220
EDWARD THE CONFESSOR: see HUMOR -
EDWARD THE CONFESSOR
EDWARD I, KING OF ENGLAND
A Gest of Robyn Hode, The Seventh
Fytte. Ox-BB:475
A Gest of Robyn Hode, The Eighth
Fytte. Ox-BB:484
EDWARD IV, KING OF ENGLAND
Bristowe Tragedie. Ox-BB:656
EDWARDS, JONATHAN
Mr. Edwards and the Spider.
R. Lowell. Br-TC:268,
Pe-OA:242, Sh-AP:230, Wi-LT:579
The Theology of Jonathan Edwards.
P. McGinley. Un-MA:596
EELS: see also HUMOR - EELS
Elvers. F. Harvey. Cl-DT:47
EERINESS: see also APPARITIONS;
GHOSTS; HALLOWEEN; HUMOR -
EERINESS
Abracadabra. D. Livesay. Do-WH:38
Carcosa. L. Carter. De-FS:47
The Carrion Crow. T. Beddoes.
Co-BBW:250, Co-PM:26, Ho-WR:211,
Rv-CB:773
The Cat. J. Brennan. Br-SM:11
Dark House in Autumn.
C. Pendleton. De-FS:148
The Demon of the Gibbet.
F. O'Brien. Co-PM:134
Devil Doll. L. Grenelle. De-FS:99
The Dream-Daemon. L. Carter.
De-FS:46
An Exceeding Great Army. E. Ayer.
De-FS:10
Gather These Bones. L. Turco.
De-FS:200
The Goblin. R. Fyleman. Ar-TP3:152,
La-PH:13
The Gourd-Heads. W. Barney.
De-FS:14
Green Candles. H. Wolfe. Co-PM:177,
Sm-MK:33, Un-MB:303
Hallowe'en. H. Behn. Ar-TP3:186,
Br-SS:65, Co-PS:135, Fe-FP:83,
Ha-YA:118, La-PH:8, La-PV:65,
Sh-RP:230
Halloween. I. Eastwick. La-PH:10

EERINESS — cont'd.
    Halloween. F. Frost.   Ja-PA:37
    Halloween. M. Pomeroy. Co-PS:138
    Halloween. Yü Kuang-chang.
      Pa-MV:189
    The Haunted House. T. Hood.
      Hi-WP I:56
    hist whist. e. e. cummings.
      Ir-BB:204, Li-TU:113, Pa-RE:43
    The Humming Stair. J. Brennan.
      De-FS:32
    I Know Some Lonely Houses.
      E. Dickinson. Co-PM:50,
      Mc-WK:129, Rv-CB:900, Un-MA:103
    In a Dark Wood. Pa-RE:116
    Invisible Painter. A. Dorn. De-FS:73
    A Lincolnshire Tale. J. Betjeman.
      De-FS:21
    The Little Fox. M. Edey and
      D. Grider. Ar-TP3:64
    Lottie Mae. S. McNail. De-FS:138
    Lunae Custodiens. L. Carter.
      De-FS:44
    The Man I Met. J. Brennan.
      De-FS:35
    Metaphor. C. Smith. De-FS:185
    Mrs. Caribou. W. Smith. Co-PM:154,
      Ir-BB:210
    The Monster. D. Quick. De-FS:151
    Moon and Fog. A. Derleth.
      De-FS:72
    News of My Friends. G. Code.
      De-FS:60
    The Night Refuses a Dreamer.
      G. Code. De-FS:62
    no time ago. e. cummings. Mc-WS:32
    October Magic. M. Livingston.
      La-PH:5, La-PV:64
    Outlaws. R. Graves. Ha-WR:58
    The Panther Possible. W. Barney.
      De-FS:13, Du-SH:115
    The Phantom Light of the Baie des
      Chaleurs. A. Eaton. Co-PM:55
    Phantoms of the Steppe.
      A. Pushkin. Ab-MO:63
    Place-Ghost. A. Derleth. De-FS:72
    Presentiment. R. Rilke. Li-TU:82
    Returning at Night. J. Harrison.
      Ca-VT:710
    Screaming Tarn. R. Bridges.
      Co-PT:26
    The Secrets of Cisterns.
      S. McNail. De-FS:138
    Shub-Ad. R. Barlow. De-FS:11
    The Silence of God. O. Sitwell.
      Mc-WK:151
    Sir Roderic's Song. W. Gilbert.
      Br-SM:10, Co-PM:75
    The Song of the Jellicles. T. Eliot.
      Bl-OB:105, Ir-BB:175, Li-LC:28,
      Li-TU:114, Lo-LL:50, Mc-WS:177,
      Ox-BC:347, Sm-LG:75, Un-GF:92

    A Spider Danced a Cosy Jig.
      I. Layton.   Do-WH:43
    The Stair. G. Claytor. De-FS:50
    The Step Mother. H. Adam. De-FS:5
    This Is Halloween. D. Thompson.
      Ar-TP3:186, Ha-YA:121, La-PH:12
    2000 A.D. B. Connelly. De-FS:68
    The Unexplored. B. Eaton.
      De-FS:82
    Warning. S. Russell. De-FS:168
    Was She a Witch? L. Richards.
      Hu-MP:446, La-PH:9, La-PV:69
    Wilderness Road. M. Keller.
      De-FS:123
    The Wind Has Wings. Do-WH:54
    Witches' Song. W. Shakespeare.
      Mc-WS:34
    The Witches' Spell.
      W. Shakespeare. Co-PM:151
    The Woods of Westermain.
      G. Meredith. Mc-WK:204
EGERIA
    Childe Harold's Pilgrimage.
      G. Byron. Al-VBP:726
EGGS: see also BIRDS - EGGS AND
      NESTS; HUMOR - EGGS
    As I Was Walking. Mo-MGT:157
    At Breakfast. M. Swenson. Pe-SS:62
    Come and See! Wy-CM:22
    The Dogmatic Egg. I. Barbu.
      Mc-AC:65
    The Egg. L. Richards. Ar-TP3:71,
      Hu-MP:239
    Fingers in the Nesting Box.
      R. Graves. Co-BBW:162
    First Lesson. N. Willard. Sc-TN:234
    Giant Turtles. G. Corso. Be-EB:14
    Hen and Cock. Gr-GB:58
    Hickety, Pickety, My Black Hen.
      Mother Goose. An-IP:(13),
      Ar-TP3:103, Au-SP:16, Bo-FP:89,
      De-PO:20, Li-LB:93, Mo-MGT:120,
      Mo-NR:23, On-TW:34, Wi-MG:11,
      Wr-RM:39
    Humpty Dumpty. Mother Goose.
      Bo-FP:29, De-PO:18, Fr-WO:32,
      Ir-BB:48, Li-LB:60, Mo-CC:(52),
      Mo-MGT:110, Mo-NR:88, Wi-MG:3,
      Wr-RM:40
    In Marble Walls. Gr-CT:11,
      Gr-GB:58, Ir-BB:51, Mo-MGT:155,
      Rv-ON:57, Sm-MK:32
    A Little Egg. T. Anthony. Le-M:30
    The Lost Egg. P. Ilott.
      Gr-EC:158, Ir-BB:63
    Riddles, II. Gr-CT:235, Gr-GB:59
EGOTISM: see CONCEIT
EGRETS: see also HERONS
    Beyond the Fog. Lo Fu. Pa-MV:115
    Egret Dyke. Wang Wei. Le-MW:11
    Egrets. J. Wright. Ad-PE:45,
      Bo-GJ:63

Far up the River. Tu Fu. Rx-OH:26
Like a Wave Crest. Emperor Uda.
    Ba-ST:48
The White Egret. Li Po. Pa-SG:98
EGYPT: see also AFRICAN VERSE -
    EGYPTIAN; NILE RIVER; and names
    of cities, as CAIRO, EGY.
Address to a Mummy. H. Smith.
    Co-RG:5
Alexandrian Kings. C. Cavafy.
    Gr-CC:109
Egypt. Z. Ghose. Ls-NY:246
The Nile. L. Hunt. Al-VBP:712,
    Ox-BN:220
The Prophecy Against Egypt. Bible.
    O.T. Isaiah. Me-PH:41
EGYPT - HISTORY AND PATRIOTISM
The Hymn to the Sun. Ab-MO:3,
    Lo-TY:21
EICHMAN, KARL ADOLPH
Poem for Adolph Eichman.
    J. Harriman. Lo-IT:42
EINSTEIN, ALBERT
Einstein (1929). A. MacLeish.
    Pl-IO:180
The Gift to Be Simple. H. Moss.
    Br-TC:307, Pl-IO:181, Tr-MR:174
Mr. Attila. C. Sandburg.
    Ha-PT:28, Pl-IO:177
Relative Sadness. C. Rowbotham.
    Gr-BT:119
EIRE: see IRELAND
EISENHOWER, DWIGHT DAVID
Eisenhower's Visit to Franco, 1959.
    J. Wright. Bl-FP:23
EL CAMINO REAL: see CAMINO REAL
EL CID: see CID
EL GRECO: see GRECO, EL
ELDON, JOHN SCOTT, 1ST EARL OF
The Masque of Anarchy. P. Shelley.
    Hi-FO:206
ELEANOR OF AQUITAINE: see also
    HENRY II, KING OF ENGLAND
Sir Aldinger. Ox-BB:23
ELDER TREES
The Elder Tree. Gr-CT:166,
    Gr-GB:307
ELECTIONS: see also HUMOR -
    ELECTIONS
The Ballot. J. Pierpont. Se-PR:200
The Poor Voter on Election Day.
    J. Whittier. Ja-PA:47, Se-PR:201,
    Vi-PP:188
ELECTRICITY: see also EDISON, THOMAS
    ALVA; HUMOR - ELECTRICITY
Death on a Live Wire. M. Baldwin.
    Ca-MB:88
The Electric Lights Shine in
    Everybody's Heart. Hs-TC:452
The Force. P. Redgrove. To-MP:178
Mazda Miracle. C. Bostelmann.
    Ke-TF:356

My Invention. S. Silverstein.
    Co-PU:29
Power: Cape Hatteras. H. Crane.
    Un-MA:528
ELEGIES: see also DIRGES; HUMOR -
    ELEGIES; SATIRE - ELEGIES
Adonais. P. Shelley. Al-VBP:759,
    Ha-PO:130, Ox-BN:287
Albert Ayler: Eulogy for a
    Decomposed Saxophone Player.
    S. Crouch. Ad-PB:486
At Laie's Tomb. O. Goga. Mc-AC:38
At Lanier's Grave. J. Tabb.
    Sh-AP:136
At the Grave of John Clare.
    C. Causley. Ma-FW:171
Ave atque Vale. A. Swinburne.
    Al-VBP:1033, Ox-BN:814
Ballade of Boot-Hill. Fi-BG:110
The Black Rock. J. Berryman.
    Ca-VT:385
Broken Promise. J. Taylor.
    Gr-BT:108
Burial of the Spirit of a Young
    Poet. R. Hughes. Un-MB:409
Bury Her at Even. M. Field.
    Sm-MK:222
Byron Recollected at Bologna.
    S. Rogers. Ox-BN:51
Charley III. S. Sandy. Ls-NY:33
Cromwell Dead. A. Marvell.
    Al-VBP:460, Gr-CT:379
Dance of the Infidels. A. Young.
    Ad-PB:363
The Death of a Negro Poet.
    C. Rivers. Ra-BP:201
Death of a Son. Bi-IT:99
Dylan, Who Is Dead. S. Allen.
    Ad-PB:167
The Eagle That Is Forgotten.
    V. Lindsay. Al-VBP:1139,
    Sh-AP:166, Tr-MR:171, Un-MA:223
Elegy. G. Byron. Pa-GTB:233
An Elegy. D. Gascoyne. Br-TC:145
Elegy. E. Millay. Un-MA:446
Elegy. A. Pope. Co-EL:141,
    De-CH:254
Elegy. Tr-US II:307
Elegy Before Death. E. Millay.
    Wi-LT:338
An Elegy for a Dead Child in the
    Street. R. Rao. Al-PI:106
Elegy for a Dead Soldier.
    K. Shapiro. Hi-TL:213, Wi-LT:541
Elegy for a Jazz Musician.
    E. Kroll. Du-SH:138
Elegy for a Nature Poet.
    H. Nemerov. Co-BN:230
Elegy for Alfred Hubbard.
    T. Connor. To-MP:101
Elegy for Chief Sealth (1786-1866).
    D. Niatum. Ni-CD:121

ELEGIES — cont'd.
  Elegy for J.F.K. W. Auden.
    Ma-FW:168
  Elegy for Jack Bowman.
    J. Bruchac. Ni-CD:32
  Elegy for Jane. T. Roethke.
    Br-TC:348, Pe-OA:204, Pe-SS:160,
    Sh-AP:213, Un-MA:598, Wi-LT:486
  Elegy for Lucy Lloyd. L. Goch.
    Pa-SG:74
  Elegy for Maria Alves. J. Cardozo.
    An-TC:33
  Elegy for Mr. Goodbeare.
    O. Sitwell. Un-MB:357
  Elegy for My Father. H. Moss.
    Wi-LT:777
  Elegy for the Rev. Mr. James B.
    Hodgson. J. Logan. St-H:111
  Elegy for the Soviet Yiddish
    Writers. C. Grade. Ho-TY:339
  Elegy of the Bird. J. Pasos.
    Be-UL:77
  Elegy on Gordon Barber. G. Derwood.
    Er-FA:193, Wi-LT:683
  Elegy on Shakespeare. W. Basse.
    Al-VBP:297, No-CL:77, Rv-CB:263
  Elegy on the Death of Mme. Anna
    Pavlova. E. Meyerstein.
    Pl-US:119
  Elegy on Thyrza. G. Byron.
    Pa-GTB:199
  Elegy over a Tomb. Lord Herbert.
    Al-VBP:296
  Elegy to the Memory of an
    Unfortunate Woman. A. Pope.
    Rv-CB:511
  Elegy Written in a Country
    Churchyard. T. Gray.
    Al-VBP:559, De-TT:83, Er-FA:462,
    Fe-PL:281, Ha-PO:144, Ma-YA:125,
    Pa-GTB:145, Rv-CB:533
  Elisa, or an Elegy upon the Unripe
    Decease of Sir Antony Irby.
    P. Fletcher. Al-VBP:291
  England Reclaimed. O. Sitwell.
    Al-VBP:1192
  Epitaph for Chaeroneia.
    Aristotle. Pa-SG:7
  The Exequy. H. King. Al-VBP:339,
    No-CL:156
  Extempore Effusion upon the Death
    of James Hogg. W. Wordsworth.
    Rv-CB:648
  For a Dead Lady. E. Robinson.
    Al-VBP:1106, Un-MA:119, Wi-LT:104
  For E. McC. E. Pound. Mo-SD:170
  For Malcolm X. M. Walker.
    Ad-PB:150, Ra-BP:157
  For Nijinsky's Tomb. F. Cornford.
    Pl-US:121
  Funeral Hymn. Pa-SG:9
  A Funerall Song. De-CH:255

  Go Thou to Rome. P. Shelley.
    Gr-CT:379
  Hawthorne — May 23, 1864.
    H. Longfellow. Rv-CB:783
  Heraclitus. W. Cory.
    Al-VBP:973, Co-EL:74, Co-PU:149,
    Hi-WP II:21, Ox-BN:648, Pa-SG:13,
    Pl-ML:143, Rv-CB:875
  His Metrical Vow. J. Graham.
    Al-VBP:425
  In Memoriam. A. Tennyson.
    Ha-PO:133, Ox-BN:494-495,
    Pa-GTB:336
  In Memoriam. Yü Ta-fu. Hs-TC:272
  In Memory of Colonel Charles Young.
    C. Cullen. Ad-PB:86
  In Memory of W. B. Yeats. W. Auden.
    Al-VBP:1228, Er-FA:41, Gr-CT:431,
    Pl-ML:163, Un-MB:459, Wi-LT:468
  John Anderson. K. Douglas.
    Cr-WS:82
  Keats. H. Longfellow. Sh-AP:39
  The Knight's Tomb. S. Coleridge.
    Cl-FC:81, Co-PU:156, Rv-CB:664,
    Sm-LG:272
  The Last Signal. T. Hardy.
    Pl-ML:159
  Little Elegy. X. Kennedy.
    Bo-GJ:234, Co-EL:78, Co-PU:157,
    Mo-BG:162
  Little Elegy. E. Wylie. Ha-LO:92
  Lycidas. J. Milton. Al-VBP:402,
    Gr-CT:250, Hi-WP II:20, Ho-P:69,
    Pa-GTB:55
  The Memory of Boxer Benny (Kid)
    Paret. F. Lima. Hu-PN:587
  Modo and Alciphron. S. Warner.
    Un-MB:375
  Mourning Hymn for the Queen of
    Sunday. R. Hayden.
    Ad-PB:117, Du-SH:105
  A Mourning Letter from Paris.
    C. Rivers. Ra-BP:199
  My Olson Elegy. I. Feldman.
    Ho-P:67
  Obit Page. P. Blackburn. Kh-VA:78
  Ode on the Death of Thomson.
    W. Collins. Rv-CB:538
  Of My Dear Son, Gervase Beaumont.
    J. Beaumont. Al-VBP:293
  On a Dead Child. R. Bridges.
    Al-VBP:1064, Ox-BN:875, Wi-LT:54
  On a Tired Housewife. Ga-S:216,
    Hi-WP I:9, Na-EO:139, Sm-MK:113
  On the Death of a Metaphysician.
    G. Santayana. Al-VBP:1088
  On the Death of a Recluse.
    G. Darley. Rv-CB:755
  On the Death of Anne Brontë
    C. Brontë. Al-VBP:916
  On the Death of Benjamin Franklin.
    P. Freneau. Hi-TL:60

On the Death of Mr. Crashaw.
A. Cowley.   Al-VBP:448
On the Death of Mr. Purcell.
J. Dryden.   Pl-US:78
On the Death of William Edward
Burghardt Du Bois by African
Moonlight and Forgotten Shores.
C. Rivers.   Ad-PB:235
On the Death of William Hervey.
A. Cowley.   Al-VBP:447,
Rv-CB:395
Praise for an Urn.   H. Crane.
Sh-AP:195, Un-MA:521, Wi-LT:394
The Quaker Graveyard in Nantucket.
R. Lowell.   Al-VBP:1248,
Pa-HT:25, Wi-LT:573
A Recluse.   W. de la Mare.
Go-BP:46
Requiem for "Bird" Parker.
G. Corso.   Hu-PN:583
Requiescat.   M. Arnold. Al-VBP:963,
Go-BP:146, Ha-PO:128
Requiescat.   O. Wilde.   Hi-WP I:21,
Ox-BN:895, Un-MB:67
Small Elegy.   M. Weisenthal.
Ls-NY:66
Thyrsis.   M. Arnold.   Ox-BN:637
The Tightrope Walker.   D. Scott.
Sa-B:121
to a poet i knew.   J. Amini.
Ad-PB:291
To an Oak Tree.   W. Scott. Ox-BN:135
To Stella.   Plato.   Al-VBP:759,
Pa-SG:13
To the Memory of Mr. Oldham.
J. Dryden.   Al-VBP:491, Ho-P:276
Tom Bowling.   C. Dibdin.   Co-SS:64,
De-TT:138, Rv-CB:556
Upon the Lines and Life of . . .
Master William Shakespeare.
H. Holland.   No-CL:82
Vaticide.   M. O'Higgins.   Ad-PB:171
A Warning to Abraham Lincoln.
J. Fombona-Pachano.   Bl-FP:29
Water Island.   H. Moss.   Ho-P:199
When Lilacs Last in the Dooryard
Bloom'd.   W. Whitman.
Al-VBP:940, Sh-AP:113, Un-MA:71,
Vi-PP:172
Wordsworth's Grave.   W. Watson.
Ox-BN:910
A Wreath.   Ho Ch'i-fang. Hs-TC:220
A Wreath for One Lost.   H. Vinal.
De-FS:208
ELEPHANTS: see also HUMOR -
ELEPHANTS
And Other Poems.   R. Morgan.
Ma-FW:95
The Big Tent under the Roof.
O. Nash.   Sh-RP:253
A Circus Garland.   R. Field.
Au-SP:124

Cradle Song of the Elephants.
A. del Valle.   Fe-FP:489,
Sh-RP:337
The Elephant.   H. Asquith.
Ar-TP3:79, Au-SP:82, St-FS:83
Elephant.   D. McFadden. Do-WH:41
Elephant.   P. Neruda.   Be-EB:48
The Elephant.   Lo-TY:3
The Elephant.   Lo-TY:11, Rd-OA:121
Elephants Are Different to
Different People.   C. Sandburg.
Un-MA:210
An Elephant Is an Odd Affair.
Z. Gay.   Sh-RP:14
The Elephant Is Slow to Mate.
D. Lawrence.   Wi-LT:221
The Elephant Knocks the Ground.
A. Mitchell.   Sm-MK:166
The Elephant's Trunk. A. Wilkins.
Ar-TP3:78, Au-SP:83
Father Elephant.   Tr-CB:34,
Tr-US I:67
The Four Friends.   A. Milne.
Un-GT:30
The Giraffe.   I. Georgoff. La-GI:55
Holding Hands.   L. Link.
Ar-TP3:78, Au-SP:81, Fe-FP:172,
Ja-PC:16, La-PP:57
Let's Pretend.   J. Tippett.
Mc-AW:80
Making Friends.   V. Lapin. Mo-MI:51
Oliphaunt.   J. Tolkien.   Cl-FC:69,
Li-LC:34
Pete at the Zoo.   G. Brooks.
Gr-EC:37, Ha-LO:8, La-PV:11
The Shape God Wears.   S. Hay.
Un-GT:82
Spiel of the Three Mountebanks.
J. Ransom.   Un-MA:411
Tit for Tat: A Tale.   J. Aikin.
Ox-BC:90
Which Animal Travels Lightest.
Re-RR:30
ELEUSIS, GR.
The Greater Mystery.   J. O'Hara.
Pa-HT:99
ELEVATED RAILROADS: see TRAINS
ELEVATORS: see also HUMOR -
ELEVATORS
The Elevator Man Adheres to Form.
M. Danner.   Ad-PB:137,
Be-MA:87, Hu-PN:161
ELIOT, THOMAS STEARNS: see also
HUMOR - ELIOT, THOMAS STEARNS
Summoned by Bells.   J. Betjeman.
Pl-ML:20
T. S. Eliot.   T. Whitbread.
Ls-NY:143
To T. S. Eliot on His Sixtieth
Birthday.   W. Auden.   Pl-ML:71

ELIZABETH, QUEEN OF BOHEMIA
On His Mistress, the Queen of
Bohemia. H. Wotton.
Al-VBP:222, Pa-GTB:73, Rv-CB:278
ELIZABETH I, QUEEN OF ENGLAND
For Soldiers. H. Gifford.
De-CH:158
The Looking Glass. R. Kipling.
Gr-CC:160, Na-EO:120
A Mirror for Poets. T. Gunn.
Pl-ML:100, Wi-LT:722
Prothalamion. E. Spenser.
Al-VBP:100, Gr-CT:298, Pa-GTB:32
To the Queen. W. Ralegh.
Rv-CB:155
ELK: see DEER
ELM TREES
Dilemma of the Elm. G. Taggard.
Un-MA:480
Elm Trees. R. Sward. St-H:224
The Fate of Elms. R. Francis.
Ls-NY:51
A Proper Place. R. Nye. Co-PU:46
ELOCUTION: see PUBLIC SPEAKING
ELOPEMENTS: see also HUMOR -
ELOPEMENTS
Allen-a-Dale. W. Scott. Co-PT:231
Bill Roy. Fi-BG:206
Earl Brand. Ox-BB:115
The Eve of St. Agnes. J. Keats.
Al-VBP:781, Fe-PL:35, Ox-BN:338
The Gaberlunzie-Man. Ox-BB:626
Katherine Jaffray. Ox-BB:300
Lochinvar. W. Scott. Co-FB:230,
Co-PT:207, Co-RG:33, Er-FA:316,
Fe-FP:504, Ga-FB:54, Gr-EC:132,
Ma-YA:143, Mc-PR:154, Na-EO:133,
Ox-BN:128, Sp-OG:126, Un-GT:134
Lord Ullin's Daughter. T. Campbell.
Co-RG:50, Fe-FP:520, Pa-GTB:182
A Love Story. O. Herford.
Co-PM:103
May Colven. Ma-BB:117, Ox-BB:49
The Skeleton in Armor.
H. Longfellow. Mc-PR:56,
Sp-OG:103, Un-GT:173
A Wedding. Bo-FP:294, Ch-B:114,
De-CH:34
ELSINORE, DEN.: see also HAMLET,
PRINCE
Conducted Tour. E. Swan. Ls-NY:306
ELVERS: see EELS
ELVES: see also HUMOR - ELVES
The Elf and the Dormouse. O. Herford.
Ar-TP3:153, Au-SP:285, Bo-FP:225,
Ch-B:60, Fe-FP:345, Hu-MP:92,
Mc-PR:31, Pa-OM:50, Pe-FB:53,
Th-AS:11, Un-GB:13, Un-GT:15
The Elf Singing. W. Allingham.
Un-GT:15
The Elfin Artist. A. Noyes. Sp-OG:168
Elfin Berries. R. Field. Ag-HE:54

The Elfin Knight.   De-CH:276,
Gr-GB:285, Ma-BB:181
Elfin Song. J. Drake. Co-PM:54
The Elves' Dance. T. Ravenscroft.
De-CH:111, De-TT:50, Fe-FP:373
Elves' Song. B. Jonson. De-TT:148
The Fairies Feast. C. Doughty.
De-CH:124
For a Mocking Voice. E. Farjeon.
Ar-TP3:148, Co-PM:60, De-CH:112
A Goblinade. F. Jaques. Ar-TP3:152
Jackie Faa. Gr-CT:162, Ma-BB:106,
Ox-BB:249
The Little Elf. J. Bangs.
Ar-TP3:153, Au-SP:287, Bo-FP:309,
Br-BC:107, Ch-B:34, Hu-MP:91,
La-PV:75, Mc-WK:106, Pe-FB:60,
Th-AS:10, Un-GB:13, Un-GT:16
Long-Nosed Elf. De-PP:30
Playground of the Pixie. G. Code.
De-FS:62
The Queen of Fairies. Al-VBP:374,
Bo-FP:318, Sm-MK:42
Red in Autumn. E. Gould. St-FS:94
Rufty and Tufty. I. Hempseed.
St-FS:69
Rutterkin. W. Cornish. Co-PM:41
The Seven Ages of Elf-Hood.
R. Field. Br-BC:6
A Surprise. E. Winton. Bo-FP:324
Thomas the Rhymer. Al-VBP:40,
De-CH:119, Fo-OG:3, Gr-CT:175,
Ha-PO:51, Ma-BB:5, Ma-FW:181,
Pa-OM:275, Rv-CB:40, Un-GT:124
The Wife of Bath's Tale.
G. Chaucer. Al-VBP:14
Wise Sarah and the Elf.
E. Coatsworth. Co-PM:36
ELYSIUM
Chorus from Oedipus at Colonus.
R. Fitzgerald. Gr-SS:58
Life after Death. Pindar. Pl-EI:5
The Poet's Paradise. M. Drayton.
Ho-WR:252
Prayer. A. Tennyson.   Go-BP:188
EMANCIPATION PROCLAMATION
Laus Deo! J. Whittier. Sh-AP:42
Little White Schoolhouse Blues.
F. Lennon. Hu-PN:514
The Proclamation. J. Whittier.
Hi-TL:116
EMBROIDERY: see NEEDLEWORK
EMERSON, RALPH WALDO
Emerson. M. Dodge. Se-PR:310
Litany of the Heroes.
V. Lindsay. Tr-MR:166
EMOTIONS
Calm after Storm. F. Yerby.
Bo-AN:138
Dead Fires. J. Fauset. Hu-PN:68
The Eye Penetrates. S. Terry.
Le-M:172
Frustration. Hu Feng. Hs-TC:376

Hope to Keep. A. Pratt. Al-WW:109
In the Spring. Ibycus. Pa-SG:86
Lemons and Apples. M. Neville.
   Ar-TP3:9
My Feelings. P. Thompson. Le-M:35
My Thoughts. S. Gristwood.
   Su-FVI:4
The Passions. W. Collins. Pa-GTB:136
Plaint. Chu Shu Chen. Rx-OH:127
The Shape of the Heart. L. Nicholl.
   Pl-IO:142
Since Feeling Is First. E. Cummings.
   Du-SH:65, Un-MA:478
The Song of the Three Songs.
   I. Minulescu. Mc-AC:43
Stanzas. E. Brontë. Go-BP:27
The Storm. H. Vaughan. Rv-CB:413
EMPERORS: see KINGS AND RULERS
EMPIRE STATE BUILDING, NEW YORK, N.Y.
   Looking at the Empire State
      Building. R. Pomeroy. Ls-NY:243
   Poem from the Empire State.
      J. Jordan. Ra-BP:247
   Rhyme of Rain. J. Holmes.
      La-OC:30, Mc-WK:36
EMUS: see HUMOR - EMUS
ENCHANTMENT: see also CHARMS;
      HUMOR - ENCHANTMENT; MAGIC;
      SATIRE - ENCHANTMENT;
      WITCHES AND WITCHCRAFT
   Abracadabra. D. Livesay. Do-WH:38
   The Adventures of Tom Bombadil.
      J. Tolkien. Li-TU:92
   Behind the Waterfall. W. Welles.
      Ar-TP3:159, Co-PM:170
   La Belle Dame sans Merci. J. Keats.
      Al-VBP:779, Bo-GJ:163, Bo-HF:22,
      De-CH:121, De-TT:200, Er-FA:409,
      Gr-CT:178, Gr-SS:108, Ha-PO:6,
      Hi-WP II:106, Ho-P:80, Mc-WK:8,
      Ni-JP:98, No-CL:65, Ox-BN:376,
      Pa-GTB:193, Rv-CB:735, Sm-LG:217,
      Sm-MK:46, Sp-OG:113, Un-GT:126
   Birthday Gifts. H. Asquith.
      Br-BC:100, Br-SS:49
   The Broomfield Hill. De-CH:292,
      Ox-BB:72
   The Brown Dwarf of Rügen.
      J. Whittier. Co-PM:171
   The Castle of Indolence. J. Thomson.
      Al-VBP:547
   The Castle Yonder. J. Dudley.
      Le-M:62
   Changeling. B. Young. Th-AS:136
   Christabel. S. Coleridge.
      De-CH:318
   A Christmas Legend. O. Herford.
      Co-PM:100
   Crab-Apple. E. Talbot. Ar-TP3:149,
      Bo-FP:328, Br-BC:8
   The Crystal Cabinet. W. Blake.
      De-CH:355, Gr-CC:1, Ox-BN:27,
      Sm-LG:217

Deeply Gone. J. Silkin. De-FS:177
The Demon Lover. Co-PM:201,
   Fo-OG:44, Ma-BB:188, Ma-FW:199,
   Ox-BB:83, Rv-CB:45
The Earl of Mar's Daughter.
   De-CH:290, Fo-OG:21, Ma-BB:146
The Erl-King. J. von Goethe.
   Sp-OG:111
The Fair Young Wife. H. Adam.
   De-FS:7
The Fairies. W. Allingham.
   Al-VBP:974, Bl-OB:92, Bo-FP:314,
   Ch-B:38, Co-PM:19, Co-RG:119,
   De-CH:114, De-TT:50, Er-FA:503,
   Fe-FP:575, Fr-WO:76, Ga-FB:172,
   Gr-CT:157, Gr-EC:160, La-PV:74,
   Li-LC:63, Na-EO:36, Ox-BC:215,
   Pa-OM:279, Pe-FB:50, Rv-CB:877,
   Sm-LG:224, Sp-OG:165
The Fairies. S. Morford. Se-PR:193
The Fairies Feast. C. Doughty.
   De-CH:124
The Fairy Thorn. S. Ferguson.
   De-CH:117, De-TT:197, Pa-OM:271
Goblin Feet. J. Tolkien.
   Co-PM:163, Fe-FP:369
The Goblin's Song. J. Telfer.
   Gr-CT:156
The Great Silkie of Sule Skerrie.
   Gr-CT:206, Gr-GB:282, Ma-BB:18
The Green Gnome. R. Buchanan.
   Co-PT:47
The Happy Townland. W. Yeats.
   Re-TW:126
The Host of the Air. W. Yeats.
   De-CH:295, Li-TU:90
Kemp Oweyne. Fo-OG:13, Ma-BB:33,
   Rv-CB:50
King Henry. Ox-BB:64
King Orfeo. Ma-BB:152, Ox-BB:62
Kubla Khan. S. Coleridge. Mc-WS:36
The Land of Heart's Desire.
   W. Yeats. Al-VBP:1090, Ma-FW:188,
   Pa-HT:162, Un-MB:109
Little Fan. J. Reeves. Co-PM:138
The Loreley. H. Heine. Sp-OG:116,
   Un-GT:137
The Lotus-Eaters. A. Tennyson.
   Al-VBP:847, Cl-FC:14, De-CH:615,
   Er-FA:76, Ga-FB:12, Ox-BN:477,
   Pa-HT:158
Madness One Monday Evening.
   J. Fields. Be-MA:150,
   Hu-NN:78, Li-TU:101
Maiden in the Moor. Ma-BB:82
Midsummer Night. M. Edey. Ha-YA:78
The Milk-White Dove. Gr-CT:159,
   Gr-GB:251
The Mystic Drum. G. Okara.
   Lo-TY:157
The Padda Song. Gr-GB:283
A Piece of Colored Cloud.
   Chien Hsu. Le-MW:35

ENCHANTMENT — cont'd.
  The Pied Piper of Hamelin.
    R. Browning.   Ar-TP3:28, Er-FA:354,
    Ox-BC:173, Sm-LG:173, Un-GT:153
  A Piper.   S. O'Sullivan.   Ar-TP3:13,
    Co-PI:186, Co-PU:131, De-CH:185,
    Fe-FP:465, Hu-MP:147, La-PV:221
  Sam.   W. de la Mare.   Ar-TP3:160,
    Co-PM:46, Co-SS:174, Ga-FB:168,
    Hi-WP I:74, Pa-OM:292, Un-MB:200
  She Wandered Through the Garden Fence.
    K. Reid.   Mo-GR:130
  The Silence of God.   O. Sitwell.
    Mc-WK:151
  The Song of Wandering Aengus.
    W. Yeats.   Ar-TP3:161, Bl-OB:91,
    Bo-GJ:142, Co-BL:165, Co-PM:196,
    De-CH:280, Gr-SS:46, Ha-LO:52,
    Ha-PO:180, Ho-LP:14, Ma-YA:230,
    Mc-WK:7, Mc-WS:33, No-CL:68,
    Re-TW:28, Sm-LG:226, Sm-MK:30,
    Th-AS:200, Un-GT:127, Un-MB:108
  The Stolen Child.   W. Yeats.
    Co-PM:197, Hu-MP:82
  The Tale the Hermit Told.   A. Reid.
    Co-PT:31
  Tam Lin.   Ma-BB:124, Ox-BB:13
  This Palace Standeth in the Air.
    M. Drayton.   De-CH:556
  Thomas the Rhymer.   Al-VBP:40,
    De-CH:119, Fo-OG:3, Gr-CT:175,
    Ha-PO:51, Ho-P:194, Ma-BB:5,
    Ma-FW:181, Pa-OM:275, Rv-CB:40,
    Un-GT:124
  The Twa Magicians.   Ox-BB:51
  Under the Moon.   W. Yeats.   Pa-HT:161
  Who Knows if the Moon's.
    E. Cummings.   Co-PM:42, Ha-LO:47
  The Woods of Westermain.
    G. Meredith.   Mc-WK:204
  Yesterday in Oxford Street.
    R. Fyleman.   Ar-TP3:147, Pe-FB:59
ENCOUNTERS: see MEETINGS (ENCOUNTERS)
ENCYLOPEDIAS: see HUMOR –
    ENCYCLOPEDIAS
END OF THE WORLD: see also HUMOR –
    END OF THE WORLD; JUDGMENT DAY;
    SATIRE – END OF THE WORLD
  Abraham Davenport.   J. Whittier.
    Sp-OG:31
  The Day of Wrath.   St. Columba.
    Ga-S:134
  Doomsday Morning.   G. Taggard.
    Un-MA:480
  Earth.   O. Herford.   Br-SM:67,
    Du-RG:81, Pe-M:84
  The Edda.   Ba-PO:125
  The End of the World.   Bible. O.T.
    Jeremiah.   Ba-PO:48, Ke-PP:2
  The End of the World. G. Bottomley.
    De-CH:390, Un-MB:212

Epitaph for the Race of Man.
    E. Millay.   Sh-AP:187
Fire and Ice.   R. Frost.
    Al-VBP:1133, Er-FA:88, Hi-WP II:3,
    Ho-LP:82, Mo-BG:186, Pe-M:97,
    Un-MA:180, Wi-LT:174
God Lay Dead in Heaven.   S. Crane.
    Ba-PO:125
The Hollow Men.   T. Eliot.
    Un-MA:395, Wi-LT:302
It Is Almost the Year Two Thousand.
    R. Frost.   Ho-TH:47
It May Be like This.   L. Lorraine.
    De-FS:134
The Kraken.   A. Tennyson.
    Ho-WR:215, Ox-BN:473
The Last Chantey.   R. Kipling.
    Sm-LG:335, Un-MB:136
The Last Day and the First.
    T. Weiss.   Br-TC:464, Ca-VT:435
The Last Riot.   V. Howard.
    Jo-VC:8
Nova.   R. Jeffers.   Pe-OA:90
Once by the Pacific.   R. Frost.
    Ca-VT:17, Pa-HT:62, Sm-PT:78,
    Un-MA:184, Wi-LT:173
Premonition.   E. Meudt. De-FS:144
Protagonist.   E. Henrich.
    Tr-MR:238
A Secret Code.   S. Kurahara.
    Sh-AM:78
Two Poems II.   R. Abrams.
    Hu-NN:111
When I Awoke.   R. Patterson.
    Ad-PB:208, Hu-NN:113
The World's Coming to an End.
    J. Bryant.   Ba-HI:45
ENDS: see MEANS AND ENDS
ENDURANCE: see PERSEVERANCE;
    SURVIVAL
ENDYMION
  Endymion.   J. Keats.   Go-BP:161
  Oh, Sleep Forever in the Latmian
    Cave.   E. Millay.   Al-VBP:1195,
    Un-MA:449, Wi-LT:339
ENEMIES: see also SATIRE – ENEMIES
  Battle Hymn.   Tr-US I:101
  The Compassionate Fool.
    N. Cameron.   Pa-GTB:499,
    Rv-CB:1000
  The Duel.   E. Dickinson. Li-TU:172
  He Got Up. Ai Ch'ing. Hs-TC:299
  Herod.   M. Martinet.   Ba-PO:144,
    Cr-WS:123
  How the Days Will Be. Bi-IT:66
  I Did Not Lose My Heart in
    Summer's Even.   A. Housman.
    Cr-WS:107, Wi-LT:67
  In the Tail of the Scorpion.
    G. Taggard.   Ca-VT:194
  The Knight Fallen on Evil Days.
    E. Wylie.   Un-MA:274

Long Feud. L. Untermeyer. Un-MA:306
Love Your Enemy. Y. Iman.
    Lo-TY:258, Ra-BP:293
The Man He Killed. T. Hardy.
    Ba-PO:131, Co-RM:218, Cr-WS:107,
    Er-FA:182, Un-MB:26, Wi-LT:18
No Enemies. C. Mackay. Un-GT:316
A Poem for a Poet. D. Lee. Ad-PB:425
a poem to complement other poems.
    D. Lee. Be-MA:158, Ra-BP:300
A Poison Tree. W. Blake. Co-PM:29,
    Er-FA:64, Ga-S:133, Gr-SS:77,
    Rv-CB:607
Reconciliation. W. Whitman.
    Ba-PO:123
The Scars Remaining. S. Coleridge.
    Ox-BN:161
Song for a Seated Dance: Victory of
    the Mea. Tr-US I:219
Strange Meeting. W. Owen. Cr-WS:85,
    Go-BP:209, Pa-GTB:452, Un-MB:367
The Taking of Life Brings Serious
    Thoughts. Bi-IT:68
To Secure Victory in Battle.
    Al-PI:18
To Those Who Fight. T'ien Chien.
    Hs-TC:322
War Song. Tr-US II:247
When We Meet the Enemy. Ho-SD:31
ENERGY: see FORCE; POWER
ENGINEERS: see also HUMOR -
    ENGINEERS; TECHNOLOGY
Casey Jones. R. Hunter. Mo-GR:52
Casey Jones. Bl-OB:76, Ga-FB:267,
    Hi-TL:141, Mc-WS:155
Engineers. J. Garthwaite.
    Au-SP:142, Ir-BB:41
The Ghost That Jim Saw. B. Harte.
    Br-SM:6, Co-PM:84
The Icosasphere. M. Moore. Pl-IO:84
Jim Bludso. J. Hay. Co-RM:234,
    Er-FA:307, Fi-BG:129, Sp-OG:34
Joseph Mica. Mo-GR:53
Requiem for a River. K. Williams.
    La-RM:40
ENGINES, RAILWAY: see ENGINEERS;
    TRAINS
ENGLAND: see also BALLADS, ENGLISH
    AND SCOTTISH; HUMOR - ENGLAND;
    SATIRE - ENGLAND; and names of
    cities and towns, as LONDON, ENG.,
    and counties, as LINCOLNSHIRE
An Airstrip in Essex. D. Hall.
    Cr-WS:168, En-PC:268, Wi-LT:727
Autumn. V. Scannell. Ma-FW:264,
    To-MP:176
Channel Crossing. G. Barker.
    Pa-GTB:533
The Daisy. A. Tennyson. Ox-BN:489
England. W. de la Mare. Pa-HT:135
England. M. Moore. Un-MA:350

England and America in 1782.
    A. Tennyson. Vi-PP:136
England, 1802. W. Wordsworth.
    Ke-PP:58, Pa-GTB:210
England! The Time Is Come.
    W. Wordsworth. Al-VBP:661
Epitaph on a Jacobite.
    T. Macaulay. Al-VBP:799,
    Cr-WS:56, De-TT:180, Ox-BN:428
Exile. D. Walcott. Sa-B:64
The Garden. A. Marvell.
    Al-VBP:457, Fe-PL:381, Ha-PO:202,
    Pa-GTB:92, Rv-CB:403
I Have Loved England. A. Miller.
    Fe-PL:181
The Island. C. Morley. Pa-HT:122
Jerusalem. W. Blake. Al-VBP:623,
    Gr-CT:295, Ox-BN:42
Lament of the Banana Man.
    E. Jones. To-MP:171
Legsby, Lincolnshire. Gr-GB:174
Letty's Globe. C. Turner.
    Rv-CB:787
London, 1802. W. Wordsworth.
    Ga-FB:225, Ma-YA:140, Ox-BN:80,
    Pa-GTB:211, Pl-ML:110
The Loyal Scot. A. Marvell.
    Al-VBP:461
Milton. W. Blake. Al-VBP:622,
    Ga-FB:223, Ha-PO:206, Hi-FO:251,
    Ke-PP:132, Na-EO:32, Ox-BN:40,
    Pl-EI:162, Rv-CB:612, Sm-LG:135
A Mirror for Poets. T. Gunn.
    Pl-ML:100, Wi-LT:722
O Thou, Whom Chance.
    T. Macaulay. De-CH:598
The Old Buccaneer. C. Kingsley.
    Co-RM:60, Na-EO:48, Un-GT:140
On Wenlock Edge the Wood's in
    Trouble. A. Housman.
    No-CL:131, Ox-BN:921, Pa-GTB:417,
    Un-MB:97
The Properties of the Shires of
    England. Gr-GB:168
Song to the Men of England.
    P. Shelley. Al-VBP:746
Southdown Summer. Sagittarius.
    Pa-HT:135
Spring 1943. R. Fuller. Wi-LT:705
Sunken Evening. L. Lee. Wi-LT:758
This England. W. Shakespeare.
    Ga-FB:223, Ke-TF:255, Ma-YA:66,
    Pa-HT:136
This Landscape, These People.
    Z. Ghose. To-MP:124
Victoria. E. Farjeon. Bl-OB:142
Watchman, What of the Night?
    A. Swinburne. Ho-WR:200
Where a Roman Villa Stood, above
    Freiburg. M. Coleridge.
    Ox-BN:927

ENGLAND — cont'd.
  The Wind at Penistone. D. Davie.
    Wi-LT:680
ENGLAND - COUNTRYSIDE: see also
    HUMOR - ENGLAND - COUNTRYSIDE
  Adlestrop. E. Thomas. Bl-OB:141,
    Bo-GJ:86, De-CH:95, Ma-FW:115,
    No-CL:253, Pa-HT:127
  Bab-Lock-Hythe. L. Binyon.
    Hi-WP II:38, Mo-SD:132
  Beeny Cliff. T. Hardy. Ox-BN:843
  Birds Waking. W. Merwin. Ca-BP:21
  Bredon Hill. A. Housman.
    Cl-DT:44, No-CL:125, Un-MB:98,
    Un-MW:99
  Brumana. J. Flecker. Pa-HT:118
  Burncombe Hollow. W. Barnes.
    Ox-BN:431
  Capturing a Spring. R. Joseph.
    Ls-NY:251
  Chaucer. H. Longfellow.
    No-CL:12, Pl-ML:98, Rv-CB:780,
    Sh-AP:39
  Cleator Moor. N. Nicholson.
    To-MP:44
  The Coracle Fishers.
    R. Bloomfield. Ox-BN:57
  Daisy. F. Thompson. Ga-FB:164,
    Ox-BN:917, Un-MB:77
  The Earthly Paradise. W. Morris.
    Al-VBP:1016
  English Downs. W. de la Mare.
    Cl-DT:65
  Fears in Solitude. S. Coleridge.
    Ox-BN:164
  From My Diary. July 1914. W. Owen.
    Un-MB:364, Wi-LT:356
  Grongar Hill. J. Dyer. Gr-CT:240
  Ha'nacker Hill. H. Belloc.
    Un-MB:170
  Haymaking. E. Thomas. Un-MB:218
  Home-Thoughts from Abroad.
    R. Browning. Bo-FP:230,
    Co-BN:19, Er-FA:266, Fe-FP:460,
    Fe-PL:376, Ga-FB:229, Ke-TF:366,
    Ma-YA:202, Mc-PR:106, Ox-BN:534,
    Pa-HT:117
  Horsey Gap. Gr-GB:172
  If I Should Ever by Chance Grow
    Rich. E. Thomas. Bl-OB:32,
    Bo-GJ:20, De-CH:518, Ox-BC:329,
    Pa-RE:73, Sm-LG:112, Un-MB:215
  In Front of the Landscape.
    T. Hardy. Ox-BN:832
  In Memoriam. A. Tennyson.
    Ox-BN:501
  In Romney Marsh. J. Davidson.
    Al-VBP:1077, Pa-HT:133
  In Terra Nostra. A. Tarbat.
    Go-BP:283
  Keats at Teignmouth. C. Causley.
    Pl-ML:122

  The Licorice Fields of Pontefract.
    J. Betjeman. To-MP:66
  Lines. W. Wordsworth. Ox-BN:66
  London Town. J. Masefield.
    Ma-YA:232
  Mamble. J. Drinkwater.
    Hi-WP I:5
  The Manor Farm. E. Thomas. Cl-FC:58
  March Evening. L. Strong. Un-MB:394
  Market Day. M. Webb. De-CH:133
  Mary, Queen of Scots. R. Burns.
    Hi-FO:125
  Meadowsweet. W. Allingham.
    Ox-BN:675
  Melhill Feast. W. Barnes.
    Ox-BN:433, Rv-CB:766
  My Early Home. J. Clare. Fe-PL:146
  Night on the Downland.
    J. Masefield. Un-MB:226,
    Wi-LT:192
  Ode. R. Fanshawe. Go-BP:19
  Ode to Evening. W. Collins.
    Al-VBP:572, Pa-GTB:143, Rv-CB:537
  The Old Squire. W. Blunt. Mo-SD:110
  The Old Vicarage, Grantchester.
    R. Brooke. Ga-FB:239, Un-MB:326
  On Eastnor Knoll. J. Masefield.
    De-CH:25, Ma-FW:122
  On the South Downs. S. Teasdale.
    Un-MA:267
  On Westwell Downs. W. Strode.
    Rv-CB:362
  The Orchard and the Heath.
    G. Meredith. Ox-BN:691
  Pont and Blyth. Gr-GB:176
  Progress of Evening. W. Landor.
    Ox-BN:186
  Puck's Song. R. Kipling.
    Ga-FB:233, Ox-BC:320, Sm-LG:136
  The Purple Island. P. Fletcher.
    Al-VBP:290
  Rain on South-East England.
    D. Davie. Ls-NY:289
  Reynard the Fox. J. Masefield.
    Al-VBP:1134
  Rivers Arise: A Fragment.
    J. Milton. Gr-CT:238
  Robin Hood and the Monk.
    Al-VBP:37, De-CH:135, Ox-BB:405
  The Rolling English Road.
    G. Chesterton. Na-EO:16,
    Sm-LG:301
  The Roman Road. T. Hardy.
    Bo-GJ:200, Gr-CC:176, Un-MB:32
  Rustic Childhood. W. Barnes.
    Ox-BN:428
  The Scholar Gypsy. M. Arnold.
    Al-VBP:964, Gr-CT:255, Ox-BN:628
  Schoolboys in Winter. J. Clare.
    Fr-WO:82, Rv-CB:732
  Shellbrook. W. Barnes. Ox-BN:434

Shooter's Hill. R. Bloomfield.
Ox-BN:55
The Shrubbery. W. Cowper. Rv-CB:547
The South Country. H. Belloc.
Un-MB:168
The Spring. W. Barnes. Co-BN:36
Spring to Winter. G. Crabbe.
Gr-CT:316
The Spring Walk. T. Miller.
De-TT:32
Stanzas from "Child Harold."
J. Clare. Ox-BN:325
Summer Images. J. Clare.
Gr-CT:117, Ox-BN:318, Rv-CB:716
Sunrise on Rydal Water.
J. Drinkwater. Wi-LT:621
Sussex. R. Kipling. Pa-HT:128
Thyrsis. M. Arnold. Ox-BN:637
A Trampwoman's Tragedy.
T. Hardy. Ox-BN:825
Traveling America. J. Struther.
Br-AF:19
Trees. W. de la Mare. Mc-PR:199
The Voices. Sp-OG:209
The West Wind. J. Masefield.
Er-FA:242, Un-MB:223, Wi-LT:188
Wiltshire Downs. A. Young.
Pa-GTB:465
Winter in the Fens. J. Clare.
Co-BN:190, Ma-FW:4
Wordsworth's Grave. W. Watson.
Ox-BN:910
ENGLAND - GOVERNMENT: see SATIRE -
ENGLAND - GOVERNMENT
ENGLAND - HISTORY AND PATRIOTISM:
see also BORDER WARS; CHARTISM;
HUMOR - ENGLAND - HISTORY AND
PATRIOTISM; MAGNA CARTA;
SATIRE - ENGLAND - HISTORY AND
PATRIOTISM; and names of rulers,
as HENRY V, KING OF ENGLAND, and
persons, as DRAKE, SIR FRANCIS
Admiral Benbow. Co-RM:66,
Rv-CB:420
Admirals All. H. Newbolt. Co-RM:51
The Admiral's Ghost. A. Noyes.
Ar-TP3:22, Co-PM:129
An American in England. E. Wylie.
Pa-HT:121
The Armada. T. Macaulay. Ox-BN:426,
Sm-LG:250
The Armada, 1588. J. Wilson.
Ox-BC:24
At Dunwich. A. Thwaite. To-MP:182
A Ballad for a Boy. W. Cory.
Ox-BC:290
The Ballad of Banners. J. Lehmann.
Ca-MB:96
The Bard. T. Gray. Pa-GTB:115
The Battle of Brunanburh.
A. Tennyson. Hi-FO:63

The Battle of Killikrankie.
W. Aytoun. Hi-FO:163
The Battle of Naseby.
T. Macaulay. Hi-FO:145
The Battle of Sole Bay. Gr-GB:189
Battle of the Baltic. T. Campbell.
Co-RG:46, Hi-FO:193, Pa-GTB:205,
Rv-CB:675
Boadicea. W. Cowper. Hi-FO:56
The Bonny Moorhen. Gr-GB:191
Bristowe Tragedie. Ox-BB:656
The Burial of Sir John Moore at
Corunna. C. Wolfe.
De-TT:139, Er-FA:285, Gr-CT:342,
Hi-FO:198, Ke-TF:165, Pa-GTB:216,
Rv-CB:693, Sp-OG:202
The Charge of the Light Brigade.
A. Tennyson. Er-FA:183,
Fe-FP:564, Ga-FB:206, Hi-FO:238,
Ma-YA:196, Mc-PR:184, Sp-OG:49
Chevy Chase. Al-VBP:43, Ma-BB:97,
Ox-BB:496
Chevy Chase, The Second Fytte.
Ma-BB:101
The Dead Heroes. I. Rosenberg.
Un-MB:352
The Death of Admiral Benbow.
Bl-OB:44, Gr-GB:239, Rv-CB:420
Drake's Drum. H. Newbolt.
Co-SS:58, De-TT:195, Hi-FO:128,
Hi-WP I:68
The Dying Patriot. J. Flecker.
Al-VBP:1156
England. E. Meyerstein.
De-TT:202
England and Switzerland, 1802.
W. Wordsworth. Li-SR:108,
Pa-GTB:209
England in 1819. P. Shelley.
Mo-GR:70
England, My England. W. Henley.
Fe-PL:179, Un-MB:56
The English Succession.
J. Marchant. Ox-BC:61
The Fairies' Farewell. R. Corbet.
Al-VBP:289, De-CH:564, Na-EO:61,
Rv-CB:321, Sm-LG:223
The Fighting Temeraire. H. Newbolt.
Sp-OG:76
For Soldiers. H. Gifford.
De-CH:158
For the Fallen. L. Binyon.
Hi-WP II:24
The Frolic Mariners of Devon.
W. Browne. Gr-CT:218
From the White Cliffs. A. Miller.
Ke-TF:254
The Golden Vanity. Bl-OB:55,
Co-SS:193, De-CH:398, Fo-OG:10,
Ho-WR:128, Rv-CB:438
The Guards Came Through. A. Doyle.
Sp-OG:52

ENGLAND - HISTORY AND PATRIOTISM —
    cont'd.
  The Gunpowder Plot.   Ma-FW:268
  Guy Fawkes Day.   Hi-FO:144,
    Li-LB:161, Mo-MGT:203
  Henry Before Agincourt. J. Lydgate.
    De-CH:179
  Ho, Brother Teig.   Gr-GB:165
  Home-Thoughts from the Sea.
    R. Browning.   Rv-CB:822
  A Horation Ode upon Cromwell.
    A. Marvell.   Al-VBP:459,
    Pa-GTB:51
  I Shall Laugh Purely.   R. Jeffers.
    Wi-LT:263
  I Travell'd among Unknown Men.
    W. Wordsworth.   Ga-FB:224,
    Mc-PR:107, Ox-BN:63, Pa-GTB:180
    Rv-CB:632
  John Dory.   Ma-BB:122
  A Joyful New Ballad.   T. Deloney.
    Al-VBP:87
  King Henry the Fifth.
    W. Shakespeare.   Co-RM:199, 200,
    Ga-FB:195, Ha-PO:255, Ke-TF:54,
    Mc-WS:100
  King John and the Abbot of
    Canterbury.   Sp-OG:147,
    Un-GT:120
  A Lamentation. T. Campion. De-CH:178
  The Land.   R. Kipling.   Ni-JP:134,
    Pa-OM:190, Un-MB:138
  Latimer and Ridley.   W. Wordsworth.
    Hi-FO:118
  The Lion and the Unicorn.
    An-IP:(29), Br-FF:9, Hi-FO:143,
    Ir-BB:270, Li-LB:80, Mo-MGT:197,
    Mo-NR:61, Na-EO:85, Pa-AP:14,
    Wr-RM:56
  London Mourning in Ashes. Hi-FO:154
  Men Who March Away.   T. Hardy.
    Cl-DT:15, De-CH:164, De-TT:137
  The Mound in the Meads.   W. Watson.
    Cr-WS:16
  The Night of Trafalgar.   T. Hardy.
    De-CH:166, Gr-CT:340, Un-MB:28
  The Norfolk Rebellion.   Gr-GB:183
  O Death, Rock Me on Sleep.
    A. Boleyn.   Gr-CT:357
  O What's the Rhyme to Porringer.
    Gr-GB:190
  Ode to Hengist and Hora.
    R. Jeffers.   Gr-SS:173
  Of the Great and Famous.
    R. Hayman.   De-CH:177
  The Other Little Boats.
    E. Shanks.   Hi-FO:267
  The Parklands.   S. Smith. Ca-MB:94
  The Parliament Soldiers. Gr-GB:189
  The Passing of Arthur.
    A. Tennyson.   Ni-JP:158,
    Ox-BN:511

  The Phantom Mail Coach.
    L. Welcome.   Co-PM:167
  A Pict Song. R. Kipling. Hi-FO:47
  Puck's Song.   R. Kipling.
    Ga-FB:233, Ox-BC:320, Sm-LG:136
  The Reeds of Runnymede.
    R. Kipling.   Hi-FO:79
  The Return. R. Kipling. Un-MB:130
  Richard III. W. Shakespeare.
    Hi-FO:102
  Robert of Gloucester's Chronicle.
    Robert of Gloucester. Ma-YA:23
  The Roman Road.   T. Hardy.
    Bo-GJ:200, Gr-CC:176, Un-MB:32
  Rule, Britannia.   J. Thomson.
    Ma-YA:121, Pa-GTB:114
  Screaming Tarn.   R. Bridges.
    Co-PT:26
  The "Shannon" and the "Chesapeake."
    De-TT:134
  Sir Andrew Bartton. Ox-BB:508
  Sir Francis Drake; or Eighty-Eight.
    Gr-GB:185
  The Soldier.   R. Brooke.
    Al-VBP:1179, Cr-WS:57, Er-FA:190,
    Fe-PL:179, Ga-FB:215, Ke-TF:169,
    Sp-OG:208, Un-MB:324, Wi-LT:612
  The Song of the Western Men.
    R. Hawker.   Co-RG:25, Hi-FO:161,
    Na-EO:109, Ox-BN:459, Rv-CB:777
  The Spires of Oxford.   W. Letts.
    Cr-WS:68, Er-FA:190, Fe-PL:178
  To the Lady Margaret Ley.
    J. Milton.   Pa-GTB:73
  Verses Written During the War,
    1756-1763.   T. Mordaunt.
    Rv-CB:544
  The Vicar of Bray.   Al-VBP:608,
    Gr-GB:198
  A War Song to Englishmen.
    W. Blake.   De-CH:157
  The Wars of the Roses. Gr-GB:183
  Watching Post.   C. Day Lewis.
    To-MP:38
  When I Have Borne in Memory.
    W. Wordsworth.   Pa-GTB:211
  Wul 'E Plaize.   De-TT:92
  Ye Mariners of England. T. Campbell.
    Mc-PR:148, Pa-GTB:204, Rv-CB:676
ENGLAND - NAVY: see also ADMIRALS;
    HUMOR - ENGLAND - NAVY
  Admirals All. H. Newbolt. Co-RM:51
  Battle of the Baltic. T. Campbell.
    Co-RG:46, Hi-FO:193, Pa-GTB:205,
    Rv-CB:675
  Cease Now the Talk of Wonders.
    De-CH:595
  1805.   R. Graves.   Co-RM:42,
    Na-EO:17, Sm-LG:155
  The Fighting Temeraire.   H. Newbolt.
    Sp-OG:76
  Messmates. H. Newbolt.   De-CH:167

Ye Mariners of England. T. Campbell.
   Mc-PR:148, Pa-GTB:204, Rv-CB:676
THE ENGLISH: see also HUMOR - THE
   ENGLISH; SATIRE - THE ENGLISH; and
   dialects of the regions of England,
   as DIALECTS, DEVON
   Bring Us In Good Ale. Al-VBP:24,
      Cl-FC:94, De-CH:64
   Colonel Fantock. E. Sitwell.
      Un-MB:334
   Elegy in a Country Churchyard.
      G. Chesterton. Al-VBP:1122,
      Mc-WS:85, Na-EO:85, Un-MB:209
   England Reclaimed. O. Sitwell.
      Al-VBP:1192
   The English Are Frosty. A. Miller.
      Fe-PL:127
   Epitaph. J. Heath-Stubbs. To-MP:74
   The Fine Old English Gentleman.
      De-CH:63
   From the White Cliffs. A. Miller.
      Ke-TF:254
   Lady Maisry. Ox-BB:295
   The Land. R. Kipling. Ni-JP:134,
      Pa-OM:190, Un-MB:138
   London, 1802. W. Wordsworth.
      Ga-FB:225, Ma-YA:140, Ox-BN:80,
      Pa-GTB:211, Pl-ML:110
   McNaughton. Ox-BB:304
   The Mayors. W. Blake. De-CH:62
   The People of Blakeney. Gr-GB:175
   The Perplexing Battler.
      H. Phillips. Ke-TF:308
   The Phantom Mail Coach. L. Welcome.
      Co-PM:167
   The South Country. H. Belloc.
      Un-MB:168
   Thirty Bob a Week. J. Davidson.
      Er-FA:271, Ox-BN:900
ENGLISH BALLADS: see BALLADS,
   ENGLISH AND SCOTTISH
ENGLISH LANGUAGE: see also HUMOR -
   ENGLISH LANGUAGE
   America. S. Dobell. Vi-PP:17
ENTERTAINMENTS: see AMUSEMENTS
ENTREATIES: see also COAXING
   Air: Catbird Singing. R. Creeley.
      Ho-P:41
   The Appeal. E. Brontë. Go-BP:149,
      Ox-BN:599
   Break of Day. J. Donne. Un-MW:76
   Come Down, O Maid. A. Tennyson.
      Al-VBP:860, Go-BP:124, Ox-BN:488,
      Rv-CB:798
   Come Hither, My Dear One. J. Clare.
      Co-BL:85
   Come, My Celia. B. Jonson.
      Ga-FB:35, Un-MW:16
   Come Night, Come Romeo.
      W. Shakespeare. Co-BL:103
   The Enchantment. T. Otway.
      Al-VBP:506

Geordie. Ox-BB:557
A Husband's Song. Bi-IT:83
Invocation of a Poet Seeking
   Inspiration, I, II. Tr-US II:28
Jerusalem. W. Blake. Gr-CT:295,
   Ox-BN:42
Johnnie Armstrang. Ox-BB:520
Longing. M. Arnold. Fe-PL:97,
   Go-BP:129, Rv-CB:867
Nexnox, Nexnox! Ho-SD:59
O Lord, Save We Beseech Thee.
   Me-PH:66
O, Open the Door to Me, O!
   R. Burns. Sm-LG:358
Ode: The Spirit Wooed. R. Dixon.
   Ox-BN:751
Please Don't Kill My Antelope.
   Le-OE:49
A Rhyme for Shrove Tuesday.
   Cl-FC:93
rusty come home damn you. D. Witt.
   Ad-II:34
A Slant of Sun. S. Crane.
   Sh-AP:145, Wi-LT:120
The Song of the Rain. Le-OE:71
Supplication. Hu P'in-ch'ing.
   Pa-MV:104
This Hour. O. La Grone.
   Hu-NN:37, Hu-PN:327
Thou Art Indeed Just, Lord, if I
   Contend. G. Hopkins.
   Pa-GTB:397, Pl-EI:88, Un-MB:39,
   Wi-LT:50
To the Muse. Hu P'in-ch'ing.
   Pa-MV:103
Two Fragments of Songs, I.
   Br-MW:48
When the Assault Was Intended to
   the City. J. Milton.
   Co-RG:23, Pa-GTB:62
Women's Song. Tr-US I:46
Young Men, Help Me. Sitting Bull.
   Da-SC:113
ENVY: see also JEALOUSY
   Adam and Eve. J. Milton. No-CL:52
   The Bishop Orders His Tomb at
      Saint Praxed's Church.
      R. Browning. Al-VBP:895,
      Mo-GR:57
   The City. E. Jarrett. Sc-TN:110
   The Cure. W. Williams. Pl-ML:28
   Envy. C. and M. Lamb. Ox-BC:140
   Envy. Y. Yevtushenko. Ma-FW:139
   The Ne'er-Do-Well. A. Sampley.
      Du-RG:61
   O for Doors to Be Open. W. Auden.
      Al-VBP:1226
   An Old Story. E. Robinson.
      Un-MA:118
   To Poets. W. Landor. Al-VBP:710
   Verses. R. Bentley. Al-VBP:510

EPICUREANISM
An Epicurean Ode. J. Hall.
  Gr-SS:49
EPIGRAMS: see also PROVERBS; WIT
An Argument Against the Empirical
  Method. W. Stafford.
  Du-SH:186
Boston. J. Bossidy. Un-GT:236
Critics. Martial. Mc-PR:21
Day-Dreamer. Ar-TP3:209
Dust to Dust. T. Hood. Br-SM:156,
  Co-FB:317, Un-GT:236
An Epigram. S. Coleridge.
  Un-GT:235
Epigram. A. Kreymborg. Co-BL:50
Epigram. Su Tung P'o. Rx-OH:84
Epigrams. J. Cunningham. Ca-VT:329
Humility. R. Herrick. Hi-WP I:138,
  Un-GT:306
Inscribed on the Collar of a Dog.
  A. Pope. Bo-FP:132, Ch-B:73,
  Gr-CT:122, Rv-CB:508, Un-GT:236
Marriage. Gr-GB:151
Ode to Maecenas. Horace.
  Pa-SG:173, Un-GT:236
On a Clergyman's Horse. Un-GT:239
On His Books. H. Belloc. Un-MB:172
A Penguin. O. Herford. Co-FB:25
Poor South. . . . J. Coogler.
  Co-FB:301
Praying and Preaching. Un-GT:238
The Secret Sits. R. Frost.
  Au-SP:184, Ha-LO:61
Senex to Matt. Prior. J. Stephen.
  Co-FB:485
Sir, I Admit Your General Rule.
  M. Prior. Co-FB:338, Pl-ML:137,
  Un-GT:236
Speak No Evil. Un-GT:238
The Spring Waters. Ping Hsin.
  Hs-TC:24
Star Guides. W. Stafford. Du-SH:186
Swan Song. S. Coleridge. Ch-B:88,
  Na-EO:101, Pl-US:60, Un-GT:236
Three Epigrams. J. Cunningham.
  Un-MA:615
Tit for Tat. Mc-WS:93
War. Samuel the Prince. Me-PH:57
Wisdom. Tr-CB:17
EPIPHANY
Ballad of the Epiphany. C. Dalmon.
  Pa-OM:360
Epiphany. R. Heber. Ke-TF:49,
  Se-PR:34
Here's to Thee. Bl-OB:139,
  Bo-FP:144, Ch-B:100, Mo-MGT:191,
  Mo-TB:120, Tu-WW:17
Twelfth Night. P. Hartnoll.
  Ga-S:110
Twelfth Night Carol. Bo-FP:206,
  Se-PR:35

Twelfth Night Song of the Camels.
  E. Coatsworth. Bo-HF:72,
  Fe-FP:171
The Twelve Days of Christmas.
  Er-FA:518, La-PH:41, Li-LB:119,
  Mo-MGT:50, On-TW:46, Sh-RP:27
Two Apple-Howling Songs, Surrey.
  Bo-FP:143
What Will Be Our Twelve, Boys.
  De-CH:629
EPITAPHS: see also HUMOR -
  EPITAPHS; SATIRE - EPITAPHS
Anonymous Gravestone. E. Kästner.
  Co-EL:77
As Toilsome I Wander'd Virginia's
  Woods. W. Whitman. Al-VBP:937,
  Sp-OG:205
Asleep, Beneath This Humble Stone.
  De-CH:653
Beneath This Yew. Co-PU:155
A Bird's Epitaph. M. Armstrong.
  De-CH:95, Re-BS:55
Braddock's Fate, with an Incitement
  to Revenge. S. Tilden. Hi-TL:33
Buckskin Sam's Tribute to Texas
  Jack. Fi-BG:174
A Dead Liar Speaks. M. Lewis.
  Un-GT:237
Do Pious Marble. F. Quarles.
  De-CH:652
Elegy for a Dead Soldier.
  K. Shapiro. Hi-TL:213, Wi-LT:541
Elegy Written in a Country Churchyard.
  T. Gray. Al-VBP:559, De-TT:83,
  Er-FA:462, Fe-PL:281, Ha-PO:144,
  Ma-YA:125, Pa-GTB:145, Rv-CB:533
Elizabeth. S. Warner. Un-MB:373
Epitaph. L. Abercrombie.
  Al-VBP:1147, Un-MB:259
Epitaph. A. Comfort. Un-MB:520
Epitaph. J. Cunningham. Co-EL:81,
  En-PC:106
An Epitaph. W. de la Mare.
  Al-VBP:1118, Co-PU:158, Un-MB:197,
  Wi-LT:132
The Epitaph. T. Gray. Mc-PR:201
An Epitaph. S. Hawes. Al-VBP:34,
  De-CH:643, Go-BP:234, Gr-CT:382,
  Rv-CB:72
Epitaph. R. Richardson. Fe-PL:285
Epitaph. R. Southey. Ox-BN:181
Epitaph. E. Wylie. Un-MA:280
Epitaph. Ba-PO:72
Epitaph for a Bigot. D. Johnson.
  Hu-PN:226
Epitaph for a Concord Boy.
  S. Young. Mc-WK:164
Epitaph for a Godly Man's Tomb.
  R. Wild. Gr-CT:379, Rv-CB:377
Epitaph for a Lighthouse-Keeper's
  Horse. J. Morton. Co-PU:156

Epitaph for a Negro Woman.
O. Dodson.   Hu-PN:301
Epitaph for a Pet.   F. Rodman.
Ke-TF:327
Epitaph for a Timid Lady.
F. Cornford.   Co-EL:85
Epitaph Intended for Sir Isaac
Newton.   A. Pope.   Al-VBP:542,
Pl-IO:157
Epitaph of a Faithful Man.
R. Mezey.   Co-EL:79
Epitaph on a Dog.   Gr-EC:86
Epitaph on a Jacobite.
T. Macaulay.   Al-VBP:799,
Cr-WS:56, De-TT:180, Ox-BN:428
Epitaph on a Tyrant.   W. Auden.
Co-EL:145, Ho-LP:90, Pe-M:69
Epitaph on an Army of Mercenaries.
A. Housman.   Al-VBP:1080
Epitaph on Dr. Johnson.
S. Jenyns.   Co-EL:69
Epitaph on Elizabeth L.H. B. Jonson.
Al-VBP:234, Ho-LP:86
An Epitaph on His Grandfather.
T. Shipman.   Rv-CB:470
Epitaph on Lady Ossory's Bullfinch.
H. Walpole.   Gr-CT:109, Rd-OA:114
An Epitaph on Salathiel Pavey.
B. Jonson.   Al-VBP:233, Ha-PO:131
Epitaph on Sir John Vanbrugh.
A. Evans.   Al-VBP:521, Co-FB:132
An Epitaph on the Admirable
Dramatic Poet, William
Shakespeare.   J. Milton.
Al-VBP:387, No-CL:82
Epitaph on the Lady Mary Villiers.
T. Carew.   Al-VBP:350
An Epitaph upon the Celebrated
Claudy Philips, Who Died Very
Poor.   S. Johnson.   Pl-US:79,
Rv-CB:527
An Epitaph upon the Right Honorable
Sir Philip Sidney.   F. Greville.
Ho-P:270
Epitaphium Citharistriae.
V. Plarr.   Al-VBP:1086
Epitaphs for Horses.   Fi-BG:98
Even Such Is Time.   W. Raleigh.
Al-VBP:97, De-CH:644, Ga-S:219,
Gr-BT:167, Gr-CT:381, Hi-WP II:169,
Na-EO:94
The Fancy Kid.   Fi-BG:56
For a Poet.   C. Cullen. Ab-MO:109,
Hu-PN:229, Lo-TY:234, Th-AS:197
For a Virgin Lady.   C. Cullen.
Un-MA:571
For an Epitaph at Fiesole.
W. Landor.   Ox-BN:195
For John Keats, Apostle of Beauty.
C. Cullen.   Ad-PB:91, Bo-AN:88

For My Grandmother.   C. Cullen.
Ad-PB:91, Bo-AN:88, ·Ca-VT:241,
Un-MA:571
For Paul Laurence Dunbar.
C. Cullen.   Ad-PB:91, Bo-AN:89,
Bo-HF:141
A Form of Epitaph.   L. Whistler.
Pa-GTB:532
Four Epitaphs.   S. Warner.
Un-MB:371
Four Texas Train Robbers.   Fi-BG:55
The Funeral of Martin Luther King,
Jr.   N. Giovanni.   Ad-BO:30,
Ra-BP:323
Gabriel John.   Rv-CB:426
Here I Lie at the Chancel Door.
Br-SM:165, Un-GT:239
Here Lies. . . .   Un-GT:237
Here Lies Father, Mother, Sister,
and I.   Un-GT:239
Here Lies Me and My Three
Daughters.   Un-GT:239
Here Lies the Body of Jonathan
Pound.   Un-GT:239
If You Should Go.   C. Cullen.
Bo-HF:32
In Memory of Ann Jones.   D. Thomas.
Un-MB:501
An Inscription by the Sea.
E. Robinson.   Co-EL:68, Co-PU:153,
Co-SS:179, Gr-CT:231
Jim Genung.   Fi-BG:55
Jno Brinlyes Body Here Doth Ly.
De-CH:653
John Bun.   Br-SM:55, Un-GT:239
John Fitzgerald Kennedy.
J. Masefield.   Vi-PP:223
King Charles upon the Scaffold.
A. Marvell.   Gr-CT:378
Lines for a Dead Poet.   D. Ferry.
Pl-ML:166
Lo, Huddled Up Together Lye.
De-CH:653
Manhattan Epitaphs: Lawyer.
A. Kreymborg.   La-OC:60
Margaret Love Peacock for Her
Tombstone, 1826.   T. Peacock.
Ox-BN:237
Minor Owens.   Fi-BG:55
Near to This Stone.   De-CH:654
A New England Bachelor.
R. Eberhart.   Un-MA:589
The Nonpareil's Grave.
M. McMahon.   Mo-SD:76
Now Full Twelve Years Twice-Told.
De-CH:639
O, Lift One Thought.
S. Coleridge.   De-CH:254
On a Dentist.   Un-GT:238
On a Doctor Named Isaac Letsome.
Co-PU:122, Un-GT:238

EPITAPHS — cont'd.
On a Man Named Meredith. Un-GT:238
On a Thieving Locksmith. Un-GT:238
On Ben Jonson. S. Godolphin.
  Rv-CB:383
On Charles II. J. Wilmot.
  Ha-PO:59
On Keats. P. Shelley. Pl-ML:151
On Leslie Moore. Un-GT:238
On Martha Snell. Bl-OB:154, Un-GT:239
On Prince Frederick. Un-GT:238
On Richard Dent, Landlord. Un-GT:238
On Skugg. B. Franklin. Un-GT:237
On Stubborn Michael Shay. Un-GT:239
On Susan Pattison. Rv-CB:416
On the Army of Spartans, Who Died
  at Thermopylae. Simonides of
  Ceos. Gr-CT:378
On the Countess Dowager of Pembroke.
  W. Browne. Al-VBP:325, Rv-CB:348
On the Death of Sir Thomas Wyatt.
  H. Howard. Rv-CB:101
On the University Carrier.
  J. Milton. Sm-LG:272
On Thomas Carew. Rv-CB:415
Padraic O'Conaire, Gaelic Storyteller.
  F. Higgins. Co-PI:63
A Placid Man's Epitaph. T. Hardy.
  Un-MB:34
Readen ov a Head-Stwone. W. Barnes.
  De-CH:264
Requiem. R. Stevenson. Al-VBP:1071,
  Bo-HF:157, Cl-FC:59, Fe-PL:286,
  Ga-FB:152, Ha-PO:138, Hu-MP:77,
  Ma-YA:220, Mc-WK:206, Ox-BN:892,
  Sm-MK:216, Sp-OG:279, Un-GT:237,
  Un-MB:59
A Robin's Epitaph. S. Rogers.
  Rv-CB:627
Slim Cunning Hands. W. de la Mare.
  Co-EL:80
Three Fingered Black Jack. Fi-BG:56
The Tragical History of Doctor
  Faustus: Epilogue. C. Marlowe.
  Al-VBP:179
Twin Epitaph. M. Katz. Ls-NY:17
Under Ben Bulben. W. Yeats.
  Pl-ML:30, Wi-LT:96
Upon a Child That Died. R. Herrick.
  De-CH:255, Sm-MK:211
Upon the Death of Sir Albert
  Morton's Wife. H. Wotton.
  Al-VBP:223, Hi-WP II:18,
  No-CL:159, Rv-CB:277
Weep Not for Her. De-CH:640
EQUALITY: see also HUMOR - EQUALITY;
  SATIRE - EQUALITY; WOMEN - EQUAL
  RIGHTS
  After They Have Tired of the
  Brilliance of Cities. S. Spender.
  Wi-LT:497

All Things Come Alike to All.
  Bible. O.T. Ecclesiastes.
  Me-PH:32
All Things Wait upon Thee.
  C. Rossetti. Sp-OG:280
Aspiration. M. de Andrade.
  Lo-TY:82
Color - Caste - Denomination.
  E. Dickinson. Pl-EI:159
Common Dust. G. Johnson.
  Ad-PB:22, Bo-AN:20, Lo-TY:209
Dark Symphony I. M. Tolson.
  Be-MA:20, Bo-AN:37, Hu-PN:136
An Equal. Wr-RM:107
The Glories of Our Blood and State.
  J. Shirley. Al-VBP:347, Ga-S:30,
  Gr-CC:107, Gr-CT:350, Ke-PP:30,
  Ni-JP:121, Pa-GTB:61, Rv-CB:360
I Am Rich. Do-CH:(18), Le-OE:122
I Would Like to Hiss This Poem.
  M. Isanos. Mc-AC:119
In the Dark None Dainty.
  R. Herrick. Co-EL:92
International Cemetery.
  Tsang K'o-chia. Hs-TC:279
It Is Not Now. Ho-SD:64
A Net to Snare the Moonlight.
  V. Lindsay. Fe-PL:420
Of Death. S. Harding. Rv-CB:458
Paternal. E. Wilson. Hu-PN:370
Poem to Negro and White.
  M. Bodenheim. Hu-PN:511
The Second Sermon on the Warpland.
  G. Brooks. Ad-PB:163, Ra-BP:171
The Tod's Hole. Gr-GB:320
The Weaker the Wine. Su Tung P'o.
  Rx-OH:72
EQUINOX
  The Equinox. H. Longfellow.
  De-TT:164
ERASMUS, DESIDERIUS
  The Sacred Order. M. Sarton.
  Pl-IO:155
ERICSON, LEIF
  The Story of Vinland. S. Lanier.
  Hi-TL:9
ERIE, LAKE
  Autumn Squall - Lake Erie.
  L. Russo. Br-AF:185
  The Great Lakes Suite, V.
  J. Reaney. Do-WH:52
ERIE CANAL
  The Erie Canal. Br-AF:66, Sh-RP:78
ERIVAN, ARMENIA: see YEREVAN,U.S.S.R.
ERLKING
  The Erl-King. J. von Goethe.
  Sp-OG:111
  Sir Olaf. J. von Herder.
  Co-PM:97, Sp-OG:108
ERMINES: see WEASELS

ERRORS: see also HUMOR - ERRORS
    From a Slip of the Foot.
        B. Franklin.   Un-GT:25
ESCALATORS: see STAIRWAYS
ESCAPE: see also HUMOR - ESCAPE;
    SATIRE - ESCAPE
    Ah . . . to the Villages!
        T. McGrath.   St-H:128
    American Nights.   R. Lattimore.
        Ha-TP:24
    And Space and Time.   V. Kovshin.
        Bo-RU:48
    Archie of Cawfield.   Ma-BB:20
    Ashima.   Hs-TC:447
    At Rest in the Blast.   M. Moore.
        Un-MA:355
    Avoidances.   R. Welburn.   Ad-PB:466
    The Ballad of Minepit Shaw.
        R. Kipling.   Co-PT:49
    The Bearer of Evil Tidings.
        R. Frost.   Rv-CB:968
    Bermudas.   A. Marvell.   Al-VBP:455,
        De-CH:362, Gr-CT:277, Hi-TL:17,
        Pa-GTB:103, Rv-CB:399, Sm-LG:296
    The Birdcage.   C. Aiken.   Re-BS:26
    Bremerton, January 18, 1969.
        A. Pratt.   Al-WW:99
    Captain Bover.   Gr-GB:238
    The Cave.   G. Dresbach.
        La-RM:35, Pe-SS:42
    The Child in School.   Le-MW:106
    Chorus.   W. Auden.   Un-MB:455
    The Coming. T. Matthews.
        Sa-B:232
    Concrete Trap.   E. Coatsworth.
        Co-BBW:41, Mo-BG:196
    Dance Song of Death.   Tr-US II:3
    The Dark Angel.   L. Johnson.
        Pa-GTB:401, Un-MB:154
    The Day I Lay Myself Down.
        P. Mayer.   St-H:131
    The Dreamer.   W. Childress.
        Du-SH:48, Pe-SS:41
    Drumdelgie.   Gr-GB:210
    Earth and Sea.   A. Pushkin.
        Pa-SG:368
    Escape.   G. Johnson.   Ad-PB:22
    Escape.   T. McGrath.   St-H:123
    The Escape. M. Van Doren.   Un-MA:468
    Escape.   E. Wylie.   Re-TW:120,
        Sh-RP:114, Un-MA:276
    Escape the Ghettos of New York.
        V. Howard.   La-IH:22
    Even from War.   Ho-SD:56
    Evening in the Village. Lu Yu.
        Rx-OH:107
    Exodus.   Caedmonian Poems.
        Ma-YA:10
    Fable for when There's No Way Out.
        M. Swenson.   Pe-M:82

    Fleeing to Safety.   R. Chettur.
        Le-M:175
    Flight.   J. Tate.   La-OC:106
    Flight of the Sparrows.
        M. Zaturenska.   Ha-TP:20
    A Gest of Robyn Hode, The Fifth
        Fytte.   Ox-BB:464
    Glimpse.   P. Lomax.   Ad-PB:503
    Halfway Down.   A. Milne.   Fe-FP:10,
        Li-LC:37
    The Harlem Dancer.   C. McKay.
        Ra-BP:59
    Harriet Tubman.   M. Walker.
        Hu-PN:320
    Haven.   A. Baconsky.   Mc-AC:134
    Herve Riel.   R. Browning.
        Co-SS:183, Pa-OM:161, Sp-OG:67
    Hobie Noble.   Ox-BB:572
    I Run, I Hide.   P. Sclafani.
        Me-WF:63
    I Wish I Could Fly.   S. Hughes.
        Me-WF:79
    I'd Leave.   A. Lang.   Fe-FP:12
    Jack and Dinah Want Freedom.
        Ra-BP:6
    Jock o' the Side.   Ox-BB:567
    John Brown's Body.   S. Benét.
        Al-VBP:1208
    Katherine Jaffray.   Ox-BB:300
    Kinmont Willie.   Ox-BB:559
    The Knight's Leap.   C. Kingsley.
        Co-PT:230
    Missing.   A. Milne.   Bo-FP:15,
        Co-IW:43, La-PP:61, La-PV:116,
        Pe-FB:9
    The Mood.   Q. Prettyman.   Ad-PB:260
    My Polish Grandma.   E. Field.
        Ho-P:73
    Northboun'.   L. Holloway.   Hu-PN:257
    O for the Wings of a Dove.
        Euripides.   Go-BP:155, Pa-SG:175
    Old Susan.   W. de la Mare.
        Se-PR:306, Un-MB:198
    On a Friend's Escape from Drowning
        off the Norfolk Coast.   G. Barker.
        To-MP:67
    The Paradox.   P. Dunbar.   Ad-PB:11
    Pinned Down. P. Horgan.   Cr-WS:86
    Poem for My Family.   J. Jordan.
        Ra-BP:245
    The Ponies.   W. Gibson.   Co-BBW:152,
        Mc-WK:74
    Portrait of a Certain Gentleman.
        S. Hay.   Ls-NY:146
    Primitives.   D. Randall. Ra-BP:139
    The Quiet Flower.   J. Johnson.
        Tr-MR:221
    The Rabbit.   A. Brownjohn.
        To-MP:109
    The Rabbits.   Bo-FP:75

ESCAPE — cont'd.
  Recitative - A Lakeshore Poem.
    M. Kaneko. Sh-AM:64
  Refugee. N. Madgett. Hu-PN:379
  The Road to Pengya. Tu Fu. Ho-P:75
  The Room. C. Day Lewis. En-PC:58
  Runagate Runagate. R. Hayden.
    Ad-PB:120, Be-MA:61, Hu-PN:293,
    Jo-SA:38, Ra-BP:128
  The Runaway Slave. W. Whitman.
    Hu-PN:467, Kr-OF:39, Un-MA:49
  The Secret Cavern. M. Widdemer.
    Fe-FP:11, Hu-MP:43, Sh-RP:110
  The Shakespearean Bear.
    A. Guiterman. Na-EO:76
  She's Leaving Home. The Beatles.
    Pe-SS:94
  The Silver Fish. S. Silverstein.
    Co-SS:178
  Solitude. A. Milne. Li-LC:14
  Somewhere. W. de la Mare. Fe-FP:8
  Song of a Fabulous Heroine Whose
    Lover Has Escaped from Captivity
    in Tonga. Tr-US II:29
  Song of the Night at Daybreak.
    A. Meynell. De-CH:444
  Song to a Runaway Slave. Ra-BP:8
  There's a Fire in the Forest.
    W. Ross. Do-WH:57
  This Old Countryside. M. Fuller.
    Ba-HI:135
  To a Fugitive. J. Wright.
    Ha-TP:40, Ho-TH:92
  To a Mole. L. Darcy. Ls-NY:198
  The Treehouse. J. Emanuel.
    Ad-PB:178, Bo-AN:174, Bo-HF:178,
    Hu-NN:21, Ra-BP:190
  Uvlunuaq's Song. Tr-US I:16
  Visit to the Monastery of Good
    Omen. Lu Chi. Rx-LT:30
  What Did You See? J. Perez.
    Me-WF:30
  Where? K. Patchen. Wi-LT:786
  Why Should I Care for the Men of
    Thames? W. Blake. Gr-CT:304,
    Rv-CB:603
  Wild Negro Bill. Ra-BP:7
  Wooden Ships. D. Crosby. Mo-GR:108
ESENIN, SERGEI ALEKSANDROVICH
  Letter to Yesenin. S. Yesenin.
    Ca-MR:108
  To Yesenin. J. Rubinstein.
    Ho-TY:239
ESKIMOS: see also DOG SLEDS; HUMOR -
    ESKIMOS; INDIANS OF NORTH
    AMERICA - VERSE - ESKIMO
  Bring Hither Your Wooden Ornament.
    Ma-BH:19
  Bring Out Your Hair Ornaments.
    Le-IB:96
  Caribou Hunting. Le-IB:71,
    Ma-BH:24, Tr-US I:13

  Come in Kayaks. Le-IB:115
  Dance Song. Le-IB:78
  Dead Man's Song. Ma-BH:31,
    Tr-US I:21
  The Dream. Le-IB:83
  Far, Far Will I Go. Ma-BH:30
  The Great Sea. Bi-IT:124, Ma-BH:18
  Hard Times, Dearth Times. Ma-BH:13
  He Is Round. Le-IB:62
  The Heavenly Song. Le-IB:124
  Hunting Songs, I. Walrus Hunting.
    Ma-BH:17, Tr-US I:12
  I Am Ashamed. Le-IB:74
  I Am Joyful. Da-SC:37, Le-IB:113
  I Sighted a Bear. Ma-BH:14
  I Want to Laugh. Ho-SD:69, Le-IB:72
  I Will Walk. Le-IB:36, Ma-BH:8
  The Kayak. Bo-FP:179, Ch-B:71,
    Fe-FP:115, Sh-RP:307
  Magic Prayer. Le-IB:30, Le-OE:19,
    Ma-BH:7, Tr-US I:9
  My Arms, They Wave High in the Air.
    Le-OE:33
  My Song Was Ready. Le-IB:79
  My Thoughts Went Constantly.
    Le-IB:99
  Old Dance Song. Tr-US I:10
  Religious Hymn to Be Sung Wearing
    a Head Decoration. Le-IB:95,
    Ma-BH:15, Tr-US I:20
  Sadness. Le-IB:115
  Song of a Dead One. Le-IB:122
  Song of the Old Woman. Le-IB:107
  There Is Fear. Ma-BH:11,
    Tr-US I:24
  There Is Joy. Do-WH:64, Ho-SD:76,
    Le-OE:104, Ma-BH:10
  Those Game Animals. Le-IB:75
  To Our Babies, I, II. Le-IB:60
  Ulivfak's Song of the Caribou.
    Le-IB:112
  When I Am a Man. Da-SC:9,
    Ho-SD:56
  When I Chance to Think of My
    Childhood. Ma-BH:29
  When I Was Young. Le-OE:119,
    Ma-BH:26
  The Wicked Little Kukook. Le-IB:87
  The Wind Has Wings. Do-WH:54
THE ESTABLISHMENT: see also SATIRE -
    THE ESTABLISHMENT
  The Daily Grind. F. Johnson.
    Bo-AN:25
  Music and Drum. A. MacLeish.
    Ho-TH:59, Tr-MR:186
ETERNITY: see also FUTURE LIFE;
    HUMOR - ETERNITY; IMMORTALITY
  Auguries of Innocence. W. Blake.
    Al-VBP:621, Ch-B:36, Co-BBW:278,
    Er-FA:69, Ga-FB:96, Ma-YA:130,
    Ox-BN:28, Pl-IO:5, Sh-RP:76,
    Sm-LG:67, Sm-MK:220, Un-GT:305

The Chariot. E. Dickinson.
  Ma-FW:164, Rv-CB:911, Sh-AP:130,
  Tr-MR:271, Un-MA:102, Wi-LT:13
The Eternal Image. R. Pitter.
  Un-MB:404
Eternity. W. Blake. Ox-BN:26
Eternity's Low Voice. M. Van Doren.
  Pl-EI:122
Exultation Is the Going. E. Dickinson.
  Rv-CB:906, Sh-AP:127
The Eye. R. Jeffers. Wi-LT:266
Holderlin. D. Schwartz. Tr-MR:285
Just Lost, When I Was Saved!
  E. Dickinson. Ho-P:22
Leave Me, O Love. P. Sidney.
  Al-VBP:130, De-CH:641, Ha-PO:168
Longing. S. Teasdale. Sm-PT:161
Our Journey Had Advanced.
  E. Dickinson. Mo-GR:127, Wi-LT:12
The Road. E. Muir. Al-VBP:1172,
  Er-FA:91, Wi-LT:246
Song. E. Sitwell. Un-MB:337
A Song in Passing. Y. Winters.
  Ca-VT:232
Time and Eternity. J. Bunyan.
  Ho-WR:248
Toward Avernus. H. Vinal. De-FS:210
The Tragical History of Doctor
  Faustus. C. Marlowe. Al-VBP:177,
  Gr-CT:151, Ma-FW:161
The World. H. Vaughan. Al-VBP:467,
  Ga-FB:93, Ga-S:6, Ho-LP:102,
  Pl-IO:7, Rv-CB:410
ETIQUETTE: see also HUMOR -
  ETIQUETTE; MANNERS AND CUSTOMS
Canterbury Tales (Prologue).
  G. Chaucer. Al-VBP:7, 9, 10, 11
The Cat's Tea-Party. F. Weatherley.
  Ar-TP3:119, Co-IW:34, Ir-BB:182,
  On-TW:22
Festive Wine. Br-FW:13
Manners at Table when Away from
  Home. Ox-BC:7
Manners in the Dining Room.
  Mother Goose. Ag-HE:75
Table Rules for Little Folks.
  Ox-BC:226
Whole Duty of Children.
  R. Stevenson. Gr-TG:14,
  Na-EO:138, Ox-BC:293
Young Roger and Dolly. Wr-RM:114
ETON, ENG.
Ode on a Distant Prospect of Eton
  College. T. Gray. Al-VBP:563,
  Pa-GTB:158
EUCHARIST: see LORD'S SUPPER
EUCLID
Euclid. V. Lindsay. Ho-LP:57,
  Li-TU:248, Pl-IO:81
Euclid Alone. E. Millay. Er-FA:88,
  Ga-FB:3, Pl-IO:75, Un-MA:448

Plane Geometry. E. Rounds.
  Li-SR:19, Pl-IO:87
EUGÉNE DE RASTIGNAC
Rastignac at 45. T. Gunn. Ha-TP:43
EUROPA (MYTH)
Europa. W. Plomer. Ca-MB:32
EUROPE
America for Me. H. Van Dyke.
  Er-FA:292, Hu-MP:403, Sh-RP:214,
  Th-AS:168, Vi-PP:39
Channel Crossing. G. Barker.
  Pa-GTB:533
Journey to a Parallel. B. Wright.
  Hu-PN:355
Pitying Europe. B. Poplavsky.
  Ca-MR:99
Snow in Europe. D. Gascoyne.
  To-MP:37
Watchman, What of the Night?
  A. Swinburne. Ho-WR:200
EUROPEAN WAR, 1914-1918: see
  WORLD WAR, 1914-1918
EUROPEAN WAR, 1939-1945: see
  WORLD WAR, 1939-1945
EURYDICE: see ORPHEUS AND
  EURYDICE
EUTAW SPRINGS, BATTLE, 1781
To the Memory of the Brave
  Americans. P. Freneau.
  Fe-PL:166, Sh-AP:14, Vi-PP:134
EUTERPE
New Chitons for Old Gods.
  D. McCord. Pl-US:142
EVANGELISTS: see REVIVALS
EVE: see ADAM AND EVE
EVENING: see also SUNSET:
  TWILIGHT
Abide with Me. H. Lyte. Er-FA:443
After Sunset. G. Conkling.
  Tr-MR:274
At Ch'en Ch'u. Wang She Ch'eng.
  Rx-LT:113
Autumn Evening Beside the Lake.
  Li Ch'ing Chao. Rx-OH:93
An Autumnal Evening. W. Sharp.
  Co-PS:123
The Beetle. J. Riley. Fe-FP:126
Blue Evening Falls. Ho-SD:49,
  Le-OE:99
A Boy. T. Miyoshi. Sh-AM:80
Chapter Two. W. Scott. Gr-CC:186
The Children's Hour. H. Longfellow.
  Bo-FP:32, Er-FA:484, Fe-FP:51,
  Fe-PL:144, Ga-FB:162, Hu-MP:109,
  Ke-TF:75, Mc-PR:208, Tu-WW:20,
  Un-GT:98
City. L. Hughes. Br-AF:209,
  Gr-EC:96, Ho-CS:7, 46,
  La-PP:33, La-PV:188, Li-LC:41
Clear Evening after Rain. Tu Fu.
  Rx-OH:27

EVENING — cont'd.
  Cloister. C. Aiken. Un-MA:436
  Come In. R. Frost. Co-BN:157,
    Ga-FB:292, Hi-WP I:4,
    Un-MA:19, Wi-LT:179
  Datur Hora Quieti. W. Scott.
    Pa-GTB:274
  The Day Is Done. H. Longfellow.
    Ch-B:68, Er-FA:488, Mc-PR:142
  Down Dip the Branches.
    M. Van Doren. Rd-SS:21
  Dream-Song. W. de la Mare.
    Sh-RP:24
  Dusk. E. Recht. Le-M:84
  Early Supper. B. Howes. Bo-GJ:27
  Elegy Written in a Country Churchyard.
    T. Gray. Al-VBP:559, De-TT:83,
    Er-FA:462, Fe-PL:281, Ha-PO:144,
    Ma-YA:125, Pa-GTB:145, Rv-CB:533
  An Enjoyable Evening in the Village
    near the Lake. Lin Ho Ching.
    Ma-FW:120
  Evening. R. Aldington. Un-MB:354
  Evening. H. Behn. Co-PU:48
  Evening. G. Byron. Mc-PR:98
  Evening. J. Cheney. Rd-SS:1
  Evening. C. Cotton. Gr-CT:400,
    Ho-WR:142
  Evening. H.D. Ca-VT:105
  Evening. A. Lutzky. Ho-TY:266
  Evening. J. Stephens. Un-MB:260
  Evening. T'ien Han. Hs-TC:27
  Evening after Rain. E. Tatum.
    Ke-TF:429
  An Evening Air. S. Sen. Al-PI:87
  Evening at the Farm. J. Trowbridge.
    Fe-FP:237, Hu-MP:308
  Evening Comes. Li Shang Yin.
    Rx-LT:78
  Evening Hymn. E. Roberts. Ar-TP3:177
  Evening in England. R. Hosken.
    Ke-TF:366
  Evening in the Village. Lu Yu.
    Rx-OH:107
  Evening Landscape. P. de Mont.
    Pa-SG:109
  Evening Lights on the River.
    Chiang She Ch'uan. Rx-LT:116
  Evening over the Forest.
    B. Mayor. Cl-FC:28
  Evening: Ponte al Mare, Pisa.
    P. Shelley. Cl-FC:30, Rv-CB:709
  Evening Settles on the Farm.
    Gr-BB:12
  The Evening Star. J. Clare.
    Gr-CT:399, Pa-GTB:320
  The Excursion. Tu Fu. Mo-SD:138
  Father Is Home. Gr-EC:220
  First Song. G. Kinnell.
    Bo-GJ:47, Br-TC:237, Ha-TP:122,
    Mo-BG:123, Wi-LT:745

  Grace Before Sleep. S. Teasdale.
    Tr-MR:52
  Green Jade Plum Trees in Spring.
    Ou Yang Hsiu. Rx-OH:53
  Hard from the Southeast Blows the
    Wind. E. Coatsworth. Ar-TP3:177
  Hardweed Path Going. A. Ammons.
    Ca-VT:552
  Hesperus. J. Stephens. Li-LC:81
  The Home. R. Tagore. Bo-GJ:xix
  I Shall Miss You Most. Ba-ST:37
  It Is a Beauteous Evening.
    W. Wordsworth. Al-VBP:659,
    De-CH:738, Fe-PL:403, Gr-CT:195,
    Pa-GTB:273, Rv-CB:646
  Lake Leman. G. Byron. Ox-BN:245
  Lightly Stepped a Yellow Star.
    E. Dickinson. Un-MA:101
  Love. A. Andritoiu. Mc-AC:142
  March Evening. L. Strong. Un-MB:394
  Margaritae Sorori. W. Henley.
    Go-BP:237, Ha-PO:127, Ox-BN:884,
    Rv-CB:948, Un-MB:57
  The Midges Dance aboon the Burn.
    R. Tannahill. Co-BN:108
  Nightfall. J. Jiménez. Pa-SG:110
  The Nightingale. M. Stearns.
    Ar-TP3:176
  The Nightingales Sing. Uko.
    Le-IS:27
  November. R. Bridges. Ox-BN:879
  Now at Evening. T. Takaori.
    Sh-AM:155
  Now Silent Falls. W. de la Mare.
    Cl-DT:26, Gr-SS:139
  Now the Day Is Over.
    S. Baring-Gould. Cl-DT:34,
    De-TT:53, Gr-TG:49, Ke-TF:79,
    Ox-BC:238, Rd-SS:42
  Ode to Evening. W. Collins.
    Al-VBP:572, Pa-GTB:143, Rv-CB:537
  On Eastnor Knoll. J. Masefield.
    De-CH:25, Ma-FW:122
  The Owl. R. Warren. Un-MA:588
  Paris. E. E. Cummings. No-CL:252
  Pastoral X. R. Hillyer. Ha-LO:84
  Il Penseroso. J. Milton. De-CH:201
  The Plower. P. Colum. Un-MB:249
  Prelude I. T. Eliot. Ar-TP3:177,
    Br-TC:103, Ca-VT:128, Hi-WP II:162,
    La-OC:130, Pe-OA:103, Sh-AP:182
  Progress of Evening. W. Landor.
    Ox-BN:186
  Reminiscence. Chu Hsiang.
    Hs-TC:99
  River Roses. D. Lawrence.
    Al-VBP:1157, Gr-SS:39
  The Rwose in the Dark. W. Barnes.
    Rv-CB:767
  Senlin. C. Aiken. Ha-LO:56
  The Shore of Life. R. Fitzgerald.
    Ca-VT:302

The Shower.   H. Vaughan.   Cl-FC:42
Small Song.   F. Frost.   Sh-RP:174
A Sound in Cambridge, Mass.
   R. Whitman.   Ls-NY:327
The Spring Waters, 42.   Ping Hsin.
   Hs-TC:23
Summer Evening.   W. de la Mare.
   Un-MB:201
The Sun Has Long Been Set.
   W. Wordsworth.   Ha-YA:72
Sunday Evening in the Common.
   J. Wheelock.   No-CL:257, Un-MA:342
Sunken Evening.   L. Lee.   Wi-LT:758
Surprised by Evening.   R. Bly.
   Ca-VT:557
To the Evening Star.   W. Blake.
   Co-BN:114, De-CH:430, Fe-PL:403,
   Ga-FB:24, Gr-CT:399, Gr-SS:131,
   Ho-WR:144
To the Evening Star.   T. Campbell.
   Pa-GTB:273
Twilight Song.   J. Hunter-Duvar.
   Do-WH:94
Village Before Sunset. F. Cornford.
   Co-BN:108, Co-PU:143, Sm-LG:50
The Water Bug.   Br-MW:96, Da-SC:87,
   Ho-SD:20, Le-OE:97
Wayfarer's Evensong II.
   J. von Goethe.   Un-R:29
Winter Landscape.   S. Spender.
   Un-MB:473
The Winter Trees.   C. Dyment.
   Cl-FC:63
EVEREST, MOUNT
Victory.   M. Miller.   Sh-RP:283
EVERGREENS: see names of individual
   species, as CEDAR TREES
EVERS, MEDGAR
Medgar Evers.   G. Brooks.   Ad-PB:158
EVIL: see also GOOD AND EVIL;
   HUMOR - EVIL; SIN; VICE
Absalom and Achitophel.
   J. Dryden.   Al-VBP:489
All Things Come Alike to All.
   Bible.   O.T.   Ecclesiastes.
   Me-PH:32
As a Plane Tree by the Water.
   R. Lowell.   Gr-SS:160,
   Un-MA:664, Wi-LT:578
Battle.   R. Jeffers.   Un-MA:371,
   Wi-LT:260
Be Still, My Soul, Be Still.
   A. Housman.   Ox-BN:923, Un-MB:101
Chorus from a Tragedy.   L. Bacon.
   Al-VBP:1173
Dalyaunce.   De-CH:26
The Dark Angel.   L. Johnson.
   Pa-GTB:401, Un-MB:154
Dirty Thoughts.   V. Contoski.
   Sc-TN:28
The End of the World. Bible. O.T.
   Jeremiah.   Ba-PO:48, Ke-PP:2

Eve.   R. Hodgson.   De-CH:465,
   Ha-PO:41, Hi-WP II:95,
   Na-EO:105, Pa-OM:286, Sm-MK:58,
   Un-MB:186, Wi-LT:123
Evil.   R. Herrick.   Ga-S:23
Evil Is Homeless.   D. Lawrence.
   Tr-MR:219
Evil Is No Black Thing.   S. Fabio.
   Ad-PB:205
For Every Evil under the Sun.
   Li-LB:161, Na-EO:161, Wr-RM:32
From My High Love.   K. Patchen.
   Un-MA:610
The Haunted Palace.   E. Poe.
   Al-VBP:875, De-CH:320, Gr-CT:160,
   Ho-WR:216, Sh-AP:54
Lost Moment.   H. Fuller.   Ad-PB:201
The Mask of Evil.   B. Brecht.
   Li-TU:177
The Pains of Sleep. S. Coleridge.
   Ox-BN:171, Rv-CB:662
Satan Is on Your Tongue.
   G. Barker.   Un-MB:493
Several Voices Out of a Cloud.
   L. Bogan.   Mo-BG:180
Since We Are Property.
   L. Lorraine.   De-FS:133
To the Reader.   C. Baudelaire.
   Mo-GR:30
The Two Spirits.   P. Shelley.
   De-CH:323, Ho-WR:189
Vampire Bride.   F. Stefanile.
   De-FS:190
EVIL SPIRITS: see DEVILS;
   WITCHES AND WITCHCRAFT
EVOLUTION: see also CREATION;
   HUMOR - EVOLUTION
Bryan's Last Battle (The Scopes
   Trial).   Em-AF:769
Each in His Own Tongue. Ke-TF:246
Evolution.   L. Smith.   Er-FA:13
Evolution.   J. Tabb.   Sh-AP:136
Fire, Hair, Meat and Bone.
   F. Johnson.   Ad-PB:391
The Fourth God.   C. Smith.
   Sm-PT:83
Here.   R. Thomas.   Pa-GTB:537
In Memoriam.   A. Tennyson.
   Pl-IO:131
Love Song to Eohippus.
   P. Viereck.   Un-MA:659
Modern Love XXX.   G. Meredith.
   Al-VBP:983
EXAGGERATION: see also BOASTING;
   TALL TALES
An Afternoon like This.   Fi-BG:82
Bitter Creek.   Fi-BG:83
The Wren Hunt.   Mo-MGT:44
EXAMINATIONS: see also STUDENTS;
   TEACHERS AND TEACHING
The Exam.   Mo-MI:85
Test.   M. Nishimura.   Le-TA:55

EXAMINATIONS — cont'd.
To a Friend on Her Examination for the Doctorate in English.
V. Cunningham. Ca-VT:325
University Examinations in Egypt.
D. Enright. Br-TC:119
EXCUSES: see also HUMOR - EXCUSES
At the Garden Gate. D. McCord.
Fe-FP:122
An Excuse for Not Returning the Visit of a Friend. Mei Yao Ch'en.
Rx-OH:37
I Meant to Do My Work Today.
R. Le Gallienne. Ar-TP3:116
Au-SP:348, Hu-MP:69, La-PP:6,
Th-AS:78, Un-GB:22, Un-GT:250
Reason. J. Miles. En-PC:107,
Mo-BG:34
EXECUTIONS AND EXECUTIONERS: see also HUMOR - EXECUTIONS AND EXECUTIONERS; SATIRE - EXECUTIONS AND EXECUTIONERS
At the Last. A. Lifschutz.
Kr-OF:125
The Ballad of Reading Gaol.
O. Wilde. Al-VBP:1072, Er-FA:87,
Un-MB:70
Ballad of the Long Drop. J. Pudney.
Co-RM:108
Billy in the Darbies. H. Melville.
Mo-BG:160, Rv-CB:835
Bristowe Tragedie. Ox-BB:656
Capital Punishment. O. Wilde.
Hi-WP II:22
Captain Hall. Gr-GB:269
The Carpenter's Son. A. Housman.
Li-SR:136, Un-MB:101
Clever Tom Clinch. J. Swift.
Co-RM:175
Click. B. Akhmadulina. Bo-RU:4
The Confessional (Spain).
R. Browning. Al-VBP:885
The Croppy Boy. Rv-CB:437
Danny Deever. R. Kipling. Co-RM:87,
Fe-PL:84, Pa-GTB:420, Un-MB:124
The Death of Lord Warriston.
Ox-BB:603
A Dream of Hanging. P. Beer.
To-MP:202
The Duchess of Malfi.
J. Webster. Gr-CT:360
Eight o' Clock. A. Housman.
Co-PU:116, Hi-WP I:22,
Un-MB:100
Elegiac Statement for Two Human Beings Named Rosenberg.
L. Hedley. Kr-OF:124
The Execution Ground.
Tsang K'o-chia. Hs-TC:286
The Execution of Montrose.
W. Aytoun. Pa-OM:96
Farewell to My Mother.
Placido. Lo-TY:99

The Hanged Thing. W. Kerr.
De-FS:127
The Hanging of Billy Budd. K. Wilson.
Sc-TN:242
Hughie Graham. Ox-BB:579
Jack Hall. Co-RM:99
King Charles upon the Scaffold.
A. Marvell. Gr-CT:378
The King of Ai. H. Plutzik.
Wi-LT:792
Last Speech to the Court.
B. Vanzetti. Mo-BG:170
Lines Before Execution.
C. Tichbourne. Al-VBP:138,
Gr-CT:324, Ha-PO:132, Rv-CB:103
Mary Hamilton. Rv-CB:131
More Light, More Light. A. Hecht.
Br-TC:182, Ca-VT:505
My Handsome Gilderoy. De-CH:78
Nathan Hale. E. Finch.
Hi-TL:53, Vi-PP:111
Nathan Hale. W. Partridge.
Vi-PP:110
The Portent. H. Melville.
Ho-WR:196, Kr-OF:109, Rv-CB:836
The Rebel. J. Fletcher. Un-MA:319
A Rope for Harry Fat. J. Baxter.
Ca-MB:85
Samuel Hall. Co-RM:98
They Are Dead Now. J. Dos Passos.
Kr-OF:120
Three Things There Be. . . .
W. Raleigh. De-CH:535, Rv-CB:159
To the Electric Chair.
E. Auerbach. Ho-TY:300
Unkept Good Fridays. T. Hardy.
Tr-MR:128
The Virginia Scaffold.
E. Proctor. Kr-OF:109
The Wake of William Orr.
W. Drennan. Ba-PO:94
See also Em-AF:730-741
EXERCISE
Athletic Employment. Mo-SD:160
EXETER CATHEDRAL
Before Exeter Church. Hsü Chih-mo
Hs-TC:81
EXILES: see also REFUGEES
And Away. B. Smith. Sa-B:72
At the Moment. M. Williams.
Sa-B:106
At Yuen Yang Lake. Wu Wei Ye.
Rx-LT:112
The Boys of Mullaghbawn. Gr-GB:256
By the Rivers of Babylon. Bible.
O.T. Psalms. Me-PH:30
Canadian Boat Song. J. Galt.
Ox-BN:204, Rv-CB:683, Sm-LG:140
Concert at the Station.
O. Mandelstam. Ca-MR:156
A Dead Turk. Li Kuang-t'ien.
Hs-TC:208

Depriving Me of Sea. . . .
  O. Mandelstam. Ca-MR:159
Epitaph on a Jacobite.
  T. Macaulay. Al-VBP:799,
  Cr-WS:56, De-TT:180, Ox-BN:428
Foreboding. G. Code. De-FS:64
Four Sheets to the Wind and a One-
  Way Ticket to France, 1933.
  C. Rivers. Ad-PB:234, Bo-AN:176,
  Hu-NN:107, Hu-PN:404, Ra-BP:199
Friends Go Away. A. Galich.
  Bo-RU:32
I Came Out of a Café.
  Wang Tu-ch'ing. Hs-TC:194
The Kalmyk Mourns for His Country.
  Tr-US II:133
A Lament for His Own Land.
  Tr-US II:114
Let Us Consider where the Great
  Men Are. D. Schwartz. Un-MA:619
Notes to the Life of Ovid.
  A. Hamori. Ls-NY:131
On the Roads of Siberia.
  H. Leivick. Ho-TY:118
Prose Poem for a Conference.
  J. LaRose. Sa-B:74
Psalm 137. L. Ryzhova. Bo-RU:70
Refugee Blues. W. Auden.
  Hi-WP I:122, Wi-LT:472
Sang-Kan River. Ya Hsüan. Pa-MV:149
Song of Exile. Tr-US I:130
Sonnet XV. Feng Chih. Hs-TC:152
A Stream of Gold Honey. . . .
  O. Mandelstam. Ca-MR:154
This Little Fellow. Wy-CM:13
Thoughts in Exile. Su Tung P'o.
  Rx-OH:81
to L.V. L. Batshev. Bo-RU:16
To Yesenin. J. Rubenstein. Ho-TY:239
Travelogue for Exiles. K. Shapiro.
  Un-MA:636
The True and Tender Wife. Al-PI:29
EXPECTATION: see ANTICIPATION
EXPERIENCE: see also HUMOR -
  EXPERIENCE; SATIRE - EXPERIENCE
  Adjuration. C. Wheeler. Bo-AN:105,
  Hu-PN:272
  After Beginning. C. Lushington.
  Sa-B:235
  Alumnus Football. G. Rice. Fe-PL:56
  L'An Trentièsme de Mon Eage.
  A. MacLeish. Ce-MV:359, Gr-SS:53,
  Un-MA:454, Wi-LT:340
  Answering a Letter from a Younger
  Poet. B. Ghiselin. En-PC:50
  Atavism. M. Sorescu. Mc-AC:157
  Carmen. V. Cruz. Ad-CI:61,
  Ad-PB:506
  Childe Harold. M. Kulbak. Ho-TY:205
  Don't Run. J. Jiménez. Le-SW:35
  Dulce Bellum Inexpertis.
  G. Gascoigne. Ba-PO:119

Even in the Darkness. H. Mullins.
  Tr-MR:227
Fiftieth Birthday. P. Viereck.
  Ls-NY:68
Four Thousand Days and Nights.
  R. Tamura. Sh-AM:125
The Four Zoas. W. Blake. Ho-P:257
Girls and Boys, Young Ladies and
  Gentlemen. R. Fernández
  Retamar. Be-UL:119
God Has Been Good to Me.
  F. Keyes. Ke-TF:454
I Am like a Distracted Child.
  J. Jiménez. Le-SW:35
In a Girl's Album. C. Dover.
  Hi-WP II:149
It Is Becoming Now to Declare My
  Allegiance. C. Day-Lewis.
  Wi-LT:425
Ithaka. C. Cavafy. Ni-JP:15
I've Seen Enough. C. Meyer.
  Jo-VC:12
A Living Pearl. K. Rexroth.
  Wi-LT:798
Man Is Nothing but.
  S. Tchernichovsky. Me-PH:76
Mohini Chatterjee. W. Yeats.
  Tr-MR:278
New Approach Is Needed. K. Amis.
  Ke-PP:89
No Reply. S. Van Ryte. Me-WF:40
Poem for Friends. Q. Troupe.
  Ad-PB:445
Poem of Angela Yvonne Davis.
  N. Giovanni. Ad-PB:458
Prospice. R. Browning. Fe-PL:287,
  Ga-FB:129, Rv-CB:829
Putting to Sea. L. Bogan. Wi-LT:381
Sonnet XIII. Feng Chih. Hs-TC:151
The Spring Waters, 146. Ping Hsin.
  Hs-TC:24
Still Branches. J. Simvovk.
  Gr-BT:156
Sweet Stay-at-Home. W. Davies.
  De-CH:36
Sword and Flower. T. Utan.
  Mc-AC:144
Thel's Motto. W. Blake. Gr-CT:432,
  Ox-BN:32
There Was a Child Went Forth.
  W. Whitman. Br-BC:128, La-RM:164,
  Un-GT:307
3 Stanzas about a Tree. M. Bell.
  Ho-P:21
Ticktacktoe. J. Wade. Sc-TN:222
Time Takes Me on Its Wing.
  Wo-HS:(58)
Titan's Lament. A. Raybin.
  Sc-TN:192
To a Child Trapped in a Barber
  Shop. P. Levine. Ca-VT:633
To Live. M. Ooka. Sh-AM:133

EXPERIENCE — cont'd.
  To the Moon. T. Hardy. Co-BN:119,
    Gr-CT:406
  Truth. J. Hearst. St-H:79
  Ulysses. A. Tennyson. Al-VBP:863,
    Ha-PO:40, Ke-TF:262, Ni-JP:16,
    Rv-CB:793
  We Play at Paste. E. Dickinson.
    Rv-CB:913
  When I Was One-and-Twenty.
    A. Housman. Al-VBP:1080,
    Bo-HF:92, Co-BL:61, Er-FA:153,
    Fe-PL:118, Ga-FB:72, Ho-LP:12,
    Ke-TF:93, Ma-YA:222, Pe-M:150,
    Un-MB:94, Un-MW:55, Wi-LT:59
  Without One Particle of Sentiment
    in His Being. M. Ooka. Sh-AM:134
  Yes, I Grew Up with the Poppies.
    Z. Stancu. Mc-AC:86
  Youth Sings a Song of Rosebuds.
    C. Cullen. Fe-PL:258, Hu-PN:234
EXPLORERS: see also DISCOVERIES;
    DISCOVERY PERIOD IN AMERICA;
    HUMOR - EXPLORERS; SPACE
    EXPLORATION; names of explorers,
    as DE SOTO, HERNANDO
  Above Pate Valley. G. Snyder.
    Mo-BG:131
  Alone. J. Farrar. Ha-YA:70,
    Hu-MP:61
  A Ballad of Sir John Franklin.
    G. Baker. Pa-OM:109
  Captain Cook. A. Domett. Hi-FO:180
  Columbus. A. Clough. Br-AF:53,
    Co-PS:131
  The English in Virginia.
    C. Reznikoff. Gr-SS:62
  The Explorer. R. Kipling.
    Sp-OG:54
  Henry Hudson's Quest, 1609.
    B. Stevenson. Vi-PP:44
  The Mediterranean. A. Tate.
    Ca-VT:219, En-PC:39, Sh-AP:205,
    Un-MA:540, Wi-LT:401
  The Night Before America.
    N. Farber. Hi-FO:106
  Sir Francis Drake. Hi-FO:224
  To the Virginian Voyage. M. Drayton.
    Al-VBP:161, Hi-TL:19, Rv-CB:184
  Voyage. J. Miles. Wi-LT:774
  The Weepers Tower in Amsterdam.
    P. Goodman. Ca-VT:334
EXPRESS HIGHWAYS: see FREEWAYS
EXPRESS SERVICE: see HUMOR -
    EXPRESS SERVICE
EXTINCT ANIMALS: see FOSSILS;
    HUMOR - EXTINCT ANIMALS;
    PREHISTORIC ANIMALS; and names
    of extinct animals, as DODOES
EXTRAVAGANCE: see WASTEFULNESS

EXTREME UNCTION
  Extreme Unction. E. Dowson.
    Ga-S:218, Un-MB:149
EYCK, JAN VAN: see HUMOR -
    EYCK, JAN VAN
EYEGLASSES: see also HUMOR -
    EYEGLASSES
  Broken Glasses. S. Takahashi.
    Sh-AM:97
  Its Curtains. T. Joans. Ad-PB:206
  Sunglasses. F. Silber. Lo-IT:125
EYES: see also HUMOR - EYES;
    SATIRE - EYES; SIGHT
  Before I Got My Eye Put Out.
    E. Dickinson. Wi-LT:5
  The Cat. W. Davies. Bl-OB:108
  Even Now. . . . Bilhana.
    Al-PI:48, Pa-SG:65
  The Eye. M. Benedikt. Mc-EA:74
  The Eye Penetrates. S. Terry.
    Le-M:172
  Eyes. T. Itozakura. Le-TA:18
  Eyes Are Lit Up. R. Coffin.
    Sm-MK:157
  Eyes That Last I Saw in Tears.
    T. Eliot. Al-VBP:1185
  For Arvia. E. Robinson. Br-BC:149
  For Damaris, about to Be Married.
    C. Walsh. St-H:241
  Her Eyes. J. Ransom. Wi-LT:316
  Merciless Beauty. G. Chaucer.
    No-CL:148, Rv-CB:59
  My Face Looks Out. E. Honig.
    Ls-NY:75
  Nocturne. O. Paz. Be-UL:69
  Older Brother. F. Yamashita.
    Le-TA:30
  A Pair of Sea-Green Eyes.
    H. MacDiarmid. Gr-CC:100
  The Snake. Kyoshi. Sh-RP:62
  Tanka. Y. Aizu. Sh-AM:142
  There Was a Man of Our Town.
    Mother Goose. Er-FA:506
  To a Child with Eyes. M. Van Doren.
    Bo-FP:95, Ha-LO:78
  To Dick, on His Sixth Birthday.
    S. Teasdale. Br-BC:59
  To Morfydd. L. Johnson.
    Re-TW:68, Un-MB:153
  A Way of Touching the World.
    Me-WF:75
  Where Is Fancy Bred.
    W. Shakespeare. Al-VBP:185,
    De-CH:197, Fe-FP:397, Hi-WP II:52,
    Ma-YA:66, Pa-GTB:30
  Women's Eyes. Bhartrihari. Pa-SG:46
FABLES: see also ALLEGORIES;
    FAIRY TALES; FOLKLORE;
    LEGENDS
  The Ant and the Cricket. Aesop.
    De-TT:59, Un-GT:78

The Ass in the Lion's Skin. Aesop.
    Gr-EC:198, Rd-OA:167
Bed-Time Story. M. Cane. Un-GT:81
The Bestiary. W. Benét. Rd-OA:126
The Black Cat. B. Okujava.
    Bo-RU:56
The Blind Men and the Elephant.
    J. Saxe. Bo-HF:73, Gr-EC:150,
    Ha-PO:302, Pa-OM:330, Un-GT:200
Blue Fly. J. de Assis. Lo-TY:81
The Brush and the Shoe.
    E. Steinberg. Ho-TY:234
The Cock and the Fox.
    J. de la Fontaine. Mc-PR:14
The Cross of Antlers.
    M. Yeryomin. Bo-RU:92
The Dog in the River. Plato.
    Mc-PR:27
Dwarf of Disintegration. O. Williams.
    En-PC:42, Wi-LT:415
The Enchanted Shirt. J. Hay.
    Ha-PO:59, Sh-RP:264, Un-GT:171
Fable. R. Emerson. Bo-FP:71,
    Bo-GJ:26, Bo-HF:69, Ch-B:27,
    Er-FA:496, Fe-FP:530, Ga-FB:317,
    Hu-MP:210, Pa-OM:333, Rd-OA:91,
    Sh-AP:27, Sp-OG:303, Un-GT:57
The Fable of the Piece of Glass
    and the Piece of Ice. Ox-BC:151
The Fox and the Grapes. J. Lauren.
    Bo-HF:70, Un-GT:170
The Frogs Who Wanted a King.
    J. Lauren. Bo-HF:94, Un-GT:170
Haukyn's Coat. W. Langland.
    Ga-S:135
The Horse and the Whip.
    E. Steinberg. Ho-TY:233
The Lion and the Mouse. J. Taylor.
    Pa-OM:328, Sh-RP:320
The Man and the Weasel. Plato.
    Mc-PR:27
The Mouse That Gnawed the Oak-Tree
    Down. V. Lindsay. Ha-LO:74
The New Duckling. A. Noyes.
    Fe-FP:283, Hu-MP:241
The Nightingale and the Glowworm.
    W. Cowper. Go-BP:76, Pa-OM:320,
    Un-GT:79
Of the Mean and Sure Estate.
    T. Wyatt. Rd-OA:98
Ogres and Pygmies. R. Graves.
    Wi-LT:376
Phoebus and Boreas.
    J. de la Fontaine. Un-R:87
The Sacrificial Knife and the
    Simple Saw. E. Steinberg.
    Ho-TY:232
The Scythian Philosopher.
    J. de la Fontaine. Un-R:79
The Sea's Prayer. V. Kalugin.
    Bo-RU:42

The Shepherd Boy and the Wolf.
    W. Leonard.   Hu-MP:406
Song about Fools. B. Okujava.
    Bo-RU:58
The Song about the Bird.
    V. Kalugin. Bo-RU:42
The Swan and Goose. Aesop.
    Fe-FP:475, Pl-US:60
The Sycophantic Fox and the
    Gullible Raven. G. Carryl.
    Co-FB:29, Co-HP:53, Er-FA:201
The Tale of the World. M. Halpern.
    Ho-TY:102
The Turtle's Song. Ra-BP:18
The Virtuous Fox and the Self-
    Righteous Cat. J. Cunningham.
    Pa-OM:334
The Washerman. U. Joshi. Al-PI:110
Zephyr. E. Ware. Fe-PL:430
FACE RHYMES
Bo Peeper. De-CH:497, De-TT:117
Brow Bender. De-PO:8, Mo-TL:45
Brow, Brow, Brenty. De-PO:6,
    Mo-TL:46
Eye Winker. De-PO:6, Mo-MGT:201
Four and Twenty White Kye.
    Gr-GB:17, Mo-TL:46
A Game with the Face. Mo-NR:8
Here Sits Farmer Giles. Mo-TL:47
Here Sits the Lord Mayor.
    De-CH:497, De-PO:6, De-TT:118,
    Ir-BB:13, Li-LB:16, Wr-RM:55
Knock at the Door. Mo-TL:46
My Mother and Your Mother.
    Mo-TL:48
Tae Titly. Ir-BB:12, Mo-TL:48
FACES: see also FACE RHYMES;
    HUMOR - FACES
Eye Winker. De-PO:6, Mo-MGT:201
Face. F. Kitagawa. Sh-AM:84
A Face. M. Moore. En-PC:11
Faces. S. McCoy. La-IH:16
Faces. S. Teasdale. La-OC:69
The Faces. P. Zweig. Mc-EA:110
Give Me the Splendid Silent Sun.
    W. Whitman. Co-BN:232, Fe-FP:263,
    Mo-BG:20, Un-MA:84
Godmother. P. Morden.. Au-SP:301,
    Th-AS:104
Houses. A. Fisher.   Au-SP:206
I See Your Face. L. Issaluk.
    Le-IB:85
In a Station of the Metro.
    E. Pound. Ad-CI:41, Ca-VT:83,
    Mo-BG:23, Sh-AP:173, Un-MA:294
In the Tube. R. Aldington.
    Hi-WP I:128
It's in Your Face. Fe-PL:299
Lament. W. Williams. Ca-VT:58
A Meeting. G. Painter. Sm-MK:40
My Face. Pa-RE:85

FACES — cont'd.
  Numbers and Faces. W. Auden.
    Pl-IO:91
  125th Street. L. Hughes. Ho-CS:13
  Phizzog. C. Sandburg.
    Ar-TP3:137, Sh-RP:141
  Pirate. S. Menashe. Sm-MK:3
  The Scarred Girl. J. Dickey.
    Du-SH:69
  The Ugly Child. E. Jennings.
    Pa-RE:31
FACTORIES: see also SATIRE -
    FACTORIES
  Autumn Begins in Martins Ferry,
    Ohio. J. Wright. Bl-FP:76,
    St-H:255
  The Factory Girl's Come-All-Ye.
    Em-AF:766
  Factory Windows Are Always Broken.
    V. Lindsay. Co-PU:72,
    Er-FA:274, La-OC:110
  Habitat. J. Anderson. Sc-TN:1
  Late Shift in the Mill.
    J. Knoepfle. St-H:94
  The Ropewalk. H. Longfellow.
    Mo-BG:12
  The Shopgirls Leave Their Work.
    C. Reznikoff. La-OC:128
  The Song of the Shirt. T. Hood.
    Hi-FO:227, Ke-PP:59, Ma-YA:188
FAILURE: see also DEFEAT;
    HUMOR - FAILURE
  As Bad as a Mile. P. Larkin.
    Co-EL:124
  Bewick Finzer. E. Robinson.
    Gr-CC:130, Un-MA:118
  Counter-Attack. S. Sassoon.
    Ba-PO:136, Co-RM:204, Cr-WS:87,
    Un-MB:312
  Dance Song. Le-IB:78
  Don't Give Up. Er-FA:8
  If There Be Sorrow. M. Evans.
    Hu-NN:22, Hu-PN:308
  In Praise of Bow and Arrow.
    Tr-CB:23, Tr-US I:54
  Losers. C. Sandburg. Un-MA:205
  Me Because. D. Witt. Ad-II:10
  My Stars. A. Ibn Ezra. Me-PH:64
  nobody loses all the time.
    E. Cummings. Br-TC:78,
    Ma-FW:132, Wi-LT:359
  A Note of Humility. A. Bontemps.
    Be-MA:46, Hu-PN:222
  The Spring Is Past. C. Tichborne.
    De-TT:181
  Success Is Counted Sweetest.
    E. Dickinson. Bo-GJ:191,
    Mo-BG:166, Rv-CB:897, Sh-AP:126,
    Un-MA:103, Wi-LT:3
  Three Things. Un-GT:306
  Those Game Animals. Le-IB:75

  To a Friend Whose Work Has Come
    to Nothing. W. Yeats.
    Un-MB:116, Wi-LT:69
  The Unfortunate Miller. A. Coppard.
    Co-PT:19
  We Never Know How High.
    E. Dickinson. Mc-WK:98, Sh-AP:131
  When I Have Fears that I May Cease
    to Be. J. Keats. Go-BP:148,
    Ha-PO:129, Ma-YA:187, No-CL:6,
    Ox-BN:369, Pa-GTB:198,
    Rv-CB:747, Un-GT:313
  When They Have Lost.
    C. Day Lewis. Un-MB:425
  The Wolf Mountain Stampede.
    Fi-BG:60
FAIRBANKS, ALSK.
  A Ballad about Nuggets.
    Y. Yevtushenko. Ca-MR:57
FAIRIES: see also BROWNIES; DWARFS
    (FAIRIES); ELVES; GNOMES;
    GOBLINS; HUMOR - FAIRIES;
    LEPRECHAUNS; MAB, QUEEN
  Alison Gross. De-CH:406, Fo-OG:36,
    Ma-BB:108, Ox-BB:54
  Ariel's Song. W. Shakespeare.
    Al-VBP:197, Bl-OB:90, Bo-FP:314,
    Bo-GJ:138, De-CH:111, De-TT:194,
    Fr-WO:87, Hu-MP:94, Li-SR:82,
    No-CL:42, Re-TW:58, Rv-CB:191,
    Sm-LG:227
  The Ballad of the Fiddler.
    S. O'Sullivan. Hu-MP:104
  La Belle Dame sans Merci. J. Keats.
    Al-VBP:779, Bo-GJ:163, Bo-HF:22,
    De-CH:121, De-TT:200, Er-FA:409,
    Gr-CT:178, Gr-SS:108, Ha-PO:6,
    Hi-WP II:106, Mc-WK:8, Ni-JP:98,
    No-CL:65, Ox-BN:376, Pa-GTB:193,
    Rv-CB:735, Sm-LG:217, Sm-MK:46,
    Sp-OG:113, Un-GT:126
  Berries. W. de la Mare. Un-MB:200
  The Best Game the Fairies Play.
    R. Fyleman. Ar-TP3:147, Au-SP:294
  The Birth of the Poet.
    Q. Prettyman. Ad-BO:18
  Bluebells. W. de la Mare. Hu-MP:87
  Buttercups. W. Thorley. Fe-FP:381
  By the Moon. T. Ravenscroft.
    De-CH:111
  The Changeling. C. Mew.
    De-CH:293, Hu-MP:95
  The Child and the Fairies. Bo-FP:310
  The Child Next Door. R. Fyleman.
    Fe-FP:302, Hu-MP:136, Th-AS:6
  Children, Children, Don't Forget.
    D. Owen. Hu-MP:84
  Could It Have Been a Shadow?
    M. Shannon. Ar-TP3:147,
    Au-SP:290, Fe-FP:390
  Crab-Apple. E. Talbot. Ar-TP3:149,
    Bo-FP:328, Br-BC:8

Day-Song for Tenio's Fete.
  Koroa.   Tr-US II:59
Faery Song.   J. Keats.   De-CH:267,
  Sp-OG:170
The Fairies.   W. Allingham.
  Al-VBP:974, Bl-OB:92, Bo-FP:314,
  Ch-B:38, Co-PM:19, Co-RG:119,
  De-CH:114, De-TT:50, Er-FA:503,
  Fe-FP:575, Fr-WO:76, Ga-FB:172,
  Gr-CT:157, Gr-EC:160, La-PV:74,
  Li-LC:63, Na-EO:36, Ox-BC:215,
  Pa-OM:279, Pe-FB:50, Rv-CB:877,
  Sm-LG:224, Sp-OG:165
Fairies.   M. Chute.   Th-AS:8
Fairies.   H. Conkling.   Ar-TP3:146,
  Th-AS:5
The Fairies.   R. Fyleman.
  Au-SP:290, Fe-FP:377, Hu-MP:89,
  Ox-BC:336, Pe-FB:54
The Fairies.   J. Herndon.   Hu-MP:105
The Fairies.   R. Herrick.   Bl-OB:90,
  Fe-FP:384, Hu-MP:87
Fairies.   Kihaku.   Hu-MP:81
Fairies.   D. Koehler.   La-GI:45
The Fairies.   S. Morford.   Se-PR:193
The Fairies' Dance.   F. Sherman.
  Sp-OG:167
The Fairies' Dance.   Hu-MP:86
The Fairies Feast.   C. Doughty.
  De-CH:124
The Fairies Have Never a Penny to
  Spend.   R. Fyleman.   Fe-FP:379,
  Hu-MP:85, Ox-BC:338, Th-AS:7
Fairies' Song.   L. Hunt.   Co-PM:106
The Fairy Fiddler.   N. Hopper.
  Al-VBP:1112
The Fairy Frolic.   J. Lyly.   Bo-FP:329
A Fairy in Armor.   J. Drake.
  Fe-FP:380
A Fairy Is like a Swan.   R. Isaac.
  La-GI:44
The Fairy King.   W. Allingham.
  Co-PM:22
Fairy Rings.   J. Clare.   Go-BP:109
Fairy Shoes.   A. Wynne.   Hu-MP:83
Fairy Song.   J. Lyly.   De-TT:112
Fairy Thief.   W. Welles.   Br-SG:84
The Fairy Thorn.   S. Ferguson.
  De-CH:117, De-TT:197, Pa-OM:271
A Fairy Voyage.   Au-SP:299, Bo-FP:309
A Fairy Went a-Marketing.   R. Fyleman.
  Au-SP:293, Ox-BC:337
The Fairy's Reply to Saturn.
  T. Hood.   Ox-BN:417
Fantasy.   R. Skidmore.   Co-PM:153
The Find.   F. Ledwidge.   Th-AS:18
The Five Little Fairies.
  H. Burnham.   Bo-FP:311
Five Little Fairies.   On-TW:23
The Flowers.   R. Stevenson.
  Fe-FP:217, Hu-MP:247

For a Child Named Katherine.
  L. Nicholl.   Th-AS:16
Goblin Feet.   J. Tolkien.
  Co-PM:163, Fe-FP:369
The Green Fiddler.   R. Field.
  Co-PT:173
Have You Watched the Fairies?
  R. Fyleman.   Ar-TP3:146,
  Au-SP:291, Pe-FB:48, Th-AS:3
Hazel Dorn.   B. Sleigh.   De-CH:558
I Keep Three Wishes Ready.
  A. Wynne.   Ar-TP3:146, Au-SP:292,
  La-PV:76, Pe-FB:49, Th-AS:9
I Like Fairies.   K. Fouchaux.
  La-GI:44
I Wish I Was Lucky.   L. Atwood.
  La-GI:45
I'd Love to Be a Fairy's Child.
  R. Graves.   Au-SP:299, Br-BC:7,
  Fe-FP:380, Ir-BB:93, La-PV:77
If You Never Talked with Fairies.
  E. Fowler.   Br-BC:133
In the Moonlight.   N. O'Connor.
  Au-SP:298
The Land of Heart's Desire.
  W. Yeats.   Al-VBP:1090,
  Ma-FW:188, Pa-HT:162, Un-MB:109
The Light-Hearted Fairy.
  Bo-FP:311, Fe-FP:378, Hu-MP:80
Little Folks in the Grass.
  A. Wynne.   Th-AS:74
Little Lad.   Br-BC:6, Ir-BB:92,
  Tu-WW:14
Lunar Moth.   R. Hillyer.   Rd-OA:9
Mab.   B. Jonson.   Ho-WR:87
Midsummer Magic.   I. Eastwick.
  Ar-TP3:148
Midsummer Night.   M. Edey.   Ha-YA:78
Mr. Moon.   B. Carman.   Fe-FP:371,
  Sh-RP:11
The Mocking Fairy.   W. de la Mare.
  Un-MB:199
My Fairy.   Ch-B:80
Night Dancers.   T. Kennedy.
  Th-AS:4
Nimphidia, the Court of Fayrie.
  M. Drayton.   Al-VBP:163
Now the Hungry Lion Roars.
  W. Shakespeare.   Al-VBP:184,
  De-CH:123, Gr-CT:154, Gr-EC:92,
  Ma-FW:125, Re-TW:29, Sm-MK:44
Oberon's Feast.   R. Herrick.
  Al-VBP:330
Of Certain Irish Fairies.
  A. Guiterman.   Fe-PL:107
One of the Sidhe.   M. Kennedy.
  De-FS:124
Over Hill, over Dale.
  W. Shakespeare.   Al-VBP:182,
  Bl-OB:90, Bo-FP:325, De-TT:113,
  Fe-FP:382, Re-TW:59

FAIRIES — cont'd.
The Peri's Lament for Hinda.
   T. Moore.   Ox-BN:217
Please.   R. Fyleman.   Hu-MP:81
The Plumpuppets.   C. Morley.
   Ar-TP3:150, Fe-FP:395, Hu-MP:117,
   Rd-SS:10
The Pointed People.   R. Field.
   Fa-FP:271, Hu-MP:86
The Pool.   L. Drake.   De-FS:77
Queen Mab.   W. Shakespeare.
   Fe-FP:382, Ma-FW:186, Un-GT:108
Queen Mab's Journey to Pigwiggen.
   M. Drayton.   Bo-FP:320
The Rainbow Fairies.   L. Hadley.
   St-FS:65
The Return of the Fairy.   H. Wolfe.
   Co-PM:178
Robin Goodfellow.   Al-VBP:371,
   Rv-CB:138
Sea Shells.   W. Goosley.   La-GI:43
The Shadow People.   F. Ledwidge.
   Bo-FP:322, Hu-MP:90, Th-AS:12
Shakespeare: The Fairies' Advocate.
   T. Hood.   Ox-BN:417
Sing a Song of Moonlight.
   I. Eastwick.   Br-SS:33
The Singing Fairy.   R. Fyleman.
   Rd-SS:35
The Sleeping Beauty.   E. Sitwell.
   Ma-FW:189
Sometimes.   R. Fyleman.   Br-SS:24
Song for Midsummer Night.
   E. Coatsworth.   Ha-YA:79
Stocking Fairy.   W. Welles.
   Ar-TP3:150, Au-SP:295, Fe-FP:378
The Stolen Child.   W. Yeats.
   Co-PM:197, Hu-MP:82
Tam Lin.   Ma-BB:124, Ox-BB:13
Tammie Doodle.   Fo-OG:12
To a Little Sister, Aged Ten.
   A. Cummings.   Br-BC:79
The Unwritten Song.   F. Ford.
   Rd-SS:9
Very Nearly.   Q. Scott-Hopper.
   Au-SP:300, Fe-FP:374, Hu-MP:81
A Violet Bank.   W. Shakespeare.
   Bo-FP:318, Co-BN:50, Fe-FP:219,
   Sh-RP:81
A Warning to Skeptics.   L. Drake.
   De-FS:76
Water Sprite.   D. Wandrei.   De-FS:211
The Wee Wee Man.   De-CH:277,
   Fo-OG:28, Gr-GB:286, Ma-BB:12,
   Ox-BB:11
When a Ring's Around the Moon.
   M. Carr.   Ar-TP3:148
When I Was Six.   Z. Cross. Fe-FP:486
When Larks Gin Sing.   De-CH:660
Where the Bee Sucks. W. Shakespeare.
   Al-VBP:199, Ar-TP3:155, Bl-OB:91,
   Bo-FP:317, Cl-DT:75, De-CH:112,
   Ga-FB:28, Hu-MP:85, La-PV:78,
   Li-LC:66, Ma-YA:70, Re-TW:60,
   Rv-CB:192, Sm-MK:33
The Wife of Bath's Tale.
   G. Chaucer.   Al-VBP:14
Yesterday in Oxford Street.
   R. Fyleman.   Ar-TP3:147,
   Pe-FB:59
You Spotted Snakes. W. Shakespeare.
   Al-VBP:183, Bl-OB:160, Fe-FP:381,
   Gr-EC:94, Mc-PR:115, Sm-MK:34,
   Un-GT:297
FAIRS: see also BAZAARS (STREET);
   MARKETS AND MARKETING
Adults Only.   W. Stafford. St-H:215
As I Was Going to Banbury.
   Ir-BB:123, Mo-MGT:185, Pa-AP:38
At the Carnival.   A. Spencer.
   Hu-PN:62
Aunt Jemima of the Ocean Waves.
   R. Hayden.   Ad-PB:125
Banbury Fair.   E. Millard. Ir-BB:238
Billy Boy.   D. King.   Ir-BB:242
Budleigh Fair.   Ir-BB:241
Caravans.   I. Thompson.   St-FS:99
Craigbilly Fair.   Gr-CT:86,
   Gr-GB:230
Fiddler's Fair.   Ju-CP:40
Gee Up, My Horse, to Budleigh Fair.
   Mo-TL:79
Jill Came from the Fair.
   E. Farjeon.   Ar-TP3:116
John-John.   T. Macdonough.
   Co-PI:105, Co-PT:194
The Lads in Their Hundreds.
   A. Housman.   Un-MB:96
Mania Went to the Fair.   Gr-BB:25
Oh! Dear, What Can the Matter Be?
   De-CH:70, Mc-WS:165, Mo-MGT:200,
   Mo-TL:34, Wr-RM:127
Richard Dick upon a Stick. Ir-BB:238
A Sheep Fair.   T. Hardy.   Ho-P:206
Sledburn Fair.   De-CH:71
Strawberry Fair.   Cl-DT:59
To-morrow's the Fair.   Gr-GB:27
Whittingham Fair.   Gr-GB:139
Widdecombe Fair.   Co-PM:213,
   De-CH:72
FAIRY TALES: see also FAIRIES;
   FOLKLORE; HUMOR - FAIRY TALES;
   LEGENDS; and names of char-
   acters in fairy tales, as
   CINDERELLA
A Ballad of China.   L. Richards.
   Sh-RP:5
The Earl of Mar's Daughter.
   De-CH:290, Fo-OG:21, Ma-BB:146
The Fairy Book. A. Brown. Hu-MP:24
Fairy Days. W. Thackeray. Un-GT:16
The Lucky Marriage.   T. Blackburn.
   Pa-GTB:546

The Mother's Tale. E. Farjeon.
   Br-BC:165
Rapunzel Song. G. Meyer. Ls-NY:93
The Singing Leaves. J. Lowell.
   Hu-MP:410
Sometimes, with Secure Delight.
   J. Milton. Hu-MP:89
The Three Singing Birds. J. Reeves.
   Co-PM:145, La-PV:216
The Two Swans. T. Hood. De-CH:282
FAIRYLAND
Ann and the Fairy Song.
   W. de la Mare. Ga-FB:170
The Brown Dwarf of Rügen.
   J. Whittier. Co-PM:171
Conversation with an April Fool.
   R. Bennett. Br-SS:146
Fairies. D. Koehler. La-GI:45
A Fairy Voyage. Au-SP:299,
   Bo-FP:309
The Little Land. R. Stevenson.
   Au-SP:213
Nimphidia, the Court of Fayrie.
   M. Drayton. Al-VBP:163
Oberon's Feast. R. Herrick.
   Al-VBP:330
Over Hill, over Dale.
   W. Shakespeare. Al-VBP:182,
   Bl-OB:90, Bo-FP:325, De-TT:113,
   Fe-FP:382, Re-TW:59
The Return of the Fairy. H. Wolfe.
   Co-PM:178
This Palace Standeth in the Air.
   M. Drayton. De-CH:556
Thomas the Rhymer. Al-VBP:40,
   De-CH:119, Fo-OG:3, Gr-CT:175,
   Ha-PO:51, Ho-P:194, Ma-BB:5,
   Ma-FW:181, Pa-OM:275, Rv-CB:40,
   Un-GT:124
Where the Bee Sucks.
   W. Shakespeare. Al-VBP:199,
   Ar-TP3:155, Bl-OB:91, Bo-FP:317,
   Cl-DT:75, De-CH:112, Ga-FB:28,
   Hu-MP:85, La-PV:78, Li-LC:66,
   Ma-YA:70, Re-TW:60, Rv-CB:192,
   Sm-MK:33
FAITH: see also ASSURANCE; CREEDS;
   HUMOR - FAITH; SATIRE - FAITH
Adon 'Olam (Lord of the World).
   Pl-EI:199
All Souls' Day. S. Sassoon.
   Tr-MR:276
All the World Moved. J. Jordan.
   Ad-PB:303
And What Will Happen.
   K. Molodowsky. Ho-TY:286
Audubon, Drafted. L. Jones.
   Lo-TY:250
Belief and Unbelief. R. Browning.
   Ga-FB:130
Bishop Blougram's Apology.
   R. Browning. Ox-BN:547

But They That Wait upon the
   Lord. . . . Bible. O.T.
   Isaiah. Ar-TP3:209
The Captain's Daughter. J. Fields.
   Er-FA:459, Fe-PL:341
Choruses from "The Rock."
   T. Eliot. Gr-CC:112
A Christmas Sonnet. E. Robinson.
   Pl-EI:89, Sm-PT:188
Civilizing the Child.
   L. Mueller. Ha-TP:118
The Collar. G. Herbert. Al-VBP:341,
   Go-BP:181, Pl-EI:92, Rv-CB:355
Columbus. J. Miller. Ar-TP3:38,
   Er-FA:298, Fe-FP:403, Ha-YA:116,
   Hi-TL:13, Hu-MP:370, Mc-PR:180,
   Mc-WK:161, Se-PR:182, Sp-OG:59,
   Vi-PP:42
Comparison. J. Bunyan. Ox-BC:36
Comparisons. C. Rossetti.
   Ox-BC:276
A Compass Needle. F. Quarles.
   Ga-S:54, Rv-CB:347
The Counsels of O'Riordan the
   Rain Maker. T. O'Bolger.
   Co-PI:149
Credo. E. Robinson. Al-AP:617,
   Un-MA:116, Wi-LT:101
Dear God. C. O'Riordan. De-CH:656
Death Is a Clean Cold Word. . . .
   R. Richmond. Go-BP:230
Defense Rests. V. Miller.
   Un-MA:680
Dover Beach. M. Arnold. Al-VBP:972,
   Cl-FC:48, Co-BL:84, Er-FA:454,
   Ga-FB:66, Go-BP:147, Ha-PO:187,
   Hi-WP II:35, Ho-P:201, Ke-PP:87,
   Ma-FW:53, Ma-YA:209, Mc-PR:70,
   Mo-GR:35, Ox-BN:645, Pa-GTB:305,
   Pl-EI:78, Rv-CB:863, Un-MW:120
The Ebb and Flow. E. Taylor.
   Sh-AP:14
Ecclesiastes. G. Chesterton.
   Un-MB:205
Epilogue. H. Melville. Pl-IO:128
Even Such Is Time. W. Raleigh.
   Al-VBP:97, De-CH:644, Ga-S:219,
   Gr-BT:167, Gr-CT:381,
   Hi-WP II:169, Na-EO:93
An Evening Thought. J. Hammon.
   Hu-PN:4
Ex Nihilo. D. Gascoyne. Pa-GTB:549
Faith Is a Fine Invention.
   E. Dickinson. Co-EL:107,
   Ga-FB:150, Rv-CB:916
The Font. C. Sansom. Ga-S:180,
   Gr-BT:5
For My Grandmother. C. Cullen.
   Ad-PB:91, Bo-AN:88, Ca-VT:241,
   Un-MA:571
Foundation of Faith.
   J. Drinkwater. Tr-MR:255

FAITH — cont'd.

French Peasants. M. Gibbon.
Ga-S:121

Fret Not Thyself Because of
Evildoers. Bible. O.T.
Psalms. Ar-TP3:210

The Fundament Is Shifted. A. Evans.
Tr-MR:238

Funeral Moment. C. Theodorescu.
Mc-AC:102

The Gate of the Year. M. Haskins.
Hi-WP II:174

Giving and Taking. J. Kirkup.
Pl-EI:47

Godhead Here in Hiding. G. Hopkins.
Ga-S:199

God's Gift. R. Southwell. Ga-S:198

Good-Bye and Keep Cold. R. Frost.
Un-GT:284

Hammer and Anvil. S. Cole.
Fe-PL:333

Hark a Thrilling Voice Is
Sounding. E. Caswall. Ga-S:57

How Firm a Foundation. Ke-TF:187

I, a Justified Sinner. A. Price.
Ls-NY:90

I Believe. A. Zeitlin. Ho-TY:321

I Need No Sky. W. Bynner. Pl-EI:3

I Never Saw a Moor. E. Dickinson.
Ar-TP3:212, Ch-B:29, Er-FA:20
Fe-FP:268, Fe-PL:345, Hu-MP:174,
Li-LC:15, Mc-PR:117, Na-EO:146,
Rv-CB:908, Th-AS:170, Un-GT:306,
Un-MA:95, Wi-LT:14

I Wage Not Any Feud with Death.
A. Tennyson. Ke-PP:79

The Impercipient (at a Cathedral
Service). T. Hardy. Al-VBP:1045

In Memoriam. A. Tennyson. Pl-IO:131

In No Strange Land. F. Thompson.
Ga-S:127, Go-BP:250, Pa-GTB:398,
Pl-EI:7, Un-MB:90

Interrogative. Sister M. Thérése.
Tr-MR:228

Jack. G. Brooks. Ha-TP:55

Journal. E. Millay. Pl-IO:133

Last Words Before Winter.
L. Untermeyer. Un-GT:285,
Un-MA:308

Lead, Kindly Light. J. Newman.
Er-FA:474, Ga-S:46, Ox-BN:436

Light Breaks where No Sun Shines.
D. Thomas. Al-VBP:1245, Un-MB:498

Light in the Darkness. A. Fisher.
Ha-YA:115, Ja-PA:30

Light Shining Out of Darkness.
W. Cowper. Er-FA:461, Ga-S:6,
Mc-PR:64, Pl-EI:210, Rv-CB:549,
Sm-LG:377

The Lights in the Sky Are Stars.
K. Rexroth. Li-TU:252

Mamma! F. Horne. Ra-BP:76

The Man Without Faith. R. Church.
Tr-MR:226

The Meaning of Atman. Al-PI:19

Meditation Eight. E. Taylor.
Sh-AP:13

A Mighty Fortress Is Our God.
M. Luther. Pl-EI:213

Mock On, Mock On. W. Blake.
Ox-BN:26

Nearer Home. P. Cary. Er-FA:456

No Coward Soul Is Mine. E. Brontë.
Al-VBP:925, Er-FA:459, Ox-BN:608,
Pl-EI:4, Rv-CB:833

O Light Invisible, We Praise Thee.
T. Eliot. Tr-MR:148

O World. G. Santayana.
Fe-PL:321, Sm-PT:168

Oh Yet We Trust that Somehow Good.
A. Tennyson. Ox-BN:498, Pl-EI:81

The One Thing Needful. V. Miller.
En-PC:226

The Pagan Isms. C. McKay. Ra-BP:64

Passage to More than India.
W. Whitman. Tr-MR:292

The Passionate Man's Pilgrimage.
W. Raleigh. Al-VBP:97, Go-BP:256,
Gr-CT:283, Hi-WP II:169, Ma-YA:59,
Rv-CB:158

Patience. F. Horne. Ra-BP:77

Poems, III. E. Blum-Alquit.
Ho-TY:263

Prospice. R. Browning. Fe-PL:287,
Ga-FB:129, Rv-CB:829

The Recovery. E. Blunden. Un-MB:398

Report on Experience. E. Blunden.
Pa-GTB:492, Rv-CB:996

Rocked in the Cradle of the Deep.
E. Willard. Er-FA:467

St. Teresa's Book-Mark.
St. Theresa. Pa-SG:191,
Pl-EI:178

Santos, New Mexico. M. Sarton.
Pl-EI:116

Shells. W. Wordsworth. Go-BP:111

Siberia. I. Emiot. Ho-TY:316

Song under Shadow. W. Benét.
Tr-MR:198

Sonnet. M. de Guevara. Ga-S:145

Sonnets. G. Hopkins. Ox-BN:870

Spring 1943. R. Fuller. Wi-LT:705

Strong Son of God, Immortal Love.
A. Tennyson. Ma-YA:193,
Pl-EI:136

That Nature Is a Heraclitean Fire
and of the Comfort of the
Resurrection. G. Hopkins.
Pa-GTB:396

The Theology of Innocence.
S. Meltzer. Ad-II:21

This above All Is Precious and
Remarkable. J. Wain.
Wi-LT:833

Though the Great Waters Sleep.
E. Dickinson. Pl-EI:91
Through the Strait Pass of
Suffering. E. Dickinson.
Ga-S:225, Tr-MR:201
To a Waterfowl. W. Bryant.
De-CH:106, De-TT:179, Er-FA:232,
Fe-PL:355, Mc-PR:55, Rv-CB:734,
Sh-AP:20, Sp-OG:295
A Tough Generation. D. Gascoyne.
Wi-LT:717
Two Poems on the Catholic
Bavarians, I, II. E. Bowers.
En-PC:220-221
Unison. J. Wheelock. Tr-MR:144
Upon the Swallow. J. Bunyan.
Ox-BC:36
Walk. F. Horne. Ra-BP:75
The Waterfall. H. Vaughan.
Al-VBP:464, Ga-S:182, Ho-WR:40
We Have Been Believers.
M. Walker. Ad-PB:145, Be-MA:76,
Hu-PN:312, Jo-SA:130
Where the Rainbow Ends. R. Lowell.
Sh-AP:230, Un-MA:665
Why Should Men Love the Church.
T. Eliot. Tr-MR:199
The World's a Sea. F. Quarles.
Gr-CT:231
Zechariah. E. Marlatt. Tr-MR:82
FAITH CURES: see HUMOR - FAITH CURES
FAITHFULNESS: see LOYALTY
FALCONRY
Hawking. M. Drayton. Mo-SD:120
September. F. da San Geminiano.
Mo-SD:122
FALCONS: see HAWKS
FALL: see AUTUMN
FALLING STARS: see METEORS
FALMOUTH, ENG.
Falmouth. W. Henley. Fe-PL:148,
Un-MB:55
FALSEHOOD: see also HUMOR -
FALSEHOOD; LIARS; SLANDER
Against Lying. De-CH:756
Cantares II. L. Speyer. Ho-TH:26
The Lie. H. Nemerov. Ls-NY:272
Lies. Y. Yevtushenko. Du-SH:106
My True Love.I.Eastwick.Br-SS:121
When My Love Swears.W.Shakespeare.
Al-VBP:209, Un-MW:183
Why Do the White Men Lie.
L. Curry. Ba-HI:118
FALSTAFF, SIR JOHN
Falstaff's Lament over Prince
Hal Become Henry V.
H. Melville. Al-VBP:958
FAME: see also GREATNESS; HONOR;
HUMOR - FAME; SATIRE - FAME
All for Love. G. Byron.
Ma-YA:174, Pa-GTB:173

All the Flowers of the Spring.
J. Webster. Al-VBP:289,
De-CH:252, Rv-CB:317
The Ballad of Dead Ladies.
F. Villon. Al-VBP:991, Er-FA:173,
Ho-WR:184
Courage Has a Crimson Coat.
N. Turner. Bo-FP:299, Th-AS:212
Elegy Written in a Country Churchyard.
T. Gray. Al-VBP:559, De-TT:83,
Er-FA:462, Fe-PL:281, Ha-PO:144,
Ma-YA:125, Pa-GTB:145, Rv-CB:533
Epistle to Dr. Arbuthnot. A. Pope.
Al-VBP:539, Gr-CT:435
Essay on Man. A. Pope. Al-VBP:537
Fame. E. Greenberg. Ho-TY:309
From a Hint in the Minor Poets.
S. Wesley. Rv-CB:515
The Glories of Our Blood and State.
J. Shirley. Al-VBP:347, Ga-S:30,
Gr-CC:107, Gr-CT:350, Ke-PP:30,
Ni-JP:121, Pa-GTB:61, Rv-CB:360
The Great Dead at Thermopylae.
Simonides. Pa-SG:8
He Comforts Himself. C. Morley.
Na-EO:54
The Motto. A. Cowley. No-CL:6
Not to Die. Simonides. Pa-SG:10
On Fame. J. Keats. Rv-CB:750
On the Bank of a Stream. Da-SC:157
One Dream All Heroes. Basho.
Be-CS:26
Settling Some Old Football Scores.
M. Bishop. Mo-SD:30
Sonnet 5. M. Drayton. Al-VBP:167
Sonnet 25. W. Shakespeare.
Rv-CB:211
To an Athlete Dying Young.
A. Housman. Ha-PO:140,
Ma-YA:223, Mo-SD:168, Ni-JP:33,
Pe-M:58, Un-MB:94, Wi-LT:60
To Franz Kafka. E. Muir. Go-BP:57
To the Memory of Master
W. Shakespeare. J. Milton.
No-CL:81
When None Shall Rail. D. Lewis.
Rv-CB:502
The White Stag. E. Pound. Ha-LO:97
FAMILY AND FAMILY LIFE: see also
HOME; HUMOR - FAMILY AND FAMILY
LIFE; MARRIAGE; PARENT AND CHILD;
SATIRE - FAMILY AND FAMILY LIFE;
and names of members of the
family, as CHILDREN, FATHERS,
MOTHERS
Achtung! Achtung! M. Hacker.
Cr-WS:1
Amusing Our Daughters. C. Kizer.
Ca-VT:542
Anton and Yaro. M. Oliver.
St-H:168

FAMILY AND FAMILY LIFE — cont'd.
  Autobiography. M. Dipoko.
    Lo-TY:142
  Boy with His Hair Cut Short.
    M. Rukeyser. Br-TC:350,
    Ca-VT:361, Co-RG:159, Wi-LT:805
  A Boy's Mother. J. Riley. Se-PR:119
  Bye, Baby Bunting. Mother Goose.
    Ar-TP3:131, Au-SP:5, Cl-DT:27,
    De-PO:6, Li-LB:12, Li-SR:126,
    Mo-MGT:134, Mo-NR:8, Wi-MG:16,
    Wr-RM:77
  Christmas Hearth Rhyme. Bo-FP:204,
    Ch-B:53
  Conversation about Christmas.
    D. Thomas. Li-TU:28, 37
  The Cotter's Saturday Night.
    R. Burns. Fe-PL:58
  Country Letter. J. Clare. Rv-CB:733
  Daddy. C. Begay. Ba-HI:91
  Daddy. Y. Kamiko. Le-TA:33
  Efficiency Apartment. G. Barrax.
    Ad-PB:217
  The Empty Woman. G. Brooks.
    Pe-SS:13
  Esthetique du Mal, V. W. Stevens.
    Wi-LT:153
  The Family. Visvaneth. Al-PI:123
  The Family Poem. M. Rawitch.
    Ho-TY:202
  Family Portrait. C. de Andrade.
    An-TC:91
  Family Prime. M. Van Doren.
    Ca-VT:195
  Father. A. Naruse. Le-TA:32
  Father Is Home. Gr-EC:220
  Father's Story. E. Roberts.
    Co-PS:101, Fe-FP:33, Hu-MP:22
  For My Father. D. Kherdian.
    Kh-VA:11
  Girl's-Eye View of Relatives.
    P. McGinley. Ke-TF:90, Mc-WS:145
  Good Times. L. Clifton. Ad-PB:306,
    Be-MA:140, Br-TC:71, Ra-BP:250
  Grace for Light. M. O'Neill.
    Th-AS:174
  How Good Are the Poor. V. Hugo.
    Ke-TF:61
  Idleness. Lu Yu. Rx-OH:109
  Infancy. C. de Andrade. An-TC:87
  The Land of Story-Books.
    R. Stevenson. Ar-TP3:114,
    Fe-FP:12, Hu-MP:23, Ja-PA:50,
    Un-GB:30, Un-GT:12
  Legend. T. Aida. Sh-AM:110
  Let's Be Merry. C. Rossetti.
    Ar-TP3:2, Fe-FP:30
  Morning Mood. M. Panegoosho.
    Le-IB:29
  Negroes. M. Bodenheim. Hu-PN:508
  New England November. D. Hall.
    Ke-TF:448

  Nikki-Rosa. N. Giovanni. Ad-CI:20,
    Ad-PB:451, Be-MA:169, Jo-SA:22
  On a Friend's Escape from Drowning
    off the Norfolk Coast.
    G. Barker. To-MP:67
  Our Family. L. Clark. Pa-RE:44
  Prayer for Difficult Days.
    E. Guest. Ke-TF:201
  Prelude to an Evening. J. Ransom.
    En-PC:12, Un-MA:418
  The Pumpkin. J. Whittier.
    Co-PS:148, Se-PR:210
  Quiet Night. Wen I-to. Hs-TC:63
  Seven Times One Are Seven.
    R. Hillyer. Br-BC:156
  Snow-Bound. J. Whittier.
    Ga-FB:302, Ho-WR:174, Mc-PR:139
  The Somerset Dam for Supper.
    J. Holmes. Ni-JP:29
  Somewhere in Tuscany.
    D. Holbrook. Ls-NY:13
  Song of War. Tr-US I:203
  The Spirit of Spring. Liu Ta-pai.
    Hs-TC:7
  Summer Remembered. I. Gardner.
    Pe-OA:235
  The Table. C. de Andrade.
    An-TC:67
  There Once Was a Man. On-TW:7
  Tired and Unhappy, You Think of
    Houses. D. Schwartz.
    Un-MA:617, Wi-LT:516
  To Aunt Rose. A. Ginsberg.
    Ca-VT:575, Wi-LT:719
  Travelling in the Family.
    C. de Andrade. An-TC:57
  Two Surprises. R. McAlpine.
    Fe-PL:88
  Under the Holly-Bough.
    C. Mackay. Ke-TF:48
  The Vixen. J. Clare. Co-BBW:33
  Washing the Dishes. C. Morley.
    Fe-PL:143
  What Does the Bee Do?
    C. Rossetti. Ar-TP3:4, Fe-FP:30,
    Ox-BC:279
  Who's In? E. Fleming. Bl-OB:145,
    Cl-FC:61, Pe-FB:22, Th-AS:41
  The Young Girl. C. Day Lewis.
    Ls-NY:223
FAMILY TREES: see ANCESTORS AND
    ANCESTRY; HERITAGE
FAMINES
  A Description of Famine. Al-PI:69
  Famine. W. Brown. Sa-B:17
  The Famine Year. Lady Wilde.
    Co-PI:197
  The Hopis and the Famine. Te-FC:35
FANS AND FANNING
  The Eagle-Feather Fan. N. Momaday.
    Ni-CD:98
  The Fan. J. Gay. Al-VBP:525

Little Maid of Far Japan.
   A. Wynne. Hu-MP:138
On a Fan That Belonged to the
   Marquise de Pompadour.
   A. Dobson.   Al-VBP:1050
A Present from the Emperor's
   New Concubine. Lady P'an.
   Rx-LT:3
FANTASY: see also HUMOR - FANTASY
   Alice 1963. G. Bishop-Dubjinsky.
   Sc-TN:11
Arizona Nature Myth. J. Michie.
   Sm-MK:187
Bedtime Story for My Son.
   P. Redgrove. Go-BP:120,
   Gr-BT:161
The Big Nasturtiums. R. Hale.
   Co-BN:50, Co-PM:83
The Birdcatcher. R. Hodgson.
   Un-MB:187
The Birds of the Air. Rv-ON:109
Bobadil. J. Reeves. Li-LC:58
Boy into Heron. C. Randall.
   Sm-MK:186
The Castle Yonder. J. Dudley.
   Le-M:62
Centaur of the Groundlevel
   Apartment. E. Pfeiffer.
   Ls-NY:337
Come, Ride with Me to Toyland.
   R. Bennett. Br-SS:103
Conceit with Aunties, Urn and
   Birds. M. Leech. Ls-NY:326
Confessions. R. Browning.
   Al-VBP:908, Pa-GTB:355
A Conversation. D. Thomas.
   La-RM:102
A Dead Bird. A. Young. Co-BBW:245,
   Re-BS:56
Dialogue - 2 Dollmakers. G. Corso.
   Kh-VA:19
Dream. S. Edwards. Hu-NN:75,
   Hu-PN:402
The Dream Woman. P. Hubbell.
   Ar-TP3:150
The Elfin Knight. De-CH:276,
   Gr-GB:285, Ma-BB:181
The Embankment. T. Hulme.
   Pa-GTB:445
Exercise Book. P. Dehn. Hi-WP II:8
Fantasia. W. Letts. Co-PI:93
Fantasy. R. Skidmore. Co-PM:153
Free Fantasia on Japanese Themes.
   A. Lowell. Un-MA:159
From Nothing Strange. G. Davidson.
   De-FS:70
From the Hills of Dream.
   F. Macleod. Th-AS:140
Green Candles. H. Wolfe. Co-PM:177,
   Sm-MK:33, Un-MB:303
The Green Dryad's Plea. T. Hood.
   Ox-BN:414

Hold Fast Your Dreams. L. Driscoll.
   Ar-TP3:214, Au-SP:356, Br-BC:123,
   Fe-FP:22, Hu-MP:73
I Stood upon a Star. S. Teasdale.
   Sh-RP:177
If You Never Talked with Fairies.
   E. Fowler. Br-BC:133
Jim Jay. W. de la Mare. Br-SS:10,
   Ir-BB:152, Sm-MK:207, Un-GT:105
Kalamazoo. V. Lindsay. Gr-CC:149,
   Pa-HT:47
Leave-Taking. Le-OE:93, Tr-US II:307
A Little Girl, Rumi's Fancy.
   N. Guha. Al-PI:81
The Man in the Ocelot Suit.
   C. Brookhouse. Ad-CI:108
Mirage. R. Church. Sm-MK:31
A Misanthrope's Serenade.
   Kuo Mo-jo. Hs-TC:36
The Night-Piece. R. Herrick.
   De-CH:275, Un-MW:21
Otherwhere. F. Gray. De-FS:98
Proposition. N. Guillén.
   Ab-MO:4, Fe-FP:487, Lo-TY:104
The Question. P. Shelley.
   De-CH:8, De-TT:141, Pa-GTB:277
The Return of the Fairy.
   H. Wolfe. Co-PM:178
Riddle of Snow and Sun. Gr-CT:395,
   Gr-GB:36, Rv-CB:444, Rv-ON:36
Shakespeare: the Fairies' Advocate.
   T. Hood. Ox-BN:417
The Shepherd and the Nymph.
   W. Landor. Ox-BN:182
Song. T. Hood. Bo-FP:322,
   Hu-MP:94
Spider Silverlegs. C. Bailey.
   Bo-FP:326
Strawberry Fields Forever.
   J. Lennon. Mo-GR:127
There Was an Old Woman. Au-SP:2,
   Bo-FP:215, Gr-EC:211, Ir-BB:252,
   La-PV:197, Li-LB:58, Mo-MGT:145,
   Mo-NR:92, Na-EO:100, Wr-RM:66
Tonight the Pacifist Moon.
   S. Alexander. Ls-NY:181
A Tree at Dusk. W. Welles.
   Hu-MP:277, Th-AS:143
A Visit from Abroad. J. Stephens.
   Co-PM:156, Ha-LO:40
Water Baby. C. O'John. Al-WW:62
The Water Lady. T. Hood.
   Al-VBP:797, De-CH:279
The Wee Wee Man. De-CH:277,
   Fo-OG:28, Gr-GB:286, Ma-BB:12,
   Ox-BB:11
FAR EAST: see ORIENT
FAREWELLS: see also HUMOR -
   FAREWELLS; LOVE - PARTING;
   PARTING; SATIRE - FAREWELLS
About to Sail for Home.
   Wang Tu-ch'ing. Hs-TC:196

FAREWELLS — cont'd.
  Ae Fond Kiss. R. Burns. Al-VBP:648,
    Er-FA:122, Hi-WP II:102, Un-MW:80
  After the Supper and Talk.
    W. Whitman. Un-MA:87
  And Now Goodnight. Mother Goose.
    Pa-AP:54
  At This Farewell. W. Wordsworth.
    Se-PR:243
  Autumn in Sigulda. A. Voznesensky.
    Ca-MR:72
  Brother Green. Em-AF:455
  Daddy. Y. Kamiko. Le-TA:33
  Departure in the Dark.
    C. Day Lewis. Br-TC:257
  Fare Thee Well. G. Byron.
    Er-FA:405, Ox-BN:251
  Fare You Well, My Darling. Em-AF:453
  The Farewell. R. Burns. Al-VBP:377,
    De-CH:175
  Farewell! G. Byron. Al-VBP:720,
    Un-MW:83
  Farewell. A. Housman. Un-MB:103
  A Farewell. C. Patmore. Ox-BN:652,
    Pa-GTB:369, Un-MW:92
  Farewell. K. Tynan. De-CH:47
  Farewell Advice. C. Kingsley.
    Ke-TF:64
  Farewell in a Dream. S. Spender.
    Un-MB:470
  Farewell! Like a Bee. Basho.
    Be-CS:62
  Farewell, My Younger Brother.
    Ho-SD:38
  Farewell of Warriors of Vavau Going
    to Fight at Sea. Tr-US II:50
  Farewell to Fan Yun at An Ch'eng.
    Shen Yueh. Rx-LT:36
  A Farewell to London. A. Pope.
    Rv-CB:513
  Farewell to My Mother. Placido.
    Lo-TY:99
  Farewell to the Farm. R. Stevenson.
    Ar-TP3:94, Fe-FP:242, Hu-MP:313
  First, Goodbye. J. Smith.
    To-MP:92
  Goin' 'Cross the Mountain.
    Em-AF:452
  Good-bye. R. Emerson. Er-FA:475
  Goodbye and Run. P. Irving.
    Al-WW:81
  Hello and Goodbye. B. Lee.
    Ja-PC:60
  How Can a Deep Love Seem Deep
    Love. Tu Mu. Le-MW:119
  Last Song. J. Guthrie. Ar-TP3:181,
    La-PV:62
  The Last Word of a Bluebird.
    R. Frost. Ar-TP3:187, Bo-GJ:13,
    Fe-FP:286, Gr-TG:33, Ir-BB:33,
    Ja-PA:8, Li-LC:55, Pa-RE:58
    Tu-WW:92

Lord Maxwell's Last Goodnight.
    Ox-BB:607
  My Bonie Mary. R. Burns.
    Al-VBP:646, Gr-CC:121, Pa-GTB:127
  My Heart's in the Highlands.
    R. Burns. Er-FA:424
  O, Fare You Well. Sp-HW:8
  Ode. C. Cotton. Al-VBP:475
  Oxford. L. Johnson. Ox-BN:949
  Prophecy. Ho Ch'i-fang. Hs-TC:218
  Shake Hands. A. Housman.
    Co-PU:146, Hi-WP I:88
  Song at the Departure of a
    Beautiful Girl. Tr-US I:170
  Song of Departure and Farewell.
    Tr-US I:245
  Song of Tukulua. Tukulua.
    Tr-US II:48
  Spanish Ladies. Sm-LG:311
  Suicide Note. S. Yesenin. Ca-MR:112
  Sweet Innisfallen. T. Moore.
    Ox-BN:215
  The Time Has Come. S. Voronov.
    Mo-MI:41
  A Traveler Departs. W. Gerry.
    Ke-TF:417
  Tristia. O. Mandelstam. Ca-MR:157
  Valediction to My Contemporaries.
    H. Gregory. Un-MA:506
  We Drink Farewell. Tu Mu.
    Rx-LT:75
  A Weary Lot Is Thine. W. Scott.
    Al-VBP:675, De-CH:174, Ox-BN:133,
    Pa-GTB:194
  When from the World. De-CH:650
  Whither Away? M. Coleridge.
    De-CH:337
  A Winter's Tale. D. Lawrence.
    Un-MB:287
  Youth. M. Tsvetayeva. Ca-MR:138
FARM LIFE: see also BARNS; COUNTRY
    LIFE; DAIRYING; FARMERS; HARVEST;
    HAY AND HAYING; HUMOR - FARM
    LIFE; PEASANTS; PLOWING; RANCH
    LIFE; SATIRE - FARM LIFE;
    TRACTORS; and names of farm
    products, as CORN
  After Apple-Picking. R. Frost.
    Al-VBP:1126, Co-RG:163, Sh-AP:146,
    Un-MA:176
  Amy Elizabeth Ermyntrude Annie.
    Q. Hopper. Ar-TP3:7
  Autumn. Ho Ch'i-fang. Hs-TC:220
  The Axe-Helve. R. Frost. Ni-JP:89
  Bent Down by a Storm. Joso.
    Be-CS:22
  Birches. R. Frost. Fe-PL:437,
    Ga-FB:299, Mo-BG:114, Pe-OA:33,
    Sm-LG:61, Sp-OG:357, Un-MA:177,
    Wi-LT:166
  Boy, Walking and Whistling.
    A. Armour. Ke-TF:82

Bread the Holy.   E. Coatsworth.
  Tr-MR:29
Burn the Cocoons.   J. Hearst.
  St-H:81
A Busy Day.   Bo-FP:68, Hi-GD:8
A Cock and Bull Story.   Sp-TM:6,
  Wr-RM:84
The Cotter's Saturday Night.
  R. Burns.   Fe-PL:58
Death of a Vermont Farm Woman.
  B. Howes.   Un-MA:653
The Death of the Hired Man.
  R. Frost.   Pe-OA:26, Un-MA:171
The Death of the Sports-Car
  Driver.   J. Aaron.   Pe-M:91
The Difficult Land.   E. Muir.
  Go-BP:228
Digging.   S. Heaney.   Br-TC:173,
  To-MP:150
Double-Damn.   Br-FW:7
Drumdelgie.   Gr-GB:210
Early Snow.   R. Huff.   St-H:84
Earth Dweller.   W. Stafford.
  Mc-EA:118
The Evacuee.   R. Thomas.   To-MP:47
Evening.   C. Cotton.   Gr-CT:400,
  Ho-WR:142
Evening at the Farm.
  J. Trowbridge.   Fe-FP:237,
  Hu-MP:308
Evening Settles on the Farm.
  Gr-BB:12
Farewell to the Farm.
  R. Stevenson.   Ar-TP3:94,
  Fe-FP:242, Hu-MP:313
The Farm.   D. Hall.   Wi-LT:727
Farm Boy after Summer.
  R. Francis.   Ha-PO:74
A Farm on the Great Plains.
  W. Stafford.   En-PC:142
Farm Wife.   R. Thomas.   Go-BP:50
Farm Yard at Evening.   J. Clare.
  Co-BBW:177
The Farmyard.   St-FS:90
A Farmyard Song.   M. Hastings.
  Au-SP:228
February.   J. Clare.   Ox-BN:309
Fence Wire.   J. Dickey.   Ca-VT:492
Fern Hill.   D. Thomas.   Al-VBP:1246,
  Bo-GJ:53, Br-TC:440, Cl-DT:63,
  Co-RG:160, Fe-PL:251, Ga-FB:166,
  Hi-WP II:46, Mc-EA:42, Mc-WK:10,
  Na-EO:45, Pa-GTB:542, Pe-SS:162,
  Re-TW:100, Sm-LG:108, Un-MB:502,
  Wi-LT:559
Fetching Cows.   N. MacCaig.
  Ma-FW:227
Fingers in the Nesting Box.
  R. Graves.   Co-BBW:162
First Song.   G. Kinnell.   Bo-GJ:47,
  Br-TC:237, Ha-TP:122, Mo-BG:123,
  Wi-LT:745

Floodtide.   A. Touré.   Ad-PB:336,
  Hu-PN:424
The Foddering Boy.   J. Clare.
  De-CH:632
Folk Wisdom.   Br-TC:242
For the Iowa Dead.   P. Engle.
  St-H:55
Foreclosure.   S. Brown.   Ad-PB:64,
  Hu-PN:170
From Plane to Plane.   R. Frost.
  Un-MA:191
The Gleaner.   J. Taylor.   Ox-BC:120
Go to the Barn for Courtesy.
  T. Coffin.   Ke-TF:339
Good-bye and Keep Cold.   R. Frost.
  Un-GT:284
The Gracious and the Gentle Thing.
  R. Coffin.   Rd-OA:84
The Happy Farmer.   Un-GT:94
Hardweed Path Going.   A. Ammons.
  Ca-VT:552
Haymaking.   E. Thomas.   Un-MB:218
Hill Farm.   K. Starbird.   Ke-TF:299
The Hill Farmer Speaks.   R. Thomas.
  To-MP:62
The Hill Wife.   R. Frost.   Wi-LT:167
The Housemaid.   R. Korn.   Ho-TY:302
How Cool Cut Hay Smells.   Boncho.
  Be-CS:16
Improved Farm Land.   C. Sandburg.
  La-RM:77
In Spring in Warm Weather.
  D. Aldis.   Br-BC:9
In the Barnyard.   D. Aldis.
  Sh-RP:330
In the Farmhouse.   G. Kinnell.
  Ha-WR:94
It Is Raining.   L. Mitchell.
  Ar-TP3:170, Au-SP:311
Kansas.   V. Lindsay.   Pa-HT:49
Labor of Fields.   E. Coatsworth.
  Mc-PR:133
Landmark.   J. Hearst.   St-H:77
Last Words Before Winter.
  L. Untermeyer.   Un-GT:285,
  Un-MA:308
Late Harvest.   J. Tate.   St-H:232
Lavender's Blue.   Ir-BB:270,
  Li-LB:28
A Leaf-Treader.   R. Frost.   Un-MA:188
Limited View.   J. Hearst.   St-H:76
Little Boy.   Gr-GB:169, Mo-MGT:62,
  Rv-ON:70
Lullaby for Ann-Lucian.   C. Forbes.
  Ad-PB:490
The Manor Farm.   E. Thomas.   Cl-FC:58
The Marital Journey.   H. Araaya.
  Pe-M:152
Maud Muller.   J. Whittier.
  Fe-PL:47, Sp-OG:271
Midsummer.   J. Scully.   Br-TC:359,
  Pe-OA:270
A Midsummer Song.   R. Gilder.
  Co-BN:92, Ke-TF:44

FARM LIFE — cont'd.
Midwife Cat. M. Van Doren.
    Rd-OA:83
Milking Time. E. Roberts.
    Bo-GJ:45, Fe-FP:239, Ma-FO:(11),
    Pa-RE:82
Minnie and Mattie. C. Rossetti.
    Ar-TP3:71, Bo-GJ:40
The Mowers. M. Benton. Ha-YA:83
Mowing. R. Frost. Ca-VT:4
My Maid Mary. Bo-FP:68, Hi-GD:11,
    Mo-MGT:149, Wr-RM:76
Nature Songs, I. Tr-US II:185
The Need of Being Versed in
    Country Things. R. Frost.
    Ha-PO:90
New England Farmhouses.
    R. Montgomery. Ke-TF:410
Night and Noises. G. Foster.
    Le-M:86
Now Gaze the Stags. E. Thurlow.
    De-CH:619
Of Bloom. L. Goldberg. Me-PH:113
Old Moon Planter. J. Knoepfle.
    St-H:94
The Old Oaken Bucket.
    S. Woodworth. Er-FA:138,
    Fe-FP:543
Oregon Rain. J. McGahey.
    Br-AF:163, Du-RG:125
Our Heritage. J. Stuart. Br-AF:4
Pagan Saturday. J. Logan. St-H:114
The Pasture. R. Frost.
    Al-VBP:1125, Ar-TP3:75, Au-SP:45,
    Bo-GJ:44, Co-BBW:162, Fe-FP:230,
    La-PP:23, La-PV:166, Li-LC:75,
    Mc-PR:121, Pa-RE:115, Pe-FB:2,
    Su-FVI:57, Th-AS:75, Un-MA:168
The Peters Family. W. Stafford,
    St-H:216
Ploughing on Sunday. W. Stevens.
    Bo-GJ:52, Fe-FP:232, Pa-RE:100,
    Re-TW:14, Sm-MK:26, We-PZ:38
Poem. P. Markish. Ho-TY:182,
    183, 184
The Poor Man's Pig. E. Blunden.
    Un-MB:396
Portrait of Life. Tsang K'o-chia.
    Hs-TC:287
Potato Digger. F. Frost. Ls-NY:152
Praise Song of the Wind.
    Tr-US II:131
The Prodigal. E. Bishop. Br-TC:52,
    Wi-LT:514
The Raggedy Man. J. Riley.
    Fe-FP:533, Hu-MP:142, Ox-BC:301,
    Un-GT:99
A Reaping Song. Tr-US II:153
The Rival. S. Warner. Un-MB:374
Sacrifice of the Sparrows of the
    Field. J. Langland.
    St-H:107

The Satin Mice Creaking Last
    Summer's Grass. R. Coffin.
    Rd-OA:90
Scythe Song. A. Lang. Sp-OG:309
She Will Weep. Br-FW:21
Sheep in Winter. J. Clare.
    Ma-FW:280
The Shepherd. W. Wordsworth.
    Ox-BN:101
The Six Badgers. R. Graves.
    Bo-GJ:76, Co-BBW:33, Co-IW:19,
    Ir-BB:22, Pa-RE:41
Snow-Bound. J. Whittier. Ga-FB:302,
    Ho-WR:174, Mc-PR:139
Snowstorm. J. Clare. Co-BN:198,
    Ho-WR:180, Ma-FW:275
The Solitary Reaper. W. Wordsworth.
    Bl-OB:146, Co-RG:122, De-CH:207,
    Go-BP:49, Ha-PO:83, Hi-WP II:142,
    Ma-YA:141, Ox-BN:77, Pa-GTB:255,
    Pl-US:50, Re-TW:114, Rv-CB:635,
    Sp-OG:336
The Song of the Banana Man.
    E. Jones. Co-RM:242, Sa-B:101
Sowing. E. Thomas. Cl-FC:29
The Steam Threshing-Machine.
    C. Tennyson-Turner. Ox-BN:470
Storm Fear. R. Frost. Al-VBP:1127
Summer Evening. W. de la Mare.
    Un-MB:201
A Time to Talk. R. Frost. Sp-OG:248
To a "Tenting" Boy.
    C. Tennyson-Turner. Ox-BN:472
Truth. J. Hearst. St-H:79
Twelve Oxen. Cl-DT:49, De-CH:139,
    Gr-CT:114, Gr-GB:53, Re-TW:78,
    Sh-RP:51
Under Your Voice, among Legends.
    P. Harris. Sc-TN:81
The Village. G. Crabbe. Ha-PO:77
Way Down Yonder in the Maple Swamp.
    Un-GT:17
The Wheel of Summer. J. Langland.
    St-H:101
When the Frost Is on the Punkin.
    J. Riley. Co-BN:134, Er-FA:132,
    Fe-PL:387, Ga-FB:298, Hu-MP:319
Where I Took Hold of Life.
    R. Coffin. Br-BC:122
Where the Hayfields Were.
    A. MacLeish. Ha-LO:80
A Whistling Girl and a Flock of
    Sheep. Sp-TM:15
White Cat. R. Knister. Do-WH:82
Wilderness. Ai Ch'ing. Hs-TC:314
A Witch. W. Barnes. Co-PM:23
The Wood-Pile. R. Frost.
    Ca-VT:8, Ni-JP:88, Sh-AP:146,
    Sp-OG:285
A Youth Mowing. D. Lawrence.
    Un-MB:285

FARMERS: see also HUMOR - FARMERS;
  PEASANTS; SATIRE - FARMERS;
  SHARECROPPERS
Above Penmaenmawr. T.Connor. To-MP:184
The Barnyard. M. Burnham.
  Ar-TP3:70, Bo-FP:105
The Crafty Farmer. Ar-TP3:16
Crossing Kansas by Train.
  D. Justice. Du-RG:45, Mc-WS:119
Cynddylan on a Tractor. R. Thomas.
  Ga-S:123, To-MP:63
The Da Pacem of the Laborer.
  Ba-PO:85
Farm Boy after Summer. R. Francis.
  Ha-PO:74
Farm Hand. J. Hearst. St-H:77
Farmer. L. Bailey. Ha-YA:108,
  Sh-RP:7
The Farmer's Boy. Cl-DT:83
A Farmer's Life. Pa-RE:24
The Farmer's Wife. A. Sexton.
  Wi-LT:816
Father. F. Frost. Ar-TP3:3,
  Br-SS:165, Fe-FP:34
Field and Forest. R. Jarrell.
  Ca-VT:403
For the Record. R. Thomas.
  Go-BP:217, To-MP:43
A Fox Started Out in a Hungry
  Plight. Mo-NR:146
The Happy Farmer. Tse Nan.
  Le-MW:115
The Happy Farmer. Un-GT:94
Hill Farm. K. Starbird. Ke-TF:299
The Hill Farmer Speaks. R. Thomas.
  Pa-GTB:536, To-MP:62
Homestead. E. Roach. Sa-B:98
I Will Go with My Father
  a-Ploughing. J. Campbell.
  Ar-TP3:202, Br-SS:166, Fe-FP:231
Imperial Valley, Calif. J. Kessler.
  Ls-NY:253
In Dessexshire as It Befell.
  Gr-GB:316
The Ox-Tamer. W. Whitman.
  Co-BBW:164, Co-RM:236, Rv-CB:857
The Ploughman. Gr-GB:211
The Plower. P. Colum. Un-MB:249
Preparation. R. Francis. Du-RG:131
Quiet Citizen. B. Cooper.
  Ke-TF:298
The Seed of All Song. Basho.
  Be-CS:18
Squatter's Rites. D. Scott. Sa-B:151
Stewards. B. Cooper. Ke-TF:299
There Lived a Little Man. St-FS:19
To the Young Pioneers of the North-
  west. Pien Chih-lin. Hs-TC:169
When Smoke Stood Up from Ludlow.
  A. Housman. Un-MB:95
You Who Cultivate Fields.
  Do-CH:(24)

FARRAGUT, DAVID GLASGOW
  Farragut. W. Meredith. Hi-TL:108
FASCISM: see also MUSSOLINI, BENITO;
  NATIONAL SOCIALISM
  Fascist Limericks. L. Bacon.
  Cr-WS:38
FASHION: see CLOTHING AND DRESS;
  DRESSMAKING; HUMOR - FASHION;
  WORTH, CHARLES FREDERICK
FASTING: see also HUMOR -
  FASTING; LENT
  This Is the Song They Sang at Fast
  Every Eight Years.. Tr-US II:278
A True Lent. R. Herrick. Se-PR:70
FATE: see also CHANCE; HUMOR - FATE;
  SATIRE - FATE
  Atavism. M. Sorescu. Mc-AC:157
  Brown Robyn's Confession.
  De-CH:399, Gr-GB:314
Dance Song of Death. Tr-US II:3
The Death of Vitellozzo Vitelli.
  I. Feldman. Br-TC:121
Design. R. Frost. Ho-LP:49,
  Pe-OA:45
Destiny. E. Arnold. Fe-PL:338
Doth Then the World Go Thus.
  W. Drummond. Pa-GTB:40
Drum Song in Three Parts from the
  Funeral Ceremony for a Hero.
  Tr-US I:56
Esthetique du Mal, XIII.
  W. Stevens. Wi-LT:158
Fate! I Have Asked. W. Landor.
  Al-VBP:704
Fear No More. W. Shakespeare.
  Al-VBP:195, Bo-HF:179, Co-RG:144,
  De-CH:250, De-TT:193, Er-FA:260,
  Gr-CT:332, Ha-PO:251, Hi-WP II:19,
  No-CL:73, Pa-GTB:28, Rv-CB:201,
  Sm-LG:267
Flux. R. Eberhart. Ca-VT:247
For I the Ballad Will Repeat.
  W. Shakespeare. Al-VBP:192
From a Hint in the Minor Poets.
  S. Wesley. Rv-CB:515
Future Simple. I. Richards. Ls-NY:120
Germinal. AE. Un-MB:146
The Glories of Our Blood and State.
  J. Shirley. Al-VBP:347, Ga-S:30,
  Gr-CC:107, Gr-CT:350, Ke-PP:30,
  Ni-JP:121, Pa-GTB:61, Rv-CB:360
Hero and Leander. C. Marlowe.
  Al-VBP:170
In the Suburbs. L. Simpson.
  Co-EL:106
The Lamentation of Enion. W. Blake.
  Ox-BN:37
The Mood. Q. Prettyman. Ad-PB:260
My Name Is Afrika. K. Kgositsile.
  Ad-PB:326
My Stars. A. Ibn Ezra. Me-PH:64
Native. N. Madgett. Be-MA:92

FATE — cont'd.
  121st Chorus. J. Kerouac.
    Ha-TP:132
  Our Little Sister Is Worried.
    Rx-LT:22
  Peruvian Dance Song.   Le-OE:133
  A Poem. B. Pasternak. Bo-RU:1
  Praise to the End. T. Roethke.
    Li-TU:214
  The Question. T. Kucherenko.
    Mo-MI:84
  Rubaiyat of Omar Khayyam.
    E. Fitzgerald. Al-VBP:832,
    Er-FA:43, Fe-FP:479, Ha-PO:210,
    Ox-BN:526, Pa-SG:120
  The Sage. D. Levertov. Kh-VA:27
  Song for the Dead. Tr-US I:53
  The Subalterns. T. Hardy. Un-MB:33
  Tired. F. Johnson. Ad-PB:24,
    Fe-PL:428, Hu-PN:88, Kr-OF:48,
    Lo-TY:210
  To Juan at the Winter Solstice.
    R. Graves. Br-TC:154,
    Ha-PO:191, Un-MB:390, Wi-LT:377
  Waiting Both. T. Hardy.
    Mc-WK:105, Un-MB:35
  Webs. C. Sandburg. Ho-TH:56
  Weep No More. J. Fletcher.
    Al-VBP:284, De-CH:420
  You Are Involved. M. Carter.
    Sa-B:135
THE FATES
  Ode. J. Bishop. Wi-LT:606
FATHERS: see also HUMOR - FATHERS;
    PARENT AND CHILD
  After Dark. A. Rich. Wi-LT:801
  Ap Huw's Testament. R. Thomas.
    Gr-BT:xv
  At the Seed and Feed. J. Simons.
    Ls-NY:235
  Becoming a Dad. E. Guest.
    Fe-PL:141
  Birthday Gift. E. de Vito.
    Br-BC:153
  Boy Driving His Father to
    Confession. S. Heaney. Gr-BT:23
  Christabel. S. Coleridge.
    Al-VBP:698
  Commander Lowell. R. Lowell.
    Ca-VT:451
  Daddy. S. Plath. Br-TC:324,
    Mc-EA:164, Wi-LT:789
  Daddy Fell into the Pond. A. Noyes.
    Co-HP:101, Fe-FP:35, Ja-PC:40,
    La-PP:45, La-PV:24, Sh-RP:140
  Daddy in the Dream. M. Yamaguchi.
    Le-TA:31
  Dirges, I. Tr-US II:41
  Elegy for My Father. H. Moss.
    Wi-LT:777
  An Evening Glow. K. Takahashi.
    Le-TA:34
  An Excuse for Not Returning the
    Visit of a Friend.
    Mei Yao Ch'en. Rx-OH:37
  Father. F. Frost. Ar-TP3:3,
    Br-SS:165, Fe-FP:34
  Father. A. Naruse. Le-TA:32
  Father. M. Weston. Co-PS:102
  Father Is Home. Gr-EC:220
  Father Son and Holy Ghost. A. Lorde.
    Ad-PB:248, Be-MA:121
  Father's Story. E. Roberts.
    Co-PS:101, Fe-FP:33, Hu-MP:22
  Father's Voice. W. Stafford.
    Mc-EA:113
  The Feast of Lanterns.
    J. Yoshimura. Le-TA:35
  Fruit of the Flower. C. Cullen.
    Fe-PL:136, Jo-SA:20
  Girl's-Eye View of Relatives.
    P. McGinley. Ke-TF:90, Mc-WS:145
  Graeme and Bewick. Ox-BB:356,
    Rv-CB:47
  Hallelujah: A Sestina. R. Francis.
    En-PC:46
  The Hero. L. Jackson. Br-SS:164
  I Sit with My Dolls. Ba-PO:179,
    Cr-WS:131
  If There Are Any Heavens.
    E. Cummings. Un-MA:476
  Kaddish. M. Rawitch. Ho-TY:203
  Lament of a Widow over Her Dead
    Husband. Tr-US I:72
  Listening. W. Stafford. Kh-VA:21
  Love from My Father. C. Clemmons.
    Ad-PB:489
  The Man of the House. D. Wagoner.
    Du-SH:52
  Mortmain. R. Warren. En-PC:74,
    Ho-P:295
  My Father. J. Sternberg. Ho-TY:194
  My Father Loved the Jumping-Off
    Place. R. Coffin. Sh-RP:309
  My Father Moved Through Dooms of
    Love. e. cummings. En-PC:22,
    Sh-AP:193
  My Father's Trunk. R. Roseliep.
    St-H:188
  My Little Son. M. Rosenfeld.
    Ho-TY:79
  Newspaper. A. Fisher. Au-SP:102
  Notes Found near a Suicide: To
    James. F. Horne. Bo-AN:45,
    Bo-HF:90, Br-BC:124, Ra-BP:73
  Oh Father. W. Rose. Ni-CD:206
  The Old and Young Courtier.
    Al-VBP:369, No-CL:229
  The Old Man and Jim. J. Riley.
    Co-PT:232, Sp-OG:197
  Our Father. R. Mathew. Ma-FW:63
  Paternal. E. Wilson. Hu-PN:370
  a poem for fathers. K. Wilson.
    Sc-TN:243

Rugby Chapel — November, 1857.
M. Arnold. Rv-CB:874
The Secret Heart. R. Coffin.
Co-PS:103, Se-PR:152
Secret Laughter. C. Morley.
Ga-FB:86
Soldier. W. Benét. Ke-TF:170
The Table. C. de Andrade. An-TC:67
Those Winter Sundays. R. Hayden.
Ad-PB:119, Du-SH:53, Jo-SA:21,
Mo-BG:75
To Sherwood Anderson in Heaven.
F. Eckman. St-H:46
Travelling in the Family.
C. de Andrade. An-TC:57
Walking. G. Glaubitz. Au-SP:108,
Mc-AW:16
The Way to Know a Father.
R. Coffin. Se-PR:151
The Western Movies. H. Ito.
Le-TA:27
What Shall They Tell That Son?
C. Sandburg. Pe-SS:10
The Wheel of Summer.
J. Langland. St-H:101
Wife and Husband. C. Day. Le-M:141
A Wonderful Man. A. Fisher.
Br-SS:164
The Workshop. A. Fisher. Au-SP:104
FATHER'S DAY: see FATHERS
FATIGUE
After I Had Worked All Day.
C. Reznikoff. Ca-VT:187
Dog-Tired. D. Lawrence. Gr-BT:50
Fatigue. P. Bacon. La-OC:62
Long Journey. Pien Chih-lin.
Hs-TC:161
Old Horse. Sun Yu-t'ang. Hs-TC:122
The Pulley. G. Herbert. Al-VBP:346,
Ga-S:52, Ha-PO:198, Mc-PR:207,
Pa-GTB:64, Pl-EI:51, Rv-CB:356
Rock Me to Sleep. E. Allen.
Er-FA:171
Supplication. J. Cotter. Hu-PN:134
Tired Tim. W. de la Mare. Ar-TP3:6,
Au-SP:133, Fe-FP:308, Hu-MP:141,
Li-LC:49, Pe-FB:27, Rd-SS:7
The Tired Worker. C. McKay.
Ra-BP:60
Tragedy. AE. Un-MB:143
FAULTFINDING: see CRITICS AND
CRITICISM
FAUNS (MYTH.)
The Faun Sees Snow for the First
Time. R. Aldington. Un-MB:354
FAUST
Faust. J. Ashbery. Br-TC:16
The Progress of Faust.
K. Shapiro. Pe-OA:220
The Tragical History of Doctor
Faustus. C. Marlowe. Al-VBP:177,
Gr-CT:151, Ma-FW:161, Ma-YA:63

FAWKES, GUY
Gunpowder Plot. V. Scannell.
Ma-FW:267, To-MP:70
Guy Fawkes Day. Hi-FO:144,
Li-LB:161, Mo-MGT:203
Wul 'E Plaize. De-TT:92
FAWNS: see DEER
FEAR: see also COURAGE;
HUMOR - FEAR
The Affliction of Margaret.
W. Wordsworth. Pa-GTB:239
Afraid. W. de la Mare. Gr-TG:58
Alan. R. Roseliep. De-FS:163
All the Roary Night. K. Patchen.
Wi-LT:786
Anne and the Field-Mouse.
I. Serraillier. Pa-RE:106
At the Keyhole. W. de la Mare.
Bl-OB:88, Un-MB:199
Autobiography. L. MacNeice.
Gr-BT:13, Ma-FW:193
Balloon. S. Tsuboi. Sh-AM:72
Between the World and Me.
R. Wright. Ad-PB:107, Bo-AN:103,
Kr-OF:158, Pe-M:92, Wi-LT:657
The Bishop Orders His Tomb at
Saint Praxed's Church.
R. Browning. Al-VBP:895,
Mo-GR:57
Black Are the Stars. R. Roseliep.
De-FS:160
Blue and Red Poem. A. Gilboa.
Me-PH:118
Both Sides of the Yellow River
Recaptured by the Imperial
Army. Tu Fu. Cr-WS:10
Bride's Song on the Way to Her
Husband's House. Tr-US II:139
Burning. G. Snyder. Ma-FW:140
Carmel Point. M. MacSweeney.
Du-RG:75
Cat and Mouse. T. Hughes. Pl-EI:127
Chant of Kororupo. Tr-US II:86
A Charm. R. Herrick. Gr-CT:167
The Child Dying. E. Muir.
Pa-GTB:468
Children at Night. S. Morse.
Ls-NY:230
A Child's Winter Evening.
G. John. De-CH:224
Chorus. W. Auden. Pa-GTB:509,
Un-MB:450
The City Is Burning. H. Lewis.
La-IH:32
The City of Dreadful Night.
J. Thomson. Ho-WR:207
The Color. J. Haines. Sc-TN:75
Corner. R. Pomeroy. Ad-CI:64,
Du-SH:39
Counterpoint. O. Dodson. Hu-PN:300,
Jo-SA:59

FEAR — cont'd

Crossing Han River. Li P'in.
  Rx-LT:88
Crystal Moment. R. Coffin.
  Gr-EC:162, Pe-SS:74
Danny Deever. R. Kipling.
  Co-RM:87, Fe-PL:84, Pa-GTB:420,
  Un-MB:124
Deep in a Windless Wood. Buson.
  Be-MC:49
The Deserted House. J. Fairbun.
  Le-M:175
A Divine Image. W. Blake.
  Ga-S:156, Gr-CT:436, Ox-BN:25
The Dream. L. Bogan. Pe-OA:146,
  Un-MA:492, Wi-LT:382
Drums and Drumming. B. Brown.
  Ba-HI:131
The End of the Weekend. A. Hecht.
  Wi-LT:731
Epilogue. W. Auden. Sm-LG:303,
  Wi-LT:465
The Exam. Mo-MI:85
Fall, 1961. R. Lowell. Ca-VT:453,
  Ha-TP:135
Falling in the Creek. I. Heke.
  Le-M:65
The Fawn in the Snow. W. Benét.
  Rd-OA:183, Un-MA:323
Fear Have I when It Comes.
  L. Curry. Jo-VC:40
Fear Is What Quickens Me.
  J. Wright. St-H:256
The Fear of Beasts. W. Meredith.
  Ha-TP:138
Fear when Coming Home Through a
  Dark Country Lane. P. Taylor.
  Le-M:207
The Field Mouse. W. Sharp.
  Co-BBW:42, Fe-FP:137, Rd-SS:34
For My Daughter. W. Kees. Mc-EA:106
Forest. J. Garrigue. Wi-LT:710
Gather These Bones. L. Turco.
  De-FS:200
The Goodnight. L. Simpson.
  To-MP:91
Gunpowder Plot. V. Scannell.
  To-MP:70
The Heavy Bear. D. Schwartz.
  Br-TC:356, Pe-OA:218, Wi-LT:520
The Hermit. W. Davies. Un-MB:176
The Hill Wife. R. Frost. Ca-VT:10
Hunger. Le-IB:93, Tr-US I:25
I Am Afraid. Ho-SD:74
I Am Frightened. V. Howard.
  Jo-VC:86, La-IH:134
I Am Nobody. . . . Who Are You?
  V. Porumbacu. Mc-AC:127
I Do Like Ogres. D. Thompson. Br-SM:1
I Dreaded That First Robin So.
  E. Dickinson. Rv-CB:919,
  Un-MA:99

I of the Owl. Ho-SD:9
I Stand Here Against This Lamp Post.
  R. Chafetz. La-IH:85
I Think I Understand. J. Mitchell.
  Mo-GR:126
I Years Had Been from Home.
  E. Dickinson. Rv-CB:917,Sh-AP:128
If on Account of the Political
  Situation. W. Auden. Ba-PO:50
Image Unreal. M. Yee. Me-WF:86
In Camera. T. Rajan. Al-PI:104
In Waste Places. J. Stephens.
  Ni-JP:35, Un-MB:266
Jack-in-the-Box. E. Olson. St-H:172
Litany for Halloween. Au-SP:371,
  Br-SM:3, Br-SS:72, Co-PS:140,
  Mo-TB:77, Se-PR:192
The Little Boy. Mo-MGT:10
A Little Maid. Mo-MGT:24
A Little While. D. Rossetti.
  Al-VBP:986
Lizards and Snakes. A. Hecht.
  Ha-TP:39
Lord, This Night. O. Mandelstam.
  Ca-MR:158
Love on the Farm. D. Lawrence.
  Ga-FB:80, Un-MB:288, Un-MW:122
The Lover's Song. I. Adigal.
  Al-PI:71
The Man-Moth. E. Bishop. En-PC:103,
  Pe-OA:213, Un-MA:612, Wi-LT:504
Midcentury Love Letter. P. McGinley.
  Al-VBP:1225, Mo-BG:91
Moscow Morning. J. Rubinstein.
  Ho-TY:239
Mother, the Wardrobe Is Full of
  Infantrymen. R. McGough.Gr-BT:117
Murder. P. Milosevic. Le-M:178
My Galley. T. Wyatt. Rv-CB:89
Nausea Has Me in Its Grip.
  A. Timofeyevsky. Bo-RU:84
The Night Is Darkening round Me.
  E. Brontë. Ho-LP:78, Ox-BN:596
The Night Mirror. J. Hollander.
  Ho-P:111
The Night of Terror.
  Wang Ya-p'ing. Hs-TC:353
Night Piece. J. Manifold.
  Un-MB:513, Wi-LT:766
Nobody. R. Graves. Ha-TP:138
An Old Soldier Dies. E. de Vito.
  Ke-TF:169
On a Certain Engagement South of
  Seoul. H. Carruth. Br-AF:89
On the Staircase. W. Wellman.
  De-FS:215
One Eyed Black Man in Nebraska.
  S. Cornish. Ad-PB:294
The Other Looks at Me.
  J. Rubinstein. Ho-TY:240
Others, I Am Not the First.
  A. Housman. Un-MB:101

Our Fear.   Z. Herbert.   Gr-BT:120
Outside.   C. McDaniels.   Me-WF:53
The Owl.   R. Warren.   Un-MA:588
Painter, Draw Me a Friend.
   M. Pavlova.   Bo-RU:64
Panic.   A. MacLeish.   Un-MA:460
The Panther Possible.   W. Barney.
   De-FS:13, Du-SH:115
Paper Men to Air Hopes and Fears.
   R. Francis.   Du-SH:92
The Pearl.   H. Andersen.   Pa-SG:49
Phantoms of the Steppe.
   A. Pushkin.   Ab-MO:63
Pike.   T. Hughes.   To-MP:83
Pinned Down.   P. Horgan.   Cr-WS:86
Pinwheel.   D. Laing.   Ls-NY:6
Poem.   E. Brathwaite.   Sa-B:169
Poem.   F. John.   Sa-B:168
Poem of the Conscripted Warrior.
   R. Nogar.   Lo-TY:187
Prelude to an Evening.   J. Ransom.
   En-PC:12, Un-MA:418
Primitives.   D. Randall.   Ra-BP:139
Professor Nocturnal.   R. Roseliep.
   De-FS:158
The Quarry Pool.   D. Levertov.
   Ca-VT:510
Recognition of Death.
   J. Brennan.   De-FS:33
The Runaway.   R. Frost.
   Ar-TP3:77, Bo-GJ:72, Br-TC:137,
   Ca-VT:16, Co-BBW:143, De-CH:24,
   Fe-FP:161, Gr-EC:39, Hu-MP:196,
   La-PV:125, Se-PR:301, Sh-RP:343,
   Sm-LG:82, Un-GT:29, Un-MA:179
The Scissors Grinder.   R. Roseliep.
   De-FS:162
The Scythe of Dreams.   J. Brennan.
   De-FS:33
See How the Doves Flutter and
   Huddle.   Do-CH:(15)
Seein' Things.   E. Field.   Hu-MP:130
Self.   N. Pritchard.   Ad-PB:359
The Shape of Fear.   S. Russell.
   De-FS:169
Shrieks at Midnight. D. Thompson.
   Br-SM:(10)
The Sleeping Giant.   D. Hall.
   Br-TC:165, Ni-JP:25
The Snare.   J. Stephens.   Ad-PE:22,
   Ar-TP3:62, Bl-OB:130, Co-BBW:21,
   Co-IW:28, De-CH:89, Gr-EC:32,
   La-PP:51, La-PV:151, Mc-WS:44,
   Se-PR:300, Sm-MK:159, Th-AS:50
Song.   Bi-IT:164, Tr-US I:27
Song Composed at the Beginning of
   an Autumn Festival.   Le-IB:106,
   Tr-US I:31
Sonnet.   P. Shelley.   Ox-BN:279
Spooks.   N. Crane.   Br-SM:4
Stone Trees.   J. Freeman.
   Co-BN:113

A Storm in Childhood.   T. Jones.
   Ma-FW:35
Story of the Pennies.   A. Lutzky.
   Ho-TY:267
Test.   M. Nishimura.   Le-TA:55
There Came a Gray Owl.   Ho-SD:17
There Is Fear.   Ma-BH:11,
   Tr-US I:24
There Is Joy.   Do-WH:64, Ho-SD:76,
   Le-OE:104, Ma-BH:10
There's a Certain Slant of Light.
   E. Dickinson.   Rv-CB:905,
   Sh-AP:128, Sm-LG:50, Un-MA:98,
   Wi-LT:4
Those Game Animals.   Le-IB:75
Thought's End.   L. Adams.   Sm-PT:136
truth.   G. Brooks.   Ho-TH:53
Twilight.   H. Longfellow.   De-CH:30
2000 A.D.   B. Connelly.   De-FS:68
Undertow.   L. Hughes.   Wi-LT:423
The Unknown Color.   C. Cullen.
   Bo-HF:55, Fe-FP:166, Gr-EC:58
The Unreturning.   W. Owen.   Un-MB:365
We Were Young.   G. Naum.   Mc-AC:116
A Wedding at Harvest Time.
   N. Bomze.   Ho-TY:227
Who but the Lord?   L. Hughes.
   Ra-BP:81
Wilderness Road.   M. Keller.
   De-FS:123
The Wind Has Wings.   Do-WH:54
A Wolf.   Ho-SD:23, Jo-TS:9
The Wolves.   A. Tate.   Wi-LT:409
The Woods Grow Darker.   De-FS:75
Words, Words.   M. Mertsalov.
   Bo-RU:51
FEASTS: see CHRISTMAS DINNERS;
   FESTIVALS; FOOD AND EATING;
   HOLIDAYS
FEATHERS
An Eagle Feather I See.   Jo-TS:20
A Garland of Peacock Feathers.
   D. ap Gwilym.   Go-BP:122
Goose Feathers.   Mo-MGT:78
Mickle, Trickle, Eat a Pickle.
   Re-RR:29
Which Weighs More.   Re-RR:34
Why Does It Snow.   L. Richards.
   Br-SS:87
FEBRUARY
February.   J. Bensel.   Un-GT:269
February.   J. Clare.   Ox-BN:309
February.   F. Sherman.   Ha-YA:170
February.   A. Whitney.   Ha-YA:169
February Birthday.   N. Turner.
   Br-BC:154
February, Tall and Trim.
   A. Gilmore.   Ha-YA:169
February Twilight.   S. Teasdale.
   Au-SP:355, Ha-YA:170, La-PP:28,
   La-PV:52, Pe-FB:82, Th-AS:27
In February.   J. Symonds.   Ha-YA:171

FEBRUARY — cont'd.
  Kingdom of Heaven.   L. Adams.
    Un-MA:547
  Late Winter.   P. Savage.   Bo-FP:180
  The Snowdrop.   A. Tennyson.
    Bo-FP:180, Se-PR:41
  The Twenty-Second of February.
    W. Bryant.   Hu-MP:329, Se-PR:57
  When.   D. Aldis.   Br-SS:125,
    Gr-EC:51, Sh-RP:191
FEEDING RHYMES
  Danty, Baby, Diddy.   Mo-NR:12
FEET: see also FOOT PLAY;
    HUMOR - FEET; TOES
  A Baby's Foot.   A. Swinburne.
    Fe-FP:38
  Do You Know What.   Re-RR:93
  Fingers and Toes.   Wr-RM:12
  From Jazz for Five, 3:Colin Barnes,
    Drums.   J. Smith.   To-MP:194
  Heavenly Grass.   T. Williams.
    Gr-EC:61
  My Feet.   G. Burgess.   Bo-FP:13,
    Ir-BB:235
  1 Black Foot + 1 Black Foot = 2
    Black Feet.   G. Solomon.
    Ba-HI:22
  Two Little Men with Equal Feet.
    Fr-WO:54
  Upon Her Feet.   R. Herrick.
    Al-VBP:335, Sm-MK:20
  Why Do You Suppose.   Re-RR:41
FELLOWSHIP: see also HUMOR -
    FELLOWSHIP
  Auld Lang Syne.   R. Burns.
    Bo-FP:209, Er-FA:425, Fe-PL:129,
    Ma-YA:133, Sp-OG:260
  Black Jackets.   T. Gunn.   Br-TC:162
  The Child's Sight.   H. Sobiloff.
    Ca-VT:354
  Dance Song.   Le-IB:100, Tr-US I:28
  de Gaulle Nods Once.   E. Brooks.
    Ls-NY:44
  Discordants.   C. Aiken.   Co-BL:35,
    Er-FA:108, Un-MA:421, Wi-LT:325
  Eve Speaks to Adam.   J. Milton.
    Gr-CT:57, Ho-WR:255
  Goodbye David Tamunoemi West.
    M. Danner.   Ra-BP:153
  The Greenwood.   W. Bowles.   Cl-FC:41
  Heart of the Woods.   W. Curtright.
    Hu-PN:280
  Heels Wear Down.   R. Roseliep.
    St-H:187
  How She Resolved to Act. M. Moore.
    Pe-SS:116, Un-MA:575, Un-MW:59
  I Want You to Read.   E. Schwager.
    Ad-II:15
  Lo Here Is Fellowship.   Ga-S:202
  Loneliness.   Cheng Min.   Hs-TC:229
  A Long Story.   F. Eckman.   St-H:51
  Losing Track. D. Levertov. Mc-EA:99

  Mad as Mist and Snow.   W. Yeats.
    Gr-CT:395
  March Weather.   S. Barker.   Ho-LP:21
  My Dead.   Rachel.   Me-PH:88
  My Fellowship with God.   J. Villa.
    Pl-EI:50
  The Night Frieda Took My Spirit by
    Surprise.   P. Mayer.   St-H:129
  The Oath.   A. Tate.   Wi-LT:408
  Old Toast.   Hi-WP II:1
  Recuerdo.   E. Millay.   Br-AF:194,
    Co-BL:108, Er-FA:110, Hi-TL:194,
    Na-EO:78, Wi-LT:337
  Six and Thirty.   D. Stevenson.
    Br-BC:65
  Some Trees.   J. Ashbery.   Mo-BG:122
  The Song of the Setting Sun.
    Hu Feng.   Hs-TC:378
  Spring Song.   R. McKuen.   Ad-CI:91
  Stillness.   J. Flecker.   Bo-GJ:126,
    De-CH:38, Un-MB:272
  The Sun Used to Shine.   E. Thomas.
    Pl-ML:41
  There Was a Man.   S. Crane.
    Un-MA:148
  To Cyriack Skinner.   J. Milton.
    Pa-GTB:66
  To His Retired Friend.   H. Vaughan.
    Al-VBP:463
  To the Rev. F. D. Maurice.
    A. Tennyson.   Pa-GTB:334
  To Wei Pa, a Retired Scholar.
    Tu Fu.   Rx-OH:11
  Tour.   In Rain.   R. Roseliep.
    De-FS:164, St-H:186
  We Go Out Together.   K. Patchen.
    Un-MA:610
  Written on the Wall at Chang's
    Hermitage.   Tu Fu.   Rx-OH:4
FENCES: see also STILES; WALLS
  Fall.   R. Francis.   Ca-VT:233
  A Fence.   C. Sandburg.   Mo-BH:33,
    Sh-AP:157
  Fence Wire.   J. Dickey.   Ca-VT:492
  Former Barn Lot.   M. Van Doren.
    Ga-FB:296, Ha-LO:53, La-PV:166,
    Un-MA:467
  Mending Wall.   R. Frost.
    Al-VBP:1128, Br-AF:125, Ca-VT:4,
    Er-FA:276, Ga-FB:285, Ha-PO:91,
    Sh-AP:145, Sh-RP:96, Un-MA:170
    Wi-LT:164
  Old Fence Post.   L. Hanes.   Gr-EC:173
  The Picket Fence.   C. Morgenstern.
    Un-R:65
  Pickety Fence.   D. McCord.   Gr-EC:194
  What Runs Around.   Re-RR:116
FENCING: see also DUELS
  For E. McC.   E. Pound.   Mo-SD:170
FENS: see MARSHES
FERGUS
  Who Goes with Fergus?   W. Yeats.
    Bo-GJ:135, Sm-LG:219

FERNS
Fern Song. J. Tabb. Sp-OG:281
The Ferns. G. Baro. Sm-MK:146
Japanese Folk-Song from Hyogo.
Pa-RE:64
Rockferns. N. Nicholson. Un-MB:505
Tillie. W. de la Mare. Ar-TP3:157,
Co-PM:49, Ir-BB:153
FERRIES: see also HUMOR - FERRIES
Back and Forth. L. Mitchell.
Fe-FP:193
The Ballad of the Merry Ferry.
E. Rounds. Hu-MP:173
By Ferry to the Island. I. Smith.
Go-BP:33, To-MP:95
Ferry-Boats. J. Tippett.
Ar-TP3:89, Au-SP:178
Ferry Me Across the Water.
C. Rossetti. Au-SP:180,
Bo-FP:128, Bo-GJ:11, Ch-B:77,
Gr-CT:9, Gr-EC:243, Hi-GD:17,
Ir-BB:240, La-PV:197, Ox-BC:277
Letter Written on a Ferry Crossing
Long Island Sound. A. Sexton.
Br-TC:365
Returning by Night to Lu-Men.
Meng Hao Jan. Rx-LT:50
The Waters of Tyne. Gr-GB:124
FESTIVALS: see also HOLIDAYS; and
names of festivals, as
HANUKKAH (FEAST OF LIGHTS)
Celebration. A. Lopez. Al-WW:3
A Celebration. V. Shepelev.
Mo-MI:24
The Ch'ing Ming Festival.
Feng Hsueh-feng. Hs-TC:368
Come, Ye Sons of Art. H. Purcell.
Pl-US:44
The Day of Cold Food.
Li Ch'ing Chao. Rx-OH:98
Divali. Ca-MU:17
Drink Deep. Br-FW:19
Feast of the Ram's Horn.
H. Shapiro. Ca-VT:530
Festival Songs, I. Tr-US II:157
For a Wine Festival. V. Watkins.
Ls-NY:301
Harvest Sacrifice. Su Tung P'o.
Rx-OH:75
Husa. F. John. Sa-B:108
Lantern Festival. Yung Tsu.
Pa-MV:202
Moon Festival. Tu Fu. Rx-OH:8
Prayer at the Burning Off a New
Communal Field. Tr-US I:168
Song at a Head-Hunting Festival.
Tr-US I:172
Song of the Priestess at a
Victory Feast. Tr-US II:302
Spring Sun. Chu Hsi.
Rx-OH:118
Sundari Mundarié. Ca-MU:20

FEUDALISM: see CHIVALRY; KNIGHTS
AND KNIGHTHOOD; PEASANTS;
SERFDOM
FEVERS: see also names of fevers,
as MALARIA
Bout with Burning. V. Miller.
Un-MA:680, Wi-LT:776
Charm to Cure Fevers. Su-FVI:48
A Dream, I. B. Akhmadulina.
Ca-MR:40
Fever 103°. S. Plath. Ca-VT:675
FICKLENESS: see also HUMOR -
FICKLENESS
Along the Field as We Came By.
A. Housman. No-CL:126, Un-MB:98
Away, Delights. J. Fletcher.
Al-VBP:284
Boatmen's Song. Tr-US I:176
The Broken-Hearted Gardener.
Gr-CT:271, Gr-GB:115
Chinook Song. Da-SC:16
The Chronicle. A. Cowley.
Al-VBP:453
The Constant Lover. J. Suckling.
Al-VBP:421, Er-FA:110, Ga-FB:42,
Ha-PO:174, Ho-LP:10, Ma-YA:99,
No-CL:186, Un-MW:43
The Coquet. A. Behn. Al-VBP:499
The Cuckoo. Rv-CB:433
The Cypress. T. Peacock.
De-CH:251, No-CL:245
Died of Love. Rv-CB:431
Down in the Meadows. Rv-CB:41
Fair Annie. De-CH:414
Faithless Nelly Gray. T. Hood.
Br-SM:33, Co-HP:78, Hi-WP I:100
False and Fickle. J. Dryden.
Un-MW:46
False Love. W. Scott. Al-VBP:675,
Gr-GB:139
False Though She Be. W. Congreve.
Al-VBP:519, Co-BL:138,
Hi-WP II:101, Rv-CB:497, Un-MW:47
Farewell, Ungrateful Traitor.
J. Dryden. Al-VBP:483, Rv-CB:462
Haul Away Joe. Co-SS:99
I Do Confess Thou Art Sae Fair.
R. Burns. Rv-CB:622
I Loved a Lass. Al-VBP:312,
De-CH:190, No-CL:121
I Loved Thee Once. R. Aytoun.
Al-VBP:224
in defense of marriage. J. Gill.
Sc-TN:67
In Love with Two. Ovid. Un-MW:69
Is It Possible. T. Wyatt. Rv-CB:93
Let Her Give Her Hand. Co-BL:56
A Light Woman. R. Browning.
No-CL:240
Little Jenny Wren. Wr-RM:71
The May Queen. A. Tennyson.
Ch-B:76, Hu-MP:336, Se-PR:111

FICKLENESS — cont'd.
The Merchant, to Secure. . . .
M. Prior.   Al-VBP:512,
Pa-GTB:130, Rv-CB:484,
Un-MW:50
The Message.   J. Donne.
Al-VBP:249, Ma-YA:80
Nobody Loves Me.   C. Zolotow.
Ho-ME:24
Oh, Think Not I Am Faithful to
a Vow!   E. Millay.   Ga-FB:85
Oh What a Thing Is Man.   De-CH:766
Phillida Flouts Me.   Al-VBP:363
Realities.   e. cummings.   Sm-PT:38
The Reconciliation.   Horace.
Un-MW:30
A Renunciation.   E. Vere.   Pa-GTB:26
A Satire.   J. Oldham.   Al-VBP:507
Sea Love.   C. Mew.   Al-VBP:1111,
Co-BL:159, Co-EL:10, Co-PU:78,
Un-MB:159, Un-MW:100
She Hugged Me and Kissed Me.
Ra-BP:16
Sigh No More, Ladies.
W. Shakespeare.   Al-VBP:185,
Co-BL:133, Rv-CB:203, Un-MW:36
Song.   S. Coleridge.   Rv-CB:769
Song of Thyrsis.   P. Freneau.
Al-VBP:606
Song to Instruments.   Tr-CB:22,
Tr-US I:48
Songs.   Tr-US II:142
Songs for a Colored Singer.
E. Bishop.   Hu-PN:551
Sonnet.   Lord Herbert.   Al-VBP:294
Sonnet.   W. Shakespeare.   Al-VBP:180
A Sweet Lullaby.   N. Breton.
Al-VBP:82
They Flee from Me.   T. Wyatt.
Al-VBP:76, Rv-CB:76, Un-MW:71
To a Lady Asking Him How Long He
Would Love Her.   G. Etheredge.
Un-MW:178
To His Mistress.   R. Herrick.
Al-VBP:326
To Myra.   F. Greville.   Al-VBP:123
To Phillis.   C. Sedley.   Co-BL:73,
No-CL:179
The Unfaithful Shepherdess.
Pa-GTB:25
Upon His Leaving His Mistress.
J. Wilmot.   Al-VBP:504
Were You on the Mountain?
Co-BL:133, Co-PU:76
Woman's Faith.   W. Scott.   Al-VBP:678
Ye Banks and Braes.   R. Burns.
Al-VBP:648, Co-BL:141, De-CH:47,
Hi-WP II:103, Pa-GTB:131, Rv-CB:615
Young John.   Ma-BB:30
FIDDLES: see VIOLINS
FIDELITY: see LOYALTY
FIELD ATHLETICS: see TRACK ATHLETICS

FIELDS AND MEADOWS
The Boy with the Little Bare Toes.
F. Harvey.   St-FS:118
The Cornfield.   E. Roberts.
Bo-GJ:46
Fairy Rings.   J. Clare.   Go-BP:109
Field and Forest.   R. Jarrell.
Ca-VT:403
The Fields of November.
M. Van Doren.   Ha-WR:85
Hayfield.   A. Fisher.   Sh-RP:206
In the Meadow.   C. Rossetti.
Ch-B:89
The Island.   D. Aldis.   Gr-EC:277
July Meadow.   L. Driscoll.   Ha-YA:82
Lives.   H. Reed.   Co-BN:67
Man Watching.   A. Brownjohn.
Ls-NY:290
Mountain Meadows.   M. Keller.
Co-BN:221
Near Mons.   N. Myers.   Ls-NY:256
Real Property.   H. Monro.
Co-BN:136, Go-BP:171
To Meadows.   R. Herrick.
Al-VBP:336, De-CH:205, Rv-CB:340
FIGHTS AND FIGHTING: see also
DUELS; HUMOR - FIGHTS AND
FIGHTING; QUARRELS
Antrim.   R. Jeffers.   Ca-VT:124
The Ballad of Pug-Nosed Lil.
R. Fletcher.   Fi-BG:231
Ballad of the Broomtails.   Fi-BG:143
Beowulf.   Al-VBP:1, Ma-YA:14
Bill Roy.   Fi-BG:206
The Combat.   E. Muir.   Un-MB:342
The Cow Girl.   Fi-BG:140
Fight.   Er-FA:215
A Gret Fight.   R. Newell.   Co-RM:179
The Man from Ironbark.
A. Peterson.   Co-RM:146
Mush, Mush.   Co-RM:114
Ranch Life.   Fi-BG:78
Robyn and Gandeleyn.   Ox-BB:374
The Shepherd and the Nymph.
W. Landor.   Ox-BN:182
Silver Jack's Religion.   J. Jones.
Fi-BG:185
The Texas Ranger.   Fi-BG:112
FILLING STATIONS: see SERVICE
STATIONS
FILUMENA, SAINT: see
PHILOMENA, SAINT
FINANCIERS: see BANKS AND BANKING;
INVESTMENTS AND INVESTORS;
MONEY; WEALTH
FINCHES: see also GOLDFINCHES;
LINNETS; REDPOLLS
Epitaph on Lady Ossory's
Bullfinch.   H. Walpole.
Gr-CT:109, Rd-OA:114
I Know the Trusty Almanac.
R. Emerson.   Re-BS:20

A Widow Bird. P. Shelley. Bl-OB:96,
   De-CH:235, De-TT:155, Fe-FP:296,
   Hi-WP I:20, Hu-MP:234, Ox-BN:303,
   Pa-GTB:275, Re-TW:69, Rv-CB:694

FINGER AND HAND PLAY
Adam and Eve Gaed up My Sleeve.
   Mo-TL:24
The Bear Went over the Mountain.
   Mo-TL:61
Can You Keep a Secret? Li-LB:18,
   Mo-TL:26
Cheetie Pussie. Mo-TL:21
Children Can Hop on One Leg.
   Mo-TL:68
Dance, Foreman, Dance. Mo-TL:50
Dance, Thumbkin, Dance.
   De-TT:117, Ir-BB:14, Li-LB:15,
   Mo-NR:34, Mo-TL:49, Wr-RM:92
Dearly Beloved Brethren, Is It
   Not a Sin. J. Tabrar.
   Co-PU:31, Mo-TL:59
Dingty Diddlety. Mo-TL:22
Finger Game. Da-SC:42
The Fingers. Mo-MGT:140
The Five Little Fairies.
   M. Burnham. Bo-FP:311
Fly Away Peter. Li-LB:15
Handy Pandy. Mo-TL:74
Here Are My Lady's Knives and
   Forks. Li-LB:18, Mo-TL:54
Here Is the Church. Mo-TL:58
Here's a Ball for Baby.
   Li-LB:17, Mo-TL:53
Here's a String of Wild Geese.
   Mo-TL:55
Hickory, Dickory, Dock. An-IP:(7),
   Au-SP:17, Bo-FP:16, De-PO:20,
   Er-FA:505, Fr-WO:17, Li-LB:102,
   Mo-CC:(15), Mo-MGT:77, Mo-NR:24,
   Mo-TL:22, Wi-MG:58, Wr-RM:125
Higgledy, Piggledy. Mo-TL:22
Hot Cross Buns. Mother Goose.
   Au-SP:11, Bo-FP:244, De-PO:10,
   Mo-MGT:109, Mo-NR:120, Mo-TL:75,
   On-TW:10, Wi-MG:39, Wr-RM:127
I Had a Little Husband.
   Er-FA:502, Ir-BB:208, Mo-MGT:84,
   Mo-TL:51, Na-EO:170
I Love a Little Pussy.
   Bo-FP:6, Li-LB:92, Mo-MGT:176,
   Mo-NR:23, Mo-TL:69, Wi-MG:59
I Put My Finger in the Woodpecker's
   Hole. Mo-TL:72
Incey, Wincey Spider, Climbed up
   the Spout. Mo-TL:52
A Little Cock Sparrow. Ir-BB:26,
   Li-LB:87, Mo-MGT:171, Mo-NR:48,
   Mo-TL:57, Wi-MG:36, Wr-RM:66
Little Miss Muffet. Au-SP:9,
   Bo-FP:103, De-PO:12, Er-FA:506,
   Li-LB:32, Mo-CC:(53), Mo-MGT:62,
   Mo-NR:30, Mo-TL:69, Pa-AP:33,
   Wi-MG:32, Wr-RM:39

The Magpie and the Raven. Gr-BB:17
Master Thumb Is First to Come.
   Mo-TL:18
The Meenister in the Poopit.
   Mo-TL:59
Mix a Pancake. C. Rossetti.
   Ag-HE:6, Au-SP:10, Bo-FP:53,
   Ch-B:80, Cl-FC:94, Li-LC:45
Nievie, Nievie, Nick, Nack.
   Mo-TL:75
Oh Where, Oh Where Has My Little
   Dog Gone. Mo-CC:(54), Mo-MGT:29,
   Mo-TL:70, Wi-MG:46
Old Davy Jones Had One Little
   Sailor. Mo-TL:60
Once I Saw a Little Bird. Fr-MP:20,
   Mo-TL:56, Wr-RM:93
One, Two Kittens That Mew.
   Mo-TL:67
One, Two, Three, Four, Five.
   Mo-TL:67, Wi-MG:30, Wr-RM:41
Pat-a-Cake, Pat-a-Cake, Baker's
   Man. Bo-FP:118, De-PO:6,
   Li-LB:18, Mo-CC:(52), Mo-MGT:5,
   Mo-NR:5, Mo-TL:74, Wi-MG:43,
   Wr-RM:14
Polly, Put the Kettle On. Mother
   Goose. Bo-FP:58, Li-LB:31,
   Mo-CC:(31), Mo-MGT:86, Mo-NR:55,
   Mo-TL:71
Pussy Cat, Pussy Cat. Mo-TL:21
Put Your Finger in Foxy's Hole.
   Li-LB:14, Mo-TL:72
Robin, Robin, Redbreast. Mo-TL:56
Roon Aboot, Roon Aboot. Mo-TL:24
Round About, Round About. Mo-TL:23
Round about There. Mo-TL:19
Round and round the Cornfield.
   Li-LB:19
Round and round Ran the Wee Hare.
   Mo-TL:19
Round and round the Garden.
   Mo-TL:19
Ten Green Bottles Hanging on
   the Wall. Mo-TL:66
Ten Little Chickadees Sitting on
   a Line. Mo-TL:62
Ten Little Injuns Standing on a
   Line. Mo-TL:64
There Was a Crooked Man.
   Au-SP:3, De-PO:22, Er-FA:506,
   Fr-WO:24, Ir-BB:216, La-PP:70,
   Li-LB:71, Mo-MGT:12, Mo-NR:86,
   Mo-TL:71, Rv-CB:457, Sm-MK:114,
   Wi-MG:15, Wr-RM:102
There Was a Man. Mo-TL:25
There Was a Wee Mouse. Mo-TL:20
This Is the Man That Broke the
   Barn. Mo-TL:18
This Is the Way We Wash Our Hands.
   Mo-NR:27
This Little Bird Flaps Its Wings.
   Mo-TL:55

FINGER AND HAND PLAY — cont'd.
  This Little Cow Eats Grass.
    Mo-TL:17
  This Little Pig Went to Market.
    Au-SP:18, Bo-FP:8, De-CH:497,
    De-PO:8, Ir-BB:10, Li-LB:20,
    Mo-CC:(48), Mo-MGT:54, Mo-NR:78,
    Mo-TL:15, Sp-TM:23, Wi-MG:73,
    Wr-RM:35
  This Old Man, He Played One.
    Au-SP:248, Ir-BB:125, Mo-TL:31
  Three French Mice.   Ir-BB:246
  Three Mice Went into a Hole to
    Spin. Mo-TL:68
  Thumb Bold. Mo-TL:18
  Tickly, Tickly. Mo-MGT:124
  Two Birds. Mo-MGT:85, On-TW:11,
    Rv-ON:14, Sp-AS:27, Wr-RM:23
  Two Little Dicky Birds. Li-LB:14,
    Mo-TL:52, On-TW:11, Wi-MG:21
  Walk down the Path. Li-LB:16
  Warm Hands, Warm. Li-LB:19
FINGERPRINTS
  Personality. C. Sandburg. Ga-S:14
FINLAND
  The Stars Go over the Lonely Ocean.
    R. Jeffers. Wi-LT:259
FINNISH VERSE
  Une Vie. P. Saarikoski. Co-EL:144
FIR TREES
  A Christmas Cross. W. Allen.
    Ke-TF:227
  A Young Firwood. D. Rossetti.
    Se-PR:98
FIRE: see also FIREPLACES; FIRES;
    HEAT; SMOKE
  Adolphus Elfinstone. G. Burgess.
    Co-BB:116, Se-PR:316
  The Armadillo. E. Bishop. Ca-VT:319
  Banking Coal. J. Toomer. Bo-HF:132,
    Hu-PN:106
  Brother Fire. L. MacNeice.
    Ba-PO:177, Ha-TP:83, Hi-FO:269
  Burning the Christmas Greens.
    W. Williams. Wi-LT:200
  Coal Fire. L. Untermeyer. Un-GT:256
  Deadfall. M. Keller. Gr-EC:272
  the discoveries of fire. L. Clifton.
    Mo-TS:32
  Earthy Anecdote. W. Stevens.
    Bo-GJ:225, Re-TW:35
  Fire. J. Craik. Le-M:126
  Fire. Feng Hsüeh-feng. Hs-TC:372
  A Fire. R. Field. Ag-HE:36
  Fire. P. Taylor. Le-M:127
  Fire and Ice. R. Frost. Al-VBP:1133,
    Er-FA:88, Hi-WP II:3, Ho-LP:82,
    Mo-BG:186, Pe-M:97, Un-MA:180,
    Wi-LT:174
  Fire Fire of the First World.
    Wo-HS:(61)

Fire Song at an Expiation
    Ceremony. Tr-US I:59
The God on My Hearth. K. Tynan.
    Go-BP:114
Hearth. P. Bacon. Fe-FP:160,
    Hu-MP:186
Hearth Song. R. Johnson. Ha-YA:128
On Lighting the Fire. M. Swenson.
    Ls-NY:276
Pictures in the Fire. P. Strong.
    Sh-RP:115
Red in the Valley. Ju-CP:10
The Sacrament of Fire. J. Oxenham.
    Ke-TF:430
Song of Sequence. Da-SC:21
Song of the Coyote Who Stole Fire.
    Da-SC:69
The Streets of Laredo.
    L. MacNeice. To-MP:45
Stuff. A. Mitchell. Sm-MK:190
There Was a Little Dog.
    Ir-BB:148, St-FS:80
To Agni. Al-PI:14
The Two Fires. J. Wright. Un-MB:515
we all joined a circle.
    M. Bergschneider. Ad-II:62
Where the Hayfields Were.
    A. MacLeish. Ha-LO:80
FIRE DEPARTMENTS: see FIREMEN; FIRES
FIRE ENGINES: see also FIREMEN
  F Is the Fighting Firetruck.
    P. McGinley. La-PP:38
  A Fire-Truck. R. Wilbur. Ha-TP:10
  The Great Figure. W. Williams.
    Su-FVI:2
FIREARMS: see ARMS AND ARMOR
FIRECRACKERS: see FIREWORKS
FIREFLIES: see also HUMOR - FIREFLIES
  Alas! The Firefly. Basho. Do-TS:21
  All about Fireflies. D. McCord.
    It-HB:11
  August Night. S. Teasdale.
    Un-MA:267
  Crawling on the Grass. M. Saito.
    Sh-AM:145
  A Dream. W. Blake. De-CH:456,
    Hu-MP:127, Rd-OA:13, Rv-CB:585
  Fire-Fly, Fire-Fly, Bright Little
    Thing. Da-SC:28
  Fireflies. A. Fisher. Au-SP:75
  Fireflies. C. Hall. Bo-FP:286,
    Fe-FP:131, Hu-MP:306
  Fireflies. W. Welles. Rd-SS:38
  Fireflies in the Garden. R. Frost.
    Rd-OA:62, We-PZ:34
  Firefly. K. Hajime. Mo-TS:63
  The Firefly. Issa. Le-IS:29,
    Sh-RP:65
  The Firefly. Li Po. Le-MW:28
  Firefly. E. Roberts. Ar-TP3:65,
    Bo-GJ:78, It-HB:60, La-PV:144,
    Li-LC:26

Firefly. E. Wood. Bo-FP:286
The Firefly Lights His Lamp.
  Au-SP:75, Hu-MP:200
Firefly Party. De-PP:63
Firefly Song. Br-MW:97
the flattered lightning bug.
  D. Marquis. Co-BBW:217
Glow-Worms. A. Young. Cl-DT:70
Goat Songs, IV. R. Drew. Kh-VA:44
I Am So Small. Re-RR:64
The Mower to the Glow-Worm.
  A. Marvell. Rv-CB:401
New Spain's Cucuio. G. Du Bartas.
  De-CH:541
The Nightingale and the Glowworm.
  W. Cowper. Go-BP:76, Pa-OM:320,
  Un-GT:79
Over in the Meadow. Au-SP:223,
  Ir-BB:24, On-TW:38
Over the Deepest. Shiyo. Be-CS:50
Phosphorescence. M. Cane. Sh-RP:83
Please Don't Go! Onitsura.
  Be-MC:33
She-Goat and Glow-Worm.
  C. Morgenstern. Rd-OA:8
The Unwritten Song. F. Ford.
  Rd-SS:9
Waiting in Darkness. Be-CS:31
FIREMEN: see also HUMOR - FIREMEN
  Number 7. L. Ferlinghetti.
  Ad-CI:18, Du-RG:102, Kh-VA:74,
  La-OC:85, Pe-SS:156
The Smithfield Market Fire.
  F. Dallas. Hi-WP I:84
FIRENZE: see FLORENCE, IT.
FIREPLACES
  A Boy's Need. H. Johnson.
  Hu-PN:283
Burning the Christmas Greens.
  W. Williams. Wi-LT:200
Fire Pictures. E. Rounds. Hu-MP:21
Winter Fancy. Yung Tzu. Pa-MV:199
Winter Night. E. Millay. Se-PR:215
A Winter Wish. R. Messinger.
  Al-VBP:882
FIRES: see also BONFIRES; FOREST
    FIRES; HUMOR - FIRES;
    PRAIRIE FIRES
Anna Imroth. C. Sandburg. Kr-OF:180
Annus Mirabilis. J. Dryden.
  Al-VBP:486
Autumn Fires. R. Stevenson.
  Ar-TP3:184, Br-SG:93, Ha-YA:101,
  Ja-PA:10, Mc-PR:100
A Ballad of Dead Girls. D. Burnet.
  Kr-OF:174
The Bells. E. Poe. Bo-FP:177,
  Bo-HF:162, Er-FA:277, Fe-FP:64,
  Fe-PL:433, Li-SR:72, Sp-OG:339
The Brooklyn Theater Fire. Em-AF:467
Chicago. B. Harte. Hi-TL:136
Chicago. J. Whittier. Se-PR:316

A Child Is Singing. A. Mitchell.
  Gr-BT:118
Church Burning: Mississippi.
  J. Emanuel. Ad-PB:178, Hu-PN:374
The City Is Burning. H. Lewis.
  La-IH:32
Elegy for the Monastery Barn.
  T. Merton. Ca-VT:420
Fire, Fire. Gr-GB:19
The Fire of Frendraught. Ox-BB:610
The Fire of London. J. Dryden.
  Gr-CT:290, Ma-FW:244
Jeremiah. Mo-MGT:111
Jim Bludso. J. Hay. Co-RM:234,
  Er-FA:307, Fi-BG:129, Sp-OG:34
Kit Carson's Ride. J. Miller.
  Fi-BG:161
London Mourning in Ashes. Hi-FO:154
Matilda. H. Belloc. Ox-BC:314
The Milwaukee Fire. Em-AF:469
The Miramichi Fire. Em-AF:464
Night Skylark. S. Tsuboi. Sh-AM:69
October Morning. J. Piatt.
  Ha-YA:109
Once Again. L. Bahe. Ni-CD:12
Running the Batteries.
  H. Melville. Hi-TL:118
The Smithfield Market Fire.
  F. Dallas. Hi-WP I:84
Some Verses upon the Burning of Our
  House, July 10th, 1666.
  A. Bradstreet. Sh-AP:10
The Supplanting. W. Berry.
  Ls-NY:115
FIREWORKS
  Choice. J. Farrar. Br-SS:175
  Fireworks. B. Deutsch. Du-RG:109
  Fireworks. E. Kroll. Du-SH:166
  Fireworks. M. Millet. Ja-HH:28
  Fireworks.` J. Reeves. Br-SG:85,
    Co-PS:117, La-PH:57
  Fireworks. M. Timm. Ho-CT:23
  Flashes of Lightning.
    H. Kawahigashi. Sh-AM:161
  Fourth of July. R. Field.
    Br-SS:173
  Fourth of July Night. D. Aldis.
    Ar-TP3:207, Br-SS:175, La-PH:56,
    Mc-AW:69
  Fourth of July Song. L. Lenski.
    Br-SS:173
  Gunpowder Plot. V. Scannell.
    Ma-FW:267, To-MP:70
  If I Had a Firecracker.
    S. Silverstein. Co-PS:116
  I've Got a Rocket. Br-SS:174
  The Pinwheel's Song. J. Ciardi. La-PV:58
FIRMAMENT: see SKY
FISH: see also AQUARIUMS; HUMOR -
    FISH; and names of fish, as TROUT
  Allie. R. Graves. Bo-GJ:81,
    Fe-FP:100, Ha-LO:103

FISH — cont'd.
  The Animal World.   Tr-CB:24
  The Aquarium Dream. F. Trefethen.
    Ls-NY:100
  As I Went up the Garden. St-FS:35
  At the Aquarium. M. Eastman.
    Fe-FP:252, Ni-JP:81
  Blow Fish. A. Congdon. Ls-NY:185
  Bread from Our Pockets. J. Rolnick.
    Ho-TY:164
  Calico Pie. E. Lear.
    Au-SP:225, Bl-OB:12, Fe-FP:356,
    Hu-MP:461, Ir-BB:88, It-HB:57,
    Li-LC:67, Lo-LL:67, Pa-RE:109,
    Rv-CB:811, Sm-LG:87, Tu-WW:114,
    Un-GB:29, Un-GF:33, Un-GT:225
  A Catch. M. Hoberman. Ag-HE:14
  A Cloud Shimmering. Shurin.
    Be-CS:14
  Eating Fish. G. Johnston. Do-WH:10
  An Exceeding Great Army. E. Ayer.
    De-FS:10
  Explanation on Coming Home Late.
    R. Hughes. Co-EL:155, Co-PU:130,
    Re-TW:8
  A Fairy Went a-Marketing. R. Fyleman.
    Au-SP:293, Ox-BC:337
  The Fish. E. Bishop. Al-VBP:1238,
    Bo-GJ:67, Co-BBW:69, Pe-OA:210,
    Un-GT:128, Un-MA:611, Wi-LT:510
  The Fish. R. Brooke. Rd-OA:148
  The Fish. M. Moore. Un-MA:350
  Fish. W. Ross. Co-BBW:76
  Fish. W. Smith. Sh-RP:328
  Fish. J. Unternecker. Sc-TN:219
  The Fish Counter at Bonneville.
    W. Stafford. Br-AF:157
  Fish Crier. C. Sandburg. Br-AF:42,
    Ga-S:123
  Fish-Eye. M. Bracker. Ls-NY:187
  Fish in Winter. I. Brodsky.
    Bo-RU:23
  Fish Market. Chung Ting-wen.
    Pa-MV:75
  Fish Peddler. Mei Yao Ch'en.
    Rx-OH:40
  Fish Riddles II. Gr-GB:73
  The Fish, the Man, and the Spirit.
    L. Hunt. Al-VBP:712, Co-FB:20,
    Co-RG:162, Gr-CT:212, Rd-OA:155,
    Sm-MK:124
  The Fish Turns into a Man.
    L. Hunt. Al-VBP:713
  Fishes. Mo-MGT:193
  The Fishes. Co-SS:107, Gr-GB:72
  Four-Footed Poems. E. Greenberg.
    Ho-TY:312
  The Gidgid-Bird. Tr-US I:245
  A Gull's Ghostly Call.
    S. Hopkins. Le-M:108
  The Hen and the Carp.
    I. Serraillier. Co-BBW:62

  Her Heards Be Thousand Fishes.
    E. Spenser. Gr-CT:199
  The Herring Loves the Merry
    Moonlight. W. Scott. Sm-LG:78
  Hovering Above. Onitsura. Be-MC:33
  How They Bite. Mo-SD:109
  I Caught a Fish. B. Murray.
    Ir-BB:65, St-FS:59
  If You Chance to Be Crossing.
    Wy-CM:17
  The Last Chance. A. Lang. Mo-SD:103
  A Little Fish. H. Farley. Le-M:111
  The Little Fish Cries. D. Recht.
    Le-M:109
  The Maldive Shark. H. Melville.
    Co-BBW:68, Rv-CB:839, Sh-AP:122,
    Sm-LG:78
  The Mock Turtle's Song. L. Carroll.
    Ir-BB:126
  The Movement of Fish. J. Dickey.
    Ca-VT:491
  One, Two, Three, Four, Five.
    Mother Goose. Mo-CC:(45),
    Mo-MGT:149, Mo-NR:34, Sm-MK:18
  Over in the Meadow. Au-SP:223,
    Ir-BB:24, On-TW:38
  Over the Green Sands. P. Bennett.
    Co-BBW:61
  The Parrot Fish. J. Merrill.
    Ls-NY:189
  The Pike. E. Blunden. Rd-OA:173
  Poor Bird. W. de la Mare. Ma-FW:93
  A Pretty Boat. N. Tolstoy.
    Mo-MI:16
  The Silver Fish. S. Silverstein.
    Co-SS:178
  Skipper. G. Brooks. Ho-ME:18
  Song of the Animal World. Ab-MO:11,
    Tr-US I:66
  Sonnet of Fishes. G. Barker.
    Ma-FW:54
  Three Movements. W. Yeats.
    Co-EL:45
  To a Fish of the Brook. J. Wolcot.
    Co-BBW:66, De-CH:491, Rv-CB:553
  A Trout Leaps High. Onitsura.
    Le-MW:7, Ma-FW:54
  We Fish. H. Melville. Un-GT:71
  What Happened. D. Aldis. Gr-EC:220
  Where the Manatee Plays and the
    Manta Ray Flutters. H. Witt.
    Ls-NY:190
FISHERMEN AND FISHING: see also FLIES,
    ARTIFICIAL; HUMOR - FISHERMEN AND
    FISHING; SPEARFISHING
  And Angling, Too. G. Byron.
    Mo-SD:109
  Angler's Choice. H. Gottlieb.
    Du-RG:105
  The Angler's Song. I. Walton.
    Fl-HH:16, Mo-SD:100

Appalachian Front. R. Weeks.
   Br-AF:135
At Ch'en Ch'u. Wang She Ch'eng.
   Rx-LT:113
At the Fishhouses. E. Bishop.
   Wi-LT:512
Ayii, Ayii (I Return). Ho-SD:78
The Bait. J. Donne. Gr-CC:189,
   Mo-SD:188, No-CL:103
Blackfriars. E. Farjeon. Ox-BC:330
The Boy Fishing. E. Scovell.
   Cl-FC:77, Sm-MK:153
The Careful Angler. R. Stevenson.
   Mo-SD:107
Carrying Their Coracles. A. Marvell.
   Gr-CT:221
The Catfish. J. Mathews. Ha-TP:115
Complaint of a Fisherman's Widow.
   Tr-US I:158
The Coracle Fishers. R. Bloomfield.
   Ox-BN:57
Cornwall. C. Bond. Le-M:33
The Coromandel Fishers. S. Naidu.
   Sh-RP:26
The Crayfish. R. Wallace.
   Co-BBW:74, Mc-WK:45
Dance to Your Daddy. Mother Goose.
   Ar-TP3:100, De-PO:6, Li-LB:10,
   Mo-MGT:181, Mo-NR:24, Mo-TL:86,
   Wr-RM:50
Dead Man's Song. Ma-BH:31,
   Tr-US I:21
Dolphin. J. Unternecker. Sc-TN:216
The Drunken Fisherman. R. Lowell.
   Ca-VT:442, Sh-AP:231, Wi-LT:577
The Fisher. L. Glazier. Du-RG:105
The Fisher. W. Renton. Hi-WP II:126
Fisher Boy. Ca-MU:14
The Fisherman. A. Brown. Fe-FP:316
The Fisherman. Li Po. Le-MW:113
The Fisherman. D. McCord. La-PV:8
Fisherman. Ou Yang Hsiu. Rx-OH:51
Fisherman. D. Scott. Sa-B:201
The Fisherman. W. Yeats. Mo-SD:192
The Fisherman. Fe-FP:473
The Fisherman. De-PP:52
Fishermen. J. Emmanuel. Bo-HF:146
The Fisher's Life. I. Walton.
   Bo-FP:255
The Fisher's Life. Gr-CT:219,
   Gr-GB:216
Fishing. E. Nevzoroff. Ba-HI:60
Fishing. A. Pratt. Al-WW:101
Fishing. D. Schmitz. St-H:195
Fishing. W. Wordsworth. Mo-SD:105
Fishing. K. Wright. Ls-NY:309
The Fishing Boat. M. Howitt.
   Mc-PR:152
Fishing Harbour Towards Evening.
   R. Kell. To-MP:133
The Fishing Pole. M. Davies.
   Fe-FP:111, Ma-FO:(24)

Fly-Fishing. J. Gay. Mo-SD:104
Fun with Fishing. E. Tietjens.
   Fe-FP:484
The Gar. C. Bell. Br-AF:141
Going Fishing. L. Griffiths.
   Pa-RE:32
A Green Stream. Wang Wêi. Mo-SD:108
He Don't Know the Inside Feel.
   H. Adams. Pe-M:24
Herring Is King. A. Graves.
   Co-PI:53
How to Catch Tiddlers. B. Jones.
   Ma-FW:55
Hush Song. E. Shane. Th-AS:34
I Return to My Little Song.
   Le-IB:76
I Went Fishing. On-TW:30
If Only the World.
   Minamoto No Sanetomo. Ba-ST:32
Instruction in the Art. P. Booth.
   Mo-SD:156
Invitation to a Young River Queen.
   D. Etter. St-H:60
Ivan and I Went Fishing. Gr-BB:10
Jim Desterland. H. Plutzik.
   Ca-VT:347, De-FS:149
Kalymniad, Part II. R. Lax.
   Sc-TN:127
The Last Chance. A. Lang. Mo-SD:103
Looking at the Moon on Putting Out
   from the Shore at Nagato.
   Ma-FW:53
Neither Hook nor Line. J. Bunyan.
   Mo-SD:158
Night at Yen Chou. Chou Shang Ju.
   Le-MW:55
The Nightfishing. W. Graham.
   Ma-FW:48
Nocturne: Georgia Coast.
   D. Hickey. Br-AF:139
Out Fishin'. E. Guest. Fe-PL:419
Out Fishing on the Ocean.
   B. Pollock. Le-M:107
The Parrot Fish. J. Merrill.
   Ls-NY:189
The Pike. J. Bruce. Mo-SD:102
Pike. J. Hollander. Wi-LT:739
The Purse-Seine. R. Jeffers.
   Pe-OA:92
The Queen of Connemara. F. Fahy.
   Co-PI:38
The Royal Fisherman. Gr-CT:128,
   Gr-GB:315
Sacrifice of a Rainbow Trout.
   J. Langland. Ha-TP:123
Salmon-Fishing. R. Jeffers.
   Mo-SD:106
A Salmon Trout to Her Children.
   Le-IB:45, Su-FVI:69, Tr-US I:3
Salutation. E. Pound.
   Ca-VT:82, Mc-EA:23, Sm-LG:390,
   Un-MA:289

FISHERMEN AND FISHING — cont'd.
  The Secrets of Angling. W. Lausen.
    De-CH:490
  Sometimes an Angler Comes.
    R. Bridges. De-CH:491
  Song of the Fishermen. Le-OE:60
  Surface Fishing. W. Moses.
    Ls-NY:305
  The Taking of the Salmon.
    T. Stoddart. Fl-HH:46
  Tommy Tittlemouse. An-IP:(11),
    De-PO:18, Mo-MGT:105, Mo-NR:58,
    Wr-RM:64
  Tricia's Fish. L. Hopkins.
    Ho-GC:32
  Two Million Two Hundred Thousand
    Fishes. D. Marcus. Le-M:66
  Uncle Roderick. N. Maccaig.
    To-MP:188
  Undersea Fever. W. Cole.
    Co-FB:455, Co-SS:168
  With the Herring Fishers.
    H. MacDiarmid. Wi-LT:627
  With the Moon. S. Ogiwara.
    Sh-AM:165
FISHING: see FISHERMEN
    AND FISHING
FITZROY, HENRY, 1ST DUKE
    OF GRAFTON
  The Duke of Grafton. Gr-CT:359,
    Gr-GB:320
FLAG DAY: see also ROSS, BETSY
    GRISCOM
  The American Flag. J. Drake.
    Er-FA:286, Sp-OG:190, Vi-PP:55
  Brother, Lift Your Flag with Mine.
    J. Bacon. Co-PS:96
  Columbia, the Gem of the Ocean.
    Vi-PP:60
  The Flag Goes By. H. Bennett.
    Ar-TP3:205, Br-SS:168, Er-FA:294,
    Fe-FP:444, Se-PR:141, Sh-RP:211,
    Vi-PP:62
  Flag Song. L. Ward. Ha-YA:76,
    Hu-MP:380, Se-PR:145
  God Bless the Flag. Se-PR:141
  God Save the Flag. O. Holmes.
    Er-FA:295
  Hang Out the Flags. J. Tippett.
    Br-SS:167
  I Am the Flag. L. Jones. Vi-PP:184
  The Old Flag. H. Bunner. Vi-PP:59
  Old Flag. H. Parker. Se-PR:142
  A Song for Our Flag. M. Sangster.
    Er-FA:288
  A Toast to the Flag. J. Daly.
    Fe-PL:160, VI-PP:57
  Your Flag and My Flag. W. Nesbit.
    Er-FA:297, Se-PR:144
FLAGS: see also FLAG DAY
  The American Flag. J. Drake.
    Er-FA:286, Sp-OG:190, Vi-PP:55

Barbara Frietchie. J. Whittier.
    Co-PS:97, Er-FA:380, Fe-FP:442,
    Fe-PL:167, Ga-FB:258, Hi-TL:112,
    Mc-PR:170, Sp-OG:40, Un-GT:190,
    Vi-PP:150
  Columbia, the Gem of the Ocean.
    Vi-PP:60
  The Flag. S. Silverstein.
    Co-PS:100
  The Flag Goes By. H. Bennett.
    Ar-TP3:205, Br-SS:168, Er-FA:294,
    Fe-FP:444, Se-PR:141, Sh-RP:211,
    Vi-PP:62
  The Flag We Fly. A. Fisher.
    Ha-YA:75
  Flags. B. Poplavsky. Ca-MR:98
  God Save the Flag. O. Holmes.
    Er-FA:295
  Hang Out the Flags. J. Tippett.
    Br-SS:167
  I Am the Flag. L. Jones. Vi-PP:184
  The Old Flag. H. Bunner. Vi-PP:59
  The Red, White, and Red. Em-AF:447
  Song for All Seas, All Ships.
    W. Whitman. Tr-MR:175
  A Song for Our Flag. M. Sangster.
    Er-FA:288
  The Star-Spangled Banner. F. Key.
    Er-FA:283, Fe-FP:401, Hi-TL:65,
    Se-PR:130, Vi-PP:53
  A Toast to the Flag. J. Daly.
    Fe-PL:160, Vi-PP:57
  A Yankee Ship Came down the
    River. Sp-HW:16
FLAMINGOS: see HUMOR – FLAMINGOS
FLANDERS: see also FLEMISH VERSE
  The Old Houses of Flanders.
    F. Hueffer. Pa-HT:112
FLANDERS – HISTORY AND PATRIOTISM
  The Belfry of Bruges.
    H. Longfellow. Pa-HT:113
FLANNAN ISLANDS
  Flannan Isle. W. Gibson.
    Bl-OB:78, Co-SS:200, De-CH:395,
    Ha-PO:154, Hi-WP I:76
FLATTERY: see also HUMOR –
    FLATTERY
  The Flattered Flying Fish. E. Rieu.
    Ar-TP3:131, Br-SM:95, La-PV:202
  The Man from Up-Country Talking.
    J. de Melo Neto. An-TC:163
  The Spider and the Fly. M. Howitt.
    De-TT:60, Er-FA:421, Fe-FP:530,
    Gr-EC:144, Ox-BC:158, Pe-FB:56
  To Celia. Rv-CB:135
FLAX
  At the End of My Yard. Gr-CT:12
  Fruit, Flower and Tree Riddles III.
    Gr-GB:71
FLEAS: see also HUMOR – FLEAS
  Eight Limericks. E. Lear. Sh-RP:128
  The Flea. J. Donne. Rv-CB:299

A Flea and a Fly in a Flue.
   Br-LL:9, Ch-B:113, Co-HP:29,
   Fe-FP:365, Gr-EC:196, Lo-LL:49,
   Mc-WS:179, Un-GT:241
Great Fleas Have Little Fleas.
   De-CH:609
Partners. J. Castillo.
   Gr-EC:15, Mc-WK:90
Restless Little Flea. Issa.
   Be-MC:17
FLEMISH VERSE
Evening Landscape. P. de Mont.
   Pa-SG:109
The Sea. H. Gorter. Pa-SG:145
To the Sun from a Flower. G. Gezelle.
   Fe-FP:471, Pa-SG:105
FLICKERS
Sitting Bull's Song. Sitting Bull.
   Da-SC:112
The Yellowhammer. J. Clare.
   Go-BP:74
FLIES: see also SATIRE -
   FLIES
The Amber Bead. R. Herrick.
   Gr-CT:109, Ho-LP:38, Ho-WR:141
The Answer to This Is. Re-RR:10
Back in My Home Town. Issa.
   Be-MC:17
Blue Fly. J. de Assis. Lo-TY:81
The Blue-Tail Fly. Er-FA:450,
   Gr-GB:324
The Cure. A. Noyes. Co-BBW:229
Fiddle-de-Dee; Fiddle-de-Dea.
   Mother Goose. Mo-NR:130, Pa-AP:48
A Flea and a Fly in a Flue.
   Br-LL:9, Ch-B:113, Co-HP:29,
   Fe-FP:365, Gr-EC:196, Lo-LL:49,
   Mc-WS:179, Un-GT:241
The Fly. W. de la Mare. Cl-DT:16
The Fly. B. Googe. De-CH:85
The Fly. O. Nash. Fe-FP:357
The Fly. K. Shapiro. Wi-LT:533
A Fly. G. Steif. La-GI:58
The Fly. S. Takahashi. Sh-AM:98
Get Drunk. Ho Ch'i-fang. Hs-TC:223
A Horsefly Mutters. Bokusui.
   Be-MC:57
How Can a Creature. Kikaku.
   Be-MC:26
I Heard a Fly Buzz when I Died.
   E. Dickinson. Mo-BG:163, Un-MA:98,
   Wi-LT:9
The Last. M. Halpern. Ho-TY:108
Little Black Bug. M. Brown.
   Fe-FP:127
Little Fly. W. Blake.
   Be-EB:36, Bl-OB:130, De-CH:539,
   Ha-PO:115, Ma-YA:128, Rv-CB:608,
   Un-GT:81
Monologue of a Dying Man.
   J. Datta. Al-PI:82
Mosca. P. Blackburn. Kh-VA:6

Mourning for Akutagawa.
   M. Saito. Sh-AM:146
Oh, Don't Strike the Fly! Issa.
   Ca-BF:31
On a Fly Drinking Out of His Cup.
   W. Oldys. Al-VBP:543, Cl-FC:96,
   Er-FA:153, Rv-CB:519, Un-GT:80
On the Farm. Re-RR:110
The Peopled Air. T. Gray.
   Rd-OA:81
The Pets. R. Farren. Gr-EC:30,
   Rd-OA:6
Precision. P. Collenette.
   Ma-FW:207
Some Western Haikus, VI. J. Kerouac.
   Kh-VA:12
The Spider and the Fly. M. Howitt.
   De-TT:60, Er-FA:421, Fe-FP:530,
   Gr-EC:144, Ox-BC:158, Pe-FB:56
The Spider and the Ghost of the
   Fly. V. Lindsay. Ca-VT:29
Stop! Don't Swat the Fly.
   Kobayashi Issa. Ma-FW:205
Truth. H. Nemerov. Wi-LT:588
Upon a Spider Catching a Fly.
   E. Taylor. Rd-OA:174, Rv-CB:476,
   Sh-AP:12
FLIES, ARTIFICIAL
Angler's Choice. E. Gottlieb.
   Du-RG:105
Fly-Fishing. J. Gay. Mo-SD:104
FLIGHT: see also AVIATORS; BIRDS -
   FLIGHT; HUMOR - FLIGHT; SPACE
   EXPLORATION
At the Airport. H. Nemerov.
   Du-SH:163, Mc-WS:115
The Blue Wings. A. Karlov.
   Mo-MI:25
Boats in a Fog. R. Jeffers.
   Mo-BG:143
The Campers at Kitty Hawk.
   J. Dos Passos. Mo-BG:59
Ceiling Unlimited. M. Rukeyser.
   Un-MA:622
Chairoplane Chant. N. Turner.
   Ir-BB:254, St-FS:107
Cockpit in the Clouds. D. Dorrance.
   Ar-TP3:88, Fe-FP:201
Ego. P. Booth. Br-TC:59,
   Du-SH:164, Pe-SS:81
Field and Forest. R. Jarrell.
   Ca-VT:403
Flight. H. Vinal. Mc-WK:208
Flying. K. Starbird. La-PV:16
Flying Crooked. R. Graves.
   Br-TC:152, Co-PU:99, Ho-LP:44,
   Ma-FW:208, Rd-OA:18, Wi-LT:371
Geography Lesson. Z. Ghose.
   To-MP:159
High Flight. J. Magee, Jr.
   Er-FA:195, Fe-FP:203, Mc-WK:209
I Had a Boat. M. Coleridge. Sm-MK:30

FLIGHT — cont'd.
  The Landscape near an Aerodrome.
    S. Spender. Un-MB:475, Wi-LT:499
  Lindbergh. Em-AF:770
  Post Early for Space.
    P. Henniker-Heaton. Br-AF:239
  Riding in an Airplane. D. Baruch.
    Fe-FP:200
  Silver Ships. M. Meigs. Ar-TP3:87,
    Fe-FP:199
  Taking Off. Ar-TP3:87, Au-SP:175,
    Mc-AW:26
  Timothy Boon. I. Eastwick.
    Au-SP:208, Ir-BB:148
  Up Silver Stairsteps. J. Stuart.
    Br-AF:237
  Winged Man. S. Benét. Un-MA:497
  Wings. Bible. O.T. Psalms.
    Bo-FP:239, Ch-B:109, Fe-FP:289
  You Were Shattered. G. Ungaretti.
    Li-TU:126
FLIRTATION: see COQUETTES;
  COURTSHIP
FLODDEN, BATTLE, 1513
  Flodden. W. Scott. Hi-FO:111
  The Flowers of the Forest.
    J. Elliott. Al-VBP:582,
    De-CH:176, Pa-GTB:120
FLOODS
  Big Dam. W. Moses. Br-AF:188
  The Boats Are Afloat. Chu Hsi.
    Le-MW:69, Rx-OH:117
  The Broken Dike, the Levee
    Washed Away. E. Millay.
    Ni-JP:128
  The Cabin Creek Flood. Em-AF:476
  The Flood. P. Ovid. Gr-CT:203
  Floodtide. A. Touré. Ad-PB:336,
    Hu-PN:424
  Foreclosure. S. Brown. Ad-PB:64,
    Hu-PN:170
  Genesis A. Ma-YA:8
  The High Tide on the Coast of
    Lincolnshire. J. Ingelow.
    De-TT:183, Pa-OM:118, Sp-OG:85
  Horsey Gap. Gr-GB:172
  I Seem to Hear the Roar of the
    Waves. Ho Ch'i-fang. Hs-TC:227
  Noah. S. Sassoon. Cl-FC:69
  Noah and the Rabbit.
    H. Chesterman. Rd-OA:12.
  One More River. Cl-DT:52
  A River. A. Ramanujan. To-MP:166
  Stratton Water. Ox-BB:680
  An Unknown Land. Tr-US I:194
  Wasn't That a Mighty Storm?
    Em-AF:471
FLORENCE, IT.
  Andrea del Sarto. R. Browning.
    Ke-TF:310
  Bat. D. Lawrence.
    Pa-GTB:458

  Bianca among the Nightingales.
    E. Browning. Pa-GTB:324
  The Old Bridge at Florence.
    H. Longfellow. Pa-HT:111
FLORIDA
  Florida. E. Bishop. Br-TC:51,
    Ca-VT:217
  Florida Road Workers. L. Hughes.
    Du-SH:145, Pe-SS:52, Un-MA:553
  Nocturne. F. Frost. Co-BN:202
  Okefenokee Swamp. D. Hickey.
    Br-AF:185
  Pursuit. R. Warren. Br-TC:454,
    Un-MA:598
  Swanee River. S. Foster.
    Er-FA:428, Se-PR:256
  Two Figures in Dense Violet Night.
    W. Stevens. No-CL:244, Un-MA:248
FLORISTS
  The Florist Shop. R. Field.
    Br-SG:75
  Winter Flower Store. D. Aldis.
    Br-SG:76
FLOUNDERS: see FISH
FLOUR MILLS: see also MILLERS (MEN)
  Five Eyes. W. de la Mare.
    Co-BBW:133, Co-IW:18, Ir-BB:28
  Lubber Breeze. T. Moore. De-CH:135
FLOWERS: see also names of flowers,
  as VIOLETS
  Adieu. P. Lewenstein. Sm-MK:212
  After the Bells Hummed. Basho.
    Be-CS:34
  And Can the Physician Make Sick
    Men Well? Bl-OB:157, Gr-EC:288,
    Re-TW:47
  Annie's Garden. E. Follen.
    Ch-B:66
  As a Flower I Come. Sundaram.
    Al-PI:112
  At Easter Time. L. Richards.
    Hu-MP:334
  Blossoms. M. Fenellosa. Bo-FP:244
  Blue Flowers. R. Field. Br-SG:32,
    Mc-PR:161
  Bonny Lassie O! J. Clare. De-CH:195
  The Breeze. Bo-FP:259, Ch-B:88
  The Broken-Hearted Gardener.
    Gr-CT:271, Gr-GB:115
  Bridal Song. J. Fletcher.
    Al-VBP:285, Rv-CB:314
  Bunch of Wild Flowers. L. Zilles.
    Sh-RP:86
  Cathemerinon. Prudentius. Pa-SG:88
  A Charm for Spring Flowers.
    R. Field. Ar-TP3:211, Tu-WW:58
  The City. D. Ignatow. Co-PU:63
  The City Child. A. Tennyson.
    Ox-BC:213
  A City Flower. A. Dobson. Go-BP:124
  A Contemplation upon Flowers.
    H. King. Co-BN:44, Rv-CB:350

A Cut Flower.   K. Shapiro. Co-BN:54
Cycle.   L. Hughes.   Fe-FP:216
Daisy.   F. Thompson.   Ga-FB:164,
   Ox-BN:917, Un-MB:77
The Death of the Flowers.
   W. Bryant.   Co-BN:188, Fe-PL:271
Directions.   Onitsura.   Au-SP:306
Dream Songs, II.   Tr-US II:248
Dreaming.   T. Miles.   Ho-CT:5
Early Spring.   M. Chute.   Br-SG:5
Envy.   C. and M. Lamb.   Ox-BC:140
Eurydice.   H.D.   Ca-VT:107
The Fall of the Flowers.   Yen Yun.
   Le-MW:73
The Flower.   V. Lapin.   Mo-MI:15
Flower Arrangement.   S. Yellen.
   Ls-NY:55
The Flower-Cart Man.   R. Field.
   Au-SP:143, Br-SG:72, Br-SS:147,
   La-OC:53
Flower Chorus.   R. Emerson.
   Bo-FP:220
Flower in the Crannied Wall.
   A. Tennyson.   Co-BN:49, Er-FA:243,
   Fe-FP:216, Fr-WO:85, Ga-FB:128,
   Hu-MP:257, Ma-YA:198, Mc-PR:137
A Flower Is Looking.   H. Monro.
   Un-MB:236
A Flower Lullaby.   De-PP:18
Flower Season.   Yeh Shan.
   Pa-MV:165
The Flower-Seller.   E. Farjeon.
   Bo-FP:123, Br-SG:74
The Flower Shop.   H. Anzai.
   Sh-AM:119
Flower Song.   Br-MW:7
The Flowering Forest.   E. Sitwell.
   Gr-SS:51
Flowers.   H. Behn.   Br-SG:54,
   Fe-FP:222
Flowers.   T. Jastrzebski.   Ho-CT:12
Flowers.   J. Rimbaud.   Ma-FW:112
The Flowers.   R. Stevenson.
   Fe-FP:217, Hu-MP:247
Flowers at Night.   A. Fisher.
   Br-SG:33
Flowers by the Sea.   W. Williams.
   Bo-GJ:86, Ho-LP:54, Mo-BG:118,
   Un-MA:261
Flowers for Heliodora.   Meleager.
   Gr-SS:83
Flowers for Sale!   Wy-CM:12
The Flowers in a Meadow.   F. Cornford.
   Gr-TG:27
Flowers Look like Balls of Wool.
   P. White.   Le-M:34
Flowers of June.   Y. Sasazawa.
   Sh-AM:75
Flowers of Middle Summer.
   W. Shakespeare.   Ha-YA:64
For a Picture of Saint Dorothea.
   G. Hopkins.   Gr-CC:140

The Garden.   J. Sylvester.
   Rv-CB:187
A Garden Song.   A. Dobson.
   Co-BN:52, Ox-BN:848
Garden Song.   A. Guiterman.
   Br-SG:63, Th-AS:48
Garden Song.   Bo-FP:253
The Gardener.   Po-Chu-I.   Co-BN:209,
   Go-BP:40, Pa-SG:166
Grandmother's Garden.   J. Tippett.
   Br-SG:40
Her Dairy.   P. Newell.   Bo-FP:83
How the Flowers Grow.   G. Setoun.
   Au-SP:307, Hu-MP:244
I Hoed and Trenched and Weeded.
   A. Housman.   Un-MB:102, Wi-LT:651
I Saw.   P. Malone.   Ho-CT:4
The Idle Flowers.   R. Bridges.
   Co-BN:45, Gr-CT:247
If I Should Ever by Chance Grow
   Rich.   E. Thomas.   Bl-OB:32,
   Bo-GJ:20, De-CH:518, Ox-BC:329,
   Pa-RE:73, Sm-LG:112, Un-MB:215
I'll Twine White Violets.   Meleager.
   Pa-SG:35
In Desert Places.   Sister M.
   Madeleva.   Un-GT:253
In Memoriam LXXXII.
   A. Tennyson.   Al-VBP:861
In the Eternal.   Ki No Tomonori.
   Ba-ST:22
In the Meadow.   C. Rossetti.
   Ch-B:89
In the Morning Unfolding.
   F. Garcia Lorca.   Le-SW:81
In the Spring.   Meleager. Pa-SG:67
In the Spring.   De-PP:57
The Last Flower.   J. Moore. Co-PS:126
Late October.   S. Teasdale.   Co-PS:125,
   Ha-YA:112
Life.   G. Herbert.   Rv-CB:353
The Lily Has an Air.   C. Rossetti.
   Br-SG:29
A Little Tune.   Tai Wang-shu.
   Hs-TC:183
Lodged.   R. Frost.   Br-SG:24,
   Sh-RP:116
The Loving Dexterity.   W. Williams.
   Ho-TH:73
The Magic Flower.   D. Marcus.
   Le-M:38
Maiden in the Moor.   Ma-BB:82
The Midges Dance aboon the Burn.
   R. Tannahill.   Co-BN:108
The Miracle of Spring.   Bahar.
   Pa-SG:82
More than Flowers We Have Brought.
   N. Turner.   Br-SS:157
Names.   D. Aldis.   Br-SG:26
A New Flower - Pure and Untorn.
   M. Korte.   Sc-TN:115
A Nosegay.   E. Spenser.   De-TT:143

FLOWERS — cont'd.
  Not Iris in Her Pride. G. Peele.
    Al-VBP:136
  The One. P. Kavanagh. Un-MB:432
  The Parliament of Bees 3. J. Day.
    Al-VBP:243
  The Picture of Little T. C. in a
    Prospect of Flowers.
    A. Marvell. Rv-CB:406
  The Procession. M. Widdemer.
    Ha-YA:19
  Prothalamion. E. Spenser.
    Al-VBP:100, Gr-CT:298, Pa-GTB:32
  The Rain Song. R. Loveman.
    Hu-MP:252
  The Round. P. Booth. Co-BN:48
  The Seeds of Love. De-TT:19,
    Gr-GB:137, Ho-WR:59, Rv-CB:428,
    Sm-LG:349
  Self-Portrait, as a Bear. D. Hall.
    Ha-TP:94
  Seventy Balconies and Not a Single
    Flower. B. Fernández Moreno.
    Be-UL:27
  The Shepherd's Calender, April.
    E. Spenser. Al-VBP:98
  Some Flowers o' the Spring.
    W. Shakespeare. Gr-CT:249
  Some Western Haikus, II.
    J. Kerouac. Kh-VA:12
  Song. T. Deloney. Al-VBP:87
  Song. Sung Tzü-hou. Pa-SG:84
  Sonnets from the Portuguese.
    E. Browning. Ox-BN:466
  A Spark in the Sun. H. Behn.
    Be-CS:3, Br-SG:24
  Spring. J. Thomson. Al-VBP:549
  The Spring Waters, 33. Ping Hsin.
    Hs-TC:22
  Summer. J. Davidson. Co-BN:100
  Summer Shower. S. Robinson.
    Th-AS:118
  A Tale. E. Thomas. Gr-CT:262
  Tapers. F. Gray. De-FS:98
  The Task. W. Cowper. Go-BP:23
  There Is a Fading Time. Ba-ST:44
  There Is a Trinity. Rippo. Le-MW:65
  They Say on Leaving Eden.
    M. Dunster. Ls-NY:47
  To Blossoms. R. Herrick.
    Co-BN:35, Pa-GTB:91, Sm-MK:5
  To Mistress Isabel Pennell.
    J. Skelton. Al-VBP:31, De-CH:34,
    Ma-FW:65, Ma-YA:51, Rv-CB:65
  To the Sun from a Flower. G. Gezelle.
    Fe-FP:471, Pa-SG:105
  The Tree. B. Björnson. Bo-FP:268,
    Hu-MP:271
  The Troll's Nosegay. R. Graves.
    En-PC:29
  The Tuft of Flowers. R. Frost.
    Rv-CB:966, Sh-AP:150, Un-MA:168

  Tule Love Song. Da-SC:16,
    Tr-US II:295
  Tumbling-Hair. E. Cummings.
    No-CL:51
  A Violet Bank. W. Shakespeare.
    Bo-FP:318, Co-BN:50, Fe-FP:219,
    Sh-RP:81
  Violets, Daffodils.
    E. Coatsworth. Ar-TP3:211,
    Co-PU:62, Mc-AW:101
  Waiting. H. Behn. Ar-TP3:199,
    Br-SG:109, Br-SS:92
  Where's My Lovely Parsley. De-CH:602
  The White Bouquet. Chung Ting-wen.
    Pa-MV:79
  A Widow's Weeds. W. de la Mare.
    Ga-FB:238
  The Wild Flower Man. Lu Yu.
    Rx-OH:103
  The Wild Flower's Song. W. Blake.
    Rv-CB:606
  The Wild Thyme. W. Blake. Ho-WR:68
  Window Boxes. E. Farjeon.
    Br-SG:29, Fe-FP:222
FLUTES: see also HUMOR - FLUTES
  Autumn Tune. Chang Hsiu-ya.
    Pa-MV:31
  Country Music. Pa-SG:132
  A Drape. Feng Chih. Hs-TC:143
  The Find. F. Ledwidge. Th-AS:18
  Flute. Chang Hsiu-ya. Pa-MV:35
  The Flute Players. J. Rabéarivelo.
    Pa-SG:130
  I Play Flute. J. Stembridge.
    Lo-IT:129
  Monk Begging, Kyoto. E. Shiffert.
    Ls-NY:140
  Neither Spirit nor Bird. Pa-SG:36
  O Moon, Why Must You. Be-CS:41
  Old Orange Flute. Gr-GB:192
  On Hearing a Flute at Night from
    the Wall of Shou-Hsiang.
    Li Yi. Pl-US:11
  Serenade. C. Brentano. Pa-SG:134
  "Two, Two!" Toots the Train.
    On-TW:8
  When I Had a Little Leisure.
    Wang Mou Fang. Le-MW:105
  Women's Dance Song. Tr-US II:151
FLYING: see FLIGHT
FLYING DUTCHMAN (LEGEND)
  The Flying Dutchman. C. Leland.
    Co-PM:121
FLYING FISH
  The Flying Fish. J. Gay. Gr-CT:213,
    Ox-BN:938
  Leaping Flying-Fish. Kôson.
    Ca-BF:47
FLYING SAUCERS
  Go Fly a Saucer. D. McCord.
    Fe-FP:198, Li-TU:47, Pl-IO:27
FLYING SQUIRRELS: see SQUIRRELS

FOAM
  Foam Flowers. Yasuhide. Le-MW:82
  Spray. D. Lawrence. Co-BN:81
  Waves Against a Dog. T. Baybars.
    Sm-MK:176
FOG: see also HAZE; MIST
  Boats in a Fog. R. Jeffers.
    Mo-BG:143
  The Breathing. D. Levertov.
    Ha-WR:73, La-RM:135
  Conversation. J. Berryman.
    Wi-LT:567
  The Cry. M. Perlberg. Co-PU:138
  Cuckoos. M. Kaneko. Sh-AM:62
  The Fog. W. Davies. Ar-TP3:172,
    La-OC:133, Mc-WK:34
  Fog. C. Garstin. Co-SS:42
  Fog. S. Ingbritson. Le-M:131
  Fog. N. Nagy. La-GI:19
  Fog. C. Sandburg.
    Ar-TP3:171, Au-SP:328, Er-FA:239,
    Fe-FP:82, Ga-FB:301, Ho-CS:34,
    Hu-MP:318, La-PP:33, Ma-FW:266,
    Pa-RE:56, Pe-FB:72, Th-AS:83,
    Un-GB:12, Un-GT:255, Un-MA:200
  Fog-Horn. W. Merwin. Mo-TS:23
  Fog, the Magician. M. Cane.
    Th-AS:122
  The Foghorn. Wang T'ung-chao.
    Hs-TC:263
  I Wonder. J. Ricci. La-GI:19
  Late Last Night. A. Gregor.
    Ca-VT:503
  My Song Was Ready. Le-IB:79
  On the White Birches.
    S. Mizuhara. Sh-AM:167
  River-Fog. Fukayabu Kiyowara.
    Fe-FP:481
  A Song from Arsut. Tr-US I:4
  The Sounding Fog. S. Pulsifer.
    La-PV:39
  We Rowed into Fog. Shiki.
    Be-CS:29
  The White Monster. T. Trubilla.
    La-GI:18
  Winter Views Serene. G. Crabbe.
    Ox-BN:9
  Yellow Fog. T. Eliot.
    Ar-TP3:171, Ha-LO:85
FOLK SONGS: see BALLADS
FOLKLORE: see also BALLADS; CHARMS;
    FABLES; FAIRIES; GHOSTS; HALLOW-
    EEN; LEGENDS; MYTHOLOGY; NURSERY
    RHYMES; REMEDIES AND CURES;
    SAYINGS AND SIGNS; SUPERSTITION;
    TALL TALES; WITCHES AND WITCHCRAFT
  The Big Rock Candy Mountain.
    Co-OH:87
  The Birth of John Henry. M. Tolson.
    Lo-TY:213, Ra-BP:118
  The Deer Live at the Deer Yawn.
    Wo-HS:(14)

  Earthquake. Kuo Mo-jo. Hs-TC:38
  John Henry. Ab-MO:81, Bo-HF:104,
    Co-RM:225, Er-FA:407, Ga-S:124,
    Hi-TL:159, Ra-BP:12
  They Have Yarns. C. Sandburg.
    Br-AF:106, Sh-RP:270, Un-GT:196,
    Un-MA:211
FONTAINEBLEAU, FR.
  Fontainebleau. S. Teasdale.
    Gr-CC:178
FOOD AND EATING: see also DIET;
    HUMOR - FOOD AND EATING; and
    names of meals, as SUPPER,
    and specific foods, as BREAD
  Address to a Haggis. R. Burns.
    Al-VBP:633
  Aiken Drum. Bl-OB:11, Ir-BB:129,
    Sm-LG:120
  Animal Crackers. C. Morley.
    Au-SP:118, Fe-FP:43, Fr-MP:5,
    Hu-MP:16, Th-AS:62
  Bacon and Greens. Co-PU:34
  The Ballad of Bouillabaisse.
    W. Thackeray. Al-VBP:879
  La Ballade. M. Bracker. Ke-TF:375
  Banquet Song. W. Gilbert.
    Gr-EC:107
  Black Man's Feast. S. Fabio.
    Ad-PB:203
  Blessing over Food. H. Bialik.
    Ha-YA:133
  Blythsome Bridal. Gr-GB:152
  Bring Us In Good Ale. Al-VBP:24,
    Cl-FC:94, De-CH:64
  Canterbury Tales. G. Chaucer.
    Al-VBP:9
  Carrying Food Home in Winter.
    M. Atwood. Mo-TS:8
  A Catch. M. Hoberman. Ag-HE:14
  Charley Wag. Mother Goose.
    Ag-HE:73, Mo-MGT:76
  Cherry-Stones. E. Farjeon. Ag-HE:52
  Chorus. T. Peacock. Al-VBP:716
  Christmas Time. W. Scott. Cl-FC:92
  Clam-Digging Song. M. Kumlin.
    Cr-SS:6
  Corn. E. Antin. Br-SG:43
  Dilly Dilly. Ag-HE:18
  Eating Fish. G. Johnston. Do-WH:10
  Egan O'Rahilly. J. Stephens.
    Rv-CB:974
  Ella. G. Brooks. Ag-HE:39
  Elvers. F. Harvey. Cl-DT:47
  Fantasia. W. Letts. Co-PI:93
  Five Little Chickens. Ch-B:85,
    Fe-FP:282, Gr-EC:182, La-PV:198,
    St-FS:78, Un-GB:15, Un-GT:67
  Food. M. Chute. Ag-HE:32,
    La-OC:81
  Food and Drink. L. Untermeyer.
    Un-MA:308

FOOD AND EATING — cont'd.
  Get 'Em Here. L. Hopkins. Ho-CS:20
  Girls and Boys, Come Out to Play.
    Ag-HE:33, Ar-TP3:98, De-TT:34,
    Hu-MP:34, Ir-BB:15, Li-LB:24,
    Mo-NR:116, Wi-MG:60, Wr-RM:17
  The Glutton. J. Oakman. Ox-BC:83
  Grace. W. de la Mare. Gr-TG:35
  The Grass on the Mountain. Bo-HF:34
  Greedy Jane. Gr-EC:106, Ox-BC:328
  Greedy Richard. J. Taylor.
    Ox-BC:121
  Greedy Tom. Ag-HE:15, Ir-BB:192,
    St-FS:11
  Handy, Pandy, Jack-a-Dandy.
    Mo-TL:73, Wr-RM:49
  Hannah Bantry. Ag-HE:17, Co-OH:52,
    Mo-MGT:77
  The Hasty Pudding. J. Barlow.
    Sm-LG:121
  Have at It! Br-FW:10
  He Who Has Never Known Hunger.
    E. Coatsworth. Ar-TP3:209
  High on the Hog. J. Fields.
    Be-MA:154
  Homely Meats. J. Davies. Sm-LG:117
  Hunger and Thirst. B. Young.
    Mc-AW:29
  Hunting Prayer. Le-OE:58
  I Must Remember. S. Silverstein.
    Co-PS:20
  I'd Like a Little. Er-FA:498
  If We Didn't Have to Eat.
    N. Waterman. Ag-HE:59, Co-FB:81
  Ivan and I Went Fishing. Gr-BB:10
  James and the Shoulder of Mutton.
    A. O'Keeffe. De-TT:46
  Late Rising. J. Prevert. Ad-CI:98
  Let Me Go Warm. L. de Góngora.
    Mc-PR:47
  Lickety-Lick. M. Justus. Fr-MP:9,
    Mc-AW:28
  The Masked Shrew. I. Gardner.
    Co-BBW:39, Pl-IO:105
  Master Jack's Song. L. Richards.
    Ag-HE:48
  A Matter of Taste. E. Merriam.
    Ag-HE:31
  Miss T. W. de la Mare. Ar-TP3:11,
    Au-SP:134, Bo-GJ:22, Hu-MP:153,
    La-PV:25, Su-FVI:22
  Mother's Biscuits. F. Quenneville.
    Du-RG:118
  My Aunt Kept Turnips in a Flock.
    R. Jarrell. Ag-HE:21
  Neighborly. V. Storey. Ar-TP3:2
  Noodle. Y. Hashimoto. Le-TA:91
  November's Come. J. Lincoln.
    Sh-RP:233
  Oberon's Feast. R. Herrick.
    Al-VBP:330
  Old Joe Jones. L. Richards. Ag-HE:17

  On Himself. J. Swift. Co-PI:183
  On the Death of an Epicure.
    R. Graves. Rv-CB:530
  Perry-the-Winkle. J. Tolkien.
    Ar-TP3:158
  Pete's Sweets. E. Merriam.
    Su-FVI:6
  A Picnic. A. Fisher. Au-SP:121
  Picnics. M. Chute. Ag-HE:36
  The Pigs. J. Taylor. De-TT:23
  Plow the Corn. Ju-CP:6
  Pretty Futility. E. Coatsworth.
    Ag-HE:46
  Puppy. A. Fisher. Au-SP:36
  Robbin and Bobbin. Mother Goose.
    Ag-HE:71, Mo-MGT:94
  Sal's Atomic Submarines.
    L. Sissman. Mo-BG:25
  Sledburn Fair. De-CH:71
  A Snack. C. Rossetti. Bo-FP:78,
    Ch-B:104
  Song in Praise of Paella.
    C. Wordsworth. Ag-HE:12,
    Co-FB:91
  A Song of Bread and Honey.
    R. Le Gallienne. Bo-FP:62
  Stool Ball. De-CH:67
  The Story of Augustus. H. Hoffmann.
    Ox-BC:205
  Survey of Literature. J. Ransom.
    Br-TC:335, Ca-VT:151, Sm-LG:36
  The Table. C. de Andrade. An-TC:67
  A Table Richly Spread. J. Milton.
    Sm-LG:119
  Taste Buds. C. Barks. Mc-EA:97
  Thanksgiving Magic. R. Bennett.
    Br-SS:82
  There Was a Young Hopeful Named
    Sam. E. Ripley. Fr-MP:5
  There Was an Old Man of the East.
    E. Lear. Ag-HE:71
  There Was an Old Person of
    Sparta. E. Lear. Ag-HE:14
  This Little Morsel of Morsels
    Here. W. de la Mare. Ag-HE:3
  Three Mice. C. Cole. Ir-BB:84,
    St-FS:63
  Through the Teeth. Su-FVI:6
  To-Morrow's the Fair. Gr-GB:27
  Tom at Dinner. A. O'Keeffe.
    De-TT:101
  Tomato Time. M. Livingston.
    Ag-HE:43, Br-SG:39
  Tummy Ache. A. Fisher. Au-SP:107
  The Two Boys. M. Lamb. Rv-CB:628
  Two Puppies. De-PP:38
  Undue Significance a Starving Man
    Attaches. E. Dickinson.
    Wi-LT:8
  Virginia. P. McGinley. Ag-HE:8
  The Visions of MacConglinne.
    Co-PI:134, De-CH:65

The Vulture.   H. Belloc.   Ag-HE:70,
   Ir-BB:77, Lo-LL:78
A Wee Little Boy Has Opened a
   Store.   Wy-CM:11
When in Rome.   M. Evans.   Bo-AN:164
Wild Duck.   T. Aida.   Sh-AM:109
FOOLS: see also HUMOR - FOOLS;
   STUPIDITY
The Cap and Bells.   W. Yeats.
   Gr-CT:71, Ma-FW:154, Pa-OM:260,
   Un-MB:110
Conversation with an April Fool.
   R. Bennett.   Br-SS:146
The Fool on the Hill.   J. Lennon.
   Mo-GR:72
The Fool's Prayer.   E. Sills.
   Fe-PL:322, Pa-OM:225, Sp-OG:137
If It Do Come to Pass.
   W. Shakespeare.   Al-VBP:187
The King of China's Daughter.
   E. Sitwell.   De-CH:186,
   Ir-BB:258, Ma-FW:185, Pa-RE:23,
   Un-MB:331
The Men of Gotham.   T. Peacock.
   Al-VBP:715, De-CH:193, Hi-WP I:91,
   Ho-WR:108, Sp-OG:344
Prayer for the Incurables.
   F. Hölderlin.   Un-R:21
Song About Fools.   B. Okujava.
   Bo-RU:58
FOOT PLAY
The Blacksmith.   Mo-TL:28,
   On-TW:8, Rv-ON:87, Wr-RM:33
Hob, Shoe, Hob.   Mo-TL:29
John Smith, Fellow Fine.   Mo-TL:28
Little Betty Blue.   Mo-NR:13,
   Wr-RM:100
Pitty Patty Polt.   Ir-BB:190,
   Mo-TL:27, St-FS:28
See-Saw, Margery Daw.   Au-SP:6,
   Ir-BB:11, Li-LB:130, Mo-MGT:28,
   Mo-NR:3, Mo-TL:16
Shoe a Little Horse.   De-PO:8,
   Li-LB:21, Mo-MGT:101, Mo-TL:29
Shoe the Pony, Shoe.   Mo-TL:32
Shoeing.   Wr-RM:100
Song to the Five Toes.   Bo-FP:8,
   Mo-TL:17
This Ain Biggit the Baurn.
   De-CH:497
This Gurt Pig.   De-CH:497
This Little Pig Got into the
   Barn.   Mo-TL:16
This Little Pig Went to Market.
   Au-SP:18, Bo-FP:8, De-CH:497,
   De-PO:8, Ir-BB:10, Li-LB:20,
   Mo-CC:(48), Mo-MGT:54,
   Mo-NR:78, Mo-TL:15, Sp-TM:23,
   Wi-MG:73, Wr-RM:35
This Old Man, He Played One.
   Au-SP:248, Ir-BB:125, Mo-TL:31
Three French Mice.   Ir-BB:236

Tit-Tat-Toe.   Mother Goose.
   Ir-BB:36, Mo-MGT:196, Mo-NR:123,
   Mo-TL:30
Wee Wiggie.   Mo-TL:17
Whose Little Pigs Are These?
   Mo-TL:16
FOOT RACING: see RUNNING
FOOTBALL: see also HUMOR - FOOTBALL;
   SATIRE - FOOTBALL
Alumnus Football.   G. Rice.
   Fe-PL:56
Football Song.   W. Scott.   Mo-SD:28
Heaps on Heaps.   M. Concanen.
   Mo-SD:28
In the Beginning Was the.
   L. Murchison.   Mo-SD:172
The Man from Inversnaid.   R. Murray.
   Mo-SD:31
Notes Found near a Suicide: To
   "Chick."   F. Horne.   Bo-AN:43,
   Ra-BP:71
The Passer.   G. Abbe.   Du-SH:77,
   Mo-SD:27
Second Half.   D. McCord.   Mo-SD:25
Settling Some Old Football Scores.
   M. Bishop.   Mo-SD:30
Street Football.   J. Gay.   Fl-HH:29,
   Mo-SD:29
Ties.   D. Stuart.   Du-SH:78,
   Mc-EA:111
Under the Goal Posts.   A. Guiterman.
   Fl-HH:39
Ways of My Exile.   R. Roseliep.
   St-H:181
FOOTPRINTS: see also ANIMAL TRACKS;
   TRACKING AND TRAILING
By One Unsure.   M. Cane.   Ls-NY:114
Evening at the Seashore.   N. Sharma.
   Al-PI:122
Footprints.   S. Kurahara.   Sh-AM:78
Goat Songs, II.   R. Drew.   Kh-VA:44
The Pigeon.   R. Church.   Hi-WP II:166
Planting Song.   Da-SC:109, Ho-SD:23
The Rabbit Leaves.   D. Schmitz.
   St-H:196
Snowy Morning.   B. Young.   Mc-AW:6
Steps.   R. Heckman.   Ba-HI:25
Strange Footprints.   V. Gouled.
   Mc-AW:87
FORBEARANCE: see PATIENCE;
   SELF-CONTROL
FORCE: see also POWER; STRENGTH
Beyond the End.   D. Levertov.
   Ca-VT:508
The Black Panther.   J. Wheelock.
   Ha-TP:94, Wi-LT:654
Native.   N. Madgett.   Be-MA:92
Of Natural Forces.   E. Chesley.
   Ls-NY:321
A Voice.   H. Leivick.   Ho-TY:124
Young Training.   L. McGaugh.
   Ad-PB:376

FORD, FORD MADOX
  Ford Madox Ford. R. Lowell.
    Br-TC:263, En-PC:163
FOREBODINGS: see PREMONITIONS
FOREFATHERS' DAY: see PILGRIM
    FATHERS
FOREIGN LEGION: see SATIRE -
    FOREIGN LEGION
FOREST FIRES
  There's a Fire in the Forest.
    W. Ross. Do-WH:57
FORESTERS AND FORESTRY
  The Jolly Forester. Pa-RE:81
FORESTS AND WOODS: see also
    HUMOR - FORESTS AND WOODS;
    LUMBERING; TREES
  After the Anonymous Swedish.
    J. Harrison. Ca-VT:711
  All That's Past. W. de la Mare.
    Al-VBP:1119, Bo-GJ:202, Re-TW:85
  All the Little Hoofprints.
    R. Jeffers. Ni-JP:109
  Autumn Woods. J. Tippett.
    Ar-TP3:184, Ja-PA:14, Mc-AW:48,
    St-FS:102
  A Ballad of Trees and the Master.
    S. Lanier. Fe-PL:345, Ke-TF:213,
    Sh-AP:134
  Bicycles. A. Voznesensky.
    Li-TU:40
  The Christmas Robin. R. Graves.
    Gr-CC:48
  Come In. R. Frost. Co-BN:157,
    Ga-FB:292, Hi-WP I:4, Un-MA:19,
    Wi-LT:179
  Dance Songs, II. Tr-US II:141
  The Deer. M. Austin. Fe-FP:171
  Easter in the Woods. F. Frost.
    Br-SS:138
  The English in Virginia.
    C. Reznikoff. Gr-SS:62
  Evening over the Forest.
    B. Mayor. Cl-FC:28
  Field and Forest. R. Jarrell.
    Ca-VT:403
  For the Nightly Ascent of Orion
    over a Forest Clearing.
    J. Dickey. Br-TC:88
  Forest. J. Garrigue. Wi-LT:710
  The Forest. D. Quick. De-FS:153
  A Forest Hymn. W. Bryant.
    Sh-AP:23
  Forest Shapes. D. Wandrei.
    De-FS:214
  The Green Dryad's Plea.
    T. Hood. Ox-BN:414
  Green Rain. M. Webb. Co-BN:21,
    De-CH:10, Fe-FP:216, Tu-WW:50
  Green Symphony. J. Fletcher.
    Un-MA:314
  Heart of the Woods.
    W. Curtright. Hu-PN:280

Holiday. E. Young. Ar-TP3:164
The Hollow Wood. E. Thomas.
  Pa-RE:10
The House in the Green Well.
  J. Wheelock. Un-MA:344
Inscription for the Entrance to
  a Wood. W. Bryant. Sh-AP:19
Lives. H. Reed. Co-BN:67
The Mass of the Grove.
  D. ap Gwilym. Go-BP:73
November Woods. H. Jackson.
  Ja-PA:42
The Ocean Wood. J. Warren.
  Rv-CB:935
Out in the Wood. C. Scollard.
  Th-AS:117
Picking Up Sticks. E. Farjeon.
  Bo-FP:67
Poem. J. Harrison. Ca-VT:710
Prologue to Evangeline.
  H. Longfellow. Li-SR:48
Prometheus Unbound. P. Shelley.
  Al-VBP:740
The Recollection. P. Shelley.
  De-CH:148
The Rescue. D. Schmitz. St-H:190
Silence. W. Turner. Un-MB:348
Solitude. A. Lampman.
  Co-BN:148, Rv-CB:955
Solitude Late at Night in the
  Woods. R. Bly. Ca-VT:558
Songs, I. Tr-US II:142
Staying Alive. D. Wagoner.
  Co-BN:160, Du-SH:183, Pe-M:38
Stopping by Woods on a Snowy
  Evening. R. Frost.
  Ad-PE:31, Al-VBP:1134, Ar-TP3:198
  Bo-FP:170, Bo-GJ:257, Br-SS:88,
  Br-TC:135, Cl-DT:20, Co-BN:151,
  Co-PS:160, De-CH:625, Er-FA:257,
  Fe-FP:67, Ga-FB:299, Gr-EC:273,
  Ha-PO:90, Ke-TF:420, La-PP:29,
  La-PV:167, Ma-FW:276, Mc-MK:32,
  Mc-PR:124, Pe-FB:80, Re-TW:123,
  Sh-AP:150, Sh-RP:52, Sm-LG:63,
  Sm-PT:8, Un-MA:187, Wi-LT:174
Summer. J. Clare. Rv-CB:718
Two Lives and Others. W. Scott.
  Du-RG:119
Under the Woods. E. Thomas.
  De-CH:50
The Voice. R. Brooke. Gr-BT:59
The Walk. W. Ross. Mo-SD:88
Walking. S. Bahe. Ba-HI:62
Warning. S. Russell. De-FS:168
A Warning to Skeptics. L. Drake.
  De-FS:76
The Way Through the Woods. R. Kipling.
  De-CH:281, Fe-FP:242, Ha-PO:154,
  Hi-WP I:107, La-RM:46, Mc-WS:31,
  Ox-BC:323, Ox-BN:932, Re-TW:128,
  Sm-LG:396

The Woodlands. W. Barnes. Co-BN:158
Woods in Winter. H. Longfellow.
   Rv-CB:781
The Woods of Westermain.
   G. Meredith. Mc-WK:204
FORGERIES: see HUMOR - FORGERIES
FORGETTING: see also HUMOR -
   FORGETTING; OBLIVION
The Absent-Minded Man.
   G. MacPherson. Ja-PC:36
Aftermath. S. Sassoon. Al-VBP:1167,
   Un-MB:314
All This Sunday Long. B. Johnson.
   Co-EL:9
Ballad of Death. G. Topirceanu.
   Mc-AC:51
Because I Liked You. A. Housman.
   Hi-WP II:108
Burial. P. Joachim. Lo-TY:146
Chucklehead. P. Robbins. Ar-TP3:61
Country Music. Plato. Pa-SG:132
Death Songs. L. Mack. Ad-PB:499
The Faery Queen. W. Raleigh.
   Al-VBP:93
Farewell to Juliet. W. Blunt.
   Al-VBP:1054
Flame-Heart. C. McKay. Bo-AN:30,
   Hu-PN:104
Forgetfulness. Chang Hsiu-ya.
   Pa-MV:33
Girls' Songs. Tr-CB:32, Tr-US I:119
Heart, We Will Forget Him!
   E. Dickinson. Al-VBP:1002
An Interlude. A. Swinburne.
   Al-VBP:1030
Leaves. C. Cullen. Bo-HF:62
Let It Be Forgotten. S. Teasdale.
   Bo-HF:127, Un-MA:266
Lethe. H.D. Al-VBP:1168,
   Ca-VT:116, Un-MA:341, Wi-LT:621
Marriage Songs. Tr-US II:159
The Missing Person. D. Justice.
   Ha-TP:41
Modern Love XII. G. Meredith.
   Al-VBP:982
Nirvana. J. Wheelock. Un-MA:343
Rococo. A. Swinburne. Al-VBP:1025
St. Anthony's Township. G. Sheldon.
   De-CH:385
So Shuts the Marigold Her Leaves.
   W. Browne. Al-VBP:321, Gr-CT:72
Song. C. Rossetti. Al-VBP:994,
   Co-BL:103, De-CH:262, Er-FA:84,
   Fe-PL:97, Ha-PO:157, Hi-WP II:21,
   Rv-CB:892, Sp-OG:278, Un-MW:91
Sonnet. T. Hood. Al-VBP:798,
   Ox-BN:424
The Unbroken Code. R. Dana. Ls-NY:95
What Lips My Lips Have Kissed.
   E. Millay. Al-VBP:1196, Pe-OA:164,
   Un-MA:445, Un-MW:102

Words. H. Brooks. Hu-NN:104,
   Hu-PN:278
FORGIVENESS
After the Pangs of a Desperate
   Love. J. Dryden. Al-VBP:480
A Ballad of a Nun. J. Davidson.
   Pa-OM:138, Un-MB:74
The Cherry-Tree Carol. Al-VBP:58,
   Ga-S:64, Gr-CT:127, Gr-GB:299,
   Ke-TF:47, Ox-BB:1, Pa-OM:349,
   Rv-CB:53
Clear Eyes. W. de la Mare.
   Al-VBP:1120
The Confidence. E. Jennings.
   Go-BP:186
Doing an Injury. . . .
   B. Franklin. Un-GT:25
Forgive, O Lord, My Little Jokes
   on Thee. R. Frost. Pl-EI:40,
   Wi-LT:188
Forgiveness. E. Sewell. Pl-EI:38
Forgiveness. Ke-TF:138
Holy Sonnets VII. J. Donne.
   Al-VBP:262, Gr-CT:382, Ma-FW:175,
   Ma-YA:81, Pl-EI:58, Rv-CB:308
The Holy Well. Gr-GB:305, Sm-LG:373
A Hymn to God the Father. J. Donne.
   Al-VBP:264, Ga-S:137, Pl-EI:206
In Place of a Curse. J. Ciardi.
   Du-SH:104
In the Deep Museum. A. Sexton.
   Un-MA:690
Lies. Y. Yevtushenko. Du-SH:106
Little Things. J. Stephens.
   Ad-PE:47, Ar-TP3:65, Bo-GJ:19,
   Br-SS:151, Co-BBW:55, Co-PU:70,
   Fe-FP:149, Gr-EC:40, Hi-WP I:33,
   Hu-MP:200, La-PV:160, Pl-EI:130,
   Un-MB:263
Love Unknown. G. Herbert. Ho-P:29
My Spectre Around Me. W. Blake.
   Rv-CB:611
Oh Thou, Who Man of Baser Earth
   Didst Make. E. Fitzgerald.
   Pl-EI:40
Of God We Ask One Favor.
   E. Dickinson. Pl-EI:71
The Proof. R. Wilbur. Pl-EI:45
The Quarrel. C. Aiken. Un-MA:430
The Quarrel. E. Farjeon. Fe-FP:41
Sonnet 34. W. Shakespeare.
   Rv-CB:216
Sonnet 35. W. Shakespeare.
   Rv-CB:217
Sonnet 40. W. Shakespeare.
   Rv-CB:219
Spring Morning. D. Lawrence.
   Co-BL:52, Un-MB:297
Still Falls the Rain. E. Sitwell.
   Br-TC:389, Ga-S:161, Tr-MR:131,
   Un-MB:336, Wi-LT:642

FORGIVENESS — cont'd.
  To Phillis. C. Sedley. Co-BL:73,
    No-CL:179
  The Toys. C. Patmore. Al-VBP:973,
    Er-FA:142, Rv-CB:876
  Under the Holly-Bough. C. Mackay.
    Ke-TF:46
  The Writing of Hezekiah, King of
    Judah, when He Was Sick. Bible.
    O.T. Isaiah. Me-PH:43
FORT HENRY, BATTLE, 1782
  Betty Zane. T. English. Vi-PP:127
FORT MCKINLEY
  Fort McKinley. Lo Men. Pa-MV:125
FORT OF RATHANGAN, IRE.
  The Fort of Rathangan. Co-PI:131,
    De-CH:181, Gr-CT:323, Ho-LP:86,
    Sm-LG:395
FORT TICONDEROGA, BATTLE, 1775
  Ticonderoga. V. Wilson. Vi-PP:122
FORTITUDE: see COURAGE
FORTUNE TELLING: see also ASTROLOGY
  Mirror, Mirror, Tell Me. Un-GT:22
  Readings, Forecasts, Personal
    Guidance. K. Fearing. Un-MA:557
FOSSILS: see also HUMOR - FOSSILS
  Footprints. S. Kurahara. Sh-AM:78
FOUNDRIES AND FOUNDING
  George. D. Randall. Ra-BP:145
  Steel-Works. M. Swann. Hi-WP I:130
FOUNTAINS
  Arethusa. P. Shelley. Ho-WR:136
  A Baroque Wall-Fountain in the
    Villa Sciarra. R. Wilbur.
    Br-TC:473, En-PC:191, Pe-OA:253
  The Bower of Bliss. E. Spenser.
    De-CH:144
  Erevan Is My City. M. Nikogosian.
    Mo-MI:21
  Flute Song. Pa-SG:150
  For More Public Fountains in New
    York City. A. Dugan. Ho-P:61
  The Fountain. al-Mu'tamid.
    Ho-LP:39
  The Fountain. D. Davie. Pa-GTB:554
  Fountain. E. Jennings. En-PC:237
  The Fountain. J. Lowell.
    Bo-FP:247, Ke-TF:50, Un-GT:315
  The Fountains. W. Rodgers.
    Co-PI:171
  Fountains. O. Sitwell. Un-MB:356
  Fountains. S. Sitwell. Un-MB:399
  The Lady Is Cold. E. White.
    Pa-HT:36
  Small Fountain. L. Abercrombie.
    De-CH:146
FOUR-LEAFED CLOVER: see CLOVER
FOURTH OF JULY: see also DECLARATION
    OF INDEPENDENCE; FIREWORKS;
    HUMOR - FOURTH OF JULY
  Fireworks. E. Kroll. Du-SH:166
  Fireworks. M. Millet. Ja-HH:26

Fourth of July. M. Chute. Br-SS:174
Fourth of July. R. Field. Br-SS:173
The Fourth of July. J. Pierpont.
  Ha-YA:85, Se-PR:157, Vi-PP:83
Fourth of July Night. D. Aldis.
  Ar-TP3:207, Br-SS:175, La-PH:56,
  Mc-AW:69
Fourth of July Ode. J. Lowell.
  Se-PR:158, Vi-PP:67
Fourth of July Song. L. Lenski.
  Br-SS:173
Grandfather Watts's Private Fourth.
  H. Bunner. Ar-TP3:8, Co-PS:113,
  Ha-PO:105
If I Had a Firecracker.
  S. Silverstein. Co-PS:116
Independence Bell. Vi-PP:80
Listen to the People. S. Benét.
  Co-PS:112
Ode. R. Emerson. Hu-MP:340,
  Se-PR:160, Vi-PP:84
Prayer on Fourth of July.
  N. Turner. Ha-YA:85
FOWLS: see CHICKENS; GUINEA FOWLS
FOX HUNTING
  A-Hunting We Will Go. H. Fielding.
    Al-VBP:551, De-TT:77
  Ballad of Red Fox. M. La Follette.
    Ad-PE:43, Ha-LO:42
  The Hunt. L. Kent. Co-BBW:53,
    Mc-WK:65
  Hunting Song. D. Finkel. Ca-MB:65,
    Co-BBW:19, Du-RG:106, We-PZ:21
  John Peel. J. Graves. De-CH:130,
    Mo-SD:113
  Listening to Foxhounds. J. Dickey.
    Ha-WR:78
  Reynard the Fox. J. Masefield.
    Al-VBP:1134
FOX INDIANS: see INDIANS OF NORTH
    AMERICA - VERSE - ALGONQUIN
FOXES: see also HUMOR - FOXES
  Ballad of Red Fox. M. La Follette.
    Ad-PE:43, Ha-LO:42
  A Call to the Wild. Lord Dunsany.
    Co-PI:36
  The Cock and the Fox.
    J. de la Fontaine. Mc-PR:14
  Concrete Trap. E. Coatsworth.
    Co-BBW:41, Mo-BG:196
  A Dog and a Cock. Ir-BB:237
  Ee-oh! De-TT:78
  The False Fox. Gr-CT:113, Gr-GB:55
  Four Little Foxes. L. Sarett.
    Ar-TP3:64, Bo-HF:71, Co-BBW:35,
    Co-PS:54, Du-RG:98, Fe-FP:173,
    Ha-YA:40, La-PV:150, La-RM:53,
    Mc-WK:64, Sh-RP:203, Un-GT:31
  The Fox. E. Ford. Ke-TF:331,
    Ls-NY:199
  The Fox. S. Kurahara. Sh-AM:77
  The Fox. K. Patchen. To-MP:32

The Fox.   I. Salomon.   Ls-NY:202
The Fox.   Bl-OB:114, Co-PT:137,
    Ha-PO:137, Un-GT:32
The Fox.   Su-FVI:62
The Fox and the Grapes.   J. Lauren.
    Bo-HF:70, Un-GT:170
The Fox and the Hedgehog.
    Archilochus.   Bo-FP:81
The Fox and the Rooster.   E. Rees.
    Ar-TP3:82
A Fox Jumped Up.   Mo-MGT:206,
    Sm-MK:72
The Fox Rhyme.   I. Serraillier.
    Co-BBW:29, Co-EL:28, Sm-MK:197
A Fox Started Out in a Hungry
    Plight.   Mo-NR:146
The Hunt.   L. Kent.   Co-BBW:53,
    Mc-WK:65
I Am the Kit Fox.   Ho-SD:10
January.   R. Thomas.   Co-BBW:49,
    Co-EL:24, Co-PU:91
The Lion and the Fox.   E. Rees.
    Ar-TP3:81
The Little Fox.   M. Edey and
    D. Grider.   Ar-TP3:64
The Magnet.   R. Stone.   Un-MA:655
Night of Wind.   F. Frost.
    Ar-TP3:64, Fe-FP:173
Nightmare.   A. Marx.   De-FS:136
Of Foxes.   B. Williams.   Co-BBW:24
Reynard the Fox.   J. Masefield.
    Al-VBP:1134, Rd-OA:51
A Ring of Silver Foxes.   Ho-SD:3
Sport.   W. Davies.   Co-BBW:47,
    Co-PU:120
Tatterdemalion.   P. Bennett.
    Co-BBW:44
The Terrible Robber Men.   P. Colum.
    Ha-LO:41
The Trap.   W. Beyer.   Du-RG:108,
    Ha-PO:127
The Vixen.   J. Clare.   Co-BBW:33
When Off This Creature's Head
    Is Cut.   Re-RR:50
Young Reynard.   G. Meredith.
    Co-BBW:38
FOXGLOVES
Four and Eight.   ff. Wolfe.
    Br-BC:76, Br-SS:43
Foxgloves.   T. Hughes.   Ha-LO:99
Summer.   R. Aldington.   Cl-FC:40
FRAGRANCE: see ODORS
FRANCE: see also DIALECTS, FRENCH;
    FOREIGN LEGION; FRENCH VERSE;
    HUMOR - FRANCE; and names of
    cities and regions, as PARIS,
    FR., and BRITTANY, FR.
England.   M. Moore.   Un-MA:350
Le Telephone.   M. Bracker.   Ke-TF:376
To Henrietta, on Her Departure for
    Calais.   T. Hood.   Ox-BC:181
Watchman, What of the Night?
    A. Swinburne.   Ho-WR:200

FRANCE - COUNTRYSIDE
France.   H. Wolfe.   Cr-WS:72
FRANCE - HISTORY AND PATRIOTISM:
    see also FRENCH REVOLUTION,
    1789-1799; and names of
    persons, as JOAN OF ARC
A Ballad for a Boy.   W. Cory.
    Ox-BC:290
The Good Joan.   L. Reese.   Ar-TP3:37,
    Fe-FP:468, Hu-MP:161, Th-AS:194
Henry VI, Part 1.   W. Shakespeare.
    Hi-FO:96
Hervé Riel.   R. Browning.
    Co-SS:183, Pa-OM:161, Sp-OG:67
Ivry.   T. Macauley.   Ga-FB:200,
    Hi-FO:131
The Map of France.   R. Duffus.
    Ke-TF:368
A St. Helena Lullaby.
    R. Kipling.   Hi-FO:176
FRANCE - SOCIAL LIFE AND CUSTOMS
1956.   D. Hoffman.   En-PC:207
FRANCESCA DA RIMINI: see PAOLO
    AND FRANCESCA
FRANCIS OF ASSISI, SAINT
A Baroque Wall-Fountain in the
    Villa Sciarra.   R. Wilbur.
    Br-TC:473, En-PC:191, Pe-OA:253
A Foreigner Comes to Earth on
    Boston Common.   H. Gregory.
    Pl-EI:111
Saint Francis.   J. Bishop.   Pl-EI:110
Saint Francis.   R. Pfingston.
    Ls-NY:112
Saint Francis and the Birds.
    S. Heaney.   Ma-FW:89
St. Francis Preaching to the
    Birds.   I. Barr.   Ke-TF:212
FRANCO, FRANCISCO (EL CAUDILLO)
Eisenhower's Visit to Franco, 1959.
    J. Wright.   Bl-FP:23
Epitaph for a Leader.   C. Norman.
    Cr-WS:36
FRANCO-PRUSSIAN WAR, 1870-1871
Before Sedan.   A. Dobson.
    Ke-TF:52
FRANKLIN, ARETHA
Poem for Aretha.   N. Giovanni.
    Ad-PB:454, Ra-BP:327
FRANKLIN, BENJAMIN
Ben Franklin's Head (1728).
    M. Howe.   Mc-WK:89
Benjamin Franklin. R. and S. Bénet.
    Ar-TP3:43, Fe-FP:424
On the Death of Benjamin Franklin.
    P. Freneau.   Hi-TL:60
FRANKLIN, SIR JOHN
A Ballad of Sir John Franklin.
    G. Baker.   Pa-OM:109
FREAKS: see also DWARFS (MIDGETS);
    GIANTS
Aunt Jemina of the Ocean Waves.
    R. Hayden.   Ad-PB:125

FREAKS — cont'd.
  The Freak Show. N. Willard.
    Sc-TN:229
FREDERICK, MD.
  Barbara Frietchie. J. Whittier.
    Co-PS:97, Er-FA:380, Fe-FP:442,
    Fe-PL:167, Ga-FB:258, Hi-TL:112,
    Mc-PR:170, Sp-OG:40, Un-GT:190,
    Vi-PP:150
FREE WILL
  Germinal. AE. Un-MB:146
  God's Thanks to Job. R. Frost.
    Tr-MR:223
  The Magnet Is Mistaken. L. Ginsburg.
    Ls-NY:322
  Man-Test. E. Markham. Tr-MR:280
  Of Natural Forces. E. Chesley.
    Ls-NY:321
  The Road Not Taken. R. Frost.
    Br-TC:136, Er-FA:180, Fe-PL:317,
    Gr-CT:314, La-RM:48, Na-EO:14,
    Sm-LG:301, Un-MA:187, Wi-LT:165
FREEDOM: see also HUMOR - FREEDOM;
    SATIRE - FREEDOM
  Against Borders. Y. Yevtushenko.
    Ad-CI:80
  America. A. Bates. Vi-PP:15
  America. B. Taylor. Vi-PP:37
  The American Freedom. M. Biller.
    Se-PR:128
  Atlantic Charter, A.D. 1620-1942.
    F. Young. Ar-TP3:39, Br-AF:86,
    Vi-PP:221
  The Bartholdi Statue. J. Whittier.
    Hi-TL:170
  The Bells of Heaven. R. Hodgson.
    Bo-GJ:20, Br-SS:152, Co-BBW:280,
    De-TT:82, Ha-PO:109, Ke-PP:104,
    Pl-EI:131, Th-AS:51, Un-MB:192,
    Wi-LT:125
  Birds. R. Fabrizio. Sm-MK:166
  A Black Man's World. L. Loflin II.
    La-IH:109
  Blue Fly. J. de Assis. Lo-TY:81
  Boston Hymn. R. Emerson. Vi-PP:76
  Brave New World. A. MacLeish.
    Sh-AP:189
  Broken-Face Gargoyles.
    C. Sandburg. Un-MA:207
  The Bruce. J. Barbour. Al-VBP:5
  Cactus Tree. J. Mitchell. Mo-GR:121
  Change. J. Donne. Al-VBP:253
  Character of a Happy Life.
    H. Wotton. Al-VBP:221,
    Ni-JP:169, Pa-GTB:63
    Ni-JP:169, Pa-GTB:63
  Choice. R. Mal'kova. Mo-MI:37
  Conclusion. W. Wordsworth.
    Ox-BN:112
  Cuba Libre. J. Miller. Hi-TL:153
  Dark Symphony I. M. Tolson.
    Be-MA:20, Bo-AN:37, Hu-PN:136
  Deer. J. Drinkwater. De-CH:282

  Dream Song. Bi-IT:128, Da-SC:100,
    Ho-SD:12, Le-OE:107
  Drums of Freedom. G. Thompson.
    Jo-VC:21
  Eloisa to Abelard. A. Pope.
    Al-VBP:535
  The Emancipation of George-Hector.
    M. Evans. Ab-MO:40, Bo-AN:165
  England and Switzerland, 1802.
    W. Wordsworth. Li-SR:108,
    Pa-GTB:209
  L'Envoi. R. Kipling. Ke-TF:140
  Esthetique du Mal, II. W. Stevens.
    Wi-LT:151
  Fable for when There's No Way Out.
    M. Swenson. Pe-M:82
  Fain Would I Live in Safest
    Freedom. A. von Platen. Pa-SG:164
  The Flower of Liberty. O. Holmes.
    Se-PR:159
  Frederick Douglass. R. Hayden.
    Ab-MO:83, Ad-PB:120, Be-MA:56,
    Bo-AN:119, Hu-PN:296, Jo-SA:41,
    Lo-TY:237
  Frederick Douglass, 1817-1895
    L. Hughes. Ra-BP:87
  Freedom. J. Barbour. Sm-LG:154
  Freedom. J. Barlow. Vi-PP:64
  Freedom. L. Hughes. Ad-PB:78
  Freedom. W. Stafford. Pe-M:29
  Freedom. Tr-CB:58, Tr-US I:64
  Freedom in Mah Soul. D. Cannon.
    Hu-PN:281
  Freedom Is Walking Toward Us.
    T'ien Chien. Hs-TC:330
  The Funeral of Martin Luther
    King, Jr. N. Giovanni.
    Ad-BO:30, Ra-BP:323
  The Glowing Years. Jen Chün.
    Hs-TC:392
  God's Thanks to Job. R. Frost.
    Tr-MR:223
  Hail, Columbia. J. Hopkinson.
    Er-FA:291, Vi-PP:32
  The Harp That Once Through Tara's
    Halls. T. Moore. Al-VBP:710,
    Co-RG:20, Fe-PL:177, Ma-YA:170,
    Ox-BN:210
  Harriet Tubman. M. Walker.
    Hu-PN:320
  The Hawk. W. Yeats. Ma-FW:92
  Hollin, Green Hollin. Gr-GB:46
  How Sadly the Bird in His Cage.
    Issa. Do-TS:23
  How Sleep the Brave. W. Collins.
    Al-VBP:572, Pa-GTB:119, Rv-CB:536,
    Sp-OG:208
  How Sweet I Roamed. W. Blake.
    Al-VBP:610, De-CH:153, Gr-CT:73,
    Ox-BN:18, Rv-CB:565, Un-MW:77
  I Am an American. E. Lieberman.
    Fe-FP:448, Fe-PL:162, Vi-PP:190

I Feel So Muggy. C. Reed.
Ad-II:14
I Have Not So Much Emulated.
W. Whitman. La-RM:170
I Lost the Love of Heaven. J. Clare.
Gr-CT:437, Ox-BN:331, Pa-GTB:321,
Rv-CB:729
I Play Flute. J. Stembridge.
Lo-IT:129
I Saw an Apple. Borya. Mo-MI:77
I Sing America Now! J. Stuart.
Br-AF:248
I Thank God I'm Free at Las'.
Ra-BP:31
If Suddenly You Come for Me.
N. Nor. Bo-RU:54
Independence. H. Thoreau.
Ba-PO:162
Jack and Dinah Want Freedom.
Ra-BP:6
Korea Bound, 1952.
W. Childress. Br-AF:87
Lafayette to Washington.
M. Anderson. Vi-PP:117
Land of My Heart. W. Foulke.
Vi-PP:21
Land of the Free. N. Hosking.
Vi-PP:22
Land of the Free. A. MacLeish.
Br-AF:243
Let America Be America Again.
L. Hughes. Hu-PN:193
Lift Every Voice and Sing.
J. Johnson. Ga-FB:277, Hu-PN:32
Little Bird. E. Murray. Me-WF:67
Lone Dog. I. McLeod. Ar-TP3:51,
Co-BBW:103, De-TT:68, Fe-FP:155,
Hu-MP:195, La-PV:108, Th-AS:186
The Lonely Traveller. K. Brew.
Lo-TY:166
The Long Shadow of Lincoln.
C. Sandburg. Ha-TP:141
The Man of Life Upright.
T. Campion. Al-VBP:219,
De-CH:637, Go-BP:44, Ha-PO:197,
Rv-CB:273
Message to Siberia.
A. Pushkin. Lo-TY:68
Midway. N. Madgett. Be-MA:93,
Hu-NN:39, Hu-PN:381, Jo-SA:126,
Kr-OF:53, Ra-BP:197
My Country Need Not Change Her
Gown. E. Dickinson. Br-AF:63
My Great-Grandfather's Slaves.
W. Berry. Mc-EA:114
Nation. C. Cobb. Ad-PB:468,
Lo-IT:17
Negro Soldier's Civil War Chant.
Ra-BP:7
No Child with Honey Heart.
L. Wolf. Ho-TY:222
Oh, Freedom. Ab-MO:53

Ode. R. Emerson. Hu-MP:340,
Se-PR:160, Vi-PP:84
The Old Stoic. E. Brontë.
Al-VBP:920, Fe-PL:308, Mc-PR:136,
Ox-BN:600
On Liberty and Slavery. G. Horton.
Hu-PN:11
On the Extinction of the Venetian
Republic. W. Wordsworth.
Al-VBP:661, Hi-FO:188, No-CL:255,
Ox-BN:79, Pa-GTB:210, Pa-HT:110
One Day You'll Be Free. L. Persons.
Me-WF:62
Plain-Chant for America. K. Chapin.
Vi-PP:34
a poem for positive thinkers.
B. Mahone. Ad-PB:473
The Ponies. W. Gibson.
Co-BBW:152, Mc-WK:74
Promises of Freedom. Ra-BP:5
Rebirth of the Muse.
Hu P'in-ch'ing. Pa-MV:105
Refugee in America. L. Hughes.
Bo-HF:44, Br-AF:249, Mc-WK:185,
Ra-BP:87
Remembering Nat Turner. S. Brown.
Ad-PB:63, Be-MA:35, Hu-PN:172
A Schoolboy's Lament. Mo-MI:85
The Sea Hawk Hunting. Taigi.
Be-CS:12
The Self-Slaved. P. Kavanagh.
Un-MB:430
She's Free. F. Harper. Kr-OF:35
Shine, Republic. R. Jeffers.
Br-AF:18, Tr-MR:188
Sing Me a New Song. J. Clarke.
Ad-PB:143
Song of Myself. W. Whitman.
Ca-BP:3
Song of the Open Road. W. Whitman.
Al-VBP:934, Ar-TP3:97, Er-FA:249,
Un-MA:63
Song of the Settlers. J. West.
Fe-FP:427
Sonnet. C. Cotton. Al-VBP:475
Sonnet on Chillon. G. Byron.
Ma-YA:173, Pa-GTB:209
The Sound Track. A. MacLeish.
Li-TU:265
The Stars Go over the Lonely
Ocean. R. Jeffers. Wi-LT:259
Stone Walls. R. Lovelace.
Hi-WP I:113
Street Demonstration. M. Walker.
Ra-BP:156
This Is a Coward's World.
Hsü Chih-mo. Hs-TC:79
The Tide River. C. Kingsley.
Co-BN:74
To a Linnet in a Cage.
F. Ledwidge. Co-RG:143

FREEDOM — cont'd.
  To Althea from Prison. R. Lovelace.
    Al-VBP:445, Ha-PO:173, Ke-TF:100,
    Ma-YA:101, Pa-GTB:81, Rv-CB:394,
    Un-MW:133
  To My Son Parker, Asleep in the
    Next Room. B. Kaufman. Ad-PB:265,
    Br-TC:230, Ca-VT:539, Jo-SA:30
  To Reckon with No One Else.
    A. Blok. Ca-MR:195
  To Vietnam. C. Cobb. Ad-PB:471
  The Virginia Scaffold. E. Proctor.
    Kr-OF:109
  Watchman, What of the Night?
    A. Swinburne. Ho-WR:200
  We Breathed Each Other In.
    A. Brooks. Ad-II:113
  We Shall Overcome. Ba-PO:199,
    Hi-TL:228, Pl-EI:165
  What Did You See? J. Perez.
    Me-WF:30
  When Virtue's Temple Falls.
    S. Little. Kr-OF:137
  Where Am I Going? L. Hargrove.
    Ba-HI:122
  Where Are You Going, Greatheart.
    J. Oxenham. Vi-PP:27
  Wild Horse. H. Allen. Le-M:99
  Wild Thyme. E. Farjeon. Br-SS:3
  The Wine Menagerie. H. Crane.
    Ca-VT:213
  With Freedom's Seed. A. Pushkin.
    Lo-TY:67
  Written at an Inn at Henley.
    W. Shenstone. Al-VBP:558
FREEPORT, ILL.
  Freeport. R. Cuscaden. St-H:31
FREEWAYS
  On the Expressway. R. Dana.
    La-OC:143
  Southbound on the Freeway.
    M. Swenson. Br-AF:236,
    Du-RG:82, Pe-SS:96
  Turnpike. R. Sward. St-H:225
FREEZING: see also FROST; ICE
  Gone Were But the Winter Cold.
    A. Cunningham. De-CH:224
FREIGHT: see CARGOES; FREIGHTERS;
    RAILROADS - FREIGHT TRAINS
FREIGHTERS: see also TUGBOATS
  Cargo-Ships. M. Press. Ke-TF:261
  Cargoes. J. Masefield.
    Ar-TP3:90, Bo-FP:134, Co-RG:56,
    Co-SS:75, Fe-FP:196, Ga-FB:182,
    Hi-WP I:109, Mc-PR:135, Th-AS:130,
    Un-MB:225, Wi-LT:189
  Freight Boats. J. Tippett.
    Cr-SS:31, Fe-FP:196,
    Hu-MP:177
  A Ship Comes In. O. Jenkins.
    Bo-FP:134

FRENCH AND INDIAN WAR, 1754-1763
  Braddock's Fate, with an Incitement
    to Revenge. S. Tilden. Hi-TL:33
  Brave Wolfe. Hi-TL:36
  Louisburg. Hi-TL:31
  Young Washington. A. Guiterman.
    Co-PS:48, Fe-FP:415, Hu-MP:379
FRENCH LANGUAGE: see HUMOR -
    FRENCH LANGUAGE
FRENCH REVOLUTION, 1789-1799: see
    also HUMOR - FRENCH REVOLUTION,
    1789-1799; NAPOLEON I, EMPEROR
    OF THE FRENCH
  The French Revolution.
    W. Wordsworth. Hi-FO:181
FRENCH VERSE: see also PROVENCAL
    VERSE
  Africa. D. Diop. Lo-TY:137
  Alons au Bois le May Cueillir.
    C. d'Orleans. Pa-SG:84
  At Early Morn. C. Mendes.
    Hu-PN:94
  The Ballad of Dead Ladies.
    F. Villon. Al-VBP:994, Er-FA:173,
    Ho-WR:184
  Ballade. E. Rostand. Co-RM:81
  Ballade for a Bridegroom.
    F. Villon. Un-MW:131
  Ballade of the Women of Paris.
    F. Villon. Un-MW:130
  Be like the Bird. V. Hugo.
    Ar-TP3:212, Ch-B:17, Ma-FO:(4)
  La Belle Saison. J. Prévert.
    Ad-CI:97
  A Black Girl Goes By. E. Roumer.
    Lo-TY:90
  The Black Man's Son. O. Durand.
    Lo-TY:91
  Black Woman. L. Senghor. Lo-TY:134
  Breath. B. Diop. Lo-TY:139
  The Bridges. J. Rimbaud. Ma-FW:265
  Burgundian Carol.
    B. de la Monnoye. Pl-US:109
  Burial. P. Joachim. Lo-TY:146
  By the River. J. Gautier.
    Gr-SS:40
  The Camel. C. de Gasztold.
    Rd-OA:161
  Cecilia. Do-WH:34
  The Child Reads On. F. Jammes.
    Fe-FP:470
  The Cock and the Fox.
    J. de la Fontaine. Mc-PR:14
  The De Pacem of the Laborer.
    Ba-PO:85
  Democracy. A. Rimbaud. Ba-PO:173
  Dry Your Tears, Africa. B. Dadie.
    Lo-TY:143
  The Dunce. J. Prévert. Ma-FW:72
  Dusky Woods. P. Quinault. Un-R:129
  Epigram. A. Lanusse. Ab-MO:30,
    Hu-PN:13, Lo-TY:96

Evening in Haiti. E. Roumer.
   Ab-MO:48
Fantasy. G. de Nerval.   Gr-SS:54
Fantasy under the Moon.
   E. Boundzekei-Dongala. Lo-TY:148
Farewell. I. L'Ouverture.
   Lo-TY:89
Flowers. J. Rimbaud.   Ma-FW:112
The Flute Players.
   J. Rabéarivelo.   Pa-SG:130
Free Pass. J. Prévert.   Ba-PO:203
The Friendly Beasts. Au-SP:376,
   Br-BC:171, Br-SS:106, Co-PS:175,
   Fe-FP:92, La-PH:28, Pa-OM:353,
   Pa-RE:88
Garden. M. Drouet.   Gr-EC:270
The Goddess. T. de Banville.
   Gr-SS:125
Good Night. V. Hugo.   Ar-TP3:219,
   Au-SP:99, Bo-FP:51, Br-SS:36,
   Ch-B:117, Fe-FP:53
Guinea. J. Roumain.   Lo-TY:92
Harlem. J. Brierre.   Lo-TY:93
He Who Has Lost All. D. Diop.
   Lo-TY:138
The Hobby Horse. Bo-FP:10
How Good Are the Poor. V. Hugo.
   Ke-TF:61
How to Paint the Portrait of a
   Bird. J. Prévert. Ma-FW:96,
   Sm-MK:168
Human Soul. R. Maran.   Lo-TY:71
I Give You Thanks My God.
   B. Dadie.   Lo-TY:144
Invitation to the Voyage.
   C. Baudelaire.   Pa-SG:56
Isabel. Do-WH:32
The Lady of the Pearls. A. Dumas.
   Lo-TY:70
Landscape. C. Baudelaire.
   Pa-SG:156
Late Rising. J. Prévert. Ad-CI:98
Legend. J. Laforgue. Ho-P:237
Loss. P. Eluard. Ho-LP:16
Lot's Wife. H. Meschonnic.
   Ba-PO:47
Love in May. J. Passerat.
   Pa-SG:32
Music. C. Baudelaire. Pa-SG:135
My Donkey. Ar-TP3:123, Ir-BB:175
The Naked World. Sully-Prudhomme.
   Pl-IO:69
Night. H. de Regnier. Pa-SG:112
Nocturne. R. Camille. Lo-TY:94
Noël. La-PH:27
Oblivion. M. Coicou. Hu-PN:69
On the Appeal from the Race of
   Sheba: II. L. Senghor. Lo-TY:134
Ophelia. A. Rimbaud. Gr-CT:78
Pan and the Cherries. P. Fort.
   Co-PM:67

Parfum Exotique.   C. Baudelaire.
   Un-MW:194
The Peasant Declares His Love.
   E. Roumer.   Lo-TY:90
The Pelican. P. de Thaun. Mc-WK:43
Phoebus and Boreas.
   J. de la Fontaine.   Un-R:87
Phrases. J. Rimbaud.   Ma-FW:100
Prayer for Peace: II. L. Senghor.
   Lo-TY:135
The Prayer of the Butterfly.
   C. Gasztold.   Li-TU:198
The Prayer of the Cat. C. Gasztold.
   Ar-TP3:82, La-PV:113
The Prayer of the Cock. C. Gasztold.
   Ar-TP3:82
The Prayer of the Donkey.
   C. Gasztold.   Ar-TP3:83
The Prayer of the Little Ducks.
   C. Gasztold. Ad-PE:38, Ar-TP3:82,
   Gr-TG:63, La-PV:131, Su-FVI:72
The Prayer of the Little Pig.
   C. Gasztold.   Li-TU:62
The Prayer of the Old Horse.
   C. Gasztold.   La-PV:126
The Prayer of the Ox.
   C. Gasztold.   Li-TU:188,
   Mc-WS:51
A Prayer to Go to Heaven with the
   Donkeys. F. Jammes.   Ar-TP3:83,
   Co-BBW:149, Go-BP:255, Pl-EI:124,
   Rd-OA:20, Tr-MR:52
Put Down. L. Damas.   Lo-TY:121
The Return of Spring. C. d'Orleans.
   Gr-CC:32
Return to My Native Land.
   A. Cesaire.   Lo-TY:123
Robinson Crusoe Returns to
   Amsterdam. F. Jammes.
   Fe-FP:472
Rondeau. C. d'Orleans. Pa-SG:79
Rondel. J. Froissart. Ho-LP:5
Roundel of Farewell. F. Villon.
   Un-MW:71
The Sailor and the Shark. P. Fort.
   Sm-MK:66
Les Salaziennes. A. Lacaussade.
   Lo-TY:69
The Schoolboy, the Pedant, and
   the Man with a Garden.
   J. de la Fontaine. Un-R:82
The Scorner. T. U Tam'si.
   Lo-TY:149
The Scythian Philosopher.
   J. de la Fontaine. Un-R:79
Since My Birth. Y. Goll. Ho-LP:18
The Sky Is Up above the Roof.
   P. Verlaine. Fe-FP:469
The Smoked Herring. C. Cros.
   Co-PT:277
Song of a Common Lover. F. Ranaivo.
   Gr-BT:54, Lo-TY:154

FRENCH VERSE — cont'd.
Song of Autumn. P. Verlaine.
Pa-SG:96
Spleen. C. Baudelaire. Un-R:77
Sunday Morning Song. Ab-MO:55
The Swallow. C. Gasztold.
Re-BS:31
Tears Flow in My Heart.
P. Verlaine. Pa-SG:184
They Came This Evening. L. Damas.
Lo-TY:120
Three French Mice. Ir-BB:236
To Make the People Happy. V. Hugo.
Ba-PO:124, Ke-PP:63
To the Castle at Gordes.
O. de Magny. Ba-PO:88,
Cr-WS:153
Totem. L. Senghor. Gr-BT:32
Verse Written in the Album of
Mademoiselle. P. Dalcour.
Ab-MO:24, Hu-PN:16, Lo-TY:97
The Virgin Martyrs.
Sigebert of Gembloux. Ga-S:226
The Vultures. D. Diop. Lo-TY:138
We Delighted, My Friend.
L. Senghor. Lo-TY:133
What Invisible Rat.
J. Rabéarivelo. Lo-TY:153
The Wheel. Sully-Prudhomme.
Pl-IO:63
The White Drake. Do-WH:35
The White Moon. P. Verlaine.
Pa-SG:143
Work Song. Ab-MO:56
FRIAR TUCK
The Friar. T. Peacock. De-TT:83,
Mo-SD:116, Un-GT:89
FRIARS: see MONKS
FRIDAY
On a Friday Morn. De-TT:130
FRIENDS: see FRIENDSHIP
**FRIENDS, SOCIETY OF: see also
PEACE**
For the Quakers. B. Bradbury.
Ba-PO:68
If Your Hands Be Full of Blood.
P. Folger. Kr-OF:100
The Martyrdom of the Quakers.
G. Joy. Kr-OF:101
Of Late. G. Starbuck.
Ca-VT:667, Cr-WS:136
**FRIENDSHIP: see also HUMOR -
FRIENDSHIP; SATIRE -
FRIENDSHIP**
Above the Bright Blue Sky.
A. Midlane. Ox-BC:229
And Yet the Earth Remains Unchanged.
Bi-IT:101
Around the Corner. C. Towne. Fe-PL:128
Auld Lang Syne. R. Burns. Bo-FP:209,
Er-FA:425, Fe-PL:129, Ma-YA:133,
Sp-OG:260

Ben Bolt. T. English. Er-FA:342
Bessy Bell and Mary Gray. De-CH:520,
Ox-BB:617
Chorus from Medea. Euripides.
Pa-SG:16
Chums. A. Guiterman. Hu-MP:135
Conversation with a Friend.
G. Abbe. Ls-NY:65
Dear Men & Women. J. Wheelock.
Ho-P:307
Death of a Comrade. M. Carter.
Sa-B:163
Early Friends. M. Mansfield.
Ke-TF:74
Elizabeth Cried. E. Farjeon.
Mc-AW:99
Empathy. A. Pratt. Al-WW:107
Farewell Once More. Tu Fu.
Rx-OH:22
For a Child. F. Davis. Fe-FP:19,
Hu-MP:287
For Jan, in Bar Maria. C. Kizer.
Ca-VT:541
For One Shortly to Die.
W. Whitman. Rv-CB:854
For Theresa. N. Giovanni. Be-MA:172
The Fountain. W. Wordsworth.
Pa-GTB:304
A Friend or Two. W. Nesbit.
Fe-PL:125
The Friend Who Just Stands By.
B. Williams. Fe-PL:126
Friends Go Away. A. Galich.
Bo-RU:32
Friendship. Bi-IT:85
From "Kleine Nachtmusik."
J. Glatstein. Ho-TY:245
From My Study at the Mouth of
the Valley. Ch'ien Ch'i.
Le-MW:53
Glass Houses. E. Robinson.
Tr-MR:161
Gnomes, II. Tr-US I:124
Gone. M. Coleridge. Ox-BN:924
Graeme and Bewick. Ox-BB:356,
Rv-CB:47
haircut. W. Packard. Ad-CI:70
The House by the Side of the Road.
S. Foss. Er-FA:18
The House of Falling Leaves.
W. Braithwaite. Hu-PN:47
How She Resolved to Act. M. Moore.
Pe-SS:116, Un-MA:575, Un-MW:59
i have friends. C. Thornton.
La-IH:70
I Hear It Was Charged Against Me.
W. Whitman. Un-MA:43
The Idiot. J. Ashberry. Ca-VT:593
If You Have a Friend. Er-FA:28
In a Child's Album. W. Wordsworth.
Bo-FP:232, Ch-B:17, Ox-BN:92

In Memoriam. A. Tennyson.
   Ox-BN:501, 507
Interlude. W. Landor. Pa-GTB:318
Isaac and Archibald. E. Robinson.
   Ni-JP:145, Pe-OA:9
James Powell on Imagination.
   L. Neal. Ra-BP:269
Just Folks. E. Guest. Er-FA:134
A Kind of Karate. D. Scott.
   Sa-B:117
Laughing. G. MacPherson. Ja-PC:10
Lines for a Young Man Who Talked.
   J. Logan. St-H:116
Long Distance. F. Eckman. St-H:49
Losing Friends. A. Gutkina.
   Mo-MI:56
Lycidas. J. Milton. Al-VBP:402,
   Gr-CT:250, Hi-WP II:20, Ho-P:69,
   Pa-GTB:55
My Dear Friend. Ho-SD:26
My Friends. R. Service. Co-RM:137
New York * December * 1931.
   B. Deutsch. Pl-IO:149
The Night Is Dark. H. Leivick.
   Ho-TY:118
The Nightingale. R. Barnefield.
   Al-VBP:265, De-CH:100, Pa-GTB:21
Oh, Suzy. B. Katz. Ho-GC:24
O Sweetheart, Hear You. J. Joyce.
   Un-MB:270, Un-MW:10
Oft, in the Stilly Night.
   T. Moore. Ho-P:309
An Old Story. E. Robinson.
   Ho-TH:19, Un-MA:118
One Time Henry Dreamed the Number.
   D. Long. Ad-PB:405, Ra-BP:310
Out Where the West Begins.
   A. Chapman. Er-FA:263
Parting. Wang Wei. Ar-TP3:97,
   Le-MW:121
Please Take Good Care of My Home.
   Hs-TC:444
Poem. L. Hughes. Li-TU:26
Poems of Two. L. Strongin.
   Sc-TN:209
The Policeman. M. Watts.
   Ar-TP3:12, Bo-FP:119
Reading the Poems of an Absent
   Friend. Ou Yang Hsiu.
   Rx-OH:57
Rediscovery. G. Awooner-Williams.
   Lo-TY:165
Remembrance. V. Zhukovsky.
   Pa-SG:15
Sat Est Scripsisse. A. Dobson.
   Go-BP:66
The Scars Remaining. S. Coleridge.
   Ox-BN:161
Seven Poems. L. Niedecker.
   Ca-VT:245
Shake Hands. A. Housman.
   Co-PU:146, Hi-WP I:88

Silet. E. Pound. Un-MA:295
Simple Verses. J. Marti. Lo-TY:100
some friends. J. Gill. Sc-TN:68
The Song of a Dream. Bi-IT:127
Song of a Visitor to a Strange
   Village. Tr-US II:309
Song of the Open Road. W. Whitman.
   Al-VBP:934, Ar-TP3:97, Er-FA:249,
   Un-MA:63
Sonnet 30. W. Shakespeare.
   Al-VBP:201, Er-FA:166, Fe-PL:130,
   Ga-FB:33, Pa-GTB:18, Rv-CB:213
Sparrows. M. Leib. Ho-TY:95
Strong Son of God, Immortal Love.
   A. Tennyson. Ma-YA:193, Pl-EI:136
Summoning the Soul. Jao Meng-k'an.
   Hs-TC:109
The Sun Used to Shine. E. Thomas.
   Pl-ML:41
The Sunlight on the Garden.
   L. MacNeice. Br-TC:279, Pa-GTB:515
They Say that in the Unchanging
   Place. H. Belloc. Fe-PL:126
Three Friends. U. Beier.
   Be-AP:31, Hu-PB:19
A Time to Talk. R. Frost.
   Sp-OG:248
To a Distant Friend. W. Wordsworth.
   Pa-GTB:189, Rv-CB:651
To a Friend. H. Coleridge.
   Fe-PL:129, Ox-BN:397, Rv-CB:757
To a Friend. A. Lowell. Fe-PL:127
To a Friend. V. Shlensky. Mo-MI:46
To a Friend. J. Valentine.
   Ha-TP:64
To a Traveller. Su Tung P'o.
   Rx-OH:77
To Chuck — Concerning a Rendezvous
   in Siam. J. Charles. Mc-MK:198
To Mary. W. Cowper. Pa-GTB:164,
   Rv-CB:550
To Mr. Lawrence. J. Milton.
   Pa-GTB:66
To the Rev. F. D. Maurice.
   A. Tennyson. Pa-GTB:334
To Wei Pa, a Retired Scholar.
   Tu Fu. Rx-OH:11
Tricia's Fish. L. Hopkins.
   Ho-GC:32
True Friendship. Pa-SG:20
Under All Change. J. Johnson.
   Tr-MR:158
Under the Holly-Bough. C. Mackay.
   Ke-TF:46
Upon the Hard Crust.
   A. Akhmatova. Pa-SG:23
Vickery's Mountain.
   E. Robinson. Un-MA:120
The Visitors. E. Jennings.
   Go-BP:140
The Warm of Heart.
   E. Coatsworth. Co-PU:66

FRIENDSHIP — cont'd.

We Saw Days. T. Palmanteer.
  Al-WW:41
Well Met. A. Evans. Co-PU:11
When I Peruse the Conquer'd
  Fame. W. Whitman. Co-EL:130,
  Co-PU:79
White Hill Looms Against the
  Black. A. Ivanov. Bo-RU:41
Whoever You Are Holding Me Now
  in Hand. W. Whitman. Ha-PO:216
A Window in the Breast.
  Gr-EC:219, Pa-SG:15
Winter. J. Hurnard. Co-PS:152
A Winter Wish. R. Messinger.
  Al-VBP:882
Wisdom. Tr-CB:17
With Rue My Heart Is Laden.
  A. Housman. Er-FA:88, Un-MB:94,
  Wi-LT:62
Words for a Friend Who Was
  Accidentally Shot. D. Etter.
  St-H:60
The World Feels Dusty.
  E. Dickinson. Un-MA:100
Young Johnstone. Ox-BB:212

FRIETCHIE, BARBARA
Barbara Frietchie. J. Whittier.
  Co-PS:97, Er-FA:380, Fe-FP:442,
  Fe-PL:167, Ga-FB:258, Hi-TL:112,
  Mc-PR:170, Sp-OG:40, Un-GT:190,
  Vi-PP:150

FRIGATE BIRDS
Man o' War Bird. D. Walcott.
  Lo-TY:112
To the Man-of-War Bird.
  W. Whitman. Sh-AP:120

FRITCHIE, BARBARA: see FRIETCHIE,
  BARBARA

FROGHOPPERS: see SPITTLE BUGS

FROGMEN: see SKIN AND SCUBA
  DIVING

FROGS: see also HUMOR - FROGS;
  TOADS
Awakened. M. Saito. Sh-AM:144
Behind His Long Face. Issa.
  Ca-BF:33
A Big Turtle. Au-SP:79, Ir-BB:75
Boys with Frogs. S. Kahn.
  Du-RG:30
Bullfrog. T. Hughes. Co-BBW:67,
  La-RM:142
Cheers. E. Merriam. Du-RG:115
"Day Darken!" Frogs Say.
  Buson. Be-CS:47
Death of a Frog. S. Hagiwara.
  Sh-AM:48
A Discovery. Yayu. Ca-BF:29
The Dormouse and the Frog.
  R. Goodchild. Ir-BB:81
A Drop of Rain! Issa.
  Ar-TP3:169, Le-IS:15

Facing Up. J. Scully. Ha-WR:18
A Fairy Went a-Marketing.
  R. Fyleman. Au-SP:293
First Song. G. Kinnell.
  Bo-GJ:47, Br-TC:237, Ha-TP:122
  Mo-BG:123, Wi-LT:745
The Frog. Issa. Le-IS:7
The Frog and the Crow. Gr-GB:67
The Frog on the Log. I. Orleans.
  Mc-AW:55
Frog-School Competing. Shiki.
  Be-CS:54
Froggie, Froggie. Wy-CM:14
Frogs. B. Bauder. La-GI:59
Frogs. B. Bose. Al-PI:78
Frogs. L. Simpson. Ho-TH:77
The Frogs' Call. De-PP:48
The Frogs Who Wanted a King.
  J. Lauren. Bo-HF:94, Un-GT:170
Goat Songs, V. R. Drew. Kh-VA:44
Grandfather Frog. L. Bechtel.
  Ar-TP3:67, Sh-RP:35
Hands Flat on the Ground. Sokan.
  Be-MC:61
Ho, for the May Rains. Sanpu.
  Be-CS:51
Hopping Frog. C. Rossetti.
  Bl-OB:132, Pa-RE:59
Hospitality. J. Tabb. Gr-EC:22
If You Chance to Be Crossing.
  Wy-CM:17
In Spring the Chirping. Onitsura.
  Be-CS:55
In the Bayou. D. Marquis.
  Br-AF:187
Little Frog. . . . Gaki. Ca-BF:17
Loving and Liking. D. Wordsworth.
  Ox-BC:129
The Marriage of the Frog and the
  Mouse. Rd-OA:64
The Mouse, the Frog, and the
  Little Red Hen. Gr-EC:31,
  Ir-BB:89
The Old Pond. Issa. Do-TS:20
Old Pond, Blackly Still. Bashô.
  Au-SP:79, Ca-BF:21
An Old Silent Pond. Bashô.
  Be-CS:8
The Padda Song. Gr-GB:283
A Pig-Tale. L. Carroll.
  Ch-B:65, Fe-FP:346, Ho-WR:80,
  Pa-RE:27, Rd-OA:94
The Puddy and the Mouse. Gr-GB:68
The Song of the Frog. De-PP:48
The Spring. R. Fyleman. Fe-FP:131
The Stone Frog. G. Pritchard.
  Co-PU:8, Ls-NY:226
A Summer Walk. E. Winton. Bo-FP:274
The Sweet o' the Year. G. Meredith.
  Co-PN:23
A Tadpole. W. Taylor. Le-M:93

Twenty Froggies. G. Cooper.
Bo-FP:76, Ch-B:108, Co-IW:10,
It-HB:49
Ways of Traveling. A. Wilkins.
Mc-AW:54
What in the World? E. Merriam.
Gr-EC:14
When Spring Is Gone. Yayu.
Be-CS:19
With That Voice. Issa. Le-MW:9
The Wood Frog. J. Hay. Ls-NY:188
You Frogs. S. Hagiwara. Sh-AM:49
FRONTIER LIFE: see PIONEERS AND
PIONEER LIFE; and names of
frontiersmen, as CROCKETT,
DAVID (DAVY)
FROST, ROBERT
For Robert Frost. G. Kinnell.
Ca-VT:600
A Letter to Robert Frost.
R. Hillyer. Un-MA:484
On Looking into Robert Frost in
Kanji. W. Meredith. Pl-ML:70
To Robert Frost. W. Snow. Ke-TF:318
FROST: see also ICE
December. J. Lowell. Un-GT:283
December. T. Ramsey. Sm-MK:137
A Devonshire Rhyme. Br-SS:89,
Hu-MP:322
Frost. W. Davies. Co-BN:185
Frost. G. Johnston. Do-WH:67
Frost. E. Pratt. Do-WH:67
The Frost. Tzu Yeh. Le-MW:86
Frost at Midnight. S. Coleridge.
Ox-BN:162, Rv-CB:661
The Frost Pane. D. McCord. Sh-RP:39
The Frost Spirit. J. Whittier.
Bo-FP:150, Ch-B:93
Frost To-Night. E. Thomas.
Sp-OG:360
Hard Frost. A. Young. Co-BN:183
Jack Frost. H. Davis. Au-SP:330,
Hu-MP:320
Jack Frost. C. Pike. St-FS:89
Jack Frost. G. Setoun. Hu-MP:320
John Frost. W. Miller. Bo-FP:150
The Last Day of the Year. A. Smart.
Bo-FP:207
Little Jack Frost. Au-SP:330
Love in Labrador. C. Sandburg.
Ca-VT:27
October Night. A. Dean. Ha-YA:111
This Evening So Cold and Chill.
Prince Shiki. Ba-ST:50
Tree in December. M. Cane.
Un-MA:235
When the Frost Lies White. Ba-ST:50
The White Chrysanthemum. Mitsune.
Ba-ST:47
Winter Morning. W. Welles. Ho-LP:33
Wizard Frost. F. Sherman. Ha-YA:147
FRUGALITY: see THRIFT

FRUIT: see also HUMOR - FRUIT;
and names of specific fruits,
as, APPLES
An Apple for the King. Rv-ON:64
Clouds' Work. F. Gullar. An-TC:171
Country Trucks. M. Shannon.
Ar-TP3:93, Fe-FP:243
The Faithful Shepherdess.
J. Fletcher. Al-VBP:286
For a Picture of Saint Dorothea.
G. Hopkins. Gr-CC:140
Fruit Song. Tr-US II:200
Fruits. C. Rossetti. Gr-EC:106
The Garden. A. Marvell.
Co-BN:43, Gr-CT:268
A Garden Song. A. Dobson.
Co-BN:52, Ox-BN:848
Market. C. Rossetti. Hi-WP I:3
Market Woman's Cries. J. Swift.
Co-PI:184
Orchard. H.D. Un-MA:337,
Wi-LT:619
The Tree. B. Björnson.
Bo-FP:268, Hu-MP:271
The Tropics in New York. C. McKay.
Ad-PB:25, Bo-AN:28, Bo-HF:167,
Hu-PN:95, Lo-TY:118
FRUSTRATION: see also DISAPPOINTMENT;
HUMOR - FRUSTRATION
Alba: Whose Muse? F. Eckman.
St-H:52
As for the World. Y. Amichai.
Me-PH:127
A Bee Thumps Against the Dusty
Window. R. Sund. Co-PU:99
Born Without a Star.
A. Ibn Ezra. Me-PH:64
Echo. W. de la Mare. Mc-WS:23
The Expense of Spirit in a Waste
of Shame. L. Mueller. St-H:146
The Field of Glory. E. Robinson.
Un-MA:125
He Died a Second Time, 7. A Glance.
Ai Ch'ing. Hs-TC:307
Her Story. N. Madgett. Ad-PB:183
The Hermit. R. Silcock. Ls-NY:321
Humpty Dumpty's Song. L. Carroll.
Bl-OB:14, Co-FB:369, Gr-CT:29,
Ir-BB:130, Pa-GTB:377, Pa-OM:11,
Un-GT:209
I Stand Here Against This Lamp
Post. R. Chafetz. La-IH:85
If There Be Sorrow. M. Evans.
Hu-NN:22, Hu-PN:308
The Invoice. R. Creeley.
Ca-VT:560, Du-SH:67
It Is Difficult to Put Words
Together. Tr-US I:16
The Leaden-Eyed. V. Lindsay.
Co-EL:136, Co-PU:150, Ke-PP:61,
Kr-OF:182, Ni-JP:32, Tr-MR:54

FRUSTRATION — cont'd.
Leaves Without Trees. Y. Amichai.
  Me-PH:130
The Mood. Q. Prettyman. Ad-PB:260
The Mouse. E. Coatsworth.
  Co-BBW:41
Myself when Young Did Eagerly
  Frequent. O. Khayyam. Pl-EI:66
The News Around Midnight.
  T. McGrath. St-H:126
The Noonday April Sun. G. Love.
  Hu-NN:69
o the world. Me-WF:90
Octaves. E. Robinson. Sm-PT:143
Orpingalik's Song: My Breath.
  Tr-US I:17
Over the Wintry. Soseki.
  Be-CS:6, La-PV:85
Sanctity. P. Kavanagh. Co-EL:45
The Streetcleaner's Lament.
  P. Hubbell. La-OC:27
Summer in the City. D. McNally.
  La-IH:64
This Last Pain. W. Empson.
  Pa-GTB:505, Wi-LT:442
To Richard Wright. C. Rivers.
  Ad-PB:234, Be-MA:105, Bo-AN:177
Waves Against a Dog. T. Baybars.
  Sm-MK:176
FUJIYAMA
Mount Fuji. M. Kaneko. Sh-AM:66
Oh, Snail. Issa. Do-TS:8
White and Wise and Old. Buson.
  Be-MC:50
FUN: see also AMUSEMENTS; GAMES;
  PLAY
For Jane, in Bar Maria. C. Kizer.
  Ca-VT:541
Glad Day. W. Robertson. Hi-GD:6
Hot Time! A. Trias. Ho-CT:18
Multi-Colored Balloon. H. Greggs.
  Ab-MO:16
FUNERALS: see also COFFINS; CREMA-
  TION; HUMOR - FUNERALS; SATIRE -
  FUNERALS; WAKES
All the Flowers of the Spring.
  J. Webster. Al-VBP:289,
  De-CH:252, Rv-CB:317
An Anniversary: A Country Burial.
  A. Stanford. Ha-TP:126
Booman. Rv-ON:95
Burial. M. Van Doren. Ca-MB:22
The Burial of Sir John Moore at
  Corunna. C. Wolfe. De-TT:139,
  Er-FA:285, Gr-CT:342, Hi-FO:198,
  Ke-TF:165, Pa-GTB:216, Rv-CB:693,
  Sp-OG:202
The Burial of the Linnet. J. Ewing.
  Ox-BC:254
Burial of the Minnisink.
  H. Longfellow. Gr-CC:122

Bury Her at Even. M. Field.
  Sm-MK:222
Cathemerinon. Prudentius.
  Pa-SG:14
Cortege. D. Scott. Sa-B:203
Country Burying. R. Warren.
  Wi-LT:837
Day of the Dead. D. Lawrence.
  Ga-S:214
Dead. L. Johnson. Ox-BN:948
The Death and Burial of Cock
  Robin. De-TT:41, Ir-BB:114,
  Mo-MGT:60, Mo-NR:143, Un-GT:62,
  Wr-RM:124
A Dirge. J. Webster. Al-VBP:288,
  Bl-OB:153, De-CH:251, Gr-CT:363,
  Pa-GTB:29, Re-TW:23, Rv-CB:315,
  Sm-LG:267
Dirge for Robin Hood. A. Munday.
  Bl-OB:152, De-CH:77, Ho-WR:116,
  Re-TW:71, Rv-CB:163
Dirge for Two Veterans. W. Whitman.
  Un-MA:77
Do Nothing till You Hear from Me.
  D. Henderson. Ad-PB:419
The Duke of Grafton. Gr-CT:359,
  Gr-GB:320
1805. R. Graves. Co-RM:42,
  Na-EO:17, Sm-LG:155
Elegy for a Dead Soldier. K. Shapiro.
  Hi-TL:213, Wi-LT:541
Emblems. A. Tate. Ca-VT:223
The Exequy. H. King. De-CH:256
The Funeral. J. Donne. Rv-CB:304
The Funeral. S. Spender. Un-MB:474
A Funeral in Tchiatura.
  A. Mezhirov. Ca-MR:89
Funeral Procession. O. de Andrade.
  An-TC:15
The Funeral Rites of the Rose.
  R. Herrick. Ha-PO:82
Funeral Song. J. Fletcher.
  Gr-CT:359
Go Down Death. J. Johnson.
  Ad-PB:6, Bo-AN:2
He Meets Two Men Carrying a Corpse
  in a Hammock. J. de Melo Neto.
  An-TC:131
Improvisation of the Dead Boy.
  M. de Andrade. An-TC:21
In These Dissenting Times.
  A. Walker. Ad-PB:475
Lament with Me. M. Tsvetayeva.
  Ca-MR:135
Magic Formula to Destroy Life.
  Bi-IT:98
Mary Passed This Morning. O.Dodson.
  Ad-PB:127
New England Protestant. R. Eberhart.
  Ho-TH:82
nobody loses all the time. E. Cummings.
  Br-TC:78, Ma-FW:132, Wi-LT:359

November Twenty-Sixth Nineteen
    Hundred and Sixty-Three.
    W. Berry. Wi-LT:662
O'Neil the Undertaker. T. Tommaro.
    Ad-II:88
The Poet's Final Instructions.
    J. Berryman. Ca-VT:384
The Rebel. M. Evans. Ad-PB:187,
    Bo-AN:163, Pe-SS:58
The Rites for Cousin Vit.
    G. Brooks. Ra-BP:167
The Sea-Ritual. G. Darley.
    De-CH:312, Gr-SS:179, Ho-WR:126,
    Ox-BN:396
Song at a Funeral. Tr-US II:90
Stop All the Clocks. W. Auden.
    Hi-WP II:29, Un-MB:465, Un-MW:103
The Streets of Laredo. Co-RM:28,
    Er-FA:337, Gr-CT:137, Gr-GB:321,
    Hi-TL:162, Mc-WK:169, Mc-WS:153
Tract. W. Williams. Br-TC:481,
    Ca-VT:52, Pe-M:102, Sh-AP:167,
    Un-MA:257, Wi-LT:195
Two Funerals. L. Untermeyer.
    Cr-WS:28
Two of the Festivities of Death.
    J. de Melo Neto. An-TC:165
Wedding and Funeral. Gr-GB:320
When I Am Dead. J. Wilson.
    Fe-PL:275
The Witch. R. Southey. Ho-WR:219
FUR: see also HUMOR - FUR
In Fur. W. Stafford. La-RM:113
FURNACES
The Drunk in the Furnace. W. Merwin.
    Br-TC:292, Wi-LT:769
FURNITURE: see HOUSEHOLD FURNISHINGS;
    and names of articles of
    furniture, as CHAIRS
FUTILITY
Cassandra. L. Bogan. Ca-VT:203,
    Un-MA:492
Chaplinesque. H. Crane. Ca-VT:212,
    Wi-LT:395
Dirge. K. Fearing. Ha-PO:247,
    Hi-TL:200, Sh-AP:207
Hast Never Come to Thee an Hour.
    W. Whitman. Rv-CB:852
Hearing of Harvests Rotting in the
    Valleys. W. Auden. Un-MB:457
The Hour. U. Greenberg. Me-PH:89
I Have Come Far to Have Found
    Nothing. C. Corman. Ca-VT:527
Invocation. C. Drewry. Tr-MR:217
Kibkarjuk Calls to Mind the
    Times. . . . Tr-US I:14
Look, How Beautiful. R. Jeffers.
    Tr-MR:148
Midnight Raffle. L. Hughes.
    La-OC:65
Missing Dates. W. Empson.
    Al-VBP:1225

O Thou Seer, Go, Flee Thee Away.
    C. Bialik. Me-PH:72.
The Pilgrim. W. Yeats. Ha-PO:248
Sailing from the United States.
    S. Moss. Ca-VT:583
The Scales. W. Empson. Wi-LT:441
The Source. P. Harris. Sc-TN:80
Speak, Parrot. J. Skelton.
    Al-VBP:29
Strange Meeting. W. Owen. Cr-WS:85,
    Go-BP:209, Pa-GTB:452, Un-MB:367
To a Dog Barking at Night.
    F. Maguire. Ls-NY:326
To Be or Not to Be.
    W. Shakespeare. Er-FA:93,
    Ha-PO:256, Ma-YA:68
To Marina Ivanovna Tsvetayeva.
    V. Kovshin. Bo-RU:48
Try Tropic. G. Taggard. Un-MA:480
Two Poems. A. Akhmatova. Ca-MR:185
Untitled Sonnet. J. Seligman.
    Cr-WS:30
Ye Hasten to the Grave!
    P. Shelley. Mo-GR:80
A Year Without Seasons.
    M. Williams. Hu-NN:68
FUTURE: see also HUMOR - FUTURE
The Burning of the Leaves.
    L. Binyon. Pa-GTB:434
Burnt Norton. T. Eliot. Wi-LT:306
Candles. C. Cavafy. Sm-MK:217
The Choice II. D. Rossetti.
    Al-VBP:990
Essay on Man. A. Pope. Al-VBP:536
For You, My Son. H. Gregory.
    Un-MA:508
The Fundament Is Shifted. A. Evans.
    Tr-MR:238
In After Time. R. Eberhart.
    Tr-MR:287
The Long Shadow of Lincoln.
    C. Sandburg. Ha-TP:141
Men at Forty. D. Justice. Ho-P:129
Poets to Come. W. Whitman. Mc-EA:25
Sonnets, vii. G. Santayana.
    Sm-PT:135
The Springfield of the Far Future.
    V. Lindsay. Tr-MR:200
They Will Appear. Bi-IT:169
To Those Born After. B. Brecht.
    Un-R:41
Unmanifest Destiny. R. Hovey.
    Vi-PP:233
Where Am I Going? L. Hargrove.
    Ba-HI:122
Written in a Time of Crisis.
    S. Benet. Vi-PP:220
FUTURE LIFE: see also ELYSIUM;
    HEAVEN; HELL; HUMOR -
    FUTURE LIFE; IMMORTALITY;
    REINCARNATION; RESURRECTION;

FUTURE LIFE — cont'd.
  SATIRE - FUTURE LIFE;
  SOUL
  Afterwards. T. Hardy. Al-VBP:1050,
    Co-BN:210, De-CH:435, Gr-CT:353,
    Ni-JP:172, No-CL:284, Ox-BN:846,
    Pa-GTB:412, Rv-CB:944, Un-MB:31,
    Wi-LT:25
  All Souls' Day. S. Sassoon.
    Tr-MR:276
  Ballade by the Fire. E. Robinson.
    Bo-HF:174
  Because that You Are Going.
    E. Dickinson. Un-MA:101
  Chorus Mysticus. J. von Goethe.
    Un-R:23
  The Dead Man Asks for a Song.
    Le-OE:129, Tr-CB:44, Tr-US I:49
  Death Song. Tr-US I:50
  Difficult Chieko. K. Takamura.
    Sh-AM:47
  The Door of Death. W. Blake.
    De-CH:753, Gr-CT:376
  Dust. R. Brooke. Un-MB:323
  For Sleep or Death. R. Pitter.
    Hi-WP I:144, Sm-MK:218
  The Heavenly Song. Le-IB:124
  Ilicet. T. Garrison. Fe-PL:306
  Invocation. S. Sassoon. Un-MB:313
  King Agongola's Song. Tr-CB:56,
    Tr-US I:55
  The Land o' the Leal. Lady Nairn.
    Pa-GTB:157
  A Lyke-Wake Dirge. De-CH:248,
    Ga-S:219, Gr-CT:366, Gr-GB:322,
    Ma-BB:236, Ma-FW:258, Na-EO:107,
    Pl-EI:139, Rv-CB:54
  A Musical Critic Anticipates
    Eternity. S. Sassoon. Pl-US:143
  My Spirit Will Not Haunt the
    Mound. T. Hardy. Ox-BN:838,
    Un-MB:32
  The New Ghost. F. Shove. Go-BP:258
  Notes on the Mystery. W. Welles.
    Sm-PT:159
  The Old Repair Man. F. Johnson.
    Bo-AN:27, Pe-M:75
  Old Shepherd's Prayer. C. Mew.
    Pl-EI:176, Un-MB:163
  Requickening. Bi-IT:162
  Second Best. R. Brooke. Un-MB:324
  She Asks for a New Earth.
    K. Tynan. Go-BP:253
  A Small Thought Speaks for the
    Flesh. C. Drewry. Tr-MR:226
  Song at a Deathbed. Tr-US I:57
  This World Is Not Conclusion.
    E. Dickinson. Pl-EI:10
  A Voice from the Waters. T. Beddoes.
    Ox-BN:449, Rv-CB:771
  Waters and Dreaming. E. Botta.
    Mc-AC:112

  The White Island. R. Herrick.
    Gr-CT:187, Ho-WR:251
  Your Last Drive. T. Hardy.
    Ox-BN:841
GABRIEL, ARCHANGEL: see also HUMOR -
  GABRIEL, ARCHANGEL
  Kingdom of Heaven. L. Adams.
    Un-MA:547
  Light the Lamps Up, Lamplighter.
    E. Farjeon. Br-SS:28, De-CH:439
  Mary and Gabriel. R. Brooke.
    Ke-TF:142
  Mary and Gabriel. Ga-S:58
  Who Did? Bu-DY:45
GAELIC LANGUAGE
  Aunt Julia. N. Maccaig. To-MP:185
GAELIC VERSE
  Charm. Ga-S:181
  Do You Remember That Night.
    Co-BL:33, Co-PI:157
  Gaelic Lullaby. Ch-B:117,
    Ke-TF:40
  Good Wish. Sm-LG:240
  Hey the Gift, Ho the Gift. Ga-S:67
  The Icebound Swans. Rd-OA:199
  In Praise of May. Re-BS:22
  The Monk and His Cat. Co-PI:43,
    De-CH:90, Pa-SG:154, Rd-OA:110,
    Sm-LG:73
  Oak-Logs Will Warm You Well.
    Mo-TB:128
  The Sea Gull. Ch-B:91, Ma-FO:(6)
  Three Blessings. Go-BP:278
  The Tiny Bird. Re-BS:30
  The Tree of Life. Re-BS:58
  Welcome to the Moon. Co-BN:117,
    Gr-CT:403
  Wrens of the Lake. Re-BS:6
GALAHAD, SIR
  Sir Galahad. A. Tennyson.
    Co-RM:78, Sp-OG:134
GALAXIES: see also STARS
  The God of Galaxies. M. Van Doren.
    Pl-IO:19, Tr-MR:138
  How Lovely. Issa. Le-IS:26
  The Lost Telescope. Chi Hsüan.
    Pa-MV:50
  When the Milky Way You Spy.
    Wy-CM:23
GALILEO
  Galileo Galilei. W. Smith.
    En-PC:168
GALLERIES: see ART GALLERIES;
  MUSEUMS
GALOSHES
  Galoshes. R. Bacmeister.
    Ar-TP3:167, Au-SP:110
GALUPPI, BALDASSARE
  A Toccata of Galuppi's.
    R. Browning. Pa-GTB:345,
    Rv-CB:814

GALVESTON, TEX.
  On Galveston Beach. B. Howes.
    Un-MA:654
  Wasn't That a Mighty Storm? Em-AF:471
GALWAY COUNTY, IRE.
  At Galway Races. W. Yeats.
    Mo-SD:191
  Galway Races. Mo-SD:65
GAMBLING
  Awakening. Lin Ling. Pa-MV:111
  Crapshooters. C. Sandburg.
    Ca-VT:22
  Don't Cry, My Little One.
    Wang T'ung-chao. Hs-TC:259
  A Hero in the Land of Dough.
    R. Clairmont. Mc-WK:93
  In Dives' Divés. R. Frost.
    Ca-VT:18
  A Nickle Bet. E. Knight. Ad-CI:43
  One Time Henry Dreamed the Number.
    D. Long. Ad-PB:405, Ra-BP:310
  Root, Hog, or Die. Fi-BG:65
  To an Avenue Sport. H. Collins.
    Hu-PN:346
GAME RHYMES
  Heel, Toe, Stamp and Over. Bu-DY:87
  Song of the Animal World. Ab-MO:11,
    Tr-US I:66
  There Was an Old Dog. De-TT:67
  See also Ju-CP
GAMES: see also CLAPPING GAMES;
    HUMOR - GAMES; SATIRE - GAMES;
    SINGING GAMES; names of games,
    as CHESS; FOOTBALL
  "A" for Apple. Bu-DY:23
  About the Bush. Wr-RM:33
  The Best Game the Fairies Play.
    R. Fyleman. Ar-TP3:147, Au-SP:294
  Bird and Toad Play Hide and Seek.
    Br-MW:50
  Blindman's Buff. W. Blake. Ho-WR:168
  A Catching Song. E. Farjeon.
    De-TT:35
  Chicken in the Bread Tray. Bu-DY:39
  Chickie, My Cranie-Crow. Ju-CP:68
  The Child's Morning. W. Scott.
    Du-RG:97
  Club Fist. Ju-CP:56
  Coo-Coo-Roo of the Girls. Do-CH:(34)
  Did You Feed My Cow? Bu-DY:11
  Fishing Simon. Bu-DY:31
  Follow the Leader. H. Behn.
    Ar-TP3:108, Au-SP:212
  Froggie in the Mill Pond. Ju-CP:70
  A Game of Tag. Bo-FP:141, Ir-BB:86
  Gee Lee, Gu Lu, Turn the Cake.
    Wy-CM:45
  Gopher Song. Da-SC:96
  The Gray Goose. Bu-DY:27, Du-RG:122
  Hand-Game Song. Da-SC:115
  I Count Ten. Ju-CP:59
  I Love Coffee. Bu-DY:84

In Just. E. Cummings. Ad-CI:72,
  Bo-FP:224, Co-HP:55, Du-RG:96,
  Fe-FP:73, Ga-FB:283, Ir-BB:25,
  Re-TW:53, Sh-RP:30, Un-GT:272,
  Un-MA:472
In My Lady's Garden. Bu-DY:14
The Land of Counterpane.
  R. Stevenson. Au-SP:205,
  Bo-FP:19, Er-FA:491, Fe-FP:48,
  Gr-EC:95, Hu-MP:52, Ke-TF:72,
  Na-EO:141
Lines and Squares. A. Milne.
  Ir-BB:18
The Lost Ball. L. Mitchell.
  Ir-BB:18
Miss Jennie Jones. Bu-DY:30
Mister Rabbit. Bu-DY:40
Motions. Bu-DY:26
My Horse. Bu-DY:38
My Mother's Lost Her Thimble.
  Ju-CP:66
Noah. Bu-DY:64
Old Hogan's Goat. Bu-DY:58,
  Co-IW:17
The Old Man's Toes. E. Farjeon.
  Ir-BB:20
Old Ponto. Bu-DY:17
Old Rattler. Bu-DY:41
The Old Woman and the Pig.
  Bu-DY:20
One Day while I Was Walking.
  Bu-DY:63
A Peacock Feather. Ir-BB:29,
  Wy-CM:46
Peep, Squirrel, Peep. Bu-DY:35
Pirate Story. R. Stevenson.
  Ar-TP3:114, Fe-FP:108, Un-GB:9,
  Un-GT:10
The Pony. Bu-DY:42
Pullman Porter. Bu-DY:36
Queen Nefertiti. Sm-MK:29
Ring-a-Ring. K. Greenaway.
  Fe-FP:101, Hu-MP:37, Ir-BB:12
Run, Squirrel, Run. Bu-DY:21
Sand Cooking. Bo-FP:279
Say There, Fellow. Bu-DY:63
See. See. Wr-RM:83
So You Be a Roller. Wy-CM:48
A Song. R. Hodgson. Bo-GJ:127
Song of the Playing Ball.
  I. Adigal. Al-PI:70
Starting Rhymes for Hide-and-Seek.
  Gr-GB:22
Statues. R. Wilbur. Ha-TP:17
Stool Ball. De-CH:67
Strut Miss Sally. Bu-DY:60
Summer's Pleasures They Are
  Gone. J. Clare. De-CH:512,
  Rv-CB:719
Ten o'Clock. P. Hubbell.
  La-OC:80
Trading. Bu-DY:43

GAMES — cont'd.
  Two Women under a Maple. R. Coffin.
    Mc-PR:147
  Up You Go. Ir-BB:107, Wy-CM:49
  We Push, We Pull. Wy-CM:47
  What's in There? De-CH:277,
    Ir-BB:143
  Where Are You Going, Ruth?
    Bu-DY:86
  Who Will. Ho-SD:83
  Whoopee-Hide. Ju-CP:58
  Woodchopper's Song. Bu-DY:32
GAMES, OLYMPIC: see OLYMPIC GAMES
GANGES RIVER
  Ganga. T. Blackburn. Ca-MB:57
GANGS: see CRIME AND CRIMINALS;
    JUVENILE DELINQUENCY
GARBAGE AND GARBAGEMEN
  Benson. J. Schevill. Du-SH:155
  Bindini. J. Schevill. Du-SH:157
  Burristrezzi. J. Schevill.
    Du-SH:153
  Duckmann. J. Schevill. Du-SH:155
  The Dustman. C. Sansom. St-FS:56
  Ferrore. J. Schevill. Du-SH:155
  Hamilton. J. Schevill. Du-SH:157
  Hanford. J. Schevill. Du-SH:156
  Jones. J. Schevill. Du-SH:155
  Like Me. D. Aldis. Mc-AW:21
  Love Lies a-Bleeding. F. Eckman.
    St-H:54
  Painter. J. Schevill. Du-SH:156
  Part of the Darkness. I. Gardner.
    St-H:73
  Swinton. J. Schevill. Du-SH:156
  Uncle Dog; the Poet at 9.
    R. Sward. Ca-VT:680
  Varge. P. Hubbell. Ar-TP3:12
GARCÍA LORCA, FEDERICO
  In Memory of the Spanish Poet
    Federico García Lorca.
    T. Merton. Pl-ML:154
  Lines to García Lorca.
    L. Jones. Hu-NN:55
GARDEN OF EDEN: see EDEN
GARDENS AND GARDENERS: see also
    FLOWERS; GREENHOUSES; HUMOR -
    GARDENS AND GARDENERS; LAWNS;
    PRUNING
  After Winter. S. Brown.
    Ad-PB:65, Be-MA:30, Bo-HF:50,
    Hu-PN:165, Jo-SA:50
  Almswomen. E. Blunden. Go-BP:51
  Annie's Garden. E. Follen.
    Ch-B:66
  Birthday Garden. I. Eastwick.
    Br-BC:58
  The Bower of Bliss. E. Spenser.
    De-CH:144
  The Breeze. Bo-FP:259, Ch-B:88
  The Broken-Hearted Gardener.
    Gr-CT:271, Gr-GB:115

The Butterbean Tent. E. Roberts.
  Bo-GJ:48, Br-SG:51
A Charleston Garden. H. Bellamann.
  Fe-PL:380
Child's Song. T. Moore.
  Al-VBP:711, Co-BN:49, Gr-CC:56,
  Gr-EC:224, Sm-MK:9
Christ Hath a Garden Walled About.
  I. Watts. Sm-LG:383
Come Visit My Garden. T. Dent.
  Hu-NN:80
A Cut Flower. K. Shapiro.
  Co-BN:54
The Dying Man in His Garden.
  G. Sewell. Pa-GTB:166
The Ecstasy. C. Lewis. Go-BP:174
Eleven. A. MacLeish. Ni-JP:26
An Enchanted Garden. C. Webb.
  Le-M:158
The Faery Queen. E. Spenser.
  Al-VBP:118
The Fairies. R. Fyleman.
  Au-SP:290, Fe-FP:377, Hu-MP:89,
  Ox-BC:336, Pe-FB:54
The Fairies' Dance. F. Sherman.
  Sp-OG:167
Flowers. H. Behn. Br-SG:54,
  Fe-FP:222
Flowers in a Garden. C. Smart.
  Gr-TG:28
For Jim. Easter Eve. A. Spencer.
  Bo-AN:17, Hu-PN:65
A Forsaken Garden. A. Swinburne.
  Ox-BN:811, Pa-GTB:385, Rv-CB:937
A Friend in the Garden. J. Ewing.
  Br-SG:64, Fe-FP:143, Hu-MP:305
The Garden. Chang Hsiu-ya.
  Pa-MV:32
Garden. M. Drouet. Gr-EC:270
The Garden. A. Marvell.
  Al-VBP:457, Co-BN:43, Fe-PL:381,
  Gr-CT:268, Ha-PO:202, Pa-GTB:92,
  Rv-CB:403
The Garden. J. Sylvester. Rv-CB:187
A Garden by the Sea. W. Morris.
  Al-VBP:1011, De-CH:461, No-CL:67,
  Ox-BN:788
The Garden Hose. B. Janosco.
  Du-RG:110
Garden Lore. J. Ewing. Ox-BC:260
The Garden of a London House.
  B. Jones. Ma-FW:110
A Garden Path. M. Justus.
  Bo-FP:241, Br-SG:49
A Garden Song. A. Dobson.
  Co-BN:52, Ox-BN:848
Garden Song. Bo-FP:253
The Gardener. L. Perkins. Bo-FP:240
The Gardener. Po-Chu-I.
  Co-BN:209, Go-BP:40, Pa-SG:166
The Gardener. R. Stevenson.
  Br-SG:25, Hu-MP:141, Ir-BB:40

The Gardener.   Gr-GB:112
The Gardens.   A. Symons.   Co-BN:44
Gardens No Emblems.   D. Davie.
   Wi-LT:680
Golden Wings.   W. Morris.
   Gr-CT:267, Ox-BN:770
Grandmother's Garden.   J. Tippett.
   Br-SG:40
Great Diocletian.   A. Cowley.
   Gr-CT:269
Green Little Gardens.   A. Machado.
   Le-SW:51
A Hint to the Wise.   P. Barret.
   Bo-FP:254
Hoeing.   J. Updike.   Mo-TS:17
Home Grown.   H. Boileau.   Mc-AW:38
How to Sow Beans.   Br-SG:11
In Marche and in Aprill.
   T. Tusser.   De-CH:481
The Indolent Gardener.   M. Kennedy.
   Co-BN:51
Inscription in a Garden.
   G. Gascoigne.   Rv-CB:145
It's Not So Easy.   Be-MC:38
just after noon with fierce
   shears.   T. Combs.   Br-TC:76
Lawn Mower.   D. Baruch.   Au-SP:104
Lesson.   H. Behn.   Br-SG:12
Little Seeds We Sow in Spring.
   E. Minarik.   Br-SG:99
Lupin.   H. Wolfe.   Gr-TG:28
Mary, Mary, Quite Contrary.
   Au-SP:7, Bo-FP:253, De-PO:12,
   Er-FA:505, Ir-BB:117, Li-LB:42,
   Mo-CC:(12), Mo-MGT:153, Mo-NR:34,
   Sp-AS:(7), Wi-MG:10, Wr-RM:90
Maytime Magic.   M. Watts.
   Br-SG:11, Mc-AW:90
My Garden.   T. Brown.   Fe-PL:380,
   Ga-FB:228, Un-GT:245
My Garden.   W. Davies.   Co-BN:52
My Garden.   Mu-tamid, King of
   Seville.   Pa-SG:29
My Master Hath a Garden.   De-CH:472
The New Garden.   R. Arkell.
   Sh-RP:205
Nightfall.   J. Jiménez.   Pa-SG:110
November Garden.   L. Driscoll.
   Ha-YA:124
No. 7, Stone Tiger Lane.
   Hsü Chih-mo.   Hs-TC:85
Old Garden.   E. Tatum.   Ke-TF:422
Old Man.   E. Thomas.   Wi-LT:646
Old Shellover.   W. de la Mare.
   Li-LC:60
The Organ Grinder's Garden.
   M. Merryman.   Au-SP:156
Our Garden.   N. Glekiva.   Mo-MI:35
The Plymouth Harvest.   W. Bradford.
   Bo-FP:154
poem.   J. Gill.
   Sc-TN:69

The Rose and the Gardener.
   H. Dobson.   Hu-MP:248
The Scythian Philosopher.
   J. de la Fontaine.   Un-R:79
The Secret Garden.   T. Kinsella.
   Br-TC:241
Seeds.   W. de la Mare.   Br-SG:13
Seventy Balconies and Not a Single
   Flower.   B. Fernández Moreno.
   Be-UL:27
A Spike of Green.   B. Baker.
   Br-SG:14
Spring.   J. Thomson.   Al-VBP:549
Spring Planting.   M. Chute.
   Br-SG:16
The Sunken Garden.   W. de la Mare.
   Cl-DT:69
The Task.   W. Cowper.   Go-BP:23
This Is the Garden.   E. Cummings.
   Un-MA:474
Time and the Garden.   Y. Winters.
   Ca-VT:230, Un-MA:550
To Any Garden.   E. Farjeon.
   Br-SG:21
Tommy.   G. Brooks.   Br-SG:15
Turkish Garden.   C. Trypanis.
   Ls-NY:238
Violets, Daffodils.   E. Coatsworth.
   Ar-TP3:211, Co-PU:62, Mc-AW:101
Vocation.   R. Tagore.   Fe-FP:484
The Walk in the Garden.   C. Aiken.
   En-PC:14
A Widow's Weeds.   W. de la Mare.
   Ga-FB:238
Window Boxes.   E. Farjeon.
   Br-SG:29, Fe-FP:222
Winter Garden.   D. Gascoyne.
   Pa-GTB:549
GARFIELD, JAMES ABRAM
   Charles Guiteau.   Em-AF:460
   Garfield's Murder.   Hi-TL:142
GARGOYLES
   Broken-Face Gargoyles.
      C. Sandburg.   Un-MA:207
   Gargoyle.   C. Sandburg.   Ba-PO:134
GARRICK, DAVID
   David Garrick.   O. Goldsmith.
      Rv-CB:543
GASOLINE: see PETROLEUM;
   SERVICE STATIONS
GAUCHOS: see COWBOYS
GAULDINGS: see HERONS
GAWAIN, SIR
   Sir Gawaine and the Green Knight.
      Y. Winters.   Ca-VT:228
GAZELLES: see ANTELOPES
GEESE: see also HUMOR - GEESE
   The Boy and the Geese.
      P. Fiacc.   Co-PI:43
   Complaint of the Wild Goose.
      Tr-US II:135
   Drifting, Feathery.   Shiki.   Be-MC:28

GEESE — cont'd.
  Fall. S. Andresen. Du-RG:123
  The False Fox. Gr-CT:113, Gr-GB:55
  A Fox Jumped Up. Mo-MGT:206,
    Sm-MK:72
  The Geese. R. Peck. Pe-SS:9
  The Goose. A. Tennyson. Gr-EC:154
  The Goose and the Gander. Gr-GB:57
  Goose Feathers. Mo-MGT:78
  Goosey, Goosey, Gander. Mother
    Goose. De-PO:28, Li-LB:84,
    Mo-MGT:21, Mo-NR:12, Wi-MG:61,
    Wr-RM:43
  The Gray Goose. Bu-DY:27, Du-RG:122
  Grey Goose and Gander. Co-PU:109,
    Gr-CT:174, Gr-GB:282, Li-LB:10,
    Pa-AP:40, Rv-ON:28
  I Too! I Too! J. Wheelock.
    Sm-MK:32
  In the Barnyard. D. Aldis.
    Sh-RP:330
  Late at Night. W. Stafford.
    La-RM:154
  The New and the Old. Shiki.
    Pa-SG:114
  Night over the Pond. Shiki.
    Be-CS:31
  The Old Grey Goose. Bl-OB:154,
    Gr-CT:108, Gr-GB:57
  Old Mother Goose. Mother Goose.
    Au-SP:2, Mo-NR:80, Wi-MG:22,
    Wr-RM:14
  Old Mother Goose and the Golden
    Egg. Li-LB:48, Mo-MGT:2
  Out of the Sky. Soin. Be-CS:49
  Pilgrims Plot Slowly. Ransetsu.
    Be-MC:46
  The Progress of Poetry. J. Swift.
    Rv-CB:491
  Ruins under the Stars. G. Kinnell.
    Ha-WR:82, La-RM:152
  Something Told the Wild Geese.
    R. Field. Ar-TP3:187, Au-SP:331,
    Br-SS:59, Co-BBW:234, Co-PS:124,
    Ha-YA:100, Ho-LP:32, La-PV:134,
    Mc-WK:27, Sm-MK:140, Tu-WW:106
  When the Rain Raineth. Gr-GB:57
  Why Does It Snow. L. Richards.
    Br-SS:87
  The Wild Geese. Ch'en Meng-chia.
    Hs-TC:113
  Wild Geese. E. Chipp. Ar-TP3:57,
    Fe-FP:284, Hu-MP:236, Sh-RP:341
  Wild Geese. Shën Yo. Pa-SG:87
  The Wild Geese. Tsumori Kunimoto.
    Ad-PE:48, Ba-ST:16, La-PV:135
    Le-MW:30
  Wild Geese. K. Tynan. Un-GT:65
  Wild Geese Flying. De-PP:37
  Wild Goose. C. Heath. Du-RG:123
GEHRIG, HENRY LOUIS (LOU)
  To Lou Gehrig. J. Kieran. Mo-SD:19

GEIGER COUNTER: see ATOMIC ENERGY;
    RADIATION
GEISHA: see THE JAPANESE
GEMS: see JEWELRY; PRECIOUS STONES
GENEALOGY: see ANCESTORS AND
    ANCESTRY; HERALDRY
GENERALS: see also SATIRE -
    GENERALS; and names of
    generals, as LEE, ROBERT
    EDWARD
  The White Horse. Tu Fu.   Gr-CT:343
GENERATION GAP: see COUNTER CULTURE;
    YOUTH AND AGE
GENEROSITY: see also GIFTS AND
    GIVING; HUMOR - GENEROSITY;
    SHARING
  A Gest of Robyn Hode, the Fourth
    Fytte. Ox-BB:452
  How Good Are the Poor. V. Hugo.
    Ke-TF:61
  Let Others Share. E. Anthony.
    Un-GT:26
  Little Gustava. C. Thaxter.
    Fe-FP:535
  A Mask Presented at Ludlow Castle.
    J. Milton. Al-VBP:399
  Mrs. Malone. E. Farjeon.
    Co-PM:61, Ox-BC:332
  Praise Song for a Chief.
    Tr-US I:94
  Preludes for Memnon. C. Aiken.
    Co-BL:49, Un-MA:434
  Substantiations. Vallana. Al-PI:40
  To God. R. Herrick. Mc-PR:69
  Unthrifty Loveliness.
    W. Shakespeare. Mo-GR:123
  Within King's College Chapel,
    Cambridge. W. Wordsworth.
    Ox-BN:81, Pa-GTB:300
GENEVA, LAKE OF
  Lake Leman. G. Byron. Ox-BN:245
GENGHIS KHAN
  The Tower of Genghis Khan.
    H. Allen. Pa-HT:85
GENIUS: see also HUMOR - GENIUS
  Prelude LVI. C. Aiken. Br-TC:7
GENOA, IT.
  Voyage. J. Miles. Wi-LT:774
GENTIANS
  Bavarian Gentians. D. Lawrence.
    Al-VBP:1159, Bo-GJ:84, Ha-PO:93,
    Pa-GTB:461, Sm-LG:57
  Blue Flowers. R. Field.
    Br-SG:32, Mc-PR:161
  Fringed Gentians. A. Lowell.
    Fe-FP:220, Hu-MP:262, Th-AS:79
  God Made a Little Gentian.
    E. Dickinson. Ga-FB:297
  To the Fringed Gentian. W. Bryant.
    Fe-PL:272, Hu-MP:262, Sh-AP:20,
    Sp-OG:288

GEOGRAPHY: see also MAPS; and
    names of countries, as
    ENGLAND, and natural
    phenomena, as MOUNTAINS
Geography. E. Farjeon. Fe-FP:80
Geography Lesson. Z. Ghose.
    To-MP:159
Physical Geography. L. Nicholl.
    Li-TU:29, Pl-IO:52
GEOLOGY: see EARTH; GEYSERS;
    HUMOR - GEOLOGY; MOUNTAINS;
    ROCKS
GEOMETRY: see also HUMOR -
    GEOMETRY
    Euclid. V. Lindsay. Ho-LP:57,
        Li-TU:248, Pl-IO:81
    The Icosasphere. M. Moore.
        Pl-IO:84
    The Point, the Line, the Surface
        and Sphere. C. Bragdon. Pl-IO:89
    The Prelude. W. Wordsworth.
        Pl-IO:85
    The Starfish. R. Coffin.
        Li-TU:43, Pl-IO:83
GEORGE, SAINT: see HUMOR -
    GEORGE, SAINT
GEORGE III, KING OF ENGLAND: see
    HUMOR - GEORGE III, KING OF
    ENGLAND
GEORGE IV, KING OF ENGLAND: see
    HUMOR - GEORGE IV, KING OF
    ENGLAND; SATIRE - GEORGE IV,
    KING OF ENGLAND
GEORGETOWN, D.C.
    Rainscapes, Hydrangeas, Roses,
        and Singing Birds.
        R. Eberhart. Un-MA:581
GEORGIA, U.S.S.R.
    And God Be Witness.
        B. Akhmadulina. Ca-MR:35
GEORGIA, U.S.A.: see also names
    of towns, as ATLANTA, GA.
    From the Flats. S. Lanier.
        Sh-AP:132
    Georgia. R. Loveman. Se-PR:258
    Georgia Dusk. J. Toomer.
        Ad-PB:29, Be-MA:17, Bo-AN:32,
        Jo-SA:102, Ra-BP:69
    Georgia Towns. D. Hickey. Br-AF:214
    In the Marble Quarry. J. Dickey.
        Br-AF:137
    The Mountain Whippoorwill. S. Benét.
        Co-PT:110
    Nocturne. F. Frost. Co-BN:202
    Nocturne: Georgia Coast. D. Hickey.
        Br-AF:139
    On Passing Two Negroes on a Dark
        Country Road Somewhere in Georgia.
        C. Rivers. Hu-NN:42
    Prayer Out of Georgia. M. Moody.
        Ke-TF:203

Ruth: or The Influence of Nature.
    W. Wordsworth. Pa-GTB:283
Song of the Chattahoochee. S. Lanier.
    Br-AF:176, Co-BN:70, Ga-FB:311,
    Mc-PR:195, Sh-AP:131
GERANIUMS
    The Geranium. T. Roethke. To-MP:141
    The Geraniums. G. Taggard.
        Ca-VT:90
    Joralemon Street. P. Hubbell.
        La-OC:22
    Red Geranium and Godly Mignonette.
        D. Lawrence. Ga-S:10, Pa-GTB:460
GERMAN LANGUAGE: see HUMOR - GERMAN
    LANGUAGE
GERMAN VERSE
    Adam. R. Rilke. Tr-MR:64
    Ane Sang of the Birth of Christ. . . .
        J. Wedderburn. Gr-CT:423
    Anonymous Gravestone. E. Kästner.
        Co-EL:77
    Approaching and Departing.
        N. Lenau. Un-R:125
    Augury. S. George. Gr-SS:68
    Autumn. R. Rilke. Pa-SG:97
    Away in a Manger. M. Luther.
        Ar-TP3:195, Bo-FP:193, Br-BC:165,
        Fe-FP:93, Gr-TG:78, Hu-MP:347,
        Ke-TF:78, La-PH:25, Mc-AW:78,
        Un-GT:301
    Aye, Even Small Things. P. Heyse.
        Un-R:113
    The Azra. H. Heine. Un-R:93
    Ballad of the Soldier. B. Brecht.
        Li-TU:231
    Bimbo's Pome. P. Klee. Ma-FW:60
    Birth of Mary. R. Rilke. Tr-MR:98
    The Boy. R. Rilke. Li-TU:170,
        Sm-MK:165
    The Call. U. Birnbaum. Un-R:78
    Capsule Conclusions, I-VIII.
        Un-MW:65
    Cats. T. Storm. Co-BBW:134
    Changing the Wheel. B. Brecht.
        Ho-LP:69
    The Chickens. Ar-TP3:71
    Children's Crusade, 1939.
        B. Brecht. Ca-MB:106
    Chorus Mysticus. J. von Goethe.
        Un-R:23
    Christmas Song. R. Leonhard.
        Un-R:57
    Christ's Descent into Hell.
        R. Rilke. Ho-P:231
    Coal for Mike. B. Brecht. Li-TU:142
    The Crow. W. Müller. Un-R:119
    Cruel Frederick. H. Hoffman.
        Li-SR:24
    Day-Dreamer. Ar-TP3:209
    Death and the Maiden. M. Claudius.
        Un-R:121

GERMAN VERSE — cont'd.
Dedication. H. von Gilm. Un-R:127
The Dewdrop and the Wave.
  G. Herwegh. Sp-OG:306
Emmaus. R. Rilke. Go-BP:302
Epimenides' Awakening. J. von Goethe.
  Un-R:27
The Erl-King. J. von Goethe.
  Sp-OG:111
Every Day. F. Mendelssohn.
  Bo-FP:300, Ch-B:97
Fain Would I Live in Safest Freedom.
  A. von Platen. Pa-SG:164
Fairest Lord Jesus. Ke-TF:184
From a Childhood. R. Rilke.
  Gr-SS:133
The Garden of Olives. R. Rilke.
  Tr-MR:124
Gasco, or The Toad. G. Grass.
  Co-EL:109
German Slumber Song. K. Simrock.
  Un-GT:301
The Glove. J. von Schiller.
  Sp-OG:138
Good-Bye Now and Good Night.
  Un-R:63
Guilt. A. Haushofer. Ba-PO:179
The Half of Life. F. Hölderlin.
  Un-R:19
The Harrowing of Hell. R. Rilke.
  Go-BP:296
Heriger, Bishop of Mainz. Li-TU:152
Home-Sickness. J. Kerner.
  Pa-SG:138
How Shall I Get Inside the Door.
  Un-R:97
In Dulci Jubilo. J. Wedderburn.
  Gr-CT:413
In Spring. E. Mörike. Pa-SG:88
Iron. B. Brecht. Ho-LP:39
Joseph's Suspicion. R. Rilke.
  Tr-MR:99
The Kings from the East. H. Heine.
  Gr-CT:424
The Knee. C. Morgenstern. Un-R:71
Korf's Joke. C. Morgenstern.
  Co-EL:49, Co-PU:33
The Last Supper. R. Rilke.
  Tr-MR:121
Lesson from a Sundial. Ar-TP3:208
Life Half Lived. J. Hölderlin.
  Gr-CT:244
The Lorelei. H. Heine. Co-PM:87,
  Sp-OG:116, Un-GT:137
Lose This Day Loitering.
  J. von Goethe. Fe-PL:438
Love. L. Tieck. Pa-SG:29
Love-Song. R. Rilke. Pa-SG:60,
  Un-MW:204
Lovely as a Flower. H. Heine.
  Pa-SG:76

The Maid Forsaken. E. Mörike.
  Un-R:111
Maiden's Song. P. Heyse. Un-R:101
Margaret at the Spinning Wheel.
  J. von Goethe. Un-R:117
The Mask of Evil. B. Brecht.
  Li-TU:177
Maxims and Mottoes. J. von Goethe.
  Un-R:31
The Men Are a Bad Lot. J. Seidl.
  Un-R:173
Mendax. Co-PU:119
The Merry-Go-Round. R. Rilke.
  Ad-CI:54, Li-TU:49
Mignon's Song. J. von Goethe.
  Co-PU:48, Pa-SG:125
Miriam's Lullaby.
  R. Beer-Hofmann. Un-R:47
Mrs. Poff. Ir-BB:148
Moon-Night. J. von Eichendorff.
  Pa-SG:113
Motto. Ar-TP3:209
The Mousetrap. C. Morgenstern.
  Rd-OA:30
My Soul, Consider! E. Mörike.
  Un-R:105
No, Really! Ir-BB:58
Nocturne. J. von Eichendorff.
  Pa-SG:111
O Woodland Cool. C. Brentano.
  Pa-SG:44
Of Swimming in Lakes and Rivers.
  B. Brecht. Mo-SD:96
Often along the Bathing Beach
  One Sees. J. Urzidil. Un-R:51
The Olive Garden. R. Rilke.
  Go-BP:293
On Fell. G. Lessing. Br-SM:104
On Lavater's Song of a Christian
  to Christ. J. von Goethe.
  Co-EL:53
On Nights like This All Cities
  Are the Same. R. Rilke.
  Gr-CC:81
The Panther. R. Rilke. Ma-FW:61,
  Rd-OA:120
The Picket Fence. C. Morgenstern.
  Un-R:65
The Pine Tree. H. Heine. Bo-FP:169
Poem. H. von Hofmannsthal.
  Pa-SG:136
The Pond. A. von Droste-Hülshoff.
  Pa-SG:188
Praise. R. Rilke. Gr-CT:446
Prayer for the Incurables.
  F. Hölderlin. Un-R:21
Presentiment. R. Rilke. Li-TU:82
The Prisoner. R. Rilke. Go-BP:213
Put Out My Eyes. R. Rilke. Ho-LP:15
Questions of a Studious Working
  Man. B. Brecht. Sm-MK:224

The Rabbits.   Bo-FP:75
The Salamander.   K. von Lemeke.
  Un-R:102
The Sea Hath Its Pearls. H. Heine.
  Pa-SG:48
Seclusion. E. Mörike. Un-R:107
Serenade. C. Brentano. Pa-SG:134
She-Goat and Glow-Worm.
  C. Morgenstern. Rd-OA:8
The Sigh. C. Morgenstein. Un-R:67
Silent Night. J. Mohr. Er-FA:515
Sleep, Baby, Sleep. Bo-FP:49,
  Fe-FP:471, Hu-MP:123, Ke-TF:40,
  Li-LB:22, Re-TW:74, Sm-MK:226,
  Un-GT:301, Wr-RM:58
The Smith. L. Uhland. Un-R:95
The Somersault. C. Morgenstern.
  Un-R:69
Song from "The Young David."
  R. Beer-Hofmann. Un-R:49
Song of Intoxication.
  F. Nietzsche. Un-R:33
Sonnets to Orpheus - Second Part.
  R. Rilke. Pl-US:101
Spring's Arrival. Fe-FP:471
The Story of Flying Robert.
  H. Hoffmann. Ir-BB:158,
  Li-SR:28
The Story of Little Suck-a-Thumb.
  H. Hoffmann. Ir-BB:95,
  Li-SR:27, Na-EO:154
Suspicious Sweetheart. H. Heine.
  Un-MW:54
Time's Mutability. B. Brecht.
  Co-EL:121
To the Sun. I. Bachmann. Co-BN:231
To Those Born After. B. Brecht.
  Un-R:41
The United States. J. von Goethe.
  Bl-FP:72
The Unnameable God. H. Brock.
  Un-R:35
Vice Versa. C. Morgenstern.
  Rd-OA:36
Vienna 1945. W. Weldin. Ba-PO:191
Wayfarer's Evensong. J. von Goethe.
  Un-R:29
We Are All Workmen. R. Rilke.
  Pl-EI:56
What They Said. Ir-BB:75
What Will You Do, God, when I Die?
  R. Rilke. Pl-EI:55
The Wheel Change. B. Brecht.
  Co-EL:104
Whenever We Happen to Kiss.
  H. Heine. Un-MW:54
Whispered on the Battlefield.
  G. Anders. Un-R:53
Who Was It. H. Heine. Pa-SG:34
The Wind's Song. E. Mörike.
  Pa-SG:140

The Wooden Crosses. H. Sahl.
  Un-R:59
The World and This Life Are So
  Scattered, They Try Me.
  H. Heine. Co-EL:102
You, Neighbor God. R. Rilke.
  Tr-MR:147
The Youth Dreams. R. Rilke.
  Pa-SG:142
GERMANY: see also DIALECTS, GERMAN;
  GERMAN VERSE; HUMOR - GERMANY;
  LEGENDS, GERMAN; NATIONAL
  SOCIALISM; SATIRE - GERMANY;
  and names of cities, as
  HAMBURG, GER., and regions, as
  BAVARIA, GER.
  Childe Harold. M. Kulbak. Ho-TY:205
  Watchman, What of the Night?
    A. Swinburne. Ho-WR:200
GERMS: see MICROBES
GERONIMO, CHIEF
  Geronimo. E. McGaffey.
    Co-RM:15, Fi-BG:48, Hi-TL:168
GERONTOLOGY: see GROWING OLD;
  OLD AGE
GETHSEMANE
  Garden of Gethsemane.
    B. Pasternak. Tr-MR:122
  The Garden of Olives. R. Rilke.
    Tr-MR:124
  The Olive Garden. R. Rilke.
    Go-BP:293
GETTYSBURG, BATTLE, 1863
  The Gettysburg Address.
    A. Lincoln. Fe-FP:443
  The High Tide at Gettysburg.
    W. Thompson. Vi-PP:153
  John Burns at Gettysburg. B. Harte.
    Sp-OG:36, Vi-PP:156
  They Will Look for a Few Words.
    N. Turner. Br-AF:71
GEYSERS: see HUMOR - GEYSERS
GHENT, TREATY, 1814
  How They Brought the Good News from
    Ghent to Aix. R. Browning.
    Ar-TP3:31, Co-RG:31, Er-FA:378,
    Gr-EC:156, Hi-WP I:66, Li-SR:12,
    Sp-OG:29, Un-GT:149
GHETTOS: see also HARLEM
  Childhood. H. Percikow. La-OC:75
  The Coat. C. Grade. Ho-TY:338
  Dark People. K. Cumbo. Ad-BO:46
  Escape the Ghettos of New York.
    V. Howard. La-IH:22
  Ghetto. R. Johnston. La-IH:50
  Here Lives the Jewish People.
    H. Leivick. Ho-TY:120
  I Will Go into the Ghetto.
    C. Reznikoff. Ca-VT:188
  Letter in Winter. R. Patterson.
    Ad-PB:211

GHETTOS — cont'd.
  Newark, for Now. C. Rodgers.
    Ad-PB:430
  Scenery. T. Joans. Ad-PB:206
  Sometimes on My Way Back Down
    to the Block. V. Cruz. Ad-BO:64
  Summertime and the Living. . . .
    R. Hayden. Ad-PB:118, Br-TC:169,
    Ra-BP:103
  Zoo. A. Boorstin. La-IH:122
GHOST TOWNS
  Ghost-Town Saloon: Winter.
    J. Brennan. De-FS:32
GHOSTS: see also APPARITIONS;
    EERINESS; HALLOWEEN; HUMOR -
    GHOSTS; VAMPIRES
  Admiral Hosier's Ghost.
    R. Glover. Al-VBP:555
  The Admiral's Ghost. A. Noyes.
    Ar-TP3:22, Co-PM:129
  Ambushed by Angels. G. Davidson.
    De-FS:71
  The Apparition. J. Donne.
    Al-VBP:250, Rv-CB:302
  Ballad. R. Fuller. Co-EL:75
  Black Are the Stars. R. Roseliep.
    De-FS:160
  Canto I. E. Pound. Ca-VT:90,
    Un-MA:297
  Charm. Tr-US II:108
  Cowboy Song. C. Causley.
    Co-RM:27, Ha-PO:10, Pe-M:36
  Daniel Webster's Horses.
    E. Coatsworth. Br-AF:116,
    Co-PM:34, De-FS:55, Un-MA:464
  Dark Hotel. A. Dorn. De-FS:74
  The Demon of the Gibbet.
    F. O'Brien. Co-PM:134
  Dream-Pedlary. T. Beddoes.
    Al-VBP:808, De-CH:429, Ho-WR:95,
    Li-LC:45, Ox-BN:455, Rv-CB:772,
    Un-GB:25
  The Druggist. L. Rubin. De-FS:167
  Elegy to the Memory of an
    Unfortunate Woman. A. Pope.
    Rv-CB:511
  Elsie's House. S. McNail. De-FS:137
  Faust. J. Ashbery. Br-TC:16
  For a Poetry Reading to Which No
    One Came. L. Rubin. De-FS:166
  The Garden Seat. T. Hardy.
    Bo-GJ:237, Gr-CC:10
  The Ghost. W. de la Mare.
    No-CL:204, Un-MB:202, Wi-LT:132
  Ghost. R. Grenville. De-FS:101
  The Ghost. J. Wright. De-FS:223
  The Ghost of Caipolicán. Bi-IT:155
  Ghost to Come. M. Widdemer.
    De-FS:219
  The Ghost Wails in the Woods at
    Night. Tu Yün-hsieh. Hs-TC:246

  The Ghostly Father. P. Redgrove.
    Ca-MB:54
  Ghosts. W. Burr. De-FS:42
  The Ghosts. T. Peacock.
    Al-VBP:719, Sm-MK:45
  Ghosts. A. Reid. De-FS:155
  The Ghost's Lament. Ma-BB:84,
    Pa-RE:105
  The Ghosts Led by Vera Preparing
    for Their Final Departure.
    Uanuku. Tr-US II:60
  The Ghosts of the Buffaloes.
    V. Lindsay. Sh-RP:46, Un-MA:223
  the ghosts of the dead.
    B. Brigham. Sc-TN:22
  Gin by Pailfuls. W. Scott.
    Gr-CT:159
  Grandfather's Ghost. J. Brennan.
    De-FS:36
  The Grave. R. Blair. Al-VBP:543
  Han Po Chops Wood. Feng Chih.
    Hs-TC:155
  The Hanged Thing. W. Kerr.
    De-FS:127
  Hangman's Tree. L. White.
    Br-AF:103
  The Haunted House. T. Hood.
    Ho-WR:192
  The Haunted Palace. E. Poe.
    Al-VBP:875, De-CH:320, Gr-CT:160,
    Ho-WR:216, Sh-AP:54
  Heman Avenue Holiday. J. Knoepfle.
    St-H:99
  The Highwayman's Ghost.
    R. Garnett. Co-PT:228
  House Ghost. L. May. Ho-CT:35
  House of Yesterday.
    W. Shedlofsky. De-FS:175
  I Saw a Ghost. J. Boilleau.
    Ar-TP3:44
  In a Dark Wood. Pa-RE:116
  In the Mind's Eye. T. Hardy.
    Gr-SS:119
  Inmate. L. Jennings. Ke-TF:411
  Is My Team Ploughing. A. Housman.
    Ha-PO:12, Hi-WP I:22, Un-MB:95,
    Un-MW:119, Wi-LT:61
  John Cherokee. Gr-GB:267
  Keith of Ravelston. S. Dobell.
    De-CH:299, De-TT:189, Ox-BN:661
  Legend of Ramapo Mountain.
    J. Palen. De-FS:144
  The Listeners. W. de la Mare.
    Al-VBP:1118, Er-FA:406, Fe-FP:513,
    Pa-OM:298, Re-TW:116, Un-MB:196,
    Wi-LT:131
  Litany for Halloween. Au-SP:371,
    Br-SM:3, Br-SS:72, Co-PS:140,
    Mo-TB:77, Se-PR:192
  Lydia Is Gone This Many a Year.
    L. Reese. Bo-GJ:236, De-CH:261,
    Gr-CC:11

Men's Song.   Tr-US I:208
Molly Means.   M. Walker. Be-MA:74,
   Bo-AN:130, Ha-PO:55, Hu-PN:309
Murder.   P. Milosevic.   Le-M:178
Murder House.   E. Coatsworth.
   De-FS:54
My Aunt's Spectre.   M. Collins.
   Co-PT:63
My Singing Aunt. J. Reeves.Br-SM:14
The New Faces.   W. Yeats. Pa-GTB:427
The New Ghost.   F. Shove. Go-BP:258
News of My Friends.G. Code.De-FS:60
Night Crow.   T. Roethke.   Ca-VT:287,
   Co-EL:38, Ho-LP:77, Re-BS:52,
   Sh-AP:213
1935.   S. Benét.   Mc-WS:107,
   Un-MA:501
Old Christmas.   R. Helton.
   Co-PM:94, Un-MA:346
The Old Ghost.   T. Beddoes.
   Ho-WR:227
The One Forgotten.   D. Sigerson.
   Se-PR:197
The Parklands.   S. Smith. Ca-MB:94
Part-Time Tenant.   E. Meudt.
   De-FS:141
The Phantom Horsewoman.   T. Hardy.
   Gr-SS:120
The Phantom Light of the Baie des
   Chaleurs.   A. Eaton.   Co-PM:55
The Phantom Mail Coach.
   L. Welcome.   Co-PM:167
The Phantom Wooer.   T. Beddoes.
   Al-VBP:811, Ho-WR:191
Place-Ghost.   A. Derleth. De-FS:72
The Portent.   H. Melville.
   Ho-WR:196, Kr-OF:109, Rv-CB:836
Proud Margret.   Ox-BB:74
A Shropshire Lad.   J. Betjeman.
   Ca-MB:70
Slave Quarter.   C. Carmer. Th-AS:208
So Ghostly Then the Girl Came In.
   R. Hillyer.   Gr-CC:7
Song of a Ghost.   Tr-US II:239
Song of Expiation.   Tr-US I:64
Song of Two Ghosts.   Tr-US II:243
Spectre.   S. Russell.   De-FS:173
Southern Mansion.   A. Bontemps.
   Ad-PB:83, Be-MA:45, Bo-AN:80,
   Br-AF:142, Hu-PN:213, Lo-TY:224,
   Wi-LT:611
Spooky.   K. Finnell.   Ho-CT:35
The Strange Visitor.   Bl-OB:86,
   De-CH:677, Gr-CT:132, Gr-GB:290
Sweet William's Ghost. De-CH:423,
   Ma-BB:115
Tenant.   F. Gray.   De-FS:97
Two Houses.   E. Thomas. Sm-LG:397
The Two Old Women of Mumbling Hill.
   J. Reeves.   Br-SM:13
The Two Wives.   D. Henderson.
   Br-SM:12

Tyrannic Love.   J. Dryden. Al-VBP:492
Waltzing Matilda.   A. Paterson.
   Gr-CT:138, Gr-GB:259, Ha-PO:238,
   Mc-WK:147
The Wandering Spectre.   Bl-OB:156,
   De-CH:314, Gr-CT:155, Gr-GB:284,
   Rv-CB:141, Sm-LG:238
The Way Through the Woods. R. Kipling.
   De-CH:281, Fe-FP:242, Ha-PO:154,
   Hi-WP I:107, La-RM:46, Mc-WS:31,
   Ox-BC:323, Ox-BN:932, Re-TW:128,
   Sm-LG:396
Wessex Heights.   T. Hardy. Ox-BN:839
When Out of the Band-Aid Box.
   Rs-PF:10
When the Tree Bares.   C. Aiken.
   Un-MA:433
The White Dress.   M. Zaturenska.
   Un-MA:560
White Rose.   S. Sitwell. Gr-SS:37
Widdecombe Fair.   Co-PM:213,
   De-CH:72
The Wife of Usher's Well.
   Ar-TP3:20, De-CH:424, De-TT:171,
   Gr-CT:134, Ma-BB:37, Ox-BB:94,
   Pa-OM:91, Rv-CB:36
Wilderness Road.   M. Keller.
   De-FS:123
The Witch of Coös.   R. Frost.
   Al-VBP:1129, Pe-OA:36, Sh-AP:147,
   Wi-LT:170
A Woman Riding.   T. Hardy. Gr-CC:8
GIANTS: see also GOLIATH; HUMOR -
   GIANTS; PAUL BUNYAN; TITANS
   The Dorchester Giant.   O. Holmes.
      Fe-FP:306, Hu-MP:414, Pa-OM:51
   Fee, Fi, Fo, Fum.   Br-FF:(3),
      Mo-MGT:26, Mo-TB:78
   Giant Thunder.   J. Reeves.
      Co-BN:176, Sm-MK:147
   The Giant's Song.   C. Carryl.
      Mc-PR:189
   In the Orchard.   J. Stephens.
      Co-RG:168, Ha-LO:11
   A Small Discovery.   J. Emanuel.
      Li-LC:13
GIBBS, JOSIAH WILLARD
   Gibbs.   M. Rukeyser. Pl-IO:178
GIFFORD, WILLIAM
   William Gifford.   W. Landor.
      Pa-GTB:317
GIFTS AND GIVING: see also
   CHRISTMAS GIFTS; HUMOR -
   GIFTS AND GIVING; SATIRE -
   GIFTS AND GIVING
   Baa, Baa, Black Sheep.
      Ar-TP3:74, Au-SP:17, Bo-FP:80,
      De-PO:18, Er-FA:506, Li-LB:89,
      Mo-MGT:11, Mo-NR:57, On-TW:15,
      Pa-AP:30, Wi-MG:66, Wr-RM:58
   Bankrupt.   C. Sayres.   Fe-PL:295
   Beowulf.   Al-VBP:1, Ma-YA:14

GIFTS AND GIVING — cont'd.
  Betsy Jane's Sixth Birthday.
    A. Noyes. Br-BC:101, Br-SS:45
  Birthday Gift. E. de Vito.
    Br-BC:153
  Birthday Gifts. H. Asquith.
    Br-BC:100, Br-SS:49
  Birthday Gifts. L. Scott. Br-BC:99
  A Birthday Song. R. Gilder.
    Se-PR:237
  Blanaid's Song. J. Campbell.
    Co-PI:19
  Broken-Face Gargoyles.
    C. Sandburg. Un-MA:207
  Burristrezzi. J. Schevill.
    Du-SH:153
  Ceremony. J. De Longchamps.
    Ls-NY:91
  A Child's Present. R. Herrick.
    Ox-BC:30
  Corinna to Tanagra. W. Landor.
    Al-VBP:708, Ox-BN:191
  Daddy. Mo-MGT:108
  Dandelions. M. Chute.
    Br-BC:102, Mc-AW:67
  Elegy for Maria Alves.
    J. Cardozo. An-TC:33
  The Fine Old English Gentleman.
    De-CH:63
  Flowers for Heliodora.
    Meleager. Gr-SS:83
  For a Birthday. E. Emans.
    Br-BC:152
  For God Hath Not Given Us the
    Gift of Fear. Bible. N.T.
    Timothy. Ar-TP3:209
  The Gift. K. Wilson. Sc-TN:239
  Gifts. H. Harris. Br-BC:32
  Gifts for a Good Boy. De-PP:20
  The Gifts of the Animals to Man.
    P. Sidney. Rd-OA:38
  Give Me the Splendid Silent Sun.
    W. Whitman. Co-BN:232, Fe-FP:263,
    Mo-BG:20, Un-MA:84
  Giving and Taking. J. Kirkup.
    Pl-EI:47
  Good King Wenceslaus. J. Neale.
    Pa-OM:355, Se-PR:234
  Henry and Mary. R. Graves.
    Bo-GJ:10, Ha-LO:46, Ir-BB:259
  Hope. G. Herbert. Gr-CC:169
  I Have Three Presents. De-CH:629
  If I Should Ever by Chance Grow
    Rich. E. Thomas. Bl-OB:32,
    Bo-GJ:20, De-CH:518, Ox-BC:329,
    Pa-RE:73, Sm-LG:112, Un-MB:215
  I'll Twine White Violets.
    Meleager. Pa-SG:35
  Interlude. E. Sitwell. Un-MB:330
  Legacy. N. Turner. Th-AS:187
  Letter. M. Strand.
    Mo-BG:102

  Little Brother's Secret.
    K. Mansfield. Ar-TP3:6,
    Fe-FP:49, Th-AS:64
  The Lovely Shall Be Choosers.
    R. Frost. Sh-AP:155, Un-MA:185
  Mania Went to the Fair. Gr-BB:25
  Mrs. Santa Claus' Christmas
    Present. A. Morris. Co-PS:166
  My Garden. Mu'tamid, King of
    Seville. Pa-SG:29
  My Gift. N. Bukhteyeva. Mo-MI:89
  Neglectful Edward. R. Graves.
    Un-MB:383
  Nursery Rhyme of Innocence and
    Experience. C. Causley.
    Bo-GJ:170, Hi-WP I:82
  Offerings. R. De Reinosa. No-CL:99
  On the Gifts of God. Bible. O.T.
    Psalms. Me-PH:29
  Parting Gift. E. Wylie. Ha-LO:7
  Phillis Inamorata. L. Andrewes.
    Gr-CC:49
  The Picture of J.T. in a Prospect
    of Stone. C. Tomlinson.
    En-PC:260
  The Poet Speaks. G. Johnson.
    Bo-AN:22
  Praise Ye the Lord. Bible. O.T.
    Psalms. Ar-TP3:188, Fe-FP:225
  Present. M. Potter. Br-BC:101
  A Present from the Emperor's New
    Concubine. Lady P'an. Rx-LT:3
  A Rare Tree. Pa-SG:69
  Reflections on a Gift of Watermelon
    Pickle Received from a Friend
    Called Felicity. J. Tobias.
    Du-RG:134
  A Sea Song from the Shore.
    J. Riley. Ch-B:37
  Seven Gifts. De-PP:33
  Seven Today. I. Eastwick.
    Br-BC:70
  Shepherd's Song at Christmas.
    L. Hughes. Ab-MO:73
  A Ship a-Sailing. G. Setoun.
    Ar-TP3:122, Au-SP:19, Bo-FP:200,
    Co-SS:85, De-TT:48, Gr-EC:242,
    Hi-GD:16, Hu-MP:175, Ir-BB:241,
    Li-LB:86, Mo-MGT:174, Mo-NR:103,
    Pa-AP:44, Sm-MK:199, Sp-HW:25,
    Wi-MG:53, Wr-RM:73
  Six Rows of Pins. Rv-ON:104
  Song of the Sky Loom. Br-MW:49,
    Da-SC:76, Le-OE:6, Tr-US II:256
  A Sonnet Sequence. R. Hillyer.
    Ho-TH:34
  Star of the East. E. Field.
    Se-PR:224
  Thank You Note. Ke-TF:127
  To His Son, Vincent Corbet.
    R. Corbet. Rv-CB:322, Sm-LG:112
  Tommy Trot. Ir-BB:42, Mo-MGT:121

The Vision of Sir Launfal.
  J. Lowell. Pa-OM:210
What Shall I Give? Ox-BC:330,
  Sm-LG:113
With Flowers. E. Dickinson.
  Sm-MK:210
You'll Find Whenever the New
  Year Comes. Wy-CM:35
GIGGLING: see LAUGHTER
GILA MONSTERS: see LIZARDS
GILBERT, SIR HUMPHREY
  Sir Francis Drake. Hi-FO:224
GILGAMESH, MYTHOLOGICAL KING
    OF BABYLON
  The Epic of Gilgamesh. Ho-P:218
GINGER (PLANT)
  Song of the Wild Ginger.
    Tr-US II:200
GIOTTO DI BONDONE: see HUMOR -
    GIOTTO DI BONDONE
GIPSIES: see GYPSIES
GIRAFFES: see also HUMOR -
    GIRAFFES
  Conversation with a Giraffe at
    Dusk in the Zoo.
    D. Livingstone. To-MP:196
  Four-Footed Poems. E. Greenberg.
    Ho-TY:312
  The Giraffe. N. Gumileo. Fe-FP:470
  Giraffe. C. McCullers. Ho-CS:24
  Giraffe. Ab-MO:39
  The Giraffe and the Tree.
    W. Turner. De-CH:279
  Giraffes. S. Kahn. Du-RG:31
  To a Giraffe. P. Hubbell.
    Su-FVI:45
GIRLS: see also CHILDREN;
    DAUGHTERS; HUMOR - GIRLS;
    SISTERS; YOUTH
  Amy Elizabeth Ermyntrude Annie.
    Q. Hopper. Ar-TP3:7
  Amy Margaret. W. Allingham.
    Br-BC:53
  Ann. K. Starbird. Gr-EC:200,
    Ho-GC:22
  Ann and the Fairy Song.
    W. de la Mare. Ga-FB:170
  Anne. Rv-ON:100
  April's Amazing Meaning.
    G. Dillon. Co-BL:17
  Around the Green Gravel. Wr-RM:88
  As Soon as Ever Twilight Comes.
    W. de la Mare. Br-SS:27
  Bailada. A. Nunez. Pa-SG:66
  A Ballad of the Mulberry Road.
    E. Pound. Ha-LO:93
  Bea's Bee. M. Ray. Ho-GC:16
  Beginning of a Girls' Song.
    Tr-US I:111
  La Belle Saison. J. Prévert.
    Ad-CI:97

Bessy Bell and Mary Gray. Bo-FP:51,
  Wr-RM:90
Betty at the Party. Br-BC:94
Billy, Billy. Wr-RM:89
Blue Girls. J. Ransom. Ca-VT:150,
  Gr-CC:79, Gr-CT:51, Ha-PO:183,
  Mc-WS:75, Pe-OA:137, Sh-AP:182,
  Un-MA:409
Boy and Girl. Mo-NR:32, Wr-RM:118
Bring Out Your Hair Ornaments.
  Le-IB:96
Buffalo Girls. Gr-EC:118
By the River. J. Gautier. Gr-SS:40
Carmen. V. Cruz. Ad-CI:61,
  Ad-PB:506
Cherry Robbers. D. Lawrence.
  Un-MB:287
Child Margaret. C. Sandburg.
  Ma-FW:74
The Children's Hour. H. Longfellow.
  Bo-FP:32, Er-FA:484, Fe-FP:51,
  Fe-PL:144, Ga-FB:162, Hu-MP:109,
  Ke-TF:75, Mc-PR:208, Tu-WW:20,
  Un-GT:98
Coo-Coo-Roo of the Girls.
  Do-CH:(34)
Counsel to Girls. R. Herrick.
  Al-VBP:328, Er-FA:104, Ga-FB:41,
  Gr-CT:51, Ha-PO:161, Hi-WP II:140,
  Li-SR:21, Ma-YA:86, Pa-GTB:71,
  Un-MW:19
Dance Songs. Tr-US II:163
Death and the Maiden. M. Claudius.
  Un-R:121
The Deserted Village.
  Feng Hsüeh-feng. Hs-TC:371
The Dessert. M. Lamb. De-TT:99
Do Those Girls. Tsurayuki.
  Ba-ST:16
Elegy for Jane. T. Roethke.
  Br-TC:348, Pe-OA:204, Pe-SS:160,
  Sh-AP:213, Un-MA:598, Wi-LT:486
Elizabeth at the Piano. H. Gregory.
  Gr-SS:134, Pl-US:20
Emmy. A. Symons. Ox-BN:934
Encouraging a Dancer. Tr-CB:18,
  Tr-US I:38
Eurasian Girl. A. Kerrigan.
  Ls-NY:139
Experience. A. Kilmer. Br-BC:46
Festive Wine. Br-FW:13
Fife Tune. J. Manifold. Bo-GJ:193,
  Er-FA:198, Ho-LP:68, Mc-WS:97,
  Sm-LG:262, Wi-LT:765
For the Girls in My Home Town.
  N. Korzhavin. Ca-MR:91
For Vicki at Seven. S. Russell.
  Br-BC:150
The Garden of Bamboos. Co-BL:27
Girl, Boy, Flower, Bicycle.
  M. Joseph. Pe-M:149

GIRLS — cont'd.
The Girl Cutting Reeds.
S. Takano.   Sh-AM:168
A Girl Skipping Rope in Flushing.
S. Stepanchev.   Ls-NY:287
Girls Can, Too.   L. Hopkins.
Ho-GC:26
Girls' Names.   E. Farjeon.   Ne-AM:18
Girls on the Yüeh River.   Li Po.
Gr-CT:62, Ho-LP:62
Gnomes, I.   Tr-US I:124
Goldenhair.   J. Joyce.   Co-BL:86,
Gr-CC:73, Gr-CT:89, Ha-LO:3,
Sh-RP:83, Th-AS:69
Gone.   C. Sandburg.   Sh-AP:156
Granny.   Ca-MU:16
Green Grow the Rashes.   R. Burns.
Al-VBP:642, Er-FA:426
Hair Ribbons.   Br-BC:47
Harlem Sweeties.   L. Hughes.
Hu-PN:190, Lo-TY:227, Wi-LT:420
Hua-La-Ma-Ch'ao.   T'ien Chien.
Hs-TC:331
I Am Rose.   G. Stein.   Ne-AM:28
I Would Like You for a Comrade.
E. Parry.   Ne-AM:20, Ox-BC:309
If No One Ever Marries Me.
L. Alma-Tadema.   Br-BC:111,
Un-GT:13
In a Girl's Album.   C. Dover.
Hi-WP II:149
In a Spring Still Not Written of.
R. Wallace.   Co-BN:20
In Spring We Gather Mulberry
Leaves.   Rx-LT:13
Isabel Jones & Curabel Lee.
D. McCord.   Un-GT:223
Jake Hates All the Girls.
E. Cummings.   Du-SH:65
Jenny White and Johnny Black.
E. Farjeon.   Fe-FP:303
July 31.   N. Jordan.   Ad-PB:323
Little Blue Ribbons.   A. Dobson.
Br-BC:54
Little Girl.   T. Iadchenko.
Mo-MI:64
A Little Girl.   Ir-BB:111,
Mo-MGT:188, Sm-MK:10
Little Girl, Be Careful What You
Say.   C. Sandburg.   Ma-FW:73
The Little Girl Found.   W. Blake.
Rv-CB:593
A Little Girl, Rumi's Fancy.
N. Guha.   Al-PI:81
The Little Girl That Lost a
Finger.   G. Mistral.   Fe-FP:491
A Little Indian Maid.   Fi-BG:196
Little Phillis.   K. Greenaway.
Br-BC:44
The Lovable Child.   A. Poulsson.
Hu-MP:331

Lucy in the Sky with Diamonds.
The Beatles.   Pe-SS:82
Lucy McLockett.   P. McGinley.
Br-BC:54
maggie and milly and molly and
may.   E. Cummings.   Co-PS:109,
Gr-BT:10, Ha-LO:15
Maiden's Song.   P. Heyse.   Un-R:101
Meeting Mary.   E. Farjeon.   Br-BC:72
Minnie.   E. Farjeon.   Un-GB:22,
Un-GT:102
Minnie and Mattie.   C. Rossetti.
Ar-TP3:71, Bo-GJ:40
Mode of Maidens.   Br-FW:5
My Turn.   M. Ray.   Ho-GC:10
New Blast Furnace.   B. Akhmadulina.
Ca-MR:37
The Night Before the Night Before
Christmas.   R. Jarrell.   Pe-M:134
November 3.   R. Brautigan.   Kh-VA:62
Oh, Fairest of the Rural Maids!
W. Bryant.   Al-VBP:767
Oh, Suzy.   B. Katz.   Ho-GC:24
On a Wet Day.   F. Sacchetti.
Co-BN:170
One and One.   C. Day-Lewis.
Pl-US:15
One, Two, Buckle My Shoe.   O. Nash.
Br-BC:44, Ir-BB:92
The Picture of Little T.C. in a
Prospect of Flowers.   A. Marvell.
Rv-CB:406
Polly.   W. Rands.   Un-GT:101
Portrait of a Girl.   C. Aiken.
Bo-GJ:123, Un-MA:425
Portrait of a Girl with a Comic
Book.   P. McGinley.   Pe-OA:198,
Pe-SS:39
Pretending.   M. Livingston.
Br-BC:75
The Ragged Girl's Sunday.
M. Bennett.   De-TT:24
The Sampler.   N. Turner.   Br-BC:80
The Scarred Girl.   J. Dickey.
Du-SH:69
Seven Today.   I. Eastwick.   Br-BC:70
She Was a Pretty Little Girl.
R. de Ayada.   Fe-FP:473
Shoplifter.   S. Edwards.   Hu-NN:82
Six Birthday Candles Shining.
M. Carr.   Br-BC:91
Song for a Kachua Dance.
Tr-US I:175
Song of a Marriageable Girl.
Tr-CB:40, Tr-US I:62
Song of Liang Chou.   Ou Yang Hsiu.
Rx-OH:55
Spring and Fall.   G. Hopkins.
Bo-GJ:249, Gr-CT:317, Ha-PO:148,
Ke-PP:99, Pa-GTB:392, Re-TW:62,
Wi-LT:44

Sunday Afternoon. D. Levertov.
  Pe-SS:55
Surprise. H. Behn. Br-BC:97
Susie Mooney. Rv-ON:85
The Sweet o' the Year. G. Meredith.
  Co-BN:23
There Was a Girl I Used to Go with.
  S. Benét. Ha-LO:4
There Was a Little Girl.
  H. Longfellow. An-IP:(12),
  Bl-OB:29, Co-BB:69, De-PO:12,
  Er-FA:492, Fr-WO:28, Mo-MGT:200,
  Na-EO:168, Ox-BC:226, Sm-LG:99,
  Un-GT:101, Wi-MG:45, Wr-RM:84
Thoughts of a Little Girl.
  M. Enriqueta. Fe-FP:489
Tilda Tilbury. L. Allen. Pa-RE:45
To a Brown Girl. O. Davis.
  Hu-PN:378
To a Child Five Years Old.
  N. Cotton. Ox-BC:66
To a Dark Girl. G. Bennett.
  Ad-PB:81
To a Girl. E. Waller. Al-VBP:385,
  Ho-WR:58, Rv-CB:364
To Charlotte Pulteney. A. Philips.
  Pa-GTB:113
To Mistress Isabel Pennell.
  J. Skelton. Al-VBP:31, De-CH:34,
  Ma-FW:65, Ma-YA:51, Rv-CB:65
To Mistress Margaret Hussey.
  J. Skelton. Al-VBP:31, Bo-GJ:109,
  Ha-PO:55, Re-TW:66, Rv-CB:66,
  Sm-LG:127, Un-GT:88
To Olivia. F. Thompson. Un-MB:90
To the Highland Girl of Inversneyde.
  W. Wordsworth. Pa-GTB:253
Tule Love Song. Da-SC:16,
  Tr-US II:295
Two Girls of Twelve or So. . . .
  C. Reznikoff. La-OC:90
Two Hundred Girls in Tights &
  Halters. D. Hoffman. Co-EL:153
The Two Little Miss Lloyds.
  E. Turner. Ox-BC:138
Us Idle Wenches. De-CH:484,
  Gr-CC:13
A Village Girl. M. Singh.
  Al-PI:144
Waking. J. Anderson. Ls-NY:19
We Keep a Dog to Guard the House.
  Wy-CM:30
What Are Little Boys Made of.
  Mother Goose. De-PO:14, Er-FA:205,
  Ir-BB:92, Mo-CC:(13), Mo-MGT:59,
  Mo-NR:111, Wi-MG:31, Wr-RM:108
Women's Song at a Girl's Initiation.
  Tr-US I:188
Wonders of Nature. Gr-TG:18
Xmas Time. W. Karsner. Co-EL:142,
  Co-PU:30

The Young Girl. C. Day Lewis.
  Ls-NY:223
Young Girl: Annam. P. Colum.
  Ha-LO:94
The Young Girl's Song. A. Gordon.
  Pe-M:140
Young Men's Song. Tr-US I:187
Youth and Age on Beaulieu River,
  Hants. J. Betjeman. Br-TC:45
GIVE-AND-TAKE
  Motto. L. Hughes. Ad-PB:75,
  Co-PU:126, Hu-PN:202, Jo-SA:118
GLACIERS: see also HUMOR - GLACIERS;
  ICE; ICEBERGS
  Message from Ohanapecosh Glacier.
  W. Ransom. Ni-CD:197
GLADNESS: see HAPPINESS; JOY
GLASS: see also WINDOWS
  Bits of Glass. S. Brown. Ho-LP:40
  The Crystal. G. Barker. Wi-LT:523
  The Fable of the Piece of Glass and
  the Piece of Ice. Ox-BC:151
GLASS BLOWERS
  The Glass Blower. J. Scully.
  Br-TC:362
  The Glassblower. G. Johnson.
  Ls-NY:308
GLASS EYES
  Iris. T. McNeill. Sa-B:6
GLENDOWER, OWEN
  The Hearth of Urien. Llywarch the
  Aged. Gr-CT:323
GLOCKENSPIELS
  The Birthday-Cake Glockenspiel.
  E. Henley. Br-BC:90
GLOUCESTER, MASS.
  Gloucester Moors. W. Moody.
  Pa-HT:19, Sp-OG:362
  Maximus of Gloucester, to You.
  C. Olson. Wi-LT:778
GLOVES
  To a Fat Lady Seen from a Train.
  F. Cornford. Bo-GJ:106,
  Co-EL:100, Co-PU:132, Hi-WP I:109,
  Li-SR:20, Sm-MK:99, Un-MB:306
  What Has Four Fingers. Re-RR:17
GLOWWORMS: see FIREFLIES
GLUTTONY: see also HUMOR - GLUTTONY
  The Glutton. J. Oakman. Ox-BC:83
  A Gluttonous Rich Man.
  G. Chaucer. Ha-PO:52
  Greedy Richard. J. Taylor. Ox-BC:121
  Griselda. E. Farjeon. Un-GB:23,
  Un-GT:100
  The Masked Shrew. I. Gardner.
  Co-BBW:39, Pl-IO:105
  The Notorious Glutton. A. Taylor.
  Ox-BC:118
  The Pigs. J. Taylor. De-TT:23
GNATS: see also HUMOR - GNATS
  The Gnat. J. Beaumont. Rv-CB:391
  Gnat. R. Moore. Un-GT:80
  The Gnats. O. Tchernine. Sm-MK:180

GNATS — cont'd.
Riddle: Gnats. Ma-YA:3
Song: One Hard Look. R. Graves.
Un-MB:388
GNOMES
The Fairies Feast. C. Doughty.
De-CH:124
The Gnome. H. Behn. Ar-TP3:151,
Au-SP:286, Fe-FP:385, La-PV:70
The Green Gnome. R. Buchanan.
Co-PT:47
A Rhyme of the Dream-Maker Man.
W. White. Fe-PL:94
Sleepyhead. W. de la Mare.
Ar-TP3:155
GNUS: see also HUMOR - GNUS
The Gnu. H. Belloc. Co-FB:34,
Co-HP:31, Co-PU:96
The Wildebeest. J. Daly. Fe-FP:479
GO-CARTS: see BABY CARRIAGES
GOALS: see AMBITION; MEANS AND ENDS
GOATS: see also HERDING; HUMOR -
GOATS
April. Y. Winters. Be-EB:20,
Co-BBW:173, Co-EL:31, Co-PU:91,
Du-RG:99, La-RM:132
Baby Goat. Z. Gay. Mc-AW:54
The Bicycle. J. Harasymowicz.
Du-SH:22
The Farmyard. St-FS:90
Goat. S. Johnson. Gr-EC:6
The Goat Paths. J. Stephens.
Ad-PE:30, Bo-GJ:56, De-CH:149,
Go-BP:93, Rd-OA:55
The Goatherd. G. Conkling.
Ar-TP3:32
Goats. L. Gibson. Co-BBW:163
The Good Shepherd with the Kid.
M. Arnold. Go-BP:286
News Report. D. Ignatov. Br-TC:214
Nosegay for a Young Goat.
W. Welles. Co-BBW:171
She-Goat and Glow-Worm.
C. Morgenstern. Rd-OA:8
To Be Sung by a Small Boy Who
Herds Goats. Y. Winters.
We-PZ:29
What Animal. Re-RR:24
Who Am I. L. Gama. Lo-TY:79
GOBLINS
The Bored Goblins. D. Thompson.
Ja-PA:38
Fire on the Hearth. R. Bennett.
Sh-RP:177
The Goblin. R. Fyleman.
Ar-TP3:152, La-PH:13
Goblin Feet. J. Tolkien.
Co-PM:163, Fe-FP:369
The Goblin's Song. J. Telfer.
Gr-CT:156
The Holiday. M. Stredder.
St-FS:53

How to Tell Goblins from Elves.
M. Shannon. Ar-TP3:154,
Fe-FP:388
In the Hours of Darkness.
J. Flexner. Fe-FP:386, Hu-MP:119
Little Orphant Annie. J. Riley.
Co-BB:113, Er-FA:493, Fe-FP:532,
Hu-MP:27, Ox-BC:300
Overheard on a Saltmarsh. H. Monro.
Ad-PE:17, Ar-TP3:153, Bo-GJ:227,
Co-PM:125, De-CH:116, Du-RG:67,
Fe-FP:388, Gr-EC:269, Li-LC:41,
Mc-WS:29, Re-TW:25, Su-FVI:16,
Th-AS:14
Polly Picklenose. L. Jackson.
Co-BB:35
Very Nearly. Q. Scott-Hopper.
Au-SP:300, Fe-FP:374, Hu-MP:81
When I Was Six. Z. Cross. Fe-FP:486
When Nights Are Murky. Re-RR:47
GOD: see also ALLAH; HUMOR - GOD;
SATIRE - GOD; TRINITY
Abide with Me. H. Lyte. Er-FA:443
Adon 'Olam (Lord of the World).
Pl-EI:199
After Reading Certain Books.
M. Coleridge. Pl-EI:74
After the Flood Went Down. Bible.
O.T. Genesis. Gr-TG:73
After the Salvo. H. Asquith.
Li-TU:243
All These Hymnings Up to God.
A. Evans. Tr-MR:197
All Things Come Alike to All.
Bible. O.T. Ecclesiastes.
Me-PH:32
The Almighty. Be-AP:18
Anactoria. A. Swinburne.
Al-VBP:1022
And the Lord Was Not in the
Whirlwind. L. MacNeice. Pl-EI:154
Apocalypse. E. Pierce. Tr-MR:262
Apology for Bad Dreams. R. Jeffers.
Sh-AP:175, Un-MA:363
As Salt Resolved in the Ocean.
Rumi. Pa-SG:202
At Evening. N. Minkoff. Ho-TY:261
At Mass. V. Lindsay. Ca-VT:30
Atalanta in Calydon. A. Swinburne.
Al-VBP:1041
Autumn. R. Rilke. Pa-SG:97
Baha'u'llah in the Garden of Ridwan.
R. Hayden. Ad-PB:122
Ballad for Gloom. E. Pound.
Un-MA:292, Wi-LT:222
The Ballad of Father Gilligan.
W. Yeats. Hi-WP I:72, Mc-MK:132,
Mc-WS:157, Pl-EI:114, Un-MB:112
A Basket of Summer Fruit. Bible.
O.T. Amos. Me-PH:49
Batter My Heart. J. Donne.
Er-FA:468, Pl-EI:52, Rv-CB:310

The Beginning.   J. Glatstein.
   Ho-TY:335
Benediction.   A. Morgan.   Ke-TF:427
Birth.   A. Gilboa.   Me-PH:116
Birth-Dues.   R. Jeffers.   Un-MA:365
The Black Cliffs, Ballybunion.
   B. Kennelly.   Co-PI:83
Blessing for Light.   Th-AS:176
The Book of Thel.   W. Blake.
   Ox-BN:32
The Burning Bush.   N. Nicholson.
   Pl-EI:57
Cabbages.   T. Hooley.   Ga-S:11
Call, and the Lord Shall Answer.
   Bible.   O.T.   Isaiah.   Gr-TG:84
A Chant Out of Doors.
   M. Wilkinson.   Th-AS:172
A Child's Prayer.   J. Tabb.
   Fe-FP:24
A Child's Thought of God.
   E. Browning.   Fe-FP:23, Hu-MP:65
Chiliasm.   R. Eberhart.   Pl-EI:77
Christ in the Universe.
   A. Meynell.   Un-MB:65
The Complaint to God.   Bible.
   O.T.   Job.   Me-PH:18
Conclusion.   W. Wordsworth.
   Ox-BN:112
Conversion.   F. Angermayer.
   Fe-PL:334
Country Thought.   S. Warner.
   Un-MB:371
The Creation.   J. Johnson.
   Ad-PB:3, Ar-TP3:214, Ga-FB:152,
   Ga-S:6, Hi-WP I:141, Jo-SA:60,
   Pe-M:76, Un-MA:149
The Creation of Man.   Ab-MO:7
The Creator.   Be-AP:19
Cry for a Dead Soldier.
   M. Inman.   Ls-NY:109
The Daily Grind.   F. Johnson.
   Bo-AN:25
The Day after Sunday.   P. McGinley.
   Un-MA:595
De Profundis.   Bible.   O.T.
   Psalms.   Ga-S:39
The Dignity of Man.   T. More.
   Ga-S:134
The Divine Image.   W. Blake.
   Al-VBP:613, Go-BP:287, Ox-BN:20,
   Rv-CB:586
Don't You Ever.   Jo-TS:7
Dread.   J. Synge.   Un-MB:182
Ducks.   F. Harvey.   Co-BBW:163
Each in His Own Tongue.   Ke-TF:246
East and West.   Ke-TF:245
The Ebb and Flow.   E. Taylor.
   Sh-AP:14
Ecclesiastes.   G. Chesterton.
   Un-MB:205
An Eclipse.   Pindar.
   Pa-SG:209

The Elixir.   G. Herbert.   Bo-FP:301,
   Ga-S:115, Gr-TG:59, Sm-LG:366
Enion Replies from the Caverns of
   the Grave.   W. Blake.   Ox-BN:39
L'Envoi.   R. Kipling.   Er-FA:10,
   Ke-TF:453
Essay on Deity.   E. Olson.   Tr-MR:141
Esthetique du Mal, III.   W. Stevens.
   Wi-LT:152
Ex Nihilo.   D. Gascoyne.   Pa-GTB:549
False Gods.   W. de la Mare.
   Pl-EI:83
Father of Night.   B. Dylan.
   Mo-GR:100
The First Autumn.   M. Schacht.
   Tr-MR:25
Foot, Fin or Feather.   C. Smart.
   Rd-OA:163
For a Child Named Katherine.
   L. Nicholl.   Th-AS:16
For God Hath Not Given Us the Gift
   of Fear.   Bible.   N.T.   Timothy.
   Ar-TP3:209
For My Funeral.   A. Housman.
   Al-VBP:1081, Go-BP:237
For the Existentialist.   W. Palmer.
   Ls-NY:339
A Forest Hymn.   W. Bryant.   Sh-AP:23
Forgive, O Lord, My Little Jokes on
   Thee.   R. Frost.   Pl-EI:40,
   Wi-LT:188
Foundation of Faith.   J. Drinkwater.
   Tr-MR:255
From Early Childhood Even as Hath
   Been Said.   W. Wordsworth.
   Go-BP:273
Frost at Midnight.   S. Coleridge.
   Ox-BN:162, Rv-CB:661
The Gate of the Year.
   M. Haskins.   Hi-WP II:174
Genesis.   Bible.   O.T.   Genesis.
   Pl-IO:14
God.   S. Hazo.   Co-EL:108
God.   Ya Hsüan.   Pa-MV:155
God, a Boy.   H. Leivick.   Ho-TY:123
God and the Holy Ghost.
   D. Lawrence.   Tr-MR:224
God Be in My Head.   Ga-S:208,
   Gr-CT:386, Pl-EI:187, Sm-MK:213
God Has Had Pity on Us.   Da-SC:121
God Is like Scissors.   J. Villa.
   Pl-EI:50
God Is Our Refuge.   Bible.   O.T.
   Psalms.   Gr-TG:84
God Makes Ducks.   G. Wall.   Le-M:105
The God of Galaxies. M. Van Doren.
   Pl-IO:19, Tr-MR:138
The God of War.   Be-AP:45
God Said.   Bible.   O.T. Joshua.
   Gr-TG:84
Godhead Here in Hiding.   G. Hopkins.
   Ga-S:199

GOD — cont'd.
God's Dark. J. Martin. Fe-PL:336
God's Gift. R. Southwell. Ga-S:198
God's Thanks to Job. R. Frost.
    Tr-MR:223
God's Virtue. B. Barnes. Go-BP:22
A Good-Night. F. Quarles. Rd-SS:41
Hammer and Anvil. S. Cole.
    Fe-PL:333
The Hands of God. D. Lawrence.
    Tr-MR:224
The Happy Land. Ga-S:21
He Giveth Snow like Wool. Bible.
    O.T. Psalms. Cl-DT:18
The Heart. F. Thompson. Pa-GTB:399,
    Un-MB:79
The History of the Flood.
    J. Heath-Stubbs. Ca-MB:40,
    Ma-FW:38
Hohiotsitsi No-Otz. Ba-PO:113
The Holy of Holies. G. Chesterton.
    Go-BP:254, Tr-MR:44
How Many Heavens. . . .
    E. Sitwell. Gr-CC:134, Tr-MR:41
How the First Hielandman of God
    Was Made of Ane Horse Turd in
    Argyll as Is Said. Gr-GB:166
Huswifery. E. Taylor. Ga-FB:95,
    Pl-EI:49, Sh-AP:12
i am a little church (no great
    cathedral). E. Cummings.
    Tr-MR:201
I Asked for Peace. D. Dolben.
    Go-BP:180
I Believe. A. Zeitlin. Ho-TY:321
I Have Sought Thee Daily.
    S. Ibn-Gabirol. Pa-SG:208
I Need No Sky. W. Bynner. Pl-EI:3
i thank You God. E. Cummings.
    Pl-EI:195, Tr-MR:22
I Vision God. Ab-MO:1, Lo-TY:196
I Will Lift Up Mine Eyes. Bible.
    O.T. Psalms. Bo-FP:305,
    Cl-DT:43, Rv-CB:129
I Wonder. J. Lawton. Le-M:170
If. R. Gutman-Jasny. Ho-TY:297
In Desert Places. Sister M.
    Madeleva. Un-GT:253
In Him We Live. J. Very. Sh-AP:66
In Memoriam. A. Tennyson.
    Ox-BN:498
In No Strange Land. F. Thompson.
    Ga-S:127, Go-BP:250, Pa-GTB:398,
    Pl-EI:7, Un-MB:90
In the Beginning. D. Thomas.
    Tr-MR:242
In the Beginning Was the Word.
    A. Tabachnik. Ho-TY:271
In Utrumque Paratus. M. Arnold.
    Ox-BN:626
The Indian upon God. W. Yeats.
    Un-MB:110

Inscription on an Altar of the
    Dead. V. Contoski. Sc-TN:32
Invocation. Pa-SG:198
Invocation. Tr-US I:76
Invocation: Hasidic Song.
    L. Isaac of Berditshev. Pl-EI:193
Invocation to the Rainbow.
    Tr-US I:63
Is God Dead? M. Radcliffe.
    La-OC:148
It Is a Beauteous Evening.
    W. Wordsworth. Al-VBP:659,
    De-CH:738, Fe-PL:403, Gr-CT:195,
    Pa-GTB:273, Rv-CB:646
Job. Bible. O.T. Job. Pl-IO:39
Job. Bible. O.T. Job. Pl-IO:45
Jonah. R. Jarrell. Tr-MR:83
Jubilate Agno. C. Smart. Pl-US:24
Justorium Animae. Apochrypha.
    Wisdom. Ga-S:51
The Lamb. W. Blake.
    Bo-FP:106, Bo-GJ:64, Co-BBW:173,
    De-CH:87, Fe-FP:165, Hi-WP I:139,
    Hu-MP:199, Li-LC:82, Ma-YA:126,
    Mc-PR:101, Mc-WK:125, Pa-RE:78,
    Pl-EI:18, Rv-CB:575, Un-GT:34
The Last Round. A. Wickham.
    Un-MB:278
Lead, Kindly Light. J. Newman.
    Er-FA:474, Ga-S:46, Ox-BN:436
The Lessons of Nature.
    W. Drummond. De-CH:153,
    Pa-GTB:39
Let Me Alone. Bible. O.T.
    Job. Ke-PP:4
Light Shining Out of Darkness.
    W. Cowper. Er-FA:461, Ga-S:6,
    Mc-PR:64, Pl-EI:210, Rv-CB:549,
    Sm-LG:377
Lightly Stepped a Yellow Star.
    E. Dickinson. Un-MA:101
The Little Boy Found. W. Blake.
    Rv-CB:582
Look, How Beautiful. R. Jeffers.
    Tr-MR:148
The Lord Shall Save. Bible.
    O.T. Psalms. Gr-TG:85
Lord, Thou Hast Been Our Dwelling
    Place. Bible. O.T. Psalms.
    Me-PH:23, Pl-EI:198
The Making of Birds. K. Tynan.
    Re-BS:54
Malachi. E. Marlatt. Tr-MR:80
Man Is God's Nature. R. Eberhart.
    Pl-EI:133, Tr-MR:287
Man-Test. E. Markham. Tr-MR:280
Mathematics of the Gift of Tongues.
    A. Branch. Pl-IO:72
A Mighty Fortress Is Our God.
    M. Luther. Pl-EI:213
Millenium. J. Kohut.
    Lo-IT:67

Morning Song from "Senlin."
   C. Aiken.   Pe-OA:141, Sh-AP:185,
   Un-MA:422, Wi-LT:325
Muhammedan Call to Prayer.
   Bilal.   Lo-TY:43
My Garden.   T. Brown.   Fe-PL:380,
   Ga-FB:228, Un-GT:245
My Soul Is Weary of My Life.
   Bible.   O.T.   Job.   Pl-EI:67
Naked and Hungry Came We into This
   World.   Gr-TG:38
Nearer to Thee.   S. Adams.
   Er-FA:481, Fe-PL:328
The Negligent Lover.   Be-AP:52
New Year's.   C. Reznikoff.   Ca-VT:189
New Year's Eve.   T. Hardy.   Un-MB:27
Night of Marvels.   Sister Violante
   do Ceo.   Ga-S:71
No Coward Soul Is Mine.   E. Brontë.
   Al-VBP:925, Er-FA:459, Ox-BN:608,
   Pl-EI:4, Rv-CB:833
Not Only Around Our Infancy.
   J. Lowell.   Er-FA:480
O God, Our Help in Ages Past.
   I. Watts.   Ke-TF:188, Pl-EI:200
O Lord, Save We Beseech Thee.
   Me-PH:66
O Stelliferi Conditor Orbis.
   Boethius.   Go-BP:240
Oh Thou, Who Man of Baser Earth
   Didst Make.   E. Fitzgerald.
   Pl-EI:40
Ode Inscribed to W. H. Channing.
   R. Emerson.   Al-VBP:800
The Old Repair Man.   F. Johnson.
   Bo-AN:27, Pe-M:75
On Another's Sorrow.   W. Blake.
   Al-VBP:614, Ga-FB:100, Rv-CB:591
On Heaven.   F. Ford.   Al-VBP:1116
On the Gifts of God.   Bible.   O.T.
   Psalms.   Me-PH:29
On the Universality and Other
   Attributes of the God of Nature.
   P. Freneau.   Sh-AP:16
The 151st Psalm.   K. Shapiro.
   Pl-EI:163
The Only One Who Understands Me.
   G. Chinchilla.   Me-WF:2
Our Father.   R. Swartz.   Tr-MR:216
Our Lords Esteemed Most High.
   Ge-TR:51
Out of Paradise.   J. Milton.
   Ga-S:35
The Pagan Isms.   C. McKay.   Ra-BP:64
The Path of the Stars.   T. Jones.
   Tr-MR:139
Peace.   H. Vaughan.   Ga-S:223,
   Gr-CC:136, Gr-CT:347, Hi-WP II:172,
   Ma-YA:105, Pa-HT:163, Pl-EI:9,
   Rv-CB:409, Sm-LG:382
Penitance.   W. Cowper.   Go-BP:179
Permit Me Voyage.   J. Agee.   Un-MA:606

Personal.   L. Hughes.   Bo-AN:66,
   Hu-PN:188
Poem.   K. Cuestas.   Jo-SA:85
Poem.   M. Yungman.   Ho-TY:364
Praise the Lord, O My Soul!
   Bible.   O.T.   Psalms.   Gr-TG:86
Prayer.   W. Bilderdÿk.   Pa-SG:200
Prayer.   L. Hughes.   Pl-EI:172
Prayer.   Bi-IT:29
Prayer on the Night Before Easter.
   J. Holmes.   Tr-MR:58
A Prayer to Be Restored to the
   Sanctuary.   Bible.   O.T.
   Psalms.   Me-PH:22
The Preacher: Ruminates Behind
   the Sermon.   G. Brooks.
   Be-MA:80, Li-TU:165
Precision.   P. Collenette.   Ma-FW:207
Prelude XIV.   C. Aiken.   Br-TC:5
Presence.   J. Moffit.   Tr-MR:146
Psalm.   T. Arghezi.   Mc-AC:30
The Pulley.   G. Herbert.   Al-VBP:346,
   Ga-S:52, Ha-PO:198, Mc-PR:207,
   Pa-GTB:64, Pl-EI:51, Rv-CB:356
Rain.   E. Benediktsson.   Pa-SG:205
The Rebellious Vine.   H. Monro.
   Go-BP:277, Mc-WK:110
Rebirth.   R. Kipling.   Ox-BN:933
Recessional.   R. Kipling.
   Al-VBP:1101, Er-FA:472, Ga-FB:242,
   Ma-YA:229, Ox-BN:867, Sp-OG:214,
   Un-MB:135
Reconciliation.   Tr-MR:250
Remember the Source.   R. Eberhart.
   Tr-MR:261
Renascence.   E. Millay.   Er-FA:95,
   Un-MA:440
Rendezvous with God.   M. Seljouk.
   Go-BP:58
Repetition.   M. Aoki.   Le-TA:85
The Ribs and Terrors.   H. Melville.
   Al-VBP:950, Pl-EI:207
The Rich Earth.   Bible.   O.T.
   Psalms.   Un-GT:245
The Rime of the Ancient Mariner.
   S. Coleridge.   Al-VBP:679,
   Bo-FP:301, Co-RG:60, Co-SS:131,
   De-CH:364, Er-FA:318, Fe-FP:147,
   Ga-FB:105, Gr-TG:61, Ha-PO:15,
   Hi-WP II:68, Ma-YA:146, Ni-JP:52,
   Ox-BN:139, Rv-CB:658, Sm-LG:312,
   Un-GT:30
Rocked in the Cradle of the Deep.
   E. Willard.   Er-FA:467
Rubaiyat of Omar Khayyam.
   E. Fitzgerald.   Al-VBP:832,
   Er-FA:43, Fe-FP:479, Ha-PO:210,
   Ox-BN:526, Pa-SG:120
The Sacrament of Fire.   J. Oxenham.
   Ke-TF:430
The Sacrament of Sleep.   J. Oxenham.
   Fe-PL:332

GOD — cont'd.
St. Patrick's Breastplate.
St. Patrick. Sm-LG:379
St. Teresa's Book-Mark. St. Theresa.
Pa-SG:191, Pl-EI:178
The Scribe. W. de la Mare.
Sm-LG:35, Tr-MR:24
The Shape God Wears. S. Hay.
Un-GT:82
Simon the Cyrenian Speaks.
C. Cullen. Be-MA:50, Bo-AN:89,
Ga-S:160, Lo-TY:235, Ra-BP:99,
Un-MA:570
Song for the Sun That Disappeared
Behind the Rainclouds.
Be-AP:22, Lo-TY:5
Song of Myself. W. Whitman.
Al-VBP:928, Er-FA:87, Mo-GR:106,
Sh-AP:69, Tr-MR:143, Un-MA:44, 61
A Song in Passing. Y. Winters.
Ca-VT:232
A Song of Thanksgiving. Bible.
O.T. Psalms. Me-PH:28
Soul's Liberty. A. Wickham.
Un-MB:282
Spring Song. H. Conkling.
Co-PS:57, Hu-MP:246
Stranger. T. Merton. Pl-EI:14
Sun, Moon and Stars. Gr-TG:68
The Sun, the Moon, the Stars,
the Seas. . . . A. Tennyson.
Go-BP:274, Li-SR:94
Tahitian Chant of Creation.
Tr-US II:67
Thanksgiving. R. Emerson.
Au-SP:373, Bo-FP:161
A Thanksgiving to God for His
House. R. Herrick. Al-VBP:337,
De-TT:168, Gr-CT:269
Theologians. W. de la Mare.
Pl-EI:20
The Theology of Innocence.
S. Meltzer. Ad-II:21
They That Go Down to the Sea.
Bible. O.T. Psalms.
Fe-FP:197, Gr-CT:217, Mc-WK:195
This Is a Poem. H. Farley. Le-M:14
Thou Art Indeed Just, Lord, if I
Contend. G. Hopkins. Pa-GTB:397,
Pl-EI:88, Un-MB:39, Wi-LT:50
Though the Great Waters Sleep.
E. Dickinson. Pl-EI:91
The Three Kings. R. Dario.
Ab-MO:74
The Tiger. W. Blake. Al-VBP:616,
Ar-TP3:80, Bl-OB:111, Co-BBW:209,
Co-RG:146, De-CH:91, Er-FA:234,
Fe-FP:178, Fe-PL:366, Ga-FB:95,
Ga-S:12, Gr-CT:115, Ha-PO:116,
Hi-WP II:171, Hu-MP:201,
Li-SR:8, Ma-YA:129, Mc-PR:158,
Ox-BN:23, Pl-EI:19, Rd-OA:118,
Rv-CB:576, Sm-LG:68, Tu-WW:108,
Un-GT:36
To a Snowflake. F. Thompson.
Co-BN:191, Ga-FB:146, Pl-IO:50,
Re-TW:90, Un-GT:248, Un-MB:78
To a Waterfowl. W. Bryant.
De-CH:106, De-TT:179, Er-FA:232,
Fe-PL:355, Mc-PR:55, Rv-CB:734,
Sh-AP:20, Sp-OG:295
To God. R. Herrick. Mc-PR:69
To the Envious. Pl-EI:25,
Tr-CB:53, Tr-US I:53
To the Stars. T. Arghezi. Mc-AC:29
To the Supreme Being.
Michelangelo. Pa-SG:198
The Triumph of Doubt. J. Bishop.
Pl-EI:90
Truth Is as Old as God.
E. Dickinson. Un-MA:103
A Turkish Legend. T. Aldrich.
Sp-OG:187
Unison. J. Wheelock. Tr-MR:144
The Universal Prayer. A. Pope.
Go-BP:271
The Unnameable God. H. Brock.
Un-R:35
The Unseen Power. Rumi. Pa-SG:192
The Valley of the Black Pig.
W. Yeats. Gr-CT:335
Vice Versa. C. Morgenstern.
Rd-OA:36
We Are All Workmen. R. Rilke.
Pl-EI:56
Wenberri's Song. Wenberri.
Tr-US I:261
What Thomas An Buile Said in a Pub.
J. Stephens. Un-MB:262
When I Consider Thy Heavens.
Bible. O.T. Psalms. Fe-FP:202,
Pl-IO:150
When Satan Fell. D. Lawrence.
Tr-MR:215
When the Lord Turned Again the
Captivity. . . . Bible. O.T.
Psalms. Go-BP:246, Me-PH:28
While Sitting Here Looking at the
Stars. L. Curry. Ba-HI:144
Who Are You - Who Are You?
D. Clarke. Jo-VC:79
The Wilderness and the Solitary
Place. . . . Bible. O.T.
Isaiah. Go-BP:263
the will's love. B. Brigham.
Sc-TN:24
Wintry Day. Bo-FP:168
With God Conversing. G. Derwood.
Tr-MR:139
Without Jews. J. Glatstein.
Ho-TY:331
The Wreck of the Deutschland.
G. Hopkins. Li-TU:220,
Ox-BN:852, Wi-LT:30

Ye That Do the Master's Will.
C. Wesley. Go-BP:181
Yet Do I Marvel. C. Cullen.
Ad-PB:87, Be-MA:50, Bo-AN:88,
Hu-PN:233, Jo-SA:128, Lo-TY:235,
Pe-SS:48, Ra-BP:100
You, Neighbor God. R. Rilke.
Tr-MR:147
You, Whose Day It Is.
Ho-SD:55, Jo-TS:1, Le-OE:16
Young. A. Sexton. To-MP:100
Zechariah. E. Marlatt. Tr-MR:82
GOD, LOVE OF
All Other Love Is like the Moon.
Ga-S:148
And She Washed His Feet with Her
Tears, and Wiped Them with the
Hairs of Her Head.
E. Sherburne. Rv-CB:396
Angels. E. Spenser. Ga-S:5
Curse God and Die, You Said
to Me. A. MacLeish. Pl-EI:69
Defense Rests. V. Miller.
Un-MA:680
Discipline. G. Herbert.
Al-VBP:342, Fe-PL:342, Mc-PR:92
The Earth. J. Very. Sh-AP:65
The Excesses of God. R. Jeffers.
Tr-MR:143
Femina Contra Mundum.
G. Chesterton. Tr-MR:249
For All Sorts and Conditions.
N. Nicholson. Pl-EI:181
From Thee to Thee. S. Gabirol.
Pl-EI:48
Giving and Taking. J. Kirkup.
Pl-EI:47
God to Be First Served.
R. Herrick. Ox-BC:31
Good Night. D. Pierce.
Ar-TP3:180, Br-SS:29
Good Night. V. Hugo.
Ar-TP3:219, Au-SP:99, Bo-FP:51,
Br-SS:36, Ch-B:117, Fe-FP:53
Grandmother Watching at Her Window.
W. Merwin. Ca-VT:616
Here Is Thy Footstool.
R. Tagore. Go-BP:288
A Hymn to Christ at the Author's
Last Going into Germany.
J. Donne. Al-VBP:263
In Most Lightsome Darkness.
M. Korte. Sc-TN:116
The Lord Is My Shepherd. Bible.
O.T. Psalms. Ar-TP3:189,
Bo-FP:107, Fe-FP:25, Fe-PL:346,
Ga-S:213, Rv-CB:130, Sh-RP:92
Love Bade Me Welcome. G. Herbert.
Al-VBP:344, De-CH:463, Fe-PL:115,
Ga-FB:92, Ga-S:138, Gr-CT:433
My Song Is Love Unknown.
S. Crossman. Ox-BC:32

The Nature of Love. J. Kirkup.
Pl-EI:91
The One. P. Kavanagh.
Un-MB:432
The One Thing Needful. V. Miller.
En-PC:226
Prayer. Chou Meng-tich. Pa-MV:71
A Prayer in Spring. R. Frost.
Ha-YA:29, Tr-MR:48
The Proof. R. Wilbur. Pl-EI:45
St. Francis and the Cloud.
M. Welch. Tr-MR:253
A Song. R. Crashaw. Al-VBP:435
Temper in October. V. Edminson.
Go-BP:31
The Vision of the Holy Church.
W. Langland. Go-BP:294
GOD - PRAISE
All People That on Earth Do Dwell.
W. Kethe. Ga-S:14
Alleluia! Alleluia! Let the Holy
Anthem Rise. Co-PS:66
Alleluia, Hearts to Heaven and
Voices Raise. C. Wordsworth.
Ke-TF:195
The Altar. G. Herbert. Ha-PO:200
Arjuna's Paean to Krishna.
Al-PI:25
Bermudas. A. Marvell. Al-VBP:455,
De-CH:362, Gr-CT:277, Hi-TL:17,
Pa-GTB:103, Rv-CB:399, Sm-LG:296
Bless the Lord, O My Soul.
Bible. O.T. Psalms. Ar-TP3:188,
Me-PH:25
Blessings for Chanukah. J. Sampter.
Ar-TP3:191
A Canticle to the Waterbirds.
Brother Antoninus. Ca-BP:11
Come and I Will Sing You. Ga-S:16
Come, Let Us Sound with Melody,
the Praises. T. Campion.
Pl-US:66
Comfort Ye My People. Bible. O.T.
Isaiah. Ga-S:65, Pl-EI:175
Count Your Blessings. Gr-TG:38
The Creation. C. Alexander.
De-TT:36, Fe-FP:260, Gr-TG:22,
Hu-MP:286, Ox-BC:200
The Creator. Bo-FP:160
The Earth Is the Lord's. Bible.
O.T. Psalms. Ar-TP3:188,
Bo-FP:249, Fe-FP:232, Pa-SG:198,
Pl-EI:214
Easter-Wings. G. Herbert.
Ha-PO:201, Ma-YA:91
Even in the Darkness. H. Mullins.
Tr-MR:227
Give Ear, O Ye Heavens. Bible.
O.T. Deuteronomy. Bo-FP:163
God Has Been Good to Me.
F. Keyes. Ke-TF:454

GOD - PRAISE — cont'd.
  God's Grandeur. G. Hopkins.
    Er-FA:467, Ox-BN:867, Tr-MR:22,
    Un-MB:42, Wi-LT:40
  The Grasshopper's Song. H. Bialik.
    Fe-FP:476, Ha-YA:65
  Heaven and Earth. James I, King
    of England. Gr-CT:235
  The Heavens Declare the Glory of
    God. Bible. O.T. Psalms.
    Fe-FP:267, Gr-CT:236
  Holy, Holy, Holy! R. Heber.
    Ke-TF:193
  The C Psalm. Bible. O.T.
    Psalms. Ma-YA:74
  Hymn. Caedmon. Ma-YA:7
  Hymn. A. Young. Pl-EI:212
  Hymn of an Inca to the God
    Viracocha. Tr-US II:299
  I Will Extol Thee, O Lord. Bible.
    O.T. Psalms. Me-PH:20
  I Will Sing Praise. Bible. O.T.
    Psalms. Fe-FP:75
  I Will Sing unto the Lord. Bible.
    O.T. Psalms. Gr-TG:85
  Kibbutz Sabbath. L. Amittai.
    Pl-EI:192
  Let All the World in Every
    Corner Sing. G. Herbert.
    Gr-TG:83
  Let the Nations Be Glad. Bible.
    O.T. Psalms. Fe-FP:495
  The Lord's Name Be Praised!
    Gr-TG:64
  Meditation Eight. E. Taylor.
    Sh-AP:13
  Mirth. C. Smart. Ox-BC:72
  Morning Hymn. T. Ken. Er-FA:455
  Never Another. M. Van Doren.
    Tr-MR:33
  O Clap Your Hands. Bible. O.T.
    Psalms. Gr-TG:85
  O Light Invisible, We Praise Thee.
    T. Eliot. Tr-MR:148
  O Sing unto the Lord a New Song.
    Bible. O.T. Psalms. Ga-S:178,
    Pl-EI:194
  O Worship the King. R. Grant.
    Ga-S:3
  Old Hundred. M. Van Doren.
    Pl-US:53
  Old Hundredth. Pl-US:52
  Pied Beauty. G. Hopkins.
    Al-VBP:1062, Bo-GJ:47, Er-FA:461,
    Ga-S:16, Hi-WP II:37, Ho-LP:47,
    Ma-FW:101, Mc-PR:182, Mc-WK:16,
    No-CL:269, Ox-BN:865, Pa-GTB:390,
    Pl-EI:124, Re-TW:89, Sm-MK:222,
    Tr-MR:25, Un-GT:246, Un-MB:39,
    Wi-LT:42
  Pleasure It Is. W. Cornish.
    Co-BN:28, De-CH:16, Ga-S:211,
    Gr-CT:39, Rv-CB:97

Praise. Bo-FP:163
Praise of Created Things.
  St. Francis of Assisi. Fe-FP:259
Praise the Lord. J. Milton.
  De-TT:116, Sm-LG:365
Praise to the Holiest. J. Newman.
  Ga-S:172
Praise Ye the Lord. Bible. O.T.
  Psalms. Ar-TP3:188, Fe-FP:225
A Psalm. Bible. O.T. Psalms.
  Au-SP:374, Se-PR:210
Psalm. M. Mendes. Tr-MR:207
Psalm Eight. Bible. O.T.
  Psalms. Pa-SG:193
Psalm. XCIX. Bible. O.T.
  Psalms. Ma-YA:75
Psalm 100. Bible. O.T. Psalms.
  Ar-TP3:188, Br-SS:81, Fe-FP:85,
  Hu-MP:287, Ma-YA:76, Pl-US:52,
  Sh-RP:92
Psalm 150. Bible. O.T. Psalms.
  Ga-S:18, Gr-CT:446, Pa-RE:126,
  Pa-SG:201, Pl-US:7
Sing a Song of Joy! T. Campion.
  Pl-US:51
Sing Merrily unto God. Bible.
  O.T. Psalms. Gr-TG:85
Singing the Reapers Homeward
  Come. Se-PR:212
The Song of Creatures.
  St. Francis of Assisi. Pa-SG:202
The Song of Honor. R. Hodgson.
  Un-MB:188
Songs and Dance Songs, III.
  Tr-US II:152
The Spacious Firmament on High.
  J. Addison. Mc-PR:202, Pl-EI:211
Stone Too Can Pray. C. Aiken.
  Pl-EI:177, Sm-MK:229, Tr-MR:23
Thanksgiving. L. Driscoll.
  Ha-YA:134, La-PH:20
A Thanksgiving. J. Taylor.
  Gr-TG:70
Thanksgiving for the Beauty of
  His Providence. T. Traherne.
  Sm-LG:381
Thanksgiving for the Earth.
  E. Goudge. Ha-YA:138
There's a Wideness in God's Mercy.
  F. Faber. Gr-TG:74
To the Name above Every Name, the
  Name of Jesus. R. Crashaw.
  Ga-S:97
Veni Creator. B. Carman. Tr-MR:26
The Voice of the Grass. S. Boyle.
  Bo-FP:228
Whether We Mutter a Thank You or
  Not. Gr-TG:39
With Rejoicing Mouth. Bi-IT:39
Wmffre the Sweep. R. Humphries.
  Pl-EI:197

Wonder. T. Traherne. De-CH:152,
    Ga-S:21, Rv-CB:472
The Wonderful World. W. Rands.
    Ar-TP3:217, Fe-FP:260, Hu-MP:284
The Writing of Hezekiah, King of
    Judah, When He Had Been Sick.
    Bible. O. T. Isaiah. Me-PH:43
You. J. Masefield. Tr-MR:32
Yours. R. Tagore. Tr-MR:33
GOD, SEARCH FOR
Ars Poetica about Ultimates.
    T. Combs. Br-TC:73
A Compass Needle. F. Quarles.
    Ga-S:54, Rv-CB:347
Crag Jack's Apostasy. T. Hughes.
    Pl-EI:86
The Created. J. Very. Sh-AP:66
Flower in the Crannied Wall.
    A. Tennyson. Co-BN:49,
    Er-FA:243, Fe-FP:216, Fr-WO:85,
    Ga-FB:128, Hu-MP:257, Ma-YA:198,
    Mc-PR:137
He Puts Me to Rest. D. Ignatow.
    Ca-VT:395
Hymn. L. Nicholl. Pl-EI:196
In Church. R. Thomas. Go-BP:226
No Beauty We Could Desire.
    C. Lewis. Go-BP:303
O Weary Pilgrims. R. Bridges.
    Un-MB:49
Perfection. F. Carlin. Er-FA:456
Redemption. G. Herbert. Ha-PO:199,
    Pl-EI:44
Son and Father. C. Day Lewis.
    Pl-EI:135
Three Elements. S. Benet. Pl-EI:183
The Way My Ideas Think Me. J. Villa.
    Pl-EI:54
GOD AND MAN
The Creditor. L. MacNeice.
    Pl-EI:41
Epilogue. F. Thompson. Un-MB:79
God's Education. T. Hardy.
    Tr-MR:221
God's Price and Man's Price.
    R. Herrick. Ga-S:167
Grace of the Way. F. Thompson.
    Un-MB:90
The Great Sad One. U. Greenberg.
    Me-PH:91
I Am the Great Sun. C. Causley.
    Ga-S:131
In Memoriam. A. Tennyson.
    Pl-IO:126
The Invitation. Bible. O.T.
    Isaiah. Me-PH:44
Like a Woman. U. Greenberg.
    Me-PH:90
Man Frail, and God Eternal.
    I. Watts. Rv-CB:499
Maxims and Mottoes. J. von Goethe.
    Un-R:31

My Fellowship with God. J. Villa.
    Pl-EI:50
Only Man. D. Lawrence. Ga-S:26
A Prayer in Darkness.
    G. Chesterton. Fe-PL:330,
    Un-MB:208
To God. R. Herrick. Ga-S:145,
    Go-BP:179
The Way My Ideas Think Me.
    J. Villa. Pl-EI:54
We Are All Workmen. R. Rilke.
    Pl-EI:56
What Will You Do, God, when I Die?
    R. Rilke. Pl-EI:55
With My God the Smith.
    U. Greenberg. Me-PH:90
GODIVA, LADY: see LEOFRIC
    AND GODIVA
GODPARENTS AND GODCHILDREN
Godmother. P. Morden. Au-SP:301,
    Th-AS:104
GODS AND GODDESSES: see also
    MYTHOLOGY; SATIRE – GODS
    AND GODDESSES; and names
    of deities, as APOLLO
Bacchus. W. Empson. En-PC:83
Blue Lake of Life. Wo-HS:(15)
Country Gods. Cométas. Sm-LG:230
Deities and Beasts. J. Updike.
    Co-EL:26
Epistle to Prometheus.
    B. Deutsch. Sm-PT:81
Evarra and His Gods. R. Kipling.
    Un-MB:134
For Once in a Dream or Trance,
    I Saw the Gods. E. Muir.
    Go-BP:155
Hymn to Proserpine. A. Swinburne.
    Hi-FO:58, Ox-BN:797
Oenone. A. Tennyson. Al-VBP:851
The Old Gods. E. Muir. Pl-EI:13
Outlaws. R. Graves. Ha-WR:58
Poem. J. Wain. En-PC:230
Proem to Hellenics. W. Landor.
    Al-VBP:702
The River God. S. Sitwell.
    Un-MB:401
The River God to Amoret.
    J. Fletcher. No-CL:104
The River-God's Song. J. Fletcher.
    Fe-FP:274, Re-TW:44, Rv-CB:312
Sabrina Fair. J. Milton.
    Al-VBP:400, De-CH:122, Rv-CB:372,
    Sm-LG:227
Second Elegy. N. Stanescu.
    Mc-AC:149
Song by Lady Happy, as a Sea-
    Goddess. M. Cavendish. Gr-SS:184
Songs from Cyprus. H.D. Un-MA:338
To the Ocean Now I Fly. J. Milton.
    Al-VBP:401

GODS AND GODDESSES — cont'd.
  We, the Few Who Believe. H. Vinal.
    De-FS:209
  The White Goddess. R. Graves.
    Un-MB:391
GODS AND GODDESSES, AFRICAN: see
    also VOODOO; and names of
    deities, as OBATALA, YORUBA
    GOD OF CREATION
  Love Song (My Boat). Lo-TY:31
  Shango I, II. Lo-TY:12
GODS AND GODDESSES, AZTEC: see
    INDIANS OF CENTRAL AMERICA -
    RELIGION AND MYTHOLOGY
GODS AND GODDESSES, EAST INDIAN:
    see also names of deities, as SHIVA
  Arjuna's Paean to Krishna. Al-PI:25
  The Birth of the Goddess Jangu Bai.
    Tr-US II:148
  The Song of Creation. Al-PI:11
  To Agni. Al-PI:14
  To the Dawn. Al-PI:15
  To the Maruts. Al-PI:13
  To the Waters. Al-PI:17
  To the Wind. Al-PI:16
GODS AND GODDESSES, EGYPTIAN:
    see HUMOR - GODS AND GODDESSES,
    EGYPTIAN; and names of deities, as RA
GODS AND GODDESSES, ESKIMO: see
    INDIANS OF NORTH AMERICA -
    RELIGION AND MYTHOLOGY
GODS AND GODDESSES, GREEK: see
    GODS AND GODDESSES
GODS AND GODDESSES, NORSE
  Erda. V. Konrick. De-FS:130
  The Song of the Reim-kennar.
    W. Scott. Ox-BN:137
GODS AND GODDESSES, NORTH AMERICAN
    INDIAN: see INDIANS OF NORTH
    AMERICA - RELIGION AND
    MYTHOLOGY
GODS AND GODGESSES, ROMAN: see
    also names of deities, as DIANA
  Hyperion, I. J. Keats. Ox-BN:362
GOETHALS, GEORGE WASHINGTON
  Goethals, the Prophet Engineer.
    P. MacKaye. Se-PR:84
GOETHE, JOHANN WOLFGANG VON:
    see also HUMOR - GOETHE,
    JOHANN WOLFGANG VON
  Sonnet XIII. Feng Chih. Hs-TC:151
GOGH, VINCENT VAN: see also
    HUMOR - GOGH, VINCENT VAN
  Farewell to Van Gogh. C. Tomlinson.
    Pa-GTB:561
  A Visit to Van Gogh. C. Causley.
    En-PC:158
GOLD (COLOR)
  Nothing Gold Can Stay. R. Frost.
    Bo-HF:56, Ca-VT:16, Mo-BG:133,
    Mo-TS:54, Un-MA:187

  What Is Gold? W. Goosley. La-GI:29
GOLD (METAL): see also CALIFORNIA -
    GOLD DISCOVERIES; KLONDIKE;
    MONEY
  Dow's Flat. B. Harte. Co-PT:86
  Epigram. J. Wolcot. Co-EL:51
  My Little Golden Sister. Wy-CM:39
  A Peck of Gold. R. Frost.
    Bo-HF:21, La-PV:196
  The Spell of the Yukon. R. Service.
    Er-FA:365
GOLD RUSHES: see CALIFORNIA - GOLD
    DISCOVERIES; KLONDIKE
GOLDEN GLOW
  The Faithless Flowers.
    M. Widdemer. Hu-MP:258, Th-AS:84
GOLDENROD
  The Golden Rod. F. Sherman.
    Fe-FP:221, Ja-PA:6
GOLDFINCHES
  A Goldfinch. W. de la Mare.
    Re-BS:38
  Goldfinches. M. Van Doren.
    Ca-BP:16
  The Hollow Wood. E. Thomas.
    Pa-RE:10
  Yellow Flutterings. J. Keats.
    Co-BBW:254
GOLDFISH: see also HUMOR -
    GOLDFISH
  Goldfish. R. Howell. Su-FVI:68
  Goldfish. H. Nemerov. Ls-NY:190
GOLF: see also HUMOR - GOLF
  The City of Golf. R. Murray.
    Mo-SD:47
  The Golf Links. S. Cleghorn.
    Er-FA:268, Fe-PL:421, Ke-PP:61,
    Kr-OF:180
  Golfers. I. Layton. Mo-SD:42
  Mullion. A. Herbert. Mo-SD:40
  A Public Nuisance. R. Arkell.
    Mo-SD:43
  Seaside Golf. J. Betjeman.
    Fl-HH:4, Ha-PP:115, Mo-SD:39
GOLGOTHA
  Golgotha Is a Mountain.
    A. Bontemps. Bo-AN:77,
    Hu-PN:219
GOLIATH
  David and Goliath. N. Crouch.
    Ox-BC:41
  Little David. Ab-MO:80
  The Pebble. E. Wylie.
    Tr-MR:156, Un-MA:281
GONGS: see BELLS
GOOD AND EVIL: see also VICE
  Borderline. R. Grenville.
    De-FS:102
  Chiliasm. R. Eberhart. Pl-EI:77
  The Counsels of O'Riordan the
    Rain Maker. T. O'Bolger.
    Co-PI:149

Erda. V. Konrick. De-FS:130

Fret Not Thyself Because of
Evildoers. Bible. O.T.
Psalms. Ar-TP3:210

Gentilesse. G. Chaucer. Rv-CB:61

Good and Bad. J. Stephens.
Un-MB:267

Haukyn's Coat. W. Langland.
Ga-S:135

I Heard an Angel Singing. W. Blake.
Rv-CB:621

In Men Whom Men Condemn as Ill.
J. Miller. Fe-PL:293

It Was Wrong to Do This, Said
the Angel. S. Crane. Sh-AP:143

Lack of Steadfastness. G. Chaucer.
Rv-CB:62

Lament. W. Williams. Ca-VT:58

Lament for One's Self. R. Pitter.
Go-BP:276

Life at War. D. Levertov.
Ca-VT:515

May. Shao Hsün-mei. Hs-TC:126

The Pardon. W. Langland.
Ga-S:126

Song under Shadow. W. Benét.
Tr-MR:198

The Two Spirits. P. Shelley.
De-CH:323, Ho-WR:189

Winter Mask. A. Tate. Ho-P:269

The World Turns. . . . T. Eliot.
Ar-TP3:210

GOOD FRIDAY: see JESUS CHRIST -
CRUCIFIXION; LENT

GOOD GROOMING: see GROOMING,
PERSONAL

GOODNESS: see also GOOD AND EVIL;
HUMOR - GOODNESS

Be Kind. Le-OE:33

Beauty. E-Yeh-Shure. Ar-TP3:213,
Fe-FP:20

Better than Gold. A. Ryan.
Er-FA:9

Blessed Are They That Sow.
A. Ben Yitzhak. Me-PH:83

Character of a Happy Life.
H. Wotton. Al-VBP:221,
Ni-JP:169, Pa-GTB:63

The Description of a Good Boy.
H. Dixon. Ox-BC:54

The Earth Is the Lord's.
Bible. O.T. Psalms.
Ar-TP3:188, Bo-FP:249, Fe-FP:232,
Pa-SG:198, Pl-EI:214

The Eternal. E. Tegner. Pa-SG:206

Fairies. M. Chute. Th-AS:8

For Modes of Faith Let Graceless
Zealots Fight. A. Pope. Go-BP:179

The Golden Rule. Ch-B:108

Good, Better, Best. Sp-AS:(35)

The Good Parson. G. Chaucer.
Go-BP:42

Here in This Book. W. Cole. Co-BB:11

I Am Waiting. V. Howard. Ba-HI:46

John Wesley's Rule. J. Wesley.
Bo-FP:301, Er-FA:29

Let Us Now Praise Famous Men.
Bible. O.T. Ecclesiastes.
Gr-CT:376

Love Thy Country. G. Dodington.
Rv-CB:514

The Man of Life Upright.
T. Campion. Al-VBP:219, De-CH:637,
Go-BP:44, Ha-PO:197, Rv-CB:273

O May I Join the Choir Invisible.
G. Eliot. Ox-BN:617

The Old Woman of Leeds. Wr-RM:97

The Rich Interior Life.
R. Eberhart. Tr-MR:250

The Sermon on the Mount. Bible.
N.T. Matthew. Un-GT:312

Shrine to What Should Be.
M. Evans. Hu-NN:77

A Song. L. Binyon. Un-MB:157

The Song of Creatures. St. Francis
of Assisi. Pa-SG:202

A Song of Nezahualcoyotl.
Nezahualcoyotl. Br-MW:26

To Be Honest, to Be Kind.
R. Stevenson. Fe-PL:311

To My Youngest Kinsman, R.L.
A. Chear. Ox-BC:34

To Theodora. Ox-BC:47

A True Story. A. Taylor. De-TT:102

Virtue. G. Herbert. Al-VBP:343,
De-CH:431, Ha-PO:199, Rv-CB:352

The Way of Life. Laotzu. Mc-MK:220

What a Piece of Work Is Man.
Sophocles. Pa-SG:194

Whatsoever Things Are True. Bible.
N.T. Philippians. Ar-TP3:210

When Mother Reads Aloud.
Fe-FP:31, Hu-MP:25

Ye That Do the Master's Will.
C. Wesley. Go-BP:181

GOPHERS

Gopher Song. Da-SC:96

A Little Gopher Man. N. Scott.
Bo-FP:97

GORILLAS: see APES

GOSSIP: see also HUMOR - GOSSIP;
SLANDER

The Cambridge Ladies. e. cummings.
Al-VBP:1202, Ha-PO:243, Ke-PP:93,
Rv-CB:991

The Continuity. P. Blackburn.
Ad-CI:105

Fire. Mo-MGT:177

Forget It. Fe-PL:294

Glass Houses. E. Robinson.
Tr-MR:161

Gossip. L. Robertson. Th-AS:205

Grandeur of Ghosts. S. Sassoon.
Un-MB:317

GOSSIP — cont'd.
  He Thinks of Those Who Have Spoken
    Evil of His Beloved. W. Yeats.
    Co-EL:37, Co-PI:206, No-CL:4
  Mrs. Mason's Basin. Br-FF:(10),
    Ir-BB:192, Mo-MGT:141, Rv-ON:86
  Mutual Charges of Molestation.
    Da-SC:45
  The Scars Remaining.
    S. Coleridge. Ox-BN:161
GOTHAM, ENG.
  The Men of Gotham. T. Peacock.
    Al-VBP:715, De-CH:193, Hi-WP I:91,
    Ho-WR:108, Sp-OG:344
GOULD, BENJAMIN APTHORP
  A Welcome to Dr. Benjamin Apthorp
    Gould. O. Holmes. Pl-IO:169
GOURDS (VINE)
  The Gourd-Heads. W. Barney.
    De-FS:14
GOVERNMENT: see also SATIRE -
    GOVERNMENT
  Builders of the State. R. Gilder.
    Se-PR:202
  Lysistrata. Aristophanes. Ba-PO:15
  Preliminary Draft of a World
    Constitution. Ba-PO:115
GOVERNMENTAL INVESTIGATIONS: see
    SATIRE - GOVERNMENTAL
    INVESTIGATIONS
GOYA Y LUCIENTES, FRANCISCO
    JOSÉ DE
  A Coney Island of the Mind.
    L. Ferlinghetti. Mo-BG:182,
    Wi-LT:701
  Disasters of War: Goya at the
    Museum. B. Deutsch. Cr-WS:35
  Goya. A. Voznesensky. Ca-MR:68
GRACE AT MEALS: see BLESSINGS
GRACKLES
  A Grackle Observed. L. Mueller.
    St-H:144
GRADUATIONS: see COMMENCEMENTS
GRAFFITI
  Aphrodite Metropolis. K. Fearing
    Ad-CI:74
  Black Is Beautiful. La-IH:99
  Inscription for the Tank.
    J. Wright. Br-TC:487
  Scribbled on a Once-Clean Wall.
    P. Christensen. La-IH:54
  Social Comment. L. Fishberg.
    La-IH:28
  Thesis, Antithesis, and Nostalgia.
    A. Dugan. Ad-CI:75
GRAFT: see CORRUPTION
GRAIL: see also ARTHUR, KING
  The Vision of Sir Launfal.
    J. Lowell.
    Pa-OM:210

GRAIN: see also names of grains,
    as WHEAT
  The Ripe and Bearded Barley.
    Cl-DT:86, Co-BN:126, Gr-CT:313,
    Gr-GB:46
GRAMMAR: see also HUMOR - GRAMMAR
  The Nine Parts of Speech. Gr-EC:135
GRANADA, SP.
  The Road to Granada. A. Ketchum.
    Pa-HT:104
GRAND CANYON
  Clouds Across the Canyon.
    J. Fletcher. Pa-HT:56
  Old Love. K. Wilson. Sc-TN:240
  View. J. Miles. Sh-RP:165
GRANDCHILDREN
  What of Olden Times. Ho-SD:57
GRANDFATHERS: see also HUMOR -
    GRANDFATHERS
  After a Line by John Peale
    Bishop. D. Justice. En-PC:228
  Anton and Yaro. M. Oliver.
    St-H:168
  Ballad of the Two Grandfathers.
    N. Guillén. Be-UL:53
  Brother. T. Ikenaga. Le-TA:23
  Camp Chums. R. Waldo. Hu-MP:41
  Direction. A. Lopez. Al-WW:10
  An Epitaph on His Grandfather.
    T. Shipman. Rv-CB:470
  Fishing. A. Pratt. Al-WW:101
  The Gardeners. D. Ignatow.
    Ls-NY:226
  Grandad's Pipe. I. Serraillier.
    St-FS:75
  Grandfather. L. Henson. Ni-CD:62
  Grandfather in the Old Men's Home.
    W. Merwin. Wi-LT:768
  Grandfather's Clock. H. Work.
    Er-FA:351
  Grandfather's Ghost. J. Brennan.
    De-FS:36
  Grandparents. R. Lowell.
    Mc-EA:106, Wi-LT:585
  I've Got a New Book from My
    Grandfather Hyde. L. Jackson.
    Br-SS:79, Fe-FP:45, Sh-RP:146
  My Last Afternoon with Uncle
    Devereux Winslow. R. Lowell.
    Ca-VT:447
  My Old Grandfather. J. Alumasa.
    Le-M:179
  The October Anniversary.
    S. Slezsky. Mo-MI:55
  Original Sin: A Short Story.
    R. Warren. Wi-LT:839
  Picture in an Old Frame.
    E. Chaffee. Ke-TF:68
  Under Your Voice, among Legends.
    P. Harris. Sc-TN:81

The Unemployed Blacksmith.
J. Woods. Mc-WS:147
GRANDMOTHERS: see also HUMOR -
GRANDMOTHERS
After My Grandfather's Death:
A Poem of the China Clock.
M. Oliver. St-H:167
Afternoon with Grandmother.
B. Huff. Fe-FP:42
Amy Elizabeth Ermyntrude Annie.
Q. Hopper. Ar-TP3:7
Crewel. N. Willard. Sc-TN:233
The Cupboard. W. de la Mare.
Ar-TP3:7, Au-SP:131, Bo-FP:51,
Fe-FP:42, Fr-MP:8, St-FS:76
The Elegance of Memory.
K. Kgositsile. Be-MA:147
For My Grandmother. C. Cullen.
Ad-PB:91, Bo-AN:88, Ca-VT:241,
Un-MA:571
Gift. C. Freeman. Ab-MO:75,
Ad-PB:397, Hu-PN:435, Lo-TY:255
Grandma Snores. N. Tolstoy.
Mo-MI:51
The Grandmother. E. Roberts.
Hu-MP:14
Grandmother Sleeps. L. Bahe.
Ni-CD:11
Grandmother's Visit. W. Wise.
Sh-RP:313
Grandparents. R. Lowell.
Mc-EA:106, Wi-LT:585
Granny. Ca-MU:16
Growing Old. R. Henderson.
Br-BC:121
I Am Ashamed. Le-IB:74
Irish Grandmother. K. Edelman.
Br-AF:43, Br-SS:136
A Juju of My Own. L. Bethune.
Ad-PB:309, Hu-PN:414
Light the Lamps Up, Lamplighter.
E. Farjeon. Br-SS:28, De-CH:439
Lineage. M. Walker. Ad-BO:59,
Ad-PB:148, Be-MA:77
Little Girl. Ir-BB:262, Mo-MGT:115
Little Maid, Little Maid, Where
Have You Been? Sp-TM:31
My Grandmother. E. Jennings.
To-MP:111
My Grandmother. K. Shapiro.
Ca-VT:372
My Grandmother's Wrinkles.
H. Nishitani. Le-TA:24
My Granny Is a Witch.
A. Mikhailov. Bo-RU:52
#4. D. Long. Ad-PB:404
Ride Away. Ar-TP3:101,
Mo-MGT:213, Mo-TL:79, St-FS:201
Somebody's Coming. J. Tippett.
Fr-MP:11

Song of a Woman Crying for the
Dead Baby Son of Her Daughter.
Tr-US I:244
GRANITE
Old New Hampshire. J. Holmes.
Se-PR:274
GRANT, ULYSSES SIMPSON
Achilles Deatheridge.
E. Masters. Br-AF:73
The Aged Stranger. B. Harte.
Br-AF:74
GRANTCHESTER, ENG.
The Old Vicarage, Grantchester.
R. Brooke. Ga-FB:239,
Hi-WP II:129, Pa-HT:120, Un-MB:326
GRAPES: see also WINE
The Fox and the Grapes. J. Lauren.
Bo-HF:70, Un-GT:170
Grapes. A. Pushkin. Ho-LP:27,
Pa-SG:98
Grapes. A. Shamri. Ho-TY:360
GRASS: see also HAY AND HAYING;
LAWNS
About the Grass. J. Weil. Ls-NY:228
Being Awakened. M. Saito. Sh-AM:145
A Blade of Grass. O. Williams.
Ls-NY:58
The Blades of Grass. S. Crane.
Sh-AP:144, Un-MA:147
Dreaming. T. Miles. Ho-CT:5
Former Barn Lot. M. Van Doren.
Ga-FB:296, Ha-LO:53, La-PV:166,
Un-MA:467
The Grass. W. Cardwell. Le-M:36
The Grass. E. Dickinson.
Fe-FP:223, Sh-RP:105
Grass. C. Sandburg. Cr-WS:19,
Fe-PL:155, Ga-FB:219, Un-MA:200
Grass Is Greener. J. Van Billiard.
La-GI:14
Grass Looks. S. Pilkington.
Le-WR:29
The Grass on the Mountain.
M. Austin. Br-AF:146
Grassroots. C. Sandburg. La-RM:75
Hayfield. A. Fisher. Sh-RP:206
Heavenly Grass. T. Williams.
Gr-EC:61
I Saw a Green Beetle. S. Kershaw.
Le-M:129
I'm Glad the Sky Is Painted Blue.
Au-SP:320, Ch-B:110, Fr-MP:12,
Lo-LL:107
Irradiations. J. Fletcher.
Un-MA:313
The Little Grass. Chu Tzu-ch'ing.
Hs-TC:12
Long Feud. L. Untermeyer.
Un-**MA**:306
Reconciliation. AE. Tr-MR:250
Residue. T. MacNeill. Sa-B:60

GRASS — cont'd.
  Song of Myself. W. Whitman.
    Al-VBP:928, Sh-AP:69, Un-MA:44,46
  Spring Grass. C. Sandburg.
    Bo-HF:53, Fe-FP:224
  The Stars. Ping Hsin. Hs-TC:21
  Stories from Kansas. W. Stafford.
    La-RM:74
  Stuff. A. Mitchell. Sm-MK:190
  Summer Is Golden. G. Sellers.
    Le-M:77
  Swinging, Swaying Grass. Issa.
    Be-MC:21
  Talking in Their Sleep. E. Thomas.
    Co-BN:29
  The Voice of the Grass. S. Boyle.
    Bo-FP:228
GRASSHOPPERS: see also HUMOR -
    GRASSHOPPERS
  An Explanation of the Grasshopper.
    V. Lindsay. Au-SP:288, Bo-FP:272,
    Fe-FP:133
  First Song of the Thunder.
    Da-SC:65, Le-OE:74
  A Game of Tag. Bo-FP:141,
    Ir-BB:86
  The Grasshopper. Anacreon.
    Un-GT:76
  The Grasshopper. A. Cowley.
    Ho-WR:64
  Grasshopper. Issa. Le-IS:5
  The Grasshopper. R. Lovelace.
    De-CH:540
  The Grasshopper. D. McCord.
    Lo-LL:21
  The Grasshopper and the Cricket.
    L. Hunt. Bo-FP:273, Co-BBW:218,
    Ox-BN:220, Un-GT:77
  Grasshopper Green. Au-SP:77,
    Bo-FP:271, Fe-FP:132, Hu-MP:304,
    It-HB:14, St-FS:111
  Grasshopper Hop-o-the Grasses.
    G. Hallock. Sh-RP:329
  The Grasshoppers. D. Aldis.
    Co-IW:24
  Grasshoppers. J. Clare. Co-BBW:224
  Grasshoppers Are Chirping.
    Chigetsu-Ni. Do-TS:30
  The Grasshopper's Song. H. Bialik.
    Fe-FP:476, Ha-YA:65
  High June. C. Morin. Ir-BB:22
  My Grasshopper. M. Livingston.
    Br-SG:53
  On the Grasshopper and Cricket.
    J. Keats. Bo-FP:272, Co-BBW:228,
    Gr-EC:6, Ho-WR:66, Rd-OA:89,
    Rv-CB:741, Sp-OG:302, Un-GT:77
  One Guess. R. Frost. Co-PU:101
  Shiv and the Grasshopper.
    R. Kipling. Go-BP:84

  The Voice That Beautifies the
    Land. Da-SC:65, Le-OE:11,
    Pa-SG:139, Tr-US II:251
  What a Burdensome Life.
    K. Tsuda. Sh-AM:174
GRATITUDE: see also SATIRE -
    GRATITUDE; THANKSGIVING DAY
  Bankrupt. C. Sayres. Fe-PL:295
  Birth. A. Gilboa. Me-PH:116
  A Boy's Prayer. H. Beeching.
    Mo-SD:193, Se-PR:313
  Bring Out Your Hair Ornaments.
    Le-IB:96
  The Earth. J. Very. Sh-AP:65
  For the Sisters of the Hôtel
    Dieu. A. Klein. Do-WH:85
  Give Ear, O Ye Heavens. Bible.
    O.T. Deuteronomy. Bo-FP:163
  God Has Been Good to Me.
    F. Keyes. Ke-TF:454
  Grace Before Sleep. S. Teasdale.
    Tr-MR:52
  The C Psalm. Bible. O.T.
    Psalms. Ma-YA:74
  Hymn. A. Young. Pl-EI:212
  i thank You God. E. Cummings.
    Pl-EI:195, Tr-MR:22
  I Will Extol Thee, O Lord. Bible.
    O.T. Psalms. Me-PH:20
  In Him We Live. J. Very. Sh-AP:66
  A Little Song of Life. L. Reese.
    Fe-FP:18, Gr-TG:23, Hu-MP:61,
    Th-AS:179
  Most She Touched Me by Her Muteness.
    E. Dickinson. Re-BS:42
  New Year's. C. Reznikoff.
    Ca-VT:189
  O Light Invisible, We Praise Thee.
    T. Eliot. Tr-MR:148
  On Re-Reading the Complete Works of
    an Elder Poet. W. Scott.
    Pl-ML:45
  A Parting Guest. J. Riley.
    Sp-OG:278
  The People of Tao-Chou. Po Chu-i.
    Gr-CT:374
  Pied Beauty. G. Hopkins.
    Al-VBP:1062, Bo-GJ:47, Er-FA:461,
    Ga-S:16, Hi-WP II:37, Ho-LP:47,
    Ma-FW:101, Mc-PR:182, Mc-WK:16,
    No-CL:269, Ox-BN:865, Pa-GTB:390,
    Pl-EI:124, Re-TW:89, Sm-MK:222,
    Tr-MR:25, Un-GT:246, Un-MB:39,
    Wi-LT:42
  Praise. Bo-FP:163
  A Prayer. R. Weston. Au-SP:356,
    Bo-FP:4
  Prayer. Bi-IT:38
  A Psalm. Bible. O.T. Psalms.
    Au-SP:374, Se-PR:210

Psalm 100. Bible. O.T. Psalms.
Ar-TP3:188, Br-SS:81, Fe-FP:85,
Hu-MP:287, Ma-YA:76, Pl-US:52,
Sh-RF:92
Remembrance. V. Zhukovsky.
Pa-SG:15
Rhapsody. W. Braithwaite.
Bo-AN:15, Bo-HF:156
Rising from Illness. Chang Hsiu-ya.
Pa-MV:30
The Sacrament of Sleep.
J. Oxenham. Fe-PL:332
Sight. W. Gibson. Un-MB:242
Singing the Reapers Homeward Come.
Se-PR:212
A Song of Thanksgiving. Bible.
O.T. Psalms. Me-PH:28
The Sunlight on the Garden.
L. MacNeice. Br-TC:279,
Pa-GTB:515
Thank You. L. Breek. Mo-MI:29
A Thank-You. W. Canton. Gr-TG:42
Thank You, Pretty Cow.
A. and J. Taylor. Bo-FP:69,
Hi-GD:9, Hu-MP:197, Ox-BC:123
Thanks. N. Gale. Un-GT:245
Thanks. An-IP:(28)
Thanks in Old Age. W. Whitman.
Ke-TF:160
Thanksgiving. L. Driscoll.
Ha-YA:134, La-PH:20
Thanksgiving. I. Eastwick.
Br-SG:103
Thanksgiving. R. Emerson.
Au-SP:373, Bo-FP:161
A Thanksgiving. J. Taylor.
Gr-TG:70
Thanksgiving for the Beauty of
His Providence. T. Traherne.
Sm-LG:38
Thanksgiving for the Earth.
E. Goudge. Ha-YA:138
A Thanksgiving to God for His
House. R. Herrick. Al-VBP:337,
De-TT:168, Gr-CT:269
This Happy Day. H. Behn.
Ar-TP3:176
To Our Babies. Le-IB:60
We Thank Thee. Fe-FP:29, Hu-MP:31
Whether We Mutter a Thank You or Not.
Gr-TG:39
GRAVEDIGGERS
Near to This Stone. De-CH:654
GRAVES, ROBERT
Poet with Sea Horse. A. Reid.
Pl-ML:52
GRAVES: see CEMETERIES; TOMBS
GRAVEYARDS: see CEMETERIES
GRAY (COLOR)
Gray Is a Feeling. C. Peifly.
La-GI:29
GREAT BEAR: see URSA MAJOR

GREAT BRITAIN: see ENGLAND;
SCOTLAND; WALES
GREAT-GRANDPARENTS
Almost Ninety. R. Whitman.
Ls-NY:134
The Sampler. N. Turner. Br-BC:80
GREAT LAKES: see names of lakes, as
ERIE, LAKE
GREAT SMOKY MOUNTAINS
Evening in the Great Smokies.
D. Heyward. Pa-HT:44
GREATNESS: see also FAME; HONOR;
HUMOR - GREATNESS; SATIRE -
GREATNESS
After-Thought. W. Wordsworth.
Ox-BN:91
The Clouds. W. Williams. Ca-VT:62
Earth. J. Wheelock. Tr-MR:42,
Un-MA:343
Grandeur of Ghosts. S. Sassoon.
Un-MB:317
The Greatest City. W. Whitman.
La-OC:71, Sh-RP:263
I Think Continually of Those Who
Were Truly Great. S. Spender.
Al-VBP:1235, Gr-CT:377, Ha-PO:222,
Pl-EI:158, Tr-MR:166, Un-MB:477,
Wi-LT:496
In a Child's Album. W. Wordsworth.
Bo-FP:232, Ch-B:17, Ox-BN:92
Let Us Consider where the Great
Men Are. D. Schwartz. Un-MA:619
The Man from the Crowd. S. Foss.
Fe-PL:422
My Olson Elegy. I. Feldman. Ho-P:67
My Sad Captains. T. Gunn.
En-PC:278, Wi-LT:726
Ode in a Night of Overhanging
Weather. V. McHugh. Mc-WK:175
Oxford. L. Johnson. Ox-BN:949
Praise of King Mtesa. Tr-US I:102
Praise Song for a Chief. Tr-US I:87
Praise Song for a Chief. Tr-US I:94
Rembrandt to Rembrandt.
E. Robinson. Sm-PT:53
The Snow. Mao Tse-tung. Hs-TC:363
Song of a Sick Chief. Tr-US I:211
A Song of Greatness. Ar-TP3:35,
Br-AF:37, Br-BC:126, Fe-FP:24,
Sh-RP:103
The Stars. Ping Hsin. Hs-TC:21
To the New King Mutara II Rwogera.
Tr-US I:97
The Yellow Crane Pavilion.
Mao Tse-tung. Hs-TC:364
GRECO, EL
El Greco. C. Trypanis. Ls-NY:177
GREECE: see also AEGEAN SEA; ELEUSIS;
GODS AND GODDESSES; GREEK VERSE;
and names of cities, as ATHENS,
GR.; and regions, as CRETE
Canto I. E.Pound. Ca-VT:90, Un-MA:297

GREECE - cont'd.
England. M. Moore. Un-MA:350
The First Day. N. Weiss. Ls-NY:240
Hellas. P. Shelley. Gr-CT:441
The Islands. H. D. Un-MA:339
The Isles of Greece.
   D. Capetanakis. Pa-GTB:524
Nemea. L. Durrell. Pa-GTB:525
Oenone. A. Tennyson. Al-VBP:851
The Oracles. A. Housman. Co-RG:24
Proem to Hellenics. W. Landor.
   Al-VBP:702
Rain Falls on Ioannina. M. Piercy.
   Sc-TN:182
A Spring Wind. B. Spencer.
   Pa-GTB:518
GREECE - HISTORY AND PATRIOTISM
Epitaph for Chaeroneia.
   Aristotle. Pa-SG:7
The Glorious Victory of Navarino.
   Hi-FO:214
The God of War. Aeschylus.
   Ke-PP:6
The Great Dead at Thermopylae.
   Simonides. Pa-SG:8
Greek War Song. K. Rigas.
   Hi-FO:212
The Isles of Greece. G. Byron.
   Al-VBP:735, Co-RG:20, Gr-CT:437,
   Ke-TF:405, Ox-BN:265, Rv-CB:690
Marco Bozzaris. F. Halleck.
   Hi-FO:208
On the Army of Spartans, Who Died
   at Thermopylae. Simonides of
   Ceos. Gr-CT:378
Variations on Simonides. G. Ely.
   Ls-NY:28
GREED: see also HUMOR - GREED;
   MISERS
The Abyss. Ya-Hsüân. Pa-MV:153
Admonition to a Traveller.
   W. Wordsworth. Pa-GTB:252
Against Exploiters. Tr-CB:33,
   Tr-US I:65
A Basket of Summer Fruit. Bible.
   O.T. Amos. Me-PH:49
Covetousness. P. Idley. Ox-BC:5
The Dance of Death.
   F. Garcia Lorca. Bl-FP:70
The Dog in the River. Plato.
   Mc-PR:27
The Goose. A. Tennyson. Gr-EC:154
The Greedy Boy. E. Turner.
   Ir-BB:96
A Greedy Friar. G. Chaucer.
   Ha-PO:51
Greedy Richard. J. Taylor.
   Ir-BB:100, Ox-BC:121
Greedy Tom. Ag-HE:15, Ir-BB:192,
   St-FS:11
Griselda. E. Farjeon. Un-GB:23,
   Un-GT:100

Hands. G. Thompson. Jo-SA:9,
   Jo-VC:15
The Mouse and the Cake. E. Cook.
   Ox-BC:209
Peter Grimes. G. Crabbe.
   Hi-WP II:65
The Prophecies Against Moab,
   Judah, and Israel. Bible.
   O.T. Amos. Me-PH:48
Thirty Bob a Week. J. Davidson.
   Co-EL:143
The White Man's Soul. J. Very.
   Kr-OF:16
Willy Wood. Ag-HE:72
Wilt Thou Lend Me Thy Mare?
   Co-EL:57, Co-PU:67, Rv-CB:423
GREEK VERSE
After the Rain. Y. Ritsos.
   Mo-TS:19
Alexandrian Kings. C. Cavafy.
   Gr-CC:109
The Ass in the Lion's Skin.
   Aesop. Gr-EC:198, Rd-OA:167
Be Still, My Soul. Archilochus.
   Pa-SG:177
The Beginning of Day. Euripides.
   Pa-SG:104
The Boar Hunt. Homer. Ma-FW:230
The Breed of Athletes. Euripides.
   Mo-SD:163
Candles. C. Cavafy. Sm-MK:217
The Children's Song. Fe-FP:476
Chorus from Medea. Euripides.
   Pa-SG:16
The Climb to Virtue. Simonides.
   Pa-SG:209
Country Music. Plato. Pa-SG:132
The Dog in the River. Plato.
   Mc-PR:27
The Dolphin's Tomb. Anyte.
   Rd-OA:147
An Eclipse. Pindar. Pa-SG:209
Epitaph for Chaeroneia.
   Aristotle. Pa-SG:7
Epitaph on a Dog. Gr-EC:86
The First Step. C. Cavafy.
   Pl-ML:34
Flowers for Heliodora. Meleager.
   Gr-SS:83
Flute Song. Pa-SG:150
Folk Song. Bo-FP:213
The Fox and the Hedgehog.
   Archilochus. Bo-FP:81
From the Greek of Julianus.
   W. Cowper. Sp-OG:49
A Garden. Sappho. Pa-SG:127
God Leads the Way. Cleanthes.
   Pl-EI:185
The God of War. Aeschylus.
   Ke-PP:6
The Grasshopper. Anacreon.
   Un-GT:76

The Great Dead at Thermopylae.
 Simonides. Pa-SG:8
The Greek Anthology. Krinagoras.
 Mo-SD:52
The Greek Anthology. Br-SM:155
Greek Anthology, I-V.
 Un-MW:173-174
Greek War Song. K. Rigas.
 Hi-FO:212
The Gusts of Winter Are Gone.
 Meleager. Pa-SG:80
Heraclitus. W. Cory. Al-VBP:973,
 Co-EL:74, Co-PU:149, Hi-WP II:21,
 Ox-BN:648, Pa-SG:13, Pl-ML:143,
 Rv-CB:875
How Can a Man Die Better.
 Tyrtaeus. Pa-SG:6
I Bless This Man. Pindar.
 Mo-SD:181
I'll Twine White Violets.
 Meleager. Pa-SG:35
In Less than Two and Twenty Years.
 Asclepiades. Ho-LP:64
In the Spring. Ibycus. Pa-SG:86
In the Spring. Meleager. Pa-SG:67
Ithaka. C. Cavafy. Ni-JP:15
The Landsman. Moschus. Pa-SG:174
A Maltese Dog. Tymnès. Ar-TP3:50,
 Co-BBW:99, Gr-EC:86, Sm-LG:85
The Man and the Weasel. Plato.
 Mc-PR:27
The Moon Has Set. Sappho.
 Gr-CT:404
Mythistorema XXIII. G. Seferis.
 Gr-BT:147
Nero's Term. C. Cavafy. Cr-WS:17
Night. Sappho. Pa-SG:63
No Joy Without Love. Mimnerus.
 Pa-SG:75
The North Wind and the Child.
 Bo-FP:174
Not to Die. Simonides. Pa-SG:10
Now This Was the Reply Odysseus
 Made. Homer. Pl-ML:7
O for the Wings of a Dove.
 Euripides. Go-BP:155, Pa-SG:175
Old Age. Sophocles. Pa-SG:182
Palm Sunday. Bo-FP:245
Plato's Tomb. Sm-LG:275
The Power of Music. Pindar.
 Pl-US:102
The Raven. Nicharchus. Pl-US:61
The Sixth Book of Homer's Iliads.
 Homer. Al-VBP:148
Sleep upon the World. Alcman.
 Gr-CT:409
The Swan and Goose. Aesop.
 Fe-FP:475, Pl-US:60
There Are No Gods. Euripides.
 Pl-EI:70
Vesper. Alcman.
 Rd-OA:206

Waiting for the Barbarians.
 C. Cavafy. Gr-CC:173
What a Piece of Work Is Man.
 Sophocles. Pa-SG:194
Where Shall Wisdom Be Found?
 Euripides. Pa-SG:186, Pl-US:108
Whoever It Was. Sophocles.
 Ba-PO:74
A Window in the Breast. Gr-EC:219,
 Pa-SG:15
A Young Bride. Sappho. Pa-SG:50
GREEKS IN THE UNITED STATES
 Consider These Greek Widows of
 America. D. Georgakas.
 Sc-TN:59
GREELEY, HORACE
 Statue in a Blizzard. R. Keener.
 Ls-NY:160
GREEN (COLOR): see also HUMOR -
 GREEN (COLOR)
 The End of Summer. Basho.
 Sh-RP:64
 Green. D. Lawrence. Co-EL:95,
 Un-MB:290
 Green Bedroom. R. Roseliep.
 St-H:182
 Green Is in Summertime Trees.
 M. Sunderland. La-GI:27
 Green Is like a Meadow of Grass.
 B. Smith. La-GI:27
 Lines. W. Williams. Su-FVI:2
 The March Problem. G. Garrett.
 Ho-LP:36
 Sir Gawain and the Green
 Knight. Ma-YA:21
GREEN MOUNTAIN BOYS: see ALLEN,
 ETHAN; FORT TICONDEROGA,
 BATTLE, 1775
GREENE, NATHANAEL
 To the Memory of the Brave
 Americans. P. Freneau.
 Fe-PL:166, Sh-AP:14, Vi-PP:134
GREENHOUSES
 Big Wind. T. Roethke. Al-VBP:1233,
 Bo-GJ:213, Ca-VT:285, Mo-BG:120
 Child on Top of a Greenhouse.
 T. Roethke. Ca-VT:286,
 Co-EL:137, Du-RG:54, Gr-BT:12,
 Ha-LO:101, Hi-WP I:110
 The Task. W. Cowper. Go-BP:23
 Trouble in the Greenhouse.
 M. Dodge. Br-SG:77
GREENLAND
 Mount Koonak: A Song of Arsut.
 Da-SC:36
 A Song from Sanerut. Da-SC:36
GREETINGS: see also HUMOR -
 GREETINGS; WELCOMES
 Anna-Marie, Love, Up Is the Sun.
 W. Scott. Al-VBP:677
 At Christmas. Cl-FC:89
 Chanticleer. W. Austin. Ga-S:77

GREETINGS — cont'd.
  The Chief Men of a Village
    Answer the Greeting of
    Travelers. Tr-US I:162
  A Cock Sat in the Yew Tree.
    De-CH:498, Ir-BB:24
  Comin' thro' the Rye. R. Burns.
    Er-FA:112
  Good Morning. M. Sipe.
    Ar-TP3:70, Au-SP:87
  Good Morning. Bo-FP:295,
    Su-FVI:48
  Good Night and Good Morning.
    R. Milnes. Ox-BC:171
  A Greeting. W. Davies. Mc-WK:82,
    Tr-MR:23, Un-MB:175
  Greeting. Gr-TG:42
  Greeting of Tane. Tr-US II:71
  Hello! L. Garnett. Br-SS:140
  Hello and Goodbye. B. Lee.
    Ja-PC:60
  I Met a Mexican. Da-SC:12
  Improvised Song of Joy. Le-IB:100,
    Tr-US I:13
  Misty-Moisty Was the Morn.
    Gr-GB:37
  The New Year. Br-FW:14
  O Mistress Mine. W. Shakespeare.
    Al-VBP:189, Bo-GJ:140, Co-BL:112,
    Er-FA:174, Ga-FB:31, Gr-CC:83,
    Hi-WP II:53, Ho-LP:7, Ke-TF:103,
    Mo-GR:125, No-CL:117, Pa-GTB:17,
    Rv-CB:194, Un-MW:183
  An Old Christmas Greeting.
    Ar-TP3:192, Br-SS:98, Ch-B:53,
    Fe-FP:88, Hu-MP:344
  One Misty, Moisty Morning.
    Mother Goose. Ar-TP3:166,
    Cl-DT:85, Ir-BB:212, La-PV:92,
    Li-LB:55, Mo-MGT:179, Mo-NR:14,
    Rv-ON:89, Wr-RM:50
  Pack, Clouds, Away! T. Heywood.
    Al-VBP:271, Bl-OB:42, De-CH:7,
    Pa-GTB:32, Re-BS:9, Re-TW:52,
    Tu-WW:11, Un-MW:6
  Song of Greeting to a Missionary's
    Wife. Tr-US I:79
  Susan Blue. K. Greenaway.
    Ar-TP3:11, Ch-B:28, Hu-MP:136
  There Were Three Sisters. On-TW:13
  This Happy Day. H. Behn.
    Ar-TP3:176
  To Miss Ferrier. R. Burns.
    Rv-CB:623
GREGORY, ANNE
  For Anne Gregory. W. Yeats.
    Co-PI:204, Er-FA:105, Gr-BT:47,
    Gr-CC:15, Ha-PO:182, Mc-WS:63,
    Wi-LT:86
GREGORY, ISABELLA AUGUSTA, LADY
    The Municipal Gallery Revisited.
    W. Yeats. Pa-GTB:432

GRENDEL
  Beowulf. Al-VBP:1, Ma-YA:14
GRENVILLE, SIR RICHARD
  The Revenge. A. Tennyson.
    Co-RM:45, Hi-FO:134, Pa-OM:154,
    Sp-OG:60
GRIEF: see also CRYING; DIRGES;
    HUMOR - GRIEF; LAMENTS;
    SATIRE - GRIEF; TEARS
  The Absent. E. Muir. Tr-MR:273
  All Day It Has Rained. A. Lewis.
    Hi-WP I:28, Pa-GTB:543
  Alone. C. Bialik. Me-PH:73
  And Be Her Mother, Just as She
    Was Mine. Ke-TF:145
  Andree Rexroth. R. Rexroth.
    Ca-VT:269
  The Animals Mourn with Eve.
    C. Rossetti. Rd-OA:197
  Annabel Lee. E. Poe. Al-VBP:877,
    Co-BL:130, Co-RG:150, De-CH:56,
    De-TT:191, Er-FA:61, Fe-FP:503,
    Hu-MP:431, Li-SR:67, No-CL:68,
    Pa-OM:258, Sh-AP:61, Sm-LG:273,
    Sp-OG:265, Un-GT:163
  Any Human to Another. C. Cullen.
    Tr-MR:160
  The Appeal. E. Brontë.
    Go-BP:149, Ox-BN:599
  Arapaho Ghost Dance Song. Ba-PO:111
  Atalanta in Calydon.
    A. Swinburne. Al-VBP:1041
  Autumn. W. de la Mare. Gr-CC:46
  Awake. M. Coleridge. Ox-BN:926
  Ayii, Ayii, Ayii (That Big Man).
    Ho-SD:79
  The Ball Poem. J. Berryman.
    La-OC:86. Un-MA:641
  Ballad. J. Gay. Al-VBP:522
  Bonnie George Campbell. Al-VBP:54,
    De-CH:41, Fo-OG:20, Gr-GB:250,
    Ox-BB:341, Rv-CB:419
  The Bourgeois Poet, #18.
    K. Shapiro. St-H:201
  Break, Break, Break. A. Tennyson.
    Bl-OB:51, Bo-GJ:182, De-CH:211,
    Ga-FB:128, Ha-PO:137, Ma-YA:192,
    Ox-BN:485, Pa-GTB:331, Sp-OG:267
  Bredon Hill. A. Housman. Cl-DT:44,
    No-CL:125, Un-MB:98, Un-MW:99
  The Broken String. Tr-CB:51,
    Tr-US I:76
  Care-Charmer Sleep. S. Daniel.
    Al-VBP:158, Pa-GTB:22, Rv-CB:180
  The Carousel. G. Oden.
    Ad-PB:185, Be-MA:95, Bo-AN:159
  Chinook Sad Song. Da-SC:16
  The Churchyard on the Sands.
    Lord De Tabley. De-CH:346,
    Ox-BN:792
  Come Up from the Fields, Father.
    W. Whitman. Ni-JP:76, Un-MA:77

The Comforters. D. Shorter.
   De-CH:259
Complaint of a Widow over Her
   Dying Son. Tr-US I:157
Composed in Spring. R. Burns.
   Co-BN:141, Rv-CB:621
Coronach. W. Scott. Al-VBP:672,
   De-CH:163, Ho-WR:119, Ma-YA:145,
   Pa-GTB:235
Corpus Christi Carol (The Falcon).
   Al-VBP:36, Ga-S:200, Gr-CC:163,
   Gr-CT:186, Gr-GB:308, Ma-FW:257,
   Rv-CB:13, Sm-MK:36
Couplets, II. Tr-US II:136
Crucifixion. R. Benally. Ba-HI:139
A Cry. F. Bianco. No-CL:261
The Cypress. T. Peacock.
   De-CH:251, No-CL:245
Daddy. C. Begay. Ba-HI:91
Dance Song on the Death of a Girl
   Named Rutenag. Tr-US II:4
Dance Songs, IV. Tr-US I:199
Dark Girl. A. Bontemps. Pe-SS:148
David's Lament. Bible. O.T.
   Samuel. Gr-CT:343
David's Lament for Jonathan.
   P. Abélard. Ga-S:162
Dead Boy. J. Ransom. Br-TC:336
Death-Bed. A. Rowse. Hi-WP II:26
Death-Dance Song. Tr-US II:243
Death Is a Clean Cold Word.
   R. Richmond. Go-BP:230
Deathwatch. M. Harper. Ad-PB:317
Desolation Is a Delicate Thing.
   E. Wylie. Un-MA:278
Dirge for Robin Hood. A. Munday.
   Bl-OB:152, De-CH:77, Ho-WR:116,
   Re-TW:71, Rv-CB:163
Ditty. W. Gibson. Ls-NY:333
Do Not Go Gentle into That Good
   Night. D. Thomas. Al-VBP:1247,
   Br-TC:439, Er-FA:40, Gr-BT:173,
   Ha-PO:126, Hi-WP II:30, Ke-PP:25,
   Un-MB:504, Wi-LT:551
Donal Oge: Grief of a Girl's
   Heart. Co-PI:56
The Dove. W. Barnes. Re-BS:36
Earth. M. Rosenfeld. Ho-TY:80
The Earth, Late Choked. T. Lodge.
   Al-VBP:132, Ha-PO:169
Echo's Lament for Narcissus.
   B. Jonson. Al-VBP:238,
   De-CH:236, Gr-CT:321
Elegy. G. Byron. Pa-GTB:233
Elegy. E. Millay. Un-MA:446
Elegy for Lucy Lloyd. L. Goch.
   Pa-SG:74
Elegy on Gordon Barber. G. Derwood.
   Er-FA:193, Wi-LT:683
Empty House. S. Spender. Hi-WP II:27
Envoy. F. Thompson. Ga-FB:335,
   Un-MB:91

Epic Song. Tr-US I:236
Epilogue to Rhymes and Rhythms.
   W. Henley. Al-VBP:1069
Escape. G. Johnson. Ad-PB:22
Eve. C. Rossetti. De-CH:166,
   Pa-GTB:375
The Exequy. H. King. Al-VBP:339,
   De-CH:256, No-CL:156
Exit. W. MacDonald. Al-VBP:1145
The Faery Queen. W. Raleigh.
   Al-VBP:93
Faery Song. J. Keats. De-CH:267,
   Sp-OG:170
Farewell to the Court. W. Ralegh.
   Rv-CB:153
Father and Son. F. Higgins.
   Co-PI:64
A Father's Notes of Woe.
   W. Scott. Ox-BN:125
Feathers and Moss. J. Ingelow.
   Li-SR:33
The First Grief. F. Hemans.
   De-CH:45
Flow Not So Fast. Al-VBP:357
The Flowers of the Forest.
   J. Elliott. Al-VBP:582,
   De-CH:176, Pa-GTB:120
Fly Hence, Shadows. J. Ford.
   Al-VBP:308
For a Child in Death. C. Mew.
   Un-MB:160
For de Lawd. L. Clifton.
   Ad-PB:306, Br-TC:71
For Johnny. J. Pudney. Hi-WP I:24
For Paul Laurence Dunbar. C. Cullen.
   Ad-PB:91, Bo-AN:89, Bo-HF:141
For Steph. W. Rose. Ni-CD:214
Four Things. P. Gearey. Ke-TF:241
Fowls in the Frith. Rv-CB:25
Fragment of a Bylina. A. Pushkin.
   Li-TU:83
The Freak Show. N. Willard.
   Sc-TN:229
Freezing Night. T'ao Hung Ching.
   Rx-LT:38
A Garden by the Sea. W. Morris.
   Al-VBP:1011, De-CH:461, No-CL:67,
   Ox-BN:788
Glories, Pleasures. J. Ford.
   Al-VBP:309
Gluskap's Hound. T. Roberts.
   Do-WH:61
Gold Wings Across the Sea.
   W. Morris. Gr-CT:74, Ox-BN:774
The Golden Net. W. Blake. Gr-SS:166
Gone. M. Coleridge. Ox-BN:924
The Grey Selchie of Sule Skerry.
   Ox-BB:91
Grief. E. Browning. Fe-PL:273,
   Ox-BN:463, Rv-CB:779
Grief. V. Contoski.
   Sc-TN:31

GRIEF — cont'd.
Grief Streams down My Chest.
   L. Jeffers. Ad-PB:173
Griefs for Dead Soldiers.
   T. Hughes. Go-BP:211
Haiku 6. E. Knight. Ra-BP:206
Harebell. J. Buxton. Sm-MK:2
The Harp That Once Through Tara's
   Halls. T. Moore. Al-VBP:710,
   Co-RG:20, Fe-PL:177, Ma-YA:170,
   Ox-BN:210
Heraclitus. W. Cory. Al-VBP:973,
   Co-EL:74, Co-PU:149, Hi-WP II:21,
   Ox-BN:648, Pa-SG:13, Pl-ML:143,
   Rv-CB:875
Hester. C. Lamb. Pa-GTB:234
Highland Mary. R. Burns.
   Al-VBP:650, Pa-GTB:151, Sp-OG:276
Hind Etin. Ox-BB:97
Home Burial. R. Frost. Pe-SS:15
How Can a Deep Love Seem Deep Love.
   Tu Mu. Le-MW:119
How Is the Gold Become Dim. Bible.
   O.T. Lamentations. Gr-CT:344
Hush. M. Leib. Ho-TY:89
Hymn of the Afflicted. Tr-US I:81
I Gazed Within. E. Brontë.
   Al-VBP:924
I Measure Every Grief I Meet.
   E. Dickinson. Un-MA:98
I Never Shall Love the Snow Again.
   R. Bridges. De-CH:258, Ga-FB:150
I Remember the Blue River.
   Mei Yao Ch'en. Rx-OH:44
I Remember the River at Wu Sung.
   Mei Yao Ch'en. Rx-OH:47
I Saw My Lady Weep. Al-VBP:355,
   Rv-CB:112
If Grief for Grief Can Touch Thee.
   E. Brontë. Ox-BN:599
If There Be Sorrow. M. Evans.
   Hu-NN:22, Hu-PN:308
Improvisation of the Dead Boy.
   M. de Andrade. An-TC:21
In London Town. M. Coleridge.
   Pa-RE:77
In Memoriam. A. Tennyson. Ha-PO:133,
   Ox-BN:493, 494, 495, Pa-GTB:336
In Memory of Ann Jones. D. Thomas.
   Un-MB:501
In Mourning for His Dead Wife.
   P'an Yueh. Rx-LT:31
In the Broad Daylight I Dream of
   My Dead Wife. Mei Yao Ch'en.
   Rx-OH:46
In the Garden at Swainston.
   A. Tennyson. Ox-BN:493
Indian Legend of the Canyon.
   J. Mahoney. Fi-BG:49
Institute Poems. M. Bruce. Ad-II:20
Isabella or The Pot of Basil.
   J. Keats. Al-VBP:783

Janet Waking. R. Ransom. Pe-SS:32,
   Re-TW:21, Sh-AP:181, Un-MA:410
John Kinsella's Lament for Mrs.
   Mary Moore. W. Yeats. Wi-LT:93
Keening. Tr-US II:309
Keith of Ravelston. S. Dobell.
   De-CH:299, De-TT:189, Ox-BN:661
Kent State, May 4, 1970.
   P. Goodman. Mo-TS:41
Lament. E. Millay. Kr-OF:183
Lament. Tr-US II:117
Lament. Tr-US II:89
Lament. Tr-US I:95
Lament. Tr-US I:86
Lament of a Widow over Her Dead
   Husband. Tr-US I:72
Lament of Huauri. Tr-US II:80
Lament: Sea-Burial of Toha's
   Daughter. Tr-US II:88
Lamentation. A. Pratt. Al-WW:108
The Last Pagan Mourns for Dark
   Rosaleen. J. Brennan. De-FS:36
The Last Quatrain of the Ballad of
   Emmett Till. G. Brooks.
   Ad-PB:155
A Leave-Taking. A. Swinburne.
   Al-VBP:1021, De-CH:340,
   Fe-PL:119, Ox-BN:795
Lesbia. R. Aldington. Fe-PL:116
The Lesson. E. Lucie-Smith.
   Br-TC:271, Gr-BT:20, To-MP:99
A Life-Lesson. J. Riley. Fe-PL:247
Lines Before Execution.
   C. Tichbourne. Al-VBP:138,
   Gr-CT:324, Ha-PO:132, Rv-CB:103
Lines on Receiving His Mother's
   Picture. W. Cowper. De-CH:38
The Little Fish Cries. D. Recht.
   Le-M:109
The Locust Swarm. Hsu Chao.
   Cr-WS:5, Rx-OH:123
London. W. Blake. Al-VBP:618,
   Gr-CT:304, Ha-PO:79, Ke-PP:49,
   Mo-GR:78, Ox-BN:24, Rv-CB:605
The Lonely Mother. F. Johnson.
   Hu-PN:91
The Lord of Biscay. A. Housman.
   Ni-JP:82
Lord, What I Most Loved You Tore
   from Me. A. Machado. Le-SW:65
Love in Exile. M. Blind. Ox-BN:849
A Lover's Lament. Pa-SG:59,
   Tr-US II:257
The Lowlands o' Holland. De-CH:345,
   Fo-OG:51, Ox-BB:348
Luck Tips the Balance. E. Greenberg.
   Ho-TY:309
Luke Havergal. E. Robinson.
   Gr-SS:138, Sh-AP:139, Sm-PT:7,
   Un-MA:123, Wi-LT:99
Lully, Lulley. De-CH:470

Lydia Is Gone This Many a Year.
L. Reese. Bo-GJ:236, De-CH:261,
Gr-CC:11

The Maid Forsaken. E. Mörike.
Un-R:111

Maiden's Song. P. Heyse. Un-R:101

Manerathiak's Song. Do-WH:54

Mariana. A. Tennyson. Al-VBP:845,
De-CH:297, Ho-WR:155, Ox-BN:473,
Rv-CB:795

Marvel No More. T. Wyatt.
Rv-CB:81

The Mask. E. Browning. Ox-BN:463,
Rv-CB:778

Mater Dolorosa. W. Barnes.
De-CH:265

Midnight Lamentation. H. Monro.
Al-VBP:1140

Mirthful Lunacy. T. Stoddart.
Ox-BN:530

The Mither's Lament. S. Smith.
Co-PU:151

Modern Love VI. G. Meredith.
Al-VBP:982

Modo and Alciphron. S. Warner.
Un-MB:375

Monna Innominata. C. Rossetti.
Al-VBP:994, Ox-BN:718

Moonlight. S. Teasdale. Ca-VT:76,
Co-PU:154

Moorland Night. C. Mew. Al-VBP:1111

The Mourning Bride. W. Congreve.
Al-VBP:520

Mourning for Akutagawa. M. Saito.
Sh-AM:146

Mourning Song. Da-SC:53

Mourning Song for Modana. Da-SC:54,
Tr-US II:217

My Grief on the Sea. Pa-SG:62

My Life Closed Twice.
E. Dickinson. Al-VBP:1000,
Ke-TF:243, Rv-CB:894, Un-MA:96,
Un-MW:89, Wi-LT:16

My November Guest. R. Frost.
Al-VBP:1125, Bo-HF:130, Fe-PL:388,
No-CL:280

Nahuatl Poem. Ho-LP:85

The Nation's Drum Has Fallen
Down. Da-SC:53

The New House. E. Thomas.
Un-MB:215

The New Pieta: For the Mothers
and Children of Detroit.
J. Jordan. Ad-PB:303

No Worst, There Is None.
G. Hopkins. Ke-PP:5, Ox-BN:870,
Pa-GTB:395, Rv-CB:944, Un-MB:46,
Wi-LT:49

Now Goeth Sun under Wood. Rv-CB:26

Oh, No More, No More. J. Ford.
Al-VBP:309

O Sing unto My Roundelay.
T. Chatterton. De-CH:249,
Ho-WR:152

O Sorrow! J. Keats. De-CH:240

O What if the Fowler? C. Dalmon.
Co-BBW:240, De-CH:337, Re-BS:24

Ode on Intimations of Immortality.
W. Wordsworth. Al-VBP:662,
Br-BC:18, Er-FA:157, Ga-FB:101,
Gr-CT:436, Ha-PO:206, Ox-BN:84,
Pa-GTB:308, Pl-EI:59

Oenone. A. Tennyson. Al-VBP:851

Of Course I Prayed.
E. Dickinson. Un-MA:97

On a Certain Ruler in Memory of
Former Rulers. Da-SC:174

On One Who Died Discovering Her
Kindness. J. Sheffield.
No-CL:74

On the Death of a New Born Child.
Mei Yao Ch'en. Rx-OH:41

On the Death of a Wife. Le-OE:133

On the Death of Anne Brontë.
C. Brontë. Al-VBP:916

On the Death of Atahualpa.
Bi-IT:154

On the Death of His Baby Son.
Su Tung P'o. Rx-OH:69

On the Death of His Wife.
Mei Yao Ch'en. Rx-OH:45

Oriflamme. J. Fauset. Ad-PB:18

The Orphan's Song. S. Dobell.
De-CH:41, Ox-BN:668

Out of the Cradle Endlessly
Rocking. W. Whitman.
Al-VBP:936, Un-MA:66

Paddling Song. Le-OE:52

Pain. M. Als. Sa-B:39

Patch-Shaneen. J. Synge. Co-PI:188

Patterns. A. Lowell. Bo-HF:116,
Co-BL:142, Cr-WS:115, Er-FA:65,
Mo-GR:39, Pa-OM:262, Pe-OA:47,
Sm-PT:18, Un-MA:156

The Pearl. M. Breslasu. Mc-AC:89

Peeling Onions. A. Rich. Mo-BG:38

Perhaps (a Dirge). Wen I-to.
Hs-TC:65

Poem. C. Herbert. Sa-B:37

Poor Crying Cricket. Kikaku.
Be-CS:23

The Precept of Silence.
L. Johnson. Al-VBP:1103,
Un-MB:155

Proud of My Broken Heart.
E. Dickinson. Al-VBP:1002

A Question. J. Synge. Co-EL:84,
Co-PI:187, Un-MB:181

Remembrance. E. Brontë. De-CH:262,
Er-FA:457, Go-BP:148, Ox-BN:601

Reuben Bright. E. Robinson.
Co-RM:233, Sh-AP:141, Un-MA:119

GRIEF — cont'd.
  The Road.   C. Aiken.   Un-MA:428
  Rose Aylmer. W. Landor. Al-VBP:705,
    Co-RG:149, De-CH:347, Er-FA:115,
    No-CL:134, Ox-BN:185, Rv-CB:667
  Sadness of Life.   Be-AP:34
  Shakespeare's Mourners. J. Tabb.
    Sh-AP:135
  She Dwelt among the Untrodden Ways.
    W. Wordsworth.   Al-VBP:656,
    Ga-FB:50, Li-SR:106, Mc-PR:179,
    Ox-BN:62, Pa-GTB:179, Rv-CB:631
  She Weeps over Rahoon. J. Joyce.
    Al-VBP:1150
  The Shower. H. Vaughan. Al-VBP:465
  Shut Out That Moon. T. Hardy.
    Al-VBP:1047
  Simple Autumnal. L. Bogan.
    Un-MA:491
  Sleep Brings No Joy. E. Brontë.
    Al-VBP:921
  The Snow. C. Dyment. Sm-MK:138
  Snowflakes. H. Longfellow.
    Bo-FP:169, Ch-B:52, Gr-CT:396,
    Ho-WR:179
  Sohrab and Rustum. M. Arnold.
    Pa-GTB:363
  Solitude. E. Wilcox. Er-FA:3,
    Fe-PL:291
  Song. W. Blunt. Al-VBP:1056
  Song. M. Holman. Jo-SA:86
  Song. A. Lewis. Wi-LT:763
  Song. P. Massinger. Al-VBP:298
  Song. E. Sitwell. Gr-CC:34
  Song from a Story. Tr-US I:30
  Song from The Bride's Tragedy.
    T. Beddoes. Gr-CC:71
  Song of a Ghost. Tr-US II:239
  Song of a Mother for Her Dead Son.
    Tr-US II:20
  Song of a Mother Whose Child Has
    Been Left Behind on the
    Caravan Trail. Tr-US I:61
  Song of a Widow. Tr-US II:18
  Song of a Woman Crying for the
    Dead Baby Son of Her Daughter.
    Tr-US I:244
  Song of Intoxication.
    F. Nietzsche. Un-R:33
  Song of the Last Moments.
    Tr-US I:58
  Song of Thyrsis. P. Freneau.
    Al-VBP:606
  Song of War. Tr-US I:203
  Sonnet. W. Drummond. Al-VBP:302
  Sonnet on the Death of His Wife.
    J. Masefield. Go-BP:150
  The Sonnets. W. Shakespeare.
    No-CL:87
  Sonnets. W. Wordsworth.
    Al-VBP:659, Ox-BN:91, Pa-GTB:198,
    Rv-CB:647

  Sonnets from the Portuguese, XXXV.
    E. Browning.   Al-VBP:817
  Sorrow. Chu Shu Chen. Rx-LT:107
  Sorrow. A. de Vere. Ho-WR:234
  Sorrow. D. Lawrence. Pa-GTB:457
  Sorrow. Mei Yao Ch'en. Rx-OH:42
  Sorrow Is the Only Faithful One.
    O. Dodson. Ad-PB:132, Bo-AN:122,
    Jo-SA:123
  The Sorrow of Love. W. Yeats.
    Un-MB:111
  The Sparrow's Dirge. J. Skelton.
    Sm-LG:85
  Spring and Fall. G. Hopkins.
    Bo-GJ:249, Gr-CT:317, Ha-PO:148,
    Ke-PP:99, Pa-GTB:392, Re-TW:62,
    Wi-LT:44
  The Spring Waters. Ping Hsin.
    Hs-TC:24
  The Stone. W. Gibson. Un-MB:241
  Stop All the Clocks. W. Auden.
    Hi-WP II:29, Un-MB:465, Un-MW:103
  Stormy Night in Autumn.
    Chu Shu Chen. Rx-OH:133
  Summer Dawn. W. Morris. Al-VBP:1010,
    Ox-BN:784, Rv-CB:930
  Sun, Moon and Stars. Gr-TG:68
  Suspiria. H. Longfellow. Al-VBP:825
  Tears Flow in My Heart.
    P. Verlaine. Pa-SG:184
  That Harp You Play So Well.
    M. Moore. Un-MA:349
  Thinking of a Friend Lost in the
    Tibetan War. Chang Chi.
    Cr-WS:8
  The Three Fishers. C. Kingsley.
    Co-SS:205, Fe-PL:418, Pa-OM:117,
    Sp-OG:91
  The Three Roses. W. Landor.
    No-CL:126
  Thyrsis. M. Arnold. Ox-BN:637
  Time Does Not Bring Relief.
    E. Millay. Ga-FB:84
  Time's Mutability. B. Brecht.
    Co-EL:121
  To an Old Tune. Hsin Ch'i Chi.
    Rx-LT:104
  To His Lute. W. Drummond.
    Al-VBP:304, Pa-GTB:24, Pl-US:13
  To His Wife. J. Skelton. Rv-CB:69
  To Mary. C. Wolfe. Al-VBP:739
  To My Brother Miguel. C. Vallejo.
    Pe-M:13
  To One in Paradise. E. Poe.
    Al-VBP:874, Fe-PL:101, Un-MW:207
  To Primroses Filled with Morning
    Dew. R. Herrick. Al-VBP:329,
    Ha-PP:258
  To the Dead. Hu Feng. Hs-TC:376
  To the Tune "A Lonely Flute on
    the Phoenix Terrace."
    Li Ch'ing Chao. Rx-LT:96

The Toys. C. Patmore. Al-VBP:973,
 Er-FA:142, Rv-CB:876
The Triumph of Time. A. Swinburne.
 Al-VBP:1017
Twice. C. Rossetti. Al-VBP:999,
 Ox-BN:714
Ulalume. E. Poe. Al-VBP:869,
 Sh-AP:58
Under the Holly-Bough.
 C. Mackay. Ke-TF:48
The Unquiet Grave. Al-VBP:39,
 De-CH:342, Gr-GB:131, Hi-WP II:17,
 Ox-BB:96, Rv-CB:51
Untitled. Wang Ching-chih.
 Hs-TC:45
Uvlunuaq's Song. Tr-US I:16
Vala, or the Four Zoas. W. Blake.
 Al-VBP:622
Venus and Adonis. W. Browne.
 No-CL:57
Victory in Defeat. E. Markham.
 Fe-PL:301
The Virgin Mother. D. Lawrence.
 Al-VBP:1157
Vittoria Colonna. H. Longfellow.
 Gr-CC:87
Wailing Song. Bi-IT:97
War. J. Langland. Du-SH:85,
 En-PC:161, Ha-TP:75
War in Chang-An City. Wang Tsan.
 Ba-PO:41, Cr-WS:12, Ke-PP:8
The Watchers. W. Braithwaite.
 Hu-PN:48
Watchman, What of the Night?
 A. Swinburne. Ho-WR:200
Weep No More. J. Fletcher.
 Al-VBP:284, De-CH:420
Weep You No More. Al-VBP:357,
 De-CH:266, Go-BP:145, Gr-CT:410
The Weeping. F. Garcia Lorca.
 Le-SW:67
Weeping Mary. Ga-S:142
When My Canary. Shiki.
 Ar-TP3:54, Be-CS:45
Where Shall the Lover Rest.
 W. Scott. Al-VBP:670,
 De-CH:263, Pa-GTB:191
Why Dost Thou Weep, My Child?
 Le-OE:29
A Widow Bird. P. Shelley. Bl-OB:96,
 De-CH:235, De-TT:155, Fe-FP:296,
 Hi-WP I:20, Hu-MP:234, Ox-BN:303,
 Pa-GTB:275, Re-TW:69, Rv-CB:694
The Widow's Lament. W. Williams.
 Wi-LT:197
The Wife of Usher's Well.
 Ar-TP3:20, De-CH:424, De-TT:171,
 Gr-CT:134, Ma-BB:37, Ox-BB:94,
 Pa-OM:91, Rv-CB:36
Willy Drowned in Yarrow. De-CH:728,
 Pa-GTB:122

Witness to Death. R. Lattimore.
 Ca-VT:282
A Woman Mourns for Her Husband.
 Kr-OF:20
The Woodspurge. D. Rossetti.
 Ox-BN:682, Pa-GTB:372, Rv-CB:886
Words for a Friend Who Was
 Accidentally Shot. D. Etter.
 St-H:60
The World's Sorrow. A. Reisen.
 Ho-TY:70
GRIFFINS
 A Gryphon Sighted in an Iowa
 Flyway. N. Westerfield.
 Ls-NY:192
 Yet Gentle Will the Griffin Be.
 V. Lindsay. Gr-EC:88, La-PV:55,
 Th-AS:19
GRINS: see SMILES
GROCERY STORES: see also HUMOR -
 GROCERY STORES
 Counters. E. Coatsworth.
 Au-SP:117, Hu-MP:146, Pe-FB:40
 Sunday. E. Coatsworth. Br-AF:213,
 La-OC:32, Mc-WK:56
GROOMING, PERSONAL: see also
 HUMOR - GROOMING, PERSONAL;
 SATIRE - GROOMING, PERSONAL
 Combing. G. Cardiff. Ni-CD:50
 Government Injunction. J. Miles.
 Hu-PN:554
 Her Powder-Box. W. Stead.
 Ls-NY:324
 Rising in Winter. Emperor Ch'ien
 Wen. Rx-LT:44
 See, I Can Do It. D. Aldis.
 Ho-GC:14
 Spring Blossom. E. Attah. Ab-MO:24
 To the Tune "Spring at Wu Ling."
 Li Ch'ing Chao. Rx-LT:94
GROSBEAKS
 Gic to Har. K. Rexroth. Ca-BP:23,
 Kh-VA:68
GROTTOES: see CAVES
GROUND: see EARTH
GROUND-HOG DAY: see CANDLEMAS
GROUND HOGS: see WOODCHUCKS
GROUSE: see PTARMIGANS
GROWING OLD: see also HUMOR -
 GROWING OLD; WRINKLES
 About Face. U. Harsen. Ke-TF:157
 Academic. T. Roethke. Co-EL:43
 After Seeing "Lear." M. Syrkin.
 Ls-NY:82
 Age in Prospect. R. Jeffers.
 Un-MA:360
 The Ageing Athlete. N. Weiss.
 Mo-SD:173
 All the World's a Stage.
 W. Shakespeare. Er-FA:151,
 Fe-PL:257, Ha-PO:257, Ma-YA:67,
 Un-GT:85

GROWING OLD — <u>cont'd</u>.
  Another and the Same. S. Rogers.
    Ox-BN:48
  April Inventory. W. Snodgrass.
    Br-TC:398, Mc-EA:148, Wi-LT:819
  At Casterbridge Fair. T. Hardy.
    Ox-BN:832
  Autumn. H. Wolfe. Fe-PL:268
  Confidential. W. Scott. Co-EL:41
  The Descent. W. Williams. En-PC:3
  The Eastern Gate. Le-MW:120,
    Ma-FW:88
  The Ebb Tide. R. Southey. Ox-BN:176
  The End of the Play. W. Thackeray.
    Er-FA:520
  The Folly of Being Comforted.
    W. Yeats. Go-BP:130
  For Jan. J. Bruchac. Ni-CD:44
  Grieve Not, Ladies. A. Branch.
    Er-FA:156
  Growing Old. M. Arnold. Er-FA:167
  Growing Older. C. Towne. Ke-TF:154
  Halcyon Days. W. Whitman. Ke-TF:155
  A Hand-Mirror. W. Whitman.
    Rv-CB:850
  I Look into My Glass. T. Hardy.
    Rv-CB:939
  I'm Just a Stranger Here, Heaven
    Is My Home. C. Clemmons.
    Ad-PB:489
  Indian Summer. M. Leib. Ho-TY:92
  It's Somebody's Birthday.
    L. Norris. Ls-NY:80
  The Lady's Complaint.
    T. Heath-Stubbs. Br-TC:178
  Lament for Old Age. Tr-US II:91
  The Last Chapter. W. de la Mare.
    Un-MB:203
  Last Days of Alice. A. Tate.
    Sh-AP:200
  Learning by Doing. H. Nemerov.
    Br-TC:313
  Let No Charitable Hope. E. Wylie.
    Ca-VT:104, Un-MA:278, Wi-LT:206
  The Long Hill. S. Teasdale.
    Un-MA:265
  Long Time a Child. H. Coleridge.
    Ox-BN:398, Rv-CB:758
  Lord! Would Men Let Me Alone.
    C. Cotton. Go-BP:20
  A Minuet on Reaching the Age of
    Fifty. G. Santayana. Er-FA:154
  My Muse and I, ere Youth and
    Spirits Fled. G. Colman.
    Co-EL:40
  Now Older Grown. M. Caruthers.
    Ke-TF:132
  Old-Age Chant. Da-SC:105
  On Falling Asleep to Birdsong.
    W. Meredith. En-PC:174
  On Growing Older. J. Wheatley.
    Ke-TF:159

  On Himself. R. Herrick. Gr-CT:272
  One Flesh. E. Jennings. To-MP:94
  Prospect Beach. L. Lipsitz.
    Ca-VT:716
  Rabbi Ben Ezra. R. Browning.
    Br-BC:142, Er-FA:175, Ga-FB:129,
    Ox-BN:578
  The Sands of Time. R. Howard.
    De-FS:107
  Second Blossoming. R. Lechlitner.
    Ke-TF:136
  Snow Storm. Tu Fu. Rx-OH:6
  Song of an Old Man. Tr-US II:144
  A Sonnet. Tai Wang-shu. Hs-TC:182
  The Soul's Dark Cottage.
    E. Waller. Gr-CT:375
  The Tea Shop. E. Pound.
    Hi-WP II:164
  Tell Me Now. Wang Chi. Sm-LG:391
  That Time of Year Thou Mayest in
    Me Behold. W. Shakespeare.
    Al-VBP:205, Ga-FB:34, Gr-CT:318,
    Ha-PO:253, No-CL:85, Pa-GTB:18,
    Rv-CB:230
  To Each His Own. M. Bracker.
    Ke-TF:138
  Too Late. F. Ludlow. Fe-PL:261
  Upon His Picture. T. Randolph.
    Rv-CB:363
  Way out West. I. Baraka. Ad-PB:252
  We Grow Old. I. Emiot. Ho-TY:316
  The Wind and the Rain.
    W. Shakespeare. Al-VBP:190,
    Hi-WP I:114, Ho-WR:21, Mc-WK:224,
    Rv-CB:204, Sm-LG:403
  Youth. M. Tsvetayeva. Ca-MR:138
GROWING UP: see also HUMOR —
    GROWING UP
  Adulthood. N. Giovanni. Be-MA:69
  Adventures. A. Kramer. Br-BC:116
  The Album. C. Day Lewis.
    Gr-BT:93
  Ambition. E. Agnew. Ar-TP3:137
  Ambition. P. George. Al-WW:120
  Answer Me This, I Pray. Re-RR:26
  Ballade of Lost Objects.
    P. McGinley. En-PC:72
  The Big Boy. Mo-MGT:76
  Birthday. E. Emans. Br-BC:138
  Birthday Garden. I. Eastwick.
    Br-BC:58
  A Certain Age. P. McGinley.
    Du-SH:44
  Child and Maiden. C. Sedley.
    Al-VBP:498, Pa-GTB:71
  Child Wife. J. Keith. De-FS:115
  The Christening. W. de la Mare.
    Br-BC:30
  Climb. W. Welles. Br-BC:128
  The Conjurer. E. Lucas. Br-BC:117,
    Co-PM:200
  Counting. H. Behn. Gr-EC:124

Dreams. N. Giovanni. Ad-PB:454
Escape. T. McGrath. St-H:123
Experience. A. Kilmer. Br-BC:46
Five-in-June. L. Borie. Br-BC:53
Five Years Old. M. Allen.
   Br-BC:52
For Maria at Four. J. Becker.
   Br-BC:52
For Theresa. N. Giovanni.
   Be-MA:172
Going into Breeches.
   C. and M. Lamb. Ox-BC:145
Going Where. P. Irving. Al-WW:78
Growing. F. Frost. Br-BC:72
Growing Up. H. Behn. Au-SP:120,
   Br-BC:118, Br-SS:47, La-PH:60,
   La-PV:163
Growing Up. A. Guiterman.
   Br-BC:81
Growing Up. A. Milne. Br-BC:107,
   Gr-TG:16
Growing Up. Br-BC:48, Fr-MP:3
Grownups. M. Duskin. Le-M:134
Growth. S. Tanikawa. Sh-AM:129
I Like. C. Tringress. St-FS:104
i remember how she sang.
   R. Penny. Ad-PB:388
If No One Ever Marries Me.
   L. Alma-Tadema. Br-BC:111,
   Un-GT:13
I'm Ceded. E. Dickinson.
   Al-VBP:1001
I'm Wife. E. Dickinson.
   Al-VBP:1002
An Impetuous Resolve. J. Riley.
   Br-BC:114, Ir-BB:43
Indian Summer. D. Parker.
   Ke-TF:128
Intaglio. H. Coulette. En-PC:252
Joan's Door. E. Farjeon. Br-BC:80
John Plans. D. Pierce. Br-BC:111
The Little Duck. Joso. Au-SP:54,
   Le-IS:9, Su-FVI:72
Long-Expected One-and-Twenty.
   S. Johnson. No-CL:118
Long Time a Child. H. Coleridge.
   Ox-BN:398, Rv-CB:758
Looking Forward. R. Stevenson.
   Ox-BC:294
Make Me a Man. P. George.
   Al-WW:121
Maturity. D. Gallup. Mc-EA:146
Measure Me, Sky. L. Speyer.
   Ad-PE:46, Br-BC:129, Fe-FP:22,
   Hu-MP:63
The Men's Turn to Cry.
   C. Brzezinski. Me-WF:84
Middle-Aged Child. I. Hogan.
   Br-BC:74
Mirror in February. T. Kinsella.
   Pa-GTB:561

Modern Love XXX. G. Meredith.
   Al-VBP:983
Mother and Son. R. Thomas.
   Gr-BT:21
My Child. Y. Amichai. Mc-EA:104
My Plan. W. Chute. Br-BC:115,
   Fe-FP:112
Nursery Rhyme of Innocence and
   Experience. C. Causley.
   Bo-GJ:170, Hi-WP I:82
Of Flesh and Bone. I. Gardner.
   St-H:67
Old-Age Chant. Da-SC:105
Older Grown. K. Greenaway.
   Br-BC:130
Plans. D. Thompson. Br-BC:114
Portrait of a Girl with a Comic
   Book. P. McGinley. Pe-OA:198,
   Pe-SS:39
Prattle. J. Ciardi. Br-BC:109
The Rebellious Vine. H. Monro.
   Go-BP:277, Mc-WK:110
The Revolutionary. V. Watkins.
   Ls-NY:118
Rising Five. N. Nicholson.
   To-MP:69
Rites of Passage. A. Lorde.
   Ad-PB:249
Seven Times One. J. Ingelow.
   Br-BC:71, Fe-FP:50, Gr-TG:47,
   Hu-MP:70, Ke-TF:41, Ox-BN:720,
   Un-GT:14
Short History of Man. J. Holmes.
   Mc-WS:138
Six in June. M. Davies. Br-BC:57
Someone. J. Ciardi. Br-BC:16
Song for Naomi. I. Layton.
   Do-WH:80
Songs, II. Tr-US II:166
The Stone Frog. G. Pritchard.
   Co-PU:8, Ls-NY:226
Sunday Afternoon. D. Levertov.
   Pe-SS:55
The Sweet Red Rose. M. Dodge.
   Br-BC:119
Then. D. Aldis. Br-BC:108
There Was a Child Went Forth.
   W. Whitman. Br-BC:128, La-RM:164,
   Un-GT:307
The Time Has Come. S. Voronov.
   Mo-MI:41
Tree Birthdays. M. Davies.
   Br-BC:9
The Vanity of Human Wishes.
   J. Leax. Pe-M:65
We Play at Paste. E. Dickinson.
   Rv-CB:913
What Does the Little Birdie Say.
   A. Tennyson. Ch-B:44, Hu-MP:214
What's a Student. A. Round.
   Ke-TF:82

GROWING UP — cont'd.
When a Fellow's Four. M. Carr.
   Br-BC:49
When I Am Big, I Mean to Buy.
   M. Dodge. Br-BC:108
When I Grow Up. R. Holland.
   Br-BC:116
When I Grow Up. W. Wise.
   Br-BC:113
When I Was a Little Boy.
   Mother Goose. Tu-WW:15
When You and I Grow Up.
   K. Greenaway. Bo-FP:135,
   Ch-B:108, Hu-MP:174
Where I Took Hold of Life.
   R. Coffin. Br-BC:122
The Wind and the Rain.
   W. Shakespeare. Al-VBP:190,
   Hi-WP I:114, Ho-WR:21, Mc-WK:224,
   Rv-CB:204, Sm-LG:403
The Wise Child. E. Lucie-Smith.
   Ls-NY:229
A Year Later. M. Hoberman.
   Ho-ME:30
A Young Birch. R. Frost. Co-BN:152
The Young Girl's Song. A. Gordon.
   Pe-M:140
Young Soul. I. Baraka. Mo-TS:3
Youth Sings a Song of Rosebuds.
   C. Cullen. Fe-PL:258, Hu-PN:234
GROWTH
The Cycle Repeated. K. Chapin.
   Ls-NY:258
Not a Tree. T. Blackburn.
   Ls-NY:171
Puzzles. J. Drinkwater. Mc-WK:107
This Compost. W. Whitman. Un-MA:86
GRUNION
Grunion. M. Livingston. La-RM:97
Grunion. W. Rose. Ni-CD:218
GRYPHONS: see GRIFFINS
GUARDS: see also HUMOR - GUARDS;
   SATIRE - GUARDS
Buckingham Palace. A. Milne.
   Ke-TF:73, La-PV:206, Ox-BC:340
Lament of a Frontier Guard.
   Rihaku. Ca-VT:83
Night Watchmen. W. Garthwaite.
   Rd-SS:15
The Picket-Guard. E. Beers.
   Er-FA:187, Sp-OG:196
Song. H. Killigrew. De-CH:447
Then. W. de la Mare. Pa-RE:114
Vocation. R. Tagore. Fe-FP:484
GUELPHS
To the Guelf Faction.
   F. da San Geminiano. Hi-FO:85
GUEST, EDGAR ALBERT
Edgar A. Guest Syndicates The Old
   Woman Who Lived in a Shoe.
   L. Untermeyer. Co-FB:232,Un-MA:311

GUESTS: see also HUMOR -
   GUESTS; INVITATIONS
Doorbells. R. Field.   Ar-TP3:9,
   Fe-FP:323
Emmaus. R. Rilke. Go-BP:302
The Guest. W. Berry. Ha-TP:96
The Guest of Twilight.
   Cheng Ch'ou-yü. Pa-MV:42
Irish-American Dignitary.
   A. Clarke. Co-PI:26
The Man from Porlock.
   H. Bevington. Na-EO:38
Miss Jennie Jones. Bu-DY:30
Somebody's Coming. J. Tippett.
   Fr-MP:11
Visitors. H. Behn. Au-SP:132
The Visitors. E. Jennings.
   Go-BP:140
GUEVARA, ERNESTO (CHÉ)
Ché. D. Walcott. Sa-B:182
The Revolutionary Core: Ché
   Guevara. A. Raymond. Sa-B:184
GUIDES AND GUIDING: see DIRECTIONS
   TO PLACES; TOURISTS
GUILT: see also HUMOR - GUILT;
   SATIRE - GUILT
At Cooloolah. J. Wright.
   Un-MB:516
Black Are the Stars. R. Roseliep.
   De-FS:160
Confession. M. Marcus. Ba-PO:36
The Dirty Word. K. Shapiro.
   En-PC:132
Eve. C. Rossetti. De-CH:466,
   Pa-GTB:375
Forgive My Guilt. R. Coffin.
   Ba-PO:165, Du-RG:76
Guilt. A. Haushofer. Ba-PO:179
The Ides of March. R. Fuller.
   En-PC:115
Jacob and the Angel.
   Brother Antoninus. Tr-MR:72
Like a Murderer. I. Manger.
   Ho-TY:272
My Grandmother. E. Jennings.
   To-MP:111
My Old Grandfather. J. Alumasa.
   Le-M:179
The Pains of Sleep.
   S. Coleridge. Ox-BN:171,
   Rv-CB:662
The Peaceable Kingdom.
   M. Piercy. Br-TC:317
Poor Naked Wretches.
   W. Shakespeare. Ke-PP:22
R. G. E. R. Eberhart. Ls-NY:72
Song by Mr. Cypress. T. Peacock.
   Ox-BN:233
Tanist. J. Stephens. Ls-NY:98
They Are Ours. A. Magil. Hu-PN:533
The Trap. W. Beyer. Du-RG:108,
   Ha-PO:127

When Lovely Woman Stoops.
    O. Goldsmith. Al-VBP:586,
    Pa-GTB:131, Rv-CB:542
You Felons on Trial in Courts.
    W. Whitman. Rv-CB:853
GUINEA, AF.
    Guinea. J. Roumain. Lo-TY:92
GUINEA FOWLS: see HUMOR -
    GUINEA FOWLS
GUINEA PIGS: see HUMOR -
    GUINEA PIGS
GUINEVERE, QUEEN
    The Boy and the Mantle. Ox-BB:31
    Lancelot. E. Robinson. Sm-PT:178
    Near Avalon. W. Morris. Rv-CB:929
GUITARS
    The Guitar. G. Dusenbery. Sc-TN:37
    The Guitarist Tunes Up.
        F. Cornford. Co-EL:20
    Herder's Song. Tr-US I:39
    The Man with the Blue Guitar.
        W. Stevens. Ha-TP:3, Pe-SS:79,
        Pl-US:126
    To a Lady with a Guitar.
        P. Shelley. Pa-GTB:257
GUITEAU, CHARLES J.
    Charles Guiteau. Em-AF:460
    Garfield's Murder. Hi-TL:142
GULLS: see also HUMOR - GULLS
    Afternoon. Amagansett Beach.
        J. Wheelock. Co-BN:79, Ha-WR:33
    Arctic Tern in a Museum.
        E. Newsome. Hu-PN:71
    The Ballet of the Fifth Year.
        D. Schwartz. Br-TC:355
    Birds. R. Jeffers. Ca-BP:29,
        Ca-VT:120
    Cape Ann. T. Eliot. Bo-GJ:53,
        Ho-LP:50, Na-EO:35, Re-TW:83,
        Sm-LG:143
    The Echoing Cliff. A. Young.
        Re-BS:33
    The Gidgid-Bird. Tr-US I:245
    Gull. W. Smith. Ar-TP3:58
    Gull. B. Stuart. Ls-NY:214
    The Gull. M. Thwaites. Ni-JP:167
    The Gull. Le-IB:68
    Gulls. L. Speyer. Ho-TH:24
    Halcyon. H. D. Un-MA:338
    The Harbor. C. Sandburg. Ho-LP:51
    The Lives of Gulls and Children.
        H. Nemerov. Ni-JP:116
    A Question. De-PP:24
    The Sea Bird to the Wave.
        P. Colum. Sh-RP:87
    The Sea Gull. L. Jackson. Ma-FO:(5)
    Sea (Gull). G. Manin. Ad-II:55
    The Sea-Gull. Gr-GB:62
    The Sea Gull. Ch-B:91, Ma-FO:(6)
    The Sea Gull Curves His Wings.
        E. Coatsworth. Ar-TP3:58,
        Co-BBW:261, Cr-SS:15, Pe-FB:15

Seagull. S. Gash. Le-M:87
The Seagull. M. Howitt. Ox-BC:161
Seagulls. R. Francis. La-RM:99
Seagulls. P. Hubbell. La-PV:136
Seagulls. F. Savage. Du-SH:159
Seascape. B. Esbensen. Ar-TP3:164
Storm's End. L. Speyer. Ho-TH:27
A Talisman. M. Moore. Al-VBP:1174,
    Bo-GJ:199, Ho-LP:52, Un-MA:349
Three Seagulls. De-PP:24
Torn Down from Glory Daily.
    A. Sexton. Ha-WR:30
A Visit from the Sea.
    R. Stevenson. Sp-OG:294
A Walk in Late Summer. T. Roethke.
    Rd-OA:3
The Waves Are So Cold. Basho.
    Be-MC:12
GUMS AND RESINS
    The Gum-Gatherer. R. Frost.
        Mo-BG:60
GUNPOWDER: see HUMOR - GUNPOWDER
GUNPOWDER PLOT: see FAWKES, GUY
GUNS: see also HUMOR - GUNS;
    SATIRE - GUNS
    A. E. F. C. Sandburg. Un-MA:203
    Arms and the Boy. W. Owen.
        Er-FA:192, Ni-JP:78, Un-MB:367,
        Wi-LT:349
    Defensive Position. J. Manifold.
        Un-MB:514
    Gnomes, I. Tr-US I:124
    Grandpa's .45. W. Ransom. Ni-CD:201
    Gunnery Practice. J. Brinnin.
        Cr-WS:64
    I Have a Six-Shooter. On-TW:24
    Illegitimate Things. W. Williams.
        Un-MA:262
    Minor Owens. Fi-BG:55
    Screw Guns. R. Kipling.
        Al-VBP:1098
    A Shiny, Long, Blue-Black Fellow.
        Re-RR:21
    The .38. T. Joans. Be-MA:102,
        Hu-NN:83
    To a Military Rifle. Y. Winters.
        Un-MA:550
    Uncle Davy. Mo-MGT:188
    What the Bullet Sang. B. Harte.
        Rv-CB:935
GUYANA
    The Eye. J. Carew. Sa-B:15
    Guyanese Reflections.
        G. Escoffery. Sa-B:95
    On the Fourth Night of Hunger
        Strike. M. Carter. Sa-B:167
    This Is the Dark Time, My Love.
        M. Carter. Sa-B:16
GWYN, ELEANOR (NELL): see also
    HUMOR - GWYN, ELEANOR (NELL)
    Tyrannic Love. J. Dryden.
        Al-VBP:492

GYPSIES
   All Your Fortunes We Can Tell Ye.
      B. Jonson. Gr-CT:162
   At Laie's Tomb. O. Goga. Mc-AC:38
   Being Gypsy. B. Young. Ar-TP3:14,
      Au-SP:212
   The Caravan. M. Nightingale.
      Hu-MP:170
   Gipsies. J. Clare. Cl-DT:81,
      Gr-CT:164
   The Gipsy Girl. R. Hodgson.
      Un-MB:193
   Gipsy Jane. W. Rands. Ar-TP3:14,
      Au-SP:149, Fe-FP:305, Pe-FB:25
   The Gipsy Laddie. Bl-OB:70,
      Sm-LG:185
   The Gipsy Trail. R. Kipling.
      Pa-HT:82
   Gypsies. R. Browning. Bo-FP:99
   Gypsies. J. Clare. De-CH:74,
      Gr-CT:165, Rv-CB:721
   The Gypsy. E. Pound. Re-TW:111
   Hawicks Crossing. J. Stuart.
      De-FS:193
   I Was Riding to Poughkeepsie.
      M. Hoberman. Gr-EC:248
   The Idlers. E. Blunden. De-CH:74
   Jackie Faa. Gr-CT:162, Ma-BB:106,
      Ox-BB:249
   Meg Merrilies. J. Keats.
      Ar-TP3:14, Bl-OB:147, Bo-FP:100,
      Cl-FC:86, Ne-AM:14, Ox-BC:147,
      Re-TW:110, Rv-CB:749, Se-PR:322,
      Sm-LG:128, Sm-MK:110, Sp-OG:249
   My Mother Said. . . . Bl-OB:28,
      De-CH:535, Gr-EC:286, Ir-BB:10,
      Mo-MGT:159, Pa-RE:55
   The Orchard and the Heath.
      G. Meredith. Ox-BN:691
   The Penny Fiddle. R. Graves.
      Gr-EC:161, Su-FVI:32
   The Princess and the Gypsies.
      F. Cornford. Co-PT:57
   The Romanies in Town.
      A. Beresford. To-MP:198
   The Scholar Gypsy. M. Arnold.
      Al-VBP:964, Gr-CT:255, Ox-BN:628
   Sons of the Kings. J. Agnew.
      Br-BC:62
   The Tale the Hermit Told.
      A. Reid. Co-PT:31
   There Cam' Seven Egyptians.
      De-CH:534
   Two Spanish Gypsy Lullabies.
      Ma-FW:66
   Where Do Gipsies Come from?
      H. Bashford. De-CH:76
   Wild Thyme. E. Farjeon. Br-SS:3
   The Wraggle Taggle Gipsies. Ar-TP3:15,
      De-Ch:75, Fe-FP:509, Ho-WR:48,
      Hu-MP:155, Mc-WS:163, Na-EO:33,
      Re-TW:124, Rv-CB:436, Un-GT:96

HABIT: see also HUMOR - HABIT
   Beyond the Snow Belt. M. Oliver.
      St-H:163
   A Builder's Lesson. J. O'Reilly.
      Fe-PL:295
   The Calf-Path. S. Foss. Fe-PL:3
   I Have to Have It. D. Aldis.
      Au-SP:185
   The Words. D. Wagoner. Du-SH:30,
      Mo-TS:52
HACKENSACK, N.J.: see HUMOR -
   HACKENSACK, N.J.
HADES: see HELL
HAGAR
   Hagar Speaks to Sarah.
      G. Howard. Ke-TF:147
   Hagar's Last Night in Abraham's
      House. I. Manger. Ho-TY:277
   Sarah Speaks to Hagar.
      G. Howard. Ke-TF:148
HAGGIS: see FOOD AND EATING;
   PUDDINGS
HAIFA, ISR.
   Jews at Haifa. R. Jarrell.
      Un-MA:649
HAIKU: see JAPANESE VERSE
HAIL: see also SLEET
   August Hail. J. Cunningham.
      Ha-PO:100
   Electrical Storm. E. Bishop.
      Ha-WR:11
   Hail. Issa. Le-MW:89
   Hail on the Pine Trees. Basho.
      Hu-MP:278
   Riddles of the Weather. Gr-GB:37
   The Whirl-Blast. W. Wordsworth.
      De-TT:162
HAIR: see also BALDNESS; BARBERS;
   HUMOR - HAIR; PIGTAILS (HAIR)
   Braid, Grow to the Waist. Gr-BB:24
   Combing. G. Cardiff. Ni-CD:50
   Goldenhair. J. Joyce.
      Co-BL:86, Gr-CC:73, Gr-CT:89,
      Ha-LO:3, Sh-RP:83, Th-AS:69
   Leofric and Godiva. W. Landor.
      Gr-CC:90
   Oh, Who Is That Young Sinner.
      A. Housman. Rv-CB:949
   On Getting a Natural. D. Randall.
      Ad-PB:141
   The Rape of the Lock. A. Pope.
      Al-VBP:531
   Songs and Dance Songs, I. Tr-US II:152
   Tell Me Now. Re-RR:9
   To a Lock of Hair. W. Scott. Pa-GTB:86
   To Amarantha. R. Lovelace.
      Al-VBP:444, Un-MW:17
HAITI
   Black Majesty. C. Cullen.
      Ad-PB:92, Ca-VT:242
   Christophe. R. Atkins. Ab-MO:82,
      Hu-PN:391

Citadel. E. Brathwaite. Sa-B:241
Evening in Haiti. E. Roumer.
  Ab-MO:48
Farewell. I. L'Ouverture.
  Lo-TY:89
Sunday Morning Song. Ab-MO:55
Work Song. Ab-MO:56
HAL, PRINCE: see HENRY V,
  KING OF ENGLAND
HALE, NATHAN
  Nathan Hale. E. Finch. Hi-TL:53,
    Vi-PP:111
  Nathan Hale. W. Partridge.
    Vi-PP:110
HALLAM, ARTHUR HENRY
  In Memoriam. A. Tennyson.
    Ha-PO:133, Ox-BN:495, Pa-GTB:336
HALLOWEEN: see also GHOSTS;
    PUMPKINS; WITCHES AND
    WITCHCRAFT
  Black and Gold. N. Turner.
    Ar-TP3:185, Au-SP:369, Ha-YA:119,
    Hu-MP:341, La-PH:16
  The Bored Goblins. D. Thompson.
    Ja-PA:38
  Frowning Jack. L. Blair. Ja-HH:39
  The Hag. R. Herrick. Bl-OB:85,
    Co-PS:137, Ho-WR:218, Ma-YA:86,
    Sm-LG:233, Sm-MK:48, Un-GT:107
  Hallowe'en. H. Behn. Ar-TP3:186,
    Br-SS:65, Co-PS:135, Fe-FP:83,
    Ha-YA:118, La-PH:8, La-PV:65,
    Sh-RP:230
  Halloween. J. Benton. Se-PR:192
  Hallowe'en. M. Capes. Th-AS:100
  Hallowe'en. M. Chute. La-PH:9
  Halloween. J. Ciardi. Ar-TP3:243
  Halloween. I. Eastwick. La-PH:10
  Halloween. F. Frost. Ja-PA:37
  Halloween. M. Lawson. Ar-TP3:237,
    Br-SS:67
  Halloween. M. Pomeroy. Co-PS:138
  Halloween. Yü Kuang-chang.
    Pa-MV:189
  Hallowe'en Charm. L. Blair.
    Ja-HH:36
  Hallowe'en Indignation Meeting.
    M. Fishback. Co-PS:139
  The Halloween Concert. A. Fisher.
    Br-SS:70
  Hallowe'en Scare. C. Cutler.
    Mc-AW:70
  Halloween Song. M. Barrows.
    Ja-PA:34
  Hempseed. Rv-ON:45
  Hey-How for Hallowe'en! Sm-LG:234
  House Ghost. L. May. Ho-CT:35
  If You've Never. E. Fowler.
    Au-SP:370
  Jack o'Lantern. A. Ayre. Au-SP:371
  Jack-o'-Lantern. A. Fisher.
    La-PH:15

Judging by Appearances.
  A. Poulsson. Hu-MP:342
Litany for Halloween. Au-SP:371,
  Br-SM:3, Br-SS:72, Co-PS:140,
  Mo-TB:77, Se-PR:192
Luck for Halloween. M. Justus.
  Ja-PA:36, Ju-CP:81
The Magic Vine. Br-SG:83
Mr. Macklin's Jack-O'-Lantern.
  D. McCord. Fe-FP:314
My Brother. D. Aldis.
  Ar-TP3:185, Au-SP:191
Not Afraid. J. Lee. Ja-HH:37
October Magic. M. Livingston.
  La-PH:5, La-PV:64
On Halloween. S. Silverstein.
  Co-PS:136
On Halloween Night. L. Blair.
  Ja-HH:34
Party Bid. A. Humphreys. De-FS:109
Pumpkin Face. L. Blair. Ja-HH:38
A Pumpkin Speaks. A. Barris.
  Bo-FP:145
Punkie Night. Su-FVI:49
So Timid. K. Dee. Ja-HH:36
Spooky. K. Finnell. Ho-CT:35
Theme in Yellow. C. Sandburg.
  Ar-TP3:186, Ha-YA:120, Hu-MP:263,
  Li-LC:77, Sh-RP:226
This Is Halloween. D. Thompson.
  Ar-TP3:186, Ha-YA:121, La-PH:12
What Am I? D. Aldis. Au-SP:369,
  Ir-BB:53, La-PH:15
What Night Would It Be? J. Ciardi.
  La-PH:6, La-PV:66
The Witches. Gr-CT:160
HALLUCINATIONS: see APPARITIONS;
    GHOSTS; ILLUSIONS; MADNESS;
    NARCOTICS
HAMBURG, GER.
  The Angels at Hamburg.
    R. Jarrell. Sh-AP:224
HAMLET, PRINCE OF DENMARK: see also
    ELSINORE, DEN.; OPHELIA
  His Choice. A. Baker. Ke-TF:252
HAMMERS
  The Hammers. R. Hodgson.
    Bo-GJ:202, Un-MB:192
  My Hammer. Alesha. Mo-MI:52
  This Old Hammer. Su-FVI:42
HAMPSHIRE, ENG.
  Youth and Age on Beaulieu River,
    Hants. J. Betjeman. Br-TC:45
HAMPTON COURT, ENG.
  Flowers at Hampton Court.
    H. Wolfe. Cr-WS:71
HAMSTERS
  Hamsters. M. Ridlon.
    Ho-ME:20
HAND PLAY: see FINGER AND
    HAND PLAY

HANDEL, GEORGE FREDERICK
  Epigram on Handel and Bononcini.
    J. Byrom. Pl-US:77, Rv-CB:517
HANDICAPPED: see also BLINDNESS;
    CRIPPLES; DEAFNESS; MENTALLY
    HANDICAPPED; SATIRE - HANDI-
    CAPPED; SOCIALLY HANDICAPPED
  An Elementary School Class Room
    in a Slum. S. Spender.
    Br-TC:403, Ke-PP:50, Un-MB:403
  The Halt. J. Miles. Co-EL:108
  The Hunchback. R. Friend.
    Ls-NY:153
  Hunchback Girl: She Thinks of
    Heaven. G. Brooks. Pe-SS:147
  Mamma! F. Horne. Ra-BP:76
  On My Short-Sightedness.
    Prem Chaya. Ma-FW:179
  Peg-Leg's Fiddle. B. Adams.
    Sh-RP:53
HANDS: see also HUMOR - HANDS;
    THUMBS
  Baby's Hands. Gomei. Hu-MP:8
  Dedication on the Gift of a
    Book to a Child. H. Belloc.
    Gr-TG:21
  Fingers and Toes. Wr-RM:12
  For Jerriann's Hands. M. Piercy.
    Sc-TN:188
  Frozen Hands. J. Bruchac.
    Ni-CD:35
  The Hand That Signed the Paper.
    D. Thomas. Mc-WS:102, Tr-MR:190,
    Un-MB:499
  Hands. G. Thompson. Jo-SA:9,
    Jo-VC:15
  Hands of a Brown Woman.
    F. Davis. Bo-HF:37
  Hold Thou My Hands. W. Canton.
    Gr-TG:80
  I Have Seen Black Hands.
    R. Wright. Ad-PB:105, Jo-SA:112
  Kashmiri Song. L. Hope. Er-FA:117
  Mother. H. Saito. Le-TA:20
  My Hands Are the Tools of My Soul.
    Wo-HS:(47)
  On a Hand. H. Belloc. Co-BL:45,
    Co-EL:13, Co-PU:77
  The Palm of the Hand. F. Saito.
    Sh-AM:150
  Songs for My Mother: Her Hands.
    A. Branch. Hu-MP:4, Se-PR:117
  Testament. Sister M. Thérése.
    Tr-MR:169
  Throwing Them Up to the Moon.
    Le-MW:124
  Torchbearer. H. Wolfe. Go-BP:245
  When Columbus Discovered America.
    Rs-RR:96
  Your Hands. A. Grimke. Ad-PB:16
HANGINGS: see EXECUTIONS AND
    EXECUTIONERS; LYNCHINGS

HANKS, NANCY: see LINCOLN,
    NANCY HANKS
HANNIBAL
  When Hannibal Crossed the Alps.
    E. Farjeon. Hi-FO:45
HANUKKAH (FEAST OF LIGHTS)
  Blessings for Chanukah.
    J. Sampter. Ar-TP3:191
  Candles. Ho-CT:43
  The Dreidel. K. Dee. Ja-HH:51
  Dreidel Song. E. Rosenzweig.
    Ar-TP3:191
  Eight Are the Lights.
    I. Orleans. Th-AS:177
  For Hanukkah. H. Bialik.
    Ar-TP3:191
  Happy Hanukkah. K. Dee. Ja-HH:49
HAPPINESS: see also CONTENTMENT;
    JOY
  The Absence. S. Warner. Un-MB:32
  Adam and Eve. J. Milton. No-CL:52
  After Dark Vapours. J. Keats.
    Ox-BN:367, Rv-CB:745
  Afternoon on a Hill. E. Millay.
    Ar-TP3:176, Au-SP:350, Cl-FC:24,
    Fe-FP:269, Hu-MP:64, La-PV:170,
    Pe-FB:75
  Afternoon with Grandmother.
    B. Huff. Fe-FP:42
  Afterwards. G. Stein. Ha-LO:76
  April Rise. L. Lee. Ma-FW:13
  Avondale. S. Smith. Pa-RE:9
  A Birthday. C. Rossetti.
    Al-VBP:997, Bl-OB:41, Co-BL:107,
    De-CH:334, Er-FA:116, Ho-WR:70,
    Re-TW:46, Un-MW:137
  The Birthday Child. R. Fyleman.
    Br-BC:3, Br-SS:50, Fe-FP:50,
    La-PH:59
  Cast Our Caps and Cares Away.
    J. Fletcher. Al-VBP:280,
    Sm-MK:17
  The Celestial Surgeon.
    R. Stevenson. Al-VBP:1070,
    Un-GT:308, Un-MB:58
  Character of a Happy Life.
    H. Wotton. Al-VBP:221,
    Ni-JP:169, Pa-GTB:63
  Cliff Klingenhagen. E. Robinson.
    Mo-BG:49, Sh-AP:140, Un-MA:117
  Consummate Happiness.
    W. Wordsworth. Ox-BN:99
  The Day with a White Mark.
    C. Lewis. Go-BP:250
  Dining-Room Tea. R. Brooke.
    Un-MB:326
  Early Spring. A. Sawai.
    Sh-AM:137
  Elegy in a Museum. P. Griffin.
    Go-BP:63
  Envoy. F. Thompson. Ga-FB:335,
    Un-MB:91

Esther. W. Blunt. Al-VBP:1051,
  Ox-BN:847
Everyone Sang. S. Sassoon.
  Co-PS:144, Ga-FB:218, Ga-S:171,
  Ha-LO:71, Mc-WK:13, Ni-JP:79,
  Pa-GTB:453, Sh-RP:88, Sm-MK:211,
  Un-MB:314
Frolic. AE. Fe-FP:99, Un-MB:144
The Golden Palace. Gr-CC:181
Good Times. S. Clifton. Ad-PB:306,
  Be-MA:140, Br-TC:71, Ra-BP:250
The Grasshopper. A. Cowley.
  Ho-WR:64
A Greeting. W. Davies. Mc-WK:82,
  Tr-MR:23, Un-MB:175
Happiness. N. Mitchell. Me-WF:38
Happiness. C. Sandburg. Ho-TH:55
Happiness Makes Up in Height for
  What It Lacks in Length.
  R. Frost. Un-MA:191
Happy. V. Windley. Ho-CT:12
The Happy Life. W. Thompson.
  Al-VBP:555
Happy Thought. R. Stevenson.
  Ar-TP3:208, Ga-S:9, Ox-BC:296,
  Sp-OG:247
Heaven. L. Hughes. Ar-TP3:214
I Thought It Was Tangiers I Wanted.
  L. Hughes. Bo-HF:84, Hu-PN:196
I'd Rather Spend My Life Quietly.
  Tai Wang-shu. Hs-TC:180
In the Spring when the Sun Never
  Sets. L. Evaloardjuak.
  Le-IB:108
Let's Be Merry. C. Rossetti.
  Ar-TP3:2, Fe-FP:30
The Light-Hearted Fairy.
  Bo-FP:311, Fe-FP:378, Hu-MP:80
Like Two Doves. Le-OE:91
A Little Song of Life. L. Reese.
  Fe-FP:18, Gr-TG:23, Hu-MP:61,
  Th-AS:179
The Means to Attain a Happy Life.
  H. Howard. Al-VBP:79
The Most. S. Suggs. Ho-CT:21
The Mother's Song. Ho-SD:75,
  Le-OE:113
My Gift. N. Bukhteyeva. Mo-MI:89
My Heart Is All Happy. Le-OE:87
New Shoes. A. Wilkins. Ar-TP3:111
New York in the Spring.
  D. Budbill. Ad-CI:3
Nikki-Rosa. N. Giovanni.
  Ad-CI:20, Ad-PB:451, Be-MA:169,
  Jo-SA:22
Ode on Solitude. A. Pope.
  Al-VBP:529, Er-FA:248, Go-BP:45,
  Ho-P:48, Ma-FW:85, Mc-PR:203,
  Ni-JP:137, Pa-GTB:110, Rv-CB:510
Ode to Maecenas. Horace.
  Pa-SG:173, Un-GT:236

On the South Downs. S. Teasdale.
  Un-MA:267
The People of Africa.
  M. Mertsalov. Bo-RU:51
The Piper. W. Blake.
  Al-VBP:611, Ar-TP3:161, Bo-GJ:131,
  Cl-FC:20, Co-RG:147, De-TT:112,
  Ga-FB:25, Hi-GD:26, Hu-MP:62,
  La-PP:vii, La-PV:xix, Li-LC:88,
  Ma-YA:126, Ox-BN:19, Pl-US:88,
  Re-TW:38, Rv-CB:566, Sm-LG:34,
  Sm-MK:14, Un-GB:17, Un-GT:11
Ploughman Singing. J. Clare.
  Go-BP:39
A Prayer for My Daughter. W. Yeats.
  Al-VBP:1090, Fe-PL:137, Tr-MR:49,
  Wi-LT:73
The Question. T. Kucherenko.
  Mo-MI:84
Recuerdo. E. Millay. Br-AF:194,
  Co-BL:108, Er-FA:110, Hi-TL:194,
  Na-EO:78, Wi-LT:337
Retirement, an Ode. T. Warton.
  Al-VBP:542
Rhapsody. W. Braithwaite.
  Bo-AN:15, Bo-HF:156
Rubaiyat. Omar Khayyam. Ba-PO:169
Rulers: Philadelphia. F. Johnson.
  Br-AF:199, Hu-PN:85
Salutation. E. Pound. Ca-VT:82,
  Mc-EA:23, Sm-LG:390, Un-MA:289
Second Night in N.Y.C. after 3
  Years. G. Corso. Gr-BT:37
Secret Laughter. C. Morley.
  Ga-FB:86
Sitting. T. Tsosie. Ba-HI:57
Solitude. E. Wilcox. Er-FA:3,
  Fe-PL:291
Song. E. Sitwell. Gr-CC:34
The Song of a Dream. Bi-IT:127
The Spring Waters. Ping Hsin.
  Hs-TC:24
The Sun. J. Drinkwater.
  Ar-TP3:175, Au-SP:344, Fe-FP:262,
  Li-LC:76, Pe-FB:62
These Are. J. Vitale. Ho-CT:8
This Happy Day. H. Behn.
  Ar-TP3:176
Thrice Happy He. W. Drummond.
  Co-BN:211
Tintern Abbey. W. Wordsworth.
  Al-VBP:667
To a Friend on His Marriage.
  F. Prince. Wi-LT:795
To One Who Has Been Long in City
  Pent. J. Keats. Go-BP:25,
  Rv-CB:738
to R. V. Erl'. Bo-RU:28
We Must Overcome the East Wind.
  Do-CH:(22)
The Wench in the Street. Rv-CB:427

HAPPINESS — cont'd.
  What Are Years? M. Moore.
    Ha-TP:140, Pe-OA:101, Pl-EI:138,
    Sh-AP:179, Sm-PT:10
  When Our Two Souls Stand Up.
    E. Browning. Al-VBP:816,
    Un-MW:206
  Where Shall Wisdom Be Found?
    Euripides. Pa-SG:186, Pl-US:108
  Whistling Boy. N. Waterman.
    Fe-PL:301
  The Work of Happiness.
    M. Sarton. Tr-MR:246
HARBORS: see also DOCKS;
    TUGBOATS
  Arrivals, Departures. P. Larkin.
    Un-MB:527
  The Bight. E. Bishop. Ha-PO:195
  Evening in England. R. Hosken.
    Ke-TF:366
  Famine. W. Brown. Sa-B:17
  Fisherman's Song. W. Brown.
    Sa-B:18
  The Harbor Dawn. H. Crane.
    Pe-OA:178, Sh-AP:198
  Interesting Things. S. Cross.
    Su-FVI:1
  Nocturne of the Wharves.
    A. Bontemps. Hu-PN:224,
    Ra-BP:93
  Old Montreal. J. Segal. Ho-TY:152
  A Sea-Chantey. D. Walcott.
    Lo-TY:111
  The Shore of Life. R. Fitzgerald.
    Ca-VT:302
  Training. D. Herrera. Lo-TY:108
  Water-Front Streets. L. Hughes.
    La-OC:38
HARDING, WARREN GAMALIEL
  Two Poems about President
    Harding. J. Wright. St-H:257
HARDY, THOMAS
  Thomas Hardy, Poet. M. Van Doren.
    Pl-ML:128
  Thoughts of Thomas Hardy.
    E. Blunden. En-PC:31
HAREBELLS: see also BLUEBELLS
  Harebell. J. Buxton. Sm-MK:2
HARES: see RABBITS
HARLEM, N.Y.: see also SATIRE -
    HARLEM, N.Y.
  African China. M. Tolson. Ad-PB:45
  beer cans. M. Goode. La-IH:47
  Bottled: New York. H. Johnson.
    Ad-PB:104
  Could Be. L. Hughes. La-OC:70
  Do Nothing till You Hear from Me.
    D. Henderson. Ad-PB:419
  Dream Deferred. L. Hughes.
    Ad-PB:76, Be-MA:42, Bo-AN:67,
    Ha-TP:21, Hu-PN:199, La-OC:149,
    Wi-LT:422

  Esthete in Harlem. L. Hughes.
    Ra-BP:57
  Harlem. J. Brierre. Lo-TY:93
  Harlem. L. Hughes. Ad-CI:32
  The Harlem Dancer. C. McKay.
    Ra-BP:59
  Harlem Freeze Frame.
    L. Bethune. Ad-PB:309
  Harlem Night Song. L. Hughes.
    La-OC:139
  Harlem 1960 & 1968. P. Bird.
    La-IH:95
  Harlem Shadows. C. McKay.
    Hu-PN:99
  Harlem Sounds: Hallelujah Corner.
    W. Browne. Bo-AN:173
  Harlem Sweeties. L. Hughes.
    Hu-PN:190, Lo-TY:227, Wi-LT:420
  January in Harlem. J. Fields.
    Ad-CI:33
  Jitterbugging in the Streets.
    C. Hernton. Ad-PB:240
  Juke Box Love Song. L. Hughes.
    Ad-PB:74
  Keep on Pushing. D. Henderson.
    Ad-PB:408
  Lenox Avenue. S. Alexander.
    Hu-PN:556
  Malcolm X — an Autobiography.
    L. Neal. Jo-SA:42, Ra-BP:269
  Movies. L. Hughes. Mo-BG:184
  Negro Servant. L. Hughes.
    Ca-VT:240
  On the Block: Another Night
    Search. J. Wright. Sc-TN:246
  Prime. L. Hughes. Ad-PB:76
  Return of the Native. I. Baraka.
    Ra-BP:222
  Simple. N. Madgett. Ad-PB:182
  Sketches of Harlem. D. Henderson.
    Hu-NN:76, Hu-PN:437
  Stars. L. Hughes. La-OC:137
  The Still Voice of Harlem.
    C. Rivers. Ad-PB:237, Be-MA:107,
    Hu-NN:44
  The Sundays of Satin-Legs Smith.
    G. Brooks. St-H:14
  Walk with de Mayor of Harlem.
    D. Henderson. Ad-PB:412
  What Now? L. Martin. La-IH:82
HARMONIA: see CADMUS AND HARMONIA
HARNESS: see HORSES
HARPERS FERRY, W.VA.
  Harpers Ferry. S. Rodman.
    Hu-PN:545
  How Old John Brown Took Harper's
    Ferry. E. Stedman. Hu-PN:493,
    Pa-OM:175
HARPS: see also HUMOR - HARPS
  The Ballad of the Harp-Weaver.
    E. Millay. Ar-TP3:156, Co-PT:64

Binnorie.   Ma-BB:25, Ox-BB:69
Frail Hands.   L. Trent.   De-FS:198
The Harp That Once Through Tara's
    Halls.   T. Moore.   Al-VBP:710,
    Co-RG:20, Fe-PL:177, Ma-YA:170,
    Ox-BN:210
The Lady of the Lake.   W. Scott.
    Al-VBP:671
The Lochnabyn Harper.   Ma-BB:208,
    Ox-BB:582
That Harp You Play So Well.
    M. Moore.   Un-MA:349
Variation on a Theme by Francis
    Kilvert.   R. Humphries.
    Pl-US:25
HARPSICHORDS
On an Air of Rameau.   A. Symons.
    Ox-BN:936
One and One.   C. Day-Lewis.
    Pl-US:15
Sonnet CXXVIII.   W. Shakespeare.
    No-CL:48
HARRIMAN, EDWARD HENRY: see
    SATIRE - HARRIMAN, EDWARD HENRY
HARRISON, WILLIAM HENRY
Old Tippecanoe.   Hi-TL:89
HARVARD UNIVERSITY
Address to the Scholars of New
    England.   J. Ransom.   Wi-LT:323
From the Harvard Yard.   D. Hall.
    Ke-TF:355
Unicorns at Harvard.   N. Farber.
    De-FS:89
HARVEST: see also HUMOR - HARVEST;
    THANKSGIVING DAY
Antique Harvesters.   J. Ransom.
    Un-MA:413
Apples in New Hampshire.
    M. Gilchrist.   Co-BN:137
August from My Desk.   R. Flint.
    Br-AF:156, Du-RG:49
The Barley Mow.   Cl-DT:84
Bread the Holy.   E. Coatsworth.
    Tr-MR:29
A Celebration.   V. Shepelev.
    Mo-MI:24
Charm of the Rice-Reapers.
    Tr-US II:207
A Child's Thought of Harvest.
    S. Coolidge.   Co-PS:121
Closing Song of a Ceremony to
    Procure Abundance.   Tr-US II:261
For a Wine Festival.   V. Watkins.
    Ls-NY:301
For All the Joys of Harvest.
    E. Vipont.   Br-SG:104
Harvest.   A. Hartich.   Ke-TF:447
Harvest.   C. Sandburg.   Ha-WR:81
Harvest.   Br-SG:89, Mo-MGT:182
Harvest Home.   H. Read.   Pa-RE:16,
    Sm-MK:180

Harvest Hymn.   J. Whittier.
    Se-PR:211
Harvest Sacrifice.   Su Tung P'o.
    Rx-OH:75
Harvest Song.   D. Georgakas.
    Sc-TN:58
Hee-Haw.   Rv-ON:40
High Wheat Country.   E. Jacobs.
    Br-AF:157
The Hock-Cart.   R. Herrick.
    Al-VBP:328, Ga-S:211
I Will Go with My Father
    a-Ploughing.   J. Campbell.
    Ar-TP3:202, Br-SS:166, Fe-FP:231
July.   J. Whittier.   Ha-YA:80
Kansas.   V. Lindsay.   Pa-HT:49
The Last Corn Shock.   G. Dresbach.
    Fe-FP:236
Many, Many Are the Songs of Good
    Harvest.   Hs-TC:442
Merry Autumn Days.   C. Dickens.
    Bo-FP:145, Ch-B:93
My Eyes Watching.   K. Nakamura.
    Sh-AM:147
The Plymouth Harvest.   W. Bradford.
    Bo-FP:154
Praise.   Bo-FP:163
Reapers.   J. Toomer.   Ad-PB:29,
    Jo-SA:63, Ra-BP:68
The Ripe and Bearded Barley.
    Cl-DT:86, Co-BN:126, Gr-CT:313,
    Gr-GB:46
Season.   W. Soyinka.   Ma-FW:127
The Sheaves.   E. Robinson.
    Ga-FB:297, Ha-PO:89, Mo-BG:140,
    Un-MA:127
Singing the Reapers Homeward
    Come.   Se-PR:212
Song.   T. Heywood.   No-CL:51
Song Concerning the Corn Harvest.
    Tr-US II:261
Song of Myself 9.   W. Whitman.
    Pa-RE:107, Sh-AP:74, Un-MA:48
The Steam Threshing-Machine.
    C. Tennyson-Turner.   Ox-BN:470
Thanksgiving.   Ja-PA:59
Their Thanksgiving Day.
    L. Driscoll.   Bo-FP:161
To Autumn.   J. Keats.   Al-VBP:777,
    Co-BN:125, Co-RG:126, De-CH:206,
    De-TT:163, Fe-PL:384, Ga-FB:225,
    Go-BP:25, Ha-PO:85, Hi-WP II:34,
    Mc-PR:84, Ox-BN:359, Pa-GTB:261,
    Rv-CB:736, Sp-OG:369, Un-GT:279
When the Frost Is on the Punkin.
    J. Riley.   Co-BN:134, Er-FA:132,
    Fe-PL:387, Ga-FB:298, Hu-MP:319
HARVEY, WILLIAM
On the Death of William Harvey.
    A. Cowley.   Al-VBP:447, Rv-CB:395
HASTE: see SPEED

HATE: see also ENEMIES;
   LOVE AND HATE;
   PREJUDICES AND
   ANTIPATHIES
   Atalanta in Calydon.
     A. Swinburne. Al-VBP:1041
   Chivalry. AE. Al-VBP:1103,
     Tr-MR:181
   Coriolanus's Farewell. . . .
     W. Shakespeare. Mc-WS:90
   The Echo. P. Solomon. Jo-VC:37
   Enslaved. C. McKay. Ra-BP:62
   Fire and Ice. R. Frost.
     Al-VBP:1133, Er-FA:88, Hi-WP II:3,
     Ho-LP:82, Mo-BG:186, Pe-M:97,
     Un-MA:180, Wi-LT:174
   Flogged Child. J. Keith. De-FS:116
   Gangrene. P. Levine. Ca-VT:628
   Hate. M. Classé. Ba-HI:35
   Hate. J. Stephens. Un-MB:265
   Hatred. G. Bennett. Ad-PB:82,
     Bo-AN:73
   I Am Frightened. V. Howard.
     Jo-VC:86, La-IH:134
   I Wish My Tongue Were a Quiver.
     L. Mackay. Mc-WS:92
   Jesus Was Crucified. C. Rodgers.
     Ad-PB:432
   Kicking Your Heels on the Dusty
     Road. P. Solomon. Jo-VC:39
   The Knight Fallen on Evil Days.
     E. Wylie. Un-MA:274
   My Enemy. L. Curry. Ba-HI:42
   Norman Conquest. P. Mackaye.
     Ke-TF:260
   Peekskill. A. Kramer. Kr-OF:162
   The Prophet's Warning or Shoot to
     Kill. Ebon. Ad-PB:434
   Remember Thee! Remember Thee!
     G. Byron. Al-VBP:721
   Strategies. W. Smith. Ad-PB:375
   Tiger. C. McKay. Ra-BP:62
   Uncle Frank. L. Bacon. Cr-WS:34
   Why. J. Velez. Ba-HI:119
HATHAWAY, ANNE
   The Path to Shottery.
     C. Skinner. Th-AS:163
HATRED: see HATE
HATS: see also HUMOR - HATS
   A City Flower. A. Dobson.
     Go-BP:124
   The Little Kittens. E. Follen.
     Ar-TP3:118
   White Cap. Mo-MGT:160
HAUNTED HOUSES: see EERINESS;
   GHOSTS
HAVANA, CUBA
   Habana. J. Bond. Hu-NN:86
   Sightseers in a Courtyard.
     N. Guillen. Lo-TY:106

HAWAII (STATE): see also COOK,
   JAMES (CAPTAIN COOK);
   POLYNESIAN VERSE - HAWAIIAN
   Our Native Land. King Kalakaua.
     Se-PR:294
   Rainbow Islands. D. Blanding.
     Ke-TF:365
HAWKING: see FALCONRY
HAWKS
   Birds. R. Jeffers. Ca-BP:29,
     Ca-VT:120
   Cold August. J. Harrison.
     Ls-NY:284
   Complaint of the Wild Goose.
     Tr-US II:135
   Corpus Christi Carol (The
     Falcon). Al-VBP:36, Ga-S:200,
     Gr-CC:163, Gr-CT:186, Gr-GB:308,
     Ma-FW:257, Rv-CB:13, Sm-MK:36
   Early Snow. R. Huff. St-H:84
   The Gay Goshawk. Ma-BB:183,
     Ox-BB:222
   A Good World. Issa. Le-MW:5
   The Hawk. H. Witt. Du-SH:161
   The Hawk. W. Yeats. Ma-FW:92
   The Hawk in the Wood. A. Morley.
     Cl-DT:58
   The Hawk Is Not a Plain Fly-
     Catching Bird. Wo-HS:(9)
   Hawk Remembered. J. Phoenice.
     Ls-NY:210
   Hawk Roosting. T. Hughes.
     Br-TC:209, Pa-GTB:564, Rd-OA:145,
     To-MP:84, Wi-LT:735
   Hawking. M. Drayton. Mo-SD:120
   Hawks. S. Bates. Ba-PO:196
   How Still the Hawk.
     C. Tomlinson. Wi-LT:830
   Hurt Hawks. R. Jeffers.
     Co-BBW:236, Ni-JP:115, Pe-SS:150,
     Sh-AP:177, Un-MA:369, Wi-LT:258
   Look Now, the Hawk. M. Parr.
     Ls-NY:212
   The Old Falcon. F. Baldwin.
     Ls-NY:107
   Old Wife's Song. E. Farjeon.
     Sh-RP:15
   The Osprey's Nest. D. Wagoner.
     Ca-BP:10
   The Penniless Hawk. De-PP:17
   Sea-Hawk. R. Eberhart. Ha-WR:40
   The Sea Hawk Hunting. Taigi.
     Be-CS:12
   Shiva. R. Jeffers. Gr-SS:69,
     Ls-NY:36
   Song. T. Beddoes. Re-BS:8
   A Sparrow-Hawk. De-CH:101
   The Windhover. G. Hopkins.
     Ox-BN:865, Pa-GTB:390, Pl-EI:129,
     Un-MB:45, Wi-LT:41
HAWTHORN TREES
   After Thunder Goes. Shiki. Be-MC:29

Alons au Bois le May Cueillir.
  C. d'Orleans. Pa-SG:84
The Fairy Thorn. S. Ferguson.
  De-CH:117, De-TT:197, Pa-OM:271
The Hawthorn. Gr-CT:46, Gr-GB:98
A Hawthorn Berry. M. Webb.
  Tu-WW:62
The Hawthorn Tree. Rv-ON:75
He Loves and Rides Away. S. Dobell.
  Ox-BN:663
I Bended unto Me. T. Brown.
  Co-PS:56
The Thorn Trees. R. Field.
  Br-SG:92
We Hurry On. D. Dolben. Ox-BN:881
HAWTHORNE, NATHANIEL
  Hawthorne — May 23, 1864.
    H. Longfellow. Rv-CB:783
HAY AND HAYING: see also SCYTHES
  An Argument Against the Empirical
    Method. W. Stafford. Du-SH:186
  The Grass. E. Dickinson.
    Fe-FP:223, Sh-RP:105
  The Hay Appeareth. Bible. O.T.
    Proverbs. Fe-FP:233
  Hay for the Horses. G. Snyder.
    Du-SH:144, Mo-BG:56
  Hay Making. Mo-MGT:115, Wr-RM:124
  Hayfield. A. Fisher. Sh-RP:206
  Haying Before Storm.
    M. Rukeyser. Ha-WR:46
  The Hayloft. R. Stevenson.
    Bo-FP:94
  Haymakers. E. Thomas. Cl-DT:66
  Haymakers, Rakers. T. Dekker.
    Al-VBP:227
  Haymaking. E. Thomas. Un-MB:218
  The Haystack. A. Young. Co-PU:50
  Haystack. Hs-TC:454
  How Cool Cut Hay Smells. Boncho.
    Be-CS:16
  Labor of Fields. E. Coatsworth.
    Mc-PR:133
  Load of Hay. Ir-BB:227, Tu-WW:16
  The Mowers. M. Benton. Ha-YA:83
  Mowing. R. Frost. Ca-VT:4
  On the Bales. E. Coupland.
    Su-FVI:65
  Song of Myself 9. W. Whitman.
    Pa-RE:107, Sh-AP:74, Un-MA:48
  The Tuft of Flowers. R. Frost.
    Rv-CB:966, Sh-AP:150, Un-MA:168
  Two Women under a Maple.
    R. Coffin. Mc-PR:147
  A Youth Mowing. D. Lawrence.
    Un-MB:285
HAYDN, FRANZ JOSEPH: see HUMOR -
    HAYDN, FRANZ JOSEPH
HAYDON, BENJAMIN ROBERT
  Addressed to Haydon. J. Keats.
    Ox-BN:335, Rv-CB:740

HAYES, ROLAND
  Singing in the Dark. I. Wassall.
    Hu-PN:546
HAYMARKET SQUARE RIOT: see
    ALTGELD, JOHN PETER
HAYSTACKS: see HAY AND HAYING
HAZE: see also FOG; MIST
  Haze. Buson. Sh-RP:62
  On the Road to Nara. Matsuo Basho.
    Ar-TP3:203, Pa-SG:91
  Woof of the Sun. H. Thoreau.
    Al-VBP:917
HAZEL TREES
  The Lazy Hours. Br-FW:4
  Nutting. W. Wordsworth. Rv-CB:637
HEAD-HUNTERS
  Chant on the Return from a
    Successful Head-Taking Raid.
    Tr-US I:142
  From an Angba. Tr-US I:181
  Song at a Head-Hunting Festival.
    Tr-US I:172
HEADS: see also HUMOR - HEADS;
    SKULLS
  The Crematory. Kuo Mo-jo.
    Hs-TC:35
  My Head. T. Fujiwara. Le-TA:88
  Painting: A Head. J. Ransom.
    Un-MA:418, Wi-LT:321
  The Well. Be-AP:69
HEALTH
  He That Would Live. De-CH:671
  A Leg in a Plaster Cast.
    M. Rukeyser. Un-MA:627
  Shooter's Hill. R. Bloomfield.
    Ox-BN:55
  Surgical Ward. W. Auden. Pe-SS:146
HEARING: see EARS; LISTENING
HEARTS: see also HUMOR - HEARTS
  Colloquy in Black Rock.
    R. Lowell. Un-MA:663
  A Correct Compassion. J. Kirkup.
    Ma-FW:141, Pl-IO:188
  Counting the Beats. R. Graves.
    Al-VBP:1206, Pa-GTB:490
  Discordants II. C. Aiken.
    Co-BL:36
  The Exchange. S. Coleridge.
    Co-FB:322
  The False Heart. H. Belloc.
    Sm-LG:391
  The Heart. S. Crane. Un-MA:148,
    Wi-LT:117
  Heart and Mind. E. Sitwell.
    Br-TC:387
  Hearts Were Made to Give Away.
    A. Wynne. Ar-TP3:200, Se-PR:53
  In This Strange House. C. Drewry.
    Tr-MR:281
  Laboratory Poem. J. Merrill.
    Br-TC:286

HEARTS — cont'd.
Monna Innominata. C. Rossetti.
Al-VBP:994, Ox-BN:718
My True Love Hath My Heart.
P. Sidney. Al-VBP:125, Bo-FP:295,
De-CH:334, Go-BP:123, Gr-CT:57,
Hi-WP II:51, Ke-TF:105, Pa-GTB:16,
Rv-CB:168, Se-PR:54, Un-MW:132
The Shape of the Heart. L. Nicholl.
Pl-IO:142
This Corruptible. E. Wylie.
Tr-MR:257, Un-MA:282
To My Heart. D. Botez. Mc-AC:62
The Voice of the Sea. Fang Wei-teh.
Hs-TC:136
HEARTSEASE: see JOHNNY-JUMP-UPS
HEAT
Autumn. J. Clare. Co-BN:135
Heat. G. Gonzalez y Contreras.
Ho-LP:24
Heat. H.D. Un-MA:336
Hot Night on Water Street.
L. Simpson. Br-TC:379
Hotness. A. Copeman. Ho-CT:19
It's Hot. A. Carrington. Ho-CT:16
June Weather. Yuan Shui-p'ai.
Hs-TC:410
The Last Bus. M. Strand.
Br-TC:422
St. Louis Midday. J. Knoepfle.
St-H:93
The Same as a Burning.
K. Takayasu. Sh-AM:157
Something in Common. R. Church.
Tr-MR:152
Tea. Ch'u Ch'uang I. Rx-LT:54
Virginia. T. Eliot. Ha-PO:94,
Sm-LG:142
HEAVEN: see also ANGELS; HUMOR –
HEAVEN
Above the Bright Blue Sky.
A. Midlane. Ox-BC:229
Again. C. Mew. Un-MB:163
The Angels Came a-Mustering.
Pl-EI:100
Arcturus Is His Other Name.
E. Dickinson. Ga-FB:148
A Ballad of Hell. J. Davidson.
Un-MB:72
The Blessed Damozel. D. Rossetti.
Li-SR:77, Ox-BN:675
The Blessed Received in Paradise.
J. Kirkup. Go-BP:259
Borderline. R. Grenville.
De-FS:102
The Cold Heaven. W. Yeats.
Pa-GTB:423
Dream with an Angel. M. Banus.
Mc-AC:113
The Dying Christian to His Soul.
A. Pope. Go-BP:235

Earth and Sky. Euripides.
Pl-EI:180
L'Envoi. R. Kipling. Er-FA:10,
Ke-TF:453
Epilogue. A. Noyes. Un-MB:248
Epilogue. F. Thompson. Un-MB:79
The Flesh and the Spirit.
A. Bradstreet. Sh-AP:9
General William Booth Enters into
Heaven. V. Lindsay. Ga-S:221,
Un-MA:221, Wi-LT:624
Grace of the Way. F. Thompson.
Un-MB:90
Heaven. G. Herbert. Gr-CC:139
Heaven. L. Hughes. Ar-TP3:214
Heaven. Fe-PL:331
The Heaven of Animals. J. Dickey.
Kh-VA:42, Wi-LT:687
Heaven-Haven. G. Hopkins.
Al-VBP:1059, Go-BP:274, Gr-BT:146,
Ha-PO:196, Hi-WP II:176,
Mc-WK:184, Ox-BN:852, Un-MB:44
Heaven Is Heaven. C. Rossetti.
Ha-YA:69
Heavenly Grass. T. Williams.
Gr-EC:61
Heriger, Bishop of Mainz. Li-TU:152
How the Gates Came Ajar. Ke-TF:42
Hunchback Girl: She Thinks of
Heaven. G. Brooks. Pe-SS:147
Hymne to God My God in My
Sicknesse. J. Donne.
Gr-CT:383, Pl-US:127
I Went to Heaven. E. Dickinson.
Ga-FB:149
I Wonder. J. Lawton. Le-M:170
If There Are Any Heavens.
E. Cummings. Un-MA:476
In No Strange Land. F. Thompson.
Ga-S:127, Go-BP:250, Pa-GTB:398,
Pl-EI:7, Un-MB:90
Jerusalem, My Happy Home.
Rv-CB:108, Sm-LG:383
Kingdom of Heaven. L. Adams.
Un-MA:547
The Land o' the Leal. Lady Nairn.
Pa-GTB:157
Mrs. Malone. E. Farjeon.
Co-PM:61, Ox-BC:332
Nearer Home. P. Cary. Er-FA:456
The New Jerusalem. Al-VBP:366,
Go-BP:263
Not Only Around Our Infancy.
J. Lowell. Er-FA:480
O Mother, Dear Jerusalem. Ke-TF:190
Old Friends. A. Muir. Co-BBW:272
On Heaven. F. Ford. Al-VBP:1116
One Stormy Night. V. Jones.
Ba-HI:130
Out of Paradise. J. Milton.
Ga-S:35

Peace. S. Speed. Go-BP:257
Peace. H. Vaughan. Ga-S:223,
   Gr-CC:136, Gr-CT:347,
   Hi-WP II:172, Ma-YA:105,
   Pa-HT:163, Pl-EI:9, Rv-CB:409,
   Sm-LG:382
A Prayer to Go to Heaven with the
   Donkeys. F. Jammes. Ar-TP3:83,
   Co-BBW:149, Go-BP:255, Pl-EI:124,
   Rd-OA:20, Tr-MR:52
The Range Rider's Soliloquy.
   Fi-BG:194
The Seekers. J. Masefield.
   Go-BP:224
She Asks for a New Earth. K. Tynan.
   Go-BP:253
Sister Lou. S. Brown. Ad-PB:66,
   Bo-AN:53, Hu-PN:174
The Spectacle. W. de la Mare.
   Go-BP:249
Sunday Morning. W. Stevens.
   Sh-AP:158, Sm-PT:121, Un-MA:242,
   Wi-LT:139
This World Is Not Conclusion.
   E. Dickinson. Pl-EI:10
When the Saints Go Marchin' In.
   Pl-EI:97
Where Is Heaven? B. Carman.
   Un-GT:309
The White Island. R. Herrick.
   Gr-CT:187, Ho-WR:251
Who Has Not Found the Heaven
   Below. E. Dickinson. Ga-S:223
You and I Shall Go.
   Bi-IT:100, Tr-US II:248
HEAVY WATER: see SATIRE -
   HEAVY WATER
HEBREW LANGUAGE: see YIDDISH
   LANGUAGE
HEBREW VERSE: see also
   YIDDISH VERSE
   Adon 'Olam (Lord of the World).
   Pl-EI:199
   The Angels Came a-Mustering.
   Pl-EI:100
   The Coming Messiah. Bible. O.T.
   Isaiah. Ba-PO:75, Ga-S:57
   David's Lament. Bible. O.T.
   Samuel II. Gr-CT:343
   The Earth Is the Lord's. Bible.
   O.T. Psalms. Ar-TP3:188,
   Bo-FP:249, Fe-FP:232, Pa-SG:198,
   Pl-EI:214
   The End of the World. Bible. O.T.
   Jeremiah. Ba-PO:48, Ke-PP:2
   For Hanukkah. H. Bialik.
   Ar-TP3:191
   For Out of Zion. Bible. O.T.
   Isaiah. Ba-PO:75
   Fret Not Thyself Because of
   Evildoers. Bible. O.T. Psalms.
   Ar-TP3:210

From Thee to Thee. S. Gabirol.
   Pl-EI:48
The Grasshopper's Song. H. Bialik.
   Fe-FP:476, Ha-YA:65
How Is the Gold Become Dim. Bible.
   O.T. Lamentations. Gr-CT:344
I Have Sought Thee Daily.
   S. Ibn-Gabirol. Pa-SG:208
Invocation: Hasidic Song.
   L. Isaac of Berditshev. Pl-EI:193
Kibbutz Sabbath. L. Amittai.
   Pl-EI:192
Man That Is Born of Woman. Bible.
   O.T. Job. Gr-CT:353
Prayer of a Woman. J. Karni.
   Un-R:75
Psalm Eight. Bible. O.T. Psalms.
   Pa-SG:193
Psalm 100. Bible. O.T. Psalms.
   Ar-TP3:188, Br-SS:81, Fe-FP:85,
   Hu-MP:287, Ma-YA:76, Pl-US:52,
   Sh-RP:92
Psalm 150. Bible. O.T. Psalms.
   Ga-S:18, Gr-CT:446, Pa-RE:126,
   Pa-SG:201, Pl-US:7
The Song of Songs. Bible. O.T.
   Song of Solomon. Pa-SG:26
Tell Him. C. Bialik. Pa-SG:52
See also Me-PH.
HEBREWS: see HEBREW VERSE; JEWS
HECTOR: see also ANDROMACHE
The Great Hector Was Killed by
   Arrows. J. Brodsky. Ca-MR:32
The Sixth Book of Homer's Iliads.
   Homer. Al-VBP:148
HEDGEHOGS: see also PORCUPINES
   Hedgehog. Chu Chen Po. Rx-LT:84
   The Hedgehog. J. Clare. Rd-OA:78
HEIDELBERG, GER.
   The Scene Pope John Wouldn't Let
   Fellini Film. D. Georgakas.
   Sc-TN:60
HELEN OF TROY: see also PARIS,
   PRINCE OF TROY; TROJAN WAR
   The Face of Helen. C. Marlowe.
   Al-VBP:176, Er-FA:106, Ga-FB:31
   Helen. H.D. Un-MA:340, Wi-LT:620
   Long-Legged Fly. W. Yeats.
   Wi-LT:92
   Love Is a Keeper of Swans.
   H. Wolfe. Un-MB:303
   No Second Troy. W. Yeats.
   Ha-PO:181, Pa-GTB:422
   To Helen. D. Schwartz. Ls-NY:26
HELEN OF TYRE
   Helen of Tyre. H. Longfellow.
   Gr-SS:78
HELICOPTERS: see also HUMOR -
   HELICOPTERS
   The Helicopter. I. Serrailler.
   Pa-RE:79

HELICOPTERS — cont'd.
Helicopter. S. Yoshino. La-TA:58
Precision. P. Collenette.
   Ma-FW:207
HELL: see also DEVILS; HADES;
   HUMOR - HELL
A Ballad of Hell. J. Davidson.
   Un-MB:72
Borderline. R. Grenville.
   De-FS:102
Canto I. E. Pound. Ca-VT:90,
   Un-MA:297
Captain Hall. Gr-GB:269
Christ's Descent into Hell.
   R. Rilke. Ho-P:231
Eurydice. H.D. Ca-VT:107
Evil Is Homeless. D. Lawrence.
   Tr-MR:219
The Good Man in Hell. E. Muir.
   Tr-MR:159, Un-MB:339
The Harrowing of Hell. R. Rilke.
   Go-BP:296
The Harrowing of Hell. Ga-S:168
Heriger, Bishop of Mainz.
   Li-TU:152
I See the World. B. Grayson.
   Me-WF:6
In Procession. R. Graves.
   Br-TC:155
In the Deep Museum. A. Sexton.
   Ho-P:229, Un-MA:690
Judging from the Pictures.
   S. Karai. Ma-FW:163
Napoleon in Hades. D. Morton.
   Cr-WS:29
No Hiding Place down There.
   Gr-GB:329
One Stormy Night. V. Jones.
   Ba-HI:130
Tenebris Interlucentem.
   J. Flecker. Rv-CB:975, Un-MB:273
Thoughts on the Christian Doctrine
   of Eternal Hell. S. Smith.
   Ke-PP:44
The Tragical History of Doctor
   Faustus. C. Marlowe. Al-VBP:177,
   Gr-CT:151, Ma-FW:161, Ma-YA:63
When Thou Must Home. Propertius.
   Al-VBP:218, Gr-CC:78, Gr-CT:73,
   Ha-PO:170, Rv-CB:270
HÉLOÏSE: see ABÉLARD AND HÉLOÏSE
HELPFULNESS: see also HUMOR -
   HELPFULNESS; SERVICE TO
   OTHERS
As I Sit. C. Begay. Ba-HI:34
Beautiful Black Women. I. Baraka.
   Ra-BP:213
For Theresa. N. Giovanni.
   Be-MA:172
i am a little church (no great
   cathedral). E. Cummings.
   Tr-MR:201

I Shall Not Pass This Way
   Again. E. York. Er-FA:10
I Will Extol Thee, O Lord.
   Bible. O.T. Psalms. Me-PH:20
The Kirk of the Birds, Beasts
   and Fishes. Gr-GB:76
Little and Great. C. Mackay.
   Fe-PL:340
Look Up! E. Hale. Er-FA:29
Not in Vain. E. Dickinson.
   Bo-HF:140, Fe-PL:297
Remember September. M. Justus.
   Br-SS:58, Ha-YA:106, Ja-PA:23
Sentimental Monologue.
   J. Wheelock. Ls-NY:339
A Solitude. D. Levertov.
   Du-SH:142, Mo-BG:36
Somebody. Er-FA:31
Somebody's Mother. M. Brine.
   Er-FA:139
Song. M. Sarton. Tr-MR:175
A Song of Thanksgiving. Bible.
   O.T. Psalms. Me-PH:28
Three Helpers in Battle.
   M. Coleridge. Pl-EI:99
Trees. H. Behn. Ar-TP3:204,
   Au-SP:368, Br-SS:144, Ha-YA:52,
   Pe-FB:74, Un-GB:10
Turn Again to Life. M. Hall.
   Fe-PL:336
The Woman Who Understands.
   L. Appleton. Fe-PL:117
Worlds of Different Sizes.
   S. McPherson. Co-PU:71
HELPLESSNESS
Acknowledgement. D. Laing.
   Co-PU:15
Balloon. S. Tsuboi. Sh-AM:72
The Donkey. Br-BC:10, Co-BBW:154,
   Gr-EC:37, Ma-FO:(31)
Girls' Songs, III. Tr-US I:119
Like a Grain of Sand.
   Tsang K'o-chia. Hs-TC:278
Little Things. J. Stephens.
   Ad-PE:47, Ar-TP3:65, Bo-GJ:19,
   Br-SS:151, Co-BBW:55, Co-PU:70,
   Fe-FP:149, Gr-EC:40, Hi-WP I:33,
   Hu-MP:200, La-PV:160, Pl-EI:130,
   Un-MB:263
Lost Moment. H. Fuller. Ad-PB:201
The Night Is Darkening round Me.
   E. Brontë. Ho-LP:78, Ox-BN:596
Night Train. Hsü Chih-mo. Hs-TC:93
Overnight in the Apartment by the
   River. Tu Fu. Gr-CT:344
The Shoemaker's Booth.
   R. Hershon. Sc-TN:92
The Snare. J. Stephens. Ad-PE:22,
   Ar-TP3:62, Bl-OB:130, Co-BBW:21,
   Co-IW:28, De-CH:89, Gr-EC:32,
   La-PP:51, La-PV:151, Mc-WS:44,
   Se-PR:300, Sm-MK:159, Th-AS:50

Songs, I. Tr-US II:170
There's Nane o' My Ain to Care.
    W. Ogilvie. De-CH:515
Thought's End. L. Adams.
    Sm-PT:136
To a Friend. J. Valentine.
    Ha-TP:64
To God. R. Herrick. Ga-S:145,
    Go-BP:179
HEMLOCK TREES
    Pastoral. R. Hillyer. Un-MA:482
HENRY II, KING OF ENGLAND:
    see also ELEANOR OF AQUITAINE
    Sir Aldinger. Ox-BB:23
HENRY V, KING OF ENGLAND
    Agincourt. M. Drayton. De-CH:501,
        Hi-FO:91, Rv-CB:183, Sm-LG:245
    Before Agincourt. W. Shakespeare.
        Gr-CT:337
    Falstaff's Lament over Prince Hal
        Become Henry V. H. Melville.
        Al-VBP:958
    Henry Before Agincourt.
        J. Lydgate. De-CH:179
    King Henry the Fifth.
        W. Shakespeare. Co-RM:199, 200,
        Ga-FB:195, Ha-PO:255, Ke-TF:54,
        Mc-WS:100
HENRY VI, KING OF ENGLAND
    Bristowe Tragedie. Ox-BB:656
HENRY VIII, KING OF ENGLAND:
    see also BOLEYN, ANNE, QUEEN
        OF ENGLAND; HUMOR - HENRY VIII,
        KING OF ENGLAND
    The Hunt Is Up. De-CH:129,
        De-TT:76
    Sir Andrew Bartton. Ox-BB:508
HENRY IV, KING OF FRANCE
    Ivry. T. Macauley. Ga-FB:200,
        Hi-FO:131
HENRY, FORT: see FORT HENRY,
    BATTLE, 1782
HENS: see CHICKENS
HERACLITUS
    Heraclitus. W. Cory. Al-VBP:973,
        Co-EL:74, Co-PU:149, Hi-WP II:21,
        Ox-BN:648, Pa-SG:13, Pl-ML:143,
        Rv-CB:875
HERALDRY: see also CHIVALRY;
    KNIGHTS AND KNIGHTHOOD
    The Lion and the Unicorn. An-IP:(29),
        Br-FF:9, Hi-FO:143, Ir-BB:270,
        Li-LB:80, Mo-MGT:197, Mo-NR:61,
        Na-EO:85, Pa-AP:14, Wr-RM:56
    Of Seals and Arms. J. Taylor.
        Rv-CB:318
HERBS
    Acon. H.D. Ca-VT:106
    And Can the Physician Make Sick
        Men Well? Bl-OB:157, Gr-EC:288,
        Re-TW:47

The Hay Appeareth. Bible. O.T.
    Proverbs. Fe-FP:233
He That Would Live. De-CH:671
Herb Pimpernell. De-CH:667
Herbs and Simples. M. Keller.
    De-FS:123
Old Man. E. Thomas. Wi-LT:646
Parsley, Sage, Rosemary and Thyme.
    Ir-BB:120
Rosemary Green. Ir-BB:118,
    Sp-AS:28
Song of the Witch of the Cloisters.
    W. Hoffman. Sc-TN:104
Tarragon, Tansy, Thyme and Teasel.
    E. Farjeon. Ir-BB:238
HERDING: see also HUMOR - HERDING
    Braggin' Bill's Fortytude.
        C. Hallock. Fi-BG:79
    Calling the Cows Home.
        J. Ingelow. Gr-TG:51
    Doney Gal. Fi-BG:165
    A Drover. P. Colum. Al-VBP:1148,
        Co-PI:26, Pa-HT:139, Un-MB:250
    Fetching Cows. N. MacCaig.
        Ma-FW:227
    The Herd-Boy's Song.
        Chen Shan-min. Pa-SG:126
    The Herdboy. Lu Yu. Gr-CT:114,
        Le-MW:110, Ma-FW:76
    Herder's Song. Be-AP:59, Tr-US I:111
    Herder's Song. Tr-US I:39
    Lament for the Cowboy Life.
        J. Mitchell. Co-RM:21
    Little Bo-Peep. Au-SP:13, Bo-FP:79,
        De-PO:14, Fr-WO:19, Ir-BB:129,
        Li-LB:40, Li-SR:126, Mo-MGT:160,
        Mo-NR:6, Wi-MG:28, Wr-RM:11
    Little Boy Blue. J. Ransom.
        We-PZ:36, Wi-LT:321
    Little Boy Blue. Au-SP:6, Bo-FP:78,
        De-PO:28, Er-FA:506, Fr-WO:10,
        Li-LB:26, Mo-MGT:15, Mo-NR:134,
        Pa-AP:42, Wi-MG:12, Wr-RM:11
    Night Herding Song. H. Stephens.
        Sh-RP:79
    Run Little Dogies. Fi-BG:156
    To Be Sung by a Small Boy Who
        Herds Goats. Y. Winters.
        We-PZ:29
    The Trail Herd. Fi-BG:145
    The Traveling Post Office.
        A. Patterson. Co-PT:290
HEREAFTER: see FUTURE LIFE;
    IMMORTALITY
HEREDITY: see also ANCESTORS AND
    ANCESTRY; HERITAGE
    Heredity. T. Hardy. Pl-IO:140,
        Rv-CB:938
HERETICS AND HERESY: see also
    CONTROVERSY; DISSENT; PROTEST
    Soul, Scorning All Measure.
        M. Tsvetayeva. Ca-MR:136

HERITAGE: see also ANCESTORS AND
   ANCESTRY; HUMOR - HERITAGE
An Afterword to My Father.
   M. Bell. Mc-EA:109
America. S. Dobell. Vi-PP:17
Ancestors. G. Cohoe. Al-WW:24
Ask the Mountains. P. George.
   Al-WW:124
An Autobiography. E. Rhys.
   Co-PU:124
Ballad of the Golden Bowl.
   S. Hay. Pa-OM:365
Ballad of the Two Grandfathers.
   N. Guillén. Be-UL:53
Black Is a Soul. J. White.
   Ad-PB:261
Black Man's Feast. S. Fabio.
   Ad-PB:203
Black Star Line. H. Dumas.
   Ad-PB:269
Black Warrior. N. Jordan.
   Ad-PB:322
The Blood Horse. B. Procter.
   Co-BBW:157
Bottled: New York. H. Johnson.
   Ad-PB:104
Breath. B. Diop. Lo-TY:139
Bwagamoyo. L. Bethune. Ad-PB:310
Carriers of the Dream Wheel.
   N. Momaday. Ni-CD:87
The Circuit. D. Wagoner. Mo-BG:66
The Congo. V. Lindsay. Er-FA:300,
   Hi-WP II:98, Hu-PN:484, Pe-OA:55,
   Sh-AP:163, Un-MA:218
Dark Symphony: Tempo Primo.
   M. Tolson. Bo-AN:39
The Descendant and the Id.
   A. Branch. Sm-PT:131
Determination. J. Clarke.
   Ad-PB:144
Digging. S. Heaney. Br-TC:173,
   To-MP:150
Each Morning. I. Baraka.
   Ad-PB:250, Hu-NN:74
Emblems. A. Tate. Ca-VT:223
England and America in 1782.
   A. Tennyson. Vi-PP:136
The Faces. P. Zweig. Mc-EA:110
A Far Cry from Africa. D. Walcott.
   Lo-TY:114
The Father and His Children.
   Ox-BC:75
Father's Voice. W. Stafford.
   Mc-EA:113
A Feller I Know. M. Austin.
   Br-AF:38, Fe-FP:306
Fire, Hair, Meat and Bone.
   F. Johnson. Ad-PB:391
For G. W. Gordon. B. Smith.
   Sa-B:224
For You, My Son. H. Gregory.
   Un-MA:508

Fruit of the Flower. C. Cullen.
   Fe-PL:136, Jo-SA:20
Grandparents. R. Lowell.
   Mc-EA:106, Wi-LT:585
Guinea. J. Roumain. Lo-TY:92
Half Black, Half Blacker.
   S. Plumpp. Ad-PB:385
He Sees Through Stone. E. Knight.
   Ad-PB:231, Be-MA:109
Here. R. Thomas. Pa-GTB:537
Heritage. G. Bennett. Ad-PB:81,
   Bo-AN:73
Heritage. C. Cullen. Ad-PB:88,
   Be-MA:47, Bo-AN:83, Ga-FB:274,
   Lo-TY:230, Ra-BP:95, Un-MA:571
Heritage. C. McKay. Be-MA:14
The Hero. L. Jackson. Br-SS:164
Homestead. E. Roach. Sa-B:98
I Went to Learn how the White
   Man Lives. Wo-HS:(37)
The Idea of Ancestry. E. Knight.
   Ad-PB:229, Be-MA:108, Ra-BP:203
An Invitation to Madison County.
   J. Wright. Ad-PB:275
I've Never Been Lost. I. Feffer.
   Ho-TY:188
JuJu. A. Touré. Ad-PB:340
Ka'Ba. I. Baraka. Ra-BP:213
Lament at Night. H. Leivick.
   Ho-TY:119
The Land. R. Kipling. Ni-JP:134,
   Pa-OM:190, Un-MB:138
Legend. T. Aida. Sh-AM:110
leroy. I. Baraka. Ad-PB:255,
   Mc-EA:105, Ra-BP:215
Men at Forty. D. Justice.
   Ho-P:129
My Fathers Came from Kentucky.
   V. Lindsay. Br-AF:131, Gr-CC:125
My Great-Grandfather's Slaves.
   W. Berry. Mc-EA:114
My Heart Leaps Up. W. Wordsworth.
   Al-VBP:655, Ar-TP3:172, Au-SP:346,
   Bo-HF:55, Br-BC:121, Co-RG:121,
   Er-FA:149, Ga-FB:22, Ha-PO:83,
   La-PP:7, Ma-YA:139, Mc-PR:169,
   Ox-BN:61, Pa-GTB:308, Rv-CB:644,
   Sp-OG:352
My Heritage. B. Smith. Sa-B:71
Nocturne. R. Camille. Lo-TY:94
now poem. for us. S. Sanchez.
   Ad-PB:290
Now We Come Southwards. Bi-IT:15
#4. D. Long. Ad-PB:404
Oh, Yes, My Dear. De-CH:584
The Old Squire. W. Blunt. Mo-SD:110
Once Again. L. Bahe. Ni-CD:12
Opinions of the New Student.
   R. Pedroso. Lo-TY:102
Piano and Drums. G. Okara.
   Lo-TY:158
poem. S. Sanchez. Ad-PB:288

Poem. M. Yungman. Ho-TY:365
A Poem for a Poet. D. Lee.
Ad-PB:425
A Prayer. D. Einhorn. Ho-TY:83
The Slave's Dream. H. Longfellow.
Hi-WP I:18, Hu-PN:459
A Song of Greatness. Ar-TP3:35,
Br-AF:37, Br-BC:126, Fe-FP:24,
Sh-RP:103
Song to the Xylophone at a
Fighting Man's Funeral. Tr-US I:42
Spit 'n Image. C. Barks. Mc-EA:101
Stark Boughs on the Family Tree.
M. Oliver. Pe-SS:14
Tauhid. A. Touré. Ad-PB:339
Testament. T. Arghezi. Mc-AC:25
To a Brown Girl. O. Davis.
Hu-PN:378
Tom Tom. B. Smith. Sa-B:73
Totem. L. Senghor. Gr-BT:32
The Valley of Men. U. Greenberg.
Me-PH:93
The Voice of My Fathers Is on the
Wind. Wo-HS:(42)
Wake-Up Niggers. D. Lee. Ad-PB:422
walking in thought. S. Ortiz.
Mc-EA:108
The Way to Know a Father.
R. Coffin. Se-PR:151
HERMES: see MERCURY (ROMAN GOD)
HERMITS
The Hermit. W. Davies. Un-MB:176
The Hermit. Hsü Pên. La-RM:168,
Le-MW:130, Ma-FW:85
The Hermit. R. Silcock. Ls-NY:321
The Hermit Picks Berries.
M. Kumin. La-RM:140
The Man Who Hid His Own Front Door.
E. MacKinstry. Fe-FP:374
The Marvellous Bear Shepherd.
Ma-FW:216
The Three Hermits. W. Yeats.
Ma-FW:86
Twilight Comes. Wang Wei. Rx-LT:57
HERMON, MOUNT
Song from "The Young David."
R. Beer-Hofmann. Un-R:49
HERO AND LEANDER: see also HUMOR -
HERO AND LEANDER
Hero and Leander. C. Marlowe.
Al-VBP:170
On an Engraved Gem of Leander.
J. Keats. Rv-CB:746
HEROD, KING OF JUDEA (THE GREAT)
The Ballad of Two Kings.
G. Code. De-FS:64
A Carol for Saint Stephen's
Day. De-CH:225, Ox-BB:3
The Crow and the Crane. Ma-BB:86
The Holy Innocents. R. Lowell.
Un-MA:663

Innocent's Song. C. Causley.
Pa-GTB:552, To-MP:105
HEROES AND HEROISM: see also
COURAGE; HUMOR - HEROES AND
HEROISM; MARTYRS; SATIRE -
HEROES AND HEROISM; and
names of men and women, as
BOONE, DANIEL; JOAN OF ARC
Admiral Benbow. Co-RM:66,
Rv-CB:420
Ballad of East and West.
R. Kipling. Ar-TP3:25, Ga-FB:211
A Ballad of Heroes. A. Dobson.
Se-PR:133
Beowulf. Al-VBP:1, Ma-YA:14
Betty Zane. T. English. Vi-PP:127
The British Grenadiers. Rv-CB:443
The Burial of Sir John Moore at
Corunna. C. Wolfe. De-TT:139,
Er-FA:285, Gr-CT:342, Hi-FO:198,
Ke-TF:165, Pa-GTB:216, Rv-CB:693,
Sp-OG:202
Casabianca. F. Hemans. Er-FA:184,
Fe-FP:552, Hi-FO:189, Un-GT:159
Character of the Happy Warrior.
W. Wordsworth. Er-FA:85
The Charge of the Light Brigade.
A. Tennyson. Er-FA:183,
Fe-FP:564, Ga-FB:206, Hi-FO:238,
Ma-YA:196, Mc-PR:184, Sp-OG:49
The Crimean War Heroes.
W. Landor. Mc-WS:104
The Dead Heroes. I. Rosenberg.
Un-MB:352
Death of an Aircraft. C. Causley.
Ca-MB:115
The Dykes. R. Kipling. Ni-JP:138
The Eagle That Is Forgotten.
V. Lindsay. Al-VBP:1139,
Sh-AP:166, Tr-MR:171, Un-MA:223
1805. R. Graves. Co-RM:42,
Na-EO:17, Sm-LG:155
Emily Geiger. Fe-PL:164, Vi-PP:124
Gunga Din. R. Kipling. Er-FA:371,
Go-BP:54, Hi-WP I:69, Ma-YA:226,
Pa-OM:230, Un-MB:122
Heroes of War and Peace.
E. Wilcox. Kr-OF:173
Heroism. R. Emerson. Al-VBP:806
Hervé Riel. R. Browning.
Co-SS:183, Pa-OM:161, Sp-OG:67
Hoffer. W. Wordsworth. Hi-FO:200
Horatius. T. Macauley. Er-FA:387,
Fe-PL:64, Hi-FO:32, Sm-LG:161
How Can a Man Die Better.
Tyrtaeus. Pa-SG:6
How Sleep the Brave. W. Collins.
Al-VBP:572, Pa-GTB:119, Rv-CB:536,
Sp-OG:208
I Think Continually of Those Who Were
Truly Great. S. Spender. Al-VBP:1235,
Gr-CT:377, Ha-PO:222, Pl-EI:158,
Tr-MR:166, Un-MB:477, Wi-LT:496

HEROES AND HEROISM — cont'd.
  Incident of the French Camp.
    R. Browning. Co-RG:28, Mc-PR:144,
    Sp-OG:43, Un-GT:148
  Ivry. T. Macaulay. Ga-FB:200,
    Hi-FO:131
  Jim Bludso. J. Hay. Co-RM:234,
    Er-FA:307, Fi-BG:129, Sp-OG:34
  Kossuth. J. Lowell. Hi-FO:231
  The Leak in the Dike. P. Cary.
    Er-FA:348, Fe-FP:554
  Lincoln, the Man of the People.
    E. Markham. Un-MA:108, Vi-PP:167
  The Lost Leader. R. Browning.
    Al-VBP:884, Hi-FO:225, Ke-TF:56,
    Pl-ML:58
  Marco Bozzaris. F. Halleck.
    Hi-FO:208
  My Sad Captains. T. Gunn.
    En-PC:278, Wi-LT:726
  Nathan Hale. W. Partridge.
    Vi-PP:110
  O Captain! My Captain!
    W. Whitman. Co-RG:38, Er-FA:282,
    Fe-FP:447, Fe-PL:171, Ga-FB:263,
    Hi-TL:121, Hu-MP:397, Ke-TF:317,
    Mc-PR:77, Se-PR:50, Sm-LG:157,
    Sp-OG:203, Un-MA:76, Vi-PP:166
  Ode in a Night of Overhanging
    Weather. V. McHugh. Mc-WK:175
  Opportunity. E. Sill. Co-RM:71,
    Sp-OG:46, Un-GT:310
  The Patriot's Pass-Word.
    J. Montgomery. Sp-OG:19
  The Revenge. A. Tennyson.
    Co-RM:45, Hi-FO:134, Pa-OM:154,
    Sp-OG:60
  The Shepherd Dog of the Pyrenees.
    E. Murray. Se-PR:302
  Song for All Seas, All Ships.
    W. Whitman. Tr-MR:175
  A Song of Greatness. Ar-TP3:35,
    Br-AF:37, Br-BC:126, Fe-FP:24,
    Sh-RP:103
  The Stampede. A. Caldwell.
    Fi-BG:100
  The Strong Swimmer. W. Benét.
    Hu-PN:500
  To Some Millions Who Survive
    Joseph E. Mander, Senior.
    S. Wright. Ad-PB:212
  Two-Gun Percy. Fi-BG:136
  Vitai Lampada. H. Newbolt.
    Sp-OG:17
  Voices of Heroes. H. Gregory.
    Gr-CC:104
  The Wrangler Kid. Fi-BG:102
HEROINES: see HEROES AND HEROISM
HERONS: see also EGRETS
  Blue Gaulding. W. Andrew.
    Sa-B:31
  Blue Water. Li Po. Le-MW:109

  Boy into Heron. C. Randall.
    Sm-MK:186
  Casida of the Golden Girl.
    F. Garcia Lorca. Le-SW:49
  The Corpus Christi Carol.
    Gr-GB:309
  The First Part of Spring.
    H. Kawahigashi. Sh-AM:161
  The Heron. T. Roethke. Co-BBW:259,
    Ho-LP:46, La-PV:137, La-RM:150,
    Re-BS:34
  The Heron. V. Watkins. Br-TC:457,
    Pa-GTB:506
  The Herons on Bo Island. E. Shane.
    Co-BBW:249
  Hidden by Darkness. Basho.
    Be-MC:11
  If the White Herons. Chiyo.
    Be-CS:50
  Look Now, the Hawk. M. Parr.
    Ls-NY:212
  May All the Earth Be Clothed in
    Light. G. Hitchcock. Ca-BP:51,
    Ca-VT:399
  Songs, II. Tr-US II:171
  With the Evening Breeze. Buson.
    Le-IS:24
HERRICK, ROBERT
  To the Author of Hesperides and
    Noble Numbers. M. Van Doren.
    Pl-ML:109
HERRING
  Fish Riddles I. Gr-GB:73
  Herring Is King. A. Graves.
    Co-PI:53
  Market Woman's Cries. J. Swift.
    Co-PI:184
  With the Herring Fishers.
    H. MacDiarmid. Wi-LT:627
HERVEY, SIR JOHN: see SATIRE -
    HERVEY, SIR JOHN
HERVEY, WILLIAM: see HARVEY,
    WILLIAM
HESIOD
  Hesiod, 1908. A. Mair. Gr-SS:60
HEYERDAHL, THOR
  The Ballad of Kon-Tiki.
    I. Serraillier. Co-SS:223
HEYWOOD, THOMAS
  Thomas Heywood. A. Swinburne.
    No-CL:15
HIAWATHA: see also HUMOR -
    HIAWATHA
  Hiawatha's Brothers.
    H. Longfellow. Bo-FP:265
  Hiawatha's Chickens.
    H. Longfellow. Bo-FP:276
  Hiawatha's Childhood.
    H. Longfellow. Ar-TP3:36,
    Fe-FP:405, Ga-FB:248, Gr-EC:100,
    Hu-MP:422, Li-SR:54, Mc-PR:80,
    Sh-RP:272

Hiawatha's Sailing.
   H. Longfellow.   Bo-FP:230
What I Think of Hiawatha.
   J. Morris.   Li-SR:61
HIBERNATION
The Dormouse.   P. Hill.   Co-BBW:56
The Dormouse.   M. Stephenson.
   St-FS:97
The Happy Hedgehog.   E. Rieu.
   Co-BBW:29, Gr-EC:276
The Jolly Woodchuck.
   M. Edey & D. Grider.   Ar-TP3:63,
   Co-IW:37, Fe-FP:169, La-PV:148
March.   J. Wright.   Ho-TH:89
Mrs. Brownish Beetle.   A. Fisher.
   It-HB:33
HICCUPS
Two Charms to Cure Hiccups,
   I, II.   Su-FVI:48
HIDING
Hide and Seek.   A. Shiffrin.
   Ir-BB:13, St-FS:68
Hiding.   D. Aldis.   Ar-TP3:113,
   Au-SP:199, Fe-FP:102, Hu-MP:45
Hiding.   M. Davidson.   Ad-II:36
In the Dark None Dainty.
   R. Herrick.   Co-EL:92
John Brown's Body.   S. Benét.
   Al-VBP:1208
The Man Who Hid His Own Front
   Door.   E. MacKinstry.   Fe-FP:374
Open to Visitors.   E. Milner.
   Co-EL:105
The Robber.   I. Eastwick.   Br-SS:119
Thief's Spell.   Tr-US I:207
HIGH SCHOOLS: see SCHOOL LIFE
HIGHWAYMEN: see OUTLAWS; THIEVES
HIGHWAYS: see ROADS; STREETS
HIKING: see WALKING
HILL, JOE: see HILLSTROM, JOSEPH
HILLS: see also HUMOR - HILLS;
   MOUNTAINS
After Sunset.   G. Conkling.
   Tr-MR:274
Archibald's Example.
   E. Robinson.   Gr-CC:183
Benediction.   A. Morgan.   Ke-TF:427
The Dark Hills.   E. Robinson.
   Bo-GJ:189, Bo-HF:133, Er-FA:196,
   Ha-PO:89, Pe-OA:22, Un-MA:126,
   Wi-LT:111
Enthralled.   C. Thaxter.   Sp-OG:252
For Me the Hills.   H. Koch.
   Ke-TF:428
Grongar Hill.   J. Dyer.   Al-VBP:544,
   Cl-FC:26, Gr-CT:240
The Hills.   F. Cornford.   Un-MB:308
The Hills.   R. Field.   Li-LC:59,
   Sh-RP:176
Hills.   G. Foster.   Le-M:122
Hills.   A. Guiterman.   Ke-TF:427,
   Sh-RP:100

How to Tell the Top of a Hill.
   J. Ciardi.   Au-SP:194
I Am Disquieted when I See Many
   Hills.   H. Plutzik.   Ca-VT:347
   Lonesome Water.   R. Helton.
      Br-AF:100, Co-PM:91, Mc-WK:200,
      Un-MA:347
   The Long Hill.   S. Teasdale.   Un-MA:265
Midnight in the Garden.
   Li Shang-Yin.   Le-MW:63
The Painted Hills of Arizona.
   E. Curran.   Pa-HT:57
The Sea and the Hills.   R. Kipling.
   Ga-FB:188
Sixteen-Syllable Stanza.
   Mao Tse-tung.   Hs-TC:362
The Sleeping Giant.   D. Hall.
   Br-TC:165, Ni-JP:25
Song of the Wild Ginger.
   Tr-US II:200
Tintock-Tap.   Gr-GB:177
Under a Small, Cold Winter Moon.
   Ransetsu.   Be-MC:47
The West Virginia Hills.   E. King.
   Se-PR:290
HILLSTROM, JOSEPH
Joe Hill.   A. Hayes.   Kr-OF:114
Last Will.   J. Hill.   Kr-OF:116
THE HIMALAYA
The Bearer of Evil Tidings.
   R. Frost.   Rv-CB:968
Himalaya.   Po Fei Huang.   Ls-NY:248
HINDUISM: see also BRAHMINS AND
   BRAHMINISM; GANGES RIVER;
   GODS AND GODDESSES, EAST
   INDIAN
Anashuya and Vijaya.   W. Yeats.
   Li-TU:146
Brahma.   R. Emerson.   Al-VBP:807,
   Mo-BG:52, Pl-EI:23, Rv-CB:776,
   Sh-AP:34
Ganga.   T. Blackburn.   Ca-MB:57
The Meaning of Atman.   Al-PI:19
Precepts.   Al-PI:24
The Song of Creation.   Al-PI:11
Thought.   Al-PI:20
To Agni.   Al-PI:14
To the Dawn.   Al-PI:15
To the Maruts.   Al-PI:13
True Religion.   Tulsidas.   Ba-PO:3
Who Is the Man of Poise?   Al-PI:26
HINDUS: see HUMOR - HINDUS
HIPPETY-HOPPETY: see HOPPING
HIPPIES: see COUNTER CULTURE
HIPPOPOTAMUSES: see also HUMOR -
   HIPPOPOTAMUSES
The Hippopotamus.   G. Durston.
   Ar-TP3:79, Ja-PC:18
The Hippopotamus.   T. Eliot.
   Ca-VT:132, Ha-PO:119
The Hippopotamus.   O. Nash.
   Ga-FB:334, Un-MA:564

HIPPOPOTAMUSES — cont'd.
Hippopotamus Hunter's Song.
Tr-US I:96
Rose's Calf. P. Bennett.
Co-BBW:189
HIROSHIMA, JAPAN
At Hiroshima. L. Hubbell.
Ba-PO:52, Cr-WS:148
Ghosts. Fire. Water. J. Kirkup.
Go-BP:215
Hiroshima. M. Rockwell. Ba-PO:53,
Ke-PP:9
Hiroshima Crewman. G. Georgakas.
Sc-TN:61
A Hiroshima Lullaby.
J. Langland. Ke-PP:131
Relative Sadness. C. Rowbotham.
Gr-BT:119
Return to Hiroshima. L. Stryk.
Cr-WS:148
To Hiroshima. Ai Ch'ing. Hs-TC:318
HISTORY: see also ARCHEOLOGY;
HUMOR - HISTORY; and also
names of battles, and wars
and names of countries, as
FRANCE - HISTORY AND PATRI-
OTISM, and names of historic
persons, as JOAN OF ARC
The Mediterranean. A. Tate.
Ca-VT:219, En-PC:39, Sh-AP:205,
Un-MA:540, Wi-LT:401
Our History. C. Coblentz. Fe-FP:80
HITCHHIKING
Dogs Have as Much Right as People
in Nevada. H. Witt. Du-SH:118
A Ride in a Blue Chevy.
J. Williams. Ls-NY:160
HITLER, ADOLF: see also NATIONAL
SOCIALISM
And Then There Were None.
E. Millay. Cr-WS:42
The Hitler Dwarf. D. Lourie.
Sc-TN:152
The Silent Generation.
L. Simpson. Hi-TL:224
HOBBIES: see also names of
hobbies, as TRAVEL AND
TRAVELERS
Beach Glass. H. Moss. Mo-BG:2
HOBBYHORSES: see also HUMOR -
HOBBYHORSES
The Centaur. M. Swenson. Br-TC:425,
Du-SH:44, Li-TU:107, Mo-BG:72
The Hobby-Horse. Ir-BB:118,
Pa-AP:24, Wr-RM:65
The Hobby Horse. Bo-FP:10
I Have a Six-Shooter. On-TW:24
Ride a Cock-Horse to Banbury Cross.
Ar-TP3:100, Au-SP:15, Bo-FP:10,
De-PO:8, Er-FA:507, Fr-WO:32,
Ir-BB:11, Li-LB:10, Mo-MGT:149,
Mo-NR:7, Mo-TL:77, Wi-MG:8,
Wr-RM:30

HOBOES: see TRAMPS
HOCKEY
Hockey. E. McLaughlin. Fl-HH:21
There's This That I Like about
Hockey, My Lad. J. Kieran.
Fl-HH:49
HOFER, ANDREAS
Hoffer. W. Wordsworth. Hi-FO:200
HOGG, JAMES
Extempore Effusion upon the Death
of James Hogg. W. Wordsworth.
Rv-CB:648
HOGS: see PIGS
HOHENLINDEN, BATTLE, 1800
Hohenlinden. T. Campbell.
Co-RG:26, De-CH:168, Gr-CT:339,
Hi-FO:191, Hi-WP I:58,
Ox-BN:195, Pa-GTB:212, Pa-OM:171,
Rv-CB:677
HOKUSAI, KATSUSHIKA
The Laughing Hyena, by Hokusai.
D. Enright. Br-TC:117
HÖLDERLIN, JOHANN CHRISTIAN
FRIEDRICH
The Death of Hoelderlin.
P. Oppenheimer. Ls-NY:167
HOLIDAY, ELEANOR (BILLIE)
Afterwards, They Shall Dance.
B. Kaufman. Br-TC:229, Ca-VT:538,
Hu-PN:409
Blues and Bitterness. L. Bennett.
Ad-PB:202, Hu-NN:53
HOLIDAYS: see also FESTIVALS;
VACATIONS; and names of
specific holidays, as
CHRISTMAS
Haymakers, Rakers. T. Dekker.
Al-VBP:227
The Hock-Cart. R. Herrick.
Al-VBP:328, Ga-S:211
Holiday Parade. E. Jay. Ja-HH:5
The Holiday Year. M. Millet.
Ja-HH:63
Holidays. H. Longfellow.
Hu-MP:326
I Must Remember. S. Silverstein.
Co-PS:20
Jolly Days. I. Eastwick. Hu-MP:326
Little Catkins. A. Blok. Pl-EI:181
Once upon a Great Holiday.
A. Wilkinson. Do-WH:15
HOLLAND: see NETHERLANDS
HOLLY TREES
Alms in Autumn. R. Fyleman.
Bo-FP:149
As the Holly Groweth Green.
Henry VIII. Al-VBP:66, Ma-FW:201
But Give Me Holly, Bold and Jolly.
C. Rossetti. Ar-TP3:192
Fruit, Flower and Tree Riddles.
Gr-GB:71
Highty, Tighty, Paradighty. Gr-CT:3

Holly and Ivy.   Rv-CB:21
The Holly and the Ivy.   De-CH:228,
   De-TT:114, Gr-CT:421, Gr-GB:301
Ivy and Holly.   E. Meyerstein.
   Co-EL:11
Nay, Ivy, Nay.   De-CH:230, Rv-CB:32
Old Polly.   Ja-HH:61
Sans Day Carol.   Ga-S:86
Song Against Children.   A. Kilmer.
   Th-AS:65
Under the Holly-Bough.
   C. Mackay.   Ke-TF:48
HOLLYHOCKS
All Day in Gray Rain.   Basho.
   Be-CS:7
Hollyhocks.   D. Etter.   St-H:61
HOLLYWOOD, CAL.
Hollywood.   K. Shapiro.   Wi-LT:537
HOLY CROSS, MOUNT OF THE
The Cross of Snow.
   H. Longfellow.   Sh-AP:40
HOLY GRAIL: see ARTHUR, KING;
   GRAIL
HOLY SPIRIT: see also SATIRE -
   HOLY SPIRIT; TRINITY
Apocalypse.   E. Pierce.   Tr-MR:262
God and the Holy Ghost.
   D. Lawrence.   Tr-MR:224
His Litany to the Holy Spirit.
   R. Herrick.   Fe-PL:343
The Spirit Dances.   T. Blackburn.
   Ga-S:191
To the Holy Spirit.   Y. Winters.
   Ca-VT:231, Un-MA:551
Veni Creator.   Ga-S:191
Veni Sancte Spiritus.   Ga-S:200
HOLY THURSDAY: see LENT
HOLY WEEK: see EASTER; JESUS
   CHRIST - CRUCIFIXION;
   LENT; RESURRECTION
HOME: see also FAMILY AND FAMILY
   LIFE; HOMECOMING; HOMESICK-
   NESS; HUMOR - HOME; MARRIAGE;
   SATIRE - HOME
Apartment House.   G. Raftery.
   Br-AF:210, Du-RG:39, La-OC:108
At Home.   J. Rolnick.   Ho-TY:166
Autumn Evening.   F. Cornford.
   De-CH:502
Benediction.   S. Kunitz.
   Ca-VT:259, Tr-MR:60
Better than Gold.   A. Ryan.
   Er-FA:9
Beyond the Snow Belt.   M. Oliver.
   St-H:163
Chorus from Medea.   Euripides.
   Pa-SG:16
Closed House.   R. Coffin. Ke-TF:416
Dear God, the Day Is Grey.
   A. Halley.   Pe-OA:287
A Deserted Home.   S. Lysaght.
   De-CH:50

Disturbances.   A. Thwaite. To-MP:137
An Empty Bed.   S. Silon.   Le-M:140
Evicted.   S. Funaroff.   Kr-OF:200
Family Prime.   M. Van Doren.
   Ca-VT:195
Fears in Solitude.   S. Coleridge.
   Ox-BN:164
Ghetto.   R. Johnston.   La-IH:50
Growing Older.   C. Towne. Ke-TF:154
Heart's Content.   Fe-PL:146
Home.   E. Montgomery.   Ba-HI:108,
   Jo-VC:29
The Home.   R. Tagore.   Bo-GJ:xix
Home, Sweet Home.   J. Payne.
   Er-FA:133
A House and Grounds.   J. Hunt.
   Rv-CB:684
House Blessing.   Bi-IT:48
The House of Christmas.
   G. Chesterton.   Tr-MR:109,
   Un-MB:210
I Saw Green Banks of Daffodils.
   E. Tennant.   Ar-TP3:201
In the Inner City.   L. Clifton.
   Be-MA:139, Mo-TS:7
Kid in the Park.   L. Hughes.
   La-OC:89
Locked Out.   R. Frost.   Li-TU:31
The Long Voyage.   M. Cowley.
   Mc-WK:182, Ni-JP:132, Pe-OA:171
Many a Mickle.   W. de la Mare.
   Ga-FB:169
The Memory-Filled House.
   M. White.   Le-M:177
My Early Home.   J. Clare. Fe-PL:146
My Home.   Ho-TY:311
Not from Here.   J. La Rose.
   Sa-B:76
Oh, Joyous House.   R. Janzen.
   Le-M:152
The Old Woman under a Hill.
   Mo-NR:66, Wr-RM:13
On Dreamland.   Cheng Ch'ou-yü.
   Pa-MV:39
On Restoring an Old House.
   E. de Liesseline.   Ke-TF:415
Our Happy Home.   De-CH:533,
   Gr-TG:68
Our House.   O. Goga.   Mc-AC:39
A Prayer for a Little Home. F. Bone.
   Bo-FP:50, Er-FA:135
Prayer for This House.
   L. Untermeyer.   Fe-FP:57,
   Fe-PL:136, Mc-PR:104
Residue.   T. MacNeill.   Sa-B:60
Return.   I. Vilariño.   Be-UL:81
Roads Go Ever Ever On. J. Tolkien.
   Ar-TP3:94, Fe-FP:183
Roofs.   J. Kilmer.   Fe-PL:135
Sold.   R. Cuscaden.   St-H:35
Song.   H. Longfellow.
   De-TT:91

HOME — cont'd.
  Song of Entering the Village.
    Da-SC:115
  Sonnet XXVI. Feng Chih. Hs-TC:154
  The Sufficient Place. E. Muir.
    Go-BP:251
  A Thanksgiving to God for His
    House. R. Herrick. Al-VBP:337,
    De-TT:168, Gr-CT:269
  There Once Was a Man. On-TW:7
  Tired and Unhappy, You Think of
    Houses. D. Schwartz. Un-MA:617,
    Wi-LT:516
  Vacation Time. R. Bennett.
    Br-SS:162
  We Shall Live Together. Wo-HS:(29)
  When the Animals Were Let Out of
    the Ark after the Flood.
    Cl-FC:76, Pa-RE:113
  Who Loves the Rain. F. Shaw.
    Hu-MP:298, Th-AS:113
  Who's In? E. Fleming. Bl-OB:145,
    Cl-FC:61, Pe-FB:22, Th-AS:41
  Winterproof. A. Guiterman.
    Ke-TF:417
  The Work of Happiness. M. Sarton.
    Tr-MR:246
  Young. A. Sexton. To-MP:100
HOMECOMING: see also SATIRE -
    HOMECOMING
  America for Me. H. Van Dyke.
    Er-FA:292, Hu-MP:403, Sh-RP:214
    Th-AS:168, Vi-PP:39
  Arrowhead Field. L. Herrick.
    Ha-TP:124
  At Night. A. Meynell. De-CH:451,
    Go-BP:133
  At Yuen Yang Lake. Wu Wei Ye.
    Rx-LT:112
  But Do You Think Our Life Is Hard.
    Sp-HW:33
  By the Deep Nine. W. Pearce.
    Gr-CT:225
  Crossing Han River. Li P'in.
    Rx-LT:88
  Daddy. Mo-MGT:108
  Datur Hora Quieti. W. Scott.
    Pa-GTB:274
  Dry Your Tears, Africa. B. Dadie.
    Lo-TY:143
  L'Envoi: The Return of Sire de
    Nesle. H. Melville. Al-VBP:956
  The Farmer's Heart with Joy Is
    Filled. Sp-HW:32
  Home Again. E. Chamberlin.
    Mc-AW:100
  Home-Coming. L. Adams. Un-MA:543
  Homecoming. Chu Hsiang. Hs-TC:100
  Homecoming. Ho Ch'e Ch'ang.
    Rx-LT:47
  homecoming. S. Sanchez.
    Ad-PB:286

Homecoming — Late at Night.
    Tu Fu. Rx-OH:31
  The Homecoming Singer. J. Wright.
    Ad-PB:279
  Homesick. Tu Yün-hsieh. Hs-TC:247
  Keepsake Mill. R. Stevenson.
    Tu-WW:27
  October Journey. M. Walker.
    Ad-PB:146
  The Old Chartist. G. Meredith.
    Hi-FO:244
  Prelude to an Evening. J. Ransom.
    En-PC:12, Un-MA:418
  Return to New York. J. Wheelock.
    Pa-HT:35
  Return to the Farm. M. Taylor.
    Ke-TF:352
  The Returned Volunteer to His
    Rifle. H. Melville. Gr-CC:114,
    Hi-TL:130
  Sailing Homeward. Chan Fang-Sheng.
    Ar-TP3:97, Le-MW:43, Pa-SG:180,
    Sm-LG:298, Th-AS:158
  The Sailor's Wife. W. Mickle.
    Al-VBP:600, De-TT:110, Pa-GTB:154
  Snow on Lotus Mountain.
    Liu Ch'ang Ch'ing. Rx-LT:68
  Sometimes on My Way Back Down
    to the Block. V. Cruz. Ad-BO:64
  Ten Days Leave. W. Snodgrass.
    Un-MA:681
  The Traveller's Return.
    R. Southey. Mc-PR:165
  Valediction to My Contemporaries.
    H. Gregory. Un-MA:506
  The Wanderer. I. Thorson. Ke-TF:418
  When Johnny Comes Marching Home.
    P. Gilmore. Co-PS:145, Hi-TL:126,
    Vi-PP:161
  When Will I Be Home? Li Shang Yin.
    Rx-LT:77
  Wilderness. Ai Ch'ing. Hs-TC:314
HOMER: see also HUMOR - HOMER;ODYSSEY
  The Epistle Dedicatory to the Iliads
    of Homer. G. Chapman. No-CL:16
  Isaiah and Homer. A. Glanz-Leyeles.
    Ho-TY:257
  The Odyssey. A. Lang. Al-VBP:1062,
    Fe-PL:433, Ox-BN:871
  On First Looking into Chapman's
    Homer. J. Keats. Al-VBP:769,
    Co-RG:17, De-CH:361, Er-FA:75,
    Ga-FB:14, Gr-CT:442, Ke-TF:61,
    Ma-YA:182, Mc-PR:78, Ni-JP:19,
    No-CL:18, Ox-BN:334, Pa-GTB:169,
    Pl-ML:91, Rv-CB:739, Sm-LG:36
  On Homer's Birthplace. T. Heywood.
    Pl-ML:90
  Paradise Regained. J. Milton.
    Al-VBP:412
  Poet. S. Halkin. Ho-TY:187

Seven Wealthy Towns.   Co-PU:68
To Homer.   J. Keats.   Rv-CB:748
HOMESICKNESS: see also HUMOR -
    HOMESICKNESS; SATIRE - HOME-
    SICKNESS
Alien.   D. Hayes.   Bo-AN:93
American Names.   S. Benét.
    Br-AF:6, Mc-WK:157, Pa-HT:3,
    Sh-AP:194, Sm-LG:145
Another Spring.   Tu Fu.   Rx-OH:24
Arizona.   Em-AF:758
At Gold Hill Monastery.
    Su Tung P'o.   Rx-OH:67
Bonnie Annie Livieston.   Ox-BB:254
Da Boy from Rome.   T. Daly.
    Fe-FP:304, Hu-MP:158
Brumana.   J. Flecker.   Pa-HT:118
By the Rivers of Babylon.   Bible.
    O.T. Psalms.   Me-PH:30
Canadian Boat Song.   J. Galt.
    Ox-BN:204, Rv-CB:683, Sm-LG:140
The Captains of Small Farms.
    R. Coffin.   Sh-RP:308
Christmas at Sea.   R. Stevenson.
    Co-SS:207, De-CH:28, Ga-FB:183,
    Ha-PO:251, Ma-YA:220, Sp-OG:257
The Cuban Emigrant.   V. Alvarez.
    Ba-HI:20
Dark Rosaleen.   J. Mangan.
    Al-VBP:812, Co-PI:128, De-CH:172
Destruction.   Chu Tzu-ch'ing.
    Hs-TC:13
Dixie.   D. Emmett.   Er-FA:290,
    Fe-FP:439
Dust.   Yu Kuang-chung.   Pa-MV:179
Epitaph on a Jacobite.
    T. Macaulay.   Al-VBP:799,
    Cr-WS:56, De-TT:180, Ox-BN:428
Exile.   V. Sheard.   Co-BBW:205
Exiled.   E. Millay.   Ni-JP:132,
    Pa-HT:7
Falmouth.   W. Henley.   Fe-PL:148,
    Un-MB:55
A Farm on the Great Plains.
    W. Stafford.   En-PC:142
For My Father.   D. Kherdian.
    Kh-VA:11
From the Flats.   S. Lanier.
    Sh-AP:132
Hame, Hame, Hame.   A. Cunningham.
    De-CH:169, De-TT:180
Home No More Home to Me.
    R. Stevenson.   De-CH:25
Home-Sick Song (Magoboreni).
    Tr- US I:97
Home-Sick Songs (Let Us).
    Tr-US I:45
Home-Sick Songs (Oh, They).
    Tr-US I:45
Home, Sweet Home.   J. Payne.
    Er-FA:133

Home-Thoughts from Abroad.
    R. Browning.   Bo-FP:230,
    Co-BN:19, Er-FA:266, Fe-FP:460,
    Fe-PL:376, Ga-FB:229, Ke-TF:366,
    Ma-YA:202, Mc-PR:106, Ox-BN:534,
    Pa-HT:117
Homesick.   Hu P'in-ch'ing.
    Pa-MV:99
Homesick Blues.   L. Hughes.
    Mc-WK:202, Un-MA:552
Hometown Name.   H. Sloanaker.
    Ke-TF:345
A Husband's Song.   Bi-IT:83
In the Highlands.   R. Stevenson.
    Cl-DT:46, Ga-FB:241
Into My Heart an Air That Kills.
    A. Housman.   Al-VBP:1080,
    Bo-GJ:199, Gr-CT:275, Na-EO:193,
    Un-MB:94, Wi-LT:62
I've Got a Home in That Rock.
    R. Patterson.   Ad-PB:209,
    Hu-PN:398
Jerusalem.   J. Halevi.   Me-PH:61
The Kalmyk Mourns for His Country.
    Tr-US II:133
Kentucky Belle.   C. Woolson.
    Ha-PO:133, Un-GT:192
Lament of the Banana Man.
    E. Jones.   To-MP:171
A Letter from Home.   M. Oliver.
    St-H:166
A Little While, a Little While.
    E. Brontë.   Al-VBP:922, Ox-BN:596
Longing for the South Country.
    Li Yu.   Le-MW:42
Mignon's Song.   J. von Goethe.
    Co-PU:48, Pa-SG:125
The Motorcyclist's Song.
    D. Bell.   Pe-M:42
The Mountains of Mourne.   P. French.
    Co-PI:46
My Heart's in the Highlands.
    R. Burns.   Bl-OB:141, Cl-FC:62,
    Fe-FP:463, Mc-PR:175, Mc-WK:192,
    Mo-SD:118, Pa-HT:149
Numerous Celts.   J. Squire.
    Li-SR:151
The Oak and the Ash. . Sm-LG:138
The Old Vicarage, Grantchester.
    R. Brooke.   Ga-FB:239,
    Hi-WP II:129, Pa-HT:120,
    Un-MB:326
On Hearing a Flute at Night from
    the Wall of Shou-Hsiang.
    Li Yi.   Pl-US:11
On His Thirty-Third Birthday.
    Ch'and Kuo Fang.   Rx-LT:118
Original Sin: A Short Story.
    R. Warren.   Wi-LT:839
The Reverie of Poor Susan.
    W. Wordsworth.   De-CH:96, De-TT:108,
    Ho-WR:155, Pa-GTB:256, Rv-CB:639

HOMESICKNESS — cont'd.
A Shropshire Lad.   A. Housman.
   Pa-HT:137
The Soldier's Dream.   T. Campbell.
   Co-RG:40, Pa-GTB:276
Song of Exile.   A. Dias.   Lo-TY:78
Song of Exile.   Tr-US I:130
Song of Young Men Working in Gold
   Mines.   Do-CH:(38)
Sonnets from the Portuguese, XXXV.
   E. Browning.   Al-VBP:817
The South Country.   H. Belloc.
   Un-MB:168
Sunday: New Guinea.   K. Shapiro.
   Br-AF:85
Swanee River.   S. Foster.
   Er-FA:428, Se-PR:256
That Mountain Far Away.   Bi-IT:47
We're Tenting To-Night.
   W. Kittredge.   Vi-PP:160
The West Wind.   J. Masefield.
   Er-FA:242, Un-MB:223, Wi-LT:188
When in Rome.   M. Evans.   Bo-AN:164
Where a Roman Villa Stood, above
   Freiburg.   M. Coleridge.
   Ox-BN:927
The Wild Trees.   L. Lee.   Go-BP:160
Willow, Bend and Weep.   H. Johnson.
   Hu-PN:285
Words from England.   D. Hall.
   Ke-TF:445
HONESTY
The Candid Man.   S. Crane.   Un-MA:147
Courage.   G. Herbert.   Bo-FP:299,
   Ch-B:97, Un-GT:305
Death Is a Clean Cold Word.
   R. Richmond.   Go-BP:230
I Like a Look of Agony.
   E. Dickinson.   Rv-CB:907
The Man of Life Upright. T. Campion.
   Al-VBP:219, De-CH:637, Go-BP:44,
   Ha-PO:197, Rv-CB:273
Truth the Best.   E. Turner.
   Ox-BC:137
HONEY: see also BEES
Brown Bear's Honey Song.
   K. Jackson.   Mc-AW:86, Sh-RP:36
Honey.   M. Cane.   Ls-NY:265
Red-Currant Jelly.   M. Stephenson.
   St-FS:67
A Song of Bread and Honey.
   R. Le Gallienne.   Bo-FP:62
Waiting.   H. Behn.   Ar-TP3:199,
   Br-SG:109, Br-SS:92
HONEYSUCKLES
Honeysuckle.   C. La Farge.
   Sm-PT:49
The Honeysuckle.   D. Rossetti.
   Rv-CB:887
The Wild Honeysuckle.   P. Freneau.
   Fe-PL:383, Rv-CB:558, Sh-AP:16

HONOR: see also FAME; MEDALS;
   SATIRE - HONOR
As a Flower I Come.   Sundaram.
   Al-PI:112
As I Was Going by Charing Cross.
   Bl-OB:146, De-CH:177, De-TT:181,
   Gr-GB:188, Ir-BB:261, Sm-LG:153
The Equilibrists.   J. Ransom.
   Pe-OA:135, Sh-AP:180, Wi-LT:319
God Give Us Men!   J. Holland.
   Se-PR:200, Vi-PP:232
A Good Name.   W. Shakespeare.
   Er-FA:75
Lady Clare.   A. Tennyson.
   Fe-FP:517, Pa-OM:253, Un-GT:144
On the Army of Spartans, Who Died
   at Thermopylae.   Simonides of
   Ceos.   Gr-CT:378
Reviewing Negro Troops Going South
   Through Washington, April 26,
   1864.   P. Horgan.   Cr-WS:23
The Sixth Book of Homer's Iliads.
   Homer.   Al-VBP:148
The Song of Honor.   R. Hodgson.
   Un-MB:188
Tételestai.   C. Aiken.   Un-MA:431,
   Wi-LT:327
To Lucasta, on Going to the Wars.
   R. Lovelace.   Al-VBP:446,
   Er-FA:116, Ga-FB:194, Gr-BT:99,
   Ke-TF:100, Ma-YA:101, Mc-WS:103,
   No-CL:191, Pa-GTB:72, Rv-CB:392,
   Un-MW:153
HOOD, THOMAS
Thomas Hood.   E. Robinson.
   Pl-ML:121
HOOPOES
The Babiaantje.   F. Prince.
   Un-MB:488
The Hoopee.   J. Becker.   Co-BBW:266
Hoopoe.   G. Darley.   Ox-BN:393
HOOVER, HERBERT CLARK: see HUMOR -
   HOOVER, HERBERT CLARK
HOPE: see also ANTICIPATION;
   SATIRE - HOPE
And the Lord Was Not in the
   Whirlwind.   L. MacNeice.
   Pl-EI:154
The Animal That Drank Up Sound.
   W. Stafford.   Ca-VT:413
Anticipation.   E. Brontë.   Ox-BN:604
As One Who Wanders into Old
   Workings.   C. Day-Lewis.
   Wi-LT:426
The Assassination.   R. Hillyer.
   Un-MA:483
Aubade for Hope. R. Warren. Un-MA:589
Both Sides of the Yellow River
   Recaptured by the Imperial
   Army.   Tu Fu.   Cr-WS:10
The Broken Dike, the Levee Washed
   Away.   E. Millay.   Ni-JP:128

Burn the Cocoons. J. Hearst.
    St-H:81
Christmas Lullaby for a New-Born
    Child. Y. Gregory. Bo-AN:153
The Coming. T. Matthews. Sa-B:232
Comparisons. C. Rossetti. Ox-BC:276
Crossing the Bar. A. Tennyson.
    Al-VBP:865, Er-FA:105, Fe-PL:286,
    Ga-FB:127, Ma-YA:199, Mc-PR:105,
    Ox-BN:526, Sp-OG:279
Dark Testament. P. Murray.
    Bo-AN:107
The Darkling Thrush. T. Hardy.
    Co-RG:170, Er-FA:455, Ha-PO:106,
    Na-EO:56, Ox-BN:824, Un-MB:25,
    Wi-LT:17
The Day Is Done. H. Longfellow.
    Ch-B:68, Er-FA:488, Mc-PR:142
Death. E. Bronte. Ox-BN:603
The Descendant and the Id.
    A. Branch. Sm-PT:131
dive for dreams. e. cummings.
    Ha-TP:139
Essay on Man. A. Pope. Al-VBP:536
Farewell and No. J. Adoum.
    Be-UL:109
A Field of Light. T. Roethke.
    Wi-LT:484
Five Short Stanzas, I. Chariot.
    Tsou Ti-fan. Hs-TC:347
For Hope. R. Crashaw. Al-VBP:436
Four Poems, I. E. Blum-Alquit.
    Ho-TY:262
Four Walls to Talk to Me.
    A. Blackwell. Jo-VC:89
The Fundament Is Shifted.
    A. Evans. Tr-MR:238
Giving and Taking. J. Kirkup.
    Pl-EI:47
The Green Spring. Shan Mei.
    Hs-TC:436
He Is Not Dead. T. Wyatt.
    Rv-CB:88
The Heather. S. Blicker.
    Pa-SG:172
Hope. R. Fanshawe. Rv-CB:368
Hope. G. Herbert. Gr-CC:169
Hope. R. Jarrell. Pe-OA:230,
    Un-MA:651
Hope and Joy. C. Rossetti.
    Ox-BC:280
A Hope for Those Separated by
    War. S. Keyes. Gr-BT:122
Hope Is the Thing with Feathers.
    E. Dickinson. Ar-TP3:217,
    Mc-PR:87, Rv-CB:914, Sh-AP:128,
    Un-MA:105
Hope's Forecast. E. Fuller.
    Sh-RP:69
I Am Tied. L. Kvitko. Ho-TY:192
I Am Waiting. V. Howard. Ba-HI:46

I Dreamed You Led Me. A. Machado.
    Le-SW:55
I Have a Dream. M. King. Lo-TY:249
I Sing of May. Jen Chun. Hs-TC:395
In No Strange Land. F. Thompson.
    Ga-S:127, Go-BP:250, Pa-GTB:398,
    Pl-EI:7, Un-MB:90
Junker Schmidt. Co-EL:101
Kicking Your Heels on the Dusty
    Road. P. Solomon. Jo-VC:39
The Last Day of the Year.
    Su Tung P'o. Rx-OH:74
The Life That Counts. Er-FA:24
Light Breaks where No Sun Shines.
    D. Thomas. Al-VBP:1245,
    Un-MB:498
Lyke as a Ship That Through the
    Ocean Wyde. E. Spenser.
    Ma-YA:55
Man Look Not Back. Ga-S:146
The Message of the March Wind.
    W. Morris. Ho-WR:27, Ox-BN:789
A Mother to Her First-Born.
    Tr-CB:27, Tr-US I:105
A Mountain Village. Shiki.
    Be-CS:30
My Magic Window. B. Carter.
    Me-WF:87
Nation. C. Cobb. Ad-PB:468,
    Lo-IT:17
The New World. A. Reisen. Ho-TY:71
Newark, for Now. C. Rodgers.
    Ad-PB:430
Night Piece. J. Manifold.
    Un-MB:513, Wi-LT:766
Night Storm. S. Murano. Sh-AM:92
Nocturne at Bethesda. A. Bontemps.
    Be-MA:43, Bo-AN:81, Hu-PN:211
Ode to the West Wind. P. Shelley.
    Al-VBP:748, Co-BN:127, De-CH:212,
    Er-FA:244, Fe-PL:390, Ga-FB:15,
    Ha-PO:96, Ma-YA:177, Ox-BN:280,
    Pa-GTB:295, Rv-CB:696
On the Beach at Night. W. Whitman.
    Gr-CT:197, Un-MA:65
On Walking to School. T. Carter.
    Me-WF:69
The Onset. R. Frost. Sh-AP:151,
    Un-MA:168
Oriflamme. J. Faucet. Ad-PB:18
Pandora. M. Livingston. Ne-AM:16
Paper Men to Air Hopes and Fears.
    R. Francis. Du-SH:92
A Pause of Thought. C. Rossetti.
    Ox-BN:708
People. Yehoash. Ho-TY:73
Poem. E. Brathwaite. Sa-B:212
Poems Addressed to Ianthe, IV.
    W. Landor. Ox-BN:188
Poems, 1930-1940. H. Gregory.
    Sm-PT:118

HOPE — cont'd.
  Poor Wayfaring Stranger. Ga-S:48
  Prayer after World War. C. Sandburg.
    Ca-VT:26
  Press Onward. Er-FA:22
  The Prisoner. E. Brontë. Ox-BN:607
  Question and Answer. L. Hughes.
    Ra-BP:89
  The Rainy Day. H. Longfellow.
    Fe-PL:303
  The Recapitulation. R. Eberhart.
    Tr-MR:284
  The Recovery. E. Blunden.
    Un-MB:398
  Remember Thy Covenant. E. Pierce.
    Tr-MR:192
  Ring Out, Wild Bells. A. Tennyson.
    Ar-TP3:240, Er-FA:522, Fe-FP:64,
    Ga-S:93, Hu-MP:328, La-PH:45,
    Se-PR:28
  Saul, Afterward, Riding East.
    J. Brinnin. Ho-P:35
  Say Not the Struggle Nought
    Availeth. A. Clough.
    Al-VBP:926, Er-FA:460, Ga-FB:132,
    Ke-TF:57, Ox-BN:610, Pa-GTB:358,
    Pl-EI:121, Rv-CB:842, Tu-WW:44
  The Singers in a Cloud.
    R. Torrence. Pl-US:56
  Socrates' Ghost Must Haunt Me Now.
    D. Schwartz. Wi-LT:518
  Solstice. M. Banus. Mc-AC:114
  Sonnet. P. Shelley. Ox-BN:279
  Sonnet XI. Feng Chih. Hs-TC:150
  Special Starlight. C. Sandburg.
    Tr-MR:101
  Spring. A. Tennyson. Al-VBP:862,
    De-TT:143, Ox-BN:507
  The Still Voice of Harlem. C. Rivers.
    Ad-PB:237, Be-MA:107, Hu-NN:44
  Straight Seeking. T. McNeill.
    Sa-B:8
  A Stroll. Wang T'ing-chao.
    Hs-TC:257
  The Sun Smashed Itself.
    V. Kalugin. Bo-RU:42
  Supernatural. J. Holland. Jo-VC:85
  Tamerlane. E. Poe. Sh-AP:42
  They Will Appear. Bi-IT:169
  Tiny World. J. Holland. Jo-VC:81
  Tomorrow. E. Garner. Ke-TF:237
  The Two Spirits: An Allegory.
    P. Shelley. Ho-P:112
  Visionary. D. Scott. Sa-B:202
  We Walk the Way of the New
    World. D. Lee. Ad-PB:428,
    Be-MA:164, Ra-BP:307
  The West Wind. P. Shelley.
    Bo-FP:167, Ch-B:72
  what if a much of a which of a
    wind. E. Cummings. Al-VBP:1203,
    Er-FA:94, Un-MA:477, Wi-LT:368

  What Should You Do. Rs-RR:32
  When My Ship Comes In. R. Burdett.
    Er-FA:30
  Where the Rainbow Ends. R. Rive.
    Ab-MO:107, Lo-TY:180
  White Night. K. Molodowsky.
    Ho-TY:288
  The Wind's Arrows Shoot
    Ceaselessly. Wang Ching-chih.
    Hs-TC:44
  Youth. L. Hughes. Bo-HF:107,
    Br-AF:243, Br-BC:134, Li-TU:266
HOPELESSNESS: see DESPAIR
HOPI INDIANS: see also INDIANS OF
    NORTH AMERICA - VERSE - HOPI
  A Dance for Rain. W. Bynner.
    Pa-HT:58
  The Hopis and the Famine. Te-FC:35
HOPKINS, GERARD MANLEY
  Poem for Gerard. E. Mayo.
    Pl-ML:127
HOPPER, EDWARD
  Edward Hopper's "House by the
    Tracks." R. Cuscaden. St-H:33
HOPPING
  Away We Go! E. Dennis. Mc-AW:14
  Hoppity. A. Milne. Ar-TP3:100,
    Ga-FB:173
HORACE
  A Classical Quotation.
    P. Goodman. Ca-VT:333
  On First Looking into Loeb's
    Horace. L. Durrell. Wi-LT:695
HORATIUS COCLES
  Horatius. T. Macauley. Er-FA:387,
    Fe-PL:64, Hi-FO:32, Sm-LG:161
HORIZON
  Each Morning. I. Baraka.
    Ad-PB:250, Hu-NN:74
  I Saw a Man Pursuing the Horizon.
    S. Crane. Mo-BG:195, Sm-LG:389,
    Un-MA:147, Wi-LT:118
HORNETS
  The Harnet and the Bittle.
    J. Akerman. Gr-CT:15
HORNS (MUSICAL INSTRUMENTS):
    see also HUMOR - HORNS
    (MUSICAL INSTRUMENTS);
    and names of musical in-
    struments, as BUGLES
  The Horn. L. Adams. Un-MA:546
HORROR: see FEAR
HORSE CHESTNUTS: see CHESTNUTS
HORSE RACING: see also HUMOR -
    HORSE RACING
  At Galway Races. W. Yeats.
    Mo-SD:191
  At Grass. P. Larkin. Ha-WR:25,
    Mo-SD:176
  Morning Workout. B. Deutsch.
    Fl-HH:33, Mo-SD:67

HORSEMANSHIP: see RIDERS AND
   RIDING; RODEOS
HORSES: see also HOBBYHORSES;
   HUMOR - HORSES
All Through the Rains. G. Snyder.
   Kh-VA:5
Annan Water. De-CH:311, Ma-BB:214
At Amberley Wild Brooks. A. Young.
   Rd-OA:193
At Grass. P. Larkin. Ha-WR:25,
   Mo-SD:176
Ballad of East and West.
   R. Kipling. Ar-TP3:25, Ga-FB:211
Birthday Gifts. L. Scott. Br-BC:99
Black Hair Rope Is What You Used.
   Ho-SD:42
A Blessing. J. Wright. Br-TC:485,
   Du-SH:122, Kh-VA:31, Ma-FW:226,
   Mc-EA:53, St-H:261
The Blood Horse. B. Procter.
   Co-BBW:157
The Broncho Buster. Fi-BG:89
The Broncho That Would Not Be
   Broken. V. Lindsay.
   Ar-TP3:255, Co-BBW:147, Co-RG:108
Broncho Versus Bicycle.
   J. Crawford. Fi-BG:117
Charley Lee. H. Knibbs. Co-RM:172,
   Mc-WK:144
Daniel Webster's Horses.
   E. Coatsworth. Br-AF:116,
   Co-PM:34, De-FS:55, Un-MA:464
The Dead Horse. C. Meireles.
   An-TC:43
The Discarded Horse. H. Anzai.
   Sh-AM:118
The Distant Runners. M. Van Doren.
   Sm-LG:81, Un-MA:467, Wi-LT:653
Doney Gal. Fi-BG:165
The Dusk of Horses. J. Dickey.
   Wi-LT:689
Epitaph for a Lighthouse-
   Keeper's Horse. J. Morton.
   Co-PU:156
Epitaphs for Horses. Fi-BG:98
Fast Rode the Knight. S. Crane.
   Li-TU:236
The Fly-Away Horse. E. Field.
   Un-GB:32, Un-GT:298
The Flying Outlaw. C. Fletcher.
   Fi-BG:94
Foal. M. Miller. Ar-TP3:77,
   Co-BBW:145, Co-IW:13, La-PV:122
The Four Horses. J. Reeves.
   Co-BBW:151
Friend. Jo-TS:20
Galloping Pony. Kyorai. Ca-BF:45
A Gigantic Beauty of a Stallion.
   W. Whitman. Co-BBW:149,
   La-PV:124
Go to the Barn for Courtesy.
   T. Coffin. Ke-TF:339

Great Aso. T. Miyoshi. Sh-AM:82
The Harness Shop. M. Moody.
   Ke-TF:353
Here Comes Our Noble Mr. Horse.
   Issa. Be-MC:22
Hey! My Pony! E. Farjeon.
   Fe-FP:482
The Horse. Bible. O.T. Job.
   Fe-FP:163, Gr-CT:264, Un-GT:28
The Horse. Cheng Min. Hs-TC:234
Horse. J. Harrison. Ha-WR:24
Horse. E. Roberts. Co-BBW:145,
   Sh-RP:38
The Horse. W. Shakespeare.
   Co-BBW:143, Un-GT:28
The Horse. W. Williams.
   Rd-OA:19, We-PZ:26
Horse and Hammer. P. Dufault.
   Co-BBW:157
The Horse and the Mule. J. Wynne.
   Ox-BC:78
The Horse and the Whip.
   E. Steinberg. Ho-TY:233
The Horse of Adonis.
   W. Shakespeare. Cl-FC:73
Horse on a City Street. S. Muano.
   Sh-AM:89
The Horse Thief. W. Benét.
   Pa-OM:300, Un-MA:324
The Horse Trader's Song. Em-AF:762
Horseback Ride. S. Johnson.
   Ho-GC:30
Horses. A. Fisher. Mc-AW:53
The Horses. T. Hughes. Go-BP:99,
   Ha-WR:74
Horses. R. Kipling. Co-PU:89
Horses. M. Mendes. An-TC:55
Horses. E. Muir. Sm-LG:80
The Horses. E. Muir. Go-BP:101,
   Ha-PO:117, Un-MB:343
The Horses. K. Wilson. Sc-TN:238
Horses and Men in the Rain.
   C. Sandburg. Fe-PL:409
The Horses of the Sea. C. Rossetti.
   Bo-GJ:42, Fe-FP:274, Li-LC:33
   Horses on the Camargue. R. Campbell.
      Pa-GTB:494, Rd-OA:153
   The Horse's Prayer. Mo-TB:123
How They Brought the Good News
   from Ghent to Aix. R. Browning.
   Ar-TP3:31, Co-RG:31, Er-FA:378,
   Gr-EC:156, Hi-WP I:66, Li-SR:12,
   Sp-OG:29, Un-GT:149
Hua-La-Ma-Ch'ao. T'ien Chien.
   Hs-TC:331
The Hush-Hush. M. Saito. Sh-AM:145
I Had a Little Pony. Mother Goose.
   Au-SP:19, Bl-OB:115, Bo-FP:131,
   De-TT:20, Li-LB:82, Mo-MGT:179,
   Mo-NR:128, Mo-TL:82, Wr-RM:83
Improvised Songs. Tr-US II:130

HORSES — cont'd.
  John Cook Had a Grey Mare.
    Bl-OB:115, De-TT:20, Mo-TL:84,
    Rv-ON:29, Wi-MG:56
  Kentucky Belle. C. Woolson.
    Ha-PO:133, Un-GT:192
  The Kentucky Thoroughbred.
    J. Riley. Co-EL:52
  The Knight's Leap. C. Kingsley.
    Co-PT:230
  Little Horse. W. Merwin. Ho-TH:87
  Little Nag. Mo-MGT:66
  A Living Pearl. K. Rexroth.
    Wi-LT:798
  The Lochmabyn Harper. Ma-BB:208,
    Ox-BB:582
  Love Song to Eohippus. P. Viereck.
    Un-MA:659
  The Man from Snowy River.
    A. Paterson. Co-RM:141,
    Hi-WP II:91
  Man Watching. A. Brownjohn.
    Ls-NY:290
  The Milkman's Horse. Au-SP:48,
    Co-IW:33
  Moss. Rv-ON:90
  A Mother Horse. Issa. Do-TS:(19),
    Le-MW:8
  The Mouse-Brown Foal. W. Renton.
    Hi-WP I:28
  My Horse. Bu-DY:38
  My Horse Took Me down the Life-
    Giving Road. Wo-HS:(45)
  My Pony. D. Aldis. Ma-FO:(33)
  My Tired Old Nag. Issa. Be-MC:20
  Noonday Sun. K. & B. Jackson.
    Ar-TP3:33, Fe-FP:161
  Old Gray Mare. Gr-GB:54
  Old Horse. Sun Yü-t'ang. Hs-TC:122
  The Old Mare. E. Coatsworth.
    Un-MA:463
  One Day. W. Horne, Jr. Ho-CT:14
  Orchard. R. Stone. Co-BBW:152
  Out of the Earth. Ho-SD:11
  Pain for a Daughter. A. Sexton.
    Mc-WS:142
  Paiute Ponies. J. Barnes.
    Ni-CD:25
  The Ponies. W. Gibson. Co-BBW:152,
    Mc-WK:74
  The Pony. Bu-DY:42
  Poor Old Horse. De-CH:84
  The Prancing Pony. De-PP:31
  The Prayer of the Old Horse.
    C. Gasztold. La-PV:126
  Prayers for the First Forty Days
    of the Dead. S. Yesenin. Ca-MR:109
  Rondeau of the Little Horses.
    M. Bandeira. An-TC:7
  The Runaway. R. Frost. Ar-TP3:77,
    Bo-GJ:72, Br-TC:137, Ca-VT:16,
    Co-BBW:143, De-CH:24, Fe-FP:161,
    Gr-EC:39, Hu-MP:196, La-PV:125,
    Se-PR:301, Sh-RP:343, Sm-LG:82,
    Un-GT:29, Un-MA:179
  Say This of Horses. M. Moody.
    Fe-PL:365
  Sheridan's Ride. T. Read.
    Er-FA:185, Ga-FB:261, Sp-OG:44
  Sir Gawain and the Green Knight.
    Ma-YA:21
  Sixteen-Syllable Stanza.
    Mao Tse-tung. Hs-TC:362
  Song of Horses. M. Beniuc.
    Mc-AC:96
  Song of the Horse. Da-SC:79,
    Le-OE:37
  Song of the Horse Society.
    Tr-US II:236
  Songs to Horses, I, II.
    Tr-US I:116
  Steeds. P. Hiebert. Do-WH:93
  The Stricken Colts. L. Peck.
    Ls-NY:211
  Sweet Wind That up the Climbing
    Road. M. Johnson. De-CH:538
  There Is an Old Horse.
    Jao Meng-k'an. Hs-TC:107
  Three Colts Exercising in a Six-
    Acre. J. Campbell. Co-PI:17
  Three Ponies. A. Guiterman.
    Gr-EC:11
  To the Four Courts, Please.
    J. Stephens. Co-PI:178,
    Ni-JP:86, Un-MB:263
  Trading Song. Tr-US II:253
  Trot Along, Pony. M. Edy &
    D. Grider. Ar-TP3:77, Au-SP:46
  Unbridled Horse, Leap. Soseki.
    Ca-BF:43
  The War God's Horse Song.
    Br-MW:60, Sm-LG:78
  The War Horse. Bible. O.T.
    Job. Co-BBW:158
  White Horses. E. Farjeon.
    La-PV:123
  The White Steed of the Prairies.
    J. Barber. Fi-BG:87
  Who'll That Be. K. Patchen.
    Mc-WK:94
  Wild Horse. H. Allen. Le-M:99
  Work Horses. E. Chase. Au-SP:47
  Your Load Being Taken Off.
    S. Ogiwara. Sh-AM:165
HORSESHOES
  Wonder Where This Horseshoe Went.
    E. Millay. Ar-TP3:94, Pe-FB:41
HOSPITALITY: see also BAUCIS AND
    PHILEMON; GUESTS; HUMOR -
    HOSPITALITY; INVITATIONS;
    SATIRE - HOSPITALITY;
    WELCOMES
  Baucis and Philemon. J. Swift.
    Sp-OG:153

The Beggar Man.   L. Aikin.
   Ox-BC:109
Canterbury Tales.   G. Chaucer.
   Al-VBP:9
The Christmas Child.   Bo-FP:189
An Easy Decision.   K. Patchen.
   Du-SH:21, Ha-LO:44
The English Are Frosty. A. Miller.
   Fe-PL:127
The Fine Old English Gentleman.
   De-CH:63
The Fire in the Snow.   V. Watkins.
   Wi-LT:454
The Golden Palace.   Gr-CC:181
The Guest.   W. Berry.   Ha-TP:96
The Hostess.   Wang Mou Fang.
   Le-MW:101
Improvised Song of Joy.
   Le-IB:100, Tr-US I:13
In the Valley of the Elwy.
   G. Hopkins.   Al-VBP:1061,
   Go-BP:30
The Lands Around My Dwelling.
   Bi-IT:49, Br-MW:141, Ma-BH:23
The Limits of Submission.
   F. Nuur.   Ab-MO:29, Lo-TY:58
Love and a Question.   R. Frost.
   Ca-MB:16
Mine Host of the "Golden Apples."
   T. Westwood.   Gr-EC:46
Preparations.   Al-VBP:353,
   De-CH:464, Ga-S:131, Hi-WP I:137,
   Na-EO:19, Pl-EI:16, Rv-CB:116,
   Sm-LG:378
A Revel.   D. Macdonagh. Co-PI:101
The Road to Pengya.   Tu Fu.
   Ho-P:75
Song.   T. Peacock.   Al-VBP:714
Stranger.   E. Roberts.   Un-MA:270
Strawberry Jam.   M. Justus.
   Fe-FP:310
A Traveler Departs.   W. Gerry.
   Ke-TF:417
The Traveller.   O. Goldsmith.
   Al-VBP:584
The Vicar.   W. Praed.   Ox-BN:445
Visit.   A. Ammons.   Br-TC:9,
   Kh-VA:25, Mo-BG:100
The Visit of the Professor of
   Aesthetics.   M. Danner.
   Ad-PB:135, Be-MA:89, Bo-AN:155,
   Hu-NN:31
Visitors.   Tu Fu.   Rx-OH:19
The Wanderer Recalls the Past.
   W. Wordsworth.   Ox-BN:92
Yussouf.   J. Lowell.   Hu-MP:409
HOSPITALS: see also ASYLUMS;
   HUMOR - HOSPITALS:
Before.   W. Henley.   Un-MB:54
Commander Death.   P. Horgan.
   Cr-WS:103

The Cottage Hospital.   J. Betjeman.
   Pa-GTB:502, Un-MB:438
The Country of a Thousand Years of
   Peace.   J. Marrill.   En-PC:240
Dedication for a Building.
   A. Dugan.   Ad-CL:89
Evening in the Sanitarium.
   L. Bogan.   Br-TC:56
A Flat One.   W. Snodgrass.
   En-PC:244, Wi-LT:822
He Died a Second Time, 2.
   Hospital. Ai Ch'ing.   Hs-TC:303
Hospital.   K. Shapiro.   Ca-VT:370
The Hospital.   S. Tanikawa.
   Sh-AM:130
Hospital Visit.   R. Roseliep.
   St-H:185
The Night Nurse Goes Her Round.
   J. Gray.   Ox-BN:940
Pilgrim State Hospital.   S. Mernit.
   Ad-II:66
Sanitorium.   H. Leivick.   Ho-TY:122
Surgical Ward.   W. Auden. Pe-SS:146
HOTELS: see HUMOR - HOTELS
HOTHOUSES: see GREENHOUSES
HOTTENTOTS: see also AFRICAN
   VERSE - HOTTENTOT
The Ancestors.   Be-AP:20
Midsummer Fantasy.   N. Levy.
   Co-PS:110
HOUNDS: see DOGS
HOURS: see TIME
HOUSEHOLD FURNISHINGS: see also
   HUMOR - HOUSEHOLD FURNISHINGS;
   and names of articles, as
   CHAIRS and RADIATORS
A Kettle for the Tea.   Gr-BB:31
Of All the Different Kinds of
   Bowls.   Gr-BB:30
HOUSEKEEPING: see also HUMOR -
   HOUSEKEEPING
Dear God, the Day Is Grey.
   A. Halley.   Pe-OA:287
The Divine Office of the Kitchen.
   C. Hallack.   Fe-PL:335
Dust.   S. Russell.   Br-SM:116,
   Du-RG:64
The Fairies.   R. Herrick.
   Bl-OB:90, Fe-FP:384, Hu-MP:87
Farm Wife.   R. Thomas.   Go-BP:50
I Like Housecleaning.
   D. Thompson.   Fe-FP:47
Mary of Bethany.   D. Lawrence.
   Ga-S:116
Mrs. Southern's Enemy.
   O. Sitwell.   Al-VBP:1190
The Monk in the Kitchen.
   A. Branch.   Un-MA:152
On a Tired Housewife.   Ga-S:216,
   Hi-WP I:9, Na-EO:139, Sm-MK:113
On an Island. J. Synge. Un-MB:181
Setting the Table.   D. Aldis.
   Ar-TP3:177, Fe-FP:44, Hu-MP:17

HOUSEKEEPING — cont'd.
  To an Isle in the Water.
    W. Yeats. Gr-TG:65, Sm-MK:8
  Washing the Dishes. C. Morley.
    Fe-PL:143
  The Week in Old New England.
    Mo-TB:111
  When Young Melissa Sweeps.
    N. Turner. Fe-FP:46
HOUSES: see also APARTMENT HOUSES;
    ATTICS; HOME;   HUMOR - HOUSES;
    SATIRE - HOUSES; TENEMENT
    HOUSES
  Animals' Houses. J. Reeves.
    St-FS:96
  Ann's House. D. Lourie. Sc-TN:151
  Appearances. R. Browning. Rv-CB:827
  Autumn. V. Contoski.   Sc-TN:27
  The Black Cottage. R. Frost.
    Ca-VT:5
  The Bourgeois Poet, #29.
    K. Shapiro. St-H:202
  The Deserted House. M. Coleridge.
    De-CH:49, De-TT:157, Pa-RE:63
    Re-TW:88
  The Deserted House. J. Fairbun.
    Le-M:175
  Empty House. E. Coatsworth.
    De-FS:52
  Even Numbers. C. Sandburg.
    La-OC:101
  A Fountain, a Bottle, a Donkey's
    Ears, and Some Books.
    R. Frost. Ca-VT:12
  The Green Afternoon. H. Rago.
    Ca-VT:425
  The Haunted House. T. Hood.
    Ho-WR:192
  The Hill Wife. R. Frost. Ca-VT:10
  The House. E. Almedingen.
    Ke-TF:412
  The House. R. Debee. Al-PI:84
  A House. Martial. Mc-PR:26
  The House. W. Williams. Ca-VT:50
  The House. R. Young Bear.
    Ni-CD:292
  A House and Grounds. J. Hunt.
    Rv-CB:684
  House Blessing. A. Guiterman.
    Ar-TP3:216
  House Dedication Prayer. Tr-US II:98
  The House in the Green Well.
    J. Wheelock. Un-MA:344
  House Moving. P. Hubbell. Su-FVI:41
  The House of Life. D. Quick.
    De-FS:151
  The House of Richesse. E. Spenser.
    De-CH:322
  The House of the Mouse. L. Mitchell.
    Ar-TP3:59, Au-SP:56, Co-IW:8,
    It-HB:59

House of Yesterday. W. Shedlofsky.
  De-FS:175
The House on Maple Hill. S. McNail.
  De-FS:139
The House on the Hill.
  E. Robinson. Bo-GJ:204,
  Bo-HF:131, Fe-FP:241, Ha-PO:156,
  Ho-TH:18, Hu-MP:77, Un-MA:118
House Song to the East. Da-SC:78
The House That Was. L. Binyon.
  Un-MB:157
The House with Nobody in It.
  J. Kilmer. Hu-MP:74, Th-AS:206
Houses. A. Fisher. Au-SP:206
Houses Bent Over. R. McBride.
  La-IH:40
Houses Have No Fun. D. Hendell.
  Me-WF:18
I Know Some Lonely Houses.
  E. Dickinson. Co-PM:50,
  Mc-WK:129, Rv-CB:900, Un-MA:103
If I Had a Cardboard Box.
  A. Fisher. Mc-AW:7
Incorporate. M. Caruthers.
  Ke-TF:414
Inmate. L. Jennings. Ke-TF:411
A Journey. Li Kuang-t'ien.
  Hs-TC:203
The Little House. Alesha.
  Mo-MI:77
Love in a Life. R. Browning.
  Ox-BN:543, Rv-CB:815
Mr. Bleaney. P. Larkin. Gr-BT:33
Murder House. E. Coatsworth.
  De-FS:54
My House. J. Krows. Au-SP:127
My Wish. Carliss St. Me-WF:19
New England Farmhouses.
  R. Montgomery. Ke-TF:410
New House. B. Buchanan. Ke-TF:409
The New House. E. Thomas.
  Un-MB:215
Not So Simple. S. Shalom.
  Me-PH:106
Oh, Joyous House. R. Janzen.
  Le-M:152
The Old Houses of Flanders.
  F. Hueffer. Pa-HT:112
Old Log House. J. Tippett.
  Fe-FP:240, Sh-RP:292
An Old Woman of the Roads.
  P. Colum. De-CH:49, Fe-FP:320,
  Hu-MP:156, Sh-RP:43, Th-AS:184,
  Un-MB:250
On Blenheim House. A. Evans.
  Rv-CB:501
On the Pagoda. Chung Ting-wen.
  Pa-MV:74
Plans. H. Brooks. Hu-NN:109,
  Hu-PN:274

Prayer for This House.
L. Untermeyer. Fe-FP:57,
Fe-PL:136, Mc-PR:104
The Quarry Pool. D. Levertov.
Ca-VT:510
Room in Darkness. M. Counselman.
De-FS:68
Ruins of a Great House. D. Walcott.
Br-TC:447
The Sea House. W. Goodreau.
Ls-NY:255
Shadowed. B. Eaton. De-FS:83
Song for a Little House. C. Morley.
Fe-FP:29, Hu-MP:3, La-PP:41
Song of Entering the Village.
Da-SC:115
Squares and Angles. A. Storni.
La-OC:100
Two Houses. E. Thomas. Sm-LG:397
Vacant House. J. Bonnette.
Du-SH:167
Victorian Parlor. E. Bohm.
Ke-TF:410
Week-End. H. Monro. Un-MB:233
When the Tree Bares. C. Aiken.
Un-MA:433
The Winter House. N. Cameron.
Rv-CB:999
HOUSMAN, ALFRED EDWARD: see also
HUMOR - HOUSMAN, ALFRED EDWARD
To A. E. Housman. W. Bynner.
Ls-NY:137
HUDSON, HENRY
Henry Hudson's Quest, 1609.
B. Stevenson. Vi-PP:44
The Weepers Tower in Amsterdam.
P. Goodman. Ca-VT:334
HUDSON RIVER
The Lordly Hudson. P. Goodman.
Ca-VT:332
The Mouth of the Hudson. R. Lowell.
Ad-CI:29, Bl-FP:79, Br-AF:181,
Ha-TP:12, La-OC:39
My Plan. W. Chute. Br-BC:115,
Fe-FP:112
New York-Albany. L. Ferlinghetti.
En-PC:171
The Returned Volunteer to His
Rifle. H. Melville. Gr-CC:114,
Hi-TL:130
HUEFFER, FORD MADOX: see FORD,
FORD MADOX
HUGHES, JOHN LANGSTON
Do Nothing till You Hear from Me.
D. Henderson. Ad-PB:419
Langston. M. Evans. Ad-BO:27
Reading Walt Whitman. C. Forbes.
Ad-PB:490
HULL, ISAAC
The Constitution and the
Guerriére. Em-AF:434
HUMAN BODY: see BODY, HUMAN

HUMAN RACE: see MAN
HUMAN RIGHTS: see CIVIL RIGHTS
HUMILIATION: see also HUMOR -
HUMILIATION; SHAME
Cassandra. R. Jeffers. Wi-LT:266
Doldrums. C. O'John. Al-WW:65
Farewell, My Nation! Farewell,
Black Hawk. Black Hawk. Kr-OF:6
From Governor Everett, Receiving
the Indians Chiefs, November,
1837. M. Fuller. Kr-OF:8
HUMILITY
The Ant's a Centaur. E. Pound.
Ha-PO:220
The Blades of Grass. S. Crane.
Sh-AP:144, Un-MA:147
Canto LXXXI. E. Pound. Al-VBP:1165,
Pe-OA:83
The Chief Men of the Village Answer
the Greeting of Travelers.
Tr-US I:162
A Contemplation upon Flowers.
H. King. Co-BN:44, Rv-CB:350
Dance Song. Le-IB:78
The Fear of God. R. Frost.
Tr-MR:225
The Feet of Judas. G. McClellan.
Hu-PN:17
From a Hint in the Minor Poets.
S. Wesley. Rv-CB:515
From Greenland to Iceland.
Er-FA:214
The Gray Monk. W. Blake. Ba-PO:9
Humility. R. Herrick. Hi-WP I:138,
Un-GT:306
I Am Disquieted when I See Many
Hills. H. Plutzik. Ca-VT:347
I Will Bow and Be Simple. Pl-EI:188
If Humility and Purity Be Not in
the Heart. T. Eliot. Ar-TP3:214
I'm Nobody! Who Are You?
E. Dickinson. Ar-TP3:211,
Bo-FP:275, Co-PU:40, La-PV:221,
Mo-BG:43, Rv-CB:912, Un-GT:91
Kibbutz Sabbath. L. Amittai.
Pl-EI:192
On a Dewy Morning. Ch'en Meng-chia.
Hs-TC:112
A Prayer to Go to Heaven with the
Donkeys. F. Jammes. Ar-TP3:83,
Co-BBW:149, Go-BP:255, Pl-EI:124,
Rd-OA:20, Tr-MR:52
Proud of My Broken Heart.
E. Dickinson. Al-VBP:1002
A Reply. Wen I-to. Hs-TC:63
The Shepherd Boy's Song.
J. Bunyan. Gr-TG:17, Pl-EI:204,
Rv-CB:459, Un-GT:308
A Song of Humility. C. Drewry.
Tr-MR:268
Sonnet IV. Feng Chih.
Hs-TC:150

HUMILITY — cont'd.
  Sonnets from the Portuguese
    XXXII. E. Browning. Al-VBP:817
  Star-Swirls. R. Jeffers. Du-SH:108
  Truth. G. Chaucer. Al-VBP:18,
    Rv-CB:60
  A Walk Late in Summer. T. Roethke.
    Rd-OA:3
  The Way of Life. Laotse. Ba-PO:7,
    Mc-WK:220
  We Are Living Humbly. Bi-IT:157
  A Wild Flower. Ch'en Meng-chia.
    Hs-TC:112
  Wisdom. L. Hughes. Ar-TP3:216
HUMMINGBIRDS
  The Container. C. Corman. Ca-VT:525
  A Crocodile. T. Beddoes. Co-BBW:84
  Garden Song. A. Guiterman.
    Br-SG:63, Th-AS:48
  The Honey Bird's Song. Tr-US I:60
  The Humming Bird. M. Howitt.
    Bo-FP:241, Ch-B:112
  The Humming Bird. H. Kemp.
    Fe-FP:291, Hu-MP:235
  Humming-Bird. D. Lawrence.
    Ca-BP:18, Wi-LT:218
  The Hummingbird. E. Dickinson.
    Sh-AP:131, Un-GT:60
  The Hummingbird. M. Kennedy.
    Co-BBW:252
  Hummingbird. R. Roseliep.
    St-H:184
  November Garden. L. Driscoll.
    Ha-YA:124
  A Prayer in Spring. R. Frost.
    Ha-YA:29, Tr-MR:48
  Song of Hummingbird. Le-OE:49
  The Storm. E. Coatsworth.
    Co-PU:100
HUMOR: see also DIALECTS;
    HUMORISTS; LIMERICKS;
    NONSENSE; PARODIES;
    TONGUE TWISTERS; WIT
  Archy Confesses. D. Marquis.
    Co-FB:359, Na-EO:142
  The Height of the Ridiculous.
    O. Holmes. Co-FB:346, Co-HP:76,
    Er-FA:221, Hu-MP:447, Mc-PR:102
HUMOR - ABBREVIATIONS
  Do You Plan to Speak Bantu?
    O. Nash. Co-FB:413
HUMOR - ABOMINABLE SNOWMEN
  The Abominable Snowman. O. Nash.
    Pa-RE:39
HUMOR - ACCIDENTS
  Accidentally. M. Kumin. Ja-PC:59
  Annabel Lee. S. Huntley. Li-SR:71
  Awkward Child. R. Fyleman.
    Ir-BB:156
  A Ballad in "G." E. Ware.
    Fe-PL:217
  Blue Bell Boy. Wr-RM:44

  Brown's Descent. R. Frost.
    Ar-TP3:145, Ha-PO:287, Na-EO:89,
    Sp-OG:234, Un-MA:178
  The Cataract at Ladore (July 3,
    1936). H. Bevington. Li-SR:88
  A Cricket Triolet. C. Kernaham.
    Hi-WP I:11
  Daddy Fell into the Pond. A. Noyes.
    Co-HP:101, Fe-FP:35, Ja-PC:40,
    La-PP:45, La-PV:24, Sh-RP:140
  A Decrepit Old Gasman. Br-LL:77,
    Co-HP:29, Er-FA:220
  Gentle Doctor Brown. B. Taylor.
    Co-OH:46
  Hallelujah! A. Housman. Br-SM:59,
    Co-FB:383, Co-PU:32, Co-OT:57
  Here's Little Jim Nast of Pawtucket.
    H. Lofting. Br-LL:75
  I Never Had a Piece of Toast.
    J. Payne. Un-GF:15
  Ladywell. E. Farjeon. Ir-BB:151
  Limericks since Lear. Un-GT:242
  A Little Boy Down in Natchez.
    Br-LL:78
  A Melancholy Song. Mo-MGT:205,
    Rv-ON:106, Wr-RM:16
  The Minister in the Pulpit.
    Co-OW:21, Su-FVI:19
  Mrs. Poff. Ir-BB:148
  Piggy on the Railway. Ir-BB:158
  A Poem to Delight My Friends
    Who Laugh at Science
    Fiction. E. Rolfe. Cr-WW:168,
    Hi-TL:234, Ke-PP:125
  Prince Tatters. L. Richards.
    Hu-MP:10
  Ring the Bells, Ring. Ir-BB:156,
    Mo-MGT:49
  Ruth and Johnnie. Br-SM:56
  Said a Foolish Young Lady of
    Wales. L. Reed. Br-LL:77
  Sir Smashum Uppe. E. Rieu.
    Co-OW:41
  There Was a Young Fellow Named
    Hall. Br-LL:73, Sm-MK:201
  There Was an Old Lady Whose
    Folly. E. Lear. Br-LL:91
  Tom Ducket. J. Jaszi. Sh-RP:135
  The Two Gray Kits. Ir-BB:153,
    Wr-RM:80
  Two Triolets. M. Baring. Ir-BB:159
  Uncle. H. Graham. Co-OT:56
HUMOR - ACHILLES
  There Was a Young Man Named
    Achilles. E. Robinson. Br-LL:65
HUMOR - ADAM AND EVE
  Eve to Her Daughters. J. Wright.
    To-MP:173
  The Lady's Maid's Song.
    J. Hollander. Wi-LT:732
  What's Wrong. Rs-PF:119

When Adam Day by Day. A. Housman.
    Co-EL:59, Co-FB:409
HUMOR - ADVENTURE AND ADVENTURERS
The Burnt Bridge. L. MacNeice.
    Gr-SS:111
The Crocodile. Co-RM:65, Rv-CB:441
Jippy and Jimmy. L. Richards.
    Ar-TP3:49, Au-SP:223, Hu-MP:453
Momotaro. Ar-TP3:136, Ir-BB:243
Sally Go round the Sun.
    Br-FF:(4), Mo-CC:(9), Mo-MGT:100,
    Mo-TL:104
There Was a Naughty Boy. J. Keats.
    Bo-FP:113, Ch-B:77, Co-HP:84,
    Fr-WO:69, Gr-EC:215, Ir-BB:97,
    Ma-YA:183, Ox-BC:148, Pl-ML:18,
    Sm-LG:291, Sm-MK:131, Un-GF:18
Three Wise Old Women. E. Corbett.
    Ox-BC:284
Upon Pagget. R. Herrick. Sm-LG:111
HUMOR - ADVERTISING
Inscription on a Klim Can.
    Yüan Shui-p'ai. Hs-TC:404
Nightmare Number Four. R. Bloch.
    De-FS:24
Summer Song. W. Watt. Co-FB:458
HUMOR - ADVICE
Advice. A. Resnikoff. Co-OH:84
Advice to a Knight. T. Jones.
    Ma-FW:245
Bringing Him Up. Lord Dunsany.
    Co-BB:15, Co-PU:4
The Devil's Advice to Story-
    Tellers. R. Graves. Rv-CB:993,
    Wi-LT:371
Epigram. A. Lanusse. Ab-MO:30,
    Hu-PN:13, Lo-TY:96
Epigram Addressed to an Artist.
    R. Burns. Co-PU:24
A Gentle Echo on Woman. J. Swift.
    Co-FB:438
Jane, Do Be Careful. I. Page.
    Co-BB:54
Jim. H. Belloc. Br-SM:113,
    Co-BB:70, Gr-CT:22, Ir-BB:161,
    Lo-LL:80, Na-EO:150
Mother, May I Go Out to Swim.
    Fe-FP:364, Ir-BB:141, Mo-MGT:37,
    Sp-AS:30
The Python. H. Belloc. Br-SM:129,
    Na-EO:166
Rules and Regulations.
    L. Carroll. Un-GF:51
Sage Counsel. A. Quiller-Couch.
    Co-HP:104, Lo-LL:27
The Story of Pauline and the
    Matches. H. Hoffman. Un-GF:56
Three Children Sliding. J. Gay.
    De-TT:39, Ir-BB:139, Li-LB:44,
    Mo-MGT:24, Un-GF:13, Wr-RM:13
Warning to Children. R. Graves.
    Bl-OB:32, Er-FA:508, Ma-FW:195,
    Sm-LG:102

HUMOR - AFFECTATION
Bunthorne's Song. W. Gilbert.
    Co-FB:349
The Lion and the Cub. J. Gay.
    Sp-OG:305
Old Man Know-All. Ra-PB:9
"Very Interesting" Death.
    Yüan Shui-p'ai. Hs-TC:408
HUMOR - AFRICA
Sadie's Playhouse. M. Danner.
    Ad-PB:138
HUMOR - AIRPLANES
Darius Green and His Flying
    Machine. J. Trowbridge.
    Fe-PL:204
The Unwinged Ones. O. Nash.
    Ke-TF:290
HUMOR - THE ALAMO
Dumbbell. W. Cole. Co-OH:59
HUMOR - ALASKA
Alaska, or Hell of the Yukon.
    Fi-BG:43
HUMOR - ALBERT, PRINCE CONSORT
    OF ENGLAND
Old England Forever, and Do It
    No More. Gr-GB:200
HUMOR - ALLITERATION
Melody for Lute and Ocarina.
    M. Bishop. Gr-EC:221
Nephelidia. A. Swinburne.
    Li-SR:144
What'll Be the Title?
    J. Richardson. Co-FB:413
HUMOR - ALPHABETS
The ABC. S. Milligan. Co-OH:20
A Ballad in "G." E. Ware.
    Fe-PL:217
Enigma on the Letter H.
    C. Fanshawe. Un-GT:229
Holy Order. J. Boothroyd.
    Co-FB:124
The Little Girl Opened the Icebox.
    Re-RR:95
A Nonsense Alphabet. E. Lear.
    Au-SP:258, Gr-EC:257, Ox-BC:192
There's a Very Mean Man of
    Belsize. Br-LL:103
What Letter Has Never Yet.
    Re-RR:84
What Word of Only Three Syllables.
    Re-RR:100
HUMOR - AMBITION
Ambition. E. Agnew. Ar-TP3:137
Ambition. Ke-TF:278
For My Contemporaries.
    J. Cunningham. Ha-PO:231,
    Mo-BG:58
Higher. Co-FB:242, Li-SR:51
Johan the Monk. Li-TU:119
Pastoral. W. Williams. Pe-SS:44
The Snail's Dream. O. Herford.
    Bo-FP:86, Ch-B:66

HUMOR - AMBITION — cont'd.
  Somebody Said that It Couldn't
    Be Done.   Co-FB:481, Co-PU:30
  Song by Isbrand.   T. Beddoes.
    Ox-BN:451
  There Once Was a Sow.   On-TW:12
  There Was a Young Maid Who Said,
    "Why. . . ."   Fr-WO:48, Ir-BB:221,
    Ja-PC:35
  Uncle Dog; the Poet at 9.   R. Sward.
    Ca-VT:680
  The Vanity of Human Wishes.
    J. Leax.   Pe-M:65
  When I Brought the News.
    J. Donleavy.   Co-PT:115
HUMOR - AMBULANCES
  Hell's Bells.   M. Fishback.
    Br-SM:139
HUMOR - AMERICA
  America, I Love You.   B. Kalmar.
    Co-FB:270
HUMOR - AMOEBAS
  Ode to the Amoeba.   A. Guiterman.
    Du-SH:123
HUMOR - ANATOMY
  Similia Similibus.   J. Morgan.
    Br-SM:111
HUMOR - ANCESTORS AND ANCESTRY
  Ancestors.   D. Randall. Ra-BP:148
  The Fall of J. W. Beane.
    O. Herford.   Co-PT:21
  Gap.   M. Horovitz.   Co-PU:16
  Then He Lay Down.   Rs-PF:83
HUMOR - ANGER
  An Indignation Dinner.
    J. Carrothers.   Hu-PN:27
HUMOR - ANIMAL COMMUNICATION
    AND SOUNDS
  I Know a Sheep.   E. Anthony.
    Ja-PC:17
HUMOR - ANIMALS
  About the Bloath.
    S. Silverstein.   Co-BBW:292
  Animal Fair.   Au-SP:30, Co-IW:7,
    La-PP:53, Mc-PR:41, Un-GT:231
  The Artful Ant.   O. Herford.
    Co-HP:74
  The Baker's Tale.   L. Carroll.
    Un-GF:28
  The Bumblebeaver.   K. Cox.
    Ar-TP3:124
  The Catipoce.   J. Reeves. Co-BBW:290
  Don't Ever Cross a Crocodile.
    K. Starbird.   Ar-TP3:130,
    La-PV:31
  A Farmer in Bungleton.   M. Dodge.
    Gr-EC:205
  Frog Went a-Courtin'.   Su-FVI:73
  The Guppy.   O. Nash.   Hi-WP II:14,
    Ir-BB:81, Ja-PC:22
  Higgledy, Piggledy, See How They Run.
    K. Greenaway. Ar-TP3:123, Ir-BB:190
  How to Tell the Wild Animals.
    C. Wells.   Ar-TP3:128, Co-FB:12,
    Co-HP:116, Er-FA:235, Fe-FP:338,
    Hu-MP:440, Ir-BB:78, Sh-RP:152,
    Un-GF:84, Un-GT:230
  I Wish I Were.   Er-FA:502
  James and the Giant Peach.
    R. Dahl.   Co-BBW:284
  The Kangarooster.   K. Cox.
    Ar-TP3:127, Ir-BB:82
  Laughing Time.   W. Smith. Au-SP:237,
    Fe-FP:327, Ir-BB:12, Ja-PC:8,
    Un-GF:91
  My Brother Bert.   T. Hughes.
    Co-BB:27
  The Nonny.   J. Reeves.   Co-BBW:293
  Not Me.   S. Silverstein. Co-BBW:285
  One Old Ox.   Gr-CT:31, On-TW:45
  Poor Old Lady.   Au-SP:251, Co-HP:22,
    Un-GT:231
  A Quadrupedremian Song.   T. Hood.
    Ir-BB:123
  The Quangle Wangle's Hat.   E. Lear.
    Ir-BB:59, Un-GF:37
  short course in natural history.
    D. Marquis.   Co-BBW:276
  The Spangled Pandemonium.   P. Brown.
    Ar-TP3:129, Co-OT:22, Lo-LL:70
  Two from the Zoo.   E. Merriam.
    Ar-TP3:102
  What They Said.   Ir-BB:75
  When Did the World Begin.
    R. Clairmont.   Au-SP:227,
    Co-HP:54, Mc-WK:102, Un-GT:230
HUMOR - ANIMALS, CRUELTY TO
  The Cruel Naughty Boy.   Co-BB:108
  Inhuman Henry.   A. Housman.
    Co-BB:25, Co-FB:101, Co-HP:80
  Run, Kitty, Run.   J. Garthwaite.
    Ir-BB:174
  To His Godson, Gerald C. A.
    Jackson.   A. Housman.   Co-PU:113
  Where Is My Butterfly Net.
    D. McCord.   Co-FB:101
HUMOR - ANIMALS - DEATH
  The Mouse.   J. Garrigue.   Br-TC:141
  O'Grady's Goat.   W. Hays. Fe-PL:214
  The Three Little Pigs.   A. Gatty.
    Ox-BC:274
HUMOR - ANIMALS, KINDNESS TO
  The Frog.   H. Belloc.   Bo-GJ:10,
    Co-FB:33, Co-HP:32, Fe-FP:344,
    Ga-FB:333, Hu-MP:456, Ir-BB:77,
    It-HB:19, Li-LC:31, Lo-LL:20,
    Ox-BC:311, Sh-RP:148
  S.P.C.A. Sermon.   S. Helmsley.
    Co-FB:21
HUMOR - ANNE, QUEEN OF ENGLAND
  Queen Anne.   Gr-CT:473, Ir-BB:265
HUMOR - ANTELOPES
  From the Sublime to the Ridiculous.
    J. Prelutsky.   Co-OW:26

HUMOR – ANTS
  The Adventures of Oberon.
    M. Drayton. Rd-OA:164
  The Ant. O. Nash. Ga-FB:334
  Ant and Eleph-Ant. S. Milligan.
    Co-OT:25
  The Artful Ant. O. Herford.
    Co-HP:74
  I Guess. Rs-PF:40
  This Here Is Hell. S. Bradley.
    De-FS:29
HUMOR – APPARITIONS
  The Apparitions. W. Yeats.
    Wi-LT:94
HUMOR – APPETITE
  Eat-It-All Elaine. K. Starbird.
    La-PV:99
  Robin the Bobbin. Ir-BB:59,
    Mo-MGT:101
  So Far, So Good. Rs-PF:41
  Wish at Meal Time. J. Farrar.
    Ja-PC:48
HUMOR – APPLE TREES
  Oh Dear! Mo-MGT:136, Wr-RM:14
HUMOR – ARCHITECTS AND
    ARCHITECTURE
  The Picket Fence. C. Morgenstern.
    Un-R:65
  See-Saw. H. Chandler. Ke-TF:270
HUMOR – ARCTIC REGIONS
  A Dash to the Pole. W. Irwin.
    Co-HP:80
HUMOR – ARISTOCRACY
  Archy, the Cockroach Speaks.
    D. Marquis. Co-HP:96, Fe-FP:338
  Here Comes Our Noble Mr. Horse.
    Issa. Be-MC:22
  My Lord Tomnoddy. R. Brough.
    Co-PU:123
HUMOR – ARITHMETIC
  Arithmetic. C. Sandburg.
    Bo-HF:108, Fe-FP:80, Ma-FW:238,
    Mc-WK:91, Pl-IO:78, Sh-RP:147
  Exercise Book. P. Dehn.
    Hi-WP II:8
  Gemini and Virgo. C. Calverley.
    Co-FB:118
  Logic. Bo-FP:11, Gr-EC:126
  A Mortifying Mistake. A. Pratt.
    Co-HP:104, Sh-RP:315
  Science and Mathematics.
    Br-LL:114, Pl-IO:80
  There Was an Old Man Who Said
    "Do." Br-LL:114, Fe-FP:361,
    Ir-BB:221, Pl-IO:79
  There Was an Old Man Who Said
    "Gee!" Br-LL:114
HUMOR – ARIZONA
  John Coil. Br-SM:156
  Someone's Opinion of Arizona.
    C. Brown. Fi-BG:42

HUMOR – ARMADILLOS
  The Arch Armadillo. C. Wells.
    Bo-FP:271, Br-LL:33
HUMOR – ARMS AND ARMOR
  Arac's Song. W. Gilbert. Co-FB:48
  Directions to the Armorer.
    E. Olson. Du-SH:99
HUMOR – ART AND ARTISTS
  Art Review. K. Fearing. Du-SH:33
  Drawing by Ronnie C., Grade One.
    R. Lechlitner. Pe-SS:24
  Poem by a Perfectly Furious
    Academician. Co-FB:334
  Remarkable Truly, Is Art.
    G. Burgess. Co-OT:69
  Sadie's Playhouse. M. Danner.
    Ad-PB:138
  Sir Joshua Reynolds. W. Blake.
    Co-EL:54, Co-FB:121, Co-PU:24
  Why I Am Not a Painter. F. O'Hara.
    Kh-VA:63
HUMOR – ASTRONAUTS
  Space. I. Hogan. Sh-RP:286
HUMOR – ASTRONOMERS AND ASTRONOMY
  The Astronomer Said. Rs-PF:39
  The Collegiate Angels.
    R. Alberti. Ma-FW:74
  Rhyme for Astronomical Baby.
    J. Cook. Li-SR:128
HUMOR – ATOMIC WEAPONS
  Respectful Request. R. Durem.
    Ab-MO:32
HUMOR – ATOMS
  Any Day Now. D. McCord. Br-SM:63
  Atomic Courtesy. E. Jacobson.
    Br-SM:63
HUMOR – AUCTIONS
  The Circuit. D. Wagoner. Mo-BG:66
HUMOR – AUKS
  The Great Auk's Ghost.
    R. Hodgson. Br-SM:3
HUMOR – AUNTS
  Chicken in the Bread Tray.
    Bu-DY:39
  Conceit with Aunties, Urn and
    Birds. M. Leech. Ls-NY:326
  My Aunt. O. Holmes. Sh-AP:62
  My Singing Aunt. J. Reeves.
    Br-SM:14
HUMOR – AUSTRALIA
  The Traveling Post Office.
    A. Patterson. Co-PT:290
  Up from Down Under. D. McCord.
    Gr-EC:187
HUMOR – AUTHORS
  Any Author to Any Friend.
    Martial. Pl-ML:66
  Archy's Autobiography. D. Marquis.
    Co-HP:97
  The Novelist. P. Lazarus. Ke-TF:278
  An Ode. J. Updike. Co-FB:363

HUMOR - AUTHORS — cont'd.
  Survey of Literature. J. Ransom.
    Br-TC:335, Ca-VT:151, Sm-LG:36
  Very like a Whale. O. Nash.
    Fe-PL:211
HUMOR - AUTOMOBILE DRIVERS
  Lather as You Go. O. Nash.
    Hi-WP II:14
  A Ride in a Blue Chevy. J. Williams.
    Ls-NY:160
HUMOR - AUTOMOBILES
  Ambition. M. Bishop. Br-AF:235
  Gentle Doctor Brown. B. Taylor.
    Co-OH:46
  In the Car. R. Margolis. Su-FVI:32
  A Tract for Autos. A. Guiterman.
    Hu-MP:441, Sh-RP:125
HUMOR - AVIATORS
  The Dying Airman. Er-FA:217
HUMOR - AWKWARDNESS
  I'm Down on You. Rs-PF:10
HUMOR - BABIES
  Is the Baby King. Rs-PF:22
  Johnnie Crack and Flossie Snail.
    D. Thomas. Bo-FP:24, Bo-GJ:150,
    Co-FB:373, Fe-FP:332, Ha-LO:21,
    La-PV:218, Li-LC:43, Pa-RE:62,
    Su-FVI:21
  Pediatric Reflections. O. Nash.
    Ke-TF:292
  Reflection on Babies. O. Nash.
    Hi-WP I:12
  Song to Be Sung by the Father of
    Infant Female Children.
    O. Nash. Un-MA:565
  A Tonversation with Baby.
    M. Bishop. Co-FB:190
  Where Is My Butterfly Net.
    D. McCord. Co-FB:101
  You Could Learn This. Re-RR:74
HUMOR - BABOONS
  A Barber Who Lived in Batavia.
    Br-LL:29
  The Big Baboon. H. Belloc.
    Co-OH:28, Un-MB:170
  The Theology of Bongwi, the
    Baboon. R. Campbell. Ga-S:194
HUMOR - BACHELORS
  The Two Old Bachelors. E. Lear.
    Co-FB:55, Co-HP:87
  Where the Single Men Go in Summer.
    N. Bourne. Co-FB:487
HUMOR - BAGPIPES
  The Piper's Progress. F. Mahony.
    Co-FB:286, Co-PI:119
HUMOR - BAKERS AND BAKERIES
  I Am a Little Baker. On-TW:36
  I Work as a Baker. Rs-PF:75
  The Merry Pieman's Song.
    J. Bennett. Lo-LL:5
HUMOR - BALDNESS
  The Bald Old Woman. Ir-BB:202

The Penalties of Baldness.
    O. Seaman. Co-FB:72
  Said the Flea. Rs-PF:20
  There Goes My Best Hat. Basho.
    Be-MC:8
  Three Men Fell Overboard. Re-RR:119
  To a Teacher. K. Aihara. Le-TA:60
HUMOR - BALLET
  Song of the Ballet. J. Morton.
    Co-FB:286
HUMOR - BALLOONS (AIRSHIPS)
  Limericks. E. Lear. Na-EO:103
HUMOR - BALLOONS (TOYS)
  Poor Percy. H. Lambert. Ir-BB:151
HUMOR - BANANAS
  In Memory of Anna Hopewell.
    Br-SM:47
HUMOR - BANDS (MUSIC)
  "And Now . . ." J. Boothroyd.
    Co-FB:275
HUMOR - BANKS AND BANKING
  The Plot to Assassinate the Chase
    Manhattan Bank. C. Larsen.
    Ke-PP:67
  Uncle Frank. M. Shannon. Ja-PC:46
HUMOR - BARBERS
  Barber, Barber, Shave a Pig.
    De-PO:18, Ir-BB:41, Li-LB:91,
    Mo-CC:(48), Mo-MGT:109,
    Mo-NR:25, Na-EO:57, On-TW:61,
    Pa-AP:28, Sp-TM:27, Wr-RM:24
  The Barber of Kew. C. Monkhouse.
    Br-LL:32, Co-HP:98, Ir-BB:223
  A Barber Who Lived in Batavia.
    Br-LL:29
  It's All Right with Me. Rs-PF:27
  A Lion. J. Francis. Br-LL:31,
    Hu-MP:457
  Mia Carlotta. T. Daly. Hi-WP I:103
  The Tales the Barbers Tell.
    M. Bishop. Co-HP:34
HUMOR - BASEBALL
  Baseball. T. Clark. Mc-EA:134
  Baseball Note. F. Adams. Mo-SD:2
  Baseball's Sad Lexicon. F. Adams.
    Er-FA:222, Mo-SD:14
  Casey at the Bat. E. Thayer.
    Bo-HF:98, Er-FA:352, Fe-FP:549,
    Mo-SD:11
  Casey's Revenge. J. Wilson.
    Pa-OM:76
  Dorlan's Home Walk.
    A. Guiterman. Co-PT:90
  The Origin of Baseball.
    K. Patchen. Mc-EA:133
  Slide, Kelly, Slide. J. Kelly.
    Er-FA:446
HUMOR - BATHS
  "Baby's" Epitaph. Co-FB:219
  The Bath. H. Graham. Br-SM:120
  In the Tub We Soak Our Skin.
    E. Horn. Co-PU:133

Miss Twye. G. Ewart. Co-FB:121
Poems in Praise of Practically
    Nothing. S. Hoffenstein.
    Na-EO:92
HUMOR - BATTLES
  Growltiger's Last Stand. T. Eliot.
    Co-RG:99, Sm-LG:198
HUMOR - BEARDS
  The Fair Circassian. R. Garnett.
    Co-PT:89
  He Was a Man. Rs-PF:107
  Old Mr. Bows. W. Horsbrugh.
    Co-OW:45, Ir-BB:149
  Song about Whiskers.
    P. Wodehouse. Co-FB:355
  There Was an Old Man in a Tree.
    E. Lear. Br-LL:46
  There Was an Old Man Named
    Michael Finnegan. Ar-TP3:132,
    Ir-BB:57, Un-GT:18
  There Was an Old Man with a Beard.
    E. Lear. Ar-TP3:133, Au-SP:243,
    Br-LL:47, Ch-B:105, Co-HP:90,
    Fr-WO:43, Gr-CT:28, Gr-EC:167,
    La-PV:35, Sh-RP:149, Un-GF:42
  The Wind and the Beard. Ja-PC:43
HUMOR - BEARS
  Adventures of Isabel. O. Nash.
    Br-SM:93, Co-HP:98, Gr-EC:202,
    Ir-BB:105, Ja-PC:26, La-PP:15,
    La-PV:32, Ne-AM:22, Un-GF:72,
    Un-MA:564
  Algy Met a Bear. Br-SM:90, Ch-B:105,
    Fe-FP:361
  B Stands for Bear. H. Belloc.
    Br-SM:91
  The Bear Hunt. M. Widdemer.
    Fe-FP:104, Hu-MP:49
  Father Goose Tells a Story.
    A. Resnikoff. Co-OH:60
  Fooba Wooba John. Co-OW:64
  Fuzzy Wuzzy. Fr-MP:21, Un-GT:18
  Grizzly Bear. M. Austin.
    Ar-TP3:127, Au-SP:85, Bo-GJ:4,
    Fe-FP:170, Gr-EC:29, Ir-BB:77,
    Ja-PC:56, La-PP:14, La-PV:32,
    Pa-RE:25
  Honey Bears; E. Lang. Ir-BB:85
  How to Tell the Wild Animals.
    C. Wells. Un-GF:84
  The Lady and the Bear. T. Roethke.
    Bo-GJ:151, Gr-EC:146
  Little Katy. Br-SM:92
  There Was an Old Person of Ware.
    E. Lear. Bo-FP:28, Ir-BB:218,
    Li-LC:47, Sh-RP:129, Un-GT:240
  When a Cub, Unaware Being Bare.
    E. Merriam. Br-LL:27
HUMOR - BEAUTY
  The Hen and the Oriole.
    D. Marquis. Co-FB:497, Co-HP:96,
    Na-EO:104

To a Lady. F. Adams. Co-FB:328
HUMOR - BEAUTY, PERSONAL
  Take Notice. R. Robin. Ls-NY:325
  W.W. I. Baraka. Ad-PB:254
  A Young Lady Sings in Our Choir.
    Br-LL:121
  Youth's Progress. J. Updike.
    Co-FB:484
HUMOR - BEDS AND BEDDING
  The Arch Armadillo. C. Wells.
    Bo-FP:271, Br-LL:33
  Bossy-Cow, Bossy-Cow, Where Do
    You Lie? Ir-BB:28
  Get Up, Get Up. Co-FB:123,
    Co-HP:22, Co-PU:5
  Goodnight. Mo-MGT:136
  A Man Was Locked Up. Re-RR:73
  A Nightmare. W. Gilbert.
    Co-HP:61, Un-GF:70
  See-Saw. Mo-NR:5, Wr-RM:33
HUMOR - BEDTIME
  Diddle, Diddle, Dumpling.
    Bo-FP:37, De-PO:28, Ir-BB:191,
    Li-LB:71, Mo-CC:(21), Mo-MGT:36,
    Mo-TL:41, Wi-MG:13, Wr-RM:37
  Fragment of an English Opera.
    A. Housman. Li-TU:22
  The Happy Family. J. Ciardi.
    Co-OW:34
  Putting on a Nightgown. Mo-MGT:120
  Weary Willie and Tired Tim.
    Ir-BB:211
HUMOR - BEECHER, HENRY WARD
  Said a Great Congregational
    Preacher. Un-GF:43, Un-GT:240
HUMOR - BEELZEBUB
  Sir Beelzebub. E. Sitwell.
    Un-MB:331
HUMOR - BEER
  Beer. C. Calverley. Co-FB:84
HUMOR - BEES
  The Adventures of Oberon.
    M. Drayton. Rd-OA:164
  The Bees' Song. W. de la Mare.
    Lo-LL:55, Mc-WS:37, Un-GF:80
  The Bumble-Bee. Ir-BB:154
  Buzz, Buzz, Buzz. Bu-DY:90
  Fooba Wooba John. Co-OW:64
  The Honey Bee. D. Marquis.
    Co-HP:96
  The Strangest Creature. Rs-PF:16
  There Once Was a Boy of Bagdad.
    Br-LL:3
  There Was an Old Man in a Tree.
    E. Lear. Ar-TP3:132, Au-SP:243
    Br-LL:4, Sh-RP:127, Un-GF:42,
    Un-GT:240
HUMOR - BEETLES
  I Knew a Black Beetle. C. Morley.
    Ir-BB:172
HUMOR - BEHAVIOR
  Abigail. K. Starbird. Ne-AM:40

HUMOR - BEHAVIOR — cont'd.
Advice to Grandsons. Co-OH:58
An Alphabet of Famous Goops.
   G. Burgess. Co-BB:81
Baby Toodles. J. Newman. Co-BB:50
Belsnickel. A. Guiterman.
   Co-BB:114
Bobby Snooks. Wr-RM:72
The Boy Who Laughed at Santa
   Claus. O. Nash. Co-BB:16,
   Ha-PO:291
The Careless Niece. C. Wells.
   Br-SM:128
Children when They're Very Sweet.
   J. Ciardi. Co-BB:40
The Conventionalist. S. Smith.
   Co-PU:39
Dan Dunder. J. Ciardi. Co-BB:34
Deborah Delora. Co-OH:19
Diddle, Diddle, Dumpling.
   Bo-FP:37, De-PO:28, Ir-BB:191,
   Li-LB:71, Mo-CC:(21), Mo-MGT:36,
   Mo-TL:41, Wi-MG:13, Wr-RM:37
A Dreadful Sight. D. Aldis.
   Co-OT:34
Eight Limericks, 6. E. Lear.
   Sh-RP:128
Eight Limericks, 7. E. Lear.
   Sh-RP:128
Extremely Naughty Children.
   E. Godley. Co-BB:65
Georgie Porgie. De-PO:16,
   Fr-WO:29, Li-LB:25, Mo-CC:44,
   Mo-MGT:80, Mo-NR:20, Wi-MG:5,
   Wr-RM:32
The Good Little Girl. A. Milne.
   Co-BB:37
Grandmother's Visit. W. Wise.
   Sh-RP:313
Grotesques. D. Marquis. Co-FB:381
Harriet Hutch. L. Richards.
   Ir-BB:97, Ne-AM:47
His Little Sub. E. Bennett.
   Ke-TF:70
Johnny Went to Church One Day.
   Co-BB:24, Co-OH:72
Josephine. A. Resnikoff. Co-OT:31
Limericks. Br-LL:109, Co-HP:29
Limericks since Lear. Co-BB:29,
   Un-GT:241
Little Orphant Annie. J. Riley.
   Co-BB:113, Er-FA:493, Fe-FP:532,
   Hu-MP:27
Little Willie. Br-SM:113
A Man's Woman. M. Davies. Fe-PL:416
Maria Jane. A. Scott-Gatty.
   Co-BB:77
Mr. Nobody. Ch-B:113, Co-PM:210,
   Fe-FP:49, Hu-MP:134
A New Song to Sing about Jonathan
   Bing. B. Brown. Au-SP:256,
   Co-OW:60

Nothing to Do? S. Silverstein.
   Co-BB:15
One Stormy Night. J. Taylor.
   Bo-FP:172, Ch-B:73, Ir-BB:166
A Parental Ode to My Son, Aged
   Three Years and Five Months.
   T. Hood. Co-FB:103, Co-HP:77,.
   Fe-FP:36, Fe-PL:139
Poems in Praise of Practically
   Nothing. S. Hoffenstein.
   Co-FB:492
Polly, Dolly, Kate and Molly.
   Co-BB:33, Ir-BB:100
Polly Picklenose. L. Jackson.
   Co-BB:35
?. E. Cummings. Co-FB:494
The Quiet Child. R. Field.
   Ne-AM:30
Random Ruthless Rhymes. Un-GF:48
Rebecca, Who Slammed Doors for
   Fun and Perished Miserably.
   H. Belloc. Ne-AM:26
Retaliation. Ja-PC:33
Rice Pudding. A. Milne. Co-BB:61
Rules and Regulations. L. Carroll.
   Un-GF:51
Sarah Cynthia Sylvia Stout.
   S. Silverstein. Co-BB:73
Scrubby Chubby. H. Lofting.
   Ir-BB:93
Sneaky Bill. W. Cole. Co-OT:30
The Story of Caspar and the Soup.
   H. Hoffman. Un-GF:55
The Story of Fidgety Philip.
   H. Hoffman. Un-GF:58
The Story of Johnny Head-in-Air.
   H. Hoffmann. Ar-TP3:135,
   Co-BB:78, Ir-BB:162
The Story of Pauline and the
   Matches. H. Hoffman. Un-GF:56
Table Manners. G. Burgess.
   Co-BB:45, Fr-MP:5
There Was a Young Lady from
   Woosester. Br-LL:70
There Was an Old Man of
   Thermopylae. E. Lear. Br-LL:67,
   Fr-WO:41, Na-EO:103
There Was an Old Person of Ischia.
   E. Lear. Br-LL:67
There Was an Old Person of
   Shoreham. E. Lear. Br-LL:68
Think of Eight Numbers.
   S. Silverstein. Co-BB:30
Those Two Boys. F. Adams.
   Co-FB:496
Three Bad Ones. Co-BB:96,
   Ir-BB:94
To a Small Boy Standing on My
   Shoes while I Am Wearing Them.
   O. Nash. Co-FB:108
A Tract for Autos. A. Guiterman.
   Hu-MP:441, Sh-RP:125

250 Willow Lane. J. Keith.
  De-FS:113
Two Limericks. Co-BB:29
The Visitor. K. Pyle. Co-BB:50
When I Was Christened. D. McCord.
  Br-BC:29
Where's Mary? I. Eastwick.
  Ne-AM:44
Willie Built a Guillotine.
  W. Engel. Co-OH:43
Young Sammy Watkins. Co-BB:94,
  Co-HP:28
HUMOR - BELLS
  The Bells. Co-FB:414
  On Bell-Ringers. Br-SM:28
  There Was an Old Man, Who Said,
    "Well!" E. Lear. Br-LL:68,
    Ir-BB:218
HUMOR - BIBLE STORIES
  Daniel. V. Lindsay. Co-RM:238,
    Ga-S:49, Gr-CT:143, Hi-WP I:80,
    Rv-CB:972, Sm-MK:75
HUMOR - BICYCLE RACING
  Bicycalamity. E. Peters. Mo-SD:59
HUMOR - BIOGRAPHY
  The Art of Biography. E. Bentley.
    Co-FB:126
HUMOR - BIRDS
  The Birds' Courting. Un-GF:81
  The King-Fisher Song. L. Carroll.
    Bl-OB:18
  Sea Change. J. Masefield.
    Co-PT:263
  Thirty Purple Birds. Hi-WP I:100
  Up from the Egg. O. Nash.
    Co-FB:30
  The Wheatear and the Snowbird.
    Da-SC:46, Le-IB:42
  A Young Lady, Whose Bonnet.
    E. Lear. Bo-FP:247, Br-LL:97
  The Zobo Bird. F. Collymore.
    Bo-GJ:156
HUMOR - BIRDS-CALLS
  Before Dawn. A. Darr. Pe-M:118
  Owls Talking. D. McCord.
    Co-BBW:254
HUMOR - BIRDS-DEATH
  A Melancholy Lay. M. Fleming.
    Co-FB:300, Re-TW:22, Sm-LG:70
  Murdered Little Bird. Co-FB:297
HUMOR - BIRDS-EGGS AND NESTS
  The Common Cormorant. Bl-OB:66,
    Co-FB:371, Co-HP:21, Gr-CT:21,
    Gr-EC:28, Ir-BB:82, Lo-LL:33,
    Pa-RE:66, Sm-LG:90, Sm-MK:192,
    Un-GT:223
  The Ostrich. O. Nash. Co-BBW:266,
    Co-OH:28
HUMOR - BIRDS-SONGS
  The Bird. S. Hoffenstein. Co-FB:21
  Frog-School Competing. Shiki.
    Be-CS:54

HUMOR - BIRTH
  Cats. T. Storm. Co-BBW:134
HUMOR - BISHOPS
  Praying and Preaching. Un-GT:238
  Robin Hood and the Bishop of
    Hereford. Bl-OB:73, Ma-BB:74
HUMOR - BISON
  The Buffalo. L. Richards.
    Co-OW:72
HUMOR - BLACKSMITHING
  The Blacksmith's Serenade.
    V. Lindsay. Co-PT:100
HUMOR - BLESSINGS
  Blessing Without Company. Ra-BP:17
  Hurly, Hurly, roon the Table.
    Sm-LG:123
  In the Morning. P. Dunbar.
    Ra-BP:51
HUMOR - BLOOD BANKS
  The Mosquito Knows.
    D. Lawrence. Rd-OA:170
HUMOR - BLUES (MUSIC)
  Request for Requiems. L. Hughes.
    Br-SM:145
HUMOR - BOA CONSTRICTORS
  Boa Constrictor. S. Silverstein.
    Co-OW:28
HUMOR - BOASTING
  Capsule Conclusions, VII. Un-MW:65
  the flattered lightning bug.
    D. Marquis. Co-BBW:217
  The Opportune Overthrow of
    Humpty Dumpty. G. Carryl.
    Co-BB:20
  small talk. D. Marquis. Co-PT:139
HUMOR - BOATS AND BOATING
  The Floating Old Man. E. Lear.
    Br-LL:76, Ho-WR:129
  The Ingenious Little Old Man.
    J. Bennett. Co-OH:28, Fe-FP:337,
    Ja-PC:42
  A Longford Legend. Co-PT:153
  Old Man Jeremy. J. Baxter.
    Gr-EC:248
HUMOR - BODY, HUMAN
  The Duchess of Malfi. J. Webster.
    Gr-CT:360
  Poor Bess. Ja-PC:39
  A Thought. D. Aldis. Ja-PC:53
HUMOR - BONES
  Bones. W. de la Mare. Br-SM:50,
    Co-FB:145, Co-HP:55, Du-RG:66
  Jerry Jones. Br-SM:138
  The Society upon the Stanislaus.
    B. Harte. Co-RM:22
HUMOR - BOOKS AND READING
  As I Was Laying on the Green.
    Co-FB:341, Co-HP:24, Mc-WS:176
  The Book-Worms. R. Burns.
    Co-EL:63, Co-FB:331, Co-PU:22,
    Gr-CT:472
  My Teddy Stands. Olga. Mo-MI:25

HUMOR - BOOKS AND READING — cont'd.
On His Books. H. Belloc. Un-MB:172
Poor South. J. Coogler. Co-FB:301
Reading Fare. L. Blair. Ja-HH:40
Sarah Byng. H. Belloc. Bo-GJ:112,
  Gr-CC:152
Shake, Mulleary and Go-ethe.
  H. Bunner. Co-FB:350
What the Book Said. Ja-HH:41
Who'd Be a Hero (Fictional)?
  M. Bishop. Co-FB:353
HUMOR - BOOMERANGS
Cassie O'Lang. Br-SM:21
HUMOR - BORDEN, LIZZIE ANDREW
Lizzie Borden. Br-SM:112,
  Er-FA:219
HUMOR - BORES AND BOREDOM
A Cheerful Old Bear at the Zoo.
  Br-LL:29, Un-GT:241
In Extremis. M. Fishback.
  Co-FB:192
On Dean Inge. H. Wolfe. Gr-CT:474
Story of Reginald. H. Phillips.
  Co-OT:59
To a Boy-Poet of the Decadence.
  O. Seaman. Co-FB:471
To a Young Lady. A. Pope.
  Hi-WP II:124
The Yak. V. Sheard. Do-WH:24
HUMOR - BORROWING AND LENDING
If I Should Die Tonight. B. King.
  Co-FB:490, Co-HP:85, Fe-PL:210
Mazilla and Mazura. Gr-CT:88
Money and the Mare. Wr-RM:14
When He Went to His Mother.
  Rs-PF:21
Wilt Thou Lend Me Thy Mare?
  Co-EL:57, Co-PU:67, Rv-CB:423
HUMOR - BOSTON, MASS.
Boston. J. Bossidy. Un-GT:236
Crispus Attucks McCoy. S. Brown.
  Ra-BP:115
His Little Sub. E. Bennett.
  Ke-TF:70
HUMOR - BOTANY
Rhyme for Botanical Baby.
  J. Cook. Li-SR:128
HUMOR - BOTTLES
Song of the Pop-Bottlers. M. Bishop.
  Co-FB:428, Co-HP:33, Fe-FP:358,
  Mc-WS:169
HUMOR - BOYS
A Boy's Head. M. Holub. Ma-FW:71
Common Carrier. R. Armour.
  Gr-EC:149
Four. E. Gibbs. Br-BC:148
Inhuman Henry. A. Housman.
  Co-BB:25, Co-FB:101, Co-HP:80
Jeremiah Obadiah. Mo-MGT:20
Life in Our Village. M. Markwei.
  Ab-MO:20

The Little Boys of Texas.
  R. Coffin. Br-SM:100, Mc-WK:167
Song to Be Sung by the Father of
  Infant Female Children.
  O. Nash. Un-MA:565
HUMOR - BRAHMS, JOHANNES
A Modern Composer Named Brahms.
  Br-LL:108
HUMOR - BRAIN
The Dinosaur. B. Taylor. Pl-IO:112
Doctor Emmanuel. J. Reeves.
  Co-PU:116
HUMOR - BREAD
I Never Had a Piece of Toast.
  J. Payne. Un-GF:15
There Was an Old Man of the Coast.
  E. Lear. Ag-HE:7, Ir-BB:218
Three Ghostesses. Ag-HE:7,
  Mo-CC:(4), Mo-MGT:209
HUMOR - BREAKFAST
Breakfast. E. Farjeon. Ag-HE:60
Breakfast with Gerard Manley
  Hopkins. A. Brode. Co-FB:253
Mummy Slept Late and Daddy Fixed
  Breakfast. J. Ciardi.
  Ar-TP3:133, La-PV:26
HUMOR - BREATHING
Hold In Your Breath. Ho-SD:59
HUMOR - BRIDES AND BRIDEGROOMS
A Ballad upon a Wedding.
  J. Suckling. Al-VBP:418,
  Rv-CB:382
Here Comes the Bride. Mo-TB:41
HUMOR - BRIDGE (GAME)
It's Three No Trumps. G. Innes.
  Co-FB:125
HUMOR - BROTHERHOOD
Friends. R. Durem. Ad-PB:150
Lines on Lands. A. Aronov.
  Bo-RU:12
People Are All Human. D. Hendell.
  Me-WF:46
HUMOR - BROTHERS
Brother and Sister. L. Carroll.
  Br-SM:122, Co-BB:89, Gr-CT:26
Careless Willie. Co-BB:95,
  Co-HP:28, Fe-FP:362
Hard Lines. T. Robinson. Br-BC:64
I Had a Little Brother. Ir-BB:92
Not Afraid. J. Lee. Ja-HH:37
Sister Nell. Co-BB:94, Co-HP:28,
  Fe-FP:362
Ten Brothers. L. Untermeyer.
  Sh-RP:9
Young Sammy Watkins. Co-BB:94,
  Co-HP:28
HUMOR - BUCKINGHAM PALACE
Malice at Buckingham Palace.
  S. Mulligan. Co-OH:24
HUMOR - BUGLES
A Bugler Named Dougal MacDougal.
  O. Nash. Br-LL:105, Lo-LL:95,
  Mc-WS:181

HUMOR - BUILDERS AND BUILDING
   Jack Straw's Castle. E. Farjeon.
      Ir-BB:34
HUMOR - BUREAUCRACY
   Departmental. R. Frost. Du-SH:114,
      Mc-WS:48, Sh-AP:154, Un-MA:190
   Lessons of the War, II. Judging
      Distances. H. Reed. Pa-GTB:538
   Old Wang Pops the Question.
      Yüan Shui-p'ai. Hs-TC:403
   There Lived a King. W. Gilbert.
      Co-FB:145, Co-PT:83
HUMOR - BUSES
   The Buses Headed for Scranton.
      O. Nash. Mc-WS:28
   Jittery Jim. W. Smith. Co-BB:33
   Roundel in the Rain. Co-FB:445
HUMOR - BUSYNESS
   Endurance Test. D. Balsdon.
      Co-FB:198
HUMOR - BUTCHERS AND BUTCHERING
   My Father Owns the Butcher Shop.
      Er-FA:499, Ir-BB:42
   Sam, Sam the Butcher Man.
      Er-FA:499, Ir-BB:41
   The Spectre Pig. O. Holmes.
      Co-RM:103
HUMOR - BUTTE, MONT.
   I'd Rather Listen. S. Hoffenstein.
      Co-FB:209
HUMOR - BUTTERFLIES
   Ways and Means. L. Carroll.
      Ag-HE:16, Co-FB:375, Co-HP:42,
      Gr-EC:206, Li-SR:112, Sm-LG:282
HUMOR - BYRON, GEORGE NOEL
      GORDON, LORD
   Sketch of Lord Byron's Life.
      J. Moore. Co-FB:301
HUMOR - CAKES AND COOKIES
   Said a Bad Little Youngster
      Named Beauchamp. C. Wells.
      Br-LL:84
HUMOR - CALENDARS
   A Man Was Locked Up. Re-RR:73
HUMOR - CALIFORNIA-GOLD DISCOVERIES
   The Arrival of the Greenhorn.
      A. Hulbert. Sh-RP:287
HUMOR - CAMELS
   Camel. M. Kumin. Ja-PC:21
   The Camel. O. Nash. Au-SP:242,
      Lo-LL:33
   The Legend of the First Cam-u-el.
      A. Guiterman. Co-HP:68
   A Pig-Tale. L. Carroll. Ch-B:65,
      Fe-FP:346, Ho-WR:80, Pa-RE:27,
      Rd-OA:94
   The Plaint of the Camel. C. Carryl.
      Au-SP:83, Co-IW:39, Fe-FP:341,
      Ir-BB:80, Na-EO:164, Ox-BC:305,
      Pe-FB:16, Th-AS:45, Un-GT:37
HUMOR - CAMPING
   The Bunyip and the Whistling
      Kettle. J. Manifold. Co-PM:123

   Eat-It-All Elaine. K. Starbird.
      La-PV:99, Ne-AM:10
HUMOR - CANARIES
   The Canary. O. Nash. Co-FB:22
HUMOR - CANDY
   Come Here. Rs-PF:33
   Reflections on Ice-Breaking.
      O. Nash. Er-FA:209, Wi-LT:629
HUMOR - CANNIBALS
   A Cannibal Chief. Rs-PF:34
   Cannibal Song. C. Dickens.
      Ir-BB:122
   Cannibalee: A Po'em of Passion.
      C. Lummis. Br-SM:84, Li-SR:71
   A Certain Young Man of Great
      Gumption. Br-LL:78, Br-SM:82
   Funebrial Reflections. O. Nash.
      Pl-IO:120
   Little Billee. W. Thackeray.
      Bl-OB:72, Br-SM:72, Co-SS:15,
      De-TT:126, Gr-EC:244, Hu-MP:452,
      Ir-BB:42, Ox-BB:678, Sm-LG:186
   The New Book for Cannibals.
      Rs-PF:104
   A Paradox. Br-SM:84
   A Reply from the Akond of Swat.
      E. Scheffauer. Br-LL:59,
      Co-FB:423
   Speak Up at Once. Re-RR:87
   The Two Little Skeezucks.
      E. Field. Hu-MP:437
   We Love All Men. Rs-PF:34
   The Yarn of the "Nancy Bell."
      W. Gilbert. Co-HP:59, Er-FA:308,
      Ga-FB:322, Na-EO:125, Sm-LG:188,
      Sp-OG:239, Un-GT:203
HUMOR - CANNING AND PRESERVING
   A Canner, Exceedingly Canny.
      C. Wells. Br-LL:69, Fe-FP:364,
      Un-GF:46
HUMOR - CAPE COD
   The Codfish Shanty. Gr-GB:179
HUMOR - CARELESSNESS
   That'll Be All Right You'll Find.
      L. Sieveking. Co-HP:112
HUMOR - CARGOES
   How Bill Went East. G. Bryan.
      Co-PT:82
   The Irish Rover. Co-SS:120
HUMOR - CARLYLE, THOMAS
   Thomas Carlyle. D. Parker.
      Co-FB:340
HUMOR - CARPENTERS AND CARPENTRY
   Industrious Carpenter Dan.
      W. Irwin. Co-SS:197
   The Walrus and the Carpenter.
      L. Carroll. Au-SP:275, Bl-OB:125,
      Co-FB:134, Co-HP:40, De-TT:95,
      Er-FA:500, Fe-FP:328, Fr-WO:59,
      Ga-FB:318, Ir-BB:245, Ox-BC:242,
      Pe-FB:103, Sp-OG:242
   When a Carpenter. Re-RR:72

HUMOR - CARRIAGES
  The Coachman. Cl-FC:29, Ir-BB:240,
    Mo-MGT:108, Rv-ON:76, Wr-RM:116
  The Deacon's Masterpiece or, The
    Wonderful "One-Hoss Shay."
    O. Holmes. Er-FA:375, Fe-PL:85,
    Sh-AP:63, Sm-LG:191, Sp-OG:229
HUMOR - CASSOWARIES
  The Cassowary. Co-OT:45
  If I Were a Cassowary.
    S. Wilberforce. Un-GF:15
HUMOR - CATS
  Beg Parding. Co-OW:71, Gr-CT:10
  The Cat and the Crocodile.
    Ca-MU:15
  A Cat Came Fiddling. Bo-FP:94,
    De-TT:29, Gr-EC:70, Ir-BB:27,
    Wi-MG:18
  A Cat in Despondency Sighed.
    Br-LL:20
  Cats. T. Storm. Co-BBW:134
  Cat's Meat. H. Monro. Ir-BB:177
  Conceit with Aunties, Urn and
    Birds. M. Leech. Ls-NY:326
  Dame Wiggins of Lee. Ir-BB:178,
    Ox-BC:153
  Diamond Cut Diamond. E. Milne.
    Ar-TP3:134, Co-BBW:123, Gr-EC:77,
    Sm-LG:76
  Fight. J. Jaszi. Sh-RP:132
  French Persian Cats Having a Ball.
    E. Morgan. To-MP:214
  Growltiger's Last Stand. T. Eliot.
    Co-RG:99, Sm-LG:198
  I Don't Much Exactly Care.
    D. McCord. Br-LL:132
  In London-Town Dame Trottypeg.
    D. Thompson. Ir-BB:167
  In Summer a Cat. Rs-PF:49
  The Kilkenny Cats. Br-LL:19,
    Br-SM:102, Co-HP:25, Er-FA:202,
    Fr-WO:31, La-PP:72, Lo-LL:32,
    Mc-PR:41, Mo-MGT:28, Un-GT:231,
    Wr-RM:87
  Kindness to Animals. L. Richards.
    Ar-TP3:122, Au-SP:236, Ir-BB:167,
    St-FS:45
  Macavity: The Mystery Cat.
    T. Eliot. Ar-TP3:121, Co-BBW:131,
    Li-TU:104, Mc-WK:53, Ox-BC:346,
    Sh-RP:321, Sm-MK:162
  Mehitabel Tries Marriage.
    D. Marquis. Hi-WP II:118
  Mother Tabbyskins. E. Hart.
    Ox-BC:268
  Oh, the Funniest Thing. Na-EO:68
  Ode on a Favourite Cat, Drowned in
    a Tub of Gold Fishes. T. Gray.
    Fe-PL:350, Ho-WR:56, Ma-YA:123,
    Pa-GTB:112, Rv-CB:531, Sp-OG:303
  Of a Sudden the Great Prima-Donna.
    P. West. Br-LL:107

  Old Woman on a Broom. Gr-EC:72,
    Ir-BB:240
  One Stormy Night. Bo-FP:172,
    Ch-B:73, Ir-BB:166
  The Owl and the Pussy-Cat. E. Lear.
    Ar-TP3:120, Au-SP:266, Bl-OB:117,
    Bo-FP:25, Bo-GJ:14, Cl-DT:30,
    Co-IW:3, Er-FA:495, Fe-FP:354,
    Fe-PL:237, Fr-WO:39, Ha-PO:239,
    Hi-WP I:94, Hu-MP:450, Ir-BB:250,
    Ke-TP:38, La-PV:204, Mc-PR:40,
    Ox-BC:185, Pa-GTB:357, Pe-FB:96,
    Rv-CB:812, Sm-LG:89, Sm-MK:200,
    St-FS:108, Un-GB:28, Un-GT:224
  The Rum Tum Tugger. T. Eliot.
    Ar-TP3:120, Fe-FP:157, Ga-FB:330,
    La-PV:110, Na-EO:21
  Run, Kitty Run. J. Garthwaite.
    Ir-BB:174
  Skimbleshanks: The Railway Cat.
    T. Eliot. Sm-LG:292
  Song. O. Herford. Li-SR:22
  the song of mehitabel.
    D. Marquis. Co-FB:62
  The Story of Pauline and the
    Matches. H. Hoffman. Un-GF:56
  The Stranger Cat. N. Babcock.
    Co-HP:30
  Tame Animals I Have Known.
    N. Waterman. Co-OW:61
  That Cat. B. King. Co-BBW:121,
    Co-FB:16, Co-HP:85
  There Was a Young Man Who Was
    Bitten. Br-LL:20
  Trouble in the Greenhouse.
    M. Dodge. Br-SG:77
  well boss mehitabel the cat.
    D. Marquis. Ke-TF:266
  What Do Children. Re-RR:117
  Where Are You Going? E. Follen.
    Au-SP:227
  Why Is a Cat. Re-RR:49
HUMOR - CAUSES (CONCERNS)
  Imaginary Figures of the Virtues.
    S. Bridges. Ha-TP:110
HUMOR - CEMENT
  A Ghoulish Old Fellow in Kent.
    M. Bishop. Br-SM:23
HUMOR - CEMETERIES
  Mary's Ghosts. T. Hood.
    Co-FB:143, Co-PT:35, Sm-MK:106
  Spooks. N. Crane. Br-SM:4
HUMOR - CENSUS
  The Puzzled Census Taker.
    J. Saxe. Co-PT:286
HUMOR - CENTAURS
  Centaur of the Groundlevel
    Apartment. E. Pfeiffer.
    Ls-NY:337
HUMOR - CENTIPEDES
  The Centipede. A. Herbert.
    Co-BBW:223

The Centipede. O. Nash. Fe-FP:352
A Centipede. Ar-TP3:129, Au-SP:231,
    Bl-OB:123, Bo-FP:89, Ch-B:40,
    Co-HP:25, Fe-FP:130, Ja-PC:11,
    Lo-LL:35, Sh-RP:143, Un-GT:77
If This Doesn't Make You Laugh.
    Re-RR:82
HUMOR - CHAIRS
Four Legs and a Back. Re-RR:42
The Perfect Reactionary. H. Mearns.
    Co-HP:97
The Table and the Chair. E. Lear.
    Au-SP:221, Bo-FP:26, Ir-BB:235,
    Hu-MP:463, Un-GB:25, Un-GT:215
HUMOR - CHAMELEONS
A Chameleon, when He's Feeling
    Blue. E. Merriam. Br-LL:13
How to Tell the Wild Animals.
    C. Wells. Un-GF:84
HUMOR - CHANCE
The Law of Averages. Troubadour.
    Co-FB:483
Luck. W. Gibson. Co-SS:72,
    Gr-EC:211, Pa-RE:98, Sm-MK:63
Oh Lucky Jim! Gr-CT:88, Gr-GB:157
One Good Turn Deserves Another.
    Br-SM:27
With a Little Bit of Luck.
    A. Lerner. Er-FA:433
HUMOR - CHANGE
Aunt Helen. T. Eliot. Ha-PO:68,
    Mc-WS:146, Pe-SS:158
The Ballad of Hagensack. W. Irwin.
    Co-PT:272
The Chameleon. A. Herbert.
    Co-BBW:94, Co-IW:44, Fe-FP:129
Changed. C. Calverley. Co-FB:74
The Convert. M. Danner. Ra-BP:149
Don't Say You Like Tchaikowsky.
    P. Rosner. Co-FB:461
On Looking Up by Chance at the
    Constellations. R. Frost.
    Li-TU:268
The Poet of Bray. J. Heath-Stubbs.
    Pl-ML:9
HUMOR - CHANGELINGS
General John. W. Gilbert.
    Co-HP:66, Un-GT:202
HUMOR - CHAOS AND ORDER
Everything in Its Place.
    A. Guiterman. Gr-EC:194
Three Hens. H. Johnstone.
    Co-OT:21
HUMOR - CHAPERONS
Life in Our Village. M. Markwei.
    Ab-MO:20
HUMOR - CHARITY
Spectator ab Extra. A. Clough.
    Pa-GTB:361
HUMOR - CHARLES II, KING OF ENGLAND
Epitaph on Charles II. J. Wilmot.
    Al-VBP:506, Co-FB:476, Hi-WP II:140,
    Mc-WS:89, Un-GT:237

Impromptu on Charles II. J. Wilmot.
    Gr-CT:473
Samuel Pepys. A. Laing. Co-FB:130
HUMOR - CHARMS
Beware, My Child. S. Silverstein.
    Co-OW:11, La-PV:30
Hallowe'en Charm. L. Blair.
    Ja-HH:36
HUMOR - CHEESE
A Cheese That Was Aged and Gray.
    Br-LL:85
Cruel Clever Cat. G. Taylor.
    Gr-CT:122
Green Cheese. Ir-BB:29
Hospitality. W. McClintic.
    Co-BBW:51
Jack and Roger. B. Franklin.
    Gr-CT:474
Queen of Cheese. J. McIntyre.
    Co-FB:295
There Was an Old Man Who Said,
    "Please." E. Knox. Br-LL:86
HUMOR - CHEMISTRY
Rhyme for a Chemical Baby.
    J. Cook. Li-SR:128
HUMOR - CHERRIES
Cherries. Ir-BB:26, Sp-AS:20
HUMOR - CHERRY TREES
In a Town Garden. D. Mattam.
    Co-EL:55, Co-FB:99, Co-PU:129
HUMOR - CHICAGO, ILL.
The Chicago Picasso. G. Brooks.
    Ra-BP:169, Wi-LT:665
HUMOR - CHICKENS
The Answer. Re-RR:64
The Chickens. Rs-PF:21
Chook-Chook-Chook. On-TW:34,
    Re-RR:85
The Cock and the Hen. Wr-RM:44
Hen Overboard. R. Coffin.
    Sh-RP:327
Henry Ward Beecher. O. Holmes.
    Br-LL:25, Gr-CT:31
I Don't Know. Ja-PC:52
The Lost Egg. P. Ilott.
    Gr-EC:158, Ir-BB:63
Peter and Michael. Ir-BB:172
The Poultries. O. Nash. Co-OT:55,
    Pa-RE:17, Un-GF:82
The Prodigal Egg. Co-HP:24
The Pullet. Bu-DY:92
A Rooster's Unruffled. Rs-PF:9
Three Hens. R. Johnstone.
    Co-OT:21
To Be or Not to Be. Co-HP:21,
    Er-FA:202, Gr-EC:168,
    Hi-WP II:12, Un-GT:228
Well I Never! Ir-BB:84
HUMOR - CHILDHOOD RECOLLECTIONS
My First Cigar. R. Burdette.
    Co-PT:278

HUMOR - CHILDREN
  Oh Come Little Children.
    P. McGinley. Ga-FB:174
  A Parental Ode to My Son, Aged
    Three Years and Five Months.
    T. Hood. Co-FB:103, Co-HP:77,
    Fe-FP:36, Fe-PL:139
HUMOR - CHIMPANZEES
  The Chimpanzee. O. Herford.
    Co-FB:26, Ga-FB:332
  The Chimpanzee. M. Sly. Co-FB:129
  Having a Wonderful Time.
    D. Wyndham Lewis. Co-FB:7
  Lord of Jesters, Prince of
    Fellows. P. Bennett, Co-BBW:191
HUMOR - CHINA
  Old Wang Pops the Question.
    Yüan Shui-p'ai. Hs-TC:403
  A Song of Reform.
    Yüan Shui-p'ai. Hs-TC:405
HUMOR - THE CHINESE
  He Shot at Lee Wing. Br-SM:53
  Plain Language from Truthful
    James. B. Harte. Co-HP:71
HUMOR - CHIVALRY
  Boys Will Be Princes. W. Heyen.
    Ls-NY:92
  The Rhyme of the Chivalrous
    Shark. W. Irwin. Br-SM:97,
    Co-HP:81
  The Troubadour. W. Gilbert.
    Co-RM:75
HUMOR - CHOICES
  Arthur Ridgewood, M.D. F. Davis.
    Be-MA:53, Ra-BP:121
  La Carte. J. Richardson. Co-EL:55
  Good Taste. C. Logue. Pa-RE:95
  In That Case. P. Solomon. Jo-VC:34
  Liberty. W. Wordsworth. Co-FB:307
  The Perils of Invisibility.
    W. Gilbert. Co-PT:299
  The Robins. Ir-BB:242, Mo-MGT:103,
    Wr-RM:52
  To the Cuckoo. F. Townsend.
    Gr-CT:21
HUMOR - CHRISTMAS
  Christmas. Au-SP:375, Mo-MGT:109,
    Wr-RM:28
  The Computer's First Christmas Card.
    E. Morgan. To-MP:215
  Simple Sam. L. Jackson. Co-PS:164
  Soliloquy of a Turkey. P. Dunbar.
    Ra-BP:47
HUMOR - CHRISTMAS CUSTOMS
  As I Went Out on Christmas Day.
    Rv-CB:20
  Jolly Jankin. Gr-GB:141
HUMOR - CHRISTMAS DINNERS
  An Indignation Dinner.
    J. Corrothers. Hu-PN:27
  Thoughts of Loved Ones.
    M. Fishback. Co-FB:85

HUMOR - CHRISTMAS ENTERTAINMENTS
  Christmas Pageant. M. Fishback.
    Co-PS:177
HUMOR - CHRISTMAS GIFTS
  Christmas Guarantee. E. Jay.
    Ja-HH:56
  Christmas Present. Ja-HH:60
  Conversation about Christmas.
    D. Thomas. Li-TU:28, 37
  Epitaph for a Christmas Gift.
    M. Bracker. Ke-TF:283
HUMOR - CHRISTMAS SHOPPING
  What Alice Wrote to Santa. E. Jay.
    Ja-HH:57
HUMOR - CHRISTMAS TREES
  Fable of the Transcendant
    Tannenbaum. S. Bates. Co-PT:307
HUMOR - CHURCHES
  Johnny Went to Church One Day.
    Co-BB:24, Co-OH:72
  The Ladies Aid. Fe-PL:415
  The New Church Organ.
    W. Carleton. Fe-PL:233
HUMOR - CIDER
  There Was a Young Lady of Ryde.
    Br-SM:74, Na-EO:169
HUMOR - CIRCLES
  Circles. H. Behn. Li-LC:36,
    Lo-LL:54
HUMOR - CIRCUSES
  The Circus Ship Euzkera.
    W. Gibson. Co-FB:151, Co-SS:146
  Johnny Morozov. B. Okujava.
    Bo-RU:55
  Our Circus. L. Randall. Ar-TP3:116
HUMOR - CITIES AND TOWNS
  A Description of a City Shower.
    J. Swift. Rv-CB:490
  The Talk of the Town.
    E. Fisher. Co-FB:361
  Yankee Doodle. De-PO:22, Gr-CT:87,
    Gr-GB:166, Ir-BB:234, Mo-CC:(17),
    Mo-MGT:162, Mo-TL:85
HUMOR - CITY TRAFFIC
  Street Scene. P. Suffolk. Co-PT:158
HUMOR - CLAMS
  Nirvana. Co-HP:24
HUMOR - CLEANLINESS
  The Battle of Clothesline Bay.
    W. Irwin. Co-SS:33
  Clean Clara. W. Rands. Co-HP:105
  Going Too Far. M. Howells.
    Ar-TP3:138, Ir-BB:203, Pa-OM:82
  Soap, the Oppressor. B. Johnson.
    Fe-PL:216
  Washing. J. Drinkwater. Fe-FP:6
  What the Book Said. Ja-HH:41
HUMOR - CLERGY
  Doctor Foster. Mo-MGT:36
  In Church. T. Hardy. Co-PT:92,
    Un-MB:29
  Limericks. R. Knox. Ke-TF:289

The Minister in the Pulpit.
  Co-OW:21, Su-FVI:19
The Vicar. W. Praed. Ox-BN:445
HUMOR - CLIMBING
  High Brow. R. Fitch. Mo-SD:93
  The Mountains. W. Gibson.
    Mo-SD:92
  Neither Hillaryous Norgay.
    G. Lewis. Co-FB:388
  Presence of Mind. H. Graham.
    Co-HP:68
  Some Families of My Acquaintance.
    L. Richards. Co-OW:18
HUMOR - CLOCKS AND WATCHES
  The Fearful Finale of the Irascible
    Mouse. G. Carryl. Co-HP:51,
    Gr-EC:18
  Oh, No! M. Dodge. Co-BB:20
  The Sad Tale of Mr. Mears.
    Co-PT:308
  This Must Be Looked Into. Rs-PF:25
HUMOR - CLOTHING AND DRESS
  All Dressed Up. A. Spilka.
    Su-FVI:14
  And . . . Co-OH:55
  The Big Baboon. H. Belloc.
    Co-OH:28, Un-MB:170
  The Bonnie Cravat. Mother Goose.
    Ar-TP3:131
  Bootless Speculations.
    P. McGinley. Ke-TF:88
  The Boy. E. Field. Gr-EC:199
  Brian O'Linn. Co-HP:26, Gr-GB:164
  Clothes. F. Frost. Sh-RP:131
  Crinolines and Bloomers. Hi-TL:174
  A Dash to the Pole. W. Irwin.
    Co-HP:80
  Diddle, Diddle, Dumpling.
    Bo-FP:37, De-PO:28, Ir-BB:191,
    Li-LB:71, Mo-CC:(21), Mo-MGT:36,
    Mo-TL:41, Wi-MG:13, Wr-RM:37
  Easter Parade. M. Chute.
    Br-SS:140, La-PH:53
  Endless Chant. Su-FVI:79
  Epitaph for a Christmas Gift.
    M. Bracker. Ke-TF:283
  The Funniest Sight That Ever I
    Saw. Un-GT:18
  Growing Up. A. Milne. Br-BC:107,
    Gr-TG:16
  I'm a Little Hindoo. Co-HP:25,
    Er-FA:498, Ir-BB:93
  Jonathan Bing. B. Brown.
    Ar-TP3:139, Au-SP:255, Co-HP:35,
    Fe-FP:335, Ir-BB:204, La-PP:68,
    La-PV:96, Lo-LL:8, Pa-OM:8,
    Pe-FB:95
  Limericks. Ke-TF:287
  Little Blue Apron. Ir-BB:94
  Midsummer Fantasy. N. Levy.
    Co-PS:110
  Mother Bulletout. Ir-BB:167

My Donkey. Ar-TP3:123, Ir-BB:175
The New Vestments. E. Lear.
  Co-HP:86, Pa-RE:118
Nothing to Wear. W. Butler.
  Fe-PL:221
Othello Jones Dresses for Dinner
  E. Roberson. Ad-PB:349, Hu-PN:429
Poems in Praise of Practically
  Nothing. S. Hoffenstein.
  Na-EO:92
Putting on a Nightgown. Mo-MGT:120
Rumbo and Jumbo. Co-HP:27
A Sleeper from the Amazon.
  Br-LL:93, Lo-LL:54, Sh-RP:144
The Soldier and the Maid. Mo-MGT:186
A Tapir Who Lived in Malay.
  O. Herford. Br-LL:33
There Was a Young Man of Bengal.
  Br-LL:93, Un-GT:242
There Was a Young Person of Crete.
  E. Lear. Br-LL:94
There Was an Old Man of the Cape.
  E. Lear. Br-LL:93, Ir-BB:219
Three Young Rats. Fr-WO:35,
  Gr-CT:31, Gr-EC:11, Gr-GB:92,
  Ir-BB:234, Lo-LL:41, Mo-MGT:187,
  On-TW:15, Sm-MK:193
To Henrietta, on Her Departure
  for Calais. T. Hood. Ox-BC:181
Tommy O'Linn. Mo-MGT:96
Wee Willie Gray. R. Burns.
  Ox-BC:92
Well I Never, Did You Ever.
  Ir-BB:192, Sm-LG:70
When a Cub, Unaware Being Bare.
  E. Merriam. Br-LL:27
Whenas in Jeans. P. Dehn. Co-FB:229
Where in the World. Rs-PF:24
Woe, Brothers, Woe! A. Kramer.
  Ke-TF:280
The Young Ones, Flip Side.
  J. Emanuel. Ab-MO:17
HUMOR - CLUMSINESS
  Love Poem. J. Nims. Mo-WS:56,
    Pe-OA:233
HUMOR - COBALT
  The Hydrogen Dog and the Cobalt
    Cat. F. Winsor. Br-SM:64
HUMOR - COCKROACHES
  Archy a Low Brow. D. Marquis.
    Co-HP:95
  Archy Confesses. D. Marquis.
    Co-FB:359, Na-EO:142
HUMOR - COCONUTS
  The Coconut. A. Milne. Co-FB:85
  Locked In. I. Gustafson.
    Co-PT:24
HUMOR - COFFEE
  The Rape of the Lock. A. Pope.
    Al-VBP:533
  While Grinding Coffee at the
    Store. W. Engel. Co-OH:53

HUMOR - COFFINS
   It Isn't the Cough.   Br-SM:136,
      Er-FA:218
HUMOR - COINS
   The Lost Farthing.   E. Farjeon.
      Ir-BB:160
HUMOR - COLD
   The Cremation of Sam McGee.
      R. Service.   Ar-TP3:143,
      Br-SM:140, Er-FA:399, Fe-PL:6,
      Ha-PO:96
   Limericks.   Ke-TF:287
   Many Are Called.   Rs-PF:42
   Morning.   C. Calverley. Co-HP:38
   There Was Once a Small Boy in
      Quebec.   R. Kipling. Br-LL:63
HUMOR - COLDS
   The Buffalo.   L. Richards. Co-OW:72
   A Child That Has a Cold. T. Dibdin.
      Co-PU:18
   Kerchoo!   M. Fishback.   Co-PS:62
   Matilda.   F. Evans.   Co-BB:84
   Old Mr. Bows.   W. Horsbrugh.
      Co-OW:45, Ir-BB:149
   Pourquoi? Co-BBW:103, Gr-CT:89,
      Gr-EC:79
   The Sniffle.   O. Nash.
      Hi-WP II:15, Mc-WS:174,
      Sh-RP:121
   Tommy Tottle.   Ja-PC:25
   Winter Is Icumen In.   B. Smith.
      Co-PS:151
HUMOR - COLLECTIVE BARGAINING
   When Serpents Bargain for the
      Right to Squirm. E. Cummings.
      Br-TC:82
HUMOR - COLLEGES AND UNIVERSITIES
   Alma Mater, Forget Me.   W. Cole.
      Co-FB:459
   as joe gould says.   E. Cummings.
      Co-FB:409
   Baccalaureate.   D. McCord.
      Li-SR:123
   Religious Emphasis Week. C. Walsh.
      St-H:242
   Song of One Eleven Years in
      Prison. G. Canning. Co-FB:429
HUMOR - COLOR
   Vegetables.   S. Silverstein.
      Co-OT:36
HUMOR - COLUMBUS, CHRISTOPHER
   Columbus Day Thought.   J. Lee.
      Ja-HH:33
   The Great Discovery.   E. Farjeon.
      Co-PS:133
   I Quite Realized. . . .   E. Bentley.
      Co-FB:126
   Short History.   Ja-HH:32
HUMOR - COMMITTEES AND COMMITTEE
      MEETINGS
   The Board Meets.   J. Gloag.
      Co-FB:461

   Clubwoman.   M. Smith.   Hu-PN:388
HUMOR - COMMONPLACENESS
   Life Cycle of Common Man.
      H. Nemerov.   To-MP:121
HUMOR - COMMUTERS
   Commuter.   E. White.   La-OC:61
HUMOR - COMPANIONSHIP OF MEN AND
      ANIMALS
   The Cow.   J. Stephens.   Gr-EC:9
   The Dog.   O. Nash.   Co-OT:68,
      Co-PU:92
   Elegy on the Death of a Mad Dog.
      O. Goldsmith.   Br-SM:103,
      Co-RG:97, Er-FA:213, Fr-WO:49,
      Ha-PO:110, Mc-WK:58, Rv-CB:540,
      Sm-LG:84, Sp-OG:237, Un-GF:17
   Kindness to Animals. L. Richards.
      Ar-TP3:122, Au-SP:236, Ir-BB:167,
      St-FS:45
   Mother Shuttle.   Ir-BB:170,
      Mo-MGT:18, Na-EO:81, Wi-MG:70
   My Uncle Jehosaphat.   Ir-BB:176,
      Ox-BC:288
   The Rhinoceros.   R. Lister.
      Co-BBW:193
   There Was a Crooked Man.
      Au-SP:3, De-PO:22, Er-FA:506,
      Fr-WO:24, Ir-BB:216, La-PP:70,
      Li-LB:71, Mo-MGT:12, Mo-NR:86,
      Mo-TL:71, Rv-CB:457, Sm-MK:114,
      Wi-MG:15, Wr-RM:102
   When It Comes to Bugs. A. Fisher.
      Ja-PC:51
HUMOR - COMPASSES
   Circles.   H. Behn.   Li-LC:36,
      Lo-LL:54
HUMOR - COMPETITION
   The Mountain Whippoorwill.
      S. Benét.   Co-PT:110
HUMOR - COMPLAINTS
   Eclogue.   E. Lear.   Li-TU:74
   Every Thing.   H. Monro. Un-MB:232
   O Why Was I Born with a Different
      Face.   W. Blake.   Co-PU:114
HUMOR - COMPOSERS
   Epigram on Handel and Bononcini.
      J. Byrom.   Pl-US:77, Rv-CB:517
   Iberia.   L. Kirschenbaum. Pl-US:93
   A Saint Cecilia's Day Epigram.
      P. Porter.   Co-EL:60
   There Was a Composer Named Bong.
      Br-LL:107
HUMOR - COMPUTERS
   The Computer's First Christmas
      Card.   E. Morgan.   To-MP:215
HUMOR - CONCEIT
   E Is the Egotist Dread. O. Herford.
      Br-LL:71
   Egoism.   W. Craddle.   Co-FB:69
   warty bliggens, the toad.
      D. Marquis.   Co-FB:14
   A Wee Little Worm. J. Riley. La-PV:33

HUMOR – CONCERTS
  The Concert. J. Newman. Co-HP:100
  Recipe for an Evening Musicale.
    P. McGinley. Pl-US:43
HUMOR – CONDORS
  Said the Condor in Tones of
    Despair. O. Herford. Br-LL:5
HUMOR – CONFESSIONS
  Adam, Lilith, and Eve.
    R. Browning. Un-MW:53
  Gentle Alice Brown. W. Gilbert.
    Co-FB:147
  My Ghostly Father. Gr-CT:59,
    Rv-CB:3
  Paddy O'Rafther. S. Lover.
    Co-PI:97, Co-PT:298
HUMOR – CONFORMITY
  Aunt Helen. T. Eliot. Ha-PO:68,
    Mc-WS:146, Pe-SS:158
  Bleat of Protest. M. Weston.
    Co-FB:208
  A Cottage in Fife. Ir-BB:139,
    Lo-LL:75, Mo-MGT:170, Wi-MG:44,
    Wr-RM:78
  Schoolmistress. C. Sansom.
    To-MP:129
  Sorrows of Werther. W. Thackeray.
    Br-SM:32, Co-FB:344, Hi-WP II:11
  They Walk under Ladders.
    C. Walsh. St-H:239
  The Vicar. W. Praed. Ox-BN:445
  Warning. J. Joseph. To-MP:161
  Yonder See. A. Housman.
    Hi-WP I:120
HUMOR – CONNECTICUT
  The Customs of the Country.
    P. McGinley. Ke-TF:343
HUMOR – CONSCIENCE
  Burglar Bill. T. Guthrie.
    Co-FB:112
  A Storm in Childhood. T. Jones.
    Ma-FW:35
HUMOR – CONSERVATISM
  Middle-Man. W. Matchett. Ha-TP:106
HUMOR – CONSPIRACY
  The Love Poems: Shepherdess.
    N. Cameron. Pa-GTB:500
HUMOR – CONSTELLATIONS
  The Man in the Moon. Mother Goose.
    Au-SP:219, Ir-BB:155, Ja-PC:55
HUMOR – CONTEMPT
  To a Cat. Co-BBW:139
HUMOR – CONTENTMENT
  The Enchanted Shirt. J. Hay.
    Ha-PO:59, Sh-RP:264, Un-GT:171
  The Fox and the Grapes. J. Lauren.
    Bo-HF:70, Un-GT:170
  The Frogs Who Wanted a King.
    J. Lauren. Bo-HF:94, Un-GT:170
  Good Times. L. Clifton. Ad-PB:306,
    Be-MA:140, Br-TC:71, Ra-BP:250

Mr. Pyme. H. Behn. Ar-TP3:139,
  Lo-LL:94
The Stars Haven't Dealt Me the
  Worst They Could Do.
  A. Housman. Co-EL:144,
  Pa-GTB:419
Suburban Vista. C. Walsh.
  St-H:238
HUMOR – CONTROVERSY
  Black Poet, White Critic.
    D. Randall. Ra-BP:33
  Then Said the Blowfly. Le-IB:43
  There Were Three Jovial Welshmen.
    Bl-OB:24, Gr-GB:86, Ir-BB:140,
    Mo-MGT:198, Pa-OM:2, Sm-MK:23,
    Sp-HW:23
HUMOR – CONVERSATION
  Arrogance Repressed. J. Betjeman.
    Co-FB:189
  Conversational. Co-BL:26,
    Co-FB:323, Co-HP:26
  Cows. J. Reeves. Bl-OB:118,
    Co-BBW:175, Co-PS:80, St-FS:85
  Don't Say You Like Tchaikowsky.
    P. Rosner. Co-FB:461
  The Feckless Dinner Party.
    W. de la Mare. Co-PT:33
  Horse. E. Roberts. Co-BBW:145,
    Sh-RP:38
  On Mrs. W. N. Bentley. Co-FB:199
  Reflections at Dawn. P. McGinley.
    Co-FB:394
  Table Talk. D. Mattam. Co-FB:191
  Talk. P. Stalker. Co-FB:482
  The Visit. O. Nash. Co-FB:498
  Wha Lies Here? Co-FB:131,
    Co-PU:159
  You'd Say It Was a Funeral.
    J. Reeves. Br-SM:119
HUMOR – CONVERSION
  Observation. D. Parker. Co-FB:396
  The Reformed Pirate. T. Roberts.
    Do-WH:20
  Silver Jack's Religion.
    J. Jones. Fi-BG:185
HUMOR – COOKS AND COOKERY
  Amelia Mixed the Mustard.
    A. Housman. Ne-AM:9
  Aunt Nerissa's Muffin. W. Irwin.
    Co-FB:88
  The Bakers. L. Blair. Ja-PC:34
  Boomer Johnson. Fi-BG:84
  Connie Likes Cookbooks. Rs-PF:93
  Mummy Slept Late and Daddy Fixed
    Breakfast. J. Ciardi.
    Ar-TP3:133, La-PV:26
  O, Dear, O! De-TT:31
  Poems in Praise of Practically
    Nothing. S. Hoffenstein.
    Na-EO:92
  Some Cook! J. Ciardi. Ag-HE:74,
    Bo-FP:52, La-PP:69, La-PV:28

HUMOR - COOKS AND COOKERY — <u>cont'd</u>.
    There Was a Young Lady of Poole.
        E. Lear.   Ag-HE:11
    There Was an Old Man of Thermopylae.
        E. Lear.   Br-LL:67, Fr-WO:41,
        Na-EO:103
    Though Some Are Fat.   Re-RR:79
HUMOR - COOPERATION
    Partners.   J. Castillo.   Gr-EC:15,
        Mc-WK:90
HUMOR - CORN
    "Ah, Ha!" Said Farmer Thorne.
        Rs-PF:44
    Autumn.   E. Roberts.   Co-PT:285,
        Ja-PA:49
    Why Are Good Farmers.   Re-RR:66
HUMOR - CORRUPTION
    The British Journalist.
        H. Wolfe.   Co-FB:472
HUMOR - COUÉ, ÉMILE
    On Monsieur Coué.   C. Inge.
        Br-LL:115, Er-FA:218
HUMOR - COUNTER CULTURE
    Portrait by a Neighbor. E. Millay.
        Ar-TP3:8, Fe-FP:312, Ha-LO:45,
        Ho-TH:22, Hu-MP:139, Mo-BG:47,
        Ne-AM:36, Pe-FB:26, Th-AS:188,
        Tu-WW:40
    Where's Mary?   I. Eastwick.
        Ne-AM:44
HUMOR - COURAGE
    Back in My Home Town.   Issa.
        Be-MC:17
    The Brave Priest.   Mo-MGT:37
    The Duke of Plaza-Toro.   W. Gilbert.
        Co-FB:70, Co-HP:63, Fe-FP:349
    The Thespians at Thermopylae.
        N. Cameron.   Pa-GTB:498
HUMOR - COURTESY
    The Courteous Knight.   Ox-BB:246
    The Gingham Umbrella.
        L. Richards.   Co-OT:67
    I Tried to Tip My Hat.
        S. Silverstein.   Co-OT:70
    Politeness.   H. Graham.   Co-OH:16
    There Was an Old Lady Who Said.
        Br-LL:62
    Tony Was a Turtle.   E. Rieu.
        Ar-TP3:130, Gr-EC:12, Ir-BB:85
HUMOR - COURTSHIP
    Before the Barn-Door Crowing.
        J. Gay.   Co-EL:14, Rv-CB:505
    The Birds' Courting.   Un-GF:81
    The Blacksmith's Serenade.
        V. Lindsay.   Co-PT:100
    Blow Me Eyes.   W. Irwin. Co-BL:166
    Brian O'Linn.   Co-HP:26, Gr-GB:164
    Conversational.   Co-BL:26,
        Co-FB:323, Co-HP:26
    The Courteous Knight.   Ox-BB:246,
    Courtship.   A. Resnikoff.
        Co-OH:18

The Courtship of the Yonghy-Bonghy-
    Bo.   E. Lear.   Ho-WR:50,
    Na-EO:171, Pa-OM:59, Un-GT:213
The Cunning Clerk.   Ox-BB:631
Duncan Gray.   R. Burns. Pa-GTB:153
Eppie Morris.   Ox-BB:251
The Fair Circassian.   R. Garnett.
    Co-PT:89
Falling in Love in Spain or
    Mexico.   R. Padgett.   Mc-EA:138
Fifteen Boys.   B. Akhmadulina.
    Bo-RU:5, Ca-MR:39, Gr-BT:65
Flight.   W. Walden.   Ls-NY:329
A Frog He Would a-Wooing Go.
    Ir-BB:114, Mo-MGT:112, Mo-NR:93
Frog Went a-Courtin'.   Un-GT:19
A Gentle Echo on Woman.   J. Swift.
    Co-FB:438
Hippopotamothalamion.
    J. Wheelock.   Co-FB:10
How a Girl Was Too Reckless of
    Grammar by Far.   G. Carryl.
    Co-FB:154
How She Resolved to Act. M. Moore.
    Pe-SS:116, Un-MA:575, Un-MW:59
A Howl about an Owl.   L. Richards.
    Ir-BB:152
In May.   J. Synge.   Un-MB:182,
    Un-MW:196
Intimates.   D. Lawrence. Co-PT:185
Kate Dalrymple.   Gr-GB:109
The King-Fisher Song.   L. Carroll.
    Bl-OB:18
Kitty of Coleraine.   Co-PT:188
The Lady and the Swine.
    Br-FF:(33), Co-OH:74, De-TT:70,
    Gr-CT:13, Gr-GB:151, Ir-BB:170,
    Mo-MGT:141
Lady Jane.   A. Quiller-Couch.
    Co-FB:443
The Lady with Technique. H. Mearns.
    Co-FB:374
A Leap-Year Episode.   E. Field.
    Co-BL:120
Little John Bottlejohn.
    L. Richards.   Co-PM:148,
    La-PV:212, Lo-LL:61, Sh-RP:252
A Little Maid.   Mo-MGT:24,
    Wr-RM:108
Love.   C. Calverley.   Co-FB:311,
    Co-HP:38
Love in a Space-Suit. J. Kirkup.
    To-MP:120
A Man and a Maid.   Mo-MGT:216,
    Wr-RM:21
Marriage.   G. Corso.   Wi-LT:673
The Marvellous Hat.
    W. Horsbrugh.   Ir-BB:200
Mia Carlotta.   T. Daly. Hi-WP I:103
The Modest Couple.   W. Gilbert.
    Co-PT:186

Moonshine.   W. de la Mare.
  Co-FB:442
The Mouse Who Lived on a Hill.
  Bu-DY:61
Old Wang Pops the Question.
  Yüan Shui-p'ai.   Hs-TC:403
The One Answer.   La-PV:209,
  Un-GT:169, Un-MW:33
The Owl and the Pussy-Cat. E. Lear.
  Ar-TP3:120, Au-SP:266, Bl-OB:117,
  Bo-FP:25, Bo-GJ:14, Cl-DT:30,
  Co-IW:3, Er-FA:495, Fe-FP:354,
  Fe-PL:237, Fr-WO:39, Ha-PO:239,
  Hi-WP I:94, Hu-MP:450, Ir-BB:250,
  Pe-FB:96, Rv-CB:812, Sm-LG:89,
  Sm-MK:200, St-FS:108, Un-GB:38,
  Un-GT:224
The Pelican Chorus.   E. Lear.
  Lo-LL:36
Pelt Kid and His Grandmother.
  Te-FC:193
A Piazza Tragedy.   E. Field.
  Co-FB:152
Prose and Poesy.   T. Ybarra.
  Co-HP:118
The Puddy and the Mouse. Gr-GB:68
Reflections on Ice-Breaking.
  O. Nash.   Er-FA:209, Wi-LT:629
Save the Tiger! A. Herbert.
  Co-HP:72
A Seaside Romance.   D. Marquis.
  Co-HP:93
A Sporty Young Man in St. Pierre.
  F. Christgau.   Br-LL:119
Squire and Milkmaid. Ox-BB:652
Sucking Cider Through a Straw.
  Gr-GB:125
There Once Was a Maiden of Siam.
  Br-LL:117
The Touchstone.   S. Bishop.
  Un-MW:41
Under the Willow-Shades.
  W. Davenant.   Un-MW:42
An Unkind Lass.   Mo-MGT:169
When Jenny Wren Was Young.
  Mother Goose.   Hu-MP:213,
  Wr-RM:23
Where Are You Going to, My
  Pretty Maid? Li-LB:145,
  Mo-MGT:204, Mo-NR:56, Wi-MG:68,
  Wr-RM:112
A Young Lady Sings in Our Choir.
  Br-LL:121
Young Roger and Dolly.   Wr-RM:114
See also Em-AF:196-227
HUMOR - COWARDICE
The Duke of Plaza-Toro. W. Gilbert.
  Co-FB:70, Co-HP:63, Fe-FP:349
Howard. A. Milne.   Co-OT:61
Impasse. L. Sarett.   Co-BBW:179
Just Behind the Battle, Mother.
  Co-FB:77

Song.   Br-MW:93
The Tale of Custard the Dragon.
  O. Nash.   Fe-FP:332, Ir-BB:170,
  Un-GB:26, Un-GT:167
HUMOR - COWBOYS
Cowboy.   Gr-CT:14
Cowboy Song.   C. Causley.
  Co-RM:27, Ha-PO:10, Pe-M:36
Silly Girl.   E. Jay.   Ja-PC:35
Tying a Knot in the Devil's Tail.
  Co-RM:35
The Zebra Dun.   Co-PT:144,
  Sh-RP:49
HUMOR - COWS
Caprice.   D. Shaw.   Co-PT:146
The Cautious Collapsible Cow.
  A. Guiterman.   Br-LL:22
The Cow.   O. Nash.   Co-BBW:167,
  Ke-TF:335
The Cow.   T. Roethke.   Co-FB:374
Cow.   W. Smith.   Co-OW:58
The Cow.   Ir-BB:141
Did You Feed My Cow? Bu-DY:11
Hey Diddle Diddle.   Ar-TP3:118,
  Au-SP:13, Bo-FP:29, De-PO:20,
  Er-FA:506, Ir-BB:14, Li-LB:104,
  Mo-CC:7, Mo-MGT:83, Mo-NR:44,
  Re-RR:111, Wi-MG:19, Wr-RM:60
I Had a Little Cow.   Ir-BB:26,
  Sp-TM:7
Jonathan.   R. Fyleman.
  Ar-TP3:133, Ja-PC:27
Life in the Country.
  M. Silverton.   Co-EL:17,
  Co-PU:139
The Moo-Cow-Moo.   E. Cooke.
  Er-FA:497
The Purple Cow.   G. Burgess.
  Ar-TP3:123, Au-SP:229, Bl-OB:21,
  Co-FB:371, Co-HP:36, Er-FA:200,
  Fe-FP:365, Fe-PL:203, Fr-WO:46,
  La-PV:33, Lo-LL:75, Un-GF:64
There Was a Piper Had a Cow.
  Ir-BB:45, Wr-RM:116
There Was an Old Man.   De-TT:45,
  Gr-EC:284, Ir-BB:29, Mo-MGT:72
There Was an Old Soldier of
  Bister.   Br-LL:22, Ir-BB:221
There Was an Old Woman Who Had
  Three Cows.   On-TW:14
What Has Two Hookers.   Re-RR:114
Why Are Good Farmers.   Re-RR:66
HUMOR - CRANES (BIRDS)
The Pelican Chorus.   E. Lear.
  Lo-LL:36
HUMOR - CREATION
How the First Hielandman of God
  Was Made of Ane Horse Turd in
  Argyll as Is Said. Gr-GB:166
Red Geranium and Godly Mignonette.
  D. Lawrence.   Ga-S:10,
  Pa-GTB:460

HUMOR - CREATION — cont'd.
  To Poor Pygmalion. E. Coatsworth.
    Co-PU:38
  When Did the World Begin.
    R. Clairmont. Au-SP:227,
    Co-HP:54, Mc-WK:102, Un-GT:230
HUMOR - CREMATION
  The Cremation of Sam McGee.
    R. Service. Ar-TP3:143,
    Br-SM:140, Er-FA:399, Fe-PL:6,
    Ha-PO:96
HUMOR - CRICKET (GAME)
  The Game of Cricket. H. Belloc.
    Co-FB:97
HUMOR - CRIME AND CRIMINALS
  Macavity: The Mystery Cat.
    T. Eliot. Ar-TP3:121, Co-BBW:131,
    Li-TU:104, Ox-BC:346, Sh-RP:321,
    Sm-MK:162
  The Policeman's Lot. W. Gilbert.
    Co-HP:59
HUMOR - CRITICS AND CRITICISM
  And Now, Kind Friends. . . .
    J. Moore. Co-FB:304
  Art Review. K. Fearing. Du-SH:33
  Black Poet, White Critic.
    D. Randall. Re-BP:33
  Cervantes. E. Bentley.
    Co-FB:127, Na-EO:54
  A Critic. W. Landor. Gr-CT:472
  Critics. Martial. Mc-PR:21
  The Disagreeable Man. W. Gilbert.
    Co-FB:66, Hu-MP:140
  A Lady There Was of Antigua.
    C. Monkhouse. Br-LL:120
  Lines Scratched in Wet Cement.
    E. Jacobson. Br-SM:23
  A Musical Critic Anticipates
    Eternity. S. Sassoon.
    Pl-US:143
  Obituary. A. Brode. Co-FB:339
  The Owl-Critic. J. Fields.
    Gr-EC:169, Ha-PO:208, Na-EO:82,
    Un-GT:200
  The Poet's Fate. T. Hood.
    Co-EL:40, Co-FB:332, Co-PU:26
HUMOR - CROCODILES
  Alligator on the Escalator.
    E. Merriam. La-OC:45
  The Cat and the Crocodile.
    Ca-MU:15
  Crocodile. K. Chukovsky.
    Gr-EC:24, 33
  The Crocodile. O. Herford.
    Co-HP:73
  The Crocodile. Co-RM:65, Rv-CB:441
  The Cruel Naughty Boy. Co-BB:108
  How to Tell the Wild Animals.
    C. Wells. Un-GF:84
  If You Should Meet a Crocodile.
    Gr-EC:29, Ir-BB:76, La-PV:30

  The Monkeys and the Crocodile.
    L. Richards. Ar-TP3:126,
    Au-SP:272, Br-SM:89, Fe-FP:175,
    Ir-BB:154, La-PP:54, Li-LB:98
  The Purist. O. Nash. Bo-GJ:111,
    Br-SM:125, Co-FB:27, Co-HP:99,
    Un-MA:569
  There Was an Old Man of Boulak.
    E. Lear. Br-LL:35
HUMOR - CROMWELL, OLIVER
  Oliver Cromwell Is Buried and
    Dead. Ir-BB:208
HUMOR - CROWDS
  Seven Limericks, 7. E. Lear.
    Sh-RP:150
HUMOR - CROWING
  Cock-a-Doodle-Do. Wr-RM:96
  To Be or Not to Be. Co-HP:21,
    Er-FA:202, Gr-EC:168,
    Hi-WP II:12, Un-GT:228
HUMOR - CROWS
  Eight Crows in a Tree. Re-RR:83
  Fooba Wooba John. Co-OW:64
  I Don't Know. Ja-PC:52
  Since You Are One Who Plainly
    Knows about Plants. Re-RR:98
  Somebody Saw a Crow. Le-IB:44
  To Be or Not to Be. Co-HP:21,
    Er-FA:202, Gr-EC:168,
    Hi-WP II:12, Un-GT:228
  Two Old Crows. V. Lindsay.
    Ha-LO:25, Sh-RP:32
HUMOR - CRUELTY
  The Nettle-Rasher. V. Vickers.
    Ir-BB:83
HUMOR - CRYING
  If I Were You. Rs-PF:54
  The Man in the Onion Bed.
    J. Ciardi. Co-OW:23
  The Sad Story of a Little Boy That
    Cried. Co-BB:36, Ir-BB:97
HUMOR - CUCKOOS
  The Oocuck. J. Richardson.
    Co-FB:3
HUMOR - CULTURE
  The Chicago Picasso. G. Brooks.
    Ra-BP:169, Wi-LT:665
  The Cultured Girl Again. B. King.
    Co-FB:396
HUMOR - CURIOSITY
  The Akond of Swat. E. Lear.
    Br-LL:55, Co-FB:421, Lo-LL:85,
    Sm-MK:100, Un-GT:226
  Questions at Night. L. Untermeyer.
    Fe-FP:264, Un-GB:31, Un-GT:20
HUMOR - CURSES
  The Albatross. R. Lister.
    Co-SS:133
  Ancient History. A. Guiterman.
    Du-RG:63, Mc-WS:172
  The Curse. J. Synge. Gr-CT:472

On Lutestrings Cat-Eaten.
   T. Masters.   No-CL:36
Samuel Hall.   Gr-CT:471
HUMOR - CYNICISM
Bagpipe Music.   L. MacNeice.
   Al-VBP:1231, Ha-PO:245,
   Pa-GTB:516, Wi-LT:458
HUMOR - DAIRYING
The Dairy's Sign.   Rs-PF:18
Her Dairy.   P. Newell.   Bo-FP:83
On the High Cost of Dairy Products.
   J. McIntyre.   Co-FB:297
HUMOR - DANCERS AND DANCING
At the Family Reunion.   Rs-PF:90
Conceit with Aunties, Urn and
   Birds.   M. Leech.   Ls-NY:326
The Dancing Cabman.   J. Morton.
   Ir-BB:213
An Epitaph.   G. Cayley.   Co-EL:49,
   Co-FB:131, Co-PU:158
A Fishy Square Dance.   E. Merriam.
   Gr-EC:116
The King Said to Salome.   Co-OH:13
Lily McQueen.   S. Jackson.
   Co-BB:159
The Lobster Quadrille.   L. Carroll.
   Bo-FP:267, Fe-FP:135, Gr-CT:29,
   Hu-MP:436, Ox-BC:240, Pe-FB:90
Off the Ground.   W. de la Mare.
   Co-PT:102, Ir-BB:60
The Potatoes' Dance.   V. Lindsay.
   Fe-FP:234, Hu-MP:311, Th-AS:96
The Zobo Bird.   F. Collymore.
   Bo-GJ:156
HUMOR - DANDELIONS
A Lucky Thing.   D. Aldis.
   Sh-RP:138
HUMOR - DANGER
The Sailor's Consolation.
   C. Dibdin.   Co-HP:103, Co-SS:56,
   De-TT:128
HUMOR - DANIEL
Daniel.   V. Lindsay.   Co-RM:238,
   Ga-S:49, Gr-CT:143, Hi-WP I:80,
   Rv-CB:972, Sm-MK:75
HUMOR - DATING (SOCIAL CUSTOM)
The Girl I Took to a Cocktail
   Party.   T. Williams.   Co-FB:391
HUMOR - DAVID, KING OF ISRAEL
King David and King Solomon.
   Sm-MK:127, Un-GF:15, Un-GT:243
HUMOR - DAYS
Fish Out of Water.   M. Fishback.
   Ke-TF:380
Query.   L. McKee.   Co-PU:11,
   Ls-NY:315
HUMOR - THE DEAD
Gentleman in Oils.   H. Vinal.
   De-FS:208
Old Roger.   Mo-MGT:143, Pa-RE:101,
   Su-FVI:23

HUMOR - DEAFNESS
Ant and Eleph-Ant.   S. Milligan.
   Co-OT:25
The Old Wife and the Ghost.
   J. Reeves.   Br-SM:16, Co-PM:140,
   Gr-EC:152, La-PV:210, Pa-RE:70
Old Woman, Old Woman, Shall We Go
   a-Shearing?   Ar-TP3:132,
   Gr-EC:214, Mo-MGT:205, Wr-RM:41
HUMOR - DEATH
Aah . . . Aargh.   V. Golyavkin.
   Bo-RU:38
Bedtime Story.   G. Macbeth.Co-PT:37
Donne Redone.   J. Tierney.Br-SM:136
The Dying Airman.   Er-FA:217
Egoism.   W. Craddle.   Co-FB:69
Jerry Jones.   Br-SM:138
Limericks.   Ke-TF:289
Lucy Lake.   E. MacIntosh. Li-SR:108
Madrigal Macabre.   S. Hoffenstein.
   Br-SM:137
Misfortunes Never Come Singly.
   H. Graham.   Er-FA:214, Un-GF:48
My Auld Wife.   Gr-GB:160
On the Death of Doctor Swift.
   J. Swift.   Al-VBP:517
One Bright Morning.   Na-EO:132
Paddy Murphy.   Co-RM:118
A Reasonable Affliction. M. Prior.
   Br-SW:127, Un-MW:51
The Rebel.   M. Evans.   Ad-PB:187,
   Bo-AN:163, Pe-SS:58
The Swift Bullets.   C. Wells.
   Br-SM:54, Ja-PC:28
There Once Was a Young Man
   Named Hall.   Br-SM:53
There Was a Young Man Who Was
   Bitten.   Br-LL:20
A Threnody.   G. Lanigan.
   Co-FB:424, Do-WH:26, Rv-CB:947
Twelve Hundred Million Men.
   R. Kipling.   Co-PU:64
An Unpopular Youth of Cologne.
   Br-LL:65
Wha Lies Here?   Co-FB:131,Co-PU:159
Willie Saw Some Dynamite.
   Fe-FP:362, Un-GF:48
HUMOR - DEATH-CHILDREN
Biby's Epitaph.   Co-FB:219
Infant Innocence.   A. Housman.
   Er-FA:219, Gr-CT:23, Sm-LG:102
The Little Peach.   E. Field.
   Ag-HE:44, Br-SM:75, Ch-B:81,
   Co-HP:57
Little Willie.   Br-SM:47,
   Mc-WS:173, Sm-MK:202, Un-GT:243
Rebecca.   H. Belloc.   Du-RG:65,
   Ir-BB:156, Tu-WW:116, Un-GF:61
Tenderheartedness.   H. Graham.
   Er-FA:214, Hi-WP I:11, Un-GF:48

HUMOR - DEATH-CHILDREN — <u>cont'd</u>.
 250 Willow Lane.   J. Keith.
  De-FS:113
 We Have Lost Our Little Hanner.
  M. Adeler.   Co-FB:306
 Willie.   M. Adeler.   Co-BB:100
HUMOR - DEBTS
 The Doctor's Story.   W. Carleton.
  Co-PT:282
 Father Will Settle the Bill.
  Ke-TF:273
 He Paid Me Seven.   Ra-BP:5
 The Mad Lover.   A. Brome. Rv-CB:398
 The Promissory Note.   B. Taylor.
  Li-SR:143
HUMOR - DECEPTION
 Afforestation.   E. Wodehouse.
  Co-FB:173, Mo-SD:44
 Bunthorne's Song.   W. Gilbert.
  Co-FB:349
 Capsule Conclusions, VI. Un-MW:65
 The Gastronomic Guile of Simple
  Simon.   G. Carryl.   Un-GT:218
 The Kiss.   C. Patmore. Un-MW:54
 Plain Language from Truthful
  James.   B. Harte.   Co-HP:71
 A Word of Encouragement. J. Pope.
  Co-EL:52, Co-FB:486, Co-PU:15
HUMOR - DEFEAT
 Procedure Is Habit.   I Affirm It.
  D. Meltzer.   Kh-VA:46
HUMOR - DE LA MARE, WALTER (JOHN)
 Mr. Walter de la Mare Makes the
  Little Ones Dizzy.
  S. Hoffenstein. Li-SR:135
 Mother Goose Up-to-Date.
  L. Untermeyer.   Un-MA:309
HUMOR - DENTISTS AND DENTISTRY
 Ode to a Dental Hygienist.
  E. Hooton.   Co-FB:397
 On a Dentist.   Un-GT:238
 Though Dentists May Not. Rs-PF:84
HUMOR - DESCARTES, RENÉ
 Theological. C. Fadiman. Co-FB:131
HUMOR - DESPAIR
 The Despairing Lover.   W. Walsh.
  Co-BL:134, Hi-WP II:113,
  No-CL:187, Sm-LG:355
 In the Dumps. Mo-MGT:167
 Sorrows of Werther. W. Thackeray.
  Br-SM:32, Co-FB:344,
  Hi-WP II:11
HUMOR - DEVILS
 Did You Ever? Bu-DY:90, Gr-GB:21
 Dinky.   T. Roethke.   Cp-OW:27,
  Li-TU:72
 Kellyburnbraes.   Ox-BB:634
 Tying a Knot in the Devil's
  Tail.   Co-RM:35
HUMOR - DIET
 Anecdotes of Four Gentlemen,
  III.   Ox-BC:152

Commissary Report.   S. King.
 Br-SM:81
Diet Riot.   J. Sartwell. Ke-TF:272
Jack Sprat.   Bo-FP:57, De-PO:24,
 Er-FA:507, Ir-BB:196, Li-LB:54,
 Mo-MGT:14, Mo-NR:4, Wi-MG:75,
 Wr-RM:47
The Man of Tobago.   Wr-RM:122
The Revolting Calory Counter.
 L. Owen.   Ke-TF:271
There Was an Old Person of Dean.
 E. Lear.   Ag-HE:20, Bl-OB:11,
 Bo-FP:56, Br-LL:88
There Was an Old Woman, and What
 Do You Think? Li-LB:67,
 Mo-NR:98, Sm-LG:118
HUMOR - DIGNITY
 A Grandfather Poem.   W. Harris.
  Ad-PB:439
 Pico della Mirandola.   M. Mason.
  Hu-PN:526
HUMOR - DIPLOMATS
 I Had a Duck-Billed Platypus.
  P. Barrington.   Co-FB:31
HUMOR - DIRECTIONS TO PLACES
 Dr. Fell and Points West.
  O. Nash.   Sh-RP:130
 Easy Directions.   M. Taylor.
  Ke-TF:282
 Hickory, Dickory, Sackory Down!
  Ir-BB:235
 Quiet Fun.   H. Graham.
  Br-SM:24, Co-HP:68
 Traveller's Curse after
  Misdirection.   R. Graves.
  Co-FB:475, Ho-LP:70, Un-MB:387,
  Wi-LT:369
HUMOR - DIRTINESS
 Soap, the Oppressor. B. Johnson.
  Fe-PL:216
HUMOR - DISASTERS
 Fielding Error.   R. Smith. Ad-CI:14
 Tilda Tilbury.   L. Allen.   Pa-RE:45
HUMOR - DISCONTENT
 As I Was Walking Slowly.
  A. Housman.   Li-TU:65
 "Day Darken!" Frogs Say.
  Buson.   Be-CS:47
 Eclogue.   E. Lear.   Li-TU:74
HUMOR - DISCRIMINATION
 Respectful Request.   R. Durem.
  Ab-MO:32
HUMOR - DISOBEDIENCE
 Disobedience.   Ca-MU:20
HUMOR - DISSENT
 Sketch from Loss of Memory.
  S. Dorman.   Pe-SS:93
HUMOR - DOGS
 An Addition to the Family: For
  M.L.   E. Morgan.   To-MP:189
 The Bandog. W. de la Mare.
  Ar-TP3:51, Na-EO:166

The Dog. O. Herford.   Ga-FB:331
The Dog. O. Nash. Co-OT:68,
   Co-PU:92
Dog and Fox. D. Ferry. Co-PU:92
A Dog in Winter. Rs-PF:73
The Dog's Cold Nose. A. Guiterman.
   Co-BBW:107, Gr-EC:84, Ha-PO:142
Eating Poetry. M. Strand. Mo-BG:7
Elegy on the Death of a Mad Dog.
   O. Goldsmith. Br-SM:103,
   Co-RG:97, Er-FA:213, Fr-WO:49,
   Ha-PO:110, Mc-WK:58, Rv-CB:540,
   Sm-LG:84, Sp-OG:237, Un-GF:17
Fashions in Dogs. E. White.
   Co-FB:8
High, Ding, Straps of Leather.
   Ir-BB:172
Howard. A. Milne. Co-OT:61
I Ask You Nicely. Re-RR:100
I Had a Little Dog, His Name Was
   Ball. Ir-BB:180
In London-Town Dame Trottypeg.
   D. Thompson. Ir-BB:167
Inscribed on the Collar of a Dog.
   A. Pope. Bo-FP:132, Ch-B:73,
   Gr-CT:122, Rv-CB:508, Un-GT:236
I've Got a Dog. Co-OT:54
Jippy and Jimmy. L. Richards.
   Ar-TP3:49, Au-SP:223, Hu-MP:453
Kindness to Animals. L. Richards.
   Ar-TP3:122, Au-SP:236, Ir-BB:167,
   St-FS:45
Little Tiny Puppy Dog. S. Milligan.
   Co-OH:31
Motto for a Dog House.
   A. Guiterman. Co-PU:21
Old Blue. Mo-SD:115
On Buying a Dog. E. Klauber.
   Co-PU:93
The Porcupine. O. Nash. Gr-EC:28
A Puppy Whose Hair Was So Flowing.
   O. Herford. Br-LL:17
The Song of the Mischievous Dog.
   D. Thomas. Er-FA:236
There Was a Young Lady of Corsica.
   E. Lear. Br-LL:19, Gr-CT:28
There Was an Old Man of
   Kamschatka. E. Lear.   Br-LL:19
Travelling. Ir-BB:234
Watchdog. R. Armour. Gr-EC:81
When a Dog Named Ben. Rs-PF:38
HUMOR - DOLPHINS
The Porpoise. O. Nash. Sh-RP:143
HUMOR - DONKEYS
The Donkey. T. Roethke. Gr-EC:23
A Donkey Eats Thistles. Rs-PF:69
HUMOR - DOORS
Godfrey Gordon Gustavus Gore.
   W. Rands. Ar-TP3:136, Co-BB:111,
   Co-OT:42, Fe-FP:308, Hu-MP:451,
   Ir-BB:109, Pe-FB:92

Rebecca. H. Belloc. Du-RG:65,
   Ir-BB:156, Ne-AM:26, Tu-WW:116,
   Un-GF:61
The Revolving Door. N. Levy.
   Br-SM:45, Co-HP:91
There Was a Young Lady of Norway.
   E. Lear. Ar-TP3:133, Br-LL:138,
   Fe-FP:360
HUMOR - DOUBT
Moll-in-the-Wad. Mo-MGT:180
HUMOR - DOVES
Mourning Dove. C. Calkins.
   Un-MW:60
HUMOR - DRAGONS
Saint George and the Dragon.
   A. Noyes. Co-RM:82, Sh-RP:139
Sir Eglamour. Bl-OB:25, Co-RM:80,
   Gr-EC:143, Mc-WK:134, Sm-LG:181
The Tale of Custard the Dragon.
   O. Nash. Fe-FP:332, Ir-BB:170,
   Un-GB:26, Un-GT:167
HUMOR - DRAMA
An Old Woman, Outside the Abbey
   Theater. L. Strong.
   Co-FB:352, Un-MB:393
pete the parrot and shakespeare.
   D. Marquis. Pl-ML:102
HUMOR - DREAMS
Caprice. D. Shaw. Co-PT:146
The Concert. J. Newman. Co-HP:100
Don't Tell Me What You Dreamt
   Last Night. F. Adams. Co-FB:261
The Dream of a Boy at Nine-Elms.
   W. Rands. Ir-BB:138
The Dream of a Girl Who Lived at
   Seven-Oaks. W. Rands. Ir-BB:138
My Dream. Ir-BB:137, Un-GT:243
A Quadrupedremian Song. T. Hood.
   Ir-BB:123
The Reformed Pirate. T. Roberts.
   Do-WH:20
Such Stuff as Dreams. F. Adams.
   Li-SR:32
There Was a Young Lady Named
   Wemyss. Br-LL:64
There Was an Old Man from Peru.
   Er-FA:222, Fr-WO:52, La-PV:35,
   Un-GF:45
When Candy Was Chocolate.
   W. Smith. Ir-BB:242
HUMOR - DRINKERS AND DRINKING
Abraham Scolds Lot. I. Manger.
   Ho-TY:274
Bobbily Boo and Wollypotump.
   L. Richards. Li-LC:46, Lo-LL:6
Captain Stratton's Fancy.
   J. Masefield. Co-SS:36, Un-MB:226
A Carrion Crow Sat on an Oak.
   Bl-OB:21, Li-LB:98, Mo-MGT:164,
   Mo-NR:132, Sm-MK:181, Wr-RM:29
Eight Limericks, 2. E. Lear.
   Sh-RP:127

HUMOR - DRINKERS AND
     DRINKING — cont'd.
  If All the World Was Apple Pie.
     An-IP:(14), Au-SP:219, Bo-FP:54,
     Er-FA:505, Lo-LL:5, Mo-NR:114,
     Un-GF:13, Wr-RM:104
  The Lacquer Liquor Locker.
     D. McCord. Co-FB:436
  Little Brown Jug. Er-FA:430
  Mr. Flood's Party. E. Robinson.
     Al-VBP:1107, Er-FA:304, Ha-PO:64,
     Na-EO:66, Ni-JP:143, Pe-M:50,
     Pe-OA:5, Sh-AP:141, Sm-PT:140,
     Un-MA:121, Wi-LT:111
  Nose, Nose, Jolly Red Nose.
     F. Beaumont and J. Fletcher.
     Cl-FC:96, Ir-BB:192, Mo-MGT:63,
     Sm-LG:120
  On an Old Toper Buried in Durham
     Churchyard, England. Br-SM:160
  The Private Dining Room. O. Nash.
     En-PC:53
  The Raven Visits Rawhide. Fi-BG:182
  Reflections on Ice-Breaking.
     O. Nash. Er-FA:209, Wi-LT:629
  R-E-M-O-R-S-E. G. Ade.
     Co-FB:90
  Said the Monkey to the Donkey.
     Er-FA:498
  Tam o'Shanter. R. Burns.
     Al-VBP:634, Sp-OG:170
  There Is an Inn, a Merry Old Inn.
     J. Tolkien. Lo-LL:98
  Tying a Knot in the Devil's Tail.
     Co-RM:35
HUMOR - DROWNING
  As I Passed By.   Ir-BB:27
  Aunt Eliza. H. Graham. Gr-CT:470,
     Mc-WS:180, Un-GF:48
  The Ballad of the Oysterman.
     O. Holmes. Er-FA:306, Sm-MK:69
  Drop Me a Line. Rs-PF:68
  The Elderly Gentleman. G. Canning.
     Gr-EC:148
  Ezra Shank.   Br-SM:51
  I Knew a Cappadocian. A. Housman.
     Co-FB:371
  Little Willie.   Br-SM:49
  Ode to Stephen Dowling Bots, Dec'd.
     M. Twain. Co-FB:304
  Old Man Know-All. Ra-BP:9
  Peg. Ir-BB:211, Mo-MGT:74
  Piano Practice. Co-BB:110
  The Ratcatcher's Daughter.
     Gr-GB:134
  Rub a Dub Dub. De-PO:16,
     Ir-BB:38, Li-LB:52, Mo-NR:18,
     Mo-TL:79, On-TW:14
  Sally Simpkin's Lament. T. Hood.
     Br-SM:57
  Silly Willy. R. L. B.   Br-SM:51

  Sister Nell.   Co-BB:94, Co-HP:28,
     Fe-FP:362
  The Stern Parent. H. Graham.
     Co-BB:99, Gr-CT:470, Un-GF:48
  Three Children Sliding.   J. Gay.
     De-TT:39, Ir-BB:139, Li-LB:44,
     Mo-MGT:24, Un-GF:13, Wr-RM:13
  Three Wise Men of Gotham.
     Er-FA:506, Li-LB:75, Mo-MGT:114,
     Mo-NR:134, Wi-MG:40, Wr-RM:25
HUMOR - DRUGS
  I Wandered Angry as a Cloud.
     P. Dehn.   Li-SR:106
HUMOR - DUCKS
  A Dappled Duck. P. Brown. Lo-LL:2
  The Duck and the Kangaroo.
     E. Lear. Ox-BC:186
  How God Hath Labored. D. Hall.
     Co-PU:107
  The Notorious Glutton. A. Taylor.
     Ox-BC:118
  There Was an Old Lady of France.
     E. Lear. Br-LL:25, Li-LC:47
  When Father Carves the Duck.
     E. Wright. Co-HP:118, Co-PS:147,
     Er-FA:136, Fe-PL:188, Ga-FB:175
HUMOR - DUELS
  Abdulla Bulbul Amir.   Co-RM:193
  The Duel. E. Field. Ar-TP3:119,
     Au-SP:273, Ch-B:42, Er-FA:496,
     Fe-FP:348, Fe-PL:202, Gr-EC:80,
     Pa-OM:40, Rd-SS:36
  The Duel. Br-SM:22
HUMOR - DUTY
  Captain Reece. W. Gilbert.
     Co-FB:57, Co-HP:62, Na-EO:156
  The Dutiful Mariner. W. Irwin.
     Co-SS:91
  Routine. A. Guiterman.
     Co-HP:70, Co-OH:70
HUMOR - DYES AND DYEING
  Teme con Variazióni.
     L. Carroll. Li-SR:65
HUMOR - EARS
  The Van Gogh Influence.
     S. Silverstein. Co-EL:64
HUMOR - EARTH
  I Quite Realized. . . .
     E. Bentley. Co-FB:126
HUMOR - EARTHQUAKES
  Let's Shake. Rs-PF:62
HUMOR - EASTER
  All Dressed Up for Easter.
     A. Fisher. Sh-RP:208
  Easter Parade. M. Chute. Br-SS:140,
     La-PH:53
  The Enormous Easter Egg Hunt.
     M. Neville. Su-FVI:29
HUMOR - EAVESDROPPING
  Child's Song. K. Greenaway.
     Bo-FP:260

Very Very. R. Margolis. Su-FVI:28
HUMOR - ECHOES
  By-Election Idyll. P. Dickinson.
    Co-FB:37
  Echo Poem. M. Allan. Co-FB:440
  A Gentle Echo on Woman. J. Swift.
    Co-FB:438
HUMOR - EDUCATION
  as joe gould says. E. Cummings.
    Co-FB:409
  A College Training. J. Lincoln.
    Co-HP:92
  The Irish Schoolmaster. J. Sidey.
    Co-FB:223, Co-HP:111
  Patrick Goes to School.
    A. Aspinwall. Hu-MP:10
  The Schoolroom Angels. R. Alberti.
    Mc-EA:147
  The Zebra Dun. Co-PT:144, Sh-RP:49
HUMOR - EDWARD THE CONFESSOR
  Edward the Confessor. E. Bentley.
    Ir-BB:260, Un-GF:49
HUMOR - EELS
  The Eel. W. de la Mare. Br-LL:37,
    Br-SM:122
  The Eel. O. Nash. Cr-SS:9,
    Fe-FP:357, Ga-FB:334
  Eels. S. Milligan. Co-OT:39
  Song of Hate for Eels.
    A. Guiterman. Co-BBW:71
HUMOR - EERINESS
  Erith on the Thames. Br-LL:66,
    Gr-CT:154, Gr-GB:171, Rv-CB:789
  Mr. Walter de la Mare Makes the
    Little Ones Dizzy.
    S. Hoffenstein. Li-SR:135
  Nightmare Number Three. S. Benét.
    Mc-WS:24, Un-MA:501
  Top Hat and Tales. L. Beers.
    De-FS:18
HUMOR - EGGS
  An Egg. A. Fisher. Ja-PC:56
  The Enormous Easter Egg Hunt.
    M. Neville. Su-FVI:29
  The Hen and the Carp.
    I. Serraillier. Co-BBW:62
  If Easter Eggs Would Hatch.
    D. Malloch. Au-SP:364, Hu-MP:335
  Limericks since Lear. Co-BB:29,
    Un-GT:241
  A Man Out Boating. Re-RR:104
  The Poultries. O. Nash. Co-OT:55,
    Pa-RE:17, Un-GF:82
  The Prodigal Egg. Co-HP:24
  Roly Poly Did Something Rash.
    Re-RR:57
  When You Buy Eggs. Re-RR:25
  You Don't Have to Break a Water
    Keg. Re-RR:116
HUMOR - ELECTIONS
  Autumn. E. Roberts. Co-PT:285,
    Ja-PA:49

HUMOR - ELECTRICITY
  Lord Finchley. H. Belloc.
    Co-EL:58, Co-FB:197
  There Was a Young Fellow Named
    Weir. Br-LL:76
  There Was an Old Lady Named
    Crockett. W. Smith. Br-LL:75,
    Br-SM:52
HUMOR - ELEGIES
  A Departed Friend. J. Moore.
    Co-FB:303
  An Elegy on the Glory of Her Sex,
    Mrs. Mary Blaize. O. Goldsmith.
    Rv-CB:541
  Elegy on the Loss of U.S. Sub-
    marine, S4. H. Canfield.
    Co-FB:299
  Ode to Stephen Dowling Bots, Dec'd.
    M. Twain. Co-FB:304
  A Serio-Comic Elegy. R. Whately.
    Br-SM:162
  A Threnody. G. Lanigan. Co-FB:424,
    Do-WH:26, Rv-CB:947
  We Have Lost Our Little Hanner.
    M. Adeler. Co-FB:306
HUMOR - ELEPHANTS
  Ant and Eleph-Ant. S. Milligan.
    Co-OT:25
  The Blind Men and the Elephant.
    J. Saxe. Bo-HF:73, Gr-EC:150,
    Ha-PO:302, Pa-OM:330, Un-GT:200
  East Is East and West Is West.
    Co-OH:86
  The Elephant. H. Belloc.
    Ar-TP3:79, Au-SP:239, Ja-PC:21,
    Lo-LL:35, Un-GF:87
  An Elephant. J. Francis. Hu-MP:457
  The Elephant, or Force of Habit.
    A. Housman. Ga-FB:329, Li-TU:116
  Eletelephony. L. Richards.
    Ar-TP3:128, Au-SP:239, Bo-GJ:7,
    Co-IW:22, Fe-FP:346, Gr-EC:186,
    Hu-MP:455, Ir-BB:56, La-PV:23,
    Lo-LL:24, Ox-BC:289, Pe-FB:102
  I Asked My Mother for Fifteen
    Cents. Ar-TP3:128, Er-FA:-498,
    Ir-BB:185, Un-GT:18
  The Indian Elephant. C. Kaberry.
    Co-FB:130
  Plain Talk for a Pachyderm.
    P. Bennett. Co-BBW:194
  Questions, Quistions, & Quoshtions.
    S. Milligan. Co-OT:12
  Rat a Tat Tat. Re-RR:84
  Riddle Me. Re-RR:67
  Some Questions to Be Asked of a
    Rajah. . . . P. Newman.
    Co-FB:419, Co-HP:101
  Way Down South. Au-SP:231,
    Ch-B:32, Co-OW:22, Ir-BB:150,
    Na-EO:75

HUMOR – ELEVATORS
  The Ups and Downs of the Elevator
    Car. C. Emerson. Ir-BB:255
HUMOR – ELIOT, THOMAS STEARNS
  Lines for Cuscuscaraway and
    Mirza Murad Ali Beg. T. Eliot.
    Co-FB:46, Li-SR:45, Pl-ML:24
HUMOR – ELOPEMENTS
  Limericks. Ke-TF:289
  Phyllis, or The Progress of Love.
    J. Swift. No-CL:226
  There Was an Old Man of Nantucket.
    Br-LL:120, Ke-TF:289
HUMOR – ELVES
  How to Treat Elves. M. Bishop.
    Co-FB:197
HUMOR – EMUS
  At the Zoo I Remarked to an Emu.
    Br-LL:9
HUMOR – ENCHANTMENT
  A Love Story. O. Herford.
    Co-PM:103
  Romantic Episode. V. Starrett.
    De-FS:187
HUMOR – ENCYCLOPEDIAS
  Epitaph on the Proofreader of the
    Encyclopedia Britannica.
    C. Morley. Br-SM:161
HUMOR – END OF THE WORLD
  The End of the World. A. MacLeish.
    Ca-VT:164, Ha-PO:48, Mc-WS:27,
    Pe-OA:162, Un-MA:457, Wi-LT:341
  Ode to the Hayden Planetarium.
    A. Guiterman. Pl-IO:29
  When Did the World Begin.
    R. Clairmont. Au-SP:227,
    Co-HP:54, Mc-WK:102, Un-GT:230
HUMOR – ENGINEERS
  Career. D. Pettiward. Ir-BB:39
  Early in the Morning. Ir-BB:248
  Horses Have Colts. Re-RR:102
HUMOR – ENGLAND
  John Bull. Mo-MGT:159
  Old England Forever, and Do It
    No More. Gr-GB:200
HUMOR – ENGLAND–COUNTRYSIDE
  A Lincolnshire Tale. J. Betjeman.
    De-FS:21
HUMOR – ENGLAND–HISTORY AND
    PATRIOTISM
  The Ballad of the Billycock.
    A. Deane. Co-SS:28
  The "Dorset Nose." C. Sansom.
    To-MP:128
  The Georges. W. Landor. Co-FB:474,
    Gr-CT:473
  Lessons. E. Farjeon. Ir-BB:111
HUMOR – ENGLAND–NAVY
  A Ballad of the Good Lord Nelson.
    L. Durrell. Wi-LT:697
  The Battle of Clothesline Bay.
    W. Irwin. Co-SS:33

  Captain Reece. W. Gilbert.
    Co-FB:57, Co-HP:62, Na-EO:156
HUMOR – THE ENGLISH
  The County Member. W. Praed.
    Ox-BN:437
  Fe, Fi, Fo, Fum. Br-SM:21,
    Na-EO:116
  Good-Night to the Season. W. Praed.
    Ox-BN:441
  Mad Dogs and Englishmen. N. Coward.
    Co-FB:204
  My Lord Tomnoddy. R. Brough.
    Co-FB:195, Co-PU:123
  There Was a Young Man Who Was
    Bitten. Br-LL:20
  The Vicar. W. Praed. Ox-BN:445
HUMOR – ENGLISH LANGUAGE
  Hints on Pronunciation for
    Foreigners. Ma-FW:237
HUMOR – EPITAPHS
  At Boot Hill in Tombstone,
    Arizona. Br-SM:54
  At Great Torrington, Devon.
    Br-SM:52
  The Author's Epitaph. Co-FB:132
  Billy Grounds. Fi-BG:55
  Cassie O'Lang. Br-SM:21
  A Curt Addendum. Br-SM:151
  Elegy Just in Case. J. Ciardi.
    Br-TC:65, Cr-WS:81
  Epitaph. R. Armour. Br-SM:55
  An Epitaph. G. Cayley. Co-EL:49,
    Co-FB:131, Co-PU:158
  Epitaph. J. Heath-Stubbs.
    To-MP:74
  Epitaph. L. Mellichamp. Br-SM:21
  Epitaph. J. Whittier. Gr-EC:78
  Epitaph. Hi-WP II:12
  Epitaph for a Grim Woman. P. Eden.
    Mc-WS:74
  Epitaph for a Horse Thief.
    Gr-EC:150
  Epitaph for a Horse Thief.
    Gr-EC:150
  Epitaph for a Postal Clerk.
    X. Kennedy. Br-SM:155
  Epitaph on Charles II. J. Wilmot.
    Al-VBP:506, Co-FB:476,
    Hi-WP II:140, Mc-WS:89, Un-GT:237
  Epitaph on John Knott. Br-SM:157,
    Gr-CT:13
  Epitaph on the Late King of the
    Sandwich Isles. W. Praed.
    Co-FB:475
  For a Lady I Know. C. Cullen.
    Ab-MO:27, Ad-PB:91, Bo-AN:89,
    Br-SM:150, Hu-PN:231, Un-MA:571
  From a Churchyard in Wales.
    Br-SM:158, Co-FB:132
  Here Lies My Wife. J. Dryden.
    Br-SM:156
  Here Lies the Body of Robert
    Low. Co-PU:157
  His Own Epitaph. J. Gay. Al-VBP:526

In Memory of Anna Hopewell.
  Br-SM:47
John Coil.   Br-SM:156
Lather as You Go. O. Nash.
  Hi-WP II:14
Missing. J. Pudney.   Hi-WP I:24
On a Lord. S. Coleridge. Co-FB:132
On a Royal Demise. T. Hood.
  Co-FB:474
On an Old Toper Buried in Durham
  Churchyard, England. Br-SM:160
On Samuel Pease. Br-SM:157
On the Author. R. Burns. Rv-CB:620
On Will Smith. Gr-EC:214
One Down. R. Armour. Mo-SD:49
Tombstone. L. and J. Hymes, Jr.
  Ar-TP3:133
Wang Peng's Recommendations for
  Improving People. P. Eldridge.
  Br-SM:165
Within This Grave Do Lie. Br-SM:158
HUMOR - EQUALITY
  Bessy Bell and Mary Gray. Bo-FP:51,
    Wr-RM:90
  Equals. L. Untermeyer. Un-MW:58
  A Marble Mausoleum. S. Jahin.
    Lo-TY:51
HUMOR - ERRORS
  Coyote's Night. P. George.
    Al-WW:128
  He Shot at Lee Wing. Br-SM:53
  Printer's Error. P. Wodehouse.
    Co-FB:334
HUMOR - ESCAPE
  As I Passed By. Ir-BB:27
  Brave Alum Bey. W. Gilbert.
    Co-SS:151
  Canopus. B. Taylor. Co-FB:486
  A Flea and a Fly in a Flue.
    Br-LL:9, Ch-B:113, Co-HP:29,
    Fe-FP:365, Gr-EC:196, Ju-CP:14,
    Lo-LL:49, Mc-WS:179, Un-GT:241
  If My Complaining Wife. Issa.
    Be-MC:19
  Intimates. D. Lawrence.
    Co-PT:185
  The Lover Rejoiceth. T. Wyatt.
    Un-MW:34
  The Man with Nought. De-TT:45,
    Mo-MGT:73, Wr-RM:88
  Run, Nigger, Run! Ra-BP:5
  The Spangled Pandemonium. P. Brown.
    Ar-TP3:129, Co-OT:22, Lo-LL:70
  When the Sline Comes to Dine.
    S. Silverstein. Co-BBW:290
  Where the Single Men Go in Summer.
    N. Bourne. Co-FB:487
HUMOR - ESKIMOS
  The Immoral Arctic. M. Bishop.
    Co-FB:214

HUMOR - ETERNITY
  Epitaph for Any New Yorker.
    C. Morley.   Br-SM:151
HUMOR - ETIQUETTE
  The Buffalo. L. Richards.
    Co-OW:72
  Etiquette. W. Gilbert. Co-FB:178,
    Co-HP:64
  Good King Wenceslas. Co-OW:75,
    Sp-OG:320
  Goodbye Now, or, Pardon My Gauntlet.
    O. Nash.   Co-FB:481
  The Guest. Br-LL:83, Co-HP:28,
    Gr-EC:213
  He'll Stand for Anything. Rs-PF:28
  I Stare at the Cow. P. Chase.
    Co-IW:42
  Limericks. Co-HP:28, Ke-TF:287
  Peas. Ch-B:113, Co-HP:23,
    Fe-FP:365, Hi-WP I:9, Ir-BB:213,
    Na-EO:72, Sh-RP:145, Sp-AS:36
  A Rather Polite Man of Hawarden.
    Br-LL:63
  The Rule of the Road Is a
    Paradox Quite. Mo-NR:134
  Table Manners. G. Burgess.
    Co-BB:45, Fr-MP:5
  There's a Dowager near Sneden
    Landing. Br-LL:63
  When Father Carves the Duck.
    E. Wright. Co-HP:118, Co-PS:147,
    Er-FA:136, Fe-PL:188, Ga-FB:175
HUMOR - EVIL
  The Evil Eye. J. Ciardi. Ca-MB:19
HUMOR - EVOLUTION
  The Chimpanzee. O. Herford.
    Co-FB:26, Ga-FB:332
  Darwinism in the Kitchen. Co-FB:380
  Ode to the Amoeba. A. Guiterman.
    Du-SH:123
  Similar Cases. C. Gilman.
    Fe-PL:191
HUMOR - EXCUSES
  Drinking. A. Cowley. Ha-PO:250,
    Hi-WP II:141, Ho-WR:64
HUMOR - EXECUTIONS AND EXECUTIONERS
  A Briton Who Shot at His King.
    D. Ross. Br-SM:26
  Samuel Hall. Gr-CT:471
  To Sit in Solemn Silence.
    W. Gilbert. Co-FB:427
  Willie Built a Guillotine.
    W. Engel. Co-OH:43
HUMOR - EXPERIENCE
  Inventory. D. Parker. Ke-TF:232
  Sophisticate. B. Young.
    Br-BC:50, Br-SM:42
  That Fond Impossibility.
    R. Lovelace. Un-MW:42
HUMOR - EXPLORERS
  A Dash to the Pole. W. Irwin.
    Co-HP:80

HUMOR - EXPLORERS — cont'd.
  This Boy Think. C. Pass. Jo-VC:3
HUMOR - EXPRESS SERVICE
  Advice to Travelers. W. Gibson.
    Du-RG:42
HUMOR - EXTINCT ANIMALS
  The Quagga. D. Enright. To-MP:112
HUMOR - EYCK, JAN VAN
  The Younger Van Eyck. E. Bentley.
    Co-FB:129
HUMOR - EYEGLASSES
  The Nose and the Eyes. W. Cowper.
    Hu-MP:449
  Peekaboo, I Almost See You.
    O. Nash. Fe-PL:260
HUMOR - EYES
  Five Eyes. W. de la Mare.
    Co-BBW:133, Co-IW:18, Ir-BB:28
  Limericks. E. Lear. Bo-GJ:9,
    Co-HP:90
  The Powerful Eyes o' Jeremy Tait.
    W. Irwin. Co-FB:135, Co-SS:79,
    Ha-PO:264
HUMOR - FACES
  The Boxer's Face. Lucilius.
    Mo-SD:79
  Curious Something. W. Welles.
    Ar-TP3:137, Ir-BB:133
  Eraser. C. Okano. Le-TA:57
  My Face. A. Euwer. Br-LL:44,
    Co-HP:57, Er-FA:222, Fe-PL:211,
    Fr-WO:44, Un-GT:241
  Overheard in the Louvre.
    X. Kennedy. Co-EL:60
  Paripace and Paripale. R. Flower.
    Ir-BB:155
  Polly Picklenose. L. Jackson.
    Co-BB:35
  There Was a Young Curate Named
    Stone. F. Cozens. Br-LL:44
  There Was a Young Lady Whose Chin.
    E. Lear. Ar-TP3:132, Au-SP:244,
    Br-LL:44, Ir-BB:218, Sh-RP:149
  There Was an Old Person of Down.
    E. Lear. Br-LL:45
  Three Wonderful Women II.
    Ox-BC:152
HUMOR - FAILURE
  Bolivar Riggin. Fi-BG:138
  nobody loses all the time.
    e. cummings. Mc-WS:139
HUMOR - FAIRIES
  The Adventures of Oberon.
    M. Drayton. Rd-OA:164
HUMOR - FAIRY TALES
  How a Girl Was Too Reckless of
    Grammar by Far. G. Carryl.
    Co-FB:154
HUMOR - FAITH
  The Theology of Bongwi, the
    Baboon. R. Campbell. Ga-S:194

HUMOR - FAITH CURES
  Faith-Healer. Br-LL:48, Er-FA:218,
    Un-GT:241
HUMOR - FALSEHOOD
  A Dead Liar Speaks. M. Lewis.
    Un-GT:237
HUMOR - FAME
  Back Room Joys. J. Richardson.
    Co-FB:485
  I'm Nobody! Who Are You?
    E. Dickinson. Ar-TP3:211,
    Bo-FP:275, Co-PU:40, La-PV:221,
    Mo-BG:43, Rv-CB:912, Un-GT:91
  Post-Obits and the Poets.
    Martial. Mc-PR:21
  ?. E. Cummings. Co-FB:494
HUMOR - FAMILY AND FAMILY LIFE
  Abigail. K. Starbird. Ne-AM:40
  Household of Eight. A. Reisen.
    Ho-TY:70
  Marriage. G. Corso. Wi-LT:673
  Our Dumb Friends. R. Wotherspoon.
    Co-BBW:113
  Our Polite Parents. C. Wells.
    Co-BB:96
  Some Families of My Acquaintance.
    L. Richards. Co-OW:18
  Such a Pleasant Familee.
    W. Irwin. Br-SM:131
HUMOR - FANTASY
  Pinkletinks. G. Allen. Gr-EC:167
HUMOR - FAREWELLS
  My Auld Wife. Gr-GB:160
HUMOR - FARM LIFE
  Ballad. C. Calverly. Co-FB:262,
    Ho-WR:56, Li-SR:34
  Bobbie Shaftoe Has a Cow. Ir-BB:30
  Cherries. Ir-BB:26, Sp-AS:20
  Cock-Crow. Mo-MGT:48, Pa-AP:18
  The Farmer and the Farmer's Wife.
    P. Hiebert. Co-FB:64
  The Happy Farmer Boy. Ke-TF:269
  Mad Farmer's Song. Ir-BB:119,
    Mo-MGT:184
  Mary Went Down to Grandpa's Farm.
    Ir-BB:30
  Nick Spence. Ir-BB:28
  The Old Man Who Lived in a Wood.
    Hu-MP:468
HUMOR - FARMERS
  Brown's Descent. R. Frost.
    Ar-TP3:145, Ha-PO:287, Na-EO:89,
    Sp-OG:234, Un-MA:178
  A Farmer in Bungleton. M. Dodge.
    Gr-EC:205
  nobody loses all the time.
    e. cummings. Mc-WS:139
  Old Farmer Buck. Co-HP:23
  The Pig and the Paddy. E. Mathias.
    Ir-BB:57
  A Rustic Song. A. Deane. Co-FB:218

HUMOR - FASHION
  Woe, Brothers, Woe! A. Kramer.
    Ke-TF:280
HUMOR - FASTING
  Ash Wednesday. W. Dunbar.
    Ga-S:142
HUMOR - FATE
  I Never Had a Piece of Toast.
    J. Payne. Un-GF:15
HUMOR - FATHERS
  The Cataract at Ladore
    (July 3, 1936).
    H. Bevington. Li-SR:88
  "Everybody Works but Father"
    as W. S. Gilbert Would Have
    Written It. A. Burgoyne.
    Co-FB:259
  Father Will Settle the Bill.
    Ke-TF:273
  Song to Be Sung by the Father
    of Infant Female Children.
    O. Nash. Un-MA:565
HUMOR - FEAR
  The Catipoce. J. Reeves.
    Co-BBW:290
  Hallowe'en Indignation Meeting.
    M. Fishback. Co-PS:139
  Horror Movie. H. Moss. Pe-M:6
  The Man with Nought. De-TT:45,
    Mo-MGT:73, Wr-RM:88
  Not Afraid. J. Lee. Ja-HH:37
  On Horror. R. Hershon. Sc-TN:94
  The Reformed Pirate. T. Roberts.
    Do-WH:20
  A Skeleton Once in Khartoum.
    Br-LL:66, Br-SM:4
  So Timid. K. Dee. Ja-HH:36
  There Lived an Old Man.
    D. Thompson. Co-OW:49,
    Ir-BB:199
  There Was an Old Man Who Said,
    "How." E. Lear. Bl-OB:17,
    Br-LL:22, Na-EO:103
  The Tiger Stalking in the Night.
    E. Horn. Co-EL:32, Co-PU:90
HUMOR - FEET
  As I Was Going Out One Day.
    Co-OW:43, Ir-BB:57
  Fate Is Unfair. D. Marquis.
    Na-EO:29
HUMOR - FELLOWSHIP
  Road Fellows. B. Young. Ir-BB:237
HUMOR - FERRIES
  I Don't Like the Ferry. Rs-PF:72
HUMOR - FICKLENESS
  I Loved Thee. R. Nugent.
    Co-FB:312
  If You Love Me. S. Hoffenstein.
    Co-FB:328
  Jenny Wren Fell Sick. Ir-BB:84,
    Mo-MGT:29, Na-EO:69, Rv-ON:116,
    Sm-MK:170

Safety at Forty. L. Sissman.
    Ho-P:243
Sonnets, xli. E. Millay. Sm-PT:33
That Fond Impossibility.
    R. Lovelace. Un-MW:42
HUMOR - FIGHTS AND FIGHTING
  Captain Carpenter. J. Ransom.
    Br-TC:387, Ha-PO:36, Un-MA:415,
    Wi-LT:314
  The Chickens. Ar-TP3:71
HUMOR - FIREFLIES
  The Adventures of Oberon.
    M. Drayton. Rd-OA:164
  The Firefly. O. Nash. Un-GF:83
  Glowworm. D. McCord. Gr-EC:130
HUMOR - FIREMEN
  Flash: The Firemen's Story.
    W. Carleton. Se-PR:317
HUMOR - FIRES
  And. . . . Co-OH:55
  Fire. Mo-MGT:177
  Flash: The Firemen's Story.
    W. Carleton. Se-PR:317
  Framed in a First-Story Winder.
    Co-OH:36
  Honesty at a Fire. J. Squire.
    Co-FB:493
  Matilda. H. Belloc. Bl-OB:30,
    Co-PT:305, Pa-OM:6, Sm-LG:100
  A New Servant Maid Named Maria.
    Br-LL:79
HUMOR - FISH
  Alas, Alack! W. de la Mare.
    Ar-TP3:124, Fe-FP:132, Hu-MP:43,
    Ir-BB:64, Na-EO:152, Ox-BC:327
  A Bit Too Sharp. Rs-PF:56
  The Cares of a Caretaker.
    W. Irwin. Co-OW:14
  The Caulker. M. Lewis. Co-PT:256
  A Fish Answers. L. Hunt.
    Al-VBP:713, Co-FB:20, Rd-OA:156
  Fish Story. R. Armour. Du-RG:104,
    Fl-HH:9
  The Fish with the Deep Sea Smile.
    M. Brown. La-PV:200
  Fishy-Fishy in the Brook.
    Un-GT:18
  A Fishy Square Dance.
    E. Merriam. Gr-EC:116
  The Flattered Flying Fish. E. Rieu.
    Ar-TP3:131, Br-SM:95, La-PV:202
  Heaven. R. Brooke. Ga-S:195,
    Un-MB:324, Wi-LT:615
  Humpty Dumpty's Song. L. Carroll.
    Ox-BC:245
  The Jam Fish. E. Parry. Ox-BC:310
  The Smoked Herring. C. Cros.
    Co-PT:277
  The Sun's Perpendicular Rays.
    W. Mansel. Gr-CT:11
  There Once Was a Bonnie Scotch
    Laddie. Br-LL:84

HUMOR - FISH — cont'd.
There Once Was a Corpulent Carp.
   C. Wells.   Br-LL:36
There Was an Old Person of Dundalk.
   E. Lear.   Co-HP:90
Tip-Toe Tale.   D. Willson.
   Ja-PC:14
To a Baked Fish.   C. Wells.
   Co-FB:88
HUMOR - FISHERMEN AND FISHING
Blackfriars. E. Farjeon. Ir-BB:212
Did You Ever Go Fishing. Ir-BB:156
The Fish with the Deep Sea Smile.
   M. Brown.   La-PV:200
Fishing Simon.   Bu-DY:31
How a Fisherman Corked Up His
   Foe in a Jar.   G. Carryl.
   Co-PM:31
The Indian and the Trout.
   E. Field.   Kr-OF:18
The Lady and the Bear. T. Roethke.
   Bo-GJ:151, Gr-EC:146
Noah an' Jonah an' Cap'n John
   Smith. D. Marquis. Co-SS:189,
   Fe-PL:198, Sm-LG:195
Some Fishy Nonsense. L. Richards.
   Ar-TP3:124, Au-SP:234, Ir-BB:107,
   St-FS:60
There Was a Young Angler of Worthing.
   Br-LL:36
Tommy Tottle.   Ja-PC:25
When a Jolly Young Fisher Named
   Fisher.   Br-LL:79
HUMOR - FLAMINGOS
F Was a Fussy Flamingo. C. Wells.
   Br-LL:9
HUMOR - FLATTERY
Said He, "Her Head."   Rs-PF:28
The Sycophantic Fox and the
   Gullible Raven.   G. Carryl.
   Co-FB:29, Co-HP:53, Er-FA:201
HUMOR - FLEAS
Archy, the Cockroach Speaks.
   D. Marquis. Co-HP:96, Fe-FP:338
The Cannibal Flea. T. Hood, Jr.
   Li-SR:68
The Flea. R. Young. Mc-WK:49
Fooba Wooba John. Co-OW:64
Great Fleas. A. de Morgan.
   Mc-WK:106, Un-GF:20
I've Got a Dog. Co-OT:54
One Two Three. Co-OW:38, On-TW:63
small talk. D. Marquis. Co-PT:139
What Great Difference Can You See.
   Re-RR:107
You've Heard Some Wild Ones.
   Re-RR:93
HUMOR - FLIGHT
Darius Green and His Flying
   Machine. J. Trowbridge.
   Fe-PL:204, Ox-BC:260

Said the Condor in Tones of Despair.
   O. Herford.   Br-LL:5
The Story of Flying Robert.
   H. Hoffmann.   Ir-BB:158,
   Li-SR:28
Uncle. H. Graham. Co-OT:56
HUMOR - FLUTES
The Amateur Flute. Li-SR:73
There Was an Old Man with a Flute.
   E. Lear.   Br-LL:11
A Tutor Who Tooted the Flute.
   C. Wells. Co-HP:119, Ke-TF:288,
   Lo-LL:49, Mc-WS:175, Un-GF:46,
   Un-GT:241
HUMOR - FOOD AND EATING
Adelaide. J. Prelutsky. Co-OH:57
After the Party. W. Wise.
   Fe-FP:359
After the Picnic. L. Blair.
   Ja-HH:30
Amelia Mixed the Mustard.
   A. Housman. Li-TU:61, Ne-AM:9
Archibishop Tait. Gr-CT:31
Baby Toodles. J. Newman. Co-BB:50
The Ballad of Culinary Frustra-
   tion. P. McGinley. Co-FB:82
Beer. C. Calverley. Co-FB:84
Bill Bet Bob that He Could Eat.
   Re-RR:101
Bobbily Boo and Wollypotump.
   L. Richards. Li-LC:46, Lo-LL:6
Book-Moth. Ma-YA:3, Rd-OA:29
Breakfast. E. Farjeon. Ag-HE:60
But What's in the Larder?
   A. Tennyson. Gr-TG:37
La Carte. J. Richardson. Co-FB:87
Cat's Meat. H. Monro. Ir-BB:177
Commissary Report. S. King.
   Br-SM:81
Courtship. C. Wells. Br-LL:123,
   Un-GT:241
A Diner while Dining at Crewe.
   Br-LL:81, Ir-BB:220, Un-GF:44
Eat-It-All Elaine. K. Starbird.
   La-PV:99, Ne-AM:10
The Eel. O. Nash. Cr-SS:9,
   Fa-FP:357, Ga-FB:334
An Epicure Dining at Crewe.
   Co-HP:28, Lo-LL:7, Un-GT:242
Folk Song. Br-SM:74
Food and Eating. Br-LL:83,
   Un-GT:242
Fussy. L. Richards. Hu-MP:446
The Giant's Song. C. Carryl.
   Mc-PR:189
The Giraffe and the Woman.
   L. Richards. Co-IW:15,
   La-PV:22
The Grandiloquent Goat. C. Wells.
   Br-LL:23, Lo-LL:18
The Greedy Boy. E. Turner. Ir-BB:96

Greedy Richard.   J. Taylor.
   Ir-BB:100, Ox-BC:121
The Groaning Board.   Co-HP:21,
   Co-PU:35
Henry King.   H. Belloc. Br-SM:118,
   Co-BB:48, Un-GF:60
How to Eat a Poem.   E. Merriam.
   Ag-HE:76, Du-RG:15
Hunting.   G. Snyder.   Mo-BG:125
I Raised a Great Hullabaloo.
   La-PV:34
I Went Fishing.   On-TW:30
Isabel Jones & Curabel Lee.
   D. McCord.   Un-GT:223
Jack and His Pony, Tom.
   H. Belloc.   Ir-BB:173
Jack Sprat.   Bo-FP:57, De-PO:24,
   Er-FA:507, Ir-BB:196, Li-LB:54,
   Mo-MGT:14, Mo-NR:4, Wi-MG:75,
   Wr-RM:47
Jelly Jake and Butter Bill.
   L. Jackson.   Co-BB:55
Johnnie Crack and Flossie Snail.
   D. Thomas.   Bo-FP:24, Bo-GJ:150,
   Co-FB:373, Fe-FP:332, Ha-LO:21,
   La-PV:218, Li-LC:43, Pa-RE:62
King Pippin.   Lo-LL:77
L Was a Lachrymose Leopard.
   C. Wells.   Br-LL:35
Latkes.   J. Lee.   Ja-HH:50
Limericks.   Ke-TF:289
Literary Dinner.   V. Nabokov.
   Co-FB:331
Little King Boggen.   Ir-BB:269,
   Rv-ON:79
Man of Derby.   Mo-MGT:23, Wr-RM:116
Mr. East's Feast.   Ag-HE:20,
   Ir-BB:193
Mr. Finney's Turnip.   Ch-B:104,
   Co-HP:22, Gr-EC:110, Lo-LL:57
Ms. Minnie McFinney, of Butte.
   Ne-AM:24
The Old Man from Dunoon.   Sm-MK:202
Only Seven.   H. Leigh.   Li-SR:118
Oodles of Noodles.
   L. and J. Hymes, Jr.   Ag-HE:11
Peas.   Ch-B:113, Co-HP:23,
   Fe-FP:365, Hi-WP I:9, Ir-BB:213,
   Na-EO:72, Sh-RP:145, Sp-AS:36
The Peasant Declares His Love.
   E. Roumer.   Lo-TY:90
Ponjoo.   W. de la Mare. Br-SM:80
The Priest and the Mulberry-Tree.
   T. Peacock.   De-TT:119,
   Ha-PO:297, Sp-OG:224
The Principal Food of the Sioux.
   Br-LL:89
The Remorseful Cakes.   E. Field.
   Ir-BB:102
Reverie.   D. Marquis.   Fe-PL:195
The Revolting Calory Counter.
   L. Owen.   Ke-TF:271

Rice Pudding.   A. Milne.   Co-BB:61
Robin the Bobbin.   Ir-BB:59,
   Mo-MGT:101
Salt, Mustard, Vinegar, Pepper.
   Su-FVI:76
Sneaky Bill.   W. Cole.   Co-OT:30
The Story of Augustus.   H. Hoffmann.
   Ag-HE:62, Ar-TP3:135, Bo-GJ:114,
   Br-SM:71, Co-BB:48, De-TT:93,
   Ir-BB:101, Li-SR:25, Ox-BC:205
The Sweet Tooth.   K. Pyle.
   Ad-HE:64, Co-BB:57
Table Manners.   G. Burgess.
   Co-BB:45, Fr-MP:5
There Is an Old Cook in N.Y.
   Br-LL:89
There Once Was a Finicky Ocelot.
   E. Merriam.   Br-LL:33
There Was a Young Lady of Corsica.
   E. Lear.   Br-LL:19, Gr-CT:28
There Was a Young Prince in
   Bombay.   W. Parke.   Br-LL:21,
   Co-HP:102
There Was an Old Man of Dumbree.
   E. Lear.   Br-LL:6, Un-GT:240
There Was an Old Person of Ewell.
   E. Lear.   Ag-HE:15
There Was an Old Person Whose
   Habits.   E. Lear.   Fe-FP:341
There Was an Old Woman, and
   What Do You Think?
   Li-LB:67, Mo-NR:98, Sm-LG:118
There Was an Old Woman Who Lived
   in the Fens.   W. de la Mare.
   Ag-HE:4
A Thousand Hairy Savages.
   S. Milligan.   Co-OW:20,
   Co-PU:134
Three Little Puffins. E. Farjeon.
   Ar-TP3:125, Lo-LL:1
The Three Unlucky Men.   J. Reeves.
   Ir-BB:151
Turtle Soup.   L. Carroll.
   Bl-OB:12, Bo-FP:57, Cl-FC:97,
   De-TT:95, Li-SR:80, Sm-MK:195
The Two Old Bachelors.   E. Lear.
   Co-FB:55, Co-HP:87
The Visitor.   K. Pyle. . Co-BB:50
The Voice of the Lobster.
   L. Carroll.   r-BB:146, Li-SR:99,
   Na-EO:39
The Waiter Said: "Try the
   Ragout."   Br-LL:85
The Walloping Window-Blind.
   C. Carryl.   Co-HP:48, Fe-FP:343,
   Hu-MP:450, Lo-LL:90, Sh-RP:123,
   Un-GF:30, Un-GT:220
Ways and Means.   L. Carroll.
   Ag-HE:16, Co-FB:375, Co-HP:42,
   Gr-EC:206, Li-SR:112, Sm-LG:282

HUMOR - FOOD AND EATING — cont'd.
 When Father Carves the Duck.
  E. Wright.   Co-HP:118,
  Co-PS:147, Er-FA:136, Fe-PL:188,
  Ga-FB:175
 When I Am Big, I Mean to Buy.
  M. Dodge.   Br-BC:108
 Wilhelmina Mergenthaler.
  H. Taber.   Co-BB:91
 Willy Wood.   Ag-HE:72
 Wish at Meal Time.   J. Farrar.
  Ja-PC:48
 Wolf and Tiger Dining, A.B.
  J. Keith.   De-FS:118
HUMOR - FOOLS
 My Father Died, but I Can't
  Tell You how.   Bl-OB:22,
  Ir-BB:124, On-TW:25, Pa-RE:46
 Old Farmer Buck.   Co-HP:23
 Sir, I Admit Your General Rule.
  M. Prior.   Co-FB:338, Pl-ML:137,
  Un-GT:236
HUMOR - FOOTBALL
 Dick Szymanski.   O. Nash.   Fl-HH:42
HUMOR - FORESTS AND WOODS
 Afforestation.   E. Wodehouse.
  Co-FB:173, Mo-SD:44
HUMOR - FORGERIES
 Aphrodite as History.   R. Francis.
  Mo-BG:188
HUMOR - FORGETTING
 Dumbbell.   W. Cole.   Co-OH:59
 Mingram Mo.   D. McCord.   Gr-EC:200
 An Odd Fellow.   L. Carroll.
  Ir-BB:209
 There Was a Young Man at the War
  Office.   J. Churton.   Br-LL:41
 There Was an Old Man of Khartoum.
  Br-LL:64
HUMOR - FOSSILS
 P Is for Paleontology.   M. Bracker.
  Co-FB:452
HUMOR - FOURTH OF JULY
 After the Picnic.   L. Blair.
  Ja-HH:30
HUMOR - FOXES
 Dog and Fox.   D. Ferry.   Co-PU:92
 The Three Foxes.   A. Milne.
  Bo-GJ:12, Ox-BC:341
HUMOR - FRANCE
 Three French Mice.   Ir-BB:236
HUMOR - FREEDOM
 When Serpents Bargain for the
  Right to Squirm.   E. Cummings.
  Br-TC:82
HUMOR - FRENCH LANGUAGE
 La Langue Francaise.   M. Bracker.
  Ke-TF:377
 Learning French.   Tr-US I:132
 To Henrietta, on Her Departure for
  Calais.   T. Hood.   Ox-BC:181

HUMOR - FRENCH REVOLUTION, 1789-1799
 La Place de la Concorde.
  M. Bracker.   Ke-TF:375
HUMOR - FRIENDSHIP
 Any Author to Any Friend.
  Martial.   Pl-ML:66
 The Chums.   T. Roethke.   Du-SH:41
 A Dedication.   G. Chesterton.
  Co-FB:378
 Epigram.   J. Swift.   Hi-WP II:123
 On the Death of Doctor Swift.
  J. Swift.   Al-VBP:518
 Sensitive Sydney.   W. Irwin.
  Co-FB:49, Co-HP:82
 There Was a Young Person Called
  Smarty.   Br-LL:61
 The Two Old Women of Mumbling
  Hill.   J. Reeves.   Br-SM:13
 Wishing.   G. MacPherson.   Ja-PC:24
HUMOR - FROGS
 As the Tadpole Said.   Rs-PF:112
 "Croak!" Said the Toad.   Bo-FP:84,
  Ch-B:61
 The Frog.   H. Belloc.   Bo-GJ:10,
  Co-FB:33, Co-HP:32, Fe-FP:344,
  Ga-FB:333, Hu-MP:456, Ir-BB:77,
  It-HB:19, Li-LC:31, Lo-LL:20,
  Ox-BC:311, Sh-RP:148
 The Frog.   Co-OW:76, Gr-EC:17
 The Frog and the Mouse.   Ho-WR:41
 A Frog He Would a-Wooing Go.
  Ir-BB:114, Mo-MGT:112, Mo-NR:93
 Frog Went a-Courtin'.   Un-GT:19
 The Frogs' Singing-School.
  E. Carbell.   Au-SP:235
 How a Girl Was Too Reckless of
  Grammar by Far.   G. Carryl.
  Co-FB:154
 A Legend of Okeefinokee.
  L. Richards.   Gr-EC:174
 Long Legs.   Re-RR:55
 Moral Song.   J. Farrar.   Sh-RP:3
 On How to Sing.   Shiki.   Le-IS:25
 A Peanut Sat.   Co-OH:38, Ir-BB:154
 Some Fishy Nonsense. L. Richards.
  Ar-TP3:124, Au-SP:234, Ir-BB:107,
  St-FS:60
HUMOR - FRUIT
 Still Lifes-I.   R. Iceland.
  Ho-TY:115
HUMOR - FRUSTRATION
 A Tragic Story.   W. Thackeray.
  Co-HP:115, De-TT:71, Fe-FP:353,
  Gr-EC:205, Hu-MP:446, Ir-BB:197,
  Pa-OM:74, Sh-RP:42, Un-GT:232
HUMOR - FUNERALS
 Just for the Ride.   Er-FA:220
 Limericks.   Br-LL:60, Br-SM:145,
  Co-HP:29
 Limericks since Lear.   Un-GT:241
 Madrigal Macabre.   S. Hoffenstein.
  Br-SM:137

Micky Thumps. Hi-WP I:15
On Seeing a Pompous Funeral for
   a Bad Husband. Br-SM:135
Perennial Mourner. S. Russell.
   De-FS:172
The Prince. W. de la Mare.
   Lo-LL:44
Rattlin' Joe's Prayer. J. Crawford.
   Fi-BG:187
Tarpauling Jacket. Co-RM:64
HUMOR - FUR
Fur Coat. E. Blunden. Co-PU:94
The Modern Hiawatha. G. Strong.
   Co-FB:415, Co-HP:115, Fe-FP:337,
   Gr-EC:192
HUMOR - FUTURE
A Father's Heart Is Touched.
   S. Hoffenstein. Co-FB:104
HUMOR - FUTURE LIFE
After. R. Hershon. Sc-TN:98
A Curt Addendum. Br-SM:151
Joshua Hight. Br-SM:149
The Origin of Baseball.
   K. Patchen. Mc-EA:133
Pity This Busy Monster, Manunkind.
   E. Cummings. Ho-LP:83, Mo-BG:197,
   Pe-SS:105, Sh-AP:192, Wi-LT:367
HUMOR - GABRIEL, ARCHANGEL
The Crusader. D. Parker. Br-SM:149
HUMOR - GAMES
Elegy on the Loss of the U.S.
   Submarine S4. H. Canfield.
   Co-FB:299
A Game of Consequences. P. Dehn.
   Co-FB:139
Life in Our Village. M. Markwei.
   Ab-MO:20
Plain Language from Truthful
   James. B. Harte. Co-HP:71
HUMOR - GARDENS AND GARDENERS
Contrary Mary. N. Turner.
   Ir-BB:104
Mr. Bidery's Spidery Garden.
   D. McCord. Un-GF:77
Old Quin Queeribus. N. Turner.
   Ar-TP3:139, Au-SP:245, Br-SG:44,
   Co-HP:116, Ir-BB:197, Ja-PC:38,
   Na-EO:77
Spring Arithmetic. Co-FB:483,
   Un-GF:75
This Season Our Tunnips Was Red.
   D. McCord. Br-LL:130
HUMOR - GEESE
Fooba Wooba John. Co-OW:64
The Grey Goose. Mc-WK:62
Some Geese. O. Herford. Co-FB:26
When a Goose Meets a Moose.
   Z. Gay. Ar-TP3:127
HUMOR - GENEROSITY
If I Were an Apple. An-IP:(4),
   Ja-PC:29

There Lived a King. W. Gilbert.
   Co-FB:145, Co-PT:83
Unselfishness. H. Graham.
   Co-OT:65
HUMOR - GENIUS
V Is a Vain Virtuoso. O. Herford.
   Br-LL:46
HUMOR - GEOLOGY
Rhyme for a Geological Baby.
   J. Cook. Li-SR:126
A Serio-Comic Elegy. R. Whately.
   Br-SM:162
HUMOR - GEOMETRY
Plane Geometry. E. Rounds.
   Li-SR:19, Pl-IO:87
Said Mrs. Isosceles Tri.
   C. Burgess. Be-LL:115
HUMOR - GEORGE, SAINT
Saint George and the Dragon.
   A. Noyes. Co-RM:82, Sh-RP:139
HUMOR - GEORGE III, KING
   OF ENGLAND
George III. E. Bentley.
   Co-FB:127, Mc-WS:84
HUMOR - GEORGE IV, KING
   OF ENGLAND
On a Royal Demise. T. Hood.
   Co-FB:474
HUMOR - GERMAN LANGUAGE
The Puzzled Census Taker. J. Saxe.
   Co-PT:286
HUMOR - GERMANY
On a German Tour. R. Porson.
   Co-FB:208
HUMOR - GEYSERS
Aunt Eliza. Br-SM:127
Clock Time by the Geyser.
   J. White. Br-SM:48
HUMOR - GHOSTS
Cape Horn Gospel. J. Masefield.
   Co-SS:171, Ha-PO:258
The Fall of J. W. Beane.
   O. Herford. Co-PT:21
Friends Beyond. T. Hardy.
   Pa-GTB:403
The Ghost That Jim Saw. B. Harte.
   Br-SM:6, Co-PM:84
Ghostesses. Gr-CT:8
Legend of the Hills. L. Lorraine.
   De-FS:135
The Lover's Ghost. L. Simpson.
   De-FS:181
Mary's Ghost. T. Hood. Co-FB:143,
   Co-PT:35, Sm-MK:106
The Old Wife and the Ghost.
   J. Reeves. Br-SM:16, Co-PM:140,
   Gr-EC:152, La-PV:210, Pa-RE:70
Sea Change. J. Masefield. Co-PT:263
Sir Roderic's Song. W. Gilbert.
   Br-SM:10, Co-PM:75
A Skeleton Once in Khartoum.
   Br-LL:66, Br-SM:4

HUMOR - GHOSTS — cont'd.
The Spectre Pig.   O. Holmes.
   Co-RM:103
Spooks. N. Crane. Br-SM:4
The Superstitious Ghost.
   A. Guiterman. Br-SM:8
Tam o' Shanter. R. Burns.
   Al-VBP:634, Sp-OG:170
There Were Three Ghostesses.
   Co-OW:32. Ir-BB:191
Three Ghostesses. Ag-HE:7,
   Mo-CC:(4), Mo-MGT:209
Unfortunate Miss Bailey. G. Colman.
   Co-FB:153, Gr-GB:293
HUMOR - GIANTS
Grombuskin. L. Richards. Ir-BB:215
HUMOR - GIFTS AND GIVING
Alma Mater, Forget Me. W. Cole.
   Co-FB:459
Courtship. Br-LL:123, Un-GT:241
I Have Four Sisters Beyond the Sea.
   On-TW:20
The Old Man.   Wr-RM:52
One Perfect Rose. D. Parker.
   Co-FB:313
HUMOR - GIOTTO DI BONDONE
When They Found Giotto. A. Laing.
   Co-FB:130
HUMOR - GIRAFFES
The Giraffe. G. Dearmer.
   Co-BBW:185, Hi-WP I:12
The Giraffe and the Woman.
   L. Richards. Co-IW:15,
   La-PV:22
I Know a Giraffe. E. Anthony.
   Ja-PC:12
There Once Was a Stately Giraffe.
   M. Vandegrift. Br-LL:30
There Was Once a Giraffe Who Said,
   "Who." O. Herford. Br-LL:29,
   Co-HP:74
The Untutored Giraffe. O. Herford.
   Br-SM:98
HUMOR - GIRLS
Bootless Speculations.
   P. McGinley. Ke-TF:88
The Comical Girl. M. Pelham.
   Co-HP:102, Ir-BB:103
Growing Up. E. Wallace.
   Br-BC:118, Th-AS:61
Life in Our Village. M. Markwei.
   Ab-MO:20
Look at That Gal. J. Bond.
   Hu-PN:434, Lo-TY:253
The Quiet Child. R. Field. Ne-AM:30
Sarah Byng. H. Belloc. Bo-GJ:112,
   Gr-CC:152
HUMOR - GLACIERS
Patience. H. Graham. Co-FB:56,
   Co-HP:67
HUMOR - GLUTTONY
Adelaide. J. Prelutsky. Co-OH:57

The Boy Stood in the Supper-Room.
   Co-OW:39
The Gastronomic Guile of Simple
   Simon. G. Carryl. Un-GT:218
Greedy Jane. Ne-AM:38
Jelly Jake and Butter Bill.
   L. Jackson. Co-BB:55
Little Thomas. F. Evans. Co-BB:45
The Sweet Tooth. K. Pyle.
   Ag-HE:64, Co-BB:57
HUMOR - GNATS
Accidentally. M. Kumin. Ja-PC:59
HUMOR - GNUS
The Gnu. S. Hoffenstein. Co-HP:76
The Gnu. T. Roethke. Gr-EC:22
One Day I Went Out to the Zoo.
   G. Johnson. Br-LL:32
HUMOR - GOATS
Billy Goats Chew. R. Emery.
   Ja-PC:23
The Grandiloquent Goat. C. Wells.
   Br-LL:23, Lo-LL:18
If a Goat Ever Swallowed. Rs-PF:99
O'Grady's Goat. W. Hays.
   Fe-PL:214
Old Hogan's Goat. Bu-DY:58,
   Co-IW:17
The Sad Goat. Fe-PL:187, Mc-WK:63
The Smile of the Goat. O. Herford.
   Co-FB:22
That Butter. Rs-PF:100
What Happened when a Lady. Re-RR:113
HUMOR - GOD
Eve to Her Daughters. J. Wright.
   To-MP:173
I Marvel at the Ways of God.
   E. White. Mc-WS:72
Monkey. J. Miles. Wi-LT:772
The Story of Samuel Jackson.
   C. Leland. Co-PT:267
The Theology of Bongwi, the Baboon.
   R. Campbell. Ga-S:194
These Bones Gwine to Rise Agin.
   Ga-S:24
Two Limericks. Ga-S:11
HUMOR - GODS AND GODDESSES,
   EGYPTIAN
I Am a Cowboy in the Boat of Ra.
   I. Reed. Ad-PB:330
HUMOR - GOETHE, JOHANN WOLFGANG VON
Shake, Mulleary, and Go-ethe.
   H. Bunner. Co-FB:350
HUMOR - GOGH, VINCENT VAN
The Van Gogh Influence.
   S. Silverstein. Co-EL:64
HUMOR - GOLDFISH
Ode on a Favorite Cat Drowned in
   a Tub of Gold Fishes. T. Gray.
   Fe-PL:350, Ho-WR:56, Ma-YA:123,
   Pa-GTB:112, Rv-CB:531, Sp-OG:303

HUMOR - GOLF
Afforestation. E. Wodehouse.
Co-FB:173, Mo-SD:44
The Ball and the Club. F. Lindsay.
Mo-SD:46
I Was Playing Golf That Day.
Co-FB:122
Magellan Went Around the World.
Rs-PF:30
One Down. R. Armour, Mo-SD:49
They Say that ex-President Taft.
Br-LL:79
HUMOR - GOODNESS
Children when They're Very Sweet.
J. Ciardi. Co-BB:40
The Good Little Girl. A. Milne.
Co-BB:37
I Am a Nice Nice Boy.
M. O'Connor. Le-M:154
HUMOR - GOSSIP
The Two Old Women of Mumbling
Hill. J. Reeves. Br-SM:13
HUMOR - GRAMMAR
As I Was Laying on the Green.
Co-FB:341, Co-HP:24, Mc-WS:176
The Cumberbunce. P. West.
Co-OH:63
Go, Little Booklet, Go. B. Nye.
Co-PU:23
A Hot-Weather Song. D. Marquis.
Co-PU:35, Sh-RP:215
How Low Is the Lowing Herd.
W. Kelly. Co-FB:122
Just Because. . . . D. McCord.
Co-OW:38, Gr-EC:128
The Naughty Preposition.
M. Bishop. Co-FB:417
Permanently. K. Koch. Mc-EA:134,
Mo-BG:93
HUMOR - GRANDFATHERS
Onto a Boy's Arm. Ho-SD:77
HUMOR - GRANDMOTHERS
Advice to Grandsons. Co-OH:58
Grandmamma's Birthday. H. Belloc.
Co-EL:56, Co-FB:189
Mr. Tom Narrow. J. Reeves.
Ir-BB:196
HUMOR - GRASSHOPPERS
Grasshopper. e. cummings.
Co-BBW:225
HUMOR - GREATNESS
Please Tell Me Just the Fabuli.
S. Silverstein. Co-EL:51,
Co-PU:19
Routine. A. Guiterman.
Co-HP:70, Co-OH:70
Soup. C. Sandburg, Sh-RP:162
HUMOR - GREED
The Greedy Man. Wr-RM:94
HUMOR - GREEN (COLOR)
Verdancy. Br-SM:75

HUMOR - GREETINGS
On Mundane Acquaintances.
H. Belloc. Co-EL:61, Co-FB:195
HUMOR - GRIEF
Alas, Alack! W. de la Mare.
Ar-TP3:124, Fe-FP:132, Hu-MP:43,
Ir-BB:64, Na-EO:152
Ko-Ko's Song. W. Gilbert. Er-FA:438
Presence of Mind. H. Graham.
Co-HP:68
Reverie. D. Marquis. Fe-PL:195
HUMOR - GROCERY STORES
The Unfortunate Grocer.
L. Richards. Co-OT:40
HUMOR - GROOMING, PERSONAL
Slovenly Peter. H. Hoffmann.
Co-BB:55
HUMOR - GROWING OLD
Changed. C. Calverley. Co-FB:74
The County Member. W. Praed.
Ox-BN:437
Fears and Tears.   Wr-RM:87
HUMOR - GROWING UP
The Birthday Bus. M. Hoberman.
Ar-TP3:92, Br-BC:98
The End. A. Milne. Br-BC:66,
Br-SS:46, Gr-TG:11
Growing Up. E. Wallace.
Br-BC:118, Th-AS:61
Hard Lines. T. Robinson.
Br-BC:64
Pelt Kid and His Grandmother.
Te-FC:193
Song to Be Sung by the Father of
Infant Female Children.
O. Nash. Un-MA:565
Sophisticate. B. Young.
Br-BC:50, Br-SS:42
There Once Was a Sow. On-TW:12
To Baby. K. Greenaway. Hu-MP:8
When I Am the President. Un-GT:17
Youth's Progress. J. Updike.
Co-FB:484
HUMOR - GUARDS
Said the Night Watchman. Rs-PF:35
HUMOR - GUESTS
Thanks Just the Same. Fe-PL:220
HUMOR - GUILT
This Is Just to Say. W. Williams.
Bo-GJ:211, Du-RG:60, Kh-VA:35,
Li-SR:100, Li-TU:24, Ma-FW:232,
Mo-BG:96, Sh-AP:169
Variations on a Theme by William
Carlos Williams. K. Koch.
Li-SR:100
HUMOR - GUINEA FOWLS
Life. A. Kreymborg. Co-BBW:235,
Co-EL:27, Co-PU:106
HUMOR - GUINEA PIGS
A Guinea-Pig Song. Ox-BC:80

HUMOR - GUINEA PIGS — cont'd.
  The Precise Guinea-Pig. Gr-EC:189,
    Ir-BB:135, Lo-LL:19, Un-GT:229
  Whoop! Little Jerry Tigg. Mother
    Goose. Ir-BB:177, Pa-AP:46
HUMOR - GULLS
  The Cares of a Caretaker.
    W. Irwin.   Co-OW:14
  Sea Change. J. Masefield.
    Co-PT:263
  The Sea-Gull. O. Nash. Er-FA:204
HUMOR - GUNPOWDER
  Limericks. Br-LL:75, Co-HP:28
HUMOR - GUNS
  The Careless Niece. C. Wells.
    Br-SM:128
HUMOR - GWYN, ELEANOR (NELL)
  Samuel Pepys. A. Laing. Co-FB:130
HUMOR - HABIT
  The Elephant, or Force of Habit.
    A. Housman. Ga-FB:329,
    Li-TU:116
  There Was an Old Person Whose
    Habits. E. Lear. Fe-FP:341
HUMOR - HACKENSACK, N.J.
  The Ballad of Hagensack.
    W. Irwin. Co-PT:272
HUMOR - HAIR
  Bought Locks. Martial. Mc-PR:20
  Cordelia Brown. Ab-MO:57
  For Anne Gregory. W. Yeats.
    Co-PI:204, Er-FA:105, Gr-BT:47,
    Gr-CC:15, Ha-PO:182, Mc-WS:63,
    Wi-LT:86
  Hair. M. Takahashi. Le-TA:59
  I'd Rather Have Fingers than Toes.
    G. Burgess. Br-LL:45, Fe-FP:365,
    Un-GF:65
  In New Orleans There Lived a Young
    Creole. Br-LL:46
  The Rape of the Lock, 3. A. Pope.
    Al-VBP:533
  Seven Limericks, 5. E. Lear.
    Sh-RP:150
HUMOR - HANDS
  The Hands They Were Made to
    Assist. A. Euwer. Br-LL:49
HUMOR - HARPS
  The Harper. Co-PI:132
  There Once Was a Corpulent Carp.
    C. Wells. Br-LL:36
HUMOR - HARVEST
  Mad Farmer's Song. Ir-BB:119,
    Mo-MGT:184
HUMOR - HATS
  Easter Bonnet. E. Jay. Ja-HH:24
  Hat Bar. M. Weston. Co-FB:401
  Hattage. A. Herbert. Co-FB:454
  The Marvellous Hat. W. Horsbrugh.
    Ir-BB:200
  Mr. Spats. S. Silverstein.
    Co-OW:46

My Hat. S. Smith. Sm-MK:78
Odd Bonnet. Ja-HH:25
Sartorial Solecism. R. Stringer.
  Co-FB:53
A Second Stanza for Dr. Johnson.
  D. Hall. Br-SM:26, Co-FB:386
There Was a Young Lady of Durban.
  Br-LL:95
There Was an Old Person of
  Fratton. Br-LL:94, Ir-BB:224
A Young Lady Whose Bonnet. E. Lear.
  Bo-FP:247, Br-LL:97
HUMOR - HAYDN, FRANZ JOSEPH
  There Was a Composer Named Haydn.
    Br-LL:109
HUMOR - HEADS
  As I Was Going Out One Day.
    Co-OW:43, Ir-BB:57
  A Boy's Head. M. Holub. Ma-FW:71
  Do You Know the Man?
    S. Silverstein. Co-OH:76
  Doctor Emmanuel. J. Reeves.
    Co-PU:116
  The Happy Family. J. Ciardi.
    Co-OW:34
  Limericks. Ke-TF:290
  Mr. Ripley Parodies Mr. Nash —
    Vice Versa. J. Brown. De-FS:40
  Mr. Spats. S. Silverstein.
    Co-OW:46
  Nicholas Ned. L. Richards.
    Ir-BB:211
  The Nose and the Eyes. W. Cowper.
    Hu-MP:449
  That Head. J. Bullmer. Co-OT:49
HUMOR - HEARTS
  Her Heart. B. Griffin. Un-MW:185
HUMOR - HEAVEN
  The Ballad of Tonopah Bill.
    Fi-BG:61
  For a Lady I Know. C. Cullen.
    Ab-MO:27, Ad-PB:91, Bo-AN:89,
    Br-SM:150, Hu-PN:231, Un-MA:571
  Heaven. R. Brooke. Ga-S:195,
    Un-MB:324, Wi-LT:615
  Hold the Wind. Gr-GB:326
  If You Want to Go to Heben.
    Gr-GB:299
  Longface Mahoney Discusses Heaven.
    H. Gregory. Ca-VT:208
  On Looking Up by Chance at the
    Constellations. R. Frost.
    Li-TU:268
  One o' These Mornin's. Ga-S:215
  Slim in Hell. S. Brown. Ra-BP:105
  tripart, 3. G. Jones. Jo-SA:13
  When de Saints Go Ma'chin' Home.
    S. Brown. Bo-AN:55
HUMOR - HELICOPTERS
  Street Scene. P. Suffolk.
    Co-PT:158

HUMOR - HELL
   Alaska, or the Hell of the Yukon.
      Fi-BG:43
   Hell in Texas.   Co-RM:30
   Lament of an Idle Demon. R. Lister.
      Co-FB:488
   May.   Shao Hsün-mei.   Hs-TC:126
   Sir Beelzebub.   E. Sitwell.
      Un-MB:331
   Slim in Hell.   S. Brown.   Ra-BP:105
   This Here Is Hell.   S. Bradley.
      De-FS:29
HUMOR - HELPFULNESS
   Oh, No!   M. Dodge.   Co-BB:20
HUMOR - HENRY VIII, KING
      OF ENGLAND
   Henry VIII.   E. and H. Farjeon.
      Co-PT:97
HUMOR - HERDING
   The Harmonious Heedlessness of
      Little Boy Blue. G. Carryl.
      Hu-MP:443
HUMOR - HERITAGE
   The "Dorset Nose."   C. Sansom.
      To-MP:128
   Gap.   M. Horovitz.   Co-PU:16
   The Heir.   Pa-RE:56
   My Father Died, but I Can't Tell
      You how.   Bl-OB:22, Ir-BB:124,
      On-TW:25, Pa-RE:46
   My Lord Tomnoddy.   R. Brough.
      Co-FB:195, Co-PU:123
   On Buying a Dog.   E. Klauber.
      Co-PU:93
   One Bowl, One Bottle.   Rv-ON:51
   Riches.   Mo-MGT:27
   When He Looked Up His Family
      Tree.   Rs-PF:30
HUMOR - HERO AND LEANDER
   Hero and Leander.   J. Newman.
      Co-FB:140
   Written after Swimming from
      Sestos to Abydos. G. Byron.
      Fl-HH:55
HUMOR - HEROES AND HEROISM
   Knight, with an Umbrella.
      E. Olson.   Co-FB:463
HUMOR - HIAWATHA
   Hiawatha's Photographing.
      L. Carroll. Co-FB:244, Li-SR:55
   The Modern Hiawatha.   G. Strong.
      Er-FA:206, Fe-FP:337, Li-SR:61
HUMOR - HILLS
   What Is the Difference. Re-RR:76
HUMOR - HINDUS
   I'm a Little Hindoo.
      Co-HP:25, Er-FA:498, Ir-BB:93
   The Poor Benighted Hindoo.
      C. Monkhouse.   Br-LL:97
HUMOR - HIPPOPOTAMUSES
   Advice to Children.   C. Wells.
      Co-OW:30

Habits of the Hippopotamus.
   A. Guiterman.   Ar-TP3:127,
   Co-FB:25, Co-HP:71, Ga-FB:333,
   Sh-RP:151
The Hippo.   T. Roethke.   Ca-VT:297,
   Co-PU:86
Hippo-Hippo-Potamuses.   Re-RR:87
Hippopotamothalamion.
   J. Wheelock.   Co-FB:10
The Hippopotamus.   H. Belloc.
   Co-FB:35, Co-HP:32
The Hippopotamus.   J. Prelutsky.
   Co-OT:75
I Had a Hippopotamus.
   P. Barrington.   Co-BBW:200,
   Ir-BB:181
The Mad Gardener's Song.
   L. Carroll.   Ja-PC:57
HUMOR - HISTORY
   Ancient History. A. Guiterman.
      Du-RG:63, Mc-WS:172
   Aphrodite as History. R. Francis.
      Mo-BG:188
   The Green Shepherd.   L. Simpson.
      Pe-OA:264
   A History Lesson.   M. Holub.
      Gr-BT:127, Ma-FW:239
   The Persian Version.   R. Graves.
      Cr-WS:31, Wi-LT:379
HUMOR - HOBBY-HORSES
   There Was a Nobby Colt. Ir-BB:177
HUMOR - HOME
   The Complacent Cliff-Dweller.
      M. Fishback.   Fe-PL:200
   Edgar A. Guest Syndicates The Old
      Woman Who Lived in a Shoe.
      L. Untermeyer.   Co-FB:232,
      Un-MA:311
   Three More Clerihews.   Un-GF:49
HUMOR - HOMER
   "Dear Me!"   E. Bentley. Co-FB:126
HUMOR - HOMESICKNESS
   Meditations of a Mariner.
      W. Irwin.   Co-SS:69
HUMOR - HOOVER, HERBERT CLARK
   Political Reflection.   O. Nash.
      Ke-TF:292
HUMOR - HORNS (MUSICAL
      INSTRUMENTS)
   An Addition to the Family: For M.L.
      E. Morgan.   To-MP:189
   The Harmonious Heedlessness of
      Little Boy Blue.   G. Carryl.
      Hu-MP:443
HUMOR - HORSE RACING
   Galway Races.   Mo-SD:65
HUMOR - HORSES
   The Diverting History of John
      Gilpin. W. Cowper. Al-VBP:588,
      Co-RG:88, Hi-WP I:47, Sp-OG:215
   Flash: The Fireman's Story.
      W. Carleton.   Se-PR:317

HUMOR - HORSES — cont'd.
  Horse & Rider. W. Robinson.
    Mo-SD:114
  The Horse's Version of the Ride
    of Paul Revere. Ke-TF:268
  Jack and His Pony. H. Belloc.
    Ir-BB:173
  On a Clergyman's Horse. Un-GT:239
  The Priest and the Mulberry Tree.
    T. Peacock. De-TT:119, Ha-PO:297,
    Sp-OG:224
  The Racing-Man. A. Herbert.
    Co-FB:23
  There Was a Young Prince in
    Bombay. W. Parke. Br-LL:21,
    Co-HP:102
  What Is the Principal. Rs-PF:105
  Why Is a Pony. Re-RR:96
HUMOR - HOSPITALITY
  The Best I Have. Basho. Be-MC:14
  Blessing Without Company. Ra-BP:17
  Guest You Are Welcome Here.
    Ke-TF:283
  Hospitality. J. Tabb. Gr-EC:22
  Old Mr. Parvenu. C. Grain.
    Co-PU:36
  Silence. M. Moore. Al-VBP:1174,
    Ha-PO:219, Ho-LP:72, Ma-FW:62,
    Mc-WS:77, Mo-BG:81
  The Woman of Exeter. Wr-RM:128
HUMOR - HOSPITALS
  Semi-Private. M. Carver. De-FS:48
HUMOR - HOTELS
  Duckmann. J. Schevill. Du-SH:155
HUMOR - HOUSEHOLD FURNISHINGS
  Every Thing. H. Monro. Un-MB:232
HUMOR - HOUSEKEEPING
  The Fresh Start. A. Wickham.
    Al-VBP:1155
  John Grumlie. A. Cunningham.
    Fe-PL:235, Gr-GB:205
  Old Farmer Grumble. Ju-CP:28
  Sisyphus. R. Burdette. Co-PT:293
  The Tidy Wife. Ir-BB:30
HUMOR - HOUSES
  The Ceiling. T. Roethke.
    Gr-EC:188, Li-LC:40
  The Floor and the Ceiling.
    W. Smith. Co-HP:113
  The Haunted House. T. Hood.
    Hi-WP I:56
  Mr. Pennycomequick. P. Stone.
    Ir-BB:234
  On Gaulston House. J. Swift.
    Rv-CB:492
HUMOR - HOUSMAN, ALFRED EDWARD
  A. E. Housman and a Few Friends.
    H. Wolfe. Co-FB:229, Li-SR:138
  What, Still Alive at Twenty Two.
    H. Kingsmill. Li-SR:137

HUMOR - HUMILIATION
  Bad Sir Brian Botany. A. Milne.
    Co-HP:97, Ir-BB:206, Mc-PR:162
  Daisy Deborah Delilah Dean.
    Co-OT:37
HUMOR - HUNTING
  The Baker's Tale. L. Carroll.
    Un-GF:26
  A Double Limerick. W. de la Mare.
    Br-LL:7
  Humorous Verse. Abu Dolama.
    Ab-MO:33, Lo-TY:43
  The Hunter. O. Nash. Co-BBW:248,
    Ke-TF:291, Mo-SD:126, Na-EO:112
  The Hunter. S. Silverstein.
    Co-RM:97
  The Hunter of Reigate. Br-LL:61,
    Wr-RM:25
  A Little Cock Sparrow. Ir-BB:26,
    Li-LB:87, Mo-MGT:171, Mo-NR:48,
    Mo-TL:57, Wi-MG:36, Wr-RM:66
  The Mighty Hunter. J. Worley.
    Fe-PL:187
  Robin-A-Bobbin. Mo-MGT:94,
    Wr-RM:33
  Safari. M. Ridlon. Ho-CS:41
  Save the Tiger! A. Herbert.
    Co-HP:72
  She Sights a Bird. E. Dickinson.
    Rd-OA:171
  That Familiar Stranger.
    F. Stefanile. De-FS:191
  There Were Three Jovial Welshmen.
    Bl-OB:24, Gr-GB:86, Ir-BB:140,
    Mo-MGT:198, Pa-OM:2, Sm-MK:23,
    Sp-HW:23
  The Three Jolly Hunters. J. Riley.
    Mc-WK:66
  Three Jolly Huntsmen. Un-GT:217
  The Wren Hunt. Mo-MGT:44
HUMOR - HUSBAND AND WIFE
  Clubwoman. M. Smith. Hu-PN:388
  A Cottage in Fife. Ir-BB:139,
    Lo-LL:75, Mo-MGT:170, Wi-MG:44,
    Wr-RM:78
  He and She. E. Ware. Fe-PL:216
  In Praise of Celibacy. Al-PI:51
  The Inventor's Wife. E. Corbett.
    Fe-PL:219
  Jack Sprat He Is So Fat. Ir-BB:199
  John, Come Sell Thy Fiddle.
    Ir-BB:208
  Johnnie Blunt. Ox-BB:630
  The Old Man Who Lived in a Wood.
    Hu-MP:468
  A Quiet Life and a Good Name.
    J. Swift. Rv-CB:493
  Thomas a Didymus, Hard of Belief.
    Ir-BB:57
  Tommy Trot. Ir-BB:42, Mo-MGT:121

HUMOR – HUSBANDS
   Epitaph. Hi-WP II:12
   Grieve Not for Me. Br-SM:159
   I Had a Little Husband.
      Er-FA:502, Ir-BB:208, Mo-MGT:84,
      Mo-TL:51, Na-EO:170
   On Seeing a Pompous Funeral for a
      Bad Husband. Br-SM:135
   The Perils of Obesity. H. Graham.
      Co-FB:121
   Stranger Call This Not. Br-SM:158
HUMOR – HYDROGEN WEAPONS
   The Hydrogen Dog and the Cobalt
      Cat. F. Winsor. Br-SM:64
   Primer of Consequences.
      V. Brasier. Br-SM:61
HUMOR – HYENAS
   The Happy Hyena. C. Wells.
      Bo-FP:29
   How to Tell the Wild Animals.
      C. Wells. Un-GF:84
   L Is for Lovable Lena. Br-LL:31
HUMOR – HYMN SINGING
   Limericks since Lear. Un-GT:242
HUMOR – HYPNOTISM
   The Powerful Eyes o' Jeremy Tait.
      W. Irwin. Co-FB:135, Co-SS:79,
      Ha-PO:264
HUMOR – ICE
   Morning Song. K. Stein. Co-FB:215
HUMOR – ICE CREAM
   Food and Eating. Br-LL:86,
      Un-GT:242
   ice cream. J. Price. Pe-SS:65
   Tableau at Twilight. O. Nash.
      Co-FB:97
HUMOR – IDLENESS
   Plucking the Rushes. Co-PU:75,
      Gr-BT:45
HUMOR – ILLUSIONS
   My Last Illusion. Dum-Dum.
      Co-FB:318
   To Cynthia, Not to Let Him Read
      the Ladies' Magazines.
      P. Hubbard. Co-FB:399
HUMOR – IMAGINATION
   B Is for Beanseed. E. Farjeon.
      Br-SG:82
   Grotesque. D. Marquis. Co-FB:381
   The Land of Ho-Ho-Hum. W. Smith.
      Ir-BB:256
   On the Beach. C. Calverley.
      Co-FB:67
   What the Lord High Chamberlain
      Said. V. Cloud. Co-BB:74
HUMOR – IMMIGRATION AND
      EMIGRATION
   Colonisation in Reverse.
      L. Bennett. Sa-B:51
HUMOR – IMPERMANENCE
   The Power of Time. J. Swift.
      Rv-CB:495

HUMOR – INDECISION
   The Ambiguous Dog. A. Guiterman.
      Co-BBW:113
   Come Along In Then, Little Girl.
      E. Millay. Bo-FP:3
   Eight Limericks, 4. E. Lear.
      Sh-RP:128
   The Platypus. O. Herford.
      Co-FB:27
   Some Families of My Acquaintance.
      L. Richards. Co-OW:18
   To Be or Not to Be. Co-HP:21,
      Er-FA:202, Gr-EC:168,
      Hi-WP II:12, Un-GT:228
HUMOR – INDIANS OF NORTH AMERICA
   The Savages. J. Miles. Wi-LT:772
HUMOR – INDIFFERENCE
   At the Ship. R. Lister. Co-FB:501
   Back Room Joys. J. Richardson.
      Co-FB:485
   Departmental. R. Frost. Du-SH:114,
      Mc-WS:48, Sh-AP:154, Un-MA:190
   Do You Love Me. Co-PS:40,
      Co-PU:19
   Don't-Care. Bl-OB:29, De-TT:23,
      Gr-EC:287, Gr-GB:17
   Friends Beyond. T. Hardy.
      Pa-GTB:403
   Pooh! W. de la Mare. Co-FB:192
   To My Friends. P. De Vries.
      Co-FB:495
HUMOR – INDIGESTION
   The Confession. R. Barham.
      Co-FB:87
HUMOR – INDIVIDUALITY
   Family Life. A. Laing. Co-FB:473
   Meditations of a Tortoise.
      E. Rieu. Ar-TP3:130, Co-BBW:82,
      Co-FB:5
   Mr. Kartoffel. J. Reeves.
      Co-OW:54, Sm-MK:116
HUMOR – INFINITY
   Science and Mathematics.
      Br-LL:114, Pl-IO:80
HUMOR – INFLUENZA
   This Troubled World Is Sighing
      Now. Un-GT:243
HUMOR – INGE, WILLIAM RALPH
   On Dean Inge. H. Wolfe. Gr-CT:474
HUMOR – INJUSTICE
   Bessy Bell and Mary Gray.
      Bo-FP:51, Wr-RM:90
HUMOR – INNOVATIONS
   The Poet of Bray. J. Heath-Stubbs.
      Pl-ML:9
HUMOR – INNS AND TAVERNS
   Lament for Lost Lodgings.
      P. McGinley. Li-SR:6
   There Is an Inn, a Merry Old Inn.
      J. Tolkien. Lo-LL:98

HUMOR - INSECTS
Concert. I. Sharaf. Ab-MO:32
A Considerable Speck. R. Frost.
   Ad-PE:23, Co-BBW:225, Un-MA:190
Fooba Wooba John. Co-OW:64
I Said to a Bug in the Sink.
   J. Ciardi. Br-LL:3
Nightmare Number Four. R. Bloch.
   De-FS:24
Tea Party. H. Behn. Li-LC:35
HUMOR - INSOMNIA
Insomnia. G. Highet. Ke-TF:285
HUMOR - INSULTS
Cromek. W. Blake. Co-FB:197,
   Gr-CT:467
Decline and Fall of a Roman
   Umpire. O. Nash. Mo-SD:7
On a Lord. S. Coleridge.
   Co-FB:132
HUMOR - INSURANCE
Epitaph. R. Armour. Br-SM:55
HUMOR - INTELLECTUALS
His Little Sub. E. Bennett.
   Ke-TF:70
Note on Intellectuals.
   W. Auden. Co-FB:500
HUMOR - INTERNATIONAL
   RELATIONS
The Copperfaces. C. Sandburg.
   Sh-RP:269
Great Lakes Suite, II. J. Reaney.
   Do-WH:49
Just Dropped In. W. Cole.
   Bo-GJ:153, Co-FB:213
HUMOR - INTERPLANETARY
   VOYAGES
A Projection. R. Whittemore.
   Mc-WK:210
HUMOR - INTOXICATION
Not Drunk Is He. T. Peacock.
   Al-VBP:716
On a German Tour. R. Porson.
   Co-FB:208
Parody on Thomas Hood's "The
   Bridge of Sighs." Co-FB:220
R-E-M-O-R-S-E. G. Ade. Co-FB:90
When They Found Giotto. A. Laing.
   Co-FB:130
William the Bastard. Lakon.
   Co-FB:131
Willie and Nellie's Wish.
   J. Moore. Co-FB:302
HUMOR - INVENTIONS
Darius Green and His Flying
   Machine. J. Trowbridge.
   Fe-PL:204, Ox-BC:260
The Inventor's Wife. E. Corbett.
The Inventor's Wife. E. Corbett.
   Fe-PL:219
Young Frankenstein's Robot Inven-
   tion. B. Braley. Br-LL:113
HUMOR - INVITATIONS
The Crocodile. O. Herford. Co-HP:73

Montezuma. A. Alderson. Gr-EC:34
HUMOR - IRASCIBILITY
Limericks since Lear. Co-BB:29,
   Un-GT:241
Temper. R. Fyleman. Ox-BC:339
HUMOR - IRELAND-HISTORY AND
   PATRIOTISM
The Irish Colonel. A. Doyle.
   Co-PU:36
HUMOR - THE IRISH
A Glass of Beer. J. Stephens.
   Co-FB:470, Mc-WS:83, Rv-CB:973,
   Un-MB:265
The Irish Rover. Co-SS:120
Numerous Celts. J. Squire. Li-SR:151
An Old Woman, Outside the Abbey
   Theater. L. Strong. Co-FB:352,
   Un-MB:393
Whack Fol the Diddle. P. Kearney.
   Co-FB:206, Co-PI:79
HUMOR - IRON
The Fable of the Magnet and the
   Churn. W. Gilbert. Fe-FP:351,
   Hu-MP:444, Pa-OM:46, Sh-RP:122
HUMOR - ITALY
Fish Out of Water. M. Fishback.
   Ke-TF:380
Italian Excursion. H. Bevington.
   Mc-WS:112
HUMOR - ITCHINESS
Eight Limericks. E. Lear. Sh-RP:128
Two Witches. A. Resnikoff.
   Co-OH:33
HUMOR - JACK THE RIPPER
Jack the Ripper. A. Laing.
   Co-FB:130
HUMOR - JAMES, HENRY
Jacobean. C. Fadiman. Co-FB:130
HUMOR - THE JAPANESE
A Globe-Trotting Man from St. Paul.
   F. Christgau. Br-LL:51
HUMOR - JEALOUSY
I Can't Think What He Sees in Her.
   A. Herbert. Co-FB:469
HUMOR - JELLYFISH
The Jellyfish. O. Nash. Co-OH:25,
   Fe-FP:341
Skip-Scoop-Anellie. T. Prideaux.
   Co-FB:373, Co-HP:104
HUMOR - JOKES
Korf's Joke. C. Morgenstern.
   Co-EL:49, Co-PU:33
HUMOR - JONAH
In the Story of Jonah. Rs-PF:48
Jonah. A. Huxley. Co-SS:173,
   Gr-CT:211
Noah an' Jonah an' Cap'n John
   Smith. D. Marquis.
   Co-SS:189, Fe-PL:198, Sm-LG:195
Who Did? Bu-DY:45

HUMOR - JOURNALISM
The British Journalist. H. Wolfe.
Co-FB:472
HUMOR - JUNGLES
The Jungle Husband. S. Smith.
Gr-BT:96
HUMOR - JUSTICE
Printer's Error. P. Wodehouse.
Co-FB:334
The Rain. Er-FA:219, Gr-EC:48
Robin Hood and the Bishop of
Hereford. Bl-OB:73, Ma-BB:74
HUMOR - KANGAROOS
The Duck and the Kangaroo.
E. Lear. Ox-BC:186
Pockets. R. Bennett. Sh-RP:129
The Sing-Song of Old Man
Kangaroo. R. Kipling. Fe-FP:174
Some Know Whom Australia.
Re-RR:103
HUMOR - KATYDIDS
To an Insect. O. Holmes. Ch-B:77
HUMOR - KIDNAPING
Kidnap Poem. N. Giovanni.
Ra-BP:326
HUMOR - KINGS AND RULERS
After Ever Happily. I. Serraillier.
Co-BL:151, Gr-EC:190, Ma-FW:145
Bobbily Boo and Wollypoturp.
L. Richards. Li-LC:46, Lo-LL:6
A Cat May Look at a King.
L. Richards. Co-IW:26
Contemporary Nursery Rhyme.
Li-SR:131
Even Before His Majesty. Dansui.
Ma-FW:139
The Frogs Who Wanted a King.
J. Lauren. Bo-HF:94, Un-GT:170
The Haughty Snail-King.
V. Lindsay. Ha-LO:58
If I Were King. A. Milne.
Sh-RP:2
If You Know Any History. Re-RR:61
King Pippin. Lo-LL:77
The King's Breakfast. A. Milne.
Ox-BC:341
Little King Boggen. Ir-BB:269,
Rv-ON:79
Montezuma. A. Alderson. Gr-EC:34
Old King Cole. Au-SP:4, De-PO:22,
Er-FA:507, Fr-WO:33, Ir-BB:265,
Li-LB:68, Mo-MGT:147, Mo-NR:137,
Wi-MG:27, Wr-RM:83
The Sailor and the Shark. P. Fort.
Sm-MK:66
Some Questions to Be Asked of a
Rajah. P. Newman. Co-FB:419,
Co-HP:101
There Lived a King. W. Gilbert.
Co-FB:145, Co-PT:83

A Threnody. G. Lanigan. Co-FB:424,
Do-WH:26, Rv-CB:947
A Toast. J. Byrom. Al-VBP:543
The Warrior's Lament. O. Seaman.
Co-FB:50
Zachary Zed. J. Reeves. Co-OH:34
HUMOR - KISSES AND KISSING
Confession. Charles d'Orleans.
Gr-CT:59, Rv-CB:3
In May. J. Synge. Un-MB:182,
Un-MW:196
Jenny Kiss'd Me. P. Dehn.
Co-FB:260, Li-SR:33
The Kiss. T. Moore. Co-BL:149
The Kiss. C. Patmore. Co-FB:324,
Un-MW:54
Kissin'. Co-BL:119, Co-FB:324,
Un-MW:34
Kissing of My Dame. Gr-GB:156,
Mo-MGT:211
Limericks. Ke-TF:288
A Melancholy Song. Mo-MGT:205,
Rv-ON:106, Wr-RM:16
She Frowned and Called Him Mr.
Br-LL:123, Fe-FP:361, Un-GT:241
Sucking Cider Through a Straw.
Gr-GB:125
The Theft. G. Wither. Un-MW:40
There Once Was a Maiden of Siam.
Br-LL:117
We're A' Dry wi' the Drinkin' o't.
Co-EL:16
Whenever We Happen to Kiss.
H. Heine. Un-MW:54
HUMOR - KIWIS
So by Chance It May Be You've Not
Heard. D. McCord. Br-LL:132
HUMOR - KLONDIKE, CAN.
The Ballad of Yukon Jake.
E. Paramore. Co-RM:133
HUMOR - KNIGHTS AND KNIGHTHOOD
Advice to a Knight. T. Jones.
Ma-FW:245
Ballad of the Mermaid.
C. Leland. Co-FB:217
The False Knight on the Road.
De-CH:316, Gr-GB:288, Ma-BB:84,
Rv-CB:52
Sir Eglamour. S. Rowlands.
Bl-OB:25, Co-RM:80, Gr-EC:143,
Mc-WK:134, Sm-LG:181
Sir Nicketty Nox. H. Chesterman.
Ir-BB:198
HUMOR - KNIVES
The Bread-Knife Ballad.
R. Service. Co-OT:72
HUMOR - KNOWLEDGE
E-MC . M. Bishop. Pl-IO:82
I Am the Great Professor Jowett.
Co-FB:76
I Want to Know. J. Drinkwater.
Fe-FP:7

HUMOR - KNOWLEDGE — cont'd.
I've Seen Everything.   J. Naito.
  Ma-FW:93
A Ride in a Blue Chevy. J. Williams.
  Ls-NY:160
HUMOR - LABOR DAY
Labor Day. E. Jay.   Ja-HH:31
HUMOR - LABOR UNIONS
A Rattlesnake Will Bite.   Rs-PF:61
HUMOR - LADDERS
How Could You Fall.   Re-RR:75
HUMOR - LAMAS
I Will Arise and Go Now.
  O. Nash. Mc-WK:86
The Llama. H. Belloc. Co-FB:37,
  Na-EO:113, Sm-LG:92
HUMOR - LAMBS
All Wool. A. Brown. Ar-TP3:123
The Lamb. O. Nash. Un-GF:83
Tame Animals I Have Known.
  N. Waterman. Co-OW:61
HUMOR - LANDLORDS AND TENANTS
On Richard Dent, Landlord.
  Un-GT:238
HUMOR - LANGUAGE
Ascot Waistcoat. D. McCord.
  Co-FB:425
Autolycus' Song in Basic English.
  R. Green. Li-SR:82
Bonne Entente. F. Scott. Co-FB:207
Les Chasse-Neige. R. Lewin.
  Co-FB:420
A False Gallop of Analogies.
  W. St. Leger. Co-FB:416
A Nocturnal Sketch. T. Hood.
  Co-FB:426
There Was an Old Maid from Peru.
  Br-LL:136
The Three Foxes. A. Milne.
  Bo-GJ:12, Ox-BC:341
Tudor Aspersions. R. Piddington.
  Co-FB:418
'Twixt Cup and Lip. M. Hollis.
  Co-FB:348
HUMOR - LATIN LANGUAGE
Amo, Amas. J. O'Keefe. Co-BL:78,
  De-CH:606, Gr-CT:60
Intramural Aestivation. O. Holmes.
  Gr-CT:5
Latin. Gr-CT:469
Sum, Es, Est. Gr-CT:469
HUMOR - LAUGHTER
The Funny Old Man and His Wife.
  Au-SP:218, Ch-B:109
I've Got the Giggles Today.
  A. Herbert. Co-FB:406
Little Tommy Grace Had a Pain
  in His Face. Ir-BB:95
HUMOR - LAUNDRY
Landscape with Figurines.
  P. McGinley. Ke-TF:344

The September Gale. O. Holmes.
  Co-FB:111, Co-HP:76
HUMOR - LAWYERS
The Briefless Barrister.
  J. Saxe. Br-SM:39
The Lawyers' Invocation to Spring.
  H. Brownell. Fe-PL:377,
  Ke-TF:279
Manhattan Epitaphs: Lawyer.
  A. Kreymborg. La-OC:60
The Nose and the Eyes. W. Cowper.
  Hu-MP:449
HUMOR - LAZINESS
The Lazy People. S. Silverstein.
  Co-OH:83
Yonder See.   A. Housman.
  Hi-WP I:120
HUMOR - LEGS
Annie Bolanny. Gr-CT:9
Bandy Legs. Ir-BB:26, Mo-MGT:136,
  Wr-RM:109
Two Legs Behind and Two Before.
  Co-OW:45
HUMOR - LENT
Ash Wednesday. W. Dunbar. Ga-S:142
HUMOR - LEONARDO DA VINCI
La Joconde. M. Bracker. Ke-TF:377
HUMOR - LEOPARDS
How to Tell the Wild Animals.
  C. Wells. Un-GF:84
L Was a Lachrymose Leopard.
  C. Wells. Br-LL:35
Little Katy. Br-SM:92
HUMOR - LETTERS AND
  LETTERWRITING
The Jungle Husband. S. Smith.
  Gr-BT:96
Lives of Great Men. Er-FA:219
Love Note to a Playwright.
  P. McGinley. Ke-TF:275
On a Very Empty Stomach. Re-RR:69
HUMOR - LETTUCE
Soliloquy of a Tortoise. E. Rieu.
  Ar-TP3:130, Br-SG:43, Co-BBW:93,
  Co-FB:4, Mc-WS:130
HUMOR - LIARS
Golly, How Truth Will Out!
  O. Nash. Un-MA:565
Lying. T. Moore. Co-FB:500,
  Co-PI:147
Matilda. H. Belloc. Bl-OB:30,
  Co-PT:305, Pa-OM:6, Sm-LG:100
Mendax. Co-PU:119
Ten Thousand Years Ago. Co-OH:26
There Was an Old Person of Gretna.
  E. Lear. Gr-CT:28
Washington and Me. E. Jay.
  Ja-HH:16
HUMOR - LIBRARIES
A Branch Library. J. Flagg. Br-LL:102
Library. R. Armour. Gr-EC:269

HUMOR - LIFE
    Donne Redone. J. Tierney. Br-SM:136
    Envoi. D. Wyndham Lewis. Co-FB:258
    I'll Eat when I'm Hungry. Un-GT:18
    Inventory. D. Parker. Ke-TF:232
    Life Cycle of Common Man.
        H. Nemerov. To-MP:121
    Solomon Grundy. Mother Goose.
        De-PO:22, Li-LB:74, Mo-MGT:140,
        Mo-NR:35, Wi-MG:42, Wr-RM:24
    There Was a Young Fellow of Perth.
        Br-LL:66
    There Was a Young Man of Cadiz.
        Br-LL:115
    well boss mehitabel the cat.
        D. Marquis. Ke-TF:266
HUMOR - LIFE AND DEATH
    Last Lauch. D. Young. Co-PU:148
    Novel. R. Lax.   Sc-TN:141
HUMOR - LIGHTNING
    At Great Torrington, Devon.
        Br-SM:52
HUMOR - LILACS
    Sam Said He Would Pick Me Some
        Lilacs. Rs-PF:12
HUMOR - LIONS
    How to Tell the Wild Animals.
        C. Wells. Un-GF:84
    Inhuman Henry. A. Housman.
        Co-BB:25, Co-FB:101, Co-HP:80
    A Lion. J. Francis. Br-LL:31,
        Hu-MP:457
    The Lion. V. Lindsay. Br-SM:92,
        Sh-RP:136
    The Lion. O. Nash. Br-SM:93
    This One Came Right Out of the
        Zoo. Re-RR:86
HUMOR - LISZT, FRANZ
    There Was a Composer Named Liszt.
        Br-LL:108
HUMOR - LITERATURE
    Survey of Literature. J. Ransom.
        Br-TC:335, Ca-VT:151, Sm-LG:36
    Very like a Whale. O. Nash.
        Fe-PL:211
HUMOR - LIZARDS
    The Lizard. T. Roethke. Co-OW:37
HUMOR - LLAMAS
    In Praise of Llamas.
        A. Guiterman. Co-FB:36, Co-HP:70
    The Llama. H. Belloc. Co-FB:37,
        Na-EO:113, Sm-LG:92
    A Llyric of the Llama.
        B. Johnson. Co-OH:30
HUMOR - LOBSTERS
    Conversion. J. Lillie. Co-BBW:74
    The Voice of the Lobster.
        L. Carroll. Ir-BB:146,
        Li-SR:99, Na-EO:39, Ox-BC:241
HUMOR - LOCKS AND KEYS
    The Bath. H. Graham.   Br-SM:120

    Common Sense. H. Graham.
        Co-FB:123, Co-HP:67, Er-FA:218,
        Un-GF:48
    On a Puritanicall Lock-Smith.
        W. Camden.   Br-SM:150
    On a Thieving Locksmith. Un-GT:238
    The Squad Car. M. Neville. Su-FVI:33
    What's Smaller than Any Mouse.
        Re-RR:114
HUMOR - LOGIC
    Abu. D. Randall. Ra-BP:147
    Goose, Moose, and Spruce.
        D. McCord. Gr-EC:127
    Jacky Jingle. Ir-BB:141, Mo-MGT:124
    Logic. Bo-FP:11, Gr-EC:126
    Scat! Scitten. D. McCord.
        Gr-EC:129
    Shoes Have Tongues. I. Orleans.
        Ir-BB:143
    There Was a Monkey. De-TT:20,
        Gr-EC:192, Ir-BB:134, Mo-MGT:81,
        Pa-RE:33
    Things to Learn About. J. Becker.
        Sh-RP:175
    Under a Hill. Li-LB:70, Mo-MGT:42
HUMOR - LONDON, ENG.
    The Ballad of Hampstead Heath.
        J. Flecker. Un-MB:275
    The Mountains of Mourne.
        P. French. Co-PI:46
    An Ode to Spring in the Metropolis.
        O. Seaman. Co-FB:234
HUMOR - LONELINESS
    Zachary Zed. J. Reeves. Co-OH:34
HUMOR - LONGFELLOW, HENRY
        WADSWORTH
    Abbreviated Interviews with a Few
        Disgruntled Literary Celebrities.
        R. Whittemore. Co-FB:343
HUMOR - LONGING
    Miniver Cheevy, Jr. D. Parry.
        Li-SR:76
HUMOR - LOVE
    A Deux. W. Wood.   Co-BL:62,
        Co-EL:7
    All or Nothing. W. Congreve.
        Un-MW:47
    Amo, Amas. J. O'Keefe. Co-BL:78,
        De-CH:606, Gr-CT:60
    And Forgive Us Our Trespasses.
        A. Behn. Un-MW:45
    Annabel Lee. S. Huntley. Li-SR:71
    As Freedom Is a Breakfastfood.
        e. cummings. Ca-VT:181,
        Wi-LT:364
    Belinda the Charitable. Un-MW:37
    The Belle of the Ball-Room.
        W. Praed. Al-VBP:799
    By What Sweet Name. S. Coleridge.
        Un-MW:52
    Capsule Conclusions, III. Un-MW:65

HUMOR - LOVE — cont'd.
    The Constant Lover. J. Suckling.
        Al-VBP:421, Er-FA:110, Ga-FB:42,
        Ha-PO:174, Ho-LP:10, Ma-YA:99,
        No-CL:186, Un-MW:43
    December 18th. A. Sexton.
        Un-MW:199
    Do You Love Me. Co-PS:40, Co-PU:19
    Elegy for a Mis-Spent Youth.
        J. Stallworthy. Un-MW:106
    Epigram. A. Kreymborg. Co-BL:50
    Evening Star. G. Barker.
        En-PC:124
    The Fired Pot. A. Wickham.
        Un-MW:125
    The Greek Anthology. Un-MW:173
    I Hear Some Say. M. Drayton.
        Un-MW:202
    In the Word Cloves. Re-RR:98
    Lily McQueen. S. Jackson. Co-BB:159
    Limericks. Ke-TF:290
    Love. Ab-MO:19, Lo-TY:198
    A Love Song. R. Patterson.
        Ad-BO:71
    Love 20¢ the First Quarter Mile.
        K. Fearing. Un-MW:104
    Love's Limit. Un-MW:31
    A Man of Experience.
        L. Mac an Bhaird. Co-PI:153
    The Manly Heart. G. Wither.
        Al-VBP:311, Co-BL:57, Ga-FB:38,
        Ma-YA:84, No-CL:185, Pa-GTB:85,
        Un-MW:40
    Men. D. Parker. Co-BL:101
    Modern Love. J. Keats.
        Ox-BN:368, Rv-CB:752
    Modern Song. Ab-MO:31
    Oh, When I Was in Love with You.
        A. Housman. Ga-FB:73,
        Hi-WP II:108, Ke-TF:92, Mc-WS:55,
        Pe-M:151, Un-MB:98, Un-MW:55
    The Olympic Girl. J. Betjeman.
        Mo-SD:34
    An Original Love Story. Co-BL:161
    Partial Comfort. D. Parker.
        Ke-TF:138
    The Sad Lover. G. Crabbe.
        Ox-BN:17
    Storm. Feng Wei-teh. Hs-TC:137
    Suspicious Sweetheart. H. Heine.
        Un-MW:54
    Three Old Brothers. F. O'Connor.
        Co-PI:150
    Versions of Love. R. Fuller.
        Wi-LT:708
    When One Loves Tensely. D. Marquis.
        Co-BL:53, Co-FB:314
    Why So Pale and Wan. J. Suckling.
        Al-VBP:423, Co-BL:136, Er-FA:115,
        Ga-FB:43, Gr-BT:75, Ma-YA:99,
        Na-EO:112, Pa-GTB:83, Rv-CB:378,
        Un-MW:44

        William Gifford. W. Landor.
            Pa-GTB:317
        See also Em-AF:196-227
HUMOR - LOVE-BASHFULNESS
    The Exchange. S. Coleridge.
        Co-FB:322
    First Person Demonstrative.
        P. McGinley. Pe-M:146
    The Modest Couple. W. Gilbert.
        Co-PT:186
    Though a Young Man of Football
        Physique. Br-LL:119
HUMOR - LOVE-BETRAYAL
    Neddy Nibble'm and Biddy Finn.
        Gr-GB:136
    The Sailor and the Shark.
        P. Fort. Sm-MK:66
    She Was Poor but She Was Honest.
        Co-FB:141, Gr-GB:260
    Unfortunate Miss Bailey. G. Colman.
        Co-FB:153, Gr-GB:293
    Whether or Not. D. Lawrence.
        Un-MB:291
HUMOR - LOVE-COMPLAINTS
    AND PROTESTS
    An Expostulation. I. Bickerstaff.
        Co-BL:137, Co-FB:326, Co-PI:10,
        Un-GF:20
    Lord, How Shall I Me Complain.
        Rv-CB:19
    Love Song. D. Parker. Mc-WS:67
    The Time I've Lost in Wooing.
        T. Moore. Un-MW:51
HUMOR - LOVE-DEVOTION
    The Ballad of the Oysterman.
        O. Holmes. Er-FA:306, Sm-MK:69
    Fifteen Boys. B. Akhmadulina.
        Bo-RU:5, Ca-MR:39, Gr-BT:65
    If You Love Me. S. Hoffenstein.
        Co-FB:328
    Lord, How Shall I Me Complain.
        Rv-CB:19
    Melody for Lute and Ocarina.
        M. Bishop. Gr-EC:221
    Oh Lucky Jim! Gr-CT:88, Gr-GB:157
    The Ratcatcher's Daughter.Gr-GB:134
    Sentimental Lines to a Young Man.
        M. Fishback. Co-FB:316
    True Love. J. Viorst. Un-MW:63
HUMOR - LOVE, FIRST
    First Love. C. Calverley. Co-FB:320
    My First Love. H. Graham. Co-FB:325

HUMOR - LOVE, FORSAKEN
    Blow Me Eyes! W. Irwin. Co-BL:166
    The Dong with the Luminous Nose.
        E. Lear. Co-PM:115, Ga-FB:325,
        Gr-CT:24, Ho-WR:228, Rv-CB:813
    This Summer. C. Smith. Me-WF:71
    Under the Drooping Willow Tree.
        Rv-CB:788
HUMOR - LOVE-OBSTACLES
    Babette's Love.W.Gilbert.Co-SS:215

Ferdinando and Elvira.
W. Gilbert.   Co-FB:170
For Anne Gregory.   W. Yeats.
Co-PI:204, Er-FA:105, Gr-BT:47,
Gr-CC:15, Ha-PO:182, Mc-WS:63,
Wi-LT:86
Gentle Alice Brown. W. Gilbert.
Co-FB:147
He Didn't Oughter. A. Herbert.
Co-FB:314
Love Poem. J. Nims. Mc-WS:56,
Pe-OA:233
A Love Story. O. Herford.
Co-PM:103
Mary's Eyes Are Blue as Azure.
S. Silverstein. Co-BL:61
The Talented Man. W. Praed.
Co-FB:403
HUMOR - LOVE-PARTING
Finis? M. Lewis. Un-MW:106
O! Susanna. S. Foster. Er-FA:431
HUMOR - LOVE-PRAISE
Lying. T. Moore. Co-FB:500,
Co-PI:147
The Merry Pieman's Song.
J. Bennett. Lo-LL:5
The Peasant Declares His Love.
E. Roumer. Lo-TY:90
Portrait of a Lady.
W. Williams. Kh-VA:41
Potpourri from a Surrey Garden.
J. Betjeman. Co-FB:326,
En-PC:81
Vista. A. Kreymborg. Co-BL:60,
Sm-MK:139
HUMOR - LOVE-PROMISES
As I Walked Out One Evening.
W. Auden. Br-TC:21, Ha-PO:189,
Un-MB:464, Wi-LT:465
HUMOR - LOVE-PROOF
Whittingham Fair. Gr-GB:139
HUMOR - LOVE-PURSUIT
The Bigger-Wiggers. P. Ilott.
Ir-BB:68
Blackbirds and Thrushes. Gr-GB:116
The Dong with the Luminous Nose.
E. Lear. Co-PM:115, Ga-FB:325,
Gr-CT:24, Ho-WR:228, Rv-CB:813
Hares on the Mountain. Rv-CB:430
On the Beach. C. Calverley.
Co-FB:67
HUMOR - LOVE, REJECTED
Antonio. L. Richards. Ar-TP3:134,
Au-SP:246, Co-HP:108, La-PV:27,
Pe-FB:93
The Courtship of Yonghy-Bonghy-Bo.
E. Lear. Ho-WR:50,
Na-EO:171, Pa-OM:59, Un-GT:213
The Despairing Lover. W. Walsh.
Co-BL:134, Hi-WP II:113,
No-CL:187, Sm-LG:355

An Expostulation. I. Bickerstaff.
Co-BL:137, Co-FB:326, Co-PI:10,
Un-GF:20
Faithless Nelly Gray. T. Hood.
Br-SM:33, Co-HP:78, Hi-WP I:100
The Jilted Nymph. T. Campbell.
Co-BL:95
Little Jenny Wren. Wr-RM:71
My Last Illusion. Dum-Dum.
Co-FB:318
The One Answer. La-PV:209,
Un-GT:169, Un-MW:33
One Day while I Was Walking.
Bu-DY:63
Polly Perkins. Co-BL:163
She Hugged Me and Kissed Me.
Ra-BP:16
To a Lost Sweetheart. D. Marquis.
Co-FB:374
Whether or Not. D. Lawrence.
Un-MB:291
HUMOR - LOVE-RENUNCIATION
See Em-AF:183-195
HUMOR - LOVE-RIVALRY
The Chinese Bumboatman. Co-SS:113
HUMOR - LOVE-TRAGEDY
Hero and Leander. J. Newman.
Co-FB:140
Lady Jane. A. Quiller-Couch.
Co-FB:443
Pyramus and Thisbe. J. Saxe.
Pa-OM:67
Sorrows of Werther. W. Thackeray.
Br-SM:32, Co-FB:344,
Hi-WP II:11
The Thorn. W. Wordsworth. Na-EO:51
HUMOR - LOVE, UNREQUITED
The Fable of the Magnet and the
Churn. W. Gilbert. Fe-FP:351,
Hu-MP:444, Pa-OM:46, Sh-RP:122
Mia Carlotta. T. Daly.
Hi-WP I:103
My Pretty Pink. Ir-BB:243
Song of One Eleven Years in
Prison. G. Canning. Co-FB:429
Were You on the Mountain?
Co-PU:76
HUMOR - LOVERS
The Thieves. R. Graves. Wi-LT:377
HUMOR - LOYALTY
The Warrior's Lament. O. Seaman.
Co-FB:50
HUMOR - LYNCHINGS
Epitaph for a Horse Thief.
Gr-EC:150
The Salvation of Texas Peters.
J. Foley. Br-SM:28
HUMOR - LYNXES
The Lesser Lynx. E. Rieu. Co-FB:13
HUMOR - MACHINERY
Epitaph. L. Mellichamp. Br-SM:21

HUMOR - MACHINERY — cont'd.
  Eve to Her Daughters. J. Wright.
    To-MP:173
  Nightmare Number Three.
    S. Benét. Mc-WS:24, Un-MA:501
  The Perforated Spirit. M. Bishop.
    Co-FB:459, Pe-M:128
  The Rhyme of the Rain Machine.
    F. Clarke. Co-BN:173
HUMOR - MACLEISH, ARCHIBALD
  Archibald MacLeish Suspends the
    Five Little Pigs.
    L. Untermeyer. Un-MA:310
HUMOR - MADNESS
  Mad as Mist and Snow. W. Yeats.
    Gr-CT:395
  The Mad Family. Br-FF:(22),
    Mo-MGT:64
  The Mad Man. Ir-BB:145,
    Mo-MGT:98, Sm-MK:193
  There Was a Man and He Was Mad.
    Gr-GB:93
HUMOR - MAGIC
  The Goose. A. Tennyson. Gr-EC:154
  Queer Things. J. Reeves. Co-PM:142
HUMOR - MAGNETS
  The Fable of the Magnet and the
    Churn. W. Gilbert. Fe-FP:351,
    Hu-MP:444, Pa-OM:46, Sh-RP:122
HUMOR - MAN
  Bedtime Story. G. Macbeth.
    Co-PT:37
  A Fish Answers. L. Hunt.
    Al-VBP:713, Co-FB:20, Rd-OA:156
  I Marvel at the Ways of God.
    E. White. Mc-WS:72
  Life Cycle of Common Man.
    H. Nemerov. To-MP:121
  Pity This Busy Monster, Manunkind.
    E. Cummings. Ho-LP:83, Mo-BG:197,
    Pe-SS:105, Sh-AP:192, Wi-LT:367
HUMOR - MAN, ISLE OF
  Courtship. L. Carroll. Br-LL:122,
    Un-GT:242
HUMOR - MAN AND WOMAN
  Breathes There a Man.
    S. Hoffenstein. Co-FB:312
HUMOR - MANNERS AND CUSTOMS
  Étude Géographique. S. King.
    Br-AF:154, Fi-BG:86
  Good-Night to the Season.
    W. Praed. Ox-BN:441
  Goodbye Now, or Pardon My Gauntlet.
    O. Nash. Co-FB:481
  Mad Dogs and Englishmen.
    N. Coward. Co-FB:204
  A Song of Reform.
    Yüan Shui-p'ai. Hs-TC:405
  There Was an Old Lady of Chertsey.
    E. Lear. Bl-OB:14, Br-LL:67,
    Sh-RP:149

A Thousand Hairy Savages.
    S. Milligan. Co-OW:20,
    Co-PU:134
HUMOR - MARATHON, BATTLE, 490 B.C.
  The Persian Version. R. Graves.
    Cr-WS:31, Wi-LT:379
HUMOR - MARCHING
  The Duke. De-TT:46, Un-GF:13
  In the Parade. L. Blair. Ja-HH:29
  Marching Song. R. Stevenson.
    Ar-TP3:112, Fe-FP:106
  O, the Grand Old Duke of York.
    Ar-TP3:100, Au-SP:4, Cl-DT:14,
    Gr-GB:197, Li-LB:51, Mo-MGT:25,
    Mo-NR:118, Wi-MG:76
HUMOR - MARRIAGE
  The Brewer's Man. L. Strong.
    Co-EL:14, Co-FB:313
  Capsule Conclusions, IV. Un-MW:65
  Dialogue Between a Newly Married
    Couple. Tr-US II:156
  Dust to Dust. T. Hood. Br-SM:156,
    Co-FB:317, Un-GT:236
  Epigram. J. Swift. Hi-WP II:123
  Eppie Morrie. Ox-BB:251
  Equals. L. Untermeyer. Un-MW:58
  Family Life. A. Laing. Co-FB:473
  Get Up and Bar the Door.
    Al-VBP:56, Ar-TP3:17, Bl-OB:19,
    Fo-OG:49, Ha-PO:75, La-PV:214,
    Pa-OM:94, Un-GT:123
  He Didn't Oughter. A. Herbert.
    Co-FB:314
  Jacky Jingle. Ir-BB:141,
    Mo-MGT:124
  Jemmy Dawson. Ir-BB:202,
    Mo-MGT:84
  A Lady There Was of Antigua.
    C. Monkhouse. Br-LL:120
  The Legend of the First Cam-u-el.
    A. Guiterman. Co-HP:68
  Little Tommy Tucker. Bo-FP:60,
    Li-LB:27, Mo-CC:(48), Mo-MGT:72,
    Mo-NR:51, Wi-MG:69, Wr-RM:110
  Love under the Republicans (or
    Democrats). O. Nash. Mc-WS:62
  The Lucky Marriage. T. Blackburn.
    Pa-GTB:546
  Marriage. G. Corso. Wi-LT:673
  A Marriage. R. Creeley. Wi-LT:679
  The Marriage of the Frog and the
    Mouse. Rd-OA:64
  Mary Ann. J. Tabrar. Co-BL:100,
    Co-PU:39
  Mehitabel Tries Marriage.
    D. Marquis. Hi-WP II:118
  Mrs. Judge Jenkins. B. Harte.
    Co-FB:238
  The Modest Couple. W. Gilbert.
    Co-PT:186
  On Marriage. T. Flatman.
    Co-EL:57, Co-FB:405

The Owl and the Pussy-Cat.
E. Lear. Ar-TP3:120, Au-SP:266,
Bl-OB:117, Bo-FP:25, Bo-GJ:14,
Cl-DT:30, Co-IW:3, Er-FA:495,
Fe-FP:354, Fe-PL:237, Fr-WO:39,
Ha-PO:239, Hi-WP I:94,Hu-MP:450,
Ir-BB:250, Ke-TP:38, La-PV:204,
Mc-PR:40, Pa-GTB:357, Pe-FB:96,
Rv-CB:812, Sm-LG:89, Sm-MK:200,
St-FS:108, Un-GB:28, Un-GT:224
Peter, Peter, Pumpkin-Eater.
An-IP:23, Au-SP:3, Bo-FP:104,
Er-FA:505, Ir-BB:196, Li-LB:61,
Mo-CC:(7), Mo-MGT:106,
Wi-MG:77, Wr-RM:98
Plan. Rod McKuen. Pe-M:3
A Reasonable Affliction. M. Prior.
Br-SM:127, Un-MW:51
A Sad Story. Mo-MGT:93
Save the Tiger! A. Herbert.
Co-HP:72
A Seaside Romance. D. Marquis.
Co-HP:93
Slave Marriage Ceremony Supplement.
Ra-BP:16
When I Was a Bachelor.
Gr-GB:147, Ir-BB:149, Li-LB:62,
Mo-NR:66, Wr-RM:118
When You Get Married. Su-FVI:78
Within This Grave Do Lie.
Br-SM:158
You'd Say It Was a Funeral.
J. Reeves. Br-SM:119
Young Bekie. Ma-BB:13, Ox-BB:103
See also Em-AF:196-227
HUMOR - MARRIAGE PROPOSALS
Antonio. L. Richards. Ar-TP3:134,
Au-SP:246, Co-HP:108, La-PV:27,
Pe-FB:93
The Lady's Song in Leap Year.
Gr-GB:107
A Leap-Year Episode. E. Field.
Co-BL:120
Li'l Liza Jane. Bu-DY:55
My Rules. S. Silverstein.
Co-PU:25
Old Wang Pops the Question.
Yüan Shui-p'ai. Hs-TC:403
Quoth John to Joan. De-CH:332
Samuel Sewall. A. Hecht.
Br-TC:181, Pe-OA:262, Wi-LT:730
Song from a Story. Tr-US I:30
HUMOR - MARSUPIALS
Are You a Marsupial? J. Becker.
Co-BBW:193, Sh-RP:145
HUMOR - MARY, QUEEN OF SCOTS
The Crossing of Mary of Scotland.
W. Smith. Co-OH:75
HUMOR - MASEFIELD, JOHN
John Masefield Relates the Story
of Tom, Tom, the Piper's Son.
L. Untermeyer. Un-MA:308

HUMOR - MASSENET, JULES ÉMILE
FRÉDÉRIC
Massenet. A. Butts. Co-FB:128
HUMOR - MATCHES
Harriet and the Matches.
H. Hoffmann. Ir-BB:157
A Little Boy Down in Natchez.
Br-LL:78
The Story of Pauline and the
Matches. H. Hoffman. Un-GF:56
HUMOR - MATHEMATICS
Hall and Knight. E. Rieu.
Co-HP:108
Hudibras. S. Butler. Pl-IO:86
HUMOR - MEALS
La Carte. J. Richardson.
Co-EL:55
Henry King. H. Belloc.
Br-SM:118, Co-BB:48, Un-GF:60
Jonathan Bing's Tea. B. Brown.
Mc-WK:117
HUMOR - MEASLES
Measles in the Ark.
S. Coolidge. Ox-BC:282
Wishing. G. MacPherson. Ja-PC:24
HUMOR - MEDICINE
The Crossing of Mary of Scotland.
W. Smith. Co-OH:75
Here Lies Me and My Three Daughters.
Un-GT:239
A Medical Student Named Elias.
Br-LL:103
What Is the Difference.
Re-RR:76
HUMOR - MEETINGS (ENCOUNTERS)
A Reunion in Kensington.
S. Cohen. Sm-MK:204
HUMOR - MELANCHOLY
M Is for Mournful Miss Molly.
I. Bellows. Br-LL:62
Melancholetta. L. Carroll.
Co-FB:182
HUMOR - MEMORIES
Reminiscence. W. Irwin. Co-FB:60
HUMOR - MEN
July 31. N. Jordan. Ad-PB:323
Man Is for the Woman Made.
P. Motteaux. Un-MW:45
A Thought. J. Stephen. Co-FB:391
HUMOR - MENTALLY HANDICAPPED
Lucy Lake. N. MacIntosh.
Li-SR:108
HUMOR - MERCHANTS
The Merchants of London.
Gr-GB:170, Ir-BB:37, Wr-RM:56
HUMOR - MERMAIDS AND MERMEN
Ballad of the Mermaid. C. Leland.
Co-FB:217
Cape Horn Gospel. J. Masefield.
Co-SS:171, Ha-PO:258

HUMOR — MERMAIDS AND
  MERMEN — cont'd.
  Little John Bottlejohn. L. Richards.
    Co-PM:148, La-PV:212, Lo-LL:61,
    Sh-RP:252
HUMOR — METHUSELAH
  Song of a Thousand Years.
    D. Marquis. Hi-WP I:98
HUMOR — MEXICO
  A Hex on the Mexican X.
    D. McCord. Co-FB:210
HUMOR — MICE
  Advice. A. Resnikoff. Co-OH:84
  A Diner while Dining at Crewe.
    Br-LL:81, Ir-BB:220, Un-GF:44
  The Fearful Finale of the
    Irascible Mouse. G. Carryl.
    Co-HP:51, Gr-EC:18
  The Frog and the Mouse. Ho-WR:41
  He Ran up the Candlestick.
    Ir-BB:84
  It's Been a Bad Year for the
    Moles. D. McCord. Br-LL:131
  Lancaster County Tragedy.
    W. Kay. Br-SM:102
  The Light-House Keeper's White
    Mouse. J. Ciardi. La-PV:199
  Malice at Buckingham Palace.
    S. Mulligan. Co-OH:24
  The Mice of Spain. E. Coatsworth.
    Lo-LL:3
  A Mouse in Her Room Woke Miss
    Dowd. Br-LL:21
  A Mouse Is like Hay. Rs-PF:23
  The Mouse Who Lived on a Hill.
    Bu-DY:61
  The Old Wife and the Ghost.
    J. Reeves. Br-SM:16,
    Co-PM:140, Gr-EC:152, La-PV:210,
    Pa-RE:70
  The Prince. W. de la Mare.
    Lo-LL:44
  The Tailor and the Mouse.
    Ir-BB:176
  Tell Me, Tell Me. M. Moore.
    Wi-LT:276
  Three French Mice. Ir-BB:236
  The Two Mice. J. Reeves.
    Ir-BB:157
  Well I Never! Ir-BB:84
HUMOR — MICROBES
  The Microbes. Co-HP:24
  Some Little Bug. R. Atwell.
    Br-SM:83, Fe-PL:230
HUMOR — MIDDLE AGE
  Peekaboo, I Almost See You.
    O. Nash. Fe-PL:260
HUMOR — MILITARY LIFE
  Captain Jinks. Er-FA:404
  The Duke of Plaza-Toro. W. Gilbert.
    Co-FB:70, Co-HP:63, Fe-FP:349

General John. W. Gilbert.
    Co-HP:66, Un-GT:202
  Lessons of the War, II. Judging
    Distances. H. Reed. Pa-GTB:538
  Naming of Parts. H. Reed.
    Al-VBP:1243, Ba-PO:189, Bo-GJ:189,
    Cr-WS:62, Hi-WP II:148, Pe-SS:134,
    To-MP:40, Un-MB:507, Wi-LT:796
  O, the Grand Duke of York.
    Ar-TP3:100, Au-SP:4, Cl-DT:14,
    Gr-GB:197, Li-LB:51, Mo-MGT:25,
    Mo-NR:118, Wi-MG:76
  On a Monument in France Which Marks
    the Last Resting Place of an
    Army Mule. Br-SM:105
HUMOR — MILKMAIDS
  Squire and Milkmaid. Ox-BB:652
HUMOR — MILKMEN
  Flash: The Fireman's Story.
    W. Carleton. Se-PR:317
  Polly Perkins. Co-BL:163
HUMOR — MILL, JOHN STUART
  John Stuart Mill. E. Bentley.
    Co-FB:126
HUMOR — MILLAY, EDNA ST. VINCENT
  Edna St. Vincent Millay Exhorts
    Little Boy Blue.
    L. Untermeyer. Un-MA:310
HUMOR — MILLS
  Two Mills. Mo-MGT:211
HUMOR — MIRRORS
  Intimates. D. Lawrence. Co-PT:185
HUMOR — MISANTHROPY
  The Complete Misanthropist.
    M. Bishop. Co-FB:471
  The Wishes of an Elderly Man.
    W. Raleigh. Co-FB:473,
    Co-HP:105, Co-PU:125, Mc-WS:88,
    Sm-LG:392, Un-GT:14
HUMOR — MISERS
  Aunt Maud. Br-SM:128, Co-HP:23
  Pa Followed the Pair to Pawtucket.
    Chicago Tribune. Br-LL:120
  There Was an Old Man of Nantucket.
    Princeton Tiger. Br-LL:120,
    Ke-TF:289
HUMOR — MISFORTUNE
  All's Well That Ends Well.
    Er-FA:211
  Dow's Flat. B. Harte. Co-PT:86
  Phyllis, or The Progress of Love.
    J. Swift. No-CL:226
  Simon Soggs' Thanksgiving.
    W. Croffut. Co-PT:120
  There Was a Young Lady of Norway.
    E. Lear. Ar-TP3:133,
    Br-LL:138, Fe-FP:360
  Trouble. D. Keppel. Er-FA:206,
    Fe-PL:229
HUMOR — MISSIONARIES
  The Cassowary. Co-OT:45
  Missionary. D. Thomas. To-MP:199

HUMOR – MISTAKEN IDENTITY
The Sweet Tooth. K. Pyle.
Ag-HE:64, Co-BB:57
HUMOR – MITTENS
The Modern Hiawatha. G. Strong.
Co-FB:415, Co-HP:115, Er-FA:206,
Fe-FP:337, Gr-EC:192, Li-SR:61
HUMOR – MOLES (ANIMALS)
It's Been a Bad Year for the Moles.
D. McCord. Br-LL:131
HUMOR – MOLIÈRE (PSEUD. OF
JEAN BAPTISTE POQUELIN)
Shake, Mulleary, and Go-ethe.
H. Bunner. Co-FB:350
HUMOR – MONEY
As I Sat at the Cafe. A. Clough.
Co-FB:496, Hi-WP I:117
I Love Sixpence. Gr-EC:226,
Ir-BB:121, Li-LB:122, Mo-NR:62,
On-TW:26, Wr-RM:77
Money. R. Armour. Er-FA:209,
Mc-WK:91
Poor Henry. L. Blair. Ja-PC:31
Squabbles. Mo-MGT:210, Wr-RM:98
Sum Fun. M. Fishback. Ke-TF:284
There Was an Old Man of Nantucket.
Br-LL:120, Ke-TF:289
HUMOR – MONKEYS
Lines on Hearing the Organ.
C. Calverley. Co-FB:279
Monkey. J. Miles. Wi-LT:772
Monkey Was a-Settin' on a Railroad
Track. Un-GT:17
The Monkeys and the Crocodile.
L. Richards. Ar-TP3:126,
Au-SP:272, Br-SM:89, Fe-FP:175,
Ir-BB:154, La-PP:54, Li-LB:98
The Ship of Rio. W. de la Mare.
Ar-TP3:126, Ir-BB:242, La-PP:52,
La-PV:203, Lo-LL:102
So Many Monkeys. M. Edey and
D. Grider. Ar-TP3:126,
Au-SP:232
HUMOR – MONKS
The Crafty Miss of London.
Ox-BB:646
The Ghosts. T. Peacock.
Al-VBP:719, Sm-MK:45
Johan the Monk. Li-TU:119
Song. T. Peacock. Al-VBP:715
HUMOR – MOON
Green Cheese. Ir-BB:29
The Man in the Moon. Mother Goose.
Au-SP:219, Ir-BB:155, Ja-PC:55
The Man in the Moon. J. Riley.
Co-HP:109
The Man in the Moon. Ir-BB:56
Poetic Thought. Co-FB:305
Target. R. Lister. Pe-SS:100
There Is an Inn, a Merry Old Inn.
J. Tolkien. Lo-LL:98

There Once Was a Knowing Raccoon.
M. Dodge. Br-LL:34
There Once Was a Man in the Moon.
D. McCord. Br-LL:131
HUMOR – MOORE, THOMAS
On Thomas Moore's Poems.
Co-FB:337
A Reply to Lines by Thomas Moore.
W. Landor. Gr-CT:470
HUMOR – MOOSE
When a Goose Meets a Moose.
Z. Gay. Ar-TP3:127
HUMOR – MORNING
Morning. C. Calverley. Co-FB:432
HUMOR – MOTHERS
There Was an Old Woman Who Lived
in a Shoe. An-IP:(27), De-PO:6,
Er-FA:505, Fr-WO:20, Ir-BB:197,
Li-LB:36, Mo-CC:(6), Mo-MGT:161,
Mo-NR:42, Wi-MG:25, Wr-RM:116
When It Comes to Bugs. A. Fisher.
Ja-PC:51
HUMOR – MOTHERS-IN-LAW
His Mother-in-Law. W. Parke.
Co-FB:392, Co-HP:102
HUMOR – MOTHS
The Hungry Moths. R. McCuaig.
Co-PU:20
HUMOR – MOTTOES
Motto. L. Hughes. Ad-PB:75,
Co-PU:126, Hu-PN:202, Jo-SA:118
well boss mehitabel the cat.
D. Marquis. Ke-TF:266
HUMOR – MOUNTAINS
After Oliver. O. Herford.
Co-HP:22
HUMOR – MOUTHS
The Sad Story of a Little Boy
That Cried. Co-BB:36, Ir-BB:97
Woman. E. Loftin. Ad-PB:514
HUMOR – MOVING PICTURES
Horror Movie. H. Moss. Pe-M:6
The Winning of the TV West.
J. Alexander. Bo-HF:97,
Br-AF:153, Mc-WK:172
HUMOR – MULES
Fooba Wooba John. Co-OW:64
Had a Little Mule. Ju-CP:2
I Had a Little Dog, His Name
Was Ball. Ir-BB:180
The Mule. Fi-BG:99
The Mule in the Mines.
Gr-CT:14, Gr-GB:222
Mules. C. Smith. Co-RM:216
My Mammy Was a Wall-Eyed Goat.
Gr-CT:14
On a Monument in France Which Marks
the Last Resting Place of an Army
Mule. Br-SM:105
Two Legs Behind and Two Before.
Co-OH:45
Whoa, Mule, Whoa. Ju-CP:32

HUMOR - MURDER
  Brave Rover. M. Beerbohm.
    Rd-OA:112
  The Dorking Thigh. W. Plomer.
    Hi-WP II:116
  He Threw Her. Rs-PF:14
  Jack the Ripper. A. Laing.
    Co-FB:130
  Lizzie Borden. Br-SM:112,
    Er-FA:219
  Printer's Error. P. Wodehouse.
    Co-FB:334
  The Salvation of Texas Peters.
    J. Foley. Br-SM:28
  Three More Clerihews. Un-GF:49
  Two Brothers There Were of
    Sioux City. Br-LL:65
  Young Sammy Watkins. Co-BB:94,
    Co-HP:28
HUMOR - MUSES
  My Muse. S. Smith. Pl-ML:17
  New Chitons for Old Gods.
    D. McCord. Pl-US:142
HUMOR - MUSIC AND MUSICIANS
  "And Now. . . ." J. Boothroyd.
    Co-FB:275
  Calypsomania. A. Brode. Co-FB:276
  The Cat Sat Asleep. De-TT:29
  Eutychides. Lucilius. Pl-US:13
  The Harmonious Heedlessness of
    Little Boy Blue. G. Carryl.
    Hu-MP:443
  I Have Heard. Co-FB:298
  J. Is for Jazz-Man. E. Farjeon.
    Su-FVI:14
  King Juke. K. Fearing.
    Mo-BG:32, Ni-JP:92
  Limericks. Br-LL:109, Co-HP:29
  Limericks since Lear. Un-GT:242
  O Moon, Why Must You. Koyo.
    Be-CS:41
  Piano Practice. I. Serraillier.
    Co-BB:110
  The Post Captain. C. Carryl.
    Co-HP:49, Co-SS:20
  Serenade. Ca-MU:9
  There Was a Composer Named Bong.
    Br-LL:107
  There Was a Young Fellow Named
    Green. Un-GF:45
  There Was an Old Lady of Steen.
    Br-LL:138
  "There's a Tune," Said a Sly
    Bengalese. J. Bennett.
    Br-LL:13
  A Tiger's Tale. J. Bennett.
    Co-HP:33
HUMOR - MUSICAL COMEDIES
  The Belle of the Balkans.
    N. Levy. Co-FB:265
HUMOR - MUSK OXEN
  The Ovibos. R. Hale. Co-FB:24

HUMOR - MYSTERY
  The Dorking Thigh. W. Plomer.
    Hi-WP II:116
  The Little Man. H. Mearns.
    Un-GF:69
  An Old Rat's Tale. Bl-OB:38,
    Ch-B:96, Gr-EC:219, Sm-MK:208
  The Twelve-Elf. C. Morgenstern.
    Un-GF:68
  Welsh Incident. R. Graves.
    Hi-WP II:114
HUMOR - MYTHICAL ANIMALS
  AND BIRDS
  The Chickamungus. J. Reeves.
    Un-GT:222
  The Doze. J. Reeves. Co-BBW:286,
    Un-GT:223
  The Flying Outlaw. C. Fletcher.
    Fi-BG:94
  The Sea Serpant. W. Irwin.
    Co-BBW:288, Co-FB:18, Co-OH:22
  The Skippery Boo. E. Newton.
    Un-GT:221
  The Wendigo. O. Nash. Gr-EC:23,
    Ir-BB:80
HUMOR - NAMES
  By What Sweet Name. S. Coleridge.
    Un-MW:52
  A Certain Young Fellow Named
    Beebee. Br-LL:122
  A Double Limerick.
    W. de la Mare. Br-LL:7
  The Frog. H. Belloc.
    Bo-GJ:10, Co-FB:33, Co-HP:32,
    Fe-FP:344, Ga-FB:333, Hu-MP:456,
    Ir-BB:77, It-HB:19, Li-LC:31,
    Lo-LL:20, Ox-BC:311, Sh-RP:148
  Geography: A Song. H. Moss.
    Ad-CI:26
  The Gnu. H. Belloc. Co-FB:34,
    Co-HP:31, Co-PU:96
  Godfrey Gordon Gustavus Gore.
    W. Rands. Ar-TP3:136, Co-BB:111,
    Co-OT:42, Fe-FP:308, Hu-MP:451,
    Ir-BB:109, Pe-FB:92
  The Ichthyosaurus. I. Bellows.
    Ch-B:48, Co-OT:27
  If I Had a Brontosaurus.
    S. Silverstein. Co-OT:44
  John Bun. Br-SM:55, Un-GT:239
  Miss James. A. Milne. Ar-TP3:11,
    Co-PU:113, Hu-MP:136
  Naming the Baby. M. Richstone.
    Br-BC:37
  Not Ragged-and-Tough. Gr-CT:4
  Ozymandias Revisited. M. Bishop.
    Co-HP:34, Li-SR:83
  Quartet. Gr-EC:199, Mo-NR:49,
    Wr-RM:28
  The Revolving Door. N. Levy.
    Br-SM:45, Co-HP:91

A Seaside Romance.   D. Marquis.
   Co-HP:93
Sing a Song of the Cities.
   M. Bishop.   Ad-CI:79
A Son Just Born.   M. Miller.
   Ar-TP3:70
Sweet Maiden of Passamaquoddy.
   J. De Mille.   Do-WH:31
There Was a Man, and His Name
   Was Dob.   De-CH:537, Gr-EC:79,
   Ir-BB:173
Tie Your Tongue, Sir?   R. Smith.
   Ad-CI:16, Gr-EC:184
Timmy Pimmy.   Gr-EC:281
To His Godson, Gerald C. A.
   Jackson.   A. Housman.   Co-PU:113
What Is It That Surely.   Re-RR:68
What's Your Name?   Un-GT:18
The Younger Van Eyck.
   E. Bentley.   Co-FB:129
Your Name's Not Jule.   Rs-PF:86
HUMOR - NAVAL BATTLES
The Ballad of the Billycock.
   A. Deane.   Co-SS:28
HUMOR - NEATNESS
The Cares of a Caretaker.
   W. Irwin.   Co-OW:14
HUMOR - NECKS
Necks.   R. Bennett.   Sh-RP:132
HUMOR - NEEDLES AND PINS
Limericks.   Ke-TF:288
HUMOR - NEEDLEWORK
Oh, the Funniest Thing.   Na-EO:68
We're Not What We Seam.   Rs-PF:58
HUMOR - NEGROES
Crispus Attucks McCoy.
   S. Brown.   Ra-BP:115
A Dance for Militant Dilettantes.
   A. Young.   Ad-PB:362
Raise a "Rucus" To-Night.
   Ra-BP:10
HUMOR - NEIGHBORS
All These Hurt.   Vainateya.
   Al-PI:58
Portrait by a Neighbor. E. Millay.
   Ar-TP3:8, Fe-FP:312, Ha-LO:45,
   Ho-TH:22, Hu-MP:139, Mo-BG:47,
   Ne-AM:36, Pe-FB:26, Th-AS:188,
   Tu-WW:40
HUMOR - NETHERLANDS
Such Is Holland.
   P. de Genestet.   Ma-FW:42
HUMOR - NEW HAMPSHIRE
The Customs of the Country.
   P. McGinley.   Ke-TF:343
HUMOR - NEW YORK, N.Y.
I'd Rather Listen.
   S. Hoffenstein.   Co-FB:209
The Talk of the Town.   E. Fisher.
   Co-FB:361
HUMOR - NEWS
Cow.   W. Smith.   Co-OW:58

News Report.   D. Ignatov.
   Br-TC:214
HUMOR - NEWSBOYS
When I Brought the News.
   J. Donleavy.   Co-PT:115
HUMOR - NEWSPAPERS
Political Reflection.
   O. Nash.   Ke-TF:292
Synchronized. L. Rubin. De-FS:165
HUMOR - NIGHT
A Nocturnal Sketch.   T. Hood.
   Co-FB:426
HUMOR - NILE RIVER
What Are the Little Rivers.
   Rs-PF:70
HUMOR - NOAH
The Dog's Cold Nose.
   A. Guiterman.   Co-BBW:107,
   Gr-EC:84, Ha-PO:142
A Long Time Ago.   Co-SS:117
Measles in the Ark.   S. Coolidge.
   Ox-BC:282
Noah.   Bu-DY:64
Noah an' Jonah an' Cap'n John
   Smith.   D. Marquis.   Co-SS:189,
   Fe-PL:198, Sm-LG:195
Wine and Water. G. Chesterton.
   Al-VBP:1121, Co-FB:83, Un-MB:209
HUMOR - NOISE
Cats Are Annoyed by Noise.
   Re-RR:122
Dan Dunder.   J. Ciardi. Co-BB:34
My Stomach Growls.
   R. Margolis.   Su-FVI:28
On the Ning Nang Nong. S. Milligan.
   Co-OW:59, St-FS:55
There Was a Young Lady of Russia.
   E. Lear.   Br-LL:69
HUMOR - NORWAY
Neal, Just Back from Norway.
   Rs-PF:16
HUMOR - NOSES
The Dog's Cold Nose.
   A. Guiterman.   Co-BBW:107,
   Gr-EC:84, Ha-PO:142
The Dong with the Luminous Nose.
   E. Lear.   Co-PM:115, Ga-FB:325,
   Gr-CT:24, Ho-WR:228, Rv-CB:813
The "Dorset Nose."   C. Sansom.
   To-MP:128
Nose, Nose, Jolly Red Nose.
   F. Beaumont and J. Fletcher.
   Cl-FC:96, Ir-BB:192, Mo-MGT:63,
   Sm-LG:120
The Song of Quoodle. G. Chesterton.
   Bo-GJ:107, Hi-WP I:10
There Was a Young Lady of Kent.
   Br-LL:41, Ke-TF:287
There Was a Young Lady Whose
   Nose.   E. Lear.   Br-LL:42,
   Fe-FP:340, Ir-BB:218, Sh-RP:127

HUMOR - NOSES — cont'd.
There Was an Old Man in a Barge.
E. Lear.   Br-LL:41, Hu-MP:461
There Was an Old Man of West
Dumpet.   E. Lear.   Br-LL:42
There Was an Old Man, on Whose
Nose.   E. Lear.   Au-SP:243
There Was an Old Man with a Nose.
E. Lear.   Br-LL:42
Tom Tickleby and His Nose.
L. Richards.   Co-OW:52
HUMOR - NUDISM
Limerick.   O. Nash.   Hi-WP I:12
HUMOR - NUMBERS
Twos.   J. Drinkwater.   Ja-PC:58
HUMOR - OBEDIENCE
Moral Song. J. Farrar. Sh-RP:3
There Was a Young Fellow of Ealing.
Br-LL:61
What the Lord High Chamberlain
Said.   V. Cloud.   Co-BB:74
HUMOR - OBSTINACY
Eppie Morris.   Ox-BB:251
Get Up and Bar the Door.
Al-VBP:56, Ar-TP3:17, Bl-OB:19,
Fo-OG:49, Ha-PO:75, La-PV:214,
Pa-OM:94, Un-GT:123
Johnnie Blunt.   Ox-BB:630
On Stubborn Michael Shay.
Un-GT:239
The Story of the Old Woman and
Her Pig.   Mo-MGT:68
HUMOR - OCCUPATIONS
An Impetuous Resolve.   J. Riley.
Br-BC:114, Ir-BB:43
John Plans.   D. Pierce.
Br-BC:111
When I Grow Up.   W. Wise.
Br-BC:113
HUMOR - OCEANS
The Uses of Ocean.   O. Seaman.
Co-FB:382, Co-HP:110, Co-SS:86
Why Does the Ocean.   Re-RR:102
HUMOR - OCELOTS
There Once Was a Finicky Ocelot.
E. Merriam.   Br-LL:33
HUMOR - OCTOPUSES
The Octopus.   O. Nash.   Ar-TP3:125,
Au-SP:78, Co-HP:99, Hi-WP II:14,
Ir-BB:78, Ja-PC:11, Mc-WS:171
The Octopussycat.   K. Cox.
Ar-TP3:125, Au-SP:78, Fe-FP:340
Ollie, What's an Octopus?
Rs-PF:96
Parkinson and the Octopus.
N. Farber.   De-FS:91
HUMOR - ODORS
"Dear Me!"   E. Bentley.   Co-FB:126
The Song of Quoodle.
G. Chesterton.   Bo-GJ:107,
Hi-WP I:10

The Tale of the Skunk and Poor Jez.
J. Becker.   Sh-RP:133
There Was an Old Man Who Said,
"Please."   E. Knox.   Br-LL:86
HUMOR - OLD AGE
The Aged Aged Man.   L. Carroll.
Ox-BC:247
The Elderly Gentleman. G. Canning.
Gr-EC:148
Father William.   L. Carroll.
Ar-TP3:139, Bo-GJ:154, Br-BC:135,
Co-FB:43, Co-HP:39, Fe-FP:350,
Fe-PL:240, Fr-WO:57, Ke-TF:273,
La-PP:71, La-PV:28, Li-SR:91,
Lo-LL:95, Ma-YA:214, Mc-WK:217,
Ox-BC:239, Sh-RP:120, Sp-OG:233,
Un-GF:24, Un-GT:206
St. Patrick's Day Jig.   J. Lee.
Ja-HH:17
Song of a Thousand Years.
D. Marquis.   Hi-WP I:98
HUMOR - ONIONS
I'm Not So Strong.   Rs-PF:15
The Man in the Onion Bed.
J. Ciardi.   Co-OW:23
The Onion.   C. Ward.   Bo-FP:158
HUMOR - OPERAS
Carmen.   N. Levy.   Co-FB:283
Fragment of an English Opera.
A. Housman.   Li-TU:22
A Musical Lady from Ga.   Br-LL:108
Operatic Note.   M. Cane.   Pl-US:61
HUMOR - OPINIONS
The Blind Men and the Elephant.
J. Saxe.   Bo-HF:73, Gr-EC:150,
Ha-PO:302, Pa-OM:330, Un-GT:200
HUMOR - OPTIMISTS AND OPTIMISM
O Is an Optimist Glad. O. Herford.
Br-LL:71
An Ode.   J. Updike.   Co-FB:363
The Optimist.   Co-PU:37
The Optimist.   Un-GT:237
Philosophy.   P. Dunbar.   Ra-BP:55
Since My House Burned Down.
Masahide.   Be-CS:43
The Sniffle.   O. Nash.   Hi-WP II:15,
Mc-WS:174, Sh-RP:121
HUMOR - ORGAN GRINDERS
Lines on Hearing the Organ.
C. Calverley.   Co-FB:279
HUMOR - ORGANS AND ORGANISTS
The New Church Organ.
W. Carleton.   Fe-PL:233
HUMOR - OUTLAWS
Bandit. A. Klein.   Do-WH:28
The Gallant Highwayman.
J. De Mille.   Do-WH:28
HUMOR - OWLS
A Howl about an Owl. L. Richards.
Ir-BB:152

The Owl-Critic.   J. Fields.
 Gr-EC:169, Ha-PO:208, Na-EO:82,
 Un-GT:200
There Was an Old Man of Dumbree.
 E. Lear.   Br-LL:6, Un-GT:240
There Was an Old Person of Crowle.
 E. Lear.   Br-LL:7
Three Wonderful Old Women.
 Ox-BC:151
HUMOR - OYSTERS
 The Oyster.   A. Herbert.   Co-BBW:63
 An Oyster from Kalamazoo.   Br-LL:36
 There's a Lady in Kalamazoo.
  W. Bellamy.   Br-LL:86
 The Walrus and the Carpenter.
  L. Carroll.   Au-SP:275,
  Bl-OB:125, Co-FB:134, Co-HP:40,
  De-TT:95, Er-FA:500, Fe-FP:328,
  Fr-WO:59, Ga-FB:318, Ir-BB:245,
  Ox-BC:242, Pe-FB:103, Sp-OG:242
 Your Case Is a Hard One.   Rs-PF:12
HUMOR - PAIN
 The Window Pain.   G. Burgess.
  Un-GF:64
HUMOR - PAINTINGS
 Limericks.   Ke-TF:290
HUMOR - PANDAS
 The Panda.   W. Smith.   Sh-RP:135
HUMOR - PANTHERS
 A Boston Boy Went Out to Yuma.
  D.D.   Br-SM:94
 Montezuma.   A. Alderson.   Gr-EC:34
 The Panther.   O. Nash.   Au-SP:239,
  Co-BBW:191, Co-OH:48, Fe-FP:331
HUMOR - PAOLO AND FRANCESCA
 Three More Clerihews.   Un-GF:49
HUMOR - PARENT AND CHILD
 The Bread-Knife Ballad.
  R. Service.   Co-OT:72
 Bringing Him Up.   Lord Dunsany.
  Co-BB:15, Co-PU:4
 A College Training.   J. Lincoln.
  Co-HP:92
 Daisy Deborah Delilah Dean.
  Co-OT:37
 A Father's Heart Is Touched.
  S. Hoffenstein.   Co-FB:104
 Fragment of an English Opera.
  A. Housman.   Li-TU:22
 Fragonard.   O. Nash.   Br-LL:60,
  Sh-RP:44
 The Happy Family.   J. Ciardi.
  Co-OW:34
 His Little Sub.   E. Bennett.
  Ke-TF:70
 Johnnie Crack and Flossie Snail.
  D. Thomas.   Bo-FP:24, Bo-GJ:150,
  Co-FB:373, Fe-FP:332, Ha-LO:21,
  La-PV:218, Li-LC:43, Pa-RE:62
 Our Polite Parents.   C. Wells.
  Co-BB:96

Pa Followed the Pair to Pawtucket.
 Chicago Tribune.   Br-LL:120
The Parent.   O. Nash.   Hi-WP I:12
A Parental Ode to My Son, Aged
 Three Years and Five Months.
 T. Hood.   Co-FB:103, Co-HP:77,
 Fe-FP:36, Fe-PL:139
Piano Practice.   I. Serraillier.
 Co-BB:110
Questions, Quistions, & Quoshtions.
 S. Milligan.   Co-OT:12
Random Ruthless Rhymes.   Un-GF:48
Social Studies.   M. Neville.
 Co-PU:65
Teme con Variazioni.   L. Carroll.
 Li-SR:65
There's Money in Mother and Father.
 M. Bishop.   Co-FB:352
Unselfishness.   H. Graham.   Co-OT:65
Willie Built a Guillotine.
 W. Engel.   Co-OH:43
HUMOR - PARIS, FR.
 Le Grand Luxe.   M. Bracker.
  Ke-TF:374
 Madame Dill.   Co-FB:295
 An Ode to Spring in the Metropolis.
  O. Seaman.   Co-FB:234
 Unromantic Song.   A. Brode.
  Co-FB:213
HUMOR - PARROTS
 The Educated Love Bird. P. Newell.
  Co-FB:216
 In London-Town Dame Trottypeg.
  D. Thompson.   Ir-BB:167
 The Old Woman of Gloucester.
  Wr-RM:112
 Parrot.   W. Smith.   Sh-RP:13
 A Sailor to His Parrot.
  W. Davies.   Al-VBP:1109
 Two and One Are a Problem.
  O. Nash.   Co-FB:17
HUMOR - PARSNIPS
 The Parsnip.   O. Nash. Hi-WP II:15
HUMOR - PARTIES (ENTERTAINMENT)
 Betty at the Party.   Br-BC:94
 The Feckless Dinner Party.
  W. de la Mare.   Co-PT:33
 The Light-House Keeper's White
  Mouse.   J. Ciardi. La-PV:199
 Literary Dinner.   V. Nabokov.
  Co-FB:331
 Little Clotilda.   Ir-BB:94
 Mae's Rent Party.   E. Wilson.
  Hu-PN:371
 Mr. Flood's Party.   E. Robinson.
  Al-VBP:1107, Er-FA:304, Ha-PO:64,
  Na-EO:66, Ni-JP:143, Pe-M:50,
  Pe-OA:5, Sh-AP:141, Sm-PT:140,
  Un-MA:121, Wi-LT:111
 The Party.   P. Dunbar.   Bo-AN:8

HUMOR - PARTIES (ENTERTAIN-
  MENT) — cont'd.
  A Party. L. Richards. Au-SP:119,
    Br-BC:93, Br-SS:49
  Party Knee. J. Updike. Co-FB:453
  Two Sad Tales. Co-OH:14
HUMOR - PARTRIDGES
  I Know a Partridge. E. Anthony.
    Ja-PC:17
HUMOR - PAST
  Miniver Cheevy, Jr. D. Parry.
    Li-SR:76
  You Were Wearing. K. Koch.
    Kh-VA:15, Mc-EA:140
HUMOR - PATIENCE
  Patience. H. Graham. Co-FB:56,
    Co-HP:67
HUMOR - PATRICK, SAINT
  St. Patrick Was a Gentleman.
    H. Bennett. Br-SS:135, Se-PR:66
HUMOR - PEACE
  Peace. Aristophanes. Ba-PO:14
HUMOR - PEANUTS
  A Peanut Sat. Co-OH:38, Ir-BB:154
  Peanuts. Co-OH:54, Er-FA:200,
    Un-GT:18
HUMOR - PELICANS
  The Pelican Chorus. E. Lear.
    Lo-LL:36
  Questions, Quistions, & Quoshtions.
    S. Milligan. Co-OT:12
  A Wonderful Bird Is the Pelican.
    D. Merritt. Br-LL:4
HUMOR - PENGUINS
  A Penguin. O. Herford. Co-FB:25
HUMOR - PEOPLE
  Lines on Lands. A. Aronov.
    Bo-RU:12
  The People of Blakeney. Gr-GB:175
  Question in a Field. L. Bogan.
    Ho-LP:65
  The Superstitious Ghost.
    A. Guiterman. Br-SM:8
HUMOR - PERFUMES
  Courtship. Br-LL:123, Un-GT:241
HUMOR - PERIODICALS
  The Sub-Average Time Reader.
    E. Wittenberg. Co-FB:360
  The Talk of the Town. E. Fisher.
    Co-FB:361
  Time like an Ever-Rolling Stream.
    P. Wodehouse. Co-FB:364
HUMOR - PERMANENCE
  Under a Hill. Li-LB:70, Mo-MGT:42
HUMOR - PERSEVERANCE
  The Grasshopper. D. McCord.
    Lo-LL:21
  Humpty Dumpty's Song. L. Carroll.
    Bl-OB:14, Co-FB:369, Gr-CT:29,
    Ir-BB:130, Pa-GTB:377, Pa-OM:11,
    Un-GT:209

The Shades of Night. A. Housman.
    Co-FB:241, Co-HP:79, Gr-CT:22,
    Li-SR:50
HUMOR - PERSONALITY
  The Disagreeable Man. W. Gilbert.
    Co-FB:66, Hu-MP:140
  O Why Was I Born with a Different
    Face? W. Blake. Co-PU:114
  The Perforated Spirit. M. Bishop.
    Co-FB:459, Pe-M:128
HUMOR - PESSIMISTS AND PESSIMISM
  For a Pessimist. C. Cullen.
    Br-SM:135
  Poems in Praise of Practically
    Nothing. S. Hoffenstein.
    Co-FB:492
  Simon Soggs' Thanksgiving.
    W. Croffut. Co-PT:120
  This Little Man Lived All Alone.
    Ir-BB:208
HUMOR - PETER I, CZAR OF RUSSIA
  (THE GREAT)
  Peterhof. E. Wilson. Bo-GJ:153
HUMOR - PETS
  Disaster. C. Calverly. Li-SR:64
  Jittery Jim. W. Smith. Co-BB:33
  Mother Balletout. Ir-BB:167
  My Brother Bert. T. Hughes.
    Co-BB:27
  Pets. D. Pettiward. Co-BBW:275
  Take One Home for the Kiddies.
    P. Larkin. Co-EL:139, Co-PU:94
  The Tiger. H. Belloc. Un-MB:171
HUMOR - PHILOSOPHY
  There Was a Young Man of Cadiz.
    Br-LL:115
HUMOR - PHOTOGRAPHERS
  AND PHOTOGRAPHY
  Hiawatha's Photographing.
    L. Carroll. Co-FB:244,
    Li-SR:55
HUMOR - PHYSICAL FITNESS
  Tom Twist. W. Butler. Co-HP:36
HUMOR - PHYSICIANS
  Bones. W. de la Mare. Br-SM:50,
    Co-FB:145, Co-HP:55, Du-RG:66
  The Doctor. G. MacPherson.
    Ja-PC:37
  A Doctor Fell in a Deep Well.
    Br-SM:49, Un-GT:243
  Doctor Foster. Bo-FP:133,
    Co-OW:42, Fr-WO:22, Ir-BB:42,
    Li-LB:70, Mo-MGT:43, Mo-NR:22,
    Wi-MG:14, Wr-RM:36
  The Doctor's Story. W. Carleton.
    Co-PT:282
  Gentle Doctor Brown. B. Taylor.
    Co-OH:46
  The Greek Anthology. Br-SM:155
  Modern Song. Ab-MO:31
  Mother Tabbykins. E. Hart.
    Ox-BC:268

My First Love. H. Graham.
    Co-FB:325
On a Doctor Named Isaac Letsome.
    Co-PU:122, Un-GT:238
Similis Similibus. J. Morgan.
    Br-SM:111
To Keep His Temper. Re-RR:74
HUMOR - PHYSICISTS AND PHYSICS
Apostrophic Notes from the New-
    World Physics. E. White.
    Pl-IO:65
E-MC . M. Bishop. Pl-IO:82
Richard Tolman's Universe.
    L. Bacon. Pl-IO:171
Science for the Young. W. Irwin.
    Br-SM:130
A Scientist Living at Staines.
    R. Hewison. Er-FA:218
HUMOR - PIANOS AND PIANISTS
A Man Was Locked in a Room.
    Re-RR:51
My Teeth Are Straight and
    Shining White. Re-RR:110
Piano Tuner, Untune Me That Tune.
    O. Nash. Pl-US:42
HUMOR - PICKLES
The Highlander's Song. C. Carryl.
    Co-HP:48
Ode on a Jar of Pickles.
    B. Taylor. Li-SR:141
Polly Picklenose. L. Jackson.
    Co-BB:35
There Was a Young Lady Named
    Perkins. Br-LL:85
HUMOR - PIES
An April First Happening.
    Ja-HH:21
Baby and I. Ir-BB:59, Mo-MGT:79
The Fastidious Serpent.
    H. Johnstone. Co-HP:83,
    Gr-EC:18, Lo-LL:25
If You Answer This. Re-RR:94
Montezuma. A. Alderson. Gr-EC:34
There Was an Old Lady of Brooking.
    Br-LL:88
There Was an Old Lady of Rye.
    Br-LL:87
HUMOR - PIGS
As I Looked Out. Ir-BB:64,
    St-FS:106
Gigl. A. Spilka. Su-FVI:72
Gregory Griggs. L. Richards.
    Au-SP:244
If Pigs Could Fly. J. Reeves.
    Ir-BB:254
Kindness to Animals. L. Richards.
    Ar-TP3:122, Au-SP:236, Ir-BB:167,
    St-FS:45
A Little Pig Found a Fifty-Dollar
    Note. Ir-BB:63
Little Piggy. T. Hood.
    Au-SP:230, Gr-EC:25, Ir-BB:67

My Uncle Jehoshaphat.
    L. Richards. Ox-BC:288
Ode to the Pig: His Tail.
    W. Brooks. Lo-LL:43
The Pig. O. Nash. Un-GF:83
The Pig and the Paddy. E. Mathias.
    Ir-BB:57
A Pig-Tale. L. Carroll.
    Ch-B:65, Fe-FP:346, Ho-WR:80,
    Pa-RE:27, Rd-OA:94
A Pig Tale. J. Reeves. Au-SP:252,
    Ir-BB:174, La-PP:16, Sm-MK:108
Pigs. J. Prelutsky. Co-OH:27
Pu-Heter Pu-Huligan. Gr-EC:8
The Spectre Pig. O. Holmes.
    Co-RM:103
A Strange Pig. Mo-MGT:37,
    Wr-RM:110
The Three Little Pigs. A. Gatty.
    Ox-BC:274
Upon a Cock-Horse to Market
    I'll Trot. Ir-BB:236
Upon My Word and Honour. Mo-NR:89
What Makes More Noise. Re-RR:95
Where Are You Going? E. Follen.
    Au-SP:227
HUMOR - PIGTAILS (HAIR)
A Tragic Story. W. Thackeray.
    Co-HP:116, De-TT:71, Fe-FP:353,
    Gr-EC:205, Hu-MP:440, Ir-BB:197,
    Pa-OM:74, Sh-RP:42, Un-GT:232
HUMOR - PILGRIM FATHERS
Thoughts for St. Stephen.
    C. Morley. Br-SM:160
HUMOR - PIPES (MUSIC)
The Cow Ate the Piper. Gr-GB:88
There Was a Piper Had a Cow.
    Ir-BB:45, Wr-RM:116
HUMOR - PIRATES
The Battle of Clothesline Bay.
    W. Irwin. Co-SS:33
The Chinese Bumboatman. Co-SS:113
The Pirate Don Durk of Dowdee.
    M. Meigs. Ar-TP3:140,
    Au-SP:270, Ir-BB:45, La-PV:94,
    Pe-FB:100
Seumas Beg. J. Stephens.
    Bl-OB:144, Co-RM:63, Fe-FP:318,
    Na-EO:155
The Tale of Custard the Dragon.
    O. Nash. Fe-FP:332, Ir-BB:170,
    Un-GB:26, Un-GT:167
HUMOR - PLANTS AND PLANTING
About the Grass. J. Weil.
    Ls-NY:228
HUMOR - PLATYPUSES
I Had a Duck-Billed Platypus.
    P. Barrington. Co-FB:31
The Platypus. O. Herford.
    Co-FB:27
HUMOR - PLUMBING
The Dripping Tap.J.Kirkup. Pa-RE:60

HUMOR - POETS AND POETRY
  Abbreviated Interviews with a Few
    Disgruntled Literary Celebrities.
    R. Whittemore. Co-FB:343
  Ah, Yes, I Wrote the "Purple Cow."
    G. Burgess. Co-FB:379, Er-FA:200
  Ain't Nature Commonplace!
    A. Guiterman. Co-FB:348
  Alas! 'Tis Very Sad to Hear.
    W. Landor. Pa-GTB:317
  Any Author to Any Friend.
    Martial. Pl-ML:66
  The Ballad of Sir Brian and the
    Three Wishes. N. Levy.
    Co-FB:271
  Breakfast with Gerard Manley
    Hopkins. A. Brode. Co-FB:253
  Calypsomania. A. Brode.
    Co-FB:276
  Catch a Little Rhyme. E. Merriam.
    La-PV:36
  Chard Whitlow. H. Reed.
    Co-FB:252, Pl-ML:72, Un-MB:508,
    Wi-LT:797
  A Decrepit Old Gasman.
    Br-LL:77, Co-HP:29, Er-FA:220
  A Departed Friend. J. Moore.
    Co-FB:303
  A Difficult Rhyme. Wr-RM:76
  Dismal Observations. J. Wheelock.
    Pl-ML:64
  La Donna E Mobile. A. K.
    Co-FB:347
  Envoi. D. Wyndham Lewis.
    Co-FB:258
  "Everybody Works but Father" as
    W. S. Gilbert Would Have
    Written It. A. Burgoyne.
    Co-FB:259
  Familiar Lines. Co-FB:342
  Famous Poet. J. Hollander.
    Wi-LT:737
  Ferdinando and Elvira. W. Gilbert.
    Co-FB:170
  Footnote to Tennyson.
    G. Bullett. Co-FB:254
  Hence These Rimes. B. Taylor.
    Co-FB:446
  Hexameter and Pentameter.
    Gr-CT:21
  Higher. Co-FB:242, Li-SR:51
  Hippopotamothalamion.
    J. Wheelock. Co-FB:10
  An Historic Moment. W. Harris.
    Co-PU:3
  If. M. Collins. Co-FB:240
  January 1940. R. Fuller.
    Wi-LT:704
  Jenny Kiss'd Me. P. Dehn.
    Co-FB:260, Li-SR:33
  John Bun. Br-SM:55, Un-GT:239

  A Limerick Shapes to the Eye.
    D. McCord. Br-LL:ix
  The Limerick's Lively to Write.
    D. McCord. Br-LL:125
  Literary Love. H. Kemp. Bo-HF:170
  Local Note. A. Guiterman.
    Co-PU:37
  Mavrone. A. Guiterman.
    Co-FB:264, Li-SR:149
  The Metre Columbian. Li-SR:48
  Mrs. Judge Jenkins. B. Harte.
    Co-FB:238
  Moonshine. W. de la Mare.
    Co-FB:442
  Myrtle. T. Roethke. Pa-RE:11
  Nonsense. N. Koralova. Mo-MI:54
  Obituary. A. Brode. Co-FB:339
  An Ode to Spring in the Metropolis.
    O. Seaman. Co-FB:234
  Of W.W. (Americanus). J. Stephen.
    Co-FB:232, Li-SR:148
  Ogden Nash Gets All the Cash.
    D. McCord. Pl-ML:69
  On a Poetess. G. Hopkins.
    Co-PU:22
  On the Poet O'Shaughnessy.
    D. Rossetti. Gr-CT:476
  Options. O. Henry. Co-FB:254
  A Parental Ode to My Son, Aged
    Three Years and Five Months.
    T. Hood. Co-FB:103, Co-HP:77,
    Fe-FP:36, Fe-PL:139
  Peter Bell. J. Reynolds.
    Ox-BN:402
  "Poet." W. Smith. Sh-RP:153
  The Poet of Bray. J. Heath-Stubbs.
    Pl-ML:9
  The Poet's Fate. T. Hood.
    Co-EL:40, Co-FB:332, Co-PU:26
  Post-Obits and the Poets.
    Martial. Mc-PR:21
  Presidential Address to a Party of
    Exiles Leaving for the Moon.
    H. Nemerov. Pl-ML:11
  The Protest of the Illiterate.
    G. Burgess. Co-FB:442,
    Co-HP:36
  P's a Poetical Bore. O. Herford.
    Br-LL:71
  A Reply to Lines by Thomas Moore.
    W. Landor. Gr-CT:470
  Rondeau. W. Smith. Co-FB:446
  A Shot at Random.
    D. Wyndham Lewis. Co-FB:252,
    Er-FA:219
  Sir, I Admit Your General Rule.
    M. Prior. Co-FB:338, Pl-ML:137,
    Un-GT:236
  The Smoked Herring. C. Cros.
    Co-PT:277
  So That's What I Remind Me of.
    O. Nash. Fe-PL:213

Some Families of My Acquaintance.
   L. Richards. Co-OW:18
Some Limericks — Most of Them,
   Reely. D. McCord. Br-LL:127
Some of Wordsworth. W. Landor.
   Gr-CT:470
Sonnet and Limerick. M. Bishop.
   Co-FB:439
Spicer's Instant Poetry. J. Reeves.
   To-MP:174
Spring Comes to Murray Hill.
   O. Nash. Co-FB:358
Squeal. L. Simpson. Co-FB:233
A Strike among the Poets.
   Co-FB:340
There Was a Naughty Boy. J. Keats.
   Bo-FP:113, Ch-B:77, Co-HP:84,
   Fr-WO:69, Gr-EC:215, Ir-BB:97,
   Ma-YA:183, Pl-ML:18, Sm-LG:291,
   Sm-MK:131, Un-GF:18
There Was a Young Bard of Japan.
   Br-LL:133, Un-GF:44
There Was a Young Poet of Kew.
   Br-LL:133
"There Was an Old Man" of Wherever.
   Br-LL:127
There Was an Old Stupid Who Wrote.
   W. Parke. Co-HP:102
Thomas Shadwell, the Poet.
   J. Dryden. Gr-CT:470
To a Child of Quality. M. Prior.
   Rv-CB:485
To Minerva. T. Hood. Co-FB:338
To Miss Ferrier. R. Burns.
   Rv-CB:623
The Translated Way. F. Adams.
   Co-FB:261
Twist-Rime on Spring.
   A. Guiterman. Co-PS:61,
   Gr-EC:44
Two Hundred Lines a Day. Martial.
   Pl-ML:65
Versions of Love. R. Fuller.
   Wi-LT:708
Very like a Whale. O. Nash.
   Fe-PL:211
W. J. Reeves. Ch-B:40,
   Gr-CT:9, Ir-BB:261
the wail of archy. D. Marquis.
   Co-FB:332
What's in the Cupboard.
   Gr-CT:8, Gr-GB:19, Ir-BB:190
Why Don't I Send My Books to You.
   Martial. Pl-ML:68
Why I Am Not a Painter.
   F. O'Hara. Kh-VA:63
Willie and Nellie's Wish.
   J. Moore. Co-FB:320
Write a Limerick Now. Say
   There Was. D. McCord. Br-LL:133
Yes, Every Poet Is a Fool.
   M. Prior. Pl-ML:136

You're a Poet. Er-FA:499
HUMOR - POISONS
   Lydia Sherman. Br-SM:24
   Terence, This Is Stupid Stuff.
      A. Housman. Ma-YA:224,
      Un-MB:100, Wi-LT:63
   Willie the Poisoner. Co-HP:28
HUMOR - POLICE
   Copper Song. E. Scheffauer.
      Co-PM:150
   I Could Learn to Be a Good
      Drummer. Rs-PF:89
   I Took a Bow and Arrow.
      J. Ciardi. Na-EO:116
   The Irate Songster. K. Patchen.
      Ca-BP:44
   Parody on Thomas Hood's "The
      Bridge of Sighs." Co-FB:220
   The Policeman's Lot. W. Gilbert.
      Co-HP:59
HUMOR - POLITICS
   By-Election Idyll. P. Dickinson.
      Co-FB:437
   Canopus. B. Taylor. Co-FB:86
   The Contemplative Sentry.
      W. Gilbert. Co-FB:491
   A Dance for Militant Dilettantes.
      A. Young. Ad-PB:362
   Middle-Man. W. Matchett. Ha-TP:106
   On a Politician. H. Belloc.
      Br-SM:155, Mc-WS:91, Un-MB:172
HUMOR - POLLUTION
   All the Smoke. E. Siegel.
      Ad-CI:46, Co-EL:103, Co-FB:123,
      Co-PU:130
HUMOR - POPE, ALEXANDER
   When Alexander Pope. E. Bentley.
      Co-FB:128, Un-GF:49
HUMOR - POPPIES
   Caprice. D. Shaw. Co-PT:146
HUMOR - PORCUPINES
   Courtship. A. Resnikoff.
      Co-OH:18
   Kag the Porcupine. A. Guiterman.
      Gr-EC:20
   The Porcupine. O. Nash. Gr-EC:28
HUMOR - PORTRAITS-MEN
   Captain Pink of the Peppermint.
      W. Irwin. Co-SS:88
   How Pleasant to Know Mr. Lear!
      E. Lear. Co-FB:45, Co-HP:90,
      Gr-CT:463, Ha-PO:240, Li-SR:43,
      Pa-GTB:356, Pl-ML:22, Rv-CB:810,
      Tu-WW:118, Un-GT:212
   Identity Parade. Sm-MK:196
   Incidents in the Life of My Uncle
      Arly. E. Lear. Co-HP:87
   The Knight's Song. L. Carroll.
      Ir-BB:142, Un-GT:210
   Me (Mr. Alexander Soames).
      K. Kuskin. Ar-TP3:138

HUMOR - PORTRAITS-MEN — cont'd.
  The Peppery Man. A. Macy. Fe-FP:319
  A Sketch. C. Rossetti. Pa-GTB:374
  The Strange Man. Fe-FP:336,
    Hu-MP:157
  There Lived an Old Man.
    D. Thompson. Co-OW:49, Ir-BB:199
  Walter Spaggot. P. Wesley-Smith.
    Pa-RE:93
HUMOR - PORTRAITS-WOMEN
  Eighteenth Century Lady.
    R. O'Neill. Ls-NY:316
  An Elegy on the Glory of Her Sex,
    Mrs. Mary Blaize. O. Goldsmith.
    Rv-CB:541
  Going Too Far. M. Howells.
    Ar-TP3:138, Ir-BB:203, Pa-OM:82
  Love Poem. J. Nims. Mc-WS:56,
    Pe-OA:233
  Lucy Lake. O. Nash. Br-SM:25
  On a Lady Who Beat Her Husband.
    Co-FB:406
  There Was a Young Lady Residing
    at Prague. Co-OW:33
HUMOR - POSTAL SERVICE
  Epitaph for a Postal Clerk.
    X. Kennedy. Br-SM:155
  The Traveling Post Office.
    A. Patterson. Co-PT:290
HUMOR - POSTURE
  Shut the Door. E. Rounds.
    Br-SM:116, Co-HP:110, Ir-BB:109
HUMOR - POTATOES
  La Ballade. M. Bracker. Ke-TF:375
HUMOR - POTS AND PANS
  A Charming Old Lady of Settle.
    E. Lear. Br-LL:96
HUMOR - POVERTY
  Here I Lie at the Chancel Door.
    Br-SM:165, Un-GT:239
  Jane Smith. R. Kipling. Li-SR:104
  The Man with Nought. De-TT:45,
    Mo-MGT:73, Wr-RM:88
HUMOR - PRAYER
  The Prayer of Cyrus Brown.
    S. Foss. Co-HP:58
HUMOR - PRAYERS
  Bruadar and Smith and Glinn.
    Co-PI:68, Mc-WS:86
  Goosey, Goosey, Gander.
    Mother Goose. De-PO:28,
    Li-LB:84, Mo-MGT:21, Mo-NR:12,
    Wi-MG:61, Wr-RM:43
  Hebrides Crofter's Prayer.
    Co-PU:71
  Holy Willie's Prayer. R. Burns.
    Al-VBP:626
  The Prayer of the Cock.
    C. Gasztold. Ar-TP3:82
  A Rat. Mo-MGT:24
  Rattlin' Joe's Prayer.
    J. Crawford. Fi-BG:187

Reb Levi Yitzkhok. I. Manger.
  Ho-TY:280
HUMOR - PREACHERS AND PREACHING
  The Preacher. Al-Mahdi. Lo-TY:45
  The Raven Visits Rawhide.
    Fi-BG:182
  This Sun Is Hot. Ra-BP:9
HUMOR - PREHISTORIC ANIMALS
  The Ichthyosaurus. I. Bellows.
    Ch-B:48, Co-OT:27
  If I Had a Brontosaurus.
    S. Silverstein. Co-OT:44
  Similar Cases. C. Gilman.
    Fe-PL:191
  There Once Was a Plesiosaurus.
    Br-LL:35
HUMOR - PREJUDICES AND
  ANTIPATHIES
  Two Sad Tales. Co-OH:14
HUMOR - PRESIDENTS-UNITED STATES
  I Am Waiting. V. Bryant. Jo-VC:6
  The Indian and the Trout.
    E. Field. Kr-OF:18
  When I Am the President. Un-GT:17
HUMOR - PRIDE
  All These Hurt. Vainateya.
    Al-PI:58
  A Bantam Rooster. Kikaku.
    Be-MC:25
  The Fall of J. W. Beane.
    O. Herford. Co-PT:21
  I Am the Great Professor Jowett.
    Co-FB:76
  Ode to the Pig: His Tail.
    W. Brooks. Lo-LL:43
HUMOR - PRIESTS
  The Priest and the Mulberry-Tree.
    T. Peacock. De-TT:119,
    Ha-PO:297, Sp-OG:224
  Robin Hood and Two Priests.
    Ma-BB:66
HUMOR - PRINCES AND PRINCESSES
  The Prince. W. de la Mare.
    Lo-LL:44
  What the Lord High Chamberlain
    Said. V. Cloud. Co-BB:74
HUMOR - PRINTING
  The Author's Epitaph. Co-FB:132
  Printer's Error. P. Wodehouse.
    Co-FB:334
  Sim Ines. J. Stubbs. Co-FB:372
HUMOR - PRISONS AND PRISONERS
  Locked In. I. Gustafson.
    Co-PT:24
  Song of One Eleven Years in
    Prison. G. Canning. Co-FB:429
  The Troubadour. W. Gilbert.
    Co-RM:75
HUMOR - PRIVACY
  The Bath. H. Graham. Br-SM:120
  Lord High-Bo. H. Belloc.
    Co-FB:456

HUMOR - PROBLEMS AND SOLUTIONS
Dilemma. D. Ignatow. Ca-VT:395
HUMOR - PROCRASTINATION
Grandpa Is Ashamed. O. Nash.
Co-PU:18
Tonight. F. Adams. Co-FB:327
HUMOR - PROGRESS
Inscription on a Klim Can.
Yüan Shui-p'ai. Hs-TC:404
It Rolls On. M. Bishop. Pl-IO:132
Pity This Busy Monster, Manunkind.
E. Cummings. Ho-LP:83,
Mo-MG:197, Pe-SS:105, Sh-AP:192,
Wi-LT:367
Progress. D. McCord. Pl-IO:130
A Song of Reform. Yüan Shui-p'ai.
Hs-TC:405
HUMOR - PRONUNCIATION
The American Indian. Co-FB:428
The Axolotl. D. McCord. Co-FB:420
Balearic Idyll. F. Packard.
Co-FB:418
Beg Parding. Co-OW:71, Gr-CT:10
Father Goose Tells a Story.
A. Resnikoff. Co-OH:60
Hints on Pronunciation for
Foreigners. Ma-FW:237
How to Tell Juan Don from Another.
G. Lewis. Co-FB:354
An Old Lady Living in Worcester.
Br-LL:25
A Sleeper from the Amazon.
Br-LL:93, Lo-LL:54, Sh-RP:144
There Was a Young Lady Named
Wemyss. Br-LL:64
The Waiter Said: "Try the Ragout."
Br-LL:85
What Word Is It. Re-RR:88
HUMOR - PROOFREADING
Epitaph on the Proofreader of
the Encyclopedia Britannica.
C. Morley. Br-SM:161
Sim Ines. J. Stubbs. Co-FB:372
HUMOR - PROPERTY
Suburban Madrigal. J. Updike.
Pe-SS:84
HUMOR - PROPHETS AND PROPHECIES
Green Grass. De-CH:191, Mo-MGT:171,
Rv-ON:16
The Rhyme of the Rain Machine.
F. Clarke. Co-BN:173
Similar Cases. C. Gilman.
Fe-PL:191
HUMOR - PROSPECTING
The Ballad of Tonopah Bill.
Fi-BG:61
Boliver Riggin. Fi-BG:138
HUMOR - PROTECTION
Directions to the Armorer.
E. Olson. Du-SH:99
Heaven Will Protect the Working
Girl. E. Smith. Co-FB:124

HUMOR - PROVERBS
Morals. J. Thurber. Ga-FB:329
HUMOR - PSYCHOANALYSIS
Ballade to My Psychoanalyst.
K. Lillington. Co-FB:457
Don't Tell Me What You Dreamt
Last Night. F. Adams. Co-FB:261
HUMOR - PSYCHOLOGY
After Reading a Book on Abnormal
Psychology. E. Moll. Co-EL:50
On Monsieur Coué. C. Inge.
Br-LL:115, Er-FA:218
HUMOR - PUBLIC SPEAKING
Casabianca. E. Bishop. Gr-SS:104
HUMOR - PUDDINGS
Puddin' Song. N. Lindsay. Co-OT:74
HUMOR - PUFFINS
The Puffin. R. Wood. Co-OH:44
There Once Was a Provident Puffin.
O. Herford. Br-LL:5
There Once Was a Puffin.
F. Jaques. Ar-TP3:124,
Au-SP:240, Fr-MP:14,
Ir-BB:89, St-FS:87
HUMOR - PUMPKINS
The Mournful Pumpkin. E. Jay.
Ja-HH:48
Peter, Peter, Pumpkin-Eater.
An-IP:23, Au-SP:3, Bo-FP:104,
Er-FA:505, Ir-BB:196, Li-LB:61,
Mo-CC:(7), Mo-MGT:106,
Wi-MG:77, Wr-RM:98
HUMOR - PUNCTUATION
I Saw a Fishpond All on Fire.
Gr-CT:153, Gr-EC:191, Gr-GB:91,
Ir-BB:143, Mo-MGT:92
I Saw a Peacock. Bl-OB:26,
Co-PM:204, De-CH:278, Gr-CC:148,
Gr-CT:154, Gr-EC:193, Gr-GB:90,
Lo-LL:66, Mo-MGT:195, Pl-IO:106,
Rv-CB:417, Sm-LG:281, Sm-MK:28,
Un-GT:228
Missing Commas. Mo-MGT:123
"Poet." W. Smith. Sh-RP:153
Triolet. P. Gilbert. Co-PU:33
HUMOR - PUNISHMENT
Captain Pink of the Peppermint.
W. Irwin. Co-SS:88
Dirge for a Bad Boy. E. Rieu.
Co-BB:105
Doctor Faustus Was a Good Man.
Mother Goose. Li-LB:66,
Mo-NR:118
Extremely Naughty Children.
E. Godley. Co-BB:65
Fie on Sinful Fantasy!
W. Shakespeare. Al-VBP:192
Go to the Bottom. Rs-PF:51
Godfrey Gordon Gustavus Gore.
W. Rands. Ar-TP3:136, Co-BB:111,
Co-OT:42, Fe-FP:308, Hu-MP:451,
Ir-BB:109, Pe-FB:92

HUMOR - PUNISHMENT — cont'd.
His Little Sub. E. Bennett.
Ke-TF:70
If You Had Your Due. Rs-PF:52
It's Better to Give. Rs-PF:95
Jimmy Refused. Rs-PF:77
Limericks. Ke-TF:288
Mutual Charges of Molestation.
Da-SC:45
Self-Sacrifice. H. Graham.
Co-BB:107
Short Poem. W. Williams.
Mo-BG:103
Speak Roughly to Your Little Boy.
L. Carroll. Bl-OB:30, Bo-FP:61,
Co-BB:105, Li-SR:4, Sm-LG:101
That's Jack. Ir-BB:100
There Was an Old Woman Who Lived
in a Shoe. An-IP:(27), De-PO:6,
Er-FA:505, Fr-WO:20, Ir-BB:197,
Li-LB:36, Mo-CC:(6), Mo-MGT:161,
Mo-NR:42, Wi-MG:25, Wr-RM:116
Thief. Co-BB:109, Co-HP:28
HUMOR - PUPPETS
Little Clown Puppet.
C. Haywood. Ir-BB:253
Mister Punchinello. Co-OW:74,
De-TT:33
HUMOR - PURGATORY
Spiritual Biography. C. Walsh.
St-H:237
HUMOR - PURITANS AND PURITANISM
Scotch Rhapsody. E. Sitwell.
Br-TC:190
HUMOR - PYRAMUS AND THISBE
Pyramus and Thisbe. J. Saxe.
Pa-OM:67
HUMOR - PYTHONS
Hello Mr. Python. S. Milligan.
Co-OH:48
The Python. H. Belloc. Br-SM:129,
Na-EO:166
The Untutored Giraffe.
O. Herford. Br-SM:98
HUMOR - QUARRELS
As I Was Going Up and Down.
Ir-BB:213
Betty, My Sister. Un-GF:12
The Duel. E. Field. Ar-TP3:119,
Au-SP:273, Ch-B:42, Er-FA:496,
Fe-FP:348, Fe-PL:202, Gr-EC:80,
Pa-OM:40, Rd-SS:36
Dust to Dust. T. Hood.
Br-SM:156, Co-FB:317, Un-GT:236
Eclogue. E. Lear. Li-TU:74
Epigram. J. Swift. Hi-WP II:123
Fight. J. Jaszi. Sh-RP:132
The Floor and the Ceiling.
W. Smith. Co-HP:113
Great Lakes Suite, II.
J. Reaney. Do-WH:49

I Never Even Suggested It.
O. Nash. Co-FB:393, Fe-PL:213
Mrs. Snipkin and Mrs. Wobblechin.
L. Richards. Ar-TP3:138,
Au-SP:247, Co-HP:107, Ir-BB:150,
Ox-BC:288
One Stormy Night. Bo-FP:172,
Ch-B:73, Ir-BB:166
Tweedledum and Tweedledee.
Bo-FP:299, Fr-WO:23, Li-LB:53,
Mo-MGT:66, Mo-NR:105, Wr-RM:13
HUMOR - QUEBÉC, CAN.
Limericks. Ke-TF:287
HUMOR - QUESTIONS AND ANSWERS
Clemo Uti — the Water Lilies.
R. Lardner. Co-FB:388
Endless Chant. Su-FVI:79
Father William. L. Carroll.
Ar-TP3:139, Bo-GJ:154, Br-BC:135,
Co-FB:43, Co-HP:39, Fe-FP:350,
Fe-PL:240, Fr-WO:57, Ke-TF:273,
La-PP:71, La-PV:28, Li-SR:91,
Lo-LL:95, Ma-YA:214, Mc-WK:217,
Sh-RP:120, Sp-OG:233, Un-GF:24,
Un-GT:206
Gemini and Virgo. C. Calverley.
Co-FB:118
The Good Little Girl. A. Milne.
Co-BB:37
Limericks. E. Lear. Bo-GJ:9
The Man in the Wilderness.
Mother Goose. Gr-EC:285,
Gr-GB:83, Li-LB:67, Mo-MGT:88,
Mo-NR:101, Sm-LG:281, Un-GF:13,
Wr-RM:89
The Old Farmer and His Young Wife.
Co-PT:311, Gr-GB:158
Question and Answer.
S. Hoffenstein. Co-FB:476
The Snuffboxes. Co-PT:304
There Was an Old Person of Burton.
E. Lear. Br-LL:68
When Did the World Begin.
R. Clairmont. Au-SP:227,
Co-HP:54, Mc-WK:102, Un-GT:230
Why? W. de la Mare. Co-FB:105
HUMOR - QUESTS
The Enormous Easter Egg Hunt.
M. Neville. Su-FVI:29
I Looked in the Mirror.
B. de Regniers. La-PV:14
HUMOR - QUIETNESS
As I Was Standing in the Street.
Co-HP:23, Co-OH:62
A Strange Old Woman. Wr-RM:57
HUMOR - RABBITS
A Baby Rabbit's Nose Is Tiny.
Re-RR:104
Fooba Wooba John. Co-OW:64
The Hare and the Tortoise.
I. Serraillier. Co-BBW:88
If a Goat Ever Swallowed. Rs-PF:99

A Peanut Sat.   Co-OH:38, Ir-BB:154
The Rabbit.   Co-FB:32
The Reason.   L. Blair.   Ja-HH:26
Story of the Man That Went Out
    Shooting.   H. Hoffmann.   Ir-BB:58
HUMOR - RACCOONS
  Raccoon on a Rail.   Ju-CP:5
  There Once Was a Knowing Raccoon.
    M. Dodge.   Br-LL:34
HUMOR - RACE RELATIONS
  African China.   M. Tolson.
    Ad-PB:45
  For a Lady I Know.   C. Cullen.
    Ab-MO:27, Ad-PB:91, Bo-AN:89,
    Br-SM:150, Hu-MP:231, Un-MA:571
  Friends.   R. Durem.   Ad-PB:150
HUMOR - RACES OF MAN
  The Human Races.   R. Lister.
    Co-FB:203
HUMOR - RADIATORS
  Radiator Lions.   D. Aldis.
    Au-SP:207, Hu-MP:50
HUMOR - RADISHES
  The Radish.   I. Quzman.   Ab-MO:31
HUMOR - RAILROADS-SLEEPING CARS
  Skimbleshanks: The Railway Cat.
    T. Eliot.   Sm-LG:292
HUMOR - RAIN
  Beyond the Window.   S. Jahin.
    Lo-TY:51
  A Description of a City Shower.
    J. Swift.   Rv-CB:490
  Doctor Foster.   Bo-FP:133,
    Co-OW:42, Fr-WO:22, Ir-BB:42,
    Li-LB:70, Mo-MGT:43, Mo-NR:22,
    Wi-MG:14, Wr-RM:36
  The Rain It Raineth.   Lord Bowen.
    Co-FB:122, Co-PU:17, Un-GF:15
  Three Large Ladies.   Re-RR:77
HUMOR - RATS
  Little Tim Sprat.   Ir-BB:177
HUMOR - REASON
  Love Not Me for Comely Grace.
    Al-VBP:360, De-CH:348, Er-FA:102,
    Fe-PL:93, Hi-WP II:51, Pa-GTB:80
HUMOR - REBELLION
  Father and Child.   W. Yeats.
    Co-PU:74
  The Rebel.   M. Evans.   Ad-PB:187,
    Bo-AN:163, Pe-SS:58
HUMOR - RED RIDING HOOD
  Little Red Riding Hood.
    G. Carryl.   Co-FB:106, Co-HP:52
HUMOR - REGRETS
  The Choice.   D. Parker.   Co-BL:95
  I Burned My Candle at Both Ends.
    S. Hoffenstein.   Co-EL:59,
    Co-FB:491
  pete the parrot and shakespeare.
    D. Marquis.   Pl-ML:102

HUMOR - RELATIVES
  Family Court.   O. Nash.
    Co-FB:488, Ke-TF:292
HUMOR - RELATIVITY
  Relativity.   A. Buller.
    Ar-TP3:132, Br-LL:138, Ch-B:65,
    Er-FA:219, Fe-FP:361, Fr-WO:55,
    Pl-IO:64
  This Dim and Ptolemaic Man.
    J. Bishop.   Pl-IO:25, Wi-LT:607
HUMOR - RELIGION
  Little Breeches.   J. Hay.   Un-GT:198
  M'Andrew's Hymn.   R. Kipling.
    Ga-S:119
  Science and Mathematics.
    Br-LL:114, Pl-IO:80
  The Seven Spiritual Ages of
    Mrs. Marmaduke Moore.   O. Nash.
    Un-MA:568
HUMOR - REMEDIES AND CURES
  An Allay for Love.   R. Burns.
    Sm-LG:236
  The Cure.   A. Noyes.   Co-BBW:229
  The Doctor's Story.   W. Carleton.
    Co-PT:282
  Ipecacuanha.   G. Canning.
    Gr-CT:14
  Matilda.   F. Evans.   Co-BB:84
  My Donkey.   Ar-TP3:123, Ir-BB:175
HUMOR - REPENTANCE
  Epigram.   A. Lanusse.
    Ab-MO:30, Hu-PN:13, Lo-TY:96
  Paddy O'Rafther.   S. Lover.
    Co-PI:97, Co-PT:298
HUMOR - REPORTERS
  A Young Reporter's "If."
    M. Driscoll.   Ke-TF:267
HUMOR - REPRIMANDS
  The Angry Lover.   M. Prior.
    Un-MW:49
  Careless Willie.   Co-BB:95,
    Co-HP:28, Fe-FP:362
  Willie the Poisoner.   Co-HP:28
HUMOR - RESCUES AND RESCUING
  The Ballad of Pug-Nosed Lil.
    R. Fletcher.   Fi-BG:231
  The Caulker.   M. Lewis.   Co-PT:256
  The Rescue.   H. Summers.   Co-PT:131
HUMOR - REST
  The Sun Was Slumbering in the
    West.   T. Hood.   Co-FB:398
HUMOR - RESTAURANTS AND BARS
  La Carte.   J. Richardson.Co-FB:87
  The Contrary Waiter. E. Parker.
    Co-OW:24
  Marble-Top.   E. White.   Co-FB:464
  November 3.   R. Brautigan.
    Kh-VA:62
HUMOR - RESURRECTION
  Maloney Remembers the Resurrection
    of Kate Finucane. B. Kennelly.
    Co-PT:108

HUMOR - RETRIBUTION
  The Cruel Naughty Boy.   Co-BB:108
  Johan the Monk.   Li-TU:119
  Little Orphant Annie.   J. Riley.
    Co-BB:113, Er-FA:493, Fe-FP:532,
    Hu-MP:27, Ox-BC:300
  Lord Waterford.   Gr-CT:472,
    Gr-GB:196
  The Opportune Overthrow of Humpty
    Dumpty.   G. Carryl.   Co-BB:20
  Retaliation.   Ja-PC:33
  Three Bad Ones.   Co-BB:96,
    Ir-BB:94
HUMOR - RETURNING
  The Ballad of Hagensack.
    W. Irwin.   Co-PT:272
HUMOR - REVENGE
  Casey's Revenge.   J. Wilson.
    Pa-OM:76
  What the Lord High Chamberlain
    Said.   V. Cloud.   Co-BB:74
HUMOR - REVERE, PAUL
  According to All Hearsay.
    Re-RR:81
  The Horse's Version of the Ride
    of Paul Revere.   Ke-TF:268
HUMOR - REVOLTS AND REVOLUTIONS
  Abu.   D. Randall.   Ra-BP:147
  Crinolines and Bloomers.
    Hi-TL:174
  Declaration of Independence.
    W. Gibbs.   Pe-SS:23
  Middle-Man.   W. Matchett.
    Ha-TP:106
  A Semi-Revolution.   R. Frost.
    Wi-LT:184
HUMOR - REWARDS
  Is There Any Reward?   H. Belloc.
    Ga-S:218
  It Pays.   A. Bennett.   Er-FA:222
  Three Actors.   V. Golyavkin.
    Bo-RU:38
HUMOR - REYNOLDS, SIR JOSHUA
  Sir Joshua Reynolds.   W. Blake.
    Co-EL:54, Co-FB:121, Co-PU:24
HUMOR - RHINOCEROSES
  The Rhinoceros.   H. Belloc.
    Fe-FP:331, Gr-CT:22
  Rhinoceroses.   Co-OH:71
HUMOR - RIDERS AND RIDING
  A Ballad in "G."   E. Ware.
    Fe-PL:217
  A Certain Young Gallant Named
    Robbie.   Br-LL:21
  The Diverting History of John
    Gilpin.   W. Cowper.   Al-VBP:588,
    Co-RG:88, Hi-WP I:47, Sp-OG:215
  How I Brought the Good News from
    Aix to Ghent (or Vice-Versa).
    R. Yeatman and W. Sellar.
    Co-FB:237, Li-SR:14, Pa-OM:80

  Hunter Trials.   J. Betjeman.
    Co-FB:98
  Just for the Ride.   Er-FA:220
  The Nut-Crackers and the Sugar
    Tongs.   E. Lear.   Fe-PL:238,
    Sm-MK:61
  Song-ily.   Gr-EC:195
  There Was an Old Person of Ickley.
    E. Lear.   Br-LL:15, Ir-BB:218,
    Na-EO:103
HUMOR - ROBINS
  Cherries.   Ir-BB:26, Sp-AS:20
  Little Brother.   A. Fisher.
    Br-BC:48, Mc-AW:91
HUMOR - ROBINSON CRUSOE
  Poor Old Robinson Crusoe.
    Ir-BB:207, Mo-NR:102, Wr-RM:76
  Robinson Crusoe's Story.
    C. Carryl.   Ar-TP3:143,
    Co-FB:168, Co-HP:49, Co-SS:143,
    Gr-EC:246, Hu-MP:466
  Why Did the Farmer.   Re-RR:24
HUMOR - ROMANCE
  The Burnt Bridge. L. MacNeice.
    Gr-SS:111
  Prose and Poesy.   T. Ybarra.
    Co-HP:118
  That Reminds Me.   O. Nash.
    Co-FB:401, Un-MW:61
HUMOR - ROME, IT.
  Says I to Myself.   E. Lear.
    Co-FB:211
HUMOR - ROME-HISTORY AND
  PATRIOTISM
  A Roman Soldier on the Wall.
    W. Auden.   Hi-WP I:122,
    Sm-MK:98
HUMOR - ROOFS
  The Roof.   G. Burgess.   Co-OT:38,
    Ir-BB:184
HUMOR - ROSES
  One Perfect Rose.   D. Parker.
    Co-FB:313
HUMOR - RUGS
  Sisyphus.   R. Burdette.   Co-PT:293
HUMOR - RUNAWAYS
  There Was a Naughty Boy. J. Keats.
    Bo-FP:113, Ch-B:77, Co-HP:84,
    Fr-WO:69, Gr-EC:215, Ir-BB:97,
    Ma-YA:183, Pl-ML:18, Sm-LG:291,
    Sm-MK:131, Un-GF:18
  Three Ponies.   A. Guiterman.
    Gr-EC:11
HUMOR - RUNNING
  Autolycus' Song in Basic English.
    R. Green.   Li-SR:82
  A Mighty Runner.   E. Robinson.
    Fl-HH:23, Mo-SD:53
  A Race.   Mrs. Molesworth.
    Ir-BB:62
  The Sluggard. Lucilius. Mo-SD:58

HUMOR - RUSKIN, JOHN
  Poem by a Perfectly Furious
    Academician.   Co-FB:334
HUMOR - SAFETY
  The Buses Headed for Scranton.
    O. Nash.   Mc-WS:28
HUMOR - SAILING
  Jippy and Jimmy. L. Richards.
    Ar-TP3:49, Au-SP:223, Hu-MP:453
  The Old Woman.   Ca-MU:27
HUMOR - SAINTS
  The Figurehead.   C. Garstin.
    Co-PT:262
HUMOR - SAND, GEORGE
  George Sand.   D. Parker. Co-FB:339
HUMOR - SANTA CLAUS
  The Death of Santa Claus.
    V. Starrett.   De-FS:188
  Santa Claws.   T. Joans.   Mc-EA:116
  Unusual Visit.   B. Lee.   Ja-HH:62
  What Alice Wrote to Santa.
    E. Jay.   Ja-HH:57
HUMOR - SAUSAGES
  Who Ever Sausage a Thing?
    Co-OH:77, Ir-BB:64, St-FS:34
HUMOR - SCARECROWS
  There Once Was a Scarecrow Named
    Joel.   D. McCord.   Br-LL:127
HUMOR - SCHOLARS AND SCHOLARSHIP
  Baccalaureate.   D. McCord.
    Li-SR:123
  A Collegiate Damsel Named Breeze.
    Br-LL:103, Un-GT:242
  Diller, Diller, Dollar.   Ju-CP:18
  Giles Johnson, Ph.D.   F. Davis.
    Ad-PB:96, Be-MA:53, Ra-BP:122
  Little Red Riding Hood.
    G. Carryl.   Co-FB:106, Co-HP:52
  Mix You into Stuffin'.   E. Lear.
    Br-SM:69
  The Owl-Critic.   J. Fields.
    Gr-EC:169, Ha-PO:208, Na-EO:82,
    Un-GT:200
  Pen Hy Cane.   M. Mason.   Hu-PN:528
  The Purist.   O. Nash.   Bo-GJ:111,
    Br-SM:125, Co-FB:27, Co-HP:99,
    Un-MA:569
  Robinson Crusoe's Story.
    C. Carryl.   Ar-TP3:143, Co-FB:168,
    Co-HP:49, Co-SS:143, Gr-EC:246,
    Hu-MP:466
  Similia Similibus.   J. Morgan.
    Br-SM:111
HUMOR - SCHOOL LIFE
  Christmas Pageant.   M. Fishback.
    Co-PS:177
  The Collegiate Angels.
    S. Alberti.   Ma-FW:74
  Have You Missed School.   Rs-PF:43
  If the Class Has a Head.   Rs-PF:74
  Johnny's Hist'ry Lesson.
    N. Waterman.   Fe-FP:189
  Patrick Goes to School.
    A. Aspinwall.   Hu-MP:10
  Schoolmistress.   C. Sansom.
    To-MP:129
  The Schoolroom Angels.
    R. Alberti.   Mc-EA:147
  Three Children Sliding.   J. Gay.
    De-TT:39, Ir-BB:139, Li-LB:44,
    Mo-MGT:24, Un-GF:13, Wr-RM:13
  Timothy Winters.   C. Causley.
    To-MP:73
HUMOR - SCHOPENHAUER, ARTHUR
  Some Geese.   O. Herford.   Co-FB:26
HUMOR - SCIENCE
  It Rolls On.   M. Bishop. Pl-IO:132
  Science for the Young. W. Irwin.
    Co-BB:92
HUMOR - SCIENCE FICTION
  A Poem to Delight My Friends Who
    Laugh at Science Fiction.
    E. Rolfe.   Cr-WS:168, Hi-TL:234,
    Ke-PP:125
HUMOR - SCORPIONS
  On Fell.   G. Lessing.   Br-SM:104
HUMOR - SCOTLAND
  There Was a Naughty Boy. J. Keats.
    Bo-FP:113, Ch-B:77, Co-HP:84,
    Fr-WO:69, Gr-EC:215, Ir-BB:97,
    Ma-YA:183, Pl-ML:18, Sm-LG:291,
    Sm-MK:131, Un-GF:18
HUMOR - SCOTSMEN
  A Bugler Named Dougal MacDougal.
    O. Nash.   Br-LL:105, Lo-LL:95,
    Mc-WS:181
  Tommy O'Linn.   Mo-MGT:96
HUMOR - SCOTT, SIR WALTER
  On Scott's Poem "The Field of
    Waterloo."   T. Erskine.
    Co-FB:337
HUMOR - SCRANTON, PA.
  The Buses Headed for Scranton.
    O. Nash.   Mc-WS:28
HUMOR - SEA URCHINS
  The Cares of a Caretaker.
    W. Irwin.   Co-OW:14
HUMOR - SEAFARING LIFE
  The Alarmed Skipper.   J. Fields.
    Co-SS:83, Un-GT:233
  Aunt Nerissa's Muffin.
    W. Irwin.   Co-FB:88
  Babette's Love.   W. Gilbert.
    Co-SS:215
  The Ballad of Hagensack.
    W. Irwin.   Co-PT:272
  Captain Pink of the Peppermint.
    W. Irwin.   Co-SS:88
  The Captain Stood on the
    Carronade.   F. Marryat.
    Co-SS:23, De-CH:597, De-TT:136,
    Ha-PO:255, Sh-RP:261
  Captain Stratton's Fancy.
    J. Masefield. Co-SS:36, Un-MB:226

HUMOR – SEAFARING LIFE — cont'd.
  The Caulker. M. Lewis. Co-PT:256
  The Dutiful Mariner. W. Irwin.
    Co-SS:91
  The Fate of the Cabbage Rose.
    W. Irwin. Co-FB:150, Co-HP:83
  The Fishes. Co-SS:107, Gr-GB:72
  The Gals o'Dublin Town. Co-SS:111
  Haul Away Joe. Co-SS:99
  Hell's Pavement. J. Masefield.
    Co-PT:272
  Hen Overboard. R. Coffin. Sh-RP:327
  The Hunting of the Snark.
    L. Carroll. Co-FB:156, Co-HP:43,
    Ox-BN:728, Pa-OM:14
  The Irish Rover. Co-SS:120
  Jack Was Every Inch a Sailor.
    Do-WH:18
  The Jumblies. E. Lear.
    Ar-TP3:141, Au-SP:267, Bl-OB:54,
    Bo-GJ:145, Co-HP:88, Er-FA:203,
    Gr-CT:6, Ho-WR:132, Ir-BB:248,
    Lo-LL:13, Na-EO:144, Ox-BC:187,
    Sm-MK:128
  Little Billee. W. Thackeray.
    Bl-OB:72, Br-SM:72, Co-SS:15,
    De-TT:126, Gr-EC:244, Hu-MP:452,
    Ir-BB:42, Ox-BB:678, Sm-LG:186
  Meditations of a Mariner.
    W. Irwin. Co-SS:69
  My Plan. W. Chute. Br-BC:115,
    Fe-FP:112
  A Nautical Ballad. K. Goodchild.
    Gr-EC:245
  A Nautical Extravaganza.
    W. Irwin. Co-PT:260
  The Post Captain. C. Carryl.
    Co-HP:49, Co-SS:20
  The Sailor's Consolation.
    C. Dibdin. Co-HP:103, Co-SS:56,
    De-TT:128
  A Sailor's Yarn. J. Roche.
    Co-SS:93
  Sea Chanty. A. Burrows. Co-SS:122
  Sheep. W. Davies. Cl-FC:68,
    Ha-PO:125, Pa-RE:29, Rd-OA:76,
    Un-MB:177, Wi-LT:618
  The Ship of Rio. W. de la Mare.
    Ar-TP3:126, Ir-BB:242, La-PP:52,
    La-PV:203, Lo-LL:102
  Tom Twist. W. Butler. Co-HP:36
  The Walloping Window-Blind.
    C. Carryl. Co-HP:48, Fe-FP:343,
    Hu-MP:450, Lo-LL:90, Sh-RP:123,
    Un-GF:30, Un-GT:220
  The Warrior's Lament. O. Seaman.
    Co-FB:50
  The Yarn of the "Nancy Bell."
    W. Gilbert. Co-HP:59, Er-FA:308,
    Ga-FB:322, Na-EO:125, Sm-LG:188,
    Sp-OG:239, Un-GT:203

HUMOR – SEAMEN
  Captain Reece. W. Gilbert.
    Co-FB:57, Co-HP:62, Na-EO:156
  The Crocodile. Co-RM:65,
    Rv-CB:441
  The Floating Old Man. E. Lear.
    Br-LL:76, Ho-WR:129
  Industrious Carpenter Dan.
    W. Irwin. Co-SS:197
  The Ingenious Little Old Man.
    J. Bennett. Co-OH:28, Fe-FP:337,
    Ja-PC:42
  The Old Sailor. A. Milne.
    Ir-BB:36
  The Post Captain. C. Carryl.
    Co-HP:49, Co-SS:20
  The Sailor and the Shark. P. Fort.
    Sm-MK:66
  A Sailor to His Parrot.
    W. Davies. Al-VBP:1109
  A Sailor Went to Sea. Ir-BB:37
  Tee-Wee's Boat. Mo-CC:(31),
    Mo-MGT:151
  There Was an Old Person of Grange.
    E. Lear. Br-LL:53
  Three Wise Men of Gotham.
    Er-FA:506, Li-LB:75, Mo-MGT:114,
    Mo-NR:134, Wi-MG:40, Wr-RM:25
HUMOR – SEAS
  O Billows Bounding Far.
    A. Housman. Co-BN:80
  There's a Tiresome Young Man in
    Bay Shore. Br-LL:119
  The Uses of Ocean. O. Seaman.
    Co-FB:382, Co-HP:110, Co-SS:86
HUMOR – SEASHORE
  The Cares of a Caretaker.
    W. Irwin. Co-OW:14
HUMOR – SEASONS
  Baseball Note. F. Adams. Mo-SD:2
  If You Don't Know. Rs-PF:86
  There Was a Young Fellow Named
    Hall. Br-LL:73, Sm-MK:201
HUMOR – SECRETS AND SECRECY
  In a Parlor Containing a Table.
    G. Kinnell. Co-EL:109,
    Co-PU:117
  The Secret Sits. R. Frost.
    Au-SP:184, Ha-LO:61, Ho-TH:46
HUMOR – SELF
  The Immoral Proposition.
    R. Creeley. Wi-LT:677
  Indian Summer. D. Parker.
    Ke-TF:128
  Investment. N. Nathan. Pe-M:125
  Middle-Man. W. Matchett.
    Ha-TP:106
  My Stomach Growls. R. Margolis.
    Su-FVI:28
  There Was a Little Woman.
    Fr-WO:26, Ir-BB:150, Mo-MGT:56,
    Sm-MK:96

There Was an Old Woman as I've
Heard Tell. Ar-TP3:132,
Co-PS:70, Co-PT:281, De-TT:69,
Gr-EC:204, Ha-PO:281, Li-LB:156,
Mo-NR:63, Pa-OM:5, Un-GT:103,
Wr-RM:71

HUMOR - SELF-CONTROL
Capsule Conclusions, II. Un-MW:64
Memorandum for Minos. R. Kell.
Co-EL:102
Sorrows of Werther. W. Thackeray.
Br-SM:32, Co-FB:344, Hi-WP II:11

HUMOR - SELF-RELIANCE
Leave Me Alone. F. Holman.
Un-GB:20

HUMOR - SERENADES
Mexican Serenade. A. Guiterman.
Co-BL:72, Co-FB:210

HUMOR - SERMONS
Rattlin' Joe's Prayer.
J. Crawford. Fi-BG:187
S.P.C.A. Sermon. S. Helmsley.
Co-FB:21

HUMOR - SERVANTS
Cock a Doodle Doodle Doo.
De-PO:14, Ir-BB:65, Mo-NR:124,
St-FS:79, Wr-RM:81
Contemporary Nursery Rhyme.
Li-SR:131
The Feckless Dinner Party.
W. de la Mare. Co-PT:33

HUMOR - SHADWELL, THOMAS
Thomas Shadwell, the Poet.
J. Dryden. Gr-CT:470

HUMOR - SHAKESPEARE, WILLIAM
Archy Confesses. D. Marquis.
Co-FB:359, Na-EO:142
Shake, Mulleary and Go-ethe.
H. Bunner. Co-FB:350
They Answer Back. Francis.
Co-FB:270

HUMOR - SHAME
I Blush for You. Rs-PF:45
The Ruined Maid. T. Hardy.
Co-FB:499

HUMOR - SHAMPOOING
Queen Caroline. Mo-MGT:196

HUMOR - SHARING
The Mouse, the Frog, and the
Little Red Hen. Gr-EC:31,
Ir-BB:89

HUMOR - SHARKS
About the Teeth of Sharks.
J. Ciardi. Co-BBW:73
The Flattered Flying Fish.
E. Rieu. Ar-TP3:131,
Br-SM:95, La-PV:202
Power Dive. N. MacCaig. Co-PU:73
The Powerful Eyes o' Jeremy Tait.
W. Irwin. Co-FB:135, Co-SS:79,
Ha-PO:254

The Rhyme of the Chivalrous Shark.
W. Irwin. Br-SM:97, Co-HP:81
The Sailor and the Shark.
P. Fort. Sm-MK:66
Sally Simpkin's Lament. T. Hood.
Br-SM:57
The Shark. L. Richards. Co-HP:107

HUMOR - SHEEP
I Know a Sheep. E. Anthony.
Ja-PC:17
Said a Sheep to Her Child, "My
Dear Ruth." J. Francis.
Br-LL:23

HUMOR - SHELLEY, PERCY BYSSHE
Shelly. J. McIntyre. Co-FB:299

HUMOR - SHEPHERDS AND
SHEPHERD LIFE
Clemo Uti — the Water Lilies.
R. Lardner. Co-FB:388

HUMOR - SHERIDAN, RICHARD
BRINSLEY
Love Note to a Playwright.
P. McGinley. Ke-TF:275

HUMOR - SHIPS
The Humbug Steamship Companies.
J. Stone. Fi-BG:134
The Ship of Rio. W. de la Mare.
Ar-TP3:126, Ir-BB:242, La-PP:52,
La-PV:203, Lo-LL:102

HUMOR - SHIPWRECKS
Brave Alum Bey. W. Gilbert.
Co-SS:151
The Castaways. E. Rieu. Co-PT:171
The Circus Ship Euzkera.
W. Gibson. Co-FB:151, Co-SS:146
Etiquette. W. Gilbert.
Co-FB:178, Co-HP:64
The Fate of the Cabbage Rose.
W. Irwin. Co-FB:150, Co-HP:83
The Figurehead. C. Garstin.
Co-PT:262
The Old Sailor. A. Milne.
Ir-BB:36
The Story of Samuel Jackson.
C. Leland. Co-PT:267
Tragedy. W. Cheney. Co-OW:57
The Wreck of the "Julie Plant."
W. Drummond. Fe-FP:491,
Ha-PO:177

HUMOR - SHOES
Bootless Speculations.
P. McGinley. Ke-TF:88
The Lost Shoe. W. de la Mare.
Ir-BB:95
There Was a Young Woman of Ayr.
Br-LL:95
There Was an Old Man of Toulouse.
E. Lear. Br-LL:95

HUMOR - SHOOTING
All of a Row.
Mo-NR:120

HUMOR - SHOOTING — cont'd.
A Carrion Crow Sat on an Oak.
Bl-OB:21, Li-LB:98, Mo-MGT:164,
Mo-NR:132, Sm-MK:181, Wr-RM:29
Country Rhyme.   Gr-EC:280
Little Dick.   Su-FVI:78
Story of the Man That Went Out
Shooting. H. Hoffmann.
Ir-BB:58
There Was a Little Man. Mother
Goose. Er-FA:505, Gr-EC:281,
Ir-BB:211, Li-LB:76, Mo-MGT:12,
Mo-NR:61, Wr-RM:36
HUMOR - SHOPPING
Le Bon Marché. M. Bracker.
Ke-TF:378
Felicia Ropps. G. Burgess.
Co-BB:40, Fe-FP:309
Nothing to Wear. W. Butler.
Fe-PL:221
HUMOR - SHRIMPS
Conversion. J. Lillie. Co-BBW:74
HUMOR - SICKNESS
A Nightmare. W. Gilbert.
Co-HP:61, Un-GF:70
Tummy Ache. A. Fisher. Au-SP:107
A Young Lady of Spain.
Co-OT:62, Sm-MK:113
HUMOR - SIGNS AND SIGNBOARDS
A Girl Caught in a Storm.
A. Lutzky. Ho-TY:266
Sarah Byng. H. Belloc.
Bo-GJ:112, Gr-CC:152
HUMOR - SILENCE
Get Up and Bar the Door.
Al-VBP:56, Ar-TP3:17, Bl-OB:19,
Fo-OG:49, Ha-PO:75, La-PV:214,
Pa-OM:94
HUMOR - SIN
And Forgive Us Our Trespasses.
A. Behn. Un-MW:45
Portrait of the Artist as a
Prematurely Old Man. O. Nash.
Er-FA:210, Pe-OA:186, Wi-LT:628
Spiritual Biography. C. Walsh.
St-H:237
HUMOR - SINGLE WOMEN
If No One Ever Marries Me.
L. Alma-Tadema. Ne-AM:12
There Was an Old Maid from Peru.
Br-LL:136
HUMOR - SIOUAN INDIANS
The American Indian. Co-FB:428
The Sioux. E. Field. Bo-GJ:154,
Co-FB:428
A Wandering Tribe Called the Sioux.
Br-LL:97
HUMOR - SIRENS
(SEA NYMPHS)
The Sirens. J. Manifold.
Un-MB:514, Wi-LT:766

HUMOR - SISTERS
As into the Garden. A. Housman.
Co-PT:296
Brother and Sister. L. Carroll.
Br-SM:122, Co-BB:89, Gr-CT:26
For Sale. S. Silverstein.
Co-OT:24
Hard Lines. T. Robinson.
Br-BC:64
My Sister Jane. T. Hughes.
Ma-FW:95
HUMOR - SITWELL, EDITH
A Thin Facade for Edith Sitwell.
J. Brinnin. Co-FB:255
HUMOR - SIZE AND SHAPE
Adelaide. J. Prelutsky. Co-OH:57
Bill's Mother Knit Him Three
Socks. Re-RR:102
The Daughter of the Farrier.
Ir-BB:27, Un-GT:243
Eight Limericks, 2. E. Lear.
Sh-RP:127
The Girl of New York.
C. Monkhouse. Br-LL:49,
Co-HP:98
His Sister Named Lucy O'Finner.
E. Lear. Br-LL:48
Horse & Rider. W. Robinson.
Mo-SD:114
I Had a Little Husband.
Er-FA:502, Ir-BB:208, Mo-MGT:84,
Mo-TL:51, Na-EO:170
I Know a Giraffe. E. Anthony.
Ja-PC:12
Jack Hall.   Ir-BB:203
Jerry Hall.   Mo-MGT:29, Wr-RM:37
John Bull.   Mo-MGT:159
Limericks.   Co-HP:28
Little Thomas. F. Evans. Co-BB:45
Min.   Gr-EC:214
Mrs. Snipkin and Mrs. Wobblechin.
L. Richards. Ar-TP3:138,
Au-SP:247, Co-HP:107, Ir-BB:150
My Brother Bert. T. Hughes.
Co-BB:27
My Sister Lois Is Plump. Rs-PF:31
Nothing-at-All. Ir-BB:60,
Mo-MGT:210, Mo-NR:128
Old Joe Brown, He Had a Wife.
Un-GT:18
The Perils of Individuality.
W. Gilbert. Co-PT:299
The Perils of Obesity.
H. Graham. Co-FB:121
A Pirate Who Hailed from
Nertskinski. Br-LL:48
Poor Henry. L. Blair. Ja-PC:31
Some Credulous Chroniclers Tell
Us. J. Riley. Br-LL:49
The Sweet Tooth. K. Pyle.
Ag-HE:64, Co-BB:57

Take the Curious Case of Tom
   Pettigrew. D. McCord.
   Br-LL:128
There Was a Maid on Scrabble Hill.
   Ir-BB:101
There Was an Old Man Who Said,
   "Hush!" E. Lear. Bo-GJ:9,
   Br-LL:5, Fr-WO:42, Un-GF:42,
   Un-GT:240
There Was an Old Man Who when
   Little. E. Lear. Br-LL:51,
   Sh-RP:150, Un-GF:42, Un-GT:240
There Was Once a Young Man of
   Oporta. L. Carroll.
   Br-LL:50, Ir-BB:223
Upon a Pipkin of Jellie.
   R. Herrick. Bo-GJ:24,
   De-CH:498, Gr-EC:291, Sm-LG:118
Whenas in Jeans. P. Dehn.
   Co-FB:229
The Young Lady of Lynn. Br-LL:136,
   Gr-CT:27, Ir-BB:219, Ke-TF:288
Your Little Hands. S. Hoffenstein.
   Co-BL:139, Co-FB:316
HUMOR - SKATING
   Golden Gates. Br-SM:48
   The Sigh. C. Morgenstern.
      Un-R:67
   There Was Once a Most Charming
      Young Miss. Br-LL:78
HUMOR - SKELETONS
   A Skeleton Once in Khartoum.
      Br-LL:66, Br-SM:4
HUMOR - SKIING
   Winter Trees. C. Diekmann.
      Fl-HH:22, Mo-SD:153
HUMOR - SKUNKS
   A Man Who Was Fond of His Skunk.
      D. McCord. Br-LL:130
   The Skunk. A. Noyes. Sh-RP:142
   The Tale of the Skunk and Poor Jez.
      J. Becker. Sh-RP:133
   There Was a Young Man from the
      City. Br-LL:20
HUMOR - SKYLARKS
   On How to Sing. Shiki. Le-IS:25
HUMOR - SLEEP
   Diddle, Diddle, Dumpling.
      Bo-FP:37, De-PO:28, Ir-BB:191,
      Li-LB:71, Mo-CC:(21), Mo-MGT:36,
      Mo-TL:41, Wi-MG:13, Wr-RM:37
   Early Rising. J. Saxe. Fe-PL:399
   Here's an Easy. Re-RR:121
   A Nightmare. W. Gilbert.
      Co-HP:61, Un-GF:70
   What Overtakes You. Re-RR:116
HUMOR - SMILES
   No Matter How Grouchy You're
      Feeling. A. Euwer. Br-LL:45
   The Smile of the Goat.
      O. Herford. Co-FB:22

The Smile of the Walrus.
   O. Herford. Co-FB:22
HUMOR - SMITH, JOHN
   Noah an' Jonah an' Cap'n John
      Smith. D. Marquis. Co-SS:189,
      Fe-PL:198, Sm-LG:195
HUMOR - SMITH, WILLIAM JAY
   Mr. Smith. W. Smith. Co-FB:47,
      Li-SR:45
HUMOR - SMOKE
   The Educated Love Bird. P. Newell.
      Co-FB:216
HUMOR - SMOKING
   The Man of Bombay. Wr-RM:75
   My First Cigar. R. Burdette.
      Co-PT:278
   Ode to Tobacco. C. Calverley.
      Co-FB:92
   There Was an Old Hag of Malacca.
      Br-LL:31
   Two Limericks. Co-BB:29
HUMOR - SNAILS
   Four and Twenty Tailors.
      Gr-GB:69, Ir-BB:41, Li-LB:87,
      Mo-MGT:117, Mo-NR:92, On-TW:60,
      Wi-MG:62, Wr-RM:88
   The Haughty Snail-King.
      V. Lindsay. Ha-LO:58
   The Periwinkle Diggers. Ir-BB:38
   Said the Snail to the Tortoise.
      O. Herford. Br-LL:15
   The Snail's Dream. O. Herford.
      Bo-FP:86, Ch-B:66
HUMOR - SNAKES
   As I Was Walking down the Lake.
      Ir-BB:19
   The Fastidious Serpent.
      H. Johnstone. Co-HP:83,
      Gr-EC:18, Lo-LL:25
   Lines to Dr. Ditmars.
      K. Robinson. Pl-IO:167
   The Little Boys of Texas.
      R. Coffin. Br-SM:100,
      Mc-WK:167
   The Serpent. T. Roethke.
      Gr-EC:19, Li-TU:71
   There Once Was a Man Who Said,
      "Why." C. Wells. Br-LL:13
   There Was an Old Man with a
      Flute. E. Lear. Br-LL:11
   "There's a Tune," Said a Sly
      Bengalese. J. Bennett.
      Br-LL:13
HUMOR - SNAPDRAGONS
   A Lucky Thing. D. Aldis. Sh-RP:136
HUMOR - SNEEZING
   That's Not to Be Sneezed At.
      Rs-PF:70
   There Once Was a Man with a
      Sneeze. M. Dodge. Br-LL:64

HUMOR - SNOBS AND SNOBBISHNESS
For a Lady I Know. C. Cullen.
Ab-MO:27, Ad-PB:91, Bo-AN:89,
Br-SM:150, Hu-MP:231, Un-MA:571
Having a Wonderful Time.
D. Wyndham Lewis. Co-FB:7
Mom Told Me. Rs-PF:21
On Buying a Dog. E. Klauber.
Co-PU:93
HUMOR - SNORING
Arthur. O. Nash. Br-LL:43,
Co-FB:52, Co-HP:100
Away with Bloodshed. A. Housman.
Br-SM:99, Li-TU:73
The Cat Sat Asleep. De-TT:29
Late Last Night. H. Graham.
Br-SM:22, Hi-WP I:11
Snoring. A. Fisher. Au-SP:96
HUMOR - SNOW
One Thousand Nine Hundred &
Sixty-Eight Winters. J. Earley.
Ab-MO:93, Jo-SA:127
HUMOR - SOAP
Soap, the Oppressor.
B. Johnson. Fe-PL:216
Social Studies. M. Neville.
Co-PU:65
HUMOR - SOCIAL CLASSES
Robert Whitmore. F. Davis.
Ad-PB:96, Be-MA:53, Hu-PN:254,
Ra-BP:121
HUMOR - SOLDIERS
Bill 'Awkins. R. Kipling.
Co-RM:214
Captain Carpenter. J. Ransom.
Br-TC:387, Ha-PO:36, Un-MA:415,
Wi-LT:314
Captain Jinks. Er-FA:404
Corporal Bull. Mo-MGT:27
The Duke of Plaza-Toro.
W. Gilbert. Co-FB:70, Co-HP:63,
Fe-FP:349
A Letter from the Front.
H. Newbolt. Cr-WS:79
O, the Grand Old Duke of York.
Ar-TP3:100, Au-SP:4, Cl-DT:14,
Gr-GB:197, Li-LB:51, Mo-MGT:25,
Mo-NR:118, Wi-MG:76
HUMOR - SOLOMON, KING OF ISRAEL
King David and King Solomon.
Sm-MK:127, Un-GF:15, Un-GT:243
HUMOR - SONGS AND SINGING
Calypsomania. A. Brode. Co-FB:276
Even among Insects. Issa.
Do-TS:17
The Frogs' Singing-School.
E. Carbell. Au-SP:235
High Notes. Ja-HH:22
I Like to Sing Also. J. Updike.
Co-FB:278
Jack the Piper. Gr-CT:88,
Gr-GB:18, Ir-BB:40
Limericks. Co-HP:29
My Singing Aunt. J. Reeves.
Br-SM:14
The New Church Organ.
W. Carleton. Fe-PL:233
Of a Sudden the Great Prima-Donna.
P. West. Br-LL:107
On How to Sing. Shiki. Le-IS:25
The Raven. Nicharchus. Pl-US:61
Schmaltztenor. M. Branch.
Co-FB:277
The Serpent. T. Roethke.
Gr-EC:19, Li-TU:71
Swan Song. S. Coleridge.
Ch-B:88, Na-EO:101, Pl-US:60,
Un-GT:236
There Was a Young Girl in the
Choir. Br-LL:107
There Was an Old Person of
Bradley. E. Lear. Pl-US:61
Try Singing These. Br-LL:135,
Un-GT:242
HUMOR - SONNETS (ABOUT)
Urceus Exit. A. Dobson. Go-BP:126
HUMOR - SOUL
Theological. C. Fadiman. Co-FB:131
HUMOR - SOUNDS
The Bees' Song. W. de la Mare.
Lo-LL:55, Mc-WS:37, Un-GF:80
HUMOR - SOUP
Baby Kate. J. Newman. Co-HP:100
Soup. C. Sandburg. Sh-RP:162
The Story of Caspar and the Soup.
H. Hoffman. Un-GF:55
HUMOR - THE SOUTH
Poor South. J. Coogler. Co-FB:301
Slim in Hell. S. Brown. Ra-BP:105
HUMOR - SPACE EXPLORATION
Interplanetary Limerick.
A. Graham. Br-LL:113
Love in a Space-Suit.
J. Kirkup. To-MP:120
The Museum of Skeletons.
M. Katsumura. Le-TA:43
Old Woman on a Broom.
Gr-EC:72, Ir-BB:240
Presidential Address to a Party
of Exiles Leaving for the
Moon. H. Nemerov. Pl-ML:11
The Scene Pope John Wouldn't
Let Fellini Film.
D. Georgakas. Sc-TN:60
Tea in a Space Ship. J. Kirkup.
To-MP:119
Unusual Visit. B. Lee. Ja-HH:62
A Week after the First Sputnik.
Mo-MI:79
HUMOR - SPANISH AMERICAN
WAR, 1898
Manila. E. Ware.
Co-FB:124

HUMOR - SPANISH LANGUAGE
   A Hex on the Mexican X.
      D. McCord.   Co-FB:210
HUMOR - SPARROWS
   The Irate Songster. K. Patchen.
      Ca-BP:44
   A Little Cock Sparrow.
      Ir-BB:26, Li-LB:87, Mo-MGT:171,
      Mo-NR:48, Mo-TL:57, Wi-MG:36,
      Wr-RM:66
   Mr. and Mrs. Spikky Sparrow.
      E. Lear.   Ox-BC:190
   Silly Willie Warden. A. Dodds.
      Hi-WP I:9
HUMOR - SPEECH
   At the Theater.   A. Herbert.
      Co-FB:476
   The Captain Stood on the
      Carronade.   F. Marryat.
      Co-SS:23, De-CH:597, De-TT:136,
      Ha-PO:255, Sh-RP:261
   La Donna E Perpetuum Mobile.
      I. Edman.   Co-FB:193
   The Girl in the Lane.   Mo-MGT:209,
      Mo-NR:30, Rv-ON:81, Wr-RM:47
   How She Resolved to Act. M. Moore.
      Pe-SS:116, Un-MA:575, Un-MW:59
   Lucinda Prattle.   P. Brown.
      Lo-LL:78
   Oh Come Little Children.
      P. McGinley.   Ga-FB:174
   The Old Woman of Gloucester.
      Wr-RM:112
   Prose and Poesy.   T. Ybarra.
      Co-HP:118
   Reflections at Dawn.
      P. McGinley.   Co-FB:394
   A Sailor to His Parrot.
      W. Davies.   Al-VBP:1109
   Talking. M. Goode.   Jo-VC:25
   To a Lady Holding the Floor.
      M. Weston.   Co-FB:196
   The Two Dogs.   Bo-FP:30, On-TW:9
   Wise Nature.   Co-PU:17
HUMOR - SPEECHES
   Some Speeches Are like the Horns
      of a Steer.   Rs-PF:55
HUMOR - SPEED
   Ambition. M. Bishop.   Br-AF:235
   A Hurrying Man He Always Was.
      Wy-CM:32
   Said a Sheep to Her Child, "My
      Dear Ruth."   J. Francis.
      Br-LL:23
   Said the Snail to the Tortoise.
      O. Herford.   Br-LL:15
   There Was an Old Man on a Hill.
      E. Lear.   Un-GF:42
   There Was an Old Person of Ickley.
      E. Lear.   Br-LL:15, Ir-BB:218,
      Na-EO:103

HUMOR - SPELLING
   Bingo.   De-CH:83, Gr-EC:82
   Bobby's First Poem.   N. Gale.
      Co-FB:105, Co-PU:7
   A Boy at Sault Ste. Marie.
      Br-LL:101
   Grasshopper.   e. cummings.
      Co-BBW:225
   I'll Bet that You.   Re-RR:95
   Laughs Anatomical.   Br-LL:51,
      Un-GT:242
   Limericks since Lear.   Un-GT:242
   A Llyric of the Llama.
      B. Johnson.   Co-OH:30
   Mr. Punchinello.   Gr-EC:281
   A Modern Composer Named Brahms.
      Br-LL:108
   A Musical Lady from Ga. Br-LL:108
   O I C.   Co-HP:24
   Old King Cole Had a Daughter.
      Re-RR:95
   An Old Lady Living in Worcester.
      Br-LL:25
   The One-L Lama.   O. Nash.
      Co-FB:38, Co-HP:98, Fe-FP:356,
      Lo-LL:21, Pa-RE:17, Sh-RP:141,
      Sm-LG:92
   The Principal Food of the Sioux.
      Br-LL:89
   The Ptarmigan.   Co-BBW:241
   Ragged Rascal.   Re-RR:68
   Rhinoceroses.   Co-OH:71
   Said a Bad Little Youngster
      Named Beauchamp.   C. Wells.
      Br-LL:84
   Said a Boy to His Teacher One
      Day.   Br-LL:101
   She Frowned and Called Him Mr.
      Br-LL:123, Fe-FP:361, Un-GT:241
   The Sioux.   E. Field.   Bo-GJ:154,
      Co-FB:428
   A Small Boy When Asked to Spell
      "Yacht."   Br-LL:101
   The Spelling Bee at Angels.
      B. Harte.   Co-PT:241
   Spelling Rhyme.   Ju-CP:6
   A Sporty Young Man in St. Pierre.
      F. Christgau.   Br-LL:119
   A Teacher Whose Spelling's
      Unique.   C. Loomis.   Br-LL:99
   Then.   D. Aldis.   Br-BC:108
   There Is an Old Cook in N.Y.
      Br-LL:89
   There Was a Composer Named Haydn.
      Br-LL:109
   There Was a Composer Named Liszt.
      Br-LL:108
   Two Brothers There Were of Sioux
      City.   Br-LL:65
   An Unpopular Youth of Cologne.
      Br-LL:65

HUMOR - SPELLING — cont'd.
A Wandering Tribe Called the
Sioux. Br-LL:97
A Young Lady Sings in Our Choir.
Br-LL:121
HUMOR - SPICES
As the Red-Hot Pepper. Rs-PF:17
HUMOR - SPIDERS
The Embarrassing Episode of
Little Miss Muffet. G. Carryl.
Ha-PO:279, Hu-MP:454, Pa-OM:38,
Sh-RP:137, Un-GF:78
When You Were a Baby. Re-RR:108
Why Might It Be Good. Re-RR:118
HUMOR - SPIES
Award. R. Durem. Ad-PB:152,
Hu-NN:33, Jo-SA:26, Ke-PP:118,
Kr-OF:54, Lo-TY:243, Ra-BP:164
HUMOR - SPINACH
There Was an Old Woman.
W. de la Mare. Br-SG:45
HUMOR - SPINES
Shut the Door. E. Rounds.
Br-SM:116, Co-HP:110, Ir-BB:109
HUMOR - SPITTING
Fascination. J. Tabb. Co-OH:80
HUMOR - SPRING (SEASON)
Kerchoo! M. Fishback. Co-PS:62
The Lawyers' Invocation to Spring.
H. Brownell. Fe-PL:377,
Ke-TF:279
Pinkletinks. G. Allen. Gr-EC:167
song. e. cummings. Mc-WS:127
Spring. M. Bishop. Mc-WS:126
HUMOR - SQUIRRELS
Of All the Idiots That Abound.
S. Hoffenstein. Sh-RP:136
HUMOR - STAIRWAYS
Alligator on the Escalator.
E. Merriam. La-OC:45
Goosey, Goosey, Gander. Mother
Goose. De-PO:28, Li-LB:84,
Mo-MGT:21, Mo-NR:12, Wi-MG:61,
Wr-RM:43
Here's Little Jim Nast of
Pawtucket. H. Lofting.
Br-LL:75
Johnnie Norrie. Mo-MGT:95
Stairs. O. Herford. Co-FB:375,
Co-HP:73, Sh-RP:147
HUMOR - STARS
Canopus. B. Taylor. Co-FB:86
La Donna E Mobile. A. K.
Co-FB:347
Earth. O. Herford. Br-SM:67,
Du-RG:81, Pe-M:84
HUMOR - STATISTICS
The Unknown Citizen. W. Auden.
Du-SH:95, Gr-BT:133, Ke-PP:33,
Mo-BG:194, Ni-JP:30, Pe-SS:106,
Tr-MR:232, Wi-LT:471

HUMOR - STATUES
Overheard in the Louvre.
X. Kennedy. Co-EL:60
HUMOR - STORMS
Brave Alum Bey. W. Gilbert.
Co-SS:151
A Nautical Extravaganza.
W. Irwin. Co-PT:260
The Sailor's Consolation. C. Dibdin.
Co-HP:103, Co-SS:56, De-TT:128
HUMOR - STORYTELLING
The Devil's Advice to Story-Tellers.
R. Graves. Rv-CB:993, Wi-LT:371
I'll Tell You a Story. Mother
Goose. Gr-EC:284, Hu-MP:152,
Li-LB:75, Mo-MGT:176, Mo-NR:4,
Wr-RM:57
Request Number. G. Sprod.
Co-FB:100, Co-HP:114, Ir-BB:109
That's All. Wr-RM:100
HUMOR - STREETCARS
There Was a Young Girl, a Sweet
Lamb. Br-LL:136, Un-GF:44
HUMOR - STRIKES
A Strike among the Poets.
Co-FB:340
HUMOR - STUPIDITY
Dick o' the Cow. Ox-BB:538
The Old Farmer and His Young.
Wife. Co-PT:311, Gr-GB:158
The Old Loony of Lyme.
Hi-WP I:100
Pelt Kid and His Grandmother.
Te-FC:193
Silly Willie Warden. A. Dodds.
Hi-WP I:9
HUMOR - STUTTERING
Pu-Heter Pu-Huligan. Gr-EC:8
There Was a Young Man of
Calcutta. Br-LL:83, Lo-LL:6
HUMOR - SUBURBAN LIFE
In the Suburbs. L. Simpson.
Ho-TH:76
Suburban Vista. C. Walsh.
St-H:238
HUMOR - SUFFERING
Anna Maria. Mo-MGT:94
Can't Understand. Yüan Shui-p'ai.
Hs-TC:411
HUMOR - SUICIDE
A Ballade of Suicide.
G. Chesterton. Co-FB:75
The Briefless Barrister.
J. Saxe. Br-SM:39
But Then. B. King. Co-PT:85
A Cat in Despondency Sighed.
Br-LL:20
The Despairing Lover. W. Walsh.
Co-BL:134, Hi-WP II:113,
No-CL:187, Sm-LG:355
Faithless Nelly Gray. T. Hood.
Br-SM:33, Co-HP:78, Hi-WP I:100

Ko-Ko's Song.   W. Gilbert.
   Er-FA:438
Life Is Fine.   L. Hughes.
   Mc-WK:95
nobody loses all the time.
   e. cummings.   Mc-WS:139
A Peanut Sat.   Co-OH:38, Ir-BB:154
The Ratcatcher's Daughter.
   Gr-GB:134
Resumé.   D. Parker.   Br-SM:27,
   Du-RG:68
Sorrows of Werther.   W. Thackeray.
   Br-SM:32, Co-FB:344,Hi-WP II:11
Too Blue.   L. Hughes.   Du-RG:73
Under the Drooping Willow Tree.
   Rv-CB:788
the wail of archy.   D. Marquis.
   Co-FB:332
HUMOR - SUN
   Monkey Sun Descends to Earth.
      Hs-TC:451
HUMOR - SUNDAY
   Sketch from Loss of Memory.
      S. Dorman.   Pe-SS:93
   Sunday Edition.   J. Keith.
      De-FS:117
HUMOR - SUNSET
   The Sunset.   H. Leigh.   Un-GF:65
HUMOR - SUPERNATURAL
   Lament for Better or Worse.
      G. Baro.   De-FS:17
   A Poem to Delight My Friends Who
      Laugh at Science Fiction.
      E. Rolfe.   Cr-WS:168, Hi-TL:234,
      Ke-PP:125
HUMOR - SUPERSTITION
   The Superstitious Ghost.
      A. Guiterman.   Br-SM:8
HUMOR - SUPPER
   Little Tommy Tucker.   Bo-FP:60,
      Li-LB:27, Mo-CC:(48),
      Mo-MGT:72, Mo-NR:51, Wi-MG:69,
      Wr-RM:110
HUMOR - SURGEONS AND SURGERY
   Jill Laughed.   Rs-PF:12
HUMOR - SURVIVAL
   Disaster.   C. Calverly. Li-SR:64
   Root, Hog, or Die.   Fi-BG:65
   'Twas Ever Thus.   H. Leigh.
      Li-SR:66
HUMOR - SUSPICION
   Much Nicer People.
      E. Coatsworth.   Co-PU:121
   Suspicious Sweetheart.   H. Heine.
      Un-MW:54
HUMOR - SUSSEX, ENG.
   Southdown Summer.   Sagittarius.
      Pa-HT:135
HUMOR - SWEET POTATOES
   A Sweet Potato Rolls off the
      Hill.   Hs-TC:454

HUMOR - SWIMMING AND DIVING
   Cold Logic.   B. Hutchinson.
      Mo-SD:142
   A Daring Young Lady of Guam.
      Br-LL:76, Un-GT:242
   Learner.   Co-OH:81
   The Little Boys of Texas.
      R. Coffin. Br-SM:100, Mc-WK:167
   Mother, May I Go Out to Swim?
      Fe-FP:364, Ir-BB:141, Mo-MGT:37,
      Sp-AS:30
   Our Silly Little Sister. D. Aldis.
      Co-HP:30, Fe-FP:40, Na-EO:118
   Written after Swimming from Sestos
      to Abydos.   G. Byron. Fl-HH:55
HUMOR - SYMPATHY
   Jane Smith. R. Kipling. Li-SR:104
HUMOR - TABLES
   Get Up, Get Up.   Co-FB:123,
      Co-HP:22, Co-PU:5
   The Table and the Chair. E. Lear.
      Au-SP:221, Bo-FP:26, Hu-MP:463,
      Ir-BB:235, Un-GB:25, Un-GT:215
HUMOR - TABLEWARE
   Alas! Alas! For Miss Mackay!
      Ir-BB:63
HUMOR - TAHITI
   Vor a Gaugin Picture zu Singen.
      K. Stein.   Co-FB:217
HUMOR - TAILORS
   Ah! Euripides? Rs-PF:70
   I Don't Think.   Rs-PF:13
   The Old Tailor.   W. de la Mare.
      Gr-EC:91, Ir-BB:41
   Remarked the Tailor.   Rs-PF:53
   Tailor of Bicester.   Ir-BB:38,
      Mo-MGT:23
   Tell Me, Tell Me.   M. Moore.
      Wi-LT:276
HUMOR - TAILS (ANIMALS)
   A Dog's Tail Is Not a Dog's
      Tail.   Rs-PF:97
   My Tale Is Told.   Rs-PF:120
   Ode to the Pig: His Tail.
      W. Brooks. Lo-LL:43
   Paripace and Paripale.
      R. Flower.   Ir-BB:155
   Pico della Mirandola.
      M. Mason.   Hu-PN:526
   Please Take Your Seats. Re-RR:116
   Riddle Me.   Re-RR:74
   Tails.   Co-HP:26
   The Tale of a Dog.
      J. Lambert, Jr.   Co-IW:16
HUMOR - TAPIRS
   A Tapir Who Lived in Malay.
      O. Herford.   Br-LL:33
HUMOR - TARIFFS
   Lines to Dr. Ditmars.
      K. Robinson.   Pl-IO:167

HUMOR - TARSIERS
  The Contrary Waiter.   E. Parker.
    Co-OW:24
HUMOR - TATTLETALES
  A Terrible Infant.
    F. Lampson-Locker.   Co-FB:100,
    Co-HP:93, Co-PU:5
HUMOR - TEA
  One Two Three.   Co-OW:38, On-TW:63
  The Rape of the Lock.   A. Pope.
    Al-VBP:531, 533
  Tea in a Space Ship.   J. Kirkup.
    To-MP:119
  Tea Party.   H. Behn.   Li-LC:35
  There Was Once a Giraffe Who
    Said, "Who."   O. Herford.
    Br-LL:29, Co-HP:74
  There's Nothing in Afternoon Tea.
    G. Burgess.   Br-LL:84
HUMOR - TEACHERS AND TEACHING
  Le Boul' Mich'.   M. Bracker.
    Ke-TF:377
  Doctor Faustus Was a Good Man.
    Mother Goose.   Li-LB:66,
    Mo-NR:118
  Doctor Foster.   Ir-BB:39
  The Irish Schoolmaster. J. Sidey.
    Co-FB:223, Co-HP:111
  Jay-Bird, Jay-Bird, Settin' on a
    Rail.   Un-GT:18
  Journey to a Parallel.
    B. Wright.   Hu-PN:355
  A Kindergarten Teacher. Rs-PF:59
  Now, Children, What Shall I Talk
    about?   Rs-PF:15
  Our Teacher's Angry Face.
    A. Mori.   Le-TA:63
  Schoolmistress.   C. Sansom.
    To-MP:129
  The Snuffboxes.   Co-PT:304
  A Teacher.   B. McGregor. Le-M:136
  A Teacher Whose Spelling's Unique.
    C. Loomis.   Br-LL:99
  Teacher's Jacket.   S. Kuroda.
    Le-TA:62
HUMOR - TEAKETTLES
  The Bunyip and the Whistling
    Kettle.   J. Manifold.
    Co-PM:123
HUMOR - TECHNOLOGY
  It Rolls On.   M. Bishop.
    Pl-IO:132
HUMOR - TEETH
  About the Teeth of Sharks.
    J. Ciardi.   Co-BBW:73
  Edie Asked Ed.   Rs-PF:28
  Reflections Dental.
    P. McGinley.   Du-RG:52, Ho-TH:70
  There Was an Old Man of Black-
    heath.   Br-LL:43, Co-HP:29,
    La-PP:70, La-PV:34, Lo-LL:56,
    Un-GF:45

There Was an Old Man of Tarentum.
    Br-LL:43, Co-HP:29, Lo-LL:7
HUMOR - TELEPHONES
  Eletelephony.   L. Richards.
    Ar-TP3:128, Au-SP:239, Bo-GJ:7,
    Co-IW:22, Fe-FP:346, Gr-EC:186,
    Hu-MP:455, Ir-BB:56, La-PV:23,
    Lo-LL:24, Ox-BC:289, Pe-FB:102
  Party Line. J. Keith.   De-FS:119
  Le Telephone. M. Bracker.
    Ke-TF:376
  The Telephone Rang.   Rs-PF:52
  Think of Eight Numbers.
    S. Silverstein.   Co-BB:30
  Woman Telephoning.   J. Keith.
    De-FS:116
HUMOR - TELEVISION
  The Man in a Picture Window
    Watching Television.
    M. Weston.   Co-EL:62
  Reflections Dental.
    P. McGinley. Du-RG:52, Ho-TH:70
HUMOR - TEMPTATION
  Temptation.   Co-EL:61
HUMOR - TENNIS
  At the Tennis Clinic.
    L. Martin.   Mo-SD:38
  Dark Eyes at Forest Hills.
    L. Martin.   Mo-SD:38
  Potpourri from a Surrey Garden.
    J. Betjeman.   Co-FB:326,
    En-PC:81
  Why Are Tennis Players. Re-RR:81
HUMOR - TENNYSON, ALFRED TENNYSON,
    1ST BARON (LORD TENNYSON)
  Abbreviated Interviews with a Few
    Disgruntled Literary Celebrities.
    R. Whittemore.   Co-FB:343
  Hornpipe.   E. Sitwell.
    Pa-GTB:472
  Sir Beelzebub.   E. Sitwell.
    Un-MB:331
  Three More Clerihews.   Un-GF:49
HUMOR - TERMITES
  The Termite.   O. Nash.
    Br-SM:101, Ke-TF:335, Un-GF:83
HUMOR - TEXAS
  Hell in Texas.   Co-RM:30
  Iowa, Kansas, Nebraska.
    G. Frumkin.   Bl-FP:22
  The Little Boys of Texas.
    R. Coffin. Br-SM:100, Mc-WK:167
HUMOR - THAWS
  The Windham Thaw.
    A. Guiterman.   Gr-EC:58
HUMOR - THEATERS
  At the Theater.   A. Herbert.
    Co-FB:476
  Le Théatre.   M. Bracker.
    Ke-TF:378

HUMOR - THIEVES
  Burglar Bill. T. Guthrie.
    Co-FB:112
  Don't Tell the Scarecrow. Yayu.
    Do-TS:31
  Epitaph for a Horse Thief.
    Gr-EC:150
  Gentle Alice Brown. W. Gilbert.
    Co-FB:147
  John Hielandman. Gr-GB:168
  Old Roger. Mo-MGT:143, Pa-RE:101,
    Su-FVI:23
  Paddy O'Rafther. S. Lover.
    Co-PI:97, Co-PT:298
  Psychological Prediction.
    V. Brasier. Co-BB:23
  The Raven Visits Rawhide.
    Fi-BG:182
  The Robber. I. Eastwick.
    Br-SS:119
  The Salvation of Texas Peters.
    J. Foley. Br-SM:28
  There Was a Robber Met a
    Robber. De-CH:533
  Thief. Co-BB:109, Co-HP:28
  The Village Blacksmith. Co-FB:53
  Warning to Book Thieves. Ju-CP:3
HUMOR - THIRST
  Song of the Seaweed. E. Cook.
    Co-FB:299
HUMOR - THOUGHT AND THINKING
  Behind His Long Face. Issa.
    Ca-BF:33
  Existentialism. L. Frankenberg.
    Co-FB:339
  Family Life. A. Laing. Co-FB:473
  Laugh, Be Jolly. A. Housman.
    Hi-WP I:120
  That Reminds Me. O. Nash.
    Co-FB:401, Un-MW:61
HUMOR - THREATS
  Dinky. T. Roethke. Co-OW:27,
    Li-TU:72
  Lullaby of the Cannibal Giants.
    Da-SC:95
HUMOR - THRIFT
  A Bachelor of Maine. E. Deland.
    Co-HP:55
  A Bugler Named Dougal MacDougal.
    O. Nash. Br-LL:105, Lo-LL:95,
    Mc-WS:181
  La Carte. J. Richardson.
    Co-FB:87
  There's a Very Mean Man of
    Belsize. Br-LL:103
  Tommy O'Linn. Mo-MGT:96
  Tommy Trot. Ir-BB:42, Mo-MGT:121
HUMOR - TIGERS
  How to Tell the Wild Animals.
    C. Wells. Un-GF:84
  O Have You Caught the Tiger?
    A. Housman. Li-SR:9

  There Was a Young Lady of Niger.
    Au-SP:244, Br-LL:136, Br-SM:94,
    Ch-B:49, Er-FA:200, Fe-FP:360,
    Fr-WO:47, Gr-EC:215, Ke-TF:287,
    Lo-LL:29
  There Was an Old Hag of Malacca.
    Br-LL:31
  The Tiger. H. Belloc. Un-MB:171
  A Tiger's Tale. J. Bennett.
    Co-HP:33
HUMOR - TIME
  Epitaph for Any New Yorker.
    C. Morley. Br-SM:151
  Fish Out of Water. M. Fishback.
    Ke-TF:380
  Jonathan Bing's Tea. B. Brown.
    Mc-WK:117
  Said a Crow in the Top of a
    Tree. J. Ciardi. Br-LL:1
  time time said old king tut.
    D. Marquis. Co-FB:125
  Why Did a Boy. Re-RR:115
HUMOR - TOADS
  As into the Garden.
    A. Housman. Co-PT:296
  "Croak!" Said the Toad.
    Bo-FP:84, Ch-B:61
  The Skunk. A. Noyes. Sh-RP:142
  warty bliggens, the toad.
    D. Marquis. Co-FB:14
  The World Has Held Great Heroes.
    K. Grahame. Bo-GJ:108,
    Co-FB:54, Co-HP:68, Fe-FP:342,
    It-HB:40, Lo-LL:12, Sh-RP:45
HUMOR - TOBACCO
  Tobacco. G. Hemminger. Fe-PL:211
HUMOR - TOES
  In the Tub We Soak Our Skin.
    E. Horn. Co-EL:124, Co-PU:133
  The Pobble Who Has No Toes.
    E. Lear. Bl-OB:16, Co-HP:89,
    Gr-EC:26, Hu-MP:465, Ir-BB:153,
    Lo-LL:72, Ox-BC:198, Sm-LG:93,
    Un-GB:24, Un-GF:34, Un-GT:212
  This Little Cow Eats Grass.
    Wy-CM:41
HUMOR - TOMBS
  St. Swithin. D. Henderson.
    Br-SM:163
  Stranger Call This Not. Br-SM:158
HUMOR - TOUCANS
  A Fellow Who Slaughtered Two
    Toucans. Br-LL:70
HUMOR - TOURISTS
  Ozymandias Revisited. M. Bishop.
    Co-HP:34, Li-SR:83
  Tourists. H. Moss. Co-FB:212
HUMOR - TOYS
  George. H. Belloc. Co-FB:109,
    Co-HP:32, Co-OH:40, Ir-BB:159,
    Un-GT:216

HUMOR - TOYS — cont'd.
  Jittery Jim. W. Smith. Co-BB:33
  Prince Tatters. L. Richards.
    Hu-MP:10
  The Squad Car. M. Neville.
    Su-FVI:33
HUMOR - TRAGEDY
  Fragment of a Greek Tragedy.
    A. Housman. Li-SR:152
  A Norrible Tale. Co-OT:76
  the wail of archy. D. Marquis.
    Co-FB:332
HUMOR - TRAINS
  The Baby Goes to Boston.
    L. Richards. Ir-BB:244
  Clinkerdump. W. Horsbrugh.
    Ir-BB:245
  Dr. Fell and Points West.
    O. Nash. Sh-RP:130
  Early in the Morning. Ir-BB:248
  The Engineer. A. Milne. Sh-RP:4
  Hallelujah! A. Housman.
    Br-SM:59, Co-FB:383, Co-OT:57,
    Co-PU:32
  Joshua Lane. Ir-BB:241
  The Passenjare. I. Bromley.
    Co-FB:430, Co-HP:35
  There Was an Old Lady Named
    Carr. Br-LL:70
  The Train to Glasgow.
    W. Horsbrugh. Ir-BB:251
HUMOR - TRANSLATING
  On Looking into Robert Frost in
    Kanji. W. Meredith. Pl-ML:70
  The Translated Way. F. Adams.
    Co-FB:261
HUMOR - TRANSPORTATION
  Punch, Brothers, Punch!
    Rv-CB:790
  The Smoking Stick. Mo-MGT:87
HUMOR - TRAPPING
  The Mousetrap. C. Morgenstern.
    Rd-OA:30
HUMOR - TRAUBEL, HELEN
  I Like to Sing Also. J. Updike.
    Co-FB:278
HUMOR - TRAVEL AND TRAVELERS
  The Humbug Steamship Companies.
    J. Stone. Fi-BG:134
  In Foreign Parts. L. Richards.
    Co-HP:106, Lo-LL:104
  Italian Excursion.
    H. Bevington. Mc-WS:112
  The Unwinged Ones. O. Nash.
    Ke-TF:290
  Why I No Longer Travel.
    L. Richards. Hu-MP:445
HUMOR - TREASON
  Treason. J. Harington.
    Co-EL:53, Co-FB:125,
    Rv-CB:177

HUMOR - TREASURE-TROVES
  Treasure Hunting. M. Justus.
    Cr-SS:24
HUMOR - TREES
  A Branch Library. J. Flagg.
    Br-LL:102
  Fraser, I Think, Tells of a Roman.
    C. Reznikoff. Kh-VA:59
  Spring Is Almost Gone. Buson.
    Be-CS:42
  What Wears Clothes in the
    Summertime. Re-RR:100
HUMOR - TRIALS
  Evidence Read at the Trial of
    the Knave of Hearts.
    L. Carroll. Er-FA:217,
    Pa-GTB:378, Un-GF:23
HUMOR - TROMBONES
  I Guess I Owe My Success.
    Rs-PF:50
HUMOR - TROUBLEMAKERS
  For a Mouthy Woman. C. Cullen.
    Ab-MO:28, Ad-PB:92, Br-SM:150
  The Little Black Dog.
    Ir-BB:82, Mo-MGT:82
  Lollocks. R. Graves. Gr-CT:155,
    Ma-FW:196, Na-EO:135
  Mr. Nobody. Ch-B:113, Co-PM:210,
    Fe-FP:49, Hu-MP:134
HUMOR - TROUSERS
  The Perils of Individuality.
    W. Gilbert. Co-PT:299
  The September Gale. O. Holmes.
    Co-FB:111, Co-HP:76
  What Can't Walk a Step. Re-RR:44
HUMOR - TRUTH
  There Was a Young Lady Named
    Ruth. Br-LL:60
HUMOR - TUNNELS
  Mister Beers. H. Lofting.
    Fe-FP:316, Ir-BB:202, Sh-RP:148
HUMOR - TURKEYS
  Soliloquy of a Turkey.
    P. Dunbar. Ra-BP:47
  Thanksgiving Drumsticks.
    L. Blair. Ja-HH:46
  Thanksgiving Gobbler. K. Dee.
    Ja-HH:47
  The Turkey. O. Nash. Sh-RP:145,
    Un-GF:82
HUMOR - TURNIPS
  If a Man Who Turnips Cries.
    Er-FA:216, Fr-WO:51, Gr-EC:286,
    Na-EO:52, Sp-TM:30, Un-GF:20
  A Mistake. Ir-BB:199
  Mr. Finney's Turnip. Ch-B:104,
    Co-HP:22, Gr-EC:110, Lo-LL:57
  What the Little Girl Said.
    L. Blair. Ja-HH:44
HUMOR - TURTLES
  The Hare and the Tortoise.
    I. Serraillier. Co-BBW:88

Meditations of a Tortoise.
E. Rieu.   Ar-TP3:130,
Co-BBW:82, Co-FB:5
Myrtle.   T. Roethke.   Pa-RE:11
Night Thoughts of a Tortoise.
E. Rieu.   Ar-TP3:131,
Co-BBW:84, Co-FB:6
Said the Snail to the Tortoise.
O. Herford.   Br-LL:15
Soliloquy of a Tortoise.
E. Rieu.   Ar-TP3:130, Br-SG:43,
Co-BBW:93, Co-FB:4, Mc-WS:170
Tony Was a Turtle.   E. Rieu.
Ar-TP3:130, Gr-EC:12, Ir-BB:85
The Turtle.   O. Nash.   Co-FB:13,
Er-FA:206, Ke-TF:334
HUMOR - TUTANKHAMEN,
KING OF EGYPT
King Tut.   X. Kennedy.   Li-TU:61
time time said old king tut.
D. Marquis.   Co-FB:125
HUMOR - TWENTIETH CENTURY
Love under the Republicans
(or Democrats).   O. Nash.
Mc-WS:62
Miniver Cheevy, Jr.   D. Parry.
Li-SR:76
HUMOR - TWINS
According to My Mother.   Rs-PF:80
Here Are the Twins.
S. Silverstein.   Co-OH:15
The Twins.   H. Leigh.   Ar-TP3:137,
Br-BC:22, Br-SM:124, Co-HP:91,
Fe-FP:355, Mc-WK:149, Un-GF:66,
Un-GT:232
HUMOR - TYPEWRITERS
Archy a Low Brow.   D. Marquis.
Co-HP:95
Dog and Fox.   D. Ferry.   Co-PU:92
Please Excuse Typing.
J. Boothroyd.   Co-FB:194
Qwerty-u-i-op.   A. Guiterman.
Co-HP:69
HUMOR - UMBRELLAS
The Rain It Raineth.   C. Bowen.
Co-FB:122, Co-PU:17, Un-GF:15
There Was a Wee Girl Named
Estrella.   M. Hill.   Br-LL:77
What Kind of Umbrella.   Re-RR:108
HUMOR - UMPIRES
Decline and Fall of a Roman
Umpire.   O. Nash.   Mo-SD:7
The Umpire.   W. Gibson.   Fl-HH:45,
Mo-SD:6
HUMOR - UNCLES
Bobby's First Poem.   N. Gale.
Co-FP:105, Co-PU:7
HUMOR - UNDERTAKERS
The Jilted Funeral.   G. Burgess.
Br-SM:139
The Undertaker's Club.   Gr-GB:325

HUMOR - UNFAITHFULNESS
Careless Talk.   M. Hollis.
Co-FB:315
Note on Intellectuals.
W. Auden.   Co-FB:500
On a Wag in Mauchline.   R. Burns.
Co-EL:54, Co-FB:322
HUMOR - UNICORNS
Inhuman Henry.   A. Housman.
Co-BB:26, Co-FB:101, Co-HP:80
HUMOR - UNITED NATIONS
Bed-Time Story.   M. Cane.   Un-GT:81
HUMOR - UNITED STATES
Stately Verse.   Ar-TP3:134,
Co-HP:25, Fe-FP:363
What a State.   L. Blair.   Ja-PC:30
HUMOR - UNITED STATES-HISTORY
AND PATRIOTISM
Johnny's Hist'ry Lesson.
N. Waterman.   Fe-FP:189
HUMOR - UNIVERSE
Earth.   O. Herford.   Br-SM:67,
Du-RG:81, Pe-M:84
Richard Tolman's Universe.
L. Bacon.   Pl-IO:171
HUMOR - VACATIONS
The Jokesmith's Vacation.
D. Marquis.   Co-FB:65,
Co-HP:94
Poor Grandpa.   R. O'Brien.
Br-SM:130
HUMOR - VALENTINE'S DAY
To My Valentine.   Au-SP:361,
Bo-FP:294, Ch-B:116, Gr-EC:223,
La-PH:47
HUMOR - VALLEYS
Between the Walls of the Valley.
E. Peck.   Br-AF:104
HUMOR - VALUE AND VALUES
Bowery.   D. Ignatow.   Pe-M:70
Investment.   N. Nathan.   Pe-M:125
Prince Tatters.   L. Richards.
Hu-MP:10
There Lived a King.   W. Gilbert.
Co-FB:145, Co-PT:83
HUMOR - VEGETABLES
Vegetables.   S. Silverstein.
Co-OT:36
HUMOR - VENUS (GODDESS)
Hornpipe.   E. Sitwell.   Pa-GTB:472
HUMOR - VICTORIA, QUEEN OF ENGLAND
Hornpipe.   E. Sitwell.   Pa-GTB:472
Old England Forever, and Do It No
More.   Gr-GB:200
HUMOR - VILLAGE LIFE
Our Village — by a Villager.
T. Hood.   Rv-CB:764
HUMOR - VILLAINS AND VILLAINY
The Ballad of Pug-Nosed Lil.
R. Fletcher.   Fi-BG:231

HUMOR - VIOLENCE
  The Bashful Man. B. Johnson.
    Co-RM:43
HUMOR - VIOLINS
  John, Come Sell Thy Fiddle.
    Ir-BB:208
  The Mountain Whippoorwill.
    S. Benét. Co-PT:110
  The Old Tailor. W. de la Mare.
    Gr-EC:71, Ir-BB:41
  Terence McDiddler. Mo-MGT:150,
    Pa-AP:26
HUMOR - VIRGINIA
  Between the Walls of the Valley.
    E. Peck. Br-AF:104
HUMOR - VOICES
  A Small Boy of Iquique. Br-LL:39
HUMOR - VOODOO
  Sermonette. I. Reed. Ad-PB:328
HUMOR - VOYAGES
  How Bill Went East. G. Bryan.
    Co-PT:82
  If Pigs Could Fly. J. Reeves.
    Ir-BB:254
  The Jumblies. E. Lear. Ox-BC:187
  The Land of Ho-Ho-Hum. W. Smith.
    Ir-BB:256
  A Long Story. Ir-BB:239
  Travel. L. Cohen. Un-MW:199
HUMOR - VULTURES
  The Vulture. H. Belloc. Ox-BC:312
HUMOR - WAFFLES
  Mummy Slept Late and Daddy Fixed
    Breakfast. J. Ciardi.
    Ar-TP3:133, La-PV:26
HUMOR - WAITERS AND WAITRESSES
  The Contrary Waiter.
    E. Parker. Co-OW:24
  To a Junior Waiter. A. Herbert.
    Co-FB:477
HUMOR - WAITING
  The Evening Out. O. Nash.
    Un-MA:567
HUMOR - WAKE-UP VERSES
  In the Morning. P. Dunbar.
    Ra-BP:51
HUMOR - WAKENING
  Before Dawn. A. Darr. Pe-M:118
  Early Rising. J. Saxe. Fe-PL:399
  A Medical Student Named Elias.
    Br-LL:103
  The Quiet One. Fang Wei-teh.
    Hs-TC:136
  Robin and Richard. Ir-BB:30,
    Mo-MGT:130, Mo-NR:131,
    On-TW:9, Wr-RM:20
  Waking. A. Higgins. Co-EL:136,
    Co-PU:3
HUMOR - WAKES
  Maloney Remembers the Resurrection
    of Kate Finucane. B. Kennelly.
    Co-PT:108

  Wake. L. Hughes. Br-SM:136
HUMOR - WALES
  Welsh Incident. R. Graves.
    Hi-WP II:114
HUMOR - WALKING
  Said Dad, "At Your Age. . . ."
    Rs-PF:88
  There Was a Young Girl of Majorca.
    E. Lear. Br-LL:69
HUMOR - WALRUSES
  The Smile of the Walrus.
    O. Herford. Co-FB:22
  The Walrus and the Carpenter.
    L. Carroll. Ar-TP3:126,
    Au-SP:275, Bl-OB:125, Co-FB:134,
    Co-HP:40, De-TT:95, Er-FA:500,
    Fe-FP:328, Fr-WO:59, Ga-FB:318,
    Ir-BB:245, Pe-FB:103, Sp-OG:242
HUMOR - WAR DEAD
  It's Three No Trumps. G. Innes.
    Co-FB:125
HUMOR - WAR WOUNDED
  Faithless Nelly Gray. T. Hood.
    Br-SM:33, Co-HP:78, Hi-WP I:100
HUMOR - WARNINGS
  Beware, My Child. S. Silverstein.
    Co-OW:11, La-PV:30
  Dinky. T. Roethke. Co-OW:27,
    Li-TU:72
  Don't Ever Cross a Crocodile.
    K. Starbird. Ar-TP3:130,
    La-PV:31
  Framed in a First-Story Winder.
    Co-OH:36
  Harriet and the Matches.
    H. Hoffmann. Ir-BB:157
  Not Again. P. Brown. Co-PU:23
  Precious Things. Lo-TY:198
  Social Note. D. Parker. Ke-TF:232
  Warning to Book Thieves. Ju-CP:3
HUMOR - WASHINGTON, GEORGE
  George Washington.
    S. Silverstein. Co-PS:46
  Leetla Giorgio Washeenton.
    T. Daly. Co-PS:46, Fe-FP:414,
    Hu-MP:377
  Washington, Man of Mystery.
    Ir-BB:214
HUMOR - WASPS
  The Adventures of Oberon.
    M. Drayton. Rd-OA:164
  A Limerick in Blank Verse.
    W. Gilbert. Br-LL:4
HUMOR - WATERLOO, BATTLE, 1815
  On Scott's Poem "The Field of
    Waterloo." T. Erskine.
    Co-FB:337
HUMOR - WAVES
  O Billows Bounding Far.
    A. Housman. Co-BN:80

HUMOR – WEALTH
  Lord Finchley. H. Belloc.
    Co-EL:58, Co-FB:197
  Love. C. Calverley. Co-FB:311,
    Co-HP:38
  The Rich Man. F. Adams. Co-FB:502,
    Co-HP:29
  Spectator ab Extra. A. Clough.
    Pa-GTB:361
HUMOR – WEASELS
  Don't Ever Seize a Weasel by the
    Tail. J. Prelutsky. Co-OW:48
  Tarragon, Tansy, Thyme and Teasel.
    E. Farjeon. Ir-BB:238
  There Was an Envious Erudite
    Ermine. O. Herford. Br-LL:34
  The Weasel. Gr-CT:11
HUMOR – WEATHER
  A Dog and a Cat Went Out Together.
    Mother Goose. Bo-FP:225,
    Ir-BB:237
  When Sally Spelled. Rs-PF:74
HUMOR – WEDDINGS
  After Ever Happily.
    I. Serraillier. Co-BL:151,
    Gr-EC:190, Ma-FW:145
  A Ballad upon a Wedding.
    J. Suckling. Al-VBP:418,
    Rv-CB:382
  Fiddle-de-Dee; Fiddle-de-Dea.
    Mother Goose. Mo-NR:130,
    Pa-AP:48
  The Frog and the Mouse. Ho-WR:41
  Frog Went a-Courtin'. Su-FVI:73
  I Mun Be Married a Sunday.
    N. Udall. Gr-CC:158
  The Mouse Who Lived on a Hill.
    Bu-DY:61
  The Owl and the Pussy-Cat. E. Lear.
    Ar-TP3:120, Au-SP:266, Bl-OB:117,
    Bo-FP:25, Bo-GJ:14, Cl-DT:30,
    Co-IW:3, Er-FA:495, Fe-FP:354,
    Fe-PL:237, Fr-WO:39, Ha-PO:239,
    Hi-WP I:94, Hu-MP:450, Ir-BB:250,
    Ke-TP:38, La-PV:204, Mc-PR:40,
    Ox-BC:185, Pa-GTB:357, Pe-FB:96,
    Rv-CB:812, Sm-LG:89, Sm-MK:200,
    St-FS:108, Un-GB:28, Un-GT:224
  There Was a Young Lady of Harwich.
    Br-LL:122
  The Wedding. Mo-MGT:208
  When Broncho Jack Was Spliced.
    J. Adams. Fi-BG:172
HUMOR – WELCOMES
  Go, Little Booklet, Go. B. Nye.
    Co-PU:23
HUMOR – WELLS
  Little Willie. Br-SM:49
HUMOR – THE WELSH
  Shon a Morgan. Gr-GB:163

HUMOR – THE WEST
  Greer County. Co-RM:15
  The Merry Miner. C. Rourke.
    Sh-RP:288
HUMOR – WESTWARD MOVEMENT
  Root, Hog, or Die. Fi-BG:65
HUMOR – WHALES AND WHALING
  If You Ever. Co-IW:23
  Jack Was Every Inch a Sailor.
    Do-WH:18
  The Powerful Eyes o' Jeremy
    Tait. W. Irwin. Co-FB:135,
    Co-SS:79, Ha-PO:264
  The Whale. T. Roethke. Co-PU:85
  The Whale. Co-SS:115, Gr-CT:208,
    Gr-GB:217
HUMOR – WHEELBARROWS
  The Old Woman of Harrow. Wr-RM:114
  Wheelbarrow. E. Farjeon. Co-FB:317
  When I Was a Bachelor.
    Gr-GB:147, Ir-BB:149, Li-LB:62,
    Mo-NR:66, Wr-RM:118
HUMOR – WHISTLES AND WHISTLING
  The Whistling Thief. Co-PT:202
HUMOR – WIGS
  The Bold Cavalier. Ox-BC:74
  A Strange Pig. Mo-MGT:37,
    Wr-RM:110
  W.W. I. Baraka. Ad-PB:254
HUMOR – WILLIAM I, KING OF
    ENGLAND (THE CONQUEROR)
  William the Bastard. Lakon.
    Co-FB:131
HUMOR – WILLS
  The Dishonest Miller. Em-AF:761
  My Uncle. Gr-EC:282
  Wills. J. Saxe. Br-SM:126,
    Er-FA:216
HUMOR – WINDS
  Granny. S. Milligan. Co-OT:71
HUMOR – WINTER
  Ancient Music. E. Pound.
    Ke-PP:111, Li-SR:124, Ma-FW:273,
    Mc-EA:45, Wi-LT:226
  Winter on Black Mingo. Co-FB:296
HUMOR – WISDOM
  Good Men. Bhartrihari. Al-PI:35
  The Man in the Moon. Mo-MGT:23
  Morals. J. Thurber. Ga-FB:329
  The Mouse. R. Vargo. La-GI:56
  There Was a Man of Our Town.
    Mother Goose. Er-FA:506
  There Was a Man of Thessaly.
    Ir-BB:208, Li-LB:54, Mo-MGT:36,
    Mo-NR:115, Rv-CB:455
  Winkelman Von Winkel. C. Lyon.
    Co-OT:20
HUMOR – WISHES
  The Chair-Mender. Mother Goose.
    Er-FA:505, Gr-EC:280, Ir-BB:40,
    Li-LB:63, Mo-MGT:124, Mo-NR:59,
    Wr-RM:19

HUMOR - WISHES — cont'd.
The False Knight on the Road.
  De-CH:316, Gr-GB:288, Ma-BB:84,
  Rv-CB:52
Plans. D. Thompson. Br-BC:114
HUMOR - WITCHES AND WITCHCRAFT
Adventures of Isabel. O. Nash.
  Br-SM:93, Co-HP:98, Gr-EC:202,
  Ir-BB:105, Ja-PC:26, La-PP:15,
  La-PV:32, Ne-AM:22, Un-GF:72,
  Un-MA:564
Dinky. T. Roethke. Co-OW:27,
  Li-TU:72
Disappearance. Ja-HH:35
The Quiet Child. R. Field.
  Ne-AM:30
Tam o'Shanter. R. Burns.
  Al-VBP:634, Sp-OG:170
HUMOR - WIVES
All's Well That Ends Well.
  Er-FA:211
A Curt Addendum. Br-SM:151
Did You See My Wife. Ir-BB:216
From a Churchyard in Wales.
  Br-SM:158, Co-FB:132
Grieve Not for Me. Br-SM:159
Here Lies My Wife. J. Dryden.
  Br-SM:156
If My Complaining Wife. Issa.
  Be-MC:19
Kellyburnbraes. Ox-BB:634
Little Dicky Dilver. Gr-CC:159,
  Ir-BB:59, Mo-MGT:16
Old Sam's Wife. Br-SM:126,
  Gr-CT:475
Three Epigrams. J. Cunningham.
  Un-MA:615
HUMOR - WOMEN
Capsule Conclusions, V. Un-MW:65
Durham Old Women. Gr-GB:175
The Evening Out. O. Nash.
  Un-MA:567
Femme Fatale. V. Starrett.
  De-FS:187
Man Is for the Woman Made.
  P. Motteaux. Un-MW:45
A Man's Woman. M. Davies.
  Fe-PL:416
On Being a Woman. D. Parker.
  Fe-PL:414
Reflections Outside of a
  Gymnasium. P. McGinley.
  Mo-SD:161
The Rhyme of the Chivalrous Shark.
  W. Irwin. Br-SM:97, Co-HP:81
The Seven Spiritual Ages of Mrs.
  Marmaduke Moore. O. Nash.
  Un-MA:568
A Thought. J. Stephen. Co-FB:391
Wise Nature. Co-PU:17

HUMOR - WOMEN-EQUAL RIGHTS
The Old Feminist. P. McGinley.
  Hi-TL:226
HUMOR - WONDERS
I Will Have the Whetstone.
  Gr-GB:87
HUMOR - WOODCHUCKS
How Much Wood Would a Woodchuck
  Chuck. Ar-TP3:123, Fe-FP:358,
  Ir-BB:188, Ju-CP:14
On Looking into Robert Frost in
  Kanji. W. Meredith. Pl-ML:70
HUMOR - WORDS
The Akond of Swat. E. Lear.
  Br-LL:55, Co-FB:421, Lo-LL:85,
  Sm-MK:100, Un-GT:226
At the Zoo. A. Milne. Fe-FP:251,
  Fr-MP:17
Crispus Attucks McCoy. S. Brown.
  Ra-BP:115
Did You Ever? Bu-DY:90,
  Gr-GB:21
The Eight Words Below. Re-RR:74
Four Quartz Crystal Clocks.
  M. Moore. Br-TC:302, Pl-IO:67
Fuzzy Wuzzy. Fr-MP:21, Un-GT:18
Goose, Moose, and Spruce.
  D. McCord. Gr-EC:127
The Guppy. O. Nash. Hi-WP II:14,
  Ir-BB:81, Ja-PC:22
In the Beginning. W. Barney.
  De-FS:16
Habits of the Hippopotamus.
  A. Guiterman. Ar-TP3:127,
  Co-FB:25, Co-HP:71, Ga-FB:333,
  Sh-RP:151
Jabberwocky. L. Carroll.
  Ar-TP3:129, Bo-GJ:148, Co-FB:433,
  Er-FA:200, Fe-FP:334, Fr-WO:64,
  Ga-FB:317, Li-SR:18, Mc-PR:42,
  Ox-BC:241, Rv-CB:925, Sp-OG:246,
  Un-GF:26, Un-GT:208
Logic. Bo-FP:11, Gr-EC:126
Logical English. Co-HP:21,
  Gr-EC:126
Merry Thoughts. L. Richards.
  Co-OW:44
Mr. Bidery's Spidery Garden.
  D. McCord. Un-GF:77
O I C. Co-HP:24
Oh Shucks, Ma'am, I Mean Excuse
  Me. O. Nash. Ke-TF:293
On a Flimmering Floom You Shall
  Ride. C. Sandburg, Gr-EC:187
Once a Big Molicepan. Fe-FP:360
An Original Love Story. Co-BL:161
Pickety Fence. D. McCord.
  Gr-EC:194
Please Tell Me Just the Fabuli.
  S. Silverstein. Co-EL:51,
  Co-PU:19

Ponjoo.   W. de la Mare.   Br-SM:80
Scat! Scitten.   D. McCord.
Gr-EC:129
Song-ily.   Gr-EC:195
Speak to Me.   Bu-DY:94
Tie Your Tongue, Sir?   R. Smith.
Ad-CI:16, Gr-EC:184
What a Beautiful Word!   W. Cole.
Co-OT:64
HUMOR - WORDSWORTH, WILLIAM
Bells for William Wordsworth.
Dom Moraes.   Go-BP:239,
Pl-ML:116
An Imitation of Wordsworth.
H. Coleridge.   Co-FB:258,
Rv-CB:760
Some of Wordsworth.   W. Landor.
Gr-CT:470
A Sonnet.   J. Stephen.
Co-FB:257, Li-SR:109, Pl-ML:115
HUMOR - WORLD
To the Terrestrial Globe.
W. Gilbert.   Li-TU:70
HUMOR - WORLD WAR, 1914-18
I Was Playing Golf That Day.
Co-FB:122
HUMOR - WORMS
The Book-Worms.   R. Burns.
Co-EL:63, Co-FB:331, Co-PU:22,
Gr-CT:472
Why?   W. de la Mare.   Co-FB:105
Will Anything Else.   Re-RR:118
You Know This.   Re-RR:104
HUMOR - WORRY
Arthur Ridgewood, M.D.   F. Davis.
Be-MA:53, Ra-BP:121
HUMOR - WORSHIP
My Cat Jeoffry.   C. Smart.
Bl-OB:107, Cl-DT:48, Co-BBW:127,
Gr-CT:120, Ha-PO:111, Ho-WR:244,
Un-GT:46
The Story of Samuel Jackson.
C. Leland.   Co-PT:267
HUMOR - WREN, SIR CHRISTOPHER
Sir Christopher Wren.
E. Bentley.   Co-FB:127
Three Clerihews.   E. Bentley.
Un-GF:49
HUMOR - YAKS
The Yak.   T. Roethke.
Gr-EC:22, Li-LC:16
The Yak.   V. Sheard.   Do-WH:24
Yak.   W. Smith.   Co-OT:26,
Ja-PC:20, Sh-RP:342, Un-GT:55
HUMOR - YALE UNIVERSITY
Monkey.   J. Miles.   Wi-LT:772
HUMOR - YOUTH
The Corner.   W. de la Mare.
Br-BC:136, Ir-BB:67
Five Years Old.   L. Borie.
Br-BC:55, Br-SS:44

HUMOR - YOUTH AND AGE
Extremely Naughty Children.
E. Godley.   Co-BB:65
Grandpa Is Ashamed.   O. Nash.
Co-PU:18
To a Child of Quality, Five Years
Old.   M. Prior.   Rv-CB:485
To a Small Boy Standing on My
Shoes while I Am Wearing Them.
O. Nash.   Co-FB:108
Uncle Frank.   M. Shannon.
Ja-PC:46
HUMOR - ZEBRAS
A Surprise.   M. Douglas.   Co-OT:48
HUMOR - ZOOS
The Prodigy.   A. Herbert.
Na-EO:132
The Zoo Club.   R. Hershon.
Sc-TN:93
HUMORISTS: see also WIT
The Humorist.   K. Preston.
Na-EO:124
The Jokesmith's Vacation.
D. Marquis.   Co-FB:65, Co-HP:94
HUNCHBACKS: see HANDICAPPED
HUNGARIANS IN THE UNITED STATES
Ode to Mayor Locker.   D. Levy.
Lo-IT:78
HUNGARY-HISTORY AND PATRIOTISM
Kossuth.   J. Lowell.   Hi-FO:231
HUNGER AND STARVATION: see also
FAMINES; POVERTY
Atman.   D. Saxon.   Lo-IT:123
Babies Are Crying.   P. John.
Ba-HI:85
A Description of Famine.
Al-PI:69
Don't Cry, My Little One.
Wang T'ung-chao.   Hs-TC:259
The Eagle.   M. Rosenfeld.   Ho-TY:81
The Famine Year.   Lady Wilde.
Co-PI:197
God to a Hungry Child.
L. Hughes.   Kr-OF:187
He Who Has Never Known Hunger.
E. Coatsworth.   Ar-TP3:209
Herod.   M. Martinet.   Ba-PO:144,
Cr-WS:123
Hunger.   B. Weinstein.   Ho-TY:291
Hunger.   Le-IB:93, Tr-US I:25
Hunger.   Lo-TY:156
Hunger Is Bad.   Do-CH:(18)
The Hungry Black Child. A. Miller.
Ad-PB:181
I Had a Dream Last Night.
C. Meyer.   Jo-VC:19
I Had Been Hungry All the Years.
E. Dickinson.   Un-MA:97,
Wi-LT:11
Is This Life?   H. Harrington.
Ba-HI:82

HUNGER AND STARVATION — cont'd.
  Late Rising. J. Prévert. Ad-CI:98
  Life. H. Harrington. Ba-HI:85
  The Little Cart. Ch'en Tzu-lung.
    Ma-FW:89
  The Lonesome Boy. V. White.
    La-IH:24
  A Long Time Ago. T'ao Ch'ien.
    Sm-LG:303
  Men Who Hunger. I. Stern.
    Ho-TY:225
  Navajo Rug. B. Lee. Ba-HI:84
  No New Music. S. Crouch.
    Ad-PB:484
  Our Doom Is in Our Being.
    J. Agee. Un-MA:605
  Poor Miner's Farewell.
    M. Jackson. Kr-OF:190
  Portrait Philippines. A. Duckett.
    Hu-PN:358
  Song for the Lazy. Do-CH:(10)
  This Little Morsel of Morsels
    Here. W. de la Mare. Ag-HE:3
  To a Starved Hare in the Garden
    in Winter. C. Turner. Sm-MK:182
  Winter in Dunover Field. T. Hardy.
    Un-MB:31
  A Winter Night. J. Velez.
    Ba-HI:72
  Yet Some Are Always Hungry.
    Gr-TG:38
HUNT, (JAMES HENRY) LEIGH
  Dedication. J. Keats. Ox-BN:334
HUNTING: see also FALCONRY;
      FOX HUNTING; HUMOR - HUNTING;
      INDIANS OF NORTH AMERICA -
      HUNTING; POACHING (LAW); SATIRE -
      HUNTING; SHOOTING; TRACKING
      AND TRAILING; TRAPPING
  After Shooting a Cock Pheasant
    Last Friday. P. Mayer.
    St-H:139
  Against Exploiters. Tr-CB:33,
    Tr-US I:65
  All in Green Went My Love Riding.
    E. Cummings. Al-VBP:1201,
    Bo-GJ:121, Ga-FB:82, Ma-FW:203,
    Mo-SD:186, No-CL:70, Re-TW:118,
    Wi-LT:357
  And Now the Hunt! Br-FW:18
  Autumn Dawning. A. Machado.
    Le-SW:71
  Ayii, Ayii, Ayii, Ayii
    (Wondering). Ho-SD:68
  Badger. J. Clare. Cl-FC:67,
    Co-BBW:50, Ho-WR:213, Rv-CB:720
  Beagles. W. Rodgers. Mo-SD:117
  Beast of the Sea. Ho-SD:79,
    Le-IB:32
  The Boar Hunt. Homer. Ma-FW:230
  Caribou Hunting. Le-IB:71,
    Ma-BH:24, Tr-US I:13

The Cheerful Horn.   De-CH:130
Chevy Chase. Al-VBP:43, Ma-BB:97,
  Ox-BB:496
The Childless Father.
  W. Wordsworth. De-CH:260
Complaint over Bad Hunting.
  Da-SC:45, Le-IB:71
Contest. F. Victor. Mo-SD:127
Crystal Moment. R. Coffin.
  Gr-EC:162, Pe-SS:74
Dance Song. Le-IB:77, 78
Day of the Wolf. K. Wilson.
  Ha-WR:76
Deer Hunt. J. Jerome. Du-RG:36
Deer Song. Da-SC:81
Encounter in the Cage Country.
  J. Dickey. Ha-TP:102
The Farmer's Gun. A. Young.
  Rd-OA:35
First They Shot. Le-IB:51
For a Hunter. Tr-CB:48,
  Tr-US I:42
Friar's Hunting Song. T. Peacock.
  De-TT:83, Mo-SD:116, Un-GT:89
The Hawk in the Wood. A. Morley.
  Cl-DT:58
Haymakers, Rakers. T. Dekker.
  Al-VBP:227
Hippopotamus Hunter's Song.
  Tr-US I:96
The Hunt Is Up. De-CH:129,
  De-TT:76
A Hunted Deer. De-PP:41
A Hunter's Pleasure. Br-FW:17
Hunter's Song. W. Scott.
  Rd-OA:176
Hunter's Song. Do-CH:(38)
Hunting. J. Aluskak. Ba-HI:67
Hunting. G. Snyder. Mo-BG:125
Hunting Song. S. Coleridge.
  Bl-OB:140, Re-TW:77
Hunting Song. W. Scott.
  Ho-WR:76, Mo-SD:181, Na-EO:13,
  Pa-GTB:241
Hunting Song. Br-MW:40,
  Le-OA:59, 61, 64,
  Tr-US II:223, 258, 271
Hunting Songs, 2. Bear Song.
  Tr-US I:12
Hunting Songs, 1. Walrus Hunting.
  Ma-BH:17, Tr-US I:12
The Hunting Tribes of Air and
  Earth. W. Scott. Rd-OA:117
I Am Ashamed. Le-IB:74
I Remember the White Bear.
  Le-IB:54
I Wanted to Use My Weapon.
  Le-IB:56
I Went to Kill the Deer.
  Wo-HS:(50)
Improvised Song of the Baby
  Coconut-Monkey. Tr-US II:202

In Praise of Bow and Arrow.
  Tr-CB:23, Tr-US I:54
India. W. Turner. Bl-OB:112,
  La-PV:155, Un-MB:348
An Interview near Florence.
  S. Rogers. Ox-BN:53
An Invitation to Phyllis.
  C. Cotton. No-CL:108
Invocation Sung by a Hunter
  Setting Out. Tr-US II:303
Johnie o'Cocklesmuir. Ox-BB:535
The Jovial Gentlemen.
  D. Hoffman. Ca-MB:62
Lament of a Widow over Her Dead
  Husband. Tr-US I:72
Landscape, Deer Season. B. Howes.
  Bo-GJ:253, Pe-M:111
Like as a Huntsman. E. Spenser.
  Ha-PO:108
Magic Words to Bring Luck when
  Hunting Caribou. Le-IB:67
The Men of Valor. Akahito.
  Ba-ST:29
Molecatcher. A. Mackie.
  Co-BBW:40
Moose Hunting. T. Willis.
  Ba-HI:65
My Song Was Ready. Le-IB:79
The Night Hunt. T. MacDonagh.
  Co-BBW:105, Co-PI:102
Nightmare. A. Marx. De-FS:136
O Have You Seen the Shah.
  Ir-BB:263, Rv-ON:30
Of the Boy and the Butterfly.
  J. Bunyan. Ox-BC:35
Old Blue. Mo-SD:115
The Old Squire. W. Blunt.
  Mo-SD:110
On His Very First Hunt.
  Le-IB:51
One-Eyed Gunner. Rv-ON:31
The Outlaw. C. Kingsley.
  Co-RM:161
Over There I Could Think of
  Nothing Else. Le-IB:50
Paddler's Song on Bad Hunting
  Weather. Da-SC:41, Le-IB:72,
  Tr-US I:7
The Pheasant. R. Coffin.
  Ar-TP3:58, Du-RG:120, Ho-TH:37
Pig-Hunting Song. Tr-US II:181
Prayer of a Hunter at a Grave of
  Heitsi-Eibib. Tr-US I:77
Prayer to the Moon. Le-OE:63
The Prehistoric Huntsman.
  D. Wandrei. De-FS:213
The Rabbit. A. Brownjohn.
  To-MP:109
The Rabbit Hunter. R. Frost.
  Be-EB:28, Ho-TH:46
The Real Slayer of the Seal.
  Da-SC:45, Le-IB:52

Religious Hymn to Be Sung Wearing
  a Head Decoration. Le-IB:95,
  Ma-BH:15, Tr-US I:20
The Revenge of Hamish. S. Lanier.
  Ni-JP:46, Sp-OG:141
A Runnable Stag. J. Davidson.
  Co-BBW:195, Ho-WR:77, Mo-SD:123,
  Na-EO:63, Rd-OA:177
Signal Song on Capture of Polar
  Bear. Le-IB:53
Simon Lee the Old Huntsman.
  W. Wordsworth. Pa-GTB:217
Song. Tr-US I:50
Song Commemorating the Death of a
  Hunter. Tr-US I:93
Song of Myself. W. Whitman.
  Un-MA:49
The Sound of a Gun. A. Taylor.
  De-TT:82
Tears. E. Thomas. Pa-GTB:441,
  Rv-CB:969
There Was a Little Man. Er-FA:505,
  Gr-EC:281, Ir-BB:211, Li-LB:76,
  Mo-MGT:12, Mo-NR:61, Wr-RM:36
Those Game Animals. Le-IB:75
To a Fugitive. J. Wright.
  Ha-TP:40, Ho-TH:92
Ulivfak's Song of the Caribou.
  Le-IB:112
Walrus Hunting. Da-SC:40,
  Le-IB:52
What Shall He Have.
  W. Shakespeare. Al-VBP:188
The White Drake. Do-WH:35
Wind Thy Horn, My Hunter Boy.
  T. Moore. Fl-HH:13
Windsor Forest. A. Pope.
  Co-PU:105, Ma-FW:127, Un-GT:64
Winter Landscape. J. Berryman.
  Br-TC:37, Mo-BG:112, Un-MA:640,
  Wi-LT:566
A Winter Legend. G. Johnson.
  De-FS:112
With Dangling Hands. Da-SC:81
Wolves. G. Kinnell. Co-RM:95
Yolp, Yolp, Yolp, Yolp. Rd-OA:50
Young Reynard. G. Meredith.
  Co-BBW:38
HURDY-GURDIES: see ORGAN GRINDERS
HURLING (GAME)
  The Convict of Clonmel.
  Co-PI:16, Mo-SD:174
HURON, LAKE
  The Great Lakes Suite, III.
  J. Reaney. Do-WH:50
HURRICANES: see also TORNADOES
  The Hurricane. H. Crane.
  Sh-AP:186, Un-MA:534
Hurricane. C. Lushington.
  Sa-B:110
The Hurricane. P. Matos.
  Fe-FP:487

HURRICANES — cont'd.
A Hurricane at Sea.
  M. Swenson. Ha-WR:34
Rain. Ca-MU:32
The West Palm Beach Story.
  Em-AF:473
HUSBAND AND WIFE: see also
  HUMOR - HUSBAND AND WIFE
Andree Rexroth. K. Rexroth.
  Ca-VT:269
Aubade. K. Shapiro. Ca-VT:376
The Boy and the Mantle. Ox-BB:31
An Elder's Reproof to His Wife.
  A. Muuse. Lo-TY:57
Epic Song. Tr-US I:236
Evening. N. Young. Ke-TF:130
The Falcon Woman. R. Graves.
  Gr-BT:89
Farm Couple, after Norman
  Rockwell. B. Spacks. Ls-NY:75
The Farmer's Wife. A. Sexton.
  Wi-LT:816
The Funny Old Man and His Wife.
  Au-SP:218, Ch-B:109
Gift of the Sego Lily.
  M. Jarvis. Fi-BG:197
Home Burial. R. Frost. Pe-SS:15
I Doubt, I Doubt. Rv-ON:67
Imperialists in Retirement.
  E. Lucie-Smith. To-MP:149
In Crisis. L. Durrell. Wi-LT:692
In the Kitchen of the Old House.
  D. Hall. To-MP:144
Jack Sprat. Bo-FP:57, De-PO:24,
  Er-FA:507, Ir-BB:196, Li-LB:54,
  Mo-MGT:14, Mo-NR:4, Wi-MG:75,
  Wr-RM:47
John Grumlie. A. Cunningham.
  Fe-PL:235, Gr-GB:205
The Jungle Husband. S. Smith.
  Gr-BT:96
A Letter to Her Husband, Absent
  upon Publick Employment.
  A. Bradstreet. Rv-CB:386
Naughty Boy. R. Creeley.
  Kh-VA:40
The Newlyweds. C. Criswell.
  Fe-PL:96
A Night Out. D. Abse. Gr-BT:158
The Old-Marrieds. G. Brooks.
  Ad-PB:154
On an Island. J. Synge. Un-MB:181
On Thomas Carew. Rv-CB:415
Patch-Shaneen. J. Synge.
  Co-PI:188
Peter, Peter, Pumpkin-Eater.
  An-IP:23, Au-SP:3, Bo-FP:104,
  Er-FA:505, Ir-BB:196, Li-LB:61,
  Mo-CC:(7), Mo-MGT:106,
  Wi-MG:77, Wr-RM:98
The Science of the Night.
  S. Kunitz. Br-TC:245, Un-MA:592

Song after a Man Dies.
  Tr-US II:293
Song of a Widow for Her Dead
  Husband. Tr-US I:242
Song to Instruments. Tr-CB:22,
  Tr-US I:48
The Tale of the Jealous Brother.
  Br-MW:120
To My Dear and Loving Husband.
  A. Bradstreet. Fe-PL:148,
  Rv-CB:385, Sh-AP:11
The True and Tender Wife.
  Al-PI:29
Une Vie. P. Saarikoski.
  Co-EL:144
Witchcraft: New Style.
  L. Abercrombie. Un-MB:256
HUSBANDS: see also HUMOR -
  HUSBANDS
Any Wife to Any Husband.
  R. Browning. Ox-BN:535
Father. Y. Urakawa. Le-TA:26
For a Husband Away. Tr-CB:45,
  Tr-US I:46
Lament. Tr-US I:86
Lament of a Widow over Her Dead
  Husband. Tr-US I:72
A Letter to Her Husband.
  A. Bradstreet. Sh-AP:11
Song from a Story. Tr-US I:30
HUTCHINSON, KANS.
Prairie Town. W. Stafford.
  St-H:210
HYACINTHS
The Babiaantje. F. Prince.
  Un-MB:488
Beauty. D. Rossetti. Al-VBP:992
Fragments of Spring. A. Pratt.
  Al-WW:108
Not by Bread Alone. J. White.
  Fe-PL:105
HYDROGEN WEAPONS: see also
  HUMOR - HYDROGEN WEAPONS;
  SATIRE - HYDROGEN WEAPONS
Japanese Fisherman Dies.
  M. Mannes. Ba-PO:57
HYENAS: see also HUMOR - HYENAS
Greed. P. Bennett. Co-BBW:184
Hyena. Lo-TY:9
The Laughing Hyena, by Hokusai.
  D. Enright. Br-TC:117
Pets. D. Pettiward. Co-BBW:275
HYGIENE: see EXERCISE; HEALTH
HYMN SINGING: see also
  HUMOR - HYMN SINGING
Mourning Hymn for the Queen of
  Sunday. R. Hayden.
  Ad-PB:117, Du-SH:105
HYMNS: see also CHRISTMAS
  SONGS
Abide with Me. H. Lyte.
  Er-FA:443

All People That on Earth Do Dwell.
W. Kethe. Ga-S:14
Alleluia! Alleluia! Let the Holy
Anthem Rise. Co-PS:66
Alleluia, Hearts to Heaven and
Voices Raise. C. Wordsworth.
Ke-TF:195
At a Solemn Musick. D. Schwartz.
Tr-MR:35
Away in a Manger. M. Luther.
Ar-TP3:195, Bo-FP:193, Br-BC:165,
Fe-FP:93, Gr-TG:78, Hu-MP:347,
Ke-TF:78, La-PH:25, Mc-AW:78,
Un-GT:301
Barthélémon at Vauxhall. T. Hardy.
Pl-US:89
Battle Hymn of the Republic.
J. Howe. De-CH:159, Er-FA:469,
Fe-FP:441, Hi-TL:100, Ke-TF:53,
Pl-EI:160, Un-GT:311, Vi-PP:145
A Candle Burning in the Night.
S. Warner. Gr-TG:46
Centennial Hymn. J. Whittier.
Vi-PP:86
The Child's Hymn. M. Howitt.
Un-GT:20
Christ Whose Glory Fills the Skies.
C. Wesley. Ga-S:178
The Creator. Bo-FP:160
The Dead Man Ariseth and Singeth
a Hymn. The Book of the Dead.
Pa-SG:210
Dear Lord and Father of Mankind.
J. Whittier. Ke-TF:206
Easter Hymn. H. Vaughan. Ga-S:171
Fairest Lord Jesus. Ke-TF:184
Father of Night. B.Dylan.Mo-GR:100
General William Booth Enters into
Heaven. V. Lindsay. Ga-S:221,
Un-MA:221, Wi-LT:624
Holy, Holy, Holy! R. Heber.
Ke-TF:193
How Firm a Foundation. Ke-TF:187
A Hymn. J. Leeson. Gr-TG:71
Hymn. L. Nicholl. Pl-EI:196
Hymn. A. Young. Pl-EI:212
Hymn for Fasting. Br-MW:32,
Da-SC:170
Hymn of an Inca to the God
Viracocha. Tr-US II:299
Hymn of the High Priest of
Xipe Totec. Da-SC:171
A Hymn to Christ at the Author's
Last Going into Germany.
J. Donne. Al-VBP:263
A Hymn to God the Father. J. Donne.
Al-VBP:264, Ga-S:137, Pl-EI:206
Hymn to the Mother of the Gods.
Tr-US II:277
The Hymn to the Sun. Ab-MO:3,
Lo-TY:21
Hymn to Tlaloc. Da-SC:169

Hymn Written after Jeremiah
Preached to Me in a Dream.
O. Dodson. Bo-AN:124
I Am the Corncob. Ge-TR:49
I Think when I Read That Sweet
Story of Old. J. Luke. Bo-FP:48
In the Isle of Dogs.
J. Davidson. Ox-BN:907
An Indian Hymn of Thanks to
Mother Corn. Bo-FP:154
Johnny Appleseed's Hymn to the
Sun. V. Lindsay. Tr-MR:29
Just as I Am, Without One Plea.
C. Elliott. Ke-TF:191
Just for Today. Ke-TF:192
The King of Love My Shepherd Is.
H. Baker. Gr-TG:40, Ke-TF:184
Lead, Kindly Light. J. Newman.
Er-FA:474, Ga-S:46, Ox-BN:436
Lead Us, O Father.
W. Burleigh. Ke-TF:189
Let All the World in Every
Corner Sing. G. Herbert.
Gr-TG:83
Lift Every Voice and Sing.
J. Johnson. Ga-FB:277,
Hu-PN:32
Maya Hymn. Br-MW:5
Morning Hymn. T. Ken. Er-FA:455
Nearer to Thee. S. Adams.
Er-FA:481, Fe-PL:328
O God, Our Help in Ages Past.
I. Watts. Ke-TF:188, Pl-EI:200
O Mother, Dear Jerusalem
Ke-TF:190
O Worship the King. R. Grant.
Ga-S:3
Onward, Christian Soldiers.
S. Baring-Gould. Bo-FP:305,
Er-FA:481, Ke-TF:186
Praise to the Holiest.
J. Newman. Ga-S:172
Recessional. R. Kipling.
Al-VBP:1101, Er-FA:472, Ga-FB:242,
Ma-YA:229, Ox-BN:867, Sp-OG:214,
Un-MB:135
Rev'rent Our Hearts. Ba-PO:113
Ride On in Majesty. H. Milman.
Ga-S:152, Ke-TF:194
Rock of Ages. A. Toplady.
Er-FA:476, Rv-CB:554
A Slant of Sun. S. Crane.
Sh-AP:145, Wi-LT:120
The Son of God Goes Forth to War.
R. Heber. Ke-TF:185
Songs in the Night.
M. Caruthers. Ke-TF:182
The Spacious Firmament on High.
J. Addison. Mc-PR:202,
Pl-EI:211
There's a Wideness in God's
Mercy. F. Faber. Gr-TG:74

HYMNS — cont'd.
  Veni Creator. Ga-S:191
  When Malindy Sings. P. Dunbar.
    Ad-PB:10, Hu-PN:37
  See also Em-AF:355-400
HYPNOTISM: see also
    HUMOR - HYPNOTISM
  Gypsy Eyes. J. Hendrix. Mo-GR:124
HYPOCRITES AND HYPOCRISY:
    see also SATIRE - HYPOCRITES
    AND HYPOCRISY
  The Abyss. Ya-Hsüan. Pa-MV:153
  Cant. W. Davies. Tr-MR:217
  The Chimney Sweeper. W. Blake.
    Ma-YA:128, Rv-CB:580
  A Denunciation of the Princes and
    the Prophets. Bible. O.T.
    Micah. Me-PH:51
  For "Mr. Dudley," a Black Spy.
    J. Emanuel. Ra-BP:191
  He Preached upon "Breadth" till
    It Argued Him Narrow.
    E. Dickinson. Sh-AP:131
  Hypocrites. "Monk." Ba-HI:28
  I Stood upon a High Place.
    S. Crane. Sh-AP:143
  In Place of a Curse. J. Ciardi.
    Du-SH:104
  The Man from Up-Country Talking.
    J. de Melo Neto. An-TC:163
  The Masque of Anarchy.
    P. Shelley. Hi-FO:206
  An Open Foe May Prove a Curse.
    B. Franklin. Un-GT:25
  The Shepherd's Dog and the Wolf.
    J. Gay. Rd-OA:132
  That Hypocrite. Ra-BP:9
  The Virtuous Fox and the Self-
    Righteous Cat. J. Cunningham.
    Pa-OM:334
  White Christmas. W. Rodgers.
    Co-PI:169, Ke-PP:29, Un-MB:482,
    Wi-LT:492
IBADAN, NIG.
  Ibadan. J. Clark. Ab-MO:44,
    Ad-CI:81
IBOS: see AFRICAN VERSE - IBO;
    BIAFRA
IBYCUS
  Ibycus. J. Heath-Stubbs.
    En-PC:165
ICARUS: see DAEDELUS AND ICARUS
ICE: see also HUMOR - ICE;
    ICICLES; SLEET
  Alaska. J. Miller. Hi-TL:133
  Answer This Riddle. Re-RR:37
  Ayii, Ayii. La-RM:108
  Brittle World. L. Sarett.
    Th-AS:91
  The Fable of the Piece of Glass
    and the Piece of Ice. Ox-BC:151

  Fire and Ice. R. Frost.
    Al-VBP:1133, Er-FA:88,
    Hi-WP II:3, Ho-LP:82, Mo-BG:186,
    Pe-M:97, Un-MA:180, Wi-LT:174
  Fire Won't Burn Me. Re-RR:118
  The Frozen Ocean. V. Meynell.
    De-CH:389
  Horses and Men in the Rain.
    C. Sandburg. Fe-PL:409
  Ice. D. Aldis. Ar-TP3:189,
    Ir-BB:15
  Ice. C. Roberts. Co-BN:184,
    Co-PU:52, Do-WH:69
  The Ice King. A. De Mille.
    Do-WH:68
  The Icebound Swans. Rd-OA:199
  Over the Sea, the Frozen Sea.
    Ho-SD:5
  Under a Spring Mist. Teitoku.
    Be-MC:56
  Winter Streams. B. Carman.
    De-TT:91, Ha-YA:149, Sp-OG:284
ICE CREAM: see also HUMOR -
    ICE CREAM
  The Good Humor Man. D. Aldis.
    Fr-MP:16
  Ice Cream. L. Mead. Ho-CT:20
  The Ice-Cream Man. R. Field.
    Au-SP:148, Br-SS:176, Fe-FP:249
ICE HOCKEY: see HOCKEY
ICE-SKATING: see SKATING
ICEBERGS
  The Berg. H. Melville.
    Rv-CB:840, Sh-AP:122
  The Imaginary Iceberg. E. Bishop.
    Un-MA:612, Wi-LT:503
ICELANDIC VERSE
  Rain. E. Benediktsson. Pa-SG:205
ICICLES
  An Icicle. Mother Goose.
    Ar-TP3:99, Au-SP:24, Wr-RM:96
  Improvisations: Light and Snow.
    C. Aiken. Co-BN:189
  Slowly Melting, Slowly Dying.
    D. Hill. Le-M:193
  A Song of Thanks. W. Cole.
    Co-OT:18
  The Thaw. J. Matthews. Ha-WR:5
  Why. Onitsura. Le-MW:89
IDA, MOUNT
  Onward to Far Ida. G. Darley.
    Ox-BN:392
IDAHO
  Here We Have Idaho. H. Powell.
    Se-PR:258
  Idaho. Gr-GB:178
  On the Trail to Idaho. Se-PR:147
IDEALS: see also SATIRE - IDEALS
  The Atlantides. H. Thoreau.
    Al-VBP:918
  By Fiat of Adoration.
    O. Williams. Wi-LT:414

dive for dreams. e. cummings.
   Ha-TP:139
Envoi. A. Wickham. Un-MB:283
The Errand Imperious. E. Markham.
   Vi-PP:72
Free at Last. A. Alenik.
   La-IH:126
Gradatim. J. Holland. Er-FA:4
Hold Fast Your Dreams.
   L. Driscoll. Ar-TP3:214,
   Au-SP:356, Br-BC:123, Fe-FP:22,
   Hu-MP:73
I Dream a World. L. Hughes.
   Bo-AN:71, Bo-HF:29
I See. A. Jewell. Me-WF:88
Idylls of the King, Guinevere.
   A. Tennyson. Ma-YA:198
If I Could Only Live at That
   Pitch That Is near Madness.
   R. Eberhart. Wi-LT:433
Kid Stuff. F. Horne. Ab-MO:76,
   Ad-PB:56, Bo-AN:41, Bo-HF:109,
   Hu-PN:148, Li-TU:247
Leave Me, O Love. P. Sidney.
   Al-VBP:130, De-CH:641, Ha-PO:168
Litany of Our Sire, Don Quixote.
   R. Darío. Be-UL:19
Mignon's Song. J. von Goethe.
   Co-PU:48, Pa-SG:125
The Music Makers.
   A. O'Shaughnessy. Al-VBP:1063,
   Co-PI:163, Ga-FB:133, Mc-PR:72,
   Se-PR:324
The Need of the Hour. E. Markham.
   Vi-PP:224
The Poet. W. Whitman. Un-MA:79
Ring Out, Wild Bells.
   A. Tennyson. Bo-FP:177,
   Fe-FP:64, Ho-WR:241
Shrine to What Should Be.
   M. Evans. Hu-NN:77
A Song. Fang Ching. Hs-TC:385
Standards. N. Crane. Un-GT:305
Ultima Thule. H. Longfellow.
   Al-VBP:829
Where Are You Going, Greatheart.
   J. Oxenham. Vi-PP:27
IDENTITY: see SELF
IDIOTS: see MENTALLY HANDICAPPED
IDLENESS: see also HUMOR -
   IDLENESS; LAZINESS
The Camel's Hump. R. Kipling.
   Ir-BB:104, Na-EO:137, Ox-BC:319
The Castle of Indolence.
   J. Thomson. Al-VBP:545
Dance Song. Le-IB:77
The Idle Life I Lead.
   R. Bridges. Wi-LT:56
An Immorality. E. Pound.
   Bo-GJ:119, Co-PU:31, Gr-CC:55,
   Ha-PO:183, Mc-WS:65, Un-MA:291,
   Wi-LT:225

Miss Norma Jean Pugh, First Grade
   Teacher. M. O'Neill. Ar-TP3:9
The Ne'er-Do-Well. A. Sampley.
   Du-RG:61
Ode on Indolence. J. Keats.
   Ox-BN:374
Sunday at the End of Summer.
   H. Nemerov. Co-BN:98
What a Wonderful. Shiki.
   Be-CS:36
When the Day Is Cloudy. Jo-TS:7
IGNORANCE: see also SATIRE -
   IGNORANCE
The Blind Wall. J. Rubinstein.
   Ho-TY:241
Dulce Bellum Inexpertis.
   G. Gascoigne. Ba-PO:119
He Who Knows. Un-GT:305
If I Know. I Men. Hs-TC:416
If Someone Asks You. M. Donian.
   Co-PS: 142
The Lamp. E. Fitzgerald.
   Ga-S:138
Melting Pot. M. Echeruo.
   Lo-TY:163
Step Out onto the Planet.
   L. Welch. Kh-VA:3
Stoplights. D. Dzwonkoski.
   Ad-II:24
IGOR, RUSSIAN PRINCE
My Tale of Igor's Men.
   V. Burich. Bo-RU:24
The Song of Igor's Campaign.
   Hi-FO:77
IGUANAS: see LIZARDS
ILLEGITIMACY: see also
   PARENT AND CHILD
The Bastard's Lot. R. Savage.
   Rv-CB:520
ILLINOIS: see also names of
   towns, as SPRINGFIELD, ILL.
Carl Hamblin. E. Masters.
   Kr-OF:113, Sh-AP:137, Wi-LT:114
Evangelist. D. Etter. Sc-TN:42
First Song. G. Kinnell.
   Bo-GJ:47, Br-TC:237, Ha-TP:122,
   Mo-BG:123, Wi-LT:745
Fragments from an Illinois
   Scrapbook. D. Etter. St-H:62
Illinois. C. Chamberlain.
   Se-PR:259
The Unfound Door. D. Etter.
   St-H:64
West of Childhood. I. Gardner.
   St-H:65
ILLNESS: see SICKNESS
ILLUMINATION OF BOOKS AND
   MANUSCRIPTS
The Book of Kells. H. Nemerov.
   Pl-EI:123

ILLUSIONS: see also CHIMERAS;
    HUMOR - ILLUSIONS;
    SATIRE - ILLUSIONS
  Alas! The Firefly. Basho.
    Do-TS:21
  An Angel in the House.
    C. Patmore. Pa-GTB:368
  At a Concert of Music. C. Aiken.
    Pl-US:148, Un-MA:430
  Autumn Window. Pien Chih-lin.
    Hs-TC:167
  The Beauty of Job's Daughters.
    J. MacPherson. En-PC:289
  Birmingham. J. Fields. Hu-PN:418
  Birth-Dues. R. Jeffers. Un-MA:365
  Bout with Burning. V. Miller.
    Un-MA:680, Wi-LT:776
  Child with Malaria. C. Mills.
    Du-SH:140
  The City of Dreadful Night.
    J. Thomson. Al-VBP:1004,
    Ox-BN:754
  The Clear Air of October.
    R. Bly. St-H:5
  Colonel Fantock. E. Sitwell.
    Un-MB:334
  The Colossus. S. Plath. Wi-LT:787
  The Counterpart. E. Jennings.
    Wi-LT:741
  Disturbances. A. Thwaite.
    To-MP:137
  Diver. P. Neruda. Li-TU:127
  Dreams. C. Cooper. Ad-PB:505
  Dwarf of Disintegration.
    O. Williams. En-PC:42, Wi-LT:415
  Edwardsville Before Sunrise.
    J. Knoepfle. St-H:97
  Fire in the Sky. Tsang K'o-chia.
    Hs-TC:280
  Four Poems, I. E. Blum-Alquit.
    Ho-TY:262
  Fueling. Chu Ta-nan. Hs-TC:130
  A Game of Glass. A. Reid.
    En-PC:242
  Go Away. Hsu Chih-mo. Hs-TC:87
  Hasbrouck and the Rose.
    H. Putnam. Al-VBP:1204
  Hello! Jao Meng-k'an. Hs-TC:108
  I Did Not Know the Truth of
    Growing Trees. D. Schwartz.
    Wi-LT:522
  I Have Been Through the Gates.
    C. Mew. Un-MB:159, Un-MW:101
  I Saw a Man Pursuing the Horizon.
    S. Crane. Mo-BG:195, Sm-LG:389,
    Un-MA:147, Wi-LT:118
  In a Mirage I Filled My Pitcher.
    V. Karandikar. Al-PI:130
  In Utrumque Paratus. M. Arnold.
    Ox-BN:626
  Insomnia. E. Bishop. Ho-TH:62
  Japan. A. Hecht. Wi-LT:728

  The Lady of Shalott.
    A. Tennyson. Er-FA:339,
    Hi-WP I:59, Ho-WR:145, Sp-OG:128
  The Last Campaign. G. Lehmann.
    Cr-WS:171
  The Lavender Kitten. A. Lopez.
    Al-WW:11
  The Lights in the Sky Are Stars.
    K. Rexroth. Li-TU:252
  A Man Saw a Ball of Gold in the
    Sky. S. Crane. Na-EO:41,
    Sh-AP:143
  The Man with the Blue Guitar.
    W. Stevens. Ha-TP:3,
    Pe-SS:79, Pl-US:126
  Mirage. R. Church. Sm-MK:31
  The Moon. Bhasa. Pa-SG:114
  The Mythos of Samuel Huntsman.
    H. Plutzik. Wi-LT:791
  New Year's Eve. J. Berryman.
    Wi-LT:570
  North on One-Eleven.
    J. Knoepfle. St-H:98
  Not Us. N. Labis. Mc-AC:151
  La Nuit Blanche. R. Kipling.
    Un-MB:134
  The Old Men Admiring Themselves
    in the Water. W. Yeats.
    Bo-GJ:198, Li-TU:140, Pe-M:57,
    Sm-LG:398
  Only the Polished Skeleton.
    C. Cullen. Ca-VT:242
  Past Arenas, Sanctuaries.
    I. Brodsky. Bo-RU:19
  Polemic. A. Ostroff. Ls-NY:67
  A Sense of Coolness. Q. Troupe.
    Ad-PB:442
  She Wandered Through the Garden
    Fence. K. Reid. Mo-GR:130
  A Snake Yarn. W. Goodge. Gr-EC:149
  A Spirit from Perfecter Ages.
    A. Clough. Ox-BN:612
  Strawberry Fields Forever.
    J. Lennon. Mo-GR:127
  The Sun Used to Shine.
    E. Thomas. Pl-ML:41
  The Tantanoola Tiger. M. Harris.
    Ca-MB:66
  The Tarnish. J. Hearst. St-H:78
  This Unimportant. Basho. Be-MC:10
  The Train Runs Late to Harlem.
    C. Rivers. Ad-PB:237
  The Triumph of Death. B. Howes.
    Un-MA:653
  A Visit from Abroad. J. Stephens.
    Co-PM:156, Ha-LO:40
  Where? K. Patchen. Wi-LT:786
  A World Without Objects Is a
    Sensible Emptiness. R. Wilbur.
    Wi-LT:594
  A Youth. S. Crane. Un-MA:148

IMAGINARY ANIMALS AND BIRDS:
    see MYTHICAL ANIMALS AND
    BIRDS
IMAGINATION: see also FANTASY;
    HUMOR - IMAGINATION; MAKE-
    BELIEVE; PLACES, MYTHICAL
    AND IMAGINARY; ROMANCE;
    VISIONS
After All and After All.
    M. Davies. Ar-TP3:117, Hu-MP:68,
    Th-AS:148
Aladdin. J. Lowell. Co-PM:122,
    Co-RG:113, Mc-WK:83, Sp-OG:335
Ann and the Fairy Song.
    W. de la Mare. Ga-FB:170
As Lucy Went a-Walking.
    W. de la Mare. Sm-MK:50
As the Sun Came Up. Wy-CM:6
The Attack. L. Clark. Pa-RE:15
The Birds Are Singing Music.
    D. Garton. Le-M:22
Breeze. M. Hourigan. Le-M:198
Brooms. D. Aldis. Au-SP:326
Byzantium. W. Yeats.
    Un-MB:117, Wi-LT:87
Candles. S. Heitler. Le-M:209
The Centaur. M. Swenson.
    Br-TC:425, Du-SH:44, Li-TU:107,
    Mo-BG:72
Check. J. Stephens. Ar-TP3:178,
    Br-SS:30, Ha-LO:65, La-PV:129,
    Pe-FB:65, Rd-SS:28, Th-AS:86
A Child-Thought. W. Thorley.
    Bo-FP:273
A Child's Winter Evening.
    G. John. De-CH:224
Clouds. P. Kuramoto. Le-M:37
Clouds in a Wild Storm. D. May.
    Le-M:50
Counters. E. Coatsworth.
    Au-SP:117, Hu-MP:146, Pe-FB:40
The Country Bedroom. F. Cornford.
    Bl-OB:137, Pa-RE:87, Un-MB:306
Country Lane. M. Darling.
    De-FS:69
Creep. L. Kershaw. Le-M:63
The Dark Gray Clouds.
    N. Belting. La-PV:40
Dialogue — 2 Dollmakers.
    G. Corso. Kh-VA:19
Digging for China. R. Wilbur.
    Bo-GJ:224, Br-TC:471, Gr-BT:11,
    Ha-LO:88, Ho-TH:66
Dreams. L. Hughes. Bo-HF:19,
    Du-RG:129, Mc-WS:38
Drop Me the Seed. J. Masefield.
    Tr-MR:56
Dvonya. L. Simpson. Mo-BG:89
Ecstacy. W. Turner. De-CH:388
An Enchanted Garden. C. Webb.
    Le-M:158

Escape. E. Wylie. Re-TW:120,
    Sh-RP:114, Un-MA:276
The Fairies. R. Fyleman.
    Au-SP:290, Fe-FP:377, Hu-MP:89,
    Ox-BC:336, Pe-FB:54
The Falcon. E. Wylie. Ha-LO:96
The Field of the Mice and the
    Marigold. E. Clarke. Le-M:40
Flight of the Roller-Coaster.
    R. Souster. Do-WH:13, Ha-PO:176
Flowers Look like Balls of Wool.
    P. White. Le-M:34
The Fly-Away Horse. E. Field.
    Un-GB:32, Un-GT:298
Fog. S. Ingbritson. Le-M:131
Foreign Lands. R. Stevenson.
    Bo-FP:86, Hu-MP:179
The Four Winds. S. Gash.
    Le-M:45, Le-WR:31
The Grass. W. Cardwell.
    Le-M:36
The Habit of Perfection.
    G. Hopkins. Al-VBP:1060,
    Go-BP:275, Pl-US:151, Un-MB:40
Hallo My Fancy. W. Cleland.
    De-CH:358
Halloween. M. Lawson.
    Ar-TP3:237, Br-SS:67
The Horseman. W. de la Mare.
    Ar-TP3:151, Au-SP:341, Bo-GJ:242,
    Cl-DT:62, La-PP:24, Sm-MK:11
Hours Are the Leaves of Life.
    S. Morrison. Le-M:121
How I Went Truant from School
    to Visit a River. M. Oliver.
    St-H:164
I Caught a Fish. B. Murray.
    Ir-BB:65, St-FS:59
I Feel Relaxed and Still.
    K. Anderson. Le-M:160
I Like to Go to the Moon.
    G. Gotthardt. La-GI:46
I Never Look out the Window.
    J. Fincher. Me-WF:13
I Would Like to Describe.
    Z. Herbert. Gr-BT:28
Imagination. J. Davidson.
    Un-MB:73
In the Car. R. Margolis.
    Su-FVI:32
In the Orchard. J. Stephens.
    Co-RG:168, Ha-LO:11
The Inner Vision. W. Wordsworth.
    Pa-GTB:278
Institute Poems, I-B. M. Bruce.
    Ad-II:19
It's Pleasant to Think.
    E. Coatsworth. Sh-RP:171
Keep a Poem in Your Pocket.
    B. de Regniers. Au-SP:97
A Kingdom of Clouds.
    M. Copeland. Le-M:83

IMAGINATION — cont'd.
The Land of Story-Books.
   R. Stevenson.   Ar-TP3:114,
   Fe-FP:12, Hu-MP:23, Ja-PA:50,
   Un-GB:30, Un-GT:12
Landscape.   C. Baudelaire.
   Pa-SG:156
Laughter.   M. Waddington.
   Do-WH:14
Let No One Suppose.   J. Reeves.
   Co-BBW:283
The Lion.   W. Turner.   Un-MB:346
A Little Girl.   Ir-BB:111,
   Mo-MGT:188, Sm-MK:10
The Little Green Orchard.
   W. de la Mare.   Hu-MP:67
The Little Land.   R. Stevenson.
   Au-SP:213
The Little Trumpet.   C. Govoni.
   Li-TU:48
The Magic Flower.   D. Marcus.
   Le-M:38
The Magic Vine.   Br-SG:83
The Mapmaker on His Art.
   H. Nemerov.   Du-SH:31
Meeting-House Hill.   A. Lowell.
   Sm-LG:146, Un-MA:155
The Mind's Liberty.   W. Davies.
   Un-MB:178
Mirror! Mirror!   D. Ensign.
   Ho-ME:7,   Le-M:64
Mrs. Alfred Uruguay.
   W. Stevens.   Br-TC:414
A Modern Dragon.   R. Bennett.
   Ar-TP3:84, Au-SP:160, La-PV:178
Moon Folly.   F. Davis.   Th-AS:24
The Moon Ship.   Hitomaro.
   Ch-B:46, Le-MW:38
Morning Moon.   V. Contoski.
   Sc-TN:29
Music.   W. de la Mare.   Se-PR:325
My Bed Is a Boat.   R. Stevenson.
   Bo-FP:40
My Father in the Night Commanding
   No.   L. Simpson.   Br-TC:380,
   Ca-VT:520, Hi-WP II:357
My Imagination.   M. Petla.
   Ba-HI:116
My Valentine.   R. Stevenson.
   Br-SS:119, Ch-B:41, Co-BL:114,
   Co-PS:37, Hu-MP:331, Mc-PR:48,
   Se-PR:52, Un-MB:59, Un-MW:139
New Year Wishes.   M. Sarton.
   Tr-MR:251
Night.   P. Hubbell.   La-PV:56
Night Clouds.   A. Lowell.
   Ho-TH:24, Mo-BG:147, Sh-RP:88,
   Th-AS:142, Un-MA:159
Night Magic.   A. Burr.
   Hu-MP:128, Th-AS:76
O for the Wings of a Dove.
   Euripides.   Go-BP:155, Pa-SG:175

Ode on Intimations of Immortality
   from Recollections of Early
   Childhood.   W. Wordsworth.
   Al-VBP:662, Er-FA:157, Ox-BN:84,
   Pa-GTB:308
On a Poet's Lips I Slept.
   P. Shelley.   Al-VBP:740,
   De-CH:681, Pa-GTB:299
On Imagination.   P. Wheatley.
   Hu-PN:9
One Day when We Went Walking.
   V. Hobbs.   Au-SP:289
The Park Is Green and Quiet.
   C. Reznikoff.   La-OC:117
Pegasus.   P. Kavanagh.   Co-PI:76
The Plumpuppets.   C. Morley.
   Ar-TP3:150, Fe-FP:395, Hu-MP:117,
   Rd-SS:10
Poem.   J. Friedman.   Ho-TY:368
Promise Me a Rose.   B. Merrill.
   Co-BL:96
The Quiet Child.   R. Field.
   Rd-SS:39
Rain Dance.   B. Krasnoff.
   Le-M:54, Le-WR:26
The Range Rider's Soliloquy.
   Fi-BG:194
The Realm of Fancy.   J. Keats.
   Pa-GTB:278
The Reverie of Poor Susan.
   W. Wordsworth.   De-CH:96,
   De-TT:108, Ho-WR:155, Pa-GTB:256,
   Rv-CB:639
Room in Darkness.   M. Counselman.
   De-FS:68
Sand Hill Road.   M. Grosser.
   Pe-SS:85
The Scared Clouds.   H. Hodgins.
   Le-M:46
School.   B. Cleave.   Ja-PA:21
Scissors.   Y. Tazaki.   Le-TA:45
Scrapyard.   M. Benson.   Le-M:71
See with Eyes Shut.   De-CH:534
The Shadow People. F. Ledwidge.
   Bo-FP:322, Hu-MP:90, Th-AS:12
Shaman Song.   G. Fowler.   Sc-TN:52
The Shell.   J. Stephens.
   Cl-DT:40, Co-BN:82, De-CH:57,
   Ma-FW:43, Ni-JP:34, Un-MB:262
A Ship a-Sailing.   G. Setoun.
   Ar-TP3:122, Au-SP:19, Bo-FP:200,
   Co-SS:85, De-TT:48, Gr-EC:242,
   Hi-GD:16, Hu-MP:175, Ir-BB:241,
   Li-LB:86, Mo-MGT:174, Mo-NR:103,
   Pa-AP:44, Sm-MK:199, Sp-HW:25,
   Wi-MG:53, Wr-RM:73
The Ships of Yule.   B. Carman.
   Br-BC:126, Do-WH:16, Sh-RP:168
A Sick Child.   R. Jarrell.
   Ca-VT:402
Silent Logs Floating.
   M. Goodson.   Le-M:90

Silver Screen. L. Clark.
Pa-RE:80
The Sleeping Giant. D. Hall.
Br-TC:165, Ni-JP:25
Solitaire. A. Lowell. Un-MA:156
Somewhere. W. de la Mare.
Fe-FP:8
Song. S. Coleridge. Co-PS:83,
De-CH:355, De-TT:148
The Squirrel. I. Serraillier.
Co-BBW:30
The Story-Teller. M. Van Doren.
Gr-EC:209, Ha-LO:39
Strange Tree. E. Roberts.
Co-BN:159, Fe-FP:208, Hu-MP:278,
Th-AS:81
The Strangers. A. Brown. Do-WH:39
Sunset on the Sea. L. Ubell.
Le-M:118
Supplication. Hu P'in-ch'ing.
Pa-MV:104
Swing Song. Bo-FP:103
Tartary. W. de la Mare.
Th-AS:146, Un-GT:105
Ten Thousand Years' Play.
N. Tozu. Le-TA:39
That Bright Chimeric Beast.
C. Cullen. Bo-AN:86
Thoughts of a Little Girl.
M. Enriqueta. Fe-FP:489
Thunder. G. Van Every. Le-M:47
Time in the Rock. C. Aiken.
Ca-VT:157
To Helen. E. Poe. Al-VBP:878,
Co-BL:76, De-CH:347, Er-FA:123,
Fe-PL:101, Fr-WO:84, Ga-FB:62,
Gr-CT:440, No-CL:56, Rv-CB:802,
Sh-AP:53, Un-MW:168
To Science. E. Poe. Ke-PP:81,
Rv-CB:805, Sh-AP:46
To the One of Fictive Music.
W. Stevens. Un-MA:241
A Tree Is a Base for Poison Ivy.
V. Williams. Le-M:32
The Tree Stands Very Straight and
Still. A. Wynne. Au-SP:288
Trees. N. Dishman. Le-M:39
Trees. S. Forman. Le-M:82
The Trouble with the Times.
T. McGrath. St-H:122
Two Million Two Hundred Thousand
Fishes. D. Marcus. Le-M:66
Underwood. H. Moss. Br-TC:308
The Unseen Playmate.
R. Stevenson. Bo-FP:101
The Wagon in the Barn.
J. Drinkwater. Pe-FB:30,
Th-AS:70
The Weaving. H. Cook. Th-AS:119
What's Night to Me. S. Gilford.
Le-M:210
When I Was Six. Z. Cross. Fe-FP:486

When Mother Reads Aloud.
Fe-FP:31, Hu-MP:25
Where. W. de la Mare. Co-PM:136,
Ir-BB:135
The Wife. R. Creeley. Ca-VT:566
Wind Is a Cat. E. Fuller.
Au-SP:327, Hu-MP:317, Th-AS:90
A Wish. T. Santos. Le-M:159
Wonder where This Horseshoe Went.
E. Millay. Ar-TP3:94, Pe-FB:41
The World Is Too Much with Us.
W. Wordsworth. Al-VBP:660,
Er-FA:267, Fe-PL:298, Gr-CT:201,
Ke-PP:53, Ox-BN:79, Pa-GTB:299,
Rv-CB:636, Sp-OG:365
Your World. G. Johnson.
Bo-AN:23, Bo-HF:170
IMMIGRATION AND EMIGRATION:
see also ALIENS; HUMOR -
IMMIGRATION AND EMIGRATION;
LIBERTY, STATUE OF; and
names of various national
groups in the United States, as
CHINESE IN THE UNITED STATES
America Greets an Alien. Vi-PP:186

At the Port. R. Iceland.
Ho-TY:116
Bermudas. A. Marvell. Al-VBP:455,
De-CH:362, Gr-CT:277, Hi-TL:17,
Pa-GTB:103, Rv-CB:399, Sm-LG:296
Burying Ground by the Ties.
A. MacLeish. Un-MA:459
Child-Mother in Metamorphosis.
S. Clarke. Sa-B:32
The Coming. T. Matthews.
Sa-B:232
The Cuban Emigrant. V. Alvarez.
Ba-HI:20
The Emigrant. J. Masefield.
Cl-FC:64
Europe and America.
D. Ignatow. Br-AF:41
Exile. D. Walcott. Sa-B:64
Faded Beauty. J. Maraj. Sa-B:87
Immigrants. N. Turner. Br-AF:35
Keorapsetse Kgositsile.
G. Brooks. Ra-BP:172
IMMORTALITY: see also FUTURE
LIFE; SOUL
Adonais. P. Shelley. Al-VBP:759,
Ha-PO:130, Ox-BN:287
And Death Shall Have No Dominion.
D. Thomas. Hi-WP II:31,
Pl-EI:60, To-MP:34, Tr-MR:291,
Un-MB:500, Wi-LT:546
Ch'eng-Hu Is Not Dead.
Liu Ta-Pai. Ox-BN:6
The Crib. C. Morley. Br-BC:157
Crossing the Bar. A. Tennyson.
Al-VBP:865, Er-FA:477, Fe-PL:286,
Ga-FB:127, Ma-YA:199, Mc-PR:105,
Ox-BN:526, Sp-OG:279

IMMORTALITY — cont'd.
  Death, Be Not Proud. J. Donne.
    Al-VBP:203, Er-FA:36, Ga-FB:91,
    Ga-S:215, Gr-CT:381, Ha-PO:143,
    Ho-LP:95, Ke-PP:24, Ma-YA:81,
    Rv-CB:309
  Divine Poems. J. Villa.
    Tr-MR:289
  Earth and Sky. Euripides.
    Pl-EI:180
  Elegy. C. Marlowe. No-CL:9
  Elegy Written in a Country
    Churchyard. T. Gray.
    Al-VBP:559, De-TT:83, Er-FA:462,
    Fe-PL:281, Ha-PO:144, Ma-YA:125,
    Pa-GTB:145, Rv-CB:533
  Everything Will Remember.
    R. Zychlinska. Ho-TY:231
  For My Grandmother.
    C. Cullen. Ad-PB:91, Bo-AN:88,
    Ca-VT:241, Un-MA:571
  Forest Leaves in Autumn.
    J. Keble. Ox-BN:306
  Go Down Death. J. Johnson.
    Ad-PB:6, Bo-AN:2
  Harder than Granite. R. Jeffers.
    Co-PU:80
  Hide-and-Seek. T. Arghezi.
    Mc-AC:27
  Holderlin. D. Schwartz.
    Tr-MR:285
  hospital/poem. S. Sanchez.
    Ad-PB:289
  How Many Foolish Things.
    M. Drayton. Rv-CB:182
  I Bring the Whirlwind. Ho-SD:14
  If I Die Tomorrow.
    G. Mahapatra. Al-PI:135
  The Immortal Past.
    A. Housman. Un-MB:97
  Immortality. F. Keyes.
    Ke-TF:178
  An Invite to Eternity. J. Clare.
    Ox-BN:330
  Magic Casements. J. Keats.
    Ga-FB:13, Ke-TF:333
  Man's Medley. G. Herbert.
    Al-VBP:340
  Monologue of a Dying Man.
    J. Datta. Al-PI:82
  No Coward Soul Is Mine. E. Brontë.
    Al-VBP:925, Er-FA:459, Ox-BN:608,
    Pl-EI:4, Rv-CB:833
  Not for That City. C. Mew.
    Un-MB:165
  Not Marble, nor the Gilded
    Monuments. W. Shakespeare.
    Al-VBP:202, Er-FA:119, Ha-PO:255,
    No-CL:8, Rv-CB:224
  Not to Die. Simonides. Pa-SG:10
  Note to Wang Wei. J. Berryman.
    Pl-ML:96

  O May I Join the Choir Invisible.
    G. Eliot. Ox-BN:617
  Ode on a Grecian Urn. J. Keats.
    Al-VBP:772, Er-FA:80, Ha-PO:228,
    Ke-TF:59, Ox-BN:355, Rv-CB:742
  Ode on Intimations of Immortality.
    W. Wordsworth. Al-VBP:662,
    Br-BC:18, Er-FA:157, Ga-FB:101,
    Gr-GT:436, Ha-PO:206, Ox-BN:84,
    Pa-GTB:308, Pl-EI:59
  On John Donne's Book of Poems.
    J. Marriot. De-CH:254
  Passage to More than India.
    W. Whitman. Tr-MR:292
  The Poet and His Book. E. Millay.
    Un-MA:443
  The Recapitulation.
    R. Eberhart. Tr-MR:284
  Second Best. R. Brooke. Un-MB:324
  Sister Lou. S. Brown. Ad-PB:66,
    Bo-AN:53, Hu-PN:174
  Smoke Stack. A. Sullivan.
    Mc-WK:20
  Song of the Ghost Dance.
    Bi-IT:171
  Song's Eternity. J. Clare.
    Mc-WK:2, Rv-CB:722, Sm-LG:32
  Songs of the Ghost Dance.
    Bi-IT:174
  Sonnets, xxiv, xxv. C. Smith.
    Sm-PT:162
  Thanatopsis. W. Bryant.
    Al-VBP:765, Co-BN:216, Er-FA:67,
    Sh-AP:17
  There Is No Death. Mc-PR:83
  They Shall Not Wither. Bi-IT:168
  This World Is Not Conclusion.
    E. Dickinson. Pl-EI:10
  Tithonus. A. Tennyson.
    Ox-BN:482, Rv-CB:792
  To a Saxon Poet. J. Borges.
    Pl-ML:92
  To Satch. S. Allen.
    Ab-MO:89, Ad-PB:167, Bo-AN:140,
    Gr-BT:178, Hu-PN:343, Jo-SA:58,
    Lo-TY:244, Mc-EA:71, Mo-SD:18
  To the Author of Hesperides and
    Noble Numbers. M. Van Doren.
    Pl-ML:109
  Torchbearer. H. Wolfe. Co-BP:245
  Two Sonnets, i. E. Robinson.
    Sm-PT:157
  The Vase. Kuo Mo-jo. Hs-TC:38
  The Village Atheist. E. Masters.
    Pl-EI:85, Sh-AP:137
  The Wanderer Recalls the Past.
    W. Wordsworth. Ox-BN:92
  The World of Light. H. Vaughan.
    Al-VBP:469, De-CH:267, Gr-CT:384,
    Rv-CB:411

IMPATIENCE
blk/rhetoric. S. Sanchez.
Be-MA:137
Brother Malcolm's Echo.
K. Kgositsile. Be-MA:146
Here I Am. A. Morrissett. Co-BL:29
James and the Shoulder of Mutton.
A. O'Keeffe. De-TT:46
Next, Please. P. Larkin. Un-MB:526
Spring Mood. V. Lapin. Mo-MI:16
There Isn't Time. E. Farjeon.
Fe-FP:323, Sh-RP:160
The Wheel Change. B. Brecht.
Co-EL:104
The Wise Child. E. Lucie-Smith.
Ls-NY:229
IMPENITENCE
The Deserter. J. Curran. Al-VBP:604
IMPERIAL VALLEY, CALIF.
Imperial Valley, Calif.
J. Kessler. Ls-NY:253
IMPERIALISM
Appeal. N. de Sousa. Lo-TY:188
Bedtime Story. G. Macbeth.
To-MP:152
Burial. P. Joachim. Lo-TY:146
The Colonial. S. Lowhar. Sa-B:79
Elegy in a Country Churchyard.
G. Chesterton. Al-VBP:1122,
Mc-WS:85. Na-EO:85, Un-MB:209
England! The Time Is Come.
W. Wordsworth. Al-VBP:661
A Far Cry from Africa.
D. Walcott. Lo-TY:114
Monangamba. A. Jacinto. Lo-TY:181
Poem of the Future Citizen.
J. Craveirinha. Ab-MO:106,
Lo-TY:186
Prayer for Peace. L. Senghor.
Lo-TY:135
Recessional. R. Kipling.
Al-VBP:1101, Er-FA:472, Ga-FB:242,
Ma-YA:229, Ox-BN:867, Sp-OG:214,
Un-MB:135
Shillin' a Day. R. Kipling.
Al-VBP:1100
Shine, Perishing Republic.
R. Jeffers. Al-VBP:1170,
Ca-VT:121, Sh-AP:177, Un-MA:369,
Wi-LT:257
The Vultures. D. Diop. Lo-TY:138
Where Are the Men Seized in This
Wind of Madness?
A. do Espirito Santo. Lo-TY:183
The Widow at Windsor. R. Kipling.
Hi-FO:249
IMPERMANENCE: see also CHANGE;
HUMOR - IMPERMANENCE; LIFE
- BREVITY
The Act. W. Williams. Ca-VT:62,
Co-EL:122

Adieu. P. Lewenstein. Sm-MK:212
Adieu: Farewell Earth's Bliss.
T. Nash. Al-VBP:211, De-CH:244,
Gr-CT:358, Ha-PO:142, Hi-FO:141,
Rv-CB:276, Sm-LG:276
Affectation and Desire. W. Ralegh.
Rv-CB:156
Alas. W. de la Mare. No-CL:71
Alexander the Great. De-CH:180
All the Flowers of the Spring.
J. Webster. Al-VBP:289,
De-CH:252, Rv-CB:317
All Things of Earth Have an End.
Le-OE:137
Another Rotating Thing.
K. Takamura. Sh-AM:45
April Mortality. L. Adams.
Un-MA:542
At Parting. A. Swinburne.
Al-VBP:1032
Autumn. Su Tung P'o. Rx-OH:88
Aztec Song. Br-WM:4, Le-OE:126
The Ballad of Banners.
J. Lehmann. Ca-MB:96
The Ballad of Dead Ladies.
F. Villon. Al-VBP:991,
Er-FA:173, Ho-WR:184
Ballade of Lost Objects.
P. McGinley. En-PC:72
Battle. R. Jeffers. Un-MA:371,
Wi-LT:260
Beauty, a Silver Dew. Rv-CB:107
Beauty Is Most at Twilight's Close.
P. Lagerkvist. Pa-SG:108
Beleaguered Cities. F. Lucas.
Cl-FC:31
A Bird Song in the Ravine.
Wang Wei. Le-MW:22
Birthright. J. Drinkwater.
De-CH:239, Gr-CC:99
Blue Girls. J. Ransom.
Ca-VT:150, Gr-CC:79, Gr-CT:51,
Ha-PO:183, Mc-WS:75, Pe-OA:137,
Sh-AP:182, Un-MA:409
The Broken Kaleidoscope.
W. de la Mare. Ls-NY:70
The Bull. R. Hodgson.
Rd-OA:122, Un-MB:190, Wi-LT:125
By World Laid Low. Gr-CT:327
Calypsos II. W. Williams.
Ho-TH:72
Chimes. D. Rossetti. Ox-BN:686
Cities and Thrones and Powers.
R. Kipling. Bo-GJ:197,
Ni-JP:123, Ox-BN:930
Clear Eyes. W. de la Mare.
Al-VBP:1120
Comparison. J. Bunyan.
Ox-BC:35
The Country in Spring. Lin Keng.
Le-MW:70

IMPERMANENCE — cont'd.
  The Crest Jewel. J. Stephens.
    Un-MB:267
  A Crown of Windflowers.
    C. Rossetti. Ox-BC:276
  A Day in Autumn. R. Thomas.
    Co-BN:139, Hi-WP II:134
  The Days and Months Do Not Last
    Long. Pai Ta-Shun. Le-MW:95
  The Dead in Europe. R. Lowell.
    Wi-LT:581
  Desolation Is a Delicate Thing.
    E. Wylie. Un-MA:278
  Dew on Young Garlic Leaves.
    T'ien Hung. Rx-LT:7
  Dirge in Dialogue. Lo-TY:3,
    Tr-US I:64
  Dirge in Woods. G. Meredith.
    Ho-WR:174, Ox-BN:699
  Do Not, Oh Do Not Prize.
    Rv-CB:122
  A Dream of Governors.
    L. Simpson. Ha-PO:224
  A Dream Within a Dream. E. Poe.
    Rv-CB:804, Sh-AP:60, Un-MW:83
  Egypt's Might Is Tumbled Down.
    M. Coleridge. De-CH:349
  Elegy. A. Pope. Co-EL:141,
    De-CH:254
  The End of the Year.
    Su Tung P'o. Rx-OH:79
  An Epitaph. W. de la Mare.
    Al-VBP:1118, Co-PU:158,
    Un-MB:197, Wi-LT:132
  The Faery Queen. E. Spenser.
    Al-VBP:119, Pl-US:40
  The Fall of the Flowers.
    Yen Yun. Le-MW:73
  Fear No More. W. Shakespeare.
    Al-VBP:195, Bo-HF:179, Co-RG:144,
    De-CH:250, De-TT:195, Er-FA:260,
    Gr-CT:332, Ha-PO:251, Hi-WP II:19,
    No-CL:73, Pa-GTB:28, Rv-CB:201,
    Sm-LG:267
  Flower Arrangement. S. Yellen.
    Ls-NY:55
  For Rhoda. D. Schwartz.
    Un-MA:617, Wi-LT:519
  The Fort of Rathangan.
    Co-PI:131, De-CH:181, Gr-CT:323,
    Ho-LP:86, Sm-LG:395
  Four Preludes on Playthings of the
    Wind: The Past Is a Bucket of
    Ashes. C. Sandburg. Un-MA:201
  The Frost. Tzu Yeh. Le-MW:86
  The Garden. J. Sylvester.
    Rv-CB:187
  The Garden of Proserpine.
    A. Swinburne. Al-VBP:1028,
    Ga-FB:138, Ox-BN:802
  The Giant Tortoise.
    E. Lucie-Smith. Co-PU:88

  The Glories of Our Blood and
    State. J. Shirley.
    Al-VBP:347, Ga-S:30, Gr-CC:107,
    Gr-CT:350, Ke-PP:30, Ni-JP:121,
    Pa-GTB:61, Rv-CB:360
  Glories, Pleasures. J. Ford.
    Al-VBP:309
  Go, Lovely Rose! E. Waller.
    Al-VBP:386, Bo-GJ:128, Ha-PO:164,
    No-CL:29, Pa-GTB:76, Rv-CB:365,
    Un-MW:162
  Gone. W. de la Mare. Bo-GJ:205,
    Gr-CC:101, Ir-BB:263
  Gone in the Wind. J. Mangan.
    Rv-CB:770
  A Great Time. W. Davies.
    Hi-WP I:1, Un-MB:178
  Grongar Hill. J. Dyer.
    Al-VBP:544, Cl-FC:26, Gr-CT:240
  Hamatreya. R. Emerson. Sh-AP:30
  The Hearth of Urien.
    Llywarch the Aged. Gr-CT:323
  Here in the Self Is All That
    Man Can Know. J. Masefield.
    Go-BP:288
  Hesitation. Ch'en Meng-chia.
    Hs-TC:112
  Hour of Memories. A. Shamri.
    Ho-TY:362
  How Time Consumeth All Earthly
    Things. T. Proctor. Gr-CT:243
  I Am of Ireland. W. Yeats.
    Co-PI:207
  I Bless This Man. Pindar.
    Mo-SD:181
  I Have Loved Flowers. R. Bridges.
    Bo-GJ:83, Un-MB:51
  I Know that All Beneath the Moon
    Decays. W. Drummond. De-CH:624
  I Saw. N. Sach. Me-PH:148
  In the Morning Unfolding.
    F. Garcia Lorca. Le-SW:81
  In the Mountain Village.
    Wang Hung Kung. Rx-LT:119
  Juan's Song. L. Bogan. Mo-BG:87
  Lalla Rookh. T. Moore. Li-SR:63
  A Lament for the Priory of
    Walsingham. Gr-CT:327
  The Last Day of the Year.
    Su Tung P'o. Rx-OH:74
  Last Lines—1916. P. Pearse.
    Co-PI:168
  Lay Your Sleeping Head, My Love.
    W. Auden. Un-MB:459
  Leaf after Leaf. W. Landor.
    Al-VBP:710
  Length of Moon. A. Bontemps.
    Hu-PN:214, Wi-LT:611
  Let All Things Pass Away.
    W. Yeats. Gr-CT:331

Let Us Now Praise Famous Men.
   Bible. O.T. Ecclesiastes.
   Gr-CT:376
Limited. C. Sandburg. Mo-BG:22,
   Sh-AP:157, Sm-LG:296, Un-MA:201
The Lion's Skeleton. C. Turner.
   Rd-OA:119
Little Dreams. L. Hughes.
   Ls-NY:53
Little Knowing. Issa. Do-TS:32
A Little While. D. Rossetti.
   Al-VBP:986
Living. D. Levertov. Ca-VT:517
Long I Have Loved to Stroll.
   T'ao Ch'ien. Gr-CT:331
Love in May. J. Passerat.
   Pa-SG:32
Love in Thy Youth. Al-VBP:363
Lullaby. L. Adams. Un-MA:548
Magdalen Walks. O. Wilde.
   Un-MB:67
Man That Is Born of Woman. Bible.
   O.T. Job. Gr-CT:353
Man's Mortality. Rv-CB:133,
   Sm-LG:400
Mist. Li Ch'ing Chao. Rx-OH:99
Modern Love. G. Meredith.
   Ox-BN:689
The Moon and the Year. Bi-IT:91
Morality. J. Garrigue. Co-EL:73
Mortality. Rv-CB:123
A Mountain Village. Shiki.
   Be-CS:30
Mozart Perhaps. J. Wheelock.
   Pl-US:81
Much Knowledge, Little Reason.
   J. Davies. Gr-CT:371
Mutability. P. Shelley.
   Al-VBP:757, Ma-YA:180, Ox-BN:296,
   Rv-CB:705
The Necromancers. J. Nims.
   En-PC:125
New Corn. T'ao Ch'ien. Pa-SG:91
New Hampshire. T. Eliot.
   Ha-LO:81, Ha-PO:94, Pa-GTB:477,
   Re-TW:98, Sm-LG:142
Night in the House by the River.
   Tu Fu. Rx-OH:29
The Night Will Never Stay.
   E. Farjeon. Au-SP:343,
   De-CH:444, Fe-FP:263, La-PP:27,
   Ox-BC:331, Pe-FB:76, Tu-WW:72
No Single Thing Abides.
   T. Lucretius Carus. Pl-IO:9
Not Marble nor the Gilded
   Monuments. A. MacLeish.
   Al-VBP:1194, Br-TC:277, Un-MW:143
Nothing Gold Can Stay. R. Frost.
   Bo-HF:56, Ca-VT:16, Mo-BG:133,
   Mo-TS:54, Un-MA:187

O Gather Me the Rose. W. Henley.
   Un-MB:56
O My Heart You Must Be Strong.
   Ge-TR:17
Oh, Why Should the Spirit of
   Mortal Be Proud? W. Knox.
   Er-FA:34
Ogier the Dane. W. Morris.
   Al-VBP:1016
Old and New Year Ditties.
   C. Rossetti. Ox-BN:713
The Old Men Admiring Themselves
   in the Water. W. Yeats.
   Bo-GJ:198, Li-TU:140, Pe-M:57,
   Sm-LG:398
Old War Song. Tr-US II:241
On the Pagoda. Chung Ting-wen.
   Pa-MV:74
On the Tombs in Westminster
   Abbey. F. Beaumont. Al-VBP:301,
   De-CH:252, Hi-WP II:18, Pa-GTB:60
On the Vanity of Earthly Greatness.
   A. Guiterman. Du-RG:63
Once. E. Batterham. De-CH:242
One Dream All Heroes. Basho.
   Be-CS:26
Ozymandias. P. Shelley.
   Co-RG:14, De-CH:384, Er-FA:83,
   Fe-PL:436, Ha-PO:208, Li-SR:83,
   Ma-YA:177, Mc-PR:186, Mc-WK:98,
   No-CL:256, Ox-BN:279, Pa-GTB:251,
   Pa-HT:91, Rv-CB:695, Sm-LG:153,
   Sp-OG:187, Un-GT:312
Panope. E. Sitwell. Un-MB:333
Passing a Ruined Palace.
   Wen T'ing Yen. Rx-LT:87
Passing and Glassing.
   C. Rossetti. Ox-BN:718
Pediment Ballet. L. Nicholl.
   Pl-US:114
The Peopled Air. T. Gray.
   Rd-OA:81
Perspectives. D. Randall.
   Bo-AN:121
Persuasions to Love. T. Carew.
   Al-VBP:348
The Poplar Field. W. Cowper.
   Co-RG:117, De-CH:46, De-TT:161,
   Gr-CT:239, Ha-PO:151, Ho-WR:159,
   Ma-FW:105, Pa-GTB:140, Rv-CB:548
A Prayer. A. Lewis. Ad-II:40
The Primrose. R. Herrick. Al-VBP:327
Proserpine. A. Swinburne.
   Gr-CT:262
Remember. G. Johnson. Hu-PN:75
Remembering Min Ch'e.
   Su Tung P'o. Rx-LT:89
The Rose and the Gardener.
   H. Dobson. Hu-MP:248
The Rose of the World. W. Yeats.
   Un-MB:111

IMPERMANENCE — cont'd.
Rubaiyat of Omar Khayyam.
   E. Fitzgerald.   Al-VBP:832,
   Er-FA:43, Fe-FP:479, Gr-CT:329,
   Ha-PO:210, Ox-BN:526, Pa-GTB:329,
   Pa-SG:120
The Ruined City.   Pao Chao.
   Ma-FW:240
Sad Song.   A. Maniu.   Mc-AC:60
Sad Songs, II, III.   Tr-US II:174
St. Anthony's Township.
   G. Sheldon.   De-CH:385
Say, Is There Aught That Can
   Convey.   De-CH:713
Security.   M. Hamburger.
   En-PC:223
See where Capella with Her Golden
   Kids.   E. Millay.   Ni-JP:122
The Shepherdess.   Cheng Ch'ou-yu.
   Pa-MV:40
Sick Love.   R. Graves.   Pa-GTB:488
Since Brass, nor Stone.
   W. Shakespeare.   Er-FA:119,
   No-CL:84, Pa-GTB:3
The Snowflake.   W. de la Mare.
   Li-LC:80
A Song.   D. Dolben.   Ox-BN:882
A Song.   P. Dunbar.   Bo-AN:13,
   Bo-HF:160
Song.   C. Mew.   Un-MB:160
Song.   Sung Tzu-hou.   Pa-SG:84
Song.   A. Tennyson.   Sm-LG:402
A Song of Nezahualcoyotl.
   Nezahualcoyotl.   Br-MW:26
Songs.   Tr-US II:170
Sonnet XVIII.   Feng Chih.
   Hs-TC:153
Sonnet 25.   W. Shakespeare.
   Rv-CB:211
Sonnets 2.   S. Daniel.   Al-VBP:157
Sonnets LXX.   E. Spenser.
   Al-VBP:98, Gr-CT:52
Spring and Fall.   G. Hopkins.
   Bo-GJ:249, Gr-CT:317, Ha-PO:148,
   Ke-PP:99, Pa-GTB:392, Re-TW:62,
   Wi-LT:44
The Spring Is Past.   C. Tichborne.
   De-TT:181
The Stars.   Ping Hsin.   Hs-TC:21
Status Quo.   B. Dismond.   Hu-PN:93
The Stuff of Dreams.
   W. Shakespeare.   Ga-FB:91,
   Mc-PR:39
Summer Holiday.   R. Jeffers.
   Pe-M:85, Un-MA:366
Summer's Pleasures They Are Gone.
   J. Clare.   De-CH:512, Rv-CB:719
Tethy's Festival.   S. Daniel.
   De-CH:154
They Are Not Long.   E. Dowson.
   Al-VBP:1102, Gr-CT:325, Ha-PO:155,
   Un-MB:151

A Thing Which Fades.
   Ono No Komachi.   Be-ST:57
This Life.   W. Drummond.
   De-CH:236, Pa-GTB:37
This Quiet Dust.   E. Dickinson.
   Al-VBP:1003, Mc-WS:80, Un-MA:100
The Tide Rises, the Tide Falls.
   H. Longfellow.   Co-SS:50,
   De-TT:183, Er-FA:260, Gr-CT:191,
   Ho-WR:135, Mc-PR:73, Pa-RE:75,
   Rv-CB:784
Time.   J. Wynne.   Ox-BC:77
Time a River.   Vainateya.
   Al-PI:45
Time Has an End They Say.   H.D.
   Ca-VT:118
Time, You Old Gipsy Man.
   R. Hodgson.   Al-VBP:1114,
   Br-SS:11, De-CH:434, Fe-FP:61,
   Mc-WK:123, Pa-HT:77, Re-TW:108,
   Un-MB:186, Wi-LT:122
To a Child Five Years Old.
   N. Cotton.   Ox-BC:66
To an Old Tune.   Lu Kuei Meng.
   Rx-LT:85
To Blossoms.   R. Herrick.
   Co-BN:35, Pa-GTB:91, Sm-MK:5
To Dianeme.   R. Herrick.
   Al-VBP:326, Pa-GTB:76, Rv-CB:335
To His Mistress.   E. Dowson.
   Co-BL:81
To Vanity.   D. Turner.   Hu-PN:401
Tomorrow and Tomorrow and Tomorrow.
   W. Shakespeare.   Er-FA:92,
   Gr-CT:367, Ma-YA:69
Torch.   W. Welles.   Sm-PT:160
Tropes of One Season.   C. Eaton.
   De-FS:85
A Turkish Legend.   T. Aldrich.
   Sp-OG:187
The Turning Year.   Su Tung P'o.
   Rx-OH:87
XXth Century.   R. Hillyer.
   Ho-TH:32
Under the Frontier Post.
   Wang Chang-Ling.   Gr-CT:340
Virtue.   G. Herbert.   Al-VBP:343,
   De-CH:431, Ha-PO:199, Rv-CB:352
Watching the Sky Fall.   P. Layton.
   Ad-II:56
When I Have Seen by Time's Fell
   Hand.   W. Shakespeare.
   Al-VBP:204, Er-FA:261, No-CL:84,
   Pa-GTB:3
Where Is Paris and Heleyne?
   Thomas of Hales.   Gr-CT:321
White Primit Falls.   Virgil.
   Gr-CT:50
The Wind and the Rain.
   W. Gibson.   Cl-FC:50
Wisdom.   F. Yerby.   Bo-AN:136
The Womanhood.   G. Brooks.   Ho-TH:52

A Year Without Seasons.
M. Williams. Hu-NN:68
Yet Ah, that Spring Should Vanish
with the Rose. O. Khayyam.
Tu-WW:45
Yollotl My Heart. Ge-TR:21
Youth. G. Johnson. Hu-PN:74
Youth's the Season. J. Gay.
Ho-WR:73
Yule's Come and Yule's Gane.
Gr-GB:49
IMPORTANCE: see GREATNESS
THE IMPOSSIBLE
Impossibilities to His Friend.
R. Herrick. Gr-SS:147
She Who Could Bind You.
S. Teasdale. Co-PU:40
Whittingham Fair. Gr-GB:139
IMPRISONMENT: see PRISONS AND
PRISONERS
INCANTATIONS: see CHARMS
INCAS: see also INDIANS OF SOUTH
AMERICA - VERSE-QUECHUA
Imperator Victus. H. Crane.
Bl-FP:36
INDECISION: see also
HUMOR - INDECISION
All Revelation. R. Frost.
Sm-PT:169
Concrete Trap. E. Coatsworth.
Co-BBW:41, Mo-BG:196
A Dialogue at Dusk.
Pien Chih-lin. Hs-TC:160
Directions to the Armorer.
E. Olson. Du-SH:99
Dream Sequence, Part 9.
N. Madgett. Ra-BP:195
Esthetique du Mal, IX.
W. Stevens. Wi-LT:156
Four III. e. cummings.
Hi-WP II:7
Four Poems, II, IV.
E. Blum-Alquit. Ho-TY:262, 264
Fragment Thirty-Six. H.D.
Ca-VT:114
I Am the Kit Fox. Ho-SD:10
Kicking Your Heels on the Dusty
Road. P. Solomon. Jo-VC:39
Kind Sir: These Woods.
A. Sexton. Ha-TP:93
Minnie. E. Farjeon. Un-GB:22,
Un-GT:102
Notes on the Mystery.
W. Welles. Sm-PT:159
The Ocean. S. Takahashi.
Sh-AM:99
Places, Loved Ones. P. Larkin.
Pe-SS:123
Portrait of a Certain Gentleman.
S. Hay. Ls-NY:146
The Robins. Ir-BB:242,
Mo-MGT:103, Wr-RM:52

Snake. D. Lawrence. Ar-TP3:68,
Co-BBW:85, Ha-PO:102, Ni-JP:112,
Wi-LT:212
Standing or Sitting. Ba-ST:31
A Thought. S. Ukachev. Mo-MI:83
To Be or Not to Be.
W. Shakespeare. Er-FA:93,
Ha-PO:256, Ma-YA:68
'Twas like a Maelstrom, with a
Notch. E. Dickinson. Wi-LT:7
The Voyage. E. Muir. Wi-LT:251
The Way. E. Muir. Gr-SS:191,
Ha-LO:75
We Saw the Swallows. G. Meredith.
Ox-BN:690, Pa-GTB:369
INDEPENDENCE: see FREEDOM;
SELF-RELIANCE
INDEPENDENCE DAY: see FOURTH
OF JULY
INDIA: see also AJANTA CAVES;
BALLADS, EAST INDIAN;
BRAHMINS AND BRAHMINISM;
COROMANDEL COAST, INDIA;
EAST INDIAN VERSE; EAST
INDIANS; HINDUISM; HINDUS;
and names of Indian cities,
as CALCUTTA, INDIA
Ballad of East and West.
R. Kipling. Ar-TP3:25,
Ga-FB:211
Cradle Song. S. Naidu.
Fe-FP:54, Hu-MP:123, Th-AS:35
Gunga Din. R. Kipling.
Er-FA:371, Go-BP:54, Hi-WP I:69,
Ma-YA:226, Pa-OM:230, Un-MB:122
The Home. R. Tagore. Bo-GJ:xix
In the Bazaars of Hyderabad.
S. Naidu. Al-PI:102, Fe-FP:489,
Sh-RP:56, Th-AS:156
India. W. Turner. Bl-OB:112,
La-PV:155, Un-MB:348
The Indolent Gardener.
M. Kennedy. Co-BN:51
The Lament of the Border Cattle
Thief. R. Kipling. Co-RM:159
Music of Stones. G. Misra.
Al-PI:137
Paper Boats. R. Tagore.
Bo-FP:108, Bo-HF:28, Fe-FP:114,
Ma-FW:236, Pa-RE:36, Th-AS:72
This Landscape, These People.
Z. Ghose. To-MP:124
To India. Yüan Shui-p'ai.
Hs-TC:413
INDIA - COUNTRYSIDE
The Cloud Messenger. Kalidasa.
Al-PI:46
INDIA - HISTORY AND
PATRIOTISM
The Rise of Shivaji. Z. Ghose.
Ca-MB:59

INDIA - SOCIAL LIFE AND CUSTOMS
Characterization. Yogesvara.
Al-PI:37
Circuit Through the Hills.
T. Singh. Al-PI:119
Conjecture. A. Raha. Al-PI:86
The Cremation Ground.
Bha Vabhuti. Al-PI:37
Divali. Ca-MU:17
The Housewife. B. Amma.
Al-PI:126
In Praise of Celibacy. Al-PI:51
Kanya-Kumari. K. Subramanyan.
Al-PI:146
The Lover's Song. I. Adigal.
Al-PI:71
Night of the Scorpion.
N. Ezekial. Al-PI:96
Observations. Naladiyar.
Al-PI:68
Patti. Ca-MU:24
The Rainy Day. R. Tagore.
Al-PI:90, Ma-FW:117
Song of the Playing Ball.
I. Adigal. Al-PI:70
The Stone-Breaker. Nirala.
Al-PI:118
Sundari Mundarié. Ca-MU:20
The Third Continent.
M. Erulkar. Al-PI:95
Wasn't It You?
K. Narasimhaswamy. Al-PI:125
INDIA - PAKISTAN WAR, 1971
A Snapshot. H. Barua. Al-PI:75
INDIAN SUMMER
Indian Summer. W. Campbell.
Do-WH:92
Indian Summer. E. Dickinson.
Un-GT:278, Un-MA:95
Indian Summer. A. Draper.
Ha-YA:102
Indian Summer. K. Jackson.
Ja-PA:60
Indian Summer. M. Leib.
Ho-TY:92
Indian Summer. M. Mansfield.
Ke-TF:446
Indian Summer. J. Whittier.
Bo-FP:152
An Indian Summer Day on the
Prairie. V. Lindsay.
La-RM:70, Mc-WK:31
INDIANA
Conservative. W. Stafford. St-H:212
Midwest. J. Nims. St-H:150
On the Banks of the Wabash, Far
Away. P. Dresser. Se-PR:260
INDIANS OF CENTRAL AMERICA: see
also names of tribes and lin-
guistic families, as AZTECS
The Beginning of Sickness.
Bi-IT:149

The Face of My Mountains.
Bi-IT:46
Hymn. Bi-IT:65
The Indians Come Down from Mixco.
M. Asturias. Mo-TS:37
The Moon and the Year. Bi-IT:91
Not Forever on Earth. Bi-IT:90
Prayer. Bi-IT:37
The Song of a Dream. Bi-IT:127
A Song of Lamentation.
Ba-PO:27, Bi-IT:137, Da-SC:175
They Came from the East.
Bi-IT:148
The Weeping Spreads. Bi-IT:147
A Woman's Complaint. Bi-IT:82
INDIANS OF CENTRAL AMERICA -
CEREMONIES AND DANCES
Dance Song of a Shaman.
Tr-US II:287
The Feast of the Great God
Tezcatlipoca. Br-MW:15
From the Aztec Ceremonial
Calendar. Br-MW:9
INDIANS OF CENTRAL AMERICA -
LEGENDS
He Wove the Strands of Our
Life. Bi-IT:8
Olowilasop Visits the Morning
Star. Tr-US II:291
Then He Descended. Bi-IT:3
Thus It Is Told. Bi-IT:6
INDIANS OF CENTRAL AMERICA -
MUSIC AND SONGS
The Bird and the Butterfly.
Tr-US II:281
Flower Song. Br-MW:7
Fragments. Br-MW:30
Hymn for Fasting. Br-MW:32,
Da-SC:170
Love Song. Tr-US II:287
Song. Br-MW:29
A Song of Nezahualcoyotl.
Br-MW:24, 26
This Is the Song They Sang at
Fast Every Eight Years.
Tr-US II:278
Tule Love Song. Da-SC:16,
Tr-US II:295
INDIANS OF CENTRAL AMERICA -
RELIGION AND MYTHOLOGY
The Feast of the Great God
Tezcatlipoca. Br-MW:15
From the Aztec Ceremonial
Calendar. Br-MW:9
From the Prophecy of Katun 9
Ahau. Br-MW:28, Da-SC:163
Hymn of the High Priest of
Xipe Totec. Da-SC:171
Hymn to the Mother of the
Gods. Tr-US II:277

Hymn to Tlaloe.   Da-SC:169
Maya Hymn.   Br-MW:5
Popul Vuh.   Da-SC:164
INDIANS OF CENTRAL AMERICA -
   SOCIAL LIFE AND CUSTOMS
The Feast of the Great God
   Tezcatlipoca.   Br-MW:15
From the Aztec Ceremonial
   Calendar.   Br-MW:9
INDIANS OF CENTRAL
   AMERICA - VERSE
—CHIBCHAN
Conversation Between a Boy and
   Two Girls Looking Through a
   Spyglass.   Tr-US II:294
Olowilasop Visits the Morning
   Star.   Tr-US II:291
Song after a Man Dies.
   Tr-US II:293
Song Before Gathering Medicinal
   Herbs for the Treatment of
   Sick Children.   Tr-US II:292
The Song of the Birds.
   Tr-US II:288
Tule Love Song.   Da-SC:16,
   Tr-US II:295
—CORA
The Eagle above Us.   Tr-US II:285
The Morning Star in the North.
   Tr-US II:286
Our Father the Sun.   Tr-US II:285
—MAYAN
The Beginning of Sickness.
   Bi-IT:149
The Face of My Mountains.
   Bi-IT:46
From the Prophecy of Katun 9
   Ahau.   Br-MW:28, Da-SC:163
Garden Song.   Bo-FP:253
Magic Formula Against Disease.
   Bi-IT:151
Maya Hymn.   Br-MW:5
The Moon and the Year.   Bi-IT:91
Plague.   Bi-IT:150
Prayer.   Bi-IT:37
Prophecy of Pech, Priest of
   Chichen-Itzá.   Da-SC:163
Ritual of the Priest Chilan.
   Bi-IT:141, Br-MW:27, Da-SC:162
Then He Descended.   Bi-IT:3
They Came from the East.
   Bi-IT:148
—MISKITO
Love Song.   Tr-US II:287
—NAHUATL
All Things of Earth Have an
   End.   Le-OE:137
And Yet the Earth Remains
   Unchanged.   Bi-IT:101
Aztec Hymn to the Virgin.
   Da-SC:15

Aztec Song.   Br-MW:4, Le-OE:128
The Bird and the Butterfly.
   Tr-US II:281
The Feast of the Great God
   Tezcatlipoca.   Br-MW:15
Flower Song.   Br-MW:7
Fragments.   Br-MW:30
Friendship.   Bi-IT:85
From the Aztec Ceremonial
   Calendar.   Br-MW:9
Grandeur of Mexico.   Bi-IT:44
He Wove the Strands of Our Life.
   Bi-IT:8
Hymn.   Bi-IT:65
Hymn for Fasting.   Br-MW:32,
   Da-SC:170
Hymn of the High Priest of
   Xipe Totec.   Da-SC:171
Hymn to the Mother of the Gods.
   Tr-US II:277
Hymn to Tlaloe.   Da-SC:169
I the Singer Stand on High on
   the Yellow Rushes.   Le-OE:20
Love Song.   Bi-IT:77
My Flowers Shall Not Perish.
   Le-OE:135
Nahuatl Poem.   Ho-LP:85
Not Forever on Earth.   Bi-IT:90
Omen.   Bi-IT:138, 139
On a Certain Ruler in Memory of
   Former Rulers.   Da-SC:174
One Poet Praises Another.
   Tr-US II:284
The Origin of Songs.
   Tr-US II:282
The Poet's Mission. Tr-US II:281
Prayer.   Bi-IT:30, Tr-US II:279
Song.   Br-MW:29
The Song of a Dream.   Bi-IT:127
A Song of Huezotzinco.   Da-SC:178
A Song of Lamentation.
   Ba-PO:27, Bi-IT:137, Da-SC:175
A Song of Nezahualcoyotl.
   Br-MW:26, Da-SC:180
A Song of the Huezotzincos.
   Da-SC:177
Songs of Birds.   Bi-IT:111
Supplication to the Rain God and
   the Spirits of Water.
   Bi-IT:105
The Surrender Speech of Cuauhtemoc.
   Cuauhtemoc.   Bi-IT:152
They Shall Not Wither.   Bi-IT:168
This Is the Song They Sang at
   Fast Every Eight Years.
   Tr-US II:278
Thus It Is Told.   Bi-IT:6
Toltec Lament.   Da-SC:167
War Song.   Tr-US II:280
A War Song of Tetlapan
   Quetzanitzin.   Da-SC:173

INDIANS OF CENTRAL
    AMERICA - VERSE-
    NAHUATL — cont'd.
  Warrior's Song. Tr-US II:280
  The Weeping Spreads. Bi-IT:147
  A Woman's Complaint. Bi-IT:82
  Words Spoken by a Mother to Her
    Newborn Son. Bi-IT:112
  See also Ge-TR
—OTOMÍ
  An Otomí Song of the Mexicans.
    Da-SC:176
  To a Woman Loved. Bi-IT:75
  A War Song of the Otomies.Da-SC:172
—QUICHÉ
  Popul Vuh. Da-SC:164
—TARAHUMARE
  Dance Song of a Shaman.Tr-US II:287
—TULE
  Love Song. Bi-IT:80
—YAQUI
  The Deer Is Taking Away. Ho-SD:19
  In Summer the Rains. Da-SC:16,
    Ho-SD:19, Le-OE:79
INDIANS OF NORTH AMERICA: see
    also HUMOR - INDIANS OF NORTH
    AMERICA; MEDICINE MEN; PEACE
    PIPES; WIGWAMS; and names of
    tribes, as NEZ PERCÉ INDIANS
    and linguistic families, as
    SIOUAN INDIANS
  After the Death of an Elder
    Klallum. D. Niatum. Ni-CD:136
  Ascent to the Sierras. R. Jeffers.
    Pa-HT:61, Sm-LG:148
  August 24, 1963 - 1:00 a.m. -
    Omaha. D. Whitewing. Al-WW:57
  Bar's Fight, August 28, 1746.
    L. Terry. Hu-PN:3, Ra-BP:37
  Brady's Bend. M. Keller. Co-PT:217
  Can You Can't. D. Whitewing.
    Al-WW:57
  Carriers of the Dream Wheel.
    N. Momaday. Ni-CD:87
  Christmas Comes to Mocassin Flat.
    J. Welch. Ni-CD:247
  Circles. C. Sandburg.
    Br-AF:38, Ma-FW:134
  Crucifixion. R. Benally.
    Ba-HI:139
  Cry Silent. D. Whitewing.
    Al-WW:56
  The Dance. H. Crane. Un-MA:526,
    Wi-LT:385
  The Discovery. J. Squire.
    Br-AF:54, Cl-FC:83, Co-PS:132,
    De-CH:361, Fe-FP:404, Mc-WK:163
  Dream Song. Bi-IT:129, 133
  The Dreamer Rides the Whirlwind.
    Bi-IT:24

The Feet of the Young Men.
    R. Kipling.   Se-PR:171
For a Winnebago Brave.
    J. Bruchac. Ni-CD:43
The Forsaken. D. Scott. Do-WH:63,
    Ha-PO:159
From the Edge of the Hole in the
    Sky. Wo-HS:(5)
The Gathering Time.
    D. Whitewing. Al-WW:52
The Ghosts of the Buffaloes.
    V. Lindsay. Sh-RP:46, Un-MA:223
Going Where. P. Irving. Al-WW:78
Grey Woman. G. Cardiff. Ni-CD:56
I Cannot Forget You. Bi-IT:78
I Went to Learn how the White Man
    Lives. Wo-HS:(37)
Immigrants. N. Turner. Br-AF:35
In My First Hard Springtime.
    J. Welch. Ni-CD:238
In Winter Time. Ho-SD:35
Indian Children. A. Wynne.
    Ar-TP3:35, Au-SP:100, Bo-FP:114,
    Hu-MP:137, Mc-AW:97
Indian Country, the Shadow-Hunter.
    L. Simpson. Mc-EA:60
Indian Names. L. Sigourney.
    Br-AF:8, Fe-FP:450, Fe-PL:412,
    Hu-MP:374, Se-PR:174, Sh-RP:305
The Indian Woman. W. Whitman.
    Bo-FP:21
Indians. J. Fandel. Br-AF:35,
    Du-RG:57, Sh-RP:112
Indians. W. Newhard. La-GI:48
A Little Indian Maid. Fi-BG:196
Little Papoose. H. Conkling.
    Fe-FP:306
Long Person. G. Cardiff.
    Ni-CD:49
Love Song. D. Whitewing.
    Al-WW:51
Love Song of a Young Man.
    Bi-IT:84
A Missouri Traveller Writes
    Home: 1830. R. Bly. Ni-JP:20
Moonlight. B. Nance. Br-AF:153
Moving in a Caravan. R. Bly.
    Mc-EA:47
My Home. J. Saltwater. Ba-HI:100
My Mother. T. Kee. Ba-HI:88
The New World. P. Engle.
    Br-AF:58
Night Blessing. F. George.
    Al-WW:118
No One Remembers Abandoning the
    Village of White Fir.
    D. Niatum. Ni-CD:124
Offering. Bi-IT:108
The Old Man Called to His Sons.
    Wo-HS:(10)

Prayer. Bi-IT:34, 38
Requickening. Bi-IT:162
The River of Stars. A. Noyes.
   Pa-OM:131
Self. P. George. Al-WW:122
Shadows and Song. P. George.
   Al-WW:123
Song. Bi-IT:45, 53
Song of a New Cradleboard.
   P. George. Al-WW:116
A Stared Story. W. Stafford.
   Ha-TP:136
Statement on Our Higher Education.
   W. Ransom. Ni-CD:198
Sweet Winds of Love. P. Irving.
   Al-WW:77
Swimmer. G. Cardiff. Ni-CD:55
The Taking of Life Brings
   Serious Thoughts. Bi-IT:68
Ten Little Indian Boys.
   M. Hutchinson. Au-SP:153,
   Ir-BB:110
Thanksgiving. K. Koch. Ca-VT:545
That Wind. Bi-IT:23
They Will Appear. Bi-IT:169
This Was Our Land. Wo-HS:(35)
To the Driving Cloud.
   H. Longfellow. Gr-CT:328
Toe'osh: A Laguna Coyote Story.
   L. Silko. Ni-CD:223
Two Indian Boys. J. Concha.
   Ba-HI:98
A Vegetable, I Will Not Be.
   D. Whitewing. Al-WW:54
Wailing Song. Bi-IT:97
We Are Living Humbly. Bi-IT:157
West of Chicago. J. Dimoff.
   Mc-EA:129
What, My Son, Does Your Blanket
   Mean? Wo-HS:(30)
The White-Footed Deer.
   W. Bryant. Sp-OG:178
Why Is Happy? D. Whitewing.
   Al-WW:56
You Shall Live. Bi-IT:170
INDIANS OF NORTH AMERICA - BATTLES:
   see INDIANS OF NORTH AMERICA -
   CHIEFS; and names of battles,
   as SAND CREEK, BATTLE, 1864;
   and names of military leaders,
   as CUSTER, GEORGE ARMSTRONG
INDIANS OF NORTH AMERICA -
   CEREMONIES AND DANCES
Arapaho Ghost Dance Song.
   Ba-PO:111
The Birth of Dawn. Br-MW:68
Buffalo Dance Song. Br-MW:72
Burial of the Minnisink.
   H. Longfellow. Gr-CC:122
Child-Naming Rite of the Bow.
   People. Da-SC:107

Closing Song of a Ceremony to
   Procure Abundance. Tr-US II:261
Concerning Wisdom. D. Yazzie.
   Br-MW:63
Corn Ceremony. Da-SC:83
Crazy Dance. Da-SC:159
A Dance for Rain. W. Bynner.
   Pa-HT:58
A Dancing Song. Br-MW:37
Dancing Song of the Skunk.
   Tr-US II:234
Dawn Boy's Song. Da-SC:64,
   Ga-FB:247
Dawn Song. Br-MW:59, Da-SC:83,
   Le-OE:17, Tr-US II:264
Discharming Song. Da-SC:85
Dry and Parched. A. Lopez.
   Al-WW:9
Far as Man Can See. Ho-SD:43
Father, the Morning Star.
   Ho-SD:25
A Feast Song. Br-MW:41
From the Medicine Lodge Initia-
   tion Ceremony. Tr-US II:231
From the New Year's Ceremony.
   Tr-US II:229
The Girl Who Took Care of the
   Turkeys. Te-FC:67
The Gourd Dancer. N. Momaday.
   Ni-CD:94
The Hako Party Presented to the
   Powers. Da-SC:102
The Hopis and the Famine.
   Te-FC:35
I Am Crying from Thirst.
   A. Lopez. Al-WW:8
I Gave Them Fruits. Bi-IT:146,
   Tr-US II:241
I Know Not if the Voice of Man.
   Da-SC:25
The Indian Burying Ground.
   P. Freneau. Fe-PL:279,
   Hi-TL:8, Rv-CB:559, Sh-AP:15
Invitation to Drink Cactus Liquor
   at a Rain-Bringing Ceremony.
   Tr-US II:269
Kachina Song. Br-MW:43, Da-SC:84,
   Pa-SG:128
Lines from the Wind Chant.
   Br-MW:64
Look, Where They Come. Ho-SD:34
Medicine Song. Br-MW:38, 39
The Parade. L. Sohappy. Al-WW:16
Prayer at the Offering of Food to
   the Ancestors. Tr-US II:255
Processional from the War Ceremony.
   Br-MW:78
Prophecy. Bi-IT:140, Br-MW:104
Proviso. P. George. Al-WW:113
Rattlesnake Ceremony Song.
   Tr-US II:249

INDIANS OF NORTH AMERICA –
  CEREMONIES AND DANCES — cont'd.
  Recitation of War Honors. Br-MW:70
  Red Rock Ceremonies. A. Probst.
    Ni-CD:164
  Rites of the Condoling Council.
    Da-SC:135
  The Rock. Br-MW:83
  Scalp Dance. Da-SC:93
  Second Skins — a Peyote Song.
    Ni-CD:42
  Shaman Song. G. Fowler. Sc-TN:53
  The Shumeekuli. Te-FC:217
  Song at the Painting of Ceremonial
    Dancers. Tr-US II:263
  Song for the Thunder Bird Dance.
    Tr-US II:216
  Song of a Chief's Daughter.
    Bi-IT:81, Ho-SD:57
  Song of QWAXILA. Da-SC:86
  Song of the Buffalo. Da-SC:157
  Song of the New-Rich. Da-SC:56
  Songs from the Deer Ceremony.
    Tr-US II:264
  Songs of the Ghost Dance.
    Bi-IT:174
  Sun Dancers. P. Irving. Al-WW:80
  The Sunbeams Stream Forward.
    Ho-SD:48, Jo-TS:1
  Taking of the Name. Bo-FP:265
  A Voice. Jo-TS:24, Tr-US II:235
  The Whirlwind. Br-MW:129,
    Da-SC:118
  The Wind Stirs the Willows.
    Bi-IT:172, Ho-SD:15
INDIANS OF NORTH AMERICA – CHIEFS:
    see also names of chiefs, as
    BLACK KETTLE, CHIEF
  Chief Leschi of the Nisqually.
    D. Niatum. Ni-CD:117
  The Death Song of White Antelope.
    White Antelope. Br-MW:92
  Elegy for Chief Sealth (1786-
    1866). D. Niatum. Ni-CD:121
  Potlatch Boasts. Br-MW:137
  Recitation of War Honors. Br-MW:70
  Rites of the Condoling Council.
    Da-SC:135
  The Tree of Great Peace.
    Dekanawideh. Br-MW:102
  The Walam Olum or Red Score.
    Da-SC:127
INDIANS OF NORTH AMERICA – DANCES:
    see INDIANS OF NORTH AMERICA –
    CEREMONIES AND DANCES
INDIANS OF NORTH AMERICA – HUNTING
  Black-Tailed Deer Song. Bi-IT:54
  Charm for Going a-Hunting.
    M. Austin. Sh-RP:341
  Hunting Song. Tr-US II:246
  The Rousing Canoe Song.
    H. Fraser. Do-WH:58

  Song of the Deer. Bi-IT:56
  Song of the Fallen Deer.
    Bi-IT:57, Da-SC:88
  Song of the Hunter. Bi-IT:55
INDIANS OF NORTH AMERICA – LEGENDS
  The Beginning. Te-FC:225
  The Boy and the Deer. Te-FC:3
  Breathe on Him. Bi-IT:20
  Buffalo Myth. Br-MW:73
  The Cannibal's Seven Sons.
    Br-MW:116
  A Chippewa Legend. J. Lowell.
    Hu-MP:425
  The Creation. Te-FC:275
  The Cussitaws Come East.
    Bi-IT:13
  Emergence Song. Bi-IT:10
  First Man Was the First to
    Emerge. Bi-IT:9, Da-SC:68
  Fragment from the Child-Naming
    Rites. Br-MW:77
  From a Legend. Br-MW:75
  The Girl Who Took Care of the
    Turkeys. Te-FC:67
  Girl's Song from a Legend.
    Da-SC:153, Tr-US II:221
  Hiawatha's Childhood.
    H. Longfellow. Ar-TP3:36,
    Fe-FP:405, Ga-FB:248, Gr-EC:100,
    Hu-MP:422, Li-SR:54, Mc-PR:80,
    Sh-RP:272
  The Hopis and the Famine.
    Te-FC:35
  Indian Legend of the Canyon.
    J. Mahoney. Fi-BG:49
  It Was the Wind. Bi-IT:19
  Legend. P. Irving. Al-WW:79
  The Little Red Spiders. Jo-TS:14
  The Man Who Married the Birds.
    Br-MW:84
  Myth. Br-MW:81
  Nespelim Man. J. Campbell.
    Al-WW:32
  Now We Come Southwards. Bi-IT:15
  Over the Water. Bi-IT:14
  Pelt Kid and His Grandmother.
    Te-FC:193
  Song of Coyote Who Stole Fire.
    Da-SC:69
  Song of Creation. Bi-IT:4,
    Ho-SD:52
  Tale. Br-MW:110
  The Tale of the Jealous Brother.
    Br-MW:120
  They Stooped Over and Came Out.
    Bi-IT:11
  This Newly Created World.
    Bi-IT:5
  Upward Going! Bi-IT:12
  Western Magic. M. Austin.
    Br-AF:99
  The Women and the Man. Te-FC:87

INDIANS OF NORTH AMERICA –
  MUSIC AND SONGS
  The Battle-Birds. Da-SC:156
  A Bedtime Song for Children.
    Br-MW:90
  Buffalo Song. Br-MW:79
  Butterfly Song. Bi-IT:110,
    Jo-TS:14, Tr-US II:259
  By What Name Is Thy Bride Known?
    Ho-SD:21
  Corn-Grinding Song. Da-SC:84
  Corn-Grinding Songs. Tr-US II:257
  Deer Song. Da-SC:81
  Discharming Song. Da-SC:85
  Down Through the Ages Vast.
    Ba-PO:113
  Drum Song about a Stupid Kayak
    Paddler. Da-SC:44
  Elegy Dream Song. Br-MW:42
  Feast Song. Br-MW:36, 41
  Festal Song. Tr-US II:265
  Foot Race Song. Da-SC:97
  From the Night Chant. Br-MW:62
  From the South. Da-SC:156
  Gambling Songs. Tr-US II:252
  Girl's Song. Tr-US II:220
  Ground-Squirrel Song.
    Da-SC:97, Le-OE:53, Tr-US II:252
  Harvest Song. D. Georgakas.
    Sc-TN:58
  A Hat of Eagle Feathers. Ho-SD:17
  Hunting Song. Br-MW:40, Da-SC:80,
    Le-OE:59, Tr-US II:258, 271
  I Am Rising. Da-SC:156
  I Sing for the Animals.
    Da-SC:23, Le-OE:36
  Indian Cradle Song. Fi-BG:220
  An Indian Hymn of Thanks to
    Mother Corn. Bo-FP:154
  Indian Lullaby. C. Myall.
    Hu-MP:124
  Kachina Song. Br-MW:43, Da-SC:84,
    Pa-SG:128
  Lament. D. Georgakas. Sc-TN:58
  Last Song of Sitting Bull.
    Kr-OF:1, Le-OE:127
  Love-Charm Songs, I, II.
    Br-MW:6
  Love Incantations. Tr-US II:232
  Love Song. Tr-US II:220, 263
  Lullaby of Nokomis.
    H. Longfellow. Bo-FP:287
  The Magpie! The Magpie!
    Da-SC:96, Ho-SD:44, Le-OE:15,
    Tr-US II:252
  Medicine Songs. Tr-US II:267
  Memorial Ode. Chief J. Buck.
    Ba-PO:107, Ho-SD:4
  A Modoc Singer. Br-MW:3
  Mourning Song. Da-SC:53
  Mutual Charges of Molestation.
    Da-SC:45

  Nith-Song of Savdlat and
    Pulangit-Sissok. Da-SC:44
  Ojibwa War Song. Da-SC:155,
    Kr-OF:1, Le-OE:120
  Oricessional Song from the Night
    Chant. Tr-US II:251
  Ouwe Dance Song for Good Crops.
    Tr-US II:259
  Owl Song. Da-SC:89
  Planting Song of Women to the
    Earth-Mother. Tr-US II:303
  The Poor Little Bee.
    Ho-SD:32, Hu-MP:304, Le-OE:51
  A Poor Man Takes the Songs.
    Ho-SD:47
  Rain Song of the Giant Society.
    Da-SC:76
  Rattlesnake Recitative. Da-SC:10
  Responsive Song for the Dead Child
    of a Chief. Tr-US II:220
  Song after Victory. Tr-US II:226
  Song at a Ceremony for Securing
    Good Crops. Tr-US II:273
  Song Concerning the Corn Harvest.
    Tr-US II:261
  Song (I Considered Myself a Wolf).
    Br-MW:93
  Song of a Bear. Tr-US II:252
  Song of a Departed Spirit.
    Tr-US II:260
  Song of Entering the Village.
    Da-SC:115
  The Song of Kuk-Ook, the Bad Boy.
    Da-SC:47
  Song of Rejection. Tr-US II:263
  Song of the Sky Loom. Da-SC:76,
    Le-OE:6, Mo-TS:16, Tr-US II:256
  Song Sung on an Expedition to
    Obtain Salt. Bi-IT:21,
    Ho-SD:51, Le-OE:73, Tr-US II:273
  The Songs Commence at Nightfall.
    Ho-SD:17
  Songs in the Garden of the House
    God. Bi-IT:115, Da-SC:86
  Swallow Song. Da-SC:97,
    Tr-US II:266
  There Came a Gray Owl. Ho-SD:17
  This Is the White Land. Ho-SD:22
  Toad Man's Song. Br-MW:59
  Trading Song. Tr-US II:253
  Two Fragments of Songs, I, II.
    Br-MW:48
  The War God's Horse Song.
    Br-MW:60, Sm-LG:78
  War Song. Tr-US II:269
  The Wind Now Commences to Sing.
    Bi-IT:22, Da-SC:88, Ho-SD:53,
    Tr-US II:268
  Winter Dance Song.
    Tr-US II:259

INDIANS OF NORTH AMERICA –
    RELIGION AND MYTHOLOGY:
    see also INDIANS OF NORTH
    AMERICA – CEREMONIES AND
    DANCES
As I Lay Sleeping.   Ho-SD:33
The Beginning.   Te-FC:225
Black Bear Song.   Da-SC:108
The Church on Comiaken Hill.
    R. Hugo.   Ho-P:123
Come On, Caddo.   Ho-SD:15
The Creation.   Te-FC:275
The Creation According to Coyote.
    S. Ortiz.   Ni-CD:144
The Father Will Descend. Ho-SD:16
Guardian-Spirit Song.   Br-MW:136
The Hako Party Presented to the
    Powers.   Da-SC:102
Ho! Ye Sun, Moon, Stars.
    Da-SC:104, Ho-SD:18
Holy Visions!   Ho-SD:32
The Hopis and the Famine. Te-FC:35
I Bring the Whirlwind.   Ho-SD:14
I Sought a Vision.   Ho-SD:14
Introduction to the Code of
    Handsome Lake.   Br-MW:105
Invocation to Dsilyi Neyani.
    Da-SC:75, Tr-US II:250
Invoking the Powers.   Br-MW:69
Let Our Children Live.   Ho-SD:28
Litany to the High Gods.
    Tr-US II:242
My Breath Became.   Bi-IT:109
The Noise of Passing Feet.
    Le-OE:8
Now I Walk with Talking God.
    Ho-SD:37
Offering of Prayer Sticks.
    Da-SC:71
A Peyote Thought.   Br-MW:66
A Peyote Vision.   Br-MW:67
Raise Your Hands to the Sky.
    A. Lopez.   Al-WW:9
The Return to the Old Gods.
    Kr-OF:21
Ritual Recitation: The Symbolic
    Painting.   Tr-US II:244
The Sacred Lands of the Blue Lake
    Forest. P. Bernal.   Br-MW:57
Skyspear.   Ho-SD:59
The Song of Bekotsidi. Da-SC:67
A Song of Nayenzgani. Da-SC:66
Song of Sequence. Da-SC:21
The Spirit Walking. Ho-SD:6,
    Le-OE:111
The Sun Priest and the Witch-
    Woman. Te-FC:135
Talking to His Drum.
    E. Mitchell.   Al-WW:96
That Woman down There. Ho-SD:71
Toward Calm and Shady Places.
    Ba-PO:114, Tr-US II:224

A Vision of Handsome Lake.
    Br-MW:108
The Walam Olum.   Da-SC:127
War Song.   Da-SC:91
White Floating Clouds. Ho-SD:29
INDIANS OF NORTH AMERICA –
    SOCIAL LIFE AND CUSTOMS
Behind Sea-Lion Town.   Ho-SD:61
The Boy and the Deer.   Te-FC:3
The Broad Woods.   Jo-TS:4
The Creation.   Te-FC:275
Dancing Teepees. C. O'John.
    Al-WW:61
An Eagle Feather I See. Jo-TS:20
Fragments.   Br-MW:130
From a Notarized Deposition Made
    by Itshas Harjo. Itshas Harjo.
    Br-MW:115
The Girl Who Took Care of the
    Turkeys.   Te-FC:67
The Hopis and the Famine.
    Te-FC:35
I Have Taken the Woman of Beauty.
    Ho-SD:62
It Is Not Now.   Ho-SD:64
Love Charm.   Br-MW:112
My Children.   Jo-TS:22
Old Man, the Sweat Lodge.
    P. George.   Al-WW:115
Once Again. L. Sohappy.
    Al-WW:17
The Path I Must Travel.
    E. Mitchell.   Al-WW:94
Pelt Kid and His Grandmother.
    Te-FC:193
The Sacred Lands of the Blue Lake
    Forest. P. Bernal.   Br-MW:57
Song Concerning a Message from
    Washington.   Tr-US II:240
The Sun Priest and the Witch-
    Woman.   Te-FC:135
Tale. Br-MW:44
Until Then. P. George. Al-WW:126
We Are Also Going to Be Invited.
    Ho-SD:60
Wolf Woman.   Da-SC:51, Ho-SD:60
Woman Song.   Da-SC:111
The Women and the Man. Te-FC:87
The Young Man Going to War.
    Jo-TS:16
INDIANS OF NORTH AMERICA – SONGS:
    see INDIANS OF NORTH AMERICA –
    MUSIC AND SONGS
INDIANS OF NORTH AMERICA –
    TREATMENT
America. W. Rose. Ni-CD:213
Bad River Reservation.
    J. Malouf. Ad-II:92
Chief Red Jacket Addresses a
    Missionary. Red Jacket.
    Kr-OF:4

Deny It, but It Is So. E. Smith.
  Kr-OF:13
Farewell, My Nation! Farewell,
  Black Hawk. Black Hawk. Kr-OF:6
The Four Directions.
  E. Mitchell. Al-WW:95
From Governor Everett, Receiving
  the Indian Chiefs, November,
  1837. M. Fuller. Kr-OF:8
Good Clean Whiteman's Fun.
  K. Ballen. Ad-II:90
Hatred of Men with Black Hair.
  R. Bly. Mc-EA:127
Heritage. G. Bowers. Ad-II:91
History of Nez Percé Indians.
  J. Reuben. Br-MW:133
In the Name of God. R. Emerson.
  Kr-OF:11
In the Oregon Country.
  W. Stafford. Bl-FP:26,
  Br-AF:162
Indian Country, Black Kettle
  Raises the Stars and Stripes.
  L. Simpson. Mc-EA:61
Indian Reservation: Caughnawaga.
  A. Klein. Wi-LT:748
John Cherokee. Gr-GB:267
The Last Reservation.
  W. Learned. Kr-OF:16
The Man from Washington.
  J. Welch. Ni-CD:248
Manifest Destiny. A. Probst.
  Ni-CD:163
My Children. Jo-TS:22
Osceola. W. Whitman. Kr-OF:9
Pirates of the Sphere.
  H. Melville. Kr-OF:18
Powwow. W. Snodgrass.
  Pe-OA:267, Pe-SS:50
The Ration Card. L. Bahe. Ni-CD:8
The Return to the Old Gods.
  Kr-OF:21
Shaman Song. G. Fowler.
  Bl-FP:78, Sc-TN:54
Song Concerning the Removal of
  the Seminole to Oklahoma.
  Tr-US II:233
Strangers in Your Town.
  P. LaFarge. Kr-OF:22
This Soil Shall Be Ours.
  Kr-OF:8
The Two Visions. H. Longfellow.
  Kr-OF:15
Wail! For Our Nation.
  J. Lowell. Kr-OF:10
The White Man's Soul. J. Very.
  Kr-OF:16
You Are Barbarians.
  R. Williams. Kr-OF:3
INDIANS OF NORTH AMERICA - VERSE
The Clear Sky. Ba-PO:113
Fragments. Br-MW:130

Lake Winnipesaukee. O. Driver.
  Sh-RP:60
Rain Song of the Giant Society.
  Da-SC:76
White Floating Clouds. Ho-SD:29
See also Ni-CD
—ABNAKI
A Ring of Silver Foxes. Ho-SD:3
We Will Watch the Northern Lights.
  Ho-SD:2, La-RM:122
—ACOMA
Butterfly Song. Bi-IT:110,
  Jo-TS:14, Tr-US II:259
Hunting Song. Tr-US II:258
The Mockingbird. Jo-TS:2
walking in thought. S. Ortiz.
  Mc-EA:108
Winter Dance Song. Tr-US II:259
—ALGONQUIN
The Death Song of White Antelope.
  White Antelope. Br-MW:92
Farewell, My Nation! Farewell,
  Black Hawk. Black Hawk.
  Kr-OF:6
Girl's Song from a Legend.
  Da-SC:153, Tr-US II:221
Hohiotsitsi No-Otz. Ba-PO:113
I Bring the Whirlwind. Ho-SD:14
Love Song. Tr-US II:222
Old War Song. Tr-US II:241
Over the Sea, the Frozen Sea.
  Ho-SD:5
Over the Water. Bi-IT:14
Song of the Ghost Dance.
  Bi-IT:171
The Song of the Stars.
  Tr-US II:221
This Soil Shall Be Ours.
  Kr-OF:8
The Walum Olum or Red Score.
  Br-MW:100, Da-SC:127
We Are Living Humbly. Bi-IT:157
Who Are They? Bi-IT:145
Wolf Song. Da-SC:112
—APACHE
Corn Ceremony. Da-SC:83
Dawn Song. Br-MW:59, Da-SC:83,
  Le-OE:17, Tr-US II:264
Deer Song. Da-SC:81
Love Song. Tr-US II:263
My Breath Became. Bi-IT:109
A Poor Man Takes the Songs.
  Ho-SD:47
Song at the Painting of Ceremonial
  Dancers. Tr-US II:263
Song of Rejection. Tr-US II:263
Songs from the Deer Ceremony.
  Tr-US II:264
The Sunbeams Stream Forward.
  Ho-SD:48, Jo-TS:1

INDIANS OF NORTH
    AMERICA - VERSE — cont'd.
—ARAPAHO
  Arapaho Ghost Dance Song.
    Ba-PO:111
  The Dreamer Rides the Whirlwind.
    Bi-IT:24
  Father, the Morning Star.
    Ho-SD:25
  I Gave Them Fruits.   Bi-IT:146,
    Tr-US II:241
  My Children, My Children.
    Da-SC:120, Ho-SD:25, Jo-TS:22,
    Le-OE:26
  A Young Man Going to War.
    Jo-TS:16
—BLACKFOOT
  Ego Swamp. K. Kuka. Al-WW:74
  A Taste of Honey. K. Kuka.
    Al-WW:73
—CADDO
  Come On, Caddo. Ho-SD:15
—CHEROKEE
  Cherokee War Song. Da-SC:154
  Formula for Obtaining Long Life.
    Da-SC:141
  Formula for Young Children.
    Da-SC:143
  Kindergarten. R. Rogers.
    Al-WW:87
  Love Charm. Br-MW:112
  Love Incantations. Tr-US II:232
  Magic Formula to Destroy Life.
    Bi-IT:98
  Magic Formula to Fix a Bride's
    Affections. Bi-IT:79
  Sioux City: January — Very
    Late. R. Rogers. Al-WW:89
  A Spell to Destroy Life.
    Br-MW:111
  Taking Off. R. Rogers. Al-WW:85
  This Is to Make Children Jump
    Down. Da-SC:143
  To Frighten a Storm. Da-SC:143
  To Shorten a Night-Goer on This
    Side. Da-SC:144
—CHEYENNE
  Hand-Game Song. Da-SC:115
—COCHITI
  The Deer. Jo-TS:4
  Ouwe Dance Song for Good Crops.
    Tr-US II:259
—ESKIMO
  Against Sickness. Da-SC:39
  Ayii, Ayii. La-RM:108
  Ayii, Ayii (The Great Sea).
    Ho-SD:80
  Ayii, Ayii, Ayii (I Am Good-
    looking). Ho-SD:82
  Ayii, Ayii (I Return). Ho-SD:78
  Ayii, Ayii (I Think). Ho-SD:76
  Ayii, Ayii (I Walked). Ho-SD:81

  Ayii, Ayii, Ayii (I Wish).
    Ho-SD:71
  Ayii, Ayii, Ayii (My Arms).
    Ho-SD:70
  Ayii, Ayii, Ayii (That Big Man).
    Ho-SD:79
  Ayii, Ayii, Ayii, Ayii
    (Wondering). Ho-SD:68
  Caribou Hunting. Le-IB:71,
    Ma-BH:24, Tr-US I:13
  Dance Song. Le-IB:77
  Drum Song about a Stupid Kayak
    Paddler. Da-SC:44
  Eskimo Chant. La-RM:125
  Finger Game. Da-SC:42
  Glorious It Is. La-RM:112
  The Great Sea. Bi-IT:124, Ma-BH:18
  A Husband's Song. Bi-IT:83
  I Am Afraid. Ho-SD:74
  I Arise with Movements. Ho-SD:77
  I Walked on the Ice of the Sea.
    Le-IB:98
  I Want to Laugh. Ho-SD:69,
    Le-IB:72
  I Wanted to Use My Weapon.
    Le-IB:56
  The Kayak Paddler's Joy at the
    Weather. Da-SC:41, Le-IB:32,
    Tr-US I:7
  Kayak Song in Dialogue. Da-SC:38,
    Le-IB:88, Tr-US I:6
  The Lands Around My Dwelling.
    Bi-IT:49, Br-MW:141, Ma-BH:23
  Magic Prayer. Le-IB:30, Le-OE:19,
    Ma-BH:7, Tr-US I:9
  Manerathiak's Song. Do-WH:54
  The Mother's Song. Ho-SD:75,
    Le-OE:113
  Mount Koonak: A Song of Arsut.
    Da-SC:36
  Mutual Charges of Molestation.
    Da-SC:45
  My Arms, They Wave High in the
    Air. Le-OE:33
  My Eyes Are Tired. Ho-SD:73
  Nith-Song of Savdlat and
    Pulangit-Sissok. Da-SC:44,
    Tr-US I:5
  Onto a Boy's Arm. Ho-SD:77
  Orpingalik's Song: My Breath.
    Tr-US I:17
  Paddler's Song on Bad Hunting
    Weather. Da-SC:41, Le-IB:72,
    Tr-US I:7
  Petting Song (Modern). Da-SC:42
  A Salmon Trout to Her Children.
    Le-IB:45, Su-FVI:69, Tr-US I:3
  The Shooting Star. Da-SC:37
  Song. Bi-IT:164, Tr-US I:27
  Song. Le-IB:86, Tr-US II:123
  Song at the Berry-Picking on the
    Mountain. Da-SC:38, Le-IB:89

Song Composed at the Beginning of an Autumn Festival. Le-IB:106, Tr-US I:31
A Song from Sanerut. Da-SC:36
Song from Southern Sermilik. Da-SC:17
Song of Caribou, Musk Oxen. Br-MW:140, Ho-SD:67, Le-IB:34, Ma-BH:21, Tr-US I:26
The Song of Kuk-Ook, the Bad Boy. Da-SC:47
Songs, I, II. Tr-US II:123
Sung by a Little Girl to Soothe a Crying Baby. Le-IB:62, Ma-BH:27, Tr-US I:10
That Woman down There. Ho-SD:71
There Is Joy. Do-WH:64, Ho-SD:76, Le-OE:104, Ma-BH:10
Ulivfak's Song of the Caribou. Le-IB:112
Uvlunuaq's Song. Tr-US I:16
Walrus Hunting. Da-SC:40, Le-IB:52
The Wheat-Ear. Da-SC:37
When I Was Young. Le-OE:119, Ma-BH:26
When the Raven. Ho-SD:80
Who Will. Ho-SD:83
The Wind Has Wings. Do-WH:54
A Woman's First Sewing after a Mourning. Da-SC:40
See also Le-IB; Tr-US I:3-34

—HAIDA
Beautiful Is She. Ho-SD:63
Behind Sea-Lion Town. Ho-SD:61
Haida Cradle-Song. Da-SC:57
I Have Taken the Woman of Beauty. Ho-SD:62
It Is His Own Fault. Ho-SD:63
It Is Not Now. Ho-SD:64
Mourning Songs. Tr-US II:215
Perhaps You Expect. Ho-SD:64
We Are Also Going to Be Invited. Ho-SD:60
Wolf Woman. Da-SC:51, Ho-SD:60

—HAVASUPAI
A Prayer. Ho-SD:24, Le-OE:7

—HOPI
Corn-Grinding Song. Da-SC:84
The Day Has Risen. Bi-IT:165
Discharming Song. Da-SC:85
Hopi Lullaby. Da-SC:95
Hopi Owl Song. Da-SC:95
Kachina Song. Br-MW:43, Da-SC:84, Pa-SG:128
The Return to the Old Gods. Kr-OF:21
Tale. Br-MW:44
There! Bi-IT:166

—IROQUOIS
At the Wood's Edge. Bi-IT:161
The Being Without Face. Bi-IT:89
The Broad Woods. Jo-TS:4

Chief Red Jacket Addresses a Missionary. Red Jacket. Kr-OF:4
Darkness Song. Da-SC:140, Le-OE:105
Death of a Son. Bi-IT:99
From the Medicine Lodge Initiation Ceremony. Tr-US II:231
From the New Year's Ceremony. Tr-US II:229
I Hear the Eagle Bird. Ho-SD:3
Introduction to the Code of Handsome Lake. Br-MW:105
Magic Formula. Bi-IT:163
Memorial Ode. Chief J. Buck. Ba-PO:107, Ho-SD:41
On the Iroquois League. Tr-US II:229
Prayer. Bi-IT:38
Prophecy. Bi-IT:140, Br-MW:104
Requickening. Bi-IT:162
Rites of the Condoling Council. Da-SC:135
The Tree of Great Peace. Dekanawideh. Br-MW:102
A Vision of Handsome Lake. Br-MW:108

—KERESAN
Bird and Toad Play Hide and Seek. Br-MW:50
Closing Song of a Ceremony to Procure Abundance. Tr-US II:261
Come You. Ho-SD:27
Let Our Children Live. Ho-SD:28
Song Concerning the Corn Harvest. Tr-US II:261
Song of a Departed Spirit. Tr-US II:260
Two Fragments of Songs, I, II. Br-MW:48

—KIOWA
Because I Am Poor. Ho-SD:16, Le-OE:55
Earth and I Gave You Turquoise. N. Momaday. Mc-EA:59
The Father Will Descend. Ho-SD:16
God Has Had Pity on Us. Da-SC:121
A Peyote Thought. Br-MW:66
A Peyote Vision. Br-MW:67
That Wind. Bi-IT:23
Warpath Song. Da-SC:112
Wind Song. Da-SC:111

—KWAKIUTL
Even from War. Ho-SD:56
Healing Song. Tr-US II:217
How Shall We Hide. Ho-SD:58
Love Song. Da-SC:51
Love Song of a Young Man. Bi-IT:84

INDIANS OF NORTH
   AMERICA - VERSE-KWAKIUTL
   — cont'd.
Love-Song of the Dead. Da-SC:54,
   Tr-US II:219
Love Songs, I, II. Tr-US II:219
Mourning Song for Modana.
   Da-SC:54, Tr-US II:217
Parting Song. Tr-US II:217
Potlatch Boasts. Br-MW:137
Shaman's Song. Da-SC:49
Song for the Thunder Bird Dance.
   Tr-US II:216
Song of a Supernatural Being.
   Tr-US II:216
Song of a Warrior for His First-
   Born Son. Tr-US II:218
Song of Parents Who Want to Wake
   Up Their Son. Da-SC:57
Song of Qwaxila. Da-SC:86
Song of the Chiefs' Daughters.
   Bi-IT:81, Ho-SD:57
Song of the Parents Who Want to
   Wake Up Their Daughter.
   Da-SC:58
To the Cedar Tree. Jo-TS:16
War Song of the Kwakiutl.
   Tr-US II:218
What of Olden Times. Ho-SD:57
When I Am a Man. Da-SC:9,
   Ho-SD:56
—MAIDU
Song of the Red Cloud.
   Tr-US II:250
—MAKAH
I Cannot Forget You. Bi-IT:78
My Little Son. Da-SC:58, Ho-SD:54
Song. Bi-IT:45
—MALECITE
Tale. Br-MW:110
—MENOMINEE
Menominee Love Songs. Da-SC:151
—MODOC
The Modoc Singer. Br-MW:3
—MUSKOGEAN
Crazy Dance. Da-SC:159
Creek Cradle Song. Da-SC:158
The Cussitaws Come East. Bi-IT:13
From a Notorized Deposition Made
   by Itshas Harjo. Itshas Harjo.
   Br-MW:115
Medicine Song for Snake Sickness.
   Da-SC:145
Poem to a Redskin. W. Rose.
   Ni-CD:205
Snake Medicine Song. Da-SC:144
Song Concerning the Removal of
   the Seminole to Oklahoma.
   Tr-US II:233
—NATCHEZ
The Cannibal's Seven Sons.
   Br-MW:116

The Tale of the Jealous Brother.
   Br-MW:120
—NAVAHO
Alone Together. G. Cohoe.
   Al-WW:26
Ancestors. G. Cohoe. Al-WW:24
Black Hair Rope Is What You Used.
   Ho-SD:42
Burro with the Long Ears.
   Fe-FP:163
Concerning Wisdom. D. Yazzie.
   Br-MW:63
The Corn Grows Up. Le-OE:78
Dawn Boy's Song. Da-SC:64,
   Ga-FB:247
Daylight Song. Da-SC:66
Far as Man Can See. Ho-SD:43
Farewell, My Younger Brother.
   Ho-SD:38
First Man Was the First to
   Emerge. Bi-IT:9, Da-SC:68
First Song of the Thunder.
   Da-SC:65, Le-OE:74
The Folding Fan. G. Cohoe.
   Al-WW:25
The Four Directions.
   E. Mitchell. Al-WW:95
From the Mountain's Summit.
   Ho-SD:40
From the Night Chant. Br-MW:62
Gambling Songs. Tr-US II:252
Gopher Song. Da-SC:96
Ground-Squirrel Song. Da-SC:97,
   Le-OE:53, Tr-US II:252
Hi-ihiya Naiho-o! Da-SC:77,
   Ho-SD:41
House Blessing. Bi-IT:48
House Song to the East. Da-SC:78
Hunting Song. Da-SC:80, Le-OE:64
In Tsegihi. Ho-SD:39
Invocation to Dailyl Neyani.
   Da-SC:75, Tr-US II:250
It Was the Wind. Bi-IT:19
Lines from the Wind Chant.
   Br-MW:64
Little Horned Toad. Fe-FP:144
Little Puppy. Fe-FP:156
Magic Formula to Make an Enemy
   Peaceful. Bi-IT:69
The Magpie! The Magpie!
   Da-SC:96, Ho-SD:44, Le-OE:15,
   Tr-US II:252
Medicine Song. Da-SC:87,
   Le-OE:98
Miracle Hill. E. Mitchell.
   Al-WW:93
Mom. G. Cohoe. Al-WW:27
My Great Corn Plants. Ho-SD:37
Navajo Prayer. E. Yeomans.
   Se-PR:170
Now I Walk with Talking God.
   Ho-SD:37

Oricessional Song from the Night
    Chant. Tr-US II:251
The Path I Must Travel.
    E. Mitchell. Al-WW:94
Prayer. Bi-IT:34
Protection Song. Da-SC:90
Song of a Bear. Tr-US II:252
The Song of Bekotsidi. Da-SC:67
A Song of Nayenzgani. Da-SC:66
Song of Sequence. Da-SC:21
Song of the Coyote Who Stole
    Fire. Da-SC:69
Song of the Flood. Da-SC:67
Song of the Horse. Da-SC:79,
    Le-OE:37
Song of the Prophet to the
    San Juan River. Bi-IT:43,
    Tr-US II:251
Song of the Sun and the Moon.
    Da-SC:68, Le-OE:3
Songs in the Garden of the House
    God. Bi-IT:115, Da-SC:86
Talking to His Drum. E. Mitchell.
    Al-WW:96
Thirst. G. Cohoe. Al-WW:23
To the Abode of the Deer I
    Came Up. Ho-SD:39
Toad Man's Song. Br-MW:59
Trading Song. Tr-US II:253
The Voice of Thunder. Ho-SD:44
The Voice That Beautifies the
    Land. Da-SC:65, Le-OE:11,
    Pa-SG:139, Tr-US II:251
The War God's Horse Song.
    Br-MW:60, Sm-LG:78
War Song. Da-SC:91
—NEZ PERCÉ
Ambition. P. George. Al-WW:120
Ask the Mountains. P. George.
    Al-WW:124
Battle Won Is Lost. P. George.
    Al-WW:114
Child Rest. P. George. Al-WW:117
Coyote's Night. P. George.
    Al-WW:128
Guardian-Spirit Song. Br-MW:136
History of the Nez Percé Indians.
    J. Reuben. Br-MW:133
I Wonder if Everyone Is Up.
    Jo-TS:2
Make Me a Man. P. George.
    Al-WW:121
Monument in Bone. P. George.
    Al-WW:122
Morning Beads. P. George.
    Al-WW:127
Night Blessing. P. George.
    Al-WW:118
Old Man, the Sweat Lodge.
    P. George. Al-WW:115
Old Man's Plea. P. George.
    Al-WW:126

Proviso. P. George. Al-WW:113
Self. P. George. Al-WW:122
Shadows and Song. P. George.
    Al-WW:123
Song of a New Cradleboard.
    P. George. Al-WW:116
Until Then. P. George. Al-WW:126
War. Chief Joseph. Ba-PO:112
—NOOTKA
Don't You Ever. Jo-TS:7
Girl's Song. Tr-US II:220
Sing Your Song. Ho-SD:55
You, Whose Day It Is. Ho-SD:55,
    Jo-TS:1, Le-OE:16
—OJIBWA
The Approach of the Storm.
    Da-SC:149, Tr-US II:224
Arrow Song. Da-SC:157
Chippewa Love Songs. Da-SC:151
Dawn Song. Tr-US II:228
Death of a Sister. Bi-IT:96
Death Song of a Warrior.
    Da-SC:157, Tr-US II:226
Dream Song. Bi-IT:130
Dream Songs, I, III. Tr-US II:224
An Eagle Feather I See. Jo-TS:20
Farewell to the Warriors. Le-OE:125
Fire-Fly, Fire-Fly, Bright Little
    Thing. Da-SC:28
Firefly Song. Br-MW:97
Hear My Voice, Birds of War!
    Da-SC:155, Ho-SD:5
Hunting Song. Tr-US II:223
I of the Owl. Ho-SD:9
It Is My Form and Person.
    Da-SC:153
A Loon I Thought It Was.
    Da-SC:151, Ho-SD:7, Le-OE:89,
    Tr-US II:225
Love-Charm Songs. Br-MW:99,
    Da-SC:152, Tr-US II:223
Love Song. Tr-US II:227
Love Song. Da-SC:152,
    Tr-US II:223
Love Songs, II, IV. Tr-US II:225
Maple Sugar. Da-SC:148
My Music Reaches to the Sky.
    Da-SC:149, Le-OE:136,
The Noise of Passing Feet.
    Le-OE:8
Oh, I Am Thinking. Ho-SD:8
Ojibwa War Song. Da-SC:155,
    Kr-OF:1, Le-OE:120
On the Bank of a Stream.
    Da-SC:157
The Red Streams of My Veins.
    Ho-SD:6
The Sioux Women. Ho-SD:9,
    Jo-TS:22, Tr-US II:226
The Sky Clears. Da-SC:147
The Sky Will Resound. Da-SC:148
Song. Bi-IT:53

INDIANS OF NORTH
    AMERICA - VERSE-OJIBWA
    — cont'd.
  Song after Victory.   Tr-US II:226
  Song of a Man Urged to Join the
    Warriors.   Tr-US II:227
  Song of a Woman when Her Lover
    Went on a Journey. Tr-US II:228
  A Song of Greatness.   Ar-TP3:35,
    Br-AF:37, Br-BC:126, Fe-FP:24,
    Sh-RP:103
  Song of One Whose Lover Is Dead.
    Tr-US II:227
  Song of the Buffalo.   Da-SC:157
  Song of the Butterfly.   Da-SC:157,
    Le-OE:39
  Song of the Thunders.   Da-SC:148
  The Spirit Walking.   Ho-SD:6,
    Le-OE:111
  Spring Song.   Bi-IT:126, Br-MW:98,
    Da-SC:148, Jo-TS:13, Tr-US II:228
  They Are Sailing on the Breeze.
    Jo-TS:20
  Three Fragments.   Br-MW:96
  Toward Calm and Shady Places.
    Ba-PO:114, Tr-US II:224
  Wailing Song.   Bi-IT:97
  War Song on a Brave Woman.
    Tr-US II:227
  War Songs.   Bi-IT:61
  What Is This.   Le-OE:19
  When I Think of Him.
    Da-SC:152, Tr-US II:225
  Who Is This? Da-SC:158, Jo-TS:9
  The Wind.   Da-SC:149, Ho-SD:7
  Woman's-Dance Song.
    Tr-US II:226
—OMAHA
  Curing Ritual.   Da-SC:110
  Death-Dance Song.   Tr-US II:243
  Litany to the High Gods.
    Tr-US II:242
  Love-Magic Song.   Tr-US II:243
  Song of Two Ghosts.
    Tr-US II:243
  Victory Song.   Tr-US II:244
  Woman Song. Da-SC:111,
    Tr-US II:244
—OSAGE
  Black Bear Song. Da-SC:108
  Child-Naming Rite of the Bow
    People. Da-SC:107
  Hunting Song.   Tr-US II:246
  Little Song of the Sun.
    Tr-US II:247
  Old-Age Chant.   Da-SC:105
  Ritual Recitation: The Symbolic
    Painting. Tr-US II:244
  War Song.   Tr-US II:247
  Woman's Song of Corn Growing.
    Tr-US II:247

—PAIUTE
  The Grass on the Mountain.
    Bo-HF:34
  Rattlesnake Recitative. Da-SC:10
  The Whirlwind.   Br-MW:129,
    Da-SC:118
  The Wind Stirs the Willows.
    Bi-IT:172, Ho-SD:15
—PALOOS
  Behold: My World. L. Sohappy.
    Al-WW:18
  Once Again. L. Sohappy. Al-WW:17
  The Parade. L. Sohappy. Al-WW:16
—PAPAGO
  At the Edge of the World.
    Jo-TS:13
  Blue Evening Falls.
    Ho-SD:49, Le-OE:99
  Celebration. A. Lopez. Al-WW:3
  A Cloud on Top of Evergreen
    Mountain. Ho-SD:47,
    Tr-US II:273
  Come All! Bi-IT:167
  Direction. A. Lopez. Al-WW:10
  Distant Train. Tr-US II:272
  Dream Song. Bi-IT:129
  Dreaming Liquor Songs.
    Tr-US II:270
  Dry and Parched. A. Lopez.
    Al-WW:9
  The Eagle. Ho-SD:50, Le-OE:13
  Eagle Flight. A. Lopez.
    Al-WW:7
  The Eagle Speaks. Jo-TS:13
  Elegy Dream Song. Br-MW:42
  Endless Search. A. Lopez.
    Al-WW:7
  Hunting Song. Tr-US II:271
  I Am Crying from Thirst.
    A. Lopez. Al-WW:8
  I Go Forth to Move about the
    Earth. A. Lopez. Al-WW:8
  I Met a Mexican. Da-SC:12
  I See a Star. A. Lopez. Al-WW:4
  In the Great Night. Bi-IT:132,
    Ho-SD:46
  In the Night. Bi-IT:107
  Invitation to Drink Cactus Liquor
    at a Rain-Bringing Ceremony.
    Tr-US II:269
  It Is Raining Up There. Ho-SD:49
  The Lavender Kitten. A. Lopez.
    Al-WW:11
  The Little Red Spiders. Jo-TS:14
  A Little Yellow Cricket. Jo-TS:14
  A Low Range of Mountains.
    Ho-SD:51, Le-OE:15
  Papago Love Song. Ho-LP:2
  A Question. A. Lopez. Al-WW:6
  Railroad Rails. Tr-US II:271

Raise Your Hands to the Sky.
   A. Lopez.   Al-WW:9
Separation.   A. Lopez.   Al-WW:4
Song at a Ceremony for Securing
   Good Crops.   Tr-US II:273
Song of Encouragement.   Bi-IT:64
Song of the Deer.   Bi-IT:56
Song of the Hunter.   Bi-IT:55
Song Sung on an Expedition to
   Obtain Salt.   Bi-IT:21, Ho-SD:51,
   Le-OE:73, Tr-US II:273
Songs Received in Dreams.
   Tr-US II:273
The Sun Is Slowly Departing.
   Ho-SD:41
The Sunrise.   Da-SC:87
Tears.   A. Lopez.   Al-WW:3
Telegraph Wires.   Tr-US II:272
Untitled.   A. Lopez.   Al-WW:5
Where Am I Running from.   Ho-SD:50
—PASSAMAQUODDY
Passamaquoddy War Song.   Da-SC:254
—PAWNEE
As I Lay Sleeping.   Ho-SD:33
The Birth of Dawn.   Br-MW:68
Breathe on Him.   Bi-IT:20
Buffalo Dance Song.   Br-MW:72
Daylight.   Da-SC:103, Hu-MP:131
Give Heed, My Child.   Ho-SD:32
The Hako Party Presented to the
   Powers.   Da-SC:102
Holy Visions!   Ho-SD:32
I Know Not if the Voice of Man.
   Da-SC:25
Invoking the Powers.   Br-MW:69
Is This Real.   Bi-IT:131,
   Da-SC:113
It Is There that Our Hearts Are
   Set.   Ho-SD:33, Le-OE:5
Look, Where They Come.   Ho-SD:34
The Morning Star.   Ho-SD:36
Recitation of War Honors.
   Br-MW:70
Rev'rent Our Hearts.   Ba-PO:113
The Sixteen Circuits of the
   Lodge.   Da-SC:103
Song of the Wolf Society.
   Tr-US II:242
Song to the Pleiades.   Da-SC:104
—PIMA
The Black Snake Wind Came to Me.
   Jo-TS:19
Black-Tailed Deer Song.   Bi-IT:54
The Bright Dawn Appears.   Ho-SD:52
The Creation of the Earth.
   Da-SC:69
A Dancing Song.   Br-MW:37
Emergence Song.   Bi-IT:10
Feast Songs.   Br-MW:36, 41
Festal Song.   Tr-US II:265

Foot Race Song.   Da-SC:97
Hunting Song.   Br-MW:40
Medicine Songs.   Br-MW:38, 39
Medicine Songs, I.   Tr-US II:267
Owl Song.   Da-SC:89
Pima War Song.   Da-SC:94
Powerless! Powerless!   Ho-SD:40
Quail Song.   Da-SC:90, Le-OE:51
Roadrunner Song.   Da-SC:89
Scalp Song.   Da-SC:93
Song of Creation.   Bi-IT:4,
   Ho-SD:52
Song of the Fallen Deer. Bi-IT:57
Swallow Song.   Da-SC:97,
   Tr-US II:266
The Taking of Life Brings Serious
   Thoughts.   Bi-IT:68
War Song.   Tr-US II:269
The Wind Now Commences to Sing.
   Bi-IT:22, Da-SC:88, Ho-SD:53,
   Tr-US II:268
—QUILEUTE
Song of the Four Little Shell-
   Animals.   Le-OE:41
—SAHAPTIN
The Surrender Speech of Chief
   Joseph.   Chief Joseph.
   Bi-IT:153, Kr-OF:19
—SALISHAN
Bremerton, January 18, 1969.
   A. Pratt.   Al-WW:99
Death Takes Only a Minute.
   A. Pratt.   Al-WW:106
Empathy.   A. Pratt.   Al-WW:107
Fishing.   A. Pratt.   Al-WW:101
Fragments of Spring.   A. Pratt.
   Al-WW:108
Hit!   T. Palmanteer.   Al-WW:39
Hope to Keep.   A. Pratt.
   Al-WW:109
I'm Only Going to Tell You Once.
   A. Pratt.   Al-WW:106
Judgment.   T. Palmanteer.
   Al-WW:46
Lamentation.   A. Pratt.   Al-WW:108
The Moccasins of an Old Man.
   R. Carden.   Al-WW:35
Nespelim Man.   J. Campbell.
   Al-WW:32
Question.   A. Pratt.   Al-WW:103
Quietly I Shout.   A. Pratt.
   Al-WW:110
Red Eagle.   J. Campbell. Al-WW:31
The Sea Is Melancholy.   A. Pratt.
   Al-WW:103
So Quickly Came Summer. A. Pratt.
   Al-WW:109
Spring Dew.   T. Palmanteer.
   Al-WW:43
The Strings of Time.
   T. Palmanteer.   Al-WW:47

INDIANS OF NORTH
    AMERICA - VERSE-SALISHAN
    — cont'd.
This Is Real.   T. Palmanteer.
    Al-WW:45
Tumbleweed.   R. Carden. Al-WW:36
Twilight's Feet.   A. Pratt.
    Al-WW:102
We Saw Days.   T. Palmanteer.
    Al-WW:41
—SHOSHONE
Neither Spirit nor Bird.   Pa-SG:36
Song of a Woman Abandoned by the
    Tribe.   Ho-LP:84
Songs of the Ghost Dance.
    Bi-IT:174
—SIOUAN
Battle Song.   Sitting Bull.
    Da-SC:113
A Bedtime Song for Children.
    Br-MW:90
Behold, This Pipe.   Bi-IT:70
Black Mouth Society Song.
    Tr-US II:234
Brave Buffalo.   Jo-TS:20
Buffalo Myth.   Br-MW:73
Buffalo Song.   Br-MW:79
Charms.   Bi-IT:92
Dancing Song of the Skunk.
    Tr-US II:234
Dream Song.   Bi-IT:128, Da-SC:100,
    Ho-SD:12, Le-OE:107
Dry Is My Tongue.   Da-SC:114
Father.   Jo-TS:4
Fragment from the Child-Naming
    Rites.   Br-MW:77
Friend.   Jo-TS:20
From a Legend.   Br-MW:75
Here Am I.   Jo-TS:9
Ho! Ye Sun, Moon, Stars.
    Da-SC:104, Ho-SD:18
Hunting Song.   Le-OE:59
I Am the Kit Fox.   Ho-SD:10
I Pass the Pipe.   Bi-IT:71
I Sing for the Animals.
    Da-SC:23, Le-OE:36
I Sought a Vision.   Ho-SD:14
If You Are Lazy.   Ho-SD:13
It Shall Be.   Ho-SD:13
Last Song of Sitting Bull.
    Sitting Bull.   Kr-OF:1,
    Le-OE:127
The Man Who Married the Birds.
    Br-MW:84
My Dear Friend.   Ho-SD:26
Myth.   Br-MW:81
Old Love Songs,   Tr-US II:238
Old Love Songs Connected with
    War, I, III. Tr-US II:238, 239
The Old Men.   Jo-TS:10,
    Tr-US II:237

Out of the Earth.   Ho-SD:11
Planting Song.   Da-SC:109,
    Ho-SD:23
Praise Song.   Tr-US II:239
Prayers.   Bi-IT:31, 32
Processional from the War
    Ceremony.   Br-MW:78
The Rising of the Buffalo Men.
    Da-SC:109, Ho-SD:23
The Rock.   Br-MW:83
Sitting Bull's Song.
    Sitting Bull.   Da-SC:112
Song.   Br-MW:93
Song Commemorating a Dead Sioux
    Warrior.   Tr-US II:235
Song Concerning a Message from
    Washington.   Tr-US II:240
Song of a Ghost.   Tr-US II:239
Song of a Medicine Man.
    Tr-US II:236
Song of a Scout Remembering
    Home.   Tr-US II:234
Song of Entering the Village.
    Da-SC:115
Song of Reproach.   Bi-IT:63
Song of the Horse Society.
    Tr-US II:236
Song of the Killing.   Da-SC:114
Song of the Maiden's Leap.
    Tr-US II:239
Song of the Pasque Flower.
    Tr-US II:235
Songs in Honor of a Prominent
    Warrior.   Tr-US II:238
Songs of a Mother Mourning Her
    Sons Killed in Battle.
    Tr-US II:237
Taking of the Name.   Bo-FP:265
They Will Appear.   Bi-IT:169
Three Fragments, II.   Br-MW:96
A Voice.   Jo-TS:24,
    Tr-US II:235
War Songs.   Bi-IT:62,
    Tr-US II:236, 237, 240
A Warrior I Have Been.   Ho-SD:12
When the Day Is Cloudy. Jo-TS:7
The Whole World Is Coming.
    Da-SC:121, Ho-SD:12
A Wolf.   Ho-SD:23, Jo-TS:9
You May Go on the Warpath.
    Da-SC:12
You Shall Live.   Bi-IT:170
Young Men, Help Me. Sitting Bull.
    Da-SC:113
—TEWA
Dead on the Warpath.   Da-SC:93,
    Tr-US II:257
A Lover's Lament.   Pa-SG:59,
    Tr-US II:257
Lullaby of the Cannibal Giants.
    Da-SC:95
Mad Coyote.   Jo-TS:10

My Sun! Jo-TS:1
Now We Come Southwards. Bi-IT:15
Prayer for Long Life.
  Tr-US II:256
San Juan Lullaby. Da-SC:17
Scalp Dance. Da-SC:93
Shadows. Da-SC:94
Song of the Sky Loom. Da-SC:76,
  Le-OE:6, Mo-TS:16, Tr-US II:256
That Mountain Far Away. Bi-IT:47
Upward Going! Bi-IT:12
Weave Us a Garment of Brightness.
  Ho-SD:45
With Dangling Hands. Da-SC:81
—TIWA
Corn-Grinding Songs, I, II.
  Tr-US II:257, 258
The Sacred Lands of the Blue Lake
  Forest. P. Bernal. Br-MW:57
See also Wo-HS
—TLINGIT
Angry Song. Da-SC:56
Carrying My Mind Around. Da-SC:53
Chinook Sad Song. Da-SC:16
Cradle-Song for a Boy. Da-SC:57,
  Ho-SD:65
Mourning Song. Da-SC:53
Mourning Song for a Brother
  Drowned at Sea. Br-MW:139
The Nation's Drum Has Fallen
  Down. Da-SC:53
Song of Hummingbird. Le-OE:49
Song of the New-Rich. Da-SC:56
Song of the Death of an Uncle.
  Tr-US II:215
When Spring Came. La-RM:124
Why Have I Come to You? Da-SC:51
Woman's Love Song. Tr-US II:215
—TSIMSHIAN
Hold In Your Breath. Ho-SD:59
Nexnox, Nexnox! Ho-SD:59
Skyspear. Ho-SD:59
—UTE
Afternoon and His Unfinished
  Poem. C. O'John. Al-WW:66
Dancing Teepees. C. O'John.
  Al-WW:61
Dirt Road. C. O'John. Al-WW:61
Doldrums. C. O'John. Al-WW:65
Half of My Life. C. O'John.
  Al-WW:64
I Am Like a Bear. Ho-SD:24
Problems. C. O'John. Al-WW:65
Speak to Me. C. O'John.
  Al-WW:64
A Tear Rolled down My Cheek.
  C. O'John. Al-WW:63
That Lonesome Place. C. O'John.
  Al-WW:68
This Day Is Over. C. O'John.
  Al-WW:67

Trees. C. O'John. Al-WW:69
Water Baby. C. O'John. Al-WW:62
You Smiled. C. O'John. Al-WW:63
—WINNEBAGO
Prayer. Bi-IT:36
This Newly Created World. Bi-IT:5
Throughout the World. Ho-SD:18,
  Le-OE:24
—WINTUN
Dream Songs. Bi-IT:125, 133,
  Tr-US II:248, 249
Lightning. Da-SC:10
The North Star. Br-MW:132
On the Stone Ridge East. Da-SC:11,
  Ho-SD:27
Polar Star. Da-SC:11, Le-OE:102,
  Tr-US II:248
Spirits. Bi-IT:94
We Spirits Dance. Bi-IT:95
You and I Shall Go.
  Bi-IT:100, Tr-US II:248
—YANAN
Curse on People That Wish One Ill.
  Bi-IT:156
—YOKUTS
Death Song of a Song Maker.
  Le-OE:118
My Words Are Tied. Ho-SD:16
Rattlesnake Ceremony Song.
  Tr-US II:249
—YUCHI
T-cho, the Sun, Said. Ho-SD:26
—YUMA
The Owl Hooted. Da-SC:88,
  Ho-SD:20, Le-OE:11
The Water Bug. Br-MW:96,
  Da-SC:87, Ho-SD:20, Le-OE:97
—ZUÑI
At the Rainbow Spring. Jo-TS:2
Beseeching the Breath. Bi-IT:25
Child of the Raven. Ho-SD:31
Corn-Grinding Song. Sh-RP:80
From a Seasonal Prayer.
  Tr-US II:254
How the Days Will Be. Bi-IT:66
In the West the Dragonfly
  Wanders. Ho-SD:30
The Locust. Fe-FP:135, Sh-RP:82
Lullaby. Le-OE:43
O, My Lovely Mountain. Ho-SD:30
Offering. Bi-IT:108
Offering of Prayer Sticks.
  Da-SC:71
Prayer at the Offering of Food to
  the Ancestors. Tr-US II:255
Prayer to a Dead Wife. Da-SC:73
Presenting an Infant to the Sun.
  Bi-IT:113
Storm Song. Bi-IT:106, Br-MW:47
They Stooped Over and Came Out.
  Bi-IT:11
When We Meet the Enemy. Ho-SD:31

INDIANS OF NORTH
    AMERICA - VERSE-ZUNI — cont'd.
  Wind-Song.   Sh-RP:82
  A Woman Mourns for Her Husband.
    Kr-OF:20
  You Talk about and Fear Me.
    Ho-SD:31
  Zuni Prayer at Sunrise.   Da-SC:70
INDIANS OF SOUTH AMERICA: see also
    names of tribes, as INCAS
  The Ghost of Caipolicán. Bi-IT:155
  Love Song.   Bi-IT:76
  On the Death of Atahualpa.
    Bi-IT:154
  Prayer.   Bi-IT:33
  A Song.   Br-MW:35
  With Rejoicing Mouth.   Bi-IT:39
INDIANS OF SOUTH AMERICA -
    CEREMONIES AND DANCES
  A Dance.   Br-MW:34
  Song of the Priestess at a
    Victory Feast.   Tr-US II:302
INDIANS OF SOUTH AMERICA - LEGENDS
  Prayer.   Bi-IT:29
INDIANS OF SOUTH AMERICA -
    MUSIC AND SONGS
  Dance Song.   Tr-US II:304
  Invocation Sung by a Hunter
    Setting Out. Tr-US II:303
  Song.   Tr-US II:301
  Song of a Visitor to a Strange
    Village.   Tr-US II:309
  Songs of Dancing Women Per-
    sonifying Birds. Tr-US II:303
  To This My Song.   Le-OE:89
INDIANS OF SOUTH AMERICA -
    RELIGION AND MYTHOLOGY
  Hymn of an Inca to the God
    Viracocha. Tr-US II:299
  Verses of an Inca Poet and
    Astrologer.   Tr-US II:300
INDIANS OF SOUTH
    AMERICA - VERSE
—ARAUCANIAN
  The Ghost of Caipolicán. Bi-IT:155
  Prayer.   Bi-IT:33
—CAINGANG
  Keening.   Tr-US II:309
—CARIBAN
  A Dance.   Br-MW:34
  A Song.   Br-MW:35
  Word of the Thunder. Tr-US II:310
—CHOROTI
  Song of a Visitor to a Strange
    Village. Tr-US II:309
—JIVARO
  Invocation Sung by a Hunter
    Setting Out. Tr-US II:303
  Planting Song of Women to the
    Earth-Mother. Tr-US II:303

Song of the Priestess at a
    Victory Feast. Tr-US II:302
Songs of Dancing Women Per-
    sonifying Birds. Tr-US II:303
—QUECHUA
  Dance Song.   Tr-US II:304
  Elegy.   Tr-US II:307
  Girl's Song. Tr-US II:306
  Hymn of an Inca to the God
    Viracocha.   Tr-US II:299
  Leave-Taking.   Le-OE:93,
    Tr-US II:307
  Like Two Doves.   Le-OE:91
  Lullaby.   Tr-US II:305
  Oh My Sun, My Moon.   Le-OE:115
  On the Death of Atahualpa.
    Bi-IT:154
  Peruvian Dance Song. Le-OE:133
  Prayer.   Bi-IT:29
  Song.   Bi-IT:123
  Song.   Tr-US II:305, 306
  To a Traitor.   Tr-US II:301
  To This My Song.   Le-OE:89
  Verses of an Inca Poet and
    Astrologer.   Tr-US II:300
  With Rejoicing Mouth.   Bi-IT:39
—TUPI
  Love Charm Songs, I, II. Br-MW:6
  Love Song.   Bi-IT:76
—WITOTO
  Song of the Victim at a Cannibal
    Feast.   Tr-US II:302
INDIFFERENCE: see also
    HUMOR - INDIFFERENCE;
    SATIRE - INDIFFERENCE
  And Now You Live Dispersed.
    T. Eliot. Ar-TP3:94
  anyone lived in a pretty how town.
    E. Cummings.   Br-TC:80,
    Ca-VT:182, Ha-PO:241, Na-EO:73,
    Pe-OA:152, Un-MA:477, Wi-LT:365
  Apology.   E. Herrick.   Ls-NY:296
  The Assassin.   D. Hall.   Ha-TP:31
  At Ease.   W. de la Mare.
    Pa-GTB:438
  At 79th and Park.   B. Howes.
    Pe-M:16
  The Ballad of Semmerwater.
    Bl-OB:81
  Ballad of the Bread Man.
    C. Causley.   To-MP:203
  Bar-Room Matins.   L. MacNeice.
    Pl-EI:152
  The Bed Sheet and the Stranger.
    R. Zychlinska.   Ho-TY:230
  Benign Neglect/Mississippi, 1970.
    P. St. John.   Ad-PB:346
  Blackout.   A. Gregor.   Gr-SS:75
  A Broken Appointment.   T. Hardy.
    Rv-CB:940

The Campus on the Hill.
W. Snodgrass. Br-TC:397
The Card Players. D. Ray.
Ca-VT:678
The Celestial Surgeon.
R. Stevenson. Al-VBP:1070,
Un-GT:308, Un-MB:58
Changing the Wheel. B. Brecht.
Ho-LP:69
A Chippewa Legend. J. Lowell.
Hu-MP:425
The Clam. S. Silverstein.
Co-BBW:72
Compromise. C. Stetson. Sp-OG:331
Confession Overheard in a Subway.
K. Fearing. Pe-SS:112,
Wi-LT:699
Could Be. L. Hughes. La-OC:70
Country Idyll. F. Cornford.
Co-BBW:176, Co-PU:95
de Gaulle Nods Once. E. Brooks.
Ls-NY:44
Droit de Seigneur. R. Murphy.
Co-PI:148
Early in the Morning.
L. Simpson. Ha-PO:158
Ecce Homo. D. Gascoyne. Wi-LT:715
The Elevator Man Adheres to Form.
M. Danner. Ad-PB:137, Be-MA:87,
Hu-PN:161
Five Vignettes, 3. J. Toomer.
Ad-PB:34
God. S. Hazo. Co-EL:108
God Bless Us. G. Bart-Williams.
Gr-BT:109
The Green Shepherd. L. Simpson.
Pe-OA:264
Guilt. A. Haushofer. Ba-PO:179
He Died a Second Time, 5. The
Posture. Ai Ch'ing. Hs-TC:305
Her Husband Asks Her to Buy a
Bolt of Silk. Ch'en T'ao.
Rx-LT:105
The Hour. U. Greenberg. Me-PH:89
Hour of Concern. L. Hubbell.
Ba-PO:52
The Idiot. J. Ashberry. Ca-VT:593
Impasse. L. Hughes. Wi-LT:424
imperial thumbprint.
T. Weatherly. Ad-PB:399
In Bertram's Garden.
S. Justice. Ca-VT:537
In Less than Two and Twenty Years.
Ascelepiades. Ho-LP:64
In Memoriam. A. Tennyson.
Ox-BN:499
In the Telegraph Office.
A. Kushner. Bo-RU:50
Innocents. K. Hopkins.
Cr-WS:130

Insensibility. W. Owen.
Ba-PO:141, Wi-LT:345
Insensibility. W. Owen.
Ba-PO:xiii
Insouciance. J. Dickson.
Du-SH:58
The Invisible. R. Kizerman.
Sa-B:107
Is My Team Ploughing. A. Housman.
Ha-PO:12, Hi-WP I:22,
Un-MB:95, Un-MW:119, Wi-LT:61
Jeff Buckner. F. Beddo. Ba-PO:77
Julius Caesar and the Honey-Bee.
C. Turner. Rd-OA:160
Killing No Murder. S. Warner.
Un-MB:375
The Lady of the Manor. G. Crabbe.
Ox-BN:2
Late Late. G. Starbuck. Ke-PP:112
Life at War. D. Levertov.
Ca-VT:515
The Looker-On. C. Stetson.
Sp-OG:325
The Lotos Eaters. A. Tennyson.
Gr-CT:278, Pa-OM:296
A Man Who Had Fallen among
Thieves. e. cummings.
Wi-LT:360
The Mountain. R. Frost. Ga-FB:292,
Pa-HT:13
Mourn Not the Dead. R. Chaplin.
Al-VBP:1147, Ba-PO:146,
Cr-WS:120, Kr-OF:117
Musée des Beaux Arts. W. Auden.
Br-TC:20, Er-FA:64, Ha-PO:223,
Pa-GTB:510, To-MP:31, Wi-LT:467
Naming of Parts. H. Reed.
Al-VBP:1243, Ba-PO:189, Bo-GJ:189,
Cr-WS:62, Hi-WP II:148, Pe-SS:134,
To-MP:40, Un-MB:507, Wi-LT:796
Neither Here nor There. W. Rodgers.
Al-VBP:1237, Wi-LT:495
Nerve. K. Ogawa. Le-TA:47
Neutral Tones. T. Hardy. Un-MB:27,
Un-MW:94
Number 5 - December. D. Henderson.
Ad-BO:69, Jo-SA:84
Of Course I Prayed. E. Dickinson.
Un-MA:97
The Orphan Girl. Em-AF:772
Our Father. R. Swartz. Tr-MR:216
Paraders for the Bomb.
S. Bernard. Ba-PO:39
A Pauper. A. Tate. Wi-LT:410
Pictures of a City. R. Fripp.
Mo-GR:78
Pilgrimage. Jao Meng-k'an.
Hs-TC:108
Poem. J. Sloman. Sc-TN:200
Poem. J. Wain. En-PC:230

INDIFFERENCE — cont'd.
A Question. A. Lopez. Al-WW:6
Question. A. Pratt. Al-WW:103
Reapers. J. Toomer. Ad-PB:29,
    Jo-SA:63, Ra-BP:68
Rondeau of the Little Horses.
    M. Bandeira. An-TC:7
A Satire. J. Oldham. Al-VBP:507
The Sea. D. Lawrence. Co-BN:76
The Sea's Prayer. V. Kalugin.
    Bo-RU:42
Sestina. Dante Alighieri.
    Gr-SS:93
The Shadow. G. Dusenbery.
    Sc-TN:37
The Silent Generation.
    L. Simpson. Hi-TL:224
Sing, Brothers, Sing! W. Rodgers.
    Un-MB:482
Song of My Indifference.
    D. Hofstein. Ho-TY:175
Street Corner College.
    K. Patchen. Un-MA:609
Suicide? J. Miles. Sa-B:178
The Suppliant. G. Johnson.
    Ad-PB:23, Hu-PN:76
There Will Come Soft Rains.
    S. Teasdale. Cr-WS:69
Thought's End. L. Adams.
    Sm-PT:136
Three Love Poems: From a Woman
    to a Greedy Lover.
    N. Cameron. Co-EL:15,
    Pa-GTB:499
Toussaint L'Ouverture.
    E. Robinson. Hu-PN:471
A True Story. A. Taylor. De-TT:102
untitled requiem for tomorrow.
    Conyus. Ad-PB:402
Vain and Careless. R. Graves.
    Ha-LO:20
Vala or the Four Zoas.
    W. Blake. Ox-BN:37
When They Call Out. S. Chudakov.
    Bo-RU:27
Who'll See Me Dive? T. McNeill.
    Sa-B:123
Why Do They? B. Wilkinson.
    La-IH:71
The Wild Flower Man. Lu Yu.
    Rx-OH:103
The Wisdom of the World.
    S. Sassoon. Un-MB:315
Your Last Drive. T. Hardy.
    Ox-BN:841
The Zero Degree of Life.
    Tsang K'o-chia. Hs-TC:289
INDIGESTION: see HUMOR -
    INDIGESTION
INDIGNATION
Grandeur of Ghosts. S. Sassoon.
    Un-MB:317

The Indignation of Taliesin.
    T. Peacock. Rv-CB:686
INDIVIDUALITY: see also HUMOR -
    INDIVIDUALITY; PERSONALITY;
    SELF
Accountability. P. Dunbar.
    Fe-PL:427
Afterwards. G. Stein. Ha-LO:76
Ballade Made in Hot Weather.
    W. Henley. Un-MB:54
Being Nobody. K. Crawford.
    Le-M:163
Beyond the Panther. J. Wade.
    Sc-TN:224
The Black Pebble. J. Reeves.
    La-PV:208
Brevities. S. Sassoon. Fe-PL:296
Character of a Happy Life.
    H. Wotton. Al-VBP:221,
    Ni-JP:169, Pa-GTB:63
The Daily Grind. F. Johnson.
    Bo-AN:25
The Dewdrop and the Wave.
    G. Herwegh. Sp-OG:306
Dick and Will. E. Roberts.
    Br-BC:25
The Distant Drum. C. Hernton.
    Ad-BO:19, Hu-NN:101, Jo-SA:97,
    Lo-TY:250
The Divine Ship Sails the Divine
    Sea for You. W. Whitman.
    Tr-MR:152
Dream-Song. P. Murtha. Ad-II:49
Ego. N. MacCaig. Pa-GTB:522
Elephants Are Different to
    Different People. C. Sandburg.
    Un-MA:210
Envy. C. and M. Lamb. Ox-BC:140
The Family. Visvaneth. Al-PI:123
For Hettie. L. Jones. Pe-SS:125
Forms of the Human. R. Eberhart.
    Ho-TH:80
Further Notice. P. Whalen.
    Ca-VT:524, Mc-EA:71
The Gardener and the Mole.
    W. Landor. Rd-OA:115
The Great Lover. R. Brooke.
    Er-FA:73, Hi-WP I:108,
    Un-MB:320, Wi-LT:613
Hallelujah: A Sestina.
    R. Francis. En-PC:46
The Hart. Gr-EC:282, Gr-GB:53,
    Mo-MGT:191, Rv-CB:448, Rv-ON:99,
    Sm-LG:291, Wr-RM:75
The Herring Loves the Merry
    Moonlight. W. Scott. Sm-LG:78
I Am as I Am. T. Wyatt.
    Rv-CB:87
I Don't Like Beetles.
    R. Fyleman. Ox-BC:338

Independence.   H. Thoreau.
   Ba-PO:162
Jenny White and Johnny Black.
   E. Farjeon.   Fe-FP:303
Let No Charitable Hope. E. Wylie.
   Ca-VT:104, Un-MA:278, Wi-LT:206
Let's Go to Bed.   Gr-CT:10,
   Rd-SS:4
maggie and milly and molly and may.
   E. Cummings.   Co-PS:109,
   Gr-BT:10, Ha-LO:15
Me. M. Goode. Ba-HI:14
The Monk and His Cat.   Co-PI:43,
   De-CH:90, Pa-SG:154, Rd-OA:110,
   Sm-LG:73
Music and Drum.   A. MacLeish.
   Ho-TH:59, Tr-MR:186
No Child with Honey Heart.
   L. Wolf.   Ho-TY:222
No Friends nor Enemies. J. Bryant.
   Jo-VC:92
Not I. R. Stevenson.   Ch-B:97,
   Hi-WP I:117
Perspective.   V. Contoski.
   Sc-TN:29
Poem to Be Read at 3 A.M.
   D. Justice.   Du-SH:29, Pe-M:130
The Problem.   R. Emerson.
   Sh-AP:26
Quiet Things.   G. Crowell.
   Fe-PL:308
The Red-Haired Man's Wife.
   J. Stephens.   Un-MB:264
Samuel Sewall. A. Hecht. Br-TC:181,
   Pe-OA:262, Wi-LT:730
The Science of the Night. S. Kunitz.
   Br-TC:245, Un-MA:592
The Sea and the Hills. R. Kipling.
   Ga-FB:188
Simple Song. M. Piercy. Mo-TS:4
Since I Left the Ocean.   Navin.
   Al-PI:120
Sisters. E. Farjeon. Fe-FP:37
Some Love Coffee, Some Love Tea.
   Ju-CP:38
Songs. L. Wolf. Ho-TY:223
Sonnet 36. W. Shakespeare.
   Rv-CB:218
Stanzas. E. Brontë.   Go-BP:27
Stuff. A. Mitchell.   Sm-MK:190
Thoughts During an Air Raid.
   S. Spender. Al-VBP:1234,
   Un-MB:479
The Tired Man. A. Wickham.
   Sm-MK:25, Un-MW:57
To a Young Brother.
   M. Jewsbury.   Ox-BC:168
To Marguerite. M. Arnold.
   Ox-BN:627, Pa-GTB:364
To My Son. Fe-PL:338

Truly My Own.   V. Howard.
   Jo-VC:83
The Twins. K. Jackson. Br-BC:24
Whoever You Are Holding Me Now
   in Hand. W. Whitman.
   Ha-PO:216
Who's Who.   W. Auden.   Mc-WS:73,
   Un-MB:450
Wishes. E. Wallace. Th-AS:57
Worms and the Wind. C. Sandburg.
   Mc-WK:48, Pa-RE:51, Rd-OA:93
Your Shadow. M. Strand. Ho-P:255
INDOLENCE: see IDLENESS; LAZINESS
INDONESIAN VERSE
   Bride's Song.   Tr-US I:166
   Curse Tabooing a Lake.
      Tr-US I:169
   Dirge.   Tr-US I:167
   Girl's Song: Refusing a Lover.
      Tr-US I:166
   Linked Pantuns.   Tr-US I:177
   Prayer at the Burning Off a New
      Communal Field. Tr-US I:168
   Song.   Tr-US I:175
   Song at a Head-Hunting Festival.
      Tr-US I:172
   Song of the Sirih-Leaf.
      Tr-US I:166
   Song of the Wild Ginger.
      Tr-US II:200
   When You Have Gone.   Le-OE:132
INDONESIAN VERSE - BATAK
   Complaint of a Fisherman's
      Widow. Tr-US I:158
   Complaint of a Widow over Her
      Dying Son. Tr-US I:157
   Dialogue.   Tr-US I:156
INDONESIAN VERSE - CERAMESE
   Boatmen's Song. Tr-US I:176
   Song for a Kachua Dance.
      Tr-US I:175
INDONESIAN VERSE - DUSUN
   Love Song.   Tr-US I:141
INDONESIAN VERSE - IFUGAO
   The Myth of Numputul, the
      Self-Beheaded. Tr-US I:178
INDONESIAN VERSE - IGOROT
   From an Angba.   Tr-US I:181
   Song.   Tr-US I:182
INDONESIAN VERSE - MALAGASY
   The Locust.   Tr-US I:116
   The Song of the Bottle.
      Tr-US I:117
   Zebu. F. Ranaivo.   Ab-MO:38
INDONESIAN VERSE - MALAY
   Charm for a Rebab. Tr-US II:207
   Charm for Striking Fear into a
      Tiger.   Tr-US II:205
   Charm for the Oil. Tr-US II:208
   Charm of the Rice-Reapers.
      Tr-US II:207

INDONESIAN VERSE - MALAY
— cont'd.
Charms Against the Demon.
Tr-US II:206
The Coconut-Monkey. Tr-US II:198
Fruit Song. Tr-US II:200
The Housewife. B. Amma. Al-PI:128
Improvised Song of the Baby
Coconut-Monkey. Tr-US II:202
Invocation to the Rice Soul at
Harvest Time. Tr-US II:204
Linked Pantuns. Tr-US II:204
Love Charm. Tr-US II:205
Magical Chant. Tr-US II:209
On the Kelantan Oboe.
Tr-US II:207
Pantuns, I-VII.
Tr-US II:203, 204
Prayer to the Goddess Ja Pudeu.
Tr-US II:202
The Pulai-Tree. Tr-US II:199
Song of a Sunrise Chinoi.
Tr-US II:201
Song of the Chinoi as They
Come Out of Flowers.
Tr-US II:201
The Tiger. Tr-US II:199
INDONESIAN VERSE - MERINA
Dialogues, I, II.
Tr-US I:118, 119
Girls' Songs. Tr-CB:32,
Tr-US I:119
INDONESIAN VERSE - MINAHASA
Song at the Departure of a
Beautiful Girl.
Tr-US I:170
Song of a Dying Girl.
Tr-US I:170
Song of a Girl to Bring Back
Her Unfaithful Lover.
Tr-US I:171
INDONESIAN VERSE - MURUT
Invitation to Drink and the
Reply. Tr-US I:145
INDONESIAN VERSE - NIAS
The Chief Men of a Village
Answer the Greeting of
Travelers. Tr-US I:162
Creation Myth. Tr-US I:159
Epilogue to a Narrative Poem.
Tr-US I:164
Song for Girl Dancers.
Tr-US I:163
Songs at a Wedding.
Tr-US I:161
INDONESIAN VERSE - SEGADA
We Pray that the Beetles
Appear. Le-OE:25
INDONESIAN VERSE - TINGUIAN
Song for a Ceremonial Dance.
Tr-US I:183

INDONESIAN VERSE - TORADJA
Harvest-Season Songs.
Tr-US I:171
INDUSTRIAL WORKERS OF THE WORLD:
see LABOR UNIONS
INFANTS: see BABIES
INFATUATION
Dance Song. Tr-US I:130
Dance Songs, III. Tr-US I:28
If. . . .   Tr-US I:121
Johnny Morozov. B. Okujava.
Bo-RU:55
INFINITY: see also HUMOR -
INFINITY
Auguries of Innocence. W. Blake.
Al-VBP:621, Ch-B:36, Co-BBW:278,
Er-FA:69, Ga-FB:96, Ma-YA:130,
Ox-BN:28, Pl-IO:5, Sh-RP:76,
Sm-LG:67, Sm-MK:220, Un-GT:305
The Choice III. D. Rossetti.
Al-VBP:990, Pa-GTB:371
Dialectics. P. Popescu. Mc-AC:166
The Infinite. G. Leopardi.
Pa-SG:170
Looking at Stars. P. Hesketh.
Cl-DT:36
The Midnight Meditation.
E. Olson. St-H:175
My Period Has Come for Prayer.
E. Dickinson. Pl-EI:171
Numbers and Faces. W. Auden.
Pl-IO:91
Prologue. A. MacLeish. Un-MA:454
Renascence. E. Millay. Er-FA:95,
Un-MA:440
Sonnet XXVII. Feng Chih.
Hs-TC:155
The Star. E. Roberts. Rd-SS:32
The Unending Sky. J. Masefield.
Ma-FW:124, Wi-LT:192
INFLUENCE
Anecdote of the Jar. W. Stevens.
Ho-LP:42, Un-MA:240
The Elegance of Memory.
K. Kgositsile. Be-MA:147
The Good Man in Hell. E. Muir.
Tr-MR:159, Un-MB:339
I Mix in Life. S. Coleridge.
Rv-CB:659
If the Heart of a Man. J. Gay.
Rv-CB:394
My Sad Captains. T. Gunn.
En-PC:278, Wi-LT:726
Old Woman. E. Jennings. Gr-BT:166
Poem for Aretha. N. Giovanni.
Ad-PB:454, Ra-BP:327
Post Mortem. R. Jeffers. Un-MA:361
Sculpture. Fe-PL:312
Some People. R. Field. Fe-FP:309,
La-PV:104

Starlight like Intuition Pierced
the Twelve. D. Schwartz.
En-PC:128, Sh-AP:222, Tr-MR:94
The Woman Who Understands.
L. Appleton. Fe-PL:117
INFLUENZA: see HUMOR - INFLUENZA
INFORMERS: see SPIES
INGE, WILLIAM RALPH: see HUMOR -
INGE, WILLIAM RALPH
INGRATITUDE
Belisarius. H. Longfellow.
Ho-WR:120
Blow, Blow, Thou Winter Wind.
W. Shakespeare. Al-VBP:187,
De-CH:232, De-TT:168, Er-FA:257,
Gr-CT:476, Hi-WP II:139,
Ho-WR:172, Mc-PR:50, Pa-GTB:26,
Rv-CB:197
Jenny Wren Fell Sick. Ir-BB:84,
Mo-MGT:29, Na-EO:69, Rv-ON:116,
Sm-MK:170
Poor Old Horse. De-CH:84
A Satire. J. Oldham. Al-VBP:507
The Tragedy of King Lear.
W. Shakespeare. Ma-FW:272
The Tree and the Lady. T. Hardy.
Un-MB:33
The Wolf and the Crane. E. Rees.
Ar-TP3:81
INHERITANCE: see HEREDITY;
HERITAGE; WILLS
INJECTIONS: see VACCINATIONS AND
INJECTIONS
INJURIES: see ACCIDENTS; SCARS;
WAR WOUNDED
INJUSTICE: see also DISCRIMINATION;
HUMOR - INJUSTICE; INDIANS OF
NORTH AMERICA - TREATMENT;
JEWS - PERSECUTION; RACE PROBLEMS
The African Affair. B. Wright.
Ad-PB:171, Hu-PN:357
Against Exploiters. Tr-CB:33,
Tr-US I:65
America. H. Dumas. Ad-BO:40,
Ad-PB:267, Co-PU:61
American History. M. Harper.
Ra-BP:291
And What Shall You Say? J. Cotter.
Ad-PB:35, Hu-PN:135, Kr-OF:49
Angola Question Mark. L. Hughes.
Lo-TY:230, Ra-BP:89
Appeal. N. de Sousa. Lo-TY:188
Are Things Really Changing?
B. Davis. Me-WF:59
Award. R. Durem. Ad-PB:152,
Hu-NN:33, Jo-SA:26, Ke-PP:118,
Kr-OF:54, Lo-TY:243, Ra-BP:164
Babylon Revisited. I. Baraka.
Ra-BP:214
The Backlash Blues. L. Hughes.
Ra-BP:90

The Ballad of Reading Gaol.
O. Wilde. Al-VBP:1072,
Er-FA:87, Un-MB:70
The Ballad of Rudolph Reed.
G. Brooks. Jo-SA:46
Ballad of the Landlord. L. Hughes.
Ha-TP:15
Banty Tim. J. Hay. Kr-OF:45
be cool, baby. R. Penny. Ad-PB:390
Be Still, My Soul, Be Still.
A. Housman. Ox-BN:923, Un-MB:101
Because He Was a Man. J. Pierpont.
Kr-OF:107
The Bird and the Tree. R. Torrence.
Hu-PN:480
Black Hieroglyph. T. Matthews.
Sa-B:230
A Black Man. S. Cornish. Ad-PB:298
A Black Man Talks of Reaping.
A. Bontemps. Ad-PB:85,
Be-MA:43, Bo-AN:75, Ho-HF:93,
Hu-PN:209, Ra-BP:94
Blackie Thinks of His Brothers.
S. Crouch. Ad-PB:484
Breaklight. K. La Fortune.
Sa-B:199
The Bridge of Sighs. T. Hood.
Pa-GTB:230
Burying Ground by the Ties.
A. MacLeish. Un-MA:459
Can't Kill Him. Chang Chih-min.
Hs-TC:426
Carl Hamblin. E. Masters.
Kr-OF:113, Sh-AP:137, Wi-LT:114
Chesterfield Cigarettes Fill the
Light-Colored Room. M. Goode.
Jo-VC:20
The Child Ate Worms. K. Ballen.
Ad-II:105
Children Are Slaves. I. Velez.
Jo-VC:32
Children's Rhymes. L. Hughes.
Ad-BO:43, Ra-BP:86
The Cold Heaven. W. Yeats.
Pa-GTB:423
The Colonial. S. Lowhar.
Sa-B:79
Colors. J. Wickersham. Ad-II:83
Coming Home from Work. E. Isac.
Mc-AC:53
The Country of a Thousand Years
of Peace. J. Marrill. En-PC:240
Credo. E. Debs. Kr-OF:117
The Cry of the Children.
E. Browning. Al-VBP:819,
Cl-FC:27
Dark Symphony III: Andante
Sostenuto. M. Tolson. Bo-AN:38
Death in Yorkville. L. Hughes.
Ad-PB:79

INJUSTICE — cont'd.
  Defeat. W. Bynner. Hu-PN:490
  Droit de Seigneur. R. Murphy.
    Co-PI:148
  The Eagle That Is Forgotten.
    V. Lindsay. Al-VBP:1139,
    Sh-AP:166, Tr-MR:171, Un-MA:223
  Execution. J. Randall. Ra-BP:277
  Factory Windows Are Always Broken.
    V. Lindsay. Co-PU:72, Er-FA:274,
    La-OC:110
  The Famine Year. Lady Wilde.
    Co-PI:197
  The Flower Market. Po-Chu-I.
    Ke-PP:10
  For Angela. Z. Gilbert. Ad-PB:196
  For My People. M. Walker.
    Ad-PB:144, Be-MA:73, Bo-AN:128,
    Hu-PN:314, Tr-MR:155
  From the Dark Tower. C. Cullen.
    Ad-PB:87, Be-MA:51, Hu-PN:235,
    Jo-SA:133, Ra-BP:100, Wi-LT:616
  Go Slow. L. Hughes. Wi-LT:424
  God Bless Us. G. Bart-Williams.
    Gr-BT:109
  Goodbye Nkrumah. D. Di Prima.
    Lo-IT:30
  The Grinders. Gr-GB:222
  Han Po Chops Wood. Feng Chih.
    Hs-TC:155
  Heroes of War and Peace.
    E. Wilcox. Kr-OF:173
  Hey There Mister. Me-WF:49
  Hospital for Defectives.
    T. Blackburn. Pa-GTB:547
  I Am a Multitude. A. De Loach.
    Lo-IT:28
  I Am a Negro. M. Al-Fituri.
    Lo-TY:54
  I Come from the Nigger Yard.
    M. Carter. Sa-B:96
  I Don't Mind. C. Jackson.
    Le-M:168
  I Had a Dream Last Night.
    C. Meyer. Jo-VC:19
  I Have Seen Black Hands.
    R. Wright. Ad-PB:105, Jo-SA:112
  I Know I'm Not Sufficiently
    Obscure. R. Durem. Ad-PB:151,
    Jo-SA:122, Ra-BP:163
  I Sit and Look Out. W. Whitman.
    Ke-PP:1, Mo-GB:177, Rv-CB:851
  I, Too, Sing America. L. Hughes.
    Ad-PB:75, Be-MA:40, Bo-AN:64,
    Ca-VT:239, Fe-PL:159, Hu-PN:182
  If It Had Been Shared with Justice.
    M. Isanos. Mc-AC:118
  Image. H. Dumas. Ad-BO:7
  In Bondage. C. McKay. Ad-PB:26
  In the Gold Mines. B. Vilakazi.
    Lo-TY:176

  An Invective Against the Wicked
    of the World. N. Breton.
    Al-VBP:85
  It Was a Funky Deal. E. Knight.
    Ad-BO:32, Ad-PB:232, Ra-BP:207
  I've Returned to My Fatherland.
    Wang Tu-ch'ing. Hs-TC:198
  Junglegrave. S. Anderson.
    Ad-PB:441
  knock on wood. H. Dumas. Ad-PB:268
  The Known Soldier. K. Patchen.
    Ba-PO:159
  Landscape near a Steel Mill.
    H. Horn. Ke-PP:110
  The Lie. W. Raleigh. Al-VBP:95,
    Gr-CT:372, Ke-PP:16, Rv-CB:157
  Lincoln . . . Today. K. Hopkins.
    Me-WF:61
  A Litany at Atlanta. W. Du Bois.
    Hu-PN:20
  A Little Boy Lost. W. Blake.
    Al-VBP:618, Rv-CB:583
  London. W. Blake. Al-VBP:618,
    Gr-CT:304, Ha-PO:79, Ke-PP:49,
    Mo-GR:78, Ox-BN:24, Rv-CB:605
  The Louisiana Weekly #4.
    D. Henderson. Ad-PB:421,
    Jo-SA:103
  Love Your Enemy. Y. Iman.
    Lo-TY:258, Ra-BP:293
  Lynched Negro. M. Bodenheim.
    Hu-PN:509
  Many Die Here. G. Jones. Jo-SA:14
  Mixed Sketches. D. Lee. Ra-BP:306
  Monangamba. A. Jacinto. Lo-TY:181
  Monument in Black. V. Howard.
    Jo-SA:3, Jo-VC:43
  My Place. M. Rosenfeld. Ho-TY:78
  Nice Day for a Lynching.
    K. Patchen. Hu-PN:555, Kr-OF:160
  O Stelliferi Conditor Orbis.
    Boethius. Go-BP:240
  Oh Why? M. Fletcher. Me-WF:23
  Ode Inscribed to W. H. Channing.
    R. Emerson. Al-VBP:800
  Old Fortunatus, 1. T. Dekker.
    Al-VBP:228
  Old Lem. S. Brown. Ad-PB:69,
    Hu-PN:167, Lo-TY:221, Ra-BP:109
  An Old Woman Remembers.
    S. Brown. Ad-PB:68
  The Orphan Girl. Em-AF:772
  The Parliament of Bees. J. Day.
    Al-VBP:243
  Pass Office Song. Lo-TY:17
  Pie in the Sky. J. Hill.
    Gr-GB:328, Ke-PP:15
  Poem for My Family. J. Jordan.
    Ra-BP:245
  Poem to Americans. G. Jackson.
    Lo-IT:58

Poor Naked Wretches.
  W. Shakespeare. Ke-PP:22
Port Authority Terminal: 9 a.m.
  Monday. C. Walsh. Ke-PP:62
Pray for Rain. M. Williams.
  Sa-B:180
Prayer for Peace: II. L. Senghor.
  Lo-TY:135
Prayer to God. Placido. Lo-TY:99
Prime. L. Hughes. Ad-PB:76
PSI. M. Tolson. Ad-BO:36
Rabbi Yussel Luksh of Chelm.
  J. Glatstein. Ho-TY:246
Reb Levi Yitzkhok. I. Manger.
  Ho-TY:280
Regeneration. W. Landor.
  Al-VBP:708
Resurrection. F. Horne. Ad-PB:56
Return to My Native Land.
  A. Cesaire. Lo-TY:123
The Ricksha Puller. Cheng Min.
  Hs-TC:233
Riot Rimes, U.S.A. R. Patterson.
  Kr-OF:57
Riots and Rituals. R. Thomas.
  Ad-PB:371
Les Salaziennes. A. Lacaussade.
  Lo-TY:69
Satire V. J. Marston.
  Al-VBP:270
Saturday's Child. C. Cullen.
  Ad-PB:86, Bo-HF:88, Wi-LT:616
Scottsboro, Too, Is Worth Its
  Song. C. Cullen. Ad-PB:93,
  Be-MA:52
Security. R. Tucker. Ke-PP:121
Sing Me a New Song. J. Clarke.
  Ad-PB:143
So Quietly. L. Hill. Ad-PB:14
The Song of the Shirt. T. Hood.
  Hi-FO:227, Ke-PP:59, Ma-YA:188
Song to the Men of England.
  P. Shelley. Al-VBP:746
Sonnet: England in 1819.
  P. Shelley. Rv-CB:699
The Soudanese. W. Watson.
  Cr-WS:159
The Spectacle. W. de la Mare.
  Go-BP:249
Speech to the Court.
  W. Lowenfels. Ke-PP:120
Strong Men. S. Brown.
  Ad-PB:60, Be-MA:27, Bo-HF:138,
  Ke-PP:127, Lo-TY:219, Ra-BP:113
Stupidity Street. R. Hodgson.
  Br-SS:149, Co-BBW:268, De-CH:103,
  De-TT:58, Ha-LO:60, La-PV:138,
  Th-AS:52, Un-MB:192, Wi-LT:125
Sweet Smiling Village.
  O. Goldsmith. Ke-PP:41

They Got You Last Night.
  A. Kurtz. Ke-PP:75
This Morning the Sun. O. Cabral.
  Ke-PP:103
To an American Poet Just Dead.
  R. Wilbur. Pl-ML:153
To Richard Wright. C. Rivers.
  Ad-PB:234, Be-MA:105, Bo-AN:177
To the White Fiends. C. McKay.
  Ad-PB:27
To Those Born After. B. Brecht.
  Un-R:41
Too Old to Work. J. Glazer.
  Hi-TL:226
Toussaint L'Ouverture.
  E. Robinson. Hu-PN:471
The Trees in the Garden Rained
  Flowers. S. Crane. Wi-LT:121
Unhappy Boston. P. Revere.
  Kr-OF:131
Untitled. J. Randall. Ra-BP:273
Vala or the Four Zoas. W. Blake.
  Al-VBP:621, Ox-BN:37
Vietnam #4. C. Major.
  Ad-BO:48, Ad-PB:298, Ba-PO:38
Vive Noir! M. Evans. Ad-PB:188
Waiting. J. Davidson.
  Al-VBP:1078
Watts. C. Rivers. Ad-BO:41,
  Ad-PB:233
We Raise de Wheat. F. Douglass.
  Ra-BP:3
We Shall Not Die in Darkness.
  E. Millay. Kr-OF:123
When Something Happens.
  J. Randall. Ra-BP:275
When Wilt Thou Save the People?
  E. Elliot. Hi-WP II:173,
  Pl-EI:157
Where Are the Men Seized in This
  Wind of Madness?
  A. do Espirito Santo. Lo-TY:183
Where? When? Which?
  L. Hughes. Ra-BP:88
The White House. C. McKay.
  Ad-PB:28, Be-MA:15, Bo-AN:31,
  Hu-PN:101, Jo-SA:119
Who Shall Die? J. Randall.
  Ra-BP:272
Why I Voted the Socialist Ticket.
  V. Lindsay. Un-MA:234
With God Conversing.
  G. Derwood. Tr-MR:139
Yet Do I Marvel. C. Cullen.
  Ad-PB:87, Be-MA:50, Bo-AN:88,
  Hu-PN:233, Jo-SA:128, Lo-TY:235,
  Pe-SS:48, Ra-BP:100
A Young David: Birmingham.
  H. Brooks. Hu-PN:276
Youth's Question - Revenge's
  Answer. R. Groppuso. Me-WF:25

INNISFREE ISLAND, IRE.
  The Lake Isle of Innisfree.
    W. Yeats. Ar-TP3:218, Co-RG:118,
    Er-FA:258, Fe-FP:464, Fr-WO:79,
    Ga-FB:242, Ma-YA:230, Mc-PR:174,
    Pa-HT:138, Th-AS:149, Un-MB:108,
    Wi-LT:68
INNOCENCE: see also SATIRE -
    INNOCENCE
  Adam and Eve. J. Milton. No-CL:52
  All the World Moved. J. Jordan.
    Ad-PB:303
  Arms and the Boy. W. Owen.
    Er-FA:192, Ni-JP:78, Un-MB:367,
    Wi-LT:349
  At the Carnival. A. Spencer.
    Hu-PN:62
  The Ballad of the Little Square.
    F. Garcia Lorca. Li-TU:222
  The Birth in a Narrow Room.
    G. Brooks. Ha-TP:117, Hu-PN:335
  Blow the Winds, I-Ho. Gr-GB:110
  The Book of Thel. W. Blake.
    Ox-BN:32
  The Boy and the Mantle. Ox-BB:31
  A Carol for Children. O. Nash.
    Pl-EI:150
  The Castle. S. Alexander.
    Hu-PN:559
  Chaplinesque. H. Crane.
    Ca-VT:212, Wi-LT:395
  Children Are Game. I. Gardner.
    St-H:66
  Daisy. F. Thompson. Ga-FB:164,
    Ox-BN:917, Un-MB:77
  An Elegy for a Dead Child in the
    Street. R. Rao. Al-PI:106
  Emmy. A. Symons. Ox-BN:934
  Epigram. Su Tung P'o. Rx-OH:84
  Eve. R. Hodgson. De-CH:465,
    Ha-PO:41, Hi-WP II:95,
    Na-EO:105, Pa-OM:286, Sm-MK:58,
    Un-MB:186, Wi-LT:123
  Fame. E. Greenberg. Ho-TY:309
  The Garden. J. Very. Sh-AP:66
  i should have caught my unicorn
    when i was. D. Witt. Ad-II:9
  Magalu. H. Johnson. Ad-PB:103,
    Hu-PN:263
  Mysteries. Y. Yevtushenko.
    Ca-MR:52
  A New Flower - Pure and Untorn.
    M. Korte. Sc-TN:115
  No Images. W. Cuney. Bo-AN:98,
    Bo-HF:92, Lo-TY:237
  Oh, Fairest of the Rural Maids!
    W. Bryant. Al-VBP:767
  O World Be Nobler. L. Binyon.
    Un-MB:156

  On a Squirrel Crossing the Road in
    Autumn, in New England.
    R. Eberhart. En-PC:60, Ho-TH:81,
    Pe-OA:196, Wi-LT:439
  On the Seashore. R. Tagore.
    Al-PI:89
  Pater Filio. R. Bridges.
    Al-VBP:1063
  The Retreat. H. Vaughan.
    Al-VBP:466, Pa-GTB:65, Rv-CB:408
  Ruth: or The Influence of Nature.
    W. Wordsworth. Pa-GTB:283
  She Walks in Beauty. G. Byron.
    Co-RG:148, Er-FA:105, Hi-WP II:54,
    Ke-TF:107, Mc-PR:91, Ni-JP:96,
    Ox-BN:251, Pa-GTB:177, Rv-CB:688,
    Sh-RP:89, Un-MW:166
  Small Colored Boy in the Subway.
    B. Deutsch. Hu-PN:513
  Snake in the Strawberries.
    J. Hearst. St-H:82
  Song. J. Dryden. Al-VBP:478,
    Rv-CB:465
  Sonnets, vii. G. Santayana.
    Sm-PT:135
  Sonnets, xxv. G. Santayana.
    Sm-PT:135
  Spring. G. Hopkins. Co-BN:25,
    Ga-FB:8, Ox-BN:864, Un-MB:42,
    Wi-LT:41
  Stoplights. D. Dzwonkoski.
    Ad-II:24
  The Tarnish. J. Hearst. St-H:78
  The Theology of Innocence.
    S. Meltzer. Ad-II:21
  Thoughts in a Garden. A. Marvell.
    Ga-S:22
  Titan's Lament. A. Raybin.
    Sc-TN:192
  To a Certain Unmarried Woman.
    M. Kaneko. Sh-AM:63
  To a Child. C. Morley. Br-BC:148
  To a Child Dancing in the Wind.
    W. Yeats. Co-PI:202
  To a Young Lady. W. Cowper.
    Pa-GTB:129
  To Olivia. F. Thompson. Un-MB:90
  Without One Particle of Sentiment
    in His Being. M. Ooka. Sh-AM:134
INNOVATIONS: see HUMOR -
    INNOVATIONS
INNS AND TAVERNS: see also HUMOR -
    INNS AND TAVERNS; and names of
    individual inns, as MERMAID TAVERN
  Elinor Rumming. J. Skelton.
    Al-VBP:27
  Tarantella. H. Belloc. De-CH:189,
    Hi-WP II:2, Li-SR:5, Pa-HT:105,
    Sm-LG:45, Th-AS:164, Un-MB:167

Thanksgiving.   K. Koch.   Ca-VT:545
A Trampwoman's Tragedy.   T. Hardy.
   Ox-BN:825
Witchcraft: New Style.
   L. Abercrombie.   Un-MB:256
Written at an Inn at Henley.
   W. Shenstone.   Al-VBP:558
INQUISITION: see SATIRE -
   INQUISITION
INSANITY: see ASYLUMS; MADNESS
INSECTS: see also HUMOR - INSECTS;
   SATIRE - INSECTS; and names of
   insects, as ANTS; BUTTERFLIES
Because the Treetops of the Peak.
   Hitomaro.   Le-MW:46
The Butterbean Tent.   E. Roberts.
   Bo-GJ:48, Br-SG:51
The Butterfly's Ball.   W. Roscoe.
   Ox-BC:131, Un-GT:74
Calico Pie.   E. Lear.
   Au-SP:225, Bl-OB:12, Fe-FP:356,
   Hu-MP:461, Ir-BB:88, It-HB:57,
   Li-LC:67, Lo-LL:67, Pa-RE:109,
   Rv-CB:811, Sm-LG:87, Tu-WW:114,
   Un-GB:29, Un-GF:33, Un-GT:225
Call It a Louse.   C. Dorman.
   Ca-VT:528
Come Visit My Garden.   T. Dent.
   Hu-NN:80
Depressed by a Book of Bad Poetry,
   I Walk Toward an Unused Pasture.
   J. Wright.   Ho-TH:90
End-of-Summer Poem.   R. Bennett.
   Br-SS:179, Fe-FP:148, Ja-PA:5
The Green Silk Bug.   A. Fisher.
   Mc-AW:61
Hey, Bug!   L. Moore.   It-HB:12
Hurt No Living Thing.
   C. Rossetti.   Au-SP:88, Bo-FP:96,
   Br-SG:50, Br-SS:149, Ch-B:16,
   Fe-FP:149, Gr-EC:39, Gr-TG:14,
   La-PV:158, Pa-RE:103, Se-PR:300
The Insect World.   J. Clare.
   Cl-DT:71
Insects! Do Not Cry!   Issa.
   Le-MW:29
Interlude III.   K. Shapiro.
   Du-RG:71
Little Black Bug.   M. Brown.
   Fe-FP:127
Little Bug.   R. Bacmeister.
   It-HB:13
Little Talk.   A. Fisher.
   Fe-FP:147, It-HB:35, La-PP:11
The Minimal.   T. Roethke.
   Li-TU:195
A Moonlight Night.   Liu Fang-P'ing.
   Le-MW:27
Nature Songs, II.   Tr-US II:186

Near Dusk.   J. Auslander.
   Fe-FP:148, Mc-PR:165
A Song of Humility.   C. Drewry.
   Tr-MR:268
The Sweet o' the Year.
   G. Meredith.   Co-BN:23
Twilight Calm.   C. Rossetti.
   Co-BN:109, Ox-BN:709
Under the Ground.
   R. Bacmeister.   It-HB:39
Who's In? E. Fleming. Bl-OB:145,
   Cl-FC:61, Pe-FB:22, Th-AS:41
With Myriad Voices Grass Was
   Filled.   C. Aiken.   Rd-OA:43
INSECURITY: see also TIMIDITY
And on This Shore.   M. Holman.
   Ad-PB:175, Hu-PN:364
By One Unsure. M. Cane. Ls-NY:114
Fall, 1961.   R. Lowell.
   Ca-VT:453, Ha-TP:135
Halcyon. H. D.   Un-MA:338
Sonnet.   A. Duckett.   Ad-PB:172,
   Hu-PN:359, Jo-SA:80
Soonest Mended.   J. Ashbery.
   Ho-P:9
Under the Moon.   Hsü Hsü.
   Hs-TC:275
Undertow. L. Hughes.   Wi-LT:423
INSOMNIA: see also HUMOR -
   INSOMNIA
The Afterwake. A. Rich.   Ho-P:211
Alone in the Night.
   Li Ch'ing Chao.   Rx-OH:96
At Night. F. Cornford.   Un-MB:307
Counting Sheep.   A. Fisher.
   Au-SP:96
Deep Night. Yuan Chi. Rx-LT:26
Dialogue at Night.   E. Greenberg.
   Ho-TY:308
In the Naked Bed, in Plato's Cave.
   D. Schwartz.   Ca-VT:365,
   Un-MA:619, Wi-LT:515
Insomnia. Lu Yu. Rx-LT:103
Luck Tips the Balance.
   E. Greenberg.   Ho-TY:309
Lying Awake. B. Young. Mc-AW:30
Midnight in the Garden.
   Li Shang-Yin.   Le-MW:63
Motionless Night.   S. Tsuboi.
   Sh-AM:74
Night-Piece.   R. Patterson.
   Ad-CI:103, Ad-PB:211
Night Thoughts. Lu Yu. Rx-OH:110
La Nuit Blanche.   R. Kipling.
   Un-MB:134
Rain on the River. Lu Yu. Rx-OH:106
Restless Little Flea.   Issa.
   Be-MC:17
A Restless Night in Camp. Tu Fu.
   Rx-OH:23

INSOMNIA — cont'd.
　The Shadow of Night. C. Patmore.
　　De-CH:452
　Sleeplessness. Tsang K'o-chia.
　　Hs-TC:279
　To Sleep. W. Wordsworth.
　　Al-VBP:691, Pa-GTB:275
　Trying to Sleep. R. Pomeroy.
　　Co-EL:105
　Waiting for Audience on a Spring
　　Night. Tu Fu. Rx-OH:10
　A Wartime Dawn. D. Gascoyne.
　　Wi-LT:713
　Winter Night. Hi-WP II:145
INSPIRATION: see also
　　IMAGINATION; MUSES
　As One Who Wanders into Old
　　Workings. C. Day-Lewis.
　　Wi-LT:426
　Bacchus. R. Emerson. Al-VBP:803,
　　Sh-AP:27
　Be Different to Trees. M. Davies.
　　Fe-FP:208, Hu-MP:269
　The Birdcatcher. R. Hodgson.
　　Un-MB:187
　A Birth. J. Dickey. Mc-EA:63
　Consummate Happiness.
　　W. Wordsworth. Ox-BN:99
　The Cure. W. Williams. Pl-ML:28
　Each in His Own Tongue. Ke-TF:246
　The Enchanted Lyre. G. Darley.
　　Ox-BN:383
　The Explorer. R. Kipling.
　　Sp-OG:54
　For Malcolm Who Walks in the
　　Eyes of Our Children.
　　Q. Troupe. Ad-PB:444
　Go to the Shine That's on a Tree.
　　R. Eberhart. Ho-LP:97, Li-TU:267,
　　Pl-US:150
　Good-Bye, My Fancy! W. Whitman.
　　Er-FA:174
　Good Company. K. Baker. Fe-FP:21
　Goodbye David Tamunoemi West.
　　M. Danner. Ra-BP:153
　I Would Like to Describe.
　　Z. Herbert. Gr-BT:28
　If I Could Only Live at That
　　Pitch That Is near Madness.
　　R. Eberhart. Wi-LT:433
　Interval. R. Humphries. Pl-ML:43
　Invocation of a Poet Seeking
　　Inspiration, I, II.
　　Tr-US II:28
　Invocation to the Muses.
　　R. Hughes. Un-MB:407
　Keorapsetse Kgositsile.
　　G. Brooks. Ra-BP:172
　King Henry the Fifth. W. Shakespeare.
　　Co-RM:199, 200, Ga-FB:195,
　　Ha-PO:255, Ke-TF:54, Mc-WS:100

　The Lady of the Lake. W. Scott.
　　Al-VBP:674, Ox-BN:132
　Lines. W. Wordsworth. Ox-BN:66
　A Little Learning. A. Pope.
　　Er-FA:99, Gr-CT:435
　Measure Me, Sky. L. Speyer.
　　Ad-PE:46, Br-BC:129, Fe-FP:22,
　　Hu-MP:63
　Miss Norma Jean Pugh, First Grade
　　Teacher. M. O'Neill. Ar-TP3:9
　The Muse. A. Akhmatova. Gr-CC:84
　My Heart Leaps Up. W. Wordsworth.
　　Al-VBP:655, Ar-TP3:172,
　　Au-SP:346, Bo-HF:55, Br-BC:121,
　　Co-RG:121, Er-FA:149, Ga-FB:22,
　　Ha-PO:83, La-PP:7, Ma-YA:139,
　　Mc-PR:169, Ox-BN:61, Pa-GTB:308,
　　Rv-CB:644, Sp-OG:352
　My Muse and I, ere Youth and Spirits
　　Fled. G. Colman. Co-EL:40
　Not Love, Not War. W. Wordsworth.
　　No-CL:10
　One Sort of Poet. A. Smith.
　　Le-NY:136
　The Person from Porlock. R. Graves.
　　Pl-ML:8
　A Pinch of Salt. R. Graves.
　　Go-BP:166, Un-MB:385
　The Poet's Voice. W. Blake.
　　Gr-CT:429, Rv-CB:567
　Prayer for a Miracle. A. Wickham.
　　Un-GT:305
　The Problem. R. Emerson.
　　Sh-AP:26
　The Progress of Poesy. T. Gray.
　　Al-VBP:566, Pa-GTB:132, Rv-CB:532
　The Radiance of Creativity.
　　O. Beshenkovskaya. Mo-MI:82
　Red Eagle. J. Campbell. Al-WW:31
　The Second Sermon on the Warpland.
　　G. Brooks. Ad-PB:163, Ra-BP:171
　Seven Poems 3. L. Niedecker.
　　Ca-VT:244
　Song of a Man Who Has Come
　　Through. D. Lawrence.
　　Al-VBP:1158, Go-BP:69, Pa-GTB:458,
　　Wi-LT:212
　Sonnet XI. Feng Chih. Hs-TC:150
　Sonnet 29. W. Shakespeare.
　　Al-VBP:200, Co-BL:117, Ga-FB:34,
　　Ha-PO:254, Ho-P:290, Ni-JP:96,
　　Pa-GTB:8, Rv-CB:212, Un-MW:181
　Sonnet 30. W. Shakespeare.
　　Al-VBP:201, Er-FA:166, Fe-PL:130,
　　Ga-FB:33, Pa-GTB:18, Rv-CB:213
　Spark of Laurel. S. Kunitz.
　　Pl-ML:36
　A Spirit from Perfecter Ages.
　　A. Clough. Ox-BN:612
　Standing on Earth. J. Milton.
　　Gr-CT:464

Star Journey. N. Madgett.
  Ra-BP:195
Sun of Blood and Stars of Sorrow.
  Y. Stefanov. Bo-RU:83
Take Back the Virgin Page.
  T. Moore. Ox-BN:211
Tauhid. A. Touré. Ad-PB:339
Thel's Motto. W. Blake.
  Gr-CT:432, Ox-BN:32
Time in the Rock. C. Aiken.
  Ca-VT:157
To the Muse. Hu P'in-ch'ing.
  Pa-MV:103
To the Muses. W. Blake.
  Al-VBP:611, Gr-CT:230, Rv-CB:561
We Are All Workmen. R. Rilke.
  Pl-EI:56
Where Didst Thou Find, Young Bard.
  J. Keats. Rv-CB:753
Within King's College Chapel,
  Cambridge. W. Wordsworth.
  Ox-BN:81, Pa-GTB:300
Yes, You Are Old. M. Breslasu.
  Mc-AC:90
INSTINCT
  The Children of the Wind.
    C. Sandburg. Hi-WP II:41,
    Re-BS:57
  Intuition. R. Grenville.
    De-FS:101
INSULTS: see also HUMOR - INSULTS
  Against Garnesche. J. Skelton.
    Al-VBP:29
  Angry Song. Da-SC:56
  Disgrace. Ab-MO:27
  Epitaph on Charles II. J. Wilmot.
    Al-VBP:506, Co-FB:476,
    Hi-WP II:140, Mc-WS:89, Un-GT:237
  An Essay on Criticism. A. Pope.
    Al-VBP:530, Ma-YA:116
  I'm Only Going to Tell You Once.
    A. Pratt. Al-WW:106
  Impromptu on Charles II.
    J. Wilmot. Gr-CT:473
  Jacob Tonson, His Publisher.
    J. Dryden. Gr-CT:470
  A Little Shrub Growing By.
    B. Jonson. Rv-CB:285
  MacFlecknoe. J. Dryden.
    Al-VBP:490
  The Master, the Swabber.
    W. Shakespeare. Al-VBP:198
  Nith-Song of Savdlat and Pulangit-
    Sissok. Da-SC:44
  Oh, Oh, You Will Be Sorry for
    That Word. E. Millay. Pe-OA:165
  On Andrew Turner. R. Burns.
    Co-PU:123
  On Noman, a Guest. H. Belloc.
    Co-PU:125

On the Death of Mr. Crashaw.
    A. Cowley. Al-VBP:448
  On the Reverend Jonathan Doe.
    Gr-CT:475
  On the Site of a Mulberry-Tree.
    D. Rossetti. Rv-CB:884
  The Rebel Scot. J. Cleveland.
    Al-VBP:441
  Song of the New-Rich. Da-SC:56
  Woman, Your Soul Is Misshapen.
    Do-CH:(28)
  You Really Resemble. Do-CH:(26)
INSURANCE: see HUMOR - INSURANCE
INTEGRATION: see RACE RELATIONS
INTEGRITY: see CHARACTER
INTELLECT: see MIND
INTELLECTUALS: see also HUMOR -
  INTELLECTUALS
  Elegy for the Rev. Mr. James B.
    Hodgson. J. Logan. St-H:111
  The Intellectuals. D. Randall.
    Ad-PB:142
INTERNATIONAL FRIENDSHIP: see
  BROTHERHOOD
INTERNATIONAL ORGANIZATION:
    see also BROTHERHOOD;
    INTERNATIONAL RELATIONS;
    UNITED NATIONS
  The Fatherland. J. Lowell.
    Se-PR:189
  Federation of the World.
    A. Tennyson. Se-PR:184
  For I Dipped into the Future.
    A. Tennyson. Fe-PL:432
INTERNATIONAL RELATIONS: see also
    ATLANTIC CHARTER; BROTHERHOOD;
    DIPLOMATS; HUMOR - INTERNA-
    TIONAL RELATIONS; INTERNA-
    TIONAL ORGANIZATION; NEUTRALITY;
    SATIRE - INTERNATIONAL RELA-
    TIONS; TREATIES; UNITED NATIONS
  Borders. S. Mosova. Mo-MI:74
  Foreign Affairs. S. Kunitz.
    Wi-LT:750
  International Hymn.
    G. Huntington. Fe-PL:161
  1956. D. Hoffman. En-PC:207
  Snow in Europe. D. Gascoyne.
    To-MP:37
  Sonnet XXX. P. Sidney. No-CL:150
  To India. Yüan Shui-p'ai.
    Hs-TC:413
INTERNMENT CAMPS: see CONCENTRA-
    TION CAMPS
INTERPLANETARY VOYAGES: see also
    HUMOR - INTERPLANETARY VOYAGES;
    SPACE EXPLORATION
  Missionary. D. Thomas. To-MP:199
  Space Travel. J. Krows. Au-SP:177
  Unknown Shores. D. Thomas.
    To-MP:209

INTOLERANCE: see PREJUDICES
AND ANTIPATHIES
INTOXICATION: see also
DRINKERS AND DRINKING;
HUMOR - INTOXICATION
Bowery.   D. Ignatow.   Pe-M:70
Get Drunk.   Ho-Ch'i-fang.
Hs-TC:223
Haiku 3.   E. Knight.   Ra-BP:206
Hail, Dionysos.   D. Randall.
Ra-BP:140
The Irresponsible Student.
Be-AP:56
Long Journey.   Pien Chih-lin.
Hs-TC:161
A Man Who Had Fallen among
Thieves.   e. cummings.   Wi-LT:360
A Note Left in Jimmy Leonard's
Shack.   J. Wright.   Ha-TP:54
INTUITION: see INSTINCT
INVALIDS: see SICKNESS
INVENTIONS: see also HUMOR -
INVENTIONS; SATIRE -
INVENTIONS
Alexander Graham Bell Did Not
Invent the Telephone.
R. Coffin.   Ar-TP3:46
And Yet Fools Say.   G. Holmes.
Ar-TP3:46
The Microscope.   M. Kumin.
Du-RG:53, Ha-PO:96
My Invention.   S. Silverstein.
Co-PU:29
INVESTMENTS AND INVESTORS
Investor's Soliloquy.   K. Ward.
Er-FA:207
INVITATIONS: see also HUMOR -
INVITATIONS
Come!   W. Barnes.   De-CH:440
Dance Songs, II.
Tr-US II:163
Invitation Standing.
P. Blackburn.   Ca-VT:556
Invitation to Miss Marianne
Moore.   E. Bishop.   Pl-ML:82
An Invite to Eternity.
J. Clare.   Ox-BN:330
Moon-Uncle.   Ca-MU:31
The Outcast.   J. Stephens.
Un-MB:267
Party Bid.   A. Humphreys.
De-FS:109
Prophecy.   Ho Ch'i-fang.
Hs-TC:218
The Telephone.   R. Frost.
No-CL:193
Visit.   A. Ammons.   Br-TC:9,
Kh-VA:25, Mo-BG:100
Who Calls.   F. Sayers.
Br-SS:130, Li-LC:89

Will You Come?   E. Thomas.
Bo-GJ:120, De-CH:439
IOWA
The Bourgeois Poet, #69.
K. Shapiro.   St-H:206
For the Iowa Dead.   P. Engle.
St-H:55
Miss Elderli Dora DesMoines —
One March.   R. Sward.   St-H:224
Pagan Saturday.   J. Logan.
St-H:114
The Song of Iowa.   S. Byers.
Se-PR:261
Words for a Friend Who Was
Accidentally Shot.
D. Etter.   St-H:60
IRANIAN VERSE - BALUCHI
Dastanghs, I, II.
Tr-US II:136, 137
IRANIAN VERSE - PASHTO
Couplets, I, II.   Tr-US II:136
Songs of Nature, I-III.
Tr-US II:137
IRANIAN VERSE - PERSIAN
As Salt Resolved in the Ocean.
Rumi.   Pa-SG:202
He Who Knows.   Un-GT:305
Heart's Desire.   Omar Khayyam.
Un-MW:193
The Miracle of Spring.   Bahar.
Pa-SG:82
A Moral Tetrastitch.   Co-PU:149
Myself when Young Did Eagerly
Frequent.   O. Khayyam.   Pl-EI:66
Perfect Love.   Sana'i.   Pa-SG:28
Rubaiyat of Omar Khayyam.
Al-VBP:832, Er-FA:43, Fe-FP:479,
Ox-BN:526, Pa-SG:120
Then from a Ruin.   Farid-uddin
Attar.   Re-BS:46
Three Things.   Un-GT:306
The Unseen Power.   Rumi.   Pa-SG:192
Yet Ah, that Spring Should Vanish
with the Rose.   O. Khayyam.
Tu-WW:45
IRASCIBILITY: see also CONTRARINESS;
HUMOR - IRASCIBILITY
Cross Patch.
De-PO:12, Gr-CT:10, Gr-GB:19,
Li-LB:55, Mo-MGT:161, Mo-NR:53,
Na-EO:73, Wi-MG:74, Wr-RM:13
Kag the Porcupine.   A. Guiterman.
Gr-EC:20
Kate.   A. Tennyson.   Co-RM:74
The Peppery Man.   A. Macy.
Fe-FP:319
Stocking Fairy.   W. Welles.
Ar-TP3:150, Au-SP:295, Fe-FP:378
Sulky Sue.   De-PO:26, Mo-CC:(50),
Mo-MGT:72, Wr-RM:68

IRELAND: see also BALLADS, IRISH;
    DIALECTS, IRISH; IRISH VERSE;
    LEGENDS, IRISH; PATRICK,
    SAINT; and names of counties,
    as GALWAY and towns, as DUBLIN
The Abbot of Inisfalen.
    W. Allingham. Pa-OM:104
The Army of the Sidhe.
    Lady Gregory. Th-AS:139
Aunt Julia. N. Maccaig. To-MP:185
Brian Boy Magee. F. Carbery.
    Co-PI:21
The Cliffs of Moher. W. Stevens.
    Ca-VT:41
Digging. S. Heaney. Br-TC:173,
    To-MP:150
Graves at Inishbofin. R. Murphy.
    Ls-NY:110
The Harp That Once Through Tara's
    Halls. T. Moore. Al-VBP:710,
    Co-RG:20, Fe-PL:177, Ma-YA:170,
    Ox-BN:210
I Am of Ireland. W. Yeats.
    Co-PI:207
In Ireland: By the Pool at the
    Third Rosses. A. Symons.
    Ox-BN:936
In Memory of W. B. Yeats.
    W. Auden. Al-VBP:1228,
    Er-FA:41, Gr-CT:431, Pl-ML:163,
    Un-MB:459, Wi-LT:468
Ireland. W. Landor. Co-PI:1,
    Pa-GTB:317
Ireland with Emily.
    J. Betjeman. Pa-GTB:500
Irish-American Dignitary.
    A. Clarke. Co-PI:26
Irish Grandmother. K. Edelman.
    Br-AF:43, Br-SS:136
The Irish Harper and His Dog.
    T. Campbell. De-CH:83, De-TT:66,
    Hu-MP:194, Rv-CB:678, Un-GT:41
Muckish Mountain (The Pig's Back).
    S. Leslie. Co-PI:92
Oh, It's Nine Years Ago I Was
    Digging in the Land. Em-AF:760
Of Certain Irish Fairies.
    A. Guiterman. Fe-PL:107
The Passage at Night - the Blaskets.
    R. Flower. Co-PI:45
Red Hanrahan's Song about Ireland.
    W. Yeats. Sm-LG:141
Sailing to an Island. R. Murphy.
    To-MP:134
Spenser's Ireland. M. Moore.
    Wi-LT:269
Sweet Innisfallen. T. Moore.
    Ox-BN:215
IRELAND - COUNTRYSIDE
The Bells of Shandon. F. Mahony.
    Co-PI:122, Co-RG:124, De-CH:197,
    Gr-CT:34, Pa-HT:141

Corrib. An Emblem. D. Davie.
    En-PC:197
A Drover. P. Colum. Al-VBP:1148,
    Co-PI:26, Pa-HT:139, Un-MB:250
The Groves of Blarney.
    R. Millikin. Rv-CB:629
In Kerry. J. Synge. Un-MB:181
The Lake Isle of Innisfree.
    W. Yeats. Ar-TP3:218, Co-RG:118,
    Er-FA:258, Fe-FP:464, Fr-WO:79,
    Ga-FB:242, Ma-YA:230, Mc-PR:174,
    Pa-HT:138, Th-AS:149, Un-MB:108,
    Wi-LT:68
Prelude. J. Synge. Co-BN:207,
    Gr-CT:235, Un-MB:180
Slieve Gua. Gr-CT:318
A Strong Wind. A. Clarke.
    Co-BN:166, Co-PI:24
The Sweetness of Nature. Gr-CC:118
IRELAND - HISTORY AND PATRIOTISM:
    see also HUMOR - IRELAND-HISTORY
    AND PATRIOTISM; SATIRE - IRELAND-
    HISTORY AND PATRIOTISM; and
    legendary heroes, as CU CHULAINN,
    MYTHICAL CELTIC HERO
The Boys of Mullaghbawn. Gr-GB:256
The Croppy Boy. Rv-CB:437
Dark Rosaleen. J. Mangan.
    Al-VBP:812, Co-PI:128, De-CH:172
The Dead at Clonmacnoise.
    T. Rolleston. Co-PI:172,
    Pa-HT:144
Easter 1916. W. Yeats. Wi-LT:70
The Famine Year. Lady Wilde.
    Co-PI:197
The Fighting Race. J. Clarke.
    Co-RM:111
The Fort of Rathangan.
    Co-PI:131, De-CH:181, Gr-CT:323,
    Ho-LP:86, Sm-LG:395
Ho, Brother Teig. Gr-GB:165
In This Year of Grace.
    J. Hewitt. Co-PI:62
An Irish Airman Foresees His
    Death. W. Yeats. Bo-GJ:191,
    Gr-CC:129, Ho-LP:87, Pa-GTB:424,
    Pe-SS:138, Sm-LG:270, Un-MB:116,
    Wi-LT:70
Irish Curse on the Occupying
    English. M. MacEntee. Co-PI:112
Lament for the Death of Eoghan
    Ruadh O'Neill. T. Davis.
    Co-PI:34, Hi-FO:148
The Lion and O'Reilly. R. Weber.
    Ke-PP:19
Lord Waterford. Gr-CT:472, Gr-GB:196
Meditations in Time of Civil War.
    W. Yeats. Pa-GTB:426
The Municipal Gallery Revisited.
    W. Yeats. Pa-GTB:432
Old Orange Flute. Gr-GB:192
Orange Lilies. J. Reaney. Do-WH:86

IRELAND - HISTORY AND
    PATRIOTISM — cont'd.
  The Orange Lily.   Gr-GB:191
  September 1913.   W. Yeats.
    Pa-GTB:422
  The Shan Van Vocht.   Gr-GB:194
  The Wake of William Orr.
    W. Drennan.   Ba-PO:94
  The Wearing of the Green. Co-PS:51,
    Er-FA:295, Gr-GB:193, Hi-FO:252
  What Will We Do for Linen?
    Gr-GB:197
IRELAND, NORTHERN: see BALLADS,
    IRISH; DIALECTS, IRISH;
    and names of counties, as
    ANTRIM, IRE., N. and towns,
    as BELFAST, IRE., N.
IRISES (FLOWERS)
  Iris.   Ar-TP3:204, Ch-B:66,
    Hu-MP:263
  Irises.   P. Colum.   Co-BN:59
  What's o'Clock.   A. Lowell.
    Ho-TH:24
  When It's Iris Time in Tennessee.
    W. Waid.   Se-PR:285
  A White Iris.   P. Barrington.
    Fe-PL:377
THE IRISH: see also DIALECTS,
    IRISH; HUMOR - THE IRISH
  Arthur McBride.   Co-RM:115,
    Gr-GB:236
  Beg-Innish.   J. Synge. Un-MB:180
  Bold O'Donahue.   Co-RM:122
  The Convict of Clonmel.   Co-PI:16,
    Mo-SD:174
  Dooley Is a Traitor.   J. Michie.
    Co-RM:119
  The Fighting Race.   J. Clarke.
    Co-RM:111
  Galway Races.   Mo-SD:65
  Go to Old Ireland.   Em-AF:759
  I Am of Ireland.   Gr-GB:164,
    Rv-CB:142, Sm-LG:141
  If Ever You Go to Dublin Town.
    P. Kavanagh.   To-MP:64
  I'll Wear a Shamrock.   M. Davies.
    Ar-TP3:200, Br-SS:134, Ha-YA:43
  Irish.   E. O'Brien.   Br-SS:136,
    La-PH:49, Th-AS:99
  The Irish Dancer.   Gr-BT:17
  The Irishman and the Lady.
    W. Maginn.   Co-RM:116
  Mush, Mush.   Co-RM:114
  An Old Woman of the Roads.
    P. Colum.   De-CH:49, Fe-FP:320,
    Hu-MP:156, Sh-RP:43, Th-AS:184,
    Un-MB:250
  Paddy Murphy.   Co-RM:118
  A Scot, a Welsh and an Irish Man.
    Gr-GB:165

Spenser's Ireland.   M. Moore.
    Wi-LT:269
  The Tarriers' Song.   T. Casey.
    Co-RM:125, Kr-OF:167
  The Tower.   W. Yeats.   Wi-LT:76
  Under Ben Bulben.   W. Yeats.
    Pl-ML:30, Wi-LT:96
IRISH REPUBLIC: see IRELAND
IRISH VERSE: see also BALLADS,
    IRISH
  Arran.   Gr-CT:238, Sm-LG:139
  Autumn.   F. O'Connor.   Co-PS:129
  The Blackbird by Belfast Lough.
    Gr-EC:167, Pa-SG:117, Re-BS:38
  Bruadar and Smith and Glinn.
    Mc-WS:86
  By World Laid Low.   Gr-CT:327
  The Convict of Clonmel.   Mo-SD:174
  Dark Rosaleen.   J. Mangan.
    Al-VBP:812, De-CH:172
  The Day of Wrath.   St. Columba.
    Ga-S:134
  The Dead at Clonmacnoise.
    T. Rolleston.   Pa-HT:144
  Dear Dark Head.   Co-BL:116,
    Pa-SG:58
  The Fort of Rathangan.   De-CH:181,
    Gr-CT:323, Ho-LP:86, Sm-LG:395
  A Glass of Beer.   J. Stephens.
    Co-FB:470, Mc-WS:83, Rv-CB:973,
    Un-MB:265
  The Green Autumn Stubble.
    Pa-SG:55
  Grief of a Girl's Heart.
    A. Gregory.   Co-BL:128, Gr-CT:76
  The Hermit's Song.   Pa-SG:158
  Kilcash.   F. O'Connor.
    Hi-WP II:132, Re-TW:86
  Lanty Leary.   Co-BL:164, Gr-CT:84
  My Grief on the Sea.   Pa-SG:62
  St. Patrick's Breastplate.
    St. Patrick.   Sm-LG:379
  Slieve Gua.   Gr-CT:318
  A Song of Winter.   De-CH:217
  Summer Is Gone.   Sm-LG:58
  The Sweetness of Nature. Gr-CC:118
  The Viking Terror.   Gr-CT:222
  The Visions of MacConglinne.
    De-CH:65
  Were You on the Mountain?
    Co-BL:133, Co-PU:76
  The Words of Finn.   Gr-CT:389
  See also Co-PI
IRON (METAL):   see also STEEL
  Charlemagne.   H. Longfellow.
    Er-FA:310
  Iron.   B. Brecht.   Ho-LP:39
  Red Iron Ore.   Ar-TP3:91
  Shovelling Iron Ore.   Gr-GB:232
  The Slave and the Iron Lace.
    M. Danner.   Bo-AN:157, Ra-BP:154

IRONSIDES: see CONSTITUTION (SHIP)
IRRITATION: see ANNOYANCE
ISAAC: see also ABRAHAM; REBEKAH
  Abraham and Isaac. Ga-S:40,
    Ma-FW:78
  Abraham Takes Isaac to the
    Sacrifice. I. Manger.
    Ho-TY:275
  The Book of Job. H. Leivick.
    Ho-TY:126
  My Father Isaac. J. Glatstein.
    Ho-TY:246
  The Parable of the Old Men and
    the Young. W. Owen. Go-BP:207,
    Ma-FW:250, Mo-GR:18
  Story of Isaac. L. Cohen.
    Mo-GR:16
ISAIAH
  Isaiah and Homer. A. Glanz-Leyeles.
    Ho-TY:257
  The Prophet. A. Pushkin. Pl-EI:98
ISAR RIVER
  River Roses. D. Lawrence.
    Al-VBP:1157, Gr-SS:39
ISHTAR, BABYLONIAN GODDESS
  The Epic of Gilgamesh. Ho-P:218
ISLAM
  Call to Prayer. Bilal. Ab-MO:61
  Lepanto. G. Chesterton.
    Ga-FB:196, Hi-FO:119, Un-MB:205
  Muhammedan Call to Prayer.
    Bilal. Lo-TY:43
ISLAND LIFE
  My Father Loved the Jumping-Off
    Place. R. Coffin. Sh-RP:309
ISLANDS: see also ISLAND LIFE;
    ISLANDS OF THE PACIFIC; and
    names of islands, as CUBA
  At Matsushima. Shiki. Pa-SG:154
  By Ferry to the Island. I. Smith.
    Go-BP:33, To-MP:95
  Fairest Isle. J. Dryden.
    Rv-CB:467
  The Islands. H. D. Un-MA:339
  Kalymniad, Part II. R. Lax.
    Sc-TN:125
  On This Island. W. Auden.
    To-MP:19
  Sailing to an Island. R. Murphy.
    To-MP:134
  The Spring Waters. Ping Hsin.
    Hs-TC:22
  To Marguerite. M. Arnold.
    Ox-BN:627, Pa-GTB:364
  Trade Winds. J. Masefield.
    Bo-HF:86, Cl-FC:56
ISLANDS OF THE PACIFIC: see also
    names of islands, as TAHITI
  Day-Song for Tenio's Fête.
    Koroa. Tr-US II:59

  Farewell of Warriors of Vavau
    Going to Fight at Sea.
    Tr-US II:50
  Fun with Fishing. E. Tietjens.
    Fe-FP:484
  Praise of Beaches. Tr-US II:47
  Priests' Chant to Usher in the
    Dawn. Tr-US II:66
  Song in Recitative Style.
    Tr-US II:45
  Song of Tukulua. Tukulua.
    Tr-US II:48
ISOLDE: see TRISTAN AND ISOLDE
ISRAEL: see also PALESTINE
  Dress Me, Dear Mother.
    A. Schlonsky. Me-PH:99
  Jezrael. A. Shlonsky. Me-PH:100
  National Thoughts. Y. Amichai.
    Me-PH:131
  New City. M. Yungman. Ho-TY:365
  The Prophecies Against Moab,
    Judah, and Israel. Bible.
    O.T. Amos. Me-PH:48
  Seeds on Cobblestones.
    A. Shamri. Ho-TY:361
  The Silver Tray. N. Alterman.
    Me-PH:112
  Your People Are Drowning in Blood.
    S. Tchernichovsky. Me-PH;80
ISRAEL - HISTORY AND PATRIOTISM
  David's Lament. Bible. O.T.
    Samuel. Gr-CT:343, Me-PH:12
  How Is the Gold Become Dim.
    Bible. O.T. Lamentations.
    Gr-CT:344
ISRAELITES: see ISRAEL; JEWS
ISRAFEL
  Israfel. E. Poe. Sh-AP:154
ITALIAN VERSE
  Alleyway. S. Quasimodo. Ma-FW:235
  And She Washed His Feet with
    Her Tears. G. Marino. Gr-CT:188
  Ballata. Pl-US:62
  Cincirinella Has a Mule. Fe-FP:475
  Confession - Gate of Purgatory.
    Dante Alighieri. Ga-S:139
  Feather. F. Bianco. No-CL:4
  First Snowfall. G. Carducci.
    Pa-SG:18
  He Compares All Things with His
    Lady and Finds Them Wanting.
    G. Cavalcanti. Pa-SG:73
  He Will Praise His Lady.
    G. Guinicelli. Pa-SG:72
  How the Gates Came Ajar. Ke-TF:42
  In Wintry Midnight, o'er a Stormy
    Main. F. Petrarch. Gr-CT:229
  The Infinite. G. Leopardi.
    Pa-SG:170
  Italian Lullaby. Fe-FP:474

ITALIAN VERSE — cont'd.
  The Little Trumpet. C. Govoni.
    Li-TU:48
  O Sorrowful and Ancient Days.
    Eugenius Vulgarius. Ba-PO:74
  On a Wet Day. F. Sacchetti.
    Co-BN:170
  Prayer of St. Francis of Assisi
    for Peace. St. Francis.
    Fe-PL:346
  Prolonged Sonnet. N. Albizzi.
    Cr-WS:20
  September. F. da San Geminiano.
    Mo-SD:122
  Sestina. Dante Alighieri.
    Gr-SS:93
  Sleep, Baby Boy. Fe-FP:475
  The Song of Creatures.
    St. Francis of Assisi.
    Pa-SG:202
  To the Guelf Faction.
    F. da San Geminiano. Hi-FO:85
  To the Supreme Being.
    Michelangelo. Pa-SG:198
  Within Her Eyes.
    Dante Alighieri. Pa-SG:61
  You Were Shattered. G. Ungaretti.
    Li-TU:126
ITALIANS IN THE UNITED STATES:
    see also DIALECTS, ITALIAN
  Da Boy from Rome. T. Daly.
    Fe-FP:304, Hu-MP:158
  Clinton South of Polk.
    C. Sandburg. Br-AF:42
  The Evil Eye. J. Ciardi. Ca-MB:19
  Italian Extravaganza. G. Corso.
    La-OC:91
ITALY: see also HUMOR - ITALY;
    ITALIAN VERSE; and names of
    towns, as VENICE, IT., and
    regions, as SICILY
  Black and White Spring.
    C. Hampton. Ls-NY:237
  Childe Harold's Pilgrimage.
    G. Byron. Al-VBP:726
  The Daisy. A. Tennyson. Ox-BN:489
  England. M. Moore. Un-MA:350
  Evening: Ponte al Mare, Pisa.
    P. Shelley. Cl-FC:30, Rv-CB:709
  Hotel Paradiso e Commerciale.
    J. Brinnin. Br-TC:61,
    En-PC:147
  Lines Written among the Euganean
    Hills. P. Shelley. Al-VBP:743,
    De-TT:144
  Tramontana at Lerici.
    C. Tomlinson. Pa-GTB:560
  Watchman, What of the Night?
    A. Swinburne. Ho-WR:200
  A Water-Colour of Venice.
    L. Durrell. Un-MB:491

ITALY - COUNTRYSIDE
  Ah, that I Were Far Away.
    A. Clough. Ox-BN:602
  For Keats and the Florentine
    Night. G. Kennedy. Ls-NY:141
  An Interview near Florence.
    S. Rogers. Ox-BN:53
  Recorders in Italy. A. Rich.
    Pl-US:19
  Somewhere in Tuscany.
    D. Holbrook. Ls-NY:13
  Two in the Campagna.
    R. Browning. Ke-TF:134,
    Ox-BN:540, Pa-GTB:348, Un-MW:114
  Up at a Villa - Down in the City.
    R. Browning. Pa-GTB:342,
    Rv-CB:824
  Written in the Euganean Hills,
    North Italy. P. Shelley.
    Pa-GTB:290
ITALY - HISTORY AND PATRIOTISM:
    see also FASCISM; GUELPHS
  On the Late Massacre in Piedmont.
    J. Milton. Al-VBP:408,
    Hi-FO:152, Pa-GTB:51, Rv-CB:376
  One Man, One Man Alone (Italy,
    1941). E. Hutton. Ke-TF:384
  To the Guelf Faction.
    F. da San Geminiano. Hi-FO:85
ITCHINESS: see also HUMOR -
    ITCHINESS
  An Itch. L. Kirkman. Ho-ME:27
ITHACA (ISLAND)
  At Ithaca. H. D. Ca-VT:112
IVES, CHARLES EDWARD
  The Feral Pioneers. I. Reed.
    Ad-PB:335, Hu-PN:415
  Ives. M. Rukeyser. Pl-US:87
IVRY, BATTLE, 1590
  Ivry. T. Macauley. Ga-FB:200,
    Hi-FO:131
IVY: see also POISON IVY
  Holly and Ivy. Rv-CB:21
  The Holly and the Ivy. De-CH:228,
    De-TT:114, Gr-CT:421, Gr-GB:301
  Ivy and Holly. E. Meyerstein.
    Co-EL:11
  The Ivy Green. C. Dickens.
    Co-BN:218
  Nay, Ivy, Nay. De-CH:230,
    Rv-CB:32
  Song. C. Rossetti. Al-VBP:995,
    Pa-GTB:374
  To the Ivy. J. Clare. Rv-CB:712
JACK-IN-THE-BOXES
  Jack-in-the-Box. E. Olson.
    St-H:172
JACK-IN-THE-PULPITS
  Jack-in-the-Pulpit. R. Bennett.
    Hu-MP:245
  Jack-in-the-Pulpit. I. Eastwick.
    Ha-YA:64

JACK O'LANTERNS: see HALLOWEEN;
PUMPKINS
JACK THE RIPPER: see HUMOR –
JACK THE RIPPER
JACKDAWS
In the Blue. A. Machado. Le-SW:75
The Jackdaw of Rheims. R. Barham.
Pa-OM:322
JACKEROOS: see KINGFISHERS
JACKSON, ANDREW
Andrew Jackson. R. Bly. Mc-EA:122
Andrew Jackson. M. Keller.
Br-AF:67, Co-RM:212, Un-GT:92
The Statue of Old Andrew Jackson.
V. Lindsay. Mc-PR:52
JACKSON, MAHALIA
When Mahalia Sings. Q. Prettyman.
Ad-PB:260, Pe-M:18
JACKSON, THOMAS JONATHAN
(STONEWALL)
Barbara Frietchie. J. Whittier.
Co-PS:97, Er-FA:380, Fe-FP:442,
Fe-PL:167, Ga-FB:258, Hi-TL:112,
Mc-PR:170, Sp-OG:40, Un-GT:190,
Vi-PP:150
The Brigade Must Not Know, Sir!
Hi-TL:120
JACOB AND RACHEL
Jacob and the Angel.
Brother Antoninus. Tr-MR:72
Poem. J. Friedman. Ho-TY:368
JADE
The Image-Maker. O. Gogarty.
Go-BP:63
Mode of Maidens. Br-FW:5
JAGUARS
The Jaguar. J. Hollander.
Wi-LT:736
JAILS: see PRISONS AND
PRISONERS
JAMAICA
And Away. B. Smith. Sa-B:72
The Coming. T. Matthews.
Sa-B:232
Homecoming. D. Scott. Sa-B:115
If There Exists a Hell.
P. Freneau. Kr-OF:27
Jamaica Market. A. Maxwell-Hall.
Ab-MO:43, Lo-TY:117
Lament of the Banana Man.
E. Jones. To-MP:171
Ode to Brother Joe. T. McNeill.
Sa-B:154
Resurrections. D. Scott.
Sa-B:205
Saint Ras. T. McNeill. Sa-B:158
The Song of the Banana Man.
E. Jones. Co-RM:242, Sa-B:101,
To-MP:168
This Land. B. Smith. Sa-B:175
The Tightrope Walker. D. Scott.
Sa-B:121

Tom Tom. B. Smith. Sa-B:73
JAMAICANS
Colonisation in Reverse..
L. Bennett. Sa-B:51
History Makers. G. Campbell.
Sa-B:33
JAMES I, KING OF ENGLAND
The Laird o' Logie. De-CH:412,
Rv-CB:49
Troynovant. T. Dekker. Gr-CT:297
JAMES, HENRY: see also HUMOR –
JAMES, HENRY
Henry James. R. Stevenson.
Ox-BN:891
I Walked over the Grave of Henry
James. R. Eberhart. Ca-VT:246
JAMES, JESSE WOODSON
Jesse James. W. Benét. Ha-PO:208,
Hi-TL:145, Un-MA:327
Jesse James. Br-AF:111
Jesse James. Ho-WR:116, Mc-WS:161
JAMS AND JELLIES
Berries. W. de la Mare. Un-MB:200
Elfin Berries. R. Field. Ag-HE:54
Master Jack's Song. L. Richards.
Ag-HE:48
Red-Currant Jelly. M. Stephenson.
St-FS:67
Strawberry Jam. M. Justus.
Fe-FP:310
JANUARY
Annual Gaiety. W. Stevens.
Un-MA:248
January. E. Coatsworth. Co-PS:156
January. S. Lambdin. Ha-YA:164
January. J. Lowell. Se-PR:26
January. M. Sendak. Ag-HE:10
January. F. Sherman. Ha-YA:161
January. J. Updike. La-PV:90
January in Harlem. J. Fields.
Ad-CI:33
January Is Here. E. Fawcett.
Ha-YA:162
January Night. R. Arrieta.
Pa-SG:30
January: Skiing Song.
M. Lewis. Un-GT:268
January Snow. A. Fisher.
Ha-YA:162
Odes of the Months. Ma-FW:4
Old January. E. Spenser.
Ha-YA:163
The Wind of January.
C. Rossetti. Ha-YA:163
Winter Nightfall. E. Olson.
St-H:171
JANUS (ROMAN GOD)
Gardener Janus Catches a
Naiad. E. Sitwell.
Un-MB:332

JAPAN: see also FUJIYAMA;
        JAPANESE VERSE; and
        names of cities and
        towns, as HIROSHIMA
    Falling Snow. K. Nakamura.
        Sh-AM:172
    The Feast of Lanterns.
        J. Yoshimura. Le-TA:35
    Free Fantasia on Japanese Themes.
        A. Lowell. Un-MA:159
    The Ghost Wails in the Woods at
        Night. Tu Yün-hsieh. Hs-TC:246
    Japan. A. Hecht. Wi-LT:728
    Kosumi, the Carver. Yehoash.
        Ho-TY:75
    Mount Fuji. M. Kaneko. Sh-AM:66
    An Old Song. S. Bloomgarden.
        Ho-TY:75, Pa-SG:147
JAPAN - COUNTRYSIDE
    Stars above Mountains.
        S. Mizuhara. Sh-AM:167
    Work to Do Toward Town.
        G. Snyder. Ca-VT:664
THE JAPANESE: see also
        HUMOR - THE JAPANESE;
        SATIRE - THE JAPANESE
    In a Bar near Shibuya Station,
        Tokyo. P. Engle. Ad-CI:84,
        Br-AF:88
    Japan. A. Hecht. Wi-LT:728
    Japanese Children. J. Kirkup.
        Ma-FW:68, Pa-RE:125
    Little Maid of Far Japan.
        A. Wynne. Hu-MP:138
    Relative Sadness. C. Rowbotham.
        Gr-BT:119
    To Those Who Fight. T'ien Chien.
        Hs-TC:322
    Under the Plane Trees.
        K. Nakamura. Sh-AM:147
JAPANESE IN THE UNITED STATES
    Reflections on a Small Parade.
        B. Kaufman. Kh-VA:8
JAPANESE VERSE
    Against the Broad Sky.
        K. Takahama. Ma-FW:273
    All That Is Left. Bashö.
        Ba-PO:25, Pa-SG:9
    At Matsushima. Shiki.
        Pa-SG:154
    The Autumn Storm. Bashö.
        Sh-RP:63
    Baby's Hands. Gomei. Hu-MP:8
    Beauty. Bashö. Au-SP:340
    Birds of Passage. Issa. Ba-PO:26
    Blossoms and Storm. Sadaiye.
        Pa-SG:90
    The Camellia. Bashö. Sh-RP:63
    Cattle. Banko. Au-SP:45,
        Hu-MP:196

    The Chicken Wants. S. Karai.
        Ma-FW:93
    Cicada-Shell. Basho. Au-SP:77
    The Cock Again. Kikaku.
        Au-SP:49
    Contentment in Poverty. Issa.
        Sh-RP:65
    Coolness. Onitsura. Pa-SG:127
    Coolness in Summer. Ryusui.
        Sh-RP:67
    Crocuses. Jösa. Ar-TP3:202,
        Hu-MP:248
    The Cuckoo's Song. Josui.
        Hu-MP:223
    Daffodils. Ar-TP3:201, Au-SP:306
    The Dragonfly. Chisoku.
        Au-SP:75
    The Earth Grown like the Moon.
        T. Kagawa. Ba-PO:126
    The End of Summer. Basho. Sh-RP:64
    Fairies. Kihaku. Hu-MP:81
    The Fall of the Plum Blossoms.
        Rankö. Ar-TP3:204
    Far Beyond Us. Pa-SG:185
    Firefly. K. Hajime. Mo-TS:63
    The Firefly Lights His Lamp.
        Au-SP:75, Hu-MP:200
    Folk Song from Fukushima.
        Ma-FW:151
    Hail on the Pine Trees. Basho.
        Hu-MP:278
    Harbingers. Basho. Sh-RP:64
    Harvest Moon. Ryota. Sh-RP:66
    Haze. Buson. Sh-RP:62
    In My New Clothing. Bashö.
        Au-SP:102, Su-FVI:10
    In the Old Man's Eyes.
        K. Takahama. Ma-FW:179
    Invisible Tree. R. Tamura.
        Mo-TS:20
    Iris. Ar-TP3:204, Ch-B:66,
        Hu-MP:263
    I've Seen Everything. J. Naito.
        Ma-FW:93
    Japanese Folk-Song from Hyogo.
        Pa-RE:64
    Judging from the Pictures.
        S. Karai. Ma-FW:163
    Late Snow. Issa. Sh-RP:65
    Late Summer. Y. Kinoshita.
        Ma-FW:115
    Leaving the House of a Friend.
        Basho. Sh-RP:63
    Lilies. Shikö. Ar-TP3:204
    The Lily Princess. Ch-B:24,
        Hu-MP:252
    Loneliness. Hashin. Au-SP:333,
        Do-TS:45, Li-TU:201, Pa-SG:185
    Looking at the Moon on Putting
        Out from the Shore at Nagato.
        Ma-FW:53

Lotus Leaves. Mitsukumi.
Pa-SG:106
Maple Leaves. Shiko. Au-SP:323,
Pa-SG:95
A Memory. Emperor Hirohito.
Th-AS:155
Mists of Daybreak. Buson.
Hu-MP:318
Momotaro. Ar-TP3:136, Ir-BB:243
The Monkey's Raincoat. Basho.
Au-SP:326, Su-FVI:67
The Moon. Ryuho. Au-SP:342
The Moon Ship. Hitomaro.
Ch-B:46, Le-MW:38
Nakatsukasa. Shüi Shü. Pa-SG:80
The New and the Old. Shiki.
Pa-SG:114
The Noisy Cricket. S. Watanabe.
Ma-FW:102
Nothing in the Voice. Basho.
Ma-FW:102
On a Bare Branch. Matsuo Basho.
Ma-FW:264
On Far Hills. K. Takahama.
Ma-FW:273
On the Mountain Pass.
Matsuo Bashö. Pa-SG:180
On the Road to Nara. Matsuo Bashö.
Ar-TP3:203, Pa-SG:91
Once Only. Ato-Tobira. Pa-SG:42
Ono Yo Yoshiki. Kokin Shü.
Ho-LP:4, Pa-SG:35
Over the Wintry. Soseki.
Be-CS:6, La-PV:85
Play About, Do. Baskö.
Au-SP:320, Le-MW:79
Plum Trees. Rankö. Au-SP:347,
Fe-FP:482, Hu-MP:274
Poems of Solitary Delights.
Tachibana Akemi. Ma-FW:235
Pole Vault. Shiro Murana.
Mo-SD:59
Poppies. Hu-MP:247
The Rain Frogs. Rogetsu.
Pa-SG:129
Rain on Castle Island.
H. Kitahara. Ma-FW:118
The Rains of Spring. Lady Ise.
Ar-TP3:170
The Red Peony. Buson. Sh-RP:62
Red Sky in the Morning.
Kobayashi Issa. Ma-FW:213
River-Fog. Fukayabu Kiyowara.
Fe-FP:481
Scampering over Saucers.
Yosa Buson. Ma-FW:266
Sheltering from the Rain.
S. Karai. Ma-FW:119
A Shower. Izembö. Ar-TP3:166
Silent, but. . . .
Tsuboi Shigeji. Ma-FW:234

The Snake. K. Takahama.
Sh-RP:62
The Snake Fled. K. Takahama.
Ma-FW:209
Snow Melting. G. Kato. Ma-FW:9
Solitary Pine. Prince Ichihara.
Pa-SG:161
Something Makes a Sound!
Boncho. Su-FVI:67
A Spark in the Sun. H. Behn.
Be-CS:3, Br-SG:24
Spring Freeze. Buson. Sh-RP:61
Spring in My Hut. Sodo.
Sh-RP:67
The Stillness. Basho. Sh-RP:64
Stop! Don't Swat the Fly.
Kobayashi Issa. Ma-FW:205
The Storm. Chora. Sh-RP:66
Suffering of This World. Issa.
Ba-PO:26
Summer Night. Ranko. Sh-RP:66
The Sun Path. Matsuo Basho.
Pa-SG:92
Taking Leave of a Friend.
Rihaku. Ho-LP:67
Tea Flowers. Rito. Hu-MP:304
Then Settle, Frost!
Otomo Oemaru. Ma-FW:264
Tolling Bells. Lady Kosa.
Pa-SG:23
Up the Barley Rows. Sora.
Au-SP:320
Wake Up! Wake Up! Basho.
Au-SP:72
The Whale. Buson. Au-SP:78
Willows in the Snow. Tsuru.
Hu-MP:273
The Wind Blows Grey.
Naito Meisetsu. Ma-FW:263
Winter. Josö. Li-TU:209,
Pa-SG:103
With His Apology. S. Karai.
Ma-FW:93
Yase: September. G. Snyder.
Mo-BG:44
See also Ba-ST, Be-CS, Be-MC,
Br-FW, Ca-BF, De-PP, Do-TS,
Le-MW, Le-TA, Sh-AM
JASON AND MEDEA
Jason and Medea. A. Lewis.
Rv-CB:1001
When I Came from Colchis.
W. Merwin. Ca-VT:612
JAYS: see also BLUE JAYS
Bird Talk. A. Fisher. Fr-MP:12
Jaybird. Co-HP:23
Squirrel with Jays. R. Souster.
Co-BBW:23
Winter in Vermont. H. Carruth.
Ca-BP:41

JAYWALKING: see CITY TRAFFIC
JAZZ MUSIC: see also BLUES
    (MUSIC)
  Battle Report.   B. Kaufman.
      Ad-CI:93, Lo-TY:252
  Frascati's.   A. Huxley.
      Al-VBP:1200
  From Jazz for Five, 3:Colin Barnes,
      Drums.   J. Smith.   To-MP:194
  From Jazz for Five, 5:Shake Keane,
      Trumpet.   J. Smith.   To-MP:195
  Haiku 9.   E. Knight.   Ra-BP:207
  Harlem Sounds: Hallelujah Corner.
      W. Browne.   Bo-AN:173
  I Too Hear America Singing.
      H. Bond.   Lo-IT:11
  J. Is for Jazz-Man.   E. Farjeon.
      Su-FVI:14
  Jazz.   F. Brown.   Hu-PN:395
  Jazz Band in a Parisian Cabaret.
      L. Hughes.   Un-MA:553
  Jazz Fantasia.   C. Sandburg.
      Hi-WP II:151, Hu-PN:483,
      La-OC:73, Un-MA:203
  The Jazz of This Hotel.
      V. Lindsay.   Bo-HF:166
  The Jazz World.   M. Gill.
      Jo-VC:26
  Jazzonia.   L. Hughes.   Bo-AN:63
  Jelly Wrote.   A. Spillman.
      Be-MA:123
  Lambda.   M. Tolson.   Be-MA:24,
      Hu-PN:141
  Lester Young.   T. Joans.   Be-MA:101,
      Bo-AN:171, Mo-BG:55
  Miles' Delight.   T. Joans.
      Hu-PN:396
  Mingus.   B. Kaufman.   Ad-PB:262,
      Be-MA:131
  Rhythm Is a Groove 2.
      L. Neal.   Jo-SA:105
  Satchmo.   M. Tolson.   Ra-BP:119
  The Sound of Afroamerican History.
      S. Anderson.   Ad-PB:441
  Sounds of Buddy Tate.   D. Rasey.
      Lo-IT:112
  Two Jazz Poems.   C. Hines, Jr.
      Bo-AN:184, Du-RG:74
  Walking Parker Home.   B. Kaufman.
      Ad-PB:265, Be-MA:130
JEALOUSY: see also ENVY;
    HUMOR - JEALOUSY
  Anashuya and Vijaya.   W. Yeats.
      Li-TU:146
  Answer to Jealousy.   M. Prior.
      Al-VBP:514, Un-MW:48
  Binnorie.   Ma-BB:25, Ox-BB:69
  Dialogues, II.   Tr-US I:119
  A Divine Image.   W. Blake.
      Ga-S:156, Gr-CT:436, Ox-BN:25

  Dread.   J. Synge.   Un-MB:182
  Fair Isabell of Rochroyall.
      Ox-BB:144
  The First Tooth.   C. and M. Lamb.
      Ox-BC:143
  How Marigolds Came Yellow.
      R. Herrick.   Ch-B:67, Gr-CT:268
  Incantation Used by a Jealous
      Woman.   Tr-US II:124
  Jealousy.   W. Davenant.   Co-BL:51
  Mary Hamilton.   Ox-BB:328
  Song of a Girl Whose Lover Has
      Married Another Woman.
      Tr-US II:195
  The Step Mother.   H. Adam.
      De-FS:5
  To a White Liberal-Minded Girl.
      J. Oliver.   Ad-II:111
  A Trampwoman's Tragedy.   T. Hardy.
      Ox-BN:825
  Turn All Thy Thoughts.   T. Campion.
      Al-VBP:215
  The Twa Sisters.   De-CH:421,
      Rv-CB:42
  Visions of the Daughters of
      Albion.   W. Blake.   Al-VBP:621
  The Wandering Gadling.
      T. Wyatt.   Rv-CB:79
  When Nightingales Burst into
      Song.   Jurin.   Be-MC:58
  Woman's Song.   Tr-US I:190
  Young Hunting.   Ox-BB:87
  Young Waters.   Fo-OG:31, Ox-BB:321
JEANNE D'ARC: see JOAN OF ARC
JEANS, SIR JAMES HOPWOOD
  Apostrophic Notes from the New-
      World Physics.   E. White.
      Pl-IO:65
JEFFERS, ROBINSON
  In Memory of Robinson Jeffers.
      E. Barker.   Ls-NY:135
JEFFERSON, THOMAS
  America Was Promises.
      A. MacLeish.   Br-AF:250,
      Vi-PP:229
  Ballad of the Common Man.
      A. Kreymborg.   Vi-PP:144
  Brave New World.   A. MacLeish.
      Sh-AP:189
  The Death of Jefferson.
      H. Butterworth.   Hi-TL:76
  Louisiana Purchase.   B. Clark.
      Ke-TF:360
  Thomas Jefferson.
      R. and S. Benét.   Ar-TP3:42,
      Fe-FP:425, Sh-RP:257
JEGON, JOHN
  Bad Bishop Jegon.   Gr-GB:186
JEHOVAH: see GOD
JEHU, KING OF ISRAEL
  Jehu.   L. MacNeice.   Wi-LT:460

JELLYFISH: see also HUMOR -
      JELLYFISH
   The Jellyfish.   G. Davis. Le-M:92
   A Jellyfish. M. Moore.   We-PZ:25
   Love Song for a Jellyfish.
      S. Hochman. Co-PU:90
   Song of a Jellyfish. M. Kaneko.
      Sh-AM:60
   Triolet. G. Chesterton. Li-LC:22
JEPHTHAH
   Jepthah's Daughter.
      A. Tennyson. Hi-FO:17
JEREZ, SP.
   Stork in Jerez. L. Lee. Go-BP:81
JEROME, SAINT
   The Thunderer. P. McGinley.
      Pl-EI:109
JERUSALEM
   The Destruction of Jerusalem by
      the Babylonian Hordes.
      I. Rosenberg. Gr-SS:172
   Jerusalem. J. Halevi. Me-PH:61
   Jerusalem: A Prisoner's Song.
      Ga-S:224
   Jerusalem Beggars. R. Potash.
      Ho-TY:357
   Mayor. Y. Amichai. Me-PH:131
   Milton. W. Blake. Al-VBP:622,
      Ga-FB:223, Ha-PO:206, Hi-FO:251,
      Ke-PP:132, Na-EO:32, Ox-BN:40,
      Pl-EI:162, Rv-CB:612, Sm-LG:135
   My Heart Is in the East.
      J. Halevi. Me-PH:61
   The New Jerusalem. Al-VBP:366,
      Go-BP:263
   O Mother, Dear Jerusalem. Ke-TF:190
   Psalm 137. L. Ryzhova. Bo-RU:70
   To a Guide in Jerusalem.
      M. Stiker. Ho-TY:283
JESTERS: see CLOWNS; FOOLS
JESUS CHRIST: see also APOSTLES;
      CHRISTMAS; EASTER; JOSEPH,
      SAINT; MARY, VIRGIN; MESSIAH;
      RESURRECTION; SATIRE - JESUS
      CHRIST; TRINITY
   Above the Bright Blue Sky.
      A. Midlane. Ox-BC:229
   Again. C. Mew. Un-MB:163
   As Kingfishers Catch Fire.
      G. Hopkins. Pl-EI:134,
      Tr-MR:286, Un-MB:45, Wi-LT:45
   At a Calvary near the Ancre.
      W. Owen. Tr-MR:187
   Baha'u'llah in the Garden of
      Ridwan. R. Hayden. Ad-PB:122
   Ballad of the Bread Man.
      C. Causley. To-MP:203
   Ballad of the Golden Bowl.
      S. Hay. Pa-OM:365
   A Ballad of Trees and the Master.
      S. Lanier. Fe-PL:345, Ke-TF:213,
      Sh-AP:134

   The Burning Babe. R. Southwell.
      Al-VBP:150, De-CH:227, Ho-P:158,
      Ma-FW:288, Rv-CB:178, Sm-LG:371
   But God's Own Descent. R. Frost.
      Pl-EI:35, Tr-MR:242
   The Calvaries. P. Williamson.
      Ls-NY:108
   Children of Love. H. Monro.
      Un-MB:235
   A Child's Present. R. Herrick.
      Ox-BC:30
   Christ Climbed Down.
      L. Ferlinghetti. Tr-MR:111
   Christ Hath a Garden Walled About.
      I. Watts. Sm-LG:383
   Christ in Alabama. L. Hughes.
      Ad-PB:73
   Christ in the Universe.
      A. Meynell. Un-MB:65
   The Christ of the Andes.
      E. Markham. Se-PR:85
   A Christmas Hymn. R. Wilbur.
      Tr-MR:99
   Christ's Descent into Hell.
      R. Rilke. Ho-P:231
   The Church. E. Muir. Tr-MR:204
   Church Burning: Mississippi.
      J. Emanuel. Ad-PB:178,
      Hu-PN:374
   The Coming Messiah. Bible. O.T.
      Isaiah. Ba-PO:75, Ga-S:57
   Comparison. J. Bunyan. Ox-BC:36
   The Confession Stone. O. Dodson.
      Ab-MO:72, Lo-TY:238
   The Conqueror. R. Tagore.
      Ga-S:151
   Cradle Song. Pl-EI:189
   Cross Talk. C. Cusack. Ls-NY:88
   The Crystal. S. Lanier. Sh-AP:133
   Defense Rests. V. Miller.
      Un-MA:680
   The Donkey's Owner. C. Sansom.
      Ga-S:152
   E Tenebris. O. Wilde. Un-MB:68
   Easter Hymn. A. Housman.
      Pl-EI:87
   Easter Song. K. Leslie. Tr-MR:134
   Emmaus. R. Rilke. Go-BP:302
   Evil Days. B. Pasternak.
      Tr-MR:119
   Father to the Man. J. Knight.
      Pl-EI:33
   The Feet of Judas. G. McClellan.
      Hu-PN:17
   The Flight into Egypt. W. Auden.
      Ga-S:113, Pl-EI:61
   Garden of Gethsemane.
      B. Pasternak. Tr-MR:122
   The Garden of Olives. R. Rilke.
      Go-BP:293, Tr-MR:124

JESUS CHRIST — cont'd.

General William Booth Enters into
  Heaven. V. Lindsay. Ga-S:221,
  Un-MA:221, Wi-LT:624
Glorious the Sun in Mid-Career.
  C. Smart. Sm-LG:376
God Abides in Men.
  C. Houselander. Ga-S:114
God Has Had Pity on Us. Da-SC:121
Godhead Here in Hiding.
  G. Hopkins. Ga-S:199
The Good Shepherd with the Kid.
  M. Arnold. Go-BP:286
Grant Me Thy Peace.
  Thomas a Kempis. Go-BP:269
The Guest. H. Monro. Go-BP:285
Haiku. R. Lockett. La-IH:132
Hail John's Army. Ga-S:76
Hark a Thrilling Voice Is Sounding.
  E. Caswell. Ga-S:57
The Harrowing of Hell. Ga-S:168
The Hollow Land. W. Morris.
  Gr-CT:48, Re-TW:80
The Holy Innocents. R. Lowell.
  Un-MA:663
A Hymn. P. Fletcher. Rv-CB:320
A Hymn to Christ at the Author's
  Last Going into Germany.
  J. Donne. Al-VBP:263
I Am the Prince. C. Causley.
  Ga-S:102
I Met the Master. Fe-PL:337
I See His Blood upon the Rose.
  J. Plunkett. De-CH:577,
  Fe-PL:331, Tr-MR:132
I Think when I Read That Sweet
  Story of Old. J. Luke.
  Bo-FP:48
I Told Jesus. S. Plumpp.
  Ad-PB:385
Iesu. G. Herbert. Ga-S:99
In Dessexshire as It Befell.
  Gr-GB:316
In the Carpenter Shop. Un-GT:92
In the Deep Museum. A. Sexton.
  Ho-P:229, Un-MA:690
In the Wilderness. R. Graves.
  De-CH:102, Ga-S:144, Pl-EI:105,
  Un-MB:388
The Innumerable Christ.
  H. MacDiarmid. Pl-EI:156
Interrogative. Sister M. Thérèse.
  Tr-MR:228
Jerusalem. W. Blake. Al-VBP:623,
  Gr-CT:295, Ox-BN:42
Jesus and His Mother. T. Gunn.
  Ke-TF:144, Pl-EI:31, To-MP:77
Johnny Appleseed's Hymn to the
  Sun. V. Lindsay. Tr-MR:29
Judas Iscariot. C. Cullen.
  Fe-PL:325

The Lamb. W. Blake. Bo-FP:106,
  Bo-GJ:64, Co-BBW:173, De-CH:87,
  Fe-FP:165, Hi-WP I:139,Hu-MP:199,
  Li-LC:82, Ma-YA:126, Mc-PR:101,
  Mc-WK:125, Ox-BC:85, Pa-RE:78,
  Pl-EI:18, Rv-CB:575, Un-GT:34
Lambs. K. Tynan. De-TT:177
Like a Murderer. I. Manger.
  Ho-TY:272
The Lily of the Valley. Ga-S:171
Lines from a Sampler. Gr-TG:82
The Litany of the Dark People.
  C. Cullen. Pl-EI:155, Tr-MR:154
The Little Black Dog.
  E. Reynolds. Fe-PL:362
Lully, Lulley. De-CH:470
Madeleine in Church. C. Mew.
  Un-MB:162
The Marigold. G. Wither. Rv-CB:333
Milton. W. Blake. Al-VBP:622,
  Ga-FB:223, Ha-PO:206, Hi-FO:251,
  Ke-PP:132, Na-EO:32, Ox-BN:40,
  Pl-EI:162, Rv-CB:612, Sm-LG:135
Miracles. C. Aiken. Un-MA:472
My Dancing Day. Rv-CB:127
My Gift. C. Rossetti.
  Br-BC:174, Br-SS:108, Ch-B:52,
  Fe-FP:23, La-PH:29, Li-LC:87
My Master Hath a Garden.
  De-CH:472
My Song Is Love Unknown.
  S. Crossman. Ox-BC:32
The Mystery. R. Hodgson.
  De-CH:143, Un-MB:192
The New Ghost. F. Shove.
  Go-BP:258
No Beauty We Could Desire.
  C. Lewis. Go-BP:303
no time ago. e. cummings.
  Mc-WS:32
On Lavater's Song of a Christian
  to Christ. J. von Goethe.
  Co-EL:53
On Seeing Two Brown Boys in a
  Catholic Church. F. Horne.
  Ad-PB:55, Hu-PN:146, Lo-TY:212
On the Swag. R. Mason. Ga-S:206
Once in Royal David's City.
  C. Alexander. Ox-BC:201
Peace. H. Vaughan. Ga-S:223,
  Gr-CC:136, Gr-CT:347,
  Hi-WP II:172, Ma-YA:105,
  Pa-HT:163, Pl-EI:9, Rv-CB:409,
  Sm-LG:382
The Pelican. P. de Thaun.
  Mc-WK:43
Pietà. C. Lewis. Go-BP:246
Praise to the Holiest.
  J. Newman. Ga-S:172

Preparations. Al-VBP:353,
   De-CH:464, Ga-S:131,
   Hi-WP I:137, Na-EO:19, Pl-EI:16,
   Rv-CB:116, Sm-LG:378
Quia Amore Langueo. Rv-CB:14
Redemption. G. Herbert. Ha-PO:199,
   Pl-EI:44
The Resurrection. J. Brooks.
   Bo-AN:95, Hu-PN:236
Resurrection. F. Horne. Ad-PB:56
Rock of Ages. A. Toplady.
   Er-FA:476, Rv-CB:554
St. Patrick's Breastplate.
   St. Patrick. Sm-LG:379
Santos, New Mexico. M. Sarton.
   Pl-EI:116
The Second Coming. W. Yeats.
   Mo-GR:89, Pa-GTB:424, Pl-EI:28,
   Tr-MR:236, Un-MB:117, Wi-LT:72
The Seven Joys. Ga-S:185
Seven Stanzas at Easter.
   J. Updike. Pl-EI:36
Sonnet. M. de Guevara. Ga-S:145
Starlight like Intuition Pierced
   the Twelve. D. Schwartz.
   En-PC:128, Sh-AP:222, Tr-MR:94
Still Falls the Rain. E. Sitwell.
   Br-TC:389, Ga-S:161, Tr-MR:131,
   Un-MB:336, Wi-LT:642
Strong Son of God, Immortal Love.
   A. Tennyson. Ma-YA:193,
   Pl-EI:136
Subversive. W. Benét. Tr-MR:116
The Supper after the Last.
   G. Kinnell. En-PC:255
Suzanne. L. Cohen. Mo-GR:33
The Temple. J. Johnson. Tr-MR:203
Through the Dear Might of Him
   Who Walked the Waves.
   J. Heath-Stubbs. Go-BP:289
To a Crucifix. A. Wickham.
   Un-MB:279
To Him That Was Crucified.
   W. Whitman. Tr-MR:177
To the Name above Every Name,
   the Name of Jesus.
   R. Crashaw. Ga-S:97
To the Sun. R. Campbell.
   Ga-S:188, Pl-EI:21
A Tolstoyan Idyll, 1917.
   M. Rawitch. Ho-TY:201
The Transfiguration. E. Muir.
   Go-BP:291
Two Funerals. L. Untermeyer.
   Cr-WS:28
Under a Wiltshire Apple Tree.
   A. De Bary. De-CH:150
Variations on a Line from
   Shakespeare's Fifty-Sixth
   Sonnet. E. Mayo. En-PC:70

What Is He That Comes? W. Herebert.
   Ga-S:187
Who Is That a-Walking in the
   Corn? F. Johnson. Gr-CC:145,
   Hu-PN:92
Who Will Be the Driver? Ga-S:187
The Words of Jesus. W. Benét.
   Tr-MR:116
JESUS CHRIST - ASCENSION
   The Ascension. J. Beaumont.
   Ga-S:187
JESUS CHRIST - CHILDHOOD
   As Mary Was a-Walking. Ga-S:107
   The Bitter Withy. Gr-CT:145,
   Gr-GB:303
   The Carpenter. P. Hartnoll.
   Ga-S:113
   A Child's Prayer. F. Thompson.
   Ga-FB:147, Ox-BC:307, Se-PR:228
   A Christmas Carol. G. Chesterton.
   Ar-TP3:196, Er-FA:517, Se-PR:233
   For a Child in Death. C. Mew.
   Un-MB:160
   The Holy Well. Gr-GB:305,
   Sm-LG:373
   Mother and Child. I. Eastwick.
   Br-SS:155
   Rocking. Cl-DT:28
JESUS CHRIST - CRUCIFIXION:
   see also THE CROSS;
   GETHSEMANE; GOLGOTHA;
   SATIRE - JESUS CHRIST -
   CRUCIFIXION
   All in the April Evening.
   K. Tynan. Gr-TG:81
   All in the Morning. Br-BC:176
   And when They Had Scourged
   Jesus. . . . W. Rodgers.
   Hi-WP I:25
   An Argument - of the Passion of
   Christ. T. Merton. Ga-S:157
   The Ballad of the Goodly Fere.
   E. Pound. Ca-MB:49, Ha-PO:8,
   Hi-FO:53, Un-MA:293, Wi-LT:223
   Calvary. E. Robinson. Un-MA:119
   Christ Crucified. R. Crashaw.
   Se-PR:73
   Christ in the Clay-Pit.
   J. Clemo. Pa-GTB:548
   Christmas Mourning. V. Miller.
   Un-MA:679
   The Cross. A. Tate. Un-MA:539
   Crucifix. E. Olson. Tr-MR:129
   Crucifixion. R. Benally.
   Ba-HI:139
   Crucifixion. Ra-BP:29
   Cruciform. W. Welles.
   Ho-LP:92, Sm-PT:137
   Early Lynching. C. Sandburg.
   Un-MA:208

JESUS CHRIST - CRUCIFIXION
  — cont'd.
  Ecce Homo. D. Gascoyne. Wi-LT:715
  The Elder Tree. Gr-CT:166,
    Gr-GB:307
  The Four Executioners. Ga-S:163
  Golgotha. J. Wheelock. Tr-MR:125
  Good Friday. Gr-CT:187
  He Is the Lonely Greatness.
    M. Rock. De-CH:249
  The Holy Cross. R. Crashaw.
    Ga-S:167
  It Is Finished. J. Wheelock.
    Tr-MR:127
  The Killing. E. Muir. Go-BP:295,
    Tr-MR:126
  Magdalene. B. Pasternak.
    Tr-MR:89
  Me Rueth Mary. Gr-GB:306
  The Moon Shines Bright. Gr-GB:297
  Never Said a Mumbalin' Word.
    Gr-GB:307
  The Pietà, Rhenish, 14th C.,
    The Cloisters. M. Van Duyn.
    Ho-P:281
  The Seven Virgins. De-CH:469,
    Ga-S:158, Gr-CT:189, Gr-GB:311
  Sheep and Lambs. K. Hinkson.
    Go-BP:91, Se-PR:74
  Simon the Cyrenian Speaks.
    C. Cullen. Be-MA:50, Bo-AN:89,
    Ga-S:160, Lo-TY:235, Ra-BP:99,
    Un-MA:570
  Stabat Mater. Jacopone da Todi.
    Ga-S:157
  Suddenly Afraid. Rv-CB:12
  There Is a Green Hill.
    C. Alexander. Ox-BC:203
  Unkept Good Fridays. T. Hardy.
    Tr-MR:128
  Untitled. D. Hine. Br-TC:188
  The Virgin Mary to Christ on the
    Cross. R. Southwell. Al-VBP:151
  The Vision of the Holy Church.
    W. Langland. Go-BP:294
  Were You There when They
    Crucified My Lord? Ra-BP:30
  What Yo' Gwine to Do when Yo'
    Lamp Burn Down? Ra-BP:29
  Woefully Arrayed. Gr-CT:385,
    Rv-CB:68
JESUS CHRIST - LAST SUPPER:
  see LORD'S SUPPER
JESUS CHRIST - LEGENDS
  The Bitter Withy. Gr-CT:145,
    Gr-GB:303
  The Holy Well. Gr-GB:305,
    Sm-LG:373

JESUS CHRIST - NATIVITY:
  see also BETHLEHEM;
    JOSEPH, SAINT; MARY,
    VIRGIN
  Adoration of the Shepherds.
    Ga-S:80
  Advent Meditation. A. Meynell.
    Tr-MR:98
  All in the Morning. Br-BC:176
  And They Came with Haste.
    Sister Mary Irma. Ke-TF:218
  Ane Sang of the Birth of
    Christ. . . . J. Wedderburn.
    Gr-CT:423
  The Annunciation. E. Jennings.
    Ga-S:63
  As I Sat on a Sunny Bank.
    Gr-CT:414, Gr-GB:300
  As Joseph Was Awakening.
    Al-VBP:59, De-TT:174, Gr-TG:75
  Away in a Manger. M. Luther.
    Ar-TP3:195, Bo-FP:193, Br-BC:165,
    Fe-FP:93, Gr-TG:78, Hu-MP:347,
    Ke-TF:78, La-PH:25, Mc-AW:78,
    Un-GT:301
  A Babe Is Born. Ga-S:100
  Ballad of the Epiphany.
    C. Dalmon. Pa-OM:360
  The Barn. E. Coatsworth.
    Au-SP:377, Br-BC:170, Un-GT:288
  Bethlehem. W. Canton. Ha-YA:158
  Bethlehem. P. Hartnoll. Ga-S:108
  Bethlehem of Judea. Br-BC:176
  Birth of Christ. R. Rilke.
    Tr-MR:103
  The Birthday of the Lord. M. Carr.
    Br-BC:161
  Birthday Presents. E. Thomas.
    Mc-AW:75
  Candle and Star. E. Coatsworth.
    Br-BC:168
  Carol. J. Short. Sm-LG:371,
    To-MP:28
  A Carol. F. Weatherly.
    Ha-YA:154
  A Carol for Saint Stephen's Day.
    De-CH:225, Ox-BB:3
  Carol of the Brown King.
    L. Hughes. La-PH:31, Li-LC:86
  The Carol of the Poor Children.
    R. Middleton. Sm-MK:219
  The Cherry-Tree Carol.
    Al-VBP:58, Ga-S:64, Gr-CT:127,
    Gr-GB:299, Ke-TF:47, Ox-BB:1,
    Pa-OM:349, Rv-CB:53
  A Child's Song of Christmas.
    M. Pickthall. Ha-YA:160
  The Christ Child. E. Fowler.
    Se-PR:226
  Christmas. A. Fair. Ho-CT:45

The Christmas Candle.   K. Brown.
  Au-SP:380, Se-PR:224
A Christmas Carol.   H. Behn.
  Br-BC:164
Christmas Carol.   K. Grahame.
  Fe-FP:88, Hu-MP:352
A Christmas Carol.   J. Lowell.
  Sp-OG:319
A Christmas Carol.   C. Rossetti.
  Br-BC:163, Rv-CB:893, Un-GT:287
A Christmas Carol.   Al-VBP:61,
  Bo-FP:202, Er-FA:516, Ga-S:88,
  Ke-TF:46
Christmas Day.   A. Young.
  Cl-DT:25
Christmas Eve.   Bible.   N.T.
  Luke.   Au-SP:381, Bo-FP:190,
  Br-BC:162, Br-SS:106, Fe-FP:91,
  Se-PR:221
Christmas Eve.   J. Davidson.
  Hu-MP:351
Christmas Eve Legend.   F. Frost.
  Br-BC:169
A Christmas Folk-Song. L. Reese.
  Ar-TP3:196, Fe-FP:93, Gr-TG:77,
  Hu-MP:348, Pa-OM:352, Se-PR:228,
  Th-AS:106
A Christmas Hymn.   R. Wilbur.
  To-MP:103
Christmas Is Remembering.
  E. Binns.   Br-BC:175, Br-SS:109
Christmas Landscape.   L. Lee.
  Go-BP:284, Ma-FW:278
Christmas Lullaby.
  U. Troubetzkoy.   Ha-YA:157
Christmas Morning.   E. Roberts.
  Bo-FP:194, Co-PS:172, Hu-MP:348,
  Sh-RP:240, Un-GT:289, Un-MA:269
Christmas Song.   B. Carman.
  Co-PS:165
Christmas Star.   B. Pasternak.
  Ma-FW:282
Christus Natus Est.   C. Cullen.
  Ab-MO:70
The Circle of a Girl's Arms.
  C. Houselander.   Ga-S:95
Come to Your Heaven.
  R. Southwell.   Ga-S:109
The Courts.   A. Meynell. Go-BP:167
Cradle Hymn.   I. Watts.   Au-SP:378,
  Gr-TG:56, Ox-BC:52, Sp-OG:312
The Crow and the Crane. Ma-BB:86
The Expectation.   R. Gales.
  Ga-S:58
First Christmas Night of All.
  N. Turner.   Br-BC:161
The First Nowell.   Al-VBP:62
The Flight in the Desert.
  Brother Antoninus.   Ca-VT:350

The Flight into Egypt.   P. Quennell.
  Wi-LT:630
The Flight into Egypt.   Ga-S:102
For the Nativity. J. Heath-Stubbs.
  Go-BP:284
The Friendly Beasts.   Au-SP:376,
  Br-BC:171, Br-SS:106, Co-PS:175,
  Fe-FP:92, La-PH:28, Pa-OM:353,
  Pa-RE:88
From Far Away.   Sp-OG:317
The Gift.   W. Williams.
  Pe-OA:76, Tr-MR:105
Go Tell It on the Mountain.
  Ab-MO:69
Good Tidings of Great Joy!
  Mrs. C. Alexander.   Gr-TG:76,
  Ke-TF:183
He Came All So Still.
  Sm-LG:368, Tu-WW:12
The House of Christmas.
  G. Chesterton.   Go-BP:254,
  Tr-MR:109, Un-MB:210
How Grand and How Bright.
  Gr-GB:302
How Many Miles to Bethlehem.
  F. Chesterton.   De-TT:176,
  Ke-TF:217
A Hymn of the Nativity.
  R. Crashaw.   Al-VBP:437
I Sing of a Maiden.   Al-VBP:20,
  De-CH:19, De-TT:175, Ma-BB:90,
  Ma-FW:288, Re-TW:65, Rv-CB:10,
  Sm-LG:367, Un-GT:288
I Wonder as I Wander.   Pl-EI:204
In Dulci Jubilo.   J. Wedderburn.
  Gr-CT:413
In Freezing Winter Night.
  R. Southwell.   Ma-FW:277,
  Re-TW:63, Un-GT:287
In Terra Nostra.   A. Tarbat.
  Go-BP:283
In the Town.   Ga-S:68
The Innkeeper's Cat.
  U. Troubetzkoy.   Ke-TF:325
Instead of Neat Inclosures.
  R. Herrick.   Gr-CT:415
It Came upon the Midnight Clear.
  E. Sears.   Bo-FP:192, Er-FA:510,
  Fe-FP:94, Ke-TF:223
The Holly and the Ivy.   De-CH:228,
  De-TT:114, Gr-CT:421, Gr-GB:301
Jolly Wat.   Al-VBP:21, Ma-BB:91
Journey of the Magi.   T. Eliot.
  Br-TC:114, Er-FA:478, Ga-S:100,
  Ha-PO:43, Hi-WP II:174,
  Pe-OA:132, Pl-EI:26, Sh-AP:184,
  Sm-LG:372, Tr-MR:107, Un-MA:397,
  Wi-LT:305
Kid Stuff.   F. Horne.   Ab-MO:76,
  Ad-PB:56, Bo-AN:41, Bo-HF:109,
  Hu-PN:148, Li-TU:247

JESUS CHRIST - NATIVITY
— cont'd.
The Kings from the East.
  H. Heine.   Gr-CT:424
The Light in the Temple.
  W. Benét.   Tr-MR:113
The Light of Bethlehem.   J. Tabb.
  Se-PR:222
Long, Long Ago.   Ar-TP3:196,
  Co-PS:176, Fe-FP:91, Hu-MP:347,
  La-PH:24, La-PV:87, Mc-AW:76,
  Pa-RE:104
Lullay, Lullay, Thou Lytil Child.
  De-CH:627
The Magi.   J. Milton.   Gr-CT:426
The Maid-Servant at the Inn.
  D. Parker.   Ke-TF:220
Mangers.   W. Davies.   Tr-MR:104
Mary and Gabriel.   Ga-S:58
Mary's Song.   E. Farjeon.
  Gr-TG:78
Masters, in This Hall.   W. Morris.
  Gr-CT:419
The Mother's Tale.   E. Farjeon.
  Br-BC:165
The Mystic Magi.   R. Hawker.
  Gr-CT:425
Nativity.   A. Laluah.   Lo-TY:164
New Year's Day.   R. Lowell.
  Wi-LT:572
Night of Marvels.
  Sister Violante do Ceo. Ga-S:71
Noël.   La-PH:27
Now Every Child.   E. Farjeon.
  Br-BC:167
Nowell Sing We.   Gr-CT:419
Ode on the Morning of Christ's
  Nativity.   J. Milton.
  Ma-YA:93, Pa-GTB:42
On Christmas Eve.   E. Pierce.
  Tr-MR:104
On Christmas Morn.   R. Sawyer.
  Fe-FP:89, La-PH:26, La-PV:88
On the Morning of Christ's
  Nativity.   J. Milton.   Sm-LG:368
Ox and Donkey's Carol.
  Sister Maris Stella.   Se-PR:223
The Oxen.   T. Hardy.   Ga-S:86,
  Go-BP:92, Ha-PO:117, No-CL:281,
  Tr-MR:109, Un-MB:33, Wi-LT:21
The Path of the Stars.   T. Jones.
  Tr-MR:139
Prayer.   J. Farrar.   Se-PR:222
Prince of Peace.   Bible. O.T.
  Isaiah.   Go-BP:283
Rest of the Nations.   G. Mellen.
  Ba-PO:69
The Riding of the Kings.
  E. Farjeon.   Ha-YA:159
St. Joseph and God's Mother.
  Ga-S:78

Sans Day Carol.   Ga-S:86
The Shepherd and the King.
  E. Farjeon.   Ar-TP3:196
The Shepherd upon a Hill. Rv-CB:11
The Shepherds at Bethlehem.
  Gr-CT:418
Shepherd's Song at Christmas.
  L. Hughes.   Ab-MO:73
The Shepherd's Tale.   J. Kirkup.
  Co-PT:62
Silent Night.   J. Mohr.   Er-FA:515
Special Starlight.   C. Sandburg.
  Tr-MR:101
The Stable.   M. Coleridge.
  Ga-S:80
Sweet Was the Song.   Co-PS:165
Take Frankincense, O God.
  C. Fitz-Geffry.   Gr-CT:426
Terly Terlow.   Rv-CB:56
The Three Kings.   R. Dario.
  Ab-MO:74
The Three Kings. H. Longfellow.
  Pa-OM:357, Sp-OG:314, Un-GT:290
To the Nativity.
  F. Gonzalez de Eslava.   Ga-S:94
Twelfth Night Song of the Camels.
  E. Coatsworth.   Bo-HF:72,
  Fe-FP:171
Unto Us a Son Is Given.
  A. Meynell.   Se-PR:227,
  Tr-MR:102
The Virgin's Slumber Song.
  F. Carlin.   Ha-YA:156
Vision and Prayer.   D. Thomas.
  Wi-LT:553
We Three Kings of Orient Are.
  J. Hopkins.   Ke-TF:229,
  La-PH:30
When Christ Was Born.   J. Tabb.
  Gr-TG:80
When Crist Was Born of Mary Free.
  Ma-YA:26
While Shepherds Watched Their
  Flocks by Night.   N. Tate.
  Bo-FP:192, Ke-TF:224
Why Do the Bells of Christmas
  Ring.   E. Field.   Ar-TP3:195,
  Au-SP:381, Bo-FP:200, Ha-YA:155,
  La-PH:23
The Witnesses.   C. Sansom.
  Ma-FW:287
JESUS CHRIST - PRAISE
Alleluia, Hearts to Heaven and
  Voices Raise. C. Wordsworth.
  Ke-TF:195
Christ Whose Glory Fills the
  Skies. C. Wesley. Ga-S:178
Fairest Lord Jesus. Ke-TF:184
Flowers in a Garden.   C. Smart.
  Gr-TG:28
Ride On in Majesty. H. Milman.
  Ga-S:152, Ke-TF:194

JESUS CHRIST - RESURRECTION:
see RESURRECTION
JEWELRY: see also BEADS;
PRECIOUS STONES
Adgulé, Madgulé. Ca-MU:8
Painter. J. Schevill. Du-SH:156
JEWS: see also HEBREW VERSE;
ISRAEL; JERUSALEM; JUDAISM;
PALESTINE; YIDDISH LANGUAGE;
YIDDISH VERSE; and names of
rulers, as DAVID, KING OF
ISRAEL, and leaders, as JOSHUA
Abraham Scolds Lot. I. Manger.
Ho-TY:274
Aishah-Schëchinah. R. Hawker.
Ox-BN:461
The Alphabet. K. Shapiro.
Tr-MR:64
At Fifty. J. Glatstein. Ho-TY:328
A Beard Wishes to Escape.
A. Lutzky. Ho-TY:265
The Beginning. J. Glatstein.
Ho-TY:335
Being a Jew. A. Zeitlin.
Ho-TY:318
By the Rivers of Babylon. Bible.
O.T. Psalms. Me-PH:30
Christmas. M. Leib. Ho-TY:93
Come Now, Let's. J. Glatstein.
Ho-TY:326
East Broadway. M. Leib. Ho-TY:92
Exodus. Caedmonian Poems.
Ma-YA:10
Feast of the Ram's Horn.
H. Shapiro. Ca-VT:530
The Funeral. M.J. Ba-PO:180
Ghetto Song. J. Glatstein.
Ho-TY:332
Go Down, Moses. Ab-MO:79,
Pl-EI:101
God of Mercy. K. Molodowsky.
Ho-TY:289
Good Night, Wide World.
J. Glatstein. Ho-TY:333
The Hebrew of Your Poets, Zion.
C. Reznikoff. Ca-VT:181
Here Lives the Jewish People.
H. Leivick. Ho-TY:120
Hugh of Lincoln. De-CH:408,
Ox-BB:317
I Believe. A. Zeitlin. Ho-TY:321
I Sit with My Dolls. Ba-PO:179,
Cr-WS:131
Inscription on My Gravestone.
M. Leib. Ho-TY:95
The Invitation. Bible. O.T.
Isaiah. Me-PH:44
Invocation: Hasidic Song.
L. Isaac of Berditshev.
Pl-EI:193
I've Never Been Lost. I. Feffer.
Ho-TY:188

Jew. J. Randall. Ra-BP:278
The Jew. I. Rosenberg. Un-MB:352
A Jew. J. Segal. Ho-TY:156
The Jew at Christmas Eve.
K. Shapiro. Ca-VT:373
A Jewish Cemetery near Leningrad.
I. Brodsky. Bo-RU:18
The Jewish Conscript. F. Frank.
Ba-PO:135
Jews at Haifa. R. Jarrell.
Un-MA:649
Kibbutz Sabbath. L. Amittai.
Pl-EI:192
The Last to Sing. D. Einhorn.
Ho-TY:82
Late Autumn in Montreal. J. Segal.
Ho-TY:153
Let Other People Come as Streams.
C. Reznikoff. Ca-VT:188
The Light of Summer's End.
I. Schwartz. Ho-TY:146
Like a Murderer. I. Manger.
Ho-TY:272
The Murder of Moses. K. Shapiro.
Pl-EI:102
My Home, Zlochev. M. Halpern.
Ho-TY:109
My Shadow. J. Rubinstein.
Ho-TY:240
National Thoughts. Y. Amichai.
Me-PH:131
The New World. A. Reisen.
Ho-TY:71
New Year's. C. Reznikoff.
Ca-VT:189
Ode for My Father's Eightieth
Birthday. R. Potash. Ho-TY:358
The 151st Psalm. K. Shapiro.
Pl-EI:163
Out of the Past. S. Halkin.
Ho-TY:186
Pictures of Jews. C. Guri.
Me-PH:122
Poem. J. Friedman. Ho-TY:367
Poem. M. Yungman. Ho-TY:365
Poem for Adolph Eichman.
J. Harriman. Lo-IT:42
Poem - 1959. S. Halkin. Ho-TY:187
Psalm 137. L. Ryzhova. Bo-RU:70
Rabbi Yussel Luksh of Chelm.
J. Glatstein. Ho-TY:246
Rejoice Not, O Israel, for Joy.
Bible. O.T. Hosea. Me-PH:46
Sabbath Is Gone. D. Hofstein.
Ho-TY:174
Sabbath Night. I. Feffer.
Ho-TY:189
The Sacrificial Knife and the
Simple Saw. E. Steinberg.
Ho-TY:232
The Silver Tray. N. Alterman.
Me-PH:112
Simple Song. B. Fundoianu. Mc-AC:78

JEWS — cont'd.
So What if I've Been Circumcised?
I. Feffer. Ho-TY:189
Song of the Sabbath.
K. Molodowsky. Ho-TY:285
A Star Blooms. N. Minkoff.
Ho-TY:260
To a Gentile Poet. M. Leib.
Ho-TY:93
To Moses Ibn Ezra in Christian
Spain. J. Halevi. Me-PH:60
To Yesenin. J. Rubinstein.
Ho-TY:239
The Valley of Men. U. Greenberg.
Me-PH:93
Vilna. M. Kulbak. Ho-TY:216
A Wedding at Harvest Time.
N. Bomze. Ho-TY:227
Weeping and Singing. C. Tiempo.
Tr-MR:85
When Israel. W. Scott. Al-VBP:676
White Night. K. Molodowsky.
Ho-TY:288
Without Jews. J. Glatstein.
Ho-TY:331
Women Songs, I. K. Molodowsky.
Ho-TY:284
A Word in Jewish Ears.
A. Galich. Bo-RU:34
Yiddish Poets in New York.
M. Stiker. Ho-TY:281
Your People Are Drowning in Blood.
S. Tchernichovsky. Me-PH:80
JEWS - HOLIDAYS: see also HANUKKAH
Blessing for Light. Th-AS:176
Blessings for Chanukah.
J. Sampter. Ar-TP3:191
Dreidel Song. E. Rosenzweig.
Ar-TP3:191
Eight Are the Lights. I. Orleans.
Th-AS:177
For Hanukkah. H. Bialik.
Ar-TP3:191
Piyyut for Rosh Hashana.
C. Guri. Me-PH:124
A Song of Always. E. Rosenzweig.
Ar-TP3:191, Th-AS:178
JEWS - PERSECUTION: see also
CONCENTRATION CAMPS;
GHETTOS; EICHMANN, KARL
ADOLF; NATIONAL SOCIALISM
At the Last. A. Lifschutz.
Kr-OF:125
Aunt Dvorah. J. Segal. Ho-TY:157
Babi Yar. Y. Yevtushenko.
Ca-MR:54
A Camp in the Prussian Forest.
R. Jarrell. Pe-OA:227,
Un-MA:644
The Coat. C. Grade. Ho-TY:338

Elegy for the Soviet Yiddish
Writers. C. Grade. Ho-TY:339
For All That Ever Has Been Ours.
Z. Landau. Ho-TY:97
The Gift. J. Ciardi. Wi-LT:670
Home. K. Gershon. Cr-WS:132
The Jewish Cemetery at Newport.
H. Longfellow. Ke-PP:69,
Pa-HT:22, Sh-AP:34
Lament at Night. H. Leivick.
Ho-TY:119
More Light, More Light. A. Hecht.
Br-TC:182, Ca-VT:505
My Father's Boots. I. Spiegel.
Ho-TY:349
My Grandmother. K. Shapiro.
Ca-VT:372
1917. P. Markish. Ho-TY:185
On Slaughter. C. Bialik. Me-PH:74
The Other Looks at Me.
J. Rubinstein. Ho-TY:240
The Permanent Delegate. Y. Suhl.
Ke-PP:71
Refugee Blues. W. Auden.
Hi-WP I:122, Wi-LT:472
Russia-1923. S. Halkin. Ho-TY:186
The Sacrificial Knife.
I. Spiegel. Ho-TY:349
Scenario. J. Segal. Ho-TY:158
Security. M. Hamburger.
En-PC:223
Smoke. J. Glatstein. Ho-TY:331
Song of My Indifference.
D. Hofstein. Ho-TY:175
They Got You Last Night. A. Kurtz.
Ke-PP:75
To the Mound of Corpses in the
Snow. U. Greenberg. Me-PH:95
Wagons. J. Glatstein. Ho-TY:330
We Were Not like Dogs.
U. Greenberg. Me-PH:98
JEZEBEL, QUEEN OF ISRAEL
Jehu. L. MacNeice. Wi-LT:460
JOAN OF ARC
The Good Joan. L. Reese.
Ar-TP3:37, Fe-FP:468, Hu-MP:161,
Th-AS:194
Henry VI, Part 1.
W. Shakespeare. Hi-FO:96
JOB
The Beauty of Job's Daughters.
J. MacPherson. En-PC:289
The Book of Job. H. Leivick.
Ho-TY:126
The Complaint to God. Bible.
O.T. Job. Me-PH:18
God's Thanks to Job. R. Frost.
Tr-MR:223
Job. E. Sewell. Pl-EI:104
My Soul Is Weary of My Life. Bible.
O.T. Job. Pl-EI:67

JOGGING RHYMES
  The Cattie Rade to Paisley.
    Mo-TL:78
  Cock-a-Doodle-Doo! Ir-BB:120,
    Li-LB:96, Mo-MGT:125, Mo-TL:88
  Dance to Your Daddy. Mother
    Goose. Ar-TP3:100, De-PO:6,
    Li-LB:10, Mo-MGT:181, Mo-NR:24,
    Mo-TL:86, Wr-RM:50
  Down at the Station, Early Every
    Morning. Mo-TL:80
  Father and Mother and Uncle John.
    Mo-TL:83, Sp-TM:17
  Gee Up, My Horse, to Budleigh
    Fair. Mo-TL:79
  Here Comes a Lady, with Her Little
    Baby. Mo-TL:82
  Here Goes My Lord. Ir-BB:235,
    Mo-TL:81, Wr-RM:21
  Hey Diddle Dinky, Poppety, Pet.
    Mo-TL:79
  Hippity-Hop to the Sweetie Shop.
    Mo-TL:79
  Husky Hi. Ar-TP3:101
  I Had a Little Pony. Mother
    Goose. Au-SP:19, Bl-OB:115,
    Bo-FP:131, De-TT:20, Li-LB:82,
    Mo-MGT:179, Mo-NR:128,
    Mo-TL:82, Wr-RM:83
  Jog On, Jog On. W. Shakespeare.
    Al-VBP:196, Ar-TP3:84, Gr-CT:49,
    Gr-GB:205, Li-SR:81, Rv-CB:206,
    Sm-LG:304, Sp-OG:249
  John Cook Had a Grey Mare.
    Bl-OB:115, De-TT:20, Mo-TL:84,
    Rv-ON:29, Wi-MG:56
  Katie Beardie Had a Cow. Mo-TL:87
  Little Johnnie Morgan. Ir-BB:234,
    Mo-TL:80
  Little Jumping Joan. Mother
    Goose. Ar-TP3:101, Ho-ME:9,
    Li-LB:43, Mo-CC:(3), Mo-MGT:21,
    Mo-NR:126, Mo-TL:88, Wr-RM:14
  Ride a Cock-Horse to Banbury Cross.
    Ar-TP3:100, Au-SP:15, Bo-FP:10,
    De-PO:8, Er-FA:507, Fr-WO:32,
    Ir-BB:11, Li-LB:10, Mo-MGT:149,
    Mo-NR:7, Mo-TL:77, Wi-MG:8,
    Wr-RM:30
  Ride Away. Ar-TP3:101, Ir-BB:236,
    Mo-MGT:213, Mo-TL:79, St-FS:201,
    Wr-RM:26
  Rub a Dub Dub. De-PO:16, Ir-BB:38,
    Li-LB:52, Mo-NR:18, Mo-TL:79,
    On-TW:14
  This Is the Way the Ladies Ride.
    Mother Goose. Ar-TP3:77,
    De-PO:10, Li-LB:11, Mo-MGT:189,
    Mo-NR:52, Mo-TL:81, Wi-MG:29,
    Wr-RM:102

  To Market, to Market. Mother Goose.
    Ar-TP3:100, Au-SP:18, Bo-FP:115,
    De-PO:8, Er-FA:507, Ir-BB:236,
    Li-LB:105, Mo-MGT:136, Mo-NR:20,
    Mo-TL:77, Sp-TM:25, 27, 33,
    Wr-RM:19
  Trit Trot to Boston. Mo-TL:78
  Trot, Trot, Horsie. Mo-TL:78
  Yankee Doodle. De-PO:22, Gr-CT:87,
    Gr-GB:166, Ir-BB:234, Mo-CC:(17),
    Mo-MGT:162, Mo-TL:85
  Yankee Doodle Is a Tune. Mo-TL:85
JOHN, SAINT (APOSTLE)
  After Reading St. John the Divine.
    G. Derwood. Wi-LT:685
  Peter and John. E. Wylie.
    Ca-MB:46, Tr-MR:87, Un-MA:279
  The Seven Virgins. De-CH:469,
    Ga-S:158, Gr-CT:189, Gr-GB:311
JOHN, SAINT (THE BAPTIST)
  Saint John. E. Coatsworth.
    Tr-MR:86
  St. John Baptist. S. Keyes.
    Ga-S:67
  Saint John the Baptist.
    W. Drummond. Ga-S:66, Pa-GTB:41,
    Pl-EI:106, Rv-CB:330
JOHN, KING OF ENGLAND
  King John and the Abbot of
    Canterbury. Sp-OG:147,
    Un-GT:120
  The Reeds of Runnymede.
    R. Kipling. Hi-FO:79
JOHN OF AUSTRIA (DON JUAN)
  Lepanto. G. Chesterton.
    'Ga-FB:196, Hi-FO:119, Un-MB:205
JOHN BARLEYCORN: see BARLEY;
    INTOXICATION
JOHN HENRY
  The Birth of John Henry. M. Tolson.
    Lo-TY:213, Ra-BP:118
  Folk-Tune. R. Wilbur. Br-AF:120
  John Henry. Br-AF:113
  John Henry. Ab-MO:81, Bo-HF:104,
    Co-RM:225, Er-FA:407, Ga-S:124,
    Hi-TL:159, Ra-BP:12
  Strange Legacies. S. Brown.
    Ad-PB:62, Lo-TY:218
JOHN SILVER
  A Ballad of John Silver.
    J. Masefield. Co-SS:13,
    Hu-MP:421, Na-EO:163
JOHNNY APPLESEED: see CHAPMAN,
    JOHN (JOHNNY APPLESEED)
JOHNNY-JUMP-UPS
  The Faithless Flowers. M. Widdemer.
    Hu-MP:258, Th-AS:84
  Wise Johnny. E. Falls.
    Ar-TP3:200, Br-SG:7, Br-SS:129
JOHNSON, JACK (JOHN ARTHUR)
  My Lord, What a Morning. W. Cuney.
    Ab-MO:90, Lo-TY:236

JOHNSON, JACK (JOHN ARTHUR)
— cont'd.
Strange Legacies. S. Brown.
Ad-PB:62, Lo-TY:218
JOHNSON, LYNDON BAINES
Ode to Mayor Locker. D. Levy.
Lo-IT:78
JOHNSON, SAMUEL (DR. JOHNSON)
Epitaph on Dr. Johnson.
S. Jenyns. Co-EL:69
JOKES: see also HUMOR - JOKES;
SATIRE - JOKES; TRICKS
Lock and Key. Wr-RM:56
JONAH: see also HUMOR - JONAH
Jonah. R. Jarrell.   Tr-MR:83
JONATHAN, SON OF SAUL
David's Lament. Bible. O.T.
Samuel. Gr-CT:343, Me-PH:17
JONES, JOHN PAUL
John Paul Jones. R. Gilder.
Se-PR:124
An Old-Time Sea Fight.
W. Whitman. Pa-OM:168,
Un-MA:57, Vi-PP:130
Paul Jones. Vi-PP:132
Paul Jones's Victory.   Em-AF:425
The Stately Southerner.
Em-AF:423
JONSON, BEN
Ah, Ben. R. Herrick.   No-CL:94
Ben Jonson Entertains a Man
from Stratford. E. Robinson.
Un-MA:127
His Prayer to Ben Jonson.
R. Herrick. Ha-PO:226,
Pl-ML:108
A Mirror for Poets. T. Gunn.
Pl-ML:100, Wi-LT:722
On Ben Jonson. S. Godolphin.
Rv-CB:383
pete the parrot and shakespeare.
D. Marquis. Pl-ML:102
To Ben Jonson. T. Randolph.
No-CL:94
JORDAN RIVER
One More River. Cl-DT:52
JOSEPH, SAINT: see also
MARY, VIRGIN
As Joseph Was Awakening.
Al-VBP:59, De-TT:174, Gr-TG:75
The Cherry-Tree Carol.
Al-VBP:58, Ga-S:64, Gr-CT:127,
Gr-GB:299, Ke-TF:47, Ox-BB:1,
Pa-OM:349, Rv-CB:53
The Flight into Egypt. Ga-S:102
In the Town. Ga-S:68
Joseph's Suspicion. R. Rilke.
Tr-MR:99
Mary and Gabriel. Ga-S:58
Mary Passed This Morning.
O. Dodson. Ad-PB:127

St. Joseph and God's Mother.
Ga-S:78
JOSHUA
Joshua Fit de Battle of Jericho.
Ra-BP:24
Little David. Ab-MO:80
JOURNALISM: see HUMOR -
JOURNALISM; NEWSPAPERS
JOURNEYS: see TRAVEL AND
TRAVELERS; VOYAGES
JOVE: see JUPITER (ROMAN GOD)
JOWETT, BENJAMIN
I Am the Great Professor Jowett.
Co-FB:76
JOY: see also HAPPINESS; LAUGHTER;
PLEASURE
Afternoon on a Hill. E. Millay.
Ar-TP3:176, Au-SP:350, Cl-FC:24,
Fe-FP:269, Hu-MP:64, La-PV:170,
Pe-FB:75
All Things Wait upon Thee.
C. Rossetti. Sp-OG:280
L'Allegro. J. Milton.
Al-VBP:389, Er-FA:37, Pa-GTB:94,
Rv-CB:369
Alleluya. R. Dario. Lo-TY:88
Amo, Amas. J. O'Keefe.
Co-BL:78, De-CH:606, Gr-CT:60
And Dancing. I. Eastwick.
Hu-MP:35
And Every Sky Was Blue and Rain.
R. Hodgson. Ha-LO:105
April. R. Emerson. Al-VBP:806
Away with Funeral Music.
R. Stevenson. Hi-WP II:1
Ayii, Ayii (The Great Sea).
Ho-SD:80
Bab-Lock-Hythe. L. Binyon.
Hi-WP II:38, Mo-SD:132
Barefoot Days. R. Field.
Fe-FP:229, Ha-YA:66
Barter. S. Teasdale. Fe-FP:21,
Ga-FB:5, Hu-MP:71, Th-AS:199
Beautiful Sunday. J. Falstaff.
Co-BN:33
The Birds. K. Finnell. Ho-CT:24
Blue Lake of Life. Wo-HS:(15)
A Boy's Summer Song. P. Dunbar.
Br-SS:171, Sh-RP:17
Bring Me the Sunset in a Cup.
E. Dickinson. Un-MA:99
Carmina Burana. Pa-SG:92
Celebrated Return. C. Major.
Be-MA:143, Bo-AN:182
Chant. O. Williams. Tr-MR:34
Chelsea Morning. J. Mitchell.
Mo-GR:119
The Cherry Tree Blossomed.
Tomonori. Le-MW:129
Christmas Carol. K. Grahame.
Fe-FP:88, Hu-MP:352

Clap Hands. D. Palmer. Sc-TN:178
Cloudy Days. A. Coor. Ho-CT:43
David's Song. R. Browning.
  Ga-FB:11
Dawn. N. Kaplan. Ad-II:33
Dawn Is a Feeling. M. Pinder.
  Mo-GR:117
Day of These Days. L. Lee.
  Co-BN:108
The Day with a White Mark.
  C. Lewis. Go-BP:250
Days Too Short. W. Davies.
  Un-MB:175
Dead Man's Song. Ma-BH:31,
  Tr-US I:21
Deciduous Spring. R. Warren.
  Un-MW:170
The Delight Song of Tsaoi-Talee.
  N. Momaday. Ni-CD:89
Do Not Expect Again a Phoenix
  Hour. C. Day Lewis.
  Un-MB:423, Wi-LT:427
Dream Variation. L. Hughes.
  Ad-PB:74, Hu-PN:183, Jo-SA:129,
  Pe-M:88
Durham Old Women. Gr-GB:175
Easter. G. Hopkins. Ga-S:179
An Easter Carol. C. Rossetti.
  Bo-FP:245, Hu-MP:334, Se-PR:77
Easter Hymn. M. Thwaites.
  Tr-MR:133
Easter Joy. N. Turner. Ha-YA:49
Ecstasy. R. Taylor. Gr-SS:107
8 May 1967. M. Korte. Sc-TN:120
Endymion. J. Keats. Al-VBP:788,
  Er-FA:264, Ma-YA:186, Mc-PR:89,
  Ox-BN:335
Eternity. W. Blake. Ox-BN:26
Everybody Laugh. L. Hale.
  Ba-HI:138
Exultation Is the Going.
  E. Dickinson. Rv-CB:906,
  Sh-AP:127
A Field of Light. T. Roethke.
  Br-TC:346
The Fisher's Life. I. Walton.
  Bo-FP:255
Freedom in Mah Soul. D. Cannon.
  Hu-PN:281
Give Me the Splendid Silent Sun.
  W. Whitman. Co-BN:232,
  Fe-FP:263, Mo-BG:20, Un-MA:84
Gladde Things. Ar-TP3:197
The Gladness of May.
  W. Wordsworth. Ha-YA:57
Go Not Too near a House of Rose.
  E. Dickinson. Un-MA:101
Good and Bad. J. Stephens.
  Un-MB:267
A Good World. Issa. Le-MW:5

The Happy World. W. Rands.
  Bo-FP:87
Have at It! Br-FW:10
He Died a Second Time, 6. In
  the Countryside. Ai-Ch'ing.
  Hs-TC:306
The Heart Asks Pleasure First.
  E. Dickinson. Ha-PO:149,
  Rv-CB:898, Un-MA:96
Hey, Nonny No! Al-VBP:353,
  De-CH:188, Gr-BT:177, Gr-CT:83,
  Sm-LG:389, Sp-OG:280
The Hill. R. Brooke. Al-VBP:1178,
  Co-BL:165, Hi-WP II:109,
  Un-MB:322, Un-MW:171
Holderlin. D. Schwartz. Tr-MR:285
Hope and Joy. C. Rossetti.
  Ox-BC:280
The Housewife. B. Amma. Al-PI:126
Hurrahing in Harvest. G. Hopkins.
  Co-BN:130, Gr-CT:313, Ma-FW:126,
  Rv-CB:946, Un-MB:43
Husa. F. John. Sa-B:108
A Hymn of Nature. R. Bridges.
  Ha-YA:107
I Feel a Bit Happier. C. Foster.
  Le-M:31
I Loved. . . . A. Seegar.
  Ke-TF:111
if up's the word and a world grows
  greener. E. Cummings. Pe-OA:150
Improvised Song of Joy. Le-IB:100,
  Tr-US I:13
In June. N. Perry. Ha-YA:72
In Time of Silver Rain. L. Hughes.
  Ab-MO:9, Ar-TP3:171, Au-SP:310
Infant Joy. W. Blake. Al-VBP:614,
  Bo-GJ:132, Br-BC:41, Br-SS:41,
  Fe-FP:37, Fe-PL:245, Ga-S:97,
  Re-TW:39, Rv-CB:571, Tu-WW:13,
  Un-GT:10
The Invitation. Bible. O.T.
  Psalms. Me-PH:44
Invitation to a Young River Queen.
  D. Etter. St-H:60
Jog On, Jog On. W. Shakespeare.
  Al-VBP:196, Ar-TP3:84, Gr-CT:49,
  Gr-GB:205, Li-SR:81, Rv-CB:206,
  Sm-LG:304, Sp-OG:249
Jonathan Bing Dances for Spring.
  B. Brown. Br-SS:131
Joy. C. Delaney. Hu-PN:180
Joy. L. Hughes. Ab-MO:21
Joy in the Morning. E. Markham.
  Fe-FP:279, Hu-MP:214, Se-PR:107
A Joyful Chant. Le-OE:82
The Juggler. R. Wilbur.
  Mo-BG:15, Sh-AP:232, Wi-LT:595
June's Here. C. Martindale.
  Ho-CT:23

JOY — cont'd.
  Just Simply Alive. Issa.
    Le-IS:21
  The Kayak Paddler's Joy at the
    Weather. Da-SC:41, Le-IB:32,
    Tr-US I:7
  Kids. W. Bynner. Hu-MP:39
  The Kitten and the Falling Leaves.
    W. Wordsworth. Bl-OB:106,
    Ch-B:23, Co-BBW:124, Fe-FP:157,
    Hu-MP:208, Un-GB:18, Un-GT:52
  Knee-Deep in June. J. Riley.
    Sp-OG:291
  L and S. M. Kulasretha.
    Al-PI:99
  Lalla Rookh. T. Moore. Li-SR:63
  Laugh and Be Merry. J. Masefield.
    Er-FA:21, Un-MB:228
  Laughing Song. W. Blake.
    Ar-TP3:117, Bo-FP:269, Bo-GJ:41,
    Co-PS:109, De-CH:187, Gr-EC:45,
    Mc-WK:26, Ox-BC:87, Re-TW:76,
    Rv-CB:587, Un-GT:11
  Laughter. M. Waddington.
    Do-WH:14
  Let Me Enjoy. T. Hardy.
    Al-VBP:1049, Ga-FB:10, Tr-MR:53
  Lighthearted William.
    W. Williams. Ha-LO:36,
    Ha-PO:76, Kh-VA:77, Mo-BG:45
  The Little Shepherd's Song.
    W. Percy. Ha-YA:67
  Love in May. J. Passerat.
    Pa-SG:32
  Lucy Lavender. I. Eastwick.
    Br-BC:47, Br-SS:42
  Lying in the Sun. I. Johnson.
    Le-M:78, Le-WR:11
  Madly Singing in the Mountains.
    Po Chü-i. Rv-CB:987
  May Song. Ga-S:184
  Measure Me, Sky! L. Speyer.
    Ad-PE:46, Br-BC:129, Fe-FP:22,
    Hu-MP:63
  Mediterranean Beach: Day after
    Storm. R. Warren. Un-MW:169
  Merry Are the Bells.
    Ar-TP3:106, De-TT:116, Hi-GD:15,
    Ir-BB:118, Lo-LL:108, Sp-AS:38
  Mirth. C. Smart. Ox-BC:72
  Morning in Spring. L. Ginsburg.
    Gr-EC:65
  A Morning Song. E. Farjeon.
    Hi-WP I:6
  The Morning-Watch. H. Vaughan.
    Al-VBP:465, Mo-GR:120
  My Limbs I Will Fling.
    W. Strode. Rv-CB:361
  My Lord, What a Morning. W. Cuney.
    Ab-MO:90, Lo-TY:236

  New Morning. B. Dylan. Mo-GR:112
  The New Year. Br-FW:14
  Night Enchantment. E. Muth.
    Br-SS:170
  Not to Sleep. R. Graves.
    Gr-BT:52
  Now the Full-Throated Daffodils.
    C. Day Lewis. Al-VBP:1224,
    Ga-S:183
  O My Love the Pretty Towns.
    K. Patchen. Ca-VT:344,
    Mc-EA:82
  O Warmth of Summer. Le-IB:37
  The October Redbreast.
    A. Meynell. Un-MB:64
  Ode on Intimations of Immortality
    from Recollections of Early
    Childhood. W. Wordsworth.
    Ho-P:88
  An Offering of Joy.
    S. Eremina. Mo-MI:61
  old laughter. G. Brooks. Ho-TH:52
  On a Bicycle. Y. Yevtushenko.
    Li-TU:19
  On Easter Day. C. Thaxter.
    Fe-FP:74, Ha-YA:51
  The Orchard and the Heath.
    G. Meredith. Ox-BN:691
  The Outcast. J. Stephens.
    Un-MB:267
  Peace and Joy. S. Silverstein.
    Co-PS:107
  Pied Beauty. G. Hopkins.
    Al-VBP:1062, Bo-GJ:47, Er-FA:461,
    Ga-S:16, Hi-WP II:37, Ho-LP:47,
    Ma-FW:101, Mc-PR:182, Mc-WK:16,
    No-CL:269, Ox-BN:865, Pa-GTB:390,
    Pl-EI:124, Re-TW:89, Sm-MK:222,
    Tr-MR:25, Un-GT:246, Un-MB:39,
    Wi-LT:42
  Poem. J. Garrigue. Ls-NY:11
  Poem in Three Parts. R. Bly.
    St-H:4
  Poem of Solitary Delights.
    Tachibana Akemi. Ma-FW:235
  The Ponies. W. Gibson.
    Co-BBW:152, Mc-WK:74
  Psalm of the Fruitful Field.
    A. Klein. Do-WH:88
  The Quartette. W. de la Mare.
    Rv-CB:963
  Rainy Song. M. Eastman.
    Bo-HF:49
  Rarely, Rarely Comest Thou.
    P. Shelley. De-CH:238,
    Ox-BN:294, Pa-GTB:225, Rv-CB:701
  Roses and Thorns. S. Betai.
    Al-PI:109
  The Seven Joys. Ga-S:185
  Silent, Silent Night. W. Blake.
    Rv-CB:604

Sinfonia Domestica. J. Untermeyer.
  Un-MA:333
Sing a Song of Moonlight.
  I. Eastwick. Br-SS:33
Sing a Song of Sunshine.
  I. Eastwick. Br-SS:16
Sometimes. R. Fyleman. Br-SS:24
Sometimes, with Secure Delight.
  J. Milton. Hu-MP:89
Sonamani's Wedding. Ca-MU:22
Song. Tr-US I:43
Song for a Camper. J. Farrar.
  Ha-YA:66
Song in the Wood. J. Fletcher.
  Re-TW:55
Song of Caribou, Musk Oxen.
  Br-MW:140, Ho-SD:67, Le-IB:34,
  Ma-BH:21, Tr-US I:26
Song of Joy. S. Vargus. Ad-II:50
The Song of the Good Samaritan.
  V. Watkins. Wi-LT:450
A Song-Offering. R. Tagore.
  Pa-SG:43
The Song on the Way. Hu-MP:289
Song Sung by a Woman Giving Birth.
  Tr-CB:55, Tr-US I:65
Songs of Joy. W. Davies.
  Un-MB:178
Songs of Nature, II. Tr-US II:137
The Spirit Dances.
  T. Blackburn. Ga-S:191
Spring. W. Blake. Ar-TP3:203,
  Ch-B:99, Fe-FP:71, Ha-YA:25,
  Li-LC:70, Sm-LG:53, Un-GB:7,
  Un-GT:271
Spring. K. Kuskin. La-PV:2
Spring Ecstasy. L. Reese.
  Un-MA:111
Spring Festival Songs. Tr-US II:172
Spring Night. Su Tung-P'o.
  Ho-P:250
Spring Ring-Jingle. M. Lewis.
  Ir-BB:121
Spring Song. W. Blake. Br-SG:3
The Star That Bids the Shepherd
  Fold. J. Milton. Sm-LG:51
Stay, Christmas! I. Eastwick.
  Br-SS:111
Summer Images. J. Clare.
  Gr-CT:117, Ox-BN:318, Rv-CB:716
Summons. R. Francis. Du-RG:62
The Sweet o' the Year.
  G. Meredith. Co-BN:23
There Is Joy. Do-WH:64, Ho-SD:76,
  Le-OE:104, Ma-BH:10
There Was a Maid Went to the Mill.
  Gr-GB:107
This Fevers Me. R. Eberhart.
  Tr-MR:38
This Wonderful World.
  M. Miller. Gr-EC:52

Three Fragments. Br-MW:96
To a Child Running with Out-
  stretched Arms in Canyon de
  Chelly. N. Momaday. Ni-CD:92
To a Poor Old Woman. W. Williams.
  Ho-LP:74, Li-TU:145
To Earthward. R. Frost. Un-MA:180
Triumph of Love. J. Wheelock.
  Un-MA:342
Tune. W. Melaney. Ad-II:51
The Turning Year. Su Tung P'o.
  Rx-OH:87
Under the Misty Sky. Shinsai.
  Le-MW:91
Untitled. Wang Ching-chih.
  Hs-TC:45
Vacation Song. E. Millay.
  Ha-YA:68
Vernal Sentiment. T. Roethke.
  Co-EL:153, Co-PU:9, Mc-WS:125
The Vesture of the Soul.
  G. Russell. Co-PI:174
Victory in Defeat. E. Markham.
  Fe-PL:301
The Vision of Sir Launfal.
  J. Lowell. Er-FA:238,
  Fe-FP:77, Ga-FB:289, Ke-TF:434,
  Mc-PR:37, Se-PR:139, Un-GT:275
Voices Gay. A. Fair. Ho-CT:8
The Waking. T. Roethke.
  Mc-WS:129, Mo-BG:127
Walking at Night. A. Hare.
  Fe-PL:405
Watching Ice Skating. Kuo Mo-jo.
  Hs-TC:42
We Wish to Be Joyful.
  Do-CH:(48)
The Weather Is Gloomy.
  A. Tarasova. Mo-MI:33
Western Town. D. Cannon.
  Hu-PN:282
What You Should Do Each Morning.
  B. Patten. Gr-BT:152
When Spring Comes. M. Patrick.
  Le-M:29
When the Lord Turned Again the
  Captivity. Bible. O.T.
  Psalms. Go-BP:246, Me-PH:28
Who Calls. F. Sayers. Br-SS:130,
  Li-LC:89
The Winter Is Past. Bible. O.T.
  Song of Solomon. Ga-S:185
Woman's Song of Corn Growing.
  Tr-US II:247
Words for the Wind. T. Roethke.
  En-PC:96
The World's Music. G. Setoun.
  Hu-MP:288
Ye That Do the Master's Will.
  C. Wesley. Go-BP:181
Young Love. S. Teasdale. Co-BL:23

JOY — cont'd.
  Youth. A.W. Hu-MP:65
  Youth's the Season. J. Gay.
    Ho-WR:73
JUDAH - HISTORY AND PATRIOTISM
  The End of the World. Bible.
    O.T. Jeremiah. Ba-PO:48,
    Ke-PP:2
  For Out of Zion. Bible. O.T.
    Isaiah. Ba-PO:75
  Judith of Bethulia. J. Ransom.
    Wi-LT:313
  The Prophecies Against Moab,
    Judah, and Israel. Bible.
    O.T. Amos. Me-PH:48
JUDAISM: see also JEWS; JEWS -
    HOLIDAYS; JEWS - PERSECUTION;
    SABBATH; SYNAGOGUES; and names
    of prophets, as ISAIAH
  Feast of the Ram's Horn.
    H. Shapiro. Ca-VT:530
  Piyyut for Rosh-Hashana.
    C. Guri. Me-PH:124
JUDAS ISCARIOT
  The Feet of Judas.
    G. McClellan. Hu-PN:17
  God's Price and Man's Price.
    R. Herrick. Ga-S:167
  Judas. V. Miller. Un-MA:680
  Judas. Ma-FW:160
  Judas Iscariot. C. Cullen.
    Fe-PL:325
  Judas Iscariot. S. Spender.
    Un-MB:478
  Like a Murderer. I. Manger.
    Ho-TY:272
JUDGES AND JUDGING: see also
    COURTS (LAW); LAW; SATIRE -
    JUDGES AND JUDGING
  A Denunciation of the Princes and
    the Prophets. Bible. O.T.
    Micah. Me-PH:51
  I Am as I Am. T. Wyatt. Rv-CB:87
  In Men Whom Men Condemn as Ill.
    J. Miller. Fe-PL:293
  The Law West of the Pecos.
    S. Barker. Fi-BG:64
  Maud Muller. J. Whittier.
    Fe-PL:47, Sp-OG:271
JUDGMENT DAY: see also END OF
    THE WORLD
  The Day of Judgment.
    H. Vaughan. Ga-S:221
  Every Day Thou Might Lere.
    Ma-YA:27
  Femina Contra Mundum.
    G. Chesterton. Tr-MR:249
  Judgment and Sunrise. Bible.
    O.T. Malachi. Me-PH:53
  The Lady's Complaint.
    T. Heath-Stubbs. Br-TC:178

  O Sinnerman. Ga-S:135
  The Plea. J. Drinkwater.
    Tr-MR:249
  Rendezvous with God.
    M. Seljouk. Go-BP:58
JUDITH AND HOLOFERNES
  Judith of Bethulia. J. Ransom.
    Wi-LT:313
JUGGLERS AND JUGGLING
  The Clown. D. Aldis. La-PV:92
  The Juggler. R. Wilbur.
    Mo-BG:15, Sh-AP:232, Wi-LT:595
JUGOSLAVIA: see YUGOSLAVIA
JUKE BOXES: see PHONOGRAPHS
JULIET: see ROMEO AND JULIET
JULIUS CAESAR: see CAESAR, GAIUS
    JULIUS
JULY: see also FOURTH OF JULY
  dry july. A. Adoff. Ad-CI:47
  Evening Clouds. Chang Ch'ou-yü.
    Pa-MV:40
  From My Diary, July 1914.
    W. Owen. Un-MB:364, Wi-LT:356
  July. J. Clare. Un-GT:276
  July. A. Dobson. Pa-RE:37
  July. S. Swett. Ha-YA:81,
    Se-PR:156
  July. L. Tatyanicheva. Pa-SG:94
  July. J. Whittier. Ha-YA:80
  July in Dutchess County.
    B. Deutsch. Ha-WR:63
  July Meadow. L. Driscoll.
    Ha-YA:82
  Labor of Fields.
    E. Coatsworth. Mc-PR:133
  The Month of the Thunder Moon.
    M. Doyle. Ha-YA:84
  The Mowers. M. Benton. Ha-YA:83
  Now Is the Time. M. Moody.
    Ke-TF:443
  The Succession of the Four Sweet
    Months. R. Herrick.
    Bo-FP:243, Fe-FP:77, Ha-YA:80,
    Ho-WR:27, Tu-WW:68
  That's July. M. Butts. Ha-YA:84
  Weekend Stroll. F. Cornford.
    Co-BN:94
JUMPING
  Is This Someone You Know?
    J. Ciardi. Un-GB:25
  Jack Be Nimble. An-IP:(15),
    Ar-TP3:101, Au-SP:7, Bo-FP:38,
    Li-LB:38, Mo-MGT:38, Mo-NR:21,
    Wi-MG:58, Wr-RM:16
  Jumping Joan. Mother Goose.
    Ne-AM:32
  The Lamb. T. Roethke. Li-LC:11
  Little Jumping Joan. Mother Goose.
    Ar-TP3:101, Ho-ME:9, Li-LB:43,
    Mo-CC:(3), Mo-MGT:21, Mo-NR:126,
    Mo-TL:88, Wr-RM:14

Spring-Heeled Jack.   J. Baxter.
   Gr-EC:120
JUMPING ROPE: see SKIPPING ROPE
JUNCOS
   Coyote and Junco.   Te-FC:77
   The Snow-Bird.   F. Sherman.
      Ar-TP3:57, Au-SP:63, Br-SS:90
JUNE
   Alone.   J. Farrar.   Ha-YA:70,
      Hu-MP:61
   The Earthly Paradise.
      W. Morris.   Al-VBP:1016
   The Fisher.   L. Glazier.   Du-RG:105
   Flowers of June.   Y. Sasazawa.
      Sh-AM:75
   In June.   N. Perry.   Ha-YA:72
   June.   M. Davies.   Br-SS:163
   June.   A. Fisher.   Ho-GC:29,
      La-PP:46, La-PV:82
   June.   N. Hopper.   Ha-YA:73
   June.   A. Levy.   Un-MW:95
   June.   D. Malloch.   Ha-YA:71
   June.   J. Reaney.   Do-WH:77
   A June Day.   S. Teasdale.
      Ha-YA:70
   June Thunder.   L. MacNeice.
      To-MP:36
   June Twilight.   J. Masefield.
      Go-BP:131
   June's Here.   C. Martindale.
      Ho-CT:23
   Knee-Deep in June.   J. Riley.
      Sp-OG:291
   Poem in June.   M. Acorn.   Do-WH:76
   Sad Green.   S. Warner.   Un-MB:373
   A Spring Lilt.   Hu-MP:303
   Stay, June, Stay! C. Rossetti.
      Ar-TP3:205, Ha-YA:74
   That's June.   M. Butts.   Ha-YA:73
   The Vision of Sir Launfal.
      J. Lowell.   Er-FA:238, Fe-FP:77,
      Ga-FB:289, Ke-TF:434, Mc-PR:37,
      Pa-OM:210, Se-PR:139, Un-GT:275
JUNGLES: see also HUMOR - JUNGLES
   Auranomoi's Song of Praise for His
      Bull Akorikono.   Tr-US I:107
   The Indolent Gardener.
      M. Kennedy.   Co-BN:51
   Jungle.   M. Smith.   Hu-PN:389
   Jungles of Grass.   A. Fisher.
      It-HB:37
   The Law of the Jungle.
      R. Kipling.   Rd-OA:128
   Morning Light.   E. Newsome.
      Ad-PB:21, Bo-AN:19, Hu-PN:70
JUNIPER TREES
   Juniper.   R. Francis.   Ca-VT:234
   Juniper.   Pa-RE:87
   The Juniper Tree.   W. Watson.
      Co-BL:162, Do-WH:36

The Juniper Tree.   N. Zabolotzky.
   Ca-MR:102
Sing a Song of Juniper.   R. Francis.
   Gr-EC:51, Ha-LO:38
Trees.   W. de la Mare.   Mc-PR:199
JUNKYARDS
   Cars Once Steel and Green, Now
      Old.   L. Zukovsky.   Ca-VT:249
   Cherrylog Road.   J. Dickey.
      Br-TC:90, Ha-TP:65
   The Deaths at Paragon, Indiana.
      J. Woods.   St-H:250
   The Drunk in the Furnace.
      W. Merwin.   Br-TC:292, Wi-LT:769
   Fast Run in the Junkyard.
      J. Nichols.   Du-SH:43
   Scrapyard.   M. Benson.   Le-M:71
JUPITER (ROMAN GOD)
   Sunday Morning.   W. Stevens.
      Sh-AP:158, Sm-PT:121, Un-MA:242,
      Wi-LT:139
JUPITER (PLANET)
   For the Conjunction of Two Planets.
      A. Rich.   Pl-IO:30
   On the Beach at Night.   W. Whitman.
      Gr-CT:197, Un-MA:65
JURIES: see COURTS (LAW)
JUSTICE: see also COURTS (LAW);
      HUMOR - JUSTICE; LAW;
      SATIRE - JUSTICE
   The Ballad of Reading Gaol.
      O. Wilde.   Al-VBP:1072,
      Er-FA:87, Un-MB:70
   Carl Hamblin.   E. Masters.
      Kr-OF:113, Sh-AP:137, Wi-LT:114
   Christ's Victory in Heaven.
      G. Fletcher, the Younger.
      Al-VBP:318
   Drums of Freedom. G. Thompson.
      Jo-VC:21
   Epimenides' Awakening.
      J. von Goethe.   Un-R:27
   Fair and Unfair.   R. Francis.
      Ca-VT:235
   Fears, Jeers, Tears.   B. Slutsky.
      Bo-RU:80
   I Have a Dream.   M. King.
      Lo-TY:249
   The Inchcape Rock.   R. Southey.
      Gr-CT:141, Un-GT:161
   Justorium Animae.   Apochrypha.
      Wisdom.   Ga-S:51
   Last Speech to the Court.
      B. Vanzetti.   Mo-BG:170
   The People of Tao-Chou.
      Po Chu-i.   Gr-CT:374
   Preliminary Draft of a World
      Constitution.   Ba-PO:115
   Robin Hood and the Widow's Three Sons.
      Ar-TP3:17, Co-PT:224, Ma-BB:70,
      Pa-OM:86, Sp-OG:157, Un-GT:119

JUSTICE — cont'd.
  Shameful Death. W. Morris.
    Gr-CT:129, Gr-SS:174, Pa-GTB:380,
    Un-GT:136
  Siberia. I. Emiot. Ho-TY:316
  Thou Art Indeed Just, Lord, if I
    Contend. G. Hopkins.
    Pa-GTB:397, Pl-EI:88, Un-MB:39,
    Wi-LT:50
  Time's Glory. W. Shakespeare.
    Gr-CT:322
JUVENILE DELINQUENCY
  The Blackstone Rangers. G. Brooks.
    Ad-CI:59, Ad-PB:159
  Hard but Soft. W. Barbour.
    La-IH:29
  Recessional for the Class of 1959
    of a School for Delinquent
    Negro Girls. J. Cowen.
    Hu-PN:575
  Street Gang. H. Webster.
    Co-RM:187
K.K.K.: see KU KLUX KLAN
KADESH, BATTLE, 1288 B.C.
  The Battle of Kadesh. Be-AP:46
KAFKA, FRANZ
  To Frank Kafka. E. Muir.
    Go-BP:57
KALAMAZOO, MICH.:
  Kalamazoo. V. Lindsay. Gr-CC:149,
    Pa-HT:47
  The Sins of Kalamazoo.
    C. Sandburg. Ca-VT:23
  What I'd Do. L. Blair. Ja-PC:5
KALMUCK VERSE: see ALTAIC
    VERSE - BURYAT
KANGAROOS: see also
    HUMOR - KANGAROOS
  The Kangaroo. E. Coatsworth.
    Ar-TP3:80
  Kangaroo. D. Lawrence. Ma-FW:214,
    Rd-OA:139
  The Kangaroo. Au-SP:86, Gr-EC:12,
    Ir-BB:74, St-FS:54
  The Kangaroo. Su-FVI:60
KANSAS
  Crossing Kansas by Train.
    D. Justice. Du-RG:45, Mc-WS:119
  A Home on the Range. J. Lomax.
    Er-FA:447, Hu-MP:204, Se-PR:262
  How Old John Brown Took Harper's
    Ferry. E. Stedman. Hu-PN:493,
    Pa-OM:175
  John Brown's Prayer. S. Benét.
    Hu-PN:517
  Kansas. V. Lindsay. Pa-HT:49
  Kansas Boy. R. Lechlitner.
    Br-AF:150, Du-RG:50
  The Peters Family. W. Stafford.
    St-H:216

  Sun City. B. Cutler. St-H:38
  Time's Exile. W. Stafford.
    St-H:210
  Where We Are. B. Cutler.
    St-H:36
KANSAS - HISTORY
  Kansas Curses the President.
    J. Howe. Kr-OF:143
  News of Blood. D. Whitney.
    Kr-OF:140
  The Ruffian Rally.
    J. Pierpont. Kr-OF:138
  While There Is a Country to Save.
    R. Emerson. Kr-OF:142
  The Wolves of the Border.
    J. Whittier. Kr-OF:147
KAREN VERSE
  Song of a War-Band Setting Out.
    Tr-US II:190
KATYDIDS: see also HUMOR -
    KATYDIDS
  To a Caty-Did. P. Freneau.
    Sh-AP:17
KAYAKS
  The Kayak. Bo-FP:179, Ch-B:71,
    Fe-FP:115, Sh-RP:307
  Listen to My Words. Le-IB:114
  Mutual Nith-Song Between Savladt
    and Pulangitsissok.
    Da-SC:44, Tr-US I:5
  Taunt Song Against a Clumsy
    Kayak Paddler. Le-IB:111,
    Tr-US I:3
KEATS, JOHN: see also BRAWNE,
    FANNY
  Adonais. P. Shelley. Al-VBP:759,
    Ha-PO:130, Ox-BN:287
  After a Lecture on Keats.
    O. Holmes. Al-VBP:831
  The Death of Keats. V. Watkins.
    Pl-ML:123
  For John Keats, Apostle of
    Beauty. C. Cullen. Ad-PB:91,
    Bo-AN:88
  For Keats and the Florentine
    Night. G. Kennedy. Ls-NY:141
  Go Thou to Rome. P. Shelley.
    Gr-CT:379
  Keats. H. Longfellow. Sh-AP:39
  Keats. J. Tabb. Sh-AP:135
  Keats at Teignmouth. C. Causley.
    Pl-ML:122
  On Keats. P. Shelley. Pl-ML:151
  On the Death of Keats. J. Logan.
    Ho-P:169
  There Was a Naughty Boy. J. Keats.
    Bo-FP:113, Ch-B:77, Co-HP:84,
    Fr-WO:69, Gr-EC:215, Ir-BB:97,
    Ma-YA:183, Ox-BC:148, Pl-ML:18,
    Sm-LG:291, Sm-MK:131, Un-GF:18

KEEPSAKES
  Broken Shell. W. Scott.
    Ls-NY:228
  Objet d' Art. L. Stryk.
    Ls-NY:264
  Spleen. C. Baudelaire. Un-R:77
KELP
  Sea-Weed. D. Lawrence. Co-BN:80
  The Tuft of Kelp. H. Melville.
    Gr-CT:197
KEMPENFELT, RICHARD
  Loss of the Royal George.
    W. Cowper. Co-RG:44, Co-SS:137,
    Pa-GTB:123, Rv-CB:552, Sp-OG:73
KENNEDY, JOHN FITZGERALD
  Channel U.S.A.—Live.
    A. Stoutenburg. Br-AF:93,
    Hi-TL:234
  Elegy for J. F. K. W. Auden.
    Ma-FW:168
  In America There Is Mourning.
    A. Karlov. Mo-MI:78
  John F. Kennedy. R. Bly.
    Mc-EA:123
  John Fitzgerald Kennedy.
    J. Masefield. Vi-PP:223
  Kennedy. M. Kazan. Pe-SS:47
  November Twenty-Sixth Nineteen
    Hundred and Sixty-Three.
    W. Berry. Wi-LT:662
KENT, ENG.
  A Knight of Cales. De-CH:607
  The Purple Island. P. Fletcher.
    Al-VBP:290
KENTUCKY
  My Fathers Came from Kentucky.
    V. Lindsay. Br-AF:131,
    Gr-CC:125
  My Old Kentucky Home. S. Foster.
    Er-FA:432, Fe-PL:143, Ga-FB:272,
    Se-PR:263
  Old Christmas. R. Helton.
    Co-PM:94, Un-MA:346
  The Swimmers. A. Tate.
    Pe-OA:180, Un-MA:540
  Uncle Ambrose. J. Still.
    Br-AF:133
  Walthena. E. Peck. Br-AF:64
KEYS: see LOCKS AND KEYS
KHMER VERSE: see CAMBODIAN
    VERSE
KIDD, WILLIAM (CAPTAIN KIDD)
  Captain Kidd. R. and S. Benét.
    Hi-TL:28, Ir-BB:40, Tu-WW:36
  My Name Is Captain Kidd.
    De-CH:536
KIDNAPING: see also HUMOR -
    KIDNAPING
  The Douglas Tragedy. Ox-BB:118,
    Un-MW:109

  Fair Annie. De-CH:414
  Hazel Dorn. B. Sleigh. De-CH:558
KIEV, U.S.S.R.
  For the Girls in My Home Town.
    N. Korzhavin. Ca-MR:91
KILIMANJARO, MOUNT
  Kilimandjaro. B. Taylor.
    Sh-AP:122
KILLDEERS: see PLOVERS
KILLIECRANKIE, BATTLE, 1689
  The Battle of Killikrankie.
    W. Aytoun. Hi-FO:163
KILROY
  Kilroy. P. Viereck. Hi-TL:211,
    Un-MA:657
KINDNESS: see also ANIMALS,
    KINDNESS TO; BIRDS,
    KINDNESS TO; FORGIVENESS;
    MERCY; SATIRE - KINDNESS
  But I Do Not Need Kindness.
    G. Corso. Kh-VA:66
  Forget It. Fe-PL:294
  I Shall Not Pass This Way Again.
    E. York. Er-FA:10
  If You Have a Friend. Er-FA:28
  In a Child's Album.
    W. Wordsworth. Bo-FP:232,
    Ch-B:17, Ox-BN:92
  Just Folks. E. Guest. Er-FA:134
  Kind and True. A. Townshend.
    Rv-CB:468
  Kindness. M. Flett. Le-M:155
  Our Saviour's Golden Rule.
    I. Watts. Ox-BC:51
  Speak Gently. D. Bates. Li-SR:3
  Success. Er-FA:17
  Sun and Rain and Dew from Heaven.
    A. Gordon. Fe-PL:313
  Trees. H. Behn. Ar-TP3:204,
    Au-SP:368, Br-SS:144, Ha-YA:52,
    Pe-FB:74, Un-GB:10
  The Warm of Heart.
    E. Coatsworth. Co-PU:66
KING, EDWARD
  Lycidas. J. Milton. Al-VBP:402,
    Gr-CT:250, Hi-WP II:20,
    Ho-P:69, Pa-GTB:55
KING, MARTIN LUTHER, JR.
  April 4, 1968. M. Goode.
    Jo-SA:6, Jo-VC:57
  Assassination. D. Lee. Ad-BO:29,
    Ad-PB:423
  Canto 7. T. Weatherly. Ad-PB:398
  Death of Dr. King. S. Cornish.
    Ad-PB:296
  The Funeral of Martin Luther
    King, Jr. N. Giovanni.
    Ad-BO:30, Ra-BP:323
  A Man in Memphis. P. Crisostomo.
    Me-WF:35

KING, MARTIN LUTHER, JR. — cont'd.
  Martin Luther King Jr. G. Brooks.
    Ad-BO:28, Ad-PB:159
  Martin's Blues. M. Harper.
    Ad-PB:312
  White Weekend. Q. Troupe.
    Kr-OF:164
KING PHILIP'S WAR, 1675-1676
  At the Indian Killer's Grave.
    R. Lowell. Ca-VT:443
KINGCUPS: see BUTTERCUPS
KINGFISHERS
  I Feel a Bit Happier. C. Foster.
    Le-M:31
  The Kingfisher.W. Davies.Go-BP:78
  The Kingfisher.A. Marvell.Gr-CT:96
  The Kingfisher. Tori. Le-MW:13
  One Kingfisher and One Yellow
    Rose. E. Brennan. Co-PI:14,
    Re-BS:41
  Sacred Song of the Jackeroo
    Cult. Tr-US I:258
KINGS AND RULERS: see also
    DICTATORS; HUMOR - KINGS
    AND RULERS; SATIRE -
    KINGS AND RULERS; and names
    of kings, as DAVID, KING OF
    ISRAEL
  After Reading Translations of
    Ancient Texts on Stone and
    Clay. C. Reznikoff. Gr-SS:170
  Alexander the Great. De-CH:180
  Alexandrian Kings. C. Cavafy.
    Gr-CC:109
  An Apple for the King. Rv-ON:64
  The Battle of Kadesh. Be-AP:46
  The Bloody Conquests of Mighty
    Tamburlaine. C. Marlowe.
    Gr-CT:335
  The Breed of Athletes.
    Euripides. Mo-SD:163
  By the Statue of King Charles at
    Charing Cross. L. Johnson.
    Co-RG:18, Ni-JP:165, Ox-BN:946,
    Un-MB:153
  By World Laid Low. Gr-CT:327
  Child's Song. K. Greenaway.
    Bo-FP:260
  The Choice. J. Masefield.
    Un-MB:229
  The Chronicle of the Drum.
    W. Thackeray. Al-VBP:878
  Dagonet's Canzonet. E. Rhys.
    Gr-SS:86
  The Death of Kings.
    W. Shakespeare. Mo-GR:93
  Dirge for a Chief. Tr-US II:116
  Earth upon Earth. Gr-CT:325,
    Rv-CB:15
  The Enchanted Shirt. J. Hay.
    Ha-PO:59, Sh-RP:264, Un-GT:171

The English Succession.
  J. Marchant. Ox-BC:61
Epilogue. L. Abercrombie.
  Un-MB:254
The Fairy King. W. Allingham.
  Co-PM:22
Fergus and the Druid. W. Yeats.
  Li-TU:166
The Fool's Prayer. E. Sills.
  Fe-PL:322, Pa-OM:225, Sp-OG:137
A Forced Music. R. Graves.
  Un-MB:389
A Foreign Ruler. W. Landor.
  Al-VBP:708
Glory to Moshesh. Be-AP:39
Gone. W. de la Mare. Bo-GJ:205,
  Gr-CC:101, Ir-BB:263
The Gray-Eyed King.
  A. Akhmatova. Ca-MR:182
Hector Protector. Gr-EC:198,
  Ir-BB:270, Mo-MGT:11, Wr-RM:89
In Honor of Senzangakona.
  Tr-US I:79
Jealousy. M. Coleridge.
  De-CH:180, Ox-BN:925
King Agongola's Song. Tr-CB:56,
  Tr-US I:55
A King Is Dead. W. Shakespeare.
  Gr-CT:357
The King of Ai. H. Plutzik.
  Wi-LT:792
King Rufus. Y. Segal. Do-WH:9
King Stephen. R. Graves.
  Mc-WK:128
The Knifesmith. D. Howard.
  Co-RM:90, Sm-MK:38
Little Girl and the Queen.
  Wr-RM:105
Men's Stick-Dance Songs.
  Tr-US II:142
The Miller of Dee. Gr-GB:214
Moon Door. M. Kennedy. Co-BL:154
Nursery Song in Pidgin English.
  Li-SR:130
O Have You Seen the Shah.
  Ir-BB:263, Rv-ON:30
The Oba of Benin. Be-AP:43
The Old and Young Courtier.
  Al-VBP:369, No-CL:229
On a Certain Ruler in Memory of
  Former Rulers. Da-SC:174
On the Tombs in Westminster
  Abbey. F. Beaumont. Al-VBP:301,
  De-CH:252, Hi-WP II:18,
  Pa-GTB:60
The Passing of Arthur.
  A. Tennyson. Ni-JP:158,
  Un-BN:511
Persepolis. C. Marlowe. No-CL:253
Praise of Chief Mosenene. Be-AP:37
Praise of King Mtesa. Tr-US I:102

Praise Song for a Chief.
  Tr-US I:87
Preparations. Al-VBP:353,
  De-CH:464, Ga-S:131,
  Hi-WP I:137, Na-EO:19,
  Pl-EI:16, Rv-CB:116, Sm-LG:378
Protus. R. Browning. Hi-FO:86
Pussy Cat, Pussy Cat, Where
  Have You Been? Ar-TP3:52,
  Au-SP:15, Bo-FP:6, De-PO:18,
  Er-FA:506, Ir-BB:269, Li-LB:88,
  Mo-MGT:163, Mo-NR:100, Pa-AP:50,
  Wi-MG:34, Wr-RM:26
Queens. J. Synge. Gr-CT:58,
  Un-MB:184
Res Publica. J. McKellar.
  Ni-JP:121
The Rubaiyat of Omar Khayyam.
  E. FitzGerald. Gr-CT:329,
  Pa-GTB:329
See where Capella with Her
  Golden Kids. E. Millay.
  Ni-JP:122
Shaka, King of the Zulus.
  Lo-TY:16
The Shepherd's Wife's Song.
  R. Greene. Al-VBP:139
Shub-Ad. R. Barlow. De-FS:11
Sing a Song of Sixpence.
  Mother Goose. Bo-FP:9,
  Br-FF:(18), De-PO:22, Fr-WO:16,
  Ir-BB:262, Li-SR:129, Mo-MGT:19,
  Mo-NR:10, On-TW:57, Sm-MK:19
The Song of Kuali. Tr-US II:98
Songs in Praise of the Chief.
  Do-CH:(42)
Tamburlaine. C. Marlowe.
  Cl-DT:13, Hi-FO:89
Tamerlane. E. Poe. Sh-AP:42
The Task. W. Cowper. Ba-PO:118
Three Kings. J. Vaughn.
  Hu-NN:24, Hu-PN:399
To Become a Chief's Favorite.
  Do-CH:(16)
To His Friend, Wei. . . .
  Li Po. Li-TU:234
To the New King Mutara II Rwogera.
  Tr-US I:97
Toltec Lament. Da-SC:167
The Trophy. E. Muir. Wi-LT:251
Two Surprises. B. McAlpine.
  Fe-PL:88
Upon the King. W. Shakespeare.
  Ke-PP:20
Waiting for Audience on a Spring
  Night. Tu Fu. Rx-OH:10
Watchman, What of the Night?
  A. Swinburne. Ho-WR:200
What I'd Do. L. Blair. Ja-PC:5
Yang-Ze-Fu. Yehoash. Ho-TY:77

KINGS RIVER CANYON, CALIF.
  Andree Rexroth. K. Rexroth.
  Ca-VT:269
KISSES AND KISSING: see also
  HUMOR - KISSES AND KISSING
  April's Amazing Meaning. G. Dillon.
  Co-BL:17
Bleeberrying. J. Denwood.
  Ca-MB:17
Come Here, My Beloved. Do-CH:(16)
A Dream. Shao Hsün-mei.
  Hs-TC:126
Dusty Miller. Mo-MGT:201
Endymion. J. Keats. Al-VBP:789
Fill a Glass with Golden Wine.
  W. Henley. Al-VBP:1068
Georgie Porgie. De-PO:16,
  Fr-WO:29, Li-LB:25, Mo-CC:44,
  Mo-MGT:80, Mo-NR:20, Wi-MG:5,
  Wr-RM:32
Girls' Songs, III. Tr-US I:119
Haidée and Don Juan. G. Byron.
  Al-VBP:731, Ox-BN:258
Her Legs. R. Herrick. Li-SR:23
I Fear Thy Kisses. P. Shelley.
  Al-VBP:754, Pa-GTB:179
In a Gondola. R. Browning.
  Al-VBP:891
In the Dark Pine-Wood. J. Joyce.
  Co-BL:113
Is It a Month. J. Synge.
  Co-PI:187
It Really Happened. E. Henley.
  Br-BC:31
It Was Out by Donnycarney.
  J. Joyce. Hi-WP I:45, Un-MB:270,
  Un-MW:10
Jenny Kissed Me. L. Hunt.
  Al-VBP:714, Br-BC:138, Co-FB:260,
  Er-FA:104, Ga-FB:51, Hi-WP I:42,
  Li-SR:32, Ma-YA:172, Un-MW:23
A Kiss. R. Argomaniz. Me-WF:22
The Kiss. T. Shipman. No-CL:127
The Kiss. S. Tanikawa. Sh-AM:130
Kiss. A. Young. Ad-PB:367
Kiss'd Yestreen. Gr-GB:101
Kisses in the Train.
  D. Lawrence. Un-MB:297
Kissing. Lord Herbert. Al-VBP:295
Kite Poem. J. Merrill. Br-TC:285
Linked Pantuns. Tr-US I:177
The Look. S. Teasdale. Bo-HF:124,
  Co-BL:91, Hi-WP I:45
Love Songs (A Javelin).
  Tr-US I:114
The Lovers. C. Aiken. Un-MW:211
Love's Philosophy. P. Shelley.
  Co-BL:40, Ga-FB:52, Hi-WP II:55,
  Pa-GTB:185, Un-MW:189
The Moth's Kiss, First!
  R. Browning. Un-MW:191

KISSES AND KISSING — cont'd.
 Nature That Gave the Bee.
  T. Wyatt. Rv-CB:84
 On a Time the Amorous Silvy.
  Al-VBP:362, No-CL:184
 Permanently. K. Koch.
  Mc-EA:135, Mo-BG:93
 Pleasures, Beauty. J. Ford.
  Al-VBP:310
 The Prodigy. A. Herbert.
  Na-EO:132
 Rondel. A. Swinburne.
  Al-VBP:1027
 Rondelay. J. Dryden. Al-VBP:479
 Scintilla. W. Braithwaite.
  Bo-AN:15
 She. T. Roethke. Co-BL:51
 Since Feeling Is First.
  E. Cummings. Du-SH:65,
  Un-MA:478
 Song. C. Cotton. Al-VBP:476
 Song. B. Jonson. Al-VBP:239
 Sonnet. W. Alexander. Al-VBP:212
 Sonnets from the Portuguese.
  E. Browning. Al-VBP:818,
  Ke-TF:109
 Such Stuff as Dreams. F. Adams.
  Li-SR:32
 Summum Bonum. R. Browning.
  Co-BL:117, Co-EL:94, Ma-YA:203
 Take, O Take Those Lips Away.
  W. Shakespeare. Al-VBP:193,
  Ga-FB:38, Pa-GTB:23, Rv-CB:199,
  Un-MW:74
 To Electra. R. Herrick.
  Ma-YA:87
 Variations. F. Garcia Lorca.
  Le-SW:57
 What Faire Pompe. T. Campion.
  Ho-P:16
 Who Was It. H. Heine. Pa-SG:34
 Willy, Willy. Wr-RM:97
 Wine and Cakes. Mo-MGT:209
 Your Kisses. A. Symons. Un-MW:24
KITCHENS: see also POTS AND PANS
 At Mrs. Appleby's. E. McWebb.
  Ar-TP3:11, Br-SS:64
 The Divine Office of the Kitchen.
  C. Hallack. Fe-PL:335
 The Monk in the Kitchen.
  A. Branch. Un-MA:152
KITES (TOYS)
 Coming along the Mountain Path.
  Taigi. Le-MW:52
 Far above an Old Hut. Issa.
  Do-TS:18
 It Has Eyes and a Nose. Wy-CM:24
 King Arthur and His Knights.
  R. Williams. Co-OT:17
 The Kite. H. Behn. Ar-TP3:163,
  Fe-FP:109, Sh-RP:55

 Kite. D. McCord. La-PV:7
 The Kite. A. O'Keeffe. De-TT:74,
  Ox-BC:125
 Kite. H. Summers. Ls-NY:268
 A Kite. Ar-TP3:163, Au-SP:196,
  Bo-FP:217, Ch-B:41
 Kite Days. M. Sawyer. Br-SS:129,
  Mc-AW:37
 Kite-Flying Song. Tr-US I:217
 A Kite Is a Victim. L. Cohen.
  Mo-SD:184
 The March Wind. J. Parr.
  La-GI:11
 The String of a Kite.
  S. Yamaguchi. Sh-AM:171
 Threnody. J. Farrar. Ja-PA:17
 The Tight Spring Broke.
  Kubonta. Be-CS:43
 Two Little Sisters Went Walking
  One Day. Wy-CM:26
 What a Pretty Kite. Issa.
  Be-CS:53
KITTENS: see CATS
KIWIS: see HUMOR - KIWIS
KLEE, PAUL
 Paul Klee. J. Haines. Sc-TN:74
KLONDIKE, CAN.: see also HUMOR -
  KLONDIKE, CAN.
 The Cremation of Sam McGee.
  R. Service. Ar-TP3:143,
  Br-SM:140, Er-FA:399,
  Fe-PL:6, Ha-PO:96
 The Klondike. E. Robinson.
  Hi-TL:171
 The Shooting of Dan McGrew.
  R. Service. Co-RM:129, Do-WH:22,
  Er-FA:382, Fe-PL:9
KNEES: see LEGS
KNIGHTS AND KNIGHTHOOD: see also
  CHIVALRY; CRUSADES; HERALDRY;
  HUMOR - KNIGHTS AND KNIGHT-
  HOOD; SATIRE - KNIGHTS AND
  KNIGHTHOOD; TOURNAMENTS;
  and names of knights, as
  GAWAIN, SIR
 Against Garnesche. J. Skelton.
  Al-VBP:29
 Corpus Christi Carol (The Falcon).
  Al-VBP:36, Ga-S:200, Gr-CC:163,
  Gr-CT:186, Gr-GB:308, Ma-FW:257,
  Rv-CB:13, Sm-MK:36
 The Corpus Christi Carol (The
  Heron). Gr-GB:309
 The Dead Knight. J. Masefield.
  De-CH:53, Pa-GTB:440
 The Eve of Crécy. W. Morris.
  Gr-SS:95
 The Faerie Queene. E. Spenser.
  Ma-YA:55
 Fairy Days. W. Thackeray.
  Un-GT:16

Fast Rode the Knight.   S. Crane.
    Li-TU:236
Flowers in the Valley.   Bl-OB:40,
    Gr-EC:136, Gr-SS:29
A Gest of Robyn Hode.   Ox-BB:420
A Gest of Robyn Hode, The
    Seconde Fytte.   Ox-BB:433
A Gest of Robyn Hode, The
    Sixth Fytte.   Ox-BB:469
The Glove.   J. von Schiller.
    Sp-OG:138
The Hart.   Gr-EC:282, Gr-GB:53,
    Mo-MGT:191, Rv-CB:448, Rv-ON:99,
    Sm-LG:291, Wr-RM:75
A Knight and a Lady.   Gr-EC:138
A Knight Came Riding from the East.
    Bl-OB:39
A Knight, Canterbury Tales.
    G. Chaucer.   Ha-PO:49, Un-GT:86
The Knight Fallen on Evil Days.
    E. Wylie.   Un-MA:274
The Knight's Leap.   C. Kingsley.
    Co-PT:230
The Knight's Tomb.
    S. Coleridge.   Cl-FC:81,
    Co-PU:156, Rv-CB:664, Sm-LG:272
The Lady of Shalott.
    A. Tennyson.   Er-FA:399,
    Hi-WP I:59, Ho-WR:145, Sp-OG:128
Lochinvar.   W. Scott.   Co-FB:230,
    Co-PT:207, Co-RG:33, Er-FA:316,
    Fe-FP:504, Ga-FB:54, Gr-EC:132,
    Ma-YA:143, Mc-PR:154, Na-EO:133,
    Ox-BN:128, Sp-OG:126, Un-GT:134
Love.   S. Coleridge.   Pa-GTB:171
Near Avalon.   W. Morris.   Rv-CB:929
The Passing of Arthur.
    A. Tennyson.   Ni-JP:158,
    Ox-BN:511
Sir Galahad.   A. Tennyson.
    Co-RM:78, Sp-OG:134
Sir Gawain and the Green Knight.
    Ma-YA:21
Sir Marmaduke.   G. Colman.
    Un-GT:94
Sir William Deloraine at the
    Wizard's Tomb.   W. Scott.
    Ox-BN:118
The Song of Finis.
    W. de la Mare.   Un-MB:196
A Squire, Canterbury Tales.
    G. Chaucer.   Hi-WP II:121,
    Un-GT:87
Three Knights from Spain.
    Bl-OB:36, De-CH:328, Fo-OG:42,
    Gr-GB:26, Rv-ON:106
The Twa Corbies.   De-CH:102,
    Ha-PO:127, Ma-BB:132, Ma-FW:256,
    Pa-GTB:90, Rv-CB:55, Sm-LG:268,
    Sp-OG:115

Two Red Roses Across the Moon.
    W. Morris.   Rv-CB:927
The Vision of Sir Launfal.
    J. Lowell.   Pa-OM:210
The Wandering Knight's Song.
    J. Lockhart.   Gr-CT:275
KNIGHTS OF THE ROUND TABLE:
    see ARTHUR, KING; and
    names of knights, as
    GAWAIN, SIR
KNITTING
    This Knot I Knot.   De-CH:668,
    Gr-GB:148
KNIVES: see also HUMOR - KNIVES;
    SATIRE - KNIVES
    Haiku 7.   E. Knight.   Ra-BP:206
    Halcyon Days.   J. Barnes.
    Ni-CD:26
    A Man Sharpening a Knife.
    K. Takamura.   Sh-AM:41
    The Sacrificial Knife and the
    Simple Saw.   E. Steinberg.
    Ho-TY:232
    The Sailor's Knife.
    Cheng Ch'ou-yü.   Pa-MV:38
    A Wonderful Man.   A. Fisher.
    Br-SS:164
KNOWLEDGE: see also HUMOR -
    KNOWLEDGE; SATIRE -
    KNOWLEDGE; SCHOLARS AND
    SCHOLARSHIP; WISDOM
    The Children.   H. Applebaum.
    Ke-TF:80
    Courage Has a Crimson Coat.
    N. Turner.   Bo-FP:299,
    'Th-AS:212
    Curiosity.   H. Behn.   Au-SP:349
    The Dunce.   W. de la Mare.
    Pl-IO:137
    Farm Child.   R. Thomas.
    Co-BN:206, Co-PU:118,
    Hi-WP II:134, Ma-FW:77
    For Scholars and Pupils.
    G. Wither.   Ox-BC:29
    Hallo My Fancy.   W. Cleland.
    De-CH:358
    In Everything I Seek to Grasp.
    B. Pasternak.   Ca-MR:167
    Intimations of Sublimity.
    W. Wordsworth.   Ox-BN:98
    The Laboratory Midnight.
    R. Denney.   Pl-IO:70
    Men Say They Know Many Things.
    H. Thoreau.   Pl-IO:124
    Numbers.   E. Roberts.   Li-LC:18
    On His Thirty-Third Birthday.
    Ch'ang Kuo Fang.   Rx-LT:118
    Portrait d'une Femme.   E. Pound.
    Br-TC:331, No-CL:239, Un-MA:295
    The Secret Sits.   R. Frost.
    Au-SP:184, Ha-LO:61, Ho-TH:46

KNOWLEDGE — cont'd.
Step Out onto the Planet.
L. Welch.   Kh-VA:3
Verse.   O. Gogarty.   Sm-LG:31
Village Portrait.   T. Duncan.
Th-AS:189
KNOXVILLE, TENN.
Knoxville, Tennessee.
N. Giovanni.   Ad-BO:58,
Ad-PB:450, Ra-BP:322
KON-TIKI (RAFT)
The Ballad of Kon-Tiki.
I. Serraillier.   Co-SS:223
KOREAN VERSE
Among Many Heaps of Ashes.
Cho Sung Kyun.   Ba-PO:156,
Cr-WS:6
KOREAN WAR, 1950-1953
Guerrilla Camp.   K. Wilson.
Ha-TP:89
Home-Coming.   P. Binford.
Ke-TF:261
Korea Bound, 1952.
W. Childress.   Br-AF:87
Ode for the American Dead in
Korea.   T. McGrath.
Bl-FP:49, Ca-VT:431
On a Certain Engagement South
of Seoul.   H. Carruth.
Br-AF:89
KOSSUTH, LAJOS (LOUIS)
Kossuth.   J. Lowell.   Hi-FO:231
KRISHNA AND RADHA
Krishna's Longing.   Jayadeva.
Al-PI:56
Song for the Feast of Krishna.
Tr-US II:139
KRISS KRINGLE: see SANTA CLAUS
KU KLUX KLAN
Elegy on a Nordic White
Protestant.   J. Fletcher.
Hu-PN:503
Ku-Klux.   M. Cawein.   Hi-TL:127
Ku Klux.   L. Hughes.   Ra-BP:81
Lynching and Burning.
P. St. John.   Ad-PB:349
Night, Death, Mississippi.
R. Hayden.   Ca-VT:357
KUBLAI KHAN
Kubla Khan.   S. Coleridge.
Al-VBP:699, Bo-GJ:222, Co-RG:15,
De-CH:386, Er-FA:361, Ga-FB:23,
Gr-CT:177, Gr-EC:140, Mc-PR:150,
Ox-BN:165, Pa-HT:154, Re-TW:132,
Rv-CB:657, Sm-LG:215
KUNMING, CHINA
I Sing of Lienta.   Cheng Min.
Hs-TC:236
KYOTO, JAP.
Monk Begging, Kyoto.   E. Shiffert.
Ls-NY:140

KYZYL VERSE
Songs, I, II.   Tr-US II:132
LABOR AND LABORERS: see also
CHILD LABOR; FACTORIES;
LABOR DAY; LABOR UNIONS;
MIGRANT LABOR; OCCUPATIONS;
SATIRE - LABOR AND LABORERS;
UNEMPLOYMENT; WORK; WORK
SONGS
After They Put Down Their Overalls.
L. Peters.   Lo-TY:170
The Banks of the Condamine.
Gr-GB:212
Boatmen.   I Men.   Hs-TC:417
The Buffalo Skinners.
Co-RM:232, Gr-GB:220, Hi-TL:150
Burying Ground by the Ties.
A. MacLeish.   Un-MA:459
The Collection.   E. Crosby.
Kr-OF:171
A Consecration.   J. Masefield.
Un-MB:221
Drumdelgie.   Gr-GB:210
The Factory Girl's Come-All-Ye.
Em-AF:766
Factory Windows Are Always
Broken.   V. Lindsay.   Co-PU:72,
Er-FA:274, La-OC:110
The Forgotten Man. E. Markham.
Fe-PL:42
Four Epitaphs.   S. Warner.
Un-MB:371
From Plane to Plane.   R. Frost.
Un-MA:191
God Made the Bees.   Bl-OB:144,
Un-GT:22
The Grinders.   Gr-GB:222
Heroes of War and Peace.
E. Wilcox.   Kr-OF:173
History Makers.   G. Campbell.
Sa-B:33
Horses and Men in the Rain.
C. Sandburg.   Fe-PL:409
A Hymn of Nature.   R. Bridges.
Ha-YA:107
I Hear America Singing.
W. Whitman.   Ar-TP3:47,
Bo-FP:304, Br-AF:44, Co-PS:118,
Er-FA:289, Fe-FP:451, Ga-FB:247,
Hu-MP:369, La-PV:103, Mc-PR:33,
Sm-LG:40, Un-GT:306, Un-MA:40,
Vi-PP:185
I Wish the Wood-Cutter Would Wake
Up.   P. Neruda.   Bl-FP:51
Iron Punts Laden with Cane.
M. Williams.   Sa-B:30
Iron Years: For Money. C. Major.
Jo-SA:89
Labor.   F. Osgood.   Se-PR:166
Labourer.   E. Brathwaite.
Sa-B:239

The Labourer.   R. Thomas.
  Go-BP:229
Living among the Toilers.
  H. Percikow.   La-OC:146
Man and Mountain.   T'ien Chien.
  Hs-TC:334
The Man with the Hoe.   E. Markham.
  Bo-HF:144, Er-FA:269, Ke-PP:108,
  Ni-JP:84, Pl-EI:142, Un-MA:107
A Man's Bread.   J. Peabody.
  Ha-YA:107
Morning Work.   D. Lawrence.
  Un-MB:298
Nocturnal Song.   Ho Ch'i-fang.
  Hs-TC:224
Psalm of Those Who Go Forth
  Before Daylight.
  C. Sandburg.   Ma-FW:129
Questions of a Studious Working
  Man.   B. Brecht.   Sm-MK:224
St. Louis Midday.   J. Knoepfle.
  St-H:93
Sugar Cane.   F. Charles.   Sa-B:185
The Tarriers' Song.   T. Casey.
  Co-RM:125, Kr-OF:167
To Labor.   C. Gilman.   Fe-PL:423
To the Young Pioneers of the
  Northwest.   Pien Chih-lin.
  Hs-TC:169
Too Old to Work.   J. Glazer.
  Hi-TL:226
Two Surprises.   R. McAlpine.
  Fe-PL:88
Under Such Blows.
  O. Mandelstam.   Ca-MR:160
Waiting.   J. Davidson.
  Al-VBP:1078
What Kind of Troops Are These.
  Chang Chih-min.   Hs-TC:430
What Shall We Do for the
  Striking Seamen? Hi-TL:199
The Worker.   R. Thomas.
  Ad-PB:370, Hu-PN:433
LABOR DAY: see also HUMOR -
  LABOR DAY
Labor.   F. Osgood.   Se-PR:166
Labor Day.   M. Pomeroy.   Co-PS:119
There You Sit.   S. Silverstein.
  Co-PS:119
To Labor.   C. Gilman.   Fe-PL:423
Work: A Song of Triumph.
  A. Morgan.   Fe-PL:439, Ke-TF:234
LABOR RELATIONS: see COLLECTIVE
  BARGAINING; SATIRE - LABOR
  RELATIONS; STRIKES
LABOR UNIONS: see also COLLECTIVE
  BARGAINING; HUMOR - LABOR
  UNIONS; SATIRE - LABOR RELA-
  TIONS; STRIKES
Before the Judge.   D. Edelshtat.
  Kr-OF:111
Joe Hill.   A. Hayes.   Kr-OF:114
Last Will.   J. Hill.   Kr-OF:116
The Mill Mother's Lament.
  E. Wiggins.   Kr-OF:191
Night Here.   G. Snyder.   Bl-FP:62
Prayer at the Graves of the
  Murdered Strikers.   C. Queens.
  Kr-OF:157
There Is Power in a Union.
  J. Hill.   Hi-TL:164
When the Cock Crows.
  A. Giovannitti.   Kr-OF:151
LABRUNIE, GÉRARD: see NERVAL,
  GÉRARD DE
LA CAMARGUE, FR.
  Horses on the Camargue.
  R. Campbell.   Pa-GTB:494,
  Rd-OA:153
LACE AND LACE MAKING
  The Lace Maker.   B. Howes.
  Ls-NY:79
LA CROSSE, WIS.
  La Crosse at Ninety Miles an
  Hour.   R. Eberhart.   Br-AF:205
LADAKHI VERSE: see TIBETAN
  VERSE - LADAKHI
LADDERS: see HUMOR - LADDERS
LADYBIRDS: see LADYBUGS
LADYBUGS
  Clock-a-Clay.   J. Clare.
  Bl-OB:119, Fe-FP:133, Ox-BN:324,
  Re-TW:95, Rv-CB:725
  Down in the Hollow.   A. Fisher.
  Au-SP:71
  Fall.   A. Fisher.   Ar-TP3:185,
  Br-SG:90, Ha-YA:113, Ja-PA:27
  Lady Bug, Lady Bug.   Wy-CM:8
  Lady-Bug, Lady-Bug! Mo-TB:89,
  Un-GT:72
  The Ladybird.   J. Clare.
  Pa-RE:86
  Ladybird.   Wr-RM:87
  Ladybird, Ladybird.   E. Eastwick.
  Br-SG:53
  Ladybird, Ladybird, Fly Away
  Home.   Mother Goose.
  Au-SP:13, Bo-FP:323, De-PO:20,
  Fe-FP:133, Ir-BB:227, Li-LB:82,
  Mo-CC:(23), Mo-MGT:115,
  Mo-NR:83, Rv-CB:449, Sm-MK:7,
  Un-GB:16, Un-GF:13, Un-GT:72
  To the Ladybug.   Mo-TB:88
LAFAYETTE, MARIE JOSEPH PAUL
  YVES ROCH GILBERT DU MOTIER,
  MARQUIS DE
  La Fayette.   D. Madison.
  Hi-TL:81, Vi-PP:118
  Lafayette to Washington.
  M. Anderson.   Vi-PP:117
LAIS
  Lais.   H.D.   Un-MA:337

LAKES: see also PONDS AND POOLS;
    and names of lakes, as
    ERIE, LAKE
  The Harbor. C. Sandburg.
    Ho-LP:51
  The Lake. J. Stephens. Un-MB:361
  The Lake. J. Tabb. Sh-AP:136
  The Lake: To. . . . E. Poe.
    Sh-AP:45
  Lakes. F. Bianco. No-CL:62
  Lying in the Sun. I. Johnson.
    Le-M:78, Le-WR:11
  On the Lake. Yung Tzu. Pa-MV:195
  Sunrise on Rydal Water.
    J. Drinkwater. Wi-LT:621
  The Winter Lakes. W. Campbell
    Co-BN:186
LAMAS: see HUMOR - LAMAS
LAMB, CHARLES
  The Lime-Tree Bower My Prison.
    S. Coleridge. Rv-CB:660
LAMBA VERSE: see AFRICAN VERSE
LAMBS: see also HUMOR - LAMBS;
    SHEEP
  All in the April Evening.
    K. Tynan. Gr-TG:81
  The Fire in the Snow.
    V. Watkins. Wi-LT:454
  First Sight. P. Larkin.
    Co-BN:192, Mo-TS:64, Rd-OA:186
  For a Lamb. R. Eberhart.
    Pe-SS:67, Wi-LT:430
  I Held a Lamb. K. Worthington.
    Au-SP:49
  The Lamb. W. Blake. Bo-FP:106,
    Bo-GJ:64, Co-BBW:173, De-CH:87,
    Fe-FP:165, Hi-WP I:139, Hu-MP:199,
    Li-LC:82, Ma-YA:126, Mc-PR:101,
    Mc-WK:125, Ox-BC:85, Pa-RE:78,
    Pl-EI:18, Rv-CB:575, Un-GT:34
  The Lamb. T. Roethke. Li-LC:11
  Lambs. K. Tynan. De-TT:177
  The Lambs of Grasmere, 1860.
    C. Rossetti. Co-BBW:165
  Leela. Ca-MU:29
  Mary's Lamb. S. Hale.
    Au-SP:17, De-PO:12, Er-FA:504,
    Fe-FP:529, Fr-WO:25, Li-LB:94,
    Mo-CC:(38), Mo-MGT:120,
    Ox-BC:166, Un-GT:34, Wi-MG:67
  The Pet Lamb. W. Wordsworth.
    De-TT:57, Ox-BC:103
  Profile. D. Morton. Ke-TF:335
  The Sale of the Pet Lamb.
    M. Howitt. De-CH:87
  Sheep and Lambs. K. Hinkson.
    Go-BP:91, Se-PR:74
  Spring. W. Blake.
    Ar-TP3:203, Ch-B:99, Fe-FP:71,
    Ha-YA:25, Li-LC:70, Sm-LG:53,
    Un-GB:7, Un-GT:271

  Young Lambs.   J. Clare. Mc-PR:55,
    Un-GT:35
  Young Lambs to Sell. De-CH:573,
    Wr-RM:65
LAMENTS: see also DIRGES;
    ELEGIES
  Aeglamour's Lament. B. Jonson.
    De-CH:334, No-CL:199
  And Will A' Not Come Again.
    W. Shakespeare. Al-VBP:192
  The Beech. A. Young. Co-BN:153
  The Broken String. Tr-CB:51,
    Tr-US I:76
  Complaint. J. Wright. Ca-VT:622
  Complaint of a Widow over Her
    Dying Son. Tr-US I:157
  David's Lament. Bible. O.T.
    Samuel. Gr-CT:343, Me-PH:17
  David's Lament for Jonathan.
    P. Abélard. Ga-S:162
  Empty Saddles. Fi-BG:192
  Fair Helen. Al-VBP:53,
    De-CH:418, Er-FA:338,
    Hi-WP I:16, Pa-GTB:89,
    Rv-CB:43
  The Fall of Kumuhonua and His
    Wife. Tr-US II:96
  The Ghost's Lament. Ma-BB:84,
    Pa-RE:105
  The Ghosts Led by Vera Preparing
    for Their Final Departure.
    Uanuku. Tr-US II:60
  Girls' Song. Tr-US I:42
  Harp Song of the Dane Women.
    R. Kipling. Co-RM:55, Ox-BN:931
  Hymn of the Afflicted.
    Tr-US I:81
  Ihunui's Lament for Her Daughter
    Rangi. Ihunui. Tr-US II:115
  In Memory. L. Johnson. Ox-BN:948
  Lament. E. Millay. Kr-OF:183
  A Lament. A. Scott. De-CH:342
  A Lament. P. Shelley. Gr-CT:318,
    Pa-GTB:307
  Lament. Tr-US I:86
  Lament. Be-AP:28
  Lament. Tr-US II:89, 95, 116,
    117, 155
  Lament for the Dead Mother.
    Be-AP:28
  Lament for the Death of Eoghan
    Ruadh O'Neill. T. Davis.
    Co-PI:34, Hi-FO:148
  Lament for the Makers. W. Dunbar.
    Pl-ML:146
  Lament for Walsingham.
    Gr-GB:184, Rv-CB:115
  Lament of a Deserted Husband.
    Moanarai. Tr-US II:69
  Lament of a Widow for Her Dead
    Husband. Tr-US I:189

Lament of a Widow over Her Dead
   Husband.   Tr-US I:72
A Lamentation.   T. Campion.
   De-CH:178
Love Songs (O merchant).
   Tr-US I:115
The Maid's Lament.   W. Landor.
   Ox-BN:189
Margaret at Her Spinning Wheel.
   J. von Goethe.   Un-R:117
Mock Lament over a Dead Slave.
   Tr-US I:55
Mourning Songs.   Tr-US II:215
On the Death of Atahualpa.
   Bi-IT:154
The Peri's Lament for Hinda.
   T. Moore.   Ox-BN:217
Pilgrims' Song.   Tr-US I:129
Powerless! Powerless! Ho-SD:40
The Rebel Soldier.   Sm-LG:261
Responsive Song for the Dead Child
   of a Chief.   Tr-US II:220
Rites of the Condoling Council.
   Da-SC:135
Song after Defeat.   Tr-US I:37
A Song Made by Dancers on Hearing
   a Woman Mourning for Her Child.
   Tr-US I:86
A Song of Huezotzinco.   Da-SC:178
A Song of Lamentation.
   Ba-PO:27, Bi-IT:137, Da-SC:175
Toltec Lament.   Da-SC:167
The Trees Are Down.   C. Mew.
   Co-BN:146, Un-MB:164
Tumea's Lament for Her Father
   Ngakauvarea.   Tumea.
   Tr-US II:54
The Wandering Spectre.
   Bl-OB:156, De-CH:314, Gr-CT:155,
   Gr-GB:284, Rv-CB:141, Sm-LG:238
The Widow's Lament.   W. Williams.
   Wi-LT:197
See also Em-AF:96-127
LAMPS AND LAMPLIGHTERS
Evening Lights on the River.
   Chiang She Ch'uan.   Rx-LT:116
Five Short Stanzas, V. Dark Night.
   Tsou Ti-fan.   Hs-TC:348
In the Darkened Fields.
   M. Nakagawa.   Sh-AM:149
The Lamp.   A. Buttigieg.
   Pa-RE:120
The Lamplighter. R. Stevenson.
   Bo-FP:31, Er-FA:486,
   Hu-MP:149, Ox-BC:297
Light the Lamps Up, Lamplighter.
   E. Farjeon.   Br-SS:28,
   De-CH:439
Rhapsody on a Windy Night.
   T. Eliot.   Sh-AP:183

Street Lamps.   D. Lawrence.
   Go-BP:163
Who Goes There.   Etsujin.
   Be-MC:54
LANCASHIRE, ENG.
Little Lad.   Br-BC:6, Ir-BB:92,
   Tu-WW:14
LANCELOT OF THE LAKE, SIR:
   see also GUINEVERE, QUEEN
The Lady of Shalott.
   A. Tennyson.   Er-FA:339,
   Hi-WP I:59, Ho-WR:145,
   Sp-OG:128
Lancelot.   E. Robinson. Sm-PT:178
LAND: see EARTH
LANDLORDS AND TENANTS: see also
   HUMOR - LANDLORDS AND TENANTS;
   SATIRE - LANDLORDS AND TENANTS;
   SHARECROPPERS
Down on Roberts' Farm. C. Reeves.
   Hi-TL:197
Hamatreya.   R. Emerson.
   Sh-AP:30
Han Po Chops Wood.   Feng Chih.
   Hs-TC:155
The Land.   R. Kipling.   Ni-JP:134,
   Pa-OM:190, Un-MB:138
The Prologue to the Canterbury
   Tales.   G. Chaucer.   Al-VBP:6,
   Gr-CT:281, Ma-FW:17, Ma-YA:28
Scenery.   T. Joans.   Ad-PB:206
Sweet Smiling Village.
   O. Goldsmith.   Ke-PP:41
LANDOR, WALTER SAVAGE
For an Epitaph at Fiesole.
   W. Landor.   Ox-BN:195
LANGO VERSE: see AFRICAN VERSE
LANGUAGE: see also CONVERSATION;
   GRAMMAR; HUMOR - LANGUAGE;
   SATIRE - LANGUAGE; SPEECH;
   TRANSLATING; WORDS; and names
   of languages, as ENGLISH
   LANGUAGE
A Bright Day.   J. Montague.
   Ls-NY:170
The Cool Web.   R. Graves.
   Pa-GTB:486
Hearing Russian Spoken.
   D. Davie.   Pa-GTB:555
The Hebrew of Your Poets, Zion.
   C. Reznikoff.   Ca-VT:181
I Know Neither English nor French.
   A. Stolzenberg.   Ho-TY:269
Philological.   J. Updike.
   Co-EL:32
Robert of Gloucester's Chronicle.
   Ma-YA:23
Their Lonely Betters.
   W. Auden.   Bo-GJ:87,
   Ha-LO:64

LANIER, SIDNEY
  At Lanier's Grave.   J. Tabb.
    Sh-AP:136
LANTERNS
  Lantern Festival.   Yung Tsu.
    Pa-MV:202
  The Lanthorn Is to Keep the
    Candle Light.   J. Bunyan.
    Gr-TG:46
  Parliament Hill.   H. Bashford.
    Hu-MP:182, Th-AS:67
LAOCOÖN
  Laokoön.   S. Doinas.   Mc-AC:129
LAOTIAN VERSE: see THAI - LAOS
    VERSE
LAPPISH VERSE
  Complaint.   Tr-US I:34
  Hymn to the Southern Mountains.
    Tr-US I:33
  Journeying to His Sweetheart.
    No-CL:265
  Songs, I.   The Wolf.   Tr-US I:33
  Songs, II.   The Reindeer Herd.
    Tr-US I:33
LAPWINGS
  O Lapwing.   W. Blake.   Gr-CT:108,
    Re-BS:27
  Two Pewits.   E. Thomas.
    De-CH:106
LAREDO, TEX.
  The Streets of Laredo.
    L. MacNeice.   Ca-MB:112,
    Gr-CT:309, To-MP:45
  The Streets of Laredo.   Co-RM:28,
    Er-FA:337, Gr-CT:137, Gr-GB:321,
    Hi-TL:162, Mc-WK:169, Mc-WS:153
LARKS: see also SKYLARKS
  Address to a Lark Singing in
    Winter.   J. Clare.   Re-BS:48
  Answer to a Child's Question.
    S. Coleridge.   Bl-OB:68,
    Co-BBW:266, Gr-EC:224, Gr-TG:67,
    Hi-GD:12, Ox-BC:111, Re-BS:10,
    Re-TW:31
  Awake!   Awake!   W. Davenant.
    Al-VBP:384, De-CH:6, Gr-CT:41,
    Un-MW:3
  Frog-School Competing.   Shiki.
    Be-CS:54
  Hark!   Hark!   The Lark.
    W. Shakespeare.   Al-VBP:194,
    Bl-OB:94, Bo-FP:234, De-CH:6,
    Er-FA:107, Fe-FP:290, Ga-FB:27
    Gr-CT:264, No-CL:269, Rv-CB:200,
    Sm-LG:49, Sm-MK:22
  A Health to the Birds.
    S. MacManus.   Co-PI:112
  Hymn for Saturday.   C. Smart.
    Ox-BC:74, Rv-CB:539, Sm-LG:68
  The Lamentation of Beulah over
    Ololon.   W. Blake.   Ho-WR:60,
    Ox-BN:41

The Lark.   I. Pillat.   Mc-AC:58
The Lark.   Gr-GB:60
The Lark.   Gr-GB:61
The Lark in the Morning.
  Gr-CT:41, Gr-GB:44, Re-BS:49
October.   D. Thomas.   Ha-YA:110
On a Birthday.   J. Synge.
  Gr-CT:42
Rabbit and Lark.   J. Reeves.
  St-FS:101
Shadows.   E. Farjeon.   De-TT:149
The Two Nests.   F. Carlin.
  Re-BS:13
The Two Stars.   W. Davies.
  Un-MB:176
Upon the Lark and the Fowler.
  J. Bunyan.   Co-BBW:256,
  De-CH:104
Who Is't Now We Hear?   J. Lyly.
  Re-BS:49
LARKSPUR
  Larkspur.   J. Haines.   Sc-TN:74
LAST SUPPER: see LORD'S SUPPER
LATENESS: see PUNCTUALITY
LATIMER, HUGH
  Latimer and Ridley.
    W. Wordsworth.   Hi-FO:118
LATIN AMERICA: see also INDIANS
    OF CENTRAL and SOUTH AMERICA;
    PAN-AMERICANISM;   SOUTH AMERICA;
    and names of Latin American
    countries, as PANAMA
  The Dictators.   P. Neruda.
    Bl-FP:41
  To Theodore Roosevelt.
    R. Dario.   Bl-FP:37
  The United Fruit Co.   P. Neruda.
    Bl-FP:39
LATIN LANGUAGE: see HUMOR -
    LATIN LANGUAGE
LATIN VERSE
  Any Author to Any Friend.
    Martial.   Pl-ML:66
  The Boat Race.   Virgil.
    Fl-HH:43, Mo-SD:64
  Bought Locks.   Martial.   Mc-PR:20
  The Boxer's Face.   Lucilius.
    Mo-SD:79
  The Boxing Match.   Virgil.
    Fl-HH:7, Mo-SD:78
  Call to Youth.   Horace.   Pa-SG:4
  Carmina Burana.   Pa-SG:92
  Cathemerinon.   Prudentius.
    Pa-SG:14, 88
  The Chariot Race.   Virgil.
    Mo-SD:69
  The Coracle.   M. Lucan.   Gr-CT:221
  The Creation.   Ovid.   Cl-FC:78
  Critics.   Martial.   Mc-PR:21
  De Coenatione Micae.   Martial.
    Sm-LG:275

Dianae Sumus in Fide. Catullus.
  Gr-CC:94
Doctor Fell. Er-FA:216, Gr-CT:467,
  Mo-MGT:177, Pl-IO:119, Un-GT:22,
  Wr-RM:60
Easter Sunday. Sedulius Scottus.
  Li-TU:218
Eutychides. Lucilius. Pl-US:13
The Flood. P. Ovid. Gr-CT:203
Gay Comes the Singer. Sm-MK:142
The Georgics. Virgil.
  Ma-FW:16, 113, 261
The Golden Mean. Horace.
  Pa-SG:176
A House. Martial. Mc-PR:26
The Housekeeper. V. Bourne.
  Fe-PL:355, Mc-PR:44, Sp-OG:300,
  Un-GT:79
Hymn to Venus. Lucretius.
  Gr-CC:96
I Must, Varus, Tell You.
  Catullus. Pl-ML:62
In Love with Two. Ovid.
  Un-MW:69
In the Woods Alone. Pa-SG:27
Intercession Against the Plague.
  Sedulius Scottus. Ga-S:44
Johan the Monk. Li-TU:119
Juliana. Co-BL:41
Let Us Live and Love. Catullus.
  Rv-CB:264, Un-MW:175
Long Have I Borne Much. Ovid.
  Un-MW:68
The New Jerusalem. Al-VBP:366,
  Go-BP:263
No Single Thing Abides.
  T. Lucretius Carus. Pl-IO:9
O Come, All Ye Faithful.
  Er-FA:514, Ke-TF:225
O Filii et Filiae. Ga-S:174
O Stelliferi Conditor Orbis.
  Boethius. Go-BP:240
Ode to Maecenas. Horace.
  Pa-SG:173, Un-GT:236
On the Gift of a Cloak.
  Hugo of Orleans. Li-TU:44
Post-Obits and the Poets.
  Martial. Mc-PR:21
The Reconciliation. Horace.
  Un-MW:30
Roast Swan Song. Ma-FW:99
The Sluggard. Lucilius.
  Mo-SD:58
The Snow Dissolv'd. Horace.
  No-CL:130
Stabat Mater. Jacopone da Todi.
  Ga-S:157
Temperament. Martial. Co-EL:156,
  Mc-PR:21
To Verse Let Kings Give Place.
  Ovid. Gr-CT:429

Two Hundred Lines a Day.
  Martial. Pl-ML:65
Veni Creator. Ga-S:191
Veni Sancte Spiritus. Ga-S:200
The Vow to Cupid. Pa-SG:68
What Man First Forged.
  Tibullus. Ba-PO:73
What Slender Youth. Horace.
  Ho-WR:185, No-CL:172
When Thou Must Home. Propertius.
  Al-VBP:218, Gr-CC:78, Gr-TC:73,
  Ha-PO:170, Rv-CB:270
White Primit Falls. Virgil.
  Gr-CT:50
Why Don't I Send My Books to You.
  Martial. Pl-ML:68
The World's Worst Boxer.
  Lucilius. Mo-SD:81
LATMUS MOUNTAINS
  Oh, Sleep Forever in the Latmian
  Cave. E. Millay. Al-VBP:1195,
  Un-MA:449, Wi-LT:339
LATTER-DAY SAINTS: see MORMONS
  AND MORMONISM
LAUGHTER: see also HUMOR -
  LAUGHTER; SATIRE - LAUGHTER;
  SMILES
  American Laughter.
    K. Robinson. Br-AF:118
  Archy Confesses. D. Marquis.
    Co-FB:359, Na-EO:142
  The Big Laugh. L. Blair.
    Ja-PC:7
  Bursting. D. Aldis. Ja-PC:6
  Celebrated Return. C. Major.
    Be-MA:143, Bo-AN:182
  A Child's Laughter. A. Swinburne.
    Br-BC:69, Fe-PL:246
  Daddy Fell into the Pond.
    A. Noyes. Co-HP:101, Fe-FP:35,
    Ja-PC:40, La-PP:45, La-PV:24,
    Sh-RP:140
  Dining-Room Tea. R. Brooke.
    Un-MB:326
  Early Supper. B. Howes.
    Bo-GJ:27
  Everybody Laugh. L. Hale.
    Ba-HI:138
  I Tell Her She Is Lovely.
    M. Gibbon. Co-PI:50
  Laugh and Be Merry. J. Masefield.
    Er-FA:21, Un-MB:228
  Laughing. G. MacPherson.
    Ja-PC:10
  Laughing Song. W. Blake.
    Ar-TP3:117, Au-SP:218, Bo-FP:269,
    Bo-GJ:41, Co-PS:109, De-CH:187,
    Gr-EC:45, Mc-WK:26, Re-TW:76,
    Rv-CB:587, Un-GT:11
  Laughter. M. Waddington.
    Do-WH:14

LAUGHTER — cont'd.
  Rainy Song. M. Eastman. Bo-HF:49
  They Say that in the Unchanging
    Place. H. Belloc. Fe-PL:126
LAUNCELOT DU LAC, SIR: see
  LANCELOT OF THE LAKE, SIR
LAUNDRY: see also HUMOR - LAUNDRY
  Bendix. J. Updike. Pe-SS:61
  The Dolls' Wash. J. Ewing.
    Ox-BC:257
  Down by the River. Mo-MGT:170
  Five Vignettes, 2. J. Toomer.
    Ad-PB:34
  In an Iridescent Time. R. Stone.
    Un-MA:655
  Laundry Song. Wen I-to.
    Hs-TC:55
  Love Calls Us to the Things of
    This World. R. Wilbur.
    Ca-VT:484, Un-MA:675
  Mar Quong, Chinese Laundryman.
    C. Morley. Hu-MP:144
  Monday. St-FS:37
  Mother and Daughter.
    J. Bovshover. Kr-OF:170
  Old Ellen Sullivan. W. Welles.
    Fe-FP:310, Hu-MP:143
  Stocking and Shirt. J. Reeves.
    Gr-EC:114
  They That Wash on Monday.
    Bl-OB:145, Ir-BB:228,
    Li-LB:163, Mo-TB:110
  Wash. J. Updike. Mo-TS:33
  Windy Wash Day. D. Aldis.
    Ar-TP3:167, Fr-MP:10, La-PP:19
LAURA (OF PETRARCH'S POEMS)
  The Faery Queen. W. Raleigh.
    Al-VBP:93
  Petrarch for Laura.
    C. McAllister. Gr-SS:101
LAUREL
  Daphne. D. Galler. Ls-NY:317
  Pennsylvania. H. Bucher.
    Se-PR:281
  Song. C. Rossetti.
    Al-VBP:995, Pa-GTB:374
LAVENDER (PLANT)
  I Planned to Have a Border of
    Lavender. P. Goodman.
    Ca-VT:336
  Lavender's Blue. Ir-BB:270,
    Li-LB:28
LAW: see also COURTS (LAW);
    LAWYERS; LEGISLATORS;
    SATIRE - LAW
  The Avengers. E. Markham.
    Un-MA:108
  The Eleventh Commandment.
    J. Holmes. Tr-MR:78
  In the State There Is the Law.
    B. Slutsky. Bo-RU:80

The Law of the Jungle.
    R. Kipling. Rd-OA:128
  Law, Say the Gardeners, Is the
    Sun. W. Auden. Un-MB:458
  The Laws of God, the Laws of Men.
    A. Housman. Un-MB:102
  Let There Be Law.
    M. Van Doren. Tr-MR:192
  Wealth. R. Emerson. Pl-IO:34
LAWES, HENRY
  Envoi. E. Pound. Ca-VT:86,
    No-CL:27, Un-MA:296
  To Mr. Henry Lawes. E. Waller.
    No-CL:28
LAWN MOWERS: see LAWNS
LAWNS
  All in the Path of a Power
    Mower. R. Gillman. Du-SH:112
  Lawn Mower. D. Baruch. Au-SP:104
  Sad Green. S. Warner. Un-MB:373
LAWRENCE, EDWARD
  To Mr. Lawrence. J. Milton.
    Pa-GTB:66
LAWYERS: see also COURTS (LAW);
    HUMOR - LAWYERS; SATIRE -
    LAWYERS
  Dialogue at Night. E. Greenberg.
    Ho-TY:308
LAZARUS: see DIVES AND LAZARUS
LAZINESS: see also HUMOR - LAZINESS
  The Ant and the Cricket. Aesop.
    De-TT:59, Un-GT:78
  Beehive. J. Toomer. Ad-PB:29,
    Be-MA:17, Lo-TY:211
  Broom, Green Broom. Bl-OB:38,
    De-CH:139, Fo-OG:8, Ha-PO:54
  Cocks Crow in the Morn.
    Ar-TP3:174, Sp-TM:1,
    Un-GT:22, Wr-RM:78
  Dame, Get Up and Bake Your Pies.
    Wi-MG:57
  Elsie Marley. Mother Goose.
    Co-BB:36, Mo-MGT:165, Mo-NR:99,
    Sp-TM:3
  Go North, South, East and West,
    Young Man. S. Milligan. Co-OT:35
  A Hot-Weather Song. D. Marquis.
    Co-PU:35, Sh-RP:215
  If You Are Lazy. Ho-SD:13
  Knee-Deep in June. J. Riley.
    Sp-OG:291
  Lazy Balan. Ca-MU:12
  The Lazy Hours. Br-FW:4
  Lazy Lou. M. Dodge. Co-BB:39
  The Lazy Man. Be-AP:57
  Lazy Mary, Will You Get Up?
    M. and M. Petersham. Sh-RP:16
  Nancy Dawson. Wr-RM:48
  Robin and Richard. Ir-BB:30,
    Mo-MGT:130, Mo-NR:131, On-TW:9,
    Wr-RM:20

See, Saw, Margery Daw.   Wi-MG:59
Sleepy John.   C. Tringress.
    St-FS:74
The Sluggard.   I. Watts.   De-CH:5,
    Gr-TG:45, Li-SR:98, Ox-BC:51
Sunning.   J. Tippett.   Ar-TP3:51,
    Br-SS:178, Du-RG:86, Gr-EC:82
Tired Tim.   W. de la Mare.
    Ar-TP3:6, Au-SP:133, Fe-FP:308,
    Hu-MP:141, Li-LC:49, Pe-FB:27
LEADERSHIP: see also SATIRE -
    LEADERSHIP
The Blackstone Rangers.   II, The
    Leaders.   G. Brooks.   Ad-PB:160
The Leader.   Bible.   O.T.
    Samuel.   Bo-FP:302
The Man from the Crowd.   S. Foss.
    Fe-PL:422
Wolf Song.   Da-SC:112
LEANDER: see HERO AND LEANDER
LEAR, EDWARD
Edward Lear.   W. Auden.   Pl-ML:95
How Pleasant to Know Mr. Lear!
    E. Lear.   Co-FB:45, Co-HP:90,
    Gr-CT:463, Ha-PO:240, Li-SR:43,
    Pa-GTB:356, Pl-ML:22, Rv-CB:810,
    Tu-WW:118, Un-GT:212
LEARNING: see EDUCATION; KNOWLEDGE;
    SCHOLARS AND SCHOLARSHIP;
    WISDOM
LEAVES
After the Storm.   Nö-in. Ba-ST:35
Autumn.   D. Dore.   Ho-CT:28
Autumn Leaves.   J. Heyward.
    Hu-MP:281
Autumn Leaves.   M. Sutphen.
    Bo-FP:147
Autumn Woods.   J. Tippett.
    Ar-TP3:184, Ja-PA:14, Mc-AW:48,
    St-FS:102
Autumnal Spring Song. V. Miller.
    Ha-PO:99
Beech Leaves.   J. Reeves.
    Pa-RE:108, Sh-RP:222
Blue Smoke.   F. Frost.   Br-SS:65,
    Sh-RP:229
The City of Falling Leaves.
    A. Lowell.   Ar-TP3:184
The College of Surgeons.
    J. Stephens.   Ha-LO:86
Color.   M. Cane.   Sh-RP:222
Come, Little Leaves.   G. Cooper.
    Bo-FP:147, Fe-FP:541, Hu-MP:280
Companions.   A. Stoutenberg.
    Ha-WR:83
Dead Metaphors.   D. Holbrook.
    Ls-NY:287
Down! Down!   E. Farjeon.
    Ar-TP3:184, Au-SP:325
A Dry Leaf Drifting.   Basho.
    Be-MC:9

A Dry Leaf Drifting.   Bokusui.
    Be-MC:57
Foam Flowers.   Yasuhide.
    Le-MW:82
Forest Leaves in Autumn. J. Keble.
    Ox-BN:306
Gathering Leaves.   R. Frost.
    Br-SG:95, Ca-VT:17, Ha-LO:34,
    Sh-RP:223
Golden Bough.   E. Wylie.
    Un-MA:276
Hospital Visit.   R. Roseliep.
    St-H:185
How the Leaves Came Down.
    S. Coolidge.   Hu-MP:281
In Storm-Tossed Grassland.
    Miyoshi.   Ca-BF:37
Invitation Standing.
    P. Blackburn.   Ca-VT:556
The Kitten.   Issa.   Do-TS:38
The Kitten and the Falling
    Leaves.   W. Wordsworth.
    Bl-OB:106, Ch-B:23, Co-BBW:124,
    Fe-FP:157, Hu-MP:208, Un-GB:18,
    Un-GT:52
The Last Leaf.   H. Behn.
    Sh-RP:231
Last Week in October.   T. Hardy.
    Co-PU:144
Leaf and Sun.   N. Farber.
    Ho-LP:99
Leaf Falling on Leaf.   Gyodai.
    Be-CS:54
A Leaf Looks Prickly.
    P. Johnson.   Le-M:124
Leaf That Falls Yellow.
    Wo-HS:(62)
A Leaf-Treader.   R. Frost.
    Un-MA:188
Leaves.   W. Barnes.   Co-BN:149,
    Gr-CT:317, Ox-BN:430
Leaves.   C. Cullen.   Bo-HF:62
Leaves.   W. Davies.   Un-MB:178
The Leaves.   O. Lermand. Ho-CT:28
Leaves.   P. Walker.   La-PV:85
The Leaves.   St-FS:125
Leaves like Fish.   G. Cardiff.
    Ni-CD:47
Looking Up at Leaves.   B. Howes.
    Co-BN:233
The Man with the Rake.   C. Morley.
    Na-EO:55
Maple Leaves.   Shiko.
    Au-SP:323, Pa-SG:95
New Leaves.   J. Jiménez.
    Le-SW:17
New York-Albany.   L. Ferlinghetti.
    En-PC:171
November Night.   A. Crapsey.
    Fe-FP:83, Hi-WP II:137,
    Ho-LP:32, Hu-MP:321, Ja-PA:41

LEAVES — cont'd.
  Nuts. De-TT:38, Ja-PA:22,
    Rv-ON:41
  The Pity of the Leaves.
    E. Robinson. Un-MA:137
  The Rain. W. Davies. Ar-TP3:171,
    Bo-FP:231
  The Room. C. Aiken. Un-MA:424,
    Wi-LT:332
  September. K. Pyle. Bo-FP:139
  Song. Tr-US I:175
  Song for a Ceremonial Dance.
    Tr-US I:183
  Spring, I Suppose. Re-RR:44
  Thorn Leaves in March. W. Merwin.
    Br-TC:289
  Thoughts of Thomas Hardy.
    E. Blunden. En-PC:31
  The Tree. B. Björnson.
    Bo-FP:268, Hu-MP:271
  The Tree Stands Very Straight
    and Still. A. Wynne. Au-SP:288
  Trees. N. Dishman. Le-M:39
  The Trees Share Their Shade.
    N. Dishman. Le-WR:11
  Two Leaves. J. Stuart. De-FS:196
  Walk on the Living. Re-RR:15
  What I Tell Him. S. Ortiz.
    Ni-CD:151
  The Whirl-Blast. W. Wordsworth.
    De-TT:162
  The Wind Brings Fallen Leaves.
    Ryokan. Do-TS:39
  You Lingering Sparse Leaves
    of Me. W. Whitman. Rv-CB:856
LEBANON
  As I Came Down from Lebanon.
    C. Scollard. Pa-HT:97
LECTURES AND LECTURING: see
    PUBLIC SPEAKING
LEDA
  Leda and the Swan. W. Yeats.
    Pa-GTB:427, Un-MB:113, Wi-LT:82
LEDBETTER, HUDDIE (LEADBELLY)
  Lead. J. Cortez. Ad-PB:343
LEE, ROBERT EDWARD
  Lee, in the Mountains, 1865-1870.
    D. Davidson. Sm-PT:92
  Robert E. Lee. J. Howe. Se-PR:36
  The Sword of Robert E. Lee.
    A. Ryan. Se-PR:36
  Uncle Frank. L. Bacon. Cr-WS:34
LEEUWENHOEK, ANTON VAN
  The Microscope. M. Kumin.
    Du-RG:53, Ha-PO:96
LEGENDS: see also CHRISTMAS LEGENDS;
    JESUS CHRIST - LEGENDS;MYTHOLOGY;
    SAINTS; TALL TALES; and names of
    legendary characters, as
    FLYING DUTCHMAN
  The Eve of St. Agnes. J. Keats.
    Al-VBP:781, Fe-PL:35, Ox-BN:338

Fourth Dance Poem. G. Barrax.
  Ad-PB:225
Helen of Tyre. H. Longfellow.
  Gr-SS:78
A Legend of the Northland.
  P. Cary. Pa-OM:317, Un-GT:139
Legend of the Waving Lady.
  E. Livingston. Sc-TN:141
Santorin. J. Flecker.
  Bo-GJ:183, Gr-CC:97, No-CL:58
LEGENDS, AFRICAN
  The Birth of Moshesh. D. Bereng.
    Lo-TY:173
  How Death Came. Lo-TY:5
LEGENDS, AMERICAN: see also
    LEGENDS, WESTERN
  The Apple-Barrel of Johnny
    Appleseed. V. Lindsay.
    Br-AF:118
  Folk-Tune. R. Wilbur. Br-AF:120
  John Henry. Br-AF:113
  Legend of Ramapo Mountain.
    J. Palen. De-FS:144
  The Mountains. W. Merwin.
    Ca-VT:614
LEGENDS, CHINESE
  Han Po Chops Wood. Feng Chih.
    Hs-TC:155
LEGENDS, EAST INDIAN
  The True and Tender Wife.
    Al-PI:29
LEGENDS, ENGLISH
  A Featherston's Doom.
    R. Hawker. Ox-BN:460
  A Winter Legend. G. Johnson.
    De-FS:112
LEGENDS, GERMAN: see also ERLKING
  The Loreley. H. Heine. Sp-OG:116,
    Un-GT:137
LEGENDS, INDIAN: see INDIANS OF
    CENTRAL and NORTH AMERICA -
    LEGENDS
LEGENDS, IRISH
  The Abbot of Inisfalen.
    W. Allingham. Pa-OM:104
  The Army of the Sidhe.
    Lady Gregory. Th-AS:139
  The Gods of the Dana. L. Drake.
    De-FS:79
  The Last Pagan Mourns for Dark
    Rosaleen. J. Brennan. De-FS:36
  Ossian. J. Brennan. De-FS:37
LEGENDS, PHILIPPINE
  The Myth of Numputul, the Self-
    Beheaded. Tr-US I:178
LEGENDS, RUSSIAN
  Babushka. E. Thomas. Hu-MP:432,
    Pa-OM:362
LEGENDS, SCOTTISH
  How the First Hielandman of God
    Was Made of Ane Horse Turd in
    Argyll as Is Said. Gr-GB:166

LEGENDS, SPANISH
  The Cid's Rising. F. Hemans.
    Hi-FO:72
LEGENDS, WEST INDIAN
  The Woman's Tongue Tree.
    A. Guiterman. Co-PM:81
LEGENDS, WESTERN
  Old North. N. Thorp. Fi-BG:131
  The White Steed of the Prairies.
    J. Barber. Fi-BG:87
  Witch of the Canyon. Fi-BG:116
LEGISLATORS: see SATIRE -
    LEGISLATORS
LEGREE, SIMON: see SIMON LEGREE
LEGS: see also HUMOR - LEGS
  The Ant. J. Kransnai. La-GI:55
  Bandy Legs. Ir-BB:26, Mo-MGT:136
  Broken Leg. S. Johnson. Ho-GC:36
  Guess This One for Me. Re-RR:26
  Her Legs. R. Herrick. Li-SR:23
  The Knee. C. Morgenstern.
    Un-R:71
  The Leg. K. Shapiro. Ha-TP:84,
    Un-MA:634
  A Leg in a Plaster Cast.
    M. Rukeyser. Un-MA:627
  The Legs. R. Graves. Ha-PO:243,
    Wi-LT:369
  Poem in Which My Legs Are Accepted.
    K. Fraser. Mc-EA:25
  Two Legs Sat upon Three Legs.
    Li-LB:167, Mo-MGT:156,
    Mo-NR:136, Rv-ON:53
LEGS, WOODEN: see HANDICAPPED
LEISURE
  Grass on the Wall. Pien Chih-lin.
    Hs-TC:165
  Leisure; W. Davies.
    Ar-TP3:213, Co-BN:205, De-CH:137,
    Er-FA:248, Fe-FP:78, Gr-EC:45,
    Hi-WP I:119, Mc-WK:22, Sh-RP:117,
    Sm-MK:177, Un-MB:179, Wi-LT:617
  The Lotos Eaters. A. Tennyson.
    Mo-GR:129
  Summer in the World. Bassho.
    Le-MW:76
  Wishes. E. Guest. Ke-TF:238
LEMAN, LAKE: see GENEVA, LAKE OF
LEMMINGS
  The Lemming's Song. Le-IB:40
LEMONADE
  August Afternoon. M. Edey.
    Ha-YA:90
  Lemonade. Gr-GB:27
  Lemonade Stand. D. Thompson.
    Br-SS:176
LEMONS
  The Land in My Mother.
    N. Hashimoto. Le-TA:17
  Lemons. P. Hubbell. Gr-EC:109

LENDING: see BORROWING AND
    LENDING
LENIN, VLADIMIR ILICH (NIKOLAI)
  Lenin. Y. Artiuschanko.
    Mo-MI:62
  The Skeleton of the Future.
    H. MacDiarmid. Un-MB:361
LENINGRAD, U.S.S.R.
  The Donkey in the Nyevsky
    Prospekt. G. Garbovsky.
    Bo-RU:35
  House in St. Petersburg.
    S. Burnshaw. Gr-SS:72
  I Am Cold. O. Mandelstam.
    Ca-MR:144
  I Return to My City.
    O. Mandelstam. Ca-MR:148
  In the Late Autumn. A. Blok.
    Ca-MR:191
  Lord, This Night. O. Mandelstam.
    Ca-MR:158
  1913. A. Akhmatova. Ca-MR:187
  The Russian Gods. D. Andreyev.
    Ca-MR:95
  St. Isaac's Church, Petrograd.
    C. McKay. Ad-PB:271, Be-MA:15,
    Bo-AN:29
  To Leningrad. N. Bugakova.
    Mo-MI:63
LENT: see also EASTER; FASTING;
    HUMOR - LENT; JESUS CHRIST -
    CRUCIFIXION; SHROVE TUESDAY
  Ash-Wednesday. T. Eliot.
    Ca-VT:134, Un-MA:398
  Ash Wednesday. L. Johnson.
    Ga-S:141
  Ash Wednesday. R. Marinoni.
    Se-PR:69
  The Corpus Christi Carol.
    Gr-GB:308
  The Donkey. G. Chesterton.
    Fe-PL:330, Ga-FB:7, Se-PR:72,
    Un-MB:209
  The Donkey's Owner. C. Sansom.
    Ga-S:152
  Elvers. F. Harvey. Cl-DT:47
  Evil Days. B. Pasternak.
    Tr-MR:119
  Holy Thursday. W. Blake.
    De-CH:62, Ma-YA:127, Rv-CB:584
  Hot Cross Buns! Mother Goose.
    Au-SP:11, Bo-FP:244, De-PO:10,
    Mo-MGT:109, Mo-NR:120, Mo-TL:75,
    On-TW:10, Wi-MG:39, Wr-RM:127
  It Is Finished. J. Wheelock.
    Tr-MR:127
  The Lent Lily. A. Housman.
    Co-PS:67, Hu-MP:250,
    Se-PR:71

LENT — cont'd.
  Palm Sunday. H. Vaughan.
    Ga-S:151
  Palm Sunday. Bo-FP:245
  A True Lent. R. Herrick.
    Se-PR:70
LEOFRIC AND GODIVA
  Leofric and Godiva. W. Landor.
    Gr-CC:90
LEONARDO DA VINCI: see HUMOR —
    LEONARDO DA VINCI
LEONIDAS, KING OF SPARTA
  The Great Dead at Thermopylae.
    Simonides. Pa-SG:8
LEOPARDS: see also HUMOR —
    LEOPARDS
  Cat. J. Tolkien. Gr-EC:68
  Color. R. Bennett. Hu-MP:185
  The Dalliance of the Leopards.
    Ho-LP:3
  Leopard. E. Braithwaite.
    Ab-MO:36
  The Snow-Leopard. R. Jarrell.
    Br-TC:221, Wi-LT:560
LEPANTO, BATTLE, 1571
  Lepanto. G. Chesterton.
    Ga-FB:196, Hi-FO:119, Un-MB:205
LEPERS
  Father Damien. J. Tabb.
    Sh-AP:136
  Sir Aldinger. Ox-BB:23
LEPRECHAUNS
  Faith, I Wish I Were a Leprechaun.
    M. Ritter. Ar-TP3:160,
    Fe-FP:389
  Goblin Feet. J. Tolkien.
    Co-PM:163, Fe-FP:369
  The Leprahaun. R. Joyce.
    Co-PM:109
  No Luck. L. Blair. Ja-HH:18
  Of Certain Irish Fairies.
    A. Guiterman. Fe-PL:107
LETTERS AND LETTER WRITING:
    see also HUMOR — LETTERS
    AND LETTER WRITING
  The Bonny Brown Girl. Ox-BB:355
  Country Letter. J. Clare.
    Rv-CB:733
  Her Letter. B. Harte. Fe-PL:20
  How to Write a Letter.
    E. Turner. Ox-BC:138
  Letter. M. Strand. Mo-BG:102
  A Letter from a Girl to Her Own
    Old Age. A. Meynell.
    Al-VBP:1065, Un-MB:63
  Letter of a Mother. R. Warren.
    Un-MA:584
  A Letter to Her Husband, Absent
    upon Publick Employment.
    A. Bradstreet. Rv-CB:386

Letter to N. Y. E. Bishop.
  Br-TC:47, Ho-TH:63, Mc-WS:116
A Letter to Robert Frost.
  R. Hillyer. Un-MA:484
Letter Written on a Ferry Crossing
  Long Island Sound. A. Sexton.
  Br-TC:365
Night Mail. W. Auden. Gr-CT:407,
  Ha-PO:44, Hi-WP I:132
The Postman's Bell Is Answered
  Everywhere. H. Gregory.
  Un-MA:512
The River Merchant's Wife: A
  Letter. Li T'ai-Po.
  Bo-HF:120, Br-TC:332, Co-BL:101,
  Gr-CC:22, Ha-PO:184, Li-TU:181,
  Mo-BG:98, Pe-SS:126, Sh-AP:171,
  Un-MA:290
A Sick Child. R. Jarrell.
  Ca-VT:402
Snow Storm. Tu Fu. Rx-OH:6
Some Foreign Letters. A. Sexton.
  En-PC:274, Un-MA:687
Sonnets from the Portuguese XXVIII.
  E. Browning. Al-VBP:816
To Miss Ferrier. R. Burns.
  Rv-CB:623
What Letter Has Never Yet.
  Re-RR:84
Young Girl: Annam. P. Colum.
  Ha-LO:94
Young Love. S. Teasdale.
  Co-BL:23
LETTUCE: see HUMOR — LETTUCE
LEVIATHAN: see MYTHICAL ANIMALS
    AND BIRDS
LEWIS AND CLARK EXPEDITION
  Empire Builders. A. MacLeish.
    Sh-AP:188
  Lewis and Clark. S. Benét.
    Sh-RP:296
LEXINGTON, BATTLE, 1775
  Lexington, April 19, 1775.
    S. Lanier. Vi-PP:100
LEY, MARGARET
  To the Lady Margaret Ley.
    J. Milton. Pa-GTB:73
LIARS: see also FALSEHOOD;
    HUMOR — LIARS
  The False Heart. H. Belloc.
    Sm-LG:391
  Heriger, Bishop of Mainz.
    Li-TU:152
  If We Want to Tell a Lie.
    Do-CH:(14)
  If You Are Lazy. Ho-SD:13
  Lord Douglas. Ox-BB:324
  Matilda. H. Belloc. Ox-BC:314
  No Matter How. S. Aleksandrovsky.
    Mo-MI:82

The Shepherd Boy and the Wolf.
    W. Leonard.   Hu-MP:406
LIBERIA
    Do. M. Tolson.   Hu-PN:143
LIBERTY: see FREEDOM
LIBERTY, STATUE OF: see also
    SATIRE - LIBERTY, STATUE OF
The Bartholdi Statue.
    J. Whittier.   Hi-TL:170
Inscription on the Statue of
    Liberty. E. Lazarus.
    Se-PR:127
The New Colossus. E. Lazarus.
    Bo-HF:35, Br-AF:247, Er-FA:289,
    Fe-FP:448, Fe-PL:153, Ga-FB:265,
    Vi-PP:187
LIBRARIES: see also HUMOR -
    LIBRARIES
    Eating Poetry. M. Strand.
    Mo-BG:7
The Library. B. Huff.   Fe-FP:250,
    Ja-PA:52
National Library.
    O. de Andrade.   An-TC:11
On a Booklover's Shelves.
    S. Coblentz.   Ke-TF:302
LICE
    Call It a Louse. C. Dorman.
    Ca-VT:528
A Louse Crept Out of My Lady's
    Shift. G. Bottomley.
    Gr-CT:85
To a Louse. R. Burns.
    Al-VBP:629, Co-BBW:221,
    Er-FA:71, Ma-YA:131, Sp-OG:300
LIDICE, CZECH.
    Lidice. E. Jebeleanu.
    Mc-AC:105
LIÈVRE RIVER
    Morning on the Lièvre.
    A. Lampman. Mo-SD:130
LIFE: see also HUMOR - LIFE;
    LIFE AND DEATH; THE
    LIVING; SATIRE - LIFE
    Age. E. Tuck. Br-BC:139,
    Fe-PL:259, Se-PR:237
All the World's a Stage.
    W. Shakespeare. Er-FA:151,
    Fe-PL:257, Ha-PO:257,
    Ma-YA:67, Un-GT:85
And Love Hung Still.
    L. MacNeice. Un-MB:443
And the Days Are Not Full
    Enough. E. Pound. Ma-FW:88
Another and the Same.
    S. Rogers. Ox-BN:48
Anthology. M. Bandeira. An-TC:5
anyone lived in a pretty how town.
    E. Cummings. Br-TC:80,
    Ca-VT:182, Ha-PO:241, Na-EO:73,
    Pe-OA:152, Un-MA:477, Wi-LT:365

As a Landscape.   F. Saito.
    Sh-AM:153
As One Who Bears Beneath His
    Neighbor's Roof. R. Hillyer.
    Un-MA:481
Atalanta in Calydon.
    A. Swinburne. Al-VBP:1040,
    Er-FA:82, Rv-CB:936
Aubade. L. MacNeice. Al-VBP:1231
Away with Funeral Music.
    R. Stevenson. Hi-WP II:1
Beseeching the Breath. Bi-IT:25
beware: do not read this poem.
    I. Reed. Ad-PB:328, Jo-SA:64,
    Ra-BP:288
The Birds of America.
    J. Broughton. Br-AF:25
Birthday. E. Emans. Br-BC:138
Blue Lake of Life. Wo-HS:(15)
The Boat. R. Pack. Ha-TP:125
Bubbles. F. Kitagawa. Sh-AM:85
The Builders. H. Longfellow.
    Er-FA:8, Sp-OG:327
Called Back. E. Dickinson.
    Un-MA:105
Canal Bank Walk. P. Kavanagh.
    Un-MB:431
Cawdor. R. Jeffers. Sm-PT:25
A Cherry Fair. Gr-CT:321
Christmas Poem. V. de Moraes.
    An-TC:101
Circumstance. A. Tennyson.
    Sp-OG:277
The Clerk. E. Robinson.
    Un-MA:126
Coexistence. M. Syrkin. Ls-NY:97
Come You Four Winds. Wo-HS:(67)
Compromise. C. Stetson.
    Sp-OG:331
A Coney Island Life. J. Weil.
    Br-AF:196, Du-RG:74
Corruption. H. Vaughan. Ho-P:296
Counterpoint. O. Dodson.
    Hu-PN:300, Jo-SA:59
David's Song. R. Browning. Ga-FB:11
death prosecuting. L. Curry.
    Jo-SA:7, Jo-VC:84
The Debt. P. Dunbar. Bo-AN:5,
    Bo-HF:176
Deliverance. Ping Hsin.
    Hs-TC:25
A Dialogue of Self and Soul.
    W. Yeats. Un-MB:118, Wi-LT:84
Dirge in Woods. G. Meredith.
    Ho-WR:174, Ox-BN:699
Discovery. H. Belloc. Al-VBP:1110
Ditty. W. Gibson. Ls-NY:333
The Dream. G. Byron. Mo-GR:118
A Dream. I. Nez. Ba-HI:129

LIFE — cont'd.
  Dreamer of Dreams. W. Carruth.
    Fe-PL:305
  Dying Speech of an Old Philosopher.
    W. Landor. Al-VBP:704,
    Gr-CT:435,Ha-PO:209, Ma-YA:169,
    Ox-BN:194, Pa-GTB:318
  Egg. M. Yoshioka. Sh-AM:112
  The End. M. Van Doren. Al-VBP:1200
  The End of the Play.
    W. Thackeray. Er-FA:520
  Enitharmon Revives with Los.
    W. Blake. Ox-BN:38
  L'Envoi. R. Kipling.
    Er-FA:10, Ke-TF:453
  Envoy. F. Thompson. Ga-FB:335,
    Un-MB:91
  Epitaph. L. Abercrombie.
    Al-VBP:1147, Un-MB:259
  Escape. R. Graves. Cr-WS:92,
    Un-MB:387
  Esther. W. Blunt. Al-VBP:1051,
    Ox-BN:847
  Esthetique du Mal, XI.
    W. Stevens. Wi-LT:157
  Even in the Darkness. H. Mullins.
    Tr-MR:227
  Even Such Is Time. W. Raleigh.
    Al-VBP:97, De-CH:644, Ga-S:219,
    Gr-BT:167, Gr-CT:381,
    Hi-WP II:169, Na-EO:93
  Everyman. S. Sassoon. Un-MB:315
  Evolution. J. Tabb. Sh-AP:136
  The Field of Glory.
    E. Robinson. Un-MA:125
  Fiftieth Birthday. P. Viereck.
    Ls-NY:68
  Fire Fire of the First World.
    Wo-HS:(61)
  Fire in the Sky. Tsang K'o-chia.
    Hs-TC:280
  The Fisher's Boy. H. Thoreau.
    Gr-CT:192
  Fleeting Signs. G. Dumitrescu.
    Mc-AC:124
  Flowers. C. Lushington. Sa-B:234
  For Life I Had Never Cared
    Greatly. T. Hardy. Wi-LT:22
  For the Moment. R. Weber.
    Co-PI:196
  For This Is Wisdom. L. Hope.
    Fe-PL:305
  Formula for Obtaining Long
    Life. Da-SC:141
  Four Walls to Talk to Me.
    A. Blackwell. Jo-VC:89
  From a Notarized Deposition Made
    by Itshas Harjo. Itshas Harjo.
    Br-MW:115
  From Jazz for Five, 3:Colin Barnes,
    Drums. J. Smith. To-MP:194

  Fulfillment. H. Johnson.
    Hu-PN:262
  The Garden of Proserpine.
    A. Swinburne. Co-PU:155
  The Goddess. T. de Banville.
    Gr-SS:125
  The Good Earth. K. Itta.
    Ba-HI:107
  Gradatim. J. Holland. Er-FA:4
  Great Man. B. Johnson. Co-EL:91
  the greedy the people.
    E. Cummings. Pe-OA:155
  Hamlet. B. Pasternak. Ca-MR:174
  The Hammers. R. Hodgson.
    Bo-GJ:202, Un-MB:192
  He Wove the Strands of Our Life.
    Bi-IT:8
  The Heart Asks Pleasure First.
    E. Dickinson. Ha-PO:149,
    Rv-CB:898, Un-MA:96
  The Hermit. Hsu Pen.
    Le-MW:130, Ma-FW:85
  Hidesong. A. Higo. Lo-TY:159
  The Hill. R. Brooke. Al-VBP:1178,
    Co-BL:165, Hi-WP II:109,
    Un-MB:322, Un-MW:171
  His Choice. A. Baker. Ke-TF:252
  The Holy of Holies. G. Chesterton.
    Go-BP:254, Tr-MR:44
  The House of Life. D. Quick.
    De-FS:151
  The Human Seasons. J. Keats.
    Er-FA:179, Ho-WR:22, Ma-YA:186,
    Pa-GTB:307
  Hymn to the Spirit of Nature.
    P. Shelley. Al-VBP:742,
    De-CH:335, Pa-GTB:281
  I Am. J. Clare. Al-VBP:764,
    Go-BP:235, Ha-PO:207, Mc-PR:109,
    Ox-BN:331, Pa-GTB:319, Rv-CB:728
  I Am like a Slip of Comet.
    G. Hopkins. Li-TU:175
  I Loved. . . . A. Seeger.
    Ke-TF:111
  I Saw from the Beach. T. Moore.
    Co-PI:144, Ox-BN:213
  I Sing No New Songs. F. Davis.
    Ad-PB:98, Hu-PN:252
  i thank You God. E. Cummings.
    Pl-EI:195, Tr-MR:22
  I Think Continually of Those Who
    Were Truly Great. S. Spender.
    Al-VBP:1235, Gr-CT:377, Ha-PO:222,
    Pl-EI:158, Tr-MR:166, Un-MB:477,
    Wi-LT:496
  I Want Time to Run. V. Lapin.
    Mo-MI:33
  If. R. Kipling. Er-FA:5,
    Hi-WP I:118, Ox-BC:324, Un-GT:314
  If It Had Been Shared with Justice.
    M. Isanos. Mc-AC:118

If They Spoke. M. Van Doren.
   Pl-IO:102
An Immorality. E. Pound.
   Bo-GJ:119, Co-PU:31, Gr-CC:55,
   Ha-PO:183, Mc-WS:65, Un-MA:291,
   Wi-LT:225
Immortality. F. Keyes. Ke-TF:178
In Due Season. W. Auden. Ho-P:15
Interlude. W. Landor. Pa-GTB:318
Intimate Parnassus.
   P. Kavanagh. Un-MB:432
Intimations of Sublimity.
   W. Wordsworth. Ox-BN:98
Invictus. W. Henley. Al-VBP:1067,
   Co-RM:245, Er-FA:460, Ga-FB:132,
   Ke-TF:253, Mc-PR:69, Ox-BN:883,
   Sp-OG:332, Un-GT:316, Un-MB:53
Is This Real. Bi-IT:131,
   Da-SC:113
It Was Wrong to Do This, Said the
   Angel. S. Crane. Sh-AP:143
It's a Gay Old World. Er-FA:12
Just Lost, when I Was Saved!
   E. Dickinson. Ho-P:22
Kimpa. Tr-US I:61
Laid in My Quiet Bed. H. Howard.
   De-CH:451
The Land of Dreams. W. Blake.
   De-CH:457
The Language of Life. B. Cutler.
   St-H:45
Let No Charitable Hope. E. Wylie.
   Ca-VT:104, Un-MA:278, Wi-LT:206
A Letter from a Girl to Her Own
   Old Age. A. Meynell.
   Al-VBP:1065, Un-MB:63
The Lien. A. Love. Th-AS:215
Life. T. Blake. Ba-HI:81
Life. Chang Hsiu-ya. Pa-MV:34
Life. Cheng Min. Hs-TC:237
Life. P. Dunbar. Bo-AN:6
Life. P. Goggins. Jo-VC:33
Life. H. Harrington. Ba-HI:85
Life. T. Kuramae. Le-TA:13
Life Is Fine. L. Hughes.
   Mc-WK:95
Life Is the Greatest Disaster.
   E. Murray. Me-WF:43
Life of Illusion.
   Nezahualcoyotl. Da-SC:180
Life's a Funny Proposition after
   All. G. Cohan. Fe-PL:309
Lines Before Execution.
   C. Tichbourne. Al-VBP:138,
   Gr-CT:324, Ha-PO:132, Rv-CB:103
A Little Song of Life. L. Reese.
   Fe-FP:18, Gr-TG:23, Hu-MP:61,
   Th-AS:179
A Little Work. G. du Maurier.
   Fe-PL:294

Loneliness. Cheng Min. Hs-TC:229
The Long Hill. S. Teasdale.
   Un-MA:265
The Lotos Eaters. A. Tennyson.
   Mo-GR:129
Lovelight. G. Johnson. Bo-AN:23
The Lovely Shall Be Choosers.
   R. Frost. Sh-AP:155, Un-MA:185
Lucinda Matlock. E. Masters.
   Ga-FB:74, Mo-BG:161, Un-MA:143,
   Wi-LT:116
Lullaby. G. Gascoigne. No-CL:232
A Man. D. Levertov. Ha-TP:132
Man. H. Wolfe. Un-MB:303
Man Is Nothing but.
   S. Tchernichovsky. Me-PH:76
Man's Medley. G. Herbert.
   Al-VBP:340
Map. M. Mendes. An-TC:49
Me. W. de la Mare. Br-BC:120,
   Fe-FP:5, Gr-TG:12
Me. J. Smith. Ad-II:13
Midnight on the Great Western.
   T. Hardy. De-CH:24
Miracles. W. Whitman.
   Ga-S:15, Li-TU:176, Ma-FW:100,
   Mc-WK:102, Sh-RP:166, Sm-MK:228,
   Tr-MR:39, Un-GT:247
Moonlight. S. Teasdale.
   Ca-VT:76, Co-PU:154
Mortification. G. Herbert.
   Al-VBP:345
Mother to Son. L. Hughes.
   Ab-MO:97, Be-MA:38, Bo-AN:67,
   Bo-HF:177, Br-BC:123, Hu-PN:186,
   Jo-SA:19, La-OC:94, Lo-TY:225,
   Pe-FB:70, Pe-SS:7
My Existence in the World.
   Tsurayuki. Ba-ST:57
My Heart Leaps Up. W. Wordsworth.
   Al-VBP:655, Ar-TP3:172, Au-SP:346,
   Bo-HF:55, Br-BC:121, Co-RG:121,
   Er-FA:149, Ga-FB:22, Ha-PO:83,
   La-PP:7, Ma-YA:139, Mc-PR:169,
   Ox-BN:61, Pa-GTB:308, Rv-CB:644,
   Sp-OG:352
My Life. J. Bryant. Jo-VC:87
My Life Has Been the Poem.
   H. Thoreau. Pl-ML:35
New England November. D. Hall.
   Ke-TF:448
New Life. J. Kariuki. Lo-TY:171
Night. R. Jeffers. Sm-PT:155,
   Un-MA:367
Not a Tree. T. Blackburn.
   Ls-NY:171
Notes Found near a Suicide: To
   Mother. F. Horne. Bo-AN:42,
   Ra-BP:71
Nova. R. Jeffers. Pe-OA:90

LIFE — cont'd.
The Oak. A. Tennyson.
  Ch-B:44, Fe-FP:212, Hu-MP:280
The Ocean. S. Takahashi.
  Sh-AM:99
Ode on Intimations of Immortality.
  W. Wordsworth. Al-VBP:662,
  Br-BC:18, Er-FA:157, Ga-FB:101,
  Gr-CT:436, Ha-PO:206, Ho-P:88,
  Ox-BN:84, Pa-GTB:308, Pl-EI:59
Ode to a Nightingale. J. Keats.
  Al-VBP:769, Er-FA:89, Gr-CT:102,
  Li-SR:138, Ox-BN:352, Pa-GTB:248
Of Flesh and Bone. I. Gardner.
  St-H:67
Old-Age Chant. Da-SC:105
On Himself. R. Herrick.
  Gr-CT:272
On Luck. M. Goldman. Ls-NY:32
On Seeming to Presume.
  L. Durrell. Wi-LT:693
On Suicide. S. Murano. Sh-AM:90
One of Us May Feel. Okura.
  Ba-ST:58
The Only Card I Got on My Birthday
  Was from an Insurance Man.
  W. Stafford. St-H:214
Our Journey Had Advanced.
  E. Dickinson. Mo-GR:127,
  Wi-LT:12
Overnight Stop. Fang Ching.
  Hs-TC:384
A Parting Guest. J. Riley.
  Sp-OG:278
Pastoral. W. Williams. Pe-SS:44
Petit, the Poet. E. Masters.
  Ha-PO:67, Ke-PP:106, Sm-LG:38,
  Un-MA:143
Poem of Angela Yvonne Davis.
  N. Giovanni. Ad-PB:458
The Poet Speaks. G. Johnson.
  Bo-AN:22
The Pope He Leads a Happy Life.
  C. Lever. Co-PI:96
Prayer for Long Life. Tr-US II:256
Preparedness. E. Markham.
  Er-FA:29, Un-MA:108
The Prodigal. E. Bishop.
  Br-TC:52, Wi-LT:514
The Proof. R. Wilbur. Pl-EI:45
A Psalm of Life. H. Longfellow.
  Er-FA:32, Fe-PL:303, Sp-OG:322
Putting to Sea. L. Bogan.
  Wi-LT:381
Quill. A. Paunescu. Mc-AC:163
Rabbi Ben Ezra. R. Browning.
  Br-BC:142, Er-FA:175, Ga-FB:129,
  Ox-BN:578
Raison d'Etre. O. Pitcher.
  Bo-AN:166, Hu-NN:115

The Rhythm. R. Creeley.
  Ha-TP:116, Wi-LT:678
Rings in a Roundness. C. Drewry.
  Ls-NY:71
The Road. C. Aiken. Un-MA:428
The Road of All Lives. Fang Ching.
  Hs-TC:388
The Road of Life. W. Morris.
  Ox-BN:786
The Room. D. Harrison. Ad-PB:394
Root Cellar. T. Roethke.
  Co-BN:219, Ho-LP:43
Royal Palms. H. Crane. Un-MA:533
Rubaiyat of Omar Khayyam.
  E. Fitzgerald. Al-VBP:832,
  Er-FA:43, Fe-FP:479, Gr-CT:329,
  Ox-BN:526, Pa-GTB:329, Pa-SG:120
Rugby Chapel—November, 1857.
  M. Arnold. Rv-CB:874
Runner. W. Auden. Mo-SD:55
Sailing to Byzantium. W. Yeats.
  Al-VBP:1093, Er-FA:152,
  Go-BP:168, Pa-GTB:425, Rv-CB:956,
  Tr-MR:290, Un-MB:114, Wi-LT:75
The Salutation of the Dawn.
  Fe-PL:397
The Sense of the Sleight-of-Hand
  Man. W. Stevens. Pe-OA:70,
  Un-MA:252, Wi-LT:147
A Song. Fang Ching. Hs-TC:385
Song. Bi-IT:164, Tr-US I:27
Song of Myself. W. Whitman.
  Al-VBP:928, Mo-GR:106,
  Sh-AP:69, Un-MA:44
A Song of Nezahualcoyotl.
  Br-MW:26
Sonnet. W. Drummond. Al-VBP:304
Sonnet. P. Shelley. Ox-BN:279
Sonnet on Life. B. Boothby.
  Al-VBP:597
The Soul's Dark Cottage.
  E. Waller. Gr-CT:375
The Source. P. Harris. Sc-TN:80
Star of the Western Skies.
  Fi-BG:193
The Strings of Time. T. Palmanteer.
  Al-WW:47
A Stroll. Wang T'ing-chao.
  Hs-TC:257
The Stuff of Dreams.
  W. Shakespeare. Ga-FB:91,
  Mc-PR:39
A Summer Night. M. Arnold.
  Rv-CB:871
Surgeons Must Be Very Careful.
  E. Dickinson. Pl-IO:144,
  Rv-CB:915
Survival This Way. S. Ortiz.
  Ni-CD:158
Symphony. F. Horne. Bo-AN:51

Tell Me, Tell Me.   E. Brontë.
    Al-VBP:920
Text.   A. Zeitlin.   Ho-TY:318
Thanks in Old Age.   W. Whitman.
    Ke-TF:160
Their Bullring.   J. La Rose.
    Sa-B:78
This Life.   W. Drummond.   De-CH:236,
    Pa-GTB:37
This Is Real.   T. Palmanteer.
    Al-WW:45
The Three Hermits.   W. Yeats.
    Ma-FW:86
3 Stanzas about a Tree.   M. Bell.
    Ho-P:21
Time Is a Pair of Scissors.
    Wang Ching-chih.   Hs-TC:44
Time Takes Me on Its Wing.
    Wo-HS:(58)
To Fling Songs into the Air.
    Y. Grizlov.   Mo-MI:34
To My Heart.   D. Botez. Mc-AC:62
To My Son.   G. Barker.   Br-TC:26
To My Son.   Fe-PL:338
To Robert Louis Stevenson.
    W. Henley.   Un-MB:56
To the Harbormaster. F. O'Hara.
    Mc-EA:168, Mo-BG:97
The Tuft of Flowers.   R. Frost.
    Rv-CB:966, Sh-AP:150, Un-MA:168
Tunnel.   F. Shimazaki.   Le-TA:96
The Twin Falls.   J. Dickey.
    Mo-BG:117
Ulysses.   A. Tennyson.
    Al-VBP:863, Ha-PO:40,
    Ke-TF:262, Ni-JP:16, Rv-CB:793
Unrest.   R. Dixon.   Ox-BN:753
The Voyage.   E. Muir.   Wi-LT:251
Walking Across Brooklyn Bridge.
    J. Marshall.   Mc-EA:78
We Wish to Be Joyful.   Do-CH:(48)
Webs.   C. Sandburg.   Ho-TH:56
West-Running Brook.   R. Frost.
    Sh-AP:151, Sm-PT:138, Un-MA:182
What Am I in Time and Space?
    A. Stolzenberg.   Ho-TY:270
What Are Years? M. Moore.
    Ha-TP:140, Pe-OA:101, Pl-EI:138,
    Sh-AP:179, Sm-PT:10, Un-MA:352
What Faire Pompe.   T. Campion.
    Ho-P:16
When Smoke Stood Up from Ludlow.
    A. Housman.   Un-MB:95
Whist.   E. Ware.   Fe-PL:311
Who's Who.   W. Auden.
    Mc-WS:73, Un-MB:450
the will's love.   B. Brigham.
    Sc-TN:24
The Wind and the Rain.
    W. Shakespeare.   Al-VBP:190,
    Hi-WP I:114, Ho-WR:21,
    Mc-WK:224, Rv-CB:204, Sm-LG:403

The World's a Sea.   F. Quarles.
    Gr-CT:231   .
Written on the Road.   M. Dodge.
    Br-BC:145
Youth.   F. Cornford.   Co-EL:128,
    Co-PU:4
LIFE - BREVITY
Abide with Me.   H. Lyte.   Er-FA:443
All the Flowers of the Spring.
    J. Webster.   Al-VBP:289,
    De-CH:252, Rv-CB:317
And Yet the Earth Remains
    Unchanged.   Bi-IT:101
As on This Day.   T. Takaori.
    Sh-AM:155
Birthright.   J. Drinkwater.
    De-CH:239, Gr-CC:99
By the Winding River.   Tu Fu.
    Rx-OH:13
Candles.   C. Cavafy.   Sm-MK:217
Capsule Conclusions, I.   Un-MW:64
The Cosmic Fabric.   Y. Polonsky.
    Pl-EI:17
Counsel to Girls.   R. Herrick.
    Al-VBP:328, Er-FA:104, Ga-FB:41,
    Gr-CT:51, Ha-PO:161, Hi-WP II:140,
    Li-SR:21, Ma-YA:86, Pa-GTB:71,
    Un-MW:19
Crawling on the Grass.   M. Saito.
    Sh-AM:145
The Cycle.   Hsü Hsü.   Hs-TC:275
The Day.   T. Spencer.
    Mo-BG:71, Ni-JP:157
Dear Child Delay No Time.
    S. Ingram.   De-CH:757
Death.   J. Clare.   Pa-GTB:319
The Death Song of White Antelope.
    White Antelope.   Br-MW:92
Everyday.   L. Curry.   Ba-HI:80
Fill a Glass with Golden Wine.
    W. Henley.   Al-VBP:1068
First Fig.   E. Millay.
    Bo-FP:45, Er-FA:220, Fe-PL:417,
    Ga-FB:3, Ho-TH:21, Sh-AP:186
Flower Song.   Br-MW:7
From Far.   A. Housman.   Go-BP:186,
    Ho-LP:103, Un-MB:102
From the Most Distant. Time.
    Emperor Wu.   Rx-LT:5
Go, Silly Worm.   J. Sylvester.
    Rv-CB:188
How Time Consumeth All Earthly
    Things.   T. Proctor.   Gr-CT:243
In Time of Pestilence.   T. Nashe.
    Ga-S:214
It Is Not Growing like a Tree.
    B. Jonson.   Co-PU:69, Gr-CT:375,
    Hi-WP I:113, Ma-YA:82, Pa-GTB:63
Jade Flower Palace. Tu Fu. Rx-OH:9
The Lament for the Makers.
    W. Dunbar.   Al-VBP:32, Gr-CT:354,
    Pl-ML:146, Rv-CB:71

LIFE - BREVITY — cont'd.
Let Me Alone. Bible. O.T.
Job. Ke-PP:4
Life Half Lived. J. Hölderlin.
Gr-CT:244
Like Flowers We Spring. Rv-CB:121
Lord, Thou Hast Been Our Dwelling
Place. Bible. O.T. Psalms.
Me-PH:23, Pl-EI:198
Loveliest of Trees. A. Housman.
Al-VBP:1079, Bl-OB:136, Bo-FP:246,
Co-BN:145, Er-FA:153, Fe-PL:371,
Ga-FB:232, Go-BP:28, Gr-CT:47,
Hu-MP:276, Ma-FW:13, Ma-YA:222,
Sh-RP:208, Sm-MK:172, Tu-WW:52,
Un-MB:95, Wi-LT:58
Man's Mortality. Rv-CB:133,
Sm-LG:400
Midnight Lamentation. H. Monro.
Al-VBP:1140
The Moon and the Year. Bi-IT:91
The Moon Shines Bright. Gr-GB:297
Mortality. Rv-CB:123
Night. Fang Ching. Hs-TC:383
Not Forever on Earth. Bi-IT:90
Nothing in the Voice. Basho.
Ma-FW:102
O My Heart You Must Be Strong.
Ge-TR:17
Oh, Why Should the Spirit of
Mortal Be Proud? W. Knox.
Er-FA:34
Old and New Year Ditties.
C. Rossetti. Ox-BN:713
On a Fly Drinking Out of His
Cup. W. Oldys. Al-VBP:543,
Cl-FC:96, Er-FA:153, Rv-CB:519,
Un-GT:80
Pear-Trees by the Fence.
Su Tung-p'o. Pa-SG:90
Poems Addressed to Ianthe, II.
W. Landor. Ox-BN:187
Remembering Min Ch'e.
Su Tung P'o. Rx-LT:89
The Repetitive Heart. D. Schwartz.
Al-VBP:1241
The River of Life. T. Campbell.
Er-FA:155, Ni-JP:156, Ox-BN:203,
Pa-GTB:306
The Rubáiyat. O. Khayyam.
Ga-FB:60
Sic Vita. H. King. Ma-YA:89
Song. T. Lodge. No-CL:117
Song of Nezahualcoyotl. Da-SC:180
Song of the Mayers. De-CH:12,
Gr-GB:42
Songs. Tr-US II:138
Spring. Su Tung P'o. Rx-OH:90
The Spring Is Past.
C. Tichborne. De-TT:181

Street Corner College.
K. Patchen. Un-MA:609
Swiftly, See, Each Moment Flies.
E. Hewitt. De-CH:757
Tears. L. Reese. Un-MA:110
They Are Not Long. E. Dowson.
Al-VBP:1102, Gr-CT:325,
Ha-PO:155, Un-MB:151
Time Is a Feathered Thing.
J. Mayne. No-CL:174
To an Old Tune. Lu Kuei Meng.
Rx-LT:85
To Blossoms. R. Herrick.
Co-BN:35, Pa-GTB:91, Sm-MK:5
To Daffodils. R. Herrick.
Al-VBP:332, Bo-GJ:70, Co-BN:55,
Hi-WP I:115, Ho-LP:94,
Na-EO:15, Pa-GTB:91, Rv-CB:342
To Wei Pa, a Retired Scholar.
Tu Fu. Rx-OH:11
Virtue. G. Herbert. Al-VBP:343,
De-CH:431, Ha-PO:199, Rv-CB:352
We Hurry On. D. Dolben. Ox-BN:881
Winter: An Ode. S. Johnson.
No-CL:128
Winter Dawn. Tu Fu. Rx-OH:5
Yet Ah, that Spring Should
Vanish with the Rose.
O. Khayyam. Tu-WW:45
Youth. G. Johnson. Hu-PN:74
LIFE AFTER DEATH: see FUTURE
LIFE; IMMORTALITY
LIFE AND DEATH: see also
HUMOR - LIFE AND DEATH
Above the Ruins. Basho. Be-CS:23
Ante Mortem. R. Jeffers.
Un-MA:360
At the Boundary of Life and Death.
J. Takami. Sh-AM:107
At the Wood's Edge. Bi-IT:161
An Autobiography. E. Rhys.
Co-PU:124
The Beach in August. W. Kees.
Mc-EA:48
Before Exeter Church. Hsü Chih-mo.
Hs-TC:81
Blind Date. C. Aiken. Al-VBP:1189
Blindman's Buff. P. Viereck.
Un-MA:659, Wi-LT:831
Border Line. L. Hughes. En-PC:49
Burning the Letters.
R. Jarrell. Un-MA:647
Chiefly to Mind Appears.
C. Day Lewis. Un-MB:423
Conclusion. S. Sassoon.
Un-MB:316
The Conclusive Voyage.
J. Jimenez. Le-SW:85
A Country Life. R. Jarrell.
Un-MA:649

Dark, Dark Night. L. Joass.
    Le-M:182
Dead Man's Song. Ma-BH:31,
    Tr-US I:21
Death at a Distance. S. Gellett.
    De-CH:757
Dew on Young Garlic Leaves.
    T'ien Hung. Rx-LT:7
Dirge in Dialogue. Lo-TY:3,
    Tr-US I:64
Divided. J. Ingelow. Ox-BN:720
Easter Eve. M. Rukeyser.
    Ca-VT:362
Elegiac Statement for Two Human
    Beings Named Rosenberg.
    L. Hedley. Kr-OF:124
Enion Replies from the Caverns
    of the Grave. W. Blake.
    Ox-BN:39
Epitaph for a Little-Known
    Gravestone. P. Mayer. St-H:135
The Eternal Image. R. Pitter.
    Un-MB:404
Farewell. F. García Lorca.
    Le-SW:83
Fear No More. W. Shakespeare.
    Al-VBP:195, Bo-HF:179, Co-RG:144,
    De-CH:250, De-TT:193, Er-FA:260,
    Gr-CT:332, Ha-PO:251, Hi-WP II:19,
    No-CL:73, Pa-GTB:28, Rv-CB:201,
    Sm-LG:267
The Feast of the Great God
    Tezcatlipoca. Br-MW:15
Flux. R. Eberhart. Ca-VT:247
For Once in a Dream or Trance,
    I Saw the Gods. E. Muir.
    Go-BP:155
For the Anniversary of My Death.
    W. Merwin. Mo-BG:165
The Four Ages of Man. W. Yeats.
    Tr-MR:269
From the Shadows. M. Beniuc.
    Mc-AC:99
Gaily I Lived. Co-EL:67
The Generous Years. S. Spender.
    En-PC:101
Hide-and-Seek. T. Arghezi.
    Mc-AC:27
Highway to Nowhere. G. Code.
    De-FS:61
How Death Came. Lo-TY:5
Hymn to Colour. G. Meredith.
    Ox-BN:700
I Have Killed the Deer. Wo-HS:(72)
I Said to the Leaf. C. Drewry.
    Tr-MR:270
If Crossed with All Mishaps.
    W. Drummond. Rv-CB:331
The Immortal Past. A. Housman.
    Un-MB:97

In Praise of Bow and Arrow.
    Tr-CB:23, Tr-US I:54
In Time of Pestilence.
    T. Nashe. Ga-S:214
Inscription on an Altar of the
    Dead. V. Contoski. Sc-TN:32
Interlude III. K. Shapiro.
    Du-RG:71
An Invite to Eternity. J. Clare.
    Ox-BN:330
Invocation. C. Drewry. Tr-MR:217
Lament for One's Self.
    R. Pitter. Go-BP:276
Last Night. D. Ignatow. Ca-VT:396
The Last Word. M. Arnold.
    Ha-PO:215, Ox-BN:647
Let This Be My Parting Word.
    R. Tagore. Tr-MR:284
Life. G. Herbert. Rv-CB:353
Life. T. Kato. Le-TA:94
Life! I Know Not What Thou Art.
    A. Barbauld. Er-FA:81,
    Pa-GTB:168
Life's Circumnavigators.
    W. Rodgers. Pa-GTB:530
Like Tiny Rain Drops. M. Bruce.
    Ad-II:17
The Lonely Say. A. Ben Yitzhak.
    Me-PH:84
Madam Life. W. Henley. Un-MB:55
Man's Going Hence. S. Rogers.
    Ox-BN:48
Memorandum. R. Graham. Hu-PN:441
Mistaken Fair. P. Stanhope.
    Rv-CB:518
Must. A. Lewis. Co-EL:80
Nearer Home. P. Cary. Er-FA:456
The Noble. W. Wordsworth.
    Gr-CT:377
On a White Beach. P. Mayer.
    St-H:138
Only the Polished Skeleton.
    C. Cullen. Ca-VT:242
Our Doom Is in Our Being.
    J. Agee. Un-MA:605
Paintings of Roses. R. Hershon.
    Sc-TN:96
The Pale Blue Casket. Q. Pitcher.
    Ad-PB:194, Hu-NN:114, Lo-TY:247
Paneled in Pine. M. George.
    De-FS:94
Pantuns, I. Tr-US II:203
The Parting Glass. P. Freneau.
    Sh-AP:15
The Passing Strange.
    J. Masefield. Un-MB:229
The Path among the Stones.
    G. Kinnell. Ho-P:135
The Poet's Testament.
    G. Santayana. Ke-TF:172

LIFE AND DEATH — cont'd.
  Post Mortem. R. Jeffers.
    Un-MA:361
  The Power of Music to Disturb.
    L. Mueller. St-H:148
  The Pythoness. K. Raine.
    Al-VBP:1233, Un-MB:485
  Question. May Swenson. Ca-VT:480,
    Wi-LT:829
  The Refugees. R. Jarrell.
    Un-MA:651
  The River. M. Arnold. Rv-CB:866
  The Rubaiyat of Omar Khayyam.
    E. Fitzgerald. Ha-PO:210
  The Sea of Death. T. Hood.
    Ox-BN:423
  Secret Prayer. Hsü Hsü. Hs-TC:274
  The Sequel. D. Schwartz. Wi-LT:522
  A Small Thought Speaks for the
    Flesh. C. Drewry. Tr-MR:226
  Song of a Dead One. Le-IB:122
  A Song of Humility. C. Drewry.
    Tr-MR:268
  A Song of Kabir. R. Tagore.
    Ga-S:126
  A Song of Lamentation. Ba-PO:27,
    Bi-IT:137, Da-SC:175
  Song of Nezahualcoyotl.
    Br-MW:24, Da-SC:180
  Song with Words. J. Agee.
    Un-MA:606
  Songs. Tr-US II:132
  Sonnet. Feng Chih. Hs-TC:148
  Sonnets I, II. J. Agee. Un-MA:604
  Sonnets, xliv. E. Millay. Sm-PT:153

  Spring Festival Songs. Tr-US II:172
  The Spring Waters. Ping Hsin.
    Hs-TC:25
  Stars, Songs, Faces. C. Sandburg.
    Ma-FW:290
  Still, Citizen Sparrow. R. Wilbur.
    Wi-LT:597
  The Sword and the Sickle. W. Blake.
    Ar-TP3:211, Gr-CT:349
  The Taking of Life Brings Serious
    Thoughts. Bi-IT:68
  Tears, Idle Tears. A. Tennyson.
    Al-VBP:859, Er-FA:150, Ha-PO:150,
    Hi-WP II:144, Ox-BN:486
  Testament. J. Holmes. Tr-MR:272
  That We Head Towards. Stephany.
    Ra-BP:333
  Those Who Go Not to Return.
    B. Galai. Me-PH:125
  A Thought. Li Chin-fa. Hs-TC:171
  Time Speaks. Chu Ta-nan. Hs-TC:133

  Time's Dedication. D. Schwartz.
    Ca-VT:367
  Tomorrow and Tomorrow and Tomorrow.
    W. Shakespeare. Er-FA:92,
    Gr-CT:367, Ma-YA:69

  The Unsettled Motorcyclist's Vision
    of His Death. T. Gunn. Mc-EA:160
  Up-Hill. C. Rossetti. Al-VBP:998,
    De-CH:462, Gr-EC:276, Ho-WR:152,
    Mc-PR:141, Ox-BN:712, Sp-OG:263
  When I Watch the Living Meet.
    A. Housman. Un-MB:96
  Why Must You Know?
    J. Wheelwright. Ca-VT:205
  Winter Mask. A. Tate. Ho-P:269
  The World a Hunting Is.
    W. Drummond. Rv-CB:329
  You Were Born; Must Die.
    S. Spender. Un-MB:478
  Your Last Drive. T. Hardy.
    Ox-BN:841
LIFE ON OTHER PLANETS
  Go Fly a Saucer. D. McCord.
    Fe-FP:198, Li-TU:47, Pl-IO:27
LIFESAVING: see also RESCUES
    AND RESCUING
  The Lifeguard. J. Dickey.
    Pe-OA:277, Pe-SS:88
LIFTS: see ELEVATORS
LIGHT
  Ark of the Covenant. L. Nicholl.
    Pl-IO:36
  Bathed Is My Blood. O. La Crone.
    Hu-NN:38
  The Blind Boy. C. Cibber.
    Co-RG:134, Ox-BC:58, Pa-GTB:111
  Cottage. S. O'Sullivan. Co-PI:165
  Eagle Song. G. Bottomley.
    Un-MB:213
  God's First Creature Was Light.
    W. Welles. Pl-IO:17
  Grace for Light. M. O'Neill.
    Th-AS:174
  The Inward Morning. H. Thoreau.
    No-CL:270, Sh-AP:67
  Let the Light Enter. F. Harper.
    Hu-PN:15
  Light. H. Hagedorn. Tr-MR:244
  Light and Water. J. Jimenez.
    Le-SW:37
  Light Breaks where No Sun Shines.
    D. Thomas. Al-VBP:1245,
    Un-MB:498
  The Light Is Sweet. Bible. O.T.
    Ecclesiastes. Fe-FP:263
  Light Wearing a Black Nightgown.
    Lo Men. Pa-MV:124
  Noon. R. Jeffers. Un-MA:361
  O Light Invisible, We Praise Thee.
    T. Eliot. Tr-MR:148
  O Virtuous Light. E. Wylie.
    Un-MA:281
  Paradise Lost. J. Milton.
    Al-VBP:408
  The Rat. W. Davies. Go-BP:91
  Revolution. A. Housman. Pl-IO:37

Song for the Sun That Disappeared
  Behind the Rainclouds.
  Be-AP:22, Lo-TY:5
A Song of Always. E. Rosenzweig.
  Ar-TP3:191, Th-AS:178
A Song-Offering. R. Tagore.
  Pa-SG:43
Storm End. J. Griffin. Mo-TS:87
Stranger. T. Merton. Pl-EI:14
This Morning. J. Wright.
  Ab-MO:105, Hu-NN:17, Jo-SA:99
To Night. J. White. Al-VBP:701,
  Co-RG:154, Ke-TF:58, Rv-CB:674
When the Light Falls. S. Kunitz.
  Un-MA:593
LIGHTHOUSES: see also LIGHTSHIPS
Epitaph for a Lighthouse-
  Keeper's Horse. J. Morton.
  Co-PU:156
Evening in England. R. Hosken.
  Ke-TF:366
Flannan Isle. W. Gibson.
  Bl-OB:78, Co-SS:200, De-CH:395,
  Ha-PO:154, Hi-WP I:76
I'd Like to Be a Lighthouse.
  R. Field. Au-SP:179, Cr-SS:14,
  La-PP:43, La-PV:182
The Light-House Keeper's White
  Mouse. J. Ciardi. Bo-FP:282,
  La-PV:199
The Lighthouse. W. Scott.
  Bo-FP:282
The Lighthouse Keeper.
  Wang Ya-p'ing. Hs-TC:352
Watching the Beams of a Light-
  house. S. Ito. Sh-AM:105
LIGHTNING: see also HUMOR -
  LIGHTNING; THUNDERSTORMS
Beyond Dark Trees. Shiki. Be-CS:15
Electrical Storm. E. Bishop.Ha-WR:11
Flashes of Lightning.
  H. Kawahigashi. Sh-AM:161
From the "Goulburn Island" Love
  Cycle. Tr-US I:246
Giant Thunder. J. Reeves.
  Co-BN:176, Sm-MK:147
Hymn to Lightning. Be-AP:24
Lightning. D. Lawrence.
  Un-MB:286
Lightning. Da-SC:10
Lightning over a Calm Sea.
  M. Ward. Ke-TF:431
The Skeptic. L. Williams.
  De-FS:220
A Storm in Childhood. T. Jones.
  Ma-FW:35
Under Oaks. J. Dickey. Ls-NY:122
War Song. Da-SC:91
LIGHTNING BUGS: see
  FIREFLIES

LIGHTS AND LIGHTING: see also
  CANDLES; LAMPS AND LAMP-
  LIGHTERS; LANTERNS;
  TRAFFIC LIGHTS
Back Yard, July Night. W. Cole.
  Co-BN:117
Beneath the Aging Buildings.
  M. Deighton. La-IH:62
City Lights. R. Field. Fe-FP:254,
  La-PP:34, La-PV:188
Coming Home. R. Humphries.
  Tr-MR:256
Eight Are the Lights. I. Orleans.
  Th-AS:177
Hidden Treasure. B. Katz.
  Ho-CS:9
Light for a Bride. De-PP:58
November Blue. A. Meynell.
  Un-MB:62
O Light Invisible, We Praise Thee.
  T. Eliot. Tr-MR:148
The Park. J. Tippett.
  Ar-TP3:176
Parliament Hill. H. Bashford.
  Hu-MP:182, Th-AS:67
The Planetary Arc-Light.
  A. Derleth. Gr-EC:164
The Shepherd's Hut. A. Young.
  Re-TW:10
Wet Night on a Pavement.
  A. Tessimond. Hi-WP I:129
W's for Windows. P. McGinley.
  Ar-TP3:176
LIGHTSHIPS: see also LIGHTHOUSES
The Eddystone Light.
  Co-SS:103, Ha-PO:271
The Lightship. J. Johnson.
  Th-AS:132
LIKES AND DISLIKES: see CHOICES;
  INDIVIDUALITY
LILACS: see also HUMOR - LILACS
As Lilacs Speak. F. Anderson.
  Ke-TF:436
The Barrel-Organ. A. Noyes.
  Ga-FB:234, Un-MB:245
Geography of Lilacs. F. Frost.
  Ke-TF:437
The Lilac. H. Wolfe. Fe-FP:221
Lilacs. A. Lowell. Un-MA:160
Lydia Is Gone This Many a Year.
  L. Reese. Bo-GJ:236, De-CH:261,
  Gr-CC:11
May Day. M. Livingston.
  Br-SG:101
Spring Lilacs. M. Moulton.
  Ke-TF:436
When Lilacs Last in the Dooryard
  Bloom'd. W. Whitman.
  Al-VBP:940, Sh-AP:113,
  Un-MA:71, Vi-PP:172

LILIES: see also EASTER;
    WATER LILIES
  At Easter Time. L. Richards.
    Hu-MP:334
  A Bulb. R. Munkittrick. Co-PU:45
  Calla Lilies in the Dusk.
    W. Struthers. Ke-TF:437
  Easter Lily. M. Miller. La-PH:51
  The Faithless Flowers.
    M. Widdemer. Hu-MP:258,
    Th-AS:84
  Gift of the Sego Lily. M. Jarvis.
    Fi-BG:192
  Lilies. Shikō. Ar-TP3:204
  The Lily. W. Blake. Sm-MK:20
  Lily Flower. M. Brownstein.
    Mc-EA:41
  The Lily Princess. Ch-B:24,
    Hu-MP:252
  Little White Lily. G. Macdonald.
    Hu-MP:251
  On Easter Day. C. Thaxter.
    Fe-FP:74, Ha-YA:51
  The Sojourners. E. Jarrett.
    Sc-TN:109
  A Spider's Web. S. Takano.
    Sh-AM:168
  Tiger-Lilies. T. Aldrich.
    Un-GT:255
  Tiger Lily. D. McCord. Ad-PE:21,
    Bo-GJ:74, La-PV:165
LILITH
  Satan's Prayer. I. Manger.
    Ho-TY:273
LIME TREES: see LINDEN TREES
LIMERICKS
  Anecdotes of Four Gentlemen.
    Ox-BC:152, 153
  An Anglican Curate in Want.
    R. Knox. Ke-TF:289
  The Arch Armadillo. C. Wells.
    Bo-FP:271
  Archbishop Tait. Gr-CT:31
  Arthur. O. Nash. Co-FB:52,
    Co-HP:100
  At the Tennis Clinic. L. Martin.
    Mo-SD:38
  Atomic Courtesy. E. Jacobson.
    Er-FA:216
  The Barber of Kew. C. Monkhouse.
    Co-HP:98, Ir-BB:223
  A Boston Boy Went Out to Yuma.
    D.D. Br-SM:94
  A Boy Who Played Tunes. Co-HP:29
  A Briton Who Shot at His King.
    D. Ross. Br-SM:26
  A Canner, Exceedingly Canny.
    C. Wells. Fe-FP:364, Un-GF:46
  The Castaways. E. Rieu.
    Co-PT:171

A Certain Young Man of Great
    Gumption. Br-SM:82
A Cheerful Old Bear at the Zoo.
    Un-GT:241
Clock Time by the Geyser.
    J. White. Br-SM:48
A Collegiate Damsel Named Breeze.
    Un-GT:242
Courtship. L. Carroll. Un-GT:242
Courtship. C. Wells. Un-GT:241
Courtship. Un-GT:241
A Daring Young Lady of Guam.
    Un-GT:242
The Daughter of the Farrier.
    Ir-BB:27, Un-GT:243
A Decrepit Old Gasman. Co-HP:29,
    Er-FA:220
The Eel. W. de la Mare.
    Br-SM:122
Eight Limericks. E. Lear.
    Sh-RP:127, 128
An Elephant. J. Francis.
    Hu-MP:457
An Epicure Dining at Crewe.
    Co-HP:28, Lo-LL:7, Un-GT:242
Faith-Healer. Er-FA:218,
    Un-GT:241
Fascist Limericks. L. Bacon.
    Cr-WS:38
A Flea and a Fly in a Flue.
    Ch-B:113, Co-HP:29, Fe-FP:365,
    Gr-EC:196, Ju-CP:14, Lo-LL:49,
    Mc-WS:179, Un-GT:241
The Floating Old Man. E. Lear.
    Ho-WR:129
Food and Eating. Un-GT:242
A Ghoulish Old Fellow in Kent.
    M. Bishop. Br-SM:23
The Girl of New York.
    C. Monkhouse. Co-HP:98
The Guest. Co-HP:28, Gr-EC:213
A Handsome Young Noble of Spain.
    Un-GF:44, Un-GT:242
The Happy Hyena. C. Wells.
    Bo-FP:29
Harriet Hutch. L. Richards.
    Ir-BB:97, Ne-AM:47
I Raised a Great Hullabaloo.
    La-PV:34
It Pays. A. Bennett. Er-FA:222
Just for the Ride. Er-FA:220
Laughs Anatomical. Un-GT:242
Limericks (From Number Nine).
    Ke-TF:290
Limericks (There Was a Young
    Lass). Ke-TF:290
Limericks (There Was a Young
    Maid). Ke-TF:288
Limericks (There Was a Young
    Man of Herne Bay). Co-HP:28

Limericks since Lear.   Co-BB:29,
    Un-GT:241, 242
The Man of Bombay.   Wr-RM:75
The Man of Tobago.   Wr-RM:122
Moonshine.   W. de la Mare.
    Co-FB:442
Ms. Minnie McFinney, of Butte.
    Ne-AM:24
The Mule in the Mines.   Gr-CT:14,
    Gr-GB:222
My Face.   A. Euwer.   Co-HP:57,
    Er-FA:222, Fe-PL:211, Fr-WO:44,
    Un-GT:241
Nonsenses.   E. Lear.   Ox-BC:183
The Old Loony of Lyme.
    Hi-WP I:100
The Old Woman from France.
    Wr-RM:52
The Old Woman of Harrow. Wr-RM:114
The Old Woman of Leeds.   Wr-RM:97
The Old Woman of Surrey.
    Wr-RM:117
The Panda.   W. Smith.   Sh-RP:135
Relativity.   A. Buller.
    Ar-TP3:132, Ch-B:65, Er-FA:219,
    Fe-FP:361, Fr-WO:55, Pl-IO:64
Said a Great Congregational
    Preacher.   Un-GF:43, Un-GT:240
Said a Sporty Young Person Named
    Groat.   Ke-TF:289
A Scientist Living at Staines.
    R. Hewison.   Er-FA:218
Seven Limericks.   E. Lear.
    Sh-RP:150
She Frowned and Called Him Mr.
    Fe-FP:361, Un-GT:241
A Silly Young Fellow Named Hyde.
    Br-SM:145, Co-HP:29
The Sioux.   E. Field.   Bo-GJ:154,
    Co-FB:428
A Tailor, Who Sailed from Quebec.
    Wi-MG:41
There Once Was a Young Man Named
    Hall.   Br-SM:53
There Was a Fair Maid Whose
    Maneuver.   Ke-TF:290
There Was a Young Fellow Named
    Green.   Un-GF:45
There Was a Young Fellow Named
    Paul.   Ke-TF:289
There Was a Young Hopeful Named
    Sam.   E. Ripley.   Fr-MP:5
There Was a Young Lady Named
    Gleedle.   Ke-TF:288
There Was a Young Lady of Corsica.
    E. Lear.   Gr-CT:28
There Was a Young Lady of Jodhpur.
    Ke-TF:289
There Was a Young Lady of Kent.
    Ke-TF:287

There Was a Young Lady of Niger.
    Au-SP:244, Br-SM:94, Ch-B:49,
    Er-FA:220, Fe-FP:360, Fr-WO:47,
    Gr-EC:215, Ke-TF:287, Lo-LL:29
There Was a Young Lady of Norway.
    E. Lear.   Ar-TP3:133, Fe-FP:360
There Was a Young Lady of Oakham.
    Co-BB:29
There Was a Young Lady of Ryde.
    Br-SM:74, Na-EO:169
There Was a Young Lady Residing
    at Prague.   Co-OW:33
There Was a Young Lady Whose Chin.
    E. Lear.   Ar-TP3:132, Au-SP:244,
    Ir-BB:218, Sh-RP:149
There Was a Young Lady Whose Eyes.
    E. Lear.   Bo-GJ:9, Co-HP:90
There Was a Young Lady Whose Nose.
    E. Lear.   Fe-FP:340, Ir-BB:218,
    Sh-RP:127
There Was a Young Maid Who Said,
    "Why. . . ."   Fr-WO:48,
    Ir-BB:221, Ja-PC:35
There Was a Young Man Named
    Ignatius.   Ke-TF:287
There Was a Young Man of Bengal.
    Un-GT:242
There Was a Young Man of Madrid.
    Ke-TF:288
There Was a Young Man of St. Bees.
    W. Gilbert.   Co-HP:67
There Was a Young Man So Benighted.
    Co-HP:28, Ke-TF:287
There Was a Young Prince in Bombay.
    W. Parke.   Co-HP:102
There Was an Old Lady Named
    Crockett.   W. Smith.   Br-SM:52
There Was an Old Lady of Chertsey.
    E. Lear.   Bl-OB:14, Sh-RP:149
There Was an Old Lady of France.
    E. Lear.   Li-LC:47
There Was an Old Man from Peru.
    Er-FA:222, Fr-WO:52, La-PV:35,
    Un-GF:45
There Was an Old Man in a Tree.
    E. Lear.   Ar-TP3:132, Au-SP:243,
    Sh-RP:127, Un-GF:42, Un-GT:240
There Was an Old Man of Black-
    heath.   Co-HP:29, La-PP:70,
    La-PV:34, Lo-LL:56, Un-GF:45
There Was an Old Man of Dumbree.
    E. Lear.   Un-GT:240
There Was an Old Man of Ibreem.
    E. Lear.   Co-HP:90, Sh-RP:150
There Was an Old Man of Nantucket.
    Princeton Tiger.   Ke-TF:289
There Was an Old Man of Tarentum.
    Co-HP:29, Lo-LL:7
There Was an Old Man of the Coast.
    E. Lear.   Ag-HE:7, Ir-BB:218

LIMERICKS — cont'd.
There Was an Old Man of the
Dargle. E. Lear. Gr-CT:28
There Was an Old Man of the
East. E. Lear. Ag-HE:71
There Was an Old Man of
Thermopylae. E. Lear. Fr-WO:41,
Na-EO:103
There Was an Old Man on a Hill.
E. Lear. Un-GF:42
There Was an Old Man on the
Border. E. Lear. Li-LC:47
There Was an Old Man, on Whose
Nose. E. Lear. Au-SP:243
There Was an Old Man Who Said
"Do." Fe-FP:361, Pl-IO:79
There Was an Old Man Who Said,
"How." E. Lear. Bl-OB:17,
Na-EO:103
There Was an Old Man Who Said,
"Hush!" E. Lear. Bo-GJ:9,
Fr-WO:42, Un-GF:42, Un-GT:240
There Was an Old Man Who when
Little. E. Lear. Sh-RP:150,
Un-GF:42, Un-GT:240
There Was an Old Man with a
Beard. E. Lear. Ar-TP3:133,
Au-SP:243, Ch-B:105, Co-HP:90,
Fr-WO:43, Gr-CT:28, Gr-EC:167,
La-PV:35, Sh-RP:149, Un-GF:42
There Was an Old Man with a Gong.
E. Lear. Bo-GJ:9
There Was an Old Person of
Bradley. E. Lear. Pl-US:61
There Was an Old Person of Dean.
E. Lear. Ag-HE:20, Bl-OB:11,
Bo-FP:56
There Was an Old Person of Diss.
E. Lear. Bo-GJ:9
There Was an Old Person of
Dundalk. E. Lear. Co-HP:90
There Was an Old Person of
Ewell. E. Lear. Ag-HE:15
There Was an Old Person of
Gretna. E. Lear. Gr-CT:28
There Was an Old Person of
Ickley. E. Lear. Na-EO:103
There Was an Old Person of Skye.
E. Lear. Gr-CT:28
There Was an Old Person of
Sparta. E. Lear. Ag-HE:14
There Was an Old Person of
Tring. Co-HP:29
There Was an Old Person of Ware.
E. Lear. Bo-FP:28, Li-LC:47,
Sh-RP:129, Un-GT:240
There Was an Old Person Whose
Habits. E. Lear. Fe-FP:341
There Was an Old Stupid Who
Wrote. W. Parke. Co-HP:102

There Was an Old Woman.
W. de la Mare. Br-SG:45
Thief. Co-BB:109, Co-HP:28
Three Wonderful Old Women.
Ox-BC:151, 152
Tom Agnew, Bill Agnew.
D. Rossetti. Gr-CT:476
Try Singing These. Un-GT:242
A Tutor Who Tooted the Flute.
C. Wells. Co-HP:119, Ke-TF:288,
Mc-WS:175, Un-GF:46, Un-GT:241
Two Limericks. Ga-S:11
The Young Lady of Lynn.
Gr-CT:27, Ke-TF:288
A Young Lady of Spain.
Co-OT:62, Sm-MK:113
See also Br-LL, Ir-BB:217-224, Ja-HH
LIMERICKS (ABOUT): see HUMOR;
POETS AND POETRY
LINCOLN, ABRAHAM: see also
EMANCIPATION PROCLAMATION;
RUTLEDGE, ANN
Abraham Lincoln. R. and S. Benét.
Ar-TP3:45, Co-PS:34, Ha-YA:176
Abraham Lincoln. M. Meigs.
Ar-TP3:45, Pe-FB:32, Vi-PP:171
Abraham Lincoln Walks at Midnight.
V. Lindsay. Ba-PO:132, Bo-HF:148,
Br-AF:82, Ca-VT:28, Er-FA:284,
Fe-FP:453, Ga-FB:263, Hi-TL:184,
Hu-MP:398, Ke-PP:21, Mc-PR:126,
Pe-OA:64, Se-PR:45, Sh-RP:311,
Tr-MR:183, Un-MA:229, Vi-PP:182
Booth Killed Lincoln. Em-AF:459
The Death of Lincoln. W. Bryant.
Sh-AP:25
For February Twelfth. M. Gessner.
Ha-YA:174, Sh-RP:189
The Gettysburg Address.
A. Lincoln. Fe-FP:443
I Saw a Ghost. J. Boilleau.
Ar-TP3:44
In Hardin County, 1809.
L. Thompson. Co-PS:32, Ha-PO:99
Kentucky Birthday, February 12,
1815. F. Frost. Br-SS:116,
Ha-YA:173
Lincoln. J. Fletcher. Se-PR:44,
Sm-PT:97, Th-AS:198, Un-MA:318
Lincoln. J. Howe. Se-PR:48
Lincoln. N. Turner. Ar-TP3:44,
Fe-FP:439, Hu-MP:396
Lincoln Monument, Washington.
L. Hughes. Li-TU:249
Lincoln, the Man of the People.
E. Markham. Un-MA:108, Vi-PP:167
Lincoln Triumphant. E. Markham.
Se-PR:44
Lincoln's Birthday. R. Stoddard.
Se-PR:49

The Long Shadow of Lincoln.
   C. Sandburg.   Ha-TP:141
The Master.   E. Robinson.
   Se-PR:46, Sh-AP:139, Un-MA:120,
   Wi-LT:101
Nancy Hanks.   R. and S. Benét.
   Ar-TP3:44, Br-SS:117, Fe-FP:438,
   Ga-FB:257, Gr-EC:233, Sh-RP:314
O Captain! My Captain!
   W. Whitman. Co-RG:38, Er-FA:282,
   Fe-FP:447, Fe-PL:171, Ga-FB:263,
   Hi-TL:121, Hu-MP:397, Ke-TF:317,
   Mc-PR:77, Se-PR:50, Sm-LG:157,
   Sp-OG:203, Un-MA:76, Vi-PP:166
On the Life-Mask of Abraham
   Lincoln.   R. Gilder. Se-PR:49
Prairie.   K. Llewellyn. Ha-YA:175
A Reply to Nancy Hanks.
   J. Silberger. Ar-TP3:44
There Was a Darkness in This Man.
   J. Fletcher. Vi-PP:169
They Will Look for a Few Words.
   N. Turner. Br-AF:71
This Dust Was Once the Man.
   W. Whitman. Se-PR:50
Two Days. M. de Veaux. Ho-CT:6
Would I Might Rouse the Lincoln
   in You All. V. Lindsay.
   Co-PS:31
LINCOLN, NANCY HANKS
   I Saw a Ghost. J. Boilleau.
   Ar-TP3:44
Nancy Hanks. R. and S. Benét.
   Ar-TP3:44, Br-SS:117, Fe-FP:438,
   Ga-FB:257, Gr-EC:233, Sh-RP:314
Nancy Hanks, Mother of Abraham
   Lincoln. V. Lindsay. Hi-TL:96
A Reply to Nancy Hanks.
   J. Silberger. Ar-TP3:44
LINCOLNSHIRE, ENG.: see also
   DIALECTS - LINCOLN
The High Tide on the Coast of
   Lincolnshire. J. Ingelow.
   De-TT:183, Pa-OM:118, Sp-OG:85
Hugh of Lincoln. De-CH:408,
   Ox-BB:317
Lincolnshire Bomber Station.
   H. Treece. Cr-WS:32
The Lincolnshire Poacher.
   Co-RM:237, De-CH:192, De-TT:79,
   Gr-GB:256, Ho-WR:75, Mo-SD:119,
   Pa-OM:188
A Lincolnshire Tale.
   J. Betjeman. De-FS:21
LINDBERGH, CHARLES AUGUSTUS
   Flight. H. Vinal. Mc-WK:208
   Lindbergh. Em-AF:770
LINDEN TREES
   The Lime. E. Farjeon.
   De-TT:162

The Lime-Tree. E. Lucie-Smith.
   Gr-BT:15
The Spring of Lime. R. Nichols.
   Pa-GTB:454
Trees. W. de la Mare. Mc-PR:199
LINDSAY, (NICHOLAS) VACHEL
   Supper with Lindsay. T. Roethke.
   Pl-ML:47
LINGG, LOUIS
   Before the Judge. D. Edelshtat.
   Kr-OF:111
LINNETS
   The Burial of the Linnet.
   J. Ewing. Ox-BC:254
The Green Linnet. W. Wordsworth.
   Pa-GTB:246, Rv-CB:650
A Health to the Birds.
   S. McManus. Co-PI:112
I Heard a Linnet Courting.
   R. Graves. Rd-OA:41, Wi-LT:51
The Linnet. R. Burns. De-TT:59,
   Re-BS:12
Song. T. Beddoes. Re-BS:8
Tenebris Interlucentem.
   J. Flecker. Rv-CB:975,
   Un-MB:273
To a Linnet in a Cage.
   F. Ledwidge. Co-RG:143
To Sparrows Fighting. W. Davies.
   Re-BS:30
LIONS: see also HUMOR - LIONS
   At the Lion's Cage.
   P. Dufault. Co-BBW:202
The Captive Lion. W. Davies.
   Co-BBW:198
Cat. J. Tolkien. Gr-EC:68
Circus Lion. C. Day Lewis.
   To-MP:114
Epigram. Viryamitra. Al-PI:39
Four-Footed Poems. E. Greenberg.
   Ho-TY:312
In Waste Places. J. Stephens.
   Ni-JP:35, Un-MB:266
Incident with Lions. S. Hay.
   Ls-NY:32
Jim. H. Belloc. Br-SM:113,
   Co-BB:70, Gr-CT:22, Ir-BB:161,
   Lo-LL:80, Na-EO:150, Ox-BC:312
Lése Majesté. O. Herford.
   Co-BBW:32
The Lion. H. Asquith. Li-TU:191
The Lion. H. Belloc. Un-MB:171
The Lion. A. Douglas. Gr-EC:10
The Lion. M. Howitt. Fe-FP:175
Lion. W. Smith. Co-BBW:183,
   We-PZ:18
Lion. M. Swenson. Pe-OA:249,
   Wi-LT:827
The Lion. W. Turner.
   Un-MB:346

LIONS — cont'd.
The Lion and the Cub. J. Gay.
Sp-OG:305
The Lion and the Fox. E. Rees.
Ar-TP3:81
The Lion and the Mouse. J. Taylor.
Pa-OM:328, Sh-RP:320
The Lion and the Unicorn.
An-IP:(29), Br-FF:9, Hi-FO:143,
Ir-BB:270, Li-LB:80, Mo-MGT:197,
Mo-NR:61, Na-EO:85, Pa-AP:14,
Wr-RM:56
The Lioness and Her Cub.
V. Lapin. Mo-MI:80
The Lion's Skeleton. C. Turner.
Rd-OA:119
Song of a Lioness Warning Her Cub.
Be-AP:60, Tr-US I:79
Why Nobody Pets the Lion at the
Zoo. J. Ciardi. Du-RG:33,
Sh-RP:344, Un-GF:88
The Wolf and the Lioness.
E. Rees. Ar-TP3:81
LIPPI, FRA FILIPPO
Fra Lippo Lippi. R. Browning.
Al-VBP:898, Ho-P:118
LISTENING
Ah, the Peasant. Hosokawa Yusai.
Le-MW:116
The Deer. T. Miyoshi. Sh-AM:83
The Eleventh Commandment.
J. Holmes. Tr-MR:78
The Listeners. W. de la Mare.
Al-VBP:1118, Er-FA:406, Fe-FP:513,
Pa-OM:298, Re-TW:116, Sh-RP:34,
Un-MB:196, Wi-LT:131
Listening. H. Behn. Un-GB:22
Listening. W. Stafford. Kh-VA:21,
La-RM:166, Mo-TS:35
Undertone. D. Quick. De-FS:153
Where's Mary? I. Eastwick.
Ar-TP3:7
A Wise Old Owl Lived in an Oak.
Er-FA:213, Li-LB:103, Mo-MGT:118,
Un-GT:22, Wi-MG:47
LISZT, FRANZ: see also HUMOR -
LISZT, FRANZ
Liszt. E. Bentley. Pl-US:34
LITANIES
Give Us the Sign! W. Du Bois.
Kr-OF:149
His Litany to the Holy Spirit.
R. Herrick. Fe-PL:343
Litany of the Lost. S. Sassoon.
Tr-MR:187
Litany to the High Gods.
Tr-US II:242
The Long Shadow of Lincoln.
C. Sandburg. Ha-TP:141
The Wet Litany. R. Kipling.
Gr-SS:189

LITERATURE: see also HUMOR -
LITERATURE
Epistle to Dr. Arbuthnot.
A. Pope. Al-VBP:539, Gr-CT:435
The Motto. A. Cowley. No-CL:6
The Writing Brush. Chung Ting-wen.
Pa-MV:75
LITTER AND LITTERING
After the Last Bulletin. R. Wilbur.
Al-VBP:1252, Un-MA:676
American Farm, 1934. G. Taggard.
Ca-VT:191
beer cans. M. Goode. La-IH:47
The Bunyip and the Whistling
Kettle. J. Manifold. Co-PM:123
Ghetto. R. Johnston. La-IH:50
Nobody Collects the Papers.
L. Warren and D. Dickson.
La-IH:53
The Produce District. T. Gunn.
Du-SH:148
Rural Dumpheap. M. Cane.
Br-AF:216
Southdown Summer. Sagittarius.
Pa-HT:135
The World Has Changed. C. Walker.
La-IH:46
LITTLE, FRANK
When the Cock Crows.
A. Giovannitti. Kr-OF:151
LITTLE, MALCOLM
Aardvark. J. Fields. Ad-BO:33
At That Moment. R. Patterson.
Ad-PB:210, Jo-SA:37
El-Hajj El-Shabazz.
R. Hayden. Ad-PB:123
For Malcolm: After Mecca.
G. Barrax. Ad-PB:224
For Malcolm Who Walks in the
Eyes of Our Children.
Q. Troupe. Ad-PB:444
For Malcolm X. N. Alba. Ad-PB:169
For Malcolm X. E. Spriggs.
Ad-CI:62
For Malcolm X. M. Walker.
Ad-PB:150, Ra-BP:157
Half Black, Half Blacker.
S. Plumpp. Ad-PB:385
i remember. . . . M. Jackson.
Ad-BO:35, Ad-PB:498
If Blood Is Black Then Spirit
Neglects My Unborn Son.
C. Rivers. Ad-PB:236
It Was a Funky Deal.
E. Knight. Ad-BO:32, Ad-PB:232,
Ra-BP:207
Malcolm. K. Cumbo. Ad-BO:34
Malcolm. S. Sanchez. Be-MA:134
malcolm. W. Smith. Ra-BP:280
Malcolm X. G. Brooks. Ab-MO:88,
Ad-PB:158, Lo-TY:246

Malcolm X - an Autobiography.
   L. Neal.   Jo-SA:42, Ra-BP:269
My Ace of Spades.   T. Joans.
   Ad-BO:31
A Poem for Black Hearts.   L. Jones.
   Ad-PB:255, Be-MA:118
Portrait of Malcolm X.   E. Knight.
   Ad-PB:232
Saint Malcolm.   J. Amini.
   Ra-BP:230
They Are Killing All the Young
   Men.   D. Henderson.   Ad-PB:414
LITTLE BIG HORN, BATTLE, 1876:
   see also SITTING BULL, CHIEF
Custer's Last Charge.
   F. Whittaker.   Fe-PL:173,
   Hi-TL:37, Pa-OM:183
LITTLE JOHN: see also
   ROBIN HOOD
A Gest of Robyn Hode, the Third
   Fytte.   Ox-BB:443
A Gest of Robyn Hode, the Fifth
   Fytte.   Ox-BB:464
LITTLE ROCK, ARK.
The Chicago Defender Sends a Man
   to Little Rock, Fall, 1957.
   G. Brooks.   Ad-PB:155,
   Be-MA:82, Bo-AN:142
THE LIVING
All Things Come Alike to All.
   Bible. O.T. Ecclesiastes.
   Me-PH:32
The Two Societies.
   J. Wheelock.   En-PC:8
LIZARDS: see also HUMOR -
   LIZARDS
Americans Are Afraid of Lizards.
   K. Shapiro.   Br-AF:45
Gecko.   N. Lloyd.   Pa-RE:18
Gila Monster.   H. Behn.
   Li-TU:191
Iguanas.   D. Atamian.   Ls-NY:194
just after noon with fierce shears.
   T. Combs.   Br-TC:76
Lizard.   D. Lawrence.   Be-EB:59
Lizard.   A. Maxwell-Hall.
   Ab-MO:35
The Lizard Is Crying.
   F. Garcia Lorca.   Le-SW:31,
   Li-TU:102, Sm-MK:155
Lizards and Snakes.   A. Hecht.
   Br-TC:183, Ha-TP:39
Lost — a Lizard.   I. Gough.
   Gr-EC:277
Oh, Oh!   Le-OE:47
On a Bougainvillea Vine at the
   Summer Palace.   B. Howes.
   Un-MA:653
Sally and Manda.   A. Campbell.
   Co-IW:32, Fr-MP:20, La-PP:72
Song.   L. Kemp.   Ls-NY:16

LLAMAS: see also HUMOR - LLAMAS
A Snap Judgment of the Llama.
   P. Bennett.   Co-BBW:209,
   Co-EL:33
LLEWELYN AB GRUFFYDD,
   WELSH PRINCE
The Fall of Llywelyn.   B. Fardd.
   Hi-FO:81
LOANS: see BORROWING AND
   LENDING
LOBSTERS: see also HUMOR -
   LOBSTERS
The Lobster.   A. Herbert.
   Ir-BB:75
The Lobster.   Un-GT:70
The Lobster Pot.   J. Arden.
   Co-EL:25
Lobsters in the Window.
   W. Snodgrass.   Du-SH:132
LOCHINVAR
Lochinvar.   W. Scott.   Co-FB:230,
   Co-PT:207, Co-RG:33, Er-FA:316,
   Fe-FP:504, Ga-FB:54, Gr-EC:132,
   Ma-YA:143, Mc-PR:154, Na-EO:133,
   Ox-BN:128, Sp-OG:126, Un-GT:134
LOCKS AND KEYS: see also HUMOR -
   LOCKS AND KEYS
The Cupboard.   W. de la Mare.
   Ar-TP3:7, Au-SP:131, Bo-FP:51,
   Fe-FP:42, Fr-MP:8, St-FS:76
The Key of the Kingdom.   Bl-OB:158,
   De-CH:3, Er-FA:202, Gr-EC:292,
   Ho-P:107, Mo-MGT:133, Re-TW:32,
   Rv-CB:31, Sm-LG:237, Sp-AS:(10)
Keys.   Yang Huan.   Pa-MV:158
The Playhouse Key.   R. Field.
   Fe-FP:107, Hu-MP:43
Sun.   D. Wakoski.   Kh-VA:13
LOCOMOTIVES: see TRAINS
LOCUSTS: see also CICADAS;
   GRASSHOPPERS
A Dewy Tree Trunk.   K. Takahama.
   Sh-AM:163
The Locust.   Fe-FP:135, Sh-RP:82
The Locust.   Tr-US I:116
The Locust Swarm.   Hsu Chao.
   Cr-WS:5, Rx-OH:123
Locusts in the Garden.   S. Ito.
   Sh-AM:106
The Stillness.   Basho.   Sh-RP:64
LODDON RIVER, ENG.
Sonnet, to the River Loddon.
   T. Warton.   Al-VBP:583
LOGIC: see also HUMOR - LOGIC;
   REASON; SATIRE - LOGIC
After a Hundred Storms.
   H. Mullins.   Ke-TF:121
Bishop Blougram's Apology.
   R. Browning.   Ox-BN:547
Esthetique du Mal, XIV.
   W. Stevens.   Wi-LT:159
Juxtaposition.   A. Clough.
   Ox-BN:613

LOGGING: see LUMBERING
LOGS: see WOOD
LONDON, ENG.: see also DIALECTS,
    COCKNEY; HUMOR - LONDON, ENG.;
    LONDON BRIDGE; THAMES RIVER;
    TOWER OF LONDON
  Annus Mirabilis. J. Dryden.
    Al-VBP:486
  As I Was Going by Charing Cross.
    Bl-OB:146, De-CH:177, De-TT:181,
    Gr-GB:188, Ir-BB:261, Sm-LG:153
  The Barrel-Organ. A. Noyes.
    Ga-FB:234, Un-MB:245
  The Bells. Wr-RM:105
  The Bells of London. Mother
    Goose. Bo-FP:125, De-PO:24,
    Gr-CT:296, Ir-BB:116, Li-LB:132,
    Mc-PR:110, Mo-MGT:138, Mo-NR:84,
    Na-EO:167
  The Children's Bells.
    E. Farjeon. De-CH:164
  A Christmas Carol. G. Thomas.
    Tr-MR:108
  Composed upon Westminster Bridge.
    W. Wordsworth. Al-VBP:660,
    Ar-TP3:173, Bo-FP:124, De-CH:524,
    Er-FA:270, Fe-PL:396, Ga-FB:224,
    Go-BP:22, Gr-CT:290, Ha-PO:80,
    Hi-WP II:126, Ke-TF:367,
    Ma-YA:139, Mc-PR:190, Ox-BN:78,
    Pa-GTB:250, Pa-HT:124, Rv-CB:645,
    Sm-LG:135
  A Farewell to London. A. Pope.
    Rv-CB:513
  The Fire of London. J. Dryden.
    Gr-CT:290, Ma-FW:244
  Holy Thursday. W. Blake.
    De-CH:62, Ma-YA:127, Rv-CB:584
  Homage to Wren. L. MacNeice.
    Cr-WS:121
  Important Statement. P. Kavanagh.
    En-PC:65
  Impression du Matin. O. Wilde.
    Un-MB:67
  Jerusalem. W. Blake. Gr-CT:295,
    Ox-BN:42
  London. W. Blake. Al-VBP:618,
    Gr-CT:304, Ha-PO:79, Ke-PP:49,
    Mo-GR:78, Ox-BN:24, Rv-CB:605
  London. J. Davidson. Ox-BN:900
  London Beautiful. R. Le Gallienne.
    Pa-HT:125
  The London Bobby.
    A. Guiterman. Pa-HT:125
  London Lackpenny. Gr-CT:305
  London Mourning in Ashes.
    Hi-FO:154
  London Nightfall. J. Fletcher.
    Un-MA:317
  London Rain. N. Turner. Th-AS:92

London Snow. R. Bridges.
    Co-BN:196, De-CH:220, Gr-CT:308,
    Ha-PO:87, Hi-WP I:126, Ho-WR:183,
    Ma-YA:218, Ni-JP:141, Ox-BN:874,
    Pa-GTB:414, Un-MB:50, Wi-LT:52
  A London Thoroughfare Two A.M.
    A. Lowell. Ni-JP:131
  London Town. J. Masefield.
    Ma-YA:232
  The Merchants of London. Gr-GB:170,
    Ir-BB:37, Wr-RM:56
  The Month of May. J. Fletcher and
    F. Beaumont. Gr-CT:44
  November Blue. A. Meynell.
    Un-MB:62
  An Ode to Mr. Anthony Stafford to
    Hasten Him into the Country.
    T. Randolph. Al-VBP:378
  Oranges and Lemons. Sm-MK:203,
    Wi-MG:79
  Parliament Hill. H. Bashford.
    Hu-MP:182, Th-AS:67
  Pussy Cat, Pussy Cat, Where Have
    You Been? Ar-TP3:52, Au-SP:15,
    Bo-FP:6, De-PO:18, Er-FA:506,
    Ir-BB:269, Li-LB:88, Mo-MGT:163,
    Mo-NR:100, Pa-AP:50, Wi-MG:34,
    Wr-RM:26
  Rain. P. Williams. Le-M:149
  The Return of the Fairy.
    H. Wolfe. Co-PM:178
  The Smithfield Market Fire.
    F. Dallas. Hi-WP I:84
  The Starling. J. Heath-Stubbs.
    Ma-FW:91
  The Streets of Laredo. L. MacNeice.
    Ca-MB:112, Gr-CT:309
  This Was That Yeere of Wonder.
    De-CH:638
  To the City of London. W. Dunbar.
    De-CH:523, Gr-CT:288, No-CL:263
  Troynovant. T. Dekker. Gr-CT:297
  Upon Paul's Steeple. Li-LB:46
  The Waste Land. T. Eliot.
    Pe-OA:112, Un-MA:386
  When the Assault Was Intended to
    the City. J. Milton.
    Co-RG:23, Pa-GTB:62
  The Wish. A. Cowley.
    Al-VBP:450, De-CH:524
  Yesterday in Oxford Street.
    R. Fyleman. Ar-TP3:147,
    Pe-FB:59
LONDON BRIDGE
  London Bridge. Bo-FP:126,
    De-CH:61, Gr-CT:287, Gr-GB:24,
    Li-LB:65, Mo-MGT:126, Mo-NR:112,
    Wr-RM:120
  Of London Bridge, and the Stupen-
    dous Sight, and Structure
    Thereof. J. Howell. Gr-CT:288

LONELINESS: see also HUMOR -
    LONELINESS; SOLITUDE
Above Tides of Leaves. Buson.
    Be-CS:10
The Aged Maple Tree.
    Chung Ting-wen. Pa-MV:76
Ah, How We Loved. O. Mandelstam.
    Ca-MR:58
Albatross. J. Collins. Mo-GR:37
The All Alone Tree.
    F. Gallagher. Bo-FP:98
Alone. C. Bialik. Me-PH:73
Alone. Chu Shu Chen. Rx-OH:134
Alone. W. de la Mare. Gr-CT:390
Alone. M. Hiers. La-IH:72
Alone. K. Mann. Ba-HI:29
Alone. E. Poe. Ha-PO:209,
    No-CL:20
Alone. K. Raikin. Mo-MI:48
Alone. S. Sassoon. Hi-WP I:121,
    Un-MB:318
Alone in the Night.
    Li Ch'ing Chao. Rx-OH:96
The Ancient Couple on Lu Mountain.
    M. Van Doren. Ca-VT:196
And All of Them Are Gone.
    D. Einhorn. Ho-TY:83
The Appeal. E. Brontë.
    Go-BP:149, Ox-BN:599
April Moon. W. de la Mare.
    Sp-OG:347
As I Sit. C. Begay. Ba-HI:34
As Long as We Are Not Alone.
    I. Emiot. Ho-TY:315
At the Edge. M. Korte. Sc-TN:116
At the Slackening of the Tide.
    J. Wright. Ca-VT:623
Aunt Jemima of the Ocean Waves.
    R. Hayden. Ad-PB:125
Autobiography. L. MacNeice.
    Gr-BT:13, Ma-FW:193
La Belle Saison. J. Prévert.
    Ad-CI:97
Bereft. R. Frost. Sm-PT:137,
    Un-MA:181, Wi-LT:174
Billboards in the Rain.
    D. Fogel. Ho-TY:236
Birds Are Flying past Me.
    D. Fong. Ba-HI:28
Break, Break, Break. A. Tennyson.
    Bl-OB:51, Bo-GJ:182, De-CH:211,
    Ga-FB:128, Ha-PO:137, Ma-YA:192,
    Ox-BN:485, Pa-GTB:331, Sp-OG:267
The Broken String. Tr-CB:51,
    Tr-US I:76
Come, It Is Late in the Day.
    Do-CH:(31)
Companions. M. Widdemer.
    De-FS:218
Complaint of a New Wife.
    Tr-US II:188

Could Be. L. Hughes. La-OC:70
Couplets, I. Tr-US II:136
Crossing the River. Pa-SG:47
Crowsfeet Splaying round His
    Eyes. L. Lloyd-Evans.
    Gr-BT:163
Cuckoos. M. Kaneko. Sh-AM:62
The Cycle. Hsü Hsü. Hs-TC:275
Dance Songs, IV. Tr-US I:199
Danse Russe. W. Williams.
    Mc-EA:68
Desert Places. R. Frost.
    Un-MA:188
The Deserted House. J. Fairbun.
    Le-M:175
Despair. I. Takenaka. Sh-AM:100
Discordants. C. Aiken. Co-BL:35,
    Er-FA:108, Un-MA:421, Wi-LT:325
Distance Spills Itself.
    Y. Bat-Miriam. Me-PH:104
The Dove's Loneliness.
    G. Darley. Ox-BN:384
Down in the Lonesome Garden.
    Ra-BP:8
Early Morning. J. Jimenez.
    Le-SW:67
Echoes. W. de la Mare. Sh-RP:105
Elegy. Tr-US II:307
An Empty Bed. S. Silon. Le-M:140
Enlightenment. Ch'en Yu Yi.
    Rx-LT:99
Etude. I. Brodsky. Bo-RU:21
Evening. A. Lutzky. Ho-TY:266
Everyone Is Asleep. Seifu-jo.
    Do-TS:37
Farewell Once More. Tu Fu.
    Rx-OH:22
Farewell to the Court.
    W. Ralegh. Rv-CB:153
The Feast of Lanterns.
    J. Yoshimura. Le-TA:35
Figure for a Landscape.
    L. Mueller. St-H:146
The Five Students. T. Hardy.
    Pa-GTB:410
The Fly. S. Takahashi.
    Sh-AM:98
For a Husband Away. Tr-CB:45,
    Tr-US I:46
The Forsaken Merman. M. Arnold.
    Al-VBP:960, Bl-OB:59, Cl-DT:41,
    Co-SS:160, Hu-MP:99, Ma-YA:205,
    Rv-CB:862, Sm-LG:339, Sm-MK:84,
    Sp-OG:117
Four and Twenty. S. Stills.
    Mo-GR:30
Four Walls to Talk to Me.
    A. Blackwell. Jo-VC:89
A Garden by the Sea. W. Morris.
    Al-VBP:1011, De-CH:461,
    No-CL:67, Ox-BN:788

LONELINESS — cont'd.

The Garden of Bamboos. Co-BL:27

Girl's Song from a Legend.
Da-SC:153, Tr-US II:221

Girls' Songs. Tr-CB:32,
Tr-US I:119

The Goat Milkers. J. Wade.
Sc-TN:223

The Great Sad One. U. Greenberg.
Me-PH:91

Harvest Sacrifice. Su Tung P'o.
Rx-OH:75

The Hill Wife. R. Frost.
Ca-VT:10, Wi-LT:167

Home. Le-MW:126, Rx-LT:9

The House of Life. K. Tynan.
Go-BP:133

The House with Nobody in It.
J. Kilmer. Hu-MP:74, Th-AS:206

How Will You Manage.
Princess Daihaku. Ba-ST:44

Hymen. H.D. Al-VBP:1169,
Gr-SS:118

I Am the Only Being. E. Brontë.
Al-VBP:923

I Break the Sky. O. Dodson.
Ad-PB:133

I Explain. S. Crane. Sh-AP:143

I Hear an Army. J. Joyce.
Al-VBP:1150, Un-MB:269, Wi-LT:623

I Know Some Lonely Houses.
E. Dickinson. Co-PM:50,
Mc-WK:129, Rv-CB:900, Un-MA:103

I Must Go Walk the Woods.
Ho-WR:158, Rv-CB:30

I of the Owl. Ho-SD:9

I Shall Miss You Most. Ba-ST:37

I Substitute for the Dead
Lecturer. L. Jones. Jo-SA:110

I Wake Up Alone. Li Shang Yin.
Rx-LT:76

The Idiot. J. Ashberry.
Ca-VT:593

In My Loneliness. Ryōzen.
Ba-ST:42

In the Empty Mountains.
Hitomaro. Ba-ST:40

In This City. A. Brownjohn.
Ad-CI:106

Inside a Deep Isolation.
S. Muro. Sh-AM:56

Into Spring Mountains.
M. Saito. Sh-AM:146

The Invisible Man. V. Kalugin.
Bo-RU:43

The Jewel. J. Dickey. Ha-TP:78

The Knight Without a Name.
Ho-WR:122

The Last Rose of Summer.
T. Moore. Co-BN:53, Er-FA:240

Late Harvest. J. Tate. St-H:232

Let's All Meet and Have a Party
Sometime. J. Birkby. Gr-BT:39

Letter from the Slough Pond.
I. Gardner. Co-EL:12, St-H:72

Little Boy Lost. W. Blake.
Rv-CB:581

Little Elegy. E. Wylie. Ha-LO:92

Little Jumping Joan. Mother
Goose. Ar-TP3:101, Ho-ME:9,
Li-LB:43, Mo-CC:(3), Mo-MGT:21,
Mo-NR:126, Mo-TL:88, Wr-RM:14

The Lives of Gulls and Children.
H. Nemerov. Ni-JP:116

Lone Dog. I. McLeod. Ar-TP3:51,
Co-BBW:103, De-TT:68, Fe-FP:155,
Hu-MP:195, La-PV:108, Th-AS:186

The Lone Tree and Others.
Liu Ta-pai. Hs-TC:9

Loneliness. Cheng Min. Hs-TC:229

Loneliness. I Men. Hs-TC:415

Loneliness. B. Jenkins. Du-RG:55,
Pe-SS:114

Loneliness. J. Pomroy. Su-FVI:11

Loneliness. A. Young. Ad-PB:368

Loneliness. Be-AP:36

The Lonely House. A. Mezquida.
Ke-TF:152

The Lonely Street. W. Williams.
Br-TC:480, Gr-CC:188

Lonely Tulip Grower.
J. Alvarez. Jo-SA:11

Lonesome. P. Dunbar. Hu-MP:29,
Se-PR:118

The Lonesome Boy. V. White.
La-IH:24

Longing. Chi Hsüan. Pa-MV:46

The Lord of Biscay. A. Housman.
Ni-JP:82

Love in a Life. R. Browning.
Ox-BN:543, Rv-CB:815

Love Song. L. Strongin.
Sc-TN:205

Love Song. Le-OE:83, Tr-US I:80

The Love Song of Har Dyal.
R. Kipling. Go-BP:150

Love Songs (Who Told). Tr-US I:131

A Lover's Lament. Pa-SG:59,
Tr-US II:257

Mariana. A. Tennyson.
Al-VBP:845, De-CH:297, Ho-WR:155,
Ox-BN:473, Rv-CB:795

Melancholy Summer. S. Ito.
Sh-AM:102

Midnight Lamentation. H. Monro.
Al-VBP:1140

Mr. Flood's Party. E. Robinson.
Al-VBP:1107, Er-FA:304, Ha-PO:64,
Na-EO:66, Ni-JP:143, Pe-M:50,
Pe-OA:5, Sh-AP:141, Sm-PT:140,
Un-MA:121, Wi-LT:111

Mnemosyne. T. Stickney.
Al-VBP:1123
The Months Go By. Rx-LT:23
The Moon Has Set. Sappho.
Gr-CT:404
Morning. Chu Shu Chen. Rx-OH:132
The Most of It. R. Frost.
Ha-PO:218, Mo-BG:104
My Friend. L. Kirkman. Ho-CS:22
My Mother Bids Me Bind My Hair.
A. Hunter. Rv-CB:555
My World. R. Diaz. Me-WF:14
Night. Fang Ching. Hs-TC:383
Night. Sappho. Pa-SG:63
Night. S. Sutu. Lo-TY:175
Night of Wind. F. Frost.
Ar-TP3:64, Fe-FP:173
Night-Piece. R. Patterson.
Ad-CI:103, Ad-PB:211
The Night Refuses a Dreamer.
G. Code. De-FS:62
Night Without End. Rx-LT:14
No Friends nor Enemies. J. Bryant.
Jo-VC:92
No Man. C. Bresher. Ad-II:121
No One. Barbara. La-IH:68
no time ago. e. cummings.
Mc-WS:32
Nobody Riding the Roads Today.
J. Jordan. Ra-BP:248
Nostalgia. K. Shapiro.
Br-TC:371
November. C. Gluck. Le-M:132
Nowhere to Turn? Br-FW:1
Number 5 - December. D. Henderson.
Ad-BO:69, Jo-SA:84
Oft in the Stilly Night.
T. Moore. Co-PI:146, De-TT:153,
Er-FA:150, Hi-WP I:116,
Ho-P:309, Ox-BN:219, Pa-GTB:224,
Rv-CB:680
Old Age. Ou Yang Hsiu.
Rx-OH:62
An Old Man's Winter Night.
R. Frost. Ca-VT:9, Ni-JP:142,
Un-MA:176
The Old Men. W. de la Mare.
Un-MB:199
Once. W. de la Mare. Go-BP:170
One. C. Rodgers. Ra-BP:261
The Only Card I Got on My Birthday
Was from an Insurance Man.
W. Stafford. St-H:214
Out of Longing. D. Fogel.
Ho-TY:238
Outcast. C. McKay. Ad-PB:25,
Be-MA:14, Bo-AN:28
Over the Paving Stones.
T. Miyoshi. Sh-AM:83
A Passing. R. Cuscaden.
St-H:31

People Are Few. Issa. Le-MW:51
Perry-the-Winkle. J. Tolkien.
Ar-TP3:158
Peter Grimes. G. Crabbe.
Ox-BN:14
Phoenix Hairpins. Lu Yu.
Rx-OH:104
The Pity of the Leaves.
E. Robinson. Un-MA:137
Plaint. Tr-US I:91
Plaint of a Woman Who Has No
Lover. Tr-US II:72
Playing. P. Costello. Le-M:74
Poem. T. Clark. Mc-EA:70
Poem. C. Herbert. Sa-B:37
Poem. D. Hofstein. Ho-TY:173
Poem. P. Markish. Ho-TY:181
Poor Fellow Me. Le-OE:123
The Poor Lonesome Cowboy.
Fi-BG:147
Prayer for Marilyn Monroe.
E. Cardenal. Be-UL:95
The Preacher: Ruminates Behind
the Sermon. G. Brooks.
Be-MA:80, Li-TU:165
A Private Letter to Brazil.
G. Oden. Bo-AN:158,
Hu-NN:91, Hu-PN:383
The Raven. E. Poe. Al-VBP:865,
Bo-GJ:165, Co-RG:103, De-CH:303,
Er-FA:312, Ga-FB:134, Sh-AP:56,
Sm-LG:207
Recitative - A Lakeshore Poem.
M. Kaneko. Sh-AM:64
Riding at Daybreak. Sun Yun Feng.
Le-MW:39, Ma-FW:129
River of Ice. S. Tsuboi.
Sh-AM:68
Rondel. W. Henley. Ox-BN:886
A Sad Song about Greenwich
Village. F. Park. La-OC:66
The Sea. Tu Yün-hsieh.
Hs-TC:250
Search. R. Souster. Co-EL:137
Separation. A. Lopez. Al-WW:4
She Dwelt among the Untrodden
Ways. W. Wordsworth.
Al-VBP:656, Ga-FB:50, Li-SR:106,
Mc-PR:179, Ox-BN:62, Pa-GTB:179,
Rv-CB:631
The Shell. J. Stephens.
Cl-DT:40, Co-BN:82, De-CH:57,
Ma-FW:43, Ni-JP:34, Un-MB:262
Siren Chorus. G. Darley.
Al-VBP:794, Gr-CT:202, Ox-BN:396
Solitude. H. Monro. Un-MB:236
Solitude. E. Wilcox. Er-FA:3,
Fe-PL:291
Sometimes I Feel. B. Congress.
Me-WF:78

LONELINESS — cont'd.
Sometimes I Feel. Y. Graham.
  Me-WF:55
Sometimes I Feel. M. Jackson.
  Me-WF:85
Sometimes I Feel. K. Ray.
  Me-WF:65
Song. W. Snodgrass. Un-MA:682
Song. Tr-US II:194
Song at the Berry-Picking on the
  Mountain. Da-SC:38, Le-IB:89
Song for a Christmas Celebration.
  Tr-US I:31
Song for Someone Who Is Absent.
  Do-CH:(42)
Song of a Scout Remembering
  Home. Tr-US II:234
Song of Hummingbird. Le-OE:49
Song of the Maiden's Leap.
  Tr-US II:239
The Sonnets. W. Shakespeare.
  No-CL:88, Pa-GTB:8, Rv-CB:237,
  Un-MW:182
Sonnets: LVII. W. Shakespeare.
  Al-VBP:203, Co-BL:60,
  No-CL:84, Pa-GTB:7
Sonnets 3. W. Wordsworth.
  Al-VBP:659, Ox-BN:91, Pa-GTB:198,
  Rv-CB:647
Sorrow. Chu Shu Chen. Rx-LT:107
Stanzas from "Child Harold."
  J. Clare. Ox-BN:325
Stanzas Written in Dejection, near
  Naples. P. Shelley. Al-VBP:745,
  Ga-FB:125, Pa-GTB:227, Rv-CB:707
Star Journey. N. Madgett.
  Ra-BP:195
The Station. J. Rathe. Le-M:173
Stormy Night in Autumn.
  Chu Shu Chen. Rx-OH:133
The Street. O. Paz. La-OC:135
A Superscription. D. Rossetti.
  Ma-YA:212, Ox-BN:686, Pa-GTB:371,
  Rv-CB:882
Tanka. Y. Aizu. Sh-AM:142
That Lonesome Place. C. O'John.
  Al-WW:68
There Once Was a Puffin.
  F. Jaques. Ar-TP3:124, Au-SP:240,
  Fr-MP:14, Ir-BB:89, St-FS:87
There's Nane o' My Ain to Care.
  W. Ogilvie. De-CH:515
This Old World. S. Cooper. Me-WF:36
The Thread of Life.
  C. Rossetti. Ox-BN:719
Three Years She Grew in Sun and
  Shower. W. Wordsworth.
  Ox-BN:63, Pa-GTB:180, Rv-CB:642
Tiny World. J. Holland. Jo-VC:81
To a Distant Friend.W. Wordsworth.
  Pa-GTB:189, Rv-CB:651

To a Traveller. Su Tung P'o.
  Rx-OH:77
To Be Alone. R. Moulder.
  Me-WF:81
To Marguerite. M. Arnold.
  Ox-BN:627, Pa-GTB:364, Rv-CB:872
To My Brother Miguel.
  C. Vallejo. Pe-M:13
Tom, Tom, the Piper's Son.
  J. Ransom. Al-VBP:1186
Tonight in This Town. Be-CS:52
The Traveler. Ho Hsun. Rx-LT:41
The Traveller. J. Berryman.
  Ca-VT:379
Two Jazz Poems. C. Hines, Jr.
  Bo-AN:184, Du-RG:74
The Unbroken Code. R. Dana.
  Ls-NY:95
Under Thin Rainfall.
  T. Takaori. Sh-AM:154
Uninhabited Island. Chi Hsüan.
  Pa-MV:49
Unwanted. E. Field. Ke-PP:78
Upon the Mountain Edge.
  Emperor Okamoto. Ba-ST:92
The Visiting Sea. A. Meynell.
  Go-BP:132
What Color Is Lonely. C. Rodgers.
  Ra-BP:265
What She Said.
  Milaipperun Kantan. Al-PI:65
When I Am Not with You.
  S. Teasdale. Co-BL:97
When I Am Outside.
  N. Blachowski. Me-WF:64
When I Was Lost. D. Aldis.
  Au-SP:117
When My Canary. Shiki.
  Ar-TP3:54, Be-CS:45
When That Beam of Light.
  M. Nakagawa. Sh-AM:149
While Enduring. S. Yamaguchi.
  Sh-AM:171
While I Stay Away. Ba-ST:44
Whoever You Are Holding Me Now
  in Hand. W. Whitman. Ha-PO:216
William Blake. J. Thomson.
  Rv-CB:931
The Wind at the Door. W. Barnes.
  Pa-GTB:321, Rv-CB:768
Winter Garden. D. Gascoyne.
  Pa-GTB:549
Winter Landscape. S. Spender.
  Un-MB:473
Winter Morning. W. Welles.
  Ho-LP:33
A Winter Night. W. Barnes.
  Gr-CT:394, Ox-BN:430
Winter Night. Hi-WP II:145
The Winter Trees. C. Dyment.
  Cl-FC:63

The Wolf.   G. Durston.   Ar-TP3:65
Women's Dance Song.
   Tr-US II:143, 151
Xmas Time.   W. Karsner.   Co-EL:142,
   Co-PU:30
You, Neighbor God.   R. Rilke.
   Tr-MR:147
Young Girl: Annam.   P. Colum.
   Ha-LO:94
LONG ISLAND, N.Y.
   Bonac.   J. Wheelock.   Pa-HT:37
LONGFELLOW, HENRY WADSWORTH:
   see also HUMOR - LONGFELLOW,
   HENRY WADSWORTH
   Longfellow.   J. Riley.   Se-PR:310
LONGING: see also HUMOR -
   LONGING
   Absence.   M. Arnold.   Rv-CB:869
   Absence.   De-TT:154
   Adrian Henri's Talking after
      Christmas Blues.   A. Henri.
      Gr-BT:73, To-MP:206
   Ah, that I Were Far Away.
      A. Clough.   Ox-BN:602
   Alun Mabon's Song.   J. Hughes.
      Hi-WP I:44
   And One Shall Live in Two.
      J. Brooks.   Hu-PN:239
   Annie of Lochroyan.   Ma-BB:202
   An Answer to Ting Yuan Ch'en.
      Ou Yang Hsiu.   Rx-OH:59
   Aromaiterai's Lament.
      Aromaiterai.   Tr-US II:68
   At the Mid Hour of Night.   T. Moore.
      Al-VBP:711, Ox-BN:210, Pa-GTB:199
   Autumn.   Tsang K'o-chia.
      Hs-TC:285
   Ayii, Ayii, Ayii (I Wish).
      Ho-SD:71
   Banquet at the Tsu Family Manor.
      Tu Fu.   Rx-OH:3
   The Bereaved.   M. Ward.   Ke-TF:176
   The Birdcage.   C. Aiken.   Re-BS:26
   Black Woman.   N. Madgett.
      Ad-PB:183
   By the Rivers of Babylon.   Bible.
      O.T. Psalms.   Me-PH:30
   Cactus Tree.   J. Mitchell.
      Mo-GR:121
   The Candle Indoors.   G. Hopkins.
      Ma-FW:124, Wi-LT:43
   Carcassonne.   G. Nadaud.
      Pa-HT:116
   Chippewa Love Songs.   Da-SC:151
   Choral Songs, II.   Tr-US II:114
   Country Lane.   M. Darling.
      De-FS:69
   Country Letter.   J. Clare.
      Rv-CB:733
   Crossing the River.   Pa-SG:47

Destruction.   Chu Tzu-ch'ing.
   Hs-TC:13
Divided.   J. Ingelow.   Ox-BN:720
Divinely Superfluous Beauty.
   R. Jeffers.   Un-MA:369
Dog-Tired.   D. Lawrence.   Gr-BT:50
A Dream at Night.   Mei Yao Ch'en.
   Rx-OH:43
Dreaming that I Went with Li and
   Yü to Visit Yüan Chên.
   Po Chü-i.   Pa-SG:19
The Drynaun Dhun.   Gr-GB:116
Dusk in War Time. S. Teasdale.
   Cr-WS:120
Each in His Own Tongue.   Ke-TF:246
Earth Trembles Waiting.
   B. Wagstaff.   Fe-PL:120
The Eve of Crécy.   W. Morris.
   Gr-SS:95
The Exile.   M. Benaya.   Ls-NY:43
The Far-Off Mountains Hide You
   from Me.   Do-CH:(34)
The First Essential.
   I. Gheorghe.   Mc-AC:152
For a Husband Away.
   Tr-CB:45, Tr-US I:46
For Carlos at War.   M. Price.
   Cr-WS:77
For Her Love I Cark and Care.
   Rv-CB:118
For the Sake of Somebody.
   R. Burns.   Hi-WP I:42
The Forsaken Merman.   M. Arnold.
   Al-VBP:960, Bl-OB:59, Cl-DT:41,
   Co-SS:160, Hu-MP:99, Ma-YA:205,
   Rv-CB:862, Sm-LG:339, Sm-MK:84,
   Sp-OG:117
From the Arabic: An Imitation.
   P. Shelley.   Rv-CB:704
A Garden by the Sea.   W. Morris.
   Al-VBP:1011, De-CH:461,
   No-CL:67, Ox-BN:788
Girls' Songs.   Tr-CB:32,
   Tr-US I:119
Golden Birds.   E. Greenberg.
   Ho-TY:314
The Grass on the Mountain.
   Bo-HF:34
The Green Autumn Stubble.
   Pa-SG:55
Home No More Home to Me.
   R. Stevenson.   De-CH:25
The Housemaid.   R. Korn.
   Ho-TY:302
Hynd Etin.   Ma-BB:192
I Am.   J. Clare.   Ho-P:37
I Can No Longer Untangle My
   Hair.   Rx-LT:17
I Closed My Shutters Fast Last
   Night.   G. Johnson.   Hu-PN:79

LONGING — cont'd.
I Saw from the Beach. T. Moore.
  Co-PI:144, Ox-BN:213
I See You Again. Ch'en Meng-chia.
  Hs-TC:114
I See Your Face. L. Issaluk.
  Le-IB:85
I Sought You. J. Wheelock.
  Co-BL:35
I Wish I Were Close. Y. Akahito.
  Li-TU:164
I'll Weave My Love a Garland.
  De-CH:695
Images. R. Aldington. Un-MB:353
Immortal Autumn. A. MacLeish.
  Gr-SS:44, Un-MA:456
In Bondage. C. McKay. Ad-PB:26
In Spring. E. Mörike. Pa-SG:88
Jean. R. Burns. Al-VBP:645,
  Hi-WP I:41, Pa-GTB:156
Jeanie with the Light Brown Hair.
  S. Foster. Er-FA:426
John Kinsella's Lament for Mrs.
  Mary Moore. W. Yeats. Wi-LT:93
June Thunder. L. MacNeice.
  To-MP:36
Krishna's Longing. Jayadeva.
  Al-PI:56
Lament. Tr-US II:78
A Lament for His Own Land.
  Tr-US II:114
last poem i'm gonna write about
  us. S. Sanchez. Be-MA:136
Letter from a Wife. S. Reese.
  Hu-PN:413
Letter from the Slough Pond.
  I. Gardner. Co-EL:12, St-H:72
A Letter to Her Husband.
  A. Bradstreet. Sh-AP:11
Lines. Shen Ch'üan-ch'i.
  Cr-WS:9
Linked Pantuns. Tr-US II:204
The Lonely House.
  A. Mezquida. Ke-TF:152
The Long Voyage. M. Cowley.
  Mc-WK:182, Ni-JP:132, Pe-OA:171
Longing. M. Arnold. Fe-PL:97,
  Go-BP:129, Rv-CB:867
Longing. Chi Hsüan. Pa-MV:46
The Lord of Biscay. A. Housman.
  Ni-JP:82
Lost Voice on This Hill.
  B. Eaton. De-FS:84
Love Longing. Tr-CB:54
Love Poem. J. Logan. St-H:115
Love Song. Tr-US II:287
The Love Song for Har Dyal.
  R. Kipling. Go-BP:150
Love Song from a Legend.
  Tr-US II:104

Mandalay. R. Kipling.
  Ga-FB:70, Un-MB:125
Mary Morison. R. Burns.
  Pa-GTB:149
Memory. C. Rossetti. Ox-BN:716
Menominee Love Songs. Da-SC:151
The Message of the Frigate Birds.
  Tr-US II:89
Missing My Daughter.
  S. Spender. Pa-GTB:521
The Moon at the Fortified Pass.
  Li Po. Cr-WS:9
Moon Door. M. Kennedy. Co-BL:154
My Heart Is in the East.
  J. Halevi. Me-PH:61
My Luve's in Germany. De-CH:172
my sweet old etcetera.
  e. cummings. Cr-WS:74,
  Mo-BG:94, Pe-SS:137
The New Wife. Ng Shao. Rx-LT:45
Night Thoughts. Lu Yu. Rx-OH:110
Nostalgia. W. Stevens. Wi-LT:134
O for the Wings of a Dove.
  Euripides. Go-BP:155, Pa-SG:175
O that 'Twere Possible.
  A. Tennyson. Rv-CB:800
O What if the Fowler? C. Dalmon.
  Co-BBW:240, De-CH:337, Re-BS:24
O Woodland Cool. C. Brentano.
  Pa-SG:44
Old Horse. Sun Yu-t'ang.
  Hs-TC:122
Old Love Songs. Tr-US II:238
Out of the Cradle Endlessly
  Rocking. W. Whitman.
  Al-VBP:936, Un-MA:66
Outcast. C. McKay. Ad-PB:25,
  Be-MA:14, Bo-AN:28
Plaint of a Woman Who Has No
  Lover. Tr-US II:72
The Plum Blossoms Have Opened.
  Ba-ST:26
Poem. L. Hughes. Li-TU:26
Pretty Polly. B. Reece.
  Co-BL:150
Psalm 137. L. Ryzhova. Bo-RU:70
Reading the Poems of an Absent
  Friend. Ou Yang Hsiu. Rx-OH:57
Red River Valley. Er-FA:445
The Return of the Marama from
  Hiti. Tr-US II:72
The River Merchant's Wife:
  A Letter. Li T'ai-Po.
  Bo-HF:120, Br-TC:332, Co-BL:101,
  Gr-CC:22, Ha-PO:184, Li-TU:181,
  Mo-BG:98, Pe-SS:126, Sh-AP:171,
  Un-MA:290
Robin Adair. C. Keppel. De-TT:154
rusty come home damn you.
  D. Witt. Ad-II:34

Sea Born.   H. Vinal.   Bo-HF:78
Sea Fever.   J. Masefield.
   Ar-TP3:90, Co-SS:55, Fe-FP:190,
   Fe-PL:440, Ga-FB:182, Hu-MP:174,
   La-PV:185, Ma-YA:232, Mc-PR:134,
   Pe-FB:43, Sh-RP:33, Th-AS:127,
   Un-MB:221
Sea (Gull).   G. Manin.   Ad-II:55
A Separation.   W. Cory.   Ox-BN:649
Separation.   M. Tsvetayeva.
   Ca-MR:137
She Thinks of Her Beloved.
   Lu Chi.   Rx-LT:28
The Skein.   C. Kizer.   Ca-VT:543
Song of a Married Woman to Her
   Lover Yuv.   Tr-US II:9
Song of a Navigator's Wife.
   Tr-US II:16
The Song of a Vagabond Son.
   Fang Ching.   Hs-TC:385
Song of a Widow.   Tr-US II:18
Song of a Widow for Her Dead
   Husband.   Tr-US II:117
Songs, I, II.   Tr-US II:123
Sonnet 30.   W. Shakespeare.
   Al-VBP:201, Er-FA:166, Fe-PL:130,
   Ga-FB:33, Pa-GTB:18, Rv-CB:213
The Sonnet-Ballad.   G. Brooks.
   Pe-SS:131
Spring.   R. Hovey.   Sh-RP:104
Spring Day on West Lake.
   Ou Yang Hsiu.   Rx-OH:60
Spring Night.   S. Teasdale.
   Co-BL:38, Un-MA:264
The Stranger.   J. Garrigue.
   Br-TC:142, Wi-LT:709
Tears, Idle Tears.
   A. Tennyson.   Al-VBP:859,
   Er-FA:150, Ha-PO:150,
   Hi-WP II:144, Ox-BN:486
Thinking of a Friend Lost in the
   Tibetan War.   Chang Chi.
   Cr-WS:8
Thoughts in Exile.   Su Tung P'o.
   Rx-OH:81
To Dream of Thee.   J. Keats.
   Un-MW:165
To Mary: It Is the Evening
   Hour.   J. Clare.   Gr-CT:264
To the Night.   P. Shelley.
   Al-VBP:755, De-CH:438, Fe-PL:401,
   Ho-WR:199, Ox-BN:292, Pa-GTB:188,
   Rv-CB:702, Sp-OG:348
To the Nyeva.   G. Garbovsky.
   Bo-RU:35
To the Tune "A Lonely Flute on the
   Phoenix Terrace."
   Li Ch'ing Chao.   Rx-LT:96
To the Tune "Cutting a Flowering
   Plum Branch." Li Ch'ing Chao.
   Rx-LT:95

To the Tune "Pear Blossoms Fall
   and Scatter." Li Ch'ing Chao.
   Rx-OH:97
To the Tune "Spring at Wu Ling."
   Li Ch'ing Chao.   Rx-LT:94
To the Tune "The Boat of Stars."
   Li Ch'ing Chao.   Rx-LT:92
Tolling Bells.   Lady Kosa.
   Pa-SG:23
Under Your Voice, among Legends.
   P. Harris.   Sc-TN:81
Unwanted.   E. Field.   Ke-PP:78
The Valley of Shadows.
   R. Dragonette.   Lo-IT:32
The Voice.   T. Hardy.   Ox-BN:842,
   Pa-GTB:406
Waiting Poem.   D. Fogel.   Ho-TY:237
Western Wind.   Al-VBP:66, Gr-GB:118,
   Li-SR:125, Rv-CB:5, Sm-LG:362,
   Un-MW:160
What the Lover Said.
   A. Nanmullaiyar.   Al-PI:63
When I Think of Him.   Da-SC:152,
   Tr-US II:225
When the Green Lies over the
   Earth.   A. Grimke.   Hu-PN:56
Where a Roman Villa Stood, above
   Freiburg.   M. Coleridge.
   Ox-BN:927
Where Is My Wandering Boy Tonight?
   Er-FA:440
While I Stay Alone.   Ba-ST:44
Why Have I Come to You?
   Da-SC:51
The Wild Trees.   L. Lee.
   Go-BP:160
Wind Song.   Da-SC:111
Winter Night.   Hi-WP II:145
Winter Remembered.   J. Ransom.
   Ca-VT:147, Rv-CB:985
Without Her.   D. Rossetti.
   Al-VBP:989, Ox-BN:685
Woman's Love Song.   Tr-US II:215
Women Songs, II.   K. Molodowsky.
   Ho-TY:285
Words.   H. Brooks.   Hu-NN:104,
   Hu-PN:278
you (her eyes, solstice).
   G. Bishop-Dubjinsky.   Sc-TN:10
Youth and Age.   G. Byron.
   Pa-GTB:221
LONGSHOREMEN: see CARGOES; DOCKS;
   STEVEDORES
LONGSPURS
   The Longspur's Incantation.
   Le-IB:44
LOOKING GLASSES: see MIRRORS
LOONS
   Chain.   P. Petrie.   Co-BBW:242
   The Loon.   L. Sarett.   Bo-HF:75

LORCA, FEDERICO GARCÍA: see
    GARCÍA LORCA, FEDERICO
LORD'S SUPPER
  Ballad of the Bread Man.
    C. Causley. To-MP:203
  The Last Supper. R. Rilke.
    Tr-MR:121
  The Last Supper. O. Williams.
    Er-FA:466, Tr-MR:120, Wi-LT:411
  No Beauty We Could Desire.
    C. Lewis. Go-BP:303
  Psalm. M. Mendes. Tr-MR:207
LORELEI
  The Lorelei. H. Heine.
    Co-PM:87, Sp-OG:116, Un-GT:137
LOS ANGELES, CALIF.: see SATIRE -
    LOS ANGELES, CALIF.; WATTS,
    CALIF.
LOSSES
  I Have Lost My Shoes.
    C. Suasnavar. Fe-FP:490
  Lines from a Sampler. Gr-TG:82
  Mary Lost Her Coat. Mother
    Goose. Mo-CC:18
LOST CHILDREN
  The Little Boy Found. W. Blake.
    Rv-CB:582
  Little Boy Lost (Father! Father!).
    W. Blake. Rv-CB:581
  A Little Boy Lost (Nought Loves
    Another). W. Blake.
    Al-VBP:618, Rv-CB:583
  Lucy Gray. W. Wordsworth.
    De-CH:222, De-TT:85, Ox-BC:98
LOT AND LOT'S WIFE
  Abraham Scolds Lot. I. Manger.
    Ho-TY:274
  Lot's Wife. H. Meschonnic.
    Ba-PO:47
LOTUSES
  Dancing. Yang Kuei-Fei.
    Fe-FP:481
  Death as the Lotus Flower.
    Be-AP:31, Lo-TY:27, Pl-EI:24
  Edge of the Lotus Pond.
    Yü Kuang-chung. Pa-MV:181
  Expression of Time.
    Li Chin-fa. Hs-TC:172
  Flower Song. De-PP:57
  The Lotus-Eaters. A. Tennyson.
    Al-VBP:847, Cl-FC:14, De-CH:615,
    Er-FA:76, Ga-FB:12, Gr-CT:278,
    Ox-BN:477, Pa-HT:158, Pa-OM:296
  The Lotus Flower. Cheng Min.
    Hs-TC:239
  Lotus Leaves. Mitsukumi. Pa-SG:106
  Waiting for You in the Rain.
    Yü Kuang-chung. Pa-MV:184
LOUISBURG, BATTLE, 1745
  Louisburg. Hi-TL:31

LOUISIANA: see also names of
    towns, as NEW ORLEANS, LA.
  In Louisiana. A. Paine. Br-AF:143
  Song of Louisiana. V. Stopher.
    Se-PR:264
LOUISIANA PURCHASE
  Louisiana Purchase. B. Clark.
    Ke-TF:360
LOVE: see also COURTSHIP;
    HUMOR - LOVE; INFATUATION;
    LONGING; LOVE SONGS;
    SATIRE - LOVE; VALENTINE'S
    DAY; and the subdivisions
    that follow LOVE
  Above the Mist. Le-IB:84
  Air and Angels. J. Donne.
    Rv-CB:295
  Alba. L. Nagan. Ad-II:53
  All the Tree's Hands.
    J. Nichols. Un-MW:146
  Amor Aeternalis. C. Smith.
    De-FS:186
  And One Shall Live in Two.
    J. Brooks. Hu-PN:239
  Appearances. R. Browning.
    Rv-CB:827
  Awake, My Heart, to Be Loved.
    R. Bridges. Pa-GTB:415,
    Un-MB:48
  The Bailiff's Daughter of
    Islington. Ox-BB:342,
    Sh-RP:250, Un-GT:114
  Baptist. S. Menashe. Sm-MK:215
  The Bead Mat. W. de la Mare.
    Rv-CB:964
  A Birthday. C. Rossetti.
    Al-VBP:997, Bl-OB:41, Co-BL:107,
    De-CH:334, Er-FA:116, Ho-WR:70,
    Re-TW:46, Un-MW:137
  Britannia's Pastorals. W. Browne.
    Al-VBP:320
  The Buried Life. M. Arnold.
    Go-BP:126
  Cakes and Ale. Er-FA:111
  Catullus de Lesbia. J. Swift.
    Rv-CB:496
  Chamber Music. J. Joyce.
    Hi-WP II:109
  Chapter Two. W. Scott. Gr-CC:186
  The Cherry-Blossom Wand.
    A. Wickham. Un-MB:281, Un-MW:25
  A Chinese Poem Written in B.C. 718.
    Hi-WP II:105
  Chippewa Love Songs. Da-SC:151
  Chisel. I. Brad. Mc-AC:141
  Come Away, My Love.
    J. Kariuki. Gr-BT:76
  Come Loose Every Sail to the
    Breeze. Co-SS:101
  Comparisons. C. Rossetti. Ox-BC:276

The Confirmation.   E. Muir.
  Hi-WP II:60
Curfew Must Not Ring Tonight.
  R. Thorpe.   Fe-FP:559
The Dead Words.   V. Watkins.
  Wi-LT:448
Death.   Wen I-to.   Hs-TC:51
A Decade.   A. Lowell.   Co-BL:109,
  Mo-BG:99, Un-MA:160
A Description of Love.
  W. Ralegh.   Fe-PL:112, Rv-CB:152
The Divine Image. W. Blake.
  Al-VBP:613, Go-BP:287, Ox-BN:20,
  Rv-CB:586
Doubt Me. . . .   E. Dickinson.
  Al-VBP:1001
Dover Beach.   M. Arnold.
  Al-VBP:972, Cl-FC:48, Co-BL:84,
  Er-FA:454, Ga-FB:66, Go-BP:147,
  Ha-PO:187, Hi-WP II:35,
  Ho-P:201, Ke-PP:87, Ma-FW:53,
  Ma-YA:209, Mc-PR:70, Mo-GR:35,
  Ox-BN:645, Pa-GTB:305, Pl-EI:78,
  Rv-CB:863, Un-MW:120
The Dream.   T. Roethke.
  Sh-AP:213
The Dream.   Le-IB:83
A Drinking Song.   W. Yeats.
  No-CL:40
The Ecstasy.   J. Donne.
  Al-VBP:250, Rv-CB:303
Edge of the Lotus Pond.
  Yü Kuang-chung.   Pa-MV:181
Eve.   Y. Fichman.   Me-PH:82
Even So.   D. Rossetti.   Ox-BN:680
Failure.   R. Brooke.   Ke-TF:122
Fain Would I Have a Pretty
  Thing.   Al-VBP:74
Fair and Fair. . . .   G. Peele.
  Al-VBP:134
The Faithful Shepherdess.
  J. Fletcher.   Al-VBP:287
Fatal Interview XI.   E. Millay.
  Ca-VT:167
The Final Word.   D. Moraes.
  Go-BP:139
For Denis Who Was a Drum.
  M. Maxwell.   Sa-B:172
For the One Who Would Take Man's
  Life in His Hands.
  D. Schwartz.   Ca-VT:366,
  Hi-TL:218, Un-MA:618, Wi-LT:517
Four Things.   P. Gearey.
  Ke-TF:241
From Pent-Up Aching Rivers.
  W. Whitman.   Al-VBP:931
Fulfilment.   T. Jones.   Ke-TF:139
The Garden of Shadow.
  E. Dowson.   Ox-BN:942
A Garland of Peacock Feathers.
  D. ap Gwilym.   Go-BP:122

Gift of the Sego Lily. M. Jarvis.
  Fi-BG:197
Girls' Songs, III. Tr-US I:119
Great Things.   T. Hardy.
  Pa-GTB:409
The Greek Room.   J. Thompson.
  Ra-BP:254
Half a Moon. R. Rozhdestvensky.
  Mo-MI:57
The Harrowing of Hell.
  W. Langland.   Go-BP:219
Hawthorn White.   C. Causley.
  Gr-BT:35
Heart Ruins.   R. House. Ke-TF:113
Hesperia.   A. Swinburne.
  Ox-BN:805
How Sweet I Roamed.   W. Blake.
  Al-VBP:610, De-CH:153, Gr-CT:73,
  Ox-BN:18, Rv-CB:565, Un-MW:77
Hymn to Colour.   G. Meredith.
  Ox-BN:700
I Am Not Yours.   S. Teasdale.
  Ca-VT:75
I Bear, in Sign of Love.
  F. Andrewes.   Re-BS:10
I Do Not Love Thee.   C. Norton.
  Hi-WP II:57
I Have Found Out a Gift for My
  Fair.   W. Shenstone.   Re-BS:11
I Know that All Beneath the Moon
  Decays.   W. Drummond.   De-CH:624
I Love You Little, I Love You Lots.
  On-TW:59
I Think the Things I Do Wrong.
  S. Hardy.   Me-WF:66
I Want to Die while You Love Me.
  G. Johnson.   Bo-AN:22
I Will Give You the Keys of
  Heaven.   Cl-DT:80
Immense Love.   G. Naum.   Mc-AC:117
In a Gondola.   R. Browning.
  Al-VBP:891
In Answer to a Question.
  W. Blunt.   Al-VBP:1053
In Spite of All This Much Needed
  Thunder.   Z. Gilbert.   Hu-PN:390
In the Merry Month of May.
  N. Breton.   Al-VBP:85,
  Ha-PO:165, Un-MW:5
In the Morning.   A. Housman.
  Hi-WP I:88
In the Silence.   Stephany.
  Ra-BP:330
Inconsistent.   M. Van Doren.
  Co-BL:74, Co-EL:95
Juan's Song.   L. Bogan.   Mo-BG:87
The Lady of the Lake. W. Scott.
  Al-VBP:673
Lay Your Sleeping Head, My Love.
  W. Auden.   Un-MB:459

LOVE — cont'd.
   Length of Moon.   A. Bontemps.
      Hu-PN:214, Wi-LT:611
   Let Me Be Held when the Longing
      Comes.   Stephany.   Ra-BP:332
   Let Us Live and Love. Catullus.
      Rv-CB:264, Un-MW:175
   Letter.   M. Strand.   Mo-BG:102
   Letter Across Doubt and Distance.
      M. Holman.   Hu-PN:363
   Light Listened.   T. Roethke.
      Un-MA:601
   Longing Pleases Me like Sweet
      Fragrance.   Do-CH:(31)
   The Looking Glass.   M. Drayton.
      No-CL:205
   Love.   S. Coleridge.   Pa-GTB:171
   Love.   T. Dent.   Hu-NN:71
   Love.   L. Tieck.   Pa-SG:29
   Love Comes Quietly.   R. Creeley.
      Co-BL:115
   Love in Exile.   M. Blind.
      Ox-BN:849
   Love in Thy Youth.   Al-VBP:363
   Love Is a Babel.   Rv-CB:126
   Love Is a Wonderful Word.
      V. Gory.   Me-WF:39
   Love Is like a Lamb.
      T. Middleton.   Co-BL:62
   Love on the Farm.   D. Lawrence.
      Ga-FB:80, Un-MB:288, Un-MW:122
   Love Song.   J. Nash.   Mo-BG:90
   Love Song.   Bi-IT:76
   Love Song.   Tr-US II:195
   Love Songs, I.   Tr-US II:171
   Lovelight.   G. Johnson.
      Bo-AN:23
   Love's Progress.   J. Donne.
      Al-VBP:257
   Lovesight.   D. Rossetti.
      Al-VBP:988, Ox-BN:683, Pa-GTB:370
   The Lowest Trees Have Tops.
      E. Dyer.   Co-BL:58, Ho-LP:6,
      Rv-CB:147
   The Maid's Thought.   R. Jeffers.
      Co-BL:21, Sm-PT:37
   The Man with a Hammer.
      A. Wickham.   Un-MW:142
   Mark Antony.   J. Cleveland.
      Al-VBP:440
   Marrow of My Bone.   M. Evans.
      Ra-BP:187
   Mary Morison.   R. Burns.
      Pa-GTB:149
   Meeting Point.   L. MacNeice.
      Hi-WP II:62
   Melander Supposed to Love Susan,
      but Did Love Ann.   E. Herbert.
      Gr-CC:186
   Midcentury Love Letter. P. McGinley.
      Al-VBP:1225, Mo-BG:91

   Midnight Lamentation.   H. Monro.
      Al-VBP:1140
   Mine.   E. Dickinson.   Un-MW:89
   Miracle.   Wen I-to.   Hs-TC:67
   Le Monocle de Mon Oncle.
      W. Stevens.   Wi-LT:135
   Much Love.   Bo-FP:295
   My Love when This Is Past.
      Stephany.   Ra-BP:332
   My Valentine.   R. Stevenson.
      Br-SS:119, Ch-B:41, Co-BL:114,
      Co-PS:37, Hu-MP:331, Mc-PR:48,
      Se-PR:52, Un-MB:59, Un-MW:139
   Neither Spirit nor Bird.
      Pa-SG:36
   The Nest.   J. de Ibarbourou.
      Be-UL:49
   The New Year's Gift to Phyllis.
      M. Prior.   Rv-CB:486
   The Newlyweds.   C. Criswell.
      Fe-PL:96
   Night Song at Amalfi.
      S. Teasdale.   Bo-HF:123,
      Sm-PT:63, Un-MA:264, Un-MW:57
   Nightfall.   Rx-LT:20
   Not a Love Poem.   Tu Yün-hsieh.
      Hs-TC:248
   Not by Bread Alone.   J. White.
      Fe-PL:105
   Not to You I Sighed.   S. Spender.
      Hi-WP II:111
   Now Ain't That Love? C. Rodgers.
      Ra-BP:260
   Now Older Grown.   W. Caruthers.
      Ke-TF:132
   Now Sleeps the Crimson Petal.
      A. Tennyson.   Al-VBP:859,
      Gr-CT:63, Hi-WP II:58,
      Ox-BN:487, Rv-CB:787, Un-MW:192
   Oh, I Am Thinking.   Ho-SD:8
   O Mistress Mine. W. Shakespeare.
      Al-VBP:189, Bo-GJ:140, Co-BL:112,
      Er-FA:174, Ga-FB:31, Gr-CC:83,
      Hi-WP II:53, Ho-LP:7, Ke-TF:103,
      Mo-GR:125, No-CL:117, Pa-GTB:17,
      Rv-CB:194, Un-MW:183
   Oh, No More, No More.   J. Ford.
      Al-VBP:309
   Oh, Think Not I Am Faithful to a
      Vow!   E. Millay.   Ga-FB:85
   O Woodland Cool.   C. Brentano.
      Pa-SG:44
   Ode on Indolence.   J. Keats.
      Ox-BN:374
   Ogier the Dane.   W. Morris.
      Al-VBP:1016
   Once as Methought Fortune Me
      Kissed.   T. Wyatt.   Rv-CB:83
   One Morning, Oh So Early!
      J. Ingelow.   Ox-BC:271

Out of the Rolling Ocean the
    Crowd.   W. Whitman. Al-VBP:933
Pantuns, III.   Tr-US II:203
Papago Love Song.   Ho-LP:2
Parlour Piece.   T. Hughes.
    Gr-BT:56
A Parting Guest.   J. Riley.
    Sp-OG:278
Passing Remark.   W. Stafford.
    Kh-VA:30
The Pearl.   H. Andersen. Pa-SG:49
Permanently.   K. Koch. Mc-EA:135,
    Mo-BG:93
Perspective.   V. Contoski.
    Sc-TN:29
Philip Sparrow.   J. Skelton.
    Al-VBP:26
Pleasures, Beauty.   J. Ford.
    Al-VBP:310
Poem Sung at a Mystical Exercise.
    Tr-US I:122
Popular Song.   Tr-US I:122
The Power of Music to Disturb.
    L. Mueller. St-H:148
The Primrose.   R. Herrick.
    Al-VBP:327
Proud Word You Never Spoke.
    W. Landor. Al-VBP:707
Psalm to My Belovèd.
    E. Tietjens. Co-BL:109
Question.   A. Pratt. Al-WW:103
A Question of Weather.
    K. Katrak. Al-PI:98
Realities. e. cummings.
    Sm-PT:38
Recessional.   G. Johnson.
    Hu-PN:80
The Reconciliation.   Horace.
    Un-MW:30
Remember.   G. Johnson. Hu-PN:75
Remember Not.   H. Johnson.
    Hu-PN:264
A Rhyme of the Dream-Maker Man.
    W. White. Fe-PL:94
The Riven Quarry.   G. Oden.
    Ad-PB:185
Rondeau for You.   M. de Andrade.
    Lo-TY:83
Rondel.   W. Henley.   Ox-BN:886
Rosalind's Madrigal.   T. Lodge.
    Al-VBP:131
Rubaiyat of Omar Khayyam.
    E. Fitzgerald.   Al-VBP:832,
    Er-FA:43, Fe-FP:479, Gr-CT:329,
    Ha-PO:210, Ox-BN:526, Pa-GTB:329,
    Pa-SG:120
Sailor.   E. Farjeon.   Pe-FB:29
The Sea Hath Its Pearls.
    H. Heine. Pa-SG:48
She Walked Unaware. P. MacDonogh.
    Co-BL:135, Co-PI:109

Silent Noon.   D. Rossetti.
    Ma-YA:211, Ox-BN:683, Un-MW:138
The Simple Ploughboy.   Sm-LG:159
Since I Saw My Love.
    A. Wickham.   Un-MW:142
Six Rows of Pins.   Rv-ON:104
The Skeleton in Armor.
    H. Longfellow. Mc-PR:56,
    Sp-OG:103, Un-GT:173
The Sleeping Beauty.   S. Rogers.
    Pa-GTB:129
So Long.   W. Stafford. Mc-EA:167
somewhere i have never travelled.
    e. cummings. Br-TC:81,
    Ca-VT:180, Mo-BG:88, Pe-SS:124,
    Un-MA:476, Un-MW:26, Wi-LT:363
Song.   R. Brooke.   Sp-OG:270
Song.   J. Dryden. Al-VBP:478,
    Rv-CB:465
Song.   A. Ginsberg.   Mc-EA:79
A Song.   R. Hodgson.   Bo-GJ:127
Song.   C. Mew.   Un-MB:160
Song.   R. Steele.   Al-VBP:520
Song.   A. Swinburne.   Un-MW:195
Song of a Young Man about to
    Be Married.   Tr-US II:186
The Song of Songs.   Bible. O.T.
    Song of Solomon.   Pa-SG:26
Song on Drums and Pipe.
    Tr-US I:124
Song to His Cynthia.
    F. Grevelle.   Al-VBP:122
Song to Steingerd.
    C. Ogmundarson.   Pa-SG:49
Songs and Dance Songs.
    Tr-US II:153
Sonnet.   C. Cullen. Pe-SS:122
Sonnet 118.   W. Shakespeare.
    Rv-CB:242
Sonnet 144.   W. Shakespeare.
    Rv-CB:252
Sonnet 147.   W. Shakespeare.
    Rv-CB:254
Sonnets, xxx.   E. Millay.
    Sm-PT:50
Sonnets, xxviii, xxxiii.
    M. Van Doren.   Sm-PT:67
Sonnets, vi, x.   E. Wylie.
    Sm-PT:70
Sonnets from the Portuguese,
    I, XXXV.   E. Browning.
    Al-VBP:817
The Spring and the Fall.
    E. Millay.   Co-BL:141
Spring Festival Songs.
    Tr-US II:173
The Spring of Love.
    W. Shakespeare. Gr-CT:55
Stanzas.   G. Byron.   Al-VBP:721
Stop Playing. Z. Shneour. Me-PH:85

LOVE — cont'd.
  Sunday up the River. J. Thomson.
    Al-VBP:1009
  Sweet Was the Song. W. Landor.
    Al-VBP:705
  Taking Heart. D. Bromige.
    Mc-EA:101
  Tell Me, O Love. W. Hammond.
    Rv-CB:414
  Thee, Thee, Only Thee. T. Moore.
    Ox-BN:214
  These Poems. D. Palmer. Sc-TN:180
  They Were Alone Once More.
    G. Byron. Ox-BN:269
  Thou Art Not Fair. T. Campion.
    Al-VBP:214
  Thus Spoke My Love. P. Hooft.
    Pa-SG:25
  Time in the Rock. C. Aiken.
    Al-VBP:1188
  The Tired Woman. A. Wickham.
    Un-MB:280, Un-MW:197
  Title Divine Is Mine.
    E. Dickinson. Al-VBP:1003
  To a Lady Asking Him How Long
    He Would Love Her.
    G. Etheredge. Un-MW:178
  To a Young Lady. R. Savage.
    Rv-CB:521
  To Althea from Prison.
    R. Lovelace. Al-VBP:445,
    Ha-PO:173, Ke-TF:100, Ma-YA:101,
    Pa-GTB:81, Rv-CB:394, Un-MW:133
  To Be in Love. G. Brooks.
    Pe-SS:120
  To Chloe, Who Wished Herself
    Young Enough for Me.
    W. Cartwright. Al-VBP:423
  To Dream of Thee. J. Keats.
    Un-MW:165
  To His Book. W. Walsh. No-CL:139
  To His Mistress. E. Dowson.
    Co-BL:81
  to L. J. Perry. Ad-PB:516
  To Mary: Of Sailing. R. Snyder.
    Ls-NY:7
  To Meet, or Otherwise. T. Hardy.
    Ox-BN:836
  To Mother and Steve. M. Evans.
    Ad-PB:191, Ra-BP:184
  To Phyllis, to Love and Live with
    Him. R. Herrick. No-CL:106
  To Virgins. R. Herrick.
    Al-VBP:331
  Today We Part. S. Doinas.
    Mc-AC:128
  Too Bright a Day. N. MacCaig.
    Pa-GTB:522
  Travel. L. Cohen. Un-MW:199
  The Triumph of Death. B. Howes.
    Un-MA:653

  The Troll's Nosegay. R. Graves.
    En-PC:29
  Tumult. C. Wheeler. Hu-PN:273
  The Turning. P. Murray.
    Ho-LP:19
  Two Guests from Alabama.
    W. Whitman. Rd-OA:27
  Understanding. P. Soroka.
    Fe-PL:105
  La Vie C'Est la Vie. J. Fauset.
    Hu-PN:67
  A Village Girl. M. Singh.
    Al-PI:144
  The Voice of the Sea.
    Fang Wei-teh. Hs-TC:136
  Waking Up from a Dream.
    Chu Ta-nan. Hs-TC:132
  We Drink Farewell. Tu Mu.
    Rx-LT:75
  We Hurry On. D. Dolben. Ox-BN:881
  We Saw the Swallows. G. Meredith.
    Ox-BN:690, Pa-GTB:369
  What Exactly Is This Thing
    Called Love? Hsü Chih-mo.
    Hs-TC:88
  What Is Once Loved.
    E. Coatsworth. Co-PU:12
  What Is the Matter with Me?
    Rx-LT:15
  When I Loved You. T. Moore.
    Co-BL:134, Ho-LP:11
  When Love Meets Love. Ke-TF:148
  When Our Two Souls Stand Up.
    E. Browning. Al-VBP:816,
    Un-MW:206
  Why Is God Love, Jack?
    A. Ginsberg. Mc-EA:84
  Why Should We Delay? E. Waller.
    Un-MW:184
  Wild Nights. E. Dickinson.
    Sh-AP:128, Un-MW:89
  The Wind's Song. E. Mörike.
    Pa-SG:140
  Winter Tryst. O. de Kay.
    Un-MW:145
  The Winter's Walk. S. Johnson.
    Rv-CB:526
  A Wish. B. Jonson. Se-PR:238
  Without One Particle of Sentiment
    in His Being. M. Ooka.
    Sh-AM:134
  Woman Song. Da-SC:111
  A Woman's Last Word. R. Browning.
    Er-FA:118, Rv-CB:823, Un-MW:190
  you (her eyes, solstice).
    G. Bishop-Dubjinsky. Sc-TN:10
  You Virgins. J. Shirley.
    Al-VBP:347
  See also Em-AF:165-173,
    228-241

LOVE - ANTICIPATION: see also
   SATIRE - LOVE - ANTICIPATION
Brown Penny. W. Yeats.
   Co-BL:18, Co-PI:203, Gr-CC:18,
   No-CL:142, Sm-LG:361
Cam' Ye By? De-CH:32, Gr-GB:105
Come Slowly, Eden! E. Dickinson.
   Un-MW:86
Dance Songs, VIII. Tr-US II:165
Dastangha, II. Tr-US II:137
The Eve of Crécy. W. Morris.
   Gr-SS:95
Expectation. R. Boureanu.
   Mc-AC:92
Here I Am. A. Morrissett.
   Co-BL:29
Hope. B. Wagstaff. Ke-TF:114
I Shall Have Had My Day.
   A. Tennyson. Un-MW:137
In Youth Is Pleasure. R. Wever.
   Gr-CT:61
Jungle Songs, I. Tr-US II:158
The Lake. M. Arnold. Rv-CB:868
Long Betwixt Love and Fear.
   J. Dryden. Al-VBP:482
A Loon I Thought It Was.
   Da-SC:151, Ho-SD:7, Le-OE:89,
   Tr-US II:225
Love among the Ruins.
   R. Browning. Ga-FB:63
Love-Magic Spell. Tr-US I:205
Love Praise. Tr-CB:42,
   Tr-US I:69
Love Song. Be-AP:51
The Lovers. J. Sabines.
   Be-UL:103
My Life's Delight. T. Campion.
   Un-MW:175
My Lover Will Soon Be Here.
   Rx-LT:21
The Necromancers. J. Nims.
   En-PC:125
Not to Sleep. R. Graves.
   Gr-BT:52
Pantuns, VII. Tr-US II:204
A Poem Looking for a Reader.
   D. Lee. Jo-SA:92
Rendezvous. Chang Chih-min.
   Hs-TC:429
signals, i. J. Amini. Ad-PB:292
Silent Is the House. E. Brontë.
   De-CH:268, Ox-BN:606
Since My Birth. Y. Goll.
   Ho-LP:18
Song. R. Milnes. De-TT:156
Song of a Fabulous Heroine Whose
   Lover Has Escaped from Captivity
   in Tonga. Tr-US II:29
Sonnet. J. Milton.
   Al-VBP:387

A Superscription. D. Rossetti.
   Ma-YA:212, Ox-BN:686, Pa-GTB:371,
   Rv-CB:882
Thunder. Fu Hsuan. Rx-LT:27
Tonight. Br-FW:8
Two Springs. Li Ch'ing Chao.
   Rx-OH:94
Visit. A. Ammons. Br-TC:9,
   Kh-VA:25, Mo-BG:100
The Voice. R. Boureanu. Mc-AC:91
The Voice. R. Brooke. Gr-BT:59
Wait. . . . P. Cummins. Gr-BT:49
Waiting. Y. Yevtushenko.
   Mc-EA:83
Wedding Morn. D. Lawrence.
   Un-MB:290
What the Girl Said. Kapilar.
   Al-PI:63
Woman's-Dance Song. Tr-US II:226
Woman's Song. Tr-US I:212
The Young Girl's Song. A. Gordon.
   Pe-M:140
The Young Man in April.
   R. Brooke. Co-BL:24
LOVE - BASHFULNESS: see also
   HUMOR - LOVE-BASHFULNESS
Because I Were Shy. Co-PT:198
"english." D. Lourie. Sc-TN:152
Girls' Songs. Tr-CB:32,
   Tr-US I:119
Go, Lovely Rose! E. Waller.
   Al-VBP:386, Bo-GJ:128, Ha-PO:164,
   No-CL:29, Pa-GTB:76, Rv-CB:365,
   Un-MW:162
I Pass in Silence. J. Clare.
   Co-BL:43
Isabella or The Pot of Basil.
   J. Keats. Al-VBP:783
Long Betwixt Love and Fear.
   J. Dryden. Al-VBP:482
The Rendezvous. P. Lal.
   Al-PI:101
Secret Love. J. Clare.
   Ga-FB:56, Hi-WP II:56,
   No-CL:147, Ox-BN:333, Rv-CB:730
Silence. A. Wickham. Co-BL:28
Song. L. Cohen. Pe-SS:119
Songs. Tr-US II:148,
To Electra. R. Herrick.
   Ma-YA:87
LOVE - BETRAYAL: see also
   HUMOR - LOVE-BETRAYAL;
   UNFAITHFULNESS
Another Dark Lady. E. Robinson.
   No-CL:203
A Ballad of Hell. J. Davidson.
   Un-MB:72
The Baron of Leys. Ox-BB:270
By the Threshold. M. Leib.
   Ho-TY:94

LOVE - BETRAYAL — cont'd.
  Clerk Colvill. Ma-BB:212,
    Ox-BB:85
  The Demon Lover. Co-PM:201,
    Fo-OG:44, Ma-BB:188, Ma-FW:199,
    Ox-BB:83, Rv-CB:45
  Died of Love. Rv-CB:431
  The Fair Flower of Northumberland.
    Ma-BB:222, Ox-BB:272
  Fair Margaret and Sweet William.
    Ox-BB:231
  Folk-Song. L. Untermeyer.
    Un-MW:102
  Frankie and Johnny. Er-FA:402
  The God. B. Akhmadulina.
    Bo-RU:2
  The Hopis and the Famine.
    Te-FC:35
  Jellon Grame. Ox-BB:164
  John Brown's Body. S. Benét.
    Ke-TF:114, Un-MA:499
  John the Innkeeper. O. Goga.
    Mc-AC:36
  The Jolly Beggar. Ox-BB:624
  Lanty Leary. Co-BL:164, Gr-CT:84
  Little Mousgrove and the Lady
    Barnet. Ox-BB:168
  Lord Randal. Cl-FC:85, Fo-OG:7,
    Ox-BB:243, Rv-CB:37, Un-MW:108
  The Men Are a Bad Lot.
    J. Seidl. Un-R:173
  O Wha Will Shoe My Bonny Foot?
    De-CH:514
  O Wha's the Bride? H. MacDiarmid.
    Wi-LT:626
  The Outlandish Knight.
    Br-SM:36, Un-GT:111
  The Puritan's Ballad. E. Wylie.
    Co-BL:92
  The Soldier and the Maid.
    Mo-MGT:186
  Song of a Woman to Her Lover.
    Tr-US II:140
  Sonnet 119. W. Shakespeare.
    Rv-CB:243
  Stratton Water. Ox-BB:680
  Waly, Waly. Al-VBP:51, Gr-GB:144,
    Ox-BB:327, Pa-GTB:87
  The Water o' Wearie's Well.
    De-CH:730
  Young Beichan. Ma-FW:146,
    Pa-OM:240
  Younge Andrew. Ox-BB:216
LOVE - COMPLAINTS AND PROTESTS:
    see also FICKLENESS; HUMOR
    - LOVE-COMPLAINTS AND
    PROTESTS
  Against Love. J. Denham.
    Rv-CB:390
  Air XXXV. J. Gay. Al-VBP:524

And Fall Shall Sit in Judgment.
    A. Lorde. Hu-NN:20
Away with Silks. R. Herrick.
    Un-MW:22
The Broken-Hearted Gardener.
    Gr-CT:271, Gr-GB:115
Complaint. Sun Yü-t'ang.
    Hs-TC:120
A Complaint. W. Wordsworth.
    Rv-CB:649
Confession of Faith. E. Wylie.
    Un-MA:278
Deep in Love. Rv-CB:432
Donald of the Isles. Ox-BB:258
The Double Rock. H. King.
    No-CL:189
Enigma. J. Fauset. Hu-PN:66
Eviction. Chu Ta-nan. Hs-TC:134
Fair Is My Love. B. Griffin.
    Al-VBP:91, Rv-CB:144
The Fatal Spell. G. Byron.
    Al-VBP:727, Ox-BN:247
The Fly. B. Googe. De-CH:85
The Greek Anthology.
    Un-MW:173-174
Greensleeves. C. Robinson.
    Un-MW:74
Human Soul. R. Maran. Lo-TY:71
Is It Not Sure? Rv-CB:8
Kind Are Her Answers. T. Campion.
    No-CL:169, Un-MW:75
Long Have I Borne Much. Ovid.
    Un-MW:68
Love Is a Sickness. S. Daniel.
    Al-VBP:154, Rv-CB:181
Love Song of a Young Man.
    Bi-IT:84
The Mad Lover. A. Brome.
    Rv-CB:398
Madrigal. Lord Herbert.
    Al-VBP:294
The Message. J. Donne.
    Al-VBP:249, Ma-YA:80
More Love or More Disdain.
    T. Carew. Al-VBP:349,
    Un-MW:177
Neglectful Edward. R. Graves.
    Un-MB:383
The Negligent Lover. Be-AP:52
No Joy Without Love. Mimnerus.
    Pa-SG:75
Odes to Nea, I. T. Moore.
    Ox-BN:205
Phillida Flouts Me. Al-VBP:363
Phoebe's Sonnet. T. Lodge.
    Al-VBP:130
Pining for Love. F. Beaumont.
    Co-BL:37, Co-PU:147
Ring Out Your Bells.
    P. Sidney. Al-VBP:128

The Sea Hath Many Thousand
   Sands.   Al-VBP:361
Sestina.   Dante Alighieri.
   Gr-SS:93
Several Girls' Songs. Do-CH:(30)
Shall I Come, Sweet Love.
   T. Campion.   Al-VBP:217
Song (Love).   A. Behn.
   Al-VBP:501, Rv-CB:473
Song (Oh, How).   T. Campbell.
   No-CL:141
Song (Go, and Catch).   J. Donne.
   Al-VBP:245, Er-FA:129, Ga-FB:37,
   Gr-BT:69, Ha-PO:175, Ke-PP:26,
   Ma-YA:79, No-CL:167, Rv-CB:290,
   Un-MW:38
Song (I Prithee).   T. Stanley.
   Al-VBP:471
Song (Why, Lovely).   R. Steele.
   Al-VBP:520
Song (Of All the Torments).
   W. Walsh.   Al-VBP:511
A Song (My Name).   Co-PU:7
Song at Separation.   Tr-US I:80
Song of a Girl to Bring Back
   Her Unfaithful Lover.
   Tr-US I:171
A Song of Fallen Leaves.
   Hsü Chih-mo.   Hs-TC:84
A Song of Marco Polo.
   T. Garrison.   Ke-TF:119
Sonnet 1.   S. Daniel.   Al-VBP:156
Sonnet.   R. Greene.   Al-VBP:144,
   No-CL:270
Sonnet.   H. King.   Al-VBP:338
Sonnet 95.   W. Shakespeare.
   Rv-CB:236
Sonnets, v.   E. Wylie.   Sm-PT:70
The Spring.   T. Carew.   Cl-FC:37,
   Co-PS:58, Gr-CC:30, Ha-PO:81,
   Ho-WR:34
Spring.   Chu Shu Chen.   Rx-OH:130
Spring Festival Songs, X.
   Tr-US II:173
Sweet, Let Me Go! Al-VBP:361,
   Gr-BT:61, Un-MW:44
Symptoms of Love.   R. Graves.
   Du-SH:60
There Was Never Nothing More Me
   Pained.   T. Wyatt.   Rv-CB:77
There's Wisdom in Women.
   R. Brooke.   Co-BL:132
The Time I've Lost in Wooing.
   T. Moore.   Co-BL:63, Co-PI:145
The Tired Woman.   A. Wickham.
   Un-MB:280, Un-MW:197
To Aurora.   W. Alexander.
   Er-FA:115, Pa-GTB:15
To His Coy Love.   M. Drayton.
   Al-VBP:160

To His Mistress Objecting to Him
   Neither Toying or Talking.
   R. Herrick.   Ga-FB:40
Two in the Campagna.
   R. Browning.   Co-BL:63
What Dreamed I? Rv-CB:104
What Is Love? A. Herbert.
   Co-BL:54
What the Lover Said.
   A. Nanmullaiyar.   Al-PI:63
When You're Away.   S. Hoffenstein.
   Co-BL:42, Co-FB:323
Who Hath Heard of Such Cruelty
   Before? T. Wyatt.   Rv-CB:78
Woman's Song.   Tr-US I:190
The Worthless Lover.   Be-AP:52,
   Lo-TY:48
LOVE - DEATH
   Ah, that I Were Far Away.
      A. Clough.   Ox-BN:602
   Along the Field as We Came By
      A. Housman.   No-CL:126,
      Un-MB:98
   And the Pear Trees Shiver.
      J. Sloan.   De-FS:182
   Annabel Lee.   E. Poe.   Al-VBP:877,
      Co-BL:130, Co-RG:150, De-CH:56,
      De-TT:191, Er-FA:61, Fe-FP:503,
      Hu-MP:431, Li-SR:67, No-CL:68,
      Pa-OM:258, Sh-AP:61, Sm-LG:273,
      Sp-OG:265, Un-GT:163
   At the Mid Hour of Night.   T. Moore.
      Al-VBP:711, Ox-BN:210, Pa-GTB:199
   At the Setting of the Sun.
      Rv-CB:440
   The Azra.   H. Heine.   Un-R:93
   Beeny Cliff.   T. Hardy.   Ox-BN:843
   Binnorie.   Ma-BB:25, Ox-BB:69
   Blindman's Buff.   P. Viereck.
      Un-MA:659, Wi-LT:831
   Bonny Barbara Allan.   De-CH:338,
      Ox-BB:353
   The Braes of Yarrow.   J. Logan.
      Pa-GTB:121
   Bredon Hill.   A. Housman.
      Cl-DT:44, No-CL:125, Un-MB:98,
      Un-MW:99
   The Bride.   D. Lawrence.
      Go-BP:244
   The Bridegroom.   R. Kipling.
      No-CL:191
   Burning the Letters.   R. Jarrell.
      Un-MA:647
   Call into Death.   D. Lawrence.
      Go-BP:245
   Ceiling Unlimited.   M. Rukeyser.
      Un-MA:622
   The Churchyard on the Sands.
      Lord De Tabley.   De-CH:346,
      Ox-BN:792

LOVE - DEATH — cont'd.

Complaint of a Fisherman's
  Widow. Tr-US I:158
Corpus Christi Carol (The
  Falcon). Al-VBP:36, Ga-S:200,
  Gr-CC:163, Gr-CT:186, Gr-GB:308,
  Ma-FW:257, Rv-CB:13, Sm-MK:36
The Cross of Snow. H. Longfellow.
  Sh-AP:40
Death. Wen I-to. Hs-TC:51
Departure. C. Patmore.
  Ox-BN:654
Dido My Dear, Alas, Is Dead.
  E. Spenser. Gr-CT:181
A Dream at Night.
  Mei Yao Ch'en. Rx-OH:43
Elegy for Lucy Lloyd. L. Goch.
  Pa-SG:74
The End of Love. K. Raine.
  Gr-BT:113
The Enemy of Life. T. Wyatt.
  Rv-CB:82
Epitaph in Sirmio. D. Morton.
  Fe-PL:106
The Exequy. H. King. Al-VBP:339,
  De-CH:256, No-CL:156
The Expiration. J. Donne.
  Rv-CB:306
Fatal Interview XIV. E. Millay.
  Ca-VT:168
Finis. W. Cuney. Bo-AN:100
The Funeral. J. Donne. Rv-CB:304
The Garden of Love. W. Blake.
  Al-VBP:617, Ga-FB:47, Rv-CB:598,
  Un-MW:78
The Gardener. Rv-CB:48
The Ghost. J. Wright. De-FS:223
Girl's Song. Tr-US I:136
The Glory of the Day Was in Her
  Face. J. Johnson. Ad-PB:5
Going Back Again. R. Lytton.
  Co-FB:306, Na-EO:47
He Has Fallen from the Height of
  His Love. W. Blunt. Al-VBP:1053
Here Lies Juliet. W. Shakespeare.
  Er-FA:127
Highland Mary. R. Burns.
  Al-VBP:650, Pa-GTB:151, Sp-OG:276
I Remember the Blue River.
  Mei Yao Ch'en. Rx-OH:44
I Shall Not Care. S. Teasdale.
  Un-MA:265
I Travell'd among Unknown Men.
  W. Wordsworth. Ga-FB:224,
  Mc-PR:107, Ox-BN:63, Pa-GTB:180,
  Rv-CB:632
I Would Like My Love to Die.
  S. Beckett. Mc-EA:39
Idolatry. A. Bontemps. Bo-AN:79,
  Hu-PN:217
In Memoriam. A. Tennyson. Ox-BN:497

In Mourning for His Dead Wife.
  P'an Yueh. Rx-LT:31
Indian Legend of the Canyon.
  J. Mahoney. Fi-BG:49
Kaddish. M. Rawitch. Ho-TY:203
Kit Carson's Ride. J. Miller.
  Fi-BG:161
The Lady of the Pearls. A. Dumas.
  Lo-TY:70
Lakes. F. Bianco. No-CL:62
Lament. Tr-US I:86
Lament. Tr-US II:155
Lament of a Widow over Her Dead
  Husband. Tr-US I:72
Lament of Huauri. Tr-US II:80
The Land o' the Leal.
  Lady Nairn. Pa-GTB:157
Lasca. F. Desprez. Fi-BG:208
Less than the Dust. L. Hope.
  Un-MW:96
Letter from Slough Pond. I. Gardner.
  Co-EL:12, St-H:72
Love and Death. B. Jonson.
  Rv-CB:288
Love Song of the Dead. Da-SC:54,
  Tr-US II:219
Love Songs. Tr-US I:126
A Lover's Lament. Pa-SG:59,
  Tr-US II:257
Love's Inspiration.
  Hsü Chih-mo. Hs-TC:96
Lowlands Away. Gr-GB:132
Lyrics. J. Agee. Un-MA:603
The Mad Maid's Song.
  R. Herrick. Al-VBP:333,
  De-CH:196, Ho-WR:88
Madrigal. R. Thomas. Co-EL:74
The Maid's Lament. W. Landor.
  Ox-BN:189
Maw Bonnie Lad. Gr-GB:133
Memorial. C. Smith. De-FS:185
A Miner Coming Home One Night.
  Gr-GB:134
The Night Has a Thousand Eyes.
  F. Bourdillon. Er-FA:104,
  Hi-WP I:89, Un-MW:209
Notes Found near a Suicide:
  To Telie. F. Horne. Bo-AN:43
O, Open the Door to Me, O!
  R. Burns. Sm-LG:358
O Sing unto My Roundelay.
  T. Chatterton. De-CH:249,
  Ho-WR:152
O Terrible Is the Highest Thing.
  K. Patchen. Ca-VT:346
On the Death of His Wife.
  Mei Yao Ch'en. Rx-OH:45
On Top of Old Smoky. Er-FA:451
Only Thy Dust. D. Marquis.
  Fe-PL:100

Ophelia. A. Rimbaud. Gr-CT:78
Ophelia's Death. W. Shakespeare.
   Gr-CT:77
Ophelia's Song. W. Shakespeare.
   Al-VBP:191, De-CH:343, De-TT:159,
   Gr-CT:77
Passer Mortuus Est. E. Millay.
   Un-MA:445
Patterns. A. Lowell. Bo-HF:116,
   Co-BL:142, Cr-WS:115, Er-FA:65,
   Mo-GR:39, Pa-OM:262, Pe-OA:47,
   Sm-PT:18, Un-MA:156
The Peri's Lament for Hinda.
   T. Moore. Ox-BN:217
Perspectives. D. Randall.
   Bo-AN:121
A Pledge. Hu P'in-ch'ing.
   Pa-MV:101
Possession. R. Aldington.
   Un-MB:355
Prescience. D. Hayes. Hu-PN:243
Pure Death. R. Graves. Pa-GTB:488
The Raven. E. Poe. Al-VBP:865,
   Bo-GJ:165, Co-RG:103, De-CH:303,
   Er-FA:312, Ga-FB:134, Sh-AP:56,
   Sm-LG:207
Remembrance. E. Brontë.
   De-CH:262, Er-FA:457, Go-BP:148,
   Ox-BN:601
Ring Out Your Bells. P. Sidney.
   Al-VBP:128
The River of Stars. A. Noyes.
   Pa-OM:131
Romance. A. Lang. Sp-OG:121
Sarcophagus Cover. R. Feldman.
   Ls-NY:18
She Weeps over Rahoon. J. Joyce.
   Al-VBP:1150
Silent Is the House. E. Brontë.
   De-CH:268, Ox-BN:606
The Sleeper. E. Poe. Rv-CB:808
Song (Oh Fly Not). W. Blunt.
   Al-VBP:1056
Song (The First). A. Lewis.
   Wi-LT:763
Song by an Unnamed Poetess.
   Tr-US II:118
Song of a Ghost. Tr-US II:239
Song of a Widow. Tr-US II:18
Song of a Widow for Her Dead
   Husband. Tr-US II:117
Song of One Whose Lover Is Dead.
   Tr-US II:227
Sonnet 32. W. Shakespeare.
   Pa-GTB:29, Pl-ML:21, Rv-CB:214
Sonnet 71. W. Shakespeare.
   Al-VBP:204, Pa-GTB:30,
   Rv-CB:229
Sonnets, xxiv, xxv. C. Smith.
   Sm-PT:162, 163

Sonnets. W. Wordsworth.
   Al-VBP:659, Ox-BN:91, Pa-GTB:198,
   Rv-CB:647
Stanzas - April, 1814. P. Shelley.
   Ox-BN:275
The Stone. W. Gibson. Un-MB:241
Sweet William's Ghost.
   De-CH:423, Ma-BB:115
That We Head Towards. Stephany.
   Ra-BP:333
Time Does Not Bring Relief.
   E. Millay. Ga-FB:84
To a Lock of Hair. W. Scott.
   Pa-GTB:86
To One in Paradise. E. Poe.
   Al-VBP:874, Fe-PL:101, Un-MW:207
A Tune. A. Symons. Co-BL:140,
   Ox-BN:937
Twin Epitaph. M. Katz. Ls-NY:17
The Unquiet Grave. Al-VBP:39,
   De-CH:342, Gr-GB:131, Hi-WP II:17,
   Ox-BB:96, Rv-CB:51
We Needs Must Be Divided.
   G. Santayana. Al-VBP:1089
Wheesht, Wheesht! H. MacDiarmid.
   Co-EL:12
When I Have Seen by Time's Fell
   Hand. W. Shakespeare.
   Al-VBP:204, Er-FA:261, No-CL:84,
   Pa-GTB:3
When Thou Must Home. Propertius.
   Al-VBP:218, Gr-CC:78, Gr-CT:73,
   Ha-PO:170, Rv-CB:270
Willy Drowned in Yarrow.
   De-CH:728, Pa-GTB:122
The Wind at the Door. W. Barnes.
   Pa-GTB:321, Rv-CB:768
Without Her. D. Rossetti.
   Ox-BN:685
The Woodlands. W. Barnes.
   Co-BN:158
The Yew-Tree. Gr-CT:80
You Would Have Understood Me.
   E. Dowson. Un-MB:149
LOVE - DECREASE
Down in the Meadows. Rv-CB:41
Fatal Interview II. E. Millay.
   Ca-VT:167
In a Drear-Nighted December.
   J. Keats. De-CH:216, Ox-BN:373,
   Pa-GTB:191, Rv-CB:737
Modern Love. G. Meredith.
   Al-VBP:984, Ox-BN:691
Neutral Tones. T. Hardy.
   Un-MB:27, Un-MW:94
Rococo. A. Swinburne. Al-VBP:1025
So We'll Go No More a-Roving.
   G. Byron. Al-VBP:723, Co-BL:64,
   De-CH:443, Er-FA:105, Fe-PL:108,
   Ga-FB:52, Gr-CC:191, Ha-PO:178,
   Hi-WP II:54, Ho-WR:163, Ma-YA:173,
   Ox-BN:257, Rv-CB:689, Un-MW:89

LOVE - DECREASE — cont'd.
  Sonnets, cxi. E. Millay.
    Sm-PT:72
  A Sorrow in the Harem.
    Wang Chang Ling. Rx-LT:61
  Why Should a Foolish Marriage Vow.
    J. Dryden. Al-VBP:481,
    Gr-BT:95, Rv-CB:463
  A Woman's Complaint. Bi-IT:82
LOVE - DEFINITIONS
  Annihilation. C. Aiken.
    Un-MA:429
  The City. E. Jarrett. Sc-TN:110
  The Clod and the Pebble. W. Blake.
    Al-VBP:615, Ga-FB:46, Ox-BN:22,
    Rv-CB:596
  A Description of Love. W. Ralegh.
    Fe-PL:112, Rv-CB:152
  Epipsychidion. P. Shelley.
    Ox-BN:286
  Fulfilment. T. Jones. Ke-TF:139
  Love. S. Bennett. Ad-II:114
  Love. Tiruvalluvar. Al-PI:67
  Love Is. A. Darr. Pe-M:119
  On the Nature of Love. W. Blunt.
    Al-VBP:1053
  Origins. K. Kgositsile.
    Ad-PB:324
  The Shepherd's Description of
    Love. W. Raleigh. Al-VBP:92
  Song. R. Brooke. Sp-OG:270
  Songs. L. Wolf. Ho-TY:223
  Sonnet. R. Brooke. Gr-BT:72,
    Rv-CB:982
  A Taste of Honey. K. Kuka.
    Al-WW:73
  Tell Me, Dearest. J. Fletcher.
    Al-VBP:283
  Though It Only Last an Instant.
    C. Alegria. Be-UL:89
  Vivien's Song. A. Tennyson.
    Ox-BN:509, Un-MW:192
  When Delia on the Plain Appears.
    G. Lyttleton. Rv-CB:528
LOVE - DENIAL
  Sonnet. R. Brooke. Gr-BT:72,
    Rv-CB:982
LOVE - DEVOTION: see also
    HUMOR - LOVE-DEVOTION
  After the Japanese. L. Strongin.
    Sc-TN:208
  Ago Love. J. Holland. Jo-VC:62
  All Year Long. Rx-LT:24
  Although I Put Away His Life.
    E. Dickinson. Un-MA:100
  Alun Mabon's Song. J. Hughes.
    Hi-WP I:44
  Amo, Amas. J. O'Keefe. Co-BL:78,
    De-CH:606, Gr-CT:60
  And So Men Say I Love Thee.
    D. Coleridge. Rv-CB:765

Appraisal. S. Teasdale.
    Un-MA:267
  As Birds Are Fitted to the
    Boughs. L. Simpson.
    Co-BL:74, Ho-LP:20
  As to His Choice of Her. W. Blunt.
    Al-VBP:1052
  Ask Me No More. A. Tennyson.
    Ox-BN:487, Un-MW:85
  Bobby Shafto. De-CH:682,
    De-TT:30, Gr-GB:104, Hu-MP:164,
    Mo-MGT:151, Wi-MG:31, Wr-RM:127
  The Bracelet: To Julia.
    R. Herrick. Un-MW:19
  Bride's Song. Tr-US I:166
  Bright Star. J. Keats.
    Al-VBP:794, De-CH:745, Ga-FB:54,
    Go-BP:108, Ke-TF:122, Ox-BN:382,
    Pa-GTB:197, Un-MW:204
  Brown Adam. Ma-BB:154, Ox-BB:162
  Brown Boy to Brown Girl.
    C. Cullen. Ad-PB:93
  Champion. Wen I-to. Hs-TC:51
  Child Waters. Ox-BB:149
  Come, My Celia. B. Jonson.
    Ga-FB:35, Un-MW:16
  The Corpus Christi Carol (The
    Heron). Gr-GB:309
  The Cripple for Life. Em-AF:457
  The Dalliance of the Leopards.
    Ho-LP:3
  Dance Songs, II. Tr-US II:146
  Dark Rosaleen. J. Mangan.
    Al-VBP:812, Co-PI:128, De-CH:172
  Day Dream. N. Cardozo. Un-MW:149
  Dear Dark Head. Co-EL:116,
    Co-PI:40, Pa-SG:58
  The Delicate Dream Beyond Chaos.
    B. Richart. Ke-TF:131
  Double-U. De-TT:28
  Dusty Miller. Mo-MGT:201,
    Wr-RM:94
  Earth and I Gave You Turquoise.
    N. Momaday. Mc-EA:59
  Embraceable You. I. Gershwin.
    Co-BL:118
  Endymion. J. Keats. Go-BP:161
  Even Now. . . . Bilhana.
    Al-PI:48, Pa-SG:65
  Evening Song. J. Toomer.
    Ra-BP:70
  Fain Would I Change. T. Hume.
    Al-VBP:358, Rv-CB:259
  Fair Annie. De-CH:414
  Faults. S. Teasdale. Mc-PR:117
  The Fisherman. Li Po. Le-MW:113
  Flowers of Darkness. F. Davis.
    Ad-IA:12, Ad-PB:95, Be-MA:55,
    Bo-AN:96, Hu-PN:255
  For Damaris, about to Be Married.
    C. Walsh. St-H:241

For the Sake of Somebody.
   R. Burns.   Hi-WP I:42
For This Is Wisdom.   L. Hope.
   Fe-PL:305
For You.   I. Horea.   Mc-AC:140
Futility.   Sister M. Madeleva.
   Ke-TF:123
Geordie.   Ox-BB:557
Gil Brenton.   Ox-BB:38
Gladly I'll Live in a Poor
   Mountain Hut.   Le-MW:111
The Good-Morrow.   J. Donne.
   Al-VBP:244, Ga-FB:36, Rv-CB:289
Gypsy Eyes.   J. Hendrix.
   Mo-GR:124
Had I a Golden Pound.
   F. Ledwidge.   Co-PI:91
Harbour.   H. Monro.   Go-BP:131
Here where the Wild Ducks.
   Taniha Omé.   Ba-ST:35
How Do I Love Thee?   E. Browning.
   Al-VBP:818, Bo-HF:112, Co-BL:91,
   Er-FA:114, Fe-PL:93, Ga-FB:57,
   Ke-TF:108, Ma-YA:191, Se-PR:54,
   Un-MW:205
How Many Times?   T. Beddoes.
   Al-VBP:807, De-CH:689, Un-MW:167
I Cannot Forget You.   Bi-IT:78
I Come to the Shore of the Yangtze
   River to Buy a Handful of Lotus
   Seeds.   Hsü Chih-mo.   Hs-TC:87
I Died True.   J. Fletcher.
   Al-VBP:277, De-CH:342
I Have No Life but This.
   E. Dickinson.   Un-MW:86
I Shall Be a Swan. . . .   Le-OE:90
I Will Give My Love an Apple.
   Bl-OB:34, Rv-CB:429
I Wish I Were Close.   Y. Akahito.
   Li-TU:164
If I Had But Two Little Wings.
   S. Coleridge.   De-CH:22
If You Become the Moon.   Le-OE:90
I'll Weave My Love a Garland.
   De-CH:695
An Immorality.   E. Pound.   Bo-GJ:119,
   Co-PU:31, Gr-CC:55, Ha-PO:183,
   Mc-WS:65, Un-MA:291, Wi-LT:225
In a Bath Teashop.   J. Betjeman.
   Co-EL:10
In the Middle of This Century.
   Y. Amichai.   Me-PH:136
In This Forest.   R. Hershon.
   Sc-TN:91
John-John.   T. Macdonough.
   Co-PI:105, Co-PT:194
The Joy of the Snowflake.
   Hsü Chih-mo.   Hs-TC:89
Juliet.   H. Belloc.   Co-BL:59,
   Co-EL:93, Co-PU:77
King Orfeo.   Ma-BB:152, Ox-BB:62

Krishna's Longing.   Jayadeva.
   Al-PI:56
The Laird o' Ochiltree Wa's.
   Ox-BB:266
The Lament of the Border Widow.
   De-CH:419, Gr-GB:246, Ox-BB:525
Lines Supposed to Have Been
   Addressed to Fanny Brawne.
   J. Keats.   Co-EL:17, Co-PU:140,
   Ox-BN:382
Love.   A. Andritoiu.   Mc-AC:142
Love among the Manchees.
   W. Dickey.   En-PC:266
Love at Sea. A. Swinburne.   Gr-SS:186
Love Continual.   T. Heywood.   Rv-CB:73
Love Not Me for Comely Grace.
   Al-VBP:360, De-CH:348, Er-FA:102,
   Fe-PL:93, Hi-WP II:51, Pa-GTB:80
Love on the Mountain.   T. Boyd.
   Co-BL:82
Love Poem.   A. Kaplan.   Mc-EA:86
Love Poem.   J. Logan.   St-H:115
Love-Song.   R. Rilke.   Pa-SG:60,
   Un-MW:204
Love Song.   Bi-IT:77
Love Song.   Le-OE:83, Tr-US I:80
The Lovers.   M. Zaturenska.
   Un-MA:559
The Lover's Shirt.   Gr-BT:53
Love's Omnipresence. J. Sylvester.
   Al-VBP:158, Pa-GTB:16
The Lowlands o'Holland.
   De-CH:345, Fo-OG:51
McNaughton.   Ox-BB:304
Madeleine in Church.   C. Mew.
   Un-MB:162
Magic Formula to Fix a Bride's
   Affections.   Bi-IT:79
The Maid Freed from the Gallows.
   Gr-EC:134
The Mask.   W. Yeats.   No-CL:202
Messages.   F. Thompson.   De-CH:246
Monna Innominata.   C. Rossetti.
   Al-VBP:993, Ox-BN:717
My True Love Hath My Heart.
   P. Sidney.   Al-VBP:125, Bo-FP:295,
   De-CH:334, Go-BP:123, Gr-CT:57,
   Hi-WP II:51, Ke-TF:105, Pa-GTB:16,
   Rv-CB:168, Se-PR:54, Un-MW:132
No, No, Fair Heretic.
   J. Suckling.   Rv-CB:379
No, No, Poor Suffering Heart.
   J. Dryden.   Al-VBP:486
Now Wolde.   De-CH:349
O gin My Love Were Yon Red Rose.
   Gr-GB:117
O, Open the Door to Me, O!
   R. Burns.   Sm-LG:358
Oh Promise Me. C. Scott. Er-FA:17
O Were My Love Yon Lilac Fair.
   R. Burns.   Gr-CT:46

LOVE - DEVOTION — cont'd.
  Oblation. A. Swinburne.
    Co-BL:59
  Of All the Souls That Stand
    Create. E. Dickinson.
    Un-MW:88
  One Word More. R. Browning.
    Al-VBP:911
  Over the Water. De-TT:30,
    Sp-HW:4, Wr-RM:85
  Pantuns. Tr-US II:203
  Perfect Love. Sana'i. Pa-SG:28
  The Philosopher to His Mistress.
    R. Bridges. Wi-LT:55
  Pippen Hill. Bl-OB:34, Ir-BB:214,
    Mo-MGT:141, Wr-RM:26
  Poem. C. Dropkin. Ho-TY:168
  The Red Streams of My Veins.
    Ho-SD:6
  Response. B. Kaufman. Ad-BO:76
  Robin Adair. C. Keppel. De-TT:154
  Rondel of Merciless Beauty.
    G. Chaucer. Un-MW:70
  Rose Aylmer. W. Landor.
    Al-VBP:705, Co-RG:149, De-CH:347,
    Er-FA:115, No-CL:134, Ox-BN:185,
    Rv-CB:667
  The Seaman's Happy Return.
    Gr-CT:64, Gr-GB:119
  Seven Times Three — Love.
    J. Ingelow. Fe-PL:103
  The Silent Lover. W. Raleigh.
    Al-VBP:93
  The Silken Tent. R. Frost.
    Br-TC:138, Un-MW:208
  Silver and Gold. E. Jebeleanu.
    Mc-AC:108
  Since First I Saw Your Face.
    Rv-CB:109
  Sir Aldinger. Ox-BB:23
  Slow Summer Twilight.
    J. Wheelock. Wi-LT:655
  So Fast Entangled. Un-MW:160
  Soft Voice. Fang Wei-teh.
    Hs-TC:137
  Song (My Dark-Headed Käthchen).
    J. Manifold. Co-BL:79
  Song (I Can't). E. Mathews.
    Er-FA:109
  Song (Why Should). E. Muir.
    Go-BP:134
  Song (When I Lie). T. Stanley.
    Al-VBP:470
  Song of the Sirih-Leaf.
    Tr-US I:166
  A Song to Amoret. H. Vaughan.
    Al-VBP:462
  Songs. Tr-US II:142-148
  Sonnet III. A. Seeger.
    Ke-TF:112

  Sonnet 44. W. Shakespeare.
    Rv-CB:223
  Sonnet CLXXVIII. V. Voiculescu.
    Mc-AC:47
  A Sonnet of the Moon. C. Best.
    De-CH:336
  Sonnet on Fidelity.
    V. de Moraes. An-TC:97
  The Sonnets (Say That).
    W. Shakespeare. No-CL:87
  The Sonnets (Why Is).
    W. Shakespeare. No-CL:86
  Sonnets: LVII.
    W. Shakespeare. Al-VBP:203,
    Co-BL:60, No-CL:84, Pa-GTB:7
  Sonnets: CX. W. Shakespeare.
    Al-VBP:208, Rv-CB:240
  Sonnets CXVI. W. Shakespeare.
    Al-VBP:208, Er-FA:126, Ga-FB:33,
    Go-BP:123, Ha-PO:253, Hi-WP II:52,
    Ke-TF:102, No-CL:90, Pa-GTB:15,
    Rv-CB:241, Un-MW:180
  Sonnets 130. W. Shakespeare.
    Bo-HF:122, Co-BL:50, Rv-CB:247
  Sonnet 141. W. Shakespeare.
    Rv-CB:250
  Sonnet XXX. P. Sidney. No-CL:150
  The Starred Coverlet. R. Graves.
    Gr-BT:77
  A Supplication. T. Wyatt.
    Al-VBP:77, Ma-YA:53, Pa-GTB:15,
    Rv-CB:86
  Sweet Afton. R. Burns. Co-BN:73,
    Er-FA:428, Mc-PR:17, Un-MW:154
  There Is a Lady Sweet and Kind.
    Co-BL:79, De-CH:348, Er-FA:102,
    Rv-CB:260, Un-MW:160
  There Is a Ship That Sails the
    Sea. Sp-HW:20
  Though It Only Last an Instant.
    C. Alegris. Be-UL:89
  The Thought. H. Wolfe. Go-BP:136
  Thus Eve to Adam. J. Milton.
    Ga-FB:42
  To----. P. Shelley. Al-VBP:758,
    Fe-PL:110, Ga-FB:53, Ox-BN:299,
    Pa-GTB:201, Rv-CB:706
  To Anthea, Who May Command Him
    Anything. R. Herrick.
    Al-VBP:335, Gr-CC:19, Pa-GTB:79,
    Rv-CB:334, Un-MW:20
  To Daisies, Not to Shut So Soon.
    R. Herrick. De-CH:430
  To Ying-hsia. Yü Ta-fu.
    Hs-TC:271
  The True and Tender Wife.
    Al-PI:29
  Two Leaves. J. Stuart. De-FS:196
  The Unquiet Grave. Al-VBP:39,
    De-CH:342, Gr-GB:131, Hi-WP II:17,
    Ox-BB:96, Rv-CB:51

A Valentine. E. Field.   Se-PR:52
Water Lilies Bloom. Emperor Wu.
   Rx-LT:40
When I Am Not with You.
   S. Teasdale. Co-BL:97
When This Cruel War Is Over.
   Em-AF:454
When Trout Swim down Great
   Ormond Street. C. Aiken.
   Ho-LP:17, Mc-WS:64
A Woman's Last Word.
   R. Browning. Al-VBP:888
The World Is a Mighty Ogre.
   F. Johnson. Bo-AN:26
You Are a Part of Me. F. Yerby.
   Bo-AN:137
You'll Love Me Yet!
   R. Browning. Un-MW:7
Young John. Ma-BB:30
LOVE, ELDERLY
Autumn. S. Smith. Co-EL:121
The Folly of Being Comforted.
   W. Yeats. Go-BP:130
October. W. Morris. Ox-BN:787
Silver Threads among the Gold.
   E. Rexford. Er-FA:427
Slow Summer Twilight.
   J. Wheelock. Wi-LT:655
Song. D. Moraes. Go-BP:138
That Time of Year Thou Mayest
   in Me Behold. W. Shakespeare.
   Al-VBP:205, Ga-FB:34, Gr-CT:318,
   Ha-PO:253, No-CL:85, Pa-GTB:18,
   Rv-CB:230
When Men Shall Find Thy Flower.
   S. Daniel. Un-MW:203
Y Is for Youth. W. Davies.
   Go-BP:145
LOVE, FIRST: see also HUMOR -
   LOVE, FIRST
Actualities, i. e. cummings.
   Sm-PT:38
Brown Penny. W. Yeats.
   Co-BL:18, Co-PI:203, Gr-CC:18,
   No-CL:142, Sm-LG:361
Changes. E. Bulwer-Lytton.
   Fe-PL:307
The Day the Weather Broke.
   A. Reid. Ha-TP:60
Don Juan. G. Byron.
   Al-VBP:729
Dream Love. C. Rossetti.
   De-CH:350
First Flame. S. Daniel. Co-BL:18
First Love. J. Clare. Gr-CT:60
Flapper. D. Lawrence. Co-BL:27
The Flight. S. Teasdale. Co-BL:23
For You I Am. R. Gutman-Jasny.
   Ho-TY:298
Freedom and Love. T. Campbell.
   Pa-GTB:184

A Girl. E. Denby.   Co-BL:94
Haidée and Don Juan. G. Byron.
   Al-VBP:731, Ox-BN:258
Hero and Leander. C. Marlowe.
   Al-VBP:170
I Gave. M. Bruce. Ad-II:47
In School Days. J. Whittier.
   Fe-FP:543, Hu-MP:406, Ox-BC:272
The Janitor's Boy. N. Crane.
   Fe-PL:236, Un-GT:165
Love and Age. T. Peacock.
   Al-VBP:717, Ox-BN:235
Love at First Sight. C. Marlowe.
   Er-FA:106, Un-MW:3
Mementos. W. Snodgrass.
   Un-MA:684, Un-MW:105
My Boy Tammy. H. Macneill.
   De-CH:33
My First Suitor. Mo-MGT:165
My Playmate. J. Whittier.
   De-TT:88
Oh, Fairest of the Rural Maids.
   W. Bryant. Al-VBP:767
The Pressures. I. Baraka.
   Ra-BP:212
The Rebirth of Spring.
   Hsü Chih-mo. Hs-TC:92
The Road to Tartary. B. Trotter.
   Ke-TF:116
The Sequel. D. Schwartz.
   Wi-LT:522
So Sweet Love Seemed. R. Bridges.
   Ga-FB:69
Songs. Tr-US II:147
Tamerlane. E. Poe. Sh-AP:42
Twice. C. Rossetti. Al-VBP:999,
   Ox-BN:714
Without Name. P. Murray.
   Ad-PB:108, Bo-AN:106, Hu-PN:279
Youth. Le-M:162
LOVE, FORSAKEN: see also HUMOR -
   LOVE, FORSAKEN
Adrian Henri's Talking after
   Christmas Blues. A. Henri.
   To-MP:206
At the Altar Rail. T. Hardy.
   Un-MB:30
Ballad of the Western Island in
   the North Country. Gr-SS:187
The Banks o' Doon. R. Burns.
   Un-MW:79
Bianca among the Nightingales.
   E. Browning. Pa-GTB:324
Billy Taylor. Rv-ON:103
Dance Song. Tr-US II:154
Dido. T. Campion. Rv-CB:266
Do You Remember the Night.
   G. Petrie. Gr-SS:33
Down by the Salley Gardens.
   W. Yeats. Co-BL:140, Un-MB:111
Early One Morning. Gr-CT:74

LOVE, FORSAKEN — cont'd.
  Excuses. Be-AP:53
  Fair Annie. Ox-BB:138
  The Forsaken Merman. M. Arnold.
    Al-VBP:960, Bl-OB:59, Cl-DT:41,
    Co-SS:160, Hu-MP:99, Ma-YA:205,
    Rv-CB:862, Sm-LG:339, Sm-MK:84,
    Sp-OG:117
  The Gipsy Laddie. Bl-OB:70,
    Sm-LG:185
  Grief of a Girl's Heart.
    A. Gregory. Co-BL:128, Gr-CT:76
  The Hope I Dreamed of.
    C. Rossetti. Un-MW:90
  The Host of the Air. W. Yeats.
    De-CH:295, Li-TU:90
  I Have Been Through the Gates.
    C. Mew. Un-MB:159, Un-MW:101
  I Loved a Lass. G. Wither.
    Al-VBP:312, De-CH:190, No-CL:121
  Improvisations: Light and Snow.
    C. Aiken. Co-BL:127
  Lament. Tr-US II:89
  Lament of a Deserted Husband.
    Moanarai. Tr-US II:69
  Lament of Hapai for Tahiki.
    Tr-US II:84
  The Letter. B. Murphy. Hu-PN:287
  Locksley Hall. A. Tennyson.
    Er-FA:56
  Loss. P. Eluard. Ho-LP:16
  Lost. Chu Shu Chen. Rx-LT:108
  Love Longing. Tr-CB:54
  Love Poem. J. Logan. St-H:115
  Love Song from New England.
    W. Welles. Un-MW:101
  The Love Song of Har Dyal.
    R. Kipling. Go-BP:150
  Love Songs. Tr-US I:114
  The Lover's Appeal. T. Wyatt.
    Ma-YA:52, Pa-GTB:21, Rv-CB:85
  The Maid Forsaken. E. Mörike.
    Un-R:111
  Man White, Brown Girl and All
    That Jazz. G. Oden. Ad-PB:186
  Margaret at the Spinning Wheel.
    J. von Goethe. Un-R:117
  Mariana. A. Tennyson.
    Al-VBP:845, De-CH:297, Ho-WR:155,
    Ox-BN:473, Rv-CB:795
  My Grief on the Sea. Pa-SG:62
  The New Wife. Ng Shao. Rx-LT:45
  Oh! Dear, What Can the Matter Be?
    De-CH:70, Mc-WS:165, Mo-MGT:200,
    Mo-TL:34, Wr-RM:127
  Oenone. A. Tennyson. Al-VBP:851
  One Word. Chang Hsiu-ya.
    Pa-MV:36
  Phoenix Hairpins. Lu Yu.
    Rx-OH:104
  The Poor Girl's Meditation.
    Co-PI:29
  A Rare Tree. Pa-SG:69
  Rarely, Rarely Comest Thou.
    P. Shelley. De-CH:238,
    Ox-BN:294, Pa-GTB:225, Rv-CB:701
  Ringleted Youth of My Love.
    D. Hyde. Co-PI:67
  Ruth, or The Influence of Nature.
    W. Wordsworth. Pa-GTB:283
  She Thinks of Her Beloved.
    Lu Chi. Rx-LT:28
  She Walked Unaware. P. MacDonogh.
    Co-BL:135, Co-PI:109
  The Shepherd's Dochter. Ox-BB:263
  Since You Left. Ch'ang Ch'u Ling.
    Rx-LT:48
  Sing, Ballad-Singer. T. Hardy.
    Un-MW:94
  Song (He Came). S. Coleridge.
    Rv-CB:769
  Song (O Lady). T. Hughes.
    Go-BP:151
  Song (Because). L. Kemp.
    Ls-NY:16
  Song (She Has Left). S. Warner.
    Un-MB:374
  Song of a Girl Abandoned by Her
    Lover. Tr-US II:118
  Song of a Girl Cast Off by Her
    Lover. Tr-US II:42
  Sonnet. W. Shakespeare.
    No-CL:87
  Sonnet 40. W. Shakespeare.
    Rv-CB:219
  Sonnets, cxvii. E. Millay.
    Sm-PT:73
  Sonnets LXXVIII. E. Spenser.
    Al-VBP:99
  They Flee from Me. T. Wyatt.
    Al-VBP:76, Rv-CB:76, Un-MW:71
  To His Lute. W. Drummond.
    Al-VBP:304, Pa-GTB:24, Pl-US:13
  To the Tune "A Lonely Flute on
    the Phoenix Terrace."
    Li Ch'ing Chao. Rx-LT:96
  To the Tune "Cutting a Flowering
    Plum Branch." Li Ch'ing Chao.
    Rx-LT:95
  To the Tune "Spring at Wu Ling."
    Li Ch'ing Chao. Rx-LT:94
  To the Tune "The Boat of Stars."
    Li Ch'ing Chao. Rx-LT:92
  Walsinghame. W. Ralegh.
    Al-VBP:73, Gr-CT:55, Ha-PO:166,
    Rv-CB:154, Sm-LG:351
  A Weary Lot Is Thine. W. Scott.
    Al-VBP:675, De-CH:174, Ox-BN:133,
    Pa-GTB:194
  What Her Friend Said.
    Varumulaiyaritti. Al-PI:64

When the Lamp Is Shattered.
  P. Shelley. Al-VBP:758,
  De-CH:241, Fe-PL:109, Ox-BN:299,
  Pa-GTB:195, Rv-CB:703
Where Have You Gone? M. Evans.
  Hu-NN:105, Hu-PN:307, Lo-TY:254,
  Pe-M:148, Ra-BP:186

LOVE - GROWTH
Evolution. L. Smith. Er-FA:13
His Picture. J. Donne. Rv-CB:307
In Going to My Naked Bed.
  R. Edwards. Rv-CB:102
Love. S. Butler. Rv-CB:387
Songs. Tr-US II:144
Sonnet 56. W. Shakespeare.
  Fe-PL:99, Rv-CB:225
Sonnet CII. W. Shakespeare.
  Al-VBP:206, No-CL:88
Sonnets, ii, ix, xviii.
  M. Van Doren. Sm-PT:65
Sonnets, xiv. E. Wylie.
  Sm-PT:71

LOVE - MEMORIES
Absence. De-TT:154
After a Journey. T. Hardy.
  Ox-BN:842, Pa-GTB:407
The Album. C. Day Lewis.
  Gr-BT:93
Anniversary. R. Lattimore.
  En-PC:87
Annunciation. Z. Stancu.
  Mc-AC:84
As in a Rose-Jar. T. Jones, Jr.
  Fe-PL:111
Ask No Return! H. Gregory.
  Ca-VT:209, Sm-PT:120, Un-MA:508
At Castle Boterel. T. Hardy.
  Ha-PO:186, Ox-BN:844, Pa-GTB:408
At the Mid Hour of Night.
  T. Moore. Al-VBP:711, Ox-BN:210,
  Pa-GTB:199
The Blossoming of Love.
  Dharmakirti. Al-PI:36
The Cameo. E. Millay. Un-MA:449
Changes. R. Bulwer-Lytton.
  Fe-PL:307
Crystal Anniversary. P. Appleman.
  Un-MW:148
The Dark Chamber. L. Untermeyer.
  Un-MA:306, Un-MW:140
Do You Remember That Night.
  Co-BL:33, Co-PI:157, Gr-SS:33
Echo. C. Rossetti. Al-VBP:998,
  De-CH:452, Ox-BN:708, Un-MW:91
False Though She Be. W. Congreve.
  Al-VBP:519, Co-BL:138, Hi-WP II:101,
  Rv-CB:497, Un-MW:47
Fatal Interview II, XIV.
  E. Millay. Ca-VT:167, 168
The First Day. C. Rossetti.
  Un-MW:8

Forget Her. Wen I-to. Hs-TC:56
A Forsaken Garden. A. Swinburne.
  Ox-BN:811, Pa-GTB:385, Rv-CB:937
The Fragment. H. Belloc.
  Co-PU:77
The Freak Show. N. Willard.
  Sc-TN:229
Go where Glory Waits Thee.
  T. Moore. Ox-BN:208
Her Letter. B. Harte. Fe-PL:20
I Come to the Shore of the Yangtze
  River to Buy a Handful of Lotus
  Seeds. Hsü Chih-mo. Hs-TC:87
I Heard You Solemn-Sweet Pipes of
  the Organ. W. Whitman.
  Rv-CB:858
In My Life. J. Lennon. Mo-GR:43
In the Mind's Eye. T. Hardy.
  Gr-SS:119
An Interlude. A. Swinburne.
  Al-VBP:1030
Kashmiri Song. L. Hope. Er-FA:117
Lines. T. Hardy. Co-BL:112
Love Song. Tr-CB:16, Tr-US I:45
A Lover's Lament. Pa-SG:59,
  Tr-US II:257
Man White, Brown Girl and All
  That Jazz. G. Oden. Ad-PB:186
Mandalay. R. Kipling. Ga-FB:70,
  Un-MB:125
Maud Muller. J. Whittier.
  Fe-PL:47, Sp-OG:271
Memory. H. Hoyt. Fe-PL:104
Music, when Soft Voices Die.
  P. Shelley. Al-VBP:757,
  Bo-HF:124, De-CH:197, Ga-FB:126,
  Ha-PO:179, Ma-YA:180, Mc-PR:82,
  Ox-BN:294, Pa-GTB:313, Un-MW:203
My Playmate. J. Whittier.
  De-TT:88
Newark Abbey. T. Peacock.
  Ox-BN:233
Non Sum Qualis Eram Bonae sub
  Regno Cynarae. E. Dowson.
  Al-VBP:1102, Co-BL:131, Er-FA:128,
  No-CL:192, Ox-BN:941, Pa-GTB:400,
  Un-MB:148, Un-MW:97
Now and Then. S. Muktibodh.
  Al-PI:132
O Lyric Love. W. Scott. Ca-VT:317
Old Love. K. Wilson. Sc-TN:240
Once I Passed Through a Populous
  City. W. Whitman. Pe-M:30
Only Thy Dust. D. Marquis.
  Fe-PL:100
Pad, Pad. S. Smith. Co-EL:131
Politics. W. Yeats. No-CL:161
Postscript for Gweno. A. Lewis.
  Hi-WP II:111, Pa-GTB:544
Pretty Polly. B. Reece. Co-BL:150

LOVE — MEMORIES — cont'd.
  The Profile on the Pillow.
    D. Randall.   Ad-PB:141, Ra-BP:147
  Rain Threads.   Cheng Ch'in-yü.
    Pa-MV:39
  Rari for O'otua.   Mahana.
    Tr-US II:93
  Remember.   G. Johnson.   Hu-PN:75
  The Rock.   Ch-B:36, Gr-CT:71
  Rococo.   A. Swinburne.   Al-VBP:1025
  Rondeau.   L. Untermeyer.   Un-MW:27
  Should You Go First.
    A. Rowswell.   Fe-PL:277
  Song Composed by a Fighting Man
    Lying Wounded in the Desert.
    Tr-US I:133
  A Song for Te Moana-Papaku.
    Topeora.   Tr-US II:118
  Song of a Scout Remembering
    Home.   Tr-US II:234
  Song of a Widow for Her Dead
    Husband.   Tr-US II:117
  Songs.   Tr-US II:143
  Songs of Nature, I-III.Tr-US II:137
  Sonnets, i. M. Van Doren. Sm-PT:64

  Souvenirs. D. Randall. Ra-BP:148
  Spleen. E. Dowson.   Un-MB:148
  The Spring of Lime. R. Nichols.
    Pa-GTB:454
  The Three Roses. W. Landor.
    No-CL:126
  Time Does Not Bring Relief.
    E. Millay.   Ga-FB:84
  The Time of Roses. T. Hood.
    De-CH:343, Un-MW:7
  To Mary: It Is the Evening
    Hour. J. Clare. Gr-CT:264
  To the Tune "Drunk under the
    Flower Shadows."
    Li Ch'ing Chao. Rx-LT:93
  A Tune. A. Symons. Co-BL:140,
    Ox-BN:937
  Under the Full Moon.
    Yü Kuang-chung. Pa-MV:182
  Viaticum. Pao Yu. Rx-LT:35
  The Voice. T. Hardy. Ox-BN:842,
    Pa-GTB:406
  The Walk on the Beach.
    J. Fletcher. Co-BL:138
  War Song. D. Parker. Cr-WS:77
  What Is Unwoven. A. Freeman.
    Ls-NY:10
  What Lips My Lips Have Kissed.
    E. Millay. Al-VBP:1196,
    Pe-OA:164, Un-MA:445, Un-MW:102
  When You Are Old. W. Yeats.
    Bo-GJ:233, Co-BL:80, Er-FA:172,
    Fe-PL:94, Ga-FB:74, Go-BP:151,
    Ha-PO:179, Hi-WP I:43, Ma-FW:289,
    Un-MB:109, Un-MW:98, Wi-LT:68

  When Will I Be Home?
    Li Shang Yim. Rx-LT:77
  The Widow of Drynam.
    P. MacDonogh. Co-PI:110
  Windy Night. Feng Chih. Hs-TC:142
  A Woman Homer Sang. W. Yeats.
    No-CL:194
  The Yew-Tree. Gr-CT:80
  You Are a Part of Me. F. Yerby.
    Bo-AN:137
  Youth and Art. R. Browning.
    Al-VBP:909
LOVE - OBSTACLES: see also HUMOR -
    LOVE-OBSTACLES; SATIRE - LOVE-
    OBSTACLES
  After the Pangs of a Desperate
    Love. J. Dryden. Al-VBP:480
  And So Men Say I Love Thee!
    D. Coleridge. Rv-CB:765
  Annan Water. De-CH:311, Ma-BB:214
  Annie of Lochroyan. Ma-BB:202
  Ballade. K. Shapiro. Un-MW:144
  Basic. R. Durem. Hu-PN:331
  The Bents and Broom. Ox-BB:187
  Bits of Straw. J. Clare. Ho-WR:187
  The Broomfield Hill. De-CH:292,
    Ox-BB:72
  Brown Robin. Ox-BB:227
  Castles and Candlelight.
    J. Reeves. Co-PT:183
  Cecilia. Do-WH:34
  The Definition of Love.
    A. Marvell. Rv-CB:405
  Deranged. P. Fiacc. Co-PI:42
  The Duke o' Athole's Nurse.
    Ox-BB:344
  The Duke of Gordon's Daughter.
    Ma-BB:217
  The Earl of Mar's Daughter.
    De-CH:290, Fo-OG:21, Ma-BB:146
  Eleventh Song. P. Sidney.
    Al-VBP:127, No-CL:170
  Erlington. Ma-BB:9
  The Eve of St. Agnes. J. Keats.
    Al-VBP:781, Fe-PL:35, Ox-BN:338
  The Famous Flower of Serving-Men.
    Ox-BB:182
  The Far-Off Mountains Hide You
    from Me. Do-CH:(34)
  Father and Child. W. Yeats.
    Co-PU:74
  Fidele's Song. A. Munday.
    Rv-CB:162
  The Gay Goshawk. Ma-BB:183,
    Ox-BB:222
  Gil Brenton. Ox-BB:38
  Hynd Horn. Ma-BB:229, Ox-BB:112
  In Love for Long. E. Muir.
    Wi-LT:256
  In Wintry Midnight, o'er a Stormy
    Main. F. Petrarch. Gr-CT:229

Katherine Jaffray. Ox-BB:300
Kemp Oweyne. Fo-OG:13, Ma-BB:33,
   Rv-CB:50
Kempion. Ox-BB:56
Kill That Crowing Cock. Rx-LT:18
King Estmere. Ma-BB:133, Ox-BB:127
King Henry. Ox-BB:64
A Knight Came Riding from the East.
   Bl-OB:39
Lady Clare. A. Tennyson.
   Co-PT:189, Fe-FP:517, Pa-OM:253,
   Sp-OG:122, Un-GT:144
Lady Elspat. Ma-BB:199
A Little While. D. Rossetti.
   Al-VBP:986
Love Lyric. Ho-LP:1
Love Song. Lo-TY:29
Love Songs. Tr-US I:131
The Lover Tells of the Rose in
   His Heart. W. Yeats.
   Al-VBP:1090, Co-PI:206, Un-MB:109
The Lover's Plea. J. Hendry.
   Ke-TF:120
McNaughton. Ox-BB:304
Maud Muller. J. Whittier.
   Fe-PL:47, Sp-OG:271
Mother, I Cannot Mind My Wheel.
   W. Landor. Un-MW:84
Muckle-Mouth Meg.
   R. Browning. Un-MW:118
My Place. M. Rosenfeld.
   Ho-TY:78
The Nymph's Reply to the Shepherd.
   W. Raleigh. Al-VBP:169,
   Ha-PO:160, No-CL:101, Rv-CB:150
On a Dream (after Reading Dante's
   Episode of Paolo and Francesca).
   J. Keats. Rv-CB:754
The Outlaw of Loch Lene.
   J. Callanan. De-CH:336
Put Out My Eyes. R. Rilke.
   Ho-LP:15
Refusal, with Wisdom. A. Armour.
   Ke-TF:118
Robin Hood and Allan a Dale.
   Gr-GB:247, Ma-BB:44, Un-GT:115
Rondel. J. Froissart. Ho-LP:5
The Simple Ploughboy. Sm-LG:359
Sir Colin. Ox-BB:20
Song. C. Sedley. Al-VBP:497
Song. Tr-US II:305
Sonnet. R. Greene. Al-VBP:144,
   No-CL:270
Sonnet 36. W. Shakespeare.
   Rv-CB:218
Sonnet 134. W. Shakespeare.
   Rv-CB:249
Spring Festival Songs, VII.
   Tr-US II:173
Story of the Flowery Kingdom.
   J. Cabell. Pa-OM:9

Stratton Water. Ox-BB:680
The Strength of Willows. A. Raybin.
   Sc-TN:194
Sweet Willie. Ox-BB:45
Tam Lin. Ma-BB:124, Ox-BB:13
To Karelana. V. Batshev.
   Bo-RU:13
To Lucasta, on Going to the Wars.
   R. Lovelace. Al-VBP:446,
   Er-FA:116, Ga-FB:194, Gr-BT:99,
   Ke-TF:100, Ma-YA:101, Mc-WS:103,
   No-CL:191, Pa-GTB:72, Rv-CB:192,
   Un-MW:153
To the Harbormaster. F. O'Hara.
   Mc-EA:168, Mo-BG:97
The Trumpeter of Fyvie. Ox-BB:349
The Twa Magicians. Ox-BB:51
Upon His Mistress Dancing.
   J. Shirley. Mc-WS:66, No-CL:188
Villikins and His Dinah.
   S. Cowell. Co-PT:184
William Bond. Ox-BB:674
You Would Have Understood Me.
   E. Dowson. Un-MB:149
Young Bekie. Ma-BB:13, Ox-BB:103
Young Benjie. Ox-BB:337
See also Em-AF:75-95
LOVE - PARENT AND CHILD
The Ancient Couple on Lu Mountain.
   M. Van Doren. Ca-VT:196
The Fortress. A. Sexton.
   Pe-OA:275, Wi-LT:814
Gil Morrice. Ox-BB:156
Maternity. A. Miller. Ke-TF:149
The Meeting. K. Tynan. Go-BP:121
A Mother to Her First-Born.
   Tr-CB:27, Tr-US I:105
The Old Woman with Four Sons.
   P. McGinley. Ke-TF:149
Song. V. de Moraes. An-TC:95
Sweetes' Li'l Feller.
   F. Stanton. Er-FA:503
Where Is My Wandering Boy
   Tonight. Er-FA:440
The Wise Mother. D. Hobson.
   Ke-TF:146
LOVE - PARTING: see also
   HUMOR - LOVE-PARTING
Absence. M. Arnold. Rv-CB:869
Absence. R. Bridges. Go-BP:130
Absence. J. Burden. Ls-NY:10
Absence. C. Mew. Un-MB:165
Adrian Henri's Talking after
   Christmas Blues. A. Henri.
   Gr-BT:73
Ae Fond Kiss. R. Burns.
   Al-VBP:648, Er-FA:122,
   Hi-WP II:102, Un-MW:80
Another Dark Lady. E. Robinson.
   No-CL:203

LOVE - PARTING — cont'd.

As You Leave Me.   E. Knight.
Be-MA:41

At a Noon Halt on a Journey.
Kanimana oult Ourzig.
Tr-US I:137

At Parting.   A. Swinburne.
Al-VBP:1032

The Banks of the Condamine.
Gr-GB:212

Because I Have Not Known.
O. Mandelstam.   Ca-MR:152

Because I Liked You.
A. Housman.   Hi-WP II:108

Black-Eyed Susan.   J. Gay.
Co-RG:82, Co-SS:66, De-TT:129,
Pa-GTB:124

Black Is the Colour.   Gr-GB:118

Break of Day.   J. Donne.
Un-MW:76

The Broken Wedding Ring.
Fi-BG:216

The Busy Heart.   R. Brooke.
Un-MB:325

A Caressing Breeze.   Mo-MI:59

A Chinese Poem Written B.C. 1121.
Hi-WP II:63

Daisy.   F. Thompson.   Ga-FB:164,
Ox-BN:917, Un-MB:77

Dance Songs.   Tr-US II:146

Dearest, Do Not You Delay Me.
J. Fletcher.   Al-VBP:280

Dedication.   H. von Gilm.
Un-R:127

Discordants.   C. Aiken.   Co-BL:37

Divided.   J. Ingelow.   Li-SR:35

Don Juan.   G. Byron.
Al-VBP:730

Drafted.   Su Wu.   Rx-LT:6

A Dream Within a Dream.   E. Poe.
Rv-CB:804, Sh-AP:60, Un-MW:83

The Drynaun Dhun.   Gr-GB:116

An Elegy.   B. Jonson.   No-CL:178

The Expiration.   J. Donne.
Rv-CB:306

Fare Thee Well.   G. Byron.
Er-FA:405, Ox-BN:251

The Farewell.   R. Burns.
Al-VBP:377, De-CH:175

Farewell!   G. Byron.   Al-VBP:720,
Un-MW:83

Farewell.   I. L'Ouverture.
Lo-TY:89

A Farewell.   C. Patmore.
Ox-BN:652, Pa-GTB:369, Un-MW:92

Farewell to Fan Yun at An Ch'eng.
Shen Yueh.   Rx-LT:36

Farewell to Shen Yueh.   Fan Yun.
Rx-LT:37

Fatal Interview XLVI.   E. Millay.
Ca-VT:170

First, Goodbye.   J. Smith.
To-MP:92

For Anne.   L. Cohen.   Co-BL:129,
Co-EL:7, En-PC:291, Pe-SS:119

For Carlos at War.   M. Price.
Cr-WS:77

From the Arabic: An Imitation.
P. Shelley.   Rv-CB:704

Going West.   Fi-BG:104

The Golden Tickseed.
G. Davidson.   Bo-HF:128

Goodbye.   A. Lewis.   To-MP:59

He Would Not Stay for Me.
A. Housman.   Hi-WP I:88

Highland Mary.   R. Burns.
Al-VBP:650, Pa-GTB:151, Sp-OG:276

His Picture.   J. Donne.   Rv-CB:307

The Housemaid.   R. Korn.   Ho-TY:302

I Cannot Live with You.
E. Dickinson.   Rv-CB:923,
Sh-AP:129, Un-MA:96, Un-MW:87

I See Your Face.   L. Isseluk.
Le-IB:85

I Will Not Let Thee Go.
R. Bridges.   Ox-BN:872

If You Should Go.   C. Cullen.
Bo-HF:32

In the Gloaming.   M. Orred.
Er-FA:490

Insects! Do Not Cry!   Issa.
Le-MW:29

An Interlude.   A. Swinburne.
Al-VBP:1030

Is It Not Sure? Rv-CB:8

Isabella.   Rv-ON:82

Jean.   R. Burns.   Al-VBP:645,
Hi-WP I:41, Pa-GTB:156

Karako Bird.   Tr-US II:90

Kashmiri Song.   L. Hope.   Er-FA:117

A Lament.   A. Scott.   De-CH:342

Lament of Taura Atua.   Taura Atua.
Tr-US II:68

Letter from a Wife.   S. Reese.
Hu-PN:413

Light Listened.   T. Roethke.
Un-MA:601

Like Two Doves.   Le-OE:91

A Little While.   D. Rossetti.
Al-VBP:986

Long Gone.   S. Brown.   Ra-BP:112

Lord Maxwell's Last Goodnight.
Ox-BB:607

The Lost Cat.   E. Rieu.
Ar-TP3:53, Co-BBW:122

The Lost Mistress.   R. Browning.
Ox-BN:532, Rv-CB:818, Un-MW:113

Love Song (Boxes).   Tr-US II:3

Love Song (My Girl).   Tr-US II:287

Love Song (Oh, How).   Da-SC:51

Love Song (I Left).   Tr-US I:129

Love Songs (O Merchant).
  Tr-US I:115
Maid of Athens. G. Byron.
  Er-FA:111, Ga-FB:51, Ni-JP:97
The Mistress. J. Wilmot.
  Al-VBP:502
Mrs. McGrath. Ba-PO:89
My Bonie Mary. R. Burns.
  Al-VBP:646, Gr-CC:121, Pa-GTB:127
My Mother Bids Me Bind My Hair.
  A. Hunter. Rv-CB:555
A Night in Florence.
  Haü Chih-mo. Hs-TC:79
O What Is That Sound. W. Auden.
  Al-VBP:1227, Gr-SS:70, Ma-FW:254,
  Pe-M:98, To-MP:29, Un-MB:455
Old Love Songs. Tr-US II:238
On Fanny Godwin. P. Shelley.
  Ox-BN:278
On the Departure Platform.
  T. Hardy. Ox-BN:829
Parting after a Quarrel.
  E. Tietjens. Co-BL:137
Parting Song. Tr-US II:217
Parting, Without a Sequel.
  J. Ransom. Mo-BG:95, Pe-OA:139,
  Un-MA:417
Poem 20. P. Neruda. Be-UL:59
Poems Addressed to Ianthe, I.
  W. Landor. Ox-BN:186
The Press-Gang. Gr-CT:223,
  Gr-GB:238
Red River Valley. Er-FA:445
Refusal, with Wisdom. A. Armour.
  Ke-TF:118
Roundel of Farewell. F. Villon.
  Un-MW:71
said don't leave me here, in a sky.
  J. Heglin. Ad-II:54
Sailing to England. D. Moraes.
  Al-PI:100
A Separation. W. Cory. Ox-BN:649
Simple Song. B. Fundoianu.
  Mc-AC:78
Since There's No Help. M. Drayton.
  Al-VBP:168, Co-BL:129, Ha-PO:167,
  Hi-WP II:101, Pa-GTB:23,
  Rv-CB:186, Un-MW:73
Since You Left. Ch'ang Ch'u Ling.
  Rx-LT:48
Song (Sweetest Love). J. Donne.
  Al-VBP:247, Rv-CB:294, Un-MW:76
A Song (Absent). J. Wilmot.
  Al-VBP:503
Song.
  Tr-US II:29, 154, 194
Song of a Married Woman to Her
  Lover Yuv. Tr-US II:9
Song of a Navigator's Wife.
  Tr-US II:16

Song of a Suitor Dismissed.
  Tr-US II:52
Song of a Woman Named Hi Pak.
  Hi Pak. Tr-US I:207
Song of a Woman when Her Lover
  Went on a Journey.
  Tr-US II:228
Sonnet LXXXIX. W. Shakespeare.
  No-CL:89
The Sonnet-Ballad. G. Brooks.
  Pe-SS:131
Sonnet on Separation.
  V. de Moraes. An-TC:111
The Sonnets. W. Shakespeare.
  No-CL:88, Pa-GTB:8, Rv-CB:237,
  Un-MW:182
Sonnets from the Portuguese VI.
  E. Browning. Al-VBP:815
Spring Festival Songs, IX.
  Tr-US II:173
The Taxi. A. Lowell. Un-MA:163
Then Go at Once. V. Bapat.
  Al-PI:129
There Ain't but the One Thing
  Grieves My Mind. Sp-HW:7
To Lucasta, on Going Beyond the
  Seas. R. Lovelace. Al-VBP:445,
  Pa-GTB:82
To Lucasta, on Going to the Wars.
  R. Lovelace. Al-VBP:446,
  Er-FA:116, Ga-FB:194, Gr-BT:99,
  Ke-TF:100, Ma-YA:101, Mc-WS:103,
  No-CL:191, Pa-GTB:72, Rv-CB:392,
  Un-MW:153
To Marguerite. M. Arnold.
  Rv-CB:872
To the Tune, "Pear Blossoms Fall
  and Scatter." Li Ch'ing Chao.
  Rx-OH:97
Today We Part. S. Doinas. Mc-AC:128
tumultuous diamond, with a spray.
  J. Heglin. Ad-II:54
Warpath Song. Da-SC:112
The Waters of Tyne. Gr-GB:124
A Weary Lot Is Thine. W. Scott.
  Al-VBP:675, De-CH:174,
  Ox-BN:113, Pa-GTB:194
What Is Unwoven. A. Freeman.
  Ls-NY:10
When We Two Parted. G. Byron.
  Al-VBP:720, Fe-PL:109,
  Hi-WP II:104, Ox-BN:237,
  Pa-GTB:190, Rv-CB:692, Un-MW:82
White in the Moon. A. Housman.
  Un-MW:98
Whither Away? M. Coleridge.
  De-CH:337
Wind Song. Da-SC:111
Without Her. D. Rossetti.
  Al-VBP:989, Rv-CB:881
Women's Dance Song. Tr-US II:143

LOVE - PERMANENCE: see also
   SATIRE - LOVE-PERMANENCE
   The Anniversary. J. Donne.
      Rv-CB:296
   An Arundel Tomb. P. Larkin.
      To-MP:79
   Believe Me, if All Those Endearing
      Young Charms. T. Moore.
      Er-FA:103, Ga-FB:50, Ma-YA:171,
      Ox-BN:212, Rv-CB:681
   Burncombe Hollow. W. Barnes.
      Ox-BN:431
   Circumstance. A. Tennyson.
      Sp-OG:277
   Dear, if You Change. Rv-CB:111
   The Delicate Dream Beyond Chaos.
      B. Richart. Ke-TF:131
   Doria. E. Pound. Ma-FW:256,
      Un-MA:294
   A Faded Rose. Wang Tu-ch'ing.
      Hs-TC:193
   Fidele's Song. A. Munday.
      Rv-CB:162
   Harbour. H. Monro. Go-BP:131
   If Thou Must Love Me. E. Browning.
      Co-BL:98, Er-FA:114, Ke-TF:108,
      Ma-YA:191, Ox-BN:466, Un-MW:205
   In Memoriam. A. Tennyson.
      Ox-BN:497
   Lament for Old Age. Tr-US II:91
   Lesbia. R. Aldington. Fe-PL:116
   Life in a Love. R. Browning.
      Ox-BN:543
   Love. Pa-SG:47
   Love Charm. Tr-US II:205
   Love Continual. T. Heywood.
      Rv-CB:73
   Love Indestructible. R. Southey.
      Ox-BN:181
   Love Lives Beyond. J. Clare.
      Gr-CT:56, Ox-BN:329
   Love Me Little, Love Me Long.
      Er-FA:112, Rv-CB:117
   A Love Poem. E. Knight. Be-MA:110
   My Light with Yours. E. Masters.
      Sm-PT:62
   Not Marble, nor the Gilded
      Monuments. W. Shakespeare.
      Al-VBP:202, Er-FA:119, Ha-PO:255,
      No-CL:8, Rv-CB:224
   Now! R. Browning. Rv-CB:828,
      Un-MW:193
   October. W. Morris. Ox-BN:787
   An Ode upon a Question Moved,
      Whether Love Should Endure
      for Ever. Lord Herbert.
      Al-VBP:297
   One Day I Wrote Her Name.
      E. Spencer. Al-VBP:99,
      No-CL:22, Rv-CB:161

   The Philosopher to His Mistress.
      R. Bridges. Wi-LT:55
   A P'i-pa Tune in an Alley at
      Midnight. Hsü Chih-mo. Hs-TC:90
   Poems Addressed to Ianthe.
      W. Landor. Ox-BN:187
   The Relic. J. Donne. Rv-CB:305
   Set Me Whereas the Sun.
      H. Howard. Al-VBP:79, Rv-CB:98
   Shall I Compare Thee to a Summer's
      Day? W. Shakespeare.
      Al-VBP:200, Er-FA:126, Fe-PL:99,
      Ga-FB:32, Ha-PO:253, Hi-WP II:53,
      Ke-TF:102, Ma-YA:65, Ni-JP:126,
      Pa-GTB:12, Rv-CB:208, Un-MW:181
   Song of a Common Lover.
      F. Ranaivo. Gr-BT:54, Lo-TY:154
   Song of a Young Man about to Be
      Married. Tr-US II:186
   Sonnet 25. W. Shakespeare.
      Rv-CB:211
   Sonnet CII. W. Shakespeare.
      Al-VBP:206, No-CL:88
   Sonnet 107. W. Shakespeare.
      Rv-CB:239
   Sonnet CXVI. W. Shakespeare.
      Al-VBP:208, Er-FA:126, Ga-FB:33,
      Go-BP:123, Ha-PO:253, Hi-WP II:52,
      Ke-TF:102, No-CL:90, Pa-GTB:15,
      Rv-CB:241, Un-MW:10
   Sonnets, xxiv, xxv. C. Smith.
      Sm-PT:162, 163
   Sonnets, viii. M. Van Doren.
      Sm-PT:65
   Sonnets, xviii. E. Wylie. Sm-PT:72
   Sudden Light. D. Rossetti. Fe-PL:98,
      Ox-BN:681, Rv-CB:885, Un-MW:207
   To a Lady Asking Him How Long He
      Sm-PT:72
   To a Lady Asking Him How Long He
      Would Love Her. G. Ethredge.
      Al-VBP:496, No-CL:196
   To Rosamund. G. Chaucer.
      Rv-CB:57
   Turn All Thy Thoughts.
      T. Campion. Al-VBP:215
   Under All Change. J. Johnson.
      Tr-MR:158
   We Live Again by the Bay and Its
      Waters. J. Brodsky. Ca-MR:32
   When Men Shall Find Thy Flower.
      S. Daniel. Un-MW:203
   When Our Two Souls Stand Up.
      E. Browning. Al-VBP:816,
      Un-MW: 206
LOVE - POWER
   The After-Glow. M. Blind.
      Ox-BN:849
   Ask No Return! H. Gregory.
      Ca-VT:209, Sm-PT:120, Un-MA:508
   Choral Songs. Tr-US II:114
   Christ's Victory on Earth.
      G. Fletcher. Al-VBP:319

De Amore. E. Dowson. Ox-BN:943
Duet from Becket. A. Tennyson.
  Gr-SS:148
Endymion. J. Keats. Al-VBP:790,
  Ox-BN:337
The Fire of Love. Bible. O.T.
  Song of Solomon. Me-PH:40
Forgiveness. Ke-TF:138
A Game of Cards. E. Jennings.
  Ls-NY:15
Love. H. Thoreau. Rv-CB:834
Love Is Enough. W. Morris.
  Hi-WP II:59
Love Songs. Tr-US I:126
Lover's Reply to Good Advice.
  R. Hughes. Un-MB:405
Love's Inspiration. Hsü Chih-mo.
  Hs-TC:96
The Morning Glory. Confucius.
  Ga-S:175, Pa-SG:50
My Ships. E. Wilcox. Fe-PL:95
The Paper Nautilus. M. Moore.
  Ca-VT:127
A Pearl, a Girl. R. Browning.
  Rv-CB:830
The Power of Love. Pa-SG:44
Salvage. E. Lieberman. Ke-TF:133
Song for an Allegorical Play.
  J. Ciardi. En-PC:150
Songs. Tr-US II:146
Songs and Dance Songs.
  Tr-US II:153
Tristram. E. Robinson. Sm-PT:63
The Woman Who Understands.
  L. Appleton. Fe-PL:117
LOVE - PRAISE: see also
  HUMOR - LOVE-PRAISE
Aeglamour's Lament. B. Jonson.
  De-CH:334, No-CL:199
After Two Years. R. Aldington.
  Un-MB:255
Ah, Were She Pitiful. R. Greene.
  Al-VBP:143
Annie Laurie. W. Douglas.
  Er-FA:425, Ga-FB:45
Appreciation. G. Meredith.
  Al-VBP:985
April Moon. W. de la Mare.
  Sp-OG:347
Arise, My Love. Bible. O.T.
  Song of Solomon. Gr-CT:42,
  Me-PH:35
As the Sun Rose over the Mountain.
  Wy-CM:33
At a Solemn Musick. D. Schwartz.
  Tr-MR:35
Autumnal. J. Wright. Ha-TP:71
Awake! Awake! W. Davenant.
  Al-VBP:384, De-CH:6, Gr-CT:41,
  Un-MW:3

The Bait. J. Donne. Gr-CC:189,
  Mo-SD:188, No-CL:103
Beauty Clear and Fair. J. Fletcher.
  Al-VBP:282, Rv-CB:313
Beauty Extolled. H. Noel.
  Gr-CT:62
Behold, Thou Art Fair. Bible.
  O.T. Song of Solomon.
  Me-PH:37, Un-MW:157
Bel M'es Quan Lo M'alena.
  A. Daniel. Pa-SG:70
The Beloved. Be-AP:50
The Bird Catcher. Be-AP:49,
  Lo-TY:28
A Black Girl Goes By. E. Roumer.
  Lo-TY:90
Black Is the Colour. Gr-GB:118
Black Magic. D. Randall.
  Ad-BO:5, Ad-PB:140
Bonnie Lesley. R. Burns.
  Pa-GTB:149, Rv-CB:625
The Bonny Keel Laddie. Gr-GB:215
The Bride. J. Suckling.
  Un-MW:18
By Fiat of Adoration.
  O. Williams. Wi-LT:414
The Call. R. Brooke. Ke-TF:110
Can Life Be a Blessing.
  J. Dryden. Al-VBP:483
The Canonization. J. Donne.
  Al-VBP:246, Rv-CB:293
Canto Amor. J. Berryman.
  Ca-VT:381, Un-MA:642
Child and Maiden. C. Sedley.
  Al-VBP:498, Pa-GTB:71
Choice. A. Morgan. Fe-PL:106,
  Ke-TF:117
The Cloud Messenger. Kalidasa.
  Al-PI:46
Come into the Garden, Maud.
  A. Tennyson. Co-BL:74,
  Ga-FB:57, Rv-CB:799
Conjured. J. Gill. Sc-TN:67
Cowboy Dance Song. Fi-BG:169
Dance Songs, IV. Tr-US II:141
Dear Dark Head. Co-BL:116,
  Pa-SG:58
Dew Sate upon Julia's Hair.
  R. Herrick. De-CH:733
A Dialogue of Watching.
  K. Rexroth. Pe-M:145
Diaphenia. H. Constable.
  Al-VBP:153, De-CH:333,
  Pa-GTB:10, Rv-CB:179
The Drynaun Dhun. Gr-GB:116
Dulce Ridentum. S. Benét.
  Ha-LO:95
The Effect of Love. T. Campion.
  Un-MW:14
Eloisa to Abelard. A. Pope.
  Al-VBP:535

LOVE - PRAISE — cont'd.
  Endymion. J. Keats.   Al-VBP:789
  L'Envoi. T. Beddoes.   Ox-BN:451
  Epilogue. L. Abercrombie.
    Un-MB:254
  Even Now. . . . Bilhana.
    Al-PI:48, Pa-SG:65
  Fain Would I Change. T. Hume.
    Al-VBP:358, Rv-CB:259
  Farewell! Thou Art Too Dear for
    My Possessing. W. Shakespeare.
    Al-VBP:205, No-CL:86, Pa-GTB:19,
    Un-MW:183
  The Fatal Spell. G. Byron.
    Al-VBP:727, Ox-BN:247
  Field of Long Grass. A. Smith.
    Co-BL:71
  The Fire of Love. Bible. O.T.
    Song of Solomon. Me-PH:40
  The First Part of Tamurlaine the
    Great. C. Marlowe.
    Al-VBP:171, 173
  Follow Thy Fair Sun. T. Campion.
    Al-VBP:213, De-CH:462, Go-BP:145,
    Rv-CB:268
  The Folly of Being Comforted.
    W. Yeats.   Go-BP:130
  For Miriam. K. Patchen.
    Un-MW:210
  Fulfillment. W. Cavendish.
    Un-MW:135
  Girl's Song. Tr-US II:21
  Give All to Love. R. Emerson.
    Al-VBP:802, Er-FA:121, Fe-PL:102,
    Mc-WK:219, No-CL:151, Sh-AP:32
  The Glory of the Day Was in Her
    Face. J. Johnson. Ad-PB:5
  The Gowden Locks of Anna.
    R. Burns. Rv-CB:624
  Greek Anthology, IV. Un-MW:174
  He Compares All Things with His
    Lady and Finds Them Wanting.
    G. Calvalcanti. Pa-SG:73
  He Will Praise His Lady.
    G. Guinicelli. Pa-SG:72
  Her, a Statue. T. Stoddart.
    Ox-BN:531
  Herder's Song. Tr-US I:39
  Herrick's Julia. H. Bevington.
    Li-SR:24
  Hide, Absolon. G. Chaucer.
    Rv-CB:63
  How Beautiful Are Thy Feet with
    Shoes. Bible. O.T. Song of
    Solomon. Me-PH:38
  How Happy the Lover. J. Dryden.
    Al-VBP:485
  How Many Foolish Things.
    M. Drayton. Rv-CB:182
  Hymn to the Spirit of Nature.
    P. Shelley. Al-VBP:742,
    De-CH:335, Pa-GTB:281

  I Have Taken the Woman of Beauty.
    Ho-SD:62
  I Knew a Woman. T. Roethke.
    Br-TC:343, Un-MA:597, Un-MW:197,
    Wi-LT:487
  I Loved a Lass. Al-VBP:312,
    De-CH:190, No-CL:121
  I Stopped in Front of You.
    L. Blaga. Mc-AC:71
  If I Have Made, My Lady.
    E. Cummings. Ga-FB:84
  Images. R. Aldington. Un-MB:353
  In Praise of Abazza Ag-Mekiia.
    Tekadeit oult Ag-Eklan.
    Tr-US I:135
  In Praise of His Love. H. Howard.
    No-CL:207
  In the Spring. Meleager. Pa-SG:67
  Ivory Masks in Orbit.
    K. Kgositsile. Ad-PB:324
  Jean. R. Burns. Al-VBP:645,
    Hi-WP I:41, Pa-GTB:156
  Kidnap Poem. N. Giovanni.
    Ra-BP:326
  Koukaa. Tr-US I:133
  The Looking Glass. M. Drayton.
    No-CL:205
  Love. P. Goggins. Jo-VC:63
  Love and Liberation. J. Wheelock.
    Un-MA:343
  Love and Sleep. A. Swinburne.
    Un-MW:195
  Love Enthroned. D. Rossetti.
    Ox-BN:682
  Love for Such a Cherry Lip.
    T. Middleton. Al-VBP:232
  Love in Her Eyes Sits Playing.
    J. Gay. Al-VBP:523
  Love in the Winds. R. Hovey.
    Co-BL:81
  Love Is Enough. W. Morris.
    Al-VBP:1017, Co-BL:113, Ga-FB:69
  Love on the Mountain. T. Boyd.
    Co-BL:82
  Love Poem. R. Bly. Co-BL:55
  Love Praise. Tr-CB:42,
    Tr-US I:69
  Love Song. D. Whitewing.
    Al-WW:51
  Love Song. Lo-TY:28, 31,
    Tr-US I:116, 141,
    Tr-US II:195
  Love Song for Nneka. Do-CH:(35)
  Love Songs. Tr-US I:129
  Love to Faults Is Always Blind.
    W. Blake. Al-VBP:620
  Lovely as a Flower. H. Heine.
    Pa-SG:76
  The Lover Praises His Lady's
    Bright Beauty. S. O'Sheel.
    Co-BL:70

The Lovers.   M. Zaturenska.
    Un-MA:559
Love's Alchemy.   J. Donne.
    Al-VBP:248
Love's Consolation.   R. Dixon.
    Ox-BN:749
Love's Harmony.   W. Shakespeare.
    No-CL:145
Love's Perjuries.   W. Shakespeare.
    Al-VBP:181, Pa-GTB:13
Magdalen Walks.   O. Wilde.
    Un-MB:67
Men's Song.   Tr-US I:209
The Miller's Daughter.
    A. Tennyson.   Rv-CB:796
Miss Melerlee.   J. Holloway.
    Hu-PN:19
More than Most Fair.   E. Spenser.
    Un-MW:151
The Morning Sun Shines.
    Emperor Wu.   Rx-LT:39
My Light Thou Art.   J. Wilmot.
    Co-BL:77, Un-MW:134
My Lord and King.   A. Tennyson.
    Gr-CT:434, Ox-BN:508
My Love.   e. cummings.   Ca-VT:171,
    Wi-LT:358
My Mistress Is as Fair as Fine.
    De-CH:333
My Sweet Sweeting.   De-CH:35
My Ulick.   C. Kickham.   Co-PI:86
My Wife.   R. Stevenson.
    Hi-WP I:43
A Night in Florence. Hsü Chih-mo.
    Hs-TC:79
Not Celia that I Juster Am.
    C. Sedley.   Al-VBP:497,
    Pa-GTB:81, Un-MW:135
A Nymph's Passion.   B. Jonson.
    No-CL:142
Oh, Fairest of the Rural Maids!
    W. Bryant.   Al-VBP:767
O Many Named Beloved.
    S. Menasha.   Sm-MK:210
O My Love the Pretty Towns.
    K. Patchen.   Ca-VT:344, Mc-EA:82
On a Girdle.   E. Waller.
    Al-VBP:385, Pa-GTB:79, Un-MW:164
On Lydia Distracted.   P. Ayres.
    Gr-SS:84
Part of Plenty.   B. Spencer.
    Wi-LT:645
Parthenope.   B. Barnes.   Rv-CB:279
Perfect Love.   Sana'i.   Pa-SG:28
Petrarch for Laura.
    C. McAllister.   Gr-SS:101
The Philosopher to His Mistress.
    R. Bridges.   Wi-LT:55
Poem.   J. Friedman.   Ho-TY:367
Poem in Prose.   A. MacLeish.
    Mc-WS:149

Poet to His Love.   M. Bodenheim.
    Co-BL:116
A Praise of His Lady.   Al-VBP:70
Prelude VI.   C. Aiken.   Un-MA:435
Puella Mea.   E. Cummings.
    No-CL:212
A Red, Red Rose.   R. Burns.
    Al-VBP:651, Ar-TP3:211, Bo-FP:292,
    Bo-HF:114, Co-BL:83, Co-PS:39,
    Er-FA:102, Fe-PL:111, Ga-FB:48,
    Gr-CT:64, Ha-PO:176, Hi-WP I:40,
    Ma-YA:136, Pa-GTB:150, Rv-CB:613,
    Se-PR:55, Sm-LG:351, Sp-OG:267,
    Un-MW:165
The Relique.   J. Donne.
    Al-VBP:252, Rv-CB:305
The Retreat.   C. Cotton.   Rv-CB:397
The Rigs o' Barley.   R. Burns.
    Al-VBP:641, Rv-CB:617
Rondel of Merciless Beauty.
    G. Chaucer.   Un-MW:70
Rosaline.   T. Lodge.   Pa-GTB:10
Rose Aylmer.   W. Landor.
    Al-VBP:705, Co-RG:149, De-CH:347,
    Er-FA:115, No-CL:134, Ox-BN:185,
    Rv-CB:667
The Rose Family.   R. Frost.
    Co-BL:85
The Rwose in the Dark.
    W. Barnes.   Rv-CB:767
Sailor and Tailor.   De-TT:127
Sally in Our Alley.   H. Carey.
    Al-VBP:527, Co-PS:38, Er-FA:125,
    Pa-GTB:126, Rv-CB:498, Sp-OG:268
A Secret Kept.   J. Al-Hariz.
    Me-PH:62
Shadows.   Da-SC:94
Shall I Compare Thee to a Summer's
    Day?   W. Shakespeare.
    Al-VBP:200, Er-FA:126, Fe-PL:99,
    Ga-FB:32, Ha-PO:253, Hi-WP II:53,
    Ke-TF:102, Ma-YA:65, Ni-JP:126,
    Pa-GTB:12, Rv-CB:208, Un-MW:181
Shall I Love Again.   W. Browne.
    Al-VBP:322
She.   T. Roethke.   Co-BL:51
She Is Not Fair.   H. Coleridge.
    Al-VBP:795, Ga-FB:56, Pa-GTB:178
She Walks in Beauty.   G. Byron.
    Co-RG:148, Er-FA:105, Hi-WP II:54,
    Ke-TF:107, Mc-PR:91, Ni-JP:96,
    Ox-BN:251, Pa-GTB:177, Rv-CB:688,
    Sh-RP:89, Un-MW:166
The Shepherd's Wife's Song.
    R. Greene.   Al-VBP:139
A Simile for Her Smile.
    R. Wilbur.   Mo-BG:92
A Simple Duty.   E. Poe.   Se-PR:55
Since Brass, nor Stone.
    W. Shakespeare.   Er-FA:119,
    No-CL:84, Pa-GTB:3

LOVE - PRAISE — cont'd.
  Since First I Saw Your Face.
    Rv-CB:109
  A Snapshot. H. Barua. Al-PI:75
  So White, So Soft, So Sweet.
    B. Jonson. De-TT:153, Sm-LG:350,
    Un-MW:16
  Song (For Her Gait). W. Brown.
    No-CL:184
  Song (Nay, but You). R. Browning.
    Al-VBP:908, Co-BL:69, Un-MW:24
  Song (Ask Me). T. Carew.
    Al-VBP:350, De-CH:144, Er-FA:107,
    Un-MW:163
  Song (Hola). Tr-US II:196
  Song (I Found Here). Le-IB:86,
    Tr-US II:123
  A Song of Marco Polo.
    T. Garrison. Ke-TF:119
  Song of the Bridegroom in Praise
    of His Bride. Tr-US I:70
  Songs. Tr-US I:168, 191,
    Tr-US II:142, 143
  Sonnet 1, 3. S. Daniel.
    Al-VBP:156, 157
  Sonnet XXX. E. Millay. Co-EL:34
  Sonnet 19. W. Shakespeare.
    Gr-CT:61, Ho-LP:8, Rv-CB:209,
    Un-MW:182
  Sonnet 20. W. Shakespeare.Rv-CB:210
  Sonnet 29. W. Shakespeare.
    Al-VBP:200, Co-BL:117, Ga-FB:34,
    Ha-PO:254, Ho-P:290, Ni-JP:96,
    Pa-GTB:8, Rv-CB:212, Un-MW:181
  Sonnet LIII. W. Shakespeare.
    Al-VBP:202, Er-FA:117
  Sonnet 91. W. Shakespeare.
    Rv-CB:234
  Sonnet CVI. W. Shakespeare.
    Al-VBP:207, Ga-FB:32, Gr-CC:80,
    No-CL:89, Pa-GTB:13, Rv-CB:238,
    Sm-LG:353
  Sonnets 1. M. Drayton.
    Al-VBP:165
  Sonnets, xvii, xxxii.
    M. Van Doren. Sm-PT:66
  Sonnets, ii. E. Wylie. Sm-PT:69
  Sourwood Mountain. Gr-GB:124
  Summum Bonum. R. Browning.
    Co-BL:117, Co-EL:94, Ma-YA:203
  The Sun Rising. J. Donne.
    Rv-CB:292, Un-MW:161
  Sweet Stay-at-Home. W. Davies.
    De-CH:36
  Take Back the Virgin Page.
    T. Moore. Ox-BN:211
  Tenderness. Li Chin-fa. Hs-TC:175
  There Be None of Beauty's Daughters.
    G. Byron. De-TT:152, Pa-GTB:176,
    Rv-CB:691

  There Is None like Her.
    A. Tennyson. Ox-BN:509
  Thou Art to Me Such a Spring.
    G. Meredith. De-CH:707
  To a Golden-Haired Girl in a
    Louisiana Town. V. Lindsay.
    Un-MA:221
  To a Woman Loved. Bi-IT:75
  To an Isle in the Water. W. Yeats.
    Gr-TG:65, Sm-MK:8
  To Be Sung on the Water.
    L. Bogan. Ca-VT:204
  To Celia. B. Jonson.
    Al-VBP:235, Bo-HF:115, Er-FA:424,
    Fe-PL:114, Ga-FB:35, Ha-PO:170,
    Ke-TF:99, Ma-YA:82, Pa-GTB:77,
    Rv-CB:286, Un-MW:152
  To Helen. E. Poe. Al-VBP:878,
    Co-BL:76, De-CH:347, Er-FA:123,
    Fe-PL:101, Fr-WO:84, Ga-FB:62,
    Gr-CT:440, No-CL:56, Rv-CB:802,
    Sh-AP:53, Un-MW:168
  To Judith Asleep. J. Ciardi.
    Wi-LT:669
  To O.E.A. C. McKay. Ra-BP:60
  To One Admiring Herself in a
    Looking Glass. T. Randolph.
    Al-VBP:381, No-CL:205
  To Phillis. C. Sedley.
    Co-BL:73, No-CL:179
  To Rosamund. G. Chaucer.
    Rv-CB:57
  To the Evening Star. T. Campbell.
    Ox-BN:196, Pa-GTB:187
  Toast. F. Horne. Hu-PN:150
  The Triumph of Charis. B. Jonson.
    Al-VBP:235, Rv-CB:283
  Triumph of Love. J. Wheelock.
    Un-MA:342
  Two Moons. Hsü Chih-mo. Hs-TC:94
  Verse Written in the Album of
    Mademoiselle. P. Dalcour.
    Ab-MO:24, Hu-PN:16, Lo-TY:97
  Verses Copied from the Window of
    an Obscure Lodging House, in
    the Neighborhood of London.
    Al-VBP:610
  A Virginal. E. Pound.
    Un-MA:291, Un-MW:209
  The Visitation. R. Graves.
    Go-BP:135
  The Visiting Sea. A. Meynell.
    Go-BP:132
  The Waggoner. Gr-GB:213
  Welcome, Welcome, Do I Sing.
    W. Browne. Al-VBP:323
  When Yon Full Moon. W. Davies.
    Un-MB:177
  Who Is Sylvia. W. Shakespeare.
    Al-VBP:180, Co-BL:71, Er-FA:431,
    Ke-TF:104

Wishes: To His Supposed Mistress.
R. Crashaw. Al-VBP:432, Pa-GTB:67
Within Her Eyes. Dante Alighieri.
Pa-SG:61
A Woman Homer Sang. W. Yeats.
No-CL:194
Words for the Wind. T. Roethke.
En-PC:96
Your Eyes Have Their Silence.
G. Barrax. Ad-PB:224
LOVE - PRAYERS
Love-Charm Songs, I, II. Br-MW:6
A Prayer for His Lady.
O. Gogarty. Ls-NY:12
LOVE - PROMISES: see also
HUMOR - LOVE-PROMISES
An Thou Were My Ain Thing.
A. Ramsay. Al-VBP:526
Another of the Same Nature.
Ignoto. No-CL:102
Bedouin Song. B. Taylor.
Co-BL:39, Sh-AP:124
Believe Me, if All Those Endearing
Young Charms. T. Moore.
Er-FA:103, Ga-FB:50, Ma-YA:171,
Ox-BN:212, Rv-CB:681
Curly Locks. Au-SP:8, Bo-FP:294,
De-PO:14, Hi-GD:10, Li-LB:45,
Mo-MGT:97, Mo-NR:130, Wi-MG:65,
Wr-RM:39
Dear, if You Change. Rv-CB:111
Declaration. A. Symons. Al-VBP:1094
Dedication. H. von Gilm. Un-R:127
The Gardener. Gr-GB:112
If Doughty Deeds. . . .
Graham of Gartmore. Pa-GTB:128
If I Were King. J. McCarthy.
Er-FA:108, Fe-PL:112
An Invitation to Phyllis.
C. Cotton. No-CL:108
Love and Life. J. Wilmot.
Al-VBP:503, No-CL:179
Love Me or Not. T. Campion.
Al-VBP:216
The Love of King David and Fair
Bethsabe. G. Peele. Al-VBP:138
The Miller. J. Clerk. Gr-CT:84
Oh! Dear, What Can the Matter Be?
De-CH:70, Mc-WS:165, Mo-MGT:200,
Mo-TL:34, Wr-RM:127
Oh Promise Me. C. Scott. Er-FA:17
O Wert Thou in the Cauld Blast.
R. Burns. Un-MW:154
Old Love Songs Connected with War,
I, III. Tr-US II:238, 239
The Passionate Shepherd to His Love.
C. Marlowe. Al-VBP:168, Bo-FP:296,
Co-BL:56, Er-FA:122, Fe-PL:113,
Ha-PO:159, Hi-WP I:37, Ke-TF:105,
Ma-YA:62, Mc-PR:16, Mc-WS:61,
No-CL:100, Pa-GTB:4, Rv-CB:149,
Un-MW:179
A Pavane for the Nursery.
W. Smith. Bo-GJ:124, Co-BL:110,
Co-PS:41, Un-MA:671
Promise Me a Rose. B. Merrill.
Co-BL:96
A Red, Red Rose. R. Burns.
Al-VBP:651, Ar-TP3:211, Bo-FP:292,
Bo-HF:114, Co-BL:83, Co-PS:39,
Er-FA:102, Fe-PL:111, Ga-FB:48,
Gr-CT:64, Ha-PO:176, Hi-WP I:40,
Ma-YA:136, Pa-GTB:150, Rv-CB:613,
Se-PR:55, Sm-LG:351, Sp-OG:267,
Un-MW:165
The Retreat. C. Cotton. Rv-CB:397
Set Me Whereas the Sun. H. Howard.
Al-VBP:79, Rv-CB:98
Silly Sweetheart. De-CH:327
Songs, III. Tr-US II:166
To Anthea, Who May Command Him
Anything. R. Herrick.
Al-VBP:335, Gr-CC:19, Pa-GTB:79,
Rv-CB:334, Un-MW:20
To Lucasta, on Going to the Wars.
R. Lovelace. Al-VBP:446,
Er-FA:116, Ga-FB:194, Gr-BT:99,
Ke-TF:100, Ma-YA:101, Mc-WS:103,
No-CL:191, Pa-GTB:72, Rv-CB:392,
Un-MW:153
Valentine Promise. Co-PS:39,
Un-MW:129
Volpone. B. Jonson. Al-VBP:240
Whenas the Rye. G. Peele.
Al-VBP:136, Rv-CB:175, Sm-LG:55
Whistle an' I'll Come. R. Burns.
Al-VBP:651, Co-BL:99,
Hi-WP I:41, Un-MW:188
LOVE - PROOF: see also
HUMOR - LOVE-PROOF
Aire & Angells. J. Donne.
Ho-P:283
Dance Song. Tr-US II:304
Jig. C. Day Lewis. Co-PI:36,
Hi-WP II:110
Love Songs (I Wish I Could Die).
Tr-US I:129
Lovers' Tasks. Gr-EC:218,
Rv-CB:446
Love's Philosophy. P. Shelley.
Co-BL:40, Ga-FB:52, Hi-WP II:55,
Pa-GTB:185, Un-MW:189
She Tells Her Love. R. Graves.
Hi-WP II:110
Songs and Dance Songs, VI.
Tr-US II:153
Villanelle of Marguerites.
E. Dowson. Un-MB:150
LOVE - PURSUIT: see also
HUMOR - LOVE-PURSUIT
The Afternoon Roads. J. Jimenez.
Le-SW:59
Albatross. J. Collins. Mo-GR:37

LOVE - PURSUIT — cont'd.
All for Love. G. Byron.
    Ma-YA:174, Pa-GTB:173
Astrophel and Stella, Sonnet I.
    P. Sidney. Al-VBP:125,
    Ma-YA:61, Rv-CB:169
Bitter Cold. Rx-LT:16
Bold O'Donahue. Co-RM:122
The Brown Dwarf of Rügen.
    J. Whittier. Co-PM:171
The Call. J. Hall. Al-VBP:471
The Chase. W. Rowley.
    De-CH:356, Gr-CT:276, Re-TW:49
The Choice. W. Letts. Co-PI:95
Circus Hand. P. Dehn. Sm-MK:164
Come Down, O Maid. A. Tennyson.
    Al-VBP:860, Go-BP:124, Ox-BN:488,
    Rv-CB:798
Come Hither, My Dear One.
    J. Clare. Co-BL:85
Come, It Is Late in the Day.
    Do-CH:(31)
Dance Songs, III. Tr-US II:141
The Doves of My Eyes.
    G. Mohanty. Al-PI:138
The Enchantment. T. Otway.
    Al-VBP:506
The False Lover. Ox-BB:277
Folk Song from Fukushima.
    Ma-FW:151
The Green Autumn Stubble. Pa-SG:55
Hawicks Crossing. J. Stuart.
    De-FS:193
I Know where I'm Going.
    Al-VBP:1122, Gr-CC:14, Gr-GB:117,
    Un-MW:189
I Sought You. J. Wheelock.
    Co-BL:35
I Stopped in Front of You.
    L. Blaga. Mc-AC:71
In Youth Is Pleasure. R. Wever.
    Rv-CB:143
Inner Temple Masque. W. Browne.
    Al-VBP:321, Gr-CT:205
Jock o' Hazeldean. W. Scott.
    De-TT:109, Pa-GTB:183
Journeying to His Sweetheart.
    No-CL:265
Juliana. Co-BL:41
Jungle Songs, III. Tr-US II:158
A Kiss in the Morning Early.
    Gr-GB:126
Love in a Life. R. Browning.
    Ox-BN:543, Rv-CB:815
Love Me, Love My Dog.
    I. Crawford. Do-WH:30
Ma Canny Hinny. Gr-GB:155
Meeting at Night. R. Browning.
    Hi-WP II:59
Persuasions to Love. T. Carew.
    Al-VBP:348

Pining for Love. F. Beaumont.
    Co-BL:37, Co-PU:147
Quest. N. Madgett. Ra-BP:194
The Question. F. Prince.
    Pa-GTB:528
St. Valentine's Day. W. Blunt.
    Al-VBP:1054
A Serenade. W. Scott. De-CH:312,
    Pa-GTB:186
Several Girls' Songs. Do-CH:(30)
The Shepherd's Dochter. Ox-BB:263
A Song of Marco Polo.
    T. Garrison. Ke-TF:119
The Song of Wandering Aengus.
    W. Yeats. Ar-TP3:161, Bl-OB:91,
    Bo-GJ:142, Co-BL:165, Co-PM:196,
    De-CH:280, Gr-SS:46, Ha-LO:52,
    Ha-PO:180, Ho-LP:14, Ma-YA:230,
    Mc-WK:7, Mc-WS:33, No-CL:68,
    Re-TW:28, Sm-LG:226, Sm-MK:30,
    Th-AS:200, Un-GT:127, Un-MB:108
Songs, I, II, III.
    Tr-US II:165, 166
Sonnet 143. W. Shakespeare.
    Rv-CB:251
Sonnets LXX. E. Spenser.
    Al-VBP:98, Gr-CT:52
The Splendor Falls on Castle Walls.
    A. Tennyson. Al-VBP:858,
    Ar-TP3:217, Bo-GJ:139, Co-RG:145,
    De-CH:113, De-TT:196, Fe-FP:373,
    Ga-FB:11, Gr-CT:444, Hi-WP I:106,
    Ho-WR:162, Hu-MP:95, Mc-PR:65,
    Ox-BN:485, Pl-US:26, Re-TW:72,
    Rv-CB:791, Sm-LG:39
Spring Night. S. Teasdale.
    Co-BL:38, Un-MA:264
Stop Playing. Z. Shneour.
    Me-PH:85
Tell Him. C. Bialik. Pa-SG:52
Three Shadows. D. Rossetti.
    Al-VBP:986
To Cupid. J. Suckling. Rv-CB:380
To Fanny. J. Keats. No-CL:155,
    Un-MW:81
To Kate, Skating Better than Her
    Date. D. Daiches. Co-FB:402,
    Mo-SD:150
To Phyllis. T. Lodge. Al-VBP:134
Two Figures in Dense Violet Night.
    W. Stevens. No-CL:244, Un-MA:248
Venus and Cupid. M. Boyd.
    Ho-P:147
LOVE, REJECTED: see also
    HUMOR - LOVE, REJECTED
The Apparition. J. Donne.
    Al-VBP:250, Rv-CB:302
The Appeal. E. Brontë. Go-BP:149,
    Ox-BN:599
An Apple Gathering. C. Rossetti.
    Co-BL:42, Gr-CC:25, Ox-BN:707

As You Leave Me.   E. Knight.
   Be-MA:41
Away, Delights.   J. Fletcher.
   Al-VBP:284
A Broken Appointment.   T. Hardy.
   Rv-CB:940
Brown Is My Love.   Rv-CB:110
The Cap and Bells.   W. Yeats.
   Gr-CT:71, Ma-FW:154, Pa-OM:260,
   Un-MB:110
Cock Robin.   De-TT:40, Ir-BB:24,
   Rv-ON:112
Composed in Spring.   R. Burns.
   Co-BN:141, Rv-CB:621
A Deep-Sworn Vow.   W. Yeats.
   Co-EL:8
Discovery.   C. Link.   Ke-TF:120
Eleventh Song.   P. Sidney.
   Al-VBP:127, No-CL:170
The False Lover.   Ox-BB:277
Farewell, Ungrateful Traitor.
   J. Dryden.   Al-VBP:483,
   Rv-CB:462
Follow Your Saint, Follow with
   Accents Sweet.   T. Campion.
   Al-VBP:213, No-CL:40, Rv-CB:269,
   Un-MW:177
The Gardener.   Rv-CB:48
The Gardener.   Gr-GB:112
Gift to a Jade.   A. Wickham.
   Co-EL:135
The Girl I Left Behind Me.
   Er-FA:129
Girl's Song: Refusing a Lover.
   Tr-US I:166
Glenlogie.   Ma-BB:120
The Glove.   J. von Schiller.
   Sp-OG:138
Go 'Way from My Window.   Ab-MO:51
Greensleeves.   No-CL:99, Rv-CB:106,
   Sm-LG:353
The Happy Shepherd.   No-CL:99
Harpalus' Complaint.   Al-VBP:67
I Asked for Peace.   D. Dolben.
   Go-BP:180
I Do Confess Thou Art Sae Fair.
   R. Burns.   Rv-CB:622
I Laid Me Down upon a Bank.
   W. Blake.   Al-VBP:619, Rv-CB:597
I Loved Thee Once.   R. Aytoun.
   Al-VBP:224
I Loved You Once.   D. Randall.
   Bo-AN:122
Importune Me No More.   Elizabeth I,
   Queen of England.   Hi-FO:139,
   Rv-CB:146
In Faith Methinks It Is No Right.
   T. Wyatt.   Rv-CB:94
John Gorham.   E. Robinson.
   Un-MA:124

The Juniper Tree.   W. Watson.
   Co-BL:162, Do-WH:36
The King of China's Daughter.
   E. Sitwell.   De-CH:186,
   Ir-BB:258, Ma-FW:185, Pa-RE:23,
   Un-MB:331
Ko-Ko's Song.   W. Gilbert.
   Er-FA:438
A Leave-Taking.   A. Swinburne.
   Al-VBP:1021, De-CH:340, Fe-PL:119,
   Ox-BN:795
Lightning.   D. Lawrence.   Un-MB:286
Literary Love.   H. Kemp.   Bo-HF:170
Love-in-Idleness.   T. Beddoes.
   Al-VBP:809
Love Rejected.   L. Clifton.
   Ra-BP:250
Love Song.   Da-SC:51
Love Song.   Tr-US II:227
Love's Epitaph.   W. Cavendish.
   Rv-CB:349
Love's Labour Lost.   R. Tofte.
   No-CL:143
Lyke as a Ship That Through the
   Ocean Wyde.   E. Spenser.
   Ma-YA:55
The Maid of Neidpath.   W. Scott.
   Pa-GTB:196
Menominee Love Songs.   Da-SC:151
Merciless Beauty.   G. Chaucer.
   No-CL:148, Rv-CB:59
A Miner Coming Home One Night.
   Gr-GB:134
Modern Love VI, XII.   G. Meredith.
   Al-VBP:982
My Lute, Awake!   T. Wyatt.
   Al-VBP:77, Rv-CB:80
My True Love.   I. Eastwick.
   Br-SS:121
Never Seek to Tell Thy Love.
   W. Blake.   Al-VBP:619,
   Co-BL:137, Er-FA:116, Ga-FB:46,
   Ha-PO:177, No-CL:146, Ox-BN:25,
   Rv-CB:595, Un-MW:23
The New Mistress.   A. Housman.
   Un-MB:103
The Nymph's Reply to the Shepherd.
   W. Raleigh.   Al-VBP:169,
   Ha-PO:160, No-CL:101, Rv-CB:150
O My Bonny, Bonny May.   Gr-GB:103
Oh, See How Thick the Goldcup
   Flowers.   A. Housman.   Co-BL:153,
   Ga-FB:72, Ke-TF:94, No-CL:129,
   Un-MB:96, Un-MW:56
Pity Me Not.   E. Millay.   Un-MA:445
Point of No Return.   M. Evans.
   Hu-NN:19
Rondelay.   J. Dryden.   Al-VBP:479
The Seeds of Love.   De-TT:19,
   Gr-GB:137, Ho-WR:59, Rv-CB:428,
   Sm-LG:349

LOVE, REJECTED — cont'd.
  Send Back My Heart. J. Suckling.
    Al-VBP:422, Un-MW:132
  Shackley-Hay. Gr-GB:119
  The Siege. J. Suckling.
    Al-VBP:416
  The Skein. C. Kizer. Ca-VT:543
  Song. W. Davenant. Al-VBP:384
  Song. P. MacDonogh. Co-PI:110
  Song of a Girl Whose Lover Has
    Married Another Woman.
    Tr-US II:195
  Song of Rejection. Tr-US II:263
  Sonnet 5. M. Drayton. Al-VBP:167
  Sonnet. Lord Herbert. Al-VBP:294
  Sonnet 33. W. Shakespeare.
    Al-VBP:201, Er-FA:262, Rv-CB:215
  Souvenirs. D. Randall. Ra-BP:148
  Speaking Twice. E. Jean-Baptiste.
    Sa-B:141
  There Gowans Are Gay. Gr-GB:97
  There Was Never Nothing More Me
    Pained. T. Wyatt. Rv-CB:77
  To a Persistent Phantom.
    F. Horne. Bo-AN:50
  To Myra. F. Greville. Al-VBP:123
  To Phyllis, the Fair Shepherdess.
    T. Lodge. Al-VBP:133
  The Triumph of Time.
    A. Swinburne. Al-VBP:1017
  Twice. C. Rossetti.
    Al-VBP:999, Ox-BN:714
  The Two Magicians. Gr-CT:68
  When Thou Must Home. Propertius.
    Al-VBP:218, Gr-CC:78, Gr-CT:73,
    Ha-PO:170, Rv-CB:270
  Where Shall the Lover Rest.
    W. Scott. Al-VBP:670,
    De-CH:263, Pa-GTB:191
  Who Hath Heard of Such Cruelty
    Before? T. Wyatt. Rv-CB:78
  The Wraggle Taggle Gipsies.
    Ar-TP3:15, De-CH:75, Fe-FP:509,
    Ho-WR:48, Hu-MP:155, Mc-WS:163,
    Na-EO:33, Re-TW:124, Rv-CB:436,
    Un-GT:96
  Ye Banks and Braes. R. Burns.
    Al-VBP:648, Co-BL:141, De-CH:47,
    Hi-WP II:103, Pa-GTB:131,
    Rv-CB:615
LOVE - RENUNCIATION: see also
    HUMOR - LOVE-RENUNCIATION
  A Denial. E. Browning. Ox-BN:467
  Farewell! Thou Art Too Dear for
    My Possessing. W. Shakespeare.
    Al-VBP:205, No-CL:86, Pa-GTB:19,
    Un-MW:183
  Ffarewell Love and All Thy Lawes
    for Ever. T. Wyatt. Ma-YA:52
  For This Is Wisdom. L. Hope.
    Fe-PL:305

  Forget Her. Wen I-to. Hs-TC:56
  It May Not Always Be So.
    E. Cummings. Ga-FB:83
  Lancelot. E. Robinson. Sm-PT:178
  Let Be at Last. E. Dowson.
    Ha-PO:155
  The Lost Mistress. R. Browning.
    Ox-BN:532, Rv-CB:818, Un-MW:113
  My Days of Love Are Over.
    G. Byron. Ox-BN:257
  Odes to Nea, I. T. Moore.
    Ox-BN:205
  Renouncement. A. Meynell.
    Al-VBP:1067, Co-BL:41, Go-BP:167,
    Ox-BN:881, Un-MB:65, Un-MW:139
  Sonnet 134. W. Shakespeare.
    Rv-CB:249
  Verses Written During the War,
    1756-1763. T. Mordaunt.
    Rv-CB:544
LOVE - RIVALRY: see also
    HUMOR - LOVE-RIVALRY
  Bill and Parson Sim. Fi-BG:199
  Hey, Wully Wine. De-CH:330
  Katherine Jaffray. Ox-BB:300
  Katherine Johnstone. Ma-BB:232
  The Landskip. W. Shenstone.
    Rv-CB:529
  A Light Woman. R. Browning.
    No-CL:240
  Lord Livingston. Ox-BB:206
  Lord Thomas and Fair Eleanor.
    Ma-FW:151
  Love Song. Be-AP:51
  The Madman Goes to a Party.
    D. Lourie. Sc-TN:153
  The Man on the Flying Trapeze.
    Co-PT:198, Er-FA:448, Sm-LG:357
  Man's Song. Tr-US I:212
  Poem. L. Cohen. Co-EL:19
  The Reconciliation. Horace.
    Un-MW:30
  The Riddling Knight. Gr-CC:165,
    Sm-LG:285
  Song. W. Walsh. Al-VBP:511
  Sonnet 42. W. Shakespeare.
    Rv-CB:221
  Sonnet 144. W. Shakespeare.
    Rv-CB:252
  The Wandering Gadling. T. Wyatt.
    Rv-CB:79
LOVE - SACRIFICES
  King Henry. Ox-BB:64
LOVE, SECRET
  At Twilight. Tr-CB:37, Tr-US I:41
  Because I Breathe Not Love to
    Every One. P. Sidney. Gr-BT:55
  Cherrylog Road. J. Dickey.
    Br-TC:90, Ha-TP:65
  The Eve of St. Agnes. J. Keats.
    Al-VBP:781, Fe-PL:35, Ox-BN:338

Fear Not, Dear Love. T. Carew.
   Un-MW:152
The Ghost. J. Wright. De-FS:223
Girl's Song. M. Zaturenska.
   Ha-TP:59
His Wife. Rachel. Me-PH:88
How Shall I Get Inside the Door.
   Un-R:97
Love Song (I Passed). Ab-MO:23,
   Lo-TY:30
Love Song (If I Beat). Tr-CB:16,
   Tr-US I:45
Love Songs (If I Might).
   Tr-US I:114
A Lovely Love. G. Brooks.
   Ra-BP:167
Menominee Love Songs. Da-SC:151
My Star. R. Browning. Fe-FP:266,
   Na-EO:156, Sp-OG:346
A Nymph's Passion. B. Jonson.
   No-CL:142
Once. W. de la Mare. Go-BP:170
Ono Yo Yoshiki. Kokin Shü.
   Ho-LP:4, Pa-SG:35
People Hide Their Love. Wu-Ti.
   Pa-SG:46
Secret Love. J. Clare. Ga-FB:56,
   Hi-WP II:56, No-CL:147,
   Ox-BN:333, Rv-CB:730
She Never Told Her Love.
   W. Shakespeare. Un-MW:73
She Was a Pretty Little Girl.
   R. de Ayada. Fe-FP:473
Silence. A. Wickham. Co-BL:28
The Silent Lover. W. Raleigh.
   Al-VBP:93
Song. R. Browning. Al-VBP:883
Songs and Dance Songs, V.
   Tr-US II:153
Sonnets, xx. M. Van Doren.
   Sm-PT:67
The Spinning Wheel. J. Waller.
   Co-BL:152, Co-PI:192, Gr-CT:405,
   Ha-PO:196
The Whisperer. M. Van Doren.
   Un-MA:465
Ye Little Birds. . . . Al-VBP:359
LOVE - TRAGEDY: see also
   HUMOR - LOVE-TRAGEDY;
   LOVE - DEATH
Aghadoe. J. Todhunter.
   Co-BL:168, Co-PI:189
Annie of Lochroyan. Ma-BB:202
As I Walked Out One Night.
   De-CH:596
At the Setting of the Sun.
   Rv-CB:440
Auld Robin Gray. A. Lindsay.
   Al-VBP:603, De-CH:344, Pa-GTB:152
Babylon. Ma-BB:143, Ox-BB:199

Balade. G. Chaucer. Gr-CT:58
Ballad. J. Gay. Al-VBP:522
Ballad. W. Soutar. Hi-WP I:89
Ballad of Another Ophelia.
   D. Lawrence. Gr-CT:79
The Ballad of Chocolate Mabbie.
   G. Brooks. Pe-SS:30
The Ballad of Reading Gaol.
   O. Wilde. Ox-BN:896
Barbara Allen. Al-VBP:55,
   Er-FA:315, Mc-PR:156, Rv-CB:434,
   Un-MW:112
La Belle Dame sans Merci. J. Keats.
   Al-VBP:779, Bo-GJ:163, Bo-HF:22,
   De-CH:121, De-TT:200, Er-FA:409,
   Gr-CT:178, Gr-SS:108, Ha-PO:6,
   Hi-WP II:106, Ho-P:80, Mc-WK:8,
   Ni-JP:98, No-CL:65, Ox-BN:376,
   Pa-GTB:193, Rv-CB:735, Sm-LG:217,
   Sm-MK:46, Sp-OG:113, Un-GT:126
Bonnie Annie Livieston.
   Ox-BB:254
Bonnie George Campbell.
   Al-VBP:54, De-CH:41, Fo-OG:20,
   Gr-GB:250, Ox-BB:341, Rv-CB:419
Bonny Barbara Allan. De-CH:338,
   Ox-BB:353
The Bonny Brown Girl. Ox-BB:355
The Bonny Earl of Livingston.
   Ox-BB:309
The Braes of Yarrow. Ox-BB:590
The Cap and Bells. W. Yeats.
   Gr-CT:71, Ma-FW:154, Pa-OM:260
Clark Sanders. Ox-BB:76, Rv-CB:34
Clyde's Waters. Ox-BB:331
Compensation. P. Dunbar.
   Bo-AN:5, Hu-PN:290, Ra-BP:56
The Confessional (Spain).
   R. Browning. Al-VBP:885
Crazy Jane and the Bishop.
   W. Yeats. Wi-LT:88
The Cruel Brother. Ma-YA:38,
   Ox-BB:236
The Death of Lord Warriston.
   Ox-BB:603
The Demon Lover. Co-PM:201,
   Fo-OG:44, Ma-BB:188, Ma-FW:199,
   Ox-BB:83, Rv-CB:45
A Development of Idiocy.
   E. Jones. Ox-BN:619
The Douglas Tragedy. Ox-BB:118,
   Un-MW:109
Down by the Salley Gardens.
   W. Yeats. Co-BL:140, Un-MB:111
The Drowned Lady. Gr-CT:139
Duriesdyke. Ox-BB:686
Dusky Woods. P. Quinault.
   Un-R:129
Fair Helen. Al-VBP:53, De-CH:418,
   Er-FA:338, Hi-WP I:16,
   Pa-GTB:89, Rv-CB:43

LOVE - TRAGEDY — <u>cont'd</u>.
  Fair Isabell of Rochroyall.
    Ox-BB:144
  Fair Janet.   Ox-BB:173
  Fair Margaret and Sweet William.
    Ox-BB:231
  The Farewell.   R. Burns.
    Al-VBP:377, De-CH:175
  The Farmer's Wife.   A. Sexton.
    Wi-LT:816
  The Fire of Frendraught.
    Ox-BB:610
  For Her Love I Cark and Care.
    Rv-CB:118
  Frankie and Johnnie.   Er-FA:402
  Ginevra.   S. Rogers.   Fe-PL:13
  Girl's Song from a Legend.
    Da-SC:153, Tr-US II:221
  Glasgerion.   Ox-BB:123
  Gold Wings Across the Sea.
    W. Morris.   Gr-CT:74, Ox-BN:774
  Green Woods.   E. Coatsworth.
    De-FS:52
  The Griesly Wife.   J. Manifold.
    Ca-MB:25, Un-MB:513
  Harpalus' Complaint.   Al-VBP:67
  The Haystack in the Floods.
    W. Morris.   Ni-JP:41, Ox-BN:779
  Here Lies Juliet.   W. Shakespeare.
    Er-FA:127
  The High Tide on the Coast of
    Lincolnshire.   J. Ingelow.
    De-TT:183, Pa-OM:118, Sp-OG:85
  The Highwayman.   A. Noyes.
    Ar-TP3:24, Co-BL:155, Er-FA:343,
    Fe-FP:449, Fe-PL:16, Un-GT:131
  I Cannot Live with You.
    E. Dickinson.   Rv-CB:923,
    Sh-AP:129, Un-MA:96, Un-MW:87
  Improvised Songs.   Tr-US II:182
  In Mourning for His Dead Wife.
    P'an Yueh.   Rx-LT:31
  Isabel.   Do-WH:32
  Isabella or The Pot of Basil.
    J. Keats.   Al-VBP:783
  June.   A. Levy.   Un-MW:95
  Kayak Song in Dialogue. Da-SC:38,
    Le-IB:88, Tr-US I:6
  Killed at the Ford.
    H. Longfellow.   Sp-OG:194
  Lady Maisry.   Ox-BB:295
  The Lady of Shalott. A. Tennyson.
    Er-FA:339, Hi-WP I:59,
    Ho-WR:145, Sp-OG:128
  The Lament of the Border Widow.
    De-CH:419, Gr-GB:246, Ox-BB:525
  The Little Moppet.   Mo-MGT:42,
    Rv-ON:88, Wr-RM:72
  The Locust Swarm.   Hsu Chao.
    Cr-WS:5, Rx-OH:123

Lord Douglas.   Ox-BB:324
Lord Livingston.   Ox-BB:206
Lord Lovel.   Co-PM:205, Fe-FP:508
Lord Randal.   Cl-FC:85, Fo-OG:7,
  Ox-BB:243, Rv-CB:37, Un-MW:108
Lord Thomas and Fair Annet.
  Ox-BB:178
Lord Thomas and Fair Eleanor.
  Ma-FW:151
Lord, What I Most Loved You Tore
  from Me.   A. Machado.   Le-SW:65
Love on the Farm.   D. Lawrence.
  Ga-FB:80, Un-MB:288, Un-MW:122
Love Song from New England.
  W. Welles.   Un-MW:101
Love Songs, II, IV.   Tr-US II:225
Love Songs (I Wish I Could Put).
  Tr-US I:126
Lowlands.   Gr-CT:229
The Lowlands o' Holland. De-CH:345,
  Fo-OG:51, Ox-BB:348
Luke Havergal.   E. Robinson.
  Gr-SS:138, Sh-AP:139, Sm-PT:7,
  Un-MA:123, Wi-LT:99
Lullaby.   Tr-US II:305
The Maid of Neidpath. T. Campbell.
  Pa-GTB:197
Modern Love.   G. Meredith.
  Al-VBP:984, Ox-BN:691
Moon-Gazing.   Hsü Chih-mo.
  Hs-TC:95
My Handsome Gilderoy.   De-CH:78
My Luve's in Germany.   De-CH:172
Naarip's Wife.   E. Isac.
  Mc-AC:54
Night Song.   Tr-US II:192
Of Love.   K. Gibran.   Fe-PL:121
On One Who Died Discovering Her
  Kindness.   J. Sheffield.
  No-CL:74
Orpheus and Eurydice.   Ovid.
  Mo-GR:21
Porphyria's Lover.   R. Browning.
  Ni-JP:36, Un-MW:116
Proud of My Broken Heart.
  E. Dickinson.   Al-VBP:1002
A Quality of Pain.   B. Holender.
  Ls-NY:14
Quia Amore Langueo.   Rv-CB:14
Rare Willie Drowned in Yarrow.
  Gr-GB:133, Ox-BB:593
The Runaway Slave at Pilgrim's
  Point.   E. Browning.   Hu-PN:448
She Is Far from the Land.
  T. Moore.   Ox-BN:212
She Dwelt among the Untrodden
  Ways.   W. Wordsworth. Al-VBP:656,
  Ga-FB:50, Li-SR:106, Mc-PR:179,
  Ox-BN:62, Pa-GTB:179, Rv-CB:631
Sir Olaf.   J. von Herder.
  Co-PM:97, Sp-OG:108

Song for a Dark Girl. L. Hughes.
   Ad-PB:73
Sonnet 133. W. Shakespeare.
   Rv-CB:248
Sonnets, xxv. E. Millay. Sm-PT:32
This Is a Coward's World.
   Hsü Chih-mo. Hs-TC:79
A Trampwoman's Tragedy. T. Hardy.
   Ox-BN:825
The True Lover. A. Housman.
   Un-MW:121
The Trumpeter of Fyvie. Ox-BB:349
Twickenham Gardens. J. Donne.
   Rv-CB:297
Two Guests from Alabama.
   W. Whitman. Rd-OA:27
A Valediction of Weeping.
   J. Donne. Rv-CB:298
Villikins and His Dinah.
   S. Cowell. Co-PT:184
Waltz. R. Sherry. De-FS:176
A Weary Song to a Slow Sad Tune.
   Li Ch'ing Chao. Rx-LT:91
Willie and Lady Margerie.
   Ox-BB:121
A Woman Mourns for Her Husband.
   Kr-OF:20
The Young Cordwainer. R. Graves.
   Ca-MB:30
Young Johnstone. Ox-BB:212
Younge Andrew. Ox-BB:216
See also Em-AF:128-152
LOVE - UNIVERSALITY
Beasts. P. Engle. En-PC:92
The Contemplative.
   Sister M. Thérése. Tr-MR:210
Fellow-Creatures. R. Pitter.
   Ls-NY:106
The Lay of the Last Minstrel.
   W. Scott. Al-VBP:670
Love Lives Beyond. J. Clare.
   Gr-CT:56, Ox-BN:329
Love Poem. K. Raine. Un-MB:485
Most Men Know Love But as a Part
   of Life. H. Timrod. Sh-AP:125
Out of Wisdom Has Come Love.
   E. Robinson. Tr-MR:162
The Rime of the Ancient Mariner.
   S. Coleridge. Al-VBP:679,
   Bo-FP:301, Co-RG:60, Co-SS:131,
   De-CH:364, Er-FA:318, Fe-FP:147,
   Ga-FB:105, Gr-TG:61, Ha-PO:15,
   Hi-WP II:68, Ma-YA:146, Ni-JP:52,
   Ox-BN:139, Rv-CB:658, Sm-LG:312,
   Un-GT:30
The Self-Slaved. P. Kavanagh.
   Un-MB:430
The Song of the Good Samaritan.
   V. Watkins. Wi-LT:450
Sonnets, i. E. Wylie. Sm-PT:69

LOVE, UNREQUITED: see also
   HUMOR - LOVE, UNREQUITED
All Seasons in One. Un-MW:31
The Bailiff's Daughter of
   Islington. Ox-BB:342, Sh-RP:250,
   Un-GT:114
Ballad. G. Mistral. Be-UL:31
Bricklayer Love. C. Sandburg.
   Sh-AP:157
A Faithful Wife. Chang Chi.
   Rx-LT:82
The False Lover. Ox-BB:277
Freezing Night. T'ao Hung Ching.
   Rx-LT:38
Greensleeves. C. Robinson.
   Un-MW:74
Impossibilities to His Friend.
   R. Herrick. Gr-SS:147
Keith of Ravelston. S. Dobell.
   De-CH:299, De-TT:189, Ox-BN:661
The Lady of Shalott.
   A. Tennyson. Er-FA:339,
   Hi-WP I:59, Ho-WR:145, Sp-OG:128
The Love-Talker. E. Carbery.
   Co-PI:20, De-CH:296, Ha-PO:192
Love Without Hope. R. Graves.
   Co-BL:38, Co-EL:18, Co-PU:146,
   Gr-CT:71, Gr-SS:99, Pa-GTB:486
The Mask. C. Delaney. Hu-PN:177
The Merryman Sings. W. Gilbert.
   Gr-EC:226
The Mirage. O. Williams.
   Wi-LT:413
The Mirror Perilous. A. Dugan.
   Br-TC:97, Wi-LT:691
My Silks and Fine Array.
   W. Blake. Gr-CT:80, No-CL:200,
   Ox-BN:19, Rv-CB:562
No Single Hour Can Stand for
   Naught. J. Clare. Ox-BN:328
Pierrot. S. Teasdale. Co-BL:100
Pretty Polly. B. Reece.
   Co-BL:150
A Pretty Wench. Mo-MGT:202
Rosaline. T. Lodge. Pa-GTB:10
Sad Songs, I. Tr-US II:174
Sometimes with One I Love.
   W. Whitman. Rv-CB:849
Song (I Went). A. O'Shaughnessy.
   Ox-BN:850
Song (Here's a Twig).
   Tr-US II:168
Song from the Bride of Smithfield.
   S. Warner. Un-MB:374
The Song of Love and Death.
   A. Tennyson. Ox-BN:510
Spring. W. Allingham. Ox-BN:673
Stanzas from "Child Harold."
   J. Clare. Ox-BN:325
Thou Art to All Lost Love the
   Best. R. Herrick. De-CH:693

LOVE, UNREQUITED — cont'd.
  Titus and Berenice.
    J. Heath-Stubbs. Pa-GTB:553
  Too Late. P. Marston. Ox-BN:887
  Ungathered Love. P. Marston.
    Ox-BN:890
  La Vie C'Est la Vie. J. Fauset.
    Hu-PN:67
  With How Sad Steps, O Moon.
    P. Sidney. Al-VBP:126, Co-BN:121,
    De-CH:442, Gr-CT:71, Un-MW:72
  Women's Song. Tr-US I:213
LOVE - WARNINGS
  As I Walked Out One Evening.
    W. Auden. Br-TC:21, Ha-PO:189,
    Un-MB:464, Wi-LT:465
  The Blossoming of Love.
    Dharmakirti. Al-PI:36
  Capsule Conclusions, I, IX.
    Un-MW:64, 65
  Generations. R. Korn. Ho-TY:304
  Hear, Ye Ladies. J. Fletcher.
    Al-VBP:278
  Hesperia. A. Swinburne.
    Ox-BN:805
  If Thou Must Love Me.
    E. Browning. Co-BL:98, Er-FA:114,
    Ke-TF:108, Ma-YA:191, Ox-BN:466,
    Un-MW:205
  Iliad. H. Wolfe. Un-MB:305
  Love Me Little, Love Me Long.
    Er-FA:112, Rv-CB:117
  The Men Are a Bad Lot.
    J. Seidl. Un-R:173
  Montrose to His Mistress.
    J. Graham. Al-VBP:424,
    Rv-CB:389
  Never Seek to Tell Thy Love.
    W. Blake. Al-VBP:619,
    Co-BL:137, Er-FA:116, Ga-FB:46,
    Ha-PO:177, No-CL:146, Ox-BN:25,
    Rv-CB:595, Un-MW:23
  No, No, Poor Suffering Heart.
    J. Dryden. Al-VBP:486
  Odes to Nea, II. T. Moore.
    Ox-BN:207
  Song of a Common Lover.
    F. Ranaivo. Gr-BT:54, Lo-TY:154
  Sonnet 95. W. Shakespeare.
    Rv-CB:236
  Sonnets 4. M. Drayton.
    Al-VBP:167
  Sweet Winds of Love.
    P. Irving. Al-WW:77
  To My Infant Daughter.
    Y. Winters. Ca-VT:226
  To One on Her Waste of Time.
    W. Blunt. Al-VBP:1055
  Water Music. L. Durrell.
    Ha-TP:60

LOVE, WEDDED: see also MARRIAGE
  All Things Come Alike to All.
    Bible. O.T.   Ecclesiastes.
    Me-PH:32
  The Anniversary. J. Donne.
    Rv-CB:296
  Any Wife to Any Husband.
    R. Browning. Ox-BN:535
  Aubade. K. Shapiro. Ca-VT:376
  Choice. J. Cunningham. Ca-VT:324
  Crystal Anniversary. P. Appleman.
    Un-MW:148
  A Dialogue of Watching.
    K. Rexroth. Pe-M:145
  Down the Mountain My Husband.
    F. Garcia Lorca. Le-SW:59
  Drafted. Su Wu. Rx-LT:6
  The Eastern Gate. Le-MW:120,
    Ma-FW:88
  Elisa, or An Elegy upon the
    Unripe Decease of Sir Antony
    Irby. P. Fletcher. Al-VBP:291
  Eulalie. E. Poe. Na-EO:140
  Evening. N. Young. Ke-TF:130
  The First Essential.
    I. Georghe. Mc-AC:152
  Her Birthday. Feng Yen-Chi.
    Le-MW:112
  His Wife's Wedding Ring.
    G. Crabbe. Rv-CB:560
  The Housewife. B. Amma.
    Al-PI:126
  A Husband's Song. Bi-IT:83
  Hynd Etin. Ma-BB:192
  I Have Taken the Woman of Beauty.
    Ho-SD:62
  I'd Rather Spend My Life Quietly.
    Tai Wang-shu. Hs-TC:180
  John Anderson, My Jo. R. Burns.
    Al-VBP:646, Ga-FB:47, Ha-PO:176,
    Pa-GTB:157, Rv-CB:619, Sp-OG:276
  The Land o' the Leal. Lady Nairn.
    Pa-GTB:157
  Legend. T. Aida. Sh-AM:110
  A Letter to Her Husband, Absent
    upon Publick Employment.
    A. Bradstreet. Rv-CB:386,
    Sh-AP:11
  A Line-Storm Song. R. Frost.
    Gr-CC:184, Pe-OA:43
  Love Song: I and Thou.
    A. Dugan. Gr-BT:139
  Love Songs, II. Tr-US II:171
  Love's Matrimony. W. Cavendish.
    Go-BP:140
  The Married Lover. C. Patmore.
    Un-MW:93
  A Mother to Her First-Born.
    Tr-CB:27, Tr-US I:105
  My Love. Wr-RM:75

Nightgown, Wife's Gown. R. Sward.
    Co-EL:9
Now Older Grown. M. Caruthers.
    Ke-TF:132
The Old Cloak. Ma-BB:226
Plum Wine. K. Takamura. Sh-AM:44
Reuben Bright. E. Robinson.
    Co-RM:233, Sh-AP:141, Un-MA:119
The River Merchant's Wife:
    A Letter. Li T'ai-Po.
    Bo-HF:120, Br-TC:332, Co-BL:101,
    Gr-CC:22, Ha-PO:184, Li-TU:181,
    Mo-BG:98, Pe-SS:126, Sh-AP:171,
    Un-MA:290
The Sailor's Wife. W. Mickle.
    De-TT:110, Pa-GTB:154
Salvage. E. Lieberman. Ke-TF:133
Seven Times Three - Love.
    J. Ingelow. Fe-PL:103
She Will Weep. Br-FW:21
Sinfonia Domestica.
    J. Untermeyer. Un-MA:333
Somewhere in Tuscany.
    D. Holbrook. Ls-NY:13
Song. Le-OE:84, Tr-US II:179
Song. Tr-US II:176
Song of an Old Man about His
    Wife. Le-IB:105
Song to the Wife of His Youth.
    N. Alterman. Me-PH:109
Sonnet on the Death of His Wife.
    J. Masefield. Go-BP:150
To My Dear and Loving Husband.
    A. Bradstreet. Fe-PL:148,
    Rv-CB:385, Sh-AP:11
To My Wife. E. Breck. Gr-BT:92
To My Wife. P. Firth. Go-BP:141
Tonight. Z. Landau. Ho-TY:98
Unfinished History. A. MacLeish.
    Ca-VT:163
Washing the Dishes. C. Morley.
    Fe-PL:143
Wasn't It You?
    K. Narasimhaswamy. Al-PI:125
The Way. R. Creeley. Wi-LT:679
Wedding Morn. D. Lawrence.
    Un-MB:290
The Wife. D. Levertov. Un-MW:147
A Wife. H. Van Dyke. Ke-TF:134
A Young Wife. D. Lawrence.
    Un-MB:287
LOVE, YOUNG
Ah, How Sweet It Is to Love.
    J. Dryden. Al-VBP:481
Aphrodite Metropolis. K. Fearing.
    Ad-CI:74
Come Night, Come Romeo.
    W. Shakespeare. Co-BL:103
The Corner of the Field.
    F. Cornford. Co-BL:123, Co-EL:8

Dear, Do Not Your Fair Beauty
    Wrong. T. May. Al-VBP:346
The Hill. R. Brooke. Al-VBP:1178,
    Co-BL:165, Hi-WP II:109,
    Un-MB:322, Un-MW:171
Kite Poem. J. Merrill. Br-TC:285
Let Not Us. Rv-CB:4
Love in the Valley. G. Meredith.
    Al-VBP:976
The Magnet. R. Stone. Un-MA:655
My Love, She's But a Lassie Yet.
    R. Burns. Al-VBP:647
Peggy. A. Ramsay. Al-VBP:526
The Picnic. J. Logan. Co-BL:24,
    Du-SH:62
Picnic to the Earth.
    S. Tanikawa. Sh-AM:132
Seen Through the Trees Behind
    Which You're Walking.
    B. Patten. Gr-BT:57
Sonnets XX. J. Agee. Un-MA:605
Spring Reminiscence. C. Cullen.
    Bo-HF:47
To Ethelinda. C. Smart.
    No-CL:190
Twice Shy. S. Heaney. Br-TC:174
Wisdom. F. Yerby. Bo-AN:136
Y Is for Youth. W. Davies.
    Go-BP:145
Young Love. T. Garrison.
    Co-PL:99
Young Love. S. Teasdale.
    Co-BL:23
LOVE AND HATE
Girls' Song at a Wedding.
    Tr-US I:128
I Murder Hate by Field or Flood.
    R. Burns. Rv-CB:618
Lines to a Critic. P. Shelley.
    Rv-CB:697
Lullaby. Tr-CB:13, Tr-US I:97
My Magic Window. B. Carter.
    Me-WF:87
No Time to Hate. E. Dickinson.
    Fe-PL:107
Pins, Pins, Falling on the Ground.
    G. Thomas. Me-WF:60
Tragedy. AE. Tr-MR:220
LOVE SONGS: see also SERENADES
At Twilight. Tr-CB:37, Tr-US I:41
A Caravan Porter's Song.
    Tr-US I:96
Courting Song and Reply.
    Tr-US I:190
Dance Songs. Tr-US I:199
Dance Songs, I. Tr-US II:145
Girls' Song (Between Gesene).
    Tr-US I:44
Girl's Song (When Our Camps).
    Tr-US II:125

LOVE SONGS — cont'd.
  Juke Box Love Song. L. Hughes.
    Ad-PB:74
  Love-Charm Songs. Br-MW:99,
    Da-SC:152, Tr-US II:223
  Love Song. Tr-US II:220, 222, 263
  Love Song (Blessed).
    Tr-US II:52
  Love Song (Elelo). Tr-US I:190
  Love Song (I Will Walk).
    Da-SC:152, Tr-US II:223
  Love Song (If I Beat).
    Tr-CB:16, Tr-US I:45
  Love Song (There Stood).
    Tr-US II:125
  Love Song (Truly Faultless).
    Tr-US I:116
  Love Song from a Legend.
    Tr-US II:104
  Love Songs, I, II.
    Tr-US II:219
  Love Songs (I Go Walking).
    Tr-US II:24
  Modern Love Songs. F. Nuur.
    Lo-TY:59
  A Negro Love Song. P. Dunbar.
    Ab-MO:21, Hu-PN:36
  Rari. Tr-US II:94
  Song. Tr-US II:305, 306
  Songs I, II. Tr-US I:191
  Songs, II. Tr-US II:132
  Tule Love Song. Da-SC:16,
    Tr-US II:295
  Woman Song. Da-SC:111,
    Tr-US II:244
  Woman's Love Song. Tr-US II:215
LOVEBIRDS: see PARROTS
LOVEJOY, ELIJAH PARISH
  Not Unavenged! W. Burleigh.
    Kr-OF:135
LOVEMAKING: see COURTSHIP
LOVERS: see also
    HUMOR - LOVERS;
    SATIRE - LOVERS
  Anashuya and Vijaya. W. Yeats.
    Li-TU:146
  At the Edge. M. Korte. Sc-TN:116
  Balade. G. Chaucer. Gr-CT:58
  Capsule Conclusions, VIII.
    Un-MW:65
  The Corner of the Field.
    F. Cornford. Co-BL:123,
    Co-EL:8
  Dance Songs. Tr-US II:140, 145
  Doomsday Morning. G. Taggard.
    Un-MA:480
  Endymion. J. Keats. Al-VBP:790,
    Ox-BN:337
  The Expense of Spirit in a Waste
    of Shame. L. Mueller. St-H:146

Fair Ladies Tall Lovers.
    E. Cummings. Gr-SS:31
The Goose Fish. H. Nemerov.
    Wi-LT:590
Hide, Absolon. G. Chaucer.
    Rv-CB:63
Ice. S. Spender. Pa-GTB:520
In Such a Night. W. Shakespeare.
    Gr-CT:171, No-CL:180
In the Dark Pine-Wood. J. Joyce.
    Co-BL:113
It Was a Lover and His Lass.
    W. Shakespeare. Al-VBP:188,
    Bo-FP:214, De-CH:188, Ma-YA:67,
    No-CL:127, Pa-GTB:6, Rv-CB:198,
    Un-MW:4
Keepsake. V. Contoski. Sc-TN:25
Love Made Me Poet. De-CH:575
Love Song. Tr-US II:174
Love Will Find Out the Way.
    Er-FA:120, Ho-WR:242, Pa-GTB:69,
    Rv-CB:132, Sm-LG:347, Un-MW:187
The Lovers. C. Aiken. Un-MW:211
The Lovers. J. Sabines. Be-UL:103
Night Ride. H. Read. Co-BL:111,
    Hi-WP II:61
The Smith. L. Uhland. Un-R:95
Song. W. Auden. Pa-GTB:511
A Song. A. Finch. Al-VBP:510
Song of a Woman to Her Lover.
    Tr-US II:140
Song to Instruments. Tr-CB:22,
    Tr-US I:48
The Starred Coverlet. R. Graves.
    Gr-BT:77
They Were Alone Once More.
    G. Byron. Ox-BN:269
Untitled. Wang Ching-chih.
    Hs-TC:45
What Slender Youth. Horace.
    Ho-WR:185, No-CL:172
A Youth Mowing. D. Lawrence.
    Un-MB:285
LOWELL, ROBERT, 1887-1950
  Commander Lowell. R. Lowell.
    Ca-VT:451
LOYALTY: see also HUMOR -
    LOYALTY; SATIRE - LOYALTY
  All Day in Gray Rain. Basho.
    Be-CS:7
  And the Pear Trees Shiver.
    J. Sloan. De-FS:182
  Answer to Jealousy. M. Prior.
    Al-VBP:514, Un-MW:48
  Any Wife to Any Husband.
    R. Browning. Ox-BN:535
  Argus and Ulysses. E. Farjeon.
    Gr-EC:84
  As the Holly Groweth Green.
    Henry VIII. Al-VBP:66, Ma-FW:201

Auld Robin Gray.   A. Lindsay.
   Al-VBP:603, De-CH:344, Pa-GTB:152
Beth Gêlert. W. Spencer. Un-GT:138
The Bonny House of Airlie.
   Ma-BB:130, Ox-BB:614
The Boy and the Mantle.   Ox-BB:31
Bright Star. J. Keats.
   Al-VBP:794, De-CH:745, Ga-FB:54,
   Go-BP:108, Ke-TF:122, Ox-BN:382,
   Pa-GTB:197, Un-MW:122
Bristowe Tragedie. Ox-BB:656
The Broken Wedding Ring. Fi-BG:216
Choice. J. Cunningham. Ca-VT:324
Coal for Mike. B. Brecht.
   Li-TU:142
Come Loose Every Sail to the
   Breeze. Co-SS:101
The Cradle Trap. L. Simpson.
   Li-TU:174
Curfew Must Not Ring Tonight.
   R. Thorpe. Fe-FP:559
The Douglas Tragedy. Ox-BB:118,
   Un-MW:109
Edom o' Gordon. Ox-BB:598
Epitaph of a Faithful Man.
   R. Mezey. Co-EL:79
Epitaph on a Jacobite.
   T. Macaulay. Al-VBP:799,
   Cr-WS:56, De-TT:180, Ox-BN:428
Eternal Masculine. W. Benét.
   Un-MA:329
Even for the Space of a Flash.
   Ba-ST:35
Fair Annie. Ox-BB:138
A Faithful Wife. Chang Chi.
   Rx-LT:82
A Far Cry from Africa.
   D. Walcott. Lo-TY:114
Faults. S. Teasdale. Mc-PR:117
Fidelity. W. Wordsworth.
   Cl-FC:70
The Flight. S. Teasdale.
   Co-BL:23
Fragment of a Bylina.
   A. Pushkin. Li-TU:83
A Gest of Robyn Hode, the Fifth
   Fytte. Ox-BB:464
A Gest of Robyn Hode, the Seventh
   Fytte. Ox-BB:475
The Girl I Left Behind Me.
   Er-FA:129
Gluskap's Hound. T. Roberts.
   Do-WH:61
The Haystack in the Floods.
   W. Morris. Ni-JP:41, Ox-BN:779
He Thinks of Those Who Have Spoken
   Evil of His Beloved. W. Yeats.
   Co-EL:37, Co-PI:206, No-CL:4
Hector the Dog. K. Barnes.
   Co-BBW:110

The House Dog's Grave. R. Jeffers.
   Co-BBW:108
Hynd Horn.   Ma-BB:229, Ox-BB:112
I Sing of Lienta. Cheng Min.
   Hs-TC:236
An Introduction to Dogs. O. Nash.
   Un-GT:38
The Irish Harper and His Dog.
   T. Campbell. De-CH:83, De-TT:66,
   Hu-MP:194, Rv-CB:678, Un-GT:41
The Juniper Tree. W. Watson.
   Co-BL:162, Do-WH:36
Kind and True. A. Townshend.
   Rv-CB:468
The Land o' the Leal. Lady Nairn.
   Pa-GTB:157
The Little Black Dog.
   E. Reynolds. Fe-PL:362
Little Mousgrove and the Lady Barnet.
   Ox-BB:168
Love Songs, I, II.   Tr-US II:171
The Loveliness of Love. G. Darley.
   Ox-BN:386, Pa-GTB:74
The Lover's Shirt.   Gr-BT:53
Love's Omnipresence. J. Sylvester.
   Al-VBP:158, Pa-GTB:16
Loyal. F. Ticknor. Sp-OG:18
Midnight Lamentation. H. Monro.
   Al-VBP:1140
Montrose to His Mistress. J. Graham.
   Al-VBP:424, Rv-CB:389
My Boy Tammy. H. Macneill.
   De-CH:33
The New Year's Gift to Phyllis.
   M. Prior. Rv-CB:486
Non Sum Qualis Eram Bonae sub
   Regno Cynarae. E. Dowson.
   Al-VBP:1102, Co-BL:131, Er-FA:128,
   No-CL:192, Ox-BN:941, Pa-GTB:400,
   Un-MB:148, Un-MW:97
Not Celia that I Juster Am.
   C. Sedley. Al-VBP:497,
   Pa-GTB:81, Un-MW:135
O Sweetheart, Hear You. J. Joyce.
   Un-MB:270, Un-MW:10
Ode to Some Pigeons. N. Parra.
   Be-UL:73
Old Dog Tray. S. Foster.
   Co-BBW:109
One Country. F. Stanton.
   Vi-PP:20
Our Old Family Dog. Issa.
   Be-MC:16
The Outlaw Murray. Ox-BB:363
Postscript for Gweno. A. Lewis.
   Hi-WP II:111, Pa-GTB:544
The River Merchant's Wife:
   A Letter. Li T'ai-Po. Bo-HF:120,
   Br-TC:332, Co-BL:101, Gr-CC:22,
   Ha-PO:184, Li-TU:181, Mo-BG:98,
   Pe-SS:126, Sh-AP:171, Un-MA:290

LOYALTY - cont'd.
  Safety at Forty. L. Sissman.
    Ho-P:243
  The Sailor's Wife. W. Mickle.
    Al-VBP:600, De-TT:110, Pa-GTB:154
  Shake Hands. A. Housman.
    Co-PU:146, Hi-WP I:88
  Sir Patrick Spens. Al-VBP:35,
    Ar-TP3:19, Bl-OB:47, Bo-GJ:159,
    Co-RG:58, Co-SS:129, De-CH:405,
    Ha-PO:3, Ma-BB:1, Ma-FW:46,
    Ma-YA:41, Ox-BB:311, Rv-CB:38,
    Sm-LG:307, Sp-OG:98
  Song. H. Longfellow. De-TT:91
  Sonnet 60. W. Shakespeare.
    Al-VBP:203, Er-FA:261, Gr-CT:196,
    Pa-GTB:19, Rv-CB:226
  Sonnets, xvi. E. Wylie.
    Sm-PT:71, Un-MA:281
  Soul Brother. H. Gordon.
    Ad-II:108
  The Three Ravens. Al-VBP:39,
    Fo-OG:34, Gr-CT:165, Gr-GB:245,
    Ox-BB:245
  Tim, an Irish Terrier. W. Letts.
    Co-BBW:104
  To a Lady Asking Him How Long He
    Would Love Her. G. Ethredge.
    Al-VBP:496, No-CL:196
  To His Mistress. R. Herrick.
    Al-VBP:326
  To Phyllis. T. Lodge. Al-VBP:134
  The True and Tender Wife.
    Al-PI:29
  True Friendship. Pa-SG:20
  Turn All Thy Thoughts. T. Campion.
    Al-VBP:215
  Two Guests from Alabama.
    W. Whitman. Rd-OA:27
  The Unchangeable. W. Shakespeare.
    No-CL:89, Pa-GTB:9
  Under All Change. J. Johnson.
    Tr-MR:158
  Upon the Weathercock. J. Bunyan.
    Ox-BC:37
  Vitai Lampada. H. Newbolt.
    Sp-OG:17
  Walsinghame. W. Ralegh.
    Al-VBP:73, Gr-CT:55, Ha-PO:166,
    Rv-CB:154, Sm-LG:351
  War Song. D. Parker. Cr-WS:77
  Warpath Song. Da-SC:112
  When Black People Are.
    A. Spellman. Ad-PB:284,
    Be-MA:127, Ra-BP:228
  When I Heard Dat White Man Say.
    Z. Gilbert. Ad-PB:195
  When I Peruse the Conquer'd Fame.
    W. Whitman. Co-EL:130, Co-PU:79
  Young Bekie. Ma-BB:13, Ox-BB:103

LUCIA, SANTA: see LUCY, SAINT
LUCIFER (SATAN)
  Birkett's Eagle. D. Howard.
    Ca-MB:27
  Divine Poems: 45. J. Villa.
    Tr-MR:214
  Lucifer. M. Anderson. Tr-MR:215
  Lucifer in Starlight. G. Meredith.
    Al-VBP:985, De-CH:314, Ha-PO:48,
    Ox-BN:693, Rv-CB:880
  Lucifer in the Train. A. Rich.
    Pl-EI:75
LUCK: see CHANCE
LUCKNOW, BATTLE, 1857
  The Pipes at Lucknow. J. Whittier.
    Hi-FO:241
  The Relief of Lucknow. R. Lowell.
    Co-PT:221
LUCY, SAINT: see also ST. LUCY'S DAY
  Prayer to St. Lucy.
    J. Heath-Stubbs. Go-BP:227
LUDLOW, ENG.
  The Lads in Their Hundreds.
    A. Housman. Un-MB:96
LULLABIES: see also
    SATIRE - LULLABIES
  All Through the Night. Ch-B:117,
    Fe-FP:466, Un-GT:301
  Away in a Manger. M. Luther.
    Ar-TP3:195, Bo-FP:193, Br-BC:165,
    Fe-FP:93, Gr-TG:78, Hu-MP:347,
    Ke-TF:78, La-PH:25, Mc-AW:78,
    Un-GT:301
  A Bedtime Song for Children.
    Br-MW:90
  Buckaroo Sandman. Fi-BG:219
  Bye, Baby Bunting. Mother Goose.
    Ar-TP3:131, Au-SP:5, Cl-DT:27,
    De-PO:6, Li-LB:12, Li-SR:126,
    Mo-MGT:134, Mo-NR:8, Wi-MG:16,
    Wr-RM:77
  Chinese Lullaby. Ir-BB:127
  Christmas Lullaby.
    U. Troubetzkoy. Ha-YA:157
  Come, Little Bird. Ca-MU:32
  Complaint of the Wild Goose.
    Tr-US II:135
  The Confession Stone. O. Dodson.
    Ab-MO:72, Lo-TY:238
  The Cottager to Her Infant.
    D. Wordsworth. De-CH:205,
    Ox-BC:127
  Coyote's Night. P. George.
    Al-WW:128
  Cradle Hymn. I. Watts. Au-SP:378,
    Gr-TG:56, Ox-BC:52, Sp-OG:312
  Cradle Song. C. Bellman.
    Fe-FP:466
  A Cradle Song. W. Blake.
    Al-VBP:612, Rv-CB:569

Cradle Song. F. Higgins. Rd-SS:17
Cradle Song. S. Naidu. Fe-FP:54,
    Hu-MP:123, Th-AS:35
A Cradle Song. W. Yeats. Li-LC:9
Cradle-Song for a Boy. Da-SC:57,
    Ho-SD:65
Creek Cradle Song. Da-SC:158
Down Dip the Branches.
    M. Van Doren. Rd-SS:21
A Dream Party. De-PP:47
Evening Song. F. Davis. Th-AS:32
A Flower Lullaby. De-PP:18
The Fly-Away Horse. E. Field.
    Un-GB:32, Un-GT:298
Fragment of a Sleepy Song.
    S. Dobell. Rd-SS:22
Gaelic Lullaby. Ch-B:117,
    Ke-TF:40
German Slumber Song. K. Simrock.
    Un-GT:301
Ghetto Song. J. Glatstein.
    Ho-TY:332
Golden Slumbers. T. Dekker.
    Al-VBP:227, Bl-OB:161, Ch-B:29,
    Co-PU:10, De-CH:265, Ox-BC:17,
    Sm-MK:216
Good Night. J. Taylor. Ch-B:109
Grey Goose and Gander. Co-PU:109,
    Gr-CT:174, Gr-GB:282, Li-LB:10,
    Pa-AP:40, Rv-ON:28
Haida Cradle-Song. Da-SC:57
How Many Miles to Bethlehem.
    F. Chesterton. De-TT:176,
    Ke-TF:217
Hush-a-Ba, Birdie. De-CH:741,
    Gr-GB:15, Mo-MGT:217, Rd-SS:20
Hush-a-Bye. Wr-RM:47
Hush-a-Bye, Baby. De-PO:8,
    Li-LB:9, Mo-CC:(8), Mo-MGT:58,
    Mo-NR:10, Mo-TL:37, Wi-MG:17,
    Wr-RM:25
Hush-a-Bye, Baby, Pussy's a Lady.
    Ir-BB:119
Hush and Baloo. Gr-GB:15
Hush, My Child. Do-CH:(5)
Hush Song. E. Shane. Th-AS:34
Hushing Song. F. Macleod.
    Th-AS:33
Indian Cradle Song. Fi-BG:220
Indian Lullaby. C. Myall.
    Hu-MP:124
Italian Lullaby. Fe-FP:474
A Juju of My Own. L. Bethune.
    Ad-PB:309, Hu-PN:414
Kahuto, the Owl. Tr-US I:214
Little Donkey, Close Your Eyes.
    M. Brown. La-PP:76, La-PV:18
Lullaby. L. Adams. Un-MA:548
Lullaby. W. Barnes. De-TT:54,
    Rd-SS:26

Lullaby. E. Coatsworth. Br-SS:38
Lullaby. P. Dunbar. Hu-MP:112
Lullaby. E. Ford. Rd-SS:25
Lullaby. G. Gascoigne. No-CL:232
Lullaby. R. Hillyer. Du-RG:111,
    Fe-FP:113, Ha-LO:22, Rd-SS:16
lullaby. Q. Prettyman. Ad-BO:75
Lullaby. Be-AP:63
Lullaby. Le-IB:63
Lullaby. Le-OE:43
Lullaby. Tr-CB:13, Tr-US I:4, 97
Lullaby. Tr-US II:35, 178, 194,
    305
Lullaby for a Baby Toad.
    S. Gibbons. Co-BBW:65, Rd-SS:23
Lullaby for a Child Whose Mother
    Has Gone to Gather Food.
    Tr-US I:218
Lullaby for Mitsura. T. Arghezi.
    Mc-AC:26
Lullaby for Peregrine. R. Coffin.
    Sh-RP:293
Lullaby of an Infant Chief.
    W. Scott. Bo-FP:45, Fe-FP:463,
    Hu-MP:122, Ox-BC:147, Un-GT:297
Lullaby of Nokomis. H. Longfellow.
    Bo-FP:287
Lullaby of the Cannibal Giants.
    Da-SC:95
Lullaby Sung by a Widow.
    Tr-US II:177
Lullay, Lullay, Thou Lytil Child.
    De-CH:627
Mammy Hums. C. Sandburg.
    Hu-PN:482
Manhattan Lullaby. R. Field.
    Br-AF:193, Br-BC:145, La-OC:127
Mary's Lullaby. I. Eastwick.
    Mc-AW:77
The Miller's Wife's Lullaby.
    Gr-GB:16
Miriam's Lullaby. R. Beer-Hofmann.
    Un-R:47
The Mouse's Lullaby. P. Cox.
    Bo-FP:16
My Little Buckaroo. Fi-BG:218
A Negro Mother's Lullaby.
    C. Cullen. Mc-PR:153
Norse Lullaby. E. Field.
    Hu-MP:125
Now Silent Falls. W. de la Mare.
    Cl-DT:26, Gr-SS:139
O Can Ye Sew Cushions? Sm-LG:97
O Sleep, My Babe. S. Coleridge.
    Ox-BN:448
O You Are like the Tender
    Cotton Worm. Le-OE:112
Orkney Lullaby. E. Field.
    Un-GT:300
Peace on Earth. W. Williams.
    Al-VBP:1153, Ha-LO:24

LULLABIES — cont'd.
Prairie Lullaby. Fi-BG:217
A Prairie Mother's Lullaby.
    E. Brininstool. Fi-BG:37
Response. B. Kaufman. Ad-BO:76
Rock-A-Bye Baby, in the Tree Top.
    Ir-BB:126, Mo-TL:36
Rock-a-Bye, Baby, Thy Cradle Is
    Green. Mother Goose.
    Bo-FP:10, Er-FA:507, Li-LB:8,
    Mo-MGT:142, Mo-NR:5, Wr-RM:89
Rocking. Cl-DT:28
A Rocking Hymn. G. Wither.
    Ox-BC:28
San Juan Lullaby. Da-SC:17
Scythe Song. A. Lang. Sp-OG:309
Seal Lullaby. R. Kipling.
    Ar-TP3:80, Co-PU:86, Fe-FP:177,
    Mc-PR:60, Mc-WS:47, Rd-SS:19
Sleep, Baby Boy. Fe-FP:475
Sleep, Baby, Sleep. Bo-FP:49,
    Fe-FP:471, Hu-MP:123, Ke-TF:40,
    Li-LB:22, Re-TW:74, Sm-MK:226,
    Un-GT:301, Wr-RM:58
Sleep Brings Pearl Necklaces. . . .
    Le-OE:100
Sleep! Sleep! Beauty Bright.
    W. Blake. Fe-PL:246, Rv-CB:570
Sleep, Sleep, Little One. . . .
    Le-OE:111
Sleepy Song. T. Aldrich.
    Un-GT:297
The Sleepy Song. J. Bacon.
    Bo-FP:48, Th-AS:36
Sleepy Song. A. Guiterman.
    Gr-EC:96
Sleepy Song. M. Kennedy.
    Mc-AW:8
Slumber Song. L. Ledoux.
    Fe-FP:56, Hu-MP:125, Rd-SS:18
Song for a Dead Mother.
    Tr-US II:181
Song of a New Cradleboard.
    P. George. Al-WW:116
The Song of the Frog. De-PP:48
Sung by a Little Girl to Soothe
    a Crying Baby. Le-IB:62,
    Ma-BH:27, Tr-US I:10
Sweet and Low. A. Tennyson.
    Bl-OB:160, Ch-B:47, Cl-DT:29,
    Co-SS:48, De-TT:84, Fe-FP:54,
    Fe-PL:245, Hu-MP:122, Ma-YA:192,
    Ox-BC:212, Re-TW:73, Sm-MK:225,
    Sp-OG:312, Un-GT:300
Sweet Baby, Sleep. G. Wither.
    Cl-DT:32
A Sweet Lullaby. N. Breton.
    Al-VBP:82
Sweet Was the Song.
    Co-PS:165

Sweetes' Li'l Feller. F. Stanton.
    Er-FA:503
Two Spanish Gypsy Lullabies.
    Ma-FW:66
The Unwritten Song. F. Ford.
    Rd-SS:9
Upon My Lap My Sovereign Sits.
    R. Rowlands. Al-VBP:210,
    De-CH:20
The Virgin's Slumber Song.
    F. Carlin. Ha-YA:156
Weep Not, My Wanton. R. Greene.
    Al-VBP:141, Rv-CB:172
What the Gray Cat Sings.
    A. Guiterman. Co-PM:80,
    Hu-MP:188, Li-TU:112, Rd-SS:24,
    Se-PR:194
What'll We Do with the Baby-O?
    Ju-CP:26
When the Sleepy Man Comes.
    C. Roberts. Hu-MP:115
Who Is This? Da-SC:158, Jo-TS:9
Willow Leaves Murmur. Wy-CM:28
Winky, Blinky. Bo-FP:44
Wynken, Blynken, and Nod.
    E. Field. Au-SP:253, Bo-FP:41,
    Ch-B:18, Er-FA:487, Fe-FP:55,
    Gr-EC:98, Hu-MP:128, Ir-BB:244,
    Ox-BC:303, Un-GT:302
You Spotted Snakes.
    W. Shakespeare. Al-VBP:183,
    Bl-OB:160, Fe-FP:381, Gr-EC:94,
    Mc-PR:115, Sm-MK:34, Un-GT:297
See also Em-AF:3-10
LUMBERING: see also DIALECTS,
    LUMBERJACK; FORESTS AND
    WOODS; TREES
Fallen Tree Elegy. V. Contoski.
    Sc-TN:30
Improved Farm Land.
    C. Sandburg. La-RM:77
When the Drive Goes Down.
    D. Malloch. Br-AF:175
Winter Night. E. Millay.
    Se-PR:215
See also Em-AF:530-559
LUMBERJACKS: see DIALECTS,
    LUMBERJACK; LUMBERING
LUNACY: see MADNESS
LUNCHROOMS: see RESTAURANTS
    AND BARS
LUNENBURG, MASS.
The Mountain. R. Frost.
    Ga-FB:292, Pa-HT:13
LUPINE
Lupin. H. Wolfe. Gr-TG:28
LUTES
Calm of Evening. Hsieh T'iao.
    Le-MW:57
Charm for a Rebab. Tr-US II:207

Music's Duel. R. Crashaw.
No-CL:31
My Lute, Awake! T. Wyatt.
Al-VBP:77, Rv-CB:80
Orpheus with His Lute.
J. Fletcher. Al-VBP:286,
Rv-CB:202, Se-PR:329, Sm-LG:38
A P'i-pa Tune in an Alley at
Midnight. Hsü Chih-mo.
Hs-TC:90
The Taming of the Shrew.
W. Shakespeare. Pl-US:14
To His Lute. W. Drummond.
Al-VBP:304, Pa-GTB:24, Pl-US:13
The Wandering Story-Teller.
Tr-CB:39, Tr-US I:46
When to Her Lute Corinna Sings.
T. Campion. Gr-CC:65, Pl-US:12
LUXURY
The Alchemist. B. Jonson.
Al-VBP:241
The Castle of Indolence.
J. Thomson. Al-VBP:547
Edward the Second. C. Marlowe.
Al-VBP:179
Le Grand Luxe. M. Bracker.
Ke-TF:374
A Table Richly Spread. J. Milton.
Sm-LG:119
LYING: see FALSEHOOD; LIARS
LYNCHINGS: see also HUMOR -
LYNCHINGS; TILL, EMMETT
Between the World and Me.
R. Wright. Ad-PB:107,
Bo-AN:103, Kr-OF:158, Pe-M:92,
Wi-LT:657
The Bird and the Tree.
R. Torrence. Hu-PN:480
blue horses. E. Roberson.
Ad-PB:351
Epitaph. D. Scott. Sa-B:4
For Mack C. Parker. P. Murray.
Ad-PB:110
Hangman's Tree. L. White.
Br-AF:103
i saw them lynch. C. Freeman.
Ad-PB:397
Jeff Buckner. F. Beddo.
Ba-PO:77
Landscape with Figures.
N. Rosten. Kr-OF:160
Lynched Negro. M. Bodenheim.
Hu-PN:509
The Lynching. C. McKay.
Ad-PB:27, Be-MA:13
Lynching. Yehoash. Ho-TY:74
The Man Hunt. M. Cawein.
Co-RM:88
A Negro Beats the Olympic Record
for the USA. A. Sperber. Mc-AC:79

Nice Day for a Lynching.
K. Patchen. Hu-PN:555,
Kr-OF:160
Plaint. C. Ford. Ke-PP:77
Remembering Nat Turner. S. Brown.
Ad-PB:63, Be-MA:35, Hu-PN:172
Safari. W. Long. Lo-IT:83
So Quietly. L. Hill. Ad-PB:14
Song for a Black Girl. L. Hughes.
Ad-PB:73
The Swimmers. A. Tate. Pe-OA:180,
Un-MA:540
Tar and Feather. J. Trumbull.
Ke-OF:131
They Got You Last Night. A. Kurtz.
Ke-PP:75
When the Cock Crows.
A. Giovanitti. Kr-OF:151
LYNXES: see HUMOR - LYNXES
LYONESSE
Sunk Lyonesse. W. de la Mare.
Wi-LT:133
When I Set Out for Lyonesse.
T. Hardy. No-CL:144, Pa-HT:156,
Un-MB:32
LYREBIRDS
Lyrebirds. J. Wright. Bo-GJ:217
MAB, QUEEN
The Fairies. R. Herrick.
Bl-OB:90, Fe-FP:384, Hu-MP:87
Mab. B. Jonson. Ho-WR:87
Nimphidia, the Court of Fayrie.
M. Drayton. Al-VBP:163
Queen Mab. T. Hood. Bo-FP:327,
Ch-B:75
Queen Mab. W. Shakespeare.
Fe-FP:382, Hu-MP:87, Ma-FW:186,
Mc-PR:28, Un-GT:108
Queen Mab's Journey to Pigwiggen.
M. Drayton. Bo-FP:320
The Queen of Fairies. Al-VBP:374,
Bo-FP:318, Sm-MK:42
MACARTHUR, DOUGLAS: see
SATIRE - MACARTHUR, DOUGLAS
McCAULEY, MARY LUDWIG HAYS
(MOLLY PITCHER)
Captain Molly. W. Collins.
Vi-PP:119
Molly Pitcher. L. Richards.
Hi-TL:55
Molly Pitcher. K. Sherwood.
Un-GT:183, Vi-PP:116
MACAWS: see PARROTS
MACHINERY: see also AUTOMATION;
COMPUTERS; CONCRETE MIXERS;
CRANES AND DERRICKS; HUMOR -
MACHINERY; SATIRE - MACHINERY;
STEAM SHOVELS
Avenger, What Wrong? J. Rorty.
Sm-PT:128

MACHINERY — cont'd.
  The Egg and the Machine.
    R. Frost.   Un-MA:186
  I Wish the Wood-Cutter Would
    Wake Up.   P. Neruda.   Bl-FP:51
  M'Andrew's Hymn.   R. Kipling.
    Ga-S:119
  La Marche des Machines.
    A. Tessimond.   To-MP:23
  On Watching the Construction
    of a Skyscraper.   B. Raffel.
    Du-RG:38, La-OC:112
  Portrait of a Machine.
    L. Untermeyer.   Pe-M:127,
    Un-MA:307,
  Say This of Horses.   M. Moody.
    Fe-PL:365
  splitting the silence.
    C. Burchardt.   Ad-II:31
  The Steam Threshing-Machine.
    C. Tennyson-Turner.   Ox-BN:470
  Steel-Works.   M. Swann.
    Hi-WP I:130
  This Excellent Machine.
    J. Lehmann.   Du-SH:87
  A Time for Building.
    M. Livingston.   Ho-CS:28,
    La-PV:191
  A Trial Run.   R. Frost.
    Hi-WP II:152
  Up to the Summer Weeds.
    S. Yamaguchi.   Sh-AM:171
McKINLEY, WILLIAM
  Zolgotz.   Em-AF:462
MACLEISH, ARCHIBALD: see
    HUMOR - MACLEISH, ARCHIBALD
MADAGASCAR: see INDONESIAN
    VERSE - MALAGASY
MADEIRA ISLANDS, PORT.
  Madeira from the Sea.
    S. Teasdale.   Pa-HT:102
MADISON, WIS.
  Morning Moon.   V. Contoski.
    Sc-TN:29
MADNESS: see also ASYLUMS;
    HUMOR - MADNESS
  Always Another Viewpoint.
    K. Patchen.   Ha-TP:40
  Borderline.   R. Grenville.
    De-FS:102
  Counting the Mad.   D. Justice.
    Ke-PP:105
  A Development of Idiocy.
    E. Jones.   Ox-BN:619
  The Farmer's Bride.   C. Mew.
    Un-MB:161
  Fighting Frenzy. Ebbeki ag Bouken.
    Tr-US I:135
  Heard in a Violent Ward.
    T. Roethke.   Pl-ML:119

  Howl.   A. Ginsberg.   Sh-AP:233
  I Am.   J. Clare.   Al-VBP:764,
    Go-BP:235, Ha-PO:207, Mc-PR:109,
    Ox-BN:331, Pa-GTB:319, Rv-CB:728
  Mad Actor.   J. Montague.   Ls-NY:136
  The Mad Maid's Song.   R. Herrick.
    Al-VBP:333, De-CH:196, Ho-WR:88
  Mad Song.   W. Blake.   Rv-CB:566
  The Mad Woman.   L. Strong.
    Co-PI:182, Un-MB:394
  Madboy's Song.   M. Rukeyser.
    Un-MA:628
  Madhouse.   C. Hernton.   Ad-PB:238,
    Hu-NN:102, Hu-PN:403, Jo-SA:81
  A Madman.   S. Dawson.   Le-M:147
  Madman.   B. O'Shea.   Le-M:146
  The Madwoman of Papine.
    S. Hopkinson.   Sa-B:21
  Mirthful Lunacy.   T. Stoddart.
    Ox-BN:530
  On Lydia Distracted.   P. Ayres.
    Gr-SS:84
  The Portrait of a Chinese Soldier.
    Wang Ya-p'ing.   Hs-TC:354
  "Praise Song" by a Woman Possessed
    by a Spirit.   Tr-US I:43
  Ringing the Bells.   A. Sexton.
    Ca-VT:635
  Ruth: or The Influence of Nature.
    W. Wordsworth.   Pa-GTB:283
  Simplicity.   L. Simpson.   Ho-P:235
  Sometimes I Go to Camarillo & Sit
    in the Lounge.   K. Lyle.
    Ad-PB:464
  The Song of the Mad Prince.
    W. de la Mare.   Bo-GJ:136,
    Gr-CC:75, Ox-BC:327, Sm-LG:287,
    Sm-MK:41
  This Is the Place to Wait.
    H. Gregory.   Un-MA:513
  To One in Bedlam.   E. Dowson.
    Un-MB:149
  Tom o' Bedlam's Song.   Al-VBP:305,
    Gr-CT:172, Ha-PO:56, Ho-WR:89,
    Na-EO:97, Rv-CB:114
MADONNA: see MARY, VIRGIN
MADRAS, INDIA
  Atman.   D. Saxon.   Lo-IT:123
MADRID, SP.
  Madrid.   F. Keyes.   Ke-TF:389
MADURAI, INDIA
  A River.   A. Ramanujan.   To-MP:166
MAGAZINES: see PERIODICALS
MAGDALENE: see MARY MAGDALENE
MAGI: see JESUS CHRIST -
    NATIVITY
MAGIC: see also CHARMS; HUMOR -
    MAGIC; MAGICIANS (ENTERTAINERS);
    WITCHES AND WITCHCRAFT
  Atlantis.   C. Aiken.   Gr-SS:180

The Big Nasturtiums. R. Hale.
Co-BN:50, Co-PM:83
Ceremonial Chant of a Shaman.
Tr-US II:126
Child of the Raven. Ho-SD:31
Cornish Magic. A. Durell.
Fe-FP:372
Crab-Apple. E. Talbot.
Ar-TP3:149, Bo-FP:328, Br-BC:8
Featherston's Doom. R. Hawker.
Ox-BN:460
Fog, the Magician. M. Cane.
Th-AS:122
A Juju of My Own. L. Bethune.
Ad-PB:309, Hu-PN:44
Ka'Ba. I. Baraka. Ra-BP:213
Lamia. J. Keats. Ma-FW:204
The Magic Seeds. J. Reeves.
Gr-EC:293, Ir-BB:62
Magic Words. Le-IB:28,
Tr-US I:9
Magical Chant. Tr-US II:209
The Magical Mouse. K. Patchen.
Ha-LO:17, We-PZ:14
Merchants from Cathay. W. Benét.
Un-MA:321
Merlin. E. Muir. Ma-FW:188,
Rv-CB:983
My Hat. S. Smith. Sm-MK:78
My Name Is John Wellington Wells.
W. Gilbert. Co-PM:72
Orpheus. E. Roberts. Un-MA:269
The Padda Song. Gr-GB:283
Powerless! Powerless! Ho-SD:40
Protection Song. Da-SC:90
The Sea-Ritual. G. Darley.
De-CH:312, Gr-SS:179, Ho-WR:126,
Ox-BN:396
The Shaman Aua's Song to Call His
Spirits. Tr-US I:10
The Sleeping Beauty. E. Sitwell.
Ma-FW:189
Songs Accompanying Healing Magic.
Do-CH:(40)
Spells. J. Reeves. Co-PM:143,
Sm-MK:54
The Story-Teller. M. Van Doren.
Ho-TH:42
The Tempest. W. Shakespeare.
Ma-FW:187
The Three Singing Birds.
J. Reeves. Co-PM:145, La-PV:216
The Two Magicians. Gr-CT:68
A Visit from Abroad. J. Stephens.
Co-PM:156, Ha-LO:40
The Water of Kane. Tr-US II:96
The Way Through the Woods.
R. Kipling. De-CH:281, Fe-FP:242,
Ha-PO:154, Hi-WP I:107, La-RM:46,
Mc-WS:31, Ox-BC:323, Ox-BN:932,
Re-TW:128, Sm-LG:396

When I Set Out for Lyonesse.
T. Hardy. No-CL:144, Pa-HT:156,
Un-MB:32
The Wife of Llew. F. Ledwidge.
Co-PI:91, Co-PM:120, No-CL:57
The Will-o'-the-Wisp.
Tr-CB:31, Tr-US I:59
The Witches' Ballad. W. Scott.
De-CH:306, Na-EO:24
Women's Song at a Dance Festival.
Tr-US I:209
The Youth and the Northwind.
J. Saxe. Co-PT:166
MAGICIANS (ENTERTAINERS)
The Conjurer. E. Lucas.
Br-BC:117, Co-PM:200
Prologue for a Magician.
A. Guiterman. Co-PM:79
MAGNA CARTA
The Reeds of Runnymede.
R. Kipling. Hi-FO:79
MAGNETS: see also COMPASSES;
HUMOR - MAGNETS
The Magnet Is Mistaken.
L. Ginsburg. Ls-NY:322
Of Natural Forces. E. Chesley.
Ls-NY:321
MAGPIES
Against the Magpie. Gr-GB:61
As Black as Ink. Rv-ON:54
Hop't She. Gr-GB:62
I Saw Seven Magpies. Mo-TB:53
The Magpie. J. Swan. Pe-OA:285
The Magpie and the Raven.
Gr-BB:17
A Magpie Bird. T. Takaori.
Sh-AM:154
A Magpie Rhyme, Northumberland.
Gr-GB:61
The Magpie Singing His Delight.
D. Campbell. Re-BS:34
The Magpie! The Magpie!
Da-SC:96, Ho-SD:44, Le-OE:15,
Tr-US II:252
Magpies. Mo-TB:52
The Marvel of Birds.
W. Langland. Ga-S:13
To the Magpie. Mo-MGT:121
MAIL SERVICE: see POSTAL
SERVICE
MAILMEN: see POSTAL SERVICE
MAINE: see also names of towns,
as PORTLAND, ME.
Exiled. E. Millay. Ni-JP:132,
Pa-HT:7
Maine. P. Booth. Br-AF:128
A Maine Roustabout. R. Eberhart.
Ha-TP:45
My Father Loved the Jumping-Off
Place. R. Coffin. Sh-RP:309

MAINE — cont'd.
  Soft Wood. R. Lowell. Wi-LT:581
  State of Maine Song. R. Snow.
    Se-PR:265
  This Is My Country. R. Coffin.
    Pa-HT:12
  Water. R. Lowell. Pe-OA:247
  Yankee Cradle. R. Coffin.
    Gr-EC:234, Na-EO:102
MAIZE: see CORN
MAKE-BELIEVE: see also DRESSING
    UP; IMAGINATION
  After All and after All.
    M. Davies. Ar-TP3:117, Hu-MP:68,
    Th-AS:148
  The Archer. C. Scollard. Fe-FP:109
  Baby Dolly. Wr-RM:17
  The Bear Hunt. M. Widdemer.
    Fe-FP:104, Hu-MP:49
  Bears. A. Rich. Ha-TP:120
  The Birthday Bus. M. Hoberman.
    Ar-TP3:92, Br-BC:98
  Blanket Street. I. Hogan.
    Br-BC:56
  Block City. R. Stevenson.
    Au-SP:210, Bo-FP:17, Fe-FP:103,
    Hu-MP:44
  Book Day. B. Lee. Ja-HH:41
  Chairoplane Chant. N. Turner.
    Ir-BB:254, St-FS:107
  Cooking. M. Livingston.
    Gr-EC:107
  Each Morning. I. Baraka.
    Ad-PB:250, Hu-NN:74
  Fairy Thief. W. Welles. Br-SG:84
  Feigned Courage. C. and M. Lamb.
    Ox-BC:146
  Fun in a Garret. E. Dowd.
    Ar-TP3:113
  The Gold-Tinted Dragon.
    K. Kuskin. Au-SP:197
  A Good Play. R. Stevenson.
    Ar-TP3:113, Fe-FP:101, Hu-MP:49,
    Ir-BB:15
  Henry and Mary. R. Graves.
    Bo-GJ:10, Ha-LO:46, Ir-BB:259
  Hiding. D. Aldis. Ar-TP3:113,
    Au-SP:199, Fe-FP:102, Hu-MP:45
  I Cannot Dance upon My Toes.
    E. Dickinson. Pl-US:116
  I Had a Little Hen. Ir-BB:66,
    Li-LB:90, Pa-AP:12, Wr-RM:21
  If All the Seas Were One Sea.
    Au-SP:220, Ir-BB:132, Lo-LL:59,
    Mo-MGT:175, Mo-NR:76, Wr-RM:53
  The Invisible Playmate.
    M. Widdemer. Fe-FP:14, Hu-MP:53
  Jeremy's Secrets. B. Todd.
    Br-BC:61
  knock on wood. H. Dumas. Ad-PB:268

  The Land of Counterpane.
    R. Stevenson. Au-SP:205,
    Bo-FP:19, Er-FA:491, Fe-FP:48,
    Gr-EC:95, Hu-MP:52, Ke-TF:72,
    Na-EO:141, Ox-BC:295
  The Land of Story-Books.
    R. Stevenson. Ar-TP3:114,
    Fe-FP:12, Hu-MP:23, Ja-PA:50,
    Un-GB:30, Un-GT:12
  Little Girl and the Queen.
    Wr-RM:105
  Make Believe. H. Behn. Sh-RP:107
  Mrs. Brown. R. Fyleman.
    Ar-TP3:115, Ox-BC:321
  My Horses. J. Jaszi. Au-SP:206
  My Shadow. R. Stevenson.
    Ox-BC:295
  Once upon a Time. Issa. Be-MC:18
  Our Circus. L. Randall.
    Ar-TP3:116
  The Party. R. Whittemore.
    Ad-CI:71
  Pirate Story. R. Stevenson.
    Ar-TP3:114, Fe-FP:108, Un-GB:9,
    Un-GT:10
  Pretending. M. Livingston.
    Br-BC:75
  Radiator Lions. D. Aldis.
    Au-SP:207, Hu-MP:50
  Romance. W. Turner. Bo-GJ:220,
    Hi-WP I:7, Mc-WS:113, Ni-JP:24,
    No-CL:251, Un-MB:345
  Safari. M. Ridlon. Ho-CS:41
  Son. J. Emmanuel. Bo-HF:24,
    Hu-PN:376
  Teddy Bear. H. Behn. Ar-TP3:105
  There Was an Old Woman. Au-SP:2,
    Bo-FP:215, Gr-EC:211, Ir-BB:252,
    La-PV:197, Li-LB:58, Mo-MGT:145,
    Mo-NR:92, Na-EO:100, Wr-RM:66
  Things to Do if You Are a Subway.
    B. Katz. Ho-CS:15
  Tired Equinox. R. Roseliep.
    St-H:183
  Toy Telephone. L. Hopkins.
    Ho-ME:23
  The Tub. G. Chappell. St-FS:91
  Us Two. A. Milne. Ar-TP3:105,
    Ox-BC:345
  When a Fellow's Four. M. Carr.
    Br-BC:49
  When I Was Six. Z. Cross.
    Br-BC:60, Fe-FP:486
  Wild Beasts. E. Stein.
    Au-SP:209, Ch-B:76, Hu-MP:208
  With a Hop, and a Skip, and a
    Jump. W. O'Neill. St-FS:4
MALACHI
  Malachi. E. Marlatt.
    Tr-MR:80

MALACHY, SAINT: see also
   ST. MALACHY'S DAY
   St. Malachy. T. Merton.
      Ca-VT:417
MALARIA
   Child with Malaria. C. Mills.
      Du-SH:140
MALAWI: see NYASALAND
MALAYA: see INDONESIAN VERSE -
   MALAY
MALCOLM X: see LITTLE, MALCOLM
MAN: see also BROTHERHOOD;
   GOD AND MAN; HUMOR - MAN;
   MAN AND WOMAN; SATIRE -
   MAN; WOMAN
   After-Thought. W. Wordsworth.
      Ox-BN:91
   Another and the Same.
      S. Rogers. Ox-BN:48
   Apology for Bad Dreams.
      R. Jeffers. Sh-AP:175,
      Un-MA:363
   Are We Their Equals?
      H. Geltman. Le-M:176
   Asides on the Oboe. W. Stevens.
      Un-MA:251
   Atalanta in Calydon.
      A. Swinburne. Al-VBP:1040,
      Er-FA:82, Rv-CB:936
   The Bear. R. Frost. Sh-AP:154,
      Un-MA:184
   The Bird-Man. W. Davies. Sm-MK:167
   The Caged Skylark. G. Hopkins.
      Un-MB:43, Wi-LT:42
   Common Dust. G. Johnson.
      Ad-PB:22, Bo-AN:20, Lo-TY:209
   The Coffin-Worm. R. Pitter.
      Un-MB:403
   Corruption. H. Vaughan. Ho-P:296
   Crude Foyer. W. Stevens.
      Wi-LT:150
   The Cussitaws Come East. Bi-IT:13
   Dialectics. P. Popescu. Mc-AC:166
   The Dignity of Man. T. More.
      Ga-S:134
   Dirge for the New Sunrise.
      E. Sitwell. Pl-EI:144, Tr-MR:189,
      Un-MB:338
   A Divine Image. W. Blake. Ga-S:156,
      Gr-CT:436, Ox-BN:25
   The Dunce. W. de la Mare.
      Pl-IO:137
   Enion Replies from the Caverns of
      the Grave. W. Blake. Ox-BN:39
   Epitaph for the Race of Man.
      E. Millay. Sh-AP:187
   Epitaph for Us. E. Masters.
      Sm-PT:158
   Essay on Man. A. Pope. Al-VBP:536,
      Er-FA:99, Ha-PO:204, Ma-YA:118,
      Ni-JP:168, Pl-IO:121

   First Man Was the First to Emerge.
      Bi-IT:9, Da-SC:68
   The Fish, the Man, and the Spirit.
      L. Hunt. Al-VBP:712, Co-FB:20,
      Co-RG:162, Gr-CT:212, Rd-OA:155,
      Sm-MK:124
   The Fish Turns into a Man.
      L. Hunt. Al-VBP:713
   Foreboding. G. Code. De-FS:64
   The Four Ages of Man. W. Yeats.
      Tr-MR:269
   Four-Footed Poems.
      E. Greenberg. Ho-TY:312
   The Fourth God. C. Smith.
      Sm-PT:83
   Genesis. Bible. O.T. Genesis.
      Pl-IO:14
   The Gifts of the Animals to Man.
      P. Sidney. Rd-OA:38
   God Is like Scissors. J. Villa.
      Pl-EI:50
   Heredity. T. Hardy. Pl-IO:140,
      Rv-CB:938
   Hymn to Earth. E. Wylie.
      Un-MA:284, Wi-LT:209
   I Know My Soul Hath Power.
      J. Davies. De-CH:585
   I Know Myself a Man. J. Davies.
      Gr-CT:371, Ni-JP:168
   If They Spoke. M. Van Doren.
      Pl-IO:102
   The Immortality of the Soul.
      J. Davies. Al-VBP:223
   In Utrumque Paratus.
      M. Arnold. Ox-BN:626
   Intimate Parnassus.
      P. Kavanagh. Un-MB:432
   It Is Big Inside a Man.
      K. Patchen. Kh-VA:50
   It Must Be Abstract. W. Stevens.
      Sm-PT:124
   Job. Bible. O.T. Job.
      Pl-IO:39
   Journal. E. Millay. Pl-IO:133
   Let Me Alone. Bible. O.T.
      Job. Ke-PP:4
   Life. Cheng Min. Hs-TC:237
   Life at War. D. Levertov.
      Ca-VT:515
   Long Feud. L. Untermeyer.
      Un-MA:306
   Man. W. Shakespeare. Ga-S:13
   Man. H. Vaughan. Rv-CB:412
   Man. H. Wolfe. Un-MB:303
   Man Carrying Bale. H. Monro.
      Un-MB:238
   Man Is God's Nature. R. Eberhart.
      Pl-EI:133, Tr-MR:287
   Man Is Nothing but.
      S. Tchernichovsky. Me-PH:76

MAN — cont'd.
  The Man-Moth. E. Bishop.
    En-PC:103, Pe-OA:213, Un-MA:612,
    Wi-LT:504
  Man-Test. E. Markham. Tr-MR:280
  Man That Is Born of Woman.
    Bible. O.T. Job. Gr-CT:353
  Man's a Bubble. R. Dodsley.
    Rv-CB:523
  Map. M. Mendes. An-TC:49
  Mars Is Out. K. Takamura.
    Sh-AM:42
  Message from Home. K. Raine.
    Pl-IO:99
  Nature or Man. P. Curry.
    Me-WF:51
  Not a Tree. T. Blackburn.
    Ls-NY:171
  O Stelliferi Conditor Orbis.
    Boethius. Go-BP:240
  Oh What a Thing Is Man. De-CH:766
  Olduvai. L. Smith, Jr. Ls-NY:81
  On Man. W. Landor. Ox-BN:185
  On Seeming to Presume.
    L. Durrell. Wi-LT:693
  Original Sin. R. Jeffers.
    Un-MA:373
  The People Will Live On.
    C. Sandburg. Un-MA:214
  Personality. C. Sandburg.
    Ga-S:14
  Psalm Eight. Bible. O.T.
    Psalms. Pa-SG:193
  The Pulley. G. Herbert.
    Al-VBP:346, Ga-S:52, Ha-PO:198,
    Mc-PR:207, Pa-GTB:64, Pl-EI:51,
    Rv-CB:356
  Rebirth. R. Kipling. Ox-BN:933
  Reluctances. H. Witt. Ls-NY:320
  Remember, Though the Telescope
    Extend. G. Dillon. Pl-IO:127
  Revolutionary Letter #36.
    D. di Prima. Kh-VA:52
  Robin and Man. R. Gordon.
    Ls-NY:342
  The Shepherd's Dog and the Wolf.
    J. Gay. Rd-OA:132
  Song. E. Sitwell. Un-MB:337
  Sonnets I, II. J. Agee. Un-MA:604
  The Spring Waters, 74. Ping Hsin.
    Hs-TC:23
  Strange Meetings. H. Monro.
    Un-MB:235
  Strong Son of God, Immortal Love.
    A. Tennyson. Ma-YA:193,
    Pl-EI:136
  The Sum of All Known Reverence.
    W. Whitman. Tr-MR:161
  They Stooped Over and Came Out.
    Bi-IT:11
  This Quiet Dust. J. Wheelock.
    Un-MA:344
  Time Takes Me on Its Wing.
    Wo-HS:(58)
  Univac to Univac. L. Salomon.
    Du-SH:89
  Up from the Bed of the River.
    J. Johnson. Pl-EI:132
  Vice Versa. C. Morgenstern.
    Rd-OA:36
  What a Piece of Work Is Man.
    Sophocles. Pa-SG:194
  What Am I, Life? E. Millay.
    Pl-IO:136
  What Are Years? M. Moore.
    Ha-TP:140, Pe-OA:101, Pl-EI:138,
    Sh-AP:179, Sm-PT:10, Un-MA:352
  what if a much of a which of a
    wind. E. Cummings. Al-VBP:1203,
    Er-FA:94, Un-MA:477, Wi-LT:368
  When I Consider Thy Heavens.
    Bible. O.T. Psalms.
    Fe-FP:202, Pl-IO:150
  With God Conversing. G. Derwood.
    Tr-MR:139
  Wolf and Tiger Dining, A.B.
    J. Keith. De-FS:118
MAN, PREHISTORIC
  The Cave-Boy. L. Richards.
    Fe-FP:17
  the discoveries of fire.
    L. Clifton. Mo-TS:32
  Evolution. L. Smith. Er-FA:13
  Prehistoric Burials.
    S. Sassoon. Un-MB:316
  The Prehistoric Huntsman.
    D. Wandrei. De-FS:213
  Similar Cases. C. Gilman.
    Fe-PL:191
  Ula Masondo's Dream. W. Plomer.
    Ca-MB:73
MAN, PRIMITIVE: see names of
    primitive tribes and peoples
MAN, ISLE OF: see also HUMOR
    - MAN, ISLE OF
  The Isle of Man. Gr-GB:166
MAN AND WOMAN: see also
    HUMOR - MAN AND WOMAN
  The Ascent. J. Wade. Sc-TN:225
  Hogamus, Higamus. Co-EL:50
  Juxtaposition. A. Clough.
    Ox-BN:613
  Man, Man, Man Is for Woman Made.
    Ho-P:264
MAN-O-WAR BIRDS: see FRIGATE BIRDS
MANCHESTER, ENG.
  Murphy in Manchester.
    J. Montague. Co-PI:142
MANDALAY, BUR.
  Mandalay. R. Kipling. Ga-FB:70,
    Un-MB:125

MANDOLINS
   At the Seed and Feed. J. Simons.
      Ls-NY:235
   A Music. W. Berry. Ca-VT:683
MANHATTAN: see NEW YORK CITY
MANHOLES
   Manhole Covers. K. Shapiro.
      Bo-GJ:214, Bo-HF:42, Br-AF:211,
      Pe-M:126
MANIPURI VERSE: see TIBETAN
   VERSE - MANIPURI
MANNERS: see ETIQUETTE
MANNERS AND CUSTOMS: see also
   CHRISTMAS CUSTOMS; ETIQUETTE;
   FESTIVALS; HOLIDAYS; HUMOR -
   MANNERS AND CUSTOMS; INDIANS
   OF NORTH AMERICA - SOCIAL LIFE
   AND CUSTOMS; RITES AND CERE-
   MONIES; SATIRE - MANNERS AND
   CUSTOMS; SOCIAL CLASSES; and
   names of countries, as
   FRANCE - SOCIAL LIFE AND
   CUSTOMS
   The Cat's Tea-Party.
      F. Weatherly. Ar-TP3:119,
      Co-IW:34, Ir-BB:182, On-TW:22
   Customs Change. Ox-BC:6
   The Dree Night. Gr-CT:364
   The Excursion. Tu Fu. Mo-SD:138
   Hannah Bantry. Ag-HE:17,
      Co-OH:52, Mo-MGT:77
   Happy New Year! Co-PS:22
   Ivy and Holly. E. Meyerstein.
      Co-EL:11
   Kowtow. Yüan Shui-p'ai.
      Hs-TC:412
   Little Girl. Ir-BB:262,
      Mo-MGT:115
   Lo-Yang. Ch'ien Wen-tu. Gr-CC:182
   A New Year Carol. Co-PS:23,
      De-CH:3, De-TT:115, Ga-S:93,
      Gr-GB:297, Mc-FW:3, Re-TW:64
   The Poor Man. Be-AP:55
   The Prologue to the Canterbury
      Tales. G. Chaucer. Al-VBP:6,
      Gr-CT:281, Ma-FW:17, Ma-YA:28
   A Song of a Men's Secret Society.
      Tr-US I:208
MANTISES
   In Storm-Tossed Grassland.
      Miyoshi. Ca-BF:37
   The Praying Mantis. O. Nash.
      Co-PU:110
   Praying Mantis. F. Stefanile.
      De-FS:189
   The Praying Mantis Visits a
      Penthouse. O. Williams.
      Er-FA:235, Wi-LT:417
   This Living Creature. M. Saito.
      Sh-AM:143

MANUSCRIPTS: see ILLUMINATION
   OF BOOKS AND MANUSCRIPTS
MANZANITA
   The Manzanita. Y. Winters.
      Ca-VT:227, Ls-NY:61
MAORIS: see also POLYNESIAN
   VERSE - MAORI
   A Rope for Harry Fat. J. Baxter.
      Ca-MB:85
MAPLE SUGAR
   Dusk in the Sugar Woods.
      C. Malam. Ls-NY:285
   Evening in a Sugar Orchard.
      R. Frost. Ha-WR:6
   Maple Feast. F. Frost.
      Br-SS:133, Sh-RP:197
   Maple Sugar. Da-SC:148
   Sap Bucket Song. L. Stoddard.
      Ls-NY:291
   Winter Sweetness. L. Hughes.
      Gr-EC:290
MAPLE TREES
   The Aged Maple Tree.
      Chung Ting-wen. Pa-MV:76
   Down at the Docks. K. Koch.
      Ca-VT:547
   Dusk in the Sugar Woods.
      C. Malam. Ls-NY:285
   The Faintly Glowing. M. Saito.
      Sh-AM:143
   Fairies. Kihaku. Hu-MP:81
   The Little Maple. C. Zolotow.
      Br-SG:106
   Maple Leaves. Shiko.
      Au-SP:323, Pa-SG:95
   October. T. Aldrich. Un-GT:278
   R.G.E. R. Eberhart. Ls-NY:72
   Swift Cloud Shadows. Shusen.
      Be-CS:51
   Trees. B. Carman. Se-PR:95
   View from the Cliffs. Tu Mu.
      Rx-LT:74
MAPS: see also GEOGRAPHY
   The Map. E. Bishop. Sh-RP:184,
      Sm-LG:300
   The Map. G. Oden. Bo-AN:161,
      Be-MA:97, Hu-NN:47, Hu-PN:385
   Map of My Country. J. Holmes.
      Br-AF:11
   The Mapmaker on His Art.
      H. Nemerov. Du-SH:31
   Maps. D. Thompson. Ar-TP3:97
   A Private Letter to Brazil.
      G. Oden. Bo-AN:158,
      Hu-NN:91, Hu-PN:383
MARATHON, BATTLE, 490 B.C.: see
   HUMOR - MARATHON, BATTLE,
   490 B.C.
MARBLE
   In the Marble Quarry. J. Dickey.
      Br-AF:137

MARBLE - cont'd.
  To the Stone-Cutters. R. Jeffers.
    En-PC:10, Ni-JP:127, Sh-AP:175,
    Un-MA:362
MARBLEHEAD, MASS.
  The Fire of Drift-Wood.
    H. Longfellow. Mo-BG:148
  Skipper Ireson's Ride.
    J. Whittier. Co-SS:147,
    Fe-PL:45, Hi-TL:73, Sh-AP:40,
    Sp-OG:226
MARC ANTONY: see ANTONY, MARK
MARCH (MONTH)
  The Children's Song. Fe-FP:476
  Counting-Out Rhyme for March.
    F. Frost. Ha-YA:37
  A Cry. F. Bianco. No-CL:261
  Evening in a Sugar Orchard.
    R. Frost. Ha-WR:6
  Facing Up. J. Scully. Ha-WR:18
  Flower Chorus. R. Emerson.
    Bo-FP:220
  Four Little Foxes. L. Sarett.
    Ar-TP3:64, Bo-HF:71, Co-BBW:35,
    Co-PS:54, Du-RG:98, Fe-FP:173,
    Ha-YA:40, La-PV:150, La-RM:53,
    Mc-WK:64, Sh-RP:203, Un-GT:31
  I Saw Green Banks of Daffodils.
    E. Tennant. Ar-TP3:201
  The Lady Is Cold. E. White.
    Pa-HT:36
  Late Winter on Our Beach.
    B. Eaton. Mc-AW:32
  March. J. Clare. Rd-OA:187
  March. E. Coatsworth. Ha-YA:39
  March. H. Crane. Co-BN:17
  March. E. Dickinson. Ha-YA:34
  March. A. Guiterman. Ha-YA:33
  March. A. Housman. Sm-LG:54
  March. L. Larcom. Bo-FP:219
  March. C. Thaxter. Un-GT:270
  March. Yung Tzu. Pa-MV:195
  March. Gr-GB:38
  March Dreams. R. Henderson.
    Th-AS:126
  March Evening. L. Strong.
    Un-MB:394
  The March Problem. G. Garrett.
    Ho-LP:36
  March Weather. S. Barker.
    Ho-LP:21
  The March Wind. J. Parr.
    La-GI:11
  March Wind. M. Uschold. Ha-YA:38
  The March Winds. G. Houghton.
    Ha-YA:35
  One March Day. Bo-FP:215, Ch-B:40
  Spring Families. F. Frost.
    Sh-RP:198
  Sunday. E. White. Mc-WS:123

  Thorn Leaves in March. W. Merwin.
    Br-TC:289
  Wild March. C. Woolson. Ha-YA:36
  Written in March. W. Wordsworth.
    Ar-TP3:202, Au-SP:317, Bo-FP:217,
    Bo-GJ:95, Co-BN:18, De-TT:37,
    Fe-FP:69, Ha-YA:36, Hu-MP:290,
    Mc-PR:36, Mc-WK:23, Na-EO:32,
    Re-TW:82, Se-PR:61, Tu-WW:66,
    Un-GT:270
MARCHING: see also HUMOR -
  MARCHING
  An Army Corps on the March.
    W. Whitman. Fe-PL:171, Vi-PP:147
  Boots. R. Kipling. Un-MB:129
  Dances. D. Meltzer. Lo-IT:90
MARCHING SONGS: see WAR SONGS
  AND CRIES
MARCO BOZZARIS: see BOZZARIS,
  MARCO
MARDI GRAS: see SHROVE TUESDAY
MARES: see HORSES
MARGARET (TUDOR), QUEEN OF
  SCOTLAND
  To the Princess Margaret Tudor.
    W. Dunbar. Gr-SS:92
MARIGOLDS
  How Marigolds Came Yellow.
    R. Herrick. Ch-B:67, Gr-CT:268
  The Marigold. G. Wither.
    Rv-CB:333
MARIN, JOHN
  Marin. P. Booth. Mo-BG:126
MARINE ANIMALS: see also names
  of animals, as CORALS
  As the Tide Goes Out. J. Fischer.
    La-GI:41
  Boy in a Pond. J. Whaler.
    Rd-OA:47
  The Coral Grove. J. Percival.
    Un-GT:262
  The Diver. R. Hayden. Be-MA:66,
    Du-SH:127, Ra-BP:136
  The Pool in the Rock.
    W. de la Mare. Cl-FC:55
  The Rock Pool. P. Hobsbaum.
    Ls-NY:215
  Song Cycle of the Moon-Bone.
    Tr-US I:246
  This Is the Sea. E. Shanks.
    De-CH:623
  Through the Dear Might of Him
    Who Walked the Waves.
    J. Heath-Stubbs. Go-BP:289
  A Water Sprite. K. Green.
    La-GI:42
  Water Sprite. M. Holub. Su-FVI:18
  The Wonder Shell. B. Holender.
    Ls-NY:166
  The World below the Brine.
    W. Whitman. Co-BN:77

MARINE PLANTS: see also KELP;
    SEAWEED
  Although both Grasses and Trees.
    Funya No Yashuhida. Ba-ST:37
  Beach Encounter. C. Wagner.
    Ls-NY:191
  The Coral Grove. J. Percival.
    Un-GT:262
  The World below the Brine.
    W. Whitman. Co-BN:77
MARION, FRANCIS (SWAMP FOX)
  Song of Marion's Men. W. Bryant.
    Hi-TL:57
MARION, O.
  Two Poems about President Harding.
    J. Wright. St-H:257
MARIONETTES: see PUPPETS
MARK, SAINT
  The Eve of Saint Mark. J. Keats.
    De-CH:447
MARK ANTONY: see ANTONY, MARK
MARK TWAIN: see CLEMENS, JANE
    LAMPTON
MARKETS AND MARKETING: see also
    BAZAARS (STREET); FAIRS;
    PEDDLERS AND PEDDLING; STORES
  At Casterbridge Fair. T. Hardy.
    Ox-BN:832
  The Child Reads On. F. Jammes.
    Fe-FP:470
  Donkey, Donkey, Do Not Bray.
    Mother Goose. Pa-AP:20
  Father and Mother and Uncle John.
    Mo-TL:83, Sp-TM:17
  In the Market on Monday Morning.
    Co-PU:6
  Jamaica Market. A. Maxwell-Hall.
    Ab-MO:43, Lo-TY:117
  Market. R. Hayden. Be-MA:65
  Market Day. M. Webb. De-CH:133
  The Market Man. J. Ratti.
    Du-SH:150
  Pushcart Row. R. Field.
    Au-SP:116, Br-SG:73
  Saturday Market. C. Mew.
    Fe-FP:244
  Saturday Shopping. K. Edelman.
    Au-SP:115
  Souk. T. Joans. Ab-MO:47
  A Supermarket in California.
    A. Ginsburg. Br-TC:149,
    Kh-VA:64, Mo-BG:185, Wi-LT:718
  To Market, to Market. Mother
    Goose. Ar-TP3:100, Au-SP:18,
    Bo-FP:115, De-PO:8, Er-FA:507,
    Ir-BB:236, Li-LB:105, Mo-MGT:136,
    Mo-NR:20, Mo-TL:77, Sp-TM:25, 27,
    33, Wr-RM:19
MARKSMANSHIP:
  see SHOOTING

MARLBOROUGH, JOHN CHURCHILL,
    1ST DUKE: see SATIRE -
    MARLBOROUGH, JOHN
    CHURCHILL, 1ST DUKE
MARLOWE, CHRISTOPHER
  Christopher Marlowe. M. Drayton.
    Gr-CT:430
MARMOTS: see WOODCHUCKS
MARRAKESH, MOR.
  Marrakech. R. Eberhart. Wi-LT:440
  Marrakech. W. Hoffman. Sc-TN:99
  Souk. T. Joans. Ab-MO:47
MARRIAGE: see also DIVORCE;
    ELOPEMENTS; HUMOR - MARRIAGE;
    HUSBAND AND WIFE; HUSBANDS;
    LOVE, WEDDED; MARRIAGE
    PROPOSALS; SATIRE - MARRIAGE;
    WEDDINGS; WIVES
  Achtung! Achtung! M. Hacker.
    Cr-WS:1
  Any Wife to Any Husband.
    R. Browning. Ox-BN:535
  Auld Robin Gray. A. Lindsay.
    Al-VBP:603, De-CH:344, Pa-GTB:152
  Ceiling Unlimited. M. Rukeyser.
    Un-MA:622
  Changes. R. Bulwer-Lytton.
    Fe-PL:307
  Circuit Through the Hills.
    T. Singh. Al-PI:119
  Complaint of a New Wife.
    Tr-US II:188
  The Conformers. T. Hardy.
    Al-VBP:1048
  Counsel to Girls. R. Herrick.
    Al-VBP:328, Er-FA:104, Ga-FB:41,
    Gr-CT:51, Ha-PO:161, Hi-WP II:140,
    Li-SR:21, Ma-YA:86, Pa-GTB:71,
    Un-MW:19
  A Decade. A. Lowell. Co-BL:109,
    Mo-BG:99, Un-MA:160
  A Development of Idiocy. E. Jones.
    Ox-BN:619
  Dialogue. Tr-US I:156
  Early Snow. R. Huff. St-H:84
  Early Thoughts of Marriage.
    N. Cotton. Ox-BC:65
  An Elder's Reproof to His Wife.
    A. Muuse. Lo-TY:57
  Eloisa to Abelard. A. Pope.
    Al-VBP:535
  Eros Turannos. E. Robinson.
    Un-MA:126, Wi-LT:109
  The Fair Young Wife. H. Adam.
    De-FS:7
  The Falcon Woman. R. Graves.
    Gr-BT:89
  The Farmer's Bride. C. Mew.
    Un-MB:161
  For Fran. P. Levine. En-PC:272

MARRIAGE — cont'd.
  For I the Ballad Will Repeat.
    W. Shakespeare. Al-VBP:192
  Fulfillment. W. Cavendish.
    Un-MW:135
  Grandmother Watching at Her
    Window. W. Merwin. Ca-VT:616
  The Griesly Wife. J. Manifold.
    Ca-MB:25, Un-MB:513
  The Hill Wife. R. Frost. Wi-LT:167
  Husbands and Wives. M. Hershenson.
    Du-RG:59, La-OC:64
  I Gave Myself. E. Dickinson.
    Ga-FB:68, Rv-CB:918
  I Refused, of Course I Did.
    Do-CH:(34)
  In Spring We Gather Mulberry
    Leaves. Rx-LT:13
  Jack Jingle. Wr-RM:98
  Jungle Songs, V. Tr-US II:160
  Last Night. D. Ignatow.
    Ca-VT:396
  Live Man's Epitaph. F. Hope.
    Gr-BT:83
  Locksley Hall. A. Tennyson.
    Er-FA:56
  The Lovely Shall Be Choosers.
    R. Frost. Sh-AP:155, Un-MA:185
  Love's Matrimony. W. Cavendish.
    Go-BP:140
  Lucinda Matlock. E. Masters.
    Ga-FB:74, Mo-BG:161, Un-MA:143,
    Wi-LT:116
  The Marital Journey. H. Araaya.
    Pe-M:152
  Marriage. Gr-GB:151
  Marriage. Tr-US II:36
  Marriage Poems, I, II, III.
    Tr-US II:162, 163
  Marriage Song. Tr-US I:201
  Marriage Songs, I. Tr-US II:159
  The Married Lover. C. Patmore.
    Un-MW:93
  The Mating of Hine and Tane-Matua.
    Tr-US II:107
  Meditation at Kew. A. Wickham.
    Gr-BT:88, Un-MB:280, Un-MW:58
  Mementos. W. Snodgrass.
    Un-MA:684, Un-MW:105
  Needles and Pins. Mo-NR:119,
    Un-GT:22, Wr-RM:92
  The Newlyweds. C. Criswell.
    Fe-PL:96
  Now You're Married You Must Obey.
    Un-GT:22
  O I Won't Lead a Homely Life.
    T. Hardy. Pl-US:33
  On the Marriage of a Beauteous
    Young Gentlewoman with an
    Ancient Man. F. Beaumont.
    Al-VBP:300

  One Flesh. E. Jennings. To-MP:94
  Our Happy Home. De-CH:533,
    Gr-TG:68
  Our Little Sister Is Worried.
    Rx-LT:22
  The Potter. Lo-TY:47
  Prelude to an Evening. J. Ransom.
    En-PC:12, Un-MA:418
  The Red-Haired Man's Wife.
    J. Stephens. Un-MB:264
  She Vowed Him This. W. Box.
    Gr-BT:90
  A Slice of Wedding Cake.
    R. Graves. Gr-BT:87
  Song. Le-OE:84, Tr-US II:179
  Song to Instruments.
    Tr-CB:22, Tr-US I:48
  Song to the Wife of His Youth.
    N. Alterman. Me-PH:109
  Songs, III. Tr-US II:144
  Songs at a Wedding, II.
    Tr-US II:167
  Les Sylphides. L. MacNeice.
    Gr-BT:81
  There Once Was a Man. On-TW:7
  Title Divine Is Mine.
    E. Dickinson. Al-VBP:1003
  To a Friend on His Marriage.
    F. Prince. Wi-LT:795
  To His Wife on the Fourteenth
    Anniversary of Her Wedding
    Day, with a Ring. S. Bishop.
    Al-VBP:596
  The True and Tender Wife.
    Al-PI:29
  Wedding Is Great Juno's Crown.
    W. Shakespeare. Al-VBP:189
  Wedding Procession. J. Emanuel.
    Hu-NN:81
  Wedding Wind. P. Larkin.
    Gr-BT:86
  West-Running Brook. R. Frost.
    Sh-AP:151, Sm-PT:138, Un-MA:182
  Why Should a Foolish Marriage Vow.
    J. Dryden. Al-VBP:481,
    Gr-BT:95, Rv-CB:463
  The Widow's Lament. W. Williams.
    Wi-LT:197
  The Wife. R. Creeley. Ca-VT:566
MARRIAGE PROPOSALS: see also
    HUMOR - MARRIAGE PROPOSALS
  Autumn. S. Smith. Co-EL:121
  Broom, Green Broom. Bl-OB:38,
    De-CH:139, Fo-OG:8, Ha-PO:54
  Cashel of Munster. Co-PI:41
  Curly Locks. Au-SP:8, Bo-FP:294,
    De-PO:14, Hi-GD:10, Li-LB:45,
    Mo-MGT:97, Mo-NR:130, Wi-MG:65,
    Wr-RM:39
  Flowers in the Valley. Bl-OB:40,
    Gr-EC:136, Gr-SS:29

The Gardener.   Rv-CB:48
I Will Give You the Keys of Heaven.
   Cl-DT:80
If I Were a Queen.   C. Rossetti.
   Br-SS:118
I'm O'er Young to Marry Yet.
   R. Burns.   Al-VBP:644
The Laird o' Cockpen.   C. Nairne.
   Co-PT:201
Leezie Lindsay.   Sm-LG:361
The One Answer.   La-PV:209,
   Un-GT:169, Un-MW:33
The Rachray Man.   M. O'Neill.
   Co-PI:162
The Riddling Knight.   Gr-CC:165,
   Sm-LG:285
The Royal Fisherman.   Gr-CT:128,
   Gr-GB:315
Ruth.   T. Hood.   Gr-CC:37,
   Ox-BN:422
Soldier, Soldier, Won't You
   Marry Me?   Bl-OB:35
Song of a Chief's Daughter.
   Bi-IT:81, Ho-SD:57
Strawberry Fair.   Cl-DT:59
Sukey, You Shall Be My Wife.
   Ir-BB:24, Mo-MGT:165
To a Lady to Answer Him Directly
   with Yea or Nay.   T. Wyatt.
   No-CL:169, Rv-CB:75
Will You?   K. Greenaway.
   Br-SS:122
MARS (PLANET)
   Mars Is Out.   K. Takamura.
   Sh-AM:42
MARSHES: see also
   OKEFENOKEE SWAMP
   In the Bayou.   D. Marquis.
   Br-AF:187
The Marsh.   W. Snodgrass.
   Co-BN:86, Ha-WR:17, Mo-BG:138
The Moor.   R. Thomas.   Go-BP:28
The One.   P. Kavanagh. Un-MB:432
Winter in the Fens.   J. Clare.
   Co-BN:190, Ma-FW:4
MARSUPIALS: see HUMOR -
   MARSUPIALS
MARTHA'S VINEYARD, MASS.
   Gay Head.   N. Abeel.   Pa-HT:30
MARTÍ, JOSÉ JULIAN
   On a Monument to Martí.
   W. Roberts.   Lo-TY:116
MARTIN, SAINT
   A Legend of Saint Martin.
   W. Bryant.   Sp-OG:151
   St. Martin and the Beggar.
   T. Gunn.   Ca-MB:51
MARTINS
   The Children of the Wind.
   C. Sandburg.   Hi-WP II:41,
   Re-BS:57

Four Birds.   W. Blake.   Gr-CT:93,
   Gr-GB:63, Gr-TG:31
MARTINS FERRY, O.:   see also
   BROWN, JOHN
   Autumn Begins in Martins Ferry,
   Ohio.   J. Wright.   Bl-FP:76,
   St-H:255
MARTINSVILLE, IND.
   The Visits of My Aunt.   J. Woods.
   St-H:244
MARTYRS: see also SATIRE -
   MARTYRS
   The Feast of the Great God
   Tezcatlipoca.   Br-MW:15
   For Andy Goodman - Michael
   Schwerner - and James Chaney.
   M. Walker.   Ra-BP:158
   Latimer and Ridley.
   W. Wordsworth.   Hi-FO:118
   The Martyrdom of the Quakers.
   G. Joy.   Kr-OF:101
   More Light, More Light.   A. Hecht.
   Br-TC:182, Ca-VT:505
   On the Late Massacre in Piedmont.
   J. Milton.   Al-VBP:408,
   Hi-FO:152, Pa-GTB:51, Rv-CB:376
   Through the Strait Pass of Suffering.
   E. Dickinson.   Ga-S:225, Tr-MR:201
   The Virgin Martyrs.
   Sigebert of Gembloux.   Ga-S:226
   Watchman, What of the Night?
   A. Swinburne.   Ho-WR:200
MARVELL, ANDREW
   You, Andrew Marvell.   A. MacLeish.
   Al-VBP:1193, Br-TC:275, Ga-FB:4,
   Mo-BG:150, Pe-OA:157, Sh-AP:134,
   Sm-PT:85, Wi-LT:342
MARY, VIRGIN: see also
   JESUS CHRIST; JOSEPH,
   SAINT
   Adam Lay Ibounden.   De-CH:468,
   Ga-S:39, Gr-CT:83, Gr-TG:82,
   Ma-YA:26, Rv-CB:9
   After Annunciation.   A. Wickham.
   Un-MB:281
   Aishah-Schechinah.   R. Hawker.
   Ox-BN:461
   The Annunciation.   E. Jennings.
   Ga-S:63
   As Joseph Was Awakening.
   Al-VBP:59, De-TT:174, Gr-TG:75
   As Mary Was a-Walking.   Ga-S:107
   Ash-Wednesday.   T. Eliot.
   Ca-VT:134, Un-MA:398
   Ave Maria.   A. Kaplan.   Mc-EA:132
   Aztec Hymn to the Virgin. Da-SC:15
   Ballad of the Bread Man.
   C. Causley.   To-MP:203
   Birth of Mary.   R. Rilke. Tr-MR:98
   Brown Robyn's Confession.
   De-CH:399, Gr-GB:314

MARY, VIRGIN — cont'd.
  The Cherry-Tree Carol. Al-VBP:58,
    Ga-S:64, Gr-CT:127, Gr-GB:299,
    Ke-TF:47, Ox-BB:1, Pa-OM:349,
    Rv-CB:53
  Church of Rose of Lima, Cincinnati.
    J. Knoepfle. St-H:95
  The Circle of a Girl's Arms.
    C. Houselander. Ga-S:95
  Conception. W. Cuney. Ab-MO:70
  The Confession Stone. O. Dodson.
    Ab-MO:72, Lo-TY:238
  The Corpus Christi Carol.
    Gr-GB:308
  The Flight into Egypt.
    P. Quennell. Wi-LT:630
  The Flight into Egypt. Ga-S:102
  He Came All So Still. Sm-LG:368,
    Tu-WW:12
  Her Nativity. R. Southwell.
    Ga-S:62
  How the Gates Came Ajar. Ke-TF:42
  I Sing of a Maiden. Al-VBP:20,
    De-CH:19, De-TT:175, Ma-BB:90,
    Ma-FW:288, Re-TW:65, Rv-CB:10,
    Sm-LG:367
  In the Town. Ga-S:68
  Jesus and His Mother. T. Gunn.
    Ke-TF:144, Pl-EI:31, To-MP:77
  Joseph's Suspicion. R. Rilke.
    Tr-MR:99
  Lully, Lulley. De-CH:470
  Mary and Gabriel. R. Brooke.
    Ke-TF:142
  Mary and Gabriel. Ga-S:58
  Mary of Nazareth. C. Sansom.
    Ga-S:64
  Mary Passed This Morning.
    O. Dodson. Ad-PB:127
  Mary's Lullaby. I. Eastwick.
    Mc-AW:77
  Me Rueth Mary. Gr-GB:306
  Miracles. C. Aiken. Un-MA:472
  Of a Rose Is All My Song.
    Ga-S:75
  On the Death of Mr. Crashaw.
    A. Cowley. Al-VBP:448
  Pietà. C. Lewis. Go-BP:246
  The Pietà, Rhenish, 14th C.,
    The Cloisters. M. Van Duyn.
    Ho-P:281
  St. Joseph and God's Mother.
    Ga-S:78
  The Seven Joys. Ga-S:185
  The Seven Virgins. De-CH:469,
    Ga-S:158, Gr-CT:189, Gr-GB:311
  Stabat Mater. Jacopone da Todi.
    Ga-S:157
  Suddenly Afraid. Rv-CB:12
  Sweet Was the Song. Co-PS:165

  The Virgin Mary to Christ on the
    Cross. R. Southwell. Al-VBP:151
  The Virgin's Slumber Song.
    F. Carlin. Ha-YA:156
  The Visitation. E. Jennings.
    Ca-MB:45
  We Have Seen Her. H.D. Ca-VT:117
MARY, QUEEN OF SCOTS: see also
    HUMOR - MARY, QUEEN OF SCOTS
  Alas! Poor Queen. M. Angus.
    Gr-SS:90
  Edinburgh. A. Noyes. Pa-HT:145
  Mary, Queen of Scots. R. Burns.
    Hi-FO:125
MARY MAGDALENE
  And She Washed His Feet with Her
    Tears. G. Marino. Gr-CT:188
  The Holy Women. W. Percy.
    Ke-TF:234
  Madeleine in Church. C. Mew.
    Un-MB:162
  Magdalene. B. Pasternak.
    Tr-MT:89
  The Weeper. R. Crashaw. Al-VBP:438
MARY AND MARTHA
  Mary of Bethany. D. Lawrence.
    Ga-S:116
MARYLAND: see also names of
    towns, as BALTIMORE, MD.
  A Cold Spring. E. Bishop.
    Br-TC:49
  The Grandmother. E. Roberts.
    Hu-MP:14
  Maryland! My Maryland!
    J. Randall. Se-PR:266
  My Maryland. J. Randall.
    Er-FA:441
  Nocturne. F. Frost. Co-BN:202
  Wild Peaches. E. Wylie.
    Pa-HT:40, Sh-AP:169
MASEFIELD, JOHN: see HUMOR -
    MASEFIELD, JOHN
MASKS (FOR THE FACE)
  Bloodtotem. K. Wilson. Sc-TN:237
  The Mask. E. Browning. Ox-BN:463,
    Rv-CB:778
  The Mask. C. Delaney. Hu-PN:177
  We Wear the Mask. P. Dunbar.
    Ad-IA:86, Ad-PB:8, Bo-AN:14,
    Bo-HF:103, Jo-SA:134, Lo-TY:208,
    Mo-BG:190
MASS: see LORD'S SUPPER
MASSACHUSETTS: see also names
    of towns, as SALEM, MASS.
  The Willows of Massachusetts.
    D. Levertov. Ha-WR:84
MASSACHUSETTS - HISTORY
  Hear, O Richmond! And Give Ear,
    O Carolina! T. Higginson.
    Kr-OF:38

Kidnappers! J. Clarke. Kr-OF:41
They Are Dead Now. J. Dos Passos.
    Kr-OF:120
Vanzetti Speaks to the Court.
    B. Vanzetti. Kr-OF:119
We Shall Not Die in Darkness.
    E. Millay. Kr-OF:123
MASSENET, JULES ÉMILE FRÉDÉRIC:
    see HUMOR - MASSENET, JULES
    ÉMILE FRÉDÉRIC
MATCHES: see HUMOR - MATCHES
MATERIALISM: see also
    WORLDLINESS
The Beast with Chrome Teeth.
    T. Snyder. Hu-NN:87
Christ Climbed Down.
    L. Ferlinghetti. Tr-MR:111
The Flesh and the Spirit.
    A. Bradstreet. Sh-AP:9
the greedy the people.
    E. Cummings. Pe-OA:155
Jehovah Buried, Satan Dead.
    E. Cummings. Pe-OA:147
Signpost. R. Jeffers. Al-VBP:1167
Statistics. S. Spender. Un-MB:471
The World Is Too Much with Us.
    W. Wordsworth. Al-VBP:660,
    Er-FA:267, Fe-PL:298, Gr-CT:201,
    Ke-PP:53, Ox-BN:79, Pa-GTB:299,
    Rv-CB:636, Sp-OG:365
MATHEMATICS: see also ARITHMETIC;
    GEOMETRY; HUMOR - MATHEMATICS
Euclid Alone. E. Millay.
    Er-FA:88, Ga-FB:3, Pl-IO:75,
    Un-MA:448
Gibbs. M. Rukeyser. Pl-IO:178
If Two's Company. Re-RR:16
Mathematics or the Gift of Tongues.
    A. Branch. Pl-IO:72
Reliques. E. Blunden. Pl-IO:71
Tulips. P. Colum. Pl-IO:76
MATHER, COTTON
Ben Franklin's Head (1728).
    M. Howe. Mc-WK:89
Cotton Mather. S. Benét.
    Hi-TL:29
MATTERHORN
Zermatt. T. Hardy. Ox-BN:823
MATURING: see CHANGE;
    GROWING UP
MAUSOLEUMS: see TOMBS
MAXIMS: see PROVERBS
MAY (MONTH): see also MAY DAY;
    SATIRE - MAY (MONTH)
And as for Me. G. Chaucer.
    Al-VBP:17, De-CH:13
Baby Seed Song. E. Nesbit.
    Bo-FP:238
Calling the Violet. L. Larcom.
    Hu-MP:249
Fairy Music. F. Ledwidge. Ha-YA:54

The Gladness of May.
    W. Wordsworth. Ha-YA:57
Here We Come a-Piping. Bl-OB:102,
    Br-SS:148, Ch-B:76, De-CH:11
Ho, for the May Rains. Sanpu.
    Be-CS:51
Hurdy-Gurdy Days. M. Clark.
    Hu-MP:293
In Praise of May. Re-BS:22
In the Merry Month of May.
    N. Breton. Al-VBP:85, Ha-PO:165,
    Un-MW:5
Lilacs. A. Lowell. Un-MA:160
Love in May. J. Passerat. Pa-SG:32
Love's Perjuries. W. Shakespeare.
    Al-VBP:181, Pa-GTB:13
The Mass of the Grove.
    D. ap Gwilym. Go-BP:73
May. W. Barnes. Gr-CT:48
May. W. Barnes. Co-PS:78
May. E. Spenser. Se-PR:110
A May Day. H. Wotton. De-CH:15
May Is Building Her House.
    R. Le Gallienne. Ha-YA:56
May Moon. O. Driver. Sh-RP:210
May Mornings. I. Eastwick.
    Br-SS:148
May 10th. M. Kumin. Co-BN:25,
    La-RM:134
May-Time. M. Gant. Bo-FP:236
Maytime Magic. M. Watts.
    Br-SG:11, Mc-AW:90
Memory. T. Aldrich. Co-BN:40,
    Fe-PL:378, Fr-WO:80
Mirth. C. Smart. Ox-BC:72
The Month of May. J. Fletcher
    and F. Beaumont. Gr-CT:44
O, the Month of May. T. Dekker.
    Al-VBP:225
Ode on the Spring. T. Gray.
    Pa-GTB:139
The Padstow Night Song.
    Gr-CT:44, Gr-GB:45
Québec May. E. Birney. Do-WH:75
Robin Hood and the Monk.
    Al-VBP:37, De-CH:135, Ox-BB:405
Song. S. Coleridge. Co-PS:83,
    De-CH:355, De-TT:148
Song for Youth. D. Burnett.
    Hu-MP:303
Song on May Morning. J. Milton.
    Cl-FC:38, Co-BN:23, De-CH:10,
    Ha-YA:55, Mc-PR:86, Se-PR:111
Spring Families. F. Frost. Sh-RP:198
A Spring Lilt. Hu-MP:303
Sunday up the River. J. Thomson.
    Al-VBP:1009
There Is But One May in the Year.
    C. Rossetti. Ar-TP3:206
'Tis Merry in Greenwood. W. Scott.
    Fe-FP:76, Hu-MP:302

MAY (MONTH) — cont'd.
  The Vow to Cupid. Pa-SG:68
MAY BASKETS: see MAY DAY
MAY DAY
  Corinna's Going a-Maying.
    R. Herrick. Co-BN:30, No-CL:278,
    Rv-CB:336, Se-PR:114
  The First of May. Bo-FP:235,
    Ir-BB:226, Mo-MGT:121, Mo-NR:91,
    Rv-ON:44, Wr-RM:66
  For a Dance. E. Farjeon.
    La-PH:55
  Hazel Dorn. B. Sleigh. De-CH:558
  The Judgment of the May.
    R. Dixon. Ox-BN:750
  The May Basket. D. Goodale.
    Bo-FP:233
  May Day. A. Fisher. La-PH:54
  May Day. M. Livingston.
    Br-SG:101
  May Day. S. Teasdale. Co-BN:39,
    Co-PS:81
  May-Day Song. Co-PS:83, Un-GT:274
  May-Pole Dance. Gr-GB:40,
    Hi-WP I:38
  The May Queen. A. Tennyson.
    Ch-B:76, Hu-MP:336, Se-PR:111
  May Song. Ga-S:184
  A Maypole. J. Swift. Rv-CB:488
  Old May Song. De-CH:12
  Sister, Awake. Co-PS:77, De-CH:11,
    Gr-CC:66
  Song of the Mayers. De-CH:12,
    Gr-GB:42
MAY QUEEN: see MAY DAY
MAYANS: see also INDIANS OF
    CENTRAL AMERICA - VERSE—
    MAYAN
  Copan. J. Rorty. Sm-PT:51
  Maya Hymn. Br-MW:5
MAYO COUNTY, IRE.
  The County Mayo. A. Raftery.
    Co-PI:179
MAYORS
  Mayor. Y. Amichai. Me-PH:131
  The Mayors. W. Blake. De-CH:62
MAYPOLES: see MAY DAY
MAZEPPA, IVAN STEPANOVICH
  Mazeppa. G. Byron. Hi-FO:169
MEADOWS: see FIELDS AND MEADOWS
MEADOWSWEET
  Meadowsweet. W. Allingham.
    Ox-BN:675
MEALS: see also HUMOR - MEALS;
    and names of meals, as
    SUPPER
  Dew-Bite. Gr-EC:110
MEANS AND ENDS
  On the Birth of My Son, Malcolm
    Coltrane. J. Lester.
    Ad-PB:356, Jo-SA:24

On the Danger of War. G. Meredith.
    Ba-PO:161, Ke-PP:90
MEASLES: see HUMOR - MEASLES
MEATH COUNTY, IRE.
  A Drover. P. Colum. Al-VBP:1148,
    Co-PI:26, Pa-HT:139, Un-MB:250
  Father and Son. F. Higgins.
    Co-PI:64
MECHANICS (PERSONS)
  Automobile Mechanics. D. Baruch.
    Ar-TP3:4, Au-SP:103, Fe-FP:35
  The Misery of Mechanics.
    P. Booth. Du-SH:151
MEDALS
  Reading a Medal. T. Tiller.
    Pa-GTB:550
MEDEA: see JASON AND MEDEA
MEDICINE: see also HUMOR -
    MEDICINE; MEDICINE MEN;
    NURSING; PHYSICIANS;
    QUACKS AND QUACKERY;
    REMEDIES AND CURES;
    SURGEONS AND SURGERY;
    VOODOO
  Some Western Haikus, VI.
    J. Kerouac. Kh-VA:12
  The Staff of Aesculapius.
    M. Moore. Pl-IO:147
  Young Lady. Do-CH:(12)
MEDICINE MEN
  Concerning Wisdom. D. Yazzie.
    Br-MW:63
  Curing Ritual. Da-SC:110
  Enchantment, II, Medicine Dance.
    L. Alexander. Ad-PB:59
  The Hopis and the Famine.
    Te-FC:35
  Lines from the Wind Chant.
    Br-MW:64
  Shaman's Song. Da-SC:49
  The Shumeekuli. Te-FC:217
  Song of a Medicine Man.
    Tr-US II:236
  The Sun Priest and the Witch-
    Woman. Te-FC:135
MEDIOCRITY: see also
    COMMONPLACENESS
  The Georgiad. R. Campbell.
    Un-MB:419
  Immolated. H. Melville.
    Al-VBP:957
MEDITATION: see THOUGHT AND
    THINKING
MEDITERRANEAN SEA
  The Mediterranean. A. Tate.
    Ca-VT:219, En-PC:39, Sh-AP:205,
    Un-MA:540, Wi-LT:401
MEDUSA (MYTH.)
  Head of Medusa. M. Zaturenska.
    Un-MA:561
  Medusa. L. Bogan. Un-MA:489

MEEKNESS: see HUMILITY;
    PATIENCE
MEETINGS (ENCOUNTERS):   see also
    HUMOR - MEETINGS (ENCOUNTERS);
    SATIRE - MEETINGS (ENCOUNTERS)
Again. C. Mew. Un-MB:163
At Dieppe: Rain on the Down.
    A. Symons. Ox-BN:934
Avoidances. R. Welburn.
    Ad-PB:466
Came You Not from Newcastle?
    Gr-GB:100
Destiny. E. Arnold. Fe-PL:338
Do You Remember That Night.
    Co-BL:33, Co-PI:157, Gr-SS:33
Dream Sequence, Part 9.
    N. Madgett. Ra-BP:195
Face to Face. A. Rich. Ha-TP:52,
    Wi-LT:803
Festival Songs, II. Tr-US II:158
The Girl by Green River. Rx-LT:19
The Great Coincidence. J. Hearst.
    St-H:80
I Met the Master. Fe-PL:337
A Joyful Chant. Le-OE:82
Juncture. R. Duncan. Hu-PN:574
Like a Sparkling Bead.
    I. Bedniakov. Mo-MI:30
Lucy in the Sky with Diamonds.
    The Beatles. Pe-SS:82
Meet-on-the-Road. Bl-OB:84,
    Co-PM:208, De-CH:674
Meeting. E. Greenberg. Ho-TY:310
A Meeting. G. Painter. Sm-MK:40
Meeting at Night. R. Browning.
    Co-BL:115, Ga-FB:62, Ho-LP:11,
    Ni-JP:98, Ox-BN:533, Rv-CB:819,
    Tu-WW:39, Un-MW:115
Meeting Mary. E. Farjeon.
    Br-BC:72
One Misty, Moisty Morning.
    Ar-TP3:166, Cl-DT:85, Ir-BB:212,
    La-PV:92, Li-LB:55, Mo-MGT:179,
    Mo-NR:14, Rv-ON:89, Wr-RM:50
A Passing. R. Cuscaden. St-H:31
Pippen Hill. Bl-OB:34, Ir-BB:214,
    Mo-MGT:141, Wr-RM:26
The Rendezvous. J. Anderson.
    Sc-TN:6
The Rendezvous. P. Lal. Al-PI:101
Small Quiet Song. R. Smith.
    Ad-CI:15
The Story of Rimini. L. Hunt.
    Na-EO:124
Time's Exile. W. Stafford.
    St-H:210
To Chuck—Concerning a Rendezvous
    in Siam. J. Charles. Mc-MK:198
To Flood Stage Again. J. Wright.
    Ho-P:319

To Meet, or Otherwise. T. Hardy.
    Ox-BN:836
To Wei Pa, a Retired Scholar.
    Tu Fu. Rx-OH:11
Vain Dream for John Clare.
    J. Hutton. Ls-NY:129
White Hill Looms Against the
    Black. A. Ivanov. Bo-RU:41
A Winter's Tale. D. Lawrence.
    Un-MB:287
MELANCHOLY: see also
    HUMOR - MELANCHOLY
Acquainted with the Night.
    R. Frost. Br-TC:135, Ca-VT:18,
    Fe-PL:402, Gr-CT:402, Ha-PO:218,
    Ha-TP:97, La-OC:136, La-PV:61,
    Mo-BG:189, Sh-AP:152, Un-MA:196,
    Wi-LT:176
Ain't Got No Home in This World
    Anymore. W. Guthrie. Kr-OF:194
Alone. Chu Shu Chen. Rx-OH:134
An Answer to Ting Yuan Ch'en.
    Ou Yang Hsiu. Rx-OH:59
At the Slackening of the Tide.
    J. Wright. Ca-VT:623
Autumn Note. G. Bacovia.
    Mc-AC:33
Autumn Song. C. Rossetti.
    Al-VBP:987, Ma-YA:212
Autumn Wind. Emperor Wu.
    Rx-LT:4, Sm-LG:398
Autumnal Ode. A. De Vere.
    Ox-BN:587
La Belle Dame sans Merci.
    Al-VBP:779, Bo-GJ:163, Bo-HF:22,
    De-CH:121, De-TT:200, Er-FA:409,
    Gr-CT:178, Gr-SS:108, Ha-PO:6,
    Hi-WP II:106, Ho-P:80, Mc-WK:8,
    Ni-JP:98, No-CL:65, Ox-BN:376,
    Pa-GTB:193, Rv-CB:735, Sm-LG:217,
    Sm-MK:46, Sp-OG:113, Un-GT:26
Blues. Q. Prettyman. Ad-BO:60
Break, Break, Break. A. Tennyson.
    Bl-OB:51, Bo-GJ:182, De-CH:211,
    Ga-FB:128, Ha-PO:137, Ma-YA:192,
    Ox-BN:485, Pa-GTB:331, Sp-OG:267
By the Winding River. Tu Fu.
    Rx-OH:13
Chimes. D. Rossetti. Ox-BN:686
A Christmas Note for Geraldine
    Udall. K. Rexroth. Bl-FP:59
The City of Dreadful Night.
    J. Thomson. Al-VBP:1007,
    Pa-GTB:382
Come Back Blues. M. Harper.
    Ad-PB:314
Complaint. Tr-US I:34
Complaint of a New Wife.
    Tr-US II:188
A Country God. E. Blunden.
    Un-MB:396

MELANCHOLY — cont'd.
The Crazy Woman.   G. Brooks.
   Ab-MO:28, Bo-HF:136, Li-TU:151
The Crescent Moon.   Mei Yao Ch'en.
   Rx-OH:40
The Cycle.   Hsü Hsü.   Hs-TC:275
D Blues.   C. Hernton.   Ad-PB:244
The Day Is Done.   J. Longfellow.
   Ch-B:68, Er-FA:488, Mc-PR:142
Death of a Friend.   P. Murray.
   Ad-PB:110
Decline.   I. Vinea.   Mc-AC:73
Dejection.   S. Coleridge.
   Ox-BN:167, Rv-CB:665
Depression.   R. Bly.   St-H:4
Desolate.   S. Dobell.   Ox-BN:659,
   Rv-CB:879
A Dirge.   P. Shelley.   Gr-CT:195,
   Ho-WR:234, Mo-GR:86
Distance Spills Itself.
   Y. Bat-Miriam.   Me-PH:104
Don't Bomb "Human Nature" Out of
   Existence.   J. Tagliabue.
   Du-SH:94
Down in the Lonesome Garden.
   Ra-BP:8
Dream-Land.   E. Poe.   Rv-CB:809,
   Sh-AP:56
Edgar Allan Poe.   R. Barlow.
   De-FS:11
Elsewhere.   G. Bacovia.   Mc-AC:33
Epistle to John Hamilton Reynolds.
   J. Keats.   Ox-BN:369
An Evening Air.   S. Sen.   Al-PI:87
Evening Comes.   Li Shang Yin.
   Rx-LT:78
Expression of Time.   Li Chin-fa.
   Hs-TC:172
Fall Down.   C. Hernton.   Ad-PB:243
Father, the Year Is Fallen.
   A. Lorde.   Ad-PB:246
Funeral March.   G. Bacovia.
   Mc-AC:34
The Garden of Proserpina.
   E. Spenser.   Gr-CT:263
Girl's Song.   Tr-US II:306
Hurting.   B. Graves.   Le-M:167
Hysteria.   Chu Shu Chen.
   Rx-OH:128
I Came Out of a Café.
   Wang Tu-ch'ing.   Hs-TC:194
I Got the Blues.   Lo-TY:203
I Know Not Why, but All This
   Weary Day.   H. Timrod.   Sh-AP:124
I Pass the Night at General
   Headquarters.   Tu Fu.   Rx-OH:25
I Walk Out into the Country at
   Night.   Lu Yu.   Rx-OH:108
Improvised Songs, II, III.
   Tr-US II:130

In Memoriam.   A. Tennyson.
   Gr-CT:315, Hi-WP II:143,
   Ox-BN:495, 500
Jade Flower Palace.   Tu Fu.
   Rx-OH:9
January 3, 1970.   M. Jackson.
   Ad-PB:499
A Journey.   Li Kuang-t'ien.
   Hs-TC:203
Kibkarjuk Calls to Mind the
   Times.   Tr-US I:14
King David.   W. de la Mare.
   Li-TU:169
The Last Day.   Wen I-to.   Hs-TC:55
Let Us.   R. Veprinski.   Ho-TY:161
Life Is Long.   Rx-LT:8
The Light of Summer's End.
   I. Schwartz.   Ho-TY:146
Little Ivory Figures Pulled with
   a String.   A. Lowell.   Al-VBP:1124
Lyke as a Ship That Through the
   Ocean Wyde.   E. Spencer.
   Ma-YA:55
Melancholy.   J. Fletcher.
   Al-VBP:281, Pa-GTB:86
Mnemosyne.   T. Stickney.
   Al-VBP:1123
Le Monocle de Mon Oncle.
   W. Stevens.   Wi-LT:135
My Eyes Watching.   K. Nakamura.
   Sh-AM:147
My Sadness Sits Around Me.
   J. Jordan.   Ra-BP:248
New Grave.   Ch'in Yzu-hao.
   Pa-MV:55
Night.   G. Bacovia.   Mc-AC:35
Night Is Still Young.
   Chang Hsiu-ya.   Pa-MV:30
Night Thoughts while Travelling.
   Tu Fu.   Rx-OH:33
No Single Hour Can Stand for
   Naught.   J. Clare.   Ox-BN:328
No Voyage.   M. Oliver.   St-H:162
November.   T. Hughes.   Pa-GTB:565
The Ocean Wood.   J. Warren.
   Rv-CB:935
Ode on Melancholy.   J. Keats.
   Al-VBP:778, Ox-BN:360, Rv-CB:744
Old Age.   Ou Yang Hsiu.   Rx-OH:62
The Old Anguish.   Chu Shu Chen.
   Rx-OH:131
The Old Clock on the Stairs.
   H. Longfellow.   Sp-OG:309
The Old Summerhouse.
   W. de la Mare.   Pa-GTB:439
On an Air of Rameau.   A. Symons.
   Ox-BN:936
The Pale Temple Bell.   Mu Mu-t'ien.
   Hs-TC:188
The Path of the Lonely Ones.
   G. Varela.   Ba-HI:87

Pear-Trees by the Fence.
  Su Tung-p'o. Pa-SG:90
Il Penseroso. J. Milton.
  Al-VBP:393, Pa-GTB:98, Rv-CB:370
Poem. P. Markish. Ho-TY:181
Poor Wayfaring Stranger. Ga-S:48
Proserpine. A. Swinburne.
  Gr-CT:262
Quail Sky. Li Ch'ing Chao.
  Rx-OH:95
The Rainy Day. H. Longfellow.
  Fe-PL:303
The Raven. E. Poe. Al-VBP:865,
  Bo-GJ:165, Co-RG:103, De-CH:303,
  Er-FA:312, Ga-FB:134, Sh-AP:56,
  Sm-LG:207
Resolution and Independence.
  W. Wordsworth. Li-SR:109
Revisiting South of the River.
  Hsü Hsü. Hs-TC:273
The River. M. Arnold. Rv-CB:866
Sabbath Stars. A. Shlonsky.
  Me-PH:101
The Sad Look of a Season.
  Tu Yûn-hsieh. Hs-TC:249
The Sad Lover. G. Crabbe.
  Ox-BN:17
Sadness. Le-IB:115
The Sands of Time. R. Howard.
  De-FS:107
Seclusion. E. Mörike. Un-R:107
Secret Prayer. Hsü Hsü. Hs-TC:274
Sept. 16, 1961, Poem. J. Kerouac.
  Kh-VA:38
Serenade of a Loyal Martyr.
  G. Darley. Ox-BN:395
The Shepherdess. Cheng Ch'ou-yü.
  Pa-MV:40
The Shrubbery. W. Cowper.
  Rv-CB:547
Snow Storm. Tu Fu. Rx-OH:6
Soft Voice. Fang Wei-teh.
  Hs-TC:137
Song. M. Holman. Jo-SA:86
Song. A. Tennyson. Ox-BN:476,
  Pa-GTB:330
Song at the Berry-Picking on the
  Mountain. Da-SC:38, Le-IB:89
Song of Autumn. P. Verlaine.
  Pa-SG:96
Sorrow of Mydath. J. Masefield.
  Un-MB:222
Soul. D. Graham. Ad-PB:482
Spleen. E. Dowson. Un-MB:148
Spring. W. Allingham. Ox-BN:673
Spring. Chu Shu Chen. Rx-OH:130
Stanzas - April, 1814.
  P. Shelley. Ox-BN:275
Stanzas from "Child Harold."
  J. Clare. Ox-BN:325

Stanzas Written in Dejection, near
  Naples. P. Shelley. Al-VBP:745,
  Ga-FB:125, Pa-GTB:227, Rv-CB:707
Tears. A. Lopez. Al-WW:3
Tears. E. Thomas. Pa-GTB:441,
  Rv-CB:969
Tears, Idle Tears. A. Tennyson.
  Al-VBP:859, Er-FA:150, Ha-PO:150,
  Hi-WP II:144, Ox-BN:486
The Terrace in the Snow.
  Su Tung P'o. Rx-OH:71
There Is a Grave. Chu Hsiang.
  Hs-TC:99
To Pi Ssu Yao. Tu Fu.
  Pl-ML:79 Rx-OH:15
The Traveler. Ho Hsun. Rx-LT:41
Travelling Northward. Tu Fu.
  Rx-OH:10
Tropes of One Season. C. Eaton.
  De-FS:85
Ulalume. E. Poe. Al-VBP:869,
  Sh-AP:58
Ungathered Love. P. Marston.
  Ox-BN:890
The Valley of Unrest. E. Poe.
  Al-VBP:872
Venice. Wang Tu-ch'ing. Hs-TC:195
Visiting Tsan, Abbot of Ta-Yun.
  Tu Fu. Rx-OH:7
A Voice from the Waters.
  T. Beddoes. Ox-BN:449, Rv-CB:771
Wait. E. Botta. Mc-AC:111
Ways of My Exile. R. Roseliep.
  St-H:181
What the Chimney Sang.
  B. Harte. Sp-OG:307
When the Moon Is in the River of
  Heaven. Ou Yang Hsiu. Rx-OH:54
William Bond. Ox-BB:674
The Window. Li Kuang-t'ien.
  Hs-TC:203
The Winter's Walk. S. Johnson.
  Rv-CB:526

MELANESIAN VERSE
  Charm to Restore a Dying Man.
    Tr-US I:189
  Courting Song and Reply.
    Tr-US I:190
  I Came from under the Earth.
    Le-OE:137
  In Honor of Maros During His
    Absence at Sea. Tr-US I:216
  Kite-Flying Song. Tr-US I:217
  Lament of a Widow for Her Dead
    Husband. Tr-US I:189
  Love Song. Tr-US I:190
  Men's Song. Tr-US I:208, 209
  Old Funeral Chant. Tr-US II:43
  A Song at a Men's Secret Society.
    Tr-US I:208

MELANESIAN VERSE — cont'd.
  Song of a Woman Named Hi Pak.
    Hi Pak.   Tr-US I:207
  Songs, I, II.   Tr-US I:191
  Woman's Song.   Tr-US I:190
  Women's Song.   Tr-US I:209
  Women's Song at a Dance Festival.
    Tr-US I:209
  Women's Song at a Wedding Feast.
    Tr-US I:208
MELANESIAN VERSE-FIJIAN
  Dance Song.   Tr-US I:232
  The Epic of Dengei.   Tr-US I:233
  Epic Song.   Tr-US I:236
  On the Pestilence That Scourged
    the Fijians after Their First
    Contact with Whites, ca. 1791.
    Tr-US I:228
  The Shades of the Newly Dead to the
    Gods.   Tr-US I:227
  Song.   Tr-US I:230
  Song on the Great Visitation of
    Measles in 1875.   Tr-US I:228
  Song on the War in the Mountains
    of Viti Levu in 1876.
    Tr-US I:229
MELANESIAN VERSE-PAPUAN
  Asking where the Thunder Peals.
    Tr-US I:195
  A Bird That Calls Before Dawn.
    Tr-US I:194
  Canoe Song.   Tr-US I:202
  Charm at a Ceremonial Bathing to
    Make One Beautiful and
    Irresistible.   Tr-US I:197
  Charm for Rain.   Tr-US I:214
  Dance Songs, IV.   Tr-US I:199
  The Dancer.   Koma Doube Pio.
    Tr-US I:192
  Dirge for a Son Killed in Battle.
    Tr-US I:187
  Incantation at First Twining Yam
    Vines.   Tr-US I:196
  Kahuto, the Owl.   Tr-US I:214
  Love Incantation.   Tr-US I:201
  Man's Song.   Tr-US I:212
  Man's Song Against a Woman.
    Tr-US I:213
  Marriage Song.   Tr-US I:201
  Song.   Koma Doube Pio.
    Tr-US I:192
  Song.   Tr-US I:202
  Song at a Public Courtship
    Ceremony.   Tr-US I:188
  Song of a Sick Chief. Tr-US I:211
  Song of Old Age and a White Head.
    Tr-US I:193
  Song of the Departed Spirit.
    Tr-US I:197
  Song Sung while Fencing a Garden.
    Tr-US I:193

  Thief's Spell.   Tr-US I:207
  An Unknown Land.   Tr-US I:194
  War Song, Sung Before Going into
    Battle.   Tr-US I:201
  Woman's Song.   Tr-US I:212, 213
  Women's Song at a Girl's Initia-
    tion.   Tr-US I:188
  The World Calling on Dawn.
    Tr-US I:195
  Young Men's Song.   Tr-US I:187
MELANESIAN VERSE-TROBRIANDAN
  A Joyful Chant.   Le-OE:82
  Love-Magic Spell.   Tr-US I:205
  Song of War.   Tr-US I:203
MELCHIZEDEK, KING OF SALEM
  Two Men.   E. Robinson.   Un-GT:91
MELONS
  The Beach.   W. Hart-Smith.
    Gr-EC:111
  Melon Girl.   Mei Yao Ch'en.
    Rx-OH:39
  My Daily Melon.
    G. Bishop-Dubjinsky.   Sc-TN:13
MELVILLE, HERMAN
  At Melville's Tomb.   H. Crane.
    Ca-VT:214, Un-MA:534
MELVILLE, THOMAS
  The Last Leaf.   O. Holmes.
    Bo-HF:134, Fe-FP:321, Fe-PL:265,
    Mc-WK:135, Sp-OG:261
MEMORIAL DAY: see also WAR DEAD
  After.   R. Kipling.   Mc-PR:66
  A Ballad of Heroes.   A. Dobson.
    Se-PR:133
  Bivouac of the Dead. T. O'Hara.
    Ke-TF:256, Se-PR:133, Vi-PP:201
  The Blue and the Gray.
    F. Finch.   Hi-TL:129, Sp-OG:206,
    Vi-PP:163
  Centennial Hymn.   J. Pierpont.
    Vi-PP:88
  Decoration Day.   H. Longfellow.
    Co-PS:90, Hu-MP:338
  Griefs for Dead Soldiers.
    T. Hughes.   Go-BP:211
  How Sleep the Brave.   W. Collins.
    Al-VBP:572, Pa-GTB:119,
    Rv-CB:536, Sp-OG:208
  May Thirtieth.   Co-PS:94
  Memorial Day.   W. Brooks.
    Se-PR:137, Vi-PP:218
  Memorial Day.   T. Garrison.
    Co-PS:94, Hu-MP:339
  Memorial Rain.   A. MacLeish.
    Un-MA:454
  Memorial Wreath.   D. Randall.
    Ad-PB:140, Hu-NN:59, Hu-PN:305
  A Monument for the Soldiers.
    J. Riley.   Se-PR:135
  More than Flowers We Have Brought.
    N. Turner.   Br-SS:157

Ode to the Confederate Dead in
  Magnolia Cemetery. H. Timrod.
  Se-PR:134, Sh-AP:126, Vi-PP:165
Remembering Day. M. Saunders.
  Ha-YA:60
Reply to "In Flanders Fields."
  J. Mitchell. Vi-PP:212
Soldier, Rest! W. Scott.
  De-CH:600, De-TT:140, Ho-PR:282,
  Mc-PR:67, Mc-WK:204, Ox-BN:130
MEMORIES: see also CHILDHOOD
  RECOLLECTIONS; HUMOR –
  MEMORIES; KEEPSAKES;
  LOVE – MEMORIES
Absence. C. Mew.   Un-MB:165
Adlestrop. E. Thomas.
  Bl-OB:141, Bo-GJ:86, De-CH:95,
  Ma-FW:115, No-CL:253, Pa-HT:127
after any sunset. M. Bruce.
  Ad-II:37
The After-Glow. M. Blind.
  Ox-BN:849
After the Visit. T. Hardy.
  Ox-BN:835
Aftermath. S. Sassoon.
  Al-VBP:1167, Un-MB:314
Afterwards. T. Hardy.
  Al-VBP:1050, Co-BN:210, De-CH:435,
  Gr-CT:353, Ni-JP:172, No-CL:284,
  Ox-BN:846, Pa-GTB:412, Rv-CB:944,
  Un-MB:31, Wi-LT:25
Against Oblivion. H. Newbolt.
  De-CH:202, De-TT:193
The Aged Maple Tree.
  Chung Ting-wen. Pa-MV:76
Akjartoq's Song of the Olden Days.
  Le-IB:110, Tr-US I:15
Alone. Chu Shu Chen. Rx-OH:134
L'An Trentièsme de Mon Eage.
  A. MacLeish. Gr-SS:53,
  Un-MA:454, Wi-LT:340
An Ancient to Ancients. T. Hardy.
  Pa-GTB:412, Wi-LT:28
Andree Rexroth. K. Rexroth.
  Ca-VT:269
An Anniversary: A Country Burial.
  A. Stanford. Ha-TP:126
Another Vexation. Hu P'in-ch'ing.
  Pa-MV:98
Antique Shop. C. Carmer.
  Fe-FP:320, Sh-RP:316, Th-AS:166
Anton and Yaro. M. Oliver.
  St-H:168
The Apple. J. Halevi. Me-PH:61
Appoggiatura. D. Hayes. Ad-PB:94,
  Bo-AN:90, Hu-PN:246
At a Concert of Music. C. Aiken.
  Pl-US:148, Un-MA:430
At Casterbridge Fair. T. Hardy.
  Ox-BN:832

At Night. A. Meynell. De-CH:451,
  Go-BP:133
August from My Desk. R. Flint.
  Br-AF:156, Du-RG:49
Auld Lang Syne. R. Burns.
  Bo-FP:209, Er-FA:425, Fe-PL:129,
  Ma-YA:133, Sp-OG:260
Aunt Jemima of the Ocean Waves.
  R. Hayden. Ad-PB:125
Autumn Wind. Emperor Wu.
  Rx-LT:4, Sm-LG:398
Autumnal Ode. A. De Vere.
  Ox-BN:587
Bacchus. R. Emerson.
  Al-VBP:803, Sh-AP:27
The Ballad of Bouillabaisse.
  W. Thackeray. Al-VBP:879
A Ballad of Remembrance.
  R. Hayden. Ad-PB:115, Bo-AN:109,
  Hu-PN:291, Ra-BP:131
The Bean Eaters. G. Brooks.
  Ad-PB:154, Be-MA:81, Jo-SA:23,
  Lo-TY:245
Beeny Cliff. T. Hardy. Ox-BN:843
Before the World Was Made.
  W. Yeats. Pa-GTB:431
Ben Bolt. T. English. Er-FA:342
Beyond the Last Lamp. T. Hardy.
  Ox-BN:837
The Bishop Orders His Tomb at
  Saint Praxed's Church.
  R. Browning. Al-VBP:895,
  Mo-GR:57
Blue and Red Poem. A. Gilboa.
  Me-PH:118
Blue Sunday. T. McNeill.
  Sa-B:5
Break, Break, Break. A. Tennyson.
  Bl-OB:51, Bo-GJ:182, De-CH:211,
  Ga-FB:128, Ha-PO:137, Ma-YA:192,
  Ox-BN:485, Pa-GTB:331, Sp-OG:267
The Brothers. E. Muir. Pa-GTB:471
Bumi. I. Baraka. Ad-PB:256
By the City Gate. Ts'ui Hao.
  Rx-LT:63
By the Exeter River. D. Hall.
  Ca-MB:21, To-MP:147
Ca'line's Prayer. L. Clifton.
  Ba-MA:141
Cat. J. Tolkien. Gr-EC:68
Chapter Two. W. Scott. Gr-CC:186
The Chinese Nightingale.
  V. Lindsay. Un-MA:229
The Ch'ing Ming Festival.
  Feng Hsüeh-feng. Hs-TC:368
A Christmas Banquet.
  C. Lushington. Sa-B:53
A Christmas Note for Geraldine
  Udall. K. Rexroth. Bl-FP:59
The Christmas Robin. R. Graves.
  Gr-CC:48

MEMORIES — cont'd.
A City by the Sea.   A. Margolin.
    Ho-TY:162
Click.   B. Akhmadulina.   Bo-RU:4
Coal for Mike.   B. Brecht.
    Li-TU:142
The Coin.   S. Teasdale.
    Ar-TP3:213, Sh-RP:108, Th-AS:217
Colder Fire.   R. Warren.
    Wi-LT:835
Confessions.   R. Browning.
    Al-VBP:908, Pa-GTB:355
The Convict of Clonmel.   Co-PI:16,
    Mo-SD:174
Cranberry Road.   R. Field.
    Th-AS:134
Crazy Jane and the Bishop.
    W. Yeats.   Wi-LT:88
A Cry.   F. Bianco.   No-CL:261
Cuckoos.   M. Kaneko.   Sh-AM:62
Daffodils.   W. Wordsworth.
    Al-VBP:657, Bl-OB:137, Bo-GJ:71,
    Bo-HF:48, Ch-B:59, Co-BN:56,
    Er-FA:258, Fe-FP:218, Ga-FB:22,
    Ha-PO:95, Hi-WP II:33, Hu-MP:252,
    Ke-TF:434, Li-SR:105, Ma-YA:140,
    Mc-PR:188, Ox-BN:65, Pa-GTB:259,
    Re-TW:102, Sm-MK:188, Sp-OG:287,
    Tu-WW:64, Un-GT:254
Dance of the Infidels.   A. Young.
    Ad-PB:363
Dark Hotel.   A. Dorn.   De-FS:74
Dark Symphony III: Andante
    Sostenuto.   M. Tolson.   Bo-AN:38
Dear Men & Women.   J. Wheelock.
    Ho-P:307
The Death of a Negro Poet.
    C. Rivers.   Ra-BP:201
Death Songs.   L. Mack.   Ad-PB:499
Death Was a Trick.   J. Mazzaro.
    Mc-EA:65
A Decanter of Madeira, Aged 86, to
    George Bancroft, Aged 86.
    S. Mitchell.   Al-VBP:992
A Deep-Sworn Vow.   W. Yeats.
    Co-EL:8
Dejection.   S. Coleridge.
    Ox-BN:167, Rv-CB:665
The Descent.   W. Williams.
    En-PC:3
A Deserted Home.   S. Lysaght.
    De-CH:50
Directive.   R. Frost.   Un-MA:195,
    Wi-LT:185
Discordants.   C. Aiken.   Co-BL:35,
    Er-FA:108, Un-MA:421, Wi-LT:325
Do You Remember Me?   W. Landor.
    Al-VBP:707, Ox-BN:188
Domination of Black.   W. Stevens.
    Ha-TP:108, Un-MA:244

A Dream.   B. Akhmadulina.
    Ca-MR:41
A Dream.   W. Allingham.   Co-PI:9,
    Co-PT:70
A Dream at Night.   Mei Yao Ch'en.
    Rx-OH:43
Dream-Land.   E. Poe.   Rv-CB:809,
    Sh-AP:56
Dusk.   L. Nathan.   Ls-NY:132
The Earthly Paradise 1.
    W. Morris.   Al-VBP:1015,
    Ox-BN:785
The Elegance of Memory.
    K. Kgositsile.   Be-MA:147
Elizabeth at the Piano.
    H. Gregory.   Gr-SS:134, Pl-US:20
Ere Sleep Comes Down to Soothe
    the Weary Eyes.   P. Dunbar.
    Hu-PN:43
Etta Moten's Attic.   M. Danner.
    Ad-PB:136, Be-MA:90, Bo-AN:156
Expression of Time.   Li Chin-fa.
    Hs-TC:172
A Falling Star.   Li Kuang-t'ien.
    Hs-TC:205
Father and Son.   S. Kunitz.
    Br-TC:247
A Few Things Explained.
    P. Neruda.   Li-TU:237
La Figlia Che Piange. T. Eliot.
    Al-VBP:1184, Ca-VT:130,
    Gr-BT:44, No-CL:246
The Fire of Drift-Wood.
    H. Longfellow.   Mo-BG:148
For All That Ever Has Been Ours.
    Z. Landau.   Ho-TY:97
For Jan.   J. Bruchac.   Ni-CD:44
For the Candle Light.   A. Grimke.
    Hu-PN:55
For the Fallen.   L. Binyon.
    Al-VBP:1109
For the Girls in My Home Town.
    N. Korzhavin.   Ca-MR:91
Forgetfulness.   Chang Hsiu-ya.
    Pa-MV:33
Four Ducks on a Pond.
    W. Allingham.   Bl-OB:66,
    Ch-B:28, De-CH:517, Du-RG:99,
    Hi-WP I:30, Re-TW:11
Four Sheets to the Wind and a
    One-Way Ticket to France, 1933.
    C. Rivers.   Ad-PB:234, Bo-AN:176,
    Hu-NN:107, Hu-PN:404, Ra-BP:199
Frail Hands.   L. Trent.   De-FS:198
Freeport.   R. Cuscaden.   St-H:31
Friar's Hunting Song. T. Peacock.
    De-TT:83, Mo-SD:116, Un-GT:89
Genealogy.   V. Felea.   Mc-AC:130
Gerontion.   T. Eliot.
    Pa-GTB:474, Wi-LT:282

Goldenhair. J. Joyce. Co-BL:86,
  Gr-CC:73, Gr-CT:89, Ha-LO:3,
  Sh-RP:83, Th-AS:69
The Gone. J. Stuart. De-FS:195
Grandfather in the Old Men's Home.
  W. Merwin. Wi-LT:768
Grandparents. R. Lowell.
  Mc-EA:106, Wi-LT:585
The Green Valley. S. Warner.
  Un-MB:377
Gunpowder Plot. V. Scannell.
  Ma-FW:267, To-MP:70
Hastings Mill. C. Smith.
  Mc-WK:196
Havana Dreams. L. Hughes.
  Hu-PN:189
He Fell among Thieves. H. Newbolt.
  Pa-OM:227, Sp-OG:47
He Has Fallen from the Height of
  His Love. W. Blunt. Al-VBP:1053
Hearing the Early Oriole.
  Po Chü-i. Pl-US:128
Hemmed-In Males. W. Williams.
  Ha-PO:74
Heraclitus. W. Cory. Al-VBP:973,
  Co-EL:74, Co-PU:149, Hi-WP II:21,
  Ox-BN:648, Pa-SG:13, Pl-ML:143,
  Rv-CB:875
Holidays. H. Longfellow.
  Hu-MP:326
Home No More Home to Me.
  R. Stevenson. De-CH:25
Hour of Memories. A. Shamri.
  Ho-TY:362
The House. R. Debee. Al-PI:84
The House of Falling Leaves.
  W. Braithwaite. Hu-PN:47
The House That Was. L. Binyon.
  Un-MB:157
I Call the Old Time Back.
  J. Whittier. Al-VBP:829
I Gazed upon the Cloudless Moon.
  E. Brontë. Gr-CT:406
i remember how she sang.
  R. Penny. Ad-PB:388
I Remember the Blue River.
  Mei Yao Ch'en. Rx-OH:44
I Remember the River at Wu Sung.
  Mei Yao Ch'en. Rx-OH:47
Imperialists in Retirement.
  E. Lucie-Smith. To-MP:149
In a Drear-Nighted December.
  J. Keats. De-CH:216, Ox-BN:373,
  Pa-GTB:191, Rv-CB:737
In a Girls' School. D. Morton.
  Se-PR:243
In Front of the Landscape.
  T. Hardy. Ox-BN:832
In Memoriam. A. Tennyson.
  Ox-BN:501, 506, 507
In Old Age. B. Chamberlain.
  Ls-NY:179
In the Garden at Swainston.
  A. Tennyson. Ox-BN:493
In the Garden of Paradise Others
  May Bask. A. Akhmatova.
  Ca-MR:186
In the Gloaming. M. Orred.
  Er-FA:490
In the Spring when the Sun Never
  Sets. L. Evaloardjuak.
  Le-IB:108
In the Third Year of the War.
  H. Treece. Cr-WS:73
Inscription for a Mirror in a
  Deserted Dwelling. W. Benét.
  Un-MA:329
Insomnia. Lu Yu. Rx-LT:103
Into My Heart an Air That Kills.
  A. Housman. Al-VBP:1080,
  Bo-GJ:199, Gr-CT:275, Na-EO:193,
  Un-MB:94, Wi-LT:62
Iris. T. McNeill. Sa-B:6
Irish Grandmother. K. Edelman.
  Br-AF:43, Br-SS:136
The Isle of Long Ago. B. Taylor.
  Er-FA:166
It Is Becoming Now to Declare
  My Allegiance. C. Day-Lewis.
  Wi-LT:425
It's a Queer Time. R. Graves.
  Un-MB:384
James Powell on Imagination.
  L. Neal. Ra-BP:269
Jeanie with the Light Brown Hair.
  S. Foster. Er-FA:426
Jenny Kissed Me. L. Hunt.
  Al-VBP:714, Br-BC:138, Co-FB:260,
  Er-FA:104, Ga-FB:51, Hi-WP I:42,
  Li-SR:32, Ma-YA:172, Un-MW:23
A Jew. J. Segal. Ho-TY:156
John Kinsella's Lament for Mrs.
  Mary Moore. W. Yeats. Wi-LT:93
John Marr. H. Melville.
  Al-VBP:952
The Journey Onwards. T. Moore.
  Pa-GTB:220
Kibkarjuk Calls to Mind the Times.
  Tr-US I:14
Kilcash. F. O'Connor. Co-PI:155,
  Hi-WP II:132, Re-TW:86
Kivers. A. Cobb. Br-AF:133
Lament for the Cowboy Life.
  J. Mitchell. Co-RM:21
The Lamentation of the Old
  Pensioner. W. Yeats.
  Co-PI:207, Ke-PP:100
The Last Day of Leave. R. Graves.
  Cr-WS:65
Lee in the Mountains, 1865-1870.
  D. Davidson. Sm-PT:92

MEMORIES — cont'd.
A Leg in a Plaster Cast.
  M. Rukeyser. Un-MA:627
Let Us Now Praise Famous Men.
  Bible. O.T. Ecclesiastes.
  Gr-CT:376
Letter to E. Franklin Frazier.
  I. Baraka. Ad-PB:253, Ra-BP:217
The Light of Summer's End.
  I. Schwartz. Ho-TY:146
Lines. W. Wordsworth. Ox-BN:66
Lines Based on a 1924 Advertisement.
  G. Lehmann. Ls-NY:264
Lines Composed above Tintern Abbey.
  W. Wordsworth. Go-BP:21,
  Ho-P:125
The Little Trumpet. C. Govoni.
  Li-TU:48
A Little While, a Little While.
  E. Brontë. Al-VBP:922,
  Ox-BN:596
Long Distance. W. Stafford.
  St-H:216
Looking for a Sunset Bird in
  Winter. R. Frost. Re-BS:17
Looking in the Album.
  V. Rutsala. Du-SH:172
Lost Voice on This Hill. B. Eaton.
  De-FS:84
Love in Exile. M. Blind.
  Ox-BN:849
Lydia Is Gone This Many a Year.
  L. Reese. Bo-GJ:236, De-CH:261,
  Gr-CC:11
Marina. T. Eliot. Pa-GTB:476,
  Sh-AP:185
Meeting. E. Greenberg. Ho-TY:310
Mementos. W. Snodgrass.
  Un-MA:684, Un-MW:105
Memorabilia. R. Browning.
  No-CL:18, Ox-BN:544, Pl-ML:124,
  Rv-CB:826
Memoranda. W. Dickey. Du-SH:173
Memories Are Great Great Things.
  "Monk." Ba-HI:32
The Memory-Filled House.
  M. White. Le-M:177
The Mill. R. Wilbur. Pe-OA:259
Mnemosyne. T. Stickney.
  Al-VBP:1123
Modern Love XII. G. Meredith.
  Al-VBP:982
The Moon Is Full. Liu Ta-Pai.
  Hs-TC:6
Musica. G. Montgomery. Lo-IT:94
Musings. W. Barnes. Ox-BN:435
My Early Home. J. Clare.
  Fe-PL:146
My Eyes Are Tired. Ho-SD:73
My Father. J. Sternberg. Ho-TY:194

My Father's Trunk. R. Roseliep.
  St-H:188
My Grandmother. K. Shapiro.
  Ca-VT:372
My Little Dreams. G. Johnson.
  Hu-PN:81
My Spirit Will Not Haunt the
  Mound. T. Hardy. Ox-BN:838,
  Un-MB:32
My Thoughts Went Constantly.
  Le-IB:99
Nahuatl Poem. Ho-LP:85
New Year's Poem. M. Avison.
  Wi-LT:661
Night in Boston. J. Harrison.
  Sc-TN:86
The Night Is Freezing Fast.
  A. Housman. Wi-LT:66
Night on the Great River.
  Meng Hao Jan. Rx-LT:49
Nocturne at Bethesda.
  A. Bontemps. Be-MA:43,
  Bo-AN:81, Hu-PN:211
Nostalgia. K. Shapiro. Br-TC:371
Nostalgia. W. Stevens. Wi-LT:134
Notes Found near a Suicide.
  F. Horne. Ad-PB:48, Bo-AN:42,
  Hu-PN:151
Notes Found near a Suicide:
  To "Chick." F. Horne.
  Bo-AN:43, Ra-BP:71
now poem. for us. S. Sanchez.
  Ad-PB:290
An Occasional Image. A. Sawai.
  Sh-AM:136
Ode on a Distant Prospect of
  Eton College. T. Gray.
  Al-VBP:563, Pa-GTB:158
Oft in the Stilly Night. T. Moore.
  Co-PI:146, De-TT:153, Er-FA:150,
  Hi-WP I:116, Ho-P:309, Ox-BN:219,
  Pa-GTB:224, Rv-CB:680
The Old Anguish. Chu Shu Chen.
  Rx-OH:131
The Old Cabin. P. Dunbar.
  Fe-PL:426
The Old Familiar Faces. C. Lamb.
  Al-VBP:701, Er-FA:168, Ha-PO:152,
  Ma-YA:168, Mo-GR:43, Pa-GTB:220,
  Rv-CB:672
Old Man, Phantom Dog. F. Eckman.
  St-H:49
An Old Man's Night Thoughts.
  Tr-US I:134
The Old Men. W. de la Mare.
  Un-MB:199
Old Ships. D. Morton. Tu-WW:34
The Old Swimmer. C. Morley.
  Mo-SD:178
The Old Times Were the Best.
  J. Riley. Er-FA:172

The Old Ute Trail.   Fi-BG:109
An Old Woman Laments in Spring-
   time.   E. Sitwell. Al-VBP:1170
An Old Woman Remembers.
   S. Brown.   Ad-PB:68
Old Women Remember. R. Boyle.
   Ls-NY:73
On a Hand. H. Belloc.   Co-BL:45,
   Co-EL:13, Co-PU:77
On Falling Asleep to Birdsong.
   W. Meredith. En-PC:174
On Hurricane Jackson. A. Dugan.
   Mo-BG:48, Mo-SD:80, Pe-M:63
On the Arizona Line. Fi-BG:36
On the Way to Kew. W. Henley.
   Al-VBP:1068, Ox-BN:885
Once. E. Batterham. De-CH:242
Once Again. L. Bahe. Ni-CD:12
Original Sin: A Short Story.
   R. Warren. Wi-LT:839
Orpingalik's Song: My Breath.
   Tr-US I:17
Parting. Y. Bat-Miriam. Me-PH:102
The People. R. Creeley.
   Bl-FP:60, Ca-VT:566
Piazza di Spagna: Early Morning.
   R. Wilbur.   Ca-VT:485
The Pity of the Leaves.
   E. Robinson. Un-MA:137
Places. S. Teasdale. Pa-HT:5
Plum Blossoms. Chang Hsiu-ya.
   Pa-MV:36
Plum Wine. K. Takamura. Sh-AM:44
Poland/1931. J. Rothenberg.
   Ho-P:217
Polo Grounds. R. Humphries.
   Mo-SD:9, Ni-JP:124
The Poplar Field. W. Cowper.
   Co-RG:117, De-CH:46, De-TT:161,
   Gr-CT:239, Ha-PO:151, Ho-WR:159,
   Ma-FW:105, Pa-GTB:140, Rv-CB:548
The Quarry Pool. D. Levertov.
   Ca-VT:510
Rain Portrait. J. Unternecker.
   Sc-TN:213
The Ramblers. V. Linton.
   Ls-NY:254
The Raven.   E. Poe.   Al-VBP:865,
   Bo-GJ:165, Co-RG:103, De-CH:303,
   Er-FA:312, Ga-FB:134, Sh-AP:56,
   Sm-LG:207
Real Property. H. Monro.
   Co-BN:136, Go-BP:171
The Reconciliation. A. MacLeish.
   Un-MA:462
Remember. C. Rossetti.
   Al-VBP:995, De-CH:264, Fe-PL:98,
   Ga-FB:68, Hi-WP I:87, Ox-BN:705,
   Un-MW:90
Remember That Country.
   J. Garrigue. Ca-VT:389

Remember Thee! Remember Thee!
   G. Byron. Al-VBP:721
Remembering Shi Ch'a Hai.
   Chang Hsiu-ya.   Pa-MV:29
Remembrance. E. Brontë.
   De-CH:262, Er-FA:457, Go-BP:148,
   Ox-BN:601
Repose of Rivers. H. Crane.
   Un-MA:518, Wi-LT:396
The Reunion.   O. Dodson.
   Bo-HF:129
Robin Hood.   J. Keats.
   Gr-CC:115, Mc-PR:34
Robinson Crusoe Returns to
   Amsterdam. F. Jammes. Fe-FP:472
Rugby Chapel—November, 1857.
   M. Arnold. Rv-CB:874
Sad Song. A. Maniu. Mc-AC:60
St. Gervais. M. Roberts.
   Sm-LG:297
Sam. W. de la Mare. Ar-TP3:160,
   Co-PM:46, Co-SS:174, Ga-FB:168,
   Hi-WP I:74, Pa-OM:292, Un-MB:200
Scintilla. W. Braithwaite.
   Bo-AN:15
Sea News. E. Barker.   Ls-NY:244
The Secret of the Sea.
   H. Longfellow. Un-GT:261
The Self-Unseeing. T. Hardy.
   Gr-CC:177, Ox-BN:825, Un-MB:34
September 1913. W. Yeats.
   Pa-GTB:422
She Came and Went. J. Lowell.
   Al-VBP:949
A Sheep Fair. T. Hardy. Ho-P:206
Shut Out That Moon. T. Hardy.
   Al-VBP:1047
The Sick Stockrider. A. Gordon.
   Hi-FO:233
Signature for Tempo. A. MacLeish.
   Ca-VT:164
The Slave's Dream. H. Longfellow.
   Hi-WP I:18, Hu-PN:459
The Snowfall. D. Justice.
   Ca-VT:536
So Shuts the Marigold Her Leaves.
   W. Browne. Al-VBP:321, Gr-CT:72
Sold. R. Cuscaden. St-H:35
The Solitary Reaper. W. Wordsworth.
   Bl-OB:146, Co-RG:122, De-CH:207,
   Go-BP:49, Ha-PO:83, Hi-WP II:142,
   Ma-YA:141, Ox-BN:77, Pa-GTB:255,
   Pl-US:50, Re-TW:114, Rv-CB:635,
   Sp-OG:336
Song. C. Rossetti. Al-VBP:994,
   Co-BL:103, De-CH:262, Er-FA:84,
   Fe-PL:97, Ha-PO:157, Hi-WP II:21,
   Rv-CB:892, Sp-OG:278, Un-MW:91
A Song for New Year's Eve.
   W. Bryant. Hu-MP:327, Se-PR:29
A Song of Nezahualcoyotl. Br-MW:26

MEMORIES — cont'd.
   Song of the Night at Daybreak.
      A. Meynell.   De-CH:444
   Sonnet. A. Nelson. Ad-PB:12,
      Hu-PN:46
   Sonnet 30. W. Shakespeare.
      Al-VBP:201, Er-FA:166, Fe-PL:130,
      Ga-FB:33, Pa-GTB:18, Rv-CB:213
   Sonnet 74. W. Shakespeare.
      Rv-CB:231
   A Sonnet. Tai Wang-shu.
      Hs-TC:182
   Sonnet, to the River Loddon.
      T. Warton. Al-VBP:583
   Sonnets at Christmas. A. Tate.
      Ca-VT:220, Sh-AP:206, Wi-LT:405
   A Sorrow in the Harem.
      Wang Chang Ling. Rx-LT:61
   Soundless. D. Witt. Ad-II:12
   Spanish Waters. J. Masefield.
      Fe-FP:514, Mc-WK:141, Pa-OM:207
   Sparrows. M. Leib. Ho-TY:95
   Spleen. C. Baudelaire. Un-R:77
   Spring Day on West Lake.
      Ou Yang Hsiu. Rx-OH:60
   Spring Reminiscence. C. Cullen.
      Bo-HF:47
   Spring Sorrow. Ch'n Ch'ang Siu.
      Rx-LT:60
   Stanzas - April, 1814.
      P. Shelley. Ox-BN:275
   Stephen's Green Revisited.
      R. Weber. Co-PI:195
   Such Lazy Shadows under the Sun.
      Tai Wang-shu. Hs-TC:179
   Summer Remembered. I. Gardner.
      Pe-OA:235
   Summer's Pleasures They Are Gone.
      J. Clare. De-CH:512, Rv-CB:719
   The Sundew. A. Swinburne.
      Ox-BN:810
   Sung in Thirty Lines.
      S. Meltzer. Ad-II:45
   The Swarming Bees. J. Laughlin.
      Ca-VT:410
   Table d'Hôte. R. Esler. Ls-NY:154
   Tarantella. H. Belloc. De-CH:189,
      Hi-WP II:2, Li-SR:5, Pa-HT:105,
      Sm-LG:45, Th-AS:164, Un-MB:167
   Tears, Idle Tears. A. Tennyson.
      Al-VBP:859, Er-FA:150, Ha-PO:150,
      Hi-WP II:144, Ox-BN:486
   Tetélestai. C. Aiken. Un-MA:431,
      Wi-LT:327
   That City. Li Kuang-t'ien.
      Hs-TC:211
   That Wind. E. Brontë.
      De-CH:215, De-TT:181
   There Is an Old Horse.
      Jao Meng-k'an. Hs-TC:107

   There Was a Girl I Used to Go with.
      S. Benét.   Ha-LO:4
   Thesis, Antithesis, and Nostalgia.
      A. Dugan.   Ad-CI:75
   Thinking of a Friend at Year's End.
      Ho Ch'i-fang.   Hs-TC:219
   This Evening So Cold and Chill.
      Prince Shiki.   Ba-ST:50
   A Thought Went up My Mind Today.
      E. Dickinson.   Sh-AP:130
   Time's Fool. R. Pitter.   Un-MB:405
   To a Lady Seen for a Few Moments at
      Vauxhall. J. Keats.   No-CL:162
   To a River in the South.
      H. Newbolt.   De-CH:48
   To an Absent Virginian.
      K. Peatross.   Ke-TF:359
   To Any Member of My Generation.
      G. Barker.   Al-VBP:1240,
      Wi-LT:529
   Tomorrow You. J. Holmes.
      Ke-TF:84
   The Tower. W. Yeats.   Wi-LT:76
   Travelling in the Family.
      C. de Andrade.   An-TC:57
   The Trees Are Down. C. Mew.
      Co-BN:146, Un-MB:164
   Trifle. G. Johnson. Bo-AN:21,
      Bo-HF:20
   The Tropics in New York. C. McKay.
      Ad-PB:25, Bo-AN:28, Bo-HF:167,
      Hu-PN:95, Lo-TY:118
   Turkestan. Ch'en T'ao. Cr-WS:8
   Twilight's Feet. A. Pratt.
      Al-WW:102
   Ulivfak's Song of the Caribou.
      Le-IB:112
   Under the Frontier Post.
      Wang Chang-Ling.   Gr-CT:340
   Under the Woods. E. Thomas.
      De-CH:50
   V. D. F. H. Wolfe. Cr-WS:76
   Vailima. R. Stevenson.
      De-CH:51, De-TT:157, Ox-BN:895
   Visiting Second Avenue.
      E. Greenberg. Ho-TY:311
   A Waltz in the Afternoon.
      B. Bentley. Co-BL:22
   The Wanderer Recalls the Past.
      W. Wordsworth. Ox-BN:92
   Water. R. Lowell. Pe-OA:247
   Water-Lilies. S. Teasdale.
      Un-MA:265
   We Have Been Here Before.
      M. Bishop. Co-FB:431, Na-EO:100
   Wessex Heights. T. Hardy.
      Ox-BN:839
   What Has Been. V. Porumbacu.
      Mc-AC:126
   When from the World. De-CH:650

When I See Pine Trees.   Ba-ST:61
When the Mint Is in the Liquor.
   C. Ouslet.   Fe-PL:417
When You Have Gone.   Le-OE:132
Where, O Where?   M. Bracker.
   Mo-SD:20
Where Shall Wisdom Be Found?
   Euripides.   Pa-SG:186, Pl-US:108
The White Dress.   M. Zaturenska.
   Un-MA:560
The Wild.   W. Berry.   Ca-VT:683
The Wind of Time.   J. Brennan.
   De-FS:37
The Window.   Li Kuang-t'ien.
   Hs-TC:203
Winter.   Chu Hsiang.   Hs-TC:103
With Rue My Heart Is Laden.
   A. Housman.   Er-FA:88, Un-MB:94,
   Wi-LT:62
The Woodlands.   W. Barnes.
   Co-BN:158
Words.   H. Brooks.   Hu-NN:104,
   Hu-PN:278
Youth and Age.   G. Byron.
   Pa-GTB:221
MEMORY
   Adieu.   P. Lewenstein.   Sm-MK:212
   Elegy for Mr. Goodbeare.
      O. Sitwell.   Un-MB:357
   Grieve Not, Ladies.   A. Branch.
      Er-FA:156
   Memory.   T. Aldrich.   Co-BN:40,
      Fe-PL:378, Fr-WO:80
   Memory.   C. Rossetti.   Ox-BN:716
   Memory.   D. Rossetti.   Rv-CB:889
   Night Is Still Young.
      Chang Hsiu-ya.   Pa-MV:30
   No Passenger Was Known to Flee.
      E. Dickinson.   Ho-LP:76
   Poem.   B. Mardhekar.   Al-PI:131
   Song.   O. Goldsmith.   Al-VBP:586
   The Time of the Barmecides.
      J. Mangan.   Co-RG:8
   To Memory.   M. Coleridge.
      Rv-CB:954
   Twenty-Five.   R. McKuen.   Du-SH:66
MEMPHIS, TENN.
   Beale Street, Memphis.
      T. Snyder.   Hu-NN:54
MEN: see also BACHELORS;
      BROTHERS; HUMOR - MEN;
      HUSBANDS; MAN AND WOMAN;
      PORTRAITS - MEN;
      SATIRE - MEN
   Abel's Bride.   D. Levertov.
      Ca-VT:514
   Advice to a Girl.   T. Campion.
      Al-VBP:215, Ma-YA:72, Un-MW:35
   All That's Past.   W. de la Mare.
      Al-VBP:1119, Bo-GJ:202, Re-TW:85

Behind Sea-Lion Town.   Ho-SD:61
The Coming American.   S. Foss.
   Br-AF:33, Mc-WK:160
Councils.   M. Piercy.   Mo-TS:44
Four Epitaphs.   S. Warner.
   Un-MB:371
God Give Us Men!   J. Holland.
   Se-PR:200, Vi-PP:232
Invitation to Drink and the Reply.
   Tr-US I:145
It Is Man Who Counts.   Do-CH:(13)
The Lady's Maid's Song.
   J. Hollander.   Wi-LT:732
Male and Female Loves in Beulah.
   W. Blake.   Ox-BN:46
Man, Man, Man.   Er-FA:444
Meditatio.   E. Pound.   Ar-TP3:132,
   Du-RG:61, Ga-S:133, Ha-LO:63,
   Hi-WP II:11, Sm-LG:390
The Men Are a Bad Lot.   J. Seidl.
   Un-R:173
The Men of Valor.   Akahito.
   Ba-ST:29
A Nation's Strength.   R. Emerson.
   Br-AF:35, Fe-FP:452, Vi-PP:65
Ode in a Night of Overhanging
   Weather.   V. McHugh.   Mc-WK:175
The Old Men.   W. de la Mare.
   Un-MB:199
The Old Men.   I. Feldman.
   Br-TC:122
That Women Are But Men's Shadows.
   B. Jonson.   Al-VBP:234,
   Rv-CB:287
The Tired Man.   A. Wickham.
   Sm-MK:25, Un-MW:57
To Men.   A. Wickham.   Un-MB:282
Windows.   J. de Melo Neto.
   An-TC:117
MENTAL HOSPITALS: see ASYLUMS
MENTALLY HANDICAPPED: see also
   HUMOR - MENTALLY HANDICAPPED
Death of a Son.   J. Silkin.
   Br-TC:375, Pa-GTB:566
Hospital for Defectives.
   T. Blackburn.   Pa-GTB:547
Rufus Prays.   L. Strong.
   Un-MB:394
Silly Sallie.   W. de la Mare.
   Bl-OB:144
Village Portrait.   T. Duncan.
   Th-AS:189
MEPHISTOPHELES: see DEVILS
MERCHANTS: see also BUSINESS;
   HUMOR - MERCHANTS; MARKETS
   AND MARKETING; SATIRE -
   MERCHANTS; STORES
The Choice. J. Masefield. Un-MB:229
The Great Merchant, Dives Prag-
   maticus, Cries His Wares.
   T. Newbery.   Ox-BC:14

MERCHANTS — cont'd.
  Merchants from Cathay. W. Benét.
    Un-MA:321
  The Prologue to the Canterbury
    Tales. G. Chaucer. Al-VBP:6,
    Gr-CT:281, Ma-FW:17, Ma-YA:28
MERCURY (ROMAN GOD)
  The Aeneid. Virgil. Al-VBP:80
MERCY: see also FORGIVENESS
  The Bridge of Sighs. T. Hood.
    Pa-GTB:230
  The Divine Image. W. Blake.
    Al-VBP:613, Go-BP:287,
    Ox-BN:20, Rv-CB:586
  I Heard an Angel Singing.
    W. Blake. Rv-CB:621
  Jonah. R. Jarrell. Tr-MR:83
  The Litany of the Dark People.
    C. Cullen. Pl-EI:155, Tr-MR:154
  Lord, Thou Hast Been Our Dwelling
    Place. Bible. O.T. Psalms.
    Me-PH:23, Pl-EI:198
  Mercy by Night. C. La Farge.
    Sm-PT:189
  The Quality of Mercy Is Not
    Strained. W. Shakespeare.
    Bo-HF:141, Er-FA:92, Mc-PR:140
  Tanka. Y. Aizu. Sh-AM:142
  When the Assault Was Intended to
    the City. J. Milton.
    Co-RG:23, Pa-GTB:62
MERIDA, SP.
  The Cycle Repeated. K. Chapin.
    Ls-NY:258
MERIONETH COUNTY, WALES
  Dead. L. Johnson. Ox-BN:948
MERLIN
  Merlin. R. Emerson. Sh-AP:32
  Merlin. E. Muir. Ma-FW:188,
    Rv-CB:983
  The Wisdom of Merlyn. W. Blunt.
    Al-VBP:1056
MERMAID TAVERN
  Lines on the Mermaid Tavern.
    J. Keats. Al-VBP:776,
    Pa-GTB:229, Pl-ML:99
  Mr. Francis Beaumont's Letter to
    Ben Jonson. F. Beaumont.
    Al-VBP:301
  pete the parrot and shakespeare.
    D. Marquis. Pl-ML:102
MERMAIDS AND MERMEN: see also
    HUMOR - MERMAIDS AND MERMEN
  Blow, Ye Winds. Co-SS:105
  Clerk Colvill. Ma-BB:212,
    Ox-BB:85
  Dream Song. Bi-IT:125
  The Eddystone Light. Co-SS:103,
    Ha-PO:271
  The Figurehead. C. Garstin.
    Co-PT:262

  The Forsaken Merman. M. Arnold.
    Al-VBP:960, Bl-OB:59, Cl-DT:41,
    Co-SS:160, Hu-MP:99, Ma-YA:205,
    Rv-CB:862, Sm-LG:339, Sm-MK:84,
    Sp-OG:117
  Genealogy of a Mermaid.
    M. Weisenthal. Ls-NY:215
  The Great Silkie of Sule Skerrie.
    Gr-CT:206, Gr-GB:282, Ma-BB:18
  I Did Not See a Mermaid.
    S. Johnson. Li-LC:61
  Kemp Oweyne. Fo-OG:13, Ma-BB:33,
    Rv-CB:50
  Little Fan. J. Reeves. Co-PM:138
  Madness One Monday Evening.
    J. Fields. Be-MA:150, Hu-NN:78,
    Li-TU:101
  A Meeting. H. Heine. Co-PM:89
  The Mermaid. A. Tennyson.
    Bo-FP:312, Co-PM:157, Fe-FP:390,
    Hu-MP:98, Li-LC:53, Un-GT:109
  The Mermaid. De-CH:403, Fo-OG:39
  The Mermaid. Co-SS:109
  The Mermaids. W. de la Mare.
    Cl-DT:42
  The Mermaids. E. Spenser.
    Gr-CT:201
  A Mermaid's Myth. Ch'in Tzu-hao.
    Pa-MV:55
  The Mermaid's Song.
    Hu P'in-ch'ing. Pa-MV:102
  The Merman. A. Tennyson.
    Bo-FP:313, Co-PM:161, Fe-FP:392,
    Un-GT:109
  Off the Ground. W. de la Mare.
    Co-PT:102, Ir-BB:60
  On a Friday Morn. De-TT:130
  Sam. W. de la Mare. Ar-TP3:160,
    Co-PM:46, Co-SS:174, Ga-FB:168,
    Hi-WP I:74, Pa-OM:292, Un-MB:200
  The Sea-Ritual. G. Darley.
    De-CH:312, Gr-SS:179, Ho-WR:126,
    Ox-BN:396
  Very Nearly. Q. Scott-Hopper.
    Au-SP:300, Fe-FP:374, Hu-MP:81
  A Vision of Mermaids. G. Hopkins.
    Gr-CT:202
MERRIMAC (SHIP)
  The Cruise of the Monitor.
    G. Boker. Hi-TL:110
  The Cumberland and the Merrimac.
    Em-AF:443
  The Cumberland's Crew. Em-AF:442
  Maggie Mac. Em-AF:445
MERRY-GO-ROUNDS
  The Carousel. G. Oden. Ad-PB:185,
    Be-MA:95, Bo-AN:159
  Counterpoint. O. Dodson.
    Hu-PN:30, Jo-SA:59
  June. M. Davies. Br-SS:163

Merry-Go-Round.   D. Baruch.
    Ar-TP3:115, Au-SP:198, Hu-MP:48,
    Ir-BB:15
The Merry-Go-Round.   E. Clark.
    Mc-AW:24
The Merry-Go-Round.   R. Rilke.
    Ad-CI:54, Li-TU:49
MESSIAH
Jerusalem Beggars.   R. Potash.
    Ho-TY:357
O Quickly, Messiah.   A. Reisen.
    Ho-TY:72
METALLURGY: see METALS
METALS: see also names of
    metals, as STEEL
A Dream of Metals.   J. Anderson.
    Sc-TN:7
METEORS
A Falling Star.   Li Kuang-t'ien.
    Hs-TC:205
The Falling Star.   S. Teasdale.
    Ar-TP3:179, Au-SP:341, La-PV:52,
    Pe-FB:71, Th-AS:30
I See You Again.   Ch'en Meng-chia.
    Hs-TC:114
The Shooting Star.   Da-SC:37
Stars, I Have Seen Them Fall.
    A. Housman.   Gr-CT:401
METHUSELAH: see HUMOR -
    METHUSELAH
MEXICAN WAR, 1846-1848
Lament for the Alamo.
    A. Guiterman.   Br-AF:69,
    Sh-RP:260
The Maid of Monterey.   Em-AF:441
Monterey.   C. Hoffman.   Hi-TL:91
O for a Man Who Is a Man!
    H. Thoreau.   Kr-OF:67
Stained with Shame.   J. Whittier.
    Kr-OF:65
The War for Slavery.   W. Garrison.
    Kr-OF:66
MEXICANS
Ai Viva Tequila.   Fi-BG:198
I Met a Mexican.   Da-SC:12
Raking Walnuts in the Rain.
    M. Shannon.   Br-SS:73
MEXICO: see also HUMOR - MEXICO;
    INDIANS OF CENTRAL and NORTH
    AMERICA; and names of towns,
    as VERACRUZ, MEX.
Concert.   R. Sward.   Ca-VT:681
The Crosses.   B. Brigham.   Sc-TN:21
Dance of Burros.   D. Laing.
    Co-BBW:155
Ear-of-Corn.   Ge-TR:39
I Am the Corncob.   Ge-TR:49
Look!   Ge-TR:27
My Daughter.   Ge-TR:44
My Son.   Ge-TR:41

O My Heart You Must Be Strong.
    Ge-TR:17
Our Lords Esteemed Most High.
    Ge-TR:51
Romance.   W. Turner.   Bo-GJ:220,
    Hi-WP I:7, Mc-WS:113, Ni-JP:24,
    No-CL:251, Un-MB:345
The Surrender Speech of Cuauhtemoc.
    Cuauhtemoc.   Bi-IT:152
Where Is the House of Quetzal
    Feathers?   Ge-TR:31
Yollotl My Heart.   Ge-TR:21
MEXICO - HISTORY AND PATRIOTISM
The Aztec City.   E. Ware.
    Pa-HT:69
A Song of Lamentation.   Ba-PO:27,
    Bi-IT:137, Da-SC:175
MICE: see also HUMOR - MICE
The Ambitious Mouse.   J. Farrar.
    Bo-FP:59
Anne and the Field-Mouse.
    I. Serraillier.   Pa-RE:106
Birthday Cake.   A. Fisher.
    Br-BC:88, La-PV:118
Calico Pie.   E. Lear.
    Au-SP:225, Bl-OB:12, Fe-FP:356,
    Hu-MP:461, Ir-BB:88, It-HB:57,
    Li-LC:67, Lo-LL:67, Pa-RE:109,
    Rv-CB:811, Sm-LG:87, Tu-WW:114,
    Un-GB:29, Un-GF:33, Un-GT:225
Cat and Mouse.   T. Hughes.
    Pl-EI:127
Cheetie Pussie.   Mo-TL:21
Christmas Mouse.   A. Fisher.
    La-PH:39
Christmas Wishes.   J. Lee.
    Ja-HH:54
The City Mouse and the Garden
    Mouse.   C. Rossetti.
    Ar-TP3:59, Bo-FP:15, Br-SG:66,
    Ch-B:25, Fe-FP:138, Hu-MP:189,
    It-HB:26, Un-GB:14, Un-GT:56
The Country Mouse and the City
    Mouse.   R. Sharpe.   Ox-BC:139
Dark Kingdom.   E. Coatsworth.
    Co-BBW:54
Death of the Cat.
    I. Serraillier.   Co-BBW:126
Deer Mouse.   A. Fisher.   It-HB:23
A Fairy Went a-Marketing.
    R. Fyleman.   Au-SP:293,
    Ox-BC:337
The Field Mouse.   W. Sharp.
    Co-BBW:42, Fe-FP:137, Rd-SS:34
The Fieldmouse.   C. Alexander.
    Ox-BC:204
Four III.   e. cummings.
    Hi-WP II:7
Good Morning.   M. Sipe.
    Ar-TP3:70, Au-SP:87

MICE — cont'd.

The Halloween Concert. A. Fisher.
Br-SS:70

Hickory, Dickory, Dock. An-IP:(7),
Au-SP:17, Bo-FP:16, De-PO:20,
Er-FA:505, Fr-WO:17, Li-LB:102,
Mo-CC:(15), Mo-MGT:77, Mo-NR:24,
Mo-TL:22, Wi-MG:58, Wr-RM:125

Hospitality. W. McClintic.
Co-BBW:51

The House of the Mouse.
L. Mitchell. Ar-TP3:59,
Au-SP:56, Co-IW:8, It-HB:59

I Wouldn't. J. Ciardi. Gr-EC:74

Kitty. E. Prentiss. Hu-MP:184

The Last Flower. J. Moore.
Co-PS:126

Lat Take a Cat. G. Chaucer.
Gr-CT:117

Lèse Majesté. O. Herford.
Co-BBW:32

The Light-Housekeeper's White-
Mouse. J. Ciardi. Bo-FP:282

The Lion and the Mouse.
J. Taylor. Pa-OM:328, Sh-RP:320

Little Black Bug. M. Brown.
Fe-FP:127

The Little Mouse. Wr-RM:117

A Little White Mouse.
M. Thomas. Le-M:95

Lullaby. E. Coatsworth. Br-SS:38

Madam Mouse Trots. S. Sitwell.
Ha-LO:9

The Magical Mouse. K. Patchen.
Ha-LO:17, We-PZ:14

The Marriage of the Frog and the
Mouse. Rd-OA:64

A Martial Mouse. S. Butler.
Rd-OA:63

The Meadow Mouse. T. Roethke.
Ad-PE:24, Mc-WS:45, Mo-TS:58,
Rd-OA:33

Mice. R. Fyleman. Ar-TP3:59,
Au-SP:55, Fe-FP:136, Hu-MP:189,
Ir-BB:79, It-HB:47, La-PV:115,
Na-EO:31, Pe-FB:7, Th-AS:43

The Miser and the Mouse.
C. Smart. Pa-RE:102

Missing. A. Milne. Bo-FP:15,
Co-IW:43, La-PP:61, La-PV:116,
Pe-FB:9

The Mouse. E. Coatsworth.
Ar-TP3:59, Au-SP:56, Co-BBW:41,
Co-IW:29, Fe-FP:136, Ir-BB:86,
Rd-SS:33, Th-AS:38

Mouse. H. Conkling.
Ar-TP3:58, Au-SP:57

The Mouse. J. Garrigue.
Br-TC:141

The Mouse. R. Isaac. La-GI:53

The Mouse. M. Stephenson.
St-FS:41

The Mouse. R. Vargo. La-GI:56

The Mouse. Bo-FP:59, Wy-CM:15

The Mouse and the Cake. E. Cook.
Ox-BC:209

The Mouse in the Wainscot.
I. Serraillier. Co-BBW:44,
La-PV:117

The Mouse That Gnawed the Oak-
Tree Down. V. Lindsay. Ha-LO:74

The Mouse, the Frog, and the
Little Red Hen. Gr-EC:31,
Ir-BB:89

The Mouse's Lullaby. P. Cox.
Bo-FP:16

Mouse's Nest. J. Clare. Cl-DT:78,
Co-BBW:20, Gr-CT:123

A Mouse's Petition. A. Barbauld.
Ox-BC:79

The Mousetrap. C. Morgenstern.
Rd-OA:30

New Strain. G. Starbuck. Br-TC:409

Of the Mean and Sure Estate.
T. Wyatt. Rd-OA:98

The Old Woman. B. Potter.
Bo-GJ:8, La-PV:118

The Old Woman and the Mouse.
Ir-BB:29, Ju-CP:5, Mo-MGT:193

Over in the Meadow. Au-SP:223,
Ir-BB:24, On-TW:38

The Pasty. Mother Goose.
Mo-MGT:158, Mo-NR:126

Poll Parrot. Mo-MGT:67

Pretty John Watts. Wr-RM:77

The Puddy and the Mouse. Gr-GB:68

Pussy Cat, Pussy Cat. Mo-TL:21

Rats and Mice. Rv-ON:24

Roon Aboot, Roon Aboot. Mo-TL:24

Santa Claus and the Mouse.
E. Poulsson. Ch-B:56

A Ship a-Sailing. G. Setoun.
Ar-TP3:122, Au-SP:19, Bo-FP:200,
Co-SS:85, De-TT:48, Gr-EC:242,
Hi-GD:16, Hu-MP:175, Ir-BB:241,
Li-LB:86, Mo-MGT:174, Mo-NR:103,
Pa-AP:44, Sm-MK:199, Sp-HW:25,
Wi-MG:53, Wr-RM:73

Six Little Mice Sat Down to Spin.
Mo-CC:(52), Mo-MGT:90,
On-TW:27, Sm-MK:192, St-FS:6

Some Little Mice Sat in a Barn
to Spin. Mo-NR:120

Song: One Hard Look.
R. Graves. Un-MB:388

Ten Little Mice. Ir-BB:25

A Thanksgiving Fable.
O. Herford. Ja-PA:58

There Was a Wee Bit Mousikie.
Bl-OB:105, De-CH:544

There Was a Wee Mouse.   Mo-TL:20
Thou Shalt See the Field-Mouse
   Peep.   J. Keats.   Rd-OA:181
Three Blind Mice.   Mother Goose.
   An-IP:(19), Li-LB:103, Mo-MGT:95,
   Mo-NR:47, Wi-MG:38, Wr-RM:35
Three Mice.   C. Cole.   Ir-BB:84,
   St-FS:63
Three Mice Went into a Hole to
   Spin.   Mo-TL:68
To a Mouse.   R. Burns.   Co-BBW:36,
   Er-FA:226, Fe-PL:367, Hu-MP:190,
   Mc-WK:60, Pa-GTB:141, Rd-OA:24,
   Rv-CB:616, Sp-OG:297
To and Fro.   E. Coatsworth.
   It-HB:31
A Waltzer in the House.
   S. Kunitz.   Co-BBW:25, We-PZ:33
What in the World?   E. Merriam.
   Gr-EC:14
Who Is So Pretty?
   E. Coatsworth.   It-HB:55
The Witch of Willoughby Wood.
   R. Bennett.   Co-PM:27, Sh-RP:228

MICHAEL, ARCHANGEL AND SAINT
   Michael, Archangel.   Alcuin.
      Ga-S:4
   Michaelmas.   N. Nicholson.
      Un-MB:506
MICHELANGELO BUONARROTI
   Long-Legged Fly.   W. Yeats.
      Wi-LT:92
   The Medici Tombs.   W. Ross.
      Ls-NY:236
   Michelangelo.   V. Voiculescu.
      Mc-AC:47
MICHELET, JULES
   The Sacred Order.   M. Sarton.
      Pl-IO:155
MICHIGAN: see also names of
      towns, as DETROIT, MICH.
   Michigan, My Michigan!
      Mrs. H. Lyster.   Se-PR:267
   The Night Frieda Took My Spirit
      by Surprise.   P. Mayer.
      St-H:129
MICHIGAN, LAKE
   Great Lakes Suite, II.
      J. Reaney.   Do-WH:49
MICROBES: see also HUMOR -
      MICROBES
   The Old Oaken Bucket.   Er-FA:208
MICRONESIAN VERSE-CAROLINE
      ISLANDS
   Boys' Dance Song on the Departure
      of an Older Girl Named Yiluai.
      Tr-US II:6
   Dance Song.   Tr-US II:7
   Dance Song of Death.
      Tr-US II:3

Dance Song on the Death of a Girl
   Named Rutenag.   Tr-US II:4
Girl's Song.   Tr-US II:21
Love Song (Boxes).   Tr-US II:3
Love Songs.   Tr-US II:24
Song of a Married Woman to Her
   Lover Yuv.   Tr-US II:9
Song of a Mother for Her Dead Son.
   Tr-US II:20
Song of a Navigator's Wife.
   Tr-US II:16
Song of a Widow.   Tr-US II:18
The Song of Senia and Monia.
   Tr-US II:25
Women's Ur-Dance Song.
   Tr-US II:12
MICRONESIAN VERSE-GILBERTESE
   Ceremonial Prayer for the
      Fructification of the
      Pandanus Tree.   Tr-US II:27
   Invocation of a Poet Seeking
      Inspiration, I, II.
      Tr-US II:28
   Satire.   Tr-US II:30
   Song.   Tr-US II:29
   Song of a Fabulous Heroine
      Whose Lover Has Escaped
      from Captivity in Tonga.
      Tr-US II:29
   Spell Called "The Lifting of the
      Head."   Tr-US II:27
MICRONESIAN VERSE-MARSHALLESE
   Storm Tide on Mejit.
      Tr-US II:31
MICROSCOPES
   Faith Is a Fine Invention.
      E. Dickinson.   Co-EL:107,
      Ga-FB:150, Rv-CB:916
   The Magnifying Glass.
      W. de la Mare.   Bl-OB:123
   The Microscope.   M. Kumin.
      Du-RG:53, Ha-PO:96
   The Two Deserts.   C. Patmore.
      Co-BN:220
MIDAS, KING OF PHRYGIA
   Epigram.   J. Wolcot.   Co-EL:51
MIDDLE AGE: see also
      HUMOR - MIDDLE AGE
   At Fifty.   J. Glatstein.   Ho-TY:328
   Men at Forty.   D. Justice.
      Ho-P:129
   Messo Cammin.   H. Longfellow.
      Rv-CB:782
   Safety at Forty.   L. Sissman.
      Ho-P:243
   The Summing Up.   S. Kunitz.
      Co-EL:125
MIDDLE AGES: see CRUSADES; DIALECTS,
      MIDDLE ENGLISH; KNIGHTS AND
      KNIGHTHOOD; MINSTRELS AND
      TROUBADOURS

THE MIDDLE WEST: see also names
     of states, as IOWA
  Ah . . . to the Villages!
     T. McGrath.   St-H:128
  A Farm on the Great Plains.
     W. Stafford.   En-PC:142
  For the Iowa Dead.   P. Engle.
     St-H:55
  Improved Farm Land.
     C. Sandburg.   La-RM:77
  Iowa, Kansas, Nebraska.
     G. Frumkin.   Bl-FP:22
  Midwest Town.   R. Peterson.
     Br-AF:219
  One Home.   W. Stafford.   Br-AF:150,
     Ca-VT:413, Kh-VA:9
  Prairie Summer.   D. Etter.
     Sc-TN:45
  The Prairies.   W. Bryant.   Sh-AP:20
  Weather.   A. MacLeish.   Un-MA:456
  West of Chicago.   J. Dimoff.
     Mc-EA:129
MIDGETS: see DWARFS (MIDGETS)
MIDNIGHT
  Five for the Grace of Man.
     W. Scott.   Ca-VT:313
  It Was Midnight.   Linda.   Le-M:211
  Midnight.   T. Middleton.   Bl-OB:140,
     Pa-RE:124, Rd-SS:35
  Midnight on March 27th.
     G. Dusenbery.   Sc-TN:36
  Natura in Urbe.   E. White.
     Mc-WK:41
  Night Plane.   F. Frost.
     Ar-TP3:88, Fe-FP:201, La-PV:60
  Sir Roderic's Song.   W. Gilbert.
     Br-SM:10, Co-PM:75
MIDSUMMER EVE
  Lord Arnaldos.   J. Flecker.
     Co-PT:266
  Midsummer Magic.   I. Eastwick.
     Ar-TP3:148
  Midsummer Night.   M. Edey.
     Ha-YA:78
  Song for Midsummer Night.
     E. Coatsworth.   Ha-YA:79
MIGNONETTE
  Red Geranium and Godly Mignonette.
     D. Lawrence.   Ga-S:10, Pa-GTB:460
MIGRANT LABOR
  Arizona.   Em-AF:758
  The Cannery.   L. Stryk.   Ls-NY:238
  The Cranberry Song.   B. Reynolds.
     Em-AF:763
  A Dream of Apricots.   J. Schevill.
     Ls-NY:304
  Kansas.   V. Lindsay.   Pa-HT:49
  Pastures of Plenty.   W. Guthrie.
     Pe-SS:53
MIGRATION: see BIRDS - MIGRATION;
     IMMIGRATION AND EMIGRATION

MIKIRIS VERSE: see TIBETAN
     VERSE-MIKIRIS
MILAN, IT.
  The Park in Milan.   W. Smith.
     Ad-CI:52
MILITARY LIFE: see also ARMIES;
     GENERALS; HUMOR - MILITARY
     LIFE; SATIRE - MILITARY LIFE;
     SOLDIERS
  All Day It Has Rained. A. Lewis.
     Hi-WP I:28, Pa-GTB:543
  An Army Corps on the March.
     W. Whitman.   Fe-PL:171,
     Vi-PP:147
  At the Lou-Shan Pass.
     Mao Tse-tung.   Hs-TC:362
  Bivouac on a Mountain Side.
     W. Whitman.   Fe-PL:170,
     Gr-CT:338, Li-TU:236, Sh-AP:118,
     Vi-PP:148
  Boots.   R. Kipling.   Un-MB:129
  Border Songs.   Lu Lun.   Le-MW:122
  Gunga Din.   R. Kipling.
     Er-FA:371, Go-BP:54, Hi-WP I:69,
     Ma-YA:226, Pa-OM:230, Un-MB:122
  Home.   Le-MW:126, Rx-LT:9
  How Goes the Night?   Le-MW:125
  I Pass the Night at General
     Headquarters.   Tu Fu.   Rx-OH:25
  In the Dordogne.   J. Bishop.
     Ca-VT:160
  Lincolnshire Bomber Station.
     H. Treece.   Cr-WS:32
  Night Encampment Outside Troy.
     A. Tennyson.   Co-RG:39
  Ode; to My Pupils.   W. Auden.
     Un-MB:451
  On the Liu-P'an Mountain.
     Mao Tse-tung.   Hs-TC:363
  The Portrait of a Chinese Soldier.
     Wang Ya-p'ing.   Hs-TC:354
  The Recruiting Sergeant.   Mo-MGT:142
  A Sight in Camp in the Daybreak
     Gray and Dim.   W. Whitman.
     Ha-PO:62
  Taps.   S. Comer.   Ad-II:99
  We're Tenting To-Night.
     W. Kittredge.   Vi-PP:160
  The Young Recruit.   A. Ficke.
     Co-EL:107
MILITARY SERVICE, COMPULSORY:
     see also CONSCIENTIOUS
     OBJECTORS; SATIRE - MILITARY
     SERVICE, COMPULSORY
  Arthur McBride.   Co-RM:115,
     Gr-GB:236
  Captain Bover.   Gr-GB:238
  Draft Notice.
     D. Mourao-Ferreira.   Cr-WS:47
  High Germany.   Hi-FO:175, Rv-CB:435
  O Cruel Was the Press Gang. Gr-GB:238

Official Visit to Shih Hao
   Village. Tu Fu. Ba-PO:154,
   Cr-WS:13
Old Mother Blinds Her Own Son.
   Yüan Shui-p'ai. Hs-TC:410
Poem of the Conscripted Warrior.
   R. Nogar. Lo-TY:187
The Press-Gang. Gr-CT:223,
   Gr-GB:238
Ugly Day. M. Levine. Ad-II:102
Without Benefit of Declaration.
   L. Hughes. Bo-AN:72, Cr-WS:47,
   Lo-TY:229
MILK
   Babies Are Crying. P. John.
      Ba-HI:85
   Buttercup Cow. E. Randall.
      Ar-TP3:74
   The Cow. C. Rossetti. Mc-PR:121
   Cushy Cow, Bonny. Gr-GB:290,
      Mo-MGT:49, Sp-TM:13, Wr-RM:32
   Inscription on a Klim Can.
      Yüan Shui-p'ai. Hs-TC:404
   A Jolly Noise. E. Jacobson.
      Mc-AW:20
   Milk. J. Schuyler. Mc-EA:142
   Milk Below. Bo-FP:129
   Milk for the Cat. H. Monro.
      Bl-OB:109, Co-BBW:137, Er-FA:233,
      Ga-BP:97, Re-TW:16, Sm-MK:160,
      Un-GT:47, Un-MB:236
   The Milk Jug. O. Herford.
      Bo-FP:56, Ch-B:43
   Milking Time. E. Roberts.
      Bo-GJ:45, Fe-FP:239,
      Ma-FO:(11), Pa-RE:82
   Thank You, Pretty Cow.
      A. and J. Taylor. Bo-FP:69,
      Hi-GD:9, Hu-MP:197, Ox-BC:123
   White Cat. R. Knister. Do-WH:82
   Witch's Milking Charm. Gr-CT:159,
      Gr-GB:290
MILKMAIDS: see also
      HUMOR - MILKMAIDS
   Dabbling in the Dew. De-CH:194
   Early Morning Meadow Song.
      C. Dalmon. De-CH:193
   Milking Pails. De-CH:67
   The Milkmaid. Mo-MGT:190
   Where Are You Going to, My Pretty
      Maid? Li-LB:145, Mo-MGT:204,
      Mo-NR:56, Wi-MG:68, Wr-RM:112
   Willy, Willy. Wr-RM:97
   The Yellow-Haired Laddie.
      Gr-GB:101
MILKMEN: see also HUMOR - MILKMEN
   The Milkman. J. Krows. Au-SP:144
   The Milkman. C. Morley.
      Hu-MP:143
   The Milkman. Mo-MGT:158
   The Milkmen. I. Gardner. St-H:70

Our Milkman. N. Duffy. Mc-AW:19
   The Strangers. A. Brown.
      Do-WH:39
MILKWEED
   Baby Seeds. Bo-FP:141, Br-SG:92,
      Ch-B:116
   Pod of the Milkweed. R. Frost.
      Wi-LT:186
   Two Voices in a Meadow. R. Wilbur.
      Pe-SS:56
MILKY WAY: see PLEIADES
MILL, JOHN STUART: see HUMOR -
      MILL, JOHN STUART
MILLAY, EDNA ST. VINCENT: see
      HUMOR - MILLAY, EDNA ST.
      VINCENT
MILLERS (MEN)
   Bingo. De-CH:83, Gr-EC:82
   Canterbury Tales (Prologue).
      G. Chaucer. Al-VBP:11,
      Gr-CT:281, Ha-PO:54, Hi-WP I:105,
      Ma-FW:17, Ma-YA:28, Un-GT:87
   The Dishonest Miller. Em-AF:761
   Dusty Miller. Mo-MGT:201,
      Wr-RM:94
   Jolly Miller. I. Bickerstaffe.
      Al-VBP:598, Co-PI:10, Li-LB:73,
      Mo-MGT:170, Un-GT:94, Wi-MG:48
   Lubber Breeze. T. Moore.
      De-CH:135
   The Mill. E. Robinson.
      Ha-PO:47, Sh-AP:142
   The Miller of Dee. Gr-GB:214
   The Old Woman and the Mouse.
      Ir-BB:29, Ju-CP:5, Mo-MGT:193
   The Reeve's Tale. G. Chaucer.
      Al-VBP:12
   There Was a Maid Went to the Mill.
      Gr-GB:107
   The Unfortunate Miller.
      A. Coppard. Co-PT:19
MILLINERY: see HATS
MILLS: see also HUMOR - MILLS;
      and names of specific mills,
      as FLOUR MILLS, WINDMILLS
   Keepsake Mill. R. Stevenson.
      Tu-WW:27
   Manor Water. Gr-GB:178
   The Mill. R. Wilbur. Pe-OA:259
   The Miller's Wife's Lullaby.
      Gr-GB:16
   The Millstream. De-PP:20
   Only the Sound Remains.
      E. Thomas. De-CH:567
   The Unfortunate Miller.
      A. Coppard. Co-PT:19
MILTON, CATHERINE WOODCOCK
   On His Deceased Wife.
      J. Milton. Er-FA:140,
      Rv-CB:375

MILTON, JOHN: see also
   KING, EDWARD
   Extempore to Voltaire Criticizing
      Milton. F. Young. Al-VBP:521
   Litany of the Heroes.
      V. Lindsay. Tr-MR:166
   London, 1802. W. Wordsworth.
      Ga-FB:225, Ma-YA:140, Ox-BN:80,
      Pa-GTB:211, Pl-ML:110
   Milton. H. Longfellow. Sh-AP:39
MILWAUKEE, WIS.
   The Milwaukee Fire.   Em-AF:469
MIMICRY
   Man, That Ape. M. Halpern.
      Ho-TY:103
MIND: see also BRAIN; MEMORY;
      SATIRE - MIND; THOUGHT AND
      THINKING; WISDOM
   The Alchemist. L. Bogan.
      Un-MA:491
   At Night. F. Cornford. Un-MB:307
   At Woodward's Gardens. R. Frost.
      Pl-IO:113
   The Atoll in the Mind.
      A. Comfort. Wi-LT:671
   The Brain Is Wider than the Sky.
      E. Dickinson. Sh-AP:129,
      Un-MA:98
   Carrying My Mind Around. Da-SC:53
   Conclusion. W. Wordsworth.
      Ox-BN:112
   A Considerable Speck. R. Frost.
      Ad-PE:23, Co-BBW:225, Un-MA:190
   The Crematory. Kuo Mo-jo.
      Hs-TC:35
   Dramatic Fragment. T. Stickney.
      Co-EL:145, Rv-CB:965
   Epilogue. S. Spender. Un-MB:472
   An Essay on Man. A. Pope.
      Pl-IO:121
   Expostulation and Reply.
      W. Wordsworth. Rv-CB:640
   Heart and Mind. E. Sitwell.
      Br-TC:387
   Homage to Aesop. C. Faerstein.
      Ls-NY:42
   How to Choose a Mistress.
      E. Prestwich. No-CL:140
   The Image-Maker. O. Gogarty.
      Go-BP:63
   In This Strange House. C. Drewry.
      Tr-MR:281
   Leave Me, O Love. P. Sidney.
      Al-VBP:130, De-CH:641, Ha-PO:168
   The Locus. C. Corman. Ca-VT:528
   The Man Who Thinks He Can.
      W. Wintle. Fe-PL:310
   Mind. R. Wilbur. Ha-PO:230
   The Mind, Intractable Thing.
      M. Moore. Wi-LT:277
   The Mind Is an Enchanting Thing.
      M. Moore. Un-MA:353
   The Mind's Liberty. W. Davies.
      Un-MB:178
   My Mind to Me a Kingdom Is.
      E. Dyer. Al-VBP:89, Ha-PO:193,
      Sp-OG:333
   My Thoughts. S. Gristwood.
      Su-FVI:4
   Nerves. E. Jennings. Ls-NY:74
   The Other Side of the Mummies.
      T. McNeill. Sa-B:208
   The Plower. P. Colum. Un-MB:249
   Remember the Source.
      R. Eberhart. Tr-MR:261
   Solitaire. A. Lowell. Un-MA:156
   Stone Walls. R. Lovelace.
      Hi-WP I:113
   Storm. R. Pitter. Go-BP:241
   Talking with Soldiers. W. Turner.
      Un-MB:346
   This Corruptible. E. Wylie.
      Tr-MR:257, Un-MA:282
   Thought. Al-PI:20
   Tramp. R. Hughes. Un-MB:407
   Twenty-Five. R. McKuen. Du-SH:66
   With God Conversing.
      G. Derwood. Tr-MR:139
MINERS AND MINING: see also
      COAL; GHOST TOWNS;
      PROSPECTING
   The Avondale Mine Disaster.
      Hi-TL:133
   A Ballad of a Mine. R. Skelton.
      Ca-MB:77
   The Blackleg Miners. Gr-GB:223
   The Book of the Dead.
      M. Rukeyser. Kr-OF:197
   Caliban in the Coal Mines.
      L. Untermeyer. Kr-OF:178,
      La-PV:102, Pe-SS:54, Un-MA:306
   Childhood. M. Walker. Ad-BO:73,
      Ad-PB:148, Be-MA:77
   Cleator Moor. N. Nicholson.
      To-MP:44
   The Collier. V. Watkins.
      Ma-FW:197, To-MP:24
   The Gresford Disaster. Gr-GB:225
   In the Gold Mines. B. Vilakazi.
      Lo-TY:176
   The Mine. B. Mason. Le-M:70
   Miners. W. Owen. Un-MB:366
   Miners. J. Wright. St-H:256
   The Mule in the Mines.
      Gr-CT:14, Gr-GB:222
   On a Miner's Lamp in Zennor
      Museum. Su-FVI:42
   The Orange Bears. K. Patchen.
      Kh-VA:7
   The Ponies. W. Gibson.
      Co-BBW:152, Mc-WK:74

Poor Miner's Farewell.
   M. Jackson. Kr-OF:190
Shoot the Beast! M. Rosenfeld.
   Kr-OF:169
Song of Young Men Working in
   Gold Mines. Do-CH:(38)
See also Em-AF:577-608
MINERVA (GODDESS)
   Reading a Medal. T. Tiller.
      Pa-GTB:550
MINES (EXPLOSIVE): see
   SATIRE - MINES (EXPLOSIVE)
MINGUS, CHARLIE
   Mingus. B. Kaufman. Ad-PB:262,
      Be-MA:131
MINISTERS OF THE GOSPEL:
   see CLERGY; PREACHERS AND
   PREACHING; PRIESTS
MINKS
   Mink. R. Lowell. Be-EB:30
MINNEAPOLIS, MINN.
   As I Step over a Puddle at the
      End of Winter I Think on an
      Ancient Chinese Governor.
      J. Wright. Kh-VA:73, St-H:254
   The Poet's Final Instructions.
      J. Berryman. Ca-VT:384
MINNESOTA: see also names of
   towns, as MINNEAPOLIS, MINN.
   By a Lake in Minnesota.
      J. Wright. Br-AF:184
   Driving Toward the Lac Qui Parle
      River. R. Bly. St-H:3
   Hail! Minnesota! T. Richard.
      Se-PR:270
   Laziness and Silence. R. Bly.
      St-H:6
MINNOWS
   Epigram. Su Tung P'o. Rx-OH:84
   From the Bridge. J. Keats.
      Bo-FP:258, Ch-B:109, Mc-PR:159
   Minnows. J. Keats. Fe-FP:134,
      Go-BP:86, Un-GT:72
MINORITIES - TREATMENT: see
   DISCRIMINATION
MINSTRELS AND TROUBADOURS:
   see also NEGRO MINSTRELS
   The Banjo Player. F. Johnson.
      Hu-PN:86
   Now This Was the Reply Odysseus
      Made. Homer. Pl-ML:7
   The Wandering Story-Teller.
      Tr-CB:39, Tr-US I:46
MIRACLES: see also
   SUPERNATURAL
   As Mary Was a-Walking. Ga-S:107
   A Ballad of a Nun. J. Davidson.
      Pa-OM:138, Un-MB:74
   The Ballad of Father Gilligan.
      W. Yeats. Hi-WP I:72, Mc-WK:132,
      Mc-WS:157, Pl-EI:114, Un-MB:112

Baucis and Philemon. J. Swift.
   Sp-OG:153
Black Rook in Rainy Weather.
   S. Plath. Wi-LT:788
Christmas. J. Betjeman.
   Hi-WP I:134
A Christmas Legend. O. Herford.
   Co-PM:100
The Crow and the Crane. Ma-BB:86
Hail John's Army. Ga-S:76
Little Breeches. J. Hay.
   Un-GT:198
Miracle. L. Bailey. Ha-YA:49
Miracle. Wen I-to. Hs-TC:67
A Miracle for Breakfast. E. Bishop.
   Mo-BG:8, Sh-AP:216
Miracles. C. Aiken. Un-MA:472
Miracles. A. Bontemps. Hu-PN:210
Miracles. W. Whitman. Ga-S:15,
   Li-TU:176, Ma-FW:100, Mc-WK:102,
   Sh-RP:166, Sm-MK:228, Tr-MR:39,
   Un-GT:247
New York * December * 1931.
   B. Deutsch. Pl-IO:149
Night of Marvels.
   Sister Violante do Ceo. Ga-S:71
Prayer. Bi-IT:32
Prayer for a Miracle. A. Wickham.
   Un-GT:305
Stone Too Can Pray. C. Aiken.
   Pl-EI:177, Sm-MK:229, Tr-MR:23
MIRAMICHI RIVER
   The Miramichi Fire. Em-AF:464
MIRIAM, SISTER OF MOSES
   The Brass Serpent. T. Carmi.
      Me-PH:143
MIRRORS: see also HUMOR - MIRRORS;
   REFLECTIONS (MIRRORED)
   A Hand-Mirror. W. Whitman.
      Rv-CB:850
   I Tell People Their Faults.
      Re-RR:28
   Inscription for a Mirror in a
      Deserted Dwelling. W. Benét.
      Un-MA:329
   The Lady Who Offers Her Looking-
      Glass. M. Prior. Al-VBP:513,
      No-CL:207, Rv-CB:487
   Lais. H.D. Un-MA:337
   Mirror. T. Itozakura. Le-TA:48
   The Mirror. B. Pasternak.
      Ca-MR:167
   Mirror. J. Updike. Mc-WK:117
   Mirror! Mirror! D. Ensign.
      Ho-ME:7, Le-M:64
   Mirror, Mirror, Tell Me.
      Un-GT:22
   Robert, Who Is Often a Stranger
      to Himself. G. Brooks.
      Ho-ME:6
MIRTH: see JOY; LAUGHTER

MISANTHROPY: see also CYNICISM;
   HUMOR - MISANTHROPY
  A Curse on the Closed Gate.
   J. Cousins.   Co-PI:32
  Much Nicer People.
   E. Coatsworth.   Co-PU:121
  Peter Grimes.   G. Crabbe.
   Hi-WP II:65
  Song.   W. Snodgrass.   Un-MA:682
  Tom, Tom, the Piper's Son.
   J. Ransom.   Al-VBP:1186
MISBEHAVIOR: see BEHAVIOR
MISCARRIAGE: see ABORTION
MISCHIEF: see BEHAVIOR;
   TROUBLEMAKERS
MISERS: see also HUMOR - MISERS
  Aaron Stark.   E. Robinson.
   Un-MA:137
  Anecdotes of Four Gentlemen IV.
   Ox-BC:153
  The Cat and the Miser.
   M. Van Doren.   Ha-TP:37
  King Agongola's Song.
   Tr-CB:56, Tr-US I:55
  The Miser and the Mouse.
   C. Smart.   Pa-RE:102
  To One on Her Waste of Time.
   W. Blunt.   Al-VBP:1055
MISFITS: see INDIVIDUALITY
MISFORTUNE: see also
   HUMOR - MISFORTUNE
  Absolutes.   G. Keyser.   Du-RG:23
  Ah, Fading Joy.   J. Dryden.
   Al-VBP:479, Gr-CT:90
  Conquest.   G. Johnson.   Bo-AN:24,
   Bo-HF:102
  The Difficult Land.   E. Muir.
   Go-BP:228
  For the Earth God.   Pl-EI:174,
   Tr-US I:52
  A Gest of Robyn Hode.   Ox-BB:420
  His Litany to the Holy Spirit.
   R. Herrick.   Fe-PL:343
  Hymn to Adversity.   T. Gray.
   Pa-GTB:161
  I to My Perils.   A. Housman.
   Al-VBP:1081
  Insouciance.   J. Dickson.
   Du-SH:58
  Life's Lesson.   Fe-PL:339
  Manerathiak's Song.   Do-WH:54
  Man's Inhumanity to Man.
   R. Burns.   Er-FA:274
  My Stars.   A. Ibn Ezra.   Me-PH:64
  Nursery Rhyme.   W. Auden.
   Gr-SS:150
  Oh My Gentle Village Fierce.
   Wo-HS:(33)
  On a Very High Mountain.
   Wy-CM:37
  Small Skill Is Gained. . . . .
   Un-GT:22
  Song of an Unlucky Man.
   Do-CH:(43)
  Sonnet.   W. Shakespeare.   No-CL:87
  Stir the Wallaby Stew.   Hi-FO:253
  Strange Legacies.   S. Brown.
   Ad-PB:62, Lo-TY:218
  Summer.   T. Tsosie.   Ba-HI:62
  To Coleridge.   P. Shelley.
   Rv-CB:700
  Troubles of the Day.   W. Barnes.
   Pa-GTB:323
  Try Smiling.   Er-FA:13
  Warning.   L. Rubin.   Du-SH:93
  When Trouble Comes to Me.
   Wo-HS:(53)
MISSIONARIES: see also
   HUMOR - MISSIONARIES;
   SATIRE - MISSIONARIES
  Song of Greeting to a Missionary's
   Wife.   Tr-US I:79
MISSIONS: see CALIFORNIA -
   MISSIONS
MISSISSIPPI: see also
   SATIRE - MISSISSIPPI
  Church Burning: Mississippi.
   J. Emanuel.   Ad-PB:178,
   Hu-PN:374
  For Andy Goodman - Michael
   Schwerner - and James Chaney.
   M. Walker.   Ra-BP:158
  An Invitation to Madison County.
   J. Wright.   Ad-PB:275
  A Little More Traveling Music.
   A. Young.   Mc-EA:28
  Night, Death, Mississippi.
   R. Hayden.   Ca-VT:357
  No New Music.   S. Crouch.
   Ad-PB:484
  Way Down South in Mississippi.
   V. Barnes.   Se-PR:271
MISSISSIPPI RIVER
  Brown River, Smile.   J. Toomer.
   Ad-PB:31, Bo-AN:34, Hu-PN:107,
   Jo-SA:72
  The Distant Runners.
   M. Van Doren.   Sm-LG:81,
   Un-MA:467, Wi-LT:653
  Down the Mississippi.   J. Fletcher.
   Br-AF:180, Pa-HT:52
  June Night on the River.
   J. Knoepfle.   St-H:99
  La Crosse at Ninety Miles
   an Hour.   R. Eberhart.
   Br-AF:205
  Missy, Missy.   Re-RR:43
  The River.   H. Crane.
   Al-VBP:1210, Sh-AP:199, Un-MA:522
  The River.   P. Lorentz.   Br-AF:169

MISSOURI: see names of cities,
    as ST. LOUIS, MO.
MISSOURI RIVER
    Foreclosure.   S. Brown.
        Ad-PB:64, Hu-PN:170
    A Missouri Traveller Writes
        Home: 1830.   R. Bly.   Ni-JP:20
    Shenandoah.   Br-AF:189
MIST: see also FOG; HAZE
    Clouds of Morning Mist.   Buson.
        Be-MC:52
    Conclusion.   W. Wordsworth.
        Ox-BN:112
    Mist.   A. Young.   Ma-FW:119
    The Mist.   Ar-TP3:99, Ir-BB:50,
        Wr-RM:39
    Mists of Daybreak.   Buson.
        Hu-MP:318
    The Morning Mist.   G. Mohanty.
        Le-M:19
    November.   J. Clare.   Ma-FW:266,
        Un-GT:282
    Riddles of the Weather IV.
        Gr-GB:37
    Rocks Partly Held in Mist.
        A. Gregor.   Ls-NY:252
    A Silver Mist Creeps along the
        Shore.   P. Irving.   Al-WW:80
    This Unimportant.   Basho. Be-MC:10
MISTAKEN IDENTITY: see also
        HUMOR - MISTAKEN IDENTITY
    The Bonny Heyn.   Ox-BB:201
    The Contretemps.   T. Hardy.
        Wi-LT:25
    The Duke o' Athole's Nurse.
        Ox-BB:344
    The Famous Flower of Serving-Men.
        Ox-BB:182
    Fa'se Footrage.   Ox-BB:279
    A Gest of Robyn Hode, the
        Seventh Fytte.   Ox-BB:475
    Little Brother.   A. Fisher.
        Br-BC:48, Mc-AW:91
    Rose the Red and White Lilly.
        Ox-BB:189
    The Shepherd's Dochter.   Ox-BB:263
MISTAKES: see ERRORS
MISTLETOE
    A Christmas Legend.   O. Herford.
        Co-PM:100
    Song Against Children.
        A. Kilmer.   Th-AS:65
    The Willow-Man.   J. Ewing.
        Ox-BC:255
MITCHELL, ARTHUR
    Arthur Mitchell.   M. Moore.
        Hu-PN:506
MITCHELL, SILAS WEIR
    A Decanter of Madeira, Aged 86, to
        George Bancroft, Aged 86.
        S. Mitchell.   Al-VBP:992

MITHRAS (PERSIAN GOD)
    A Song to Mithras.   R. Kipling.
        Hi-FO:61
MITTENS: see also HUMOR - MITTENS
    The Little Kittens.   E. Follen.
        Ar-TP3:118
    The Mitten Song.   M. Allen.
        Ar-TP3:189, Au-SP:107, Ir-BB:122
    Presents.   M. Chute.   Br-SS:109,
        La-PH:36, La-PP:60, Na-EO:130
    The Three Little Kittens.
        An-IP:(16), Au-SP:22, Bo-FP:91,
        Fe-FP:526, Li-LB:146, Mo-MGT:212,
        Mo-NR:15, On-TW:16
MOAB
    The Prophecies Against Moab,
        Judah, and Israel.   Bible.
        O.T. Amos.   Me-PH:48
MOBILE BAY, BATTLE, 1864
    Craven.   H. Newbolt.   Sp-OG:78
    Farragut.   W. Meredith.   Hi-TL:108
MOBS: see CROWDS, PEOPLE
MOCCASINS
    The Moccasins of an Old Man.
        R. Carden.   Al-WW:35
    Morning Beads.   P. George.
        Al-WW:127
MOCKINGBIRDS
    After Yesterday.   A. Ammons.
        Mo-TS:50
    A Legend of Lake Okeefinokee.
        L. Richards.   Gr-EC:174
    Look at Six Eggs.   C. Sandburg.
        Fe-FP:291
    The Mockingbird.   R. Jarrell.
        La-RM:146, Li-TU:189, Rd-OA:203
    The Mockingbird.   Jo-TS:2
    Silence.   E. McCarthy.   Co-PU:104
MODENA, IT.
    Ginevra.   S. Rogers.   Fe-PL:13
MODERATION
    Choose Something like a Star.
        R. Frost.   En-PC:1, Un-MA:195
    Chorus from Medea.   Euripides.
        Pa-SG:16
    Christian Ethics.   T. Traherne.
        Pl-US:140
    A Counsel of Moderation.
        F. Thompson.   Un-MB:85
    The Golden Mean.   Horace.
        Pa-SG:176
    Name or Person.   Lao Tzu.
        Sm-MK:223
    Who Is the Man of Poise?
        Al-PI:26
MODRED, SIR: see
        MORDRED, SIR
MOHAMMEDANISM: see ISLAM
MOLE (AFRICAN PEOPLE):   see
        AFRICAN VERSE - MOSSI

MOLES (ANIMALS):   see also
    HUMOR - MOLES (ANIMALS)
  All but Blind.   W. de la Mare.
    Fe-FP:138, Ga-S:48, Hi-WP I:121,
    La-PV:152, Mc-WK:99, Ni-JP:82,
    Un-MB:291
  A Dead Mole.   A. Young.
    Co-BBW:43, Pa-GTB:466
  The Eagle and the Mole. E. Wylie.
    Al-VBP:1166, Rd-OA:158,
    Un-MA:274, Wi-TL:205
  The Gardener and the Mole.
    W. Landor. Rd-OA:115
  If You Crawled in a Hole.
    Re-RR:23
  Laziness and Silence. R. Bly.
    St-H:6
  The Mole. R. Daniells. Do-WH:83
  The Mole. W. Matchett. Ha-WR:62
  The Mole. E. Mayo. Mc-WK:68
  The Mole. I. Orleans. Br-SG:67
  Mole. W. Smith. Sh-RP:44
  A Mole-Catcher Am I. De-CH:612
  Molecatcher. A. Mackie. Co-BBW:40
  Moles. W. Stafford. La-RM:147
  Over in the Meadow. Au-SP:223,
    Ir-BB:24, On-TW:38
  To a Mole. L. Darcy. Ls-NY:198
  The Women and the Man. Te-FC:87
MOLIÈRE (PSEUD. OF JEAN BAPTISTE
    POQUELIN):   see HUMOR -
    MOLIÈRE (PSEUD. OF JEAN
    BAPTISTE POQUELIN)
MOLLUSKS: see SHELLS (SEA)
MOLOCH (SEMITIC GOD)
  Howl, Part II. A. Ginsberg.
    En-PC:234
MOMUS (GREEK GOD)
  Momus. E. Robinson.
    Al-VBP:1106
MONADNOCK, MOUNT
  New England Landscape.
    D. Heyward. Pa-HT:17
MONARCHS: see KINGS AND RULERS
MONASTERIES: see also CONVENTS
    AND NUNNERIES; MONKS
  Amongst the Cliffs. Han Yu.
    Rx-LT:69
  A Drape. Feng Chih. Hs-TC:143
  Lament for Walsingham.
    Gr-GB:184, Rv-CB:115
  Leaving the Monastery Early in
    the Morning. Lu Yu.
    Rx-OH:105
  Mont-Saint-Michel. C. Stork.
    Ke-TF:380
  Newark Abbey. T. Peacock.
    Ox-BN:233
  Twilight Comes. Wang Wei.
    Rx-LT:57

  Visit to the Monastery of Good
    Omen. Lu Chi. Rx-LT:30
MONEY: see also BANKS AND
    BANKING; COINS; HUMOR -
    MONEY; INVESTMENTS AND
    INVESTORS; SATIRE - MONEY;
    WEALTH
  America. H. Dumas. Ad-BO:40,
    Ad-PB:267, Co-PU:61
  At the Bank. R. Field. Mc-PR:183
  Basic. R. Durem. Hu-PN:331
  The City. E. Jarrett. Sc-TN:110
  The Complaint of Chaucer to His
    Purse. G. Chaucer. Al-VBP:19,
    Ma-YA:36, No-CL:11
  Epigram. J. Wolcot. Co-EL:51
  The Hardship of Accounting.
    R. Frost. Er-FA:214, Sm-LG:390
  An Invective Against the Wicked
    of the World. N. Breton.
    Al-VBP:85
  Old Fortunatus, 1600. T. Dekker.
    Al-VBP:230
  On a Halfpenny. . . .
    H. Fielding. Rv-CB:524
  Painter. J. Schevill. Du-SH:156
  Proposition. N. Guillen.
    Ab-MO:4, Fe-FP:487, Lo-TY:104
  Wilt Thou Lend Me Thy Mare?
    Co-EL:57, Co-PU:67, Rv-CB:423
MONGOLIA: see also ALTAIC
    VERSE - MONGOLIAN
  Mongolian Pastoral. Hs-TC:446
  Wind on an Inner Mongolian Desert.
    Wang T'ung-chao. Hs-TC:262
MONITOR (SHIP)
  The Cruise of the Monitor.
    G. Boker. Hi-TL:110
MONKEYS: see also
    HUMOR - MONKEYS
  The Animal World. Tr-CB:24
  At Woodward's Gardens.
    R. Frost. Pl-IO:113
  Ay Me, Alas. De-CH:85, Sm-LG:69
  Black Monkeys. R. Ainsworth.
    St-FS:8
  The Coconut-Monkey. Tr-US II:198
  Colobus Monkey. Be-AP:61
  The First Rain of Winter.
    Basho. Do-TS:40
  Improvised Song of the Baby
    Coconut-Monkey. Tr-US II:202
  The Long Night. Shiki. Le-MW:33
  Monkeys. P. Colum. Co-BBW:203
  Monkeys. J. Miller. Bo-FP:266,
    Rd-OA:125
  Monkeys. S. Read. Pa-RE:112
  The Monkeys. E. Thompson.
    Ar-TP3:79
  The Monkey's Raincoat. Basho.
    Au-SP:326, Su-FVI:67

The Organ Grinder's Garden.
   M. Merryman.   Au-SP:156
Paddling Song.   Le-OE:52
The Road Song of the Bander Log.
   R. Kipling.   Go-BP:96
Song of the Animal World.
   Ab-MO:11, Tr-US I:66
Swell People.   C. Sandburg.
   Ha-LO:59
To a Monkey.   M. Fleming.
   Co-FB:300, Er-FA:227, Un-GT:55
Well I Never, Did You Ever.
   Ir-BB:192, Sm-LG:70
What in the World?   E. Merriam.
   Gr-EC:14
MONKS: see also HUMOR - MONKS;
   MONASTERIES; SATIRE - MONKS
The Abbot of Inisfalen.
   W. Allingham.   Pa-OM:104
Blackfriars.   E. Farjeon.
   Ox-BC:330
A Christmas Legend.   O. Herford.
   Co-PM:100
Fra Lippo Lippi.   R. Browning.
   Al-VBP:898
Friar's Hunting Song. T. Peacock.
   De-TT:83, Mo-SD:116, Un-GT:89
The Ghostly Father.   P. Redgrove.
   Ca-MB:54
The Gray Monk.   W. Blake.
   Ba-PO:9
A Greedy Friar.   G. Chaucer.
   Ha-PO:51
In Praise of Celibacy.   Al-PI:51
A Monk.   Pien Chih-lin.   Hs-TC:161
Monk Begging, Kyoto. E. Shiffert.
   Ls-NY:140
The Monk in the Kitchen.
   A. Branch.   Un-MA:152
Robin Hood and the Curtal Friar.
   Ma-BB:48
Robin Hood and the Monk.
   Al-VBP:37, De-CH:135, Ox-BB:405
Sir William Deloraine at the
   Wizard's Tomb.   W. Scott.
   Ox-BN:118
Spring Comes to a Little Temple.
   Ch'en Meng-chia.   Hs-TC:117
Stanzas from the Grande Chartreuse.
   M. Arnold.   Al-VBP:971
Ten of Chaucer's People: A
   Sporting Monk.   G. Chaucer.
   Ha-PO:51
The Wife of Bath's Tale.
   G. Chaucer.   Al-VBP:14
MONMOUTH COURTHOUSE, BATTLE, 1778
Captain Molly.   W. Collins.
   Vi-PP:119
Molly Pitcher.   K. Sherwood.
   Un-GT:183, Vi-PP:116

MONROE, MARILYN
   Prayer for Marilyn Monroe.
   E. Cardenal.   Be-UL:95
MONS, BELG.
   Near Mons.   N. Myers.   Ls-NY:256
MONT-SAINT-MICHEL, FR.
   Mont-Saint-Michel.   C. Stork.
   Ke-TF:380
MONTANA: see also names of
   towns, as BUTTE, MONT.
   Indian Summer, Montana, 1950.
   W. Ransom.   Ni-CD:199
   Montana.   C. Cohan.   Se-PR:272
   Montana Fifty Years Ago.
   J. Cunningham.   Ho-P:47
   Montana Pastoral. J. Cunningham.
   Ca-VT:324, Un-MA:615
   Montana Wives.   G. Haste.
   Br-AF:159
MONTEREY, BATTLE, 1846
   Monterey.   C. Hoffman.   Hi-TL:91
MONTGOMERY, ALA.
   It Happened in Montgomery.
   P. Petrie.   Ab-MO:86
   Montgomery.   S. Cornish.
   Ad-PB:293
MONTHS: see also names of
   months, as MAY (MONTH)
   The Garden Year.   S. Coleridge.
   Ar-TP3:183, Bo-FP:204, Ch-B:30,
   De-TT:35, Hu-MP:289, Ir-BB:227,
   Mc-PR:30, Ox-BC:169, Sh-RP:188,
   Un-GB:8, Un-GT:268
   Labours of the Months.   Gr-GB:205
   March Will Search Ye.   De-CH:566
   The Months.   C. Rossetti.
   Fe-FP:62, Mc-PR:49
   The Months.   R. Sheridan.
   Bo-FP:178
   The Months.   Gr-CT:425
   Months for Marriage.   Mo-TB:42
   The Succession of the Four Sweet
   Months.   R. Herrick.   Bo-FP:243,
   Fe-FP:77, Ha-YA:80, Ho-WR:27,
   Tu-WW:68
   There's Nothing like the Sun.
   E. Thomas.   Ga-FB:6
   Thirty Days Hath September.
   Au-SP:323, Bo-FP:139, Li-LB:165,
   Mo-MGT:172, Mo-NR:101, On-TW:59,
   Un-GT:22, Wi-MG:30, Wr-RM:17
MONTREAL, CAN.
   Late Autumn in Montreal.
   J. Segal.   Ho-TY:153
   Old Montreal.   J. Segal.   Ho-TY:152
   A Psalm of Montreal.
   S. Butler.   Rv-CB:933
MONTROSE, JAMES GRAHAM,
   1ST MARQUIS
   The Execution of Montrose.
   W. Aytoun.   Pa-OM:96

MONUMENTS: see also SATIRE -
   MONUMENTS; TOMBS
  A Monument for the Soldiers.
     J. Riley.   Se-PR:135
  Monument to Pushkin. I. Brodsky.
     Bo-RU:22
  To My Son Parker, Asleep in the
     Next Room. B. Kaufman.
     Ad-PB:265, Br-TC:230,
     Ca-VT:539, Jo-SA:30
  Washington Monument by Night.
     C. Sandburg. Co-PS:45,
     Fe-FP:452
MOODS: see EMOTIONS
MOON: see also DIANA (GODDESS);
   ECLIPSES; HUMOR - MOON;
   MOONRISE; MOONSET; SATIRE -
   MOON; SELENE (GODDESS)
  Above the Dock. T. Hulme.
     Pa-GTB:445
  After Working. R. Bly. Ha-WR:47
  Aiken Drum. Bl-OB:11, Ir-BB:129,
     Sm-LG:120
  All Hail to Thee Moon. De-CH:668
  Arizona Nature Myth. J. Michie.
     Sm-MK:187
  Auctioneer. C. Sandburg.
     La-PV:57
  Autumn. T. Hulme. Al-VBP:1152,
     Ha-LO:102, Ja-PA:7, Sm-MK:13
  The Bad Kittens. E. Coatsworth.
     Fe-FP:160, Hu-MP:186, Se-PR:195,
     Sh-RP:40, Th-AS:105
  The Barn Owl. S. Butler.
     Sm-MK:149
  Bedtime. Bo-FP:108, Mo-MGT:207,
     Rd-SS:5, Wr-RM:101
  Behind Me the Moon. Kikaku.
     Be-CS:11
  Brimming Water. Tu Fu. Rx-OH:34
  Broken and Broken. Chosu.
     Be-CS:48
  A Buddhist Hymn. Feng Wei-teh.
     Hs-TC:138
  A Caravan from China Comes.
     R. Le Gallienne. Th-AS:152
  Cast upon the Ground.
     T. Takaori. Sh-AM:154
  The Cat and the Moon. W. Yeats.
     Bo-FP:92, Bo-GJ:245, Co-BBW:135,
     Co-PI:200, Co-PM:194, Co-RG:102,
     Ha-LO:30, Hi-WP I:2, Li-TU:200,
     Ma-FW:57, Re-TW:18, Sm-LG:72
  The City of Stones. Liu Yu-Hsi.
     Le-MW:62
  Clear Evening after Rain. Tu Fu.
     Rx-OH:27
  The Clouds Have Left the Sky.
     R. Bridges. De-CH:448
  Coolness in Summer. Ryusui.
     Sh-RP:67

  Crescent Moon.   E. Roberts.
     Ar-TP3:180, Mc-AW:84
  Dejection. S. Coleridge.
     Ox-BN:167, Rv-CB:665
  Dog at Night. L. Untermeyer.
     Pe-M:110, Un-GT:42
  Dusk. E. Recht. Le-M:84
  The Early Morning. H. Belloc.
     Co-BN:122, Gr-EC:104, Gr-TG:41,
     Mc-WK:4
  Esthetique du Mal, II.
     W. Stevens.   Wi-LT:151
  Ethinthus, Queen of Waters.
     W. Blake. Gr-CT:402
  Euclid. V. Lindsay. Ho-LP:57,
     Li-TU:248, Pl-IO:81
  Evening. R. Aldington. Un-MB:354
  Everyone Is Asleep. Seifu-jo.
     Do-TS:37
  The Faraway Moon. R. Gutman-Jasny.
     Ho-TY:298
  Foxgloves. T. Hughes. Ha-LO:99
  The Freedom of the Moon.
     R. Frost. Ho-LP:55
  Full Moon. W. de la Mare.
     Ar-TP3:180, Co-BN:118, Gr-EC:89,
     Hi-WP I:32
  Full Moon. R. Hayden. Ra-BP:135
  Full Moon. Tu Fu. Rx-OH:28
  A Full Moon Comes Up. Shiki.
     Be-MC:30
  The Full Moon Whispered to the
     World. J. Rathe. Le-M:204
  Full Moonlight in Spring.
     W. Merwin. Co-PU:46, Ho-TH:86
  Goat Songs, I, III. R. Drew.
     Kh-VA:44
  Half Moon. F. Garcia Lorca.
     La-RM:155, Le-SW:77, Li-TU:205
  Harbingers. Basho. Sh-RP:64
  Harvest Moon. Ryota. Sh-RP:66
  The Harvest Moon. Sodo.
     Do-TS:36
  Here Am I. Jo-TS:9
  High Tide. J. Untermeyer.
     Un-MA:331
  Homage to Diana. W. Raleigh.
     Ho-WR:38
  The Hour of Magic. W. Davies.
     Un-MB:175
  A Hungry Owl Hoots. Joso.
     Be-CS:14
  Hungry Tree. N. Altshuler.
     Le-M:205
  Hymn to Diana. B. Jonson.
     Al-VBP:239, De-CH:441, Gr-CT:403,
     Ho-WR:39, Ma-YA:83, Pa-GTB:67,
     Rv-CB:281
  I Am Round like a Ball.
     St-FS:39

I Gazed upon the Cloudless Moon.
  E. Brontë. Gr-CT:406
I Like to Play with the Moon.
  F. Gonzalez. La-GI:46
I See the Moon. Ar-TP3:180,
  Au-SP:94, Bo-FP:47, De-CH:743,
  Gr-GB:39, Mo-MGT:207, Rd-SS:32,
  Sm-MK:215, Un-GT:23
In My Delight. . . . Ba-ST:61
In the Car. R. Margolis.
  Su-FVI:32
In the Moon. D. Stelaru.
  Mc-AC:120
In the Moonlight. N. O'Connor.
  Au-SP:298
Insomnia. E. Bishop. Ho-TH:62
It Was the Lovely Moon.
  J. Freeman. Co-BN:119
Jack o'Lantern. A. Ayre.
  Au-SP:371
Judging by Appearances.
  A. Poulsson. Hu-MP:342
Lady Moon. Lord Houghton.
  Bo-FP:47
Lady Moon. R. Milnes. Ox-BC:171
The Lake. J. Stephens. Un-MB:361
Last Song. J. Guthrie.
  Ar-TP3:181, La-PV:62
The Leaves. St-FS:125
Lightly a New Moon. Kyoshi.
  Be-CS:26
Lines for a Night Driver.
  P. Dufault. Ha-WR:53
Little Miss Moon. De-PP:20
Look, the Sea! W. Zorach.
  Ad-PE:12
Looking at the Moon and Thinking
  of One Far Away.
  Chang Ching-ling. Pa-SG:145
Love in Moonlight. Bhartrihari.
  Pa-SG:64
Lovers, Forget the Moon.
  C. Norman. Cr-WS:121
Low Clouds Are Shattered.
  Basho. Be-MC:9
Lunae Custodiens. L. Carter.
  De-FS:44
A Magic Landscape. A. Fet.
  Mo-MI:13, Pa-SG:103
The Man in the Moon. Ir-BB:149,
  Li-LB:59, Mo-MGT:23, Wr-RM:73
May Moon. O. Driver. Sh-RP:210
A Midnight Memory. Lu Li.
  Hs-TC:422
Milk-White Moon, Put the Cows to
  Sleep. C. Sandburg. Fe-FP:164
Mr. Moon. B. Carman. Fe-FP:371,
  Sh-RP:11
Mockery. K. Riggs. Hu-MP:111,
  Pe-FB:69, Th-AS:22

Moist Moon People. C. Sandburg.
  Un-MA:209
Mon, in the Mone. De-CH:742
Moon. N. Alterman. Me-PH:108
The Moon. Bhasa. Pa-SG:114
The Moon. E. Coatsworth.
  Sh-RP:174
The Moon. R. Creeley. Ca-VT:569
The Moon. W. Davies. Un-MB:175
The Moon. E. Follen. Hi-GD:24,
  Hu-MP:120
The Moon. L. Garnett. Br-SS:32
The Moon. Ryuho. Au-SP:342
The Moon. Ab-MO:3, Be-AP:68
Moon. Mo-MGT:166
The Moon and the Nightingale.
  J. Milton. Gr-CT:401
The Moon and the Yew Tree.
  S. Plath. Mo-BG:146, To-MP:96
The Moon Cannot Fight. Le-OE:103
Moon Festival. Tu Fu. Rx-OH:8
Moon Folly. F. Davis. Th-AS:24
Moon-Gazing. Hsü Chih-mo.
  Hs-TC:95
The Moon in the Mountains.
  Chen Shan-min. Pa-SG:165
The Moon in the Water. Ryota.
  Au-SP:342, Le-IS:26
Moon, O Mother Moon. Le-OE:5
Moon Poem. S. Sharp. Ab-MO:5
Moon Song. H. Conkling.
  Th-AS:20
Moon-Uncle. Ca-MU:31, 32
Moonlit Apples. J. Drinkwater.
  Co-BN:132, Go-BP:113
Moons. J. Haines. Sc-TN:71
The Moon's Funeral. H. Belloc.
  Th-AS:145
The Moon's the North Wind's Cooky.
  V. Lindsay. Au-SP:327,
  Er-FA:499, Fe-FP:265, La-PP:26,
  La-PV:54, Li-LC:62, Na-EO:170,
  Th-AS:21, Un-GB:12, Un-GT:258
Morning Moon. V. Contoski.
  Sc-TN:29
Mother Moon, Bless Baby.
  Le-OE:104
My Wish. P. Strong. Sh-RP:114
The New Moon. W. Bryant.
  De-TT:85
New Moon. D. Lawrence. Co-BN:122
New Moon. Tu Fu. Rx-OH:17
New Moon Come Out. Le-OE:70
Night. P. Hubbell. La-PV:56
Night Clouds. A. Lowell.
  Ho-TH:24, Mo-BG:147, Sh-RP:88,
  Th-AS:142, Un-MA:159
The Night of the Full Moon.
  L. Frankenberg. Co-BL:114
Night Riddle. Gr-EC:92

MOON — cont'd.
  Night Song. F. Cornford.
    Co-BBW:112, Co-IW:41
  O Lady Moon. C. Rossetti.
    Bo-FP:285, De-CH:690, De-TT:84,
    Ox-BC:277, Rd-SS:32
  O Moon, Why Must You. Koyo.
    Be-CS:41
  Oh My Sun, My Moon! Le-OE:115
  O That Moon Last Night!
    Teitoku. Be-MC:56
  The Old Coon-Dog Dreams.
    K. Porter. Un-GT:40
  The Old Man in the Moon.
    Bo-FP:325, Rd-SS:30
  Old Moon Planter. J. Knoepfle.
    St-H:94
  On the Sea of Heaven. Hitomaro.
    Ba-ST:32
  The Pale Cold Moon. W. Renton.
    Hi-WP II:127
  The Path on the Sea. I. Muller.
    Mo-MI:28
  Phases of the Moon.
    R. Browning. Gr-CT:406
  Prayer to the Moon. Be-AP:23
  Proposition. N. Guillén.
    Ab-MO:4, Fe-FP:487, Lo-TY:104
  The Ragged Phantom. Boncho.
    Be-MC:36
  Reason Has Moons. . . .
    R. Hodgson. Sm-LG:203, Un-MB:186
  Riddle. Gr-CT:402, Gr-GB:39
  Riddle #29. Bo-GJ:244
  A Ring of Silver Foxes. Ho-SD:3
  The Rising Moon. Fang Hsin.
    Pa-MV:82
  River Moons. C. Sandburg.
    Ma-FW:123
  The Robber. W. Turner. Un-MB:345
  Saturday Night. Mo-MGT:167
  The Sea Was Calm. C. Minor.
    Ba-HI:103, Jo-VC:71
  Seven Times One. J. Ingelow.
    Br-BC:71, Fe-FP:50, Gr-TG:47,
    Hu-MP:70, Ke-TF:41, Ox-BN:720,
    Un-GT:14
  Shiny. J. Reeves. Sh-RP:181
  Silver. W. de la Mare.
    Ar-TP3:181, Br-SS:32, Co-BN:121,
    Co-PM:48, Fe-FP:265, Mc-WK:5,
    Rd-SS:27, Sp-OG:308, Un-GB:12,
    Un-GT:262, Un-MB:202
  Since My House Burned Down.
    Masahide. Be-CS:43
  Sing a Song of Moonlight.
    I. Eastwick. Br-SS:33
  Sleepyhead. W. de la Mare.
    Ar-TP3:155
  A Small Hungry Child. Basho.
    Be-CS:58

  Snail, Moon, and Rose.
    J. Kenward. Sm-MK:55
  Song. Tr-US I:182
  Song Cycle of the Moon-Bone.
    Tr-US I:246
  Song of Creation. Bi-IT:4,
    Ho-SD:52
  The Song of Creatures.
    St. Francis of Assisi.
    Pa-SG:202
  A Song of the Moon. C. McKay.
    Hu-PN:98
  Song of the Sun and the Moon.
    Da-SC:68, Le-OE:3
  Songs and Dance Songs, III.
    Tr-US II:152
  A Sonnet of the Moon. C. Best.
    De-CH:336
  The Spacious Firmament on High.
    J. Addison. Mc-PR:202,
    Pl-EI:211
  The Spring Waters. Ping Hsin.
    Hs-TC:22
  Stars and Moon on the River.
    Tu Fu. Rx-OH:32
  The Storm. Chora. Sh-RP:66
  Summer Moonlight. P. Strong.
    Sh-RP:216
  Summer Night. Ranko. Sh-RP:66
  Summer Song. W. Williams.
    Ha-WR:54
  Tailor's Song. P. Dehn.
    Sm-MK:178
  There Is a Trinity. Rippo.
    Le-MW:65
  There Is Fear. Ma-BH:11,
    Tr-US I:24
  There Was a Thing. Mo-MGT:157
  Thousands of Shining Knights.
    Re-RR:100
  To a Solitary Disciple.
    W. Williams. Ca-VT:54
  To the Moon. T. Hardy. Co-BN:119,
    Gr-CT:406
  To the Moon. P. Shelley.
    Al-VBP:754, Co-BN:120,
    Pa-GTB:275, Sh-RP:74, Sm-MK:6
  To the Moon. W. Wordsworth.
    Rv-CB:653
  Tom o' Bedlam. De-CH:275,
    Ho-PR:51, Mc-WK:5, Sm-LG:203
  The Traveler. V. Lindsay.
    Un-MA:225
  Turning from Watching. Shiki.
    Be-CS:40
  The Twelfth Moon Came.
    Wo-HS:(16)
  Two Mad Songs, II. E. Jarrett.
    Sc-TN:109
  Two Moons. Hsü Chih-mo.
    Hs-TC:94

Under the Full Moon.
Yü Kuang-chung. Pa-MV:182
The Wandering Moon. J. Reeves.
Sh-RP:85
The Waning Moon. P. Shelley.
De-CH:443, Sm-LG:52
Watching the Moon. D. McCord.
Ha-YA:103, Ja-PA:20, Sh-RP:221
Waves Coming Up Against the Rocks.
Le-OE:85, Tr-US I:244
We Have Seen the Sun.
Emperor Tenchi. Ba-ST:32
The Weaving. H. Cook. Th-AS:119
A Weeping Child. Issa. Le-MW:102
Welcome to the Moon. Co-BN:117,
Gr-CT:403
We're like Two Flowers. Re-RR:92
What Can You See. Re-RR:76
What Invisible Rat.
J. Rabéarivelo. Lo-TY:153
A White Blossom. D. Lawrence.
Un-MB:290
The White Moon. P. Verlaine.
Pa-SG:143
The White Window. J. Stephens.
Ar-TP3:180
Who Knows if the Moon's.
E. Cummings. Co-PM:42, Ha-LO:47
Wind and Silver. A. Lowell.
Co-PU:140, Mo-BG:152, Un-MA:159
The Wind and the Moon.
G. MacDonald. Bo-GJ:35,
Ir-BB:127, Li-LC:79, Pa-OM:268,
Un-GT:258
Winter Moon. L. Hughes. Ab-MO:4
A Wish. T. Santos. Le-M:159
With How Sad Steps, O Moon.
P. Sidney. Al-VBP:126,
Co-BN:121, De-CH:442,
Gr-CT:71, Un-MW:72
With the Moon's Ax. J. Sternberg.
Ho-TY:196
The World's Wanderers.
P. Shelley. Al-VBP:755
Yet Gentle Will the Griffin Be.
V. Lindsay. Gr-EC:88,
La-PV:55, Th-AS:19
MOONRISE
Aware. D. Lawrence. Co-BN:118,
Co-PU:57, Un-MB:297
Golden Moonrise. W. Braithwaite.
Ad-PB:14
Moonrise. G. Hopkins. Un-MB:43
Moonrise. D. Lawrence. Wi-LT:211
Shadows. Le-MW:59
Sun Low in the West. Buson.
Be-CS:27
Waiting. Le-MW:59
MOONSET
Aware. D. Lawrence. Co-BN:118,
Co-PU:57, Un-MB:297

Moon Moves down the Sky. Buson.
Be-MC:51
Now the Moon Goes Down. Buson.
Be-CS:59
The Sunrise. Da-SC:87
MOORE, SIR JOHN
The Burial of Sir John Moore at
Corunna. C. Wolfe.
De-TT:139, Er-FA:285, Gr-CT:342,
Hi-FO:198, Ke-TF:165, Pa-GTB:216,
Rv-CB:693, Sp-OG:202
MOORE, MARIANNE CRAIG
Invitation to Miss Marianne Moore.
E. Bishop. Pl-ML:82
MOORE, THOMAS: see also
HUMOR - MOORE, THOMAS
To Thomas Moore. G. Byron.
Pl-ML:78
MOORHENS: see WATER BIRDS
MOORS: see MARSHES
MOORS (ARABS): see also
BEDOUINS
The Moors Fight on the Side of
God. C. Norman. Cr-WS:37
The Preacher. Al-Mahdi.
Lo-TY:45
Pretences. Ibn Rashiq.
Lo-TY:44
The Sword. Abu Bakr. Lo-TY:44
MOOSE: see HUMOR - MOOSE
MORALITY: see GOODNESS;
VALUE AND VALUES
MORDRED, SIR
The Passing of Arthur.
A. Tennyson. Ni-JP:158,
Ox-BN:511
MORGAN, SIR HENRY
The Sack of Old Panama.
D. Burnet. Co-RM:56
MORGAN'S RAIDS, 1862-1864
Kentucky Belle. C. Woolson.
Ha-PO:133, Un-GT:192
MORMONS AND MORMONISM
Old North. N. Thorp. Fi-BG:131
See also Em-AF:611-626
MORNING: see also DAWN;
HUMOR - MORNING;
WAKE-UP VERSES
The Aïr to Gi'e Your Cheäks
a Hue. W. Barnes. De-CH:614
And Love Hung Still.
L. MacNeice. Un-MB:443
And Now the Hunt! Br-FW:18
Anna-Marie, Love, Up Is the
Sun. W. Scott. Al-VBP:677
Annual Gaiety. W. Stevens.
Un-MA:248
The Answer. J. Wheelock. Ha-WR:80
At Half-Past Three a Single Bird.
E. Dickinson. Un-MA:105

MORNING — cont'd.
Aubade.   E. Sitwell.
    Hi-WP II:6, Un-MB:330
Autumn Morning.   F. Frost.
    Sh-RP:225
The Avenue Bearing the Initial
    of Christ into the New World.
    G. Kinnell.   Ad-CI:11, Wi-LT:746
Awake! Awake!   W. Davenant.
    Al-VBP:384, De-CH:6, Gr-CT:41,
    Un-MW:3
Awake, My Heart, to Be Loved.
    R. Bridges.   Pa-GTB:415,
    Un-MB:48
Awaken.   S. Bingham.   Le-M:21
Barefoot Days.   R. Field.
    Fe-FP:229, Ha-YA:66
The Beginning of Day.
    Euripides.   Pa-SG:104
Beyond Dawn.   Lo Fu.   Pa-MV:117
The Birds Are Singing Music.
    D. Garton.   Le-M:22
Business Girls.   J. Betjeman.
    Hi-WP II:167
Cambridge.   F. Cornford.   Cl-FC:57
Ceiling Unlimited.
    M. Rukeyser.   Un-MA:622
Chelsea Morning.   J. Mitchell.
    Mo-GR:119
City.   L. Hughes.   Br-AF:209,
    Gr-EC:96, Ho-CS:7, 46, La-PP:33,
    La-PV:188, Li-LC:41
Cockcrow Song.   Le-MW:40
Composed upon Westminster Bridge.
    W. Wordsworth.   Al-VBP:660,
    Ar-TP3:173, Bo-FP:124, De-CH:524,
    Er-FA:270, Fe-PL:396, Ga-FB:224,
    Go-BP:22, Gr-CT:290, Ha-PO:80,
    Hi-WP II:126, Ke-TF:367, Ma-YA:139,
    Mc-PR:190, Ox-BN:78, Pa-GTB:250,
    Pa-HT:124, Rv-CB:645, Sm-LG:135
Day of These Days.   L. Lee.
    Co-BN:108
A Description of the Morning.
    J. Swift.   Al-VBP:515, Ho-P:62
Discovering God Is Waking One
    Morning.   J. L'Heureux.
    Co-BN:92
Early Astir.   H. Read.   Co-PU:132
Early Morn.   W. Davies.   De-CH:6
Early Morning.   J. Jimenez.
    Le-SW:67
East Anglian Bathe.   J. Betjeman.
    Mo-SD:144
Easter.   E. Coatsworth.   Ha-YA:50
Easter.   G. Herbert.   Bo-FP:248,
    De-CH:16, Ga-S:173
8 May 1967.   M. Korte.   Sc-TN:120
Epitaph for a Little-Known
    Gravestone.   P. Mayer.   St-H:135

The Eye.   J. Carew.   Sa-B:15
Fairy Music.   F. Ledwidge.
    Ha-YA:54
Fall Mornings.   M. Cannon.
    Ja-PA:28
A Field of Light.   T. Roethke.
    Br-TC:346
Getting Up.   R. Burgunder.
    Ar-TP3:175
The Golden Net.   W. Blake.
    Gr-SS:166
Good Night and Good Morning.
    R. Milnes.   Ox-BC:171
A Greeting.   W. Davies.   Mc-WK:82,
    Tr-MR:23, Un-MB:175
The Heart of the Ancient City.
    Pien Chih-lin.   Hs-TC:166
Impression du Matin.   O. Wilde.
    Un-MB:67
The Imprisoned.   R. Fitzgerald.
    Br-TC:127
In Fields of Summer.   G. Kinnell.
    Co-BN:99, Ha-WR:22, La-RM:144
In Memoriam.   A. Tennyson.
    Gr-CT:315, Hi-WP II:143,
    Ox-BN:495
In My House.   Sodo.   Be-MC:15
In the Naked Bed, in Plato's
    Cave.   D. Schwartz.   Ca-VT:365,
    Un-MA:619, Wi-LT:515
Kill That Crowing Cock.   Rx-LT:18
The Lime Avenue.   S. Sitwell.
    Ha-LO:48
Listen.   Put On Morning.
    W. Graham.   Wi-LT:720
A Little Morning Music.
    D. Schwartz.   Co-BN:212
Love in May.   J. Passerat.
    Pa-SG:32
May Mornings.   I. Eastwick.
    Br-SS:148
Merry Sunshine.   Ch-B:25, Hu-MP:132
The Minstrel.   J. Beattie.
    Al-VBP:598
Moon-Come-Out.   E. Farjeon.
    Ar-TP3:179, Mc-AW:12
Morning.   E. Dickinson.   Au-SP:343,
    Br-SS:15, Fe-FP:261, Pe-FB:68
Morning.   D. Gallagher.   Br-SS:20
Morning.   J. Harrison.   Ha-WR:44
Morning.   J. Keats.   Sp-OG:349
Morning at the Window.   T. Eliot.
    Ad-CI:10, Ho-LP:73
Morning Hymn.   T. Ken.   Er-FA:455
Morning in Spring.   L. Ginsburg.
    Gr-EC:65
The Morning Mist.   G. Mohanty.
    Le-M:19
Morning on the Liévre.
    A. Lampman.   Mo-SD:130

Morning Overture: Chorus of
  Dogs. P. Strachan. Un-GT:42
Morning Song. A. Dugan.
  Ad-CI:13, Co-EL:99
A Morning Song. E. Farjeon.
  Hi-WP I:6
Morning Song from "Senlin."
  C. Aiken. Pe-OA:141,
  Sh-AP:185, Un-MA:422, Wi-LT:325
The Morning-Watch. H. Vaughan.
  Al-VBP:465, Mo-GR:120
Neighborhood. G. Isaacs.
  La-IH:43
New Morning. B. Dylan. Mo-GR:112
No Time for Poetry. J. Fields.
  Be-MA:149, Bo-AN:183
Not Ideas about the Thing, but the
  Thing Itself. W. Stevens.
  Al-VBP:1145
November Morning. E. Stein.
  Ha-YA:127
Oh My Sun, My Moon! Le-OE:115
October. R. Frost. Bo-GJ:251,
  Gr-CC:41
On the Staircase. E. Farjeon.
  Br-SS:35
Once. W. de la Mare. Go-BP:170
One Misty, Moisty Morning.
  Ar-TP3:166, Cl-DT:85, Ir-BB:212,
  La-PV:92, Li-LB:55, Mo-MGT:179,
  Mo-NR:14, Rv-ON:89, Wr-RM:50
One Star Lingering. H. Behn.
  Be-MC:5
Open, Open the Gates. Tatya.
  Mo-MI:19
Open the Door. M. Edey. Ar-TP3:182,
  Br-SS:18
The Owl. A. Tennyson. Bl-OB:65,
  Bo-FP:285, Bo-GJ:73, Ch-B:112,
  De-CH:98, De-TT:80, Fe-FP:293,
  Gr-EC:176, Hu-MP:238, Ir-BB:23,
  Re-TW:24, Rv-CB:794, Sm-LG:88,
  Tu-WW:90, Un-GB:17, Un-GT:65
Pack, Clouds, Away! T. Heywood.
  Al-VBP:271, Bl-OB:42, De-CH:7,
  Pa-GTB:32, Re-BS:9, Re-TW:52,
  Tu-WW:11, Un-MW:6
Parting at Morning. R. Browning.
  Ga-FB:63, Ho-WR:135, Ni-JP:98,
  Ox-BN:534, Rv-CB:820
Pippa's Song. R. Browning.
  Bo-FP:213, Bo-GJ:96, Ch-B:98,
  Cl-DT:45, Er-FA:20, Fe-FP:72,
  Ha-YA:28, Hu-MP:291, Ke-TF:434,
  La-PV:81, Li-LC:72, Ma-YA:200,
  Mc-PR:95, Mo-GR:113, Rv-CB:816,
  Se-PR:68, Sp-OG:215, Tu-WW:60,
  Un-GT:273
Ploughman Singing. J. Clare.
  Go-BP:39

Preludes II. T. Eliot. Br-TC:105,
  Ca-VT:129, Pe-OA:103, Sh-AP:182
Preludes III. T. Eliot. Br-TC:105,
  Ca-VT:129, Sh-AP:182
A Red Morning Sky. Issa.
  Le-IS:4
Resolution and Independence.
  W. Wordsworth. Co-BN:214,
  Ma-FW:36, Ox-BN:71, Rv-CB:654
Reveillé. A. Housman. Er-FA:20,
  Fe-PL:398, No-CL:121, Un-MB:93,
  Wi-LT:59
Rich Morning. R. Farren.
  Co-PI:39
Rising from Illness.
  Chang Hsiu-ya. Pa-MV:30
The Rivals. J. Stephens.
  Fe-FP:280, Mc-PR:191, Pa-RE:42,
  Re-BS:43, Th-AS:53
Sing a Song of Sunshine.
  I. Eastwick. Br-SS:16
Sister, Awake. Co-PS:77,
  De-CH:11, Gr-CC:66
Small Song. F. Frost. Sh-RP:174
Snowy Morning. L. Moore.
  Un-GB:11
Softly, Drowsily. W. de la Mare.
  Ar-TP3:175, Au-SP:98
Song. T. Shadwell. Al-VBP:502
Song. G. Vicente. Pa-SG:148
The Song of Songs. Bible. O.T.
  Song of Solomon. Pa-SG:26
Song on May Morning. J. Milton.
  Cl-FC:38, Co-BN:23, De-CH:10,
  Ha-YA:55, Mc-PR:86, Se-PR:111
Spring Morning - Santa Fe.
  L. Riggs. Pa-HT:57
A Summer Morning. R. Field.
  Ar-TP3:175, Au-AP:319,
  La-PV:48, Pe-FB:86
Summer Morning. B. Young.
  Mc-AW:40
Summons to Love. W. Drummond.
  Al-VBP:303, Pa-GTB:1
The Sunbeams Stream Forward.
  Ho-SD:48, Jo-TS:1
Sunday. V. Rutsala. Du-SH:101
Sunday up the River.
  J. Thomson. Al-VBP:1009
This Morning. J. Wright.
  Ab-MO:105, Hu-NN:17, Jo-SA:99
To a Solitary Disciple.
  W. Williams. Ca-VT:54
To My Wife. J. Simcock. Gr-BT:91
The Trumpet. E. Thomas.
  Gr-SS:169, Un-MB:216
Twinkling Stars. Ca-MU:10
Unrest. R. Dixon. Ox-BN:753
Very Early. K. Kuskin.
  Au-SP:41, La-PV:49

MORNING — cont'd.
  Weaving the Morning.
    J. de Melo Neto. An-TC:151
  What You Should Do Each Morning.
    B. Patten. Gr-BT:152
  A Wood Song. R. Hodgson.
    Bo-GJ:96
MORNING-GLORIES
  Ah! I Am Eating My Breakfast.
    Basho. Do-TS:34
  Five Short Stanzas, II. The
    Morning Glory. Tsou Ti-fan.
    Hs-TC:347
  I Must Go Begging. Chiyo.
    Be-CS:55
  Morning-Glories. De-PP:57
  Morning Glory. P. Roche.
    Sm-MK:174
MORONS: see MENTALLY HANDICAPPED
MORTICIANS: see UNDERTAKERS
MORTON, FERDINAND (JELLY ROLL)
  Jelly Wrote. A. Spellman.
    Be-MA:125
MOSCOW, U.S.S.R.
  Early Train. B. Pasternak.
    Ca-MR:173
  Moscow Morning. J. Rubinstein.
    Ho-TY:239
  The Other Looks at Me.
    J. Rubinstein. Ho-TY:240
  People, Listen! A. Shchukin.
    Bo-RU:73
  A Wondrous City Is Moscow.
    Taniusha. Mo-MI:63
MOSES: see also MIRIAM,
  SISTER OF MOSES
  The Angels Came a-Mustering.
    Pl-EI:100
  An Ante-Bellum Sermon.
    P. Dunbar. Ra-BP:44
  The Burning Bush.
    N. Nicholson. Pl-EI:57
  The Eleventh Commandment.
    J. Holmes. Tr-MR:78
  Go Down, Moses. Ab-MO:79,
    Ga-S:45, Pl-EI:101, Ra-BP:23
  The Jew. I. Rosenberg. Un-MB:352
  Moses. Mo-MGT:202
  Mount Avarim. J. Halevi.
    Me-PH:60
  The Murder of Moses. K. Shapiro.
    Pl-EI:102
MOSLEMISM: see ISLAM
MOSQUITOES
  The Best I Have. Basho. Be-MC:14
  The Mosquito. J. Updike.
    Du-SH:110, Ma-FW:206
  The Mosquito Knows. D. Lawrence.
    Rd-OA:170
  Onto a Boy's Arm. Ho-SD:77

MOSSES
  Moss-Gathering. T. Roethke.
    La-RM:49
  Tale. W. Merwin. Ho-TH:86
MOTHER GOOSE (ABOUT)
  Old Mother Goose. Mother Goose.
    Au-SP:2, Mo-NR:80, Wi-MG:22,
    Wr-RM:14
  Old Mother Goose and the Golden
    Egg. Li-LB:48, Mo-MGT:2
MOTHER GOOSE RHYMES: see
  NURSERY RHYMES
MOTHERS: see also FAMILY AND
  FAMILY LIFE; HUMOR -
  MOTHERS; MOTHERS-IN-LAW;
  PARENT AND CHILD; SATIRE -
  MOTHERS; STEPMOTHERS
  The Adversary. P. McGinley.
    Mc-WS:144
  The Affliction of Margaret.
    W. Wordsworth. Pa-GTB:239
  And Be Her Mother, Just as She
    Was Mine. Ke-TF:145
  Ap Huw's Testament. R. Thomas.
    Gr-BT:xv
  A Baby-Tending Song. S. Muro.
    Sh-AM:54
  Baking Day. R. Joseph. To-MP:142
  The Ballad of the Harp-Weaver.
    E. Millay. Ar-TP3:156, Co-PT:64
  The Bents and Broom. Ox-BB:187
  Big Momma. D. Lee. Ra-BP:304
  A Boatwoman. Chao Yeh. Le-MW:114
  The Bonny Earl of Livingston.
    Ox-BB:309
  A Boy's Mother. J. Riley.
    Se-PR:119
  C.L.M. J. Masefield. Un-MB:225,
    Wi-LT:190
  Child and Mother. E. Field.
    Hu-MP:126
  The Child and the Snake. M. Lamb.
    De-TT:63, Ox-BC:142
  Christmas Lullaby for a New-Born
    Child. Y. Gregory. Bo-AN:153
  Clyde's Waters. Ox-BB:331
  Complaint of a Widow over Her
    Dying Son. Tr-US I:157
  The Constancy. J. Miller.
    Sc-TN:171
  The Critic. J. Farrar. Au-SP:92
  Dance Songs, IV. Tr-US I:199
  Dandelions. M. Chute. Br-BC:102,
    Mc-AW:67
  A Dream. W. Allingham. Co-PI:9,
    Co-PT:70
  The Dream. J. Bishop. Wi-LT:608
  Edward, Edward. De-CH:410,
    Ha-PO:1, Ma-BB:39, Ox-BB:239,
    Rv-CB:39

Esthetique du Mal, X.   W. Stevens.
   Wi-LT:156
Eyes.   T. Itozakura.   Le-TA:18
Fair Isabell of Rochroyall.
   Ox-BB:144
The Family Poem.   M. Rawitch.
   Ho-TY:202
For a Very New Angel.   V. Storey.
   Ke-TF:200
For Me Again.   T. Joans.   Be-MA:100
The Forsaken.   D. Scott.   Do-WH:63,
   Ha-PO:159
Fruit of the Flower.   C. Cullen.
   Fe-PL:136, Jo-SA:20
The Gift of God.   E. Robinson.
   Un-MA:135
Ginger Bread Mama.   D. Long.
   Ad-PB:404, Ra-BP:310
Girl's-Eye View of Relatives.
   P. McGinley.   Ke-TF:90,
   Mc-WS:145
Green Afternoon.   F. Frost.
   Ar-TP3:76
Greens.   D. Ray.   Ca-VT:678
Heart-Summoned.   J. Stuart.
   De-FS:195
Her Words.   A. Branch.   Ar-TP3:4,
   Br-SS:154, Fe-FP:32, Ha-YA:59
The Hero.   S. Sassoon.   Co-RM:208
His Mother's Wedding Ring.
   G. Crabbe.   Ox-BN:18
The Housewife.   B. Amma.   Al-PI:126
How's My Boy?   S. Dobell.   De-CH:31
I Look Hard at This World.
   V. Burich.   Bo-RU:26
I See a Star.   A. Lopez.   Al-WW:4
If I Look out My Window.
   C. Weaver.   Me-WF:47
If I Were a Wind.   Y. Aji.
   Le-TA:19
If There Are Any Heavens.
   E. Cummings.   Un-MA:476
If Your Mother Has Set Out to
   Fish.   Do-CH:(7)
I'm Just a Stranger Here,
   Heaven Is My Home. C. Clemmons.
   Ad-PB:489
In an Iridescent Time.   R. Stone.
   Un-MA:655
In These Dissenting Times.
   A. Walker.   Ad-PB:475
Interior.   P. Colum.   Co-PI:28,
   Un-MB:250
Jean Richepin's Song.   H. Trench.
   Co-PI:191, Co-PT:25, Gr-EC:127
Jesus and His Mother.   T. Gunn.
   Ke-TF:144, Pl-EI:31
Jesus Was Crucified.   C. Rodgers.
   Ad-PB:432
Kaddish.   A. Ginsberg.   Lo-IT:58

Keening.   Tr-US II:309
Lament for the Dead Mother.
   Be-AP:28
leroy.   I. Baraka.   Ad-PB:255,
   Mc-EA:105, Ra-BP:215
A Lesson for Mamma.   S. Dayre.
   Ox-BC:286
Lines on Receiving His Mother's
   Picture.   W. Cowper.   De-CH:38
The Lonely Mother.   F. Johnson.
   Hu-PN:91
Lonesome.   P. Dunbar.   Hu-MP:29,
   Se-PR:118
Lullaby.   Le-IB:63
McDonogh Day in New Orleans.
   M. Christian.   Bo-AN:52,
   Hu-PN:157
Mamma!   F. Horne.   Ra-BP:76
Mammy Hums.   C. Sandburg.
   Hu-PN:482
Mater Dolorosa.   W. Barnes.
   De-CH:265
Maternity.   A. Miller.   Ke-TF:149
The Mither's Lament.   S. Smith.
   Co-PU:151
Mom.   G. Cohoe.   Al-WW:27
Mother.   R. Fyleman.   Br-SS:152,
   Hu-MP:5
Mother.   T. Helburn.   Fe-FP:31
Mother.   H. Saito.   Le-TA:20
Mother and Child.   I. Eastwick.
   Br-SS:155
Mother and Slave Raiders.
   Tr-US I:90
The Mother Bird.   W. de la Mare.
   Sp-OG:297
Mother Dear.   Do-CH:(8)
The Mother in the House.
   H. Hagedorn.   Se-PR:116
A Mother Is a Sun.   P. Bennett.
   Co-PS:85
Mother o' Mine.   R. Kipling.
   Er-FA:136
Mother of the House.   Bible.
   O.T.   Proverbs.   Co-PS:88,
   Un-GT:91
A Mother Praises Her Baby.
   Tr-US I:77
A Mother to Her First-Born.
   Tr-CB:27, Tr-US I:105
Mother to Son.   L. Hughes.
   Ab-MO:97, Be-MA:38, Bo-AN:67,
   Bo-HF:177, Br-BC:123, Hu-PN:186,
   Jo-SA:19, La-OC:94, Lo-TY:225,
   Pe-FB:70, Pe-SS:7
Mother's Day.   A. Fisher. Mc-AW:68
Mother's Day.   Y. Takeuchi.
   Le-TA:22
The Mother's Song.   Ho-SD:75,
   Le-OE:113

MOTHERS — cont'd.
My Mamma Has Been Clever. Anya.
    Mo-MI:59
My Mamma Moved among the Days.
    L. Clifton. Ad-PB:308,
    Be-MA:139
My Mother. C. Grade. Ho-TY:220
My Mother. T. Kee. Ba-HI:88
My Mother. A. Taylor. Ox-BC:114
My Mother's Breast. J. Okito.
    Le-TA:21
My Old Mother Stands. T. Tsosie.
    Ba-HI:90
My Trust. J. Whittier. Se-PR:118
Nancy Hanks. R. and S. Benét.
    Ar-TP3:44, Br-SS:117, Fe-FP:438,
    Ga-FB:257, Gr-EC:233, Sh-RP:314
Nancy Hanks, Mother of Abraham
    Lincoln. V. Lindsay. Hi-TL:96
The New Pieta: For the Mothers
    and Children of Detroit.
    J. Jordan. Ad-PB:303
Night and Morning. D. Aldis.
    Co-PS:89, Ha-YA:58
O Sleep My Babe. S. Coleridge.
    Ox-BN:448
Oh, Yes, My Dear. De-CH:584
Old Mother Blinds Her Own Son.
    Yüan Shui-p'ai. Hs-TC:410
Only One Mother. G. Cooper.
    Bo-FP:38, Br-SS:153, Ch-B:116,
    Fe-FP:31, Hu-MP:4
Oriflamme. J. Fauset. Ad-PB:18
Our Mother's Tunes. E. Farjeon.
    Hu-MP:6
Over the Hills to the Poor-House.
    W. Carleton. Er-FA:266
The Potter. Lo-TY:47
Prince Robert. Ox-BB:203
A Riddle. M. Nikogosian.
    Mo-MI:55
Rufus Prays. L. Strong. Un-MB:394
Second Air Force. R. Jarrell.
    Wi-LT:563
The Sick Child. R. Stevenson.
    Co-PS:87, De-CH:37, De-TT:151
Sleep, Sleep, Little One. . . .
    Le-OE:111
Somebody's Mother. M. Brine.
    Er-FA:139
Song of a Mother for Her Dead
    Son. Tr-US II:20
Song of a Mother Whose Child Has
    Been Left Behind on the Caravan
    Trail. Tr-US I:61
The Song of a Vagabond Son.
    Fang Ching. Hs-TC:385
Song of Exile. Tr-US I:130
The Song of the Old Mother.
    W. Yeats. Co-PI:208, Ha-LO:98,
    Un-MB:112

Song Sung by a Woman Giving Birth.
    Tr-CB:55, Tr-US I:65
Songs for My Mother: Her Hands.
    A. Branch. Hu-MP:4, Se-PR:117
Songs in the Night.
    M. Caruthers. Ke-TF:182
Songs of a Mother Mourning Her
    Sons Killed in Battle.
    Tr-US II:237
Sonnet to My Mother. G. Barker.
    Al-VBP:1240, Br-TC:24, Er-FA:138,
    Ma-FW:63, Pe-SS:155, Wi-LT:528
The Spring Waters. Ping Hsin.
    Hs-TC:24
sugarfields. B. Mahone. Ad-PB:473
The Time Has Come. S. Voronov.
    Mo-MI:41
To My Mother. Y. Amichai.
    Me-PH:133
To My Mother. L. Ginsberg.
    Co-PS:86
To My Mother. T. Moore. Se-PR:120
To Our Babies, I, II. Le-IB:60
Two Mothers. I. Sheyanova.
    Mo-MI:45
Two Mounds. J. Glatstein.
    Ho-TY:326
Upon My Lap My Sovereign Sits.
    R. Rowlands. Al-VBP:210,
    De-CH:20
Upstream. C. Sandburg. Pe-M:45,
    Tr-MR:176, Un-MA:209
Uvlunuaq's Song. Tr-US I:16
Valentine for My Mother.
    H. Lee. Hu-MP:331
Virginia. E. Loftin. Ad-PB:514
Waking Time. J. Eastwick.
    Ar-TP3:239, Br-SS:7
What My Child Learns of the Sea.
    A. Lorde. Ad-PB:247
What Rules the World.
    W. Wallace. Se-PR:120
When I Read My Poems.
    H. Takai. Le-TA:36
When Mother Reads Aloud.
    Fe-FP:31, Hu-MP:25
Why Do You Cry? Do-CH:(4)
Wife and Husband. C. Day.
    Le-M:141
The Wife of Usher's Well.
    Ar-TP3:20, De-CH:424, De-TT:171,
    Gr-CT:134, Ma-BB:37, Ox-BB:94,
    Pa-OM:91, Rv-CB:36
The Wise Mother. D. Hobson.
    Ke-TF:146
Wishing. W. Allingham. Hu-MP:69
The Wolf and the Lioness.
    E. Rees. Ar-TP3:81
Young Companions. Fi-BG:211
MOTHER'S DAY: see MOTHERS

MOTHERS-IN-LAW: see also
    HUMOR - MOTHERS-IN-LAW
  Sweet Willie. Ox-BB:45
MOTHS: see also HUMOR - MOTHS
  Design. R. Frost. Ho-LP:49,
    Pe-OA:45
  Green Moth. W. Welles.
    Ar-TP3:66, Fe-FP:139, Rd-SS:8
  Inquiry into the Nature of
    Cruelty. L. Cohen. Be-EB:30
  Lunar Moth. R. Hillyer. Rd-OA:9
  Lying Awake. W. Snodgrass.
    Un-MA:684
  Moth. K. Alling. Ho-LP:46
  The Moths. W. Matchett.
    Ha-WR:48
  Where More Is Meant. C. Morley.
    Sh-RP:70
MOTION
  Fishes Swim in Water Clear.
    Mother Goose. Pa-AP:10
  Flight. S. Allen. Du-SH:158
  Motions. Bu-DY:26
  The Pleasures of Merely
    Circulating. W. Stevens.
    Ha-LO:12
  Tumbling. Ox-BC:60
  With a Hop, and a Skip, and a
    Jump. W. O'Neill. St-FS:4
MOTION PICTURES: see MOVING
    PICTURES
MOTORCYCLES
  Fifteen. W. Stafford. Ad-CI:66,
    Du-RG:70, Pe-SS:40
  On the Move. T. Gunn. Br-TC:159,
    Wi-LT:723
  Sketch from Loss of Memory.
    S. Dorman. Pe-SS:93
  305 Honda. G. Fowler. Sc-TN:49
  The Unsettled Motorcyclist's
    Vision of His Death. T. Gunn.
    Mc-EA:160
MOTTOES: see also EPIGRAMS;
    HUMOR - MOTTOES; PROVERBS;
    SAYINGS AND SIGNS
  Good, Better, Best. Sp-AS:(35)
  Lesson from a Sundial. Ar-TP3:208
  Motto. Ar-TP3:209
MOUNT VERNON, VA.
  At Mount Vernon. T. Clark.
    Vi-PP:140
  Mount Vernon, the Home of
    Washington. W. Day. Se-PR:60
MOUNTAIN ASH TREES
  A Red Cluster. M. Tsvetayeva.
    Ca-MR:134
MOUNTAIN CLIMBING: see CLIMBING
MOUNTAIN LIFE
  Appalachian Front. R. Weeks.
    Br-AF:135

I Am the Mountainy Singer.
  J. Campbell. Un-MB:251
Mountain Meadows. M. Keller.
  Co-BN:221
The Mountain Whippoorwill.
  S. Benét. Co-PT:110
MOUNTAIN LIONS
  The Glory Trail. B. Clark.
    Co-PT:129
  Mountain Lion. D. Lawrence.
    La-RM:20
  The Women and the Man. Te-FC:87
MOUNTAIN SHEEP: see BIGHORNS
MOUNTAINS: see also HILLS;
    HUMOR - MOUNTAINS;
    VOLCANOES; and names of
    mountains, as FUJIYAMA
    and ranges of mountains,
    as HIMALAYA
  Above Pate Valley. G. Snyder.
    Mo-BG:131
  Above Tides of Leaves. Buson.
    Be-CS:10
  Alpine. R. Thomas. Co-BN:220,
    La-RM:42
  Alpine Spirit's Song. T. Beddoes.
    Ox-BN:457
  At Feng Ting Temple. Li Po.
    Le-MW:41
  Because the Mist.
    Kiyowara Fukayabu. Ba-ST:37
  Because the Treetops of the
    Peak. Hitomaro. Le-MW:46
  Benediction. A. Morgan. Ke-TF:427
  The Birthplace. R. Frost.
    Sm-LG:110
  Burning. G. Snyder. Ma-FW:140
  The Ching-Ting Mountain.
    Li Po. Li-TU:39
  Come Down, O Maid. A. Tennyson.
    Al-VBP:860, Go-BP:124, Ox-BN:488,
    Rv-CB:798
  Conclusion. W. Wordsworth.
    Ox-BN:112
  Conversation in the Mountains.
    Li Po. Pa-SG:192
  The Death Song of White Antelope.
    White Antelope. Br-MW:92
  18,000 Feet. E. Roberson.
    Hu-PN:430
  Emigrant's Iconoclasm.
    T. Baybars. Ls-NY:249
  Enthralled. C. Thaxter.
    Sp-OG:252
  Epistle to Prometheus.
    B. Deutsch. Sm-PT:81
  Evening Shadows Touch.
    Buson. Be-CS:39
  Every Morning I Walk into the
    Tent. Wo-HS:(46)

MOUNTAINS — cont'd.
  Fable. R. Emerson. Bo-FP:71,
    Bo-GJ:26, Bo-HF:69, Ch-B:27,
    Er-FA:496, Fe-FP:530, Ga-FB:317,
    Hu-MP:210, Pa-OM:333, Rd-OA:91,
    Sh-AP:27, Sp-OG:303, Un-GT:57
  The Face of My Mountains.
    Bi-IT:46
  Far up the River. Tu Fu.
    Rx-OH:26
  From Garden to Garden, Ridge to
    Ridge. J. Muir. La-RM:43
  From the Highest Camp. T. Gunn.
    Br-TC:163
  Golgotha Is a Mountain.
    A. Bontemps. Bo-AN:77, Hu-PN:219
  The Grass on the Mountain.
    M. Austin. Br-AF:146
  Hearing of Harvests Rotting in the
    Valleys. W. Auden. Un-MB:457
  Here in Katmandu. D. Justice.
    La-RM:38
  High on a Mountain. Basho.
    Be-CS:21
  Holding the Sky. W. Stafford.
    La-RM:37
  Hymn to the Southern Mountains.
    Tr-US I:33
  In a Desert Town. L. Stevenson.
    Br-AF:217
  In a Mountain Cabin in Norway.
    R. Bly. La-RM:23
  In My Mountains. J. Yokomizo.
    Ba-HI:102
  In the Country. Lu Yu. Rx-LT:101
  In the Mountains on a Summer Day.
    Li Po. Ma-FW:116, Mo-SD:93
  In Time like Glass. W. Turner.
    Un-MB:347
  The Kalmyk Mourns for His Country.
    Tr-US II:133
  Languishing. Br-FW:2
  Low Clouds Are Shattered. Basho.
    Be-MC:9
  A Low Range of Mountains.
    Ho-SD:51, Le-OE:15
  Morning Prayer. Do-CH:(46)
  Morning Star. T. Ferril.
    Ca-VT:200
  Mount Kuanyin. Yu Kuang-chung.
    Pa-MV:188
  Mount T'ai P'ing. Ch'ien Ch'i.
    Rx-LT:66
  The Mountain. R. Frost.
    Ga-FB:292, Pa-HT:13
  The Mountain Afterglow.
    J. Laughlin. Ca-VT:409
  The Mountain Sat upon a Plain.
    E. Dickinson. Ga-FB:283
  The Mountains Are a Lonely Folk.
    H. Garland. Sh-RP:76
  The Mountains Grow Unnoticed.
    E. Dickinson. Mc-PR:138,
    Un-MA:103
  Mountains of Discontent.
    Wo-HS:(56)
  Mountains on Mountains. De-PP:42
  Muckish Mountain (The Pig's Back).
    S. Leslie. Co-PI:92
  My Heart's in the Highlands.
    R. Burns. Er-FA:424
  My Help Is in the Mountain.
    Wo-HS:(55)
  Night Practice. M. Swenson.
    Li-TU:168
  On a Mountain Road.
    Wu Ch'ing-jen. Pa-SG:99
  On Hardscrabble Mountain.
    G. Kinnell. La-RM:28
  Open Range. K. and B. Jackson.
    Ar-TP3:34, Fe-FP:271
  The Peaks. S. Crane. Sh-AP:144
  The Poem That Took the Place of
    a Mountain. W. Stevens.
    Pl-ML:13
  River-Fog. Fukayabu Kiyowara.
    Fe-FP:481
  A River Leaping. Meisetsu.
    Be-CS:20
  St. Gervais. M. Roberts.
    Sm-LG:297
  Seascape. B. Esbensen. Ar-TP3:164
  A Song from Arsut. Tr-US I:4
  Songs. Tr-US II:138
  A Story. W. Stafford. La-RM:30
  Strength Through Joy.
    K. Rexroth. Ca-VT:268
  Summer Solstice. A. Garner.
    Gr-BT:155
  That Dark Other Mountain.
    R. Francis. Mo-SD:169, Pe-SS:8
  That Mountain Far Away.
    Bi-IT:47
  This Unimportant. Basho.
    Be-MC:10
  To Miss Blackett on Her First
    Ascent of Helvellyn.
    W. Wordsworth. No-CL:109
  The Topography of History.
    T. McGrath. St-H:119
  View from the Cliffs.Tu Mu. Rx-LT:74
  Water and Shadow.
    M. Zaturenska. Gr-SS:132
MOURNING: see GRIEF
MOUTHS: see also HUMOR –
  MOUTHS; TEETH; TONGUES
  Cherry-Ripe. T. Campion.
    Al-VBP:217, Bo-GJ:125, De-CH:142,
    Ke-TF:98, Pa-GTB:77, Re-TW:67,
    Rv-CB:267
  I Have a Pink Pen. Re-RR:34
  Life. T. Kuramae. Le-TA:13

The Mouth and the Body.
  P. Mwanikih.   Le-M:169
Mouths. D. Aldis.   Ag-HE:75
MOVING (HOUSEHOLD)
  The 1st. L. Clifton.   Mo-TS:6
  House Moving. P. Hubbell.
    Su-FVI:41
  The Move Continuing. A. Young.
    Ad-PB:365
  Moving. E. Tietjens.   Ar-TP3:93
  Moving. R. Wallace.   Du-SH:170
  Moving Day. H. Hartman.   Se-PR:177
  October 1. K. Shapiro.   Un-MA:637
  Rich. A. Fisher.   Hu-MP:138
MOVING PICTURES: see also HUMOR -
    MOVING PICTURES; SATIRE -
    MOVING PICTURES; and names of
    actors, as CHAPLIN, CHARLES
  At the Silent Movies. Z. Landau.
    Ho-TY:101
  Autobiographical Note.
    V. Scannell. To-MP:127
  Hollywood. K. Shapiro. Wi-LT:537
  Movie. J. Nims. St-H:153
  A Night Out. D. Abse. Gr-BT:158
  Reel One. A. Stoutenburg.
    Du-SH:40, Pe-M:4
  The Western Movies. H. Ito.
    Le-TA:27
MOWING: see HAY AND HAYING
MOZAMBIQUE
  Poem of the Conscripted Warrior.
    R. Nogar. Lo-TY:187
  Poem of the Future Citizen.
    J. Craveirinha. Ab-MO:106,
    Lo-TY:186
MOZART, WOLFGANG AMADEUS
  Mozart. J. Mayhall. Ls-NY:132
  Mozart, 1935. W. Stevens.
    Sh-AP:161
MUD
  April Showers. T. Tribilla.
    La-GI:24
  Catherine. K. Kuskin.   La-PV:97
  Colloquy in Black Rock.
    R. Lowell. Un-MA:663
  Cooking. M. Livingston.
    Gr-EC:107
  Mud. P. Boyden. Ar-TP3:167,
    Au-SP:187, Ga-FB:168,
    Hu-MP:298, Ir-BB:101
  Mud in Vietnam. J. Lester.
    Jo-SA:66
  Mud Pie. K. Fraser. Ho-CS:43
  The Puddle. M. Caroprese.
    La-GI:25
  Puddles. D. Ricker. La-GI:26
  Who Likes the Rain.
    C. Bates. Ar-TP3:167,
    Bo-FP:226, St-FS:18

MUHAMMED ALI: see CLAY,
    CASSIUS MARCELLUS
MUIR, JOHN
  Burning. G. Snyder. Ma-FW:140
MULBERRY TREES
  Banjo Boomer. W. Stevens.
    Mc-WK:37
  On the Site of a Mulberry-Tree.
    D. Rossetti. Rv-CB:884
MULES: see also HUMOR - MULES
  Boliver Riggin. Fi-BG:138
  Cincirinella Has a Mule.
    Fe-FP:475
  The Erie Canal. Br-AF:66,
    Sh-RP:78
  Ever Since. E. Coatsworth.
    Br-SS:123
  Farm Hand. J. Hearst. St-H:77
  Four-Footed Poems. E. Greenberg.
    Ho-TY:312
  The Horse and the Mule.
    J. Wynne. Ox-BC:78
  Mule Song. A. Guiterman.
    Co-BBW:144
  The Old Mare. E. Coatsworth.
    Un-MA:463
  On the Road to Cook's Peak.
    Fi-BG:135
  The Train. Pien Chih-lin.
    Hs-TC:164
MULLEIN
  A Flower of Mullein. L. Reese.
    Un-MA:112
MULLINS, PRISCILLA: see
    ALDEN, JOHN
MUMMIES
  Address to a Mummy. H. Smith.
    Co-RG:5
  Why Were the Egyptians.
    Re-RR:36
MUMPS
  Mumps. E. Roberts. Au-SP:106,
    Fe-FP:47, Hu-MP:13, Ja-PC:50,
    Lo-LL:58, Mc-AW:92
MURDER: see also ASSASSINATIONS;
    HUMOR - MURDER; LYNCHINGS;
    SATIRE - MURDER
  At That Moment. R. Patterson.
    Ad-PB:210, Jo-SA:37
  The Ballad of Reading Gaol.
    O. Wilde. Ox-BN:896
  Bill and Parson Sim. Fi-BG:199
  Black Bart. Fi-BG:139
  The Bonny Earl of Murray.
    Bl-OB:152, Co-RM:206, Ma-BB:36,
    Ox-BB:594, Rv-CB:35, Sm-LG:271
  The Brothers. A. Groesbeck.
    De-FS:102
  Cain and Abel. I. Manger.
    Ho-TY:278

MURDER — cont'd.
 Captain Hall. Gr-GB:269
 The Cruel Brother. Ma-YA:38,
  Ox-BB:236
 The Death of Lord Warriston.
  Ox-BB:603
 Derelict. Y. Allison. Co-SS:17.
  Er-FA:436, Pa-OM:204
 Edward, Edward. De-CH:410,
  Ha-PO:1, Ma-BB:39, Ox-BB:239,
  Rv-CB:39
 Epitaph. Ba-PO:72
 Fair Flowers in the Valley.
  Rv-CB:46
 The Fancy Kid. Fi-BG:56
 For Andy Goodman - Michael
  Schwerner - and James Chaney.
  M. Walker. Ra-BP:158
 For the One Who Would Take Man's
  Life in His Hands.
  D. Schwartz. Ca-VT:366,
  Hi-TL:218, Un-MA:618, Wi-LT:517
 Green Woods. E. Coatsworth.
  De-FS:52
 Hanging Johnny. Gr-GB:271
 The Hunting Tribes of Air and
  Earth. W. Scott. Rd-OA:117
 Ibycus. J. Heath-Stubbs. En-PC:165
 James Powell on Imagination.
  L. Neal. Ra-BP:269
 Judith of Bethulia. J. Ransom.
  Wi-LT:313
 The Knifesmith. D. Howard.
  Co-RM:90, Sm-MK:38
 The Laboratory. R. Browning.
  Ni-JP:38
 The Lady Isabella's Tragedy.
  Gr-GB:251
 Lamkin. Ox-BB:313, Rv-CB:44
 The Last Quatrain of the Ballad
  of Emmett Till. G. Brooks.
  Ad-PB:155
 Lord Maxwell's Last Goodnight.
  Ox-BB:607
 Martyrdom. R. Thomas. Ad-PB:370
 Mary Hamilton. Rv-CB:131
 A Mother Speaks. M. Harper.
  Ra-BP:291
 Mourning Hymn for the Queen of
  Sunday. R. Hayden. Ad-PB:117,
  Du-SH:105
 A Murder. L. Wolf. Ho-TY:224
 Old Christmas. R. Helton.
  Co-PM:94, Un-MA:346
 On the Birth of My Son, Malcolm
  Coltrane. J. Lester.
  Ad-PB:356, Jo-SA:24
 One-Sided Shoot-Out. D. Lee.
  Ad-PB:423, Ra-BP:302
 The Outlandish Knight.
  Br-SM:36, Un-GT:111

 Panther. S. Cornish.   Ad-PB:297
 The Parklands. S. Smith.
  Ca-MB:94
 Porphyria's Lover. R. Browning.
  Ni-JP:36, Un-MW:116
 Prince Robert. Ox-BB:203
 The Rise of Shivaji. Z. Ghose.
  Ca-MB:59
 A Rope for Harry Fat. J. Baxter.
  Ca-MB:85
 The Runaway Slave at Pilgrim's
  Point. E. Browning. Hu-PN:448
 Samuel Hall. Co-RM:98
 Screaming Tarn. R. Bridges.
  Co-PT:26
 Sir Halewyn. Ox-BB:690
 Song David. Ox-BB:241
 Stranger Bride. J. Sloan. De-FS:182
 The .38. T. Joans. Be-MA:102,
  Hu-NN:83
 Tim Turpin. T. Hood. Ho-WR:84
 The True Import of Present
  Dialogue: Black vs. Negro.
  N. Giovanni. Ad-PB:451, Ra-BP:318
 The Twa Sisters. De-CH:421,
  Rv-CB:42
 Two Ponies Shy. Fi-BG:142
 Verses on Daniel Good. Ox-BB:654
 Une Vie. P. Saarikoski.
  Co-EL:144
 Waltz. R. Sherry. De-FS:176
 Waring of Sonoratown. H. Knibbs.
  Fi-BG:141
 The Workhouse Boy. Gr-GB:265
 Young Benjie. Ox-BB:337
 Young Hunting. Ox-BB:87
 Young Waters. Fo-OG:31, Ox-BB:321
 See also Em-AF:670-701
MUSES: see also HUMOR - MUSES;
  INSPIRATION; PEGASUS
 The Dark and the Fair.
  S. Kunitz. En-PC:67
 Invocation to the Muses.
  R. Hughes. Un-MB:407
 The Muse. A. Akhmatova. Pl-ML:32
 The Muse in the New World.
  W. Whitman. Un-MA:41
 A Muse of Fire. W. Shakespeare.
  Gr-CT:429
 Rebirth of the Muse.
  Hu P'in-ch'ing. Pa-MV:105
 The Song of the Muses. M. Arnold.
  Gr-CT:444, Ho-WR:249
 Standing on Earth. J. Milton.
  Gr-CT:464
 To the Muses. W. Blake.
  Al-VBP:611, Gr-CT:230,
  Rv-CB:561

MUSEUMS: see also ART GALLERIES;
   PLANETARIUMS; and names of
   museums, as BRITISH MUSEUM
The Dinosaur Bones. C. Sandburg.
   Du-SH:108, Ho-TH:56
The Dodo. H. Belloc. Co-OH:68,
   Gr-CT:21, Ir-BB:82, Lo-LL:69
Elegy in a Museum. P. Griffin.
   Go-BP:63
Museums. L. MacNeice.
   Pe-SS:83, Un-MB:444
Visit to a Museum. A. Ficke.
   Ls-NY:209
The War Museum at Nagasaki.
   C. Higham. Ls-NY:30
MUSHROOMS
The Elf and the Dormouse.
   O. Herford. Ar-TP3:153,
   Au-SP:285, Bo-FP:225, Ch-B:60,
   Fe-FP:345, Hu-MP:92, Mc-PR:31,
   Pa-OM:50, Pe-FB:53, Th-AS:11,
   Un-GB:13, Un-GT:15
Morels. W. Smith. Co-BN:224,
   La-RM:50
Mushrooms. S. Plath. Co-BN:222,
   Sm-MK:184
On an Old Rotted Stump. Gr-BB:6
Round about the Mushroom Ring.
   L. Haberly. Cl-DT:77
Toadstools. E. Fleming. St-FS:61
MUSIC AND MUSICIANS: see also
   BANDS (MUSIC); COMPOSERS;
   CONCERTS; EUTERPE; HUMOR -
   MUSIC AND MUSICIANS; JAZZ
   MUSIC; OPERAS; ORCHESTRAS;
   ROCK MUSIC AND SONG; SONGS
   AND SINGING; and names of
   composers, musicians, and
   musical instruments
After a Music Concert. S. Muro.
   Sh-AM:52
After a Symphony Concert.
   V. Uflyand. Bo-RU:86
Albert Ayler: Eulogy for a
   Decomposed Saxophone Player.
   S. Crouch. Ad-PB:486
Alexander's Feast. J. Dryden.
   Ho-WR:100, Ma-YA:107, Pa-GTB:105
All These Hymnings Up to God.
   A. Evans. Tr-MR:197
Anthem for St. Cecilia's Day.
   W. Auden. Br-TC:20
At a Concert of Music. C. Aiken.
   Pl-US:148, Un-MA:430
At a Solemn Music. J. Milton.
   Pa-GTB:104, Pl-US:131
At a Solemn Musick. D. Schwartz.
   Tr-MR:35
At Laie's Tomb. O. Goga.
   Mc-AC:38

At My Wedding. J. Segal.
   Ho-TY:151
At the Symphony. R. Nathan.
   Se-PR:326
The Aura. J. Dickey. Du-SH:55
The Barrel-Organ. A. Noyes.
   Ga-FB:234, Un-MB:245
Beautiful Black Men. N. Giovanni.
   Ra-BP:320
Beethoven's Ninth Symphony in
   Wartime. E. Pierce. Cr-WS:59
Birmingham. J. Fields. Hu-PN:418
Blues Note. B. Kaufman.
   Ad-PB:263, Be-MA:131, Jo-SA:36
The Castle of Indolence.
   J. Thomson. Al-VBP:547
Closing Cadence. J. Moffit.
   Tr-MR:262
Come, Let Us Sound with Melody,
   the Praises. T. Campion.
   Pl-US:66
Come, Ye Sons of Art. H. Purcell.
   Pl-US:44
The Commendation of Music.
   W. Strode. No-CL:39
The Concert. P. McGinley.
   Ha-YA:47
Concert Interpretation (Le Sacre
   du Printemps). S. Sassoon.
   Rv-CB:981
The Desert Music. W. Williams.
   Pl-US:5
Duke of Parma's Ear. E. Siegel.
   Co-EL:154
Elizabeth at the Piano.
   H. Gregory. Gr-SS:134, Pl-US:20
End-of-Summer Poem. R. Bennett.
   Br-SS:179, Fe-FP:148, Ja-PA:5
Enitharmon's Song. W. Blake.
   Gr-CT:174
An Epitaph upon the Celebrated
   Claudy Philips, Who Died Very
   Poor. S. Johnson. Pl-US:79,
   Rv-CB:527
Esthetique du Mal, IV. W. Stevens.
   Wi-LT:153
The Faery Queen. E. Spenser.
   Al-VBP:119, Pl-US:40
The Fairy Fiddler. N. Hopper.
   Al-VBP:1112
Fantasy. G. de Nerval. Gr-SS:54
The Fiddle and the Bow. H. Wolfe.
   Go-BP:225
Fiddler Jones. E. Masters.
   Mo-BG:158, Pl-US:31, Sh-AP:136,
   Sm-LG:41
First Song. G. Kinnell.
   Bo-GJ:47, Br-TC:237, Ha-TP:122,
   Mo-BG:123, Wi-LT:745
Five Little Fairies. On-TW:23

MUSIC AND MUSICIANS — cont'd.
  Flute. Chang Hsiu-ya. Pa-MV:35
  The Flute Players. J. Rabéarivelo.
    Pa-SG:130
  Flute Song. Pa-SG:150
  For Marian Anderson. F. Bock.
    Ls-NY:159
  For the Eightieth Birthday of a
    Great Singer. E. Shanks.
    Pl-US:58
  From Jazz for Five, 5:Shake Keane,
    Trumpet. J. Smith. To-MP:195
  The Green Fiddler. R. Field.
    Co-PT:173
  Guide to the Symphony. W. Kees.
    Ca-VT:405
  The Guitarist Tunes Up.
    F. Cornford. Co-EL:20
  The Habit of Perfection.
    G. Hopkins. Al-VBP:1060,
    Go-BP:275, Pl-US:151, Un-MB:40
  The Harper of Chao. Po Chü-i.
    Pl-US:23
  Henry Purcell. G. Hopkins.
    Pl-US:80
  Home-Sickness. J. Kerner. Pa-SG:138
  I Heard You Solemn-Sweet Pipes
    of the Organ. W. Whitman.
    Rv-CB:858
  I Saw Three Ships Come Sailing By.
    Mo-NR:50
  I Too Hear America Singing.
    H. Bond. Lo-IT:11
  If All the Unplayed Pianos.
    W. Scott. Du-SH:169
  If Music and Sweet Poetry.
    R. Barnefield. Al-VBP:266
  In Such a Night. W. Shakespeare.
    Gr-CT:171, No-CL:180
  Inside a Deep Isolation.
    S. Muro. Sh-AM:56
  Italian Music in Dakota.
    W. Whitman. Sh-AP:120
  Italian Opera. J. Miller.Pl-US:35
  Ives. M. Rukeyser. Pl-US:87
  Jno Brinlyes Body Here Doth Ly.
    De-CH:653
  Kubla Khan. S. Coleridge.
    Al-VBP:699, Bo-GJ:222, Co-RG:15,
    De-CH:386, Er-FA:361, Ga-FB:23,
    Gr-CT:177, Gr-EC:140, Mc-PR:150,
    Ox-BN:165, Pa-HT:154, Re-TW:132,
    Rv-CB:657, Sm-LG:215
  Lester Young. T. Joans.
    Be-MA:101, Bo-AN:171, Mo-BG:55
  A Lost Chord. A. Procter.
    Er-FA:437, Sp-OG:338
  Love. L. Tieck. Pa-SG:29
  A Man with a Little Pleated
    Piano. W. Welles. Fe-FP:249
  Many a Mickle. W. de la Mare.
    Ga-FB:169
  Me, in Kulu Se & Karma.
    C. Rodgers. Ad-PB:432
  Merlin. R. Emerson. Sh-AP:32
  Moths. J. Fields. Ad-PB:320,
    Hu-PN:417
  The Mourning Bride. W. Congreve.
    Al-VBP:520
  Mozart, 1935. W. Stevens.
    Sh-AP:162
  Mozart Perhaps. J. Wheelock.
    Pl-US:81
  Music. C. Baudelaire. Pa-SG:135
  A Music. W. Berry. Ca-VT:683
  Music. H. Conkling. Hu-MP:72
  Music. W. de la Mare. Se-PR:325
  Music. R. Emerson. Ga-FB:13,
    Un-GT:309
  The Music Makers. A. O'Shaughnessy.
    Al-VBP:1063, Co-PI:163, Ga-FB:133,
    Mc-PR:72, Se-PR:324
  The Music of a Tree. W. Turner.
    Un-MB:347
  Music Room. E. Pierce. Cr-WS:59
  Music, when Soft Voices Die.
    P. Shelley. Al-VBP:757,
    Bo-HF:124, De-CH:197, Ga-FB:126,
    Ha-PO:179, Ma-YA:180, Mc-PR:82,
    Ox-BN:294, Pa-GTB:313, Un-MW:203
  A Musical Critic Anticipates
    Eternity. S. Sassoon. Pl-US:143
  A Musical Instrument. E. Browning.
    Fe-FP:384, Ho-WR:36, Mc-PR:122,
    Pa-OM:284, Se-PR:327, Sp-OG:343
    Un-GT:162
  Musician. L. Bogan. Bo-GJ:132,
    Pl-US:28
  The Musician. R. Lister.
    Pl-US:6
  Musicians Wrestle Everywhere.
    E. Dickinson. Pl-US:144
  Musicks Empire. A. Marvell.
    Gr-CC:60
  My Music Reaches to the Sky.
    Da-SC:149, Le-OE:136
  Notes Found near a Suicide:
    To Catalina. F. Horne. Bo-AN:43
  O I Won't Lead a Homely Life.
    T. Hardy. Pl-US:33
  Ode on a Grecian Urn. J. Keats.
    Al-VBP:772, Er-FA:80, Ha-PO:228,
    Ke-TF:59, Ox-BN:355, Rv-CB:742
  Ode to a Nightingale. J. Keats.
    Al-VBP:769, Er-FA:89, Gr-CT:102,
    Li-SR:138, Ox-BN:352, Pa-GTB:248
  Old King Cole. Au-SP:4, De-PO:22,
    Er-FA:507, Fr-WO:33, Ir-BB:265,
    Li-LB:68, Mo-MGT:147, Mo-NR:137,
    Wi-MG:27, Wr-RM:83

On a Piece of Music. G. Hopkins.
   Pl-US:94
On an Air of Rameau. A. Symons.
   Ox-BN:936
On Hearing a Symphony of Beethoven.
   E. Millay. Pl-US:85, Un-MA:448,
   Wi-LT:339
On Music. W. Landor. Bo-GJ:140,
   Gr-CC:67
On the Death of Mr. Purcell.
   J. Dryden. Pl-US:78
On the Praise of Poetry and Music.
   A. Cowley. No-CL:30
Onion Bucket. L. Thomas.
   Ad-PB:483
Orpheus with His Lute.
   J. Fletcher. Al-VBP:286,
   Rv-CB:202, Se-PR:329, Sm-LG:38
Over His Keys. J. Lowell.
   Se-PR:327
The Passions. W. Collins. Pa-GTB:136
Pediment Ballet. L. Nicholl.
   Pl-US:114
Peter Quince at the Clavier.
   W. Stevens. Al-VBP:1142,
   Br-TC:415, Gr-CC:62, No-CL:43,
   Pe-OA:66, Un-MA:240, Wi-LT:142
Piano after War. G. Brooks.
   Bo-AN:142
The Players Ask for a Blessing on
   the Psalteries and on Themselves.
   W. Yeats. Pl-US:10
Poem. H. Johnson. Ad-PB:93,
   Bo-AN:100
Poem for Aretha. N. Giovanni.
   Ad-PB:454, Ra-BP:327
The Power of Music. Pindar.
   Pl-US:102
The Power of Music to Disturb.
   L. Mueller. St-H:148
Program Notes on Sibelius.
   D. Babcock. Pl-US:73
The Progress of Poesy. T. Gray.
   Al-VBP:566, Pa-GTB:132, Rv-CB:532
The Quarrel. C. Aiken. Un-MA:430
The Remote Bermudas: Ferdinand.
   W. Shakespeare. No-CL:43,
   Pl-US:130
Serenade. C. Brentano. Pa-SG:134
Sheldonian Symphony. S. Sassoon.
   Pl-US:82
The Shooting of Dan McGrew.
   R. Service. Co-RM:129, Do-WH:22,
   Er-FA:382, Fe-PL:9
Singing. P. Shelton. Le-M:137
A Song for St. Cecilia's Day,
   1687. J. Dryden. Pa-GTB:49,
   Pl-US:152, Rv-CB:466
Song from a County Fair. L. Adams.
   Bo-GJ:234

The Song of Shadows.
   W. de la Mare.   Un-MB:202
Sonnet VIII. W. Shakespeare.
   Al-VBP:199
Sonnet CXXVIII. W. Shakespeare.
   No-CL:48
The Sound of Afroamerican History.
   S. Anderson. Ad-PB:441
String Quartet. B. Deutsch.
   Pl-US:36
Strings in the Earth and Air.
   J. Joyce. Ha-LO:6, Ma-FW:120,
   No-CL:46, Un-MB:269
Symphony: First Movement.
   J. Wheelock. Pl-US:38
There Be None of Beauty's Daughters.
   G. Byron. De-TT:152, Pa-GTB:176,
   Rv-CB:691
To — . W. Braithwaite. Ad-PB:13
To a Lady, with a Guitar.
   P. Shelley. Pa-GTB:257
To J. S. Bach. M. Thwaites.
   Tr-MR:196
To Mr. Henry Lawes. E. Waller.
   No-CL:28
To Musique, to Becalme His Fever.
   R. Herrick. Bo-GJ:133,
   Pl-US:136
To the One of Fictive Music.
   W. Stevens. Un-MA:241
A Toccata of Galuppi's.
   R. Browning. Pa-GTB:345,
   Rv-CB:814
T'Other Little Tune. Pl-US:32,
   Rv-ON:102, Wr-RM:53
Twelfth Night. W. Shakespeare.
   Pl-US:39
Two Hundred Girls in Tights &
   Halters. D. Hoffman. Co-EL:153
Undersong. M. Van Doren.
   En-PC:25
Up in Heaven. On-TW:29
Variation on a Theme by Francis
   Kilvert. R. Humphries.
   Pl-US:25
Variations for Two Pianos.
   D. Justice. Du-SH:168
The Violin. R. Gilder.   Se-PR:326
What Kind of Music? J. Reeves.
   Sh-RP:69
When a Ring's Around the Moon.
   M. Carr. Ar-TP3:148
When de Saints Go Ma'chin' Home.
   S. Brown. Bo-AN:55
Where the Rainbow Ends. R. Rive.
   Ab-MO:107, Lo-TY:180
Ya Se Van los Pastores.
   D. Fitts. Gr-CC:172
Yardbird's Skull. O. Dodson.
   Ad-PB:132, Bo-AN:125, Ca-VT:387

MUSIC AND MUSICIANS — cont'd.
You Are Alms. J. Thompson.
Ad-PB:270
Youth and Art. R. Browning.
Al-VBP:909
MUSIC BOXES
Alle Vögel Sind Schon Da.
F. Chesterton. Pl-US:64
MUSICAL COMEDIES: see
HUMOR - MUSICAL COMEDIES
MUSICAL INSTRUMENTS: see also
names of instruments, as
FLUTES
Battle Report. B. Kaufman.
Ad-CI:93, Lo-TY:252
Come, Ye Sons of Art. H. Purcell.
Pl-US:44
The Fairy Queen. E. Spenser.
Cl-DT:13
Guide to the Symphony. W. Kees.
Ca-VT:405
Hymne to God My God in My
Sicknesse. J. Donne.
Gr-CT:383, Pl-US:127
The Instruments. C. Smart.
Ho-WR:97
Italian Opera. J. Miller.
Pl-US:35
The Jazz of This Hotel.
V. Lindsay. Bo-HF:166
Jubilate Agno. C. Smart.
Pl-US:24
Musicks Empire. A. Marvell.
Gr-CC:60
Psalm 150. Bible. O.T. Psalms.
Ga-S:18, Gr-CT:446, Pa-RE:126,
Pa-SG:201, Pl-US:7
Samisen. J. Kirkup. Ls-NY:324
A Song for St. Cecilia's Day,
1687. J. Dryden. Pa-GTB:49,
Pl-US:152, Rv-CB:466
We Can Play the Big Bass Drum.
Mo-TL:105
Ya Se Van los Pastores. D. Fitts.
Gr-CC:172
MUSICIANS: see MUSIC AND
MUSICIANS; and names of
musicians, as ARMSTRONG,
LOUIS (SATCHMO)
MUSK OXEN: see also HUMOR -
MUSK OXEN
Ayii, Ayii, Ayii (I Wish).
Ho-SD:71
Song of Caribou, Musk Oxen.
Br-MW:140, Ho-SD:67, Le-IB:34,
Ma-BH:21, Tr-US I:26
MUSKRATS
The Lost Son. T. Roethke.
Li-TU:217
MUSLIMISM: see ISLAM

MUSSOLINI, BENITO: see SATIRE -
MUSSOLINI, BENITO
MUSTARD
Amelia Mixed the Mustard.
A. Housman. Ne-AM:9
MUTESA, KING OF BUGANDA
Stanley Meets Mutesa.
J. Rubadiri. Bo-HF:150,
MYSTERY: see also HUMOR -
MYSTERY; SECRETS AND SECRECY
Adjuration. F. Long. De-FS:130
Against Oblivion. H. Newbolt.
De-CH:202, De-TT:193
Alan. R. Roseliep. De-FS:163
And in the Hanging Gardens.
C. Aiken. Co-PT:45, Un-MA:426
Another September. T. Kinsella.
En-PC:270
As I Looked Out. Ir-BB:64,
St-FS:106
At the Keyhole. W. de la Mare.
Bl-OB:88, Un-MB:199
Avery Anameer. J. Brennan.
De-FS:38
The Ballad of Minepit Shaw.
R. Kipling. Co-PT:49
Beyond the Last Lamp. T. Hardy.
Ox-BN:837
Boys Will Be Princes. W. Heyen.
Ls-NY:92
Building of Sand. G. Code.
De-FS:65
Carcosa. L. Carter. De-FS:47
The Cat. W. Davies. Bl-OB:108
The Chestnut Roasters. J. Brennan.
De-FS:34
Christabel. S. Coleridge.
De-CH:318
The Clean Gentleman. G. Abbe.
De-FS:4
Dark Yuggoth. L. Carter.
De-FS:48
Deadfall. M. Keller. Gr-EC:272
Dear Beauteous Death. H. Vaughan.
Ga-S:36
The Desert. S. Crane. Wi-LT:119
Doth Not a Tenarif. J. Donne.
Gr-CT:209
Dream-Song. W. de la Mare.
Sh-RP:24
Empty House. E. Coatsworth.
De-FS:52
Enchantment, Night.
L. Alexander. Ad-PB:58
The End of the Weekend. A. Hecht.
Wi-LT:731
Enigma. K. Reeves. De-FS:154
Flannan Isle. W. Gibson.
Bl-OB:78, Co-SS:200, De-CH:395,
Ha-PO:154, Hi-WP I:76

Forest Shapes. D. Wandrei.
De-FS:214
The Fruit Plucker. S. Coleridge.
De-CH:320, De-TT:150, Ox-BN:175,
Sm-LG:110
Godhead Here in Hiding.
G. Hopkins. Ga-S:199
Going Back Again. R. Lytton.
Co-FB:306, Na-EO:47
Grand Finale. S. Carleton.
De-FS:43
The Greater Mystery. J. O'Hara.
Pa-HT:99
The Green Door. L. Drake.
Br-BC:155
A Greyport Legend. B. Harte.
Sp-OG:83
Grim and Gloomy. J. Reeves.
Sh-RP:183
The Haunted House. T. Hood.
Ho-WR:192
Hear, Sweet Spirit. S. Coleridge.
Al-VBP:700, De-CH:313
Hello! Jao Meng-k'an. Hs-TC:108
The High Place at Marib.
G. Code. De-FS:58
Highway to Nowhere. G. Code.
De-FS:61
The House of Life. D. Quick.
De-FS:151
The House of Richesse. E. Spenser.
De-CH:322
The House on Maple Hill.
S. McNail. De-FS:139
Hymn to Colour. G. Meredith.
Ox-BN:700
I See. A. Jewell. Me-WF:88
Ibant Obscurae. T. Brown. Ox-BN:722
In Due Season. W. Auden. Ho-P:15
Intuition. R. Grenville.
De-FS:101
The Invaders. J. Sloan. De-FS:183
An Invite to Eternity. J. Clare.
Ox-BN:330
Isabel Sparrow. M. Oliver.
Ls-NY:145
Jim Desterland. H. Plutzik.
Ca-VT:347, De-FS:149
A Lady Comes to an Inn.
E. Coatsworth. Ar-TP3:32,
Co-PT:39, Un-MA:465
The Lady of Shalott. A. Tennyson.
Er-FA:339, Hi-WP I:59,
Ho-WR:145, Sp-OG:128
Late at Night. Hsü Chih-mo.
Hs-TC:82
The Listeners. W. de la Mare.
Al-VBP:1118, Er-FA:406, Fe-FP:513,
Pa-OM:298, Re-TW:116, Sh-RP:34,
Un-MB:196, Wi-LT:131

Lost. E. Recht. Le-M:194
Lunae Custodiens. L. Carter.
De-FS:44
Meet-on-the Road. Bl-OB:84,
Co-PM:208, De-CH:674
Merchants from Cathay. W. Benét.
Un-MA:321
Midnight. T. Middleton. Bl-OB:140,
Pa-RE:124, Rd-SS:35
The Mistress of Vision.
F. Thompson. De-CH:269
Mockery. K. Riggs. Hu-MP:111,
Pe-FB:69, Th-AS:22
The Mocking Fairy. W. de la Mare.
Un-MB:199
The Motive for Metaphor.
W. Stevens. Un-MA:253
Mysteries. Y. Yevtushenko.
Ca-MR:52
The Mystery. R. Hodgson.
De-CH:143, Un-MB:192
Night. Fang Ching. Hs-TC:383
Night Peril. S. Russell.
De-FS:167
Nocturne. C. Garstin. De-CH:454
O World. G. Santayana.
Fe-PL:321, Sm-PT:168
The Old City. R. Manning-Sanders.
De-CH:322
Old Garden. E. Tatum. Ke-TF:422
Old Meg of Kitrann. J. Keith.
De-FS:119
On a Night of Snow. E. Coatsworth.
Co-BBW:123, Du-RG:91, Un-GT:48,
Un-MA:465
On the Eclipse of the Moon of
October 1865. C. Tennyson-Turner.
Ox-BN:471
On Yes Tor. E. Gosse. De-CH:301
One Day of Rain. J. Brennan.
De-FS:31
Opening Door. W. Burr. De-FS:41
Otherwise. A. Fisher. Au-SP:355
Out in the Dark. E. Thomas.
Cl-DT:35, De-CH:453, Pa-GTB:444,
Un-MB:218, Wi-LT:647
Out of Bounds. J. Stallworthy.
Ha-TP:121
The Package. A. Fisher. Au-SP:101
Perseus. L. MacNeice. Wi-LT:457
The Planetary Arc-Light.
A. Derleth. Gr-EC:164
The Pool. L. Drake. De-FS:77
The Question in the Cobweb.
A. Reid. Mc-WK:114
Rainy Night. Feng Chih. Hs-TC:141
Rapunzel Song. G. Meyer. Ls-NY:93
The Raven. E. Poe. Al-VBP:865,
Bo-GJ:165, Co-RG:103, De-CH:303,
Er-FA:312, Ga-FB:134, Sh-AP:56,
Sm-LG:207

MYSTERY — cont'd.
The Rider. W. Burford. Ls-NY:85
Romance. A. Lang. Sp-OG:121
Room in Darkness. M. Counselman.
   De-FS:68
The Rowers. L. Benét. De-FS:19
The Scholar Gypsy. M. Arnold.
   Al-VBP:964, Gr-CT:255, Ox-BN:628
The Sea House. W. Goodreau.
   Ls-NY:255
The Sea Wolf. V. McDougal.
   Hu-MP:177
Secrets. M. McArthur. De-TT:34
Shadowed. B. Eaton. De-FS:83
Shadows and Song. P. George.
   Al-WW:123
The Shape of Fear. S. Russell.
   De-FS:169
Sheath and Knife. De-CH:54
The Shell. J. Stephens.
   Cl-DT:40, Co-BN:82, De-CH:57,
   Ma-FW:43, Ni-JP:34, Un-MB:262
The Silence of God. O. Sitwell.
   Mc-WK:151
Silent Is the House. E. Brontë.
   De-CH:268, Ox-BN:606
Sir William Deloraine at the
   Wizard's Tomb. W. Scott.
   Ox-BN:118
So Long. W. Stafford. Mc-EA:167
So Separate and Strange.
   F. Stefanile. De-FS:192
Some One. W. de la Mare.
   Ar-TP3:155, Au-SP:284, Fe-FP:370,
   Hu-MP:84, La-PV:72, Li-LC:50,
   St-FS:110, Th-AS:2, Un-MB:198
Song. A. Noyes. De-CH:142
The Spring Waters. Ping Hsin.
   Hs-TC:24
A Strange Place. P. Rake. Le-M:157
Tenant. F. Gray. De-FS:97
That Familiar Stranger.
   F. Stefanile. De-FS:191
There Gowans Are Gay. Gr-GB:97
Three Kings. J. Vaughn.
   Hu-NN:24, Hu-PN:399
To Juan at the Winter Solstice.
   R. Graves. Br-TC:154,
   Ha-PO:191, Un-MB:390, Wi-LT:377
Tom o' Bedlam. De-CH:275,
   Mc-WK:5, Sm-LG:203
The Two Wives. D. Henderson.
   Br-SM:12
Unwelcome. M. Coleridge.
   De-CH:301, Ox-BN:926
Valentine. C. Wilson. Fr-MP:8
The Valley of White Poppies.
   F. Macleod. Th-AS:141
Vendor. R. Roseliep.
   De-FS:157, St-H:179
Visit. E. Recht. Le-M:202

A Warning to Skeptics. L. Drake.
   De-FS:76
Was It the Sound. E. Ramal.
   De-CH:659
Was She a Witch? L. Richards.
   Hu-MP:446, La-PH:9, La-PV:69
The Wave. D. Hine. Ho-P:99
The Way Through the Woods.
   R. Kipling. De-CH:281,
   Fe-FP:242, Ha-PO:154, Hi-WP I:107,
   Mc-WS:31, Ox-BN:932, Re-TW:128,
   Sm-LG:396
The Western Hill. Ch'en Meng-chia.
   Hs-TC:116
When I Set Out for Lyonesse.
   T. Hardy. No-CL:144, Pa-HT:156,
   Un-MB:32
The Wind Skrieked Loud.
   E. Coatsworth. De-FS:53
The Word of Willow. L. Drake.
   De-FS:78
The World of Light. H. Vaughan.
   Al-VBP:469, De-CH:267,
   Gr-CT:384, Rv-CB:411
The Yellow Cat. L. Jennings.
   De-FS:110
MYSTIC RIVER
Mystic River. J. Ciardi.
   Sh-AP:228
MYSTICISM
For a Marriage of St. Catherine.
   D. Rossetti. Gr-SS:162
Time in the Rock. C. Aiken.
   Ca-VT:153
Unity. AE. Tr-MR:283
MYTHICAL ANIMALS AND BIRDS:
   see also HUMOR - MYTHICAL
   ANIMALS AND BIRDS; and
   names of mythical animals
   and birds, as CENTAURS
   and ROCS
The Bunyip. D. Stewart. Rd-OA:66
A Gryphon Sighted in an Iowa
   Flyway. N. Westerfield.
   Ls-NY:192
The Huge Leviathan. E. Spenser.
   Gr-CT:207
Kiph. W. de la Mare. Ar-TP3:151
The Kraken. A. Tennyson.
   Ho-WR:215, Ox-BN:473
Leviathan. L. Untermeyer.
   Un-GT:36
Sea Monsters. E. Spenser.
   Gr-CT:207
Song for the Thunder Bird Dance.
   Tr-US II:216
The Unicorn. E. Young. Ar-TP3:161,
   Au-SP:357, Fe-FP:394
The White Steed of the Prairies.
   J. Barber. Fi-BG:87

MYTHOLOGY: see also CONSTELLA-
    TIONS; CREATION; FOLKLORE;
    GODS AND GODDESSES; MYTHICAL
    ANIMALS AND BIRDS; PLACES,
    MYTHICAL AND IMAGINARY; and
    names of heroes and mythical
    characters, as ECHO (NYMPH),
    ULYSSES
  The Aeneid. Virgil. Al-VBP:80
  Arethusa. P. Shelley. Ho-WR:136
  Atalanta in Calydon. A. Swinburne.
    Al-VBP:1038, Ga-FB:230, Ha-PO:237,
    Ma-YA:216, Na-EO:58, Pa-GTB:388
  Country Gods. Cométas. Sm-LG:230
  Deirdre. J. Stephens.
    Al-VBP:1151, Gr-CC:91
  The Life and Death of Jason.
    W. Morris. Al-VBP:1011
  Mackado, Fustian and Motley.
    J. Taylor. Rv-CB:319
  The Ring of. C. Olson. Ca-VT:305
  Satire V. J. Marston. Al-VBP:270
  Solar Myth. G. Taggard. Un-MA:479
MYTHS: see MYTHOLOGY
NA-KHI VERSE: see TIBETAN
    VERSE - NA-KHI
NAGA VERSE: see TIBETAN
    VERSE - NAGA
NAGASAKI, JAP.
  In a Surrealist Year.
    L. Ferlinghetti. Ke-PP:3
  The War Museum at Nagasaki.
    C. Higham. Ls-NY:30
NAIADS: see NYMPHS
NAILS (CARPENTERS')
  A Ship's Nail. Wr-RM:96
NAMES: see also BAPTISM; HUMOR -
    NAMES; NICKNAMES; PLACE NAMES
  A B C of Names. Ir-BB:96
  American Names. S. Benét.
    Br-AF:6, Mc-WK:157, Pa-HT:3,
    Sh-AP:194, Sm-LG:145
  The Baby's Name. T. Jenks.
    Br-BC:37
  Bartholomew. N. Gale. Br-BC:42,
    Th-AS:54
  The Blind Man. A. Young. Re-BS:41
  Boys' Names. E. Farjeon.
    Ar-TP3:6, Br-BC:36
  Choosing a Name. C. and M. Lamb.
    Ox-BC:141
  The Christening. A. Milne.
    Br-BC:38
  Dorset. J. Betjeman. To-MP:20
  Étude Géographique. S. King.
    Br-AF:154, Fi-BG:86
  The Evil Eye. J. Ciardi. Ca-MB:19
  The Faithless Flowers. M. Widdemer.
    Hu-MP:258, Th-AS:84
  The Fingers. Mo-MGT:140

  Five Hens. Gr-GB:58, Mo-MGT:135
  From the Highest Camp. T. Gunn.
    Br-TC:163
  Gentle Name. S. Robinson.
    Th-AS:68
  Georgia Towns. D. Hickey.
    Br-AF:214
  Gifts. H. Harris. Br-BC:32
  GraceAnAnne. L. Borie. Br-BC:26,
    Sh-RP:317
  Girls' Names. E. Farjeon.
    Ar-TP3:6, Ne-AM:18
  Hallelujah: A Sestina.
    R. Francis. En-PC:46
  I Am Rose. G. Stein. Ne-AM:28
  I Have to Be a Lively Hood.
    T. Hood. Un-GT:95
  If I Should Ever by Chance Grow
    Rich. E. Thomas. Bl-OB:32,
    Bo-GJ:20, De-CH:518, Ox-BC:329,
    Pa-RE:73, Sm-LG:112, Un-MB:215
  Indian Names. L. Sigourney.
    Br-AF:8, Fe-FP:450, Fe-PL:412,
    Hu-MP:374, Se-PR:174, Sh-RP:305
  Infant Joy. W. Blake. Al-VBP:614,
    Bo-GJ:132, Br-BC:41, Br-SS:41,
    Fe-FP:37, Fe-PL:245, Ga-S:97,
    Re-TW:39, Rv-CB:571, Tu-WW:13,
    Un-GT:10
  Jest 'fore Christmas. E. Field.
    Er-FA:513, Fe-FP:538, Fe-PL:201,
    Ga-FB:176, Hu-MP:359
  Little Bird Got a Name. J. Vega.
    Ad-II:110
  Little Brother. A. Fisher.
    Br-BC:48, Mc-AW:91
  Little Phillis. K. Greenaway.
    Br-BC:44
  Localities. C. Sandburg.
    Br-AF:7
  Maiden Name. P. Larkin.
    Pa-GTB:556
  Mamble. J. Drinkwater.
    Hi-WP I:5
  A Man Rode to Town. Re-RR:12
  Melander Supposed to Love Susan,
    but Did Love Ann. E. Herbert.
    Gr-CC:186
  Mima. W. de la Mare. Br-BC:38
  A Mother to Her First-Born.
    Tr-CB:27, Tr-US I:105
  Mythological Sonnets, VIII.
    R. Fuller. Pa-GTB:527
  Names. D. Aldis. Br-SG:26
  Names. L. Mueller. Ha-TP:104
  Names from the War. B. Catton.
    Br-AF:78
  The Naming of Cats. T. Eliot.
    Bo-FP:7, Co-HP:56, Sh-RP:324,
    We-PZ:17

NAMES — cont'd.
  The Old Man Called to His Sons.
    Wo-HS:(10)
  Riding Across John Lee's Finger.
    S. Crouch. Ad-PB:485
  Romance. W. Turner. Bo-GJ:220,
    Hi-WP I:7, Mc-WS:113, Ni-JP:24,
    No-CL:251, Un-MB:345
  Star Thistle. R. Sund. Co-PU:62
  Taking of the Name. Bo-FP:265
  There Was an Old Dog. De-TT:67
  Two Men. E. Robinson. Un-GT:91
  The Umpire. M. Bracker.
    Mo-SD:5
  Victoria. E. Farjeon. Bl-OB:142
  Weather Words. D. McCord.
    Pl-IO:51
  Yankee Cradle. R. Coffin.
    Gr-EC:234, Na-EO:102
NANTUCKET, MASS.
  The Quaker Graveyard in Nantucket.
    R. Lowell. Al-VBP:1248,
    Pa-HT:25, Wi-LT:573
  Square-Toed Princes. R. Coffin.
    Br-AF:129
NAPLES, IT.
  Esthetique du Mal, I. W. Stevens.
    Wi-LT:151
NAPOLEON I, EMPEROR OF THE
    FRENCH: see also BORODINO,
    BATTLE, 1812
  Giant Bonaparte. Mo-MGT:166
  Incident of the French Camp.
    R. Browning. Co-RG:28, Mc-PR:144,
    Sp-OG:43, Un-GT:148
  The March to Moscow. R. Southey.
    Hi-FO:201
  Men Who March Away. T. Hardy.
    Cl-DT:15, De-CH:164, De-TT:137
  Napoleon. W. de la Mare.
    Sm-LG:157
  Napoleon in Hades. D. Morton.
    Cr-WS:29
  A St. Helena Lullaby.
    R. Kipling. Hi-FO:176
  The Sphinx Speaks. F. Saltus.
    Pa-HT:90
  Toussaint L'Ouverture.
    E. Robinson. Hu-PN:471
NARCISSUS (MYTH.)
  Echo's Lament for Narcissus.
    B. Jonson. Al-VBP:238,
    De-CH:236, Gr-CT:321
NARCISSUSES (FLOWER):
    see DAFFODILS
NARCOTICS: see also
    HALLUCINATIONS
  Addict. M. Carver. De-FS:49
  The Addict. A. Sexton.
    Ha-TP:47

Afterwards, They Shall Dance.
    B. Kaufman. Br-TC:229,
    Ca-VT:538, Hu-PN:409
  Casey Jones. R. Hunter. Mo-GR:52
  Cocaine Lil. Gr-GB:266, Pe-M:138
  Escape the Ghettos of New York.
    V. Howard. La-IH:22
  A Flat One. W. Snodgrass.
    En-PC:244, Wi-LT:822
  The Idea of Ancestry. E. Knight.
    Ad-PB:229, Be-MA:108, Ra-BP:203
  Junior Addicts. L. Hughes.
    Ra-BP:85
  Lacrimas or There Is a Need to
    Scream. K. Lyle. Ad-PB:466
  Letter to Duncan. G. Dusenbery.
    Sc-TN:36
  Lunar Baedeker. M. Loy. Ca-VT:43
  Slave. L. Hughes. Wi-LT:423
  summer words of a sistuh addict.
    S. Sanchez. Ra-BP:237
  This Old World. S. Cooper.
    Me-WF:36
  To Mother and Steve. M. Evans.
    Ad-PB:191, Ra-BP:184
  Willy the Weeper. Gr-GB:270
NARWHALS: see WHALES
NASBY, BATTLE, 1645
  The Battle of Naseby. T. Macaulay.
    Hi-FO:145
NASH, OGDEN
  Ogden Nash Gets All the Cash.
    D. McCord. Pl-ML:69
NASTURTIUMS
  The Big Nasturtiums. R. Hale.
    Co-BN:50, Co-PM:83
  Lines to a Nasturtium. A. Spencer.
    Bo-AN:18, Hu-PN:64
  Nasturtium. M. Miller. Br-SG:31
NATIONAL SOCIALISM: see also
    FASCISM; HITLER, ADOLF;
    JEWS - PERSECUTION
  Daddy. S. Plath. Br-TC:324,
    Mc-EA:164, Wi-LT:789
  Footnote. C. Norman. Cr-WS:46
  On the Eyes of an SS Officer.
    R. Wilbur. Cr-WS:42
  Prologue. K. Barnes. Cr-WS:45
  Refugee Blues. W. Auden.
    Hi-WP I:122, Wi-LT:472
  Scenario. J. Segal. Ho-TY:158
NATIONAL SONGS
  America. S. Smith. Er-FA:293,
    Fe-FP:423, Fe-PL:158, Se-PR:131,
    Vi-PP:11
  America the Beautiful. K. Bates.
    Bo-FP:302, Er-FA:293, Fe-FP:402,
    Ga-FB:278, Hu-MP:363, Pl-EI:164,
    Se-PR:127, Vi-PP:30
  The Epic of Dengei. Tr-US I:233

Epic Song.   Tr-US I:236
A National Hymn.   J. DeForest.
   Vi-PP:13
National Hymn.   D. Roberts.
   Vi-PP:41
"National Song" of the Matabele.
   Tr-US I:85
The Star-Spangled Banner.   F. Key.
   Er-FA:283, Fe-FP:401, Hi-TL:65,
   Se-PR:130, Vi-PP:107
Waltzing Matilda. A. Paterson.
   Gr-CT:138, Gr-GB:259,
   Ha-PO:238, Mc-WK:147
Yankee Doodle.   Em-AF:427,
   Er-FA:434, Fe-FP:422,
   Se-PR:162, Vi-PP:107
NATIVITY: see BIRTH; JESUS
   CHRIST - NATIVITY
NATURALNESS
   Naturally.   A. Lorde.   Be-MA:122,
   Jo-SA:87
   Re-Act for Action. D. Lee.Ra-BP:296
NATURE: see also COMPANIONSHIP
      OF MAN AND NATURE; COUNTRY
      LIFE; NATURE - BEAUTY;
      NATURE, UNAPPRECIATED;
      OUTDOOR LIFE; SATIRE - NATURE
   Adonais.   P. Shelley.   Al-VBP:759,
   Ha-PO:130, Ox-BN:287
   All Things Are Current Found.
   H. Thoreau.   Al-VBP:919
   All Things Wait upon Thee.
   C. Rossetti.   Sp-OG:280
   The Apology.   R. Emerson.No-CL:273
   Ask No Return!   H. Gregory.
   Ca-VT:209, Sm-PT:120, Un-MA:508
   Away, Away!   P. Shelley.   Un-GT:249
   Ayii, Ayii (The Great Sea).Ho-SD:80
   The Barefoot Boy.   J. Whittier.
   Ch-B:65, Fe-FP:544, Fe-PL:249
   Bring Me the Sunset in a Cup.
   E. Dickinson.   Un-MA:99
   A Chant Out of Doors.
   M. Wilkinson.   Th-AS:172
   The Comforters.   D. Shorter.
   De-CH:259
   Composed in Spring.   R. Burns.
   Co-BN:141, Rv-CB:621
   Contemplation.   F. Thompson.
   Ox-BN:920
   Death.   E. Brontë.   Ox-BN:603
   Debate Question, Quarry Dream.
   R. Warren.   Ca-VT:277
   Edict.   H. Vinal.   Ls-NY:49
   Elegy for a Nature Poet.
   H. Nemerov.   Co-BN:230
   The Fall of the Leaf.
   H. Thoreau.   Sh-AP:68
   Father.   Jo-TS:4
   February.   J. Clare.   Ox-BN:309

Field-Glasses.   A. Young.
   Pa-GTB:467, Rv-CB:979
The Fiftieth Birthday of Agassiz.
   H. Longfellow.   Pl-IO:161
Fishing.   W. Wordsworth. Mo-SD:105
Fleeing to Safety.   R. Chettur.
   Le-M:175
Flower in the Crannied Wall.
   A. Tennyson.   Co-BN:49,
   Er-FA:243, Fe-FP:216, Fr-WO:85,
   Ga-FB:128, Hu-MP:257, Ma-YA:198,
   Mc-PR:137
For a Child.   F. Davis.   Fe-FP:19,
   Hu-MP:287
The Force that Through the Green
   Fuse.   D. Thomas.   Al-VBP:1244,
   Pl-IO:98, Rv-CB:1002,
   Un-MB:499, Wi-LT:545
Forest.   J. Garrigue.   Wi-LT:710
Foundation of Faith.
   J. Drinkwater.   Tr-MR:255
The Fresh Air.   H. Monro.
   De-CH:9
The Georgics.   Virgil.   Ma-FW:261
The Goddess.   D. Levertov.
   Wi-LT:759
The Golden Hive.   H. Behn.
   Ar-TP3:218
Good Company.   K. Baker.   Fe-FP:21
Gravelly Run.   A. Ammons.   Ho-P:3
A Green Place.   W. Smith.
   Sh-RP:95
Green Red Brown and White.
   M. Swenson.   Ca-VT:481
Hal's Birthday.   L. Larcom.
   Br-BC:51
The Hermit.   Hsu Pen.   Le-MW:130,
   Ma-FW:85
Hie Away.   W. Scott.   Al-VBP:676,
   Ar-TP3:95, Bo-FP:309, Hu-MP:63,
   Sm-MK:183
How They Came from the Blue Snows.
   A. Kenseth.   Ke-PP:54
The Hunting Tribes of Air and
   Earth.   W. Scott.   Rd-OA:117
I Dreaded That First Robin So.
   E. Dickinson.   Rv-CB:919,
   Un-MA:99
I Saw a Green Beetle.
   S. Kershaw.   Le-M:129
I See His Blood upon the Rose.
   J. Plunkett.   De-CH:577,
   Fe-PL:331, Tr-MR:132
In Memoriam.   A. Tennyson.
   Ox-BN:499
In Spring.   E. Mörike.   Pa-SG:88
Intimations of Sublimity.
   W. Wordsworth.   Ox-BN:98
The Inward Morning.   H. Thoreau.
   No-CL:270, Sh-AP:67

NATURE — cont'd.
    July.   J. Clare.   Un-GT:276
    The Lamentation of Enion.
        W. Blake.   Ox-BN:37
    The Language of Life. B. Cutler.
        St-H:45
    Legacy.   C. Morley.   Du-RG:130
    Lilian's Song. G. Darley. Ox-BN:386
    Lines Composed above Tintern
        Abbey. W. Wordsworth. Go-BP:21,
        Ho-P:125
    Love Poem.   K. Raine.   Un-MB:485
    Lycidas. J. Milton. Al-VBP:402,
        Gr-CT:250, Hi-WP II:20, Ho-P:69,
        Pa-GTB:55
    A Mask Presented at Ludlow Castle.
        J. Milton.   Al-VBP:399
    Measure Me, Sky. L. Speyer.
        Ad-PE:46, Br-BC:129, Fe-FP:22,
        Hu-MP:63
    The Midges Dance aboon the Burn.
        R. Tannahill.   Co-BN:108
    Midnight.   T. Sackville.
        De-CH:107, De-TT:150, Rd-OA:205
    Miracles.   W. Whitman.   Ga-S:15,
        Li-TU:176, Ma-FW:100, Mc-WK:102,
        Sh-RP:166, Sm-MK:228, Tr-MR:39,
        Un-GT:247
    Modern Love. G.Meredith.Ox-BN:689
    Morning on the Lièvre.   A. Lampman.
        Mo-SD:130
    My Love Is in a Light Attire.
        J. Joyce.   Ha-LO:91
    My Words Are Tied.   Ho-SD:16
    Nature.   S. Kuroda.   Sh-AM:117
    Nature.   H. Longfellow.   Co-BN:229,
        Fe-PL:280
    Nature at Three. B. Breeser. Br-BC:46
    Nature or Man. P. Curry.   Me-WF:51
    Not Only Around Our Infancy.
        J. Lowell.   Er-FA:480
    Nothing Gold Can Stay. R. Frost.
        Bo-HF:56, Ca-VT:16, Mo-BG:133,
        Mo-TS:54, Un-MA:187
    O Dear Me! W. de la Mare.
        Ar-TP3:184, Sm-MK:3
    O Wearisome Condition. F. Greville.
        Al-VBP:124, Rv-CB:265
    Ode. G. Santayana. Al-VBP:1087
    Ode on Intimations of Immortality.
        W. Wordsworth. Al-VBP:662,
        Br-BC:18, Er-FA:157, Ga-FB:101,
        Gr-GT:436, Ha-PO:206, Ho-P:88,
        Ox-BN:84, Pa-GTB:308, Pl-EI:59
    Of Gold and Jewels. Yuan Chieh.
        Le-MW:6
    Of Man and Nature. H. Mungin.
        Ad-BO:44
    Offering.   Bi-IT:108

    Out in the Woods with Father.
        D. McCord.   Gr-TG:24
    Paradise Lost.   J. Milton.
        Al-VBP:410
    The Peace of Wild Things.
        W. Berry.   Ca-VT:685, Ls-NY:62
    Poet and Goldsmith. V. Watkins.
        En-PC:89
    The Point, the Line, the Surface
        and Sphere. C. Bragdon.
        Pl-IO:89
    Prelude. J. Synge.   Co-BN:207,
        Gr-CT:235, Un-MB:180
    Proem. M. Cawein.   Co-BN:213
    The Pulse. M. Van Doren.
        Un-MA:467
    The Question in the Cobweb.
        A. Reid.   Mc-WK:114
    Resolution and Independence.
        W. Wordsworth. Co-BN:214,
        Ma-FW:36, Ox-BN:71, Rv-CB:654
    The Return. E. Millay.   Un-MA:450
    The Rime of the Ancient Mariner.
        S. Coleridge. Al-VBP:679,
        Bo-FP:301, Co-RG:60, Co-SS:131,
        De-CH:364, Er-FA:318, Fe-FP:147,
        Ga-FB:105, Gr-TG:61, Ha-PO:15,
        Hi-WP II:68, Ma-YA:146, Ni-JP:52,
        Ox-BN:139, Rv-CB:658, Sm-LG:312,
        Un-GT:30
    Ruth: or The Influence of Nature.
        W. Wordsworth. Pa-GTB:283
    The Secret Song. M. Brown.
        La-PP:3, La-PV:222
    Self-Portrait, as a Bear.
        D. Hall.   Ha-TP:94
    Sewing.   Ch-B:97
    The Sky Is Low. E. Dickinson.
        Co-BN:183, Co-EL:113, Ga-FB:301,
        Mc-PR:169, Rv-CB:904, Un-MA:95
    Song. R. Hogg.   Do-WH:81
    Song: Fish in the Unruffled Lakes.
        W. Auden.   Un-MB:464
    Song in Spring. L. Ginsberg.
        Ha-YA:31
    Song of Myself. W. Whitman.
        Ca-BP:3
    Song to David. C. Smart.
        Al-VBP:575, Gr-CT:447, Pl-US:72
    Sonnet. J. Masefield. Un-MB:228,
        Wi-LT:191
    Stanzas. E. Brontë. Go-BP:27
    Stanzas from "Child Harold."
        J. Clare.   Ox-BN:325
    Stillness. M. Leaso. Le-M:130
    Summer. J. Clare. Co-BN:95
    A Summer Commentary. Y. Winters.
        Wi-LT:656
    Summer Images. J. Clare.
        Gr-CT:117, Ox-BN:318, Rv-CB:716

Summer Morning. J. Ingelow.
  Gr-TG:43
The Summer Rain. H. Thoreau.
  Sh-AP:67
Sun, Moon and Stars. Gr-TG:68
The Sweetness of Nature. Gr-CC:118
The Symphony. S. Lanier.
  Al-VBP:1058
The Tables Turned. W. Wordsworth.
  Rv-CB:641
Tell Me Not Here, It Needs Not
  Saying. A. Housman. Hi-WP II:40,
  Ox-BN:923, Pa-GTB:418, Rv-CB:950,
  Wi-LT:66
Thanatopsis. W. Bryant.
  Al-VBP:765, Co-BN:216, Er-FA:67,
  Sh-AP:17
Thank You. L. Breek. Mo-MI:29
Thanksgiving. I. Eastwick.
  Br-SG:103
There Will Come Soft Rains.
  S. Teasdale. Cr-WS:69
This Compost. W. Whitman. Un-MA:86
Tintern Abbey. W. Wordsworth.
  Al-VBP:667
To Look at Any Thing. J. Moffitt.
  Du-RG:21
To Walk on Hills. R. Graves.
  Mo-SD:90
Under the Greenwood Tree.
  W. Shakespeare.
  Al-VBP:186, Ar-TP3:204, Bo-FP:259,
  Co-BN:206, De-CH:134, De-TT:147,
  Er-FA:263, Fe-FP:211, Gr-EC:48,
  Ho-WR:74, Hu-MP:268, Mc-PR:30,
  Pa-GTB:5, Rv-CB:196, Tu-WW:61
Understanding. T. Traherne.
  Go-BP:107, Mo-SD:84
Unstill Life. V. Huidobro. Be-UL:41
Vain Dream for John Clare.
  J. Hutton. Ls-NY:129
Vala or the Four Zoas. W. Blake.
  Al-VBP:621, Ox-BN:37
We Are. R. Hershon. Sc-TN:92
Wealth. R. Emerson. Pl-IO:34
Weave Us a Garment of Brightness.
  Ho-SD:45
William Jones. E. Masters.Pl-IO:166
With a Daisy. E. Dickinson.
  Pl-IO:141
Written in Early Spring.
  W. Wordsworth. Fe-PL:372,
  Pa-GTB:282, Rv-CB:633
You. J. Masefield. Tr-MR:32

NATURE - BEAUTY
  After. R. Hodgson.
  Afternoon on a Hill. E. Millay.
  Ar-TP3:176, Au-SP:350, Cl-FC:24,
  Fe-FP:269, Hu-MP:64, La-PV:170,
  Pe-FB:75

L'Allegro. J. Milton. Al-VBP:389,
  Er-FA:37, Ga-FB:26, Pa-GTB:94,
  Rv-CB:369
Alpine Spirit's Song. T. Beddoes.
  Ox-BN:457
Apology for Bad Dreams. R. Jeffers.
  Sh-AP:175, Un-MA:363
April Rise. L. Lee. To-MP:57
August. H. Winslow. Ha-YA:86
Autumn Evening Beside the Lake.
  Li Ch'ing Chao. Rx-OH:93
Autumnal Ode. A. De Vere.
  Ox-BN:587
Autumn's Fete. A. McGeorge.
  Ha-YA:96
Beauty. E-Yeh-Shure. Ar-TP3:213,
  Fe-FP:20
Beauty Once Shared. H. Tappan.
  Ke-TF:442
Before I Got My Eye Put Out.
  E. Dickinson. Wi-LT:5
Behold: My World. L. Sohappy.
  Al-WW:18
The Brook. A. Tennyson. Bl-OB:134,
  Bo-FP:72, Bo-GJ:42, Cl-DT:60,
  Cl-FC:51, Co-BN:64, De-TT:145,
  Er-FA:259, Fe-FP:272, Ga-FB:227,
  Hu-MP:293, Mc-PR:99, Sp-OG:282
Childhood and School-Time.
  W. Wordsworth. Ox-BN:93
Clifton Grove. H. White.
  Ox-BN:228
Composed while under Arrest.
  M. Lermontov. Pa-SG:204
Conversion. T. Hulme. Al-VBP:1152
Country of No Lack.
  J. Untermeyer. Un-MA:333
The Creation. C. Alexander.
  De-TT:36, Fe-FP:260, Gr-TG:22,
  Hu-MP:286, Ox-BC:200
Credo. R. Jeffers. Un-MA:366
The Dawn. W. Yeats. Mo-GR:73
Days Too Short. W. Davies.
  Un-MB:175
Discovering God Is Waking One
  Morning. J. L'Heureux.
  Co-BN:92
Each Season More Lovely.
  Yakamocho. Ba-ST:11
Esthetique du Mal, XV.
  W. Stevens. Wi-LT:160
Eve Speaks to Adam. J. Milton.
  Gr-CT:57, Ho-WR:255
Even Stones. Onitsura. Be-CS:37
Evening after Rain. E. Tatum.
  Ke-TF:429
The Excesses of God. R. Jeffers.
  Tr-MR:143
A Field of Light. T. Roethke.
  Br-TC:346

NATURE — BEAUTY — cont'd.

The Field of the Mice and the
    Marigold. E. Clarke. Le-M:40
A Fine Day. M. Drayton. Bo-FP:239
First Note. J. Miller. Sc-TN:168
The Fool on the Hill. J. Lennon.
    Mo-GR:72
For a Dewdrop. E. Farjeon.
    De-TT:62
From Garden to Garden, Ridge to
    Ridge. J. Muir. La-RM:43
From My Study at the Mouth of the
    Valley. Ch'ien Ch'i. Le-MW:53
Ghoul Care. R. Hodgson. Un-MB:193
The Glory of Nature. F. Tennyson.
    Ox-BN:469
God's World. E. Millay.
    Co-PS:124, Ga-FB:3, Sh-RP:103,
    Tr-MR:26, Tu-WW:48, Un-GT:245,
    Un-MA:443
A Great Time. W. Davies.
    Hi-WP I:1, Un-MB:178
Green Little Gardens. A. Machado.
    Le-SW:51
Hope. W. Shenstone. Co-BN:215
How Still, How Happy! E. Brontë.
    Ox-BN:598
Hymn to the Spirit of Nature.
    P. Shelley. Al-VBP:742,
    De-CH:335, Pa-GTB:281
I Love. . . . T. Mitrofanova.
    Mo-MI:60
I Shall Not Pass This Way Again.
    E. York. Er-FA:10
The Idle Flowers. R. Bridges.
    Co-BN:45, Gr-CT:247
I'm Glad the Sky Is Painted Blue.
    Au-SP:320, Ch-B:110, Fr-MP:12,
    Lo-LL:107
Immalee. C. Rossetti. Bl-OB:136,
    Co-BN:207, Re-TW:61
In My Mountains. J. Yokomizo.
    Ba-HI:102
In the Fields. C. Mew. Co-BN:208,
    Sm-MK:221, Un-MB:159
Inscription for the Entrance to a
    Wood. W. Bryant. Sh-AP:19
Isle of Arran. A. Reid. Ha-WR:19
It Is a Beauteous Evening.
    W. Wordsworth. Al-VBP:659,
    De-CH:738, Fe-PL:403, Gr-CT:195,
    Pa-GTB:273, Rv-CB:646
A June Day. S. Teasdale. Ha-YA:70
Lake Leman. G. Byron. Ox-BN:245
Leisure. W. Davies.
    Ar-TP3:213, Co-BN:205, De-CH:137,
    Er-FA:248, Fe-FP:78, Gr-EC:45,
    Hi-WP I:119, Mc-WK:22, Sh-RP:117,
    Sm-MK:177, Un-MB:179, Wi-LT:617
Lines. W. Wordsworth. Ox-BN:66

Lines Written among the Euganean
    Hills. P. Shelley.
    Al-VBP:743, De-TT:144
Little Children. T. Tsosie.
    Ba-HI:142
Loveliest of Trees. A. Housman.
    Al-VBP:1079, Bl-OB:136,
    Bo-FP:246, Co-BN:145, Er-FA:153,
    Fe-PL:371, Ga-FB:232, Go-BP:28,
    Gr-CT:47, Hu-MP:276, Ma-FW:13,
    Ma-YA:222, Sh-RP:208, Sm-MK:172,
    Tu-WW:52, Un-MB:95, Wi-LT:58
Magdalen Walks. O. Wilde.
    Un-MB:67
A Magic Landscape. A. Fet.
    Mo-MI:13, Pa-SG:103
The Maid's Thought. R. Jeffers.
    Co-BL:21, Sm-PT:37
May. W. Barnes. Co-PS:78
Maÿ Day. S. Teasdale. Co-BN:39,
    Co-PS:81
Morning. J. Keats. Sp-OG:349
A Morning Song. E. Farjeon.
    Hi-WP I:6
Morning Song from "Senlin."
    C. Aiken. Pe-OA:141, Sh-AP:185,
    Un-MA:422, Wi-LT:325
My Heart Leaps Up. W. Wordsworth.
    Al-VBP:655, Ar-TP3:172,
    Au-SP:346, Bo-HF:55, Br-BC:121,
    Co-RG:121, Er-FA:149, Ga-FB:22,
    Ha-PO:83, La-PP:7, Ma-YA:139,
    Mc-PR:169, Ox-BN:61, Pa-GTB:308,
    Rv-CB:644, Sp-OG:352
Mysteries. E. Dickinson.
    Un-MA:96
Nature. J. Clare. Rv-CB:713
Night on the Downland.
    J. Masefield. Un-MB:226,
    Wi-LT:192
The Nymphs. J. Hunt. Ox-BN:221
Ode: The Spirit Wooed. R. Dixon.
    Ox-BN:751
A Page's Road Song. W. Percy.
    Ha-YA:32, Ke-TF:201
Pied Beauty. G. Hopkins.
    Al-VBP:1062, Bo-GJ:47,
    Er-FA:461, Ga-S:16, Hi-WP II:37,
    Ho-LP:47, Ma-FW:101, Mc-PR:182,
    Mc-WK:16, No-CL:269, Ox-BN:865,
    Pa-GTB:390, Pl-EI:124, Re-TW:89,
    Sm-MK:222, Tr-MR:25, Un-GT:246,
    Un-MB:39, Wi-LT:42
Pleasure It Is. W. Cornish.
    Co-BN:28, De-CH:16, Ga-S:211,
    Gr-CT:39, Rv-CB:97
The Poem of Ten "Ones." Ho P'ei Yu.
    Le-MW:44, Ma-FW:237
A Prayer in Spring. R. Frost.
    Ha-YA:29, Tr-MR:48

The Prelude.   W. Wordsworth.
  Ma-FW:121
Press Close Bare-Bosom'd Night.
  W. Whitman.   Un-MW:169
Pruning Trees.   Po Chu-i.
  Ma-FW:107, Pa-SG:169
The Rat.   W. Davies.   Go-BP:91
The Sacrament.   R. Coffin.
  Ho-TH:38
The Scribe.   W. de la Mare.
  Sm-LG:35, Tr-MR:24
The Sense of the Sleight-of-Hand
  Man.   W. Stevens.   Pe-OA:70,
  Un-MA:252, Wi-LT:147
Sinners.   D. Lawrence.   Al-VBP:1158
A Small Hungry Child.   Basho.
  Be-CS:58
Song.   J. Jiménez.   Le-SW:57
Song for Youth.   D. Burnett.
  Hu-MP:303
Song of Myself.   W. Whitman.
  Ar-TP3:216, Sh-AP:87, Un-MA:56
Song of the Open Road.   O. Nash.
  Mo-BG:121
The Song on the Way.   Hu-MP:289
The Spring.   A. Cowley.   No-CL:274
Spring Morning.   D. Lawrence.
  Co-BL:52, Un-MB:297
Spring Walk to the Pavilion of
  Good Crops and Peace.
  Ou Yang Hsiu.   Rx-OH:52
Summer Afternoon.   R. Souster.
  Co-BN:98, Ls-NY:292
Summer Song.   E. Nesbit.   Co-PS:105
Sun Low in the West.   Buson.
  Be-CS:27
This Fevers Me.   R. Eberhart.
  Tr-MR:38
Thus Eve to Adam.   J. Milton.
  Ga-FB:42
'Tis Merry in Greenwood. W. Scott.
  Fe-FP:76, Hu-MP:302
To Autumn.   J. Keats.   Al-VBP:777,
  Co-BN:125, Co-RG:126, De-CH:206,
  De-TT:163, Fe-PL:384, Ga-FB:225,
  Go-BP:25, Ha-PO:85, Hi-WP II:34,
  Mc-PR:84, Ox-BN:359, Pa-GTB:261,
  Rv-CB:736, Sp-OG:369, Un-GT:279
To Jane: The Invitation.
  P. Shelley.   Re-TW:91
The Trees Are a Beautiful Sight.
  M. Lasanta.   Ba-HI:63
The Vision of Sir Launfal.
  J. Lowell.   Er-FA:238, Fe-FP:77,
  Ga-FB:289, Ke-TF:434, Mc-PR:37,
  Se-PR:139, Un-GT:275
Visit to the Hermit Ts'ui.
  Ch'ien Ch'i.   Rx-LT:67
The Voice That Beautifies the
  Land.   Da-SC:65, Le-OE:11,
  Pa-SG:139, Tr-US II:251

The Walk in the Garden.   C. Aiken.
  En-PC:14
Wantage Bells.   J. Betjeman.
  Hi-WP I:111
The Western Hill.
  Ch'en Meng-chia.   Hs-TC:116
White Horses.   W. Howard.
  Au-SP:296
Whose Are This Pond and House?
  Chang Liang-Ch'en.   Le-MW:68
Wonder.   T. Traherne.   De-CH:152,
  Ga-S:21, Rv-CB:472
The World Is Too Much with Us.
  W. Wordsworth.   Al-VBP:660,
  Er-FA:267, Fe-PL:298, Gr-CT:201,
  Ke-PP:53, Ox-BN:79, Pa-GTB:299,
  Rv-CB:636, Sp-OG:365
Zummer Stream.   W. Barnes.
  Co-BN:93
NATURE, UNAPPRECIATED
  The Glory of Nature.
    F. Tennyson.   Ox-BN:469
  In Memoriam.   A. Tennyson.
    Ox-BN:506
  A Mask Presented at Ludlow Castle.
    J. Milton.   Al-VBP:399
  Spring Walk to the Pavilion of
    Good Crops and Peace.
    Ou Yang Hsiu.   Rx-OH:52
  To a Fat Lady Seen from a Train.
    F. Cornford.   Bo-GJ:106,
    Co-EL:100, Co-PU:132, Hi-WP I:109,
    Li-SR:20, Sm-MK:99, Un-MB:306
  The Woman at Banff.   W. Stafford.
    Ha-TP:46
NAUTILUSES
  The Chambered Nautilus.
    O. Holmes.   Er-FA:479,
    Fe-PL:297, Mc-PR:130,
    Sh-AP:63, Sp-OG:366
  The Paper Nautilus.   M. Moore.
    Ca-VT:127
NAVAHO INDIANS: see also INDIANS
    OF NORTH AMERICA - VERSE—
    NAVAHO
  Ancestors.   G. Cohoe.   Al-WW:24
  My People.   B. George.   Ba-HI:17
  The Navajo.   E. Coatsworth.
    Br-AF:36
  Navajo Children, Canyon de Chelly,
    Arizona.   C. Middleton.
    Ma-FW:69
  Navajo Rug.   B. Lee.   Ba-HI:84
  The Proud Navajo. P. Kee. Ba-HI:21
  To the Abode of the Deer I Came Up.
    Ho-SD:39
NAVAL BATTLES: see also HUMOR -
    NAVAL BATTLES; and battles, as
    TRAFALGAR, BATTLE, 1805
  Admiral Hosier's Ghost.
    R. Glover.   Al-VBP:555

NAVAL BATTLES — cont'd.
  The Armada. T. Macaulay.
    Ox-BN:426, Sm-LG:250
  The Armada, 1588. J. Wilson.
    Ox-BC:24
  A Ballad for a Boy. W. Cory.
    Ox-BC:290
  The Banks of Champlain. Em-AF:436
  The Battle of Sole Bay. Gr-GB:189
  The Captain Stood on the
    Carronade. F. Marryat.
    Co-SS:23, De-CH:597, De-TT:136,
    Ha-PO:255, Sh-RP:261
  The Coasts of High Barbary.
    Bl-OB:50
  The Cruise of the Monitor.
    G. Boker. Hi-TL:110
  The Cumberland and the Merrimac.
    Em-AF:443
  The Cumberland's Crew. Em-AF:442
  The Death of Admiral Benbow.
    Bl-OB:44, Co-RM:66, Gr-GB:239,
    Rv-CB:420
  Farragut. W. Meredith. Hi-TL:108
  Hervé Riel. R. Browning.
    Co-SS:183, Pa-OM:161, Sp-OG:67
  James Bird. Em-AF:438
  Lepanto. G. Chesterton.
    Ga-FB:196, Hi-FO:119, Un-MB:205
  Maggie Mac. Em-AF:445
  An Old-Time Sea Fight.
    W. Whitman. Pa-OM:168,
    Un-MA:57, Vi-PP:130
  Paul Jones. Vi-PP:132
  Pilots, Man Your Planes.
    R. Jarrell. Un-MA:645
  The Revenge. A. Tennyson.
    Co-RM:45, Hi-FO:134,
    Pa-OM:154, Sp-OG:60
  The "Shannon" and the "Chesapeake."
    De-TT:134
  Ye Parliament of England.
    Em-AF:433
NAVARINO, BATTLE, 1827
  The Glorious Victory of Navarino.
    Hi-FO:214
NAZI MOVEMENT: see NATIONAL
    SOCIALISM; JEWS - PERSECUTION
NEATNESS: see HUMOR - NEATNESS
NEBO, MOUNT: see ABARIM
    MOUNTAINS
NEBRASKA
  My Nebraska. T. Diers. Se-PR:273
  Nebraska. J. Swan. Ha-WR:43,
    La-RM:76
  Under Your Voice, among Legends.
    P. Harris. Sc-TN:81
NEBUCHADNEZZAR, KING OF BABYLON
  Nebuchadnezzar. E. Wylie.
    Un-MA:277

NECKS: see HUMOR - NECKS
NECKTIES AND CRAVATS: see
    CLOTHING AND DRESS
NEEDLES AND PINS: see also
    HUMOR - NEEDLES AND PINS
  About Buttons. D. Aldis.
    Th-AS:59
  All Are Cold and Very Skinny.
    Re-RR:88
  An Argument Against the Empirical
    Method. W. Stafford.
    Du-SH:186
  I Can Prick Your Finger. St-FS:39
  Old Mother Twitchett. Mother
    Goose. Ar-TP3:99, Au-SP:26,
    Ir-BB:50, Li-LB:169, Mo-MGT:157,
    Wr-RM:30
  The Pin. A. Taylor. Ox-BC:117
  A Riddle. C. Rossetti. Ox-BC:279
  See a Pin and Pick It Up.
    Ir-BB:226, Li-LB:161, Mo-MGT:172,
    Mo-NR:119, Mo-TB:55, Un-GT:23,
    Wr-RM:41
NEEDLEWORK: see also DRESSMAKING;
    HUMOR - NEEDLEWORK; KNITTING;
    LACE AND LACEMAKING; TAPESTRY
  Aunt Jennifer's Tigers. A. Rich.
    Ha-TP:52
  Crewel. N. Willard. Sc-TN:233
  A Drape. Feng Chih. Hs-TC:143
  The King's Young Dochter.
    De-CH:602
  The Sampler. N. Turner.
    Br-BC:80
  Sewing. Ch-B:97
  Stitching. C. Rossetti.
    Ch-B:97
  Talents Differ. L. Richards.
    Ar-TP3:55
  A Woman's First Sewing after a
    Mourning. Da-SC:40
NEFERTITI, QUEEN OF EGYPT
  Queen Nefertiti. Ne-AM:42,
    Sm-MK:29
NEGRO BALLADS: see BALLADS, NEGRO
NEGRO MINSTRELS
  Buckdancer's Choice. J. Dickey.
    Hu-PN:579
NEGRO MUSIC: see JAZZ MUSIC;
    NEGRO MINSTRELS; NEGROES
    - SONGS; SPIRITUALS
NEGROES: see also BALLADS, NEGRO;
    BLACK PANTHERS; DIALECTS, NEGRO;
    HARLEM, N.Y.; HUMOR - NEGROES;
    RACE PROBLEMS; RACE RELATIONS;
    SATIRE - NEGROES; SLAVERY; and
    names of Negroes, as DOUGLASS,
    FREDERICK
  Abu. D. Randall. Ra-BP:147
  Adulthood. N. Giovanni. Be-MA:69

after kent state. L. Clifton.
Be-MA:142
Alabama Centennial. N. Madgett.
Ra-BP:197
The Alarm Clock. M. Evans.
Ad-BO:6
Amen. R. Thomas. Ad-PB:372
America. B. Hamilton. Ad-BO:41
America. C. McKay. Ad-PB:26,
Be-MA:15, Bo-HF:40, Hu-PN:100,
Lo-TY:119
America. J. Whitfield. Ba-PO:17,
Ra-BP:35
American Heartbreak. L. Hughes.
Ra-BP:87, Wi-LT:422
American History. M. Harper.
Ra-BP:291
Ancestors. D. Randall. Ra-BP:148
And Through the Caribbean Sea.
M. Danner. Ra-BP:152
And Was Not Improved. L. Bennett.
Ad-PB:203
and we conquered. R. Penny.
Ad-PB:391
Angola Question Mark. L. Hughes.
Lo-TY:230, Ra-BP:89
Are Things Really Changing?
B. Davis. Me-WF:59
As I Grew Older. L. Hughes.
Ha-TP:101
Awareness. D. Lee. Ad-BO:2,
Ad-PB:421
Babylon Revisited. I. Baraka.
Ra-BP:214
Back Again, Home. D. Lee.
Ra-BP:295
The Backlash Blues. L. Hughes.
Ra-BP:90
Ballad of Birmingham. D. Randall.
Be-MA:71, Ra-BP:143
The Ballad of Chocolate Mabbie.
G. Brooks. Pe-SS:30
A Ballad of Remembrance.
R. Hayden. Ad-PB:115,
Bo-AN:109, Hu-PN:291, Ra-BP:131
The Ballad of Rudolph Reed.
G. Brooks. Jo-SA:46
Ballad of the Landlord. L. Hughes.
Ha-TP:15
Banty Tim. J. Hay. Kr-OF:45
Baptism. C. Bell. Br-AF:140
Barricades. M. Harper. Ad-PB:316
be cool, baby. R. Penny.
Ad-PB:390
Beautiful Black Men. N. Giovanni.
Ra-BP:320
Beautiful Black Women. I. Baraka.
Ra-BP:213
The Beginning of a Long Poem on why
I Burned the City. L. Benford.
Kr-OF:55, Lo-TY:257

Between the World and Me.
R. Wright. Ad-PB:107, Bo-AN:103,
Kr-OF:158, Pe-M:92, Wi-LT:657
Beyond the Nigger. S. Plumpp.
Ad-PB:387
Big Momma. D. Lee. Ra-BP:304
Birmingham 1963. R. Patterson.
Ad-PB:209, Kr-OF:163
Black All Day. R. Patterson.
Ad-BO:4, Ad-PB:212
Black Bourgeoisie. I. Baraka.
Ra-BP:223
Black Child. P. Solomon.
Jo-VC:51
De Black Girl. Gr-GB:224
Black Hieroglyph. T. Matthews.
Sa-B:230
Black Is a Soul. J. White.
Ad-PB:261
Black Is Beautiful. A. Burns.
Ba-HI:18
Black Is Best. L. Thompson.
Ad-BO:2, Ad-PB:512
Black Lover Lead Man. L. Curry.
Jo-VC:65
Black Magic. D. Randall.
Ad-BO:5, Ad-PB:140
Black Majesty. C. Cullen.
Ad-PB:92, Ca-VT:242
A Black Man. S. Cornish. Ad-PB:298
A Black Man Talks of Reaping.
A. Bontemps. Ad-PB:85, Be-MA:43,
Bo-AN:75, Bo-HF:93, Hu-PN:209,
Ra-BP:94
A Black Man's World.
L. Loflin II. La-IH:109
Black Narcissus. G. Barrax.
Ad-PB:223
Black Nights. R. Williams. Me-WF:45
Black People. J. Bryant.
Jo-VC:53
A Black Poetry Day. A. Johnson.
Ad-PB:13
Black Power. A. Saxon. Ad-PB:493
Black Star Line. H. Dumas.
Ad-PB:269
Black Warrior. N. Jordan.
Ad-PB:322
Black Woman. L. Curry. Jo-VC:64
Black Woman. N. Madgett.
Ad-PB:183
Black Woman. L. Senghor.
Lo-TY:134
Blackie Thinks of His Brothers.
S. Crouch. Ad-PB:484
Blackman/an unfinished history.
D. Lee. Be-MA:161
The Blackstone Rangers. The
Leaders. G. Brooks. Ad-PB:160
Blind and Deaf Old Woman.
C. Major. Ad-PB:300, Jo-SA:49

NEGROES — cont'd.
  blk/rhetoric. S. Sanchez.
    Be-MA:137
  The Blue-Tail Fly. Er-FA:450,
    Gr-GB:324
  Blues and Bitterness. L. Bennett.
    Ad-PB:202, Hu-NN:53
  Booker T. and W.E.B. D. Randall.
    Ab-MO:84, Be-MA:69
  Bottled: New York. H. Johnson.
    Ad-PB:104
  Bound No'th Blues. L. Hughes.
    Bo-AN:65
  Brass Spittoons. L. Hughes.
    Bo-AN:61, Un-MA:552
  Breakthrough. C. Rodgers.
    Ra-BP:263
  Brother Malcolm's Echo.
    K. Kgositsile. Be-MA:146
  But He Was Cool. D. Lee.
    Ad-PB:426, Be-MA:160, Ra-BP:299
  Canto 4. T. Weatherly. Ad-PB:397
  Carol of the Brown King.
    L. Hughes. La-PH:31, Li-LC:86
  Cathexis. F. Bryant. Ad-PB:406
  Children's Rhymes. L. Hughes.
    Ad-BO:43, Ra-BP:86
  Christ in Alabama. L. Hughes.
    Ad-PB:73
  The Citizen. V. Howard. Hu-NN:58
  Close Your Eyes! A. Bontemps.
    Ad-PB:86, Bo-AN:76, Hu-PN:218
  Coal. A. Lorde. Ad-PB:244,
    Be-MA:121, Jo-SA:95
  Color. L. Hughes. Ad-BO:3
  The Colored Band. P. Dunbar.
    Hu-MP:149
  Colors. J. Wickersham. Ad-II:83
  The Congo. V. Lindsay. Er-FA:300,
    Hi-WP.II:98, Hu-PN:484, Pe-OA:55,
    Sh-AP:163, Un-MA:218
  Cross. L. Hughes. Ad-PB:73,
    Be-MA:39, Bo-AN:62, Fe-PL:428,
    Wi-LT:421
  Crow, with Shiny Clothes.
    B. Jones. Ba-HI:19
  Cultural Exchange. L. Hughes.
    Ad-PB:76, Hu-PN:203, Ra-BP:83
  Dance of the Abakweta. M. Danner.
    Ad-PB:134, Be-MA:88, Bo-AN:154,
    Hu-NN:30, Hu-PN:163
  The Dancer. A. Young. Ad-PB:364
  Dancing in the Streets.
    A. Young. Mc-EA:51
  Dangerous Toy. H. Gordon.
    Ad-II:109
  Dark Girl. A. Bontemps.
    Pe-SS:148
  Dark People. K. Cumbo.
    Ad-BO:46

  Dark Symphony: Allegro Moderato.
    M. Tolson. Be-MA:20, Bo-AN:37,
    Hu-PN:136
  Dark Symphony: Andante Sostenuto.
    M. Tolson. Bo-AN:38
  Dark Symphony: Larghetto.
    M. Tolson. Bo-AN:40
  Dark Symphony: Lento Grave.
    M. Tolson. Bo-AN:38
  Dark Symphony: Tempo di Marcia.
    M. Tolson. Bo-AN:40
  Dark Symphony: Tempo Primo.
    M. Tolson. Bo-AN:39
  Dark Testament. P. Murray.
    Bo-AN:107
  The Day-Breakers. A. Bontemps.
    Ad-PB:84, Be-MA:43, Bo-AN:76,
    Hu-PN:223
  The Days of My People. M. Gill.
    Jo-VC:54
  Death as History. J. Wright.
    Ad-PB:280, Sc-TN:249
  Death in Yorkville. L. Hughes.
    Ad-PB:79
  The Death of a Negro Poet.
    C. Rivers. Ra-BP:201
  Dedication to a Final Confronta-
    tion. Djangatolum. Ad-PB:512,
    Jo-SA:12
  definition for blk/children.
    S. Sanchez. Ad-PB:288
  Determination. J. Clarke.
    Ad-PB:144
  A Different Image. D. Randall.
    Ra-BP:142
  Dinner Guest: Me. L. Hughes.
    Ra-BP:78
  Dirge. Q. Troupe. Ad-PB:442
  Dream Deferred. L. Hughes.
    Ad-PB:76, Be-MA:42, Bo-AN:67,
    Ha-TP:21, Hu-PN:199, La-OC:149,
    Wi-LT:422
  Dream Variation. L. Hughes.
    Ad-PB:74, Hu-PN:183,
    Jo-SA:129, Pe-M:88
  The Easter Bunny Blues or All I
    Want for Xmas Is the Loop.
    Ebon. Ad-PB:436
  Elephant Rock. P. St. John.
    Ad-PB:347
  Enslaved. C. McKay. Ra-BP:62
  Execution. J. Randall. Ra-BP:277
  A Far Cry from Africa. D. Walcott.
    Lo-TY:114
  Finally. H. Gordon. Ad-II:107
  Fire, Hair, Meat and Bone.
    F. Johnson. Ad-PB:391
  Florida Road Workers.
    L. Hughes. Du-SH:145, Pe-SS:52,
    Un-MA:553

Flowers of Darkness.   F. Davis.
   Ad-IA:12, Ad-PB:95, Be-MA:55,
   Bo-AN:96, Hu-PN:255
For Angela.   Z. Gilbert.   Ad-PB:196
For Bill Hawkins, a Black Militant.
   W. Harris.   Ad-PB:439
For Black Poets Who Think of
   Suicide.   E. Knight.   Ad-PB:253,
   Be-MA:112
For de Lawd.   L. Clifton.
   Ad-PB:306, Br-TC:71
For Denis Who Was a Drum.
   M. Maxwell.   Sa-B:172
For Eusi, Ayi Kwei & Gwen Brooks.
   K. Kgositsile.   Ad-PB:325
for h. w. fuller.   C. Rodgers.
   Ra-BP:262
For My People.   M. Walker.
   Ad-PB:144, Be-MA:73, Bo-AN:128,
   Hu-PN:314, Tr-MR:155
for Nina Simone wherever you are.
   L. Curry.   Jo-VC:46
For Some Poets.   M. Jackson.
   Ad-BO:16, Ad-PB:497
For Stephen Dixon.   Z. Gilbert.
   Ad-PB:195
For the Union Dead.   R. Lowell.
   Br-TC:265, Pe-OA:244, Wi-LT:583
Four Sheets to the Wind and a
   One-Way Ticket to France, 1933.
   C. Rivers.   Ad-PB:234, Bo-AN:176,
   Hu-NN:107, Hu-PN:404, Ra-BP:199
Frederick Douglass.   R. Hayden.
   Ab-MO:83, Ad-PB:120, Be-MA:56,
   Bo-AN:119, Hu-PN:296, Jo-SA:41,
   Lo-TY:237
Freedom.   L. Hughes.   Ad-PB:78
From the Dark Tower.   C. Cullen.
   Ad-PB:87, Be-MA:51, Hu-PN:235,
   Jo-SA:133, Ra-BP:100, Wi-LT:616
The Funeral of Martin Luther
   King, Jr.   N. Giovanni.
   Ad-BO:30, Ra-BP:323
Garnishing the Aviary.   M. Danner.
   Ad-PB:134, Be-MA:88, Bo-AN:153,
   Hu-NN:29, Ra-BP:149
Giles Johnson, Ph.D.   F. Davis.
   Ad-PB:96, Be-MA:53, Ra-BP:122
Ginger Bread Mama.   D. Long.
   Ad-PB:404, Ra-BP:310
Go Down Death.   J. Johnson.
   Ad-PB:6, Bo-AN:2
Go Slow.   L. Hughes.   Wi-LT:424
Good Times.   L. Clifton.
   Ad-PB:306, Be-MA:140, Br-TC:71,
   Ra-BP:250
Goodbye David Tamunoemi West.
   M. Danner.   Ra-BP:153
Greek Anthology, IV.   Un-MW:174
Grief Streams down My Chest.
   L. Jeffers.   Ad-PB:173

Half Black, Half Blacker.
   S. Plumpp.   Ad-PB:385
Hands of a Brown Woman.   F. Davis.
   Bo-HF:37
Hard but Soft.   W. Barbour.
   La-IH:29
Harlem.   L. Hughes.   Ad-CI:32
Harlem Freeze Frame.   L. Bethune.
   Ad-PB:309
Harlem 1960 & 1968.   P. Bird.
   La-IH:95
Harlem Sweeties.   L. Hughes.
   Hu-PN:190, Lo-TY:227, Wi-LT:420
He Rather Die.   K. Jones.
   Jo-VC:55
He Sees Through Stone.   E. Knight.
   Ad-PB:231, Be-MA:109
Her Story.   N. Madgett.   Ad-PB:183
Heritage.   G. Bennett.
   Ad-PB:81, Bo-AN:73
Heritage.   C. Cullen.   Ad-PB:88,
   Be-MA:47, Bo-AN:83, Ga-FB:274,
   Lo-TY:230, Ra-BP:95, Un-MA:571
High on the Hog.   J. Fields.
   Be-MA:154
Hokku Poems.   R. Wright.
   Bo-AN:105, Mo-BG:74
Hold the Wind.   Gr-GB:326
Holyghost Woman.   C. Major.
   Jo-SA:52
homecoming.   S. Sanchez.
   Ad-PB:286
The Homecoming Singer.
   J. Wright.   Ad-PB:279
Honky.   C. Cooper.   Ad-PB:504
hospital/poem.   S. Sanchez.
   Ad-PB:289
How High the Moon.   L. Jeffers.
   Ad-PB:172
Howdy, Honey, Howdy.   P. Dunbar.
   Fe-PL:425
I Am a Black Man.   B. Lewis.
   Ba-HI:15
I Am a Negro.   M. Al-Fituri.
   Lo-TY:54
I Am Cool Brother Cool.
   W. McLean.   Ad-II:116
I Came to the New World Empty-
   Handed.   H. Swift.   Br-AF:40
I Come from the Nigger Yard.
   M. Carter.   Sa-B:96
I Don't Mind.   C. Jackson.
   Le-M:168
I Give You Thanks My God.
   B. Dadie.   Lo-TY:144
I Have a Dream.   M. King.   Lo-TY:249
I Have Seen Black Hands. R. Wright.
   Ad-PB:105, Jo-SA:112
I Know I'm Not Sufficiently Obscure.
   R. Durem.   Ad-PB:151, Jo-SA:122,
   Ra-BP:163

NEGROES — cont'd.

I Love Those Little Booths at
   Benvenutt's. G. Brooks.
   St-H:10
I Play Flute. J. Stembridge.
   Lo-IT:129
I Saw Someone Just like Me.
   T. Heard. Me-WF:44
I Told Jesus. S. Plumpp.
   Ad-PB:385
I Too Hear America Singing.
   H. Bond. Lo-IT:11
I, Too, Sing America. L. Hughes.
   Ad-PB:75, Be-MA:40, Bo-AN:64,
   Ca-VT:239, Fe-PL:159, Hu-PN:182
i used to wrap my white doll up in.
   M. Jackson. Ad-BO:72, Ad-PB:498
Idle Chatter. C. Cooper.
   Ad-BO:8
The Idiot. D. Randall. Ra-BP:144
If Everybody Was Black.
   J. Holland. Jo-VC:50
If I Ride This Train. J. Johnson.
   Ad-PB:384
If the Stars Should Fall.
   S. Allen. Ad-PB:168, Hu-NN:95
If We Must Die. C. McKay.
   Ad-PB:25, Be-MA:13, Bo-AN:31,
   Ga-FB:277, Hu-PN:102, Jo-SA:135,
   Kr-OF:48, Lo-TY:118, Ra-BP:63
If You Saw a Negro Lady. J. Meyer.
   Jo-SA:54, Lo-IT:92
imperial thumbprint.
   T. Weatherly. Ad-PB:399
In Bondage. C. McKay. Ad-PB:26
in defense of black poets.
   C. Rivers. Ad-BO:20, Ra-BP:200
in orangeburg my brothers did.
   A. Spellman. Ad-PB:285,
   Ra-BP:229
In Texas Grass. Q. Troupe.
   Ad-PB:443
In These Dissenting Times.
   A. Walker. Ad-PB:475
Incident. C. Cullen.
   Ab-MO:94, Ad-PB:91, Be-MA:51,
   Ca-VT:241, Ho-LP:58, Hu-PN:232,
   Jo-SA:107, Kr-OF:50, Mo-BG:78,
   Pe-OA:190, Ra-BP:98, Th-AS:193
interlude. W. Smith. Ad-PB:374
The Invisible Man. C. Rivers.
   Be-MA:105
An Invitation to Madison County.
   J. Wright. Ad-PB:275
Its Curtains. T. Joans. Ad-PB:206
I've Seen Enough. C. Meyer.
   Jo-VC:12
January 3, 1970. M. Jackson.
   Ad-PB:499
Jeff Buckner. F. Beddo. Ba-PO:77

Jelly Wrote. A. Spellman.
   Be-MA:125
Jesus Was Crucified. C. Rodgers.
   Ad-PB:432
JuJu. A. Touré. Ad-PB:340
Junior Addict. L. Hughes.
   Ra-BP:85
Justice. L. Hughes. Ra-BP:87
Ka'Ba. I. Baraka. Ra-BP:213
Keorapsetse Kgositsile.
   G. Brooks. Ra-BP:172
knock on wood. H. Dumas.
   Ad-PB:268
Ku Klux. L. Hughes. Ra-BP:81
Lady, Lady. A. Spencer. Ad-PB:17
Landscape with Figures. N. Rosten.
   Kr-OF:160
The Last Empty Seat. R. Goodkin.
   La-IH:112
Last Night Somebody Called Me
   Darky. N. Guillen. Ab-MO:95
The Last Quatrain of the Ballad
   of Emmett Till. G. Brooks.
   Ad-PB:155
The Last Riot. V. Howard.
   Jo-VC:8
Legacy: My South. D. Randall.
   Ad-PB:138, Be-MA:71, Hu-NN:43,
   Hu-PN:306
leroy. I. Baraka. Ad-PB:255,
   Mc-EA:105, Ra-BP:215
Letter from a Black Soldier.
   B. Anderson. Ca-VT:625
Lincoln . . . Today.
   K. Hopkins. Me-WF:61
Listen, Lord - A Prayer.
   J. Johnson. Ra-BP:41
The Litany of the Dark People.
   C. Cullen. Pl-EI:155, Tr-MR:154
The Little Black Boy. W. Blake.
   De-CH:20, Hu-PN:445, Ox-BC:85,
   Ox-BN:21, Rv-CB:590, Sm-LG:106
A Little More Traveling Music.
   A. Young. Mc-EA:28
Lost Moment. H. Fuller.
   Ad-PB:201
The Louisiana Weekly. D. Henderson.
   Ad-PB:421, Jo-SA:103
Love Your Enemy. Y. Iman.
   Lo-TY:258, Ra-BP:293
Lynching. Yehoash. Ho-TY:74
Lynching and Burning.
   P. St. John. Ad-PB:349
A Man of the Middle Class.
   G. Brooks. St-H:12
Many Die Here. G. Jones.
   Jo-SA:14
Marginalia for Solo Voice and
   Tom-Tom; the Negroes Sing.
   A. Voznesensky. Ca-MR:75

Martin's Blues. M. Harper.
Ad-PB:312
Me. M. Goode. Ba-HI:14
The Melting Pot. D. Randall.
Ra-BP:141
Memorial Wreath. D. Randall.
Ad-PB:140, Hu-NN:59, Hu-PN:305
Middle Passage. R. Hayden.
Ad-PB:110, Be-MA:56, Bo-AN:113,
Ra-BP:123
Midway. N. Madgett.
Be-MA:93, Hu-NN:39, Hu-PN:381,
Jo-SA:126, Kr-OF:53, Ra-BP:197
Militant. L. Hughes. Ad-PB:80
Mister Banjo. Ab-MO:52
Mr. Roosevelt Regrets.
P. Murray. Ad-PB:109
Mixed Sketches. D. Lee. Ra-BP:306
A Moment Please. S. Allen.
Ad-PB:166, Bo-AN:138
Monument in Black. V. Howard.
Jo-SA:3, Jo-VC:43
Most Lovely Shade. E. Sitwell.
Pa-GTB:473
A Mother Speaks. M. Harper.
Ra-BP:291
Motto. L. Hughes. Ad-PB:75,
Co-PU:126, Hu-PN:202, Jo-SA:118
Mourning Hymn for the Queen of
Sunday. R. Hayden.
Ad-PB:117, Du-SH:105
A Mourning Letter from Paris.
C. Rivers. Ra-BP:199
Move Un-noticed to Be Noticed.
N. Giovanni. Be-MA:166
Movies. L. Hughes. Mo-BG:184
My Ace of Spades. T. Joans.
Ad-BO:31
My Black Boy. C. Wade. La-IH:102
My Blackness Is the Beauty of
This Land. L. Jeffers.
Ad-PB:173
My Heritage. B. Smith. Sa-B:71
My Mama Moved among the Days.
L. Clifton. Ad-PB:308,
Be-MA:139
My Name Was Legion. H. Swift.
Br-AF:39
My People. L. Hughes. Jo-SA:18
My Poem. N. Giovanni.
Ad-BO:22, Ad-PB:453, Ra-BP:319
My Soul Speaks Spanish.
M. Lasanta. Jo-VC:49
Narrative. R. Atkins. Ad-PB:198
Nation. C. Cobb. Ad-PB:468,
Lo-IT:17
Naturally. A. Lorde. Be-MA:122,
Jo-SA:87
Negritude. J. Emanuel. Ra-BP:189
The Negro. J. Emanuel. Ra-BP:188

A Negro Beats the Olympic Record
for the USA. A. Sperber.
Mc-AC:79
Negro Dreams. D. Long. Ad-PB:405
Negro Hero. G. Brooks. St-H:8
A Negro Mother's Lullaby.
C. Cullen. Mc-PR:153
A Negro Peddler's Song.
F. Johnson. Bo-AN:26
Negro Servant. L. Hughes.
Ca-VT:240
Negro Women. L. Alexander.
Ad-PB:58
The Negro's Tragedy. C. McKay.
Ra-BP:63
The New Integrationist.
D. Lee. Ad-BO:56
The New Math. V. Howard.
Jo-VC:44
nigger. S. Sanchez. Ra-BP:232
Night, Death, Mississippi.
R. Hayden. Ca-VT:357
Nikki-Rosa. N. Giovanni.
Ad-CI:20, Ad-PB:451,
Be-MA:169, Jo-SA:22
No Joke. F. John. Sa-B:143
No. No. C. Bresher. Ad-II:120
No Way Out. L. Curry.
Jo-SA:8, Jo-VC:82
Nocturne at Bethesda. A. Bontemps.
Be-MA:43, Bo-AN:81, Hu-PN:211
Now, All You Children. R. Durem.
Jo-SA:106
now poem. for us. S. Sanchez.
Ad-PB:290
#4. D. Long. Ad-PB:404
Numbers, Letters. I. Baraka.
Ra-BP:218
O Black and Unknown Bards.
J. Johnson. Ad-PB:2, Bo-AN:1,
Hu-PN:29, Lo-TY:206, Pl-US:74,
Ra-BP:42
O Daedalus, Fly Away Home.
R. Hayden. Ad-PB:116, Bo-HF:158,
Hu-PN:288, Jo-SA:120
O Great Black Masque. T. Joans.
Be-MA:104
Okay "Negroes." J. Jordan.
Ra-BP:243
Old Black Joe. S. Foster.
Er-FA:441
Old Black Men Say. J. Emanuel.
Ad-PB:180
The Old Cabin. P. Dunbar.
Fe-PL:426
Old Lem. S. Brown. Ad-PB:69,
Hu-PN:167, Lo-TY:221, Ra-BP:109
An Old Woman Remembers.
S. Brown. Ad-PB:68
On a Picture by Pippin, Called
"The Den." S. Rodman. Hu-PN:544

NEGROES — cont'd.
On Being Brought from Africa to
America. P. Wheatley.
Lo-TY:205
On Getting a Natural. D. Randall.
Ad-PB:141
On Passing Two Negroes on a Dark
Country Road Somewhere in
Georgia. C. Rivers. Hu-NN:42
On the Birth of My Son, Malcolm
Coltrane. J. Lester.
Ad-PB:356, Jo-SA:24
On the Block: Another Night
Search. J. Wright. Sc-TN:246
Once. A. Walker. Ad-PB:474
1 Black Foot + 1 Black Foot = 2
Black Feet. G. Solomon.
Ba-HI:22
One Eyed Black Man in Nebraska.
S. Cornish. Ad-PB:294
One Flower. M. Malik. Sa-B:146
One-Sided Shoot-Out. D. Lee.
Ad-PB:423, Ra-BP:302
One Thousand Nine Hundred &
Sixty-Eight Winters. J. Earley.
Ab-MO:93, Jo-SA:127
Oriflamme. J. Faucet. Ad-PB:18
Outcast. C. McKay. Ad-PB:25,
Be-MA:14, Bo-AN:28
Panther. S. Cornish. Ad-PB:297
Panther Man. J. Emanuel.
Ra-BP:192
The Party. P. Dunbar. Bo-AN:8
Paul Robeson. G. Brooks.
Ad-PB:165
Pavlov. N. Madgett. Ra-BP:196
Poem. E. Brathwaite. Sa-B:212
Poem. J. Fields. Be-MA:151
Poem. H. Johnson. Ad-PB:93,
Bo-AN:100
poem. S. Sanchez. Ad-PB:288
A Poem for a Poet. D. Lee.
Ad-PB:425
Poem for Aretha. N. Giovanni.
Ad-PB:454, Ra-BP:327
Poem for Black Boys. N. Giovanni.
Ra-BP:325
Poem for Flora. N. Giovanni.
Ad-PB:456, Ne-AM:34
Poem for Friends. Q. Troupe.
Ad-PB:445
Poem for My Family. J. Jordan.
Ra-BP:245
A Poem Looking for a Reader.
D. Lee. Jo-SA:92
Poem (No Name No. 2).
N. Giovanni. Ad-BO:9
A Poem Some People Will Have to
Understand. I. Baraka.
Ra-BP:216

Poem to Americans. G. Jackson.
Lo-IT:58
a poem to complement other poems.
D. Lee. Be-MA:158, Ra-BP:300
poll. E. Roberson. Ad-PB:350
Prayer for Peace: II.
L. Senghor. Lo-TY:135
Prayer Out of Georgia. M. Moody.
Ke-TF:203
Prime. L. Hughes. Ad-PB:76
The Primitive. D. Lee. Ra-BP:297
The Prophet's Warning, or Shoot
to Kill. Ebon. Ad-PB:434
Prose Poem for a Conference.
J. LaRose. Sa-B:74
PSI. M. Tolson. Ad-BO:36
Query. Ebon. Ad-PB:435
The Question. V. Howard.
Jo-VC:45
Question and Answer. L. Hughes.
Ra-BP:89
The Race Question. N. Madgett.
Be-MA:93, Ra-BP:196
Rain. C. Minor. Jo-VC:67
The Rainwalkers. D. Levertov.
Ad-CI:109, Du-SH:145
Re-Act for Actions. D. Lee.
Ra-BP:296
The Rebel. M. Evans. Ad-PB:187,
Bo-AN:163, Pe-SS:58
Return of the Native. I. Baraka.
Ra-BP:222
Return to My Native Land.
A. Cesaire. Lo-TY:123
Resurrection. F. Horne. Ad-PB:56
Reviewing Negro Troops Going
South Through Washington,
April 26, 1864. P. Horgan.
Cr-WS:23
Rhythm Is a Groove. L. Neal.
Jo-SA:105
Riding Across John Lee's Finger.
S. Crouch. Ad-PB:485
right on: white america.
S. Sanchez. Ad-BO:42, Ad-PB:287,
Be-MA:135, Jo-SA:104
Riot. G. Brooks. Ad-PB:164,
Ra-BP:175
Riot Rimes, U.S.A.
R. Patterson. Kr-OF:57
Riots and Rituals. R. Thomas.
Ad-PB:371
Rites of Passage. A. Lorde.
Ad-PB:249
Robert Whitmore. F. Davis.
Ad-PB:96, Be-MA:53, Hu-PN:254,
Ra-BP:121
Roses and Revolutions.
D. Randall. Ad-PB:142,
Ra-BP:142

Rulers: Philadelphia. F. Johnson.
Br-AF:199, Hu-PN:85
SOS. I. Baraka. Ad-PB:257,
Ra-BP:181
Salute. O. Pitcher. Ad-PB:193
Santa Claws. T. Joans. Mc-EA:116
Scottsboro, Too, Is Worth Its Song.
C. Cullen. Ad-PB:93, Be-MA:52
The Self-Hatred of Don L. Lee.
D. Lee. Ra-BP:297
The Sermon on the Warpland.
G. Brooks. Ad-PB:163, Ra-BP:170,
Wi-LT:666
She Came with Lips of Brown.
B. Cox. La-IH:100
signals, i. J. Amini. Ad-PB:292
Simon the Cyrenian Speaks.
C. Cullen. Be-MA:50, Bo-AN:89,
Ga-S:160, Lo-TY:235, Ra-BP:99,
Un-MA:570
Simple. N. Madgett. Ad-PB:182
Sketches of Harlem. D. Henderson.
Hu-NN:76, Hu-PN:437
Sleeping Beauty. C. Johnson.
La-IH:104
So I'm Still a Negro. Nathaniel.
La-IH:101
Song for a Dark Girl. L. Hughes.
Ad-PB:73
A Song in the Front Yard.
G. Brooks. Ad-PB:153, Bo-HF:101
The Song of the Smoke.
W. Du Bois. Ad-PB:1
Sonnet to a Negro in Harlem.
H. Johnson. Bo-AN:102, Mo-BG:27
Sonnet to Negro Soldiers.
J. Cotter. Ad-PB:35
Sorrow Is the Only Faithful One.
O. Dodson. Ad-PB:132,
Bo-AN:122, Jo-SA:123
Soul. D. Graham. Ad-PB:482
Soul Brother. H. Gordon. Ad-II:108
The Sound of Afroamerican History.
S. Anderson. Ad-PB:440, 441
Southern Road. S. Brown.
Ad-PB:67, Be-MA:29, Ra-BP:111
The Southern Road. D. Randall.
Ad-PB:139, Be-MA:70, Hu-NN:41
The Spade. E. Brathwaite.
Sa-B:43
Special Bulletin. L. Hughes.
Ad-PB:80
Spirits Unchained.
K. Kgositsile. Ad-PB:323
Stevedore. L. Collins. Bo-AN:127
The Still Voice of Harlem.
C. Rivers. Ad-PB:237, Be-MA:107,
Hu-NN:44
A Strange Meeting. W. Davies.
Bl-OB:148

Strategies. W. Smith. Ad-PB:375
Street Demonstration. M. Walker.
Ra-BP:156
Strong Men. S. Brown. Ad-PB:60,
Be-MA:27, Bo-HF:138, Ke-PP:127,
Lo-TY:219, Ra-BP:113
Summertime and the Living.
R. Hayden. Ad-PB:118,
Br-TC:169, Ra-BP:103
The Sundays of Satin-Legs Smith.
G. Brooks. St-H:14
Sympathy. P. Dunbar. Ad-PB:8,
Bo-AN:13, Hu-PN:34
Tauhid. A. Touré. Ad-PB:339
Taxes. D. Lee. Ad-BO:56
Theme One: The Variations.
A. Wilson. Ad-PB:491
They Are Killing All the Young
Men. D. Henderson. Ad-PB:414
They Got You Last Night.
A. Kurtz. Ke-PP:75
The Third Sermon on Warpland.
G. Brooks. Ra-BP:176
This Is a Black Room.
T. Beasley. La-IH:110
This Is an African Worm.
M. Danner. Ra-BP:151
Those Boys That Ran Together.
L. Clifton. Ad-PB:307
The Thoughts of a Child.
D. Embry. La-IH:94
Tiger. C. McKay. Ra-BP:62
Time to Die. R. Dandridge.
Ad-PB:18
Tired. F. Johnson. Ad-PB:24,
Fe-PL:428, Hu-PN:88, Kr-OF:48,
Lo-TY:210
To a Dark Girl. G. Bennett.
Ad-PB:81
To a White Liberal-Minded Girl.
J. Oliver. Ad-II:111
To Certain Critics. C. Cullen.
Ra-BP:101
to L. J. Perry. Ad-PB:516
To Richard Wright. C. Rivers.
Ad-PB:234, Be-MA:105, Bo-AN:177
To the White Fiends. C. McKay.
Ad-PB:27
To Vietnam. C. Cobb. Ad-PB:471
tomorrow the heroes. A. Spellman.
Ad-PB:285
tony get the boys. D. Graham.
Ad-PB:480
The Train Runs Late to Harlem.
C. Rivers. Ad-PB:237
Tripart, 2. G. Jones. Jo-SA:13
The True Import of Present
Dialogue: Black vs. Negro.
N. Giovanni. Ad-PB:451,
Ra-BP:318

NEGROES — <u>cont'd</u>.
  Trumpet Player. L. Hughes.
    Ha-TP:50, Lo-TY:226
  26 Ways of Looking at a Blackman.
    R. Patterson. Jo-SA:109
  224 Stoop. V. Cruz. Ad-BO:68
  Uncle Bull-Boy. J. Jordan.
    Ad-PB:304, Jo-SA:28
  The Unsung Heroes. P. Dunbar.
    Ra-BP:54
  Untitled. J. Randall. Ra-BP:273
  Vet's Rehabilitation. R. Durem.
    Ad-PB:150
  Vietnam #4. C. Major. Ad-BO:48,
    Ad-PB:298, Ba-PO:38
  Vive Noir! M. Evans. Ad-BO:52,
    Ad-PB:188
  WALK TALL MY BLACK CHILDREN.
    S. Boone. La-IH:114
  Walk Together Children. Ra-BP:1
  Warning. L. Hughes. Ra-BP:91
  Washiri. K. Cumbo. Ad-BO:12
  We Dance like Ella Riffs.
    C. Rodgers. Ad-PB:431
  We Have Been Believers.
    M. Walker. Ad-PB:145,
    Be-MA:76, Hu-PN:312, Jo-SA:130
  We Live in a Cage. W. Harris.
    Ad-PB:438
  We Own the Night. I. Baraka.
    Ad-BO:7, Ad-PB:257
  We Wear the Mask. P. Dunbar.
    Ad-IA:86, Ad-PB:8, Bo-AN:14,
    Bo-HF:103, Jo-SA:134,
    Lo-TY:208, Mo-BG:190
  The Weary Blues. L. Hughes.
    Be-MA:39, Ga-FB:276, Hu-PN:184,
    Pl-US:90
  Wednesday Night Prayer Meeting.
    J. Wright. Ad-PB:272
  Weeksville Women. E. Loftin.
    Ad-PB:515
  We're Free. C. Williams.
    Ba-HI:124
  What's Black Power.
    L. Baez. Jo-VC:47
  When Black People Are.
    A. Spellman. Ad-PB:284,
    Be-MA:127, Ra-BP:228
  When de Saints Go Ma'chin' Home.
    S. Brown. Bo-AN:55
  When Dey 'Listed Colored Soldiers.
    P. Dunbar. Ra-BP:48
  When I Heard Dat White Man Say.
    Z. Gilbert. Ad-PB:195
  When Mahalia Sings.
    Q. Prettyman. Ad-PB:260,
    Pe-M:18

  When Something Happens.
    J. Randall. Ra-BP:275
  When Sue Wears Red. L. Hughes.
    Lo-TY:228
  Where? When? Which?
    L. Hughes. Ra-BP:88
  The White House. C. McKay.
    Ad-PB:28, Be-MA:15, Bo-AN:31,
    Hu-PN:101, Jo-SA:119
  White Man and Black Man Are
    Talking. M. Goode. Jo-VC:48
  Who Am I. L. Gama. Lo-TY:79
  Who Are You - Who Are You?
    D. Clarke. Jo-VC:79
  Who but the Lord? L. Hughes.
    Ra-BP:81
  Why Do They Stare? W. Rountree.
    La-IH:93
  Why Prejudice. B. Chase.
    Ba-HI:24
  Why Try? T. Joans. Br-MA:101
  Will I Make It? J. Holland.
    Jo-VC:91
  Yes, I Am a Negro. J. West.
    La-IH:96
  Yes, This Is a Black Room.
    D. Dixon. La-IH:111
  Yet Do I Marvel. C. Cullen.
    Ad-PB:87, Be-MA:50, Bo-AN:88,
    Hu-PN:233, Jo-SA:128, Lo-TY:235,
    Pe-SS:48, Ra-BP:100
  You Know, Joe. R. Durem.
    Ad-BO:47, Hu-PN:330
  You're Nothing but a Spanish
    Colored Kid. F. Luciano.
    Ad-PB:501
  Youth's Question - Revenge's
    Answer. R. Groppuso. Me-WF:25
  Yuh Lookin GOOD. C. Rodgers.
    Ra-BP:266
NEGROES - HISTORY
  Black Man's Feast. S. Fabio.
    Ad-PB:203
  Effendi. M. Harper. Ad-PB:318
  The Living Truth. S. Plumpp.
    Ad-PB:388
  Sing Me a New Song. J. Clarke.
    Ad-PB:143
NEGROES - SONGS: see also BALLADS,
    NEGRO; SPIRITUALS
  Dixie. D. Emmett. Er-FA:290,
    Fe-FP:439
  My Old Kentucky Home.
    S. Foster. Er-FA:432, Fe-PL:143,
    Ga-FB:272, Se-PR:263
  Negro Spirituals. R. and S. Benét.
    Br-AF:110, Fe-FP:440
  We Shall Overcome. Ba-PO:199,
    Hi-TL:228, Pl-EI:165

NEIGHBORS: see also HUMOR -
    NEIGHBORS
  The Bourgeois Poet, #29.
    K. Shapiro.   St-H:202
  Brief Biography. M. George.
    De-FS:94
  The Child Next Door. R. Fyleman.
    Fe-FP:302, Hu-MP:136, Th-AS:6
  Exercise No. 2. W. Williams.
    Ho-TH:73
  How Good Are the Poor.
    V. Hugo. Ke-TF:61
  Just Folks. E. Guest. Er-FA:134
  Mending Wall. R. Frost.
    Al-VBP:1128, Br-AF:125,
    Ca-VT:4, Er-FA:276, Ga-FB:285,
    Ha-PO:91, Sh-AP:145, Sh-RP:96,
    Un-MA:170, Wi-LT:164
  Near and Far. K. Goddard.
    Fr-MP:12
  Neighboring. C. Rossetti.
    Bo-FP:80
  Neighborly. V. Storey. Ar-TP3:2
  Neighbors. Tu Fu. Le-MW:117
  A New Friend. M. Anderson.
    Fr-MP:10, Mc-AW:13
  The New Little Boy. H. Behn.
    Li-LC:48
  The New Neighbor. R. Fyleman.
    Ar-TP3:10, Au-SP:132
  Next Door. Mei Yao Ch'en.
    Rx-OH:38
  A Sad Song about Greenwich
    Village. F. Park. La-OC:66
  Summer Storm. R. Cuscaden.
    St-H:32
  Un-Birthday Cake. A. Fisher.
    Br-BC:89
  Welcome. R. Waldo. Au-SP:133,
    Hu-MP:38
NELSON, HORATIO NELSON, VISCOUNT
  The Admiral's Ghost. A. Noyes.
    Ar-TP3:22, Co-PM:129
  A Ballad of the Good Lord Nelson.
    L. Durrell. Wi-LT:697
  Battle of the Baltic.
    T. Campbell. Co-RG:46, Hi-FO:193,
    Pa-GTB:205, Rv-CB:675
  1805. R. Graves. Co-RM:42,
    Na-EO:17, Sm-LG:155
  Nelson and Pitt. W. Scott.
    Hi-FO:196
  The Night of Trafalgar.
    T. Hardy. De-CH:166, Gr-CT:340,
    Un-MB:28
NEPAL - COUNTRYSIDE
  Here in Katmandu. D. Justice.
    La-RM:38
NEPTUNE (GOD)
  In Praise of Neptune. T. Campion.
    Co-BN:63, Ho-WR:117, Rv-CB:271

NERO, ROMAN EMPEROR
  Nero's Term. C. Cavafy. Cr-WS:17
NERVAL, GÉRARD DE
  In a Warm Chicken House.
    J. Wright. Ls-NY:303
NETHERLANDIC VERSE: see DUTCH
    VERSE
NETHERLANDS: see also THE DUTCH;
    DUTCH VERSE; HUMOR - NETHER-
    LANDS; and names of towns, as
    AMSTERDAM, NETH.
  The Character of Holland.
    A. Marvell. Gr-CT:204
  The Little Toy Land of the Dutch.
    Hu-MP:181
  Tulip Beds in Holland.
    A. Morgan. Ke-TF:435
NETHERLANDS - HISTORY AND
    PATRIOTISM
  The Leak in the Dike. P. Cary.
    Er-FA:348, Fe-FP:554
NETTLES
  Nettles. Rv-ON:48
  Tall Nettles. E. Thomas.
    Co-EL:114, Gr-CT:237,
    Rv-CB:970, Un-MB:215
NEUTRALITY: see also
    INTERNATIONAL RELATIONS
  The Conflict. C. Day Lewis.
    Un-MB:424, Wi-LT:429
  Neutrality. S. Keyes. Un-MB:523
NEVA RIVER
  To the Nyeva. G. Garbovsky.
    Bo-RU:35
NEVADA
  Dogs Have as Much Right as
    People in Nevada.
    H. Witt. Du-SH:118
  Home Means Nevada.
    B. Raffetto. Se-PR:273
  Vacation. W. Stafford.
    Br-AF:149
  You Are on U.S. 40 Headed West.
    V. White. Br-AF:234
NEW BRITAIN
  Thief's Spell. Tr-US I:207
NEW CALEDONIA
  Lullaby for a Child Whose Mother
    Has Gone to Gather Food.
    Tr-US I:218
  Song for a Seated Dance: Victory
    of the Mea. Tr-US I:219
NEW ENGLAND: see also
    DIALECTS, NEW ENGLAND; and
    names of cities and states,
    as BOSTON, MASS and MAINE
  Address to the Scholars of New
    England. J. Ransom. Wi-LT:323
  An American in England.
    E. Wylie. Pa-HT:121

NEW ENGLAND — cont'd.
   Brown's Descent. R. Frost.
      Ar-TP3:145, Ha-PO:287, Na-EO:89,
      Sp-OG:234, Un-MA:178
   The Captains of Small Farms.
      R. Coffin. Sh-RP:308
   Citizens in the Round. R. Coffin.
      Sh-RP:290
   Clipper Ships and Captains.
      S. Benét. Sh-RP:298
   Cousin Nancy. T. Eliot.
      Ha-PO:68
   Covered Bridge. R. Coffin.
      Br-AF:125
   The Customs of the Country.
      P. McGinley. Ho-TH:70
   Falling Asleep over the Aeneid.
      R. Lowell. Un-MA:666
   Gay Head. N. Abeel. Pa-HT:30
   Geography of Lilacs. F. Frost.
      Ke-TF:437
   Gloucester Moors. W. Moody.
      Pa-HT:19, Sp-OG:362
   Graveyard. R. Coffin. Br-AF:127
   Jehu. L. MacNeice. Wi-LT:460
   The Landing of the Pilgrim
      Fathers. F. Hemans.
      Ar-TP3:39, Bo-FP:159, Er-FA:296,
      Fe-FP:409, Ga-FB:252, Gr-EC:228,
      Hi-TL:23, Se-PR:217, Sp-OG:23,
      Un-GT:176, Vi-PP:50
   Lilacs. A. Lowell. Un-MA:160
   New England. B. Bradbury.
      Ke-TF:346
   New England. E. Forbes. Ke-TF:347
   New England. E. Robinson.
      Sh-AP:141, Un-MA:135
   New England Churchyard. M. Adams.
      Ke-TF:349
   New England Farmer. C. Smith.
      Sm-PT:96
   New England Farmhouses.
      R. Montgomery. Ke-TF:410
   New England Landscape.
      E. Chaffee. Ke-TF:348
   New England Landscape.
      D. Heyward. Pa-HT:17
   New England November. D. Hall.
      Ke-TF:448
   New England Village, 1942.
      M. Bracker. Ke-TF:260
   Nocturne. F. Frost. Co-BN:202
   Skunk Hour. R. Lowell. Un-MA:669
   Square-Toed Princes. R. Coffin.
      Br-AF:129
   The Star-Splitter. R. Frost.
      Pl-IO:173
   To Robert Frost. W. Snow.
      Ke-TF:318
   Two Women under a Maple.
      R. Coffin. Mc-PR:147

   Voices of Heroes. H. Gregory.
      Gr-CC:104
   The Week in Old New England.
      Mo-TB:111
NEW ENGLAND - HISTORY
   I Am for Peace. P. Folger.
      Kr-OF:61
   If Your Hands Be Full of Blood.
      P. Folger. Kr-OF:100
   New England Lamented. J. Saffin.
      Kr-OF:102
   Tar and Feather. J. Trumbull.
      Kr-OF:131
NEW ENGLANDERS: see NEW ENGLAND
NEW GUINEA: see also MELANESIAN
      VERSE-PAPUAN
   Sunday: New Guinea.
      K. Shapiro. Br-AF:85
   See also Tr-US I:187-195
NEW HAMPSHIRE: see also HUMOR -
      NEW HAMPSHIRE
   Apples in New Hampshire.
      M. Gilchrist. Co-BN:137
   New Hampshire. T. Eliot.
      Ha-LO:81, Ha-PO:94, Pa-GTB:477,
      Re-TW:98, Sm-LG:142
   New Hampshire. D. Hall. Mo-BG:145
   New Hampshire Moon. F. Frost.
      Ke-TF:351
   Old New Hampshire. J. Holmes.
      Se-PR:274
   Spring in New Hampshire. C. McKay.
      Bo-HF:52, Hu-PN:97, Ra-BP:59
NEW HEBRIDES
   Kite-Flying Song. Tr-US I:217
NEW JERSEY: see also SATIRE -
      NEW JERSEY; and names of towns,
      as NEWARK, N.J.
   Legend. J. Weaver. Br-AF:197
   Ode to New Jersey. E. Carr.
      Se-PR:275
NEW MEXICO: see also names of
      towns, as SANTA FE, N.M.
   New Mexico. P. Boyden.
      Ar-TP3:33
   O, Fair New Mexico. E. Garrett.
      Se-PR:276
   The Railroad Cars Are Coming.
      Br-AF:228, Fe-FP:437, Hu-MP:395
   Rain in the Southwest.
      R. Kelley. Br-AF:147
   The Sound of Morning in New
      Mexico. R. Kelley. Br-AF:145
NEW ORLEANS, LA.
   The Cathedral of St. Louis.
      C. Carmer. Th-AS:167
   New Orleans. H. Carruth.
      Br-AF:201
   Vieux Carre. W. Roberts. Hu-PN:84
NEW ORLEANS, BATTLE, 1815
   The Battle of New Orleans.
      T. English. Hi-TL:67

The Battle of New Orleans.
Em-AF:439
The Statue of Old Andrew Jackson.
V. Lindsay. Mc-PR:52
NEW YEAR: see also SATIRE -
NEW YEAR
As New Year's Day Dawns.
Ransetsu. Be-MC:48
At Christmas. Cl-FC:89
At the New Year. K. Patchen.
Wi-LT:784
Death of the Old Year.
A. Tennyson. Co-PS:25
Early January. W. Merwin.
Ca-VT:621
The End of the Year.
Su Tung P'o. Rx-OH:79
Farewell to the Old Year.
E. Farjeon. Br-SS:112
From the New Year's Ceremony.
Tr-US II:229
Happy New Year. M. Roberts.
Mc-AW:64
Happy New Year! Co-PS:22
I Saw Three Ships Come Sailing By.
Mo-NR:50
In Memoriam (Dip Down).
A. Tennyson. Al-VBP:861
In Trust. M. Dodge. Br-SS:113
January! M. Millet. Ja-HH:6
January 1. M. Pomeroy. Co-PS:26
The Last Day of the Year.
A. Smart. Bo-FP:207
The Last Day of the Year.
Su Tung P'o. Rx-OH:74
Midnight Mass for the Dying Year.
H. Longfellow. Se-PR:31
The Moon Shines Bright. Gr-GB:297
The New Year. D. Cooke.
Hu-MP:327
The New Year. D. Craik.
Bo-FP:207, Ha-YA:167, Hu-MP:327
A New Year. M. Davies. Ha-YA:168
The New Year. H. Powers.
Se-PR:33
A New Year. D. Shorter. Ha-YA:167
New Year. Wang Ya-p'ing.
Hs-TC:352
The New Year. Br-FW:14
The New Year Came. Ja-HH:7
A New Year Carol. Co-PS:23,
De-CH:3, De-TT:115, Ga-S:93,
Gr-GB:297, Ma-FW:3, Re-TW:64
New Year Ditty. C. Rossetti.
Se-PR:29
A New Year Idyl. E. Field.
Co-PS:28
New Year Song. E. Miller.
Se-PR:27
New Year Wishes. M. Sarton.
Tr-MR:251

New Year's. G. Dusenbery. Sc-TN:35
New Year's. C. Reznikoff.
Ca-VT:189
New Year's Day. R. Field.
Ar-TP3:198, Au-SP:360, La-PH:44
New Year's Day. R. Lowell.
Wi-LT:572
New Year's Eve. J. Berryman.
Wi-LT:570
New Year's Eve. T. Hardy. Un-MB:27
New Year's Poem. M. Avison.
Wi-LT:661
New Year's Resolution. B. Lee.
Ja-HH:7
News! News! E. Farjeon. Br-SS:114

Old Father Annum. L. Jackson.
Br-SS:113
Our Cat. V. Lapin. Mo-MI:30
Resolution. T. Berrigan.
Mc-EA:39
Ring Out, Wild Bells. A. Tennyson.
Ar-TP3:240, Bo-FP:177, Er-FA:522,
Fe-FP:64, Ga-S:93, Ho-WR:241,
Hu-MP:328, La-PH:45, Se-PR:28
Song. A. Tennyson. Ox-BN:476,
Pa-GTB:330
Song for December Thirty-First.
F. Frost. Ha-YA:165
A Song for New Year's Eve.
W. Bryant. Hu-MP:327, Se-PR:29
Twelfth Night Carol. Bo-FP:206,
Se-PR:35
Up the Hill, down the Hill.
E. Farjeon. Co-PS:27
Welcome to the New Year.
E. Farjeon. Ha-YA:166, Th-AS:109

Winter Dawn. Tu Fu. Rx-OH:5
Years-End. R. Wilbur. Wi-LT:596
You'll Find Whenever the New
Year Comes. Wy-CM:35
NEW YORK (STATE): see names of
cities, as BUFFALO, N.Y.
NEW YORK, N.Y.: see also EAST
RIVER, N.Y.; EMPIRE STATE
BUILDING, NEW YORK, N.Y.;
HARLEM, N.Y.; HUMOR - NEW
YORK, N.Y.; SATIRE - NEW
YORK, N.Y.; WASHINGTON
SQUARE, NEW YORK, N.Y.
The Avenue Bearing the Initial of
Christ into the New World.
G. Kinnell. Ad-CI:11, Wi-LT:746
Broadway: Twilight.
T. Prideaux. La-OC:19
Brooklyn Bridge at Dawn.
R. LeGallienne. Ar-TP3:173
Central Park. R. Lowell. Wi-LT:586
Central Park Tourney. M. Weston.
Br-AF:195, Du-RG:47, La-OC:123,
Pe-M:129

NEW YORK, N.Y. — cont'd.
  Chapter Two. W. Scott. Gr-CC:186
  Dedication for a Building.
    A. Dugan. Ad-CI:89
  Dive. L. Hughes. Ad-CI:51
  East Broadway. M. Leib. Ho-TY:92
  For More Public Fountains in New
    York City. A. Dugan. Ho-P:61
  Give Me the Splendid Silent Sun.
    W. Whitman. Co-BN:232,
    Fe-FP:263, Mo-BG:20, Un-MA:84
  The Harbor Dawn. H. Crane.
    Pe-OA:178, Sh-AP:198
  Hearing Men Shout at Night on
    MacDougal Street. R. Bly.
    Ad-CI:34, Mc-EA:117
  Here Lives the Jewish People.
    H. Leivick. Ho-TY:120
  How Come? D. Ignatow. Ad-CI:110
  Invitation to Miss Marianne
    Moore. E. Bishop. Pl-ML:82
  The Lady Is Cold. E. White.
    Pa-HT:36
  Letter to New York. E. Bishop.
    Br-TC:47, Ho-TH:63, Mc-WS:116
  The Light of Summer's End.
    I. Schwartz. Ho-TY:146
  Love in a City in Spring.
    A. Miller. Ke-TF:358
  Manhattan. M. Beer. Br-AF:193
  Mannahatta. W. Whitman. Un-MA:43
  Mazda Miracle. C. Bostelmann.
    Ke-TF:356
  Metromania. B. Braley. Ke-TF:356
  Metropolitan Nightmare. S. Benét.
    Pl-IO:115
  My City. J. Johnson. Bo-HF:41,
    Hu-PN:31
  New York. V. Jones. Me-WF:12
  New York in the Spring.
    D. Budbill. Ad-CI:3
  New York Skyscrapers. J. Mbiti.
    Ab-MO:49
  Pennsylvania Station. L. Hughes.
    Bo-AN:71
  Polo Grounds. R. Humphries.
    Mo-SD:9, Ni-JP:124
  A Private Letter to Brazil.
    G. Oden. Bo-AN:158, Hu-NN:91,
    Hu-PN:383
  Reading Yeats I Did Not Think.
    L. Ferlinghetti. Pl-ML:117
  Return to New York.
    J. Wheelock. Pa-HT:35
  Review from Staten Island.
    G. Oden. Ad-PB:184, Be-MA:95,
    Hu-NN:90
  Rhyme of Rain. J. Holmes.
    La-OC:30, Mc-WK:36
  Riverside Drive. J. Rolnick.
    Ho-TY:166

  Second Night in N.Y.C. after 3
    Years. G. Corso. Gr-BT:37
  Song of the Witch of the Cloisters.
    W. Hoffman. Sc-TN:104
  Sounds of Buddy Tate. D. Rasey.
    Lo-IT:112
  A Step Away from Them. F. O'Hara.
    Ca-VT:586
  The Stone. P. Blackburn. Du-SH:24
  Summer: West Side. J. Updike.
    Pe-SS:68
  They Are Killing All the Young
    Men. D. Henderson. Ad-PB:414
  Trinity Place. P. McGinley.
    La-OC:120, Un-MA:596
  The Tropics in New York.
    C. McKay. Ad-PB:25, Bo-AN:28,
    Bo-HF:167, Hu-PN:95, Lo-TY:118
  The Unicorn. W. Hoffman. Sc-TN:105
  Uptown. A. Ginsburg. Br-TC:150
  Van Winkle. H. Crane. Ga-FB:269,
    Sh-AP:199, Un-MA:521
  Visiting Second Avenue.
    E. Greenberg. Ho-TY:311
  When Dawn Comes to the City:
    New York. C. McKay.
    Bo-HF:30, La-OC:138
  Wonderful New York. C. Meyer.
    Jo-VC:11
  Yiddish Poets in New York.
    M. Stiker. Ho-TY:281
NEW YORK, N.Y. - HISTORY
  As Tawny Tigers. H. Melville.
    Kr-OF:148
  School Days in New Amsterdam.
    A. Guiterman. Fe-FP:411
NEW ZEALAND: see also MAORIS
  Old Dance Song. Tr-US II:110
NEW ZEALAND - HISTORY AND
    PATRIOTISM
  The Song of the Aotea Canoe.
    Tr-US II:108
NEWARK, N.J.
  Newark, for Now. C. Rodgers.
    Ad-PB:430
NEWFOUNDLAND, CAN.: see also
    DIALECTS - NEWFOUNDLAND
  The Way of Cape Race.
    E. Pratt. Do-WH:47
NEWPORT, R.I.
  The Jewish Cemetery at Newport.
    H. Longfellow. Ke-PP:69,
    Pa-HT:22, Sh-AP:34
NEWS: see also HUMOR - NEWS;
    REPORTERS; SATIRE - NEWS
  Brazilian Happenings.
    R. O'Connell. Du-SH:97
  How They Brought the Good News
    from Ghent to Aix. R. Browning.
    Ar-TP3:31, Co-RG:31, Er-FA:378,
    Gr-EC:156, Hi-WP I:66, Li-SR:12,
    Sp-OG:29, Un-GT:149

News. E. Auerbach. Ho-TY:299
Night Mail. W. Auden. Gr-CT:407,
Ha-PO:44, Hi-WP I:132
Sing, Brothers, Sing! W. Rodgers.
Un-MB:482
Song to Accompany the Bearer of
Bad News. D. Wagoner.
Mo-BG:192
To the Electric Chair.
E. Auerbach. Ho-TY:300
What's the News? Mo-MGT:102
NEWSBOYS: see also HUMOR - NEWSBOYS
Nestus Gurley. R. Jarrell.
Br-TC:216
New Paper Boy. A. Cresson.
Ke-TF:301
NEWSPAPERS: see also HUMOR -
NEWSPAPERS; REPORTERS;
SATIRE - NEWSPAPERS
After the Last Bulletin.
R. Wilbur. Al-VBP:1252,
Un-MA:676
Carl Hamblin. E. Masters.
Kr-OF:113, Sh-AP:137, Wi-LT:114
Coming and Going. N. Goodman.
Ca-VT:497
The Daily Globe. H. Nemerov.
Ha-TP:16
The Day after Sunday.
P. McGinley. Un-MA:595
Editor-Weekly Journal. C. Hyde.
Ke-TF:297
The Morning Star. P. St. John.
Ad-PB:346
The News Stand. D. Berrigan.
Ad-CI:35
Newspaper. A. Fisher. Au-SP:102
Not Unavenged! W. Burleigh.
Kr-OF:135
The War for Truth. W. Bryant.
Kr-OF:133
What's in the Newspaper Tonight?
R. Holzinger. La-IH:17
When Virtue's Temple Falls.
S. Little. Kr-OF:137
NEWTON, SIR ISAAC
Epitaph Intended for Sir Isaac
Newton. A. Pope.
Al-VBP:542, Pl-IO:157
Letter to Alex Comfort.
D. Abse. Br-TC:1
Newton. W. Wordsworth.
Pl-IO:158
To the Memory of Sir Isaac
Newton. J. Thomson. Pl-IO:159
NEWTON, IA.
Hometown Name. H. Sloanaker.
Ke-TF:345
NEWTS: see
SALAMANDERS

NEZ PERCÉ INDIANS: see also INDIANS
OF NORTH AMERICA - VERSE—NEZ
PERCÉ
History of Nez Percé Indians.
J. Reuben. Br-MW:133
NIAGARA FALLS
The Great Lakes Suite, V.
J. Reaney. Do-WH:52
The River of Stars. A. Noyes.
Pa-OM:131
NICHOLAS, SAINT: see SANTA CLAUS
NICKNAMES
Mima. W. de la Mare. Br-BC:38
Quartet. Gr-EC:199, Mo-NR:49,
Wr-RM:28
NIGHT: see also BEDTIME; EVENING;
HUMOR - NIGHT; MIDNIGHT
Acceptance. R. Frost. Tr-MR:275
Acquainted with the Night.
R. Frost. Br-TC:135, Ca-VT:18,
Fe-PL:402, Gr-CT:402, Ha-PO:218,
Ha-TP:97, La-OC:136, La-PV:61,
Mo-BG:189, Sh-AP:152, Un-MA:196,
Wi-LT:176
The Aeneid. H. Howard. Ma-YA:54
After Working. R. Bly. Ha-WR:47
The Afterwake. A. Rich. Ho-P:211
An Arab Love-Song. F. Thompson.
Un-MB:78, Un-MW:168
Arizona Village. R. Davieau.
Br-AF:148
At the Airport. H. Nemerov.
Du-SH:163, Mc-WS:115
At the Time That Turned the Beat.
Le-OE:97
At the Time when the Earth.
Le-OE:2
August Night. E. Roberts.
Ha-YA:89
August Night. S. Teasdale.
Un-MA:267
Autumn. T. Hulme. Al-VBP:1152,
Ha-LO:102, Ja-PA:7, Sm-MK:13
Back Yard, July Night. W. Cole.
Co-BN:117
Beale Street, Memphis.
T. Snyder. Hu-NN:54
The Bear. J. Carpenter.
Ls-NY:86
Beasts. R. Wilbur. Br-TC:472
Beauty Once Shared. H. Tappan.
Ke-TF:442
Bedtime. E. Coatsworth.
Gr-TG:52
Beginning. J. Wright. St-H:260
Begonias. Su Tung P'o. Rx-OH:86
Between Motions. J. Mazzaro.
Ls-NY:297
The Bird. R. Tagore.
Pa-SG:132

NIGHT — cont'd.
  Bird and Waterfall Music.
    Wang Wei. Rx-LT:59
  Black-Out. R. Jeffers. Wi-LT:262
  Blind Angel. D. Rokeah. Me-PH:119
  Blue Water. Li Po. Le-MW:109
  Boats at Night. E. Shanks.
    De-CH:313, Ma-FW:54
  The Bridge of Dreams. Teika.
    Ba-ST:25
  Brownstone. R. McKuen. Ha-TP:8
  Bussy d'Ambois. G. Chapman.
    Al-VBP:146
  By Night. R. Francis. Ca-VT:233
  By the Fire. E. Coatsworth.
    Sh-RP:72
  By T'ing Yang Waterfall.
    Hsieh Ling Yuen. Rx-LT:34
  Check. J. Stephens. Ar-TP3:178,
    Br-SS:30, Ha-LO:65, La-PV:129,
    Pe-FB:65, Rd-SS:28, Th-AS:86
  A Child's Winter Evening.
    G. John. De-CH:224
  Chimes. A. Meynell. De-CH:202,
    Tu-WW:70, Un-MB:62
  City Number. C. Sandburg.
    La-OC:109
  The Clock. J. Jaszi. Au-SP:97
  The Clouds Have Left the Sky.
    R. Bridges. De-CH:448
  The Cock. M. Mota. An-TC:113
  Come Night, Come Romeo.
    W. Shakespeare. Co-BL:103
  Coming Home. R. Humphries.
    Tr-MR:256
  Crossing the Bar. A. Tennyson.
    Al-VBP:865, Er-FA:477, Fe-PL:286,
    Ga-FB:127, Ma-YA:199, Mc-PR:105,
    Ox-BN:526, Sp-OG:279
  Curfew. H. Longfellow. Mc-WK:33
  Dance Songs, VIII. Tr-US II:165
  Dark Fills the Sky. B. Dinsdale.
    Le-M:203
  Darkness. Murari. Al-PI:38
  The Darkness Darts. Janine.
    Le-M:214
  Darkness Song. Da-SC:140,
    Le-OE:105
  Dawn Has Yet to Ripple In.
    M. Cane. Un-MA:236
  Day and Night. A. Lindsay.
    Gr-TG:41
  Day That I Have Loved.
    R. Brooke. Fe-PL:400
  The Day's No Rounder than Its
    Angles Are. P. Viereck.
    Sh-AP:229
  Death Songs. L. Mack. Ad-PB:499
  December Stillness. S. Sassoon.
    Tr-MR:57

  Deep Night. Yuan Chi. Rx-LT:26
  The Deer Is Taking Away.
    Ho-SD:19
  Desert Places. R. Frost.
    Un-MA:188
  Domination of Black. W. Stevens.
    Ha-TP:108, Un-MA:244
  Dover Beach. M. Arnold.
    Al-VBP:972, Cl-FC:48, Co-BL:84,
    Er-FA:454, Ga-FB:66, Go-BP:147,
    Ha-PO:187, Hi-WP II:35, Ho-P:201,
    Ke-PP:87, Ma-FW:53, Ma-YA:209,
    Mc-PR:70, Mo-GR:35, Ox-BN:645,
    Pa-GTB:305, Pl-EI:78, Rv-CB:863,
    Un-MW:120
  Down the Glimmering Staircase.
    S. Sassoon. Fe-PL:413
  Dream Song. Bi-IT:128, Da-SC:100,
    Ho-SD:12, Le-OE:107
  Dream Variation. L. Hughes.
    Ad-PB:74, Hu-PN:183, Jo-SA:129,
    Pe-M:88
  Driving to Town Late to Mail a
    Letter. R. Bly. Ca-VT:558,
    Co-BN:201, Co-EL:156, Mo-TS:55
  Enchantment, Night. L. Alexander.
    Ad-PB:58
  Envoy, Passages. R. Duncan.
    Ca-VT:467, Mc-EA:159
  Evening. T. Miller. Ox-BC:210
  Evening Song. J. Toomer.
    Ra-BP:70
  Far Beyond Us. Pa-SG:185
  Fear when Coming Home Through a
    Dark Country Lane. P. Taylor.
    Le-M:207
  The Field Mouse. W. Sharp.
    Co-BBW:42, Fe-FP:137, Rd-SS:34
  Finis. H. Newbolt. Ar-TP3:181
  The First Night of Fall and
    Falling Rain. D. Schwartz.
    Ls-NY:298
  First Note. J. Miller. Sc-TN:168
  Fishing. K. Wright. Ls-NY:309
  Five Short Stanzas, Dark Night.
    Tsou Ti-fan. Hs-TC:348
  Fixer of Midnight. R. Denney.
    Du-SH:54
  Flowers at Night. A. Fisher.
    Br-SG:33
  Flowers of Darkness. F. Davis.
    Ad-IA:12, Ad-PB:95, Be-MA:55,
    Bo-AN:96, Hu-PN:255
  Folding the Flocks. J. Fletcher.
    De-CH:437, De-TT:113
  For Bill Hawkins, a Black Militant.
    W. Harris. Ad-PB:439
  For the Nightly Ascent of Orion
    over a Forest Clearing.
    J. Dickey. Br-TC:88

Four Glimpses of Night. F. Davis.
  Ab-MO:103, Ad-PB:97, Be-MA:54,
  Bo-AN:97, Hu-PN:250
Freezing Night. T'ao Hung Ching.
  Rx-LT:38
The Full Heart. R. Nichols.
  Co-BN:116, Co-PU:58
God's Dark. J. Martin. Fe-PL:336
God's Virtue. B. Barnes.
  Go-BP:22
Going to Sleep in the Country.
  H. Moss. En-PC:204
Good Hours. R. Frost.
  Gr-SS:45, Sp-OG:247
Good Night. V. Hugo.
  Ar-TP3:219, Au-SP:99, Bo-FP:51,
  Br-SS:36, Ch-B:117, Fe-FP:53
Good Night. D. Pierce.
  Ar-TP3:180, Br-SS:29
Good Night and Good Morning.
  R. Milnes. Ox-BC:172
A Goodnight. W. Williams.
  Un-MA:259
Goodnight, Little People.
  T. Hood. Fr-MP:23
The Grave. R. Blair. Al-VBP:543
Harlem Night Song. L. Hughes.
  La-OC:139
Hearing Men Shout at Night on
  McDougal Street. R. Bly.
  Ad-CI:34, Mc-EA:117
Hello! Jao Meng-k'an. Hs-TC:108
Herder's Song. Tr-US I:39
Hidden Treasure. B. Katz.
  Ho-CS:9
Hold Back Thy Hours.
  J. Fletcher. Al-VBP:276
Homecoming - Late at Night.
  Tu Fu. Rx-OH:31
The Horseman. W. de la Mare.
  Ar-TP3:151, Au-SP:341, Bo-GJ:242,
  Cl-DT:62, La-PP:24, Sm-MK:11
Hot Night on Water Street.
  L. Simpson. Br-TC:379
How Goes the Night? Le-MW:125
Hymn to Night. M. Cane. Un-MA:236
Hymn to the Night. H. Longfellow.
  Al-VBP:823, Sh-AP:35
Hymn to the Sun. Be-AP:22,
  Le-OE:9
I Am He That Walks with the
  Tender and Growing Night.
  W. Whitman. Gr-CT:236
I Walk Out into the Country at
  Night. Lu Yu. Rx-OH:108
If the Owl Calls Again.
  J. Haines. Co-BN:107
Illness. B. Pasternak. Ca-MR:170
Impressions. E. Cummings.
  Ad-CI:6, Sm-PT:80, Un-MA:470

In Most Lightsome Darkness.
  M. Korte. Sc-TN:116
In Such a Night. W. Shakespeare.
  Gr-CT:171, No-CL:180
In the Dark None Dainty.
  R. Herrick. Co-EL:92
In the Great Night.
  Bi-IT:132, Ho-SD:46
In the Naked Bed, in Plato's Cave.
  D. Schwartz. Ca-VT:365,
  Un-MA:619, Wi-LT:515
In the Silent Night. J. Yokomizo.
  Ba-HI:71
In the Summer. D. Aldis.
  Mc-AW:41
The Interrupted Concert.
  F. García Lorca. Le-SW:79
Inversely, as the Square of Their
  Distances Apart. K. Rexroth.
  Mo-TS:24
The Isle of Portland. A. Housman.
  Un-MB:102
It Is a Night of Milky Clouds.
  S. Gash. Le-WR:25
It's Cool. J. Sternberg. Ho-TY:196
January Night. R. Arrieta.
  Pa-SG:30
The Journey. Hu Feng. Hs-TC:375
June Night on the River.
  J. Knoepfle. St-H:99
Kill That Crowing Cock. Rx-LT:18
Late at Night. Hsü Chih-mo.
  Hs-TC:82
Light the Lamps Up, Lamplighter.
  E. Farjeon. Br-SS:28, De-CH:439
Lines for a Bed at Kelmscott
  Manor. W. Morris. De-CH:445,
  Ho-WR:235, Rd-SS:14
The Little Fox. M. Edey and
  D. Grider. Ar-TP3:64
The Little Green Orchard.
  W. de la Mare. Ar-TP3:159,
  Na-EO:86
Little Ivory Figures Pulled with
  String. A. Lowell. Al-VBP:1124
A Little Night Music.
  F. Stefanile. De-FS:188
Little Song of the Sun.
  Tr-US II:247
A London Thoroughfare Two A.M.
  A. Lowell. Ni-JP:131
Looking at the Moon and Thinking
  of One Far Away.
  Chang Ching-Ling. Pa-SG:145
Love in Moonlight. Bhartrihari.
  Pa-SG:64
Lullaby. E. Ford. Rd-SS:25
Mad Song. W. Blake. Rv-CB:566
Madam Mouse Trots. S. Sitwell.
  Ha-LO:9

NIGHT — <u>cont'd</u>.
A Mask Presented at Ludlow
    Castle. J. Milton.
    Al-VBP:397, Sm-LG:51
Medicine Song. Da-SC:87, Le-OE:98
Meeting at Night. R. Browning.
    Co-BL:115, Ga-FB:62, Ho-LP:11,
    Ni-JP:98, Ox-BN:533, Rv-CB:819,
    Tu-WW:39, Un-MW:115
Metaphor. C. Smith. De-FS:185
Midnight. T. Sackville. De-CH:107,
    De-TT:150, Rd-OA:205
Midnight in the Garden.
    Li Shang-Yin. Le-MW:63
A Midnight Memory. Lu Li.
    Hs-TC:422
Moon. N. Alterman. Me-PH:108
Moon and Fog. A. Derleth.
    De-FS:72
The Moon and the Nightingale.
    J. Milton. Gr-CT:401
Moon-Come-Out. E. Farjeon.
    Ar-TP3:179, Mc-AW:12
The Moon Has Set. Sappho.
    Gr-CT:404
Moon-Night. J. von Eichendorff.
    Pa-SG:113
The Moon Ship. Hitomaro.
    Ch-B:46, Le-MW:38
Moonlight. B. Nance. Br-AF:153
A Moonlight Night.
    Liu Fang-P'ing. Le-MW:27
Moonlight . . . Scattered Clouds.
    R. Bloomfield. Ox-BN:55
Moonlit Apples. J. Drinkwater.
    Co-BN:132, Go-BP:113
A Moth Flies round the Window.
    J. Bairstow. Le-M:201
Motionless Night. S. Tsuboi.
    Sh-AM:74
My Imagination. M. Petla.
    Ba-HI:116
Negro Woman. L. Alexander.
    Ad-PB:58
Night. Ai Mu. Hs-TC:436
Night. G. Bacovia. Mc-AC:35
Night. W. Benét. Un-MA:322
Night. W. Blake. Br-SC:33,
    Ch-B:13, Co-BN:111, De-CH:432,
    Fe-FP:53, Fe-PL:404, Ho-WR:197,
    Ox-BC:88, Rd-SS:29, Rv-CB:592,
    Un-GT:263
Night. C. Bullwinkle. Bo-FP:45
Night. M. Butts. Rd-SS:11
Night. H. de Regnier. Pa-SG:112
Night. Fang Ching. Hs-TC:383
Night. D. Hayes. Rd-SS:5
Night. P. Hubbell. La-PV:56
Night. R. Jeffers. Sm-PT:155,
    Un-MA:367

The Night. M. Livingston.
    La-PV:54
Night. T. McGrath. Bl-FP:48
Night. L. McKay. Br-SS:30
Night. C. Sandburg. La-OC:132
Night. Sappho. Pa-SG:63
Night. S. Sutu. Lo-TY:175
Night Airs. W. Landor.
    Co-BN:118, Gr-CT:402
Night and a Distant Church.
    R. Atkins. Ad-PB:198
Night and Morning. D. Aldis.
    Co-PS:89, Ha-YA:58
Night at Anchor by Maple Bridge.
    Chang Chi. Rx-LT:64
Night at Yen Chou.
    Chou Shang Ju. Le-MW:55
Night Blessing. P. George.
    Al-WW:118
Night, Death, Mississippi.
    R. Hayden. Ca-VT:357
Night Enchantment. E. Muth.
    Br-SS:170
A Night Frozen Hard. S. Ito.
    Sh-AM:103
Night Has Come. Gr-BB:32
Night in Boston. J. Harrison.
    Sc-TN:86
Night in November. D. McCord.
    Ls-NY:147
Night in the Desert. R. Southey.
    Mc-PR:146
Night Is Still Young.
    Chang Hsiu-ya. Pa-MV:30
Night Journey. T. Roethke.
    Bl-FP:80, Bo-HF:36, Br-AF:231,
    Gr-EC:239, Ha-TP:25
Night Magic. A. Burr.
    Hu-MP:128, Th-AS:76
Night Mail. W. Auden. Gr-CT:407,
    Ha-PO:44, Hi-WP I:132
Night of Spring. T. Westwood.
    Rv-CB:832
The Night of the Full Moon.
    L. Frankenberg. Co-BL:114
Night of Wind. F. Frost.
    Ar-TP3:64, Fe-FP:173
Night on the Downland.
    J. Masefield. Un-MB:226,
    Wi-LT:192
Night on the Great River.
    Meng Hao Jan. Rx-LT:49
Night on the Prairies. W. Whitman.
    La-RM:68, Tr-MR:288
Night over the Pond. Shiki.
    Be-CS:31
Night-Piece. L. Adams. Un-MA:548
Night Ride. H. Read. Co-BL:111,
    Hi-WP II:61
The Night Scene. Ho Ch'i-fang.
    Hs-TC:222

Night Song. L. Hughes. Ab-MO:99
Night Things Are Soft and Loud.
   Z. Gay. Sh-RP:12
Night Time. P. Wisdom. Le-M:199
Night Train. R. Francis.
   Ar-TP3:84, Ha-LO:87
Night Train. Hsü Chih-mo.
   Hs-TC:93
The Night Will Never Stay.
   E. Farjeon. Au-SP:343,
   De-CH:444, Fe-FP:263, La-PP:27,
   Ox-BC:331, Pe-FB:76, Tu-WW:72
The Night Wind. E. Field.
   Fe-FP:70
Night, Window, Wind.
   J. Anderson. Sc-TN:5
Nightfall. J. Jimenez. Le-SW:75
The Nightingale near the House.
   H. Monro. Un-MB:239
Nocturne. R. Camille. Lo-TY:94
Nocturne. J. von Eichendorff.
   Pa-SG:111
Nocturne. C. Garstin. De-CH:454
Nocturne. O. Paz. Be-UL:69
Nocturne. I. Pillat. Mc-AC:58
Nocturne in a Deserted Brickyard.
   C. Sandburg. Un-MA:201
Nod. W. de la Mare. Rd-SS:12,
   Re-TW:113, Un-GT:303, Un-MB:203
North on One-Eleven.
   J. Knoepfle. St-H:98
November Night. A. Crapsey.
   Fe-FP:83, Hi-WP II:37,
   Ho-LP:32, Hu-MP:321, Ja-PA:41
Now Close the Windows. R. Frost.
   Ha-LO:5
Now Fall Asleep. E. Coatsworth.
   Rd-SS:19
Now Sleeps the Crimson Petal.
   A. Tennyson. Al-VBP:859,
   Gr-CT:63, Hi-WP II:58, Ox-BN:487,
   Rv-CB:787, Un-MW:192
Now the Hungry Lion Roars.
   W. Shakespeare. Al-VBP:184,
   De-CH:123, Gr-CT:154, Gr-EC:92,
   Ma-FW:125, Re-TW:29, Sm-MK:44
Now the Moon Goes Down. Buson.
   Be-SC:59
O Daedalus, Fly Away Home.
   R. Hayden. Ad-PB:116,
   Bo-HF:158, Hu-PN:288, Jo-SA:120
Old Shellover. W. de la Mare.
   Li-LC:60
On a Night of Snow. E. Coatsworth.
   Co-BBW:123, Du-RG:91, Un-GT:48,
   Un-MA:465
On Nights like This All Cities Are
   the Same. R. Rilke. Gr-CC:81
On Visiting a Clear Spring.
   Li Po. Le-MW:56

Orange Tree by Night.
   S. Sitwell. Gr-CC:55
Out in the Dark. E. Thomas.
   Cl-DT:35, De-CH:453, Pa-GTB:444,
   Un-MB:218, Wi-LT:647
Outlaws. R. Graves. Ha-WR:58
Over a Ruined Temple.
   K. Takahama. Sh-AM:162
Paradigm of a Hero. J. Mathews.
   Ha-TP:56
Pardon, Goddess of the Night.
   W. Shakespeare. Al-VBP:186
Peace. W. de la Mare. Ni-JP:79,
   Un-MB:203
Peace on Earth. W. Williams.
   Al-VBP:1153, Ha-LO:24
Peitou Valley. Chang Ch'ou-yü.
   Pa-MV:38
Pine Tree Tops. G. Snyder.
   Ho-P:249
Poem. P. Markish. Ho-TY:181
Poem to Be Read at 3 A.M.
   D. Justice. Du-SH:29, Pe-M:130
Press Close Bare-Bosomed Night.
   W. Whitman. Un-MW:169
Questions at Night.
   L. Untermeyer. Fe-FP:264,
   Un-GB:31, Un-GT:20
Quiet Night. Liu Ta-pai.
   Hs-TC:8
Rainy Night. Feng Chih. Hs-TC:141
Rapunzel Song. G. Meyer. Ls-NY:93
Relieving Guard. B. Harte.
   Co-RG:37, Cr-WS:26, Sp-OG:204
Returning. Ch'en Fu. Le-MW:54
Returning at Night. J. Harrison.
   Ca-VT:710
Rhapsody on a Windy Night.
   T. Eliot. Sh-AP:183
River Moons. C. Sandburg.
   Ma-FW:123
The Robber. W. Turner. Un-MB:345
Seein' Things. E. Field. Hu-MP:130
The Shadow of Night. C. Patmore.
   De-CH:452
The Shopgirls Leave Their Work.
   C. Reznikoff. La-OC:128
Shut Out That Moon. T. Hardy.
   Al-VBP:1047
Silent, Silent Night. W. Blake.
   Rv-CB:604
Sing a Song of Moonlight.
   I. Eastwick. Br-SS:33
Sleep and Dreams. P. Kelso.
   Le-M:212
Sleep upon the World. Alcman.
   Gr-CT:409
Snail, Moon, and Rose. J. Kenward.
   Sm-MK:55
So in the Empty Sky the Stars
   Appear. J. Masefield. Go-BP:109

NIGHT — cont'd.
  So Long. W. Stafford. Mc-EA:167
  So We'll Go No More a-Roving.
    G. Byron. Al-VBP:723, Co-BL:64,
    De-CH:443, Er-FA:105, Fe-PL:108,
    Ga-FB:52, Gr-CC:191, Ha-PO:178,
    Hi-WP II:54, Ho-WR:163, Ma-YA:173,
    Ox-BN:257, Rv-CB:689, Un-MW:89
  Solitaire. A. Lowell. Un-MA:156
  Solitude. H. Monro. Un-MB:236
  Solitude Late at Night in the
    Woods. R. Bly. Ca-VT:558
  Sometimes. R. Fyleman. Br-SS:24
  Song. G. Chapman. Al-VBP:145
  Song. Br-MW:93
  The Song of Shadows.
    W. de la Mare. Un-MB:202
  Song of the Night at Daybreak.
    A. Meynell. De-CH:444
  Song to Night. E. Coatsworth.
    Mc-WK:33
  Sonnets. M. Drayton. Al-VBP:168
  Souls Lake. R. Fitzgerald.
    Br-TC:128
  The Sound of Night. M. Kumin.
    Co-BN:116
  Spring Night. Su Tung P'o.
    Ho-P:250, Rx-OH:89
  Spring Night. S. Teasdale.
    Co-BL:38, Un-MA:264
  Spring River Flowers Moon Night.
    The Emperor Yang. Rx-LT:46
  The Star That Bids the Shepherd
    Fold. J. Milton. Sm-LG:51
  Stars. S. Teasdale. Tr-MR:45
  Stars and Moon on the River.
    Tu Fu. Rx-OH:32
  Stillness. J. Flecker.
    Bo-GJ:126, De-CH:38, Un-MB:272
  Stone Trees. J. Freeman. Co-BN:113
  Stopping by Woods on a Snowy Evening.
    R. Frost. Ad-PE:31, Al-VBP:1134,
    Ar-TP3:198, Bo-FP:170, Bo-GJ:257,
    Br-SS:88, Br-TC:135, Cl-DT:20,
    Co-BN:151, Co-PS:160, De-CH:625,
    Er-FA:257, Fe-FP:67, Ga-FB:299,
    Gr-EC:273, Ha-PO:90, Ke-TF:420,
    La-PP:29, La-PV:167, Ma-FW:276,
    Mc-PR:124, Mc-WK:32, Pe-FB:80,
    Re-TW:123, Sh-AP:150, Sh-RP:52,
    Sm-LG:63, Sm-PT:8, Un-MA:187,
    Wi-LT:174
  The Storm Is Over. R. Bridges.
    Pa-GTB:416, Wi-LT:56
  The Street. O. Paz. La-OC:135
  Street Lamps. D. Lawrence.
    Go-BP:163
  Summer Night. V. Contoski.
    Sc-TN:31
  Summer Night. A. Machado. Le-SW:41

  Summer Stars. C. Sandburg.
    Ha-LO:33
  The Sun Has Set. E. Brontë.
    Al-VBP:921
  Sunday at Hampstead. J. Thomson.
    Al-VBP:1010, Sm-MK:12, Sp-OG:345
  Tailor's Song. P. Dehn. Sm-MK:178
  Tanka. Y. Aizu. Sh-AM:142
  That Wind. E. Brontë. De-CH:215,
    De-TT:181
  There Is a Grave. Chu Hsiang.
    Hs-TC:99
  Thorn Leaves in March. W. Merwin.
    Br-TC:289
  Thought's End. L. Adams.
    Un-MA:543
  The Tide Rises, the Tide Falls.
    H. Longfellow. Co-SS:50,
    De-TT:183, Er-FA:260, Gr-CT:191,
    Ho-WR:135, Mc-PR:73, Pa-RE:75,
    Rv-CB:784
  Tiptoe Night. J. Drinkwater.
    Br-SS:29
  The Tired Worker. C. McKay.
    Ra-BP:60
  To Daisies, Not to Shut So Soon.
    R. Herrick. De-CH:430
  To Jane. P. Shelley. Re-TW:106
  To Night. J. White. Al-VBP:701,
    Co-RG:154, Ke-TF:58, Rv-CB:674
  To the Night. P. Shelley.
    Al-VBP:755, De-CH:438, Fe-PL:401,
    Ho-WR:199, Ox-BN:292, Pa-GTB:188,
    Rv-CB:702, Sp-OG:348
  Tolling Bells. Lady Kosa.
    Pa-SG:23
  Tom o' Bedlam. De-CH:275,
    Ho-PR:51, Mc-WK:5, Sm-LG:203
  Tracking Rabbits: Night.
    J. Barnes. Ni-CD:20
  Tree-Sleeping. R. Coffin.
    Ha-LO:54
  The Turning Year. Su Tung P'o.
    Rx-OH:87
  Two Countries. J. Marti.
    Lo-TY:101
  Two Figures in Dense Violet
    Night. W. Stevens. No-CL:244,
    Un-MA:248
  The Two Spirits. P. Shelley.
    De-CH:323, Ho-WR:189
  Two Splendid Horses. Re-RR:88
  The Two Stars. W. Davies.
    Un-MB:176
  Turned Towards the Moon.
    Yakamochi. Ba-ST:35
  Under a Winter Moon.
    S. Yamaguchi. Sh-AM:171
  Under the Moon. Ho Ch'i-fang.
    Hs-TC:221

Vel. M. Bruce. Ad-II:48
Walking at Night. A. Hare.
  Fe-PL:405
Walking into the Woods. J. Bender.
  Le-M:189
Wanderer's Night Song. M. Bacon.
  Rd-SS:26
Watchman, What of the Night?
  A. Swinburne. Ho-WR:200
We Own the Night. I. Baraka.
  Ad-BO:7, Ad-PB:257
We Will Watch the Northern
  Lights. Ho-SD:2, La-RM:122
Wet Night on a Pavement.
  A. Tessimond. Hi-WP I:129
What's Night to Me. S. Gilford.
  Le-M:210
What's o'Clock XV. A. Lowell.
  Ho-TH:24
When Night Comes. A. Jones.
  Me-WF:56
When That Beam of Light.
  M. Nakagawa. Sh-AM:149
When the Light of Day Fades.
  N. Zabolotzky. Ca-MR:100
The White Moon. P. Verlaine.
  Pa-SG:143
Who Calls. F. Sayers.
  Br-SS:130, Li-LC:89
Who Steals round the House by
  Night? Ir-BB:211
Wind and Silver. A. Lowell.
  Co-PU:140, Mo-BG:152, Un-MA:159
Wind Tossed Dragons. Hsieh Ngao.
  Rx-LT:110
Windy Nights. R. Stevenson.
  Ar-TP3:165, Bo-GJ:35, Br-SS:34,
  De-TT:163, Gr-CC:9, Gr-EC:56,
  Ir-BB:241, Ja-PA:44, Ox-BC:294,
  Sp-OG:307, Tu-WW:25
Winter. W. de la Mare.
  Gr-CT:394, Ha-YA:144
A Winter Night. W. Barnes.
  Gr-CT:394, Ox-BN:430
Winter Night. M. Butts.
  Ar-TP3:198
A Winter Night. B. Pasternak.
  Ca-MR:174
Winter Nightfall. R. Bridges.
  Un-MB:50
Winter Walk. K. van der Veer.
  Ke-TF:86
With the Moon. S. Ogiwara.
  Sh-AM:165
You, Andrew Marvell. A. MacLeish.
  Al-VBP:1193, Br-TC:275,
  Ga-FB:4, Mo-BG:150, Pe-OA:157,
  Sh-AP:134, Sm-PT:85, Wi-LT:342
Young. A. Sexton.
  To-MP:100

NIGHT CLUBS
  Ballad of the Ten Casino Dancers.
    C. Meireles. An-TC:39
  The Imprisoned III.
    R. Fitzgerald. Br-TC:126
  Jazz Band in a Parisian Cabaret.
    L. Hughes. Un-MA:553
  Jazzonia. L. Hughes. Bo-AN:63
NIGHTINGALE, FLORENCE
  Santa Filomena.
    H. Longfellow. Se-PR:63
NIGHTINGALES
  Bianca among the Nightingales.
    E. Browning. Pa-GTB:324
  The Chinese Nightingale.
    V. Lindsay. Un-MA:229
  Come, Come Away! R. Brome.
    Re-BS:22
  The Fields Abroad with Spangled
    Flowers. Gr-CT:106
  For Keats and the Florentine
    Night. G. Kennedy. Ls-NY:141
  Four-Footed Poems.
    E. Greenberg. Ho-TY:312
  The Happy Nightingale.
    Ox-BC:70
  Heaven Is Heaven.
    C. Rossetti. Ha-YA:69
  I Rose Anon. J. Lydgate.
    De-CH:489
  In the Fields of Spring. Ba-ST:19
  Itylus. A. Swinburne. Gr-CT:104
  King David. W. de la Mare.
    Li-TU:169
  Magic Casements. J. Keats.
    Ga-FB:13, Ke-TF:333
  The Moon and the Nightingale.
    J. Milton. Gr-CT:401
  Music's Duel. R. Crashaw.
    No-CL:31
  Nakatsukasa. Shüi Shü. Pa-SG:80
  The Nightingale. R. Barnefield.
    Al-VBP:265, De-CH:100, Pa-GTB:21
  The Nightingale. S. Coleridge.
    De-TT:152
  The Nightingale. M. Stearns.
    Ar-TP3:176
  The Nightingale and the Glowworm.
    W. Cowper. Go-BP:76, Pa-OM:320,
    Un-GT:79
  The Nightingale near the House.
    H. Monro. Un-MB:239
  Nightingales. R. Bridges.
    Gr-SS:52, Ox-BN:877, Rd-OA:194,
    Un-MB:51, Wi-LT:57
  Nightingales. S. Coleridge.
    Gr-CT:102
  Nightingales. Ca-MU:30
  The Nightingales Sing. Uko.
    Le-IS:27

The Nightingale's Song Is
   Beautiful. Issa.   Do-TS:29
Nocturne. J. von Eichendorff.
   Pa-SG:111
Ode to a Nightingale. J. Keats.
   Al-VBP:769, Er-FA:89, Gr-CT:102,
   Li-SR:138, Ox-BN:352, Pa-GTB:248
Peacock and Nightingale.
   R. Finch. Co-BBW:248
Philomela. J. Ransom. Gr-CT:106,
   Sh-AP:179
Prometheus Unbound. P. Shelley.
   Al-VBP:741
The Shadow of Night. C. Patmore.
   De-CH:452
Songs from Cyprus. H.D.
   Gr-CC:21, Un-MA:338
Sonnet. J. Milton. Al-VBP:387
A Sparrow-Hawk. De-CH:101
Sweeney among the Nightingales.
   T. Eliot. Wi-LT:285
To See a Nightingale. De-PP:33
Town and Country. De-PP:36
When Nightingales Burst into
   Song. Jurin. Be-MC:58
A Winter's Dream. De-PP:45
NIGHTMARES
Nightmare. J. Brennan. De-FS:39
Nightmare. R. Grenville.
   De-FS:100
Nightmare. A. Marx. De-FS:136
The Pains of Sleep. S. Coleridge.
   Ox-BN:171, Rv-CB:662
Scenes from a Text. R. Sward.
   St-H:220
Vampire. W. Kerr. De-FS:127
NIJINSKY, VASLAV
For Nijinsky's Tomb.
   F. Cornford. Pl-US:121
Homage to Vaslav Nijinsky.
   J. Kirkup. Pl-US:120
NILE RIVER: see also
   HUMOR - NILE RIVER
Above the Nile. H. Hamilton.
   Ls-NY:245
The Nile. E. Coatsworth.
   Pa-HT:89
The Nile. L. Hunt.
   Al-VBP:712, Ox-BN:220
NKRUMAH, KWAME
Goodbye Nkrumah. D. Di Prima.
   Lo-IT:30
NOAH: see also HUMOR - NOAH
And Did the Animals.
   M. Van Doren. Ca-VT:196
The Animals in the Ark.
   Gr-CT:93, Gr-GB:74
The Ballad of Mrs. Noah.
   R. Duncan. To-MP:106
Ballad of the Flood. E. Muir.
   Ca-MB:34

Genesis A. Ma-YA:8
The History of the Flood.
   J. Heath-Stubbs. Ca-MB:40,
   Ma-FW:38
In Come de Animuls Two by Two.
   Gr-GB:75
Incident with Lions. S. Hay.
   Ls-NY:32
The Mystic Magi. R. Hawker.
   Gr-CT:425
Noah. W. Brown. Sa-B:218
Noah. R. Daniells. Do-WH:45
Noah. H. Hagedorn. Tr-MR:66
Noah. S. Sassoon. Cl-FC:69
Noah and the Rabbit.
   H. Chesterman. Rd-OA:12
Old Noah's Ark. Co-BBW:271
One More River. Cl-DT:52
Parley of Beasts. H. MacDiarmid.
   Rd-OA:22, Un-MB:359
Still, Citizen Sparrow.
   R. Wilbur. Wi-LT:597
NOAH'S ARK: see NOAH
NOBILITY: see ARISTOCRACY;
   HERALDRY; KINGS AND RULERS;
   KNIGHTS AND KNIGHTHOOD
NOISE: see also HUMOR - NOISE;
   SONIC BOOMS; SOUNDS
Bang Street. L. Welch. Er-FA:218
Based on City Rhythms.
   L. McDowell. Me-WF:7
Beech Leaves. J. Reeves.
   Pa-RE:108, Sh-RP:222
Bim, Bam, Blamity, Blee. Re-RR:13
City Afternoon. B. Howes.
   Br-AF:211, Ha-TP:9
Companions. M. Widdemer.
   De-FS:218
Extremes. J. Riley.
   Bo-FP:18, Ch-B:80, Fe-FP:104,
   Gr-EC:201, Hu-MP:55
King Juke. K. Fearing.
   Mo-BG:32, Ni-JP:92
Naughty Donna. L. Hopkins.
   Ho-GC:39
The Pier. E. Lozada. Le-M:117
Rest Hour. G. Johnston.
   Do-WH:10
Roller Skates. J. Farrar.
   Fe-FP:106
Sound. J. Harrison. Ca-VT:711
Wind Song. L. Moore.
   Un-GB:11
NOMADS: see also BEDOUINS;
   GYPSIES
Dastangha. Tr-US II:136
NONENTITY: see also
   ANONYMITY
Poem. I. Charik.
   Ho-TY:191

NONSENSE: see also LIMERICKS;
  and subheadings under HUMOR
Advice. A. Resnikoff. Co-OH:84
After Ever Happily.
  I. Serraillier. Co-BL:151,
  Gr-EC:190, Ma-FW:145
The Akond of Swat. E. Lear.
  Br-LL:55, Co-FB:421, Lo-LL:85,
  Sm-MK:100, Un-GT:226
Alas, Alack! W. de la Mare.
  Ar-TP3:124, Fe-FP:132, Hu-MP:43,
  Ir-BB:64, Na-EO:152, Ox-BC:327
Alas! Alas! For Miss Mackay!
  Ir-BB:63
All Dressed Up. A. Spilka.
  Su-FVI:14
All I Need to Make Me Happy.
  Un-GT:18
America, I Love You. B. Kalmar.
  Co-FB:270
Animal Fair. Au-SP:30, Co-IW:7,
  La-PP:53, Mc-PR:41, Un-GT:231
As Freedom Is a Breakfastfood.
  e. cummings. Ca-VT:181,
  Wi-LT:364
As I Was Going Out One Day.
  Co-OW:43, Ir-BB:57
As I Was Walking Along in the
  Fields. Ir-BB:62
Ascot Waistcoat. D. McCord.
  Co-FB:425
The Axolotl. D. McCord.
  Co-FB:420
The Baker's Tale. L. Carroll.
  Un-GF:28
Ballad. C. Calverly. Co-FB:262,
  Ho-WR:56, Li-SR:34
The Ballad of Sir Brian and the
  Three Wishes. N. Levy.
  Co-FB:271
Barney Bodkin. Ir-BB:135,
  Rv-ON:80
The Bigger-Wiggers. P. Ilott.
  Ir-BB:68
Billy and the Butterfly.
  Ir-BB:163
Boston Charlie. W. Kelly.
  Bo-GJ:152, Co-FB:269
Brave Alum Bey. W. Gilbert.
  Co-SS:151
Brian O'Linn. Co-HP:26,
  Gr-GB:164
Buzz, Buzz, Buzz. Bu-DY:90
Calico Pie. E. Lear.
  Au-SP:225, Bl-OB:12, Fe-FP:356,
  Hu-MP:461, Ir-BB:88, It-HB:57,
  Li-LC:67, Lo-LL:67, Pa-RE:109,
  Rv-CB:811, Sm-LG:87, Tu-WW:114,
  Un-GB:29, Un-GF:33, Un-GT:225
Carry and Kate. W. Rands. Ir-BB:94

Catch a Little Rhyme.
  E. Merriam. La-PV:36
The Ceiling. T. Roethke.
  Gr-EC:188, Li-LC:40
Les Chasse-Neige. R. Lewin.
  Co-FB:420
The Chickamungus. J. Reeves.
  Un-GT:222
Chicken Come Clock. Rv-ON:27
Chorus. W. Rands. Ox-BC:233
Cinderella. Co-OW:36
Clara Codd and Frederick Friddle.
  M. Michaels. Un-GF:67
Cold Are the Crabs. E. Lear.
  Bo-GJ:39
The Comical Girl. M. Pelham.
  Co-HP:102, Ir-BB:103
The Common Cormorant.
  Bl-OB:66, Co-FB:371, Co-HP:21,
  Gr-CT:21, Gr-EC:28, Ir-BB:82,
  Lo-LL:33, Pa-RE:66, Sm-LG:90,
  Sm-MK:192, Un-GT:223
The Corner. W. de la Mare.
  Br-BC:136, Ir-BB:67
A Cottage in Fife. Ir-BB:139,
  Lo-LL:75, Mo-MGT:170, Wi-MG:44,
  Wr-RM:78
The Courtship of the Yonghy-
  Bonghy-Bo. E. Lear. Ho-WR:50,
  Na-EO:171, Pa-OM:59, Un-GT:213
Cow. W. Smith. Co-OW:58
The Cumberbunce. P. West.
  Co-OH:63
The Dame of Dundee. Ir-BB:208
A Dash to the Pole. W. Irwin.
  Co-HP:80
Dicky Dan. Ir-BB:211
Dinky. T. Roethke. Co-OW:27,
  Li-TU:72
Dismal Observations.
  J. Wheelock. Pl-ML:64
Do You Know the Man? Co-OH:76
Do You Plan to Speak Bantu?
  O. Nash. Co-FB:413
The Dong with the Luminous Nose.
  E. Lear. Co-PM:115, Ga-FB:325,
  Gr-CT:24, Ho-WR:228, Rv-CB:813
The Dormouse and the Frog.
  R. Goodchild. Ir-BB:81
The Doze. J. Reeves.
  Co-BBW:286, Un-GT:223
A Dream. M. Stiker. Ho-TY:281
The Duck and the Kangaroo.
  E. Lear. Ox-BC:186
Eeka, Neeka. W. de la Mare.
  Ir-BB:133, Mc-WK:105
Evidence Read at the Trial of
  the Knave of Hearts. L. Carroll.
  Er-FA:217, Pa-GTB:378, Un-GF:23
A False Gallop of Analogies.
  W. St. Leger. Co-FB:416

NONSENSE — <u>cont'd</u>.

Fascination. J. Tabb. Co-OH:80

Father Goose Tells a Story.
A. Resnikoff. Co-OH:60

A Flea and a Fly in a Flue.
Br-LL:9, Ch-B:113, Co-HP:29,
Fe-FP:365, Gr-EC:196, Lo-LL:49,
Mc-WS:179, Un-GT:241

The Folk Who Live in Backward
Town. M. Hoberman. Ar-TP3:135

For Every Evil under the Sun.
Li-LB:161, Na-EO:161, Wr-RM:32

The Frog. Co-OW:76, Gr-EC:17

The Funny Beasts. Ir-BB:82

A Funny Man. N. Joan. Ir-BB:214

Fussy. L. Richards. Hu-MP:446

The Gardener's Song. L. Carroll.
Co-FB:384, Co-HP:40, Gr-CC:155,
Ir-BB:144, Na-EO:52, Ox-BC:249

The Giraffe and the Tree.
W. Turner. De-CH:279

Glue. G. Burgess. Co-OH:69

Goody Goody Gout. Bu-DY:91

The Great Panjandrum. S. Foote.
Bl-OB:13, Co-HP:57, Fe-PL:230,
Gr-EC:189, Ir-BB:64, Lo-LL:62,
Sm-LG:282

The Ha! Ha! V. Vickers.
Ir-BB:83

Had a Little Mule. Ju-CP:2

Harriet Hutch. L. Richards.
Ir-BB:97, Ne-AM:47

Hexameter and Pentameter.
Gr-CT:21

Hey Diddle Diddle. Ar-TP3:118,
Au-SP:13, Bo-FP:29, De-PO:20,
Er-FA:506, Ir-BB:14, 203,
Li-LB:104, Mo-CC:(7), Mo-MGT:83,
Mo-NR:44, Re-RR:111, Wi-MG:19,
Wr-RM:60

Higgledy, Piggledy, See How They
Run. K. Greenaway.
Ar-TP3:123, Ir-BB:190

The High Barbaree. L. Richards.
Au-SP:281

Hokey Pokey. Bu-DY:90

The Horny-Goloch. Co-BBW:292,
Ir-BB:88, Lo-LL:71

A Horse and a Flea. Er-FA:499

The Horses Run Around. Co-OH:78

How Pleasant to Know Mr. Lear!
E. Lear. Co-FB:45, Co-HP:90,
Gr-CT:463, Ha-PO:240, Li-SR:43,
Pa-GTB:356, Pl-ML:22, Rv-CB:810,
Tu-WW:118, Un-GT:212

How to Recognize a Snark.
L. Carroll. Hu-MP:462

Humpty Dumpty's Song. L. Carroll.
Bl-OB:14, Co-FB:369, Gr-CT:29,
Ir-BB:130, Ox-BC:245, Pa-GTB:377,
Pa-OM:11, Un-GT:209

The Hunting of the Snark.
L. Carroll. Co-FB:156,
Co-HP:43, Ox-BN:728, Pa-OM:14

Hycokkalorum. V. Vickers.
Ir-BB:83

I Have Three Presents. De-CH:629

I Knew a Cappadocian.
A. Housman. Co-FB:371

I Know a Funny Thing. Ju-CP:6

I Saw a Dog. I. Orleans.
Ir-BB:79

I Saw a Fishpond All on Fire.
Gr-CT:153, Gr-EC:191, Gr-GB:91,
Ir-BB:143, Mo-MGT:92

I Saw a Peacock.
Bl-OB:26, Co-PM:204, De-CH:278,
Gr-CC:148, Gr-CT:154, Gr-EC:193,
Gr-GB:90, Lo-LL:66, Mo-MGT:195,
Pl-IO:106, Rv-CB:417, Sm-LG:281,
Sm-MK:28, Un-GT:226

I Saw an Old Man. Ir-BB:236

I Stood on the Bridge at Midnight.
Er-FA:499

I Think So: Don't You? Ir-BB:132

I Went down the Garden. Ir-BB:136

I Went Downtown. Ir-BB:145

I Wish that My Room Had a Floor.
G. Burgess. Br-LL:111,
Co-FB:387, Co-HP:36, Fr-WO:45,
La-PP:73, Lo-LL:76, Sh-RP:144,
Un-GF:64, Un-GT:241

Ibbity, Bibbity, Sibbity.
Bu-DY:91, Ir-BB:19, Su-FVI:80

If a Man Who Turnips Cries.
Er-FA:216, Fr-WO:51, Gr-EC:286,
Na-EO:52, Sp-TM:30, Un-GF:20

If All the World Was Apple Pie.
An-IP:(14), Au-SP:219, Bo-FP:54,
Er-FA:505, Lo-LL:5, Mo-NR:114,
Un-GF:13, Wr-RM:104

If All the World Were Paper.
Ag-HE:27, Bl-OB:20, Gr-GB:91,
Ir-BB:119, Mo-MGT:99, Rv-CB:139,
Sp-HW:6, Wi-MG:59

If Buttercups Buzz'd after the Bee.
Sm-LG:281

In the Beginning. W. Barney.
De-FS:16

Jabberwocky. L. Carroll.
Ar-TP3:129, Bo-GJ:148, Co-FB:433,
Er-FA:200, Fe-FP:334, Fr-WO:64,
Ga-FB:317, Li-SR:18, Mc-PR:42,
Ox-BC:241, Rv-CB:925, Sp-OG:246,
Un-GF:26, Un-GT:208

The Jam Fish. E. Parry.
Ox-BC:310

Jim Jay. W. de la Mare.
Br-SS:10, Ir-BB:152,
Sm-MK:207, Un-GT:105

Johnnie Crack and Flossie Snail.
  D. Thomas. Bo-FP:24, Bo-GJ:150,
  Co-FB:373, Fe-FP:332, Ha-LO:21,
  La-PV:218, Li-LC:43, Pa-RE:62,
  Su-FVI:21
Jonathan. R. Fyleman.
  Ar-TP3:133, Ja-PC:27
Josephine. A. Resnikoff.
  Co-OT:31
The Jumblies. E. Lear.
  Ar-TP3:141, Au-SP:267, Bl-OB:54,
  Bo-GJ:145, Co-HP:88, Er-FA:203,
  Gr-CT:6, Ho-WR:132, Ir-BB:248,
  Lo-LL:13, Na-EO:144, Ox-BC:187,
  Sm-MK:128
Just like Me. Wr-RM:28
The Knight's Song. L. Carroll.
  Ir-BB:142, Un-GT:210
Ladies and Gentlemen. Bu-DY:93
The Land of Bumbley Boo.
  S. Milligan. St-FS:115
Little Dicky Dilver. Gr-CC:159,
  Ir-BB:59, Mo-MGT:16
The Little Green Blackbird.
  K. Patchen. En-PC:109
Little Man. I. Orleans.
  Ir-BB:146
The Little Man Who Wasn't There.
  H. Mearns. Au-SP:284, Co-HP:97,
  Er-FA:217, Fe-FP:362, Fe-PL:232,
  Fr-WO:53, Ir-BB:203, Un-GF:69
A Little Pig Found a Fifty-Dollar
  Note. Ir-BB:63
The Lobster Quadrille. L. Carroll.
  Bo-FP:267, Fe-FP:135, Gr-CT:29,
  Hu-MP:436, Ox-BC:240, Pe-FB:90
Logical English. Co-HP:21,
  Gr-EC:126
The Lost Egg. P. Ilott.
  Gr-EC:158, Ir-BB:63
Lovers, and a Reflection.
  C. Calverly. Li-SR:40
A Man in Our Town. Wr-RM:30
The Man in the Moon.
  Ir-BB:149, Li-LB:59, Wr-RM:73
A Man of Words. Bl-OB:156,
  De-TT:72, Er-FA:274, Gr-EC:208,
  Rv-CB:450, Rv-ON:115, Sm-LG:235,
  Sp-AS:35
Master Riddle-Me-Roo. Ir-BB:198
The Men of Gotham. T. Peacock.
  Al-VBP:715, De-CH:193,
  Hi-WP I:91, Ho-WR:108,
  Sp-OG:344
Merry Are the Bells. Ar-TP3:106,
  De-TT:116, Hi-GD:15, Ir-BB:118,
  Lo-LL:108, Sp-AS:38
Merry Thoughts. L. Richards.
  Co-OW:44
Missing Commas. Mo-MGT:123

Mr. and Mrs. Spikky Sparrow.
  E. Lear. Ox-BC:190
Mr. Kartoffel. J. Reeves.
  Co-OW:54, Sm-MK:116
Mixed. Ir-BB:71
The Mock Turtle's Song.
  L. Carroll. Ir-BB:126
The Monotony Song. T. Roethke.
  Co-OT:14, Li-TU:63
The Moon Bird. V. Vickers.
  Ir-BB:83
My Mother Bought a Donkey.
  Ir-BB:155
My Name Is Sittiest Ditty. Bu-DY:93
Myrtle. T. Roethke. Pa-RE:11
The Nettle-Rasher. V. Vickers.
  Ir-BB:83
A New Song to Sing about
  Jonathan Bing. B. Brown.
  Au-SP:256, Co-OW:60
No, Really! Ir-BB:58
Nonsense. N. Koralova. Mo-MI:54
A Nonsense Alphabet. E. Lear.
  Au-SP:258, Gr-EC:257, Ox-BC:192
A Nonsense Song. S. Benét.
  Tu-WW:113
Nonsenses. E. Lear. Ox-BC:183
A Norrible Tale. Co-OT:76
Nottamun Town. Bl-OB:23
Nursery Rhyme. W. Auden. Gr-SS:150
O! Susanna. S. Foster. Er-FA:431
Old Joe Clarke. Co-OH:82
Old Quin Queeribus. N. Turner.
  Ar-TP3:139, Au-SP:245, Br-SG:44,
  Co-HP:116, Ir-BB:197, Ja-PC:38,
  Na-EO:77
On a Flimmering Floom You Shall
  Ride. C. Sandburg. Gr-EC:187
On Christmas Eve I Turned the
  Spit. Ir-BB:135
On the Ning Nang Nong.
  S. Milligan. Co-OW:59, St-FS:55
One Bright Morning. Na-EO:132
Order in the Court. Co-OW:63,
  Su-FVI:6
Outside My Door I Heard Someone
  Say. Wy-CM:38
The Owl and the Eel and the
  Warming-Pan. L. Richards.
  Na-EO:72
The Owl and the Pussy-Cat. E. Lear.
  Ar-TP3:120, Au-SP:266, Bl-OB:117,
  Bo-FP:25, Bo-GJ:14, Cl-DT:30,
  Co-IW:3, Er-FA:495, Fe-FP:354,
  Fe-PL:237, Fr-WO:39, Ha-PO:239,
  Hi-WP I:94, Hu-MP:450, Ir-BB:250,
  Ke-TF:38, La-PV:204, Mc-PR:40,
  Ox-BC:185, Pa-GTB:357, Pe-FB:96,
  Rv-CB:812, Sm-LG:89, Sm-MK:200,
  St-FS:108, Un-GB:28, Un-GT:224

NONSENSE — cont'd.
Paripace and Paripale. R. Flower.
    Ir-BB:155
A Peanut Sat.   Co-OH:38, Ir-BB:154
The Perfect Reactionary.
    H. Mearns.   Co-HP:97
Peter and Michael.   Ir-BB:172
Pick Me Up.   W. Smith.   Ir-BB:136,
    Sh-RP:134
The Pig and the Paddy.
    E. Mathias.   Ir-BB:57
A Pig-Tale.   L. Carroll.   Ch-B:65,
    Fe-FP:346, Ho-WR:80, Pa-RE:27,
    Rd-OA:94
A Pin Has a Head.   C. Rossetti.
    Ir-BB:132
The Pobble Who Has No Toes.
    E. Lear.   Bl-OB:16, Co-HP:89,
    Gr-EC:26, Hu-MP:465, Ir-BB:153,
    Lo-LL:72, Ox-BC:198, Sm-LG:93,
    Un-GB:24, Un-GF:34, Un-GT:212
Pocket Full of Rocks.   Ju-CP:2
Poor Bess.   Ja-PC:39
Poor Old Lady.   Au-SP:251,
    Co-HP:22, Un-GT:231
porky & porkie.   e. cummings.
    Li-TU:215
Possum up a Gum Tree.   Ju-CP:2
Praise to the End. T. Roethke.
    Li-TU:214
The Precise Guinea-Pig.
    Gr-EC:189, Ir-BB:135,
    Lo-LL:19, Un-GT:229
Pudden Tame.   Gr-CT:27
The Purple Cow.   G. Burgess.
    Ar-TP3:123, Au-SP:229, Bl-OB:21,
    Co-FB:371, Co-HP:36, Er-FA:200,
    Fe-FP:365, Fe-PL:203, Fr-WO:46,
    La-PV:33, Lo-LL:75, Un-GF:64
A Quadrupedremian Song.
    T. Hood.   Ir-BB:123
The Quangle Wangle's Hat.
    E. Lear.   Ir-BB:59, Un-GF:37
Raccoon on a Rail.   Ju-CP:5
A Race.   Mrs. Molesworth.
    Ir-BB:62
Rain.   S. Silverstein. Co-OT:11
A Reunion in Kensington.
    S. Cohen.   Sm-MK:204
The Riot.   Ir-BB:141, Mo-MGT:168
Robin the Bobbin.   Ir-BB:59,
    Mo-MGT:101
A Sad Case of Misapplied Concen-
    tration.   L. Sieveking.
    Co-HP:112
A Seaside Romance.   D. Marquis.
    Co-HP:93
Sheep-Skin and Bee's Wax.
    Ir-BB:127, Pa-RE:76
The Silly.   De-TT:118

The Skippery Boo.   E. Newton.
    Un-GT:221
The Soft-Nosed Wollop.
    V. Vickers.   Ir-BB:83
Some Fishy Nonsense. L. Richards.
    Ar-TP3:124, Au-SP:234,
    Ir-BB:107, St-FS:60
Some Sights Sometimes Seen and
    Seldom Seen.   W. Cole.
    Co-OH:85
Song for Joey.   M. Browne.
    Co-OT:47
A Song of Thanks.   W. Cole.
    Co-OT:18
The Song of the Dumb Waiter.
    J. Reeves.   Ir-BB:118
The Spangled Pandemonium. P. Brown.
    Ar-TP3:129, Co-OT:22, Lo-LL:70
Speak to Me.   Bu-DY:94
Stalky Jack.   W. Rands.   Ir-BB:102
Story of the Man That Went Out
    Shooting.   H. Hoffmann.
    Ir-BB:58
A Strange Man.   Ir-BB:66
The Sun's Perpendicular Rays.
    W. Mansel.   Gr-CT:11
Surreal Adventure.
    L. Untermeyer.   Un-GF:62
The Swank.   V. Vickers.   Ir-BB:83
The Table and the Chair.   E. Lear.
    Au-SP:221, Bo-FP:26, Ir-BB:235,
    Hu-MP:463, Un-GB:25, Un-GT:215
The Tailor and the Mouse.
    Ir-BB:176
Tea Party.   H. Behn.   Li-LC:35
Teapots and Quails.   E. Lear.
    Bo-GJ:6
Ten Thousand Years Ago.   Co-OH:26
That'll Be All Right You'll Find.
    L. Sieveking.   Co-HP:112
There I Saw.   E. Farjeon.
    Ir-BB:139
There Was a Man of Double Deed.
    De-CH:658, Gr-GB:93, Ir-BB:137,
    Mo-MGT:169, Sm-MK:35
There Was a Man of Thessaly.
    Ir-BB:208, Li-LB:54, Mo-MGT:36,
    Mo-NR:115, Rv-CB:455
There Was a Young Lady Whose
    Chin.   E. Lear.   Ar-TP3:132,
    Au-SP:244, Ir-BB:218, Sh-RP:149
There Was an Old Man of the
    Dargle.   E. Lear.   Gr-CT:28
There Was an Old Man of
    Thermopylae.   E. Lear.
    Fr-WO:41, Na-EO:103
There Was an Old Man on the
    Border.   E. Lear.   Li-LC:47
There Was an Old Person of Skye.
    E. Lear.   Gr-CT:28

There Was an Old Woman Sat
   Spinning. Mo-MGT:193, Un-GT:18
There Were Three Jovial Welshmen.
   Bl-OB:24, Gr-GB:86, Ir-BB:140,
   Mo-MGT:198, Pa-OM:2, Sm-MK:23,
   Sp-HW:23
Thomas a Didymus, Hard of Belief.
   Ir-BB:57
Three Children Sliding. J. Gay.
   De-TT:39, Ir-BB:139, Li-LB:44,
   Mo-MGT:24, Un-GF:13, Wr-RM:13
The Three Foxes. A. Milne.
   Bo-GJ:12, Ox-BC:341
Three Wise Men of Gotham.
   Er-FA:506, Li-LB:75, Mo-MGT:114,
   Mo-NR:134, Wi-MG:40, Wr-RM:25
Three Young Rats. Fr-WO:35,
   Gr-CT:31, Gr-EC:11, Gr-GB:92,
   Ir-BB:234, Lo-LL:41, Mo-MGT:187,
   On-TW:15, Sm-MK:193
Time upon a Once. R. Smith.
   Gr-EC:185
Timmy Pimmy. Gr-EC:281
'Tis Midnight. Co-OW:70
To Be or Not to Be. Co-HP:21,
   Er-FA:202, Gr-EC:168,
   Hi-WP II:12, Un-GT:228
Tonight at Noon. A. Henri.
   To-MP:192
Topsy-Turvy Land. H. Wilkinson.
   Au-SP:256, Ir-BB:56, 71
Topsy-Turvy World. W. Rands.
   Gr-EC:186, Hu-MP:439, Ir-BB:134,
   Mc-PR:176, Ox-BC:232, Un-GF:21
A Tragic Story. W. Thackeray.
   Co-HP:115, De-TT:71, Fe-FP:353,
   Gr-EC:205, Hu-MP:446, Ir-BB:197,
   Pa-OM:74, Sh-RP:42, Un-GT:232
The Train Pulled in the Station.
   Co-OW:50
Tricketty Trock. Ir-BB:71
Tudor Aspersions.
   R. Piddington. Co-FB:418
Tumbling Jack. Ir-BB:213
The Twelve-Elf. C. Morgenstern.
   Un-GF:68
Twelve Huntsmen with Horns and
   Hounds. Ir-BB:141, Pa-RE:54
The Twins. H. Leigh. Ar-TP3:137,
   Br-BC:22, Br-SM:124, Co-HP:91,
   Fe-FP:355, Mc-WK:149, Un-GF:66,
   Un-GT:232
Two Little Men with Equal Feet.
   Fr-WO:54
The Two Old Bachelors. E. Lear.
   Co-FB:55, Co-HP:87
Two or Three. J. Keats.
   Sm-MK:206
Unholy Missions. B. Kaufman.
   Lo-TY:253

Up and down the City Road.
   Mo-CC:(42). Mo-MGT:100,
   Na-EO:175
Up from Down Under. D. McCord.
   Gr-EC:187
The Voice of the Lobster.
   L. Carroll. Ir-BB:146,
   Li-SR:99, Na-EO:39
The Walloping Window-Blind.
   C. Carryl. Co-HP:48, Fe-FP:343,
   Hu-MP:450, Lo-LL:90, Sh-RP:123,
   Un-GF:30, Un-GT:220
The Walrus and the Carpenter.
   L. Carroll. Au-SP:275,
   Bl-OB:125, Co-FB:134, Co-HP:40,
   De-TT:95, Er-FA:500, Fe-FP:328,
   Fr-WO:59, Ga-FB:318, Ir-BB:245,
   Ox-BC:242, Pe-FB:103, Sp-OG:242
Walter Spaggot. P. Wesley-Smith.
   Pa-RE:93
Well I Never! Ir-BB:84
We're All in the Dumps. Bl-OB:10,
   Gr-GB:93, Ir-BB:133
What They Said. Ir-BB:75
What You Will Learn about the
   Brobinyak. J. Ciardi.
   Na-EO:40
What'll Be the Title?
   J. Richardson. Co-FB:413
The Whatnot. V. Vickers.
   Ir-BB:83
When Candy Was Chocolate.
   W. Smith. Ir-BB:242
When Cold December. E. Sitwell.
   Mc-WS:133
When Fishes Set Umbrellas Up.
   C. Rossetti. Ir-BB:132
When I Was a Lad. Br-FF:(16),
   Ir-BB:137
Who Ever Sausage a Thing?
   Co-OH:77, Ir-BB:64, St-FS:34
Why I No Longer Travel.
   L. Richards. Hu-MP:445
Wibbleton and Wobbleton.
   Mo-CC:(47), Mo-MGT:196
Willie Saw Some Dynamite.
   Fe-FP:362, Un-GF:48
Yak. W. Smith. Co-OT:26,
   Ja-PC:20, Sh-RP:342, Un-GT:55
You Look. Bu-DY:94
The Zobo Bird. F. Collymore.
   Bo-GJ:156
See also Em-AF:16-26
NOON
   High Noon! A Hot Sun. Hajime.
      Ca-BF:15
   Noon. R. Jeffers. Un-MA:361
   The Tower of Genghis Khan.
      H. Allen. Pa-HT:85
   Village Noon: Mid-Day Bells.
      M. Moore. Un-MA:576

NORSEMEN: see NORTHMEN
NORTH, CHRISTOPHER, pseud.:
      see WILSON, JOHN
THE NORTH: see also
      SATIRE - THE NORTH
   In the Garden of Paradise Others
      May Bask.   A. Akhmatova.
      Ca-MR:186
   North Wind.   Tr-US II:38
   Northboun'.   L. Holloway.
      Hu-PN:257
   Northbound.   L. Rubin.   Ls-NY:292
   Northern View.   H. Plimpton.
      Ls-NY:293
   you (her eyes, solstice).
      G. Bishop-Dubjinsky.   Sc-TN:10
NORTH AMERICAN INDIANS:
      see INDIANS OF NORTH AMERICA
NORTH CAROLINA
   Brother Jonathan's Lament for
      Sister Caroline.   O. Holmes.
      Hi-TL:102
   Nocturne.   F. Frost.   Co-BN:202
   The Old North State.   W. Gaston.
      Se-PR:277
   Report from the Carolinas.
      H. Bevington.   Br-AF:136
NORTH CAROLINA - HISTORY
   Prayer at the Graves of the
      Murdered Strikers.
      C. Queens.   Kr-OF:157
NORTH DAKOTA
   August from My Desk.   R. Flint.
      Br-AF:156, Du-RG:49
   North Dakota Hymn.   J. Foley.
      Se-PR:278
   Outside Fargo, North Dakota.
      J. Wright.   Kh-VA:10
NORTH SEA
   At Dunwich.   A. Thwaite.   To-MP:182
NORTH STAR
   The North Star.   Br-MW:132
   Polar Star.   Da-SC:11, Le-OE:102,
      Tr-US II:248
NORTHERN CROWN
   Visiting Tsan, Abbot of Ta-Yun.
      Tu Fu.   Rx-OH:7
NORTHERN IRELAND:
      see IRELAND, NORTHERN
NORTHERN LIGHTS: see AURORAS
NORTHMEN
   Beowulf's Voyage to Denmark.
      Ma-FW:45
   The Parklands.   S. Smith.
      Ca-MB:94
   Rumilda's Chant.   G. Darley.
      Co-PI:33, Co-SS:31, Gr-CT:222
   The Story of Vinland.   S. Lanier.
      Hi-TL:9
   The Viking Terror.   Co-PI:138,
      Gr-CT:222

NORTHUMBERLAND, ENG.:   see also
      DIALECTS - NORTHUMBERLAND
   A. U. Hinny Bird.   Gr-GB:170
NORTHWEST PASSAGE: see
      ARCTIC REGIONS
NORWAY: see also HUMOR -
      NORWAY; NORWEGIAN VERSE
   In a Mountain Cabin in Norway.
      R. Bly.   La-RM:23
NORWEGIAN VERSE
   The Call.   B. Björnson.   Ch-B:16
   Husky Hi.   Ar-TP3:101
   Like an April Day.
      J. Wellhaven.   Pa-SG:30
   The Tree.   B. Björnson.   Bo-FP:268,
      Co-PS:75, Fe-FP:467, Hu-MP:271
NOSES: see also HUMOR - NOSES
   Life.   T. Kuramae.   Le-TA:13
   My Nose.   D. Aldis.   Ho-ME:14
   Peter White's Nose.   Ir-BB:199,
      Mo-MGT:73
   Smell.   W. Williams.   Un-MA:259
   Sniff.   F. Frost.   Ar-TP3:113,
      Br-SS:161
   Though It's Close.   Re-RR:12
   Why Do You Suppose.   Re-RR:41
NOSTALGIA: see CHILDHOOD
   RECOLLECTIONS; HOMESICKNESS;
   MEMORIES
NOTHINGNESS: see also
      ANONYMITY; NONENTITY
   The Abyss.   C. Baudelaire.
      Mo-GR:29
   Alone.   K. Taguchi.   Le-TA:93
   The Day We Die.   Le-OE:130
   Death Songs.   L. Mack.   Ad-PB:499
   The Emptiness of Man.
      J. de Melo Neto.   An-TC:159
   Handfuls of Wind. Y. Mar. Me-PH:126
   I Have Come Far to Have Found
      Nothing.   C. Corman.   Ca-VT:527
   Mars Is Out.   K. Takamura.
      Sh-AM:42
   Montana Fifty Years Ago.
      J. Cunningham.   Ho-P:47
   Neither Here nor There.
      W. Rodgers.   Al-VBP:1237,
      Wi-LT:495
   Nothing Is.   Sun Ra.   Ad-PB:207
   Two Poems, II.   R. Abrams.
      Hu-NN:111
   Upon Nothing.   J. Wilmot.
      Al-VBP:504
   The Waste Land.
      T. Eliot.   Pe-OA:112,
      Un-MA:386
   When I Watch the Living
      Meet.   A. Housman.
      Un-MB:96

NOVEMBER
The Crazy Woman. G. Brooks.
   Ab-MO:28, Bo-HF:136, Li-TU:151
The Fields of November.
   M. Van Doren. Ha-WR:85
Harvest. C. Sandburg. Ha-WR:81
Hearth Song. R. Johnson.
   Ha-YA:128
Invisible Painter. A. Dorn.
   De-FS:73
The Mist and All. D. Willson.
   Au-SP:329, Fe-FP:82, Ha-YA:129,
   Hu-MP:318, Ja-PA:43, Pe-FB:88
My November Guest. R. Frost.
   Al-VBP:1125, Bo-HF:130,
   Fe-PL:388, No-CL:280
New England November. D. Hall.
   Ke-TF:448
Night in November. D. McCord.
   Ls-NY:147
No! T. Hood. Bl-OB:99, Co-FB:435,
   Co-HP:78, Gr-CT:392, Mc-PR:51,
   Un-GT:280
November. R. Bridges. Ox-BN:879
November (I Love). J. Clare.
   Bo-FP:148, Ch-B:92, Cl-FC:44
November (The Landscape).
   J. Clare. Ma-FW:266, Un-GT:282
November. E. Coatsworth.
   Ha-YA:130, Ja-PA:46
November. A. Fisher. Br-SS:84
November. C. Gluck. Le-M:132
November. G. Hahn. Ke-TF:449
November. T. Hughes. Pa-GTB:565
November. C. Rossetti. Ha-YA:122
November Day. E. Averitt.
   Du-RG:121
November Garden. L. Driscoll.
   Ha-YA:124
November Glow. H. Rostron.
   St-FS:57
November Morning. E. Blunden.
   Hi-WP II:132
November Morning. E. Stein.
   Ha-YA:127
November Night. A. Crapsey.
   Fe-FP:83, Hi-WP II:137,
   Ho-LP:32, Hu-MP:321, Ja-PA:41
The November Shine.
   R. Humphries. Mo-BG:137
November Wears a Paisley Shawl.
   H. Morris. Bo-FP:148, Ha-YA:126
November Woods. H. Jackson.
   Ja-PA:42
November's Come. J. Lincoln.
   Sh-RP:233
The Pity of the Leaves.
   E. Robinson. Un-MA:137
Sonnet: November. H. Coleridge.
   Ox-BN:398, Se-PR:196

There's Nothing like the Sun.
   E. Thomas. Ga-FB:6
Ways of My Exile. R. Roseliep.
   St-H:181
Weather Vanes. F. Frost.
   Br-SS:72
Winter Landscape. S. Spender.
   Un-MB:473
NUCLEAR ENERGY: see
   ATOMIC ENERGY
NUDISM: see also
   HUMOR - NUDISM
L'Ile du Levant; the Nudist
   Colony. B. Howes. En-PC:137
Mr. Lerner. J. Keith. De-FS:115
NUMBERS: see also
   HUMOR - NUMBERS
Child Margaret. C. Sandburg.
   Ma-FW:74
Counting. H. Behn. Gr-EC:124
A Counting Rhyme. M. Stephenson.
   St-FS:9
The Dream of a Boy Who Lived at
   Nine Elms. W. Rands. Ox-BC:235
The Dream of a Girl Who Lived at
   Seven Oaks. W. Rands. Ox-BC:235
Half of a Quartet Is Twins.
   On-TW:24
I Love You Little, I Love You
   Lots. On-TW:59
The Ideal Age for a Man.
   M. Shannon. Br-BC:43
In the Wood, a Stand of Pine.
   On-TW:32
Mathematics of the Gift of
   Tongues. A. Branch. Pl-IO:72
Nine Times Nine. On-TW:33
Numbers. E. Roberts. Li-LC:18
Numbers and Faces. W. Auden.
   Pl-IO:91
One, Two. R. Ainsworth. St-FS:10
One, Two, Buckle My Shoe.
   Ar-TP3:104, Au-SP:21, Bo-FP:5,
   De-PO:14, Ir-BB:34, Mo-NR:31,
   On-TW:50, Wi-MG:30, Wr-RM:80
One, Two, Three, Four, Five.
   Ar-TP3:103, On-TW:56
One, Two, Three, Four, Five,
   Six, Seven. On-TW:62
One's None. Rv-ON:13
This Old Man, He Played One.
   Au-SP:248, Ir-BB:125, Mo-TL:31
Two or Three. J. Keats.
   Sm-MK:206
What Number Is Larger. Re-RR:114
NUNNERIES: see CONVENTS
   AND NUNNERIES
NUNS
A Ballad of a Nun. J. Davidson.
   Pa-OM:138, Un-MB:74

NUNS — cont'd.
A Drape. Feng Chih. Hs-TC:143
For the Sisters of the Hôtel Dieu.
  A. Klein. Do-WH:85
Four Lovely Sisters. C. Trypanis.
  Co-EL:138
Heaven-Haven. G. Hopkins.
  Al-VBP:1059, Go-BP:274,
  Gr-BT:146, Ha-PO:196,
  Hi-WP II:176, Mc-WK:184,
  Ox-BN:852, Un-MB:44
Letter Written on a Ferry
  Crossing Long Island Sound.
  A. Sexton. Br-TC:365
Nuns at Eve. J. Brinnin.
  Br-TC:64
On a Row of Nuns in a Cemetery.
  R. Howarth. Co-EL:80
The Prologue to the Canterbury
  Tales. G. Chaucer.
  Al-VBP:6, 7, Gr-CT:281,
  Ha-PO:50, Ma-FW:17, Ma-YA:28
Street Scene. R. Mezey. Wi-LT:770
The Wreck of the Deutschland.
  G. Hopkins. Li-TU:220,
  Ox-BN:852, Wi-LT:30
NURSERIES (FOR CHILDREN)
The Nursery. C. Aiken. Ha-LO:10
NURSERY PLAY: see
  ACTION RHYMES
NURSERY RHYME CHARACTERS
Archibald MacLeish Suspends the
  Five Little Pigs.
  L. Untermeyer. Un-MA:310
Contemporary Nursery Rhyme.
  Li-SR:131
Edgar A. Guest Syndicates the
  Old Woman Who Lived in a Shoe.
  L. Untermeyer. Co-FB:232,
  Un-MA:311
Edna St. Vincent Millay Exhorts
  Little Boy Blue.
  L. Untermeyer. Un-MA:310
The Embarrassing Episode of
  Little Miss Muffet.
  G. Carryl. Ha-PO:279,
  Hu-MP:454, Pa-OM:38, Sh-RP:137,
  Un-GF:78
The Gastronomic Guile of Simple
  Simon. G. Carryl. Un-GT:218
Girls and Boys, Come Out to
  Play. I. Serraillier. Ir-BB:17
Hey Diddle Diddle. P. Dehn.
  Co-FB:451, Du-RG:80
John Masefield Relates the Story
  of Tom, Tom, the Piper's Son.
  L. Untermeyer. Un-MA:308
Little Boy Blue. J. Ransom.
  We-PZ:36, Wi-LT:321
Mother Goose (Circa 2054).
  I. Sekula. Br-SM:65

Walter de la Mare Tells the
  Listener about Jack and Jill.
  L. Untermeyer. Un-MA:309
NURSERY RHYMES: see also FOLKLORE;
  NURSERY RHYME CHARACTERS
A Was an Archer. Gr-EC:253,
  Ir-BB:43, Li-LB:110, Mo-NR:28
All I Need to Make Me Happy.
  Un-GT:18
Animal Fair. Au-SP:30, Co-IW:7,
  La-PP:53, Mc-PR:41, Un-GT:231
As I Was Going to St. Ives.
  Au-SP:26, Cl-DT:61, Ir-BB:54,
  Li-LB:168, Mo-NR:122, On-TW:29
As I Was Walking Along in the
  Fields. Ir-BB:62
As I Went up the Garden. St-FS:35
As We Were Going Along, Long, Long.
  Sp-AS:(8)
Baa, Baa, Black Sheep.
  Ar-TP3:74, Au-SP:17, Bo-FP:80,
  De-PO:18, Er-FA:506, Li-LB:89,
  Mo-NR:57, On-TW:15, Pa-AP:30
Bell Horses, Bell Horses, What
  Time of Day. Ar-TP3:174,
  Bo-FP:123, Br-SS:5, Ir-BB:190
Belle Isle. Rv-ON:68
Betty, My Sister. Un-GF:12
Bobbie Shaftoe Has a Cow. Ir-BB:30
Bossy-Cow, Bossy-Cow, Where Do
  You Lie? Ir-BB:28
Brandy Hill. Ir-BB:185, Rv-CB:445,
  Rv-ON:69
Buckee Bene. De-CH:276
Bye, Baby Bunting. Mother Goose.
  Ar-TP3:131, Au-SP:5, Cl-DT:27,
  De-PO:6, Li-LB:12, Li-SR:126,
  Mo-NR:8
Charley, Charley. Br-FF:14
The Clucking Hen. A. Hawkshawe.
  Ch-B:45, Ir-BB:28
Cock a Doodle Doodle Doo.
  De-PO:14, Ir-BB:65,
  Mo-NR:124, St-FS:79
Come On In. Mo-SD:141
Counting Out Rhyme. Li-SR:125
Cry, Baby. Mo-NR:58, Un-GT:17
The Death and Burial of Cock Robin.
  De-TT:41, Ir-BB:114, Mo-MGT:60,
  Mo-NR:143, Un-GT:62, Wr-RM:124
Elder Belder. Rv-ON:61
The Electric Lights Shine in
  Everybody's Heart. Hs-TC:452
Every Time I Come to Town.
  Un-GT:18
Fishy-Fishy in the Brook. Un-GT:18
Frog Went a-Courtin'.
  Su-FVI:73, Un-GT:19
The Funniest Sight That Ever
  I Saw. Un-GT:18

Fuzzy Wuzzy.   Fr-MP:21, Un-GT:18
Green Cheese.   Ir-BB:29
Hark, Hark, the Dogs Do Bark.
  An-IP:(20), Ar-TP3:132,
  Bo-FP:114, Br-FF:(31),
  Cl-DT:16, De-PO:20, Gr-GB:228,
  Li-LB:74, Mo-NR:56
Here Comes a Poor Woman. Ir-BB:96
Hickety, Pickety, My Black Hen.
  Mother Goose.   An-IP:(13),
  Ar-TP3:103, Au-SP:16, Bo-FP:89,
  De-PO:20, Li-LB:93, Mo-NR:23,
  On-TW:34
Higgledy, Piggledy, See How They
  Run.   K. Greenaway. Ar-TP3:123,
  Ir-BB:190
High in the Pine Tree. Sp-AS:(27)
Hippety Hop to the Barber Shop.
  Ar-TP3:100, Au-SP:9, Ir-BB:13
Hot Cockles.   Rv-ON:64
I Asked My Mother for Fifteen
  Cents. Ar-TP3:128, Er-FA:498,
  Ir-BB:185, Un-GT:18
I Doubt, I Doubt.   Rv-ON:67
I Like Coffee, I Like Tea.
  Er-FA:499
I'll Eat when I'm Hungry.
  Un-GT:18
Intery, Mintery, Cutery Corn.
  Ar-TP3:103, Bo-FP:140, Cl-FC:19,
  De-TT:28, Gr-EC:283, Tu-WW:15
Jack Straw's Castle.   E. Farjeon.
  Ir-BB:34
Jacky's Fiddle.   Pl-US:34,
  Rv-ON:101
Jay-Bird, Jay-Bird, Settin' on a
  Rail. Un-GT:18
Jim Jay.   W. de la Mare. Br-SS:10,
  Ir-BB:152, Sm-MK:207, Un-GT:105
Jumping Joan.   Mother Goose.
  Ne-AM:32
Lady-Bug, Lady-Bug! Mo-TB:89,
  Un-GT:72
Ladybird, Ladybird, Fly Away
  Home. Mother Goose. Au-SP:13,
  Bo-FP:323, De-PO:20, Fe-FP:133,
  Ir-BB:227, Li-LB:82, Mo-CC:(23),
  Mo-NR:83, Rv-CB:449, Sm-MK:7,
  Un-GB:16, Un-GF:13, Un-GT:72
Leela.   Ca-MU:29
A Little Old Man Came Riding By.
  Un-GT:18
Load of Hay.   Ir-BB:227, Tu-WW:16
Mary Lost Her Coat. Mother Goose.
  Mo-CC:(18)
Mary, Mary, Quite Contrary.
  Au-SP:7, Bo-FP:253, De-PO:12,
  Er-FA:505, Ir-BB:117, Li-LB:42,
  Mo-CC:(12), Mo-NR:34,
  Sp-AS:(7)

Mary Went Down to Grandpa's
  Farm.   Ir-BB:30
Matthew, Mark, Luke and John.
  Bo-FP:36, De-CH:446, De-PO:28,
  De-TT:202, Gr-GB:298, Gr-TG:55,
  Hi-GD:23, Mo-NR:99, On-TW:18,
  Rd-SS:40, Rv-CB:451, Sm-LG:385,
  Un-GT:23
The Merchants of London.
  Gr-GB:170, Ir-BB:37
Mr. East's Feast.   Ag-HE:20,
  Ir-BB:193
Mix a Pancake.   C. Rossetti.
  Ag-HE:6, Au-SP:10, Bo-FP:53,
  Ch-B:80, Cl-FC:94, Li-LC:45
Monkey Was a-Settin' on a
  Railroad Track.   Un-GT:17
Multiplication Is Vexation.
  Un-GT:23
My Father Owns the Butcher Shop.
  Er-FA:499, Ir-BB:42
Old Joe Brown, He Had a Wife.
  Un-GT:18
Old King Cole.
  Au-SP:4, De-PO:22, Er-FA:507,
  Fr-WO:33, Ir-BB:265, Li-LB:68
Old Mother Hubbard.   An-IP:(8),
  Au-SP:3, Fr-WO:21, Ir-BB:171,
  Li-LB:153, Mo-NR:108, Ox-BC:126,
  Pa-OM:336, Un-GT:102
The Old Woman.   B. Potter.
  Bo-GJ:8, La-PV:118
The Old Woman.   Ca-MU:27
The Old Woman and the Mouse.
  Ir-BB:29, Ju-CP:5
Once I Saw a Little Bird.
  Fr-MP:20, Mo-TL:56
One Misty, Moisty Morning.
  Ar-TP3:166, Cl-DT:85, Ir-BB:212,
  La-PV:92, Li-LB:55, Mo-NR:14,
  Rv-ON:89
One to Make Ready. Mother Goose.
  Bo-FP:264, Li-LB:118, Mo-NR:25,
  Mo-SD:68, Pa-AP:5
Peanuts.   Co-OH:54, Er-FA:200,
  On-GT:18
The Peddler.   E. Farjeon.
  Ir-BB:39
The Periwinkle Diggers.
  Ir-BB:38
Pussy Cat, Pussy Cat. Where Have
  You Been? Ar-TP3:52, Au-SP:15,
  Bo-FP:6, De-PO:18, Er-FA:506,
  Ir-BB:269, Li-LB:88, Mo-NR:100,
  Pa-AP:50
Rain, Rain, Go Away.   Mother
  Goose. An-IP:(25), Ar-TP3:166,
  Au-SP:315, De-PO:26, Mo-CC:(50)
A Rhyme for Shrove Tuesday.
  Cl-FC:93

NURSERY RHYMES — cont'd.

Ride a Cock-Horse to Banbury
Cross.   Ar-TP3:100, Au-SP:15,
Bo-FP:10, De-PO:8, Er-FA:507,
Fr-WO:32, Ir-BB:11, Li-LB:10,
Mo-NR:7, Mo-TL:77

Said the Monkey to the Donkey.
Er-FA:498

A Sailor Went to Sea.   Ir-BB:37

Sam, Sam the Butcher Man.
Er-FA:499, Ir-BB:41

Simple Simon.   Au-SP:9,
De-PO:16, Fr-WO:18, Ir-BB:205,
Li-LB:30, Mo-NR:89, Un-GT:104

The Star.   J. Taylor.
Ar-TP3:178, Au-SP:340, Bo-FP:46,
Cl-DT:37, Er-FA:491, Fe-FP:525,
Gr-EC:90, Gr-TG:50, Hu-MP:121,
Li-SR:93, Mo-CC:(37), Sm-MK:179

Star Light, Star Bright.
Ar-TP3:178, Au-SP:20, Bo-FP:46,
Gr-EC:88, Ir-BB:227, Mo-TB:6,
Tu-WW:16

There Was a Bee Sat on a Wall.
Sp-AS:(8)

There Was a Man of Double Deed.
De-CH:658, Gr-GB:93, Ir-BB:137,
Sm-MK:35

There Was a Man of Our Town.
Mother Goose.   Er-FA:506

There Was a Piper Had a Cow.
Ir-BB:45

There Was an Old Man Named
Michael Finnegan.
Ar-TP3:132, Ir-BB:57, Un-GT:18

There Was an Old Woman as I've
Heard Tell.   Ar-TP3:132,
Co-PS:70, Co-PT:281, De-TT:69,
Gr-EC:204, Ha-PO:281, Li-LB:156,
Mo-NR:63, Pa-OM:5, Un-GT:103

There Was an Old Woman Sat
Spinning.   Un-GT:18

There Was an Owl.   Un-GF:13

This Little Pig Went to Market.
Au-SP:18, Bo-FP:8, De-CH:497,
De-PO:8, Ir-BB:10, Li-LB:20,
Mo-CC:(48), Mo-NR:78,
Mo-TL:15, Sp-TM:23

Three Blind Mice.   An-IP:(19),
Li-LB:103, Mo-NR:47

Three Mice.   C. Cole.   Ir-BB:84,
St-FS:63

The Tokens of Love.   Gr-GB:85,
Ir-BB:44

Tom He Was a Piper's Son. Mother
Goose. Ar-TP3:118, Bo-FP:77,
Gr-GB:99, Ir-BB:31, Mo-NR:64

Tom Tinker's Ground.   Rv-ON:71

Tommy Trot.   Ir-BB:42

T'Other Little Tune.   Pl-US:32,
Rv-ON:102

Two Little Men with Equal Feet.
Fr-WO:54

Way Down Yonder in the Maple
Swamp.   Un-GT:17

Wee Willie Winkie.   Au-SP:8,
Bo-FP:39, Br-SS:36, Cl-DT:31,
De-PO:28, Er-FA:492, Li-LB:39,
Mo-CC:(36), Mo-NR:106,
Ox-BC:172, Rd-SS:7

Went to the River, Couldn't Get
Across.   Un-GT:18

What's Your Name?   Un-GT:18

When I Am the President.
Un-GT:17

When I Was a Little Boy.
Mother Goose.   Tu-WW:15

William McTrimbletoe.   Ir-BB:39

Yes, by Golly.   Mo-SD:141

See also Mo-MGT, Op-ON, Sp-HW,
Sp-TM, Wi-MG, Wr-RM

NURSING: see also NIGHTINGALE,
FLORENCE; RED CROSS

For the Sisters of the Hôtel
Dieu.   A. Klein.   Do-WH:85

He Died a Second Time, 3.
The Hand.   Ai Ch'ing.   Hs-TC:304

The Night Nurse Goes Her Round.
J. Gray.   Ox-BN:940

NUTMEG TREES

I Had a Little Nut-Tree.
An-IP:(20), Ar-TP3:154,
Au-SP:24, Br-FF:(34),
De-CH:186, De-TT:19, Gr-EC:294,
Gr-GB:18, Ir-BB:264, Li-LB:33,
Mo-MGT:148, Rv-CB:453, Sm-MK:7

The King of China's Daughter.
E. Sitwell.   De-CH:186,
Ir-BB:258, Ma-FW:185, Pa-RE:23,
Un-MB:331

NUTS: see also names of nuts,
as ACORNS

Chucklehead.   P. Robbins.   Ar-TP3:61

Nuts.   De-TT:38, Ja-PA:22,
Rv-ON:41

Nutting.   W. Wordsworth.   Rv-CB:637

NYASALAND

Stanley Meets Mutesa.
J. Rubadiri.   Bo-HF:150

NYMPHS (MYTH.)

Gardener Janus Catches a Naiad.
E. Sitwell.   Un-MB:332

The Green Dryad's Plea.
T. Hood.   Ox-BN:414

The Nymph Complaining for the
Death of Her Fawn. A. Marvell.
De-CH:92, Rd-OA:191, Rv-CB:402,
Sm-LG:71

The Nymphs.   J. Hunt.   Ox-BN:221

Oread.   H.D.   Bo-GJ:177, Sh-RP:80,
Un-MA:336

Overheard on a Saltmarsh. H. Monro.
   Ad-PE:17, Ar-TP3:153, Bo-GJ:227,
   Co-PM:125, De-CH:116, Du-RG:67,
   Fe-FP:388, Gr-EC:269, Li-LC:41,
   Mc-WS:29, Re-TW:25, Su-FVI:16,
   Th-AS:14
The Shepherd and the Nymph.
   W. Landor.   Ox-BN:182
The Spirit of the Birch. A. Ketchum.
   Hu-MP:274, Th-AS:135
To the Water Nymphs, Drinking at
   the Fountain. R. Herrick.
   Al-VBP:334
The Water Lady. T. Hood.
   Al-VBP:797, De-CH:279
You Nymphs, Called Naiads.
   W. Shakespeare. Al-VBP:198
OAK TREES: see also ACORNS
Autumn Scene. B. Dowling.
   Co-BN:133
Bearded Oaks. R. Warren.
   Br-TC:451, Sh-AP:211, Un-MA:589,
   Wi-LT:840
Beech and Oak. T. Peacock.
   Rv-CB:687
Dodona's Oaks Were Still.
   P. MacDonogh.   Co-PI:107
The Lazy Hours. Br-FW:4
The Oak. A. Tennyson.
   Ch-B:44, Fe-FP:212, Hu-MP:280
The Oak of Guernica.
   W. Wordsworth. Hi-FO:262
The Raven. S. Coleridge.
   Ho-WR:212
Spring Oak. G. Kinnell.
   Co-BN:40, Co-EL:114, Co-PU:45
The Stump. D. Hall. Du-RG:126,
   Pe-M:81
Sundown. L. Adams. Un-MA:548
Symmetries and Asymmetries.
   W. Auden. Ma-FW:109
To the Oaks of Glencree. J. Synge.
   Co-EL:69, Un-MB:189
Vaunting Oak. J. Ransom.
   Ca-VT:148
Woodchopper's Song. Bu-DY:32
OBATALA, YORUBAN GOD OF CREATION
Invocation of the Creator.
   Be-AP:17
OBEDIENCE: see also HUMOR -
   OBEDIENCE; SATIRE - OBEDIENCE
I Will Bow and Be Simple.
   Pl-EI:188
The Law of the Jungle.
   R. Kipling.   Rd-OA:128

Love Bade Me Welcome. G. Herbert.
   Al-VBP:344, De-CH:463, Fe-PL:115,
   Ga-FB:92, Ga-S:138, Gr-CT:433
The Main Truck; or a Leap for Life.
   G. Morris.   Fe-PL:55
Song for the Heroes. A. Comfort.
   Cr-WS:163, Un-MB:521
Variations on Simonides.
   G. Ely.   Ls-NY:28
OBESITY: see SIZE AND SHAPE
OBLIVION
Go By. A. Tennyson.   Ox-BN:484
Great Aso. T. Miyoshi.   Sh-AM:82
In Ireland: By the Pool at the
   Third Rosses. A. Symons.
   Ox-BN:936
The Lotus-Eaters. A. Tennyson.
   Al-VBP:847, Cl-FC:14, De-CH:615,
   Er-FA:76, Ga-FB:12, Gr-CT:278,
   Ox-BN:477, Pa-HT:158, Pa-OM:296
Meeting Point. L. MacNeice.
   Hi-WP II:62
Oblivion. M. Coicou.   Hu-PN:69
Remembering Min Ch'e.
   Su Tung P'o. Rx-LT:89
To Everlasting Oblivion.
   J. Marston. Rv-CB:311
To the Stone-Cutters. R. Jeffers.
   En-PC:10, Ni-JP:127, Sh-AP:175,
   Un-MA:362
Wants. P. Larkin.   Pa-GTB:556
OBOES
On the Kelantan Oboe. Tr-US II:207
OBSTINACY: see also CONTRARINESS;
   HUMOR - OBSTINACY
A'Dappled Duck. P. Brown. Lo-LL:2
Steel. Rege. Al-PI:134
Time Out. J. Montague.
   Co-PI:143, Ls-NY:196
OCCUPATIONS: see also HUMOR -
   OCCUPATIONS; and names of
   specific occupations, as
   NURSING
The Imprisoned. R. Fitzgerald.
   Br-TC:127
The Outlaw. C. Kingsley.
   Co-RM:161
Sext. W. Auden. Ga-S:118,
   Li-TU:180
Song of Myself. W. Whitman.
   Un-MA:50
OCEANIA: see ISLANDS OF THE
   PACIFIC
OCEANS: see also HUMOR - OCEANS;
   NEPTUNE (GOD); SEAS; TIDES;
   WAVES; and names of oceans,
   as ATLANTIC OCEAN
Are We Their Equals? H. Geltman.
   Le-M:176
Ark of the Covenant. L. Nicholl.
   Pl-IO:36

OCEANS — cont'd.
  At the Edge. M. Korte. Sc-TN:116
  By the Deep Sea. G. Byron.
    Ox-BN:249
  Continent's End. R. Jeffers.
    Ga-FB:312, Pl-IO:53
  The Frozen Ocean. V. Meynell.
    De-CH:389
  The Horses of the Sea.
    C. Rossetti. Bo-GJ:42,
    Fe-FP:274, Li-LC:33
  My Rough Sketch. M. Abvakana.
    Ba-HI:43
  The Ocean. G. Byron. Al-VBP:728,
    Co-SS:46, Ga-FB:181, Gr-CT:193
  Since I Left the Ocean. Navin.
    Al-PI:120
  Songs Received in Dreams.
    Tr-US II:273
  Winter Ocean. J. Updike.
    Co-EL:116, Co-PU:53, Co-SS:41
OCELOTS: see HUMOR - OCELOTS
O'CONNOR, FRANK, PSEUD.
  Light Dying. B. Kennelly.
    Co-PI:84
OCTOBER
  A Bowl of October. H. Bevington.
    Sh-RP:129
  The Clear Air of October.
    R. Bly. St-H:5
  Color. M. Cane. Sh-RP:222
  Especially when the October
    Wind. D. Thomas. Go-BP:68,
    Un-MB:500
  Fall. A. Fisher. Ar-TP3:185,
    Br-SG:90, Ha-YA:113, Ja-PA:27
  The Great Scarf of Birds.
    J. Updike. Mo-BG:134
  In October. B. Carman. Ha-YA:110
  Last Week in October. T. Hardy.
    Co-PU:144
  Late October. S. Teasdale.
    Co-PS:125, Ha-YA:112
  Letter from Fort Scott.
    B. Cutler. St-H:44
  October. T. Aldrich. Un-GT:278
  October. R. Frost. Bo-GJ:251,
    Gr-CC:41
  October. R. Fyleman. Br-SG:94,
    Br-SS:61, Ja-PA:25, Sh-RP:225
  October. P. Hubbell. Ja-PA:26
  October. P. Kavanagh. Pa-GTB:514
  October. H. McMahan. Se-PR:176
  October. W. Morris. Ox-BN:787
  October. D. Thomas. Ha-YA:110
  October. W. Trask. No-CL:279
  October Journey. M. Walker.
    Ad-PB:146, Bo-AN:132, Hu-PN:317
  October Magic. M. Livingston.
    La-PH:5, La-PV:64
  October Morning. J. Piatt.
    Ha-YA:109
  October 1. K. Shapiro. Un-MA:637
  October Winds. V. Randall.
    Ha-YA:114
  October's Bright Blue Weather.
    H. Jackson. Co-PS:128
  October's Party. G. Cooper.
    Br-SS:60, Fe-PL:386, Sh-RP:227
  Ox Driver. B. Cutler. St-H:40
  Poem in October. D. Thomas.
    Gr-CC:42, Hi-WP II:135, To-MP:54
  Temper in October.
    V. Edminson. Go-BP:31
  Ulalume. E. Poe. Al-VBP:869,
    Sh-AP:58
  A Vagabond Song. B. Carman.
    Co-PS:122, Fe-FP:81, Hu-MP:316,
    Sh-RP:116, Sp-OG:251, Un-GT:277
  Was Not the Lost Dauphin.
    R. Warren. Be-EB:40
  The Wild Swans at Coole. W. Yeats.
    Go-BP:79, Gr-CT:97, Hi-WP II:128,
    Ma-FW:260, Pa-HT:143, Un-MB:112
  Words from England. D. Hall.
    Ke-TF:445
OCTOPUSES: see also
  HUMOR - OCTOPUSES
  Devilfish. W. Brown. Sa-B:161
  Inkfish. Ch'in Tzu-hao. Pa-MV:61
ODESSA, U.S.S.R.
  Dvonya. L. Simpson. Mo-BG:89
ODORS: see also HUMOR - ODORS
  After the Bells Hummed.
    Basho. Be-CS:34
  Alien. D. Hayes. Bo-AN:93
  All Tropic Places Smell of Mold.
    K. Shapiro. Ca-VT:375
  Blossom Themes. C. Sandburg.
    Pe-M:8
  Digging. E. Thomas. Un-MB:216
  Exit Molloy. D. Mahon. Co-PI:119
  Hokku Poems. R. Wright. Bo-AN:105
  Love Song. W. Williams. Un-MA:255
  Plum Trees. Rankö. Au-SP:347,
    Fe-FP:482, Hu-MP:274
  The Scent of Autumn.
    Li Kuang-t'ien. Hs-TC:202
  Smell. W. Williams. Un-MA:259
  Smells. C. Morley. Bo-HF:161,
    Mc-PR:206
  Smells. K. Worth. Sh-RP:209
  Smells (Junior). C. Morley.
    Ar-TP3:3, Hu-MP:14
  Sniff. F. Frost. Ar-TP3:113,
    Br-SS:161
  The Stinky City. R. Isaac.
    La-GI:49
  There Was an Old Woman.
    Mother Goose. Ag-HE:22

To the Most Fair and Lovely
  Mistress, Anne Soame, Now
  Lady Abdie. R. Herrick.
  Al-VBP:332
Two Songs of Spring Wandering, II.
  Wang Wei. Le-MW:72
When the Moon Is in the River of
  Heaven. Ou Yang Hsiu.
  Rx-OH:54
The World Is Full of Wonderful
  Smells. Z. Gay. Ar-TP3:111
ODYSSEUS: see ULYSSES
ODYSSEY
  The Odyssey. A. Lang.
  Al-VBP:1062, Fe-PL:433,
  Ox-BN:871
OFFICE WORKERS: see also
    CLERKS AND CLERKING
  The Stenographers. P. Page.
  Wi-LT:782
  Thirty Bob a Week. J. Davidson.
  Er-FA:271, Ox-BN:900
OGRES (MYTH.)
  I Do Like Ogres. D. Thompson.
  Br-SM:1
OHIO: see also names of towns,
    as MARION, O.
  Anton and Yaro. M. Oliver.
  St-H:168
  The Founders of Ohio.
  W. Venable. Hi-TL:85
  A Poem for Home. M. Oliver.
  St-H:161
  To Sherwood Anderson in Heaven.
  F. Eckman. St-H:46
OHIO RIVER
  Why Should I Care for the Men
  of Thames? W. Blake.
  Gr-CT:304, Rv-CB:603
OIL: see PETROLEUM
OJIBWA INDIANS: see also
    INDIANS OF NORTH AMERICA -
    VERSE—OJIBWA
  A Chippewa Legend. J. Lowell.
  Hu-MP:425
OKEFENOKEE SWAMP
  A Legend of Lake Okeefinokee.
  L. Richards. Gr-EC:174
  Okefenokee Swamp. D. Hickey.
  Br-AF:185
OKLAHOMA
  Arizona. Em-AF:758
  Oklahoma. H. Camden. Se-PR:279
OLD AGE: see also GROWING
    OLD; HUMOR - OLD AGE;
    SATIRE - OLD AGE;
    WRINKLES; YOUTH AND AGE
  After a Line by John Peale
  Bishop. D. Justice.
  En-PC:228

After Long Silence. W. Yeats.
  Co-EL:122, Wi-LT:89
After My Grandfather's Death:
  A Poem of the China Clock.
  M. Oliver. St-H:167
After Seeing "Lear."
  M. Syrkin. Ls-NY:82
Age. W. Landor. Co-EL:123,
  Co-PU:150
Age. E. Tuck. Br-BC:139,
  Fe-PL:259, Se-PR:237
Akjartoq's Song of the Olden
  Days. Le-IB:110, Tr-US I:15
All Gone. W. de la Mare.
  Go-BP:233
Almost Ninety. R. Whitman.
  Ls-NY:134
Almswomen. E. Blunden. Do-BP:51
An Ancient Virgin. G. Crabbe.
  Ox-BN:4
Angry Old Men. B. Payne.
  Co-PI:167
The Apparitions. W. Yeats.
  Wi-LT:94
Aunt Alice in April. W. Matchett.
  Ha-TP:128
Autumn Leaves. J. Heyward.
  Hu-MP:281
Autumn Thoughts. Lu Yu.
  Rx-OH:112
Autumn Wind. Emperor Wu.
  Rx-LT:4, Sm-LG:398
The Autumnal. J. Donne. Al-VBP:254
The Bean Eaters. G. Brooks.
  Ad-PB:154, Be-MA:81, Jo-SA:23,
  Lo-TY:245
The Bear. N. Momaday. Ni-CD:91
The Beekeeper. J. Matthews.
  Ls-NY:138
Before the World Was Made.
  W. Yeats. Pa-GTB:431
Belisarius. H. Longfellow.
  Ho-WR:120
By the Exeter River. D. Hall.
  Ca-MB:21, To-MP:147
Ca'line's Prayer. L. Clifton.
  Be-MA:141
Casual Lines. Su Shih.
  Le-MW:128, Ma-FW:87
The Cherry Tree Blossomed.
  Tomonori. Le-MW:129
Clear Eyes. W. de la Mare.
  Al-VBP:1120
Clipper Captain. S. Barker.
  Mc-WK:183
Colonel Fantock. E. Sitwell.
  Un-MB:334
Complaint. Tr-US I:34
Confessions. R. Browning.
  Al-VBP:908, Pa-GTB:355

OLD AGE — cont'd.
  Crowsfeet Splaying round His
    Eyes. L. Lloyd-Evans.
    Gr-BT:163
  A Cry. F. Bianco. No-CL:261
  Danny Murphy. J. Stephens.
    Co-RG:165
  De Profundis. L. Blaga. Mc-AC:72
  A Decanter of Madeira, Aged 86, to
    George Bancroft, Aged 86.
    S. Mitchell. Al-VBP:992
  Do Not Go Gentle into That Good
    Night. D. Thomas. Al-VBP:1247,
    Br-TC:439, Er-FA:40, Gr-BT:173,
    Ha-PO:126, Hi-WP II:30,
    Ke-PP:25, Un-MB:504, Wi-LT:551
  Dying Speech of an Old Philosopher.
    W. Landor. Al-VBP:704,
    Gr-CT:435, Ha-PO:209, Ma-YA:169,
    Ox-BN:194, Pa-GTB:318
  Envy the Old. M. Van Doren.
    Ho-P:275
  Evening in the Great Smokies.
    D. Heyward. Pa-HT:44
  The Fairy King. W. Allingham.
    Co-PM:22
  Farewell to Fan Yun at An Ch'eng.
    Shen Yueh. Rx-LT:36
  Fate! I Have Asked. W. Landor.
    Al-VBP:704
  Feather. F. Bianco. No-CL:4
  Five Vignettes, 3. J. Toomer.
    Ad-PB:34
  A Flat One. W. Snodgrass.
    En-PC:244, Wi-LT:822
  For William Edward Burghardt
    Dubois on His Eightieth
    Birthday. B. Latimer.
    Ad-PB:199, Hu-PN:392
  Formula for Old Age. U. Harsen.
    Ke-TF:161
  The Fountain. W. Wordsworth.
    Pa-GTB:304
  A Friend Advises Me to Stop
    Drinking. Mei Yao Ch'en.
    Rx-OH:48
  From My Window. M. Coleridge.
    Ox-BN:927
  Gerontion. T. Eliot.
    Pa-GTB:474, Wi-LT:282
  Grandfather in the Old Men's
    Home. W. Merwin. Wi-LT:768
  The Guest of Twilight.
    Cheng Ch'ou-yü. Pa-MV:42
  He Sees Through Stone.
    E. Knight. Ad-PB:231, Be-MA:109
  His Wish to God. R. Herrick.
    Go-BP:234
  Homecoming. Ho Ch'e Ch'ang.
    Rx-LT:47

  The Horse Show. W. Stevens.
    Ca-VT:66, Pe-OA:79
  I Am Old Now and Covered with
    My Life. Wo-HS:(69)
  I Am Raftery. A. Raftery.
    Co-PI:181
  I Get Up at Dawn. Lu Yu.
    Rx-OH:111
  I Have Been a Forester.
    Gr-GB:151, Rv-CB:22
  Imperialists in Retirement.
    E. Lucie-Smith. To-MP:149
  In a Poor Old Village. Lida.
    Mo-MI:82
  In the Old Man's Eyes.
    K. Takahama. Ma-FW:179
  In These Dissenting Times.
    A. Walker. Ad-PB:475
  Isaac and Archibald.
    E. Robinson. Ni-JP:145,
    Pe-OA:9
  It Is Too Late. H. Longfellow.
    Fe-PL:304
  John Anderson, My Jo. R. Burns.
    Al-VBP:646, Ga-FB:47, Ha-PO:176,
    Pa-GTB:157, Rv-CB:619, Sp-OG:276
  Kibkarjuk Calls to Mind the
    Times. Tr-US I:14
  King Lear. W. Shakespeare.
    Ho-P:94
  The Lamentation of the Old
    Pensioner. W. Yeats.
    Co-PI:207, Ke-PP:100
  The Last Leaf. O. Holmes.
    Bo-HF:134, Fe-FP:321, Fe-PL:265,
    Mc-WK:135, Sp-OG:261
  A Letter from a Girl to Her Own
    Old Age. A. Meynell.
    Al-VBP:1065, Un-MB:63
  The Lime-Tree Bower My Prison.
    S. Coleridge. Rv-CB:660
  Long Time a Child.
    H. Coleridge. Ox-BN:398,
    Rv-CB:758
  Love and Age. T. Peacock.
    Al-VBP:717, Ox-BN:235
  Love in Thy Youth. Al-VBP:363
  The Love Song of J. Alfred
    Prufrock. T. Eliot.
    Al-VBP:1180, Br-TC:106, Pe-OA:105,
    Rv-CB:986, Un-MA:379, Wi-LT:278
  Man's Going Hence. S. Rogers.
    Ox-BN:48
  Mild Is the Parting Year.
    W. Landor. Rv-CB:669
  Minerva's Shield. I. Pillat.
    Mc-AC:57
  Miss Rosie. L. Clifton.
    Ad-PB:307, Be-MA:139,
    Br-TC:69

Mr. Flood's Party. E. Robinson.
    Al-VBP:1107, Er-FA:304,
    Ha-PO:64, Na-EO:66, Ni-JP:143,
    Pe-M:50, Pe-OA:5, Sh-AP:141,
    Sm-PT:140, Un-MA:121, Wi-LT:111
The Moccasins of an Old Man.
    R. Carden. Al-WW:35
Moo! R. Hillyer. Co-BBW:170,
    Ho-TH:33
Moonlight. S. Teasdale.
    Ca-VT:76, Co-PU:154
The Moor. R. Hodgson.   Un-MB:187
The Musician. R. Lister.
    Pl-US:6
My Birthday. T. Moore. Se-PR:239
My Eyes Are Tired. Ho-SD:73
My Horse Took Me down the Life-
    Giving Road. Wo-HS:(45)
My Tired Old Nag. Issa.
    Be-MC:20
The New House. E. Thomas.
    Un-MB:215
The News Stand. D. Berrigan.
    Ad-CI:35
Notes to the Life of Ovid.
    A. Hamori. Ls-NY:131
October. W. Morris. Ox-BN:787
Of an Ancient Spaniel in Her
    Fifteenth Year. C. Morley.
    Mc-WK:57
Of the Last Verses in the Book.
    E. Waller. Al-VBP:386
Old Age. Ou Yang Hsiu.
    Rx-OH:62
Old Age. Sophocles. Pa-SG:182
Old Age. Al-PI:22
Old-Age Chant. Da-SC:105
Old Black Joe. S. Foster.
    Er-FA:441
Old Black Men. G. Johnson.
    Ad-PB:21, Hu-PN:77
Old Black Men Say. J. Emmanuel.
    Ad-PB:180
Old Dan'l. L. Strong.
    Cl-FC:36, Co-EL:125, Co-PS:64,
    Co-PU:122, Sm-MK:104, Un-MB:393
Old Dog. A. Covici. Ch-B:29
The Old Falcon. E. Baldwin.
    Ls-NY:107
Old Gray Mare. Gr-GB:54
The Old Knight. G. Peele.
    Al-VBP:135, Gr-CT:346,
    Ha-PO:172, Rv-CB:173
Old Man. J. Siegal. Le-M:150
An Old Man. W. Wordsworth.
    Go-BP:40, Sm-LG:129
Old Man, Phantom Dog.
    F. Eckman. St-H:49
Old Man Pondered. J. Ransom.
    Un-MA:416

The Old Man's Comforts and How
    He Gained Them. R. Southey.
    Li-SR:90, Ma-YA:167, Ox-BC:93
An Old Man's Night Thoughts.
    Tr-US I:134
Old Man's Plea. P. George.
    Al-WW:126
An Old Man's Winter Night.
    R. Frost. Ca-VT:9, Ni-JP:142,
    Un-MA:176
The Old Man's Wish. W. Pope.
    Go-BP:47
The Old Mare. E. Coatsworth.
    Un-MA:463
The Old Men. W. de la Mare.
    Un-MB:199
The Old Men. I. Feldman.
    Br-TC:122
Old Men. O. Nash. Na-EO:20
The Old Men Admiring Themselves
    in the Water. W. Yeats.
    Bo-GJ:198, Li-TU:140, Pe-M:57,
    Sm-LG:398
Old Men and Old Women Going
    Home on the Street Car.
    M. Moore. Un-MA:574
The Old Men. J. Campbell.
    Al-VBP:1148, Un-MB:252
Old Woman. E. Jennings. Gr-BT:166
Old Woman Awaiting the Greyhound
    Bus. D. Niatum. Ni-CD:127
An Old Woman Laments in Spring-
    time. E. Sitwell. Al-VBP:1170
Old Woman Sitting in the Sun.
    M. Inman. Ls-NY:78
Old Women Remember. R. Boyle.
    Ls-NY:73
On Growing Old. J. Masefield.
    Al-VBP:1136, Er-FA:149, Fe-PL:263,
    Tr-MR:55, Un-MB:227, Wi-LT:193
On the Death of Doctor Swift.
    J. Swift. Al-VBP:516
Once. E. Batterham. De-CH:242
Orpingalik's Song: My Breath.
    Tr-US I:17
Outdistanced. L. Rubin. Du-SH:49
Over the Hills to the Poor-House.
    W. Carleton. Er-FA:266
Papa John. J. de Lima. Lo-TY:84
A Parting Guest. J. Riley.
    Sp-OG:278
Pastoral. W. Williams. Br-TC:479
A Pauper. A. Tate. Wi-LT:410
Persuasions to Love. T. Carew.
    Al-VBP:348
Piazza Piece. J. Ransom.
    Gr-SS:122, Ha-PO:46, Rv-CB:984,
    Un-MA:414
Poor Fellow Me. Le-OE:123
The Prayer of the Old Horse.
    C. Gasztold. La-PV:126

OLD AGE — cont'd.
Promise of Peace. R. Jeffers.
   Un-MA:365, Wi-LT:258
Provide, Provide. R. Frost.
   Br-TC:139, Sh-AP:153
Rain. P. Williams. Le-M:149
The Red Cliff. Su Tung P'o.
   Rx-OH:65
Reflections in a Little Park.
   B. Deutsch. Co-EL:100
Remember Now Thy Creator.
   Bible. O.T. Ecclesiastes.
   Gr-CT:322, Mc-PR:18, Me-PH:34
Resolution and Independence.
   W. Wordsworth. Li-SR:109
Senex to Matt. Prior.
   J. Stephen. Co-FB:485
The Sign-Post. E. Thomas.
   Al-VBP:1136
Silver and Gold. E. Jebeleanu.
   Mc-AC:108
Silver Threads among the Gold.
   E. Rexford. Er-FA:427
Some Foreign Letters. A. Sexton.
   En-PC:274, Un-MA:687
Song. C. Rossetti.
   Al-VBP:995, Pa-GTB:374
Song after Defeat. Tr-US I:37
Song for September.
   R. Fitzgerald. Ca-VT:301
A Song for Simeon. T. Eliot.
   Gr-BT:174, Pl-EI:202
Song of a Woman Abandoned by
   the Tribe. Ho-LP:84
Song of an Old Man about His
   Wife. Le-IB:105
Song of Old Age and a White
   Head. Tr-US I:193
The Song of the Old Mother.
   W. Yeats. Co-PI:208,
   Ha-LO:98, Un-MB:112
Song of the Old Woman. Le-IB:107
Sonnets 2. S. Daniel. Al-VBP:157
The Span of Life. R. Frost.
   Ma-FW:228, Wi-LT:179
Spring Day on West Lake.
   Ou Yang Hsiu. Rx-OH:60
Sweet Cupid, Ripen Her Desire.
   Al-VBP:362
Sweet Was the Song. W. Landor.
   Al-VBP:705
Terminus. R. Emerson. Fe-PL:266
Testament. Sister M. Thérése.
   Tr-MR:169
Thanks in Old Age. W. Whitman.
   Ke-TF:160
That Time of Year Thou Mayest in
   Me Behold. W. Shakespeare.
   Al-VBP:205, Ga-FB:34, Gr-CT:318,
   Ha-PO:253, No-CL:85, Pa-GTB:18,
   Rv-CB:230

This Room Is Full of Clocks.
   I. Gardner. St-H:74
Three Old Brothers. F. O'Connor.
   Co-PI:150
Three Portraits. G. Hitchcock.
   Ca-VT:392
The Time of the Barmecides.
   J. Mangan. Co-RG:8
Time Speaks. Chu Ta-nan.
   Hs-TC:133
'Tis Late and Cold. J. Fletcher.
   Al-VBP:281
To an Old Lady. W. Empson.
   Pa-GTB:504
To an Old Lady Asleep at a Poetry
   Reading. J. Kirkup. Go-BP:53
To Mary. W. Cowper. Pa-GTB:164,
   Rv-CB:550
To the Four Courts, Please.
   J. Stephens. Co-PI:178,
   Ni-JP:86, Un-MB:263
Tomorrow. J. Collins. Pa-GTB:167
Too Old to Work. J. Glazer.
   Hi-TL:226
The Tower. W. Yeats. Wi-LT:76
Twenty Years Hence.
   W. Landor. Al-VBP:706
The Two Old Women. Ke-TF:158
Ulivfak's Song of the Caribou.
   Le-IB:112
Ulysses. A. Tennyson.
   Al-VBP:863, Ha-PO:40, Ke-TF:262,
   Ni-JP:16, Rv-CB:793
Uncle Ambrose. J. Still. Br-AF:133
A Valentine. J. Cournos.
   No-CL:221
We Are Never Old. R. Emerson.
   Se-PR:238
Weeksville Women. E. Loftin.
   Ad-PB:515
Western Ch'ang-An Street.
   Pien Chih-lin. Hs-TC:162
When I Do Count the Clock.
   W. Shakespeare. Al-VBP:200,
   Er-FA:262, Rv-CB:207
When My Love Swears.
   W. Shakespeare. Al-VBP:209,
   Un-MW:183
When You Are Old. W. Yeats.
   Bo-GJ:233, Co-BL:80, Er-FA:172,
   Fe-PL:94, Ga-FB:74, Go-BP:151,
   Ha-PO:179, Hi-WP I:43, Ma-FW:289,
   Un-MB:109, Un-MW:98, Wi-LT:68
The WhenIwas. D. Lourie. Sc-TN:150
Wisdom. S. Teasdale. Mc-PR:63
Years, Many Parti-Colored Years.
   W. Landor. Al-VBP:705, Rv-CB:671
Yes, You Are Old. M. Breslasu.
   Mc-AC:90
You Lingering Sparse Leaves of Me.
   W. Whitman. Rv-CB:856

OLD ENGLISH VERSE: see
   ANGLO-SAXON VERSE
OLD IRONSIDES: see
   CONSTITUTION (SHIP)
OLD MAIDS: see SINGLE WOMEN
OLD NORSE VERSE
   The Edda. Ba-PO:125
   Song to Steingerd.
      C. Ogmundarson. Pa-SG:49
OLD PRETENDER: see STUART,
   JAMES FRANCIS EDWARD
   (OLD PRETENDER)
OLIVE TREES
   Aye, Even Small Things.
      P. Heyse. Un-R:113
   The Olive Tree. N. Alterman.
      Me-PH:107
OLSON, CHARLES
   My Olson Elegy. I. Feldman.
      Ho-P:67
OLYMPIC GAMES
   The Greek Anthology.
      Krinagoras. Mo-SD:52
   A Negro Beats the Olympic
      Record for the USA.
      A. Sperber. Mc-AC:79
OMENS: see PREMONITIONS
O'NEILL, OWEN ROE
   Lament for the Death of Eoghan
      Ruadh O'Neill. T. Davis.
      Co-PI:34, Hi-FO:148
ONIONS: see also HUMOR - ONIONS
   Market Woman's Cries.
      J. Swift. Co-PI:184
   Peeling Onions. A. Rich. Mo-BG:38
   The Routine. P. Blackburn. Co-EL:118
   Vegetable Fantasies. H. Hoyt.
      Ir-BB:16, 17
ONTARIO, LAKE
   The Great Lakes Suite, VI.
      J. Reaney. Do-WH:53
OPERAS: see also HUMOR - OPERAS
   Faust. J. Ashbery. Br-TC:16
   Matinees. J. Merrill.
      Ho-P:187
OPERATIONS: see SURGEONS AND
   SURGERY
OPHELIA: see also HAMLET,
   PRINCE OF DENMARK
   Ballad of Another Ophelia.
      D. Lawrence. Gr-CT:79
   Ophelia. A. Rimbaud. Gr-CT:78
   Ophelia's Death. W. Shakespeare.
      Gr-CT:77
OPINIONS: see HUMOR - OPINIONS
OPOSSUMS
   The Opossum. M. Pomeroy.
      Co-BBW:34
   Opossum. W. Smith. Un-GT:56
   Over in the Meadow. Au-SP:223,
      Ir-BB:24, On-TW:38

The Possum Tree. I. Gough.
   Gr-EC:50
OPPORTUNITY: see also
   SATIRE - OPPORTUNITY
After Beginning. C. Lushington.
   Sa-B:235
America Was Promises. A. MacLeish.
   Br-AF:250, Vi-PP:229
Be Daedalus. N. Alba. Ad-PB:169,
   Hu-PN:329
The Chambered Nautilus. O. Holmes.
   Er-FA:479, Fe-PL:297, Mc-PR:130,
   Sh-AP:63, Sp-OG:366
Dancing. A. Young. Mc-EA:88
Days. R. Emerson. Al-VBP:805,
   Mo-BG:136, Ni-JP:30, Rv-CB:775
An Elementary School Class Room
   in a Slum. S. Spender.
   To-MP:26
For Eusi, Ayi Kwei & Owen Brooks.
   K. Kgositsile. Ad-PB:325
Freedom in Mah Soul. D. Cannon.
   Hu-PN:281
I Am Tied. L. Kvitko. Ho-TY:192
I Sing America Now! J. Stuart.
   Br-AF:248
Inscription on the Statue of
   Liberty. E. Lazarus. Se-PR:127
It Is Big Inside a Man.
   K. Patchen. Kh-VA:50
Let America Be America Again.
   L. Hughes. Hu-PN:193
A Lost Chord. A. Procter.
   Er-FA:437, Sp-OG:338
Miracle Hill. E. Mitchell.
   Al-WW:93
The New World. E. Masters.
   Br-AF:246
A New Year. M. Davies. Ha-YA:168
The Nonconformist. A. Ivanushkin.
   Mo-MI:38
Opportunity. J. Ingalls.
   Er-FA:6, Fe-PL:411
Opportunity. E. Sill. Co-RM:71,
   Sp-OG:46, Un-GT:310
People. Yehoash. Ho-TY:73
Poem. E. Brathwaite.
   Sa-B:212, 215
Poem. J. Friedman. Ho-TY:368
A Psalm of Life. H. Longfellow.
   Er-FA:32, Fe-PL:303, Sp-OG:322
"pygmies are pygmies still, though
   percht on Alps." G. Brooks.
   Hu-PN:336
Rebirth. R. Kipling. Ox-BN:933
Return of the Native. I. Baraka.
   Ra-BP:222
SOS. I. Baraka. Ad-PB:257,
   Ra-BP:181
The Salutation of the Dawn.
   Fe-PL:397

OPPORTUNITY — <u>cont'd.</u>
The Sermon on the Warpland.
G. Brooks. Ad-PB:163,
Ra-BP:170, Wi-LT:666
Song of a Man Who Has Come
Through. D. Lawrence.
Al-VBP:1158, Go-BP:69,
Pa-GTB:458, Wi-LT:212
Southern Ships and Settlers,
1606-1732. R. and S. Benét.
Br-AF:56
To Odessa. L. Kvitko. Ho-TY:192
The United States.
J. von Goethe. Bl-FP:72
Urgency. S. Wright. Hu-PN:270
Walter Bradford. G. Brooks.
Ra-BP:174
The World Looks On. L. Newman.
Hu-PN:515
Written on the Road. M. Dodge.
Br-BC:145
You, Whoever You Are.
W. Whitman. Br-AF:49
Youth. L. Hughes. Bo-HF:107,
Br-AF:243, Br-BC:134, Li-TU:266
OPPRESSION: see also TYRANNY
Bad Bishop Jegon. Gr-GB:186
A Basket of Summer Fruit. Bible.
O.T. Amos. Me-PH:49
The Blackleg Miners. Gr-GB:223
Caliban in the Coal Mines.
L. Untermeyer. Kr-OF:178,
La-PV:102, Pe-SS:54, Un-MA:306
Commission. E. Pound. Br-TC:329
A Consecration. J. Masefield.
Un-MB:221
Dark Symphony: Andante Sostenuto.
M. Tolson. Bo-AN:38
Drumdelgie. Gr-GB:210
Go Down, Moses. Ab-MO:79,
Pl-EI:101
The Grinders. Gr-GB:222
The Labourer. R. Thomas. Go-BP:229
The Man with the Hoe. E. Markham.
Bo-HF:144, Er-FA:269, Ke-PP:108,
Ni-JP:84, Pl-EI:142, Un-MA:107
Odell. J. Stephens. Un-MB:265
The Rest. E. Pound.
Sh-AP:173, Un-MA:296
The Road. C. Aiken. Un-MA:428
A Song of Huezotzinco. Da-SC:178
Thirty Bob a Week. J. Davidson.
Co-EL:143
Under Such Blows. O. Mandelstam.
Ca-MR:160
Vala, or the Four Zoas.
W. Blake. Al-VBP:622
Waiting. J. Davidson.
Al-VBP:1078

OPTIMISTS AND OPTIMISM: see also
HUMOR - OPTIMISTS AND OPTIMISM;
SATIRE - OPTIMISTS AND OPTIMISM
All's Well. J. Whittier.
Rv-CB:785
Comparison. M. Hoberman.
Br-BC:110
David's Song. R. Browning.
Ga-FB:11
dive for dreams. e. cummings.
Ha-TP:139
Dust of Snow. R. Frost.
Ad-PE:19, Ar-TP3:212, Hi-WP I:4,
La-PV:133, Mo-TS:22, Re-BS:52,
Tu-WW:42
Epilogue. R. Browning.
Al-VBP:916, Ga-FB:131,
Ox-BN:586
A Greeting. W. Davies. Mc-WK:82,
Tr-MR:23, Un-MB:175
The Heather. S. Blicker.
Pa-SG:172
I Heard a Bird Sing. O. Herford.
Ar-TP3:212, Au-SP:352, Br-SS:88,
Co-BBW:256, Fe-PL:389, Ha-YA:151,
La-PP:8, La-PV:128, Li-LC:71,
Th-AS:49
Ianthe's Troubles. W. Landor.
Al-VBP:706, Ox-BN:188
Laugh and Be Merry. J. Masefield.
Er-FA:21, Un-MB:228
Legend. J. Wright. Co-PT:179,
Ma-FW:192
Life's Lesson. Fe-PL:339
A Little Old Man Came Riding By.
Un-GT:18
Look Up! E. Hale. Er-FA:29
The Man. S. Brooks. Ad-II:77
121st Chorus. J. Kerouac.
Ha-TP:132
Pippa's Song. R. Browning.
Bo-FP:213, Bo-GJ:96, Ch-B:98,
Cl-DT:45, Er-FA:20, Fe-FP:72,
Ha-YA:28, Hu-MP:291, Ke-TF:434,
La-PV:81, Li-LC:72, Ma-YA:200,
Mc-PR:95, Mo-GR:113, Rv-CB:816,
Se-PR:68, Sp-OG:215, Tu-WW:60,
Un-GT:273
Rabbi Ben Ezra. R. Browning.
Br-BC:142, Er-FA:175, Ga-FB:129,
Ox-BN:578
Shadows. A. Peel. Th-AS:203
Solitude. E. Wilcox. Er-FA:3,
Fe-PL:291
'Twixt Optimist and Pessimist.
Un-GT:24
The Two Spirits. P. Shelley.
De-CH:323, Ho-P:112
Ho-WR:189

The Weather Is Gloomy.
   A. Tarasova.   Mo-MI:33
What a Pretty Kite.   Issa.
   Be-CS:53
When My Ship Comes In.
   R. Burdett.   Er-FA:30
ORANG-UTANS
The Orang Utan. E. Lucie-Smith.
   Co-PU:89
ORANGE TREES
My Old Grandfather. J. Alumasa.
   Le-M:179
Orange Tree by Night.
   S. Sitwell.   Gr-CC:55
The Red-Gold Rain. S. Sitwell.
   Gr-CC:54, Un-MB:400
Tampa Robins.   S. Lanier.
   Se-PR:108
ORANGEBURG, S.C.
in orangeburg my brothers did.
   A. Spellman.   Ad-PB:285,
   Ra-BP:229
When Black People Are.
   A. Spellman.   Ad-PB:284,
   Be-MA:127, Ra-BP:228
ORANGEMAN'S DAY: see IRELAND -
   HISTORY AND PATRIOTISM
ORANGES
As I Went over London Bridge.
   Gr-CT:11, Ir-BB:49
Oranges.   De-TT:93,
   Mo-MGT:18, Sp-AS:(24)
Tangerines.   A. Karanikas.
   Bo-HF:99
When the Old Hen Laid.   Re-RR:26
ORATORS AND ORATORY: see SPEECHES;
   and names of orators, as
   WEBSTER, DANIEL
ORCHARDS: see also FRUIT;
   and names of fruit trees,
   as APPLE TREES
Apple Season.   F. Frost.   Br-SS:64
Fairies' Song.   L. Hunt.   Co-PM:106
Good-bye and Keep Cold.   R. Frost.
   Un-GT:284
I Have an Orchard.   C. Marlowe.
   Gr-CT:272
In the Apple Orchard. I. Schwartz.
   Ho-TY:149
The Little Green Orchard.
   W. de la Mare.   Ar-TP3:159,
   Hu-MP:67, Na-EO:86
Orchard.   H.D.   Un-MA:337,
   Wi-LT:619
The Orchard and the Heath.
   G. Meredith.   Ox-BN:691
A Prayer in Spring.   R. Frost.
   Ha-YA:29, Tr-MR:48
ORCHESTRAS
At the Symphony.   R. Nathan.
   Se-PR:326

The Children's Orchestra.
   M. Johnson.   De-CH:710
Concert Interpretation
   (Le Sacre du Printemps).
   S. Sassoon.   Rv-CB:981
Guide to the Symphony.   W. Kees.
   Ca-VT:405
ORCHIDS
The Bee-Orchis.   A. Young.
   Cl-DT:79, Gr-CT:249 ·
By Chance I Walk. Yuan Mei. Pe-M:7
Discovery.   Yuan Mei.   Le-MW:26
ORDER: see CHAOS AND ORDER
ORDINARINESS: see COMMONPLACENESS
OREGON
Oregon Rain.   J. McGahey.
   Br-AF:163, Du-RG:125
Oregon State Song.   J. Buchanan.
   Se-PR:280
OREGON TRAIL: see also
   LEWIS AND CLARK EXPEDITION
The Oregon Trail, 1843.
   A. Guiterman.   Fe-FP:432,
   Hu-MP:392
ORGAN GRINDERS: see also
   HUMOR - ORGAN GRINDERS
The Barrel-Organ.   A. Noyes.
   Ga-FB:234, Un-MB:245
Hurdy-Gurdy Days.   M. Clark.
   Hu-MP:293
In the Isle of Dogs.
   J. Davidson.   Ox-BN:907
The Organ Grinder's Garden.
   M. Merryman.   Au-SP:156
The Shower.   B. Eve.   De-TT:159
Singing.   R. Stevenson. Gr-TG:23
ORGANS AND ORGANISTS: see also
   HUMOR - ORGANS AND ORGANISTS
Charles.   L. Clark.   Ma-FW:180
Over His Keys.   J. Lowell.
   Se-PR:327
ORIENT: see also names of
   countries, as INDIA
A Caravan from China Comes.
   R. Le Gallienne.   Th-AS:152
England.   M. Moore. Un-MA:350
ORIOLES
Far up the River.   Tu Fu.
   Rx-OH:26
Hearing the Early Oriole.
   Po Chü-i.   Pl-US:128
Kriss Kringle.   T. Aldrich.
   Hu-MP:360
Nesting Time.   A. Guiterman.
   Gr-EC:180
Oriole.   E. Fawcett.   Un-GT:59
Orioles. J. Langland. Ha-WR:12
Spring.   Shao Hsün-mei. Hs-TC:125
A Spring Lilt.   Hu-MP:303
Spring Sorrow.   Ch'n Ch'ang Siu.
   Rx-LT:60

ORIOLES — cont'd.
  To Hear an Oriole Sing.
    E. Dickinson. Pl-US:129
ORION (CONSTELLATION)
  For the Nightly Ascent of Orion
    over a Forest Clearing.
    J. Dickey. Br-TC:88
  Look at Orion. F. Saito.
    Sh-AM:151
  The Star-Splitter. R. Frost.
    Pl-IO:17
ORPHANS
  Alice Fell. W. Wordsworth.
    De-TT:105, Li-SR:102
  Come and Let Us Play.
    Issa. Ca-BF:35
  Little Orphant Annie. J. Riley.
    Co-BB:113, Er-FA:493, Fe-FP:532,
    Hu-MP:27, Ox-BC:300
  The Orphan Girl. Em-AF:772
  The Orphan's Song. S. Dobell.
    De-CH:41, Ox-BN:668
ORPHEUS AND EURIDYCE
  Eurydice. H.D. Ca-VT:107
  From the Underworld.
    H. Blaikley. Mo-GR:20
  The Life and Death of Jason.
    W. Morris. Al-VBP:1011
  On the Praise of Poetry and
    Music. A. Cowley. No-CL:30
  Orpheus. E. Roberts. Un-MA:269
  Orpheus. Y. Winters. Ca-VT:227
  Orpheus and Eurydice. Ovid.
    Mo-GR:21
  Orpheus' Dream. E. Muir.
    Gr-SS:113
  Orpheus with His Lute.
    J. Fletcher. Al-VBP:286,
    Rv-CB:202, Se-PR:329, Sm-LG:38
  Wedding Song. N. Willard.
    Sc-TN:231
OSCEOLA, SEMINOLE LEADER
  Osceola. W. Whitman. Kr-OF:9
O'SHAUGHNESSY, ARTHUR WILLIAM
  EDGAR: see SATIRE -
    O'SHAUGHNESSY, ARTHUR
    WILLIAM EDGAR
OSHKOSH, WIS.
  Kalamazoo. V. Lindsay.
    Gr-CC:149, Pa-HT:47
OSPREYS: see HAWKS
OSTENTATION: see BOASTING;
    SATIRE - OSTENTATION
OSTRICHES
  The Ostrich. O. Nash. Co-BBW:266,
    Co-OH:28
  The Ostrich. Tr-CB:21, Tr-US I:75
  The Ostrich Is a Silly Bird.
    M. Freeman. Ar-TP3:131,
    Au-SP:242, Ch-B:112, Co-HP:58,
    Ja-PC:12, Lo-LL:42, Mc-WK:73

OTTERBURN, BATTLE, 1388
  The Battle of Otterburn.
    Ox-BB:491, Pa-OM:148
  Chevy Chase. Al-VBP:43, Ma-BB:97,
    Ox-BB:496
OTTERS
  River-Mates. P. Colum.
    Co-BBW:64, Co-PI:28, Rd-OA:45
OUSELS: see OUZELS
OUTDOOR LIFE: see also CAMPING; COM-
    PANIONSHIP OF MAN AND NATURE;
    COUNTRY LIFE; NATURE; NATURE -
    BEAUTY; and names of outdoor
    sports, as FISHERMEN AND FISHING
  Above Pate Valley. G. Snyder.
    Mo-BG:131
  Afar in the Desert. T. Pringle.
    Rd-OA:168
  Afternoon on a Hill. E. Millay.
    Ar-TP3:176, Au-SP:350, Cl-FC:24,
    Fe-FP:269, Hu-MP:64, La-PV:170,
    Pe-FB:75
  All Morning. T. Roethke.
    Ca-BP:48
  Alone. J. Farrar. Ha-YA:70,
    Hu-MP:61
  At Cove on the Crooked River.
    W. Stafford. Wi-LT:825
  Autumn. F. O'Connor. Co-PS:129
  Autumn! N. Turner. Ha-YA:95,
    Ja-PA:10
  Bab-Lock-Hythe. L. Binyon.
    Hi-WP II:38, Mo-SD:132
  The Bear. J. Carpenter. Ls-NY:86
  Before the Coming of Winter.
    D. Schmitz. St-H:198
  Behold: My World. L. Sohappy.
    Al-WW:18
  Blackberrying. S. Plath. To-MP:98
  The Brook-Song. J. Riley.
    Sp-OG:281
  Bunch of Wild Flowers. L. Zilles.
    Sh-RP:86
  Camping Out on Rainy Mountain.
    J. Barnes. Ni-CD:19
  A Chant Out of Doors.
    M. Wilkinson. Th-AS:172
  The Concert. P. McGinley.
    Ha-YA:47
  Country Summer. L. Adams.
    Al-VBP:1218, Bo-GJ:98,
    Un-MA:546, Wi-LT:604
  The Dance. H. Crane. Un-MA:526,
    Wi-LT:385
  Daniel Boone, 1735-1820.
    R. and S. Benét. Br-AF:63,
    Ho-LP:89
  Dark Danny. I. Eastwick.
    Ar-TP3:14, Fe-FP:397
  The Dawn. W. Yeats. Mo-GR:73

Day of These Days. L. Lee.
   Co-BN:108
The day we went out.
   M. Bergschneider. Ad-II:61
Dream Song. Bi-IT:133
Enthralled. C. Thaxter. Sp-OG:252
Fain Would I Live in Safest
   Freedom. A. von Platen.
   Pa-SG:164
Fall. R. Francis.   Ca-VT:233
Far from the Madding Crowd.
   N. Waterman. Hu-MP:60
Farm Child. R. Thomas.
   Co-BN:206, Co-PU:118,
   Hi-WP II:134, Ma-FW:77
Father. M. Weston. Co-PS:102
The Feet of the Young Men.
   R. Kipling. Se-PR:171
The Field Mouse. W. Sharp.
   Co-BBW:42, Fe-FP:137, Rd-SS:34
Field of Autumn. L. Lee.
   Wi-LT:757
The Fisher's Life. I. Walton.
   Bo-FP:255
Fishing. D. Schmitz. St-H:195
The Flowers in a Meadow.
   F. Cornford. Gr-TG:27
Gipsies. J. Clare. Cl-DT:81,
   Gr-CT:164
Going to Sleep in the Country.
   H. Moss. En-PC:204
The Golden Hive. H. Behn.
   Ar-TP3:218
A Green Place. W. Smith.
   Sh-RP:95
Harvest Home. A. Guiterman.
   Ha-YA:109
Hie Away. Al-VBP:676, Ar-TP3:95,
   Bo-FP:309, Hu-MP:63, Sm-MK:183
Hiking. J. Bruchac. Ni-CD:38
Hot Sun Sounds. M. Sheedy.
   Ad-II:59
How I Went Truant from School to
   Visit a River. M. Oliver.
   St-H:164
I Dreamed You Led Me.
   A. Machado. Le-SW:55
I Meant to Do My Work Today.
   R. Le Gallienne. Ar-TP3:116,
   Au-SP:348, Hu-MP:69, La-PP:6,
   Th-AS:78, Un-GB:22, Un-GT:250
In Dreamy Swoon. G. Darley.
   Ox-BN:388
In June. N. Perry. Ha-YA:72
In Response to a Question.
   W. Stafford. Mc-EA:54, St-H:213
Interruption. R. Graves.
   Wi-LT:372
Jack-in-the-Pulpit.
   I. Eastwick. Ha-YA:64

Joy.   O. Wilde.   Bo-FP:221
July Meadow. L. Driscoll.
   Ha-YA:82
The Kayak Paddler's Joy at the
   Weather. Da-SC:41, Le-IB:32,
   Tr-US I:7
Keeping Store. M. Butts.
   Bo-FP:140
The Language of Life. B. Cutler.
   St-H:45
A Letter from Home. M. Oliver.
   St-H:166
The Little Green Orchard.
   W. de la Mare. Ar-TP3:159,
   Hu-MP:67, Na-EO:86
The Little Shepherd's Song.
   W. Percy. Ha-YA:67
Love on the Farm. D. Lawrence.
   Ga-FB:80, Un-MB:288, Un-MW:122
Love Song. W. Williams. Un-MA:255
May All the Earth Be Clothed in
   Light. G. Hitchcock.
   Ca-BP:51, Ca-VT:399
Meg Merrilies. J. Keats.
   Ar-TP3:14, Bl-OB:147, Bo-FP:100,
   Cl-FC:86, Ne-AM:14, Ox-BC:147,
   Re-TW:110, Rv-CB:749, Se-PR:322,
   Sm-LG:128, Sm-MK:110, Sp-OG:249
Mid-August at Sourdough Mountain
   Lookout. G. Snyder. Kh-VA:28,
   Mc-EA:41
Millions of Strawberries.
   G. Taggard. Ar-TP3:206,
   Du-RG:114, Fe-FP:233, Hu-MP:310,
   Un-GB:8, Un-GT:252
The Month of the Thunder Moon.
   M. Doyle. Ha-YA:84
My Valentine. R. Stevenson.
   Br-SS:119, Ch-B:41, Co-BL:114,
   Co-PS:37, Hu-MP:331, Mc-PR:48,
   Se-PR:52, Un-MB:59, Un-MW:139
New Hampshire. D. Hall. Mo-BG:145
New Morning. B. Dylan. Mo-GR:112
No Title. L. Nagan. Ad-II:74
October's Bright Blue Weather.
   H. Jackson. Co-PS:128
Of the Surface of Things.
   W. Stevens. Co-EL:46
On Hardscrabble Mountain.
   G. Kinnell. Du-SH:107, La-RM:28
Onward to Far Ida. G. Darley.
   Ox-BN:392
Out in the Woods with Father.
   D. McCord. Gr-TG:24
Peace. Bhartrihari. Pa-SG:161
The Peace of Wild Things. W. Berry.
   Ca-VT:685, Ls-NY:62
The Peasant Poet. J. Clare.
   Ox-BN:332
Peter Grimes. G. Crabbe. Ox-BN:14

OUTDOOR LIFE — cont'd.
The Pike. E. Blunden. Wi-LT:609
Prelude. J. Synge. Co-BN:207,
  Gr-CT:235, Un-MB:180
Prothalamion. R. Hillyer.
  Un-MA:482
Psalm of the Fruitful Field.
  A. Klein. Do-WH:88
Quaker Hill. H. Crane. Wi-LT:389
A Rainy Day. J. Lincoln.
  Sh-RP:198
Remember September. M. Justus.
  Br-SS:58, Ha-YA:106, Ja-PA:23
The Rescue. D. Schmitz. St-H:190
Reynard the Fox. J. Masefield.
  Rd-OA:51
The Riders. A. Stanford.
  Ha-TP:118
Scene in a Garden. R. Browning.
  Bo-FP:142
September. E. Reed. Ha-YA:105,
  Hu-MP:314
Sometimes, with Secure Delight.
  J. Milton. Hu-MP:89
Song in Spring. L. Ginsberg.
  Ha-YA:31
A Song of Bread and Honey.
  R. Le Gallienne. Bo-FP:62
Song of Myself. W. Whitman.
  Ca-BP:3, Un-MA:49
Song of the Open Road.
  W. Whitman. Al-VBP:934,
  Ar-TP3:97, Er-FA:249, Un-MA:63
Spring. R. Hovey. Sh-RP:104
Spring. J. Lowell. Ga-FB:287
Stay Thu Soft Murmuring.
  E. Darwin. Rd-OA:189
The Stone Harp. J. Haines.
  Sc-TN:75
A Summer Commentary. Y. Winters.
  Wi-LT:656
Summer Morning. J. Ingelow.
  Gr-TG:43
Sun. J. Duffey. Ad-II:60
Suspense. A. Stoutenberg.
  Ha-WR:50
they are closing in.
  E. Livingston. Sc-TN:147
Time Is the Mercy of Eternity.
  K. Rexroth. Ca-VT:272
To Jane: The Invitation.
  P. Shelley. Re-TW:91
To K. de M. R. Stevenson.
  Ox-BN:891
To Walk on Hills. R. Graves.
  Mo-SD:90
Toad Man's Song. Br-MW:59
Tramp. R. Hughes. Un-MB:407
Two Lives and Others. W. Scott.
  Du-RG:119

Under the Greenwood Tree.
  W. Shakespeare. Al-VBP:186,
  Ar-TP3:204, Bo-FP:259, Co-BN:206,
  De-CH:134, De-TT:147, Er-FA:263,
  Fe-FP:211, Gr-EC:48, Ho-WR:74,
  Hu-MP:268, Mc-PR:30, Pa-GTB:5,
  Rv-CB:196, Tu-WW:61
Understanding. T. Traherne.
  Go-BP:107, Mo-SD:84
Vacation Song. E. Millay.
  Ha-YA:68
A Valentine. E. Hammond.
  Ar-TP3:200, Ha-YA:179, Sh-RP:191
Valentine's Day. A. Fisher.
  Ha-YA:178, La-PH:46
Vesper. Alcman. Rd-OA:206
The Waking. T. Roethke. La-RM:128
Walk in the Rain. F. Frost.
  Ke-TF:85
Water Ouzel. W. Matchett.
  En-PC:213, Ni-JP:107
When Gathering Up on a Wet
  Mountain Morning. G. Dubrow.
  Ad-II:46
Winter in the Wood.
  I. Eastwick. Ha-YA:142
With Myriad Voices Grass Was
  Filled. C. Aiken. Rd-OA:43
With the Roses. J. Jiménez.
  Le-SW:19, Li-TU:207
OUTER SPACE: see SPACE
OUTLAWS: see also HUMOR —
  OUTLAWS; PIRATES; and
  names of outlaws, as
  BONNEY, WILLIAM H.
  (BILLY THE KID), and
  ROBIN HOOD
As Tawny Tigers. H. Melville.
  Kr-OF:148
The Ballad of Billy the Kid.
  H. Knibbs. Fi-BG:179
Ballade of Boot-Hill. Fi-BG:110
The Baron of Braikley. Ox-BB:618
Belle Starr. Fi-BG:225
Billy the Kid. Co-RM:164,
  Fi-BG:53, Hi-TL:144
Brennan on the Moor.
  Co-RM:165, Gr-GB:254
The Bushrangers.
  E. Harrington. Co-PT:244
Clever Tom Clinch. J. Swift.
  Co-RM:175
The Death of Ben Hall.
  W. Ogilvie. Co-PT:214
Dust or Bust. Fi-BG:51
Hangman's Tree. L. White. Br-AF:103
The Highwayman. J. Gay. Ho-WR:45
The Highwayman. A. Noyes.
  Ar-TP3:24, Co-BL:155, Er-FA:343,
  Fe-FP:449, Fe-PL:16, Un-GT:131

The Highwayman's Ghost.
   R. Garnett.   Co-PT:228
Jesse James.   W. Benét. Ha-PO:208,
   Hi-TL:145, Un-MA:327
Jesse James.   Br-AF:111,
   Ho-WR:116, Mc-WS:161
Jim Genung.   Fi-BG:55
Kinmont Willie.   Ox-BB:559
News of Blood.   D. Whitney.
   Kr-OF:140
The Outlaw.   C. Kingsley.
   Co-RM:161
The Outlaw.   W. Scott. Pa-GTB:174
The Outlaw Murray.   Ox-BB:363
The Outlaw of Loch Lene.
   J. Callanan.   De-CH:336
The Outlaw's Song.   J. Baillie.
   Sp-OG:161
Parcy Reed.   Ox-BB:586
Queen of the Desperados.
   Fi-BG:227, 229
The Ruffian Rally.   J. Pierpont.
   Kr-OF:138
Spanish Johnny.   W. Cather.
   Co-RM:26, Fe-FP:436, Hu-MP:154,
   Mc-WK:140, Mc-WS:160, Sh-RP:41
Three Fingered Black Jack.
   Fi-BG:56
The Two-Gun Man.   Fi-BG:54
Two Ponies Shy.   Fi-BG:142
The Wild Colonial Boy.   Co-RM:171
The Wolves of the Border.
   J. Whittier.   Kr-OF:147
See also Em-AF:702-729
OUZELS
   The Tiny Bird.   Re-BS:30
   The Water-Ousel.   M. Webb.
      De-CH:99, Tu-WW:94
   Water Ouzel.   D. McCord. Co-BBW:258
   Water Ouzel.   W. Matchett.
      En-PC:213, Ni-JP:107
OVENBIRDS
   The Oven Bird.   R. Frost.
      Pl-US:63
OVERALLS: see CLOTHING AND DRESS
OVERLAND JOURNEYS TO THE PACIFIC:
      see LEWIS AND CLARK EXPEDITION;
      also names of routes, as
      OREGON TRAIL
OVIBOSES: see MUSK OXEN
OVID
   Notes to the Life of Ovid.
      A. Hamori.   Ls-NY:131
   Ovid's Island.
      C. Theodorescu.   Mc-AC:101
OWLS: see also
      HUMOR - OWLS
   Alabama.   J. Fields.
      Ad-PB:319, Hu-PN:420

All But Blind.   W. de la Mare.
   Fe-FP:138, Ga-S:48, Hi-WP I:121,
   La-PV:152, Mc-WK:99, Ni-JP:82,
   Un-MB:291
The Aziola.   P. Shelley.   Gr-SS:67,
   Rv-CB:710
The Barn Owl.   S. Butler.
   De-TT:81, Sm-MK:149
The Bird of Night.   R. Jarrell.
   Ad-PE:32, La-RM:55, Mo-TS:65,
   Re-BS:45
The Bonny, Bonny Owl.   W. Scott.
   Re-BS:46
The Boy in the Barn.   Wr-RM:97
Come On, Owl.   Issa.   Le-IS:16
Disturbances.   A. Thwaite.
   To-MP:137
Flight.   W. Walden.   Ls-NY:329
Four-Footed Poems.
   E. Greenberg.   Ho-TY:312
The Frog on the Log.
   I. Orleans.   Mc-AW:55
The Great Brown Owl.   J. Browne.
   Ox-BC:225
Hopi Owl Song.   Da-SC:95
A Hungry Owl Hoots.   Joso.
   Be-CS:14
I of the Owl.   Ho-SD:9
If the Owl Calls Again.
   J. Haines.   Co-BN:107
Kahuto, the Owl.   Tr-US I:214
The Little Boy.   Mo-MGT:10
The Little Fox.   M. Edey and
   D. Grider.   Ar-TP3:64
Love Song.   Tr-US II:222
Nay, Ivy, Nay.   De-CH:230,
   Rv-CB:32
Once I Was a Monarch's Daughter.
   De-CH:98, De-TT:81
Over in the Meadow.   Au-SP:223,
   Ir-BB:24, On-TW:38
Owl.   E. Braithwaite.   Ls-NY:203
Owl.   G. Macbeth.   To-MP:154
The Owl.   B. Procter.   Co-BBW:262
The Owl.   W. Smith.   Co-IW:21,
   La-PV:134
The Owl.   A. Tennyson.   Bl-OB:65,
   Bo-FP:285, Bo-GJ:73, Ch-B:112,
   De-CH:98, De-TT:80, Fe-FP:293,
   Gr-EC:176, Hu-MP:238, Ir-BB:23,
   Re-TW:24, Rv-CB:794, Sm-LG:88,
   Tu-WW:90, Un-GB:17, Un-GT:65
The Owl.   E. Thomas.   Gr-CT:107,
   Ha-PO:105, Ni-JP:86,
   Pa-GTB:441, Re-BS:47
The Owl.   R. Warren.   Un-MA:588
The Owl.   Mo-MGT:207
The Owl.   Ca-MU:30
Owl, Crevice-Sitter.   Le-OE:42

OWLS — cont'd.
  The Owl Hooted.   Da-SC:88,
    Ho-SD:20, Le-OE:11
  Owl Song.   Da-SC:89
  Owls Talking.   D. McCord.
    Co-BBW:254
  Prayer to the Snowy Owl.
    J. Haines.   Co-PU:107
  Questioning Faces.   R. Frost.
    Co-BBW:233, Co-EL:28, Co-PU:106
  The Snowy Owl.   E. Kroll.
    Co-BBW:244
  Song.   Br-MW:93
  Song from a Story.   Tr-US I:30
  Sweet Suffolk Owl.   T. Vautor.
    De-CH:97, Gr-CT:107, Rv-CB:262
  Then from a Ruin.
    Farid-uddin Attar.   Re-BS:46
  There Came a Gray Owl.   Ho-SD:17
  There Was a Boy.   W. Wordsworth.
    Go-BP:119, Ox-BN:101, Sm-LG:107
  There Was an Owl.   Un-GF:13
  "Two, Two!" Toots the Train.
    On-TW:8
  The Unwise Owl.   Ir-BB:124
  The White Owl.   G. Meredith.
    Gr-CT:108
  The White Owl.   F. Patmore.
    Co-PM:136, De-CH:548
  Who Is This?   Da-SC:158, Jo-TS:9
  Who? Who?   De-CH:98
  Winter.   W. Shakespeare.
    Al-VBP:182, Bl-OB:98, Bo-FP:178,
    Bo-GJ:252, Co-BN:181, Co-PS:157,
    Co-RG:129, De-CH:230, Fe-FP:65,
    Gr-CT:392, Ha-PO:252, Ho-WR:171,
    Hu-MP:323, Ma-YA:65, Mc-WK:29,
    Pa-GTB:17, Re-TW:102, Rv-CB:190,
    Sm-LG:59, Sp-OG:286, Tu-WW:74
  A Wise Old Owl Lived in an Oak.
    Er-FA:213, Li-LB:103, Mo-MGT:118,
      Un-GT:22, Wi-MG:47
  The Women and the Man.   Te-FC:87
OWNERSHIP: see POSSESSIONS;
  PROPERTY
OXEN: see also MUSK OXEN
  Crossing the Plains.   J. Miller.
    Gr-CC:127
  The Herd-Boy's Song.
    Chen Shan-min.   Pa-SG:126
  The Herdboy.   Lu Yu.
    Gr-CT:114, Le-MW:110, Ma-FW:76
  Love Songs.   Tr-US I:114
  The Old Cowboy.   Kao Chi.
    Rx-LT:111
  Old North.   N. Thorp.   Fi-BG:131
  The Ox.   S. Murano.   Sh-AM:96
  The Ox-Tamer.   W. Whitman.
    Co-BBW:164, Co-RM:236,
    Rv-CB:857

  The Oxen.   T. Hardy.   Ga-S:86,
    Go-BP:92, Ha-PO:117, No-CL:281,
    Tr-MR:109, Un-MB:33, Wi-LT:21
  Partners.   J. Castillo.
    Gr-EC:15, Mc-WK:90
  The Prayer of the Ox.
    C. Gasztold.   Li-TU:188, Mc-WS:51
  Twelve Oxen.   Cl-DT:49, De-CH:139,
    Gr-CT:114, Gr-GB:53, Re-TW:78,
    Sh-RP:51
  When Off This Creature's Head
    Is Cut.   Re-RR:50
  Zebu.   F. Ranaivo.   Ab-MO:38
OXFORD, ENG.
  Duns Scotus's Oxford.
    G. Hopkins.   Pa-GTB:391
  Oxford.   R. Aldridge.   Ls-NY:247
  The Scholar Gypsy.   M. Arnold.
    Al-VBP:964, Gr-CT:255, Ox-BN:628
  Thyrsis. M. Arnold.   Ox-BN:637
OXFORD UNIVERSITY
  Oxford.   L. Johnson.   Ox-BN:949
  The Spires of Oxford.   W. Letts.
    Cr-WS:68, Er-FA:190, Fe-PL:178
  V.D.F.   H. Wolfe.   Cr-WS:76
OXUS RIVER
  Sohrab and Rustum.   M. Arnold.
    Pa-GTB:363
OYSTER RIVER
  Meditation at Oyster River.
    T. Roethke.   Un-MA:601
OYSTERS: see HUMOR - OYSTERS
PACIFIC OCEAN: see also
    ISLANDS OF THE PACIFIC
  The Eye.   R. Jeffers.   Wi-LT:266
  Night.   R. Jeffers.   Sm-PT:155,
    Un-MA:367
  Ocean.   R. Jeffers.   Pe-OA:87
  Once by the Pacific. R. Frost.
    Ca-VT:17, Pa-HT:62, Sm-PT:78,
    Un-MA:184, Wi-LT:173
  Prayer to the Pacific.   L. Silko.
    Ni-CD:226
  Sea Surface Full of Clouds.
    W. Stevens.   Ca-VT:32, Un-MA:245
PACIFISTS: see CONSCIENTIOUS
    OBJECTORS; FRIENDS, SOCIETY OF
PADSTOW, ENG.
  The Padstow Night Song.
    Gr-CT:44, Gr-GB:45
PAGODAS: see TEMPLES
PAIGE, LEROY ROBERT (SATCHEL)
  To Satch.   S. Allen.
    Ab-MO:89, Ad-PB:167, Bo-AN:140,
    Gr-BT:178, Hu-PN:343, Jo-SA:58,
    Lo-TY:244, Mc-EA:71, Mo-SD:18
PAIN: see also HUMOR - PAIN;
    SUFFERING
  After Great Pain a Formal Feeling
    Comes. E. Dickinson. Un-MA:100

A Baby Asleep after Pain.
D. Lawrence. Go-BP:117
A Charm Against the Stitch.
Ma-FW:233
A Commemoration for the Physicist
X. P. Oppenheimer. Ls-NY:130
Curious Exposure. G. Sardiff.
Ni-CD:53
Epitaph. E. Wylie. Un-MA:280
Esthetique du Mal, I. W. Stevens.
Wi-LT:151
Flash Crimson. C. Sandburg.
Un-MA:207
A Flat One. W. Snodgrass.
En-PC:244
Four Things. P. Gearey.
Ke-TF:241
He Knoweth Not that the Dead Are
Thine. M. Coleridge.
Co-EL:11, Ox-BN:925
The Heart Asks Pleasure First.
E. Dickinson. Ha-PO:149,
Rv-CB:898, Un-MA:96
Hospital. K. Shapiro. Ca-VT:370
Hurt Hawks. R. Jeffers.
Co-BBW:236, Ni-JP:115, Pe-SS:150,
Sh-AP:177, Un-MA:369, Wi-LT:258
I Like a Look of Agony.
E. Dickinson. Rv-CB:907
Love Songs. Tr-US I:126
My Donkey. Ar-TP3:123, Ir-BB:175
Notes Found near a Suicide:
To Mother. F. Horne. Bo-AN:42,
Ra-BP:71
Only Seven. H. Leigh. Li-SR:118
Pain. AE. Un-MB:142
Pain. M. Als. Sa-B:39
Pain Has an Element of Blank.
E. Dickinson. Rv-CB:901,
Un-MA:104, Wi-LT:12
A Quality of Pain. B. Holender.
Ls-NY:14
Quietly I Shout. A. Pratt.
Al-WW:110
Surgical Ward. W. Auden.
Pe-SS:146
Threnody. D. Hayes. Bo-AN:93
To Earthward. R. Frost. Un-MA:180
Weltschmerz. F. Yerby. Bo-AN:136
The Wound-Dresser. W. Whitman.
Al-VBP:937
PAINE, THOMAS
America Was Promises. A. MacLeish.
Br-AF:250, Vi-PP:229
Citizen Paine. J. Daugherty.
Gr-EC:230
PAINTING,
INDUSTRIAL
The El-Painter's Daughter.
M. Kessler. Ls-NY:222

PAINTINGS: see also ART AND
ARTISTS; HUMOR - PAINTINGS
Abstract Painter in Spring.
R. Haas. Ls-NY:151
The Auction Sale. H. Reed.
Un-MB:509
Before a Saint's Picture.
W. Landor. Ox-BC:170
La Creazione degli Animale.
J. Brinnin. Ls-NY:174
Don't Let That Horse.
L. Ferlinghetti. Mo-BG:82
Elegiac Stanzas. W. Wordsworth.
Ox-BN:81, Pa-GTB:297
Fra Lippo Lippi. R. Browning.
Ho-P:118
Gentleman in Oils. H. Vinal.
De-FS:208
Ginevra. S. Rogers. Fe-PL:13
Giocanni da Fiesole on the
Sublime. R. Howard. Ho-P:117
A Glance. Cheng Min. Hs-TC:235
The Horses. K. Wilson. Sc-TN:238
How to Paint the Portrait of a
Bird. J. Prévert.
Ma-FW:96, Sm-MK:168
Hunters in the Snow: Brueghel.
J. Langland. Wi-LT:753
I Paint What I See. E. White.
Mo-BG:64
In Santa Maria del Popolo.
T. Gunn. Pa-GTB:563
Intaglio. H. Coulette. En-PC:252
The Lotus Flower. Cheng Min.
Hs-TC:239
Marin. P. Booth. Mo-BG:126
The Municipal Gallery Revisited.
W. Yeats. Pa-GTB:432
Mural of Borodino. L. Adler.
Ls-NY:175
Musée des Beaux Arts. W. Auden.
Br-TC:20, Er-FA:64, Ha-PO:223,
Pa-GTB:510, To-MP:31, Wi-LT:467
My Last Duchess. R. Browning.
Er-FA:374, Fe-PL:82, Ha-PO:39,
Ma-YA:200, Ni-JP:40, Ox-BN:545,
Pa-GTB:350
On a Portrait by Copley.
A. Freeman. Co-RM:215, Cr-WS:54
The Peaceable Kingdom. M. Piercy.
Br-TC:317
Picasso's "Portrait de Femme."
I. Feldman. Ls-NY:89
Portrait of a Lady. W. Praed.
No-CL:235
Postcard. E. Livingston. Sc-TN:144
Retort to the Anti-Abstractionists.
E. Jennings. Go-BP:64
So-and-So Reclining on Her Couch.
W. Stevens. Wi-LT:149

PAINTINGS — cont'd.
  To the Portrait of an Unknown Man.
    A. Scruggs. Ls-NY:144
  Untitled. D. Hine. Br-TC:188
  Upon His Picture. T. Randolph.
    Rv-CB:363
  We Have Seen Her. H.D. Ca-VT:117
  Wild Beasts. Cheng Min. Hs-TC:240
  Winter Landscape. J. Berryman.
    Br-TC:37, Mo-BG:112, Un-MA:640,
    Wi-LT:566
  The Woman at the Window.
    D. Wandrei. De-FS:212
PAIUTE INDIANS: see INDIANS OF
    NORTH AMERICA - VERSE—PAIUTE
PALACES: see also CASTLES
  Epilogue. L. Abercrombie.
    Un-MB:254
  The Haunted Palace. E. Poe.
    Al-VBP:875, De-CH:320, Gr-CT:160,
    Ho-WR:216, Sh-AP:54
  On a Bougainvillea Vine at the
    Summer Palace. B. Howes.
    Un-MA:653
  The Parliament of Bees.
    J. Day. Al-VBP:242
  Tamurlaine the Great. C. Marlowe.
    Al-VBP:175
  This Palace Standeth in the Air.
    M. Drayton. De-CH:556
PALANQUINS
  Palanquin Bearers. S. Naidu.
    Th-AS:154
PALEONTOLOGY: see FOSSILS;
    PREHISTORIC ANIMALS
PALESTINE: see also ISRAEL
  John Brown. V. Lindsay.
    Un-MA:227
PALESTRINA, GIOVANNI
    PIERLUIGI DA
  Duke of Parma's Ear. E. Siegel.
    Co-EL:154
PALLAS ATHENE: see MINERVA
PALM SUNDAY: see LENT
PALM TREES
  Ceremonial Prayer for the
    Fructification of the
    Pandanus Tree. Tr-US II:27
  The Palm. R. Campbell.
    Un-MB:417
  Royal Palms. H. Crane. Un-MA:533
  Song of the Departed Spirit.
    Tr-US I:197
PAN (GOD):
  The Forest. D. Quick. De-FS:153
  The God of Sheep. J. Fletcher.
    Sm-LG:228
  Hymn of Pan. P. Shelley.
    Sm-LG:229

  A Musical Instrument.
    E. Browning. Fe-FP:384,
    Ho-WR:36, Mc-PR:122, Pa-OM:284,
    Se-PR:327, Sp-OG:343, Un-GT:162
  Pan and the Cherries. P. Fort.
    Co-PM:67
  Pan's Syrinx Was a Girl.
    J. Lyly. Al-VBP:122
  Sing His Praises. J. Fletcher.
    Al-VBP:277
PAN-AMERICANISM
  The Christ of the Andes.
    E. Markham. Se-PR:85
  Hymn of the New World.
    P. MacKaye. Se-PR:82
  Panama. J. Roche. Se-PR:83
  South American Sway. M. Byers.
    Gr-EC:120
PANAMA
  Beyond the Chagres. J. Gilbert.
    Fe-PL:429
  Panama. J. Roche. Se-PR:83
  The Sack of Old Panama.
    D. Burnet. Co-RM:56
PANAMA CANAL
  Goethals, the Prophet Engineer.
    P. MacKaye. Se-PR:84
  A Song of Panama. A. Runyon.
    Hi-TL:158
PANCAKES: see CAKES AND COOKIES
PANDANUS TREES: see PALM TREES
PANDAS: see HUMOR - PANDAS
PANDORA
  Pandora. M. Livingston. Ne-AM:16
  Pandora and the Moon. M. Moore.
    Un-MA:576
PANTHEISM
  Essay on Deity. E. Olson.
    Tr-MR:141
  How Many Heavens. E. Sitwell.
    Gr-CC:134, Tr-MR:41
  Lines Composed above Tintern
    Abbey. W. Wordsworth.
    Go-BP:21, Ho-P:125
  Song of Myself. W. Whitman.
    Er-FA:87, Tr-MR:143, Un-MA:61
PANTHERS: see also HUMOR -
    PANTHERS
  The Panther. R. Rilke. Ma-FW:61,
    Rd-OA:120
  The Panther Possible. W. Barney.
    De-FS:13, Du-SH:115
PAOLO AND FRANCESCA: see also
    HUMOR - PAOLO AND FRANCESCA
  The Story of Rimini. L. Hunt.
    Na-EO:124
PAPER
  Paper. C. Sandburg. Ho-TH:57
  A Paper Suicide. A. Lutzky.
    Ho-TY:265

The Term. W. Williams. Mo-TS:34
PAPER NAUTILUSES: see NAUTILUSES
PARABLES: see ALLEGORIES; FABLES
PARACHUTES
The Parachutes. C. Gullans.
Ls-NY:31
Sky Diver. A. Stoutenburg.
Mo-TS:14
PARADES
The Circus Parade. O. Miller.
Ar-TP3:115, Au-SP:126
Dances. D. Meltzer. Lo-IT:90
Listen to the People. S. Benét.
Co-PS:112
A Parade. M. Rose. Au-SP:122
Paraders for the Bomb.
S. Bernard. Ba-PO:39
PARADISE: see EDEN;
ELYSIUM; HEAVEN
PARASITES
The First Animal. V. Contoski.
Sc-TN:25
PARASOLS: see UMBRELLAS
PARENT AND CHILD: see also
DAUGHTERS; FAMILY AND FAMILY
LIFE; FATHERS; HUMOR - PARENT
AND CHILD; ILLEGITIMACY;
MOTHERS; SATIRE - PARENT AND
CHILD; SONS
Abraham and Isaac. Ga-S:40,
Ma-FW:78
Abraham Takes Isaac to the
Sacrifice. I. Manger.
Ho-TY:275
The Affliction of Margaret.
W. Wordsworth. Pa-GTB:239
After Dark. A. Rich. Wi-LT:801
An Afterword to My Father.
M. Bell. Mc-EA:109
Alec Yeaton's Son. T. Aldrich.
Sp-OG:92
Am I Stupid? H. Ooguro.
Le-TA:92
Amelia Mixed the Mustard.
A. Housman. Ne-AM:9
Among School Children. W. Yeats.
Pa-GTB:428, Un-MB:114, Wi-LT:72
Amusing Our Daughters. C. Kizer.
Ca-VT:542
And What about Children.
A. Lorde. Ad-PB:247
Andre. G. Brooks. Ar-TP3:5,
Sh-RP:97
Annie of Lochroyan. Ma-BB:202
At My Father's Grave.
H. MacDiarmid. Co-EL:70,
Pa-GTB:486
At the Washing of My Son.
Su Tung P'o.
Rx-OH:84

Automobile Mechanics. D. Baruch.
Ar-TP3:4, Au-SP:103, Fe-FP:35
Babies: Just Babies.
M. Fishback. Gr-EC:21
A Baby Asleep after Pain.
D. Lawrence. Go-BP:117
The Ballad of the Harp-Weaver.
E. Millay. Ar-TP3:156, Co-PT:64
Bartholomew. N. Gale. Br-BC:42,
Th-AS:54
Bats. R. Jarrell. To-MP:156
Bedtime. K. Goddard. Fr-MP:22
Before Sedan. A. Dobson.
Ke-TF:52
Big Momma. D. Lee. Ra-BP:304
Birmingham 1963. R. Patterson.
Ad-PB:209, Kr-OF:163
"Blackened-Face" Dirge - Proper
for Atiroa. Koroneu.
Tr-US II:64
The Boat. R. Pack. Ha-TP:125
A Boy. B. Graves. Le-M:142
The Boy and the Deer. Te-FC:3
Broken Shell. W. Scott. Ls-NY:228
Broom, Green Broom. Bl-OB:38,
De-CH:139, Fo-OG:8, Ha-PO:54
Burial. R. Raymond. Ls-NY:224
By the Exeter River. D. Hall.
Ca-MB:21
The Cannibal's Seven Sons.
Br-MW:116
Child and Mother. E. Field.
Hu-MP:126
The Child and the Snake. M. Lamb.
De-TT:63, Ox-BC:142
A Child Half-Asleep. T. Connor.
Go-BT:8
The Childless Father.
W. Wordsworth. De-CH:260
The Children's Hour. H. Longfellow.
Bo-FP:32, Er-FA:484, Fe-FP:51,
Fe-PL:144, Ga-FB:162, Hu-MP:109,
Ke-TF:75, Mc-PR:208, Tu-WW:20,
Un-GT:98
The Chimney Sweeper. W. Blake.
Ma-YA:128, Rv-CB:580
The Circle of Weeping. A. Gilboa.
Me-PH:117
Civilizing the Child. L. Mueller.
Ha-TP:118
Colder Fire. R. Warren. Wi-LT:835
Commander Lowell. R. Lowell.
Ca-VT:451
The Confession Stone. O. Dodson.
Ab-MO:72, Lo-TY:238
The Constancy. J. Miller.
Sc-TN:171
The Cottager to Her Infant.
D. Wordsworth. De-CH:205,
Ox-BC:127

PARENT AND CHILD — cont'd.
  The Crib. C. Morley. Br-BC:157
  The Cruel Mother. Ox-BB:68
  Daddy. R. Fyleman. Br-SS:165
  Daddy. S. Plath. Br-TC:324,
    Mc-EA:164, Wi-LT:789
  Daddy in the Dream.
    M. Yamaguchi. Le-TA:31
  Daedalus and Icarus. L. Coxe.
    Ls-NY:228
  Dance Songs, IV. Tr-US I:199
  Death of a Son. Bi-IT:99
  Deathwatch. M. Harper. Ad-PB:317
  Declaration of Independence.
    W. Gibbs. Pe-SS:23
  The Dishonest Miller. Em-AF:761
  Dress Me, Dear Mother.
    A. Schlonsky. Me-PH:99
  Dusk. L. Nathan. Ls-NY:132
  Earth. M. Rosenfeld. Ho-TY:80
  Edward, Edward. De-CH:410,
    Ha-PO:1, Ma-BB:39, Ox-BB:239,
    Rv-CB:39
  Efficiency Apartment. G. Barrax.
    Ad-PB:217
  The El-Painter's Daughter.
    M. Keesler. Ls-NY:222
  Elegy for My Father. H. Moss.
    Wi-LT:777
  The Empty Woman. G. Brooks.
    Pe-SS:13
  Epic Song. Tr-US I:236
  The Erl-King. J. von Goethe.
    Sp-OG:111
  An Excuse for Not Returning the
    Visit of a Friend.
    Mei Yao Ch'en. Rx-OH:37
  The Exhortation of a Father to
    His Children. R. Smith.
    Ox-BC:13
  The Family Poem. M. Rawitch.
    Ho-TY:202
  The Farewell. J. Whittier.
    Hu-PN:461, Kr-OF:29
  Farewell to My Mother.
    Placido. Lo-TY:99
  Father and Child. W. Yeats.
    Co-PU:74
  Father and Son. F. Higgins.
    Co-PI:64
  Father and Son. S. Kunitz.
    Br-TC:247
  A Father Swings His Child.
    W. Snodgrass. Mc-WS:141
  A Father's Notes of Woe.
    W. Scott. Ox-BN:125
  Father's Voice. W. Stafford.
    La-RM:167
  find my father with freedom.
    L. Curry. Jo-VC:38

  A Flower Given to My Daughter.
    J. Joyce. Go-BP:117
  Follower. S. Heaney. Co-PI:59
  For a Fatherless Son. S. Plath.
    Mc-EA:98, Mo-TS:36
  For a Junior School Poetry Book.
    C. Middleton. Ma-FW:70,
    To-MP:151
  For My Daughter. W. Kees.
    Mc-EA:106
  For My Father. P. Whalen.
    Mc-EA:112
  For You, My Son. H. Gregory.
    Un-MA:508
  Forming Child Poems. S. Ortiz.
    Ni-CD:153
  The Forsaken. D. Scott.
    Do-WH:63, Ha-PO:159
  From a Childhood. R. Rilke.
    Gr-SS:133
  From the Greek of Julianus.
    W. Cowper. Sp-OG:49
  Frost at Midnight. S. Coleridge.
    Ox-BN:162, Rv-CB:661
  A Frosty Night. R. Graves.
    Ca-MB:15, De-CH:215, Un-MB:388
  Fruit of the Flower. C. Cullen.
    Fe-PL:136, Jo-SA:20
  GI. R. Roseliep. De-FS:164
  Generations. R. Korn. Ho-TY:304
  The Gift of God. E. Robinson.
    Un-MA:135
  Ginger Bread Mama. D. Long.
    Ad-PB:404, Ra-BP:310
  Give Heed, My Child. Ho-SD:32
  Going to the Heavenly Bridge.
    Li Kuang-t'ien. Hs-TC:205
  The Goodnight. L. Simpson.
    To-MP:91
  Graeme and Bewick. Ox-BB:356,
    Rv-CB:47
  Grandmother Watching at Her
    Window. W. Merwin.
    Ca-VT:616
  Greens. D. Ray. Ca-VT:678
  Ha Ha Thisaway. Bu-DY:33
  Hallelujah: A Sestina.
    R. Francis. En-PC:46
  Henry C. Calhoun. E. Masters.
    Sh-AP:138, Wi-LT:115
  Hide-and-Seek. T. Arghezi.
    Mc-AC:27
  Homecoming. A. Kramer. Ls-NY:94
  The Horse Show. W. Stevens.
    Ca-VT:66, Pe-OA:79
  How the Gates Came Ajar.
    Ke-TF:42
  Hynd Etin. Ma-BB:192
  I Have Breakfast, Dinner, Tea.
    Gr-TG:36

I Walk Out into the Country at
   Night. Lu Yu. Rx-OH:108
I Wanted to Come Home. Wen I-to.
   Hs-TC:59
If I Should Ever by Chance Grow
   Rich. E. Thomas. Bl-OB:32,
   Bo-GJ:20, De-CH:518, Ox-BC:329,
   Pa-RE:73, Sm-LG:112, Un-MB:215
If I Were a Wind. Y. Aji.
   Le-TA:19
In Memoriam. Yu Tu-fu. Hs-TC:272
It Shall Be. Ho-SD:13
Jean Richepin's Song. H. Trench.
   Co-PI:191, Co-PT:25, Gr-EC:127
Jepthah's Daughter. A. Tennyson.
   Hi-FO:17
Jesus and His Mother. T. Gunn.
   Ke-TF:144, Pl-EI:31, To-MP:77
Jesus Was Crucified. C. Rodgers.
   Ad-PB:432
Johnny Shall Have a New Bonnet.
   Mo-NR:46, Wr-RM:45
The Kid Has Gone to the Colors.
   W. Herschell. Fe-PL:163
King Lear. W. Shakespeare.
   Ho-P:94
Lady Elspat. Ma-BB:199
Lament. Tr-US II:117
Lament. Tr-US II:78
Lament of Huauri. Tr-US II:80
Lament: Sea-Burial of Toha's
   Daughter. Tr-US II:88
The Last Quatrain of the Ballad
   of Emmett Till. G. Brooks.
   Ad-PB:155
Leave Me Alone. F. Holman.
   Un-GB:20
Letter of a Mother. R. Warren.
   Un-MA:584
Lines on Receiving His Mother's
   Picture. W. Cowper. De-CH:38
The Lioness and Her Cub.
   V. Lapin. Mo-MI:80
The Little Boy Found. W. Blake.
   Rv-CB:582
Little Boy Lost. W. Blake.
   Rv-CB:581
Little Brand New Baby.
   T. Paxton. Pe-SS:3
Little Brown Baby. P. Dunbar.
   Ab-MO:100, Hu-PN:40
The Little Girl Found. W. Blake.
   Rv-CB:593
Little Jack Horner. De-TT:49,
   Li-LB:42
The Lonely Mother. F. Johnson.
   Hu-PN:91
Lord Christ, My Darling Is So
   Dear. C. Hansen-Bay.
   Gr-TG:66

the lost baby poem. L. Clifton.
   Be-MA:141
McDonogh Day in New Orleans.
   M. Christian. Bo-AN:52,
   Hu-PN:157
McNaughton. Ox-BB:304
Mamma! F. Horne. Ra-BP:76
March 18. Jao Meng-k'an.
   Hs-TC:106
Margaret Love Peacock for Her
   Tombstone, 1826. T. Peacock.
   Ox-BN:237
Mary Hamilton. Ox-BB:328
The Message of the Frigate Birds.
   Tr-US II:89
Milking Pails. De-CH:67
The Mill Mother's Lament.
   E. Wiggins. Kr-OF:191
Morning Song. S. Plath.
   Mc-EA:103
Mortmain. R. Warren. En-PC:74,
   Ho-P:295
Mother and Daughter.
   J. Bovshover. Kr-OF:170
Mother and Slave Raiders.
   Tr-US I:90
Mother and Son. A. Tate.
   Un-MA:538
Mother and Son. R. Thomas.
   Gr-BT:21
A Mother Horse. Issa.
   Do-TS:(19), Le-MW:8
A Mother Praises Her Baby.
   Tr-US I:77
Mother, the Wardrobe Is Full
   of Infantrymen.
   R. McGough. Gr-BT:117
Mother to Son. L. Hughes.
   Ab-MO:97, Be-MA:38, Bo-AN:67,
   Bo-HF:177, Br-BC:123, Hu-PN:186,
   Jo-SA:19, La-OC:94, Lo-TY:225,
   Pe-FB:70, Pe-SS:7
Mother's Advice. Em-AF:771
Mother's Day. Y. Takeuchi.
   Le-TA:22
The Mother's Song. Ho-SD:75,
   Le-OE:113
Mount Fuji. M. Kaneko. Sh-AM:66
Mousemeal. H. Nemerov. Br-TC:315
Muse Late in November.
   J. Brooks. Hu-PN:240
My Child. Y. Amichai. Mc-EA:104
My Daughter. Ge-TR:44
My Father in the Night Commanding
   No. L. Simpson. Br-TC:380,
   Ca-VT:520, Hi-WP II:357
My Father Loved the Jumping-Off
   Place. R. Coffin. Sh-RP:309
My Little Son. M. Rosenfeld.
   Ho-TY:79

PARENT AND CHILD — cont'd.
My Little Son. Da-SC:58, Ho-SD:54
My Mamma Has Been Clever. Anya.
    Mo-MI:59
My Mamma Moved among the Days.
    L. Clifton. Ad-PB:308,
    Be-MA:139
My Mother and Me. Mo-MI:45
My Papa's Waltz. T. Roethke.
    Ca-VT:286, Ha-PO:71, Ma-FW:64,
    Mo-BG:79, Pe-OA:206, Pe-SS:12,
    Sh-AP:213, Wi-LT:478
My Son. Ge-TR:41
My Sun! Jo-TS:1
The Name. R. Creeley. Pe-SS:4
A Negro Soldier's Viet Nam Diary.
    H. Martin. Ad-PB:227
The New Pieta: For the Mothers
    and Children of Detroit.
    J. Jordan. Ad-PB:303
Newspaper. A. Fisher. Au-SP:102
Nightmare. A. Marx. De-FS:136
Noodle. Y. Hashimoto. Le-TA:91
Not from Here. J. La Rose.
    Sa-B:76
Notes Found near a Suicide:
    To James. F. Horne. Bo-AN:45,
    Bo-HF:90, Br-BC:124, Ra-BP:73
Notes Found near a Suicide:
    To Mother. F. Horne.
    Bo-AN:42, Ra-BP:71
Now the Man Has a Child.
    S. Karai. Ma-FW:67
O Sleep, My Babe. S. Coleridge.
    Ox-BN:448
Ode for My Father's Eightieth
    Birthday. R. Potash. Ho-TY:358
The Old Man and Jim. J. Riley.
    Co-PT:232, Sp-OG:197
Old Mother Goose and the Golden
    Egg. Li-LB:48, Mo-MGT:2
On the Birth of His Son.
    Su Tung-P'o. Gr-BT:7
On the Death of His Baby Son.
    Su Tung P'o. Rx-OH:69
On the Staircase. W. Wellman.
    De-FS:215
On Visiting My Son, Port Angeles,
    Washington. D. Niatum.
    Ni-CD:130
The Only Son. H. Newbolt.
    Sp-OG:200
Oriflamme. J. Fauset. Ad-PB:18
Our Father. R. Mathew. Ma-FW:63
Our Hired Man. M. Shannon.
    Fe-FP:313
Out in the Woods with Father.
    D. McCord. Gr-TG:24
Papa, Mama. C. Belli.
    Be-UL:115

Pater Filio. R. Bridges.
    Al-VBP:1063
Paternal. E. Wilson. Hu-PN:370
The Phoenix Self-Born. J. Dryden.
    Gr-CT:100
The Picture of J.T. in a Prospect
    of Stone. C. Tomlinson.
    En-PC:260
a poem for fathers. K. Wilson.
    Sc-TN:243
Poems for My Daughter.
    H. Gregory. Un-MA:505
Polly. W. Rands. Un-GT:101
A Prayer for My Daughter.
    W. Yeats. Al-VBP:1090,
    Fe-PL:37, Tr-MR:49, Wi-LT:73
Preface to a Twenty Volume
    Suicide Note. L. Jones.
    Ad-PB:250, Hu-PN:406, Jo-SA:33,
    Kh-VA:18, Lo-TY:251, Pe-SS:43
Presenting an Infant to the
    Sun. Bi-IT:113
Proud Motherhood. F. Lucas.
    Hi-FO:263
Quiet Citizen. B. Cooper.
    Ke-TF:298
The Rainy Day. R. Tagore.
    Al-PI:90, Ma-FW:117
Readen ov a Head-Stwone.
    W. Barnes. De-CH:264
Requiem of a War-Baby.
    J. Watton. Co-PI:193
The Return of the Marama from
    Hiti. Tr-US II:72
The Runaway Slave at Pilgrim's
    Point. E. Browning. Hu-PN:448
Second Son. B. Weinstein.
    Ho-TY:292
The Secret Heart. R. Coffin.
    Co-PS:103, Se-PR:152
Secret Laughter. C. Morley.
    Ga-FB:86
A Sense of Property. A. Thwaite.
    To-MP:139
Sick Boy. A. Ridler. Ls-NY:225
The Sick Child. R. Stevenson.
    Co-PS:87, De-CH:37, De-TT:151
Silly Song. F. Garcia Lorca.
    Le-SW:25, Li-TU:68
Six and Thirty. D. Stevenson.
    Br-BC:65
Sohrab and Rustum. M. Arnold.
    Pa-GTB:363
Something Peaceful.
    T. Tsyganok. Mo-MI:69
Son and Father. C. Day Lewis.
    Pl-EI:135
Song David. Ox-BB:241
Song of a Lioness Warning Her
    Cub. Be-AP:60, Tr-US I:79

Song of a Mother for Her Dead
  Son. Tr-US II:20
Song of a New Cradleboard.
  P. George. Al-WW:116
Song of a Warrior for His First-
  Born Son. Tr-US II:218
Song of Parents Who Want to Wake
  Up Their Son. Da-SC:57
Song of the Parents Who Want to
  Wake Up Their Daughter.
  Da-SC:58
A Song of Wetting the Bed.
  Y. Tanaka. Le-TA:87
Songs for My Mother: Her Hands.
  A. Branch. Hu-MP:4, Se-PR:117
The Spring Waters. Ping Hsin.
  Hs-TC:24
Squatter's Rites. D. Scott.
  Sa-B:151
Step on His Head. J. Laughlin.
  Ca-VT:411
Stewards. B. Cooper. Ke-TF:299
Supper. Y. Ashibe. Le-TA:25
Sword and Flower. T. Utan.
  Mc-AC:144
tell our daughters. B. Brigham.
  Sc-TN:17
There Was an Old Woman Who Lived
  in a Shoe. An-IP:(27), De-PO:6,
  Er-FA:505, Fr-WO:20, Ir-BB:197,
  Li-LB:36, Mo-CC:(6), Mo-MGT:161,
  Mo-NR:42, Wi-MG:25, Wr-RM:116
The Three Roses. W. Landor.
  No-CL:126
The Three Sons. Wr-RM:80
To Be Sung. P. Viereck.
  Ga-FB:86
To Children. L. McGaugh.
  Ad-PB:377
To His Son, Vincent Corbet.
  R. Corbet. Ox-BC:25, Rv-CB:322,
  Sm-LG:112
To Mother and Steve. M. Evans.
  Ad-PB:191, Ra-BP:184
To My Infant Daughter.
  Y. Winters. Ca-VT:226
To My Mother. Y. Amichai.
  Me-PH:133
To My Son. G. Barker. Br-TC:26
To My Son. S. Sassoon. Mc-WS:137
The Toys. C. Patmore.
  Al-VBP:973, Er-FA:142, Rv-CB:876
Upon My Lap My Sovereign Sits.
  R. Rowlands. Al-VBP:210, De-CH:20
Upon the Water. K. Takayasu.
  Sh-AM:157
Uvlunuaq's Song. Tr-US I:16
Verses for a First Birthday.
  G. Barker. Un-MB:495
Virginia. E. Loftin. Ad-PB:514

The Vow. A. Hecht. Ho-P:93
Waldheim Cemetery. R. Sward.
  St-H:217
What I Tell Him. S. Ortiz.
  Ni-CD:151
What My Child Learns of the Sea.
  A. Lorde. Ad-PB:247
What Shall I Give? E. Thomas.
  Ox-BC:330, Sm-LG:113
What Shall They Tell That Son?
  C. Sandburg. Pe-SS:10
When I Am a Man. Da-SC:9,
  Ho-SD:56
When I Am in Grief.
  Yamanoue no Okura. Le-MW:121
Where the Hayfields Were.
  A. MacLeish. Ha-LO:80
White Cat. R. Knister. Do-WH:82
Who Is a Son of My Father.
  Gr-BB:31
The Widow of Drynam. P. MacDonogh.
  Co-PI:110
The Wife of Usher's Well.
  Ar-TP3:20, De-CH:424, De-TT:171,
  Gr-CT:134, Ma-BB:37, Ox-BB:94,
  Pa-OM:91, Rv-CB:36
The Wild Flower and the Rose.
  D. Nikogosian. Mo-MI:80
the will's love. B. Brigham.
  Sc-TN:24
With Kit, Age 7, at the Beach.
  W. Stafford. La-RM:92
Words Spoken by a Mother to Her
  Newborn Son. Bi-IT:112
Young Woman at a Window.
  W. Williams. La-OC:56
Younge Andrew. Ox-BB:216

PARET, BERNARDO (KID)
  The Memory of Boxer Benny (Kid)
    Paret. F. Lima. Hu-PN:587
PARIS, PRINCE OF TROY
  Oenone. A. Tennyson. Al-VBP:851
PARIS, FR.: see also
    HUMOR - PARIS, FR.
  About to Sail for Home.
    Wang Tu-ch'ing. Hs-TC:196
  All Tropic Places Smell of Mold.
    K. Shapiro. Ca-VT:375
  Les Arbres. M. Bracker. Ke-TF:377
  The Ballad of Bouillabaisse.
    W. Thackeray. Al-VBP:879
  Ballade of the Women of Paris.
    F. Villon. Un-MW:130
  Le Bois. M. Bracker. Ke-TF:376
  Le Bon Marché. M. Bracker.
    Ke-TF:378
  Four Sheets to the Wind and a
    One-Way Ticket to France, 1933.
    C. Rivers. Ad-PB:234, Bo-AN:176,
    Hu-NN:107, Hu-PN:404, Ra-BP:199

PARIS, FR. — cont'd.
Homesick. Hu-P'in-ch'ing.
Pa-MV:99
A Mourning Letter from Paris.
C. Rivers. Ra-BP:199
Paris. G. Corso. Ca-VT:656
Paris. E. Cummings. No-CL:252
Paris. A. Seeger. Ke-TF:372
La Place de la Concorde.
M. Bracker. Ke-TF:375
Printemps. M. Bracker. Ke-TF:373
Le Sightseeing. M. Bracker.
Ke-TF:375
Ungainly Things. R. Wallace.
Du-SH:34
PARKER, CHARLES
CHRISTOPHER (BIRD)
Yardbird's Skull. O. Dodson.
Ad-PB:132, Bo-AN:125, Ca-VT:387
PARKS: see also PLAYGROUNDS;
SATIRE - PARKS; ZOOS
Babies: Just Babies.
M. Fishback. Gr-EC:21
Le Bois. M. Bracker. Ke-TF:376
Central Park. R. Lowell.
Wi-LT:586
A City Park. A. Brody. La-OC:118
Central Park Tourney. M. Weston.
Br-AF:195, Du-RG:47, La-OC:123,
Pe-M:129
Chapter Two. W. Scott. Gr-CC:186
Ellis Park. H. Hoyt. Th-AS:120
I Walked Across the Park.
B. Douglas. Me-WF:1
In the Boston Public Garden.
S. Gottlieb. Ke-TF:354
Kid in the Park. L. Hughes.
La-OC:89
My Friend. L. Kirkman. Ho-CS:22
On the Fine Arts Garden, Cleveland.
R. Atkins. Ad-PB:197
The Park. J. Tippett. Ar-TP3:176
The Park. M. Wolfe. Ho-CT:30
The Park in Milan. W. Smith.
Ad-CI:52
The Park Is Green and Quiet.
C. Reznikoff. La-OC:117
Park Play. J. Tippett. Mc-AW:4
Reflections in a Little Park.
B. Deutsch. Co-EL:100
South End. C. Aiken. Pe-OA:144
Spring. P. Larkin.
Un-MB:527
The Swings in the Park.
C. McGlynn. La-IH:67
Water Picture. M. Swenson.
Co-BN:85, La-OC:121
PARNASSUS, MOUNT
Mount Parnassus. A. Clarke.
Ls-NY:88

PARODIES
A. E. Housman and a Few Friends.
H. Wolfe. Co-FB:229, Li-SR:138
Alaska, or Hell of the Yukon.
Fi-BG:43
The Amateur Flute. Li-SR:73
America, I Love You. B. Kalmar.
Co-FB:270
Ancient Music. E. Pound.
Ke-PP:111, Li-SR:124, Ma-FW:273,
Mc-EA:45, Wi-LT:226
And. . . . Co-OH:55
Annabel Lee. S. Huntley.
Li-SR:71
Archibald MacLeish Suspends the
Five Little Pigs.
L. Untermeyer. Un-MA:310
Autolycus' Song in Basic English.
R. Green. Li-SR:82
Baccalaureate. D. McCord.
Li-SR:123
The Ball and the Club.
F. Lindsay. Mo-SD:46
Ballad. C. Calverly. Co-FB:262,
Ho-WR:56, Li-SR:34
The Ballad of Sir Brian and the
Three Wishes. N. Levy.
Co-FB:271
The Belle of the Balkans.
N. Levy. Co-FB:265
Bird Thou Never Wert. P. Bennett.
Co-BBW:204
The Boy Stood in the Supper-Room.
Co-OW:204
Breakfast with Gerard Manley
Hopkins. A. Brode. Co-FB:253
Breathes There a Man.
S. Hoffenstein. Co-FB:312
The Cannibal Flea. T. Hood, Jr.
Li-SR:68
Cannibalee: A Po'em of Passion.
C. Lummis. Br-SM:84, Li-SR:71
Casabianca. E. Bishop.
Gr-SS:104
Casey Jones, the Union Scab.
J. Hill. Kr-OF:177
The Cataract at Ladore (July 3,
1936). H. Bevington. Li-SR:88
Chard Whitlow. H. Reed.
Co-FB:252, Pl-ML:72, Un-MB:508,
Wi-LT:797
A Christmas Carol. G. Chesterton.
Ga-S:88
A Classic Waits for Me.
E. White. Li-SR:146
Contemporary Nursery Rhyme.
Li-SR:131
Cowboy Song. C. Causley.
Co-RM:27, Ha-PO:10, Pe-M:36
Disaster. C. Calverly.
Li-SR:64
Donne Redone. J. Tierney. Br-SM:136

Don't Tell Me What You Dreamt
   Last Night. F. Adams. Co-FB:261
Edgar A. Guest Syndicates The Old
   Woman Who Lived in a Shoe.
   L. Untermeyer. Co-FB:232,
   Un-MA:311
Edna St. Vincent Millay Exhorts
   Little Boy Blue.
   L. Untermeyer. Un-MA:310
The Embarrassing Episode of
   Little Miss Muffet. G. Carryl.
   Ha-PO:279, Hu-MP:454, Pa-OM:38,
   Sh-RP:137, Un-GF:78
Envoi. D. Wyndham Lewis. Co-FB:258
"Everybody Works but Father" as
   W. S. Gilbert Would Have Written
   It. A. Burgoyne. Co-FB:259
Familiar Lines. Co-FB:342
Father William. L. Carroll.
   Ar-TP3:139, Bo-GJ:154, Br-BC:135,
   Co-FB:43, Co-HP:39, Fe-FP:350,
   Fe-PL:240, Fr-WO:57, Ke-TF:273,
   La-PP:71, La-PV:28, Li-SR:91,
   Lo-LL:95, Ma-YA:214, Mc-WK:217,
   Ox-BC:239, Sh-RP:120, Sp-OG:233,
   Un-GF:24, Un-GT:206
Footnote to Tennyson. G. Bullett.
   Co-FB:254
Fragment of a Greek Tragedy.
   A. Housman. Li-SR:152
The Funny Beasts. Ir-BB:82
Futurama Love Song.
   N. Rosten. Cr-WS:146
The Gastronomic Guile of Simple
   Simon. G. Carryl. Un-GT:218
Geiger, Geiger, Ticking Slow.
   P. Dehn. Li-SR:9
Good King Wenceslas.
   Co-OW:75, Sp-OG:320
He Paid Me Seven. Ra-BP:5
Herrick's Julia. H. Bevington.
   Li-SR:24
Hey Diddle Diddle. P. Dehn.
   Co-FB:451, Du-RG:80
Hiawatha's Photographing.
   L. Carroll. Co-FB:244, Li-SR:55
Higher. Co-FB:242, Li-SR:51
The Higher Pantheism in a
   Nutshell. A. Swinburne. Li-SR:95
Holy Order. J. Boothroyd.
   Co-FB:124
The Horse's Version of the Ride of
   Paul Revere. Ke-TF:268
How Doth the Little Crocodile.
   L. Carroll. Ar-TP3:125, Au-SP:233,
   Bl-OB:116, Bo-FP:88, Br-SM:89,
   Ch-B:83, Er-FA:209, Fe-FP:352,
   Gr-EC:9, Hu-MP:455, La-PP:55,
   Li-LC:25, Li-SR:98, Lo-LL:34,
   Ma-YA:214, Sm-LG:91, Un-GT:70

How I Brought the Good News from
   Aix to Ghent (or Vice-Versa).
   R. Yeatman and W. Sellar.
   Co-FB:237, Li-SR:14, Pa-OM:80
I Burned My Candle at Both Ends.
   S. Hoffenstein. Co-EL:59,
   Co-FB:491
I Stood on the Bridge at Midnight.
   Er-FA:499
I Wandered Angry as a Cloud.
   P. Dehn. Li-SR:106
If. M. Collins. Co-FB:240
An Imitation of Wordsworth.
   H. Coleridge. Co-FB:258,
   Rv-CB:760
In a Town Garden. D. Mattam.
   Co-EL:55, Co-FB:99, Co-PU:129
Investor's Soliloquy. K. Ward.
   Er-FA:207
Jane Smith. R. Kipling. Li-SR:104
Jenny Kiss'd Me. P. Dehn.
   Co-FB:260, Li-SR:33
John Masefield Relates the Story
   of Tom, Tom, the Piper's Son.
   L. Untermeyer. Un-MA:308
Just Behind the Battle, Mother.
   Co-FB:77
The King of Love My Shepherd Is.
   H. Baker. Gr-TG:40, Ke-TF:184
Lament for Lost Lodgings.
   P. McGinley. Li-SR:6
A Leaden Treasury of Verse.
   P. Dehn. Co-FB:464
Lewis Carroll. E. Farjeon.
   Ox-BC:331
Lines for Cuscuscaraway and
   Mirza Murad Ali Beg. T. Eliot.
   Co-FB:46, Li-SR:45, Pl-ML:24
Little Boy Blue. J. Ransom.
   We-PZ:36, Wi-LT:321
The Little Star. Li-SR:93
Lives of Great Men. Er-FA:219
Love under the Republicans (or
   Democrats). O. Nash.
   Mc-WS:62
Lovers, and a Reflection.
   C. Calverly. Li-SR:40
Lucy Lake. N. MacIntosh.
   Li-SR:108
M-Day's Child. M. Rukeyser.
   Kr-OF:89
The Mad Hatter's Song. L. Carroll.
   Bo-FP:82, Ir-BB:121
The Man from Inversnaid.
   R. Murray. Mo-SD:31
Mavrone. A. Guiterman.
   Co-FB:264, Li-SR:149
The Messed Damozel. C. Towne.
   Li-SR:75
The Metre Columbian. Li-SR:48

PARODIES — cont'd.
  Miniver Cheevy, Jr.   D. Parry.
    Li-SR:76
  Mrs. Judge Jenkins.   B. Harte.
    Co-FB:238
  The Modern Hiawatha.   G. Strong.
    Co-FB:415, Co-HP:115, Er-FA:206,
    Fe-FP:337, Gr-EC:192, Li-SR:61
  Morning Song.   K. Stein. Co-FB:215
  Mother Goose (Circa 2054).
    I. Sekula. Br-SM:65
  Nephelidia.   A. Swinburne.
    Li-SR:144
  Now We Are Sick.   J. Morton.
    Co-PU:29, Li-SR:63
  Nursery Song in Pidgin English.
    Li-SR:130
  O Have You Caught the Tiger?
    A. Housman. Li-SR:9
  The Octopussycat.   K. Cox.
    Ar-TP3:125, Au-SP:78, Fe-FP:340
  Ode on a Jar of Pickles.
    B. Taylor. Li-SR:141
  An Ode to Spring in the Metropolis.
    O. Seaman. Co-FB:234
  Of W.W. (Americanus).   J. Stephen.
    Co-FB:232, Li-SR:148
  The Old Oaken Bucket.   Er-FA:208
  On a Military Graveyard.
    K. Rexroth. Cr-WS:173
  On a Ruined House in a Romantic
    Country.   S. Coleridge.
    Un-GF:16
  On Being Chosen Poet of Vermont.
    R. Frost. Pl-ML:25
  On Mrs. W—.   N. Bentley. Co-FB:199
  Only Seven.   H. Leigh. Li-SR:118
  Options.   O. Henry. Co-FB:254
  Our New National Anthem.
    W. Eggleston. Ba-PO:80,
    Cr-WS:155
  Ozymandias Revisited.   M. Bishop.
    Co-HP:34, Li-SR:83
  Parody on Thomas Hood's "The
    Bridge of Sighs." Co-FB:220
  Peanuts. Co-OH:54, Er-FA:200,
    Un-GT:18
  Pentagonia.   G. Bates. Li-SR:133
  Peter Bell.   J. Reynolds.
    Ox-BN:402
  Pie in the Sky.   J. Hill.
    Gr-GB:328, Ke-PP:15
  The Poet of Bray.
    J. Heath-Stubbs. Pl-ML:9
  Poker. Fi-BG:205
  Prayer in Blackout.   G. Code.
    De-FS:66
  The Promissory Note.   B. Taylor.
    Li-SR:143
  Rhyme for a Chemical Baby.
    J. Cook. Li-SR:128

Rhyme for Astronomical Baby.
    J. Cook. Li-SR:128
  Rhyme for Botanical Baby.
    J. Cook. Li-SR:128
  Ring-a-Ring o' Neutrons.   P. Dehn.
    Li-SR:129
  The Shades of Night.   A. Housman.
    Co-FB:241, Co-HP:79, Gr-CT:22,
    Li-SR:50
  A Shot at Random. D. Wyndham Lewis.
    Co-FB:252, Er-FA:219
  Song.   O. Herford. Li-SR:22
  Song to Be Sung by the Father of
    Infant Female Children.
    O. Nash. Un-MA:565
  A Sonnet.   J. Stephen. Co-FB:257,
    Li-SR:109, Pl-ML:115
  Speak Roughly to Your Little Boy.
    L. Carroll. Bl-OB:30, Bo-FP:61,
    Co-BB:105, Li-SR:4, Sm-LG:101
  Squeal.   L. Simpson. Co-FB:233
  Such Stuff as Dreams.   F. Adams.
    Li-SR:32
  A Supermarket in California.
    A. Ginsburg. Br-TC:149,
    Kh-VA:64, Mo-BG:185, Wi-LT:718
  Teme con Variazióni.   L. Carroll.
    Li-SR:65
  There Lived among the Untrodden
    Ways.   H. Coleridge. Li-SR:107
  They Answer Back.   Francis.
    Co-FB:270
  A Thin Facade for Edith Sitwell.
    J. Brinnin. Co-FB:255
  The Translated Way.   F. Adams.
    Co-FB:261
  Turtle Soup.   L. Carroll.
    Bl-OB:12, Bo-FP:57, Cl-FC:97,
    De-TT:95, Li-SR:80, Sm-MK:195
  'Twas Ever Thus.   H. Leigh.
    Li-SR:66
  Twinkle, Twinkle, Little Star.
    P. Dehn. Li-SR:93
  Variations on a Theme by William
    Carlos Williams.   K. Koch.
    Li-SR:100
  The Village Blacksmith. Co-FB:53
  The Voice of the Lobster.
    L. Carroll. Ir-BB:146,
    Li-SR:99, Na-EO:39
  Walter de la Mare Tells The
    Listener about Jack and Jill.
    L. Untermeyer. Un-MA:309
  What, Still Alive at Twenty-Two.
    H. Kingsmill. Li-SR:137
  Whenas in Jeans. P. Dehn. Co-FB:229
  Where Is My Butterfly Net.
    D. McCord. Co-FB:101
  Winter Is Icumen In.   B. Smith.
    Co-PS:151

Winter Trees. C. Diekmann.
  Fl-HH:22, Mo-SD:153
Woe, Brothers, Woe! A. Kramer.
  Ke-TF:280
A Word of Encouragement. J. Pope.
  Co-EL:52, Co-FB:486, Co-PU:15
A Young Reporter's "If."
  M. Driscoll. Ke-TF:267
PARROTS: see also HUMOR - PARROTS
The Boy and the Parrot.
  J. Frere. Ox-BC:150
Clothed in Yellow, Red, and
  Green. Mo-MGT:155
Decoration. L. Bogan. Un-MA:490
Little Miss and Her Parrot.
  J. Marchant. Ox-BC:61
My Little Parrot. W. Wood.
  Co-PU:103
Never Get Up till the Sun
  Gets Up. Do-CH:(11)
The Parrot. Ca-MU:11
Parrot, Parrot. Ca-MU:21
The Parrots. W. Gibson.
  Co-RG:107, De-CH:384
Poll Parrot. Mo-MGT:67
Psittachus Eois Imitatrix
  Ales ab Indis. S. Sitwell.
  Un-MB:400
The Red Cockatoo. Po Chu-i.
  Co-PU:105, Gr-CT:98, Rd-OA:37
PARSNIPS: see HUMOR - PARSNIPS
PARTIES (ENTERTAINMENT):
  see also HUMOR - PARTIES
  (ENTERTAINMENT)
Another Birthday. B. Jonson.
  Ho-WR:71
Banquet at the Tsu Family
  Manor. Tu Fu. Rx-OH:3
The Butterfly's Ball. W. Roscoe.
  Ox-BC:131, Un-GT:74
The Cats Have Come to Tea.
  K. Greenaway. Bo-FP:58,
  Ch-B:101
The Cat's Tea-Party.
  F. Weatherley. Ar-TP3:119,
  Co-IW:34, Ir-BB:182, On-TW:22
The Cocktail Party. H. Zinnes.
  Ls-NY:302
I Live with Your Picture.
  B. Pasternak. Co-MR:166
I Would Like to Be a Bee.
  D. Baruch. Br-BC:92
Isabel Jones & Curabel Lee.
  D. McCord. Un-GT:223
Luther Leavitt Is a Whale Hunter.
  A. Brower. Ba-HI:55
October's Party. G. Cooper.
  Br-SS:60, Fe-PL:386, Sh-RP:227
The Party. R. Whittemore.
  Ad-CI:71

The Peacock "At Home."
  C. Dorset. Ox-BC:132
A Revel. D. Macdonagh.
  Co-PI:101
Waiting. J. Reeves. St-FS:71
PARTING: see also FAREWELLS;
  LOVE - PARTING
Adieu. J. Clare. Ma-FW:170
Adieu. P. Lewenstein. Sm-MK:212
After the Supper and Talk.
  W. Whitman. Un-MA:87
Afterwards. T. Hardy. Al-VBP:1050,
  Co-BN:210, De-CH:435, Gr-CT:353,
  Ni-JP:172, No-CL:284, Ox-BN:846,
  Pa-GTB:412, Rv-CB:944, Un-MB:31,
  Wi-LT:25
The Ancient Couple on Lu Mountain.
  M. Van Doren. Ca-VT:196
Approaching and Departing.
  N. Lenau. Un-R:125
Arrivals, Departures. P. Larkin.
  Un-MB:527
At the Time when Blossoms.
  Le-MW:20
At This Farewell. W. Wordsworth.
  Se-PR:243
Away, Rio. Sm-LG:338
The Beginning. W. Stevens.
  Ca-VT:40, Ha-TP:70
The Closing of the Rodeo.
  W. Smith. Br-TC:395, Ho-LP:73,
  Mc-WS:111, Mo-SD:70, Sh-RP:306
The Conclusive Voyage.
  J. Jimenez. Le-SW:85
Courtship and Wedding Songs.
  Tr-US I:99
Departure in the Dark.
  C. Day Lewis. Br-TC:257
Divided. J. Ingelow. Ox-BN:720
Dusk in War Time. S. Teasdale.
  Cr-WS:120
Elisa, or An Elegy upon the
  Unripe Decease of Sir Antony
  Irby. P. Fletcher. Al-VBP:291
The Emigrant. J. Masefield.
  Cl-FC:64
The End of the Year.
  Su Tung P'o. Rx-OH:79
The Escape. M. Van Doren.
  Un-MA:468
Eyes That Last I Saw in Tears.
  T. Eliot. Al-VBP:1185
The Farewell. J. Whittier.
  Hu-PN:461, Kr-OF:29
Farewell! Like a Bee. Basho.
  Be-CS:62
Farewell Once More. Tu Fu.
  Rx-OH:22
Fate! I Have Asked. W. Landor.
  Al-VBP:704

PARTING — cont'd.
  La Figlia Che Piange. T. Eliot.
    Al-VBP:1184, Ca-VT:130, Gr-BT:44,
    No-CL:246
  First Departure. F. Frost.
    Br-SS:57
  Gone. C. Sandburg. Sh-AP:156
  Good-Bye Now and Good Night.
    Un-R:63
  Good Night. P. Shelley.
    Al-VBP:755
  Hymen. H.D. Al-VBP:1169,
    Gr-SS:118
  i wish i could stay with you
    awhile. D. Witt. Ad-II:35
  In and Out: Severance of
    Connections, 1946. L. Sissman.
    Br-TC:384
  John Gorham. E. Robinson.
    Un-MA:124
  Jungle Songs, IV. Tr-US II:160
  Korea Bound, 1952.
    W. Childress. Br-AF:87
  The Last Day. Wen I-to.
    Hs-TC:55
  Leave Her, Johnny. Sm-MK:71
  A Leave-Taking. A. Swinburne.
    Al-VBP:1021, De-CH:340,
    Fe-PL:119, Ox-BN:795
  Leave-Taking. Tr-US I:74
  Leave-Taking. Le-OE:93,
    Tr-US II:307
  Leavetaking. E. Merriam.
    La-PV:17
  Like My Cupped Hands.
    Tsurayuki. Ba-ST:32
  Mother's Advice. Em-AF:771
  My Life Closed Twice.
    E. Dickinson. Al-VBP:1000,
    Ke-TF:243, Rv-CB:894, Un-MA:96,
    Un-MW:89, Wi-LT:16
  No Voyage. M. Oliver.   St-H:162
  Now All at Once It Is Colder.
    M. Piercy. Sc-TN:183
  Oh, Suzy. B. Katz. Ho-GC:24
  On Leaving Bruges. D. Rossetti.
    Rv-CB:883
  Parting. Y. Bat-Miriam.
    Me-PH:102
  Parting. Wang Wei. Ar-TP3:97,
    Le-MW:121
  Parting as Descent. J. Berryman.
    Un-MA:641
  Parting at Morning. R. Browning.
    Ga-FB:63, Ho-WR:135, Ni-JP:98,
    Ox-BN:534, Rv-CB:820
  Partings. M. Jewsbury.
    Ox-BC:167
  Pattern. E. Pierce.
    Cr-WS:50

  Reluctance.   R. Frost. Un-MA:170
  Remembrance.   V. Zhukovsky.
    Pa-SG:15
  Sailing from the United States.
    S. Moss. Ca-VT:583
  The Sailor's Knife. Cheng Ch'ou-yü.
    Pa-MV:38
  Second Farewell to Cambridge.
    Hsü Chih-mo. Hs-TC:83
  The Send-Off. W. Owen.
    Cr-WS:61, Un-MB:368
  Separation. M. Tsvetayeva.
    Ca-MR:137
  So Long! W. Whitman. Sh-AP:111
  Song at Separation. Tr-US I:80
  Song at the Departure of a
    Beautiful Girl. Tr-US I:170
  The Song of Youth. Ai Ch'ing.
    Hs-TC:297
  Songs at a Wedding, I.
    Tr-US II:166
  Spring Departing. Basho.
    Le-MW:74
  Stephen's Green Revisited.
    R. Weber. Co-PI:195
  Sweet Innisfallen. T. Moore.
    Ox-BN:215
  Taking Leave of a Friend.
    Rihaku. Ho-LP:67
  The Time Has Come. S. Voronov.
    Mo-MI:41
  To Coleridge in Sicily.
    W. Wordsworth. Ox-BN:103
  To Moses Ibn Ezra in Christian
    Spain. J. Halevi. Me-PH:60
  To New York Town We Bid Adieu.
    Sp-HW:20
  Tristia. O. Mandelstam.
    Ca-MR:157
  Upon His Leaving His Mistress.
    J. Wilmot. Al-VBP:504
  The Walk. L. Adams. Gr-CC:45
  What Her Friend Said.
    Varumulaiyaritti. Al-PI:64
  Winterproof. A. Guiterman.
    Ke-TF:417
  A Winter's Tale. D. Lawrence.
    Un-MB:287
  Ya Se Van los Pastores. D. Fitts.
    Gr-CC:172
PARTRIDGES: see also
    HUMOR - PARTRIDGES
  June. D. Malloch.
    Ha-YA:71
  One Day I Went Down in the Golden
    Harvest Field. Gr-GB:65
PASHTO VERSE: see
    IRANIAN VERSE - PASHTO
PASQUE FLOWERS:
    see ANEMONES

PAST: see also HUMOR - PAST;
   SATIRE - PAST
All That's Past. W. de la Mare.
   Al-VBP:1119, Bo-GJ:202,
   Re-TW:85
An Ancient to Ancients. T. Hardy.
   Pa-GTB:412, Wi-LT:28
Antique Shop. C. Carmer.
   Fe-FP:320, Sh-RP:316, Th-AS:166
Antrim. R. Jeffers. Ca-VT:124
Babylon. S. Sassoon. Tr-MR:235
The Ballad of Dead Ladies.
   F. Villon. Al-VBP:991,
   Er-FA:173, Ho-WR:184
Beach from the Past.
   V. Teodorescu. Mc-AC:103
The Buffalo Coat. T. McGrath.
   St-H:124
The Burning of the Leaves.
   L. Binyon. Pa-GTB:434
Burnt Norton. T. Eliot.
   Wi-LT:306
The Campfire Has Gone Out.
   B. Arnold. Fi-BG:106
Candles. C. Cavafy. Sm-MK:217
Chaucer's Thames. W. Morris.
   Cl-FC:25
The Crosses. B. Brigham.
   Sc-TN:21
Dear Men & Women. J. Wheelock.
   Ho-P:307
Death of the Old Year.
   A. Tennyson. Co-PS:25
Directive. R. Frost. Un-MA:195,
   Wi-LT:185
Distress. S. Tanikawa. Sh-AM:131
East Coker. T. Eliot. Ca-VT:140
Endymion. J. Keats. Al-VBP:790,
   Ox-BN:337
Essay on Man. A. Pope.
   Al-VBP:536
Fantasy. G. de Nerval. Gr-SS:54
The Flowering Past. M. Lowry.
   Ls-NY:180
For Rhoda. D. Schwartz.
   Un-MA:617, Wi-LT:519
Fragments from an Illinois
   Scrapbook. D. Etter.
   St-H:62
Ghost Church. H. Elliott.
   Ke-TF:423
Gone. W. de la Mare.
   Bo-GJ:205, Gr-CC:101, Ir-BB:263
Gone in the Wind. J. Mangan.
   Rv-CB:770
The Good Old Days of Adam and
   Eve. Fi-BG:105
The Green Valley. S. Warner.
   Un-MB:377
Growth. S. Tanikawa.   Sh-AM:129

Hellas. P. Shelley.   Gr-CT:441
Heritage. C. McKay.   Be-MA:14
The House. E. Almedingen.
   Ke-TF:412
Incorporate. M. Caruthers.
   Ke-TF:414
Indian Children. A. Wynne.
   Ar-TP3:35, Au-SP:100, Bo-FP:114,
   Hu-MP:137, Mc-AW:97
Jade Flower Palace. Tu Fu.
   Rx-OH:9
Line-Up for Yesterday. O. Nash.
   Mo-SD:21
The Long Shadow of Lincoln.
   C. Sandburg. Ha-TP:141
Love among the Ruins.
   R. Browning. Ga-FB:63
The Mediterranean. A. Tate.
   Ca-VT:219, En-PC:39, Sh-AP:205,
   Un-MA:540, Wi-LT:401
Men at Forty. D. Justice.
   Ho-P:129
Midnight Mass for the Dying
   Year. H. Longfellow. Se-PR:31
The Mighty Thoughts of an Old
   World. T. Beddoes. Bo-GJ:201,
   Gr-SS:63
Miniver Cheevy. E. Robinson.
   Er-FA:384, Fe-PL:33, Ga-FB:328,
   Gr-CT:467, Ha-PO:63, Li-SR:75,
   No-CL:243, Pe-OA:3, Rv-CB:958,
   Sm-LG:130, Un-MA:117, Wi-LT:103
My Sad Captains. T. Gunn.
   En-PC:278, Wi-LT:726
Never to Return. Li-Chin-fa.
   Hs-TC:174
New England Farmer. C. Smith.
   Sm-PT:96
New Excavations. L. Speyer.
   Ho-TH:27
Night on the Downland.
   J. Masefield. Un-MB:226,
   Wi-LT:192
Night Thoughts. Lu Yu.
   Rx-OH:110
Nostalgia. W. Stevens.
   Wi-LT:134
Nostalgia. Yang Huan. Pa-MV:159
The Old Cabin. P. Dunbar.
   Fe-PL:426
Old Garden. E. Tatum. Ke-TF:422
Old Things. D. Quick. Ke-TF:415
The Old Times Were the Best.
   J. Riley. Er-FA:172
Orient Wheat. A. Rich. Mo-BG:39
Oxford. L. Johnson. Ox-BN:949
The Past. R. Emerson. Sh-AP:34,
   Sm-LG:395
Progress. D. McCord. Pl-IO:130
Ravenna. A. Blok. Ca-MR:196

PAST — cont'd.
  The Red Cliff. Su Tung P'o.
    Rx-OH:65
  Remember That Country.
    J. Garrigue. Ca-VT:389
  Robin Hood. J. Keats. Gr-CC:115,
    Mc-PR:34
  St. Anthony's Township.
    G. Sheldon. De-CH:385
  Shootin' Up the Trail.
    G. Shumway. Fi-BG:107
  The Snow. Mao Tse-tung.
    Hs-TC:363
  Sonnets, vii. G. Santayana.
    Sm-PT:135
  A Spirit from Perfecter Ages.
    A. Clough. Ox-BN:612
  A Stared Story. W. Stafford.
    Ha-TP:136
  Summer's Pleasures They Are
    Gone. J. Clare. De-CH:512,
    Rv-CB:719
  The Sun-Dial. T. Peacock.
    Ox-BN:231
  Then. W. de la Mare. Pa-RE:114
  There Is an Old Horse.
    Jao Meng-k'an. Hs-TC:107
  Time's Exile. W. Stafford.
    St-H:210
  To England. R. Brautigan.
    Mc-EA:142
  The Too-Late Born. A. MacLeish.
    Bo-GJ:192, Gr-CC:111, Sh-AP:188,
    Un-MA:458, Wi-LT:340
  The Train. Pien Chih-lin.
    Hs-TC:164
  Unfathomed Past. R. Tagore.
    Al-PI:88
  Victorian Parlor. E. Bohm.
    Ke-TF:410
  We Have Been Here Before.
    M. Bishop. Co-FB:431, Na-EO:100
  Welsh Landscape. R. Thomas.
    To-MP:58
  Western Ch'ang-An Street.
    Pien Chih-lin. Hs-TC:162
  You, Andrew Marvell. A. MacLeish.
    Al-VBP:1193, Br-TC:275, Ga-FB:4,
    Mo-BG:150, Pe-OA:157, Sh-AP:134,
    Sm-PT:85, Wi-LT:342
PASTORAL LIFE: see also
    SATIRE - PASTORAL LIFE
  Another of the Same Nature.
    Ignoto. No-CL:102
  Arcades: Second Song. J. Milton.
    Al-VBP:388, Re-TW:51
  Arcades: Third Song. J. Milton.
    Al-VBP:389, Rv-CB:373
  The Castle of Indolence.
    J. Thomson. Al-VBP:545

Daphnis Came on a Summer's Day.
    Al-VBP:354
Daphnis to Ganymede.
    R. Barnfield. Re-TW:42
Diaphenia. H. Constable.
    Al-VBP:153, De-CH:333,
    Pa-GTB:10, Rv-CB:179
Dido My Dear, Alas, Is Dead.
    E. Spenser. Gr-CT:181
A Dirge. W. Cory. Ox-BN:648
Fair and Fair. G. Peele.
    Al-VBP:134
The Faithful Shepherdess.
    J. Fletcher. Al-VBP:287
The Green Shepherd.
    L. Simpson. Pe-OA:264
In the Merry Month of May.
    N. Breton. Al-VBP:85, Ha-PO:165,
    Un-MW:5
An Invitation to Phyllis.
    C. Cotton. No-CL:108
Lycidas. J. Milton. Al-VBP:402,
    Gr-CT:250, Hi-WP II:20,
    Ho-P:69, Pa-GTB:55
On a Time the Amorous Silvy.
    Al-VBP:362, No-CL:184
Paradise Lost. J. Milton.
    Al-VBP:410
The Passionate Shepherd to His
    Love. C. Marlowe.
    Al-VBP:168, Bo-FP:296, Co-BL:56,
    Er-FA:122, Fe-PL:113, Ha-PO:159,
    Hi-WP I:37, Ke-TF:105, Ma-YA:62,
    Mc-PR:16, Mc-WS:61, No-CL:100,
    Pa-GTB:4, Rv-CB:149, Un-MW:179
Phillida Flouts Me. Al-VBP:363
The Shepherd's Garland.
    M. Drayton. Al-VBP:159
Sing His Praises. J. Fletcher.
    Al-VBP:277
To Phyllis, to Love and Live with
    Him. R. Herrick. No-CL:106
The Unfaithful Shepherdess.
    Pa-GTB:25
You Nymphs, Called Naiads.
    W. Shakespeare. Al-VBP:198
PASTORS: see CLERGY
PASTRY: see CAKES AND COOKIES; PIES
PASTURES: see FARM LIFE;
    FIELDS AND MEADOWS
PATHS: see TRAILS
PATIENCE: see also HUMOR -
    PATIENCE; SATIRE - PATIENCE
  Battle. R. Jeffers. Un-MA:371,
    Wi-LT:260
  Certain Mercies. R. Graves.
    Pa-GTB:489
  Courage Has a Crimson Coat.
    N. Turner. Bo-FP:299, Th-AS:212
  Crucifixion. Ra-BP:29

Drums of Freedom.   G. Thompson.
   Jo-VC:21
for h. w. fuller.   C. Rodgers.
   Ra-BP:262
Gargoyle.   C. Sandburg.   Ba-PO:134
The Honest Whore.   T. Dekker.
   Al-VBP:231
I Am Joyful.   Da-SC:37, Le-IB:113
Never Said a Mumbalin' Word.
   Gr-GB:307
On His Blindness.   J. Milton.
   Al-VBP:408, Er-FA:31, Fe-PL:321,
   Ga-FB:92, Gr-CT:434, Ke-TF:58,
   Ma-FW:181, Ma-YA:93, Mc-PR:79,
   Pa-GTB:62, Rv-CB:374, Sp-OG:332
Patience.   F. Horne.   Ra-BP:77
Patience, Hard Thing. G. Hopkins.
   Ho-P:212
Pebbles.   F. Sherman.   Mc-PR:29
Sonnets.   G. Hopkins.   Ox-BN:871
Tom at Dinner.   A. O'Keeffe.
   De-TT:101
Waiting.   R. Jacob.   Br-BC:103
PATRICK, SAINT: see also
   HUMOR - PATRICK, SAINT;
   ST. PATRICK'S DAY
The Birth of Saint Patrick.
   S. Lover.   Co-PS:50, Se-PR:65
The Green Little Shamrock of
   Ireland.   A. Cherry.
   Hu-MP:333, Se-PR:67
St. Patrick's Breastplate.
   St. Patrick.   Sm-LG:379
PATRIOTIC SONGS: see NATIONAL
   SONGS; STATE SONGS
PATRIOTISM: see also HEROES
   AND HEROISM; PLACES, LOVE
   OF; SATIRE - PATRIOTISM;
   and names of countries with
   subdivision - HISTORY AND
   PATRIOTISM
Barbara Frietchie.   J. Whittier.
   Co-PS:97, Er-FA:380, Fe-FP:442,
   Fe-PL:167, Ga-FB:258, Hi-TL:112,
   Mc-PR:170, Sp-OG:40, Un-GT:190,
   Vi-PP:150
Columbia.   Em-AF:430
Concord Hymn.   R. Emerson.
   Al-VBP:805, Br-AF:61, Er-FA:188,
   Fe-FP:422, Hi-TL:52, Hu-MP:379,
   Ke-TF:256, Mc-PR:22, Pa-HT:18,
   Se-PR:87, Sh-AP:25, Sp-OG:193,
   Tu-WW:30, Vi-PP:99
Dear Land of All My Love.
   S. Lanier.   Hu-MP:404
Debs.   J. Oppenheim.   Kr-OF:118
Grandfather Watts's Private
   Fourth.   H. Bunner.   Ar-TP3:8,
   Co-PS:113, Ha-PO:105
The Hero.   A. Bierce.   Se-PR:121

I Hear America Singing. W. Whitman.
   Ar-TP3:47, Bo-FP:304, Br-AF:44,
   Co-PS:118, Er-FA:289, Fe-FP:451,
   Ga-FB:247, Hu-MP:369, La-PV:103,
   Mc-PR:33, Sm-LG:40, Un-GT:306,
   Un-MA:40, Vi-PP:185
Incident of the French Camp.
   R. Browning.   Co-RG:28,
   Mc-PR:144, Sp-OG:43, Un-GT:148
Jolly Soldier.   Em-AF:432
The Kid Has Gone to the Colors.
   W. Herschell.   Fe-PL:163
My Native Land.   W. Scott.
   Er-FA:286, Hu-MP:362, Mc-PR:32,
   Ox-BN:127, Pa-HT:147, Sp-OG:188,
   Vi-PP:25
New England Village, 1942.
   M. Bracker.   Ke-TF:260
Night Journey.   T. Roethke.
   Bl-FP:80, Bo-HF:36, Br-AF:231,
   Gr-EC:239, Ha-TP:25
Our Heritage.   J. Stuart.
   Br-AF:4
Paul Revere's Ride. H. Longfellow.
   Ar-TP3:40, Er-FA:368, Fe-FP:418,
   Ga-FB:254, Hi-TL:48, Se-PR:90,
   Sh-RP:278, Sm-LG:258, Sp-OG:24,
   Un-GT:184, Vi-PP:94
Please Take Good Care of My Home.
   Hs-TC:444
Pro Patria Mori.   T. Moore.
   Pa-GTB:215
Prologue to a Yomeh Ballad.
   Tr-US I:44
The River.   H. Crane.   Bl-FP:81
Song for a War Dance. Tr-US I:92
Tempt Me No More.   C. Day Lewis.
   Un-MB:423
Verse on the Wall.
   Chang Chih-min.   Hs-TC:431
The War for Slavery.
   W. Garrison.   Kr-OF:66
PAUL, SAINT
Out of Wisdom Has Come Love.
   E. Robinson.   Tr-MR:162
The Three Taverns.
   E. Robinson.   Sm-PT:186
PAUL BUNYAN
Folk-Tune.   R. Wilbur.   Br-AF:120
Paul Bunyan.   A. Bourinot.
   Br-AF:114, Fe-FP:494
PAVLOVA, ANNA
Elegy on the Death of Mme.
   Anna Pavlova. E. Meyerstein.
   Pl-US:119
PAWNBROKERS
Street Window. C. Sandburg.La-OC:51
PAWNEE INDIANS: see also INDIANS OF
   NORTH AMERICA - VERSE—PAWNEE
   The Morning Star.   Ho-SD:36

PEACE: see also ARMISTICES;
    HUMOR - PEACE; PEACE OF
    MIND; SATIRE - PEACE
A.E.F.   C. Sandburg.   Un-MA:203
Ain' Go'n' to Study War No Mo'.
    Ba-PO:167
The Arsenal at Springfield.
    H. Longfellow. Ba-PO:96,
    Cr-WS:24
At Peace. Rumi. Pa-SG:163
A Baby-Sermon. G. MacDonald.
    Ox-BC:274
Bang. J. Blair. Ad-II:96
Beasts. R. Wilbur. Br-TC:472
The Bells of Peace. A. Fisher.
    Br-SS:75
Bookra. C. Warner. Cr-WS:20
A Christmas Carol. J. Lowell.
    Sp-OG:319
Christmas 1945. A. Hine.
    Hi-TL:219
The City Is Big. T. Heard.
    Me-WF:10
The Clear Sky. Ba-PO:113
The Coming Messiah. Bible. O.T.
    Isaiah. Ba-PO:75, Ga-S:57
Dawn over the Mountains. Tu Fu.
    Rx-OH:30
Dead Sea. Sun Yü-t'ang. Hs-TC:123
Dear Lord and Father of Mankind.
    J. Whittier. Ke-TF:206
Disarmament. J. Whittier.
    Ba-PO:103, Cr-WS:157
Down Through the Ages Vast.
    Ba-PO:113
Easter Eve. M. Rukeyser.
    Ca-VT:362
The Easterner's Prayer. Fe-PL:130,
    Ke-TF:208
The Echo. P. Solomon. Jo-VC:37
The Faintly Glowing. M. Saito.
    Sh-AM:143
A Flower Has Opened. S. Sassoon.
    Ga-S:182
For I Dipped into the Future.
    A. Tennyson. Fe-PL:432
For Once in a Dream or Trance,
    I Saw the Gods. E. Muir.
    Go-BP:155
For Out of Zion. Bible. O.T.
    Isaiah. Ba-PO:75
From the Walum Olum. Br-MW:100
Full Moon. Tu Fu. Rx-OH:28
The Golden Hour. T. Moore.
    Ox-BN:216
Golden Wings. W. Morris.
    Gr-CT:267, Ox-BN:770
The Harrowing of Hell.
    W. Langland.
    Go-BP:219

Heaven-Haven. G. Hopkins.
    Al-VBP:1059, Go-BP:274,
    Gr-BT:146, Ha-PO:196,
    Hi-WP II:176, Mc-WK:184,
    Ox-BN:852, Un-MB:44
Hohiotsitsi No-Otz. Ba-PO:113
Hope's Forecast. E. Fuller.
    Sh-RP:69
The Hundred Names. Ba-PO:117
Hymn to the Night. H. Longfellow.
    Al-VBP:823, Sh-AP:35
I Go Forth to Move about the
    Earth. A. Lopez. Al-WW:8
I Heard an Angel Singing. W. Blake.
    Rv-CB:621
I Sing of Anshan Steel. Feng Chih.
    Hs-TC:158
In Any Soul There Is a Bright
    Country. A. Yaskolka. Bo-RU:91
In Memoriam. A. Tennyson.
    Gr-CT:315, Hi-WP II:143,
    Ox-BN:495, 500
International Hymn. G. Huntington.
    Fe-PL:161
Jehu. L. MacNeice. Wi-LT:460
Jhesu, for Thy Wondes Fyff.
    Ba-PO:6
Kid Stuff. F. Horne.
    Ab-MO:76, Ad-PB:56, Bo-AN:41,
    Bo-HF:109, Hu-PN:148, Li-TU:247
Lake Leman. G. Byron. Ox-BN:245
Last Night I Had the Strangest
    Dream. E. McCurdy. Ba-PO:198
Magic Formula to Make an Enemy
    Peaceful. Bi-IT:69
The Men of War. H. Vaughan. Ba-PO:6
The Music Makers. A. O'Shaughnessy.
    Al-VBP:1063, Co-PI:163,
    Ga-FB:133, Mc-PR:72, Se-PR:324
November Eleventh. K. Burton.
    Se-PR:204
November Moratorium, Washington.
    C. Burchardt. Ad-II:32
Oh World. L. Blair. Ja-PA:33
An Old Song. S. Bloomgarden.
    Ho-TY:75, Pa-SG:147
On Wearing Ears. W. Harris.
    Ad-BO:70
One Morning the World Woke Up.
    O. Williams. Ba-PO:192,
    Er-FA:197
Pastoral. V. Wilder. Ke-TF:442
Pause. R. Marinoni. De-FS:136
Pax Nobiscum. E. Marlett. Tr-MR:188
Peace. W. de la Mare. Ni-JP:79,
    Un-MB:203
Peace. G. Herbert. Go-BP:297,
    Gr-CT:347
Peace. G. Hopkins. Pa-GTB:391
Peace. C. Scollard. Se-PR:188

Peace. H. Vaughan. Ga-S:223,
  Gr-CC:136, Gr-CT:347,
  Hi-WP II:172, Ma-YA:105,
  Pa-HT:163, Pl-EI:9,
  Rv-CB:409, Sm-LG:382
Peace and Rest. W. Davies.
  Go-BP:29
Peace in the World.
  J. Galsworthy. Fe-PL:181
Peace, like a Lamb. L. Clark.
  Hi-WP I:110
Peace Universal. A. Thorne.
  Se-PR:186
Prayer. J. Kirkup. Go-BP:218
A Prayer for Peace.
  Charles d'Orleans. Ba-PO:20
Prayer for Peace. Tr-US II:54
Prayer of St. Francis of Assisi
  for Peace. St. Francis.
  Fe-PL:346
Preliminary Draft of a World
  Constitution. Ba-PO:115
Prospect. T. Clark. Se-PR:187
The Recollection. P. Shelley.
  Ox-BN:300, Pa-GTB:270
Rest of the Nations. G. Mellen.
  Ba-PO:69
Returning by Night to Lu-Men.
  Meng Hao Jan. Rx-LT:50
Shooter's Hill. R. Bloomfield.
  Ox-BN:55
Sleep and Dreams. P. Kelso.
  Le-M:212
Something Peaceful.
  T. Tsyganok. Mo-MI:69
The Song of Momus to Mars.
  J. Dryden. Rv-CB:468
Spring River Flowers Moon Night.
  The Emperor Yang. Rx-LT:46
Sunset. E. Muir. Go-BP:29
The Sword and the Sickle.
  W. Blake. Ar-TP3:211, Gr-CT:349
Tenting on the Old Camp Ground.
  W. Kittredge. Ba-PO:198
Three Blessings. Go-BP:278
3 Meditations. G. Fowler.
  Sc-TN:55
To the Castle at Gordes.
  O. de Magny. Ba-PO:88,
  Cr-WS:153
Tolstoi Is Plowing Yet.
  V. Lindsay. Ba-PO:133
Toward Calm and Shady Places.
  Ba-PO:114, Tr-US II:224
The Tree of Great Peace.
  Dekanawideh. Br-MW:102
Under the Holly-Bough.
  C. Mackay. Ke-TF:48
The War God. S. Spender.
  Tr-MR:180

War-Monger. Kr-OF:96
We Shall Live Together. Wo-HS:(29)
We Shall Overcome. Ba-PO:199,
  Hi-TL:228, Pl-EI:165
A Whim of Time. S. Spender.
  Un-MB:471
The Wilderness and the Solitary
  Place. Bible. O.T. Isaiah.
  Go-BP:263
The Winds of God. C. Scollard.
  Se-PR:188
The Wolf Also Shall Dwell. Bible.
  O.T. Isaiah. Fe-FP:179,
  Go-BP:103, La-PV:158
Wordsworth's Grave.
  W. Watson. Ox-BN:910
PEACE OF MIND: see also
  CONTENTMENT; SATIRE -
  PEACE OF MIND
Advice to Dreamers.
  R. Frederick. Ke-TF:237
After Dark Vapours. J. Keats.
  Ox-BN:367, Rv-CB:745
After Drinking All Night with a
  Friend. R. Bly. St-H:7
Amours de Voyage. A. Clough.
  Pa-GTB:360
As It Looked Then. E. Robinson.
  Sm-PT:189
A Chant. W. Davies. Go-BP:51
Cloister. C. Aiken. Un-MA:436
Composed while under Arrest.
  M. Lermontov. Pa-SG:204
Contentment. N. Cotton. Ox-BC:64
Conversation in the Mountains.
  Li Po. Pa-SG:192
Elegiac Stanzas. W. Wordsworth.
  Ox-BN:81, Pa-GTB:297
Enigma. J. Fauset. Hu-PN:66
Eternity's Low Voice.
  M. Van Doren. Pl-EI:122
Every Morning I Walk into the
  Tent. Wo-HS:(46)
The Face. E. Muir. Pa-GTB:467
For Jim. Easter Eve. A. Spencer.
  Bo-AN:17, Hu-PN:65
For Sleep or Death. R. Pitter.
  Hi-WP I:144, Sm-MK:218
For You. C. Sandburg.
  Mc-WK:214, Tr-MR:61, Un-MA:210
From My Window.
  M. Coleridge. Ox-BN:927
Give Me Peace. A. Voznesensky.
  Gr-BT:148
Grant Me Thy Peace.
  Thomas a Kempis. Go-BP:269
I Feel So Muggy. C. Reed.
  Ad-II:14
Immense Hour. J. Jiménez.
  Pa-SG:166

PEACE OF MIND — cont'd.
   In Ireland: By the Pool at the
      Third Rosses. A. Symons.
      Ox-BN:936
   The Kingdom. L. MacNeice.
      Wi-LT:463
   Lord! Would Men Let Me Alone.
      C. Cotton. Go-BP:20
   A Mad Poem Addressed to My
      Nephews and Nieces. Po Chü-i.
      Gr-BT:165
   The Music of a Tree. W. Turner.
      Un-MB:347
   An Old Man. W. Wordsworth.
      Go-BP:40, Sm-LG:129
   Peace. Bhartrihari. Pa-SG:161
   Peace. J. Clare. Go-BP:23
   Peace. S. Speed. Go-BP:257
   Penitence. W. Cowper. Go-BP:179
   Promise of Peace. R. Jeffers.
      Un-MA:365, Wi-LT:258
   Psalm to My Belovèd.
      E. Tietjens. Co-BL:109
   Ship of Death. D. Lawrence.
      Al-VBP:1160, Pa-GTB:462,
      Un-MB:299
   The Sky Clears. Da-SC:147
   The Small Task. M. Lindsay.
      Ke-TF:241
   Spring Quiet. C. Rossetti.
      Co-BN:16, De-CH:235, Gr-TG:26,
      Pa-GTB:373, Re-BS:21
   The Sufficient Place. E. Muir.
      Go-BP:251
   A Sunday. W. de la Mare.
      Ls-NY:50
   Sunset. Tai Wang-shu.
      Hs-TC:182
   Temper in October. V. Edminson.
      Go-BP:31
   Visiting Tsan, Abbot of Ta-Yun.
      Tu Fu. Rx-OH:7
   Who Is Sad? E. Coatsworth.
      Gr-EC:38
   Written in the Euganean Hills,
      North Italy. P. Shelley.
      Pa-GTB:290
   The Young Recruit. A. Ficke.
      Co-EL:107
PEACE PIPES
   Behold, This Pipe. Bi-IT:70
   I Pass the Pipe. Bi-IT:71
PEACH BLOSSOMS
   By the City Gate. Ts'ui Hao.
      Rx-LT:63
   Flying Petals.
      Emperor Ch'ien Wen. Rx-LT:43
   Peach Blossoms after Rain. Le-MW:20
   The Purple Peach Tree.
      Su Tung P'o. Rx-OH:78

   Spring Ending. Hsü Chih-mo.
      Hs-TC:92
PEACH TREES
   Hokku Poems. R. Wright. Bo-AN:105
   Peach Tree in the Garden of an
      Empty House. J. Press.
      Ls-NY:307
   Peach Tree with Fruit.
      P. Colum. Co-BN:156
   The Purple Peach Tree.
      Su Tung P'o. Rx-OH:78
PEACHES
   The Little Peach. E. Field.
      Ag-HE:44, Br-SM:75, Ch-B:81,
      Co-HP:57
   Peach Tree with Fruit. P. Colum.
      Co-BN:156
PEACOCKS
   Bird Riddles III. Gr-GB:65
   Domination of Black. W. Stevens.
      Ha-TP:108, Un-MA:244
   For the Peacock Dance.
      Tr-US II:169
   Peacock. S. Allen. Ke-TF:334
   The Peacock. I. Barbu. Mc-AC:63
   Peacock and Nightingale.
      R. Finch. Co-BBW:248
   The Peacock of Java. W. Smith.
      Sh-RP:168
   A Riddle. Ca-MU:18
   Swell People. C. Sandburg.
      Ha-LO:59
   Truth. W. Cowper. Co-BBW:267
   Why Do You Think. Re-RR:112
PEANUTS: see HUMOR - PEANUTS
PEAR BLOSSOMS
   Night Storm. S. Murano. Sh-AM:92
   Spring. Su Tung P'o. Rx-OH:90
PEAR TREES
   Pear Tree. H.D. Un-MA:336
   The Pear Tree. E. Millay.
      Un-MA:442
   The Pear Tree. Gr-GB:140
   Pear-Trees by the Fence.
      Su Tung-p'o. Pa-SG:90
PEARLS
   Aye, Even Small Things.
      P. Heyse. Un-R:113
   The Necklace of Pearls.
      H. Longfellow. Kr-OF:106
   The Oyster. A. Herbert.
      Co-BBW:63
   The Pearl. H. Andersen.
      Pa-SG:49
   A Pearl, a Girl. R. Browning.
      Rv-CB:830
PEARS
   I Had Eight Pairs of Pears.
      On-TW:30
   Pairs or Pears. Wr-RM:81

The Pear.   V. de Moraes.   An-TC:99
Pretty Futility.   E. Coatsworth.
    Ag-HE:46
Sickle Pears.   O. Dodson.
    Bo-AN:124
PEAS
A Seasonable Song.   Wr-RM:12
PEASANTS
Coming Home from Work.   E. Isac.
    Mc-AC:53
The Deserted Village.
    O. Goldsmith.   Al-VBP:585,
    Er-FA:410, Hi-FO:178
Exiles.   AE.   Un-MB:145
French Peasants.   M. Gibbon.
    Ga-S:121
The Peasants.   A. Lewis.   Wi-LT:764
The Sandaled Soldier.
    Tu Yün-hsieh.   Hs-TC:245
The Serf.   R. Campbell.   Ni-JP:85,
    Pa-GTB:494, Un-MB:419
The Story of Soutine.
    J. Schevill.   En-PC:188
PEBBLES: see ROCKS
PEDDLERS AND PEDDLING:
    see also STREET CRIES
Bread and Cherries.
    W. de la Mare.   Br-SG:71
Chestnut Stands.   R. Field.
    Br-SS:73
Come Buy My Nice Muffins.
    Bo-FP:129
Fine Knacks for Ladies.   Al-VBP:356,
    De-CH:70, Ho-WR:46, Rv-CB:113
Fish Crier.   C. Sandburg.
    Br-AF:42, Ga-S:123
Fish Peddler.   Mei Yao Ch'en.
    Rx-OH:40
The Flower-Cart Man.   R. Field.
    Au-SP:143, Br-SG:72, Br-SS:147,
    La-OC:53
The Flower-Seller.   E. Farjeon.
    Bo-FP:123, Br-SG:74
Flowers for Sale!   Wy-CM:12
The Good Humor Man.   D. Aldis.
    Fr-MP:16
The Horse Trader's Song.   Em-AF:762
The Ice-Cream Man.   R. Field.
    Au-SP:148, Br-SS:176, Fe-FP:249
Milk Below.   Bo-FP:129
A Negro Peddler's Song.
    F. Johnson.   Bo-AN:26
Old Joe Jones.   L. Richards.
    Ag-HE:17
The Peddler.   E. Farjeon.   Ir-BB:39
The Peddler of Spells.   Lu Yu.
    Le-MW:127
The Peddler's Caravan.   W. Rands.
    Au-SP:150, Bl-OB:145, Bo-FP:130,
    Hu-MP:166, Ox-BC:233

The Pedlar.   W. de la Mare.
    Sp-OG:181
Tha Pedlar.   W. Shakespeare.
    Al-VBP:196, De-CH:70, Ho-WR:46,
    Mc-PR:49
Pushcart Row.   R. Field.
    Au-SP:116, Br-SG:73
Return to the North.   Yu P'ing-po.
    Hs-TC:17
The Rice Seller.   Bo-FP:129
The Scissors Grinder.
    R. Roseliep.   De-FS:162
Several Individuals.   Pien Chih-lin.
    Hs-TC:164
Three Portraits.   G. Hitchcock.
    Ca-VT:392
V Is for Vendor.   P. McGinley.
    Br-SG:71
Vendor.   R. Roseliep.   De-FS:157,
    St-H:179
Vocation.   R. Tagore.   Fe-FP:484
The Wild Flower Man.   Lu Yu.
    Rx-OH:103
Will You Buy Any Tape.
    W. Shakespeare.   Al-VBP:197
PEDIGREES: see ANCESTORS AND
    ANCESTRY; HERALDRY
PEEKSKILL, N.Y.
Peekskill.   A. Kramer.   Kr-OF:162
PEGASUS (MYTH.)
At Amberley Wild Brooks.
    A. Young.   Rd-OA:193
Pegasus.   E. Farjeon.   Sm-MK:49
Pegasus Lost.   E. Wylie.
    Un-MA:275
PEKING, CHINA
Going to the Heavenly Bridge.
    Li Kuang-t'ien.   Hs-TC:205
The Night Scene.   Ho Ch'i-fang.
    Hs-TC:222
Remembering Shi Ch'a Hai.
    Chang Hsiu-ya.   Pa-MV:29
To the Dead.   Hu-Feng.   Hs-TC:376
PELICANS: see also
    HUMOR - PELICANS
The Pelican.   P. de Thaun.
    Mc-WK:43
Pelicans.   R. Jeffers.   Un-MA:366
The Reason for the Pelican.
    J. Ciardi.   Au-SP:233,
    La-PP:17, La-PV:29
Skin Diving in the Virgins.
    J. Brinnin.   Pe-OA:238
PEMBROKE, MARY HERBERT,
    COUNTESS OF
On the Countess Dowager of Pembroke.
    W. Browne.   Al-VBP:325, Rv-CB:348
PENCILS
It Lies in the Groove.
    N. Qualthrough.   Le-M:26

PENELOPE
  At Ithaca. H.D. Ca-VT:112
PENGUINS: see also
    HUMOR - PENGUINS
  Enigma Sartorial. L. Rhu.
    Ir-BB:79
  The Penguin and I.
    A. Glanz-Leyeles. Ho-TY:258
  Seven Themes from the Zoo,
    No. 2. J. Bennett. Ls-NY:208
  The View from Here. W. Stafford.
    Co-EL:29, La-RM:123
PENITENCE: see REPENTANCE
PENMANSHIP: see ALPHABETS;
    CALLIGRAPHY; ILLUMINATION
    OF BOOKS AND MANUSCRIPTS
PENNIES: see COINS
PENNINE CHAIN
  Pennines in April. T. Hughes.
    Hi-WP II:49
PENNSYLVANIA: see also names of
    towns, as PITTSBURGH, PA.
  Nocturne. F. Frost. Co-BN:202
  Pennsylvania. H. Bucher.
    Se-PR:281
PENNSYLVANIA DUTCH: see DIALECTS,
  PENNSYLVANIA DUTCH
PENNY ARCADES
  Penny Arcade. J. Nims. St-H:151
PENTLAND HILLS
  The Pentland Hills. Gr-GB:175
PEONIES
  Drinking with Friends Amongst
    the Blooming Peonies.
    Liu Yu Hsi. Rx-LT:71
  Flower Song. De-PP:57
  Leaving the House of a Friend.
    Basho. Sh-RP:63
  The Peony Was as Big as This.
    Issa. Do-TS:3
  The Red Peony. Buson. Sh-RP:62
  A White Peony. K. Takahama.
    Sh-AM:162
PEOPLE: see also CROWDS;
    HUMOR - PEOPLE
  All the World's a Stage.
    W. Shakespeare. Er-FA:151,
    Fe-PL:257, Ha-PO:257,
    Ma-YA:67, Un-GT:85
  As I Step over a Puddle at the
    End of Winter I Think on an
    Ancient Chinese Governor.
    J. Wright. Kh-VA:73, St-H:254
  Bird Talk. A. Fisher. Fr-MP:12
  Blythsome Bridal. Gr-GB:152
  But Outer Space. R. Frost.
    Li-TU:252
  The City. J. Bryant. Ba-HI:109,
    La-IH:15
  The Clown. N. Alexander. Me-WF:78

  Esthetique du Mal, XII.
    W. Stevens. Wi-LT:158
  Faces. S. McCoy. La-IH:16
  A Lazy Thought. E. Merriam.
    La-OC:44
  The Leaders of the Crowd.
    W. Yeats. Un-MB:116
  The Noise of Passing Feet.
    Le-OE:8
  The People. R. Creeley.
    Bl-FP:60, Ca-VT:566
  People. L. Lenski. Au-SP:130,
    Fe-FP:247, Ho-CS:16, La-OC:43
  People. D. Morris. Me-WF:34
  The People. E. Roberts. Bo-GJ:105
  People. O. Rock. Ba-HI:90
  People Talks. P. Harrison.
    Ba-HI:89
  People Who Must. C. Sandburg.
    La-OC:48, La-PV:190
  The People Will Live On.
    C. Sandburg. Un-MA:214
  The Suburban Train.
    A. Voznesensky. Ca-MR:69
  Walk down My Street. V. Dorset.
    La-IH:39
  What Are Little Boys Made of.
    De-PO:14, Er-FA:205, Ir-BB:92,
    Mo-CC:(13), Mo-MGT:59, Mo-NR:111,
    Wi-MG:31, Wr-RM:108
  When Wilt Thou Save the People?
    E. Elliot. Hi-WP II:173,
    Pl-EI:157
  The World. T. Peacock. Co-PU:61
  The World So Big. A. Fisher.
    Au-SP:184
PEPPER PLANTS
  Mist. Li Ch'ing Chao. Rx-OH:99
PEPPER TREES
  Scenes from the Life of the
    Peppertrees. D. Levertov.
    Wi-LT:761
PERCY, SIR HENRY, 1st EARL
  OF NORTHUMBERLAND
  The Battle of Otterburn.
    Ox-BB:491, Pa-OM:148
  Chevy Chase. Al-VBP:43,
    Ma-BB:97, Ox-BB:496
  Chevy Chase, The Second Fytte.
    Ma-BB:101
  Northumberland Betrayd by Dowglas.
    Ox-BB:526
PERFECTION: see also
  SATIRE - PERFECTION
  The Habit of Perfection.
    G. Hopkins. Al-VBP:1060,
    Go-BP:275, Pl-US:151, Un-MB:40
  Her Perfections. P. Sidney.
    No-CL:208
  In Utrumque Paratus. M. Arnold.
    Ox-BN:626

Perfection. F. Carlin. Er-FA:456
PERFUMES: see also
HUMOR - PERFUMES
Another on Her. R. Herrick.
Li-SR:23
Essential Oils Are Wrung.
E. Dickinson. Rv-CB:921
Parfum Exotique. C. Baudelaire.
Un-MW:194
To the Most Fair and Lovely
Mistress, Anne Soame, Now
Lady Abdie. R. Herrick.
Al-VBP:332
PERIODICALS: see HUMOR -
PERIODICALS; JOURNALISM;
NEWSPAPERS
PERIS: see FAIRIES
PERIWINKLES: see FLOWERS;
SNAILS
PERMANENCE: see also HUMOR -
PERMANENCE; SATIRE -
PERMANENCE
The Adamant. T. Roethke.
Ls-NY:25
After-Thought. W. Wordsworth.
Ox-BN:91
And Yet the Earth Remains
Unchanged. Bi-IT:101
As on This Day. T. Takaori.
Sh-AM:155
Audubon, Drafted. L. Jones.
Lo-TY:250
The Ballad of Banners.
J. Lehmann. Ca-MB:96
Black Mouth Society Song.
Tr-US II:234
The Brook. A. Tennyson.
Bl-OB:134, Bo-FP:72, Bo-GJ:42,
Cl-DT:60, Cl-FC:51, Co-BN:64,
De-TT:145, Er-FA:259, Fe-FP:272,
Ga-FB:227, Hu-MP:293, Mc-PR:99,
Sp-OG:282
Buddha. S. Hagiwara. Sh-AM:51
Can It Be. Narihira. Ba-ST:21
Canto LXXXI. E. Pound.
Al-VBP:1165, Pe-OA:83
The City of Stones. Liu Yu-Hsi.
Le-MW:62
Credo. R. Jeffers. Un-MA:366
East Coker. T. Eliot. Ca-VT:140
Endymion. J. Keats. Al-VBP:788,
Er-FA:264, Ma-YA:186, Mc-PR:89,
Ox-BN:335
The Eternal. E. Tegnér. Pa-SG:206
I Shall Go Back. E. Millay.
Sm-PT:170, Un-MA:446
In Time like Glass. W. Turner.
Un-MB:347
In Time of "The Breaking of
Nations." T. Hardy. Ha-PO:185,
Tr-MR:188, Un-MB:25, Wi-LT:23

Leave Me, O Love. P. Sidney.
Al-VBP:130, De-CH:641, Ha-PO:168
The Lost Telescope. Chi Hsuan.
Pa-MV:50
Morality. J. Garrigue. Co-EL:73
A Mountain Spring. Ch'u Ch'uang I.
Rx-LT:51
My Flowers Shall Not Perish.
Le-OE:135
The Ocean. G. Byron. Al-VBP:728,
Co-SS:46, Ga-FB:181, Gr-CT:193
The Old Men. Jo-TS:10,
Tr-US II:237
Old War Song. Tr-US II:241
On the Beach at Night. W. Whitman.
Gr-CT:197, Un-MA:65
On the Praise of Poetry and
Music. A. Cowley. No-CL:30
Pediment Ballet. L. Nicholl.
Pl-US:114
Present in Absence. Pa-GTB:6
Puzzles. J. Drinkwater.
Mc-WK:107
The Reunion. O. Dodson.
Bo-HF:129
A River Leaping. Meisetsu.
Be-CS:20
The Rock. Br-MW:83
Smoke Stack. A. Sullivan.
Mc-WK:20
The Spring Waters. Ping Hsin.
Hs-TC:22
Stone Angel. A. Ridler. Pl-EI:11
To Me, Fair Friend, You Never
Can Be Old. W. Shakespeare.
Al-VBP:207, Ho-P:130, Pa-GTB:9
To the Stone-Cutters.
R. Jeffers. En-PC:10, Ni-JP:127,
Sh-AP:175, Un-MA:362
Wherever Beauty Has Been Quick
in Clay. J. Masefield.
Tr-MR:41
PERPETUAL MOTION
The Wheelgoround. R. Clairmont.
Co-PM:33
PERSECUTION: see also JEWS -
PERSECUTION; MARTYRS
A Hope for Those Separated by
War. S. Keyes. Gr-BT:122
If Your Hands Be Full of Blood.
P. Folger. Kr-OF:100
The Place's Fault. P. Hobsbaum.
To-MP:131
Soul, Scorning All Measure.
M. Tsvetayeva. Ca-MR:136
PERSEPHONE: see PROSERPINA
PERSEPOLIS, PERSIA
Persepolis. C. Marlowe. No-CL:253
PERSEUS (MYTH.)
Perseus. L. MacNeice. Wi-LT:457

PERSEVERANCE: see also
    DETERMINATION; DILIGENCE;
    HUMOR - PERSEVERANCE
Adam. R. Rilke. Tr-MR:64
Athletes. W. Gibson. Mo-SD:177
The Beetle in the Country Bathtub.
    J. Wheelock. Ha-WR:65
Before a Saint's Picture.
    W. Landor. Ox-BC:170
Beyond the Fog. Lo Fu.
    Pa-MV:115
Columbus. J. Miller. Ar-TP3:38,
    Er-FA:298, Fe-FP:403, Ha-YA:116,
    Hi-TL:13, Hu-MP:370, Mc-PR:180,
    Mc-WK:161, Se-PR:182, Sp-OG:59,
    Vi-PP:42
The Difficult Land. E. Muir.
    Go-BP:228
Don't Give Up. P. Cary.
    Ch-B:81
Don't Give Up. Er-FA:8
Excelsior. H. Longfellow.
    Fe-FP:566, Li-SR:49, Pa-OM:223
Fare Well. W. de la Mare.
    Pa-GTB:439
For de Lawd. L. Clifton.
    Ad-PB:306, Br-TC:71
A Hope for Those Separated by
    War. S. Keyes. Gr-BT:122
It Couldn't Be Done. E. Guest.
    Er-FA:7
Keep a-Goin'. F. Stanton.
    Er-FA:27
Keep a Stiff Upper Lip. P. Cary.
    Er-FA:19
Keep the Glad Flag Flying.
    Er-FA:486
Little Strokes. B. Franklin.
    Un-GT:25
A Man Sharpening a Knife.
    K. Takamura. Sh-AM:41
The Mouse That Gnawed the Oak-
    Tree Down. V. Lindsay.
    Ha-LO:74
O Thou Seer, Go, Flee Thee Away.
    C. Bialik. Me-PH:72
Ode to Joy. M. Holub. Gr-BT:150
The Old Man Called to His Sons.
    Wo-HS:(10)
A Pause of Thought. C. Rossetti.
    Ox-BN:708
Preface. T. Weiss. Ca-VT:433
Shall I Love Again. W. Browne.
    Al-VBP:322
Stick to It. E. Guest. Er-FA:23
Tomorrow. J. Masefield. Un-MB:222
The Tortoise. I. Alexandru.
    Mc-AC:160
Try, Try Again. Er-FA:27,
    Fe-FP:540, Sh-RP:93

Vicarious Atonement.
    R. Aldington. Un-MB:354
PERSIA: see BARMECIDES;
    IRANIAN VERSE - PERSIAN
PERSIMMON TREES
    The Persimmon Tree. Gr-GB:71
PERSONALITY: see also
    HUMOR - PERSONALITY;
    INDIVIDUALITY; SELF
Ann's House. D. Lourie.
    Sc-TN:151
Even Numbers. C. Sandburg.
    La-OC:101
The Eye. M. Benedikt. Mc-EA:74
The Four Horses. J. Reeves.
    Co-BBW:151
I Am. H. Conkling. Ar-TP3:208,
    Fe-FP:18
Me. J. Smith. Ad-II:13
My Inside Self. R. Field.
    Fe-FP:6
My Star. R. Browning. Fe-FP:266,
    Na-EO:156, Sp-OG:346
Temperament. Martial. Co-EL:156,
    Mc-PR:21
Thanksgiving. A. Guiterman.
    Co-PU:67
PERUGIA, IT.
    A Night in Perugia. R. Church.
    Ke-TF:382
PESSIMISTS AND PESSIMISM:
    see also HUMOR - PESSIMISTS
    AND PESSIMISM
The Chestnut Casts His Flambeaux.
    A. Houseman. No-CL:132,
    Un-MB:99
Dover Beach. M. Arnold.
    Al-VBP:972, Cl-FC:48, Co-BL:84,
    Er-FA:454, Ga-FB:66, Go-BP:147,
    Ha-PO:187, Hi-WP II:35,Ho-P:201,
    Ke-PP:87, Ma-FW:53, Ma-YA:209,
    Mc-PR:70, Mo-GR:35, Ox-BN:645,
    Pa-GTB:305, Pl-EI:78, Rv-CB:863,
    Un-MW:120
Fragment of a Lost Gnostic Poem.
    H. Melville. Al-VBP:956
If Crossed with All Mishaps.
    W. Drummond. Rv-CB:331
Ninth Philosopher's Song.
    A. Huxley. Al-VBP:1199
The One Certainty. C. Rossetti.
    Ox-BN:711
The Pessimist. B. King.
    Bl-OB:14, Co-HP:84, Er-FA:205,
    Hi-WP II:13, Mc-WK:85,
    Sm-MK:115
Solitude. E. Wilcox.
    Er-FA:3, Fe-PL:291
'Twixt Optimist and Pessimist.
    Un-GT:24

The Two Spirits. P. Shelley.
    De-CH:323, Ho-P:112, Ho-WR:189
The World a Hunting Is.
    W. Drummond. Rv-CB:329
PESTILENCE: see PLAGUES
PETALS
    At the Time when Blossoms.
        Le-MW:20
    Peach Blossoms after Rain.
        Le-MW:20
PETER, SAINT
    In the Servant's Quarters.
        T. Hardy. Tr-MR:92, Un-MB:26
    The Lord Looks at Peter.
        J. Gray. Ga-S:160
    Peter. E. Marlatt. Tr-MR:93
    Peter and John. E. Wylie.
        Ca-MB:46, Tr-MR:87, Un-MA:279
    Roosters. E. Bishop.
        Wi-LT:506
PETER I, CZAR OF RUSSIA
        (THE GREAT): see HUMOR -
        PETER I, CZAR OF RUSSIA
        (THE GREAT)
PETRARCH: see also LAURA
        (OF PETRARCH'S POEMS)
    Petrarch for Laura.
        C. McAllister. Gr-SS:101
PETROGRAD: see LENINGRAD,
        U.S.S.R.
PETROLEUM: see also SERVICE
        STATIONS
    Night Fire. J. Knoepfle.
        St-H:96
    To a Tidelands Oil Pump.
        B. Janosca. Du-SH:160
PETS: see also HUMOR - PETS;
        also names of animals,
        as CATS
    The Animal Store. R. Field.
        Ar-TP3:52, Au-SP:88, Co-IW:45,
        La-PP:58, La-PV:106
    Bow, Wow, Wow. Ar-TP3:48,
        Bo-FP:115, De-PO:18,
        Mo-CC:(52), Mo-MGT:16
    A Boy and a Pup. A. Guiterman.
        Hu-MP:40
    The Canary. E. Turner.
        Ox-BC:136
    A Child's Pet. W. Davies.
        Co-BBW:174, De-CH:89
    Chums. A. Guiterman. Fr-MP:20
    The Dog and the Cat.
        G. Hallock. Sh-RP:330
    Dogs. F. Cornford. Gr-TG:25,
        Ma-FO:(15), St-FS:25
    Epitaph for a Pet. F. Rodman.
        Ke-TF:327
    Familiar Friends. J. Tippett.
        Au-SP:42, St-FS:120

Four-Paws. H. Eden. De-TT:65
Hint Heavenward. A. Peach.
    Ke-TF:207
I Bought Me a Cat. Su-FVI:52
I Had a Little Doggy.
    Ch-B:43, Hu-MP:191
Janet Waking. J. Ransom.
    Pe-SS:32, Re-TW:21, Sh-AP:181,
    Un-MA:410
Mary's Canary. De-TT:38,
    Sp-AS:23, Wr-RM:93
Mother Shuttle. Ir-BB:170,
    Mo-MGT:18, Na-EO:81, Wi-MG:70
My Dog. M. Chute. Ar-TP3:50,
    Au-SP:37, Fe-FP:154, La-PV:107,
    Mc-AW:52, Pe-FB:20, Th-AS:40
My Dog. S. Lewis. St-FS:98
My Dog. J. Robinson. Au-SP:39
My Father Kept a Horse. Gr-GB:54
My Kitten. Mo-TL:43, Wr-RM:53
Notice. D. McCord. Au-SP:72
Oh Where, Oh Where Has My Little
    Dog Gone. Mother Goose.
    Mo-CC:(54), Mo-MGT:29,
    Mo-TL:70, Wi-MG:46
Open the Door. M. Edey.
    Ar-TP3:182, Br-SS:18
The Pet Lamb. W. Wordsworth.
    De-TT:57, Ox-BC:103
Pet Shop. R. Sward. Co-EL:23
The Pets. R. Farren. Gr-EC:30,
    Rd-OA:6
The Sale of the Pet Lamb.
    M. Howitt. De-CH:87
Samuel. B. Katz. Ho-GC:19
Sonnet: To Tartar, a Terrier
    Beauty. T. Beddoes. Ox-BN:455
The Story of the Baby Squirrel.
    D. Aldis. Ar-TP3:60
Vern. G. Brooks. Ar-TP3:50,
    Ho-CS:36, La-OC:82
Whoop! Little Jerry Tigg.
    Mother Goose. Ir-BB:177,
    Pa-AP:46
The Woodman's Dog. W. Cowper.
    Bo-FP:101, Co-BBW:108, Co-EL:33,
    Co-PU:93, De-TT:69
PETS, CARE OF
    Mary and Her Kitten. E. Farjeon.
        De-TT:29
PEWITS: see LAPWINGS
PHANTOMS: see GHOSTS
PHARAOHS: see KINGS AND RULERS
PHARMACISTS
    Drug Store. J. Weaver. Hi-TL:192
    The Druggist. L. Rubin.
        De-FS:167
PHEASANTS
    After Shooting a Cock Pheasant Last
        Friday. P. Mayer. St-H:139

PHEASANTS — cont'd.
  The Pheasant. R. Coffin.
    Ar-TP3:58, Du-RG:120, Ho-TH:37
  Windsor Forest. A. Pope.
    Co-PU:105, Ma-FW:127, Un-GT:64
PHEBES: see PHOEBES
PHILADELPHIA, PA.
  Independence Bell. Vi-PP:80
  The Little Black-Eyed Rebel.
    W. Carleton. Fe-FP:551,
    Un-GT:188
  Rulers: Philadelphia.
    F. Johnson. Br-AF:199,
    Hu-PN:85
PHILANTHROPY: see
    GIFTS AND GIVING
PHILEMON: see BAUCIS
    AND PHILEMON
PHILIPPINES: see also
    INDONESIAN VERSE;
    LEGENDS, PHILIPPINE
  From an Angba. Tr-US I:181
  Portrait Philippines.
    A. Duckett. Hu-PN:358
  Song. Tr-US I:182
  Song for a Ceremonial Dance.
    Tr-US I:183
PHILOMENA, SAINT
  Santa Filomena. H. Longfellow.
    Se-PR:63
PHILOSOPHY: see also
    HUMOR - PHILOSOPHY;
    SATIRE - PHILOSOPHY
  African China. M. Tolson.
    Ad-PB:45
  Asides on the Oboe. W. Stevens.
    Un-MA:251
  Conclusion. W. Wordsworth.
    Ox-BN:112
  Credo. R. Jeffers. Un-MA:366
  Dodona's Oaks Were Still.
    P. MacDonogh. Co-PI:107
  For Simone Weil.
    Sister M. Thérése. Tr-MR:172
  Ghazal. J. Morabandi.
    Al-PI:151
  Homage to the Philosopher.
    B. Deutsch. Pl-IO:179
  Juxtaposition. A. Clough.
    Ox-BN:613
  The Philosopher and the Lover.
    W. Davenant. Ho-P:315
  Sonnet XIII. Feng Chih.
    Hs-TC:151
  The Weaker the Wine. Su Tung P'o.
    Rx-OH:72
PHOEBES
  I Was a Phoebe. E. Dickinson.
    Re-BS:29
  Nesting Time. A. Guiterman.
    Gr-EC:180

PHOENIX
  I Saw a Phoenix in the Wood
    Alone. E. Spenser. Gr-CT:99
  News of the Phoenix.
    A. Smith. Co-EL:147
  The Phoenix. G. Darley.
    De-CH:579, Gr-CC:180, Gr-CT:99,
    Ho-WR:142, Ox-BN:390, Rv-CB:756,
    Sm-LG:205
  The Phoenix. H. Nemerov.
    Wi-LT:592
  The Phoenix. S. Sassoon.
    Gr-CT:101
  Phoenix. M. Stiker. Ho-TY:282
  The Phoenix and the Turtle.
    W. Shakespeare. Rv-CB:256
  The Phoenix Self-Born.
    J. Dryden. Gr-CT:100
PHONOGRAPHS
  King Juke. K. Fearing.
    Mo-BG:32, Ni-JP:92
PHOSPHORESCENCE
  The Signature of All Things.
    K. Rexroth. Co-BN:214
PHOTOGRAPHERS AND PHOTOGRAPHY:
    see also HUMOR -
    PHOTOGRAPHERS AND PHOTOGRAPHY
  Looking in the Album.
    V. Rutsala. Du-SH:172
  Looking into History.
    R. Wilbur. Ca-VT:485
  Photograph. S. Ishikawa.
    Le-TA:41
  Photograph. Q. Prettyman.
    Ad-PB:258
  To a Photograph. J. Tabb.
    Sh-AP:135
  Vacation Snapshot.
    M. LaFollette. Ls-NY:310
PHYSICAL FITNESS: see
    HUMOR - PHYSICAL FITNESS
PHYSICIANS: see also HUMOR -
    PHYSICIANS; MEDICINE MEN;
    SATIRE - PHYSICIANS;
    SURGEONS AND SURGERY
  Country Doctor. I. Gridley.
    Ke-TF:296
  The Deaths at Paragon, Indiana.
    J. Woods. St-H:250
  The Doctor Who Sits at the
    Bedside of a Rat.
    J. Miles. Ca-VT:339
  From Plane to Plane.
    R. Frost. Un-MA:191
  In the Evening. T. Hardy.
    Pl-IO:183
  Pursuit. R. Warren. Br-TC:454,
    Un-MA:598
  The White-Haired Man: For
    Richard Cabot. M. Sarton.
    Tr-MR:173

You, Doctor Martin.   A. Sexton.
    Un-MA:686
PHYSICISTS AND PHYSICS: see also
    HUMOR - PHYSICISTS AND PHYSICS;
    SATIRE - PHYSICISTS AND PHYSICS
A Commemoration for the Physicist.
    P. Oppenheimer.   Ls-NY:130
Poets and Physicists.
    B. Slutzky.   Ca-MR:93
PIANOS AND PIANISTS: see also
    CLAVICHORDS; HARPSICHORDS;
    HUMOR - PIANOS AND PIANISTS;
    TUNING
Elizabeth at the Piano.
    H. Gregory.   Gr-SS:134,
    Pl-US:20
Haiku 2.   E. Knight.   Ra-BP:206
Has Eighty-Eight Keys.   Re-RR:38
If All the Unplayed Pianos.
    W. Scott.   Du-SH:169
Liszt.   E. Bentley.   Pl-US:34
Mozart Perhaps.   J. Wheelock.
    Pl-US:81
Notes Found near a Suicide:
    To Catalina.   F. Horne.
    Bo-AN:43
Piano.   D. Lawrence.   Pa-GTB:457,
    Rv-CB:977, Un-MB:289
Piano after War.   G. Brooks.
    Bo-AN:142
Piano and Drums.   G. Okara.
    Lo-TY:158
Pyrargyrite Metal, 9.
    C. Meireles.   An-TC:47
Recital.   L. Nicholl.   Pl-US:22
To—.   W. Braithwaite.
    Ad-PB:13
Variations for Two Pianos.
    D. Justice.   Du-SH:168
Woman at the Piano.
    M. Zaturenska.   Un-MA:562
PICASSO, PABLO: see also CUBISM
Picasso's "Portrait de Femme."
    I. Feldman.   Ls-NY:89
PICKAXES
Bam, Bam, Bam.   E. Merriam.
    La-PV:193
PICKETING: see LABOR UNIONS;
    PROTEST; STRIKES
PICKLES: see HUMOR - PICKLES
PICNICS
Beach Fire.   F. Frost.
    Ar-TP3:110, Pe-FB:24
By Ferry to the Island.   I. Smith.
    Go-BP:33, To-MP:95
The Excursion.   Tu Fu.   Mo-SD:138
Growing Up.   H. Behn.   Au-SP:120,
    Br-BC:118, Br-SS:47, La-PH:60,
    La-PV:163
In Memoriam.   A. Tennyson.   Ox-BN:501

The Picnic.   D. Aldis.
    Ar-TP3:109, Fr-MP:15, Mc-AW:17
A Picnic.   A. Fisher.   Au-SP:121
Picnic.   H. Lofting.   Bo-GJ:4,
    Ir-BB:100
The Picnic.   J. Logan.   Co-BL:24,
    Du-SH:62
The Picnic Box.   A. Fisher.
    Mc-AW:60
Picnic Day.   R. Field.
    Ar-TP3:109, Au-SP:122, Br-SS:172
Picnic: The Liberated.
    M. Holman.   Ad-PB:176, Hu-PN:367
Picnics.   M. Chute.   Ag-HE:36
Somewhere in Tuscany.
    D. Holbrook.   Ls-NY:13
Trebetherick.   J. Betjeman.
    Na-EO:160
PICO DELLA MIRANDOLA,
    GIOVANNI
Pico della Mirandola.
    M. Mason.   Hu-PN:526
PICTURE GALLERIES:
    see ART GALLERIES
PICTURES: see PAINTINGS
PIERROT AND PIERRETTE
Pierrot.   S. Teasdale.
    Co-BL:100
PIES: see also HUMOR -
    PIES; TARTS (FOOD)
A Was an Apple-Pie.   Bo-FP:55,
    Gr-EC:251, Li-LB:108,
    Mo-MGT:137
Little Jack Horner.   De-TT:49,
    Li-LB:42
Nursery Song in Pidgin English.
    Li-SR:130
The Pasty.   Mother Goose.
    Mo-MGT:158, Mo-NR:126
The Pie.   Mo-MGT:14
The Pumpkin.   J. Whittier.
    Co-PS:148, Se-PR:210
Simple Simon.   Mother Goose.
    Au-SP:9, De-PO:16, Fr-WO:18,
    Ir-BB:205, Li-LB:30, Mo-MGT:34,
    Mo-NR:89, Un-GT:104, Wi-MG:55,
    Wr-RM:35
Sing a Song of Sixpence.
    Mother Goose.   Bo-FP:9,
    Br-FF:(18), De-PO:22, Fr-WO:16,
    Ir-BB:262, Li-SR:129, Mo-MGT:19,
    Mo-NR:10, On-TW:57, Sm-MK:19
There Was an Old Woman.
    Mother Goose.   Ag-HE:22
PIETY: see SATIRE - PIETY
PIGEONS: see also DOVES
All Morning.   T. Roethke.   Ca-BP:48
The Ballad of the Light-Eyed
    Little Girl.   G. Brooks.
    Li-TU:140, Pe-SS:28

PIGEONS — cont'd.
  The Cock Crows. Ca-MU:11
  Country Rhyme. Gr-TG:30
  The Epic of Dengei.
    Tr-US I:233
  Mrs. Peck-Pigeon. E. Farjeon.
    Ar-TP3:56, Au-SP:62, La-PV:189
  Park Pigeons. M. Cane.
    Ad-CI:49
  The People. E. Roberts.
    Bo-GJ:105
  Perfect. G. Jones. Ma-FW:92
  The Pigeon. R. Church.
    Hi-WP II:166
  Pigeon. M. Van Doren. Ca-BP:17
  Pigeon English. S. Hay. Re-BS:32
  Pigeon Playmates. De-PP:54
  Pigeon Woman. M. Swenson.
    Mo-BG:50
  The Pigeons. M. Burnham.
    Bo-FP:219
  Pigeons. W. Hart-Smith.
    Co-PU:138
  Pigeons. R. Kell. Sm-MK:171
  Pigeons. B. Meyers. Ca-BP:32
  Pigeons. A. Reid. Br-TC:341
  The Produce District. T. Gunn.
    Du-SH:148
  Trinity Place. P. McGinley.
    La-OC:120, Un-MA:596
  Two Pigeons. Mo-MGT:172,
    Wr-RM:55
  Winter in Dunover Field.
    T. Hardy. Un-MB:31
PIGS: see also BOARS;
    HUMOR - PIGS
  Anyone if He Will Try. Ju-CP:13
  Archibald MacLeish Suspends the
    Five Little Pigs.
    L. Untermeyer. Un-MA:310
  Betty Pringle's Pig. Gr-EC:111
  A Cock Sat in the Yew Tree.
    De-CH:498, Ir-BB:24
  A Counting Rhyme.
    M. Stephenson. St-FS:9
  The Flying Pig. De-PO:18,
    Mo-MGT:67, Wi-MG:6, Wr-RM:24
  Grig's Pig. Mo-MGT:20
  Hardweed Path Going. A. Ammons.
    Ca-VT:552
  Higglety, Pigglety, Pop!
    Ir-BB:184, Lo-LL:30,
    Mo-MGT:129, St-FS:22
  Jiggity-Jig, Jiggity-Jig.
    Ju-CP:11
  Just Born Pig. F. Lape.
    Co-PU:8
  The Lady and the Swine. Br-FF:(33),
    Co-OH:74, De-TT:70, Gr-CT:13,
    Gr-GB:151, Ir-BB:170, Mo-MGT:141

  Litter of Pigs. F. Lape.
    Co-BBW:161
  Little Dame Crump. Bo-FP:89,
    Pa-RE:91
  The Little Kittens. E. Follen.
    Ar-TP3:118
  The Old Woman and the Pig.
    Bu-DY:20
  Over in the Meadow. Au-SP:223,
    Ir-BB:24, On-TW:38
  Pearls among Swine. P. Bennett.
    Co-BBW:172
  The Pigs. J. Taylor. De-TT:23
  Pigs o' Pelton. Gr-GB:176
  The Poor Man's Pig.
    E. Blunden. Un-MB:396
  The Prayer of the Little Pig.
    C. Gasztold. Li-TU:62
  A Pretty Wench. Mo-MGT:202
  The Prodigal. E. Bishop.
    Br-TC:52, Wi-LT:514
  Song to the Five Toes.
    Bo-FP:8, Mo-TL:17
  Tale of a Pig. Ju-CP:42
  There Once Was a Sow. On-TW:12
  There Was a Pig. Rv-ON:110
  This Little Pig Got into the
    Barn. Mo-TL:16
  Three Young Rats.
    Fr-WO:35, Gr-CT:31, Gr-EC:11,
    Gr-GB:92, Ir-BB:234, Lo-LL:41,
    Mo-MGT:187, On-TW:15, Sm-MK:193
  To Market, to Market. Mother
    Goose. Ar-TP3:100, Au-SP:18,
    Bo-FP:115, De-PO:8, Er-FA:507,
    Ir-BB:236, Li-LB:105,
    Mo-MGT:136, Mo-NR:20, Mo-TL:77,
    Sp-TM:25, 27, 33, Wr-RM:19
  The Unknown Color. C. Cullen.
    Bo-HF:55, Fe-FP:166, Gr-EC:58
  View of a Pig. T. Hughes.
    Br-TC:210, Ma-FW:229, Wi-LT:738
  We Keep a Dog to Guard the
    House. Wy-CM:30
  Wee Wiggie. Mo-TL:17
  The Wheel of Summer.
    J. Langland. St-H:101
  Whose Little Pigs Are These?
    Mo-TL:16
PIGTAILS (HAIR): see HUMOR -
    PIGTAILS (HAIR)
PIKE (FISH)
  From a Porthole in the Ice.
    W. Sieller. Ls-NY:192
  The Pike. E. Blunden.
    Rd-OA:173, Wi-LT:609
  The Pike. J. Bruce. Mo-SD:102
  Pike. J. Hollander.
    Wi-LT:739
  Pike. T. Hughes. To-MP:83

PILGRIM FATHERS: see also
    HUMOR - PILGRIM FATHERS;
    PURITANS AND PURITANISM
  American History. M. Adams.
    Se-PR:219
  Atlantic Charter, A.D. 1620-1942.
    F. Young. Ar-TP3:39, Br-AF:86,
    Vi-PP:221
  The First Thanksgiving Day.
    M. Preston. Hi-TL:24
  If I Were a Pilgrim Child.
    R. Bennett. Ha-YA:137,
    Sh-RP:304
  The Landing of the Pilgrim
    Fathers. F. Hemans. Ar-TP3:39,
    Bo-FP:159, Er-FA:296, Fe-FP:409,
    Ga-FB:252, Gr-EC:228, Hi-TL:23,
    Se-PR:217, Sp-OG:23, Un-GT:176,
    Vi-PP:50
  Lullaby for Peregrine. R. Coffin.
    Sh-RP:293
  New England Farmer. C. Smith.
    Sm-PT:96
  The Pilgrim Fathers.
    W. Wordsworth. Se-PR:219
  The Pilgrims Came. A. Wynne.
    Hu-MP:344, Ja-PA:54, Mc-AW:71
  Plymouth Rock. O. Driver.
    Sh-RP:234
  The Word of God to Leyden Came.
    J. Rankin. Se-PR:216, Vi-PP:48
PILGRIMS AND PILGRIMAGES:
    see also CRUSADES
  The Golden Journey to Samarkand.
    J. Flecker. Ga-S:227
  O Weary Pilgrims. R. Bridges.
    Un-MB:49
  The Passionate Man's Pilgrimage.
    W. Raleigh. Al-VBP:97,
    Go-BP:256, Gr-CT:283,
    Hi-WP II:169, Ma-YA:59,
    Rv-CB:158
  The Pilgrim. J. Bunyan.
    Ar-TP3:210, Cl-FC:22, De-TT:178,
    Ho-WR:47, Mc-WK:207, Na-EO:96,
    Rv-CB:460
  Pilgrimage. Jao Meng-k'an.
    Hs-TC:108
  A Pilgrim's Journey. Ke-TF:247
  Pilgrims Plod Slowly. Ransetsu.
    Be-MC:46
  Pilgrims' Song. Tr-US I:129
  The Prologue to the Canterbury
    Tales. G. Chaucer. Al-VBP:6,
    Gr-CT:281, Ha-PO:50, Ma-FW:17,
    Ma-YA:28
PINDAR
  The Honeybee.H. Bevington.Ls-NY:174
  The Progress of Poesy. T. Gray.
    Al-VBP:566, Pa-GTB:132, Rv-CB:532

PINE TREES
  Butterflies, Beware! Shosen.
    Be-MC:55
  Come, Companions. Okura.
    Ba-ST:31
  Dirge in Woods. G. Meredith.
    Ho-WR:174, Ox-BN:699
  A Drowsy Breeze Sighs.
    Onitsura. Be-MC:32
  Green Symphony. J. Fletcher.
    Un-MA:314
  Hail on the Pine Trees.
    Basho. Hu-MP:278
  Harvest Moon. Ryota. Sh-RP:66
  In Autumn. T. Dinsburg.
    Mo-MI:21
  In the Wood, a Stand of Pine.
    On-TW:32
  The Least of Breezes.
    Onitsura. Be-CS:46
  O Pine Tree Standing. Hakatsu.
    Ba-ST:58
  The Pine Bough. R. Aldridge.
    Co-PS:151, Ho-LP:36
  The Pine Tree. H. Heine.
    Bo-FP:169
  Pine Tree Tops. G. Snyder.
    Ho-P:249
  The Pine Trees. M. Caroprese.
    La-GI:15
  The Pine-Trees in the Courtyard.
    Po Chu-i. Pa-SG:162
  When I See Pine Trees. Ba-ST:61
PINS: see NEEDLES AND PINS
PIONEER DAY: see PIONEERS
    AND PIONEER LIFE
PIONEERS AND PIONEER LIFE:
    see also COLONIAL PERIOD IN
    AMERICA; COWBOYS; GHOST TOWNS;
    SATIRE - PIONEERS AND PIONEER
    LIFE; WESTWARD MOVEMENT; and
    names of frontiersmen, as
    BOONE, DANIEL
  The Arrival of the Greenhorn.
    A. Hulbert. Sh-RP:287
  The Ballad of William Sycamore.
    S. Benét. Co-RM:228, Hu-MP:387
    Un-MA:498
  Between the Walls of the Valley.
    E. Peck. Br-AF:104
  The Buffalo Coat. T. McGrath.
    St-H:124
  The Cimarron. B. Cutler. St-H:42
  The Circuit. D. Wagoner. Mo-BG:66
  Conquest. E. Coatsworth.
    Br-AF:59, Fe-FP:411, Hu-MP:362
  Cumberland Gap. Br-AF:112
  Daniel Boone. A. Guiterman.
    Fe-FP:428, Hu-MP:385
  The Explorer. R. Kipling. Sp-OG:54

PIONEERS AND PIONEER LIFE — cont'd.
  For February Twelfth. M. Gessner.
    Ha-YA:174, Sh-RP:189
  The Founders of Ohio. W. Venable.
    Hi-TL:85
  Gift of the Sego Lily. M. Jarvis.
    Fi-BG:197
  Hangman's Tree. L. White.
    Br-AF:103
  Hill People. H. Blackwell.
    Br-AF:132
  In the Days when the Cattle Ran.
    H. Garland. Hu-MP:205,
    Sh-RP:268
  John Day, Frontiersman.
    Y. Winters. Ha-PO:73
  Johnny Appleseed. S. Benét.
    Hu-MP:390
  Kentucky Birthday, February 12,
    1815. F. Frost. Br-SS:116,
    Ha-YA:173
  Land of the Free. A. MacLeish.
    Br-AF:243
  Laramie Trail. J. Hanson.
    Fi-BG:57
  Letter from Fort Scott.
    B. Cutler. St-H:44
  Lucinda Matlock. E. Masters.
    Ga-FB:74, Mo-BG:161,
    Un-MA:143, Wi-LT:116
  Lullaby for Peregrine. R. Coffin.
    Sh-RP:293
  Men. A. MacLeish. Br-AF:95
  Missouri Rhapsody.
    J. Daugherty. Sh-RP:299
  A Missouri Traveller Writes
    Home: 1830. R. Bly. Ni-JP:20
  Moonlight. B. Nance. Br-AF:153
  My Father Loved the Jumping-Off
    Place. R. Coffin. Sh-RP:309
  Names from the War. B. Catton.
    Br-AF:78
  New City. M. Yungman. Ho-TY:365
  O Pioneers! J. Bishop. Ca-VT:161
  Old Dolores. Pe-M:34
  Old Log House. J. Tippett.
    Fe-FP:240, Sh-RP:292
  On the Trail to Idaho. Se-PR:147
  The Oregon Trail, 1843.
    A. Guiterman. Fe-FP:432,
    Hu-MP:392
  The Pioneer. A. Guiterman.
    Ar-TP3:37, Hu-MP:394
  The Pioneer. W. Ruggles.
    Gr-EC:233
  The Pioneer Woman - in the North
    Country. E. Tietjens. Br-AF:158
  Pioneers! O Pioneers! W. Whitman.
    Hu-MP:381
  Prairie. K. Llewellyn. Ha-YA:175

  Song of the Settlers. J. West.
    Fe-FP:427
  Spanish Johnny. W. Cather.
    Co-RM:26, Fe-FP:436, Hu-MP:154,
    Mc-WK:140, Mc-WS:160, Sh-RP:41
  Starting from Paumanok.
    W. Whitman. Al-VBP:927
  The Streets of Laredo.
    L. MacNeice. Ca-MB:112,
    Gr-CT:309, To-MP:45
  Trail Breakers. J. Daugherty.
    Br-AF:226, Sh-RP:302
  Walthena. E. Peck. Br-AF:64
  We Put on the Buffalo.
    R. Coffin. Sh-RP:289
  Western Wagons. S. Benét.
    Mc-WK:165
  Wheel Ruts. J. Daugherty.
    Sh-RP:301
  Young Washington. A. Guiterman.
    Co-PS:48, Fe-FP:415, Hu-MP:379
PIPAS: see LUTES
PIPES: see PEACE PIPES; SMOKING
PIPES (MUSIC): see also BAGPIPES;
    HUMOR - PIPES (MUSIC)
  Flute Song. Pa-SG:150
  Hymn of Pan. P. Shelley.
    Sm-LG:229
  The Magic Piper. E. Marsh.
    Br-SS:131
  A Musical Instrument. E. Browning.
    Fe-FP:384, Ho-WR:36, Mc-PR:122,
    Pa-OM:284, Se-PR:327, Sp-OG:343,
    Un-GT:162
  The Musician. R. Lister.
    Pl-US:6
  Ode on a Grecian Urn. J. Keats.
    Al-VBP:772, Er-FA:80, Ha-PO:228,
    Ke-TF:59, Ox-BN:355, Rv-CB:742
  Pan's Syrinx Was a Girl.
    J. Lyly. Al-VBP:122
  The Pied Piper of Hamelin.
    R. Browning. Ar-TP3:28,
    Er-FA:354, Ox-BC:173, Sm-LG:173,
    Un-GT:153
  The Piper. W. Blake. Al-VBP:611,
    Ar-TP3:161, Bo-GJ:131, Cl-FC:20,
    Co-RG:147, De-TT:112, Ga-FB:25,
    Hi-GD:26, Hu-MP:62, La-PP:vii,
    La-PV:xix, Li-LC:88, Ma-YA:126,
    Ox-BC:84, Ox-BN:19, Pl-US:88,
    Re-TW:38, Rv-CB:566, Sm-LG:34,
    Sm-MK:14, Un-GB:17, Un-GT:11
  A Piper. S. O'Sullivan.
    Ar-TP3:13, Co-PI:186, Co-PU:131,
    De-CH:185, Fe-FP:465, Hu-MP:147,
    La-PV:221
  Piping. Ir-BB:41
  Recorders in Italy. A. Rich.
    Pl-US:19

Tom He Was a Piper's Son.
Mother Goose. Ar-TP3:118,
Bo-FP:77, Gr-GB:99, Ir-BB:31,
Mo-NR:64
PIPPIN, HORACE
On a Picture by Pippin, Called
"The Den." S. Rodman.
Hu-PN:544
PIRATES: see also HUMOR - PIRATES;
and names of pirates, as
KIDD, WILLIAM (CAPTAIN KIDD)
A Ballad of John Silver.
J. Masefield. Co-SS:13,
Hu-MP:421, Na-EO:163
Captain Kidd. R. and S. Benét.
Hi-TL:28, Ir-BB:40, Tu-WW:36
The Coasts of High Barbary.
Bl-OB:50
Derelict. Y. Allison.
Co-SS:17, Er-FA:436, Pa-OM:204
Henry Martyn. Fo-OG:18, Rv-CB:439
The Old Buccaneer. G. Kingsley.
Co-RM:60, Na-EO:48, Un-GT:140
One-Eyed Jack. On-TW:6
Pirate. S. Menashe. Sm-MK:3
Pirate Story. R. Stevenson.
Ar-TP3:114, Fe-FP:108,
Un-GB:9, Un-GT:10
The Reformed Pirate.
T. Roberts. Do-WH:20
The Sack of Old Panama.
D. Burnet. Co-RM:56
The Salcombe Seaman's Flaunt to
the Proud Pirate. Gr-CT:224
Sir Andrew Bartton. Ox-BB:508
Spanish Waters. J. Masefield.
Fe-FP:514, Mc-WK:141, Pa-OM:207
The Tarry Buccaneer.
J. Masefield. Co-PT:213
PISGAH, MOUNT: see ABARIM
MOUNTAINS
PITCHER, MOLLY: see McCAULEY,
MARY LUDWIG HAYS (MOLLY
PITCHER)
PITT, WILLIAM (THE YOUNGER PITT)
Nelson and Pitt. W. Scott.
Hi-FO:196
PITTSBURGH, PA.
Pittsburgh. W. Bynner. Br-AF:200
PITY: see also SYMPATHY
The Ballad of Father Gilligan.
W. Yeats. Hi-WP I:72,
Mc-MK:132, Mc-WS:157,
Pl-EI:114, Un-MB:112
Chaplinesque. H. Crane.
Ca-VT:212, Wi-LT:395
Could Man Be Drunk for Ever.
A. Housman. Wi-LT:65
Dear Lord. W. Mann.
Me-WF:20

The Divine Image. W. Blake.
Al-VBP:613, Go-BP:287,
Ox-BN:20, Rv-CB:586
Dream Song. Bi-IT:130
I Heard an Angel Singing.
W. Blake. Rv-CB:621
Jack and Gye. Mo-MGT:183
Me Rueth Mary. Gr-GB:306
Merciless Beauty. G. Chaucer.
No-CL:148, Rv-CB:59
On the Swag. R. Mason. Ga-S:206
Pitying Europe. B. Poplavsky.
Ca-MR:99
Poem. J. Wain. En-PC:230
The Ruthless Moon. B. Reece.
Ls-NY:99
There Was One I Met upon the
Road. S. Crane. Pl-EI:72
To a Dog Injured in the Street.
W. Williams. Wi-LT:203
PIXIES: see ELVES; FAIRIES
PLACE NAMES: see also names of
cities and towns, as
BOSTON, MASS.
American Names. S. Benét.
Br-AF:6, Mc-WK:157, Pa-HT:3,
Sh-AP:194, Sm-LG:145
As I Went Down by Havre de Grace.
E. Wylie. Pa-HT:6
PLACES, LOVE OF: see also
NATIONAL SONGS; PATRIOTISM;
STATE SONGS
An American in England.
E. Wylie. Pa-HT:121
And God Be Witness.
B. Akhmadulina. Ca-MR:35
Aromaiterai's Lament. Tr-US II:68
As I Went Down by Havre de Grace.
E. Wylie. Pa-HT:6
At St Jerome. F. Harrison.
Do-WH:74
Avila. F. Keyes. Ke-TF:395
Blue Sunday. T. McNeill.
Sa-B:5
Bonac. J. Wheelock. Pa-HT:37
Burning in the Night. T. Wolfe.
Br-AF:14
Bury Me. Chu Hsiang.
Hs-TC:98
Calcutta. A. Chakravarty.
Al-PI:77
Canadian Boat Song. J. Galt.
Ox-BN:204, Rv-CB:683, Sm-LG:140
Charleston - Post Confederate.
A. Deas. Ke-TF:360
City Child. E. McCormick.
La-IH:83
Clifton Grove. H. White.
Ox-BN:228
Closed House. R. Coffin. Ke-TF:416

PLACES, LOVE OF — cont'd.
  Come Back, Paddy Reilly.
    P. French. Co-PI:48
  Composed upon Westminster Bridge.
    W. Wordsworth. Al-VBP:660,
    Ar-TP3:173, Bo-FP:124, De-CH:524,
    Er-FA:270, Fe-PL:396, Ga-FB:224,
    Go-BP:22, Gr-CT:290, Ha-PO:80,
    Hi-WP II:126, Ke-TF:367,
    Ma-YA:139, Mc-PR:190, Ox-BN:78,
    Pa-GTB:250, Pa-HT:124, Rv-CB:645,
    Sm-LG:135
  The Conclusive Voyage.
    J. Jimenez. Le-SW:85
  Conservative. W. Stafford.
    St-H:212
  The County Mayo. A. Raftery.
    Co-PI:179
  Cranberry Road. R. Field.
    Th-AS:134
  The Daisy. A. Tennyson. Ox-BN:489
  Dakota, the Beauty of the West.
    Fi-BG:74
  Drifting. T. Read. Pa-HT:107
  Dusk. D. Heyward. Pa-HT:43
  England. W. de la Mare.
    Pa-HT:135
  England, My England. W. Henley.
    Fe-PL:179, Un-MB:56
  Epitaph on a Jacobite.
    T. Macaulay. Al-VBP:799,
    Cr-WS:56, De-TT:180, Ox-BN:428
  Exiled. E. Millay. Ni-JP:132,
    Pa-HT:7
  The Face of My Mountains.
    Bi-IT:46
  Falmouth. W. Henley.
    Fe-PL:148, Un-MB:55
  Farewell. I. L'Ouverture.
    Lo-TY:89
  Farewell. K. Tynan. De-CH:47
  The Farm by the Lake. Chu Hsi.
    Rx-OH:119
  Fears in Solitude.
    S. Coleridge. Ox-BN:164
  A Few Things Explained.
    P. Neruda. Li-TU:237
  Four Sheets to the Wind and a
    One-Way Ticket to France.
    C. Rivers. Ad-PB:234,
    Bo-AN:176, Hu-NN:107,
    Hu-PN:404, Ra-BP:199
  From the Flats. S. Lanier.
    Sh-AP:132
  From the Harvard Yard. D. Hall.
    Ke-TF:355
  Ghost to Come. M. Widdemer.
    De-FS:219
  Hemmed-In Males. W. Williams.
    Ha-PO:74

  Himalaya. Po Fei Huang.
    Ls-NY:248
  Home-Sick Song. Tr-US I:97
  Home, Sweet Home. J. Payne.
    Er-FA:133
  Home-Thoughts from Abroad.
    R. Browning. Bo-FP:230,
    Co-BN:19, Er-FA:266, Fe-FP:460,
    Fe-PL:376, Ga-FB:229, Ke-TF:366,
    Ma-YA:202, Mc-PR:106, Ox-BN:534,
    Pa-HT:117
  Homecoming. D. Scott. Sa-B:115
  Homesick. Hu P'in-ch'ing.
    Pa-MV:99
  Homesick. Tu Yün-hsieh.
    Hs-TC:247
  Hometown Name. H. Sloanaker.
    Ke-TF:345
  The House. E. Almedingen.
    Ke-TF:412
  I Have Loved England. A. Miller.
    Fe-PL:181
  I Return to My City.
    O. Mandelstam. Ca-MR:148
  I Return to the Place where
    I Was Born. T'ao Yuan Ming.
    Rx-LT:33
  I Saw Green Banks of Daffodils.
    E. Tennant. Ar-TP3:201
  I Travell'd among Unknown Men.
    W. Wordsworth. Ga-FB:224,
    Mc-PR:107, Ox-BN:63, Pa-GTB:180,
    Rv-CB:632
  I Was Born upon Thy Bank, River.
    H. Thoreau. Co-EL:129,
    Co-PU:50
  Improvised Song of Joy.
    Le-IB:100, Tr-US I:13
  In My Life. J. Lennon. Mo-GR:43
  In My Mountains. J. Yokomizo.
    Ba-HI:102
  In the Highlands. R. Stevenson.
    Cl-DT:46, Ga-FB:241
  The Intruder. B. Smith. Sa-B:140
  Invocation. S. Benét. Br-AF:10,
    Hu-MP:364, Sm-PT:99, Vi-PP:226
  The Island. C. Morley. Pa-HT:122
  The Islands. H.D. Un-MA:339
  Isle of the Dragonfly. Br-FW:12
  I've Got a Home in That Rock.
    R. Patterson. Ad-PB:209,
    Hu-PN:398
  Jerusalem. W. Blake.
    Gr-CT:295, Ox-BN:42
  Jerusalem. J. Halevi. Me-PH:61
  The Kalmyk Mourns for His Country.
    Tr-US II:133
  Keziah. G. Brooks. Un-GB:21
  Kilcash. F. O'Connor. Co-PI:155,
    Hi-WP II:132, Re-TW:86

The Lake Isle of Innisfree.
  W. Yeats.   Ar-TP3:218,
  Co-RG:118, Er-FA:258, Fe-FP:464,
  Fr-WO:79, Ga-FB:242, Ma-YA:230,
  Mc-PR:174, Pa-HT:138, Th-AS:149,
  Un-MB:108, Wi-LT:68
Lake Leman.   G. Byron.   Ox-BN:245
A Lament for His Own Land.
  Tr-US II:114
The Landskip.   W. Shenstone.
  Rv-CB:529
Lines.   W. Wordsworth.   Ox-BN:66
Lines on Leaving a Scene in
  Bavaria.   T. Campbell.
  Ox-BN:198
A Little While, a Little While.
  E. Brontë.   Al-VBP:922, Ox-BN:596
Localities.   C. Sandburg.   Br-AF:7
London Beautiful. R. Le Gallienne.
  Pa-HT:125
London Town.   J. Masefield.
  Ma-YA:232
Lonesome Water.   R. Helton.
  Br-AF:100, Co-PM:91,
  Mc-WK:200, Un-MA:347
The Long Voyage.   M. Cowley.
  Mc-WK:182, Ni-JP:132, Pe-OA:171
Longing for the South Country.
  Li Yu.   Le-MW:42
The Lordly Hudson.   P. Goodman.
  Ca-VT:332
Love Song.   R. Whittemore.
  Br-AF:27
Madrid.   F. Keyes.   Ke-TF:389
Map of My Country.   J. Holmes.
  Br-AF:11
Mignon's Song.   J. von Goethe.
  Co-PU:48, Pa-SG:125
Mont-Saint-Michel.   C. Stork.
  Ke-TF:380
Mountain Meadows.   M. Keller.
  Co-BN:221
My Heart Is in the East.
  J. Halevi.   Me-PH:61
My Heart's in the Highlands.
  R. Burns.   Bl-OB:141,
  Cl-FC:62, Er-FA:424, Fe-FP:463,
  Mc-PR:175, Mc-WK:192, Mo-SD:118,
  Pa-HT:149
My Home.   Ho-TY:311
My Land.   T. Davis.   Hu-MP:373,
  Vi-PP:24
My Land Is Fair for Any Eyes to
  See. J. Stuart. Ar-TP3:218,
  Fe-FP:229
My Lost Youth.   H. Longfellow.
  Al-VBP:825, Bo-GJ:178, Co-RG:114,
  Er-FA:163, Fe-FP:547, Fe-PL:253,
  Ga-FB:160, Hu-MP:73, No-CL:257,
  Pa-HT:9

My Maryland. J. Randall.   Er-FA:441
My Native Land.   W. Scott.
  Er-FA:286, Hu-MP:362, Mc-PR:32,
  Ox-BN:127, Pa-HT:147, Sp-OG:188,
  Vi-PP:25
My Prairies.   H. Garland.
  Fe-FP:268
My South.   D. West.   Hu-PN:547
My Spirit Will Not Haunt the
  Mound.   T. Hardy.   Ox-BN:838,
  Un-MB:32
Never Shall I Leave the Places
  That I Love.   Wo-HS:(71)
next to of course god.
  e. cummings.   Br-AF:14,
  Ca-VT:178, Pe-SS:101,
  Sh-AP:192, Wi-LT:361
A Night in Perugia.   R. Church.
  Ke-TF:382
Not in the Guide-Books.
  E. Jennings.   Wi-LT:742
The Oak and the Ash.   Sm-LG:138
The Old Buccaneer. C. Kingsley.
  Co-RM:60, Na-EO:48, Un-GT:140
The Old Chartist. G. Meredith.
  Hi-FO:244
The Old Squire.   W. Blunt.
  Mo-SD:110
The Old Vicarage, Grantchester.
  R. Brooke.   Ga-FB:239,
  Hi-WP II:129, Pa-HT:120,
  Un-MB:326
On the Arizona Line.   Fi-BG:36
On the Frisco River.   Fi-BG:46
Our Heritage.   J. Stuart. Br-AF:4
Out where the West Begins.
  A. Chapman.   Er-FA:263
Oxford.   L. Johnson.   Ox-BN:949
Paris.   A. Seeger.   Ke-TF:372
The Pinta, the Nina and the
  Santa Maria; and Many Other
  Cargoes of Light.
  J. Tagliabue.   Br-AF:23
Places.   S. Teasdale.   Pa-HT:5
A Poem for Home.   M. Oliver.
  St-H:161
Praise of Beaches.   Tr-US II:47
Printemps.   M. Bracker.   Ke-TF:373 [3]
Prologue to a Yomeh Ballad.
  Tr-US I:44
Return to Chartres.   M. Sarton.
  Ke-TF:379
The Reverie of Poor Susan.
  W. Wordsworth.   De-CH:96,
  De-TT:108, Ho-WR:155,
  Pa-GTB:256, Rv-CB:639
The Sacred Lands of the Blue Lake
  Forest.   P. Bernal.   Br-MW:57
Sailing Homeward.   Chan Fang-Sheng.
  Ar-TP3:97, Le-MW:43, Pa-SG:180,
  Sm-LG:298, Th-AS:158

PLACES, LOVE OF — <u>cont'd.</u>
  Salamanca. F. Keyes. Ke-TF:393
  Sea Born. H. Vinal. Bo-HF:78
  Second Farewell to Cambridge.
    Hsü Chih-mo. Hs-TC:83
  Segovia. F. Keyes. Ke-TF:391
  Sevilla. F. Keyes. Ke-TF:401
  Shellbrook. W. Barnes. Ox-BN:434
  Siena, from a Northern Slope.
    J. Ackerson. Ke-TF:381
  Six o' Clock. O. Dodson. Hu-PN:298
  The Snow. Mao Tse-tung. Hs-TC:363
  Some Refrains at the Charles
    River. P. Viereck. En-PC:154
  Song. Bi-IT:45
  The Song of a Vagabond Son.
    Fang Ching. Hs-TC:385
  The Song of Cove Creek Dam.
    Em-AF:757
  The Song of Iowa. S. Byers.
    Se-PR:261
  Songs, I. Tr-US II:135
  South. E. Brathwaite. Sa-B:46
  The Southern Road. D. Randall.
    Ad-PB:139, Be-MA:70, Hu-NN:41
  The Spell of the Yukon.
    R. Service. Er-FA:365
  A Sweet Country Life. Rv-ON:42
  Sweet Innisfallen. T. Moore.
    Ox-BN:215
  Table d'Hote. R. Esler. Ls-NY:154
  There Is a Charming Land.
    A. Oehlenschlager. Fe-FP:467
  There Is a Land. J. Montgomery.
    Vi-PP:26
  This England. W. Shakespeare.
    Ga-FB:223, Ke-TF:255,
    Ma-YA:66, Pa-HT:136
  This Land. I. Mudie. Gr-BT:30
  This Landscape, These People.
    Z. Ghose. To-MP:124
  This Was Our Land. Wo-HS:(35)
  Thoughts in Exile. Su Tung P'o.
    Rx-OH:81
  To a River in the South.
    H. Newbolt. De-CH:48
  To an Absent Virginian.
    K. Peatross. Ke-TF:359
  To the Nyeva. G. Garbovsky.
    Bo-RU:35
  Trade Winds. J. Masefield.
    Bo-HF:86, Cl-FC:56
  The Unfound Door. D. Etter.St-H:64
  Vailima. R. Stevenson.
    De-CH:51, De-TT:157, Ox-BN:895
  Valencia. F. Keyes. Ke-TF:397
  Watching Post. C. Day Lewis.
    To-MP:38
  Waters and Dreaming. E. Botta.
    Mc-AC:112

  We Who Were Born. E. Lewis.
    Br-BC:11, Fe-FP:465
  When the Mint Is in the Liquor.
    C. Ouslet. Fe-PL:417
  Where a Roman Villa Stood, above
    Freiburg. M. Coleridge.
    Ox-BN:927
  Wild Peaches. E. Wylie.
    Pa-HT:40, Sh-AP:169
  The Wild Trees. L. Lee. Go-BP:160
  Winterproof. A. Guiterman.
    Ke-TF:417
  With My Maimed Hand.
    Tai Wang-Shu. Hs-TC:185
  Words from England. D. Hall.
    Ke-TF:445
  Yankee Cradle. R. Coffin.
    Gr-EC:234, Na-EO:102
PLACES, MYTHICAL AND IMAGINARY
  The Atlantides. H. Thoreau.
    Al-VBP:918
  Atlantis. C. Aiken. Gr-SS:180
  The City of Dreadful Night.
    J. Thomson. Ho-WR:207
  Forty Singing Seamen. A. Noyes.
    Pa-OM:197
  The Golden City of St. Mary.
    J. Masefield. Bo-HF:82,
    Pa-HT:157
  The Happy Townland. W. Yeats.
    Re-TW:126
  Kiph. W. de la Mare. Ar-TP3:151
  Kubla Khan. S. Coleridge.
    Al-VBP:699, Bo-GJ:222, Co-RG:15,
    De-CH:386, Er-FA:361, Ga-FB:23,
    Gr-CT:177, Gr-EC:140, Mc-PR:150,
    Ox-BN:165, Pa-HT:154, Re-TW:132,
    Rv-CB:657, Sm-LG:215
  The Lotus-Eaters. A. Tennyson.
    Al-VBP:847, Cl-FC:14, De-CH:615,
    Er-FA:76, Ga-FB:12, Gr-CT:278,
    Ox-BN:477, Pa-HT:158, Pa-OM:296
  Somewhere. W. de la Mare.Fe-FP:8
  Under the Moon. W. Yeats.
    Pa-HT:161
  When I Set Out for Lyonesse.
    T. Hardy. No-CL:144, Pa-HT:156,
    Un-MB:32
PLAGIARISM
  An Advertisement to the Reader.
    J. Bunyan. De-CH:616
  A Coat. W. Yeats.
    Pl-ML:33, Wi-LT:69
PLAGUES
  Adieu; Farewell Earth's Bliss.
    T. Nashe. Al-VBP:211, De-CH:244,
    Gr-CT:356, Ha-PO:142, Hi-FO:141,
    Rv-CB:276, Sm-LG:276
  Bessy Bell and Mary Gray.
    De-CH:520, Ox-BB:617

The Coming of the Plague.
  W. Kees. Ca-VT:407, Du-SH:109
Go Down, Moses. Ab-MO:79,
  Ga-S:45, Pl-EI:101, Ra-BP:23
Intercession Against the Plague.
  Sedulius Scottus. Ga-S:44
The Old City. R. Manning-Sanders.
  De-CH:322
On the Pestilence That Scourged
  the Fijians after Their First
  Contact with Whites, ca. 1791.
  Tr-US I:228
Plague. Bi-IT:150
Plague Charm. Hi-FO:153
Song on the Great Visitation of
  Measles in 1875. Tr-US I:228
This Was That Yeere of Wonder.
  De-CH:638
PLAINS: see PRAIRIES
PLANE TREES: see SYCAMORE TREES
PLANETARIUMS
  Ode to the Hayden Planetarium.
  A. Guiterman. Pl-IO:29
PLANETS: see also names of
    planets, as JUPITER (PLANET)
  Among the Stars. W. Blake.
    Re-TW:129, Un-GT:264
  An Astrologer's Song.
    R. Kipling. Un-MB:135
  Dark Yuggoth. L. Carter.
    De-FS:48
  Hudibras. S. Butler. Pl-IO:23
  Night. S. Teasdale. Ar-TP3:211,
    Au-SP:340, Fe-FP:264,
    Pe-FB:63, Th-AS:31
PLANTS, MEDICINAL: see REMEDIES
    AND CURES
PLANTS AND PLANTING: see also
    HUMOR - PLANTS AND PLANTING;
    and names of plants, as FERNS
  The Anxious Farmer. B. Johnson.
    Co-BN:37
  Eastward I Stand, Mercies I Beg.
    Pl-EI:173
  Fairy Rings. J. Clare. Go-BP:109
  Forms of the Human.
    R. Eberhart. Ho-TH:80
  Green Things Growing. D. Craik.
    Er-FA:247
  The Idle Flowers. R. Bridges.
    Co-BN:45, Gr-CT:247
  In a Warm Chicken House.
    J. Wright. Ls-NY:303
  Planting Song of Women to the
    Earth-Mother. Tr-US II:303
  Seed Leaves. R. Wilbur. Co-BN:38
  Seeds. W. de la Mare.
    Ar-TP3:202, Sh-RP:204
  Song of a Hebrew. D. Abse.
    Sm-MK:214

Songs in the Garden of the House
    God. Bi-IT:115, Da-SC:86
The Sower. R. Olivares Figueroa.
    Fe-FP:490, Ho-LP:38
The Task. W. Cowper. Go-BP:23
Transplanting. T. Roethke.
    Ha-WR:14
We've Plowed Our Land, We've
  Sown Our Seed. Sp-AS:(36)
PLASTICS
  Stuff. A. Mitchell. Sm-MK:190
PLATO
  Among School Children. W. Yeats.
    Pa-GTB:428, Un-MB:114, Wi-LT:72
  Plato's Tomb. Sm-LG:275
PLATYPUSES: see HUMOR - PLATYPUSES
PLAY: see also ACTION RHYMES;
    AMUSEMENTS; DRESSING UP;
    GAMES; MAKE-BELIEVE; PLAY-
    GROUNDS; PLAYHOUSES; PLAY-
    MATES; SWINGS AND SWINGING;
    TOYS
  All Work and No Play. Mo-MGT:187
  As Soon as Ever Twilight Comes.
    W. de la Mare. Br-SS:27
  Baby Playing. R. Clarke.
    Le-M:73
  The Bear Hunt. M. Widdemer.
    Fe-FP:104, Hu-MP:49
  Billy, Billy. Wr-RM:89
  Block City. R. Stevenson.
    Au-SP:210, Bo-FP:17, Fe-FP:103,
    Hu-MP:44
  Boys and Girls, Come Out to Play.
    De-CH:742, Mo-CC:(56),
    Mo-MGT:181, Sm-MK:136
  A Boy's Song. J. Hogg.
    Bl-OB:138, Bo-FP:258, Ch-B:62,
    De-CH:132, De-TT:75, Fe-FP:301,
    Ho-WR:69, Ke-TF:45, Mc-PR:114,
    Mc-WK:84, Ox-BC:156
  Creep. L. Kershaw. Le-M:63
  Drawing upon the Ground.
    S. Ogiwara. Sh-AM:165
  Following the Music. H. Rostron.
    St-FS:21
  Frolic. AE. Fe-FP:99, Un-MB:144
  Fun in a Garret. E. Dowd.
    Ar-TP3:113
  Fun with My Shadow. C. Tringress.
    St-FS:16
  Girls and Boys, Come Out to Play.
    I. Serrailler. Ir-BB:17
  Girls and Boys, Come Out to Play.
    Ag-HE:33, Ar-TP3:98, De-TT:34,
    Hu-MP:34, Ir-BB:15, Li-LB:24,
    Mo-NR:116, Wi-MG:60, Wr-RM:17
  A Good Play. R. Stevenson.
    Ar-TP3:113, Fe-FP:101,
    Hu-MP:49, Ir-BB:15

PLAY — cont'd.
  Hide and Seek. A. Shiffrin.
    Ir-BB:13, St-FS:68
  Hiding. D. Aldis. Ar-TP3:113,
    Au-SP:199, Fe-FP:102, Hu-MP:45
  Holiday. E. Young. Ar-TP3:164
  How Many Days Has My Baby to
    Play? Mother Goose.
    Ar-TP3:183, Ir-BB:10, Mo-NR:8,
    Wr-RM:28
  Keeping Store. M. Butts.
    Bo-FP:140
  Kick a Little Stone. D. Aldis.
    Au-SP:185
  Kids. W. Bynner. Hu-MP:39
  The Kitten and the Falling
    Leaves. W. Wordsworth.
    Bl-OB:106, Ch-B:23, Co-BBW:124,
    Fe-FP:157, Hu-MP:208, Un-GB:18,
    Un-GT:52
  Lamplighter Barn. M. Livingston.
    Ar-TP3:105
  The Little Jumping Girls.
    K. Greenaway. Ar-TP3:101,
    Fe-FP:105, Hu-MP:38, Ir-BB:14,
    St-FS:43
  Mackado, Fustian and Motley.
    J. Taylor. Rv-CB:319
  Marching Song. R. Stevenson.
    Ar-TP3:112, Fe-FP:106
  My Shadow. R. Stevenson.
    Ar-TP3:112, Au-SP:189, Bo-FP:112,
    Fe-FP:13, Ga-FB:167, Hu-MP:72,
    Ir-BB:102, Ke-TF:71, La-PP:74,
    La-PV:12, Pe-FB:36
  My Taxicab. J. Tippett. Hu-MP:46
  Nurse's Song. W. Blake.
    Cl-FC:60, De-CH:433, De-TT:89,
    Fe-FP:99, Hu-MP:109, Ox-BC:88,
    Rd-SS:6, Re-TW:75, Rv-CB:574,
    Un-GT:11
  On a Wet Day. F. Sacchetti.
    Co-BN:170
  One, Two, Three. H. Bunner.
    Bo-FP:20, Fe-FP:537, Fe-PL:12,
    Hu-MP:54
  Our Circus. L. Randall.
    Ar-TP3:116
  Pagan Saturday. J. Logan.
    St-H:114
  Park Play. J. Tippett.
    Mc-AC:4
  Play Song. P. Clarke.
    Ab-MO:10
  The Postman. L. Richards.
    Ar-TP3:10, Au-SP:137
  School Is Over. K. Greenaway.
    Ar-TP3:98, Ch-B:114
  Step on His Head. J. Laughlin.
    Ca-VT:411

  Ten Thousand Years' Play.
    N. Tozu. Le-TA:39
  Upside Down. R. Burgunder.
    Ar-TP3:108
  Where Go the Boats? R. Stevenson.
    Ar-TP3:110, Au-SP:201, Bo-GJ:177,
    Hu-MP:173, Li-LC:74, Mc-PR:132,
    Ox-BC:294, Sm-LG:103
  Windy Morning. H. Behn.
    Ar-TP3:164
  With a Hop, and a Skip, and a
    Jump. W. O'Neill. St-FS:4
  You Do It, Too. M. Langford.
    St-FS:23
PLAYGROUNDS
  Black Clouds. T. Brame.
    Pa-RE:72
  It Is an Outfielder.
    R. Loewinsohn. Kh-VA:76
  Old Playground. M. Wada.
    Le-TA:49
PLAYHOUSES
  A House of Cards. C. Rossetti.
    Bo-FP:18
  The Playhouse Key. R. Field.
    Fe-FP:107, Hu-MP:43
  Sand Castles. W. Robertson.
    Hu-MP:42
  September. K. Pyle. Bo-FP:139
PLAYMATES
  Invitation. R. Torrence.
    Bo-FP:103
  The Unseen Playmate.
    R. Stevenson. Bo-FP:101
PLAYS: see DRAMA
PLEASURE: see also SATIRE -
    PLEASURE
  A Boat, a Boat. Rv-CB:425
  Cakes and Ale. Er-FA:111
  The Choice. D. Rossetti.
    Al-VBP:989
  Christian Ethics. T. Traherne.
    Pl-US:140
  Edward the Second. C. Marlowe.
    Al-VBP:179
  The Garden. J. Sylvester.
    Rv-CB:187
  In Youth Is Pleasure. R. Wever.
    Rv-CB:143
  Invitation to the Voyage.
    C. Baudelaire. Pa-SG:56
  King Agongola's Song.
    Tr-CB:56, Tr-US I:55
  A Mask Presented at Ludlow
    Castle. J. Milton. Al-VBP:399
  The Merry Country Lad. N. Breton.
    Al-VBP:84, De-CH:137, Rd-OA:39,
    Rv-CB:148
  Song of Intoxication.
    F. Nietzsche. Un-R:33

Tame Cat. E. Pound. Co-EL:89
Tethy's Festival. S. Daniel.
De-CH:154
PLEIADES
Native-Cat Songs. Tr-US I:254
The Pleiades. E. Coatsworth.
Pl-IO:31
Song to the Pleiades. Da-SC:104
The Turning Year. Su Tung P'o.
Rx-OH:87
You and I Shall Go. Bi-IT:100,
Tr-US II:248
PLOVERS
Forgive My Guilt. R. Coffin.
Ba-PO:165, Du-RG:76
The Nesting Ground. D. Wagoner.
En-PC:249
The Plover. Pa-SG:134
PLOWING
Follower. S. Heaney. Co-PI:59
Go, Ploughman, Plough.
J. Campbell. Hu-MP:395
Horses. E. Muir. Sm-LG:80
Ploughing on Sunday. W. Stevens.
Bo-GJ:52, Fe-FP:232, Pa-RE:100,
Re-TW:14, Sm-MK:26, We-PZ:38
Ploughman Singing. J. Clare.
Go-BP:39
The Plower. P. Colum. Un-MB:249
Portrait of Life.
Tsang K'o-chia. Hs-TC:287
The Serf. R. Campbell. Ni-JP:85,
Pa-GTB:494, Un-MB:419
To the Man after the Harrow.
P. Kavanagh. Pa-GTB:514
Tubal Cain. C. Mackay. Hu-MP:407
PLUM BLOSSOMS
Even Stones. Onitsura. Be-CS:37
The Fall of the Plum Blossoms.
Rankō. Ar-TP3:204
In the Fields of Spring.
Ba-ST:19
Plum Blossoms. Chang Hsiu-ya.
Pa-MV:36
The Plum Blossoms Have Opened.
Ba-ST:26
These Flowers of the Plum.
Izen. Le-MW:78
The Vase. Kuo Mo-jo. Hs-TC:38
Warbler, Wipe Your Feet. Issa.
Be-MC:23
Wild Plum. O. Johns. Bo-HF:65
PLUM CAKE
The Mouse and the Cake.
E. Cook. Ox-BC:209
To Market, to Market. Mo-NR:17
PLUM TREES
The Backyard on Fulton Street.
G. Dusenbery. Sc-TN:35
Harbingers. Basho. Sh-RP:64

Plum Trees. Rankō. Au-SP:347,
Fe-FP:482, Hu-MP:274
The Vase. Kuo Mo-jo. Hs-TC:38
PLUMBING: see also HUMOR -
PLUMBING
Elegy for Alfred Hubbard.
T. Connor. To-MP:101
PLUMS
This Is Just to Say.
W. Williams. Bo-GJ:211,
Du-RG:60, Kh-VA:35, Li-SR:100,
Li-TU:24, Ma-FW:232, Mo-BG:96,
Sh-AP:169
To a Poor Old Woman.
W. Williams. Ho-LP:74,
Li-TU:145
PLYMOUTH ROCK
Plymouth Rock. O. Driver.
Sh-RP:234
POACHING (LAW)
The Ballad of Minepit Shaw.
R. Kipling. Co-PT:49
The Lincolnshire Poacher.
Co-RM:237, De-CH:192, De-TT:79,
Gr-GB:256, Ho-WR:75, Mo-SD:119,
Pa-OM:188
POCAHONTAS
Pocahontas. W. Thackeray.
Br-AF:55, Fe-FP:408, Hi-TL:21,
Hu-MP:429, Pa-OM:129, Un-GT:177,
Vi-PP:46
POCKETS
It Pays. A. Bennett. Er-FA:222
Lucy Locket. Bo-FP:121, De-PO:18,
Hi-FO:160, Li-LB:45, Mo-MGT:132,
Wr-RM:23
Pockets. R. Bennett. Sh-RP:129
Pockets. S. Williams. St-FS:51
Timothy Dan. J. Sheridan.
St-FS:47
POE, EDGAR ALLAN
Abbreviated Interviews with a Few
Disgruntled Literary Celebrities.
R. Whittemore. Co-FB:343
Edgar Allan Poe. R. Barlow.
De-FS:11
Edgar Allan Poe. C. Lanier.
Se-PR:311
POETS AND POETRY: see also CALYPSOS;
CHILDREN AS POETS; HUMOR - POETS
AND POETRY; LIMERICKS (ABOUT);
MINSTRELS AND TROUBADOURS;
PARODIES; SATIRE - POETS AND
POETRY; SONNETS (ABOUT); names of
language and ethnic verse, as
AFRICAN VERSE, and names of poets,
as WHITMAN, WALT
About Myself. S. Mernit. Ad-II:16
Adam's Curse. W. Yeats.
Co-PI:205

POETS AND POETRY — cont'd.
   Adonais. P. Shelley. Al-VBP:759,
      Ha-PO:130, Ox-BN:287
   Afternoon and His Unfinished
      Poem. C. O'John. Al-WW:66
   Afterwards, They Shall Dance.
      B. Kaufman. Br-TC:229,
      Ca-VT:538, Hu-PN:409
   Ah, Ben. R. Herrick. No-CL:94
   Alba: Whose Muse? F. Eckman.
      St-H:52
   All Things Can Tempt Me.
      W. Yeats. Co-PI:204
   America. S. Dobell. Vi-PP:17
   American Poetry. L. Simpson.
      Co-EL:42, Ho-TH:76
   Anactoria. A. Swinburne.
      Al-VBP:1022
   And Thus in Ninevah. E. Pound.
      Ca-VT:80
   Answer to Jealousy. M. Prior.
      Al-VBP:514, Un-MW:48
   Answering a Letter from a
      Younger Poet.
      B. Ghiselin. En-PC:50
   Apology for Apostasy?
      E. Knight. Be-MA:111
   The Argument of His Book.
      R. Herrick. Al-VBP:325
   Der Arme Poet. M. Roberts.
      Pl-ML:16
   Ars Poetica. A. MacLeish.
      Bo-HF:168, Ho-TH:60, Sh-AP:187,
      Un-MA:453, Wi-LT:341
   Ars Poetica about Ultimates.
      T. Combs. Br-TC:73
   Astrophel and Stella, Sonnet I.
      P. Sidney. Al-VBP:125,
      Ma-YA:61, Rv-CB:169
   At Lanier's Grave. J. Tabb.
      Sh-AP:136
   At the Edge. M. Korte. Sc-TN:116
   At the Grave of John Clare.
      C. Causley. Ma-FW:171
   Austerity of Poetry. M. Arnold.
      No-CL:20
   Ave atque Vale. A. Swinburne.
      Al-VBP:1033, Ox-BN:814
   Ballade. K. Shapiro. Un-MW:144
   The Balloon. A. Tennyson.
      Co-RG:137
   Banquet at the Tau Family Manor.
      Tu Fu. Rx-OH:3
   The Bard. T. Gray. Pa-GTB:115
   The Bard. M. Leib. Ho-TY:94
   The Bards. R. Graves. Wi-LT:368
   Baudelaire. D. Schwartz.
      Br-TC:357, Pl-ML:14
   The Bear. G. Kinnell. Ca-VT:605,
      La-RM:25, Mc-EA:55

   Ben Jonson Entertains a Man from
      Stratford. E. Robinson.
      Un-MA:127
   beware: do not read this poem.
      I. Reed. Ad-PB:328, Jo-SA:64,
      Ra-BP:288
   The Birth of the Poet.
      Q. Prettyman. Ad-BO:18
   A Black Poetry Day. A. Johnson.
      Ad-PB:13
   The Bourgeois Poet, #27.
      K. Shapiro. St-H:201
   The Bourgeois Poet, #59.
      K. Shapiro. St-H:207
   Breakthrough. C. Rodgers.
      Ra-BP:263
   Broken Promise. J. Taylor.
      Gr-BT:108
   Burial of the Spirit of a Young
      Poet. R. Hughes. Un-MB:409
   Butterfly Bones. M. Avison.
      Wi-LT:661
   Butterfly, These Words.
      Soseki. Be-CS:18
   By a Rich Fast Moving Stream.
      J. Tagliabue. Co-EL:39
   Camoëns. H. Melville. Al-VBP:957
   Camoëns in the Hospital (After).
      H. Melville. Al-VBP:958
   A Caution to Poets.
      M. Arnold. Rv-CB:873
   Chaos and Exactitude.
      M. Paraschivescu. Mc-AC:110
   Chaucer. H. Longfellow.
      No-CL:12, Pl-ML:98,
      Rv-CB:780, Sh-AP:39
   A Choice of Weapons. S. Kunitz.
      Wi-LT:749
   Christopher Marlowe. M. Drayton.
      Gr-CT:430
   Cincophrenicpoet. B. Kaufman.
      Hu-PN:411
   The Circuit. D. Wagoner.
      Mo-BG:66
   A Classical Quotation. P. Goodman.
      Ca-VT:333
   A Coat. W. Yeats. Pl-ML:33,
      Wi-LT:69
   Come, Serene Plainness.
      M. Leib. Ho-TY:89
   Commission. E. Pound.
      Br-TC:329
   Compensation. P. Dunbar.
      Bo-AN:5, Hu-PN:290, Ra-BP:56
   Concert. R. Sward. Ca-VT:681
   The Confession. Wen Yi-tuo.
      Gr-CT:463
   Confidential. W. Scott. Co-EL:41
   Contemplation. F. Thompson.
      Ox-BN:920

The Counterpart. E. Jennings.
   Wi-LT:741
The Courts. A. Meynell. Go-BP:167
The Crack. T. McNeill. Sa-B:207
Crepuscular. R. Howard. Br-TC:199
The Crickets Are Saying.
   Kikaku. Be-MC:27
The Critic. J. Farrar. Au-SP:92
The Cure. W. Williams. Pl-ML:28
The Day Is Done. H. Longfellow.
   Ch-B:68, Er-FA:488, Mc-PR:142
The Dead Poet. A. Douglas.
   Al-VBP:1110, No-CL:19
Dedication of the Cook.
   A. Wickham. Un-MB:279
Les Deux Arts. M. Ward.
   Ke-TF:242
Diamond Cut Diamond. E. Milne.
   Ar-TP3:134, Co-BBW:123,
   Gr-EC:77, Sm-LG:76
A Different Speech. L. Nicholl.
   Pl-IO:26
The Distant Drum. C. Hernton.
   Ad-BO:19, Hu-NN:101, Jo-SA:97,
   Lo-TY:250
Dylan Thomas. S. Spender.
   Pl-ML:160
Dylan, Who Is Dead. S. Allen.
   Ad-PB:167
Earth. J. Wheelock.
   Tr-MR:42, Un-MA:343
The Earthly Paradise. W. Morris.
   Al-VBP:1015, Ox-BN:785
Eating Poetry. M. Strand.
   Mo-BG:7
Edgar Allan Poe. C. Lanier.
   Se-PR:311
The Egg Boiler. G. Brooks.
   Ad-PB:154
Elegy. C. Marlowe. No-CL:9
Elegy. A. Pope. Co-EL:141,
   De-CH:254
Elegy for a Nature Poet.
   H. Nemerov. Co-BN:230
Elegy for Minor Poets.
   L. MacNeice. Pl-ML:144
Elegy for the Soviet Yiddish
   Writers. C. Grade. Ho-TY:339
The Enchanted Lyre. G. Darley.
   Ox-BN:383
Enlightenment. Ch'en Yu Yi.
   Rx-LT:99
Envoi. E. Pound. Ca-VT:86,
   No-CL:27, Un-MA:296
The Epistle Dedicatory to the
   Iliads of Homer. G. Chapman.
   No-CL:16
Epistle to Dr. Arbuthnot.
   A. Pope. Al-VBP:539, Gr-CT:435
Epitaph. A. Comfort. Un-MB:520

Epitaph. R. Thomas. Hi-WP II:146
Especially when the October Wind.
   D. Thomas. Go-BP:68, Un-MB:500
Essentials. R. Fulton. Co-PU:42
Extempore Effusion upon the
   Death of James Hogg.
   W. Wordsworth. Rv-CB:648
Fears, Jeers, Tears.
   B. Slutsky. Bo-RU:80
Feather. F. Bianco. No-CL:4
The First Step. C. Cavafy. Pl-ML:34
Fish in Winter. I. Brodsky. Bo-RU:23
The Fishes and the Poet's Hands.
   F. Yerby. Bo-AN:134, Hu-PN:332
The Flowering Past. M. Lowry.
   Ls-NY:180
For a Poet. C. Cullen. Ab-MO:109,
   Hu-PN:229, Lo-TY:234, Th-AS:197
For a Poetry Reading to Which No
   One Came. L. Rubin. De-FS:166
For a Wordfarer. R. Humphries.
   Pl-ML:6
For Black Poets Who Think of
   Suicide. E. Knight. Ad-PB:253,
   Be-MA:112
For John Keats, Apostle of
   Beauty. C. Cullen.
   Ad-PB:91, Bo-AN:88
For My Contemporaries.
   J. Cunningham. Ha-PO:231,
   Mo-BG:58
For Poets. A. Young. Ad-PB:361,
   La-RM:178, Mc-EA:21
For Robert Frost. G. Kinnell.
   Ca-VT:600
For Saundra. N. Giovanni.
   Lo-TY:256, Ra-BP:321
For Some Poets. M. Jackson.
   Ad-BO:16, Ad-PB:497
For There Is an Upstart Crow.
   R. Greene. Pl-ML:57
Forming Child Poems. S. Ortiz.
   Ni-CD:153
A Fountain, a Bottle, a Donkey's
   Ears, and Some Books.
   R. Frost. Ca-VT:12
Four Thousand Days and Nights.
   R. Tamura. Sh-AM:125
XIV. A. Caiero. Mo-TS:92
Fragments. Br-MW:30
The Fresh Start. A. Wickham.
   Al-VBP:1155
From the Shadows. M. Beniuc.
   Mc-AC:99
Further Instructions.
   E. Pound. Br-TC:329
Genesis. E. Sewall. Pl-ML:12
George Crabbe. E. Robinson.
   Pl-ML:113, Un-MA:122, Wi-LT:100
The Gift. J. Ciardi. Wi-LT:670

POETS AND POETRY — cont'd.

Goat Songs, I, III. R. Drew.
Kh-VA:44

Gone Forever. B. Mills.
Du-RG:18

Good-Bye, My Fancy! W. Whitman.
Er-FA:174

Great Elegy for John Donne.
J. Brodsky. Ca-MR:27

Haiku 9. E. Knight. Ra-BP:207

Harder than Granite. R. Jeffers.
Co-PU:80

He Comforts Himself. C. Morley.
Na-EO:54

He Thinks of Those Who Have
Spoken Evil of His Beloved.
W. Yeats. Co-EL:37, Co-PI:206,
No-CL:4

Heard in a Violent Ward.
T. Roethke. Pl-ML:119

The Hebrew of Your Poets, Zion.
C. Reznikoff. Ca-VT:181

Heels Wear Down. R. Roseliep.
St-H:187

A High-Toned Old Christian
Woman. W. Stevens. Pe-OA:71

His Prayer to Ben Jonson.
R. Herrick. Ha-PO:226,
Pl-ML:108

An Historic Moment. W. Harris.
Ad-BO:15, Co-PU:3

Homage to Mistress Bradstreet.
J. Berryman. Sh-AP:225

The Honeybee. H. Bevington.
Ls-NY:174

The Honor Done to Poets of Old
and Modern Poets.
T. Heywood. No-CL:13

House: A Reply. R. Browning.
No-CL:91

The House of Life.
D. Rossetti. Al-VBP:988,
Ma-YA:211

How Many Foolish Things.
M. Drayton. Rv-CB:182

How the Sestina (Yawn) Works.
A. Waldman. Mc-EA:23

How to Eat a Poem. E. Merriam.
Ag-HE:76, Du-RG:15

How You Feel. V. Cruz. Mc-EA:31

Hyperion. J. Keats. Al-VBP:793

I Am. M. Leib. Ho-TY:87

I Am the Mountainy Singer.
J. Campbell. Un-MB:251

I Am Raftery. A. Raftery.
Co-PI:181

I Am the Poet, Davies, William.
W. Davies. Rv-CB:960

I Carried with Me Poems.
G. Dusenbery. Sc-TN:34

I Have Loved Flowers. R. Bridges.
Bo-GJ:83, Un-MB:51

I Hear Some Say. M. Drayton.
Un-MW:202

I Hoed and Trenched and Weeded.
A. Housman. Un-MB:102, Wi-LT:65

I Know that All Beneath the Moon
Decays. W. Drummond. De-CH:624

I Must, Varus, Tell You.
Catullus. Pl-ML:62

I Reckon, when I Count at All.
E. Dickinson. Un-MA:101

"I," Says the Poem. Ar-TP3:222

Ibycus. J. Heath-Stubbs.
En-PC:165

If All the Pens That Ever Poets
Held. C. Marlowe. Gr-CT:431

If I Have Made, My Lady.
E. Cummings. Ga-FB:84

If Music and Sweet Poetry.
R. Barnefield. Al-VBP:266

Iliad. H. Wolfe. Un-MB:305

In a Spring Still Not Written of.
R. Wallace. Co-BN:20

in defense of black poets.
C. Rivers. Ad-BO:20, Ra-BP:200

In Full Voice. V. Mayakovsky.
Ca-MR:121

In Memory of W. B. Yeats.
W. Auden. Al-VBP:1228,
Er-FA:41, Gr-CT:431, Pl-ML:163,
Un-MB:459, Wi-LT:468

In My Craft or Sullen Art.
D. Thomas. Ha-PO:230,
No-CL:21, Pa-GTB:541, Wi-LT:552

In My Desk. J. Brodsky.
Ca-MR:26

In Some Seer's Cloud Car.
C. Middleton. Br-TC:293

In the Time of Revolution.
J. Lester. Ad-PB:354, Lo-IT:75

Inside a Poem. E. Merriam.
Ar-TP3:XVI

Interval. R. Humphries. Pl-ML:43

Intimate Parnassus.
P. Kavanagh. Un-MB:432

Invocation of a Poet Seeking
Inspiration, I, II.
Tr-US II:28

Invocation to the Social Muse.
A. MacLeish. Wi-LT:344

Is Poetry Always Worthy when It's
Old. Kalidasa. Gr-BT:i

It Is Becoming Now to Declare My
Allegiance. C. Day-Lewis.
Wi-LT:425

It Is Difficult to Put Words
Together. Tr-US I:16

It Must Be Abstract.
W. Stevens. Sm-PT:55

Ité. E. Pound. Un-MA:297
Keats. J. Tabb. Sh-AP:135
Keep a Poem in Your Pocket.
  B. de Regniers. Au-SP:97
Kidnap Poem. N. Giovanni.
  Ra-BP:326
Lament for the Makers. W. Dunbar.
  Pl-ML:146
Lately Our Poets Loiter'd in
  Green Lanes. W. Landor.
  Pa-GTB:318
Let the Light Enter. F. Harper.
  Hu-PN:15
Letter to E. Franklin Frazier.
  I. Baraka. Ad-PB:253, Ra-BP:217
A Letter to Robert Frost.
  R. Hillyer. Un-MA:484
A Letter to Yvor Winters.
  K. Rexroth. Pl-ML:53
Life. Lu Li. Hs-TC:422
Light Dying. B. Kennelly.
  Co-PI:84
The Light of Summer's End.
  I. Schwartz. Ho-TY:146
A Little Tune. Tai Wang-shu.
  Hs-TC:183
Limitations. S. Sassoon. Un-MB:316
Lines for a Dead Poet. D. Ferry.
  Pl-ML:166
Lines on the Mermaid Tavern.
  J. Keats. Al-VBP:776,
  Pa-GTB:229, Pl-ML:99
Lines Written in Windsor Forest.
  A. Pope. Gr-SS:100
Listen! Ge-TR:13
Litany of Our Sire, Don Quixote.
  R. Dario. Be-UL:19
Literature: The God, Its Ritual.
  M. Moore. Du-SH:28
A Little More Traveling Music.
  A. Young. Mc-EA:28
Locusts in the Garden. S. Ito.
  Sh-AM:106
Loneliness. A. Young. Ad-PB:368
Look, Hart, That Horse You Ride
  Is Wood. P. Vierick. Pl-ML:156
The Loser. C. Bukowski. Pe-M:64
Lost Joy. A. Onyezhskaya.
  Bo-RU:60
Love. A. Andritoiu. Mc-AC:142
Love Made Me Poet. De-CH:575
Love Poem. A. Kaplan. Mc-EA:86
Lu Yün's Lament. H. Read. Pl-ML:26
Madly Singing in the Mountains.
  Po Chü-i. Rv-CB:987
The Maker. R. Thomas. Co-EL:37
The Makers. R. Kell. Co-PI:82
The Man with the Rake. C. Morley.
  Na-EO:55
Mandela's Sermon. K. Kgositsile.
  Be-MA:146

Manifesto. N. Parra. Mo-TS:93
Many a Night. A. Reisen. Ho-TY:69
Metrical Feet. S. Coleridge.
  Ox-BC:112
Mid-Winter Waking. R. Graves.
  Go-BP:136
Minor Game. I. Barbu. Mc-AC:64
The Minstrel Responds to Flattery.
  W. Scott. Ox-BN:126
A Mirror for Poets. T. Gunn.
  Pl-ML:100, Wi-LT:722
Misapprehension. P. Dunbar.
  Ra-BP:46
Mr. Whittier. W. Scott. Ca-VT:315
Mrs. Arbuthnot. S. Smith.
  Ls-NY:127
Momus. E. Robinson. Al-VBP:1106
Le Monocle de Mon Oncle.
  W. Stevens. Wi-LT:135
Mugala's Song. Tr-CB:14,
  Tr-US I:92
The Muse. A. Akhmatova.
  Pl-ML:32
The Music Makers.
  A. O'Shaughnessy. Al-VBP:1063,
  Co-PI:163, Ga-FB:133, Mc-PR:72,
  Se-PR:324
My Last Poem. M. Bandeira.
  An-TC:3
My Life Has Been the Poem.
  H. Thoreau. Pl-ML:35
My Poem. N. Giovanni. Ad-BO:22,
  Ad-PB:453, Ra-BP:319
My Poem. E. Hewell. Le-M:16
Myself when I Am Real. A. Young.
  Ad-PB:365
The Night Frieda Took My Spirit
  by Surprise. P. Mayer.
  St-H:129
Night in the House by the River.
  Tu Fu. Rx-OH:29
Night Thoughts while Traveling.
  Tu Fu. Rx-OH:33
No Time for Poetry. J. Fields.
  Be-MA:149, Bo-AN:183
"Not Marble nor the Gilded
  Monuments." A. MacLeish.
  Al-VBP:1194, Br-TC:277,
  Un-MW:143
Not Marble, nor the Gilded
  Monuments. W. Shakespeare.
  Al-VBP:202, Er-FA:119, Ha-PO:255,
  No-CL:8, Rv-CB:224
Note to Wang Wei. J. Berryman.
  Pl-ML:96
Notes Found near a Suicide: To
  the Poets. F. Horne.
  Bo-AN:46
O, Lift One Thought.
  S. Coleridge. De-CH:254

POETS AND POETRY — cont'd.
  O the Beatniks Never Win.
    C. Larsen.   Lo-IT:71
  Ode of the Angels of Chicago
    Who Move Perpetually.
    P. Carroll.   St-H:20
  Ode on Indolence. J. Keats.
    Ox-BN:374
  Ode on the Death of Thomson.
    W. Collins. Rv-CB:538
  Ode on the Poets. J. Keats.
    Al-VBP:775, Pa-GTB:169
  Ode: Salute to the French
    Negro Poets. F. O'Hara.
    Hu-PN:581
  Ode to the West Wind. P. Shelley.
    Al-VBP:748, Co-BN:127, De-CH:212,
    Er-FA:244, Fe-PL:390, Ga-FB:15,
    Ha-PO:96, Ma-YA:177, Ox-BN:280,
    Pa-GTB:295, Rv-CB:696
  The Odyssey. A. Lang.
    Al-VBP:1062, Fe-PL:433,
    Ox-BN:871
  Of Modern Poetry. W. Stevens.
    Sh-AP:161
  On a Poet's Lips I Slept.
    P. Shelley. Al-VBP:740,
    De-CH:681, Pa-GTB:299
  On a Prohibitionist Poem.
    G. Chesterton. Al-VBP:1122
  On Being Asked for a War Poem.
    W. Yeats. Co-PI:201
  On Being Chosen Poet of Vermont.
    R. Frost. Pl-ML:25
  On Donne's Poetry.
    S. Coleridge. Rv-CB:663
  On First Looking into Chapman's
    Homer. J. Keats. Al-VBP:769,
    Co-RG:17, De-CH:361, Er-FA:75,
    Ga-FB:14, Gr-CT:442, Ke-TF:61,
    Ma-YA:182, Mc-PR:78, Ni-JP:19,
    No-CL:18, Ox-BN:334, Pa-GTB:169,
    Pl-ML:91, Rv-CB:739, Sm-LG:36
  On Hearing Someone Sing a Poem
    by Yüan Chen. Po Chü-i.
    Pl-ML:150
  On John Donne's Book of Poems.
    J. Marriot. De-CH:254
  On Looking into E. V. Rieu's
    Homer. P. Kavanagh. Pl-ML:46
  On Re-Reading the Complete Works
    of an Elder Poet. W. Scott.
    Pl-ML:45
  On Seeing a Poet of the First
    World War on the Station at
    Abbeville. C. Causley. Wi-LT:667
  On the Death of Mr. Crashaw.
    A. Cowley. Al-VBP:448
  On the Oxford Book of Victorian
    Verse. H. MacDiarmid. Un-MB:360

  On the Praise of Poetry and
    Music. A. Cowley. No-CL:30
  One Day I Wrote Her Name.
    E. Spenser. Al-VBP:99,
    No-CL:22, Rv-CB:161
  One Poet Praises Another.
    Tr-US II:284
  One Sort of Poet. A. Smith.
    Ls-NY:136
  One Word More. R. Browning.
    Al-VBP:911
  Only Be Willing to Search for
    Poetry. Yuan Mei. La-PV:224
  The Origin of Songs.
    Tr-US II:282
  An Otomí Song of the Mexicans.
    Da-SC:176
  Paddler's Song on Bad Hunting
    Weather. Da-SC:41, Le-IB:72,
    Tr-US I:7
  Paschal Poem, III. L. Strongin.
    Sc-TN:205
  Past Ruined Ilion. W. Landor.
    Al-VBP:706, Ha-PO:178,
    No-CL:5, Ox-BN:187, Rv-CB:670
  Paul Laurence Dunbar.
    J. Corrothers. Hu-PN:25
  The Peasant Poet. J. Clare.
    Ox-BN:332
  pete the parrot and shakespeare.
    D. Marquis. Pl-ML:102
  Petit, the Poet. E. Masters.
    Ha-PO:67, Ke-PP:106, Sm-LG:38,
    Un-MA:143
  The Philosopher and the Lover.
    W. Davenant. Ho-P:315
  A Pinch of Salt. R. Graves.
    Go-BP:166, Un-MB:385
  The Planet on the Table.
    W. Stevens. Pl-ML:3
  Please. R. Creeley. Kh-VA:47,
    Pl-ML:54
  Poem. I. Charik. Ho-TY:191
  Poem. J. Fields. Be-MA:151
  Poem. W. Williams. Ca-VT:67
  The Poem on the Wall.
    Po Chü-i. Pl-ML:85
  The Poem That Took the Place of a
    Mountain. W. Stevens. Pl-ML:13
  Poem to Be Cast into the Sea in
    a Bottle. J. Kirkup. Go-BP:217
  Poem to Be Read at 3 A.M.
    D. Justice. Du-SH:29, Pe-M:130
  Poems. P. Kelso. Le-M:15
  The Poet. P. Dunbar. Ra-BP:52
  Poet. D. Hayes. Bo-AN:92,
    Hu-PN:242
  The Poet. R. Holden. Sm-PT:56
  Poet. K. Shapiro. Un-MA:638,
    Wi-LT:539

Poet. P. Viereck. Un-MA:660
The Poet. W. Whitman. Un-MA:79
Poet and Goldsmith. V. Watkins.
 En-PC:89
The Poet and His Book.
 E. Millay. Un-MA:443
The Poet and His Song. P. Dunbar.
 Bo-HF:154, Se-PR:329
Poet in Winter. E. Lucie-Smith.
 Br-TC:273
Poet to Dancer. B. Kavinsky.
 Pl-US:122
Poetic Art. I. Pillat. Mc-AC:58
Poetry. M. Moore. Al-VBP:1175,
 Ha-PO:232, Mc-EA:21, Mo-TS:90,
 Pl-ML:4, Sh-AP:178, Un-MA:351,
 Wi-LT:267
Poetry. Yang Huan. Pa-MV:159
The Poets. M. Morris. Sa-B:10
Poets and Physicists. B. Slutzky.
 Ca-MR:93
Poets Hitchhiking on the Highway.
 G. Corso. Du-RG:19
The Poets Light But Lamps.
 E. Dickinson. Pl-ML:89
Poets Love Nature. J. Clare.
 Rv-CB:727
The Poet's Mission. Tr-US II:281
The Poets of Peace and Gladness.
 M. Korte. Sc-TN:120
The Poet's Paradise.
 M. Drayton. Ho-WR:252
Poets to Come. W. Whitman. Mc-EA:25
The Poet's Voice. W. Blake.
 Gr-CT:429, Rv-CB:567
Poietes Apoietes. H. Coleridge.
 Ox-BN:399
Portrait of the Boy as an Artist.
 B. Howes. Un-MA:653
Praise. R. Rilke. Gr-CT:446
Preface. T. Weiss. Ca-VT:433
Prelude LVI. C. Aiken. Br-TC:7
Procedure Is Habit. I Affirm It.
 D. Meltzer. Kh-VA:46
Proem. M. Cawein. Co-BN:213
The Progress of Poesy. T. Gray.
 Al-VBP:566, Pa-GTB:132,
 Rv-CB:532
Prologue to Aureng-zebe.
 J. Dryden. Rv-CB:464
Reading the Poems of an Absent
 Friend. Ou Yang Hsiu. Rx-OH:57
Reading Walt Whitman. C. Forbes.
 Ad-PB:490
Resolution and Independence.
 W. Wordsworth. Pl-ML:114
Rhymes. Y. Segal. Do-WH:6,
 Ho-TY:153
Roethke. H. Healy. Ls-NY:134
Saadi. R. Emerson. Sh-AP:28

san francisco county jail cell b-6.
 Conyus. Ad-PB:400
A Satire. J. Oldham. Al-VBP:507
Scorn Not the Sonnet.
 W. Wordsworth. No-CL:90
Silet. E. Pound. Un-MA:295
The Singer. A. Wickham.
 Un-MB:283
Six Lines Unheard.
 D. Hovanessian. Ls-NY:173
Soldier, There Is a War Between
 the Mind. W. Stevens.
 Wi-LT:163
A Song of the Huezotzincos.
 Da-SC:177
The Song of the Three Songs.
 I. Minulescu. Mc-AC:43
Song of Tukulua. Tr-US II:48
Song to David. C. Smart.
 Al-VBP:575, Gr-CT:447, Pl-US:72
Sonnet 3. S. Daniel. Al-VBP:157
Sonnets. M. Drayton. Al-VBP:166
Sonnet 32. W. Shakespeare.
 Pa-GTB:29, Pl-ML:21, Rv-CB:214
Sonnets LIV. W. Shakespeare.
 Al-VBP:202
Sonnet 107. W. Shakespeare.
 Rv-CB:239
The Sonnets (Alack!).
 W. Shakespeare. No-CL:89
The Sonnets (Why).
 W. Shakespeare. No-CL:86
Sonnets. W. Wordsworth.
 Al-VBP:658
Spark of Laurel. S. Kunitz.
 Pl-ML:36
Spring Morning. Ch'en Yu Yi.
 Rx-LT:98
Spring Poem: Brown's Town.
 T. McNeill. Sa-B:209
Standing on Earth. J. Milton.
 Gr-CT:464
Starting from Paumanok.
 W. Whitman. Al-VBP:927
The Steel Pen. Chung Ting-wen.
 Pa-MV:76
Summer Storm. R. Cuscaden.
 St-H:32
Supper with Lindsay. T. Roethke.
 Pl-ML:47
T. S. Eliot. T. Whitbread.
 Ls-NY:143
Ten Definitions of Poetry.
 C. Sandburg. Un-MA:199
Terence, This Is Stupid Stuff.
 A. Housman. Ma-YA:224,
 Un-MB:100, Wi-LT:63
Testament. T. Arghezi. Mc-AC:25
That Bright Chimeric Beast.
 C. Cullen. Bo-AN:86

POETS AND POETRY — cont'd.
There's a Little Ambiguity over
There among the Bluebells.
R. Krauss.   Mc-EA:75
These Poems.   D. Palmer. Sc-TN:180
They Say My Verse Is Sad.
A. Housman. Hi-WP I:23
This Room Is Full of Clocks.
I. Gardner. St-H:74
This Was a Poet. E. Dickinson.
Pl-ML:5
Thomas Heywood. A. Swinburne.
No-CL:15
Time and the Garden. Y. Winters.
Ca-VT:230, Un-MA:550
To a Child. C. Morley. Br-BC:148
To a Dead Poet, His Book.
D. Berrigan. Pl-ML:147
To a Gentile Poet. M. Leib.
Ho-TY:93
To a Lady Friend. W. Davies.
Un-MB:179
To a Poet a Thousand Years Hence.
J. Flecker. Gr-CT:433, Un-MB:274
to a poet i knew. J. Amini.
Ad-PB:291
To a Poet Who Has Had a Heart
Attack. R. Eberhart. Pl-ML:55
To a Poet, Who Would Have Me
Praise Certain Bad Poets.
W. Yeats. Co-PI:203, Pl-ML:60
To a Saxon Poet. J. Borges.
Pl-ML:92
To a War Poet, on Teaching Him a
New Country. D. Enright.
Pl-ML:138
To an American Poet Just Dead.
R. Wilbur. Pl-ML:153
To an Old Lady Asleep at a
Poetry Reading. J. Kirkup.
Go-BP:53
To Ben Jonson. T. Randolph.
No-CL:94
To Calliope. R. Graves. Ls-NY:165
To E. T. R. Frost. Pl-ML:162
To Ethelinda. C. Smart. No-CL:190
To Everlasting Oblivion.
J. Marston. Rv-CB:311
To Homer. J. Keats. Rv-CB:748
To Mr. Henry Lawes. E. Waller.
No-CL:28
To My Friends. N. Nor. Bo-RU:54
To Pi Ssu Yao. Tu Fu. Pl-ML:79,
Rx-OH:15
To Poets. W. Landor.
Al-VBP:710
To R. B. G. Hopkins. Pa-GTB:398,
Pl-ML:50, Rv-CB:943
To Robert Browning. W. Landor.
Al-VBP:702, Se-PR:307

To Science. E. Poe.   Ke-PP:81,
Rv-CB:805, Sh-AP:46
To Sherwood Anderson in Heaven.
F. Eckman. St-H:46
To Swinburne. Shao Hsün-mei.
Hs-TC:128
To the Author of Hesperides and
Noble Numbers. M. Van Doren.
Pl-ML:109
To the Memory of My Beloved, the
Author Mr. William Shakespeare.
B. Jonson. Gr-CT:432, Pl-ML:148
To the Poets of India. F. Scott.
Ls-NY:168
To the Stone-Cutters. R. Jeffers.
En-PC:10, Ni-JP:127,
Sh-AP:175, Un-MA:362
To Verse Let Kings Give Place.
Ovid. Gr-CT:429
To Virgil. A. Tennyson.
Gr-CT:442, Pa-GTB:340
To W. H. Auden on His Fiftieth
Birthday. B. Howes. Pl-ML:76
To Wordsworth. P. Shelley.
No-CL:264, Se-PR:312
To Yesenin. J. Rubinstein.
Ho-TY:239
To Yvor Winters, 1955. T. Gunn.
Pa-GTB:562
today is a day of great joy.
V. Cruz. Lo-TY:260, Mc-EA:22
Tonight the Pacifist Moon.
S. Alexander. Ls-NY:181
The Truth. T. Joans. Ad-BO:14,
Be-MA:100, Bo-AN:172, Lo-TY:247
Tyrannic Love. J. Dryden.
Al-VBP:492
Under Ben Bulben. W. Yeats.
Pl-ML:30, Wi-LT:96
Unfolding Bud. N. Koriyama.
Du-RG:17
Urceus Exit. A. Dobson. Go-BP:126
The Vase. Kuo Mo-jo. Hs-TC:38
Verse. O. Gogarty. Sm-LG:31
The Victory. J. Gelman. Be-UL:123
Villanelle. W. Skeat. Co-FB:441
Voronezh. A. Akhmatova. Ca-MR:185
Was It the Proud Full Sail of His
Great Verse. W. Shakespeare.
Pl-ML:56, Rv-CB:233
Washiri. K. Cumbo.
Ad-BO:12
We Poets Speak. F. Thompson.
Ga-FB:7
What Curious Dresses All Men
Wear. D. Schwartz. Co-EL:38
What Is Poetry? E. Farjeon.
Ha-YA:(5)
What the Chimney Sang. B. Harte.
Sp-OG:307

When I Die. F. Johnson. Hu-PN:90
When I Read My Poems. H. Takai.
  Le-TA:36
When the Light of Day Fades.
  N. Zabolotzky. Ca-MR:100
Where Didst Thou Find, Young
  Bard. J. Keats. Rv-CB:753
Who Translates a Poet Badly.
  G. Prado. Co-EL:39
William Blake. J. Thomson.
  Rv-CB:931
A Word. K. Ozaki. Sh-AM:57
Words. E. Thomas. Hi-WP II:4
The Words. D. Wagoner.
  Du-SH:30, Mo-TS:52
Words in Time. A. MacLeish.
  En-PC:20
The Words Will Resurrect.
  J. de Lima. Lo-TY:83
Wordsworth's Grave. W. Watson.
  Ox-BN:910
Yes, the Secret Mind Whispers.
  A. Young. Ad-PB:367
Yes, You Are Old. M. Breslasu.
  Mc-AC:90
Yet Do I Marvel. C. Cullen.
  Ad-PB:87, Be-MA:50, Bo-AN:88,
  Hu-PN:233, Jo-SA:128, Lo-TY:235,
  Pe-SS:48, Ra-BP:100
Yiddish Poets in New York.
  M. Stiker. Ho-TY:281
Young Poet. M. O'Higgins.
  Ad-PB:170, Hu-PN:351
POINSETTIAS
  Flame-Heart. C. McKay.
  Bo-AN:30, Hu-PN:104
POISON GASES
  Christmas: 1924. T. Hardy.
  Ba-PO:170, Cr-WS:2, Gr-BT:114
  James Honeyman. W. Auden.
  Ca-MB:100, Sm-MK:117
POISON IVY
  Poison Ivy! K. Gallagher. Br-SS:172
  Poison Ivy. Mo-TB:132
POISONS: see also HUMOR - POISONS
  Herbs and Simples. M. Keller.
  De-FS:123
  The Laboratory. R. Browning.
  Ni-JP:38
  Lord Randal. Cl-FC:85, Fo-OG:7,
  Ox-BB:243, Rv-CB:37, Un-MW:108
  Missing Dates. W. Empson.
  Al-VBP:1225, Wi-LT:445
  A Poison Tree. W. Blake.
  Co-PM:29, Er-FA:64, Ga-S:133,
  Gr-SS:77, Rv-CB:607
POKER (GAME): see CARD GAMES
POLAND: see also POLISH VERSE
  An Airstrip in Essex. D. Hall.
  Cr-WS:168, En-PC:268, Wi-LT:727

Children's Crusade, 1939.
  B. Brecht. Ca-MB:106
Poland/1931. J. Rothenberg.
  Ho-P:217
POLAR BEARS: see BEARS
POLAR REGIONS: see ARCTIC REGIONS
POLAR STAR: see NORTH STAR
POLICE: see also HUMOR - POLICE;
    SATIRE - POLICE
  Arrest. Tsang K'o-chia.
  Hs-TC:287
  Bobby Blue. J. Drinkwater.
  Au-SP:135, Fe-FP:247
  Corner. R. Pomeroy. Ad-CI:64,
  Du-SH:39
  The Death of the Sheriff.
  R. Lowell. Un-MA:664
  High Tide. D. Palmer. Sc-TN:179
  I'm the Police Cop Man, I Am.
  M. Morrison. Au-SP:204
  knock on wood. H. Dumas.
  Ad-PB:268
  Like Me. D. Aldis. Mc-AW:21
  The London Bobby. A. Guiterman.
  Pa-HT:125
  My Policeman. R. Fyleman.
  Au-SP:136
  Newsletter from My Mother.
  M. Harper. Ad-PB:315
  Night Constable. J. Woods.
  St-H:247
  Panther. S. Cornish. Ad-PB:297
  People Who Must. C. Sandburg.
  La-OC:48, La-PV:190
  Police Station. D. Dzwonkoski.
  Ad-II:86
  The Policeman. M. Watts.
  Ar-TP3:12, Bo-FP:119
  P's the Proud Policeman.
  P. McGinley. Ar-TP3:11,
  Au-SP:135
POLISH VERSE
  The Bicycle. J. Harasymowicz.
  Du-SH:22
  The Funeral. M. J. Ba-PO:180
  I Would Like to Describe.
  Z. Herbert. Gr-BT:28
  Our Fear. Z. Herbert.
  Gr-BT:120
  To Sleep. J. Kochanowski.
  Pa-SG:178
POLITENESS: see COURTESY
POLITICS: see also
    ELECTIONS;
    HUMOR - POLITICS;
    SATIRE - POLITICS
  Free Silver. Em-AF:768
  Politics. A. Tennyson. Se-PR:203
  Politics. W. Yeats. Co-PI:202,
  No-CL:161

POLLUTION: see also HUMOR -
POLLUTION; LITTER AND
LITTERING; SATIRE -
POLLUTION
Above the Moving River.
D. Kherdian. Kh-VA:72
America the Beautiful.
J. Streich. Ad-II:80
Beleaguered Cities. F. Lucas.
Cl-FC:31
The Bourgeois Poet. K. Shapiro.
St-H:204
City. J. Bruchac. Ni-CD:39
Get the Gasworks. D. Ignatow.
Kh-VA:57, Mo-BG:181
God's Grandeur. G. Hopkins.
Er-FA:467, Ox-BN:867, Tr-MR:22,
Un-MB:42, Wi-LT:40
The Great Lakes Suite, IV.
J. Reaney. Do-WH:51
Habitat. J. Anderson. Sc-TN:1
The Hermit. R. Silcock.
Ls-NY:321
How Come? D. Ignatow.
Ad-CI:110, Bl-FP:24
In the Cities. D. Lawrence.
Hi-WP II:161
The Land. V. Cruz. Lo-TY:26
London. J. Davidson. Ox-BN:900
Mystic River. J. Ciardi.
Sh-AP:228
Nature Poem. G. Mende. La-IH:121
New York Skyscrapers. J. Mbiti.
Ab-MO:49
On the Beach. Ch'in Tzu-hao.
Pa-MV:57
The Orange Bears. K. Patchen.
Kh-VA:7
The Peaceable Kingdom.
M. Piercy. Br-TC:317
Poem from the Empire State.
J. Jordan. Ra-BP:247
Revolutionary Letter #16.
D. di Prima. Kh-VA:69
Rural Dumpheap. M. Cane.
Br-AF:216
Sarah Cynthia Sylvia Stout.
S. Silverstein. Co-BB:73
The Stinky City. R. Isaac.
La-GI:49
A Street Is a River. C. Mcgee.
La-IH:44
The Streetcleaner's Lament.
P. Hubbell. La-OC:27
Sunrise. F. Garcia Lorca. Bl-FP:84
The Tide River. C. Kingsley.
Co-BN:74, Ox-BC:227
Window, 3rd Story, 5th to the
Right, Morning. R. Drapeau.
La-IH:56

Wooden Ships. D. Crosby.
Mo-GR:108
POLO (GAME)
Polo Player. D. Hicky. Th-AS:192
POLYHYMNIA (MUSE)
Rebirth of the Muse.
Hu P'in-ch'ing. Pa-MV:105
POLYNESIAN VERSE
Aromaiterai's Lament.
Tr-US II:68
Birth. Tr-US II:36
"Blackened-Face" Dirge - Proper
for Atiroa. Koroneu.
Tr-US II:64
Chant of Kororupo.
Tr-US II:86
Creation Chant. Tr-US II:79
Day-Song for Tenio's Fête.
Koroa. Tr-US II:59
Dirges, I, II. Tr-US II:41, 42
Dream Song of a Canoe-Builder.
Tr-US II:72
East Wind. Tr-US II:38
The Ghosts Led by Vera Preparing
for Their Final Departure.
Uanuku. Tr-US II:60
Greeting of Tane. Tr-US II:71
I Would I Were. Le-OE:43
Incantation Used by Rangitokona
to Create Man. Tr-US II:120
Ironical Song of the Intoler-
ance of Missionaries and
Converts. Tr-US II:42
Lament. Tr-US II:78, 89
Lament for Old Age.
Tr-US II:91
Lament of a Deserted Husband.
Moanarai. Tr-US II:69
Lament of Hapai for Tahiki.
Tr-US II:84
Lament of Huauri. Tr-US II:80
Lament of Taura Atua.
Tr-US II:68
Lament: Sea-Burial of Toga's
Daughter. Tr-US II:88
Lullaby. Tr-US II:35
Lullaby for a Child Whose Mother
Has Gone to Gather Food.
Tr-US I:218
Marriage. Tr-US II:36
The Message of the Frigate Birds.
Tr-US II:89
Mu. Ma'u. Tr-US II:95
North Wind. Tr-US II:38
The Overthrow of Ruanae.
Potiki. Tr-US II:56
Plaint of a Woman Who Has No
Lover. Tr-US II:72
Prayer for Peace.
Tr-US II:54

Prayer over a Human Sacrifice to
Rongo.   Tr-US II:53
Priests' Chant to Usher in the
Dawn.   Tr-US II:66
Rari about the Faufe's Bird.
Puko'i.   Tr-US II:93
Rari for O'otua.   Mahana.
Tr-US II:93
Rari for the Americans.   Eina'a.
Tr-US II:94
The Return of the Marama from
Hiti.   Tr-US II:72
The Rich and the Poor.
Tr-US II:92
Sea Chant.   Tr-US II:35
Song at a Funeral.   Tr-US II:90
Song for a Seated Dance:
Victory of the Mea.
Tr-US I:219
Song of a Girl Cast Off by Her
Lover.   Tr-US II:42
Song of a Returning Voyager.
Tr-US II:41
South Wind.   Tr-US II:39
Tumea's Lament for Her Father
Ngakauvarea.   Tr-US II:54
West Wind.   Tr-US II:40
POLYNESIAN VERSE - HAWAIIAN
At the Time when the Earth.
Le-OE:2
The Beautiful.   Le-OE:138
Chant of Welcome to a Kinsman
or Friend.   Tr-US II:103
Dirge.   Tr-US II:103
The Fall of Kumuhonua and His
Wife.   Tr-US II:96
House Dedication Prayer.
Tr-US II:98
Love Song from a Legend.
Tr-US II:104
Phases of the Sea. Tr-US II:102
Song for the Hula Ala'a-Papa.
Tr-US II:101
The Song of Kuali.   Tr-US II:98
Storm Scene.   Tr-US II:102
Tahitian Chant of Creation.
Tr-US II:67
Taunt Song.   Tr-US II:105, 112
The Water of Kane.
Tr-US II:96
POLYNESIAN VERSE - MAORI
At the Time That Turned the
Beat.   Le-OE:97
Charm.   Tr-US II:108
Cosmogony.   Tr-US II:106
Ihunui's Lament for Her Daughter
Rangi.   Tr-US II:115
A Joyous Reveling Song Sung
by the Wood Rats.
Su-FVI:59

The Mating of Hine and Tane-Matua.
Tr-US II:107
Old Dance Song.   Tr-US II:110
The Song of the Aotea Canoe.
Tr-US II:108
Vaunt of the Hero Whakatau on
Going into Battle.
Tr-US II:110
See also Tr-US II:112-119
POLYNESIAN VERSE - MARQUESAN
When a Man's Body Is Young.
Le-OE:109
POLYNESIAN VERSE - SAMOAN
See Tr-US II:51-52
POLYNESIAN VERSE - TONGAN
Farewell of Warriors of Vavau
Going to Fight at Sea.
Tr-US II:50
Mother and Slave Raiders.
Tr-US I:90
Praise of Beaches. Tr-US II:47
Recitative.   Tr-US II:45
Song in Recitative Style.
Tr-US II:45
Song of Tukulua. Tr-US II:48
POMEGRANATE TREES
The Deserted Village.
Feng Hsüeh-feng.   Hs-TC:371
Men's Song at a Wedding.
Tr-US I:127
POMONA (GODDESS)
Pomona.   W. Morris.   Ho-LP:37,
Ho-WR:160
POMPADOUR, MARQUISE DE
On a Fan That Belonged to the
Marquise de Pompadour.
A. Dobson.   Al-VBP:1050
POMPEII, IT.
New Excavations.   L. Speyer.
Ho-TH:27
A Poem on the Nuclear War,
from Pompeii.   R. Tillinghast.
Ba-PO:55
PONDS AND POOLS
After the Anonymous Swedish.
J. Harrison.   Ca-VT:711
Atavism.   E. Wylie.   De-FS:225
Dipping My Feet in Water.
Cheng Min.   Hs-TC:240
Edge of the Lotus Pond.
Yü Kuang-chung.   Pa-MV:181
Forest Pools.   L. Clark.
Cl-DT:67
Here where the Wild Ducks.
Taniha Omé.   Ba-ST:35
The Mirror Perilous.   A. Dugan.
Br-TC:97, Wi-LT:691
Nocturne in a Deserted Brickyard.
C. Sandburg.
Un-MA:201

PONDS AND POOLS — cont'd.
  Old Pond, Blackly Still. Bashô.
    Au-SP:79, Ca-BF:21
  The Pond. A. von Droste-Hülshoff.
    Pa-SG:188
  The Pond. M. Morris. Sa-B:63
  The Pool. L. Drake. De-FS:77
  The Pool in the Rock.
    W. de la Mare. Cl-FC:55
  Remembering Shi Ch'a Hai.
    Chang Hsiu-ya. Pa-MV:29
  The Rock Pool. P. Hobsbaum.
    Ls-NY:215
  Small Fountain. L. Abercrombie.
    De-CH:146
  The Spring Waters. Ping Hsin.
    Hs-TC:22
  Suicide Pond. K. McLaughlin.
    Du-SH:137
  Thoughts while Reading.
    Chu Hsi. Rx-OH:120
  Three Riddles: Whose. Mo-TS:77
  Thunder Pools. R. Coffin.
    Ha-LO:70
  Under the Full Moon.
    Yu Kuang-chung. Pa-MV:182
  Water Picture. M. Swenson.
    Co-BN:85, La-OC:121
  Wind and Silver. A. Lowell.
    Co-PU:140, Mo-BG:152, Un-MA:159
  Wrinkles Run down the Pool.
    R. Cowie. Le-WR:12
PONIES: see HORSES
PONTEFRACT, ENG.
  The Licorice Fields of Pontefract.
    J. Betjeman. To-MP:66
PONY EXPRESS
  The Pony Express. D. Thompson.
    Br-AF:227
  Young Jack Snyder. J. Adams.
    Fi-BG:223
POOL (GAME): see also BILLIARDS
  Rotation. J. Bond. Hu-NN:67
  We Real Cool. G. Brooks.
    Ab-MO:96, Ad-PB:157, Be-MA:81,
    Bo-HF:106, Gr-BT:22, Ha-TP:21,
    La-OC:59, Lo-TY:245
POOLS: see PONDS AND POOLS
THE POOR: see POVERTY
POORHOUSES: see POVERTY
POPCORN
  A Pop Corn Song. N. Turner.
    Fe-FP:45, Hu-MP:21
POPE, ALEXANDER: see also
    HUMOR - POPE, ALEXANDER
  Mr. Pope. A. Tate. Br-TC:429,
    Ca-VT:223, Pl-ML:112
  When None Shall Rail.
    D. Lewis. Rv-CB:502
POPES: see SATIRE - POPES

POPLAR TREES
  The Interrupted Concert.
    F. García Lorca. Le-SW:79
  New Leaves. J. Jiménez. Le-SW:17
  The Poplar. R. Aldington.
    Bo-HF:60
  The Poplar Field. W. Cowper.
    Co-RG:117, De-CH:46, De-TT:161,
    Gr-CT:239, Ha-PO:151, Ho-WR:159,
    Ma-FW:105, Pa-GTB:140, Rv-CB:548
  The Poplars. T. Garrison.
    Se-PR:97
  To a Late Poplar. P. Kavanagh.
    Co-PI:75
POPPIES: see also HUMOR - POPPIES
  Baby Seed Song. E. Nesbit.
    Fe-FP:215, Hu-MP:246, Th-AS:73
  In Flanders Fields. J. McCrae.
    Al-VBP:1115, Br-SS:76, Er-FA:189,
    Ga-FB:217, Hu-MP:342, Se-PR:207,
    Sp-OG:212, Th-AS:196, Vi-PP:211
  In Poppy Fields. E. Markham.
    Mc-PR:160
  Just Simply Alive. Issa. Le-IS:21
  Poppies. Hu-MP:247
  The Poppy. F. Thompson. Un-MB:80
  The Rock-a-By Lady. E. Field.
    Bo-FP:43, Hu-MP:116
  The Valley of White Poppies.
    F. Macleod. Th-AS:141
POPULATION: see PEOPLE
PORCELAIN: see POTTERY
PORCUPINES: see also HEDGEHOGS;
    HUMOR - PORCUPINES
  The Fox and the Hedgehog.
    Archilochus. Bo-FP:81
  The Happy Hedgehog. E. Rieu.
    Co-BBW:29, Gr-EC:276
  The Last Flower. J. Moore.
    Co-PS:126
  Little Billy Breek. Ir-BB:51,
    Mo-MGT:156
  Meeting. C. Dyment. Co-BBW:46
  Mister Rusticap. Mo-MGT:188
  Porcupine. B. Meyers. Co-BBW:57
  The Porcupine Asked the Rabbit.
    Gr-BB:18
  porky & porkie. e. cummings.
    Li-TU:215
  What Did the Near-Sighted
    Porcupine Say. Re-RR:24
PORPOISES: see also DOLPHINS
  I Did Not See a Mermaid.
    S. Johnson. Li-LC:61
PORT ANGELES, WASH.
  On Visiting My Son, Port
    Angeles, Washington.
    D. Niatum. Ni-CD:130
PORT BOU, SP.
  Port Bou. S. Spender. Br-TC:404

PORTAPOVITCH, STANISLAW
  To Potapovitch. H. Crane.
    Pl-US:117
PORTINARI, BEATRICE:
    see BEATRICE
PORTLAND, ME.
  My Lost Youth. H. Longfellow.
    Al-VBP:825, Bo-GJ:178, Co-RG:114,
    Er-FA:163, Fe-FP:547, Fe-PL:253,
    Ga-FB:160, Hu-MP:73, No-CL:257,
    Pa-HT:9
PORTRAITS - MEN: see also
    HUMOR - PORTRAITS-MEN
  Aaron Stark. E. Robinson.
    Un-MA:137
  Absalom and Achitophel.
    J. Dryden. Al-VBP:489
  Academic. J. Reeves. To-MP:72
  After the Death of an Elder
    Klallum. D. Niatum. Ni-CD:136
  All the Little Hoofprints.
    R. Jeffers. Ni-JP:109
  Alphabet Spring. L. Nagan.
    Ad-II:72
  American Primitive. W. Smith.
    Br-TC:393, Ke-PP:46, Un-MA:670
  And Mr. Ferritt. J. Wright.
    Un-MB:516
  Angry Old Men. B. Payne.
    Co-PI:167
  Appraisal. S. Teasdale. Un-MA:267
  Archibald's Example. E. Robinson.
    Gr-CC:183
  The Beekeeper. J. Matthews.
    Ls-NY:138
  Bewick Finzer. E. Robinson.
    Gr-CC:130, Un-MA:118
  Black Bourgeoisie. I. Baraka.
    Ra-BP:223
  Black Lover Lead Man.
    L. Curry. Jo-VC:65
  Blue Blood. J. Stephens.
    Un-MB:266
  Bottled: New York. H. Johnson.
    Ad-PB:104
  The Bourgeois Poet. K. Shapiro.
    St-H:205
  Bran. G. Moore. Ls-NY:162
  Brevities. S. Sassoon. Fe-PL:296
  Brown's Descent. R. Frost.
    Ar-TP3:145, Ha-PO:287, Na-EO:89,
    Sp-OG:234, Un-MA:178
  Brutus. W. Shakespeare.
    Er-FA:63, Un-GT:85
  Canterbury Tales. G. Chaucer.
    Al-VBP:8, Go-BP:42, Gr-CT:281,
    Ha-PO:51, 54, Hi-WP I:105,
    Ma-FW:17, Ma-YA:28, Un-GT:87
  The Captive. R. Kipling. Go-BP:53
  The Circuit. D. Wagoner. Mo-BG:66

  The Clean Gentleman. G. Abbe.
    De-FS:4
  Cliff Klingenhagen. E. Robinson.
    Mo-BG:49, Sh-AP:140, Un-MA:117
  Colonel Fantock. E. Sitwell.
    Un-MB:334
  A Commemoration for the
    Physicist X. P. Oppenheimer.
    Ls-NY:130
  Danny Murphy. J. Stephens.
    Co-RG:165
  Death. W. Williams. Ca-VT:51
  The Death of the Hired Man.
    R. Frost. Pe-OA:25, Un-MA:171
  Diary of a Nondescript.
    G. Oppenheim. Ls-NY:148
  Dinky. T. Roethke. Co-OW:27,
    Li-TU:72
  The Disagreeable Man. W. Gilbert.
    Co-FB:66, Hu-MP:140
  A Disappearance in West Cedar
    Street. L. Sissman. Br-TC:383
  Dreaming in the Shanghai
    Restaurant. D. Enright.
    To-MP:123
  The Drum Maker. J. Bruchac.
    Mo-TS:28
  An Elegy. D. Gascoyne. Br-TC:145
  Elegy for Mr. Goodbeare.
    O. Sitwell. Un-MB:357
  Elegy for the Rev. Mr. James B.
    Hodgson. J. Logan. St-H:111
  The Elevator Man Adheres to
    Form. M. Danner. Ad-PB:137,
    Be-MA:87, Hu-PN:161
  The Emperor's Double.
    R. Gittings. Ls-NY:142
  The Epitaph. T. Gray. Mc-PR:201
  Eros Turannos. E. Robinson.
    Un-MA:126, Wi-LT:109
  Evening. B. Smith. Sa-B:36
  The Fisherman. W. Yeats.
    Mo-SD:192
  Flammonde. E. Robinson. Wi-LT:105
  For Denis Who Was a Drum.
    M. Maxwell. Sa-B:172
  From My Window. M. Coleridge.
    Ox-BN:927
  The Gardener. R. Stevenson.
    Br-SG:25, Hu-MP:141, Ir-BB:40
  George. D. Randall. Ra-BP:145
  A Gluttonous Rich Man.
    G. Chaucer. Ha-PO:52
  The Goatherd. G. Conkling.
    Ar-TP3:32
  The Gum-Gatherer. R. Frost.
    Mo-BG:60
  He Sees Through Stone. E. Knight.
    Ad-PB:231, Be-MA:109
  Heimdall. H. Vinal. De-FS:210

PORTRAITS - MEN — cont'd.
  How Beastly the Bourgeois Is.
    D. Lawrence.   Gr-CT:468,
    Wi-LT:219
  How It Strikes a Contemporary.
    R. Browning.   Pa-GTB:352
  The Hunchback in the Park.
    D. Thomas.   Br-TC:437,
    Un-MB:504
  If Ever You Go to Dublin Town.
    P. Kavanagh.   To-MP:64
  Immortality. F. Keyes. Ke-TF:178
  In Praise of Abazza Ag-Mekiia.
    Tekadeit oult Ag-Eklan.
    Tr-US I:135
  Iowa, Kansas, Nebraska.
    G. Frumkin.   Bl-FP:22
  The Irishman and the Lady.
    W. Maginn.   Co-RM:116
  Isaac and Archibald. E. Robinson.
    Ni-JP:145, Pe-OA:9
  Jack. G. Brooks. Ha-TP:55
  Jacob Tonson, His Publisher.
    J. Dryden.   Gr-CT:470
  James Wetherell.   E. Robinson.
    Un-MA:117
  John Brown's Body. S. Benét.
    Ke-TF:303
  John Burns of Gettysburg.
    B. Harte.   Sp-OG:36, Vi-PP:156
  John Mouldy. W. de la Mare.
    Ox-BC:326
  A Kind of Hero. V. Scannell.
    Co-RM:207
  A Knight. G. Chaucer.
    Ha-PO:49, Un-GT:86
  Labourer. E. Brathwaite.
    Sa-B:239
  The Last Leaf. O. Holmes.
    Bo-HF:134, Fe-FP:321, Fe-PL:265,
    Mc-WK:135, Sp-OG:261
  A Little Shrub Growing By.
    B. Jonson.   Rv-CB:285
  A Long Story. F. Eckman. St-H:51
  A Maine Roustabout. R. Eberhart.
    Ha-TP:45
  The Man from Up-Country Talking.
    J. de Melo Neto.   An-TC:163
  The Man in the Bowler Hat.
    P. Black.   Gr-BT:135
  A Man Sharpening a Knife.
    K. Takamura.   Sh-AM:41
  The Market Man. J. Ratti. Du-SH:150
  The Marquis of Carabas.
    R. Brough.   Co-FB:200
  Miniver Cheevy. E. Robinson.
    Er-FA:384, Fe-PL:33, Ga-FB:328,
    Gr-CT:467, Ha-PO:63, Li-SR:75,
    No-CL:243, Pe-OA:3, Rv-CB:958,
    Sm-LG:130, Un-MA:117, Wi-LT:103

Mister Banjo.   Ab-MO:52
Mr. Bleaney. P. Larkin. Gr-BT:33
Mr. Coggs, Watchmaker.   E. Lucas.
  Fe-FP:315, Hu-MP:145
Mr. Flood's Party.   E. Robinson.
  Al-VBP:1107, Er-FA:304, Ha-PO:64,
  Na-EO:66, Ni-JP:143, Pe-M:50,
  Pe-OA:5, Sh-AP:141, Sm-PT:140,
  Un-MA:121, Wi-LT:111
Mr. Wells. E. Roberts. Fe-FP:314
Mortmain. R. Warren. En-PC:74,
  Ho-P:295
My Father Moved Through Dooms of
  Love. e. cummings. En-PC:22,
  Sh-AP:193
My Father's Trunk. R. Roseliep.
  St-H:188
My Last Duchess. R. Browning.
  Er-FA:374, Fe-PL:82, Ha-PO:39,
  Ma-YA:200, Ni-JP:40, Ox-BN:545,
  Pa-GTB:350, Rv-CB:817
A New England Bachelor.
  R. Eberhart.   Un-MA:589
The News Stand. D. Berrigan.
  Ad-CI:35
Night Constable. J. Woods.
  St-H:247
Nimium Fortunatus. R. Bridges.
  Un-MB:51
Of All the Men. T. Moore.
  Co-FB:52
Ogun. E. Brathwaite. Sa-B:48
Old Abram Brown. De-TT:45,
  Rv-ON:93
Old Dan'l. L. Strong.
  Cl-FC:36, Co-EL:125, Co-PS:64,
  Co-PU:122, Sm-MK:104, Un-MB:393
Old Grimes. Wr-RM:87
Old Jack Noman. E. Thomas.
  Bl-OB:147
Old Jake Sutter. K. Starbird.
  Ar-TP3:13
Old Man. J. Siegal. Le-M:150
An Old Man. W. Wordsworth.
  Go-BP:40, Sm-LG:129
An Old Man's Winter Night.
  R. Frost. Ca-VT:9, Ni-JP:142,
  Un-MA:176
The Old Squire. W. Blunt.
  Mo-SD:110
O'Neil the Undertaker.
  T. Tommaro. Ad-II:88
Oriki Erinle. Lo-TY:11
Our Father. R. Mathew. Ma-FW:63
Our Hired Man. M. Shannon.
  Fe-FP:313
Padraic O'Conaire, Gaelic Story-
  teller. F. Higgins. Co-PI:63
Papa John. J. de Lima.
  Lo-TY:84

The Parson. O. Goldsmith.
  Hi-WP II:125
Peerless Jim Driscoll.
  V. Scannell. Co-RM:231
Peter Grimes. G. Crabbe.
  Hi-WP II:65
Poor White. A. Planz.   Lo-IT:104
Portrait. K. Fearing.
  Pe-OA:184, Un-MA:556
Portrait of a Certain Gentleman.
  S. Hay. Ls-NY:146
The Prologue to the Canterbury
  Tales. G. Chaucer. Al-VBP:6,
  Gr-CT:281, Ma-FW:17, Ma-YA:28
The Puritan. K. Shapiro.
  Un-MA:635
The Raggedy Man. J. Riley.
  Fe-FP:533, Hu-MP:142,
  Ox-BC:301, Un-GT:99
Rain or Hail. E. Cummings.
  Du-SH:136
A Recluse. W. de la Mare.
  Go-BP:46
The Reeve's Tale. G. Chaucer.
  Al-VBP:12
Rendezvous with God.
  M. Seljouk. Go-BP:58
Resolution and Independence.
  W. Wordsworth. Li-SR:109
Reuben Bright. E. Robinson.
  Co-RM:233, Sh-AP:141, Un-MA:119
Richard Cory. E. Robinson.
  Co-PT:107, Er-FA:336, Fe-PL:33,
  Ho-TH:19, Pe-M:62, Sh-AP:140,
  Sm-LG:131, Un-MA:118, Wi-LT:100
The Ricksha Puller.
  Tsang K'o-chia. Hs-TC:281
A Ruffian. T. Beddoes. Co-PU:115
Sailing from the United States.
  S. Moss. Ca-VT:583
Saint Ras. T. McNeill. Sa-B:158
Say Good-Bye to Big Daddy.
  R. Jarrell. Hu-PN:567
The Scholar Gypsy. M. Arnold.
  Al-VBP:964, Gr-CT:255, Ox-BN:628
The Schoolmaster. J. Whittier.
  Un-GT:90
Schoolmaster. Y. Yevtushenko.
  Li-TU:136, Ma-FW:137
Self-Portrait. L. Blaga.
  Mc-AC:72
Sestina of the Tramp Royal.
  R. Kipling. Ni-JP:18, Un-MB:137
Seumas Beg. J. Stephens.
  Bl-OB:144, Co-RM:63,
  Fe-FP:318, Na-EO:155
Shot Who? Jim Lane!
  M. Moore. Un-MA:574
Simon Lee the Old Huntsman.
  W. Wordsworth. Pa-GTB:217

the singer. K. Wilson. Sc-TN:240
Sir Gawain and the Green Knight.
  Ma-YA:21
Sir Marmaduke. G. Colman.
  Un-GT:94
Sonnet to a Negro in Harlem.
  H. Johnson. Bo-AN:102, Mo-BG:27
The Spade. E. Brathwaite.
  Sa-B:43
Spanish Johnny. W. Cather.
  Co-RM:26, Fe-FP:436, Hu-MP:154,
  Mc-WK:140, Mc-WS:160, Sh-RP:41
Spiritual Biography. C. Walsh.
  St-H:237
A Squire. G. Chaucer.
  Hi-WP II:121, Un-GT:87
The Star-Splitter. R. Frost.
  Pl-IO:173
A Strange Funeral in Braddock.
  M. Gold. Kr-OF:184
The Sub-Average Time Reader.
  E. Wittenberg. Co-FB:360
The Sundays of Satin-Legs Smith.
  G. Brooks. St-H:14
Sweeney among the Nightingales.
  T. Eliot. Wi-LT:285
The Table. C. de Andrade.
  An-TC:67
The Talented Man. W. Praed.
  Co-FB:403
To a Rogue. J. Addison. Co-PU:115
To Don at Salaam. G. Brooks.
  Ra-BP:173
To the Four Courts, Please.
  J. Stephens. Co-PI:178,
  Ni-JP:86, Un-MB:263
To the Portrait of an Unknown
  Man. A. Scruggs. Ls-NY:144
Tom, Tom, the Piper's Son.
  J. Ransom. Al-VBP:1186
A True Story. J. Smith.
  Sm-MK:111
The Uncle. J. Whittier.
  Un-GT:89
Uncle Ananias. E. Robinson.
  Un-MA:137
Uncle Bull-Boy. J. Jordan.
  Ad-PB:304, Jo-SA:28
Uncle Roderick. N. Maccaig.
  To-MP:188
The Unemployed Blacksmith.
  J. Woods. Mc-WS:147
The Unknown Citizen. W. Auden.
  Du-SH:95, Gr-BT:133, Ke-PP:33,
  Mo-BG:194, Ni-JP:30, Pe-SS:106,
  Tr-MR:232, Wi-LT:471
Vendor. R. Roseliep. De-FS:157,
  St-H:179
The Vicar. G. Crabbe.
  Ox-BN:7

PORTRAITS - MEN — cont'd.
  Vickery's Mountain.
    E. Robinson. Un-MA:120
  The Village Blacksmith.
    H. Longfellow.
    Ch-B:86, Er-FA:275, Fe-FP:545,
    Sp-OG:323, Tu-WW:22, Un-GT:96
  The Vinegar Man. R. Mitchell.
    Hu-MP:147, Th-AS:182
  Who's Who. W. Auden. Mc-WS:73,
    Un-MB:450
  William Jones. E. Masters.
    Pl-IO:166
  Witchcraft: New Style.
    L. Abercrombie. Un-MB:256
  The Worthless Lover.
    Be-AP:52, Lo-TY:48
PORTRAITS - WOMEN: see also
    HUMOR - PORTRAITS-WOMEN
  Abandoned. V. Howard. Jo-VC:66
  An Adventure with a Lady.
    D. Hall. Ha-TP:64
  Albatross. J. Collins. Mo-GR:37
  Almswomen. E. Blunden. Go-BP:51
  Always Another Viewpoint.
    K. Patchen. Ha-TP:40
  An Ancient Virgin. G. Crabbe.
    Ox-BN:4
  Appoggiatura. D. Hayes.
    Ad-PB:94, Bo-AN:90, Hu-PN:246
  Aunt Edna. J. Tate. St-H:229
  Aunt Jane Allen. F. Johnson.
    Ad-PB:24, Hu-PN:89
  Aunt Jennifer's Tigers.
    A. Rich. Ha-TP:52
  The Autumnal. J. Donne.
    Al-VBP:254
  Balcony. F. Garcia Lorca.
    Le-SW:53, Li-TU:124
  Beautiful Is She. Ho-SD:63
  The Beloved. Be-AP:50
  Bessie Bobtail. J. Stephens.
    Co-PI:177
  Big Momma. D. Lee. Ra-BP:304
  The Black Cottage. R. Frost.
    Ca-VT:5
  Black Woman. L. Curry. Jo-VC:64
  Blind and Deaf Old Woman.
    C. Major. Ad-PB:300, Jo-SA:49
  Canterbury Tales (Prologue).
    G. Chaucer. Al-VBP:7, Ha-PO:50
  Canto Amor. J. Berryman.
    Ca-VT:381, Un-MA:642
  Catherine Takes a Stroll.
    J. Cournos. No-CL:203
  A Chant. W. Davies. Go-BP:51
  Choral Songs, III. Tr-US II:114
  A City Flower. A. Dobson. Go-BP:124
  Dagonet's Canzonet.
    E. Rhys. Gr-SS:86

The Death of the Hired Man.
    R. Frost. Pa-OA:26, Un-MA:171
Elegy to the Memory of an Un-
    fortunate Woman. A. Pope.
    Rv-CB:511
Epithalamion. E. Spenser.
    Al-VBP:104
Eros Turannos. E. Robinson.
    Un-MA:126, Wi-LT:109
The Eternal Image. R. Pitter.
    Un-MB:404
Eurasian Girl. A. Kerrigan.
    Ls-NY:139
The Evacuee. R. Thomas. To-MP:47
The Farmer's Bride. C. Mew.
    Un-MB:161
Femme Fatale. V. Starrett.
    De-FS:187
For a Dead Lady. E. Robinson.
    Al-VBP:1106, Un-MA:119,
    Wi-LT:104
For Fran. P. Levine. En-PC:272
A Fountain, a Bottle, a Donkey's
    Ears, and Some Books.
    R. Frost. Ca-VT:12
Foxey Lady. P. Solomon. Jo-SA:4
The Gallery. A. Marvell.
    Gr-SS:87
The Garden. E. Pound. Br-TC:331,
    Un-MA:289
A Gesture by a Lady with an
    Assumed Name. J. Wright.
    Wi-LT:846
Goodbye Now, or Pardon My
    Gauntlet. O. Nash. Co-FB:481
Grey Woman. G. Cardiff. Ni-CD:56
The Henchman. J. Whittier.
    No-CL:64
Her Eyes. J. Ransom. Wi-LT:316
Here Lies a Lady. J. Ransom.
    Ca-VT:150, Na-EO:21, Un-MA:410,
    Wi-LT:312
Here Lies Sweet Isabell in Bed.
    M. Fleming. De-CH:733
Herrick's Julia. H. Bevington.
    Li-SR:24
The Hill Wife. R. Frost.
    Wi-LT:167
Holyghost Woman. C. Major.
    Jo-SA:52
How a Girl Was Too Reckless of
    Grammar by Far. G. Carryl.
    Co-FB:154
I Call the Old Time Back.
    J. Whittier. Al-VBP:829
I Knew a Woman. T. Roethke.
    Br-TC:343, Un-MA:597,
    Un-MW:197, Wi-LT:487
If You Saw a Negro Lady.
    J. Meyer. Jo-SA:54, Lo-IT:92

In Memory of Ann Jones. D. Thomas.
Un-MB:501
The Indian Woman. W. Whitman.
Bo-FP:21
Insouciance. J. Dickson.
Du-SH:58
Interior. P. Colum. Co-PI:28,
Un-MB:250
Isabel Sparrow. M. Oliver.
Ls-NY:145
John Brown's Body. S. Benét.
Ke-TF:303
Kate. A. Tennyson. Co-RM:74
The Ladies. R. Kipling.
Ke-TF:243, Un-MB:128
A Lady. A. Lowell. Un-MA:156
A Lady Comes to an Inn.
E. Coatsworth. Ar-TP3:32,
Co-PT:39, Un-MA:465
Lady Feeding Cats. D. Stewart.
Ma-FW:61
Lady, Lady. A. Spencer. Ad-PB:17
The Lady's Complaint.
T. Heath-Stubbs. Br-TC:178
Lines on Receiving His Mother's
Picture. W. Cowper. De-CH:38
Lines to a Nasturtium.
A. Spencer. Bo-AN:18, Hu-PN:64
Louisa. W. Wordsworth. Gr-CC:24
Love in the Valley. G. Meredith.
Al-VBP:976
Lucinda Matlock. E. Masters.
Ga-FB:74, Mo-BG:161,
Un-MA:143, Wi-LT:116
The Mad Woman. L. Strong.
Co-PI:182, Un-MB:394
Martha. W. de la Mare.
Un-MB:198
Meg Merrilies. J. Keats.
Ar-TP3:14, Bl-OB:147, Bo-FP:100,
Cl-FC:86, Ne-AM:14, Ox-BC:147,
Re-TW:110, Rv-CB:749, Se-PR:322,
Sm-LG:128, Sm-MK:110, Sp-OG:249
Mis' Smith. A. Paine. Fe-PL:415
Miss Rosie. L. Clifton. Ad-PB:307,
Be-MA:139, Br-TC:69
Miss Thompson Goes Shopping.
M. Armstrong. Hi-WP II:153
Mrs. Southern's Enemy. O. Sitwell.
Al-VBP:1190
Montana Wives. G. Haste. Br-AF:159
Mother of the House. Bible. O.T.
Proverbs. Co-PS:88, Un-GT:91
Movie Queen. J. Vaughn. Hu-NN:62
My Aunt's Spectre. M. Collins.
Co-PT:63
My Last Duchess. R. Browning.
Er-FA:374, Fe-PL:82, Ha-PO:39,
Ma-YA:200, Ni-JP:40, Ox-BN:545,
Pa-GTB:350, Rv-CB:817

"Not Marble nor the Gilded
Monuments." A. MacLeish.
Al-VBP:1194, Br-TC:277,
Un-MW:143
Now She Is like the White Rose
Tree. C. Day Lewis. Un-MB:422
O Catch Miss Daisy Pinks.
A. Campbell. Pe-M:136
O Ruddier than the Cherry.
J. Gay. Al-VBP:524
Old Ellen Sullivan. W. Welles.
Fe-FP:310, Hu-MP:143
Old Meg of Kitrann. J. Keith.
De-FS:119
Old Tityrus to Eugenia.
C. Cotton. Al-VBP:474
The Old Woman. J. Campbell.
Al-VBP:1148, Un-MB:252
Old Woman. E. Jennings.
Gr-BT:166
Old Woman Awaiting the Greyhound
Bus. D. Niatum. Ni-CD:127
An Old Woman Laments in Spring-
time. E. Sitwell. Al-VBP:1170
On a Certain Lady at Court.
A. Pope. Rv-CB:512
On a Virtuous Young Gentlewoman
That Died Suddenly.
W. Cartwright. Rv-CB:384
On Mrs. W—. N. Bentley. Co-FB:199
Part of Plenty. B. Spencer.
Wi-LT:645
Petrarch for Laura.
C. McAllister. Gr-SS:101
Pigeon Woman. M. Swenson.
Mo-BG:50
The Pioneer Woman - in the
North Country. E. Tietjens.
Br-AF:158
The Planter's Daughter.
A. Clarke. Co-PI:25
Poem. J. Garrigue. Ls-NY:11
Pooh! W. de la Mare. Co-FB:192
Portrait by a Neighbor.
E. Millay. Ar-TP3:8,
Fe-FP:312, Ha-LO:45, Ho-TH:22,
Hu-MP:139, Mo-BG:47, Ne-AM:36,
Pe-FB:26, Th-AS:188, Tu-WW:40
Portrait d'une Femme. E. Pound.
Br-TC:331, No-CL:239, Un-MA:295
Portrait of a Lady. W. Praed.
No-CL:235
Portrait of a Lady. W. Williams.
Kh-VA:41
Potato Digger. F. Frost. Ls-NY:152
A Praise of His Lady. Al-VBP:70
The Prince's Progress.
C. Rossetti. Al-VBP:995
The Princess of Scotland.
R. Taylor. Gr-SS:123

PORTRAITS - WOMEN — cont'd.
  The Prologue to the Canterbury
    Tales. G. Chaucer. Al-VBP:6,
    Gr-CT:281, Ma-FW:17, Ma-YA:28
  Queens. J. Synge. Gr-CT:58,
    Un-MB:184
  Rainy Song. M. Eastman. Bo-HF:49
  The Rape of the Lock. A. Pope.
    Al-VBP:531
  The Reeve's Tale. G. Chaucer.
    Al-VBP:12
  Resolution in Four Sonnets.
    C. Cotton. Ho-P:244, No-CL:233
  Resurrections. D. Scott.
    Sa-B:205
  The Rites for Cousin Vit.
    G. Brooks. Ra-BP:167
  The Rival. S. Warner. Un-MB:374
  Rondeau for You. M. de Andrade.
    Lo-TY:83
  Samela. R. Greene. Al-VBP:141
  Saralinda. L. Sheppard. Le-M:138
  Self-Analysis. A. Wickham.
    Un-MB:277
  Sestina. Dante Alighieri.
    Gr-SS:93
  She Walked Unaware. P. MacDonogh.
    Co-BL:135, Co-PI:109
  She Walks in Beauty. G. Byron.
    Co-RG:148, Er-FA:105,
    Hi-WP II:54, Ke-TF:107,
    Mc-PR:91, Ni-JP:96, Ox-BN:251,
    Pa-GTB:177, Rv-CB:688,
    Sh-RP:89, Un-MW:166
  She Was a Phantom of Delight.
    W. Wordsworth. Al-VBP:656,
    Er-FA:109, Ga-FB:49,
    Pa-GTB:178, Rv-CB:638
  The Shepherd's Garland.
    M. Drayton. Al-VBP:159
  The Silken Tent. R. Frost.
    Br-TC:138, Un-MW:208
  A Sketch from Private Life.
    G. Byron. Ox-BN:253
  Skunk Hour. R. Lowell. Un-MA:660
  Slim Cunning Hands.
    W. de la Mare. Co-EL:80
  So White, So Soft, So Sweet.
    B. Jonson. De-TT:153,
    Sm-LG:350, Un-MW:16
  The Solitary Reaper. W. Wordsworth.
    Bl-OB:146, Co-RG:122, De-CH:207,
    Go-BP:49, Ha-PO:83, Hi-WP II:142,
    Ma-YA:141, Ox-BN:77, Pa-GTB:255,
    Pl-US:50, Re-TW:114, Rv-CB:635,
    Sp-OG:336
  Song. H.D. Un-MA:337, Wi-LT:618
  Song. M. Sarton. Tr-MR:175
  Sonnet. R. Greene. Al-VBP:144,
    No-CL:270

  Sonnet to My Mother. G. Barker.
    Al-VBP:1240, Br-TC:24, Er-FA:138,
    Ma-FW:63, Pe-SS:155, Wi-LT:528
  Still Life: Lady with Birds.
    Q. Prettyman. Ad-CI:50,
    Ad-PB:259
  Strawberry Jam. M. Justus.
    Fe-FP:310
  The Street Angel. Tsang K'o-chia.
    Hs-TC:283
  Suzanne. L. Cohen. Mo-GR:33
  Tamurlaine the Great.
    C. Marlowe. Al-VBP:171, 173
  Ten of Chaucer's People: The
    Wife of Bath. G. Chaucer.
    Ha-PO:53, Hi-WP I:122
  That Ever I Saw. Rv-CB:7
  Three Years She Grew in Sun and
    Shower. W. Wordsworth.
    Ox-BN:63, Pa-GTB:180, Rv-CB:642
  To a Fat Lady Seen from a Train.
    F. Cornford. Bo-GJ:106,
    Co-EL:100, Co-PU:132, Hi-WP I:109,
    Li-SR:20, Sm-MK:99, Un-MB:306
  To a Lady. F. Adams. Co-FB:328
  To a Lady. W. Dunbar. No-CL:149
  To a Young Lady. R. Savage.
    Rv-CB:521
  To an Isle in the Water. W. Yeats.
    Gr-TG:65, Sm-MK:8
  To an Old Lady. W. Empson.
    Pa-GTB:504
  To Aunt Rose. A. Ginsberg.
    Ca-VT:575, Wi-LT:719
  To Cynthia. F. Kynaston.
    Al-VBP:310
  To Helen. E. Poe.
    Al-VBP:878, Co-BL:76, De-CH:347,
    Er-FA:123, Fe-PL:101, Fr-WO:84,
    Ga-FB:62, Gr-CT:440, No-CL:56,
    Rv-CB:802, Sh-AP:53, Un-MW:168
  To Mistress Isabel Pennell.
    J. Skelton. Al-VBP:31, De-CH:34,
    Ma-FW:65, Ma-YA:51, Rv-CB:65
  To Mistress Margery Wentworth.
    J. Skelton. Al-VBP:30,
    Go-BP:118, Rv-CB:67
  Two Ladies Bidding Us "Good
    Morning." J. Vaughn. Hu-NN:63
  The Two Old Women. Ke-TF:158
  Unamina. B. Vilikazi. Pa-SG:38
  Upon His Julia. R. Herrick. Li-SR:23
  The Visitation. R. Graves.
    Go-BP:135
  The Visits of My Aunt.
    J. Woods. St-H:244
  Weeksville Women. E. Loftin.
    Ad-PB:515
  What She Did in the Morning I
    Wouldn't Know. M. Moore. Du-SH:57

Who Is Sylvia? W. Shakespeare.
   Al-VBP:180, Co-BL:71,
   Er-FA:431, Ke-TF:104
The Widows. D. Hall. Du-SH:57
Wishes! To His Supposed Mistress.
   R. Crashaw. Al-VBP:432,
   Pa-GTB:67
Witch of the Canyon. Fi-BG:116
Witchcraft: New Style.
   L. Abercrombie. Un-MB:256
Within Her Eyes. Dante Alighieri.
   Pa-SG:61
The Woman at Banff. W. Stafford.
   Ha-TP:46
The Woman at the Window.
   D. Wandrei. De-FS:212
A Woman Riding. T. Hardy.
   Gr-CC:8
Yase: September. G. Snyder.
   Mo-BG:44
PORTS: see HARBORS
PORTUGUESE VERSE
Appeal. N. de Sousa. Lo-TY:188
Aspiration. M. de Andrade.
   Lo-TY:82
Bailada. A. Nunez. Pa-SG:66
Blue Fly. J. de Assis. Lo-TY:81
Draft Notice. D. Mourao-Ferreira.
   Cr-WS:47
The Fisherman. Fe-FP:473
XIV. A. Caiero. Mo-TS:92
Good Saint Benedict. Ab-MO:58
Monangamba. A. Jacinto.
   Lo-TY:181
Night of Marvels.
   Sister Violante do Ceo.
   Ga-S:71
Papa John. J. de Lima. Lo-TY:84
Poem of the Conscripted Warrior.
   R. Nogar. Lo-TY:187
Rondeau for You. M. de Andrade.
   Lo-TY:83
Sea Horse. Ab-MO:60
Song. G. Vicente. Pa-SG:41
Song of Exile. A. Dias.
   Lo-TY:78
To the Wayfarer. Ar-TP3:217,
   Br-SS:144
Where Are the Men Seized in This
   Wind of Madness?
   A. do Espirito Santo. Lo-TY:183
Who Am I. L. Gama. Lo-TY:79
Woman. V. Malangatana. Lo-TY:190
The Words Will Resurrect.
   J. de Lima. Lo-TY:83
See also An-TC
POSSESSIONS: see also PROPERTY;
   SATIRE - POSSESSIONS
At Home. J. Rolnick. Ho-TY:166
Auction. J. Holmes. Mc-WK:88

Cottage. E. Farjeon. St-FS:72
Father. Jo-TS:4
Hawthorn White. C. Causley.
   Gr-BT:35
His Grange or Private Wealth.
   R. Herrick. Bo-FP:65, Bo-GJ:22,
   Ma-YA:88
Legal Fiction. W. Empson.
   Wi-LT:442
Mine. L. Moore. Cr-SS:16
My First Suitor. Mo-MGT:165
Poverty. T. Traherne. Ho-P:11
Residue. T. MacNeill. Sa-B:60
This Fall of New Snow.
   Kikaku. Be-CS:30
Tree Climbing. K. Fraser.
   Ho-ME:10
The Twig. J. Rolnick. Ho-TY:165
What Do You Do with a Woman's
   Things? A. Miller. Ke-TF:175
What Is Once Loved.
   E. Coatsworth. Co-PU:12
POSSUMS: see OPOSSUMS
POSTAL CARDS
Poem. W. Williams. Ca-VT:67
Postcard. E. Livingston.
   Sc-TN:144
To a Post-Office Inkwell.
   C. Morley. Fe-PL:411
POSTAL SERVICE: see also HUMOR -
   POSTAL SERVICE; PONY EXPRESS
Begins with a P. Re-RR:32
Conversation about Christmas.
   D. Thomas. Li-TU:123
The Highwayman's Ghost.
   R. Garnett. Co-PT:228
Like Me. D. Aldis. Mc-AW:21
Night Mail. W. Auden. Gr-CT:407,
   Ha-PO:44, Hi-WP I:132
Old Postmaster. A. Higbee.
   Ke-TF:297
On Their Appointed Rounds.
   Fe-FP:248
The Phantom Mail Coach.
   L. Welcome. Co-PM:167
The Pony Express. D. Thompson.
   Br-AF:227
The Postman. L. Richards.
   Ar-TP3:10, Au-SP:137
The Postman. C. Rossetti.
   Ar-TP3:10, Bo-FP:4
The Postman. Fe-FP:248
To a Post-Office Inkwell.
   C. Morley. Fe-PL:411
U.S. Mail. F. Mastin. Ke-TF:302
POSTMEN: see POSTAL SERVICE
POSTURE: see HUMOR - POSTURE
POTATOES: see also HUMOR - POTATOES;
   SWEET POTATOES
Have You Seen Old Lovell? Br-SG:45

POTATOES — cont'd.
  Mr. East's Feast. Ag-HE:20,
    Ir-BB:193
  Potato Digger. F. Frost. Ls-NY:152
  The Potatoes' Dance. V. Lindsay.
    Fe-FP:234, Hu-MP:311, Th-AS:96
  Ulysses. I. Voronca. Mc-AC:87
POTLATCHES: see INDIANS OF NORTH
    AMERICA - CEREMONIES AND DANCES
POTOMAC, BATTLE, 1861
  The Red, White, and Red. Em-AF:447
POTOMAC RIVER
  Potomac Town in February.
    C. Sandburg. Li-LC:67,
    Mc-WK:104, Na-EO:117
POTS AND PANS: see HUMOR -
    POTS AND PANS
POTTERY
  Cups Without Wine. J. Halevi.
    Me-PH:62
  Girls' Song for the Game of
    "Pots." Do-CH:(32), Tr-CB:46,
    Tr-US I:109
  The Potter. Lo-TY:47
  To a Lady on Her Passion for
    Old China. J. Gay. Er-FA:141
POULTICES: see REMEDIES AND CURES
POULTRY: see CHICKENS; DUCKS;
    GEESE; TURKEYS;
POUND, EZRA LOOMIS
  Asylum. D. Clark. Ke-PP:52
  Visits to St. Elizabeths.
    E. Bishop. Ca-VT:320, Mc-EA:154
POVERTY: see also COST OF LIVING;
    GHETTOS; HUMOR - POVERTY;
    HUNGER AND STARVATION; SLUMS
    AND SLUM LIFE
  Alice Fell. W. Wordsworth.
    De-TT:105, Li-SR:102
  Almswomen. E. Blunden. Go-BP:51
  Der Arme Poet. M. Roberts.
    Pl-ML:16
  Aspiration. M. de Andrade.
    Lo-TY:82
  Babies Are Crying. P. John.
    Ba-HI:85
  The Ballad of the Harp-Weaver.
    E. Millay. Ar-TP3:156,
    Co-PT:64
  The Bean Eaters. G. Brooks.
    Ad-PB:154, Be-MA:81,
    Jo-SA:23, Lo-TY:245
  La Belle Saison. J. Prévert.
    Ad-CI:97
  Bessie Bobtail. J. Stephens.
    Co-PI:177
  Boy with His Hair Cut Short.
    M. Rukeyser. Br-TC:350,
    Ca-VT:361, Co-RG:159,
    Wi-LT:805

  Brass Spittoons. L. Hughes.
    Bo-AN:61, Un-MA:552
  By the Winding River. Tu Fu.
    Rx-OH:13
  Can't Kill Him. Chang Chih-min.
    Hs-TC:426
  Caravaners. Tr-CB:26,
    Tr-US I:113
  Carol. J. Short. Sm-LG:371,
    To-MP:28
  The Carol of the Poor Children.
    R. Middleton. Sm-MK:219
  Childhood. H. Percikow.
    La-OC:75
  The Child's Hymn. M. Howitt.
    Un-GT:20
  The Complaint of Chaucer to
    His Purse. G. Chaucer.
    Al-VBP:19, Ma-YA:36, No-CL:11
  The Death and Life of a Severino.
    J. de Melo Neto. An-TC:127
  Ditty. W. Gibson. Ls-NY:333
  Don't Cry, My Little One.
    Wang T'ung-chao. Hs-TC:259
  Down on Roberts' Farm.
    C. Reeves. Hi-TL:197
  Elegy Written in a Country
    Churchyard. T. Gray.
    Al-VBP:559, De-TT:83, Er-FA:462,
    Fe-PL:281, Ha-PO:144, Ma-YA:125,
    Pa-GTB:145, Rv-CB:533
  An Elementary School Class Room
    in a Slum. S. Spender.
    Br-TC:403, Ke-PP:50, Un-MB:403
  The Embankment. T. Hulme.
    Co-EL:123
  The Enchanted Shirt. J. Hay.
    Ha-PO:59, Sh-RP:264, Un-GT:171
  Face of Poverty. L. Smith.
    Hu-NN:45, Hu-PN:267
  The Flower Market. Po-Chu-I.
    Ke-PP:10
  For My Unborn & Wretched Children.
    A. Spellman. Ad-PB:283
  Fra Lippo Lippi. R. Browning.
    Al-VBP:898
  Get This Garbage Out of My Life.
    P. Goggins. Ba-HI:132
  The Gleaner. J. Taylor. Ox-BC:120
  Go to Old Ireland. Em-AF:759
  The Golf Links. S. Cleghorn.
    Er-FA:268, Fe-PL:421,
    Ke-PP:61, Kr-OF:180
  Hard Times. Em-AF:767
  Hard Times, Dearth Times. Ma-BH:13
  He Meets Two Men Carrying a Corpse
    in a Hammock. J. de Melo Neto.
    An-TC:131
  Her Husband Asks Her to Buy a Bolt
    of Silk. Ch'en T'ao. Rx-LT:105

Hey There Mister.   Me-WF:49
History Makers.   G. Campbell.
   Sa-B:33
How Good Are the Poor.   V. Hugo.
   Ke-TF:61
I Have a Garment.   A. Ibn Ezra.
   Me-PH:65
If Things Were Better.   Issa.
   Be-CS:32
An Invective Against the Wicked
   of the World.   N. Breton.
   Al-VBP:85
Just Making It.   R. Thomas.
   Hu-PN:432
The Laborer.   R. Thomas.   Go-BP:229
Laventville.   D. Walcott.   Sa-B:24
Legend.   T. Aida.   Sh-AM:110
Letter in Winter.   R. Patterson.
   Ad-PB:211
Life.   H. Harrington.   Ba-HI:85
London.   S. Johnson.
   Al-VBP:553, Gr-CT:303
the lost baby poem.   L. Clifton.
   Be-MA:141
The Lovers of the Poor.
   G. Brooks.   Be-MA:83
Market.   R. Hayden.   Be-MA:65
The Mayors.   W. Blake.   De-CH:62
The Mill Mother's Lament.
   E. Wiggins.   Kr-OF:191
Miss Rosie.   L. Clifton.
   Ad-PB:307, Be-MA:139, Br-TC:69
Moving Through the Silent Crowd.
   S. Spender.   To-MP:22
Nobody Collects the Papers.
   L. Warren and D. Dickson.
   La-IH:53
Nostalgia.   Yang Huan.   Pa-MV:159
Oh Why?   M. Fletcher.   Me-WF:23
Odyssey of a Slum.   V. Howard.
   La-IH:124
An Old Woman of the Roads.
   P. Colum.   De-CH:49, Fe-FP:320,
   Hu-MP:156, Sh-RP:43, Th-AS:184,
   Un-MB:250
On Passing Two Negroes on a Dark
   Country Road Somewhere in
   Georgia.   C. Rivers.   Hu-NN:42
Over the Hills to the Poor-House.
   W. Carleton.   Er-FA:266
Papa, Mama.   C. Belli.   Be-UL:115
Park Bench.   L. Hughes.   Kr-OF:188
The Pauper's Funeral.   G. Crabbe.
   Ox-BN:1
Plot Improbable, Character Un-
   sympathetic. E. Olson.   St-H:173
Poem for the Subterranean Poor.
   D. di Prima.   Kh-VA:53
The Poor.   W. Williams.
   Un-MA:261

The Poor Girl's Meditation.
   Co-PI:29
The Poor Man.   Be-AP:55
Poor Naked Wretches.
   W. Shakespeare.   Ke-PP:22
Poor People.   R. Zychlinska.
   Ho-TY:230
Poor White.   A. Planz.   Lo-IT:104
Poverty.   T. Traherne.   Ho-P:11
The Princess of Scotland.
   R. Taylor.   Gr-SS:123
Puerto Ricans in New York.
   C. Reznikoff.   Kh-VA:60
The Rage That Shatters Man into
   Children.   C. Vallejo.
   Be-UL:41
The Rich and the Poor.
   Tr-US II:92
Saturday's Child.   C. Cullen.
   Ad-PB:86, Bo-HF:88, Wi-LT:616
Search.   R. Souster.   Co-EL:137
Sightseers in a Courtyard.
   N. Guillen.   Lo-TY:106
Simon Lee the Old Huntsman.
   W. Wordsworth.   Pa-GTB:217
A Slum Dwelling.   G. Crabbe.
   Ox-BN:11
Song of the Poor Man.   Lo-TY:49
Song to the Wife of His Youth.
   N. Alterman.   Me-PH:109
The Sorrow of Shanghai.
   Wang Tu-ch'ing.   Hs-TC:198
Sweet, Smiling Village.
   O. Goldsmith.   Ke-PP:41
Taught Me Purple.   E. Hunt.
   La-OC:93, Pe-SS:6
Thirty Bob a Week. J. Davidson.
   Er-FA:271, Ox-BN:900
This Place.   C. Graves.   La-IH:133
Times Are Gettin' Hard.   L. Mays.
   Kr-OF:168
Timothy Winters.   C. Causley.
   Sm-MK:123, To-MP:73
To an Unborn Pauper Child.
   T. Hardy.   Al-VBP:1046,
   Pa-GTB:405
To the Four Courts, Please.
   J. Stephens.   Co-PI:178,
   Ni-JP:86, Un-MB:263
The Vesture of the Soul.
   G. Russell.   Co-PI:174
Waiting.   J. Davidson.
   Al-VBP:1078
We're Free.   C. Williams.
   Ba-HI:124
A Winter Night.   J. Velez.
   Ba-HI:72
The World.   G. Abraham.   Me-WF:48
Xmas Time.   W. Karsner.
   Co-EL:142, Co-PU:30

POWELL, ADAM CLAYTON, JR.
  For "Mr. Dudley," a Black Spy.
    J. Emanuel. Ra-BP:191
POWER: see also INFLUENCE;
    LOVE - POWER; SATIRE -
    POWER; STRENGTH
  And Whoever Brings. A. Tabachnik.
    Ho-TY:271
  The Arrow and the Song.
    H. Longfellow. Er-FA:16,
    Sp-OG:337
  Birthday Verses Written in a
    Child's Album. J. Lowell.
    Ox-BC:282
  The Bloody Conquests of Mighty
    Tamburlaine. C. Marlowe.
    Gr-CT:335
  Bronzeville Man with a Belt in
    the Back. G. Brooks. Ad-PB:157
  The Bull. R. Hodgson. Rd-OA:122,
    Un-MB:190, Wi-LT:125
  The Death of Justice. W. Hawkins.
    Ad-PB:20
  Energy. V. Cruz. Ad-PB:507
  The Force. P. Redgrove.
    To-MP:178
  Fountain. E. Jennings. En-PC:237
  Good Wish. Sm-LG:240
  The Hand That Rocks the Cradle Is
    the Hand That Rules the World.
    W. Wallace. Er-FA:135, Fe-PL:149
  The Hand That Signed the Paper.
    D. Thomas. Mc-WS:102, Tr-MR:190,
    Un-MB:499
  Hands. G. Thompson. Jo-SA:9,
    Jo-VC:15
  Hymn to Intellectual Beauty.
    P. Shelley. Ox-BN:276
  In Honor of Senzangakona.
    Tr-US I:79
  Man Is a Lumpe where All Beasts
    Kneaded Be. C. Lewis.
    Go-BP:102
  Men's Stick-Dance Songs.
    Tr-US II:142
  Music and Drum. A. MacLeish.
    Ho-TH:59, Tr-MR:186
  Night Practice. M. Swenson.
    Li-TU:168
  No Man Exists. Do-CH:(16)
  The Oba of Benin. Be-AP:43
  On the Vanity of Earthly Great-
    ness. A. Guiterman. Du-RG:63
  Poem. H. Carberry. Sa-B:142
  Power: Cape Hatteras.
    H. Crane. Un-MA:528
  Praise of Chief Mosenene.
    Be-AP:37
  Praise Song for a Chief.
    Tr-US I:87

  Sext. W. Auden. Ga-S:118,
    Li-TU:180
  Song David. Ox-BB:241
  Song of a Supernatural Being.
    Tr-US II:216
  The Stars Go over the Lonely
    Ocean. R. Jeffers. Wi-LT:259
  The Time of Ede. Be-AP:42
  To My Friends. N. Nor. Bo-RU:54
  Two Voices in a Meadow.
    R. Wilbur. Pe-SS:56
  Variations on a Line from
    Shakespeare's Fifty-Sixth
    Sonnet. E. Mayo. En-PC:70
  What Rules the World.
    W. Wallace. Se-PR:120
  Wisdom. Tr-CB:17
  Witchcraft: New Style.
    L. Abercrombie. Un-MB:256
PRAIRIE DOGS
  Prairie-Dog Town. M. Austin.
    Ar-TP3:631, Fe-FP:176
  Prairie Town. W. Stafford.
    St-H:210
PRAIRIE FIRES
  Kit Carson's Ride. J. Miller.
    Fi-BG:161
  The Wrangler Kid. Fi-BG:102
PRAIRIES
  Bury Me Not on the Lone Prairie.
    Er-FA:445, Ga-FB:269
  In the Days when the Cattle Ran.
    H. Garland. Hu-MP:205,
    Sh-RP:268
  An Indian Summer Day on the
    Prairie. V. Lindsay.
    La-RM:70, Mc-WK:31
  Letter from Fort Scott.
    B. Cutler. St-H:44
  My Prairies. H. Garland.
    Fe-FP:268
  Night on the Prairies.
    W. Whitman. La-RM:68,
    Tr-MR:288
  Open Range. K. and B. Jackson.
    Ar-TP3:34, Fe-FP:271
  The Peters Family. W. Stafford.
    St-H:216
  Prairie Town. W. Stafford.
    St-H:210
  The Prairies. W. Bryant.
    Sh-AP:20
  A Sound from the Earth.
    W. Stafford. La-RM:82
  Spring Song. Bi-IT:126,
    Br-MW:98, Da-SC:148, Jo-TS:13,
    Tr-US II:228
  Swallows. T. Ferril. La-RM:83
  To Make a Prairie.
    E. Dickinson. Bo-HF:21

West of Chicago.   J. Dimoff.
   La-RM:81
Wires.   P. Larkin.   Pe-M:32
PRAISE: see GOD - PRAISE;
      JESUS CHRIST - PRAISE;
      LOVE - PRAISE
PRAXITELES
   The Statue.   R. Humphries. Ni-JP:127
PRAYER: see also HUMOR - PRAYER;
      SATIRE - PRAYER; WORSHIP
   Jubilate Agno.   C. Smart. Ho-P:165
   Leofric and Godiva.   W. Landor.
      Gr-CC:90
   Muhammedan Call to Prayer.
      Bilal.   Lo-TY:43
   My Period Has Come for Prayer.
      E. Dickinson.   Pl-EI:171
   Of Course I Prayed.
      E. Dickinson.   Un-MA:97
   The Pains of Sleep.
      S. Coleridge.   Ox-BN:171,
      Rv-CB:662
   Prayer.   L. Hughes.   Pl-EI:172
   Prayer.   A. Tennyson.
      Ga-S:208, Go-BP:188
   Proof.   E. Fuller.   Th-AS:171
   Saying a Prayer.   R. Bennett.
      Hu-MP:108
   Song of a Hebrew. D. Abse. Sm-MK:214
PRAYERS: see also BLESSINGS;
      CHRISTMAS PRAYERS; HUMOR -
      PRAYERS; LITANIES; LOVE -
      PRAYERS; SATIRE - PRAYERS;
      WORSHIP
   Abide with Me.   H. Lyte. Er-FA:443
   Adieu; Farewell Earth's Bliss.
      T. Nashe.   Al-VBP:211, De-CH:244,
      Gr-CT:358, Ha-PO:142, Hi-FO:141,
      Rv-CB:276, Sm-LG:276
   Afraid.   W. de la Mare.   Gr-TG:58
   All Souls.   L. Romano.   De-FS:156
   America.   J. Whitfield.
      Ba-PO:17, Ra-BP:35
   Anashuya and Vijaya.   W. Yeats.
      Li-TU:146
   And Be Her Mother, Just as She
      Was Mine.   Ke-TF:145
   And Now, O Father.   Ke-TF:214
   Ash-Wednesday.   T. Eliot.
      Ca-VT:134, Un-MA:398
   At a Child's Baptism. V. Miller.
      Bo-GJ:28, Ls-NY:119
   At the New Year.   K. Patchen.
      Wi-LT:784
   Battle Hymn.   Tr-US I:101
   The Bells of Heaven. R. Hodgson.
      Bo-GJ:20, Br-SS:152, Co-BBW:280,
      De-TT:82, Ha-PO:109, Ke-PP:104,
      Pl-EI:131, Th-AS:51, Un-MB:192,
      Wi-LT:125

   Benediction.   D. Hayes.
      Bo-AN:91, Hu-PN:248
   Benediction.   S. Kunitz.
      Ca-VT:259, Tr-MR:60
   Birthday Sonnet.   W. Wylie.
      Un-MA:280
   A Boy's Prayer.   H. Beeching.
      Mo-SD:193, Se-PR:313
   Call to Prayer.   Bilal. Ab-MO:61
   The Camel.   C. de Gasztold.
      Rd-OA:161
   The Celestial Surgeon.
      R. Stevenson.   Al-VBP:1070,
      Un-GT:308, Un-MB:58
   Centennial Hymn.   J. Whittier.
      Vi-PP:86
   Ceremonial Chants of a Shaman.
      Tr-US II:126, 128
   Ceremonial Prayer for the
      Fructification of the Pandanus
      Tree.   Tr-US II:27
   A Child's Evening Prayer.
      S. Coleridge.   Ox-BC:112
   A Child's Prayer.   J. Tabb.
      Fe-FP:24
   A Child's Prayer.   F. Thompson.
      Ga-FB:147, Ox-BC:307, Se-PR:228
   A Child's Prayer at Evening.
      C. Roberts.   Rd-SS:41
   Closing Cadence.   J. Moffit.
      Tr-MR:262
   The Conversation of Prayer.
      D. Thomas.   Pa-GTB:540
   Conversion.   F. Angermayer.
      Fe-PL:334
   Cry for a Dead Soldier.
      M. Inman.   Ls-NY:109
   The Da Pacem of the Laborer.
      Ba-PO:85
   De Profundis.   Bible.   O.T.
      Psalms.   Ga-S:39
   The Dead in Europe.   R. Lowell.
      Wi-LT:581
   Dear Father.   M. Brown.   La-PV:140
   Dear God.   C. O'Riordan. De-CH:656
   Dear God, the Day Is Grey.
      A. Halley.   Pe-OA:287
   Dear Lord and Father of Mankind.
      J. Whittier.   Ke-TF:206
   Easter Hymn.   A. Housman. Pl-EI:87
   The Easterner's Prayer.   Fe-PL:130,
      Ke-TF:208
   Eastward I Stand, Mercies I Beg.
      Pl-EI:173
   Envoi.   A. Wickham.   Un-MB:283
   Evening.   T. Miller.   Ox-BC:210
   An Evening Hymn.   T. Ken.
      Ox-BC:34
   An Evening Thought.   J. Hammon.
      Hu-PN:4

PRAYERS — cont'd.
  Every Morning when I Wake.
    D. Thomas. Ha-LO:66
  Father. Jo-TS:4
  The Fool's Prayer. E. Sills.
    Fe-PL:322, Pa-OM:225, Sp-OG:137
  For a Very New Angel. V. Storey.
    Ke-TF:200
  For All Sorts and Conditions.
    N. Nicholson. Pl-EI:181
  For All That Ever Has Been Ours.
    Z. Landau. Ho-TY:97
  For Sleep or Death. R. Pitter.
    Hi-WP I:144, Sm-MK:218
  For Strength. R. Tagore.
    Tr-MR:52
  For the Earth God. Pl-EI:174,
    Tr-US I:52
  From a Seasonal Prayer.
    Tr-US II:254
  From the New Year's Ceremony.
    Tr-US II:229
  Gentle Jesus, Meek and Mild.
    C. Wesley. Ox-BC:59
  God Be in My Head. Ga-S:208,
    Gr-CT:386, Pl-EI:187, Sm-MK:213
  God Bless the Work. B. O'Higgins.
    Ke-TF:205
  God of Mercy. K. Molodowsky.
    Ho-TY:289
  Good Night! J. Tabb. Gr-TG:56
  Good Reader, Warn All Men and
    Women. De-CH:653
  Grace Before Sleep. S. Teasdale.
    Tr-MR:52
  Grant Me Thy Peace.
    Thomas à Kempis. Go-BP:269
  Grant Us, O Lord. Ke-TF:202
  Guide, O Christ, This Little
    Hand. Gr-TG:59
  Hippopotamus Hunter's Song.
    Tr-US I:96
  Hold Thou My Hands. W. Canton.
    Gr-TG:80
  Holy Visions! Ho-SD:32
  The Horse's Prayer. Mo-TB:123
  House Dedication Prayer.
    Tr-US II:98
  A Hymn. P. Fletcher. Rv-CB:320
  A Hymn to God the Father.
    J. Donne. Al-VBP:264,
    Ga-S:137, Pl-EI:206
  I, a Justified Sinner. A. Price.
    Ls-NY:90
  I Fled from Desolation.
    R. Korn. Ho-TY:306
  I Have a Garment. A. Ibn Ezra.
    Me-PH:65
  I Walked on the Ice of the Sea.
    Le-IB:98

  I Will Bow and Be Simple.
    Pl-EI:188
  I Will Extol Thee, O Lord.
    Bible. O.T. Psalms. Me-PH:20
  The Icebound Swans. Rd-OA:199
  Intercession Against the Plague.
    Sedulius Scottus. Ga-S:44
  Invocation. Tr-US I:76
  Invocation to Dsilyi Neyani.
    Da-SC:75, Tr-US II:250
  Invocation to the Rainbow.
    Tr-US I:63
  Invocation to the Rice Soul at
    Harvest Time. Tr-US II:204
  Jesus, Tender Shepherd, Hear Me.
    M. Duncan. Gr-TG:57
  Jhesu, for Thy Wondes Fyff.
    Ba-PO:6
  John Brown's Prayer. S. Benét.
    Hu-PN:517
  Johnny Appleseed's Hymn to the
    Sun. V. Lindsay. Tr-MR:29
  Just for Today. Ke-TF:192
  Keep Hidden from Me. R. Korn.
    Ho-TY:306
  The King of Ai. H. Plutzik.
    Wi-LT:792
  Lament at Night. H. Leivick.
    Ho-TY:119
  Lead Us, O Father. W. Burleigh.
    Ke-TF:189
  Let Our Children Live. Ho-SD:28
  Let the Light Enter. F. Harper.
    Hu-PN:15
  Listen, Lord - a Prayer.
    J. Johnson. Ra-BP:41
  A Litany at Atlanta.
    W. Du Bois. Hu-PN:20
  Litany for Halloween.
    Au-SP:371, Br-SM:3, Br-SS:72,
    Co-PS:140, Mo-TB:77, Se-PR:192
  Little Things. J. Stephens.
    Ad-PE:47, Ar-TP3:65, Bo-GJ:19,
    Br-SS:151, Co-BBW:55, Co-PU:70,
    Fe-FP:149, Gr-EC:40, Hi-WP I:33,
    Hu-MP:200, La-PV:160, Pl-EI:130,
    Un-MB:263
  Lord Christ, My Darling Is So
    Dear. C. Hansen-Bay. Gr-TG:66
  The Lord Is My Shepherd. Bible.
    O.T. Psalms. Ar-TP3:189,
    Bo-FP:107, Fe-FP:25, Fe-PL:346,
    Ga-S:213, Rv-CB:130, Sh-RP:92
  Lord, Look upon a Little Child.
    J. Taylor. Gr-TG:59
  Lord of All Pots and Pans. Ke-TF:205
  Lord, This Night. O. Mandelstam.
    Ca-MR:158
  The Lord's Prayer. Bible. N.T.
    Matthew. Fe-PL:345, Pl-EI:169

Love Song.   Bi-IT:76
Loving Jesus, Gentle Lamb.
   C. Wesley.   Gr-TG:59
Lullaby for Mitsura. T. Arghezi.
   Mc-AC:26
The Marital Journey.   H. Araaya.
   Pe-M:152
may my heart always be open to
   little. E. Cummings. Tr-MR:48
Moon, O Mother Moon.   Le-OE:5
A Morning Hymn.   C. Smart.
   Ox-BC:71
Morning Prayer.   O. Nash.
   Ox-BC:349
Morning Prayer.   Do-CH:(46)
My Brother the Star.   Wo-HS:(32)
My Dog Is Dead. Ke-TF:207
My Shadow. J. Rubenstein.
   Ho-TY:240
My Sun! Jo-TS:1
A National Hymn.   J. DeForest.
   Vi-PP:13
National Hymn. D. Roberts.
   Vi-PP:41
The Newer Vainglory.
   A. Meynell.   Tr-MR:218
Now and Afterwards. D. Craik.
   Fe-PL:329
Now I Lay Me Down to Sleep.
   Au-SP:94, Ch-B:117, Er-FA:466,
   Gr-GB:298, Mo-MGT:173, Sm-MK:213
Now the Day Is Over.
   S. Baring-Gould.   Cl-DT:34,
   De-TT:53, Gr-TG:49, Ke-TF:79,
   Ox-BC:238, Rd-SS:42
O Father, Bless Me Good or Bad.
   Gr-TG:60
O Father Give Me Grace and
   Sense.   Gr-TG:60
O Jesus, Keep My Candle Burning
   Bright.   Gr-TG:46
O Lord, Save We Beseech Thee.
   Me-PH:66
Oh My Gentle Village Fierce.
   Wo-HS:(33)
O Terrible Is the Highest Thing.
   K. Patchen.   Ca-VT:346
Offering. Bi-IT:108
Offering of Prayer Sticks.
   Da-SC:71
Ombrure Calls Up the Forest
   Spirits.   Tr-US I:60
On Restoring an Old House.
   E. de Liesseline.   Ke-TF:415
Overtones. W. Percy. Bo-HF:136
A Page's Road Song. W. Percy.
   Ha-YA:32, Ke-TF:201
Prayer. W. Bilderdÿk. Pa-SG:200
Prayer. I. Brown. Hu-NN:61,
   Hu-PN:341

Prayer.   Chou Meng-tich. Pa-MV:71
A Prayer. D. Einhorn. Ho-TY:83
Prayer. J. Kirkup. Go-BP:218
A Prayer. E. Markham. Se-PR:320
Prayer. T. Roethke. Br-TC:345
Prayer. L. Untermeyer. Un-GT:308,
   Un-MA:305
A Prayer. V. Watkins.   Tr-MR:50
A Prayer. R. Weston. Au-SP:356,
   Bo-FP:4
Prayer. J. Wheelock. Ls-NY:105,
   Pl-EI:182
Prayer. Be-AP:19
Prayer. Bi-IT:29, 30, 31, 33,
   34, 36, 37, 38
A Prayer. Ho-SD:24, Le-OE:7
Prayer. Tr-US I:279
Prayer after World War.
   C. Sandburg. Ca-VT:26
Prayer at the Burning Off a New
   Communal Field. Tr-US I:168
Prayer at the Graves of the
   Murdered Strikers.   C. Queens.
   Kr-OF:157
Prayer at the Offering of Food
   to the Ancestors.
   Tr-US II:255
Prayer Before Birth. L. MacNeice.
   Br-TC:282, Co-PI:117, Gr-BT:183,
   Pa-GTB:517, Pe-SS:34, To-MP:52
A Prayer for a Little Home.
   F. Bone. Bo-FP:50, Er-FA:135
Prayer for a Miracle.
   A. Wickham. Un-GT:305
Prayer for a Night of Snow.
   D. Hickey. Ke-TF:209
Prayer for a Pilot. C. Roberts.
   Fe-FP:202
Prayer for Difficult Days.
   E. Guest. Ke-TF:201
Prayer for Fine Weather.
   S. Leslie. Co-PI:92
A Prayer for Little Things.
   E. Farjeon. Gr-TG:62,
   St-FS:119
Prayer for Long Life.
   Tr-US II:256
Prayer for Marilyn Monroe.
   E. Cardenal. Be-UL:95
A Prayer for Our Nation. Ba-PO:70
A Prayer for Peace.
   Charles d'Orleans. Ba-PO:20
Prayer for Peace. L. Senghor.
   Lo-TY:135
Prayer for Peace. Tr-US II:54
Prayer for Rain. H. Palmer.
   Hi-WP II:42
Prayer for Reptiles.
   P. Hubbell. Ad-PE:42,
   La-PV:153

PRAYERS — cont'd.
  Prayer for Thanksgiving.
    E. Voswinkel. Ke-TF:209
  Prayer for This House.
    L. Untermeyer. Fe-FP:57,
    Fe-PL:136, Mc-PR:104
  Prayer in Blackout. G. Code.
    De-FS:66
  A Prayer in Darkness.
    G. Chesterton. Fe-PL:330,
    Un-MB:208
  A Prayer in Spring. R. Frost.
    Ha-YA:29, Tr-MR:48
  Prayer of a Hunter at a Grave
    of Heitsi-Eibib. Tr-US I:77
  Prayer of a Woman. J. Karni.
    Un-R:75
  The Prayer of Columbus.
    W. Whitman. Se-PR:180
  Prayer of St. Francis of Assisi
    for Peace. St. Francis.
    Fe-PL:346
  The Prayer of the Butterfly.
    C. Gasztold. Li-TU:198
  The Prayer of the Cat.
    C. Gasztold. Ar-TP3:82,
    La-PV:113
  The Prayer of the Donkey.
    C. Gasztold. Ar-TP3:83
  The Prayer of the Little Ducks.
    C. Gasztold. Ad-PE:38,
    Ar-TP3:82, Gr-TG:63,
    La-PV:131, Su-FVI:72
  The Prayer of the Little Pig.
    C. Gasztold. Li-TU:62
  The Prayer of the Old Horse.
    C. Gasztold. La-PV:126
  The Prayer of the Ox.
    C. Gasztold. Li-TU:188,
    Mc-WS:51
  Prayer on Fourth of July.
    N. Turner. Ha-YA:85
  Prayer on the Night Before
    Easter. J. Holmes. Tr-MR:58
  Prayer Out of Georgia. M. Moody.
    Ke-TF:203
  Prayer to a Dead Wife. Da-SC:73
  A Prayer to Be Delivered from
    Liars and Warmongers. Bible.
    O.T. Psalms. Me-PH:27
  A Prayer to Be Restored to the
    Sanctuary. Bible. O.T.
    Psalms. Me-PH:22
  A Prayer to Be Said when Thou
    Goest to Bed. F. Seager.
    Ox-BC:12
  A Prayer to Go to Heaven with the
    Donkeys. F. Jammes.
    Ar-TP3:83, Co-BBW:149, Go-BP:255,
    Pl-EI:124, Rd-OA:20, Tr-MR:52

  Prayer to God. Placido. Lo-TY:99
  Prayer to the Creator.
    Tr-US II:124
  Prayer to the God Thot. Be-AP:18,
    Lo-TY:28
  Prayer to the Goddess Ja Pudeu.
    Tr-US II:202
  Prayer to the Moon. Be-AP:23
  Prayers of Steel. C. Sandburg.
    Fe-FP:255, Hu-MP:403, La-OC:151,
    La-PV:194, Mo-BG:26, Un-MA:203
  Presenting an Infant to the Sun.
    Bi-IT:113
  Rufus Prays. L. Strong. Un-MB:394
  St. Patrick's Breastplate.
    St. Patrick. Sm-LG:379
  Satan's Prayer. I. Manger.
    Ho-TY:273
  Self. P. George. Al-WW:122
  Shaman's Address to His Spirits.
    Tr-US II:125
  Six Birthday Candles Shining.
    M. Carr. Br-BC:91
  A Slant of Sun. S. Crane.
    Sh-AP:145, Wi-LT:120
  Small Prayer. W. Kees. Ca-VT:408
  A Small Thought Speaks for the
    Flesh. C. Drewry. Tr-MR:226
  Soldier Asleep. P. McGinley.
    Cr-WS:60
  Soldier's Prayer. A. Giles.
    Ke-TF:203
  A Song for Simeon. T. Eliot.
    Gr-BT:174, Pl-EI:202
  Sonnet XXII. Feng Chih.
    Hs-TC:153
  Storm Song. Bi-IT:106, Br-MW:47
  Sun, God of Living. J. Nez.
    Ba-HI:145
  Supplication to the Rain God and
    the Spirits of Water.
    Bi-IT:105
  The Sword of Surprise.
    G. Chesterton. Tr-MR:57,
    Un-MB:210
  The Teacher. L. Hill. Hu-PN:52
  A Thank-You. W. Canton.
    Gr-TG:42
  Thanks. N. Gale. Un-GT:245
  Thanksgiving. L. Driscoll.
    Ha-YA:134, La-PH:20
  Thanksgiving. R. Emerson.
    Au-SP:373, Bo-FP:161
  A Thanksgiving. J. Taylor.
    Gr-TG:70
  There Is an Umbrella.
    V. Cokeham. Le-M:60
  This Little Cloud, and This.
    Do-CH:(19)
  Three Elements. S. Benét. Pl-EI:183

To Agni. Al-PI:14
To Destiny. Pl-EI:184
To the Dawn. Al-PI:15
To the Sun-God. Tr-CB:52,
  Tr-US I:52
To the Supreme Being.
  Michelangelo. Pa-SG:198
To the Waters. Al-PI:17
To the Wind. Al-PI:16
The Unforeseen. C. Roxlo.
  Tr-MR:58
The Universal Prayer. A. Pope.
  Go-BP:271
Veni Sancte Spiritus. Ga-S:200
Very Close to Death. M. Saito.
  Sh-AM:144
Vespers. A. Milne. Ke-TF:77,
  Li-SR:62, Ox-BC:344
Vision and Prayer. D. Thomas.
  Wi-LT:553
We Are Living Humbly. Bi-IT:157
We Pray that the Beetles Appear.
  Le-OE:25
We Thank Thee. Fe-FP:29,
  Hu-MP:31
When Wilt Thou Save the People?
  E. Elliot. Hi-WP II:173,
  Pl-EI:157
White Floating Clouds. Ho-SD:29
Who First Began. D. Lindsey.
  Ba-PO:73
The Will-o'-the-Wisp.
  Tr-CB:31, Tr-US I:59
Without Ceremony. V. Miller.
  Un-MA:679
Women's Song for Fighting Men
  Delayed on a Raid. Tr-US I:95
Work. H. Van Dyke. Ke-TF:204,
  Se-PR:67, Th-AS:209
The Worm. C. Applegate. La-GI:54
The Wreckers' Prayer.
  T. Roberts. Co-SS:127
Zuñi Prayer at Sunrise. Da-SC:70
PRAYING MANTISES: see MANTISES
PREACHERS AND PREACHING:
    see also HUMOR - PREACHERS
    AND PREACHING; SERMONS
  The Circuit. D. Wagoner. Mo-BG:66
  The Deserted Village. O. Goldsmith.
    Al-VBP:585, Er-FA:410, Hi-FO:178
  Evangel. J. Burden. Ls-NY:147
  Legend of the Hills.
    L. Lorraine. De-FS:135
  A Revivalist in Boston.
    A. Rich. Pl-EI:107
  The Theology of Jonathan Edwards.
    P. McGinley. Un-MA:596
PRECIOUS STONES: see also names of
  precious stones, as PEARLS
  Flint. C. Rossetti. Ox-BC:277

Mine Argosy from Alexandria.
  C. Marlowe. Gr-CT:219
Precious Stones. C. Rossetti.
  Ar-TP3:210, De-TT:62, Un-GT:306
Ruby, Amethyst, Emerald, Diamond.
  De-CH:752
Yellow Stones on Sunday.
  Mo-TB:113
PREEXISTENCE
  Ode on Intimations of Immortality.
    W. Wordsworth. Al-VBP:662,
    Br-BC:18, Er-FA:157, Ga-FB:101,
    Gr-CT:436, Ha-PO:206, Ho-P:88,
    Ox-BN:84, Pa-GTB:308, Pl-EI:59
  Pre-Existence. F. Cornford.
    Mc-WK:107
  Sudden Light. D. Rossetti.
    Fe-PL:98, Ox-BN:681,
    Rv-CB:885, Un-MW:207
PREFERENCES: see CHOICES
PREGNANCY: see also
    ABORTION; THE UNBORN
  Fertility. Tr-US II:144
  For Karen. D. Hughes. Ls-NY:21
  Now that I Am Forever with
    Child. A. Lorde. Ad-PB:246
  Poem. C. Dropkin. Ho-TY:168
  Prayer of a Woman. J. Karni.
    Un-R:75
  The Pregnant Woman. Tr-US I:90
  Song of Joy. S. Vargus.
    Ad-II:50
  The Visitation. E. Jennings.
    Ca-MB:45
  With Child. G. Taggard.
    Un-MA:478
PREHISTORIC ANIMALS: see also
    DINOSAURS; HUMOR - PRE-
    HISTORIC ANIMALS
  Evolution. L. Smith.
    Er-FA:13
PREHISTORIC MAN: see MAN,
    PREHISTORIC
PREJUDICES AND ANTIPATHIES:
    see also DISCRIMINATION;
    HUMOR - PREJUDICES AND
    ANTIPATHIES; RACE
    PROBLEMS; SATIRE -
    PREJUDICES AND ANTIPATHIES
  Against Women Either Good or
    Bad. Al-VBP:72
  America. A. Ginsberg. Bl-FP:64
  As Soon as He Learned.
    D. Georgakas. Sc-TN:59
  The Color. J. Haines. Sc-TN:75
  Doctor Fell. Er-FA:216, Gr-CT:467,
    Mo-MGT:177, Pl-IO:119, Un-GT:22,
    Wr-RM:60
  Epitaph for a Bigot.
    D. Johnson. Hu-PN:226

PREJUDICES AND ANTIPATHIES — cont'd.
  Gangrene. P. Levine. Ca-VT:628
  Hatred of Men with Black Hair.
    R. Bly. Mc-EA:127
  He Rather Die. K. Jones.
    Jo-VC:55
  I Love Those Little Booths at
    Benvenutt's. G. Brooks.
    St-H:10
  Improvised Song Against a White
    Man. Tr-US I:118
  In Distrust of Merits. M. Moore.
    Al-VBP:1176, Pl-EI:146, Se-PR:207,
    Sm-PT:126, Un-MA:354, Wi-LT:272
  Jake Hates All the Girls.
    E. Cummings. Du-SH:65
  Jitterbugging in the Streets.
    C. Hernton. Ad-PB:240
  The Last Empty Seat.
    R. Goodkin. La-IH:112
  Manners. M. Van Rensselaer.
    Fe-FP:44, Hu-MP:16
  Negro Hero. G. Brooks. St-H:8
  Oh, Who Is That Young Sinner.
    A. Housman. Rv-CB:949
  Poor White. A. Planz. Lo-IT:104
  Prejudice. G. Johnson.
    Ad-PB:23, Bo-AN:24
  Ringless. D. Wakoski. Ho-P:287
  The Thoughts of a Child.
    D. Embry. La-IH:94
  Uptown. A. Ginsberg. Br-TC:150
  You've Got to Be Taught.
    O. Hammerstein II. Br-AF:46
PREMONITIONS
  Bad Moon Rising. J. Fogerty.
    Mo-GR:85
  Battle Song. Sitting Bull.
    Da-SC:113
  Before the Charge. P. MacGill.
    Cr-WS:90
  Foreboding. G. Code. De-FS:64
  Girl's Song. Tr-US II:306
  Gunnery Practice. J. Brinnin.
    Cr-WS:64
  The Hill. R. Brooke.
    Al-VBP:1178, Co-BL:165,
    Hi-WP II:109, Un-MB:322,
    Un-MW:171
  Ihunui's Lament for Her Daughter
    Rangi. Tr-US II:115
  The Lake: To —. E. Poe.
    Sh-AP:45
  Leaving the Monastery Early in the
    Morning. Lu Yu. Rx-OH:105
  The New House. E. Thomas.
    Un-MB:215
  Night Crow. T. Roethke.
    Ca-VT:287, Co-EL:38, Ho-LP:77,
    Re-BS:52, Sh-AP:213

  Night Train. R. Francis.
    Ar-TP3:84, Ha-LO:87
  1913. A. Akhmatova. Ca-MR:187
  Omen. Bi-IT:138, 139
  On a Friday Morn. De-TT:130
  Once by the Pacific. R. Frost.
    Ca-VT:17, Pa-HT:62, Sm-PT:78,
    Un-MA:184, Wi-LT:173
  The Owl. E. Thomas.
    Gr-CT:107, Ha-PO:105, Ni-JP:86,
    Pa-GTB:441, Re-BS:47
  A Poem for Emily. R. Cuscaden.
    St-H:33
  Poems for My Brother Kenneth.
    O. Dodson. Ad-PB:131,
    Hu-PN:304
  Presentiment. E. Dickinson.
    Co-EL:84, Ho-LP:77, Rv-CB:903
  Prophecy. W. Shedlofsky.
    De-FS:175
  The Shadow. G. Dusenbery.
    Sc-TN:37
  Shapes and Signs. J. Mangan.
    Co-PI:124
  The Sleeping House.
    A. Tennyson. Ox-BN:508
  Song for a Seated Dance:
    Victory of the Mea.
    Tr-US I:219
  Strange Fits of Passion.
    W. Wordsworth. Al-VBP:655,
    Ox-BN:61, Rv-CB:630
  There's Something Uneasy.
    I. Kharabov. Bo-RU:45
  To Any Member of My Generation.
    G. Barker. Al-VBP:1240,
    Wi-LT:529
  Today. L. Hughes. Ca-VT:240
  The Wolves. A. Tate. Wi-LT:409
PRESENT: see also
  SATIRE - PRESENT
  Burnt Norton. T. Eliot.
    Wi-LT:306
  The Good Old Days of Adam and
    Eve. Fi-BG:105
  Here and Now. C. Cater.
    Bo-AN:140, Hu-PN:340
  Love and Life. J. Wilmot.
    Al-VBP:503, No-CL:179
  Nostalgia. Yang Huan. Pa-MV:159
  The Sun-Dial. T. Peacock.
    Ox-BN:231
  The Train. Pien Chih-lin.
    Hs-TC:164
  Unfathomed Past. R. Tagore.
    Al-PI:88
PRESENTS: see
  GIFTS AND GIVING
PRESERVING: see
  CANNING AND PRESERVING

PRESIDENTS - UNITED STATES: see
HUMOR - PRESIDENTS - UNITED
STATES; SATIRE - PRESIDENTS -
UNITED STATES; and names of
Presidents, as LINCOLN,
ABRAHAM
PRESIDENTS - UNITED STATES -
INAUGURATION
God Save Our President.
F. Janvier. Vi-PP:70
Inauguration Day. R. Gilder.
Se-PR:38
PRESTER JOHN
Forty Singing Seamen.
A. Noyes. Pa-OM:197
PRETENDING: see MAKE-BELIEVE
PRETENSE: see AFFECTATION;
DECEPTION
PRETZELS
The Pretzel Man. R. Field.
Au-SP:148
PRIDE: see also DIGNITY;
HUMOR - PRIDE; SATIRE -
PRIDE; SELF-RESPECT
Auranomoi's Song of Praise for
His Bull Akorikono.
Tr-US I:107
Awareness. D. Lee. Ad-BO:2,
Ad-PB:421
The Bishop Orders His Tomb at
Saint Praxed's Church.
R. Browning. Al-VBP:895,
Mo-GR:57
Black Is Best. L. Thompson.
Ad-BO:2, Ad-PB:512
Black People. J. Bryant.
Jo-VC:53
Black Star Line. H. Dumas.
Ad-PB:269
Canto 4. T. Weatherly.
Ad-PB:397
Color. L. Hughes. Ad-BO:3
Cynddylan on a Tractor. R. Thomas.
Ga-S:123, To-MP:63
The Days of My People. M. Gill.
Jo-VC:54
Despisals. M. Rukeyser.
Ho-P:223
Do Not, Oh Do Not Prize.
Rv-CB:122
Do You Remember Me?
W. Landor. Al-VBP:707,
Ox-BN:188
Evarra and His Gods. R. Kipling.
Un-MB:134
A Game of Tag. Bo-FP:141,
Ir-BB:86
Half Black, Half Blacker.
S. Plumpp.
Ad-PB:385

I Hear America Singing.
W. Whitman. Ar-TP3:47,
Bo-FP:304, Br-AF:44, Co-PS:118,
Er-FA:289, Fe-FP:451, Ga-FB:247,
Hu-MP:369, La-PV:103, Mc-PR:33,
Sm-LG:40, Un-GT:306, Un-MA:40,
Vi-PP:185
I Saw Someone Just like Me.
T. Heard. Me-WF:44
I, Too, Sing America. L. Hughes.
Ad-PB:75, Be-MA:40, Bo-AN:64,
Ca-VT:239, Fe-PL:159, Hu-PN:182
Invitation to Drink and the Reply.
Tr-US I:145
Leave Me Alone. M. Lasanta.
Ba-HI:16
The Lion and the Cub. J. Gay.
Sp-OG:305
The Little Duck. Joso. Au-SP:54,
Le-IS:9, Su-FVI:72
My Blackness Is the Beauty of
This Land. L. Jeffers.
Ad-PB:173
My Soul Speaks Spanish.
M. Lasanta. Jo-VC:49
The Mysterious Cat. V. Lindsay.
Ar-TP3:54, Au-SP:33, Bo-GJ:88,
Co-IW:12, Fe-FP:158, Gr-CT:119,
Hu-MP:167, Ir-BB:174, Pe-FB:10,
Th-AS:42
The Newer Vainglory. A. Meynell.
Tr-MR:218
The Old Cloak. Ma-BB:226
One Thousand Nine Hundred &
Sixty-Eight Winters. J. Earley.
Ab-MO:93, Jo-SA:127
poem. S. Sanchez. Ad-PB:288
Poem for Flora. N. Giovanni.
Ad-PB:456, Ne-AM:34
Pride Is Out. Rv-CB:16
The Princess of Scotland.
R. Taylor. Gr-SS:123
Proud Maisie. W. Scott.
De-CH:339, Gr-CT:364, Ox-BN:136,
Pa-GTB:229, Rv-CB:655, Sm-LG:269
Proud Margret. Ox-BB:74
The Proud Navajo. P. Kee.
Ba-HI:21
Proud of My Broken Heart.
E. Dickinson. Al-VBP:1002
Proud Word You Never Spoke.
W. Landor. Al-VBP:707
The Question. V. Howard. Jo-VC:45
The Reeve's Tale. G. Chaucer.
Al-VBP:12
Revolt. Rachel. Me-PH:87
Song. Tr-US I:123
The Song of the Banana Man.
E. Jones. Co-RM:242, Sa-B:101,
To-MP:168

PRIDE — cont'd.
  Speed. W. Davies. Tr-MR:268
  The Thoughts of a Child.
    D. Embry. La-IH:94
  Throughout the World. Ho-SD:18,
    Le-OE:24
  To a Louse. R. Burns.
    Al-VBP:629, Co-BBW:221,
    Er-FA:71, Ma-YA:131, Sp-OG:300
  To Dianeme. R. Herrick.
    Al-VBP:326, Pa-GTB:76, Rv-CB:335
  Truth. W. Cowper. Co-BBW:267
  224 Stoop. V. Cruz. Ad-BO:68
  Vive Noir! M. Evans. Ad-PB:188
  WALK TALL MY BLACK CHILDREN.
    S. Boone. La-IH:114
  What's Black Power. L. Baez.
    Jo-VC:47
  The Wife of Bath. G. Chaucer.
    Ha-PO:53, Hi-WP II:122
  Wisdom. Tr-CB:17
  The Woman of Three Cows.
    Co-PI:125
  Worms and the Wind. C. Sandburg.
    Mc-WK:48, Pa-RE:51, Rd-OA:93
  Yes, I Am a Negro. J. West.
    La-IH:96
PRIESTS: see also CLERGY;
    HUMOR - PRIESTS
  The Ballad of Father Gilligan.
    W. Yeats. Hi-WP I:72,
    Mc-WK:132, Mc-WS:157,
    Pl-EI:114, Un-MB:112
  Ballad of the Priest of Rudeni.
    G. Topirceanu. Mc-AC:49
  Beneath This Yew. Co-PU:155
  The Choice. J. Masefield.
    Un-MB:229
  The Confessional (Spain).
    R. Browning. Al-VBP:885
  Eddi's Service. R. Kipling.
    Go-BP:41
  Father O'Flynn. A. Graves.
    Co-PI:54
  Morning at the Temple of Kobai.
    E. Shiffert. Ls-NY:257
  On a Mountain Top.
    K. Nakamura. Sh-AM:147
  Tanka. M. Ota. Sh-AM:141
  Ten of Chaucer's People:
    A Parson. G. Chaucer.
    Go-BP:42, Ha-PO:53
  Vendor. R. Roseliep.
    De-FS:157, St-H:179
  The Wolf Has Come. Wy-CM:42
PRIMITIVE MAN: see names
    of primitive tribes
    and peoples
PRIMITIVE RELIGIONS: see
    RELIGIONS, PRIMITIVE

PRIMROSES
  The Evening Primrose. J. Clare.
    De-CH:434
  Peep-Primrose. E. Farjeon.
    Br-SG:6
  The Primrose. R. Herrick.
    Al-VBP:327
  To a Primrose. J. Clare.
    Ma-FW:10
  To an Early Primrose. H. White.
    Ox-BN:230
  To Primroses Filled with Morning
    Dew. R. Herrick.
    Al-VBP:329
PRINCES AND PRINCESSES: see also
    HUMOR - PRINCES AND PRINCESSES
  After All and after All.
    M. Davies. Ar-TP3:117,
    Hu-MP:68, Th-AS:148
  The Azra. H. Heine. Un-R:93
  Castles and Candlelight.
    J. Reeves. Co-PT:183
  I Had a Little Nut-Tree.
    An-IP:(20), Ar-TP3:154, Au-SP:24,
    Br-FF:(34), De-CH:186, De-TT:19,
    Gr-EC:294, Gr-GB:18, Ir-BB:264,
    Li-LB:33, Mo-MGT:148, Rv-CB:453,
    Sm-MK:7
  The King of China's Daughter.
    E. Sitwell. De-CH:186,
    Ir-BB:258, Ma-FW:185,
    Pa-RE:23, Un-MB:331
  King Tekla Haimont Learns that
    His Daughter Mentaub Has Been
    Captured by the Enemy.
    Tr-US I:112
  The King's Young Dochter.
    De-CH:602
  Look! Ge-TR:27
  Sheath and Knife. De-CH:54
  Sons of the Kings. J. Agnew.
    Br-BC:62
  The Whummil Bore. De-CH:329
PRINTING: see also
    HUMOR - PRINTING; PROOFREADING
  Avenger, What Wrong? J. Rorty.
    Sm-PT:128
  News. E. Auerbach. Ho-TY:299
PRISONS AND PRISONERS: see also
    CONCENTRATION CAMPS; CRIME
    AND CRIMINALS; HUMOR -
    PRISONS AND PRISONERS;
    SATIRE - PRISONS AND
    PRISONERS; and names of
    prisons and prisoners, as
    ATTICA, N.Y., BONNIVARD,
    FRANCOIS DE
  Ashima. Hs-TC:447
  At the Railway Station,
    Upway. T. Hardy. Ma-FW:71

The Ballad of Reading Gaol.
  O. Wilde. Al-VBP:1072,
  Er-FA:87, Ox-BN:896, Un-MB:70
Big Man. M. Mason. Hu-PN:524
Birmingham Jail. Er-FA:235,
  Gr-GB:264
Brazilian Happenings.
  R. O'Connell. Du-SH:97
Capital Punishment. O. Wilde.
  Hi-WP II:22
The Captive. R. Kipling.
  Go-BP:53
Captivity. S. Rogers. Ox-BN:47
Cell Song. E. Knight. Ad-PB:228
The Convict of Clonmel.
  Co-PI:16, Mo-SD:174
Even Now. . . . Bilhana.
  Al-PI:48, Pa-SG:65
find my father with freedom.
  L. Curry. Jo-VC:38
Girl Held Without Bail.
  M. Walker. Ad-PB:148,
  Ra-BP:156
The Gaol Song. Gr-GB:263
Haiku 1, 3. E. Knight. Ra-BP:206
Hyperion. J. Keats. Ox-BN:365
The Idea of Ancestry. E. Knight.
  Ad-PB:229, Be-MA:108, Ra-BP:203
If Suddenly You Come for Me.
  N. Nor. Bo-RU:54
In Prison. W. Morris. Rv-CB:928
Inscription for the Tank.
  J. Wright. Br-TC:487
Inscription from a Convict's
  Cell. Co-RM:164
The Isle of Portland.
  A. Housman. Un-MB:102
King Tekla Haimont Learns that
  His Daughter Mentaub Has Been
  Captured by the Enemy.
  Tr-US I:112
The Lament of the Border Cattle
  Thief. R. Kipling. Co-RM:159
Listen. Ai Ch'ing. Hs-TC:297
Mary, Queen of Scots. R. Burns.
  Hi-FO:125
Message to Siberia. A. Pushkin.
  Lo-TY:68
My Friends. R. Service.
  Co-RM:137
Ode to Brother Joe. T. McNeill.
  Sa-B:154
Pardon. B. Krasnoff. Ad-II:87
Portrait. A. Dugan. Ha-TP:49
The Prisoner. M. Ana.
  Co-BP:213
The Prisoner. E. Brontë.
  Ox-BN:607
The Prisoner. D. Mahon.
  Co-PI:118

The Prisoner. R. Rilke.
  Go-BP:213
The Prisoner of Chillon.
  G. Byron. Fe-PL:22
The Prisoners. S. Spender.
  Un-MB:473
The Ropewalk. H. Longfellow.
  Mo-BG:12
Samson Agonistes. J. Milton.
  Al-VBP:413, Ga-S:47
san francisco county jail cell b-6.
  Conyus. Ad-PB:400
Serenade of a Loyal Martyr.
  G. Darley. Ox-BN:395
Sonnet on Chillon. G. Byron.
  Ma-YA:173, Pa-GTB:209
Sonnets, vii. G. Santayana.
  Sm-PT:135
Southern Road. S. Brown.
  Ad-PB:67, Be-MA:29, Ra-BP:111
The State Has Need of Me.
  L. Batshev. Bo-RU:14
Stir the Wallaby Stew. Hi-FO:253
Stone Walls. R. Lovelace.
  Hi-WP I:113
To Althea from Prison.
  R. Lovelace. Al-VBP:445,
  Ha-PO:173, Ke-TF:100, Ma-YA:101,
  Pa-GTB:81, Rv-CB:394, Un-MW:133
To Karelana. V. Batshev.
  Bo-RU:13
Toussaint L'Ouverture.
  J. Carew. Sa-B:11
Words, Words. M. Mertsalov.
  Bo-RU:51
The Workhouse Boy. Gr-GB:265
Written on a Prison Wall.
  Tai Wang-shu. Hs-TC:184
PRIVACY: see also
  HUMOR - PRIVACY
  The Call of Himself. A. Freeman.
    Br-TC:131
  Eulogy for Populations.
    R. Welburn. Ad-PB:467
  Kindly Refrain. Br-FW:11
  Open to Visitors. E. Milner.
    Co-EL:105
  Talk. D. Lawrence. Cl-FC:21
  Trespass. R. Frost. Ga-FB:286
  We Live in a Cage. W. Harris.
    Ad-PB:438
PRIZE FIGHTING: see BOXING
PRIZES: see REWARDS
PROBLEMS AND SOLUTIONS: see also
  HUMOR - PROBLEMS AND SOLUTIONS;
  SATIRE - PROBLEMS AND SOLUTIONS
  Dinner Guest: Me.
    L. Hughes. Ra-BP:78
  The Great Magicians.
    C. Day Lewis. Pl-EI:82

PROBLEMS AND SOLUTIONS — cont'd.
  The Image. R. Fuller. Pa-GTB:526
  Man Flies Through the Universe.
    M. Goode. Jo-VC:5
  Problems. C. O'John. Al-WW:65
  This Hour. O. La Grone.
    Hu-NN:37, Hu-PN:327
  U.S. Mail. F. Mastin. Ke-TF:302
PROCESSIONS: see PARADES
PROCNE (MYTH.)
  Procne. P. Quennell.
    Un-MB:426, Wi-LT:632
PROCRASTINATION: see also
    HUMOR - PROCRASTINATION
  Around the Corner. C. Towne.
    Fe-PL:128
  Around the World. K. Greenaway.
    Ch-B:85, Fe-FP:38
  But That Was Yesterday.
    A. Fisher. Au-SP:203
  Going to Bed. M. Chute.
    Ho-GC:42, La-PP:66, La-PV:20
  Lose This Day Loitering.
    J. von Goethe. Fe-PL:438
  The Prince's Progress.
    C. Rossetti. Al-VBP:995
  The Slow Starter. L. MacNeice.
    To-MP:89
  Three Things. Un-GT:306
  Tomorrow I'll Reform.
    B. Franklin. Un-GT:25
PRODIGAL SON
  The Prodigal. E. Bishop.
    Br-TC:52, Wi-LT:514
  The Prodigal Son. E. Robinson.
    Un-MA:136
PROFESSORS: see SCHOLARS AND
    SCHOLARSHIP; TEACHERS AND
    TEACHING
PROFITS: see SATIRE - PROFITS
PROGRESS: see also HUMOR -
    PROGRESS; SATIRE - PROGRESS
  Blackman/an unfinished history.
    D. Lee. Be-MA:161
  Conquest. E. Coatsworth.
    Br-AF:59, Fe-FP:411, Hu-MP:362
  Corruption. H. Vaughan.
    Ho-P:296
  Dark Symphony: Tempo di Marcia.
    M. Tolson. Bo-AN:40
  Dark Symphony: Tempo Primo.
    M. Tolson. Bo-AN:39
  Life. Lu Li. Hs-TC:422
  Measure Me, Sky. L. Speyer.
    Ad-PE:46, Br-BC:129,
    Fe-FP:22, Hu-MP:63
  Once to Every Man and Nation.
    J. Lowell. Vi-PP:68
  Progress. E. Agnew.
    Br-AF:233

  Signatures. C. Stevenson. Br-AF:28
  Verse on the Wall. Chang Chih-min.
    Hs-TC:431
PROMETHEUS
  Epistle to Prometheus.
    B. Deutsch. Sm-PT:81
PROMISES: see also LOVE - PROMISES
  After the Flood Went Down. Bible.
    O.T. Genesis. Gr-TG:73
  America Was Promises. A. MacLeish.
    Br-AF:250, Vi-PP:229
  America's Answer. R. Lilliard.
    Vi-PP:215
  Around the World. K. Greenaway.
    Ch-B:85, Fe-FP:38
  Black-Eyed Susan. J. Gay. Co-RG:82,
    Co-SS:66, De-TT:129, Pa-GTB:124
  Broken-Face Gargoyles.
    C. Sandburg. Un-MA:207
  The Fortress. A. Sexton.
    Pe-OA:275, Wi-LT:814
  Gifts for a Good Boy. De-PP:20
  Grief of a Girl's Heart.
    A. Gregory. Co-BL:128, Gr-CT:76
  If I Were a Queen.
    C. Rossetti. Br-SS:118
  Judgment and Sunrise. Bible.
    O.T. Malachi. Me-PH:53
  A Legacy. J. Tabb. Mc-PR:147
  The Love of King David and the
    Fair Bethsabe. G. Peele.
    Al-VBP:137
  Morning Prayer. O. Nash. Ox-BC:349
  Mulholland's Contract.
    R. Kipling. Co-SS:210
  My Mamma Has Been Clever.
    Anya. Mo-MI:59
  My Mother Sent Me for Some
    Water. Sp-HW:6
  Pippen Hill. Bl-OB:34, Ir-BB:214,
    Mo-MGT:141, Wr-RM:26
  A Promise Made. Er-FA:215
  Promises of Freedom. Ra-BP:5
  The Rubaiyat of Omar Khayyam.
    E. Fitzgerald. Gr-CT:329,
    Pa-GTB:329
  She Vowed Him This. W. Box.
    Gr-BT:90
  Stopping by Woods on a Snowy Evening.
    R. Frost. Ad-PE:31, Al-VBP:1134,
    Ar-TP3:198, Bo-FP:170, Bo-GJ:257,
    Br-SS:88, Br-TC:135, Cl-DT:20,
    Co-BN:151, Co-PS:160, De-CH:625,
    Er-FA:257, Fe-FP:67, Ga-FB:299,
    Gr-EC:273, Ha-PO:90, Ke-TF:420,
    La-PP:29, La-PV:167, Ma-FW:276,
    Mc-PR:124, Mc-WK:32, Pe-FB:80,
    Re-TW:123, Sh-AP:150, Sh-RP:52,
    Sm-LG:63, Sm-PT:8, Un-MA:187,
    Wi-LT:174

Tamurlaine the Great. C. Marlowe.
   Al-VBP:175
To Chuck—Concerning a Rendezvous
   in Siam. J. Charles. Mc-WK:198
To Destiny. Pl-EI:184
What Is This. Le-OE:19
Why Are Promises.   Re-RR:88
Will You? K. Greenaway.
   Br-SS:122
PRONUNCIATION: see
   HUMOR - PRONUNCIATION
PROOFREADING: see
   HUMOR - PROOFREADING
PROPERTY: see also
   HUMOR - PROPERTY;
   SATIRE - PROPERTY
The House. W. Williams.
   Ca-VT:50
Kindly Refrain.   Br-FW:11
Real Property. H. Monro.
   Co-BN:136, Go-BP:171
Trespass. R. Frost.   Ga-FB:286
The Woman of Three Cows.
   Co-PI:125
PROPHETS AND PROPHECIES:
   see also ASTROLOGY; FORTUNE
   TELLING; HUMOR - PROPHETS
   AND PROPHECIES; PREMONITIONS;
   SATIRE - PROPHETS AND
   PROPHECIES
Advice to a Prophet. R. Wilbur.
   Tr-MR:233, Un-MA:677
Balaam. J. Keble. Ox-BN:304
A Basket of Summer Fruit.
   Bible. O.T. Amos. Me-PH:49
Boadicea. W. Cowper. Hi-FO:56
Cassandra. R. Jeffers. Wi-LT:266
Clarel. H. Melville. Ba-PO:91
The Coming Messiah. Bible. O.T.
   Isaiah. Ba-PO:75, Ga-S:57
The End of the World. Bible.
   O.T. Jeremiah. Ba-PO:48,
   Ke-PP:2
For I Dipped into the Future.
   A. Tennyson. Fe-PL:432
For Out of Zion. Bible. O.T.
   Isaiah. Ba-PO:75
I Sought a Vision. Ho-SD:14
Judgment and Sunrise. Bible.
   O.T. Malachi. Me-PH:53
Locksley Hall. A. Tennyson.
   Er-FA:56
The Luck of Edenhall.
   H. Longfellow. Co-PT:151
My Name Is John Wellington
   Wells. W. Gilbert. Co-PM:72
Noah. H. Hagedorn. Tr-MR:66
The Oracles. A. Housman. Co-RG:24
Prince of Peace. Bible. O.T.
   Isaiah.   Go-BP:283

The Prophecies Against Moab, Judah,
   and Israel. Bible. O.T. Amos.
   Me-PH:48
The Prophecy Against Egypt. Bible.
   O.T. Isaiah. Me-PH:41
Prophecy of Pech, Priest of
   Chichen-Itzá. Da-SC:163
The Prophet. A. Pushkin.
   Pl-EI:98
Prophets for a New Day.
   M. Walker. Ra-BP:160
Proud Maisie. W. Scott.
   De-CH:339, Gr-CT:364, Ox-BN:136,
   Pa-GTB:229, Rv-CB:655, Sm-LG:269
Rebecca. V. Andreyev. Ca-MR:97
Ritual of the Priest Chilan.
   Bi-IT:141, Br-MW:27, Da-SC:162
So Long! W. Whitman. Sh-AP:111
Subversive. W. Benét. Tr-MR:116
Vision of Belshazzar. G. Byron.
   Co-RG:3, Hi-FO:30, Pa-OM:115
Watchman, What of the Night?
   A. Swinburne. Ho-WR:200
PROPOSALS: see MARRIAGE
   PROPOSALS
PROSERPINA
The Garden of Proserpine.
   A. Swinburne. Al-VBP:1028,
   Ga-FB:138, Gr-CT:262, Ox-BN:802
The Garden of Proserpina.
   E. Spenser. Gr-CT:263
Hymn to Proserpine. A. Swinburne.
   Hi-FO:58, Ox-BN:797
PROSPECTING: see also
   HUMOR - PROSPECTING;
   MINERS AND MINING
A Ballad about Nuggets.
   Y. Yevtushenko. Ca-MR:57
Sunstrike. D. Livingstone.
   To-MP:165
The Wolf Mountain Stampede.
   Fi-BG:60
PROSPERITY: see also
   SATIRE - PROSPERITY;
   SUCCESS; WEALTH
We Pray that the Beetles Appear.
   Le-OE:25
PROTECTION: see also
   HUMOR - PROTECTION;
   SATIRE - PROTECTION
Birthday Sonnet. E. Wylie.
   Un-MA:280
Chorus. W. Auden. Pa-GTB:509,
   Un-MB:450
Color. R. Bennett. Hu-MP:185
For a Child Named Katherine.
   L. Nicholl. Th-AS:16
A Frosty Night. R. Graves.
   Ca-MB:15, De-CH:215, Un-MB:388
The Golden Net. W. Blake. Gr-SS:166

PROTECTION — cont'd.

A Good-Night. F. Quarles.
Rd-SS:41

His Shield. M. Moore. Wi-LT:275

The Hollow Land. W. Morris.
Gr-CT:48, Re-TW:80

The House. R. Young Bear.
Ni-CD:292

I Will Lift Up Mine Eyes.
Bible. O.T. Psalms.
Bo-FP:305, Cl-DT:43, Rv-CB:129

A Mighty Fortress Is Our God.
M. Luther. Pl-EI:213

The Nesting Ground. D. Wagoner.
En-PC:249

Noon Hour. J. Finnigan.
Gr-BT:115

The North Wind and the Child.
Bo-FP:174

The Paper Nautilus. M. Moore.
Ca-VT:127

Prayer of a Woman. J. Karni.
Un-R:75

Protection Song. Da-SC:90

Psalm Concerning the Castle.
D. Levertov. Br-TC:256

The Reason. D. Aldis.
Ar-TP3:167

The River-God's Song. J. Fletcher.
Fe-FP:274, Re-TW:44, Rv-CB:312

Songs in Praise of the Chief.
Do-CH:(42)

The Spirit Walking. Ho-SD:6,
Le-OE:111

To Destiny. Pl-EI:184

To Nowhere. D. Ignatow.
Ad-CI:44

The Tortoise in Eternity.
E. Wylie. Fe-FP:145, Ho-LP:48,
Pl-IO:18, Rd-OA:150

The Tree. A. Hopewell. Pa-RE:123

PROTEST: see also BLACK PANTHERS;
CONSCIENTIOUS OBJECTORS;
COUNTER CULTURE; DISSENT;
SATIRE - PROTEST; STRIKES

Ain' Go'n' to Study War No Mo'.
Ba-PO:167

The Air Is Dirty. G. Thompson.
Jo-SA:10, Jo-VC:73

Alabama Centennial. N. Madgett.
Ra-BP:197

America. A. Ginsberg. Bl-FP:64

April 4, 1968. M. Goode.
Jo-SA:6, Jo-VC:57

The Articles of War. R. Francis.
Cr-WS:64

Bad Bishop Jegon. Gr-GB:186

Bang. J. Blair. Ad-II:96

Barricades. M. Harper.
Ad-PB:316

Black Warrior. N. Jordan.
Ad-PB:322

A Boy. B. Graves. Le-M:142

Bremerton, January 18, 1969.
A. Pratt. Al-WW:99

Cable Cars. S. Tsuboi. Sh-AM:71

Childe Harold. M. Kulbak.
Ho-TY:205

The Children. T. McNeill.
Sa-B:211

A Christmas Banquet.
C. Lushington. Sa-B:53

A Coat. W. Yeats. Pl-ML:33,
Wi-LT:69

Come Live with Me and Be My
Love. C. Day Lewis. No-CL:111

Commission. E. Pound. Br-TC:329

Conscientious Objector.
E. Millay. Ba-PO:4, Cr-WS:137

The Conscientious Objector.
K. Shapiro. Ba-PO:166,
Pe-SS:140

The Country of a Thousand Years
of Peace. J. Marrill. En-PC:240

Crispus Attucks McCoy. S. Brown.
Ra-BP:115

A Curse. B. Gibson. Ba-PO:170

Damn! E. Jenkins. Ad-II:23

The Days of My People.
M. Gill. Jo-VC:54

Deathwatch. M. Harper. Ad-PB:317

Democracy. A. Rimbaud. Ba-PO:173

Dirge Without Music. E. Millay.
Ke-PP:80, Tr-MR:266

Disarmament. J. Whittier.
Ba-PO:103, Cr-WS:157

Do Not Trust the Disciples.
D. Samoilov. Bo-RU:72

The Duel. E. Dickinson.
Li-TU:172

Eighth Air Force. R. Jarrell.
En-PC:140, Mo-BG:172

Epitaph. Ba-PO:72

Expression. I. Rosenberg.
Un-MB:350

The Factory Girl's Come-All-Ye.
Em-AF:766

Farewell and No. J. Adoum.
Be-UL:109

A Flat One. W. Snodgrass.
En-PC:244, Wi-LT:822

For G. W. Gordon. B. Smith.
Sa-B:224

for h. w. fuller. C. Rodgers.
Ra-BP:262

Girl Held Without Bail. M. Walker.
Ad-PB:148, Ra-BP:156

Good Night, Wide World.
J. Glatstein. Ho-TY:333

Goya. A. Voznesensky. Ca-MR:68

The Grass on the Mountain.
    Bo-HF:34
the greedy the people.
    E. Cummings. Pe-OA:155
High on the Hog. J. Fields.
    Be-MA:154
How High the Moon. L. Jeffers.
    Ad-PB:172
Howl. A. Ginsberg. Sh-AP:233
I Ain't Marchin' Any More.
    P. Ochs. Ba-PO:199
I Am a Negro. M. Al-Fituri.
    Lo-TY:54
If. R. Gutman-Jasny. Ho-TY:297
In Any Soul There Is a Bright
    Country. A. Yaskolka.
    Bo-RU:91
In the Mourning Time.
    R. Hayden. Ra-BP:138
Irish Curse on the Occupying
    English. M. MacEntee.
    Co-PI:112
Is This Life? H. Harrington.
    Ba-HI:82
It Happened in Montgomery.
    O. Petrie. Ab-MO:86
It Is Time. T. Joans. Hu-NN:34
Jail. T. Barnes. La-IH:131
Lamentations. S. Sassoon.
    Cr-WS:119
Let Me Alone. Bible. O.T.
    Job. Ke-PP:4
The Lie. W. Raleigh. Al-VBP:95,
    Gr-CT:372, Ke-PP:16, Rv-CB:157
The Lion and O'Reilly.
    R. Weber. Ke-PP:19
The Lions of Fire Shall Have
    Their Hunting. K. Patchen.
    Ba-PO:159, Ca-VT:343
Listening to Foxhounds.
    J. Dickey. Ha-WR:78
London. S. Johnson.
    Al-VBP:553, Gr-CT:303
Malcolm. S. Sanchez. Be-MA:134
Manifesto of Man.
    Y. Galanskov. Bo-RU:29
Many Die Here. G. Jones.
    Jo-SA:14
March on the Delta. A. Berger.
    Lo-IT:9
Midway. N. Madgett.
    Be-MA:93, Hu-NN:39, Hu-PN:381,
    Jo-SA:126, Kr-OF:53, Ra-BP:197
Militant. L. Hughes. Ad-PB:80
Milton. W. Blake. Al-VBP:622,
    Ga-FB:223, Ha-PO:206, Hi-FO:251,
    Ke-PP:132, Na-EO:32, Ox-BN:40,
    Pl-EI:162, Rv-CB:612, Sm-LG:135
Monument in Black. V. Howard.
    Jo-SA:3, Jo-VC:43

The Moral Warfare. J. Whittier.
    Vi-PP:231
Mourn Not the Dead. R. Chaplin.
    Al-VBP:1147, Ba-PO:146,
    Cr-WS:120, Kr-OF:117
My Blackness Is the Beauty of
    This Land. L. Jeffers. Ad-PB:173
My People. D. Palmer. Sc-TN:175
Negro Hero. G. Brooks. St-H:8
Newsletter from My Mother.
    M. Harper. Ad-PB:315
No Matter if You Remain
    Unaffected by. B. Patten.
    Gr-BT:129
Norman Morrison. D. Ferguson.
    Ba-PO:34
O the Beatniks Never Win.
    C. Larsen. Lo-IT:71
Odell. J. Stephens. Un-MB:265
Of Late. G. Starbuck.
    Ca-VT:667, Cr-WS:136
On Thanksgiving for a National
    Victory. R. Burns. Ba-PO:192
Our New National Anthem.
    W. Eggleston. Ba-PO:80,
    Cr-WS:155
Panther Man. J. Emanuel. Ra-BP:192
Papa, Mama. C. Belli. Be-UL:115
The Plot to Assassinate the
    Chase Manhattan Bank.
    C. Larsen. Ke-PP:67
Poem. J. Fields. Be-MA:151
Poem. J. Sloman. Sc-TN:200
Poem to Be Cast into the Sea
    in a Bottle. J. Kirkup.
    Go-BP:217
Poem to Czechoslovakia.
    M. Tsvetayeva. Ca-MR:139
Port Authority Terminal:
    9 a.m. Monday. C. Walsh.
    Ke-PP:62
Pray for Rain. M. Williams.
    Sa-B:180
A Protest in the Sixth Year of
    Chi'en Fu. Ts'ao Sung. Ga-FB:193
The Rage That Shatters Man into
    Children. C. Vallejo. Be-UL:41
The Revolutionary. V. Watkins.
    Ls-NY:118
The Rickshaw Puller. Cheng Min.
    Hs-TC:233
Riot. G. Brooks. Ad-PB:164,
    Ra-BP:175
St. Dexter's Fire. D. Etter.
    Sc-TN:43
Security. R. Tucker. Ke-PP:121
The Silent Generation.
    L. Simpson. Hi-TL:224
Sing Me a New Song.
    J. Clarke. Ad-PB:143

PROTEST — cont'd.
Soul, Scorning All Measure.
M. Tsvetayeva.   Ca-MR:136
Speech to the Court.
W. Lowenfels.   Ke-PP:120
Spring Poem: Brown's Town.
T. McNeill.   Sa-B:209
Street Demonstration. M. Walker.
Ra-BP:156
There Is Power in a Union.
J. Hill.   Hi-TL:164
The Third Sermon on the Warpland.
G. Brooks.   Ra-BP:176
This Hour. O. La Grone.
Hu-NN:37, Hu-PN:327
This Morning the Sun.   O. Cabral.
Ke-PP:103
To My Generation.
A. Onyezhskaya.   Bo-RU:61
To the Dead. Hu Feng.   Hs-TC:376
To Those Born After. B. Brecht.
Un-R:41
Tommy. R. Kipling.   Ga-FB:209,
Un-MB:127
Until They Have Stopped.
S. Wright.   Ad-PB:215
Variations on a Line from
Shakespeare's Fifty-Sixth
Sonnet. E. Mayo.   En-PC:70
The War God. S. Spender.
Tr-MR:180
We Can Be Together.
P. Kantner.   Mo-GR:105
We Have Been Believers.
M. Walker.   Ad-PB:145,
Be-MA:76, Hu-PN:312, Jo-SA:130
White Magic. W. Braithwaite.
Hu-PN:49
Who First Began. D. Lindsay.
Ba-PO:73
Why. J. Velez.   Ba-HI:119
Why I Voted the Socialist Ticket.
V. Lindsay.   Un-MA:234
Why Prejudice. B. Chase.
Ba-HI:24
Winter in the City.
Wang Ya-p'ing.   Hs-TC:351
Yes, I Am a Negro. J. West.
La-IH:96
See also Kr-OF
PROUST, MARCEL
Marcel Proust. W. Smith. Ls-NY:149
PROVENÇAL VERSE
Bel M'es quan Lo M'alena.
A. Daniel.   Pa-SG:70
The Happy Shepherd. No-CL:99
PROVENCE, FR.: see also
PROVENÇAL VERSE
A Visit to Van Gogh.
C. Causley.   En-PC:158

PROVERBS: see also EPIGRAMS;
FOLKLORE; HUMOR - PROVERBS;
SAYINGS AND SIGNS
A Baker's Duzzen uv Wize Saws.
E. Sill.   Er-FA:214
For Want of a Nail.   Gr-EC:130,
Ir-BB:134, Li-LB:166, Mo-MGT:132,
Mo-NR:103, Un-GT:305, Wr-RM:101
Four Things.   Bible.   O.T.
Proverbs. Fe-FP:124, Un-GT:30
Gnomic Verse from Cotton
Manuscript. Ma-YA:4
A Promise Made.   Er-FA:215
A Proverb.   Co-BL:55
Proverbs. B. Franklin.
Un-GT:25-26
Proverbs of King Alfred.
King Alfred.   Mc-WK:222
St. Gregory's Day.   Bo-FP:217
Thirty-Three Triads.   Co-PI:87
Today Well, Tomorrow Cold in
the Mouth. J. Gill.   Sc-TN:66
Where There's a Will There's
a Way. E. Cook.   Er-FA:26
PRUNING
Pruning Trees. Po Chu-i.
Ma-FW:107, Pa-SG:169
PSALMS (ABOUT)
The Psalms of David . . . Are
Ended. M. Taylor.   Ke-TF:210
PSYCHE (MYTH.)
Ode to Psyche. J. Keats.
Al-VBP:773, Ox-BN:357, Rv-CB:743
Ulalume. E. Poe.   Al-VBP:869,
Sh-AP:58
PSYCHOANALYSIS: see also
HUMOR - PSYCHOANALYSIS
Analysands. D. Randall.   Ra-BP:139
PSYCHOLOGY: see HUMOR - PSYCHOLOGY
PTARMIGANS
The Ptarmigan. Co-BBW:241
PUBLIC OPINION: see
SATIRE - PUBLIC OPINION
PUBLIC SPEAKING: see
HUMOR - PUBLIC SPEAKING
PUBLICITY: see
SATIRE - PUBLICITY
PUDDINGS: see also
HUMOR - PUDDINGS
Address to a Haggis. R. Burns.
Al-VBP:633
The Christmas Pudding.
Ar-TP3:192, La-PH:35
Flour of England.
Ir-BB:51, Mo-MGT:155,
Wr-RM:55
The Hasty Pudding. J. Barlow.
Sm-LG:121
Three Cooks.   Ir-BB:37,
Mo-MGT:75

When Good King Arthur Ruled.
Bo-FP:53, Br-FF:(6), De-TT:93,
Ir-BB:272, Li-LB:50, Mo-MGT:168,
Mo-NR:54, On-TW:13
PUERTO RICANS
My Soul Speaks Spanish.
M. Lasanta. Jo-VC:49
You're Nothing but a Spanish
Colored Kid. F. Luciano.
Ad-PB:501
PUERTO RICANS IN THE
UNITED STATES
Puerto Ricans in New York.
C. Reznikoff. Kh-VA:60
PUERTO RICO
The Land. V. Cruz. Lo-IT:26
Spanish Waters. J. Masefield.
Fe-FP:514, Mc-WK:141, Pa-OM:207
PUFFINS: see also
HUMOR - PUFFINS
Three Little Puffins. E. Farjeon.
Ar-TP3:125, Lo-LL:1
PUGILISM: see BOXING
PUMAS: see PANTHERS
PUMPKINS: see also HALLOWEEN;
HUMOR - PUMPKINS
Building Pumpkin Trellis.
Hs-TC:453
Corn Ceremony. Da-SC:83
Frowning Jack. L. Blair.
Ja-HH:39
Jack o'Lantern. A. Ayre.
Au-SP:371
Judging by Appearances.
A. Poulsson. Hu-MP:342
Little Jack Pumpkin Face.
Bo-FP:156
The Magic Vine. Br-SG:83
The Pumpkin. R. Graves.
Br-SG:41, Co-PM:76,
Ir-BB:65, La-PV:67
The Pumpkin. S. Orlov. Mo-MI:22
The Pumpkin. J. Whittier.
Co-PS:148, Se-PR:210
Pumpkin Face. L. Blair. Ja-HH:38
A Pumpkin Speaks. A. Barris.
Bo-FP:145
Pumpkins. J. Cotton. Co-BN:139
Theme in Yellow. C. Sandburg.
Ar-TP3:186, Ha-YA:120, Hu-MP:263,
Li-LC:77, Sh-RP:226
What Am I? D. Aldis. Au-SP:369,
Ir-BB:53, La-PH:15
PUNCH AND JUDY: see PUPPETS
PUNCTUALITY
The Alarum. S. Warner.
Un-MB:372
Cocks Crow in the Morn.
Ar-TP3:174, Sp-TM:1,
Un-GT:22, Wr-RM:78

A Dillar, a Dollar.
Ar-TP3:131, De-PO:18, Er-FA:505,
Li-LB:43, Mo-MGT:152, Mo-NR:60,
Wi-MG:26, Wr-RM:94
Do It Now. Er-FA:24
He That Would Thrive. Ir-BB:229,
Mo-MGT:131, Sp-TM:1
Lightly Stepped a Yellow Star.
E. Dickinson. Un-MA:101
Punctuality. Mo-MGT:133
Tardiness. G. Burgess. Co-BB:36
PUNCTUATION: see HUMOR - PUNCTUATION
PUNISHMENT: see also EXECUTIONS
AND EXECUTIONERS; HUMOR -
PUNISHMENT; PRISONS AND
PRISONERS; RETRIBUTION;
SATIRE - PUNISHMENT
The Ballad of Semmerwater.
W. Watson. Bl-OB:81
A Basket of Summer Fruit. Bible.
O.T. Amos. Me-PH:49
The Black Martyr. R. Dickens.
La-IH:106
The Boy Who Laughed at Santa
Claus. O. Nash. Co-BB:16,
Ha-PO:291
Bump, Bump, Please Go Away.
Wy-CM:36
Character Building. E. Anthony.
Un-GT:26
The Cold Heaven. W. Yeats.
Pa-GTB:423
The End of the World. Bible.
O.T. Jeremiah. Ba-PO:48,
Ke-PP:2
Eve. C. Rossetti. De-CH:466,
Pa-GTB:375
In Dessexshire as It Befell.
Gr-GB:316
The Inky Boys. H. Hoffman. De-TT:21
Jack Jelf. Wr-RM:45
Jim Jones at Botany Bay.
Co-RM:139, Gr-GB:257
Little Polly Flinders. Mother
Goose. Li-LB:26, Mo-MGT:87,
Mo-NR:90, Wi-MG:64, Wr-RM:26
Nick Spence. Ir-BB:28
Pussy-Cat Mew. Bo-FP:30,
Ir-BB:167, Wr-RM:83
The Queen of Hearts.
An-IP:(24), Bo-FP:54,
Br-FF:(26), Ir-BB:263,
Li-LB:56, Mo-MGT:122, Mo-NR:59,
Wi-MG:71, Wr-RM:107
The Revenge of Hamish. S. Lanier.
Ni-JP:46, Sp-OG:141
Skipper Ireson's Ride.
J. Whittier. Co-SS:147,
Fe-PL:45, Hi-TL:73,
Sh-AP:40, Sp-OG:226

PUNISHMENT — <u>Cont'd</u>.
There Was a Little Girl.
H. Longfellow. An-IP:(12),
Bl-OB:29, Co-BB:69, De-PO:12,
Er-FA:492, Fr-WO:28, Mo-MGT:200,
Na-EO:168, Ox-BC:226, Sm-LG:99,
Un-GT:101, Wi-MG:45, Wr-RM:84
There Was a Presbyterian Cat.
Sm-LG:77
This Little Fellow. Wy-CM:13
Tom, Tom, the Piper's Son.
Li-LB:34, Mo-MGT:22, Mo-NR:64,
Wi-MG:7, Wr-RM:77
Upon Pagget. R. Herrick.
Sm-LG:111
You, North Must Go.
Ir-BB:17, St-FS:32
PUNS
After Oliver. O. Herford.
Co-HP:22
All Wool. A. Brown. Ar-TP3:123
As I Was Going o'er Yon Moor of
Moss. De-CH:676
Baby Kate. J. Newman. Co-HP:100
Baby Toodles. J. Newman.
Co-BB:50
Boston, Lincolnshire. Gr-GB:174
A Branch Library. J. Flagg.
Br-LL:102
The Briefless Barrister.
J. Saxe. Br-SM:39
A Briton Who Shot at His King.
D. Ross. Br-SM:26
A Canner. Exceedingly Canny.
C. Wells. Br-LL:69, Fe-FP:364,
Un-GF:46
Career. D. Pettiward. Ir-BB:39
Cautionary Verses to Youth of
Both Sexes. T. Hook. Ox-BC:157
A Certain Young Gallant Named
Robbie. Br-LL:21
A Certain Young Man of Great
Gumption. Br-LL:78, Br-SM:82
Cold Logic. B. Hutchinson.
Mo-SD:142
A Collegiate Damsel Named Breeze.
Br-LL:103, Un-GT:242
Courtship. L. Carroll.
Br-LL:122, Un-GT:242
Courtship. C. Wells. Br-LL:123,
Un-GT:241
Courtship. Br-LL:123, Un-GT:241
The Cow Slips Away. B. King.
Co-HP:85, Gr-EC:195
A Doctor Fell in a Deep Well.
Br-SM:49, Un-GT:243
The Duel. Br-SM:22
The Dutiful Mariner. W. Irwin.
Co-SS:91
Epitaph. R. Armour. Br-SM:55
Epitaph on John Knott. Br-SM:157,
Gr-CT:13
Faithless Nelly Gray. T. Hood.
Br-SM:33, Co-HP:78, Hi-WP I:100
A Fishy Square Dance. E. Merriam.
Gr-EC:116
A Flea and a Fly in a Flue.
Br-LL:9, Ch-B:113, Co-HP:29,
Fe-FP:365, Gr-EC:196, Ju-CP:14,
Lo-LL:49, Mc-WS:179, Un-GT:241
Flight. W. Walden. Ls-NY:329
A Handsome Young Noble of Spain.
Br-LL:32, Un-GF:44, Un-GT:242
Henry Ward Beecher. O. Holmes.
Br-LL:25, Gr-CT:31
How Much Wood Would a Woodchuck
Chuck. Ar-TP3:123, Fe-FP:358,
Ir-BB:188, Ju-CP:14
A Hymn to God the Father.
J. Donne. Al-VBP:264, Ga-S:137,
Pi-EI:206
I Don't Know. Ja-PC:52
I Have to Be a Lively Hood.
T. Hood. Un-GT:95
It Isn't the Cough. Br-SM:136,
Er-FA:218
It Was Shut. J. Greenleaf.
Co-OW:62
Japanesque. O. Herford.
Co-FB:209, Co-HP:74
The Jellyfish. O. Nash.
Co-OH:25, Fe-FP:341
Little Willie. Br-SM:47, 49,
Mc-WS:173, Sm-MK:202, Un-GT:243
The Lost Egg. P. Ilott.
Gr-EC:158, Ir-BB:63
Manila. E. Ware. Co-FB:124
Mary's Ghosts. T. Hood.
Co-FB:143, Co-PT:35, Sm-MK:106
Melancholetta. L. Carroll.
Co-FB:182
The Microbes. Co-HP:24
Motto for a Dog House.
A. Guiterman. Co-PU:21
Neither Hillaryous Norgay.
G. Lewis. Co-FB:388
No! T. Hood. Bl-OB:99,
Co-FB:435, Co-HP:78, Gr-CT:392,
Mc-PR:51, Un-GT:280
On a Dentist. Un-GT:238
On a Man Named Meredith.
Un-GT:238
On Dr. Lettsom, by Himself.
J. Lettsom. Co-PU:122
On His Books. H. Belloc.
Un-MB:172
On Leslie Moore. Un-GT:238
On Martha Snell. Bl-OB:154,
Un-GT:239
On Samuel Pease. Br-SM:157

One Day I Went Out to the Zoo.
G. Johnson.   Br-LL:32
The Opportune Overthrow of
Humpty Dumpty.   G. Carryl.
Co-BB:20
Pa Followed the Pair to Pawtucket.
Chicago Tribune.   Br-LL:120
A Paradox.   Br-SM:84
Ruth and Johnnie.   Br-SM:56
Said a Great Congregational
Preacher.   Un-GF:43, Un-GT:240
Sally Simpkin's Lament.
T. Hood.   Br-SM:57
She Frowned and Called Him Mr.
Br-LL:123, Fe-FP:361, Un-GT:241
Silly Girl.   E. Jay.   Ja-PC:35
Similia Similibus.   J. Morgan.
Br-SM:111
Some Questions to Be Asked of a
Rajah.   P. Newman.
Co-FB:419, Co-HP:101
Spring Comes to Murray Hill.
O. Nash.   Co-FB:358
Stately Verse.   Ar-TP3:134,
Co-HP:25, Fe-FP:363
The Sunset.   H. Leigh.   Un-GF:65
The Swift Bullets.   C. Wells.
Br-SM:54, Ja-PC:28
Tame Animals I Have Known.
N. Waterman.   Co-OW:61
Theological.   C. Fadiman.
Co-FB:131
There Once Was a Young Man
Named Hall.   Br-SM:53
There Was a Young Fellow Named
Hall.   Br-LL:73, Sm-MK:201
There Was a Young Lady from
Woosester.   Br-LL:70
There Was an Old Man of Nantucket.
Princeton Tiger.   Br-LL:120,
Ke-TF:289
Tim Turpin.   T. Hood.   Ho-WR:84
To Minerva.   T. Hood.   Co-FB:338
The Train Pulled in the Station.
Co-OW:50
A Tutor Who Tooted the Flute.
C. Wells.   Co-HP:119, Ke-TF:288,
Lo-LL:49, Mc-WS:175, Un-GF:46,
Un-GT:241
What a State.   L. Blair.   Ja-PC:30
When a Jolly Young Fisher Named
Fisher.   Br-LL:79
Wills.   J. Saxe.   Br-SM:126,
Er-FA:216
The Window Pain.   G. Burgess.
Un-GF:64
See also Re-RR, Rs-PF
PUPPETS: see also HUMOR - PUPPETS
The Marionette.   I. Feldman.
Ls-NY:318

Punch and Judy.   Mo-MGT:43
The Puppet Play.   P. Colum.
Co-RG:166
Variations.   R. Jarrell.   Ca-VT:400
Young Master's Account of a
Puppet Show.   J. Marchant.
Ox-BC:63
PUPPIES: see DOGS
PURCELL, HENRY
Henry Purcell.   G. Hopkins.
Pl-US:80
On the Death of Mr. Purcell.
J. Dryden.   Pl-US:78
PURGATORY: see also
HUMOR - PURGATORY
Confession - Gate of Purgatory.
Dante Alighieri.   Ga-S:139
Presences Perfected.
S. Sassoon.   Un-MB:318
PURITANS AND PURITANISM:
see also HUMOR - PURITANS
AND PURITANISM; SATIRE -
PURITANS AND PURITANISM;
and names of puritans, as
BRADSTREET, ANNE; MATHER,
COTTON
At the Indian Killer's Grave.
R. Lowell.   Ca-VT:443
The Fairies' Farewell.
R. Corbet.   Al-VBP:289,
De-CH:564, Na-EO:61,
Rv-CB:321, Sm-LG:223
Homage to Mistress Bradstreet.
J. Berryman.   Sh-AP:225
Jonas Kindred's Household.
G. Crabbe.   Ox-BN:15
The Puritan.   K. Shapiro.
Un-MA:635
A Puritan Lady.   L. Reese.
Un-MA:111
Puritan Sonnet.   E. Wylie.
Pe-OA:86, Sh-AP:170, Un-MA:277
PURPLE (COLOR)
Violet Spring.   Chi Hsüan.
Pa-MV:48
PURSUIT: see HUNTING;
LOVE - PURSUIT
PUSHKIN, ALEKSANDR SERGEYEVICH
Monument to Pushkin.
I. Brodsky.   Bo-RU:22
PUSSY WILLOWS
April Fool!   B. Lee.   Ja-HH:20
Catkin.   Au-SP:308, Hu-MP:260,
Ir-BB:22, St-FS:29
Little Catkins.   A. Blok.
Pl-EI:181
Pussy Willow Song.   Co-OW:53
Pussy-Willows. A. Fisher. Sh-RP:200
Pussy Willows.   M. Plummer.
Hu-MP:272

PUTNAM, ISRAEL
  Death and General Putnam.
    A. Guiterman. Co-PM:77,
    Co-RM:219, Cr-WS:55
PYLOS: see NAVARINO, BATTLE, 1827
PYRAMUS AND THISBE: see
    HUMOR - PYRAMUS AND THISBE
PYTHAGORAS
  Among School Children.
    W. Yeats. Pa-GTB:428,
    Un-MB:114, Wi-LT:72
PYTHONS: see HUMOR - PYTHONS
QUACKS AND QUACKERY
  Witch Doctor. R. Hayden.
    Bo-AN:110
QUAILS
  As Evening Falls. Shunzei.
    Ba-ST:39
  Bob White. G. Cooper.
    Hu-MP:226, Un-GT:60
  Bobwhite. R. Hillyer.
    Co-BBW:254
  Quail Song. Da-SC:90, Le-OE:51
QUAKERS: see FRIENDS, SOCIETY OF
QUAKING ASPEN TREES: see
    ASPEN TREES
QUARRELS: see also FIGHTS AND
    FIGHTING; HUMOR - QUARRELS
  Camp Fever. J. Blight. Co-RM:96
  Clinton South of Polk.
    C. Sandburg. Br-AF:42
  Coffee and Tea. Wr-RM:83
  Comparison. J. Bunyan.
    De-CH:734
  Discord in Childhood. D. Lawrence.
    Co-EL:147, Rv-CB:978
  Fable. R. Emerson. Bo-FP:71,
    Bo-GJ:26, Bo-HF:69, Ch-B:27,
    Er-FA:496, Fe-FP:530, Ga-FB:317,
    Hu-MP:210, Pa-OM:333, Rd-OA:91,
    Sh-AP:27, Sp-OG:303, Un-GT:57
  In Going to My Naked Bed.
    R. Edwards. Rv-CB:102
  Infidelities. D. Scott. Sa-B:3
  Love Lies a-Bleeding.
    F. Eckman. St-H:54
  The Lovers. W. Rodgers.
    Hi-WP II:147
  Parting after a Quarrel.
    E. Tietjens. Co-BL:137
  Party Line. J. Keith. De-FS:119
  The Quarrel. C. Aiken. Un-MA:430
  The Quarrel. E. Farjeon.
    Fe-FP:41
  Quarrels Never Could Last Long.
    B. Franklin. Un-GT:25
  The Society upon the Stanislaus.
    B. Harte. Co-RM:22
  Squabbles. Mo-MGT:210, Wr-RM:98
  Young Benjie. Ox-BB:337

QUARRYING
  In the Marble Quarry. J. Dickey.
    Br-AF:137
QUASARS
  Quasi-Stellar Radio Sources.
    H. McCord. Ls-NY:323
QUÉBEC, CAN.: see also
    HUMOR - QUÉBEC, CAN.
  Québec May. E. Birney.
    Do-WH:75
QUÉBEC, BATTLE, 1759
  Montcalm and Wolfe. Em-AF:419
QUEEN ANNE'S LACE
  I Need No Sky. W. Bynner.
    Pl-EI:3
  Queen Anne's Lace. M. Newton.
    Fe-FP:219, Hu-MP:257, Th-AS:80
  Queen Anne's Lace. W. Williams.
    Un-MA:256
  Wild Carrot. J. Moreland.
    Ls-NY:47
QUEENS: see KINGS AND RULERS;
    and names of queens, as
    ELIZABETH I, QUEEN OF ENGLAND
QUESTIONS AND ANSWERS: see also
    CURIOSITY; HUMOR - QUESTIONS
    AND ANSWERS; SATIRE -
    QUESTIONS AND ANSWERS
  Advice to a Prophet. R. Wilbur.
    Tr-MR:233, Un-MA:677
  After the Visit. T. Hardy.
    Ox-BN:835
  All Revelation. R. Frost.
    Sm-PT:169
  Alone. M. Hiers. La-IH:72
  At the Bottom of the Well.
    L. Untermeyer. Bo-GJ:218
  Aunt Selina. C. Haynes.
    Hu-MP:15, Ja-PC:44
  Baby. G. Macdonald. Br-BC:14,
    Er-FA:485, Fe-FP:528, Hu-MP:7
  Before Exeter Church.
    Hsü Chih-mo. Hs-TC:81
  But How It Came from Earth.
    C. Aiken. Un-MA:434
  Came You Not from Newcastle?
    Gr-GB:100
  Casual Lines. Yü P'ing-po.
    Hs-TC:18
  Cause and Effect. M. Swenson.
    Ha-TP:97
  Channel Crossing. G. Barker.
    Pa-GTB:533
  Christmas Lullaby for a New-
    Born Child. Y. Gregory. Bo-AN:153
  Clootie. Ma-BB:94
  The Crematory. Chung Ting-wen.
    Pa-MV:78
  Curiosity. H. Behn.
    Au-SP:349

The Cutty Wren.   Gr-GB:63,
  Rv-CB:418, Rv-ON:117
Despair.   I. Takenaka.   Sh-AM:100
Dialogue.   Tr-US I:156
A Dialogue at Dusk.
  Pien Chih-lin.   Hs-TC:160
A Disappearance in West Cedar
  Street.   L. Sissman.   Br-TC:383
The Doctor Who Sits at the Bedside
  of a Rat.   J. Miles.   Ca-VT:339
The Dunce.   W. de la Mare.
  Pl-IO:137
An Epicurean Ode.   J. Hall.
  Gr-SS:49
Expostulation and Reply.
  W. Wordsworth.   Rv-CB:640
The False Knight upon the Road.
  De-CH:316, Gr-GB:288
For Arvia.   E. Robinson.
  Br-BC:149
For Vicki at Seven.   S. Russell.
  Br-BC:150
The Giant Turtle Grants an
  Interview.   J. Brinnin.
  Be-EB:46
God's Education.   T. Hardy.
  Tr-MR:221
Granny.   Ca-MU:16
Hard Questions.   M. Tsuda.
  La-RM:172
How Shall I Get Inside the Door.
  Un-R:97
The Humming Stair.   J. Brennan.
  De-FS:32
I Don't Know Why.
  M. Livingston.   Br-SG:81
I Want to Know. J. Drinkwater.
  Fe-FP:7
I Wonder Why.   E. Lee.   Ba-HI:115
Interrogative. Sister M. Thérèse.
  Tr-MR:228
Is My Team Ploughing. A. Housman.
  Ha-PO:12, Hi-WP I:22, Un-MB:95,
  Un-MW:119, Wi-LT:61
Isabel Sparrow.   M. Oliver.
  Ls-NY:145
I've Got to Know.   W. Guthrie.
  Pe-SS:142
Jig Time: Not for Love.
  T. McGrath.   Ca-VT:427
John Brown.   V. Lindsay. Un-MA:227
A Knight Came Riding from the
  East.   Bl-OB:39
Little Boy.   Gr-GB:169, Mo-MGT:62,
  Rv-ON:70
Love and a Question.   R. Frost.
  Ca-MB:16
Ma Canny Hinny.   Gr-GB:155
March 18.   Jao Meng-k'an.
  Hs-TC:106

Meet-on-the-Road.   Bl-OB:84,
  Co-PM:208, De-CH:674
Moment.   D. Berrigan.   Be-EB:41
Mother's Party.   A. Fisher.
  Br-BC:17
My Life.   J. Bryant.   Jo-VC:87
The New Neighbor.   R. Fyleman.
  Ar-TP3:10, Au-SP:132
No Reply.   S. Van Ryte.   Me-WF:40
Oh Why? M. Fletcher. Me-WF:23
Once a Child.   E. Dickinson.
  Pl-IO:21
Poem.   S. Clarke.   Sa-B:105
Portrait of a Lady.   W. Praed.
  No-CL:235
Pudden Tame.   Gr-CT:27
A Question.   R. Frost.   Ho-TH:46
The Question.   T. Kucherenko.
  Mo-MI:84
The Question.   F. Prince.
  Pa-GTB:528
Question.   M. Swenson.   Ca-VT:480,
  Wi-LT:829
A Question.   De-PP:24
A Question.   Rv-CB:136
Question and Answer.
  K. Raine.   Un-MB:484
The Question in the Cobweb.
  A. Reid.   Mc-WK:114
Questions of a Studious Working
  Man.   B. Brecht.   Sm-MK:224
Prattle.   J. Ciardi.   Br-BC:109
Rat Riddles.   C. Sandburg.
  Be-EB:60, La-OC:102
Sea-Sand and Sorrow.
  C. Rossetti.   Gr-CT:193
Son and Father.   C. Day Lewis.
  Pl-EI:135
Song of a Marriageable Girl.
  Tr-CB:40, Tr-US I:62
Special Starlight.   C. Sandburg.
  Tr-MR:101
Stopping.   C. Scott.   Ad-II:30
Teddy's Wonderings.   J. Bangs.
  Br-BC:109
To Be Answered in Our Next
  Issue.   Mc-WK:111
To Clarissa Scott Delany.
  A. Grimke.   Bo-AN:15
The Twa Brothers.   De-CH:52,
  Ox-BB:234
Unison.   J. Wheelock.   Tr-MR:144
The Universe.   M. Swenson.
  Ha-TP:131
What in the World?   E. Merriam.
  Gr-EC:14
What Were They Like?
  D. Levertov.   Ba-PO:33,
  Ca-VT:517, Cr-WS:53,
  Ke-PP:38, Kr-OF:94

QUESTIONS AND ANSWERS — cont'd.
  What's in There? Mo-MGT:176,
    Pa-RE:74, Rv-ON:72
  When Delia on the Plain Appears.
    G. Lyttleton. Rv-CB:528
  Where Am I Going? L. Hargrove.
    Ba-HI:122
  Where Did You Come from, Baby
    Dear? G. Macdonald.
    Ox-BC:273
  Who Am I? F. Holman. La-RM:162
  Why. V. Howard. Ba-HI:120
  Why. J. Velez. Ba-HI:119
  Why. L. Wolf. Ho-TY:222
  Why Did I Laugh Tonight?
    J. Keats. Rv-CB:751
  Why Do They Stare? W. Rountree.
    La-IH:93
  Why Isn't the World Happy?
    R. Lewis. Ba-HI:117
QUESTS: see also
    HUMOR - QUESTS;
    LOVE - PURSUIT
  An Abandoned Road to the Chi-Ming
    Temple. Ch'en Meng-chia.
    Hs-TC:115
  Comparison. J. Bunyan.
    Ox-BC:36
  Death Song of a Song Maker.
    Le-OE:118
  Debate Question, Quarry Dream.
    R. Warren. Ca-VT:277
  Eldorado. E. Poe. Ho-WR:248,
    Mc-PR:177, Mc-WK:174, Mo-BG:11,
    Pa-HT:153, Sh-RP:284, Sm-LG:204
  Facing West from California's
    Shores. W. Whitman. Un-MA:70
  The Flaming Circle. J. Maraj.
    Sa-B:86
  Four Quartets. T. Eliot. Pl-IO:6
  Further West. Fi-BG:111
  Heart's Content. Fe-PL:146
  The Heart's Desire Is Full of
    Sleep. R. Pitter. Go-BP:223
  Home-Sickness. J. Kerner.
    Pa-SG:138
  I Know Not What I Seek Eternally.
    R. de Castro. Pa-SG:137
  I Want to Find the Essence.
    B. Pasternak. Mo-MI:31
  I Thought It Was Tangiers I
    Wanted. L. Hughes.
    Bo-HF:84, Hu-PN:196
  i wish i could stay with you
    awhile. D. Witt.
    Ad-II:35
  In Search of a Bright Star.
    Hsü Chih-mo. Hs-TC:86
  In the Night Fields.
    W. Merwin. En-PC:258

  The Key of the Kingdom. Bl-OB:158,
    De-CH:3, Er-FA:202, Gr-EC:292,
    Ho-P:107, Mo-MGT:133, Re-TW:32,
    Rv-CB:31, Sm-LG:237, Sp-AS:(10)
  The Little Girl Found.
    W. Blake. Rv-CB:593
  A Living Pearl. K. Rexroth.
    Wi-LT:798
  The Lost Tribe. R. Pitter.
    Ho-LP:80
  Number 5 - December. D. Henderson.
    Ad-BO:69, Jo-SA:84
  Prayer. L. Untermeyer.
    Un-GT:308, Un-MA:305
  Prelude. C. Aiken. Br-TC:5
  Psalm. T. Arghezi. Mc-AC:30
  Roadways. J. Masefield.
    Pa-HT:78, Sh-RP:157
  Running to Paradise. W. Yeats.
    Ha-LO:13
  The Seekers. J. Masefield.
    Go-BP:224
  A Song. Fang Ching. Hs-TC:385
  The Song of Wandering Aengus.
    W. Yeats. Ar-TP3:161, Bl-OB:91,
    Bo-GJ:142, Co-BL:165, Co-PM:196,
    De-CH:280, Gr-SS:46, Ha-LO:52,
    Ha-PO:180, Ho-LP:14, Ma-YA:230,
    Mc-WK:7, Mc-WS:33, No-CL:68,
    Re-TW:28, Sm-LG:226, Sm-MK:30,
    Th-AS:200, Un-GT:127, Un-MB:108
  Sonnet. J. Masefield.
    Un-MB:228, Wi-LT:191
  Space. W. Burford. Ho-LP:81
  The Stars Have Departed.
    C. Okigbo. Ab-MO:6
  Suzanne. L. Cohen. Mo-GR:33
  To Somewhere. L. Nathan.
    Ls-NY:96
  Tony O. C. Francis. Bl-OB:19,
    Ch-B:72, Co-PU:147, De-CH:357
  The Untold Want. W. Whitman.
    Un-MA:87
  What Did I Lose? Sun Yü-t'ang.
    Hs-TC:119
  Where? K. Patchen. Wi-LT:786
  The White Goddess. R. Graves.
    Un-MB:391
  Who Is That a-Walking in the
    Corn? F. Johnson.
    Gr-CC:145, Hu-PN:92
QUETZALS
  Listen! Ge-TR:13
  A Song of Lamentation. Ba-PO:27,
    Bi-IT:137, Da-SC:175
QUICKSAND: see SAND
QUIETNESS: see also HUMOR -
    QUIETNESS; SILENCE
  The Anchorage. P. Wilson. Co-SS:172
  Autumn. R. Tagore. Go-BP:26

Bearded Oaks. R. Warren.
  Br-TC:451, Sh-AP:211,
  Un-MA:589, Wi-LT:840
Beyond Stillness. Kyorai.
  Be-MC:42
The Breathing. D. Levertov.
  Ha-WR:73, La-RM:135
A Butterfly's. K. Takahama.
  Sh-AM:163
Calm. M. Drayton. De-TT:73
A Cave. J. Kirkup. Go-BP:32
Deep in a Windless Wood.
  Buson. Be-MC:49
A Dewy Tree Trunk. K. Takahama.
  Sh-AM:163
Early Morning. J. Jiménez.
  Le-SW:67
The Ecstasy. C. Lewis.
  Go-BP:174
Evening Landscape. P. de Mont.
  Pa-SG:109
Extremes. J. Riley.
  Bo-FP:18, Ch-B:80, Fe-FP:104,
  Gr-EC:201, Hu-MP:55
Feather or Fur. J. Becker.
  Ar-TP3:65, Bo-FP:75, Fe-FP:121,
  Ma-FO:(1), Sh-RP:25
Give Me Peace. A. Voznesensky.
  Gr-BT:148
The Goat Paths. J. Stephens.
  Ad-PE:30, Bo-GJ:56, De-CH:149,
  Go-BP:93, Rd-OA:55
High Noon! A Hot Sun. Hajime.
  Ca-BF:15
The House Was Quiet and the
  World Was Calm. W. Stevens.
  Ca-VT:40
How Still, How Happy! E. Brontë.
  Ox-BN:598
The Hush-Hush. M. Saito.
  Sh-AM:145
Immense Hour. J. Jiménez.
  Pa-SG:166
In Memoriam. A. Tennyson.
  Gr-CT:315, Hi-WP II:143,
  Ox-BN:495
It Is a Beauteous Evening.
  W. Wordsworth. Al-VBP:659,
  De-CH:738, Fe-PL:403, Gr-CT:195,
  Pa-GTB:273, Rv-CB:646
It Is Our Quiet Time.
  Wo-HS:(26)
Lightning Flickering. Basho.
  Be-CS:10
The Mirror. A. Milne.
  Gr-EC:268
The Mouse. M. Stephenson.
  St-FS:41
Nemea. L. Durrell.
  Pa-GTB:525

Ode on Solitude. A. Pope.
  Al-VBP:529, Er-FA:248, Go-BP:45,
  Ho-P:48, Ma-FW:85, Mc-PR:203,
  Ni-JP:137, Pa-GTB:110, Rv-CB:510
Over Coarse Rock in the Middle of
  the Square. A. Machado.
  Le-SW:63
Peace and Rest. W. Davies.
  Go-BP:29
The Plants Stand Silent round Me.
  J. Jorgensen. Ho-LP:22,
  Pa-SG:155
Q Is for Quietness. P. McGinley.
  La-OC:31
The Quiet Flower. J. Johnson.
  Tr-MR:221
Quiet Night. Liu Ta-pai.
  Hs-TC:8
Quiet Please. E. Hilsabeck.
  Mc-AW:18
Quiet Things. G. Crowell.
  Fe-PL:308
The Recollection. P. Shelley.
  Ox-BN:300, Pa-GTB:270
Repose of Rivers. H. Crane.
  Un-MA:518, Wi-LT:396
Resurrection. Fang Hsin.
  Pa-MV:87
Riding at Daybreak. Sun Yun Feng.
  Le-MW:39, Ma-FW:129
River Travel. Ts'ui Hao.
  Le-MW:82
Sea Calm. L. Hughes.
  Ha-LO:69, Li-TU:210
"Sh." J. Tippett. Ar-TP3:3
Silence. W. Williams. Re-BS:53
The Sleeper. W. de la Mare.
  Un-MB:198
Snow. A. Wilkins. Ar-TP3:190,
  Mc-AW:96
The Snow Fall. A. MacLeish.
  Ha-LO:51
Snowy Morning. L. Moore.
  Un-GB:11
Solitude. A. Lampman.
  Co-BN:148, Rv-CB:955
Song for a Summer Afternoon.
  V. Miller. Ca-BP:46
The Spring Waters. Ping Hsin.
  Hs-TC:23
A Still Day. J. Cherwinski.
  Sh-RP:196
Stillness. Chora. Le-IS:17
Stillness. M. Leaso. Le-M:130
A Summer's Day. A. Hume.
  De-CH:136
The Sun Is a Globe of Fire.
  A. Machado. Le-SW:45
The Sunken Garden.
  W. de la Mare. Cl-DT:69

QUIETNESS — cont'd.
  Sunset. E. Muir. Go-BP:29
  Tanka. M. Ota. Sh-AM:141
  Thoughts in a Garden.
    A. Marvell. Ga-S:22
  The Tired Man. A. Wickham.
    Sm-MK:25, Un-MW:57
  Up Here Is Quiet. Wo-HS:(47)
  Variations. F. Garcia Lorca.
    Le-SW:57
  Virginia. T. Eliot.
    Ha-PO:94, Sm-LG:142
  Waiting. Le-MW:59
  Wayfarer's Evensong.
    J. von Goethe. Un-R:29
  A Wise Old Owl Lived in an Oak.
    Er-FA:213, Li-LB:103, Mo-MGT:118,
    Un-GT:22, Wi-MG:47
  Wisteria Trellis. Fang Hsin.
    Pa-MV:84
QUILTS: see BEDS AND BEDDING
QUIXOTE, DON: see DON QUIXOTE
RA (EGYPTIAN GOD)
  The Dead Man Ariseth and Singeth
    a Hymn. The Book of the Dead.
    Pa-SG:210
  The Hymn to the Sun. Ab-MO:3,
    Lo-TY:21
RABBITS: see also HUMOR -
    RABBITS
  Annus Mirabilis. J. Dryden.
    Co-BBW:46
  Belief. E. Jay. Ja-HH:27
  Birthdays. M. Chute.
    Br-BC:78, Br-SS:48
  Bye, Baby Bunting. Mother
    Goose. Ar-TP3:131, Au-SP:5,
    Cl-DT:27, De-PO:6, Li-LB:12,
    Li-SR:126, Mo-NR:8, Wi-MG:16,
    Wr-RM:77
  Do Rabbits Have Christmas?
    A. Fisher. Mc-AW:82
  Done For. W. de la Mare.
    Bl-OB:131
  Down a Sunny Easter Meadow.
    N. Turner. Au-SP:363,
    Br-SS:140
  Dream Song. J. Berryman.
    Br-TC:38
  Easter Morning. A. Fisher.
    La-PH:52
  Fireflies. W. Welles. Rd-SS:38
  Four-Footed Poems. E. Greenberg.
    Ho-TY:312
  Four Things. Bible. O.T.
    Proverbs. Fe-FP:124, Un-GT:30
  The Hare. W. de la Mare.
    Ar-TP3:62, Sp-OG:299, Tu-WW:98
  Hares at Play. J. Clare.
    Rd-OA:44, Rv-CB:717

  The Hart. Gr-EC:282, Gr-GB:53,
    Mo-MGT:191, Rv-CB:448, Rv-ON:99,
    Sm-LG:291, Wr-RM:75
  Legs like a Kangaroo. Re-RR:52
  Medicine Songs. Tr-US II:267
  Meeting the Easter Bunny.
    R. Bennett. Ar-TP3:203,
    Au-SP:365, Br-SS:139
  Mr. Rabbit. D. Wilson. Fr-MP:21
  Mister Rabbit. Bu-DY:40
  Noah and the Rabbit.
    H. Chesterman. Rd-OA:12
  On a Hare. W. Cowper. Bl-OB:121,
    Co-BBW:47, Go-BP:94
  One, Two, Three, Four, Five.
    Ar-TP3:103, On-TW:56
  The Outdoor Christmas Tree.
    A. Fisher. Br-SS:102
  The Persimmon Tree. Gr-GB:71
  The Porcupine Asked the Rabbit.
    Gr-BB:18
  The Rabbit. A. Brownjohn.
    To-MP:109
  The Rabbit. W. Davies.
    Hi-WP I:32
  The Rabbit. G. Durston.
    Au-SP:58
  The Rabbit. E. King. Au-SP:58
  The Rabbit. P. McIntyre. Le-M:96
  The Rabbit. E. Millay.
    Co-BBW:28
  The Rabbit. E. Roberts.
    Ar-TP3:61, Au-SP:59, Br-SG:63,
    Co-BBW:23, Hu-MP:201, La-PP:50,
    Ma-FO:25, Pe-FB:8, Tu-WW:102,
    Un-GT:55
  Rabbit. T. Robinson. Fe-FP:166
  Rabbit and Lark. J. Reeves.
    St-FS:101
  The Rabbit as King of the Ghosts.
    W. Stevens. Rd-OA:143, Re-TW:20
  The Rabbit Hunter. R. Frost.
    Be-EB:28, Ho-TH:46
  The Rabbit Leaves. D. Schmitz.
    St-H:196
  The Rabbit Man. Mo-MGT:114
  Rabbits. D. Baruch. Au-SP:61
  Rabbits. R. Fabrizio. Sm-MK:156
  The Rabbits. Bo-FP:75
  The Rabbits' Song Outside the
    Tavern. E. Coatsworth. Ar-TP3:62
  Resolution and Independence.
    W. Wordsworth. Co-BN:214,
    Ma-FW:36, Ox-BN:71, Rv-CB:654
  Round About, Round About. Mo-TL:23
  The Snare. J. Stephens. Ad-PE:22,
    Ar-TP3:62, Bl-OB:130, Co-BBW:21,
    Co-IW:28, De-CH:89, Gr-EC:32,
    La-PP:51, La-PV:151, Mc-WS:44,
    Se-PR:300, Sm-MK:159, Th-AS:50

A Story in the Snow. P. Crouch.
 Ar-TP3:62, Au-SP:60, Hu-MP:322
Three Riddles: When. B. Swann.
 Mo-TS:79
Time for Rabbits. A. Fisher.
 La-PH:50
To a Starved Hare in the Garden
 in Winter. C. Turner. Sm-MK:182
To Three Small Rabbits in a
 Burrow. M. Kennedy. Co-BBW:34
Twin Lakes Hunter. A. Guthrie.
 Du-RG:127, Ha-PO:143
Two Songs of a Fool. W. Yeats.
 Rd-OA:14
Vice Versa. C. Morgenstern.
 Rd-OA:36
What in the World? E. Merriam.
 Gr-EC:14
The White Rabbit. E. Rieu.
 Sm-MK:198
White Season. F. Frost.
 Ar-TP3:62, Co-BBW:38, Fe-FP:167
Why Rabbits Jump. De-PP:50
Yolp, Yolp, Yolp, Yolp. Rd-OA:50
RACCOONS: see also
 HUMOR - RACCOONS
Babies: Just Babies.
 M. Fishback. Gr-EC:21
Mill Valley. M. Livingston.
 La-RM:156
The Persimmon Tree. Gr-GB:71
Raccoon. K. Rexroth. Co-FB:488
Raccoon on the Road. J. Brennan.
 Gr-EC:40
Raccoons. A. Fisher. La-PP:47,
 La-PV:149
S F. E. Leverett. Co-PU:135
RACE PROBLEMS: see also
 DISCRIMINATION; LYNCHINGS
Alabama Centennial. N. Madgett.
 Ra-BP:197
The Ballad of Chocolate Mabbie.
 G. Brooks. Pe-SS:30
The Ballad of Joe Meek.
 S. Brown. Be-MA:31
Barricades. M. Harper. Ad-PB:316
Bedtime Story. L. Lipsitz.
 Ca-VT:717
The Beginning of a Long Poem on
 why I Burned the City.
 L. Benford. Kr-OF:55,
 Lo-TY:257
Beyond the Nigger. S. Plumpp.
 Ad-PB:387
Birmingham 1963. R. Patterson.
 Ad-PB:209, Kr-OF:163
The Black Man's Son.
 O. Durand. Lo-TY:91
Black Muslim Boy in a Hospital.
 J. Emanuel. Hu-PN:375

blk/rhetoric. S. Sanchez.
 Be-MA:137
Broken Heart, Broken Machine.
 R. Grant. Ad-PB:505
Brother Malcolm's Echo.
 K. Kgositsile. Be-MA:146
The Chicago Defender Sends a
 Man to Little Rock, Fall, 1957.
 G. Brooks. Ad-PB:155,
 Be-MA:82, Bo-AN:142
Children's Rhymes. L. Hughes.
 Ad-BO:43, Ra-BP:86
Colors. J. Wickersham.
 Ad-II:83
Cross. L. Hughes. Ad-PB:73,
 Be-MA:39, Bo-AN:62,
 Fe-PL:428, Wi-LT:421
A Dab of Color. T. Weiss.
 Ca-VT:435
The Dancer. A. Young. Ad-PB:364
Dangerous Toy. H. Gordon.
 Ad-II:109
Dark Symphony: Allegro Moderato.
 M. Tolson. Be-MA:20, Bo-AN:37,
 Hu-PN:136
Dinner Guest: Me. L. Hughes.
 Ra-BP:78
Enslaved. C. McKay. Ra-BP:62
The Fishes and the Poet's Hands.
 Bo-AN:134, Hu-PN:332
For My People. M. Walker.
 Ad-PB:144, Be-MA:73, Bo-AN:128,
 Hu-PN:314, Tr-MR:155
Frederick Douglass. R. Hayden.
 Ab-MO:83, Ad-PB:120, Be-MA:56,
 Bo-AN:119, Hu-PN:296, Jo-SA:41,
 Lo-TY:237
Give Us the Sign! W. Du Bois.
 Kr-OF:149
God Give to Men. A. Bontemps.
 Hu-PN:225, Ra-BP:92
He Rather Die. K. Jones.
 Jo-VC:55
Honky. C. Cooper. Ad-PB:504
I Don't Mind. C. Jackson.Le-M:168
I Gave Them Fruits. Bi-IT:146,
 Tr-US II:241
In the Gold Mines. B. Vilakazi.
 Lo-TY:176
Incident. C. Cullen. Ab-MO:94,
 Ad-PB:91, Be-MA:51, Ca-VT:241,
 Ho-LP:58, Hu-PN:232, Jo-SA:107,
 Kr-OF:50, Mo-BG:78, Pe-OA:190,
 Ra-BP:98, Th-AS:193
Landscape with Figures.
 N. Rosten. Kr-OF:160
The Last Riot. V. Howard. Jo-VC:8
Legacy: My South. D. Randall.
 Ad-PB:138, Be-MA:71, Hu-NN:43,
 Hu-PN:306

RACE PROBLEMS — cont'd.

Let America Be America Again.
L. Hughes.   Hu-PN:193

Lincoln . . . Today.
K. Hopkins.   Me-WF:61

A Litany at Atlanta. W. Du Bois.
Hu-PN:20

The Louisiana Weekly.
D. Henderson.   Ad-PB:421,
Jo-SA:103

March on the Delta.   A. Berger.
Lo-IT:9

Marginalia for Solo Voice and
Tom-Tom; the Negroes Sing.
A. Voznesensky.   Ca-MR:75

Monument in Black.   V. Howard.
Jo-SA:3, Jo-VC:43

Move Un-noticed to Be Noticed.
N. Giovanni.   Be-MA:166

Nation.   C. Cobb.   Ad-PB:468,
Lo-IT:17

The New Math.   V. Howard.
Jo-VC:44

Night, Death, Mississippi.
R. Hayden.   Ca-VT:357

No Way Out.   L. Curry.
Jo-SA:8, Jo-VC:82

O Great Black Masque.   T. Joans.
Be-MA:104

Oh Why?   M. Fletcher.   Me-WF:23

One Eyed Black Man in Nebraska.
S. Cornish.   Ad-PB:294

Outcast.   C. McKay.   Ad-PB:25,
Be-MA:14, Bo-AN:28

Pass Office Song.   Lo-TY:17

Poem to Negro and White.
M. Bodenheim.   Hu-PN:511

poll.   E. Roberson.   Ad-PB:350

Question and Answer. L. Hughes.
Ra-BP:89

The Race Question. N. Madgett.
Be-MA:93, Ra-BP:196

right on: white america.
S. Sanchez.   Ad-BO:42,
Ad-PB:287, Be-MA:135, Jo-SA:104

Riot Rimes, U.S.A.
R. Patterson.   Kr-OF:57

Les Salaziennes. A. Lacaussade.
Lo-TY:69

Snapshots of the Cotton South.
F. Davis.   Ad-PB:98

Song for Aimé Césaire.
K. Kgositsile.   Be-MA:146

The Southern Road. D. Randall.
Ad-PB:139, Be-MA:70, Hu-NN:41

Strong Men.   S. Brown.
Ad-PB:60, Be-MA:27, Bo-HF:138,
Ke-PP:127, Lo-TY:219, Ra-BP:113

Tenebris.   A. Grimke.
Ad-PB:15, Hu-PN:58

They Got You Last Night.
A. Kurtz.   Ke-PP:75

Tiger.   C. McKay.   Ra-BP:62

To a Negro Boy Graduating.
E. Maleska.   Hu-PN:569

To a White Liberal-Minded Girl.
J. Oliver.   Ad-II:111

To Columbus.   R. Dario. Lo-TY:86

To the White Fiends.   C. McKay.
Ad-PB:27

Tripart, I. G. Jones.   Jo-SA:13

26 Ways of Looking at a Blackman.
R. Patterson.   Jo-SA:109

Watts.   C. Rivers.   Ad-BO:41,
Ad-PB:233

The White City.   C. McKay.
Ra-BP:61

White Man and Black Man Are
Talking. M. Goode.   Jo-VC:48

Who Shall Die?   J. Randall.
Ra-BP:272

You're Nothing but a Spanish Kid.
F. Luciano.   Ad-PB:501

Youth's Question - Revenge's
Answer.   R. Groppuso.
Me-WF:25

RACE RELATIONS: see also
DISCRIMINATION; HUMOR -
RACE RELATIONS; SATIRE
- RACE RELATIONS

Bedtime Story.   L. Lipsitz.
Ca-VT:717

Black Narcissus.   G. Barrax.
Ad-PB:223

Booker T. and W.E.B.   D. Randall.
Ab-MO:84, Be-MA:69

The Castle.   S. Alexander.
Hu-PN:559

Circles.   C. Sandburg.
Br-AF:38, Ma-FW:134

Daybreak in Alabama. L. Hughes.
Br-AF:47

Go Slow.   L. Hughes.   Wi-LT:424

Here where Coltrane Is.
M. Harper.   Ad-PB:313

I Went to Learn how the White
Man Lives.   Wo-HS:(37)

If Everybody Was Black.
J. Holland.   Jo-VC:50

I'll Wear Me a Cotton Dress.
Ra-BP:11

imperial thumbprint.
T. Weatherly.   Ad-PB:399

The Inky Boys. H. Hoffman. De-TT:21

The Invisible Man.   C. Rivers.
Be-MA:105

Jesus Was Crucified.   C. Rodgers.
Ad-PB:432

Lenox Avenue.   S. Alexander.
Hu-PN:556

A Moment Please. S. Allen.
  Ad-PB:166, Bo-AN:138
Montgomery. S. Cornish. Ad-PB:293
Move Un-noticed to be Noticed.
  N. Giovanni. Be-MA:166
My Black Boy. C. Wade. La-IH:102
Nice Day for a Lynching.
  K. Patchen. Hu-PN:555,
  Kr-OF:160
O White Mistress. D. Johnson.
  Hu-NN:40
Ode: Salute to the French Negro
  Poets. F. O'Hara. Hu-PN:581
A Poem for Integration.
  A. Saxon. Ad-PB:495
The Prophet's Warning, or Shoot
  to Kill. Ebon. Ad-PB:434
Query. Ebon. Ad-PB:435
Re-Act for Actions. D. Lee.
  Ra-BP:296
The Riddle. G. Johnson.
  Ad-PB:23
Sleeping Beauty. C. Johnson.
  La-IH:104
So I'm Still a Negro. Nathaniel.
  La-IH:101
Subway Rush Hour. L. Hughes.
  La-OC:63
The Subway Witnesses.
  L. Thomas. Ad-PB:482
Tableau. C. Cullen.
  Ad-PB:92, Br-AF:248
This Is a Black Room. T. Beasley.
  La-IH:110
To a Single Shadow Without Pity.
  S. Cornish. Ad-PB:294
To Richard Wright.
  C. Rivers. Ad-PB:234,
  Be-MA:105, Bo-AN:177
Totem. L. Senghor.
  Gr-BT:32
Undertow. L. Hughes.
  Wi-LT:423
Vietnam. C. Major.
  Ad-PB:299
Vive Noir! M. Evans. Ad-BO:52
We Wear the Mask. P. Dunbar.
  Ad-IA:86, Ad-PB:8, Bo-AN:14,
  Bo-HF:103, Jo-SA:134, Lo-TY:208,
  Mo-BG:190
Where the Rainbow Ends. R. Rive.
  Ab-MO:107, Lo-TY:180
Who Am I. L. Gama. Lo-TY:79
Why Do the White Men Lie.
  L. Curry. Ba-HI:118
Why Isn't the World Happy?
  R. Lewis. Ba-HI:117
Why Prejudice. B. Chase. Ba-HI:24
Yes, This Is a Black Room.
  D. Dixon. La-IH:111

RACES OF MAN: see also
    CIVILIZATION; FOLKLORE;
    HUMOR - RACES OF MAN;
    MANNERS AND CUSTOMS;
    SATIRE - RACES OF MAN
  All of Us a Family. C. Meyer.
    Jo-VC:18
  A Baby Is a European. Be-AP:64
  Brown River, Smile. J. Toomer.
    Ad-PB:31, Bo-AN:34, Hu-PN:107,
    Jo-SA:72
  The City Is Big. T. Heard.
    Me-WF:10
  The European. Be-AP:56
  The People of Africa.
    M. Mertsalov. Bo-RU:51
  Song. Be-AP:63
  Then as Now. W. de la Mare.
    Li-TU:250, Mc-WK:116
  This Is a World Full. . . .
    D. Peterson. Ba-HI:41
  To My Son Parker, Asleep in the
    Next Room. B. Kaufman.
    Ad-PB:265, Br-TC:230,
    Ca-VT:539, Jo-SA:30
  Wake-Up Niggers. D. Lee.
    Ad-PB:422
  white people. D. Henderson.
    Ad-PB:420
RACHEL: see JACOB AND RACHEL
RACINE, JEAN BAPTISTE
  I Shall Not See the Famous
    Phedre. O. Mandelstam.
    Ca-MR:150
RACING: see AUTOMOBILE RACING;
    BICYCLE RACING; BOAT RACING;
    CHARIOT RACING; HORSE
    RACING; RUNNING
RADAR
  Radar. A. Ross. Pe-OA:281
RADHA: see KRISHNA AND RADHA
RADIATION: see also
    SATIRE - RADIATION
  Hey Diddle Diddle. P. Dehn.
    Co-FB:451, Du-RG:80
RADIATORS: see also
    HOUSEHOLD FURNISHINGS;
    HUMOR - RADIATORS
  The Steam Family.
    G. Pangborn. Ke-TF:69
RADIO
  Proof. E. Fuller. Th-AS:171
  Static. R. Humphries. Pl-US:41
  Swinton. J. Schevill. Du-SH:156
RADISHES: see also
    HUMOR - RADISHES
  The Gardeners. D. Ignatow.
    Ls-NY:226
  Vegetable Fantasies. H. Hoyt.
    Ir-BB:16-17

RAFTERY, ANTHONY
  I Am Raftery. A. Raftery.
    Co-PI:181
RAGE: see ANGER
RAGWORTS
  The Ragwort. J. Clare. Gr-CT:255
RAIDS: see also MORGAN'S
    RAIDS, 1862-1864
  Brian Boy Magee. F. Carbery.
    Co-PI:21
  How Old John Brown Took Harper's
    Ferry. E. Stedman.
    Hu-PN:493, Pa-OM:175
  Running the Batteries.
    H. Melville. Hi-TL:118
  The Sack of Old Panama.
    D. Burnet. Co-RM:56
  The War-Song of Dinas Vawr.
    T. Peacock. Al-VBP:716,
    Ha-PO:220, Ho-WR:106, Mc-WS:105,
    Na-EO:110, Pa-OM:197
RAILROADS: see also ENGINEERS;
    EXPRESS SERVICE; TRAINS;
    WESTWARD MOVEMENT
  The Bourgeois Poet.
    K. Shapiro. St-H:205
  Burying Ground by the Ties.
    A. MacLeish. Un-MA:459
  Carshops at Centralia.
    R. Cuscaden. St-H:30
  Casey Jones, the Union Scab.
    J. Hill. Kr-OF:177
  Homesick Blues. L. Hughes.
    Mc-WK:202, Un-MA:552
  In Texas Grass. Q. Troupe.
    Ad-PB:443
  I've Been Workin' on the Railroad.
    Er-FA:440
  John Henry. Ab-MO:81, Bo-HF:104,
    Co-RM:225, Er-FA:407, Ga-S:124,
    Hi-TL:159, Ra-BP:12
  Landscape as Metal and Flowers.
    W. Scott. Bo-GJ:209, Br-AF:232
  Long Gone. S. Brown. Ra-BP:112
  The Old and the New. Q.B.M.
    Au-SP:175, Pa-SG:114
  Old Davenport Days. R. Cuscaden.
    St-H:34
  The Old Section Boss. Ra-BP:17
  A Passing. R. Cuscaden.
    St-H:31
  The Railroad Cars Are Coming.
    Br-AF:228, Fe-FP:437, Hu-MP:395
  Railroad Rails. Tr-US II:271
  Rhyme of the Rails. J. Saxe.
    Fe-PL:80
  The Spiritual Railway. Ga-S:146
  The Tay River Bridge Disaster.
    W. McGonagall. Na-EO:78
  Tracks. E. Schwager. Ad-CI:36

What's the Railroad to Me?
  H. Thoreau. Co-EL:117,
    Ga-FB:265, Hi-TL:140, Mo-BG:116
Where We Are. B. Cutler.
  St-H:36
See also Em-AF:656-669
RAILROADS - FREIGHT TRAINS
  Crossing. P. Booth. Br-AF:229
    Du-RG:43
  Engine. J. Tippett. Au-SP:172
  The Freight Train. R. Bennett.
    La-PP:39, La-PV:179, Sh-RP:178
RAILROADS - SLEEPING CARS: see
    HUMOR - RAILROADS - SLEEPING CARS
RAILROADS - STATIONS
  Concert at the Station.
    O. Mandelstam. Ca-MR:156
  Depot in a River Town.
    M. Williams. Du-SH:131
  For the New Railway Station in
    Rome. R. Wilbur. Pe-OA:257
  Pennsylvania Station.
    L. Hughes. Bo-AN:71
  The Railway Junction.
    W. de la Mare. Rv-CB:962
  The Station. K. Parsons.
    Bo-FP:119
  The Station. J. Rathe. Le-M:173
  Stop. R. Wilbur. Ha-WR:87
RAILS (BIRDS)
  The Corncrake. J. Cousins.
    Co-PI:31
RAILWAYS: see RAILROADS
RAIN: see also FLOODS;
    HUMOR - RAIN
  After the Rain. Y. Ritsos.
    Mo-TS:19
  All Day It Has Rained. A. Lewis.
    Hi-WP I:28, Pa-GTB:543
  The Alley in the Rain.
    Tai Wang-shu. Hs-TC:180
  And Then It Rained.
    M. Van Doren. Co-BN:171
  April Rain Song. L. Hughes.
    Ar-TP3:170, Fe-FP:74, La-PP:21,
    La-PV:41, Li-LC:73, Pe-FB:87
  April Showers. T. Tribilla.
    La-GI:24
  At Dieppe: Rain on the Down.
    A. Symons. Ox-BN:934
  Autumn Rain. A. Fisher.
    Sh-RP:220
  Bare Almond-Trees. D. Lawrence.
    Ma-FW:274
  Bouncing Ball. S. Watson.
    Au-SP:193
  Brightly the Sun Shines.
    Ontei. Be-CS:47
  Brownstone. R. McKuen. Ha-TP:8
  Buckets. R. Padgett. Mc-EA:38

A Child Stretched Forth. Torai.
   Le-MW:71
City Rain. R. Field. Ar-TP3:169,
   Au-SP:309, Gr-EC:63
Clear Evening after Rain. Tu Fu.
   Rx-OH:27
A Cloud on Top of Evergreen
   Mountain. Ho-SD:47,
   Tr-US II:273
Come On, Owl. Issa. Le-IS:16
Coming from Nowhere. B. Jones.
   Ba-HI:68
Consciousness. R. Nickens.
   La-IH:116
Corn-Grinding Song. Da-SC:84
The Corn Grows Up. Le-OE:78
A Dance for Rain. W. Bynner.
   Pa-HT:58
Dance Songs. Tr-US II:163
Darkling Summer, Ominous Dusk,
   Rumerous Rain. D. Schwartz.
   Ha-WR:67
The Day the Weather Broke.
   A. Reid. Ha-TP:60
The day we went out.
   M. Bergschneider. Ad-II:61
Deadfall. M. Keller. Gr-EC:272
Deluge. J. Clare. Co-BN:169
A Description of a City Shower.
   J. Swift. Al-VBP:515
Desolate. S. Dobell. Ox-BN:659,
   Rv-CB:879
A Dog and a Cat Went Out Together.
   Mother Goose. Bo-FP:225,
   Ir-BB:237
Down the Rain Falls.
   E. Coatsworth. Au-SP:314
A Drop of Rain! Issa.
   Ar-TP3:169, Le-IS:15
Dry and Parched. A. Lopez.
   Al-WW:9
Earth Cure Me. Earth Receive
   My Woe. Wo-HS:(55)
Far as Man Can See. Ho-SD:43
Fern Song. J. Tabb. Sp-OG:281
The First Night of Fall and
   Falling Rain. D. Schwartz.
   Ls-NY:298
The First Rain of Winter.
   Basho. Do-TS:40
Fisherman. Ou Yang Hsiu.
   Rx-OH:51
Flute-Priest Song for Rain.
   A. Lowell. Pl-US:132
Footwear. M. Justus. Au-SP:332,
   Ha-YA:18
Four Things. P. Gearey. Ke-TF:241
From a Seasonal Prayer.Tr-US II:254
From the Rain-Making Ceremony.
   Tr-US I:104

Glass Falling. L. MacNeice.
   Co-PI:114, Pa-RE:45
Great Aso. T. Miyoshi.
   Sh-AM:82
The Happy Farmer. Tse Nan.
   Le-MW:115
Hi-ihiya Naiho-o! Da-SC:77,
   Ho-SD:41
Ho, for the May Rains. Sanpu.
   Be-CS:51
Hokku Poems. R. Wright.
   Bo-AN:105
Horses and Men in the Rain.
   C. Sandburg. Fe-PL:409
How Gray the Rain. E. Coatsworth.
   Ar-TP3:216, Au-SP:344
I Am Crying from Thirst.
   A. Lopez. Al-WW:8
I Saw God Wash the World.
   W. Stidger. Hu-MP:285
In the Night. Bi-IT:107
In the Spring Rain. Chiyo-Ni.
   Do-TS:10
In Time of Silver Rain.
   L. Hughes. Ab-MO:9,
   Ar-TP3:171, Au-SP:310
Irradiations. J. Fletcher.
   Un-MA:313
It Is Nice to Read. Onitsura.
   Be-CS:5
It Is Raining. L. Mitchell.
   Ar-TP3:170, Au-SP:311
It Rained in the Night.
   J. Carrera Andrade. Ho-LP:28
Jardins sous la Pluie.
   J. Redwood-Anderson. Cl-FC:46
Job. Bible. O.T. Job.
   Pl-IO:45
The Journey of a Raindrop.
   Wo-HS:(7)
June Thunder. L. MacNeice.
   To-MP:36
The Last Sunday. Wang Tu-ch'ing.
   Hs-TC:194
The Latter Rain. J. Very.
   Sh-AP:65
Leaf Falling on Leaf. Gyodai.
   Be-CS:54
The Lime Avenue. S. Sitwell.
   Ha-LO:48
A Line-Storm Song. R. Frost.
   Gr-CC:184, Pe-OA:43
Little Rain. E. Roberts.
   Ar-TP3:169, Au-SP:321,
   Br-SG:52, Ir-BB:33
The Little Rain. Tu Fu. Fe-FP:480
Little Rain Men. R. Hussey.
   Bo-FP:263
Little Raindrops. J. Browne.
   Ox-BC:224

RAIN — <u>cont'd</u>.
  London Rain. N. Turner. Th-AS:92
  Many Shiver. J. Klein. Le-M:57,
    Le-WR:24
  Mechanical Landscape. I. Minulescu.
    Mc-AC:42
  Memorial Rain. A. MacLeish.
    Un-MA:454
  The Monkey's Raincoat. Basho.
    Au-SP:326, Su-FVI:67
  Moods. S. Teasdale. Mc-PR:62
  Moods of Rain. V. Scannell.
    Co-BN:172
  The Narba-Bird. Tr-US I:245
  Near the West Lake. Kuo Mo-jo.
    Hs-TC:37
  New Life. J. Kariuki. Lo-TY:171
  New Moon Come Out. Le-OE:70
  Night, Window, Wind.
    J. Anderson. Sc-TN:5
  No Drip of Rain. I. Eastwick.
    Mc-AW:80
  Noah. H. Hagedorn. Tr-MR:66
  November Rain. M. Uschold.
    Ha-YA:123
  Now a Spring Rain Falls. Chiyo.
    Be-MC:40
  O, My Lovely Mountain. Ho-SD:30
  Ode to Rain. Bo-FP:222
  Old Man Rain. M. Cawein.
    Co-PS:58
  Ombres Chinoises. B. Deutsch.
    Ha-TP:23
  Oregon Rain. J. McGahey.
    Br-AF:163, Du-RG:125
  Others. H. Behn. Au-SP:114
  Ouwe Dance Song for Good Crops.
    Tr-US II:259
  Over the Sun-Darkened River
    Sands. Le-OE:73
  Owl, Crevice-Sitter. Le-OE:42
  Pearls on the Grass.
    G. Mohanty. Le-M:59
  Prayer for Rain. H. Palmer.
    Hi-WP II:42
  Rain. E. Benediktsson. Pa-SG:205
  Rain. L. Coxe. Ls-NY:62
  The Rain. R. Creeley.
    Ca-VT:563, Mc-EA:37
  The Rain. W. Davies. Ar-TP3:171,
    Bo-FP:231, De-TT:160
  Rain. R. Drillich. Le-M:53
  Rain. B. Eng. Ba-HI:68
  Rain. J. Fegley. La-GI:20
  Rain. L. Heron. Le-M:81
  Rain. C. Minor. Jo-VC:67
  Rain. Mother Goose. Ar-TP3:166,
    Mo-CC:(51), Mo-MGT:74
  Rain. S. O'Sullivan. Co-PI:165
  Rain. R. Parmenter. Ls-NY:57

  The Rain. J. Parr. La-GI:25
  Rain. J. Riley. Co-BN:169
  Rain. S. Silverstein. Co-OT:11
  Rain. A. Smith. Le-M:56
  Rain. R. Stevenson. Ar-TP3:166,
    Au-SP:312, Bo-FP:223, Bo-GJ:34,
    Ch-B:60, Gr-EC:48, Hu-MP:297
  Rain. A. Stoutenburg. La-PV:41
  Rain. M. Taylor. Ba-HI:69
  Rain. P. Williams. Le-M:149
  Rain. E. Young. Ar-TP3:170
  The Rain. Ch-B:84
  Rain after a Vaudeville Show.
    S. Benét. Mo-BG:29, Un-MA:497
  Rain Before Seven. Ir-BB:231,
    Ju-CP:72, Mo-MGT:19, Un-GT:23
  Rain Clouds. R. Harding.
    Ho-CT:2
  Rain Dance. B. Krasnoff.
    Le-M:54, Le-WR:26
  The Rain Falls. I. Luciano.
    La-GI:26
  The Rain Frogs. Rogetsu.
    Pa-SG:129
  Rain in Summer. H. Longfellow.
    Bo-FP:262, Ch-B:103
  Rain in the Night. A. Burr.
    Ar-TP3:168, Hu-MP:130,
    Th-AS:89
  Rain in the Southwest.
    R. Kelley. Br-AF:147
  The Rain-Man Praises Himself.
    Tr-CB:38, Tr-US I:71
  Rain Music. J. Cotter. Bo-FP:223
  Rain on Castle Island.
    H. Kitahara. Ma-FW:118
  Rain on South-East England.
    D. Davie. Ls-NY:289
  Rain on the Housetops. La-GI:22
  Rain on the River. Lu Yu.
    Rx-LT:100, Rx-OH:106
  Rain Poem. E. Coatsworth.
    Gr-EC:53
  rain rain falling down.
    T. Randle. Me-WF:32
  Rain, Rain, Go Away. Mother
    Goose. An-IP:25, Ar-TP3:166,
    Au-SP:315, De-PO:26, Mo-CC:(50)
  Rain, Rain, Go to Spain.
    Mo-NR:35, Wi-MG:59, Wr-RM:50
  Rain Riddle. De-PP:53
  Rain Riders. C. Scollard.
    Ar-TP3:171, Au-SP:314
  Rain Sizes. J. Ciardi. Au-SP:112
  Rain Song. J. Garrigue.
    Ls-NY:52
  The Rain Song. R. Loveman.
    Hu-MP:252
  Rain Song of the Giant Society.
    Da-SC:76

The Rain Walked with Long Legs.
   Wo-HS:(61)
Rain Went Sweeping On.   Sho-U.
   Be-CS:35
Raindrops.   K. Dickinson.
   Le-M:58, Le-WR:22
Raindrops.   Bo-FP:262
Raindrops.   Ch-B:84
The Rains of Spring.   Lady Ise.
   Ar-TP3:170
Rainscapes, Hydrangeas, Roses,
   and Singing Birds.
   R. Eberhart.   Un-MA:581
The Rainstorm.   Ca-MU:23
The Rainwalkers.   D. Levertov.
   Ad-CI:109, Du-SH:145
A Rainy Day.   J. Lincoln.
   Sh-RP:198
The Rainy Day.   H. Longfellow.
   Fe-PL:303
The Rainy Day.   R. Tagore.
   Al-PI:90, Ma-FW:117
Rainy Day Song.   V. Storey.
   Ha-YA:28
Rainy Night.   Feng Chih.
   Hs-TC:141
A Rainy Scene.   Chu Hsiang.
   Hs-TC:104
Rainy Song.   M. Eastman.   Bo-HF:49
The Rainy Summer.   A. Meynell.
   Bo-GJ:99, Gr-SS:42
The Reason.   D. Aldis.   Ar-TP3:167
Rhyme of Rain.   J. Holmes.
   La-OC:30, Mc-WK:36
The Rhyme of the Rain Machine.
   F. Clarke.   Co-BN:173
Sacrifice of the Sparrows of the
   Field.   J. Langland.   St-H:107
The Sad Look of a Season.
   Tu Yün-hsieh.   Hs-TC:249
St. Malachy.   T. Merton.
   Ca-VT:417
St. Swithin's Day. . . .
   Ir-BB:231, Li-LB:161, Un-GT:23
See This Beautiful Rainy Day.
   A. Grover.   Le-M:55, Le-WR:19
A Sheep Fair.   T. Hardy.   Ho-P:206
Sheltering from the Rain.
   S. Karai.   Ma-FW:119
A Shower.   Izembō.   Ar-TP3:166
The Shower.   H. Vaughan.   Al-VBP:465,
   Cl-FC:42, Co-BN:175, Co-PU:49,
   Gr-CT:237, Ma-FW:116
Signs of Rain.   E. Jenner.
   Co-BN:165, De-TT:73
Slanting, Windy Rain.   Buson.
   Be-MC:49
Slowly Slowly the Drip Drip Drop.
   J. Lloyd.   Le-WR:18
Small Rain.   A. Gould.   Th-AS:114

Some Western Haikus, IV.
   J. Kerouac.   Kh-VA:12
Song.   W. Watson.   Co-PS:53,
   Ga-FB:232, Se-PR:79, Un-GT:273
Song for the Hula Ala'a-Papa.
   Tr-US II:101
Song in the Rain.   Yang Huan.
   Pa-MV:159
Song of Sequence.   Da-SC:21
The Song of the Rain.   Le-OE:71
Song Sung on an Expedition to
   Obtain Salt.   Bi-IT:21,
   Ho-SD:51, Le-OE:73,
   Tr-US II:273
Songs in the Garden of the
   House God.   Bi-IT:115, Da-SC:86
The Songs of Spring (II).
   Feng Hsüeh-feng.   Hs-TC:368
The Sower.   R. Olivares Figueroa.
   Fe-FP:490, Ho-LP:38
Splish Splosh.   S. Martul.
   Le-M:49
Spring Rain.   H. Behn.
   Ar-TP3:169, Pe-FB:85
Spring Rain.   Chiyo-Ni.
   Ba-ST:21, Le-MW:93, Ma-FW:34
Spring Rain.   M. Chute.
   Ar-TP3:167, Fr-MP:13, La-PP:20,
   Mc-AW:81
Spring Rain.   Tu Fu.   Pa-SG:83,
   Rx-LT:62
Squirrel in the Rain.   F. Frost.
   Sh-RP:334
The Story of Flying Robert.
   H. Hoffmann.   Ir-BB:158,
   Li-SR:28
The Story of Rain.   L. Atwood.
   La-GI:21
A Stray Cat.   Taigi.   Do-TS:7
Sudden Shower.   J. Clare.
   Co-PS:61, Mc-PR:178, Rv-CB:715
Sudden Storm.   E. Coatsworth.
   Ho-CS:38
Summer in the Rain.   Yung Tzu.
   Pa-MV:196
Summer Rain.   E. Coatsworth.
   Br-SS:179, Sh-RP:217
Summer Rain.   Lin Keng.   Le-MW:77
Summer Rain.   E. Merriam.
   La-PV:40
Summer Rain.   H. Read.   Wi-LT:632
Summer Shower.   E. Dickinson.
   Co-BN:102
Summer Shower.   S. Robinson.
   Th-AS:118
A Sunshiny Shower.   Mother Goose.
   Bo-FP:227, Ir-BB:231, Li-LB:161,
   Mo-NR:122, Un-GT:22, Wr-RM:122
Tears Flow in My Heart.
   P. Verlaine.   Pa-SG:184

RAIN — cont'd.
  There Goes My Best Hat. Basho.
    Be-MC:8
  There Is an Umbrella. V. Cokeham.
    Le-M:60
  Thirst. G. Cohoe. Al-WW:23
  Thunder Pools. R. Coffin.
    Ha-LO:70
  Tippity-Tap. K. Fouchaux.
    La-GI:24
  To the Tune "The Fair Maid of Yu."
    Chiang Chieh. Rx-LT:109
  Tour. In Rain. R. Roseliep.
    De-FS:164, St-H:186
  Traveling Storm. M. Van Doren.
    Th-AS:116
  Two Sewing. H. Hall. Th-AS:112
  U Is for Umbrellas. P. McGinley.
    Ar-TP3:167
  An Umbrella and a Raincoat.
    Buson. Do-TS:11
  The Umbrella Brigade. L. Richards.
    Ar-TP3:168, Au-SP:113
  Under Oaks. J. Dickey. Ls-NY:122
  The Unknown Dead. H. Timrod.
    Sh-AP:126
  Waiting for You in the Rain.
    Yü Kuang-chung. Pa-MV:184
  Walking at Night. A. Hare.
    Fe-PL:405
  We Must Overcome the East Wind.
    Do-CH:(22)
  Weathers. T. Hardy. Bl-OB:96,
    Bo-FP:73, De-CH:9, De-TT:145,
    Ga-FB:229, Hi-WP I:30, Na-EO:42,
    Sh-RP:23, Sm-LG:64, Sm-MK:143,
    Tu-WW:28, Un-GB:18, Un-MB:28
  Wet Weather. P. Low. Ca-VT:670
  What a Terrible Day. B. Ovens.
    Le-WR:23
  What's o'Clock XVI. A. Lowell.
    Ho-TH:24
  When the Rain. P. Romanick.
    La-GI:20
  When the Rain Raineth. Gr-GB:57
  Who Is Tapping at My Window.
    A. Deming. Au-SP:313, Ch-B:84
  Who Loves the Rain. F. Shaw.
    Hu-MP:298, Th-AS:113
  Who Walks There? K. Patchen.
    Ha-WR:13
  A Whole Sheet of Solitude.
    Liu Ta-Pai. Hs-TC:6
  The Wind and the Rain.
    W. Gibson. Cl-FC:50
  The Wind Begun to Rock the Grass.
    E. Dickinson. Co-BN:172,
    Gr-CC:28, Gr-EC:60
  The Wind Blows the Rain into Our
    Faces. C. Reznikoff. La-OC:29

  Window, 3rd Story, 5th to the
    Right, Morning. R. Drapeau.
    La-IH:56
  Winter in the Fens. J. Clare.
    Co-BN:190, Ma-FW:4
  Winter Rain. C. Rossetti.
    Co-BN:184, Ho-WR:24
  With a Hey, Ho, the Wind and
    the Rain. W. Shakespeare.
    Ar-TP3:112
RAIN CROWS: see CUCKOOS
RAINBOWS
  After the Rain. Chang Chih-min.
    Hs-TC:426
  An Angel in the House.
    C. Patmore. Pa-GTB:368
  Boats Sail on the Rivers.
    C. Rossetti. Ar-TP3:172,
    Bo-FP:263, Ox-BC:278, Pe-FB:73
  The Cloud. P. Shelley.
    Al-VBP:752, Bo-FP:261, Fe-FP:76,
    Hu-MP:295, Pl-IO:46, Rv-CB:708,
    Sh-RP:67, Sp-OG:349
  Death of an Evening Rainbow.
    Cheng Ch'ou-yü. Pa-MV:41
  The Door. L. Strong. Un-MB:394
  A Great Time. W. Davies.
    Hi-WP I:1, Un-MB:178
  The History of the Flood.
    J. Heath-Stubbs. Ca-MB:40,
    Ma-FW:38
  How Gray the Rain. E. Coatsworth.
    Ar-TP3:216, Au-SP:344
  Invocation to the Rainbow.
    Tr-US I:63
  Legend. J. Wright. Co-PT:179,
    Ma-FW:192
  More Riddles I. Gr-GB:39
  My Heart Leaps Up. W. Wordsworth.
    Al-VBP:655, Ar-TP3:172, Au-SP:346,
    Bo-HF:55, Br-BC:121, Co-RG:121,
    Er-FA:149, Ga-FB:22, Ha-PO:83,
    La-PP:7, Ma-YA:139, Mc-PR:169,
    Ox-BN:61, Pa-GTB:308, Rv-CB:644,
    Sp-OG:352
  Pink and Violet. Re-RR:52
  Purple, Yellow, Red, and Green.
    Ir-BB:51, Mo-MGT:155
  The Rainbow. W. de la Mare.
    Ar-TP3:172, Au-SP:345
  The Rainbow. D. Lawrence.
    Ma-FW:118
  The Rainbow. D. McCord.
    Au-SP:316, Fe-FP:75
  Rainbow. Ca-MU:26
  Rainbow at Night. Bo-FP:261,
    Gr-EC:65, Ir-BB:230, Un-GT:22
  The Rainbow Fairies.
    L. Hadley. St-FS:65
  A Rainbow Is Just. Wo-HS:(16)

Up High the Ribbons Descend.
Gr-BB:22
Which Is the Bow?   Gr-GB:38
Who Am I?   Ca-MU:18
Women's Song at a Wedding Feast.
Tr-US I:208
You, Whose Day It Is.   Ho-SD:55,
Jo-TS:1, Le-OE:16
RAINE, KATHLEEN
For K. R. on Her Sixtieth
Birthday.   R. Wilbur. Pl-ML:77
RAJAHS: see KINGS AND RULERS
RAMEAU, JEAN PHILIPPE
On an Air of Rameau. A. Symons.
Ox-BN:936
RAMS: see SHEEP
RANCH LIFE: see also AUSTRALIA;
CATTLE; COWBOYS; DIALECTS,
WESTERN; SHEEP; THE WEST
The High Loping Cowboy.
C. Fletcher. Fi-BG:76
Indian Summer, Montana, 1950.
W. Ransom. Ni-CD:199
Montana Pastoral. J. Cunningham.
Ca-VT:324, Un-MA:615
On the Trail from a Puncher's
Point of View. Fi-BG:149
The Philosophical Cowboy.
J. H. S. Fi-BG:148
Ranch at Twilight. Fi-BG:75
RAPHAEL
One Word More.   R. Browning.
Al-VBP:911
RAPUNZEL
Rapunzel Song.   G. Meyer.
Ls-NY:93
RATHANGAN, FORT OF: see FORT OF
RATHANGAN, IRE.
RATISBON, BATTLE, 1809
Incident of the French Camp.
R. Browning. Co-RG:28,
Mc-PR:144, Sp-OG:43, Un-GT:148
RATS: see also HUMOR - RATS;
WATER RATS
Assailant.   J. Raven. Ra-BP:258
Bishop Hatto.   R. Southey.
Gr-CT:130, Ha-PO:78, Pa-OM:125
Break of Day in the Trenches.
I. Rosenberg. Al-VBP:1190,
Ba-PO:138, Hi-FO:257,
Pa-GTB:446, Un-MB:351
The Doctor Who Sits at the Bedside
of a Rat. J. Miles. Ca-VT:339
Fire Island Walking Song.
E. Kinkead. Co-BBW:56
Five Eyes.   W. de la Mare.
Co-BBW:133, Co-IW:18, Ir-BB:28
Four Preludes on Playthings of the
Wind: The Past Is a Bucket of
Ashes. C. Sandburg. Un-MA:201

freddy the rat perishes.
D. Marquis. La-OC:103,
Pe-M:120
In a Deep Museum.   A. Sexton.
Ho-P:229, Un-MA:690
A Joyous Reveling Song Sung
by the Wood Rats.
Su-FVI:59, Tr-US II:113
Limits.   R. Emerson. Rd-OA:170
An Old Rat's Tale.   Bl-OB:38,
Ch-B:96, Gr-EC:219, Sm-MK:208
The Pied Piper of Hamelin.
R. Browning. Ar-TP3:28,
Er-FA:354, Ox-BC:173,
Sm-LG:173, Un-GT:153
Pretty John Watts.   Wr-RM:77
The Puddy and the Mouse. Gr-GB:68
The Rat.   W. Davies. Go-BP:91
The Rat.   A. Young. Hi-WP II:43
A Rat.   Mo-MGT:24
Rat Riddles.   C. Sandburg.
Be-EB:60, La-OC:102
The Rats.   R. Browning.
Cl-DT:17, Co-BBW:31
Rats and Mice.   Rv-ON:24
Scampering over Saucers.
Yosa Buson. Ma-FW:266
The Sheaf.   A. Young. Gr-CT:123
Song Cycle of the Moon-Bone.
Tr-US I:246
this big rat.   Me-WF:41
Three Young Rats.
Fr-WO:35, Gr-CT:31, Gr-EC:11,
Gr-GB:92, Ir-BB:234, Lo-LL:41,
Mo-MGT:187, On-TW:15, Sm-MK:193
The Two Gray Kits.   Ir-BB:153,
Wr-RM:80
Visit to a Museum.   A. Ficke.
Ls-NY:209
What Became of Them? Ox-BC:289
RATTLESNAKES: see SNAKES
RAVENNA, IT.
Ravenna.   A. Blok. Ca-MR:196
RAVENS
Each Time a Wave Breaks.
Nissha. Le-MW:12
A Farmer Went Trotting.
Ar-TP3:122, Br-FF:(28),
Gr-EC:285, Li-LB:144, Mo-MGT:129,
Mo-NR:67, Na-EO:123, Wr-RM:123
The Magpie and the Raven.
Gr-BB:17
Over in the Meadow.   Au-SP:223,
Ir-BB:24, On-TW:38
The Raven.   S. Coleridge. Ho-WR:212
The Raven.   Nicharchus. Pl-US:61
The Raven.   E. Poe.
Al-VBP:865, Bo-GJ:165, Co-RG:103,
De-CH:303, Er-FA:312, Ga-FB:134,
Sh-AP:56, Sm-LG:207

RAVENS — cont'd.
   The Raven's Song.   Le-IB:40
   When the Raven.   Ho-SD:80
READING: see BOOKS AND READING
REAL ESTATE: see PROPERTY
REALITY: see also SATIRE - REALITY
   After Christmas.   W. Auden.
      Ga-S:90, Un-MB:467
   Dance Songs, IV.   Tr-US I:29
   Doubts.   T. Tzara.   Mc-AC:75
   A Dream Within a Dream.
      E. Poe.   Gr-CT:193
   Early Waking.   L. Adams.
      Wi-LT:603
   L'Envoi.   R. Kipling.
      Er-FA:10, Ke-TF:453
   Esthetique du Mal, VIII, IX.
      W. Stevens.   Wi-LT:155, 156
   Go Away.   Hsü Chih-mo.
      Hs-TC:87
   Heels Wear Down.   R. Roseliep.
      St-H:187
   I Did Not Know the Truth of
      Growing Trees.   D. Schwartz.
      Wi-LT:522
   I Have Folded My Sorrows.
      B. Kaufman.   Ad-PB:264
   If I Could Only Live at That
      Pitch That Is near Madness.
      R. Eberhart.   Wi-LT:433
   In the Third Year of the War.
      H. Treece.   Cr-WS:73
   Is This Real.   Bi-IT:131,
      Da-SC:113
   Leaving the Monastery Early in
      the Morning.   Lu Yu.   Rx-OH:105
   Metonymy as an Approach to the
      Real World.   W. Bronk.
      Ca-VT:455
   Mrs. Alfred Uruguay.   W. Stevens.
      Br-TC:414
   My Existence in the World.
      Tsurayuki.   Ba-ST:57
   The New Faces.   W. Yeats.
      Pa-GTB:427
   Not Ideas about the Thing, but
      the Thing Itself.   W. Stevens.
      Al-VBP:1145
   The Nymph's Reply to the Shepherd.
      W. Raleigh.   Al-VBP:169,
      Ha-PO:160, No-CL:101, Rv-CB:150
   O Pine Tree Standing.   Hakatsu.
      Ba-ST:58
   One Day when We Went Walking.
      V. Hobbs.   Au-SP:289
   One of Us May Feel.   Okura.
      Ba-ST:58
   Pegasus Lost.   E. Wylie.
      Un-MA:275
   Polemic.   A. Ostroff.   Ls-NY:67

   Positives: For Sterling Plumpp.
      D. Lee.   Ad-PB:427
   The Prejudice Against the Past.
      W. Stevens.   Wi-LT:161
   Since I Am Convinced.
      Saigyo Hishi.   Ba-ST:58
   So-and-So Reclining on Her
      Couch.   W. Stevens.   Wi-LT:149
   Sonnet XV.   Feng Chih.   Hs-LT:152
   Sonnets 130.   W. Shakespeare.
      Bo-HF:122, Co-BL:50, Rv-CB:247
   A Spade Is Just a Spade.
      W. Hawkins.   Ad-PB:19
   Strawberry Fields Forever.
      J. Lennon.   Mo-GR:127
   The Tapestry.   H. Nemerov.
      Ho-P:205
   Tired and Unhappy, You Think of
      Houses.   D. Schwartz.
      Un-MA:617, Wi-LT:516
   To a Child with Eyes.
      M. Van Doren.   Bo-FP:95,
      Ha-LO:78
   truth.   G. Brooks.   Ho-TH:53
   We Play at Paste.
      E. Dickinson.   Rv-CB:913
   You Shout about Freedom.
      Wilburt.   La-IH:57
REASON: see also HUMOR - REASON;
   LOGIC
   Much Knowledge, Little Reason.
      J. Davies.   Gr-CT:371
   Reason.   A. Stolzenberg.
      Ho-TY:270
   Reason Has Moons.   R. Hodgson.
      Sm-LG:203, Un-MB:186
   Religio Laici.   J. Dryden.
      Al-VBP:491
REBEKAH, WIFE OF ISAAC
   Rebecca.   V. Andreyev.   Ca-MR:97
REBELLION: see also HUMOR -
   REBELLION; PROTEST
   Alabama Centennial.
      N. Madgett.   Ra-BP:197
   America.   C. McKay.   Ad-PB:26,
      Be-MA:15, Bo-HF:40,
      Hu-PN:100, Lo-TY:119
   and we conquered.   R. Penny.
      Ad-PB:391
   Angola Question Mark.   L. Hughes.
      Lo-TY:230, Ra-BP:89
   Applebaum's Sunday.   A. Magil.
      Kr-OF:192
   As I Lay with My Head in Your Lap
      Camerado.   W. Whitman.   Gr-BT:27
   Atalanta in Calydon.
      A. Swinburne.   Al-VBP:1041
   The Beginning of a Long Poem
      on why I Burned the City.
      L. Benford.   Kr-OF:55, Lo-TY:257

Beyond the Nigger.   S. Plumpp.
   Ad-PB:387
Black Muslim Boy in a Hospital.
   J. Emmanuel.   Hu-PN:375
Cousin Nancy.   T. Eliot.
   Ha-PO:68
Crack in the Wall Holds Flowers.
   A. Miller.   Ad-PB:181
The Cricket.   Hsü Chih-mo.
   Hs-TC:91
Dark Testament.   P. Murray.
   Bo-AN:107
Dawn in the Heart of Africa.
   P. Lumumba.   Lo-TY:150
The Day-Breakers.   A. Bontemps.
   Ad-PB:84, Be-MA:43, Bo-AN:76,
   Hu-PN:223
The Day I Lay Myself Down.
   P. Mayer.   St-H:131
Death of Dr. King.   S. Cornish.
   Ad-PB:296
Elegy on a Nordic White
   Protestant.   J. Fletcher.
   Hu-PN:503
England and America in 1782.
   A. Tennyson.   Vi-PP:136
Eugene Carman.   E. Masters.
   Kr-OF:181
For Saundra.   N. Giovanni.
   Lo-TY:256, Ra-BP:321
High on the Hog.   J. Fields.
   Be-MA:154
How Old John Brown Took Harper's
   Ferry.   E. Stedman.
   Hu-PN:493, Pa-OM:175
Hugh Selwyn Mauberley.   E. Pound.
   Ba-PO:149, Ca-VT:84, Ha-PO:122,
   Hi-TL:186, Un-MA:301, Wi-LT:232
The Hungry Black Child.
   A. Miller.   Ad-PB:181
Hurricane.   C. Lushington.
   Sa-B:110
I Know I'm Not Sufficiently
   Obscure.   R. Durem.   Ad-PB:151,
   Jo-SA:122, Ra-BP:163
If We Cannot Live as People.
   C. Lynch.   Ad-PB:461
If We Must Die.   C. McKay.
   Ad-PB:25, Be-MA:13, Bo-AN:31,
   Ga-FB:277, Hu-PN:102, Jo-SA:135,
   Kr-OF:48, Lo-TY:118, Ra-BP:63
in defense of black poets.
   C. Rivers.   Ad-BO:20, Ra-BP:200
in orangeburg my brothers did.
   A. Spellman.   Ad-PB:285,
   Ra-BP:229
In the State There Is the Law.
   B. Slutsky.   Bo-RU:80
In This Hotel.   E. Carnaval.
   Gr-SS:141

In This Year of Grace.
   J. Hewitt.   Co-PI:62
Incident with Lions.   S. Hay.
   Ls-NY:32
It Was a Funky Deal.   E. Knight.
   Ad-BO:32, Ad-PB:232, Ra-BP:207
Jim Jones at Botany Bay.
   Co-RM:139, Gr-GB:257
Jitterbugging in the Streets.
   C. Hernton.   Ad-PB:240
John Brown's Prayer.   S. Benét.
   Hu-PN:517
Kent State, May 4, 1970.
   P. Goodman.   Mo-TS:41
The Laws of God, the Laws of Men.
   A. Housman.   Un-MB:102
The Limits of Submission.
   F. Nuur.   Ab-MO:29, Lo-TY:58
mayday.   E. Roberson.   Ad-PB:350
Men Who Hunger.   I. Stern.
   Ho-TY:225
Moths.   J. Fields.   Ad-PB:320,
   Hu-PN:417
My Place.   M. Rosenfeld.   Ho-TY:78
Narrative.   R. Atkins.   Ad-PB:198
The New Duckling.   A. Noyes.
   Fe-FP:283, Hu-MP:241
The Night of Terror.
   Wang Ya-p'ing.   Hs-TC:353
No More Dams I'll Make.
   W. Shakespeare.   Al-VBP:198
The Norfolk Rebellion.   Gr-GB:183
Oh, Oh, You Will Be Sorry for
   That Word.   E. Millay.   Pa-OA:165
On the Fourth Night of Hunger
   Strike.   M. Carter.   Sa-B:167
One Who Mobs the Mob.
   R. Emerson.   Kr-OF:136
Opinions of the New Student.
   R. Pedroso.   Lo-TY:102
Park Bench.   L. Hughes.   Kr-OF:188
Patterns.   A. Lowell.
   Bo-HF:116, Co-BL:142, Cr-WS:115,
   Er-FA:65, Mo-GR:39, Pa-OM:262,
   Pe-OA:47, Sm-PT:18, Un-MA:156
A Pict Song.   R. Kipling.
   Hi-FO:47
Plot Improbable, Character Un-
   sympathetic.   E. Olson.   St-H:173
a poem to complement other poems.
   D. Lee.   Be-MA:158, Ra-BP:300
The Rebel.   J. Fletcher.   Un-MA:319
The Rebel.   I. Randolph.
   Co-RM:208, Hi-TL:128
The Rebellious Vine.   H. Monro.
   Go-BP:277, Mc-WK:110
The Red-Haired Man's Wife.
   J. Stephens.   Un-MB:264
Resolution of Dependence.
   G. Barker.   Wi-LT:524

REBELLION — cont'd.
  Revolutionary Letter No. 29.
    D. Di Prima. Mc-EA:77
  Riot. G. Brooks. Ad-PB:164,
    Ra-BP:175
  Riot Laugh & I Talk.
    D. Henderson. Jo-SA:109
  Riot Rimes, U.S.A.
    R. Patterson. Kr-OF:57
  Riots and Rituals. R. Thomas.
    Ad-PB:371
  Salute. O. Pitcher. Ad-PB:193
  Songs for a Colored Singer, IV.
    E. Bishop. Hu-PN:552
  Sonnets. G. Hopkins. Ox-BN:871
  Street Law. S. Bennett. Ad-II:115
  Thanksgiving. A. Guiterman.
    Co-PU:67
  The Third Sermon on the Warpland.
    G. Brooks. Ra-BP:176
  Tired. F. Johnson.
    Ad-PB:24, Fe-PL:428, Hu-PN:88,
    Kr-OF:48, Lo-TY:210
  To Toussaint L'Ouverture.
    W. Wordsworth. Hi-FO:185,
    Hu-PN:447, Ox-BN:80
  The Trophy. E. Muir. Wi-LT:251
  The True Import of Present
    Dialogue: Black vs. Negro.
    N. Giovanni. Ad-PB:451, Ra-BP:318
  Vive Noir! M. Evans.
    Ad-BO:52, Ad-PB:188
  Walk with de Mayor of Harlem.
    D. Henderson. Ad-PB:412
  The Wall. G. Brooks. Hu-PN:338
  the west ridge is menthol-cool.
    D. Graham. Ad-PB:480
  When Something Happens.
    J. Randall. Ra-BP:275
  With the Moon's Ax.
    J. Sternberg. Ho-TY:196
  Yuh Lookin GOOD. C. Rodgers.
    Ra-BP:266
RECKLESSNESS
  Ballad of the Soldier.
    B. Brecht. Li-TU:231
  New Blast Furnace.
    B. Akhmadulina. Ca-MR:37
RECOMPENSE: see RETRIBUTION;
    REWARDS
RECONSTRUCTION: see CIVIL WAR –
    UNITED STATES – RECONSTRUCTION
RECORD PLAYERS: see PHONOGRAPHS
RECORDERS: see PIPES (MUSIC)
RECREATION: see AMUSEMENTS
RED (COLOR)
  King Rufus. Y. Segal. Do-WH:9
  November Glow. H. Rostron.
    St-FS:57
  Red. A. Faldich. Ba-HI:36
  The Red Nude. D. Etter. Sc-TN:42
  When Sue Wears Red. L. Hughes.
    Lo-TY:228
RED CROSS
  The Red Cross. E. Jacques.
    Se-PR:62
RED RIDING HOOD: see HUMOR – RED
    RIDING HOOD
RED RIVER
  Red River Valley. Er-FA:445
REDBIRDS: see CARDINALS (BIRDS)
REDPOLLS
  Winter in Vermont.
    H. Carruth. Ca-BP:41
REDWINGS: see BLACKBIRDS
REDWOOD TREES: see SEQUOIA TREES
REFINERIES (PETROLEUM)
  Night Fire. J. Knoepfle.
    St-H:96
REFLECTIONS (MIRRORED)
  Beyond Dark Trees. Shiki.
    Be-CS:15
  Broken and Broken. Chosu.
    Be-CS:48
  Casida of the Golden Girl.
    F. García Lorca. Le-SW:49
  City River. S. Muro. Sh-AM:55
  A Cloud Shimmering.
    Shurin. Be-CS:14
  A Coffeepot Face. A. Fisher.
    Hu-MP:20
  Coolness in Summer. Ryusui.
    Sh-RP:67
  The Crystal. G. Barker.
    Wi-LT:523
  Dipping My Feet in Water.
    Cheng Min. Hs-TC:240
  The Freedom of the Moon.
    R. Frost. Ho-LP:55
  The Hunchback. R. Friend.
    Ls-NY:153
  Inscription for a Mirror in a
    Deserted Dwelling.
    W. Benét. Un-MA:329
  It Looks like Your Twin. Re-RR:97
  The Kingfisher. Tori. Le-MW:13
  The Lady of Shalott.
    A. Tennyson. Er-FA:339,
    Hi-WP I:59, Ho-WR:145, Sp-OG:128
  The Lake. J. Stephens. Un-MB:361
  The Lake. J. Tabb. Sh-AP:136
  Lament. W. Williams. Ca-VT:58
  The Mirror. W. Davies. Th-AS:214
  The Mirror. A. Milne. Gr-EC:268
  The Mirror. B. Pasternak.
    Ca-MR:167
  Mirror. J. Updike.
    Mc-WK:117
  Mirror in February. T. Kinsella.
    Pa-GTB:561

The Mirror Perilous.   A. Dugan.
    Br-TC:97, Wi-LT:691
The Moon in the Water.   Ryota.
    Au-SP:342, Le-IS:26
The Night Mirror.   J. Hollander.
    Ho-P:111
The Pond.   M. Morris.   Sa-B:63
Rain Went Sweeping On.   Sho-U.
    Be-CS:35
Reflection.   M. Livingston.
    Fr-MP:4
Reflection.   Tomonori.   Le-MW:83
The River.   D. Davie.   Ls-NY:259
The River Is a Piece of the Sky.
    J. Ciardi.   Ar-TP3:243,
    Au-SP:200, La-PV:183
River Moons.   C. Sandburg.
    Ma-FW:123
Song.   Co-PU:109, Rv-CB:137
Suburban Madrigal.   J. Updike.
    Pe-SS:84
Thoughts while Reading.   Chu Hai.
    Rx-OH:120
Three Riddles: Whose.   Mo-TS:77
Thunder Pools.   R. Coffin.
    Ha-LO:70
A Trout Leaps High.   Onitsura.
    Le-MW:7, Ma-FW:54
Walking by the Stream.
    Hsin Ch'i-Chi.   Le-MW:47
Water Picture.   M. Swenson.
    Co-BN:85, La-OC:121
Yang-Ze-Fu.   Yehoash.   Ho-TY:77
REFRIGERATORS
The Refrigerator.   A. Genikova.
    Mo-MI:50
REFUGEES: see also EXILES
Exodus.   J. Bodet.   Cr-WS:125
Home.   K. Gershon.   Cr-WS:132
Poem.   P. Markish.   Ho-TY:180
Refugee Blues.   W. Auden.
    Hi-WP I:122, Wi-LT:472
The Refugees.   R. Jarrell.Un-MA:651
The Refugees.   H. Read.   Cr-WS:124
To Another Poet a Thousand Years
    Hence.   C. Norman.   Cr-WS:131
War in Chang-An City.   Wang Tsan.
    Ba-PO:41, Cr-WS:12, Ke-PP:8
REFUSE AND REFUSE DISPOSAL:
    see also GARBAGE AND GARBAGEMEN;
    JUNKYARDS; LITTER AND LITTERING;
    POLLUTION; STREET CLEANING
The Fate of a Broom—an Anticipa-
    tion. T. Peacock. Rv-CB:685
REGRETS: see also APOLOGIES;
    HUMOR - REGRETS
After He Has Gone.   S. Warner.
    Un-MB:373
Around the Corner.   C. Towne.
    Fe-PL:128

As One Who Bears Beneath His
    Neighbor's Roof.
    R. Hillyer.   Un-MA:481
Camp Fever.   J. Blight.   Co-RM:96
The Carpenter's Son.   A. Housman.
    Li-SR:136, Un-MB:101
The Cypress.   T. Peacock.
    De-CH:251, No-CL:245
Dejection.   S. Coleridge.
    Ox-BN:167, Rv-CB:665
The Double Shame.   S. Spender.
    Wi-LT:502
England, 1802.   W. Wordsworth.
    Ke-PP:58, Pa-GTB:210
A Faithful Wife.   Chang Chi.
    Rx-LT:82
The Fish Weeps.   Rx-LT:11
For the Girls in My Home Town.
    N. Korzhavin.   Ca-MR:91
Forgiven.   A. Milne.   Au-SP:73,
    Pe-FB:18
The Gipsy Laddie.   Bl-OB:70,
    Sm-LG:185
Gone.   C. Sandburg.   Sh-AP:156
Greedy Richard.   J. Taylor.
    Ox-BC:121
Hélas.   O. Wilde.   Un-MB:67
Henry C. Calhoun.   E. Masters.
    Sh-AP:138, Wi-LT:115
Her Letter.   B. Harte.   Fe-PL:20
I Wanted to Come Home.
    Wen I-to.   Hs-TC:59
Immolated.   H. Melville.   Al-VBP:957
Importune Me No More.
    Elizabeth I, Queen of England.
    Hi-FO:139, Rv-CB:146
In My Own Album.   C. Lamb.
    Rv-CB:673
In the Room of the Bride-Elect.
    T. Hardy.   Gr-BT:84
Incident on a Journey.
    T. Gunn.   To-MP:75
Into My Heart an Air That Kills.
    A. Housman.   Al-VBP:1080,
    Bo-GJ:199, Gr-CT:275, Na-EO:193,
    Un-MB:94, Wi-LT:62
Last Song of Sitting Bull.
    Kr-OF:1, Le-OE:127
The Maid's Lament.   W. Landor.
    Ox-BN:189
Man Look Not Back.   Ga-S:146
Maud Muller.   J. Whittier.
    Fe-PL:47, Sp-OG:271
Meeting.   E. Greenberg.   Ho-TY:310
Mild Is the Parting Year.
    W. Landor.   Rv-CB:669
the mother.   G. Brooks.   Be-MA:79
Mu. Ma'u.   Tr-US II:95
My Little Dreams.   G. Johnson.
    Hu-PN:81

REGRETS — cont'd.
  The Old Familiar Faces. C. Lamb.
    Al-VBP:701, Er-FA:168, Ha-PO:152,
    Ma-YA:168, Mo-GR:43, Pa-GTB:220,
    Rv-CB:672
  An Old Story. E. Robinson.
    Ho-TH:19, Un-MA:118
  Orient Wheat. A. Rich. Mo-BG:39
  The Rachray Man. M. O'Neill.
    Co-PI:162
  Remorse. J. Betjeman. Un-MB:440
  The Rotten-Wooded Willow.
    Suguwara No Michizane. Ba-ST:21
  Sold. R. Cuscaden. St-H:35
  Sonnet 30. W. Shakespeare.
    Al-VBP:201, Er-FA:166, Fe-PL:130,
    Ga-FB:33, Pa-GTB:18, Rv-CB:213
  Sonnet 34. W. Shakespeare.
    Rv-CB:216
  The Stenographers. P. Page.
    Wi-LT:782
  Title Divine Is Mine.
    E. Dickinson. Al-VBP:1003
  Too Late. P. Marston. Ox-BN:887
  The Tortoise. C. Corman.
    Ca-VT:527
  A Wasted Day. F. Cornford.
    Un-MB:306
REINCARNATION
  Another Song of a Fool.
    W. Yeats. Rd-OA:195
  A Creed. J. Masefield. Tr-MR:278
  Dew on a Dusty Heart.
    J. Untermeyer. Un-MA:333
  reincarnation. M. Jackson.
    Ad-PB:498
REINDEER: see DEER
RELATIVES: see also HUMOR -
    RELATIVES; and specific
    relatives, as COUSINS
  Dvonya. L. Simpson. Mo-BG:89
  Girl's-Eye View of Relatives.
    P. McGinley. Ke-TF:90,
    Mc-WS:145
  The Idea of Ancestry. E. Knight.
    Ad-PB:229, Be-MA:108, Ra-BP:203
  Stark Boughs on the Family Tree.
    M. Oliver. Pe-SS:14
RELATIVITY: see also HUMOR -
    RELATIVITY
  The Day. T. Spencer.
    Mo-BG:71, Ni-JP:157
RELIGION: see also FAITH; GOD;
    HUMOR - RELIGION; HYMNS;
    PRAYER; SATIRE - RELIGION;
    WORSHIP; and places of worship,
    as TEMPLES and names of religions
    as listed under the heading -
    RELIGIONS
  Baptism. C. Bell.   Br-AF:140

  The Belfry. R. Thomas. Ga-BP:189
  Bishop Blougram's Apology.
    R. Browning. Ox-BN:547
  Bryan's Last Battle (The Scopes
    Trial). Em-AF:769
  Chief Red Jacket Addresses a
    Missionary. Red Jacket.
    Kr-OF:4
  Church Going. P. Larkin.
    Br-TC:251, Pa-GTB:557,
    Un-MB:528, Wi-LT:754
  The Congo. V. Lindsay.
    Er-FA:300, Hi-WP II:98,
    Hu-PN:484, Pe-OA:55,
    Sh-AP:163, Un-MA:218
  Cowboy's Salvation Song.
    R. Carr. Fi-BG:191
  The Dilly Song. Gr-GB:28
  East and West. Ke-TF:245
  Epilogue. H. Melville. Pl-IO:128
  Harlem Sounds: Hallelujah
    Corner. W. Browne. Bo-AN:173
  Holyghost Woman. C. Major.
    Jo-SA:52
  In California There Are Two
    Hundred Fifty-Six Religions.
    R. Albert. Du-SH:102
  Incense. V. Lindsay. Tr-MR:196
  Innate Helium. R. Frost.
    Pl-IO:104
  Ireland with Emily.
    J. Betjeman. Pa-GTB:500
  Jesus Was Crucified.
    C. Rodgers. Ad-PB:432
  The Loyal Scot. A. Marvell.
    Al-VBP:461
  Marion at the Pentacostal
    Meeting. A. Knowlan.
    Co-EL:142
  Ode to Brother Joe. T. McNeill.
    Sa-B:154
  On the Death of Mr. Crashaw.
    A. Cowley. Al-VBP:448
  The Passionate Man's Pilgrimage.
    W. Raleigh. Al-VBP:97,
    Go-BP:256, Gr-CT:283,
    Hi-WP II:169, Ma-YA:59, Rv-CB:158
  Personal. L. Hughes.
    Bo-AN:66, Hu-PN:188
  Religio Laici. J. Dryden.
    Al-VBP:491
  Saint Ras. T. McNeill. Sa-B:158
  Santos, New Mexico. M. Sarton.
    Pl-EI:116
  Son and Father. C. Day Lewis.
    Pl-EI:135
  The Spiritual Railway. Ga-S:146
  Sunday Morning. W. Stevens.
    Sh-AP:158, Sm-PT:121, Un-MA:242,
    Wi-LT:139

Theologians.   W. de la Mare.
  Pl-EI:20
Time in the Rock.   C. Aiken.
  Ca-VT:153
Trinity Sunday.   V. Kovshin.
  Bo-RU:47
The Unnameable God.   H. Brock.
  Un-R:35
Upon a Ring of Bells.
  J. Bunyan.   De-CH:198
When Mahalia Sings.   Q. Prettyman.
  Ad-PB:260, Pe-M:18
Why Should Men Love the Church.
  T. Eliot.   Tr-MR:199
Within King's College Chapel,
  Cambridge.   W. Wordsworth.
  Ox-BN:81, Pa-GTB:300
The Word of God to Leyden Came.
  J. Rankin.   Se-PR:216, Vi-PP:48
RELIGIONS: see BRAHMINS AND
  BRAHMINISM; BUDDHISM; CHRISTI-
  ANITY; HINDUISM; INDIANS OF
  NORTH AMERICA - RELIGION AND
  MYTHOLOGY; ISLAM; JUDAISM;
  MYTHOLOGY; TAOISM; and names of
  religious leaders, as MOSES
RELIGIONS, PRIMITIVE: see also
  HEAD-HUNTERS; SACRIFICES; and
  names of primitive tribes and
  peoples
  See Tr-US II:53, 54, 64
REMBRANDT, HARMENSZOON VAN RIJN
  A Glance.   Cheng Min.   Hs-TC:235
  Rembrandt to Rembrandt.
  E. Robinson.   Sm-PT:53
REMEDIES AND CURES: see also
  CHARMS; HUMOR - REMEDIES
  AND CURES; MEDICINE
Acon.   H.D.   Ca-VT:106
Against Sickness.   Da-SC:39
And Can the Physician Make Sick
  Men Well?   Bl-OB:157, Gr-EC:288,
  Re-TW:47
Bump on My Knee.   M. Livingston.
  Ho-ME:26
Curing Ritual.   Da-SC:110
Curious Exposure.   G. Sardiff.
  Ni-CD:53
The Death of Robin Hood.
  Ma-BB:77, Ma-FW:156
Earth Cure Me.   Earth Receive
  My Woe.   Wo-HS:(55)
Formula for Young Children.
  Da-SC:143
Healing Song.   Tr-US II:217
Indian Brew.   Ju-CP:4
Medicine Song for Snake Sickness.
  Da-SC:145
Mountain Medicine.   E. Long.
  Br-AF:109

My Help Is in the Mountain.
  Wo-HS:(55)
Shaman's Song.   Da-SC:49
Sheep-Skin and Bee's Wax.
  Ir-BB:127, Pa-RE:76
Snake Medicine Song.   Da-SC:144
Song Before Gathering Medicinal
  Herbs for the Treatment of
  Sick Children.   Tr-US II:292
Songs Accompanying Healing Magic.
  Do-CH:(40)
Sonnet 118.   W. Shakespeare.
  Rv-CB:242
That Little Black Cat.
  D. Thompson.   Ox-BC:231
To Shorten a Night-Goer on
  This Side.   Da-SC:144
Try Tropic.   G. Taggard.
  Un-MA:480
Winifred Waters.   W. Rands.
  Ox-BC:237
See also Mo-TB:97-104
RENEWAL
After I Had Worked All Day.
  C. Reznikoff.   Ca-VT:187
And Every Sky Was Blue and
  Rain.   R. Hodgson.   Ha-LO:105
And Now in Age I Bud Again.
  G. Herbert.   Rv-CB:357
The Animal That Drank Up
  Sound.   W. Stafford.   Ca-VT:413
But They That Wait upon the
  Lord.   Bible.   O.T.   Isaiah.
  Ar-TP3:209
Cities and Thrones and Powers.
  R. Kipling.   Bo-GJ:197,
  Ni-JP:123, Ox-BN:930
Deliverance.   L. Lee.   Go-BP:238
Former Barn Lot.   M. Van Doren.
  Ga-FB:296, Ha-LO:53, La-PV:166,
  Un-MA:467
The Goddess.   T. de Banville.
  Gr-SS:125
He Is Not Dead.   T. Wyatt.
  Rv-CB:88
The Last Day and the First.
  T. Weiss.   Br-TC:464, Ca-VT:435
Light.   H. Hagedorn.   Tr-MR:244
My Heart Has Known Its Winter.
  A. Bontemps.   Be-MA:45
Noah.   S. Sassoon.   Cl-FC:69
The Old Repair Man.   F. Johnson.
  Bo-AN:27, Pe-M:75
The Onset.   R. Frost.   Sh-AP:151,
  Un-MA:168
Panic.   A. MacLeish.   Un-MA:460
The Pythoness.   K. Raine.
  Al-VBP:1233, Un-MB:485
Renascence.   E. Millay.
  Er-FA:95, Un-MA:440

RENEWAL — cont'd.
  Rumination. R. Eberhart.
    Ho-LP:96, Sm-MK:214, Wi-LT:433
  Seeds. T. Snyder. Hu-NN:88
  Small Prayer. W. Kees.
    Ca-VT:408
  Spring Morning. D. Lawrence.
    Co-BL:52, Un-MB:297
  The Spring Will Come. H. Lowry.
    Co-BN:17, Co-PU:9
  Storm. R. Pitter. Go-BP:241
  Struggle. S. Lanier. Rv-CB:943
  This Compost. W. Whitman.
    Un-MA:86
  Tree in December. M. Cane.
    Un-MA:235
  When They Have Lost.
    C. Day Lewis. Un-MB:425
  The Whirlwind. Br-MW:129,
    Da-SC:118
  Wind in the Grass.
    M. Van Doren. Ga-FB:296
  Winter Rain. C. Rossetti.
    Co-BN:184, Ho-WR:24
RENUNCIATION: see also LOVE —
    RENUNCIATION
  For a Virgin Lady. C. Cullen.
    Un-MA:571
  Renunciation. E. Dickinson.
    Un-MA:104
  To a Persistent Phantom.
    F. Horne. Bo-AN:50
REPAIRING
  Fixer of Midnight. R. Denney.
    Du-SH:54
  The Man of the House.
    D. Wagoner. Du-SH:52
  Sunday at the End of Summer.
    H. Nemerov. Co-BN:98
REPENTANCE: see also HUMOR —
    REPENTANCE
  Adam Bell, Clym of the Clough,
    and William of Cloudesley.
    Ma-BB:157, Ox-BB:380
  Adieu; Farewell Earth's Bliss.
    T. Nashe. Al-VBP:211,
    De-CH:244, Gr-CT:356, Ha-PO:142,
    Hi-FO:141, Rv-CB:276, Sm-LG:276
  Batter My Heart. J. Donne.
    Er-FA:468, Pl-EI:52, Rv-CB:310
  Brazen Tongue. W. Benét.
    Un-MA:327
  The Cherry-Tree Carol. Al-VBP:58,
    Ga-S:64, Gr-CT:127, Gr-GB:299,
    Ke-TF:47, Ox-BB:1, Pa-OM:349,
    Rv-CB:53
  Dance Song. Tr-US I:232
  Ghosts. Fire. Water.
    J. Kirkup. Go-BP:215
  The Heir of Linne. Ma-BB:110

Hind Etin.   Ox-BB:97
Holy Sonnets. J. Donne.
  Al-VBP:262, Gr-CT:382, Ma-FW:175,
  Ma-YA:81, Pl-EI:58, Rv-CB:308
A Hymn. P. Fletcher. Rv-CB:320
Jacob and the Angel.
  Brother Antoninus. Tr-MR:72
Jerusalem. W. Blake. Al-VBP:623,
  Gr-CT:295, Ox-BN:42
Just as I Am, Without One Plea.
  C. Elliott. Ke-TF:191
Lord, Thou Hast Been Our Dwelling
  Place. Bible. O.T. Psalms.
  Me-PH:23, Pl-EI:198
Penitence. W. Cowper.   Go-BP:179
Proud Margret. Ox-BB:74
The Queen of Hearts. An-IP:(24),
  Bo-FP:54, Br-FF:(26), Ir-BB:263,
  Li-LB:56, Mo-MGT:122, Mo-NR:59,
  Wi-MG:71, Wr-RM:107
To Heaven. R. Herrick. Ga-S:142
Upon the Image of Death.
  R. Southwell. De-CH:244
Walk, Damn You, Walk!
  W. De Vere. Fe-PL:51
REPORTERS: see HUMOR - REPORTERS;
  JOURNALISM; NEWSPAPERS
REPRIMANDS: see also HUMOR -
  REPRIMANDS
  Am I Stupid? H. Ooguro.
    Le-TA:92
  An Elder's Reproof to His Wife.
    A. Muuse. Lo-TY:57
  I and I. H. Sanuki. Le-TA:54
  The Midnight Snack.
    J. Merrill. Mo-BG:80
  The Poetess Reproaches Mohammed
    ag Mekiia. Eberkaou oult
    Beleou. Tr-US I:136
  Song of Reproach. Bi-IT:63
  Songs at a Wedding, I.
    Tr-US II:166
REPROACHES: see REPRIMANDS
REPTILES: see also CROCODILES;
  LIZARDS; SNAKES
  Prayer for Reptiles. P. Hubbell.
    Ad-PE:42, La-PV:153
REPUTATION: see FAME
RESCUES AND RESCUING: see also
  HUMOR - RESCUES AND RESCUING;
  LIFESAVING
  Alice Brand. W. Scott. Pa-OM:248
  Boot and Saddle. R. Browning.
    Bo-FP:300
  Geordie. Ox-BB:557
  It Shall Be. Ho-SD:13
  The Little Dog under the Wagon.
    Fe-PL:360
  The Maid Freed from the Gallows.
    Gr-EC:134

The Main Truck; or a Leap for
    Life. G. Morris. Fe-PL:55
The Rescue. J. Logan. St-H:117
The Rescue. D. Schmitz.
    St-H:190
Robin Hood and the Widow's Three
    Sons. Ar-TP3:17, Co-PT:224,
    Ma-BB:70, Pa-OM:86, Sp-OG:157,
    Un-GT:119
The Story of Johnny Head-in-Air.
    H. Hoffmann. Ox-BC:206
REST: see also HUMOR - REST; SLEEP
    Bearded Oaks. R. Warren.
        Br-TC:451, Sh-AP:211,
        Un-MA:589, Wi-LT:840
    Chipmunk, Chipmunk.
        M. Van Doren. Rd-SS:20
    Endymion. J. Keats. Go-BP:161
    Evening. G. Byron. Mc-PR:98
    Lines for a Bed at Kelmscott
        Manor. W. Morris. De-CH:445,
        Ho-WR:235, Rd-SS:14
    The Lotos Eaters. A. Tennyson.
        Mo-GR:129
    On a Tired Housewife. Ga-S:216,
        Hi-WP I:9, Na-EO:139, Sm-MK:113
    Rest. C. Rossetti. Ox-BN:712
    Rest Hour. G. Johnston.
        Do-WH:10
    Siesta. S. Hazo. Ls-NY:53
RESTAURANTS AND BARS: see also
    HUMOR - RESTAURANTS AND BARS;
    INNS AND TAVERNS
    A Ballad about Nuggets.
        Y. Yevtushenko. Ca-MR:57
    Emmy. A. Symons. Ox-BN:934
    Frascati's. A. Huxley.
        Al-VBP:1200
    The Geraniums. G. Taggard.
        Ca-VT:90
    Hemmed-In Males. W. Williams.
        Ha-PO:74
    Lunch at the Coq d'Or.
        P. Davison. Br-TC:85
    R Is for the Restaurant.
        P. McGinley. Ar-TP3:90
    Three Poems for the Indian
        Steelworkers in a Bar where
        I Used to Drink.
        J. Bruchac. Ni-CD:36
    Uptown. A. Ginsberg. Br-TC:150
RESURRECTION: see also EASTER;
    FUTURE LIFE; HUMOR - RESURREC-
    TION; JESUS CHRIST
    Canticle of the Sun Dancing on
        Easter Morning.
        J. Heath-Stubbs. Go-BP:298
    Doubting Thomas. Ga-S:176
    Easter Hymn. A. Housman. Pl-EI:87
    Easter Hymn. M. Thwaites. Tr-MR:133

Even Such Is Time.   Al-VBP:97,
    De-CH:644, Ga-S:219, Gr-BT:167,
    Gr-CT:381, Hi-WP II:169,
    Na-EO:93
O Filii et Filiae. Ga-S:174
Prayer to the Moon. Be-AP:23
The Resurrection. J. Brooks.
    Bo-AN:95, Hu-PN:236
The Sacrament of Sleep.
    J. Oxenham. Fe-PL:332
Seven Stanzas at Easter.
    J. Updike. Pl-EI:36
Softly Through the Mellow
    Starlight. Se-PR:77
That Nature Is a Heraclitean
    Fire and of the Comfort of
    the Resurrection.
    G. Hopkins. Pa-GTB:396
To Bring the Dead to Life.
    R. Graves. Un-MB:390
Verses Composed on the Eve of
    His Execution. J. Graham.
    Gr-CT:383, Rv-CB:388
The Yew Tree. V. Watkins.
    Pl-EI:6
RETIREMENT: see also OLD AGE
    At Grass. P. Larkin.
        Ha-WR:25, Mo-SD:176
    The Calls. W. Owen. Go-BP:48
    I Have Been a Forester.
        Gr-GB:151, Rv-CB:22
    Jim at the Corner. E. Farjeon.
        Au-SP:151
    The Old Falcon. E. Baldwin.
        Ls-NY:107
    A Schoolmaster Retires.
        E. Lieberman. Ke-TF:156
    Shillin' a Day. R. Kipling.
        Al-VBP:1100
    Swineherd. E. Chuilleanáin.
        Co-PI:24
    To One Planning Retirement.
        E. Lieberman. Ke-TF:157
    Too Old to Work. J. Glazer.
        Hi-TL:226
    Upon the Downs. G. Etherege.
        Al-VBP:495
RETRIBUTION: see also HUMOR -
    RETRIBUTION; PUNISHMENT;
    REVENGE
    Barbara Allen. Al-VBP:55,
        Er-FA:315, Mc-PR:156,
        Rv-CB:434, Un-MW:112
    Bishop Hatto. R. Southey.
        Gr-CT:130, Ha-PO:78, Pa-OM:125
    Black All Day. R. Patterson.
        Ad-BO:4, Ad-PB:212
    The Bushrangers. E. Harrington.
        Co-PT:244
    A Creed. J. Masefield. Tr-MR:278

RETRIBUTION — cont'd.
  Dere's No Hidin' Place down Dere.
    Ra-BP:25
  Dives and Lazarus. Ga-S:202,
    Ma-FW:165, Ox-BB:5
  Esthetique du Mal, XIII.
    W. Stevens. Wi-LT:158
  A Gest of Robyn Hode, The Second
    and Third Fyttes.
    Ox-BB:433, 443
  The Hound. S. Lanier. Co-PM:113
  Image. H. Dumas. Ad-BO:7
  The Inchcape Rock. R. Southey.
    Gr-CT:141, Un-GT:161
  Lamkin. Ox-BB:313, Rv-CB:44
  A Lyke-Wake Dirge.
    De-CH:248, Ga-S:219, Gr-CT:366,
    Gr-GB:322, Ma-BB:236, Ma-FW:258,
    Na-EO:107, Pl-EI:139, Rv-CB:54
  The Marvellous Bear Shepherd.
    Ma-FW:216
  My Thirty Years. J. Manzano.
    Lo-TY:98
  On Calvary's Lonely Hill.
    H. Johnson. Hu-PN:286
  Psalm 137. L. Ryzhova. Bo-RU:70
  Rejoice Not, O Israel, for Joy.
    Bible. O.T. Hosea. Me-PH:46
  The Rime of the Ancient Mariner.
    S. Coleridge. Al-VBP:679,
    Co-RG:60, Co-SS:131, De-CH:364,
    Er-FA:318, Ga-FB:105, Ha-PO:15,
    Hi-WP II:68, Ma-YA:146, Ni-JP:52,
    Ox-BN:139, Rv-CB:658, Sm-LG:312
  Sonnets at Christmas. A. Tate.
    Hu-PN:520
  Tale. Br-MW:44
  Tit for Tat. W. de la Mare.
    Co-BBW:273
  The Tragedy of King Lear.
    W. Shakespeare. Ma-FW:272
  Two Ponies Shy. Fi-BG:142
  The White-Footed Deer.
    W. Bryant. Sp-OG:178
  Young Benjie. Ox-BB:337
  Younge Andrew. Ox-BB:216
RETURNING: see also HOMECOMING;
    HUMOR - RETURNING; SATIRE -
    RETURNING
  After a Journey. T. Hardy.
    Ox-BN:842, Pa-GTB:407
  After the Visit. T. Hardy.
    Ox-BN:835
  Arriving in the Country Again.
    J. Wright. Co-PU:139
  Autobiography: Last Chapter.
    J. Barnes. Ni-CD:27
  Both Sides of the Yellow River
    Recaptured by the Imperial
    Army. Tu Fu. Cr-WS:10

  Celebrated Return. C. Major.
    Be-MA:143, Bo-AN:182
  Circle One. O. Dodson. Bo-HF:172
  Convalescence. A. Rau. Mc-AC:145
  Discovery. Wen I-to. Hs-TC:58
  A Dream. B. Akhmadulina. Ca-MR:41
  Exile. D. Scott. Sa-B:59
  For Me Again. T. Joans.
    Be-MA:100
  For the Girls in My Home Town.
    N. Korzhavin. Ca-MR:91
  Frail Hands. L. Trent.
    De-FS:198
  The Gone. J. Stuart. De-FS:195
  Guinea. J. Roumain. Lo-TY:92
  Heman Avenue Holiday.
    J. Knoepfle. St-H:99
  Home. Le-MW:126, Rx-LT:9
  I Return to My City.
    O. Mandelstam. Ca-MR:148
  I Return to the Place where I
    Was Born. T'ao Yuan Ming.
    Rx-LT:33
  I Shall Go Back. E. Millay.
    Sm-PT:170, Un-MA:446
  I Years Had Been from Home.
    E. Dickinson. Rv-CB:917,
    Sh-AP:128
  In and Out: Severance of
    Connections, 1946.
    L. Sissman. Br-TC:384
  Jimmy's Father. J. Wade.
    Sc-TN:225
  Johnny, I Hardly Knew Ye.
    Gr-GB:241
  My Spirit Will Not Haunt the
    Mound. T. Hardy.
    Ox-BN:838, Un-MB:32
  Newark Abbey. T. Peacock.
    Ox-BN:233
  A Note of Humility. A. Bontemps.
    Be-MA:46, Hu-PN:222
  Odysseus. C. Guri. Me-PH:121
  Our House. O. Goga. Mc-AC:39
  Picnic to the Earth.
    S. Tanikawa. Sh-AM:132
  Puzzle. S. Cooksley. Ls-NY:17
  The Quarry Pool. D. Levertov.
    Ca-VT:510
  Resolve. V. Miller. Ha-TP:106
  The Return. A. Bontemps.
    Ad-PB:84, Hu-PN:215
  The Return. E. Dickinson.
    Un-MA:103
  The Return. R. Kipling. Un-MB:130
  Returning. Ch'en Fu. Le-MW:54
  The Seaman's Happy Return.
    Gr-CT:64, Gr-GB:119
  Second Night in N.Y.C. after 3
    Years. G. Corso. Gr-BT:37

The Ship. J. Squire. De-CH:402,
  De-TT:133
Song of a Returning Voyager.
  Tr-US II:41
Song of Entering the Village.
  Da-SC:115
Songs, I. Tr-US II:135
The Southern Road. D. Randall.
  Ad-PB:139, Be-MA:70, Hu-NN:41
Soviet Russia. S. Yesenin.
  Ca-MR:110
To Where My Own Teacups.
  S. Ogiwara. Sh-AM:165
Viaticum. Pao Yu. Rx-LT:35
Walking Across Brooklyn Bridge.
  J. Marshall. Mc-EA:78
Wessex Heights. Ox-BN:839
Woodstock. J. Mitchell.
  Mo-GR:102
REVENGE: see also HUMOR - REVENGE
  Birkett's Eagle. D. Howard.
    Ca-MB:27
  Braddock's Fate, with an Incite-
    ment to Revenge. S. Tilden.
    Hi-TL:33
  Brady's Bend. M. Keller.
    Co-PT:217
  Brian Boy Magee. F. Carbery.
    Co-PI:21
  Can't Kill Him. Chang Chih-min.
    Hs-TC:426
  El Capitan-General. C. Leland.
    Co-SS:25
  The Challenger. D. Wandrei.
    De-FS:214
  The Congo. V. Lindsay.
    Er-FA:300, Hi-WP II:98, Hu-PN:484,
    Pe-OA:55, Sh-AP:163, Un-MA:218
  The Death of Lord Warriston.
    Ox-BB:603
  'Dobe Bill. Co-RM:31
  Doing an Injury. B. Franklin.
    Un-GT:25
  1867. J. Plunkett. Co-PI:169
  find my father with freedom.
    L. Curry. Jo-VC:38
  The Fire of Frendraught.
    Ox-BB:610
  Flogged Child. J. Keith.
    De-FS:116
  For Stephen Dixon. Z. Gilbert.
    Ad-PB:195
  A Gest of Robyn Hode, The Sixth
    Fytte. Ox-BB:469
  He Got Up. Ai Ch'ing.
    Hs-TC:299
  Henry C. Calhoun. E. Masters.
    Sh-AP:138, Wi-LT:115
  Jackie Faa. Gr-CT:162,
    Ma-BB:106, Ox-BB:249

Jamie Telfer and the Fair Dodhead.
  Ox-BB:549
Jellon Grame. Ox-BB:164
Judith of Bethulia.
  J. Ransom. Wi-LT:313
The Laboratory. R. Browning.
  Ni-JP:38
The Laily Worm and the Machrel of
  the Sea. Gr-CT:135, Ox-BB:59,
  Rd-OA:200
The Lament of the Border Cattle
  Thief. R. Kipling. Co-RM:159
Lamkin. Ox-BB:313, Rv-CB:44
Little Mousgrove and the Lady
  Barnet. Ox-BB:168
Lord Maxwell's Last Goodnight.
  Ox-BB:607
The Lord of Lorn and the Fals
  Steward. Ox-BB:285
Old Christmas. R. Helton.
  Co-PM:94, Un-MA:346
The Outlandish Knight.
  Br-SM:36, Un-GT:111
Passamaquoddy War Song.
  Da-SC:254
Poem for Adolph Eichman.
  J. Harriman. Lo-IT:42
Prelude. C. Rivers. Ad-PB:233,
  Be-MA:107
The Raven. S. Coleridge.
  Ho-WR:212
The Revenge of Hamish. S. Lanier.
  Ni-JP:46, Sp-OG:141
Revolt. Rachel. Me-PH:87
The River of Stars. A. Noyes.
  Pa-OM:131
Shameful Death. W. Morris.
  Gr-CT:129, Gr-SS:174,
  Pa-GTB:380, Un-GT:136
The Shooting of Dan McGrew.
  R. Service. Co-RM:129,
  Do-WH:22, Er-FA:382, Fe-PL:9
Sir Halewyn. Ox-BB:690
A Song of Huezotzinco. Da-SC:178
Song of Revenge. Tr-US II:113
Song of the Last Moments.
  Tr-US I:58
Speak No Evil. Un-GT:238
The Subway Witnesses.
  L. Thomas. Ad-PB:482
Taffy Was a Welshman.
  Co-BB:83, Gr-GB:163, Mo-MGT:53,
  Mo-NR:98, Wr-RM:113
The Three Songs. B. Taylor.
  Co-PT:237
Tit for Tat: A Tale.
  J. Aikin. Ox-BC:90
To a Traitor. Tr-US II:301
tony get the boys. D. Graham.
  Ad-PB:480

REVENGE — cont'd.

Tyson's Corner. P. St. John.
Ad-PB:345

The Women and the Man. Te-FC:87

Young Benjie. Ox-BB:337

Younger Brother. T. Suzuki.
Le-TA:28

Yussouf. J. Lowell. Hu-MP:409

REVERE, PAUL: see also HUMOR -
REVERE, PAUL

Paul Revere's Ride. H. Longfellow.
Ar-TP3:40, Er-FA:368, Fe-FP:418,
Ga-FB:254, Hi-TL:48, Se-PR:90,
Sh-RP:278, Sm-LG:258, Sp-OG:24,
Un-GT:184, Vi-PP:278

REVERENCE: see WORSHIP

REVIVALS: see also SATIRE - REVIVALS

Evangel. J. Burden. Ls-NY:147

Evangelist. D. Etter. Sc-TN:42

A Revivalist in Boston. A. Rich.
Pl-EI:107

REVOLTS AND REVOLUTIONS: see also
FRENCH REVOLUTION, 1789-1799;
HUMOR - REVOLTS AND REVOLUTIONS;
REBELLION; REVOLUTIONARY WAR IN
AMERICA, 1776-1781; RUSSIAN
REVOLUTION, 1917-1921; SATIRE -
REVOLTS AND REVOLUTIONS

Black Hieroglyph. T. Matthews.
Sa-B:230

Dedication to a Final Confrontation. Djangatolum.
Ad-PB:512, Jo-SA:12

The Glowing Years. Jen Chün.
Hs-TC:392

How the Sestina (Yawn) Works.
A. Waldman. Mc-EA:23

I Am a Multitude. A. De Loach.
Lo-IT:28

In the State There Is the Law.
B. Slutsky. Bo-RU:80

In the Time of Revolution.
J. Lester. Ad-PB:354, Lo-IT:75

The Last Riot. V. Howard.
Jo-VC:8

A Litany at Atlanta.
W. Du Bois. Hu-PN:20

Manifesto of Man. Y. Galanskov.
Bo-RU:29

March 18. Jao Meng-k'an.
Hs-TC:106

Musical Vietnams. B. Allen. Lo-IT:4

My Poem. N. Giovanni.
Ad-BO:22, Ad-PB:453, Ra-BP:319

1905. B. Pasternak. Ca-MB:171

On the Birth of My Son, Malcolm
Coltrane. J. Lester.
Ad-PB:356, Jo-SA:24

Only the Beards Are Different.
B. Dawe. Cr-WS:44

Poem. M. Als. Sa-B:226

Poem for Black Boys.
N. Giovanni. Ra-BP:325

The Rendezvous. B. Spencer.
Pa-GTB:519

The Revolutionary Core:
Che Guevara. A. Raymond.
Sa-B:184

Roses and Revolutions. D. Randall.
Ad-PB:142, Ra-BP:142

The Second Coming. W. Yeats.
Mo-GR:89, Pa-GTB:424, Pl-EI:28,
Tr-MR:236, Un-MB:117, Wi-LT:72

The Second Sermon on the Warpland.
G. Brooks. Ad-PB:163, Ra-BP:171

Simon: How Many Bolivars?
C. Lushington. Sa-B:194

Smash the Blockade. Jen Chün.
Hs-TC:398

Song after Defeat. Tr-US I:37

The Song of the Western Men.
R. Hawker. Co-RG:25, Hi-FO:161,
Na-EO:109, Ox-BN:459, Rv-CB:777

Song to the Men of England.
P. Shelley. Al-VBP:746

Ten Years: 1959-1969.
J. Carew. Sa-B:189

The Terror Spreads like Fire.
Kuo Mo-jo. Hs-TC:40

Toussaint L'Ouverture.
E. Robinson. Hu-PN:471

When Black People Are.
A. Spellman. Ad-PB:284,
Be-MA:127, Ra-BP:228

Why Should I Want. W. Harris.
Ad-PB:439

REVOLUTIONARY WAR IN AMERICA,
1776-1781: see also BOSTON TEA
PARTY, 1773; FOURTH OF JULY; and
names of persons, as ALLEN,
ETHAN; and names of battles, as
LEXINGTON, BATTLE, 1775

After. R. Kipling. Mc-PR:66

Captain Molly. W. Collins.
Vi-PP:119

Carmen Bellicosum. G. McMaster.
Vi-PP:114

Citizen Paine. J. Daugherty.
Gr-EC:230

Concord Hymn. R. Emerson.
Al-VBP:805, Br-AF:61, Er-FA:188,
Fe-FP:422, Hi-TL:52, Hu-MP:379,
Ke-TF:256, Mc-PR:22, Pa-HT:18,
Se-PR:87, Sh-AP:25, Sp-OG:193,
Tu-WW:30, Vi-PP:99

Death and General Putnam.
A. Guiterman. Co-PM:77,
Co-RM:219, Cr-WS:55

The Dying Sergeant.
Em-AF:420

Emily Geiger.   Fe-PL:164, Vi-PP:124
Epitaph for a Concord Boy.
   S. Young.   Mc-WK:164
Jolly Soldier.   Em-AF:432
The Little Black-Eyed Rebel.
   W. Carleton.   Fe-FP:551,
   Un-GT:188
Major Andre.   Em-AF:428
Molly Pitcher.   L. Richards.
   Hi-TL:55
My Country Need Not Change Her
   Gown.   E. Dickinson. Br-AF:63
New England's Chevy Chase.
   E. Hale. Se-PR:88, Vi-PP:103
Paul Jones.   Vi-PP:132
Paul Jones's Victory.   Em-AF:425
Paul Revere's Ride. H. Longfellow.
   Ar-TP3:40, Er-FA:368, Fe-FP:418,
   Ga-FB:254, Hi-TL:48, Se-PR:90,
   Sh-RP:278, Sm-LG:258, Sp-OG:24,
   Un-GT:184, Vi-PP:278
Prophecy in Flame.   F. Howard.
   Br-AF:62
Song of Marion's Men.
   W. Bryant.   Hi-TL:57
The Stately Southerner. Em-AF:423
To the Memory of the Brave
   Americans.   P. Freneau.
   Fe-PL:166, Sh-AP:14, Vi-PP:134
Yankee Doodle.   Em-AF:427,
   Er-FA:434, Fe-FP:422,
   Se-PR:162, Vi-PP:107
REWARDS: see also HUMOR –
   REWARDS; MEDALS
The Beatific Vision.
   G. Chesterton.   Tr-MR:244
Brown Robyn's Confession.
   De-CH:399, Gr-GB:314
Cast They Bread upon the Waters.
   Bible.   O.T.   Ecclesiastes.
   Ar-TP3:209
L'Envoi.   R. Kipling.
   Er-FA:10, Ke-TF:453
The Forgotten Man. E. Markham.
   Fe-PL:42
Go to Bed First.   Gr-CT:410
   Gr-GB:17, Mo-MGT:39, On-TW:63,
   Rd-SS:7, Rv-ON:46
If You Would Reap Praise.
   B. Franklin.   Un-GT:26
The Jolly Thresherman.   Em-AF:773
Justorium Animae.   Apochrypha.
   Wisdom.   Ga-S:51
A Man's Bread.   J. Peabody.
   Ha-YA:107
Momotaro.   Ar-TP3:136, Ir-BB:243
Not Only Around Our Infancy.
   J. Lowell.   Er-FA:480
The Sermon on the Mount. Bible.
   N.T.   Matthew.   Un-GT:312

A Smuggler's Song. R. Kipling.
   Bl-OB:52, Ha-PO:43
Tom Tinker's Ground.   Rv-ON:71
Two Surprises. R. McAlpine.
   Fe-PL:88
When Jacky's a Very Good Boy.
   Ag-HE:61, Mo-MGT:107, Na-EO:70
REYNOLDS, SIR JOSHUA: see HUMOR –
   REYNOLDS, SIR JOSHUA
RHINE RIVER
   Childe Harold's Pilgrimage.
   G. Byron.   Al-VBP:725
   The Lorelei.   H. Heine.
   Co-PM:87, Sp-OG:116, Un-GT:137
RHINOCEROSES: see also HUMOR –
   RHINOCEROSES
The Rhino Stands Still in a
   Field of Lilies. N. O'Gorman.
   Be-EB:56
The Rhinoceros.   R. Lister.
   Co-BBW:193
The Rhinoceros.   O. Nash.
   Co-FB:7, Co-HP:100, Sh-RP:142,
   Un-GT:37, Un-MA:564
RHODE ISLAND: see also names of
   towns, as NEWPORT, R.I.
   Rhode Island.   T. Brown.
   Se-PR:282
RHODODENDRONS
   Green Symphony.   J. Fletcher.
   Un-MA:314
RHODORAS
   The Rhodora.   R. Emerson.
   Co-BN:59, De-CH:577, Er-FA:468,
   Ga-FB:289, Hu-MP:264, Sp-OG:359,
   Un-GT:257
RHYTHM
   Metrical Feet. S. Coleridge.
   Ox-BC:112
   The Pulse.   M. Van Doren.
   Un-MA:467
   The Room.   D. Harrison. Ad-PB:394
RIBBONS
   Hair Ribbons.   Br-BC:47
   Little Blue Ribbons. A. Dobson.
   Br-BC:54
   Why Do Girls.   Re-RR:45
RICE
   Before the Shrine.   Br-FW:3
   Invocation to the Rice Soul
   at Harvest Time.
   Tr-US II:204
   Mud in Vietnam.   J. Lester.
   Jo-SA:66
   The Rice Seller.   Bo-FP:129
RICHARD III, KING OF
   ENGLAND
   Richard III.   W. Shakespeare.
   Hi-FO:102
RICHES: see WEALTH

RIDDLES

Although It Never Asked a Thing.
    Ju-CP:13
Anyone if He Will Try.   Ju-CP:13
Around the Rick.   Mo-MGT:155
As Black as Ink.   Rv-ON:54
As I Looked Out o' My Chamber
    Window.   De-CH:676
As I Was Going o'er London Bridge.
    De-CH:675, Mo-MGT:156
As I Was Going o'er Yon Moor of
    Moss.   De-CH:676
As I Was Going to St. Ives.
    Au-SP:26, Cl-DT:61, Li-LB:168,
    Mo-NR:122, On-TW:29
As I Was Walking.   Mo-MGT:157
As I Went over London Bridge.
    Gr-CT:11
As White as Milk.   De-TT:31
At the End of My Yard.   Gr-CT:12
Big and Gray.   Gr-BB:15
Bird Riddles.   Gr-GB:65
Black, but Not a Raven.   Gr-BB:14
Black I Am.   Mo-MGT:154
Black Within.   De-CH:676, Gr-GB:17,
    Mo-MGT:155, Wr-RM:87
A Book.   H. More.   Co-PS:141,
    Se-PR:306
Book-Moth.   Ma-YA:3, Rd-OA:29
Bridges Great, Bridges Small.
    Ju-CP:13
A Bright Red Flower He Wears
    on His Head.   Wy-CM:20
The Broad Water.   Rv-ON:58
Busy Craftsmen in Their Homes.
    Gr-BB:15
A Cherry.   Wr-RM:121
A Child That Has a Cold.
    T. Dibdin.   Co-PU:18,
    Gr-CT:392
Clothed in Yellow, Red, and
    Green.   Mo-MGT:155
Come a Riddle.   De-CH:676
Crooked as a Rainbow.
    Ju-CP:10
Dreaming of Apples.   De-CH:676
Enigma on the Letter H.
    C. Fanshawe.   Un-GT:229
An Equal.   Wr-RM:107
The Fiddler and His Wife.
    De-CH:675
The Fields Are Golden. Gr-BB:20
Fish Riddles, I, II.   Gr-GB:73
The Five. J. Swift. Gr-EC:124
A Flock of White Sheep. De-TT:31
Flour of England.   Mo-MGT:155,
    Wr-RM:55
Four Stiff-Standers. Br-FF:(42),
    Gr-CT:13, Gr-GB:17, 58,Li-LB:168,
    Mo-MGT:157, Mo-TL:46, Sp-TM:13

Fruit, Flower and Tree Riddles.
    Gr-GB:71, 72
Goes Through the Mud.   Mo-MGT:157
He Went to the Wood.
    Gr-GB:210, Mo-MGT:156
High It Flies.   Ju-CP:12
Highty, Tighty, Paradighty.
    Gr-CT:3
A House Full, a Yard Full.
    De-CH:675, Li-LB:169,
    Mo-MGT:154, Rv-ON:55
How Many Birds? Rv-ON:54
Humpty Dumpty.   Mother Goose.
    Bo-FP:29, De-PO:18, Fr-WO:32,
    Li-LB:60, Mo-CC:(52),
    Mo-MGT:110, Mo-NR:88, Wi-MG:3,
    Wr-RM:40
I Am Round like a Ball. St-FS:39
I Can Prick Your Finger.
    St-FS:39
I Can Walk on This.   St-FS:40
I Have a Little Sister.
    Ar-TP3:99, De-CH:675, De-TT:32,
    Li-LB:169, Mo-MGT:156,Re-RR:46,
    Rv-ON:58
I Have a Young Sister.
    De-CH:55, Gr-GB:84
I Have Four Sisters Beyond the
    Sea.   On-TW:20
I Have Legs.   St-FS:38
I Have No Wings, but Yet I Fly.
    M. Austin.   Ar-TP3:99
I Have Teeth.   St-FS:38
An Icicle.   Mother Goose.
    Ar-TP3:99, Au-SP:24, Wr-RM:96
If You Are Wise.   Ju-CP:12
I'm Called by the Name of a
    Man.   Gr-GB:65, Mo-MGT:154
In Marble Walls.   Gr-CT:11,
    Gr-GB:58, Mo-MGT:155,
    Rv-ON:57, Sm-MK:32
In Spring I Look Gay.
    Mo-MGT:155
Insect Riddles.   Gr-GB:70
It Has Eyes and a Nose.
    Wy-CM:24
It Is in the Rock.   Gr-CT:10
It Is Smooth and Round and
    Red.   Gr-BB:9
It Never Moves by Day or Night.
    Ju-CP:11
I've Seen You where You Never
    Was.   De-TT:32
Jiggity-Jig, Jiggity-Jig.
    Ju-CP:11,
A Kettle for the Tea. Gr-BB:31
King John and the Abbot of
    Canterbury. Sp-OG:147, Un-GT:120
The Land Was White.   Gr-CT:10,
    Mo-MGT:156

A Lane.   Bo-FP:38
Little Billy Breek.   Mo-MGT:156
Little Nancy Etticoat.
    Ar-TP3:99, Au-SP:25, Bo-FP:36,
    Gr-CT:3, Li-LB:169, Mo-MGT:154,
    Mo-NR:99, Wr-RM:39
A Little Red Shirt.   Gr-BB:8
The Meadows Are Snowy. Gr-BB:20
The Mist.   Ar-TP3:99, Wr-RM:39
More Riddles.   Gr-GB:39
My Boat Is Turned Up at Both
    Ends.   Wy-CM:18
Night Riddle.   Gr-EC:92
Oh Send to Me an Apple That
    Hasn't Any Kernel.   Sm-LG:286
Of All the Different Kinds of
    Bowls.   Gr-BB:30
Old Chang, the Crab.
    Bo-FP:279, Wy-CM:16
Old Mother Twitchett.
    Ar-TP3:99, Au-SP:26, Li-LB:169,
    Mo-MGT:157, Wr-RM:30
Old or Young.   Ju-CP:10
On Yonder Hill There Is a Red
    Deer.   Gr-CT:11, Gr-GB:39
One Day I Went Down in the
    Golden Harvest Field.
    Gr-GB:65
One Guess.   R. Frost.   Co-PU:101
Over the Ground.   Ju-CP:11
Pairs or Pears.   Wr-RM:81
Purple, Yellow, Red, and Green.
    Mo-MGT:155
A Puzzling Example.
    V. Benjamin.   Br-BC:55
Quartet.   Gr-EC:199, Mo-NR:49,
    Wr-RM:28
Red in the Valley.   Ju-CP:10
Rhyming Riddle.   M. Austin.
    Ar-TP3:99, Au-SP:27, Co-BN:193
A Riddle.   C. Fanshawe.   Gr-CT:36
A Riddle.   G. Macbeth.   Mo-TS:83
A Riddle.   M. Nikogosian.
    Mo-MI:55
Riddle.   C. Rossetti.   Au-SP:372,
    Ox-BC:279
A Riddle.   Ca-MU:18
Riddle.   Gr-CT:402, Gr-GB:39
Riddle.   Gr-GB:91
Riddle.   Su-FVI:47
A Riddle from the Old English.
    Gr-CT:97
Riddle: Gnats.   Ma-YA:3
Riddle Me.   Mo-MGT:154
Riddle of Snow and Sun.
    Gr-CT:395, Gr-GB:36,
    Rv-CB:444, Rv-ON:36
Riddles.   Au-SP:26, On-TW:19
Riddles.   Gr-Ct:235, 395
Riddles.   Gr-GB:37, 39, 59, 71, 323

The Riddling Knight.
    Gr-CC:165, Sm-LG:285
Round as a Marble.   Gr-BB:9
Round as a Moon.   Gr-BB:23
Runs All Day and Never Walks.
    R. Wood.   Ar-TP3:99
The Rye Fields Are Ripening.
    Gr-BB:21
Seven Brothers Have One Sister.
    Gr-BB:30
A Ship's Nail.   Wr-RM:96
A Sieve.   Ar-TP3:99, Wr-RM:76
The Snow Is Thawing. Gr-BB:21
Something Very Elegant.
    A. Fisher.   Br-BC:74
Standing in the Fields.
    Gr-BB:22
A Star.   Ar-TP3:99,
    Mo-MGT:157, Wr-RM:94
Sunshine.   Ar-TP3:99, Wr-RM:97
There Was a Knight.
    De-CH:315, Gr-GB:277
There Was a Little Green House.
    De-TT:31
There Was a Thing.   Mo-MGT:157
They Ripen in the Sun.
    Gr-BB:8
Thirty-Two White Calves.
    Ju-CP:10
Thirty White Horses.
    Ar-TP3:99, Au-SP:25, Mo-MGT:154,
    Rv-ON:57, Wr-RM:52
This Is as Plain as the End of
    Your Nose.   Ju-CP:12
A Thorn.   Wr-RM:117
Three More Riddles.   Gr-CT:12
Three Riddles: Garden.
    Mo-TS:78
Three Riddles: When. B. Swann.
    Mo-TS:79
Three Riddles: Whose.
    Mo-TS:77
Tobacco.   Mo-MGT:192
The Tokens of Love.   Gr-GB:85,
    Ir-BB:44
Tongs.   Gr-GB:18, Li-LB:169,
    Mo-NR:34, Wr-RM:98
Two Brothers We Are.   Mo-MGT:155
Two Legs Sat upon Three Legs.
    Li-LB:167, Mo-MGT:156,
    Mo-NR:136, Rv-ON:53
Up and down the Road It Goes.
    Ju-CP:11
Up High the Ribbons Descend.
    Gr-BB:22
Very Nice, Very Neat. Ju-CP:13
A Walnut.   Gr-GB:71, Li-LB:168,
    Mo-MGT:189, Wr-RM:73
Wee Man o'Leather.   Gr-CT:12,
    Gr-GB:70

RIDDLES — cont'd.

A Well. Ar-TP3:99, Mo-MGT:157,
  Wr-RM:83
What Am I? D. Aldis. Au-SP:369,
  La-PH:15
What Happens in a Minute.
  Ju-CP:13
What Has Feet like Plum Blossoms.
  Wy-CM:20
What Is It That Sits. Ju-CP:12
What Is the Difference?
  Su-FVI:47
What Won't Go up a Chimney Up.
  Ju-CP:10
What's My Thought like?
  T. Moore. Rv-CB:682
Which Is the Bow? Gr-GB:38
Who? Ca-MU:19
Who Am I? Ca-MU:18
Who Is a Son of My Father.
  Gr-BB:31
Who Was It? Ca-MU:19
The Wind. J. Reeves.
  Co-PU:55, Gr-EC:56
The Wind. Gr-CT:389, Gr-GB:37,
  Sm-LG:64
Without Hammer or Hands.
  Gr-BB:14
You Can See Me in the Country.
  St-FS:39
See also Cr-ST, Ir-BB:47-54,
  Re-RR

RIDERS AND RIDING: see also HUMOR -
  RIDERS AND RIDING; RODEOS
Afar in the Desert. T. Pringle.
  Rd-OA:168
Beyond the Whip. Lo Fu.
  Pa-MV:118
The Boy. R. Rilke. Li-TU:170,
  Sm-MK:165
The Cattie Rade to Paisley.
  Mo-TL:78
Charley Lee. H. Knibbs.
  Co-RM:172, Mc-WK:144
Dogs Have as Much Right as
  People in Nevada. H. Witt.
  Du-SH:118
Gee Up, My Horse, to Budleigh
  Fair. Mo-TL:79
Here Comes a Lady, with Her
  Little Baby. Mo-TL:82
Here Goes My Lord. Ir-BB:235,
  Mo-TL:81, Wr-RM:21
Hey! My Pony! E. Farjeon.
  Fe-FP:482
The Hobby Horse. Bo-FP:10
The Horse Thief. W. Benét.
  Pa-OM:300, Un-MA:324
Horseback Ride. S. Johnson.
  Ho-GC:30

The Horseman. W. de la Mare.
  Ar-TP3:151, Au-SP:341, Bo-GJ:242,
  Cl-DT:62, La-PP:24, Sm-MK:11
How They Brought the Good News
  from Ghent to Aix. R. Browning.
  Ar-TP3:31, Co-RG:31, Er-FA:378,
  Gr-EC:156, Hi-WP I:66, Li-SR:12,
  Sp-OG:29, Un-GT:149
Hua-La-Ma-Ch'ao. T'ien Chien.
  Hs-TC:331
Husky Hi. Ar-TP3:101
I Had a Little Pony. Mother Goose.
  Au-SP:19, Bl-OB:115, Bo-FP:131,
  De-TT:20, Li-LB:82, Mo-MGT:179,
  Mo-NR:128, Mo-TL:82, Wr-RM:83
Image from d'Orleans. E. Pound.
  Ha-LO:67, Ma-FW:15
John Cook Had a Grey Mare.
  Bl-OB:115, De-TT:20, Mo-TL:84,
  Rv-ON:29, Wi-MG:56
Kit Carson's Ride. J. Miller.
  Fi-BG:161
Little Nag. Mo-MGT:66
The Man from Snowy River.
  A. Paterson. Co-RM:141,
  Hi-WP II:91
Master I Have. Ar-TP3:101,
  Wr-RM:41
Mazeppa. G. Byron.
  Hi-FO:169
Mirage. R. Church. Sm-MK:31
Mrs. Alfred Uruguay. W. Stevens.
  Br-TC:414
My Horse Clip-Clopping.
  Basho. Be-CS:19
My Horses. J. Jaszi. Au-SP:206
Night of Spring. T. Westwood.
  Rv-CB:832
Paul Revere's Ride. H. Longfellow.
  Ar-TP3:40, Er-FA:368, Fe-FP:418,
  Ga-FB:254, Hi-TL:48, Se-PR:90,
  Sh-RP:278, Sm-LG:258, Sp-OG:24,
  Un-GT:184, Vi-PP:94
The Phantom Horsewoman. T. Hardy.
  Gr-SS:120
Proud Riders. H. Davis. Co-RM:24
Ride Away. Ar-TP3:101, Ir-BB:236,
  Mo-MGT:213, Mo-TL:79, St-FS:201,
  Wr-RM:26
The Rider. W. Burford.
  Ls-NY:85
Riding. W. Allingham. Ox-BC:216
Riding in the Rain. M. Kumin.
  La-RM:148
Riding Together. W. Morris.
  Cl-FC:79
St. Valentine's Day. W. Blunt.
  Al-VBP:1054
The Scout. R. Church. Hi-WP I:74
Silver Screen. L. Clark. Pa-RE:80

Sketch from Loss of Memory.
  S. Dorman.   Pe-SS:93
Skipper Ireson's Ride. J. Whittier.
  Co-SS:147, Fe-PL:45, Hi-TL:73,
  Sh-AP:40, Sp-OG:226
Tamburlaine. C. Marlowe.
  Cl-DT:13
This Is the Way the Ladies Ride.
  Mother Goose. Ar-TP3:77,
  De-PO:10, Li-LB:11, Mo-MGT:189,
  Mo-NR:52, Mo-TL:81, Wi-MG:29,
  Wr-RM:102
To Bella Akhmadulina.
  A. Voznesensky. Ca-MR:79
Trit Trot to Boston. Mo-TL:78
Trot, Trot, Horsie. Mo-TL:78
Upon the Horse and His Rider.
  J. Bunyan. Ox-BC:38
Will You Come? E. Thomas.
  Bo-GJ:120, De-CH:439
Windy Nights. R. Stevenson.
  Ar-TP3:165, Bo-GJ:35, Br-SS:34,
  De-TT:163, Gr-CC:9, Gr-EC:56,
  Ir-BB:241, Ja-PA:44, Ox-BC:294,
  Sp-OG:307, TU-WW:25
A Woman Riding. T. Hardy.
  Gr-CC:8
Yankee Doodle. De-PO:22,
  Gr-CT:87, Gr-GB:166, Ir-BB:234,
  Mo-CC:(17), Mo-MGT:162,
  Mo-TL:85
Young Jack Snyder. J. Adams.
  Fi-BG:223
The Youth Dreams. R. Rilke.
  Pa-SG:142
RIDICULE: see CONTEMPT
RIDLEY, NICHOLAS
  Latimer and Ridley.
    W. Wordsworth. Hi-FO:118
RIEU, EMILE VICTOR
  On Looking into E. V. Rieu's
    Homer. P. Kavanagh. Pl-ML:46
RIGHTS, CIVIL: see CIVIL RIGHTS
RIMBAUD, ARTHUR
  Prelude LVI. C. Aiken.
    Br-TC:7
RINGS: see also SATIRE - RINGS
  Go Little Ring. Rv-CB:29
  His Mother's (Wife's) Wedding
    Ring. G. Crabbe.
    Ox-BN:18, Rv-CB:560
  A Pearl, a Girl. R. Browning.
    Rv-CB:830
  To His Wife on the Fourteenth
    Anniversary of Her Wedding
    Day, with a Ring. S. Bishop.
    Al-VBP:596
  The Two Wives. D. Henderson.
    Br-SM:12

RIO DE JANEIRO, BRAZIL
  The Last Bus. M. Strand. Br-TC:422
  Rolling Down to Rio. R. Kipling.
    Pa-HT:71
RIOTS: see CROWDS; REBELLION;
  REVOLTS AND REVOLUTIONS
RIP VAN WINKLE
  Van Winkle. H. Crane.
    Ga-FB:269, Sh-AP:199, Un-MA:521
RITES AND CEREMONIES: see also
  BAPTISM; FUNERALS; INDIANS OF
  NORTH AMERICA - CEREMONIES AND
  DANCES; MANNERS AND CUSTOMS;
  SATIRE - RITES AND CEREMONIES;
  WEDDINGS; and names of countries
  with subheading SOCIAL LIFE AND
  CUSTOMS, as INDIA - SOCIAL LIFE
  AND CUSTOMS
  Song for a Ceremonial Dance.
    Tr-US I:183
RITUALS: see LITANIES; RITES AND
  CEREMONIES; WORSHIP
RIVALRY: see COMPETITION;
  LOVE - RIVALRY
RIVER LIFE
  Down the Mississippi. J. Fletcher.
    Br-AF:180, Pa-HT:52
RIVERA, DIEGO
  I Paint What I See. E. White.
    Mo-BG:64
RIVERS: see also DAMS; FLOODS;
  and names of rivers, as
  THAMES RIVER
  American Child. P. Engle. Br-AF:170
  Big Dam. W. Moses. Br-AF:188
  The Boats Are Afloat. Chu Hsi.
    Le-MW:69, Rx-OH:117
  The Bothie of Tober-na-Vuolich.
    A. Clough. Co-BN:69
  Brimming Water. Tu Fu. Rx-OH:34
  Bubbles. F. Kitagawa. Sh-AM:85
  By Sandy Waters. J. Stuart.
    Br-AF:178
  The Chiming River. Rokwa. Be-MC:53
  City River. S. Muro. Sh-AM:55
  Crooked as a Mountain Railroad.
    Re-RR:71
  Detroit. D. Hall. Br-AF:203
  The Dry Salvages. T. Eliot.
    Ar-TP3:173, Sm-PT:171
  Explanation on Coming Home Late.
    R. Hughes. Co-EL:155,
    Co-PU:130, Re-TW:8
  Falling in the Creek.
    I. Heke. Le-M:65
  First Praise. W. Williams.
    Ca-VT:50
  Flowing On By. K. Takahama.
    Sh-AM:163
  IV. J. Bruchac. Ni-CD:40

RIVERS — cont'd.
  From the Bridge. J. Keats.
    Bo-FP:258, Ch-B:109, Mc-PR:159
  The Gleaming Stream. C. Minor.
    Ba-HI:64
  A Green Stream. Wang Wêi.
    Mo-SD:108
  I Came from under the Earth.
    Le-OE:137
  I Was Born upon Thy Bank, River.
    H. Thoreau. Co-EL:129,
    Co-PU:50
  In the Evening I Walk by the
    River. Hsiu Ou-Yang.
    Le-MW:88, Rx-OH:51
  It Is the Key. S. Schmitz.
    St-H:195
  Kubla Khan. S. Coleridge.
    Al-VBP:699, Bo-GJ:222, Co-RG:15,
    De-CH:386, Er-FA:361, Ga-FB:23,
    Gr-CT:177, Gr-EC:140, Mc-PR:150,
    Ox-BN:165, Pa-HT:154, Re-TW:132,
    Rv-CB:657, Sm-LG:215
  Lives. H. Reed. Co-BN:67
  Long Person. G. Cardiff.
    Ni-CD:49
  The Millstream. De-PP:20
  The Negro Speaks of Rivers.
    L. Hughes. Ad-PB:72, Be-MA:38,
    Br-AF:176, Hu-PN:187, Li-TU:179,
    Lo-TY:225, Mo-TS:38, Pe-SS:49,
    Ra-BP:78
  No Moon No Star. B. Deutsch.
    Ha-WR:52
  The Old Bridge. H. Conkling.
    Hu-MP:172, Th-AS:95
  On the Bridge. K. Greenaway.
    Hu-MP:66
  Pont and Blyth. Gr-GB:176
  The Rapid. C. Sangster.
    Do-WH:72
  Repose of Rivers. H. Crane.
    Un-MA:518, Wi-LT:396
  Requiem for a River.
    K. Williams. La-RM:40
  The River. H. Crane. Bl-FP:81
  The River. D. Davie. Ls-NY:259
  The River. P. Lorentz.
    Br-AF:169, 182
  The River. J. Stephens. Gr-EC:274
  The River. Tsou Ti-fan. Hs-TC:338
  The River Don. Gr-GB:175
  The River God. S. Sitwell.
    Un-MB:401
  The River God to Amoret.
    J. Fletcher. No-CL:104
  The River-God's Song. J. Fletcher.
    Fe-FP:274, Re-TW:44, Rv-CB:312
  The River in the Meadows.
    L. Adams. Un-MA:546

  The River Is a Piece of the Sky.
    J. Ciardi. Ar-TP3:243,
    Au-SP:200, La-PV:183
  A River Leaping. Meisetsu.
    Be-CS:20
  River Night. F. Frost. La-OC:36
  The River of Rivers in Connecticut.
    W. Stevens. Ca-VT:42
  Rivers Arise: A Fragment.
    J. Milton. Gr-CT:238
  The Rivers Remember. N. Turner.
    Br-AF:170
  Runs All Day and Never Walks.
    R. Wood. Ar-TP3:99, Ir-BB:48
  Sampan. Hi-WP I:1
  Sang-Kan River. Ya Hsüan.
    Pa-MV:149
  Six o' Clock. O. Dodson.
    Hu-PN:298
  Song of the Prophet to the San
    Juan River. Bi-IT:43,
    Tr-US II:251
  The Tide River. C. Kingsley.
    Co-BN:74, Ox-BC:227
  To a River in the South.
    H. Newbolt. De-CH:48
  Too Anxious for Rivers.
    R. Frost. Rv-CB:967
  The Topography of History.
    T. McGrath. St-H:119
  Twilight in the River Pavilion.
    Chiang She Ch'uan. Rx-LT:117
  Under a Winter Moon.
    S. Yamaguchi. Sh-AM:171
  Upon Boys Diverting Themselves
    in the River. T. Foxton.
    Ox-BC:55
  Virginia. T. Eliot.
    Ha-PO:94, Sm-LG:142
  Walking by the Stream.
    Hsin Ch'i-Chi. Le-MW:47
  Water Baby. C. O'John.
    Al-WW:62
  Water Ouzel. W. Matchett.
    En-PC:213, Ni-JP:107
  The Weepers Tower in Amsterdam.
    P. Goodman. Ca-VT:334
  When a Bank Goes Broke.
    Re-RR:14
  When the Drive Goes Down.
    D. Malloch. Br-AF:175
  Where Do Rivers Go? De-PP:24
  Where Go the Boats? R. Stevenson.
    Ar-TP3:110, Au-SP:201, Bo-GJ:177,
    Hu-MP:173, Li-LC:74, Mc-PR:132,
    Ox-BC:294, Sm-LG:103
  White Stone Bank. Wang Wei.
    Le-MW:118
  Wilderness Rivers.
    E. Coatsworth. Br-AF:173

Winter Streams. B. Carman.
    De-TT:91, Ha-YA:149, Sp-OG:284
Zummer Stream. W. Barnes. Co-BN:93
ROADRUNNERS
    The Mind, Intractable Thing.
        M. Moore. Wi-LT:277
    The Road-Runner. P.Whalen. Kh-VA:37
    Roadrunner Song. Da-SC:89
ROADS: see also CAMINO REAL;
        FREEWAYS; TRAILS
    And Now You Live Dispersed.
        T. Eliot. Ar-TP3:94
    The Autostrada. G. Johnson.
        Ls-NY:250
    Bound No'th Blues. L. Hughes.
        Bo-AN:65
    The Calf-Path. S. Foss. Fe-PL:3
    City Streets and Country Roads.
        E. Farjeon. Ar-TP3:93,
        Au-SP:165, Pe-FB:46
    Cranberry Road. R. Field.
        Th-AS:134
    Florida Road Workers. L. Hughes.
        Du-SH:145, Pe-SS:52, Un-MA:553
    Gathering Seaweed. S. Suyama.
        Le-TA:81
    How Sad This Road. Mitsune.
        Ba-ST:52
    In the Middle of the Road.
        C. de Andrade. An-TC:89
    It Never Moves by Day or Night.
        Ju-CP:11
    A Lane. Bo-FP:38
    Late Last Night. A. Gregor.
        Ca-VT:503
    The Motorcyclist's Song.
        D. Bell. Pe-M:42
    The Old Walking Song. J. Tolkien.
        La-RM:159
    On a Mountain Road.
        Wu Ch'ing-jen. Pa-SG:99
    Puzzle. S. Cooksley. Ls-NY:17
    The Road. C. Aiken. Un-MA:428
    The Road. H. Johnson. Hu-PN:266
    A Road Might Lead to Anywhere.
        R. Field. Au-SP:166, Fe-FP:183,
        La-PV:168, Mc-WK:199, Pe-FB:45,
        St-FS:124
    The Road Not Taken. R. Frost.
        Br-TC:136, Er-FA:180, Fe-PL:317,
        Gr-CT:314, La-RM:48, Na-EO:14,
        Sm-LG:301, Un-MA:187
    The Road to Anywhere. B. Taylor.
        Hu-MP:165
    Roads Go Ever Ever On. J. Tolkien.
        Ar-TP3:94, Fe-FP:183
    The Roads into the Country.
        T. McGrath. St-H:121
    Roadways. J. Masefield.
        Pa-HT:78, Sh-RP:157

    The Rolling English Road.
        G. Chesterton. Na-EO:16,
        Sm-LG:301
    The Roman Road. T. Hardy.
        Bo-GJ:200, Gr-CC:176, Un-MB:32
    Song of the Open Road.
        W. Whitman. Al-VBP:934,
        Ar-TP3:97, Er-FA:249, Un-MA:63
    Stray Roads. H. Welshimer.
        Ke-TF:239
    The Temple Bells of Yun Sui.
        Yang Wan-Li. Le-MW:48
    Through Lane It Lay.
        E. Dickinson. Gr-SS:80
    To Somewhere. L. Nathan.
        Ls-NY:96
    Tour 5. R. Hayden. Be-MA:64
    The Unexplorer. E. Millay.
        Ha-LO:62, Sh-RP:102
    Up-Hill. C. Rossetti.
        Al-VBP:998, De-CH:462, Gr-EC:276,
        Ho-WR:152, Mc-PR:141, Ox-BN:712,
        Sp-OG:263
    Wanderer's Song. A. Symons.
        Al-VBP:1095
    The Way. E. Muir. Gr-SS:191,
        Ha-LO:75
    The Way Through the Woods.
        R. Kipling. De-CH:281,
        Fe-FP:242, Ha-PO:154,Hi-WP I:107,
        La-RM:46, Mc-WS:31, Ox-BC:323,
        Ox-BN:932, Re-TW:128, Sm-LG:396
    What Crosses the Land. Re-RR:68
    With Wavering Feet I Walked.
        V. Solovyov. Pa-SG:118
    You Are on U.S. 40 Headed West.
        V. White. Br-AF:234
ROAMING: see WANDERERS AND WANDERING
ROBBERS: see THIEVES
ROBERT I (ROBERT THE BRUCE),
        KING OF SCOTLAND
    Freedom. J. Barbour. Sm-LG:154
    Scots Wha Hae. R. Burns.
        Hi-FO:83, Ma-YA:135, Sm-LG:154,
        Sp-OG:189
ROBESON, PAUL
    Paul Robeson. G. Brooks.
        Ad-PB:165
    Until They Have Stopped.
        S. Wright. Ad-PB:215
ROBIN GOODFELLOW
    Robin Goodfellow. Al-VBP:371,
        Rv-CB:138
ROBIN HOOD: see also ALLEN-A-DALE;
        FRIAR TUCK; LITTLE JOHN;
        SHERWOOD FOREST
    The Birth of Robin Hood.
        Al-VBP:37, Ma-BB:41, Ox-BB:377
    The Death of Robin Hood.
        E. Field. Co-PT:239

ROBIN HOOD — cont'd.
  The Death of Robin Hood.
    Al-VBP:38, Ma-BB:77, Ma-FW:156
  Dirge for Robin Hood. A. Munday.
    Bl-OB:152, De-CH:77, Ho-WR:116,
    Re-TW:71, Rv-CB:163
  A Gest of Robyn Hode, I-VIII.
    Ox-BB:420-484
  A Lytell Geste of Robyn Hode.
    Ma-YA:43
  Robin Hood. J. Keats.
    Gr-CC:115, Mc-PR:34
  Robin Hood and Allan a Dale.
    Gr-GB:247, Ma-BB:44, Un-GT:115
  Robin Hood and Guy of Gisborne.
    Ma-BB:54
  Robin Hood and Little John.
    Bo-FP:218, Ir-BB:122, Wr-RM:50
  Robin Hood and the Bishop of
    Hereford. Bl-OB:73, Ma-BB:74
  Robin Hood and the Butcher.
    Ma-BB:62
  Robin Hood and the Curtal Friar.
    Ma-BB:48
  Robin Hood and the Monk.
    Al-VBP:37, De-CH:135, Ox-BB:405
  Robin Hood and the Widow's Three
    Sons. Ar-TP3:17, Co-PT:224,
    Ma-BB:70, Pa-OM:86, Sp-OG:157,
    Un-GT:119
  Robin Hood and Two Priests.
    Ma-BB:66
  Rose the Red and White Lilly.
    Ox-BB:189
  A Song of Sherwood. A. Noyes.
    Ar-TP3:20, Fe-FP:461, Hu-MP:417,
    Mc-PR:192, Th-AS:160, Un-MB:244
  When Terry Reads. B. Lee.
    Ja-HH:42
ROBINS: see also HUMOR - ROBINS
  Always with Us! - the Black
    Preacher. H. Melville. Re-BS:51
  The Babes in the Wood.
    Bl-OB:70, De-CH:546, De-TT:44,
    Gr-EC:152, Ox-BC:97
  Bird Talk. A. Fisher. Fr-MP:12
  The Blossom. W. Blake.
    Bo-GJ:97, Re-TW:39, Rv-CB:577
  The Cat and the Bird. G. Canning.
    Gr-CT:118, Gr-EC:76, Re-BS:4
  The Christmas Robin. R. Graves.
    Gr-CC:48
  Cock Robin. De-TT:40, Ir-BB:24,
    Rv-ON:112
  The Death and Burial of Cock
    Robin. De-TT:41, Ir-BB:114,
    Mo-MGT:60, Mo-NR:143, Un-GT:62,
    Wr-RM:124
  Desolate. S. Dobell. Ox-BN:659,
    Rv-CB:879

  Four Birds. W. Blake. Gr-CT:93,
    Gr-GB:63, Gr-TG:31
  I'm Called by the Name of a Man.
    Gr-GB:65, Mo-MGT:154
  Jenny Wren Fell Sick.
    Ir-BB:84, Mo-MGT:29, Na-EO:69,
    Rv-ON:116, Sm-MK:170
  Little Bob Robin. Rv-ON:113
  Little Robin Redbreast.
    De-PO:28, Ir-BB:24
  Nesting-Time. C. Rossetti.
    Ar-TP3:55, Bo-FP:227, Ch-B:16
  The North Wind Doth Blow.
    Au-SP:62, Bl-OB:97, Bo-FP:152,
    Cl-DT:19, De-CH:625, Hi-GD:21,
    Ir-BB:29, Li-LB:102, Mo-MGT:20,
    Mo-NR:86, Pa-AP:16, Sm-MK:2,
    Wi-MG:20, Wr-RM:114
  The October Redbreast.
    A. Meynell. Un-MB:64
  Proud Maisie. W. Scott.
    De-CH:339, Gr-CT:364, Ox-BN:136,
    Pa-GTB:229, Rv-CB:655, Sm-LG:269
  The Red Robin. J. Clare.
    Pa-RE:30, Re-BS:4
  A Robin. W. de la Mare.
    Cl-DT:21, Gr-CT:393, Re-BS:3
  The Robin. E. Dickinson.
    Ga-FB:284, Re-BS:1
  The Robin. T. Hardy. Pa-RE:14
  Robin and Man. R. Gordon.
    Ls-NY:342
  The Robin and the Cows.
    W. Howells. Un-GT:60
  Robin Redbreast. W. Allingham.
    Hi-WP I:28, Hu-MP:222,
    Ja-PA:16, Ox-BC:219, Re-BS:2
  Robin Redbreast. S. Kunitz.
    Ho-P:151
  Robin Redbreast. Co-BBW:243
  Robin Redbreast. Hu-MP:185,
    Li-LB:83, Wr-RM:14
  Robin Redbreast's Testament.
    Gr-GB:66
  The Robins. Ir-BB:242,
    Mo-MGT:103, Wr-RM:52
  A Robin's Epitaph. S. Rogers.
    Rv-CB:627
  The Robin's Last Will.
    Rv-ON:114
  The Robin's Song. R. Honeywood.
    Gr-EC:222, Pa-RE:83
  Robin's Song. E. King.
    Ar-TP3:201
  The Secret. Ar-TP3:55, Au-SP:64,
    Gr-EC:172, Hu-MP:213
  Sir Robin. L. Larcom. Hu-MP:221
  A Spring Lilt. Hu-MP:303
  Talents Differ. L. Richards.
    Ar-TP3:55

Tampa Robins.   S. Lanier.
  Se-PR:108
Three Little Trees.   Ch-B:67
Three o'Clock in the Morning.
  Hu-MP:216
Three Things to Remember.
  W. Blake. Br-SS:150, Ch-B:89,
  Fe-FP:280, Gr-EC:178, Gr-TG:31,
  Hi-GD:13, Hi-WP II:170
Traveling Light. M. Upton.
  Bo-FP:151
What the Robin Told. G. Cooper.
  Ar-TP3:55, Ch-B:67, Fe-FP:285,
  Hu-MP:221
When Jenny Wren Was Young.
  Mother Goose. Hu-MP:213,
  Wr-RM:23
When the Snow Is on the Ground.
  Wr-RM:128
The Wind of January.
  C. Rossetti. Ha-YA:163
Winter. W. de la Mare.
  Gr-CT:394, Ha-YA:144
Winter. J. Thomson.
  Al-VBP:550
ROBINSON CRUSOE: see also HUMOR -
  ROBINSON CRUSOE
Robinson Crusoe Returns to
  Amsterdam. F. Jammes.
  Fe-FP:472
ROBUSTI, JACOPO: see TINTORETTO
ROCK MUSIC AND SONGS
  Albatross. J. Collins. Mo-GR:37
  Bad Moon Rising. J. Fogerty.
  Mo-GR:85
  Bishop Cody's Last Request.
  T. Paxton. Mo-GR:55
  Cactus Tree. J. Mitchell.
  Mo-GR:121
  Casey Jones. R. Hunter. Mo-GR:52
  Chelsea Morning. J. Mitchell.
  Mo-GR:119
  The Continuing Story of Bungalow
  Bill. J. Lennon. Mo-GR:75
  Dawn Is a Feeling. M. Pinder.
  Mo-GR:117
  The Day They Busted the Grateful
  Dead. R. Brautigan.
  Mc-EA:130
  Father of Night. B. Dylan.
  Mo-GR:100
  The Fool on the Hill.
  J. Lennon. Mo-GR:72
  Four and Twenty. S. Stills.
  Mo-GR:30
  From the Underworld.
  H. Blaikley. Mo-GR:20
  Gypsy Eyes. J. Hendrix. Mo-GR:124
  I Think I Understand.
  J. Mitchell. Mo-GR:126

In My Life. J. Lennon. Mo-GR:43
The King Must Die. B. Taupin.
  Mo-GR:91
Lucy in the Sky with Diamonds.
  The Beatles. Pe-SS:82
Masters of War. B. Dylan.
  Mo-GR:68
New Morning. B. Dylan. Mo-GR:112
The Observation. D. Leitch.
  Mo-GR:80
Pictures of a City. R. Fripp.
  Mo-GR:78
She Wandered Through the Garden
  Fence. K. Reid. Mo-GR:130
She's Leaving Home.
  The Beatles. Pe-SS:94
Stories of the Street. L. Cohen.
  Mo-GR:88
Story of Isaac. L. Cohen.
  Mo-GR:16
Strawberry Fields Forever.
  J. Lennon. Mo-GR:127
Suzanne. L. Cohen. Mo-GR:33
Tales of Brave Ulysses.
  E. Clapton. Mo-GR:11
We Can Be Together.
  P. Kantner. Mo-GR:105
Wooden Ships. D. Crosby.
  Mo-GR:108
Woodstock. J. Mitchell.
  Mo-GR:102
ROCKEFELLER, NELSON ALDRICH
  I Paint What I See.
  E. White. Mo-BG:64
ROCKETS (AERONAUTICS)
  Fueled. M. Hans. Du-RG:83,
  Pe-M:80
  The Old and the New.
  Q. B. M. Au-SP:175
  Vapor Trails. G. Snyder.
  Du-SH:166, Mo-BG:129
ROCKING RHYMES
  Dance a Baby Diddy. Mo-TL:35
  Diddle-Me-Diddle-Me-Dandy-O!
  Mo-TL:38
  Dormy, Dormy, Dormouse.
  Mo-TL:35
  Hoolie, the Bed'll Fall!
  Mo-TL:38
  Hush-a-Bye, Baby. De-PO:8,
  Li-LB:9, Mo-CC:(8), Mo-MGT:58,
  Mo-NR:10, Mo-TL:37, Wi-MG:17,
  Wr-RM:25
  Oh! Dear, What Can the Matter
  Be? De-CH:70, Mc-WS:165,
  Mo-MGT:200, Mo-TL:34, Wr-RM:127
  Rock-a-Bye Baby, in the Tree Top.
  Ir-BB:126, Mo-TL:36
  A Rocking Hymn. G. Wither.
  Ox-BC:28

ROCKING RHYMES — cont'd.
  See-Saw, Margery Daw.
    Au-SP:6, Ir-BB:11, Li-LB:130,
    Mo-MGT:28, Mo-NR:3, Mo-TL:16
  Up and Down Again. Mo-TL:35
ROCKS: see also varieties of rocks,
    as GRANITE
  As a Huge Stone Is Sometimes
    Seen to Lie. W. Wordsworth.
    De-CH:601
  As to the Restless Brook.
    J. Bangs. Co-OW:53
  The Captive Stone. J. Barnes.
    Ni-CD:23
  Ceremony. J. De Longchamps.
    Ls-NY:91
  Dirt Road. C. O'John. Al-WW:61
  Double-Damn. Br-FW:7
  Earth Cure Me. Earth Receive
    My Woe. Wo-HS:(55)
  Education by Stone.
    J. de Melo Neto. An-TC:149
  Explanation on Coming Home Late.
    R. Hughes. Co-EL:155,
    Co-PU:130, Re-TW:8
  Forms of the Earth at Abiquiu.
    N. Momaday. Ni-CD:88
  The Friendly Rock. S. Pulsifer.
    La-PP:43
  He Went to the Wood.
    Gr-GB:210, Mo-MGT:156
  How Happy Is the Little Stone.
    E. Dickinson. Sh-AP:131
  In the Middle of the Road.
    C. de Andrade. An-TC:89
  I've Got a Home in That Rock.
    R. Patterson. Ad-PB:209,
    Hu-PN:398
  Kick a Little Stone. D. Aldis.
    Au-SP:185
  La Crosse at Ninety Miles an
    Hour. R. Eberhart. Br-AF:205
  Music of Stones. G. Misra.
    Al-PI:137
  Old War Song. Tr-US II:241
  On Yes Tor. E. Gosse.
    De-CH:301
  The Path among the Stones.
    G. Kinnell. Ho-P:135
  Pebbles. F. Sherman. Mc-PR:29
  The Picture of J.T. in a Prospect
    of Stone. C. Tomlinson. En-PC:260
  Rock. K. Raine. Pl-IO:42
  The Rock. Br-MW:83
  Rocks Partly Held in Mist.
    A. Gregor. Ls-NY:252
  Runes. E. Jarrett. Kh-VA:4
    Sc-TN:106
  Sea Holly. C. Aiken. Wi-LT:331
  The Stone. P. Blackburn. Du-SH:24

  Stone Giant. J. Bruchac.
    Ni-CD:34
  This Is My Rock. D. McCord.
    Br-SS:27, Fe-FP:10, La-PV:169
  To Ailsa Rock. J. Keats.
    Ox-BN:373
  Two Voices in a Meadow.
    R. Wilbur. Pe-SS:56
  The Words. G. Fowler. Sc-TN:49
ROCKY MOUNTAIN SHEEP: see BIGHORNS
ROCKY MOUNTAINS
  Dancing Teepees. C. O'John.
    Al-WW:61
  Gates of the Rockies.
    J. Daugherty. Sh-RP:301
ROCS
  Roc's Brood. S. Bradley.
    De-FS:30
RODEOS: see also COWBOYS; HORSES
  The Closing of the Rodeo.
    W. Smith. Br-TC:395, Ho-LP:73,
    Mc-WS:111, Mo-SD:70, Sh-RP:306
  Cowboys: One, Two, Three.
    R. McKuen. Pe-M:66-68
  Idaho Jack. J. Lee. Fi-BG:90
  Rodeo. E. Lueders.
    Co-RM:24, Du-RG:133
ROETHKE, THEODORE
  Roethke. H. Healy. Ls-NY:134
ROLLER COASTERS
  The Contraption. M. Swenson.
    Ha-TP:10
  Flight of the Roller-Coaster.
    R. Souster. Do-WH:13, Ha-PO:176
ROLLER-SKATING: see SKATING
ROMAN CATHOLIC CHURCH: see
    CATHOLIC CHURCH
ROMAN WALLS
  A Roman Soldier on the Wall
    W. Auden. Hi-WP I:122,
    Sm-MK:98
  The Wind and the Rain.
    W. Gibson. Cl-FC:50
ROMANCE: see also HUMOR - ROMANCE;
    IMAGINATION; LOVE
  Aladdin. J. Lowell. Co-PM:122,
    Co-RG:113, Mc-WK:83, Sp-OG:335
  As I Came Down from Lebanon.
    C. Scollard. Pa-HT:97
  The Bearer of Evil Tidings.
    R. Frost. Rv-CB:968
  A Caravan from China Comes.
    R. Le Gallienne. Th-AS:152
  Cargoes. J. Masefield.
    Ar-TP3:90, Bo-FP:134, Co-RG:56,
    Co-SS:75, Fe-FP:196, Ga-FB:182,
    Hi-WP I:109, Mc-PR:135,
    Th-AS:130, Un-MB:225, Wi-LT:189
  The Chinese Nightingale.
    V. Lindsay. Un-MA:229

Coole Park and Ballylee, 1931.
    W. Yeats.   Pa-GTB:430
Dark Kingdom.   E. Coatsworth.
    Co-BBW:54
Endymion.   J. Keats.   Al-VBP:788,
    Er-FA:264, Ma-YA:186, Mc-PR:89,
    Ox-BN:335
Evening.   W. Turner.   Pa-HT:103
Evening Clouds.   D. Bharati.
    Al-PI:114
The Golden City of St. Mary.
    J. Masefield.   Bo-HF:82,
    Pa-HT:157
The Golden Journey to Samarkand.
    J. Flecker.   Bo-GJ:228,
    Pa-HT:91
Golden Wings.   W. Morris.
    Gr-CT:267, Ox-BN:770
The Green Valley.   S. Warner.
    Un-MB:377
Horses and Men in the Rain.
    C. Sandburg.   Fe-PL:409
I Had a Little Nut-Tree.
    An-IP:(20), Ar-TP3:154,
    Au-SP:24, Br-FF:(34), De-CH:186,
    De-TT:19, Gr-EC:294, Gr-GB:18,
    Ir-BB:264, Li-LB:33, Mo-MGT:148,
    Rv-CB:453, Sm-MK:7
In Procession.   R. Graves.
    Br-TC:155
The Janitor's Boy.   N. Crane.
    Fe-PL:236, Un-GT:165
The King of China's Daughter.
    E. Sitwell.   De-CH:186, Ir-BB:258,
    Ma-FW:185, Pa-RE:23, Un-MB:331
Love at Sea.   A. Swinburne.
    Gr-SS:186
Meeting-House Hill. A. Lowell.
    Sm-LG:146, Un-MA:155
Merchants from Cathay.
    W. Benét.   Un-MA:321
The Mistress of Vision.
    F. Thompson.   De-CH:269
The Old Ships.   J. Flecker.
    Co-RG:57, De-CH:363, De-TT:194,
    Go-BP:156, Hi-FO:15, Na-EO:114,
    No-CL:254, Pa-HT:95, Un-MB:272
The Outlaw.   W. Scott.
    Pa-GTB:174
The Padda Song.   Gr-GB:283
A Piper.   S. O'Sullivan.
    Ar-TP3:13, Co-PI:186, Co-PU:131,
    De-CH:185, Fe-FP:465, Hu-MP:147,
    La-PV:221
The River in the Meadows.
    L. Adams.   Un-MA:546
Romance.   E. Poe.   Rv-CB:806
Romance.   W. Turner.
    Bo-GJ:220, Hi-WP I:7, Mc-WS:113,
    Ni-JP:24, No-CL:251, Un-MB:345

The Royal Fisherman.
    Gr-CT:128, Gr-GB:315
Sailing to Byzantium.   W. Yeats.
    Al-VBP:1093, Er-FA:152,
    Go-BP:168, Pa-GTB:425, Rv-CB:956,
    Tr-MR:290, Un-MB:114, Wi-LT:75
San Francisco.   W. Roberts.
    Hu-PN:82
The Secret of the Sea.
    H. Longfellow.   Un-GT:261
A Ship Comes In.   O. Jenkins.
    Bo-FP:134
The Ships of Yule. B. Carman.
    Br-BC:126, Do-WH:16, Sh-RP:168
The Song of Wandering Aengus.
    W. Yeats.   Ar-TP3:161, Bl-OB:91,
    Bo-GJ:142, Co-BL:165, Co-PM:196,
    De-CH:280, Gr-SS:46, Ha-LO:52,
    Hà-PO:180, Ho-LP:14, Ma-YA:230,
    Mc-WK:7, Mc-WS:33, No-CL:68,
    Re-TW:28, Sm-LG:226, Sm-MK:30,
    Th-AS:200, Un-GT:127, Un-MB:108
Spanish Waters.   J. Masefield.
    Fe-FP:514, Mc-WK:141, Pa-OM:207
The Splendor Falls on Castle
    Walls.   A. Tennyson.
    Al-VBP:858, Ar-TP3:217, Bo-GJ:139,
    Co-RG:145, De-CH:113, De-TT:196,
    Fe-FP:373, Ga-FB:11, Gr-CT:444,
    Hi-WP I:106, Ho-WR:162, Hu-MP:95,
    Mc-PR:65, Ox-BN:485, Pl-US:26,
    Re-TW:72, Rv-CB:791, Sm-LG:39
Sunk Lyonesse. W. de la Mare.
    Wi-LT:133
The Tarry Buccaneer.
    J. Masefield.   Co-PT:213
Tartary.   W. de la Mare.
    Th-AS:146, Un-GT:105
Uncle Ananias.   E. Robinson.
    Un-MA:137
Under the Moon.   Ho Ch'i-fang.
    Hs-TC:221
Water-Front Streets.
    L. Hughes.   La-OC:38
When I Set Out for Lyonesse.
    T. Hardy.   No-CL:144,
    Pa-HT:156, Un-MB:32
Yarrow Visited, September, 1814.
    W. Wordsworth.   Pa-GTB:266
ROMANIA: see RUMANIA and subheadings
ROMANS
    Lincolnshire Bomber Station.
        H. Treece.   Cr-WS:32
ROME, IT.:   see also HUMOR -
    ROME, IT.
    Adonais.   P. Shelley.   Al-VBP:759,
        Ha-PO:130, Ox-BN:287
    For the New Railway Station
        in Rome.   R. Wilbur.
        Pe-OA:257

ROME, IT. — cont'd.
  Go Thou to Rome. P. Shelley.
    Gr-CT:379
  Long Ago I Went to Rome.
    M. Furse. De-CH:578
  Morality. J. Garrigue. Co-EL:73
  On the Death of Keats.
    J. Logan. Ho-P:169
  Piazza di Spagna: Early Morning.
    R. Wilbur. Ca-VT:485
  Rome. T. Hardy. No-CL:255
  Rome. M. Stiker. Ho-TY:282
  So Not Seeing I Sung. A. Clough.
    Ox-BN:615, Pa-GTB:360
  Sonnet. D. Cory. Ke-TF:309
  The Thief. S. Kunitz.
    Ca-VT:261, Un-MA:593
ROME - HISTORY AND PATRIOTISM:
    see also ATTILA; CONSTANTINE I,
    THE GREAT; HUMOR - ROME -
    HISTORY AND PATRIOTISM; and
    names of Romans, as CAESAR,
    GAIUS JULIUS
  Call to Youth. Horace. Pa-SG:4
  Elene. Cynewulf. Ma-YA:11
  Horatius. T. Macauley.
    Er-FA:387, Fe-PL:64, Hi-FO:32,
    Sm-LG:161
  Julius Caesar. W. Shakespeare.
    Hi-FO:49
  Nero's Term. C. Cavafy.
    Cr-WS:17
  The Roman Road. D. Davidson.
    Cr-WS:17
  Romulus and Remus. R. Kipling.
    Hi-FO:25
  Vae Victis. R. Humphries.
    Ni-JP:123
  Waiting for the Barbarians.
    C. Cavafy. Gr-CC:173
  When Hannibal Crossed the Alps.
    E. Farjeon. Hi-FO:45
ROMEO AND JULIET
  Come Night, Come Romeo.
    W. Shakespeare. Co-BL:103
  Farewell to Juliet.
    W. Blunt. Al-VBP:1054
  Here Lies Juliet.
    W. Shakespeare. Er-FA:127
ROMNEY, ENG.
  In Romney Marsh. J. Davidson.
    Al-VBP:1077, Pa-HT:133
ROMULUS AND REMUS
  Romulus and Remus. R. Kipling.
    Hi-FO:25
RONCESVALLES, SP.
  The Too-Late Born. A. MacLeish.
    Bo-GJ:192, Gr-CC:111, Sh-AP:188,
    Un-MA:458, Wi-LT:340
RONCEVAUX: see RONCESVALLES, SP.

ROOFS: see also HUMOR - ROOFS
  On the Pagoda. Chung Ting-wen.
    Pa-MV:74
  Roof Tops. K. Gorkos.
    La-GI:50
ROOKS (BIRDS)
  Black Rook in Rainy Weather.
    S. Plath. Wi-LT:788
  The Farmer's Gun. A. Young.
    Rd-OA:35
  The Late, Last Rook.
    R. Hodgson. Un-MB:190
  Lines Written among the Euganean
    Hills. P. Shelley.
    Al-VBP:743, De-TT:144
  On a Bare Branch. Basho.
    Ma-FW:264
  Rookery: Brookfield Zoo.
    L. Mueller. St-H:143
  The Rooks. J. Browne. Ox-BC:223
  Rooks. C. Sorley. Un-MB:380
  Thaw. E. Thomas. Co-EL:116,
    Ho-LP:37, Ma-FW:10, Pa-GTB:443,
    Re-BS:18, Un-MB:217
  Winter Field. A. Coppard.
    Re-BS:16
  Winter in Dunover Field.
    T. Hardy. Un-MB:31
ROOMS: see HOUSES
ROOSEVELT, FRANKLIN DELANO:
    see also SATIRE - ROOSEVELT,
    FRANKLIN DELANO
  At Warm Springs. W. Benét.
    Se-PR:39
  Franklin Delano Roosevelt.
    J. Masefield. Ke-TF:319
ROOSEVELT, THEODORE
  Our Colonel. A. Guiterman.
    Se-PR:190
  Sagamore. C. Robinson. Se-PR:190
  Theodore Roosevelt. R. Bly.
    Mc-EA:122
  To Theodore Roosevelt.
    R. Dario. Bl-FP:37
ROOSTERS: see CHICKENS
ROOTS
  Birch. Br-FW:15
  Fear of the Earth. A. Comfort.
    Un-MB:519
  Grassroots. C. Sandburg. La-RM:75
  A Spark in the Sun. H. Behn.
    Be-CS:3, Br-SG:24
  There Is a Fading Time. Ba-ST:44
  These Days. C. Olsen. Mo-TS:48
  Wild Horses. C. Sandburg.
    Sh-RP:173
ROSEMARY
  Time Has an End They Say.
    H.D. Ca-VT:118

ROSENBERG, JULIUS AND ETHEL
  At the Last. A. Lifschutz.
    Kr-OF:125
  Elegiac Statement for Two Human
    Beings Named Rosenberg.
    L. Hedley. Kr-OF:124
ROSES: see also HUMOR - ROSES
  The Act. W. Williams.
    Ca-VT:62, Co-EL:122
  Aye, Even Small Things.
    P. Heyse. Un-R:113
  Blanaid's Song. J. Campbell.
    Co-PI:19
  A Bowl of Roses. W. Henley.
    Un-MB:54, Un-MW:9
  Comparisons. C. Rossetti.
    Ox-BC:276
  Essential Oils Are Wrung.
    E. Dickinson. Rv-CB:921
  A Faded Rose. Wang Tu-ch'ing.
    Hs-TC:193
  A Flower Given to My Daughter.
    J. Joyce. Go-BP:117
  The Funeral Rites of the Rose.
    R. Herrick. Ha-PO:82
  Go, Lovely Rose! E. Waller.
    Al-VBP:386, Bo-GJ:128, Ha-PO:164,
    No-CL:29, Pa-GTB:76, Rv-CB:365,
    Un-MW:162
  Go Not Too near a House of Rose.
    E. Dickinson. Un-MA:101
  Here's a Thorny Sort of Riddle.
    Re-RR:28
  How Roses Came Red. R. Herrick.
    Ch-B:96, Gr-CT:268
  I Am Rose. G. Stein. Sm-MK:18
  June. D. Malloch. Ha-YA:71
  Kinship. M. Doyle. Ke-TF:439
  The Lady of the Lake. W. Scott.
    Al-VBP:673
  Landscape as Metal and Flowers.
    W. Scott. Bo-GJ:209, Br-AF:232
  The Last Rose of Summer.
    T. Moore. Co-BN:53, Er-FA:240
  The Lily. W. Blake. Sm-MK:20
  The Lily Has an Air.
    C. Rossetti. Br-SG:29
  The Little Rose Tree. R. Field.
    Ar-TP3:206, Br-SG:28, Fe-FP:217
  The Mystery. R. Hodgson.
    De-CH:143, Un-MB:192
  Of a Rose Is All My Song. Ga-S:75
  One Kingfisher and One Yellow
    Rose. E. Brennan.
    Co-PI:14, Re-BS:41
  The Ramblers. V. Linton. Ls-NY:254
  Rising from Illness. Chang Hsiu-ya.
    Pa-MV:30
  The Rose. W. Browne.
    Al-VBP:324, De-CH:143

  The Rose. R. Lovelace.
    Al-VBP:443
  The Rose and the Gardener.
    H. Dobson. Hu-MP:248
  The Rose Family. R. Frost.
    Co-BL:85
  Roses and Thorns. S. Beţai.
    Al-PI:109
  Roses Only. M. Moore. Wi-LT:268
  The Rose's Scent. Ho-WR:60,
    Rv-CB:28
  The Rwose in the Dark. W. Barnes.
    Rv-CB:767
  Second Rose Motif.
    C. Meireles. An-TC:35
  A Sepal, Petal, and a Thorn.
    E. Dickinson. Br-SG:30
  The Sick Rose. W. Blake.
    Al-VBP:617, Gr-CT:68, Ha-PO:205,
    Ox-BN:22, Rv-CB:578
  Song. A. Noyes. De-CH:142
  Song. C. Rossetti. Al-VBP:995,
    Pa-GTB:374
  Song. Tr-US I:121
  A Summer Wish. C. Rossetti.
    Ox-BN:706
  The Time of Roses. T. Hood.
    De-CH:343, Un-MW:7
  To Flossie. W. Williams. Ho-TH:74
  Tuppence Ha'penny Farden.
    Mo-MGT:163
  White Rose. S. Sitwell. Gr-SS:37
  Wild Briar-Roses. R. Coffin.
    Ke-TF:441
  Women and Roses. R. Browning.
    Al-VBP:890
  Yellow Rose. M. Hopkins.
    Ke-TF:439
ROSS, BETSY GRISCOM
  Betsy's Battle Flag.
    M. Irving. Se-PR:145
ROSS, DONALD: see YELLOW FEVER
ROUND TABLE: see ARTHUR, KING
ROUNDUPS: see RODEOS
ROWING: see BOATS AND BOATING
ROYAL GEORGE (SHIP)
  Loss of the Royal George.
    W. Cowper. Co-RG:44, Co-SS:137,
    Pa-GTB:123, Rv-CB:552, Sp-OG:73
RUGS: see also HUMOR - RUGS
  I'll Give You a Hug. Re-RR:26
RUINS: see also GHOST TOWNS
  Ancient Temple. I. Pillat.
    Mc-AC:58
  The Aztec City. E. Ware. Pa-HT:69
  The Ebb Tide. R. Southey. Ox-BN:176
  Four Preludes on Playthings of
    the Wind: The Past Is a
    Bucket of Ashes.
    C. Sandburg. Un-MA:201

RUINS — cont'd.
In Texas Grass. Q. Troupe.
   Ad-PB:443
Jade Flower Palace. Tu Fu.
   Rx-OH:9
Kilcash. F. O'Connor. Co-PI:155,
   Hi-WP II:132, Re-TW:86
Love among the Ruins.
   R. Browning. Ga-FB:63
Never to Return. Li-Chin-fa.
   Hs-TC:174
Newark Abbey. T. Peacock.
   Ox-BN:233
Passing a Ruined Palace.
   Wen T'ing Yen. Rx-LT:87
Pastoral. P. Mowrer. Cr-WS:70
Remember That Country.
   J. Garrigue. Ca-VT:389
The Ruin. Ma-YA:4
Ruins. E. Pierce. Cr-WS:51
Ruins of a Great House.
   D. Walcott. Br-TC:447
A Tale. E. Thomas. Gr-CT:262
The Temple. J. Johnson.
   Tr-MR:203
RULERS: see KINGS AND RULERS
RUM
Captain Stratton's Fancy.
   J. Masefield. Co-SS:36,
   Un-MB:226
RUMANIA - COUNTRYSIDE
Mechanical Landscape.
   I. Minulescu. Mc-AC:42
On the Other Bank of the Danube.
   V. Voiculescu. Mc-AC:46
The Vineyard. I. Pillat.
   Mc-AC:56
Waters and Dreaming. E. Botta.
   Mc-AC:112
RUMANIA - HISTORY AND PATRIOTISM
Sunny Land. H. Imre. Mc-AC:93
RUMANIAN VERSE: see also BALLADS,
   RUMANIAN
See Mc-AC
RUNAWAYS: see also HUMOR - RUNAWAYS
The Bus. L. Cohen. Ad-CI:9
How I Went Truant from School
   to Visit a River. M. Oliver.
   St-H:164
I Wonder in What Fields Today.
   Kaga no Chiyo.
   Le-MW:99
The Path of the Lonely Ones.
   G. Varela. Ba-HI:87
Poetry of Departures.
   P. Larkin. Br-TC:249
The Runaway Boy. J. Riley.
   Hu-MP:30
A Summer Walk. E. Winton.
   Bo-FP:274

RUNNING: see also HUMOR - RUNNING;
   SKIPPING
Bell Horses, Bell Horses, What
   Time of Day. Ar-TP3:174,
   Bo-FP:123, Br-SS:5, Ir-BB:190,
   Mo-MGT:173, Wr-RM:113
The Chase. W. Rowley.
   De-CH:356, Gr-CT:276, Re-TW:49
Foot Race Song. Da-SC:97
The Greek Anthology. Krinagoras.
   Mo-SD:52
The Hundred-Yard Dash.
   W. Lindsey. Fl-HH:61
Jenny. Mo-MGT:183
A Negro Beats the Olympic Record
   for the USA. A. Sperber.
   Mc-AC:79
Notes Found near a Suicide:
   To James. F. Horne. Bo-AN:45,
   Bo-HF:90, Br-BC:124, Ra-BP:73
One to Make Ready. Mother
   Goose. Bo-FP:264, Li-LB:118,
   Mo-MGT:173, Mo-NR:25, Mo-SD:68,
   Pa-AP:5
Race Starting. Mo-MGT:173,
   On-TW:62
Runner. W. Auden. Mo-SD:55
The Runner. W. Whitman.
   Fl-HH:51, Mo-SD:53, Pe-M:53
The Song of the Ungirt Runners.
   C. Sorley. Un-MB:379
The Sprinters. L. Murchison.
   Mo-SD:54
RUNNYMEDE, ENG.
The Reeds of Runnymede.
   R. Kipling. Hi-FO:79
RUSKIN, JOHN: see HUMOR -
   RUSKIN, JOHN
RUSSIA: see also BOLSHEVISM;
   SATIRE - RUSSIA; SIBERIA,
   U.S.S.R.; and names of
   cities, as MOSCOW, U.S.S.R.,
   and soviets, as GEORGIA,
   U.S.S.R.
Babi Yar. Y. Yevtushenko.
   Ca-MR:54
Do Not Trust the Disciples.
   D. Samoilov. Bo-RU:72
Do the Russians Want War?
   Y. Yevtushenko. Mo-MI:67
Down by the Volga.
   I. Kharabov. Bo-RU:45
Friends Go Away. A. Galich.
   Bo-RU:32
Good Morning! T. Nichiporum.
   Mo-MI:66
The House. E. Almedingen.
   Ke-TF:412
I'm Like a Count. L. Batshev.
   Bo-RU:15

In the State There Is the Law.
    B. Slutsky. Bo-RU:80
Letter to Yesenin. S. Yesenin.
    Ca-MR:108
Lost Joy. A. Onyezhskaya.
    Bo-RU:60
Manifesto of Man. Y. Galanskov.
    Bo-RU:29
Poem. D. Hofstein. Ho-TY:173
Russia-1923. S. Halkin.
    Ho-TY:186
Russia, Your Image. Y. Stefanov.
    Bo-RU:83
Sabbath Is Gone. D. Hofstein.
    Ho-TY:174
The Scythians. A. Blok.
    Ca-MR:198
Silence Is Gold. A. Galich.
    Bo-RU:33
The Size of Him! A. Kotul'sky.
    Mo-MI:27
Song of My Indifference.
    D. Hofstein. Ho-TY:175
Trinity Sunday. V. Kovshin.
    Bo-RU:47
Two Mothers. I. Sheyanova.
    Mo-MI:45
A Word in Jewish Ears.
    A. Galich. Bo-RU:34
Words, Words. M. Mertsalov.
    Bo-RU:51
RUSSIA - COUNTRYSIDE
O Fields. S. Yesenin. Ca-MR:108
RUSSIA - HISTORY AND PATRIOTISM
The Descent into Hell.
    Y. Stefanov. Bo-RU:81
Granada. M. Svetlov. Ca-MR:86
The March to Moscow.
    R. Southey. Hi-FO:201
Mural of Borodino. L. Adler.
    Ls-NY:175
My Tale of Igor's Men.
    V. Burich. Bo-RU:24
1905. B. Pasternak. Ca-MR:171
The October Anniversary.
    S. Slezsky. Mo-MI:55
The Russian Gods. D. Andreyev.
    Ca-MR:95
Snow in the Caucasus.
    Y. Gillespie. Ls-NY:29
The Song of Igor's Campaign.
    Hi-FO:77
The Tale of Bogolyubovo.
    A. Vasyutkov. Bo-RU:87
The Trojan Horse. L. Shkol'nik.
    Bo-RU:78
The Word. A. Timofeyevsky.Bo-RU:84
RUSSIA - STALIN ERA, 1925-1953
All We Who in His Name.
    P. Antokol'sky. Bo-RU:7

The Black Cat. B. Okujava.
    Bo-RU:56
House in St. Petersburg.
    S. Burnshaw. Gr-SS:72
I Return to My City.
    O. Mandelstam. Ca-MR:148
I Wouldn't Go, Man. A. Aronov.
    Bo-RU:8
Moscow Gold. A. Onyezhskaya.
    Bo-RU:60
The Pipe. H. Plisetsky. Bo-RU:65
RUSSIAN LANGUAGE
Hearing Russian Spoken.
    D. Davie. Pa-GTB:555
RUSSIAN REVOLUTION, 1917-1921:
    see also BOLSHEVISM; and
    names of revolutionary leaders,
    as LENIN, VLADIMIR ILICH
    (NIKOLAI)
Bolsheviks. A. Stolzenberg.
    Ho-TY:269
1917. P. Markish. Ho-TY:185
Ringed. V. Mayakovsky.
    Ca-MR:83
Soviet Russia. S. Yesenin.
    Ca-MR:110
To Odessa. L. Kvitko. Ho-TY:192
A Tolstoyan Idyll, 1917.
    M. Rawitch. Ho-TY:201
The Twelve. A. Blok. Ca-MR:200
RUSSIAN VERSE: see also ALTAIC
    VERSE; BALLADS, RUSSIAN
Against Borders. Y. Yevtushenko.
    Ad-CI:80
Baby Camel. V. Korostylev.
    Co-BBW:186
Bicycles. A. Voznesensky.
    Li-TU:40
Black Diamond. N. Gumilyov.
    Pa-SG:24
Brooklyn Bridge. V. Mayakovsky.
    Li-TU:254
Christmas Star. B. Pasternak.
    Ma-FW:282
The Companion. Y. Yevtushenko.
    Cr-WS:127, Ma-FW:252
Composed while under Arrest.
    M. Lermontov. Pa-SG:204
Crocodile. K. Chukovsky.
    Gr-EC:24, 33
Eagles. V. Bashkin. Co-BBW:239
Earth and Sea. A. Pushkin.
    Pa-SG:168
Envy. Y. Yevtushenko. Ma-FW:139
Evil Days. B. Pasternak.
    Tr-MR:119
Fifteen Boys. B. Akhmadulina.
    Gr-BT:65
Fragment of a Bylina.
    A. Pushkin. Li-TU:83

RUSSIAN VERSE — cont'd.
  Garden of Gethsemane.
    B. Pasternak.   Tr-MR:122
  The Giraffe.   N. Gumileo.
    Fe-FP:470
  Give Me Peace.
    A. Voznesensky.   Gr-BT:148
  Goya.   A. Voznesensky.   Ca-MR:68
  Grapes.   A. Pushkin.
    Ho-LP:27, Pa-SG:98
  In the Clear Cold.   S. Yesenin.
    Pa-SG:100
  July.   L. Tatyanicheva.
    Pa-SG:94
  Lies.   Y. Yevtushenko.
    Du-SH:106
  Little Catkins.   A. Blok.
    Pl-EI:181
  Magdalene.   B. Pasternak.
    Tr-MR:89
  A Magic Landscape.   A. Fet.
    Pa-SG:103
  Message to Siberia.
    A. Pushkin.   Lo-TY:68
  The Muse.   A. Akhmatova.
    Gr-CC:84, Pl-ML:32
  An Ocean Holds the Globe.
    F. Tyutchev.   Pa-SG:124
  Ode to Rain.   Bo-FP:222
  On a Bicycle.   Y. Yevtushenko.
    Li-TU:19
  Phantoms of the Steppe.
    A. Pushkin.   Ab-MO:63
  The Prophet.   A. Pushkin.
    Pl-EI:98
  Remembrance.   V. Zhukovsky.
    Pa-SG:15
  Rooster.   F. Belkin.   Co-BBW:172
  Schoolmaster.   Y. Yevtushenko.
    Li-TU:136, Ma-FW:137
  Silentium.   F. Tyutchev.
    Pa-SG:123
  Someone Is Beating a Woman.
    A. Voznesensky.   Gr-BT:125
  The Song of Igor's Campaign.
    Hi-FO:77
  Spring.   V. Mayakovsky.   Ad-CI:90
  Spring Song.   Bo-FP:236
  Twilight.   F. Tyutchev.   Pa-SG:107
  Upon the Hard Crust.
    A. Akhmatova.   Pa-SG:23
  With Freedom's Seed.
    A. Pushkin.   Lo-TY:67
  With Wavering Feet I Walked.
    V. Solovyov.   Pa-SG:118
  Zima Junction.
    Y. Yevtushenko.   Li-TU:31
  The Zoo.   B. Pasternak.   Ma-FW:221
  See also   Bo-RU, Ca-MR, Gr-BB,
    Mo-MI

RUSSIANS: see also COSSACKS
  Early Train.   B. Pasternak.
    Ca-MR:173
  The Lads.   L. Shkol'nik.   Bo-RU:78
  Merry Tale.   A. Aronov.   Bo-RU:9
  People, Listen!   A. Shchukin.
    Bo-RU:73
  The People of Africa.
    M. Mertsalov.   Bo-RU:51
  The Pipe.   H. Plisetsky.   Bo-RU:65
  The Suburban Train.
    A. Voznesensky.   Ca-MR:69
  To My Generation.
    A. Onyezhskaya.   Bo-RU:61
RUTH
  Ruth.   T. Hood.   Gr-CC:37,
    Ox-BN:422
RUTLEDGE, ANN
  Anne Rutledge.   E. Masters.
    Br-AF:82, Co-PS:33, Er-FA:287,
    Ha-PO:66, Hi-TL:116, Mo-BG:164,
    Sh-AP:137, Un-MA:144, Wi-LT:116
SABBATH
  Kibbutz Sabbath.   L. Amittai.
    Pl-EI:192
  Sabbath Stars.   A. Shlonsky.
    Me-PH:101
  Song of the Sabbath.
    K. Molodowsky.   Ho-TY:285
SABRINA
  Sabrina Fair.   J. Milton.
    Al-VBP:400, De-CH:122,
    Rv-CB:372, Sm-LG:227
SACCO-VANZETTI CASE
  Justice Denied in Massachusetts.
    E. Millay.   Un-MA:447
  Last Speech to the Court.
    B. Vanzetti.   Mo-BG:170
  They Are Dead Now.   J. Dos Passos.
    Kr-OF:120
  Vanzetti Speaks to the Court.
    B. Vanzetti.   Kr-OF:119
  We Shall Not Die in Darkness.
    E. Millay.   Kr-OF:123
SACRAMENTS: see BAPTISM; EXTREME
    UNCTION; LORD'S SUPPER; MARRIAGE
SACRIFICE: see also LOVE -
    SACRIFICES
  Abraham and Isaac.   Ga-S:40,
    Ma-FW:78
  The Book of Job.   H. Leivick.
    Ho-TY:126
  The Descent into Hell.
    Y. Stefanov.   Bo-RU:81
  The Forsaken.   D. Scott.
    Do-WH:63, Ha-PO:159
  Inscription on an Altar of
    the Dead.   V. Contoski.   Sc-TN:32
  Invocation to Dsilyi Neyani.
    Da-SC:75, Tr-US II:250

Jepthah's Daughter. A. Tennyson.
  Hi-FO:17
McDonogh Day in New Orleans.
  M. Christian.   Bo-AN:52,
  Hu-PN:157
Memorial to the Great Big
  Beautiful Self-Sacrificing
  Advertisers. E. Ebright.
  Hi-TL:207
My Father Isaac. J. Glatstein.
  Ho-TY:246
Norman Morrison. D. Ferguson.
  Ba-PO:34
The Parable of the Old Men and
  the Young. W. Owen.
  Go-BP:207, Ma-FW:250, Mo-GR:18
Prayer for Peace.   Tr-US II:54
Prayer over a Human Sacrifice to
  Rongo. Tr-US II:53
Prayer to the Sea.   Tr-US II:124
Quia Amore Langueo. Rv-CB:14
Res Publica. J. McKellar.
  Ni-JP:121
Sonnets, xvi. E. Wylie.
  Sm-PT:71, Un-MA:281
A Spell. J. Dryden. Gr-SS:153,
  Ho-WR:226
Story of Isaac. L. Cohen.
  Mo-GR:16
Tempt Me No More. C. Day Lewis.
  Un-MB:423
Time to Die. R. Dandridge.
  Ad-PB:18
SADNESS: see MELANCHOLY
SAFETY: see also HUMOR - SAFETY;
  RESCUES AND RESCUING; SATIRE -
  SAFETY; SECURITY
All Through the Night.
  Ch-B:117, Fe-FP:466, Un-GT:301
The Attack. L. Clark.
  Pa-RE:15
The Bell-Man. R. Herrick.
  De-CH:202, Rv-CB:341
Earth and Sea. A. Pushkin.
  Pa-SG:168
The Fox and the Rooster.
  E. Rees. Ar-TP3:82
German Slumber Song.
  K. Simrock. Un-GT:301
Hidden by Darkness. Basho.
  Be-MC:11
The Lanthorn Is to Keep the
  Candle Light. J. Bunyan.
  Gr-TG:46
Leap Before You Look. W. Auden.
  Ha-TP:137
The Lion and the Fox. E. Rees.
  Ar-TP3:81
The Little Girl Found. W. Blake.
  Rv-CB:593

Old Man Pondered.   J. Ransom.
  Un-MA:416
The Old Man's Comforts and How
  He Gained Them. R. Southey.
  Li-SR:90, Ma-YA:167, Ox-BC:93
The Owl. E. Thomas.
  Gr-CT:107, Ha-PO:105, Ni-JP:86,
  Pa-GTB:441, Re-BS:47
Reconnaissance. A. Bontemps.
  Bo-AN:80, Bo-HF:54, Ra-BP:92
Seaside Storm. M. Craig.
  Cr-SS:18
The Ship. J. Squire.
  De-CH:402, De-TT:133
Sleep, Baby, Sleep.
  Bo-FP:49, Fe-FP:471, Hu-MP:123,
  Ke-TF:40, Li-LB:22, Re-TW:74,
  Sm-MK:226, Un-GT:301, Wr-RM:58
A Story. W. Stafford.
  Co-PT:142
This Is a Poem. H. Farley.
  Le-M:14
To Nowhere. D. Ignatow.
  Ad-CI:44
Twice Shy. S. Heaney. Br-TC:174
Vessels Large. B. Franklin.
  Un-GT:26
The Viking Terror. Co-PI:138,
  Gr-CT:222
SAILING: see also BOATS AND
  BOATING; HUMOR - SAILING;
  YACHTS AND YACHTING
The Ballad of Kon-Tiki.
  I. Serraillier. Co-SS:223
Dreams of a Summer Night.
  G. Barker. Ma-FW:51
Drifting. T. Read. Pa-HT:107
Idly My Ship Glides. Otsuji.
  Be-CS:44
Offshore. P. Booth.
  Mo-SD:137
A Passer-By. R. Bridges.
  Ho-WR:125, Ox-BN:873,
  Un-MB:48, Wi-LT:52
Puffed by a Wind. Kyorai.
  Be-CS:33
River Travel. Ts'ui Hao.
  Le-MW:82
Sailboat, Your Secret.
  R. Francis. Mo-SD:140
Sailing. Ch-B:36
Sailing in Autumn. K. Nakamura.
  Sh-AM:172
Sailing to an Island. R. Murphy.
  To-MP:134
Sailing upon the River.
  G. Crabbe. Ox-BN:10
Sampan. Hi-WP I:1
The Spring Waters. Ping Hsin.
  Hs-TC:23

SAILING — cont'd.
  Swedish Folk Song. Bo-FP:280
  To Mary: Of Sailing.
    R. Snyder. Ls-NY:7
  Vacationer. W. Gibson.
    Mo-SD:139
  The Yachts. W. Williams.
    Al-VBP:1154, Fl-HH:27, Ma-FW:51,
    Pe-OA:73, Pe-SS:72, Sm-PT:112,
    Un-MA:262, Wi-LT:194
  Youth and Age on Beaulieu River,
    Hants. J. Betjeman. Br-TC:45
SAILORS: see SEAMEN
ST. AGNES'S EVE
  The Eve of St. Agnes. J. Keats.
    Al-VBP:781, Fe-PL:35, Ox-BN:338
ST. ANDREWS, SCOT.
  The City of Golf. R. Murray.
    Mo-SD:47
ST. CLAIR, LAKE
  The Great Lakes Suite, IV.
    J. Reaney. Do-WH:51
ST. DAVID'S DAY
  There Were Three Jovial
    Welshmen. Bl-OB:24, Gr-GB:86,
    Ir-BB:140, Mo-MGT:198, Pa-OM:2,
    Sm-MK:23, Sp-HW:23
ST. GERVAIS, FR.
  St. Gervais. M. Roberts.
    Sm-LG:297
ST. GREGORY'S DAY
  St. Gregory's Day. Bo-FP:217
ST. JEROME, CAN.
  At St Jerome. F. Harrison.
    Do-WH:74
ST. JOHN'S EVE: see MIDSUMMER EVE
ST. LOUIS, MO.
  St. Louis Midday. J. Knoepfle.
    St-H:93
  Sunset, St. Louis.
    S. Teasdale. Pa-HT:51
ST. LUCY'S DAY
  A Nocturnal upon Saint Lucy's
    Day. J. Donne. Rv-CB:301
  Prayer to St. Lucy.
    J. Heath-Stubbs. Go-BP:227
ST. MALACHY'S DAY: see also
    MALACHY, SAINT
  St. Malachy. T. Merton.
    Ca-VT:417
ST. PATRICK'S DAY: see also
    PATRICK, SAINT
  Dawn Song - St. Patrick's Day.
    V. Storey. Ha-YA:42
  I'll Wear a Shamrock.
    M. Davies. Ar-TP3:200,
    Br-SS:134, Ha-YA:43
  No Luck. L. Blair. Ja-HH:18
  St. Patrick's Day Jig.
    J. Lee. Ja-HH:17

Wearing of the Green. A. Fisher.
    Ha-YA:41, La-PH:48
  The Wearing of the Green.
    Co-PS:51, Er-FA:295, Gr-GB:193,
    Hi-FO:252
ST. PETER'S CHURCH
  Ah, that I Were Far Away.
    A. Clough. Ox-BN:602
ST. PETERSBURG: see LENINGRAD,
    U.S.S.R.
SAINT-SAENS, (CHARLES) CAMILLE
  The Carnival of Animals.
    O. Nash. Pl-US:92
ST. STEPHEN'S DAY
  The Cutty Wren. Gr-GB:63,
    Rv-CB:418, Rv-ON:117
ST. VALENTINE'S DAY: see
    VALENTINE'S DAY
SAINTS: see also APOSTLES; HUMOR -
    SAINTS; MARTYRS; SATIRE -
    SAINTS; and names of saints,
    as CECILIA, SAINT
  Benediction. D. Quick.
    Ke-TF:211
  By a Chapel as I Came.
    Gr-CT:43, Gr-GB:313
  God's Saints Are Shining Lights.
    H. Vaughan. Gr-TG:57
  Matthew, Mark, Luke and John.
    Bo-FP:36, De-CH:446, De-PO:28,
    De-TT:202, Gr-GB:298, Gr-TG:55,
    Hi-GD:23, Mo-MGT:28, Mo-NR:99,
    On-TW:18, Rd-SS:40, Rv-CB:451,
    Sm-LG:385, Un-GT:23
  Saints. G. Garrett. Pl-EI:117
  Sanctity. P. Kavanagh.
    Co-EL:45
  The Virgin Martyrs.
    Sigebert of Gembloux. Ga-S:226
  When the Saints Go Marchin' In.
    Pl-EI:97
SALAMANCA, SP.
  Salamanca. F. Keyes. Ke-TF:393
SALAMANDERS
  The Newt. D. McCord. Ar-TP3:68
  The Salamander. K. von Lemeke.
    Un-R:102
  Salamander. M. Rukeyser.
    Ha-WR:71
  Samuel. B. Katz. Ho-GC:19
  Summer. D. Wakoski. Ca-VT:714
SALEM, MASS.: see also SATIRE -
    SALEM, MASS.
  Salem. R. Lowell. Mo-BG:141
  The Witch. S. McNail. De-FS:140
SALESMEN: see also SATIRE -
    SALESMEN
  Sale. J. Miles. Du-SH:152
SALOONS: see RESTAURANTS
    AND BARS

SALT
  On Salt Plains. D. Coldiron.
    Fi-BG:47
  Salt. R. Francis. Ls-NY:167
  Song Sung on an Expedition to
    Obtain Salt. Bi-IT:21, Ho-SD:51,
    Le-OE:73, Tr-US II:273
SALT LAKE CITY, UTAH
  Salt Lake City. H. Carruth.
    Br-AF:207
SALVATION: see also CONVERSION
  The Brass Serpent. T. Carmi.
    Me-PH:143
  Done Found My Lost Sheep.
    Ga-S:147
  An Evening Thought.
    J. Hammon. Hu-PN:4
  Glorious the Sun in Mid-Career.
    C. Smart. Sm-LG:376
  Hold the Wind. Gr-GB:326
  Love Unknown. G. Herbert.
    Ho-P:29
  Rock of Ages. A. Toplady.
    Er-FA:476, Rv-CB:554
  Songs Between the Soul and the
    Bridegroom. St. John of the
    Cross. Ga-S:139
  The Spirit Dances. T. Blackburn.
    Ga-S:191
  That Nature Is a Heraclitean
    Fire and of the Comfort of
    the Resurrection. G. Hopkins.
    Pa-GTB:396
  When Wilt Thou Save the People?
    E. Elliot. Hi-WP II:173,
    Pl-EI:157
  Woodstock. J. Mitchell.
    Mo-GR:102
SALVATION ARMY
  General William Booth Enters
    into Heaven. V. Lindsay.
    Ga-S:221, Un-MA:221, Wi-LT:624
SAMARKAND
  The Bloody Conquests of Mighty
    Tamburlaine. C. Marlowe.
    Gr-CT:335
  The Golden Journey to Samarkand.
    J. Flecker. Bo-GJ:228,
    Pa-HT:91
SAMISENS
  Samisen. J. Kirkup. Ls-NY:324
SAMPANS: see BOATS AND BOATING
SAMSON
  Death of Samson. J. Milton.
    Gr-CT:378
  How Samson Bore Away the Gates
    of Gaza. V. Lindsay. Tr-MR:76
  Samson Agonistes. J. Milton.
    Al-VBP:413, Ga-S:47, Hi-FO:20,
    Ma-FW:173

SAN FRANCISCO, CALIF.
  On the Eve. L. Simpson. Bl-FP:56
  San Francisco. W. Roberts.
    Hu-PN:82
  Scenic. J. Updike. Ad-CI:87,
    Ke-TF:364
  305 Honda. G. Fowler. Sc-TN:49
  Trip: San Francisco.
    L. Hughes. Br-AF:209
SAN PEDRO SULA, HOND.
  I Have Lost My Shoes.
    C. Suasnavar. Fe-FP:490
SANATORIUMS: see HOSPITALS
SAND, GEORGE: see HUMOR –
    SAND, GEORGE
SAND
  By the Swimming. R. Sward.
    Du-SH:130
  Five. C. Tringress. St-FS:3
  I Can Walk on This. St-FS:40
  Little Drops of Water.
    Sp-HW:33
  The Lost Dancer. J. Toomer.
    Ad-PB:34
  Mine. L. Moore. Cr-SS:16
  The Sandcastle. M. Stephenson.
    St-FS:58
  The Stars. Ping Hsin. Hs-TC:21
  White Sand and Grey Sand.
    Rv-CB:422
SAND CREEK, BATTLE, 1864
  Black Kettle Raises the Stars
    and Stripes. L. Simpson.
    Cr-WS:24
  The Death Song of White Antelope.
    White Antelope. Br-MW:92
SAND DUNES
  Culbin Sands. A. Young.
    Pa-GTB:466
  Sand Dunes. R. Frost.
    La-RM:94, Un-MA:185
SANDMAN
  I Feel Relaxed and Still.
    K. Anderson. Le-M:160
SANDPIPERS
  The Sandpiper. F. Frost.
    Cr-SS:10
  The Sandpiper. C. Thaxter.
    Fe-FP:292, Hu-MP:234,
    Mc-PR:19, Ox-BC:281
  Sandpipers. H. Nemerov.
    Mo-BG:130
  Sandpipers. C. Sandburg.
    Re-BS:37
SANDWICH ISLANDS: see HAWAII (STATE)
SANDWICHES
  When Crossing a Desert. Re-RR:20
SANITARIUMS: see HOSPITALS
SANSKRIT: see EAST INDIAN
    VERSE – SANSKRIT

SANTA ANNA, ANTONIO LOPEZ DE
  The Defence of the Alamo.
    J. Miller. Pa-OM:173
SANTA BARBARA, CALIF.
  The Santa Barbara Earthquake.
    Em-AF:472
SANTA CLAUS: see also CHRISTMAS;
    HUMOR - SANTA CLAUS; SATIRE -
    SANTA CLAUS
  The Boy Who Laughed at Santa
    Claus. O. Nash. Co-BB:16,
    Ha-PO:291
  Christmas Eve Rhyme.
    C. McCullers. Ho-ME:28
  Christmas Guarantee. E. Jay.
    Ja-HH:56
  Conversation Between Mr. and
    Mrs. Santa Claus. R. Bennett.
    Ar-TP3:237, Br-SS:110
  Kriss Kringle. T. Aldrich.
    Hu-MP:360
  Mrs. Claus. B. Lee. Ja-HH:59
  Santa Claus and the Mouse.
    E. Poulsson. Ch-B:56
  Santa's Ride. J. Lee.
    Ja-HH:59
  A Visit from St. Nicholas.
    C. Moore. Ar-TP3:193, Bo-FP:187,
    Br-SS:104, Er-FA:511, Fe-FP:86,
    Ga-FB:177, Hu-MP:357, Ox-BC:154,
    Pa-OM:346, Sh-RP:242, Un-GT:292
SANTA FE, N.M.
  Spring Morning - Santa Fe.
    L. Riggs. Pa-HT:57
SANTAYANA, GEORGE
  For George Santayana.
    R. Lowell. Ca-VT:446
  Sonnet. D. Cory. Ke-TF:309
SANTIAGO, SP.
  Madrigal to the City of Santiago.
    F. Garciá Lorca. Ad-CI:86
SAPPHO
  Anactoria. A. Swinburne.
    Al-VBP:1022
SARACENS
  War Song of the Saracens.
    J. Flecker. Ga-FB:193,
    Hi-FO:65, Un-MB:273
SARAH, WIFE OF ABRAHAM
  Hagar Speaks to Sarah.
    G. Howard. Ke-TF:147
  Sarah Speaks to Hagar.
    G. Howard. Ke-TF:148
SARAJEVO, YUGOS.
  Sarajevo. L. Durrell.
    Pa-GTB:525
SARDANAPALUS, KING OF ASSYRIA
  Sardanapalus. H. Howard.
    Hi-FO:29
SARIS: see CLOTHING AND DRESS; INDIA

SARTO, ANDREA DEL: see
    ANDREA DEL SARTO
SASSAFRAS
  Sassafras Tea. M. Newsome.
    Gr-EC:111
  Witchwood. M. Justus. Br-SS:68,
    Ju-CP:75
SASSOON, SIEGFRIED
  Broken Promise. J. Taylor.
    Gr-BT:108
SATAN: see DEVILS; LUCIFER (SATAN)
SATELLITES, ARTIFICIAL: see
    ARTIFICIAL SATELLITES
SATIRE - ADDISON, JOSEPH
  Atticus. A. Pope. Ha-PO:60
SATIRE - ADVENTURE AND ADVENTURERS
  A Day with the Foreign Legion.
    R. Whittemore. Wi-LT:842
SATIRE - ADVERTISING
  Advertisement. O. de Andrade.
    An-TC:13
  Brainwashing Dramatized.
    D. Johnson. Hu-PN:436
  Headline Music. Yüan Shui-p'ai.
    Hs-TC:402
  It Is Not Enough.
    D. Henderson. Ke-PP:98
  Memorial to the Great Big
    Beautiful Self-Sacrificing
    Advertisers. E. Ebright.
    Hi-TL:207
  Poem, or Beauty Hurts Mr. Vinal.
    E. Cummings. Sh-AP:191,
    Un-MA:474
  The River. H. Crane. Al-VBP:1210,
    Sh-AP:199, Un-MA:522
SATIRE - ADVICE
  Lord Thomas and Fair Annet.
    Ox-BB:178
  Signpost. R. Jeffers.
    Al-VBP:1167
SATIRE - AMBITION
  As I Grew Older. L. Hughes.
    Ha-TP:101
  Babylon. L. Benét. De-FS:20
  Comparison. J. Bunyan.
    Ox-BC:35
  The Cowboy's Wishes. D. White.
    Fi-BG:72
  Go, Silly Worm. J. Sylvester.
    Rv-CB:188
  Hollyhocks. D. Etter. St-H:61
  Jack and the Beanstalk.
    P. Goedicke. Du-SH:50
  Misdirection. E. Slator.
    Th-AS:216
  Negro Dreams. D. Long.
    Ad-PB:405
  Watering the Horse. R. Bly.
    St-H:5

SATIRE - AMERICA
America. A. Ginsberg. Bl-FP:64
America. B. Hamilton. Ad-BO:41
America. W. Rose. Ni-CD:213
America. J. Whitfield. Ha-PO:17,
  Ra-BP:35
American History. M. Harper.
  Ra-BP:291
Benediction. B. Kaufman.
  Be-MA:132, Hu-PN:412, Lo-IT:66
black power poem. I. Reed.
  Ra-BP:288
Blue Ruth: America. M. Harper.
  Ad-PB:317
Brave New World. A. MacLeish.
  Sh-AP:189
Children's Rhymes. L. Hughes.
  Ad-BO:43, Ra-BP:86
A Coney Island of the Mind.
  L. Ferlinghetti. Mo-BG:182,
  Wi-LT:701
The Dance of Death.
  F. Garciá Lorca. Bl-FP:70
Empire Builders. A. MacLeish.
  Sh-AP:188
Love Your Enemy. Y. Imam.
  Lo-TY:258, Ra-BP:293
My Blackness Is the Beauty of
  This Land. L. Jeffers.
  Ad-PB:173
Paterson. W. Williams. Bl-FP:61
Poem, or Beauty Hurts Mr. Vinal.
  E. Cummings. Sh-AP:191,
  Un-MA:474
The Primitive. D. Lee. Ra-BP:297
A Projection. R. Whittemore.
  Mc-WK:210
right on: white america.
  S. Sanchez. Ad-BO:42,
  Ad-PB:287, Be-MA:135, Jo-SA:104
Special Bulletin. L. Hughes.
  Ad-PB:80
A Supermarket in California.
  A. Ginsberg. Br-TC:149,
  Kh-VA:64, Mo-BG:185, Wi-LT:718
Those Being Eaten by America.
  R. Bly. Mc-EA:126
tomorrow the heroes.
  A. Spellman. Ad-PB:285
Vive Noir! M. Evans. Ad-PB:188
What Is America? J. Velez.
  Ba-HI:110
When Something Happens. J. Randall.
  Ra-BP:275
Will the Wig Be Big Enough?
  P. Crawford. La-IH:128
SATIRE - AMERICANS
Hour of Concern. L. Hubbell.
  Ba-PO:52

SATIRE - ANIMALS - DEATH
Rhymes for a Modern Nursery.
  P. Dehn. Co-FB:451
SATIRE - ANONYMITY
Riding Across John Lee's Finger.
  S. Crouch. Ad-PB:485
They Are Killing All the Young
  Men. D. Henderson. Ad-PB:414
SATIRE - ANTICIPATION
Before the Charge. P. MacGill.
  Cr-WS:90
SATIRE - APPROVAL
After Goliath. K. Amis. En-PC:194
SATIRE - ARMS AND ARMOR
Arms and the Boy. W. Owen.
  Er-FA:192, Ni-JP:78,
  Un-MB:367, Wi-LT:349
SATIRE - ARNOLD, MATTHEW
The Dover Bitch. A. Hecht.
  Ca-VT:504
SATIRE - ART AND ARTISTS
Icarus. H. Sabgir. Bo-RU:71
SATIRE - ASTRONOMERS AND ASTRONOMY
When I Heard the Learn'd
  Astronomer. W. Whitman.
  Ho-LP:56, Rv-CB:860,
  Sm-LG:53, Un-MA:42
SATIRE - ATOMIC ENERGY
Atomic Courtesy. E. Jacobson.
  Er-FA:216
Geiger, Geiger, Ticking Slow.
  P. Dehn. Li-SR:9
It Is Not Only the Dead.
  F. Long. De-FS:132
A Leaden Treasury of Verse.
  P. Dehn. Co-FB:464
SATIRE - ATOMIC WEAPONS
Contemplating More Bomb Tests.
  E. Merriam. Ba-PO:60
5 Ways to Kill a Man. E. Brock.
  Co-WS:145, Mo-TS:39
Futurama Love Song. N. Rosten.
  Cr-WS:146
Harry. N. Rosten. Cr-WS:147
Norris Dam. S. Rodman.
  Hu-PN:542
On Shooting Particles Beyond the
  World. R. Eberhart.
  Wi-LT:434
Return to Hiroshima. L. Stryk.
  Cr-WS:148
Talking Atom. Ba-PO:198
SATIRE - ATOMS
Song, on Reading that the Cyclotron
  Has Produced Cosmic Rays.
  S. Hoffenstein. Br-SM:66
SATIRE - AUTHORS
A Farewell to London. A. Pope.
  Rv-CB:513

SATIRE - AUTHORS — cont'd.
On Some South African Novelists.
R. Campbell.   Pa-GTB:496
A Plea to Boys and Girls.
R. Graves.   Pa-GTB:491
SATIRE - AVIATION
What Bright Pushbutton?
S. Allen.   Hu-PN:344
SATIRE - BARTON, BRUCE
Empire Builders.   A. MacLeish.
Sh-AP:188
SATIRE - BATTLES
Breakfast.   W. Gibson.
Cr-WS:104
SATIRE - BEAUTY
The Pawnshop.   Chu Hsiang.
Hs-TC:104
The Washerman.   U. Joshi.
Al-PI:110
SATIRE - BEAUTY, PERSONAL
Corinna, Pride of Drury-Lane.
J. Swift.   Ke-PP:34
The Question.   N. Gale.
Co-EL:19, Co-FB:473
SATIRE - BIRTH
Slap Happy.   E. Glenn.   Lo-IT:41
SATIRE - BISHOPS
Bad Bishop Jegon.   Gr-GB:186
Bishop Cody's Last Request.
T. Paxton.   Mo-GR:55
Crazy Jane and the Bishop.
W. Yeats.   Wi-LT:88
SATIRE - BLESSINGS
Blessing the Battle. W. Tappan.
Cr-WS:140
Grace to Be Said at the
Supermarket.   H. Nemerov.
To-MP:118
SATIRE - BOMBS
My Spoon Was Lifted.
N. Replansky.   Co-PU:73
The Unexploded Bomb. C. Lewis.
Ha-TP:28
SATIRE - BOOKS AND READING
A Classic Waits for Me.
E. White.   Li-SR:146
SATIRE - BOSTON, ENG.
Boston, Lincolnshire.
Gr-GB:174
SATIRE - BOSTON, MASS.
As a Plane Tree by the Water.
R. Lowell.   Gr-SS:160,
Un-MA:664, Wi-LT:578
SATIRE - BOWS AND ARROWS
Brave Old World.   F. Lambert.
Er-FA:216
SATIRE - BREAKFAST
Breakfast. W. Gibson.   Cr-WS:104
SATIRE - BROTHERHOOD
A Black Man. S. Cornish. Ad-PB:298

Boogie-Woogie Ballads.
S. McKelway.   Hu-PN:534
Cold Term.   I. Baraka.
Ra-BP:220
Defeat.   W. Bynner.   Hu-PN:490
Don't Ask Me Who I Am.
J. Randall.   Ra-BP:274
Frontier Guard.   T. Wright.
Cr-WS:141
Geography Lesson.   Z. Ghose.
To-MP:159
interlude.   W. Smith.   Ad-PB:374
International Conference.
C. Ellis.   Cr-WS:138
On the Eve of New Wars.
L. Untermeyer.   Ba-PO:164
Report from a Planet.
R. Lattimore.   Ba-PO:201
Sapphics.   G. Canning.   Hi-FO:186
The Trophy.   E. Muir.   Wi-LT:251
The Unexploded Bomb.   C. Lewis.
Ha-TP:28
The U.S. Sailor with the Japanese
Skull.   W. Scott.   Pe-OA:207,
Wi-LT:812
Who Shall Die?   J. Randall.
Ra-BP:272
SATIRE - BUREAUCRACY
Barricades.   M. Harper.
Ad-PB:316
The Final Toast.   T. Veitch.
Mc-EA:131
Her Beauty Is Hidden.
Li Shang Yin.   Rx-LT:79
Letter to the City Clerk.
F. Wright.   Er-FA:224
Ode for the Burial of a Citizen.
J. Ciardi.   Wi-LT:668
Pass Office Song.   Lo-TY:17
Refugee Blues.   W. Auden.
Hi-WP I:122, Wi-LT:472
SATIRE - BUSINESS
Dolor.   T. Roethke.   Ha-PO:225,
Ke-PP:116, Sh-AP:212, Wi-LT:478
SATIRE - BUSYNESS
Character Sketch.   G. Howard.
Ke-TF:174
Leisure.   W. Davies.   Ar-TP3:213,
Co-BN:205, De-CH:137, Er-FA:248,
Fe-FP:78, Gr-EC:45, Hi-WP I:119,
Mc-WK:22, Sh-RP:117, Sm-MK:177,
Un-MB:179, Wi-LT:617
SATIRE - CALIFORNIA
Sand Hill Road.   M. Grosser.
Pe-SS:85
SATIRE - CEMETERIES
Visiting a Dead Man on a Summer
Day.   M. Piercy.   Lo-IT:102
SATIRE - CHANGE
The Early Rebels. W. Morris. Sa-B:9

Noah.   W. Brown.   Sa-B:218
Passing and Glassing.
   C. Rossetti.   Ox-BN:718
Quaker Hill.   H. Crane.
   Wi-LT:389
Sonnet XV.   Feng Chih.   Hs-TC:152
"They."   S. Sassoon.   Cr-WS:118
SATIRE - CHARITY
The Lovers of the Poor.
   G. Brooks.   Be-MA:83
On the Gift of a Cloak.
   Hugo of Orleans.   Li-TU:44
Sapphics.   G. Canning.   Hi-FO:186
Zoo.   A. Boorstin.   La-IH:122
SATIRE - CHICAGO, ILL.
Chicago.   Ya Hsuan.   Pa-MV:145
Chicago.   Yu Kuang-chung.
   Pa-MV:180
SATIRE - CHILDHOOD
The Leaden-Eyed.   V. Lindsay.
   Co-EL:136, Co-PU:150, Ke-PP:61,
   Kr-OF:182, Ni-JP:32, Tr-MR:54
SATIRE - CHINA
New Year.   Yüan Shui-p'ai.
   Hs-TC:407
Strange Tales, Domestic Vintage.
   Yüan Shui-p'ai.   Hs-TC:406
SATIRE - CHIVALRY
Hudibras.   S. Butler.   Al-VBP:426
SATIRE - CHRISTIANITY
Christmas.   M. Leib.   Ho-TY:93
Dawn in the Heart of Africa.
   P. Lumumba.   Lo-TY:150
Ecce Homo.   D. Gascoyne.   Wi-LT:715
From the Prophecy of Katun 9 Ahau.
   Br-MW:28, Da-SC:163
The Gray Squirrel.   H. Wolfe.
   Bo-GJ:65, Co-BBW:39, Un-MB:303
Magalu.   H. Johnson.
   Ad-PB:103, Hu-PN:263
On Seeing Two Brown Boys in a
   Catholic Church.   F. Horne.
   Ad-PB:55, Hu-PN:146, Lo-TY:212
The Only Man That E'er I Knew.
   W. Blake.   Co-PU:16
Our New National Anthem.
   W. Eggleston.   Ba-PO:80,
   Cr-WS:155
The Return to the Old Gods.
   Kr-OF:21
Thoughts on the Christian Doctrine
   of Eternal Hell.   S. Smith.
   Ke-PP:44
We Were Not like Dogs.
   U. Greenberg.   Me-PH:98
Ye Ancient Divine Ones.
   A. Clough.   Ox-BN:611
SATIRE - CHRISTMAS
A Carol for Children.   O. Nash.
   Pl-EI:150

Christ Climbed Down.
   L. Ferlinghetti.   Tr-MR:111
Christmas.   M. Leib.   Ho-TY:93
Christmas Eve under Hooker's
   Statue.   R. Lowell.
   Ba-PO:202, Hi-TL:214
Karma.   E. Robinson.
   Sm-PT:142, Un-MA:138
No Man.   C. Bresher.   Ad-II:121
Santa Claus.   H. Nemerov.
   Pe-OA:252
White Christmas.   W. Rodgers.
   Co-PI:169, Ke-PP:29,
   Un-MB:482, Wi-LT:492
SATIRE - CHRISTMAS SONGS
A Christmas Carol.
   G. Chesterton.   Ga-S:88
SATIRE - CHURCHES
Church on the Corner of Union
   and Third.   I. Smith.
   Lo-IT:126
Legsby, Lincolnshire.   Gr-GB:174
SATIRE - CITIES AND TOWNS
All the Mornings.   R. Sward.
   St-H:219
Answer.   D. Quick.   Ke-TF:425
Birmingham.   L. MacNeice.
   Un-MB:445
City.   J. Bruchac.   Ni-CD:39
The City.   Yüan Shui-p'ai.
   Hs-TC:402
Hard Questions.   M. Tsuda.
   La-RM:172
Howl, Part II.   A. Ginsberg.
   En-PC:234
In the Cities.   D. Lawrence.
   Hi-WP II:161
The Man in the Ocelot Suit.
   C. Brookhouse.   Ad-CI:108
The Mayors.   W. Blake.   De-CH:62
Metromania.   B. Braley.   Ke-TF:356
A Northern Suburb. J. Davidson.
   Ox-BN:904
Pictures of a City.   R. Fripp.
   Mo-GR:78
Poem.   M. Halpern.   Ho-TY:114
Poem.   T. McGrath.   St-H:125
Song: Weekend's Over.
   M. Halpern.   Ho-TY:106
The Soul of Shanghai.
   Shao Hsün-mei.   Hs-TC:127
Stories of the Streets.
   L. Cohen.   Mo-GR:88
Terminal Theater.   R. Sward.
   St-H:218
The Thrush in February.
   G. Meredith.
   Ox-BN:694
Today Tomorrow?   S. Cybulski.
   Me-WF:83

SATIRE - CITIZENSHIP
  Confession Overheard in a Subway.
    K. Fearing. Pe-SS:112,
    Wi-LT:699
SATIRE - CIVIL RIGHTS
  Black Backlash. C. Snipe.
    Lo-IT:128
  We Live in a Cage. W. Harris.
    Ad-PB:438
  What Ever Happened to America.
    R. Patterson. Kr-OF:127
SATIRE - CIVIL WAR - UNITED STATES,
  1861-1865
  Death in Yorkville. L. Hughes.
    Ad-PB:79
  This Newer Bondage. P. Dunbar.
    Kr-OF:47
SATIRE - CIVILIZATION
  Battle. R. Jeffers. Un-MA:371,
    Wi-LT:260
  The Beast with Chrome Teeth.
    T. Snyder. Hu-NN:87
  Book Allargando. A. Franklyn.
    Lo-IT:35
  Boom! H. Nemerov. Ba-PO:193,
    Wi-LT:589
  Burial. P. Joachim. Lo-TY:146
  Chorus for a Phonograph.
    K. Congdon. Lo-IT:21
  Dirge. K. Fearing. Ha-PO:247,
    Hi-TL:200, Sh-AP:207
  The Earth Grown like the Moon.
    T. Kagawa. Ba-PO:126
  Eve to Her Daughters.
    J. Wright. To-MP:173
  The Fury of Aerial Bombardment.
    R. Eberhart. Ba-PO:178,
    Ca-VT:248, Sh-AP:209, Wi-LT:438
  The Great Society. J. Haines.
    Sc-TN:76
  Headline History. W. Plomer.
    Hi-FO:261
  Howl. A. Ginsberg. En-PC:234,
    Sh-AP:233
  Hugh Selwyn Mauberley. E. Pound.
    Ba-PO:149, Ca-VT:84, Ha-PO:122,
    Hi-TL:185, Un-MA:301, Wi-LT:232
  I Shall Laugh Purely. R. Jeffers.
    Wi-LT:263
  If There Was Peace. S. Jahin.
    Lo-TY:52
  Jehovah Buried, Satan Dead.
    E. Cummings. Pe-OA:147
  The Land. V. Cruz. Lo-IT:26
  Litany of the Lost. S. Sassoon.
    Tr-MR:187
  Maxims of Gloucester, to You.
    C. Olson. Wi-LT:778
  Menagerie. I. Van Sertima.
    Sa-B:40

Mission Uncontrolled. R. Peck.
    Pe-M:86
Missionary. D. Thomas. To-MP:199
Nature or Man. P. Curry. Me-WF:51
Nightmare with Angels. S. Benét.
    Ba-PO:12
Ogres and Pygmies. R. Graves.
    Wi-LT:376
Prayer Before Birth. L. MacNeice.
    Br-TC:282, Co-PI:117, Gr-BT:183,
    Pa-GTB:517, Pe-SS:34, To-MP:52
The Primitive. D. Lee. Ra-BP:297
Report from a Planet.
    R. Lattimore. Ba-PO:201
Simple Beast. M. Van Doren.
    Ho-TH:43
Stories of the Street. L. Cohen.
    Mo-GR:88
Summer Holiday. R. Jeffers.
    Pe-M:85, Un-MA:366
Tired. F. Johnson. Ad-PB:24,
    Fe-PL:428, Hu-PN:88, Kr-OF:48,
    Lo-TY:210
The Tribes. R. Fuller.
    Wi-LT:706
12 Gates to the City.
    N. Giovanni. Ad-PB:457
The Vultures. D. Diop.
    Lo-TY:138
A Winter Scene. Kuo Mo-jo.
    Hs-TC:37
Woodstock. J. Mitchell.
    Mo-GR:102
SATIRE - CLERGY
  Captain Hall. Gr-GB:269
  Clerical Oppressors.
    J. Whittier. Ke-PP:73
  The Dodger. Gr-GB:201
  Friars. W. Langland. Ke-PP:14
  God. Ya Hsüan. Pa-MV:155
  Lycidas. J. Milton. Al-VBP:402,
    Gr-CT:250, Hi-WP II:20,
    Ho-P:69, Pa-GTB:55
  On the Gift of a Cloak.
    Hugo of Orleans. Li-TU:44
  Pie in the Sky. J. Hill.
    Gr-GB:328, Ke-PP:15
  The Smooth Divine. T. Dwight.
    Ke-PP:43
  Spring 1942. R. Fuller. Wi-LT:705
  The Vicar. G. Crabbe. Ox-BN:7
  The Vision of William Concerning
    Piers the Plowman.
    W. Langland. Ma-YA:37
SATIRE - CLERKS AND CLERKING
  What Was Her Name? J. Ciardi.
    Pe-M:137
SATIRE - COLLEGES AND UNIVERSITIES
  The Academy Disporting.
    J. Nims. St-H:159

Examiner. F. Scott. Ke-PP:123
SATIRE - COLONIAL PERIOD IN AMERICA
The Beginning of Sickness.
   Bi-IT:149
I Gave Them Fruits. Bi-IT:146,
   Tr-US II:241
Pirates of the Sphere.
   H. Melville. Kr-OF:18
Plague. Bi-IT:150
The Surrender Speech of Chief
   Joseph. Chief Joseph.
   Bi-IT:153, Kr-OF:19
The Surrender Speech of Cuauhtemoc.
   Bi-IT:152
They Came from the East.
   Bi-IT:148
To Columbus. R. Dario. Lo-TY:86
The Weeping Spreads. Bi-IT:147
SATIRE - COLOR
colors for mama. B. Mahone.
   Ad-PB:473
SATIRE - COMMUNICATION
The Bourgeois Poet, #14.
   K. Shapiro. St-H:199
SATIRE - COMMUNISM
In Full Voice. V. Mayakovsky.
   Ca-MR:121
SATIRE - COMPANIONSHIP OF MAN
     AND NATURE
R.G.E. R. Eberhart. Ls-NY:72
SATIRE - COMPANIONSHIP OF MEN
     AND ANIMALS
Albert. D. Abse. Sm-MK:109
The Distances They Keep.
   H. Nemerov. Ca-BP:40
Spaniel's Sermons. C. Ellis.
   Cr-WS:138
SATIRE - COMPUTERS
Evolution. E. Brock. To-MP:212
SATIRE - CONFORMITY
America. A. Ginsberg. Bl-FP:64
Asylum. D. Clark. Ke-PP:52
Black Bourgeoisie. I. Baraka.
   Ra-BP:223
Borderline Ballad. R. Weber.
   Ke-PP:117
The Cambridge Ladies. e. cummings.
   Al-VBP:1202, Ha-PO:243, Ke-PP:93,
   Rv-CB:991
The Conformers. T. Hardy.
   Al-VBP:1048
The Conscientious Objector.
   K. Shapiro. Ba-PO:166,
   Pe-SS:140
Directions to a Rebel.
   W. Rodgers. Wi-LT:488
Dolor. T. Roethke. Ha-PO:225,
   Ke-PP:116, Sh-AP:212, Wi-LT:478
The Dome of Sunday. K. Shapiro.
   Un-MA:637, Wi-LT:532

Don'ts. D. Lawrence. Wi-LT:220
The Educators. D. Black.
   To-MP:210
Fish in Winter. I. Brodsky.
   Bo-RU:23
For the Time Being. W. Auden.
   Wi-LT:476
The Forgotten Graveyard.
   D. Etter. St-H:63
The Martyrdom of the Quakers.
   G. Joy. Kr-OF:101
The Negro. J. Emanuel.
   Ra-BP:188
Night Here. G. Snyder.
   Bl-FP:62
Oh, Oh, You Will Be Sorry for
   That Word. E. Millay.
   Pe-OA:165
The Odyssey of a Snail.
   F. Garcia Lorca. Ma-FW:211
The Old Agitator. W. Leonard.
   Ba-PO:147
The Paper Soldier. B. Okujava.
   Bo-RU:55
Plot Improbable, Character
   Unsympathetic. E. Olson.
   St-H:173
The Plot to Assassinate the
   Chase Manhattan Bank.
   C. Larsen. Ke-PP:67
Poem. T. McGrath. St-H:125
Port Authority Terminal:
   9 a.m. Monday. C. Walsh.
   Ke-PP:62
Problem in Social Geometry -
   The Inverted Square.
   R. Durem. Ad-PB:151
The Road to Tartary.
   B. Trotter. Ke-TF:116
The Romanies in Town.
   A. Beresford. To-MP:198
Shame. R. Wilbur. Cr-WS:173
The Trees. W. Williams.
   Sm-PT:17
Verses on Accepting the World.
   I. Brodsky. Bo-RU:20
What Soft, Cherubic Creatures.
   E. Dickinson. Ke-PP:92,
   Un-MA:102
SATIRE - CONQUESTS
The Soudanese. W. Watson.
   Cr-WS:159
The Tale of the World.
   M. Halpern. Ho-TY:102
SATIRE - CONSCIENCE
Karma. E. Robinson.
   Sm-PT:142, Un-MA:138
The Whipping.
   R. Hayden. Ad-PB:119,
   Pe-M:14

SATIRE - CONVERSATION
Dinner at Eight. K. Louchheim.
Ls-NY:332
Two Friends. D. Ignatow.
Du-SH:59
SATIRE - COST OF LIVING
Can't Afford to Live.
Yüan Shui-p'ai. Hs-TC:412
SATIRE - COUNTER CULTURE
Problem in Social Geometry -
The Inverted Square.
R. Durem. Ad-PB:151
SATIRE - COUNTRY LIFE
Sand Hill Road. M. Grosser.
Pe-SS:85
SATIRE - COURAGE
Tell Brave Deeds of War.
S. Crane. Cr-WS:158
SATIRE - COURTS (LAW)
London Lackpenny. Gr-CT:305
New England Lamented. J. Saffin.
Kr-OF:102
The Old Agitator. W. Leonard.
Ba-PO:147
The People vs. the People.
K. Fearing. Un-MA:555
Tar and Feather. J. Trumbull.
Kr-OF:131
SATIRE - CREATION
God. S. Hazo. Co-EL:108
SATIRE - CRITICS AND CRITICISM
Lines to a Don. H. Belloc.
Un-MB:171
Misapprehension. P. Dunbar.
Ra-BP:46
On Kuan Shan-Yüeh's Painting.
Kuo Mo-jo. Hs-TC:42
The Poet. P. Dunbar. Ra-BP:52
Poetry. M. Moore. Al-VBP:1175,
Ha-PO:232, Mc-EA:21, Mo-TS:90,
Pl-ML:4, Sh-AP:178, Un-MA:351,
Wi-LT:267
Three Epigrams. J. Cunningham.
Un-MA:615
To a Captious Critic. P. Dunbar.
Ab-MO:33, Ra-BP:50
SATIRE - CUBISM
The Messed Damozel. C. Towne.
Li-SR:75
SATIRE - CULTURE
Cultural Exchange.
L. Hughes. Ad-PB:76,
Hu-PN:203, Ra-BP:83
The Story of the Zeros.
V. Cruz. Ad-PB:510
Under Which Lyre. W. Auden.
Un-MB:415
SATIRE - DANCERS AND DANCING
A Victory Dance. A. Noyes.
Fe-PL:153

SATIRE - DEATH
Buffalo Bill's. E. Cummings.
Br-AF:113, Ca-VT:172, Gr-CC:128,
Ho-LP:91, Li-TU:144, Mc-EA:158,
Mo-BG:157, Mo-GR:76, Un-MA:473
Death Takes Only a Minute.
A. Pratt. Al-WW:106
Is My Team Ploughing. A. Housman.
Ha-PO:12, Hi-WP I:22,
Un-MB:95, Un-MW:119, Wi-LT:61
Ode for the Burial of a Citizen.
J. Ciardi. Wi-LT:668
On the Death of Doctor Swift 3-5.
J. Swift. Al-VBP:517, 519
Photographs: A Vision of
Massacre. M. Harper.
Ad-PB:313
Pornography of Death.
S. Gavronsky. Lo-IT:38
Song, on Reading that the
Cyclotron Has Produced
Cosmic Rays.
S. Hoffenstein. Br-SM:66
"Very Interesting" Death.
Yüan Shui-p'ai. Hs-TC:408
What Was Her Name? J. Ciardi.
Pe-M:137
SATIRE - DEMOCRACY
America. B. Hamilton.
Ad-BO:41
The Body Politic. D. Hall.
Br-TC:167, Pe-OA:272, Pe-SS:104
Democracy. A. Rimbaud. Ba-PO:173
SATIRE - DETROIT, MICH.
To the New Annex to the Detroit
County Jail. R. Thomas.
Ad-PB:373
SATIRE - DICTATORS
The Dictators. P. Neruda.
Bl-FP:41
Fascist Limericks. L. Bacon.
Cr-WS:38
The United Fruit Co.
P. Neruda. Bl-FP:39
SATIRE - DINNERS
Dinner at Eight. K. Louchheim.
Ls-NY:332
SATIRE - DIRGES
Ode for the Burial of a Citizen.
J. Ciardi. Wi-LT:668
SATIRE - DISCRIMINATION
And Was Not Improved.
L. Bennett. Ad-PB:203
SATIRE - EASTER
The Easter Bunny Blues or All
I Want for Xmas Is the Loop.
Ebon. Ad-PB:436
SATIRE - EDUCATION
The Educators. D. Black. To-MP:210
Examiner. F. Scott. Ke-PP:123

Little White Schoolhouse Blues.
F. Lennon.   Hu-PN:514
Prologue. K. Barnes.   Cr-WS:45
Recessional for the Class of
1959 of a School for Delin-
quent Negro Girls.
J. Cowen.   Hu-PN:575
The Student. M. Moore. Br-TC:300
You've Got to Be Taught.
O. Hammerstein II.   Br-AF:46
SATIRE - ELEGIES
Here Lies a Lady. J. Ransom.
Ca-VT:150, Na-EO:21, Un-MA:410,
Wi-LT:312
On the Grave of a Young Cavalry
Officer Killed in the Valley
of Virginia. H. Melville.
Cr-WS:103
A Satyrical Elegy. J. Swift.
Hi-FO:173
SATIRE - ENCHANTMENT
Disenchanted. L. Untermeyer.
Un-GT:168
SATIRE - END OF THE WORLD
Nos Moraturi Te Salutamus.
G. Code. De-FS:66
SATIRE - ENEMIES
Death, Look to Your Domain.
C. Norman. Cr-WS:172
The Fury of Aerial Bombardment.
R. Eberhart. Ba-PO:178,
Ca-VT:248, Sh-AP:209, Wi-LT:438
The Last Campaign. G. Lehmann.
Cr-WS:171
On the Death of a Murderer.
L. Wain. Cr-WS:113
Strange Meeting. W. Owen.
Ba-PO:140
SATIRE - ENGLAND
Autobiography. C. Causley.
Wi-LT:668
England. Co-EL:56, Rv-CB:140
Sonnet: England in 1819.
P. Shelley. Rv-CB:699
SATIRE - ENGLAND - GOVERNMENT
The Ballad of Hampstead Heath.
J. Flecker. Un-MB:275
SATIRE - ENGLAND - HISTORY AND
PATRIOTISM
The Fine Old English Gentleman.
C. Dickens. Hi-FO:223
SATIRE - THE ENGLISH
The English. Gr-GB:163
The Fine Old English Gentleman.
C. Dickens. Hi-FO:223
How Beastly the Bourgeois Is.
D. Lawrence. Gr-CT:468, Wi-LT:219
Put Down. L. Damas. Lo-TY:121
The True-Born Englishman.
D. Defoe. Hi-FO:69

SATIRE - EPITAPHS
Bona de Mortuis. T. Beddoes.
Co-EL:77
Fragment. T. Beddoes.
Co-EL:83
Now that He Is Safely Dead.
C. Hines. Bo-HF:157
SATIRE - EQUALITY
Boogie-Woogie Ballads.
S. McKelway. Hu-PN:534
A Communication to Nancy Cunard.
K. Boyle. Hu-PN:530
Is It True? N. Rosten.
Kr-OF:201
Little White Schoolhouse Blues.
F. Lennon.   Hu-PN:514
The New Math. V. Howard.
Jo-VC:44
Picnic: The Liberated. M. Holman.
Ad-PB:176, Hu-PN:367
Riot Rimes, U.S.A. R. Patterson.
Kr-OF:57
You Know, Joe. R. Durem.
Ad-BO:47, Hu-PN:330
SATIRE - ESCAPE
Knowlt Hoheimer. E. Masters.
Ba-PO:81, Ho-LP:89
Newsreel. C. Day Lewis.
Un-MB:425
SATIRE - THE ESTABLISHMENT
Borderline Ballad. R. Weber.
Ke-PP:117
Clerical Oppressors.
J. Whittier. Ke-PP:73
Give Way. D. Finkel. Ke-PP:122
he's doing natural life.
Conyus. Ad-PB:403
Landscape near a Steel Mill.
H. Horn. Ke-PP:110
The Lie. W. Raleigh. Al-VBP:95,
Gr-CT:372, Ke-PP:16, Rv-CB:157
The Plot to Assassinate the Chase
Manhattan Bank. C. Larsen.
Ke-PP:67
Song. W. Auden. Pa-GTB:511
They Got You Last Night.
A. Kurtz. Ke-PP:75
Two Bums Walk Out of Eden.
R. Francis. Ke-PP:23
SATIRE - EXECUTIONS AND EXECUTIONERS
Jig Time: Not for Love.
T. McGrath. Ca-VT:427
SATIRE - EXPERIENCE
We Shall Not Go down Broadway.
N. Nor. Bo-RU:54
SATIRE - EYES
On the Eyes of an SS Officer.
R. Wilbur. Cr-WS:42
SATIRE - FACTORIES
Anna Imroth. C. Sandburg. Kr-OF:180

SATIRE - FACTORIES — cont'd.
A Ballad of Dead Girls.
D. Burnet. Kr-OF:174
The Mill Mother's Lament.
E. Wiggins. Kr-OF:191
SATIRE - FAITH
Elephant Rock. P. St. John.
Ad-PB:347
From the Fang of Time.
S. Jahin. Lo-TY:51
I Believe. A. Zeitlin. Ho-TY:321
In Humbleness. D. Hoffman.
Cr-WS:139
The New Platitudes.
R. Whittemore. Ba-PO:28
We, the Few Who Believe.
H. Vinal. De-FS:209
SATIRE - FAME
Fame. W. Landor. Co-PU:19
Lately Our Poets Loiter'd in Green
Lanes. W. Landor. Pa-GTB:318
Now that He Is Safely Dead.
C. Hines. Bo-HF:147
Seven Wealthy Towns. Co-PU:68,
Pl-ML:90
To the Stone-Cutters.
R. Jeffers. En-PC:10,
Ni-JP:127, Sh-AP:175, Un-MA:362
SATIRE - FAMILY AND FAMILY LIFE
An Inconvenience. J. Raven.
Ra-BP:258
A Quiet Life and a Good Name.
J. Swift. Rv-CB:493
SATIRE - FAREWELLS
To Certain Ladies on Going to
the Wars. H. Treece.
Cr-WS:48
SATIRE - FARM LIFE
American Farm, 1934. G. Taggard.
Ca-VT:191
The Old Oaken Bucket.
Er-FA:208
SATIRE - FARMERS
The Dodger. Gr-GB:201
SATIRE - FATE
Hap. T. Hardy. Ke-PP:94,
Pl-EI:65, Un-MB:35
SATIRE - FLIES
In a Garden. A. Herbert.
Co-BBW:220
SATIRE - FOOTBALL
Football. W. Mason. Mo-SD:26
SATIRE - FOREIGN LEGION
A Day with the Foreign Legion.
R. Whittemore. Wi-LT:842
SATIRE - FREEDOM
American Heartbreak. L. Hughes.
Ra-BP:87, Wi-LT:422
An Ante-Bellum Sermon.
P. Dunbar. Ra-BP:44

Children's Rhymes. L. Hughes.
Ad-BO:43, Ra-BP:86
Death in Yorkville. L. Hughes.
Ad-PB:79
Landscape with Figures.
N. Rosten. Kr-OF:160
Liberty for All. W. Garrison.
Kr-OF:30
My Name Was Legion. H. Swift.
Br-AF:39
No Chains. H. Jones. La-IH:107
October 16: The Raid.
L. Hughes. Ad-BO:36, Ad-PB:78
Pastures of Plenty. W. Guthrie.
Pe-SS:53
The Ropewalk. H. Longfellow.
Mo-BG:12
The Runaway Slave at Pilgrim's
Point. E. Browning. Hu-PN:448
Special Bulletin. L. Hughes.
Ad-PB:80
Stanzas on Freedom. J. Lowell.
Hu-PN:464, Kr-OF:31
We're Free. C. Williams.
Ba-HI:124
When a Man Hath No Freedom to
Fight for at Home. G. Byron.
Fe-PL:178, Ha-PO:249
Wires. P. Larkin. Pe-M:32
You Shout about Freedom.
Wilburt. La-IH:57
SATIRE - FRIENDSHIP
Blow, Blow, Thou Winter Wind.
W. Shakespeare. Al-VBP:187,
De-CH:232, De-TT:168, Er-FA:257,
Gr-CT:476, Hi-WP II:139,
Ho-WR:172, Mc-PR:50, Pa-GTB:26,
Rv-CB:197
A Friend. M. Power. Er-FA:212
Villains. Abhinanda. Al-PI:38
SATIRE - FUNERALS
Italian Extravaganza. G. Corso.
La-OC:91
The Lady of the Manor. G. Crabbe.
Ox-BN:2
The Pauper's Funeral. G. Crabbe.
Ox-BN:1
A Strange Funeral in Braddock.
M. Gold. Kr-OF:184
SATIRE - FUTURE LIFE
Life after Death. R. Thomas.
Ad-PB:373
SATIRE - GAMES
Poem for Black Boys. N. Giovanni.
Ra-BP:325
SATIRE - GENERALS
The Benediction. M. English.
Cr-WS:37
The Crimean War Heroes.
W. Landor. Mc-WS:104

Forgive Me, Sire. N. Cameron.
  Pa-GTB:499
The General. S. Sassoon.
  Co-EL:83, Co-FB:470, Co-PU:119,
  Cr-WS:78, Ga-FB:218, Wi-LT:641
General Monk. Mo-MGT:48
The Generals. S. Silverstein.
  Co-OT:50
On a Portrait by Copley.
  A. Freeman. Co-RM:215,
  Cr-WS:54
Two Funerals. L. Untermeyer.
  Cr-WS:28
Two Wise Generals. T. Hughes.
  Ca-MB:98
SATIRE - GEORGE IV, KING OF ENGLAND
  Epitaph on the Late King of
    the Sandwich Isles. W. Praed.
  Co-FB:475
SATIRE - GERMANY
  Footnote. C. Norman. Cr-WS:46
  No Quarrel. A. Herbert.
    Cr-WS:39
  Speech by Moonlight. C. Norman.
    Cr-WS:54
SATIRE - GIFTS AND GIVING
  Gift to a Jade. A. Wickham.
    Co-EL:135
  Obituary. K. Fearing.
    Ca-VT:237
SATIRE - GOD
  Blessing the Battle. W. Tappan.
    Cr-WS:140
  In Humbleness. D. Hoffman.
    Cr-WS:139
  The Moors Fight on the Side of
    God. C. Norman. Cr-WS:37
  Peyote Poem, I. A. Fowler.
    Lo-IT:33
  The Plot to Assassinate the Chase
    Manhattan Bank. C. Larsen.
    Ke-PP:67
  Third Enemy Speaks. C. Day Lewis.
    Pl-EI:42
  The Young Man. C. Houselander.
    Ga-S:196
SATIRE - GODS AND GODDESSES
  Black Trumpeter. H. Dumas.
    Ad-PB:267
SATIRE - GOVERNMENT
  Bellies. J. Waters. Kr-OF:182
  The Body Politic. D. Hall.
    Br-TC:167, Pe-OA:272, Pe-SS:104
  Mr. Roosevelt Regrets.
    P. Murray. Ad-PB:109
  The Night There Was Dancing in the
    Streets. E. Olson. St-H:174
  Old Dance Song. Tr-US II:110
  On the Birth of His Son.
    Su Tung-P'o. Gr-BT:7

To the States. W. Whitman.
  Bl-FP:21
SATIRE - GOVERNMENTAL INVESTIGATIONS
  Un-American Investigators.
    L. Hughes. Ra-BP:79
SATIRE - GRATITUDE
  Naked and Hungry Came We into
    This World. Gr-TG:38
  Tommy. R. Kipling. Ga-FB:209,
    Un-MB:127
SATIRE - GREATNESS
  Autumn Thoughts. Lu Yu.
    Rx-OH:112
  Egypt's Might Is Tumbled Down.
    M. Coleridge. De-CH:349
  The Preacher: Ruminates Behind
    the Sermon. G. Brooks.
    Be-MA:80, Li-TU:165
  A Tall Man Executes a Jig.
    I. Layton. En-PC:119
  What Am I in Time and Space?
    A. Stolzenberg. Ho-TY:270
SATIRE - GRIEF
  Clear Bright. Huang T'ing Ch'ien.
    Rx-LT:90
SATIRE - GROOMING, PERSONAL
  Advertisement. O. de Andrade.
    An-TC:13
SATIRE - GUARDS
  If We Cannot Live as People.
    C. Lynch. Ad-PB:461
SATIRE - GUILT
  Revolutionary Letter #36.
    D. di Prima. Kh-VA:52
  We Didn't Know. T. Paxton.
    Ke-PP:129
SATIRE - GUNS
  Naming of Parts. H. Reed.
    Al-VBP:1243, Ba-PO:189, Bo-GJ:189,
    Cr-WS:62, Hi-WP II:148, Pe-SS:134,
    To-MP:40, Un-MB:507, Wi-LT:796
SATIRE - HANDICAPPED
  Vet's Rehabilitation. R. Durem.
    Ad-PB:150
SATIRE - HARLEM, N.Y.
  For "Mr. Dudley," a Black Spy.
    J. Emanuel. Ra-BP:191
SATIRE - HARRIMAN, EDWARD HENRY
  Empire Builders. A. MacLeish.
    Sh-AP:188
SATIRE - HEAVY WATER
  Rhymes for a Modern Nursery.
    P. Dehn. Co-FB:451
SATIRE - HEROES AND HEROISM
  The Ash and the Oak. L. Simpson.
    Cr-WS:3, Mo-BG:168
  The Hometown Hero Come Home.
    D. Etter. Cr-WS:15, St-H:58
  Saints and Heroes You Dare Say.
    C. Day Lewis. Go-BP:184

SATIRE - HEROES AND HEROISM — cont'd.
  To Make the People Happy.
    V. Hugo. Ba-PO:124, Ke-PP:63
  Veteran. L. Bacon. Cr-WS:34
SATIRE - HERVEY, SIR JOHN
  Sporus. A. Pope. Gr-CT:474
SATIRE - HOLY SPIRIT
  The Young Man. C. Houselander.
    Ga-S:196
SATIRE - HOME
  The Realm of Fancy. J. Keats.
    Pa-GTB:278
  She's Leaving Home. The Beatles.
    Pe-SS:94
SATIRE - HOMECOMING
  Birmingham. M. Walker.
    Ad-PB:149
  Fight to a Finish. S. Sassoon.
    Cr-WS:142
  Home Leave. B. Howes. Br-TC:306
SATIRE - HOMESICKNESS
  The Last. M. Halpern. Ho-TY:108
  My Home, Zlochev. M. Halpern.
    Ho-TY:109
SATIRE - HONOR
  Advice to a Knight. T. Jones.
    Ma-FW:245
  On Homer's Birthplace. T. Heywood.
    Co-PU:68, Pl-ML:90
  On the Setting Up of Mr. Butler's
    Monument in Westminster Abbey.
    S. Wesley. Ke-PP:51,
    Rv-CB:516
SATIRE - HOPE
  Noah. W. Brown. Sa-B:218
SATIRE - HOSPITALITY
  I Gave Them Fruits. Bi-IT:146,
    Tr-US II:241
  In the Town. Ga-S:68
  The Mayors. W. Blake. De-CH:62
SATIRE - HOUSES
  Seventy Balconies and Not a
    Single Flower.
    B. Fernández Moreno. Be-UL:27
SATIRE - HUNTING
  The Chase. A. Gregor. Gr-CC:114
  The Continuing Story of Bungalow
    Bill. J. Lennon. Mo-GR:75
  The Fox. K. Patchen. To-MP:32
  Peace. C. Bukowski.
    Kh-VA:32
  The Rabbit Hunter. R. Frost.
    Be-EB:28, Ho-TH:46
  Sport. W. Davies. Co-BBW:47,
    Co-PU:120
  Vice Versa. C. Morgenstern.
    Rd-OA:36
SATIRE - HYDROGEN WEAPONS
  Brave Old World.   F. Lambert.
    Er-FA:216

SATIRE - HYPOCRITES AND HYPOCRISY
  Address to the Unco Guid or the
    Rigidly Righteous. R. Burns.
    Al-VBP:631
  Holy Willie's Prayer. R. Burns.
    Al-VBP:626
SATIRE - IDEALS
  Walking Past. L. Martinez.
    La-IH:87
SATIRE - IGNORANCE
  The Color. J. Haines.
    Sc-TN:75
  If I Had Known. M. Davies.
    Ke-TF:129
SATIRE - ILLUSIONS
  Black Power. A. Saxon. Ad-PB:493
  An Old Story. H. Nemerov.
    Co-PU:74
  Penny Arcade. J. Nims. St-H:151
  Turning Away from Lies. R. Bly.
    Mc-EA:120
  Until They Have Stopped.
    S. Wright. Ad-PB:215
SATIRE - INDIFFERENCE
  Speech to the Court.
    W. Lowenfels. Ke-PP:120
  The U.S. Sailor with the Japanese
    Skull. W. Scott. Pe-OA:207,
    Wi-LT:812
  We Didn't Know. T. Paxton.
    Ke-PP:129
SATIRE - INNOCENCE
  A Dream. Shao Hsün-mei.
    Hs-TC:126
  Innocence. T. Gunn. Wi-LT:724
SATIRE - INQUISITION
  Dialect Quatrain. M. Christian.
    Bo-AN:53
SATIRE - INSECTS
  Nos Moraturi Te Salutamus.
    G. Coade. De-FS:66
SATIRE - INTERNATIONAL RELATIONS
  communication in white.
    D. Lee. Ra-BP:299
  Great Powers Conference.
    E. Pierce. Cr-WS:160
  The Green Shepherd.
    L. Simpson. Pe-OA:264
  Rain Falls on Ioannina.
    M. Piercy. Sc-TN:182
SATIRE - INVENTIONS
  Brave Old World. F. Lambert.
    Er-FA:216
  Little Johnny's Foolish
    Invention. B. Patten.
    Gr-BT:142
SATIRE - IRELAND - HISTORY
    AND PATRIOTISM
  Whack Fol the Diddle. P. Kearney.
    Co-FB:206, Co-PI:79

SATIRE - THE JAPANESE
Yen Hai-shan's Tax Agent.
Lin Chia. Hs-TC:434
SATIRE - JESUS CHRIST
Here Comes Jesus, Lowly Jesus.
W. MacDonald. Ba-PO:6
Mandylion. P. Harris.
Sc-TN:78
New Approach Is Needed. K. Amis.
Ke-PP:89
SATIRE - JESUS CHRIST - CRUCIFIXION
5 Ways to Kill a Man. E. Brock.
Cr-WS:145, Mo-TS:39
SATIRE - JOKES
The Joke. W. Gibson. Cr-WS:105
SATIRE - JUDGES AND JUDGING
Jig Time Not for Love.
T. McGrath. Ca-VT:427
Western Justice. A. Rafter.
Fi-BG:63
SATIRE - JUSTICE
A Communication to Nancy Cunard.
K. Boyle. Hu-PN:530
The Day They Busted the Grateful
Dead. R. Brautigan. Mc-EA:130
The Death of Justice.
W. Hawkins. Ad-PB:20
Doth Then the World Go Thus.
W. Drummond. Pa-GTB:40
A Dream of Hanging. P. Beer.
To-MP:202
Finally. H. Gordon. Ad-II:107
Give Us the Sign! W. Du Bois.
Kr-OF:149
If We Cannot Live as People.
C. Lynch. Ad-PB:461
In the Dock. W. de la Mare.
Wi-LT:133
The Inquest. W. Davies.
Pa-GTB:435, Rv-CB:961
Justice. L. Hughes. Ra-BP:87
London Lackpenny. Gr-CT:305
The Necklace of Pearls.
H. Longfellow. Kr-OF:106
New England Lamented. J. Saffin.
Kr-OF:102
Now, All You Children. R. Durem.
Jo-SA:106
Oh, Who Is That Young Sinner.
A. Housman. Rv-CB:949
The Old Agitator. W. Leonard.
Ba-PO:147
Pardon. B. Krasnoff.
Ad-II:87
Poem of Angela Yvonne Davis.
N. Giovanni. Ad-PB:458
A Rope for Harry Fat. J. Baxter.
Ca-MB:85
Salute. O. Pitcher. Ad-PB:193
Sermonette. I. Reed. Ad-PB:328

Sonnet. W. Shakespeare.
Al-VBP:204, Er-FA:120, No-CL:85,
Pa-GTB:40, Rv-CB:227
Tar and Feather. J. Trumbull.
Kr-OF:131
The Trial. M. Rukeyser.
Hu-PN:560
Upside Down Hotel. E. Bastien.
Sa-B:28
What Ever Happened to America.
R. Patterson. Kr-OF:127
When the Cock Crows.
A. Giovannitti. Kr-OF:151
SATIRE - KINDNESS
But I Do Not Need Kindness.
G. Corso. Kh-VA:66
SATIRE - KINGS AND RULERS
Cities and Thrones and Powers.
R. Kipling. Bo-GJ:197,
Ni-JP:123, Ox-BN:930
A Denunciation of the Princes
and the Prophets. Bible.
O.T. Micah. Me-PH:51
The Duchess of Malfi.
J. Webster. Gr-CT:360
Elegy in a Country Churchyard.
G. Chesterton. Al-VBP:1122,
Mc-WS:85, Na-EO:85, Un-MB:209
England in 1819. P. Shelley.
Mo-GR:70, Rv-CB:699
The Fort of Rathangan.
Co-PI:131, De-CH:181, Gr-CT:323,
Ho-LP:86, Sm-LG:395
The King Must Die. B. Taupin.
Mo-GR:91
The Kings Are Passing Deathward.
D. Morton. Cr-WS:29
Lése Majesté. O. Herford.
Co-BBW:32
Master of War. B. Dylan.
Mo-GR:68
My Lord Tomnoddy. R. Brough.
Co-FB:195, Co-PU:123
Of the Death of Kings.
W. Shakespeare. Gr-CT:368
Ozymandias. P. Shelley.
Co-RG:14, De-CH:384, Er-FA:83,
Fe-PL:436, Ha-PO:208, Li-SR:83,
Ma-YA:177, Mc-PR:186, Mc-WK:98,
No-CL:256, Ox-BN:279, Pa-GTB:251,
Pa-HT:91, Rv-CB:695, Sm-LG:153,
Sp-OG:187, Un-GT:312
Pretences. Ibn Rashiq. Lo-TY:44
Song Composed under a Tyrannical
King. Tr-US I:102
War Is the Statesman's Game.
P. Shelley. Ba-PO:157, Ke-PP:57
SATIRE - KNIGHTS AND KNIGHTHOOD
A Dream of Governors.
L. Simpson. Ha-PO:224

SATIRE - KNIGHTS AND KNIGHTHOOD —
    cont'd.
  Hudibras. S. Butler.
    Al-VBP:426
SATIRE - KNIVES
  The Sacrificial Knife.
    I. Spiegel. Ho-TY:349
SATIRE - KNOWLEDGE
  On Shooting Particles Beyond the
    World. R. Eberhart.
    Wi-LT:434
  The Philosopher and the Lover.
    W. Davenant. Ho-P:315
SATIRE - LABOR AND LABORERS
  Applebaum's Sunday. A. Magil.
    Kr-OF:192
  Ode on the Last International.
    A. Zeitlin. Ho-TY:319
  The Perpetual Worker.
    G. Garbovsky. Bo-RU:37
  The Ricksha Puller. Cheng Min.
    Hs-TC:233
  A Strange Funeral in Braddock.
    M. Gold. Kr-OF:184
  The Sweatshop. M. Rosenfeld.
    Ho-TY:78, Kr-OF:170
SATIRE - LABOR RELATIONS
  Anna Imroth. C. Sandburg.
    Kr-OF:180
  A Ballad of Dead Girls.
    D. Burnet. Kr-OF:174
  Bread and Roses. J. Oppenheim.
    Kr-OF:179
  Casey Jones, the Union Scab.
    J. Hill. Kr-OF:177
SATIRE - LANDLORDS AND TENANTS
  Ballad of the Landlord.
    L. Hughes. Ha-TP:15
  Ch'eng-Hu Is Not Dead.
    Liu Ta-Pai. Ox-BN:6
  The Lady of the Manor.
    G. Crabbe. Ox-BN:2
  A Slum Dwelling. G. Crabbe.
    Ox-BN:11
  zapata & the landlord.
    A. Spellman. Ad-PB:282
SATIRE - LANGUAGE
  Dr. Hu. N. Mailer. Co-EL:103
  Language Has Not the Power.
    J. Clare. Ox-BN:333
SATIRE - LAUGHTER
  Slap Happy. E. Glenn.
    Lo-IT:41
SATIRE - LAW
  The Law West of the Pecos.
    S. Barker. Fi-BG:64
  Legal Fiction. W. Empson.
    Wi-LT:442
  Recapitulations. K. Shapiro.
    Hu-PN:563

SATIRE - LAWYERS
  The Dodger. Gr-GB:201
SATIRE - LEADERSHIP
  The Leaders of the Crowd.
    W. Yeats. Un-MB:116
  A Learned Man. S. Crane.
    Un-MA:148
  Satire. Tr-US II:30
SATIRE - LEGISLATORS
  The Cure All. D. Lee. Ad-CI:30
SATIRE - LIBERTY, STATUE OF
  On a Chilean Cigarette Package.
    Ai Ch'ing. Hs-TC:317
SATIRE - LIFE
  The Brand. Tsang K'o-chia.
    Hs-TC:280
  Can't Afford to Live.
    Yüan Shui-p'ai. Hs-TC:412
  For One Moment. D. Ignatow.
    Ha-TP:99
  Here Dead Lie We. A. Housman.
    Cr-WS:135, Fe-PL:156
  The Human Fold. E. Muir.
    Wi-LT:247
  If I Ride This Train.
    J. Johnson. Ad-PB:384
  I've Never Been Lost. I. Feffer.
    Ho-TY:188
  The Leaden-Eyed. V. Lindsay.
    Co-EL:136, Co-PU:150, Ke-PP:61,
    Kr-OF:182, Ni-JP:32, Tr-MR:54
  Life. Lord Bacon. Pa-GTB:38
  The Love Song of J. Alfred
    Prufrock. T. Eliot. Al-VBP:1180,
    Br-TC:106, Pe-OA:105, Rv-CB:986,
    Un-MA:379, Wi-LT:278
  Ninth Philosopher's Song.
    A. Huxley. Al-VBP:1199
  No Escape. L. Lorraine. De-FS:133
  Poems, 1930-1940. H. Gregory.
    Sm-PT:118
  Prayer Before Birth. L. MacNeice.
    Br-TC:282, Co-PI:117, Gr-BT:183,
    Pa-GTB:517, Pe-SS:34, To-MP:52
  Preface. Shao Hsün-mei.
    Hs-TC:127
  A Reflection on the Course of
    Human Life. W. Lloyd. Co-PU:159
  Slap Happy. E. Glenn. Lo-IT:41
  Song. Br-MW:29
  Song, on Reading that the
    Cyclotron Has Produced
    Cosmic Rays. S. Hoffenstein.
    Br-SM:66
  Sonnet 66. W. Shakespeare.
    Al-VBP:204, Er-FA:120, No-CL:85,
    Pa-GTB:40, Rv-CB:227
  Sunday: Outskirts of Knoxville,
    Tennessee. J. Agee. Mo-BG:178
  Sunrise. F. García Lorca. Bl-FP:84

To the Reader. C. Baudelaire.
   Mo-GR:30
The Vow. A. Hecht. En-PC:199
The World Is a Beautiful Place.
   L. Ferlinghetti. Pe-M:10
Ye Hasten to the Grave!
   P. Shelley. Mo-GR:80
The Young Man. C. Houselander.
   Ga-S:196
SATIRE - LOGIC
Rabbi Yussel Luksh of Chelm.
   J. Glatstein. Ho-TY:246
SATIRE - LOS ANGELES, CALIF.
Los Angeles. F. Alexander.
   Bl-FP:63
SATIRE - LOVE
Come Live with Me and Be My
   Love. C. Day Lewis. No-CL:111
Experience. D. Parker.
   Co-BL:102
He Abjures Love. T. Hardy.
   Ox-BN:830
Modern Love. G. Meredith.
   Ox-BN:690
Three Love Poems: From a Woman
   to a Greedy Lover. N. Cameron.
   Co-EL:15, Pa-GTB:499
Three Love Poems: In the
   Queen's Room. N. Cameron.
   Pa-GTB:500
The Waste Land. T. Eliot.
   Pe-OA:112, Un-MA:386
When the Lad for Longing Sighs.
   A. Housman. Un-MB:97
SATIRE - LOVE - ANTICIPATION
War Poem. H. Treece. Cr-WS:108
SATIRE - LOVE - OBSTACLES
Speech by Moonlight.
   C. Norman. Cr-WS:54
SATIRE - LOVE - PERMANENCE
Song. A. O'Shaughnessy.
   Ox-BN:850
Unknown Shores. D. Thomas.
   To-MP:209
You Swear by the Sun. Wen I-to.
   Hs-TC:59
SATIRE - LOVERS
The Dodger. Gr-GB:201
SATIRE - LOYALTY
Un-American Investigators.
   L. Hughes. Ra-BP:79
SATIRE - LULLABIES
A Lullaby. G. Glasgow. Sp-OG:210
Lullaby. E. Sitwell.
   Wi-LT:644
Songs for a Colored Singer, III.
   E. Bishop. Hu-PN:550
SATIRE - MACARTHUR, DOUGLAS
The Formalities. J. Ciardi.
   Cr-WS:143

SATIRE - MACHINERY
Cape Hatteras. H. Crane.
   Sm-PT:130
The Worker. R. Thomas.
   Ad-PB:370, Hu-PN:433
SATIRE - MAN
Apostrophe to Man. E. Millay.
   Du-SH:86
By the Deep Sea. G. Byron.
   Ox-BN:249
Cold-Blooded Creatures.
   E. Wylie. Pl-IO:103
The Conqueror Worm. E. Poe.
   Sh-AP:55
The Emptiness of Man.
   J. de Melo Neto. An-TC:159
The Fairy's Reply to Saturn.
   T. Hood. Ox-BN:417
The Hollow Men. T. Eliot.
   Un-MA:395, Wi-LT:302
The Human Fold. E. Muir.
   Wi-LT:247
In the Beginning Was the Word.
   A. Tabachnik. Ho-TY:271
Man Is But a Castaway. J. Day.
   Pl-IO:125
A Man Said to the Universe.
   S. Crane. Pl-IO:139,
   Wi-LT:120
Man, That Ape. M. Halpern.
   Ho-TY:103
Man, the Man-Hunter. C. Sandburg.
   Kr-OF:156
Ode Inscribed to W. H. Channing.
   R. Emerson. Al-VBP:800
Of Man and Nature. H. Mungin.
   Ad-BO:44
On Shooting Particles Beyond Our
   World. R. Eberhart. Wi-LT:434
Rearmament. R. Jeffers. Bl-FP:50
Reserved. W. de la Mare.
   Pa-GTB:437
Song of Myself. W. Whitman.
   Be-EB:44, Ca-BP:3,
   Co-BBW:271, 274, Er-FA:225,
   Ke-PP:85, Li-TU:187, Ni-JP:101,
   Rv-CB:895, Sh-AP:87, Sm-MK:158,
   Un-MA:56
Written in Early Spring.
   W. Wordsworth. Fe-PL:372,
   Pa-GTB:282, Rv-CB:633
SATIRE - MANNERS AND CUSTOMS
The Rape of the Lock.
   A. Pope. Al-VBP:531
The Sundays of Satin-Legs Smith.
   G. Brooks. St-H:14
SATIRE - MARLBOROUGH, JOHN
   CHURCHILL, 1ST DUKE
A Satyrical Elegy. J. Swift.
   Hi-FO:173

SATIRE - MARRIAGE
  Her Beauty Is Hidden.
    Li Shang Yin. Rx-LT:79
  In Praise of Celibacy. Al-PI:51
  Made in Heaven. P. Porter.
    Ke-PP:35
  Marriage. A. Clarke.
    Pa-GTB:493
  My Last Duchess. R. Browning.
    Er-FA:374, Fe-PL:82, Ha-PO:39,
    Ma-YA:200, Ni-JP:40, Ox-BN:545,
    Pa-GTB:350, Rv-CB:817
SATIRE - MARTYRS
  now. A. Toegemann. Ad-II:63
SATIRE - MAY (MONTH)
  Nuts in May. L. MacNeice.
    Un-MB:446
SATIRE - MEETINGS (ENCOUNTERS)
  Good Ships. J. Ransom.
    Ha-TP:53
  Lunch at the Coq d'Or.
    P. Davison. Br-TC:85
SATIRE - MEN
  Experience. D. Parker.
    Co-BL:102
  His Answer to the Critics.
    S. Ibn Gabirol. Me-PH:57
  The Ladies Aid. Fe-PL:415
  The Lords of Creation. Fe-PL:63
  Of Seals and Arms. J. Taylor.
    Rv-CB:318
  A Slice of Wedding Cake.
    R. Graves. Gr-BT:87
SATIRE - MERCHANTS
  The Dodger. Gr-GB:201
SATIRE - MILITARY LIFE
  Base Details. S. Sassoon.
    Cr-WS:78, Un-MB:311
  Free Pass. J. Prévert. Ba-PO:203
  Oh, It's Nine Years Ago I Was
    Digging in the Land. Em-AF:760
  O What Is That Sound. W. Auden.
    To-MP:29
  Pocket Guide for Servicemen.
    H. Creekmore. Ba-PO:190
  The Sergeant Major. K. Hopkins.
    Cr-WS:63
SATIRE - MILITARY SERVICE,
    COMPULSORY
  Draft Dodger Rag. P. Ochs.
    Ba-PO:200
  Poem for the Subterranean Poor.
    D. di Prima. Kh-VA:53
SATIRE - MIND
  In a Hard Intellectual Light.
    R. Eberhart. Wi-LT:432
  James Honeyman. W. Auden.
    Ca-MB:100, Sm-MK:117
  On a Prohibitionist Poem.
    G. Chesterton. Al-VBP:1122

SATIRE - MINES (EXPLOSIVE)
  Mined Country. R. Wilbur.
    Cr-WS:129
  Rhymes for a Modern Nursery.
    P. Dehn. Co-FB:451,
    Co-PU:32, Er-FA:429
SATIRE - MISSIONARIES
  Ironical Song of the Intolerance
    of Missionaries. Tr-US II:42
  The Missionary. Tr-CB:20,
    Tr-US I:82
  The Return to the Old Gods.
    Kr-OF:21
  They Came from the East.
    Bi-IT:148
SATIRE - MISSISSIPPI
  Benign Neglect/Mississippi,
    1970. P. St. John.
    Ad-PB:346
SATIRE - MONEY
  Bewick Finzer. E. Robinson.
    Gr-CC:130, Un-MA:118
  Cassandra. E. Robinson.
    Ke-PP:101, Wi-LT:108
  Jack and the Beanstalk.
    P. Goedicke. Du-SH:50
  London Lackpenny. Gr-CT:305
  Money. V. Contoski. Sc-TN:27
SATIRE - MONKS
  Friars. W. Langland. Ke-PP:14
  A Gest of Robyn Hode, The Seconde
    and Fourth Fyttes.
    Ox-BB:433, 452
  A Walk in the Country.
    Su Tung P'o. Rx-OH:76
SATIRE - MONUMENTS
  On the Setting Up of Mr. Butler's
    Monument in Westminster Abbey.
    S. Wesley. Ke-PP:51, Rv-CB:516
SATIRE - MOON
  In Dispraise of the Moon.
    M. Coleridge. Co-BN:122,
    De-CH:443
SATIRE - MOTHERS
  Bedtime Tales. J. Keith.
    De-FS:114
SATIRE - MOVING PICTURES
  A Day with the Foreign Legion.
    R. Whittemore. Wi-LT:842
  Headline Music. Yüan Shui-p'ai.
    Hs-TC:402
  Movies. L. Hughes. Mo-BG:184
  Newsreel. C. Day Lewis. Un-MB:425
  Newsreel in Wartime. A. Stoutenburg.
    Ba-PO:35, Cr-WS:99
  Prayer for Marilyn Monroe.
    E. Cardenal. Be-UL:95
SATIRE - MURDER
  Five Ways to Kill a Man.
    E. Brock. Cr-WS:145, Mo-TS:39

Recruiting Drive. C. Causley.
   Ha-TP:85, Ke-PP:115
SATIRE - MUSSOLINI, BENITO
One Man, One Man Alone (Italy,
   1941). E. Hutton.
   Ke-TF:384
SATIRE - NATURE
Beach Glass. H. Moss. Mo-BG:2
Definition of Nature. E. Redmond.
   Ad-PB:311
In a Wood. T. Hardy. Ox-BN:821
Nature Poem. G. Mende.
   La-IH:121
Reserved. W. de la Mare.
   Pa-GTB:437
SATIRE - NEGROES
Brainwashing Dramatized.
   D. Johnson. Hu-PN:436
he's doing natural life.
   Conyus. Ad-PB:403
Poem to a Nigger Cop. B. Hamilton.
   Lo-TY:255
SATIRE - NEW JERSEY
The Invention of New Jersey.
   J. Anderson. Sc-TN:3
SATIRE - NEW YEAR
New Year. Yüan Shui-p'ai.
   Hs-TC:407
SATIRE - NEW YORK, N.Y.
Empire City. G. Georgakas.
   Sc-TN:61
Saturday in New York.
   A. Beresford. To-MP:197
Song: Weekend's Over.
   M. Halpern. Ho-TY:106
Sunrise. F. García Lorca.
   Bl-FP:84
Thanksgiving. K. Koch.
   Ca-VT:545
SATIRE - NEWS
In Hardin County, 1809.
   L. Thompson. Co-PS:32,
   Ha-PO:99
Newsreel. C. Day Lewis. Un-MB:425
Smoke. C. Sandburg. Ba-PO:134
They Are Killing All the Young
   Men. D. Henderson. Ad-PB:414
The Zero Degree of Life.
   Tsang K'o-chia. Hs-TC:289
SATIRE - NEWSPAPERS
Headline History. W. Plomer.
   Hi-FO:261
The Newspaper. G. Crabbe.
   Ke-PP:47
A Newspaper. S. Crane.
   Al-VBP:1114, Sh-AP:144
Sunday Edition. J. Keith.
   De-FS:117
SATIRE - THE NORTH
Migration. C. Clemmons. Ad-PB:489

SATIRE - OBEDIENCE
On a Military Graveyard.
   K. Rexroth. Cr-WS:173
SATIRE - OLD AGE
Tithonus. A. Tennyson.
   Ox-BN:482, Rv-CB:792
SATIRE - OPPORTUNITY
Noah. W. Brown. Sa-B:218
Okay "Negroes." J. Jordan.
   Ra-BP:243
The Ricksha Puller. Cheng Min.
   Hs-TC:233
The Sun Came. E. Knight.
   Ad-PB:229
Thirty Bob a Week. J. Davidson.
   Er-FA:271, Ox-BN:900
SATIRE - OPTIMISTS AND OPTIMISM
In Tenebris. T. Hardy. Wi-LT:16
SATIRE - O'SHAUGHNESSY, ARTHUR
   WILLIAM EDGAR
On the Poet O'Shaughnessy.
   D. Rossetti. Gr-CT:476
SATIRE - OSTENTATION
New Blast Furnace.
   B. Akhmadulina. Ca-MR:37
Power Dive. N. MacCaig.
   Co-PU:73
SATIRE - PARENT AND CHILD
Bedtime Tales. J. Keith.
   De-FS:114
The Gate. E. Muir. Wi-LT:250
Home. K. Gershon. Cr-WS:132
She's Leaving Home. The Beatles.
   Pe-SS:94
Song for Mother's Day.
   T. Matthews. Co-EL:140
SATIRE - PARKS
Two Bums Walk Out of Eden.
   R. Francis. Ke-PP:23
SATIRE - PAST
The Lesson for Today. R. Frost.
   Wi-LT:180
The School Boy Reads His Iliad.
   D. Morton. Cr-WS:135
SATIRE - PASTORAL LIFE
The Village. G. Crabbe.
   Ha-PO:77
SATIRE - PATIENCE
The Bird. M. Halpern.   Ho-TY:104
SATIRE - PATRIOTISM
The Butchers at Prayer.
   D. Marquis. Cr-WS:138
Draft Dodger Rag. P. Ochs.
   Ba-PO:200
Dulce et Decorum Est. W. Owen.
   Ba-PO:139, Co-RM:210, Cr-WS:98,
   Ga-FB:217, Ke-PP:58, Rv-CB:990,
   Un-MB:364, Wi-LT:351
Gone Away Blues. T. McGrath.
   Cr-WS:174

SATIRE - PATRIOTISM — cont'd.
  Harry Wilmans. E. Masters.
    Ke-PP:7, Kr-OF:81
  If War Should Come. B. Musser.
    Ba-PO:168
  International Conference.
    C. Ellis. Cr-WS:138
  Knowlt Hoheimer. E. Masters.
    Ba-PO:81, Ho-LP:89
  Lamentations. S. Sassoon.
    Cr-WS:119
  Let Us Now Passionately Remember.
    e. cummings. Kr-OF:84
  Poem, or Beauty Hurts Mr. Vinal.
    E. Cummings. Sh-AP:191,
    Un-MA:474
  When the Cock Crows.
    A. Giovannitti. Kr-OF:151
SATIRE - PEACE
  Bethlehem. P. Hartnell. Ga-S:108
  Christmas. O. Lermand. Ho-CT:45
  Christmas: 1924. T. Hardy.
    Ba-PO:170, Cr-WS:2, Gr-BT:114
  communication in white. D. Lee.
    Ra-BP:299
  The Formalities. J. Ciardi.
    Cr-WS:143
  Great Powers Conference.
    E. Pierce. Cr-WS:160
  Jonas Kindred's Household.
    G. Crabbe. Ox-BN:15
  A Legend of Versailles.
    M. Tolson. Ra-BP:118
  The Night There Was Dancing in
    the Streets. E. Olson.
    St-H:174
  On a Shield Representing the
    Birth of Christ. Ba-PO:5
  Peace Was My Earliest Love.
    E. Millay. Ls-NY:35
  The Peaceable Kingdom. M. Piercy.
    Br-TC:317
  Redeployment. H. Nemerov.
    Ba-PO:193, Hi-TL:222, Wi-LT:591
  The Snare. P. MacDonough.
    Co-BBW:55
  Under Which Lyre. W. Auden.
    Un-MB:415
  The Watchman. A. Reisen.
    Ba-PO:205
SATIRE - PERFECTION
  The Gemlike Flame. R. Lister.
    Co-FB:345
SATIRE - PERMANENCE
  Vanity. R. Graves. Pa-GTB:487
SATIRE - PHILOSOPHY
  The Higher Pantheism in a Nutshell.
    A. Swinburne. Li-SR:95
  The Scythian Philosopher.
    J. de la Fontaine. Un-R:79

SATIRE - PHYSICIANS
  The Dodger. Gr-GB:201
  On Dr. Lettsom, by Himself.
    J. Lettsom. Co-PU:122
SATIRE - PHYSICISTS AND PHYSICS
  Hey Diddle Diddle. P. Dehn.
    Co-FB:451, Du-RG:80
SATIRE - PIETY
  There Was A Presbyterian Cat.
    Sm-LG:77
SATIRE - PIONEERS AND PIONEER LIFE
  right on: white america.
    S. Sanchez. Ad-BO:42,
    Ad-PB:287, Be-MA:135, Jo-SA:104
SATIRE - PLEASURE
  Nero's Term. C. Cavafy. Cr-WS:17
  Pleasures of the Soul.
    Z. Landau. Ho-TY:99
SATIRE - POETS AND POETRY
  The Bourgeois Poet. K. Shapiro.
    St-H:199
  His Answer to the Critics.
    S. Ibn Gabirol. Me-PH:57
  I Know I'm Not Sufficiently
    Obscure. R. Durem. Ad-PB:151,
    Jo-SA:122, Ra-BP:163
  An Idle Poet. C. Patmore.
    Al-VBP:973, De-CH:584,
    Ox-BN:652, Pa-GTB:367
  The Indignation of Taliesin.
    T. Peacock. Rv-CB:686
  The Line of an American Poet.
    R. Whittemore. Ke-PP:107
  Lovers, and a Reflection.
    C. Calverly. Li-SR:40
  Memo from the Desk of X.
    D. Justice. Br-TC:223
  On Homer's Birthplace.
    T. Heywood. Co-PU:68, Pl-ML:90
  On Professor Drennan's Verse.
    R. Campbell. Pa-GTB:496
  The Progress of Poetry.
    J. Swift. Rv-CB:491
  Short Song to Greet the New
    Year. Tsang K'o-chia.
    Hs-TC:291
  There Lived among the Untrodden
    Ways. H. Coleridge. Li-SR:107
  Trench Poets. E. Rickword.
    Cr-WS:97
  The Volunteer's Reply to the Poet
    ("Will It Be So Again?")
    R. Campbell. Al-VBP:1222
  We Must Start All Over Again.
    V. Batshev. Bo-RU:13
  William Lisle Bowles. G. Byron.
    Ox-BN:239
SATIRE - POLICE
  Assassination. D. Lee.
    Ad-BO:29, Ad-PB:423

Bim Bam. D. Rosenberg. Hu-PN:571
definition for blk/children.
   S. Sanchez. Ad-PB:288
A Gest of Robyn Hode, the Third
   and Sixth Fyttes. Ox-BB:443, 469
The Idiot. D. Randall. Ra-BP:144
Jazz. F. Brown. Hu-PN:395
Keep on Pushing. D. Henderson.
   Ad-PB:408
Love. P. Solomon. Jo-VC:4
A Mother Speaks. M. Harper.
   Ra-BP:291
O the Beatniks Never Win.
   C. Larsen. Lo-IT:71
Once. A. Walker. Ad-PB:474
The Poo-lice. N. Brown. Ad-II:84
Watch Dog. T. Barnes. La-IH:127
Who but the Lord? L. Hughes.
   Ra-BP:81
SATIRE - POLITICS
By the Winding River. Tu Fu.
   Rx-OH:14
The County Member. W. Praed.
   Ox-BN:437
Dinner at Eight. K. Louchheim.
   Ls-NY:332
The Dodger. Gr-GB:201
East Wind. Ou Yang Hsiu. Rx-OH:52
Similes for Two Political
   Characters of 1819. P. Shelley.
   Rv-CB:698
To Become a Chief's Favorite.
   Do-CH:(16)
The Way to Hump a Cow.
   E. Cummings. Sh-AP:193
SATIRE - POLLUTION
Contemplating More Bomb Tests.
   E. Merriam. Ba-PO:60
SATIRE - POPES
The Benediction. M. English.
   Cr-WS:37
SATIRE - POSSESSIONS
An Ancient Virgin. G. Crabbe.
   Ox-BN:4
The Bird. M. Halpern. Ho-TY:104
Having. I. Schneider. Kr-OF:196
Suburbia. M. Martinez. Hu-PN:408
SATIRE - POWER
Against Exploiters. Tr-CB:33,
   Tr-US I:65
By World Laid Low. Gr-CT:327
Cassandra. E. Robinson.
   Ke-PP:101, Wi-LT:108
Dark with Power. W. Berry.
   Mc-EA:119
Fear No More. W. Shakespeare.
   Al-VBP:195, Bo-HF:179, Co-RG:144,
   De-CH:250, De-TT:193, Er-FA:260,
   Gr-CT:332, Ha-PO:251, Hi-WP II:19,
   No-CL:73, Pa-GTB:28, Rv-CB:201,
   Sm-LG:267

For and Against. C. Norman.
   Cr-WS:162
The Glories of Our Blood and
   State. J. Shirley.
   Al-VBP:347, Ga-S:30, Gr-CC:107,
   Gr-CT:350, Ke-PP:30, Ni-JP:121,
   Pa-GTB:61, Rv-CB:360
Goodbye Nkrumah. D. di Prima.
   Lo-IT:30
He Who Pursues Force.
   Kuo Mo-jo. Hs-TC:40
I Gave Them Fruits. Bi-IT:146,
   Tr-US II:241
I Saw an Army. G. Abbe.
   Ba-PO:11
In Distrust of Merits. M. Moore.
   Al-VBP:1176, Pl-EI:146, Se-PR:207,
   Sm-PT:126, Un-MA:354, Wi-LT:272
Independence. H. Thoreau.
   Ba-PO:162
Jungle. M. Smith. Hu-PN:389
King of the Castle. Mo-MGT:29
The Last Conqueror. J. Shirley.
   Pa-GTB:60, Rv-CB:359
Masters of War. B. Dylan.
   Mo-GR:68
Of the Death of Kings.
   W. Shakespeare. Gr-CT:368
Ozymandias. P. Shelley.
   Co-RG:14, De-CH:384, Er-FA:83,
   Fe-PL:436, Ha-PO:208, Li-SR:83,
   Ma-YA:177, Mc-PR:186, Mc-WK:98,
   No-CL:256, Ox-BN:279, Pa-GTB:251,
   Pa-HT:91, Rv-CB:695, Sm-LG:153,
   Sp-OG:187, Un-GT:312
The Peaceful Shepherd. R. Frost.
   Tr-MR:191, Un-MA:181
Prophecy. Bi-IT:140, Br-MW:104
Ringless. D. Wakoski.
   Ho-P:287
The Rubaiyat of Omar Khayyam.
   E. FitzGerald. Gr-CT:329,
   Pa-GTB:329
Sweet, Smiling Village.
   O. Goldsmith. Ke-PP:41
There Are No Good Giants.
   W. Benton. Cr-WS:52
To Theodore Roosevelt. R. Daric.
   Bl-FP:37
The Trees in the Garden Rained
   Flowers. S. Crane. Wi-LT:121
The United Fruit Co.
   P. Neruda. Bl-FP:39
Upon the King.
   W. Shakespeare. Ke-PP:20
War Is the Statesman's Game.
   P. Shelley. Ba-PO:157, Ke-PP:57
SATIRE - PRAYER
In Westminster Abbey.
   J. Betjeman. Ba-PO:183

SATIRE - PRAYERS
   The Butchers at Prayer.
      D. Marquis.   Cr-WS:138
SATIRE - PREJUDICES AND ANTIPATHIES
   Lady Maisry.   Ox-BB:295
   Race Prejudice.   A. Kreymborg.
      Co-EL:63, Co-PU:21
SATIRE - PRESENT
   The Lesson for Today. R. Frost.
      Wi-LT:180
SATIRE - PRESIDENTS - UNITED STATES
   in the master bedroom of the
      white house.   D. Lourie.
      Sc-TN:156
   A Poem Beginning with a Line
      from Pindar.   R. Duncan.
      Bl-FP:74
   To the States.   W. Whitman.
      Bl-FP:21
   Two Poems about President
      Harding.   J. Wright. St-H:257
SATIRE - PRIDE
   Gnomes, III.   Tr-US I:125
   The Wild Flower and the Rose.
      D. Nikogosian.   Mo-MI:80
SATIRE - PRISONS AND PRISONERS
   If We Cannot Live as People.
      C. Lynch.   Ad-PB:461
   to Bobby Seale.   L. Clifton.
      Ad-PB:308
SATIRE - PROBLEMS AND SOLUTIONS
   It Is Time.   T. Joans.
      Hu-NN:34
   Like in the Movies.
      F. Eckman.   St-H:53
SATIRE - PROFITS
   The Collection.   E. Crosby.
      Kr-OF:171
SATIRE - PROGRESS
   Always the Following Wind.
      W. Auden.   Un-MB:454
   Change Is Not Always Progress.
      D. Lee.   Be-MA:163
   The Dam.   P. Dickinson.
      Co-PT:165
   Homo Faber: The Shell Game.
      M. Piercy.   Sc-TN:190
   Jehovah Buried, Satan Dead.
      E. Cummings.   Pe-OA:147
   No Curtain.   F. Scott. Ls-NY:277
   Parkinson and the Octopus.
      N. Farber.   De-FS:91
   Powers and Times Are Not Gods.
      W. Auden.   Tr-MR:237
   A Pretty Pot of Gray.
      E. Jean-Baptiste.   Sa-B:222
   Progress.   S. Hoffenstein.
      Hi-TL:223
   The Purse-Seine.   R. Jeffers.
      Pe-OA:92

Requiem for a River.   K. Williams.
      La-RM:40
   Shootin' Up the Trail.
      G. Shumway.   Fi-BG:107
   Strange Tales, Domestic Vintage.
      Yüan Shui-p'ai.   Hs-TC:406
   Trail Breakers.   J. Daugherty.
      Br-AF:226, Sh-RP:302
   The War Against Trees.
      S. Kunitz.   Ke-PP:42
SATIRE - PROPERTY
   Choosing a Homesite.   P. Booth.
      Ha-TP:13
SATIRE - PROPHETS AND PROPHECIES
   A Denunciation of the Princes
      and the Prophets.   Bible. O.T.
      Micah.   Me-PH:51
SATIRE - PROSPERITY
   Boom!   H. Nemerov.   Ba-PO:193,
      Wi-LT:589
SATIRE - PROTECTION
   My Parents Kept Me from Children
      Who Were Rough.   S. Spender.
      Ho-LP:59, Ma-FW:62, Pe-SS:26
SATIRE - PROTEST
   The Early Rebels.   W. Morris.
      Sa-B:9
SATIRE - PUBLIC OPINION
   The People vs. the People.
      K. Fearing.   Un-MA:555
SATIRE - PUBLICITY
   The Preview.   W. Benton.
      Cr-WS:166
SATIRE - PUNISHMENT
   Flogged Child.   J. Keith.
      De-FS:116
   They Are Killing All the Young
      Men.   D. Henderson. Ad-PB:414
   The Whipping.   R. Hayden.
      Ad-PB:119, Pe-M:14
SATIRE - PURITANS AND PURITANISM
   Address to the Unco Guid or the
      Rigidly Righteous.   R. Burns.
      Al-VBP:631
SATIRE - QUESTIONS AND ANSWERS
   Some Litanies.   M. Benedikt.
      Br-TC:33
SATIRE - RACE RELATIONS
   And Was Not Improved.
      L. Bennett.   Ad-PB:203
   The Beast Section.   W. Smith.
      Ad-PB:374
   Boogie-Woogie Ballads.
      S. McKelway.   Hu-PN:534
   Cultural Exchange.   L. Hughes.
      Ad-PB:76, Hu-PN:203, Ra-BP:83
   Deathwatch.   M. Harper.
      Ad-PB:317
   i saw them lynch.   C. Freeman.
      Ad-PB:397

I Told Jesus. S. Plumpp.
  Ad-PB:385
i used to wrap my white doll
  up in. M. Jackson. Ad-BO:72,
  Ad-PB:498
Jitterbugging in the Streets.
  C. Hernton. Ad-PB:240
Keep on Pushing. D. Henderson.
  Ad-PB:408
Negro Hero. G. Brooks. St-H:8
The Negro's Tragedy. C. McKay.
  Ra-BP:63
Norris Dam. S. Rodman. Hu-PN:542
Old Lem. S. Brown. Ad-PB:69,
  Hu-PN:167, Lo-TY:221, Ra-BP:109
Once. A. Walker. Ad-PB:474
PSI. M. Tolson. Ad-BO:36
Recapitulations. K. Shapiro.
  Hu-PN:563
Slave Story. H. Carter.
  Hu-PN:540
Strategies. W. Smith. Ad-PB:375
Telephone Conversation.
  W. Soyinka. Lo-TY:161,
  Ma-FW:134
The Third Sermon on the Warpland.
  G. Brooks. Ra-BP:176
Today Tomorrow? S. Cybulski.
  Me-WF:83
Upstairs Downstairs. H. Allen.
  Hu-PN:507
Vet's Rehabilitation. R. Durem.
  Ad-PB:150
We Raise de Wheat. F. Douglass.
  Ra-BP:3
You Know, Joe. R. Durem.
  Ad-BO:47, Hu-PN:330
SATIRE - RACES OF MAN
12 Gates to the City.
  N. Giovanni. Ad-PB:457
SATIRE - RADIATION
Futurama Love Song. N. Rosten.
  Cr-WS:146
Geiger, Geiger, Ticking Slow.
  P. Dehn. Li-SR:9
It Is Not Only the Dead.
  F. Long. De-FS:132
SATIRE - REALITY
Matinees. J. Merrill. Ho-P:187
SATIRE - RELIGION
At a Calvary near the Ancre.
  W. Owen. Tr-MR:187
Bethlehem. P. Hartnoll.
  Ga-S:108
The Church on Comiaken Hill.
  R. Hugo. Ho-P:123
Church on the Corner of Union
  and Third. L. Smith. Lo-IT:126
Clerical Oppressors. J. Whittier.
  Ke-PP:73

A High-Toned Old Christian Woman.
  W. Stevens. Pe-OA:71
The Hippopotamus. T. Eliot.
  Ca-VT:132, Ha-PO:119
Hudibras 2. S. Butler.
  Al-VBP:422, Hi-FO:150
In the Deep Museum. A. Sexton.
  Ho-P:229, Un-MA:690
Ironical Song of the Intolerance
  of Missionaries and Converts.
  Tr-US II:42
Millenium. J. Kohut. Lo-IT:67
A Psalm of Montreal. S. Butler.
  Rv-CB:933
Second Elegy. N. Stanescu.
  Mc-AC:149
The Vicar. G. Crabbe. Ox-BN:7
Wednesday Night Prayer Meeting.
  J. Wright. Ad-PB:272
The Young Man. C. Houselander.
  Ga-S:196
SATIRE - RETURNING
Bim Bam. D. Rosenberg. Hu-PN:571
Exile. D. Walcott. Sa-B:64
The Hometown Hero Come Home.
  D. Etter. Cr-WS:15, St-H:58
Yorkville. D. Aldan. Lo-IT:3
SATIRE - REVIVALS
An Imitator of Billy Sunday.
  J. Jiménez. Bl-FP:69
Pie in the Sky. J. Hill.
  Gr-GB:328, Ke-PP:15
SATIRE - REVOLTS AND REVOLUTIONS
People, Listen! A. Shchukin.
  Bo-RU:73
SATIRE - RINGS
Ringless. D. Wakoski. Ho-P:287
SATIRE - RITES AND CEREMONIES
Upon the King. W. Shakespeare.
  Ke-PP:20
SATIRE - ROOSEVELT, FRANKLIN DELANO
Mr. Roosevelt Regrets.
  P. Murray. Ad-PB:109
SATIRE - RUSSIA
After a Symphony Concert.
  V. Uflyand. Bo-RU:86
Elegy for the Soviet Yiddish
  Writers. C. Grade. Ho-TY:339
The Hothouse. A. Shchukin.
  Bo-RU:76
You and I Are Almost Cripples.
  V. Kovshin. Bo-RU:47
SATIRE - SAFETY
Documentary. R. Beum.
  Cr-WS:130
To Another Poet a Thousand Years
  Hence. C. Norman. Cr-WS:131
SATIRE - SAINTS
Saints and Heroes You Dare Say.
  C. Day Lewis. Go-BP:184

SATIRE - SALEM, MASS.
  Salem of Oppression. J. Keith.
    De-FS:118
  Witching Hour. N. Farber.
    De-FS:91
SATIRE - SALESMEN
  A Salesman Is an It That Stinks
    Excuse. E. Cummings. Sh-AP:192
  Tom Agnew, Bill Agnew.
    D. Rossetti. Gr-CT:476
SATIRE - SANTA CLAUS
  Christ Climbed Down.
    L. Ferlinghetti. Tr-MR:111
  The Jew at Christmas Eve.
    K. Shapiro. Ca-VT:373
  Santa Claus. H. Nemerov.
    Pe-OA:252
SATIRE - SCHOLARS AND SCHOLARSHIP
  The Dawn. W. Yeats. Mo-GR:73
  Dr. Hu. N. Mailer. Co-EL:103
  For My Shakespeare Class.
    V. Adrian. Ls-NY:341
  A Learned Man. S. Crane.
    Un-MA:148
  Lines to a Don. H. Belloc.
    Un-MB:171
  Man Is But a Castaway. C. Day.
    Pl-IO:125
  Mr. Attila. C. Sandburg.
    Ha-PT:28, Pl-IO:177
  On Professor Drennan's Verse.
    R. Campbell. Pa-GTB:496
  The Scholars. W. Yeats.
    Pl-ML:61
  Under Which Lyre. W. Auden.
    Un-MB:415
  The World and This Life Are So
    Scattered, They Try Me.
    H. Heine. Co-EL:102
SATIRE - SCIENCE
  Earth. J. Wheelock. Cr-WS:175,
    Du-RG:81, Wi-LT:655
  James Honeyman. W. Auden.
    Ca-MB:100, Sm-MK:117
  Stop, Science - Stop!
    A. Herbert. Co-FB:452
  The Washerman. U. Joshi.
    Al-PI:110
  With a Daisy. E. Dickinson.
    Pl-IO:141
SATIRE - SECURITY
  The Gate. E. Muir. Wi-LT:250
  Give Way. D. Finkel. Ke-PP:122
  Horses and Men in the Rain.
    C. Sandburg. Fe-PL:409
  A Lullaby. G. Glasgow.
    Sp-OG:210
  Outside. P. Harris. Sc-TN:80
  Sanctuary. J. Boothroyd.
    Co-FB:28

Security. M. Hamburger.
    En-PC:223
Security. R. Tucker. Ke-PP:121
The Window. E. Muir. Wi-LT:255
SATIRE - SELF-DENIAL
  Four Lovely Sisters. C. Trypanis.
    Co-EL:138
SATIRE - SERENADES
  The Guitar. G. Dusenbery.
    Sc-TN:37
SATIRE - SERVANTS
  Girls Mocking White Men's
    Serving Boys. Tr-CB:50,
    Tr-US I:52
SATIRE - SHOOTING
  First Blood. J. Stallworthy.
    Ha-TP:104
SATIRE - SILENCE
  Silence Is Gold. A. Galich.
    Bo-RU:33
SATIRE - SIRENS (SEA NYMPHS)
  Nearing Again the Legendary
    Isle. C. Day Lewis. Un-MB:421
SATIRE - SNOW
  The Snow Shovel. C. Walsh.
    St-H:235
SATIRE - SOCIAL WORKERS
  Feeding the Lions. N. Jordan.
    Ad-BO:45, Ad-PB:322, Kr-OF:56
SATIRE - SOLDIERS
  Forgive Me, Sire. N. Cameron.
    Pa-GTB:499
  I Know Something. C. Sandburg.
    Kr-OF:88
  I'll Get Me Cap and Jacket.
    B. Okujava. Bo-RU:58
  Innocence. T. Gunn. Wi-LT:724
  Insensibility. W. Owen.
    Ba-PO:141, Wi-LT:345
  Knowlt Hoheimer. E. Masters.
    Ba-PO:81, Ho-LP:89
  Lt. Cmdr. T. E. Sanderson.
    J. Scully. Ha-TP:87
  On the Fourth Night of Hunger
    Strike. M. Carter. Sa-B:167
  The Paper Soldier. B. Okujava.
    Bo-RU:55
  The Picket-Guard. E. Beers.
    Er-FA:187, Sp-OG:196
  Pocket Guide for Servicemen.
    H. Creekmore. Ba-PO:190
  Recruiting Drive. C. Causley.
    Ha-TP:85, Ke-PP:115
  The Roman Road. D. Davidson.
    Cr-WS:17
  Sergeant Major Money.
    R. Graves. Co-RM:220
  Soldiers Who Wish.
    Ba-PO:92, Cr-WS:61
    Gr-GB:242

A Song of Liang Chou. Wang Han.
   Cr-WS:11
A Song of War Chariots. Tu Fu.
   Cr-WS:10
To a Conscript of 1940. H. Read.
   Wi-LT:633
To the Warmakers. E. Pierce.
   Cr-WS:26
Veteran. L. Bacon. Cr-WS:34
We're Here Because. Ba-PO:93
SATIRE - SONS
   Bedtime Tales. J. Keith.
      De-FS:114
SATIRE - THE SOUTH
   Birmingham. M. Walker.
      Ad-PB:149
   Boogie-Woogie Ballads.
      S. McKelway. Hu-PN:534
   Elegy on a Nordic White
      Protestant. J. Fletcher.
      Hu-PN:503
   Migration. C. Clemmons.
      Ad-PB:489
   Picnic: The Liberated.
      M. Holman. Ad-PB:176, Hu-PN:367
   A Reunion. J. Schuyler.
      Mc-EA:136
   Safari. W. Long. Lo-IT:83
   Snapshots of the Cotton South.
      F. Davis. Ad-PB:98
   The Southerner. K. Shapiro.
      Hu-PN:565
SATIRE - SOUTH AFRICA
   In the Gold Mines. B. Vilakazi.
      Lo-TY:176
SATIRE - SPANIARDS IN AMERICA
   Imperator Victus. H. Crane.
      Bl-FP:36
SATIRE - SPEECH
   The Voices of Peace Are Hushed.
      S. Himmell. Cr-WS:165
SATIRE - SPORTSMANSHIP
   The Real Slayer of the Seal.
      Da-SC:45, Le-IB:52
SATIRE - SPRING (SEASON)
   Spring MCMXL. D. Gascoyne.
      Cr-WS:70
SATIRE - STATISTICS
   Meditation on Statistical
      Method. J. Cunningham.
      Ca-VT:328
SATIRE - STATUES
   Icarus. H. Sabgir. Bo-RU:71
SATIRE - STEWART, ROBERT,
      VISCOUNT CASTLEREAGH
   What's My Thought Like?
      T. Moore. Rv-CB:682
SATIRE - STOICISM
   The Scythian Philosopher.
      J. de la Fontaine. Un-R:79

SATIRE - SUBMISSIVENESS
   The Idiot. D. Randall.
      Ra-BP:144
   A Quiet Life and a Good Name.
      J. Swift. Rv-CB:493
SATIRE - SUCCESS
   Black Bourgeoisie. I. Baraka.
      Ra-BP:223
   The City of Satisfactions.
      D. Hoffman. Ho-P:105
   Robert Whitmore. F. Davis.
      Ad-PB:96, Be-MA:53,
      Hu-PN:254, Ra-BP:121
SATIRE - SUICIDE
   "Very Interesting" Death.
      Yüan Shui-p'ai. Hs-TC:408
SATIRE - SUPERMARKETS
   Grace to Be Said at the
      Supermarket. H. Nemerov.
      To-MP:118
   A Supermarket in California.
      A. Ginsberg. Br-TC:149,
      Kh-VA:64, Mo-BG:185, Wi-LT:718
SATIRE - SURVIVAL
   Return to Hiroshima. L. Stryk.
      Cr-WS:148
   Roc's Brood. S. Bradley.
      De-FS:30
   A Survivor. K. Hopkins.
      Cr-WS:112
SATIRE - SWORDS
   What Man First Forged.
      Tibullus. Ba-PO:73
SATIRE - SYMPATHY
   Don't Ask Me Who I Am.
      J. Randall. Ra-BP:274
   Serves You Right, Beggar.
      Hsü Chih-mo. Hs-TC:77
SATIRE - TAXES AND TAX COLLECTORS
   A Ballad on the Taxes.
      E. Ward. Ke-PP:11
   Taxes. D. Lee. Ad-BO:56
   Yen Hsi-shan's Tax Agent.
      Liu Chia. Hs-TC:434
SATIRE - TEACHERS AND TEACHING
   Children Are Slaves. I. Velez.
      Jo-VC:32
   He Don't Know the Inside Feel.
      H. Adams. Pe-M:24
   The Schoolboy, the Pedant, and
      the Man with a Garden.
      J. de la Fontaine. Un-R:82
   The Schoolmaster. Gr-GB:28
SATIRE - TELEPHONES
   The Bestfriend. D. Lourie. Sc-TN:150
SATIRE - TELEVISION
   Conversation Piece. P. Hobsbaum.
      Ls-NY:319
   The Electric Cop. V. Cruz.
      Ad-PB:507

SATIRE - TEN COMMANDMENTS
The Latest Decalogue. A. Clough.
Al-VBP:926, Gr-CT:475,
Ox-BN:609, Pa-GTB:358, Rv-CB:841
SATIRE - TOLERANCE
The Angry Man. P. McGinley.
Pe-SS:108
Riot. G. Brooks. Ad-PB:164,
Ra-BP:175
SATIRE - TOMBS
The Unknown Soldier. W. Benton.
Cr-WS:106
SATIRE - TOURISTS
Adina. H. Telemaque.
Lo-TY:110
I Love Those Little Booths at
Benvenutt's. G. Brooks.
St-H:10
Sightseers in a Courtyard.
N. Guillen. Lo-TY:106
SATIRE - TOYS
Epitaph for a Wooden Soldier.
G. Code. De-FS:67
Misericordia. A. Lowell.
Cr-WS:67
SATIRE - TREATIES
Two Wise Generals. T. Hughes.
Ca-MB:98
SATIRE - TRUMAN, HARRY S
Harry. N. Rosten. Cr-WS:147
SATIRE - TRUMPETS
The Trumpet. K. Douglas.
Cr-WS:75
SATIRE - TWENTIETH CENTURY
Boom! H. Nemerov. Ba-PO:193,
Wi-LT:589
Chorus for a Phonograph.
K. Congdon. Lo-IT:21
A Coney Island of the Mind.
L. Ferlinghetti. Mo-BG:182,
Wi-LT:701
Desolation Row. B. Dylan.
Mc-EA:33
Five Ways to Kill a Man.
E. Brock. Cr-WS:145, Mo-TS:39
The Holy Innocents. R. Lowell.
Un-MA:663
I Run, I Hide. P. Sclafani.
Me-WF:63
I Shall Laugh Purely. R. Jeffers.
Wi-LT:263
If You've Never Been in a Con-
centration Camp. A. Mikhailov.
Bo-RU:53
The Invention of New Jersey.
J. Anderson. Sc-TN:3
It Was a Goodly Co.
e. cummings. Wi-LT:366
The Observation. D. Leitch.
Mo-GR:80

Prayer for Marilyn Monroe.
E. Cardenal. Be-UL:95
Rearmament. R. Jeffers. Bl-FP:50
Several Voices Out of a Cloud.
L. Bogan. Mo-BG:180
Simple Beast. M. Van Doren.
Ho-TH:43
XXth Century. R. Hillyer. Ho-TH:32
Vil for the Layman. M. Piercy.
Sc-TN:187
The Zero Degree of Life.
Tsang K'o-chia. Hs-TC:289
SATIRE - UNITED STATES
America Bleeds. A. Lewis.
Ad-II:79, Ad-PB:513
America the Beautiful. J. Streich.
Ad-II:80
April 1962. P. Goodman. Ca-VT:336
Black-Out. R. Jeffers. Wi-LT:262
Boom! H. Nemerov. Ba-PO:193,
Wi-LT:589
Canto 89. E. Pound. Bl-FP:27
Cassandra. E. Robinson.
Ke-PP:101, Wi-LT:108
Dancing. A. Young. Mc-EA:88
Dancing in the Streets.
A. Young. Mc-EA:51
Dark Symphony: Larghetto.
M. Tolson. Bo-AN:40
Dark with Power. W. Berry.
Mc-EA:119
Dear America. R. Peterson.
Ke-PP:48, Kr-OF:92
Eagle Valor, Chicken Mind.
R. Jeffers. Ba-PO:185,
Co-EL:138
Elephant Rock. P. St. John.
Ad-PB:347
Forsworn to the People.
W. Whitman. Kr-OF:41
The Gangster's Death. I. Reed.
Ad-PB:331
Goodby Nkrumah. D. di Prima.
Lo-IT:30
Hatred of Men with Black Hair.
R. Bly. Mc-EA:127
I Have Seen Black Hands.
R. Wright. Ad-PB:105, Jo-SA:112
I Hear America Griping.
M. Bishop. Br-AF:43
I Know I'm Not Sufficiently
Obscure. R. Durem.
Ad-PB:151, Jo-SA:122, Ra-BP:163
In a Surrealist Year.
L. Ferlinghetti. Ke-PP:3
in the master bedroom of the white
house. D. Lourie. Sc-TN:156
Is It True? N. Rosten. Kr-OF:201
It Is Not Enough. D. Henderson.
Ke-PP:98

It Is Time. T. Joans. Hu-NN:34
Late Late. G. Starbuck.
  Ke-PP:112
Lincoln . . . Today. K. Hopkins.
  Me-WF:61
The Melting Pot. D. Randall.
  Ra-BP:141
Mr. Roosevelt Regrets.
  P. Murray. Ad-PB:109
Negro Hero. G. Brooks. St-H:8
Ode. R. Emerson. Ke-PP:65,
  Sh-AP:31
Old Lem. S. Brown. Ad-PB:69,
  Hu-PN:167, Lo-TY:221, Ra-BP:109
Pastures of Plenty. W. Guthrie.
  Pe-SS:53
Plan. R. McKuen. Pe-M:3
A Poem Beginning with a Line by
  Pindar. R. Duncan. Bl-FP:74
A Pretty Pot of Grey.
  E. Jean-Baptiste. Sa-B:222
Rain Rain on Splintered Girl.
  I. Reed. Ad-PB:327
Recessional for the Class of
  1959 of a School for Delin-
  quent Negro Girls.
  J. Cowen. Hu-PN:575
Red Atlantis. J. Haines. Sc-TN:77
The Runaway Slave at Pilgrim's
  Point. E. Browning. Hu-PN:448
This Morning the Sun. O. Cabral.
  Ke-PP:103
To the States. W. Whitman.
  Bl-FP:21
The United Fruit Co.
  P. Neruda. Bl-FP:39
Until They Have Stopped.
  S. Wright. Ad-PB:215
The Village Fish. D. Hall.
  Ba-PO:40
We Have Been Believers. M. Walker.
  Ad-PB:145, Be-MA:76,
  Hu-PN:312, Jo-SA:130
White Weekend. Q. Troupe.
  Kr-OF:164
Who Shall Die? J. Randall.
  Ra-BP:272
SATIRE - UNITED STATES - CONSTITUTION
  1776-1970. J. Zeier. Ad-II:93
SATIRE - UNITED STATES - HISTORY
    AND PATRIOTISM
  Again They Surround Thee.
    W. Whitman. Kr-OF:105
  The Dred Scott Decision. W. Bryant.
    Kr-OF:108
  I Sing of Olaf. e. cummings.
    Ca-VT:179, Ke-PP:113, Sh-AP:190,
    Wi-LT:362
  On American Island Wars. W. Moody.
    Bl-FP:33

Patriotic Poem. D. Wakoski.
  Ca-VT:712
Stanzas to an Alien. P. Freneau.
  Kr-OF:103
Wail! For Our Nation.
  J. Lowell. Kr-OF:10
The War for Slavery. W. Garrison.
  Kr-OF:66
SATIRE - UNITED STATES - SOCIAL
    LIFE AND CUSTOMS
  Blueprint. J. Sloman. Sc-TN:204
SATIRE - USEFULNESS
  The Conversation. A. Raybin.
    Sc-TN:193
SATIRE - VALUE AND VALUES
  How They Came from the Blue
    Snows. A. Kenseth. Ke-PP:54
  Me Again. K. Rexroth. Kh-VA:36
  Reserved. W. de la Mare.
    Pa-GTB:437
  Seventy Balconies and Not a
    Single Flower.
    B. Fernández Moreno. Be-UL:27
  The War Against Trees.
    S. Kunitz. Ke-PP:42
SATIRE - VAN BUREN, MARTIN
  Canto 89. E. Pound. Bl-FP:27
SATIRE - VANDERBILT, CORNELIUS
  Empire Builders. A. MacLeish.
    Sh-AP:188
SATIRE - VICTORIA, QUEEN OF ENGLAND
  The Widow at Windsor. R. Kipling.
    Hi-FO:249
SATIRE - VICTORY
  The Battle of Blenheim. R. Southey.
    Cr-WS:21, Fe-PL:182, Ga-FB:203,
    Ha-PO:13, Hi-FO:165, Ox-BN:177,
    Pa-GTB:213, Sp-OG:184, Un-GT:146
  Conquerors. H. Treece.
    Co-RM:210, To-MP:51
  Defeat. W. Bynner. Hu-PN:490
  Hawks. S. Bates. Ba-PO:196
  On a Victory. Tr-US I:127
  Peace. L. Hughes. Ra-BP:82
  Triumphal Entry. C. Norman.
    Cr-WS:125
  A Victory Dance. A. Noyes.
    Fe-PL:153
  The War Year. Ts'ao Sung.
    Ba-PO:172, Cr-WS:15, Ke-PP:12
SATIRE - VIETNAMESE WAR, 1957-1975
  The Gangster's Death. I. Reed.
    Ad-PB:331
  Of Late. G. Starbuck.
    Ca-VT:667, Cr-WS:136
  Vietnam #4. C. Major. Ad-BO:48,
    Ad-PB:298, Ba-PO:38
SATIRE - VILLAGE LIFE
  Acton Beauchamp, Herefordshire.
    Gr-GB:174

SATIRE - VILLAGE LIFE — cont'd.
  The Song of Youth. Ai Ch'ing.
    Hs-TC:297
SATIRE - VILLIERS, GEORGE, 2ND DUKE
    OF BUCKINGHAM
  George Villiers, Duke of
    Buckingham. J. Dryden.
    Ha-PO:61
SATIRE - WAITING
  Commander Death. P. Horgan.
    Cr-WS:103
  War Poem. H. Treece. Cr-WS:108
SATIRE - WAR
  Achtung! Achtung! M. Hacker.
    Cr-WS:1
  Advent 1966. D. Levertov.
    Ho-P:157
  After the War. G. Garbovsky.
    Bo-RU:36
  Air Raid Across the Bay of
    Plymouth. S. Spender. Ha-TP:80
  All the World over. R. Kipling.
    Go-BP:216
  And There Was a Great Calm.
    T. Hardy. Gr-CT:345, Tr-MR:181,
    Wi-LT:26
  The Articles of War. R. Francis.
    Cr-WS:64
  Asking for It. S. Sassoon.
    Tr-MR:185
  At Carnoy. S. Sassoon.
    Cr-WS:84
  Attila. W. Everson. Cr-WS:4
  B-52's. A. Kenseth. Ke-PP:84
  The Battle of Blenheim. R. Southey.
    Cr-WS:21, Fe-PL:182, Ga-FB:203,
    Ha-PO:13, Hi-FO:165, Ox-BN:177,
    Pa-GTB:213, Sp-OG:184, Un-GT:146
  Battle Won Is Lost. P. George.
    Al-WW:114
  The Bayonet. D. Marquis.
    Cr-WS:99
  Blessing the Battle. W. Tappan.
    Cr-WS:140
  Break of Day in the Trenches.
    I. Rosenberg. Al-VBP:1190,
    Bo-PO:138, Hi-FO:257,
    Pa-GTB:446, Un-MB:351
  Buttons. C. Sandburg.
    Kr-OF:83
  By the Deep Sea. G. Byron.
    Ox-BN:249
  Cable Cars. S. Tsuboi. Sh-AM:71
  Channel Firing. T. Hardy.
    Ke-PP:96
  Christmas Eve under Hooker's
    Statue. R. Lowell.
    Ba-PO:202, Hi-TL:214
  Clear Today. N. Kaplan.
    Ad-II:103

  Cleator Moor. N. Nicholson.
    To-MP:44
  Clover Swaths. J. Hearst.
    St-H:83
  Communiqué from an Army Deserter
    Probably Italian. S. Moss.
    Cr-WS:91
  Condemnation. Thich Nhat Hanh.
    Ke-PP:40
  Conquerors. H. Treece.
    To-MP:51
  Counter-Attack. S. Sassoon.
    Ba-PO:136, Co-RM:204,
    Cr-WS:87, Un-MB:312
  The Coward. E. Merriam.
    Ba-PO:204
  A Curse. B. Gibson. Ba-PO:170
  The Curse of Cain.
    H. Longfellow. Kr-OF:62
  Dead Soldier. N. Guillén.
    Ba-PO:42, Lo-TY:105
  Dear America. R. Peterson.
    Ke-PP:48, Kr-OF:92
  The Death-Bed. S. Sassoon.
    Wi-LT:640
  Death, Look to Your Domain.
    C. Norman. Cr-WS:172
  The Death of the Ball Turret
    Gunner. R. Jarrell.
    Ba-PO:186, Ca-VT:400, Co-EL:82,
    Cr-WS:100, Pe-SS:138, Un-MA:647,
    Wi-LT:561
  Dido of Tunisia. P. McGinley.
    Cr-WS:18
  Disarmament. J. Whittier.
    Ba-PO:103, Cr-WS:157
  Disasters of War: Goya at the
    Museum. B. Deutsch.
    Cr-WS:35
  Dulce et Decorum Est. W. Owen.
    Ba-PO:139, Co-RM:210, Cr-WS:98,
    Ga-FB:217, Ke-PP:58, Rv-CB:990,
    Un-MB:364, Wi-LT:351
  Eagle Valor, Chicken Mind.
    R. Jeffers. Ba-PO:185,
    Co-EL:138
  Ecce Homo. D. Gascoyne.
    Wi-LT:715
  Eighth Air Force. R. Jarrell.
    En-PC:140, Mo-BG:172
  Epitaph for a Wooden Soldier.
    G. Code. De-FS:67
  Exposure. W. Owen.
    Go-BP:207
  The Fairy's Reply to Saturn.
    T. Hood. Ox-BN:417
  Fast Rode the Knight. S. Crane.
    Li-TU:236
  The Fifth Sense. P. Beer.
    Ca-MB:120

First Blood. J. Stallworthy.
    Ha-TP:104
5 Ways to Kill a Man. E. Brock.
    Cr-WS:145, Mo-TS:39
For the Minority. R. Peterson.
    Kr-OF:93
Fragment from a Poem, "Another
    Late Edition." P. Cabral.
    Ke-OF:89
Frontier Guard. T. Wright.
    Cr-WS:141
The Fury of Aerial Bombardment.
    R. Eberhart. Ba-PO:178,
    Ca-VT:248, Sh-AP:209, Wi-LT:438
The Gardener and the Mole.
    W. Landor. Rd-OA:115
The Generals. S. Silverstein.
    Co-OT:50
the ghosts of the dead.
    B. Brigham. Sc-TN:22
The Glories of Our Blood and
    State. J. Shirley. Al-VBP:347,
    Ga-S:30, Gr-CC:107, Gr-CT:350,
    Ke-PP:30, Ni-JP:121, Pa-GTB:61,
    Rv-CB:360
The God of War. Aeschylus.
    Ke-PP:6
Goya. A. Voznesensky. Ca-MR:68
The Gray Monk. W. Blake.
    Ba-PO:9
Gunner. R. Jarrell. Mc-EA:125
The Happy Warrior. H. Read.
    Cr-WS:119
Harry Wilmans. E. Masters.
    Ke-PP:7, Kr-OF:81
Heartbreak Ridge. E. Pierce.
    Cr-WS:142
Here Dead We Lie. A. Housman.
    Cr-WS:135, Fe-PL:156
Herod. M. Martinet.
    Ba-PO:144, Cr-WS:123
Hiroshima. M. Rockwell.
    Ba-PO:53, Ke-PP:9
A History Lesson. M. Holub.
    Gr-BT:127, Ma-FW:239
The Hometown Hero Come Home.
    D. Etter. Cr-WS:15, St-H:58
How Is the Gold Become Dim.
    Bible. O.T. Lamentations.
    Gr-CT:344
Hugh Selwyn Mauberley. E. Pound.
    Ba-PO:149, Ca-VT:84, Ha-PO:122,
    Hi-TL:186, Un-MA:301, Wi-LT:232
I Am for Peace. W. Tappan.
    Ba-PO:101, Cr-WS:151
I Know Something. C. Sandburg.
    Kr-OF:88
I Saw an Army. G. Abbe. Ba-PO:11
If There Were Not a War.
    J. Lester. Jo-SA:70

If War Should Come. B. Musser.
    Ba-PO:168
Imperator Victus. H. Crane.
    Bl-FP:36
In Distrust of Merits. M. Moore.
    Al-VBP:1176, Pl-EI:146, Se-PR:207,
    Sm-PT:126, Un-MA:354, Wi-LT:272
Insensibility. W. Owen.
    Ba-PO:141, Wi-LT:345
I've Got to Know. W. Guthrie.
    Pe-SS:142
The Jewish Conscript. F. Frank.
    Ba-PO:135
The Joke. W. Gibson. Cr-WS:105
The Known Soldier. K. Patchen.
    Ba-PO:159
Lamentations. S. Sassoon.
    Cr-WS:119
The Last Campaign. G. Lehmann.
    Cr-WS:171
The Last Laugh. W. Owen.
    Cr-WS:94
A Letter to the Young Men.
    K. Patchen. Mc-EA:124
Lines for an Interment.
    A. MacLeish. Kr-OF:87
The Lions of Fire Shall Have
    Their Hunting. K. Patchen.
    Ba-PO:159, Ca-VT:343
Losses. R. Jarrell.
    Sh-AP:223, Wi-LT:562
M-Day's Child. M. Rukeyser.
    Kr-OF:89
Masters of War. B. Dylan.
    Mo-GR:68
Me Again. K. Rexroth. Kh-VA:36
Misericordia. A. Lowell.
    Cr-WS:67
Moon Festival. Tu Fu. Rx-OH:8
The Moors Fight on the Side of
    God. C. Norman. Cr-WS:37
Mount Fuji. M. Kaneko.
    Sh-AM:66
Mourn Not the Dead. R. Chaplin.
    Al-VBP:1147, Ba-PO:146,
    Cr-WS:120, Kr-OF:117
Music Room. E. Pierce.
    Cr-WS:59
Musical Vietnams. B. Allen.
    Lo-IT:4
The Nefarious War. Li Po.
    Ba-PO:153, Cr-WS:14, Li-TU:241
A Negro Soldier's Viet Nam Diary.
    H. Martin. Ad-PB:227
Newscast. A. Kramer. Kr-OF:91
Newsreel in Wartime. A. Stoutenberg.
    Ba-PO:35, Cr-WS:99
Night. T. McGrath. Bl-FP:48
Nightmare with Angels.
    S. Benét. Ba-PO:12

SATIRE - WAR — cont'd.
  1935. S. Benét. Mc-WS:107,
    Un-MA:501
  Official Visit to Shih Hao
    Village. Tu Fu.
    Ba-PO:154, Cr-WS:13
  An Old Man Reviews the Wars.
    W. Bynner. Cr-WS:2
  The Old Men and the Young Men.
    W. Bynner. Cr-WS:162
  On a Shield Representing the
    Birth of Christ. Ba-PO:5
  On a Very Young, Very Dead
    Soldier. R. Gillman.
    Cr-WS:101
  On American Island Wars.
    W. Moody. Bl-FP:33
  On Seeing a Poet of the First
    World War on the Station at
    Abbeville. C. Causley.
    Wi-LT:667
  On Thanksgiving for a National
    Victory. R. Burns. Ba-PO:169
  On the Danger of War. G. Meredith.
    Ba-PO:161, Ke-PP:90
  On the Death of a Murderer.
    J. Wain. Cr-WS:113
  On the Eve of New Wars.
    L. Untermeyer. Ba-PO:164
  On War. C. Kilgore. Ha-TP:82
  The Origin of Baseball.
    K. Patchen. Mc-EA:133
  Our New National Anthem.
    W. Eggleston. Ba-PO:80,
    Cr-WS:155
  The Peasants. A. Lewis.
    Wi-LT:764
  The Philippine Conquest.
    E. Masters. Kr-OF:80
  plato told. e. cummings.
    Ba-PO:187, Br-AF:84,
    Cr-WS:95, Hi-TL:209
  Recalling War. R. Graves.
    Wi-LT:373
  Recruiting Drive. C. Causley.
    Ha-TP:85, Ke-PP:115
  Remembering That Island.
    T. McGrath. Cr-WS:161, Ke-PP:91
  The Savage Century. C. Norman.
    Cr-WS:132
  The School Boy Reads His Iliad.
    D. Norton. Cr-WS:135
  Schoolday in Man Quang. D. Knight.
    Kr-OF:90
  The Send-Off. W. Owen. Cr-WS:61,
    Un-MB:368
  The Shield of Achilles. W. Auden.
    Pa-GTB:512
  Simple Statement. E. Thorne.
    Kr-OF:95

A Song of War Chariots. Tu Fu.
  Cr-WS:10
Spaniel's Sermons. C. Ellis.
  Cr-WS:138
The State. R. Jarrell.
  Wi-LT:564
Strange Meeting. W. Owen.
  Ba-PO:140
Swell's Soliloquy. Co-FB:222
Tell Brave Deeds of War.
  S. Crane. Cr-WS:158
There Was Crimson Clash of War.
  S. Crane. Cr-WS:158
"They." S. Sassoon. Cr-WS:118
They Say the Last Supper Is Badly
  Damaged. S. Yellen. Cr-WS:133
This Morning the Sub. O. Cabral.
  Ke-PP:103
To a Conscript of 1940. H. Read.
  Wi-LT:633
To a War Poet, on Teaching Him a
  New Country. D. Enright.
  Pl-ML:138
To Any Dead Officer. S. Sassoon.
  Cr-WS:111
To Make the People Happy. V. Hugo.
  Ba-PO:124, Ke-PP:63
To the Warmakers. E. Pierce.
  Cr-WS:26
To Touch. V. Schafer. Ad-II:97
The Trumpet. K. Douglas.
  Cr-WS:75
The Turkish Trench Dog. G. Dearmer.
  Co-BBW:101
Twenty Million. A. Kreymborg.
  Kr-OF:83
Ultima Ratio Regum. S. Spender.
  Er-FA:196, Pe-SS:139,
  To-MP:33, Wi-LT:501
The U.S. Sailor with the Japanese
  Skull. W. Scott. Pe-OA:207,
  Wi-LT:812
The Unkillable Knowledge.
  W. Everson. Ba-PO:181
The Unknown Soldier. B. Rose.
  Vi-PP:209
Unseen Fire. R. Currey. To-MP:42
Untitled Sonnet. J. Seligman.
  Cr-WS:30
The Voices of Peace Are Hushed.
  S. Himmell. Cr-WS:165
War Is Kind. S. Crane.
  Al-VBP:1113, Ba-PO:83, Cr-WS:158,
  Fe-PL:175, Hi-TL:155, Kr-OF:75,
  Mo-BG:169, Vi-PP:203, Wi-LT:118
War Is the Statesman's Game.
  P. Shelley. Ba-PO:157, Ke-PP:57
War-Monger. Kr-OF:96
War Song. J. Davidson.
  Ox-BN:905

The War-Song of Dinas Vawr.
  T. Peacock. Al-VBP:716,
  Ha-PO:220, Ho-WR:106, Mc-WS:105,
  Na-EO:110, Pa-OM:197
The War with Spain. B. Shadwell.
  Kr-OF:79
The War Year. Ts'ao Sung.
  Ba-PO:172, Cr-WS:15, Ke-PP:12
What Man First Forged.
  Tibullus. Ba-PO:73
When after Many Battles Past.
  Ba-PO:170
A Winter Scene. Kuo Mo-jo.
  Hs-TC:37
World War. Er-FA:206
ygUDuh. e. cummings. Ba-PO:188
You at Washington. E. Crosby.
  Kr-OF:71
SATIRE - WAR DEAD
  Draft Notice. D. Mourão-Ferreira.
    Cr-WS:47
  Let Us Now Passionately Remember.
    e. cummings. Kr-OF:84
  Lt. Cmdr. T. E. Sanderson.
    J. Scully. Ha-TP:87
  Lines for an Interment.
    A. MacLeish. Kr-OF:87
  Memo. C. Lynch. Ad-PB:461
  Odor of Blood. T. McGrath.
    Bl-FP:45
  The Only Son. H. Newbolt.
    Sp-OG:200
SATIRE - WAR SONGS AND CRIES
  All the Hills and Vales.
    C. Sorley. Un-MB:380
SATIRE - WAR WOUNDED
  Disabled. W. Owen.
    Co-PT:235, Wi-LT:354
  Does It Matter? S. Sassoon.
    Ke-PP:13, Un-MB:313
  Guerrilla Camp. K. Wilson.
    Ha-TP:89
  He Died a Second Time, 7.
    A Glance. Ai Ch'ing.
    Hs-TC:307
  Let Us Now Passionately Remember.
    e. cummings. Kr-OF:84
SATIRE - WASHINGTON, GEORGE
  Cameo No. II. J. Jordan.
    Ra-BP:243
  Patriotic Poem. D. Wakoski.
    Ca-VT:712
SATIRE - WASHINGTON, D.C.
  Bellies. J. Waters. Kr-OF:182
SATIRE - WEALTH
  American Primitive. W. Smith.
    Br-TC:393, Ke-PP:46, Un-MA:670
  The Cricket. Hsü Chih-mo. Hs-TC:91
  The Flower Market. Po-Chu-I.
    Ke-PP:10

God Made the Bees. Bl-OB:144,
  Un-GT:22
God to a Hungry Child.
  L. Hughes. Kr-OF:187
The Golf Links. S. Cleghorn.
  Er-FA:268, Fe-PL:421,
  Ke-PP:61, Kr-OF:180
Is It True? N. Rosten.
  Kr-OF:201
Metrum V. H. Vaughan. Ke-PP:32
Park Bench. L. Hughes.
  Kr-OF:188
Power Dive. H. MacCaig.
  Co-PU:73
SATIRE - WEDDINGS
  In the Room of the Bride-Elect.
    T. Hardy. Gr-BT:84
SATIRE - WELCOMES
  Homecoming. Chu Hsiang.
    Hs-TC:100
SATIRE - WELLS
  The Old Oaken Bucket. Er-FA:208
SATIRE - WESTWARD MOVEMENT
  Canto 89. E. Pound. Bl-FP:27
  The Indian and the Trout.
    E. Field. Kr-OF:18
  The Last Reservation.
    W. Learned. Kr-OF:16
SATIRE - WILDLIFE
  Part of the Darkness.
    I. Gardner. St-H:73
SATIRE - WILLIAM III AND MARY II,
    RULERS OF ENGLAND
  O What's the Rhyme to Porringer.
    Gr-GB:190
SATIRE - WILLS
  The Will. M. Halpern. Ho-TY:112
SATIRE - WISDOM
  Song about Fools. B. Okujava.
    Bo-RU:58
  The Young Man. C. Houselander.
    Ga-S:196
SATIRE - WISHES
  A Legend of Saint Martin.
    W. Bryant. Sp-OG:151
SATIRE - WITCHES AND WITCHCRAFT
  Salems of Oppression. J. Keith.
    De-FS:118
SATIRE - WOMEN
  The Cambridge Ladies.
    e. cummings. Al-VBP:1202,
    Ha-PO:243, Ke-PP:93, Rv-CB:991
  Choral Songs, III. Tr-US II:114
  I Look Hard at This World.
    V. Burich. Bo-RU:26
  To the Ladies. A. Kenseth. Ke-PP:27
  Two Ladies Bidding Us "Good
    Morning." J. Vaughn. Hu-NN:63
  What Soft, Cherubic Creatures.
    E. Dickinson. Ke-PP:92,Un-MA:102

SATIRE - WORDSWORTH, WILLIAM
  Peter Bell.   J. Reynolds.
    Ox-BN:402
  There Lived among the Untrodden
    Ways. H. Coleridge.
    Li-SR:107
SATIRE - WORK
  Mother and Daughter.
    J. Bovshover.   Kr-OF:170
  A Northern Suburb.
    J. Davidson.   Ox-BN:904
SATIRE - WORLD
  Reflections.   V. Howard.
    Jo-SA:2
  This Is a Coward's World.
    Hsü Chih-mo.   Hs-TC:79
SATIRE - WORLD WAR, 1939-1945
  Black-Out.   R. Jeffers.
    Wi-LT:262
  For the Lost Generation.
    G. Kinnell.   Ke-PP:58
  Hiroshima Crewman.
    G. Georgakas.   Sc-TN:61
  In a Surrealist Year.
    L. Ferlinghetti.   Ke-PP:3
SATIRE - WORSHIP
  In Westminster Abbey.
    J. Betjeman.   Ba-PO:183
  The Pipe.   H. Plisetsky.
    Bo-RU:65
SATIRE - YOUTH
  Clover Swaths.   J. Hearst.
    St-H:63
  To the Warmakers.   E. Pierce.
    Cr-WS:26
SATIRE - YOUTH AND AGE
  The Early Rebels.   M. Morris.
    Sa-B:9
  Of the Great White War.
    T. Burke.   Cr-WS:143
  The Old Men and the Young Men.
    W. Bynner.   Cr-WS:162
SATIRE - ZOOS
  Rimbaud Jingle.   T. McNeill.
    Sa-B:61
SATURDAY
  At Home.   Mo-MI:47
  Hymn for Saturday.   C. Smart.
    Ox-BC:74, Rv-CB:539, Sm-LG:68
  Laziness and Silence.
    R. Bly.   St-H:6
  Saturday in the County Seat.
    E. Jacobs.   Br-AF:220
  Saturday Shopping. K. Edelman.
    Au-SP:115
  Saturday, Sunday.   Wr-RM:69
  Saturday's Child.   C. Cullen.
    Ad-PB:86, Bo-HF:88, Wi-LT:616
  This Is Silver Saturday.
    Sp-TM:35

SATURN (GOD)
  The Green Dryad's Plea. T. Hood.
    Ox-BN:414
  Hyperion, I. J. Keats.
    Ox-BN:362
SATYRS
  The Crackling Twig. J. Stephens.
    Co-EL:158, Co-PU:134
  Holy Satyr.   H. D.   Un-MA:339
SAUK INDIANS: see INDIANS OF NORTH
    AMERICA - VERSE—ALGONQUIN
SAUL, KING OF ISRAEL
  David's Lament.   Bible. O.T.
    Samuel.   Gr-CT:343, Me-PH:12
  Saul.   R. Browning.   Hi-FO:23
SAUSAGES: see HUMOR - SAUSAGES
SAVING: see THRIFT
SAWS (TOOLS)
  Busy Carpenters.   J. Tippett.
    Au-SP:138
  Carpenters.   Ch-B:41
  Runs East and West.   Re-RR:71
  The Sacrificial Knife and the
    Simple Saw.   E. Steinberg.
    Ho-TY:232
  Sixth-Month Song in the Foothills.
    G. Snyder.   Ha-WR:7
  The Stump.   D. Hall.
    Du-RG:126, Pe-M:81
SAXOPHONES
  Albert Ayler: Eulogy for a
    Decomposed Saxophone Player.
    S. Crouch.   Ad-PB:486
SAYINGS AND SIGNS: see also
    EPIGRAMS; FOLKLORE; PROVERBS
  Adjuration.   F. Long.   De-FS:130
  And, to Make Trebly Sure.
    De-CH:635
  As Wet as a Fish.   Ir-BB:133,
    Un-GT:24
  August.   M. Lewis.   Un-GT:277
  The Beetle in the Wood.
    B. Reece.   Co-PT:40
  Birds of a Feather.   Un-GT:22,
    Wr-RM:93
  Blue Is True.   Un-GT:22
  Buttercup.   M. Dodge.   Gr-EC:291
  A Charm for Spring Flowers.
    R. Field.   Ar-TP3:211, Tu-WW:58
  Cheese and Bread for Gentlemen.
    Sp-TM:31
  Cocks Crow in the Morn.
    Ar-TP3:174, Sp-TM:1,
    Un-GT:22, Wr-RM:78
  The Cuckoo.   Ir-BB:76, Li-LB:164,
    Mo-MGT:20
  A Description of a City Shower.
    J. Swift.   Rv-CB:490
  Dream Signs.   Ju-CP:82
  Dreams.   Wr-RM:84

The Dree Night.   Gr-CT:364
Early to Bed.   An-IP:(10),
    Bo-FP:36, Ch-B:117, Li-LB:162,
    Mo-NR:122
Easter Gloves.   Bo-FP:246, De-PO:24
Epistle to Be Left in the Earth.
    A. MacLeish.   Pl-IO:55,
    Sm-PT:114, Un-MA:458
Evening Red and Morning Gray.
    Un-GT:22
The First of May.   Bo-FP:235,
    Mo-MGT:121, Mo-NR:91, Rv-ON:44,
    Wr-RM:66
For Every Evil under the Sun.
    Li-LB:161, Na-EO:161, Wr-RM:32
The Four Winds.   Bo-FP:217
Gnomic Verse from Cotton Manu-
    script.   Ma-YA:4
Go to Bed First.   Gr-CT:410,
    Gr-GB:17, Mo-MGT:39, On-TW:63,
    Rd-SS:7, Rv-ON:46
God Made the Bees.
    Bl-OB:144, Un-GT:22
Guy Fawkes Day.   Hi-FO:144,
    Li-LB:161, Mo-MGT:203
He That Would Thrive.
    Mo-MGT:131, Sp-TM:1
Hearthfire.   Ju-CP:81
Hee-Haw.   Rv-ON:40
Here Stand I Ever Lonely.
    De-CH:484
Hours of Sleep.   Un-GT:24
How They Bite.   Mo-SD:109
How to Sleep Easy.   Ag-HE:71,
    Mo-MGT:22
If Bees Stay at Home.   Un-GT:23
If Candlemas Day Be Fair and
    Bright.   Co-PS:30, Se-PR:42
If Ifs and Ands Were Pots and
    Pans.   Li-LB:160
If Wishes Were Horses.
    De-PO:22, Li-LB:160, Mo-MGT:97,
    Mo-NR:119, Wi-MG:31, Wr-RM:19
In Winter Time.   Ho-SD:35
The Little Red Spiders.   Jo-TS:14
Little Ships Must Keep the
    Shore.   Sp-HW:9
Lullaby for Ann-Lucian.
    C. Forbes.   Ad-PB:490
Mackerel Skies and Mares' Tails.
    Sp-HW:11
A Magpie Rhyme, Northumberland.
    Gr-GB:61
A Man of Words.   Bl-OB:156, De-TT:72,
    Er-FA:274, Gr-EC:208, Rv-CB:450,
    Rv-ON:115, Sm-LG:235, Sp-AS:35
March Will Search Ye.   De-CH:566
March Winds.   Au-SP:317, Br-SG:22,
    De-PO:26, Li-LB:160, Mo-MGT:148,
    Mo-NR:118, Un-GT:23, Wr-RM:120

Mirror, Mirror, Tell Me.   Un-GT:22
Monday's Child.   Au-SP:5,
    De-PO:14, Gr-EC:129, Li-LB:164,
    Mo-CC:(11), Mo-MGT:16,
    Mo-NR:19, Rv-CB:452, Sm-LG:97,
    Un-GT:22, Wi-MG:58, Wr-RM:87
Multiplication Is Vexation.
    Un-GT:23, Wr-RM:113
Needles and Pins.   Mo-NR:119,
    Un-GT:22, Wr-RM:92
Now You're Married You Must Obey.
    Un-GT:22
O Lady Moon.   C. Rossetti.
    Bo-FP:285, De-CH:690, De-TT:84,
    Ox-BC:277, Rd-SS:32
Observations.   Naladiyar.
    Al-PI:68
Old Jack Noman.   E. Thomas.
    Bl-OB:147
A Promise Made.   Er-FA:215
A Pullet in the Pen.   Ag-HE:19
Punctuality.   Mo-MGT:133
Putting on a Nightgown.
    Mo-MGT:120
Rain Before Seven.   Ju-CP:72,
    Mo-MGT:19, Un-GT:23
Rain, Rain, Go to Spain.
    Mo-NR:35, Wi-MG:59, Wr-RM:50
Rainbow at Night.   Bo-FP:261,
    Gr-EC:65, Un-GT:22
A Red Sky at Night.   Li-LB:161,
    Mo-MGT:103, Mo-NR:131
The Robin and the Wren.
    Bl-OB:64, Ch-B:49, De-TT:43
The Robin of the Red Breast.
    Co-PM:212, De-CH:547
Rock, Ball, Fiddle.   De-CH:446,
    De-TT:52, Mo-MGT:39, Rv-CB:454
St. Swithin's Day.   Li-LB:161,
    Un-GT:23
The Sea-Gull.   Gr-GB:62
See a Pin and Pick It Up.
    Li-LB:161, Mo-MGT:172, Mo-NR:119,
    Un-GT:23, Wr-RM:41
Seven Little Blackbirds.
    Ju-CP:77
Signs of Rain.   E. Jenner.
    Co-BN:165, De-TT:73
Signs of Winter.   J. Clare.
    Co-BN:201, Co-PS:150,
    Ho-LP:300, Ho-WR:168
Small Skill Is Gained.   Un-GT:22
Sneeze on Monday.   Ju-CP:80,
    Li-LB:165, Mo-NR:91, Na-EO:19,
    Wr-RM:128
The Stern Parent.   H. Graham.
    Co-BB:99, Gr-CT:470, Un-GF:48
Sticks and Stones May Break
    My Bones.   Mo-CC:(44)
Storms, Winds, Clouds.   Rv-ON:39

SAYINGS AND SIGNS — cont'd.
  Straws. E. Coatsworth.
    Br-AF:109
  Sunday Sail, Never Fail.
    Sp-HW:10
  A Sunshiny Shower. Bo-FP:227,
    Li-LB:161, Mo-NR:122,
    Un-CT:22, Wr-RM:122
  A Swarm of Bees in May.
    Li-LB:160, Wr-RM:17
  Ten Commandments, Seven Deadly
    Sins, and Five Wits. Gr-CT:168
  They That Wash on Monday.
    Bl-OB:145, Li-LB:163, Mo-TB:110
  Thirty Days Hath September.
    Au-SP:323, Bo-FP:139, Li-LB:165,
    Mo-MGT:172, Mo-NR:101, On-TW:59,
    Un-GT:22, Wi-MG:30, Wr-RM:17
  Thirty-Three Triads. Co-PI:87
  'Tis a Sin. De-CH:569
  To Be Said when Popping Corn.
    Rv-ON:45, Su-FVI:47
  To Kill the Eagle. Wo-HS:(54)
  To the Magpie. Mo-MGT:121
  Upon a Pipkin of Jellie.
    R. Herrick. Bo-GJ:24, De-CH:498,
    Gr-EC:291, Sm-LG:118
  Weather Rhymes. Ju-CP:72
  A Weather Rule. Hu-MP:285
  Wedding and Funeral. Gr-GB:320
  When Clouds Appear. Un-GT:23
  When Sea Birds Fly to Land.
    Sp-HW:11
  When Signs You See. Ju-CP:72
  When the Days Begin to Lengthen.
    Un-GT:22
  When the Milky Way You Spy.
    Wy-CM:23
  When the Rain Raineth.
    Gr-GB:57
  When the Wind Is in the East.
    Bo-FP:264, Li-LB:160, Mo-MGT:152,
    Mo-NR:91, Un-GT:23
  Wherever the Cat of the House.
    De-CH:545
  A Whistling Girl and a Flock of
    Sheep. Sp-TM:15
  White Horses. E. Farjeon.
    La-PV:123
  Wilful Waste Brings Woeful Want.
    Ag-HE:63
  Winter's Thunder. Li-LB:161,
    Rv-ON:37, Un-GT:23
  Witchwood. M. Justus.
    Br-SS:68, Ju-CP:75
  Yesterday Returneth Not. De-CH:485
  See also Ir-BB:226-231, Mo-TB
SCARECROWS: see also HUMOR -
    SCARECROWS
  Automation. P. Hubbell. Su-FVI:67

Don't Tell the Scarecrow.
    Yayu.   Do-TS:31
  Even Before His Majesty. Dansui.
    Ma-FW:139
  Grasshoppers Are Chirping.
    Chigetsu-Ni.   Do-TS:30
  The Lonely Scarecrow. J. Kirkup.
    Bl-OB:139, La-PV:69, Pa-RE:22
  The Scarecrow. W. de la Mare.
    Un-MB:202
  A Tumbled-Down Scarecrow.
    S. Saito. Sh-AM:170
  A Wintry Blizzard. Kyoroku.
    Be-MC:60
  With a Whispering Hiss. Boncho.
    Be-MC:36
SCARS
  Memoranda. W. Dickey. Du-SH:173
  R. G. E. R. Eberhart. Ls-NY:72
  The Scarred Girl. J. Dickey.
    Du-SH:69
  Stone Giant. J. Bruchac.
    Ni-CD:34
SCENTS: see ODORS
SCHOLARS AND SCHOLARSHIP: see also
    HUMOR - SCHOLARS AND SCHOLAR-
    SHIP; INTELLECTUALS; SATIRE -
    SCHOLARS AND SCHOLARSHIP
  Academic. J. Reeves. To-MP:72
  John Anderson. K. Douglas.
    Cr-WS:82
  Nor Let Them Fall under Discour-
    agement. J. Bunyan. De-CH:568
  On the Death of a Metaphysician.
    G. Santayana. Al-VBP:1088
  Professor Nocturnal.
    R. Roseliep. De-FS:158
  The Prologue to the Canterbury
    Tales. G. Chaucer. Al-VBP:6, 9,
    Gr-CT:281, Ha-PO:50, Ma-FW:17,
    Ma-YA:28
  The Sacred Order. M. Sarton.
    Pl-IO:155
  The Scholar. R. Southey.
    Pa-GTB:228
  A Scholar and His Dog.
    J. Marston. Go-BP:98
  The Scholar Gypsy. M. Arnold.
    Al-VBP:964, Gr-CT:255, Ox-BN:628
  Some Boys Have Wit Enough.
    De-CH:568
  Stanzas from the Grande
    Chartreuse. M. Arnold.
    Al-VBP:971
  To a Friend on Her Examination
    for the Doctorate in English.
    V. Cunningham.
    Ca-VT:325
  Verses. R. Bentley.
    Al-VBP:510

SCHOOL LIFE: see also COMMENCEMENTS;
    DROPOUTS; HUMOR - SCHOOL LIFE;
    STUDENTS; TEACHERS AND TEACHING
The Accident. R. Patterson.
    Ad-CI:102
After School: Room Three.
    W. Stafford. Ls-NY:221
Among School Children. W. Yeats.
    Pa-GTB:428, Un-MB:114, Wi-LT:72
At School. D. Marstiller.
    Ho-CT:31
At This Farewell. W. Wordsworth.
    Se-PR:243
The Ballad of Chocolate Mabbie.
    G. Brooks. Pe-SS:30
Big Brother. E. Roberts.
    Fe-FP:41, Hu-MP:9
Blue Girls. J. Ransom.
    Ca-VT:150, Gr-CC:79, Gr-CT:51,
    Ha-PO:183, Mc-WS:75, Pe-OA:137,
    Sh-AP:182, Un-MA:409
The Brothers. A. Groesbeck.
    De-FS:102
The Campus on the Hill.
    W. Snodgrass. Wi-LT:821
Cathexis. F. Bryant.
    Ad-PB:406
The Child in School. Le-MW:106
The Description of a Good Boy.
    H. Dixon. Ox-BC:54
An Elementary School Class
    Room in a Slum. S. Spender.
    Br-TC:403, Ke-PP:50,
    To-MP:26, Un-MB:403
First Departure. F. Frost.
    Br-SS:57
For a Junior School Poetry
    Book. C. Middleton.
    Ma-FW:70, To-MP:151
Gee, You're So Beautiful
    that It's Starting to Rain.
    R. Brautigan. Kh-VA:14
The General Public. S. Benét.
    Pl-ML:125
Getting Back. D. Thompson.
    Br-SS:56
Graduation. J. Heinegg.
    Ad-II:64
Ha Ha Thisaway. Bu-DY:33
Harvest. A. Hartich. Ke-TF:447
The High School Band.
    R. Whittemore. Pe-M:9
In a Girls' School. D. Morton.
    Se-PR:243
It Lies in the Groove.
    N. Qualthrough. Le-M:26
Kindergarten. R. Rogers.
    Al-WW:87
The Lesson. E. Lucie-Smith.
    Br-TC:271, Gr-BT:20, To-MP:99

London Snow. R. Bridges.
    Co-BN:196, De-CH:220, Gr-CT:308,
    Ha-PO:87, Hi-WP I:126, Ho-WR:183,
    Ma-YA:218, Ni-JP:141, Ox-BN:874,
    Pa-GTB:414, Un-MB:50, Wi-LT:52
Mary's Lamb. S. Hale. Au-SP:17,
    De-PO:12, Er-FA:504, Fe-FP:529,
    Fr-WO:25, Li-LB:94, Mo-CC:(38),
    Mo-MGT:120, Ox-BC:166, Un-GT:34,
    Wi-MG:67
Noon Hour. J. Finnigan.
    Gr-BT:115
Ode on a Distant Prospect of
    Clapham Academy. T. Hood.
    Rv-CB:763
Ode on a Distant Prospect of
    Eton College. T. Gray.
    Al-VBP:563, Pa-GTB:158
Our Teacher's Angry Face.
    A. Mori. Le-TA:63
Patti. Ca-MU:24
The Plaza and the Flaming Orange
    Trees. A. Machado. Le-SW:23
School. B. Cleave. Ja-PA:21
School-Bell. E. Farjeon.
    Br-SS:55, Fe-FP:19
School Days in New Amsterdam.
    A. Guiterman. Fe-FP:411
The School Servant. Suifu.
    Le-MW:107
The Schoolboy. W. Blake.
    Co-BN:95, De-CH:131,
    Ma-FW:136, Rv-CB:594
A Schoolboy's Lament. Mo-MI:85
A Schoolmaster's Admonition.
    Ox-BC:21
A Schoolmaster's Precepts.
    J. Penkethman. Ox-BC:26
Sing-Song Rhyme. Br-SS:58
A Snowy Day in School.
    D. Lawrence. Ma-FW:75
Timothy Winters. C. Causley.
    Sm-MK:123, To-MP:73
Tripart, I. G. Jones. Jo-SA:13
Twenty Froggies. G. Cooper.
    Bo-FP:76, Ch-B:108,
    Co-IW:10, It-HB:49
The Unhappy Schoolboy.
    Ox-BC:11
Van Winkle. H. Crane.
    Ga-FB:269, Sh-AP:199, Un-MA:521
The Village Schoolmaster.
    O. Goldsmith. Ha-PO:76
Vitai Lampada. H. Newbolt.
    Sp-OG:17
The Wind Was Bringing Me to
    School. J. Snyder. Le-M:25
SCHOOLHOUSES: see also SCHOOL LIFE
In School Days. J. Whittier.
    Fe-FP:543, Hu-MP:406, Ox-BC:272

SCHOPENHAUER, ARTHUR: see HUMOR -
   SCHOPENHAUER, ARTHUR
SCHUBERT, FRANZ PETER
   For M.S. Singing Frühlingsglaube
      in 1945. F. Cornford. Pl-US:65
SCIENCE: see also HUMOR - SCIENCE;
   SATIRE - SCIENCE; and names of
   scientists, as EINSTEIN, ALBERT
   Arcturus Is His Other Name.
      E. Dickinson. Ga-FB:148
   Dr. Sigmund Freud Discovers the
      Sea Shell. A. MacLeish.
      Ke-PP:82, Pe-OA:160
   Epilogue. H. Melville.
      Pl-IO:128
   The Gift to Be Simple. H. Moss.
      Br-TC:307, Pl-IO:181, Tr-MR:174
   The Laboratory Midnight.
      R. Denney. Pl-IO:70
   Laboratory Poem. J. Merrill.
      Br-TC:286
   Letter to Alex Comfort.
      D. Abse. Br-TC:1
   New York * December * 1931.
      B. Deutsch. Pl-IO:149
   No Single Thing Abides.
      T. Lucretius Carus. Pl-IO:9
   Poems, 1930-1940. H. Gregory.
      Sm-PT:118
   Science in God. R. Herrick.
      Pl-IO:61
   To Science. E. Poe. Ke-PP:81,
      Rv-CB:805, Sh-AP:46
   The Two Deserts. C. Patmore.
      Co-BN:220
SCIENCE FICTION: see HUMOR -
   SCIENCE FICTION
SCISSORS
   North, South. Re-RR:90
   The Scissor-Man. M. Nightingale.
      Ar-TP3:10, Hu-MP:145, Ir-BB:118
   Scissors. Y. Tazaki. Le-TA:45
   The Scissors Grinder. R. Roseliep.
      De-FS:162
SCOLDING: see REPRIMANDS
SCORN: see CONTEMPT
SCORPIONS: see also HUMOR -
   SCORPIONS
   Night of the Scorpion.
      N. Ezekial. Al-PI:96
   The Scorpion. H. Belloc. Ir-BB:75
   The Scorpion. Ca-MU:16
SCOTLAND: see also BAGPIPES;
   BALLADS, ENGLISH AND SCOTTISH;
   HUMOR - SCOTLAND; and names of
   Scottish towns, as EDINBURGH,
   SCOT.
   Childhood. Ma-FW:67
   The Cotter's Saturday Night.
      R. Burns. Fe-PL:58

   The Loyal Scot. A. Marvell.
      Al-VBP:461
   My Native Land. W. Scott.
      Er-FA:286, Hu-MP:362, Mc-PR:32,
      Ox-BN:127, Pa-HT:147, Sp-OG:188,
      Vi-PP:25
   The Princess of Scotland.
      R. Taylor. Gr-SS:123
   The Rebel Scot. J. Cleveland.
      Al-VBP:441
   Scotland. H. MacDiarmid.
      Un-MB:359
SCOTLAND - CLANS
   The Bonny House of Airlie.
      Ma-BB:130, Ox-BB:614
   Lullaby of an Infant Chief.
      W. Scott. Bo-FP:45, Fe-FP:463,
      Hu-MP:122, Ox-BC:147, Un-GT:297
   March, March. W. Scott.
      Al-VBP:678
   Pibroch of Donuil Dhu. W. Scott.
      Hi-FO:100, Pa-GTB:202
   The Pipes at Lucknow.
      J. Whittier. Hi-FO:241
SCOTLAND - COUNTRYSIDE
   The Dreary Change. W. Scott.
      Ox-BN:134
   In the Highlands. R. Stevenson.
      Cl-DT:46, Ga-FB:241
   Inversnaid. G. Hopkins.
      Fr-WO:88, Pa-GTB:393, Un-MB:45,
      Wi-LT:45
   My Heart's in the Highlands.
      R. Burns. Bl-OB:141, Cl-FC:62,
      Er-FA:424, Fe-FP:463, Mc-PR:175,
      Mc-WK:192, Mo-SD:118, Pa-HT:149
   O Alva Hills Is Bonny. De-CH:518
   Rannoch, by Glencoe. T. Eliot.
      Sm-LG:143
   The River Don. Gr-GB:175
   Sweet Afton. R. Burns. Co-BN:73,
      Er-FA:428, Mc-PR:17, Un-MW:154
   Tintock-Tap. Gr-GB:177
   Yarrow Unvisited, 1803.
      W. Wordsworth. Pa-GTB:264
SCOTLAND - HISTORY AND PATRIOTISM:
   see also BORDER WARS
   The Battle of Killikrankie.
      W. Aytoun. Hi-FO:163
   The Bonny Earl of Murray.
      Bl-OB:152, Co-RM:206, Ma-BB:36,
      Ox-BB:594, Rv-CB:35, Sm-LG:271
   The Bonny Moorhen. Gr-GB:191
   Canadian Boat Song. J. Galt.
      Ox-BN:204, Rv-CB:683, Sm-LG:140
   Charlie, He's My Darling. R. Burns.
      Al-VBP:652, De-CH:174
   Edinburgh. A. Noyes. Pa-HT:145
   The Execution of Montrose.
      W. Aytoun. Pa-OM:96

The Farewell. R. Burns.
Al-VBP:377, De-CH:175
Flodden. W. Scott. Hi-FO:111
The Flowers of the Forest.
J. Elliott. Al-VBP:582,
De-CH:176, Pa-GTB:120
The Lady of the Lake. W. Scott.
Al-VBP:671
The Laird o' Logie. De-CH:412,
Rv-CB:49
Lament for Culloden. R. Burns.
Pa-GTB:119, Rv-CB:614
March, March. W. Scott.
Al-VBP:678
Moy Castle. Un-GT:112
Pibroch of Donuil Dhu. W. Scott.
Hi-FO:100, Pa-GTB:202
Scots Wha Hae. R. Burns.
Hi-FO:83, Ma-YA:135,
Sm-LG:154, Sp-OG:189
Sir Andrew Bartton. Ox-BB:508
There'll Never Be Peace.
R. Burns. Rv-CB:626
SCOTSMEN: see also DIALECTS,
SCOTTISH; HUMOR - SCOTSMEN;
and names of famous Scots-
men, as BURNS, ROBERT
Bonnie Annie Livieston.
Ox-BB:254
Ech, Sic a Pairish. Co-FB:222
Lady Maisry. Ox-BB:295
The Revenge of Hamish. S. Lanier.
Ni-JP:46, Sp-OG:141
A Scot, a Welsh and an Irish Man.
Gr-GB:165
Scotch Rhapsody. E. Sitwell.
Br-TC:190
SCOTT, SIR WALTER: see also HUMOR -
SCOTT, SIR WALTER
Edinburgh. A. Noyes. Pa-HT:145
SCOTT-MONCRIEFF, ANN
For Ann Scott-Moncrieff. E. Muir.
Gr-SS:119, Pa-GTB:469
SCOTTISH BALLADS: see BALLADS,
ENGLISH AND SCOTTISH
SCOTTSBORO CASE
A Communication to Nancy Cunard.
K. Boyle. Hu-PN:530
first monday scottsboro alabama.
T. Weatherly. Ad-PB:399
Scottsboro, Too, Is Worth Its
Song. C. Cullen. Ad-PB:93,
Be-MA:52
They Are Ours. A. Magil. Hu-PN:533
The Trial. M. Rukeyser. Hu-PN:560
SCOUTS AND SCOUTING: see BOY SCOUTS;
and names of famous scouts, as
BOONE, DANIEL
SCRANTON, PA.: see HUMOR -
SCRANTON, PA.

SCRATCHING: see ITCHINESS
SCRIBES
The Scribe. W. de la Mare.
Sm-LG:35, Tr-MR:24
SCULPTORS AND SCULPTURE: see also
STATUES; and names of sculptors,
as MICHELANGELO BUONARROTI
An Artist. R. Jeffers.
Ca-VT:122
Chisel. I. Brad. Mc-AC:141
Divina Commedia. H. Longfellow.
Sh-AP:36
Ecstacy. W. Turner. De-CH:388
For Jerriann's Hands. M. Piercy.
Sc-TN:188
The Image-Maker. O. Gogarty.
Go-BP:63
Lapis Lazuli. W. Yeats.
Wi-LT:89
The Medici Tombs. W. Ross.
Ls-NY:236
The Prisoner. I. Stark.
Ls-NY:180
Sculpture. Fe-PL:312
The Statue. R. Humphries.
Ni-JP:127
SCYTHES
Scythe Song. A. Lang. Sp-OG:309
SCYTHIANS
The Scythians. A. Blok.
Ca-MR:198
SEA ANEMONES
By the Sea. C. Rossetti.
Co-BN:75
Carmel Point. M. MacSweeney.
Du-RG:75
SEA CHANTEYS: see SEA SONGS
SEA GULLS: see GULLS
SEA HOLLY
Sea Holly. C. Aiken.
Wi-LT:331
SEA HORSES (FISH)
Sea Horse. Ab-MO:60
SEA SHELLS: see SHELLS (MOLLUSKS)
SEA SONGS
As I Walked Out One Sunny Morn.
Sp-HW:28
Away, Rio. Sm-LG:338
The Ballad of Hagensack.
W. Irwin. Co-PT:272
A Ballad of John Silver.
J. Masefield. Co-SS:13,
Hu-MP:421, Na-EO:163
Blow, Ye Winds. Co-SS:105
By the Deep Nine. W. Pearce.
Gr-CT:225
The Chinese Bumboatman. Co-SS:113
The Clipper Dunbar to the Clipper
Cutty Sark. E. Anderson.
Co-PT:249

SEA SONGS — cont'd.
  The Codfish Shanty. Gr-GB:179
  Come Loose Every Sail to the
    Breeze. Co-SS:101
  The Coxswain's Line. H. Cressman.
    Sh-RP:255
  Derelict. Y. Allison. Co-SS:17,
    Er-FA:436, Pa-OM:204
  The Eddystone Light. Co-SS:103,
    Ha-PO:271
  The Fishes. Co-SS:107, Gr-GB:72
  The Gals o' Dublin Town.
    Co-SS:111
  Hanging Johnny. Gr-GB:271
  Haul Away Joe. Co-SS:99
  Hell's Pavement. J. Masefield.
    Co-PT:272
  The Irish Rover. Co-SS:120
  Jack Was Every Inch a Sailor.
    Do-WH:18
  John Cherokee. Gr-GB:267
  The Last Chantey. R. Kipling.
    Sm-LG:335, Un-MB:136
  Lowlands. Gr-CT:229
  Mariners' Carol. W. Merwin.
    Pl-EI:208
  The Mermaid. Co-SS:109
  The Queen of Connemara.
    F. Fahy. Co-PI:38
  The Salcombe Seaman's Flaunt to
    the Proud Pirate. Gr-CT:224
  Sea Chant. Tr-US II:35
  A Sea-Chantey. D. Walcott.
    Lo-TY:111
  Sea Chanty. A. Burrows.
    Co-SS:122
  Spanish Ladies. Sm-LG:311
  Stormey's Dead. De-CH:709
  Tarpauling Jacket. Co-RM:64
  The Walloping Window-Blind.
    C. Carryl. Co-HP:48, Fe-FP:343,
    Hu-MP:450, Lo-LL:90, Sh-RP:123,
    Un-GF:30, Un-GT:220
  The Whale. Co-SS:115, Gr-CT:208,
    Gr-GB:217
  See also Em-AF:479-529
SEA URCHINS: see HUMOR - SEA
    URCHINS
SEAFARING LIFE: see also ADMIRALS;
    HUMOR - SEAFARING LIFE; NAVAL
    BATTLES; RIVER LIFE; SEAMEN;
    SHIPS
  Alec Yeaton's Son. T. Aldrich.
    Sp-OG:92
  The Anchorage. P. Wilson.
    Co-SS:172
  Another Song from Arsut.
    Tr-US I:5
  At Melville's Tomb. H. Crane.
    Ca-VT:214, Un-MA:534

At the Fishhouses. E. Bishop.
  Wi-LT:512
Away, Rio. Sm-LG:338
Ballad. W. Soutar. Hi-WP I:89
The Ballad of Kon-Tiki.
  I. Serraillier. Co-SS:223
The Ballad of the "Bolivar."
  R. Kipling. Sp-OG:79
The Banks of Newfoundland.
  Gr-GB:219
Beowulf's Voyage to Denmark.
  Ma-FW:45
Billy in the Darbies. H. Melville.
  Mo-BG:160, Rv-CB:835
Boats in a Fog. R. Jeffers.
  Mo-BG:143
Brown Robyn's Confession.
  De-CH:399, Gr-GB:314
By the Deep Nine. W. Pearce.
  Gr-CT:225
El Capitan-General. C. Leland.
  Co-SS:25
The Captains of Small Farms.
  R. Coffin. Sh-RP:308
Cargoes. J. Masefield.
  Ar-TP3:90, Bo-FP:134, Co-RG:56,
  Co-SS:75, Fe-FP:196, Ga-FB:182,
  Hi-WP I:109, Mc-PR:135,
  Th-AS:130, Un-MB:225, Wi-LT:189
The Castaway. W. Cowper.
  Ha-PO:135, Rv-CB:551
The Child and the Mariner.
  W. Davies. De-CH:383
Christmas at Sea. R. Stevenson.
  Co-SS:207, De-CH:28, Ga-FB:183,
  Ha-PO:251, Ma-YA:220, Sp-OG:257
Citizens in the Round.
  R. Coffin. Sh-RP:290
Clipper Ships and Captains.
  S. Benét. Sh-RP:298
Complaint of a Fisherman's
  Widow. Tr-US I:158
The Country Bedroom.
  F. Cornford. Bl-OB:137,
  Pa-RE:87, Un-MB:306
The Coxswain's Line. H. Cressman.
  Sh-RP:255
The Deckhands. Co-RM:53
Derelict. Y. Allison. Co-SS:17,
  Er-FA:436, Pa-OM:204
Drake's Drum. H. Newbolt.
  Co-SS:58, De-TT:195,
  Hi-FO:128, Hi-WP I:68
Dreams of a Summer Night.
  G. Barker. Ma-FW:51
Duriesdyke. Ox-BB:686
The Fire of Drift-Wood.
  H. Longfellow. Mo-BG:148
The First Essential.
  I. Gheorghe. Mc-AC:152

Fisherman's Song. W. Brown.
Sa-B:18
Fishing Harbour Towards Evening.
R. Kell. To-MP:133
Fog. C. Garstin. Co-SS:42
The Frolic Mariners of Devon.
W. Browne. Gr-CT:218
The Golden City of St. Mary.
J. Masefield. Bo-HF:82, Pa-HT:157
The Great Sea. Bi-IT:124,
Ma-BH:18
A Greyport Legend. B. Harte.
Sp-OG:83
The Hanging of Billy Budd.
K. Wilson. Sc-TN:242
How Good Are the Poor. V. Hugo.
Ke-TF:61
How's My Boy? S. Dobell. De-CH:31
In Wintry Midnight, o'er a Stormy
Main. F. Petrarch. Gr-CT:229
John Marr. H. Melville. Al-VBP:952
Kalymniad, Part II. R. Lax.
Sc-TN:127
The Last Chantey. R. Kipling.
Sm-LG:335, Un-MB:136
Leave Her, Johnny. Sm-MK:71
Life's Circumnavigators.
W. Rodgers. Pa-GTB:530
The Long Trail. R. Kipling.
Al-VBP:1095, Ga-FB:185, Sp-OG:253
Looking at the Moon on Putting
Out from the Shore at Nagato.
Ma-FW:53
The Lowlands of Holland.
Ox-BB:348
Luck. W. Gibson. Co-SS:72,
Gr-EC:211, Pa-RE:98, Sm-MK:63
M'Andrew's Hymn. R. Kipling.
Ga-S:119
Mariners' Carol. W. Merwin.
Pl-EI:208
Maximus of Gloucester, to You.
C. Olson. Wi-LT:778
Mulholland's Contract.
R. Kipling. Co-SS:210
Nearing La Guaira. D. Walcott.
Lo-TY:113
The Nightfishing. W. Graham.
Ma-FW:48
The North Ship. P. Larkin.
Ma-FW:50
Old Gray Squirrel. A. Noyes.
Co-SS:215
The Old Ships. J. Flecker.
Co-RG:57, De-CH:363, De-TT:194,
Go-BP:156, Hi-FO:15, Na-EO:114,
No-CL:254, Pa-HT:95, Un-MB:272
On a Friday Morn. De-TT:130
On a Steamer. D. Baruch.
Fe-FP:192

The Rime of the Ancient Mariner.
S. Coleridge. Al-VBP:679,
Bo-FP:301, Co-RG:60, Co-SS:131,
De-CH:364, Er-FA:318, Fe-FP:147,
Ga-FB:105, Gr-TG:61, Ha-PO:15,
Hi-WP II:68, Ma-YA:146, Ni-JP:52,
Ox-BN:139, Rv-CB:658, Sm-LG:312,
Un-GT:30
Roadways. J. Masefield.
Pa-HT:78, Sh-RP:157
Rounding the Horn. J. Masefield.
Un-MB:223
Rumilda's Chant. G. Darley.
Co-PI:33, Co-SS:31, Gr-CT:222
The Sailor's Wife. W. Mickle.
Al-VBP:600, De-TT:110, Pa-GTB:154
Salem. R. Lowell. Mo-BG:141
Sea Change. J. Masefield.
Co-PT:263
Sea Chant. Tr-US II:35
Sea Fever. J. Masefield.
Ar-TP3:90, Co-SS:55, Fe-FP:190,
Fe-PL:440, Ga-FB:182, Hu-MP:174,
La-PV:185, Ma-YA:232, Mc-PR:134,
Pe-FB:43, Sh-RP:33, Th-AS:127,
Un-MB:221
The Sea Gypsy. R. Hovey.
Co-SS:76, Fe-FP:191, La-PV:186,
Sh-RP:285, Un-GT:261
Sea Song. T. Beddoes.
De-CH:364, Un-GT:262
The Seafarer. E. Pound.
Sh-AP:171
The Seafarer. Ma-YA:5
The Seaman's Happy Return.
Gr-CT:64, Gr-GB:119
The Secret of the Sea.
H. Longfellow. Un-GT:261
She Is Far from the Land.
T. Hood. Ho-WR:129
The Ship. J. Squire.
De-CH:402, De-TT:133
A Ship for Singapore.
D. Hicky. Th-AS:129
The Ships of Yule. B. Carman.
Br-BC:126, Do-WH:16, Sh-RP:168
Song for All Seas, All Ships.
W. Whitman. Tr-MR:175
Song of a Navigator's Wife.
Tr-US II:16
Song of a Returning Voyager.
Tr-US II:41
Song of a Woman Named Hi Pak.
Hi Pak. Tr-US I:207
Song of the Galley-Slaves.
R. Kipling. Gr-CT:223,
Pa-GTB:421
The Sound of the Wind.
C. Rossetti. Ar-TP3:165,
Bl-OB:58

SEAFARING LIFE — cont'd.
  Spanish Ladies. Sm-LG:311
  Spanish Waters. J. Masefield.
    Fe-FP:514, Mc-WK:141, Pa-OM:207
  Square-Toed Princes. R. Coffin.
    Br-AF:129
  Storm at Sea. W. Davenant.
    Co-RG:43, Co-RM:41
  The Story of Vinland.
    S. Lanier. Hi-TL:9
  Sweet and Low. A. Tennyson.
    Bl-OB:160, Ch-B:47, Cl-DT:29,
    Co-SS:48, De-TT:84, Fe-FP:54,
    Fe-PL:245, Hu-MP:122, Ma-YA:192,
    Ox-BC:212, Re-TW:73, Sm-MK:225,
    Sp-OG:312, Un-GT:300
  The Tarry Buccaneer.
    J. Masefield. Co-PT:213
  The Three Fishers. C. Kingsley.
    Co-SS:205, Fe-PL:418,
    Pa-OM:117, Sp-OG:91
  To the Harbormaster. F. O'Hara.
    Mc-EA:168, Mo-BG:97
  Twilight. H. Longfellow.
    De-CH:30
  Ulysses. A. Tennyson.
    Al-VBP:863, Ha-PO:40, Ke-TF:262,
    Ni-JP:16, Rv-CB:793
  Voices. J. Hearst. Th-AS:128
  A Wanderer's Song. J. Masefield.
    Sh-RP:158, Tu-WW:32, Un-MB:222
  The Way of Cape Race.
    E. Pratt. Do-WH:47
  We'll Go to Sea No More.
    Co-SS:62, Gr-CT:220, Gr-GB:215
  The Wet Litany. R. Kipling.
    Gr-SS:189
  A Wet Sheet and a Flowing Sea.
    A. Cunningham. Ar-TP3:89,
    Bl-OB:46, Bo-FP:280, Cl-FC:54,
    Co-RG:49, Mc-PR:167, Mc-WK:193,
    Pa-GTB:203, Sp-OG:82
  Where Lies the Land? A. Clough.
    Co-SS:73, Gr-CT:217,
    Ox-BN:78, Sm-LG:299
  Who Pilots Ships. D. Hickey.
    Th-AS:131
  Wind. T. Hughes. Ma-FW:37
  Wind, Waves, and Sails.
    M. La Rue. Co-SS:70
  A Windy Day. W. Howard. Fe-FP:191
  Winter Views Serene. G. Crabbe.
    Ox-BN:9
  Women's Ur-Dance Song. Tr-US II:12
  The World's a Sea. F. Quarles.
    Gr-CT:231
  The Yarn of the Loch Achray.
    J. Masefield. Co-SS:139,
    Ha-PO:252
  See also Sp-HW

SEALE, BOBBY G.
  to Bobby Seale. L. Clifton.
    Ad-PB:308
SEALS (ANIMALS)
  At the Fishhouses. E. Bishop.
    Wi-LT:512
  The Dancing Seal. W. Gibson.
    Co-PU:68, Pa-OM:289
  Deeply Gone. J. Silkin.
    De-FS:177
  The Great Silkie of Sule Skerrie.
    Gr-CT:206, Gr-GB:282,
    Ma-BB:18, Ox-BB:91
  Hard Times, Dearth Times.
    Ma-BH:13
  The Moon-Child. F. Macleod.
    De-CH:402
  Orphan. Le-IB:69
  Orpingalik's Song: My Breath.
    Tr-US I:17
  The Real Slayer of the Seal.
    Da-SC:45, Le-IB:52
  Religious Hymn to Be Sung
    Wearing a Head Decoration.
    Le-IB:95, Ma-BH:15, Tr-US I:20
  Seal. W. Smith. Co-BBW:63,
    Du-RG:29, La-RM:101, Un-GT:68
  Seal Lullaby. R. Kipling.
    Ar-TP3:80, Co-PU:86, Fe-FP:177,
    Mc-PR:60, Mc-WS:47, Rd-SS:19
  The Seals. D. Aldis.
    Ar-TP3:80
  The Seals in Penobscot Bay.
    D. Hoffman. Br-TC:191
  Seals, Terns, Time. R. Eberhart.
    Un-MA:580, Wi-LT:436
  Soft Wood. R. Lowell.
    Wi-LT:581
SEAMEN: see also DIALECTS, SEAMAN;
    HUMOR - SEAMEN; SEAFARING LIFE;
    SHIPS
  Admiral Death. H. Newbolt.
    Co-RM:62
  Admirals All. H. Newbolt.
    Co-RM:51
  As I Walked Out One Night.
    De-CH:596
  As I Went up the Garden.
    St-FS:35
  At the Port. R. Iceland. Ho-TY:116
  Awake, Awake, You Weary Sleepers.
    Sp-HW:14
  A Ballad of Sir John Franklin.
    G. Baker. Pa-OM:109
  The Ballad of the "Bolivar."
    R. Kipling. Sp-OG:79
  The Banks of Newfoundland. Gr-GB:219
  Billy Taylor. Rv-ON:103
  Black-Eyed Susan. J. Gay. Co-RG:82,
    Co-SS:66, De-TT:129, Pa-GTB:124

Bobby Shafto.   De-CH:682, De-TT:30,
    Gr-GB:104, Hu-MP:164, Mo-MGT:151,
    Wi-MG:31, Wr-RM:127
But Do You Think Our Life Is Hard.
    Sp-HW:33
Cam' Ye By?   De-CH:32, Gr-GB:105
The Child and the Mariner.
    W. Davies.   De-CH:383
Clipper Captain.   S. Barker.
    Mc-WK:183
The Coromandel Fishers.
    S. Naidu.   Sh-RP:26
The Coxswain's Line.   H. Cressman.
    Sh-RP:255
The Deckhands.   Co-RM:53
The Farmer's Heart with Joy Is
    Filled.   Sp-HW:32
For the Unknown Seamen of the
    1939-45 War Buried in Iona
    Churchyard.   I. Smith.
    Go-BP:212
Forty Singing Seamen.   A. Noyes.
    Pa-OM:197
Harp Song of the Dane Women.
    R. Kipling.   Co-RM:55, Ox-BN:931
How's My Boy?   S. Dobell.
    De-CH:31
I Sing for You.   Lin Ling.
    Pa-MV:109
In the Late Autumn.   A. Blok.
    Ca-MR:191
Jim at the Corner.   E. Farjeon.
    Au-SP:151
Kingdoms.   O. Gogarty.   Pa-RE:90
The Knight Without a Name.
    Ho-WR:122
Leave Her, Johnny.   Sm-MK:71
Loss of the Royal George.
    W. Cowper.   Co-RG:44, Co-SS:137,
    Pa-GTB:123, Rv-CB:552, Sp-OG:73
Luck.   W. Gibson.   Co-SS:72,
    Gr-EC:211, Pa-RE:98, Sm-MK:63
A Maine Roustabout.   R. Eberhart.
    Ha-TP:45
Mariners.   M. Morris.   Sa-B:160
The Men of Gotham.   T. Peacock.
    Al-VBP:715, De-CH:193,
    Hi-WP I:91, Ho-WR:108, Sp-OG:344
Messmates.   H. Newbolt.   De-CH:167
My Mother Sent Me for Some
    Water.   Sp-HW:6
Neglectful Edward.   R. Graves.
    Un-MB:383
The Night a Sailor Came to Me in
    a Dream.   D. Wakoski.   Ca-VT:714
Nursery Rhyme of Innocence and
    Experience.   C. Causley.
    Bo-GJ:170, Hi-WP I:82
O, Fare You Well.
    Sp-HW:8

O Kitty Karson, Jilted the
    Parson.   Sp-HW:29
Over the Water.   De-TT:30,
    Sp-HW:4, Wr-RM:85
Peg-Leg's Fiddle.   B. Adams.
    Sh-RP:53
Posted as Missing.   J. Masefield.
    Bl-OB:51
The Puritan's Ballad.   E. Wylie.
    Co-BL:92
Putting to Sea.   L. Bogan.
    Wi-LT:381
The Quaker Graveyard in Nantucket.
    R. Lowell.   Al-VBP:1248,
    Pa-HT:25, Wi-LT:573
Rari for the Americans.   Eina'a.
    Tr-US II:94
Rasta Fishermen.   W. Brown.
    Sa-B:70
Red Iron Ore.   Ar-TP3:91
The Return of the Marama from
    Hiti.   Tr-US II:72
The Rime of the Ancient Mariner.
    S. Coleridge.   Al-VBP:679,
    Co-RG:60, Co-SS:131, De-CH:364,
    Er-FA:318, Ga-FB:105, Ha-PO:15,
    Hi-WP II:68, Ma-YA:146,
    Ni-JP:52, Ox-BN:139, Rv-CB:658,
    Sm-LG:312
Rounding the Horn.   J. Masefield.
    Un-MB:223
Rousecastle.   D. Wright.
    Ca-MB:81, Co-SS:195
Sailor.   E. Farjeon.   Pe-FB:29
Sailor.   L. Hughes.   Bo-HF:80,
    Gr-EC:210
Sailor and Tailor.   De-TT:127
Sailor on Leave.   O. Dodson.
    Bo-AN:126
Sailors.   B. Weinstein.
    Ho-TY:293
Sea Fever.   J. Masefield.
    Ar-TP3:90, Co-SS:55, Fe-FP:190,
    Fe-PL:440, Ga-FB:182, Hu-MP:174,
    La-PV:185, Ma-YA:232, Mc-PR:134,
    Pe-FB:43, Sh-RP:33, Th-AS:127,
    Un-MB:221
A Sea Song from the Shore.
    J. Riley.   Ch-B:37
Seumas Beg.   J. Stephens.   Bl-OB:144,
    Co-RM:63, Fe-FP:318, Na-EO:155
Song for All Seas, All Ships.
    W. Whitman.   De-CH:167, Tr-MR:175
Spanish Ladies.   Sm-LG:311
There Ain't but the One Thing
    Grieves My Mind.   Sp-HW:7
To New York Town We Bid Adieu.
    Sp-HW:20
Watson and the Shark.
    P. Petrie.   Ls-NY:37

SEAMEN — cont'd.
  What Shall We Do for the Striking
    Seamen? Hi-TL:199
  Ye Mariners of England.
    T. Campbell. Mc-PR:148,
    Pa-GTB:204, Rv-CB:676
SEARCHES: see QUESTS
SEARCHING AND FINDING RHYMES
  My Little Maid. Wr-RM:101
SEAS: see also HUMOR - SEAS;
    NEPTUNE; OCEANS; SEASHORE;
    TIDES; WAVES; and names of
    seas, as CARIBBEAN SEA
  Absences. P. Larkin.
    En-PC:202
  At Dunwich. A. Thwaite.
    Ca-MB:89
  The Atheist's Tragedy.
    C. Tourneur. Al-VBP:273
  Beach Glass. H. Moss. Mo-BG:2
  The Beginning of Day. Euripides.
    Pa-SG:104
  Beginning to Squall. M. Swenson.
    Ls-NY:308
  Break, Break, Break.
    A. Tennyson. Bl-OB:51,
    Bo-GJ:182, De-CH:211, Ga-FB:128,
    Ha-PO:137, Ma-YA:192, Ox-BN:485,
    Pa-GTB:331, Sp-OG:267
  Broken and Broken. Chosu.
    Be-CS:48
  By the Sea. C. Rossetti.
    Co-BN:75
  The Canefield and the Sea.
    J. de Melo Neto. An-TC:153
  The Character of Holland.
    A. Marvell. Gr-CT:204
  A Conversation. D. Thomas.
    La-RM:102
  The Coral Grove. J. Percival.
    Un-GT:262
  The Dancing Sea. J. Davies.
    Gr-CT:191
  Dead Sea. Sun Yü-t'ang.
    Hs-TC:123
  Doth Not a Tenarif. J. Donne.
    Gr-CT:209
  Dover Beach. M. Arnold.
    Al-VBP:972, Cl-FC:48, Co-BL:84,
    Er-FA:454, Ga-FB:66, Go-BP:147,
    Ha-PO:187, Hi-WP II:35, Ho-P:201,
    Ke-PP:87, Ma-FW:53, Ma-YA:209,
    Mc-PR:70, Mo-GR:35, Ox-BN:645,
    Pa-GTB:305, Pl-EI:78, Rv-CB:863,
    Un-MW:120
  Duet from Becket. A. Tennyson.
    Gr-SS:148
  Earth and Sea. A. Pushkin. Pa-SG:368
  Echoes. W. de la Mare. Sh-RP:105
  The Even Sea. M. Swenson. Ha-WR:37

  The Exile. M. Benaya. Ls-NY:43
  The Face. E. Muir. Pa-GTB:467
  Far Beyond Us. Pa-SG:185
  The Fish. M. Moore. Un-MA:350
  Flood. J. Joyce. Un-MB:271
  The Flying Sea. R. Mortimer.
    Le-M:115
  Garden. M. Drouet. Gr-EC:270
  The Gravedigger. B. Carman.
    Co-BN:72
  A Great Green House. Re-RR:31
  Grim and Gloomy. J. Reeves.
    Sh-RP:183
  Halcyon. H.D. Un-MA:338
  Harp Song of the Dane Women.
    R. Kipling. Co-RM:55,
    Ox-BN:931
  Harvest-Season Songs.
    Tr-US I:171
  Her Heards Be Thousand Fishes.
    E. Spenser. Gr-CT:199
  The House in the Green Well.
    J. Wheelock. Un-MA:344
  How Can the Sea Be Dark and Gray?
    S. Horton. Le-M:113
  A Hurricane at Sea. M. Swenson.
    Ha-WR:34
  I Explain. S. Crane.
    Sh-AP:143
  I Stand as One. W. Whitman.
    La-RM:86
  I Started Early, Took My Dog.
    E. Dickinson. Re-TW:122,
    Rv-CB:920, Wi-LT:10
  I Walked on the Ice of the Sea.
    Le-IB:98
  The Idea of Order at Key West.
    W. Stevens. Sh-AP:160,
    Un-MA:349
  It Is a Beauteous Evening.
    W. Wordsworth. Al-VBP:659,
    De-CH:738, Fe-PL:403, Gr-CT:195,
    Pa-GTB:273, Rv-CB:646
  It Is Raining. L. Mitchell.
    Ar-TP3:170, Au-SP:311
  Kansas Boy. R. Lechlitner.
    Br-AF:150, Du-RG:50
  The Knight Without a Name.
    Ha-WR:122
  The Kraken. A. Tennyson.
    Ho-WR:215, Ox-BN:473
  The Landsman. Moschus. Pa-SG:174
  Long Trip. L. Hughes. Ar-TP3:97
  Look, the Sea! W. Zorach. Ad-PE:12
  The Main-Deep. J. Stephens.
    Un-MB:266
  Mediterranean Beach: Day after
    Storm. R. Warren. Un-MW:169
  The Mermaids. W. de la Mare.
    Cl-DT:42

A Mermaid's Myth.   Ch'in Tzu-hao.
    Pa-MV:55
A Misanthrope's Serenade.
    Kuo Mo-jo.   Hs-TC:36
The Moldering Hulk. A. Machado.
    Pa-SG:144
Mythistorema XXIII.   G. Seferis.
    Gr-BT:147
Native-Cat Songs.   Tr-US I:254
Neither Out Far nor In Deep.
    R. Frost.   Gr-CT:192, Sh-AP:153
New Auld Lang Syne. Kuo Mo-jo.
    Hs-TC:34
The Old Churchyard at Bonchurch.
    P. Marston.   Ox-BN:888
Old Deep Sing-Song.
    C. Sandburg.   Ma-FW:43
On the Sea. J. Keats. Al-VBP:779,
    Ma-YA:182, Sp-OG:365
Oread.   H.D.   Bo-GJ:177, Sh-RP:80,
    Un-MA:336
Patrolling Barnegat.
    W. Whitman.   Rv-CB:848
Phases of the Sea.   Tr-US II:102
Plague of Dead Sharks. A. Dugan.
    Wi-LT:692
Prayer to the Sea.   Tr-US II:124
A Pretty Boat.   N. Tolstoy.
    Mo-MI:16
Rocked in the Cradle of the
    Deep. E. Willard.   Er-FA:467
Rousecastle.   D. Wright.
    Ca-MB:81, Co-SS:195
Sam. W. de la Mare. Ar-TP3:160,
    Co-PM:46, Co-SS:174, Ga-FB:168,
    Hi-WP I:74, Pa-OM:292, Un-MB:200
Sand Dunes.   R. Frost.
    La-RM:94, Un-MA:185
The Sea.   S. Kuroda.   Sh-AM:116
The Sea.   D. Lawrence.
    Co-BN:76
The Sea.   J. Reeves.   Co-SS:51
The Sea.   S. Shoenblum. Le-M:116
The Sea.   Suzanne G.   Le-M:104
The Sea.   Tu Yün-hsieh.
    Hs-TC:250
The Sea and the Canefield.
    J. de Melo Neto.   An-TC:147
The Sea and the Hills. R. Kipling.
    Ga-FB:188
Sea Born. H. Vinal.   Bo-HF:78
Sea Calm. L. Hughes.
    Ha-LO:69, Li-TU:210
A Sea-Change: For Harold.
    J. Langland.   Wi-LT:752
The Sea Eats the Land at Home.
    K. Awoonor.   Ad-CI:82
The Sea Gypsy. R. Hovey.
    Co-SS:76, Fe-FP:191, La-PV:186,
    Sh-RP:285, Un-GT:261

The Sea Is Melancholy. A. Pratt.
    Al-WW:103
Sea Love. C. Mew.   Al-VBP:1111,
    Co-BL:159, Co-EL:10, Co-PU:78,
    Un-MB:159, Un-MW:100
Sea Lullaby. E. Wylie.
    Co-BN:78
The Sea of Death.   De-CH:389
The Sea Princess. K. Pyle.
    Au-SP:297, Bo-FP:83
The Sea-Ritual.   G. Darley.
    De-CH:312, Gr-SS:179,
    Ho-WR:126, Ox-BN:396
Sea Surface Full of Clouds.
    W. Stevens.   Ca-VT:32, Un-MA:245
The Sea Was Calm.   C. Minor.
    Ba-HI:103, Jo-VC:71
Sea-Wash. C. Sandburg.   Mc-PR:61
The Seafarer. E. Pound. Sh-AP:171
The Seagull. M. Howitt. Ox-BC:161
Seal Lullaby. R. Kipling.
    Ar-TP3:80, Co-PU:86, Fe-FP:177,
    Mc-PR:60, Mc-WS:47, Rd-SS:19
Seascape. B. Esbensen.
    Ar-TP3:164
Silences. E. Pratt.   En-PC:5
Sketch. C. Sandburg. Bo-HF:83
Song by Lady Happy, as a Sea-
    Goddess. M. Cavendish.
    Gr-SS:184
Song from Southern Sermilik.
    Da-SC:17
The Song of Kuali.   Tr-US II:98
Song Sung on an Expedition to
    Obtain Salt. Bi-IT:21, Ho-SD:51,
    Le-OE:73, Tr-US II:273
South. E. Brathwaite.   Sa-B:46
Storm at Sea. W. Davenant.
    Co-RG:43, Co-RM:41
Storm at Sea. A. Kotul'sky.
    Mo-MI:18
A Storm at Sea. D. Valentin.
    Le-M:52, Le-WR:21
Storm Scene. Tr-US II:102
Sunset on the Sea. L. Ubell.
    Le-M:3
The Tempest. W. Smith.
    Un-MA:672
They That Go Down to the Sea.
    Bible. O.T. Psalms.
    Fe-FP:197, Gr-CT:217, Mc-WK:195
This Is the Sea. E. Shanks.
    De-CH:623
Three Kings. J. Vaughn.
    Hu-NN:24, Hu-PN:399
Through the Dear Might of Him
    Who Walked the Waves.
    J. Heath-Stubbs.   Go-BP:289
To Helen. D. Schwartz. Ls-NY:26
Training. D. Herrera.   Lo-TY:108

SEAS — cont'd.
  The Triumph of Time. A. Swinburne.
    Al-VBP:1017
  Umbara's Song. Umbara.
    Tr-US I:260
  Underneath. T. Folk. La-GI:40
  Undersea. M. Chute. Ja-PC:54,
    La-PP:42
  Until I Saw the Sea. L. Moore.
    Cr-SS:5
  Vista. A. Kreymborg.
    Co-BL:60, Sm-MK:139
  Wading at Wellfleet. E. Bishop.
    Sh-AP:216
  The Water Wants All Sea.
    L. Frankenberg. Ls-NY:270
  We Rowed into Fog. Shiki.
    Be-CS:29
  Week-End by the Sea.
    E. Masters. Un-MA:140
  Who Are the Two from Whom We
    Beg. Re-RR:31
  A Windy Day. W. Howard.
    Fe-FP:191
  The World below the Brine.
    W. Whitman. Co-BN:77
  Young Sea. C. Sandburg.
    Sh-RP:172
SEASHORE: see also HUMOR -
    SEASHORE; OCEANS; SAND DUNES
  Afternoon, Amagansett Beach.
    J. Wheelock. Co-BN:79,
    Ha-WR:33
  Alien. D. Hayes. Bo-AN:93
  Apology for Bad Dreams.
    R. Jeffers. Sh-AP:175,
    Un-MA:363
  At the Fishhouses. E. Bishop.
    Wi-LT:512
  At the Sea-Side. R. Stevenson.
    Ar-TP3:109, Cl-DT:39, Fe-FP:113,
    Hu-MP:48, Li-LC:76, Ox-BC:293
  At the Slackening of the Tide.
    J. Wright. Ca-VT:623
  Autumn in Carmel. G. Sterling.
    Pa-HT:63
  The Beach. W. Hart-Smith.
    Gr-EC:111
  Beach Fire. F. Frost. Ar-TP3:110,
    Pe-FB:24
  Beech Leaves. J. Reeves.
    Pa-RE:108, Sh-RP:222
  Beside the Sierra in Flower.
    A. Machado. Le-SW:43
  The Bight. E. Bishop. Ha-PO:195
  Bits of Glass. S. Brown. Ho-LP:40
  The Black Cliffs, Ballybunion.
    B. Kennelly. Co-PI:83
  Black-Out. R. Jeffers.
    Wi-LT:262

  The Black Pebble. J. Reeves.
    La-PV:208
  Blind Angel. D. Rokeah.
    Me-PH:119
  The Bones. W. Merwin. Wi-LT:767
  Bran. G. Moore. Ls-NY:162
  By the Sea. R. Dixon. Ox-BN:750
  A Canticle to the Waterbirds.
    Brother Antoninus. Ca-BP:11
  Clam-Digging Song. M. Kumin.
    Cr-SS:6
  The Cliff-Top. R. Bridges.
    Co-BN:83
  Conjured. J. Gill. Sc-TN:67
  Continent's End. R. Jeffers.
    Ga-FB:312, Pl-IO:53
  The Cry. M. Perlberg. Co-PU:138
  The Door. L. Strong. Un-MB:394
  The Dykes. R. Kipling. Ni-JP:138
  East Anglian Bathe. J. Betjeman.
    Mo-SD:144
  Eel-Grass. E. Millay. Mo-BG:142
  Epitaph. A. Comfort. Un-MB:520
  Evening at the Seashore.
    N. Sharma. Al-PI:122
  Exiled. E. Millay. Ni-JP:132,
    Pa-HT:7
  The First Day. N. Weiss.
    Ls-NY:240
  The Fisher's Boy. H. Thoreau.
    Gr-CT:192
  Flowers by the Sea. W. Williams.
    Bo-GJ:86, Ho-LP:54,
    Mo-BG:118, Un-MA:261
  High Tide. J. Untermeyer.
    Un-MA:331
  I Shall Go Back. E. Millay.
    Sm-PT:170, Un-MA:446
  I'm a Newcomer. Chung Hsüan.
    Hs-TC:433
  Late Winter on Our Beach.
    B. Eaton. Mc-AW:32
  The Lie. H. Moss. Wi-LT:776
  Little Blue Apron. Ir-BB:94
  The Lover's Song. I. Adigal.
    Al-PI:71
  maggie and milly and molly and
    may. E. Cummings. Co-PS:109,
    Gr-BT:10, Ha-LO:15
  A Maine Roustabout. R. Eberhart.
    Ha-TP:45
  Marooned. R. Field.
    Sh-RP:165
  Meditation at Oyster River.
    T. Roethke. Un-MA:601
  Mine. L. Moore. Cr-SS:16
  Morning on the White Sands.
    A. Rau. Mc-AC:146
  Neither Out Far nor In Deep.
    R. Frost. Gr-CT:192, Sh-AP:153

The Ocean Wood.   J. Warren.
  Rv-CB:935
Often along the Bathing Beach
  One Sees.   J. Urzidil.
  Un-R:51
On a White Beach.   P. Mayer.
  St-H:138
On Galveston Beach.   B. Howes.
  Un-MA:654
On the Beach.   Ch'in Tzu-hao.
  Pa-MV:57
On the Beach.   C. Parker.
  Le-M:106
On the Beach at Fontana.
  J. Joyce.   Li-TU:216,
  Un-MB:270
On the Seashore.   Ca-MU:14
On the Shore.   D. Baruch.
  Cr-SS:12
On This Island.   W. Auden.
  Ma-FW:44, Pa-GTB:510,
  To-MP:19, Un-MB:457
Once by the Pacific.   R. Frost.
  Ca-VT:17, Pa-HT:62, Sm-PT:78,
  Un-MA:184, Wi-LT:173
The Parting.   A. Rich.   Ha-WR:41
Patrolling Barnegat.
  W. Whitman.   Rv-CB:848
pete at the seashore. D. Marquis.
  Co-BBW:115
The Picnic.   D. Aldis. Ar-TP3:109,
  Fr-MP:15, Mc-AW:17
The Pier.   E. Lozada.   Le-M:117
Potpourri at Granite Hill.
  Ch'in Tzu-hao.   Pa-MV:52
Pre-Existence.   F. Cornford.
  Mc-WK:107
Prelude.   R. Gilder.   Fe-PL:395
Prospect Beach.   L. Lipsitz.
  Ca-VT:716
Recited Before Going to the Beach
  to Fish.   Tr-US I:241
The Recollection.   P. Shelley.
  De-CH:148
Reed-Leaf Boat.   Pien Chih-lin.
  Hs-TC:165
Riding in a Motor Boat.
  D. Baruch.   Fe-FP:194,
  Hu-MP:171
The Rock Pool.   P. Hobsbaum.
  Ls-NY:215
Sacred Song of the Avocet Cult.
  Tr-US I:256
Sand Castles.   W. Robertson.
  Hu-MP:42
Sand Cooking.   Bo-FP:279
The Sandcastle.   M. Stephenson.
  St-FS:58
The Sandpiper.   F. Frost.
  Cr-SS:10

The Sandpiper.   C. Thaxter.
  Fe-FP:292, Hu-MP:234,
  Mc-PR:19, Ox-BC:281
Sandpipers.   C. Sandburg.
  Re-BS:37
The Sands of Dee. C. Kingsley.
  Bl-OB:153, Cl-FC:88, Co-PM:111,
  Co-SS:43, De-CH:211, De-TT:182,
  Fe-FP:511, Hu-MP:430, Sp-OG:84
Scattered on the Sand.   Basho.
  Be-MC:13
The Sea.   H. Gorter.   Pa-SG:145
The Sea.   Suzanne G.   Le-M:104
The Sea Boy.   W. de la Mare.
  Cr-SS:32
A Sea-Change: For Harold.
  J. Langland.   Wi-LT:752
Sea Holly.   C. Aiken.
  Wi-LT:331
Sea News.   E. Barker.
  Ls-NY:244
Seaside Storm.   M. Craig.
  Cr-SS:18
The Shell.   J. Stephens.
  Cl-DT:40, Co-BN:82, De-CH:57,
  Ma-FW:43, Ni-JP:34, Un-MB:262
Shore.   M. Miller.   Ar-TP3:110,
  Mc-AW:43
Sitting in the Sand. K. Kuskin.
  Cr-SS:8
Skeleton.   S. Barry.   Le-M:110
Skin Diving in the Virgins.
  J. Brinnin.   Pe-OA:238
Skipping Along Alone. W. Welles.
  Ar-TP3:110, Au-SP:296
Slave of the Moon.   M. Yarmon.
  Le-M:112
A Song from Arsut. Tr-US I:4
Song Sung on an Expedition to
  Obtain Salt.   Bi-IT:21, Ho-SD:51,
  Le-OE:73, Tr-US II:273
Songs from Cyprus.   H.D.
  Gr-CC:21, Un-MA:338
Summer Song.   J. Ciardi.
  Gr-EC:43
This Is the Sea.   E. Shanks.
  De-CH:623
Tidal.   R. Ballak.   Cr-SS:28
The Tide.   M. Wilson.   Bo-FP:284
The Tide Rises, the Tide Falls.
  H. Longfellow.   Co-SS:50,
  De-TT:183, Er-FA:260, Gr-CT:191,
  Ho-WR:135, Mc-PR:73, Pa-RE:75,
  Rv-CB:784
Torn Down from Glory Daily.
  A. Sexton.   Ha-WR:30
Treasure Hunting.   M. Justus.
  Cr-SS:24
Treasures.   M. Thayer.
  Au-SP:349, Hu-MP:176

SEASHORE — cont'd.
  Trebetherick. J. Betjeman.
    Na-EO:160
  Tree-Sleeping. R. Coffin.
    Ha-LO:54
  Trying Too Hard to Write a Poem
    Sitting on the Beach.
    P. Whalen. Mc-EA:44
  Upon the Beach. I. Orleans.
    Ar-TP3:109
  A Very Odd Fish. D. Thompson.
    Ox-BC:232
  The Visiting Sea. A. Meynell.
    Go-BP:132
  Voyages I. H. Crane.
    Ca-VT:215, Mo-BG:132
  Water. R. Lowell. Pe-OA:247
  The Water Wants All Sea.
    L. Frankenberg. Ls-NY:270
  The Wave. H. Behn. Cr-SS:22
  The Wave. D. Hine. Ho-P:99
  Waves Against a Dog.
    T. Baybars. Sm-MK:176
  Waves Coming Up Against the
    Rocks. Le-OE:85, Tr-US I:244
  Waves Slap on the Shore.
    C. Moore. Le-M:114
  We Lying by Seasand. D. Thomas.
    Go-BP:84
  Week-End by the Sea.
    E. Masters. Un-MA:140
  Wind, Waves, and Sails.
    M. La Rue. Co-SS:70
  With Kit, Age 7, at the Beach.
    W. Stafford. La-RM:92
  Would My House. Ba-ST:31
SEASONS: see also HUMOR - SEASONS;
    and names of seasons, as AUTUMN
  Aella. T. Chatterton. Al-VBP:606
  All Seasons in One. Un-MW:31
  All Year Long. Rx-LT:24
  As Imperceptibly as Grief.
    E. Dickinson. Wi-LT:15
  The Banks of Newfoundland.
    Gr-GB:219
  The Calendar. B. Todd.
    Ir-BB:23
  Change of Seasons. J. Smith.
    Mc-AW:33
  Eros and Agape. C. Walsh.
    St-H:240
  Four Seasons. R. Bennett.
    Br-SS:8
  The Golden Rod. F. Sherman.
    Fe-FP:221, Ja-PA:6
  How Still, How Happy!
    E. Brontë. Ox-BN:598
  The Human Seasons. J. Keats.
    Er-FA:179, Ho-WR:22,
    Ma-YA:186, Pa-GTB:307

  In Due Season. W. Auden.
    Ho-P:15
  In Due Season. J. Drinkwater.
    Ke-TF:240
  Leaves. W. Barnes. Co-BN:149,
    Gr-CT:317, Ox-BN:430
  Marjorie's Almanac. T. Aldrich.
    Br-SG:101, Fe-FP:62, Hu-MP:298
  Merry Autumn Days. C. Dickens.
    Bo-FP:145, Ch-B:93
  The Mountain God. Ya Hsuan.
    Pa-MV:147
  Northern View. H. Plimpton.
    Ls-NY:293
  O Dear Me! W. de la Mare.
    Ar-TP3:184, Sm-MK:3
  Ode to Winter, Germany, December,
    1800. T. Campbell. Pa-GTB:262
  The Procession. M. Widdemer.
    Ha-YA:19
  Seasons. H. Carruth. Ls-NY:290
  The Seasons. K. Kuskin.
    Br-SG:105
  The Seasons. Ar-TP3:182,
    Au-SP:306, Gr-EC:42, Ir-BB:185
  Seasons. C. Rossetti. Ha-YA:18
  Signs of the Seasons. Gr-EC:42
  Sing a Song of Seasons.
    R. Stevenson. Ch-B:92
  The Snow Dissolv'd. Horace.
    No-CL:130
  So Quickly Came Summer.
    A. Pratt. Al-WW:109
  Solace. C. Delany. Ad-PB:71,
    Bo-AN:59, Hu-PN:178
  The Song of the Four Winds.
    T. Peacock. Ho-WR:22
  Song of the Seasons. B. Lofton.
    Ha-YA:17
  Sonnet. J. Masefield.
    Un-MB:228, Wi-LT:191
  Spring Song. Bi-IT:126,
    Br-MW:98, Da-SC:148,
    Jo-TS:13, Tr-US II:228
  Spring to Winter. G. Crabbe.
    Gr-CT:316
  Summer. C. Rossetti.
    Co-BN:91, Rv-CB:890
  Summer Sunshine. M. Lathbury.
    Ha-YA:184
  There Is a Trinity. Rippo.
    Le-MW:65
  Therefore All Seasons Shall Be
    Sweet to Thee. S. Coleridge.
    Cl-DT:22, De-CH:632
  This Measure. L. Adams. Un-MA:547
  Times o' Year. W. Barnes.
    Co-BN:226
  To a Certain Unmarried Woman.
    M. Kaneko. Sh-AM:63

The Tree. B. Björnson.
    Bo-FP:268, Co-PS:75,
    Fe-FP:467, Hu-MP:271
The Wheel. W. Yeats.   Pa-GTB:427
Winter Night. C. Hutchison.
    Ar-TP3:199
Winter Will Follow. R. Dixon.
    De-CH:208, Pa-GTB:380
The Year's Round. C. Patmore.
    Br-SG:100, De-TT:170,
    Re-TW:92, Se-PR:25
SEAWEED: see also KELP
Flood. J. Joyce. Un-MB:271
Gathering Seaweed. S. Suyama.
    Le-TA:81
Seaweed. M. Livingston.
    Cr-SS:21
SECAUCUS, N.J.
In a Prominent Bar in Secaucus
    One Day. X. Kennedy.
    En-PC:284
SECESSION: see CIVIL WAR - UNITED
    STATES, 1861-1865
SECRETS AND SECRECY: see also
    HUMOR - SECRETS AND SECRECY;
    LOVE, SECRET
A Divine Image. W. Blake.
    Ga-S:156, Gr-CT:436, Ox-BN:25
Eulogy for Populations.
    R. Welburn. Ad-PB:467
Flammonde. E. Robinson.
    Wi-LT:105
Gone. M. Coleridge. Ox-BN:924
Heather Ale. R. Stevenson.
    Co-PT:117, Sp-OG:162
House: A Reply. R. Browning.
    No-CL:91
Jeremy's Secrets. B. Todd.
    Br-BC:61
Keziah. G. Brooks. Un-GB:21
Little Brother's Secret.
    K. Mansfield. Ar-TP3:6,
    Fe-FP:49, Th-AS:64
Sabbath Is Gone. D. Hofstein.
    Ho-TY:174
The Secret. Ar-TP3:55, Au-SP:64,
    Gr-EC:172, Hu-MP:213
The Secret Cavern. M. Widdemer.
    Fe-FP:11, Hu-MP:43, Sh-RP:110
The Secret Song. M. Brown.
    La-PP:3, La-PV:222
Secrets. E. Fowler. Br-BC:102
Secrets. M. McArthur. De-TT:34
The Secrets of Cisterns.
    S. McNail. De-FS:138
Sonnets. M. Drayton. Al-VBP:166
A Strange Place. P. Rake.
    Le-M:157
Three Little Trees.
    Ch-B:67

SECURITY: see also SAFETY;
    SATIRE - SECURITY
Abide with Me. H. Lyte. Er-FA:443
Arrows of Love.   Chauras.
    Pa-SG:51
An Astrologer's Song.
    R. Kipling. Un-MB:135
At Rest in the Blast. M. Moore.
    Un-MA:355
The Beautiful American Word,
    Sure. D. Schwartz. Ca-VT:366
A Child Half-Asleep. T. Connor.
    Go-BT:8
The Cottager to Her Infant.
    D. Wordsworth. De-CH:205,
    Ox-BC:127
Cradle Song. F. Higgins.
    Rd-SS:17
Evening. T. Miller. Ox-BC:210
God Is Our Refuge. Bible. O.T.
    Psalms. Gr-TG:84
Good Night. J. Taylor. Ch-B:109
I Got a Home in Dat Rock.
    Ra-BP:25
Kindness. M. Flett. Le-M:155
The King of Love My Shepherd Is.
    H. Baker. Gr-TG:40, Ke-TF:184
Lines for a Bed at Kelmscott
    Manor. W. Morris. De-CH:445,
    Ho-WR:235, Rd-SS:14
Locked Out. R. Frost. Li-TU:31
Lullaby. W. Barnes. De-TT:54,
    Rd-SS:26
Man Frail, and God Eternal.
    I. Watts. Rv-CB:499
Matthew, Mark, Luke and John.
    Bo-FP:36, De-CH:446, De-PO:28,
    De-TT:202, Gr-GB:298, Gr-TG:55,
    Hi-GD:23, Mo-NR:99, On-TW:18,
    Rd-SS:40, Rv-CB:451, Sm-LG:385,
    Un-GT:23
Midnight. T. Sackville.
    De-CH:107, De-TT:150, Rd-OA:205
The Nest. J. de Ibarbourou.
    Be-UL:49
The Night Is Come. T. Browne.
    De-CH:748
Nimble Rays of Day Bring Oxygen
    to Her Blood. T. Clark.
    Mc-EA:102
O God, Our Help in Ages Past.
    I. Watts. Ke-TF:188, Pl-EI:200
Of All the Faces. R. Zychlinska.
    Ho-TY:231
Old Cat Care. R. Hughes.
    Rd-SS:13, Re-TW:15
On a Quiet Conscience. Charles I.
    De-CH:446
The Owl. E. Thomas.
    Ni-JP:86

SECURITY — cont'd.
  Provide, Provide. R. Frost.
    Br-TC:139, Sh-AP:153
  Psalm Concerning the Castle.
    D. Levertov. Br-TC:256
  Rocked in the Cradle of the Deep.
    E. Willard. Er-FA:467
  Sanctuary. E. Wylie. Un-MA:276
  The Secret Heart. R. Coffin.
    Co-PS:103, Se-PR:152
  Song. H. Killigrew. De-CH:447
  The Sparrow. Bible. O.T.
    Psalms. Fe-FP:294
  A Story. W. Stafford.
    La-RM:30
  A Thank-You. W. Canton. Gr-TG:42
  To a Waterfowl. W. Bryant.
    De-CH:106, De-TT:179, Er-FA:232,
    Fe-PL:355, Mc-PR:55, Rv-CB:734,
    Sh-AP:20, Sp-OG:295
  Windy Night. Feng Chih.
    Hs-TC:142
  Women. L. Bogan. Br-TC:55,
    Ca-VT:202, Mc-EA:87, Un-MA:490
  Your Hands. A. Grimke. Ad-PB:16
SEDAN, FR.
  Before Sedan. A. Dobson.
    Ke-TF:52
SEEDS
  The Anxious Farmer.
    B. Johnson. Co-BN:37
  B Is for Beanseed. E. Farjeon.
    Br-SG:82
  Baby Seed Song. E. Nesbit.
    Bo-FP:238, Fe-FP:215,
    Hu-MP:246, Th-AS:73
  Baby Seeds. Bo-FP:141,
    Br-SG:92, Ch-B:116
  Fueled. M. Hans. Du-RG:83,
    Pe-M:80
  The Holy of Holies. G. Chesterton.
    Go-BP:254, Tr-MR:44
  I Hoed and Trenched and Weeded.
    A. Housman. Un-MB:102,
    Wi-LT:65
  In the Heart of a Seed.
    K. Brown. Sh-RP:201
  Lesson. H. Behn. Br-SG:12
  The Magic Seeds. J. Reeves.
    Gr-EC:293, Ir-BB:62
  The Magic Vine. Br-SG:83
  The Seed Eaters. R. Francis.
    Ca-BP:7
  Seed Journey. G. Corso. Ca-VT:660
  Seed Leaves. R. Wilbur. Co-BN:38
  The Seed Shop. M. Stuart.
    Co-BN:229, Un-GT:257
  Seeds. L. Blaga. Mc-AC:69
  Seeds. W. de la Mare. Ar-TP3:202,
    Br-SG:13, Sh-RP:204

  Seeds. J. Reeves. Gr-EC:293
  Seeds. T. Snyder. Hu-NN:88
  Spring Planting. M. Chute.
    Br-SG:16
  Street Lamps. D. Lawrence.
    Go-BP:163
  Talking in Their Sleep.
    E. Thomas. Co-BN:29
  There Was a Young Farmer of
    Leeds. Br-LL:62, Ir-BB:220
  To the Man after the Harrow.
    P. Kavanagh. Pa-GTB:514
  Tommy. G. Brooks. Br-SG:15
SEESAWS
  See-Saw, Margery Daw. Au-SP:6,
    Ir-BB:11, Li-LB:130, Mo-MGT:28,
    Mo-NR:3, Mo-TL:16
  White Cap. Mo-MGT:160
SEGOVIA, SP.
  Segovia. F. Keyes. Ke-TF:391
SEGREGATION: see DISCRIMINATION
SELENE (GODDESS): see ENDYMION
SELF: see also HUMOR - SELF;
  INDIVIDUALITY; PERSONALITY
  Africa's Plea. R. Dempster.
    Lo-TY:168
  An Agony. As Now. I. Baraka.
    Ra-BP:211, Wi-LT:743
  All That He Is. E. de Vito.
    Ke-TF:127
  Alone. S. Sassoon.
    Hi-WP I:121, Un-MB:318
  Alone. K. Taguchi. Le-TA:93
  And Through the Caribbean Sea.
    M. Danner. Ra-BP:152
  Animals. L. Anderson. Me-WF:91
  Answering a Letter from a Younger
    Poet. B. Ghiselin. En-PC:50
  Apologies. M. Piercy. Sc-TN:186
  The Arrow and the Song.
    H. Longfellow. Er-FA:16,
    Sp-OG:337
  As Kingfishers Catch Fire.
    G. Hopkins. Pl-EI:134,
    Tr-MR:286, Un-MB:45, Wi-LT:45
  be cool, baby. R. Penny.
    Ad-PB:390
  Be True. W. Shakespeare.
    Bo-FP:306, Ch-B:89
  Bear. S. Tsuboi. Sh-AM:74
  Being. K. Ozaki. Sh-AM:59
  Bill. J. Salzburg. Br-BC:50
  bitchice. E. Jenkins. Ad-II:22
  The Black Me. Chi Hsüan. Pa-MV:46
  The Black Panther. J. Wheelock.
    Ha-TP:94, Wi-LT:654
  Blackie Thinks of His Brothers.
    S. Crouch. Ad-PB:484
  Both Water and the Earth.
    F. Saito. Sh-AM:152

Breakthrough. C. Rodgers.
  Ra-BP:263
Bumi. I. Baraka. Ad-PB:256
The Buried Life. M. Arnold.
  Go-BP:126
Canto 4. T. Weatherly.
  Ad-PB:397
Cawdor. R. Jeffers. Sm-PT:25
A Child-Thought. W. Thorley.
  Bo-FP:273
Coming Home. R. Humphries.
  Tr-MR:256
Confession. Wen I-to. Hs-TC:57
Consciousness. R. Nickens.
  La-IH:116
Consummate Happiness.
  W. Wordsworth. Ox-BN:99
The Crack. T. McNeill.
  Sa-B:207
The Crystal Gazer. S. Teasdale.
  Un-MA:266
Dancing. A. Young. Mc-EA:88
Danse Russe. W. Williams.
  Mc-EA:68
The Day I Lay Myself Down.
  P. Mayer. St-H:131
The Delight Song of Tsaoi-Talee.
  N. Momaday. Ni-CD:89
Deliverance. Ping Hsin.
  Hs-TC:25
The Descendant and the Id.
  A. Branch. Sm-PT:131
Destruction. Chu Tzu-ch'ing.
  Hs-TC:13
A Devil. Y. Kurihara. Le-TA:90
A Dialogue of Self and Soul.
  W. Yeats. Un-MB:118, Wi-LT:84
A Different Image. D. Randall.
  Ra-BP:142
Direction. A. Lopez. Al-WW:10
The Distant Drum. C. Hernton.
  Ad-BO:19, Hu-NN:101,
  Jo-SA:97, Lo-TY:250
The Divine Ship Sails the Divine
  Sea for You. W. Whitman.
  Tr-MR:152
Don't Run. J. Jimenez.
  Le-SW:35
Doubts. R. Brooke. De-CH:247,
  Gr-SS:117
Dramatic Fragment. T. Stickney.
  Co-EL:145, Rv-CB:965
The Drayman. W. Whitman.
  Hu-PN:469
Eclipse. E. Roberson. Hu-PN:431
Ego Swamp. K. Kuka. Al-WW:74
The Electric Train. M. Nakagiri.
  Sh-AM:120
Endless Search. A. Lopez. Al-WW:7
L'Envoi. R. Kipling. Ke-TF:140

Epitaph. J. Cunningham.
  Co-EL:81, En-PC:106
Esthetique du Mal, IV, XII.
  W. Stevens. Wi-LT:153, 158
Everybody Says. D. Aldis.
  Fe-FP:5, Ho-ME:17, Th-AS:55
Extracts from Addresses to the
  Academy of Fine Ideas.
  W. Stevens. Wi-LT:148
Fisherman. D. Scott. Sa-B:201
The Flower Shop. H. Anzai.
  Sh-AM:119
Flowers. C. Lushington.
  Sa-B:234
For the Existentialist.
  W. Palmer. Ls-NY:339
Forty Years Ago. J. Perrault.
  Mc-EA:66
The Fox. S. Kurahara. Sh-AM:77
Full Moon. E. Wylie.
  Ca-VT:103, Un-MA:280
Ghazal. J. Morabandi. Al-PI:151
God and the Holy Spirit.
  D. Lawrence. Tr-MR:224
Gravelly Run. A. Ammons. Ho-P:3
The Hands of God. D. Lawrence.
  Tr-MR:224
The Harlem Dancer. C. McKay.
  Ra-BP:59
The Heart. F. Thompson.
  Pa-GTB:399, Un-MB:79
The Heavy Bear. D. Schwartz.
  Br-TC:356, Pe-OA:218, Wi-LT:520
Here in the Self Is All That Man
  Can Know. J. Masefield.
  `Go-BP:288
Hoc Est Corpus. A. Comfort.
  Wi-LT:672
Holy Sonnet V. J. Donne.
  Ma-FW:175
Hot Sun Sounds. M. Sheedy.
  Ad-II:59
Hymn for Fasting. Br-MW:32,
  Da-SC:170
Hysteria. Chu Shu Chen.
  Rx-OH:128
I, a Justified Sinner. A. Price.
  Ls-NY:90
I Am. J. Clare. Al-VBP:764,
  Go-BP:235, Ha-PO:207, Ho-P:37,
  Mc-PR:109, Ox-BN:331, Pa-GTB:319,
  Rv-CB:728
I Am. H. Conkling. Ar-TP3:208,
  Fe-FP:18
I Am a Parcel of Vain Strivings
  Still. H. Thoreau. No-CL:242
I Am Nobody . . . Who Are You?
  V. Porumbacu. Mc-AC:127
I and I. H. Sanuki.
  Le-TA:54

SELF — cont'd.
  I Give You Thanks My God.
    B. Dadie. Lo-TY:144
  I Go Forth to Move about the
    Earth. A. Lopez. Al-WW:8
  I Might Repeat.
    S. Aleksandrovsky. Mo-MI:35
  I Substitute for the Dead
    Lecturer. L. Jones. Jo-SA:110
  I Think. Tai Wang-shu. Hs-TC:184
  I Walk These Many Rooms.
    C. Day Lewis. Go-BP:185
  I Want Time to Run. V. Lapin.
    Mo-MI:33
  Identity. D. Botez. Mc-AC:61
  The Ides of March. R. Fuller.
    En-PC:115
  If, My Darling. P. Larkin.
    Wi-LT:756
  I'm Nobody! Who Are You?
    E. Dickinson. Ar-TP3:211,
    Bo-FP:275, Co-PU:40, La-PV:221,
    Mo-BG:43, Rv-CB:912, Un-GT:91
  Imaginary Figures of the Virtues.
    S. Bridges. Ha-TP:110
  Impasse. L. Hughes. Wi-LT:424
  In a Dark Time. T. Roethke.
    Pl-EI:46, Un-MA:600
  In Response to a Question.
    W. Stafford. Mc-EA:54,
    St-H:213
  In the Waiting Room. E. Bishop.
    Ho-P:27
  The Informing Spirit.
    R. Emerson. Mc-PR:137
  Inside a Deep Isolation. S. Muro.
    Sh-AM:56
  Intervals. R. Creeley. Ha-TP:107
  The Invention of Comics.
    I. Baraka. Ad-PB:251, Bo-AN:179,
    Wi-LT:744
  The Invisible. R. Kizerman.
    Sa-B:107
  It Must Give Pleasure. W. Stevens.
    Sm-PT:28
  It's a Gay Old World. Er-FA:12
  Journey to the Interior.
    T. Roethke. Ca-VT:297
  Keeping Things Whole. M. Strand.
    Mc-EA:66
  Kind Sir: These Woods.
    A. Sexton. Ha-TP:93
  The Kingdom. L. MacNeice.
    Wi-LT:463
  The Knowledge of Light.
    H. Rago. En-PC:144
  Last Words. S. Plath. Mc-EA:157
  Little Bird Got a Name.
    J. Vega. Ad-II:110
  Loneliness. Cheng Min. Hs-TC:229

  Look at That Gal. J. Bond.
    Hu-PN:434, Lo-TY:253
  Look, See the Cat. N. Price.
    Ls-NY:99
  A Man. D. Levertov. Ha-TP:132
  Man Is God's Nature. R. Eberhart.
    Pl-EI:133, Tr-MR:287
  The Man on My Back. P. Sen.
    Gr-BT:136
  Me. Danny. La-IH:89
  Me. W. de la Mare. Br-BC:120,
    Fe-FP:5, Gr-TG:12
  Me. M. Giloni. Me-WF:10
  Me to You. A. Raybin. Sc-TN:196
  A Meeting. G. Painter.
    Sm-MK:40
  The Melting Pot. D. Randall.
    Ra-BP:141
  Memory. C. Rossetti.
    Ox-BN:716
  Miracle Hill. E. Mitchell.
    Al-WW:93
  Mirror. R. Potash. Ho-TY:359
  The Missing Person. D. Justice.
    Ha-TP:41
  The Most Important. D. Almore.
    Me-WF:11
  Motto. L. Hughes. Ad-PB:75,
    Co-PU:126, Hu-PN:202, Jo-SA:118
  Mountains, Give Me a Body.
    L. Blaga. Mc-AC:68
  My Inside Self. R. Field.
    Fe-FP:6
  My Own Heart. G. Hopkins.
    Un-MB:46, Wi-LT:49
  Myself. De-TT:70, Gr-CT:12,
    Hu-MP:61, Mo-MGT:208,
    Rv-ON:83, Wr-RM:85
  Myself when I Am Real. A. Young.
    Ad-PB:365
  News. E. Auerbach. Ho-TY:299
  The Night Before the Night
    Before Christmas. R. Jarrell.
    Pe-M:134
  The No-Color Man. D. Hall.
    Mc-EA:153
  No Finis. D. Schubert.
    Mc-EA:169
  Notes Toward a Supreme Fiction.
    W. Stevens. Wi-LT:162
  Numbers, Letters. I. Baraka.
    Ra-BP:218
  Oh Father. W. Rose. Ni-CD:206
  An Occasional Image. A. Sawai.
    Sh-AM:136
  Of Flesh and Bone. I. Gardner.
    St-H:67
  On a Dewy Morning. Ch'en Meng-chia.
    Hs-TC:112
  Out. H. McCord. Mc-EA:73

Pavlov. N. Madgett. Ra-BP:196
Phantom. S. Coleridge.
  Gr-SS:116
The Planet on the Table.
  W. Stevens. Pl-ML:3
Poem. T. Clark. Mc-EA:70
Poem. S. Clarke. Sa-B:229
Poem. F. John. Sa-B:168
Poem. J. La Rose. Sa-B:38
Poem for Friends. Q. Troupe.
  Ad-PB:445
Poem for Half White College
  Students. I. Baraka.
  Be-MA:118, Ra-BP:225
a poem for positive thinkers.
  B. Mahone. Ad-PB:473
Poem of the Future Citizen.
  J. Craveirinha. Ab-MO:106,
  Lo-TY:186
Poems of Shape and Motion.
  M. Carter. Sa-B:136
The Poet and His Book.
  E. Millay. Un-MA:443
Portrait of a Certain Gentleman.
  S. Hay. Ls-NY:146
Positives: For Sterling Plumpp.
  D. Lee. Ad-PB:427
Prelude. C. Aiken. Br-TC:5
The Repetitive Heart.
  D. Schwartz. Sh-AP:221
The Ritual to Read to Each Other.
  W. Stafford. Pe-SS:115
Robert, Who Is Often a Stranger
  to Himself. G. Brooks.
  Ho-ME:6
The Room. C. Day Lewis.
  En-PC:58
St. Dexter's Fire. D. Etter.
  Sc-TN:43
Self. P. George. Al-WW:122
Self-Analysis. A. Wickham.
  Un-MB:277
Self-Portrait. N. Cassian.
  Mc-AC:132
The Self-Slaved. P. Kavanagh.
  Un-MB:430
A Simple Duty. E. Poe. Se-PR:55
Sketch for a Self-Portrait.
  A. Philippide. Mc-AC:81
So-and-So Reclining on Her
  Couch. W. Stevens. Wi-LT:149
some friends. J. Gill. Sc-TN:68
A Song of Diana. L. Nagan.
  Ad-II:52
Song of Myself. W. Whitman.
  Mo-GR:101
Sonnet XVI, XVIII, XXII.
  Feng Chih. Hs-TC:152, 153
Sonnets. G. Hopkins.
  Ox-BN:870

Sonnets, vii. G. Santayana.
  Sm-PT:135
Souls. F. Davis. Th-AS:202
The Spectacle. W. de la Mare.
  Go-BP:249
The Spring Waters. Ping Hsin.
  Hs-TC:24
Star Journey. N. Madgett.
  Ra-BP:195
The Stars Have Departed.
  C. Okigbo. Ab-MO:6
Street Law. S. Bennett.
  Ad-II:115
Sun Poem XV. W. Harris.
  Sa-B:85
The Sunday Driver in Search of
  Himself. J. Tate. St-H:233
Swallow the Lake. C. Major.
  Ad-PB:302
The Sword of Surprise.
  G. Chesterton. Tr-MR:57,
  Un-MB:210
Tanist. J. Stephens. Ls-NY:98
Tea at the Palaz of Hoon.
  W. Stevens. Rv-CB:971
Their Bullring. J. La Rose.
  Sa-B:78
This Is Real. T. Palmanteer.
  Al-WW:45
A Thought. A. Milne. Gr-TG:20
The Thread of Life.
  C. Rossetti. Ox-BN:719
To Sherwood Anderson in Heaven.
  F. Eckman. St-H:46
Touch Me Not. P. Solomon.
  Jo-VC:77
Two Deep Clear Eyes.
  W. de la Mare. Gr-TG:10
The Unsettled Motorcyclist's
  Vision of His Death.
  T. Gunn. Mc-EA:160
Untitled. Kao Meng-k'an.
  Hs-TC:106
Valley Prince. M. Morris.
  Sa-B:125
A Vegetable, I Will Not Be.
  D. Whitewing. Al-WW:54
Volcano. I. Van Sertima.
  Sa-B:41
Want to Be Someone. H. Yazzie.
  Ba-HI:15
What Am I in Time and Space?
  A. Stolzenberg. Ho-TY:270
What Am I, Life? E. Millay.
  Pl-IO:136
What Are Years? M. Moore.
  Ha-TP:140, Pe-OA:101, Pl-EI:138,
  Sh-AP:179, Sm-PT:10, Un-MA:352
What I Am I Must Become.
  Wo-HS:(70)

SELF — cont'd.
Who Am I? F. Holman. La-RM:162
Who Am I. S. Mancillas.
    La-IH:61
who are you, little i.
    e. cummings. Li-LC:21
Who Are You - Who Are You?
    D. Clarke. Jo-VC:79
Why. P. Irving. Al-WW:81
Why Is God Love, Jack?
    A. Ginsberg. Mc-EA:84
Wisdom. H. Sobiloff. Ca-VT:355
With God Conversing.
    G. Derwood. Tr-MR:139
With My God the Smith.
    U. Greenberg. Me-PH:90
Without One Particle of Senti-
    ment in His Being.
    M. Ooka. Sh-AM;134
Would and Dream. A. Shamri.
    Ho-TY:360
You Ask My Age.
    Sister M. Madeleva. Ke-TF:152
Young Soul. I. Baraka.
    Mc-EA:32, Ra-BP:220
Zalka Peetruza. R. Dandridge.
    Ad-PB:19
SELF-CONFIDENCE: see SELF-RELIANCE
SELF-CONTROL: see also HUMOR -
    SELF-CONTROL
Ah, Poverties, Wincings, and
    Sulky Retreats. W. Whitman.
    Rv-CB:855
Childhood's Trials.
    Mrs. C. Alexander. Gr-TG:20
Controlling the Tongue.
    G. Chaucer. Ox-BC:3
Discretion. Rv-CB:18
Epigram. Viryamitra. Al-PI:39
The Epistle Dedicatory to the
    Iliads of Homer. G. Chapman.
    No-CL:16
Forbearance. R. Emerson.
    Al-VBP:801, Hu-MP:307, Se-PR:314
He That Is Slow to Anger.
    Bible. O.T. Proverbs.
    Ar-TP3:209, Fe-FP:24
Institute Poems, I-A. M. Bruce.
    Ad-II:18
The Mouth and the Body.
    P. Mwanikih. Le-M:169
Norman Conquest. P. Mackaye.
    Ke-TF:260
Silence. M. Moore. Al-VBP:1174,
    Ha-PO:219, Ho-LP:72, Ma-FW:62,
    Mc-WS:77, Mo-BG:81
They That Have the Power to
    Hurt. W. Shakespeare.
    Al-VBP:206, Ha-PO:254,
    Pa-GTB:20, Rv-CB:235

To His Little Son Benedict from
    the Tower of London.
    J. Hoskyns. Ox-BC:21
Tolerance. T. Hardy. Tr-MR:158
The White House. C. McKay.
    Ad-PB:28, Be-MA:15, Bo-AN:31,
    Hu-PN:101, Jo-SA:119
Who Is the Man of Poise?
    Al-PI:26
Zone. L. Bogan. En-PC:33
SELF-DENIAL: see also SATIRE -
    SELF-DENIAL
The Heart of a Woman. G. Johnson.
    Fe-PL:416, Hu-PN:73
The Old Cloak. Ma-BB:226
Sonnet IV. Feng Chih. Hs-TC:150
SELF-RELIANCE: see also HUMOR -
    SELF-RELIANCE
Ballad for Gloom. E. Pound.
    Un-MA:292, Wi-LT:222
Baptism. C. McKay. Hu-PN:103
Close Your Eyes! A. Bontemps.
    Ad-PB:86, Bo-AN:76, Hu-PN:218
Confidence. M. Lasants.
    Ba-HI:33
Conquest. G. Johnson.
    Bo-AN:24, Bo-HF:102
The Garden. E. Pound.
    Br-TC:331, Un-MA:289
His Shield. M. Moore. Wi-LT:275
I May, I Might, I Must. M. Moore.
    Co-EL:103, Mc-WS:118,
    Mo-BG:63, Sh-RP:303
In Waste Places. J. Stephens.
    Ni-JP:35, Un-MB:266
Invictus. W. Henley. Al-VBP:1067,
    Co-RM:245, Er-FA:460, Ga-FB:132,
    Ke-TF:253, Mc-PR:69, Ox-BN:883,
    Sp-OG:332, Un-GT:316, Un-MB:53
Life. Cheng Min. Hs-TC:237
A Maine Roustabout. R. Eberhart.
    Ha-TP:45
The Man Who Thinks He Can.
    W. Wintle. Fe-PL:310
My Own Hallelujahs. Z. Gilbert.
    Ad-PB:194
Octaves. E. Robinson. Sm-PT:143
Overnight Stop. Fang Ching.
    Hs-TC:384
Paddle Your Own Canoe. S. Bolton.
    Er-FA:25
See, I Can Do It. D. Aldis.
    Ho-GC:14
The Sense of Comedy. J. Wright.
    Sc-TN:252
Silence. M. Moore. Al-VBP:1174,
    Ha-PO:219, Ho-LP:72, Ma-FW:62,
    Mc-WS:77, Mo-BG:81
The Solitary. S. Teasdale.
    Un-MA:266

Song of Myself. W. Whitman.
  Ho-P:139
The Soul Selects Her Own Society.
  E. Dickinson. Sh-AP:128,
  Un-MA:96, Un-MW:86
Speech to a Crowd. A. MacLeish.
  Un-MA:462
Straight Seeking. T. McNeill.
  Sa-B:8
The Suppliant. G. Johnson.
  Ad-PB:23, Hu-PN:76
The Tame Stag. J. Gay. Rv-CB:503
To My Son. Fe-PL:338
To My Son Parker, Asleep in the
  Next Room. B. Kaufman.
  Ad-PB:265, Br-TC:230,
  Ca-VT:539, Jo-SA:30
A Tough Generation. D. Gascoyne.
  Wi-LT:717
Ulysses. A. Tennyson.
  Al-VBP:863, Ha-PO:40, Ke-TF:262,
  Ni-JP:16, Rv-CB:793
Upstream. C. Sandburg. Pe-M:45,
  Tr-MR:176, Un-MA:209
Who Bides His Time. J. Riley.
  Sp-OG:329
A Willing Suspension. J. Holmes.
  En-PC:62
SELF-RESPECT: see also DIGNITY
  Haven. D. Hayes. Bo-AN:92,
  Hu-PN:245
  I Am a Black Man. B. Lewis.
  Ba-HI:15
  No Joke. F. John. Sa-B:143
  The Self-Hatred of Don L. Lee.
  D. Lee. Ra-BP:297
  The Song of the Banana Man.
  E. Jones. Co-RM:242, Sa-B:101
  Sonnet 121. W. Shakespeare.
  Rv-CB:244
  Throughout the World. Ho-SD:18,
  Le-OE:24
SELF-SATISFACTION: see SMUGNESS
SELFISHNESS
  Bar-Room Matins. L. MacNeice.
  Pl-EI:152
  Cant. W. Davies. Tr-MR:217
  "Don't Care" and "Never Mind."
  J. Bangs. Er-FA:16
  The Man and the Weasel. Plato.
  Mc-PR:27
  Montrose to His Mistress.
  J. Graham. Al-VBP:424, Rv-CB:389
  The Mouse and the Cake. E. Cook.
  Ox-BC:209
  The Revenger's Tragedy.
  C. Tourneur. Al-VBP:275
  The Sea. D. Lawrence. Co-BN:76
  Sitting upon the Koala Bear
  Statue. J. Tomasello. La-IH:120

SELKIRK, ALEXANDER: see also
  ROBINSON CRUSOE
  Alexander Selkirk. W. Cowper.
  Co-RG:130, Fe-PL:292,
  Hi-FO:168, Pa-GTB:162
SELMA, ALA.
  American History. M. Harper.
  Ra-BP:291
SEMINOLE WARS
  From Governor Everett, Receiving
  the Indian Chiefs, November,
  1837. M. Fuller. Kr-OF:8
  Osceola. W. Whitman. Kr-OF:9
  This Soil Shall Be Ours. Kr-OF:8
SEMPACH, BATTLE, 1386
  The Patriot's Pass-Word.
  J. Montgomery. Sp-OG:19
SENEGAL
  He Who Has Lost All. D. Diop.
  Lo-TY:138
  On the Appeal from the Race of
  Sheba: II. L. Senghor.
  Lo-TY:134
  Song. Tr-US I:43
SENNACHERIB, KING OF ASSYRIA
  The Destruction of Sennacherib.
  G. Byron. Er-FA:347, Fe-FP:511,
  Fe-PL:431, Hi-FO:27, Hu-MP:416,
  Mc-PR:25, Na-EO:50, Ni-JP:75,
  Pa-OM:146, Sm-LG:256, Sp-OG:183,
  Un-GT:143
SENSES AND SENSATIONS: see also
  names of senses, as SIGHT
  Ballade Made in Hot Weather.
  W. Henley. Un-MB:54
  The Celestial Surgeon.
  R. Stevenson. Al-VBP:1070,
  Un-GT:308, Un-MB:58
  Destruction. Chu Tzu-ch'ing.
  Hs-TC:13
  Details. L. Zilles. Sh-RP:84
  Esthetique du Mal, XV.
  W. Stevens. Wi-LT:160
  The Fifth Sense. P. Beer.
  Ca-MB:120
  Gone Away. D. Levertov.
  Pe-SS:57
  A Goodnight. W. Williams.
  Un-MA:259
  The Great Lover. R. Brooke.
  Er-FA:73, Hi-WP I:108,
  Un-MB:320, Wi-LT:613
  High on Life. B. Kaufman.
  Be-MA:132
  Honeysuckle. C. La Farge.
  Sm-PT:49
  Inside a Poem. E. Merriam.
  Ar-TP3:XVI
  Invitation to the Voyage.
  C. Baudelaire. Pa-SG:56

SENSES AND SENSATIONS — cont'd.
  The Lady with the Unicorn.
    V. Watkins. Br-TC:459
  Little Eyes See Pretty Things.
    Wy-CM:10
  Me, in Kulu Se & Karma.
    C. Rodgers. Ad-PB:432
  A Midnight Interior.
    S. Sassoon. Tr-MR:55
  Out of Blindness. L. Blades.
    Du-SH:141
  The Poet. R. Holden. Sm-PT:56
  Prayer. T. Roethke. Br-TC:345
  Song of Myself. W. Whitman.
    Un-MA:44
  Storm End. J. Griffin. Mo-TS:87
  Strangeness of Heart.
    S. Sassoon. Tr-MR:260
  Things of Summer. K. Jackson.
    Br-SG:27, Mc-AW:44
  To Live. M. Ooka. Sh-AM:133
  Understanding. T. Traherne.
    Go-BP:107, Mo-SD:84
  When All My Five and Country
    Senses See. D. Thomas.
    Un-MB:497
  You, Andrew Marvell. A. MacLeish.
    Al-VBP:1193, Br-TC:275,
    Ga-FB:4, Mo-BG:150, Pe-OA:157,
    Sh-AP:134, Sm-PT:85, Wi-LT:342
SENSITIVITY: see SENSES AND
  SENSATIONS
SEPTEMBER
  Autumn. I. Vinea. Mc-AC:74
  Green Little Gardens. A. Machado.
    Le-SW:51
  Harvest. C. Sandburg. Ha-WR:81
  Parameter. M. Reis. An-TC:169
  Remember September. M. Justus.
    Br-SS:58, Ha-YA:106, Ja-PA:23
  The Ripe and Bearded Barley.
    Cl-DT:86, Co-BN:126,
    Gr-CT:313, Gr-GB:46
  Season of Amber. D. Quick.
    Ke-TF:444
  September. M. Brown.
    Mc-AW:47
  September. F. da San Geminiano.
    Mo-SD:122
  September. E. Fallis. Br-SG:102,
    Ha-YA:103
  September. M. Howitt.
    Ja-PA:19
  September. T. Hughes. Gr-SS:43
  September. H. Jackson.
    Bo-GJ:250, Fe-FP:76, Fe-PL:385,
    Ha-YA:104, Hu-MP:315, Mc-PR:93,
    Se-PR:165, Un-GT:277
  September. E. Reed. Ha-YA:105,
    Hu-MP:314

September Day. L. Blaga.
  Mc-AC:71
Song for September. R. Fitzgerald.
  Ca-VT:301
Tell Me Not Here, It Needs Not
  Saying. A. Housman.
  Hi-WP II:40, Ox-BN:923,
  Pa-GTB:418, Rv-CB:950, Wi-LT:66
Watching the Moon. D. McCord.
  Ha-YA:103, Ja-PA:20, Sh-RP:221
SEQUOIA TREES
  California Winter. K. Shapiro.
    Br-AF:164
  The Red Woods. D. Quick.
    Ke-TF:426
  The Redwoods. L. Simpson.
    Br-AF:164, Ho-TH:78, Ma-FW:106
SERAVEZZA, IT.
  Seravezza. H. Fuller. Ad-PB:200
SERBO-CROATIAN VERSE
  Donkey. V. Popa. Mo-TS:70
SERENADES: see also HUMOR -
  SERENADES; LOVE SONGS;
  SATIRE - SERENADES
  An Arab Love-Song. F. Thompson.
    Un-MB:78, Un-MW:168
  Bedouin Song. B. Taylor.
    Co-BL:39, Sh-AP:124
  The Indian Serenade. P. Shelley.
    Al-VBP:751, Co-BL:44,
    Pa-GTB:176, Un-MW:166
  Pierrot. S. Teasdale.
    Co-BL:100
  Serenade. H. Longfellow.
    Al-VBP:824
  A Serenade. W. Scott.
    De-CH:312, Pa-GTB:186
  Summons to Love. W. Drummond.
    Al-VBP:303, Pa-GTB:1
SERENITY: see CONTENTMENT;
  PEACE OF MIND
SERFDOM
  The Serf. R. Campbell. Ni-JP:85,
    Pa-GTB:494, Un-MB:419
SERMONS: see also HUMOR - SERMONS;
  PREACHERS AND PREACHING
  An Ante-Bellum Sermon.
    P. Dunbar. Ra-BP:44
  The Creation. J. Johnson.
    Ad-PB:3, Ar-TP3:214, Ga-FB:152,
    Ga-S:6, Hi-WP I:141, Jo-SA:60,
    Pe-M:76, Un-MA:149
  The Day after Sunday.
    P. McGinley. Un-MA:595
  Eddi's Service. R. Kipling.Go-BP:41
  A Foreigner Comes to Earth on
    Boston Common. H. Gregory.
    Pl-EI:111
  Go Down Death. J. Johnson.
    Ad-PB:6, Bo-AN:2

How Samson Bore Away the Gates
   of Gaza. V. Lindsay. Tr-MT:76
Mr. Edwards and the Spider.
   R. Lowell. Br-TC:268, Pe-OA:242,
   Sh-AP:230, Wi-LT:579
Simon Legree—a Negro Sermon.
   V. Lindsay. Co-RM:182,
   Sm-LG:183, Un-MA:226
SERVANTS: see also HUMOR - SERVANTS;
   SATIRE - SERVANTS
Aubade. E. Sitwell. Hi-WP II:6,
   Un-MB:330
A Boy Serving at Table.
   J. Lydgate. Ox-BC:4
The Housemaid. R. Korn. Ho-TY:302
John Brown's Body. S. Benét.
   Ke-TF:303
Master I Have. Ar-TP3:101,Wr-RM:41
Mrs. Southern's Enemy.
   O. Sitwell. Al-VBP:1190
Negro Servant. L. Hughes.
   Ca-VT:240
SERVICE STATIONS
Ex-Basketball Player. J. Updike.
   Du-SH:79, Ha-TP:38, Mo-BG:53,
   Ni-JP:32, Pe-M:60
A Valedictory to Standard Oil of
   Indiana. D. Wagner. Du-SH:146
SERVICE TO OTHERS
And to the Young Men.
   M. Moore. Un-MA:577
A Chant. W. Davies. Go-BP:51
The Divine Office of the
   Kitchen. C. Hallack. Fe-PL:335
I Walk These Many Rooms.
   C. Day Lewis. Go-BP:185
In a Child's Album.
   W. Wordsworth. Bo-FP:232,
   Ch-B:17, Ox-BN:92
Morning Light. E. Newsome.
   Ad-PB:21, Bo-AN:19, Hu-PN:70
Now and Afterwards. D. Craik.
   Fe-PL:329
The Ploughman. Gr-GB:211
Service Is No Heritage. Rv-CB:17
Songs in Praise of the Chief.
   Do-CH:(42)
Sonnets: LVII. W. Shakespeare.
   Al-VBP:203, Co-BL:60,
   No-CL:84, Pa-GTB:7
Those Winter Sundays. R. Hayden.
   Ad-PB:119, Du-SH:53,
   Jo-SA:21, Mo-BG:75
True Religion. Tulsidas. Ba-PO:3
Vicarious Atonement. R. Aldington.
   Un-MB:354
The White-Haired Man: For Richard
   Cabot. M. Sarton. Tr-MR:173
Written in the Album of a Child.
   W. Wordsworth. Ox-BC:105

SEVEN DEADLY SINS: see SIN
SEVEN YEARS' WAR, 1756-1763
Verses Written During the War,
   1756-1763. T. Mordaunt.
   Rv-CB:544
SEVERN RIVER
Elvers. F. Harvey. Cl-DT:47
Sabrina Fair. J. Milton.
   Al-VBP:400, De-CH:122,
   Rv-CB:372, Sm-LG:227
The Severn. M. Drayton.
   Gr-CT:239
SEVILLE, SP.
Sevilla. F. Keyes. Ke-TF:401
SEWALL, SAMUEL
Samuel Sewall. A. Hecht.
   Br-TC:181, Pe-OA:262, Wi-LT:730
SEWING: see NEEDLEWORK
SEXES: see MAN AND WOMAN; MEN;
   WOMEN
SHADOWS
Behind Me the Moon. Kikaku.
   Be-CS:11
Cast upon the Ground.
   T. Takaori. Sh-AM:154
Coming Home. R. Humphries.
   Tr-MR:256
Cottage. S. O'Sullivan.
   Co-PI:165
Could It Have Been a Shadow?
   M. Shannon. Ar-TP3:147,
   Au-SP:290, Fe-FP:390
Down a Sunny Easter Meadow.
   N. Turner. Au-SP:363, Br-SS:140
Follow Thy Fair Sun. T. Campion.
   Al-VBP:213, De-CH:462,
   Go-BP:145, Ho-P:42, Rv-CB:268
Fun with My Shadow. C. Tringress.
   St-FS:16
Haiku 5. E. Knight. Ra-BP:206
Halloween. F. Frost. Ja-PA:37
The Harvest Moon. Sodo.
   Do-TS:36
Human Made Shade. S. Clemons.
   Me-WF:8
I Fear. K. Hanis. Me-WF:9
Little Birches. E. Newsome.
   Hu-PN:72
Lonely Walk. G. McBride. Me-WF:3
Look. C. Zolotow. Ho-ME:8
My Shadow. J. Rubinstein.
   Ho-TY:240
My Shadow. R. Stevenson.
   Ar-TP3:112, Au-SP:189, Bo-FP:112,
   Fe-FP:13, Ga-FB:167, Hu-MP:72,
   Ir-BB:102, Ke-TF:71, La-PP:74,
   La-PV:12, Ox-BC:295, Pe-FB:36
Nocturne Varial. L. Alexander.
   Ad-PB:60, Hu-PN:158
Shadow. Ch'en Meng-chia. Hs-TC:116

SHADOWS — cont'd.
  The Shadow. Chung Ting-wen.
    Pa-MV:74
  Shadow. P. Parmar. Le-M:165
  Shadow and Shade. A. Tate.
    Al-VBP:1215, Ca-VT:222
  Shadow Dance. I. Eastwick.
    Ar-TP3:112, Au-SP:188, La-PP:75
  The Shadow of Flowers.
    Su Tung P'o. Rx-OH:78
  Shadows. E. Farjeon. De-TT:149
  Shadows. P. Hubbell. Su-FVI:12
  Shadows. A. Peel. Th-AS:203
  Shadows. Le-MW:59
  The Sky. E. Roberts. Un-MA:269
  Step on His Head. J. Laughlin.
    Ca-VT:411
  Swift Cloud Shadows. Shusen.
    Be-CS:51
  Tenebris. A. Grimke.
    Ad-PB:15, Hu-PN:58
  The Trees Share Their Shade.
    N. Dishman. Le-WR:11
  Turning from Watching. Shiki.
    Be-CS:40
  Uninhabited Island. Chi Hsüan.
    Pa-MV:49
  Water and Shadow. M. Zaturenska.
    Gr-SS:132
  Wind Tossed Dragons. Hsieh Ngao.
    Rx-LT:110
  Your Shadow. M. Strand.
    Ho-P:255
  Zebra. I. Dinesen. Ad-PE:35,
    Be-EB:17, Bo-GJ:88, La-RM:72,
    Pe-M:107
SHADRACH, MESHACH, AND ABEDNEGO
  Warm Babies. K. Preston.
    Co-FB:225, Ga-S:53
SHADWELL, THOMAS: see also HUMOR -
    SHADWELL, THOMAS
  MacFlecknoe. J. Dryden. Al-VBP:490
SHAKESPEARE, WILLIAM: see also
    HATHAWAY, ANNE; HUMOR -
    SHAKESPEARE, WILLIAM
  Ben Jonson Entertains a Man from
    Stratford. E. Robinson.
    Un-MA:127
  Bishop Blougram's Apology.
    R. Browning. Ox-BN:547
  Elegy on Shakespeare. W. Basse.
    Al-VBP:297, No-CL:77, Rv-CB:263
  An Epitaph on the Admirable
    Dramatic Poet, William
    Shakespeare. J. Milton.
    Al-VBP:387, No-CL:82
  For My Shakespeare Class.
    V. Adrian. Ls-NY:341
  For There Is an Upstart Crow.
    R. Greene. Pl-ML:57

  The King Must Die. B. Taupin.
    Mo-GR:91
  On the Site of a Mulberry-Tree.
    D. Rossetti. Rv-CB:884
  The Path to Shottery. C. Skinner.
    Th-AS:163
  pete the parrot and shakespeare.
    D. Marquis. Pl-ML:102
  The Progress of Poesy. T. Gray.
    Al-VBP:566, Pa-GTB:132,
    Rv-CB:532
  Shakespeare. M. Arnold.
    Al-VBP:959, Go-BP:66, No-CL:83,
    Rv-CB:864, Se-PR:311
  Shakespeare. M. Sorescu.
    Mc-AC:156
  Shakespeare: The Fairies'
    Advocate. T. Hood. Ox-BN:417
  Shakespeare's Mourners.
    J. Tabb. Sh-AP:135
  This Figure. B. Jonson.
    No-CL:93
  To the Memory of Master W.
    Shakespeare. J. Milton.
    No-CL:81
  To the Memory of . . . Mr.
    William Shakespeare.
    B. Jonson. Al-VBP:236,
    Gr-CT:432, No-CL:78, Pl-ML:148
  To the Memory of the Deceased
    Author, Master W. Shakespeare.
    L. Digges. No-CL:80
SHAME: see also GUILT; HUMOR -
    SHAME
  The Confidence. E. Jennings.
    Go-BP:186
  Deceptions. P. Larkin.
    Pa-GTB:557
  Horse and Hammer. P. Dufault.
    Co-BBW:157
  Hymn Written after Jeremiah
    Preached to Me in a Dream.
    O. Dodson. Bo-AN:124
  I Sit and Look Out. W. Whitman.
    Ke-PP:1, Mo-GB:177, Rv-CB:851
  Ichabod. J. Whittier. Kr-OF:33,
    Rv-CB:786, Sh-AP:40
  Lines for a Young Man Who Talked.
    J. Logan. St-H:116
  Militant. L. Hughes. Ad-PB:80
  Reflections. V. Howard. Jo-SA:2
  Requiem of a War-Baby.
    J. Watton. Co-PI:193
  When We Two Parted. G. Byron.
    Al-VBP:720, Fe-PL:109,
    Hi-WP II:104, Ox-BN:237,
    Pa-GTB:190, Rv-CB:692, Un-MW:82
  Where Shall the Lover Rest.
    W. Scott. Al-VBP:670,
    De-CH:263, Pa-GTB:191

SHAMPOOING: see also HUMOR –
SHAMPOOING
Sacrifice of the Sparrows of
the Field. J. Langland.
St–H:107
SHAMROCKS
The Green Little Shamrock of
Ireland. A. Cherry.
Hu–MP:333, Se–PR:67
I'll Wear a Shamrock. M. Davies.
Ar–TP3:200, Br–SS:134, Ha–YA:43
The Wearing of the Green.
Co–PS:51, Er–FA:295,
Gr–GB:193, Hi–FO:252
SHANGHAI, CHINA
The Battle Hymn of Shanghai.
Wang T'ung-chao. Hs–TC:269
An Impression of Shanghai.
Kuo Mo-jo. Hs–TC:36
I've Returned to My Fatherland.
Wang Tu-ch'ing. Hs–TC:198
Smash the Blockade. Jen Chün.
Hs–TC:398
The Sorrow of Shanghai.
Wang Tu-ch'ing. Hs–TC:198
The Soul of Shanghai.
Shao Hsün-mei. Hs–TC:127
SHANTEYS: see SEA SONGS
SHAPE: see SIZE AND SHAPE
SHARECROPPERS
Ain't Got No Home in This World
Anymore. W. Guthrie. Kr–OF:194
Down on Roberts' Farm.
C. Reeves. Hi–TL:197
Floodtide. A. Touré.
Ad–PB:336, Hu–PN:424
These Old Cumberland Mountain
Farms. Kr–OF:189
SHARING: see also HUMOR – SHARING
Betsy Jane's Sixth Birthday.
A. Noyes. Br–BC:101, Br–SS:45
For Them. E. Farjeon. Gr–TG:72
I Have Breakfast, Dinner, Tea.
Gr–TG:36
If You Have a Friend. Er–FA:28
St. Martin and the Beggar.
T. Gunn. Ca–MB:51
A Snack. C. Rossetti.
Bo–FP:78, Ch–B:104
SHARKS: see also HUMOR – SHARKS
The Birth of a Shark.
D. Wevill. Br–TC:465
The Maldive Shark. H. Melville.
Co–BBW:68, Rv–CB:839,
Sh–AP:122, Sm–LG:78
Plague of the Dead Sharks.
A. Dugan. Wi–LT:692
The Sea Turtle and the Shark.
M. Tolson. Ad–PB:44, Ad–PE:40
The Shark. J. Ciardi. Pe–M:114

The Shark. E. Pratt. Do–WH:46
The Shark's Parlor. J. Dickey.
Pe–M:116
Watson and the Shark.
P. Petrie. Ls–NY:37
SHAW, ROBERT GOULD
For the Union Dead. R. Lowell.
Br–TC:265, Pe–OA:244, Wi–LT:583
My Hero. B. Brawley. Hu–PN:59
SHEBA, QUEEN OF
Poem for Flora. N. Giovanni.
Ad–PB:456, Ne–AM:34
The Puppet Dreams. C. Aiken.
Un–MA:425
Solomon and the Bees. J. Saxe.
Un–GT:142
Song. L. Abercrombie.
Un–MB:253
SHEEP: see also BIGHORNS; HERDING;
HUMOR – SHEEP; LAMBS
All in the April Evening.
K. Tynan. Gr–TG:81
Baa, Baa, Black Sheep.
Ar–TP3:74, Au–SP:17, Bo–FP:80,
De–PO:18, Er–FA:506, Li–LB:89,
Mo–NR:57, On–TW:15, Pa–AP:30,
Wi–MG:66, Wr–RM:58
The Borrowing Days. Gr–GB:38
A Child's Pet. W. Davies.
Co–BBW:174, De–CH:89
The Derby Ram. Gr–GB:81, Ir–BB:70,
Lo–LL:64, Mo–MGT:144, Wr–RM:64
The Good Shepherd with the Kid.
M. Arnold. Go–BP:286
The Happy Sheep. W. Thorley.
Au–SP:48, Bo–FP:79,
Ch–B:88, Ma–FO:(7)
The Kill. D. Hall. Ha–WR:45
The Lily. W. Blake. Sm–MK:20
Little Bo-Peep. Au–SP:13,
Bo–FP:79, De–PO:14, Fr–WO:19,
Ir–BB:129, Li–LB:40, Li–SR:126,
Mo–MGT:160, Mo–NR:6, Wi–MG:28,
Wr–RM:11
The Magnet. R. Stone. Un–MA:655
On Westwell Downs. W. Strode.
Rv–CB:362
The One-Horned Ewe.
Gr–GB:82
The Pentland Hills. Gr–GB:175
Sheep. W. Davies. Cl–FC:68,
Ha–PO:125, Pa–RE:29, Rd–OA:76,
Un–MB:177, Wi–LT:618
The Sheep. A. Taylor. Hu–MP:199,
Ox–BC:123
A Sheep Fair. T. Hardy. Ho–P:206
Sheep in Winter. J. Clare.
Ma–FW:280
Sheep Shearing. F. Lape.
Co–BBW:168

SHEEP — cont'd.
  Sleep, Baby, Sleep.
    Bo-FP:49, Fe-FP:471, Hu-MP:123,
    Ke-TF:40, Li-LB:22, Re-TW:74,
    Sm-MK:226, Un-GT:301, Wr-RM:58
  The Sleepy Song. J. Bacon.
    Bo-FP:48, Th-AS:36
  Slumber Song. L. Ledoux.
    Fe-FP:56, Hu-MP:125, Rd-SS:18
  There Was a Pig. Rv-ON:110
  Truth Will Out. P. Bennett.
    Co-BBW:201
  The War-Song of Dinas Vawr.
    T. Peacock. Al-VBP:716,
    Ha-PO:220, Ho-WR:106, Mc-WS:105,
    Na-EO:110, Pa-OM:197
  When Christ Was Born. J. Tabb.
    Gr-TG:80
  Who Goes round My Pinfold Wall?
    Gr-GB:24
  The Wild Boar and the Ram.
    J. Gay. Ke-PP:37
SHELLEY, PERCY BYSSHE: see also
    HUMOR - SHELLEY, PERCY BYSSHE
  The Fishes and the Poet's Hands.
    F. Yerby. Bo-AN:134, Hu-PN:332
  The General Public. S. Benét.
    Pl-ML:125
  Memorabilia. R. Browning.
    No-CL:18, Ox-BN:544,
    Pl-ML:124, Rv-CB:826
  Percy Bysshe Shelley. E. Masters.
    Pl-ML:152
  Shelley's Skylark. T. Hardy.
    Ga-FB:21
  To Shelley. W. Landor.
    Al-VBP:703
SHELLS (MOLLUSKS)
  Broken Shell. W. Scott.
    Ls-NY:228
  By the Sea. C. Rossetti.
    Co-BN:75
  Dr. Sigmund Freud Discovers the
    Sea Shell. A. MacLeish.
    Ke-PP:82, Pe-OA:160
  Footnote to History.
    E. Coatsworth. Br-SS:124
  Frutta di Mare. G. Scott.
    Co-SS:166, Gr-CT:196, Gr-SS:185
  I Have the Shells Now in a
    Leather Box. E. Jennings.
    Go-BP:111
  Lacy Sea Shell. D. Seip.
    La-GI:42
  Reed-Leaf Boat. Pien Chih-lin.
    Hs-TC:165
  Scattered on the Sand. Bashö.
    Be-MC:13
  The Sea. H. Gorter.
    Pa-SG:145

Sea Shell. A. Lowell. Bo-FP:279,
  Bo-HF:81, Fe-FP:274, Hu-MP:176,
  Li-LC:39, Mc-PR:61, Sh-RP:81
Sea Shells. W. Goosley.
  La-GI:43
See What a Lovely Shell.
  A. Tennyson. Bo-GJ:185,
  Co-BN:84
See What I Found. M. Livingston.
  Cr-SS:20
She Sells Sea Shells. Mo-MGT:197,
  Sp-HW:27
The Shell. D. McCord. Li-LC:38
The Shell. J. Stephens.
  Cl-DT:40, Co-BN:82, De-CH:57,
  Ma-FW:43, Ni-JP:34
Shells. K. Raine. Pl-IO:43
Shells. W. Wordsworth.
  Go-BP:111
The Wonder Shell. B. Holender.
  Ls-NY:166
See also La-GI:36-39
SHENANDOAH RIVER
  Shenandoah. Br-AF:189
SHEPHERDS AND SHEPHERD LIFE:
    see also HERDING; HUMOR -
    SHEPHERDS AND SHEPHERD LIFE;
    JESUS CHRIST - NATIVITY;
    PASTORAL LIFE
  The Banks of the Condamine.
    Gr-GB:212
  Blow the Winds, I-Ho. Gr-GB:110
  Break of Day. J. Clare.
    Rv-CB:731
  Fidelity. W. Wordsworth.
    Cl-FC:70
  Folding the Flocks. J. Fletcher.
    De-CH:437, De-TT:113
  The Happy Shepherd. No-CL:99
  A Hymn. J. Leeson. Gr-TG:71
  The Jolly Shepherd. W. Shakespeare.
    Bo-FP:264
  The King of Love My Shepherd Is.
    H. Baker. Gr-TG:40, Ke-TF:184
  The Lambs of Grasmere, 1860.
    C. Rossetti. Co-BBW:165
  Little Bo-Peep. Au-SP:13,
    Bo-FP:79, De-PO:14, Fr-WO:19,
    Ir-BB:129, Li-LB:40, Li-SR:126,
    Mo-MGT:160, Mo-NR:6, Wi-MG:28,
    Wr-RM:11
  Little Boy Blue. J. Ransom.
    We-PZ:36, Wi-LT:321
  The Little Shepherd's Song.
    W. Percy. Ha-YA:67
  The Lord Is My Shepherd.
    Bible. O.T. Psalms.
    Ar-TP3:189, Bo-FP:107, Fe-FP:25,
    Fe-PL:346, Ga-S:213, Rv-CB:130,
    Sh-RP:92

Moonlight . . . Scattered Clouds.
  R. Bloomfield. Ox-BN:55
Old Shepherd's Prayer. C. Mew.
  Pl-EI:176, Un-MB:163
Pastoral. W. Trask. No-CL:262
The Purple Island. P. Fletcher.
  Al-VBP:290
The Sheepherder. L. Sarett.
  Br-AF:161, Fe-FP:317
The Shepherd. J. Baxter.Gr-EC:216
The Shepherd. W. Blake.
  Ar-TP3:13, Go-BP:39, Re-TW:40,
  Rv-CB:588, Un-GT:11
The Shepherd. W. Wordsworth.
  Ox-BN:101
The Shepherd and the Nymph.
  W. Landor. Ox-BN:182
Shepherd's Song. J. Quinn.
  Ke-TF:336
The Shepherd's Wife's Song.
  R. Greene. Al-VBP:139
Sleep, Baby, Sleep.
  Bo-FP:49, Fe-FP:471, Hu-MP:123,
  Ke-TF:40, Li-LB:22, Re-TW:74,
  Sm-MK:226, Un-GT:301, Wr-RM:58
Ya Se Van los Pastores.
  D. Fitts. Gr-CC:172
SHERIDAN, PHILIP HENRY
  Sheridan's Ride. T. Read.
    Er-FA:185, Ga-FB:261, Sp-OG:44
SHERIDAN, RICHARD BRINSLEY: see
    HUMOR — SHERIDAN, RICHARD
    BRINSLEY
SHERIFFS: see POLICE
SHERMAN, TEX.
  The Sherman Cyclone. Em-AF:471
SHERWOOD FOREST
  A Song of Sherwood. A. Noyes.
    Ar-TP3:20, Fe-FP:461, Hu-MP:417,
    Mc-PR:192, Th-AS:160, Un-MB:244
SHILOH, BATTLE, 1862
  The Battle of Shiloh. Em-AF:448
  The Drummer Boy of Shiloh.
    Em-AF:450
  Shiloh, a Requiem. H. Melville.
    Al-VBP:952, Br-AF:72, Ho-WR:120,
    Pa-HT:42, Rv-CB:838, Vi-PP:149
SHIPS: see also BOATS AND BOATING;
    FREIGHTERS; HUMOR — SHIPS; YACHTS
    AND YACHTING
  After the Sea Ship. W. Whitman.
    Co-SS:49, Rv-CB:844
  The Anchorage. P. Wilson. Co-SS:172
  The Captain's Daughter. J. Fields.
    Er-FA:459, Fe-PL:341
  Cargoes. J. Masefield. Ar-TP3:90,
    Bo-FP:134, Co-RG:56, Co-SS:75,
    Fe-FP:196, Ga-FB:182,
    Hi-WP I:109, Mc-PR:135,
    Th-AS:130, Un-MB:225, Wi-LT:189

Celebrated Return. C. Major.
  Be-MA:143, Bo-AN:182
The Dismantled Ship. W. Whitman.
  Cl-FC:87, Ho-LP:53, Rv-CB:846
The Enormous Hand. J. de Lima.
  An-TC:19
The Golden Vanity. Bl-OB:55,
  Co-SS:193, De-CH:398, Fo-OG:10,
  Ho-WR:128, Rv-CB:438
Hastings Mill. C. Smith.
  Mc-WK:196
A Horse Would Tire.
  E. Coatsworth. Ar-TP3:90
A Hurricane at Sea. M. Swenson.
  Ha-WR:34
I Explain. S. Crane. Sh-AP:143
Leave Her, Johnny. Sm-MK:71
The Liner She's a Lady.
  R. Kipling. Ga-FB:189
Little Ships Must Keep the Shore.
  Sp-HW:9
Middle Passage. R. Hayden.
  Ad-PB:110, Be-MA:56,
  Bo-AN:113, Ra-BP:123
Mine Argosy from Alexandria.
  C. Marlowe. Gr-CT:219
The Moldering Hulk. A. Machado.
  Pa-SG:144
My Ships. E. Wilcox. Fe-PL:95
Near Avalon. W. Morris.
  Rv-CB:929
Nocturne of the Wharves.
  A. Bontemps. Hu-PN:224, Ra-BP:93
The Old Ships. J. Flecker.
  Co-RG:57, De-CH:363, De-TT:194,
  Go-BP:156, Hi-FO:15, Na-EO:114,
  No-CL:254, Pa-HT:95, Un-MB:272
Old Ships. D. Morton. Tu-WW:34
An Old Song Re-Sung. J. Masefield.
  Gr-EC:243, Na-EO:68
On a Steamer. D. Baruch. Fe-FP:192
A Passer-By. R. Bridges.
  Ho-WR:125, Ox-BN:873,
  Un-MB:48, Wi-LT:52
Posted as Missing. J. Masefield.
  Bl-OB:51
S.S. Lusitania. M. Arnold.
  Rv-CB:865
Sailing. Ch-B:36
She Is Far from the Land.
  T. Hood. Ho-WR:129
The Ship. J. Squire. De-CH:402,
  De-TT:133
A Ship a-Sailing. G. Setoun.
  Ar-TP3:122, Au-SP:19, Bo-FP:200,
  Co-SS:85, De-TT:48, Gr-EC:242,
  Hi-GD:16, Hu-MP:175, Ir-BB:241,
  Li-LB:86, Mo-MGT:174, Mo-NR:103,
  Pa-AP:44, Sm-MK:199, Sp-HW:25,
  Wi-MG:53, Wr-RM:73

SHIPS — cont'd.
  The Ship Moves. W. Williams.
    Su-FVI:41
  Ships. N. Turner. Au-SP:179
  The Silence of God. O. Sitwell.
    Mc-WK:151
  The Tempest. W. Smith.
    Un-MA:672
  There Is a Ship That Sails the
    Sea. Sp-HW:20
  There Were Three Jovial Welshmen.
    Bl-OB:24, Gr-GB:86, Ir-BB:140,
    Mo-MGT:198, Pa-OM:2, Sm-MK:23,
    Sp-HW:23
  They That Go Down to the Sea.
    Bible. O.T. Psalms.
    Fe-FP:197, Gr-CT:217, Mc-WK:195
  The Water Is Wide. Sp-HW:1
  The Wet Litany. R. Kipling.
    Gr-SS:189
  When My Ship Comes In.
    R. Burdett. Er-FA:30
  A Yankee Ship Came down the
    River. Sp-HW:16
SHIPWRECKS: see also HUMOR -
    SHIPWRECKS; and names of
    wrecked ships, as TITANIC
    (SHIP)
  Alec Yeaton's Son. T. Aldrich.
    Sp-OG:92
  Alexander Selkirk. W. Cowper.
    Co-RG:130, Fe-PL:292,
    Hi-FO:168, Pa-GTB:162
  The Berg. H. Melville.
    Rv-CB:840, Sh-AP:122
  The Bones. W. Merwin.
    Wi-LT:767
  The Clipper Dunbar to the
    Clipper Cutty Sark.
    E. Anderson. Co-PT:249
  The Convergence of the Twain.
    T. Hardy. Ni-JP:119,
    Un-MB:35, Wi-LT:19
  The Diver. R. Hayden.
    Be-MA:66, Du-SH:127, Ra-BP:136
  A Dream of Wrecks. W. Shakespeare.
    Gr-CT:229
  Duriesdyke. Ox-BB:686
  The Gravedigger. B. Carman.
    Co-BN:72
  A Greyport Legend. B. Harte.
    Sp-OG:83
  Henry Martyn. Fo-OG:18,
    Rv-CB:439
  Her Sails Were Old. Sp-HW:17
  The Inchcape Rock. R. Southey.
    Gr-CT:141, Un-GT:161
  The Lowlands o' Holland.
    De-CH:345, Fo-OG:51, Ox-BB:348
  Marooned. R. Field. Sh-RP:165

  Naarip's Wife. E. Isac. Mc-AC:54
  Nearing La Guaira. D. Walcott.
    Lo-TY:113
  An Old Song Re-Sung. J. Masefield.
    Gr-EC:243, Na-EO:68
  On a Friday Morn. De-TT:130
  One Friday Morn. De-CH:400,
    Pa-OM:294
  The Phantom Light of the Baie
    des Chaleurs. A. Eaton.
    Co-PM:55
  The Raven. S. Coleridge.
    Ho-WR:212
  S.S. Lusitania. M. Arnold.
    Rv-CB:865
  Sir Patrick Spens. Al-VBP:35,
    Ar-TP3:19, Bl-OB:47, Bo-GJ:159,
    Co-RG:58, Co-SS:129, De-CH:405,
    Ha-PO:3, Ma-BB:1, Ma-FW:46,
    Ma-YA:41, Ox-BB:311, Rv-CB:38,
    Sm-LG:307, Sp-OG:98
  Skipper Ireson's Ride. J. Whittier.
    Co-SS:147, Fe-PL:45, Hi-TL:73,
    Sh-AP:40, Sp-OG:226
  The Titanic. Co-SS:135
  The Watchers. W. Braithwaite.
    Hu-PN:48
  The Wreck of the Deutschland.
    G. Hopkins. Li-TU:220,
    Ox-BN:852, Wi-LT:30
  The Wreck of the Hesperus.
    H. Longfellow. Er-FA:385,
    Fe-FP:561, Sp-OG:94
  The Wreckers' Prayer.
    T. Roberts. Co-SS:127
  The Yarn of the Loch Achray.
    J. Masefield. Co-SS:139,
    Ha-PO:252
SHIRLEY, MYRA BELLE: see STARR, BELLE
SHIVA (HINDU GOD)
  Shiv and the Grasshopper.
    R. Kipling. Go-BP:84
SHOEMAKERS
  Amends to the Tailors and
    Soutars. W. Dunbar.
    Rv-CB:70
  At the Keyhole. W. de la Mare.
    Bl-OB:88, Un-MB:199
  Cobbler. P. Bacon. La-OC:54
  The Cobbler. E. Chaffee.
    Ar-TP3:12, Au-SP:141
  The Cobbler. St-FS:131
  Cobbler, Cobbler, Mend My
    Shoe. Ir-BB:45, Li-LB:131,
    Mo-MGT:146, Mo-TL:100, Wi-MG:49
  I Am. M. Leib. Ho-TY:87
  A Kiss in the Morning Early.
    Gr-GB:126
  Proletarian Portrait. W. Williams.
    La-OC:49, Pe-M:135

Reynard the Fox. J. Masefield.
    Al-VBP:1134, Rd-OA:51
Riddles. Au-SP:26, Ir-BB:51,
    On-TW:19
The Shoemaker. Au-SP:141,
    Fe-FP:316
The Shoemaker's Booth.
    R. Hershon. Sc-TN:92
SHOES: see also BOOTBLACKS;
    GALOSHES; HUMOR - SHOES;
    MOCCASINS
The Barefoot Bat. De-PP:17
The Brush and the Shoe.
    E. Steinberg. Ho-TY:234
Children, Children, Don't
    Forget. D. Owen. Hu-MP:84
Chinka-Pen. Re-RR:36
Choosing Shoes. F. Wolfe.
    Ar-TP3:111, Au-SP:111, St-FS:77
Cobbler. P. Bacon. La-OC:54
Fairy Shoes. A. Wynne.
    Hu-MP:83
Footwear. M. Justus.
    Au-SP:332, Ha-YA:18
Full All Day. Re-RR:18
Here's Finikey Hawkes. Bo-FP:121,
    Ir-BB:37, Mo-CC:(19)
I Have Lost My Shoes.
    C. Suasnavar. Fe-FP:490
The Lost Shoe. Wr-RM:121
My Father's Boots.
    I. Spiegel. Ho-TY:349
New Shoes. M. Watts. Au-SP:110,
    Bo-FP:116, Fr-MP:4
New Shoes. A. Wilkins. Ar-TP3:111
Over the Ground. Ju-CP:11
Proletarian Portrait. W. Williams.
    La-OC:49, Pe-M:135
Sale. J. Miles. Du-SH:152
Searching for the Visitor's
    Shoes. Koka. Le-MW:103
Shoes. T. Robinson. Ar-TP3:3,
    Au-SP:109
Two Brothers We Are. Mo-MGT:155
SHOOTING: see also HUMOR -
    SHOOTING; HUNTING; SATIRE -
    SHOOTING
The Ballad of Billy the Kid.
    H. Knibbs. Fi-BG:179
The Ballad of Joe Meek.
    S. Brown. Be-MA:31
Grandpa's .45. W. Ransom.
    Ni-CD:201
Ho, Brother Teig. Gr-GB:165
Pizen Pete's Mistake. M. Honey.
    Fi-BG:67
A Shooting Song. W. Rands.
    Ox-BC:234
Shot Who? Jim Lane! M. Moore.
    Un-MA:574

SHOOTING GALLERIES
Travelogue in a Shooting-Gallery.
    K. Fearing. Ni-JP:93
SHOOTING STARS: see METEORS
SHOPPING: see also CHRISTMAS
    SHOPPING; HUMOR - SHOPPING
Miss Thompson Goes Shopping.
    M. Armstrong. Hi-WP II:153
Shop Windows. R. Fyleman.
    Ar-TP3:3, Au-SP:115
The Shopman. E. Farjeon.
    Bo-FP:117
A Sonnet Sequence. R. Hillyer.
    Ho-TH:34
SHOPS AND SHOPKEEPERS: see BAZAARS
    (STREET); GROCERY STORES;
    MARKETS AND MARKETING; STORES
SHOTTERY, ENG.
The Path to Shottery.
    C. Skinner. Th-AS:163
SHOW-OFFS: see BOASTING;
    OSTENTATION
SHREWS (ANIMALS)
The Masked Shrew. I. Gardner.
    Co-BBW:39, Pl-IO:105
Small, Smaller. R. Hoban.
    Co-PU:83
SHREWSBURY, JOHN TALBOT, 1ST EARL OF
Lord Waterford. Gr-CT:472,
    Gr-GB:196
SHRIMPS: see HUMOR - SHRIMPS
SHROPSHIRE, ENG.
A Shropshire Lad. J. Betjeman.
    Ca-MB:70
A Shropshire Lad. A. Housman.
    Pa-HT:137
A Shropshire Lad. Gr-CT:12
SHROVE TUESDAY
A Rhyme for Shrove Tuesday.
    Cl-FC:93
SHRUBS
Little Bush. E. Roberts.
    Li-LC:12
Three Fragments. Br-MW:96
SHYNESS: see LOVE - BASHFULNESS;
    TIMIDITY
SIBELIUS, JEAN
Program Notes on Sibelius.
    D. Babcock. Pl-US:73
SIBERIA, U.S.S.R.: see also ALTAIC
    VERSE; CHUKCHI VERSE; VOGUL
    VERSE; YUKAGHIR VERSE
Message to Siberia. A. Pushkin.
    Lo-TY:68
On the Roads of Siberia.
    H. Leivick. Ho-TY:118
Siberia. J. Mangan.
    Co-RG:132, Hi-FO:221
to L.V. L. Batshev.
    Bo-RU:16

SICILY: see also names of towns, as
    SYRACUSE, SIC.
  Bare Almond-Trees. D. Lawrence.
    Ma-FW:274
  Snake. D. Lawrence. Ar-TP3:68,
    Co-BBW:85, Ha-PO:102,
    Ni-JP:112, Wi-LT:212
SICKNESS: see also HUMOR -
    SICKNESS; and names of diseases,
    as COLDS and FEVERS
  Acon. H.D. Ca-VT:106
  After the Party. W. Wise.
    Fe-FP:359
  Against Sickness. Da-SC:39
  Dusk. L. Nathan. Ls-NY:132
  Evening in the Sanitarium.
    L. Bogan. Br-TC:56
  Felix Randal. G. Hopkins.
    Co-RG:158, Ox-BN:866, Pa-GTB:392,
    Un-MB:44, Wi-LT:43
  Here Lies a Lady. J. Ransom.
    Ca-VT:150, Na-EO:21,
    Un-MA:410, Wi-LT:312
  Hospital. K. Shapiro.
    Ca-VT:370
  How Annandale Went Out.
    E. Robinson. Un-MA:125
  Hymne to God My God in My
    Sicknesse. J. Donne.
    Gr-CT:383, Pl-US:127
  Illness. B. Pasternak. Ca-MR:170
  In the Hospital. D. Laing.
    Ls-NY:73
  Inevitable. J. Betjeman.
    Un-MB:440
  The Land of Counterpane.
    R. Stevenson. Au-SP:205,
    Bo-FP:19, Er-FA:491, Fe-FP:48,
    Gr-EC:95, Hu-MP:52, Ke-TF:72,
    Na-EO:141, Ox-BC:295
  Magic Formula Against Disease.
    Bi-IT:151
  Mother and Son. A. Tate.
    Un-MA:538
  Nerves. E. Jennings. Ls-NY:74
  Night Sweat. R. Lowell.
    Ca-VT:454
  La Nuit Blanche. R. Kipling.
    Un-MB:134
  On the Pestilence That Scourged
    the Fijians after Their First
    Contact with Whites, ca. 1791.
    Tr-US I:228
  The Potter. Lo-TY:47
  Pursuit. R. Warren. Br-TC:454,
    Un-MA:598
  Sick Boy. A. Ridler.
    Ls-NY:225
  A Sick Child. R. Jarrell.
    Ca-VT:402

  The Sick Child. R. Stevenson.
    Co-PS:87, De-CH:37, De-TT:151
  The Soliloquy of an Invalid.
    Harata Tangikuku. Tr-US II:119
  Song of a Sick Chief.
    Tr-US I:211
  Spring Voices. J. Stuart.
    De-FS:196
  The Subalterns. T. Hardy.
    Un-MB:33
  Try Tropic. G. Taggard.
    Un-MA:480
  The Visitors. E. Jennings.
    Go-BP:140
  The Watch. F. Cornford. Un-MB:306
  The Writing of Hezekiah, King of
    Judah, when He Had Been Sick.
    Bible. O.T. Isaiah. Me-PH:43
SIDE SHOWS: see CIRCUSES; FAIRS;
    FREAKS
SIDE-WHEELERS: see BOATS AND
    BOATING
SIDMOUTH, HENRY ADDINGTON, VISCOUNT
  The Masque of Anarchy.
    P. Shelley. Hi-FO:206
SIDNEY, SIR PHILIP
  An Epitaph upon the Right
    Honorable Sir Philip Sidney.
    F. Greville. Ho-P:270
  A Funerall Song. De-CH:255
  Was Never Eie. E. Spenser.
    De-CH:647
SIENA, IT.
  Siena, from a Northern Slope.
    J. Ackerson. Ke-TF:381
SIERRA LEONE: see BALLADS,
    SIERRA LEONE
SIERRA NEVADA
  Ascent to the Sierras.
    R. Jeffers. Pa-HT:61,
    Sm-LG:148
SIEVES
  A Sieve. Ar-TP3:99, Ir-BB:51,
    Wr-RM:76
SIGHT
  The Cross-Eyed Lover. D. Finkel.
    Ho-P:79
  Esthetique du Mal, XV.
    W. Stevens. Wi-LT:160
  I've Seen a Dying Eye.
    E. Dickinson. Fe-PL:285
  My Face Looks Out. E. Honig.
    Ls-NY:75
  On My Short-Sightedness.
    Prem Chaya. Ma-FW:179
  Sight. W. Gibson. Un-MB:242
  The Tint I Cannot Take Is Best.
    E. Dickinson. Un-MA:99
  A Way of Touching the World.
    Me-WF:75

SIGHTSEERS: see TOURISTS
SIGNPOSTS: see SIGNS AND SIGNBOARDS
SIGNS (OMENS): see SAYINGS AND
   SIGNS
SIGNS AND SIGNBOARDS: see also
   HUMOR - SIGNS AND SIGNBOARDS
  Always. L. Pepper. Ho-CT:32
  Billboards in the Rain.
   D. Fogel. Ho-TY:236
  The Sign-Post. E. Thomas.
   Al-VBP:1136
  Song of the Open Road. O. Nash.
   Mo-BG:121
  There Are. D. Taylor. Ho-CT:33
SIGULDA, U.S.S.R.
  Autumn in Sigulda.
   A. Voznesensky. Ca-MR:72
SILENCE: see also HUMOR - SILENCE;
   QUIETNESS; SATIRE - SILENCE
  Acknowledgement. D. Laing.
   Co-PU:15
  Advice to Dreamers.
   R. Frederick. Ke-TF:237
  As Long as We Are Not Alone.
   I. Emiot. Ho-TY:315
  Being Awakened. M. Saito.
   Sh-AM:145
  A Camel. S. Muro. Sh-AM:54
  Carving Away in the Mist.
   M. Padgaonkar. Al-PI:133
  Casual Lines. Yu P'ing-po.
   Hs-TC:18
  A Cave. J. Kirkup. Go-BP:32
  Cloister. C. Aiken. Un-MA:436
  The Dumb Soldier.
   R. Stevenson. Un-GT:164
  Elected Silence. S. Sassoon.
   Un-MB:315
  Envy the Old. M. Van Doren.
   Ho-P:275
  Faint Music. W. de la Mare.
   Sm-LG:39
  Frost at Midnight. S. Coleridge.
   Ox-BN:162, Rv-CB:661
  Haiku 6. E. Knight. Ra-BP:206
  Hide and Seek. S. Kuroda.
   Sh-AM:117
  The House in the Green Well.
   J. Wheelock. Un-MA:344
  Hush. M. Leib. Ho-TY:89
  The Interrupted Concert.
   F. García Lorca. Le-SW:79
  Into Spring Mountains.
   M. Saito. Sh-AM:146
  Let Be at Last. E. Dowson.
   Ha-PO:155
  The Listeners. W. de la Mare.
   Al-VBP:1118, Er-FA:406, Fe-FP:513,
   Pa-OM:298, Re-TW:116, Sh-RP:34,
   Un-MB:196, Wi-LT:131

Monna Innominata. C. Rossetti.
  Al-VBP:994, Ox-BN:718
Moth. K. Alling. Ho-LP:46
My Existence. S. Mizuhara.
  Sh-AM:167
A Night Frozen Hard. S. Ito.
  Sh-AM:103
Night Song at Amalfi.
  S. Teasdale. Bo-HF:123,
  Sm-PT:63, Un-MA:264, Un-MW:57
Night Time. P. Wisdom.
  Le-M:199
Nightfall. C. Ricardo.
  An-TC:27
Now Close the Windows.
  R. Frost. Ha-LO:5
Now Fall Asleep. E. Coatsworth.
  Rd-SS:19
An Old Silent Pond. Basho.
  Be-CS:8
The Old Sweet Dove of Wiveton.
  S. Smith. Rd-OA:4
Onion Bucket. L. Thomas.
  Ad-PB:483
Orders. A. Klein. Do-WH:5
Pastourelle. D. Hayes. Bo-AN:94
Peace, like a Lamb. L. Clark.
  Hi-WP I:110
Poetic Art. I. Pillat. Mc-AC:58
The Precept of Silence.
  L. Johnson. Al-VBP:1103,
  Un-MB:155
The Recollection. P. Shelley.
  De-CH:148
Silence. T. Hood. Al-VBP:798,
  `De-CH:385, Ox-BN:425, Rv-CB:762
Silence. E. Masters. Un-MA:144
Silence. M. Moore. Al-VBP:1174,
  Ha-PO:219, Ho-LP:72, Ma-FW:62,
  Mc-WS:77, Mo-BG:81
Silence. A. Pritam. Al-PI:141
Silence. W. Turner. Un-MB:348
Silence. J. Wheelock. Wi-LT:654
Silences. A. O'Shaughnessy.
  Ox-BN:851
Silences. E. Pratt. En-PC:5
Silent, but. . . . Tsuboi Shigeji.
  Ma-FW:234
Silent Noon. D. Rossetti.
  Ma-YA:211, Ox-BN:683, Un-MW:138
Silentium. F. Tyutchev.
  Pa-SG:123
Sleep upon the World. Alcman.
  Gr-CT:409
Song. R. Milnes. De-TT:156
The Spring Waters, 43, 168.
  Ping Hsin. Hs-TC:23, 24
The Stillness. Basho. Sh-RP:64
Stillness. J. Flecker.
  Bo-GJ:126, De-CH:38, Un-MB:272

SILENCE — cont'd.
Undertone. D. Quick. De-FS:153
Walk on a Winter Day. S. Allen.
   Ha-YA:143
The Wave. D. Hine. Ho-P:99
What Is So Airy. Re-RR:66
A Winter Twilight. A. Grimke.
   Ad-PB:16, Hu-PN:54
A Wise Old Owl Lived in an Oak.
   Er-FA:213, Li-LB:103, Mo-MGT:118,
   Un-GF:13, Un-GT:22, Wi-MG:47
Your Eyes Have Their Silence.
   G. Barrax. Ad-PB:224
SILICA
The Book of the Dead.
   M. Rukeyser. Kr-OF:197
SILKWORMS
The Silkworms. D. Stewart.Ma-FW:205
SILVER, JOHN: see JOHN SILVER
SILVER (COLOR)
Silver. W. de la Mare.
   Ar-TP3:181, Br-SS:32, Co-BN:121,
   Co-PM:48, Fe-FP:265, Mc-WK:5,
   Rd-SS:27, Sp-OG:308, Un-GB:12,
   Un-GT:262, Un-MB:202
Washed in Silver. J. Stephens.
   Co-EL:151
SILVER (METAL)
The Fable of the Magnet and the
   Churn. W. Gilbert. Fe-FP:351,
   Hu-MP:444, Pa-OM:46, Sh-RP:122
SIMEON (BIBLE. N.T.)
The Light in the Temple.
   W. Benét. Tr-MR:113
A Song for Simeon. T. Eliot.
   Gr-BT:174, Pl-EI:202
SIMON LEGREE
Simon Legree - a Negro Sermon.
   V. Lindsay. Co-RM:182,
   Sm-LG:183, Un-MA:226
SIMON MAGUS: see HELEN OF TYRE
SIMON, THE CYRENIAN
Simon the Cyrenian Speaks.
   C. Cullen. Be-MA:50, Bo-AN:89,
   Ga-S:160, Lo-TY:235, Ra-BP:99,
   Un-MA:570
SIMONE, NINA
for Nina Simone wherever you are.
   L. Curky. Jo-VC:46
SIMPLE LIFE: see also COMMONPLACE-
   NESS; SIMPLICITY
The American Freedom. M. Biller.
   Se-PR:128
Better than Gold. A. Ryan. Er-FA:9
Character of a Happy Life.
   H. Wotton. Al-VBP:221,
   Ni-JP:169, Pa-GTB:63
The Commonplace. W. Whitman.
   Un-MA:42
Country Cottage. Tu Fu. Rx-PH:20

Elegy Written in a Country
   Churchyard. T. Gray.
   Al-VBP:559, De-TT:83, Er-FA:462,
   Fe-PL:281, Ha-PO:144, Ma-YA:125,
   Pa-GTB:145, Rv-CB:533
Evening in the Village. Lu Yu.
   Rx-OH:107
French Peasants. M. Gibbon.
   Ga-S:121
Gladly I'll Live in a Poor
   Mountain Hut. Le-MW:111
Good-bye. R. Emerson.
   Er-FA:475
The Happy Life. W. Thompson.
   Al-VBP:555
I Eat a Slice of Bread. P. Mayer.
   St-H:132
I Love All Natural Things.
   V. Burich. Bo-RU:26
If I Were King. J. McCarthy.
   Er-FA:108, Fe-PL:112
The Jolly Thresherman. Em-AF:773
The Man of Life Upright.
   T. Campion. Al-VBP:219,
   De-CH:637, Go-BP:44,
   Ha-PO:197, Rv-CB:273
Metrum V. H. Vaughan. Ke-PP:32
A Mind Content. R. Greene.
   Al-VBP:142
Not Self-Denial. E. Gibbs.
   Ls-NY:334
O Happy! De-TT:105, Sp-AS:28
Quiet Citizen. B. Cooper.
   Ke-TF:298
Resolve. V. Miller. Ha-TP:106
The Shepherd Boy's Song.
   J. Bunyan. Gr-TG:17, Pl-EI:204,
   Rv-CB:459, Un-GT:308
The Sky Is Up above the Roof.
   P. Verlaine. Fe-FP:469
Spring Comes to a Little Temple.
   Ch'en Meng-chia. Hs-TC:117
A Thanksgiving to God for His
   House. R. Herrick. Al-VBP:337,
   De-TT:168, Gr-CT:269
To a Mouse. R. Burns.
   Co-BBW:36, Er-FA:226, Fe-PL:367,
   Hu-MP:190, Mc-WK:60, Pa-GTB:141,
   Rd-OA:24, Rv-CB:616, Sp-OG:297
To Mr. Izaak Walton. C. Cotton.
   Al-VBP:472, Go-BP:19
Turf-Stacks. L. MacNeice.
   Wi-LT:455
Under the Greenwood Tree.
   W. Shakespeare. Al-VBP:186,
   Ar-TP3:204, Bo-FP:259, Co-BN:206,
   De-CH:134, De-TT:147, Er-FA:263,
   Fe-FP:211, Gr-EC:48, Ho-WR:74,
   Hu-MP:268, Mc-PR:30, Pa-GTB:5,
   Rv-CB:196, Tu-WW:61

Visitors. Tu Fu. Rx-OH:19
What Makes Me Different.
   B. Akhmadulina. Bo-RU:6
When We Court and Kiss.
   T. Campion. Al-VBP:220,
   Un-MW:176
Where Is Heaven? B. Carman.
   Un-GT:309
The Wish. A. Cowley.
   Al-VBP:450, De-CH:524
SIMPLICITY: see also COMMONPLACE-
   NESS; SIMPLE LIFE
The Carpenter. P. Hartnoll.
   Ga-S:113
Come, Serene Plainness.
   M. Leib. Ho-TY:89
Contentment in Poverty. Issa.
   Sh-RP:65
The Gift to Be Simple.
   H. Moss. Br-TC:307, Pl-IO:181,
   Tr-MR:174
How Happy Is the Little Stone.
   E. Dickinson. Sh-AP:131
The Kingdom. L. MacNeice.
   Wi-LT:463
A Midnight Interior. S. Sassoon.
   Tr-MR:55
Not in the Guide-Books.
   E. Jennings. Wi-LT:742
Puritan Sonnet. E. Wylie.
   Pe-OA:86, Sh-AP:170, Un-MA:277
When Jenny Wren Was Young.
   Hu-MP:213, Wr-RM:23
Wild Peaches. E. Wylie.
   Pa-HT:40, Sh-AP:169
SIN: see also GOOD AND EVIL;
   HUMOR - SIN; IMPENITENCE; VICE
Adam Lay Ibounden.
   De-CH:468, Ga-S:39, Gr-CT:83,
   Gr-TG:82, Ma-YA:26, Rv-CB:9
The Black Riders. S. Crane.
   Sh-AP:144
Duessa's Coach. E. Spenser.
   Ga-S:27
Ecclesiastes. G. Chesterton.
   Un-MB:205
Forgive My Guilt. R. Coffin.
   Ba-PO:165, Du-RG:76
God and the Holy Ghost.
   D. Lawrence. Tr-MR:224
I Asked for Peace. D. Dolben.
   Go-BP:180
In Answer to a Question.
   W. Blunt. Al-VBP:1053
In My Own Album. C. Lamb. Rv-CB:673
A Leg in a Plaster Cast.
   M. Rukeyser. Un-MA:627
Lord, Thou Hast Been Our Dwelling
   Place. Bible. O.T. Psalms.
   Me-PH:23, Pl-EI:198

My Spectre Around Me. W. Blake.
   Rv-CB:611
Original Sin. R. Jeffers.
   Un-MA:373
Original Sin: A Short Story.
   R. Warren. Wi-LT:839
Rejoice Not, O Israel, for Joy.
   Bible. O.T. Hosea.
   Me-PH:46
Sin. G. Herbert. Al-VBP:344
Sinners. D. Lawrence. Al-VBP:1158
There Was One I Met upon the Road.
   S. Crane. Pl-EI:72
Young Companions. Fi-BG:211
SINGAPORE
A Ship for Singapore. D. Hicky.
   Th-AS:129
SINGING: see SONGS AND SINGING
SINGING GAMES: see also CLAPPING
   GAMES
All the Birdies in the Air.
   Mo-TL:101
Alligoshee. Mo-MGT:203
American Jump! Mo-TL:104
Among the Little White Daisies.
   Ju-CP:48
Bagpipes. Mo-MGT:205
Bangles. Ca-MU:17
The Bells of London.
   Bo-FP:125, De-PO:24, Gr-CT:296,
   Ir-BB:116, Li-LB:132, Mc-PR:110,
   Mo-MGT:138, Mo-NR:84, Na-EO:167
Blind Man's Buff. Mo-MGT:189
Bluebird, Blackbird. Ju-CP:44
Bobby Shafto. De-CH:682,
   De-TT:30, Gr-GB:104, Hu-MP:164,
   Mo-MGT:151, Wi-MG:31, Wr-RM:127
Cobbler, Cobbler, Mend My Shoe.
   Ir-BB:45, Li-LB:131, Mo-MGT:146,
   Mo-TL:100, Wi-MG:49
Didn't It Rain? Bu-DY:52
Do You Know the Muffin Man.
   Mo-TL:90
Dollar, Dollar. Ju-CP:31
Down in Yonder Meadow.
   De-CH:331, Ir-BB:32
Ducks and Drakes. De-CH:685,
   Ir-BB:33, Wr-RM:104
The Farmer in His Den.
   Mo-TL:91
Girls' Song for the Game of
   "Pots." Do-CH:(32),
   Tr-CB:46, Tr-US I:109
Go in and out the Window.
   Ju-CP:52
Great A. De-PO:8, Li-LB:106,
   Mo-MGT:146, Mo-NR:49, Wr-RM:55
Green Grass. De-CH:191, Gr-GB:25,
   Mo-MGT:171, Rv-ON:16
Green Gravel. Ju-CP:54

SINGING GAMES — cont'd.
  Here Come the Dukes. Ju-CP:46
  Here Comes a Lusty Wooer.
    De-CH:327
  Here We Come Gathering Nuts in
    May. Li-LB:136, Mo-TL:95,
    Na-EO:119
  Here We Go round the Mulberry
    Bush. De-PO:26, Li-LB:128,
    Mo-MGT:178, Mo-NR:26,
    Mo-TL:94, Wr-RM:65
  Hey, Wully Wine. De-CH:330
  I'm the Wee Mouse. Mo-TL:97
  The Jolly Miller. Ju-CP:51
  The King of France. Wr-RM:105
  London Bridge. Bo-FP:126,
    De-CH:61, Gr-CT:287, Gr-GB:24,
    Li-LB:65, Mo-MGT:126, Mo-NR:112,
    Wr-RM:120
  Looby Loo. Au-SP:21, Ir-BB:14,
    Mo-TL:102
  Mary Brown. Su-FVI:77
  The Merry-Ma-Tanzie. Gr-GB:22,
    Rv-ON:15
  My Bangelory Man. Gr-EC:223,
    Ir-BB:241, Rv-ON:18
  Nay, Ivy, Nay. De-CH:230,
    Rv-CB:32
  Now You're Married You Must
    Obey. Un-GT:22
  Polly Perkin, Hold on to My
    Jerkin. Mo-TL:96
  Pop! Goes the Weasel. Au-SP:250,
    Bu-DY:53, Ir-BB:125, Mo-CC:(42),
    Mo-MGT:100, Na-EO:175, Pa-AP:52
  Ring-a-Ring o' Roses. De-PO:(3),
    Ir-BB:11, Li-LB:13, Li-SR:129,
    Mo-CC:(21), Mo-MGT:173,
    Mo-NR:107, Mo-TL:89
  Ring-Around-a-Rosy. Au-SP:20
  Rules of Contrary. Rv-ON:20
  Run a Little. J. Reeves.
    Ir-BB:11, St-FS:70
  Sally down Our Alley. Ju-CP:50
  Sally Go round the Sun.
    Br-FF:(4), Mo-CC:(9),
    Mo-MGT:100, Mo-TL:104
  Skip to My Lou. Gr-EC:236
  Swinging. Mo-MGT:201
  There Was a Farmer Had a Dog.
    Mo-TL:102
  Three Knights from Spain.
    Bl-OB:36, De-CH:328, Fo-OG:42,
    Gr-CB:26, Rv-ON:106
  Three Times Round Went Our Gallant,
    Gallant Ship. Mo-TL:99
  We Are Off to Timbuctoo.
    Mo-TL:96
  We Can Play the Big Bass Drum.
    Mo-TL:105

  A Wedding. Bo-FP:294, Ch-B:114,
    De-CH:34
  When I Was a Baby. Mo-TL:98
  The Whummil Bore. De-CH:329
SINGLE MEN: see BACHELORS
SINGLE WOMEN: see also HUMOR -
    SINGLE WOMEN; WIDOWS
  An Ancient Virgin. G. Crabbe.
    Ox-BN:4
  Four Epitaphs. S. Warner.
    Un-MB:371
  If No One Ever Marries Me.
    L. Alma-Tadema. Br-BC:111,
    Un-GT:13
  Miss Thompson Goes Shopping.
    M. Armstrong. Hi-WP II:153
  My Aunt. O. Holmes.
    Sh-AP:62
  My Old Maid Aunt. D. Schultz.
    Du-SH:137
  What She Did in the Morning I
    Wouldn't Know. M. Moore.
    Du-SH:57
  The Yellow Cat. L. Jennings.
    De-FS:110
SIOUAN INDIANS: see also HUMOR -
    SIOUAN INDIANS; INDIANS OF
    NORTH AMERICA - VERSE-SIOUAN
  Cottonwood Leaves. B. Clark.
    Ar-TP3:35
  The Sioux Women. Ho-SD:9,
    Jo-TS:22, Tr-US II:226
SIRENS (SEA NYMPHS): see also
    HUMOR - SIRENS (SEA NYMPHS)
  The Life and Death of Jason.
    W. Morris. Al-VBP:1011
  Siren Chorus. G. Darley.
    Al-VBP:794, Gr-CT:202, Ox-BN:396
  The Sirens' Song. Homer.
    Mo-GR:13
  Tales of Brave Ulysses.
    E. Clapton. Mo-GR:11
  Ulysses and the Siren.
    S. Daniel. Al-VBP:154
SIRMIONE, IT.
  Frater Ave atque Vale.
    A. Tennyson. Gr-CT:444,
    Pa-GTB:341
SISTERS: see also HUMOR - SISTERS
  Around the World. K. Greenaway.
    Ch-B:85, Fe-FP:38
  Babylon. Ma-BB:143, Ox-BB:199
  Binnorie. Ma-BB:25,
    Ox-BB:69
  The Bonny Heyn. Ox-BB:201
  Boy with His Hair Cut Short.
    M. Rukeyser. Br-TC:350,
    Ca-VT:361, Co-RG:159, Wi-LT:805
  Brother and Sister.
    W. Wordsworth. De-TT:33

The Ch'ing Ming Festival.
  Feng Hsüeh-feng.   Hs-TC:368
Clootie.   Ma-BB:94
Coffee and Tea.   Wr-RM:83
Cradle-Song for a Boy.
  Da-SC:57, Ho-SD:65
The Cruel Brother.   Ma-YA:38,
  Ox-BB:236
Death of a Sister.   Bi-IT:96
Dirges, II.   Tr-US II:42
Fair Annie.   De-CH:414, Ox-BB:138
Girl's-Eye View of Relatives.
  P. McGinley.   Ke-TF:90,
  Mc-WS:145
Hymn of the Afflicted.
  Tr-US I:81
I Would Like to Be a Bee.
  D. Baruch.   Br-BC:92
Joan's Door.   E. Farjeon.   Br-BC:80
Little.   D. Aldis.   Ar-TP3:5,
  Fe-FP:38
Older Brother.   T. Maruyama.
  Le-TA:29
On the Death of Anne Brontë.
  C. Brontë.   Al-VBP:916
Our Silly Little Sister.
  D. Aldis.   Co-HP:30,
  Fe-FP:40, Na-EO:118
A Puzzling Example.
  V. Benjamin.   Br-BC:55
Resolution in Four Sonnets.
  C. Cotton.   Ho-P:244, No-CL:233
Seven Brothers Have One Sister.
  Gr-BB:30
Sisters.   E. Farjeon.   Fe-FP:37
Song.   Tr-US I:230
Swinging on a Gate.   On-TW:31
To a Little Sister, Aged Ten.
  A. Cummings.   Br-BC:79
Triolet Against Sisters.
  P. McGinley.   Pe-M:133
The Truth about My Sister and
  Me.   A. Probst.   Ni-CD:166
The Twa Sisters.   De-CH:421,
  Rv-CB:42
Young Johnstone.   Ox-BB:212
SISTERS-IN-LAW
  Her Sister-in-Law Answers the
    Greeting Song.   Tr-CB:36,
    Tr-US I:93
SITTING BULL, CHIEF
  Last Song of Sitting Bull.
    Kr-OF:1, Le-OE:127
  Sitting Bull's Song.   Da-SC:112
SITWELL, EDITH: see HUMOR -
    SITWELL, EDITH
SIZE AND SHAPE: see also HUMOR -
    SIZE AND SHAPE
  Aye, Even Small Things.
    P. Heyse.   Un-R:113

City Blockades.   L. Hopkins.
  Ho-CS:33
Comparison.   M. Hoberman.
  Br-BC:110
The Difference.   E. Chaffee.
  Br-BC:75
The Fly.   W. de la Mare.
  Cl-DT:16
Four and Eight.   ff. Wolfe.
  Br-BC:76, Br-SS:43
Gnat.   R. Moore.   Un-GT:80
If All the Seas Were One Sea.
  Au-SP:220, Ir-BB:132, Lo-LL:59,
  Mo-MGT:175, Mo-NR:76, Wr-RM:53
Little Bug.   R. Bacmeister.
  It-HB:13
The Little Elf.   J. Bangs.
  Ar-TP3:153, Au-SP:287, Bo-FP:309,
  Br-BC:107, Ch-B:34, Hu-MP:91,
  La-PV:75, Mc-WK:106, Pe-FB:60,
  Th-AS:10, Un-GB:13, Un-GT:16
Measurement.   A. Sullivan.
  Mc-WK:18, Sh-RP:71
One.   A. Young.   La-IH:21
The Peony Was as Big as This.
  Issa.   Do-TS:3
People.   L. Lenski.   Au-SP:130,
  Fe-FP:247, Ho-CS:16, La-OC:43
Playgrounds.   L. Alma-Tadema.
  Bo-FP:270, Mc-AW:93
Rain Sizes.   J. Ciardi.
  Au-SP:112
Small, Smaller.   R. Hoben.
  Co-PM:83
Teacher.   T. Kobayashi.
  Le-TA:53
A Wee Little Boy Has Opened a
  Store.   Wy-CM:11
What Are Heavy?   C. Rossetti.
  Ox-BC:278
The World So Big.   A. Fisher.
  Au-SP:184
SKATING: see also HUMOR - SKATING
  Answer This Riddle.   Re-RR:37
  Black Water and Bright Air.
    C. Carrier.   Mo-SD:194
  Ice-Skates.   E. Olson.   Mo-SD:145
  The Midnight Skaters. E. Blunden.
    Bo-GJ:235, Hi-WP II:145,
    Pa-GTB:491, Un-MB:398
  Rink.   D. Lourie.   Sc-TN:151
  River Skater.   W. Welles.
    Mo-SD:151
  Roller Skates. J. Farrar. Fe-FP:106
  The Skaters.   J. Fletcher.
    Mo-SD:149, Un-MA:318
  The Skaters.   J. Williams.
    Fl-HH:15, Mo-SD:179
  A Skater's Valentine.
    A. Guiterman.   Br-SS:120

SKATING — cont'd.
  Skating. H. Asquith. Ar-TP3:106,
    Au-SP:194, Fe-FP:116
  Skating. R. Kipling. Mo-SD:151
  Skating. W. Wordsworth.
    De-CH:219, Mo-SD:148,
    Sm-LG:60, Un-GT:281
  Skating Song. C. Morley.
    Bo-FP:180
  Snow. W. Rodgers. Wi-LT:491
  To Kate, Skating Better than
    Her Date. D. Daiches.
    Co-FB:402, Mo-SD:150
  Watching Ice Skating.
    Kuo Mo-jo. Hs-TC:42
  Wings and Wheels. N. Turner.
    Ar-TP3:107, Au-SP:168
SKELETONS: see also BONES; HUMOR -
    SKELETONS; SKULLS
  Danse Macabre. A. Schwab.
    De-FS:174
  In the Museum. I. Gardner.
    Co-EL:78
  The Lion's Skeleton. C. Turner.
    Rd-OA:119
  Ode to Hengist and Hora.
    R. Jeffers. Gr-SS:173
  On Finding a Bird's Bones in
    the Woods. L. Mueller.
    St-H:144
  Skeleton. S. Barry. Le-M:110
  The Witch of Coös. R. Frost.
    Al-VBP:1129, Pe-OA:36,
    Sh-AP:147, Wi-LT:170
  You Earth. Le-IB:119
SKIING: see also HUMOR - SKIING
  Hunger. L. Bruce. Pe-M:46
  January: Skiing Song.
    M. Lewis. Un-GT:268
  Out Skiing. L. Shakhovich.
    Mo-MI:19
  Skier. R. Francis. Fl-HH:31,
    Ho-LP:61, La-RM:31, Mo-SD:152
  Skiing. M. Chute. La-PP:31
SKILL
  Civilities. T. Whitbread.
    Mo-SD:164
  Of Kings and Things.
    L. Morrison. Ad-CI:67
  On His Very First Hunt.
    Le-IB:51
  The Passer. G. Abbe.
    Du-SH:77, Mo-SD:27
  Rue St. Honore. P. Williamson.
    Ls-NY:242
SKIMMERS (BIRDS)
  Skimmers. P. Newman. Ca-BP:47
SKIN
  Covering the Subject. R. Armour.
    Mc-WK:47, Sh-RP:146

SKIN AND SCUBA DIVING
  Diver. P. Neruda. Li-TU:127
  Skin Diving in the Virgins.
    J. Brinnin. Pe-OA:238
  Underseas Fever. W. Cole.
    Co-FB:455, Co-SS:168
SKINNER, CYRIACK
  To Cyriack Skinner. J. Milton.
    Pa-GTB:66
SKIPPING
  Hippety Hop to the Barber Shop.
    Ar-TP3:100, Au-SP:9, Ir-BB:13
  Skipping Along Alone. W. Welles.
    Ar-TP3:110, Au-SP:296
  Skipping Song. Ju-CP:69
SKIPPING ROPE
  All in Together. Bu-DY:88
  Charlie Chaplin Went to France.
    Er-FA:499
  Dolly Mariar. Ju-CP:8
  A Girl Skipping Rope in Flushing.
    S. Stepanchev. Ls-NY:287
  The High Skip. Li-LB:129
  I Like Coffee, I Like Tea.
    Er-FA:499
  The Little Jumping Girls.
    K. Greenaway. Ar-TP3:101,
    Fe-FP:105, Hu-MP:38,
    Ir-BB:14, St-FS:43
  Order in the Court. Co-OW:63,
    Su-FVI:6
  See also Bu-DY:70-84, Wo-JR
SKULLS
  The Relic. R. Hillyer.
    Pl-US:145
  The Revenger's Tragedy.
    C. Tourneur. Al-VBP:274
  The U.S. Sailor with the
    Japanese Skull. W. Scott.
    Pe-OA:207, Wi-LT:812
  Upon the Image of Death.
    R. Southwell. De-CH:244
  Yardbird's Skull. O. Dodson.
    Ad-PB:132, Bo-AN:125, Ca-VT:387
SKUNKS: see also HUMOR - SKUNKS
  Dancing Song of the Skunk.
    Tr-US II:234
  The Skunk. D. Baruch.
    Au-SP:70
  The Skunk. R. Coffin.
    Ar-TP3:63, Fe-FP:168
  Skunk Hour. R. Lowell. Un-MA:669
  The Wood-Weasel. M. Moore.
    Be-EB:18, Rd-OA:46
SKY
  As I Row over the Plain.
    Fujiwara no Tadamichi.
    Ba-ST:31
  An Astrologer's Song.
    R. Kipling. Un-MB:135

Evening over the Forest.
   B. Mayor. Cl-FC:28
The God of Galaxies. M. Van Doren.
   Pl-IO:19, Tr-MR:138
He Wishes for the Cloths of
   Heaven. W. Yeats. Go-BP:130,
   Ho-LP:13, Th-AS:144, Un-MB:108
The Heavens Declare the Glory of
   God. Bible. O.T. Psalms.
   Fe-FP:267, Gr-CT:236
I Break the Sky. O. Dodson.
   Ad-PB:133
I Have a Garden. Re-RR:31
I'll Sail upon the Dog-Star.
   T. Durfey. Ir-BB:107, Pa-RE:89,
   Rv-CB:481, Sm-LG:205
I'm Glad the Sky Is Painted Blue.
   Au-SP:320, Ch-B:110,
   Fr-MP:12, Lo-LL:107
It Is There that Our Hearts Are
   Set. Ho-SD:33, Le-OE:5
Little Garaine. G. Parker.
   Fe-FP:302
Lost in Heaven. R. Frost.
   Un-MA:188
Love in Labrador. C. Sandburg.
   Ca-VT:27
A Misanthrope's Serenade.
   Kuo Mo-jo. Hs-TC:36
The Moon Ship. Hitomaro.
   Ch-B:46, Le-MW:38
No Moon No Star. B. Deutsch.
   Ha-WR:52
O Sky. O. Mandelstam.
   Ca-MR:150
On the Sea of Heaven.
   Hitomaro. Ba-ST:32
Peace on Earth. W. Williams.
   Al-VBP:1153, Ha-LO:24
Polar Star. Da-SC:11,
   Le-OE:102, Tr-US II:248
Preludes for Memnon. C. Aiken.
   Co-BL:49, Un-MA:434
Rabbit and Lark. J. Reeves.
   St-FS:101
Recitative. Tr-US II:45
Sea (Gull). G. Manin.
   Ad-II:55
The Sky. E. Roberts. Un-MA:269
The Sky. Ab-MO:6, Be-AP:64,
   Le-OE:109, Lo-TY:8
The Sky Is Up above the Roof.
   P. Verlaine. Fe-FP:469
The Sky Will Resound. Da-SC:148
Song of the Sky Loom. Da-SC:76,
   Le-OE:6, Mo-TS:16, Tr-US II:256
The Spacious Firmament on High.
   J. Addison. Mc-PR:202, Pl-EI:211,
Star of the Evening. J. Sayles.
   Li-SR:79

Star of the Western Skies.
   Fi-BG:193
The Starlight Night. G. Hopkins.
   Al-VBP:1061, Cl-DT:38, Pa-GTB:389,
   Re-TW:84, Un-MB:42, Wi-LT:40
Sunday at Hampstead. J. Thomson.
   Al-VBP:1010, Sm-MK:12, Sp-OG:345
Twilit Revelation. L. Adams.
   Un-MA:545
The Unending Sky. J. Masefield.
   Ma-FW:124, Wi-LT:192
When I Consider Thy Heavens.
   Bible. O.T. Psalms.
   Fe-FP:202, Pl-IO:150
SKYLARKS: see also HUMOR - SKYLARKS
Above the Meadow. Chiyo.
   Be-MC:40
The Caged Skylark. G. Hopkins.
   Un-MB:43, Wi-LT:42
Heaven Is Heaven. C. Rossetti.
   Ha-YA:69
High on a Mountain. Basho.
   Be-CS:21
Lark Ascending. G. Meredith.
   Ho-WR:66, Rd-OA:53
Night Skylark. S. Tsuboi.
   Sh-AM:69
Ode on the Pleasure Arising from
   Vicissitude. T. Gray.
   Pa-GTB:109
Shelley's Skylark. T. Hardy.
   Ga-FB:21
The Skylark. J. Hogg.
   Co-BBW:235
The Skylark. C. Rossetti.
   Pa-RE:26, Un-GT:61
Skylark. Seien. Le-MW:24
There, where the Skylark's
   Singing. Kyorai. Be-MC:43
Three Things. J. Auslander.
   Hu-MP:198
Three Things to Remember.
   W. Blake. Br-SS:150, Ch-B:89,
   Fe-FP:280, Gr-EC:178, Gr-TG:31,
   Hi-GD:13, Hi-WP II:170
To a Skylark. P. Shelley.
   Co-RG:139, Er-FA:228, Fe-FP:293,
   Fe-PL:356, Ga-FB:18, Hu-MP:230,
   Ox-BN:283, Pa-GTB:243, Sp-OG:353
To the Skylark. W. Wordsworth.
   Er-FA:227, Pa-GTB:242
An Unseen Skylark. Shiki.
   Be-CS:17
Voices. Kyoroku. Le-IS:13
SKYROS
Scyros. K. Shapiro.
   Wi-LT:536
SKYSCRAPERS
Building a Skyscraper.
   J. Tippett. Hu-MP:399

SKYSCRAPERS — cont'd.
Elegy on an Empty Skyscraper.
J. Fletcher. Sh-AP:173
People Who Must. C. Sandburg.
La-OC:48, La-PV:190
Prayers of Steel. C. Sandburg.
Fe-FP:255, Hu-MP:403, La-OC:151,
La-PV:194, Mo-BG:26, Un-MA:203
Skyscraper Is a City's House.
C. Lambert. Hu-MP:400
Skyscrapers. R. Field. Fe-FP:244,
Fr-MP:16, Gr-EC:278
Song of the Builders. J. Murton.
Br-AF:212
Summon the Workers. C. Lambert.
Hu-MP:400
Tall City. S. Pulsifer.
La-OC:99
To a Giraffe. P. Hubbell.
Su-FVI:45
SKYWRITING
The Pens. W. Merwin. Ho-TH:86
Sky Valentine. E. Jay. Ja-HH:13
SLANDER: see also GOSSIP
He Thinks of Those Who Have
Spoken Evil of His Beloved.
W. Yeats. Co-EL:37, Co-PI:206,
No-CL:4
Mutual Charges of Molestation.
Da-SC:45
On Censure. J. Swift. Rv-CB:494
SLAVERY: see also EMANCIPATION
PROCLAMATION; SERFDOM;
TURNER, NAT
Advice to the Slave-Drivers of
America. J. Barlow. Kr-OF:29
Africa. D. Diop. Lo-TY:137
The African Affair. B. Wright.
Ad-PB:171, Hu-PN:357
Again They Surround Thee.
W. Whitman. Kr-OF:105
America. J. Whitfield.
Ba-PO:17, Ra-BP:35
American History. M. Harper.
Ra-BP:291
As Tawny Tigers. H. Melville.
Kr-OF:148
Ballad of the Two Grandfathers.
N. Guillén. Be-UL:53
Brown of Ossawatomie.
J. Whittier. Hi-TL:98
Bury Me in a Free Land.
F. Harper. Ra-BP:40
Bwagamoyo. L. Bethune. Ad-PB:310
Cameo No. II. J. Jordan.
Ra-BP:243
Children Are Slaves. I. Velez.
Jo-VC:32
The Colonial. S. Lowhar.
Sa-B:79

Dark Symphony: Andante Sostenuto.
M. Tolson. Bo-AN:38
Dark Symphony: Lento Grave.
M. Tolson. Bo-AN:38
Down in the Lonesome Garden.
Ra-BP:8
The Dred Scott Decision.
W. Bryant. Kr-OF:108
Epitaph. D. Scott. Sa-B:4
Ethiopia Saluting the Colors.
W. Whitman. Hu-PN:470,
Sh-AP:119
The Farewell. J. Whittier.
Hu-PN:461, Kr-OF:29
Formerly a Slave. H. Melville.
Hu-PN:466
Forsworn to the People.
W. Whitman. Kr-OF:41
Frederick Douglass. S. Cornish.
Ad-PB:294
The Fugitive Slave Law.
A. Preston. Kr-OF:34
Georgia Dusk. J. Toomer.
Ad-PB:29, Be-MA:17, Bo-AN:32,
Jo-SA:102, Ra-BP:69
Gloucester Moors. W. Moody.
Pa-HT:19, Sp-OG:362
Go Down, Moses. Ga-S:45, Ra-BP:23
Harriet Tubman. M. Walker.
Hu-PN:320
He Who Has Lost All. D. Diop.
Lo-TY:138
Hear, O Richmond! And Give Ear,
O Carolina! T. Higginson.
Kr-OF:38
Homo Faber: The Shell Game.
M. Piercy. Sc-TN:190
How Old John Brown Took Harper's
Ferry. E. Stedman. Hu-PN:493,
Pa-OM:175
If There Exists a Hell.
P. Freneau. Kr-OF:27
Jack and Dinah Want Freedom.
Ra-BP:6
January 3, 1970. M. Jackson.
Ad-PB:499
Kansas Curses the President.
J. Howe. Kr-OF:143
Kidnappers! J. Clarke.
Kr-OF:41
Lament of the Slave. Ab-MO:54
Little Bird Got a Name. J. Vega.
Ad-II:110
Love Your Enemy. Y. Iman.
Lo-TY:258, Ra-BP:293
Middle Passage. R. Hayden.
Ad-PB:110, Be-MA:56,
Bo-AN:113, Ra-BP:123
Mother and Slave Raiders.
Tr-US I:90

My Great-Grandfather's Slaves.
  W. Berry. Mc-EA:114
My Name Was Legion. H. Swift.
  Br-AF:39
My Thirty Years. J. Manzano.
  Lo-TY:98
Negro Soldier's Civil War Chant.
  Ra-BP:7
News of Blood. D. Whitney.
  Kr-OF:140
No More Auction Block. Ra-BP:21
Not Unavenged! W. Burleigh.
  Kr-OF:135
O for a Man Who Is a Man!
  H. Thoreau. Kr-OF:67
Oh, Freedom. Ab-MO:53
Ode Inscribed to W. H. Channing.
  R. Emerson. Al-VBP:800
The Old Cabin. P. Dunbar.
  Fe-PL:426
Old Marse John. Lo-TY:198
On Liberty and Slavery.
  G. Horton. Hu-PN:11
On Listening to Spirituals.
  L. Jeffers. Ad-PB:173
One Who Mobs the Mob.
  R. Emerson. Kr-OF:136
Papa John. J. de Lima.
  Lo-TY:84
The People of Tao-Chou.
  Po Chu-i. Gr-CT:374
Peter Grimes. G. Crabbe.
  Hi-WP II:65
Poem for My Family. J. Jordan.
  Ra-BP:245
Prayer for Peace. L. Senghor.
  Lo-TY:135
Promises of Freedom. Ra-BP:5
Return to My Native Land.
  A. Césaire. Lo-TY:123
A Reunion. J. Schuyler.
  Mc-EA:136
The Ruffian Rally. J. Pierpont.
  Kr-OF:138
Runagate Runagate. R. Hayden.
  Ad-PB:120, Be-MA:61, Hu-PN:293,
  Jo-SA:38, Ra-BP:128
The Runaway Slave. W. Whitman.
  Hu-PN:467, Kr-OF:39, Un-MA:49
The Runaway Slave at Pilgrim's
  Point. E. Browning. Hu-PN:448
She's Free. F. Harper. Kr-OF:35
Sitting on the Dock. C. Meyer.
  Jo-VC:52
The Slave and the Iron Lace.
  M. Danner. Bo-AN:157, Ra-BP:154
The Slave Auction. F. Harper.
  Hu-PN:14, Lo-TY:205, Ra-BP:39
Slave Marriage Ceremony Supple-
  ment. Ra-BP:16

Slave Quarter. C. Carmer.
  Th-AS:208
Slavery. W. Bryant.
  Kr-OF:44
Slavery. T. Dwight.
  Kr-OF:28
The Slave's Dream. H. Longfellow.
  Hi-WP I:18, Hu-PN:459
Song of a Mother Whose Child Has
  Been Left Behind on the Caravan
  Trail. Tr-US I:61
Song of the Galley-Slaves.
  R. Kipling. Gr-CT:223,
  Pa-GTB:421
Song of the Son. J. Toomer.
  Ad-PB:30, Be-MA:18,
  Bo-AN:33, Jo-SA:32
Song to a Runaway Slave.
  Ra-BP:8
Southern Mansion. A. Bontemps.
  Ad-PB:83, Be-MA:45, Bo-AN:80,
  Br-AF:142, Hu-MP:213, Lo-TY:224,
  Wi-LT:611
Stanzas on Freedom. J. Lowell.
  Hu-PN:464, Kr-OF:31
Strong Men. S. Brown.
  Ad-PB:60, Be-MA:27, Bo-HF:138,
  Ke-PP:127, Lo-TY:219, Ra-BP:113
Sugar Cane Man. F. Charles.
  Sa-B:88
This Newer Bondage. P. Dunbar.
  Kr-OF:47
This Noble Head. R. Emerson.
  Kr-OF:141
This Sun Is Hot. Ra-BP:9
To the Right Honorable William,
  Earl of Dartmouth. P. Wheatley.
  Lo-TY:204, Ra-BP:38
Vala, or the Four Zoas.
  W. Blake. Al-VBP:622
The War for Slavery. W. Garrison.
  Kr-OF:66
The War for Truth. W. Bryant.
  Kr-OF:133
Webster. F. Douglass. Kr-OF:32
When Virtue's Temple Falls.
  S. Little. Kr-OF:137
While There Is a Country to Save.
  R. Emerson. Kr-OF:142
White Magic. W. Braithwaite.
  Hu-PN:49
Wild Negro Bill. Ra-BP:7
The Wolves of the Border.
  J. Whittier. Kr-OF:147
The Wounded Person. W. Whitman.
  Hu-PN:468
SLAVES: see SLAVERY
SLEDS AND SLEIGHS: see also DOG SLEDS
  The Bells. E. Poe. Bo-FP:177,
  Bo-HF:162, Er-FA:277, Fe-FP:64,
  Fe-PL:433, Li-SR:72, Sp-OG:339

SLED AND SLEIGHS — cont'd.
  Jingle Bells. J. Pierpont.
    Er-FA:510, Mo-CC:(35),
    Mo-MGT:158
  The Little Red Sled. J. Bush.
    Ar-TP3:106, Au-SP:197
  A Sledding Song. N. Schlichter.
    Fe-FP:115
  Sleigh Bells at Night.
    E. Coatsworth. Br-SS:95
  Thanksgiving Day. L. Child.
    Bo-FP:156, Br-SS:83, Ch-B:94,
    Fe-FP:84, Gr-EC:232, Hu-MP:343,
    La-PH:18, Un-GT:278
  A Valentine. E. Field.
    Se-PR:52
SLEEP: see also BEDTIME; DREAMS;
    DROWSINESS; HUMOR - SLEEP;
    LULLABIES; SANDMAN
  The Aeneid. H. Howard.
    Ma-YA:54
  Air. J. Gay. Al-VBP:524
  Angel Spirits of Sleep. R. Bridges.
    De-CH:455
  At Night. F. Cornford. Un-MB:307
  The Bellman's Song. Rd-SS:4
  Buckaroo Sandman. Fi-BG:219
  Caesar and Pompey. G. Chapman.
    Al-VBP:146
  Care-Charmer Sleep. S. Daniel.
    Al-VBP:158, Pa-GTB:22, Rv-CB:180
  Care-Charming Sleep. J. Fletcher.
    Al-VBP:279
  Come, Sleep. J. Fletcher.
    De-CH:745
  Come Sleep. P. Sidney.
    Al-VBP:126, Rv-CB:170
  A Cradle Song. W. Blake.
    Al-VBP:612, Rv-CB:569
  Cradle Song. F. Higgins.
    Rd-SS:17
  Cradle Song. S. Naidu. Fe-FP:54,
    Hu-MP:123, Th-AS:35
  Dance Songs. Tr-US II:140, 145
  Doubts. R. Brooke. De-CH:247,
    Gr-SS:117
  Down Dip the Branches.
    M. Van Doren. Rd-SS:21
  The Dream. G. Byron. Mo-GR:118
  Endless Sleep. C. Minor.
    Jo-VC:68
  Endymion. J. Keats. Go-BP:161
  Ere Sleep Comes Down to Soothe
    the Weary Eyes. P. Dunbar.
    Hu-PN:43
  Evening Song. F. Davis. Th-AS:32
  Falling Asleep. S. Sassoon.
    Un-MB:315
  The Final Hunger. V. Miller.
    Wi-LT:775

  For Sleep or Death. R. Pitter.
    Hi-WP I:144, Sm-MK:218
  Going to Sleep in the Country.
    H. Moss. En-PC:204
  Good Night. D. Pierce.
    Ar-TP3:180, Br-SS:29
  A Goodnight. W. Williams.
    Un-MA:259
  Great Elegy for John Donne.
    J. Brodsky. Ca-MR:27
  Green Bedroom. R. Roseliep.
    St-H:182
  Hours of Sleep. Ir-BB:229,
    Un-GT:24
  How They Sleep. Ch-B:28
  If I Had But Two Little Wings.
    S. Coleridge. De-CH:22
  In the Smoking Car. R. Wilbur.
    Un-MA:677, Wi-LT:599
  Inner Temple Masque. W. Browne.
    Al-VBP:322
  The Land of Nod. R. Stevenson.
    Hu-MP:108, Ir-BB:256, Un-GT:303
  Laura Sleeping. C. Cotton.
    Al-VBP:476
  Lights Out. E. Thomas. Ma-FW:177
  Little Donkey, Close Your Eyes.
    M. Brown. La-PP:76, La-PV:18
  Lying Awake. B. Young.
    Mc-AW:30
  Minnie and Winnie. A. Tennyson.
    Ch-B:118, Ir-BB:199, Ox-BC:214
  Miriam's Lullaby.
    R. Beer-Hofmann. Un-R:47
  Night. M. Butts. Rd-SS:11
  The Night Is Come. T. Browne.
    De-CH:748
  Nightgown, Wife's Gown.
    R. Sward. Co-EL:9
  Nocturne. E. Davison. De-CH:161
  Nod. W. de la Mare. Rd-SS:12,
    Re-TW:113, Un-GT:303, Un-MB:203
  Now Fall Asleep. E. Coatsworth.
    Rd-SS:19
  On a Quiet Conscience.
    Charles I. De-CH:446
  Pastoral. R. Hillyer.
    Un-MA:482
  The Rime of the Ancient Mariner.
    S. Coleridge. Al-VBP:679,
    Bo-FP:301, Co-RG:60, Co-SS:131,
    De-CH:364, Er-FA:318, Fe-FP:147,
    Ga-FB:105, Gr-TG:61, Ha-PO:15,
    Hi-WP II:68, Ma-YA:146, Ni-JP:52,
    Ox-BN:139, Rv-CB:658, Sm-LG:312,
    Un-GT:30
  Rocked in the Cradle of the Deep.
    E. Willard. Er-FA:467
  The Sacrament of Sleep.
    J. Oxenham. Fe-PL:332

Serenade. H. Longfellow.
   Al-VBP:824
The Siesta. Pa-SG:149
Sleep. A. Cowley. Gr-CT:409
Sleep Brings No Joy. E. Brontë.
   Al-VBP:921
Sleep Is like a Bridge.
   J. Jimenez. Le-SW:83
The Sleeper. W. de la Mare.
   Un-MB:198
Sleeping Beauty. C. Johnson.
   La-IH:104
The Sleeping Beauty. S. Rogers.
   Pa-GTB:129
The Sleeping Fury. L. Bogan.
   Wi-LT:380
The Sleeping House. A. Tennyson.
   Ox-BN:508
The Sleepy Song. J. Bacon.
   Bo-FP:48, Th-AS:36
Sleepy Song. A. Guiterman.
   Gr-EC:96
Sleepyhead. W. de la Mare.
   Ar-TP3:155
Slumber Song. L. Ledoux.
   Fe-FP:56, Hu-MP:125, Rd-SS:18
Slumber Song. A. Noyes.
   Rd-SS:9
Song Sung while Fencing a Garden.
   Tr-US I:193
Sonnet to Sleep. J. Keats.
   Al-VBP:779, Gr-CT:409,
   Ma-FW:178
Summer Day. Yuan Mei.
   Rx-LT:114
The Sweetest Thing. Ab-MO:102,
   Be-AP:68, Lo-TY:7
Talking in Their Sleep.
   E. Thomas. Co-BN:29
To an Old Lady Asleep at a
   Poetry Reading. J. Kirkup.
   Go-BP:53
To Judith Asleep. J. Ciardi.
   Wi-LT:669
To Sleep. J. Kochanowski.
   Pa-SG:178
To Sleep. W. Wordsworth.
   Al-VBP:691, Pa-GTB:275
Touch. T. Gunn. To-MP:180
Tree-Sleeping. R. Coffin.
   Ha-LO:54
The Unwritten Song. F. Ford.
   Rd-SS:9
Vesper. Alcman. Rd-OA:206
Wanderer's Night Song. M. Bacon.
   Rd-SS:26
The Waterfowl. Ginko.
   Le-MW:15
Weep You No More. Al-VBP:357,
   De-CH:266, Go-BP:145, Gr-CT:410

When the Day Is Cloudy. Jo-TS:7
Where Are You Now? M. Miller.
   Gr-EC:102
Wind Song. C. Sandburg.
   Pe-OA:54, Un-MA:206
Wynken, Blynken, and Nod. E. Field.
   Au-SP:253, Bo-FP:41, Ch-B:18,
   Er-FA:487, Fe-FP:55, Gr-EC:98,
   Hu-MP:128, Ir-BB:244, Ox-BC:303,
   Un-GT:302
SLEEPLESSNESS: see INSOMNIA
SLEET
   Sleet Storm. J. Tippett.
   Br-SS:92, Pe-FB:78
SLEIGHS: see SLEDS AND SLEIGHS
SLIDES AND SLIDING
   Sliding. M. Chute. Mc-AW:14
   Sliding. M. Cohn. Ar-TP3:102,
   Br-SS:94
SLIPPERS: see SHOES
SLOTHS
   The Sloth. T. Roethke.
   Co-BBW:192, Co-FB:14, Mc-WK:52,
   Un-GF:89, We-PZ:11
SLOWNESS: see SPEED
SLUMS AND SLUM LIFE: see also
   GHETTOS; TENEMENT HOUSES
   Assailant. J. Raven. Ra-BP:258
   Birthplace Revisited. G. Corso.
   Ad-CI:63, Ca-VT:655,
   Kh-VA:65, La-OC:58
   The Days of My People. M. Gill.
   Jo-VC:54
   An Elementary School Class Room
   in a Slum. S. Spender.
   ·To-MP:26
   In the Isle of Dogs.
   J. Davidson. Ox-BN:907
   An Inconvenience. J. Raven.
   Ra-BP:258
   Laventville. D. Walcott.
   Sa-B:24
   Little Dreams. L. Hughes.
   Ls-NY:53
   The Lovers of the Poor.
   G. Brooks. Be-MA:83
   Mixed Sketches. D. Lee.
   Ra-BP:306
   Nikki-Rosa. N. Giovanni.
   Ad-CI:20, Ad-PB:451,
   Be-MA:169, Jo-SA:22
   Nobody Collects the Papers.
   L. Warren and D. Dickson.
   La-IH:53
   Sightseers in a Courtyard.
   N. Guillen. Lo-TY:106
   A Slum Dwelling. G. Crabbe.
   Ox-BN:11
   The Spawn of Slums.
   J. Thompson. Ra-BP:254

SLUMS AND SLUM LIFE — cont'd.
  What Now? L. Martin. La-IH:82
  When Something Happens.
    J. Randall. Ra-BP:275
  Who Am I. S. Mancillas.
    La-IH:61
  Yorkville. D. Aldan. Lo-IT:3
SMILES: see also HUMOR - SMILES
  Get Up or You'll Be Late for
    School, Silly. J. Ciardi.
    Gr-EC:103
  Growing Smiles. Fe-PL:430
  In Schrafft's. W. Auden.
    Mc-WS:76
  The Mask. E. Browning.
    Ox-BN:463, Rv-CB:778
  She Is Not Fair. H. Coleridge.
    Al-VBP:795, Ga-FB:56,
    Pa-GTB:178
  A Simile for Her Smile.
    R. Wilbur. Mo-BG:92
  Smile. Chu Ta-nan. Hs-TC:133
  Smile. M. O'Neill. Ja-PC:6
  The Snowman's Resolution.
    A. Fisher. Au-SP:337, Pe-FB:84
  Song: One Hard Look.
    R. Graves. Un-MB:388
  Try Smiling. Er-FA:13
  Waiting in Darkness. Be-CS:31
  When This Conundrum You Have
    Heard. Re-RR:59
  You Smiled. C. O'John. Al-WW:63
SMITH, BESSIE
  Blues for Bessie. M. O'Higgins.
    Hu-PN:347, Kr-OF:50
  Homage to the Empress of the
    Blues. R. Hayden. Ad-PB:117,
    Be-MA:64, Hu-PN:290, Mo-BG:46
  Salute. O. Pitcher. Ad-PB:193
SMITH, JOHN: see also HUMOR -
    SMITH, JOHN
  Pocahontas. W. Thackeray.
    Br-AF:55, Fe-FP:408, Hi-TL:21,
    Hu-MP:429, Pa-OM:129, Un-GT:177,
    Vi-PP:46
SMITH, WILLIAM JAY: see HUMOR -
    SMITH, WILLIAM JAY
SMOKE: see also HUMOR - SMOKE
  All the Smoke. E. Siegel.
    Ad-CI:46, Co-EL:103,
    Co-FB:123, Co-PU:130
  Are You Able to Guess. Re-RR:58
  From a Naturalist's Notebook:
    Smoke. B. Cutler. St-H:41
  High It Flies. Ju-CP:12
  A House Full, a Yard Full.
    De-CH:675, Li-LB:169,
    Mo-MGT:154, Rv-ON:55
  Light-Winged Smoke. H. Thoreau.
    Al-VBP:919

  The Ship Moves. W. Williams.
    Su-FVI:41
  Smoke. J. Glatstein. Ho-TY:331
  Smoke. P. Murphy. Me-WF:37
  Smoke and Steel. C. Sandburg.
    Un-MA:204
  Smoke Animals. R. Bennett.
    Sh-RP:179
  The Song of the Smoke.
    W. Du Bois. Ad-PB:1
  Trails of Smoke. R. Bennett.
    Hu-MP:78
SMOKING: see also HUMOR - SMOKING;
    TOBACCO
  Anecdotes of Four Gentlemen.
    Ox-BC:152
  Grandad's Pipe. I. Serraillier.
    St-FS:75
  Homely Meats. J. Davies.
    Sm-LG:117
SMOKY MOUNTAINS: see GREAT SMOKY
    MOUNTAINS
SMUGGLING
  A Smuggler's Song. R. Kipling.
    Bl-OB:52, Ha-PO:43, Ox-BC:322
SMUGNESS
  Easter Parade. M. Chute.
    Br-SS:140, La-PH:53
  I Am a Nice Nice Boy.
    M. O'Connor. Le-M:154
  The Ragged Girl's Sunday.
    M. Bennett. De-TT:24
  Salutation. E. Pound. Ca-VT:82,
    Mc-EA:23, Sm-LG:390, Un-MA:289
SNAILS: see also HUMOR - SNAILS
  Consider This Odd Little Snail.
    D. McCord. Br-LL:128
  Considering the Snail. T. Gunn.
    Br-TC:163, Ha-WR:16,
    Ma-FW:211, Wi-LT:725
  Even a Wise Man. Kyorai.
    Be-MC:41
  A Garden Path. M. Justus.
    Bo-FP:241, Br-SG:49
  The Garden Snail. R. Wallace.
    Co-BBW:81
  Hokku Poems. R. Wright.
    Bo-AN:104
  The Housekeeper. V. Bourne.
    Fe-PL:355, Mc-PR:44,
    Sp-OG:300, Un-GT:79
  Little Snail. H. Conkling.
    Ar-TP3:66, Fe-FP:140,
    Hu-MP:305, It-HB:20
  Midsummer. S. Calverley. Re-BS:23
  Nursery Snail. R. Herschberger.
    Ad-PE:25
  Oh, Snail. Issa. Do-TS:8
  The Odyssey of a Snail.
    F. García Lorca. Ma-FW:211

A Red Morning Sky. Issa.
    Le-IS:4, Ma-FW:213
The Shape God Wears. S. Hay.
    Un-GT:82
The Snail. G. Conkling.
    Br-SG:57
The Snail. W. Cowper. Bo-FP:84,
    Co-BBW:91, Mc-WK:51, Un-GT:79
Snail. J. Drinkwater.
    Au-SP:71, Bo-GJ:85, Ir-BB:74,
    Li-LC:32, Pa-RE:76
Snail. F. García Lorca.
    Le-SW:27
Snail. L. Hughes.
    Ab-MO:36, Ar-TP3:67, Br-SG:55,
    Fe-FP:140, Mc-WS:52
Snail. D. McCord. Sh-RP:134
The Snail. J. Reeves.
    Bl-OB:123, Br-SG:56, Co-BBW:92,
    Gr-EC:27, It-HB:42, Sh-RP:325
The Snail. Bo-FP:85, Wy-CM:19
Snail, Moon, and Rose. J. Kenward.
    Sm-MK:55
Snakes and Snails. G. Hallock.
    Sh-RP:331
Summer Rain. Lin Keng.
    Le-MW:77
There Was an Old Person of
    Sparta. E. Lear. Ag-HE:14
To the Snail. Mo-MGT:49
Upon the Snail. J. Bunyan.
    Co-BBW:94, Go-BP:85,
    Gr-CT:116, Ox-BC:36
Well! Hello down There.
    Issa. Be-CS:25
Where Can He Be Going. Issa.
    Do-TS:(6), Le-MW:31, Ma-FW:213
The Widow's Yard. I. Gardner.
    St-H:71
SNAKES: see also HUMOR - SNAKES;
    and names of specific snakes,
    as PYTHONS
The Black Snake. P. Hubbell.
    La-PV:154
The Brass Serpent. T. Carmi.
    Me-PH:143
Cheers. E. Merriam. Du-RG:115
The Child and the Snake. M. Lamb.
    De-TT:63, Ox-BC:142
The Death of a Snake. W. Plomer.
    Co-EL:23
The Deer and the Snake.
    K. Patchen. Un-MA:609
The Desert. S. Crane. Wi-LT:119
Empedocles on Etna. M. Arnold.
    Pa-GTB:366
Eve. R. Hodgson. De-CH:465,
    Ha-PO:41, Hi-WP II:95, Na-EO:105,
    Pa-OM:286, Sm-MK:58, Un-MB:186,
    Wi-LT:123

Eve. C. Rossetti. De-CH:466,
    Pa-GTB:375
Fishing for Snakes. R. Eberhart.
    Li-TU:30
Growing Old. S. Takayanagi.
    Sh-AM:175
Hospitality. J. Tabb.
    Gr-EC:22
Lizards and Snakes. A. Hecht.
    Br-TC:183, Ha-TP:39
A Narrow Fellow in the Grass.
    E. Dickinson. Ad-PE:20,
    Bo-GJ:65, Co-BBW:90, Er-FA:233,
    Fe-PL:349, Li-TU:190, Ma-FW:210,
    Mc-PR:166, Rd-OA:136, Rv-CB:896,
    Un-GB:17, Un-GT:68, We-PZ:12,
    Wi-LT:14
On a Little Boy Endeavouring to
    Catch a Snake. T. Foxton.
    Ox-BC:56
On Time. R. Hughes. Un-MB:409
Pit Viper. N. Momaday. Ni-CD:100
The Rattlesnake. J. and A. Lomax.
    Sh-RP:19
The Rattlesnake. A. Purdy.
    Do-WH:91
Rattlesnake Ceremony Song.
    Tr-US II:249
Rattlesnake Recitative. Da-SC:10
The Serpent Waits. J. Brennan.
    De-FS:35
The Silent Snake. Ar-TP3:240,
    Fe-FP:140
The Snake. M. Kerecz. La-GI:52
The Snake. K. Kuskin.
    Br-SG:66, La-PP:12
The Snake. Kyoshi. Sh-RP:62
Snake. D. Lawrence.
    Ar-TP3:68, Co-BBW:85,
    Ha-PO:102, Ni-JP:112, Wi-LT:212
The Snake. A. Maniu. Mc-AC:59
Snake. T. Roethke. Be-EB:55,
    Co-BBW:82, Gr-EC:32, La-RM:143,
    Ma-FO:(28), Rd-OA:138
The Snake. Valerie. Su-FVI:64
The Snake Charmer. Ca-MU:28
The Snake Is a Ribbon of Riches.
    Wo-HS:(9)
Snake Medicine Song.
    Da-SC:144
The Snake Trying. W. Ross.
    Co-BBW:83
Snakes and Snails. G. Hallock.
    Sh-RP:331
Swan. E. Lowbury.
    Pa-GTB:535
Thou Shalt See the Field-Mouse
    Peep. J. Keats. Rd-OA:181
To a Fair Lady, Playing with a
    Snake. E. Waller. Gr-CC:86

SNAKES — cont'd.
   To the Snake. D. Levertov.
      Co-BBW:92, Wi-LT:760
   Underneath This Hazelin Mote.
      De-CH:670
   The Viper. R. Pitter. Gr-CC:144
   Viper. Be-AP:62
   Warning to Snake-Killers.
      R. Barlow. De-FS:12
   Water Snake. E. Jacobson.Ls-NY:188

SNAPDRAGONS: see HUMOR -
   SNAPDRAGONS
SNARING: see TRAPPING
SNEEZING: see also HUMOR - SNEEZING
   Sneeze Between Twelve and One.
      Mo-TB:54
   Sneeze on Monday. Ir-BB:228,
      Ju-CP:80, Li-LB:165, Mo-NR:91,
      Mo-TB:108, Na-EO:19, Wr-RM:128
   Sneezing. M. Allen. Au-SP:105
   Sneezing. Mo-TB:54, Wr-RM:128
   Speak Roughly to Your Little Boy.
      L. Carroll. Bl-OB:30, Bo-FP:61,
      Co-BB:105, Li-SR:4, Sm-LG:101
   You Know the Moon. Re-RR:54
SNIPES (BIRDS)
   To the Snipe. J. Clare. Ox-BN:313
   Washing My Rice Hoe. Buson.
      Be-CS:13
SNOBS AND SNOBBISHNESS: see also
   HUMOR - SNOBS AND SNOBBISHNESS
   Boston. J. Bossidy. Br-AF:198,
      Un-GT:236
   I Love Those Little Booths at
      Benvenutt's. G. Brooks.
      St-H:10
   Inscribed on the Collar of a Dog.
      A. Pope. Bo-FP:132, Ch-B:73,
      Gr-CT:122, Rv-CB:508, Un-GT:236
   The Mysterious Cat. V. Lindsay.
      Ar-TP3:54, Au-SP:33, Bo-GJ:88,
      Co-IW:12, Fe-FP:158, Gr-CT:119,
      Hu-MP:167, Ir-BB:174, Pe-FB:10,
      Th-AS:42
   Outwitted. E. Markham. Co-EL:110,
      Co-PU:25, Un-MA:106
   To a Louse. R. Burns. Al-VBP:629,
      Co-BBW:221, Er-FA:71, Ma-YA:131,
      Sp-OG:300
SNORING: see also HUMOR - SNORING
   Grandma Snores. N. Tolstoy.
      Mo-MI:51
   To an Old Lady Asleep at a Poetry
      Reading. J. Kirkup. Go-BP:53
SNOW: see also HUMOR - SNOW;
   SATIRE - SNOW; SLEDS AND
   SLEIGHS; SLEET; SNOWMEN
   Annual Gaiety. W. Stevens. Un-MA:248
   Approach to a City. W. Williams.
      Ad-CI:25

Beauty. Bashö. Au-SP:340
Because the Songbird.
   T. Takaori. Sh-AM:155
Birds at Winter Nightfall.
   T. Hardy. Co-EL:25, Un-MB:31
Butterflies Dancing. Oemaru.
   Do-TS:46
Chapter Two. W. Scott. Gr-CC:186
The Christmas Robin. R. Graves.
   Gr-CC:48
A Comparison. J. Farrar.
   Fe-FP:214, Hu-MP:277
Cynthia in the Snow. G. Brooks.
   Ar-TP3:190, Li-LC:79
Dark. S. Partridge. De-TT:87
Deadfall. M. Keller. Gr-EC:272
December. A. Fisher. Br-SS:95,
   La-PH:21
December. S. Vanderbilt.
   La-OC:79
Desert Places. R. Frost.
   Un-MA:188
A Devonshire Rhyme. Br-SS:89,
   Hu-MP:322
A Dove of New Snow. V. Lindsay.
   Un-MA:228
Drifting, Feathery. Shiki.
   Be-MC:28
Dust of Snow. R. Frost. Ad-PE:19,
   Ar-TP3:212, Hi-WP I:4, La-PV:133,
   Mo-TS:22, Re-BS:52, Tu-WW:42
The End of the World.
   G. Bottomley. De-CH:390,
   Un-MB:212
Even as the Snow Fell. Issa.
   Le-MW:68
Falling Snow. Ar-TP3:190,
   Au-SP:336, Mo-CC:(28),
   Pe-FB:81
Falling Snow. De-PP:26
Farm Couple, after Norman Rockwell.
   B. Spacks. Ls-NY:75
The Faun Sees Snow for the First
   Time. R. Aldington. Un-MB:354
Feathers of Snow. Gr-GB:36
The Fire in the Snow.
   V. Watkins. Wi-LT:454
First Sight. P. Larkin.
   Co-BN:192, Mo-TS:64, Rd-OA:186
First Snow. M. Allen.
   Ar-TP3:189, Au-SP:333
First Snow. I. Eastwick.
   Ar-TP3:190
First Snow. F. Frost. Ke-TF:449
The First Snow-Fall. J. Lowell.
   Co-PS:158, Fe-FP:65, Sp-OG:264
First Snow in Lake Country.
   L. Mueller. St-H:142
The First Snow Is So Beautiful.
   Kikaku. Do-TS:42

First Winter's Day. D. Aldis.
   Au-SP:334
For Snow. E. Farjeon. De-CH:221
From the Highest Camp. T. Gunn.
   Br-TC:163
Gone Were But the Winter Cold.
   A. Cunningham. De-CH:224
Haiku 6. E. Knight. Ra-BP:206
Has a Drift of Snow. Bashö.
   Be-MC:7
He Giveth Snow like Wool. Bible.
   O.T. Psalms. Cl-DT:18
Hi There, Friend or Foe.
   I. Ivanova. Mo-MI:50
Hills Have Disappeared. Joso.
   Be-MC:45
Hokku Poems. R. Wright.
   Bo-AN:105, Mo-BG:74
I Could Eat It! Issa. Do-TS:43,
   Le-MW:87, Ma-FW:276
I Never Shall Love the Snow
   Again. R. Bridges. De-CH:258,
   Ga-FB:150
Ice Cold. D. Adams. Ho-CT:40
If the White Herons. Chiyo.
   Be-CS:50
In Memory of Robinson Jeffers.
   E. Barker. Ls-NY:135
In the Evening I Walk by the
   River. Hsiu Ou-Yang.
   Le-MW:88, Rx-OH:51
It Was I Who Did Command.
   Lady Fujiwara. Ba-ST:48
It's Snowing. P. Romanick.
   La-GI:7
January. E. Coatsworth.
   Co-PS:156
The Joy of the Snowflake.
   Hsü Chih-mo. Hs-TC:89
Late Snow. Issa. Sh-RP:65
Late Snowflakes.
   Kiyowara no Fukayabu. Le-MW:90
Letter from a Black Soldier.
   B. Anderson. Ca-VT:625
Little White Birds. Re-RR:19
London Snow. R. Bridges.
   Co-BN:196, De-CH:220, Gr-CT:308,
   Ha-PO:87, Hi-WP I:126, Ho-WR:183,
   Ma-YA:218, Ni-JP:141, Ox-BN:874,
   Pa-GTB:414, Un-MB:50, Wi-LT:52
Loneliness. Hashin. Au-SP:333,
   Do-TS:45, Li-TU:201, Pa-SG:185
A Lost Snowflake. De-PP:56
Magnificent Snow. Emperor Temmu.
   Ba-ST:48
A Mountain Village. Shiki.
   Be-CS:30
My Birthday's in Winter.
   Z. Gay. Br-BC:59
New Snow. C. Rowles. Ha-YA:141

The Onset. R. Frost. Sh-AP:151,
   Un-MA:168
The Open Door. E. Coatsworth.
   Gr-EC:76
A Patch of Old Snow. R. Frost.
   Co-PU:53, Du-RG:130, La-OC:35
The Pine Bough. R. Aldridge.
   Co-PS:151, Ho-LP:36
The Pine Tree. H. Heine. Bo-FP:169
Pine Tree Tops. G. Snyder.
   Ho-P:249
Rhyming Riddle. M. Austin.
   Ar-TP3:99, Au-SP:27, Co-BN:193
Riddle of Snow and Sun.
   Gr-CT:395, Gr-GB:36,
   Rv-CB:444, Rv-ON:36
Riddles. Gr-CT:395
The Runaway. R. Frost.
   Ar-TP3:77, Bo-GJ:72, Br-TC:137,
   Ca-VT:16, Co-BBW:143, De-CH:24,
   Fe-FP:161, Gr-EC:39, Hu-MP:196,
   La-PV:125, Se-PR:301, Sh-RP:343,
   Sm-LG:82, Un-GT:29, Un-MA:179
Russian Snow. O. Teitelman.
   Mo-MI:29
Snow. D. Aldis. Ar-TP3:190,
   Co-PU:51, La-PV:42
The Snow. T. Batchelor.
   Ho-CT:39
Snow. E. Coatsworth. Be-SS:115
The Snow. E. Dickinson.
   Sh-RP:237, Un-GT:248
The Snow. C. Dyment. Sm-MK:138
The Snow. D. Hall. Mc-EA:49
The Snow. R. Herman. La-GI:8
Snow. J. Kelleher. Co-EL:116
Snow. K. Orendurff. Le-M:191
Snow. W. Rodgers. Wi-LT:491
Snow. E. Thomas. Co-PU:51
Snow. A. Wilkins. Ar-TP3:190,
   Mc-AW:96
Snow. Gr-GB:36
Snow Advent. J. Auslander.
   Th-AS:94
Snow-Bound. J. Whittier.
   Ga-FB:302, Ho-WR:174, Mc-PR:139
Snow Everywhere. I. Eastwick.
   Fr-MP:21
The Snow Fall. A. MacLeish.
   Ha-LO:51
Snow Fell until Dawn. Rokwa.
   Be-CS:24
Snow Harvest. A. Young.
   Cl-FC:34, Co-BN:191
Snow in Europe. D. Gascoyne.
   To-MP:37
Snow in Spring. I. Eastwick.
   La-PV:43
Snow in the Caucasus. Y. Gillespie.
   Ls-NY:29

SNOW — cont'd.
  Snow in the City. R. Field.
    Ar-TP3:190, Gr-EC:63, La-PP:32
  Snow in the Suburbs. T. Hardy.
    Bo-GJ:254, Co-BN:192,
    Hi-WP I:127, Re-TW:105, Un-MB:34
  Snow, Softly, Slowly. Oeharu.
    Be-MC:61
  Snow Toward Evening. M. Cane.
    Ar-TP3:178, La-PV:44
  The Snowfall. D. Justice.
    Ca-VT:536
  The Snowflake. W. de la Mare.
    Li-LC:80
  Snowflakes. M. Chute.
    La-PP:30, La-PV:42
  Snowflakes. G. Cohoe. Al-WW:27
  Snowflakes. M. Dodge. Hu-MP:323
  Snowflakes. M. Kennedy.
    Mc-AW:49
  Snowflakes. H. Longfellow.
    Bo-FP:169, Ch-B:52,
    Gr-CT:396, Ho-WR:179
  Snowman. De-PP:32
  Snowstorm. J. Clare. Co-BN:198,
    Ho-WR:180, Ma-FW:275
  The Snowstorm. R. Emerson.
    Ar-TP3:191, Bo-FP:169, Co-BN:195,
    Fe-PL:388, Ho-P:5, Sh-AP:26
  A Snowy Day. D. ap Gwilym.
    Pa-SG:100
  Snowy Morning. L. Moore.
    Un-GB:11
  Snowy Morning. B. Young.
    Mc-AW:6
  Song from "The Young David."
    R. Beer-Hofmann. Un-R:49
  The Spring Waters. Ping Hsin.
    Hs-TC:22, 23
  Statue in a Blizzard.
    R. Keener. Ls-NY:160
  A Still Day. J. Cherwinski.
    Sh-RP:196
  Stopping by Woods on a Snowy
    Evening. R. Frost.
    Ad-PE:31, Al-VBP:1134, Ar-TP3:198,
    Bo-FP:170, Bo-GJ:257, Br-SS:88,
    Br-TC:135, Cl-DT:20, Co-BN:151,
    Co-PS:160, De-CH:625, Er-FA:257,
    Fe-FP:67, Ga-FB:299, Gr-EC:273,
    Ha-PO:90, Ke-TF:420, La-PP:29,
    La-PV:167, Ma-FW:276, Mc-PR:124,
    Mc-WK:32, Pe-FB:80, Re-TW:123,
    Sh-AP:150, Sh-RP:52, Sm-LG:63,
    Sm-PT:8, Un-MA:187, Wi-LT:174
  Strange Footprints. V. Gouled.
    Mc-AW:87
  The Terrace in the Snow.
    Su Tung P'o.
    Rx-OH:71

Thaw. W. Gibson. Co-EL:73,
  Co-PU:75
There Blooms No Bud in May.
  W. de la Mare. Un-MB:201
There Is a Trinity. Rippo.
  Le-MW:65
This Fall of New Snow. Kikaku.
  Be-CS:30
To a Snowflake. F. Thompson.
  Co-BN:191, Ga-FB:146, Pl-IO:50,
  Re-TW:90, Un-GT:248, Un-MB:78
To the City in Snow.
  A. Ruggeri. Th-AS:125
To the Snow. Br-FF:(24),
  Mo-CC:(30), Mo-MGT:17
Total Calm. P. Booth.
  Ha-WR:88
Tracks in the Snow. M. Chute.
  Br-SS:90
Velvet Shoes. E. Wylie.
  Ad-PE:37, Ar-TP3:199, Au-SP:354,
  Bo-FP:174, Bo-GJ:255, Br-SS:89,
  De-CH:221, Fe-FP:66, Hu-MP:324,
  Pe-FB:83, Th-AS:124, Un-MA:276
Vista. A. Kreymborg.
  Co-BL:60, Sm-MK:139
Watering the Horse. R. Bly.
  St-H:5
When It Snows. G. Jacoby.
  La-GI:9
The Whirlwind. Br-MW:129,
  Da-SC:118
White Fields. J. Stephens.
  Au-SP:335, Br-SS:91, Co-BN:199,
  Co-PS:159, Fe-FP:66, Gr-EC:84,
  Mc-AW:50
White Season. F. Frost.
  Ar-TP3:62, Co-BBW:38, Fe-FP:167
Who Can Stay Indoors. Kikaku.
  Be-MC:24
Why Does It Snow. L. Richards.
  Br-SS:87
Willows in the Snow. Tsuru.
  Hu-MP:273
Winter. W. de la Mare.
  Gr-CT:394, Ha-YA:144
Winter. M. Hicks. Ho-CT:40
Winter. Jŏsŏ. Li-TU:209,
  Pa-SG:103
Winter Circus. A. Fisher.
  Ha-YA:148
The Winter House. N. Cameron.
  Rv-CB:999
A Winter Hymn - To the Snow.
  E. Jones. Ox-BN:623
Winter Morning. W. Smith. Co-BN:197
A Winter Night. B. Pasternak.
  Ca-MR:174
Winter Noon. S. Teasdale.
  Ha-YA:146, Sh-RP:238

Without an Ending. S. Saito.
   Sh-AM:170
Yonder on the Plum Tree.
   Ba-ST:48
You Light the Fire. Basho.
   Le-MW:89
SNOWBIRDS: see JUNCOS
SNOWDROPS
   The First Bee. M. Webb.
      De-TT:55
   The Snowdrop. A. Tennyson.
      Bo-FP:180, Se-PR:41
SNOWFLAKES: see SNOW
SNOWMEN
   Boy at the Window. R. Wilbur.
      Ho-TH:65, Pe-SS:27
   The Snowman. R. Ainsworth.
      St-FS:26
   The Snowman.   Ch-B:72
   Snowman. De-PP:32
   The Snowman's Resolution.
      A. Fisher.   Au-SP:337, Pe-FB:84
   Snowman's Valentine. K. Dee.
      Ja-HH:11
SOAP: see also HUMOR - SOAP
   How Come? D. Ignatow.
      Ad-CI:110, Bl-FP:24
   A Riddle. G. Macbeth.
      Mo-TS:83
   The Voyage of Jimmy Poo.
      J. Emanuel. Bo-AN:174,
      Hu-NN:97, Ls-NY:220
SOAP BUBBLES
   Mrs. Gilfillan. J. Reeves.
      Ir-BB:212, Li-TU:150
SOCIABILITY: see FELLOWSHIP
SOCIAL CLASSES: see also ARISTOCRACY;
      HUMOR - SOCIAL CLASSES
   Beverly Hills, Chicago.
      G. Brooks. Ca-VT:439
   De Black Girl. Gr-GB:224
   Four Lovely Sisters.
      C. Trypanis. Co-EL:138
   The Garden. E. Pound.
      Br-TC:331, Un-MA:289
   Lines Based on a 1924 Advertise-
      ment. G. Lehmann. Ls-NY:264
   Snapshots of the Cotton South.
      F. Davis. Ad-PB:98
   A Song in the Front Yard.
      G. Brooks. Ad-PB:153,
      Bo-HF:101
   Vergidemiarum. J. Hall.
      Al-VBP:267
SOCIAL PROBLEMS: see DISCRIMI-
      NATION; DIVORCE; INDIANS OF
      NORTH AMERICA - TREATMENT;
      INJUSTICE; POLLUTION;
      POVERTY; RACE PROBLEMS;
      SLAVERY; UNEMPLOYMENT; WAR

SOCIAL WORKERS: see also SATIRE -
      SOCIAL WORKERS
   The WhenIwas. D. Lourie.
      Sc-TN:150
SOCIALLY HANDICAPPED
   The Death and Life of a Severino.
      J. de Melo Neto. An-TC:127
   An Elementary School Class Room
      in a Slum. S. Spender.
      Br-TC:403, Ke-PP:50,
      To-MP:26, Un-MB:403
   Here Is Thy Footstool. R. Tagore.
      Go-BP:288
   I Will Go into the Ghetto.
      C. Reznikoff. Ca-VT:188
   The Labourer. R. Thomas.
      Go-BP:229
   The Two Boys. M. Lamb.
      Rv-CB:628
SOCRATES
   For the One Who Would Take Man's
      Life in His Hands. D. Schwartz.
      Ca-VT:366, Hi-TL:218,
      Un-MA:618, Wi-LT:517
   Paradise Regained. J. Milton.
      Al-VBP:412
   Socrates' Ghost Must Haunt Me Now.
      D. Schwartz. Wi-LT:518
SODOM
   Ballad of the Trial of Sodom.
      V. Watkins. Tr-MR:68
SOLDIERS: see also HUMOR -
      SOLDIERS; KILROY; SATIRE -
      SOLDIERS; WARRIORS; and
      names of soldiers, as
      SASSOON, SIEGFRIED
   À Terre. W. Owen. Wi-LT:352
   All the Hills and Vales.
      C. Sorley. Un-MB:380
   All the World over. R. Kipling.
      Go-BP:216
   Apologia pro Poemate Meo.
      W. Owen. Un-MB:363, Wi-LT:347
   An Army Corps on the March.
      W. Whitman. Fe-PL:171,
      Vi-PP:147
   As Toilsome I Wander'd Virginia's
      Woods. W. Whitman.
      Al-VBP:937, Sp-OG:205
   The Ash and the Oak. L. Simpson.
      Cr-WS:3, Mo-BG:168
   At the British War Cemetery,
      Bayeux. C. Causley.
      Go-BP:210
   Ballad of the Soldier. B. Brecht.
      Li-TU:231
   The Battle. L. Simpson.
      Cr-WS:84, Du-SH:82, Ha-TP:76
   Boots. R. Kipling. Un-MB:129
   A Boy. S. Teasdale. Cr-WS:51

SOLDIERS — cont'd.
The Brave at Home. T. Read.
Sp-OG:201
Break of Day in the Trenches.
I. Rosenberg. Al-VBP:1190,
Ba-PO:138, Hi-FO:257,
Pa-GTB:446, Un-MB:351
The British Grenadiers.
Rv-CB:443
Budmouth Dears. T. Hardy.
De-CH:165
Character of the Happy Warrior.
W. Wordsworth. Er-FA:85
Charlie He's My Darling. De-CH:174
Christmas Song. R. Leonhard.
Un-R:57
Confession. M. Marcus. Ba-PO:36
The Constant Bridegrooms.
K. Patchen. Wi-LT:785
Conversion. F. Angermayer.
Fe-PL:334
Counter-Attack. S. Sassoon.
Ba-PO:136, Co-RM:204,
Cr-WS:87, Un-MB:312
Custer's Last Fight. Fi-BG:114
Dan Ellis's Boys. Em-AF:452
Danny Deever. R. Kipling.
Co-RM:87, Fe-PL:84,
Pa-GTB:420, Un-MB:124
Dark Rosaleen. J. Mangan.
Al-VBP:812, Co-PI:128, De-CH:172
The Day of Battle. A. Housman.
Cr-WS:90
Do Li A. Gr-GB:236
Drafted. Su Wu. Rx-LT:6
Dreamers. S. Sassoon.
Cr-WS:83, Un-MB:310
The Drum. J. Scott. Al-VBP:588,
Ba-PO:67, Ke-PP:39, Rv-CB:545
The Dug-Out. S. Sassoon.
De-CH:160, Ma-FW:252, Un-MB:313
Dulce et Decorum Est. W. Owen.
Ba-PO:139, Co-RM:210, Cr-WS:98,
Ga-FB:217, Ke-PP:58, Rv-CB:990,
Un-MB:364, Wi-LT:351
Elegy for a Dead Soldier.
K. Shapiro. Hi-TL:213,
Wi-LT:541
Epitaph for a Concord Boy.
S. Young. Mc-WK:164
Epitaph on an Army of Mercenaries.
A. Housman. Al-VBP:1080
Exposure. W. Owen.
Go-BP:207
Fight to a Finish. S. Sassoon.
Cr-WS:142
Fighting South of the Ramparts.
Cr-WS:7, Ma-FW:249, Pa-SG:3
The First Division Marches.
G. Rice. Vi-PP:216

For and Against. C. Norman.
Cr-WS:162
For Lover Man and All Other Young
Men Who Failed to Return from
World War II. M. Williams.
Cr-WS:109, Hu-NN:56
For the Fallen. L. Binyon.
Al-VBP:1109
For the Union Dead. R. Lowell.
Br-TC:265, Pe-OA:244, Wi-LT:583
For to Admire. R. Kipling.
Un-MB:140
The Forty-Second. Gr-GB:235
Fuzzy-Wuzzy. R. Kipling.
Un-MB:126
Graduation. D. Richardson.
Ke-TF:87
Grass Withers. Ba-PO:92
The Grenadier. Gr-GB:238
Griefs for Dead Soldiers.
T. Hughes. Go-BP:211
The Guards Came Through.
A. Doyle. Sp-OG:52
Gunga Din. R. Kipling.
Er-FA:371, Go-BP:54, Hi-WP I:69,
Ma-YA:226, Pa-OM:230, Un-MB:122
Hame, Hame, Hame. A. Cunningham.
De-CH:169, De-TT:180
The Happy Warrior. H. Read.
Cr-WS:119
He Died a Second Time, 4.
Healing. Ai Ch'ing. Hs-TC:304
He Died a Second Time, 5.
The Posture. Ai Ch'ing.
Hs-TC:305
He Died a Second Time, 6.
In the Countryside.
Ai Ch'ing. Hs-TC:306
He Died a Second Time, 8.
Exchange. Ai Ch'ing.
Hs-TC:308
He Died a Second Time, 9.
Send-off. Ai Ch'ing.
Hs-TC:308
He Died a Second Time, 10.
A Thought. Ai Ch'ing.
Hs-TC:309
The Heart of a Warrior.
Tsang K'o-chia. Hs-TC:284
The Hero. S. Sassoon. Co-RM:208
The Heroes. L. Simpson.
Cr-WS:92, Du-SH:83, Pe-SS:145
Ho, Brother Teig. Gr-GB:165
Homecoming. Chü Hsiang. Hs-TC:100
How Happy the Soldier. Sm-LG:262
Hugh Selwyn Mauberley. E. Pound.
Ba-PO:149, Ca-VT:84, Ha-PO:122,
Hi-TL:186, Un-MA:301, Wi-LT:232
I Heard a Soldier. H. Trench.
De-CH:160

If There Were Not a War.
   J. Lester.   Jo-SA:70
An Infantryman.   E. Blunden.
   Al-VBP:1208
Jack Ellyat Heard the Guns.
   S. Benét.   Fe-PL:172
Johnny, I Hardly Knew Ye.
   Gr-GB:241
Journey to a Parallel.
   B. Wright.   Hu-PN:355
The Kid Has Gone to the Colors.
   W. Herschell.   Fe-PL:163
Killed at the Ford.
   H. Longfellow.   Sp-OG:194
Lancer.   A. Housman.
   Un-MB:99
The Last Day of Leave.
   R. Graves.   Cr-WS:65
Letter from a Black Soldier.
   B. Anderson.   Ca-VT:625
Looking into History.
   R. Wilbur.   Ca-VT:485
The Man He Killed.   T. Hardy.
   Ba-PO:131, Co-RM:218, Cr-WS:107,
   Er-FA:182, Un-MB:26, Wi-LT:18
Mandalay.   R. Kipling.
   Ga-FB:70, Un-MB:125
The March into Virginia.
   H. Melville.   Al-VBP:951,
   Sh-AP:121
Memories of a Lost War.
   L. Simpson.   Ca-VT:519
Mrs. McGrath.   Ba-PO:89
The Moon at the Fortified Pass.
   Li Po.   Cr-WS:9
Mount Fuji.   M. Kaneko.   Sh-AM:66
My Luve's in Germany.   De-CH:172
my sweet old etcetera.
   e. cummings.   Cr-WS:74,
   Mo-BG:94, Pe-SS:137
The Nefarious War.   Li Po.
   Ba-PO:153, Cr-WS:14, Li-TU:241
New England Village, 1942.
   M. Bracker.   Ke-TF:260
The New Mistress.   A. Housman.
   Un-MB:103
Nocturne.   E. Davison.   De-CH:161
O What Is That Sound.   W. Auden.
   Al-VBP:1227, Gr-SS:70, Ma-FW:254,
   Pe-M:98, To-MP:29, Un-MB:455
Ode; to My Pupils.   W. Auden.
   Un-MB:451
The Old Man and Jim.   J. Riley.
   Co-PT:232, Sp-OG:197
Old Soldier.   I Men.   Hs-TC:419
An Old Soldier Dies.   E. de Vito.
   Ke-TF:169
On a Soldier Fallen in the
   Philippines.   W. Moody.
   Cr-WS:155, Hi-TL:156

On the Idle Hill of Summer.
   A. Housman.   Ox-BN:922,
   Un-MB:98
One-and-Twenty.   Em-AF:458
The Parliament Soldiers.
   Gr-GB:189
Pattern.   E. Pierce.   Cr-WS:50
Please Take Good Care of My
   Home.   Hs-TC:444
Port Bou.   S. Spender.
   Br-TC:404
Prayer Out of Georgia.   M. Moody.
   Ke-TF:203
Prolonged Sonnet.   N. Albizzi.
   Cr-WS:20
The Rebel Soldier.   Sm-LG:261
The Recruiting Sergeant.
   Mo-MGT:142
Relieving Guard.   B. Harte.
   Co-RG:37, Cr-WS:26, Sp-OG:204
The Returned Volunteer to His
   Rifle.   H. Melville.
   Gr-CC:114, Hi-TL:130
Reviewing Negro Troops Going
   South Through Washington,
   April 26, 1864.   P. Horgan.
   Cr-WS:23
A Roman Soldier on the Wall.
   W. Auden.   Hi-WP I:122,
   Sm-MK:98
The Sandaled Soldier.
   Tu Yün-hsieh.   Hs-TC:245
Screw Guns.   R. Kipling.
   Al-VBP:1098
The Send-Off.   W. Owen.
   Cr-WS:61, Un-MB:368
Shillin' a Day.   R. Kipling.
   Al-VBP:1100
Sixteen-Syllable Stanza.
   Mao Tse-tung.   Hs-TC:362
The Size of Him!   A. Kotul'sky.
   Mo-MI:27
The Sniper.   Tu Yün-hsieh.
   Hs-TC:246
Soldier.   W. Benét.   Ke-TF:170
The Soldier.   R. Brooke.
   Al-VBP:1179, Cr-WS:57, Er-FA:190,
   Fe-PL:179, Ga-FB:215, Ke-TF:169,
   Sp-OG:208, Un-MB:324, Wi-LT:612
The Soldier and the Maid.
   Mo-MGT:186
Soldier Asleep.   P. McGinley.
   Cr-WS:60
Soldier, Rest!   W. Scott.
   De-CH:600, De-TT:140, Ho-PR:282,
   Mc-PR:67, Mc-WK:204, Ox-BN:130
Soldier, There Is a War Between
   the Mind. W. Stevens. Wi-LT:163
Soldiers Bathing.   F. Prince.
   Pa-GTB:528, Un-MB:486, Wi-LT:793

SOLDIERS — cont'd.
  The Soldier's Dream. T. Campbell.
    Co-RG:40, Pa-GTB:276
  Soldier's Prayer. A. Giles.
    Ke-TF:203
  Soldier's Song. T. Hume.
    Co-RM:216, Ho-WR:118
  Song for the Heroes. A. Comfort.
    Cr-WS:163, Un-MB:521
  Song of Reproach. Bi-IT:63
  Song of War. T. Tzara.
    Mc-AC:76
  Sonnet to Negro Soldiers.
    J. Cotter. Ad-PB:35
  The Spires of Oxford. W. Letts.
    Cr-WS:68, Er-FA:190, Fe-PL:178
  Spring Offensive. W. Owen.
    Pa-GTB:451
  Tears. E. Thomas. Pa-GTB:441,
    Rv-CB:969
  These Are the Boys. A. Herbert.
    Cr-WS:123
  To Certain Ladies on Going to the
    Wars. H. Treece. Cr-WS:48
  To E. T. R. Frost. Pl-ML:162
  Tommy. R. Kipling.
    Ga-FB:209, Un-MB:127
  The Twelve. A. Blok. Ca-MR:200
  Tywater. R. Wilbur.
    Ha-PO:124, Wi-LT:593
  Ultima Ratio Regum. S. Spender.
    Er-FA:196, Pe-SS:139, Wi-LT:501
  Untitled Sonnet. J. Seligman.
    Cr-WS:30
  "Vale" from Carthage.
    P. Viereck. Cr-WS:102,
    Pe-OA:238, Un-MA:658, Wi-LT:832
  Variations on Simonides.
    G. Ely. Ls-NY:28
  Vergissmeinicht. K. Douglas.
    Cr-WS:80, Pa-GTB:545
  Verses Written During the War,
    1756-1763. T. Mordaunt.
    Rv-CB:544
  The Volunteer's Reply to the
    Poet. R. Campbell. Al-VBP:1222
  War. J. Langland. Du-SH:85,
    En-PC:161, Ha-TP:75
  A War Game. A. Richards.
    La-IH:130
  War Song. D. Parker.
    Cr-WS:77
  War Story. J. Stallworthy.
    Co-EL:82
  The Warrior Bards. H. Treece.
    Pl-ML:94
  We Be Soldiers Three. Gr-CC:119,
    Gr-CT:87, Gr-GB:235
  Western Ch'ang-An Street.
    Pien Chih-lin. Hs-TC:162

  Whispered on the Battlefield.
    G. Anders. Un-R:53
  The Widow at Windsor.
    R. Kipling. Hi-FO:249
  Without Benefit of Declaration.
    L. Hughes. Bo-AN:72,
    Cr-WS:47, Lo-TY:229
  The Wound-Dresser. W. Whitman.
    Al-VBP:937
  Ypres. I. Gurney. Hi-FO:259
SOLITUDE: see also HERMITS
  Alexander Selkirk. W. Cowper.
    Co-RG:130, Fe-PL:292,
    Hi-FO:168, Pa-GTB:162
  Amongst the Cliffs. Han Yu.
    Rx-LT:69
  The Apology. R. Emerson. No-CL:273
  As I Step over a Puddle at the
    End of Winter I Think on an
    Ancient Chinese Governor.
    J. Wright. Kh-VA:73, St-H:254
  The Bad Thing. J. Wain. Gr-BT:38
  Bird and Waterfall Music.
    Wang Wei. Rx-LT:59
  Bits of Straw. J. Clare.
    Ho-WR:187
  Brevities. S. Sassoon. Fe-PL:296
  By All Means Use Sometimes to Be
    Alone. G. Herbert. Co-PU:69
  By the Deep Sea. G. Byron.
    Ox-BN:249
  Childhood and School-Time.
    W. Wordsworth. Ox-BN:93
  Cloister. C. Aiken. Un-MA:436
  Compensation. R. Jeffers.
    Un-MA:359
  The Conquered One. D. Jackson.
    Ba-HI:30
  Daffodils. W. Wordsworth.
    Al-VBP:657, Bl-OB:137, Bo-GJ:71,
    Bo-HF:48, Ch-B:59, Co-BN:56,
    Er-FA:258, Fe-FP:218, Ga-FB:22,
    Ha-PO:95, Hi-WP II:33, Hu-MP:252,
    Ke-TF:434, Li-SR:105, Ma-YA:140,
    Mc-PR:188, Ox-BN:65, Pa-GTB:259,
    Re-TW:102, Sm-MK:188, Sp-OG:287,
    Tu-WW:64, Un-GT:254
  Deep in the Mountain Wilderness.
    Wang Wei. Rx-LT:58
  Dodona's Oaks Were Still.
    P. MacDonogh. Co-PI:107
  The Dove's Loneliness. G. Darley.
    Ox-BN:384
  The Dreamer. W. Childress.
    Du-SH:48, Pe-SS:41
  The Eagle and the Mole. E. Wylie.
    Al-VBP:1166, Rd-OA:158,
    Un-MA:274, Wi-TL:205
  Elected Silence. S. Sassoon.
    Un-MB:315

Essay on Solitude. A. Cowley.
   Al-VBP:451
Fain Would I Live in Safest
   Freedom. A. von Platen.
   Pa-SG:164
Far from the Madding Crowd.
   N. Waterman. Hu-MP:60
A Forest Hymn. W. Bryant.
   Sh-AP:23
Frost at Midnight. S. Coleridge.
   Ox-BN:162, Rv-CB:661
The Garden. A. Marvell.
   Al-VBP:457, Co-BN:43, Fe-PL:381,
   Gr-CT:268, Ho-PO:202, Pa-GTB:92,
   Rv-CB:403
The Goat Paths. J. Stephens.
   Ad-PE:30, Bo-GJ:56, De-CH:149,
   Go-BP:93, Rd-OA:55
Good-bye. R. Emerson. Er-FA:475
The Hermit's Song. Pa-SG:158
Hibernation. Chi Hsuan.
   Pa-MV:48
Hollin, Green Hollin. Gr-GB:46
I Break the Sky. O. Dodson.
   Ad-PB:133
I Built My Hut. Tao Ch'ien.
   Pa-SG:157
In the Mountains as Autumn
   Begins. Wen T'ing Yen.
   Rx-LT:86
In the Woods Alone. Pa-SG:27
Intimations of Sublimity.
   W. Wordsworth. Ox-BN:98
The Invaders. J. Sloan.
   De-FS:183
Isle of Arran. A. Reid.
   Ha-WR:19
Landscape. C. Baudelaire.
   Pa-SG:156
Lines on Leaving a Scene in
   Bavaria. T. Campbell.
   Ox-BN:198
Little Bush. E. Roberts.
   Li-LC:12
Lord! Would Men Let Me Alone.
   C. Cotton. Go-BP:20
Love in Moonlight. Bhartrihari.
   Pa-SG:64
The Milkmen. I. Gardner.
   St-H:70
Night. R. Jeffers. Sm-PT:155,
   Un-MA:367
Nocturne. O. Paz.
   Be-UL:69
Ode on Solitude. A. Pope.
   Al-VBP:529, Er-FA:248, Go-BP:45,
   Ho-P:48, Ma-FW:85, Mc-PR:203,
   Ni-JP:137, Pa-GTB:110, Rv-CB:510
Ode to Evening. W. Collins.
   Al-VBP:572, Pa-GTB:143, Rv-CB:537

Ode to Solitude. J. Grainger.
   Al-VBP:570
On Dreamland. Cheng Ch'ou-yü.
   Pa-MV:39
Peace. Bhartrihari. Pa-SG:161
Il Penseroso. J. Milton.
   Al-VBP:393, Pa-GTB:98, Rv-CB:370
The Plants Stand Silent round Me.
   J. Jorgensen. Ho-LP:22,
   Pa-SG:155
A Recluse. W. de la Mare.
   Go-BP:46
The Recollection. P. Shelley.
   De-CH:148, Ox-BN:300, Pa-GTB:270
Retirement, an Ode. T. Warton.
   Al-VBP:542
The Room. C. Day Lewis. En-PC:58
The Rustic Temple Is Hidden.
   Chu Chen Po. Rx-LT:83
The Scholar Gypsy. M. Arnold.
   Al-VBP:964, Gr-CT:255, Ox-BN:628
Seclusion. E. Mörike.
   Un-R:107
Skipping Along Alone. W. Welles.
   Ar-TP3:110, Au-SP:296
The Solitary. S. Teasdale.
   Un-MA:266
The Solitary Reaper. W. Wordsworth.
   Bl-OB:146, Co-RG:122, De-CH:207,
   Go-BP:49, Ha-PO:83, Hi-WP II:142,
   Ma-YA:141, Ox-BN:77, Pa-GTB:255,
   Pl-US:50, Re-TW:114, Rv-CB:635,
   Sp-OG:336
Solitude. A. Milne. Li-LC:14
Solitude. H. Monro. Un-MB:236
Solitude Late at Night in the
   Woods. R. Bly. Ca-VT:558
The Spring Waters. Ping Hsin.
   Hs-TC:24
Stranger. T. Merton. Pl-EI:14
The Thread of Life.
   C. Rossetti. Ox-BN:719
Thrice Happy He. W. Drummond.
   Co-BN:211
To Mr. Izaak Walton. C. Cotton.
   Al-VBP:472, Go-BP:19
Tudor Church Music. S. Warner.
   Pl-US:16
Visit to the Hermit Ts'ui.
   Ch'ien Ch'i. Rx-LT:67
Walking at Night. A. Hare.
   Fe-PL:405
Wants. P. Larkin. Pa-GTB:556
The Well. Tu Yün-hsieh. Hs-TC:249
White Butterfly. Tai Wang-shu.
   Hs-TC:184
A Whole Sheet of Solitude.
   Liu Ta-Pai. Hs-TC:6
Written on the Wall at Chang's
   Hermitage. Tu Fu. Rx-OH:4

SOLOMON, KING OF ISRAEL: see also
    HUMOR - SOLOMON, KING OF ISRAEL
  Solomon and the Bees.   J. Saxe.
    Un-GT:142
SOLOMON ISLANDS
  See Tr-US I:211-214
SOMERSAULTS
  Somersault.   D. Aldis.   Au-SP:186
  The Somersault.   C. Morgenstern.
    Un-R:69
SOMME RIVER
  Hospital Barge at Cerisy.
    W. Owen.   Rv-CB:988
SONGS AND SINGING: see also BALLADS;
    CALYPSOS; CHOIRS (MUSIC);
    CHRISTMAS SONGS; DRINKING SONGS;
    HUMOR - SONGS AND SINGING; HYMNS;
    INDIANS OF NORTH AMERICA - MUSIC
    AND SONGS; INDIANS OF SOUTH
    AMERICA - MUSIC AND SONGS; LOVE
    SONGS; LULLABIES; NATIONAL SONGS;
    NEGROES - SONGS; ROCK MUSIC AND
    SONGS; SEA SONGS; SERENADES;
    SINGING GAMES; SPIRITUALS; STATE
    SONGS; WAR SONGS AND CRIES;
    WORK SONGS
  And the Old Women Gathered.
    M. Evans.   Ad-PB:187, Hu-NN:79
  The Animal World.   Tr-CB:24
  Ann and the Fairy Song.
    W. de la Mare.   Ga-FB:170
  As I Was Going Along. Mo-CC:(16),
    Sp-AS:(8), Wr-RM:89
  As I Went Singing over the Earth.
    M. Coleridge.   Pl-US:57
  At a Solemn Music.   J. Milton.
    Pa-GTB:104, Pl-US:131
  At the Mid Hour of Night.
    T. Moore.   Al-VBP:711,
    Ox-BN:210, Pa-GTB:199
  Aye, Even Small Things.
    P. Heyse.   Un-R:113
  A Baby-Tending Song.   S. Muro.
    Sh-AM:54
  Balcony.   F. Garcia Lorca.
    Le-SW:53, Li-TU:124
  Ballata.   Pl-US:62
  The Bellman's Song.   Rd-SS:4
  The Bishop of Atlanta: Ray
    Charles.   J. Bond.
    Bo-AN:184, Mo-BG:54
  The Blue-Tail Fly.
    Er-FA:450, Gr-GB:324
  Blues and Bitterness. L. Bennett.
    Ad-PB:202, Hu-NN:53
  Bold O'Donahue.   Co-RM:122
  Bring the Soul Blocks.   V. Cruz.
    Ad-CI:60
  Canadian Boat Song.   J. Galt.
    Ox-BN:204, Rv-CB:683, Sm-LG:140
  Carriers of the Dream Wheel.
    N. Momaday.   Ni-CD:87
  Celia Singing.   T. Carew.
    No-CL:41
  Characterization.   Yogesvara.
    Al-PI:37
  Cino.   E. Pound.   Ca-VT:78
  Come and I Will Sing You.
    Ga-S:16
  Coridon's Song.   J. Chalkhill.
    Al-VBP:271
  Country Words.   W. Stevens.
    Ls-NY:328
  Cowboy Dance Song.   Fi-BG:169
  The Crazy Woman.   G. Brooks.
    Ab-MO:28, Bo-HF:136, Li-TU:151
  The Cutty Wren.   Gr-GB:63,
    Rv-CB:418, Rv-ON:117
  Dance Song.   Le-IB:100,
    Tr-US I:28
  Dark Symphony: Lento Grave.
    M. Tolson.   Bo-AN:38
  The Day Before April.   M. Davies.
    Fe-FP:20, Th-AS:71
  The Dead Man Asks for a Song.
    Le-OE:129, Tr-CB:44,
    Tr-US I:49
  The Deil's Awa wi' the Exciseman.
    R. Burns.   Al-VBP:649
  Dew on a Dusty Heart.
    J. Untermeyer.   Un-MA:333
  The Dick Johnson Reel.
    J. Falstaff.   Co-RM:14,
    Na-EO:94
  Diller, Diller, Dollar.
    Ju-CP:18
  The Dilly Song.   Gr-GB:28
  Donkey Riding.   Do-WH:19,
    Ir-BB:253, Pa-RE:49, St-FS:125
  Envoi.   E. Pound.   Ca-VT:86,
    No-CL:27, Un-MA:296
  Envoy.   F. Thompson.   Ga-FB:335,
    Un-MB:91
  Everyone Sang.   S. Sassoon.
    Co-PS:144, Ga-FB:218, Ga-S:171,
    Ha-LO:71, Mc-WK:13, Ni-JP:79,
    Pa-GTB:453, Sh-RP:88, Sm-MK:211,
    Un-MB:314
  Fa La La.   De-CH:187
  Fair and Fair.   G. Peele.
    Al-VBP:134
  A Farmyard Song.   M. Hastings.
    Au-SP:228
  Fiddler's Fair.   Ju-CP:40
  Fire Island Walking Song.
    E. Kinkead.   Co-BBW:56
  Football Song.   W. Scott.
    Mo-SD:28
  For M.S. Singing Frülinġsġlaube
    in 1945.   F. Cornford. Pl-US:65

for Nina Simone wherever you are.
L. Curry. Jo-VC:46
For the Eightieth Birthday of a
Great Singer. E. Shanks.
Pl-US:58
A Forced Music. R. Graves.
Un-MB:389
Georgia Dusk. J. Toomer.
Ad-PB:29, Be-MA:17, Bo-AN:32,
Jo-SA:102, Ra-BP:69
Goldenhair. J. Joyce.
Co-BL:86, Gr-CC:73, Gr-CT:89,
Ha-LO:3, Sh-RP:83, Th-AS:69
The Good Old Days of Adam and
Eve. Fi-BG:105
The Hawthorn Tree. Rv-ON:75
A Health unto His Majesty.
J. Savile. Gr-CT:83
The Herd-Boy's Song.
Chen Shan-min. Pa-SG:126
Hey, Nonny No! Al-VBP:353,
De-CH:188, Gr-BT:177, Gr-CT:83,
Sm-LG:389, Sp-OG:280
Holy Thursday. W. Blake.
De-CH:62, Ma-YA:127, Rv-CB:584
Homage to the Empress of the
Blues. R. Hayden. Ad-PB:117,
Be-MA:64, Hu-PN:290, Mo-BG:46
How to Sing or Read.
R. Stevenson. Gr-EC:128
I Am the Duke of Norfolk.
Gr-GB:197
I Loved a Lass. G. Wither.
Al-VBP:312, De-CH:190, No-CL:121
I the Singer Stand on High on
the Yellow Rushes. Le-OE:20
I Will Go with My Father
a-Ploughing. J. Campbell.
Ar-TP3:202, Br-SS:166, Fe-FP:231
The Idea of Order at Key West.
W. Stevens. Sh-AP:160,
Un-MA:349
In the Evening. G. Chesterton.
Li-TU:220
The Inheritance. Ir-BB:122,
St-FS:127
Invitation. R. Torrence.
Bo-FP:103
Irish. E. O'Brien. Br-SS:136,
La-PH:49, Th-AS:99
Jean Richepin's Song. H. Trench.
Co-PI:191, Co-PT:25, Gr-EC:127
John Brown. V. Lindsay.
Un-MA:227
The Joy of Church Fellowship.
E. Taylor. Rv-CB:475, Sh-AP:14
Ko-Ko's Song. W. Gilbert.
Er-FA:438
Little Hoe-Down Jordan.
Ju-CP:20

A Little More Traveling Music.
A. Young. Mc-EA:28
The Little Shepherd's Song.
W. Percy. Ha-YA:67
Lost Voice on This Hill.
B. Eaton. De-FS:84
M., Singing. L. Bogan.
Bo-GJ:137
The Mad Maid's Song. R. Herrick.
Al-VBP:333, De-CH:196, Ho-WR:88
Maiden's Song. P. Heyse.
Un-R:101
Marginalia for Solo Voice and
Tom-Tom; the Negroes Sing.
A. Voznesensky. Ca-MR:75
May-Day Song. Co-PS:83, Un-GT:274
Mazilla and Mazura. Gr-CT:88
Merlin. R. Emerson. Sh-AP:32
The Merryman Sings. W. Gilbert.
Gr-EC:226
Mush, Mush. Co-RM:114
Music and Words. E. Jennings.
Pl-US:48
The Music Makers. A. O'Shaughnessy.
Al-VBP:1063, Co-PI:163, Ga-FB:133,
Mc-PR:72, Se-PR:324
A New Year Carol. Co-PS:23,
De-CH:3, De-TT:115, Ga-S:93,
Gr-GB:297, Ma-FW:3, Re-TW:64
O Black and Unknown Bards.
J. Johnson. Ad-PB:2, Bo-AN:1,
Hu-PN:29, Lo-TY:206, Pl-US:74,
Ra-BP:42
The October Redbreast.
A. Meynell. Un-MB:64
Old Dance Song. Tr-US I:10
Old Farmer Grumble. Ju-CP:28
Old Hundred. M. Van Doren.
Pl-US:53
On a Fair Morning. Al-VBP:355
On Visiting a Clear Spring.
Li Po. Le-MW:56
Orpheus. E. Roberts. Un-MA:269
Our Mother's Tunes. E. Farjeon.
Hu-MP:6
Our Songs Make the Yangtze
River Flow Backward. Hs-TC:444
Parsley, Sage, Rosemary and
Thyme. Ir-BB:120
Peekskill. A. Kramer. Kr-OF:162
The Piper. W. Blake. Al-VBP:611,
Ar-TP3:161, Bo-GJ:131, Cl-FC:20,
Co-RG:147, De-TT:112, Ga-FB:25,
Hi-GD:26, Hu-MP:62, La-PP:vii,
La-PV:xix, Li-LC:88, Ma-YA:126,
Ox-BC:84, Ox-BN:19, Pl-US:88,
Re-TW:38, Rv-CB:566, Sm-LG:34,
Sm-MK:14, Un-GB:17, Un-GT:11
The Poet and His Song. P. Dunbar.
Bo-HF:154, Se-PR:329

SONGS AND SINGING — cont'd.
  Psalm 100. Bible. O.T. Psalms.
    Ar-TP3:188, Br-SS:81, Fe-FP:85,
    Hu-MP:287, Ma-YA:76, Pl-US:52,
    Sh-RP:92
  The Quartette. W. de la Mare.
    Rv-CB:963
  The Reaper. R. Duncan. Gr-CC:68
  Ringely, Ringely. E. Follen.
    Br-BC:15
  The Rivals. J. Stephens.
    Fe-FP:280, Mc-PR:191, Pa-RE:42,
    Re-BS:43, Th-AS:53
  Robin Hood. J. Keats.
    Gr-CC:115, Mc-PR:34
  Robin Hood and Little John.
    Bo-FP:218, Ir-BB:122, Wr-RM:50
  Sally in Our Alley. H. Carey.
    Al-VBP:527, Co-PS:38, Er-FA:125,
    Pa-GTB:126, Rv-CB:498, Sp-OG:268
  Saul. R. Browning. Hi-FO:23
  Sea Shell. A. Lowell. Bo-FP:279,
    Bo-HF:81, Fe-FP:274, Hu-MP:176,
    Li-LC:39, Mc-PR:61, Sh-RP:81
  The Seed of All Song. Basho.
    Be-CS:18
  Sheep-Skin and Bee's Wax.
    Ir-BB:127, Pa-RE:76
  Sing a Song of Joy! T. Campion.
    Pl-US:51
  Sing Song Merry Go Round.
    Ir-BB:124
  Singing. P. Shelton. Le-M:137
  Singing (The Children Sing).
    R. Stevenson. Gr-TG:23
  Singing (Of Speckled Eggs).
    R. Stevenson. Bo-FP:133,
    Fr-MP:13
  The Singing Bird. Ju-CP:36
  The Singing Fairy. R. Fyleman.
    Rd-SS:35
  Singing in the Dark.
    I. Wassall. Hu-PN:546
  Singing-Time. R. Fyleman.
    Ar-TP3:175, Br-SS:15,
    Fr-MP:3, Mc-AW:3
  The Sirens' Song. Homer.
    Mo-GR:13
  Skipping Song. Ju-CP:69
  A Sledding Song. N. Schlichter.
    Fe-FP:115
  The Solitary Reaper.
    W. Wordsworth. Bl-OB:146,
    Co-RG:122, De-CH:207, Go-BP:49,
    Ha-PO:83, Hi-WP II:142,
    Ma-YA:141, Ox-BN:77, Pa-GTB:255,
    Pl-US:50, Re-TW:114, Rv-CB:635,
    Sp-OG:336
  Song. T. Peacock.
    Al-VBP:714

Song for Everyone. R. Smith.
  Gr-EC:2
Song from The Bride's Tragedy.
  T. Beddoes. Gr-CC:71
Song in the Wood. J. Fletcher.
  Re-TW:55
The Song Maker. A. Wickham.
  Un-MB:279
Song of a Hebrew. D. Abse.
  Sm-MK:214
The Song of Honor. R. Hodgson.
  Un-MB:188
The Song of the Banana Man.
  E. Jones. Co-RM:242,
  Sa-B:101, To-MP:168
The Song of the Muses. M. Arnold.
  Gr-CT:444, Ho-WR:249
Song of the Son. J. Toomer.
  Ad-PB:30, Be-MA:18,
  Bo-AN:33, Jo-SA:32
The Song of the Toad.
  J. Burroughs. Fe-FP:142
Songs, I, II. Tr-US II:123
Song's Eternity. J. Clare.
  Mc-WK:2, Rv-CB:722, Sm-LG:32
Songs of Joy. W. Davies.
  Un-MB:178
The Souling Song. Gr-SS:151
South American Sway. M. Byers.
  Gr-EC:120
Spanish Folk Song. Cl-FC:17
Spanish Johnny. W. Cather.
  Co-RM:26, Fe-FP:436, Hu-MP:154,
  Mc-WK:140, Mc-WS:160, Sh-RP:41
Swing Song. H. Behn. Ar-TP3:108
Tale of a Pig. Ju-CP:42
Taunt Song Against a Clumsy
  Kayak Paddler. Le-IB:111,
  Tr-US I:3
Threnody. D. Hayes. Bo-AN:93
To Colin Clout. A. Munday.
  Al-VBP:120, Pa-GTB:12, Rv-CB:164
To Jane. P. Shelley. Re-TW:106
To Our Babies, I, II. Le-IB:60
Turkey in the Straw. Er-FA:434,
  Gr-GB:209
Under the Greenwood Tree.
  W. Shakespeare. Al-VBP:186,
  Ar-TP3:204, Bo-FP:259, Co-BN:206,
  De-CH:134, De-TT:147, Er-FA:263,
  Fe-FP:211, Gr-EC:48, Ho-WR:74,
  Hu-MP:268, Mc-PR:30, Pa-GTB:5,
  Rv-CB:196, Tu-WW:61
Weltschmerz. F. Yerby. Bo-AN:136
Whack Fol the Diddle. P. Kearney.
  Co-FB:206, Co-PI:79
When a Man's Body Is Young.
  Le-OE:109
When Mahalia Sings. Q. Prettyman.
  Ad-PB:260, Pe-M:18

When Malindy Sings. P. Dunbar.
    Ad-PB:10, Hu-PN:37
When to Her Lute Corinna Sings.
    T. Campion. Gr-CC:65, Pl-US:12
The Whistle-Pig Song.
    Ju-CP:19
Who Will Shoe My Little Feet.
    Ju-CP:24
The Winter's Tale.
    W. Shakespeare. Pl-US:102
Wishing Song. Ju-CP:23
Witches' Song. E. Coatsworth.
    Co-PM:38
Woman at the Piano.
    M. Zaturenska. Un-MA:562
Yankee Doodle. De-PO:22,
    Gr-CT:87, Gr-GB:166, Ir-BB:234,
    Mo-CC:(17), Mo-MGT:162,
    Mo-TL:85
SONIC BOOMS
Sonic Boom. J. Updike.
    Du-RG:78, Ha-TP:26, Pe-SS:64
SONNETS (ABOUT): see also HUMOR -
    SONNETS (ABOUT)
The House of Life. D. Rossetti.
    Al-VBP:988, Ma-YA:211
Scorn Not the Sonnet.
    W. Wordsworth. No-CL:90
Sonnets. W. Wordsworth.
    Al-VBP:658
SONS: see also SATIRE - SONS
Ap Huw's Testament. R. Thomas.
    Gr-BT:xv
At the Washing of My Son.
    Su Tung P'o. Rx-OH:84
The Aura. J. Dickey. Du-SH:55
Bartholomew. N. Gale.
    Br-BC:42, Th-AS:54
Boy Driving His Father to Con-
    fession. S. Heaney.
    Gr-BT:23
The Constancy. J. Miller.
    Sc-TN:171
Death of a Son. J. Silkin.
    Br-TC:375, Pa-GTB:566
Death of a Son. Bi-IT:99
Dirge. Tr-US II:146
Dirge for a Son Killed in Battle.
    Tr-US I:187
For a Fatherless Son. S. Plath.
    Mc-EA:98, Mo-TS:36
For My Father. P. Whalen.
    Mc-EA:112
The Gift of God. E. Robinson.
    Un-MA:135
Hind Etin. Ox-BB:97
Letter of a Mother.
    R. Warren. Un-MA:584
The Meeting. K. Tynan. Go-BP:121
My Son.   Ge-TR:41

Of My Dear Son, Gervase Beaumont.
    J. Beaumont. Al-VBP:293
The Old and Young Courtier.
    Al-VBP:369, No-CL:229
The Old Woman with Four Sons.
    P. McGinley. Ke-TF:149
On Visiting My Son, Port Angeles,
    Washington. D. Niatum.
    Ni-CD:130
A Prayer. V. Watkins. Tr-MR:50
The Son. R. Torrence. Mc-WK:131
Song after Defeat. Tr-US I:37
The Three Sons. Wr-RM:80
To His Son, Vincent Corbet.
    R. Corbet. Ox-BC:25, Rv-CB:322,
    Sm-LG:112
To My Son. S. Sassoon. Mc-WS:137
The Toys. C. Patmore. Al-VBP:973,
    Er-FA:142, Rv-CB:876
Uvlunuaq's Song. Tr-US I:16
The Wife of Usher's Well.
    Ar-TP3:20, De-CH:424, De-TT:171,
    Gr-CT:134, Ma-BB:37, Ox-BB:94,
    Pa-OM:91, Rv-CB:36
SOPHISTICATION
i should have caught my unicorn.
    D. Witt. Ad-II:9
Thoughts while Driving Home.
    J. Updike. Pe-SS:111
SOPHOCLES
Wind, Gentle Evergreen.
    Rv-CB:424
SORCERY: see WITCHES AND WITCHCRAFT
SORROW: see GRIEF
SOTO, HERNANDO DE: see DE SOTO,
    HERNANDO
SOUDAN: see SUDAN
SOUL: see also HUMOR - SOUL
Address to My Soul. E. Wylie.
    Tr-MR:252, Wi-LT:208
All That Was Mortal.
    S. Teasdale. Tr-MR:286
The Black Me. Chi Hsüan.
    Pa-MV:46
Bring the Soul Blocks.
    V. Cruz. Ad-CI:60
The Brook of the Heart.
    E. Dickinson. Co-BL:28,
    Gr-FB:67
By the Sea. R. Dixon. Ox-BN:750
The Caged Skylark. G. Hopkins.
    Un-MB:43, Wi-LT:42
The Crematory. Kuo Mo-jo.
    Hs-TC:35
The Crest Jewel. J. Stephens.
    Un-MB:267
Darest Thou Now O Soul.
    W. Whitman. Al-VBP:948
The Descendant and the Id.
    A. Branch. Sm-PT:131

SOUL — cont'd.
A Dialogue of Self and Soul.
    W. Yeats. Un-MB:118, Wi-LT:84
The Door of Death. W. Blake.
    De-CH:753, Gr-CT:376
Doubts. R. Brooke. De-CH:247,
    Gr-SS:117
The Dying Christian to His Soul.
    A. Pope. Go-BP:235
The Ecstasy. J. Donne.
    Al-VBP:250, Rv-CB:303
Expectans Expectavi. C. Sorley.
    Sm-LG:379
The Fish Turns into a Man.
    L. Hunt. Al-VBP:713
The Flesh and the Spirit.
    A. Bradstreet. Sh-AP:9
Ghoul Care. R. Hodgson.
    Un-MB:193
High on Life. B. Kaufman.
    Be-MA:132
The House of Life. K. Tynan.
    Go-BP:133
I Know My Soul. C. McKay.
    Ra-BP:65
The Immortal Spirit. S. Spender.
    Tr-MR:289
The Immortality of the Soul.
    J. Davies. Al-VBP:223
In a Dark Time. T. Roethke.
    Pl-EI:46, Un-MA:600
In Due Season. J. Drinkwater.
    Ke-TF:240
In My Own Album. C. Lamb.
    Rv-CB:673
The Informing Spirit.
    R. Emerson. Mc-PR:137
The Invention of Comics.
    I. Baraka. Ad-PB:251,
    Bo-AN:179, Wi-LT:744
Longing. S. Teasdale. Sm-PT:161
My Soul, Consider! E. Mörike.
    Un-R:105
The Negro Speaks of Rivers.
    L. Hughes. Ad-PB:72, Be-MA:38,
    Br-AF:176, Hu-PN:187, Li-TU:179,
    Lo-TY:225, Mo-TS:38, Pe-SS:49,
    Ra-BP:78
A Noiseless Patient Spider.
    W. Whitman. Ha-PO:107,
    Ho-WR:141, Mc-PR:112, Na-EO:44,
    Tr-MR:281, Un-MA:42
Palladium. M. Arnold.
    Ox-BN:646, Pa-GTB:366
Passage to More than India.
    W. Whitman. Tr-MR:292
Pegasus. P. Kavanagh.
    Co-PI:76
Phantom. S. Coleridge. Gr-SS:116
Poem. K. Cuestas. Jo-SA:85

Prometheus Unbound. P. Shelley.
    Al-VBP:742, Mo-GR:110
Ship of Death. D. Lawrence.
    Al-VBP:1160, Pa-GTB:462,
    Un-MB:299
Song of a Jellyfish. M. Kaneko.
    Sh-AM:60
Song of Myself. W. Whitman.
    Er-FA:87, Tr-MR:143, Un-MA:61
Sonnet 146. W. Shakespeare.
    Al-VBP:209, Pa-GTB:38,
    Pl-EI:53, Rv-CB:253
Sonnets from the Portuguese.
    E. Browning. Al-VBP:815
Soul, Scorning All Measure.
    M. Tsvetayeva. Ca-MR:136
The Soul Selects Her Own Society.
    E. Dickinson. Sh-AP:128,
    Un-MA:96, Un-MW:86
Souls. F. Davis. Th-AS:202
Struggle. S. Lanier. Rv-CB:943
The Sun, the Moon, the Stars,
    the Seas. A. Tennyson.
    Go-BP:274, Li-SR:94
This Corruptible. E. Wylie.
    Tr-MR:257, Un-MA:282
This Soul. J. Cendejas.
    Me-WF:68
SOUNDS: see also HUMOR - SOUNDS;
    NOISE
Aeroplane. M. Greene.
    Ar-TP3:87, Au-SP:174, Pe-FB:44
After the Bells Hummed.
    Basho. Be-CS:34
Alike. D. Aldis. Sh-RP:216
Alleyway. S. Quasimodo.
    Ma-FW:235
The Animal That Drank Up Sound.
    W. Stafford. Ca-VT:413
August 24, 1963 - 1:00 a.m. -
    Omaha. D. Whitewing.
    Al-WW:57
The Avenue Bearing the Initial
    of Christ into the New World.
    G. Kinnell. Ad-CI:11, Wi-LT:746
Blue Water. Li Po. Le-MW:109
Boats at Night. E. Shanks.
    De-CH:313, Ma-FW:54
Broadway: Twilight.
    T. Prideaux. La-OC:19
By Night. R. Francis.
    Ca-VT:233
A Child's Laughter. A. Swinburne.
    Br-BC:69, Fe-PL:246
City Trees. E. Millay. Bo-HF:64,
    Fe-FP:250, La-OC:23, Sh-RP:108
Crickets. D. McCord.
    Ja-PA:22, La-PV:145
Dawn Has Yet to Ripple In.
    M. Cane. Un-MA:236

A Different Speech.   L. Nicholl.
   Pl-IO:26
Down the Rain Falls.
   E. Coatsworth.   Au-SP:314
The Express.   S. Spender.
   Bo-GJ:210, Br-TC:401, Co-RG:157,
   To-MP:21, Un-MB:474, Wi-LT:498
The Faery Queen.   E. Spenser.
   Al-VBP:119, Pl-US:40
Faint Music.   W. de la Mare.
   Sm-LG:39
Flight.   J. Tate.   La-OC:106
Going to Sleep in the Country.
   H. Moss.   En-PC:204
A Goodnight.   W. Williams.Un-MA:259
The Greenwood.   W. Bowles.Cl-EC:41
The Harbor Dawn.   H. Crane.
   Pe-OA:178, Sh-AP:198
Hearing the Wind at Night.
   M. Swenson.   Co-BN:166, Ha-WR:55
The Hermit.   W. Davies.   Un-MB:176
The House in the Green Well.
   J. Wheelock.   Un-MA:344
The Interrupted Concert.
   F. García Lorca.   Le-SW:79
A Jolly Noise.   E. Jacobson.
   Mc-AW:20
The Lady of the Lake.   W. Scott.
   Al-VBP:674, Ox-BN:132
Lilian's Song.   G. Darley.
   Ox-BN:386
Listen.   Ai Ch'ing.   Hs-TC:297
Listening.   W. Stafford.
   Kh-VA:21, La-RM:166, Mo-TS:35
A Loon I Thought It Was.
   Da-SC:151, Ho-SD:7,
   Le-OE:89, Tr-US II:225
Many a Mickle.   W. de la Mare.
   Ga-FB:169
Midnight.   T. Middleton.
   Bl-OB:140, Pa-RE:124, Rd-SS:35
Midnight on March 27th.
   G. Dusenbery.   Sc-TN:36
Night and a Distant Church.
   R. Atkins.   Ad-PB:198
Night and Noises.   G. Foster.
   Le-M:86
Night Magic.   A. Burr.
   Hu-MP:128, Th-AS:76
Night Things Are Soft and Loud.
   Z. Gay.   Sh-RP:12
The Noise of Waters.   J. Joyce.
   Ar-TP3:173, Fe-FP:271, Ho-LP:79,
   Li-TU:206, Ma-FW:34, Sm-LG:344,
   Un-MB:270
The Noise That Time Makes.
   M. Moore.   Un-MA:577
November Night.   A. Crapsey.
   Fe-FP:83, Hi-WP II:137,
   Ho-LP:32, Hu-MP:321, Ja-PA:41

November Woods.   H. Jackson.
   Ja-PA:42
On Watching the Construction of
   a Skyscraper.   B. Raffel.
   Du-RG:38, La-OC:112
Only the Sound Remains.   E. Thomas.
   De-CH:567
Pastoral.   E. Millay.
   Sh-RP:218
Peace, like a Lamb.   L. Clark.
   Hi-WP I:110
Il Penseroso.   J. Milton.
   De-CH:201
Pleasant Sounds.   J. Clare.
   Go-BP:110, Rv-CB:723
Proem.   M. Cawein.   Co-BN:213
Railroad Reverie.   E. Young.
   Gr-EC:241
River of Ice.   S. Tsuboi.
   Sh-AM:68
The Shell.   J. Stephens.
   Cl-DT:40, Co-BN:82, De-CH:57,
   Ma-FW:43, Ni-JP:34, Un-MB:262
Song for a Summer Afternoon.
   V. Miller.   Ca-BP:46
Song of the Train.   D. McCord.
   Au-SP:166, Fe-FP:188
Sonnet II.   G. Bennett.
   Ad-PB:82, Bo-AN:75, Hu-PN:206
A Sound from the Earth.
   W. Stafford.   La-RM:82
A Sound in Cambridge, Mass.
   R. Whitman.   Ls-NY:327
The Sound of Night.   M. Kumin.
   Co-BN:116
The Sound of Trees.   R. Frost.
   Bo-HF:58, Sm-PT:11
The Sounding Fog.   S. Pulsifer.
   La-PV:39
Static.   R. Humphries.
   Pl-US:41
Summer Remembered.   I. Gardner.
   Pe-OA:235
Symphony.   Li Kuang-t'ien.
   Hs-TC:204
To Autumn.   J. Keats.   Cl-FC:43
Tortoise Shout.   D. Lawrence.
   Wi-LT:215
An Unfinished Poem.   S. Muro.
   Sh-AM:56
Uninhabited Island.   Chi Hsüan.
   Pa-MV:49
Very Early.   K. Kuskin.
   Au-SP:41, La-PV:49
Was It the Sound.   E. Ramal.
   De-CH:659
Water Noises.   E. Roberts.
   Co-BN:68, Mc-AW:42, Th-AS:82
A Way of Touching the World.
   Me-WF:75

SOUNDS — cont'd.
  What Is Buzz? M. O'Neill.
    It-HB:50
  When Dawn Comes to the City:
    New York. C. McKay.
    Bo-HF:30, La-OC:138
  Wind. A. Fisher. Sh-RP:159
  Wrinkles Run down the Pool.
    R. Cowie. Le-WR:12
SOUNION, CAPE: see SUNIUM, CAPE
SOUP: see also HUMOR - SOUP
  January. M. Sendak. Ag-HE:10
  The Story of Augustus.
    H. Hoffmann. Ag-HE:62,
    Ar-TP3:135, Bo-GJ:114, Br-SM:71,
    Co-BB:48, De-TT:93, Ir-BB:101,
    Li-SR:25, Ox-BC:205
  Turtle Soup. L. Carroll.
    Bl-OB:12, Bo-FP:57, Cl-FC:97,
    De-TT:95, Li-SR:80, Sm-MK:195
THE SOUTH: see also CONFEDERATE
    STATES OF AMERICA; CREOLES;
    HUMOR - THE SOUTH; SATIRE -
    THE SOUTH; and names of states,
    as VIRGINIA, and cities, as
    NEW ORLEANS, LA.
  A Ballad of Remembrance. R. Hayden.
    Ad-PB:115, Bo-AN:109,
    Hu-PN:291, Ra-BP:131
  Childhood. M. Walker. Ad-BO:73,
    Ad-PB:148, Be-MA:77
  Christ in Alabama. L. Hughes.
    Ad-PB:73
  Crape Myrtles in the South.
    E. Tatum. Ke-TF:440
  Emblems. A. Tate. Ca-VT:223
  The Gar. C. Bell. Br-AF:141
  Dixie. D. Emmett.
    Er-FA:290, Fe-FP:439
  Green Symphony. J. Fletcher.
    Un-MA:314
  John Brown's Body. S. Benét.
    Ke-TF:303
  Lee in the Mountains, 1865-1870.
    D. Davidson. Sm-PT:92
  Legacy: My South. D. Randall.
    Ad-PB:138, Be-MA:71,
    Hu-NN:43, Hu-PN:306
  Moths. J. Fields. Ad-PB:320,
    Hu-PN:417
  My South. D. West. Hu-PN:547
  Northboun'. L. Holloway. Hu-PN:257
  Northbound. L. Rubin. Ls-NY:292
  October Journey. M. Walker.
    Ad-PB:146, Bo-AN:132, Hu-PN:317
  An Old Woman Remembers. S. Brown.
    Ad-PB:68
  Poem. D. Walcott. Sa-B:67
  reincarnation. M. Jackson.
    Ad-PB:498

Song for a Dark Girl.
  L. Hughes. Ad-PB:73
South Wind. Tr-US II:39
Southern Mansion. A. Bontemps.
  Ad-PB:83, Be-MA:45, Bo-AN:80,
  Br-AF:142, Hu-PN:213,
  Lo-TY:224, Wi-LT:611
The Southern Road. D. Randall.
  Ad-PB:139, Be-MA:70, Hu-NN:41
the west ridge is menthol-cool.
  D. Graham. Ad-PB:480
When the Mint Is in the Liquor.
  C. Ouslet. Fe-PL:417
you (her eyes, solstice).
  G. Bishop-Dubjinsky. Sc-TN:10
SOUTH AFRICA: see also SATIRE -
    SOUTH AFRICA
  Drummer Hodge. T. Hardy.
    Pa-GTB:404
  The Flaming Terrapin.
    R. Campbell. Co-BBW:210,
    Rd-OA:134
SOUTH AFRICAN WAR, 1899-1902: see
    BOER WAR, 1899-1902
SOUTH AMERICA: see also INDIANS OF
    SOUTH AMERICA; and names of
    countries, as BRAZIL
  South American Sway. M. Byers.
    Gr-EC:120
SOUTH CAROLINA: see also names of
    cities and towns, as
    CHARLESTON, S.C.
  Brother Jonathan's Lament for
    Sister Caroline. O. Holmes.
    Hi-TL:102
  Carolina. H. Timrod. Se-PR:283
  Report from the Carolinas.
    H. Bevington. Br-AF:136
SOUTH DAKOTA
  Dakota Badlands.
    E. Landweweer. Br-AF:155
  Dakota, the Beauty of the West.
    Fi-BG:74
  Hail! South Dakota.
    D. Hammitt. Se-PR:284
SOUTH SEA ISLANDS: see ISLANDS
    OF THE PACIFIC
SOUTHERN CROSS
  Nocturne. C. Garstin.
    De-CH:454
THE SOUTHWEST: see also names of
    states, as ARIZONA
  Git Along, Cayuse. H. Knibbs.
    Fi-BG:202
  New Mexico. P. Boyden. Ar-TP3:33
  On the Arizona Line. Fi-BG:36
  On the Frisco River. Fi-BG:46
  A Prairie Mother's Lullaby.
    E. Brininstool. Fi-BG:37
  A Pretty Woman. S. Ortiz. Ni-CD:150

Waring of Sonoratown.
  H. Knibbs. Fi-BG:141
Western Magic. M. Austin.
  Br-AF:99
The Wide Land. A. Ammons.
  Br-TC:11
SOUTHWOLD (SOLE) BAY, BATTLE, 1672
  The Battle of Sole Bay.
    Gr-GB:189
SOUTINE, CHAIM
  The Story of Soutine.
    J. Schevill. En-PC:188
SOVIET UNION: see RUSSIA
SPACE (OUTER)
  But Outer Space. R. Frost.
    Li-TU:252
  Earth's Bondman. B. Dabney.
    Gr-EC:275
  Post Early for Space.
    P. Henniker-Heaton. Br-AF:239
  Space Travel. J. Krows.
    Au-SP:177
SPACE EXPLORATION: see also
    ARTIFICIAL SATELLITES; HUMOR -
    SPACE EXPLORATION
  Among the Stars. W. Blake.
    Re-TW:129, Un-GT:264
  Little Satellite. J. Krows.
    Au-SP:176
  Man Flies Through the Universe.
    M. Goode. Jo-VC:5
  Mission Uncontrolled. R. Peck.
    Pe-M:86
  Moon Poem. S. Sharp. Ab-MO:5
  The Shore of the Universe.
    K. Zinoviev. Mo-MI:88
  Space. W. Burford. Ho-LP:81
  Space Pilot. J. Blackie.
    Ga-S:125
SPAIN: see also SPANISH VERSE; and
    names of towns, as SEVILLE, SP.
  Eisenhower's Visit to Franco, 1959.
    J. Wright. Bl-FP:23
  Evening. W. Turner. Pa-HT:103
  Over Coarse Rock in the Middle of
    the Square. A. Machado.
    Le-SW:63
  The Plaza and the Flaming Orange
    Trees. A. Machado. Le-SW:23
  Summer Night. A. Machado. Le-SW:41
  The Tale the Hermit Told.
    A. Reid. Co-PT:31
  Tarantella. H. Belloc. De-CH:189,
    Hi-WP II:2, Li-SR:5, Pa-HT:105,
    Sm-LG:45, Th-AS:164, Un-MB:167
  Three Knights from Spain.
    Bl-OB:36, De-CH:328, Fo-OG:42,
    Gr-GB:26, Rv-ON:106
SPAIN - COUNTRYSIDE
  Autumn Dawning. A. Machado.Le-SW:71

Figures in the Field Against the
    Sky. A. Machado. Le-SW:61
SPAIN - HISTORY AND PATRIOTISM
  El Archivo General de Indias.
    I. Wright. Ke-TF:386
  The Moors Fight on the Side of
    God. C. Norman. Cr-WS:37
  The Oak of Guernica.
    W. Wordsworth. Hi-FO:262
SPAIN - HISTORY AND PATRIOTISM-
    CIVIL WAR, 1936-1939
  The Benediction. M. English.
    Cr-WS:37
  Bombing Casualties: Spain.
    H. Read. Ke-PP:64
  Epitaph for a Leader.
    C. Norman. Cr-WS:36
  A Few Things Explained.
    P. Neruda. Li-TU:237
  In Memory of the Spanish Poet
    Federico García Lorca.
    T. Merton. Pl-ML:154
  Port Bou. S. Spender. Br-TC:404
  Proud Motherhood. F. Lucas.
    Hi-FO:263
  To Aunt Rose. A. Ginsberg.
    Ca-VT:575, Wi-LT:719
  Toledo. R. Campbell. Un-MB:419
  Two Armies. S. Spender. Ba-PO:121
SPANIARDS
  Little Senorita. C. Divine.
    Hu-MP:159
  Song in Praise of Paella.
    C. Wordsworth.Ag-HE:12,Co-FB:91
  Tarantella. H. Belloc.
    De-CH:189, Hi-WP II:2, Li-SR:5,
    Pa-HT:105, Sm-LG:45, Th-AS:164,
    Un-MB:167
SPANIARDS IN AMERICA: see also
    CALIFORNIA - MISSIONS; CAMINO
    REAL; SATIRE - SPANIARDS
    IN AMERICA; and names of ex-
    plorers, as DE SOTO, HERNANDO
  Conquistador. E. Coatsworth.
    Un-GT:93
  Conquistador.A. MacLeish.Hi-TL:15
  A Feller I Know. M. Austin.
    Br-AF:38, Fe-FP:306
  Las Trampas, U.S.A.
    C. Tomlinson. Br-TC:443
  Leave Me Alone. M. Lasanta.
    Ba-HI:16
  Spanish Johnny. W. Cather.
    Co-RM:26, Fe-FP:436, Hu-MP:154,
    Mc-WK:140, Mc-WS:160, Sh-RP:41
SPANISH AMERICA: see LATIN AMERICA
SPANISH-AMERICAN WAR, 1898: see
    also HUMOR - SPANISH-AMERICAN
    WAR, 1898
  Harry Wilmans. E. Masters.
    Ke-PP:7, Kr-OF:81

SPANISH-AMERICAN WAR, 1898 — cont'd.
Knowlt Hoheimer. E. Masters.
  Ba-PO:81, Ho-LP:89
On a Soldier Fallen in the
  Philippines. W. Moody.
  Cr-WS:155, Hi-TL:156
On American Island Wars.
  W. Moody. Bl-FP:33
On the Road to Santiago.
  S. Crane. Kr-OF:74
Our New National Anthem.
  W. Eggleston. Ba-PO:80,
  Cr-WS:155
The Philippine Conquest.
  E. Masters. Kr-OF:80
War Is Kind. S. Crane.
  Al-VBP:1113, Ba-PO:83, Cr-WS:158,
  Fe-PL:175, Hi-TL:155, Kr-OF:75,
  Mo-BG:169, Vi-PP:203, Wi-LT:118
The War with Spain.
  R. Shadwell. Kr-OF:79
You at Washington. E. Crosby.
  Kr-OF:71
SPANISH ARMADA
The Armada. T. Macaulay.
  Ox-BN:426, Sm-LG:250
The Armada, 1588. J. Wilson.
  Ox-BC:24
Sir Francis Drake; or Eighty-
  Eight. Gr-GB:185
SPANISH LANGUAGE: see also
  HUMOR - SPANISH LANGUAGE
My Soul Speaks Spanish.
  M. Lasanta. Jo-VC:49
SPANISH VERSE: see also BALLADS,
  SPANISH
Alleluya. R. Dario. Lo-TY:88
An Arrow Flying Past.
  G. Becquér. Pa-SG:181
Artichoke. P. Neruda. Li-TU:53
As Mary Was a-Walking. Ga-S:107
Balcony. F. García Lorca.
  Le-SW:53, Li-TU:124
The Ballad of the Little Square.
  F. García Lorca. Li-TU:222
The Christmas Child. Bo-FP:189
The Coming Star. J. Jiménez.
  Li-TU:196
Concert. I. Sharaf. Ab-MO:32
Cradle Song of the Elephants.
  A. del Valle. Fe-FP:489,
  Sh-RP:337
The Dance of Death.
  F. García Lorca. Bl-FP:70
Dawn. O. Paz. Mo-TS:86
Dead Soldier. N. Guillén.
  Ba-PO:42, Lo-TY:105
The Dictators. P. Neruda. Bl-FP:41
Diver. P. Neruda. Li-TU:127
Elephant. P. Neruda. Be-EB:48
Exodus. J. Bodet. Cr-WS:125

Farewell to My Mother.
  Placido. Lo-TY:99
A Few Things Explained.
  P. Neruda. Li-TU:237
Guadalupe, W.I. N. Guillén.
  Ab-MO:45, Lo-TY:104
Half Moon. F. García Lorca.
  La-RM:155, Le-SW:77, Li-TU:205
Heat. G. Gonzalez y Contreras.
  Ho-LP:24
The Hurricane. P. Matos.
  Fe-FP:487
I Have Lost My Shoes.
  C. Suasnavar. Fe-FP:490
I Know Not What I Seek Eternally.
  R. de Castro. Pa-SG:137
I Wish the Wood-Cutter Would
  Wake Up. P. Neruda. Bl-FP:51
An Imitator of Billy Sunday.
  J. Jiménez. Bl-FP:69
Immense Hour. J. Jiménez.
  Pa-SG:166
The Indians Come Down from
  Mixco. M. Asturias.
  Mo-TS:37
It Rained in the Night.
  J. Carrera Andrade. Ho-LP:28
January Night. R. Arrieta.
  Pa-SG:30
Lament of the Slave. Ab-MO:54
Last Night Somebody Called Me
  Darky. N. Guillén. Ab-MO:95
Let Me Go Warm.
  L. de Góngora. Mc-PR:47
The Little Girl That Lost a
  Finger. G. Mistral. Fe-FP:491
Little Songs for the Children
  of the Antilles. N. Guillén.
  Ab-MO:14
The Lizard Is Crying.
  F. García Lorca. Le-SW:31,
  Li-TU:102, Sm-MK:155
Madrigal to the City of Santiago.
  F. García Lorca. Ad-CI:86
The Moldering Hulk.
  A. Machado. Pa-SG:144
My Thirty Years. J. Manzano.
  Lo-TY:98
My Voice. J. Jiménez. Li-TU:213
Nightfall. J. Jiménez. Pa-SG:110
The Odyssey of a Snail.
  F. García Lorca. Ma-FW:211
Offerings. R. De Reinosa.
  No-CL:99
On Christmas Morn. Fe-FP:89,
  La-PH:26, La-PV:88
Opinions of the New Student.
  R. Pedroso. Lo-TY:102
Prayer to God. Placido.
  Lo-TY:99

Proposition. N. Guillén.
   Ab-MO:4, Fe-FP:487, Lo-TY:104
Psalm. M. Mendes. Tr-MR:207
The Radish. I. Quzman.
   Ab-MO:31
Rumba. J. Tallet. Lo-TY:102
St. Joseph and God's Mother.
   Ga-S:78
St. Teresa's Book-Mark.
   St. Theresa. Pa-SG:191,
   Pl-EI:178
She Was a Pretty Little Girl.
   R. de Ayada. Fe-FP:473
The Siesta. Pa-SG:149
Sightseers in a Courtyard.
   N. Guillén. Lo-TY:106
Silly Song. F. García Lorca.
   Le-SW:25, Li-TU:68
Simple Verses. J. Marti.
   Lo-TY:100
Song. G. Vicente. Pa-SG:148
Songs Between the Soul and the
   Bridegroom. St. John of the
   Cross. Ga-S:139
Sonnet. M. de Guevara.
   Ga-S:145
The Sower. R. Olivares Figueroa.
   Fe-FP:490, Ho-LP:38
Spanish Folk Song. Cl-FC:17
Squares and Angles. A. Storni.
   La-OC:100
The Street. O. Paz. La-OC:135
Sunrise. F. García Lorca.
   Bl-FP:84
Thoughts of a Little Girl.
   M. Enriqueta. Fe-FP:489
The Three Kings. R. Dario.
   Ab-MO:74
To a Saxon Poet. J. Borges.
   Pl-ML:92
To Columbus. R. Dario. Lo-TY:86
To Miss Rapida. J. Jiménez.
   Li-TU:178
To My Brother Miguel.
   C. Vallejo. Pe-M:13
To the Nativity.
   F. Gonzalez de Eslava.
   Ga-S:94
To Theodore Roosevelt.
   R. Dario. Bl-FP:37
Two Countries. J. Marti.
   Lo-TY:101
Two Spanish Gypsy Lullabies.
   Ma-FW:66
The Unforeseen. C. Roxlo.
   Tr-MR:58
The United Fruit Co. P. Neruda.
   Bl-FP:39
Walnut. J. Andrade.   Co-EL:118,
   Co-PU:129

Weeping and Singing. C. Tiempo.
   Tr-MR:85
Well I Never! Ir-BB:84
Where Shall We Dance?
   G. Mistral. Pa-SG:119
Who Translates a Poet Badly.
   G. Prado. Co-EL:39
With the Roses. J. Jiménez.
   Le-SW:19, Li-TU:207
See also Be-UL, Le-SW
SPANKINGS: see PUNISHMENT
SPARROWS: see also HUMOR - SPARROWS
All at Once the Storm. Buson.
   Ca-BF:13
And Other Poems. R. Morgan.
   Ma-FW:95
As New Year's Day Dawns.
   Ransetsu. Be-MC:48
At Last the Sparrows. Onitsura.
   Be-CS:39
The Bee, the Ant, and the Sparrow.
   N. Cotton. Ox-BC:67
The Blind Sparrow. Gyodai.
   Le-IS:23
The Blossom. W. Blake.
   Bo-GJ:97, Re-TW:39, Rv-CB:577
The Child and the Sparrow.
   T. Westwood. Re-BS:39
City Sparrow. A. Kreymborg.
   La-OC:119
Claritas. D. Levertov.
   Ca-BP:27, Ca-VT:512
Come and Let Us Play. Issa.
   Ca-BF:35
A Day of Spring. Onitsura.
   Le-IS:10
The Dead Sparrow. W. Cartwright.
   De-CH:95
Dream Songs, III. Tr-US II:249
Flight of the Sparrows.
   M. Zaturenska. Ha-TP:20
I Know the Trusty Almanac.
   R. Emerson. Re-BS:20
Let Ye Then My Birds Alone.
   J. Clare. Re-BS:27
The Liberator. Wu-ti. Re-BS:25
Look Out, My Sparrow. Issa.
   Ca-BF:27
The Nightingale's Song Is
   Beautiful. Issa. Do-TS:29
No Mother! No Father! Issa.
   Do-TS:2
Pastoral. W. Williams. Br-TC:479
Philipp Sparrowe. J. Skelton.
   Gr-EC:177
The Praise of Philip Sparrow.
   G. Gascoigne. Al-VBP:81,
   De-CH:93, Rd-OA:102
Sacrifice of the Sparrows of the
   Field. J. Langland. St-H:107

SPARROWS — cont'd.
  Sleepy Sparrows.   De-PP:16
  Some Brown Sparrows.   B. Fearing.
    Co-BBW:258, Du-RG:27
  Song.   T. Beddoes.   Re-BS:8
  The Song Sparrow.   H. Van Dyke.
    Hu-MP:229
  Sparrow.   W. Berry.   Ca-BP:26
  The Sparrow.   Bible.   O.T.
    Psalms.   Fe-FP:294
  The Sparrow.   W. Williams.
    Ca-BP:35, Ca-VT:71
  Sparrow Queen.   Ca-MU:23
  Sparrows.   M. Leib.   Ho-TY:95
  The Sparrow's Dirge.   J. Skelton.
    Sm-LG:85
  The Sparrows Fighting.
    W. Davies.   Re-BS:30
  Sparrows or Butterflies?
    De-PP:23
  The Sparrow's Skull.   R. Pitter.
    Pl-EI:141
  Still, Citizen Sparrow.
    R. Wilbur.   Wi-LT:597
  There Was a Pig.   Rv-ON:110
  Two Sparrows.   H. Wolfe.
    Sm-MK:173
  When Nightingales Burst into
    Song.   Jurin.   Be-MC:58
SPARTA, GR.
  From the Greek of Julianus.
    W. Cowper.   Sp-OG:49
SPEARFISHING
  Tarpon.   L. Lieberman.
    Du-SH:124
SPEARS
  Spear-Blessing.   Tr-US I:103
SPECTACLES: see EYEGLASSES
SPECULATION (FINANCIAL)
  The South Sea Bubble.
    Anne, Countess of Winchelsea.
    Rv-CB:482
SPEECH: see also HUMOR - SPEECH;
    SATIRE - SPEECH; STUTTERING
  After a Line by John Peale
    Bishop.   D. Justice.   En-PC:228
  Controlling the Tongue.
    G. Chaucer.   Ox-BC:3
  Goodbye Now, or, Pardon My
    Gauntlet.   O. Nash.
    Co-FB:481
  I Went to Noke.   Gr-GB:172
  Kalymniad, Part II.   R. Lax.
    Sc-TN:131, 136
  The Man from Up-Country Talking.
    J. de Melo Neto.   An-TC:163
  On a Child Beginning to Talk.
    T. Bastard.   Rv-CB:261
  One Bowl, One Bottle.
    Rv-ON:51

  Precious Moments.   C. Sandburg.
    Un-MA:208
  To His Little Son Benedict from
    the Tower of London.
    J. Hoskyns.   Ox-BC:21
  Without a Speaking Tongue.
    W. Sorell.   Ls-NY:120
SPEECHES: see also HUMOR -
    SPEECHES; TOASTS
  Corner Meeting.   L. Hughes.
    Ad-CI:31
SPEED: see also HUMOR - SPEED
  Haste.   B. Franklin.
    Un-GT:26
  Highway: Michigan.   T. Roethke.
    Du-SH:68
  How Many Miles to Babylon?
    Bo-FP:30, Cl-DT:33, De-PO:10,
    Gr-GB:25, Ir-BB:241, Ke-TF:69,
    Li-LB:38, Mo-MGT:108, Mo-NR:105,
    On-TW:61, Rv-CB:456, Sm-LG:241,
    Tu-WW:14, Wr-RM:57
  The Hurrier.   H. Monro.
    Un-MB:240
  A Hurry-Up Word.   E. Hilsabeck.
    Mc-AW:15
  Jungle Songs, II.   Tr-US II:158
  A Lazy Thought.   E. Merriam.
    La-OC:44
  The Leg in the Subway.
    O. Williams.   Wi-LT:418
  On the Move.   T. Gunn.
    Br-TC:159, Wi-LT:723
  One Day.   W. Horne, Jr.
    Ho-CT:14
  Portrait.   M. Chute.   Mc-AW:15
  Reluctances.   H. Witt.   Ls-NY:320
  Rides.   G. Derwood.   Wi-LT:686
  The Sloth.   T. Roethke.
    Co-BBW:192, Co-FB:14, Mc-WK:52,
    Un-GF:89, We-PZ:11
  Slow Pokes.   L. Arlon.   Mo-AW:56
  Slowly.   J. Reeves.   Bl-OB:138
  Someone Slow.   J. Ciardi.
    Un-GB:21
  Song in the Rain.   Yang Huan.
    Pa-MV:159
  Swift Things Are Beautiful.
    E. Coatsworth.   Ar-TP3:213,
    Du-RG:101
  They Are Sailing on the Breeze.
    Jo-TS:20
  To Bella Akhmadulina.
    A. Voznesensky.   Ca-MR:79
  To Miss Rapida.   J. Jiménez.
    Li-TU:178
  The Tortoise.   C. Corman.
    Ca-VT:527
  Train.   K. Baba.   Le-TA:95
  XXth Century.   R. Hillyer.   Ho-TH:32

SPELLING: see also HUMOR - SPELLING
   Anyone if He Will Try.   Ju-CP:13
   Bea's Bee. M. Ray.   Ho-GC:16
   A Farmer's Dog. Bl-OB:115
   Jack Jelf. Wr-RM:45
   May Thirtieth. Co-PS:94
   There Was an Old Dog. De-TT:67
   Tobacco. Mo-MGT:192
SPELLS: see CHARMS; MAGIC
SPHINXES
   The Sphinx. O. Wilde. Un-MB:69
   The Sphinx Speaks. F. Saltus.
      Pa-HT:90
SPICEBUSH
   Spicewood. L. Reese.
      Un-MA:111
SPICES: see HUMOR - SPICES;
      and names of specific spices,
      as CLOVES
SPIDER WEBS: see COBWEBS
SPIDERS: see also COBWEBS; HUMOR -
      SPIDERS; TARANTULAS
   A.E.F. C. Sandburg. Un-MA:203
   Arachnida, Female. A. Humphreys.
      De-FS:109
   Cold Snuggle. J. Lloyd.
      Le-WR:33
   The Cure. A. Noyes. Co-BBW:229
   Design. R. Frost.
      Ho-LP:49, Pe-OA:45
   Four Things. Bible. O.T.
      Proverbs. Fe-FP:124, Un-GT:30
   The Huntress. G. Johnston.
      Do-WH:90
   The Image. R. Fuller. Pa-GTB:526
   Incantation at First Twining Yam
      Vines. Tr-US I:196
   Ipsey Wipsey. Mo-MGT:13
   The Lily Princess. Ch-B:24,
      Hu-MP:252
   Lined Up One by One. Shiki.
      Ca-BF:19
   Little City. R. Horan. Co-BBW:219
   Little Miss Muffet. Au-SP:9,
      Bo-FP:103, De-PO:12, Er-FA:506,
      Li-LB:32, Mo-CC:(53),Mo-MGT:62,
      Mo-NR:30, Mo-TL:69, Pa-AP:33,
      Wi-MG:32, Wr-RM:39
   The Little Red Spiders. Jo-TS:14
   Mr. Edwards and the Spider.
      R. Lowell. Br-TC:268,
      Pe-OA:242, Sh-AP:230, Wi-LT:579
   Mrs. Spider. M. Livingston.
      La-PV:146
   A Noiseless Patient Spider.
      W. Whitman. Ha-PO:107, Ho-WR:141,
      Mc-PR:112, Na-EO:44, Tr-MR:281,
      Un-MA:42
   Now the Pond Is Still. Aohôzuki.
      Ca-BF:25

Of a Spider. W. Thorley.
   Fe-FP:141, La-PV:146
The Orb Weaver. R. Francis.
   Du-SH:111, Ke-PP:95, Rd-OA:172
The Spider. R. Coffin.
   Mc-PR:113, Pl-IO:108
Spider. P. Colum. Co-RG:85
Spider. M. Foster. Le-M:200
The Spider. A. Herbert.
   Ir-BB:103
The Spider. J. Jenkins.
   Le-M:91
A Spider. E. Schramm. La-GI:58
The Spider. Rv-ON:34
The Spider and the Fly. M. Howitt.
   De-TT:60, Er-FA:421, Fe-FP:530,
   Gr-EC:144, Ox-BC:158, Pe-FB:56
The Spider and the Ghost of the
   Fly. V. Lindsay. Ca-VT:29
Spider Silverlegs. C. Bailey.
   Bo-FP:326
The True Story of Web-Spinner.
   M. Howitt. De-TT:122
Upon a Spider Catching a Fly.
   E. Taylor. Rd-OA:174,
   Rv-CB:476, Sh-AP:12
Webs. C. Sandburg. Ho-TH:56
With the Pine-Tree Wind.
   K. Takahama. Sh-AM:163
You Water Spider. M. Saito.
   Sh-AM:143
SPIES: see also HUMOR - SPIES
   German Eyes. R. Hershon.
      Sc-TN:95
   How It Strikes a Contemporary.
      R. Browning. Pa-GTB:352
   The Unbroken Code. R. Dana.
      Ls-NY:95
SPINACH: see HUMOR - SPINACH
SPINES: see HUMOR - SPINES
SPINNING
   The Inheritance. Ir-BB:122,
      St-FS:127
   Maiden's Song. P. Heyse.
      Un-R:101
   The Spinners. De-PP:36
   The Spinning Wheel. J. Waller.
      Co-BL:152, Co-PI:192,
      Gr-CT:405, Ha-PO:196
SPINSTERS: see SINGLE WOMEN
SPIRES: see STEEPLES
SPIRITS: see APPARITIONS; GHOSTS;
      and names of alcoholic
      beverages, as RUM
SPIRITUALISM: see also
      APPARITIONS; GHOSTS
   The Clouds. W. Williams. Ca-VT:62
   spirits. V. Cruz. Ad-PB:509
   Voices from the Other World.
      J. Merrill. Br-TC:287

SPIRITUALISM —— cont'd.
   The Witch of Coös. R. Frost.
      Al-VBP:1129, Pe-OA:36,
      Sh-AP:147, Wi-LT:170
SPIRITUALS
   Ain' Go'n' to Study War No Mo'.
      Ba-PO:167
   Dark Symphony: Lento Grave.
      M. Tolson. Bo-AN:38
   Deep River. Ra-BP:26
   Dere's No Hidin' Place down
      Dere. Ra-BP:25
   Dives and Laz'us. Lo-TY:197
   Done Found My Lost Sheep.
      Ga-S:147
   Echoes of Childhood. A. Corbin.
      Hu-PN:491
   Give Me Jesus. Re-BP:28
   Go Down, Moses. Ab-MO:79,
      Ga-S:45, Pl-EI:101, Ra-BP:23
   Go Tell It on the Mountain.
      Ab-MO:69
   The Gospel Train. Bo-FP:120,
      Ra-BP:27
   Hail John's Army. Ga-S:76
   Hold the Wind. Gr-GB:326
   I Got a Home in Dat Rock.
      Ra-BP:25
   I Know de Moonlight.
      Ra-BP:23
   I Thank God I'm Free at Las'.
      Ra-BP:31
   In Come de Animuls Two by Two.
      Gr-GB:75
   Joshua Fit de Battle of Jericho.
      Ra-BP:24
   The Lily of the Valley.
      Ga-S:171
   Little David. Ab-MO:80
   Lonesome Valley. Ga-S:34
   Mary Passed This Morning.
      O. Dodson. Ad-PB:127
   Negro Spiritual. P. Trott.
      Hu-PN:548
   Negro Spirituals.
      R. and S. Benét. Br-AF:110,
      Fe-FP:440
   Never Said a Mumbalin' Word.
      Gr-GB:307, Ra-BP:29
   No More Auction Block. Ra-BP:21
   O Black and Unknown Bards.
      J. Johnson. Ad-PB:2, Bo-AN:1,
      Hu-PN:29, Lo-TY:206,
      Pl-US:74, Ra-BP:42
   O Sinnerman. Ga-S:135
   De Ole Sheep Dey Know de Road.
      Ra-BP:32
   One More River. Cl-DT:52
   Poor Wayfaring Stranger.
      Ga-S:48
   A Spiritual. P. Dunbar.
      Ra-BP:53
   Steal Away to Jesus. Ra-BP:27
   Swing Low, Sweet Chariot.
      Br-AF:111, Fe-FP:441,
      Gr-GB:327, Sm-LG:386
   These Bones Gwine to Rise Again.
      Ga-S:24
   Walk Together Children. Ra-BP:1
   Weeping Mary. Ga-S:142
   Were You There when They Crucified
      My Lord? Ra-BP:30
   What Yo' Gwine to Do when Yo'
      Lamp Burn Down? Ra-BP:29
   When the Saints Go Marchin' In.
      Pl-EI:97
   Who Will Be the Driver? Ga-S:187
SPITTING: see HUMOR - SPITTING
SPITTLEBUGS
   The Spit-Bug. W. Matchett.
      Mc-WK:50
SPLEENWORTS: see FERNS
SPOCK, BENJAMIN MCLANE
   Doctor Spock. Y. Yevtushenko.
      Ca-MR:60
SPORTS: see also OLYMPIC GAMES;
      and names of specific sports,
      as BASEBALL
   I Bless This Man. Pindar.
      Mo-SD:181
   Reflections Outside of a Gymnasium.
      P. McGinley. Mo-SD:161
   Spring Is a Looping-Free Time.
      M. Robbins. Mo-SD:185
   Sweating. H. Linton. Ho-CT:23
SPORTSMANSHIP: see also SATIRE -
      SPORTSMANSHIP
   Vitai Lampada. H. Newbolt.
      Sp-OG:17
   Who Misses or Who Wins.
      W. Thackeray. Mo-SD:160
SPRING (SEASON): see also EQUINOX;
      HUMOR - SPRING (SEASON); SATIRE
      - SPRING (SEASON); and names of
      months, as APRIL
   Above the Water. Prince Shiki.
      Ba-ST:15
   After Winter. C. Bailey. Bo-FP:181
   After Winter. S. Brown.
      Ad-PB:65, Be-MA:30, Bo-HF:50,
      Hu-PN:165, Jo-SA:50
   All. N. Labis. Mc-AC:151
   All Through the Rains.
      G. Snyder. Kh-VA:5
   Alons au Bois le May Cueillir.
      C. d'Orleans. Pa-SG:84
   And Every Sky Was Blue and Rain.
      R. Hodgson. Ha-LO:105
   Another Spring. Tu Fu. Rx-OH:24
   Apology. E. Herrick. Ls-NY:296

April. R. Emerson. Al-VBP:806
April. M. Masters. Du-RG:95
April. S. Teasdale. Ar-TP3:203,
 Au-SP:319, Bo-FP:222, Co-PS:54,
 Fe-FP:74, Ha-YA:45, La-PV:81
April. E. Tietjens. Au-SP:347,
 Ha-YA:47
April Rise. L. Lee. To-MP:57
As We Dance Round. De-CH:11
Aunt Alice in April. W. Matchett.
 Ha-TP:128
Autumnal Spring Song.
 V. Miller. Ha-PO:99
The Barrel-Organ. A. Noyes.
 Ga-FB:234, Un-MB:245
Barren Spring. D. Rossetti.
 Ox-BN:685
Beautiful Sunday. J. Falstaff.
 Co-BN:33
Blossom Themes. C. Sandburg.
 Pe-M:8
Blue-Butterfly Day. R. Frost.
 Br-SG:4, La-RM:133
Blue Flowers. R. Field.
 Br-SG:32, Mc-PR:161
The Boats Are Afloat. Chu Hsi.
 Le-MW:69, Rx-OH:117
The Brown Bear. M. Austin.
 Co-PS:62, Fe-FP:169, Hu-MP:202,
 Mc-PR:118, Mc-WK:70
Bus Ride. S. Robinson. Fe-FP:246
Carmina Burana. Pa-SG:92
Change Toward Certainty.
 J. Hearst. St-H:79
The Children's Song. Fe-FP:476
The Child's Morning. W. Scott.
 Du-RG:97
The Christmas Present. P. Hubbell.
 La-PV:86
Clearing at Dawn. Li T'ai-po.
 Pa-SG:83
The Clouds of Springtime.
 M. Saito. Sh-AM:145
A Cold Spring. E. Bishop.
 Br-TC:49
Coming. P. Larkin. Un-MB:526
The Coming of Spring. N. Perry.
 Au-SP:318, Ha-YA:27
The Country in Spring. Lin Keng.
 Le-MW:70
Crocus. S. Day. Hu-MP:248
The Cuckoo. Gr-CT:49
Cuckoos. A. Young. Gr-CT:50
The Day Before April. M. Davies.
 Fe-FP:20, Th-AS:71
The Day of Cold Food.
 Li Ch'ing Chao. Rx-OH:98
A Day of Spring. Onitsura. Le-IS:10
Days Too Short. W. Davies.
 Un-MB:175

December. S. Vanderbilt.
 La-OC:79
Deciduous Spring. R. Warren.
 Un-MW:170
The Dress of Spring. M. Justus.
 Ha-YA:55
Eager Spring. G. Bottomley.
 Un-MB:213
Early Spring. M. Chute.
 Br-SG:5
Early Spring. A. Sawai.
 Sh-AM:137
East Wind. Ou Yang Hsiu.
 Rx-OH:52
Easter. J. Kilmer. Ar-TP3:204,
 Au-SP:366, Hu-MP:333, La-PH:51,
 La-PV:82
The Echoing Green. W. Blake.
 Bo-FP:237, Ch-B:115, Co-PS:59,
 De-CH:21, Ho-WR:161, Rv-CB:589
Edict. H. Vinal. Ls-NY:49
Even as the Snow Fell. Issa.
 Le-MW:68
The Fall of the Flowers. Yen Yun.
 Le-MW:73
The First Part of Spring.
 H. Kawahigashi. Sh-AM:161
The First Spring Day.
 C. Rossetti. Ho-WR:35
The First Spring Morning.
 R. Bridges. Co-BN:15,
 Ha-YA:26, Sm-MK:144
The Fisherman. Li Po. Le-MW:113
Five Short Stanzas, III. Spring.
 Tsou Ti-fan. Hs-TC:348
Flapping into a Fog. Gyodai.
 Be-MC:53
The Flower-Cart Man. R. Field.
 Au-SP:143, Br-SG:72,
 Br-SS:147, La-OC:53
Flowers. T. Jastrzebski.
 Ho-CT:12
The Flowers to the Tree's Root.
 Emperor Sûtoku. Ba-ST:26
For, Lo, the Winter Is Past.
 Bible. O.T. Song of Solomon.
 Ar-TP3:201, Au-SP:317, Bo-FP:231,
 Ch-B:98, Fe-FP:71, Ha-YA:27,
 La-PP:9, La-PV:80, Mc-AW:33,
 Tu-WW:78
Four Ducks on a Pond.
 W. Allingham. Hi-WP I:30
Four Little Foxes. L. Sarett.
 Ar-TP3:64, Bo-HF:71, Co-BBW:35,
 Co-PS:54, Du-RG:98, Fe-FP:173,
 Ha-YA:40, La-PV:150, La-RM:53,
 Mc-WK:64, Sh-RP:203, Un-GT:31
Fragments of Spring. A. Pratt.
 Al-WW:108
The Gardener. L. Perkins. Bo-FP:240

SPRING (SEASON) — cont'd.
   Gay Comes the Singer. Sm-MK:142
   The Georgics. Virgil. Ma-FW:11
   Getting Up Early on a Spring
     Morning. Po Chu-i. Ma-FW:9
   Glad Earth. E. Forbes. Ha-YA:24
   Grave Visiting. S.Murano. Sh-AM:88
   A Great Time. W. Davies.
     Hi-WP I:1, Un-MB:178
   Green Jade Plum Trees in Spring.
     Ou Yang Hsiu. Rx-OH:53
   Green Song. P. Booth. Co-BN:27
   The Green Spring. Shan Mei.
     Hs-TC:436
   The Gusts of Winter Are Gone.
     Meleager. Pa-SG:80
   Happy. V. Windley. Ho-CT:12
   Harbingers. Basho. Sh-RP:64
   Hello! L. Garnett. Br-SS:140
   Here Is Spring Again. L. Letay.
     Mc-AC:137
   Here We Come a-Piping. Bl-OB:102,
     Br-SS:148, Ch-B:76, De-CH:11
   Hokku Poems. R. Wright. Bo-AN:105
   The Hollow Land. W.Morris. Gr-CT:48
   Home-Thoughts from Abroad.
     R. Browning. Bo-FP:230,
     Co-BN:19, Er-FA:266, Fe-FP:460,
     Fe-PL:376, Ga-FB:229, Ke-TF:366,
     Ma-YA:202, Mc-PR:106, Ox-BN:534,
     Pa-HT:117
   How Do I Know It Is Spring?
     Wo-HS:(40)
   How Do You Know It's Spring?
     M. Brown. Br-SG:102
   How Many Heavens. E. Sitwell.
     Gr-CC:134, Tr-MR:41
   I Feel a Bit Happier.
     C. Foster. Le-M:31
   I Heard It in the Valley.
     A. Wynne. Th-AS:77
   I Saw. P. Malone. Ho-CT:4
   I Saw Green Banks of Daffodils.
     E. Tennant. Ar-TP3:201
   Idleness. Lu Yu. Rx-OH:109
   If I Should Ever by Chance Grow
     Rich. E. Thomas. Bl-OB:32,
     Bo-GJ:20, De-CH:518, Ox-BC:329,
     Pa-RE:73, Sm-LG:112, Un-MB:215
   if up's the word and a world grows
     greener. E. Cummings. Pe-OA:150
   In a Spring Still Not Written Of.
     R. Wallace. Co-BN:20
   In Early Spring. R. Aldridge.
     Ls-NY:295
   In Just. E. Cummings. Ad-CI:72,
     Bo-FP:224, Co-HP:55, Du-RG:96,
     Fe-FP:73, Ga-FB:283, Ir-BB:25,
     Re-TW:53, Sh-RP:30, Un-GT:272,
     Un-MA:472

   In Memoriam. A. Tennyson.
     Al-VBP:861
   In My House. Sodo. Be-MC:15
   In Spring. E. Mörike. Pa-SG:88
   In Spring in Warm Weather.
     D. Aldis. Br-BC:9
   In the Eternal. Ki no Tomonori.
     Ba-ST:22
   In the Spring. Ibycus.
     Pa-SG:86
   In the Spring. Meleager.
     Pa-SG:67
   In the Spring. A. Tennyson.
     Co-BN:35
   In the Spring. De-PP:57
   In the Spring Rain. Chiyo-Ni.
     Do-TS:10
   In the Spring when the Sun Never
     Sets. L. Evaloardjuak.
     Le-IB:108
   In the Woods Alone. Pa-SG:27
   The Invitation. P. Shelley.
     De-CH:146, Pa-GTB:269
   It Was a Lover and His Lass.
     W. Shakespeare. Al-VBP:188,
     Bo-FP:214, De-CH:188, Ma-YA:67,
     No-CL:127, Pa-GTB:6, Rv-CB:198,
     Un-MW:4
   Jonathan Bing Dances for Spring.
     B. Brown. Br-SS:131
   Joy. O. Wilde. Bo-FP:221
   Juliana. Co-BL:41
   Just a Mile Beyond. A. Fisher.
     Sh-RP:196
   The King's Young Dochter.
     De-CH:602
   Kite Days. M. Sawyer.
     Br-SS:129, Mc-AW:37
   The Lamentation of Beulah over
     Ololon. W. Blake.
     Ho-WR:60, Ox-BN:41
   Late Snow. Issa. Sh-RP:65
   Lenten Is Come. Al-VBP:4
   Lighthearted William. W. Williams.
     Ha-LO:36, Ha-PO:76,
     Kh-VA:77, Mo-BG:45
   Little Children. T. Tsosie.
     Ba-HI:142
   The Little Grass.
     Chu Tzu-ch'ing. Hs-TC:12
   Little Seeds We Sow in Spring.
     E. Minarik. Br-SG:99
   A Little Song of Spring.
     M. Austin. Ha-YA:26
   Look, Spring Is Coming. Gr-BB:11
   Love in May. J. Passerat.
     Pa-SG:32
   Magdalen Walks. O. Wilde. Un-MB:67
   The Magic Flower. D. Marcus.
     Le-M:38

The Magic Piper. E. Marsh.
  Br-SS:131
March. H. Crane. Co-BN:17
March. A. Housman. Sm-LG:54
March. C. Thaxter. Un-GT:270
March Winds. Au-SP:317, Br-SG:22,
  De-PO:26, Li-LB:160, Mo-MGT:148,
  Mo-NR:118, Un-GT:23, Wr-RM:120
Majorie's Almanac. T. Aldrich.
  Br-SG:101, Fe-FP:62, Hu-MP:298
May 10th. M. Kumin. Co-BN:25,
  La-RM:134
The Message of the March Wind.
  W. Morris. Ho-WR:27,
  Ox-BN:789
Miracle. L. Bailey. Ha-YA:49
The Miracle of Spring. Bahar.
  Pa-SG:82
Mist. Li Ch'ing Chao.
  Rx-OH:99
A Moonlight Night. Liu Fang-P'ing.
  Le-MW:27
Morning in Spring. L. Ginsburg.
  Gr-EC:65
My Heart Has Known Its Winter.
  A. Bontemps. Be-MA:45
Nakatsukasa. Shüi Shü. Pa-SG:80
Nature Songs, I. Tr-US II:185
New Hampshire. T. Eliot.
  Ha-LO:81, Ha-PO:94, Pa-GTB:477,
  Re-TW:98, Sm-LG:142
New Leaves. J. Jiménez. Le-SW:17
New York in the Spring.
  D. Budbill. Ad-CI:3
Night of Spring. T. Westwood.
  Rv-CB:832
The Noonday April Sun. G. Love.
  Hu-NN:69
Now a Spring Rain Falls. Chiyo.
  Be-MC:40
now i lay (with everywhere around).
  e. cummings. Mc-EA:40
Now It Is Spring. Yakamochi.
  Ba-ST:16
Now the Full-Throated Daffodils.
  C. Day Lewis. Al-VBP:1224,
  Ga-S:183
Now the Lusty Spring.
  J. Fletcher. Al-VBP:278
Ode on the Spring. T. Gray.
  Pa-GTB:139
Old Dan'l. L. Strong.
  Cl-FC:36, Co-EL:125, Co-PS:64,
  Co-PU:122, Sm-MK:104, Un-MB:393
On a Mountain Top. K. Nakamura.
  Sh-AM:147
On the Road to Nara. Basho.
  Ar-TP3:203, Pa-SG:91
On the Siu Cheng Road.
  Su Tung P'o. Rx-OH:80

Only the Wind Says Spring.
  H. Miller. Un-GT:260
The Onset. R. Frost.
  Sh-AP:151, Un-MA:168
Out of One Wintry. Ransetsu.
  Be-CS:38
Out of the Sky. Soin. Be-CS:49
A Page's Road Song. W. Percy.
  Ha-YA:32, Ke-TF:201
Perfection. G. Ost'or. Mo-MI:87
Phoenix Hairpins. Lu Yu.
  Rx-OH:104
Pippa's Song. R. Browning.
  Bo-FP:213, Bo-GJ:96, Ch-B:98,
  Cl-DT:45, Er-FA:20, Fe-FP:72,
  Ha-YA:28, Hu-MP:291, Ke-TF:434,
  La-PV:81, Li-LC:72, Ma-YA:200,
  Mc-PR:95, Mo-GR:113, Rv-CB:816,
  Se-PR:68, Sp-OG:215, Tu-WW:60,
  Un-GT:273
Place Midnight in the Care of My
  Hands. Y. Vinokurov. Ca-MR:88
poem. J. Gill. Sc-TN:69
Poem for the Subterranean Poor.
  D. di Prima. Kh-VA:51
A Prayer in Spring. R. Frost.
  Ha-YA:29, Tr-MR:48
Prothalamion. R. Hillyer.
  Un-MA:482
Rain Music. J. Cotter.
  Bo-FP:223
Rainy Day Song. V. Storey.
  Ha-YA:28
The Rebirth of Spring.
  Hsü Chih-mo. Hs-TC:92
The Return of Spring.
  C. d'Orleans. Gr-CC:32
Rich Morning. R. Farren.
  Co-PI:39
Robin's Song. E. King.
  Ar-TP3:201
Rondeau. C. d'Orleans. Pa-SG:70

The Saddest Noise, the Sweetest
  Noise. E. Dickinson.
  Cl-FC:39
St. Gregory's Day. Bo-FP:217
St. Ursanne. M. Roberts.
  Wi-LT:635
St. Valentine's Day. W. Blunt.
  Al-VBP:1054
Sap Bucket Song. L. Stoddard.
  Ls-NY:291
Scarcely Spring. L. Untermeyer.
  Un-GT:270
Screw Spring. W. Hoffman.
  Sc-TN:102
Seeds. W. de la Mare. Br-SG:13
The Seeds of Love. De-TT:19,
  Gr-GB:137, Ho-WR:59, Rv-CB:428,
  Sm-LG:349

SPRING (SEASON) — <u>cont'd.</u>
  Slow Spring. S. Tremayne.
    Sm-MK:141
  Smells. K. Worth. Sh-RP:209
  The Snow Is Thawing. Gr-BB:21
  Some Flowers o' the Spring.
    W. Shakespeare. Gr-CT:249
  Someone I Know. Mo-MI:36
  Somewhere in Tuscany.
    D. Holbrook. Ls-NY:13
  Song. Sung Tzü-hou. Pa-SG:84
  Song in Spring. L. Ginsberg.
    Ha-YA:31
  Song of Liang Chou.
    Ou Yang Hsiu. Rx-OH:55
  The Song of Songs. Bible. O.T.
    Song of Solomon. Pa-SG:26
  Song of the Pasque Flower.
    Tr-US II:235
  Song on May Morning. J. Milton.
    Cl-FC:38, Co-BN:23, De-CH:10,
    Ha-YA:55, Mc-PR:86, Se-PR:111
  The Songs of Spring.
    Feng Hsüeh-feng. Hs-TC:368
  Sonnets. XCVIII.
    W. Shakespeare. Al-VBP:206,
    Gr-CT:46
  Sonnets LXX. E. Spenser.
    Al-VBP:98, Gr-CT:52
  The Spirit of Spring.
    Liu Ta-pai. Hs-TC:7
  The Spring. W. Barnes. Co-BN:36
  Spring. H. Behn. Ar-TP3:201,
    La-PP:22
  Spring. W. Blake. Ar-TP3:203,
    Ch-B:99, Fe-FP:71, Ha-YA:25,
    Li-LC:70, Sm-LG:53, Un-GB:7,
    Un-GT:271
  The Spring. T. Carew.
    Cl-FC:37, Co-PS:58, Gr-CC:30,
    Ha-PO:81, Ho-WR:34
  Spring. Chu Shu Chen. Rx-OH:130
  Spring. M. Chute.
    Br-SG:17, Mc-AW:39
  The Spring. A. Cowley.
    No-CL:274
  Spring. A. De Vere.
    Ox-BN:586
  Spring. G. Hopkins.
    Co-BN:25, Ga-FB:8, Ox-BN:864,
    Un-MB:42, Wi-LT:41
  Spring. H. Howard. Ma-FW:6,
    Ma-YA:54, Rd-OA:188
  Spring. K. Kuskin. La-PV:2
  Spring. P. Larkin. Un-MB:527
  Spring. J. Lowell. Ga-FB:287
  Spring. V. Mayakovsky. Ad-CI:90
  Spring. E. Millay. Gr-BT:132,
    Mo-BG:113, Un-MA:444
  Spring. W. Miller. Co-PS:60

  Spring. T. Nashe. Al-VBP:210,
    Bl-OB:102, Bo-FP:235, Co-BN:21,
    De-CH:14, De-TT:55, Ho-WR:35,
    Ma-FW:6, Ma-YA:73, Pa-GTB:1,
    Pa-RE:82, Rv-CB:275, Tu-WW:57
  Spring. C. Rossetti. Ox-BN:704
  Spring. Shao Hsün-mei. Hs-TC:125
  Spring. J. Subits. La-GI:10
  Spring. A. Tennyson. Al-VBP:862,
    De-TT:143, Ox-BN:507
  Spring. J. Thomson. Al-VBP:549
  Spring. C. Wilson. Ba-HI:52
  Spring Air. G. Derwood.
    Er-FA:113
  Spring and All. W. Williams.
    Ha-PO:221, Un-MA:256, Wi-LT:198
  The Spring and the Fall.
    E. Millay. Co-BL:141
  Spring Cricket. F. Rodman.
    Br-SS:141, Fe-FP:128
  Spring Day on West Lake.
    Ou Yang Hsiu. Rx-OH:60
  Spring Days. Ya Hsüan.
    Pa-MV:153
  Spring Departing. Basho.
    Le-MW:74
  Spring Dew. T. Palmanteer.
    Al-WW:43
  Spring Ecstasy. L. Reese.
    Un-MA:111
  Spring, etc. R. Whittemore.
    Mc-WK:24
  Spring Goeth All in White.
    R. Bridges. Co-BN:28,
    Gr-CT:47
  Spring Grass. C. Sandburg.
    Bo-HF:53, Fe-FP:224
  Spring Has Come. A. Machado.
    Le-SW:15
  Spring in Hiding. F. Frost.
    Ha-YA:23
  Spring in My Hut. Sodo.
    Sh-RP:67
  Spring in New Hampshire. C. McKay.
    Bo-HF:52, Hu-PN:97, Ra-BP:59
  Spring Is a Hooping-Free Time.
    M. Robbins. Mo-SD:185
  Spring Is in the Making.
    N. Duffy. Ha-YA:172
  spring is like a perhaps hand.
    e. cummings. Ca-VT:175,
    Ma-FW:7
  A Spring Lilt. Hu-MP:303
  Spring Mood. V. Lapin. Mo-MI:16
  Spring Morning. Ch'en Yu Yi.
    Rx-LT:98
  Spring Morning. D. Lawrence.
    Co-BL:52, Un-MB:297
  Spring Night. Su Tung P'o.
    Ho-P:250, Rx-OH:89

Spring Oak.   G. Kinnell.
Co-BN:40, Co-EL:114, Co-PU:45
Spring Quiet.   C. Rossetti.
Co-BN:16, De-CH:235, Gr-TG:26,
Pa-GTB:373, Re-BS:21
Spring Rain.   H. Behn.
Ar-TP3:169, Pe-FB:85
Spring Rain.   Chiyo-Ni.
Ba-ST:21, Le-MW:93, Ma-FW:34
Spring Rain.   Tu Fu.
Pa-SG:83, Rx-LT:62
Spring Reminiscence.   C. Cullen.
Bo-HF:47
Spring Ring-Jingle.   M. Lewis.
Ir-BB:121
Spring Song.   W. Blake.
Br-SG:3
Spring Song.   H. Conkling.
Co-PS:57, Hu-MP:246
Spring Song.   W. Griffith.
Hu-MP:291
Spring Song.   M. Justus.
Mc-AW:35
Spring Song.   R. McKuen.
Ad-CI:91
Spring Song.   Bi-IT:126,
Br-MW:98, Da-SC:148,
Jo-TS:13, Tr-US II:228
Spring Song.   Bo-FP:229, 236
A Spring Song.   Fe-PL:371
Spring Stops Me Suddenly.
V. Iremonger.   Co-PI:73
Spring Sun.   Chu Hsi.   Rx-OH:118
Spring Thunder.   M. Van Doren.
Bo-HF:46, Ha-WR:9, Ho-TH:43
Spring Voices.   L. MacNeice.
Hi-WP II:45
Spring Walk to the Pavilion of
Good Crops and Peace.
Ou Yang Hsiu.   Rx-OH:52
The Spring Waters, 11, 43.
Ping Hsin.   Hs-TC:22, 23
The Spring Will Come. H. Lowry.
Co-BN:17, Co-PU:9
Spring Wind.   K. Agrawal.
Al-PI:115
Spring Wind.   N. Turner.
Br-SS:133
Spring's Arrival.   Fe-FP:471
Sun and Rain and Dew from
Heaven.   A. Gordon.   Fe-PL:313
Sunday: Outskirts of Knoxville,
Tennessee.   J. Agee.
Mo-BG:178
Surprise.   B. Martin.   Mc-AW:34
The Sweet o' the Year.
G. Meredith.   Co-BN:23
Tardy Spring.   G. Meredith.
Cl-FC:35
Tell of Spring.   Br-FW:6

Thaw.   E. Thomas.   Co-EL:116,
Ho-LP:37, Ma-FW:10, Pa-GTB:443,
Re-BS:18, Un-MB:217
This Fevers Me.   R. Eberhart.
Tr-MR:38
Time for Rabbits.   A. Fisher.
La-PH:50
The Time of the Singing Birds.
Bible.   O.T.   Song of Solomon.
Gr-TG:29
Tired Equinox.   R. Roseliep.
St-H:183
'Tis Merry in Greenwood.
W. Scott.   Fe-FP:76, Hu-MP:302
To a Primrose.   J. Clare.
Ma-FW:10
To Spring.   W. Blake.   Co-BN:18,
Fe-PL:373, Ho-WR:33, Rv-CB:563
A Tree Frog Trilling.   Rogetsu.
Be-CS:7
Twist-Rime on Spring.
A. Guiterman.   Co-PS:61,
Gr-EC:44
Two Poems.   R. Abrams.   Hu-NN:111
Two Sewing.   H. Hall.   Th-AS:112
Two Songs of Spring Wandering.
Wang Wei.   Le-MW:72
Two Springs.   Li Ch'ing Chao.
Rx-OH:94
Under a Spring Mist.   Teitoku.
Be-MC:56
Under the Misty Sky.   Shinsai.
Le-MW:91
The Unicorn.   W. Hoffman. Sc-TN:105
upon leaving the parole board
hearing.   Conyus.   Ad-PB:401
Vernal Equinox.   R. Stone.
Un-MA:655
Vernal Sentiment. T. Roethke.
Co-EL:153, Co-PU:9, Mc-WS:125
Violet Spring.   Chi Hsüan.
Pa-MV:48
Voices Gay.   A. Fair.   Ho-CT:8
Waiting for the Bus.
H. Ishida.   Sh-AM:173
The Waking Year.
E. Dickinson.   Co-BN:26
A Walk in the Country.
Su Tung P'o.   Rx-OH:76
Water-Front Streets.
L. Hughes.   La-OC:38
West of Childhood.   I. Gardner.
St-H:65
The West Wind.   P. Shelley.
Bo-FP:167, Ch-B:72
What Bird So Sings.   J. Lyly.
Al-VBP:121, Bl-OB:67,
De-CH:14, Re-TW:54
When Daisies Pied. W. Shakespeare.
Al-VBP:181, Re-TW:56, Rv-CB:189

SPRING (SEASON) — cont'd.
  When Faces Called Flowers.
    E. Cummings. Co-BN:22
  When Green Buds Hang in the
    Elms like Dust.
    A. Housman. Go-BP:28
  When I Went Out. Akahito.
    Ba-ST:19, Le-MW:71
  When Spring Came. La-RM:124
  When Spring Comes. M. Patrick.
    Le-M:29
  When the. V. Fraser. Ho-CT:5
  When the Green Lies over the
    Earth. A. Grimke. Hu-PN:56
  The White Fury of the Spring.
    L. Reese. Gr-SS:36
  White Primit Falls. Virgil.
    Gr-CT:50
  Who Calls. F. Sayers.
    Br-SS:130, Li-LC:89
  Whose Are This Pond and House?
    Chang Liang-Ch'en. Le-MW:68
  Why Chidest Thou the Tardy
    Spring. R. Emerson. Re-BS:19
  Wild Geese. Shēn Yo. Pa-SG:87
  The Winter Is Past. Bible. O.T.
    Song of Solomon. Ga-S:185
  Wisdom. S. Teasdale. Un-MA:266
  Wise Johnny. E. Fallis.
    Ar-TP3:200, Br-SG:7, Br-SS:129
  Written in March. W. Wordsworth.
    Ar-TP3:202, Au-SP:317, Bo-FP:217,
    Bo-GJ:95, Co-BN:18, De-TT:37,
    Fe-FP:69, Ha-YA:36, Hu-MP:290,
    Mc-PR:36, Mc-WK:23, Na-EO:32,
    Re-TW:82, Se-PR:61, Tu-WW:66,
    Un-GT:270
  Young Lambs. J. Clare.
    Mc-PR:55, Un-GT:35
SPRINGBOKS
  Prayer to the Moon. Le-OE:63
SPRINGFIELD, ILL.
  Abraham Lincoln Walks at Midnight.
    V. Lindsay. Ba-PO:132,
    Bo-HF:148, Br-AF:82, Ca-VT:28,
    Er-FA:284, Fe-FP:453, Ga-FB:263,
    Hi-TL:184, Hu-MP:398, Ke-PP:21,
    Mc-PR:126, Pe-OA:64, Se-PR:45,
    Sh-RP:311, Tr-MR:183, Un-MA:229,
    Vi-PP:182
  On the Building of Springfield.
    V. Lindsay. Tr-MR:247
  The Springfield of the Far Future.
    V. Lindsay. Tr-MR:200
SPRINGFIELD, MASS.
  The Arsenal at Springfield.
    H. Longfellow. Ba-PO:96,
    Cr-WS:24
SPRINGS (WATER): see also WELLS
  Capturing a Spring. R. Joseph.
    Ls-NY:251

The Enchanted Spring. G. Darley.
  Co-BN:32
An Offering of Joy. S. Eremina.
  Mo-MI:61
On Visiting a Clear Spring.
  Li Po. Le-MW:56
The Pasture. R. Frost.
  Al-VBP:1125, Ar-TP3:75, Au-SP:45,
  Bo-GJ:44, Co-BBW:162, Fe-FP:230,
  La-PP:23, La-PV:166, Li-LC:75,
  Mc-PR:121, Pa-RE:115, Pe-FB:2,
  Su-FVI:57, Th-AS:75, Un-MA:168
The Spring. R. Fyleman. Fe-FP:131
SPRINKLERS
  Sprinkling. D. Pierce.
    Ar-TP3:206
SPRITES: see ELVES; FAIRIES;
    GOBLINS
SPRUCE TREES
  Christmas Tree. A. Fisher.
    La-PH:38, La-PV:173
SPURGES
  The Woodspurge. D. Rossetti.
    Ox-BN:682, Pa-GTB:372, Rv-CB:886
SPYGLASSES: see TELESCOPES
SQUALOR
  The Air Is Dirty. G. Thompson.
    Jo-SA:10, Jo-VC:73
  Kitchenette Building. G. Brooks.
    Hu-PN:334, Ra-BP:166
SQUARE DANCING
  At a Cowboy Dance. J. Adams.
    Sh-RP:22
  A Cowboy Dance. N. Bachman.
    Fi-BG:167
  Cowboy Dance Call. Fi-BG:170
  Skip to My Lou. Su-FVI:56
  See also Em-AF:51-57
SQUASH (GAME)
  After a Game of Squash.
    S. Albert. Fl-HH:35
  Civilities. T. Whitbread.
    Mo-SD:164
SQUIRRELS: see also HUMOR —
    SQUIRRELS
  Autumn. W. Smith. Sh-RP:219
  Boy with a Toy. Re-RR:58
  Chucklehead. P. Robbins.
    Ar-TP3:61
  The Curliest Thing. St-FS:58
  Don't Tell Me. D. Aldis.
    Ma-FO:(20)
  Fable. R. Emerson. Bo-FP:71,
    Bo-GJ:26, Bo-HF:69, Ch-B:27,
    Er-FA:496, Fe-FP:530, Ga-FB:317
    Hu-MP:210, Pa-OM:333, Rd-OA:91,
    Sh-AP:27, Sp-OG:303, Un-GT:57
  Five Eager Little Squirrels.
    On-TW:23
  Five Little Squirrels.
    Ir-BB:81

Fred. D. McCord. Ar-TP3:61
The Gray Squirrel. H. Wolfe.
   Bo-GJ:65, Co-BBW:39, Un-MB:303
Ground-Squirrel Song. Da-SC:97,
   Le-OE:53, Tr-US II:252
Joe. D. McCord. Ar-TP3:60
A Little Squirrel. Ar-TP3:60
The Migration of the Grey
   Squirrels. W. Howitt.
   Ox-BC:164
On a Squirrel Crossing the Road
   in Autumn. R. Eberhart.
   En-PC:60, Ho-TH:81,
   Pe-OA:196, Wi-LT:439
Peep, Squirrel, Peep.
   Bu-DY:35
Questions for a Flying Squirrel
   to Answer. R. Field.
   Sh-RP:336
Remembering the Winter.
   R. Bennett. Br-SS:74
Run, Squirrel, Run.
   Bu-DY:21
The Squirrel. W. Cowper.
   Un-GT:57
The Squirrel. I. Serraillier.
   Co-BBW:30
Squirrel. J. Tippett.
   Sh-RP:335
The Squirrel. Ar-TP3:60,
   Au-SP:68, Fe-FP:167, Ir-BB:77,
   La-PV:141, Ma-FO:(19),
   Su-FVI:58
The Squirrel. De-TT:19, Mo-MGT:97
The Squirrel and the Wind.
   Bo-FP:153
Squirrel in Sunshine. W. Cowper.
   Co-BBW:35, Co-PU:84
Squirrel in the Rain. F. Frost.
   Sh-RP:334
Squirrel with Jays. R. Souster.
   Co-BBW:23
Squirrels' Thanksgiving.
   K. Dee. Ja-HH:43
The Story of the Baby Squirrel.
   D. Aldis. Ar-TP3:60
Ten Little Squirrels. St-FS:7
To a Squirrel at Kyle-Na-No.
   W. Yeats. Ad-PE:28, Be-EB:38,
   Bl-OB:131, Co-BBW:43, Co-PU:85,
   Fe-FP:167, La-PV:140, Li-LC:23,
   Re-TW:34
To a Winter Squirrel. G. Brooks.
   Bo-HF:76
STAFFA, SCOT.
   Staffa. J. Keats. Gr-SS:163
STAGECOACHES
   Black Bart. Fi-BG:139
   Californy Stage. Fi-BG:132
   On the Road to Cook's Peak.
      Fi-BG:135

STAIRWAYS: see also HUMOR -
      STAIRWAYS
   All Around the Town. P. McGinley.
      Ar-TP3:93, Fr-MP:16,
      Lo-LL:90, Mc-AW:22
   Halfway Down. A. Milne.
      Fe-FP:10, Li-LC:37
   i have friends. C. Thornton.
      La-IH:70
   On the Staircase. E. Farjeon.
      Br-SS:35
   Plans. H. Brooks. Hu-NN:109,
      Hu-PN:274
   The Stair. G. Claytor.
      De-FS:50
   Wooden Hill. Mo-MGT:169
STALIN, JOSEPH
   Stalin. O. Mandelstam.
      Ca-MR:151
STALLIONS: see HORSES
STAMMERING: see STUTTERING
STAMPEDES: see CATTLE
STANLEY, SIR HENRY MORTON
   Stanley Meets Mutesa.
      J. Rubadiri. Bo-HF:150
STARFISH
   Five. C. Tringress.
      St-FS:3
   The Starfish. R. Coffin.
      Li-TU:43, Pl-IO:83
   Starfish. W. Welles.
      Br-SS:31, Fe-FP:141
   A Turkey's Tail Spread Out.
      J. Amoroso. La-GI:37
STARLINGS
   And Other Poems. R. Morgan.
      Ma-FW:95
   Fluttering Helplessly.
      T. Boughton. Le-M:187
   The Great Scarf of Birds.
      J. Updike. Mo-BG:134
   Let Us Go, Then, Exploring.
      V. Woolf. Co-BN:90
   The Manoeuvre. W. Williams.
      Ha-LO:28
   The Park Is Green and Quiet.
      C. Reznikoff. La-OC:117
   A Smoke of Birds. M. Cowley.
      Mo-TS:18
   Spring Song. J. Simpson.
      Sm-MK:150
   The Starling. J. Heath-Stubbs.
      Ma-FW:91, To-MP:115
   Starlings. M. Webb. Tu-WW:100
   Winter Field. A. Coppard.
      Re-BS:16
   Winter in Dunover Field.
      T. Hardy. Un-MB:31
STARR, BELLE
   Belle Starr. Fi-BG:225
   Queen of the Desperados. Fi-BG:227,229

STARS: see also HUMOR - STARS;
    JESUS CHRIST - NATIVITY;
    METEORS; and names of stars,
    as NORTH STAR
  An Astrologer's Song. R. Kipling.
    Un-MB:135
  At Peace.   Rumi.   Pa-SG:163
  At the Bottom of the Well.
    L. Untermeyer.   Bo-GJ:218
  August Night. E. Roberts.Ha-YA:89
  Autumn. T. Hulme. Al-VBP:1152,
    Ha-LO:102, Ja-PA:7, Sm-MK:13
  Baby Toes. C. Sandburg.
    Fe-FP:267, Li-LC:42
  Blow the Stars Home.
    E. Farjeon.   La-PV:45
  The Book of How. M. Moore.Un-MA:577
  Bright Star. J. Keats.
    Al-VBP:794, De-CH:745,
    Ga-FB:54, Go-BP:108, Ke-TF:122,
    Ox-BN:382, Pa-GTB:197, Un-MW:204
  Broadway Twilight. T. Prideaux.
    La-OC:19
  Choose Something like a Star.
    R. Frost. En-PC:1, Un-MA:195
  The Coming Star. J. Jiménez.
    Li-TU:196
  Counting. F. Johnson.Bo-AN:27
  Daisies. F. Sherman. Ch-B:88
  Daisies. A. Young. Bo-GJ:241
  Darkness. Murari. Al-PI:38
  Day Song. E. Hammond. Mc-AW:13
  Earth and Sky. E. Farjeon.
    Br-SG:108, Co-PS:173
  Escape at Bedtime. R. Stevenson.
    Ar-TP3:178, Bo-FP:34,
    Pe-FB:64, Rd-SS:31, Un-GT:13
  The Evening Star. J. Clare.
    Gr-CT:399, Pa-GTB:320
  Evening Star. E. Poe. Sh-AP:45
  February Twilight. S. Teasdale.
    Au-SP:355, Ha-YA:170, La-PP:28,
    La-PV:52, Pe-FB:82, Th-AS:27
  Fireflies in the Garden.
    R. Frost. Rd-OA:62, We-PZ:34
  The Flowering Forest.
    E. Sitwell. Gr-SS:51
  For Life I Had Never Cared
    Greatly. T. Hardy. Wi-LT:22
  For the Conjunction of Two
    Planets. A. Rich. Pl-IO:30
  Fragment from the Child-Naming
    Rites. Br-MW:77
  From a Legend. Br-MW:75
  The Full Heart. R. Nichols.
    Co-BN:116, Co-PU:58
  A Full Moon Comes Up. Shiki.
    Be-MC:30
  The Great Bear. J. Hollander.
    Br-TC:196, Wi-LT:733

  El Hombre. W. Williams. Ho-LP:56
  I Gathered Stars. R. Kresensky.
    Ke-TF:421
  I Have a Garden. Re-RR:31
  I Have a Garment. A. Ibn Ezra.
    Me-PH:65
  I Have a Little Sister. Ar-TP3:99,
    De-CH:675, De-TT:32, Li-LB:169,
    Mo-MGT:156, Re-RR:46, Rv-ON:58
  I Know a Star. P. Nardella.
    La-GI:47
  I See a Star. A. Lopez.
    Al-WW:4
  I Stood upon a Star.
    S. Teasdale.   Sh-RP:177
  In the Silent Night.
    J. Yokomizo. Ba-HI:71
  In Time like Glass. W. Turner.
    Un-MB:347
  The Jolly Company. R. Brooke.
    Sp-OG:346
  Last Song. J. Guthrie.
    Ar-TP3:181, La-PV:62
  Light the Lamps Up, Lamplighter.
    E. Farjeon. Br-SS:28, De-CH:439
  Little Garaine. G. Parker.
    Fe-FP:302
  The Little Star. Li-SR:93
  Looking at Stars. P. Hesketh.
    Cl-DT:36
  The Lost Telescope. Chi Hsüan.
    Pa-MV:50
  Lucifer in Starlight.
    G. Meredith. Al-VBP:985,
    De-CH:314, Ha-PO:48,
    Ox-BN:693, Rv-CB:880
  Moon Song. H. Conkling.
    Th-AS:20
  Moon-Uncle. Ca-MU:31, 32
  The Morning Star. E. Brontë.
    Gr-CT:389
  Morning Star. T. Ferril.
    Ca-VT:200
  The Morning Star. Ho-SD:36
  The Morning Star in the North.
    Tr-US II:286
  Mythological Sonnets, VIII.
    R. Fuller. Pa-GTB:527
  Night. S. Teasdale. Ar-TP3:211,
    Au-SP:340, Fe-FP:264,
    Pe-FB:63, Th-AS:31
  Night on the Prairies. W. Whitman.
    La-RM:68, Tr-MR:288
  Night Train. Hsü Chih-mo. Hs-TC:93
  Nova. R. Jeffers. Pe-OA:90
  O Stelliferi Conditor Orbis.
    Boethius. Go-BP:240
  Offshore. P. Booth. Mo-SD:137
  On Looking Up by Chance at the
    Constellations. R. Frost.Li-TU:268

On the Beach at Night.
  W. Whitman.   Gr-CT:197, Un-MA:65
On the Sea of Heaven.   Hitomaro.
  Ba-ST:32
The Path of the Stars.   T. Jones.
  Tr-MR:139
The Peaceful Shepherd.   R. Frost.
  Tr-MR:191, Un-MA:181
The Pleiades.   E. Coatsworth.
  Pl-IO:31
Polar Star.   Da-SC:11, Le-OE:102,
  Tr-US II:248
Preludes for Memnon.   C. Aiken.
  Co-BL:49, Un-MA:434
The Shape Called Star.
  L. Nicholl.   Ho-LP:98
Silver Sheep.   A. Payne.
  Br-SS:23
Skating.   W. Wordsworth.
  De-CH:219, Mo-SD:148
So in the Empty Sky the Stars
  Appear.   J. Masefield.
  Go-BP:109
Song Cycle of the Moon-Bone.
  Tr-US I:246
Special Starlight.   C. Sandburg.
  Tr-MR:101
The Spring Waters, 60, 65.
  Ping Hsin.   Hs-TC:23
The Star.   E. Roberts.   Rd-SS:32
The Star.   J. Taylor.
  Ar-TP3:178, Au-SP:340, Bo-FP:46,
  Cl-DT:37, Er-FA:491, Fe-FP:525,
  Gr-EC:90, Gr-TG:50, Hu-MP:121,
  Li-SR:93, Mo-CC:(37),
  Mo-MGT:24, Ox-BC:122, Sm-MK:179
A Star.   Ar-TP3:99, Mo-MGT:157,
  Wr-RM:94
Star Guides.   W. Stafford.
  Du-SH:186
Star Light, Star Bright.
  Ar-TP3:178, Au-SP:20, Bo-FP:46,
  Gr-EC:88, Ir-BB:227, Mo-MGT:172,
  Mo-TB:6, Tu-WW:16
Star of the East.   E. Field.
  Se-PR:224
Star of the Evening.   J. Sayles.
  Li-SR:79
Star of the Western Skies.
  Fi-BG:193
Star Talk.   R. Graves.   Bo-GJ:242,
  Co-BN:115, Un-MB:385
The Star Watcher.   P. Davison.
  Br-TC:86
The Starlight Night.   G. Hopkins.
  Al-VBP:1061, Cl-DT:38, Pa-GTB:389,
  Re-TW:84, Un-MB:42, Wi-LT:40
The Starlighter.   A. Guiterman.
  Be-SS:31, Th-AS:26
Stars.   R. Bacmeister.   Fr-MP:23

Stars.   F. Edsall.   Th-AS:88
The Stars.   D. ap Gwilym.
  Go-BP:107
Stars.   L. Hughes.   La-OC:137
Stars.   C. Sandburg.   Li-TU:204
The Stars.   C. Smart.   Gr-CT:401
Stars.   S. Teasdale.   Ar-TP3:179,
  Fe-FP:266, Th-AS:28, Tr-MR:45
The Stars.   Tsang K'o-chia.
  Hs-TC:288
Stars at Night.   I. Takenaka.
  Sh-AN:101
The Stars Were Packed So Close
  That Night.   G. Hopkins.
  Li-TU:204
Stars Wheel in Purple.   H.D.
  Gr-CC:29, Un-MA:337
Summer Stars.   C. Sandburg.
  Ad-PE:16, Ha-LO:33, Ha-YA:69,
  La-RM:69, Sh-RP:218
Sunday at Hampstead. J. Thomson.
  Al-VBP:1010, Sm-MK:12, Sp-OG:345
Thought's End.   L. Adams.
  Un-MA:543
Thousands of Shining Knights.
  Re-RR:100
The Three Kings. H. Longfellow.
  Pa-OM:357, Sp-OG:314, Un-GT:290
To Night.   J. White.   Al-VBP:701,
  Co-RG:154, Ke-TF:58, Rv-CB:674
To the Evening Star.   W. Blake.
  Co-BN:114, De-CH:430, Fe-PL:403,
  Ga-FB:24, Gr-CT:399, Gr-SS:131,
  Ho-WR:144
To the Evening Star. T. Campbell.
  Ox-BN:196, Pa-GTB:187, 273
Tousle-Haired Star.
  M. Tsvetayeva.   Ca-MR:138
Tragedy.   AE.   Un-MB:143
The Twelfth Moon Came.   Wo-HS:(16)
Twilit Revelation.   L. Adams.
  Un-MA:545
Twinkle, Twinkle, Little Star.
  P. Dehn.   Li-SR:93
Twinkling Stars.   Ca-MU:10
The Two Stars.   W. Davies.
  Un-MB:176
The Unknown God.   AE.   Un-MB:144
Until We Built a Cabin.
  A. Fisher.   Ar-TP3:179
Waiting Both.   T. Hardy.
  Mc-WK:105, Un-MB:35
When I Heard the Learn'd
  Astronomer.   W. Whitman.
  Ho-LP:56, Rv-CB:860,
  Sm-LG:53, Un-MA:42
When the Light of Day Fades.
  N. Zabolotzky.   Ca-MR:100
With Flowers.   E. Dickinson.
  Sm-MK:210

STARS — cont'd.
  The World's Wanderers. P. She
    Al-VBP:755
STARVATION: see HUNGER AND
    STARVATION
THE STATE: see GOVERNMENT
STATE SONGS
  Alabama. J. Tutwiler. Se-PR:250
  Alaska. Se-PR:293
  Arizona. M. Clifford. Se-PR:252
  The Arkansas Traveler.
    S. Faulkner. Se-PR:253
  Carolina. H. Timrod. Se-PR:283
  Carry Me Back to Old Virginny.
    J. Bland. Er-FA:444,
    Ga-FB:273, Se-PR:289
  Georgia. R. Loveman. Se-PR:258
  Hail! Minnesota! T. Rickard.
    Se-PR:270
  Hail! South Dakota. D. Hammitt.
    Se-PR:284
  Hail, Vermont! J. Perry.
    Se-PR:288
  Here We Have Idaho. H. Powell.
    Se-PR:258
  Home Means Nevada. B. Raffetto.
    Se-PR:273
  A Home on the Range. J. Lomax.
    Er-FA:447, Hu-MP:204, Se-PR:262
  Illinois. C. Chamberlain.
    Se-PR:259
  Maryland! My Maryland!
    J. Randall. Se-PR:266
  Michigan, My Michigan!
    Mrs. H. Lyster. Se-PR:267
  Montana. C. Cohan. Se-PR:272
  My Nebraska. T. Diers.
    Se-PR:273
  My Old Kentucky Home. S. Foster.
    Er-FA:432, Fe-PL:143,
    Ga-FB:272, Se-PR:263
  North Dakota Hymn. J. Foley.
    Se-PR:278
  O, Fair New Mexico. E. Garrett.
    Se-PR:276
  Ode to New Jersey. E. Carr.
    Se-PR:275
  Oklahoma. H. Camden. Se-PR:279
  Old New Hampshire. J. Holmes.
    Se-PR:274
  The Old North State. W. Gaston.
    Se-PR:277
  On the Banks of the Wabash, Far
    Away. P. Dresser. Se-PR:260
  Oregon State Song. J. Buchanan.
    Se-PR:280
  Our Delaware. G. Hynson.
    Se-PR:255
  Our Native Land.
    King Kalakaua. Se-PR:294
  Pennsylvania. H. Bucher. Se-PR:281

  Rhode Island. T. Brown. Se-PR:282
  The Song of Iowa. S. Byers. Se-PR:261
  Song of Louisiana. V. Stopher.
    Se-PR:264
  State of Maine Song. R. Snow.
    Se-PR:265
  The State We Honor. F. Crosby.
    Se-PR:254
  Swanee River. S. Foster.
    Er-FA:428, Se-PR:256
  Texas, Our Texas. G. Wright.
    Se-PR:286
  Utah, We Love Thee. E. Stephens.
    Se-PR:287
  Washington's Song. E. Meany.
    Se-PR:290
  Way Down South in Mississippi.
    V. Barnes. Se-PR:271
  The West Virginia Hills.
    E. King. Se-PR:290
  When It's Iris Time in Tennessee.
    W. Waid. Se-PR:285
  Wyoming. C. Winter. Se-PR:292
THE STATES: see UNITED STATES;
    and names of states
STATESMEN: see DIPLOMATS; and names
    of statesmen, as CHURCHILL,
    WINSTON LEONARD SPENCER
STATISTICS: see HUMOR - STATISTICS;
    SATIRE - STATISTICS
STATUE OF LIBERTY: see LIBERTY,
    STATUE OF
STATUES: see also HUMOR - STATUES;
    SATIRE - STATUES; and names of
    statues, as LIBERTY, STATUE OF
  A Boy Looking at Big David.
    M. Swenson. Li-TU:52
  By the Statue of King Charles at
    Charing Cross. L. Johnson.
    Co-RG:18, Ni-JP:165, Ox-BN:946,
    Un-MB:153
  The Carver and the Rock Are One.
    B. Brigham. Sc-TN:31
  Caryatid. L. Adams. Wi-LT:603
  Charing Cross. Rv-CB:447
  The Christ of the Andes.
    E. Markham. Se-PR:85
  The Convert. M. Danner. Ra-BP:149
  For the Union Dead. R. Lowell.
    Br-TC:265, Pe-OA:244, Wi-LT:583
  Green Mountain Boy. F. Smyth.
    Gr-EC:231
  Lincoln Monument, Washington.
    L. Hughes. Li-TU:249
  Ozymandias. P. Shelley. Co-RG:14,
    De-CH:384, Er-FA:83, Fe-PL:436,
    Ha-PO:208, Li-SR:83, Ma-YA:177,
    Mc-PR:186, Mc-WK:98, No-CL:256,
    Ox-BN:279, Pa-GTB:251, Pa-HT:91,
    Rv-CB:695, Sm-LG:153, Sp-OG:187,
    Un-GT:312

Pediment Ballet. L. Nicholl.
   Pl-US:114
Protus. R. Browning. Hi-FO:86
A Psalm of Montreal. S. Butler.
   Rv-CB:933
The Rider Victory. E. Muir.
   Wi-LT:254
Saint Francis. R. Pfingston.
   Ls-NY:112
The Statue. R. Humphries.
   Ni-JP:127
Statue and Birds. L. Bogan.
   Un-MA:491
Statue in a Blizzard.
   R. Keener. Ls-NY:160
The Statue of Old Andrew Jackson.
   V. Lindsay. Mc-PR:52
Statues. R. Wilbur. Ha-TP:17
Stone Angel. A. Ridler.
   Pl-EI:11
Ye Ancient Divine One.
   A. Clough. Ox-BN:611
STEALING: see THIEVES
STEAM
   The Steam Family.
      G. Pangborn. Ke-TF:69
STEAM ROLLERS
   To a Steam Roller. M. Moore.
      Ca-VT:126, Mo-BG:62, Un-MA:349
STEAM SHOVELS
   Steam Shovel. C. Malam.
      Du-RG:37
STEEL
   I Sing of Anshan Steel.
      Feng Chih. Hs-TC:158
   John Henry. Co-RM:225
   Late Shift in the Mill.
      J. Knoepfle. St-H:94
   Prayers of Steel. C. Sandburg.
      Fe-FP:255, Hu-MP:403, La-OC:151,
      La-PV:194, Mo-BG:26, Un-MA:203
   Smoke and Steel. C. Sandburg.
      Un-MA:204
   Steel-Works. M. Swann.
      Hi-WP I:130
   A Strange Funeral in Braddock.
      M. Gold. Kr-OF:184
STEEPLES
   The Belfry. R. Thomas. Ga-BP:189
   To a Solitary Disciple.
      W. Williams. Ca-VT:54
STEERS: see CATTLE
STEPMOTHERS
   Kemp Oweyne. Fo-OG:13,
      Ma-BB:33, Rv-CB:50
   Kempion. Ox-BB:56
   The Lady Isabella's Tragedy.
      Gr-GB:251
   Rose the Red and White Lilly.
      Ox-BB:189

The Step Mother. H. Adam.
   De-FS:5
STEVEDORES: see also CARGOES; DOCKS
   Stevedore. L. Collins. Bo-AN:127
STEVENS, WALLACE
   To Wallace Stevens. D. Berrigan.
      Pl-ML:161
STEVENSON, ROBERT LOUIS
   Edinburgh. A. Noyes. Pa-HT:145
STEWART, JAMES, EARL OF MORAY
   The Bonny Earl of Murray.
      Bl-OB:152, Co-RM:206, Ma-BB:36,
      Ox-BB:594, Rv-CB:35, Sm-LG:271
STEWART, ROBERT, VISCOUNT
      CASTLEREAGH: see also SATIRE -
      STEWART, ROBERT, VISCOUNT
      CASTLEREAGH
   The Masque of Anarchy.
      P. Shelley. Hi-FO:206
STICKBALL: see also BASEBALL
   Of Kings and Things.
      L. Morrison. Ad-CI:67
   Stickball. L. Thompson.
      Ad-II:117
STILES
   Leg over Leg. Li-LB:83, Mo-NR:67,
      Mo-TL:39, Wr-RM:23
STINGINESS: see MISERS
STITCHERY: see NEEDLEWORK
STOATS: see WEASELS
STOCKINGS: see also CHRISTMAS
      STOCKINGS
   Stocking Fairy. W. Welles.
      Ar-TP3:150, Au-SP:295, Fe-FP:378
STOCKRIDERS: see COWBOYS
STOICISM: see also SATIRE -
      STOICISM
   Boys Don't Cry. L. Martinez.
      La-IH:80
   The Old Stoic. E. Brontë.
      Al-VBP:920, Fe-PL:308,
      Mc-PR:136, Ox-BN:600
STOMACHS
   Stomach. H. Kuroiwa.
      Le-TA:42
STONECHATS: see THRUSHES
STONEHENGE, ENG.
   Prehistoric Burials.
      S. Sassoon. Un-MB:316
STONES: see QUARRYING; ROCKS
STONES, PRECIOUS: see PRECIOUS
      STONES
STORES: see also GROCERY STORES;
      MARKETS AND MARKETING; SHOPPING
   Alligator on the Escalator.
      E. Merriam. La-OC:45
   At the Seed and Feed.
      J. Simons. Ls-NY:235
   Bus Ride. S. Robinson.
      Fe-FP:246

STORES — <u>cont'd.</u>
  Eighth Street West. R. Field.
    Br-SS:100
  Emma's Store. D. Aldis.
    La-OC:46
  General Store. R. Field.
    Au-SP:210, Hu-MP:34, Tu-WW:18
  The Harness Shop. M. Moody.
    Ke-TF:353
  The Novelty Shop. D. Niatum.
    Ni-CD:132
  The Pennycandystore Beyond the El.
    L. Ferlinghetti. Ad-CI:17,
    Mo-BG:19, Pe-SS:80
  Shops. W. Letts.   Th-AS:180
STORKS
  As the Stately Stork.
    Okamoto Kanoko. Le-MW:16
  Spring Song. Bo-FP:229
  Stork in Jerez. L. Lee.
    Go-BP:81
STORMS: see also HUMOR - STORMS;
    HURRICANES; THUNDERSTORMS;
    TORNADOES
  All at Once the Storm. Buson.
    Ca-BF:13
  The Autumn Storm. Basho.
    Sh-RP:63
  The Ballad of the Bolivar.
    R. Kipling. Sp-OG:79
  Before the Big Storm.
    W. Stafford. St-H:214
  Before the Summer Downpour.
    S. Kolosova. Mo-MI:26
  Beginning to Squall. M. Swenson.
    La-RM:88, Ls-NY:308
  Bent Down by a Storm. Joso.
    Be-CS:22
  Big Wind. T. Roethke.
    Al-VBP:1233, Bo-GJ:213,
    Ca-VT:285, Mo-BG:120
  By the Swimming. R. Sward.
    Du-SH:130
  The Captain's Daughter. J. Fields.
    Er-FA:459, Fe-PL:341
  Charm for Rain. Tr-US I:214
  Christmas at Sea. R. Stevenson.
    Co-SS:207, De-CH:28, Ga-FB:183,
    Ha-PO:251, Ma-YA:220, Sp-OG:257
  City-Storm. H. Monro. Un-MB:239
  Clouds in a Wild Storm.
    D. May. Le-M:50
  Deluge. J. Clare. Co-BN:169
  Dream in a Storm. Chu Ta-nan.
    Hs-TC:131
  During a Storm. Mo-TB:130
  Eastern Tempest. E. Blunden.
    Un-MB:398
  Eleven Horsemen. Shiki.
    Be-MC:29

The Enormous Hand. J. de Lima.
  An-TC:19
The Equinox. H. Longfellow.
  De-TT:164
A Flash of Lightning. Buson.
  Le-IS:15
Found in a Storm. W. Stafford.
  La-RM:36
The Fugitives. P. Shelley.
  Bo-FP:281
The Georgics. Virgil. Ma-FW:261
God's Little Mountain. G. Hill.
  Go-BP:173
Hatteras Calling. C. Aiken.
  Co-BN:178
Haying Before Storm.
  M. Rukeyser. Ha-WR:46
The Heather. S. Blicker. Pa-SG:172
In Memoriam. A. Tennyson. Ox-BN:496
In Winter. R. Wallace. Co-BN:182
Little Exercise. E. Bishop.
  Un-MA:614
Lodged. R. Frost. Br-SG:24,
  Sh-RP:116
Looking from the Pavilion over the
  Lake. Su Tung P'o. Rx-OH:82
My Breath Became. Bi-IT:109
Naarip's Wife. E. Isac. Mc-AC:54
Night Storm. S. Murano. Sh-AM:92
Now Close the Windows.
  G. Hopkins. Hi-WP II:37
On Wenlock Edge the Wood's in
  Trouble. A. Housman. No-CL:131,
  Ox-BN:921, Pa-GTB:417, Un-MB:97
One A.M. X. Kennedy.
  Co-EL:115, Ls-NY:54
Passing of the Wrangler.
  H. Fellow. Fi-BG:151
Patrolling Barnegat.
  W. Whitman. Rv-CB:848
Rainscapes, Hydrangeas, Roses,
  and Singing Birds.
  R. Eberhart. Un-MA:581
Rounding the Horn. J. Masefield.
  Un-MB:223
Sailing to an Island.
  R. Murphy. To-MP:134
Sea News. E. Barker. Ls-NY:244
Seaside Storm. M. Craig. Cr-SS:18
She Thinks of Her Beloved.
  Lu Chi. Rx-LT:28
Sir Patrick Spens. Al-VBP:35,
  Ar-TP3:19, Bl-OB:47, Bo-GJ:159,
  Co-RG:58, Co-SS:129, De-CH:405,
  Ha-PO:3, Ma-BB:1, Ma-FW:46,
  Ma-YA:41, Ox-BB:311, Rv-CB:38,
  Sm-LG:307, Sp-OG:98
The Sky Is Low. E. Dickinson.
  Co-BN:183, Co-EL:113, Ga-FB:301,
  Mc-PR:169, Rv-CB:904, Un-MA:95

Sleet Storm. J. Tippett.
  Br-SS:92, Pe-FB:78
Snow-Bound. J. Whittier.
  Ga-FB:302, Ho-WR:174, Mc-PR:139
Snowstorm. J. Clare. Co-BN:198,
  Ho-WR:180, Ma-FW:275
The Snowstorm. R. Emerson.
  Ar-TP3:191, Bo-FP:169, Co-BN:195,
  Fe-PL:388, Ho-P:5, Sh-AP:26
Song Composed at the Beginning of
  an Autumn Festival. Le-IB:106,
  Tr-US I:31
Spate in Winter Midnight.
  N. MacCaig. Pa-GTB:523
Spring Thunder. M. Van Doren.
  Bo-HF:46, Ha-WR:9
The Stampede. F. Miller.
  Fi-BG:159
Stone Trees. J. Freeman.
  Co-BN:113
Storm. H. Aldington. Ar-TP3:166
The Storm. Chora. Sh-RP:66
The Storm. E. Dickinson.
  Sm-MK:175
Storm. R. Pitter. Go-BP:241
The Storm. H. Vaughan.
  Rv-CB:413
Storm at Sea. W. Davenant.
  Co-RG:43, Co-RM:41
Storm at Sea. A. Kotul'sky.
  Mo-MI:18
A Storm at Sea. D. Valentin.
  Le-M:52, Le-WR:21
Storm Fear. R. Frost.
  Al-VBP:1127
A Storm in Childhood.
  T. Jones. Ma-FW:35
The Storm Is Over. R. Bridges.
  Pa-GTB:416, Wi-LT:56
Storm Scene. Tr-US II:102
Storm Song. Bi-IT:106, Br-MW:47
A Story for a Child. B. Taylor.
  Co-BBW:188
Sudden Gale in Spring.
  M. Thomas. Gr-EC:61
Sunday at the End of Summer.
  H. Nemerov. Co-BN:98
A Tailor, Who Sailed from Quebec.
  Wi-MG:41
The Tay River Bridge Disaster.
  W. McGonagall. Na-EO:78
The Tempest. W. Smith. Un-MA:672
The Tempest. M. Zaturenska.
  Un-MA:562
There. R. Mezey. Mo-TS:5
Thunder. W. de la Mare. Co-BN:176
To Chloris. W. Drummond.
  No-CL:143
To Frighten a Storm. G. Cardiff.
  Ni-CD:54

To Frighten a Storm. Da-SC:143
To the Maruts. Al-PI:13
Total Calm. P. Booth. Ha-WR:88
Traveling Storm. M. Van Doren.
  Th-AS:116
The Viking Terror. Co-PI:138,
  Gr-CT:222
Wind. T. Hughes. Ma-FW:37,
  To-MP:81
The Wind Begun to Rock the
  Grass. E. Dickinson. Co-BN:172,
  Gr-CC:28, Gr-EC:60
The Wind Now Commences to Sing.
  Bi-IT:22, Da-SC:88,
  Ho-SD:53, Tr-US II:268
Wind on an Inner Mongolian
  Desert. Wang T'ung-chao.
  Hs-TC:262
Winter. J. Thomson. Al-VBP:550
The Wreck of the Hesperus.
  H. Longfellow. Er-FA:385,
  Fe-FP:561, Sp-OG:94
The Wreck of the Julie Plant.
  W. Drummond. Fe-FP:491,
  Ha-PO:177
STORYBOOKS: see BOOKS AND READING
STORYTELLING: see also HUMOR -
  STORYTELLING
  Centaur of the Groundlevel
    Apartment. E. Pfeiffer.
    Ls-NY:337
  Colonel Fantock. E. Sitwell.
    Un-MB:334
  Father's Story. E. Roberts.
    Co-PS:101, Fe-FP:33, Hu-MP:22
  King Stephen. R. Graves.
    Mc-WK:128
  Little Orphant Annie. J. Riley.
    Co-BB:113, Er-FA:493, Fe-FP:532,
    Hu-MP:27, Ox-BC:300
  Martha. W. de la Mare. Un-MB:198
  The Mother's Tale. E. Farjeon.
    Br-BC:165
  Old Joan. K. Greene. Bo-FP:127
  Padraic O'Conaire, Gaelic Story-
    teller. F. Higgins. Co-PI:63
  The Somerset Dam for Supper.
    J. Holmes. Ni-JP:29
  The Story-Teller. M. Van Doren.
    Gr-EC:209, Ha-LO:39, Ho-TH:42
  Uncle Ananias. E. Robinson.
    Un-MA:137
  When I Was a Little Girl.
    A. Milligan. Co-PI:139
STOWE, HARRIET BEECHER
  Harriet Beecher Stowe.
    P. Dunbar. Ra-BP:47
STRANGERS: see also ALIENS
  The Bed Sheet and the Stranger.
    R. Zychlinska. Ho-TY:230

STRANGERS — cont'd.
Fifteen Poems of My Heart.
Juan Chi. Ma-FW:184
From Country to Town.
H. Coleridge. Rv-CB:759
An Invitation to Madison County.
J. Wright. Ad-PB:275
The New Little Boy. H. Behn.
Li-LC:48
O Country People. J. Hewitt.
Co-PI:60
A Passing. R. Cuscaden.
St-H:31
Poem. E. Brathwaite. Sa-B:169
Song of a Visitor to a Strange
Village. Tr-US II:309
Stranger. E. Roberts. Un-MA:270
The Strangers. J. Very.
Rv-CB:831
The Warm of Heart.
E. Coatsworth. Co-PU:66
STRAVINSKY, IGOR FEDOROVICH
Concert Interpretation
(Le Sacre du Printemps).
S. Sassoon. Rv-CB:981
STRAWBERRIES
The Dead Volcano. D. Iida.
Sh-AM:166
A Little Red Shirt. Gr-BB:8
Millions of Strawberries.
G. Taggard. Ar-TP3:206,
Du-RG:114, Fe-FP:233, Hu-MP:310,
Un-GB:8, Un-GT:252
Strawberries. E. Farjeon.
Ag-HE:53
That You Know This. Re-RR:87
Wild Strawberries. R. Graves.
Sm-LG:31
STREAMS: see BROOKS; RIVERS
STREET CLEANING
The Streetcleaner's Lament.
P. Hubbell. La-OC:27
Work for Yobo. J. Bautista.
La-GI:51
STREET CRIES
Beggar's Rhyme. Ar-TP3:192,
Au-SP:375, Bo-FP:181, Cl-DT:23,
La-PH:33, Mo-MGT:109, Wr-RM:123
The Bell-Man. R. Herrick.
De-CH:202, Rv-CB:341
Bread and Cherries.
W. de la Mare. Br-SG:71
The Button-Seller. Ir-BB:36,
Wr-RM:61
The Call of Life. Tsang K'o-chia.
Hs-TC:284
The Chair-Mender.
Er-FA:505, Gr-EC:280, Ir-BB:40,
Li-LB:63, Mo-MGT:124, Mo-NR:59,
Wr-RM:19

Cherries a Ha'penny a Stick.
De-CH:573
Come Buy My Nice Muffins.
Bo-FP:129
Fine Sevil Oranges. De-CH:572
Fish Crier. C. Sandburg.
Br-AF:42, Ga-S:123
Get 'Em Here. L. Hopkins.
Ho-CS:20
Flowers for Sale! Wy-CM:12
The Great Merchant, Dives
Pragmaticus, Cries His Wares.
T. Newbery. Ox-BC:14
Hot Cross Buns!
Au-SP:11, Bo-FP:244, De-PO:10,
Mo-MGT:109, Mo-NR:120, Mo-TL:75,
On-TW:10, Wi-MG:39, Wr-RM:127
I Have Screenes. De-CH:572
Lemonade Stand. D. Thompson.
Br-SS:176
Market. C. Rossetti. Hi-WP I:3
Market Woman's Cries. J. Swift.
Co-PI:184
Milk Below. Bo-FP:129
A Negro Peddler's Song.
F. Johnson. Bo-AN:26
Old Joe Jones. L. Richards.
Ag-HE:17
One a Penny, Poker. De-CH:573
The Rabbit Man. Mo-MGT:114
Return to the North.
Yü P'ing-po. Hs-TC:17
The Rice Seller. Bo-FP:129
Room for a Jovial Tinker.
Ox-BB:636
Round and Sound. De-CH:572
The Scissors Grinder.
R. Roseliep. De-FS:162
Several People. Pien Chih-Lin.
Le-MW:108
Strawberries. E. Farjeon.
Ag-HE:53
Summer Rain. Lin Keng. Le-MW:77
Toys for Sale. Gr-EC:284,
Ir-BB:36
Turn, Cheeses, Turn. Rv-ON:17
V Is for Vendor. P. McGinley.
Br-SG:71
The Watercress Seller.
T. Miller. Ox-BC:211
The Wench in the Street.
Rv-CB:427
Who Liveth So Merry.
De-CH:573
Young Lambs to Sell.
De-CH:573, Wr-RM:65
STREETCARS: see also HUMOR -
STREETCARS
Ballad of Tramway Art.
A. Aronov. Bo-RU:8

STREETS: see also CITY TRAFFIC;
   MANHOLES; ROADS
  Approach to a City. W. Williams.
    Ad-CI:25
  Bang Street. L. Welch.   Er-FA:218
  Beale Street, Memphis.
    T. Snyder. Hu-NN:54
  beer cans. M. Goode. La-IH:47
  Blue Island Intersection.
    C. Sandburg. Un-MA:203
  City Streets and Country Roads.
    E. Farjeon. Ar-TP3:93,
    Au-SP:165, Pe-FB:46
  Dive. L. Hughes. Ad-CI:51
  Eighth Street West. R. Field.
    Br-SS:100
  Five for the Grace of Man.
    W. Scott. Ca-VT:313
  Good Green Bus. R. Field.
    Mc-PR:95
  It Is Raining. L. Mitchell.
    Ar-TP3:170, Au-SP:311
  Joralemon Street. P. Hubbell.
    La-OC:22
  A London Thoroughfare Two A.M.
    A. Lowell. Ni-JP:131
  Neighborhood. G. Isaacs.
    La-IH:43
  New York in the Spring.
    D. Budbill. Ad-CI:3
  125th Street. L. Hughes.
    Ho-CS:13
  The Rainwalkers. D. Levertov.
    Ad-CI:109, Du-SH:145
  Several People. Pien Chih-Lin.
    Le-MW:108
  The Stone. P. Blackburn.
    Du-SH:24
  The Street. O. Paz.   La-OC:135
  A Street Is a River. C. Mcgee.
    La-IH:44
  The Term. W. Williams.
    Du-RG:77, La-OC:25, Li-TU:106,
    Re-TW:97, Mo-TS:34, Sh-RP:161
  There Are. D. Taylor. Ho-CT:33
  Walk down My Street.
    V. Dorset. La-IH:39
  What They Are for. D. Aldis.
    Au-SP:188
  You Shout about Freedom.
    Wilburt. La-IH:57
STRENGTH
  For Strength. R. Tagore. Tr-MR:52
  George. D. Randall. Ra-BP:145
  I Fled from Desolation.
    R. Korn. Ho-TY:306
  Orator. R. Emerson. Co-PU:16
  Palladium. M. Arnold.
    Ox-BN:646, Pa-GTB:366
  Poem. H. Carberry. Sa-B:142

  Samson Agonistes. J. Milton.
    Hi-FO:20, Ma-FW:173
  Strong Men, Riding Horses.
    G. Brooks. Ad-PB:157
  The Strongest. Yehoash.Ho-TY:73
  Upstream. C. Sandburg. Pe-M:45,
    Tr-MR:176, Un-MA:209
  The Wee Wee Man. De-CH:277,
    Fo-OG:28, Gr-GB:286,
    Ma-BB:12, Ox-BB:11
STRIKES: see also HUMOR - STRIKES
  Bread and Roses. J. Oppenheim.
    Kr-OF:179
  Casey Jones, the Union Scab.
    J. Hill. Kr-OF:177
  Prayer at the Graves of the
    Murdered Strikers.
    C. Queens. Kr-OF:157
  Shoot the Beast! M. Rosenfeld.
    Kr-OF:169
  What Shall We Do for the
    Striking Seamen? Hi-TL:199
STUART, CHARLES EDWARD (BONNIE
    PRINCE CHARLIE)
  Moy Castle. Un-GT:112
STUART, JAMES FRANCIS EDWARD
    (THE OLD PRETENDER)
  The Bonny Moorhen. Gr-GB:191
  There'll Never Be Peace.
    R. Burns. Rv-CB:626
STUBBORNNESS: see OBSTINACY
STUDENTS: see also COLLEGES
    AND UNIVERSITIES; SCHOOL LIFE
  Beginning My Studies.
    W. Whitman. Rv-CB:861
  Blue Girls. J. Ransom.
    Ca-VT:150, Gr-CC:79, Gr-CT:51,
    Ha-PO:183, Mc-WS:75, Pe-OA:137,
    Sh-AP:182, Un-MA:409
  The Description of a Good Boy.
    H. Dixon. Ox-BC:54
  The Dunce. J. Prévert. Ma-FW:72
  Duty of the Student.
    E. Anthony. Un-GT:26
  Elegy for Jane. T. Roethke.
    Br-TC:348, Pe-OA:204, Pe-SS:160,
    Sh-AP:213, Un-MA:598, Wi-LT:486
  Expostulation and Reply.
    W. Wordsworth. Rv-CB:640
  For Scholars and Pupils.
    G. Wither. Ox-BC:29
  Henry's Secret. D. Kilner.Ox-BC:82
  Love Sonnet to My Students.
    J. Solovay. Ke-TF:83
  My Students. R. Sward. St-H:223
  Religious Emphasis Week.
    C. Walsh. St-H:242
  The Student. M. Moore. Br-TC:300
  Three Portraits. G. Hitchcock.
    Ca-VT:392

STUDENTS — cont'd.
  The Unhappy Schoolboy. Ox-BC:11
  What's a Student. A. Round.
    Ke-TF:82
  While Enduring. S. Yamaguchi.
    Sh-AM:171
STUPIDITY: see also FOOLS;
    HUMOR - STUPIDITY
  John Wesley Gaines. Co-EL:62,
    Co-FB:478, Co-PU:121
  My Father Died, but I Can't
    Tell You How. Bl-OB:22,
    Ir-BB:124, On-TW:25, Pa-RE:46
  The Silly. De-TT:118
  Simple Sam. L. Jackson.
    Co-PS:164
  Simple Simon. Au-SP:9,
    De-PO:16, Fr-WO:18, Ir-BB:205,
    Li-LB:30, Mo-NR:89, Un-GT:104
  When I Was a Little Boy.
    Mo-MGT:105, Rv-ON:62
STUTTERING: see also HUMOR -
    STUTTERING
  Praise to the Stutterer.
    M. Katz. Ls-NY:110
SUBMISSIVENESS: see also
    SATIRE - SUBMISSIVENESS
  Easter Song. K. Leslie. Tr-MR:134
  The Ebb and Flow. E. Taylor.
    Sh-AP:14
  The End of the Play.
    W. Thackeray. Er-FA:520
  Grant Me Thy Peace.
    Thomas à Kempis. Go-BP:269
  Heaven-Haven. G. Hopkins.
    Go-BP:182
  In This Hour. J. Johnson.
    Tr-MR:232
  Judas Iscariot. C. Cullen.
    Fe-PL:325
  Letter to My Sister. A. Spencer.
    Ad-PB:16, Bo-AN:19, Hu-PN:61
  Permit Me Voyage. J. Agee.
    Un-MA:606
  Silence Is Gold. A. Galich.
    Bo-RU:33
  Veni Creator. B. Carman. Tr-MR:26
  We Wear the Mask. P. Dunbar.
    Ad-IA:86, Ad-PB:8, Bo-AN:14,
    Bo-HF:103, Jo-SA:134, Lo-TY:208,
    Mo-BG:190
  A Word in Jewish Ears. A. Galich.
    Bo-RU:34
SUBURBAN LIFE: see HUMOR -
    SUBURBAN LIFE
SUBWAYS
  City Afternoon. B. Howes.
    Br-AF:211, Ha-TP:9
  Early Train. B. Pasternak.
    Ca-MR:173

  Husbands and Wives. M. Hershenson.
    Du-RG:59, La-OC:64
  The Imprisoned I. R. Fitzgerald.
    Br-TC:125
  In the Street I Have Just Left.
    C. Reznikoff. La-OC:26
  In the Tube. R. Aldington.
    Hi-WP I:128
  The Leg in the Subway.
    O. Williams. Wi-LT:418
  Rapid Transit. J. Agee.
    Un-MA:607
  Riding the "A." M. Swenson.
    Ad-CI:37, Mo-BG:24
  The Subway. C. Rivers.
    Be-MA:106
  Subway Ride on a Summer Day.
    D. Solomon. La-IH:27
  Subway Rush Hour. L. Hughes.
    La-OC:63
  Things to Do if You Are a
    Subway. B. Katz. Ho-CS:15
  Tired and Unhappy, You Think
    of Houses. D. Schwartz.
    Un-MA:617, Wi-LT:516
  The Tunnel. H. Crane.
    Sh-AP:203, Un-MA:529
  Walk about the Subway Station.
    C. Reznikoff. Ad-CI:42
SUCCESS: see also ACHIEVEMENT;
    GREATNESS; SATIRE - SUCCESS
  Don't Give Up. Er-FA:8
  Reliance. H. Van Dyke.
    Er-FA:29
  Success. Er-FA:17
  Success Is Counted Sweetest.
    E. Dickinson. Bo-GJ:191,
    Mo-BG:166, Rv-CB:897, Sh-AP:126,
    Un-MA:103, Wi-LT:3
SUCKLING, SIR JOHN
  Brief Lines in Not So Brief.
    O. Nash. Pl-ML:111
SUDAN
  Fuzzy-Wuzzy. R. Kipling.
    Un-MB:126
  The Soudanese. W. Watson.
    Cr-WS:159
SUFFERING: see also HUMOR -
    SUFFERING; PAIN
  After Great Pain a Formal Feeling
    Comes. E. Dickinson. Un-MA:100
  An Agony. As Now. I. Baraka.
    Ra-BP:211, Wi-LT:743
  The Book of Job. H. Leivick.
    Ho-TY:126
  Christ in Alabama. L. Hughes.
    Ad-PB:73
  City Life. D. Lawrence.
    Ad-CI:88
  Deliverance. L. Lee. Go-BP:238

Do Not Believe Your Shakespear's
  Grief. C. Aiken. Co-PU:68,
  Rd-OA:32
Epilogue. S. Kwartler.
  Jo-SA:4
Five Vignettes, 4. J. Toomer.
  Ad-PB:35
A Flat One. W. Snodgrass.
  En-PC:244, Wi-LT:822
For Annie. E. Poe. Sh-AP:60
The Garden of Olives. R. Rilke.
  Go-BP:293, Tr-MR:124
Gargoyle. C. Sandburg.
  Ba-PO:134
The Heart Asks Pleasure First.
  E. Dickinson. Ha-PO:149,
  Rv-CB:898, Un-MA:96
How Annandale Went Out.
  E. Robinson. Un-MA:125
How It Is. U. Greenberg.
  Me-PH:91
I've Seen Enough. C. Meyer.
  Jo-VC:12
Labourer. E. Brathwaite.
  Sa-B:239
Lacrimas or There Is a Need to
  Scream. K. Lyle. Ad-PB:466
Lines Written During a Period of
  Insanity. W. Cowper. Ho-P:183
Musée des Beaux Arts. W. Auden.
  Br-TC:20, Er-FA:64, Ha-PO:223,
  Pa-GTB:510, To-MP:31, Wi-LT:467
Negro Woman. L. Alexander.
  Ad-PB:58
New Approach Is Needed.
  K. Amis. Ke-PP:89
Night of the Scorpion.
  N. Ezekial. Al-PI:96
Pain for a Daughter.
  A. Sexton. Mc-WS:142
A Poem. B. Pasternak. Bo-RU:1
Poem. J. Wain. En-PC:230
Purgatory. Sun Yü-t'ang.
  Hs-TC:121
The Road. C. Aiken. Un-MA:428
Rubaiyat. Omar Khayyam. Ba-PO:169
The Seer. L. Turco. De-FS:199
Still Here. L. Hughes.
  Gr-BT:151, Rs-BP:83
Suffering of This World.
  Issa. Ba-PO:26
Through the Strait Pass of
  Suffering. E. Dickinson.
  Ga-S:225, Tr-MR:201
To Certain Critics. C. Cullen.
  Ra-BP:101
Unkept Good Fridays. T. Hardy.
  Tr-MR:128
Vicarious Atonement.
  R. Aldington. Un-MB:354

We Wear the Mask. P. Dunbar.
  Ad-IA:86, Ad-PB:8, Bo-AN:14,
  Bo-HF:103, Jo-SA:134, Lo-TY:208,
  Mo-BG:190
What Now? L. Martin. La-IH:82
The World's Sorrow. A. Reisen.
  Ho-TY:70
Yet Do I Marvel. C. Cullen.
  Ad-PB:87, Be-MA:50, Bo-AN:88,
  Hu-PN:233, Jo-SA:128, Lo-TY:235,
  Pe-SS:48, Ra-BP:100
SUFFOLK, ENG.
  At Dunwich. A. Thwaite.
  Ca-MB:89
SUGAR CANE
  The Canefield and the Sea.
  J. de Melo Neto. An-TC:153
  Labourer. E. Brathwaite.
  Sa-B:239
  The Sea and the Canefield.
  J. de Melo Neto. An-TC:147
  Sugar Cane. F. Charles.
  Sa-B:185
  sugarfields. B. Mahone.
  Ad-PB:473
SUICIDE: see also HUMOR - SUICIDE;
  SATIRE - SUICIDE
  Albert Ayler: Eulogy for a De-
  composed Saxophone Player.
  S. Crouch. Ad-PB:486
  Avery Anameer. J. Brennan.
  De-FS:38
  A Ballad of Hell. J. Davidson.
  Un-MB:72
  Bill and Parson Sim. Fi-BG:199
  The Bridge of Sighs. T. Hood.
  Pa-GTB:230
  Dirges, I, II. Tr-US II:41, 42
  A Dispute over Suicide.
  Lo-TY:26
  Improvised Songs. Tr-US II:182
  Junker Schmidt. Co-EL:101
  Look, Hart, That Horse You Ride
  Is Wood. P. Vierick. Pl-ML:156
  The Mill. E. Robinson.
  Ha-PO:47, Sh-AP:142
  A Miner Coming Home One Night.
  Gr-GB:134
  Night Song. Tr-US II:192
  Norman Morrison. D. Ferguson.
  Ba-PO:34
  Notes Found near a Suicide.
  F. Horne. Ad-PB:48,
  Bo-AN:42, Hu-PN:151
  Notes Found near a Suicide:
  To the Poets. F. Horne.
  Bo-AN:46
  Of Late. G. Starbuck.
  Ca-VT:667, Cr-WS:136
  On Suicide. S. Murano. Sh-AM:90

SUICIDE — cont'd.
  A Paper Suicide. A. Lutzky.
    Ho-TY:265
  Prayer for Marilyn Monroe.
    E. Cardenal. Be-UL:95
  Richard Cory. E. Robinson.
    Co-PT:107, Er-FA:336, Fe-PL:33,
    Ho-TH:19, Pe-M:62, Sh-AP:140,
    Sm-LG:131, Un-MA:118, Wi-LT:100
  Rousecastle. D. Wright.
    Ca-MB:81, Co-SS:195
  Sardanapalus. H. Howard.
    Hi-FO:29
  The Seer. L. Turco. De-FS:199
  Ship of Death. D. Lawrence.
    Al-VBP:1160, Pa-GTB:462,
    Un-MB:299
  Song. Tr-US I:230
  Song for a Suicide. L. Hughes.
    Hu-PN:198
  Suicide? J. Miles. Sa-B:178
  Suicide Note. S. Yesenin.
    Ca-MR:112
  To Be or Not to Be.
    W. Shakespeare. Er-FA:93,
    Ha-PO:256, Ma-YA:68
  The Unfortunate Miller.
    A. Coppard. Co-PT:19
  Way out West. I. Baraka.
    Ad-PB:252
  Who'll See Me Dive? T. McNeill.
    Sa-B:123
SUMATRA: see also INDONESIAN VERSE
  Complaint of a Fisherman's
    Widow. Tr-US I:158
  Complaint of a Widow over Her
    Dying Son. Tr-US I:157
  Dialogue. Tr-US I:156
SUMMER
  Alike. D. Aldis. Sh-RP:216
  Arabesque. F. Johnson.
    Ad-PB:393
  As Imperceptibly as Grief.
    E. Dickinson. Wi-LT:15
  At Last the Sparrows.
    Onitsura. Be-CS:39
  August. M. Lewis. Un-GT:277
  August Afternoon. M. Edey.
    Ha-YA:90
  August Hail. J. Cunningham.
    Ha-PO:100
  Barefoot Days. R. Field.
    Fe-FP:229, Ha-YA:66
  Bed in Summer. R. Stevenson.
    Bo-FP:35, Bo-GJ:100, De-TT:90,
    Fr-WO:34, Ke-TF:71
  The Beginning. W. Stevens.
    Ca-VT:40, Ha-TP:70
  Between Motions. J. Mazzaro.
    Ls-NY:297

  Birds in Summer. M. Howitt.
    Hu-MP:215
  The Birks of Aberfeldy.
    R. Burns. Al-VBP:643
  Blue Flowers. R. Field.
    Br-SG:32, Mc-PR:161
  A Boy's Song. J. Hogg.
    Bl-OB:138, Bo-FP:258, Ch-B:62,
    De-CH:132, De-TT:75, Fe-FP:301,
    Ho-WR:69, Ke-TF:45, Mc-PR:114,
    Mc-WK:84, Ox-BC:156
  A Boy's Summer Song. P. Dunbar.
    Br-SS:171, Sh-RP:17
  The Breeze. Bo-FP:259, Ch-B:88
  The Call. B. Björnson. Ch-B:16
  Cicadas Buzzing. Basho.
    Be-CS:9
  Country Summer. L. Adams.
    Al-VBP:1218, Bo-GJ:98,
    Un-MA:546, Wi-LT:604
  Daisy. W. Williams. Un-MA:257
  The Deceptive Present, the
    Phoenix Year. D. Schwartz.
    Co-BN:99
  A Dog Day. R. Field. Br-SS:178
  The End of Summer. E. Millay.
    Co-BN:102
  Fern Hill. D. Thomas.
    Al-VBP:1246, Bo-GJ:53, Br-TC:440,
    Cl-DT:63, Co-RG:160, Fe-PL:251,
    Ga-FB:166, Hi-WP II:46, Mc-EA:42,
    Mc-WK:10, Na-EO:45, Pa-GTB:542,
    Pe-SS:162, Re-TW:100, Sm-LG:108,
    Un-MB:502, Wi-LT:559
  The Field Madonna. S. Mernit.
    Ad-II:42
  Flowers of Middle Summer.
    W. Shakespeare. Ha-YA:64
  Grasshopper Green. Au-SP:77,
    Bo-FP:271, Fe-FP:132, Hu-MP:304,
    It-HB:14, St-FS:111
  The Greenwood. W. Bowles.
    Cl-FC:41
  The Half of Life. F. Hölderlin.
    Un-R:19
  Heat. G. Gonzalez y Contreras.
    Ho-LP:24
  High Summer. J. Clare. Gr-CC:35
  The Hollow Land. W. Morris.
    Gr-CT:48, Re-TW:80
  Hot Time! A. Trias. Ho-CT:18
  Hotness. A. Copeman. Ho-CT:19
  Hymn to the Sun. M. Roberts.
    Sm-LG:56
  In Fields of Summer. G. Kinnell.
    Co-BN:99, Ha-WR:22, La-RM:144
  In Summer the Rains. Da-SC:16,
    Ho-SD:19, Le-OE:79
  In the Mountains on a Summer Day.
    Li Po. Ma-FW:116, Mo-SD:93

In the Summer. D. Aldis.
   Mc-AW:41
July. J. Clare. Un-GT:276
July in Dutchess County.
   B. Deutsch. Ha-WR:63
June. A. Fisher. Ho-GC:29,
   La-PP:46, La-PV:82
June's Here. C. Martindale.
   Ho-CT:23
Knoxville, Tennessee.
   N. Giovanni. Ad-BO:58,
   Ad-PB:450, Ra-BP:322
Late Summer. Y. Kinoshita.
   Ma-FW:115
Late Summer Evening. Shiki.
   Be-MC:28
Lemonade Stand. D. Thompson.
   Br-SS:176
Let Us Go, Then, Exploring.
   V. Woolf. Co-BN:90
Long Summer. L. Lee. Co-BN:89
Lying in the Sun. I. Johnson.
   Le-M:78, Le-WR:11
Marjorie's Almanac. T. Aldrich.
   Br-SG:101, Fe-FP:62, Hu-MP:298
Melancholy Summer. S. Ito.
   Sh-AM:102
Midsummer. J. Scully.
   Br-TC:359, Pe-OA:270
Midsummer Jingle. N. Levy.
   Co-BN:96, Co-PU:47
Midsummer Pause. F. Lape.
   Co-PS:107
A Midsummer Song. R. Gilder.
   Co-BN:92, Ke-TF:44
The Milkman's Horse. Au-SP:48,
   Co-IW:33
The Most. S. Suggs. Ho-CT:21
Night Enchantment. E. Muth.
   Br-SS:170
Now Welcome Summer. G. Chaucer.
   Rv-CB:58
Number 7. L. Ferlinghetti.
   Ad-CI:18, Du-RG:102, Kh-VA:74,
   La-OC:85, Pe-SS:156
O Warmth of Summer. Le-IB:37
On Summer Nights. Tsurayuki.
   Ba-ST:29
On the Lake. Yung Tzu.
   Pa-MV:195
Pastoral X. R. Hillyer.
   Ha-LO:84
Prairie Summer. D. Etter.
   Sc-TN:45
Rain Portrait. J. Unternecker.
   Sc-TN:213
The Rainy Summer. A. Meynell.
   Bo-GJ:99, Gr-SS:42
The Riders. A. Stanford. Ha-TP:118
Rondel. W. Henley. Ox-BN:886

The Rye Fields Are Ripening.
   Gr-BB:21
The Schoolboy. W. Blake.
   Co-BN:95, De-CH:131,
   Ma-FW:136, Rv-CB:594
Secret. E. Doolittle.   Ha-YA:63
September. E. Fallis.
   Br-SG:102, Ha-YA:103
So Quickly Came Summer.
   A. Pratt. Al-WW:109
Song. E. Sitwell. Gr-CC:34
Song for a Summer Afternoon.
   V. Miller. Ca-BP:46
Sonnet. J. Masefield.
   Un-MB:228, Wi-LT:191
South Wind. Tu Fu. Ar-TP3:203,
   Le-MW:75, Ma-FW:100, Rx-OH:24
Spring Stops Me Suddenly.
   V. Iremonger. Co-PI:73
Subway Ride on a Summer Day.
   D. Solomon. La-IH:27
Sumer Is Icumen In.
   Al-VBP:2, Bo-FP:241, Fr-WO:74,
   Gr-CT:48, Gr-GB:40, Li-SR:123,
   Ma-FW:34, Ma-YA:25, Rv-CB:1
Summer. R. Aldington. Cl-FC:40
Summer. Bana. Al-PI:35
Summer (How Sweet). J. Clare.
   Co-BN:95
Summer (The Woodman's Axe).
   J. Clare. Rv-CB:718
Summer. J. Davidson. Co-BN:100
Summer. E. Hillery. Ho-CT:18
Summer. C. Rossetti.
   Co-BN:91, Rv-CB:890
Summer. T. Tsosie. Ba-HI:62
Summer Afternoon. R. Souster.
   Co-BN:98, Ls-NY:292
Summer and Winter. P. Shelley.
   Co-BN:101
Summer Comes. E. Agnew.Br-SS:169
The Summer Countries. H. Rago.
   Ca-VT:425
Summer Day. Yuan Mei. Rx-LT:114
Summer Evening. W. de la Mare.
   Un-MB:201
Summer Images. J. Clare.
   Gr-CT:117, Ox-BN:318, Rv-CB:716
Summer in the City. D. McNally.
   La-IH:64
Summer in the Rain. Yung Tzu.
   Pa-MV:196
Summer in the World.Bassho.Le-MW:76
Summer Is Golden. G. Sellers.
   Le-M:77
Summer Morning. J. Clare.
   Co-PS:111, Rv-CB:714
A Summer Morning. R. Field.
   Ar-TP3:175, Au-SP:319,
   La-PV:48, Pe-FB:86

SUMMER — cont'd.
  Summer Rain. E. Coatsworth.
    Br-SS:179, Sh-RP:217
  Summer Remembered. I. Gardner.
    Pe-OA:235
  Summer Shower. E. Dickinson.
    Co-BN:102
  Summer Solstice. A. Garner.
    Gr-BT:155
  Summer Song. J. Ciardi. Gr-EC:43
  Summer Song. E. Nesbit. Co-PS:105
  Summer Song. W. Williams.
    Ha-WR:54
  Summer Stars. C. Sandburg.
    Ad-PE:16, Ha-LO:33, Ha-YA:69,
    La-RM:69, Sh-RP:218
  Summer Sun. R. Stevenson.
    Ch-B:15, Un-MB:58
  Summer: West Side. J. Updike.
    Pe-SS:68
  A Summer's Day. A. Hume.
    De-CH:136
  Summertime and the Living.
    R. Hayden. Ad-PB:118,
    Br-TC:169, Ra-BP:103
  Sun. J. Duffey. Ad-II:60
  The Sun Is a Globe of Fire.
    A. Machado. Le-SW:45
  Sunning. J. Tippett.
    Ar-TP3:51, Br-SS:178,
    Du-RG:86, Gr-EC:82
  Sweating. H. Linton. Ho-CT:23
  Swinging, Swaying Grass. Issa.
    Be-MC:21
  There Is Joy. Do-WH:64,
    Ho-SD:76, La-RM:125,
    Le-OE:104, Ma-BH:10
  Things of Summer. K. Jackson.
    Br-SG:27, Mc-AW:44
  This Summer. C. Smith. Me-WF:71
  The Throstle. A. Tennyson.
    Co-BBW:241, Co-BN:97, Co-PS:106,
    Fe-FP:294, Mc-WK:25, Se-PR:155
  A Time. T. Chambers. Ho-CT:20
  To Summer. W. Blake. Ho-WR:63
  Two Little Birds Fly. Gr-BB:26
  Under the Boughs. G. Baro.
    Co-BN:156
  Under the Greenwood Tree.
    Gr-GB:44
  Under the Plane Trees.
    K. Nakamura. Sh-AM:147
  Upside Down. R. Burgunder.
    Ar-TP3:108
  Virginia. T. Eliot.
    Ha-PO:94, Sm-LG:142
  The Visitor. M. Goldman.
    Ha-WR:69
  The Waking. T. Roethke.
    La-RM:128, Mc-WS:129, Mo-BG:127

  Weekend Stroll. F. Cornford.
    Co-BN:94
  When Daffodils Begin to Peer.
    W. Shakespeare. Al-VBP:195,
    Gr-CT:42, Rv-CB:205, Sm-LG:55
  Where the Single Men Go in
    Summer. N. Bourne. Co-FB:487
  Winter and Summer. S. Spender.
    Un-MB:480
  Woof of the Sun. H. Thoreau.
    Al-VBP:917
SUMMERSAULTS: see SOMERSAULTS
SUMNER, CHARLES
  This Noble Head. R. Emerson.
    Kr-OF:141
SUN: see also ECLIPSES;
    HUMOR - SUN
  Adoration of the Disk.
    King Akhnaten and Princess
    Nefer Neferiu Aten. Fe-FP:478
  After the Black Nights.
    C. McElrath. Me-WF:70
  All Day in Gray Rain. Basho.
    Be-CS:7
  And Then It Rained.
    M. Van Doren. Co-BN:171
  Arizona Nature Myth. J. Michie.
    Sm-MK:187
  As the Sun Came Up. Wy-CM:6
  The Brave Man. W. Stevens.
    Li-TU:206
  Breakfast Time. J. Stephens.
    Gr-EC:66
  Brightly the Sun Shines.
    Ontei. Be-CS:47
  A Buddhist Hymn. Feng Wei-teh.
    Hs-TC:138
  Calypsos II. W. Williams.
    Ho-TH:72
  Canticle of the Sun Dancing on
    Easter Morning.
    J. Heath-Stubbs. Go-BP:298
  Day Song. E. Hammond. Mc-AW:13
  Earth Cure Me. Earth Receive
    My Woe. Wo-HS:(55)
  Esthetique du Mal, VI.
    W. Stevens. Wi-LT:154
  Followe Thy Faire Sunne.
    T. Campion. Al-VBP:213,
    Ho-P:42
  The Force. P. Redgrove. To-MP:178
  Give Me the Splendid Silent Sun.
    W. Whitman. Co-BN:232,
    Fe-FP:263, Mo-BG:20, Un-MA:84
  Go Down, Old Hannah. Lo-TY:200
  High Noon! A Hot Sun. Hajime.
    Ca-BF:15
  Hudibras. S. Butler. Pl-IO:23
  The Hymn to the Sun.
    Ab-MO:3, Lo-TY:21

Hymn to the Sun.   Be-AP:22,
   Le-OE:9
I Hear the Eagle Bird. Ho-SD:3
I Love I Love the Sun Above.
   C. Cox.   Me-WF:24
In Time like Glass. W. Turner.
   Un-MB:347
An Indian Summer Day on the
   Prairie. V. Lindsay.
   La-RM:70, Mc-WK:31
The Inward Morning. H. Thoreau.
   No-CL:270, Sh-AP:67
It's a Sunny, Sunny Day Today.
   S. Gatti. Le-M:24
Johnny Appleseed's Hymn to the
   Sun. V. Lindsay.   Tr-MR:29
The Lamp.   A. Buttigieg.
   Pa-RE:120
Last Song.   J. Guthrie.
   Ar-TP3:181, La-PV:62
Leaf and Sun.   N. Farber. Ho-LP:99
A Little Morning Music.
   D. Schwartz.   Co-BN:212
Little Song of the Sun.
   Tr-US II:247
Long Summer. L. Lee. Co-BN:89
Look! J. Smith. Sm-MK:4
Look, the Sea! W. Zorach.
   Ad-PE:12
Metric Figure. W. Williams.
   Un-MA:255
Morning Sun. L. MacNeice.
   Br-TC:281, Un-MB:445
The Nature of Love. J. Kirkup.
   Pl-EI:91
Nova.   R. Jeffers.   Pe-OA:90
Oh My Sun, My Moon! Le-OE:115
October. W. Trask.   No-CL:279
The Old Man Called to His Sons.
   Wo-HS:(10)
Omen.   B. Diop.   Ho-LP:25,
   Ma-FW:103
On Yonder Hill There Is a Red
   Deer. Gr-CT:11, Gr-GB:39
Once. W. de la Mare. Go-BP:170
Our Father the Sun. Tr-US II:285
Over the Hill the Sun's Crown.
   V. Erl'. Bo-RU:28
Phoebus and Boreas.
   J. de la Fontaine.   Un-R:87
Pieces of Sun on the Lake of
   My Spirits. Wo-HS:(28)
A Prayer. Ho-SD:24, Le-OE:7
Revolution. A. Housman. Pl-IO:37
Riddle #29. Bo-GJ:244
Riddle of Snow and Sun.
   Gr-CT:395, Gr-GB:36,
   Rv-CB:444, Rv-ON:36
Riddles, III.   Gr-CT:235,
   Gr-GB:39

Shine Out Fair Sun.   Ma-FW:5
Shiny. J. Reeves. Sh-RP:181
Silver Sheep. A. Payne.
   Br-SS:23
Snow Fell until Dawn. Rokwa.
   Be-CS:24
So in the Empty Sky the Stars
   Appear. J. Masefield.
   Go-BP:109
Solar Myth. G. Taggard.
   Un-MA:479
Some Say the Sun Is a Golden
   Earring. N. Belting.
   La-PV:50
Song of Creation. Bi-IT:4,
   Ho-SD:52
The Song of Creatures.
   St. Francis of Assisi.
   Pa-SG:202
Song of the Sun and the Moon.
   Da-SC:68, Le-OE:3
Sonnet 33. W. Shakespeare.
   Al-VBP:201, Er-FA:262,
   Rv-CB:215
The Spacious Firmament on High.
   J. Addison. Mc-PR:202,
   Pl-EI:211
Sprinkling. D. Pierce.
   Ar-TP3:206
Summer Sun. R. Stevenson.
   Ch-B:15, Un-MB:58
Summons to Love. W. Drummond.
   Al-VBP:303, Pa-GTB:1
The Sun. J. Drinkwater.
   Ar-TP3:175, Au-SP:344, Fe-FP:262,
   Li-LC:76, Pe-FB:62
The Sun. F. Thompson. Un-MB:82
The Sun. W. Turner. Un-MB:349
Sun. D. Wakoski. Kh-VA:13
The Sun. Be-AP:64
Sun City. B. Cutler. St-H:38
Sun, God of Living. J. Nez.
   Ba-HI:145
The Sun Is a Shapely Fire.
   A. Seymour. Sa-B:82
The Sun Is Today. I. Muller.
   Mo-MI:64
The Sun Path. Matsuo Basho.
   Pa-SG:92
The Sun Rising. J. Donne.
   Rv-CB:292, Un-MW:161
The Sun Tries. M. Ware. Le-WR:37
The Sunbeams. L. Pidgeon. Le-M:23
The Sunbeams Stream Forward.
   Ho-SD:48, Jo-TS:1
Sunflower No. 1. Ch'in Tzu-hao.
   Pa-MV:60
The Sun's Travels. R. Stevenson.
   Fe-FP:262, Hu-MP:115
T-cho, the Sun, Said. Ho-SD:26

SUN — cont'd.
Tell of Spring. Br-FW:6
There's Nothing like the Sun.
  E. Thomas. Ga-FB:6
This Happy Day. H. Behn.
  Ar-TP3:176
Thousands of Shining Knights.
  Re-RR:100
To the Envious. Pl-EI:25,
  Tr-CB:53, Tr-US I:53
To the Sun. I. Bachmann.
  Co-BN:231
To the Sun. R. Campbell.
  Ga-S:188, Pl-EI:21
To the Sun from a Flower.
  G. Gezelle. Fe-FP:471,
  Pa-SG:105
To the Sun-God. Tr-CB:52,
  Tr-US I:52
truth. G. Brooks. Ho-TH:53
The Twelfth Moon Came.
  Wo-HS:(16)
Two Mad Songs, I. E. Jarrett.
  Sc-TN:108
We're like Two Flowers.
  Re-RR:92
Who Can Stay Indoors. Kikaku.
  Be-MC:24
The Women and the Man. Te-FC:87
Woof of the Sun. H. Thoreau.
  Al-VBP:917
Zuñi Prayer at Sunrise. Da-SC:70
SUN GLASSES: see EYEGLASSES
SUNAPEE, LAKE
  Pier. J. Scully. Ha-WR:21
SUNDAY: see also HUMOR - SUNDAY;
  SABBATH
Applebaum's Sunday. A. Magil.
  Kr-OF:192
Beautiful Sunday. J. Falstaff.
  Co-BN:33
Morning Song. A. Dugan.
  Ad-CI:13, Co-EL:99
Ploughing on Sunday. W. Stevens.
  Bo-GJ:52, Fe-FP:232, Pa-RE:100,
  Re-TW:14, Sm-MK:26, We-PZ:38
Q Is for Quietness. P. McGinley.
  La-OC:31
The Ragged Girl's Sunday.
  M. Bennett. De-TT:24
Saturday, Sunday. Wr-RM:69
Sunday. E. Coatsworth. Br-AF:213,
  La-OC:32, Mc-WK:56
A Sunday. W. de la Mare.
  Ls-NY:50
Sunday. V. Rutsala. Du-SH:101
Sunday Morning. L. MacNeice.
  Un-MB:444
Sunday Morning. W. Moreland.
  Ad-PB:502

Sunday Morning. W. Stevens.
  Sh-AP:158, Sm-PT:121,
  Un-MA:242, Wi-LT:139
Sunday Morning Song. Ab-MO:55
Sunday: New Guinea.
  K. Shapiro. Br-AF:85
Those Winter Sundays. R. Hayden.
  Ad-PB:119, Du-SH:53,
  Jo-SA:21, Mo-BG:75
Veracruz. R. Hayden. Bo-AN:119
SUNDAY SCHOOLS: see CHURCHES
SUNDEW
The Sundew. A. Swinburne.
  Ox-BN:810
SUNDIALS
Here Stand I Ever Lonely.
  De-CH:484
Lesson from a Sundial. Ar-TP3:208
On a Sundial. H. Belloc.
  Co-PU:18
On Man. W. Landor. Ox-BN:185
The Sun-Dial. T. Peacock.
  Ox-BN:231
SUNFLOWERS
Ah! Sun-Flower. W. Blake.
  Al-VBP:617, Co-EL:85, Gr-CT:255,
  Ox-BN:24, Rv-CB:610
Baby Seed Song. E. Nesbit.
  Fe-FP:215, Hu-MP:246, Th-AS:73
O My Heart You Must Be Strong.
  Ge-TR:17
Round as a Moon. Gr-BB:23
Sunflower. S. Tsuboi. Sh-AM:69
Sunflower. J. Updike. Co-BN:60
Sunflower No. 1. Ch'in Tzu-hao.
  Pa-MV:60
Sunflowers. C. Scollard.
  Hu-MP:261
SUNIUM, CAPE
The First Day. N. Weiss.
  Ls-NY:240
Temple Fever: Sounion.
  J. De Longchamps. Ls-NY:231
SUNRISE: see also DAWN; MORNING
African Sunrise. G. Lutz.
  Du-RG:46
Early, Early Easter Day.
  A. Fisher. Br-SS:137, Mc-AW:66
From the Sacred Dulngulg Cycle.
  Tr-US I:243
El Hombre. W. Williams.
  Ho-LP:56
I Am like a Bear. Ho-SD:24
I'll Tell You how the Sun Rose.
  E. Dickinson. Br-SS:23,
  Ga-FB:291, La-PV:47, Re-TW:36,
  Sh-RP:167, Un-GT:251
A Miracle for Breakfast.
  E. Bishop. Mo-BG:8, Sh-AP:216
Morning. W. Blake. Sm-LG:49

Plainview. N. Momaday. Ni-CD:103
Prelude. R. Gilder. Fe-PL:395
Priests' Chant to Usher in the
  Dawn. Tr-US II:66
Riverside Drive. J. Rolnick.
  Ho-TY:166
Rubaiyat of Omar Khayyam.
  E. Fitzgerald. Al-VBP:832,
  Er-FA:43, Fe-FP:479, Gr-CT:329,
  Ha-PO:210, Ox-BN:526, Pa-GTB:329,
  Pa-SG:120
Song of a Sunrise Chinoi.
  Tr-US II:201
Sunday up the River.
  J. Thomson. Al-VBP:1009
Sunrise. F. Garcia Lorca.
  Bl-FP:84
Sunrise. C. Wood. Un-GT:250
The Sunrise. Da-SC:87
Sunrise on the Sea.
  W. Shakespeare. Gr-CT:198
SUNSET: see also EVENING; HUMOR -
  SUNSET; TWILIGHT
The After-Glow. M. Blind.
  Ox-BN:849
Any Sunset. L. Untermeyer.
  Un-GT:251
Archibald's Example. E. Robinson.
  Gr-CC:183
Autumn Tune. Chang Hsiu-ya.
  Pa-MV:31
born of leaf and branch.
  M. D'Elia. Ad-II:38
Calm of Evening. Hsieh T'iao.
  Le-MW:57
A Cautious Crow. Basho.
  Be-CS:35
Choral Songs, II, III.
  Tr-US II:114
Country Cottage. Tu Fu. Rx-OH:20
The Dark Hills. E. Robinson.
  Bo-GJ:189, Bo-HF:133, Er-FA:196,
  Ha-PO:89, Pe-OA:22, Un-MA:126,
  Wi-LT:111
Dusk. E. Recht. Le-M:84
Evening. J. Stephens. Un-MB:260
An Evening Glow. K. Takahashi.
  Le-TA:34
Evening Gold. J. Rolnick.
  Ho-TY:164
The Evening Sun. N. Akukawa.
  Sh-AM:121
The Evening Sun. E. Brontë.
  De-CH:429
God's Virtue. B. Barnes. Go-BP:22
Human Things. H. Nemerov. Co-BN:200
I'll Tell You how the Sun Rose.
  E. Dickinson. Br-SS:23,
  Ga-FB:291, La-PV:47, Re-TW:36,
  Sh-RP:167, Un-GT:251

June Twilight. J. Masefield.
  Go-BP:131
The Late, Last Rook. R. Hodgson.
  Un-MB:190
Legend. J. Weaver. Br-AF:197
Margaritae Sorori. W. Henley.
  Go-BP:237, Ha-PO:127, Ox-BN:884,
  Rv-CB:948, Un-MB:57
Metaphor. C. Smith. De-FS:185
The Mountain Afterglow.
  J. Laughlin. Ca-VT:409
New Auld Lang Syne. Kuo Mo-jo.
  Hs-TC:34
Of the Going Down of the Sun.
  J. Bunyan. De-CH:431
On a River in Late Autumn.
  Liu Ta-pai. Hs-TC:8
On Eastnor Knoll. J. Masefield.
  De-CH:25, Ma-FW:122
Overlooking the Desert. Tu Fu.
  Rx-OH:18
The Red Sun Sinks Low. Boncho.
  Be-CS:11
Sailing on the Lake to the Ching
  River. Lu Yu. Rx-OH:113
The Setting of the Sun.
  M. Copeland. Le-M:197
The Song of the Setting Sun.
  Hu Feng. Hs-TC:378
The Spring Waters. Ping Hsin.
  Hs-TC:22
The Stone Harp. J. Haines.
  Sc-TN:75
The Sun Is Slowly Departing.
  Ho-SD:41
Sun Low in the West. Buson.
  Be-CS:27
Sunset. E. Cummings. Un-MA:470
Sunset. V. Lindsay. Rd-SS:5
Sunset. E. Muir. Go-BP:29
Sunset. Tai Wang-shu. Hs-TC:182
Sunset on the Sea. L. Ubell.
  Le-M:118
Sunset over the Aegean.
  G. Byron. Ox-BN:240
Sunsets. C. Sandburg. Un-MA:210
Tailor's Song. P. Dehn.
  Sm-MK:178
This Is My Rock. D. McCord.
  Br-SS:27, Fe-FP:10, La-PV:169
To Amoret Gone from Him.
  H. Vaughan. Rv-CB:407
Trees and Evening Sky.
  N. Momaday. Ni-CD:102
We Have Seen the Sun.
  Emperor Tenchi. Ba-ST:32
who are you, little i.
  e. cummings. Li-LC:21
SUNSHINE
  Merry Sunshine. Ch-B:25, Hu-MP:132

SUNSHINE — <u>cont'd</u>.
  Sing a Song of Sunshine.
    I. Eastwick. Br-SS:16
  The Sun. L. Handcock. Mc-AW:45
  Sunlight. Chang Hsiu-ya.
    Pa-MV:33
  The Sun's Frolic. C. Tringress.
    St-FS:116
  Sunshine. Ar-TP3:99, Wr-RM:97
  There's a Certain Slant of Light.
    E. Dickinson. Rv-CB:905,
    Sh-AP:128, Sm-LG:50,
    Un-MA:98, Wi-LT:4
  What Can Go Through. Re-RR:24
  Winter Nightfall. E. Olson.
    St-H:171
SUPERIOR, LAKE
  The Great Lake Suite, I.
    J. Reaney. Do-WH:48
SUPERMARKETS: see SATIRE –
    SUPERMARKETS
SUPERNATURAL: see also CHARMS;
    GHOSTS; HUMOR – SUPERNATURAL;
    MAGIC; MIRACLES; WITCHES AND
    WITCHCRAFT
  Ambushed by Angels. G. Davidson.
    De-FS:71
  The High Place at Marib.
    G. Code. De-FS:58
  Mythological Episode.
    R. Barlow. De-FS:13
  Ritual Song. Tr-US I:62
  The Skeptic. L. Williams.
    De-FS:220
  The Watcher. S. Coblentz.
    De-FS:57
SUPERSTITION: see also ASTROLOGY;
    CHARMS; FOLKLORE; FORTUNE
    TELLING; GHOSTS; HUMOR –
    SUPERSTITION; WITCHES AND
    WITCHCRAFT
  Atavism. E. Wylie. De-FS:225
  The Beetle in the Wood.
    B. Reece. Co-PT:40
  Church Going. P. Larkin.
    Br-TC:251, Pa-GTB:557,
    Un-MB:528, Wi-LT:754
  The Evil Eye. J. Ciardi.
    Ca-MB:19
  Flannan Isle. W. Gibson.
    Bl-OB:78, Co-SS:200, De-CH:395,
    Ha-PO:154, Hi-WP I:76
  Full Moon. R. Hayden.
    Ra-BP:135
  He Who Hanged Himself.
    Tsou Ti-fan. Hs-TC:341
  I Am a Cowboy in the Boat of Ra.
    I. Reed. Ad-PB:330
  The Jovial Gentlemen.
    D. Hoffman. Ca-MB:62

  The Land in My Mother.
    N. Hashimoto. Le-TA:17
  Night of the Scorpion. N. Ezekial.
    Al-PI:96
  Old Moon Planter. J. Knoepfle.
    St-H:94
  Old Wife's Song. E. Farjeon.
    Sh-RP:15
  The Rime of the Ancient Mariner.
    S. Coleridge. Al-VBP:679,
    Bo-FP:301, Co-RG:60, Co-SS:131,
    De-CH:364, Er-FA:318, Fe-FP:147,
    Ga-FB:105, Gr-TG:61, Ha-PO:15,
    Hi-WP II:68, Ma-YA:146, Ni-JP:52,
    Ox-BN:139, Rv-CB:658, Sm-LG:312,
    Un-GT:30
  Runes IX. H. Nemerov. Du-SH:100
  Tapers. F. Gray. De-FS:98
  This Is Halloween. D. Thompson.
    Ar-TP3:186, Ha-YA:121, La-PH:12
  The Wife of Bath's Tale.
    G. Chaucer. Al-VBP:14
  Witchwood. M. Justus.
    Br-SS:68, Ju-CP:75
SUPPER: see also HUMOR – SUPPER
  Alice's Supper. L. Richards.
    Hu-MP:18
  Hot Boiled Beans. Wr-RM:61
  How to Sleep Easy. Ag-HE:71,
    Mo-MGT:22
  The Somerset Dam for Supper.
    J. Holmes. Ni-JP:29
SURFING
  Song for a Surf-Rider.
    S. Allen. Cr-SS:30
SURGEONS AND SURGERY: see also
    AMPUTATIONS; HUMOR – SURGEONS
    AND SURGERY; PHYSICIANS
  Before. W. Henley. Un-MB:54
  A Correct Compassion.
    J. Kirkup. Ma-FW:141,
    Pl-IO:188
  In a Surgery Room.
    T. Yamamoto. Sh-AM:128
  Surgeons Must Be Very Careful.
    E. Dickinson. Pl-IO:144,
    Rv-CB:915
SURPRISES
  Anna Elise. Gr-EC:115, Ir-BB:145,
    Lo-LL:84
  Gnomes, II. Tr-US I:124
  O Stay, Sweet Love. Un-MW:32
  The Pasty. Mo-MGT:158, Mo-NR:126
  Present. M. Potter. Br-BC:101
  Surprise. H. Behn. Br-BC:97
  Surprises. J. Soule. Br-BC:97
  The Unforeseen. C. Roxlo. Tr-MR:58
SURREY, ENG.
  Potpourri from a Surrey Garden.
    J. Betjeman. Co-FB:326, En-PC:81

SURVEYING
  The Survey. D. Walcott. Sa-B:217
SURVIVAL: see also HUMOR -
    SURVIVAL; SATIRE - SURVIVAL
  Aware, Aware. T. Combs. Br-TC:75
  For de Lawd. L. Clifton.
    Ad-PB:306, Br-TC:71
  I Shall Laugh Purely. R. Jeffers.
    Wi-LT:263
  The Lost Dancer. J. Toomer.
    Ad-PB:34
  Midsummer. J. Scully.
    Br-TC:359, Pe-OA:270
  Nature or Man. P. Curry.
    Me-WF:51
  Root Cellar. T. Roethke.
    Co-BN:219, Ho-LP:43
  The Scythians. A. Blok.
    Ca-MR:198
  The Sea Turtle and the Shark.
    M. Tolson. Ad-PB:44, Ad-PE:40
  Soviet Russia. S. Yesenin.
    Ca-MR:110
  Staying Alive. D. Wagoner.
    Co-BN:160, Du-SH:183, La-RM:61,
    Mo-TS:9, Pe-M:38
  Still Here. L. Hughes.
    Gr-BT:151, Ra-BP:83
  Survival. J. Welch. Ni-CD:239
  Survival This Way. S. Ortiz.
    Ni-CD:158
  Under Oaks. J. Dickey.
    Ls-NY:122
SUSANNA AND THE ELDERS
  Peter Quince at the Clavier.
    W. Stevens. Al-VBP:1142,
    Br-TC:415, Gr-CC:62, No-CL:43,
    Pe-OA:66, Un-MA:240, Wi-LT:142
SUSPENSE
  As I Step over a Puddle at the End
    of Winter I Think on an Ancient
    Chinese Governor. J. Wright.
    Kh-VA:73, St-H:254
  Foul Shot. E. Hoey. Du-RG:112,
    Fl-HH:53
  Volcano. I. Van Sertima. Sa-B:41
  Welsh Incident. R. Graves.
    Hi-WP II:114
SUSPICION: see also DOUBT;
    HUMOR - SUSPICION
  Corner. R. Pomeroy.
    Ad-CI:64, Du-SH:39
  A Joyous Reveling Song Sung by
    the Wood Rats. Su-FVI:59,
    Tr-US II:113
  Mary and Gabriel. Ga-S:58
  Poem. E. Brathwaite. Sa-B:169
  Simile. N. Momaday. Ni-CD:101
  Small Change. T. Ostrovskaya.
    Mo-MI:86

SUSSEX, ENG.: see also HUMOR -
    SUSSEX, ENG.
  On the South Downs.
    S. Teasdale. Un-MA:267
  St. Valentine's Day.
    W. Blunt. Al-VBP:1054
  The South Country. H. Belloc.
    Un-MB:168
  Sussex. R. Kipling. Pa-HT:128
SUTTER, JOHN AUGUSTUS
  John Sutter. Y. Winters.
    Ha-PO:72, Un-MA:549
SUWANEE RIVER
  Swanee River. S. Foster.
    Er-FA:428, Se-PR:256
SWAGMEN: see TRAMPS
SWALLOWS
  Barn Swallow. C. Bell.
    Ls-NY:208
  Bat. D. Lawrence. Pa-GTB:458
  The Children's Song.
    Fe-FP:476
  Description Is a Bird.
    M. Ondaatje. Ca-BP:8
  The Emperor's Bird's-Nest.
    H. Longfellow. Hu-MP:419,
    Re-BS:14
  Folk Song. Bo-FP:213
  Four Birds. W. Blake. Gr-CT:93,
    Gr-GB:63, Gr-TG:31
  Itylus. A. Swinburne. Gr-CT:104
  The Red-Throated. M. Saito.
    Sh-AM:144
  Sixth-Month Song in the Foothills.
    G. Snyder. Ha-WR:7
  Song. T. Beddoes. Re-BS:8
  The Swallow. L. Aikin. Ox-BC:110
  The Swallow. C. Gasztold.
    Re-BS:31
  The Swallow. Otsuyu. Le-MW:30
  The Swallow. C. Rossetti.
    Un-GB:16, Un-GT:64
  Swallow Song. Da-SC:97,
    Tr-US II:266
  Swallow Tails. T. Robinson.
    Fe-FP:294
  The Swallows. E. Arnold.
    Se-PR:109
  The Swallows. E. Coatsworth.
    Li-LC:32
  Swallows. T. Ferril. Ca-BP:20,
    Du-RG:27, La-RM:83
  The Swallows. A. Young.
    Co-BBW:245
  To Sparrows Fighting. W. Davies.
    Re-BS:30
  Upon the Swallow. J. Bunyan.
    Ox-BC:36
  We Saw the Swallows. G. Meredith.
    Ox-BN:690, Pa-GTB:369

SWAMPS: see MARSHES
SWANEE RIVER: see SUWANEE RIVER
SWANS
  And Other Poems. R. Morgan.
    Ma-FW:95
  The Boy and the Geese.
    P. Fiacc. Co-PI:43
  Down the Stream the Swans All
    Glide. S. Milligan.
    Co-OT:60, St-FS:62
  The Dying Swan. A. Tennyson.
    Ho-WR:139
  The Dying Swan. Gr-CT:98
  Gates of the Rockies.
    J. Daugherty. Sh-RP:301
  The Half of Life. F. Hölderlin.
    Un-R:19
  Horsey Gap. Gr-GB:172
  Hour for Swans. H. Vinal.
    Ke-TF:332
  The Icebound Swans. Rd-OA:199
  Leda and the Swan. W. Yeats.
    Pa-GTB:427, Un-MB:113,
    Wi-LT:82
  Love Is a Keeper of Swans.
    H. Wolfe. Un-MB:303
  Love the Wild Swan. R. Jeffers.
    Un-MA:367
  A Madrigal. R. Greene.
    Al-VBP:144
  No Swan So Fine. M. Moore.
    Gr-CC:179
  A Riddle from the Old English.
    Gr-CT:97
  Ritual. G. Davidson. Ls-NY:71
  Roast Swan Song. Ma-FW:99
  The Silver Swan. Co-PU:145,
    Gr-CT:98, Gr-SS:25, Sm-LG:91
  Sitting Pretty. M. Fishback.
    Fe-PL:201
  Song. Co-PU:109, Rv-CB:137
  Song: Fish in the Unruffled
    Lakes. W. Auden. Un-MB:464
  Swan. E. Lowbury. Pa-GTB:535
  The Swan. Ch-B:61, Fe-FP:364,
    Gr-CT:11, Wr-RM:122
  The Swan. De-TT:58
  The Swan Bathing. R. Pitter.
    Un-MB:405
  Swan Curse. A. Sullivan.
    Ls-NY:213
  Swans. L. Durrell. Un-MB:489
  The Swans. A. Young. Hi-WP II:43
  Swans at Night. M. Gilmore.
    Co-BBW:239
  The Swan's Nest. P. Griffin.
    Go-BP:80
  Tell Me, O Swan. Kabir. Al-PI:55
  This Room Is Full of Clocks.
    I. Gardner. St-H:74
  We Saw the Swallows. G. Meredith.
    Ox-BN:690, Pa-GTB:369
  Wild Swans. E. Millay.
    Un-MA:443
  The Wild Swans at Coole.
    W. Yeats. Go-BP:79, Gr-CT:97,
    Hi-WP II:128, Ma-FW:260,
    Pa-HT:143, Un-MB:112
SWEDEN: see also SWEDISH VERSE
  A Carriage from Sweden. M. Moore.
    Br-TC:297, Wi-LT:271
SWEDISH VERSE
  Beauty Is Most at Twilight's
    Close. P. Lagerkvist.
    Pa-SG:108
  Cradle Song. C. Bellman.
    Fe-FP:466
  The Eternal. E. Tegnér.
    Pa-SG:206
  Locked In. I. Gustafson.
    Co-PT:24
  Swedish Folk Song. Bo-FP:280
SWEET PEAS
  Air. T. Clark. Mc-EA:50
  Sweet Peas. J. Keats. Bo-FP:254,
    Br-SG:32, Ch-B:60, Hu-MP:245
SWEET POTATOES: see HUMOR -
    SWEET POTATOES
SWIFT, JONATHAN
  On the Death of Doctor Swift 3-5.
    J. Swift. Al-VBP:517, 519
SWIFTNESS: see SPEED
SWIMMING AND DIVING: see also
    HUMOR - SWIMMING AND DIVING;
    SKIN AND SCUBA DIVING
  At the Carnival. A. Spencer.
    Hu-PN:62
  Come On In. Mo-SD:141
  The Dive. C. Gould. Fl-HH:11
  The Diver. R. Hayden. Be-MA:66,
    Du-SH:127, Ra-BP:136
  The Diver. W. Ross. Do-WH:44
  The Divers. P. Quennell.
    Un-MB:427
  Diving. S. Murano. Sh-AM:87
  Duck-Chasing. G. Kinnell.
    Br-TC:238, Ca-VT:599
  East Anglian Bathe. J. Betjeman.
    Mo-SD:144
  Evening Gold. J. Rolnick. Ho-TY:164
  First Lesson. P. Booth.
    Br-TC:60, Mo-SD:165
  400-Meter Freestyle. M. Kumin.
    Mo-SD:60
  High Diver. R. Francis.
    Mo-SD:142
  Kalymniad, Part II. R. Lax.
    Sc-TN:129
  The Lesson. J. Krows.
    Au-SP:186

The Lifeguard. J. Dickey.
  Pe-OA:277, Pe-SS:88
Of Swimming in Lakes and
  Rivers. B. Brecht. Mo-SD:96
The Old Swimmer. C. Morley.
  Mo-SD:178
The Old Swimmin'-Hole. J. Riley.
  Er-FA:241
The River. D. Short. Du-SH:129
A Shropshire Lad. J. Betjeman.
  Ca-MB:70
Song for a Camper. J. Farrar.
  Ha-YA:66
The Strong Swimmer. W. Benét.
  Hu-PN:500
The Swimmer. S. Hagiwara.
  Sh-AM:48
The Swimmer. J. Ransom.
  Mo-SD:98
Swimmers. L. Untermeyer.
  Mo-SD:143
Swimming. C. Scollard.
  Fe-FP:112, Hu-MP:41
A Year Later. M. Hoberman.
  Ho-ME:30
SWINBURNE, ALGERNON CHARLES
To Swinburne. Shao Hsün-mei.
  Hs-TC:128
SWINE: see PIGS
SWINGS AND SWINGING
The Big Swing-Tree Is Green
  Again. M. Carr. Br-SS:158
The Child Sways on the Swing.
  Issa. Le-MW:104
A Father Swings His Child.
  W. Snodgrass. Mc-WS:141
How Can You Travel. Re-RR:53
On a Fat and Spiny Pine.
  Gr-BB:7
Swing. H. Ohashi. Le-TA:40
The Swing. R. Stevenson.
  Ar-TP3:107, Au-SP:196, Bo-FP:102,
  Bo-GJ:25, Er-FA:485, Fr-MP:19,
  Hu-MP:35, La-PP:64, La-PV:5,
  Li-LC:20, Pe-FB:28
A Swing Song. W. Allingham.
  Ch-B:111, Fe-FP:110,
  Hu-MP:35, Pe-FB:66
Swing Song. H. Behn. Ar-TP3:108
Swing Song. Bo-FP:103
Swing Swong. Gr-EC:286
Swinging. Mo-MGT:201
Swinging on a Gate. On-TW:31
The Swings in the Park.
  C. McGlynn. La-IH:67
SWITHIN, SAINT
St. Swithin. D. Henderson.
  Br-SM:163
St. Swithin's Day. Ir-BB:231,
  Li-LB:161, Un-GT:23

SWITZERLAND: see also names of
  towns, as ZERMATT, SWITZ.
The Country of a Thousand Years
  of Peace. J. Merrill.
  En-PC:240
SWITZERLAND - HISTORY AND
PATRIOTISM
England and Switzerland, 1802.
  W. Wordsworth. Li-SR:108,
  Pa-GTB:209
The Patriot's Pass-Word.
  J. Montgomery. Sp-OG:19
SWORDS: see also SATIRE - SWORDS
Ballade. E. Rostand. Co-RM:81
The Knifesmith. D. Howard.
  Co-RM:90, Sm-MK:38
An Old Song. E. Bloomgarden.
  Ho-TY:75, Pa-SG:147
The Sword. Abu Bakr. Lo-TY:44
The Sword of Robert E. Lee.
  A. Ryan. Se-PR:36
Tubal Cain. C. Mackay. Hu-MP:407
SYCAMORE TREES
A London Plane-Tree. A. Levy.
  Hi-WP I:125
Love Song. Lo-TY:29
The Trees Are Down. C. Mew.
  Co-BN:146, Un-MB:164
Two Limericks. Ga-S:11
SYMBOLS
The Counterpart. E. Jennings.
  Wi-LT:741
The Dilly Song. Gr-GB:28
Fleeting Signs. G. Dumitrescu.
  Mc-AC:124
I Am the Flag. L. Jones.
  Vi-PP:184
What, My Son, Does Your Blanket
  Mean? Wo-HS:(30)
SYMPATHY: see also COMFORT;
  CONCERN (CARE); HUMOR -
  SYMPATHY; PITY; SATIRE -
  SYMPATHY
Afterwards. T. Hardy.
  Al-VBP:1050, Co-BN:210, De-CH:435,
  Gr-CT:353, Ni-JP:172, No-CL:284,
  Ox-BN:846, Pa-GTB:412, Rv-CB:944,
  Un-MB:31, Wi-LT:25
Alice Fell. W. Wordsworth.
  De-TT:105, Li-SR:102
And to the Young Men. M. Moore.
  Un-MA:577
The Animals Mourn with Eve.
  C. Rossetti. Rd-OA:197
Any Human to Another.
  C. Cullen. Tr-MR:160
As Long as We Are Not Alone.
  I. Emiot. Ho-TY:315
At the Lion's Cage.
  P. Dufault. Co-BBW:202

SYMPATHY — cont'd.

Awareness. D. Lee. Ad-BO:2,
   Ad-PB:421
Because I Am Poor. Ho-SD:16,
   Le-OE:55
The Bed Sheet and the Stranger.
   R. Zychlinska. Ho-TY:230
The Book of Job. H. Leivick.
   Ho-TY:126
Boy at the Window. R. Wilbur.
   Ho-TH:65, Pe-SS:27
The Children of the Poor.
   G. Brooks. Be-MA:80,
   En-PC:157, Ra-BP:166
Come, Serene Plainness. M. Leib.
   Ho-TY:89
The Comforters. D. Shorter.
   De-CH:259
A Development of Idiocy.
   E. Jones. Ox-BN:619
"Don't Care" and "Never Mind."
   J. Bangs. Er-FA:16
Esthetique du Mal, V.
   W. Stevens. Wi-LT:153
A Flower. D. Battiato.
   Me-WF:73
For Steph. W. Rose. Ni-CD:214
The Friend Who Just Stands By.
   B. Williams. Fe-PL:126
A Gest of Robyn Hode. Ox-BB:443
The Golden Net. W. Blake.
   Gr-SS:166
The Halt. J. Miles. Co-EL:108
Hard but Soft. W. Barbour.
   La-IH:29
Having Eyes That See. M. Morris.
   Sa-B:221
The Holy Women. W. Percy.
   Ke-TF:234
Home Burial. R. Frost.
   Pe-SS:15
I Know Neither English nor
   French. A. Stolzenberg.
   Ho-TY:269
I Want You to Read. E. Schwager.
   Ad-II:15
If Grief for Grief Can Touch
   Thee. E. Brontë. Ox-BN:599
If I Had Known. M. Davies.
   Ke-TF:129
If You Have a Friend. Er-FA:28
Interracial. G. Johnson.
   Hu-PN:78, Lo-TY:210
Is There No Thread to Bind Us?
   M. Peake. Gr-BT:102
The Jolly Company. R. Brooke.
   Sp-OG:346
Lamentation. A. Pratt. Al-WW:108
Loneliness. B. Jenkins.
   Du-RG:55, Pe-SS:114

The Loveliness of Love. G. Darley.
   Ox-BN:386, Pa-GTB:74
The Meadow Mouse. T. Roethke.
   Ad-PE:24, Mc-WS:45,
   Mo-TS:58, Rd-OA:33
Monkeys. P. Colum. Co-BBW:203
The Night Is Dark. H. Leivick.
   Ho-TY:118
Not in Vain. E. Dickinson.
   Bo-HF:140, Fe-PL:297
On Another's Sorrow. W. Blake.
   Al-VBP:614, Ga-FB:100,
   Rv-CB:591
Pain for a Daughter. A. Sexton.
   Mc-WS:142
Painter, Draw Me a Friend.
   M. Pavlova. Bo-RU:64
The Parson. O. Goldsmith.
   Hi-WP II:125
Poem. J. Wain. En-PC:230
Poet. D. Hayes. Bo-AN:92,
   Hu-PN:242
Porgy, Maria, and Bess.
   D. Heyward. Hu-PN:499
Prescience. D. Hayes. Hu-PN:243
Renascence. E. Millay.
   Er-FA:95, Un-MA:440
The Ritual to Read to Each
   Other. W. Stafford. Pe-SS:115
Santos, New Mexico. M. Sarton.
   Pl-EI:116
Search. R. Souster. Co-EL:137
She Came with Lips of Brown.
   B. Cox. La-IH:100
somewhere i have never traveled.
   e. cummings. Br-TC:81,
   Ca-VT:180, Mo-BG:88, Pe-SS:124,
   Un-MA:476, Un-MW:26, Wi-LT:363
Song. M. Holman. Jo-SA:86
Soundless. D. Witt. Ad-II:12
Strangeness of Heart.
   S. Sassoon. Tr-MR:260
Sympathy. P. Dunbar. Ad-PB:8,
   Bo-AN:13, Hu-PN:34
The Telephone. R. Frost. No-CL:193
There Was a Man. S. Crane.
   Un-MA:148
There's Snow on the Fields.
   C. Rossetti. De-TT:39
To Coleridge in Sicily.
   W. Wordsworth. Ox-BN:103
To One in Bedlam. E. Dowson.
   Un-MB:149
The Truth the Dead Know.
   A. Sexton. Un-MA:689
Walking Past. L. Martinez.
   La-IH:87
A Wanderer. N. Ayukawa. Sh-AM:123
The Wanderer Recalls the Past.
   W. Wordsworth. Ox-BN:92

The Warm of Heart. E. Coatsworth.
   Co-PU:66
West-Running Brook. R. Frost.
   Sh-AP:151, Sm-PT:138, Un-MA:182
A Window in the Breast.
   Gr-EC:219, Pa-SG:15
Without One Particle of Sentiment
   in His Being. M. Ooka.Sh-AM:134
The World and I. A. Reisen.
   Ho-TY:69
Worlds of Different Sizes.
   S. McPherson. Co-PU:71
Young Soul. I. Baraka.
   Mc-EA:32, Mo-TS:3, Ra-PB:220
Youth. Le-M:162
SYMPHONY ORCHESTRAS: see MUSIC
   AND MUSICIANS; ORCHESTRAS
SYNAGOGUES
   Vilna. M. Kulbak. Ho-TY:216
SYNGE, JOHN MILLINGTON
   A Memory. L. Strong. Co-PI:181
   The Municipal Gallery Revisited.
      W. Yeats. Pa-GTB:432
SYRACUSE, SIC.
   Syracuse. E. Coatsworth.Pa-HT:102
SYRINX (NYMPH): see PAN (GOD)
TABLE ETIQUETTE: see ETIQUETTE
TABLES: see HUMOR - TABLES
TABLEWARE: see HUMOR - TABLEWARE
TACT
   Civilities. T. Whitbread.Mo-SD:164
   Duty of the Student.
      E. Anthony. Un-GT:26
TADPOLES: see FROGS; TOADS
TAHITI: see also HUMOR - TAHITI
   Americans Are Afraid of Lizards.
      K. Shapiro. Br-AF:45
TAI SHAN (MOUNTAIN)
   The Most-Sacred Mountain.
      E. Tietjens. Pa-HT:87,
      Tr-MR:202
TAILORS: see also HUMOR - TAILORS
   Amends to the Tailors and
      Soutars. W. Dunbar. Rv-CB:70
   Sailor and Tailor. De-TT:127
   Tailor. E. Farjeon. Ox-BC:331
   The Tradesman. Bo-FP:116
TAILS (ANIMALS): see also HUMOR -
   TAILS (ANIMALS)
   Ducks' Ditty. K. Grahame.
      Ar-TP3:73, Au-SP:51, Bo-FP:68,
      Bo-GJ:50, Co-BBW:169, Fe-FP:182,
      Hu-MP:241, Ir-BB:78, La-PP:4,
      La-PV:130, Mc-WK:40, Ox-BC:328,
      Pe-FB:12, Tu-WW:84
   Holding Hands. L. Link.
      Ar-TP3:78, Au-SP:81, Fe-FP:172,
      Ja-PC:16, La-PP:57
   In the Fashion. A. Milne.
      La-PP:56, Sh-RP:31

Little Bo-Peep. Au-SP:13, Bo-FP:79,
   De-PO:14, Fr-WO:19, Ir-BB:129,
   Li-LB:40, Li-SR:126, Mo-MGT:160,
   Mo-NR:6, Wi-MG:28, Wr-RM:11
Tails. R. Bennett. Sh-RP:334
Tails. I. Russell. St-FS:64
TALIESIN (WELSH BARD)
   The Indignation of Taliesin.
      T. Peacock. Rv-CB:686
TALISMANS: see CHARMS; MAGIC
TALKATIVENESS: see SPEECH
TALL TALES
   The Ballad of Yukon Jake.
      E. Paramore. Co-RM:133
   Braggin' Bill's Fortytude.
      C. Hallock. Fi-BG:79
   The Caulker. M. Lewis. Co-PT:256
   The Cow Ate the Piper. Gr-GB:88
   The Coxswain's Line. H. Cressman.
      Sh-RP:255
   The Crocodile. Co-RM:65,Rv-CB:441
   Daley's Dorg Wattie. W. Goodge.
      Co-BBW:106
   The Derby Ram. Gr-GB:81, Ir-BB:70,
      Lo-LL:64, Mo-MGT:144, Wr-RM:64
   The Gray Goose. Bu-DY:27,
      Du-RG:122, Mc-WK:62
   A Gret Fight. R. Newell. Co-RM:179
   Idaho. Gr-GB:178
   Jack Was Every Inch a Sailor.
      Do-WH:18
   John Henry. Ab-MO:81, Bo-HF:104,
      Co-RM:225, Er-FA:407, Ga-S:124,
      Hi-TL:159, Ra-BP:12
   My Hat. S. Smith. Sm-MK:78
   A Nautical Extravaganza.
      W. Irwin. Co-PT:260
   Noah an' Jonah an' Cap'n John
      Smith. D. Marquis. Co-SS:189,
      Fe-PL:198, Sm-LG:195
   A Sailor's Yarn. J. Roche.
      Co-SS:93
   A Spider Danced a Cosy Jig.
      I. Layton. Do-WH:43
   The Story of Samuel Jackson.
      C. Leland. Co-PT:267
   Ten Thousand Years Ago. Co-OH:26
   They Have Yarns. C. Sandburg.
      Br-AF:106, Sh-RP:270,
      Un-GT:196, Un-MA:211
   Tywater. R. Wilbur. Ha-PO:124,
      Wi-LT:593
   Unholy Missions. B. Kaufman.
      Lo-TY:253
TALLNESS: see SIZE AND SHAPE
TAMALPAIS, MOUNT
   Andree Rexroth. K. Rexroth.
      Ca-VT:269
TAMAZUNCHALE, MEX.
   Tamazunchali. W. Bynner. Ls-NY:244

TAMERLANE
  The Bloody Conquests of Mighty
    Tamburlaine. C. Marlowe.
    Gr-CT:335
  Persepolis. C. Marlowe. No-CL:253
  Tamburlaine. C. Marlowe.
    Cl-DT:13, Hi-FO:89
  Tamburlaine the Great.
    C. Marlowe. Al-VBP:171
  Tamerlane. E. Poe. Sh-AP:42
TANAGRA, GR.
  Corinna to Tanagra. W. Landor.
    Al-VBP:708, Ox-BN:191
TANGERINES: see ORANGES
TANKA: see JAPANESE VERSE
TANZANIA
  Blue Tanganyika. L. Bethune.
    Ad-PB:311
TAOISM
  The Way of Life. Laotse.
    Ba-PO:7, Mc-WK:220
TAOS INDIANS: see also INDIANS
    OF NORTH AMERICA - VERSE-TIWA
  The Sacred Lands of the Blue
    Lake Forest. P. Bernal.
    Br-MW:57
TAPESTRY
  Crewel. N. Willard. Sc-TN:233
  The Lady with the Unicorn.
    V. Watkins. Br-TC:459
  The Tapestry. H. Nemerov.
    Ho-P:205
TAPIRS: see HUMOR - TAPIRS
TARANTELLAS: see DANCERS AND
    DANCING
TARANTULAS
  freddy the rat perishes.
    D. Marquis. La-OC:103,
    Pe-M:120
TARDINESS: see PUNCTUALITY
TARIFFS: see HUMOR - TARIFFS;
    SMUGGLING
TARPON
  Tarpon. L. Lieberman. Du-SH:124
TARSIERS: see HUMOR - TARSIERS
TARTARY
  Tartary. W. de la Mare.
    Ox-BC:325, Th-AS:146, Un-GT:105
  Turkestan. Ch'en T'ao. Cr-WS:8
TARTS (FOOD): see also PIES
  The Queen of Hearts.
    An-IP:(24), Bo-FP:54, Br-FF:(26),
    Ir-BB:263, Li-LB:56, Mo-MGT:122,
    Mo-NR:59, Wi-MG:71, Wr-RM:107
TATTLETALES: see also HUMOR -
    TATTLETALES
  Tell Tale, Tit. Mo-NR:101
TATTOOING
  Blackie, the Electric Rembrandt.
    T. Gunn. Ma-FW:130

TAURUS MOUNTAINS
  A Stream of Gold Honey.
    O. Mandelstam. Ca-MR:154
TAVERNS: see INNS AND TAVERNS
TAXCO, MEX.
  Taxco, Mexico. M. Uschold.
    Ke-TF:365
TAXES AND TAX COLLECTORS: see also
    SATIRE - TAXES AND TAX
    COLLECTORS
  The Deil's Awa wi' the Exciseman.
    R. Burns. Al-VBP:649
  Odell. J. Stephens. Un-MB:265
  The Toll Taker. P. Hubbell.
    Ar-TP3:13, Ho-CS:19
TAXICABS
  Can't Walk. Re-RR:40
  My Taxicab. J. Tippett. Hu-MP:46
    Hu-MP:46
  Taxis. R. Field. Ar-TP3:92,
    Au-SP:164, Fe-FP:245,
    Hu-MP:160, La-PP:36
TAY RIVER
  The Tay River Bridge Disaster.
    W. McGonagall. Na-EO:78
TEA: see also HUMOR - TEA;
    TEAKETTLES
  Canadian Folk Song.
    W. Campbell. Bo-FP:171
  The Cats Have Come to Tea.
    K. Greenaway. Bo-FP:58, Ch-B:101
  Coffee and Tea. Wr-RM:83
  Dining-Room Tea. R. Brooke.
    Un-MB:326
  The Five Little Fairies.
    M. Burnham. Bo-FP:311
  The Light-Housekeeper's
    White-Mouse. J. Ciardi.Bo-FP:282
  Milk for the Cat. H. Monro.
    Bl-OB:109, Co-BBW:137, Er-FA:233,
    Ga-BP:97, Re-TW:16, Sm-MK:160,
    Un-GT:47, Un-MB:236
  Polly and Sukey. Wr-RM:124
  Polly, Put the Kettle On.
    Bo-FP:58, Li-LB:31, Mo-CC:(31),
    Mo-MGT:86, Mo-NR:55, Mo-TL:71
  The Radish Is Blooming.
    Irina. Mo-MI:20
  Tea. Ch'u Ch'uang I. Rx-LT:54
  Tea Flowers. Rito. Hu-MP:304
  The Tea Party. K. Greenaway.
    Hu-MP:50
  The Tea Roaster. De-PP:36
TEA PARTIES: see PARTIES (ENTER-
    TAINMENT)
TEACHERS AND TEACHING: see also
    HUMOR - TEACHERS AND TEACHING;
    SATIRE - TEACHERS AND
    TEACHING; STUDENTS
  Academic. J. Reeves. To-MP:72

America Was Schoolmasters.
    R. Coffin. Mc-WK:173, Vi-PP:191
April Inventory. W. Snodgrass.
    Br-TC:398, Mc-EA:148, Wi-LT:819
At School-Close. J. Whittier.
    Se-PR:241
The Brothers. A. Groesbeck.
    De-FS:102
The Campus on the Hill.
    W. Snodgrass. Br-TC:397
Dame Duck's Lecture. St-FS:94
Death of a Schoolteacher.
    B. Hirshberg. Ke-TF:171
Desert School Ma'am. S. Andrews.
    Fi-BG:195
The Deserted Village.
    O. Goldsmith. Al-VBP:585,
    Er-FA:410, Hi-FO:178
Don Juan. G. Byron. Al-VBP:731
The Dunce. J. Prévert.
    Ma-FW:72
Elegy for Jane. T. Roethke.
    Br-TC:348, Pe-OA:204, Pe-SS:160,
    Sh-AP:213, Un-MA:598, Wi-LT:486
Elegy for the Rev. Mr. James B.
    Hodgson. J. Logan. St-H:111
First Lesson. P. Booth.
    Br-TC:60, Mo-SD:165
Hiawatha's Childhood.
    H. Longfellow. Ar-TP3:36,
    Fe-FP:405, Ga-FB:248, Gr-EC:100,
    Hu-MP:422, Li-SR:54, Mc-PR:80,
    Sh-RP:272
I Wish. N. Turner. Br-SS:156
In a Spring Still Not Written Of.
    R. Wallace. Co-BN:20
Instruction in the Art.
    P. Booth. Mo-SD:156
Love Sonnet to My Students.
    J. Solovay. Ke-TF:83
The Master. C.G.L. Pl-IO:185
Miss Norma Jean Pugh, First
    Grade Teacher. M. O'Neill.
    Ar-TP3:9
My Students. R. Sward. St-H:223
Nocturnal Song. Ho Ch'i-fang.
    Hs-TC:224
Our Teacher's Face. T. Yoshida.
    Le-TA:61
The Pay Is Good. R. Kell. To-MP:132
The Poet. W. Whitman.
    Un-MA:79
Religious Emphasis Week.
    C. Walsh. St-H:242
The Schoolmaster. J. Whittier.
    Un-GT:90
Schoolmaster. Y. Yevtushenko.
    Li-TU:136, Ma-FW:137
A Schoolmaster's Admonition.
    Ox-BC:21

A Schoolmaster's Precepts.
    J. Penkethman.   Ox-BC:26
Snowstorm. M. Kuramitsu.
    Le-TA:64
The Star Watcher. P. Davison.
    Br-TC:86
Subversive. W. Benét. Tr-MR:116
The Teacher. L. Hill. Hu-PN:52
Teacher. T. Kobayashi.
    Le-TA:53
teechur. D. Higgins. Pe-M:25
The Vanity of Human Wishes.
    J. Leax. Pe-M:65
Vergidemiarum. J. Hall.
    Al-VBP:267
The Village Schoolmaster.
    O. Goldsmith. Ha-PO:76
TEAKETTLES: see also HUMOR –
    TEAKETTLES
The Teakettle. V. Lapin.
    Mo-MI:52
TEARS
Hours of Idleness. G. Byron.
    Na-EO:71
Peeling Onions. A. Rich.
    Mo-BG:38
A Tear Rolled down My Cheek.
    C. O'John. Al-WW:63
Tears. W. Kraus. Su-FVI:10
Tears. L. Reese. Un-MA:110
Tears, Flow No More.
    Lord Herbert. Rv-CB:323
Tears, Idle Tears. A. Tennyson.
    Al-VBP:859, Er-FA:150, Ha-PO:150,
    Hi-WP II:144, Ox-BN:486
A Valediction of Weeping.
    J. Donne. Rv-CB:298
Waldheim Cemetery. R. Sward.
    St-H:217
The Weeper. R. Crashaw.
    Al-VBP:438
Why Is Happy? D. Whitewing.
    Al-WW:56
TEASING
For a Mocking Voice. E. Farjeon.
    Ar-TP3:148, Co-PM:60, De-CH:112
A Girl Speaks to Her Playmate.
    Al-PI:66
The Inky Boys. H. Hoffman.
    De-TT:21
Loneliness. J. Pomroy.Su-FVI:11
The Monkeys and the Crocodile.
    L. Richards. Ar-TP3:126,
    Au-SP:272, Br-SM:89, Fe-FP:175,
    Ir-BB:154, La-PP:54, Li-LB:98
Silly Sallie. W. de la Mare.
    Bl-OB:144
TECHNOLOGY: see also HUMOR –
    TECHNOLOGY
Outward. L. Simpson. Li-TU:253

TEDDY BEARS: see TOYS
TEEN AGE: see ADOLESCENCE; YOUTH
TEETH: see also DENTISTS AND
   DENTISTRY; HUMOR - TEETH
   A Charm Against the Toothache.
      J. Heath-Stubbs. Br-TC:177,
      Go-BP:49, Ma-FW:231, Sm-MK:194
   Ditty for a Child Losing His
      First Tooth. Do-CH:(7)
   I Have a Pink Pen. Re-RR:34
   I Know a Little Fence. Re-RR:28
   Little Tin. V. Burich.
      Bo-RU:26
   Thirty-Two White Calves.
      Ju-CP:10
   Thirty White Horses. Ar-TP3:99,
      Au-SP:25, Mo-MGT:154,
      Rv-ON:57, Wr-RM:52
   This Tooth. L. Hopkins.
      Ho-ME:15
TELEGRAPH: see also CABLES,
   SUBMARINE
   In the Telegraph Office.
      A. Kushner. Bo-RU:50
   The Line-Gang. R. Frost.
      Ma-FW:109
   Song of the Telegraph.
      Tr-US I:51
   Telegram. W. Wise. Ar-TP3:105
   Telegraph Poles. P. Dehn.
      Sm-MK:172
   Telegraph Wires. Tr-US II:272
   To a Vine-Clad Telegraph Pole.
      L. Untermeyer. Un-MA:307
   The Wires Are So Still and High.
      A. Wynne. Bo-FP:131
TELEPHONES: see also HUMOR -
   TELEPHONES; SATIRE - TELEPHONES
   Alexander Graham Bell Did Not
      Invent the Telephone.
      R. Coffin. Ar-TP3:46
   The Line-Gang. R. Frost.
      Ma-FW:109
   Long Distance. F. Eckman.
      St-H:49
   Manual System. C. Sandburg.
      Ar-TP3:13
   The Telephone. E. Field.
      Ad-CI:104
   Telephone Poles. J. Updike.
      Ma-FW:108, Mo-BG:119
   Toy Telephone. L. Hopkins.
      Ho-ME:23
   What Never Asks. Re-RR:18
TELESCOPES
   Conversation Between a Boy and
      Two Girls Looking Through a
      Spyglass. Tr-US II:294
   Field-Glasses. A. Young.
      Pa-GTB:467, Rv-CB:979
   Spyglass. H. Gregory. Ha-TP:133
   The Two Deserts. C. Patmore.
      Co-BN:220
TELEVISION: see also HUMOR -
   TELEVISION; SATIRE - TELEVISION
   Almost Any Evening. P. McGinley.
      Ho-TH:70
   Aunts Watching Television.
      J. Pudney. To-MP:71
   The Forecast. D. Jaffe.
      Du-RG:117
   How the Sestina (Yawn) Works.
      A. Waldman. Mc-EA:23
   Mousemeal. H. Nemerov.
      Br-TC:315
   Watching Television. R. Bly.
      Ha-TP:27
   The Western Movies. H. Ito.
      Le-TA:27
   The Winning of the TV West.
      J. Alexander. Bo-HF:97,
      Br-AF:153, Mc-WK:172
TELLING TIME: see also CLOCKS AND
   WATCHES; SUNDIALS
   Bell Horses, Bell Horses, What
      Time of Day. Ar-TP3:174,
      Bo-FP:123, Br-SS:5, Ir-BB:190,
      Mo-MGT:173, Wr-RM:113
   The Chronometer. A. Sullivan.
      Mc-WK:120
TÉMÉRAIRE (SHIP)
   The Fighting Téméraire.
      H. Newbolt. Sp-OG:76
TEMPER: see IRASCIBILITY
TEMPLES: see also SYNAGOGUES
   At Feng Ting Temple. Li Po.
      Le-MW:41
   The Bat. Sun Yü-t'ang. Hs-TC:119
   The First Day. N. Weiss.
      Ls-NY:240
   Hero and Leander. C. Marlowe.
      Al-VBP:170
   Kanya-Kumari. K. Subramanyan.
      Al-PI:146
   A Monk. Pien Chih-lin. Hs-TC:161
   Morning at the Temple of Kobai.
      E. Shiffert. Ls-NY:257
   On the Pagoda. Chung Ting-wen.
      Pa-MV:74
   Over a Ruined Temple.
      K. Takahama. Sh-AM:162
   Over the Paving Stones.
      T. Miyoshi. Sh-AM:83
   The Pale Temple Bell.
      Mu Mu-t'ien. Hs-TC:188
   Pilgrimage. Jao Meng-k'an.
      Hs-TC:108
   A Prayer to Be Restored to the
      Sanctuary. Bible. O.T.
      Psalms. Me-PH:22

The Problem. R. Emerson.
  Sh-AP:26
Spring Comes to a Little Temple.
  Ch'en Meng-chia. Hs-TC:117
Tanka. Y. Aizu. Sh-AM:142
The Temple. J. Johnson.
  Tr-MR:203
Temple Fever: Sounion.
  J. De Longchamps. Ls-NY:231
A Temple Room. S. Takano.
  Sh-AM:168
Visiting Tsan, Abbot of Ta-Yun.
  Tu Fu. Rx-OH:7
TEMPTATION: see also HUMOR -
  TEMPTATION
After Reading Certain Books.
  M. Coleridge. Pl-EI:74
Alison Gross. De-CH:406,
  Fo-OG:36, Ma-BB:108, Ox-BB:54
A Ballad of a Nun. J. Davidson.
  Pa-OM:138, Un-MB:74
The Book of Job. H. Leivick.
  Ho-TY:126
Brown Adam. Ma-BB:154,
  Ox-BB:162
Dabbling in the Dew. De-CH:194
Eve. Y. Fichman. Me-PH:82
Eve. R. Hodgson. De-CH:465,
  Ha-PO:41, Hi-WP II:95,
  Na-EO:105, Pa-OM:286,Sm-MK:58,
  Un-MB:186, Wi-LT:123
From the Underworld.
  H. Blaikley. Mo-GR:20
The Girl Who Took Care of the
  Turkeys. Te-FC:67
Greek Anthology, III. Un-MW:174
Hugh of Lincoln. De-CH:408,
  Ox-BB:317
I Almost Did — Very Nigh.
  E. Turner. Gr-TG:15
I Meant to Do My Work Today.
  R. Le Gallienne. Ar-TP3:116,
  Au-SP:348, Hu-MP:69, La-PP:6,
  Th-AS:78, Un-GB:22, Un-GT:250
The Life and Death of Jason.
  W. Morris. Al-VBP:1011
The Mocking Bird. Ir-BB:126,
  Mo-MGT:89
Now the Lusty Spring.
  J. Fletcher. Al-VBP:278
Odes to Nea, II. T. Moore.
  Ox-BN:207
Orpheus and Eurydice. Ovid.
  Mo-GR:21
Parfum Exotique.
  C. Baudelaire. Un-MW:194
The Pedlar. W. de la Mare.
  Sp-OG:181
The Quip. G. Herbert.
  Ma-YA:92, Rv-CB:354

The Sirens' Song. Homer.
  Mo-GR:13
Song of Liang Chou.
  Ou Yang Hsiu. Rx-OH:55
Sonnet 41. W. Shakespeare.
  Rv-CB:220
The Spider and the Fly.
  M. Howitt. De-TT:60,
  Er-FA:421, Fe-FP:530, Gr-EC:144,
  Ox-BC:158, Pe-FB:56
Tales of Brave Ulysses.
  E. Clapton. Mo-GR:11
Ulysses and the Siren.
  S. Daniel. Al-VBP:154
Wise Sarah and the Elf.
  E. Coatsworth. Co-PM:36
TEN COMMANDMENTS: see also
  SATIRE - TEN COMMANDMENTS
The Jew. I. Rosenberg.Un-MB:352
The Ten Commandments. Ox-BC:57
TENANTS: see LANDLORDS AND TENANTS
TENEMENT HOUSES
All the Mornings. R. Sward.
  St-H:219
The Imprisoned II.
  R. Fitzgerald. Br-TC:126
Sitting upon the Koala Bear
  Statue. J. Tomasello.La-IH:120
TENNESSEE: see also names of
  towns, as MEMPHIS, TENN.
Anecdote of the Jar. W. Stevens.
  Ho-LP:42, Un-MA:240
The Homecoming Singer.
  J. Wright. Ad-PB:279
Kentucky Belle. C. Woolson.
  Ha-PO:133, Un-GT:192
Street Scene - 1946.
  K. Porter. Hu-PN:539
These Old Cumberland Mountain
  Farms. Kr-OF:189
When It's Iris Time in Tennessee.
  W. Waid. Se-PR:285
TENNESSEE VALLEY AUTHORITY
The Song of Cove Creek Dam.
  Em-AF:757
TENNIS: see also HUMOR - TENNIS;
  SQUASH (GAME)
Adulescentia. R. Fitzgerald.
  Mo-SD:33
A Ballade of Lawn Tennis.
  F. Adams. Mo-SD:32
Old Tennis Player. G. Brooks.
  Mo-SD:158
The Olympic Girl. J. Betjeman.
  Mo-SD:34
A Snapshot for Miss Bricka.
  R. Wallace. Mo-SD:35
A Subaltern's Love-Song.
  J. Betjeman. Br-TC:43,
  Mc-WS:58, Na-EO:147, Un-MW:62

TENNIS — cont'd.
  Tennis. M. Avison. Fl-HH:37
  Tennis in San Juan. R. Denney.
    Mo-SD:36
TENNYSON, ALFRED TENNYSON, 1ST BARON
    (LORD TENNYSON): see HUMOR-
    TENNYSON, ALFRED TENNYSON, 1ST
    BARON (LORD TENNYSON)
TEPEES: see WIGWAMS
TERMITES: see also HUMOR - TERMITES
  Metropolitan Nightmare.
    S. Benét. Pl-IO:115
  The Termites. R. Hillyer.
    Rd-OA:159
TERNS: see GULLS
TERRAPINS: see TURTLES
TERROR: see FEAR
TERTULLIAN
  The Good Shepherd with the Kid.
    M. Arnold. Go-BP:286
TESTS: see EXAMINATIONS
TEVIOT RIVER
  A Father's Notes of Woe.
    W. Scott. Ox-BN:125
TEXAS: see also THE ALAMO; BEAN,
    ROY; HUMOR - TEXAS; and names
    of towns, as GALVESTON, TEX.
  Ballade of Boot-Hill. Fi-BG:110
  Cattle. B. Nance. Fi-BG:35
  In Texas. M. Sarton. Ke-TF:362
  In Texas Grass. Q. Troupe.
    Ad-PB:443
  Lasca. F. Desprez. Fi-BG:208
  Texas. A. Lowell. Br-AF:143
  Texas Bus Ride. K. Porter.
    Ke-TF:363
  Texas, Our Texas. O. Wright.
    Se-PR:286
  Texas Trains and Trails.
    M. Austin. Ar-TP3:85, Au-SP:154
THAI-LAOS VERSE
  Dialogue. Tr-US II:192
  Night Song. Tr-US II:192
  On My Short-Sightedness.
    Prem Chaya. Ma-FW:179
THAI-SIAMESE VERSE
  Funeral Poem. Tr-US II:191
THAÏS
  Alexander's Feast. J. Dryden.
    Ho-WR:100, Ma-YA:107, Pa-GTB:105
THAMES RIVER
  Bab-Lock-Hythe. L. Binyon.
    Hi-WP II:38, Mo-SD:132
  Ballad of the Two Tapsters.
    V. Watkins. Ca-MB:91
  Chaucer's Thames. W. Morris.
    Cl-FC:25
  Cooper's Hill. J. Denham. Al-VBP:442
  Impression du Matin. O. Wilde.
    Un-MB:67
  The Lover to the Thames of
    London. G. Turberville.
    Gr-CT:298
  On the Way to Kew. W. Henley.
    Al-VBP:1068, Ox-BN:885
  Prothalamion. E. Spenser.
    Al-VBP:100, Gr-CT:298,
    Pa-GTB:32
  Why Should I Care for the Men
    of Thames? W. Blake.
    Gr-CT:304, Rv-CB:603
THANKFULNESS: see GRATITUDE
THANKSGIVING DAY
  The Feast Day. A. McDonnall.
    Bo-FP:159
  The First Thanksgiving.
    N. Turner. Ha-YA:136, Ja-PA:56
  The First Thanksgiving Day.
    M. Preston. Hi-TL:24
  First Thanksgiving of All.
    N. Turner. Br-SS:80, Fe-FP:410,
    Sh-RP:232, Vi-PP:52
  Harvest Hymn. J. Whittier.
    Se-PR:211
  If I Were a Pilgrim Child.
    R. Bennett. Ha-YA:137,
    Sh-RP:304
  The Little Girl and the Turkey.
    D. Aldis. Ag-HE:9
  The Mournful Pumpkin. E. Jay.
    Ja-HH:48
  November's Come. J. Lincoln.
    Sh-RP:233
  The Pilgrims Came. A. Wynne.
    Hu-MP:344, Ja-PA:54, Mc-AW:71
  Prayer for Thanksgiving.
    E. Voswinkel. Ke-TF:209
  The Pumpkin. J. Whittier.
    Co-PS:148, Se-PR:210
  Simon Soggs' Thanksgiving.
    W. Croffut. Co-PT:120
  Squirrels' Thanksgiving.
    K. Dee. Ja-HH:43
  Thanksgiving. I. Eastwick.
    Br-SG:103
  Thanksgiving. R. Emerson.
    Au-SP:373, Bo-FP:161
  Thanksgiving. Ja-PA:59
  Thanksgiving Day. L. Child.
    Bo-FP:156, Br-SS:83, Ch-B:94,
    Fe-FP:84, Gr-EC:232, Hu-MP:343,
    La-PH:18, Un-GT:278
  Thanksgiving Drumsticks.
    L. Blair. Ja-HH:46
  A Thanksgiving Fable.
    O. Herford. Ja-PA:58
  Thanksgiving Gobbler. K. Dee.
    Ja-HH:47
  Thanksgiving Magic. R. Bennett.
    Br-SS:82

Thanksgiving Time. Au-SP:372,
  Bo-FP:155
Thanksgiving Wishes.
  A. Guiterman. Co-PS:146
Their Thanksgiving Day.
  L. Driscoll. Bo-FP:161
Turkey Time. Bo-FP:156, Ch-B:92
What the Little Girl Said.
  L. Blair. Ja-HH:44
THAWS: see also HUMOR - THAWS
  March 8, 1849. H. Thoreau.
    La-RM:158
  Snow Harvest. A. Young.
    Cl-FC:34, Co-BN:191
  The Snow Is Thawing. Gr-BB:21
  The Snow Thaws. Issa.
    Le-MW:90, Ma-FW:11
  Thaw. W. Gibson. Co-EL:73,
    Co-PU:75
  The Thaw. J. Matthews. Ha-WR:5
  Thaw. E. Thomas. Co-EL:116,
    Ho-LP:37, Ma-FW:10, Pa-GTB:443,
    Re-BS:18, Un-MB:217
  Thaw. E. Tietjens. Mc-AW:6
  To the Thawing Wind. R. Frost.
    Ha-LO:82
  A Warm Winter Day. J. Cooper.
    Co-BN:187
THEATERS: see also ACTORS AND
    ACTING; HUMOR - THEATERS;
    PUPPETS
  At the Theater. R. Field.
    Fe-FP:252, Hu-MP:55
  Faust. J. Ashbery. Br-TC:16
  I Shall Not See the Famous
    Phedre. O. Mandelstam.
    Ca-MR:150
THEOTOCOPOULOS, KYRIAKOS:
    see GRECO, EL
THERESA, SAINT (1515-1582):
    see also AVILA, SP.
  Conversation in Avila.
    P. McGinley. Pl-EI:108
THERMOPYLAE, GR.
  The Great Dead at Thermopylae.
    Simonides. Pa-SG:8
  On the Army of Spartans, Who
    Died at Thermopylae.
    Simonides of Ceos. Gr-CT:378
  Thermopylae 1941. C. Trypanis.
    Cr-WS:33
  The Thespians at Thermopylae.
    N. Cameron. Pa-GTB:498
THIEVES: see also HUMOR - THIEVES
  Ballad of the Broomtails.
    Fi-BG:143
  Black Bart. Fi-BG:139
  The Boys and the Apple-Tree.
    A. O'Keeffe. De-TT:120
  Buckinghamshire. Gr-GB:169

The Cat and the Miser.
  M. Van Doren. Ha-TP:37
Charley, Charley. Br-FF:14
The Crafty Farmer. Ar-TP3:16
Cruel Tom. Rv-ON:94
Dick o' the Cow. Ox-BB:538
Dingty Diddlety. Mo-TL:22
Dust or Bust. Fi-BG:51
Effort at Speech. W. Meredith.
  Ho-P:181
Four Texas Train Robbers.
  Fi-BG:55
The Hold-Up. D. Wagoner.
  Ha-TP:19
The Horse Thief. W. Benét.
  Pa-OM:300, Un-MA:324
I Stole Brass. Gr-CT:10
Jack Hall. Co-RM:99
Jamie Telfer of the Fair Dodhead.
  Ox-BB:549
The Lament of the Border Cattle
  Thief. R. Kipling. Co-RM:159
Man of Derby. Mo-MGT:23,
  Wr-RM:116
The Man with Nought. De-TT:45,
  Mo-MGT:73, Wr-RM:88
Men's Song at a Wedding.
  Tr-US I:127
A Murder. L. Wolf. Ho-TY:224
Nauty Pauty. Ag-HE:38, Mo-MGT:135
Noonday Sun. K. and B. Jackson.
  Ar-TP3:33, Fe-FP:161
The Queen of Hearts. An-IP:(24),
  Bo-FP:54, Br-FF:(26), Ir-BB:263,
  Li-LB:56, Mo-MGT:122, Mo-NR:59,
  Wi-MG:71, Wr-RM:107
Robbers. Gr-EC:282
Shoplifter. S. Edwards.
  Hu-NN:82
Shub-Ad. R. Barlow. De-FS:11
Somebody Stole. Ju-CP:34
Taffy Was a Welshman.
  Co-BB:83, Gr-GB:163, Mo-MGT:53,
  Mo-NR:98, Wr-RM:113
The Terrible Robber Men.
  P. Colum. Ha-LO:41
The Thief. S. Kunitz.
  Ca-VT:261, Un-MA:593
Thief's Spell. Tr-US I:207
Tom, Tom, the Piper's Son.
  Li-LB:34, Mo-MGT:22,
  Mo-NR:64, Wi-MG:7, Wr-RM:77
Two-Gun Percy. Fi-BG:136
Waltzing Matilda. A. Paterson.
  Gr-CT:138, Gr-GB:259,
  Ha-PO:238, Mc-WK:147
Who Goes round My Pinfold Wall?
  Gr-GB:24
THINKING: see THOUGHT AND
  THINKING

THINNESS: see SIZE AND SHAPE
THIRST: see also HUMOR - THIRST
  Drinking. A. Cowley. Ha-PO:250,
    Hi-WP II:141, Ho-WR:64
  Dry Is My Tongue. Da-SC:114
  Green, Green, Is El Aghir.
    N. Cameron. Ca-MB:114
  The Rime of the Ancient Mariner.
    S. Coleridge. Al-VBP:679,
    Bo-FP:301, Co-RG:60, Co-SS:131,
    De-CH:364, Er-FA:318, Fe-FP:147,
    Ga-FB:105, Gr-TG:61, Ha-PO:15,
    Hi-WP II:68, Ma-YA:146,
    Ni-JP:52, Ox-BN:139, Rv-CB:658,
    Sm-LG:312, Un-GT:30
THISTLEDOWN: see THISTLES
THISTLES
  Thistledown. L. Reese. Ha-YA:87
  Thistles. T. Hughes. To-MP:179
THOMAS, SAINT (APOSTLE)
  Doubting Thomas. Ga-S:176
THOMAS, DYLAN
  Afterwards, They Shall Dance.
    B. Kaufman. Br-TC:229,
    Ca-VT:538, Hu-PN:409
  Dylan Thomas. S. Spender.
    Pl-ML:160
  Dylan, Who Is Dead. S. Allen.
    Ad-PB:167
THOMAS, EDWARD
  All Day It Has Rained.
    A. Lewis. Hi-WP I:28,
    Pa-GTB:543
  To E.T. R. Frost. Pl-ML:162
THOMSON, JAMES (1700-1748)
  Ode on the Death of Thomson.
    W. Collins. Rv-CB:538
THOREAU, HENRY DAVID
  The Articles of War.
    R. Francis. Cr-WS:64
THORNS
  He Went to the Wood.
    Gr-GB:210, Mo-MGT:156
  Roses and Thorns. S. Betai.
    Al-PI:109
  Roses Only. M. Moore.
    Wi-LT:268
  A Thorn. Wr-RM:117
  Thorn Song. De-PP:28
THOTH (EGYPTIAN GOD)
  Prayer to the God Thot.
    Be-AP:18, Lo-TY:28
THOUGHT AND DEED
  Action. S. Davis. Ke-TF:251
  blk/rhetoric. S. Sanchez.
    Be-MA:137
  A Dialogue of Self and Soul.
    W. Yeats. Un-MB:118, Wi-LT:84
  Speak, Parrot. J. Skelton.
    Al-VBP:29

THOUGHT AND THINKING: see also
    HUMOR - THOUGHT AND THINKING;
    LOGIC
  The Climate of Thought. R. Graves.
    Al-VBP:1205, Go-BP:169
  Coffee. J. Cunningham.
    Ca-VT:325, Un-MA:615
  Crude Foyer. W. Stevens.
    Wi-LT:150
  Day-Dreamer. Ar-TP3:209
  Days. K. Baker. Ar-TP3:213,
    Sh-RP:112, Th-AS:204
  Gone Forever. B. Mills.
    Du-RG:18
  I Have. Fang Wei-teh.
    Hs-TC:136
  The Inner Vision.
    W. Wordsworth. Pa-GTB:278
  Lack of Communication.
    A. Philippide. Mc-AC:82
  Il Penseroso. J. Milton.
    Al-VBP:393, Pa-GTB:98,
    Rv-CB:370
  Sunday Morning. W. Stevens.
    Sh-AP:158, Sm-PT:121,
    Un-MA:242, Wi-LT:139
  Thought. Al-PI:20
  Throughout the World. T. Wyatt.
    Co-EL:43, Rv-CB:95
  Ulysses Pondering. S. Plumley.
    Ls-NY:336
THOUGHTS
  Bundles. C. Sandburg. Un-MA:209
  The Busy Heart. R. Brooke.
    Un-MB:325
  Butterflies. W. Davies. Go-BP:83
  Days. K. Baker. Ar-TP3:213,
    Sh-RP:112, Th-AS:204
  Deer. J. Drinkwater. De-CH:282
  It's Pleasant to Think.
    E. Coatsworth. Sh-RP:171
  My Garden. Mu'tamid, King of
    Seville. Pa-SG:29
  The Night. A. Goodman. Le-M:213
  Orders. A. Klein. Do-WH:5
  A Real Dream. S. Brown. Ba-HI:133
  The Shepherdess. A. Meynell.
    Sp-OG:335, Un-MB:61
  The Thought. H. Wolfe. Go-BP:136
  A Thought Went up My Mind Today.
    E. Dickinson. Sh-AP:130
  To the Tune "Glittering Sword
    Hilts." Liu Yo Hsi. Rx-LT:72
  Whatsoever Things Are True. Bible.
    N.T. Philippians. Ar-TP3:210
THREATS: see also HUMOR - THREATS
  The Apparition. J. Donne.
    Al-VBP:250, Rv-CB:302
  The Backlash Blues. L. Hughes.
    Ra-BP:90

Charleston. H. Timrod. Sh-AP:125
The Fall of Hyperion. J. Keats.
  Ox-BN:379
Fee, Fi, Fo, Fum. Br-FF:(3),
  Br-SM:21, Mo-MGT:26,
  Mo-TB:78, Na-EO:116
For Stephen Dixon. Z. Gilbert.
  Ad-PB:195
Giant Bonaparte. Mo-MGT:166
Irritable Song. R. Atkins.
  Bo-AN:170
Ku-Klux. M. Cawein. Hi-TL:127
My Mother Said. Bl-OB:28,
  De-CH:535, Gr-EC:286, Ir-BB:10,
  Mo-MGT:159, Pa-RE:55
Song of a Girl Whose Lover Has
  Married Another Woman.
  Tr-US II:195
A Strange Meeting. W. Davies.
  Bl-OB:148
Warning. L. Hughes. Ra-BP:91
When We Meet the Enemy.
  Ho-SD:31
The Wicked Little Kukook.
  Le-IB:87
THREE MUSKETEERS
  D'Artagnan. V. Starrett.
  Cr-WS:17
THRIFT: see also HUMOR - THRIFT
  The Ant and the Cricket. Aesop.
  De-TT:59, Un-GT:78
  Candle-Saving. De-TT:63,
  Wr-RM:85
  Maine. P. Booth. Br-AF:128
  See a Pin and Pick It Up.
  Ir-BB:226, Li-LB:161, Mo-MGT:172,
  Mo-NR:119, Mo-TB:55, Un-GT:23,
  Wr-RM:41
  Wilful Waste Brings Woeful Want.
  Ag-HE:63
THROSTLES: see THRUSHES
THRUSHES
  The Brown Thrush. L. Larcom.
  Fe-FP:295, Hu-MP:224
  Come In. R. Frost. Co-BN:157,
  Ga-FB:292, Hi-WP I:4,
  Un-MA:19, Wi-LT:179
  The Darkling Thrush. T. Hardy.
  Co-RG:170, Er-FA:455, Ha-PO:106,
  Na-EO:56, Ox-BN:824, Un-MB:25,
  Wi-LT:17
  A Health to the Birds. S. MacManus.
  Co-PI:112
  In the Swamp. W. Whitman.
  La-RM:151
  Last Rites. C. Rossetti. Ox-BC:280
  Malison of the Stone-Chat.
  Gr-GB:63
  Midsummer. S. Calverley.
  Re-BS:23

The Missel-Thrush. A. Young.
  Re-BS:37
Nesting Time. A. Guiterman.
  Gr-EC:180
The Relic. R. Hillyer.
  Pl-US:145
The Reverie of Poor Susan.
  W. Wordsworth. De-CH:96,
  De-TT:108, Ho-WR:155,
  Pa-GTB:256, Rv-CB:639
The Throstle. A. Tennyson.
  Co-BBW:241, Co-BN:97, Co-PS:106,
  Fe-FP:294, Mc-WK:25, Se-PR:155
Thrush. C. Simic. Mc-EA:39
A Thrush Before Dawn.
  A. Meynell. Un-MB:64
Thrush for Hawk. J. Fandel.
  Ls-NY:117
The Thrush in February.
  G. Meredith. Ox-BN:694
The Thrush's Nest. J. Clare.
  Bl-OB:67, Bo-GJ:91, Ha-PO:84,
  Ma-FW:12, Re-TW:94, Se-PR:109,
  Sm-MK:143, Un-GT:64
The Thrush's Nest. R. Ryan.
  Co-PI:174
The Thrush's Song. W. McGillivray.
  De-CH:97, Un-GT:64
Two Sparrows. H. Wolfe. Sm-MK:173
Watching Bird. L. Coxe. Co-BBW:260
The Wheat-Ear. Da-SC:37
When Lilacs Last in the Dooryard
  Bloom'd. W. Whitman.
  Al-VBP:940, Un-MA:71
Winter. D. Rossetti. Rv-CB:888
THUCYDIDES
  The Night There Was Dancing in
  the Streets. E. Olson.
  St-H:174
THUMBS
  The Story of Little Suck-a-Thumb.
  H. Hoffmann. Ir-BB:95,
  Li-SR:27, Na-EO:154
THUNDERBIRDS: see MYTHICAL
  ANIMALS AND BIRDS
THUNDERSTORMS: see also LIGHTNING
  The Approach of the Storm.
  Da-SC:149, Tr-US II:224
  Asking where the Thunder
  Peals. Tr-US I:195
  A Baby-Sermon. G. MacDonald.
  Ox-BC:274
  Chiefly to Mind Appears.
  C. Day Lewis. Un-MB:423
  Dream Songs, I, III.
  Tr-US II:224
  Electrical Storm. E. Bishop.
  Ha-WR:11
  First Song of the Thunder.
  Da-SC:65, Le-OE:74

THUNDERSTORMS — <u>cont'd.</u>
  Giant Thunder.   J. Reeves.
    Co-BN:176, Sm-MK:147
  Hot Afternoons.   P. Blackburn.
    Ca-VT:555
  Over the Sun-Darkened River
    Sands.   Le-OE:73
  Rain on the Housetops.   La-GI:22
  Song of the Thunders.   Da-SC:148
  The Storm.   E. Shanks.
    Co-BN:177, De-TT:161
  Thunder!   P. Arenstein.
    Ho-CT:26
  Thunder.   W. de la Mare.
    Co-BN:176
  Thunder.   Fu Hsuan.   Rx-LT:27
  Thunder.   G. Van Every.
    Le-M:47
  A Thundery Day.   S. Meader.
    Le-M:48, Le-WR:16
  The Voice of Thunder.   Ho-SD:44
  The Voice That Beautifies the
    Land.   Da-SC:65, Le-OE:11,
    Pa-SG:139, Tr-US II:251
  Winter's Thunder.   Li-LB:161,
    Rv-ON:37, Un-GT:23
  Word of the Thunder.   Tr-US II:310
TIBETAN VERSE – LADAKHI
  Songs.   Tr-US II:138
TIBETAN VERSE – MANIPURI
  O You Are like the Tender Cotton
    Worm.   Le-OE:112
TIBETAN VERSE – MIKIRIS
  Sleep Brings Pearl Necklaces.
    Le-OE:100
TIBETAN VERSE – NA-KHI
  Improvised Songs.   Tr-US II:182
TIBETAN VERSE – NAGA
  Long Song.   Tr-US II:174
  Lullaby Sung by a Widow.
    Tr-US II:177
  The Road Looks Longer.   Le-OE:85
  Song.   Tr-US II:176
  Song Contest.   Tr-US II:175
TICKLING GAMES
  Adam and Eve Gaed up My Sleeve.
    Mo-TL:24
  Can You Keep a Secret?
    Li-LB:18, Mo-TL:26
  Cheetie Pussie.   Mo-TL:21
  Dingty Diddlety.   Mo-TL:22
  Hickory, Dickory, Dock.
    An-IP:(7), Au-SP:17, Bo-FP:16,
    De-PO:20, Er-FA:505, Fr-WO:17,
    Li-LB:102, Mo-CC:(15), Mo-MGT:77,
    Mo-NR:24, Mo-TL:22, Wi-MG:58,
    Wr-RM:125
  Higgledy, Piggledy.   Mo-TL:22
  If You Are a Gentleman.
    Mo-TL:26

Lady, Lady, in the Land.   Mo-TL:26
Pussy Cat, Pussy Cat.   Mo-TL:21
Round About, Round About.
  Mo-TL:23
Round about There.   Mo-TL:19
Round and Round Ran the Wee Hare.
  Mo-TL:19
Round and round the Garden.
  Mo-TL:19
A Sure Test.   Wr-RM:56
There Was a Man.   Mo-TL:25
There Was a Wee Mouse.   Mo-TL:20
Three Straws.   Wr-RM:122
Tickly, Tickly, in Your Hand.
  Mo-TL:26
TICONDEROGA: see FORT TICONDEROGA,
  BATTLE, 1775
TIDAL WAVES: TSUNAMIS
TIDES: see also HUMOR – TIDES
  As the Tide Goes Out.
    J. Fischer.   La-GI:41
  Continent's End.   R. Jeffers.
    Ga-FB:312, Pl-IO:53
  The Dancing Sea.   J. Davies.
    Gr-CT:191
  The Ebb Tide.   R. Southey.
    Ox-BN:176
  German Shepherd.   M. Livingston.
    La-RM:96
  Here, in This Little Bay.
    C. Patmore.   Co-BN:81,
    Ox-BN:633, Pa-GTB:368
  High Tide.   J. Untermeyer.
    Un-MA:331
  I Started Early, Took My Dog.
    E. Dickinson.   Re-TW:122,
    Rv-CB:920, Wi-LT:10
  Night.   R. Jeffers.   Sm-PT:155,
    Un-MA:367
  One Day I Wrote Her Name.
    E. Spenser.   Al-VBP:99,
    No-CL:22, Rv-CB:161
  A Question.   De-PP:24
  Sketch.   C. Sandburg.   Bo-HF:83
  Slave of the Moon.   M. Yarmon.
    Le-M:112
  A Song of Thanks.   W. Cole.
    Co-OT:18
  A Sonnet of the Moon.   C. Best.
    De-CH:336
  Storm Tide on Mejit.   Tr-US II:31
  Tidal.   R. Ballak.   Cr-SS:28
  The Tide.   M. Wilson.   Bo-FP:284
  The Tide in the River.   E. Farjeon.
    Ar-TP3:172, Bl-OB:136, Sm-MK:13
  The Tide Rises, the Tide Falls.
    H. Longfellow.   Co-SS:50,
    De-TT:183, Er-FA:260, Gr-CT:191,
    Ho-WR:135, Mc-PR:73, Pa-RE:75,
    Rv-CB:784

Tides of a Spring Sea. Buson.
  Be-MC:52
Time and Tide. H. LaMarre.
  Hu-PN:360
Water. K. Raine. Pl-IO:44
Waves Coming Up Against the
  Rocks. Le-OE:85, Tr-US I:244
TIGER LILIES: see LILIES
TIGERS: see also HUMOR - TIGERS
  The Baby Tigers. K. Raikin.
    Mo-MI:53
  Color. R. Bennett. Hu-MP:185
  The Fear of Beasts. W. Meredith.
    Ha-TP:138
  Four-Footed Poems. E. Greenberg.
    Ho-TY:312
  Good Taste. C. Logue.
    Pa-RE:95
  Here She Is. M. Miller.
    Ad-PE:34, Ar-TP3:80
  India. W. Turner. Bl-OB:112,
    La-PV:155, Un-MB:348
  The Shape God Wears. S. Hay.
    Un-GT:82
  Softly. P. Sandell. Su-FVI:67
  The Tantanoola Tiger.
    M. Harris. Ca-MB:66
  The Tiger. W. Blake. Al-VBP:616,
    Ar-TP3:80, Bl-OB:111, Co-BBW:209,
    Co-RG:146, De-CH:91, Er-FA:234,
    Fe-FP:178, Fe-PL:366, Ga-FB:95,
    Ga-S:12, Gr-CT:115, Ha-PO:116,
    Hi-WP II:171, Hu-MP:201, Li-SR:8,
    Ma-YA:129, Mc-PR:158, Ox-BN:23,
    Pl-EI:19, Rd-OA:118, Rv-CB:576,
    Sm-LG:68, Tu-WW:108, Un-GT:36
  Tiger. W. Brown. Sa-B:68
  The Tiger. Tr-US II:199
  The Tiger Stalking in the Night.
    E. Horn. Co-EL:32, Co-PU:90
  The Tigress. R. Pitter. Ls-NY:196
TILL, EMMETT
  Emmett Till. J. Emanuel. Ad-PB:179
  The Last Quatrain of the Ballad of
    Emmett Till. G. Brooks.
    Ad-PB:155
TILL RIVER
  The Two Rivers. Co-BN:79,
    De-CH:404, Gr-CT:165, Gr-GB:176,
    Ma-BB:83, Rv-CB:119
TIMBUKTU, MALI
  Timbuctu. E. Brathwaite.
    To-MP:164
TIME: see also CALENDARS; CLOCKS AND
  WATCHES; FUTURE; HUMOR - TIME;
  PAST; PRESENT; SUNDIALS; TELLING
  TIME
  The Alarum. S. Warner. Un-MB:372
  Are We Their Equals? H. Geltman.
    Le-M:176

As I Walked Out One Evening.
  W. Auden. Br-TC:21, Ha-PO:189,
  Un-MB:464, Wi-LT:465
August. L. MacNeice. Wi-LT:456
Bell Horses, Bell Horses, What
  Time of Day. Ar-TP3:174,
  Bo-FP:123, Br-SS:5, Ir-BB:190,
  Mo-MGT:173, Wr-RM:113
Bell Speech. R. Wilbur.
  Un-MA:675
The Builders. H. Longfellow.
  Er-FA:8, Sp-OG:327
Burial. P. Joachim. Lo-TY:146
Burnt Norton. T. Eliot.
  Wi-LT:306
The City of Dreadful Night XIII.
  J. Thomson. Al-VBP:1007
Clear Eyes. W. de la Mare.
  Al-VBP:1120
The Clerks. E. Robinson.
  Un-MA:126
Come, Break with Time. L. Bogan.
  Un-MA:492
Continental Crossing.
  D. Thompson. Br-AF:233
The Corner. W. de la Mare.
  Br-BC:136, Ir-BB:67
Counsel to Girls. R. Herrick.
  Al-VBP:328, Er-FA:104, Ga-FB:41,
  Gr-CT:51, Ha-PO:161, Hi-WP II:140,
  Li-SR:21, Ma-YA:86, Pa-GTB:71,
  Un-MW:19
Cow Time. M. Shannon. Br-SS:9
Dawn Is a Feeling. M. Pinder.
  Mo-GR:117
The Day. T. Spencer.
  Mo-BG:71, Ni-JP:157
Days. R. Emerson. Al-VBP:805,
  Mo-BG:136, Ni-JP:30, Rv-CB:775
Days. P. Larkin. Sm-MK:212
The Dream. G. Byron. Mo-GR:118
Eight o' Clock. A. Housman.
  Co-PU:116, Hi-WP I:22, Un-MB:100
Epilogue. S. Spender. Un-MB:472
Esthetique du Mal, VII.
  W. Stevens. Wi-LT:155
The Eye. R. Jeffers. Wi-LT:266
Fingernails of the Dead.
  J. Takami. Sh-AM:108
Flowers at an Airport.
  W. Stafford. Mc-EA:128
For You. I. Horea. Mc-AC:140
Four Preludes on Playthings of the
  Wind: The Past Is a Bucket of
  Ashes. C. Sandburg. Un-MA:201
Four Quartz Crystal Clocks.
  M. Moore. Br-TC:302, Pl-IO:67
From the Most Distant Time.
  Emperor Wu. Rx-LT:5
The Frost. Tzu Yeh. Le-MW:86

TIME — cont'd.
  Gallop, Gallop to a Rhyme.
    M. Shannon. Br-SS:4
  The Gathering. W. Scott.
    Al-VBP:672, Ox-BN:131
  The Gathering Time.
    D. Whitewing. Al-WW:52
  Grass on the Wall.
    Pien Chih-lin. Hs-TC:165
  Here Stand I Ever Lonely.
    De-CH:484
  Hidesong. A. Higo. Lo-TY:159
  Hours Are the Leaves of Life.
    S. Morrison. Le-M:121
  Housekeeping Problems.
    L. Haft. Le-M:139
  How Many Seconds in a Minute?
    C. Rossetti. Br-SS:5, Mc-PR:198
  How Soon Hath Time. J. Milton.
    Al-VBP:388, Ma-YA:93
  How Time Consumeth All Earthly
    Things. T. Proctor. Gr-CT:243
  I Am Disquieted when I See Many
    Hills. H. Plutzik. Ca-VT:347
  I Could Give All to Time.
    R. Frost. Sm-PT:169, Tr-MR:283
  I Will Sing You One-O.
    R. Frost. Sm-PT:78
  In Time like Glass. W. Turner.
    Un-MB:347
  The Incubus of Time. C. Smith.
    De-FS:184
  The Isle of Long Ago. B. Taylor.
    Er-FA:166
  It Must Give Pleasure.
    W. Stevens. Sm-PT:28
  Jim Jay. W. de la Mare.
    Br-SS:10, Ir-BB:152,
    Sm-MK:207, Un-GT:105
  The Lamentation of the Old
    Pensioner. W. Yeats.
    Co-PI:207, Ke-PP:100
  The Lonely Say. A. Ben Yitzhak.
    Me-PH:84
  Long Time a Child. H. Coleridge.
    Ox-BN:398, Rv-CB:758
  Meeting Point. L. MacNeice.
    Hi-WP II:62
  The Melodies of Time. T. Hood.
    Ox-BN:413
  The Mount. L. Adams. Un-MA:541
  The Mouse Whose Name Is Time.
    R. Francis. Ha-LO:29
  My Father's Watch. J. Ciardi.
    Pl-IO:24
  The Noise That Time Makes.
    M. Moore. Un-MA:577
  Ode on a Grecian Urn. J. Keats.
    Al-VBP:772, Er-FA:80, Ha-PO:228,
    Ke-TF:59, Ox-BN:355, Rv-CB:742

  The Old Clock on the Stairs.
    H. Longfellow. Sp-OG:309
  On Time. R. Hughes. Un-MB:409
  Pause of the Clock.
    F. García Lorca. Le-SW:43
  Pinwheel. D. Laing. Ls-NY:6
  The Power of Time. J. Swift.
    Rv-CB:495
  The Prejudice Against the Past.
    W. Stevens. Wi-LT:161
  Prologue. A. MacLeish.
    Un-MA:454
  The Reconciliation. A. MacLeish.
    Un-MA:462
  Reply to Mr. Wordsworth.
    A. MacLeish. Pl-IO:62
  Ritual. G. Davidson.
    Ls-NY:71
  The River of Life. T. Campbell.
    Er-FA:155, Ni-JP:156,
    Ox-BN:203, Pa-GTB:306
  The Road. E. Muir. Al-VBP:1172,
    Er-FA:91, Wi-LT:246
  The Rose and the Gardener.
    H. Dobson. Hu-MP:248
  St. Anthony's Township.
    G. Sheldon. De-CH:385
  Say, Is There Aught That Can
    Convey. De-CH:713
  September. T. Hughes. Gr-SS:43
  Signature for Tempo.
    A. MacLeish. Ca-VT:164
  Since Brass, nor Stone.
    W. Shakespeare. Er-FA:119,
    No-CL:84, Pa-GTB:3
  The Slow Starter. L. MacNeice.
    To-MP:89
  Slowly. J. Reeves. Bl-OB:138
  The Snow Fall. A. MacLeish.
    Ha-LO:51
  The Song of Finis.
    W. de la Mare. Un-MB:196
  Song of the Riders. S. Benét.
    Un-MA:501
  Sonnet 19. W. Shakespeare.
    Gr-CT:61, Ho-LP:8,
    Rv-CB:209, Un-MW:182
  Sonnet 60. W. Shakespeare.
    Al-VBP:203, Er-FA:261,
    Gr-CT:196, Pa-GTB:19, Rv-CB:226
  Sonnet LXIV. W. Shakespeare.
    Al-VBP:204
  Spidersilk. J. Nixon, Jr.
    Ls-NY:294
  Stanzas. G. Byron. Al-VBP:721
  Star-Swirls. R. Jeffers. Du-SH:108
  A Stopwatch and an Ordnance Map.
    S. Spender. Ca-MB:99
  The Sun's Travels. R. Stevenson.
    Fe-FP:262, Hu-MP:115

Symphony.   Li Kuang-t'ien.
  Hs-TC:204
This Room Is Full of Clocks.
  I. Gardner.   St-H:74
Time.   R. Graves.   Wi-LT:375
Time.   R. Hodgson.   Pa-GTB:36
Time.   R. McCoy.   Ba-HI:77
Time.   P. Shelley.   Fe-PL:302,
  Ma-YA:181
Time.   J. Wynne.   Ox-BC:77
Time a River.   Vainateya.
  Al-PI:45
Time and Eternity.   J. Bunyan.
  Ho-WR:248
Time and the Garden.   Y. Winters.
  Ca-VT:230, Un-MA:550
Time and Tide.   H. LaMarre.
  Hu-PN:360
Time Is a Feathered Thing.
  J. Mayne.   No-CL:174
Time Is a Pair of Scissors.
  Wang Ching-chih.   Hs-TC:44
Time Is the Mercy of Eternity.
  K. Rexroth.   Ca-VT:272
Time Speaks.   Chu Ta-nan.
  Hs-TC:133
Time Takes Me on Its Wing.
  Wo-HS:(58)
Time, You Old Gipsy Man.
  R. Hodgson.   Al-VBP:1114,
  Br-SS:11, De-CH:434, Fe-FP:61,
  Mc-WK:123, Pa-HT:77, Re-TW:108,
  Un-MB:186, Wi-LT:122
Time's Dedication.   D. Schwartz.
  Ca-VT:367
Time's Glory.   W. Shakespeare.
  Gr-CT:322
To His Coy Mistress. A. Marvell.
  Al-VBP:456, Er-FA:123, Fe-PL:115,
  Ga-FB:44, Ha-PO:162, Ma-YA:103,
  No-CL:176, Rv-CB:400, Un-MW:185
To His Watch.   G. Hopkins.
  Un-MB:44
To Miss Rapida.   J. Jiménez.
  Li-TU:178
Toward Avernus.   H. Vinal.
  De-FS:210
Trap.   W. Kerr.   De-FS:128
The Unbeseechable.
  F. Cornford.   Un-MB:307
Uncle Time.   D. Scott.   Sa-B:153
Upon the Water.   K. Takayasu.
  Sh-AM:157
Villanelle.   W. Auden.   Un-MB:456
The Walk in the Garden.
  C. Aiken.   En-PC:14
What Time Is It.   Re-RR:14
When I Do Count the Clock.
  W. Shakespeare.   Al-VBP:200,
  Er-FA:262, Rv-CB:207

Who Was It.   H. Heine.   Pa-SG:34
Wild Thyme.   E. Farjeon.
  Br-SS:3
Winter: An Ode.   S. Johnson.
  No-CL:128
Words in Time.   A. MacLeish.
  En-PC:20
The World.   H. Vaughan.
  Al-VBP:467, Ga-FB:93, Ga-S:6,
  Ho-LP:102, Pl-IO:7, Rv-CB:410
Ye Should Stay Longer.
  F. Beaumont.   Al-VBP:299
You Ask My Age.
  Sister M. Madeleva.   Ke-TF:152
TIMIDITY: see also LOVE -
    BASHFULNESS
  The Bashful Man.   B. Johnson.
    Co-RM:43
  Epitaph for a Timid Lady.
    F. Cornford.   Co-EL:85
  The Farmer's Bride.   C. Mew.
    Un-MB:161
  Frightened Flower.   W. Harris.
    Ad-BO:69
  The Garden Snail.   R. Wallace.
    Co-BBW:81
  I Shook His Hand.   N. Noffke.
    Le-M:161
  I'm O'er Young to Marry Yet.
    R. Burns.   Al-VBP:644
  Institute Poems.   M. Bruce.
    Ad-II:20
  Like an April Day.   J. Wellhaven.
    Pa-SG:30
  Small Quiet Song.   R. Smith.
    Ad-CI:15
  To an Isle in the Water. W. Yeats.
    Gr-TG:65, Sm-MK:8
  Two Kinds, Bold and Shy.
    J. Holmes.   Mc-WS:71
TIMOTHEUS, 446-357 B.C.
  Alexander's Feast.   J. Dryden.
    Ho-WR:100, Ma-YA:107, Pa-GTB:105
TIMUR THE LAME: see TAMERLANE
TINKERS
  The Tradesman.   Bo-FP:116
TINTORETTO
  La Creazione degli Animale.
    J. Brinnin.   Ls-NY:174
TIPPERARY COUNTY. IRE.
  The Two Travellers.   C. Boland.
    Co-PI:11
TIPTOEING
  Tiptoe.   K. Kuskin.
    Ar-TP3:102, La-PV:3
TITANIC (SHIP)
  The Convergence of the Twain.
    T. Hardy.   Ni-JP:119,
    Un-MB:35, Wi-LT:35
  The Titanic.   Co-SS:135

TITANS
  Hyperion. J. Keats. Ox-BN:365
TITHONUS
  Tithonus. A. Tennyson.
    Ox-BN:482, Rv-CB:792
TITMICE
  Dead Titmouse. E. Gullevic.
    Be-EB:26
TITUS AND BERENICE
  Titus and Berenice.
    J. Heath-Stubbs. Pa-GTB:553
TOADS: see also FROGS;
    HUMOR - TOADS
  At the Garden Gate. D. McCord.
    Fe-FP:122
  Bedtime. E. Coatsworth.
    Gr-TG:52
  Bird and Toad Play Hide and
    Seek. Br-MW:50
  The Death of a Toad. R. Wilbur.
    Sh-AP:231, Wi-LT:598
  Folk Wisdom. Br-TC:242
  A Friend in the Garden. J. Ewing.
    Br-SG:64, Fe-FP:143,
    Hu-MP:305, Ox-BC:256
  A Garden Path. M. Justus.
    Bo-FP:241, Br-SG:49
  Gasco, or The Toad. G. Grass.
    Co-EL:109
  Hop Out of My Way. Chora.
    Be-CS:27
  Hoppity Toads. A. Fisher.
    Sh-RP:75
  Little Horned Toad. Fe-FP:144
  The Little Red Spiders. Jo-TS:14
  Loving and Liking. D. Wordsworth.
    Ox-BC:129
  Lullaby for a Baby Toad.
    S. Gibbons. Co-BBW:65, Rd-SS:23
  Our Mr. Toad. D. McCord.
    Ar-TP3:67, It-HB:24, Ma-FO:(30)
  Over in the Meadow. Au-SP:223,
    Ir-BB:24, On-TW:38
  The Proud Toad. G. Hallock.
    Sh-RP:329
  The Rain Frogs. Rogetsu. Pa-SG:129
  Seven Poems, 2. L. Niedecker.
    Ca-VT:243
  The Song of the Toad. J. Burroughs.
    Fe-FP:142
  The Toad. E. Coatsworth.
    It-HB:53
  The Toad! Issa. Le-IS:8
  The Toad. Ca-MU:23
  A Tree Frog Trilling. Rogetsu.
    Be-CS:7
  The Tree Toad. M. Shannon.
    Ar-TP3:124, Fe-FP:142, Hu-MP:457
  Ungainly Things. R. Wallace.
    Du-SH:34

TOADSTOOLS: see MUSHROOMS
TOAST: see BREAD
TOASTERS: see also HUMOR - TOASTERS
  The Toaster. W. Smith.
    Ag-HE:6, Ar-TP3:113, Au-SP:100,
    Co-HP:114, Du-RG:37, Ir-BB:173
TOASTS
  The Barley Mow. Cl-DT:84
  The Blacksmith's Song. Gr-GB:208
  The Brown Jug. F. Fawkes.
    Al-VBP:570, Rv-CB:534
  A Health unto His Majesty.
    J. Savile. Gr-CT:83
  Here Is a Toast That I Want to
    Drink. W. Lathrop. Fe-PL:424
  Here's to the Maiden.
    R. Sheridan. Al-VBP:605,
    Ke-TF:277, Rv-CB:557
  Old Toast. Hi-WP II:1
  A Toast. J. Byrom. Al-VBP:543
  Toast. F. Horne. Hu-PN:150
  Verse, Violence, and the Vine.
    J. Cunningham. Ls-NY:330
TOBACCO: see HUMOR - TOBACCO;
    SMOKING
TODAY
  Morning Mood. M. Panegoosho.
    Le-IB:29
  Ode to Maecenas. Horace.
    Pa-SG:173, Un-GT:236
  Today Well, Tomorrow Cold in
    the Mouth. J. Gill. Sc-TN:66
TOES: see also HUMOR - TOES
  A Bunch of Roses. J. Tabb.
    Th-AS:58
  Moses. Mo-MGT:202
TOLEDO, SP.
  Toledo. R. Campbell. Un-MB:419
TOLERANCE: see SATIRE - TOLERANCE
TOLLS: see TAXES AND TAX COLLECTORS
TOLMAN, RICHARD CHACE
  Richard Tolman's Universe.
    L. Bacon. Pl-IO:171
TOLSTOI, COUNT LEO, PÈRE
  Tolstoi Is Plowing Yet.
    V. Lindsay. Ba-PO:133
TOLTECS: see also INDIANS OF
    CENTRAL AMERICA - VERSE-NAHUATL
  The Toltecs Were Wise. Ge-TR:35
TOMATOES
  If Three Ripe Tomatoes. Re-RR:86
    love apple. M. Scheiner. La-IH:41
  A Song of Thanks. W. Cole.
    Co-OT:18
  Tomato Time. M. Livingston.
    Ag-HE:43, Br-SG:39
TOMBS: see also EPITAPHS; HUMOR -
    TOMBS; SATIRE - TOMBS
  A Solis Ortus Cardine. F. Ford.
    Al-VBP:1118

Above the Nile. H. Hamilton.
  Ls-NY:245
Address to a Mummy. H. Smith.
  Co-RG:5
After a Lecture on Keats.
  O. Holmes. Al-VBP:831
Agamemnon's Tomb. S. Sitwell.
  Un-MB:402
Ample Make This Bed.
  E. Dickinson. Un-MA:100
An Arundel Tomb. P. Larkin.
  To-MP:79
As Toilsome I Wander'd Virginia's
  Woods. W. Whitman.
  Al-VBP:937, Sp-OG:205
At the Grave of Henry Vaughan.
  S. Sassoon. Pa-GTB:454,
  Pl-EI:8
Ave Maria. A. Kaplan. Mc-EA:132
The Bishop Orders His Tomb at
  Saint Praxed's Church.
  R.Browning. Al-VBP:895,Mo-GR:57
The Bourne. C. Rossetti.Ox-BN:715
Bury Me Not on the Lone Prairie.
  Er-FA:445, Ga-FB:269
The Cemetery. M. Tsvetayeva.
  Ca-MR:133
Clear Bright. Huang T'ing Ch'ien.
  Rx-LT:90
Cool Tombs. C. Sandburg.
  Al-VBP:1138, Fe-PL:276, Sh-AP:157,
  Un-GB:159, Un-MA:200, Vi-PP:194
De Coenatione Micae. Martial.
  Sm-LG:275
A Dead Soldier Abandoned on the
  Roadside. Tu Yün-hsieh.
  Hs-TC:251
The Death of Robin Hood. E. Field.
  Co-PT:239
Dirge. T. Beddoes. Ho-WR:188,
  Ox-BN:453
Dirge in Cymbeline. W. Collins.
  Al-VBP:574, No-CL:63
Discordants. C. Aiken. Co-BL:36
An Exceeding Great Army. E. Ayer.
  De-FS:10
The Faery Queen. W. Raleigh.
  Al-VBP:93
The Grave. R. Blair. Al-VBP:543
The Grave. T. Jones. Pa-SG:179
The Grave. Gr-CT:367
Graves. M. Ibn Ezra. Me-PH:59
Graves at Inishbofin.
  R. Murphy. Ls-NY:110
Here Lies a Prisoner. C. Mew.
  Un-MB:165
I Found Her out There. T. Hardy.
  De-CH:257
I Walked over the Grave of Henry
  James. R. Eberhart. Ca-VT:246

Inscription on My Gravestone.
  M. Leib. Ho-TY:95
Invocation. H. Johnson.
  Bo-AN:102, Hu-PN:265
The Knight's Tomb. S. Coleridge.
  Cl-FC:81, Co-PU:156,
  Rv-CB:664, Sm-LG:272
Last Words. S. Plath. Mc-EA:157
A Little Shrub Growing By.
  B. Jonson. Rv-CB:285
Losers. C. Sandburg. Un-MA:205
May the Gravedigger Not Bury Me.
  Do-CH:(48)
The Medici Tombs. W. Ross.
  Ls-NY:236
Mom. G. Cohoe. Al-WW:27
My Soul, Consider! E. Mörike.
  Un-R:105
New Grave. Ch'in Yzu-hao.
  Pa-MV:55
On the Tombs in Westminster
  Abbey. F. Beaumont.
  Al-VBP:301, De-CH:252,
  Hi-WP II:18, Pa-GTB:60
Panope. E. Sitwell.
  Un-MB:333
Pilgrims' Song. Tr-US I:129
Plato's Tomb. Sm-LG:275
The Poet's Final Instructions.
  J. Berryman. Ca-VT:384
Rome. T. Hardy. No-CL:255
Safe in Their Alabaster Chambers.
  E. Dickinson. Rv-CB:924
Sarcophagus Cover. R. Feldman.
  Ls-NY:18
Sir William Deloraine at the
  Wizard's Tomb. W. Scott.
  Ox-BN:118
The Skeleton of the Future.
  H. MacDiarmid. Un-MB:361
A Street in Bronzeville:
  Southeast Corner. G. Brooks.
  Ca-VT:439
To the Oaks of Glencree. J. Synge.
  Co-EL:69, Un-MB:189
tomb. B. Brigham. Sc-TN:23
Vailima. R. Stevenson. De-CH:51,
  De-TT:157, Ox-BN:895
A Voice from the Waters.
  T. Beddoes. Ox-BN:449, Rv-CB:771
Wake, All the Dead! W. Davenant.
  De-CH:639, Rv-CB:366, Sm-LG:277
When I Am Dead. J. Wilson.
  Fe-PL:275
Wind, Gentle Evergreen. Rv-CB:424
TOMORROW
  Hurry Tomorrow. I. Eastwick.
    Br-BC:43
  If Cats Have Many Kittens.
    Re-RR:82

TOMORROW — <u>cont'd</u>.
  Night Piece. J. Manifold.
    Un-MB:513, Wi-LT:766
  Today Well, Tomorrow Cold in
    the Mouth. J. Gill. Sc-TN:66
  Tomorrow. E. Garner. Ke-TF:237
  Tomorrow. J. Masefield.
    Un-MB:222
  Youth. L. Hughes. Bo-HF:107,
    Br-AF:243, Br-BC:134, Li-TU:266
TONGUE TWISTERS
  Betty Botter's Batter. Mo-MGT:182
  Cats Are Annoyed by Noise.
    Re-RR:122
  Davy Doldrum Dreamed He Drove a
    Dragon. Pa-AP:36
  Eletelephony. L. Richards.
    Ar-TP3:128, Au-SP:239, Bo-GJ:7,
    Co-IW:22, Fe-FP:346, Gr-EC:186,
    Hu-MP:455, Ir-BB:56, La-PV:23,
    Lo-LL:24, Ox-BC:289, Pe-FB:102
  A Flea and a Fly in a Flue.
    Br-LL:9, Ch-B:113, Co-HP:29,
    Fe-FP:365, Gr-EC:196, Ju-CP:14,
    Lo-LL:49, Mc-WS:179, Un-GT:241
  How Much Wood Would a Woodchuck
    Chuck. Ar-TP3:123, Fe-FP:358,
    Ir-BB:188, Ju-CP:14
  Jumble Jingle. L. Richards.
    Co-OW:62
  My Dame Hath a Lame Tame Crane.
    Pa-AP:34
  One Old Ox. Gr-CT:31, On-TW:45
  Peter Piper. Er-FA:507,
    Fe-FP:358, Li-LB:66, Mo-MGT:184,
    Mo-NR:42, Wi-MG:58, Wr-RM:107
  Robert Rowley. Rv-ON:52
  The Rugged Rock. Mo-CC:(53),
    Mo-MGT:197
  She Sells Sea Shells.
    Mo-MGT:197, Sp-HW:27
  Song of the Pop-Bottlers.
    M. Bishop. Co-FB:428, Co-HP:33,
    Fe-FP:358, Mc-WS:169
  The Swan. Ch-B:61, Fe-FP:364,
    Gr-CT:11, Wr-RM:122
  Theophilus Thistledown.
    Lo-LL:53
  There Was a Man, and His Name
    Was Dob. De-CH:537, Gr-EC:79,
    Ir-BB:173
  Three Crooked Cripples. Rv-ON:52
  A Tutor Who Tooted the Flute.
    C. Wells. Co-HP:119, Ke-TF:288,
    Lo-LL:49, Mc-WS:175, Un-GF:46,
    Un-GT:241
  Twister Twisting Twine. J. Wallis.
    Gr-CT:3
  "Two, Two!" Toots the Train.
    On-TW:8

TONGUES
  I Have a Pink Pen.   Re-RR:34
  Thirty-Two White Calves.
    Ju-CP:10
TOOLS
  Eleven. A. MacLeish. Ni-JP:26
  No Curtain. F. Scott. Ls-NY:277
  The Workshop. A. Fisher.
    Au-SP:104
TOOTHACHE: see TEETH
TOOTHPASTE: see TEETH
TOPS (TOYS)
  The Dreidel. K. Dee. Ja-HH:51
  If I Were a Top. E. Frey.
    La-GI:48
  Time. R. Hodgson. Pa-GTB:436
  You've Had One. Re-RR:91
TORMENT: see SUFFERING
TORNADOES: see also HURRICANES
  The Sherman Cyclone. Em-AF:471
  Tornado. W. Stafford.
    Ha-WR:51, St-H:211
  The Tupelo Disaster. Em-AF:474
TORTOISES: see TURTLES
TOSSING AND CATCHING RHYMES
  Catch Him, Crow! Br-FF:(20),
    Gr-EC:287, Mo-MGT:185, Mo-TL:36
  A Catching Song. E. Farjeon.
    De-TT:35
  Dance, Little Baby. A. Taylor.
    De-PO:6, Gr-EC:119,
    Ox-BC:120, Wr-RM:101
TOUCANS: see HUMOR — TOUCANS
TOURISTS: see also HUMOR —
    TOURISTS; SATIRE — TOURISTS;
    TRAVEL AND TRAVELERS
  Indian Reservation: Caughnawaga.
    A. Klein. Wi-LT:748
  The Permanent Tourists.
    P. Page. Wi-LT:783
  The Tourist from Syracuse.
    D. Justice. Br-TC:226
  Tudor Church Music. S. Warner.
    Pl-US:16
TOURNAMENTS
  The Faery Queen. E. Spenser.
    Al-VBP:116
  Sir Galahad. A. Tennyson.
    Co-RM:78, Sp-OG:134
  The Tournament. P. Sidney.
    Ma-YA:61, No-CL:64
TOUSSAINT L'OUVERTURE, PIERRE
    FRANCOIS DOMINIQUE
  Black Majesty. C. Cullen.
    Ad-PB:92, Ca-VT:242
  To Toussaint L'Ouverture.
    W. Wordsworth. Hi-FO:185,
    Hu-PN:447, Ox-BN:80
  Toussaint L'Ouverture. J. Carew.
    Sa-B:11

Toussaint L'Ouverture.
E. Robinson. Hu-PN:471
TOWER OF LONDON
Tears. E. Thomas. Pa-GTB:441,
Rv-CB:969
TOWERS
The Broken Tower. H. Crane.
Sh-AP:196, Un-MA:535, Wi-LT:399
The Clock Tower. C. Thibaudeau.
Do-WH:87
The Tower. Y. Sasasawa.
Sh-AM:76
The Tower of Genghis Khan.
Pa-HT:85
TOWNS: see CITIES AND TOWNS
TOYS: see also HUMOR - TOYS;
SATIRE - TOYS; and names
of toys, as KITES (TOYS)
Acorn Bill. R. Ainsworth.
St-FS:15
Come, Ride with Me to Toyland.
R. Bennett. Br-SS:103
The Dumb Soldier. R. Stevenson.
Ox-BC:299, Un-GT:164
The Engineer. A. Milne.
Sh-RP:4
Fuzzy Wuzzy. Fr-MP:21, Un-GT:18
Little Boy Blue. E. Field.
Er-FA:490, Fe-FP:536, Fe-PL:248
My Teddy Bear. B. Olgin.
Mc-AW:10
My Teddy Stands. Olga. Mo-MI:25
Naughty Donna. L. Hopkins.
Ho-GC:39
Night Watchmen. W. Garthwaite.
Rd-SS:15
Our Birthday. M. Edey.
Br-BC:57, Br-SS:44
Teddy Bear. H. Behn. Ar-TP3:105
The Toys. C. Patmore. Al-VBP:973,
Er-FA:142, Rv-CB:876
Toys for Sale. Gr-EC:284,
Ir-BB:36
TRACK ATHLETICS: see also RUNNING
After the Record Is Broken.
J. Emanuel. Ls-NY:40
Challenge. S. Hazo. Mo-SD:58
The Hundred-Yard Dash.
W. Lindsey. Fl-HH:61
Notes Found near a Suicide: To
James. F. Horne. Bo-AN:45,
Bo-HF:90, Br-BC:124, Ra-BP:73
Notes on a Track Meet.
D. McCord. Mo-SD:57
Pole Vault. Shiro Murana.
Mo-SD:59
The Pole-Vaulter.
Fl-HH:57
The Sprinters. L. Murchison.
Mo-SD:54

TRACKING AND TRAILING: see also
ANIMAL TRACKS; FOOTPRINTS
A Bedtime Song for Children.
Br-MW:90
Tracking Rabbits: Night.
J. Barnes. Ni-CD:20
White Fields. J. Stephens.
Au-SP:335, Br-SS:91, Co-BN:199,
Co-PS:159, Fe-FP:66, Gr-EC:84,
Mc-AW:50
TRACTORS
Cynddylan on a Tractor. R. Thomas.
Ga-S:123, To-MP:63
New Farm Tractor. C. Sandburg.
Fe-FP:230
TRADE: see BUSINESS; CARGOES;
MARKETS AND MARKETING
TRADE UNIONS: see LABOR UNIONS
TRADES: see OCCUPATIONS
TRAFALGAR, BATTLE, 1805
A Ballad of the Good Lord
Nelson. L. Durrell. Wi-LT:697
The Night of Trafalgar. T. Hardy.
De-CH:166, Gr-CT:340, Un-MB:28
TRAFFIC: see CITY TRAFFIC
TRAFFIC LIGHTS
Stoplights. D. Dzwonkoski.
Ad-II:24
Traffic Light. N. Duffy.
Mc-AW:25
Urgency. S. Wright. Hu-PN:270
TRAGEDY: see also HUMOR - TRAGEDY;
LOVE - TRAGEDY
And in the Hanging Gardens.
C. Aiken. Co-PT:45, Un-MA:426
Ballad. Tr-US I:125
The Bonny Heyn. Ox-BB:201
Bristowe Tragedie. Ox-BB:656
The Castle. S. Alexander.
Hu-PN:559
Cumnor Hall. W. Mickle.
Al-VBP:599, Ox-BB:670
Edom o' Gordon. Ox-BB:598
The Famous Flower of Serving-Men.
Ox-BB:182
Gil Morrice. Ox-BB:156
Graeme and Bewick. Ox-BB:356,
Rv-CB:47
Green Valley. D. Johnson.
Hu-PN:227
The Grey Selchie of Sule Skerry.
Ox-BB:91
I Sit and Look Out. W. Whitman.
Ke-PP:1, Mo-GB:177, Rv-CB:851
In Search of a Bright Star.
Hsü Chih-mo. Hs-TC:86
London. W. Blake. Al-VBP:618,
Gr-CT:304, Ha-PO:79, Ke-PP:49,
Mo-GR:78, Ox-BN:24, Rv-CB:605
Mary Hamilton. Ox-BB:328

TRAGEDY — <u>cont'd.</u>
  Paradise Regained. J. Milton.
    Al-VBP:412
  Prince Robert. Ox-BB:203
  Up-Hill. C. Rossetti. Al-VBP:998,
    De-CH:462, Gr-EC:276, Ho-WR:152,
    Mc-PR:141, Ox-BN:712, Sp-OG:263
  Young Waters. Fo-OG:31, Ox-BB:321
TRAILERS: see AUTOMOBILES -
    TRAILERS
TRAILS: see also names of trails,
    as OREGON TRAIL
  A Garden Path. M. Justus.
    Bo-FP:241, Br-SG:49
  Laramie Trail. J. Hanson.
    Fi-BG:57
  The Old Ute Trail. Fi-BG:109
  The Pioneer. A. Guiterman.
    Ar-TP3:37, Hu-MP:394
  Shootin' Up the Trail.
    G. Shumway. Fi-BG:107
  Song. Tr-US I:182
  Star of the Western Skies.
    Fi-BG:193
  The Trail. Anil. Al-PI:128
TRAINS: see also ENGINEERS;
    EXPRESS SERVICE; HUMOR -
    TRAINS; RAILROADS
  As a Landscape. F. Saito.
    Sh-AM:153
  The Bourgeois Poet. K. Shapiro.
    St-H:205
  The Brothers: Two Saltimbanques.
    J. Logan. Du-SH:46
  Casey Jones. R. Hunter.
    Mo-GR:52
  Casey Jones. Bl-OB:76, Ga-FB:267,
    Hi-TL:141, Mc-WS:155
  The City of Satisfactions.
    D. Hoffman. Ho-P:105
  Coal for Mike. B. Brecht.
    Li-TU:142
  Crossing Kansas by Train.
    D. Justice. Du-RG:45,
    Mc-WS:119
  Distant Train. Tr-US II:272
  Down at the Station, Early
    Every Morning. Mo-TL:80
  The El-Painter's Daughter.
    M. Kessler. Ls-NY:222
  The Electric Train. M. Nakagiri.
    Sh-AM:120
  Elevated. J. Nims. St-H:154
  The Express. S. Spender.
    Bo-GJ:210, Br-TC:401, Co-RG:157,
    To-MP:21, Un-MB:474, Wi-LT:498
  From a Railway Carriage.
    R. Stevenson. Ar-TP3:86,
    Cl-DT:62, Fa-FP:189, La-PV:180,
    Ox-BC:298, Pe-FB:42

  The Ghost That Jim Saw. B. Harte.
    Br-SM:6, Co-PM:84
  Habitat. J. Anderson. Sc-TN:1
  Hoar-Frost, Station Smoke, Rusty
    Tracks. R. Cuscaden. St-H:34
  I Like to See It Lap the Miles.
    E. Dickinson. Fe-FP:187,
    Ga-FB:265, Hu-MP:166, La-PV:177,
    Mc-PR:43, Rv-CB:895, Sh-RP:180,
    Sm-LG:295, Un-MA:96, Wi-LT:11
  I Wish. R. Mortimer. Le-M:72
  In the Smoking Car. R. Wilbur.
    Un-MA:677, Wi-LT:599
  It's Here in the. R. Atkins.
    Ad-PB:197, Bo-AN:171,
    Jo-SA:98, Pe-SS:149
  Limited. C. Sandburg. Mo-BG:22,
    Sh-AP:157, Sm-LG:296, Un-MA:201
  Midnight on the Great Western.
    T. Hardy. De-CH:24
  A Modern Dragon. R. Bennett.
    Ar-TP3:84, Au-SP:160, La-PV:178
  Morning Express. S. Sassoon.
    Hi-WP II:165
  My Imagination. M. Petla.
    Ba-HI:116
  Night Journey. T. Roethke.
    Bl-FP:80, Bo-HF:36, Br-AF:231,
    Gr-EC:239, Ha-TP:25
  Night Mail. W. Auden. Gr-CT:407,
    Ha-PO:44, Hi-WP I:132
  Night Train. R. Francis.
    Ar-TP3:84, Ha-LO:87
  Night Train. Hsü Chih-mo.
    Hs-TC:93
  Nobody. J. Wade. Sc-TN:222
  On the El. Z. Landau. Ho-TY:100
  The Orient Express. R. Jarrell.
    Sh-AP:224
  Outside Fargo, North Dakota.
    J. Wright. Kh-VA:10
  Passenger Train. E. Chase.
    Au-SP:169
  Prayers for the First Forty Days
    of the Dead. S. Yesenin.
    Ca-MR:109
  Pullman Porter. Bu-DY:36
  Railroad Reverie. E. Young.
    Gr-EC:241
  The Railway Train. Tr-US I:260
  Reading Yeats I Did Not Think.
    L. Ferlinghetti. Pl-ML:117
  Riding the "A." M. Swenson.
    Ad-CI:37, Mo-GB:24
  The River. H. Crane. Al-VBP:1210,
    Bl-FP:81, Sh-AP:199, Un-MA:522
  Runaway Engine. M. Clarke.
    St-FS:33
  The Sea. Suzanne G.
    Le-M:104

A Siding near Chillicothe.
   R. Lattimore.   Br-AF:202
Song.   Tr-US II:150
Song of the Train.   D. McCord.
   Au-SP:166, Fe-FP:188
Stop.   R. Wilbur.   Ha-WR:87
The Suburban Train.
   A. Voznesensky.   Ca-MR:69
Sun City.   B. Cutler.
   St-H:38
Sunday at Hampstead. J. Thomson.
   Al-VBP:1010, Sm-MK:12, Sp-OG:345
Texas Trains and Trails.
   M. Austin.   Ar-TP3:85,
   Au-SP:154
Tracks.   E. Schwager.   Ad-CI:36
Train.   K. Baba.   Le-TA:95
The Train.   Be-AP:35
The Train.   Lo-TY:9
Train Tune.   L. Bogan.
   Gr-EC:240
Trains.   R. Burgunder.
   Ar-TP3:85
The Trains.   R. Spencer.
   Le-M:135
Trains.   J. Tippett.   Ar-TP3:86,
   Au-SP:171, Fe-FP:188, Fr-MP:18
Trains at Night.   F. Frost.
   Ar-TP3:86
Transcontinent.   D. Hall.
   Du-RG:41, La-OC:145, Pe-M:31
Travel.   E. Millay.   Ar-TP3:87,
   Bo-HF:43, Fe-FP:190, Hu-MP:169,
   La-PP:40, Sh-RP:99, Th-AS:151
"Two, Two!" Toots the Train.
   On-TW:8
Vacation.   W. Stafford.
   Br-AF:149
Vendor.   R. Roseliep.
   De-FS:157, St-H:179
The Ways of Trains.
   E. Coatsworth.   Ar-TP3:86,
   Au-SP:170
TRAITORS: see TREASON
TRAMPS
   Ballad of Death.
      G. Topirceanu.   Mc-AC:51
   The Big Rock Candy Mountain.
      Gr-CT:280, Gr-GB:228,
      Hi-WP I:96, Pe-SS:86
   Bowery.   D. Ignatow.
      Pe-M:70
   Bums, on Waking.   J. Dickey.
      Mo-TS:29
   The Dead Swagman.   N. Cato.
      Co-RM:140
   Five for the Grace of Man.
      W. Scott.   Ca-VT:312
   Hallelujah, Bum Again.
      Gr-GB:231

Moving Through the Silent Crowd.
   S. Spender.   To-MP:22
November.   T. Hughes.
   Pa-GTB:565
On the Swag.   R. Mason.
   Ga-S:206
The River.   H. Crane.   Al-VBP:1210,
   Sh-AP:199, Un-MA:522
The Road to Vagabondia.   D. Burnet.
   Fe-PL:410
Shovelling Iron Ore.   Gr-GB:232
The Swagman.   C. Dennis.
   Gr-EC:212
Things of the Spirit.
   M. Mason.   Hu-PN:527
Tramp.   R. Hughes.   Un-MB:407
A Trampwoman's Tragedy.
   T. Hardy.   Ox-BN:825
Two Bums Walk Out of Eden.
   R. Francis.   Ke-PP:23
Two Girls of Twelve or So.
   C. Reznikoff.   La-OC:90
Two Tramps in Mud Time.
   R. Frost.   Un-MA:189, Wi-LT:176
Waltzing Matilda. A. Paterson.
   Gr-CT:138, Gr-GB:259,
   Ha-PO:238, Mc-WK:147
TRANQUILITY: see PEACE OF MIND;
   QUIETNESS
TRANSIENCE: see IMPERMANENCE;
   LIFE, BREVITY
TRANSLATING: see also HUMOR -
   TRANSLATING
   Homage to Arthur Waley.
      R. Fuller.   Pl-ML:51
   Who Translates a Poet Badly.
      G. Prado.   Co-EL:39
TRANSPORTATION: see also HUMOR -
   TRANSPORTATION; and various
   means of transportation, as
   RAILROADS
   Down the Stream the Swans All
      Glide.   S. Milligan.
      Co-OT:60, St-FS:62
   Progress.   E. Agnew.
      Br-AF:233
   There Are So Many Ways of
      Going Places.   L. Thompson.
      Au-SP:161, Fe-FP:184
TRAPPING: see also HUMOR - TRAPPING
   The Boys and the Apple-Tree.
      A. O'Keeffe.   De-TT:120
   Chain.   P. Petrie.   Co-BBW:242
   A Change of Heart.   V. Hobbs.
      Br-SS:151
   The Fox.   I. Salomon.   Ls-NY:202
   Hunter's Song.   Do-CH:(38)
   The Lobster Pot.   J. Arden.
      Co-EL:25
   Mink.   R. Lowell.   Be-EB:30

TRAPPING — cont'd.
A Mole-Catcher Am I.   De-CH:612
Myxomatosis. P. Larkin.
  Co-EL:30
The Rabbit. W. Davies.
  Hi-WP I:32
The Snare. P. MacDonough.
  Co-BBW:55
The Snare. J. Stephens. Ad-PE:22,
  Ar-TP3:62, Bl-OB:130, Co-BBW:21,
  Co-IW:28, De-CH:89, Gr-EC:32,
  La-PP:51, La-PV:151, Mc-WS:44,
  Se-PR:300, Sm-MK:159, Th-AS:50
The Trap. W. Beyer. Du-RG:108,
  Ha-PO:127
Trap. W. Kerr. De-FS:128
Upon the Lark and the Fowler.
  J. Bunyan. Co-BBW:256,
  De-CH:104
TRAUBEL, HELEN: see HUMOR –
  TRAUBEL, HELEN
TRAVEL AND TRAVELERS: see also
  HUMOR – TRAVEL AND TRAVELERS;
  TOURISTS; VOYAGES; WANDERLUST
America for Me. H. Van Dyke.
  Er-FA:292, Hu-MP:403, Sh-RP:214,
  Th-AS:168, Vi-PP:39
Babylon. Gr-CT:275
Chorus. W. Auden. Un-MB:455
The Daisy. A. Tennyson.
  Ox-BN:489
Dance Songs, II. Tr-US I:28
Driving Cross-Country.
  X. Kennedy. Br-TC:234
Exile. D. Scott. Sa-B:59
From a Railway Carriage.
  R. Stevenson. Ar-TP3:189,
  Cl-DT:62, Fe-FP:189, La-PV:180,
  Ox-BC:298, Pe-FB:42
God Has Been Good to Me.
  F. Keyes. Ke-TF:454
The Guest of Twilight.
  Cheng Ch'ou-yü. Pa-MV:42
I Have Lost My Shoes.
  C. Suasnavar. Fe-FP:490
I Thought It Was Tangiers I
  Wanted. L. Hughes.
  Bo-HF:84, Hu-PN:196
Johnny Fife and Johnny's Wife.
  M. Merryman. Ar-TP3:95,
  Au-SP:161
Journey Song. Tr-US I:74
The Listeners. W. de la Mare.
  Al-VBP:1118, Er-FA:406, Fe-FP:513,
  Pa-OM:298, Re-TW:116, Sh-RP:34,
  Un-MB:196, Wi-LT:131
Long Journey. Pien Chih-lin.
  Hs-TC:161
The Mapmaker on His Art.
  H. Nemerov. Du-SH:31

Morning Express. S. Sassoon.
  Hi-WP II:165
Night Journey. T. Roethke.
  Bl-FP:80, Bo-HF:36, Br-AF:231,
  Gr-EC:239, Ha-TP:25
O Dreams, O Destinations, 9.
  C. Lewis. Pa-GTB:497
October Journey. M. Walker.
  Ad-PB:146, Bo-AN:132, Hu-PN:317
On His Thirty-Third Birthday.
  Ch'ang Kuo Fang. Rx-LT:118
Post Early for Space.
  P. Henniker-Heaton. Br-AF:239
Returning at Night.
  Chang Hsiu-ya. Pa-MV:34
Rides. G. Derwood. Wi-LT:686
A Road Might Lead to Anywhere.
  R. Field. Au-SP:166,
  Fe-FP:183, La-PV:168, Mc-WK:199,
  Pe-FB:45, St-FS:124
Some Foreign Letters. A. Sexton.
  En-PC:274, Un-MA:687
Song of the Blue Roadster.
  R. Field. Fe-FP:184
The Swallow. L. Aikin. Ox-BC:110
Sweet Stay-at-Home. W. Davies.
  De-CH:36
To Henrietta, on Her Departure
  for Calais. T. Hood. Ox-BC:181
The Trains. R. Spencer. Le-M:135
Travel. E. Millay. Ar-TP3:87,
  Bo-HF:43, Fe-FP:190, Hu-MP:179,
  La-PP:40, Sh-RP:99, Th-AS:151
The Traveler. Ho Hsun. Rx-LT:41
The Traveller. J. Berryman.
  Ca-VT:379
The Traveller. O. Goldsmith.
  Al-VBP:584
Vacation Time. R. Bennett.
  Br-SS:162
When You and I Grow Up.
  K. Greenaway. Bo-FP:135,
  Ch-B:108, Hu-MP:174
Where I Went. Mo-MGT:190
Wonder where This Horseshoe Went.
  E. Millay. Ar-TP3:94, Pe-FB:41
TRAVIS, WILLIAM BARRETT
The Defence of the Alamo.
  J. Miller. Pa-OM:173
TREACHERY: see also BETRAYAL;
  CONSPIRACY; LOVE – BETRAYAL;
  TREASON
Admiral Hosier's Ghost.
  R. Glover. Al-VBP:555
Aghadoe. J. Todhunter.
  Co-BL:168, Co-PI:189
And Then There Were None.
  E. Millay. Cr-WS:42
Ballad. Tr-US I:125
The Baron of Braikley. Ox-BB:618

Black Kettle Raises the Stars
and Stripes. L. Simpson.
Cr-WS:24
The Braes of Yarrow. Ox-BB:590
Clyde's Waters. Ox-BB:331
Consider These, for We Have
Condemned Them. C. Day-Lewis.
Wi-LT:428
Czecho-Slovakia. E. Millay.
Cr-WS:45
The Death of Ben Hall.
W. Ogilvie. Co-PT:214
The Death of Lord Warriston.
Ox-BB:603
Dialogues, II. Tr-US I:119
The Dodger. Em-AF:755
Edom o' Gordon. Ox-BB:598
Fair Isabell of Rochroyall.
Ox-BB:144
Fa'se Footrage. Ox-BB:279
A Gest of Robyn Hode, The Fifth
and Eighth Fyttes.
Ox-BB:464, 484
Glasgerion. Ox-BB:123
The Golden Vanity. Bl-OB:55,
Co-SS:193, De-CH:398, Fo-OG:10,
Ho-WR:128, Rv-CB:438
Jamie Telfer and the Fair
Dodhead. Ox-BB:549
Jesse James. Br-AF:111,
Ho-WR:116, Mc-WS:161
Johnie o'Cocklesmuir. Ox-BB:535
Lord Douglas. Ox-BB:324
The Lord of Lorn and the Fals
Steward. Ox-BB:285
Lord Thomas and Fair Annet.
Ox-BB:178
A Lytell Geste of Robyn Hode.
Ma-YA:43
Northumberland Betrayd by
Dowglas. Ox-BB:526
Parcy Reed. Ox-BB:586
Radhadevi's Dance.
Nayacandra Suri. Al-PI:53
The Rise of Shivaji. Z. Ghose.
Ca-MB:59
Sea Lullaby. E. Wylie. Co-BN:78
Sir Aldinger. Ox-BB:23
A Sketch from Private Life.
G. Byron. Ox-BN:253
Stratton Water. Ox-BB:680
The Three Butchers. Co-RM:102
Two Wise Generals. T. Hughes.
Ca-MB:98
Young Johnstone. Ox-BB:212
TREASON: see also HUMOR - TREASON;
TREACHERY
The Deserter. J. Curran.
Al-VBP:604
John Dory. Ma-BB:122

Major Andre. Em-AF:428
To a Traitor. Tr-US II:301
TREASURE-TROVES: see also HUMOR -
TREASURE-TROVES
Spanish Waters. J. Masefield.
Fe-FP:514, Mc-WK:141, Pa-OM:207
TREASURES: see also KEEPSAKES
Treasure. E. Long. Br-BC:65
Treasures in Heaven. Bible.
N.T. Matthew. Un-GT:309
TREATIES: see also SATIRE -
TREATIES
Atlantic Charter, A.D. 1620-1942.
F. Young. Ar-TP3:39, Br-AF:86,
Vi-PP:221
The Hand That Signed the Paper.
D. Thomas. Mc-WS:102,
Tr-MR:190, Un-MB:499
TREE FROGS: see TOADS
TREE TOADS: see TOADS
TREES: see also ARBOR DAY;
CHRISTMAS TREES; FORESTS
AND WOODS; HUMOR - TREES;
LEAVES; LUMBERING; WOOD;
and names of individual
trees, as OAK TREES
Against the Broad Sky.
Takahama Kyoshi. Ma-FW:273
The All Alone Tree.
F. Gallagher. Bo-FP:98
All the Tree's Hands.
J. Nichols. Un-MW:146
Alone Together. G. Cohoe.
Al-WW:26
Arbor Day. D. Thompson.
Br-SG:100, Br-SS:141, Mc-AW:94
An Arbor Day Tree. Sh-RP:207
Arbor Vitae. C. Patmore.
Ox-BN:656
Les Arbres. M. Bracker. Ke-TF:377
Archibald's Example.
E. Robinson. Gr-CC:183
Autumn Colors. Wen I-to.
Hs-TC:52
Autumn Fancies. Fe-FP:212,
Hu-MP:279, Ja-PA:15
Autumn Fashions. E. Thomas.
Ha-YA:99
Balme. E. Spenser. De-CH:471
Be Different to Trees. M. Davies.
Fe-FP:208, Hu-MP:269
Bedtime. E. Coatsworth.
Gr-TG:52
Before Exeter Church.
Hsu Chih-mo. Hs-TC:81
Benediction. A. Morgan.
Ke-TF:427
The Botticellian Trees.
W. Williams. Sh-AP:168
Brooms. D. Aldis. Au-SP:326

TREES — cont'd.
A Child-Thought. W. Thorley.
  Bo-FP:273
Child's Song in Spring.
  E. Nesbit. Ox-BC:308
A City Park. A. Brody.
  La-OC:118
City Trees. E. Millay.
  Bo-HF:64, Fe-FP:250,
  La-OC:23, Sh-RP:108
Climbing. A. Fisher. Ar-TP3:102
Coolness. Onitsura. Pa-SG:127
Cry Silent. D. Whitewing.
  Al-WW:56
The Dead Branch. D. Gibson.
  Ls-NY:77
The Deceptive Present, the
  Phoenix Year. D. Schwartz.
  Co-BN:99
Deliverance. L. Lee.
  Go-BP:238
During a Storm. Mo-TB:130
Every Time I Climb a Tree.
  D. McCord. Ar-TP3:103,
  Au-SP:192, Ho-GC:34, La-PP:62,
  La-PV:4, Un-GT:253
The Fallen Tree. A. Young.
  Co-BN:148
Fallen Tree Elegy. V. Contoski.
  Sc-TN:30
Fear of the Earth. A. Comfort.
  Un-MB:519
Fed. E. Bragdon. Ke-TF:426
Foreign Lands. R. Stevenson.
  Bo-FP:86, Hu-MP:179
Forester's Song. A. Coppard.
  Fe-FP:214, Hu-MP:279
The Gardener. Po-Chu-I.
  Co-BN:209, Go-BP:40, Pa-SG:166
A Ghost Story. De-PP:40
Golden Bough. E. Wylie.
  Un-MA:276
Good Company. K. Baker.
  Fe-FP:21
The Green Grass Growing All
  Around. Gr-EC:47, Hu-MP:237
Grongar Hill. J. Dyer.
  Al-VBP:544, Cl-FC:26, Gr-CT:240
Haiku 5. E. Knight. Ra-BP:206
How the Leaves Came Down.
  S. Coolidge. Hu-MP:281
Hungry Tree. N. Altshuler.
  Le-M:205
I Did Not Know the Truth of
  Growing Trees. D. Schwartz.
  Wi-LT:522
I Sit Cooling Beneath It.
  Kyoroku. Do-TS:5
I Stand under the Naked Tree.
  L. McCall. Le-M:188

If You Are Wise. Ju-CP:12
In a Wood. T. Hardy. Ox-BN:821
In Praise of Johnny Appleseed.
  V. Lindsay. Se-PR:99
In Spring I Look Gay. Mo-MGT:155
Into the Vast Sky. K. Takahama.
  Sh-AM:163
Irradiations. J. Fletcher.
  Un-MA:313
It Is Raining. L. Mitchell.
  Ar-TP3:170, Au-SP:311
A Lady Stays. Re-RR:12
Learning by Doing. H. Nemerov.
  Br-TC:313
The Lone Tree and Others.
  Liu Ta-pai. Hs-TC:9
Motto for a Tree-Planting.
  R. Gilder. Se-PR:95
The Music of a Tree.
  W. Turner. Un-MB:347
The Nest. J. de Ibarbourou.
  Be-UL:49
The Old Tree. A. Young.
  Bo-GJ:49
On Killing a Tree. G. Patel.
  Al-PI:104
Outside the Door. A. Wynne.
  Au-SP:334
Planting a Tree. N. Turner.
  Ha-YA:53, Sh-RP:209
Planting Trees. V. Friedlaender.
  Co-BN:146
A Proper Place. R. Nye.
  Co-PU:46
Pruning Trees. Po Chu-i.
  Ma-FW:107, Pa-SG:169
Rain Portrait. J. Untermeyer.
  Sc-TN:213
The Recovery. E. Blunden.
  Un-MB:398
The Robber. W. Turner. Un-MB:345
The Room. C. Aiken.
  Un-MA:424, Wi-LT:332
Sleep Impression. C. Sandburg.
  Sh-RP:60
Solace. C. Delany. Ad-PB:71,
  Bo-AN:59, Hu-PN:178
Some Trees. J. Ashbery.
  Mo-BG:122
Song. R. Dixon. Gr-CT:316
Song. Sung Tzu-hou. Pa-SG:84
Song of the Open Road.
  O. Nash. Mo-BG:121
Song to a Tree. E. Markham.
  Fe-FP:207, Hu-MP:268
Sonnet III. Feng Chih. Hs-TC:149
The Sound of Trees. R. Frost.
  Bo-HF:58, Sm-PT:11
Speak to Me. C. O'John.
  Al-WW:64

Strange Tree. E. Roberts.
   Co-BN:159, Fe-FP:208,
   Hu-MP:278, Th-AS:81
Symmetries and Asymmetries.
   W. Auden. Ma-FW:107
Tapestry Trees. W. Morris.
   Co-BN:150, Fe-FP:209, Hu-MP:270
Three Little Trees. Ch-B:67
To My Wife. J. Simcock.
   Gr-BT:91
To the Wayfarer. Ar-TP3:217,
   Br-SS:144
The Tree. B. Björnson.
   Bo-FP:268, Co-PS:75,
   Fe-FP:467, Hu-MP:271
The Tree. A. Hopewell.
   Pa-RE:123
Tree. J. Hunter. Le-M:123
The Tree. J. Rose. La-GI:16
The Tree. J. Very. Co-PS:72,
   Se-PR:96, Un-GT:254
The Tree and the Lady.
   T. Hardy. Un-MB:33
Tree at My Window. R. Frost.
   Bo-HF:59, Co-BN:149, Un-MA:182
Tree Birthdays. M. Davies.
   Br-BC:9
Tree Climbing. K. Fraser.
   Ho-ME:10
A Tree Design. A. Bontemps.
   Bo-HF:66
Tree in December. M. Cane.
   Un-MA:235
A Tree Is a Base for Poison Ivy.
   V. Williams. Le-M:32
Tree-Sleeping. R. Coffin.
   Ha-LO:54
A Tree with No Leaves.
   J. Gonzalez. Jo-VC:72
Trees. H. Behn. Ar-TP3:204,
   Au-SP:368, Br-SS:144, Ha-YA:52,
   Pe-FB:74, Un-GB:10
Trees. S. Coleridge. Bo-FP:229,
   Ch-B:26, Hu-MP:266, Ox-BC:170
Trees. N. Dishman. Le-M:39
Trees. S. Forman. Le-M:82
Trees. R. Johnson. Me-WF:5
Trees. J. Kilmer. Er-FA:247,
   Fe-FP:207, Hu-MP:266, Sp-OG:357
Trees. H. Nemerov. Co-BN:159
Trees. C. O'John. Al-WW:69
The Trees. A. Rich. Ha-WR:56
The Trees. W. Williams.
   Sm-PT:17
Trees and Evening Sky.
   N. Momaday. Ni-CD:102
The Trees Are a Beautiful Sight.
   M. Lasanta. Ba-HI:63
Trees in the Garden.
   D. Lawrence. Un-MB:298

The Trees Share Their Shade.
   N. Dishman. Le-WR:11
The Twig. J. Rolnick.
   Ho-TY:165
The Two Old Women of Mumbling
   Hill. J. Reeves. Br-SM:13
Undertone. D. Quick. De-FS:153
The War Against Trees.
   S. Kunitz. Ke-PP:42
What Do We Plant? H. Abbey.
   Ar-TP3:205, Fe-FP:211, Hu-MP:269
Winter Branches. M. Widdemer.
   Sh-RP:98
Winter Night. C. Hutchison.
   Ar-TP3:199
The Winter Trees. C. Dyment.
   Cl-FC:63
Woodman, Spare That Tree.
   G. Morris. Er-FA:243,
   Fe-FP:546, Hu-MP:267
TRELAWNY, SIR JONATHAN
   The Song of the Western Men.
   R. Hawker. Co-RG:25, Hi-FO:161,
   Na-EO:109, Ox-BN:459, Rv-CB:777
TREVES, SIR FREDERICK
   In the Evening. T. Hardy.
   Pl-IO:183
TRIALS: see also HUMOR - TRIALS
   Garfield's Murder. Hi-TL:142
   Tim Turpin. T. Hood.
   Ho-WR:84
TRICKS: see also APRIL FOOL'S DAY;
   HALLOWEEN; HIDING
   The Alarmed Skipper. J. Fields.
   Co-SS:83, Un-GT:233
   All Your Fortunes We Can Tell Ye.
   B. Jonson. Gr-CT:162
   As I Was Walking Slowly.
   A. Housman. Li-TU:65
   Ballad. Tr-US I:125
   Bandy Legs. Ir-BB:26, Mo-MGT:136,
   Wr-RM:109
   Bat, Bat. Ir-BB:191, Mo-MGT:85,
   Wr-RM:73
   Brown Robin. Ox-BB:227
   A Children's Don't.
   H. Graham. Co-BB:90
   Clootie. Ma-BB:94
   Conversion. J. Lillie. Co-BBW:74
   Coyote and Junco. Te-FC:77
   The Crafty Miss of London.
   Ox-BB:646
   Dick o' the Cow. Ox-BB:538
   A Dog and a Cock. Ir-BB:237
   Dwarves' Song. J. Tolkien.
   Li-TU:89
   The Enormous Easter Egg Hunt.
   M. Neville. Su-FVI:29
   The Fair Flower of Northumberland.
   Ma-BB:222, Ox-BB:272

TRICKS — cont'd.
  The Fair Lass of Islington.
    Ox-BB:649
  The Fox and the Hedgehog.
    Archilochus. Bo-FP:81
  The Gay Goshawk. Ma-BB:183,
    Ox-BB:222
  Get Up and Bar the Door.
    Al-VBP:56, Ar-TP3:17, Bl-OB:19,
    Fo-OG:49, Ha-PO:75, La-PV:214,
    Pa-OM:94, Un-GT:123
  The Hare and the Tortoise.
    I. Serraillier. Co-BBW:88
  Hobie Noble. Ox-BB:572
  How a Fisherman Corked Up His
    Foe in a Jar. G. Carryl.
    Co-PM:31
  If I Had a Firecracker.
    S. Silverstein. Co-PS:116
  Jock o' the Side. Ox-BB:567
  The Leprahaun. R. Joyce.
    Co-PM:109
  Little Jenny Wren. Wr-RM:71
  Lizards and Snakes. A. Hecht.
    Br-TC:183, Ha-TP:39
  The Lochmabyn Harper.
    Ma-BB:208, Ox-BB:582
  A Melancholy Song. Mo-MGT:205,
    Rv-ON:106, Wr-RM:16
  The Merchant and the Fidler's
    Wife. Ox-BB:640
  Mrs. Mason's Basin. Br-FF:(10),
    Ir-BB:192, Mo-MGT:141, Rv-ON:86
  Old Sir Simon the King.
    Br-FF:(12), Ir-BB:270,
    Mo-MGT:180
  The Pullet. Bu-DY:92
  Robin and Richard. Ir-BB:30,
    Mo-MGT:130, Mo-NR:131,
    On-TW:9, Wr-RM:20
  Robin Hood and the Butcher.
    Ma-BB:62
  Robin Hood and Two Priests.
    Ma-BB:66
  Room for a Jovial Tinker. Ox-BB:36
  The Seals. D. Aldis. Ar-TP3:80
  The Shepherd Boy and the Wolf.
    W. Leonard. Hu-MP:406
  The Silver Fish. S. Silverstein.
    Co-SS:178
  Tatterdemalion. P. Bennett.
    Co-BBW:44
  There Was a Little Woman. Fr-WO:26,
    Ir-BB:150, Mo-MGT:56, Sm-MK:96
  There Was an Old Woman as I've
    Heard Tell. Ar-TP3:132,
    Co-PS:70, Co-PT:281, De-TT:69,
    Gr-EC:204, Ha-PO:281, Li-LB:156,
    Mo-NR:63, Pa-OM:5, Un-GT:103,
    Wr-RM:71

  Tom's Little Dog. W. de la Mare.
    Ar-TP3:50, Co-BBW:99
  The Unfortunate Miller.
    Ox-BB:643
  The Youth and the Northwind.
    J. Saxe. Co-PT:166
  See also Em-AF:174-182
TRINIDAD (ISLAND)
  Cordelia Brown. Ab-MO:57
  Husa. F. John. Sa-B:108
  Laventville. D. Walcott.
    Sa-B:24
  Poem. M. Als. Sa-B:226
TRINITY: see also GOD; HOLY SPIRIT;
    JESUS CHRIST
  It Really Happened. E. Henley.
    Br-BC:31
  St. Patrick's Breastplate.
    St. Patrick. Sm-LG:379
  Trinity. W. Langland. Ga-S:193
TRINITY BAY, CAN.
  The Cable Hymn. J. Whittier.
    Hi-TL:131
TRISTAN AND ISOLDE
  Tristram. E. Robinson.
    Sm-PT:63
TRISTAN DA CUNHA
  Tristan da Cunha. R. Campbell.
    Co-RG:52, Un-MB:411
TRIUMPH: see VICTORY
TROJAN WAR: see also names of
    Greeks, as ULYSSES and
    Trojans, as HECTOR
  Because I Have Not Known.
    O. Mandelstam. Ca-MR:152
  The God of War. Aeschylus.
    Ke-PP:6
  Night Encampment Outside Troy.
    A. Tennyson. Co-RG:39
  Palladium. M. Arnold.
    Ox-BN:646, Pa-GTB:366
  To Helen. D. Schwartz.
    Ls-NY:26
TROLLS
  Perry-the-Winkle. J. Tolkien.
    Ar-TP3:158
  The Stone Troll. J. Tolkien.
    Li-TU:110, Lo-LL:9
TROMBONES: see also HUMOR -
    TROMBONES
  New Orleans. H. Carruth. Br-AF:201
TROPICS: see also JUNGLES
  All Tropic Places Smell of Mold.
    K. Shapiro. Ca-VT:375
  Down and Out. C. Hay.
    Co-RM:151
  Reconnaissance. A. Bontemps.
    Bo-AN:80, Bo-HF:54, Ra-BP:92
TROUBADOURS: see MINSTRELS AND
    TROUBADOURS

TROUBLEMAKERS: see also HUMOR -
   TROUBLEMAKERS
  The Bold Unbiddable Child.
    W. Letts. Co-PI:94
  Foxgloves. T. Hughes. Ha-LO:99
  A Kind of Hero. V. Scannell.
    Co-RM:207
TROUBLES: see MISFORTUNE
TROUSERS: see HUMOR - TROUSERS
TROUT
  Johnshaven. Gr-GB:178
  Ocean. R. Jeffers. Pe-OA:87
  Sacrifice of a Rainbow Trout.
    J. Langland. Ha-TP:123
  A Salmon Trout to Her Children.
    Le-IB:45, Su-FVI:69, Tr-US I:3
  The Trout. D. Hine. Ls-NY:186
  The Trout. J. Montague.
    Co-PI:141
  Trout Shadows. S. Muro.
    Sh-AM:53
TROY: see also TROJAN WAR
  The Sirens' Song. Homer.
    Mo-GR:13
  Troynovant. T. Dekker. Gr-CT:297
TRUANCY: see RUNAWAYS
TRUCKS
  Country Trucks. M. Shannon.
    Ar-TP3:93, Fe-FP:243
  The Grumbling Truck. R. Bennett.
    Hu-MP:164
  Song of the Truck. D. Frankel.
    Br-AF:235
  A Trucker. T. Gunn. Ha-TP:26
  Trucks. J. Tippett. Fe-FP:186
TRUMAN, HARRY S: see SATIRE -
   TRUMAN, HARRY S
TRUMPETS: see also SATIRE -
   TRUMPETS
  From Jazz for Five, 5: Shake
    Keane, Trumpet. J. Smith.
    To-MP:195
  How High the Moon. L. Jeffers.
    Ad-PB:172
  Jubilate Agno. C. Smart.
    Pl-US:24
  Lewis Has a Trumpet. K. Kuskin.
    La-PV:93
  The Little Trumpet. C. Govoni.
    Li-TU:48
  Satchmo. M. Tolson.
    Ra-BP:119
  See the Conquering Hero Comes.
    N. Lee. Cl-DT:12
  A Song for St. Cecilia's Day.
    J. Dryden. Pa-RE:97
  Trumpet Player. L. Hughes.
    Ha-TP:50, Lo-TY:226
  Two Jazz Poems. C. Hines, Jr.
    Bo-AN:184, Du-RG:74

TRUST: see FAITH
TRUSTWORTHINESS
  Be True. W. Shakespeare.
    Bo-FP:306, Ch-B:89
  Casabianca. F. Hemans.
    Er-FA:184, Fe-FP:552,
    Hi-FO:189, Un-GT:159
  Lack of Steadfastness.
    G. Chaucer. Rv-CB:62
  Stars Wheel in Purple. H.D.
    Gr-CC:29, Un-MA:337
  To a Friend. A. Lowell.
    Fe-PL:127
  To Fling Songs into the Air.
    Y. Grizlov. Mo-MI:34
  A Trial Run. R. Frost.
    Hi-WP II:152
TRUTH: see also HONESTY; HUMOR -
   TRUTH; REALITY
  The Adamant. T. Roethke.
    Ls-NY:25
  Against Lying. De-CH:756
  The Battle-Field. W. Bryant.
    Fe-PL:176, Vi-PP:197
  Cassandra. R. Jeffers. Wi-LT:266
  The City of Dreadful Night.
    J. Thomson. Al-VBP:1004,
    Ox-BN:754
  Courage. G. Herbert. Bo-FP:299,
    Ch-B:97, Un-GT:305
  Each and All. R. Emerson.
    Sh-AP:25
  Ending. N. Jordan. Hu-PN:423
  Epipsychidion. P. Shelley.
    Ox-BN:286
  The Eternal. E. Tegnér.
    Pa-SG:206
  Here, in This Little Bay.
    C. Patmore. Co-BN:81,
    Ox-BN:633, Pa-GTB:368
  I Died for Beauty. E. Dickinson.
    Er-FA:85, Un-MA:95, Wi-LT:9
  If We Want to Tell a Lie.
    Do-CH:(14)
  It Must Be Abstract.
    W. Stevens. Sm-PT:124
  The Leaders of the Crowd.
    W. Yeats. Un-MB:116
  Memory. C. Rossetti. Ox-BN:716
  My Ace of Spades. T. Joans.
    Ad-BO:31
  No Matter How. S. Aleksandrovsky.
    Mo-MI:82
  On the Road Home. W. Stevens.
    Sm-PT:123
  Once to Every Man and Nation.
    J. Lowell. Vi-PP:68
  One Thread of Truth in a Shuttle.
    Do-CH:(14)
  The Pardon. W. Langland. Ga-S:126

TRUTH — cont'd.
  The Rebel. J. Fletcher.
    Un-MA:319
  Rubaiyat of Omar Khayyam.
    E. Fitzgerald. Al-VBP:832,
    Er-FA:43, Fe-FP:479, Gr-CT:329,
    Ox-BN:526, Pa-GTB:329, Pa-SG:120
  Song under Shadow. W. Benét.
    Tr-MR:198
  Sonnets LIV. W. Shakespeare.
    Al-VBP:202
  Soonest Mended. J. Ashbery.
    Ho-P:9
  Tell All the Truth but Tell It
    Slant. E. Dickinson. Wi-LT:15
  To My Son. Fe-PL:338
  Truth. G. Chaucer.
    Al-VBP:18, Rv-CB:60
  Truth. C. McKay. Ra-BP:64
  Truth Is as Old as God.
    E. Dickinson. Un-MA:103
  The Truth Is Quite Messy.
    W. Harris. Ad-BO:15
  The Wayfarer. S. Crane.
    Mc-WK:96, Mo-BG:57, Un-MA:147
  We Shall Overcome. Ba-PO:199,
    Hi-TL:228, Pl-EI:165
  A World Without Objects Is a
    Sensible Emptiness.
    R. Wilbur. Wi-LT:594
  Zola. E. Robinson. Hi-FO:255
TSUNAMIS
  The High Tide on the Coast of
    Lincolnshire. J. Ingelow.
    De-TT:183, Pa-OM:118, Sp-OG:85
TUAREG VERSE: see AFRICAN VERSE –
  BERBER
TUBMAN, HARRIET ROSS
  Harriet Tubman. M. Walker.
    Hu-PN:320
  Runagate, Runagate. R. Hayden.
    Ad-PB:120, Be-MA:61, Hu-PN:293,
    Jo-SA:38, Ra-BP:128
TUCK, FRIAR: see FRIAR TUCK
TUGBOATS
  Tugs. J. Tippett. Fe-FP:195
TULIP TREES
  Tulip Trees. S. Sitwell.
    Un-MB:401
TULIPS
  Lonely Tulip Grower. J. Alvarez.
    Jo-SA:11
  Tulip. W. Smith. Sh-RP:206
  Tulip. H. Wolfe. Un-MB:303
  Tulip Beds in Holland.
    A. Morgan. Ke-TF:435
  Tulips. P. Colum. Pl-IO:76
TUMBLEWEEDS
  Tumbleweed. R. Carden. Al-WW:36
  Tumbleweed. D. Wagoner. Co-BN:228

Tumbling Mustard. M. Cowley.
  Br-AF:102
TUNING
  Pyrargyrite Metal, 9.
    C. Meireles. An-TC:47
TUNNELS: see also HUMOR – TUNNELS;
  SUBWAYS
  Because a Tunnel. F. Saito.
    Sh-AM:152
  Tunnel. F. Shimazaki. Le-TA:96
TUPELO, MISS.
  The Tupelo Destruction.
    Em-AF:474
TURKEY: see also BYZANTIUM;
  TURKISH VERSE
  Turkish Garden. C. Trypanis.
    Ls-NY:238
TURKEY – HISTORY AND PATRIOTISM
  Lepanto. G. Chesterton.
    Ga-FB:196, Hi-FO:119, Un-MB:205
TURKEYS: see also HUMOR – TURKEYS
  The Girl Who Took Care of the
    Turkeys. Te-FC:67
  The Little Girl and the Turkey.
    D. Aldis. Ag-HE:9
  A Melancholy Lay. M. Fleming.
    Co-FB:300, Re-TW:22, Sm-LG:70
  November's Come. J. Lincoln.
    Sh-RP:233
  Turkeys Observed. S. Heaney.
    Ma-FW:98
  When Nights Are Murky. Re-RR:47
TURKISH VERSE
  A Proverb. Co-BL:55
TURNER, NAT
  The Ballad of Nat Turner.
    R. Hayden. Ca-VT:358,
    Ra-BP:133
  Remembering Nat Turner. S. Brown.
    Ad-PB:63, Be-MA:35, Hu-PN:172
TURNIPS: see also HUMOR – TURNIPS
  My Aunt Kept Turnips in a Flock.
    R. Jarrell. Ag-HE:21
  Vegetable Fantasies. H. Hoyt.
    Ir-BB:16, 17
TURQUOISE
  The Serenity in Stones.
    S. Ortiz. Ni-CD:156
TURTLES: see also HUMOR – TURTLES
  Baby Tortoise. D. Lawrence.
    Go-BP:86
  A Big Turtle. Au-SP:79, Ir-BB:75
  A Discovery. A. Knipe.
    Ma-FO:(22)
  The Egg and the Machine.
    R. Frost. Un-MA:186
  The Emancipation of George-Hector.
    M. Evans. Ab-MO:40, Bo-AN:165
  Fire Fire of the First World.
    Wo-HS:(61)

The Giant Tortoise.
  E. Lucie-Smith. Co-PU:88
The Giant Turtle Grants an
  Interview. J. Brinnin.
  Be-EB:46
Giant Turtles. G. Corso.
  Be-EB:14
Hunter's Chant Sung while
  Spearing Turtles. Tr-US I:241
The Little Turtle. V. Lindsay.
  Ar-TP3:67, Au-SP:79, Bo-FP:74,
  Bo-GJ:79, Fe-FP:145, La-PV:120,
  Li-LC:24, Pa-RE:50, Su-FVI:69,
  Th-AS:39
Living Tenderly. M. Swenson.
  Ad-PE:9, Mc-EA:100
Mud Turtles. G. Hallock.
  Sh-RP:330
Out in the Woods. Re-RR:114
Over in the Meadow. Au-SP:223,
  Ir-BB:24, On-TW:38
Paddling We Saw That Turtle.
  Le-OE:45
The Sea Turtle and the Shark.
  M. Tolson. Ad-PB:44, Ad-PE:40
Slow Pokes. L. Arlon. Mc-AW:56
Song Cycle of the Moon-Bone.
  Tr-US I:246
The Tortoise. I. Alexandru.
  Mc-AC:160
The Tortoise in Eternity.
  E. Wylie. Fe-FP:145, Ho-LP:48,
  Pl-IO:18, Rd-OA:150
Tortoise Shell. D. Lawrence.
  Go-BP:89
Tortoise Shout. D. Lawrence.
  Wi-LT:215
The Turtle's Song. Ra-BP:18
TUSKEGEE INSTITUTE
  Tuskegee. L. Hill. Hu-PN:53
TUTANKHAMEN, KING OF EGYPT: see
  HUMOR - TUTANKHAMEN, KING OF
  EGYPT
TWAIN, MARK: see CLEMENS, JANE
  LAMPTON
TWEED RIVER
  The Two Rivers. Co-BN:79,
  De-CH:404, Gr-CT:165, Gr-GB:176,
  Ma-BB:83, Rv-CB:119
TWELFTH NIGHT: see EPIPHANY
TWELVE DISCIPLES: see APOSTLES
TWENTIETH CENTURY: see also
  HUMOR - TWENTIETH CENTURY;
  SATIRE - TWENTIETH CENTURY
  If I Were a Pilgrim Child.
  R. Bennett. Ha-YA:137,
  Sh-RP:304
  Nature or Man. P. Curry. Me-WF:51
  Stars at Night. I. Takenaka.
  Sh-AM:101

Sunflower. C. Bukowski.
  Kh-VA:48
TWILIGHT
  As Now I Come. Nöin. Ba-ST:25
  As Soon as Ever Twilight Comes.
  W. de la Mare. Br-SS:27
  At Twilight. Shiki. Be-MC:31
  At Twilight. Tr-CB:37, Tr-US I:41
  Autumn Twilight in the Mountains.
  Wang Wei. Rx-LT:55
  Beauty Is Most at Twilight's
  Close. P. Lagerkvist.
  Pa-SG:108
  Calm of Evening. Hsieh T'iao.
  Le-MW:57
  Day That I Have Loved.
  R. Brooke. Fe-PL:400
  Death of an Evening Rainbow.
  Cheng Ch'ou-yü. Pa-MV:41
  Evening Shadows Touch. Buson.
  Be-CS:39
  February Twilight. S. Teasdale.
  Au-SP:355, Ha-YA:170, La-PP:28,
  La-PV:52, Pe-FB:82, Th-AS:27
  Frolic. AE. Fe-FP:99, Un-MB:144
  Georgia Dusk. J. Toomer.
  Ad-PB:29, Be-MA:17, Bo-AN:32,
  Jo-SA:102, Ra-BP:69
  The Great Breath. AE. Un-MB:143
  Greek Epigram. E. Pound.
  Un-MA:292
  Home-Coming. L. Adams. Un-MA:543
  Immense Hour. J. Jiménez.
  Pa-SG:166
  In My Loneliness. Ryözen.
  Ba-ST:42
  In the Evening. G. Chesterton.
  Li-TU:220
  June Twilight. J. Masefield.
  Go-BP:131
  London Nightfall. J. Fletcher.
  Un-MA:317
  Miracles. C. Aiken. Un-MA:472
  Mise en Scene. R. Fitzgerald.
  Ca-VT:303
  The Mountain Afterglow.
  J. Laughlin. Ca-VT:409
  Near Dusk. J. Auslander.
  Fe-FP:148, Mc-PR:165
  Ranch at Twilight. Fi-BG:75
  The Rising Moon. Fang Hsin.
  Pa-MV:82
  The Sea in the Dusk. Basho.
  Be-CS:28
  So Ghostly Then the Girl Came In.
  R. Hillyer. Gr-CC:7
  Sundown. L. Adams. Un-MA:548
  A Tree at Dusk. W. Welles.
  Hu-MP:277, Th-AS:143
  Twilight. F. Tyutchev. Pa-SG:107

TWILIGHT — cont'd.
  Twilight Calm.   C. Rossetti.
    Co-BN:109, Ox-BN:709
  Twilight Comes.   Wang Wei.
    Rx-LT:57
  The Twilight Darkness.
    K. Takahama.   Sh-AM:164
  Twilights.   I. Stern.   Ho-TY:226
  Twilit Revelation.   L. Adams.
    Un-MA:545
  The Unknown God.   AE.   Un-MB:144
  Winter Nightfall.   E. Olson.
    St-H:171
  A Winter Twilight.   A. Grimke.
    Ad-PB:16, Hu-PN:54
TWINS: see also HUMOR - TWINS
  Being Twins.   K. Jackson.
    Br-BC:21
  Betwixt and Between.   H. Lofting.
    Br-BC:26
  Dick and Will.   E. Roberts.
    Br-BC:25
  A Flight Shot.   M. Thompson.
    Co-RM:72
  GraceAnAnne.   L. Borie.
    Br-BC:26, Sh-RP:317
  The Twins.   D. Aldis.
    Br-BC:23
  The Twins.   K. Jackson.
    Br-BC:24
  Twins.   L. Perkins.   Co-OT:32
  The Twins.   E. Roberts.
    Ar-TP3:6, Br-BC:21, Mc-AW:96
  The Twins.   K. Shapiro.
    Ha-PO:70, Un-MA:636
  Twins.   De-PP:21
  The Two Little Miss Lloyds.
    E. Turner.   Ox-BC:138
TYNE RIVER
  The Waters of Tyne.   Gr-GB:124
TYPEWRITERS: see also HUMOR -
    TYPEWRITERS
  Underwood.   H. Moss.   Br-TC:308
TYRANNY
  Advice to the Slave-Drivers of
    America.   J. Barlow.   Kr-OF:29
  The Bard.   T. Gray.   Pa-GTB:115
  Determination.   J. Clarke.
    Ad-PB:144
  Epitaph on a Tyrant.   W. Auden.
    Co-EL:145, Ho-LP:90, Pe-M:69
  A Foreign Ruler.   W. Landor.
    Al-VBP:708
  The Gray Monk.   W. Blake.
    Ba-PO:9
  Howl.   A. Ginsberg.   En-PC:234,
    Sh-AP:233
  Lines on Leaving a Scene in
    Bavaria.   T. Campbell.
    Ox-BN:198

  The Prisoner.   E. Brontë.   Ox-BN:607
  Regeneration.   W. Landor.
    Al-VBP:708
  Song Composed under a Tyrannical
    King.   Tr-US I:102
  This Is the Dark Time, My Love.
    M. Carter.   Sa-B:16
TYRE, PHOENICIA
  The Old Ships.   J. Flecker.
    Co-RG:57, De-CH:363, De-TT:194,
    Go-BP:156, Hi-FO:15, Na-EO:114,
    No-CL:254, Pa-HT:95, Un-MB:272
UFO: see FLYING SAUCERS
U.N.:   see UNITED NATIONS
U.S.S.R. (UNION OF SOCIALIST SOVIET
    REPUBLICS):   see RUSSIA
UCALEGON
  Two Men.   E. Robinson.   Un-GT:91
UCHEE INDIANS: see INDIANS OF
    NORTH AMERICA - VERSE-YUCHI
UGANDA: see MUTESA, KING OF BUGANDA
UGLINESS (APPEARANCE)
  Disgrace.   Ab-MO:27
  Positives: For Sterling Plumpp.
    D. Lee.   Ad-PB:427
  The Ugly Child.   E. Jennings.
    Pa-RE:31
UKRAINE, U.S.S.R.
  The Grave.   S. Tchernichovsky.
    Me-PH:79
ULYANOV, VLADIMIR ILICH: see
    LENIN, VLADIMIR ILICH (NIKOLAI)
ULYSSES
  And Space and Time.
    V. Kovshin.   Bo-RU:48
  Argus and Ulysses.   E. Farjeon.
    Gr-EC:84
  Canto I.   E. Pound.   Ca-VT:90,
    Un-MA:297
  Ithaka.   C. Cavafy.   Ni-JP:15
  Odysseus.   C. Guri.   Me-PH:121
  The Sirens.   J. Manifold.
    Un-MB:514, Wi-LT:766
  Tales of Brave Ulysses.
    E. Clapton.   Mo-GR:11
  Ulysses.   A. Tennyson.
    Al-VBP:863, Ha-PO:40,
    Ke-TF:262, Ni-JP:16, Rv-CB:793
  Ulysses and the Siren.
    S. Daniel.   Al-VBP:154
  Ulysses Pondering.   S. Plumley.
    Ls-NY:336
UMBRELLAS: see also HUMOR -
    UMBRELLAS
  The Elf and the Dormouse.
    O. Herford.   Ar-TP3:153,
    Au-SP:285, Bo-FP:225, Ch-B:60,
    Fe-FP:345, Hu-MP:92, Mc-PR:31,
    Pa-OM:50, Pe-FB:53, Th-AS:11,
    Un-GB:13, Un-GT:15

No Drip of Rain.   I. Eastwick.
Mc-AW:80
The Story of Flying Robert.
H. Hoffmann.   Ir-BB:158,
Li-SR:28
Sudden Storm.   E. Coatsworth.
Ho-CS:38
U Is for Umbrellas. P. McGinley.
Ar-TP3:167
An Umbrella and a Raincoat.
Buson.   Do-TS:11
The Umbrella Brigade. L. Richards.
Ar-TP3:168, Au-SP:113
What Is It.   Re-RR:63
What Won't Go up a Chimney Up.
Ju-CP:10
You Can See Me in the Country.
St-FS:39
UMPIRES: see also HUMOR – UMPIRES
Hits and Runs.   C. Sandburg.
Fl-HH:41, Mo-SD:3
The Umpire.   M. Bracker.
Mo-SD:5
UNBELIEF
Belief and Unbelief.
R. Browning.   Ga-FB:130
Church Going.   P. Larkin.
Br-TC:251, Pa-GTB:557,
Un-MB:528, Wi-LT:754
Crag Jack's Apostasy. T. Hughes.
Pl-EI:86
Didymus.   L. MacNeice.
Pl-EI:84
The God.   B. Akhmadulina.
Bo-RU:2
The Great Magicians.
C. Day Lewis.   Pl-EI:82
Jesus Was Crucified.
C. Rodgers.   Ad-PB:432
The Man Without Faith.
R. Church.   Tr-MR:226
To the Stars.   T. Arghezi.
Mc-AC:29
When I Pray.   M. Classé.
Ba-HI:141
THE UNBORN: see also ABORTION;
PREGNANCY
The Abortion.   A. Sexton.
Ca-VT:636
Behind Memory.
M. Montes de Oca.   Be-UL:127
The Child Unborn.   H. Wolfe.
Gr-BT:164
Counting.   F. Johnson.
Bo-AN:27
For a Child Expected. A. Ridler.
Gr-BT:3, Wi-LT:804
the lost baby poem.   L. Clifton.
Be-MA:141
the mother.   G. Brooks.   Be-MA:79

Prayer Before Birth. L. MacNeice.
Br-TC:282, Co-PI:117, Gr-BT:183,
Pa-GTB:517, Pe-SS:34, To-MP:52
To an Unborn Pauper Child.
T. Hardy.   Al-VBP:1046,
Pa-GTB:405
Two Poems, II.   R. Abrams.
Hu-NN:111
The Vow.   A. Hecht.   Ho-P:93
UNCERTAINTY: see DOUBT; INDECISION
UNCLES: see also HUMOR - UNCLES
The Fox Rhyme.   I. Serraillier.
Co-BBW:29, Co-EL:28, Sm-MK:197
In These Dissenting Times.
A. Walker.   Ad-PB:475
Kiph.   W. de la Mare.
Ar-TP3:151
Manners.   M. Van Rensselaer.
Fe-FP:44, Hu-MP:16
My Last Afternoon with Uncle
Devereux Winslow. R. Lowell.
Ca-VT:447
My Uncle.   Gr-EC:282
The Swarming Bees.   J. Laughlin.
Ca-VT:410
A True Story.   J. Smith.Sm-MK:111
'Twas Ever Thus.   H. Leigh.
Li-SR:66
Uncle.   J. Tate.   St-H:228
The Uncle. J. Whittier. Un-GT:89
Uncle Roderick.   N. Maccaig.
To-MP:188
Zima Junction. Y. Yevtushenko.
Li-TU:31
UNDERGROUND RAILROAD: see SLAVERY;
TUBMAN, HARRIET ROSS
UNDERPRIVILEGED: see SOCIALLY
HANDICAPPED
UNDERSTANDING: see BROTHERHOOD;
SYMPATHY
UNDERTAKERS: see also HUMOR –
UNDERTAKERS
The Death of the Sheriff.
R. Lowell.   Un-MA:664
The Funeral Home.   R. Mezey.
Wi-LT:771
O'Neil the Undertaker.
T. Tommaro.   Ad-II:88
UNEMPLOYMENT
Boy with His Hair Cut Short.
M. Rukeyser.   Br-TC:350,
Ca-VT:361, Co-RG:159, Wi-LT:805
Moving Through the Silent Crowd.
S. Spender.   To-MP:22
No. No. C. Bresher. Ad-II:120
six ten sixty-nine. Conyus.Ad-PB:401
UNFAITHFULNESS: see also HUMOR –
UNFAITHFULNESS; LOVE - BETRAYAL
The Baron of Leys.   Ox-BB:270
False Gods. W. de la Mare. Pl-EI:83

UNFAITHFULNESS — cont'd.
  The Font. C. Sansom.
    Ga-S:180, Gr-BT:5
  The Hopis and the Famine. Te-FC:35
  The Nightingale. R. Barnefield.
    Al-VBP:265, De-CH:100, Pa-GTB:21
  Ruth: or The Influence of
    Nature. W. Wordsworth.
    Pa-GTB:283
  Song (Go, and Catch). J. Donne.
    Al-VBP:245, Er-FA:129, Ga-FB:37,
    Gr-BT:69, Ha-PO:175, Ke-PP:26,
    Ma-YA:79, No-CL:167, Rv-CB:290,
    Un-MW:38
  Sonnet 41. W. Shakespeare.
    Rv-CB:220
  The Twa Corbies. De-CH:102,
    Ha-PO:127, Ma-BB:132, Ma-FW:256,
    Pa-GTB:90, Rv-CB:55, Sm-LG:268,
    Sp-OG:115
UNHAPPINESS: see DESPAIR; GRIEF;
  MELANCHOLY
UNICORNS: see also HUMOR - UNICORNS
  Gazelles and Unicorn. J. Gay.
    Gr-CT:115
  i should have caught my unicorn.
    D. Witt. Ad-II:9
  The Lion and the Unicorn.
    An-IP:(29), Br-FF:9, Hi-FO:143,
    Ir-BB:270, Li-LB:80, Mo-MGT:197,
    Mo-NR:61, Na-EO:85, Pa-AP:14,
    Wr-RM:56
  Senlin. C. Aiken. Ha-LO:56
  The Strangers. A. Brown. Do-WH:39
  The Unicorn. G. Darley.
    Gr-CT:116, Ox-BN:394
  Unicorn. N. Gray. Gr-EC:38
  The Unicorn. W. Hoffman. Sc-TN:105
  The Unicorn. R. Pitter. Un-MB:404
  The Unicorn. E. Rieu. Co-BBW:286
  The Unicorn. E. Young. Ar-TP3:161,
    Au-SP:357, Fe-FP:394
  Unicorns at Harvard. N. Farber.
    De-FS:89
  The Unicorn's Hoofs. Rd-OA:169,
    Sm-LG:43
UNIFORMS
  It Lies in the Groove.
    N. Qualthrough. Le-M:26
UNION OF SOVIET SOCIALIST REPUBLICS:
  see RUSSIA
UNITED NATIONS: see HUMOR - UNITED
  NATIONS
UNITED STATES: see also AMERICA;
  AMERICANS; BALLADS, AMERICAN;
  HUMOR - UNITED STATES; SATIRE
  - UNITED STATES; and names of
  states, as OHIO and regions,
  as THE WEST
  All One People. C. Sandburg.Br-AF:33

  America. A. Bates. Vi-PP:15
  America Is Corn. R. Coffin.
    Mc-WK:158
  American Letter. A. MacLeish.
    Br-AF:3
  The Birds of America.
    J. Broughton. Br-AF:25
  Burning in the Night.
    T. Wolfe. Br-AF:14
  Centennial Hymn. J. Whittier.
    Vi-PP:86
  The Errand Imperious. E. Markham.
    Vi-PP:72
  The Flag. S. Silverstein.
    Co-PS:100
  I Am the United States.
    J. Ackerson. Ke-TF:343
  I Came to the New World Empty-
    Handed. H. Swift. Br-AF:40
  If I Was President. M. Cowan.
    Jo-VC:7
  If Miss Issippi. Re-RR:14
  Keorapsetse Kgositsile.
    G. Brooks. Ra-BP:172
  Localities. C. Sandburg.
    Br-AF:7
  Love Song. R. Whittemore.
    Br-AF:27
  Map of My Country. J. Holmes.
    Br-AF:11
  The Motorcyclist's Song.
    D. Bell. Pe-M:42
  Our Country. J. Howe. Vi-PP:18
  Quilt. J. Updike. Mc-WK:156
  Shine, Perishing Republic.
    R. Jeffers. Al-VBP:1170,
    Ca-VT:121, Sh-AP:177,
    Un-MA:369, Wi-LT:257
  Signatures. C. Stevenson.
    Br-AF:28
  A Song for the States.
    W. Whitman. Se-PR:246
  Tribute to America. P. Shelley.
    Vi-PP:36
UNITED STATES - AIR FORCE
  The U.S. Air Force.
    R. Crawford. Se-PR:125
UNITED STATES - ARMY
  The Caisson Song. E. Gruber.
    Vi-PP:107
  The First Division Marches.
    G. Rice. Vi-PP:216
UNITED STATES - CAVALRY
  Cavalry Crossing a Ford.
    W. Whitman. Co-PU:137,
    Gr-CT:338, Mo-BG:167, Ni-JP:76,
    Rv-CB:847, Sh-AP:118, Sh-RP:312
UNITED STATES - CONSTITUTION: see
  SATIRE - UNITED STATES - CON-
  STITUTION

UNITED STATES - COUNTRYSIDE
  Traveling America. J. Struther.
    Br-AF:19
UNITED STATES - HISTORY AND PATRI-
  OTISM: see also CIVIL WAR -
    UNITED STATES, 1861-1865;
    COLONIAL PERIOD IN AMERICA;
    DECLARATION OF INDEPENDENCE;
    EMANCIPATION PROCLAMATION;
    FLAG DAY; FOURTH OF JULY;
    HUMOR - UNITED STATES - HISTORY
    AND PATRIOTISM; MEMORIAL DAY;
    MEXICAN WAR, 1846-1848; REVOLU-
    TIONARY WAR IN AMERICA, 1776-
    1781; SATIRE - UNITED STATES -
    HISTORY AND PATRIOTISM; SPANISH-
    AMERICAN WAR, 1898; VETERANS DAY;
    WAR OF 1812; WESTWARD MOVEMENT;
    WORLD WAR, 1914-1918; WORLD WAR,
    1939-1945; and names of persons,
    as FRANKLIN, BENJAMIN
  America. S. Smith. Er-FA:293,
    Fe-FP:423, Fe-PL:158, Se-PR:131,
    Vi-PP:11
  America. B. Taylor. Vi-PP:37
  America the Beautiful. K. Bates.
    Bo-FP:302, Er-FA:293, Fe-FP:402,
    Ga-FB:278, Hu-MP:363, Pl-EI:164,
    Se-PR:127, Vi-PP:30
  The American Flag. J. Drake.
    Er-FA:286, Sp-OG:190, Vi-PP:55
  The American Freedom. M. Biller.
    Se-PR:128
  American Laughter. K. Robinson.
    Br-AF:118
  American Names. S. Benét.
    Br-AF:6, Mc-WK:157, Pa-HT:3,
    Sh-AP:194, Sm-LG:145
  Another Reply to "In Flanders
    Fields." J. Armstrong.
    Vi-PP:214
  Centennial Hymn. J. Pierpont.
    Vi-PP:88
  A Christmas Note for Geraldine
    Udall. K. Rexroth. Bl-FP:59
  Columbia, the Gem of the Ocean.
    Vi-PP:60
  Concord Hymn. R. Emerson.
    Al-VBP:805, Br-AF:61, Er-FA:188,
    Fe-FP:422, Hi-TL:52, Hu-MP:379,
    Ke-TF:256, Mc-PR:22, Pa-HT:18,
    Se-PR:87, Sh-AP:25, Sp-OG:193,
    Tu-WW:30, Vi-PP:99
  Eagle Plain. R. Francis. Br-AF:24
  The Flag Goes By. H. Bennett.
    Ar-TP3:205, Br-SS:168, Er-FA:294,
    Fe-FP:444, Se-PR:141, Sh-RP:211,
    Vi-PP:62
  The Flower of Liberty. O. Holmes.
    Se-PR:159

  The Fourth of July. J. Pierpont.
    Ha-YA:85, Se-PR:157, Vi-PP:83
  The Gift Outright. R. Frost.
    Br-AF:29, Mc-WK:184, Mo-BG:109,
    Sh-AP:153, Sh-RP:267, Sm-LG:144,
    Un-MA:195, Vi-PP:29, Wi-LT:179
  God Save the Flag. O. Holmes.
    Er-FA:295
  Hail, Columbia. J. Hopkinson.
    Er-FA:291, Vi-PP:32
  His Excellency General Washington.
    P. Wheatley. Hu-PN:7
  I Am an American. E. Lieberman.
    Fe-FP:448, Fe-PL:162, Vi-PP:190
  In Praise of Johnny Appleseed.
    V. Lindsay. Se-PR:99
  Invocation. S. Benét. Br-AF:10,
    Hu-MP:364, Sm-PT:99, Vi-PP:226
  it occurred to me that we were
    driving. M. Gorlin. Ad-II:82
  Land of My Heart. W. Foulke.
    Vi-PP:21
  Land of the Free. N. Hosking.
    Vi-PP:22
  Louisiana Purchase. B. Clark.
    Ke-TF:360
  The Marines' Hymn. Se-PR:124,
    Vi-PP:206
  Men. A. MacLeish. Br-AF:95
  Names. L. Mueller. Ha-TP:104
  Nathan Hale. E. Finch.
    Hi-TL:53, Vi-PP:111
  A Nation's Strength. R. Emerson.
    Br-AF:35, Fe-FP:452, Vi-PP:65
  The Need of the Hour.
    E. Markham. Vi-PP:224
  New England's Chevy Chase.
    E. Hale. Se-PR:88, Vi-PP:103
  next to of course god.
    e. cummings. Br-AF:14,
    Ca-VT:178, Pe-SS:101,
    Sh-AP:192, Wi-LT:361
  Oh Mother of a Mighty Race.
    W. Bryant. Vi-PP:73
  The Old Flag. H. Bunner.
    Vi-PP:59
  Old Flag. H. Parker. Se-PR:142
  Old Ironsides. O. Holmes.
    Co-SS:60, Er-FA:189, Fe-FP:548,
    Hi-TL:82, Mc-PR:23, Se-PR:123,
    Sp-OG:75, Vi-PP:195
  One Country. F. Stanton. Vi-PP:20
  The Pinta, the Nina and the Santa
    Maria; and Many Other Cargoes
    of Light. J. Tagliabue.
    Br-AF:23
  The Reveillé. B. Harte. Se-PR:121,
    Sp-OG:192, Vi-PP:199
  The Shannon and the Chesapeake.
    De-TT:134

UNITED STATES — HISTORY AND
    PATRIOTISM — cont'd.
  Shine, Republic. R. Jeffers.
    Br-AF:18, Tr-MR:188
  The Ship of State. H. Longfellow.
    Er-FA:294, Fe-FP:455, Vi-PP:215
  A Song for Our Flag. M. Sangster.
    Er-FA:288
  The Star-Spangled Banner. F. Key.
    Er-FA:283, Fe-FP:401, Hi-TL:65,
    Se-PR:130, Vi-PP:53
  Star-Spangled Ode. P. McGinley.
    Hi-TL:235
  The Statue of Old Andrew Jackson.
    V. Lindsay. Mc-PR:52
  A Toast to Our Native Land.
    R. Bridges. Vi-PP:75
  Unmanifest Destiny. R. Hovey.
    Vi-PP:233
  Voices of Heroes. H. Gregory.
    Gr-CC:104
  Whenever I Say "America."
    N. Turner. Ha-YA:77
  Written in a Time of Crisis.
    S. Benét. Vi-PP:220
UNITED STATES - MARINE CORPS
  The Mariners' Hymn.
    Se-PR:124, Vi-PP:206
UNITED STATES - SOCIAL LIFE AND
    CUSTOMS: see also SATIRE -
    UNITED STATES - SOCIAL LIFE
    AND CUSTOMS
  Invocation to the Social Muse.
    A. MacLeish. Wi-LT:344
  The Opening Session of Congress
    Rock and Roll. G. Dusenbery.
    Sc-TN:38
UNIVERSALITY: see also LOVE -
    UNIVERSALITY
  Dear Men & Women. J. Wheelock.
    Ho-P:307
  Each and All. R. Emerson.
    Sh-AP:25
  Earth. J. Wheelock. Tr-MR:42,
    Un-MA:343
  Enion Replies from the Caverns of
    the Grave. W. Blake. Ox-BN:39
  Enitharmon Revives with Los.
    W. Blake. Ox-BN:38
  Epitaph for Us. E. Masters.
    Sm-PT:158
  The Expectation. R. Gales. Ga-S:58
  The Force That Through the Green
    Fuse. D. Thomas. Al-VBP:1244,
    Pl-IO:98, Rv-CB:1002, Un-MB:499,
    Wi-LT:545
  Gravelly Run. A. Ammons.
    Ho-P:3
  Hot Sun Sounds. M. Sheedy.
    Ad-II:59

  The Hour of Death. F. Hemans.
    Ox-BN:307
  Hymn to Intellectual Beauty.
    P. Shelley. Ox-BN:276
  I Am the Prince. C. Causley.
    Ga-S:102
  In the Waiting Room. E. Bishop.
    Ho-P:27
  It Is Nice to Read. Onitsura.
    Be-CS:5
  Message from Home. K. Raine.
    Pl-IO:99
  Mountains, Give Me a Body.
    L. Blaga. Mc-AC:68
  Ode of the Angels of Chicago Who
    Move Perpetually. P. Carroll.
    St-H:20
  On the Universality and Other
    Attributes of the God of
    Nature. P. Freneau. Sh-AP:16
  Poet and Goldsmith. V. Watkins.
    En-PC:89
  Singing. R. Stevenson. Gr-TG:23
  Song of Myself. W. Whitman.
    Al-VBP:928, Ho-P:139, Mo-GR:101,
    Sh-AP:69, Un-MA:44, 46
  Sonnet XVI, XVIII, XXII.
    Feng Chih. Hs-TC:152, 153
  To the Garden of the World.
    W. Whitman. Mo-GR:103
  Two Sonnets. E. Robinson.
    Sm-PT:148
  Unison. J. Wheelock.
    Tr-MR:144
  Unstill Life. V. Huidobro.
    Be-UL:41
  We Are. R. Hershon. Sc-TN:92
  You. J. Masefield. Tr-MR:32
UNIVERSE: see also EARTH; HUMOR -
    UNIVERSE; LIFE ON OTHER
    PLANETS; WORLD
  Auguries of Innocence. W. Blake.
    Al-VBP:621, Ch-B:36, Co-BBW:278,
    Er-FA:69, Ga-FB:96, Ma-YA:130,
    Ox-BN:28, Pl-IO:5, Sh-RP:76,
    Sm-LG:67, Sm-MK:220, Un-GT:305
  Blue Lake of Life. Wo-HS:(15)
  Christ in the Universe.
    A. Meynell. Un-MB:65
  Housemates. O. Shepard.
    Tr-MR:192
  I Will Sing You One-O.
    R. Frost. Sm-PT:78
  In No Strange Land. F. Thompson.
    Ga-S:127, Go-BP:250, Pa-GTB:398,
    Pl-EI:7, Un-MB:90
  The Innumerable Christ.
    H. MacDiarmid. Pl-EI:156
  Job. Bible. O.T. Job.
    Pl-IO:39

Lightly Stepped a Yellow Star.
E. Dickinson.   Un-MA:101
A Man Said to the Universe.
S. Crane.   Pl-IO:139, Wi-LT:120
Measurement.   A. Sullivan.
Mc-WK:18, Sh-RP:71
The Motion of the Earth.
N. Nicholson.   Li-TU:251,
Pl-IO:38
Night on the Prairies.
W. Whitman.   La-RM:68,
Tr-MR:288
No Single Thing Abides.
T. Lucretius Carus.   Pl-IO:9
Prometheus Unbound. P. Shelley.
Pl-IO:12
Quasi-Stellar Radio Sources.
H. McCord.   Ls-NY:323
Renascence.   E. Millay.
Er-FA:95, Un-MA:440
Shells.   W. Wordsworth.
Go-BP:111
The Shore of the Universe.
K. Zinoviev.   Mo-MI:88
A Slumber Did My Spirit Seal.
W. Wordsworth.   Al-VBP:657,
Hi-WP I:20, Ma-FW:176, Ox-BN:65,
Pa-GTB:181, Rv-CB:643, Sm-LG:275
The Spring Waters, 33.   Ping Hsin.
Hs-TC:22
The Sun, the Moon, the Stars, the
Seas.   A. Tennyson.
Go-BP:274, Li-SR:94
Thanatopsis.   W. Bryant.
Al-VBP:765, Co-BN:216,
Er-FA:67, Sh-AP:17
The Universe.   M. Swenson.
Ha-TP:131
The Watcher.   S. Coblentz.
De-FS:57
THE UNKNOWN
All the Roary Night. K. Patchen.
Wi-LT:786
Conversation.   J. Berryman.
Wi-LT:567
Darest Thou Now O Soul.
W. Whitman.   Al-VBP:948
Epilogue.   W. Auden.
Sm-LG:303, Wi-LT:465
Nature.   H. Longfellow.
Co-BN:229, Fe-PL:280
no dawns.   J. Perry. Ad-PB:516
Nobody.   R. Graves.   Ha-TP:138
Sonnet XXVI. Feng Chih. Hs-TC:154
There's Something Uneasy.
I. Kharabov.   Bo-RU:45
To What Shore Would You Cross.
Kabir.   Al-PI:59
Upstairs.   J. Wade.   Sc-TN:223
Villanelle. W. Auden. Un-MB:456

UNKNOWN SOLDIER
The Unknown Soldier.   W. Benton.
Cr-WS:106
The Unknown Soldier.   A. Lewis.
Un-MB:518
The Unknown Soldier.   B. Rose.
Vi-PP:209
UNMARRIED WOMEN: see SINGLE WOMEN
UNWIN, MARY
To Mary.   W. Cowper.
Pa-GTB:164, Rv-CB:550
To Mary Unwin.   W. Cowper.
Pa-GTB:164
UNWORTHINESS
Always Before Your Voice.
E. Cummings.   Un-MA:472
Bricklayer Love. C. Sandburg.
Sh-AP:157
Dear God, the Day Is Grey.
A. Halley.   Pe-OA:287
Drum Song about a Stupid Kayak
Paddler.   Da-SC:44
Hugh Selwyn Mauberley. E. Pound.
Ba-PO:149, Ca-VT:84, Ha-PO:122,
Hi-TL:186, Un-MA:301, Wi-LT:232
St. Francis and the Cloud.
M. Welch.   Tr-MR:253
The Sonnets (Alack!).
W. Shakespeare.   No-CL:89
Sonnets (When Thou).
W. Shakespeare.   No-CL:86
The Visit of the Professor of
Aesthetics.   M. Danner.
Ad-PB:135, Be-MA:89,
Bo-AN:155, Hu-NN:31
URSA MAJOR
The Great Bear.   J. Hollander.
Br-TC:196, Wi-LT:733
The Lost Telescope.   Chi Hsüan.
Pa-MV:50
Ursa Major.   J. Kirkup. Pl-IO:32
Winter.   W. de la Mare.
Gr-CT:394, Ha-YA:144
USEFULNESS: see also SATIRE -
USEFULNESS
At Woodward's Gardens.
R. Frost.   Pl-IO:113
The Book of Thel.   W. Blake.
Ox-BN:32
Let Ye Then My Birds Alone.
J. Clare.   Re-BS:27
Of What Use Are Twigs.
Buson.   Be-CS:15
Prayers of Steel.   C. Sandburg.
Fe-FP:255, Hu-MP:403, La-OC:151,
La-PV:194, Mo-BG:26, Un-MA:203
Precious Stones.   C. Rossetti.
Ar-TP3:210, De-TT:62, Un-GT:306
We Keep a Dog to Guard the House.
Wy-CM:30

USELESSNESS: see FUTILITY;
   HELPLESSNESS
USK RIVER
   Usk.   T. Eliot.   Sm-LG:143
USURY
   Canto XLV.   E. Pound.
   Wi-LT:244
UTAH: see also names of towns,
   as SALT LAKE CITY, UTAH
   Gift of the Sego Lily.
   M. Jarvis.   Fi-BG:197
   Utah, We Love Thee.
   E. Stephens.   Se-PR:287
UTE INDIANS: see also INDIANS OF
   NORTH AMERICA - VERSE-UTE
   The Old Ute Trail.   Fi-BG:109
UTOPIAS
   The Big Rock Candy Mountain.
   Gr-CT:280, Gr-GB:228,
   Hi-WP I:96, Pe-SS:86
   Heart's Content.   Fe-PL:146
   An Invitation to Lubberland.
   Gr-GB:226
   Ode on the Last International.
   A. Zeitlin.   Ho-TY:319
VACATIONS: see also HUMOR -
   VACATIONS
   Camp Chums.   R. Waldo.
   Hu-MP:41
   Getting Back.   D. Thompson.
   Br-SS:56
   I Wish.   N. Turner.   Br-SS:156
   The Last Day of Leave.
   R. Graves.   Cr-WS:65
   The Lonely Street. W. Williams.
   Br-TC:480, Gr-CC:188
   The Most.   S. Suggs.   Ho-CT:21
   Peace and Joy.   S. Silverstein.
   Co-PS:107
   School Is Out.   F. Frost.
   Br-SS:161, Sh-RP:213
   School Is Over. K. Greenaway.
   Ar-TP3:98, Ch-B:114
   Summer Song.   J. Ciardi.
   Gr-EC:43
   Vacation Snapshot.
   M. LaFollette.   Ls-NY:310
   Vacation Time. R. Bennett.
   Br-SS:162
   Vacationer. W. Gibson.
   Mo-SD:139
   Week-End. H. Monro.
   Un-MB:233
VACCINATIONS AND INJECTIONS
   Injection. Y. Keneko.
   Le-TA:56
VAGABONDS: see GYPSIES; TRAMPS;
   WANDERLUST
VALENCIA, SP.
   Valencia. F. Keyes.   Ke-TF:397

VALENTINE'S DAY: see also HUMOR -
   VALENTINE'S DAY
   The Cardinal's Valentine.
   Ja-HH:14
   Counting Valentines.
   J. Lee.   Ja-HH:10
   For a Valentine. M. Newell.
   Bo-FP:293
   Good Bishop Valentine.
   E. Farjeon.   Co-PS:40
   Good Morning. Bo-FP:295,
   Su-FVI:48
   Hail, Bishop Valentine.
   J. Donne.   Gr-CT:39
   Hearts Were Made to Give Away.
   A. Wynne.   Ar-TP3:200,
   Se-PR:53
   A Little Valentine.   E. Winton.
   Bo-FP:293
   The Lovable Child.   A. Poulsson.
   Hu-MP:331
   My Valentine.   K. Parsons.
   Ar-TP3:200, Au-SP:361
   My Valentine.   R. Stevenson.
   Br-SS:119, Ch-B:41, Co-BL:114,
   Co-PS:37, Hu-MP:331, Mc-PR:48,
   Se-PR:52, Un-MB:59, Un-MW:139
   Phillis Inamorata.
   L. Andrewes.   Gr-CC:49
   Quite a Clown.   J. Lee.
   Ja-HH:12
   St. Valentine's Day. W. Blunt.
   Al-VBP:1054
   Saint Valentine's Day.
   C. Patmore.   Ox-BN:657
   A Skater's Valentine.
   A. Guiterman.   Br-SS:120
   Sky Valentine. E. Jay.
   Ja-HH:13
   Snowman's Valentine. K. Dee.
   Ja-HH:11
   Song.   W. Shakespeare.
   Br-SS:118
   Special Delivery.   E. Winton.
   Bo-FP:292
   A Sure Sign.   N. Turner.
   Ar-TP3:199, Au-SP:360,
   Bo-FP:291
   Tomorrow.   De-CH:490
   Tomorrow Is St. Valentine's Day.
   W. Shakespeare.   Al-VBP:191,
   Ch-B:81, Fe-FP:68,
   Hu-MP:330, Li-LC:71
   Valentine.   C.T.   Ha-YA:178,
   Sh-RP:192
   A Valentine. E. Field. Se-PR:52
   A Valentine.   E. Hammond.
   Ar-TP3:200, Ha-YA:179, Sh-RP:191
   A Valentine.   L. Richards.
   Ha-YA:180, Hu-MP:332

Valentine. S. Silverstein.
Co-PS:43
Valentine. C. Wilson. Fr-MP:8
Valentine for My Mother.
H. Lee. Hu-MP:331
Valentine Greetings. K. Sexton.
La-PH:47
Valentine's Day. A. Fisher.
Ha-YA:178, La-PH:46
Valentine's Day. Ja-HH:10
The Vinegar Man. R. Mitchell.
Hu-MP:147, Th-AS:182
When You Send a Valentine.
M. Hill. Mc-AW:65
VALLEYS: see also HUMOR - VALLEYS
Birmingham Jail. Er-FA:235,
Gr-GB:264
The Combe. E. Thomas. Pa-GTB:443
Come Down, O Maid. A. Tennyson.
Al-VBP:860, Go-BP:124,
Ox-BN:488, Rv-CB:798
The Green Valley. S. Warner.
Un-MB:377
Hearing of Harvests Rotting in
the Valleys. W. Auden.
Un-MB:457
Here in Katmandu. D. Justice.
La-RM:38
Night Practice. M. Swenson.
Li-TU:168
The Valley of Unrest. E. Poe.
Al-VBP:872
The Valley's Singing Day.
R. Frost. Pl-US:54
VALUE AND VALUES: see also HUMOR -
VALUE AND VALUES; SATIRE -
VALUE AND VALUES
The Answer. R. Jeffers. Tr-MR:222
April Inventory. W. Snodgrass.
Br-TC:398, Mc-EA:148, Wi-LT:819
Auction. J. Holmes. Mc-WK:88
Barter. S. Teasdale. Fe-FP:21,
Ga-FB:5, Hu-MP:71, Th-AS:199
The Bloody Sire. R. Jeffers.
Cr-WS:88, Wi-LT:261
Character of the Happy Warrior.
W. Wordsworth. Er-FA:85
The Commonplace. W. Whitman.
Un-MA:42
The Cricket. Hsü Chih-mo.
Hs-TC:91
England, 1802. W. Wordsworth.
Ke-PP:58, Pa-GTB:210
Father's Voice. W. Stafford.
La-RM:167
For the Moment. R. Weber.
Co-PI:196
For Want of a Nail. Gr-EC:130,
Ir-BB:134, Li-LB:166, Mo-MGT:132,
Mo-NR:103, Un-GT:305, Wr-RM:101

Four Things. H. Van Dyke.
Fe-PL:291, Un-GT:305
Good-bye. R. Emerson. Er-FA:475
I Reckon, when I Count at All.
E. Dickinson. Un-MA:101
I Want to Find the Essence.
B. Pasternak. Mo-MI:31
If Humility and Purity Be Not
in the Heart. T. Eliot.
Ar-TP3:214
It Is Man Who Counts. Do-CH:(13)
Leisure. W. Davies.
Ar-TP3:213, Co-BN:205, De-CH:137,
Er-FA:248, Fe-FP:78, Gr-EC:45,
Hi-WP I:119, Mc-WK:22, Sh-RP:117,
Sm-MK:177, Un-MB:179, Wi-LT:617
The Lien. A. Love. Th-AS:215
The Life That Counts. Er-FA:24
Little Things. J. Carney.
An-IP:(31), Ch-B:89, Er-FA:239,
Fe-FP:540, Mo-CC:(2), Ox-BC:182,
Sp-HW:33, Un-GT:306
London, 1802. W. Wordsworth.
Ga-FB:225, Ma-YA:140, Ox-BN:80,
Pa-GTB:211, Pl-ML:110
Love Enthroned. D. Rossetti.
Ox-BN:682
A Man's a Man for A' That.
R. Burns. Al-VBP:653,
Bo-HF:142, Er-FA:268, Sp-OG:330
Mary of Bethany. D. Lawrence.
Ga-S:116
The Measure of a Man. Fe-PL:312
Medgar Evers. G. Brooks.
Ad-PB:158
My Ships. E. Wilcox. Fe-PL:95
Name or Person. Lao Tzu.
Sm-MK:223
The Newlyweds. C. Criswell.
Fe-PL:96
O May I Join the Choir Invisible.
G. Eliot. Ox-BN:617
O World Be Nobler. L. Binyon.
Un-MB:156
Ode. G. Santayana. Al-VBP:1087
Of Gold and Jewels. Yuan Chieh.
Le-MW:6
Petit, the Poet. E. Masters.
Ha-PO:67, Ke-PP:106,
Sm-LG:38, Un-MA:143
The Poet. W. Whitman. Un-MA:79
Practical Concerns. W. Harris.
Ad-PB:440
A Prayer. V. Watkins. Tr-MR:50
A Question. R. Frost. Ho-TH:46
The Rich Interior Life.
R. Eberhart. Tr-MR:250
Some Verses upon the Burning of
Our House, July 10th, 1666.
A. Bradstreet. Sh-AP:10

VALUE AND VALUES — cont'd.
  Sonnet. W. Drummond. Al-VBP:304
  Sonnet XXX. E. Millay. Co-BL:34
  Soul's Liberty. A. Wickham.
    Un-MB:282
  Special Starlight. C. Sandburg.
    Tr-MR:101
  Statistics. S. Spender. Un-MB:471
  Stop Playing. Z. Shneour.
    Me-PH:85
  They Say that in the Unchanging
    Place. H. Belloc. Fe-PL:126
  Threes. C. Sandburg. Fe-PL:409
  To a Poet a Thousand Years Hence.
    J. Flecker. Gr-CT:433,
    Un-MB:274
  Treasures in Heaven. Bible.
    N.T. Matthew. Un-GT:309
  Turf-Stacks. L. MacNeice.
    Wi-LT:455
  Undue Significance a Starving
    Man Attaches. E. Dickinson.
    Wi-LT:8
  Victory in Defeat. E. Markham.
    Fe-PL:301
  The Way of Life. Laotzu.
    Mc-WK:220
  Winter Mask. A. Tate. Ho-P:269
  A Word Fitly Spoken. Bible.
    O.T. Proverbs. Fe-FP:16
  The World Is Too Much with Us.
    W. Wordsworth. Al-VBP:660,
    Er-FA:267, Fe-PL:298, Gr-CT:201,
    Ke-PP:53, Ox-BN:79, Pa-GTB:299,
    Rv-CB:636, Sp-OG:365
  You Tell Me that Times Are
    Changing. Wo-HS:(38)
VAMPIRES: see also GHOSTS
  So Separate and Strange.
    F. Stefanile. De-FS:192
  Vampire Bride. F. Stefanile.
    De-FS:190
VANBRUGH, SIR JOHN
  Epitaph on Sir John Vanbrugh.
    A. Evans. Al-VBP:521,
    Co-FB:132
VAN BUREN, MARTIN: see SATIRE –
  VAN BUREN, MARTIN
VANDERBILT, CORNELIUS: see SATIRE –
  VANDERBILT, CORNELIUS
VAN DOREN, MARK
  A Ballad of Remembrance. R. Hayden.
    Ad-PB:115, Bo-AN:109,
    Hu-PN:291, Ra-BP:131
VAN EYCK, JAN: see EYCK, JAN VAN
VAN GOGH, VINCENT: see GOGH,
  VINCENT VAN
VANITY: see CONCEIT; PRIDE
VANZETTI, BARTOLOMEO: see SACCO-
  VANZETTI CASE

VATICAN: see ST. PETER'S CHURCH
VAUDEVILLE
  Rain after a Vaudeville Show.
    S. Benét. Mo-BG:29, Un-MA:497
  Vaudeville Dancer. J. Wheelock.
    Pl-US:112
VAUGHAN, HENRY
  At the Grave of Henry Vaughan.
    S. Sassoon. Pa-GTB:454, Pl-EI:8
VEERIES: see THRUSHES
VEGETABLES: see also GARDENERS
  AND GARDENING; HUMOR –
  VEGETABLES; and names of
  vegetables, as POTATOES
  After Winter. S. Brown.
    Ad-PB:65, Be-MA:30, Bo-HF:50,
    Hu-PN:165, Jo-SA:50
  Country Vegetables. E. Farjeon.
    Bo-FP:83, Br-SG:37, Fe-FP:233
  Grandmother's Garden.
    J. Tippett. Br-SG:40
  The Plymouth Harvest.
    W. Bradford. Bo-FP:154
  poem. J. Gill. Sc-TN:69
  Vegetables. R. Field.
    Au-SP:118, Br-SG:38
VENGEANCE: see REVENGE
VENICE, IT.
  Childe Harold's Pilgrimage.
    G. Byron. Al-VBP:726
  The City of Falling Leaves.
    A. Lowell. Ar-TP3:184
  In a Gondola. R. Browning.
    Al-VBP:891
  On the Extinction of the Venetian
    Republic. W. Wordsworth.
    Al-VBP:661, Hi-FO:188, No-CL:255,
    Ox-BN:79, Pa-GTB:210, Pa-HT:110
  A Toccata of Galuppi's.R. Browning.
    Pa-GTB:345, Rv-CB:814
  Venice. Wang Tu-ch'ing. Hs-TC:195
  A Water-Colour of Venice.
    L. Durrell. Un-MB:491
  Written in the Euganean Hills,
    North Italy. P. Shelley.
    Pa-GTB:290
VENTRILOQUISTS
  Uncle. J. Tate. St-H:228
VENUS (GODDESS): see also HUMOR –
  VENUS (GODDESS)
  Anthem for St. Cecilia's Day.
    W. Auden. Br-TC:20
  Cupid's Mistaken. M. Prior.
    Al-VBP:513
  Hymn to Venus. Lucretius. Gr-CC:96
  Reading a Medal. T. Tiller.
    Pa-GTB:550
  The Ring of. C. Olson. Ca-VT:305
  Tales of Brave Ulysses.
    E. Clapton. Mo-GR:11

Venus and Adonis. W. Browne.
    No-CL:57
Venus with Young Adonis.
    B. Griffin. Al-VBP:91
VENUS (PLANET)
    For the Conjunction of Two
      Planets. A. Rich. Pl-IO:30
    Golden Venus. T. Miyoshi.
      Sh-AM:81
VERACRUZ, MEX.
    Veracruz. R. Hayden. Bo-AN:119
VERGIL
    The Motto. A. Cowley. No-CL:6
    To Virgil. A. Tennyson.
      Gr-CT:442, Pa-GTB:340
VERLAINE, PAUL
    Prelude LVI. C. Aiken.
      Br-TC:7
VERMONT
    Butternuts. E. Astley.
      Ke-TF:446
    Fall Comes to Back-Country
      Vermont. R. Warren.
      Ca-VT:278
    Green Mountain Latitudes.
      F. Frost. Ke-TF:350
    Hail, Vermont! J. Perry.
      Se-PR:288
    Landscape with Figurines.
      P. McGinley. Ke-TF:344
    Lullaby for a Vermont Town.
      F. Frost. Ke-TF:350
    On Being Chosen Poet of Vermont.
      R. Frost. Pl-ML:25
    The Windham Thaw.
      A. Guiterman. Gr-EC:58
VERSAILLES, FR.
    No Swan So Fine. M. Moore.
      Gr-CC:179
VESUVIUS, IT.
    Drifting. T. Read. Pa-HT:107
VETERANS DAY
    America's Answer. R. Lilliard.
      Vi-PP:215
    Another Reply to "In Flanders
      Fields." J. Armstrong.
      Vi-PP:214
    Armistice Day. R. Montgomery.
      Se-PR:205
    Everyone Sang. S. Sassoon.
      Co-PS:144, Ga-FB:218, Ga-S:171,
      Ha-LO:71, Mc-WK:13, Ni-JP:79,
      Pa-GTB:453, Sh-RP:88, Sm-MK:211,
      Un-MB:314
    It Shall Not Be Again.
      T. Clark. Se-PR:205
    November Eleventh. K. Burton.
      Se-PR:204
    Reply to "In Flanders Fields."
      J. Mitchell. Vi-PP:212

The Warmest and Coldest Day
      Ever. A. Kreymborg. Kr-OF:84
    When Johnny Comes Marching Home.
      P. Gilmore. Co-PS:145,
      Hi-TL:126, Vi-PP:161
VICARS: see CLERGY
VICE: see also CRIME AND CRIMINALS;
    SIN
    Vice. A. Pope. Co-EL:107
VICTORIA, QUEEN OF ENGLAND: see
    also HUMOR - VICTORIA, QUEEN
    OF ENGLAND; SATIRE - VICTORIA,
    QUEEN OF ENGLAND
    Queen Victoria. Hi-FO:218
VICTORY: see also SATIRE - VICTORY
    And Death Shall Have No Dominion.
      D. Thomas. Hi-WP II:31,
      Pl-EI:60, To-MP:34, Tr-MR:291,
      Un-MB:500, Wi-LT:546
    At the Lou-Shan Pass.
      Mao Tse-tung. Hs-TC:362
    Ghoul Care. R. Hodgson. Un-MB:193
    Last Speech to the Court.
      B. Vanzetti. Mo-BG:170
    Lines. Shen Ch'üan-ch'i.
      Cr-WS:9
    Memory. C. Rossetti. Ox-BN:716
    Notes Found near a Suicide: To
      James. F. Horne. Bo-AN:45,
      Bo-HF:90, Br-BC:124, Ra-BP:73
    Query. Ebon. Ad-PB:435
    Song after Victory. Tr-US II:226
    The Victorious Fighting Man's
      Home-Coming. Tr-US I:113
    Victory of the Mea. Tr-US I:219
    Victory Song. Tr-US II:244
VIENNA, AUS.
    Vienna 1945. W. Weldin. Ba-PO:191
VIETNAM: see also VIETNAMESE VERSE
    Mud in Vietnam. J. Lester.
      Jo-SA:66
    To Vietnam. C. Cobb. Ad-PB:471
THE VIETNAMESE
    What Were They Like? D. Levertov.
      Ba-PO:33, Ca-VT:517, Cr-WS:53,
      Ke-PP:38, Kr-OF:94
VIETNAMESE VERSE
    Condemnation. Thich Nhat Hanh.
      Ke-PP:40
    Love Song. Tr-US II:195
    Lullaby. Tr-US II:194
    Prayer at the Sacrifice Before
      the Coffin. Tr-US II:196
    Song of a Girl Whose Lover Has
      Married Another Woman.
      Tr-US II:195
    Song of Coughing. Tr-US II:195
VIETNAMESE WAR, 1957-1975: see
    also AIR RAIDS; SATIRE -
    VIETNAMESE WAR, 1957-1975
    Advent 1966. D. Levertov. Ho-P:157

VIETNAMESE WAR, 1957-1975 — cont'd.
  A Bummer. M. Casey. Mo-TS:43
  The Children of Vietnam.
    O. Teitelman. Mo-MI:71
  Condemnation. Thich Nhat Hanh
    Ke-PP:40
  "Containing Communism."
    C. Cobb. Ad-PB:472
  Fragment from a Poem, "Another
    Late Edition." O. Cabral.
    Kr-OF:89
  Gods in Vietnam. E. Redmond.
    Ad-PB:312
  Grief Streams down My Chest.
    L. Jeffers. Ad-PB:173
  He Killed Many of My Men.
    J. Bennett. Gr-BT:110
  Hit! T. Palmanteer. Al-WW:39
  If You Love Your Uncle Sam.
    P. Seeger. Ba-PO:199
  It Is Not Enough.
    D. Henderson. Ke-PP:98
  Junglegrave. S. Anderson.
    Ad-PB:441
  Life at War. D. Levertov.
    Ca-VT:515
  March on the Delta. A. Berger.
    Lo-IT:9
  Musical Vietnams. B. Allen.
    Lo-IT:4
  A Negro Soldier's Viet Nam
    Diary. H. Martin. Ad-PB:227
  Newscast. A. Kramer. Kr-OF:91
  Norman Morrison. D. Ferguson.
    Ba-PO:34
  On the Eve. L. Simpson.
    Bl-FP:56
  Paraders for the Bomb.
    S. Bernard. Ba-PO:39
  Schoolday in Man Quang.
    D. Knight. Kr-OF:90
  Simple Statement. E. Thorne.
    Kr-OF:95
  This Morning the Sun. O. Cabral.
    Ke-PP:103
  Vapor Trail Reflected in the
    Frog Pond. G. Kinnell.
    Ca-VT:604, Pe-SS:102
  Vietnam. C. Major. Ad-PB:299
  The Village Fish. D. Hall.
    Ba-PO:40
  The War Dead. B. Krasnoff.
    Ad-II:101
  War Poem. R. West. Hi-FO:270
  We Saw Days. T. Palmanteer.
    Al-WW:41
  What Were They Like? D. Levertov.
    Ba-PO:33, Ca-VT:517, Cr-WS:53,
    Ke-PP:38, Kr-OF:94
VIKINGS: see NORTHMEN

VILLAGE LIFE: see also HUMOR -
    VILLAGE LIFE; SATIRE - VILLAGE
    LIFE
  Ah . . . to the Villages!
    T. McGrath. St-H:128
  Almswomen. E. Blunden. Go-BP:51
  American Nights. R. Lattimore.
    Ha-TP:24
  At the Seed and Feed.
    J. Simons. Ls-NY:235
  The Campus on the Hill.
    W. Snodgrass. Br-TC:397
  Clear Night. Ai Ch'ing.
    Hs-TC:295
  Concert. R. Sward. Ca-VT:681
  Courthouse Square. H. Merrill.
    Br-AF:218
  A Dead Turk. Li Kuang-t'ien.
    Hs-TC:208
  The Deserted Village.
    O. Goldsmith. Al-VBP:585,
    Er-FA:410, Hi-FO:178
  Emigrant's Iconoclasm.
    T. Baybars. Ls-NY:249
  Prairie Summer. D. Etter.
    Sc-TN:45
  St. Ursanne. M. Roberts.
    Wi-LT:635
  Saturday in the County Seat.
    E. Jacobs. Br-AF:220
  Village at Dusk. Mu Mu-t'ien.
    Hs-TC:187
  Village Noon: Mid-Day Bells.
    M. Moore. Un-MA:576
  Western Town. D. Cannon.
    Hu-PN:282
VILLAINS AND VILLAINY: see also
    HUMOR - VILLAINS AND VILLAINY
  Between the Acts. S. Kunitz.
    Co-EL:101
  Bishop Hatto. R. Southey.
    Gr-CT:130, Ha-PO:78, Pa-OM:125
  Consider These, for We Have
    Condemned Them. C. Day-Lewis.
    Wi-LT:428
  Down and Out. C. Hay. Co-RM:151
  Knock, Knock, Knock, Knock.
    On-TW:18
  The Outlandish Knight.
    Br-SM:36, Un-GT:111
  The Pied Piper of Hamelin.
    R. Browning. Ar-TP3:28,Er-FA:354,
    Ox-BC:173, Sm-LG:173, Un-GT:153
  Ruth: or The Influence of Nature.
    W. Wordsworth. Pa-GTB:283
  Simon Legree—a Negro Sermon.
    V. Lindsay. Co-RM:182,
    Sm-LG:183, Un-MA:226
  Stagolee. Lo-TY:201
  The Wheel. R. Hayden. Ra-BP:137

VILLIERS, GEORGE, 2ND DUKE OF
    BUCKINGHAM: see SATIRE -
    VILLIERS, GEORGE, 2ND DUKE
    OF BUCKINGHAM
VILLIERS, LADY MARY
  Epitaph on the Lady Mary Villiers.
    T. Carew. Al-VBP:350
VILNA, U.S.S.R.
  Vilna. M. Kulbak. Ho-TY:216
VINCI, LEONARDO DA: see LEONARDO
    DA VINCI
VINES: see also names of vines,
    as IVY
  B Is for Beanseed. E. Farjeon.
    Br-SG:82
  The Butterbean Tent. E. Roberts.
    Bo-GJ:48, Br-SG:51
  The Magic Vine. Br-SG:83
  The Rebellious Vine. H. Monro.
    Go-BP:277, Mc-WK:110
  To a Vine-Clad Telegraph Pole.
    L. Untermeyer. Un-MA:307
VIOLENCE: see also HUMOR -
    VIOLENCE; RAIDS
  The Abyss. Ya-Hsüan. Pa-MV:153
  Angola Question Mark. L. Hughes.
    Lo-TY:230, Ra-BP:89
  Avenger, What Wrong? J. Rorty.
    Sm-PT:128
  Ballad of Birmingham. D. Randall.
    Be-MA:71, Ra-BP:143
  Benign Neglect/Mississippi, 1970.
    P. St. John. Ad-PB:346
  Billy the Kid. Co-RM:164,
    Fi-BG:53, Hi-TL:144
  Birmingham 1963. R. Patterson.
    Ad-PB:209, Kr-OF:163
  The Bloody Sire. R. Jeffers.
    Cr-WS:88, Wi-LT:261
  Brazilian Happenings. R. O'Connell.
    Du-SH:97
  Camp Fever. J. Blight.
    Co-RM:96
  Carl Hamblin. E. Masters.
    Kr-OF:113, Sh-AP:137, Wi-LT:114
  The Dance of Death.
    F. García Lorca. Bl-FP:70
  For Stephen Dixon. Z. Gilbert.
    Ad-PB:195
  Free at Last. A. Alenik. La-IH:126
  He Fell among Thieves. H. Newbolt.
    Pa-OM:227, Sp-OG:47
  in orangeburg my brothers did.
    A. Spellman. Ad-PB:285,
    Ra-BP:229
  In This Hour. J. Johnson. Tr-MR:232
  The Intellectuals. D. Randall.
    Ad-PB:142
  Jitterbugging in the Streets.
    C. Hernton. Ad-PB:240

  Ku-Klux. M. Cawein. Hi-TL:127
  Life Is the Greatest Disaster.
    E. Murray. Me-WF:43
  Lost Moment. H. Fuller.
    Ad-PB:201
  Lynching and Burning.
    P. St. John. Ad-PB:349
  Mr. Roosevelt Regrets. P. Murray.
    Ad-PB:109
  Mousemeal. H. Nemerov.
    Br-TC:315
  Newsletter from My Mother.
    M. Harper. Ad-PB:315
  An Old Woman Remembers. S. Brown.
    Ad-PB:68
  Onion Bucket. L. Thomas.
    Ad-PB:483
  Parable. P. Bennett. Co-EL:137
  Photographs: A Vision of
    Massacre. M. Harper. Ad-PB:313
  Plot Improbable, Character Un-
    sympathetic. E. Olson.
    St-H:173
  Prelude. C. Rivers. Ad-PB:233,
    Be-MA:107
  Prologue. K. Barnes. Cr-WS:45
  Silences. E. Pratt. En-PC:5
  Street Gang. H. Webster. Co-RM:187
  Third Degree. L. Hughes.
    Gr-BT:123, Ra-BP:80
  The .38. T. Joans. Be-MA:102,
    Hu-NN:83
  Time in the Rock. C. Aiken.
    Al-VBP:1188
  tony get the boys. D. Graham.
    Ad-PB:480
  The War-Song of Dinas Vawr.
    T. Peacock. Al-VBP:716,
    Ha-PO:220, Ho-WR:106, Mc-WS:105,
    Na-EO:110, Pa-OM:197
  the west ridge is menthol-cool.
    D. Graham. Ad-PB:480
  What's Black Power. L. Baez.
    Jo-VC:47
  The Wild Boar and the Ram.
    J. Gay. Ke-PP:37
VIOLETS
  Calling the Violet. L. Larcom.
    Hu-MP:249
  On the Mountain Pass.
    Matsuo Bashō. Pa-SG:180
  Rolling down the Hill. Baken.
    Do-TS:25
  Song. L. Cohen. Pe-SS:119
  Song. C. Rossetti. Al-VBP:995,
    Pa-GTB:374
  Sonnet. A. Nelson. Ad-PB:12,
    Hu-PN:46
  Surprise. B. Martin.
    Mc-AW:34

VIOLETS — cont'd.
  To Violets. R. Herrick.
    Al-VBP:327, Tu-WW:56
  The Violet. W. Wordsworth.
    Bo-FP:244, Ch-B:38
  Violets. C. Rossetti. Mc-PR:161
  When I Went Out. Akahito.
    Ba-ST:19, Le-MW:71
  The Yellow Violet. W. Bryant.
    Fe-PL:373
VIOLINS: see also HUMOR - VIOLINS
  At Laie's Tomb. O. Goga.
    Mc-AC:38
  At My Wedding. J. Segal.
    Ho-TY:151
  At the Railway Station, Upway.
    T. Hardy. Ma-FW:71
  The Ballad of the Fiddler.
    S. O'Sullivan. Hu-MP:104
  Cottage. S. O'Sullivan.
    Co-PI:165
  The Drowned Lady. Gr-CT:139
  The Fairy Fiddler. N. Hopper.
    Al-VBP:1112
  The Fiddle and the Bow.
    H. Wolfe. Go-BP:225
  A Fiddler. W. de la Mare.
    Ha-LO:32, Pl-US:30
  Fiddler Jones. E. Masters.
    Mo-BG:158, Pl-US:31,
    Sh-AP:136, Sm-LG:41
  The Fiddler of Dooney. W. Yeats.
    Ar-TP3:15, Pl-US:113, Sm-LG:42
  The Green Fiddler. R. Field.
    Co-PT:173
  Green Sleeves. Gr-GB:102
  Jacky's Fiddle. Pl-US:34,
    Rv-ON:101, Wr-RM:61
  Old King Cole. Au-SP:4,
    De-PO:22, Er-FA:507, Fr-WO:33,
    Ir-BB:265, Li-LB:68, Mo-NR:137,
    Wi-MG:27, Wr-RM:83
  On the Tuareg Violin. Tr-US I:133
  Peg-Leg's Fiddle. B. Adams.
    Sh-RP:53
  The Penny Fiddle. R. Graves.
    Gr-EC:161, Su-FVI:32
  The Seven Fiddlers. S. Evans.
    Co-PM:57, Pa-OM:282
  Stranger. E. Roberts.
    Un-MA:270
  String Quartet. B. Deutsch.
    Pl-US:36
  The Violin. R. Gilder.
    Se-PR:326
VIRGIL: see VERGIL
VIRGIN ISLANDS
  Skin Diving in the Virgins.
    J. Brinnin. Pe-OA:238
VIRGIN MARY: see MARY, VIRGIN

VIRGINIA: see also HUMOR -
    VIRGINIA; and names of
    towns, as MT. VERNON, VA.
  Carry Me Back to Old Virginny.
    J. Bland. Er-FA:444,
    Ga-FB:273, Se-PR:289
  The English in Virginia.
    C. Reznikoff. Gr-SS:62
  Life-Long, Poor Browning.
    A. Spencer. Hu-PN:60
  Nocturne. F. Frost. Co-BN:202
  To an Absent Virginian.
    K. Peatross. Ke-TF:359
  To the Virginian Voyage.
    M. Drayton. Al-VBP:161,
    Hi-TL:19, Rv-CB:184
  Virginia. T. Eliot.
    Ha-PO:94, Sm-LG:142
  Virginia. P. McGinley.
    Ag-HE:8
  Virginia's Bloody Soil. Em-AF:446
VIRGINIA (SHIP): see MERRIMAC
    (SHIP)
VIRGINS
  The Golden Net. W. Blake.
    Gr-SS:166
  The Virgin. Gr-GB:303
VIRTUE: see GOODNESS
VISIONS: see also DREAMS
  Abou Ben Adhem. L. Hunt.
    Er-FA:6, Fe-FP:565, Ga-FB:127,
    Gr-EC:142, Ma-YA:172, Mc-PR:187,
    Sp-OG:321, Un-GT:315
  After Reading St. John the Divine.
    G. Derwood. Wi-LT:685
  The Alley in the Rain.
    Tai Wang-shu. Hs-TC:180
  Apocalypse. E. Pierce. Tr-MR:262
  Autumnal Ode. A. De Vere.
    Ox-BN:587
  The Ballad of Nat Turner.
    R. Hayden. Ca-VT:358, Ra-BP:133
  The Beatific Vision.
    G. Chesterton. Tr-MR:244
  The Book of Thel. W. Blake.
    Ox-BN:32
  Cable Cars. S. Tsuboi. Sh-AM:71
  The Call. U. Birnbaum. Un-R:78
  The Chinese Nightingale.
    V. Lindsay. Un-MA:229
  Christmas Lullaby for a New-Born
    Child. Y. Gregory. Bo-AN:153
  Cities and Seas. N. Jordan.
    Hu-PN:422
  The City in the Sea. E. Poe.
    Al-VBP:873, Gr-SS:182,
    Rv-CB:807, Sh-AP:53
  The City of Dreadful Night.
    J. Thomson. Al-VBP:1007,
    Ho-WR:207, Pa-GTB:382

The Crystal Cabinet. W. Blake.
De-CH:355, Gr-CC:1,
Ox-BN:27, Sm-LG:217
Dark Testament. P. Murray.
Bo-AN:107
Death. J. Milton. Ga-S:29
A Dream. M. Arnold. Pa-GTB:362
The Dream. J. Bishop. Wi-LT:608
The Dream. G. Byron. Mo-GR:118
Dream-Land. E. Poe.
Rv-CB:809, Sh-AP:56
The Dream of the Rood. Ga-S:153
Dream with an Angel. M. Banus.
Mc-AC:113
Dreams of a Summer Night.
G. Barker. Ma-FW:51
Duessa's Coach. E. Spenser.
Ga-S:27
England. E. Meyerstein.
De-TT:202
Enion Replies from the Caverns
of the Grave. W. Blake.
Ox-BN:39
Enitharmon Revives with Los.
W. Blake. Ox-BN:38
Epistle to John Hamilton
Reynolds. J. Keats. Ox-BN:369
Ere Sleep Comes Down to Soothe
the Weary Eyes. P. Dunbar.
Hu-PN:43
The Eternal Image. R. Pitter.
Un-MB:404
The Eve of Saint Mark. J. Keats.
De-CH:447
The Fall of Hyperion. J. Keats.
Ox-BN:379
Fantasy under the Moon.
E. Boundzekei-Dongala. Lo-TY:148
The Flaming Terrapin. R. Campbell.
Ga-S:3
Flash Crimson. C. Sandburg.
Un-MA:207
For My People. M. Walker.
Ad-PB:144, Be-MA:73, Bo-AN:128,
Hu-PN:314, Tr-MR:155
Galileo Galilei. W. Smith.
En-PC:168
God's Little Mountain. G. Hill.
Go-BP:173
Green Valley. D. Johnson.
Hu-PN:227
The Grove. E. Muir. Wi-LT:249
The Happy Land. Ga-S:21
The Haunted Palace. E. Poe.
Al-VBP:875, De-CH:320, Gr-CT:160,
Ho-WR:216, Sh-AP:54
The Hitler Dwarf. D. Lourie.
Sc-TN:152
The Homecoming Singer. J. Wright.
Ad-PB:279

I Have a Dream. M. King. Lo-TY:249
Ibant Obscurae. T. Brown.
Ox-BN:722
If Suddenly You Come for Me.
N. Nor. Bo-RU:54
Incident on a Journey. T. Gunn.
To-MP:75
Instantaneous. V. Ayres. Hu-NN:85
Introduction to the Code of Hand-
some Lake. Br-MW:105
Jerusalem. W. Blake. Gr-CT:295,
Ox-BN:42
Jerusalem. A. Rich. Mc-EA:121
Jerusalem: A Prisoner's Song.
Ga-S:224
Jim Desterland. H. Plutzik.
Ca-VT:347, De-FS:149
Kingdom of Heaven. L. Adams.
Un-MA:547
Kubla Khan. S. Coleridge.
Al-VBP:699, Bo-GJ:222, Co-RG:15,
De-CH:386, Er-FA:361, Ga-FB:23,
Gr-CT:177, Gr-EC:140, Mc-PR:150,
Ox-BN:165, Pa-HT:154, Re-TW:132,
Rv-CB:657, Sm-LG:215
Lacrimas or There Is a Need to
Scream. K. Lyle. Ad-PB:466
The Leg in the Subway.
O. Williams. Wi-LT:418
Let This Be My Parting Word.
R. Tagore. Tr-MR:284
Locksley Hall. A. Tennyson.
Er-FA:56
Male and Female Loves in Beulah.
W. Blake. Ox-BN:46
The Mental Traveller. W. Blake.
Mo-GR:131
The Midnight Meditation.
E. Olson. St-H:175
The Mirage. O. Williams.
Wi-LT:413
The Mistress of Vision.
F. Thompson. De-CH:269
The Moment of Vision.
R. Eberhart. Tr-MR:243
The Motion of the Earth.
N. Nicholson. Li-TU:251,
Pl-IO:38
The New Ghost. F. Shove.
Go-BP:258
O World. G. Santayana.
Fe-PL:321, Sm-PT:168
Ode on Indolence. J. Keats.
Ox-BN:374
On the Building of Springfield.
V. Lindsay. Tr-MR:247
One Flower. M. Malik.
Sa-B:146
The Pains of Sleep. S. Coleridge.
Ox-BN:171, Rv-CB:662

VISIONS — cont'd.
  The Path among the Stones.
    G. Kinnell. Ho-P:135
  Recompense. L. Williams.
    De-FS:222
  Renunciation. E. Dickinson.
    Un-MA:104
  The Rime of the Ancient Mariner.
    S. Coleridge. Al-VBP:679,
    Bo-FP:301, Co-RG:60, Co-SS:131,
    De-CH:364, Er-FA:318, Fe-FP:147,
    Ga-FB:105, Gr-TG:61, Ha-PO:15,
    Hi-WP II:68, Ma-YA:146, Ni-JP:52,
    Ox-BN:139, Rv-CB:658, Sm-LG:312,
    Un-GT:30
  Roses and Revolutions. D. Randall.
    Ad-PB:142, Ra-BP:142
  Saints and Heroes You Dare Say.
    C. Day Lewis. Go-BP:184
  The Sea of Death. T. Hood.
    Ox-BN:423
  The Second Coming. W. Yeats.
    Mo-GR:89, Pa-GTB:424, Pl-EI:28,
    Tr-MR:236, Un-MB:117, Wi-LT:72
  Shapes and Signs. J. Mangan.
    Co-PI:124
  Sometimes I Go to Camarillo &
    Sit in the Lounge. K. Lyle.
    Ad-PB:464
  Songs for a Colored Singer, IV.
    E. Bishop. Hu-PN:552
  The Springfield of the Far
    Future. V. Lindsay. Tr-MR:200
  Spyglass. H. Gregory. Ha-TP:133
  A Stared Story. W. Stafford.
    Ha-TP:136
  Tell Me, O Swan. Kabir. Al-PI:55
  They Sometimes Call Me.
    W. Rose. Ni-CD:216
  The Transfiguration. E. Muir.
    Go-BP:291
  Truth. H. Nemerov. Wi-LT:588
  The Two April Mornings.
    W. Wordsworth. Pa-GTB:302
  Ultima Thule. H. Longfellow.
    Al-VBP:829
  Unity. AE. Tr-MR:283
  A Vision of Handsome Lake.
    Br-MW:108
  The Vision of Sir Launfal.
    J. Lowell. Pa-OM:210
  The Visions of MacConglinne.
    Co-PI:134, De-CH:65
  What Has Been. V. Porumbacu.
    Mc-AC:126
  White Night. K. Molodowsky.
    Ho-TY:288
  The Wilderness and the Solitary
    Place. Bible. O.T.
    Isaiah. Go-BP:263

  Wmffre the Sweep. R. Humphries.
    Pl-EI:197
  The World. H. Vaughan.
    Al-VBP:467, Ga-FB:93, Ga-S:6,
    Ho-LP:102, Pl-IO:7, Rv-CB:410
  Zechariah. E. Marlatt.
    Tr-MR:82
VOCABULARY: see WORDS
VOCATIONS: see OCCUPATIONS
VOGUL VERSE
  Dance Song. Tr-US II:127
VOICES: see also HUMOR - VOICES
  Bedtime Story for My Son.
    P. Redgrove. Go-BP:120,
    Gr-BT:161
  Spring Voices. J. Stuart.
    De-FS:196
  The Voice. R. Brooke. Gr-BT:59
  The Voice of My Fathers Is on
    the Wind. Wo-HS:(42)
  Voices. W. Bynner. Bo-FP:158
  Voices from the Other World.
    J. Merrill. Br-TC:287
VOLCANOES: see also EARTHQUAKES
  The Dead Volcano. D. Iida.
    Sh-AM:166
  Esthetique du Mal, I.
    W. Stevens. Wi-LT:151
  Volcano. I. Van Sertima.
    Sa-B:41
VOLTAIRE (FRANCOIS MARIE AROUET)
  Extempore to Voltaire Criticizing
    Milton. F. Young. Al-VBP:521
  Voltaire at Ferney. W. Auden.
    Wi-LT:470
VOLVOX: see MARINE PLANTS
VOODOO: see also HUMOR - VOODOO
  The Congo. V. Lindsay.
    Er-FA:300, Hi-WP II:98, Hu-PN:484,
    Pe-OA:55, Sh-AP:163, Un-MA:218
  He Sees Through Stone. E. Knight.
    Ad-PB:231, Be-MA:109
  A Juju of My Own. L. Bethune.
    Ad-PB:309, Hu-PN:414
  off d pig. I. Reed. Jo-SA:90
  Trap. W. Kerr. De-FS:128
VORONEZH, U.S.S.R.
  Voronezh. A. Akhmatova.
    Ca-MR:185
VOYAGES: see also HUMOR - VOYAGES;
    SEAFARING LIFE; TRAVEL AND
    TRAVELERS
  The Child and the Mariner.
    W. Davies. De-CH:383
  The Emigrant. J. Masefield.
    Cl-FC:64
  The Exile. M. Benaya.
    Ls-NY:43
  Facing West from California's
    Shores. W. Whitman. Un-MA:70

In Honor of Maros During His
   Absence at Sea. Tr-US I:216
Ithaka. C. Cavafy. Ni-JP:15
Leaving Harbor. N. Ayukawa.
   Sh-AM:122
A Long Time Ago. T'ao Ch'ien.
   Sm-LG:303
The Long Trail. R. Kipling.
   Al-VBP:1095, Ga-FB:185,
   Sp-OG:253
Maps. D. Thompson. Ar-TP3:97
Song of a Woman Crying for the
   Dead Baby Son of Her Daughter.
   Tr-US I:244
Trains. R. Burgunder. Ar-TP3:85
The Voyage. E. Muir. Wi-LT:251
The Wandering Knight's Song.
   J. Lockhart. Gr-CT:275
VULTURES: see also CONDORS;
   HUMOR - VULTURES
The Drafted Vultures.
   J. de Melo Neto. An-TC:161
For the Vulture Dance.
   Tr-US II:169
Still, Citizen Sparrow.
   R. Wilbur. Wi-LT:597
The Vulture. H. Belloc.
   Ag-HE:70, Ir-BB:77, Lo-LL:78
WABANAKI INDIANS: see INDIANS OF
   NORTH AMERICA - VERSE-ABNAKI
WABASH RIVER
On the Banks of the Wabash, Far
   Away. P. Dresser. Se-PR:260
WADING
Crossing a Creek. H. Johnson.
   Hu-PN:284
Inviting, Rippling Waters.
   M. Bendig. Le-M:79
What Happiness. Buson. Le-MW:78
WAFFLES: see HUMOR - WAFFLES
WAGONS
The Gold-Tinted Dragon.
   K. Kuskin. Au-SP:197
Old or Young. Ju-CP:10
The Peddler's Caravan. W. Rands.
   Au-SP:150, Bl-OB:145, Bo-FP:130,
   Hu-MP:166, Ox-BC:233
Star of the Western Skies.
   Fi-BG:193
The Waggoner. Gr-GB:213
The Wagon in the Barn.
   J. Drinkwater. Pe-FB:30,Th-AS:70
WAGTAILS
Little Trotty Wagtail. J. Clare.
   Bl-OB:65, Fe-FP:296,
   Ir-BB:32, Rv-CB:724
WAITERS AND WAITRESSES: see also
   HUMOR - WAITERS AND WAITRESSES
The Deaths at Paragon, Indiana.
   J. Woods. St-H:250

In This Hotel. E. Carnaval.
   Gr-SS:141
Table d'Hote. R. Esler.
   Ls-NY:154
WAITING: see also HUMOR - WAITING;
   SATIRE - WAITING
After Two Years. R. Aldington.
   Un-MB:255
The Afterwake. A. Rich. Ho-P:211
Alabama Centennial. N. Madgett.
   Ra-BP:197
Alphabet Spring, n. L. Nagan.
   Ad-II:72
Among the Lions Night Is Still.
   M. Korte. Sc-TN:119
Another Song from Arsut.
   Tr-US I:5
Darkness Song. Da-SC:140,
   Le-OE:105
Earth Trembles Waiting.
   B. Wagstaff. Fe-PL:120
Eight o' Clock. A. Housman.
   Co-PU:116, Hi-WP I:22,
   Un-MB:100
Evening Appointment. Cheng Min.
   Hs-TC:242
For a Child Named Katherine.
   L. Nicholl. Th-AS:16
From the Dark Tower. C. Cullen.
   Ad-PB:87, Be-MA:51, Hu-PN:235,
   Jo-SA:133, Ra-BP:100, Wi-LT:616
The Gathering Time.
   D. Whitewing. Al-WW:52
Haven. A. Baconsky. Mc-AC:134
Hoar-Frost, Station Smoke, Rusty
   Tracks. R. Cuscaden. St-H:34
I Am Waiting. M. Goode.
   Jo-SA:5, Jo-VC:88
I Am Waiting. V. Howard.
   Ba-HI:46
The Juniper Tree. W. Watson.
   Co-BL:162, Do-WH:36
Letter from a Wife. S. Reese.
   Hu-PN:413
Lines for Marking Time.
   R. Hill. Ni-CD:78
A Loon I Thought It Was.
   Da-SC:151, Ho-SD:7,
   Le-OE:89, Tr-US II:225
A Man Waiting for the Sunrise.
   M. Beniuc. Mc-AC:98
Miracle. Wen I-to. Hs-TC:67
The Morning Glory. Confucius.
   Ga-S:175, Pa-SG:50
Oh! Dear, What Can the Matter
   Be? De-CH:70, Mc-WS:165,
   Mo-MGT:200, Mo-TL:34, Wr-RM:127
Pantuns, VI. Tr-US II:203
The Rendezvous. J. Anderson.
   Sc-TN:6

WAITING — __cont'd.__
Rendezvous. Chang Chih-min.
Hs-TC:429
The Serpent Waits. J. Brennan.
De-FS:35
Seven Times Three—Love.
J. Ingelow. Fe-PL:103
Sheltering from the Rain.
S. Karai. Ma-FW:119
signals, i. J. Amini. Ad-PB:292
Summoning the Soul.
Jao Meng-k'an. Hs-TC:109
Tell Him. C. Bialik. Pa-SG:52
The Unexplored. B. Eaton.
De-FS:82
The Voice. R. Boureanu.
Mc-AC:91
Wait. P. Cummins. Gr-BT:49
Waiting. J. Freeman. De-CH:36
Waiting. R. Jacob. Br-BC:103
Waiting. J. Kirkup. Ma-FW:138
Waiting. J. Reeves. St-FS:71
Waiting Both. T. Hardy.
Mc-WK:105, Un-MB:35
Waiting for You in the Rain.
Yü Kuang-chung. Pa-MV:184
Waiting Poem. D. Fogel.
Ho-TY:237
The Watchers. W. Braithwaite.
Hu-PN:48
Where We Are. B. Cutler. St-H:36
WAKE-UP VERSES: see also HUMOR -
WAKE-UP VERSES
Anna-Marie, Love, Up Is the Sun.
W. Scott. Al-VBP:677
Aubade. E. Sitwell.
Hi-WP II:6, Un-MB:330
Awake! Awake! W. Davenant.
Al-VBP:384, De-CH:6,
Gr-CT:41, Un-MW:3
Awake, Awake, You Weary Sleepers.
Sp-HW:14
Awake, My Heart, to Be Loved.
R. Bridges. Pa-GTB:415,
Un-MB:48
Bonny at Morn. Gr-GB:15
Chanticleer. J. Farrar.
Ar-TP3:72, Au-SP:50, Bo-FP:65
The Cock. Ar-TP3:174, Bo-FP:65
The Cock Crows. Ca-MU:11
Corinna's Going a-Maying.
R. Herrick. Co-BN:30,
No-CL:278, Rv-CB:336, Se-PR:114
Dawn Song. Tr-US II:104
Daylight. Da-SC:103, Hu-MP:131
The Donkey. Ir-BB:33, Mo-MGT:213,
Sp-AS:20, Wr-RM:104
Early to Bed. An-IP:(10),
Bo-FP:36, Ch-B:117, Ir-BB:231,
Li-LB:162, Mo-NR:122

Get Up or You'll Be Late for
School, Silly. J. Ciardi.
Gr-EC:103
Getting Out of Bed. E. Farjeon.
Br-SS:22
Getting-Up Time. De-PP:40
Hark! Hark! the Lark.
W. Shakespeare. Al-VBP:194,
Bl-OB:94, Bo-FP:234, De-CH:6,
Er-FA:107, Fe-FP:290, Ga-FB:27,
Gr-CT:264, No-CL:269, Rv-CB:200,
Sm-LG:49, Sm-MK:22
I Wonder if Everyone Is Up.
Jo-TS:2
Lazy Mary, Will You Get Up?
M. and M. Petersham. Sh-RP:16
Little Boy Blue. Au-SP:6,
Bo-FP:78, De-PO:28, Er-FA:506,
Fr-WO:10, Li-LB:26, Mo-MGT:15,
Mo-NR:134, Pa-AP:42, Wi-MG:12,
Wr-RM:11
Love in May. J. Passerat.
Pa-SG:32
Magic Song for Him Who Wishes to
Live. Le-IB:27, Tr-US I:3
May-Day Song. Co-PS:83,
Un-GT:274
Minnie and Winnie. A. Tennyson.
Ch-B:118, Ir-BB:199, Ox-BC:214
O Thou That Sleep'st.
W. Davenant. Rv-CB:367
Reveillé. A. Housman.
Er-FA:20, Fe-PL:398, No-CL:121,
Un-MB:93, Wi-LT:59
Sister, Awake. Co-PS:77,
De-CH:11, Gr-CC:66
Sleepy Sparrows. De-PP:16
Somewhere Town. K. Greenaway.
Ch-B:14, Ir-BB:136
Song. G. Vicente. Pa-SG:148
Song of Parents Who Want to
Wake Up Their Daughter.
Da-SC:58
Song of Parents Who Want to
Wake Up Their Son. Da-SC:57
A Summer Morning. R. Field.
Ar-TP3:175, Au-SP:319,
La-PV:48, Pe-FB:86
Summons. R. Francis. Du-RG:62
Time to Get Up. R. Stevenson.
Bo-FP:3, Br-SS:22,
Gr-TG:44, Ox-BC:298
To Jane: The Invitation.
P. Shelley. Re-TW:91
The Trumpet. E. Thomas.
Gr-SS:169, Un-MB:216
Wake Up! Wake Up! Bashö.
Au-SP:72
A Wood Song. R. Hodgson.
Bo-GJ:96

WAKENING: see also HUMOR - WAKENING
And Love Hung Still.
    L. MacNeice.   Un-MB:443
Another September.   T. Kinsella.
    En-PC:270
Awaken.   S. Bingham.   Le-M:21
Being Awakened.   M. Saito.
    Sh-AM:145
Beyond Dawn.   Lo Fu.   Pa-MV:117
Chanticleer.   K. Tynan.
    Ar-TP3:72, Hu-MP:219, Tu-WW:86
Chelsea Morning.   J. Mitchell.
    Mo-GR:119
Coffee.   J. Cunningham.
    Ca-VT:325, Un-MA:615
Cold Blows the Wind.   J. Hamilton.
    De-CH:218
Dawn.   O. Paz.   Mo-TS:86
Daybreak.   H. Longfellow.
    De-TT:54, Fe-PL:399, Mc-WK:30
Discovering God Is Waking One
    Morning.   J. L'Heureux.
    Co-BN:92
Early Morn.   W. Davies.   De-CH:6
Early Waking.   L. Adams.   Wi-LT:603
Edwardsville Before Sunrise.
    J. Knoepfle.   St-H:97
For Sleep or Death.   R. Pitter.
    Hi-WP I:144, Sm-MK:218
Getting Up.   R. Burgunder.
    Ar-TP3:175
Getting Up Early on a Spring
    Morning.   Po Chu-i.   Ma-FW:9
Green Sleeves.   Gr-GB:102
Green Song.   P. Booth.   Co-BN:27
The Huntsmen.   W. de la Mare.
    Ar-TP3:109, Br-SS:37
I Pray You, Rooster.   Br-FW:9
I Wake Up Alone.   Li Shang Yin.
    Rx-LT:76
I Wonder if Everyone Is Up.
    Jo-TS:2
If I Had But Two Little Wings.
    S. Coleridge.   De-CH:22
In the Naked Bed, in Plato's
    Cave.   D. Schwartz.   Ca-VT:365,
    Un-MA:619, Wi-LT:515
Love Calls Us to the Things of
    This World.   R. Wilbur.
    Ca-VT:484, Un-MA:675
Magic Prayer.   Ho-SD:77, Le-IB:30,
    Le-OE:19, Ma-BH:7, Tr-US I:9
Magic Song for Him Who Wishes to
    Live.   Le-IB:27, Tr-US I:3
Mid-Winter Waking.   R. Graves.
    Go-BP:136
Morning at the Temple of Kobai.
    E. Shiffert.   Ls-NY:257
Morning Hymn.   T. Ken.
    Er-FA:455

Morning Mood.   M. Panegoosho.
    Le-IB:29
Morning Song.   S. Plath.
    Mc-EA:103
Not Ideas about the Thing, but
    the Thing Itself.   W. Stevens.
    Al-VBP:1145
Pack, Clouds, Away!   T. Heywood.
    Al-VBP:271, Bl-OB:42, De-CH:7,
    Pa-GTB:32, Re-BS:9, Re-TW:52,
    Tu-WW:11, Un-MW:6
Parched by the Shrill Song.
    Soseki.   Be-MC:37
Pastoral.   R. Hillyer.   Un-MA:482
Poem in Three Parts.   R. Bly.
    St-H:4
Prelude.   W. Gibson.   Un-MB:241
Preludes I-III.   T. Eliot.
    Ar-TP3:177, Br-TC:103, 105,
    Ca-VT:128, 129, Hi-WP II:162,
    La-OC:130, Pe-OA:103, Sh-AP:182
Ripeness.   R. Whitman.   Mo-TS:85
Rising in the Morning.
    H. Rhodes.   Ox-BC:12
Rising in Winter.
    Emperor Ch'ien Wen.   Rx-LT:44
Singing-Time.   R. Fyleman.
    Ar-TP3:175, Br-SS:15,
    Fr-MP:3, Mc-AW:3
Sleepy John.   C. Tringress.
    St-FS:74
Softly, Drowsily.   W. de la Mare.
    Ar-TP3:175, Au-SP:98
Sun City.   B. Cutler.   St-H:38
Talking in Their Sleep.
    E. Thomas.   Co-BN:29
Very Early.   K. Kuskin.
    Au-SP:41, La-PV:49
Waking.   J. Anderson.   Ls-NY:19
Waking Time.   J. Eastwick.
    Ar-TP3:239, Br-SS:7
Wide Awake.   M. Livingston.
    Ho-GC:8
WAKES: see also HUMOR - WAKES
My Old Maid Aunt.
    D. Schultz.   Du-SH:137
WALES: see also BALLADS, WELSH;
    HUMOR - WALES; THE WELSH;
    WELSH VERSE; and names of
    counties, as MERIONETH
    COUNTY, WALES
The Cutty Wren.   Gr-GB:63,
    Rv-CB:418, Rv-ON:117
In the Valley of the Elwy.
    G. Hopkins.   Al-VBP:1061,
    Go-BP:30
Peace in the Welsh Hills.
    V. Watkins.   Pa-GTB:507
A Storm in Childhood.
    T. Jones.   Ma-FW:35

WALES - COUNTRYSIDE
The Artist on Penmaenmawr.
  C. Tennyson-Turner. Ox-BN:471
The Collier. V. Watkins.
  Ma-FW:197, To-MP:24
Cynddylan on a Tractor. R. Thomas.
  Ga-S:123, To-MP:63
Fern Hill. D. Thomas. Al-VBP:1246,
  Bo-GJ:53, Br-TC:440, Cl-DT:63,
  Co-RG:160, Fe-PL:251, Ga-FB:166,
  Hi-WP II:46, Mc-EA:42, Mc-WK:10,
  Na-EO:45, Pa-GTB:542, Pe-SS:162,
  Re-TW:100, Sm-LG:108, Un-MB:502,
  Wi-LT:559
Meandering Wye. R. Bloomfield.
  Ox-BN:59
Poem in October. D. Thomas.
  Gr-CC:42, Hi-WP II:135,
  To-MP:54
Usk. T. Eliot. Sm-LG:143
Wales Visitation. A. Ginsberg.
  Ho-P:85
WALES - HISTORY AND PATRIOTISM: see
  also names of historic persons,
  as GLENDOWER, OWEN
The Bard. T. Gray. Pa-GTB:115
The Fall of Llywelyn. B. Fardd.
  Hi-FO:81
The Hearth of Urien.
  Llywarch the Aged. Gr-CT:323
Welsh Landscape. R. Thomas.
  To-MP:58
WALEY, ARTHUR (DAVID)
Homage to Arthur Waley.
  R. Fuller. Pl-ML:51
WALKING: see also HITCHHIKING;
  HUMOR - WALKING; TIPTOEING
A Black Girl Goes By.
  E. Roumer. Lo-TY:90
Catherine Takes a Stroll.
  J. Cournos. No-CL:203
A Devonshire Rhyme.
  Br-SS:89, Hu-MP:322
Figure for a Landscape.
  L. Mueller. St-H:146
Food. M. Chute. Ag-HE:32,
  La-OC:81
Good Hours. R. Frost.
  Gr-SS:45, Sp-OG:247
Heavenly Grass. T. Williams.
  Gr-EC:61
The Hike. N. Weiss. Mo-SD:87
I Have to Have It. D. Aldis.
  Au-SP:185
I Will Walk. Le-IB:36, Ma-BH:8
It May Be. Re-RR:16
Jump or Jingle. E. Beyer.
  Ar-TP3:102, Au-SP:85, Ir-BB:74
Kick a Little Stone.
  D. Aldis. Au-SP:185

Little Blue Shoes. K. Greenaway.
  Ar-TP3:5, Hu-MP:8
Lonely Walk. G. McBride.
  Me-WF:3
A Modoc Singer. Br-MW:3
Paradigm of a Hero. J. Mathews.
  Ha-TP:56
The Rescue. D. Schmitz.
  St-H:190
Song of the Open Road.
  W. Whitman. Al-VBP:934,
  Ar-TP3:97, Er-FA:249,
  La-RM:163, Un-MA:63
The Spring Walk. T. Miller.
  De-TT:32
The Street. O. Paz. La-OC:135
Sunday. E. White. Mc-WS:123
Susan Blue. K. Greenaway.
  Ar-TP3:11, Ch-B:28, Hu-MP:136
Taking Steps at Thirteen Months.
  H. Miller. Ls-NY:219
To Walk on Hills. R. Graves.
  Mo-SD:90
Two Lives and Others. W. Scott.
  Du-RG:119
Understanding. T. Traherne.
  Go-BP:107, Mo-SD:84
Walk. F. Horne. Ra-BP:75
The Walk. W. Ross. Mo-SD:88
Walk in the Rain. F. Frost.
  Ke-TF:85
Walk on a Winter Day.
  S. Allen. Ha-YA:143
Walking. S. Bahe. Ba-HI:62
Walking. G. Glaubitz.
  Au-SP:108, Mc-AW:16
Walking. T. Tsosie. Ba-HI:56
Walking at Night. A. Hare.
  Fe-PL:405
Walking Song. W. Hickson.
  Ox-BC:230
When You Walk. J. Stephens.
  Gr-EC:64, La-PV:189, Mc-WK:21
Winter Walk. K. van der Veer.
  Ke-TF:86
Wonder Wander. L. Kandel. Du-RG:51
WALL OF CHINA
At the Great Wall of China.
  E. Blunden. Pa-GTB:492
Under the Frontier Post.
  Wang Chang-Ling. Gr-CT:340
The Wall of China. P. Colum.
  Co-RG:110
WALLPAPER
On Gay Wallpaper. W. Williams.
  Un-MA:257
WALLS: see also FENCES; GRAFFITI;
  STILES
The City of Stones. Liu Yu-Hsi.
  Le-MW:62

If It Isn't Your Desire.
   Re-RR:98
Mending Wall.   R. Frost.
   Al-VBP:1128, Br-AF:125, Ca-VT:4,
   Er-FA:276, Ga-FB:285, Ha-PO:91,
   Sh-AP:145, Sh-RP:96, Un-MA:170,
   Wi-LT:164
Next Time at the Shore.   Re-RR:28
Regarding a Door.   D. Antin.
   Du-SH:26
Social Comment.   L. Fishberg.
   La-IH:28
The Wall.   A. Brownjohn.
   Ls-NY:260
When I Look Outside My Window.
   M. Liu.   Me-WF:57
You, Neighbor God.   R. Rilke.
   Tr-MR:147
WALNUTS
   Raking Walnuts in the Rain.
      M. Shannon.   Br-SS:73
   Riddles, I.   Gr-CT:235, Gr-GB:71
   Tell Me What Nut.   Re-RR:54
   Walnut.   J. Andrade.   Co-EL:118,
      Co-PU:129
   A Walnut.   Gr-GB:71, Li-LB:168,
      Mo-MGT:189, Wr-RM:73
WALRUSES: see also HUMOR - WALRUSES
   Hunting Songs, 1.   Walrus Hunting.
      Ma-BH:17, Tr-US I:12
   Walrus Hunting.   Da-SC:40,
      Le-IB:52
WALSINGHAM, ENG.
   A Lament for the Priory of
      Walsingham.   Gr-CT:327
   Lament for Walsingham.
      Gr-GB:184, Rv-CB:115
   Walsinghame.   W. Ralegh.
      Al-VBP:73, Gr-CT:55, Ha-PO:166,
      Rv-CB:154, Sm-LG:351
WANDERERS AND WANDERING: see also
      GYPSIES; NOMADS; TRAMPS
   Abraham.   E. Muir.   Tr-MR:67
   Cino.   E. Pound.   Ca-VT:78
   The City Child.   A. Tennyson.
      Ox-BC:213
   Dawn Boy's Song.   Da-SC:64,
      Ga-FB:247
   Dream Song.   Bi-IT:128, 129,
      Da-SC:100, Ho-SD:12, Le-OE:107
   Hollin, Green Hollin.   Gr-GB:46
   The Knight Without a Name.
      Ho-WR:122
   Over Hill, over Dale.
      W. Shakespeare.   Al-VBP:182,
      Bl-OB:90, Bo-FP:325, De-TT:113,
      Fe-FP:382, Re-TW:59
   Song of Two Ghosts.   Tr-US II:243
   Tom o' Bedlam.   De-CH:275,
      Ho-PR:51, Mc-WK:5, Sm-LG:203

Two Indian Boys.   J. Concha.
   Ba-HI:98
Where Is My Wandering Boy Tonight.
   Er-FA:440
WANDERLUST: see also ADVENTURE AND
      ADVENTURERS; SEAFARING LIFE;
      TRAVEL AND TRAVELERS
   Anton and Yaro.   M. Oliver.
      St-H:168
   At Dover Cliffs, July 20, 1787.
      W. Bowles.   Al-VBP:654
   Autobiography.   C. Causley.
      Wi-LT:668
   The Big Rock Candy Mountain.
      Gr-CT:280, Gr-GB:228,
      Hi-WP I:96, Pe-SS:86
   Brumana.   J. Flecker.   Pa-HT:118
   The Caravan.   M. Nightingale.
      Hu-MP:170
   Connecticut Road Song.
      A. Branch.   Pa-HT:31
   Departure.   E. Millay.   Un-MA:446
   Far, Far Will I Go.   Ma-BH:30
   The Feet of the Young Men.
      R. Kipling.   Se-PR:171
   The Gipsy Trail.   R. Kipling.
      Pa-HT:82
   Git Along, Cayuse.   H. Knibbs.
      Fi-BG:202
   Harp Song of the Dane Women.
      R. Kipling.   Co-RM:55,
      Ox-BN:931
   I Sing for You.   Lin Ling.
      Pa-MV:109
   I Thought It Was Tangiers I
      Wanted.   L. Hughes.
      Bo-HF:84, Hu-PN:196
   I Too!   I Too!   J. Wheelock.
      Sm-MK:32
   I Want to Go Wandering.
      V. Lindsay.   Pa-HT:72
   Identity.   D. Botez.   Mc-AC:61
   John-John.   T. Macdonough.
      Co-PI:105, Co-PT:194
   Long Gone.   S. Brown.   Ra-BP:112
   The Long Trail.   R. Kipling.
      Al-VBP:1095, Ga-FB:185, Sp-OG:253
   Nocturne of the Wharves.
      A. Bontemps.   Hu-PN:224,
      Ra-BP:93
   Ride Along, My Friend.
      T. Tsosie.   Ba-HI:97
   The Road to Anywhere.   B. Taylor.
      Hu-MP:165
   The Road to Vagabondia.
      D. Burnet.   Fe-PL:410
   Roadways.   J. Masefield.
      Pa-HT:78, Sh-RP:157
   Rolling Down to Rio.
      R. Kipling.   Pa-HT:71

WANDERLUST — cont'd.
  Romance. W. Turner. Bo-GJ:220,
    Hi-WP I:7, Mc-WS:113, Ni-JP:24,
    No-CL:251, Un-MB:345
  Roofs. J. Kilmer. Fe-PL:135
  Sacred Song of the Jackeroo Cult.
    Tr-US I:258
  Sailor. E. Farjeon. Pe-FB:29
  The Sea Gypsy. R. Hovey.
    Co-SS:76, Fe-FP:191, La-PV:186,
    Sh-RP:285, Un-GT:261
  Sea Way! S. Briody. Ho-CT:34
  The Seafarer. Ma-YA:5
  Sestina of the Tramp Royal.
    R. Kipling. Ni-JP:18, Un-MB:137
  A Ship Comes In. O. Jenkins.
    Bo-FP:134
  The Ships of Yule. B. Carman.
    Br-BC:126, Do-WH:16, Sh-RP:168
  The Sign-Post. E. Thomas.
    Al-VBP:1136
  Song. G. Vicente. Pa-SG:148
  The Song of a Vagabond Son.
    Fang Ching. Hs-TC:385
  Song of the Open Road.
    W. Whitman. Al-VBP:934,
    Ar-TP3:97, Er-FA:249, Un-MA:63
  A Song of the Road. R. Stevenson.
    Sp-OG:250
  The Sound of Trees. R. Frost.
    Bo-HF:58, Sm-PT:11
  Starting from Paumanok.
    W. Whitman. Al-VBP:927
  The Texas Ranger. Fi-BG:112
  Time, You Old Gipsy Man.
    R. Hodgson. Al-VBP:1114,
    Br-SS:11, De-CH:434, Fe-FP:61,
    Mc-WK:123, Pa-HT:77, Re-TW:108,
    Un-MB:186, Wi-LT:122
  To Chuck—Concerning a Rendezvous
    in Siam. J. Charles. Mc-WK:198
  Travel. R. Stevenson. Ar-TP3:96,
    Bo-HF:26, Fe-FP:459, Hu-MP:178,
    Mc-WK:190, Pa-HT:84, Sm-LG:104,
    Un-GT:263
  The Traveller. O. Goldsmith.
    Al-VBP:584
  Tumbling Mustard. M. Cowley.
    Br-AF:102
  Ulysses. A. Tennyson.
    Al-VBP:863, Ha-PO:40, Ke-TF:262,
    Ni-JP:16, Rv-CB:793
  The Vagabond. R. Stevenson.
    Al-VBP:1070, Cl-DT:62,
    Pa-HT:80, Se-PR:314
  A Vagabond Song. B. Carman.
    Co-PS:122, Fe-FP:81, Hu-MP:316,
    Sh-RP:116, Sp-OG:251, Un-GT:277
  Wander-Thirst. G. Gould.
    Ar-TP3:96, Cl-FC:59, Pa-HT:79

  The Wanderer. I. Thorson.
    Ke-TF:418
  A Wanderer's Song. J. Masefield.
    Sh-RP:158, Tu-WW:32, Un-MB:222
  Wanderer's Song. A. Symons.
    Al-VBP:1095
  The Water Is Wide. Sp-HW:1
  Western Star. S. Benét.
    Br-AF:225
  When Green Buds Hang in the Elms
    like Dust. A. Housman.
    Go-BP:28
  When I Grow Up. R. Holland.
    Br-BC:116
  Where Lies the Land? A. Clough.
    Co-SS:73, Gr-CT:217,
    Ox-BN:78, Sm-LG:299
  The Wraggle Taggle Gipsies.
    Ar-TP3:15, De-CH:75, Fe-FP:509,
    Ho-WR:48, Hu-MP:155, Mc-WS:163,
    Na-EO:33, Re-TW:124, Rv-CB:436,
    Un-GT:96
WAR: see also AIR RAIDS; ARMIES;
    ARMISTICES; ARMS AND ARMOR;
    BATTLES; CIVIL DEFENSE; CON-
    SCIENTIOUS OBJECTORS; NAVAL
    BATTLES; SATIRE - WAR;
    SOLDIERS; WAR DEAD; WAR WOUNDED;
    and names of battles, as SAND
    CREEK, BATTLE, 1864, and wars,
    as KOREAN WAR, 1950-1953
  Addition Problem. M. Goode.
    Jo-VC:17
  After the Salvo. H. Asquith.
    Li-TU:243
  Ain' Go'n' to Study War No Mo'.
    Ba-PO:167
  All Day It Has Rained. A. Lewis.
    Hi-WP I:28, Pa-GTB:543
  Apologia pro Poemate Meo.
    W. Owen. Un-MB:363, Wi-LT:347
  The Arsenal at Springfield.
    H. Longfellow. Ba-PO:96,
    Cr-WS:24
  The Ash and the Oak. L. Simpson.
    Cr-WS:3, Mo-BG:168
  Awake! W. Rodgers. Wi-LT:493
  The Battle. L. Simpson.
    Cr-WS:84, Du-SH:82, Ha-TP:76
  The Battle-Field. W. Bryant.
    Fe-PL:176, Vi-PP:197
  The Battle Hymn of Shanghai.
    Wang T'ung-chao. Hs-TC:269
  Beautiful Is the Land South of
    the Yangtse River.
    Wang T'ung-chao. Hs-TC:265
  Before the Charge. P. MacGill.
    Cr-WS:90
  Biafra. N. Kaplan.
    Ad-II:104

The Biglow Papers. J. Lowell.
  Ba-PO:98, Cr-WS:154, Ke-PP:83
The Bloody Sire. R. Jeffers.
  Cr-WS:88, Wi-LT:261
Boots. R. Kipling. Un-MB:129
Both Sides of the Yellow River
  Recaptured by the Imperial
  Army. Tu Fu. Cr-WS:10
The Brave at Home. T. Read.
  Sp-OG:201
Call to Youth. Horace. Pa-SG:4
The Captain. J. White. Co-RM:201
Cargo-Ships. M. Press. Ke-TF:261
The Century when Even Death Died.
  K. Patchen. Ba-PO:ix
Chivalry. AE. Al-VBP:1103,
  Tr-MR:181
The Chronicle of the Drum.
  W. Thackeray. Al-VBP:878
Clarel. H. Melville. Ba-PO:91
Come to the Stone. R. Jarrell.
  Ca-VT:399
The Conflict. C. Day Lewis.
  Un-MB:424, Wi-LT:429
Conquerors. H. Treece.
  Co-RM:210, To-MP:51
Conscientious Objector.
  E. Millay. Ba-PO:4, Cr-WS:137
Conversion. F. Angermayer.
  Fe-PL:334
The Cross-Roads of the World.
  M. Dragomir. Mc-AC:121
Curs'd Is the Man. Homer.Ba-PO:169
The Da Pacem of the Laborer.
  Ba-PO:85
Dead Cow Farm. R. Graves.
  Li-TU:244
Dead Man's Dump. I. Rosenberg.
  Pa-GTB:446, Wi-LT:636
The Deserted Village.
  Feng Hsüeh-feng. Hs-TC:371
Do the Russians Want War?
  Y. Yevtushenko. Mo-MI:67
Dooley Is a Traitor. J. Michie.
  Co-RM:119
Dreamers. S. Sassoon.
  Cr-WS:83, Un-MB:310
The Drum. J. Scott. Al-VBP:588,
  Ba-PO:67, Ke-PP:39, Rv-CB:545
Dulce Bellum Inexpertis.
  G. Gascoigne. Ba-PO:119
Dusk in War Time. S. Teasdale.
  Cr-WS:120
Dwarf of Disintegration. O. Williams.
  En-PC:42, Wi-LT:415
The Edda. Ba-PO:125
The Effect. S. Sassoon.
  Cr-WS:89, Gr-BT:107
Th Eleventh Hour. F. Morris.
  Hi-WP II:146

Embassy. W. Auden.   Du-SH:81
The Epic of Dengei.
  Tr-US I:233
Epitaph for Chaeroneia.
  Aristotle. Pa-SG:7
The Eve of Waterloo. G. Byron.
  Al-VBP:723, Er-FA:362, Ga-FB:205,
  Hi-FO:204, Ox-BN:243
Evening at the Sunset. W. Melaney.
  Ad-II:100
Exodus. J. Bodet. Cr-WS:125
A Farm Boy's Answer. J. Lowell.
  Kr-OF:63
The Field of Glory. E. Robinson.
  Un-MA:125
The Field of Waterloo. T. Hardy.
  Sm-LG:257
Fighting South of the Ramparts.
  Cr-WS:7, Ma-FW:249, Pa-SG:3
For Carlos at War. M. Price.
  Cr-WS:77
For the Fallen. L. Binyon.
  Al-VBP:1109
For the Record. R. Thomas.
  Go-BP:217, To-MP:43
A Front. R. Jarrell.
  Ca-VT:399
God Bless Us. G. Bart-Williams.
  Gr-BT:109
The God of War. Be-AP:45
Granada. M. Svetlov.
  Ca-MR:86
Greater Love. W. Owen.
  Al-VBP:1196, Er-FA:198,
  Pa-GTB:449, Un-MB:366,
  Wi-LT:348
Gunpowder Plot. V. Scannell.
  Ma-FW:267, To-MP:70
Hear a War Drum Sound.
  S. Takayanagi. Sh-AM:176
High Germany. Hi-FO:175,
  Rv-CB:435
A Horation Ode upon Cromwell.
  A. Marvell. Al-VBP:459,
  Pa-GTB:51
The Horses. E. Muir. Go-BP:101,
  Ha-PO:117, Un-MB:343
The House Is in Ruins.
  I. Ivanova. Mo-MI:70
Housemates. O. Shepard. Tr-MR:192
I Ain't Marchin' Any More.
  P. Ochs. Ba-PO:199
I Am for Peace. P. Folger.
  Kr-OF:61
I Have a Rendezvous with Death.
  A. Seeger. Al-VBP:1179,
  Cr-WS:58, Er-FA:191, Ga-FB:216,
  Hi-TL:182, Ke-TF:168, Sp-OG:211
I Hear an Army. J. Joyce.
  Al-VBP:1150, Un-MB:269, Wi-LT:623

WAR — cont'd.
  I Heard a Young Man Saying.
    J. Fields. Be-MA:149,
    Hu-NN:110
  I Know. K. Canter. Ad-II:98
  If on Account of the Political
    Situation. W. Auden.
    Ba-PO:50
  In Any Soul There Is a Bright
    Country. A. Yaskolka.
    Bo-RU:91
  In the Mourning Time. R. Hayden.
    Ra-BP:138
  In the Third Year of the War.
    H. Treece. Cr-WS:73
  Innocents. K. Hopkins.
    Cr-WS:130
  Insensibility. W. Owen.
    Ba-PO:xiii
  Into the Salient. E. Blunden.
    Al-VBP:1207
  Iron Virgin. Kuo Mo-jo.
    Hs-TC:41
  It Shall Not Be Again. T. Clark.
    Se-PR:205
  Jerusalem. W. Blake.
    Al-VBP:623, Gr-CT:295, Ox-BN:42
  Jerusalem. A. Rich. Mc-EA:121
  The Jewel. J. Dickey. Ha-TP:78
  Kid Stuff. F. Horne.
    Ab-MO:76, Ad-PB:56, Bo-AN:41,
    Bo-HF:109, Hu-PN:148, Li-TU:247
  Lament of a Frontier Guard.
    Rihaku. Ca-VT:83
  Letter from a Black Soldier.
    B. Anderson. Ca-VT:625
  A Letter from the Front.
    H. Newbolt. Cr-WS:79
  Life at War. D. Levertov.
    Ca-VT:515
  The Long War. L. Lee.
    Go-BP:216, Br-BT:100
  Lovers, Forget the Moon.
    C. Norman. Cr-WS:121
  A Lullaby. G. Glasgow. Sp-OG:210
  Lysistrata. Aristophanes.
    Ba-PO:15
  The Man He Killed. T. Hardy.
    Ba-PO:131, Co-RM:218, Cr-WS:107,
    Er-FA:182, Un-MB:26, Wi-LT:18
  A Man-Made World. S. Spender.
    Tr-MR:185
  Memorial to the Great Big
    Beautiful Self-Sacrificing
    Advertisers. E. Ebright.
    Hi-TL:207
  Memories of a Lost War.
    L. Simpson. Ca-VT:519
  The Men of War. H. Vaughan.
    Ba-PO:6

  Men's Stick-Dance Songs, I.
    Tr-US II:142
  The Metamorphoses. R. Jarrell.
    Ha-TP:87
  The Moral Warfare. J. Whittier.
    Vi-PP:231
  Mother, the Wardrobe Is Full of
    Infantrymen. R. McGough.
    Gr-BT:117
  My Friend, You Must Have Smelt
    This Stench. Wang T'ung-chao.
    Hs-TC:267
  my sweet old etcetera.
    e. cummings. Cr-WS:74,
    Mo-BG:94, Pe-SS:137
  Names. L. Mueller. Ha-TP:104
  Night. Ai Mu. Hs-TC:436
  No Matter if You Remain
    Unaffected by. B. Patten.
    Gr-BT:129
  Nocturne. E. Davison. De-CH:161
  Not the Deeds of Blood!
    H. Longfellow. Kr-OF:66
  Notes for a Movie Script.
    M. Holman. Ad-PB:174,
    Bo-AN:151, Hu-PN:362
  Notes for My Son. A. Comfort.
    Un-MB:520, Wi-LT:672
  November Eleventh. K. Burton.
    Se-PR:204
  Nuts in May. L. MacNeice.
    Un-MB:446
  O Sorrowful and Ancient Days.
    Eugenius Vulgarius. Ba-PO:74
  O What Is That Sound. W. Auden.
    Al-VBP:1227, Gr-SS:70, Ma-FW:254,
    Pe-M:98, To-MP:29, Un-MB:455
  Ode; to My Pupils. W. Auden.
    Un-MB:451
  Of Bombs and Boys. R. Corbin.
    Pe-SS:136
  An Old Song. S. Bloomgarden.
    Ho-TY:75, Pa-SG:147
  On a Certain Engagement South of
    Seoul. H. Carruth. Br-AF:89
  On Receiving News of the War.
    I. Rosenberg. Un-MB:357
  Overnight in the Apartment by
    the River. Tu Fu. Gr-CT:344
  The Parable of the Old Men and
    the Young. W. Owen.
    Go-BP:207, Ma-FW:250, Mo-GR:18
  Pastoral. P. Mowrer. Cr-WS:70
  Patterns. A. Lowell.
    Bo-HF:116, Co-BL:142, Cr-WS:115,
    Er-FA:65, Mo-GR:39, Pa-OM:262,
    Pe-OA:47, Sm-PT:18, Un-MA:156
  Pause. R. Marinoni. De-FS:136
  The Peaceful Shepherd. R. Frost.
    Tr-MR:191, Un-MA:181

Piano after War.   G. Brooks.
   Bo-AN:142
Pinned Down.   P. Horgan.
   Cr-WS:86
Poem to Be Cast into the Sea in
   a Bottle.   J. Kirkup.   Go-BP:217
A Prayer for Peace.
   Charles d'Orleans.   Ba-PO:20
Processional from the War Ceremony.
   Br-MW:78
Prospect.   T. Clark.   Se-PR:187
A Protest in the Sixth Year of
   Chi'en Fu.   Ts'ao Sung.
   Ga-FB:193
Range-Finding.   R. Frost.
   Ha-TP:77
The Rear Guard.   S. Sassoon.
   Un-MB:311
Recitative - A Lakeshore Poem.
   M. Kaneko.   Sh-AM:64
Reconciliation.   W. Whitman.
   Ba-PO:123
A Restless Night in Camp.
   Tu Fu.   Rx-OH:23
The Reveille.   B. Harte.
   Se-PR:121, Sp-OG:192, Vi-PP:199
Sailor on Leave.   O. Dodson.
   Bo-AN:126
Sang-Kan River.   Ya Hsüan.
   Pa-MV:149
The Shadow.   G. Dusenbery.
   Sc-TN:37
The Show.   W. Owen.   Al-VBP:1197,
   Un-MB:368, Wi-LT:350
Smoke.   C. Sandburg.   Ba-PO:134
Soldier, There Is a War Between
   the Mind.   W. Stevens.
   Wi-LT:163
Soldiers Bathing.   F. Prince.
   Pa-GTB:528, Un-MB:486, Wi-LT:793
Soldier's Song.   T. Hume.
   Co-RM:216, Ho-WR:118
Something Peaceful.
   T. Tsyganok.   Mo-MI:69
Song in Recitative Style.
   Tr-US II:45
The Song of Momus to Mars.
   J. Dryden.   Rv-CB:468
Song of the Exposition.
   W. Whitman.   Ba-PO:123
Song of War.   T. Tzara.
   Mc-AC:76
Songs for a Colored Singer, III.
   E. Bishop.   Hu-PN:550
The Sonnet-Ballad.   G. Brooks.
   Pe-SS:131
Spring MCMXL.   D. Gascoyne.
   Cr-WS:70
Spring Offensive.   W. Owen.
   Pa-GTB:451

Stars in a May Night.
   Wang T'ung-chao.   Hs-TC:266
Strength Through Joy.
   K. Rexroth.   Ca-VT:268
The Sun Used to Shine.   E. Thomas.
   Pl-ML:41
Sunset Horn.   M. O'Higgins.
   Bo-AN:146, Hu-PN:352
The Sword and the Sickle.
   W. Blake.   Ar-TP3:211,
   Gr-CT:349
The Task.   W. Cowper.   Ba-PO:118
There Will Come Soft Rains.
   S. Teasdale.   Cr-WS:69
This Excellent Machine.
   J. Lehmann.   Du-SH:87
This Hour.   O. La Grone.
   Hu-NN:37, Hu-PN:327
The Time of Ede.   Be-AP:42
To a Military Rifle.
   Y. Winters.   Un-MA:550
To His Friend, Wei.   Li Po.
   Li-TU:234
To Lucasta, on Going to the Wars.
   R. Lovelace.   Al-VBP:446,
   Er-FA:116, Ga-FB:194, Gr-BT:99,
   Ke-TF:100, Ma-YA:101, Mc-WS:103,
   No-CL:191, Pa-GTB:72, Rv-CB:392,
   Un-MW:153
To the Castle at Gordes.
   O. de Magny.   Ba-PO:88,
   Cr-WS:153
The Triumph of Freedom.
   W. Garrison.   Ba-PO:100
Triumphal Entry.   C. Norman.
   Cr-WS:125
Tubal Cain.   C. Mackay.
   Hu-MP:407
The Twelve.   A. Blok.   Ca-MR:200
Ugly Day.   M. Levine.   Ad-II:102
Vala or the Four Zoas.   W. Blake.
   Al-VBP:621, Ox-BN:37
The Voices.   Sp-OG:209
The Volunteer's Reply to the Poet.
   R. Campbell.   Al-VBP:1222
War.   Chief Joseph.   Ba-PO:112
War.   J. Langland.   Du-SH:85,
   En-PC:161, Ha-TP:75
War.   Li Po.   Gr-CT:341
War.   W. McLean.   Ad-BO:53
War.   S. Mason.   Le-M:148
War.   D. Roth.   Du-RG:71
War.   Samuel the Prince.   Me-PH:57
War Begets Poverty.
   F. Pastorius.   Ba-PO:169
A War Between Two Races of Ants.
   H. Thoreau.   Kr-OF:69
A War Game. A. Richards. La-IH:130
The War God. S. Spender. Tr-MR:180
The War God. Ya Hsüan.   Pa-MV:148

WAR — cont'd.
A War Song of Tetlapan
  Quetzahitzin. Da-SC:173
A War Song of the Otomies.
  Da-SC:172
What the Old Women Say.
  A. MacLeish. Ha-TP:76
Where Have All the Flowers Gone?
  P. Seeger. Pe-SS:132
Who First Began. D. Lindsay.
  Ba-PO:73
Whoever It Was. Sophocles.
  Ba-PO:74
Without Benefit of Declaration.
  L. Hughes. Bo-AN:72,
  Cr-WS:47, Lo-TY:229
See also Em-AF:165-173
WAR - AFTERMATH
An Airstrip in Essex. D. Hall.
  Cr-WS:168, En-PC:268, Wi-LT:727
Among Many Heaps of Ashes.
  Cho Sung Kyun. Ba-PO:156,
  Cr-WS:6
Christmas 1945. A. Hine.
  Hi-TL:219
The Decision. O. Dodson.
  Hu-PN:302
One Morning the World Woke Up.
  O. Williams. Ba-PO:192,
  Er-FA:197
Redeployment. H. Nemerov.
  Ba-PO:193, Hi-TL:222, Wi-LT:591
Vienna 1945. W. Waldin.
  Ba-PO:191
With My Maimed Hand.
  Tai Wang-Shu. Hs-TC:185
WAR DEAD: see also HUMOR - WAR
  DEAD; MEMORIAL DAY; SATIRE
  - WAR DEAD; UNKNOWN SOLDIER
À Terre. W. Owen. Wi-LT:352
After. R. Kipling. Mc-PR:66
All Day It Has Rained. A. Lewis.
  Hi-WP I:28, Pa-GTB:543
All That Is Left. Basho.
  Ba-PO:25, Pa-SG:9
America's Answer. R. Lilliard.
  Vi-PP:215
Another Reply to "In Flanders
  Fields." J. Armstrong.
  Vi-PP:214
Another Song. D. Justice.
  Ca-VT:536
Anthem for Doomed Youth.
  W. Owen. Al-VBP:1198,
  Bo-HF:173, Cr-WS:67, Er-FA:195,
  Gr-BT:106, Gr-CT:349, Ma-FW:250,
  Na-EO:81, Pa-GTB:450, Un-MB:363,
  Wi-LT:350
Armistice Day. R. Montgomery.
  Se-PR:205

As Toilsome I Wander'd Virginia's
  Woods. W. Whitman. Al-VBP:937,
  Sp-OG:205
Asleep. W. Owen. Hi-WP II:25
At the British War Cemetery,
  Bayeux. C. Causley. Go-BP:210
At War. R. Atkins. Bo-AN:169
A Ballad of Heroes. A. Dobson.
  Se-PR:133
The Battle-Field. W. Bryant.
  Fe-PL:176, Vi-PP:197
The Battle of Antietam Creek.
  Em-AF:451
Beach Burial. K. Slessor.
  Cr-WS:96
Before Sedan. A. Dobson. Ke-TF:52
Bivouac of the Dead. T. O'Hara.
  Ke-TF:256, Se-PR:133, Vi-PP:201
The Blue and the Gray.
  F. Finch. Hi-TL:129,
  Sp-OG:206, Vi-PP:163
Breakfast. W. Gibson. Cr-WS:104
The Brigade Must Not Know, Sir!
  Hi-TL:120
Carentan O Carentan. L. Simpson.
  Bl-FP:46, Ca-MB:117, Co-RM:202
Charley III. S. Sandy. Ls-NY:33
The Children's Bells.
  E. Farjeon. De-CH:164
Come Up from the Fields, Father.
  W. Whitman. Ni-JP:76, Un-MA:77
Commander Death. P. Horgan.
  Cr-WS:103
Confession. M. Marcus. Ba-PO:36
Counter-Attack. S. Sassoon.
  Ba-PO:136, Co-RM:204,
  Cr-WS:87, Un-MB:312
The Crowns. J. Freeman. De-CH:163
Cry for a Dead Soldier.
  M. Inman. Ls-NY:109
Custer's Last Fight. Fi-BG:114
David's Lament. Bible. O.T.
  Samuel. Gr-CT:343, Me-PH:12
The Dead. R. Brooke. De-CH:161,
  Se-PR:136, Sp-OG:213
The Dead Heroes. I. Rosenberg.
  Un-MB:352
The Dead in Europe. R. Lowell.
  Wi-LT:581
Dead Man's Dump. I. Rosenberg.
  Pa-GTB:446, Wi-LT:636
Dead on the Warpath.
  Da-SC:93, Tr-US II:257
Dead Soldier. N. Guillén.
  Ba-PO:42, Lo-TY:105
A Dead Soldier Abandoned on the
  Roadside. Tu Yün-hsieh.
  Hs-TC:251
The Death-Bed. S. Sassoon.
  Wi-LT:640

The Death of the Ball Turret
    Gunner.   R. Jarrell. Ba-PO:186,
    Ca-VT:400, Co-EL:82, Cr-WS:100,
    Pe-SS:138, Un-MA:647, Wi-LT:561
Dick Milburn.   W. Gibson.
    Cr-WS:105
Dirge for a Son Killed in Battle.
    Tr-US I:187
Dirge for Two Veterans.
    W. Whitman.   Un-MA:77
The Dying Sergeant.   Em-AF:420
Easter 1916.   W. Yeats.
    Wi-LT:70
The Effect.   S. Sassoon.
    Cr-WS:89, Gr-BT:107
Elegy for a Dead Soldier.
    K. Shapiro.   Hi-TL:213,
    Wi-LT:541
The End.   W. Owen.   De-CH:162
Epitaph for a Concord Boy.
    S. Young.   Mc-WK:164
Esthetique du Mal, VII.
    W. Stevens.   Wi-LT:155
A Father's Notes of Woe.
    W. Scott.   Ox-BN:125
The Fighting Race.   J. Clarke.
    Co-RM:111
Fighting South of the Ramparts.
    Cr-WS:7, Ma-FW:249, Pa-SG:3
The First Division Marches.
    G. Rice.   Vi-PP:216
The Flowers of the Forest.
    J. Elliott.   Al-VBP:582,
    De-CH:176, Pa-GTB:120
For and Against.   C. Norman.
    Cr-WS:162
For Lover Man and All Other Young
    Men Who Failed to Return from
    World War II.   M. Williams.
    Cr-WS:109, Hu-NN:56
For the Fallen.   L. Binyon.
    Al-VBP:1109, Hi-WP II:24
For the Iowa Dead.   P. Engle.
    St-H:55
For the Unknown Seamen of the
    1939-45 War Buried in Iona
    Churchyard.   I. Smith.
    Go-BP:212
The Formalities.   J. Ciardi.
    Cr-WS:143
Fort McKinley.   Lo Men. Pa-MV:125
Funeral Hymn.   Pa-SG:9
GI.   R. Roseliep.   De-FS:164
Ghosts. Fire. Water.
    J. Kirkup.   Go-BP:215
Grass.   C. Sandburg.
    Cr-WS:19, Fe-PL:155,
    Ga-FB:219, Un-MA:200
The Great Dead at Thermopylae.
    Simonides.   Pa-SG:8

Greater Love.   W. Owen.
    Al-VBP:1196, Er-FA:198,
    Pa-GTB:449, Un-MB:366,
    Wi-LT:348
Griefs for Dead Soldiers.
    T. Hughes.   Go-BP:211
Hanging Corpse.   Ch'in Tzu-hao.
    Pa-MV:54
He Died a Second Time, 10.
    A Thought.   Ai Ch'ing.
    Hs-TC:309
He Died a Second Time, 12.
    He Fell. Ai Ch'ing. Hs-TC:311
He Killed Many of My Men.
    J. Bennett.   Gr-BT:110
Heartbreak Ridge.   E. Pierce.
    Cr-WS:142
Here Dead Lie We.   A. Housman.
    Cr-WS:135, Fe-PL:156
Home-Coming.   P. Binford.
    Ke-TF:261
How Can a Man Die Better.
    Tyrtaeus.   Pa-SG:6
How Sleep the Brave. W. Collins.
    Al-VBP:572, Pa-GTB:119,
    Rv-CB:536, Sp-OG:208
I Did Not Lose My Heart in
    Summer's Even.   A. Housman.
    Cr-WS:107, Wi-LT:67
I May Not Know Them All by
    Name.   Mo-MI:70
In Distrust of Merits. M. Moore.
    Al-VBP:1176, Pl-EI:146,
    Se-PR:207, Sm-PT:126,
    Un-MA:354, Wi-LT:272
In Flanders Fields.   J. McCrae.
    Al-VBP:1115, Br-SS:76, Er-FA:189,
    Ga-FB:217, Hu-MP:342, Se-PR:207,
    Sp-OG:212, Th-AS:196, Vi-PP:211
In Memoriam (Easter 1915).
    E. Thomas.   Pa-GTB:444
In Memory of Colonel Charles
    Young. C. Cullen.   Ad-PB:86
In the Dordogne.   J. Bishop.
    Ca-VT:160
The Investiture.   S. Sassoon.
    Cr-WS:110
It Shall Not Be Again.
    T. Clark.   Se-PR:205
Jack Ellyat Heard the Guns.
    S. Benét.   Fe-PL:172
John Anderson.   K. Douglas.
    Cr-WS:82
The Joke. W. Gibson. Cr-WS:105
A Kind of Hero.   V. Scannell.
    Co-RM:207
Knowlt Hoheimer.   E. Masters.
    Ba-PO:81, Ho-LP:89
Lancer. A. Housman.   Un-MB:99
The Last Fierce Charge. Em-AF:456

WAR DEAD — cont'd.
  The Last Laugh. W. Owen.
    Cr-WS:94
  The Last Soldier. S. Morozov.
    Mo-MI:72
  The Locust Swarm. Hsu Chao.
    Cr-WS:5, Rx-OH:123
  Losses. R. Jarrell.
    Sh-AP:223, Wi-LT:562
  Lullaby Sung by a Widow.
    Tr-US II:177
  The Man in the Dead Machine.
    D. Hall. Bl-FP:73, Du-SH:96
  The Man in White. W. Percy.
    Ke-TF:166
  The March. J. Squire. Co-PS:91
  Memorial. Tr-US I:126
  Memorial Day. W. Brooks.
    Se-PR:137, Vi-PP:218
  Memorial Rain. A. MacLeish.
    Un-MA:454
  Memorial Wreath. D. Randall.
    Ad-PB:140, Hu-NN:59, Hu-PN:305
  The Messages. W. Gibson.
    Co-RM:221
  Messmates. H. Newbolt. De-CH:167
  The Mither's Lament. S. Smith.
    Co-PU:151
  A Monument for the Soldiers.
    J. Riley. Se-PR:135
  More than Flowers We Have Brought.
    N. Turner. Br-SS:157
  The Mound in the Meads.
    W. Watson. Cr-WS:16
  My Friend, You Must Have Smelt
    This Stench. Wang T'ung-chao.
    Hs-TC:267
  My Luve's in Germany. De-CH:172
  Near Mons. N. Myers. Ls-NY:256
  1935. S. Benét. Mc-WS:107,
    Un-MA:501
  Not to Die. Simonides. Pa-SG:10
  Notes for a Movie Script.
    M. Holman. Ad-PB:174,
    Bo-AN:151, Hu-PN:362
  Ode for the American Dead in
    Korea. T. McGrath.
    Bl-FP:49, Ca-VT:431
  Ode to the Confederate Dead.
    A. Tate. Al-VBP:1215,
    Un-MA:536, Wi-LT:402
  Ode to the Confederate Dead in
    Magnolia Cemetery.
    H. Timrod. Se-PR:134,
    Sh-AP:126, Vi-PP:165
  Old Funeral Chant. Tr-US II:43
  The Old Man and Jim. J. Riley.
    Co-PT:232, Sp-OG:197
  On a Military Graveyard.
    K. Rexroth. Cr-WS:173

  On a Soldier Fallen in the
    Philippines. W. Moody.
    Cr-WS:155, Hi-TL:156
  On a Very Young, Very Dead
    Soldier. R. Gillman.
    Cr-WS:101
  On a Victory. Tr-US I:127
  On the Grave of a Young Cavalry
    Officer Killed in the Valley
    of Virginia. H. Melville.
    Cr-WS:103
  On the Road to Santiago.
    S. Crane. Kr-OF:74
  The Overthrow of Ruanae.
    Potiki. Tr-US II:56
  Peace. W. de la Mare.
    Ni-JP:79, Un-MB:203
  The Performance. J. Dickey.
    Wi-LT:688
  Philip Dagg. W. Gibson.
    Cr-WS:106
  The Picket-Guard. E. Beers.
    Er-FA:187, Sp-OG:196
  Poem of the Conscripted Warrior.
    R. Nogar. Lo-TY:187
  Praise Song. Tr-US II:239
  A Private. E. Thomas. Pa-GTB:444
  Proud Motherhood. E. Lucas.
    Hi-FO:263
  Quintana Lay in the Shallow
    Grave of Coral. K. Shapiro.
    Ca-VT:374
  The Rear Guard. S. Sassoon.
    Un-MB:311
  Reply to "In Flanders Fields."
    J. Mitchell. Vi-PP:212
  The Send-Off. W. Owen.
    Cr-WS:61, Un-MB:368
  Seravezza. H. Fuller. Ad-PB:200
  She Is Far from the Land.
    T. Moore. Ox-BN:212
  She Said . . . J. Brooks.
    Hu-PN:241
  Shiloh, a Requiem. H. Melville.
    Al-VBP:952, Br-AF:72, Ho-WR:120,
    Pa-HT:42, Rv-CB:838, Vi-PP:149
  The Show. W. Owen. Al-VBP:1197,
    Un-MB:368, Wi-LT:350
  Sic Transit Gloria. E. Pierce.
    Cr-WS:109
  A Sight in Camp in the Daybreak
    Gray and Dim. W. Whitman.
    Ha-PO:62
  the singer. K. Wilson. Sc-TN:240
  The Singers in a Cloud.
    R. Torrence. Pl-US:56
  The Sioux Women. Ho-SD:9,
    Jo-TS:22, Tr-US II:226
  Sohrab and Rustum. M. Arnold.
    Pa-GTB:363

The Soldier. R. Brooke.
  Al-VBP:1179, Cr-WS:57, Er-FA:190,
  Fe-PL:179, Ga-FB:215, Ke-TF:169,
  Sp-OG:208, Un-MB:324, Wi-LT:612
Song after Defeat. Tr-US I:37
Song Commemorating a Dead Sioux
  Warrior. Tr-US II:235
Song for All Seas, All Ships.
  W. Whitman. De-CH:167,
  Tr-MR:175
Song for the Heroes. A. Comfort.
  Cr-WS:163, Un-MB:521
Songs in Honor of a Prominent
  Warrior. Tr-US II:238
Songs of a Mother Mourning Her
  Sons Killed in Battle.
  Tr-US II:237
The Spires of Oxford. W. Letts.
  Cr-WS:68, Er-FA:190, Fe-PL:178
The Spring Waters, 176.
  Ping Hsin. Hs-TC:25
A Stopwatch and an Ordnance Map.
  S. Spender. Ca-MB:99
Strange Meeting. W. Owen.
  Cr-WS:85, Go-BP:209,
  Pa-GTB:452, Un-MB:367
The Street of Crosses.
  A. Stringer. Ke-TF:179
Sunset Horn. M. O'Higgins.
  Bo-AN:146, Hu-PN:352
A Survivor. K. Hopkins.
  Cr-WS:112
To Any Dead Officer. S. Sassoon.
  Cr-WS:111
To E. T. R. Frost. Pl-ML:162
To the Memory of the Brave
  Americans. P. Freneau.
  Fe-PL:166, Sh-AP:14, Vi-PP:134
Toledo. R. Campbell. Un-MB:419
The Too-Late Born. A. MacLeish.
  Bo-GJ:192, Gr-CC:111, Sh-AP:188,
  Un-MA:458, Wi-LT:340
Trench Poets. E. Rickword.
  Cr-WS:97
Tumea's Lament for Her Father
  Ngakauvarea. Tr-US II:54
Turkestan. Ch'en T'ao. Cr-WS:8
Tywater. R. Wilbur. Ha-PO:124,
  Wi-LT:593
Ultima Ratio Regum. S. Spender.
  Er-FA:196, Pe-SS:139,
  To-MP:33, Wi-LT:501
The Unknown Dead. H. Timrod.
  Sh-AP:126
The Unknown Soldier. A. Lewis.
  Un-MB:518
The Unsung Heroes. P. Dunbar.
  Ra-BP:54
V.D.F. H. Wolfe.
  Cr-WS:76

"Vale" from Carthage. P. Viereck.
  Cr-WS:102, Pe-OA:238, Un-MA:658,
  Wi-LT:832
Variations on Simonides. G. Ely.
  Ls-NY:28
A Victory Dance. A. Noyes.
  Fe-PL:153
Vigil Strange I Kept on the
  Field One Night. W. Whitman.
  Un-MA:78
Voices of Heroes. H. Gregory.
  Gr-SS:104
War. J. Langland. Du-SH:85,
  En-PC:161, Ha-TP:75
The War Dead. B. Krasnoff.
  Ad-II:101
The War God. Ya Hsüan. Pa-MV:148
The War Museum at Nagasaki.
  C. Higham. Ls-NY:30
War Poem. H. Treece. Cr-WS:108
War Story. J. Stallworthy.
  Co-EL:82
When Dey 'Listed Colored Soldiers.
  P. Dunbar. Ra-BP:48
Where Have All the Flowers Gone?
  P. Seeger. Pe-SS:132
A Whim of Time. S. Spender.
  Un-MB:471
Willie Mackintosh. Ma-BB:8,
  Ox-BB:597, Rv-CB:125
The Wooden Crosses. H. Sahl.
  Un-R:59
WAR OF 1812: see also CONSTITUTION
  (SHIP); GHENT, TREATY OF, 1814;
  and names of historic persons,
  as HARRISON, WILLIAM HENRY
Andrew Jackson. M. Keller.
  Br-AF:67, Co-RM:212, Un-GT:92
The Banks of Champlain. Em-AF:436
The Battle of New Orleans.
  Em-AF:439
The Constitution and the
  Guerriére. Em-AF:434
James Bird. Em-AF:438
The Star-Spangled Banner. F. Key.
  Er-FA:283, Fe-FP:401, Hi-TL:65,
  Se-PR:130, Vi-PP:53
Ye Parliament of England.
  Em-AF:433
WAR SONGS AND CRIES: see also
  SATIRE – WAR SONGS AND CRIES
The Battle-Birds. Da-SC:156
Battle Hymn. Tr-US I:101
Battle Hymn of the Republic.
  J. Howe. De-CH:159, Er-FA:469,
  Fe-FP:441, Hi-TL:100, Ke-TF:53,
  Pl-EI:160, Un-GT:311, Vi-PP:145
Boots. R. Kipling. Un-MB:129
The British Grenadiers.
  Rv-CB:443

WAR SONGS AND CRIES — cont'd.
  The Caisson Song. E. Gruber.
    Vi-PP:107
  Carry Me Back. J. Holmes.
    Br-AF:21
  Do Li A. Gr-GB:236
  Fife Tune. J. Manifold.
    Bo-GJ:193, Er-FA:198, Ho-LP:68,
    Mc-WS:97, Sm-LG:262, Wi-LT:765
  For Soldiers. H. Gifford.
    De-CH:158
  The Forty-Second. Gr-GB:235
  From the South. Da-SC:156
  Goin' 'cross the Mountain.
    Em-AF:452
  Greek War Song. K. Rigas.
    Hi-FO:212
  He Died a Second Time, 11.
    Forward March. Ai Ch'ing.
    Hs-TC:310
  Hear My Voice, Birds of War!
    Da-SC:155, Ho-SD:5
  The Hearse Song. Ba-PO:198
  How the Days Will Be. Bi-IT:66
  Hymn. Bi-IT:65
  I Am Rising. Da-SC:156
  If You Love Your Uncle Sam.
    P. Seeger. Ba-PO:199
  Last Night I Had the Strangest
    Dream. E. McCurdy. Ba-PO:198
  Look! Ge-TR:27
  March, March. W. Scott.
    Al-VBP:678
  Men Who March Away. T. Hardy.
    Cl-DT:15, De-CH:164, De-TT:137
  The Night of Trafalgar. T. Hardy.
    De-CH:166, Gr-CT:340, Un-MB:28
  Ojibwa War Song. Da-SC:155,
    Kr-OF:1, Le-OE:120
  The Old Men. Jo-TS:10,
    Tr-US II:237
  Old War Song. Tr-US I:132
  Old War Song. Tr-US II:241
  Passamaquoddy War Song.
    Da-SC:254
  Pibroch of Donuil Dhu. W. Scott.
    Hi-FO:100, Pa-GTB:202
  Pima War Song. Da-SC:94
  Protection Song. Da-SC:90
  The Romance of Antar. Antar.
    Ab-MO:66
  Scalp Song. Da-SC:93
  Screw Guns. R. Kipling.
    Al-VBP:1098
  Song for a War Dance. Tr-US I:92
  Song of a Man Urged to Join the
    Warriors. Tr-US II:227
  Song of a War-Band Setting Out.
    Tr-US II:190
  Song of Encouragement. Bi-IT:64

  Song of the Brave. L. Altgood.
    Vi-PP:205
  Song of the Killing. Da-SC:114
  Song of War. Tr-US I:203
  Song on the War in the Mountains
    of Vita Levu in 1876.
    Tr-US I:229
  Spear-Blessing. Tr-US I:103
  To Those Who Fight.
    T'ien Chien. Hs-TC:322
  Victory of the Mea. Tr-US I:219
  War Chant. Be-AP:45
  War Song. Da-SC:91
  War Song. Tr-US I:40
  War Song. Tr-US II:247, 269, 280
  The War-Song of Dinas Vawr.
    T. Peacock. Al-VBP:716,
    Ha-PO:220, Ho-WR:106, Mc-WS:105,
    Na-EO:110, Pa-OM:197
  War Song of Goloane. Goloane.
    Tr-US I:82
  A War Song of Tetlapan
    Quetzanitzin. Da-SC:173
  War Song of the Kwakiutl.
    Tr-US II:218
  War Song of the Nkuna Clan.
    Tr-US I:89
  A War Song of the Otomies.
    Da-SC:172
  War Song of the Saracens.
    J. Flecker. Ga-FB:193,
    Hi-FO:65, Un-MB:273
  War Song on a Brave Woman.
    Tr-US II:227
  War Song, Sung Before Going into
    Battle. Tr-US I:201
  A War Song to Englishmen.
    W. Blake. De-CH:157
  War Songs. Bi-IT:61, 62,
    Tr-US II:236, 237, 240
  The Warrior Bards. H. Treece.
    Pl-ML:94
  Warrior's Song. Tr-US II:280
  When Johnny Comes Marching Home.
    P. Gilmore. Co-PS:145,
    Hi-TL:126, Vi-PP:161
  Women's Song for Fighting Men
    Delayed on a Raid. Tr-US I:95
  You Shall Live. Bi-IT:170
  Young Men, Help Me. Sitting Bull.
    Da-SC:113
WAR WOUNDED: see also AMPUTATIONS;
    HUMOR – WAR WOUNDED; SATIRE –
    WAR WOUNDED
  À Terre. W. Owen. Wi-LT:352
  Brother Green. Em-AF:455
  The Cripple for Life.
    Em-AF:457
  Dead Man's Dump. I. Rosenberg.
    Pa-GTB:446, Wi-LT:636

Esthetique du Mal, VII.
  W. Stevens. Wi-LT:155
Futility. W. Owen. Gr-BT:112,
  Ho-LP:93, Pa-GTB:450,
  Rv-CB:989, Un-MB:362
Greater Love. W. Owen.
  Al-VBP:1196, Er-FA:198,
  Pa-GTB:449, Un-MB:366,
  Wi-LT:348
He Died a Second Time, 1.
  On the Litter. Ai Ch'ing.
  Hs-TC:302
He Died a Second Time, 2.
  Hospital. Ai Ch'ing. Hs-TC:303
He Died a Second Time, 3.
  The Hand. Ai Ch'ing. Hs-TC:304
He Died a Second Time, 4.
  Healing. Ai Ch'ing. Hs-TC:304
He Died a Second Time, 5.
  The Posture. Ai Ch'ing.
  Hs-TC:305
The Heroes. L. Simpson.
  Cr-WS:92, Du-SH:83, Pe-SS:145
Hit! T. Palmanteer. Al-WW:39
In a Bar near Shibuya Station,
  Tokyo. P. Engle. Ad-CI:84,
  Br-AF:88
In the Ambulance. W. Gibson.
  Cr-WS:94
Johnny, I Hardly Knew Ye.
  Gr-GB:241
The Maid of Monterey. Em-AF:441
A Man. N. Cassian. Mc-AC:132
On a Victory. Tr-US I:127
On the Road to Santiago.
  S. Crane. Kr-OF:74
One-and-Twenty. Em-AF:458
A Pilot from the Carrier.
  R. Jarrell. Ha-TP:79
The Portrait of a Chinese
  Soldier. Wang Ya-p'ing.
  Hs-TC:354
Recalling War. R. Graves.
  Wi-LT:373
The Show. W. Owen. Al-VBP:1197,
  Un-MB:368, Wi-LT:350
Song Composed by a Fighting Man
  Lying Wounded in the Desert.
  Tr-US I:133
"They." S. Sassoon. Cr-WS:118
A War Game. A. Richards.
  La-IH:130
Whispered on the Battlefield.
  G. Anders. Un-R:53
Whisperin' Bill. I. Bacheller.
  Fe-PL:156
With My Maimed Hand.
  Tai Wang-Shu. Hs-TC:185
The Wound-Dresser. W. Whitman.
  Al-VBP:937

WARBLERS
  A Baby Warbler. Kikaku.
    Be-CS:42
  June. D. Malloch. Ha-YA:71
  Perch in My Plum Tree.
    Onitsura. Be-MC:32
  The Pettichap's Nest. J. Clare.
    Go-BP:74
  Sedge-Warblers. E. Thomas.
    Re-BS:33
  Warbler, Wipe Your Feet. Issa.
    Be-MC:23
  Yonder on the Plum Tree.
    Ba-ST:48
WARM SPRINGS, GA.: see ROOSEVELT,
  FRANKLIN DELANO
WARNINGS: see also HUMOR -
  WARNINGS; LOVE - WARNINGS;
  PREMONITIONS
  About an Excavation. C. Reznikoff.
    Ca-VT:188, Co-PU:137
  After Seeing "Lear." M. Syrkin.
    Ls-NY:82
  All in the Path of a Power Mower.
    R. Gillman. Du-SH:112
  At a Noon Halt on a Journey.
    Kanimana oult Ourzig.
    Tr-US I:137
  At the Setting of the Sun.
    Rv-CB:440
  Awake! W. Rodgers. Wi-LT:493
  The Banks of Newfoundland.
    Gr-GB:219
  Be Still, My Child. Do-CH:(6)
  Blue Girls. J. Ransom.
    Ca-VT:150, Gr-CC:79, Gr-CT:51,
    Ha-PO:183, Mc-WS:75, Pe-OA:137,
    Sh-AP:182, Un-MA:409
  The Calls. W. Owen. Go-BP:48
  A Caution to Poets. M. Arnold.
    Rv-CB:873
  Celanta at the Well of Life.
    G. Peele. Bl-OB:158, Gr-CT:174
  Controlling the Tongue.
    G. Chaucer. Ox-BC:3
  Courtship and Wedding Songs.
    Tr-US I:99
  Dance Songs, V. Tr-US II:141
  Directions to a Rebel.
    W. Rodgers. Wi-LT:488
  Do Not Dream. N. Zach. Gr-BT:160
  During a Storm. Mo-TB:130
  Every Day Thou Might Lere.
    Ma-YA:27
  The Fairies' Dance. Hu-MP:86
  The Hanged Thing. W. Kerr.
    De-FS:127
  Hope. R. Fanshawe. Rv-CB:368
  A Hungry Wolf. Irina.
    Mo-MI:48

WARNINGS — cont'd.
  I Went to Kill the Deer.
    Wo-HS:(50)
  Improvised Song Against a White
    Man.   Tr-US I:118
  The Invaders.   J. Sloan.
    De-FS:183
  Jerusalem.   W. Blake.   Gr-CT:295,
    Ox-BN:42
  Johnie o'Cocklesmuir.   Ox-BB:535
  Johnny Rover.   Rv-ON:84
  A Joyous Reveling Song Sung by
    the Wood Rats.   Su-FVI:59,
    Tr-US II:113
  Kite Poem.   J. Merrill.   Br-TC:285
  The Lake.   M. Arnold.   Rv-CB:868
  The Lark.   Gr-GB:60
  Look Not Thou.   W. Scott.
    Rv-CB:656
  A Man of Words.   Bl-OB:156,
    De-TT:72, Er-FA:274, Gr-EC:208,
    Rv-CB:450, Rv-ON:115, Sm-LG:235,
    Sp-AS:35
  Midsummer Magic.   I. Eastwick.
    Ar-TP3:148
  Misgivings.   H. Melville.
    Rv-CB:837
  Moon Poem.   S. Sharp.   Ab-MO:5
  The Moon Shines Bright.   Gr-GB:297
  My Children, My Children.
    Da-SC:120, Ho-SD:25, Jo-TS:22,
    Le-OE:26
  Notes for My Son.   A. Comfort.
    Un-MB:520, Wi-LT:672
  One of the Sidhe.   M. Kennedy.
    De-FS:124
  Our Fear.   Z. Herbert.   Gr-BT:120
  The Pedlar.   W. de la Mare.
    Sp-OG:181
  Please.   R. Fyleman.   Hu-MP:81
  Pride Is Out.   Rv-CB:16
  Prophecy of Pech, Priest of
    Chichen-Itzá.   Da-SC:163
  The Question in the Cobweb.
    A. Reid.   Mc-WK:114
  Resolution.   T. Berrigan.
    Mc-EA:39
  A Salmon Trout to Her Children.
    Le-IB:45, Su-FVI:69, Tr-US I:3
  A Schoolmaster's Admonition.
    Ox-BC:21
  The Sea Gull Curves His Wings.
    E. Coatsworth.   Ar-TP3:58,
    Co-BBW:261, Cr-SS:15, Pe-FB:15
  The Seals in Penobscot Bay.
    D. Hoffman.   Br-TC:191
  Sing, Brothers, Sing!
    W. Rodgers.   Un-MB:482
  A Song for St. Cecilia's Day.
    J. Dryden.   Pa-RE:97

  Song of a Lioness Warning Her
    Cub.   Be-AP:60, Tr-US I:79
  The Spangled Pandemonium.
    P. Brown.   Ar-TP3:129,
    Co-OT:22, Lo-LL:70
  This Hour.   O. La Grone.
    Hu-NN:37, Hu-PN:327
  Though Ye Suppose.   J. Skelton.
    Rv-CB:64
  To His Little Son Benedict from
    the Tower of London.
    J. Hoskyns.   Ox-BC:21
  To My Youngest Kinsman, R. L.
    A. Chear.   Ox-BC:34
  The Tupelo Destruction.
    Em-AF:474
  The Unquiet Grave.   Al-VBP:39,
    De-CH:342, Gr-GB:131,
    Hi-WP II:17, Ox-BB:96,
    Rv-CB:51
  Vegetable Fantasies.   H. Hoyt.
    Ir-BB:16, 17
  Villains.   Abhinanda.   Al-PI:38
  Voyages I.   H. Crane.   Ca-VT:215,
    Mo-BG:132
  Walk, Damn You, Walk!
    W. De Vere.   Fe-PL:51
  Warning.   L. Rubin.   Du-SH:93
  A Warning to Crows.   De-PP:36
  When I Was a Little Girl.
    A. Milligan.   Co-PI:139
  The Whole World Is Coming.
    Da-SC:121, Ho-SD:12
  The Witch.   E. Farjeon.
    Co-OT:33, Su-FVI:18
  Women Songs, I.   K. Molodowsky.
    Ho-TY:284
  Young Poet.   M. O'Higgins.
    Ad-PB:170, Hu-PN:351
WARREN, JOSEPH
  Warren's Address at Bunker Hill.
    J. Pierpont.   Vi-PP:106
WARRIORS: see also names of individ-
    ual warriors, as SITTING BULL
  Chant on the Return from a Suc-
    cessful Head-Taking Raid.
    Tr-US I:142
  Death Song of a Warrior.
    Da-SC:157, Tr-US II:226
  Farewell of Warriors of Vavau
    Going to Fight at Sea.
    Tr-US II:50
  From an Angba.   Tr-US I:181
  Girls' Song.   Tr-US I:44
  Home-Coming Song of Fighting
    Men after a Raid.
    Tr-US I:69
  Last Song of Sitting Bull.
    Kr-OF:1, Le-OE:127
  Look!   Ge-TR:27

The Mu'allaqa of Antar. Antar.
Lo-TY:37
Ojibwa War Song. Da-SC:155,
Kr-OF:1, Le-OE:120
Old Love Songs. Tr-US II:238
Old Love Songs Connected with
War, I, III. Tr-US II:238, 239
On the Bank of a Stream.
Da-SC:157
The Overthrow of Ruanae.
Potiki. Tr-US II:56
Shaka, King of the Zulus.
Lo-TY:16
Song of a Warrior for His First-
Born Son. Tr-US II:218
Song of the Butterfly.
Da-SC:157, Le-OE:39
Song of the Maiden's Leap.
Tr-US II:239
Songs to Horses, I, II.
Tr-US I:116
Tumea's Lament for Her Father
Ngakauvarea. Tr-US II:54
Vaunt of the Hero Whakatau on
Going into Battle.
Tr-US II:110
The Victorious Fighting Man's
Home-Coming. Tr-US I:113
Victory Song. Tr-US II:244
A Warrior I Have Been. Ho-SD:12
Watchman, What of the Night?
A. Swinburne. Ho-WR:200
You May Go on the Warpath.
Da-SC:12
WARTS
Charm to Cure Warts. Su-FVI:49
WASHING MACHINES: see LAUNDRY
WASHINGTON, BOOKER TALIAFERRO
Alabama Earth. L. Hughes.
Br-AF:48
Booker T. and W.E.B. D. Randall.
Ab-MO:84, Be-MA:69
WASHINGTON, DINAH
To Dinah Washington. E. Knight.
Ad-PB:230
WASHINGTON, GEORGE: see also HUMOR
- WASHINGTON, GEORGE; MOUNT
VERNON, VA.; SATIRE - WASHINGTON,
GEORGE; WASHINGTON MONUMENT
The Boy Washington. D. Thompson.
Br-SS:122
Crown Our Washington.
H. Butterworth. Se-PR:58
Ever Since. E. Coatsworth.
Br-SS:123
First President. Ja-HH:15
Footnote to History.
E. Coatsworth. Br-SS:124
George Washington.
R. and S. Benét. Fe-FP:416

George Washington. J. Ingham.
Vi-PP:139
George Washington. J. Tippett.
Ha-YA:182, Sh-RP:194
George Washington. Hu-MP:375
Hail, Columbia. J. Hopkinson.
Er-FA:291, Vi-PP:32
His Excellency General Washington.
P. Wheatley. Hu-PN:7
Inscription at Mount Vernon.
Se-PR:59
Lafayette to Washington.
M. Anderson. Vi-PP:117
Mount Vernon. Em-AF:433
The Name of Washington. A. Field.
Vi-PP:141
Ours, and All Men's. J. Lowell.
Sh-RP:193, Vi-PP:138
Picture People. R. Bennett.
Ha-YA:181, Hu-MP:32
The Rivers Remember.
N. Turner. Br-AF:170
The Twenty-Second of February.
W. Bryant. Hu-MP:329,
Se-PR:57
Washington. G. Byron.
Se-PR:58, Vi-PP:137
Washington. H. Monroe.
Se-PR:56
Washington. D. O'Crowley.
Se-PR:56
Washington. N. Turner. Ar-TP3:92,
Au-SP:362, Fe-FP:413, Gr-EC:230,
Ha-YA:183, Hu-MP:376, Pe-FB:33
Washington and Me. E. Jay.
Ja-HH:16
Young Washington. A. Guiterman.
Co-PS:48, Fe-FP:415, Hu-MP:379
WASHINGTON, MARTHA
Picture People. R. Bennett.
Ha-YA:181, Hu-MP:32
WASHINGTON, D.C.: see also GEORGE-
TOWN, D.C.; SATIRE - WASHINGTON,
D.C.; WASHINGTON MONUMENT
July in Washington. R. Lowell.
Ho-P:175
View of the Capitol from the
Library of Congress.
E. Bishop. Br-AF:200
WASHINGTON MONUMENT
Washington Monument by Night.
C. Sandburg. Co-PS:45, Fe-FP:452
WASHINGTON SQUARE, NEW YORK, N.Y.
An Imitator of Billy Sunday.
J. Jiménez. Bl-FP:69
Villanelle of Washington Square.
W. Roberts. Hu-PN:83
WASHINGTON (STATE)
Washington's Song. E. Meany.
Se-PR:290

WASPS: see also HUMOR - WASPS
  New Hampshire, February.
    R. Eberhart. Br-TC:99,
    Wi-LT:438
  Upon a Spider Catching a Fly.
    E. Taylor. Rd-OA:174,
    Rv-CB:476, Sh-AP:12
  Upon a Wasp Chilled with Cold.
    E. Taylor. Rv-CB:474
  The Wasp. W. Sharp. Fe-FP:146
  The Wasp's Nest. G. MacBeth.
    Ma-FW:128
WASTEFULNESS
  Achtung! Achtung! M. Hacker.
    Cr-WS:1
  The Heir of Linne. Ma-BB:110
  On the Coming of Age of a Rich
    Extravagant Young Man.
    S. Johnson. Al-VBP:554
  Sonnets 4. M. Drayton.
    Al-VBP:167
  Walk, Damn You, Walk.
    W. De Vere. Fe-PL:51
WATCHES: see CLOCKS AND WATCHES
WATCHMEN: see GUARDS
WATER: see also BROOKS; FLOODS;
    FOUNTAINS; LAKES; PONDS AND
    POOLS; RIVERS; SPRINGS (WATER);
    WATERFALLS; WAVES; WELLS
  Appoggiatura. D. Hayes.
    Ad-PB:94, Bo-AN:90, Hu-PN:246
  Baptist. S. Menashe. Sm-MK:215
  By the Swimming. R. Sward.
    Du-SH:130
  Clear Water. Br-FW:16
  Dead Water. Wen I-to. Hs-TC:65
  Fed. E. Bragdon. Ke-TF:426
  Fire. P. Taylor. Le-M:127
  Fire Fire of the First World.
    Wo-HS:(61)
  The Fires of Life. B. Cutler.
    St-H:40
  From the Bridge. J. Keats.
    Bo-FP:258, Ch-B:109, Mc-PR:159
  The Full Heart. R. Nichols.
    Co-BN:116, Co-PU:58
  A Garden. Sappho. Pa-SG:127
  Green, Green, Is El Aghir.
    N. Cameron. Ca-MB:114
  Gunga Din. R. Kipling.
    Er-FA:371, Go-BP:54, Hi-WP I:69,
    Ma-YA:226, Pa-OM:230, Un-MB:122
  I Tremble and Shake. Re-RR:12
  A Jolly Noise. E. Jacobson.
    Mc-AW:20
  Light and Water. J. Jiménez.
    Le-SW:37
  Little Drops of Water. Sp-HW:33
  The Movement of Fish. J. Dickey.
    Ca-VT:491

The Noise of Waters. J. Joyce.
    Ar-TP3:173, Fe-FP:271, Ho-LP:79,
    Li-TU:206, Ma-FW:34, Sm-LG:344,
    Un-MB:270
  Number 7. L. Ferlinghetti.
    Ad-CI:18, Du-RG:102, Kh-VA:74,
    La-OC:85, Pe-SS:156
  October. W. Trask. No-CL:279
  Physical Geography. L. Nicholl.
    Li-TU:29, Pl-IO:52
  Rain. L. Coxe. Ls-NY:62
  A Song of Nayenzgani. Da-SC:66
  Song on the Water. T. Beddoes.
    Sm-LG:52
  Stuff. A. Mitchell. Sm-MK:190
  Tell Me the Answer. Re-RR:14
  To Morfydd. L. Johnson.
    Re-TW:68, Un-MB:153
  To the Waters. Al-PI:17
  The Walk. L. Adams. Gr-CC:45
  Water. H. Conkling. Ar-TP3:162
  Water. K. Raine. Pl-IO:44
  Water and Shadow. M. Zaturenska.
    Gr-SS:132
  Water Noises. E. Roberts.
    Co-BN:68, Mc-AW:42, Th-AS:82
  The Water of Kane. Tr-US II:96
  The Water Wants All Sea.
    L. Frankenberg. Ls-NY:270
  The Well-Finder. H. Vinal.
    De-FS:211
  Well Water. R. Jarrell.
    Ca-VT:403
WATER BIRDS: see also names of
    water birds, as GULLS
  Birds in Fens. M. Drayton.
    Gr-CT:95
  A Canticle to the Waterbirds.
    Brother Antoninus. Ca-BP:11
  October Textures. M. Swenson.
    Ca-BP:31
  Old Mother Minchin.
    J. Kenward. Sm-MK:126
  To a Waterfowl. W. Bryant.
    De-CH:106, De-TT:179, Er-FA:232,
    Fe-PL:355, Mc-PR:55, Rv-CB:734,
    Sh-AP:20, Sp-OG:295
  To the Snipe. J. Clare.
    Ox-BN:313
  The Waterfowl. Ginko. Le-MW:15
WATER HYACINTHS
  The River's Breadth. T. Takaori.
    Sh-AM:156
WATER LILIES
  The Past Three Mornings.
    B. Tsuchiya. Sh-AM:148
  Reflection. L. Sarett. Th-AS:87
  Water-Lilies. S. Teasdale.Un-MA:265
  Water Lilies Bloom. Emperor Wu.
    Rx-LT:40

WATER OUZELS: see OUZELS
WATER RATS
  The Old Chartist. G. Meredith.
    Hi-FO:244
WATERFALLS: see also names of
    waterfalls, as NIAGARA FALLS
  Behind the Falls. W. Stafford.
    La-RM:60
  Behind the Waterfall. W. Welles.
    Ar-TP3:159, Co-PM:170
  Bird and Waterfall Music.
    Wang Wei. Rx-LT:59
  Bridge and Waterfall.
    Wang T'ung-chao. Hs-TC:261
  The Cataract at Ladore
    (July 3, 1936). H. Bevington.
    Li-SR:88
  The Cataract of Ladore.
    R. Southey. Li-SR:84,
    Ox-BC:94
  Contentment in Poverty. Issa.
    Sh-RP:65
  Fragment. J. Clark. Co-BN:78
  Going to Sleep in the Country.
    H. Moss. En-PC:204
  Song. W. Turner. Bo-GJ:253,
    Un-MB:345
  The Twin Falls. J. Dickey.
    Mo-BG:117
  Waterfall. Issa. Be-MC:24
  The Waterfall. Pai Ch'in.
    Pa-MV:141
  The Waterfall. H. Vaughan.
    Al-VBP:464, Ga-S:182, Ho-WR:40
WATERFORD, LORD: see SHREWSBURY,
    JOHN TALBOT, 1ST EARL OF
WATERLOO, BATTLE, 1815: see also
    HUMOR - WATERLOO, BATTLE, 1815
  The Eve of Waterloo. G. Byron.
    Al-VBP:723, Er-FA:362,
    Ga-FB:205, Hi-FO:204, Ox-BN:243
  The Field of Waterloo. T. Hardy.
    Sm-LG:257
WATERMELONS
  Reflections on a Gift of Water-
    melon Pickle Received from a
    Friend Called Felicity.
    J. Tobias. Du-RG:134
  It Is Smooth and Round and Red.
    Gr-BB:9
  The Land in My Mother.
    N. Hashimoto. Le-TA:17
  The Watermelon.
    L. Alaverdoshvili. Mo-MI:28
  Watermelon. T. Joans. Mc-EA:28
WATTS, CALIF.
  Watts. A. Saxon. Ad-PB:494
WATUSIS
  African Memories.
    J. Oppenheimer. Lo-IT:100

Dance of the Abakweta. M. Danner.
    Ad-PB:134, Be-MA:88, Bo-AN:154,
    Hu-NN:30, Hu-PN:163
WAVES: see also HUMOR - WAVES;
    TSUNAMIS
  As I Row over the Plain.
    Fujiwara no Tadamichi. Ba-ST:31
  After the Sea Ship. W. Whitman.
    Co-SS:49, Rv-CB:844
  Atlantic Ocean. V. Mayakovsky.
    Ca-MR:118
  Broken and Broken. Chosu.
    Be-CS:48
  The Dewdrop and the Wave.
    G. Herwegh. Sp-OG:306
  The Dykes. R. Kipling. Ni-JP:138
  Each Time a Wave Breaks. Nissha.
    Le-MW:12
  The Even Sea. M. Swenson.
    Ha-WR:37
  German Shepherd. M. Livingston.
    La-RM:96
  The Great Lakes Suite, VI.
    J. Reaney. Do-WH:53
  The Horses of the Sea.
    C. Rossetti. Bo-GJ:42,
    Fe-FP:274, Li-LC:33
  How Everything Happens.
    M. Swenson. La-RM:90
  The Hungry Waves. D. Aldis.
    Sh-RP:181
  I Explain. S. Crane. Sh-AP:143
  I Hear an Army. J. Joyce.
    Al-VBP:1150, Un-MB:269,
    Wi-LT:623
  Imitation of Water.
    J. de Melo Neto. An-TC:141
  Lightly a New Moon. Kyoshi.
    Be-CS:26
  The Main-Deep. J. Stephens.
    Un-MB:266
  My Rough Sketch. M. Abvakana.
    Ba-HI:43
  Prelude. W. Gibson. Un-MB:241
  The Sea Bird to the Wave.
    P. Colum. Sh-RP:87
  Sea-Wash. C. Sandburg.
    Mc-PR:61
  Sketch. C. Sandburg. Bo-HF:83
  Spray. D. Lawrence. Co-BN:81
  There Are Big Waves.
    E. Farjeon. St-FS:62
  This Is the Sea. E. Shanks.
    De-CH:623
  Underneath. T. Folk. La-GI:40
  Wading at Wellfleet. E. Bishop.
    Sh-AP:216
  The Wave. H. Behn. Cr-SS:22
  Waves. M. Miller. Sh-RP:73
  The Waves. W. Smith. Co-SS:45

WAVES — cont'd.
  Waves Against a Dog. T. Baybars.
    Sm-MK:176
  Waves Coming Up Against the
    Rocks. Le-OE:85, Tr-US I:244
  Waves Slap on the Shore.
    C. Moore. Le-M:114
  When I Count.
    Minamoto no Shitagö. Ba-ST:39
  White Horses. W. Howard.
    Au-SP:296
  Wind in the Trees. Robyn.
    Le-M:51
  With Kit, Age 7, at the Beach.
    W. Stafford. La-RM:92
  Would My House. Ba-ST:31
WEAKNESS: see also HELPLESSNESS
  Academic. T. Roethke. Co-EL:43
  As Bad as a Mile. P. Larkin.
    Co-EL:124
  Girls' Song. Tr-CB:32,
    Tr-US I:119
  I Know Myself a Man. J. Davies.
    Gr-CT:371, Ni-JP:168
  Reliance. H. Van Dyke.
    Er-FA:29
  The Tight Spring Broke.
    Kubonta. Be-CS:43
WEALTH: see also HUMOR - WEALTH;
    MONEY; SATIRE - WEALTH
  Beverly Hills, Chicago.
    G. Brooks. Ca-VT:439
  The Earth Is Not an Old Woman.
    D. Satyarthi. Al-PI:142
  The Fairies Have Never a
    Penny to Spend. R. Fyleman.
    Fe-FP:379, Hu-MP:85,
    Ox-BC:338, Th-AS:7
  A Gluttonous Rich Man.
    G. Chaucer. Ha-PO:52
  Hard Times, Dearth Times.
    Ma-BH:13
  Her Letter. B. Harte. Fe-PL:20
  Legacy. N. Turner. Th-AS:187
  Minstrel's Song. Do-CH:(39)
  Nostalgia. Yang Huan. Pa-MV:159
  Old Fortunatus, 1600.
    T. Dekker. Al-VBP:230
  The Rich and the Poor.
    Tr-US II:92
  Richer. A. Fisher. Br-BC:5
  A True Story. A. Taylor.
    De-TT:102
WEAPONS: see ARMS AND ARMOR; also
    names of weapons, as ATOMIC
    WEAPONS, HYDROGEN WEAPONS
WEARINESS: see FATIGUE
WEASELS: see also HUMOR - WEASELS;
    SKUNKS
  The Bestiary. W. Benét. Rd-OA:126

The Man and the Weasel. Plato.
    Mc-PR:27
O Foolish Ducklings. Buson.
    Be-CS:59
Under the Woods. E. Thomas.
    De-CH:50
Weasel. S. Read. Pa-RE:113
WEATHER: see also CLOUDS; COLD;
    HUMOR - WEATHER; RAIN; SNOW;
    STORMS; WINDS
April. T. Robinson. Un-GT:273
The Borrowing Days. Gr-GB:38
Ceiling Unlimited.
    M. Rukeyser. Un-MA:622
Clouds. J. Reaney. Do-WH:79
Cold's the Wind. T. Dekker.
    Al-VBP:226
Dejection. S. Coleridge.
    Ox-BN:167, Rv-CB:665
Dogs and Weather. W. Welles.
    Ar-TP3:51, Fe-FP:155,
    Ma-FO:(18)
The Dormouse. M. Stephenson.
    St-FS:97
The Elements. W. Davies.
    Mc-WK:19, Sh-RP:111, Un-MB:178
Evening Red and Morning Gray.
    Ir-BB:230, Un-GT:22
Glass Falling. L. MacNeice.
    Co-PI:114, Pa-RE:45
Ground Hog Day. M. Pomeroy.
    Co-BBW:32, Co-PS:29, Co-PU:83
Happiness Makes Up in Height for
    What It Lacks in Length.
    R. Frost. Un-MA:191
Hymn to the Sun. M. Roberts.
    Sm-LG:56
I Am Joyful. Da-SC:37, Le-IB:113
If Bees Stay at Home. Ir-BB:230,
    Un-GT:23
If Candlemas Day Be Fair and
    Bright. Co-PS:30, Se-PR:42
The Kayak Paddler's Joy at the
    Weather. Da-SC:41, Le-IB:32,
    Tr-US I:7
March Winds. Au-SP:317, Br-SG:22,
    De-PO:26, Li-LB:160, Mo-MGT:148,
    Mo-NR:118, Un-GT:23, Wr-RM:120
Michaelmas. N. Nicholson.
    Un-MB:506
Misty-Moisty Was the Morn.
    Gr-GB:37
On Leaving Bruges. D. Rossetti.
    Rv-CB:883
Prayer for Fine Weather.
    S. Leslie. Co-PI:92
Rain Before Seven. Ir-BB:231,
    Ju-CP:72, Mo-MGT:19, Un-GT:23
Rainbow at Night. Bo-FP:261,
    Gr-EC:65, Ir-BB:230, Un-GT:22

A Rainy Day.   J. Lincoln.
   Sh-RP:198
The Rainy Summer.   A. Meynell.
   Bo-GJ:99, Gr-SS:42
A Red Sky at Night.   Li-LB:161,
   Mo-MGT:103, Mo-NR:131
Sadness.   Le-IB:115
St. Swithin's Day.   Ir-BB:231,
   Li-LB:161, Un-GT:23
Slow Spring.   S. Tremayne.
   Sm-MK:141
Solution.   L. Jacobs.
   Fr-MP:4
Song Composed at the Beginning
   of an Autumn Festival.
   Le-IB:106, Tr-US I:31
Storms, Winds, Clouds.
   Rv-ON:39
A Sunshiny Shower.   Bo-FP:227,
   Ir-BB:231, Li-LB:161, Mo-NR:122,
   Un-GT:22, Wr-RM:122
Synchronized.   L. Rubin.
   De-FS:165
Today.   L. Hughes.   Ca-VT:240
Tree at My Window.   R. Frost.
   Bo-HF:59, Co-BN:149, Un-MA:182
Weather.   H. Conkling.
   Ar-TP3:162
Weather.   A. MacLeish.
   Un-MA:456
The Weather.   N. Taalak.
   Ba-HI:76
Weather Ear.   N. Nicholson.
   To-MP:68
Weather Rhymes.   Ju-CP:72
A Weather Rule.   Hu-MP:285
Weathers.   T. Hardy.   Bl-OB:96,
   Bo-FP:73, De-CH:9, De-TT:145,
   Ga-FB:229, Hi-WP I:30,
   Na-EO:42, Sh-RP:23, Sm-LG:64,
   Sm-MK:143, Tu-WW:28, Un-GB:18,
   Un-MB:28
Wet Weather.   P. Low.   Ca-VT:670
What Is This.   Le-OE:19
When Clouds Appear.   Un-GT:23
When the Milky Way You Spy.
   Wy-CM:23
When the Wind Is in the East.
   Bo-FP:264, Ir-BB:230, Li-LB:160,
   Mo-MGT:152, Mo-NR:91, Un-GT:23
The Wind and the Rain.
   W. Gibson.   Cl-FC:50
The Windham Thaw.
   A. Guiterman.   Gr-EC:58
The Winds.   T. Tusser.   Ho-WR:25
you (her eyes, solstice).
   G. Bishop-Dubjinsky.   Sc-TN:10
You, Whose Day It Is.   Ho-SD:55,
   Jo-TS:1, Le-OE:16
See also Mo-TB:135-148

WEATHER VANES
   The Gnome.   H. Behn.   Ar-TP3:151,
      Au-SP:286, Fe-FP:385, La-PV:70
   Straws.   E. Coatsworth.   Br-AF:109
   Upon the Weathercock.   J. Bunyan.
      Ox-BC:37
WEAVING
   At Ithaca.   H.D.   Ca-VT:112
   The Ballad of the Harp-Weaver.
      E. Millay.   Ar-TP3:156,
      Co-PT:64
   Her Husband Asks Her to Buy a
      Bolt of Silk.   Ch'en T'ao.
      Rx-LT:105
   Navajo Rug.   B. Lee.   Ba-HI:84
   Song of the Sky Loom. Da-SC:76,
      Le-OE:6, Mo-TS:16, Tr-US II:256
   What the Gray Cat Sings.
      A. Guiterman.   Co-PM:80,
      Hu-MP:188, Li-TU:112,
      Rd-SS:24, Se-PR:194
WEBSTER, DANIEL
   Daniel Webster's Horses.
      E. Coatsworth.   Br-AF:116,
      Co-PM:34, De-FS:55, Un-MA:464
   1854.   R. Emerson.   Kr-OF:37
   Ichabod.   J. Whittier.
      Kr-OF:33, Rv-CB:786, Sh-AP:40
   Webster.   F. Douglass.   Kr-OF:32
WEDDING RINGS: see RINGS
WEDDINGS: see also BRIDES AND
      BRIDEGROOMS; HUMOR - WEDDINGS;
      SATIRE - WEDDINGS
   The Bells.   E. Poe.   Bo-FP:177,
      Bo-HF:162, Er-FA:277, Fe-FP:64,
      Fe-PL:433, Li-SR:72, Sp-OG:339
   Blythsome Bridal.   Gr-GB:152
   Courtship and Wedding Songs.
      Tr-US I:99
   The Cruel Brother.   Ma-YA:38,
      Ox-BB:236
   Epithalamion.   E. Spenser.
      Al-VBP:104
   Epithalamium.   R. Crashaw.
      Al-VBP:430
   Girls' Song at a Wedding.
      Tr-US I:128
   I Saw Three Ships Come Sailing By.
      Mo-NR:50
   Men's Song at a Wedding.
      Tr-US I:127
   Months for Marriage.   Mo-TB:42
   Nuptial Song.   J. Warren.
      Pa-GTB:384
   Saturday, Sunday.   Wr-RM:69
   Shaman's Chant at a Wedding.
      Tr-US II:134
   Sonamani's Wedding.   Ca-MU:22
   Song.   G. Chapman.
      Al-VBP:145

WEDDINGS — cont'd.
  Song for the Arrival of Guests
    and the Bride. Tr-US II:134
  Song of Myself. W. Whitman.
    Ca-BP:3, Un-MA:49
  Songs, II. Tr-US II:132
  Songs at a Wedding. Tr-US I:161
  Wedding and Funeral. Gr-GB:320
  A Wedding at Harvest Time.
    N. Bomze. Ho-TY:227
  Wedding Procession. J. Emanuel.
    Hu-NN:81
  Wedding Song. Tr-US I:102, 201
  Women's Song at a Wedding Feast.
    Tr-US I:208
WEDDINGS - ANNIVERSARIES
  The Diverting History of John
    Gilpin. W. Cowper.
    Al-VBP:588, Co-RG:88,
    Hi-WP I:47, Sp-OG:215
  To His Wife on the Fourteenth
    Anniversary of Her Wedding
    Day, with a Ring. S. Bishop.
    Al-VBP:596
WEEDS: see also names of individual
    weeds, as NETTLES
  Poor Bird. W. de la Mare.
    Ma-FW:93
  Preface. T. Weiss. Ca-VT:433
  Sonnet IV. Feng Chih.
    Hs-TC:150
  The Weed. R. Pitter. Sm-MK:79
  Weeds. F. Kitagawa. Sh-AM:86
WEEKENDS
  Week-End. H. Monro. Un-MB:233
WEEKS
  Hope. R. Jarrell. Pe-OA:230,
    Un-MA:651
  Seven Days in the Week. On-TW:28
WEEPING: see CRYING
WEEVILS: see BOLL WEEVILS
WEIL, SIMONE
  For Simone Weil.
    Sister M. Thérése. Tr-MR:172
WELCOMES: see also HUMOR -
    WELCOMES; SATIRE - WELCOMES
  America Greets an Alien. Vi-PP:186
  Chant of Welcome to a Kinsman or
    Friend. Tr-US II:103
  The Fire in the Snow. V. Watkins.
    Wi-LT:454
  Her Sister-in-Law Answers the
    Greeting Song. Tr-CB:36,
    Tr-US I:93
  The Hostess. Wang Mou Fang.
    Le-MW:101
  Howdy, Honey, Howdy. P. Dunbar.
    Fe-PL:425
  The Lands Around My Dwelling.
    Bi-IT:49, Br-MW:141, Ma-BH:23

Preparations. Al-VBP:353,
    De-CH:464, Ga-S:131,
    Hi-WP I:137, Na-EO:19, Pl-EI:16,
    Rv-CB:116, Sm-LG:378
  The Return. E. Dickinson.
    Un-MA:103
  The Sailor's Wife. W. Mickle.
    Al-VBP:600, De-TT:110, Pa-GTB:154
  Shadows. Le-MW:59
  Sitalkas. H.D. Al-VBP:1168
  Song for the Arrival of Guests
    and the Bride. Tr-US II:134
  Summoning the Soul.
    Jao Meng-k'an. Hs-TC:109
  Welcome. R. Waldo.
    Au-SP:133, Hu-MP:38
  Welcome to the New Year.
    E. Farjeon. Ha-YA:166,
    Th-AS:109
  Welcome, Welcome, Do I Sing.
    W. Browne. Al-VBP:323
  When Johnny Comes Marching
    Home. P. Gilmore. Co-PS:145,
    Hi-TL:126, Vi-PP:161
  When Rosy Plumelets. A. Tennyson.
    Al-VBP:862, Ox-BN:503
WELFARE: see POVERTY; SLUMS AND
    SLUM LIFE; SOCIAL WORKERS
WELLINGTON, ARTHUR WELLESLEY,
    1ST DUKE OF (IRON DUKE):
    see also WATERLOO, BATTLE, 1815
  Wellington. B. Disraeli.
    Hi-FO:237
WELLS: see also HUMOR - WELLS;
    SATIRE - WELLS
  At the Bottom of the Well.
    L. Untermeyer. Bo-GJ:218
  Have You Heard the Yarn.
    Re-RR:44
  I Break the Sky. O. Dodson.
    Ad-PB:133
  The Old Oaken Bucket. S. Woodworth.
    Er-FA:138, Fe-FP:543
  Round as a Wheel. Re-RR:36
  The Secrets of Cisterns.
    S. McNail. De-FS:138
  The Way-Side Well. J. Cotter.
    Hu-PN:18
  The Well. Tu Yün-hsieh.
    Hs-TC:249
  A Well. Ar-TP3:99, Mo-MGT:157,
    Wr-RM:83
  Well Water. R. Jarrell.
    Ca-VT:403
THE WELSH: see also HUMOR -
    THE WELSH
  Death of a Peasant. R. Thomas.
    Ma-FW:168
  A Scot, a Welsh and an Irish
    Man. Gr-GB:165

There Were Three Jovial Welshmen.
    Bl-OB:24, Gr-GB:86, Ir-BB:140,
    Mo-MGT:198, Pa-OM:2, Sm-MK:23,
    Sp-HW:23
Variation on a Theme by Francis
    Kilvert. R. Humphries.
    Pl-US:25
Welsh Landscape. R. Thomas.
    To-MP:58
WELSH VERSE: see also BALLADS, WELSH
    Elegy for Lucy Lloyd. L. Goch.
        Pa-SG:74
    The Fall of Llywelyn. B. Fardd.
        Hi-FO:81
    A Garland of Peacock Feathers.
        D. ap Gwilym. Go-BP:122
    The Grave. T. Jones. Pa-SG:179
    The Hearth of Urien.
        Llywarch the Aged. Gr-CT:323
    The Lover's Shirt. Gr-BT:53
    The Mass of the Grove.
        D. ap Gwilym. Go-BP:73
    My Heart Moves as Heavy.
        Co-EL:139, Co-PU:66
    Oh Send to Me an Apple That
        Hasn't Any Kernel. Sm-LG:286
    Odes of the Months. Ma-FW:4
    Robin Redbreast. Co-BBW:243
    The Rock. Ch-B:36, Gr-CT:71
    A Snowy Day. D. ap Gwilym.
        Pa-SG:100
    The Stars. D. ap Gwilym.
        Go-BP:107
    Traveller's Curse after Mis-
        direction. R. Graves.
        Co-FB:475, Ho-LP:70,
        Un-MB:387, Wi-LT:369
    The Yew-Tree. Gr-CT:80
WEMYSS, SIR JOHN
    The Laird o' Logie. De-CH:412,
        Rv-CB:49
WESLEY, CHARLES
    Wesley in Heaven. T. Brown.
        Ox-BN:722
WESSEX: see DORSETSHIRE, ENG.;
    HAMPSHIRE, ENG.; WILTSHIRE, ENG.
THE WEST: see also DIALECTS,
    WESTERN; HUMOR - THE WEST;
    LEGENDS, WESTERN; and names
    of states, as UTAH
    At Cove on the Crooked River.
        W. Stafford. Wi-LT:825
    The Buffalo Skinners.
        Gr-GB:220, Hi-TL:150
    The Bullwhacker.
        Co-RM:18
    Charley Lee. H. Knibbs.
        Co-RM:172, Mc-WK:144
    Cowboy Song. C. Causley.
        Co-RM:27, Ha-PO:10, Pe-M:36

Desert School Ma'am. S. Andrews.
    Fi-BG:195
Étude Géographique. S. King.
    Br-AF:154
The Ghosts of the Buffaloes.
    V. Lindsay. Sh-RP:46, Un-MA:223
The Horse Thief. W. Benét.
    Pa-OM:300, Un-MA:324
In the Oregon Country.
    W. Stafford. Bl-FP:26,
    Br-AF:162
The Insult. Co-RM:20
Lament for the Cowboy Life.
    J. Mitchell. Co-RM:21
A Living Pearl. K. Rexroth.
    Wi-LT:798
O Pioneers! J. Bishop. Ca-VT:161
Open Range. K. and B. Jackson.
    Ar-TP3:34, Fe-FP:271
Out where the West Begins.
    A. Chapman. Er-FA:263
Proud Riders. H. Davis.
    Co-RM:24
The Sheepherder. L. Sarett.
    Br-AF:161, Fe-FP:317
Spanish Johnny. W. Cather.
    Co-RM:26, Fe-FP:436, Hu-MP:154,
    Mc-WK:140, Mc-WS:160, Sh-RP:41
Strong Men, Riding Horses.
    G. Brooks. Ad-PB:157
Sunrise. C. Wood. Un-GT:250
Traveling America. J. Struther.
    Br-AF:19
West of Your City.
    W. Stafford. Wi-LT:825
West Wind. Tr-US II:40
Western Town. D. Cannon.
    Hu-PN:282
Wild West. R. Boylan. Du-SH:134
See also Fi-BG
WEST INDIAN VERSE
    See Sa-B
WEST INDIANS: see also DIALECTS,
    WEST INDIAN
    Upside Down Hotel. E. Bastien.
        Sa-B:28
WEST INDIES: see also BARBADOS;
    CREOLES; CUBA; PUERTO RICO;
    WEST INDIAN VERSE
    Adina. H. Telemaque. Lo-TY:110
    The Air Plant. H. Crane.
        Un-MA:533
    Black Hieroglyph. T. Matthews.
        Sa-B:230
    Breaklight. K. La Fortune.
        Sa-B:199
    Child-Mother in Metamorphosis.
        S. Clarke. Sa-B:32
    A Christmas Banquet.
        C. Lushington. Sa-B:53

WEST INDIES — cont'd.
  Faded Beauty. J. Maraj. Sa-B:87
  Guadalupe, W.I. N. Guillén.
    Ab-MO:45, Lo-TY:104
  Haunted Caudillo. F. Charles.
    Sa-B:187
  Little Songs for the Children
    of the Antilles. N. Guillén.
    Ab-MO:14
  Poem. S. Clarke. Sa-B:229
  Prose Poem for a Conference.
    J. LaRose. Sa-B:74
  A Sea-Chantey. D. Walcott.
    Lo-TY:111
  Song of Dry Bones. T. Matthews.
    Sa-B:92
  South. E. Brathwaite. Sa-B:46
  Ten Years: 1959-1969.
    J. Carew. Sa-B:189
WEST PALM BEACH, FLA.
  The West Palm Beach Story.
    Em-AF:473
WEST VIRGINIA: see also names of
    towns, as HARPERS FERRY, W.V.
  The Book of the Dead.
    M. Rukeyser. Kr-OF:197
  The West Virginia Hills.
    E. King. Se-PR:290
WESTERNS: see COWBOYS; MOVING
    PICTURES
WESTMINSTER ABBEY
  The Duke of Grafton.
    Gr-CT:359, Gr-GB:320
  In Westminster Abbey.
    J. Betjeman. Ba-PO:183
  On the Tombs in Westminster
    Abbey. F. Beaumont.
    Al-VBP:301, De-CH:252,
    Hi-WP II:18, Pa-GTB:60
WESTWARD MOVEMENT: see also CUM-
    BERLAND GAP; HUMOR - WESTWARD
    MOVEMENT; OREGON TRAIL;
    RAILROADS; SATIRE - WESTWARD
    MOVEMENT
  The Ballad of William Sycamore.
    S. Benét.   Co-RM:228, Hu-MP:387,
    Un-MA:498
  Chorus for Survival. H. Gregory.
    Sm-PT:115
  Crossing the Plains. J. Miller.
    Gr-CC:127
  Emblems. A. Tate.
    Ca-VT:223
  Further West. Fi-BG:111
  In Praise of Johnny Appleseed.
    V. Lindsay. Se-PR:99
  Johnny Appleseed. S. Benét.
    Hu-MP:390
  Land of the Free. A. MacLeish.
    Br-AF:243

  Laramie Trail. J. Hanson.
    Fi-BG:57
  My Fathers Came from Kentucky.
    V. Lindsay. Br-AF:131,
    Gr-CC:125
  The Oregon Trail, 1843.
    A. Guiterman. Fe-FP:432,
    Hu-MP:392
  The Pioneer. W. Ruggles.
    Gr-EC:233
  Pioneers! O Pioneers!
    W. Whitman. Hu-MP:381
  Times Are Gettin' Hard. L. Mays.
    Kr-OF:168
  Trail Breakers. J. Daugherty.
    Br-AF:226, Sh-RP:302
  Verses on the Prospect of Planting
    Arts and Learning in America.
    G. Berkeley. Al-VBP:521,
    Er-FA:458
  Waltz Against the Mountains.
    T. Ferril. Ca-VT:197
  Western Wagons. S. Benét.
    Mc-WK:165
  See also Em-AF:627-634
WHALES AND WHALING: see also
    HUMOR - WHALES AND WHALING
  For a Coming Extinction.
    W. Merwin. Mo-TS:72
  The Harpooning. T. Walker.
    Ha-WR:38
  Luther Leavitt Is a Whale Hunter.
    A. Brower. Ba-HI:55
  My Eyes Are Tired. Ho-SD:73
  Ocean. R. Jeffers. Pe-OA:87
  The Ribs and Terrors. H. Melville.
    Al-VBP:950, Pl-EI:207
  The Song of the Whale. G. Dearmer.
    Cr-SS:26, Ir-BB:76
  Square-Toed Princes. R. Coffin.
    Br-AF:129
  The Triumph of the Whale.
    C. Lamb. Pl-IO:110
  Whale. W. Benét. Sm-PT:22,
    Un-MA:323
  The Whale. Buson. Au-SP:78
  The Whale. E. Darwin. Un-GT:69
  The Whale. J. Donne. Cl-DT:74,
    Gr-CT:210, Ha-PO:108
  The Whale. T. Roethke.
    Co-OT:63, Co-PU:85
  The Whale. Rd-OA:151
  The Whale, His Bulwark.
    D. Walcott. Lo-TY:113
  Whale Hunting. S. Nashookpuk.
    Ba-HI:54
  Whales. T. Sakeagak. Ba-HI:53
  Wind in the Trees. Robyn.
    Le-M:51
WHARVES: see DOCKS, HARBORS

WHEAT: see also FLOUR MILLS
  High Wheat Country. E. Jacobs.
    Br-AF:157
  Immortal. M. Van Doren.
    Un-MA:467
  Kansas. V. Lindsay. Pa-HT:49
  The Sheaves. E. Robinson.
    Ga-FB:297, Ha-PO:89,
    Mo-BG:140, Un-MA:127
  A Vegetable, I Will Not Be.
    D. Whitewing. Al-WW:54
  Wheat. R. Cuscaden. St-H:35
WHEATEARS: see THRUSHES
WHEELBARROWS: see also HUMOR -
    WHEELBARROWS
  Goes Through the Mud. Mo-MGT:157
  The Red Wheelbarrow. W. Williams.
    Ma-FW:111, Mc-EA:52, Mo-TS:49,
    Na-EO:115, Re-TW:12, Un-MA:261,
    Wi-LT:199
WHEELS
  The Wheel. Sully-Prudhomme.
    Pl-IO:63
  The Wheelgoround. R. Clairmont.
    Co-PM:33
WHIPPOORWILLS
  Chuck Will's Widow Song. Ra-BP:19
  The Mountain Whippoorwill.
    S. Benét. Co-PT:110
  On Falling Asleep to Birdsong.
    W. Meredith. En-PC:174
  Whippoorwill. M. Miller.
    Co-BBW:247
WHIRLWINDS: see WINDS
WHISKERS: see BEARDS
WHISPERING
  Whispers. M. Livingston.
    La-PV:220, Li-LC:19
WHISTLES AND WHISTLING: see also
    HUMOR - WHISTLES AND WHISTLING
  Boy, Walking and Whistling.
    A. Armour. Ke-TF:82
  The Little Whistler. F. Frost.
    Ar-TP3:111, Au-SP:190,
    La-PV:9, Pe-FB:37
  Lost. C. Sandburg. Du-RG:69,
    La-PV:184, Mc-PR:108, Sh-RP:76
  Night Train. R. Francis.
    Ar-TP3:84, Ha-LO:87
  The Penny Whistle. E. Thomas.
    Un-MB:216
  The Tin-Whistle Player.
    P. Colum. Pl-US:27
  Trains at Night. F. Frost.
    Ar-TP3:86
  When I Learned to Whistle.
    G. Lea. Le-M:67
  Whistle. Wr-RM:113
  Whistles. D. Aldis.
    Ja-PC:47, La-PP:67

  Whistles. R. Field. Ar-TP3:89
  Whistling Boy. J. Quinn.
    Br-BC:77
  Whistling Boy. N. Waterman.
    Fe-PL:301
  Wonders of Nature. Gr-TG:18
WHITE, PEREGRINE
  Lullaby for Peregrine. R. Coffin.
    Sh-RP:293
WHITE (COLOR)
  If the White Herons. Chiyo.
    Be-CS:50
  Music of Colours. V. Watkins.
    Wi-LT:453
  Spring Ecstasy. L. Reece.
    Un-MA:111
  Spring Goeth All in White.
    R. Bridges. Co-BN:28, Gr-CT:47
  What Is White? R. Mudri.
    La-GI:28
  A White Peony. K. Takahama.
    Sh-AM:162
WHITEHEAD, ALFRED NORTH
  Homage to the Philosopher.
    B. Deutsch. Pl-IO:179
WHITMAN, WALT
  Cape Hatteras. H. Crane.
    Sm-PT:10, 102
  Old Walt. L. Hughes. Pl-ML:132
  A Pact. E. Pound. Co-EL:41,
    Pl-ML:129, Rv-CB:976
  Reading Walt Whitman.
    C. Forbes. Ad-PB:490
  A Supermarket in California.
    A. Ginsberg. Br-TC:149,
    Kh-VA:64, Mo-BG:185, Wi-LT:718
  Walt Whitman. E. Robinson.
    Sh-AP:142
  Walt Whitman at Bear Mountain.
    L. Simpson. En-PC:216,
    Pl-ML:130, Wi-LT:817
WHITTIER, JOHN GREENLEAF
  Mr. Whittier. W. Scott.
    Ca-VT:315
  White Magic. W. Braithwaite.
    Hu-PN:49
WHITTLING
  Halcyon Days. J. Barnes.
    Ni-CD:26
  Picture in an Old Frame.
    E. Chaffee. Ke-TF:68
  A Wonderful Man. A. Fisher.
    Br-SS:164
WIDOW BIRDS: see FINCHES
WIDOWS
  Complaint of a Fisherman's
    Widow. Tr-US I:158
  Consider These Greek Widows of
    America. D. Georgakas.
    Sc-TN:59

WIDOWS — cont'd.
  Elisa, or An Elegy upon the
    Unripe Decease of Sir
    Antony Irby. P. Fletcher.
    Al-VBP:291
  Hymn of the Afflicted. Tr-US I:81
  Lady of the Land. Rv-ON:100
  Lament of a Widow for Her Dead
    Husband. Tr-US I:189
  Song of a Widow. Tr-US II:18
  Song of a Widow for Her Dead
    Husband. Tr-US II:117
  Whether or Not. D. Lawrence.
    Un-MB:291
  The Widow of Drynam.
    P. MacDonogh. Co-PI:110
  The Widows. D. Hall. Du-SH:57
  Widows. E. Masters. Un-MA:141
  Widows. R. Veprinski. Ho-TY:160
  A Widow's Weeds. W. de la Mare.
    Ga-FB:238
WIGS: see also HUMOR - WIGS
  Gregory Griggs. Ir-BB:213,
    Mo-MGT:63, On-TW:60
  The Little Kittens. E. Follen.
    Ar-TP3:118
  Samuel Sewall. A. Hecht.
    Br-TC:181, Pe-OA:262, Wi-LT:730
WIGWAMS
  Dancing Teepees. C. O'John.
    Al-WW:61
WILD GEESE: see GEESE
WILD HORSES: see HORSES
WILDE, OSCAR
  The Arrest of Oscar Wilde at the
    Cadogan Hotel. J. Betjeman.
    Un-MB:440
WILDEBEESTS: see GNUS
WILDERNESS
  Conquest. E. Coatsworth.
    Br-AF:59, Fe-FP:411, Hu-MP:362
  In the Wilderness. R. Graves.
    De-CH:102, Ga-S:144,
    Pl-EI:105, Un-MB:388
  Playground of the Pixie. G. Code.
    De-FS:62
  The Wild. W. Berry. Ca-VT:683
  Wilderness Rivers. E. Coatsworth.
    Br-AF:173
WILDLIFE: see also SATIRE -
    WILDLIFE
  Hard Questions. M. Tsuda. La-RM:172
  Horses on the Camargue.
    R. Campbell. Pa-GTB:494,
    Rd-OA:153
  The Rocky Mountain Sheep.
    M. Austin. Hu-MP:206
  We Need the Tonic of Wildness.
    H. Thoreau. La-RM:174
WILDNESS: see FREEDOM

WILL-O'-THE-WISP
  The Will-o'-the-Wisp. Tr-CB:31,
    Tr-US I:59
WILLIAM I, KING OF ENGLAND (THE CON-
    QUEROR): see HUMOR - WILLIAM I,
    KING OF ENGLAND (THE CONQUEROR)
WILLIAM III AND MARY II, RULERS
    OF ENGLAND: see also SATIRE -
    WILLIAM III AND MARY II, RULERS
    OF ENGLAND
  The Duke of Grafton. Gr-CT:359,
    Gr-GB:320
  Orange Lilies. J. Reaney.
    Do-WH:86
WILLIAMS, THEODORE SAMUEL (TED)
  Dream of a Baseball Star.
    G. Corso. Ca-VT:658,
    Fl-HH:18, Mo-SD:17
WILLIAMS, WILLIAM CARLOS
  Obit Page. P. Blackburn.
    Kh-VA:78
  On Re-Reading the Complete
    Works of an Elder Poet.
    W. Scott. Pl-ML:45
WILLINGNESS
  Lucy Gray. W. Wordsworth.
    De-CH:222, De-TT:85, Ox-BC:98
  Old and New Year Ditties.
    C. Rossetti. Ox-BN:713
WILLOW TREES
  Because the Songbird.
    T. Takaori. Sh-AM:155
  Dancing. Yang Kuei-Fei.
    Fe-FP:481
  Hunting Pheasants in a Cornfield.
    R. Bly. St-H:2
  The Rotten-Wooded Willow.
    Suguwara no Michizane.
    Ba-ST:21
  Saying. A. Ammons. Mo-TS:51
  The Songs of Spring.
    Feng Hsüeh-feng. Hs-TC:368
  Spring. Su Tung P'o.
    Rx-OH:90
  Tell of Spring. Br-FW:6
  Thou Art to All Lost Love the
    Best. R. Herrick. De-CH:693
  To a Weeping Willow.
    L. Untermeyer. Un-MW:141
  Trees. W. de la Mare. Mc-PR:199
  Under Thin Rainfall.
    T. Takaori. Sh-AM:154
  The Willow. Tu Fu.
    Rx-OH:21
  Willow, Bend and Weep.
    H. Johnson. Hu-PN:285
  The Willow-Man. J. Ewing.
    Ox-BC:255
  The Willow Switch. D. Gibson.
    Ls-NY:269

The Willows. W. Eaton.
    Fe-FP:213, Hu-MP:273
Willows in the Snow. Tsuru.
    Hu-MP:273
The Willows of Massachusetts.
    D. Levertov. Ha-WR:84
The Word of Willow. L. Drake.
    De-FS:78
WILLS: see also HUMOR - WILLS;
    SATIRE - WILLS
The Cruel Brother. Ma-YA:38,
    Ox-BB:236
Holographic Testament.
    S. Salazar Bondy. Be-UL:85
Last Will. J. Hill. Kr-OF:116
Robin Redbreast's Testament.
    Gr-GB:66
The Robin's Last Will. Rv-ON:114
The Tower. W. Yeats. Wi-LT:76
WILSON, JOHN (CHRISTOPHER NORTH,
    PSEUD.)
To Christopher North. A. Tennyson.
    Co-FB:337, Co-PU:26, Na-EO:117
WILTSHIRE, ENG.: see DIALECTS, WILTS.
WINDMILLS
The Windmill. H. Longfellow.
    Cl-DT:73
The Windmill. E. Lucas.
    De-TT:165
WINDOW BOXES
Window Boxes. E. Farjeon.
    Br-SG:29, Fe-FP:222
WINDOWS
The Church Windows. G. Herbert.
    Rv-CB:351
Divina Commedia. H. Longfellow.
    Sh-AP:37
Factory Windows Are Always Broken.
    V. Lindsay. Co-PU:72, Er-FA:274,
    La-OC:110
The Forgotten Window.
    M. Donohue. Me-WF:15
From My. A. Dunlap. La-IH:55
The Frost Pane. D. McCord.
    Sh-RP:39
I Did Not Know the Truth of
    Growing Trees. D. Schwartz.
    Wi-LT:522
The Magic Window. E. Hammond.
    Hu-MP:3, St-FS:84
o the world. Me-WF:90
Three Riddles: Garden. Mo-TS:78
What Has Panes. Re-RR:72
What Part of a Room. Re-RR:50
Window, 3rd Story, 5th to the Right,
    Morning. R. Drapeau. La-IH:56
W's for Windows. P. McGinley.
    Ar-TP3:176
Young Woman at a Window.
    W. Williams. La-OC:56

WINDS: see also HUMOR - WINDS;
    HURRICANES; TORNADOES;
    WEATHER VANES
Address to a Child During a
    Boisterous Winter Evening.
    D. Wordsworth. Bl-OB:100,
    Ox-BC:128
Aeolus. R. Humphries. Sh-RP:164
After He Had Gone. S. Warner.
    Un-MB:373
Are We Their Equals? H. Geltman.
    Le-M:176
At Brill. Gr-GB:172, Mo-MGT:211,
    Rv-ON:47
At Matsushima. Shiki. Pa-SG:154
The Autumn Wind. J. Clare.
    Co-BN:130
Awake! Bible. O.T. Song of
    Solomon. Br-SG:22, Fe-FP:72
Awake! W. Rodgers. Wi-LT:493
A Beard Wishes to Escape.
    A. Lutzky. Ho-TY:265
The Beggar Wind. M. Austin.
    Co-BN:165
Big Wind. T. Roethke.
    Al-VBP:1233, Bo-GJ:213.
    Ca-VT:285, Mo-BG:120
The Black Snake Wind Came to Me.
    Mo-TS:19
Blow, Blow, Thou Winter Wind.
    W. Shakespeare. Al-VBP:187,
    De-CH:232, De-TT:168, Er-FA:257,
    Gr-CT:476, Hi-WP II:139,
    Ho-WR:172, Mc-PR:50, Pa-GTB:26,
    Rv-CB:197
Blow the Stars Home. E. Farjeon.
    La-PV:45
Blow, Wind, Blow. Ar-TP3:163,
    Au-SP:11, Bo-FP:77, De-PO:26,
    Mo-MGT:88
Breeze. M. Hourigan. Le-M:198
The Breeze. Bo-FP:259, Ch-B:88
Brooms. D. Aldis. Au-SP:326
The Butterfly. J. Benitez.
    Me-WF:26
Child on Top of a Greenhouse.
    T. Roethke. Ca-VT:286,
    Co-EL:137, Du-RG:54, Gr-BT:12,
    Ha-LO:101, Hi-WP I:110
Cold Blows the Wind. J. Hamilton.
    De-CH:218
Come You Four Winds. Wo-HS:(67)
Comes In at Every Door.
    Re-RR:64
Coming from Nowhere. B. Jones.
    Ba-HI:68
Coolness. Onitsura. Pa-SG:127
Cruel Winter Wind. J. James.
    Ba-HI:75
The Day We Die. Le-OE:130

WINDS — cont'd.
  Daybreak. H. Longfellow.
    De-TT:54, Fe-PL:399, Mc-WK:30
  Deadfall. M. Keller.   Gr-EC:272
  Do You Fear the Wind?
    H. Garland.   Ar-TP3:165,
    Hu-MP:317, Ja-PA:45, Th-AS:115
  Dream Song. Bi-IT:128, Da-SC:100,
    Ho-SD:12, Le-OE:107
  The Dreamer Rides the Whirlwind.
    Bi-IT:24
  East Wind.   Tr-US II:38
  Every Morning I Walk into the
    Tent. Wo-HS:(46)
  The Fickle Wind.   C. Schonhaut.
    Le-M:128
  The Field of the Mice and the
    Marigold. E. Clarke.   Le-M:40
  The Force. P. Redgrove.
    To-MP:178
  The Four Winds. S. Gash.
    Le-M:45, Le-WR:31
  The Four Winds. Bo-FP:217
  Four Winds Blow the Wide World
    o'er.   On-TW:19
  The Full Heart. R. Nichols.
    Co-BN:116, Co-PU:58
  Gale in April. R. Jeffers.
    Un-MA:362
  Happy Wind. W. Davies.
    Bo-FP:243, Sm-MK:6
  Harvest-Season Songs.
    Tr-US I:171
  Hayfield. A. Fisher.   Sh-RP:206
  Hearing the Wind at Night.
    M. Swenson. Co-BN:166,
    Ha-WR:55
  Hide and Seek. S. Kuroda.
    Sh-AM:117
  Holiday. E. Young. Ar-TP3:164
  The Hummingbird. E. Dickinson.
    Sh-AP:131, Un-GT:60
  I Am Tired of the Wind.
    J. Smith. Sm-MK:151
  I Called to the Wind.   Kyorai.
    Be-MC:41
  I Saw the Wind Today.   P. Colum.
    Bo-GJ:34, Co-RG:169, Gr-EC:55,
    Ha-LO:83, La-PV:46, Pa-RE:38
  I Wonder What the Wind Would Say.
    K. Revingston. Me-WF:33
  In the Evening.
    Minamoto no Tsunenobu. Ba-ST:42
  In the Mountain Village.
    Minamoto no Morotada. Ba-ST:40
  It Was the Wind.   Bi-IT:19
  January. W. Williams.
    Un-MA:256
  The Last Sunday. Wang Tu-ch'ing.
    Hs-TC:194

A Leaf Looks Prickly. P. Johnson.
  Le-M:124
The Least of Breezes.   Onitsura.
  Be-CS:46
The Leaves.   St-FS:125
Leaves like Fish.   G. Cardiff.
  Ni-CD:47
A Line-Storm Song.   R. Frost.
  Gr-CC:184, Pe-OA:43
Little Wind.   K. Greenaway.
  Ar-TP3:162, Bo-GJ:33, Ch-B:50,
  La-PP:18, Pa-RE:99
Lobster Cove Shindig.
  L. Morrison.   Co-BN:82
Long-Nosed Elf.   De-PP:30
Lost.   E. Recht.   Le-M:194
The Love of King David and Fair
  Bethsabe.   G. Peele.
  Al-VBP:138
Lying in the Sun.   I. Johnson.
  Le-M:78, Le-WR:11
Mad Coyote.   Jo-TS:10
A Man Is Buried where the Cold
  Winds Blow.   D. Matumeak.
  Ba-HI:73
Man Is Nothing but.
  S. Tchernichovsky.   Me-PH:76
Many a Mickle.   W. de la Mare.
  Ga-FB:169
The March Wind.   J. Parr. La-GI:11
March Wind.   M. Uschold.
  Ha-YA:38
The March Winds.   G. Houghton.
  Ha-YA:35
The Message of the March Wind.
  W. Morris.   Ho-WR:27, Ox-BN:789
Mid-Country Blow. T. Roethke.
  Co-BN:167, Co-PU:56
The Moon's the North Wind's
  Cooky. V. Lindsay. Au-SP:327,
  Er-FA:499, Fe-FP:265, La-PP:26,
  La-PV:54, Li-LC:62, Na-EO:170,
  Th-AS:21, Un-GB:12, Un-GT:258
My Children, My Children.
  Da-SC:120, Ho-SD:25, Jo-TS:22,
  Le-OE:26
My Lady Wind.   Bo-FP:215,
  Gr-EC:57, Mo-MGT:177
My Love Is in a Light Attire.
  J. Joyce.   Ha-LO:91
Nebraska.   J. Swan.   Ha-WR:43,
  La-RM:76
The New House.   E. Thomas.
  Un-MB:215
Night Airs.   W. Landor.
  Co-BN:118, Gr-CT:402
Night and a Distant Church.
  R. Atkins.   Ad-PB:198
The Night Wind.   E. Brontë.
  Co-RG:152, Gr-CT:403, Ha-PO:138

The Night Wind.   E. Field.
   Fe-FP:70
Night, Window, Wind. J. Anderson.
   Sc-TN:5
The North Wind.   L. Reis.
   Bo-FP:153
North Wind.   Tr-US II:38
The North Wind and the Child.
   Bo-FP:174
The North Wind Cries Aloud.
   L. Weg.   Le-WR:38
The North Wind Doth Blow.
   Au-SP:62, Bl-OB:97, Bo-FP:152,
   Cl-DT:19, De-CH:625, Hi-GD:21,
   Ir-BB:29, Li-LB:102, Mo-MGT:20,
   Mo-NR:86, Pa-AP:16, Sm-MK:2,
   Wi-MG:20, Wr-RM:114
November.   J. Clare.   Bo-FP:148,
   Ch-B:92, Cl-FC:44
November Day.   E. Averitt.
   Du-RG:121
Now Close the Windows.
   R. Frost.   Ha-LO:5
O Wind, Why Do You Never Rest.
   C. Rossetti.   Ar-TP3:166
October Winds.   V. Randall.
   Ha-YA:114
Ode to the West Wind. P. Shelley.
   Al-VBP:748, Co-BN:127, De-CH:212,
   Er-FA:244, Fe-PL:390, Ga-FB:15,
   Ha-PO:96, Ma-YA:177, Ox-BN:280,
   Pa-GTB:295, Rv-CB:696
Old Man Jeremy.   J. Baxter.
   Gr-EC:248
Old Man Rain.   M. Cawein.
   Co-PS:58
Old Mother Wind.   Bo-FP:259
On a Windy Day.   Z. Gay. Sh-RP:14
On Wenlock Edge the Wood's in
   Trouble.   A. Housman. No-CL:131,
   Ox-BN:921, Pa-GTB:417, Un-MB:97
One March Day.   Bo-FP:215,
   Ch-B:40
Only the Wind Says Spring.
   H. Miller.   Un-GT:260
Over the Wintry.   Soseki.
   Be-CS:6, La-PV:85
The Parting.   A. Rich.   Ha-WR:41
Phoebus and Boreas.
   J. de la Fontaine.   Un-R:87
Picking Up Sticks.   E. Farjeon.
   Bo-FP:67
Pirate Wind.   M. Carr.
   Br-SS:53
The Pity of the Leaves.
   E. Robinson.   Un-MA:137
Praise Song of the Wind.
   Tr-US II:131
Rain.   E. Young.   Ar-TP3:170
Rain Riddle.   De-PP:53

Rounding the Horn. J. Masefield.
   Un-MB:223
Secret Intimations. J. Wheelock.
   Co-PU:54
The Siesta.   Pa-SG:149
Small Song. A. Ammons. Co-PU:54
Snowstorm.   J. Clare.   Co-BN:198,
   Ho-WR:180, Ma-FW:275
Softly. Issa.   Le-MW:17
Song.   Tr-US I:121
The Song of the Four Winds.
   T. Peacock.   Ho-WR:22
A Sound from the Earth.
   W. Stafford.   La-RM:82
The Sound of the Wind.
   C. Rossetti.   Ar-TP3:165,
   Bl-OB:58
The South Wind.   R. Bridges.
   Ox-BN:877
South Wind.   Tu Fu.   Ar-TP3:203,
   Le-MW:75, Ma-FW:100, Rx-OH:24
South Wind.   Tr-US II:39
Spring Air.   G. Derwood.
   Er-FA:113
Spring Breeze.   Buson.   Sh-RP:61
Spring Breeze.   Ho Hsun. Rx-LT:42
The Squirrel and the Wind.
   Bo-FP:153
Stillness.   M. Leaso.   Le-M:130
Stocking and Shirt.   J. Reeves.
   Gr-EC:114
The Stone Harp.   J. Haines.
   Sc-TN:75
The Story of Flying Robert.
   H. Hoffmann.   Ir-BB:158,
   Li-SR:28
Straws. E. Coatsworth. Br-AF:109
A Strong Wind.   A. Clarke.
   Co-BN:166, Co-PI:24
Sudden Gale in Spring.
   M. Thomas.   Gr-EC:61
Sunset.   E. Cummings.   Un-MA:470
Swallows.   T. Ferril.   Ca-BP:20,
   Du-RG:27, La-RM:83
The Tempest. W. Smith. Un-MA:672
The Term.   W. Williams.
   Du-RG:77, La-OC:25, Li-TU:106,
   Mo-TS:34, Re-TW:97, Sh-RP:161
That Wind.   E. Brontë.
   De-CH:215, De-TT:181
That Wind.   Bi-IT:23
Thoughts of a Little Girl.
   M. Enriqueta.   Fe-FP:489
To Morfydd.   L. Johnson.
   Re-TW:68, Un-MB:153
To the Thawing Wind.   R. Frost.
   Ha-LO:82
To the Wind.   Al-PI:16
To the Wind at Morn.   W. Davies.
   Co-EL:140

WINDS — cont'd.
  Trade Winds. J. Masefield.
    Bo-HF:86, Cl-FC:56
  Tramontana at Lerici.
    C. Tomlinson. Pa-GTB:560
  Traveling Storm. M. Van Doren.
    Th-AS:116
  Two Ducks. Hiroshige. Le-MW:14
  Two Sewing. H. Hall. Th-AS:112
  The Unknown Color. C. Cullen.
    Bo-HF:55, Fe-FP:166, Gr-EC:58
  Untitled. Chung Ting-wen.
    Pa-MV:74
  Vernal Equinox. R. Stone.
    Un-MA:655
  The Villain. W. Davies.
    Un-MB:175
  We Must Overcome the East Wind.
    Do-CH:(22)
  Weather. A. MacLeish. Un-MA:456
  Weather Words. D. McCord.
    Pl-IO:51
  Wedding Wind. P. Larkin.
    Gr-BT:86
  The West Wind. J. Masefield.
    Er-FA:242, Un-MB:223, Wi-LT:188
  The West Wind. P. Shelley.
    Bo-FP:167, Ch-B:72
  West Wind. Tr-US II:40
  What the Chimney Sang.
    B. Harte. Sp-OG:307
  When the Wind Is in the East.
    Bo-FP:264, Ir-BB:230, Li-LB:160,
    Mo-MGT:152, Mo-NR:91, Un-GT:23
  When You Walk. J. Kemp. Le-WR:41
  The Whirlwind. Br-MW:129,
    Da-SC:118
  White Cap. Mo-MGT:160
  Who? Ca-MU:19
  Who Has Seen the Wind?
    C. Rossetti. Ar-TP3:163,
    Bl-OB:96, Bo-FP:216, Bo-GJ:33,
    Ch-B:50, De-TT:166, Fe-FP:69,
    Gr-EC:54, Hi-GD:20, Hu-MP:66,
    La-PV:45, Li-LC:78, Mc-AW:95,
    Ox-BC:278, Pe-FB:67
  Whose Scarf Could This Be.
    Buson. Be-CS:56
  The Wide Land. A. Ammons.
    Br-TC:11
  Wild Horses. C. Sandburg.
    Sh-RP:173
  Wild March. C. Woolson.
    Ha-YA:36
  Wind. L. Feeney. Un-GT:260
  Wind. A. Fisher. Sh-RP:159
  Wind. T. Hughes. Ma-FW:37
  The Wind. K. Itta. Ba-HI:74
  The Wind. J. Reeves.
    Co-PU:55, Gr-EC:56

The Wind. J. Stephens.
  Co-BN:165, Co-EL:117, Co-PI:177,
  Co-PU:57, Fr-WO:81, Li-TU:210
The Wind. R. Stevenson.
  Ar-TP3:163, Au-SP:353,
  Bo-FP:216, Hu-MP:36
The Wind. C. Wilson. La-GI:17
The Wind. Da-SC:149, Ho-SD:7
The Wind. Gr-CT:389, Gr-GB:37,
  Sm-LG:64
The Wind and the Moon.
  G. MacDonald. Bo-GJ:35,
  Ir-BB:127, Li-LC:79, Pa-OM:268,
  Un-GT:258
The Wind and the Rain.
  W. Gibson. Cl-FC:50
The Wind at Penistone.
  D. Davie. Wi-LT:680
The Wind at the Door. W. Barnes.
  Pa-GTB:321, Rv-CB:768
The Wind in a Frolic. W. Howitt.
  Ox-BC:162
Wind in the Grass.
  M. Van Doren. Ga-FB:296
Wind in the Trees. Robyn.
  Le-M:51
Wind Is a Cat. E. Fuller.
  Au-SP:327, Hu-MP:317, Th-AS:90
Wind Is a World. A. Hall.
  Le-WR:34
The Wind Is Half the Flower.
  D. Cairns. Le-M:43, Le-WR:34
The Wind Is like the Yeast in
  Bread. R. Tanaka. Le-M:44,
  Le-WR:14
Wind Message. De-PP:40
The Wind Now Commences to Sing.
  Bi-IT:22, Da-SC:88,
  Ho-SD:53, Tr-US II:268
The Wind of January.
  C. Rossetti. Ha-YA:163
The Wind Shrieked Loud.
  E. Coatsworth. De-FS:53
Wind Song. L. Moore. Un-GB:11
Wind Song. C. Sandburg.
  Pe-OA:54, Un-MA:206
Wind-Song. Sh-RP:82
The Wind Tapped like a Tired
  Man. E. Dickinson. Un-MA:105
The Wind Took Up the Northern
  Things. E. Dickinson.
  Mc-PR:54
Wind Tossed Dragons.
  Hsieh Ngao. Rx-LT:110
The Wind Was Bringing Me to
  School. J. Snyder. Le-M:25
The Wind Was Once a Man.
  Le-OE:106
Wind Whining. J. Evans.
  Le-WR:28

Wind—Wolves. W. Sargent.
    Ar-TP3:165, Hu-MP:316
The Winds. T. Tusser. Ho-WR:25
The Winds. Wr-RM:26
The Wind's Song. E. Mörike.
    Pa-SG:140
A Windy Day. W. Howard.
    Fe-FP:191
A Windy Day. A. Young.
    Re-TW:93, Un-GT:259
Windy Morning. H. Behn.
    Ar-TP3:164
Windy Nights. R. Stevenson.
    Ar-TP3:165, Bo-GJ:35, Br-SS:34,
    De-TT:163, Gr-CC:9, Gr-EC:56,
    Ir-BB:241, Ja-PA:44, Ox-BC:294,
    Sp-OG:307, Tu-WW:25
Windy Wash Day. D. Aldis.
    Ar-TP3:167, Fr-MP:10, La-PP:19
Winter Morning. W. Smith.
    Co-BN:197
With a Hey, Ho, the Wind and the
    Rain. W. Shakespeare.
    Ar-TP3:112
Wondering. K. Windsor. Le-M:156
The World Has Changed.
    C. Walker. La-IH:46
The World's Wanderers.
    P. Shelley. Al-VBP:755
The Youth and the Northwind.
    J. Saxe. Co-PT:166
Zephyr. E. Ware. Fe-PL:430
WINE
Ballad of the Two Tapsters.
    V. Watkins. Ca-MB:91
A Boat, a Boat. Rv-CB:425
The Bottle of Chianti.
    R. Souster. Co-EL:154
Bubbling Wine. Abu Zakariya.
    Lo-TY:46
Chorus. T. Peacock. Al-VBP:716
Cups Without Wine. J. Halevi.
    Me-PH:62
A Decanter of Madeira, Aged 86,
    to George Bancroft, Aged 86.
    S. Mitchell. Al-VBP:992
Drink Deep. Br-FW:19
Drink To-Day. J. Fletcher.
    Al-VBP:282
A Drinking Song. W. Yeats.
    No-CL:40
Drums into Mortars. Br-FW:20
Endymion. J. Keats. Al-VBP:790
Festive Wine. Br-FW:13
God Lyaeus, Ever Young.
    J. Fletcher. Al-VBP:279
The Hostess. Wang Mou Fang.
    Le-MW:101
The Irresponsible Student.
    Be-AP:56

Mazilla and Mazura.   Gr-CT:88
My Heart Got Stuck. S. Jahin.
    Lo-TY:51
Ode. C. Cotton. Al-VBP:477
On a Prohibitionist Poem.
    G. Chesterton. Al-VBP:1122
The Parliament of Bees.
    J. Day. Al-VBP:243
Plum Wine. K. Takamura. Sh-AM:44
Rubaiyat of Omar Khayyam.
    E. Fitzgerald. Al-VBP:832,
    Er-FA:43, Fe-FP:479, Gr-CT:329,
    Ha-PO:210, Ox-BN:526, Pa-GTB:329,
    Pa-SG:120
Stork in Jerez. L. Lee.
    Go-BP:81
A Stream of Gold Honey.
    O. Mandelstam. Ca-MR:154
Sunset. Tu Fu. Rx-OH:21
Verse, Violence, and the Vine.
    J. Cunningham. Ls-NY:330
Wine and Water. G. Chesterton.
    Al-VBP:1121, Co-FB:83,
    Un-MB:209
The Wine Menagerie. H. Crane.
    Ca-VT:213
WINKELREID, ARNOLD VON: see
    SWITZERLAND - HISTORY AND
    PATRIOTISM
WINNEPESAUKEE, LAKE
Lake Winnipesaukee. O. Driver.
    Sh-RP:60
WINTER: see also COLD; FROST;
    HUMOR - WINTER; ICE; SLEET; SNOW
Address to a Lark Singing in
    Winter. J. Clare. Re-BS:48
After the Winter. C. McKay.
    Ad-PB:28, Hu-PN:96
Against the Broad Sky.
    Takahama Kyoshi. Ma-FW:273
Alone. W. de la Mare. Gr-CT:390
An Answer to Ting Yuan Ch'en.
    Ou Yang Hsiu. Rx-OH:59
Bear. S. Tsuboi. Sh-AM:74
Benediction. F. Ebright.
    Ls-NY:288
Beyond the Snow Belt.
    M. Oliver. St-H:163
Birds at Winter Nightfall.
    T. Hardy. Co-EL:25, Co-PU:101,
    Re-BS:19, Un-MB:31
Blow, Blow, Thou Winter Wind.
    W. Shakespeare. Al-VBP:187,
    De-CH:232, De-TT:168, Er-FA:257,
    Gr-CT:476, Hi-WP II:139,
    Ho-WR:172, Mc-PR:50, Pa-GTB:26,
    Rv-CB:197
Blue Winter. R. Francis. Ho-LP:34
Brittle World. L. Sarett.
    Th-AS:91

WINTER — cont'd.
  The Brook in February. C. Roberts.
    Co-BN:68, Do-WH:71
  Canadian Folk Song. W. Campbell.
    Bo-FP:171
  Cat & the Weather. M. Swenson.
    Co-BBW:120, Ha-WR:90, Pe-M:108
  A Child's Winter Evening.
    G. John. De-CH:224
  Christmas in the Woods.
    F. Frost. Ar-TP3:197
  The Christmas Present. P. Hubbell.
    La-PV:86
  Cloudy Days. A. Coor. Ho-CT:43
  Cold Blows the Wind. J. Hamilton.
    Cl-FC:33, De-CH:218
  Cold Winter Now Is in the Wood.
    E. Coatsworth. Ar-TP3:198,
    Tu-WW:77
  The Crocus. N. Nicholson.
    Go-BP:113
  Cruel Winter Wind. J. James.
    Ba-HI:75
  Crumbs. W. de la Mare. Au-SP:66
  The Darkling Thrush. T. Hardy.
    Co-RG:170, Er-FA:455, Ha-PO:106,
    Na-EO:56, Ox-BN:824, Un-MB:25,
    Wi-LT:17
  December. A. Fisher. Br-SS:95,
    La-PH:21
  A December Day. S. Teasdale.
    Ha-YA:151, Se-PR:214
  The Deceptive Present, the
    Phoenix Year. D. Schwartz.
    Co-BN:99
  Deliverance. L. Lee. Go-BP:238
  Driving to Town Late to Mail a
    Letter. R. Bly. Ca-VT:558,
    Co-BN:201, Co-EL:156, Mo-TS:55
  The Fawn in the Snow. W. Benét.
    Rd-OA:183, Un-MA:323
  February. J. Bensel. Un-GT:269
  The First Rain of Winter.
    Basho. Do-TS:40
  First Snowfall. G. Carducci.
    Pa-SG:18
  First Winter's Day. D. Aldis.
    Au-SP:334
  Flight. G. Johnston. Do-WH:66
  The Foddering Boy. J. Clare.
    De-CH:632
  Good-bye and Keep Cold.
    R. Frost. Un-GT:284
  Good Hours. R. Frost.
    Gr-SS:45, Sp-OG:247
  The Grass on the Mountain.
    M. Austin. Bo-HF:34, Br-AF:146
  Haiku. D. Lippa. Le-M:192
  The Half of Life. F. Hölderlin.
    Un-R:19

  Hard Frost. A. Young. Co-BN:183
  Heart's Needle: Child of My
    Winter. W. Snodgrass.
    Un-MA:682
  Hibernation. Chi Hsuan. Pa-MV:48
  Hot Cake. Shu Hsi. Cl-FC:90,
    Ma-FW:280
  How Many Nights. G. Kinnell.
    Ca-BP:45
  Human Things. H. Nemerov.
    Co-BN:200
  I Walked on the Ice of the Sea.
    Le-IB:98
  Ice. D. Aldis. Ar-TP3:189,
    Ir-BB:15
  Ice. C. Roberts. Co-BN:184,
    Co-PU:52, Do-WH:69
  Ice-Skates. E. Olson. Mo-SD:145
  In the Blue. A. Machado. Le-SW:75
  In the Evening I Walk by the
    River. Hsiu Ou-Yang.
    Le-MW:88, Rx-OH:51
  In the Farmhouse. G. Kinnell.
    Ha-WR:94
  In Winter. R. Wallace. Co-BN:182
  Into the Vast Sky. K. Takahama.
    Sh-AM:163
  It Is the Quiet Time of Winter.
    Wo-HS:(22)
  It Is Winter I Know. M. Moore.
    Un-MA:574
  January. J. Lowell. Se-PR:26
  January. M. Sendak. Ag-HE:10
  January. J. Updike. La-PV:90
  January: Skiing Song. M. Lewis.
    Un-GT:268
  Jingle Bells. J. Pierpont.
    Er-FA:510, Mo-CC:(35),
    Mo-MGT:158
  Just a Mile Beyond. A. Fisher.
    Sh-RP:196
  Last Words Before Winter.
    L. Untermeyer. Un-GT:285,
    Un-MA:308
  Late Winter. Laksmidhara.
    Al-PI:41
  Looking for a Sunset Bird in
    Winter. R. Frost. Re-BS:17
  Mad as Mist and Snow. W. Yeats.
    Gr-CT:395
  A Magic Landscape. A. Fet.
    Pa-SG:103
  Marjorie's Almanac. T. Aldrich.
    Br-SG:101, Fe-FP:62, Hu-MP:298
  The Meadows Are Snowy. Gr-BB:20
  Midwinter. O. Wilde. Bo-FP:179
  The Milkman's Horse. Au-SP:48,
    Co-IW:33
  The Miracle of Spring. Bahar.
    Pa-SG:82

The Morning Star.   E. Brontë.
    Gr-CT:389
My Birthday's in Winter. Z. Gay.
    Br-BC:59
No Possum, No Sop, No Taters.
    W. Stevens. Ca-VT:38, Sh-AP:162
A Nocturnal upon Saint Lucy's Day.
    J. Donne. Rv-CB:301
Nocturne. F. Frost.   Co-BN:202
The North Wind Doth Blow.
    Au-SP:62, Bl-OB:97, Bo-FP:152,
    Cl-DT:19, De-CH:625, Hi-GD:21,
    Ir-BB:29, Li-LB:102, Mo-MGT:20,
    Mo-NR:86, Pa-AP:16, Sm-MK:2,
    Wi-MG:20, Wr-RM:114
Ode to Winter, Germany, December,
    1800. T. Campbell. Pa-GTB:262
An Old Man's Winter Night.
    R. Frost. Ca-VT:9, Ni-JP:142,
    Un-MA:176
Old Song. Bo-FP:181, Ch-B:73
Old Winter. T. Noël.   Co-PS:152
On a Night of Snow. E. Coatsworth.
    Co-BBW:123, Du-RG:91,
    Un-GT:48, Un-MA:465
On Far Hills.   Takahama Kyoshi.
    Ma-FW:273
On Leaving Bruges. D. Rossetti.
    Rv-CB:883
Oregon Rain. J. McGahey.
    Br-AF:163, Du-RG:125
The Organ Grinder's Garden.
    M. Merryman. Au-SP:156
Out Skiing. L. Shakhovich.
    Mo-MI:19
Outside the Door. A. Wynne.
    Au-SP:334
Over the Wintry. Soseki.
    Be-CS:6, La-PV:85
Pencil and Paint. E. Farjeon.
    La-PV:86
Perfection. G. Ost'or. Mo-MI:87
Poem. D. Hofstein. Ho-TY:173
Poet in Winter. E. Lucie-Smith.
    Br-TC:273
Prayer for a Night of Snow.
    D. Hickey. Ke-TF:209
Prediction. B. Esbensen.
    Ar-TP3:187
Preludes. T. Eliot. Ar-TP3:177,
    Br-TC:103, Ca-VT:128,
    Hi-WP II:162, La-OC:130,
    Pe-OA:103, Sh-AP:182
Rag Doll and Summer Birds.
    O. Dodson. Hu-PN:299
The Redwing. P. Dickinson. Go-BP:77
Saint Valentine's Day.
    C. Patmore. Ox-BN:657
Scampering over Saucers. Yosa Buson.
    Ma-FW:266

Schoolboys in Winter.   J. Clare.
    Fr-WO:82, Rv-CB:732
The Seed Eaters. R. Francis.
    Ca-BP:7
The Sense of the Sleight-of-Hand
    Man. W. Stevens. Pe-OA:70,
    Un-MA:252, Wi-LT:147
Sheep in Winter. J. Clare.
    Ma-FW:280
Shine Out, Fair Sun, with All
    Your Heat. G. Chapman. Gr-CT:414
Signs of Winter. J. Clare.
    Co-BN:201, Co-PS:150,
    Ho-LP:300, Ho-WR:168
Skating. W. Wordsworth. De-CH:219,
    Mo-SD:148, Sm-LG:60, Un-GT:281
A Sledding Song. N. Schlichter.
    Fe-FP:115
Snow.   D. Aldis. Ar-TP3:190,
    Co-PU:51, La-PV:42
The Snow. T. Batchelor. Ho-CT:39
The Snow. Mao Tse-tung. Hs-TC:363
Snow. K. Orendurff. Le-M:191
Snow-Bound. J. Whittier. Ga-FB:302
    Ho-WR:174, Mc-PR:139
The Snow Man. W. Stevens. Bo-GJ:226
Snow on Lotus Mountain.
    Liu Ch'ang Ch'ing. Rx-LT:68
Snowstorm. J. Clare. Co-BN:198,
    Ho-WR:180, Ma-FW:275
A Snowy Day. D. ap Gwilym.
    Pa-SG:100
Somehow You Know when It Arrives.
    E. Livingston. Sc-TN:148
Song. A. Tennyson. Ox-BN:476,
    Pa-GTB:330
Song. W. Turner. Bo-GJ:253,
    Un-MB:345
A Song of Winter. De-CH:217
Sonnet. Feng Chih. Hs-TC:148
The Sorceress. L. Pazharskaya.
    Mo-MI:22
Spidersilk. J. Nixon. Ls-NY:294
The Spring. T. Carew. Cl-FC:37,
    Co-PS:58, Gr-CC:30, Ha-PO:81,
    Ho-WR:34
A Still Day.J. Cherwinski.Sh-RP:196
Stop. R. Wilbur. Ha-WR:87
Stopping by Woods on a Snowy
    Evening. R. Frost. Ad-PE:31,
    Al-VBP:1134, Ar-TP3:198,
    Bo-FP:170, Bo-GJ:257, Br-SS:88,
    Br-TC:135, Cl-DT:20, Co-BN:151,
    Co-PS:160, De-CH:625, Er-FA:257,
    Fe-FP:67, Ga-FB:299, Gr-EC:273,
    Ha-PO:90, Ke-TF:420, La-PP:29,
    La-PV:167, Ma-FW:276, Mc-PR:124,
    Mc-WK:32, Pe-FB:80, Re-TW:123,
    Sh-AP:150, Sh-RP:52, Sm-LG:63,
    Sm-PT:8, Un-MA:187, Wi-LT:174

WINTER — cont'd.
  Storm Fear. R. Frost. Al-VBP:1127
  Street Scene. R. Mezey. Wi-LT:770
  Summer and Winter. P. Shelley.
    Co-BN:101
  Summer Comes. E. Agnew. Br-SS:169
  Summer Is Gone. Co-PI:158,
    Sm-LG:58
  Supplication. Hu P'in-ch'ing.
    Pa-MV:104
  The Terrace in the Snow.
    Su Tung P'o. Rx-OH:71
  That Wind. E. Brontë.
    De-CH:215, De-TT:181
  There Is Fear. Ma-BH:11,
    Tr-US I:24
  There Is Joy. Do-WH:64, Ho-SD:76,
    La-RM:125, Le-OE:104, Ma-BH:10
  Therefore All Seasons Shall Be
    Sweet to Thee. S. Coleridge.
    Cl-DT:22, De-CH:632
  There's a Certain Slant of
    Light. E. Dickinson.
    Rv-CB:905, Sh-AP:128, Sm-LG:50,
    Un-MA:98, Wi-LT:4
  These. W. Williams. Un-MA:261
  Thinking of a Friend at Year's
    End. Ho Ch'i-fang. Hs-TC:219
  Those Wild Geese. M. Saito.
    Sh-AM:144
  Three Kinds of Pleasure. R. Bly.
    Mo-BG:110, St-H:1
  To Winter. W. Blake. Ho-WR:167
  The Tree and the Lady. T. Hardy.
    Un-MB:33
  Tree in December. M. Cane.
    Un-MA:235
  A Tree with No Leaves.
    J. Gonzalez. Jo-VC:72
  Triolet on a Dark Day.
    M. Fishback. Co-PS:161
  Twin Lakes Hunter. A. Guthrie.
    Du-RG:127, Ha-PO:143
  Two Little Birds Fly. Gr-BB:26
  Under a Small, Cold Winter Moon.
    Ransetsu. Be-MC:47
  Up in the Morning Early.
    R. Burns. Bl-OB:98, Bo-FP:168,
    Co-PS:160, De-TT:91
  Upon the Hard Crust.
    A. Akhmatova. Pa-SG:23
  The Vision of Sir Launfal.
    J. Lowell. Pa-OM:210
  Visitors. H. Behn. Au-SP:132
  Walk on a Winter Day.
    S. Allen. Ha-YA:143
  Walking into the Woods.
    J. Bender. Le-M:189
  A Warm Winter Day. J. Cooper.
    Co-BN:187

  Weather Chant. Le-IB:118
  Welcome, Winter Guest. Gr-BB:29
  The West Wind. P. Shelley.
    Bo-FP:167, Ch-B:72
  What Can I Give Him? C. Rossetti.
    Cl-DT:19, Gr-CT:422, Gr-TG:79
  When Daisies Pied. W. Shakespeare.
    Al-VBP:181, Re-TW:56, Rv-CB:189
  When the Days Begin to Lengthen.
    Un-GT:22
  When the Snow Is on the Ground.
    Wr-RM:128
  White Fields. J. Stephens.
    Au-SP:335, Br-SS:91, Co-BN:199,
    Co-PS:159, Fe-FP:66, Gr-EC:84,
    Mc-AW:50
  A Widow Bird. P. Shelley.
    Bl-OB:96, De-CH:235, De-TT:155,
    Fe-FP:296, Hi-WP I:20,
    Hu-MP:234, Ox-BN:303, Pa-GTB:275,
    Re-TW:69, Rv-CB:694
  The Wind Blows Cold. De-CH:633
  The Wind Blows Grey.
    Naito Meisetsu. Ma-FW:263
  The Windham Thaw. A. Guiterman.
    Gr-EC:58
  Winter. T. Campion. Al-VBP:218,
    Ma-FW:277, No-CL:280, Rv-CB:272
  Winter. Chu Hsiang. Hs-TC:103
  Winter. J. Constant. Le-M:190
  Winter. A. Crapsey. Hu-MP:322
  Winter (Clouded). W. de la Mare.
    Cl-DT:18
  Winter (Green Mistletoe).
    W. de la Mare. Gr-CT:394,
    Ha-YA:144
  Winter. M. Hicks. Ho-CT:40
  Winter. R. Hughes. Re-TW:112
  Winter. G. Humphrey. Le-M:185
  Winter. J. Hurnard. Co-PS:152
  Winter. J. Jaszi. Au-SP:333
  Winter. Jösö. Li-TU:209,
    Pa-SG:103
  Winter. C. Mair. Co-PS:153
  Winter. C. Patmore. Ox-BN:655
  Winter. D. Rossetti. Rv-CB:888
  Winter. W. Shakespeare.
    Al-VBP:182, Bl-OB:98, Bo-FP:178,
    Bo-GJ:252, Co-BN:181, Co-PS:157,
    Co-RG:129, De-CH:230, Fe-FP:65,
    Gr-CT:392, Ha-PO:252, Ho-WR:171,
    Hu-MP:323, Ma-YA:65, Mc-WK:29,
    Pa-GTB:17, Re-TW:102, Rv-CB:190,
    Sm-LG:59, Sp-OG:286, Tu-WW:74
  Winter. R. Stevenson.
    Hi-WP I:31
  Winter. A. Tennyson.
    Bo-FP:176
  Winter. J. Thomson.
    Al-VBP:550, De-TT:167

Winter. De-TT:39, Mo-MGT:178,
  Wr-RM:12
Winter: An Ode. S. Johnson.
  No-CL:128
Winter and Summer. S. Spender.
  Un-MB:480
Winter Branches. M. Widdemer.
  Sh-RP:98
Winter Circus. A. Fisher.
  Ha-YA:148
Winter Fancy. Yung Tzu.
  Pa-MV:199
Winter Feast. F. Frost.
  Br-SG:107, Ha-YA:146
Winter Field. K. Ozaki.
  Sh-AM:58
Winter Has Come. K. Takamura.
  Sh-AM:46
Winter Holding off the Coast of
  North America. N. Momaday.
  Ni-CD:91
The Winter House. N. Cameron.
  Rv-CB:999
A Winter Hymn - To the Snow.
  E. Jones. Ox-BN:623
Winter in Alaska. F. Washington.
  Ba-HI:70
Winter in Dunover Field.
  T. Hardy. Un-MB:31
Winter in the City.
  Wang Ya-p'ing. Hs-TC:351
Winter in the Fens. J. Clare.
  Co-BN:190, Ma-FW:4
Winter in the Wood.
  I. Eastwick. Ha-YA:142
Winter in Vermont. H. Carruth.
  Ca-BP:41
The Winter Lakes. W. Campbell.
  Co-BN:186
Winter Landscape. J. Berryman.
  Br-TC:37, Mo-BG:112,
  Un-MA:640, Wi-LT:566
Winter Landscape. S. Spender.
  Un-MB:473
Winter Morning. W. Smith.
  Co-BN:197
Winter Morning. W. Welles.
  Ho-LP:33
A Winter Night. W. Barnes.
  Gr-CT:394, Ox-BN:430
Winter Night. M. Butts.
  Ar-TP3:198
Winter Night. E. Millay.
  Se-PR:215
A Winter Night. B. Pasternak.
  Ca-MR:174
A Winter Night. J. Velez.
  Ba-HI:72
Winter Nightfall. R. Bridges.
  Un-MB:50

Winter Noon. S. Teasdale.
  Ha-YA:146, Sh-RP:238
Winter Portrait. R. Southey.
  Co-BN:184, Co-PU:52
Winter Rain. C. Rossetti.
  Co-BN:184, Ho-WR:24
Winter Remembered. J. Ransom.
  Ca-VT:147, Rv-CB:985
Winter Song. J. Jimenez.
  Le-SW:73
Winter Stormed In. S. Jahin.
  Lo-TY:52
Winter Streams. B. Carman.
  De-TT:91, Ha-YA:149, Sp-OG:284
Winter, the Huntsman.
  O. Sitwell. Bl-OB:99,
  Cl-FC:32, Hi-WP I:34
Winter-Time. R. Stevenson.
  Ox-BC:298, Un-GT:280, Un-MB:58
The Winter Trees. C. Dyment.
  Cl-FC:63
A Winter Twilight. A. Grimke.
  Ad-PB:16, Hu-PN:54
Winter Views Serene. G. Crabbe.
  Ox-BN:9
Winter Walk. K. van der Veer.
  Ke-TF:86
A Winter's Tale. D. Lawrence.
  Un-MB:287
Winter's Thunder. Li-LB:161,
  Rv-ON:37, Un-GT:23
Winter's Troops. C. Cotton.
  Gr-CT:390
The Winter's Walk. S. Johnson.
  Rv-CB:526
A Wintry Blizzard. Kyoroku.
  Be-MC:60
Wintry Day. Bo-FP:168
The Wolf Cry. L. Sarett.
  Fe-FP:179
Woods in Winter. H. Longfellow.
  Rv-CB:781
The Words of Finn. Gr-CT:389
Years-End. R. Wilbur. Wi-LT:596
WINTER SPORTS: see names of par-
  ticular sports, as SKATING
WINTERS, (ARTHUR) YVOR
  A Letter to Yvor Winters.
  K. Rexroth. Pl-ML:53
  To Yvor Winters, 1955. T. Gunn.
  Pa-GTB:562
WIRE
  The Wires Are So Still and High.
  A. Wynne. Bo-FP:131
WISCONSIN: see also names of towns,
  as OSHKOSH, WIS.
  Eros and Agape. C. Walsh. St-H:240
  The Snow Shovel.C. Walsh. St-H:235
  Two Beers in Argyle, Wisconsin.
  D. Etter. St-H:62

WISCONSIN, UNIVERSITY OF
  Valediction to My Contemporaries.
    H. Gregory. Un-MA:506
WISDOM: see also COMMON SENSE;
    HUMOR - WISDOM; MINERVA
    (GODDESS); SATIRE - WISDOM;
    THOTH (EGYPTIAN GOD)
  After Long Silence. W. Yeats.
    Co-EL:122, Wi-LT:89
  Auguries of Innocence. W. Blake.
    Al-VBP:621, Ch-B:36, Co-BBW:278,
    Er-FA:69, Ga-FB:96, Ma-YA:130,
    Ox-BN:28, Pl-IO:5, Sh-RP:76,
    Sm-LG:67, Sm-MK:220, Un-GT:305
  Bacchus. R. Emerson.
    Al-VBP:803, Sh-AP:27
  The Book of Wisdom. S. Crane.
    Un-MA:147
  Concerning Wisdom. D. Yazzie.
    Br-MW:63
  The Dark and the Fair. S. Kunitz.
    En-PC:67
  Don't Tell All You Know. Bo-FP:119
  An Elegy for a Dead Child in the
    Street. R. Rao. Al-PI:106
  Epistle to Be Left in the Earth.
    A. MacLeish. Pl-IO:55,
    Sm-PT:114, Un-MA:458
  Essay on Man. A. Pope. Al-VBP:537
  Fergus and the Druid. W. Yeats.
    Li-TU:166
  Flower in the Crannied Wall.
    A. Tennyson. Co-BN:49,
    Er-FA:243, Fe-FP:216, Fr-WO:85,
    Ga-FB:128, Hu-MP:257, Ma-YA:198,
    Mc-PR:137
  The Fool on the Hill. J. Lennon.
    Mo-GR:72
  For This Is Wisdom. L. Hope.
    Fe-PL:305
  For William Edward Burghardt
    Dubois on His Eightieth
    Birthday. B. Latimer.
    Ad-PB:199, Hu-PN:392
  The Four Zoas. W. Blake.
    Ho-P:257
  He Who Knows. Un-GT:305
  I Go Forth to Move about the
    Earth. A. Lopez. Al-WW:8
  I Thee Advise. G. Turberville.
    De-CH:621
  If I Know. I Men. Hs-TC:416
  It Must Be Abstract.
    W. Stevens. Sm-PT:124
  The Lamp. E. Fitzgerald.
    Ga-S:138
  A Little Learning. A. Pope.
    Er-FA:99, Gr-CT:435
  Lone Founts. H. Melville.
    Al-VBP:955

  The Man of Life Upright.
    T. Campion. Al-VBP:219,
    De-CH:637, Go-BP:44,
    Ha-PO:197, Rv-CB:273
  My Son. Ge-TR:41
  O Virtuous Light. E. Wylie.
    Un-MA:281
  O World. G. Santayana.
    Fe-PL:321, Sm-PT:168
  Old Fortunatus. T. Dekker.
    Al-VBP:229
  On Growing Old. J. Masefield.
    Al-VBP:1136, Er-FA:149, Fe-PL:263,
    Tr-MR:55, Un-MB:227, Wi-LT:193
  Orator. R. Emerson. Co-PU:16
  Rumination. R. Eberhart.
    Ho-LP:96, Sm-MK:214, Wi-LT:433
  The Sacred Order. M. Sarton.
    Pl-IO:155
  The Same Old Law. W. Whitman.
    Rd-OA:23
  Senex to Matt. Prior. J. Stephen.
    Co-FB:485
  Solomon and the Bees. J. Saxe.
    Un-GT:142
  Some Refrains at the Charles
    River. P. Viereck. En-PC:154
  Song of a Woman Abandoned by
    the Tribe. Ho-LP:84
  The Spring Waters. Ping Hsin.
    Hs-TC:24
  Time in the Rock. C. Aiken.
    Al-VBP:1188
  To Juan at the Winter Solstice.
    R. Graves. Br-TC:154,
    Ha-PO:191, Un-MB:390, Wi-LT:377
  Unison. J. Wheelock. Tr-MR:144
  The Way of Life. Laotse.
    Ba-PO:7, Mc-WK:220
  What Are Years? M. Moore.
    Ha-TP:140, Pe-OA:101, Pl-EI:138,
    Sh-AP:179, Sm-PT:10, Un-MA:352
  Where Shall Wisdom Be Found?
    Euripides. Pa-SG:186, Pl-US:108
  Wisdom. L. Hughes. Ar-TP3:216
  Wisdom. H. Sobiloff. Ca-VT:355
  Wisdom (It Was a Night).
    S. Teasdale. Un-MA:266
  Wisdom (When I Have Ceased).
    S. Teasdale. Mc-PR:63
  Wisdom. Tr-CB:17
  The Wisdom of Merlyn. W. Blunt.
    Al-VBP:1056
  The Wisdom of the World.
    S. Sassoon. Un-MB:315
  The Wise. C. Cullen.
    Hu-PN:230
  A Wise Old Owl Lived in an Oak.
    Er-FA:213, Li-LB:103, Mo-MGT:118,
    Un-GF:13, Un-GT:22, Wi-MG:47

WISE MEN: see JESUS CHRIST -
   NATIVITY
WISHES: see also HUMOR - WISHES;
   LONGING; SATIRE - WISHES
  Being Gypsy. B. Young.
     Ar-TP3:14, Au-SP:212
  Bouncing Ball. S. Watson.
     Au-SP:193
  Cake. M. Potter. Br-BC:85
  Children, Children, Don't Forget.
     D. Owen. Hu-MP:84
  The Christening. W. de la Mare.
     Br-BC:30
  Christmas Wishes. J. Lee.
     Ja-HH:54
  A Death Song. P. Dunbar.
     Fe-PL:274, Hu-PN:42
  Departure. E. Millay. Un-MA:446
  Faith, I Wish I Were a Leprechaun.
     M. Ritter. Ar-TP3:160,
     Fe-FP:389
  The Falling Star. S. Teasdale.
     Ar-TP3:179, Au-SP:341, La-PV:52,
     Pe-FB:71, Th-AS:30
  The False Knight upon the Road.
     De-CH:316, Gr-GB:288
  The Fisherman. D. McCord.
     La-PV:8
  Five Little Chickens. Ch-B:85,
     Fe-FP:282, Gr-EC:182, La-PV:198,
     St-FS:78, Un-GB:15, Un-GT:67
  Going Fishing. L. Griffiths.
     Pa-RE:32
  Harvest Moon. Ryota. Sh-RP:66
  The Haughty Snail-King.
     V. Lindsay. Ha-LO:58
  He Wishes for the Cloths of
     Heaven. W. Yeats. Go-BP:130,
     Ho-LP:13, Th-AS:144, Un-MB:108
  Her Birthday. Feng Yen-Chi.
     Le-MW:112
  I Bid You Keep Some Few Small
     Dreams. H. Frazee-Bower.
     Th-AS:210
  I Keep Three Wishes Ready.
     A. Wynne. Ar-TP3:146,
     Au-SP:292, La-PV:76,
     Pe-FB:49, Th-AS:9
  I Wish. R. Mortimer. Le-M:72
  I Wish I Was Lucky. L. Atwood.
     La-GI:45
  I Would I Were. Le-OE:43
  I'd Leave. A. Lang.
     Fe-FP:12
  If Easter Eggs Would Hatch.
     D. Malloch. Au-SP:364, Hu-MP:335
  If I Was President. M. Cowan.
     Jo-VC:7
  If Only the World.
     Minamoto no Sanetomo. Ba-ST:32

  I'm Wishing the Whole World
     Christmas. A. Wynne.
     Th-AS:108
  A Kite. Ar-TP3:163, Au-SP:196,
     Bo-FP:217, Ch-B:41
  Let There Always Be a Sky.
     K. Barannikov. Mo-MI:90
  Load of Hay. Ir-BB:227, Tu-WW:16
  Lullaby for Mitsura. T. Arghezi.
     Mc-AC:26
  My Ships. E. Wilcox. Fe-PL:95
  My Wish. Carliss St Me-WF:19
  My Wish. P. Strong. Sh-RP:114
  New Year Wishes. M. Sarton.
     Tr-MR:251
  Nursery Rhyme of Innocence and
     Experience. C. Causley.
     Bo-GJ:170, Hi-WP I:82
  O for Doors to Be Open.
     W. Auden. Al-VBP:1226
  Oh, that I Were. Mo-MGT:180
  Old Fortunatus. T. Dekker.
     Al-VBP:229
  The Old Man's Wish. W. Pope.
     Go-BP:47
  An Old Woman of the Roads.
     P. Colum. De-CH:49, Fe-FP:320,
     Hu-MP:156, Sh-RP:43, Th-AS:184,
     Un-MB:250
  On the Shore. D. Baruch. Cr-SS:12
  On This Island. W. Auden.
     Ma-FW:44, Pa-GTB:510,
     To-MP:19, Un-MB:457
  Otherwhere. F. Gray. De-FS:98
  Poem. C. Dropkin. Ho-TY:168
  Rathers. M. Austin. Fe-FP:15
  The Retreat. H. Vaughan.
     Al-VBP:466, Pa-GTB:65, Rv-CB:408
  A Sea Song from the Shore.
     J. Riley. Ch-B:37
  She Asks for a New Earth.
     K. Tynan. Go-BP:253
  The Silver Fish. S. Silverstein.
     Co-SS:178
  The Singing Leaves. J. Lowell.
     Hu-MP:410
  Song of a Dying Girl. Tr-US I:170
  Spring. C. Clemmons. Ad-PB:488
  Star Light, Star Bright.
     Ar-TP3:178, Au-SP:20, Bo-FP:46,
     Gr-EC:88, Ir-BB:227, Mo-MGT:172,
     Mo-TB:6, Tu-WW:16
  A Summer Wish. C. Rossetti.
     Ox-BN:706
  Thanksgiving Wishes.
     A. Guiterman. Co-PS:146
  To a Friend on His Marriage.
     F. Prince. Wi-LT:795
  To a Little Sister, Aged Ten.
     A. Cummings. Br-BC:79

WISHES — cont'd.
To His Son, Vincent Corbet.
R. Corbet. Ox-BC:25, Rv-CB:322,
Sm-LG:112
To Patricia on Her Christening
Day. E. Price. Br-BC:29
Varge. P. Hubbell. Ar-TP3:12
Vocation. R. Tagore. Fe-FP:484
The Wants of Man. J. Adams.
Fe-PL:315
The Way-Side Well. J. Cotter.
Hu-PN:18
We Wish to Be Joyful. Do-CH:(48)
Where Is Fancy Bred.
W. Shakespeare. Al-VBP:185,
De-CH:197, Fe-FP:397, Hi-WP II:52,
Ma-YA:66, Pa-GTB:30
White Horses. E. Farjeon.
La-PV:123
Who Wants a Birthday? D. McCord.
Br-BC:3
The Wish. A. Cowley. Al-VBP:450,
De-CH:524
The Wish. A. Friday. La-PH:58
A Wish. S. Rogers. Pa-GTB:143
A Wish Is Quite a Tiny Thing.
A. Wynne. Hu-MP:69, Th-AS:110
Wish Rhyme. Ju-CP:76
Wishes. E. Wallace. Th-AS:57
Wishes: To His Supposed Mistress.
R. Crashaw. Al-VBP:432,
Pa-GTB:67
Wishing. W. Allingham. Fe-FP:14,
Hu-MP:69, Ox-BC:218
Wishing Song. Ju-CP:23
WISTERIA
Clear Is the Bottom of the Lake.
Yakanochi. Ba-ST:19
Wisteria Trellis. Fang Hsin.
Pa-MV:84
WIT: see also EPIGRAMS; HUMOR
Art Thou That She. Al-VBP:353
Mr. Francis Beaumont's Letter
to Ben Jonson. F. Beaumont.
Al-VBP:301
WITCHES AND WITCHCRAFT: see also
CHARMS; EERINESS; ENCHANTMENT;
HALLOWEEN; HUMOR - WITCHES AND
WITCHCRAFT; SATIRE - WITCHES
AND WITCHCRAFT; VOODOO
Abracadabra. D. Livesay. Do-WH:38
Against Witches. Gr-GB:290
Alison Gross. De-CH:406, Fo-OG:36,
Ma-BB:108, Ox-BB:54
All. All a-Lonely. Gr-CT:159
Ambushed by Angels. G. Davidson.
De-FS:71
And Can the Physician Make Sick
Men Well? Bl-OB:157, Gr-EC:288,
Re-TW:47

Annan Water. De-CH:311, Ma-BB:214
As Lucy Went a-Walking.
W. de la Mare. Sm-MK:50
The Beginning. Te-FC:225
La Belle Dame sans Merci. J. Keats.
Al-VBP:779, Bo-GJ:163, Bo-HF:22,
De-CH:121, De-TT:200, Er-FA:409,
Gr-CT:178, Gr-SS:108, Ha-PO:6,
Hi-WP II:106, Ho-P:80, Mc-WK:8,
Ni-JP:98, No-CL:65, Ox-BN:376,
Pa-GTB:193, Rv-CB:735, Sm-LG:217,
Sm-MK:46, Sp-OG:113, Un-GT:126
Bewitched. W. de la Mare.
Co-PM:44
The Broomstick Train. O. Holmes.
Ch-B:45, Co-PM:105, Fe-FP:395
A Charm Against the Stitch.
Ma-FW:233
Cotton Mather. S. Benét.
Hi-TL:29
A Country Witch. W. Barnes.
Un-GT:106
The Demon Lover. Co-PM:201,
Fo-OG:44, Ma-BB:188, Ma-FW:199,
Ox-BB:83, Rv-CB:45
The Demon of the Gibbet.
F. O'Brien. Co-PM:134
Evocation. H. King. De-FS:129
The Fairy King. W. Allingham.
Co-PM:22
The False Knight upon the Road.
De-CH:316, Gr-GB:288
First Travels of Max. J. Ransom.
Un-MA:412
The Flying Dutchman. C. Leland.
Co-PM:121
Giles Corey. Hi-TL:28
The Hag. R. Herrick. Bl-OB:85,
Co-PS:137, Ho-WR:218, Ma-YA:86,
Sm-LG:233, Sm-MK:48, Un-GT:107
Hallowe'en. M. Chute. La-PH:9
Halloween. J. Ciardi. Ar-TP3:243
Halloween. I. Eastwick. La-PH:10
Halloween. M. Lawson. Ar-TP3:237,
Br-SS:67
The Hare. W. de la Mare.
Ar-TP3:62, Sp-OG:299, Tu-WW:98
Hazel Dorn. B. Sleigh. De-CH:558
Her Kind. A. Sexton.
Br-TC:368, Wi-LT:813
Herbs and Simples. M. Keller.
De-FS:123
Hey-How for Hallowe'en! Sm-LG:234
Hinx, Minx. Ir-BB:185, Mo-CC:(33),
Mo-MGT:145, Rv-ON:74
How a Fisherman Corked Up His Foe
in a Jar. G. Carryl. Co-PM:31
The Laily Worm and the Machrel of
the Sea. Gr-CT:135, Ox-BB:59,
Rd-OA:200

Learning the Spells: A Diptych.
A. Probst. Ni-CD:170
The Little Creature.
W. de la Mare. Na-EO:149
The Lorelei. H. Heine.
Co-PM:87, Sp-OG:116, Un-GT:137
The Love-Talker. E. Carbery.
Co-PI:20, De-CH:296, Ha-PO:192
Meet-on-the-Road. Bl-OB:84,
Co-PM:208, De-CH:674
The Mermaid. De-CH:403, Fo-OG:39
Mrs. Caribou. W. Smith.
Co-PM:154, Ir-BB:210
Molly Means. M. Walker. Be-MA:74,
Bo-AN:130, Ha-PO:55, Hu-PN:309
The Moon-Child. F. Macleod.
De-CH:402
Mother Maudlin the Witch.
B. Jonson. Gr-CT:160
My Name Is John Wellington Wells.
W. Gilbert. Co-PM:72
The Nativity Chant. W. Scott.
Gr-CT:167, Sm-LG:233
On Halloween Night. L. Blair.
Ja-HH:34
Once upon a Time. Issa.
Be-MC:18
One Friday Morn. De-CH:400,
Pa-OM:294
A Poison Tree. W. Blake.
Co-PM:29, Er-FA:64, Ga-S:133,
Gr-SS:77, Rv-CB:607
The Quiet Child. R. Field.
Rd-SS:39
The Ride-by-Nights. W. de la Mare.
Ar-TP3:186, Br-SS:66, Fe-FP:394
The Sabbat. L. Carter. De-FS:47
Sir Olaf. J. von Herder.
Co-PM:97, Sp-OG:108
Sir William Deloraine at the
Wizard's Tomb. W. Scott.
Ox-BN:118
Soucouyant. F. Charles. Sa-B:131
Spooky. K. Finnell. Ho-CT:35
The Stone. W. Kerr. De-FS:128
The Stone Troll. J. Tolkien.
Li-TU:110, Lo-LL:9
The Strange Visitor. Bl-OB:86,
De-CH:677, Gr-CT:132, Gr-GB:290
The Sun Priest and the Witch-
Woman. Te-FC:135
There Cam' Seven Egyptians.
De-CH:534
There Was a Knight. De-CH:315,
Gr-GB:277
This Is Halloween. D. Thompson.
Ar-TP3:186, Ha-YA:121, La-PH:12
The Three Cats.De-TT:30,Rv-ON:120
Tillie. W. de la Mare.
Ar-TP3:157, Co-PM:49, Ir-BB:153

To Shorten a Night-Goer on This
Side. Da-SC:144
Trap. W. Kerr. De-FS:128
The Turn of the Road.
J. Stephens. Li-TU:97
Unwelcome. M. Coleridge.
De-CH:301, Ox-BN:926
Was She a Witch? L. Richards.
Hu-MP:446, La-PH:9, La-PV:69
What the Gray Cat Sings.
A. Guiterman. Co-PM:80,
Hu-MP:188, Li-TU:112,
Rd-SS:24, Se-PR:194
A Witch. W. Barnes. Co-PM:23
The Witch. E. Farjeon.
Co-OT:33, Su-FVI:18
The Witch. P. Ilott. Ja-PA:40
The Witch. S. McNail. De-FS:140
The Witch. P. Thornton.
Le-M:208
Witch Cat. R. Bennett. Br-SS:69
The Witch of Coös. R. Frost.
Al-VBP:1129, Pe-OA:36,
Sh-AP:147, Wi-LT:170
The Witch of Willoughby Wood.
R. Bennett. Co-PM:27, Sh-RP:228
The Witches. L. Drake. De-FS:80
Witches. Linden. Le-M:206
The Witches. Gr-CT:160
The Witches' Ballad. W. Scott.
De-CH:306, Na-EO:24
Witches' Charm (The Owl).
B. Jonson. Bl-OB:88, Sm-LG:234
The Witches' Charms (Dame).
B. Jonson. Co-PM:107, Re-TW:26
The Witches' Ride. K. Kuskin.
La-PH:14, La-PV:68
Witches' Song. E. Coatsworth.
Co-PM:38
The Witches' Song. B. Jonson.
De-CH:302
Witches' Song. W. Shakespeare.
Mc-WS:34
The Witches' Spell.
W. Shakespeare. Co-PM:151
Witching Hour. N. Farber.
De-FS:91
Witch's Broomstick Spell.
Gr-GB:290
Witch's Milking Charm.
Gr-CT:159, Gr-GB:290
The Witch's Ride.
Bo-FP:146
The Witch's Song.
Mo-MGT:192
Witchwood. M. Justus.
Br-SS:68, Ju-CP:75
The Woman's Tongue Tree.
A. Guiterman. Co-PM:81
See also Mo-TB:79-81

WIVES: see also HUMOR - WIVES;
   HUSBAND AND WIFE; WIDOWS
   Against Women Either Good or Bad.
      Al-VBP:72
   Any Wife to Any Husband.
      R. Browning.   Ox-BN:535
   Ap Huw's Testament.   R. Thomas.
      Gr-BT:xv
   At Flock Mass.   F. Higgins.
      Co-PI:65
   Complaint.   J. Wright.   Ca-VT:622
   Creatrix.   A. Wickham.   Un-MB:277
   Difficult Chieko.   K. Takamura.
      Sh-AM:47
   A Dream at Night.   Mei Yao Ch'en.
      Rx-OH:43
   Farm Wife.   R. Thomas.   Go-BP:50
   Father.   Y. Urakawa.   Le-TA:26
   For Fran.   P. Levine.   En-PC:272
   For Hettie.   L. Jones.   Pe-SS:125
   Fulfillment.   W. Cavendish.
      Un-MW:135
   Gladly I'll Live in a Poor Moun-
      tain Hut.   Le-MW:111
   His Wife.   Rachel.   Me-PH:88
   I Remember the River at Wu Sung.
      Mei Yao Ch'en.   Rx-OH:47
   In the Broad Daylight I Dream of
      My Dead Wife.   Mei Yao Ch'en.
      Rx-OH:46
   Kayak Song in Dialogue.   Da-SC:38,
      Le-IB:88, Tr-US I:6
   Love Song: I and Thou.
      A. Dugan.   Gr-BT:139
   Love's Matrimony.   W. Cavendish.
      Go-BP:140
   Meditation at Kew.   A. Wickham.
      Gr-BT:88, Un-MB:280, Un-MW:58
   Mother of the House.   Bible.
      O.T.   Proverbs.   Co-PS:88,
      Un-GT:91
   My Auld Wife.   Gr-GB:160
   My Wife.   R. Stevenson.
      Hi-WP I:43
   O I Won't Lead a Homely Life.
      T. Hardy.   Pl-US:33
   Oh, Oh, You Will Be Sorry for
      That Word.   E. Millay.
      Pe-OA:165
   On His Deceased Wife. J. Milton.
      Er-FA:140, Rv-CB:375
   On Susan Pattison.   Rv-CB:416
   On the Death of a Wife.
      Le-OE:133
   On the Death of His Wife.
      Mei Yao Ch'en.   Rx-OH:45
   Plum Wine.   K. Takamura.
      Sh-AM:44
   Poem in Prose.   A. MacLeish.
      Mc-WS:149

   Prayer to a Dead Wife.   Da-SC:73
   The Red-Haired Man's Wife.
      J. Stephens.   Un-MB:264
   The Silken Tent.   R. Frost.
      Br-TC:138, Un-MW:208
   Sinfonia Domestica.
      J. Untermeyer.   Un-MA:333
   Song.   Le-OE:84, Tr-US II:179
   Song.   Tr-US I:230
   Sonnet on the Death of His Wife.
      J. Masefield.   Go-BP:150
   The Tired Man.   A. Wickham.
      Sm-MK:25, Un-MW:57
   To His Wife.   J. Skelton.
      Rv-CB:69
   To My Wife.   P. Firth.   Go-BP:141
   T'Other Little Tune.   Pl-US:32,
      Rv-ON:102, Wr-RM:53
   The Two Wives.   D. Henderson.
      Br-SM:12
   Two Women under a Maple.
      R. Coffin.   Mc-PR:147
   Upon the Death of Sir Albert
      Morton's Wife.   H. Wotton.
      Al-VBP:223, Hi-WP II:18,
      No-CL:159, Rv-CB:277
   The Wife.   R. Creeley.   Ca-VT:566
   A Wife.   H. Van Dyke.   Ke-TF:134
   The Wife of Llew.   F. Ledwidge.
      Co-PI:91, Co-PM:120, No-CL:57
   A Young Wife.   D. Lawrence.
      Un-MB:287
WIZARDS: see WITCHES AND WITCHCRAFT
WOLFE, JAMES
   Brave Wolfe.   Hi-TL:36
   Montcalm and Wolfe.   Em-AF:419
WOLSEY, THOMAS
   Why Come Ye Not to Courte.
      J. Skelton.   Hi-FO:113
WOLVES
   Big and Gray.   Gr-BB:15
   A Chippewa Legend.   J. Lowell.
      Hu-MP:425
   Day of the Wolf.   K. Wilson.
      Ha-WR:76
   The Fair Young Wife.   H. Adam.
      De-FS:7
   A Hungry Wolf.   Irina.   Mo-MI:48
   I Give to You.   Re-RR:27
   The Law of the Jungle.
      R. Kipling.   Rd-OA:128
   Myth.   Br-MW:81
   A Night with a Wolf.
      B. Taylor.   Un-GT:33
   A North Pole Story. M. Smedley.
      Ox-BC:251
   The Sea Wolf.   V. McDougal.
      Hu-MP:177
   The Shepherd's Dog and the Wolf.
      J. Gay.   Rd-OA:132

Song of the Wolf. Sitting Bull.
   Da-SC:113
Songs, I. The Wolf. Tr-US I:33
A Story for a Child. B. Taylor.
   Co-BBW:188
The Tantanoola Tiger. M. Harris.
   Ca-MB:66
The Wolf. G. Durston. Ar-TP3:65
The Wolf and the Crane. E. Rees.
   Ar-TP3:81
The Wolf and the Lioness.
   E. Rees. Ar-TP3:81
The Wolf Cry. L. Sarett.
   Fe-FP:179
WOMEN: see also HUMOR - WOMEN;
   MOTHERS; PORTRAITS - WOMEN;
   SATIRE - WOMEN; SINGLE WOMEN;
   SISTERS; WIDOWS; WIVES
Abel's Bride. D. Levertov.
   Ca-VT:514
Aella. T. Chatterton. Al-VBP:606
Against Women Either Good or Bad.
   Al-VBP:72
And There Was Mary Magdalene and
   the Other Mary, Sitting Over
   Against the Sepulchre.
   W. Rodgers. Hi-WP II:147
At the Silent Movies. Z. Landau.
   Ho-TY:101
The Ballad of Dead Ladies.
   F. Villon. Al-VBP:991,
   Er-FA:173, Ho-WR:184
Beautiful Black Women.
   I. Baraka. Ra-BP:213
Behind Sea-Lion Town. Ho-SD:61
Bring Hither Your Wooden
   Ornament. Ma-BH:19
C.L.M. J. Masefield.
   Un-MB:225, Wi-LT:190
Changes. R. Bulwer-Lytton.
   Fe-PL:307
Characterization. Yogesvara.
   Al-PI:37
The Chronicle. A. Cowley.
   Al-VBP:453
Cino. E. Pound. Ca-VT:78
Councils. M. Piercy. Mo-TS:44
Creatrix. A. Wickham. Un-MB:277
Dakota, the Beauty of the West.
   Fi-BG:74
Esthetique du Mal, X.
   W. Stevens. Wi-LT:156
The Girl I Left Behind Me.
   Er-FA:129
Great Man. B. Johnson. Co-EL:91
Grieve Not, Ladies. A. Branch.
   Er-FA:156
The Hand That Rocks the Cradle Is
   the Hand That Rules the World.
   W. Wallace. Er-FA:135, Fe-PL:149

The Heart of a Woman. G. Johnson.
   Fe-PL:416, Hu-PN:73
Her Kind. A. Sexton. Br-TC:368,
   Wi-LT:813
Here's to the Maiden. R. Sheridan.
   Al-VBP:605, Ke-TF:277, Rv-CB:557
I Am as Light as Any Roe.
   Al-VBP:23, Gr-GB:207
I Am Waiting. V. Bryant.
   Jo-VC:6
If the Heart of a Man. J. Gay.
   Rv-CB:394
The Ladies Aid. Fe-PL:415
The Lady's Maid's Song.
   J. Hollander. Wi-LT:732
The Lords of Creation. Fe-PL:63
Lovely Dames. W. Davies.
   Gr-SS:103
The Lovely Shall Be Choosers.
   R. Frost. Sh-AP:155, Un-MA:185
Love's Alchemy. J. Donne.
   Al-VBP:248
Love's Progress. J. Donne.
   Al-VBP:257
Male and Female Loves in Beulah.
   W. Blake. Ox-BN:46
Man, Man, Man. Er-FA:444
Meditation at Kew. A. Wickham.
   Gr-BT:88, Un-MB:280, Un-MW:58
The Men of Valor. Akahito.
   Ba-ST:29
The Old Woman and the Pig.
   Bu-DY:20
Old Woman Sitting in the Sun.
   M. Inman. Ls-NY:78
Old Women Remember. R. Boyle.
   Ls-NY:73
Passing and Glassing.
   C. Rossetti. Ox-BN:718
Puella Mea. E. Cummings.
   No-CL:212
A Puritan Lady. L. Reese.
   Un-MA:111
A Renunciation. E. Vere.
   Pa-GTB:26
The Revenger's Tragedy.
   C. Tourneur. Al-VBP:275
A Slice of Wedding Cake.
   R. Graves. Gr-BT:87
Someone Is Beating a Woman.
   A. Voznesensky. Gr-BT:125
Song (Go, and Catch). J. Donne.
   Al-VBP:245, Er-FA:129, Ga-FB:37,
   Gr-BT:69, Ha-PO:175, Ke-PP:26,
   Ma-YA:79, No-CL:167, Rv-CB:290,
   Un-MW:38
Sonnet 20. W. Shakespeare.
   Rv-CB:210
Tame Cat. E. Pound. Co-EL:89
The Tame Stag. J. Gay. Rv-CB:503

WOMEN — cont'd.
  Tell Me, Dearest. J. Fletcher.
    Al-VBP:283
  Tell Me, O Love. W. Hammond.
    Rv-CB:414
  That Women Are But Men's Shadows.
    B. Jonson. Al-VBP:234,
    Rv-CB:287
  To a Young Lady. W. Cowper.
    Pa-GTB:129
  To Woman. G. Byron. Al-VBP:719
  The Tribute. C. Patmore.
    Ox-BN:651
  What Do You Do with a Woman's
    Things? A. Miller. Ke-TF:175
  When Thy Beauty Appears.
    T. Parnell. Rv-CB:500
  Woman. V. Malangatana. Lo-TY:190
  Woman Recipe. V. de Moraes.
    An-TC:105
  The Woman Who Understands.
    L. Appleton. Fe-PL:117
  Women. L. Bogan. Br-TC:55,
    Ca-VT:202, Mc-EA:87, Un-MA:490
  Women. M. Swenson. Ho-P:263
  Women and Roses. R. Browning.
    Al-VBP:890
  Women Songs, II. K. Molodowsky.
    Ho-TY:285
  Women Transport Corps. Hs-TC:441
WOMEN—EQUAL RIGHTS: see also
    BLOOMER, AMELIA JENKS; HUMOR —
    WOMEN—EQUAL RIGHTS
  The Rights of Women. W. Cowper.
    Rv-CB:546
  To Men. A. Wickham. Un-MB:282
WOMEN'S LIBERATION MOVEMENT: see
    WOMEN—EQUAL RIGHTS
WONDER: see also CURIOSITY;
    IMAGINATION
  At Feng Ting Temple. Li Po.
    Le-MW:41
  Ayii, Ayii. Ho-SD:81
  Books. E. Farjeon. Ha-YA:132
  A Boundless Moment. R. Frost.
    Ke-TF:420
  The Child and the Mariner.
    W. Davies. De-CH:383
  A Different Speech. L. Nicholl.
    Pl-IO:26
  The Door. L. Strong.
    Un-MB:394
  Dreams. L. Hughes. Bo-HF:19,
    Du-RG:129, Mc-WS:38
  Fifth Birthday Gift. M. Lederer.
    Br-BC:104
  For Arvia. E. Robinson.
    Br-BC:149
  The God of Galaxies. M. Van Doren.
    Pl-IO:19, Tr-MR:138

God's World. E. Millay. Co-PS:124,
  Ga-FB:3, Sh-RP:103, Tr-MR:26,
  Tu-WW:48, Un-GT:245, Un-MA:443
The Hatch. N. Farber.   Ho-LP:100
I Don't Know Why. M. Livingston.
  Br-SG:81
I Shook His Hand. N. Noffke.
  Le-M:161
I Wonder Why. E. Lee. Ba-HI:115
In Procession. R. Graves.
  Br-TC:155
The Laboratory Midnight.
  R. Denney. Pl-IO;70
Legend. J. Weaver. Br-AF:197
The Magnifying Glass.
  W. de la Mare. Bl-OB:123
Miracle. Wen I-to. Hs-TC:67
On First Looking into Chapman's
  Homer. J. Keats. Al-VBP:769,
  Co-RG:17, De-CH:361, Er-FA:75,
  Ga-FB:14, Gr-CT:442, Ke-TF:61,
  Ma-YA:182, Mc-PR:78, Ni-JP:19,
  No-CL:18, Ox-BN:334, Pa-GTB:169,
  Pl-ML:91, Rv-CB:739, Sm-LG:36
Once a Child. E. Dickinson.
  Pl-IO:21
Once by the Pacific. R. Frost.
  Ca-VT:17, Pa-HT:62, Sm-PT:78,
  Un-MA:184, Wi-LT:173
Out in the Wood. C. Scollard.
  Th-AS:117
Pastoral. W. Williams. Br-TC:479
Personality. C. Sandburg.
  Ga-S:14
Praise to the Stutterer.
  M. Katz. Ls-NY:110
The Shape Called Star.
  L. Nicholl. Ho-LP:98
Song of a Man Who Has Come
  Through. D. Lawrence.
  Al-VBP:1158, Go-BP:69,
  Pa-GTB:458, Wi-LT:212
Summer Song. E. Nesbit. Co-PS:105
Teddy's Wonderings. J. Bangs.
  Br-BC:109
Thanksgiving for the Body.
  T. Traherne. Pl-IO:145
There Is Fear. Ma-BH:11,
  Tr-US I:24
The Tiger. W. Blake. Al-VBP:616,
  Ar-TP3:80, Bl-OB:111, Co-BBW:209,
  Co-RG:146, De-CH:91, Er-FA:234,
  Fe-FP:178, Fe-PL:366, Ga-FB:95,
  Ga-S:12, Gr-CT:115, Ha-PO:116,
  Hi-WP II:171, Hu-MP:201, Li-SR:8,
  Ma-YA:129, Mc-PR:158, Ox-BN:23,
  Pl-EI:19, Rd-OA:118, Rv-CB:576,
  Sm-LG:68, Tu-WW:108, Un-GT:36
The Two Deserts. C. Patmore.
  Co-BN:220

Warning to Children. R. Graves.
  Bl-OB:32, Er-FA:508,
  Ma-FW:195, Sm-LG:102
Wonder. T. Traherne. De-CH:152,
  Ga-S:21, Rv-CB:472
Wondering. K. Windsor. Le-M:156
WONDERS: see also HUMOR - WONDERS;
  MIRACLES
But how It Came from Earth.
  C. Aiken. Un-MA:434
Kingdoms. O. Gogarty. Pa-RE:90
The Mighty Thoughts of an Old
  World. T. Beddoes.
  Bo-GJ:201, Gr-SS:63
Pastourelle. D. Hayes. Bo-AN:94
Seven Poems. L. Niedecker.
  Ca-VT:243
Song of Myself. W. Whitman.
  Ar-TP3:216, Sh-AP:87, Un-MA:56
This Wonderful World. M. Miller.
  Gr-EC:52
Who'll That Be. K. Patchen.
  Mc-WK:94
WOOD: see also LUMBERING
The Dead Branch. D. Gibson.
  Ls-NY:77
Down at the Docks. K. Koch.
  Ca-VT:547
Fifty Faggots. E. Thomas.
  Un-MB:217
Getting Wood. J. Tritt.
  Ba-HI:59
Hearthfire. Ju-CP:81
Iron. B. Brecht. Ho-LP:39
Oak-Logs Will Warm You Well.
  Mo-TB:128
Silent Logs Floating.
  M. Goodson. Le-M:90
A Snake Yarn. W. Goodge.
  Gr-EC:149
Stuff. A. Mitchell. Sm-MK:190
Two Tramps in Mud Time. R. Frost.
  Un-MA:189, Wi-LT:176
Winter Night. E. Millay.
  Se-PR:215
The Wood-Pile. R. Frost.
  Ca-VT:8, Ni-JP:88, Sh-AP:146,
  Sp-OG:285
Woodchopper's Song. Bu-DY:32
WOOD THRUSHES: see THRUSHES
WOODCHUCKS: see also HUMOR -
  WOODCHUCKS
Clover for Breakfast.
  F. Frost. Sh-RP:333
A Drumlin Woodchuck. R. Frost.
  Mc-WK:69
The Groundhog. R. Eberhart.
  Er-FA:62, Ha-PO:121,
  Pe-OA:192, Sh-AP:208,
  Un-MA:579, Wi-LT:430

The Jolly Woodchuck. M. Edey and
  D. Grider. Ar-TP3:63, Co-IW:37,
  Fe-FP:169, La-PV:148
Song of the Animal World.
  Ab-MO:11, Tr-US I:66
The Whistle-Pig Song. Ju-CP:19
WOODPECKERS
Like They Say. R. Creeley.
  Co-EL:29, Co-PU:104
On the Extinction of a Species.
  D. Hoffman. Be-EB:54
River Roads. C. Sandburg.
  Ca-VT:22
When Cherry Trees Bloom. Joso.
  Be-MC:45
Who's There? F. Frost.
  Gr-EC:181, Sh-RP:332
The Woodpecker. A. Marvell.
  Gr-CT:96, Re-BS:28
The Woodpecker. E. Roberts.
  Ar-TP3:56, Fe-FP:297,
  Hu-MP:224, La-PP:49
WOODS: see FORESTS AND WOODS
WOODWORK
Ogun. E. Brathwaite. Sa-B:48
Picture Framing. B. Meyers.
  Co-EL:106
WOOL
Baa, Baa, Black Sheep.
  Ar-TP3:74, Au-SP:17, Bo-FP:80,
  De-PO:18, Er-FA:506, Li-LB:89,
  Mo-MGT:11, Mo-NR:57, On-TW:15,
  Pa-AP:30, Wi-MG:66, Wr-RM:58
WORDS: see also HUMOR - WORDS
Blum. D. Aldis. Co-HP:30,
  Gr-EC:188, Ir-BB:13,
  Li-LC:16, Mc-AW:83
Book-Moth. Ma-YA:3, Rd-OA:29
Brazen Tongue. W. Benét.
  Un-MA:327
A Bright Day. J. Montague.
  Ls-NY:170
Bright Is the Ring of Words.
  R. Stevenson. Mc-PR:63,
  Ox-BN:893, Un-GT:309
Coal. A. Lorde. Ad-PB:244,
  Be-MA:121, Jo-SA:95
Country Words. W. Stevens.
  Ls-NY:328
The Customs of the Country.
  P. McGinley. Ho-TH:70
The Dead Words. V. Watkins.
  Wi-LT:448
Death Is a Clean Cold Word.
  R. Richmond. Co-BP:230
The Dirty Word. K. Shapiro.
  En-PC:132
Especially when the October
  Wind. D. Thomas. Go-BP:68,
  Un-MB:500

WORDS — cont'd.

Expression. I. Rosenberg.
Un-MB:350

The Final Word. D. Moraes.
Go-BP:139

For a Wordfarer. R. Humphries.
Pl-ML:6

A Grandfather Poem. W. Harris.
Ad-PB:439

He Knoweth Not that the Dead
Are Thine. M. Coleridge.
Co-EL:11, Ox-BN:925

Her Words. A. Branch. Ar-TP3:4,
Br-SS:154, Fe-FP:32, Ha-YA:59

A Hurry-Up Word. E. Hilsabeck.
Mc-AW:15

I Would Like to Describe.
Z. Herbert. Gr-BT:28

If Ifs and Ands Were Pots and
Pans. Li-LB:160

In One Petal. Hirotsugu.
Ba-ST:22

Little Girl, Be Careful What
You Say. C. Sandburg.
Ma-FW:73

Loving and Liking. D. Wordsworth.
Ox-BC:129

The Mouth and the Body.
P. Mwanikih. Le-M:169

nigger. S. Sanchez. Ra-BP:232

Nightfall. C. Ricardo. An-TC:27

On the Road Home. W. Stevens.
Sm-PT:123

Poems. P. Kelso. Le-M:15

Precious Moments. C. Sandburg.
Un-MA:208

Preludes for Memnon. C. Aiken.
Co-BL:49, Un-MA:434

Pretty Words. E. Wylie.
Sh-RP:170

Primer Lesson. C. Sandburg.
Fe-FP:19, Ho-TH:57, Sh-RP:162,
Tu-WW:37, Un-MA:206

Refugee in America. L. Hughes.
Bo-HF:44, Br-AF:249,
Mc-WK:185, Ra-BP:87

Shaman Song. G. Fowler. Sc-TN:52

Small Rain. A. Gould. Th-AS:114

A Soft Answer Turneth Away Wrath.
Bible. O.T. Proverbs.
Ar-TP3:209

The Spring Waters. Ping Hsin.
Hs-TC:23

Stop Playing. Z. Shneour.
Me-PH:85

Tangling Words. E. Schwager.
Ad-II:71

Their Lonely Betters. W. Auden.
Bo-GJ:87, Ha-LO:64

Threes. C. Sandburg. Fe-PL:409

Throughout the World. T. Wyatt.
Co-EL:43, Rv-CB:95

to R. V. Erl'. Bo-RU:28

To the Tune "Glittering Sword
Hilts." Liu Yo Hsi. Rx-LT:72

The Twins. E. Roberts.
Ar-TP3:6, Br-BC:21, Mc-AW:96

Within One Petal. Ba-ST:22

A Word. E. Dickinson. Ar-TP3:217

A Word. K. Ozaki. Sh-AM:57

The Word. A. Timofeyevsky.
Bo-RU:84

A Word Fitly Spoken. Bible.
O.T. Proverbs. Fe-FP:16

The Words. G. Fowler. Sc-TN:49

Words. K. Iijima. Le-TA:89

Words. D. Quick. Ke-TF:129

Words. S. Spender. Sm-MK:158

Words. E. Thomas. Hi-WP II:4

The Words. D. Wagoner.
Du-SH:30, Mo-TS:52

Words. Fe-PL:418

The Words Will Resurrect.
J. de Lima. Lo-TY:83

Words, Words. M. Mertsalov.
Bo-RU:51

WORDSWORTH, WILLIAM: see also
HUMOR - WORDSWORTH, WILLIAM;
SATIRE - WORDSWORTH, WILLIAM

In These Fair Vales.
W. Wordsworth. Rv-CB:652

The Lost Leader. R. Browning.
Al-VBP:884, Hi-FO:225,
Ke-TF:56, Pl-ML:58

Resolution of Dependence.
G. Barker. Wi-LT:524

To Wordsworth. P. Shelley.
No-CL:264, Se-PR:312

Wordsworth's Grave. W. Watson.
Ox-BN:910

WORK: see also BUSYNESS; LABOR AND
LABORERS; SATIRE - WORK; WORK
SONGS

Adam's Curse. W. Yeats. Co-PI:205

All Things Come Alike to All.
Bible. O.T. Ecclesiastes.
Me-PH:32

All Work and No Play. Mo-MGT:187

The Ant and the Cricket. Aesop.
De-TT:59, Un-GT:78

Brass Spittoons. L. Hughes.
Bo-AN:61, Un-MA:552

The Camel's Hump. R. Kipling.
Ir-BB:104, Na-EO:137, Ox-BC:319

The Cry of the Children.
E. Browning. Al-VBP:819,
Cl-FC:27

Do It Now. Er-FA:24

Dress Me, Dear Mother.
A. Schlonsky. Me-PH:99

The Father and His Children.
    Ox-BC:75
Florida Road Workers. L. Hughes.
    Du-SH:145, Pe-SS:52, Un-MA:553
The Forgotten Man. E. Markham.
    Fe-PL:42
Getting Wood. J. Tritt. Ba-HI:59
Go, Silly Worm. J. Sylvester.
    Rv-CB:188
God Bless the Work. B. O'Higgins.
    Ke-TF:205
Good Advice. L. Untermeyer.
    Ar-TP3:209
Hay for the Horses. G. Snyder.
    Du-SH:144, Mo-BG:56
Hoo, Suffolk. Gr-GB:175
I'm a Newcomer. Chung Hsüan.
    Hs-TC:433
Jezrael. A. Shlonsky. Me-PH:100
John Grumlie. A. Cunningham.
    Fe-PL:235, Gr-GB:205
Labours of the Months. Gr-GB:205
The Ladies Aid. Fe-PL:415
Lazy Balan. Ca-MU:12
Lose This Day Loitering.
    J. von Goethe. Fe-PL:438
Motto. Ar-TP3:209
Old Farmer Grumble. Ju-CP:28
On a Tired Housewife.
    Ga-S:216, Hi-WP I:9,
    Na-EO:139, Sm-MK:113
Potato Digger. F. Frost.
    Ls-NY:152
Quiet Work. M. Arnold.
    Ma-YA:205, Se-PR:167
The Rival. S. Warner. Un-MB:374
The Road. C. Aiken. Un-MA:428
Seven Days in the Week. On-TW:28
The Silver Tray. N. Alterman.
    Me-PH:112
The Small Task. M. Lindsay.
    Ke-TF:241
Song for the Lazy. Do-CH:(10)
Song of a Hebrew. D. Abse.
    Sm-MK:214
The Song of the Old Mother.
    W. Yeats. Co-PI:208,
    Ha-LO:98, Un-MB:112
The Song of the Shirt. T. Hood.
    Hi-FO:227, Ke-PP:59, Ma-YA:188
Stevedore. L. Collins.
    Bo-AN:127
Sunday at the End of Summer.
    H. Nemerov. Co-BN:98
Testament. Sister M. Thérése.
    Tr-MR:169
This Is Silver Saturday.
    Sp-TM:35
To Labor. C. Gilman.
    Fe-PL:423

Two Tramps in Mud Time. R. Frost.
    Un-MA:189, Wi-LT:176
Verse on the Wall.
    Chang Chih-min. Hs-TC:431
Verses. R. Bentley. Al-VBP:510
Work. K. Cox. Se-PR:166
Work. D. Lawrence. Ga-S:117
Work. J. Lowell. Co-PS:120
Work. H. Van Dyke. Ke-TF:204,
    Se-PR:67, Th-AS:209
Work: A Song of Triumph.
    A. Morgan. Fe-PL:439,
    Ke-TF:234
Work Horses. E. Chase. Au-SP:47
WORK SONGS
    A Big Mountain Is Moved Away.
        Hs-TC:442
    Cotton Songs. J. Toomer.
        Ra-BP:68
    Go Down, Old Hannah. Lo-TY:200
    Haul on the Bow-Line. Sp-HW:21
    Haystack. Hs-TC:454
    I Stand on Mountain High.
        Hs-TC:450
    I'm a Longshoreman. Hs-TC:451
    It Can Bend the Huge River.
        Hs-TC:443
    I've Been Workin' on the Railroad.
        Er-FA:440
    Many, Many Are the Songs of Good
        Harvest. Hs-TC:442
    One Step Covers Ten Thousand Li.
        Hs-TC:452
    Our Songs Make the Yangtze River
        Flow Backward. Hs-TC:444
    Songs. Tr-US II:142
    Southern Road. S. Brown.
        Ad-PB:67, Be-MA:29, Ra-BP:111
    Tomorrow We Take Over the
        Heavenly Palace. Hs-TC:443
    Water Flows Around Our Village.
        Hs-TC:450
    With One Stroke I Dig Through
        the Crystal Palace. Hs-TC:442
    Women Transport Corps. Hs-TC:441
    Work Song. Ab-MO:56
    See also Em-AF:648-655
WORLD: see also EARTH; HUMOR –
    WORLD; SATIRE – WORLD
    Ark of the Covenant. L. Nicholl.
        Pl-IO:36
    The Boy from Nowhere. R. Peace.
        Me-WF:82
    Casual Lines. Yü P'ing-po.
        Hs-TC:18
    A Change of World. A. Rich.
        Ha-TP:33
    The Creation. C. Alexander.
        De-TT:36, Fe-FP:260, Gr-TG:22,
        Hu-MP:286, Ox-BC:200

WORLD — cont'd.
  The Daily Globe. H. Nemerov.
    Ha-TP:16
  Dalyaunce. De-CH:26
  Dear Lord. W. Mann. Me-WF:20
  Fear Have I when It Comes.
    L. Curry. Jo-VC:40
  Four Winds Blow the Wide World
    o'er. On-TW:19
  From My High Love. K. Patchen.
    Un-MA:610
  God's Grandeur. G. Hopkins.
    Er-FA:467, Ox-BN:867, Tr-MR:22,
    Un-MB:42, Wi-LT:40
  I Love the World. P. Wollner.
    Le-M:153
  I Often Wonder. "Monk."
    Ba-HI:121
  I See the World. B. Grayson.
    Me-WF:6
  Identity. D. Botez. Mc-AC:61
  In No Strange Land. F. Thompson.
    Ga-S:127, Go-BP:250, Pa-GTB:398,
    Pl-EI:7, Un-MB:90
  In the Middle of This Century.
    Y. Amichai. Me-PH:136
  It's a Gay Old World. Er-FA:12
  The Lessons of Nature.
    W. Drummond. De-CH:153,
    Pa-GTB:39
  Letty's Globe. C. Turner.
    Rv-CB:787
  Moment. D. Berrigan. Be-EB:41
  My World. R. Diaz. Me-WF:14
  New Year's Eve. T. Hardy.
    Un-MB:27
  Oh World. L. Blair. Ja-PA:33
  Poem for Psychologists and/or
    Theologians. C. Lewis.
    Go-BP:159
  Preliminary Draft of a World
    Constitution. Ba-PO:115
  The Rich Earth. Bible. O.T.
    Psalms. Un-GT:245
  Six Weeks Old. C. Morley.
    Br-BC:41
  Snow. L. MacNeice. Wi-LT:458
  The Song on the Way. Hu-MP:289
  This Is a World Full. . . .
    D. Peterson. Ba-HI:41
  This Wonderful World.
    M. Miller. Gr-EC:52
  To What Shall I Compare. Mansei.
    Ba-ST:55
  Too Anxious for Rivers. R. Frost.
    Rv-CB:967
  Undersong. M. Van Doren.
    En-PC:25
  The Vanity of the World.
    F. Quarles. Ke-PP:28

  Warning to Children. R. Graves.
    Bl-OB:32, Er-FA:508,
    Ma-FW:195, Sm-LG:102
  Water. H. Conkling. Ar-TP3:162
  The Wonderful World. W. Rands.
    Ar-TP3:217, Fe-FP:260,
    Hu-MP:284, Ox-BC:236
  The World. T. Peacock. Co-PU:61
  The World. D. Speaks. Me-WF:4
  The World out There Called to My
    Son. Wo-HS:(36)
  The World So Big. A. Fisher.
    Au-SP:184
  The World's Music. G. Setoun.
    Hu-MP:288
WORLD FEDERATION: see INTERNATIONAL
    ORGANIZATION
WORLD FRIENDSHIP: see BROTHERHOOD
WORLD WAR, 1914-1918: see also
    HUMOR - WORLD WAR, 1914-1918;
    and names of battles, as YPRES,
    BATTLES, 1914-1918 and names of
    persons, as SASSOON, SIEGFRIED
  Abraham Lincoln Walks at Midnight.
    V. Lindsay. Ba-PO:132,
    Bo-HF:148, Br-AF:82, Ca-VT:28,
    Er-FA:284, Fe-FP:453, Ga-FB:263,
    Hi-TL:184, Hu-MP:398, Ke-PP:21,
    Mc-PR:126, Pe-OA:64, Se-PR:45,
    Sh-RP:311, Tr-MR:183, Un-MA:229,
    Vi-PP:182
  Aftermath. S. Sassoon.
    Al-VBP:1167, Un-MB:314
  America's Answer. R. Lilliard.
    Vi-PP:215
  And There Was a Great Calm.
    T. Hardy. Gr-CT:345, Tr-MR:181,
    Wi-LT:26
  Another Reply to "In Flanders
    Fields." J. Armstrong.
    Vi-PP:214
  Anthem for Doomed Youth. W. Owen.
    Al-VBP:1198, Bo-HF:173,
    Cr-WS:67, Er-FA:195, Gr-BT:106,
    Gr-CT:349, Ma-FW:250, Na-EO:81,
    Pa-GTB:450, Un-MB:363, Wi-LT:350
  Armistice Day. R. Montgomery.
    Se-PR:205
  As the Team's Head-Brass.
    E. Thomas. Pa-GTB:442
  Attack. S. Sassoon. Un-MB:311
  Break of Day in the Trenches.
    I. Rosenberg. Al-VBP:1190,
    Ba-PO:138, Hi-FO:257,
    Pa-GTB:446, Un-MB:351
  Buttons. C. Sandburg. Kr-OF:83
  The Children's Bells. E. Farjeon.
    De-CH:164
  Counter-Attack. S.Sassoon. Ba-PO:136,
    Co-RM:204, Cr-WS:87, Un-MB:312

The Crowns. J. Freeman.
  De-CH:163
The Dead. R. Brooke. De-CH:161,
  Se-PR:136, Sp-OG:213
Dead Man's Dump. I. Rosenberg.
  Pa-GTB:446, Wi-LT:636
Dreamers. S. Sassoon.
  Cr-WS:83, Un-MB:310
The Dug-Out. S. Sassoon.
  De-CH:160, Ma-FW:252, Un-MB:313
Dulce et Decorum Est. W. Owen.
  Ba-PO:139, Co-RM:210, Cr-WS:98,
  Ga-FB:217, Ke-PP:58, Rv-CB:990,
  Un-MB:364, Wi-LT:351
The End. W. Owen. De-CH:162
Everyone Sang. S. Sassoon.
  Co-PS:144, Ga-FB:218, Ga-S:171,
  Ha-LO:71, Mc-WK:13, Ni-JP:79,
  Pa-GTB:453, Sh-RP:88, Sm-MK:211,
  Un-MB:314
The First Division Marches.
  G. Rice. Vi-PP:216
For the Fallen. L. Binyon.
  Hi-WP II:24
Greater Love. W. Owen.
  Al-VBP:1196, Er-FA:198,
  Pa-GTB:449, Un-MB:366,
  Wi-LT:348
The Guards Came Through.
  A. Doyle. Sp-OG:52
In Flanders Fields. J. McCrae.
  Al-VBP:1115, Br-SS:76, Er-FA:189,
  Ga-FB:217, Hu-MP:342, Se-PR:207,
  Sp-OG:212, Th-AS:196, Vi-PP:211
In the Dordogne. J. Bishop.
  Ca-VT:160
An Infantryman. E. Blunden.
  Al-VBP:1208
Into the Salient. E. Blunden.
  Al-VBP:1207
It's a Queer Time. R. Graves.
  Un-MB:384
Lines for an Interment.
  A. MacLeish. Kr-OF:87
The Map of France. R. Duffus.
  Ke-TF:368
Old Funeral Chant. Tr-US II:43
The Pity of It. T. Hardy.
  Wi-LT:23
Reply to "In Flanders Fields."
  J. Mitchell. Vi-PP:212
The Roman Road. D. Davidson.
  Cr-WS:17
Sergeant Major Money. R. Graves.
  Co-RM:220
Twenty Million. A. Kreymborg.
  Kr-OF:83
Veteran. L. Bacon. Cr-WS:34
When the Cock Crows.
  A. Giovannitti. Kr-OF:151

WORLD WAR, 1939-1945: see also AIR
  RAIDS; CONCENTRATION CAMPS;
  SATIRE - WORLD WAR, 1939-1954;
  and names of battles and engage-
  ments, as DUNKIRK, FR. and per-
  sons, as CHURCHILL, SIR WINSTON
  LEONARD SPENCER
The Angels at Hamburg. R. Jarrell.
  Sh-AP:224
An Austrian Army. Co-FB:415,
  Gr-CT:336
Battle. R. Jeffers. Un-MA:371,
  Wi-LT:260
Blackout. A. Gregor. Gr-SS:75
Brother Fire. L. MacNeice.
  Ba-PO:177, Ha-TP:83, Hi-FO:269
A Camp in the Prussian Forest.
  R. Jarrell. Pe-OA:227,
  Un-MA:644
Carentan O Carentan. L. Simpson.
  Bl-FP:46, Ca-MB:117,
  Co-RM:202, To-MP:49
Children's Crusade, 1939.
  B. Brecht. Ca-MB:106
Christmas Song. R. Leonhard.
  Un-R:57
The Companion. Y. Yevtushenko.
  Cr-WS:127, Ma-FW:252
Death of an Aircraft.
  C. Causley. Ca-MB:115
Documentary. R. Beum.
  Cr-WS:130
The Fifth Sense. P. Beer.
  Ca-MB:120
Flowers at Hampton Court.
  H. Wolfe. Cr-WS:71
For Lover Man and All Other
  Young Men Who Failed to
  Return from World War II.
  M. Williams. Cr-WS:109,
  Hu-NN:56
The Formalities. J. Ciardi.
  Cr-WS:143
The Funeral. M.J. Ba-PO:180
The Ghost Wails in the Woods at
  Night. Tu Yün-hsieh.
  Hs-TC:246
Ghosts. Fire. Water.
  J. Kirkup. Go-BP:215
The Good Joan. L. Reese.
  Ar-TP3:37, Fe-FP:468,
  Hu-MP:161, Th-AS:194
Hiroshima. M. Rockwell.
  Ba-PO:53, Ke-PP:9
I Sit with My Dolls. Ba-PO:179,
  Cr-WS:131
I Wish the Wood-Cutter Would Wake
  Up. P. Neruda. Bl-FP:51
In a Bar near Shibuya Station, Tokyo.
  P. Engle. Ad-CI:84, Br-AF:88

WORLD WAR, 1939-1945 — cont'd.
  In Crisis. L. Durrell. Wi-LT:692
  In Westminster Abbey. J. Betjeman.
    Ba-PO:183
  Journey to a Parallel. B. Wright.
    Hu-PN:355
  Lidice. E. Jebeleanu. Mc-AC:105
  The Man in the Dead Machine.
    D. Hall. Bl-FP:73, Du-SH:96
  The Map of France. R. Duffus.
    Ke-TF:368
  The Moon and the Night and the
    Men. J. Berryman. Ca-VT:380
  On the Death of a Murderer.
    J. Wain. Cr-WS:113
  The Other Little Boats. E. Shanks.
    Hi-FO:267
  The Other Looks at Me.
    J. Rubinstein. Ho-TY:240
  Pilots, Man Your Planes.
    R. Jarrell. Un-MA:645
  Protocols. R. Jarrell. Ca-VT:308
  Quintana Lay in the Shallow Grave
    of Coral. K. Shapiro.
    Ca-VT:374
  The Russian Gods. D. Andreyev.
    Ca-MR:95
  Scyros. K. Shapiro. Wi-LT:536
  Second Air Force. R. Jarrell.
    Wi-LT:563
  September 1, 1939. W. Auden.
    Un-MB:461
  She Said. . . . J. Brooks.
    Hu-PN:241
  Speech by Moonlight. C. Norman.
    Cr-WS:54
  Spring 1943. R. Fuller.
    Wi-LT:705
  The Stars Go over the Lonely
    Ocean. R. Jeffers. Wi-LT:259
  Still Falls the Rain. E. Sitwell.
    Br-TC:389, Ga-S:161, Tr-MR:131,
    Un-MB:336, Wi-LT:642
  The Strong Swimmer. W. Benét.
    Hu-PN:500
  Sunday: New Guinea. K. Shapiro.
    Br-AF:85
  Thermopylae 1941. C. Trypanis.
    Cr-WS:33
  They Say the Last Supper Is Badly
    Damaged. S. Yellen. Cr-WS:133
  Thoughts During an Air Raid.
    S. Spender. Al-VBP:1234,
    Un-MB:479
  To the Mound of Corpses in
    the Snow. U. Greenberg.
    Me-PH:95
  "Vale" from Carthage. P. Viereck.
    Cr-WS:102, Pe-OA:238,
    Un-MA:658, Wi-LT:832

  Vergissmeinicht. K. Douglas.
    Cr-WS:80, Pa-GTB:545
  The War Museum at Nagasaki.
    C. Higham. Ls-NY:30
  A Wartime Dawn. D. Gascoyne.
    Wi-LT:713
  Whispered on the Battlefield.
    G. Anders. Un-R:53
  Written on a Prison Wall.
    Tai Wang-shu. Hs-TC:184
WORLDLINESS
  The Wisdom of the World.
    S. Sassoon. Un-MB:315
WORMS: see also HUMOR – WORMS
  Book-Moth. Ma-YA:3, Rd-OA:29
  The Book of Thel. W. Blake.
    Ma-FW:209
  The Coffin-Worm. R. Pitter.
    Un-MB:403
  The Conqueror Worm. E. Poe.
    Sh-AP:55
  I Can Climb Our Apple Tree.
    J. Jones. Sh-RP:106
  I Walked Across the Park.
    B. Douglas. Me-WF:1
  Inch-Worm. D. Aldis. Ho-GC:20
  A Long and Legless Fellow.
    Re-RR:66
  Our Little Kinsmen. E. Dickinson.
    Fe-FP:121, Pl-IO:107
  This Is an African Worm.
    M. Danner. Ra-BP:151
  A Wee Little Worm. J. Riley.
    La-PV:33
  The Wind Blows the Rain into
    Our Faces. C. Reznikoff.
    La-OC:29
  The Worm. C. Applegate. La-GI:54
  The Worm. R. Bergengren.
    Br-SG:60, Br-SS:137
  The Worm. E. Roberts. Br-SG:59
  The Worm. R. Souster. Do-WH:71
  The Worm. A. Taylor. Br-SG:58
  Worms and the Wind. C. Sandburg.
    Mc-WK:48, Pa-RE:51, Rd-OA:93
WORRY: see also HUMOR – WORRY
  As I Sit. C. Begay. Ba-HI:34
  Dead Man's Song. Ma-BH:31,
    Tr-US I:21
  For Her Love I Cark and Care.
    Rv-CB:118
  Girl's-Eye View of Relatives.
    P. McGinley. Ke-TF:90, Mc-WS:145
  The Hurrier. H. Monro. Un-MB:240
  I Am Ashamed. Le-IB:74
  Mrs. Gilfillan. J. Reeves.
    Ir-BB:212, Li-TU:150
  Old Cat Care. R. Hughes.
    Rd-SS:13, Re-TW:15
  The Old Woman of Surrey. Wr-RM:117

Out in the Fields with God.
L. Guiney. Hu-MP:64,
Mc-PR:183, Un-GT:264
Song of a Dead One. Le-IB:122
Too Anxious for Rivers. R. Frost.
Rv-CB:967
WORSHIP: see also HUMOR - WORSHIP;
HYMNS; LITANIES; PRAYERS;
SATIRE - WORSHIP
Address on the Talking Drums to
Asase Yaa, the Spirit of Earth.
Tr-US I:47
Adoration of the Disk. King
Akhnaten and Princess Nefer
Neferiu Aten. Fe-FP:478
The Altar. G. Herbert. Ha-PO:200
Ars Poetica about Ultimates.
T. Combs. Br-TC:73
At Mass. V. Lindsay. Ca-VT:30
Beauteous, Yea Beauteous More
than These. C. Smart.
Pl-EI:97
The Belfry. L. Binyon. De-CH:200
Building in Stone. S. Warner.
Un-MB:377
The Church Windows. G. Herbert.
Rv-CB:351
Cradle Song. Pl-EI:189
The Dead Man Ariseth and Singeth
a Hymn. The Book of the Dead.
Pa-SG:210
Divina Commedia. H. Longfellow.
Al-VBP:828, Sh-AP:37, 38
The Divine Office of the Kitchen.
C. Hallack. Fe-PL:335
Dog, Dog in My Manger.
G. Barker. Wi-LT:531
The Ebb and Flow. E. Taylor.
Sh-AP:14
Father of Night. B. Dylan.
Mo-GR:100
For the Lord's Day Evening.
I. Watts. Ox-BC:50
A Forest Hymn. W. Bryant.
Sh-AP:23
Good Friday. Gr-CT:187
Holy Thursday. W. Blake.
De-CH:62, Ma-YA:127, Rv-CB:584
Hurrahing in Harvest.
G. Hopkins. Co-BN:130,
Gr-CT:313, Ma-FW:126,
Rv-CB:946, Un-MB:43
I Am the Corncob. Ge-TR:49
I Have Sought Thee Daily.
S. Ibn Gabirol. Pa-SG:208
In Church. W. Barnes.
Hi-WP I:140
In the Morning I Look for You.
S. Ibn Gabirol. Me-PH:58
In Tsegihi. Ho-SD:39

Incense. V. Lindsay. Tr-MR:196
The Joy of Church Fellowship.
E. Taylor. Rv-CB:475, Sh-AP:14
Keep Hidden from Me. R. Korn.
Ho-TY:306
Kibbutz Sabbath. L. Amittai.
Pl-EI:192
The Lover Tells of the Rose in
His Heart. W. Yeats.
Al-VBP:1090, Co-PI:206,
Un-MB:109
Malachi. E. Marlatt. Tr-MR:80
The Mass of the Grove.
D. ap Gwilym. Go-BP:73
The Moor. R. Thomas. Go-BP:28
The Morning-Watch. H. Vaughan.
Al-VBP:465, Mo-GR:120
My Period Has Come for Prayer.
E. Dickinson. Pl-EI:171
My Words Are Tied. Ho-SD:16
New York-Albany. L. Ferlinghetti.
En-PC:171
Noon. R. Jeffers. Un-MA:361
Now I Walk with Talking God.
Ho-SD:37
O Come, All Ye Faithful.
Er-FA:514, Ke-TF:225
Ode to Psyche. J. Keats.
Al-VBP:773, Ox-BN:357, Rv-CB:743
Old Hundred. M. Van Doren.
Pl-US:53
On Christmas Morn. Fe-FP:89,
La-PH:26, La-PV:88
Our Lords Esteemed Most High.
Ge-TR:51
Out of the Past. S. Halkin.
Ho-TY:186
Overtones. W. Percy. Bo-HF:136
The Peaks. S. Crane. Sh-AP:144
The Poets of Peace and Gladness.
M. Korte. Sc-TN:120
Prayer. I. Brown. Hu-NN:61,
Hu-PN:341
Religious Hymn to Be Sung Wearing
a Head Decoration. Le-IB:95,
Ma-BH:15, Tr-US I:20
The Sacrament of Fire.
J. Oxenham. Ke-TF:430
St. Isaac's Church, Petrograd.
C. McKay. Ad-PB:271,
Be-MA:15, Bo-AN:29
The Shepherds at Bethlehem.
Gr-CT:418
Some Keep Their Sabbath Going to
Church. E. Dickinson. Un-MA:104
Song for the Feast of Krishna.
Tr-US II:139
Sunday Morning. W. Stevens.
Sh-AP:158, Sm-PT:121,
Un-MA:242, Wi-LT:139

WORSHIP — cont'd.
  They Came This Evening. L. Damas.
    Lo-TY:120
  The Unnameable God. H. Brock.
    Un-R:35
  When Mahalia Sings. Q. Prettyman.
    Ad-PB:260, Pe-M:18
  Yollotl My Heart. Ge-TR:21
WORTH, CHARLES FREDERICK
  Crinolines and Bloomers.
    Hi-TL:174
WOUNDS: see ACCIDENTS; SCARS;
    WAR WOUNDED
WRECKS: see ACCIDENTS; SHIPWRECKS
WREN, SIR CHRISTOPHER: see HUMOR -
    WREN, SIR CHRISTOPHER
WRENS
  Cock Robin. De-TT:40, Ir-BB:24,
    Rv-ON:112
  Country Rhyme. Gr-TG:30
  The Cutty Wren. Gr-GB:63,
    Rv-CB:418, Rv-ON:117
  The Dove and the Wren. De-TT:38,
    Mo-MGT:17, On-TW:56, Wr-RM:41
  Four Birds. W. Blake.
    Gr-CT:93, Gr-GB:63, Gr-TG:31
  Go Now, My Song. A. Young.
    Gr-CT:93
  Jenny Wren. W. Davies.
    Co-BBW:257, Re-BS:7, Un-MB:176
  Jenny Wren. W. de la Mare.
    Re-BS:5
  Jenny Wren. Wr-RM:110
  Jenny Wren Fell Sick. Ir-BB:84,
    Mo-MGT:29, Na-EO:69, Rv-ON:116,
    Sm-MK:170
  Little Lady Wren. T. Robinson.
    Ar-TP3:55, Fe-FP:297
  Nesting Time. A. Guiterman.
    Gr-EC:180
  Nesting-Time. C. Rossetti.
    Ar-TP3:55, Bo-FP:227, Ch-B:16
  No Communication. M. Van Doren.
    Re-BS:6
  Old Fence Post. L. Hanes.
    Gr-EC:173
  The Pets. R. Farren.
    Gr-EC:30, Rd-OA:6
  Sing a Song of Sixpence. Au-SP:16,
    Li-LB:100, Wi-MG:72, Wr-RM:62
  Sudden Shower. J. Clare.
    Co-PS:61, Mc-PR:178, Rv-CB:715
  Three Things to Remember.
    W. Blake. Br-SS:150, Ch-B:89,
    Fe-FP:280, Gr-EC:178, Gr-TG:31,
    Hi-GD:13, Hi-WP II:170
  The Two Nests. F. Carlin. Re-BS:13
  Two Wrens. Ir-BB:26
  When Jenny Wren Was Young.
    Hu-MP:213, Wr-RM:23

  The Wren.   Ox-BC:82
  Wrens of the Lake. Re-BS:6
WRESTLING
  The Twa Brothers. De-CH:52,
    Ox-BB:234
  Wrestlers. M. Drayton. Mo-SD:81
WRIGHT, ORVILLE AND WILBUR
  The Campers at Kitty Hawk.
    J. Dos Passos. Mo-BG:59
WRIGHT, RICHARD (NATHANIEL)
  A Mourning Letter from Paris.
    C. Rivers. Ra-BP:199
  To Richard Wright. C. Rivers.
    Ad-PB:234, Be-MA:105, Bo-AN:177
WRINKLES
  My Grandmother's Wrinkles.
    H. Nishitani. Le-TA:24
WRITERS AND WRITING: see AUTHORS;
    JOURNALISM; POETS AND POETRY
WRITING: see ALPHABETS; CALLIGRAPHY
WYATT, SIR THOMAS
  On the Death of Sir Thomas Wyatt.
    H. Howard. Rv-CB:101
WYE RIVER
  Lines. W. Wordsworth. Ox-BN:66
  Meandering Wye. R. Bloomfield.
    Ox-BN:59
WYOMING
  Snow Country. D. Etter. Br-AF:160
  Wyoming. C. Winter. Se-PR:292
X RAYS
  The Book of the Dead.
    M. Rukeyser. Kr-OF:197
  X-Ray. L. Speyer. Pl-IO:146
YACHTS AND YACHTING
  The Yachts. W. Williams.
    Al-VBP:1154, Fl-HH:27, Ma-FW:51,
    Pe-OA:73, Pe-SS:72, Sm-PT:112,
    Un-MA:262, Wi-LT:194
YAKS: see also HUMOR - YAKS
  Bird Thou Never Wert.
    P. Bennett. Co-BBW:204
  The Yak. H. Belloc. Bl-OB:117,
    Bo-FP:28, Co-HP:31, Fe-FP:340,
    Ga-FB:332, Hu-MP:456, Ir-BB:166,
    Ox-BC:310, Un-GF:90, Un-MB:170
YAKUT VERSE: see ALTAIC VERSE-YAKUT
YALE UNIVERSITY: see HUMOR - YALE
    UNIVERSITY
YANGTZE RIVER
  After Swimming Across the Yangtze
    River. Mao Tse-tung. Hs-TC:365
  At Gold Hill Monastery.
    Su Tung P'o. Rx-OH:67
  Autumn on the Yangtze River.
    Chi Hsüan. Pa-MV:46
  Beautiful Is the Land South of the
    Yangtze River. Wang T'ung-chao.
    Hs-TC:265
  Our Songs Make the Yangtze River
    Flow Backward. Hs-TC:444

YARROW (PLANT)
Yarrow, Sweet Yarrow.   De-CH:669
YARROW RIVER
The Braes of Yarrow.   J. Logan.
Pa-GTB:121
The Braes of Yarrow.   Ox-BB:590
Rare Willie Drowned in Yarrow.
Gr-GB:133, Ox-BB:593
Willy Drowned in Yarrow.
De-CH:728, Pa-GTB:122
Yarrow Unvisited, 1803.
W. Wordsworth.   Pa-GTB:264
Yarrow Visited, September, 1814.
W. Wordsworth.   Pa-GTB:266
YAWNING
Accidentally.   M. Kumin.   Ja-PC:59
The Yawn.   P. Blackburn.
Co-EL:93, Kh-VA:58
YEARS
During Wind and Rain.   T. Hardy.
Ha-PO:153, Pa-GTB:411
Farewell to the Old Year.
E. Farjeon.   Br-SS:112
Pinwheel.   D. Laing.   Ls-NY:6
Song of the Riders.   S. Benét.
Un-MA:501
Sonnets from the Portuguese.
E. Browning.   Al-VBP:815,
Ox-BN:465, 466
Years, Many Parti-Colored Years.
W. Landor.   Al-VBP:705,
Rv-CB:671
You Ask My Age.
Sister M. Madeleva.   Ke-TF:152
YEASTS
There Once Was a Pious Young
Priest.   Br-LL:88
YEATS, WILLIAM BUTLER
In Memory of W. B. Yeats.
W. Auden.   Al-VBP:1228,
Er-FA:41, Gr-CT:431, Pl-ML:163,
Un-MB:459, Wi-LT:468
Reading Yeats I Did Not Think.
L. Ferlinghetti.   Pl-ML:117
Under Ben Bulben.   W. Yeats.
Pl-ML:30, Wi-LT:96
YELLOW (COLOR)
How Marigolds Came Yellow.
R. Herrick.   Ch-B:67,
Gr-CT:268
Symphony in Yellow.   O. Wilde.
Bo-FP:127, Un-MB:69
We Lying by Seasand.   D. Thomas.
Go-BP:84
A Yell for Yellow.   E. Merriam.
Gr-EC:112
Yellow Is Tons of Corn.
W. Newhard.   La-GI:31
Yellow Spring.   J. Jimenez.
Le-SW:21

YELLOW FEVER
Lines Written after the Discovery
by the Author of the Germ of
Yellow Fever.   R. Ross.
Pl-IO:187
YELLOWHAMMERS: see FLICKERS
YEREVAN, U.S.S.R.
Erevan Is My City. M. Nikogosian.
Mo-MI:21
YESININ, SERGEI ALEKSANDROVICH: see
ESENIN, SERGEI ALEKSANDROVICH
YESTERDAY
Yesterday.   H. Chesterman.
Br-SS:8
Yesterday Returneth Not.
De-CH:485
YEW TREES
A Fallen Yew.   F. Thompson.
Un-MB:83
The Moon and the Yew Tree.
S. Plath.   Mo-BG:146, To-MP:96
Trees.   W. de la Mare.
Mc-PR:199
The Yew Tree.   V. Watkins.
Pl-EI:6
YIDDISH LANGUAGE
The Light of Summer's End.
I. Schwartz.   Ho-TY:146
Teaching Yiddish.   J. Segal.
Ho-TY:155
YIDDISH VERSE
I Sit with My Dolls.
Ba-PO:179, Cr-WS:131
King Rufus.   Y. Segal. Do-WH:9
The Permanent Delegate.
Y. Suhl.   Ke-PP:71
Rhymes.   Y. Segal.   Do-WH:6
The Watchman.   A. Reisen.
Ba-PO:205
See also Ho-TY
YORKVILLE, N.Y.
Death in Yorkville.   L. Hughes.
Ad-PB:79
Yorkville.   D. Aldan.   Lo-IT:3
YOUNG, LESTER WILLIS
Lester Young.   T. Joans.
Be-MA:101, Bo-AN:171, Mo-BG:55
YOUTH: see also ADOLESCENCE; BOYS;
GIRLS; HUMOR - YOUTH; JUVENILE
DELINQUENCY; LOVE, YOUNG;
SATIRE - YOUTH; YOUTH AND AGE
Air Burial. J. Rorty.   Sm-PT:162
Always Before Your Voice.
E. Cummings.   Un-MA:472
A Boy.   S. Teasdale.   Cr-WS:51
A Boy's Prayer.   H. Beeching.
Mo-SD:193, Se-PR:313
Call to Youth.   Horace.   Pa-SG:4
Childe Harold.   M. Kulbak.
Ho-TY:205

YOUTH — cont'd.
  The Conventionalist. S. Smith.
    Co-PU:39
  A Cry. F. Bianco. No-CL:261
  Cub. D. Scott. Sa-B:119
  Death and the Maiden.
    M. Claudius. Un-R:121
  Exit. W. MacDonald. Al-VBP:1145
  Fern Hill. D. Thomas. Al-VBP:1246,
    Bo-GJ:53, Br-TC:440, Cl-DT:63,
    Co-RG:160, Fe-PL:251, Ga-FB:166,
    Hi-WP II:46, Mc-EA:42, Mc-WK:10,
    Na-EO:45, Pa-GTB:542, Pe-SS:162,
    Re-TW:100, Sm-LG:108, Un-MB:502,
    Wi-LT:559
  Fifteen. W. Stafford. Ad-CI:66,
    Du-RG:70, Pe-SS:40
  For Ann Scott-Moncrieff. E. Muir.
    Gr-SS:119, Pa-GTB:469
  For the Fallen. L. Binyon.
    Al-VBP:1109
  Going Where. P. Irving. Al-WW:78
  Here Dead Lie We. A. Housman.
    Cr-WS:135, Fe-PL:156
  How Can a Man Die Better.
    Tyrtaeus. Pa-SG:6
  How Soon Hath Time. J. Milton.
    Al-VBP:388, Ma-YA:93
  A Human Instinct. C. Morley.
    Na-EO:54
  I Roam Through. Y. Yevtushenko.
    Ca-MR:52
  I'm O'er Young to Marry Yet.
    R. Burns. Al-VBP:644
  In an Age of Fops and Toys.
    R. Emerson. Fe-FP:167
  In Clementina's Artless Mien.
    W. Landor. Al-VBP:704
  In Youth Is Pleasure. R. Wever.
    Gr-CT:61, Rv-CB:143
  Intimations of Sublimity.
    W. Wordsworth. Ox-BN:98
  Jeremy's Secrets. B. Todd.
    Br-BC:61
  The Lads. L. Shkol'nik.
    Bo-RU:78
  The Lads in Their Hundreds.
    A. Housman. Un-MB:96
  The Leaden-Eyed. V. Lindsay.
    Co-EL:136, Co-PU:150, Ke-PP:61,
    Kr-OF:182, Ni-JP:32, Tr-MR:54
  A Letter from a Girl to Her Own
    Old Age. A. Meynell.
    Al-VBP:1065, Un-MB:63
  Lies. Y. Yevtushenko. Du-SH:106
  Love in Thy Youth. Al-VBP:363
  The March into Virginia.
    H. Melville. Al-VBP:951,
    Sh-AP:121

  may my heart always be open to
    little. E. Cummings. Tr-MR:48
  O Mistress Mine. W. Shakespeare.
    Al-VBP:189, Bo-GJ:140, Co-BL:112,
    Er-FA:174, Ga-FB:31, Gr-CC:83,
    Hi-WP II:53, Ho-LP:7, Ke-TF:103,
    Mo-GR:125, No-CL:117, Pa-GTB:17,
    Rv-CB:194, Un-MW:183
  Old Tityrus to Eugenia.
    C. Cotton. Al-VBP:474
  On a Very Young, Very Dead
    Soldier. R. Gillman. Cr-WS:101
  On This Day I Complete My Thirty-
    Sixth Year. G. Byron.
    Al-VBP:738, Ma-YA:175
  Pater Filio. R. Bridges.
    Al-VBP:1063
  Piazza Piece. J. Ransom.
    Gr-SS:122, Ha-PO:46,
    Rv-CB:984, Un-MA:414
  Pride of Youth. D. Rossetti.
    Ox-BN:684
  Promise of Peace. R. Jeffers.
    Un-MA:365, Wi-LT:258
  Recuerdo. E. Millay. Br-AF:194,
    Co-BL:108, Er-FA:110, Hi-TL:194,
    Na-EO:78, Wi-LT:337
  The Revolutionary. V. Watkins.
    Ls-NY:118
  San Francisco. W. Roberts.
    Hu-PN:82
  Shellbrook. W. Barnes. Ox-BN:434
  The Silver Tray. N. Alterman.
    Me-PH:112
  Small Elegy. M. Weisenthal.
    Ls-NY:66
  Son and Father. C. Day Lewis.
    Pl-EI:135
  The Song of Youth. Ai Ch'ing.
    Hs-TC:297
  Sonnets, xxv. G. Santayana.
    Sm-PT:135
  Spring and Fall. G. Hopkins.
    Bo-GJ:249, Gr-CT:317, Ha-PO:148,
    Ke-PP:99, Pa-GTB:392, Re-TW:62,
    Wi-LT:44
  A Squire. G. Chaucer.
    Hi-WP II:121, Un-GT:87
  Stoplights. D. Dzwonkoski.
    Ad-II:24
  The Summing Up. S. Kunitz.
    Co-EL:125
  Sweet Cupid, Ripen Her Desire.
    Al-VBP:362
  Tell Me, Tell Me. E. Brontë.
    Al-VBP:920
  There Was a Boy. W. Wordsworth.
    Go-BP:119, Ox-BN:101, Sm-LG:107
  This Morning Our Boat Left.
    Rx-LT:10

To a Girl. E. Waller.
    Al-VBP:385, Ho-WR:58, Rv-CB:364
To a Very Young Lady. G. Etherege.
    Al-VBP:496
To an Athlete Dying Young.
    A. Housman. Ha-PO:140,
    Ma-YA:223, Mo-SD:168, Ni-JP:33,
    Pe-M:58, Un-MB:94, Wi-LT:60
To Any Member of My Generation.
    G. Barker. Al-VBP:1240,
    Wi-LT:529
To the Young Pioneers of the
    Northwest. Pien Chih-lin.
    Hs-TC:169
Ultima Ratio Regum. S. Spender.
    Er-FA:196, Pe-SS:139,
    To-MP:33, Wi-LT:501
Waking. J. Anderson. Ls-NY:19
A Waltz in the Afternoon.
    B. Bentley. Co-BL:22
We Hurry On. D. Dolben.
    Ox-BN:881
We Were Young. G. Naum.
    Mc-AC:116
What Makes Life Interesting.
    M. Montgomery. Ls-NY:340
When a Man's Body Is Young.
    Le-OE:109
When I Was One-and-Twenty.
    A. Housman. Al-VBP:1080,
    Bo-HF:92, Co-BL:61, Er-FA:153,
    Fe-PL:118, Ga-FB:72, Ho-LP:12,
    Ke-TF:93, Ma-YA:222, Pe-M:150,
    Un-MB:94, Un-MW:55, Wi-LT:59
The Wind's Arrows Shoot Cease-
    lessly. Wang Ching-chih.
    Hs-TC:44
The Young Girl. C. Day Lewis.
    Ls-NY:223
The Young Ones, Flip Side.
    J. Emanuel. Ab-MO:17
Young Soul. I. Baraka.
    Mc-EA:32, Mo-TS:3, Ra-BP:220
Youth. F. Cornford.
    Co-EL:128, Co-PU:4
A Youth. S. Crane. Un-MA:148
Youth. L. Hughes. Bo-HF:107,
    Br-AF:243, Br-BC:134, Li-TU:266
Youth. G. Johnson. Hu-PN:74
Youth and Art. R. Browning.
    Al-VBP:909
Youth Sings a Song of Rosebuds.
    C. Cullen. Fe-PL:258, Hu-PN:234
Youth's the Season. J. Gay.
    Ho-WR:73
YOUTH AND AGE: see also COUNTER
    CULTURE; HUMOR - YOUTH AND AGE;
    SATIRE - YOUTH AND AGE
  Adolescent with Bear. A. Storni.
    Be-UL:35

Age. E. Tuck. Br-BC:139,
    Fe-PL:259, Se-PR:237
Age in Prospect. R. Jeffers.
    Un-MA:360
Aladdin. J. Lowell. Co-PM:122,
    Co-RG:113, Mc-WK:83, Sp-OG:335
All the World's a Stage.
    W. Shakespeare. Er-FA:151,
    Fe-PL:257, Ha-PO:257,
    Ma-YA:67, Un-GT:85
An Ancient to Ancients. T. Hardy.
    Pa-GTB:412, Wi-LT:28
The Angel. W. Blake. De-CH:454
Anticipation. E. Brontë.
    Ox-BN:604
Aristotle to Phyllis. J. Hollander.
    En-PC:280
Aunt Selina. C. Haynes.
    Hu-MP:15, Ja-PC:44
Battle Won Is Lost.
    P. George. Al-WW:114
Building of Sand. G. Code.
    De-FS:65
The Campus on the Hill.
    W. Snodgrass. Wi-LT:821
change-up. D. Lee. Ad-PB:428
Child Rest. P. George. Al-WW:117
The Children. H. Applebaum.
    Ke-TF:80
The Children of the Poor.
    G. Brooks. Be-MA:80, En-PC:157,
    Ra-BP:166
Clothes. E. Jennings. Pa-RE:61
Counsel to Girls. R. Herrick.
    Al-VBP:328, Er-FA:104, Ga-FB:41,
    Gr-CT:51, Ha-PO:161,
    Hi-WP II:140, Li-SR:21, Ma-YA:86,
    Pa-GTB:71, Un-MW:19
Crabbed Age and Youth.
    W. Shakespeare. Al-VBP:91,
    Ma-YA:71, Pa-GTB:5
The Dance. R. Thomas. Go-BP:118
The Difference. E. Chaffee.
    Br-BC:75
Dream with an Angel. M. Banus.
    Mc-AC:113
The Echoing Green. W. Blake.
    Bo-FP:237, Ch-B:115, Co-PS:59,
    De-CH:21, Ho-WR:161, Rv-CB:589
Egan O'Rahilly. J. Stephens.
    Rv-CB:974
The Fair Young Wife. H. Adam.
    De-FS:7
For a Junior School Poetry Book.
    C. Middleton. Ma-FW:70,
    To-MP:151
Furniture. P. Harris.
    Ha-TP:32
The Generation Gap. E. Alexander.
    La-IH:86

YOUTH AND AGE — cont'd.
  Girls and Boys, Young Ladies
    and Gentlemen.
    R. Fernández Retamar. Be-UL:119
  Girl's Song. Tr-US II:220
  Girls' Song at a Wedding.
    Tr-US I:128
  Great Aunts. S. O'Críadáin.
    Co-PI:157
  Grown Folks. H. Leivick.
    Ho-TY:123
  Grownups. M. Duskin. Le-M:134
  He Abjures Love. T. Hardy.
    Ox-BN:830
  I Dreamed You Led Me.
    A. Machado. Le-SW:55
  I Saw from the Beach. T. Moore.
    Co-PI:144, Ox-BN:213
  If Souls Should Only Shine as
    Bright. W. Barnes. De-CH:636
  In Less than Two and Twenty
    Years. Asclepiades. Ho-LP:64
  Intimations of an Autobiography.
    J. Tate. St-H:226
  Jesus Was Crucified.
    C. Rodgers. Ad-PB:432
  Kids. W. Bynner. Hu-MP:39
  Laid in My Quiet Bed.
    H. Howard. De-CH:451
  A Lesson. W. Wordsworth.
    Pa-GTB:222
  Life Is Long. Rx-LT:8
  Listen to My Words. Le-IB:114
  Man's Going Hence. S. Rogers.
    Ox-BN:48
  Meeting Mary. E. Farjeon.
    Br-BC:72
  The Mind. M. Donohue. Me-WF:42
  A Moral Tetrastitch. Co-PU:149
  Mother's Party. A. Fisher.
    Br-BC:17
  Musings. W. Barnes. Ox-BN:435
  My Son. Ge-TR:41
  No Joy Without Love. Mimnerus.
    Pa-SG:75
  The Oak-Tree. Rv-CB:33
  Ode on Intimations of Immortality.
    W. Wordsworth. Al-VBP:662,
    Br-BC:18, Er-FA:157, Ga-FB:101,
    Gr-CT:436, Ha-PO:206, Ho-P:88,
    Ox-BN:84, Pa-GTB:308, Pl-EI:59
  Old Men and Young Men. J. Holmes.
    Mc-WK:216, Mc-WS:78
  On the Marriage of a Beauteous
    Young Gentlewoman with an
    Ancient Man. F. Beaumont.
    Al-VBP:300
  One, Two, Three. H. Bunner.
    Bo-FP:20, Fe-FP:537,
    Fe-PL:12, Hu-MP:54

The Orchard and the Heath.
    G. Meredith. Ox-BN:691
  Outdistanced. L. Rubin. Du-SH:49
  Playgrounds. L. Alma-Tadema.
    Bo-FP:270, Mc-AW:93
  Poems Addressed to Ianthe.
    W. Landor. Ox-BN:187
  Points of View. A. Lowell.
    Co-PU:63, Ha-LO:37
  Politics. W. Yeats.
    Co-PI:202, No-CL:161
  The Poppy. F. Thompson.
    Un-MB:80
  Rabbi Ben Ezra. R. Browning.
    Br-BC:142, Er-FA:175,
    Ga-FB:129, Ox-BN:578
  The River of Life. T. Campbell.
    Er-FA:155, Ni-JP:156,
    Ox-BN:203, Pa-GTB:306
  The Road of Life. W. Morris.
    Ox-BN:786
  The Roads into the Country.
    T. McGrath. St-H:121
  Sailing to Byzantium. W. Yeats.
    Al-VBP:1093, Er-FA:152, Go-BP:168,
    Pa-GTB:425, Rv-CB:956, Tr-MR:290,
    Un-MB:114, Wi-LT:75
  Sair Fyel'd, Hinny. Gr-GB:319
  Sentimental Monologue. J. Wheelock.
    Ls-NY:339
  Seumas Beg. J. Stephens.
    Bl-OB:144, Co-RM:63,
    Fe-FP:318, Na-EO:155
  so shy shy shy.
    e. cummings. Ha-TP:63
  Something Very Elegant.
    A. Fisher. Br-BC:74
  A Song. D. Dolben. Ox-BN:882
  Song. D. Moraes. Go-BP:138
  Song of the Pasque Flower.
    Tr-US II:235
  The Tea Shop. E. Pound.
    Hi-WP II:164
  That Is Tad. M. Korte. Sc-TN:118
  These Are the Boys. A. Herbert.
    Cr-WS:123
  Time. R. Graves. Wi-LT:375
  Time's Mutability. B. Brecht.
    Co-EL:121
  To an Old Tune. Hsin Ch'i Chi.
    Rx-LT:104
  To Chloe, Who Wished Herself
    Young Enough for Me.
    W. Cartwright. Al-VBP:423
  To the Tune "The Fair Maid of Yu."
    Chiang Chieh. Rx-LT:109
  V.D.F. H. Wolfe. Cr-WS:76
  A Valentine. J. Cournos. No-CL:221
  The Victory. J. Gelman. Be-UL:123
  Waiting. J. Kirkup. Ma-FW:138

we all joined a circle.
  M. Bergschneider.   Ad-II:62
We, the Young. M. Gurvich.
  Mo-MI:40
What Did I Lose?
  Sun Yü-t'ang.   Hs-TC:119
Whom the Gods Love. M. Bruner.
  Fe-PL:261
Young and Old. C. Kingsley.
  Al-VBP:949, Er-FA:148, Fe-PL:253,
  Ma-YA:204, Mc-PR:135, Mc-WK:203,
  Ox-BC:228, Rv-CB:843, Sp-OG:260
Youth. A.W.   Hu-MP:65
Youth and Age. G. Byron.
  Pa-GTB:221
Youth and Age. T. Campion.
  Rv-CB:265
Youth and Age. S. Coleridge.
  Fe-PL:256, Ox-BN:173, Pa-GTB:300
Youth and Age. W. Yeats.
  Co-EL:135
Youth and Age on Beaulieu River,
  Hants. J. Betjeman. Br-TC:45
Youth's Agitations. M. Arnold.
  Rv-CB:870
YPRES, BATTLES, 1914-1918
  Ypres. I. Gurney. Hi-FO:259
YUCCA
  The Boy and the Deer. Te-FC:3
YUCCA FLATS, NEV.
  Back Again from Yucca Flats.
    R. Kelley. Br-AF:92
YUGOSLAVIA: see SERBO-CROATIAN
  VERSE
YUKAGHIR VERSE
  See Tr-US II:125
YUKON, CAN.
  The Spell of the Yukon.
    R. Service. Er-FA:365
YULE: see CHRISTMAS
ZANE, ELIZABETH
  Betty Zane. T. English.
    Vi-PP:127
ZEBRAS: see also HUMOR - ZEBRAS
  This One's Known. Re-RR:56
  Zebra. I. Dinesen.
    Ad-PE:35, Be-EB:17, Bo-GJ:88,
    La-RM:72, Pe-M:107
  The Zebras. R. Campbell.
    Al-VBP:1222, Co-BBW:192,
    Un-MB:410
ZEBUS: see OXEN
ZECHARIAH
  Zechariah. E. Marlatt. Tr-MR:82
ZEPPELINS: see AIRSHIPS
ZERMATT, SWITZ.
  Zermatt. T. Hardy.   Ox-BN:823
ZEUS: see JUPITER
ZODIAC
  The Zodiac Rhyme.   Gr-GB:35

ZOLA, ÉMILE
  Zola. E. Robinson.   Hi-FO:255
ZOOS: see also ANIMALS, CAPTIVE;
    HUMOR - ZOOS; SATIRE - ZOOS
  At the Zoo. A. Milne.
    Fe-FP:251, Fr-MP:17
  At the Zoo. W. Thackeray.
    Ox-BC:223
  Ballade of a Zoo Buff.
    M. Bracker. Co-BBW:279
  Best Loved of Africa. M. Danner.
    Ad-PB:137, Hu-PN:162
  Excuse Us, Animals in the Zoo.
    A. Wynne. Ar-TP3:78
  False Country of the Zoo.
    J. Garrigue. Wi-LT:711
  Giraffe. C. McCullers. Ho-CS:24
  The Jaguar. J. Hollander.
    Wi-LT:736
  Mr. Zookeeper. L. Hopkins.
    Ho-CS:27
  The Park in Milan. W. Smith.
    Ad-CI:52
  Rookery: Brookfield Zoo.
    L. Mueller. St-H:143
  Seven Themes from the Zoo.
    J. Bennett. Ls-NY:208
  Some Brown Sparrows. B. Fearing.
    Co-BBW:258, Du-RG:27
  Truth Will Out. P. Bennett.
    Co-BBW:201
  Two from the Zoo. E. Merriam.
    Ar-TP3:102
  Willy. R. Moore. Du-SH:117
  The Woman at the Washington
    Zoo. R. Jarrell.
    Br-TC:220, Wi-LT:565
  Zoo. A. Boorstin. La-IH:122
  The Zoo. B. Pasternak.
    Ma-FW:221
  The Zoo. H. Wolfe.
    Co-HP:117, Mc-WK:78
  Zoo Manners. E. Mathias.
    St-FS:52
ZUÑI INDIANS: see INDIANS OF
    NORTH AMERICA - VERSE-ZUÑI